Liquidity

Working capital	Current assets − Current liabilities	p. 59
Current ratio	$\dfrac{\text{Current assets}}{\text{Current liabilities}}$	p. 59
Current cash debt coverage ratio	$\dfrac{\text{Cash provided by operations}}{\text{Average current liabilities}}$	p. 607
Inventory turnover ratio	$\dfrac{\text{Cost of goods sold}}{\text{Average inventory}}$	p. 281
Days in inventory	$\dfrac{\text{365 days}}{\text{Inventory turnover ratio}}$	p. 281
Receivables turnover ratio	$\dfrac{\text{Net credit sales}}{\text{Average net receivables}}$	p. 388
Average collection period	$\dfrac{\text{365 days}}{\text{Receivables turnover ratio}}$	p. 388

Solvency

Debt to total assets ratio	$\dfrac{\text{Total liabilities}}{\text{Total assets}}$	p. 60
Cash debt coverage ratio	$\dfrac{\text{Cash provided by operations}}{\text{Average total liabilities}}$	p. 608
Times interest earned ratio	$\dfrac{\text{Net income + Interest expense + Tax expense}}{\text{Interest expense}}$	p. 493
Free cash flow	Cash provided by operations − Capital expenditures − Cash dividends	p. 63

Profitability

Earnings per share	$\dfrac{\text{Net income − Preferred stock dividends}}{\text{Average common shares outstanding}}$	p. 55
Price-earnings ratio	$\dfrac{\text{Stock price per share}}{\text{Earnings per share}}$	p. 662
Gross profit rate	$\dfrac{\text{Gross profit}}{\text{Net sales}}$	p. 234
Profit margin ratio	$\dfrac{\text{Net income}}{\text{Net sales}}$	p. 235
Return on assets ratio	$\dfrac{\text{Net income}}{\text{Average total assets}}$	p. 437
Asset turnover ratio	$\dfrac{\text{Net sales}}{\text{Average total assets}}$	p. 439
Payout ratio	$\dfrac{\text{Cash dividends declared on common stock}}{\text{Net income}}$	p. 556
Return on common stockholders' equity ratio	$\dfrac{\text{Net income − Preferred stock dividends}}{\text{Average common stockholders' equity}}$	p. 558

RAPID REVIEW
Chapter Content

ACCOUNTING CONCEPTS (Chapters 1–4)

Characteristics	Assumptions	Principles	Constraints
Relevance	Monetary unit	Revenue recognition	Materiality
Reliability	Time period	Full disclosure	Conservatism
Comparability	Economic entity	Matching	
Consistency	Going concern	Cost	

INVENTORY (Chapters 5 and 6)

Ownership

Freight Terms	Ownership of goods on public carrier resides with:
FOB Shipping point	Buyer
FOB Destination	Seller

BASIC ACCOUNTING EQUATION (Chapter 3)

ADJUSTING ENTRIES (Chapter 4)

	Type	Adjusting Entry	
Prepayments	1. Prepaid expenses	Dr. Expenses	Cr. Assets
	2. Unearned revenues	Dr. Liabilities	Cr. Revenues
Accruals	1. Accrued revenues	Dr. Assets	Cr. Revenues
	2. Accrued expenses	Dr. Expenses	Cr. Liabilities

Note: Each adjusting entry will affect one or more income statement accounts and one or more balance sheet accounts.

Interest Computation

Interest = Face value of note × Annual interest rate × Time in terms of one year

CLOSING ENTRIES (Chapter 4)

Purpose

1. Update the Retained Earnings account in the ledger by transferring net income (loss) and dividends to retained earnings.
2. Prepare the temporary accounts (revenue, expense, dividends) for the next period's postings by reducing their balances to zero.

ACCOUNTING CYCLE (Chapter 4)

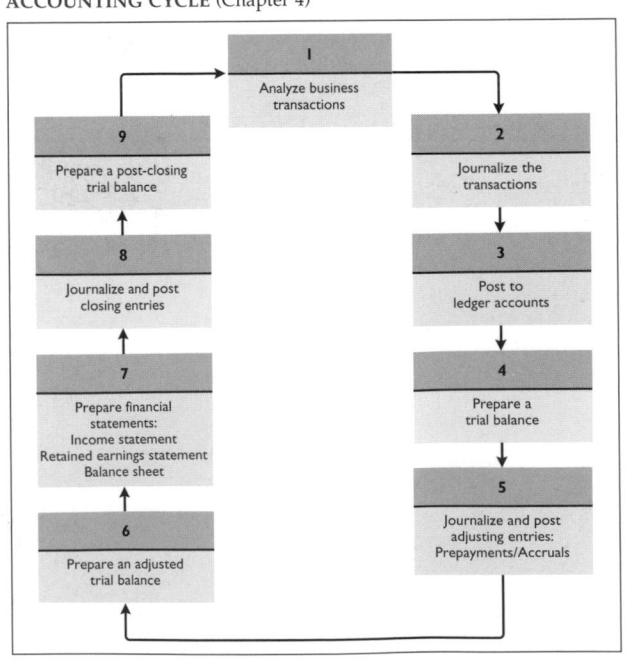

Perpetual vs. Periodic Journal Entries

Event	Perpetual	Periodic
Purchase of goods	Inventory Cash (A/P)	Purchases Cash (A/P)
Freight (shipping point)	Inventory Cash	Freight In Cash
Return of goods	Cash (or A/P) Inventory	Cash (or A/P) Purchase Returns and Allowances
Sale of goods	Cash (or A/R) Sales Cost of Goods Sold Inventory	Cash (or A/R) Sales No entry
End of period	No entry	Closing or adjusting entry required

INTERNAL CONTROL AND CASH (Chapter 7)

Principles of Internal Control

Establishment of responsibility
Segregation of duties
Documentation procedures
Physical, mechanical, and electronic controls
Independent internal verification
Other controls

Bank Reconciliation

Bank	Books
Balance per bank statement Add: Deposits in transit	Balance per books Add: Unrecorded credit memoranda from bank statement
Deduct: Outstanding checks	Deduct: Unrecorded debit memoranda from bank statement
Adjusted cash balance	Adjusted cash balance

Note: 1. Errors should be offset (added or deducted) on the side that made the error.
2. Adjusting journal entries should only be made for items affecting books.

STOP AND CHECK: Does the adjusted cash balance in the Cash account equal the reconciled balance?

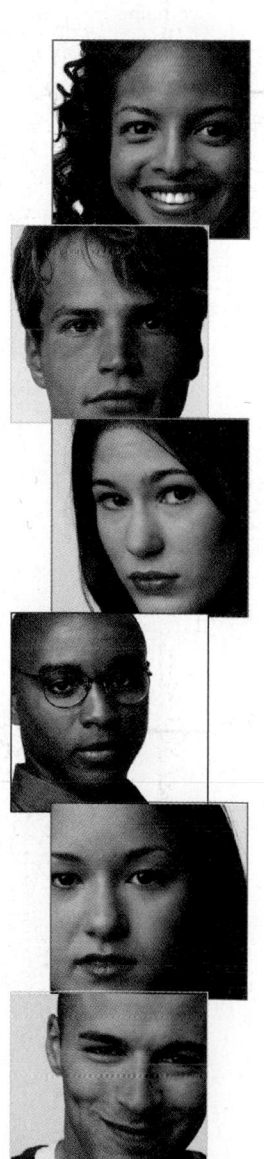

Prepare & Present

Create outstanding class presentations using a wealth of resources, such as PowerPoint™ slides, image galleries, interactive simulations, and more. Plus you can easily upload any materials you have created into your course, and combine them with the resources Wiley provides you with.

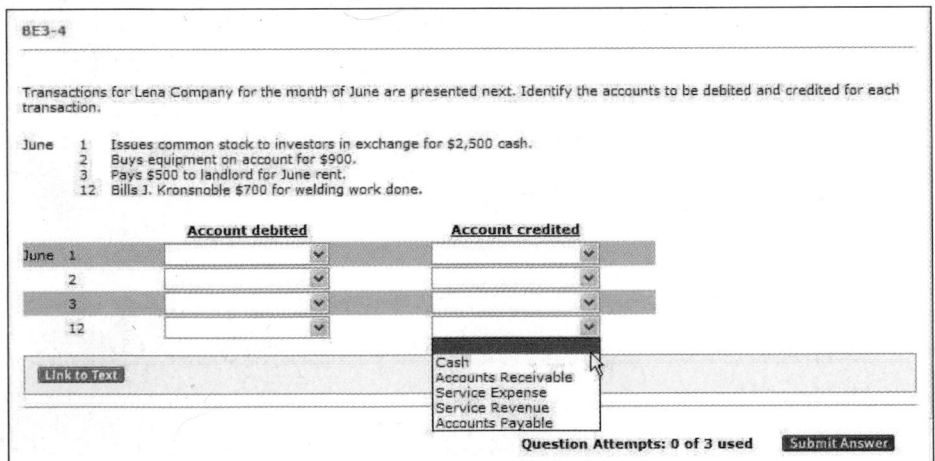

Create Assignments

Automate the assigning and grading of homework or quizzes by using the provided question banks, or by writing your own. Student results will be automatically graded and recorded in your gradebook. *WileyPLUS* also links homework problems to relevant sections of the online text, hints, or solutions—context-sensitive help where students need it most!

*Based on a spring 2005 survey of 972 student users of *WileyPLUS*

TO THE STUDENT

You have the potential to make a difference!

Will you be the first person to land on Mars? Will you invent a car that runs on water? But, first and foremost, will you get through this course?

WileyPLUS is a powerful online system packed with features to help you make the most of your potential, and get the best grade you can!

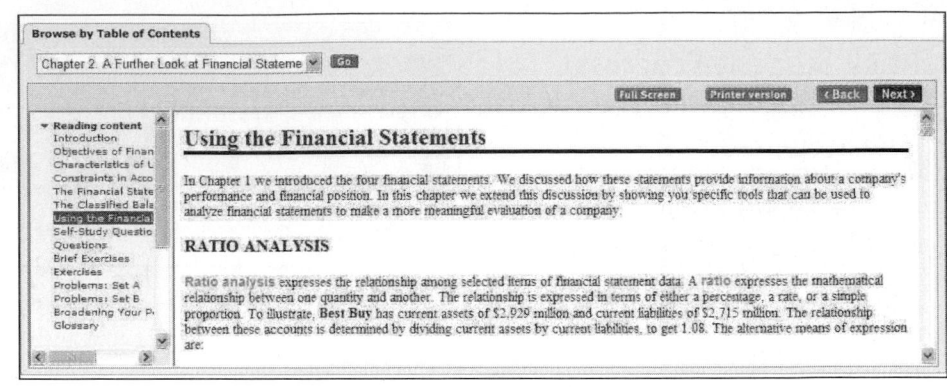

With Wiley**PLUS** you get:

A complete online version of your text and other study resources

Study more effectively and get instant feedback when you practice on your own. Resources like self-assessment quizzes, tutorials, and animations bring the subject matter to life, and help you master the material.

Problem-solving help, instant grading, and feedback on your homework and quizzes

You can keep all of your assigned work in one location, making it easy for you to stay on task. Plus, many homework problems contain direct links to the relevant portion of your text to help you deal with problem-solving obstacles at the moment they come up.

The ability to track your progress and grades throughout the term.

A personal gradebook allows you to monitor your results from past assignments at any time. You'll always know exactly where you stand.

If your instructor uses *WileyPLUS*, you will receive a URL for your class. If not, your instructor can get more information about *WileyPLUS* by visiting www.wiley.com/college/wileyplus

---

"It has been a great help, and I believe it has helped me to achieve a better grade."

Michael Morris, *Columbia Basin College*

69% of students surveyed said it helped them get a better grade.*

Accounting

Tools for Business Decision Making
2nd Edition

PAUL D. KIMMEL, PHD, CPA

Associate Professor of Accounting
University of Wisconsin—Milwaukee

JERRY J. WEYGANDT PHD, CPA

Arthur Andersen Alumni Professor of Accounting
University of Wisconsin

DONALD E. KIESO PHD, CPA

KPMG Peat Marwick Emeritus Professor of Accountancy
Northern Illinois University

BICENTENNIAL
1807
WILEY
2007
BICENTENNIAL

John Wiley & Sons, Inc.

Dedicated to
our parents and in-laws,
our families,
and most especially our spouses,
   Merlynn
   Enid
   Donna

PUBLISHER	Donald Fowley
EXECUTIVE EDITOR	Christopher M. DeJohn
ASSOCIATE EDITOR	Brian Kamins
DEVELOPMENT EDITOR	Ann Torbert
SENIOR PRODUCTION EDITOR	Valerie A. Vargas
EXECUTIVE MARKETING MANAGER	Clay Stone
CREATIVE DIRECTOR	Harry Nolan
SENIOR DESIGNER	Kevin Murphy
SENIOR MEDIA EDITOR	Allie K. Morris
PROJECT EDITOR	Ed Brislin
SENIOR ILLUSTRATION EDITOR	Sandra Rigby
SENIOR PHOTO EDITOR	Elle Wagner
EDITORIAL ASSISTANT	Karolina Zarychta
MARKETING ASSISTANT	Tierra Morgan
PRODUCTION SERVICES MANAGEMENT	Ingrao Associates
COVER DESIGN	David Levy
COVER PHOTO	Philip and Karen Smith/Photodisc/Getty Images, Inc.

This book was set in New Aster by Techbooks and printed and bound by Von Hoffmann. The cover was printed by Von Hoffmann.

This book is printed on acid free paper. ∞

To order books or for customer service, please call 1-800-CALL WILEY (225-5945).

ISBN-13-978-0470-08744-2

Printed in the United States of America

10 9 8 7 6 5 4 3 2 1

Paul D. Kimmel, PhD, CPA, received his bachelor's degree from the University of Minnesota and his doctorate in accounting from the University of Wisconsin. He is an Associate Professor at the University of Wisconsin—Milwaukee, and has public accounting experience with Deloitte & Touche (Minneapolis). He was the recipient of the UWM School of Business Advisory Council Teaching Award, the Reggie Taite Excellence in Teaching Award, and a three-time winner of the Outstanding Teaching Assistant Award at the University of Wisconsin. He is also a recipient of the Elijah Watts Sells Award for Honorary Distinction for his results on the CPA exam. He is a member of the American Accounting Association and the Institute of Management Accountants and has published articles in *Accounting Review, Accounting Horizons, Advances in Management Accounting, Managerial Finance, Issues in Accounting Education, Journal of Accounting Education,* as well as other journals. His research interests include accounting for financial instruments and innovation in accounting education. He has published papers and given numerous talks on incorporating critical thinking into accounting education, and helped prepare a catalog of critical thinking resources for the Federated Schools of Accountancy.

Jerry J. Weygandt, PhD, CPA, is Arthur Andersen Alumni Professor of Accounting at the University of Wisconsin—Madison. He holds a Ph.D. in accounting from the University of Illinois. Articles by Professor Weygandt have appeared in the *Accounting Review, Journal of Accounting Research, Accounting Horizons, Journal of Accountancy,* and other academic and professional journals. These articles have examined such financial reporting issues as accounting for price-level adjustments, pensions, convertible securities, stock option contracts, and interim reports. Professor Weygandt is author of other accounting and financial reporting books and is a member of the American Accounting Association, the American Institute of Certified Public Accountants, and the Wisconsin Society of Certified Public Accountants. He has seved on numerous committees of the American Accounting Association and as a member of the editorial board of the *Accounting Review;* he also has served as President and Secretary-Treasurer of the American Accounting Association. In addition, he has been actively involved with the American Institute of Certified Public Accountants and has been a member of the Accounting Standards Executive Committee (AcSEC) of that organization. He has served on the FASB task force that examined the reporting issues related to accounting for income taxes and served as a trustee of the Financial Accounting Foundation. Professor Weygandt has received the Chancellor's Award for Excellence in Teaching and the Beta Gamma Sigma Dean's Teaching Award. He is on the board of directors of M & I Bank of Southern Wisconsin. He is the recipient of the Wisconsin Institute of CPA's Outstanding Educator's Award and the Lifetime Achievement Award. In 2001 he received the American Accounting Association's Outstanding Accounting Educator Award.

Donald E. Kieso, PhD, CPA, received his bachelor's degree from Aurora University and his doctorate in accounting from the University of Illinois. He has served as chairman of the Department of Accountancy and is currently the KPMG Emeritus Professor of Accountancy at Northern Illinois University. He has public accounting experience with Price Waterhouse & Co. (San Francisco and Chicago) and Arthur Andersen & Co. (Chicago) and research experience with the Research Division of the American Institute of Certified Public Accountants (New York). He has done postdoctorate work as a Visiting Scholar at the University of California at Berkeley and is a recipient of NIU's Teaching Excellence Award and four Golden Apple Teaching Awards. Professor Kieso is the author of other accounting and business books and is a member of the American Accounting Association, the American Institute of Certified Public Accountants, and the Illinois CPA Society. He has served as a member of the Board of Directors of the Illinois CPA Society, the AACSB's Accounting Accreditation Committees, the State of Illinois Comptroller's Commission, as Secretary-Treasurer of the Federation of Schools of Accountancy, and as Secretary-Treasurer of the American Accounting Association. Professor Kieso is currently serving on the Board of Trustees and Executive Committee of Aurora University, as a member of the Board of Directors of Kishwaukee Community Hospital, and as Treasurer and Director of Valley West Community Hospital. From 1989 to 1993 he served as a charter member of the national Accounting Education Change Commission. He is the recipient of the Outstanding Accounting Educator Award from the Illinois CPA Society, the FSA's Joseph A. Silvoso Award of Merit, the NIU Foundation's Humanitarian Award for Service to Higher Education, a Distinguished Service Award from the Illinois CPA Society, and in 2003 an honorary doctorate from Aurora University.

The goal of this text is to introduce students to accounting in a way that demonstrates the importance of accounting to society and the relevance of accounting to their future careers. We strive to teach the students those things that they really need to know and to do it in a way that maximizes their opportunities for successful completion of the course. To accomplish these goals, the foundation of this text relies on a few key beliefs.

"It really matters." The collapse of Enron, WorldCom, Arthur Andersen, and others had devastating consequences. A number of the book's features are designed to reveal accounting's critical role to society. Some of the *Feature Stories*, the *Business Insight—Ethics Perspective* boxes, and end-of-chapter *Ethics Cases* and *Research Cases* introduce students to the important effects of accounting on business and society. In short, it has never been more clear that accounting really matters.

"Less is more." Our instructional objective is to provide students with an understanding of those core concepts that are fundamental to the use of accounting. Most students will forget procedural details within a short period of time. On the other hand, students should remember well-taught core concepts for a lifetime. Concepts are especially important in a world where the details are constantly changing.

Decision Checkpoints

"Don't just sit there—do something." The overriding pedagogical objective of this book is to provide students with continual opportunities for active learning. One of the best tools for active learning is strategically placed questions. Our discussions are framed by questions, often beginning with rhetorical questions and ending with review questions. Also, our analytical devices, called *Decision Toolkits*, use key questions to demonstrate the purpose of each.

"Get real." Students will be most willing to commit time and energy to a topic when they believe that it is relevant to their future careers. There is no better way to demonstrate relevance than to ground discussions in the real world. We do this in several ways: First, we use high-profile companies such as Nike, Microsoft, and Intel to frame out discussion of accounting issues.

Second, the book employs a "macro" approach in its first two chapters, teaching students how to understand and use the real financial statements of Tootsie Roll, Hershey, and Best Buy, before teaching how to record transactions. Many students determine their opinion of a course during the initial weeks, and this macro approach clearly demonstrates the relevance of accounting while students are forming impressions of the course.

Accounting across the Organization boxes connect accounting to business functions such as finance, marketing, and management and show uses of accounting for students with business majors other than accounting. In addition, because the economy has shifted toward service industries, we have included more examples and homework materials related to service companies.

"Make a decision." All business people must make decisions. Decision making involves critical evaluation and analysis of the information at hand, and this takes practice. We have integrated important analytical tools throughout the book. After each new decision tool is presented, we summarize the key features of that tool in a *Decision Toolkit*. At the end of each chapter we provide a comprehensive demonstration of an analysis of a real company using the decision tools presented in the chapter.

"It's a small world." The Internet has made it possible for even small businesses to sell their products virtually anywhere in the world. Few business decisions can be made without consideration of international factors. To heighten student awareness of international issues, we have many references to international companies and issues, and many *Interpreting Financial Statements* problems have an international focus.

TOOLS FOR STUDENT SUCCESS

Accounting 2e provides many proven pedagogical tools to help students learn accounting concepts and apply them to decision making in the business world. This pedagogical framework emphasizes the *processes* students undergo as they learn. Turn to the **Student Owner's Manual** on page XX to see all the learning tools of the book in detail. Here are a few key features.

Learning How to Use the Text

- The **Student Owner's Manual**, p. xxi, and notes in red in Chapter 1, explain to students how to take advantage of the text's learning tools to help achieve success in the course.

- A **Learning Styles Quiz**, p. xxx, includes tips on in-class and at-home learning strategies.

- **The Navigator** guides students through each chapter by pulling all the learning tools together into a learning system. Throughout the chapter, **The Navigator** prompts students to use the learning aids and to set priorities as they study.

Understanding the Context

- **Study Objectives**, listed at the beginning of each chapter, reappear in the margins and again in the **Summary of Study Objectives**.

- A **Feature Story** helps students picture how the chapter topic relates to the real world of accounting and business and serves as a recurrent example.

- A **Chapter Preview** links the Feature Story to the major topics of the chapter and provides a road map to the chapter.

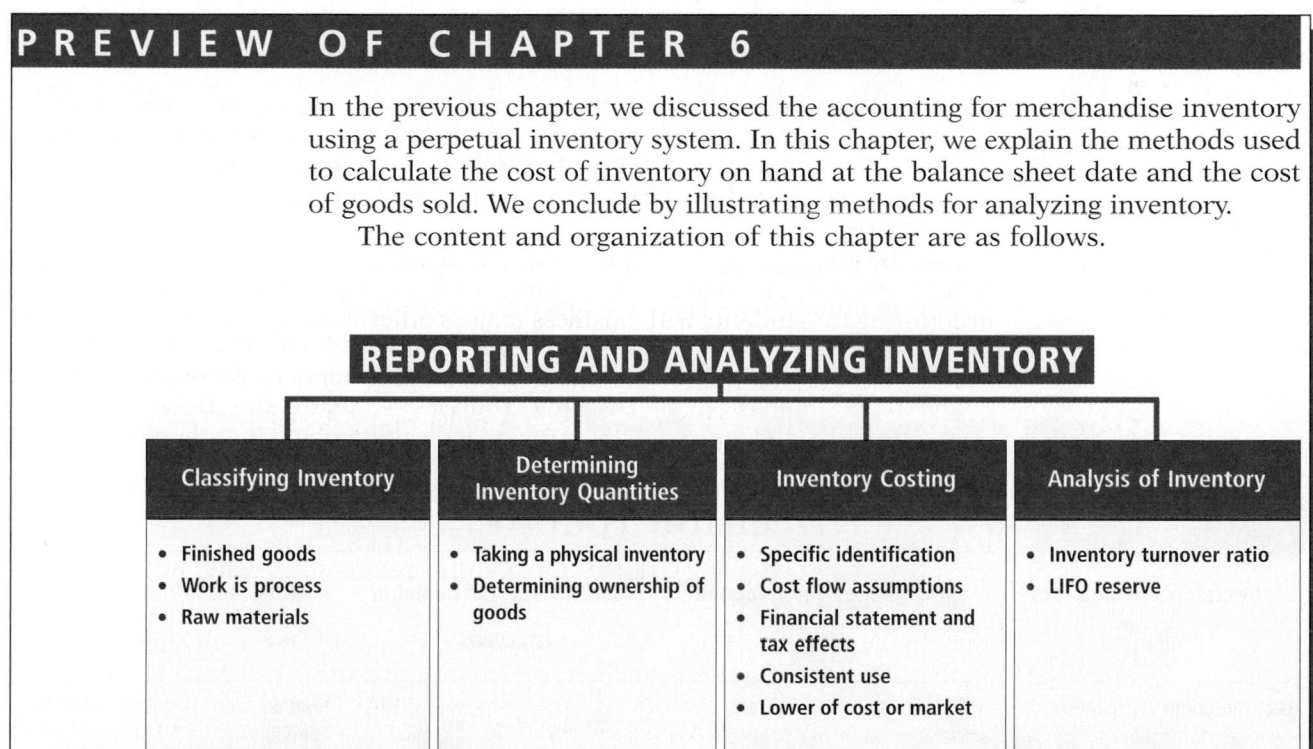

PREVIEW OF CHAPTER 6

In the previous chapter, we discussed the accounting for merchandise inventory using a perpetual inventory system. In this chapter, we explain the methods used to calculate the cost of inventory on hand at the balance sheet date and the cost of goods sold. We conclude by illustrating methods for analyzing inventory. The content and organization of this chapter are as follows.

REPORTING AND ANALYZING INVENTORY

Classifying Inventory	Determining Inventory Quantities	Inventory Costing	Analysis of Inventory
• Finished goods • Work is process • Raw materials	• Taking a physical inventory • Determining ownership of goods	• Specific identification • Cost flow assumptions • Financial statement and tax effects • Consistent use • Lower of cost or market	• Inventory turnover ratio • LIFO reserve

TOOLS FOR STUDENT SUCCESS

Learning the Material

- The text emphasizes accounting experiences of **real companies and business situations throughout**.

- Different types of **Business Insight** boxes—highlighting ethics, investor, international, management, and e-business perspectives—give students glimpses into how real companies make decisions using accounting information. In addition, new **Accounting across the Organization** boxes give glimpses of how businesspeople in non-accounting functions use accounting information in their decision making.

- The **Business Insight** boxes and the new **Accounting across the Organization** boxes in the financial chapters end with a question, to encourage students to think about and apply the information in the box. **Guidelines answers** for these questions appear at the end of the Broadening Your Perspective section, at the end of the chapter.

- **Color illustrations**, including **infographics**, create "visual anchors" that help students visualize and apply accounting concepts.

- **Before You Go On** sections provide learning checks (**Review It**) and mini demonstration problems (**Do It**). Questions marked with the **Tootsie Roll** send students to find information in Tootsie Roll's 2004 annual report printed in Appendix A at the back of the book.

BEFORE YOU GO ON . . .

▶ Review It

1. What are the phases of the product life cycle, and how do they affect the statement of cash flows?

2. Based on its statement of cash flows, in what stage of the product life cycle is Tootsie Roll Industries? The answer to this question appears on page 643.

3. What are the three major steps in preparing a statement of cash flows?

A	= L +	SE
		−150 Exp
−150		

Cash Flows
−150

- **Accounting Equation analyses** in the margin next to journal entries reinforce understanding of the impact of an accounting transaction on the financial statements. They report the **cash effect** of each transaction to reinforce understanding of the difference between cash effects and accrual accounting.

- **Helpful Hints, Alternative Terminology**, and highlighted **key terms and concepts** help focus students on key concepts as they study the material.

- **International Notes** provide a convenient way to expose students to international issues.

- **Decision tools** useful for analyzing and solving business problems are presented and then summarized in **Decision Toolkits**. A **Using the Decision Toolkit** exercise asks students to use the decision tools presented in the chapter and takes them through the problem-solving steps.

Decision Toolkit

Decision Checkpoints	Info Needed for Decision	Tool to Use for Decision	How to Evaluate Results
Can the company meet its near-term obligations?	Current assets and current liabilities	$\text{Current ratio} = \dfrac{\text{Current assets}}{\text{Current liabilities}}$	Higher ratio suggests favorable liquidity.
Can the company meet its long-term obligations?	Total debt and total assets	$\text{Debt to total assets ratio} = \dfrac{\text{Total liabilities}}{\text{Total assets}}$	Lower value suggests favorable solvency.

TOOLS FOR STUDENT SUCCESS

Putting It Together

At the end of each chapter are several features useful for review and reference.

- A **Summary of Study Objectives** reviews the main points of the chapter.
- The **Decision Toolkit—A Summary** presents in one place the decision tools used throughout the chapter.
- A **Glossary** of key terms gives definitions with page references to the text.
- A **Demonstration Problem** with an **Action Plan** gives students another opportunity to refer to a detailed solution to a representative problem before they do homework assignments.

Demonstration Problem

Trillo Company's bank statement for May 2007 shows these data.

Balance May 1	$12,650	Balance May 31	$14,280
Debit memorandum:		Credit memorandum:	
NSF check	175	Collection of note receivable	505

The cash balance per books at May 31 is $13,319. Your review of the data reveals the following.

1. The NSF check was from Hup Co., a customer.
2. The note collected by the bank was a $500, 3-month, 12% note. The bank charged a $10 collection fee. No interest has been accrued.

Action Plan

- Follow the four steps used in reconciling items (p. 330).
- Work carefully to minimize mathematical errors in the reconciliation.
- Prepare entries based on reconciling items per books.

Developing Skills Through Practice

Each chapter is supported by a full complement of homework material. **Self-Study Questions, Questions, Brief Exercises, Exercises**, and three sets of **Problems** (one of which is at the book's website) are all keyed to the Study Objectives. In addition:

- Certain Questions, Exercises, and Problems in the financial accounting chapters use the decision tools presented in the chapter. These are marked with the icon ⊙▭━━ℂ. Also, certain Questions, Exercises, and Problems show applications of accounting issues for business functions across the organization. These are marked with the icon ▰▶.

- A new **Comprehensive Problem** (in Chapters 5–11) combines material of the current chapter with previous chapters so that students understand "how it all fits together." Each of these problems requires the recording of transaction and adjusting entries, and culminates in the preparation of financial statements.

- A new Continuing Cookie Chronicle problem (in Chapters 1–13) traces the growth of an entrepreneurial venture. Each week students apply their newly acquired accounting skills to solve the financial reporting issues faced by this small business.

Continuing Cookie Chronicle
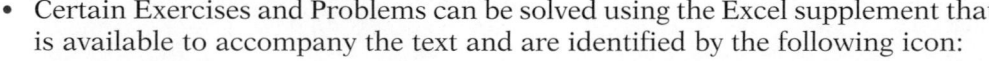

(*Note:* This is a continuation of the Cookie Chronicle from Chapter 1.)

CCC2 After investigating the different forms of business organization, Natalie Koebel decides to operate her business as a corporation, Cookie Creations Inc., and she begins the process of getting her business running.

- Certain Exercises and Problems can be solved using the Excel supplement that is available to accompany the text and are identified by the following icon:

- Other Exercises and Problems can be solved with the **General Ledger Software** available with the text and are marked with the icon 𝗚𝗟𝗦.

TOOLS FOR STUDENT SUCCESS

Expanding and Applying Knowledge

Broadening Your Perspective at the end of each chapter offers a wealth of resources for those instructors who want to broaden the learning experience by brining in more real-world decision making, analysis, and critical thinking activities.

BROADENING YOUR PERSPECTIVE

Financial Reporting and Analysis

FINANCIAL REPORTING PROBLEM: *Tootsie Roll Industries*

BYP3-1   The financial statements of Tootsie Roll in Appendix A at the back of this book contain the following selected accounts, all in thousands of dollars.

In the Financial Accounting chapters–

- A **Financial Reporting Problem** directs students to study various aspects of the financial statements of Tootsie Roll Industries, Inc., which are printed in Chapter 1 (in simplified form) and in Appendix A (in full).

- A **Comparative Analysis Problem** offers the opportunity to compare and contrast the financial reporting of Tootsie Roll Industries, Inc., with a competitor, Hershey Foods Corporation.

- **Interpreting Financial Statements** problems offer mini-cases that ask students to read parts of financial statements of actual companies and use the decision tools of the chapter to interpret them. Some of these cases, indicated by a globe icon, focus on specific situations faced by actual international companies.

In the Managerial Accounting chapters–

- **Managerial Analysis** assignments build analytical and decision-making skills in situations encountered by managers.

- **Real-World Focus** problems ask students to apply techniques and concepts presented in the chapter to specific situations faced by actual companies.

Throughout the book–

- **Research Cases** direct students to the *Wall Street Journal* and other business periodical for further study and analysis of key topics.

- **Group Decision Cases** help promote group collaboration and build decision-making and business communication skills by requiring teams of students to evaluate a manager's decision.

- **Exploring the Web exercises** guide students to websites from which they can mine and analyze information related to the chapter topic.

- **Communication Activities** provide practice in written communication, a skill much in demand among employers.

- **Ethics Cases** ask students to analyze situations, identify the ethical issues involved, and decide on an appropriate course of action.

In the spirit of continuous improvement, we have made many changes to this edition. These changes come in response to suggestions made by reviewers, focus group participants, and users. We sincerely appreciate their input.

Major Changes in This Edition

- First, we changed the book's title, from *Principles of Accounting* to *Accounting*. The impetus behind this decision was the desire for the title to better reflect the flexible nature of the text. The teaching of the introductory accounting course sequence continues to evolve. In the past, schools could be easily categorized as using either a Principles approach (65 percent financial and 35 percent managerial) or a financial/managerial approach (50 percent financial and 50 percent managerial). The approach now used at many schools can be characterized as a hybrid between these two.

  As a result of these and other changes in the accounting curriculum, the range of topics mentioned by instructors for inclusion in the introductory sequence has increased. While some of these topics have widespread instructor support for inclusion, others receive more limited mention. The challenge for us as authors is to support diverse instructor demands while avoiding the temptation of simply providing an incohesive smorgasbord of topics. We want to provide flexibility to instructors, allowing them to tailor the course as they desire. But we are equally concerned that the end result should provide a logical story for the student.

  Based on survey results and discussions with users, we decided to make three very distinct changes to the text to addresses the evolving needs of instructors. First, an increasing number of schools are no longer covering investments in the introductory sequence. As a consequence, we chose to move that topic into an end-of-book appendix (Appendix H). Second, activity-based costing, with the related topic of activity-based management, has increased in use. Many instructors requested that we provide an easily-understood introduction to the basic concepts underlying ABC (Chapter 17). Finally, to support those managerial accounting instructors who are expanding the decision-making emphasis, we provided a chapter that discusses variable costing (Chapter 19), with an emphasis on its use in decision making, as well as expanded coverage of break-even analysis.

- In order to illustrate the importance of accounting knowledge to non-accounting majors, we have added 35 **Accounting across the Organization** boxes which demonstrate the use of accounting to address issues in marketing, finance, management, and other functional areas of business.

- To reflect recent events affecting financial reporting, we created numerous new **Business Insight** boxes. As suggested by users of the book, we actually reduced the total number of Business Insight boxes, and instead inserted more of the "real-world references" directly into the text discussion.

- The Accounting across the Organization and Business Insight boxes in the financial chapters now end with a question to test student understanding. Guideline answers are provided at the end of the Broadening Your Perspective section, at the end of the chapter.

- We added a new set of problems—**Problems: Set C**—to expand the homework options available to the instructor. The C Problems, which are available on book's website, parallel the A and B problem sets.

- Over 400 **new questions** are included in this edition of the Test Bank. Each test item is classified by test study objective. New to this edition is the classification by Bloom's taxonomy.

- In addition, more than 150 new Exercises and Problems are included in this edition of the text.

- To enhance students' conceptual understanding of the impact of transactions, the accounting equation analyses in the margins next to each journal entry have been redesigned so that the effect on each account is more clearly associated with the accounting equation.

- We discuss the financial reporting implications of the Sarbanes–Oxley Act at numerous points throughout the text.

- We have added **Comprehensive Problems** to Chapters 5-11. These new problems require students to record transactions and adjusting entries and prepare financial statements. They are designed to reinforce the students' understanding of the accounting cycle throughout the course.

- We have added a **Continuing Cookie Chronicle** problem to every financial accounting chapter. This problem illustrates the usefulness of accounting in a small-business setting throughout the various stages of a company's formation and growth, and it provides a comprehensive review of topics.

- We have entirely rewritten Chapter 12, on the statement of cash flows, to provide a significantly shorter, more streamlined presentation of the basic concepts needed to prepare and understand that statement. In addition, we moved the presentation of the direct approach to an end-of-chapter appendix.
- We have **increased emphasis on the use of spreadsheets,** by employing spreadsheets in our illustrations and significantly increasing the amount of end-of-chapter material that is supported by spreadsheets.
- Finally, but by no means the least significant of the changes in this edition, we have made various improvement in the technology available with the textbook, as a way to enrich the learning environment. The most exciting technological development of this edition is **WileyPLUS.** WileyPLUS is a Web-based product that provides an integrated suite of learning resources via a unique class homepage. Through this homepage students can access the following: the full content of the textbook, assignments, selected solutions, exams created by the instructor, and an online gradebook to monitor progress.

As a result of these changes, as well as the many other changes discussed below, we are very excited about this edition of the text and its ability to meet your needs in teaching today's accounting principles curriculum.

Key Features of Each Chapter

Our "focus companies" are again Tootsie Roll Industries and Hershey Foods. They have high name recognition with students, they operate primarily in a single industry, and they have relatively simple financial statements. This edition of the book uses the companies' **2004 annual reports.** We have updated the **Review It** questions related to Tootsie Roll and the **Broadening Your Perspective** problems related to both companies to reflect the new data.

FINANCIAL CHAPTERS

Chapter 1, Introduction to Financial Statements

- Explains the purpose of each financial statement.
- Uses financial statements of a hypothetical company (to keep it simple), followed by those for a real company, Tootsie Roll Industries (to make it relevant).
- *Changes:* Added new Feature Story on open-book management; added new section, "Accounting and You"; revised ethics section with emphasis on Sarbanes-Oxley; moved section on assumptions and principles to Chapter 2.

Chapter 2 A Further Look at Financial Statements

- Discusses revenue, expenses, assets, and liabilities.
- Presents the classified balance sheet.
- Applies ratio analysis (current ratio, debt to total assets, earnings per share, and free cash flow) to real companies—Best Buy and Circuit City.
- *Changes:* Moved "The Financial Statements Revisited" section to beginning of chapter; deleted some ratios (P-E, current cash debt coverage, and current cash coverage) and added free cash flow; added section on assumptions and principles (from Chapter 1).

Chapter 3 The Accounting Information System

- Covers transaction analysis—emphasizes fundamentals while avoiding unnecessary detail.

Chapter 4 Accrual Accounting Concepts

- Emphasizes difference between cash and accrual accounting.
- Discusses how some companies manage earnings through accrual practices.
- Presents minimal discussion of closing and work sheets; provides additional detail on work sheets in an appendix.
- *Changes:* Added section on quality of earnings; simplified text presentation in several places.

Chapter 5 Merchandising Operations and the Multiple-Step Income Statement

- Introduces merchandising concepts using the perpetual inventory approach.
- Presents the multiple-step income statement.
- Applies ratio analysis (gross profit rate and profit margin ratio) to real companies—Target and Wal-Mart.

Chapter 6 Reporting and Analyzing Inventory

- Covers cost flow assumptions and their implications for financial reporting, emphasizing the periodic approach (for simplicity).
- Applies ratio analysis (inventory turnover) to real companies—Target and Wal-Mart.
- Discusses implication of LIFO reserve for real company—Caterpillar Inc.
- Covers in an appendix cash flow assumptions under perpetual inventory systems.
- *Changes:* Slightly expanded discussion of lower of cost or market, including a numeric example.

Chapter 7 Internal Control and Cash

- Covers internal control concepts and implications of control failures.
- Presents bank reconciliation as a control device.

- Discusses cash management, including operating cycle and cash budgeting.
- *Changes:* Added new Feature Story; added new section on Sarbanes-Oxley.

Chapter 8 Reporting and Analyzing Receivables

- Presents the basics of account and notes receivable, bad debt estimation, and interest calculations.
- Discusses receivables management, including determining to whom to extend credit, establishing the payment period, monitoring collections, evaluating the receivables balance, and accelerating receipts.
- Applies ratio analysis (receivables turnover) to a real company—McKesson.
- *Changes:* Added new financial statement disclosure for receivables.

Chapter 9 Reporting and Analyzing Long-Lived Assets

- Covers the basics of plant assets and intangible assets.
- Discusses the basics of the buy or lease decision.
- Covers the implications of depreciation method choice; shows details of accelerated methods in an appendix.
- Applies ratio analysis (asset turnover and return on assets) to real companies—Southwest Airlines and AirTran.
- Demonstrates implications of estimated useful life for amortization of intangibles.
- Discusses the statement of cash flows presentation of fixed-asset transactions.
- *Changes:* Updated discussion and analysis of return on assets, and updated section on intangible assets.

Chapter 10 Reporting and Analyzing Liabilities

- Covers current liabilities: notes payable, sales taxes, payroll, unearned revenues, and current maturities of long-term debt.
- Covers long-term liabilities, bond pricing, and various types of bonds.
- Presents straight-line amortization and the effective-interest method in a chapter-end appendix.
- Includes present value discussion in an appendix at the back of the book.
- Discusses the basics of contingent liabilities, lease obligations, and off-balance-sheet financing.
- Applies ratio analysis (current ratio, debt to total assets ratio, and times interest earned) to real companies—Ford and General Motors.
- Discusses the statement of cash flows presentation of debt transactions.

- *Changes:* Moved the key points from the appendix on contingent liabilities and leases into the text, and eliminated the remainder of that appendix.

Chapter 11 Reporting and Analyzing Stockholders' Equity

- Presents pros and cons of the corporate form of organization.
- Covers issues related to common and preferred stock, and reasons companies purchase treasury stock.
- Explains reasons for cash dividends, stock dividends, and stock splits, and implications for analysis.
- Discusses the debt versus equity choice.
- Applies ratio analysis (return on common stockholders' equity and payout ratio) to real companies—Nike and Reebok.
- Discusses the statement of cash flows presentation of equity transactions.

Chapter 12 Statement of Cash Flows

- Explains the purpose and usefulness of the statement of cash flows.
- Presents the indirect method in the body of the chapter and the direct method in a chapter-end appendix.
- Applies ratio analysis (free cash flow, current cash debt coverage ratio, and cash debt coverage ratio) to real companies—Microsoft, Oracle, AMD, and Intel.
- *Changes:* Shortened coverage of preparing operating activities section, for both methods; condensed presentation from two years to one year; moved the direct method into an appendix.

Chapter 13 Financial Analysis: The Big Picture

- Capstone chapter—presents some new tools, and reinforces previous analytical tools and demonstrates their interrelationships.
- Demonstrates horizontal and vertical analysis of Kellogg.
- Discusses "sustainable income" and implications of discontinued operations, extraordinary items, accounting changes, nonrecurring charges, and comprehensive earnings.
- Discusses factors that affect the quality of earnings.
- In an appendix, applies comprehensive ratio analysis to real companies—Kellogg and General Mills.
- *Changes:* Added new section on the price-earnings ratio; rewrote coverage of changes in accounting principle to reflect the new FASB standard.

Managerial Chapters

Chapter 14 Managerial Accounting

- Compares and contrasts managerial accounting with financial accounting.
- Identifies three broad functions of management.
- Defines three classes of manufacturing costs, organizational structure, and business ethics issues.
- Distinguishes between product costs and period costs.
- Presents the costs of goods manufactured section of the income statement.
- Presents an overview of trends in managerial accounting, including the shift toward service industries, value chain management, enterprise resource planning, just-in-time inventory, activity-based costing, theory of constraints, and the balanced scorecard.
- *Changes:* Added new discussion of the changing role of managerial accountants; new section on organizational structure; new section on business ethics; and new material on the value chain, theory of constraints, and balanced scorecard.

Chapter 15 Job Order Costing

- Provides an overview of cost accounting systems.
- Illustrates the flow of costs in a job order cost system and basic entries.
- Presents use of job cost sheets.
- Demonstrates use of predetermined overhead rate.
- Provides simple presentation of overapplied and underapplied overhead.
- *Changes:* Two new Business Insight boxes on job order costing software and use of job order costing by service companies.

Chapter 16 Process Costing

- Explains the difference between job order and process costing systems.
- Illustrates the flow of costs and end-of-period accounting procedures for process costing.
- Demonstrates computation of physical units of production, equivalent units of production, and unit costs.
- Shows how to assign costs to units of output and prepare a production cost report.
- *Changes:* Revised illustrations for clarity, and presented some illustrations as spreadsheets.

Chapter 17 Activity-Based Costing

- Explains the need for activity-based costing (ABC).
- Contrasts ABC to traditional costing systems.
- Identifies numerous activities, activity cost pools, and cost drivers.

- Discusses implications of value-added and non-value-added activities.
- Illustrates use of ABC in service industries.
- Reviews the benefits and limitations of ABC.
- Discusses the implications of activity levels.
- End-of-chapter appendix illustrates use of just-in-time inventory systems.
- *Changes:* Moved section on classification of activity levels from the appendix into the chapter; moved section on just-in-time inventory into chapter-end appendix; revised illustrations for clarity and presented some illustrations as spreadsheets.

Chapter 18 Cost-Volume-Profit

- Distinguishes between variable and fixed costs, and explains relevant range and mixed costs.
- Identified components and assumptions of CVP analysis.
- Discusses concept of contribution margin and illustrates CVP income statement.
- Illustrates calculation of break-even point.
- Discusses margin of safety and target net income.
- *Changes:* Moved section on target net income forward to better integrate with discussion on break-even analysis; moved appendix on variable costing to new chapter on variable costing (Chapter 19); and presented some illustrations as spreadsheets.

Chapter 19 Variable Costing: A Decision-Making Perspective

Entirely new chapter that:

- Explains the difference between absorption costing and variable costing.
- Discusses the effect that changes in production level and sales level have on net income measured under absorption costing versus variable costing.
- Discusses the relative merits of absorption costing versus variable costing for management decision making.
- Explains sales mix and its effect on break-even analysis.
- Promotes understanding of how operating leverage affects profitability.

Chapter 20 Budgetary Planning

- Discusses benefits of budgeting.
- Illustrates the process of assembling information for a master budget.
- Prepares budgeted income statement, balance sheet, and cash budget.
- Discusses use of budgets in merchandising, service, and not-for-profit enterprises.
- *Changes:* Added new discussions of participative budgeting and budgetary slack; added new

Business Insight boxes on participative budgeting at Time Warner and cash budgeting by engineering firm Alstom; and presented some illustrations as spreadsheets.

Chapter 21 Budgetary Control and Responsibility Accounting

- Explains how companies use budgets to control costs and operations.
- Contrasts static and flexible budgets.
- Uses a case study to illustrate usefulness of flexible budgets.
- Illustrates responsibility reporting systems.
- Defines cost centers, profit centers, and investment centers.
- Illustrates the computation and use of return on investment and (in a chapter appendix) residual income.
- *Changes:* Presented some illustrations as spreadsheets.

Chapter 22 Standard Costs and Balanced Scorecard

- Differentiates between a standard and a budget.
- Discusses advantages of standard costs and methods of computing.
- Illustrates computation of direct material variances, direct labor variances, and manufacturing overhead variance.
- Demonstrates analysis through comparison of actual with standard.
- Discusses basic features and usefulness of the balanced scorecard.
- Appendix illustrates the journal entries for a standard cost system.
- *Changes:* Added new section on balanced scorecard; added new *Business Insight* boxes on the development of shared industrial standards and the use of balanced scorecard at United Airlines; and presented some illustrations as spreadsheets.

Chapter 23 Incremental Analysis and Capital Budgeting

- Explains the concepts of relevant cost, opportunity cost, and sunk cost.
- Applies incremental analysis in the following decision settings: accept an order at a special price; make or buy; sell or process further, including discussion of joint costs; retain or replace equipment; eliminate an unprofitable segment, and allocate limited resources.
- Describes and illustrates four methods of evaluating capital expenditures: cash payback, net present value, internal rate of return, and annual rate of return.

- *Changes:* Added discussion on theory of constraints; added new *Business Insight* box on make-or-buy decision; added new *Accounting across the Organization* box on incremental analysis and off-shoring; added new *Business Insight* box on building risk into capital budgeting decisions; and presented some illustrations as spreadsheets.

Appendix A Specimen Financial Statements: Tootsie Roll Industries, Inc.

- Presents 2004 annual report, including notes, of Tootsie Roll Industries.

Appendix B Specimen Financial Statements: Hershey Food Corporation

- Presents key 2004 financial statements of Hershey Food.

Appendix C Time Value of Money

- Discusses simple and compound interest; presents tools for finding future value and present value of both single sums and annuities.

Appendix D Payroll Accounting

- Discusses internal control of payroll, determining and recording the payroll, and employer payroll taxes.

Appendix E Subsidiary Ledgers and Special Journals

- Discusses the nature and purpose of subsidiary ledgers; discusses use of special journals (sales, cash receipts, purchases, and cash payments journals), and the effects of special journals on the general journal.

Appendix F Accounting for Sole Proprietorships

- Discusses topics specific to accounting for sole proprietorships: increases and decreases in owner's equity, recording transactions, preparing financial statements, closing the books, and preparing a post-closing trial balance.

Appendix G Accounting for Partnerships

- Discusses the accounting for partnerships: forming partnerships and the partnership agreement, accounting for partnership formation, division of net income, financial statements, admission and withdrawal of partners, and liquidation.

Appendix H Investments

- Provides a comprehensive discussion of reporting and analyzing investments; discusses statement of cash flows presentation of investments.

Active Teaching and Learning Supplementary Material

Accounting 2e features a full line of teaching and learning resources. Driven by the same basic beliefs as the textbook, these supplements provide a consistent and well-integrated learning system. This hands-on, real-world package guides instructors through the process of *active learning and gives them the tools to create an interactive learning environment. With its emphasis on activities, exercises, and the Internet, the package encourages students to take an active role in the course and prepares them for decision making in a real-world context.*

 ## Kimmel's Integrated Technology Solutions

WileyPLUS—For Instructors. WileyPLUS is an online suite of resources that contains online homework, drill, and practice activities with access to an online version of the text. WileyPLUS gives instructors the technology to create an environment where students reach their full potential and experience academic success. Instructor resources include a wealth of presentation and preparation tools, easy-to-navigate assignment and assessment tools, and a complete system to administer and manage the course exactly as an instructor wishes. In addition, a premium version of WileyPLUS is available that will include selected problems powered by new general ledger software and Excel Working Papers.

WileyPLUS is built around the activities instructors regularly perform:

- **Prepare and present class presentations** using relevant Wiley resources such as PowerPoint™ slides, image galleries, animations, and other WileyPLUS materials. Instructors can also upload their own resources or web pages to use in conjunction with Wiley materials.

- **Create assignments** by choosing from end-of-chapter exercises, problems, and test bank questions organized by chapter, study objective, level of difficulty, and source—or add one's own questions. Algorithmic versions are available for each exercise and problems, allowing for additional drill and practice. WileyPLUS automatically grades students' homework and quizzes and records the results in an instructor's gradebook.

- **Offer context-sensitive help to students, 24/7.** When the instructor assigns homework or quizzes, he or she decides if and when students get access to hints, solutions, or answers where appropriate. Or students can be linked to relevant sections of their complete, online text for additional help whenever and wherever they need it most.

- **Track student progress.** Instructors can analyze students' results and assess their level of understanding on an individual and class level using the WileyPLUS gradebook, and can export data to their own personal gradebooks.

Seamlessly integrate all of the rich WileyPLUS content and resources with the power and convenience of a **WebCT or Blackboard course**—with a single sign-on.

WileyPLUS—For Students. WileyPLUS for students offers **"Read, Study, and Practice"** resources that can include the entire online textbook, select interactive, and end-of-chapter demonstration problems. Additional resources can include interactive chapter reviews, web-based tutorials, and other problem-solving resources.

- An **"Assignment"** area helps students stay "on task" by containing all homework assignments in one location. Many homework problems contain a link to the relevant sections of the ebook, providing students with context-sensitive help that allows them to conquer problem-solving obstacles.

- A **Personal Gradebook** will allow each student to view results from past assignments at any time.

Book Companion Site–for Instructors. On this website instructors will find electronic versions of the Solutions Manual, Test Bank, Instructor's Manual, Computerized Test Bank, and other resources.

Book Companion Site–for Students. The *Accounting* student website provides a wealth of support materials that will help students develop their conceptual understanding of class material and increase their ability to solve problems. On this website students will find Excel templates, PowerPoint presentations, web quizzing, and other resources. In addition, the new Problems: Set C can be accessed at this site.

Instructor's Active Teaching Aids

We offer useful supplements for instructors with varying levels of experience and different instructional circumstances.

Instructor's Resource CD. The Instructor's Resource CD (IR CD) contains an electronic version of all instructor supplements.

Solutions Manual, Volumes I and II. The Solutions Manual contains detailed solutions to all questions, brief exercises, exercises, and problems in the textbook as well as suggested answers to the questions and cases. Each chapter includes an *assignment classification table*, an *assignment characteristics table*, and a *Bloom's taxonomy table*. Print is large and bold for easy readability in lecture settings. A team of independent accuracy checkers carefully verified the Solutions Manual.

Solution Transparencies, Volumes I and II. The solution transparencies feature detailed solutions to brief exercises, exercises, problems, and Broadening Your Perspectives activities. They feature large, bold type for better projection and easy readability in large-classroom settings.

Instructor's Manual, Volumes I and II. Included in each chapter are lecture outlines with teaching tips, and review quizzes.

Teaching Transparencies. The teaching transparencies are four-color acetate images detailing important concepts in each chapter.

Test Bank, Volumes I and II. With *over 400 new questions*, the test bank allows instructors to tailor examinations according to study objectives and Bloom's taxonomy. Achievement tests, comprehensive examinations, and a final exam are included.

Computerized Test Bank. The computerized test bank allows instructors to create and print multiple versions of the same test by scrambling the order of all questions found in the print test bank. The computerized test bank also allows users to customize exams by altering or adding new problems.

PowerPoint™ Presentation Material. The PowerPoint™ presentations contain a combination of key concepts, images, and problems from the textbook. New review exercises are included in each chapter to encourage classroom participation.

WebCT and Blackboard. WebCT or Blackboard offer an integrated set of course management tools that enable instructors to easily design, develop, and manage Web-based and Web-enhanced courses.

Student Active Learning Aids

The Accounting Principles Website. The student website at **www.wiley.com/college/kimmel** provides a wealth of support materials that will help students develop their conceptual understanding of course concepts and increase their ability to solve problems. On this website students will find PowerPoint™ presentations, Excel workbook and templates, web quizzing, and other resources. Also included there are the C Problems.

Working Papers. Working Papers are templates for end-of-chapter brief exercises, exercises, problems, and cases. A convenient resource for organizing and completing homework assignments, they demonstrate how to correctly present homework solutions.

Excel Working Papers. An electronic version of the print working papers, these Excel-formatted templates help students properly format and present end-of-chapter textbook solutions.

Study Guide, Volumes I and II. Each study guide chapter contains a detailed chapter review, demonstration problems, true/false, multiple-choice, and matching questions, as well as comprehensive exercises. Solutions are provided.

GLS General Ledger Software. General ledger software allows students to solve select end-of-chapter text problems using a computerized accounting system. Problems available in general ledger software are identified by an icon next to end-of-chapter textbook exercises and problems.

Excel Workbook and Templates. This online manual and collection of Excel templates allow students to complete select end-of-chapter exercises and problems identified by a spreadsheet icon in the textbook.

Acknowledgments

We benefited greatly from the input of focus group participants, manuscript reviewers, ancillary authors, and proofers. We greatly appreciate the constructive suggestions and innovative ideas of the reviewers and the creativity and accuracy of the ancillary authors and checkers.

Ancillary Authors, Contributors, and Proofers

Sheila Ammons, *Austin Community College* – Test Bank and Instructor's Manual author

John Borke, *University of Wisconsin – Platteville* – Text and Solutions Manual proofer

Molly Brown, *James Madison University* – Test Bank author

Lee Cannell, *El Paso Community College* – Test Bank author

James M. Emig, *Villanova University* – Solutions Manual and Test Bank proofer

James M. Emig, *Villanova University* – Solutions Manual, Test Bank, and Study Guide proofer

Larry R. Falcetto, *Emporia Sate University* – Test Bank and Checklist author, Text and Solutions Manual proofer

Janet Farler, *Pima Community College* – Test Bank author

Cecelia M. Fewox, *College of Charleston* – Study Guide author

Jessica Frazier, *Eastern Kentucky University* – Instructor's Manual author

Carol Hartley, *Providence College* – PowerPoint author

Douglas W. Kieso, *Aurora University* – Study Guide author

Laura McNally – WileyPLUS author and proofer

Patricia Mounce, *University of Central Arkansas* – Instructor's Manual author

Rex Schildhouse, *San Diego Community College* – Excel Workbook and Templates author

Alice Sineaath, *Forsyth Technical Community College* – Test Bank proofer

Eileen Shifflett, *James Madison University* – Test Bank author

Teresa Speck, *St. Mary's University* – Text and Solutions Manual proofer

Ellen L. Sweatt, *Georgia Perimeter College* – PowerPoint author

Diane Tanner, *University of North Florida* – Test Bank author

Sheila Viel, *University of Wisconsin– Milwaukee* – Text and Solutions Manual proofer

Dan R. Ward, *University of Louisiana at Lafayette* – PowerPoint author

Suzanne Ward, *University of Louisiana at Lafayette* – PowerPoint author

Dick D. Wasson, *Southwestern College* – Working Papers and Excel Working Papers author, Text and Solutions Manual proofer

Melanie Yan – WileyPLUS author and proofer

We appreciate the exemplary support and professional commitment given us by our publisher Don Fowley, executive editor Chris DeJohn, marketing manager Clay Stone, associate director of marketing Frank Lyman, assistant editor Brian Kamins, project editor Ed Brislin, editorial assistant Karolina Zarychta, program assistant Kristin Babroski, senior media editor Allie Morris, development editor Ann Torbert, vice-president of higher education production and manufacturing Ann Berlin, illustration editor Anna Melhorn, photo editor Elle Wagner, senior production editor Valerie Vargas, outside project manager Suzanne Ingrao, product manager Jane Shifflet at TechBooks, and manuscript assistant Cassie Schulenburg.

We welcome your thoughts and suggestions about the book. You can send your thought to us via email at *AccountingAuthors@yahoo.com*.

PAUL D. KIMMEL
Milwaukee, Wisconsin

JERRY J. WEYGANDT
Madison, Wisconsin

DONALD E. KIESO
DeKalb, Illinois

Study Objectives at the beginning of each chapter give you a framework for learning the specific concepts covered in the chapter. Each study objective reappears in the margin where the concept is discussed. You can review the concepts related to the study objectives in the **Summary** at the end of the chapter text.

The Navigator is a learning system designed to guide you through each chapter and help you succeed in learning the material. It consists of (1) a checklist at the beginning of the chapter, which outlines text features and study aids you will need, and (2) a series of check boxes that prompt you to use the learning aids in the chapter and set priorities as you study.

CHAPTER 1

Introduction to Financial Statements

STUDY OBJECTIVES

After studying this chapter, you should be able to:

1 Describe the primary forms of business organization.
2 Identify the users and uses of accounting information.
3 Explain the three principal types of business activity.
4 Describe the content and purpose of each of the financial statements.
5 Explain the meaning of assets, liabilities, and stockholders' equity, and state the basic accounting equation.
6 Describe the components that supplement the financial statements in an annual report.

THE NAVIGATOR

- Scan Study Objectives
- Read Feature Story
- Read Preview
- Read text and answer Before You Go On p. 11 p. 17 p. 24
- Work Using the Decision Toolkit
- Review Summary of Study Objectives
- Work Demonstration Problem
- Answer Self-Study Questions
- Complete Assignments

FEATURE STORY

Knowing the Numbers

Many students who take this course do not plan to be accountants. If you are in that group, you might be thinking, "If I'm not going to be an accountant, why do I need to know accounting?" In response, consider this quote from Harold Geneen, the former chairman of IT&T: "To be good at your business, you have to know the numbers—cold." Success in any business comes back to the numbers. You will rely on them to make decisions, and managers will use them to evaluate your performance. That is true whether your job involves marketing, production, management, or information systems.

In business, accounting and financial statements are the means for communicating the numbers. If you don't know how to read financial statements, you can't really know your business.

Many companies spend significant resources teaching their employees basic accounting so that they can read financial statements and understand how their actions affect the company's financial results. One such company is Springfield ReManufacturing Corporation (SRC). When Jack Stack and 11 other managers purchased SRC for 10 cents a share, it was a failing division of International Harvester. Jack had 119 employees who were counting on him for their livelihood, and he knew that the new com-

The **Feature Story** helps you picture how the chapter topic relates to the real world of accounting and business. References in the chapter to the Feature Story will help you put new ideas in context, organize them, and remember them.

PREVIEW OF CHAPTER 1

How do you start a business? How do you make it grow into a widely recognized brand name like Tootsie Roll? How do you determine whether your business is making or losing money? When you need to expand your operations, where do you get money to finance expansion—should you borrow, should you issue stock, should you use your own funds? How do you convince lenders to lend you money or investors to buy your stock? Success in business requires making countless decisions, and decisions require financial information.

The purpose of this chapter is to show you what role accounting plays in providing financial information. The content and organization of the chapter are as follows.

INTRODUCTION TO FINANCIAL STATEMENTS

Forms of Business Organization	Users and Uses of Financial Information	Business Activities	Communicating with Users	A Quick Look at Tootsie Roll's Financial Statements
• Sole proprietorship • Partnership • Corporation	• Internal users • External users • Ethics in financial reporting	• Financing • Investing • Operating	• Income statement • Retained earnings statement • Balance sheet • Statement of cash flows • Interrelationships of statements	• Income statement • Retained earnings statement • Balance sheet • Statement of cash flows • Other elements of an annual report

THE NAVIGATOR

The **Preview** links the Feature Story with the major topics of the chapter and describes the purpose of the chapter. It then outlines the topics that are discussed. This narrative and visual preview helps you organize the information you are learning.

Accounting across the Organization

Accounting can even serve as a useful recruiting tool for the human resources department. **Rhino Foods**, located in Burlington, VT, is a manufacturer of specialty ice cream novelties and ice cream ingredients. Its corporate website includes the following paragraphs:

"Wouldn't it be great to work where you were part of a team? Where your input and hard work made a difference? Where you weren't kept in the dark about what management was thinking?

Well—it's not a dream! It's the way we do business at Rhino Foods on Industrial Parkway in Burlington. Rhino Foods believes in family, honesty and open communication—we really care about and appreciate our employees—and it shows. Operating results are posted and monthly group meetings inform all employees about what's happening in the Company. Employees also share in the Company's profits, in addition to having an excellent comprehensive *benefits* package."

Source: www.rhinofoods.com/workforus/workforus.html.

 What are the benefits to the company and to the employees of making the financial statements available to all employees?

EXTERNAL USERS

There are several types of **external users** of accounting information. **Investors** (owners) use accounting information to make decisions to buy, hold, or sell stock. **Creditors** such as suppliers and bankers use accounting information to evaluate the risks of granting credit or lending money. Some questions that investors and creditors may ask about a company are shown in Illustration 1-3.

The information needs and questions of other external users vary considerably. **Taxing authorities,** such as the Internal Revenue Service, want to know whether the company complies with the tax laws. **Customers** are interested in whether

Illustration 1-3

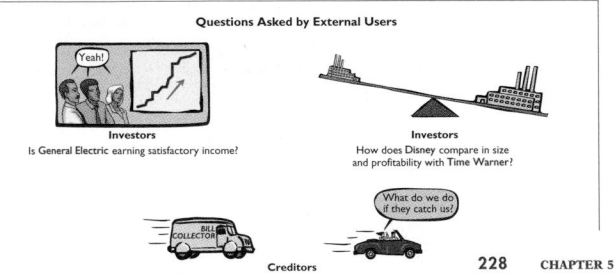

Questions Asked by External Users

Investors
Is General Electric earning satisfactory income?

Investors
How does Disney compare in size and profitability with Time Warner?

Creditors
Will United Airlines be able to pay its debts as they come due?

Accounting across the Organization boxes demonstrate the use of accounting to address issues in marketing, finance, management, and other functional areas of business. If you are not an accounting major, these should be of particular interest. (A guideline answer to the question at the end of boxes appears near the end of the chapter.)

Color illustrations, such as this **infographic,** help you visualize and apply information as you study. They reinforce important concepts and therefore often contain material that may appear on exams.

---

228   CHAPTER 5   Merchandising Operations and the Multiple-Step Income Statement

Junot Diaz Company

Sept.	5	Accounts Receivable	1,500	
		Sales		1,500
		(To record credit sale)		
	5	Cost of Goods Sold	800	
		Merchandise Inventory		800
		(To record cost of goods sold on account)		
Sept.	8	Sales Returns and Allowances	200	
		Accounts Receivable		200
		(To record credit granted for receipt of returned goods)		
	8	Merchandise Inventory	105	
		Cost of Goods Sold		105
		(To record cost of goods returned)		

THE NAVIGATOR

Income Statement Presentation

Companies widely use two forms of the income statement. One is the **single-step income statement.** The statement is so named because only one step, subtracting total expenses from total revenues, is required in determining net income (or net loss).

In a single-step statement, all data are classified into two categories: (1) **revenues,** which include both operating revenues and nonoperating revenues and gains (for example, interest revenue and gain on sale of equipment); and (2) **expenses,** which include cost of goods sold, operating expenses, and non-operating expenses and losses (for example, interest expense, loss on sale of equipment, or income tax expense). The single-step income statement is the form we have used thus far in the text. Illustration 5-5 shows a single-step statement for Wal-Mart.

STUDY OBJECTIVE 4

Distinguish between a single-step and a multiple-step income statement.

Study Objectives reappear in the margins where the related topic is discussed. End-of-chapter assignments are keyed to study objectives.

Financial statements appear regularly throughout the book. Those from actual companies are identified by a logo or photo. Often, numbers or categories are highlighted in red to draw your attention to key information.

Illustration 5-5
Single-step income statements

WAL★MART
ALWAYS LOW PRICES. *Always*

WAL-MART STORES, INC.
Income Statements
(in millions)

	For the years ended January 31	
	2004	**2003**
Revenues		
Net sales	$256,329	$229,616
Other revenues, net	2,352	1,961
	258,681	231,577
Expenses		
Cost of goods sold	198,747	178,299
Selling, general, and administrative expenses	44,909	39,983
Interest expense	832	927
Other expense	21	56
Income taxes	5,118	4,357
	249,627	223,622
Net income	$ 9,054	$ 7,955

Business Insight
Ethics Perspective

Allegations of abuse of the revenue recognition principle have become all too common in recent years. For example, it was alleged that Krispy Kreme sometimes doubled the number of doughnuts shipped to wholesale customers at the end of a quarter to boost quarterly results. The customers shipped the unsold doughnuts back after the beginning of the next quarter for a refund. Conversely, Computer Associates International was accused of backdating sales—that is, saying that a sale that occurred at the beginning of one quarter occurred at the end of the previous quarter in order to achieve the previous quarter's sales targets.

 What motivates sales executives and finance and accounting executives to participate in activities that result in inaccurate reporting of revenues?

BEFORE YOU GO ON . . .

▶Review It

1. What are the revenue recognition and matching principles?
2. What are the differences between the cash and accrual bases of accounting?

THE NAVIGATOR

The Basics of Adjusting Entries

In order for revenues to be recorded in the period in which they are earned, and for expenses to be recognized in the period in which they are incurred, companies make adjusting entries. **Adjusting entries ensure that the revenue recognition and matching principles are followed**.

Adjusting entries are necessary because the **trial balance**—the first pulling together of the transaction data—may not contain up-to-date and complete data. This is true for several reasons:

1. Some events are not recorded daily because it is not efficient to do so. Examples are the use of supplies and the earning of wages by employees.
2. Some costs are not recorded during the accounting period because these costs expire with the passage of time rather than as a result of recurring

STUDY OBJECTIVE

Explain why adjusting entries are needed, and identify the major types of adjusting entries.

> **Business Insight** boxes give you more glimpses into how actual companies make decisions using accounting information. These high-interest boxes are classified by different points of view—ethics, investor, international, the management and e-business perspectives. Questions at the end of boxes test your understanding. (Guideline answers appear near the end of the chapter.)

> **Key terms** and concepts are printed in blue where they are first explained in the text. They are listed and defined again in the end-of-chapter **Glossary**.

---

224 **CHAPTER 5** Merchandising Operations and the Multiple-Step Income Statement

When an invoice is paid within the discount period, the amount of the discount decreases Merchandise Inventory. Why? Because the merchandiser records inventory at its cost and, by paying within the discount period, it has reduced that cost. To illustrate, assume Sauk Stereo pays the balance due of $3,500 (gross invoice price of $3,800 less purchase returns and allowances of $300) on May 14, the last day of the discount period. The cash discount is $70 ($3,500 × 2%), and the amount of cash Sauk Stereo paid is $3,430 ($3,500 − $70). The entry Sauk makes to record its May 14 payment decreases Accounts Payable by the amount of the gross invoice price, reduces Merchandise Inventory by the $70 discount, and reduces Cash by the net amount owed.

A = L + SE
−3,500
−3,430
−70

Cash Flows
−3,430

May 14	Accounts Payable	3,500	
	Cash		3,430
	Merchandise Inventory		70
	(To record payment within discount period)		

If Sauk Stereo failed to take the discount and instead made full payment of $3,500 on June 3, Sauk would debit Accounts Payable and credit Cash for $3,500 each.

A = L + SE
−3,500
−3,500

Cash Flows
−3,500

June 3	Accounts Payable	3,500	
	Cash		3,500
	(To record payment with no discount taken)		

A merchandising company usually should take all available discounts. Passing up the discount may be viewed as **paying interest** for use of the money. For example, passing up the discount offered by PW Audio would be like Sauk Stereo paying an interest rate of 2% for the use of $3,500 for 20 days. This is the equivalent of an annual interest rate of approximately 36.5% (2% × 365/20). Obviously, it would be better for Sauk Stereo to borrow at prevailing bank interest rates of 6% to 10% than to lose the discount.

> **Accounting equation analyses** appear in the margin next to key journal entries. They will help you understand the impact of an accounting transaction on the financial statements and on the company's cash flows.

---

of rising prices. For example, at Houston Electronics, income taxes are $7 under LIFO, compared to $990 under FIFO. The tax savings of $240 makes cash available for use in the business.

Decision Toolkit

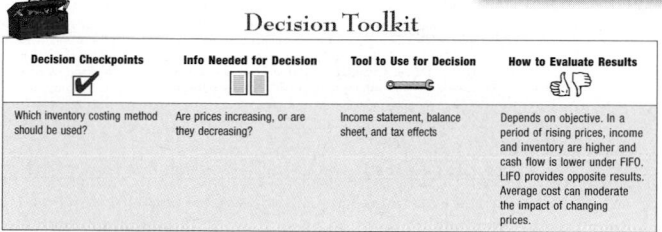

Decision Checkpoints	Info Needed for Decision	Tool to Use for Decision	How to Evaluate Results
Which inventory costing method should be used?	Are prices increasing, or are they decreasing?	Income statement, balance sheet, and tax effects	Depends on objective. In a period of rising prices, income and inventory are higher and cash flow is lower under FIFO. LIFO provides opposite results. Average cost can moderate the impact of changing prices.

USING INVENTORY COST FLOW METHODS CONSISTENTLY

Whatever cost flow method a company chooses, it should use that method consistently from one accounting period to another. Consistent application enhances the comparability of financial statements over successive time periods. In contrast, using the FIFO method one year and the LIFO method the next year would make it difficult to compare the net incomes of the two years.

Although consistent application is preferred, it does not mean that a company may *never* change its method of inventory costing. When a company adopts a different method, it should disclose in the financial statements the change and its effects on net income. A typical disclosure is shown in Illustration 6-14, using information from recent financial statements of the Quaker Oats Company.

Helpful Hint As you learned in Chapter 2, consistency and comparability are important characteristics of accounting information.

> Each chapter presents **decision tools** that help decision makers analyze and solve business problems. At the end of the text discussion, a **Decision Toolkit** summarizes the key features of a decision tool, and it reviews why and how you would use it.

> **Helpful Hints** in the margins are like having an instructor with you as you read. They further clarify concepts being discussed.

STOCKHOLDERS' EQUITY

Stockholders' equity consists of two parts: common stock and retained earnings. Companies record as **common stock** the investments of assets into the business by the stockholders. They record as **retained earnings** the income retained for use in the business. These two parts, combined, make up **stockholders' equity** on the balance sheet. In Illustration 2-2 Franklin reported common stock of $14,000 and retained earnings of $20,050.

Alternative Terminology
Common stock is sometimes called *capital stock.*

> **Alternative Terminology** notes present synonymous terms that you may come across in practice.

BEFORE YOU GO ON . . .

▶**Review It**

1. What are the major sections in a classified balance sheet?
2. What is the primary determining factor to distinguish current assets from long-term assets?
3. What was Tootsie Roll's largest current asset at December 31, 2004? (The answer to this question appears on page 97.)
4. Where on the balance sheet do companies report accumulated depreciation?

▶**Do It**

Baxter Hoffman recently received the following information related to Hoffman Corporation's December 31, 2007, balance sheet.

Prepaid expenses	$ 2,300	Inventory	$3,400
Cash	800	Accumulated depreciation	2,700
Property, plant, and equipment	10,700	Accounts receivable	1,100

Prepare the assets section of Hoffman Corporation's balance sheet.

Action Plan

• Present current assets first. Current assets are cash and other resources that the company reasonably expects to consume in one year.
• Present current assets in the order in which the company expects to convert them into cash.
• Subtract accumulated depreciation from property, plant, and equipment to determine net property, plant, and equipment.

Solution

HOFFMAN CORPORATION
Balance Sheet (partial)
December 31, 2007

Assets

Current assets		
Cash	$ 800	
Accounts receivable	1,100	
Inventory	3,400	
Prepaid expenses	2,300	
Total current assets		$ 7,600
Property, plant, and equipment	10,700	
Less: Accumulated depreciation	2,700	8,000
Total assets		$15,600

THE NAVIGATOR

> **Before You Go On** sections follow each key topic. *Review It* questions prompt you to stop and review the key points you have just studied. If you cannot answer these questions, you should go back and read the section again. *Review It* questions marked with the Tootsie Roll icon direct you to find information in Tootsie Roll Industries' 2004 Annual Report, printed in Appendix A. Answers appear at the end of the chapter.

> Brief *Do It* exercises ask you to put to work your newly acquired knowledge. They outline an **Action Plan** necessary to complete the exercise and show a **Solution**.

> A **Using the Decision Toolkit** exercise follows the final set of *Review It* questions in the chapter. It asks you to use business information and the decision tools presented in the chapter. You should think through the questions related to the decision before you study the **Solution** provided.

Using the Decision Toolkit

Reebok remains one of Nike's fiercest competitors. In such a competitive and rapidly changing environment, one wrong step can spell financial disaster. After bottoming out at the end of 1999, Reebok's stock has rebounded sharply.

Instructions

The following facts are available for Reebok. Using this information, evaluate its (1) dividend record and (2) earnings performance, and contrast them with those for Nike for 2003 and 2004. Nike's earnings per share were $3.59 in 2004 and $2.80 in 2003.

(in thousands except per share data)	2004	2003	2002
Dividends declared	$ 17,839	$ 8,847	0
Net income	$ 192,425	$ 157,254	$126,458
Preferred stock dividends	0	0	0
Shares outstanding at end of year	101,827	101,081	99,235
Common stockholders' equity	$1,219,956	$1,033,710	$884,570

Solution

1. *Dividend record:* A measure to evaluate dividend record is the payout ratio. For Reebok, this measure in 2004 and 2003 is calculated as shown below.

	2004	2003
Payout ratio	$\dfrac{\$17,839}{\$192,425} = 9.3\%$	$\dfrac{\$8,847}{\$157,254} = 5.6\%$

Nike's payout ratio remained nearly constant at 21%. Reebok's payout ratio increased significantly from 2003 to 2004 but was still less than half Nike's ratio.

2. *Earnings performance:* There are many measures of earnings performance. Some of those presented thus far in the book were earnings per share (page 55) and the return on common stockholders' equity ratio (this chapter). These measures for Reebok in 2004 and 2003 are calculated as shown here.

	2004	2003
Earnings per share	$\dfrac{\$192,425 - 0}{(101,827 + 101,081)/2} = \$1.90$	$\dfrac{\$157,254 - 0}{(101,081 + 99,235)/2} = \$1.57$
Return on common stockholders' equity ratio	$\dfrac{\$192,425 - 0}{(\$1,219,956 + \$1,033,710)/2} = 17.1\%$	$\dfrac{\$157,254 - 0}{(\$1,033,710 + \$884,570)/2} = 16.4\%$

From 2003 to 2004, Reebok's net income improved 22% and its earnings per share increased 21%. During the same time period Nike's earnings per share increased 28%.

Reebok's return on common stockholders' equity increased from 16.4% to 17.1%. While this represents a healthy increase, it is still less than Nike's 21.6%.

THE NAVIGATOR

The **Summary of Study Objectives** reviews the main points related to the Study Objectives. It provides you with another opportunity to review what you have learned as well as to see how the key topics within the chapter fit together.

---

130 **CHAPTER 3** The Accounting Information System

Summary of Study Objectives

1 *Analyze the effect of business transactions on the basic accounting equation.* Each business transaction must have a dual effect on the accounting equation. For example, if an individual asset is increased, there must be a corresponding (a) decrease in another asset, or (b) increase in a specific liability, or (c) increase in stockholders'equity.

2 *Explain what an account is and how it helps in the recording process.* An account is an individual accounting record of increases and decreases in specific asset, liability, and stockholders' equity items.

3 *Define debits and credits and explain how they are used to record business transactions.* The terms *debit* and *credit* are synonymous with *left* and *right*. Assets, dividends, and expenses are increased by debits and decreased by credits. Liabilities, common stock, retained earnings, and revenues are increased by credits and decreased by debits.

4 *Identify the basic steps in the recording process.* The basic steps in the recording process are: (a) analyze each transaction in terms of its effect on the accounts, (b) enter the transaction information in a journal, and (c) transfer the journal information to the appropriate accounts in the ledger.

5 *Explain what a journal is and how it helps in the recording process.* The initial accounting record of a transaction is entered in a journal before the data are entered in the accounts. A journal (a) discloses in one place the complete effect of a transaction, (b) provides a chronological record of transactions, and (c) prevents or locates errors because the debit and credit amounts for each entry can be readily compared.

6 *Explain what a ledger is and how it helps in the recording process.* The entire group of accounts maintained by a company is referred to collectively as a ledger. The ledger keeps in one place all the information about changes in specific account balances.

7 *Explain what posting is and how it helps in the recording process.* Posting is the procedure of transferring journal entries to the ledger accounts. This phase of the recording process accumulates the effects of journalized transactions in the individual accounts.

8 *Explain the purposes of a trial balance.* A trial balance is a list of accounts and their balances at a given time. The primary purpose of the trial balance is to prove the mathematical equality of debits and credits after posting. A trial balance also uncovers errors in journalizing and posting and is useful in preparing financial statements.

THE NAVIGATOR

The **WileyPLUS** icon at the chapter Summary and other places in the assignment materials indicates electronic book content that will enable you to review the text and complete homework online.

At the end of each chapter, the **Decision Toolkit— A Summary** reviews the techniques for decision making that were covered in the chapter.

Decision Toolkit—A Summary

Decision Checkpoints	Info Needed for Decision	Tool to Use for Decision	How to Evaluate Results
Has an accounting transaction occurred?	Details of the event	Accounting equation	If the event affected assets, liabilities, or stockholders' equity, then record as a transaction.
How do you determine that debits equal credits?	All account balances	Trial balance	List the account titles and their balances; total the debit and credit colums; verify equality.

Glossary

Account An individual accounting record of increases and decreases in specific asset, liability, or stockholders' equity items. (p. 108)

Accounting information system The system of collecting and processing transaction data and communicating financial information to interested parties. (p. 100)

Accounting transactions Events that require recording in the financial statements because they affect assets, liabilities, or stockholders' equity. (p. 101)

Chart of accounts A list of a company's accounts. (p. 118)

Credit The right side of an account. (p. 109)

Debit The left side of an account. (p. 109)

Double-entry system A system that records the dual effect of each transaction in appropriate accounts. (p. 109)

General journal The most basic form of journal. (p. 114)

General ledger A ledger that contains all asset, liability, and stockholders' equity accounts. (p. 117)

The **Glossary** defines all the **key terms** and **concepts** introduced in the chapter. Page references help you find any terms you need to study further.

Demonstration Problem

Rolman Corporation is authorized to issue 1,000,000 shares of $5 par value common stock. In its first year the company has the following stock transactions.

Jan. 10 Issued 400,000 shares of stock at $8 per share.
Sept. 1 Purchased 10,000 shares of common stock for the treasury at $9 per share.
Dec. 24 Declared a cash dividend of 10 cents per share on common stock outstanding.

Instructions
(a) Journalize the transactions.
(b) Prepare the stockholders' equity section of the balance sheet assuming the company had retained earnings of $150,600 at December 31.

Action Plan
• When common stock has a par value, credit Common Stock for par value and Paid-in Capital in Excess of Par Value for the amount above par value.
• Debit the Treasury Stock account at cost.

Solution to Demonstration Problem

(a) Jan. 10	Cash	3,200,000	
	Common Stock		2,000,000
	Paid-in Capital in Excess of Par Value		1,200,000
	(To record issuance of 400,000 shares of $5 par value stock)		
Sept. 1	Treasury Stock	90,000	
	Cash		90,000
	(To record purchase of 10,000 shares of treasury stock at cost)		
Dec. 24	Retained Earnings	39,000	
	Dividends Payable		39,000
	(To record declaration of 10 cents per share cash dividend)		

(b)
ROLMAN CORPORATION
Balance Sheet (partial)

Stockholders' equity
Paid-in capital
Capital stock
Common stock, $5 par value, 1,000,000 shares
authorized, 400,000 shares issued, 390,000 outstanding $2,000,000
Additional paid-in capital in excess of par value 1,200,000
Total paid-in capital 3,200,000
Retained earnings 150,600
Total paid-in capital and retained earnings 3,350,600
Less: Treasury stock (10,000 shares) 90,000
Total stockholders' equity $3,260,600

THE NAVIGATOR

A **Demonstration Problem** is the final step before you begin homework. These sample problems provide you with an **Action Plan** in the margin that lists the strategies needed to approach and solve the problem. The **Solution** demonstrates both the form and content of complete answers.

Self-Study Questions provide a practice test, keyed to Study Objectives, that gives you an opportunity to check your knowledge of important topics. Answers appear at the end of the chapter. Additional opportunities for self-testing are available through WileyPLUS.

Questions allow you to explain your understanding of concepts and relationships from the chapter. Use them to help prepare for class discussion and tests.

Brief Exercises help you focus on one Study Objective at a time and thus help you build confidence in your basic skills and knowledge.

Exercises, which are more difficult than Brief Exercises, help you continue to build confidence in your ability to use the material learned in the chapter.

This icon indicates review and homework material that relates to issues in marketing, finance, management, and other business areas other than accounting.

The tool icon ⚬━━━⚬ indicates review and homework material that asks you to use the **decision tools** presented in the chapter.

Certain Exercises and Problems, marked with a pencil icon ◁▭▭▭ help you practice **business writing skills,** which are much in demand among employers.

Questions 31

Self-Study Questions

Answers are at the end of the chapter.

(SO 1) **1.** Which is *not* one of the three forms of business organization?
(a) Sole proprietorship. (c) Partnership.
(b) Creditorship. (d) Corporation.

(SO 1) **2.** Which is an advantage of corporations relative to partnerships and sole proprietorships?
(a) Lower taxes.
(b) Harder to transfer ownership.
(c) Reduced legal liability for investors.
(d) Most common form of organization.

(SO 2) **3.** Which statement about users of accounting information is *incorrect*?
(a) Management is considered an internal user.
(b) Taxing authorities are considered external users.
(c) Present creditors are considered external users.
(d) Regulatory authorities are considered internal users.

(SO 3) **4.** Which is *not* one of the three primary business activities?
(a) Financing. (c) Advertising.
(b) Operating. (d) Investing.

(SO 3, 4) **5.** Net income will result during a time period when:
(a) assets exceed liabilities.

(c) The financing section.
(d) The cash flow statement does not give this information.

(SO 5) **7.** Which financial statement reports assets, liabilities, and stockholders' equity?
(a) Income statement.
(b) Retained earnings statement.
(c) Balance sheet.
(d) Statement of cash flows.

(SO 5) **8.** Stockholders' equity represents:
(a) claims of creditors.
(b) claims of employees.
(c) the difference between revenues and expenses.
(d) claims of owners.

(SO 5) **9.** As of December 31, 2007, Stoneland Corporation has assets of $3,500 and stockholders' equity of $2,000. What are the liabilities for Stoneland Corporation as of December 31, 2007?
(a) $1,500. (c) $2,500.
(b) $1,000. (d) $2,000.

(SO 6) **10.** ⚬━━━⚬ The segment of a corporation's annual report that describes the corporation's accounting methods is the:
(a) notes to the financial statements.
(b) management discussion and analysis.
(c) auditor's report.
(d) income statement.

Go to the book's website, **www.wiley.com/college/kimmel**, to access additional Self-Study Questions.

Questions

1. What are the three basic forms of business organizations?

2. What are the advantages to a business of being formed as a corporation? What are the disadvantages?

3. What are the advantages to a business of being formed as a partnership or sole proprietorship? What are the disadvantages?

4. "Accounting is ingrained in our society and is vital to our economic system." Do you agree? Explain.

5. Who are the internal users of accounting data? How does accounting provide relevant data to the internal users?

6. Who are the external users of accounting data? Give examples.

7. What are the three main types of business activity? Give examples of each activity.

8. Listed here are some items found in the financial statements of Ellyn Toth, Inc. Indicate in which financial statement(s) each item would appear.
(a) Service revenue. (d) Accounts receivable.
(b) Equipment. (e) Common stock.
(c) Advertising expense. (f) Wages payable.

9. ⚬━━━⚬ Why would a bank want to monitor the dividend payment practices of the corporations it lends money to?

---

78 CHAPTER 2 A Further Look at Financial Statements

Brief Exercises

Classify accounts on balance sheet.
(SO 1)

BE2-1 The following are the major balance sheet classifications:

Current assets (CA)   Current liabilities (CL)
Long-term investments (LTI) Long-term liabilities (LTL)
Property, plant, and equipment (PPE) Common stock (CS)
Intangible assets (IA)   Retained earnings (RE)

Match each of the following accounts to its proper balance sheet classification.

___ Accounts payable   ___ Income tax payable
___ Accounts receivable   ___ Investment in long-term bonds
___ Accumulated depreciation ___ Land
___ Building   ___ Merchandise inventory
___ Cash   ___ Patent
___ Goodwill   ___ Supplies

Identify placement of items on a multiple-step income statement.
(SO 4)

BE5-6 Explain where each of these items would appear on a multiple-step income statement: gain on sale of equipment, cost of goods sold, depreciation expense, and sales returns and allowances.

Compute net purchases and cost of goods purchased.
(SO 5)

BE5-7 Assume that Roshek Company uses a periodic inventory system and has these account balances: Purchases $424,000; Purchase Returns and Allowances $11,000; Purchase Discounts $7,000; and Freight-in $16,000. Determine net purchases and cost of goods purchased.

---

194 CHAPTER 4 Accrual Accounting Concepts

Exercises

Identify point of revenue recognition.
(SO 1)

E4-1 The following independent situations require professional judgement for determining when to recognize revenue from the transactions.
(a) Southwest Airlines sells you an advance-purchase airline ticket in September for your flight home at Christmas.
(b) Ultimate Electronics sells you a home theatre on a "no money down, no interest, and no payments for one year" promotional deal.
(c) The Toronto Blue Jays sell season tickets online to games in the Skydome. Fans can purchase the tickets at any time, although the season doesn't officially begin until April. The major league baseball season runs from April through October.
(d) You borrow money in August from RBC Financial Group. The loan and the interest are repayable in full in November.
(e) In August, you order a sweater from Sears using its online catalog. The sweater arrives in September, and you charge it to your Sears credit card. You receive and pay the Sears bill in October.

Instructions
Identify when revenue should be recognized in each of the above situations.

Each **Problem** helps you pull together and apply several concepts from the chapter. Two sets of **Problems—A** and **B**—are keyed to the same Study Objectives and provide additional opportunities for practice.

Problems: Set A

P3-1A On April 1 Far and Wide Travel Agency Inc. was established. These transactions were completed during the month.

Analyze transactions and compute net income.
(SO 1)

1. Stockholders invested $20,000 cash in the company in exchange for common stock.
2. Paid $900 cash for April office rent.
3. Purchased office equipment for $2,800 cash.
4. Purchased $200 of advertising in the *Chicago Tribune*, on account.
5. Paid $500 cash for office supplies.
6. Earned $9,000 for services provided: Cash of $1,000 is received from customers, and the balance of $8,000 is billed to customers on account.
7. Paid $400 cash dividends.
8. Paid *Chicago Tribune* amount due in transaction (4).
9. Paid employees' salaries $1,200.
10. Received $8,000 in cash from customers who have previously been billed in transaction (6).

Instructions
(a) Prepare a tabular analysis of the transactions using these column headings: Cash, Accounts Receivable, Supplies, Office Equipment, Accounts Payable, Common Stock, and Retained Earnings. Include margin explanations for any changes in Retained Earnings.
(b) From an analysis of the column Retained Earnings, compute the net income or net loss for April.

(a) Cash $23,000
Ret. earnings $ 6,300

P3-2A Marie Blaesing started her own consulting firm, Blaesing Consulting Inc., on May 1, 2007. The following transactions occurred during the month of May.

Analyze transactions and prepare financial statements.
(SO 1)

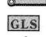

Spreadsheet Exercises and **Problems**, identified by an icon, can be solved using the Excel spreadsheet workbook and templates.

Problems: Set B

P5-1B Midwest Distributing Company completed these merchandising transactions in the month of April. At the beginning of April, the ledger of Midwest showed Cash of $9,000 and Common Stock of $9,000.

Journalize, post, prepare partial income statement, and calculate ratios.
(SO 2, 3, 4, 6)

Apr.	2	Purchased merchandise on account from Kane Supply Co. $6,300, terms 2/10, n/30.
	4	Sold merchandise on account $5,000, terms 2/10, n/30. The cost of the merchandise sold was $3,700.
	5	Paid $200 freight on April 4 sale.
	6	Received credit from Kane Supply Co. for merchandise returned $300.
	11	Paid Kane Supply Co. in full, less discount.
	13	Received collections in full, less discounts, from customers billed on April 4.
	14	Purchased merchandise for cash $4,700.
	16	Received refund from supplier for returned merchandise on cash purchase of April 14, $500.
	18	Purchased merchandise from Great Plains Distributors $4,500, terms 2/10, n/30.
	20	Paid freight on April 18 purchase $100.
	23	Sold merchandise for cash $8,300. The cost of the merchandise sold was $5,820.
	26	Purchased merchandise for cash $2,300.
	27	Paid Great Plains Distributors in full, less discount.
	29	Made refunds to cash customers for returned merchandise $180. The returned merchandise had a cost of $120.
	30	Sold merchandise on account $3,980, terms n/30. The cost of the merchandise sold was $2,500.

Midwest Distributing Company's chart of accounts includes Cash, Accounts Receivable, Merchandise Inventory, Accounts Payable, Common Stock, Sales, Sales Returns and Allowances, Sales Discounts, Cost of Goods Sold, and Freight-out.

Check figures in the margin provide key numbers to let you know you're on the right track as you do assignments.

General Ledger Problems, identified by an icon, are selected problems that can be solved using the *General Ledger Software* package.

A set of **C Problems** is available at the book's website.

A **Comprehensive Problem** (in Chapters 5–11) combines material from the current and previous chapters, to show "how it all fits together."

Problems: Set C

Go to the book's website, **www.wiley.com/college/kimmel**, to access a set of C Problems.

Comprehensive Problem

CP10 Crow Corporation's balance sheet at December 31, 2006, is presented below.

CROW CORPORATION
Balance Sheet
December 31, 2006

Cash	$30,500	Accounts payable	$13,750
Inventory	25,750	Bond interest payable	3,000
Prepaid insurance	5,600	Bonds payable	50,000
Equipment	38,000	Common stock	20,000
	$99,850	Retained earnings	$13,100
			$99,850

During 2007, the following transactions occurred.
1. Crow paid $3,000 interest on the bonds on January 1, 2007.
2. Crow purchased $241,100 of inventory on account.
3. Crow sold for $400,000 cash inventory which cost $240,000. Crow also collected $24,000 sales taxes.
4. Crow paid $230,000 on accounts payable.
5. Crow paid $3,000 interest on the bonds on July 1, 2007.
6. The prepaid insurance ($5,600) expired on July 31.
7. On August 1, Crow paid $10,800 for insurance coverage from August 1, 2007, through July 31, 2008.
8. Crow paid $17,000 sales taxes to the state.
9. Paid other operating expenses, $91,000.
10. Retired the bonds on December 31, 2007, by paying $48,000 plus $3,000 interest.
11. Issued $70,000 of 8% bonds on December 31, 2007, at 104. The bonds pay interest every June 30 and December 31.

Continuing Cookie Chronicle

(*Note:* This is a continuation of the Cookie Chronicle from Chapter 1.)

CCC2 After investigating the different forms of business organization, Natalie Koebel decides to operate her business as a corporation, Cookie Creations Inc., and she begins the process of getting her business running.

While at a trade show, Natalie is introduced to Gerry Richards, operations manager of "Biscuits," a national food retailer. After much discussion, Gerry asks Natalie to consider being Biscuits' major supplier of oatmeal chocolate chip cookies. He provides Natalie with the most recent copy of the financial statements of Biscuits. He expects that Natalie will need to supply Biscuits' Watertown warehouse with approximately 1,500 dozen cookies a week. Natalie is to send Biscuits a monthly invoice, and she will be paid approximately 30 days from the date the invoice is received in Biscuits' Chicago office.

Natalie is thrilled with the offer. However, she has recently read in the newspaper that Biscuits has a reputation for selling cookies and donuts with high amounts of sugar and fat, and as a result, consumer demand for the company's products has decreased.

Instructions
Natalie has several questions. Answer the following questions for Natalie.
(a) What type of information does each financial statement provide?
(b) How can Natalie evaluate whether Biscuits will be able to pay her invoices? What type of information can financial statements give that will reassure her that Biscuits will pay her invoices?
(c) Will Biscuits have enough cash to meet its current liabilities? Where can she find this information?
(d) Will Biscuits be able to survive over a long period of time? Where can she find this information?
(e) Is Biscuits profitable? Where can she find this information?
(f) Does Biscuits have any debt? Is Biscuits able to pay off both its debt and the interest on it? Where can she find this information?
(g) Does Biscuits pay any dividends? Where can she find this information?
(h) In deciding whether to go ahead with this opportunity, are there other areas of concern that she should be aware of?

The **Continuing Cookie Chronicle** (in Chapters 1–13) traces the growth of a small business and the financial reporting issues it encounters.

94   CHAPTER 2   A Further Look at Financial Statements

BROADENING YOUR PERSPECTIVE

FINANCIAL REPORTING PROBLEM: *Tootsie Roll Industries, Inc.*

BYP2-1   The financial statements of Tootsie Roll Industries, Inc., are presented in Appendix A at the end of this book.

Instructions
Answer the following questions using the Consolidated Balance Sheet and the Notes to Consolidated Financial Statements section.
(a) What were Tootsie Roll's total current assets at December 31, 2004, and December 31, 2003?
(b) Are the assets included in current assets listed in the proper order? Explain.
(c) How are Tootsie Roll's assets classified?
(d) What were Tootsie Roll's current liabilities at December 31, 2004, and December 31, 2003?

COMPARATIVE ANALYSIS PROBLEM: *Tootsie Roll vs. Hershey Foods*

BYP2-2   The financial statements of Hershey Foods are presented in Appendix B, following the financial statements for Tootsie Roll in Appendix A. Hershey's average number of shares outstanding was 253,881,000, and Tootsie Roll's was 52,366,000.

Instructions
(a) For each company calculate the following values for 2004.
   (1) Working capital.   (4) Free cash flow.
   (2) Current ratio.   (5) Earnings per share.
   (3) Debt to total assets ratio

   (*Hint:* When calculating free cash flow, consider business acquisitions to be part of capital expenditures.)

(b) Based on your findings above, discuss the relative liquidity, solvency, and profitability of the two companies.

RESEARCH CASE

BYP2-3   The March 2, 2004, issue of the *Wall Street Journal* includes an article by Mitchell Pacelle and Matthew Karnitschnig titled "Spiegel's European Owner Gets a Hard Lesson in U.S. Business."

Instructions
Read the article and answer the following.
(a) Mr. Otto controls 89 companies. What was unique about Spiegel, and how did this get him into trouble?
(b) Mr. Otto is German and is accustomed to the regulatory environment in Germany. How does the German regulatory environment differ from that of the U.S.? According to the article, how is the German regulatory environment changing?
(c) Briefly explain what is meant by the "going concern assumption."
(d) Explain why Spiegel's violation of its loan agreements caused its auditor to say that it would most likely issue an audit opinion that questioned the company's ability to continue as a going concern.
(e) How would the company's creditors react to the news that the auditor questioned the company's ability to continue as a going concern?
(f) Briefly explain the "full disclosure principle" and discuss whether Spiegel appears to have violated this principle.

...by Gap, Inc. in its 2004 annual report.

	2002	2001	2000
	$10,283	$8,096	$7,387
	$2,972	$1,018	$(153)
	2.08:1	1.48:1	0.95:1
	.66:1	.64:1	.62:1
	$0.55	$(0.03)	$0.99

INTERPRETING FINANCIAL STATEMENTS

BYP5-4   Recently it was announced that two giant French retailers, Carrefour SA and Promodes SA, would merge. A headline in the *Wall Street Journal* blared, "French Retailers Create New Wal-Mart Rival." While Wal-Mart's total sales would still exceed those of the combined company, Wal-Mart's international sales are far less than those of the combined company. This is a serious concern for Wal-Mart, since its primary opportunity for future growth lies outside of the United States.
   Below are basic financial data for the combined corporation (in euros) and Wal-Mart (in U.S. dollars). Even though their results are presented in different currencies, by employing ratios we can make some basic comparisons.

	Carrefour (in millions)	Wal-Mart (in millions)
Sales	euros 70,486	$256,329
Cost of goods sold	54,630	198,747
Net income	1,738	9,054
Total assets	39,063	104,912
Current assets	14,521	34,421
Current liabilities	13,660	37,418
Total liabilities	29,434	61,289

FINANCIAL ANALYSIS ON THE WEB

BYP6-5   *Purpose:* Use SEC filings to learn about a company's inventory accounting practices.

Address: http://biz.yahoo.com/p/_capgds-bldmch.html
   (or go to www.wiley.com/college/kimmel)

Steps
1. Go to this site and click on the name of an equipment manufacturer other than those discussed in the chapter.
2. Click on **SEC filings**.
3. Under "Recent filings" choose **Form 10K** (annual report) and click on **Full Filing at Edgar Online**.
4. Choose option "3", **Online HTML Version**.
If the 10K is not listed among the recent filings then click on **View All Filings on EDGAR Online**.

Instructions
Review the 10K to answer the following questions.
(a) What is the name of the company?
(b) How has its inventory changed from the previous year?
(c) What is the amount of raw materials, work in process, and finished goods inventory?
(d) What inventory method does the company use?
(e) Calculate the inventory turnover ratio and days in inventory for the current year.
(f) If the company uses LIFO, what was the amount of its LIFO reserve?

The **Broadening Your Perspective** section helps you pull together concepts from the chapter and apply them to real-world business situations.

In the **Financial Reporting Problem** you study the financial statements of Tootsie Roll Industries, which are printed in Chapter 1 (in simplified form) and in Appendix A (in full).

A **Comparative Analysis Problem** compares and contrasts the financial reporting of Tootsie Roll with a competitor, Hershey Foods (whose financial statements appear in Appendix B).

Research Cases direct you to the *Wall Street Journal* and other business periodicals for further study and analysis of key topics.

Interpreting Financial Statements are mini-cases that ask you to read parts of financial statements of actual companies and use the decision tools from the chapter to interpret this information. Those identified by a globe icon ask you to apply concepts to specific situations faced by actual foreign companies.

Financial Analysis on the Web exercises guide you to websites where you can find and analyze information related to the chapter topic.

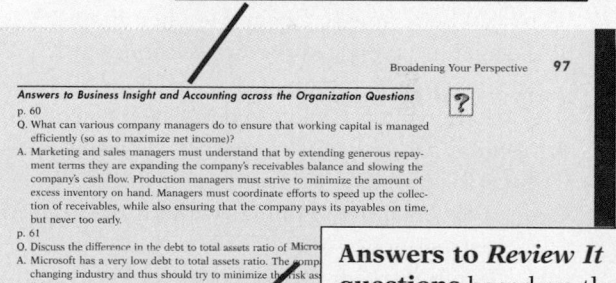

44 CHAPTER 1 Introduction to Financial Statements

(d) What are the names of four companies in this industry?
(e) Choose one of the competitors. What is this competitor's name? What were its sales? What was its net income?

Critical Thinking

DECISION MAKING ACROSS THE ORGANIZATION

BYP1-6 Kim Perkins recently accepted a job in the production department at Tootsie Roll. Before she starts work, she decides to review the company's annual report to better understand its operations.

Instructions
Use the annual report provided in Appendix A to answer the following questions.
(a) What CPA firm performed the audit of Tootsie Roll's financial statements?
(b) What was the amount of Tootsie Roll's earnings per share in 2004?
(c) What are the company's net sales in foreign countries?
(d) What did management suggest as the cause of the increase in the sales in 2004?
(e) What were net sales in 2000?
(f) How many shares of Class B common stock have been authorized?
(g) How much cash was spent on capital expenditures in 2004?
(h) Over what life does the company depreciate its buildings?
(i) What was the value of raw material inventories in 2003?

COMMUNICATION ACTIVITY

BYP1-7 Carol Young is the bookkeeper for Evans Company, Inc. Carol has been trying to get the company's balance sheet to balance. She finally got it to balance, but she still isn't sure that it is correct.

EVANS COMPANY, INC.
Balance Sheet
For the Month Ended December 31, 2007

Assets		Liabilities and Stockholders' Equity	
Equipment	$20,500	Common stock	$11,000
Cash	10,500	Accounts receivable	(3,000)
Supplies	2,000	Dividends	(2,000)
Accounts payable	(5,000)	Notes payable	12,000
Total assets	$28,000	Retained earnings	10,000
		Total liabilities and stockholders' equity	$28,000

Instructions
Explain to Carol Young in a memo (a) the purpose of a balance sheet, and (b) why this balance sheet is incorrect and what she should do to correct it.

ETHICS CASE

BYP1-8 Rules governing the investment practices of individual certified public accountants prohibit them from investing in the stock of a company that their firm audits. The Securities and Exchange Commission became concerned that some accountants were violating this rule. In response to an SEC investigation, PricewaterhouseCoopers fired 10 people and spent $25 million educating employees about the investment rules and installing an investment tracking system.

Instructions

...auditors from investing in companies that
...be allowed to invest in a company's stock
...n working on the company's audit or con-

The **Decision Making across the Organization** cases help you build decision-making skills. They require you to consider the perspectives of various business functions. They also give practice in building communication skills.

Communication Activities help you build business communication skills by asking you to engage in real-world business situations using writing, speaking, or presentation skills.

Answers to Business Insight and **Accounting across the Organization Questions** offer guideline answers for questions that appear in the chapter's boxed real-world examples (in chapters 1–13).

Through the **Ethics Cases**, you will reflect on typical ethical dilemmas, analyze the issues involved, and decide on an appropriate course of action.

Broadening Your Perspective **97**

Answers to Business Insight and Accounting across the Organization Questions

p. 60
Q. What can various company managers do to ensure that working capital is managed efficiently (so as to maximize net income)?
A. Marketing and sales managers must understand that by extending generous repayment terms they are expanding the company's receivables balance and slowing the company's cash flow. Production managers must strive to minimize the amount of excess inventory on hand. Managers must coordinate efforts to speed up the collection of receivables, while also ensuring that the company pays its payables on time, but never too early.

p. 61
Q. Discuss the difference in the debt to total assets ratio of Micro...
A. Microsoft has a very low debt to total assets ratio. The comp... changing industry and thus should try to minimize the risk ass... debt. Also, because Microsoft generates significant amounts of... needs for large investments in plant assets, it does not need... General Motors needs to make huge investments in plant ass... large credit operation. Thus it has large borrowing needs.

p. 66
Q. What problems might Best Buy's year-end create for analysts...
A. First, if Best Buy's competitors use a different year-end, then... their financial results, you are not comparing performance o... time or financial position at the same point in time. Also, by no... particular date, the number of weeks in Best Buy's fiscal year will change. For example, fiscal years 2002, 2003, and 2004 had 52 weeks, but fiscal year 2001 had 53 weeks.

Answer to Tootsie Roll Review It Question 3, p. 53
Tootsie Roll's largest current asset at December 31, 2004, was cash and cash equivalents, at $56,989,000.

Answers to Self-Study Questions
1. d 2. a 3. b 4. a 5. c 6. b 7. d 8. a 9. a 10. c 11. c 12. c

Answers to *Review It* questions based on the Tootsie Roll financial statements appear here.

Answers to Self-Study Questions provide feedback on your understanding of concepts in the Self-Study quiz.

After you complete your homework assignments, it's a good idea to go back to **The Navigator** checklist at the start of the chapter to see if you have used all the chapter's study aids.

This questionaire aims to find out something about your preferences for the way you work with information. You will have a preferred learning style and one part of that learning style is your preference for the intake and the output of ideas and information.

Circle the letter of the answer that best explains your preference. Circle more than one if a single answer does not match your perception. Leave blank any question that does not apply.

1. You are about to give directions to a person who is standing with you. She is staying in a hotel in town and wants to visit your house later. She has a rental car. Would you
   a. draw a map on paper?
   b. tell her the directions?
   c. write down the directions (without a map)?
   d. pick her up at the hotel in your car?

2. You are not sure whether a word should be spelled "dependent" or "dependant." Do you
   c. look it up in the dictionary?
   a. see the word in your mind and choose by the way it looks?
   b. sound it out in your mind?
   d. write both versions down on paper and choose one?

3. You have just received a copy of your itinerary for a world trip. This is of interest to a friend. Would you
   b. call her immediately and tell her about it?
   c. send her a copy of the printed itinerary?
   a. show her on a map of the world?
   d. share what you plan to do at each place you visit?

4. You are going to cook something as a special treat for your family. Do you
   d. cook something familiar without the need for instructions?
   a. thumb through the cookbook looking for ideas from the pictures?
   c. refer to a specific cookbook where there is a good recipe?

5. A group of tourists has been assigned to you to find out about wildlife reserves or parks. Would you
   d. drive them to a wildlife reserve or park?
   a. show them slides and photographs?
   c. give them pamphlets or a book on wildlife reserves or parks?
   b. give them a talk on wildlife reserves or parks?

6. You are about to purchase a new CD player. Other than price, what would most influence your decision?
   b. The salesperson telling you what you want to know.
   c. Reading the details about it.
   d. Playing with the controls and listening to it.
   a. Its fashionable and upscale appearance.

7. Recall a time in your life when you learned how to do something like playing a new board game. Try to avoid choosing a very physical skill, e.g. riding a bike. How did you learn best? By
   a. visual clues—pictures, diagrams, charts?
   c. written instructions?
   b. listening to somebody explaining it?
   d. doing it or trying it?

8. You have an eye problem. Would you prefer that the doctor
   b. tell you what is wrong?
   a. show you a diagram of what is wrong?
   d. use a model to show what is wrong?

9. You are about to learn to use a new program on a computer. Would you
   d. sit down at the keyboard and begin to experiment with the program's features?
   c. read the manual that comes with the program?
   b. call a friend and ask questions about it?

10. You are staying in a hotel and have a rental car. You would like to visit friends whose address/location you do not know. Would you like them to
    a. draw you a map on paper?
    b. tell you the directions?
    c. write down the directions (without a map)?
    d. pick you up at the hotel in their car?

11. Apart from price, what would most influence your decision to buy a particular book?
    d. You have used a copy before.
    b. A friend talking about it.
    c. Quickly reading parts of it.
    a. The appealing way it looks.

12. A new movie has arrived in town. What would most influence your decision to go (or not go)?
    b. You heard a radio review about it.
    c. You read a review about it.
    a. You saw a preview of it.

13. Do you prefer a lecturer or teacher who likes to use
    c. a textbook, handouts, readings?
    a. flow diagrams, charts, graphs?
    d. field trips, labs, practical sessions?
    b. discussion, guest speakers?

Count your choices:

	a.	b.	c.	d.
	❏	❏	❏	❏
	V	A	R	K

Now match the letter or letters you have recorded most to the same letter or letters in the Learning Styles Chart. You may have more than one learning style preference—many people do. Next to each letter in the Chart are suggestions that will refer you to different learning aids throughout this text.

LEARNING STYLES CHART

	Intake: To take in the information	To make a study package

Visual

Intake:
- Pay close attention to charts, drawings, and handouts your instructors use.
- Underline.
- Use different colors.
- Use symbols, flow charts, graphs, different arrangements on the page, white spaces.

To make a study package:
Convert your lecture notes into "page pictures." To do this:
- Use the "Intake" strategies.
- Reconstruct images in different ways.
- Redraw pages from memory.
- Replace words with symbols and initials.
- Look at your pages.

Aural

Intake:
- Attend lectures and tutorials.
- Discuss topics with students and instructors.
- Explain new ideas to other people.
- Use a tape recorder.
- Leave spaces in your lecture notes for later recall.
- Describe overheads, pictures, and visuals to somebody who was not in class.

To make a study package:
You may take poor notes because you prefer to listen. Therefore:
- Expand your notes by talking with others and with information from your textbook.
- Tape-record summarized notes and listen.
- Read summarized notes out loud.
- Explain your notes to another "aural" person.

Reading/ Writing

Intake:
- Use lists and headings.
- Use dictionaries, glossaries, and definitions.
- Read handouts, textbooks, and supplementary library readings.
- Use lecture notes.

To make a study package:
- Write out words again and again.
- Reread notes silently.
- Rewrite ideas and principles into other words.
- Turn charts, diagrams, and other illustrations into statements.

Kinesthetic

Intake:
- Use all your senses.
- Go to labs, take field trips.
- Listen to real-life examples.
- Pay attention to applications.
- Use hands-on approaches.
- Use trial-and-error methods.

To make a study package:
You may take poor notes because topics do not seem concrete or relevant. Therefore:
- Put examples in your summaries.
- Use case studies and applications to help with principles and abstract concepts.
- Talk about your notes with another "kinesthetic" person.
- Use pictures and photographs that illustrate an idea.

Source: Adapted from VARK pack. © Copyright 2001–2006 Neil D. Fleming. This material may be used for faculty or student development if attribution is given. It may not be published in either paper or electronic form without consent of the authors. There is a VARK website at **www.vark-learn.com**.

Text features that may help you the most	Output: To do well on exams	
The Navigator/Feature Story/Preview Infographics/Illustrations Accounting Equation Analyses Highlighted words Decision Toolkits Demonstration Problem/Action Plan Questions/Exercises/Problems Financial Reporting Problem Comparative Analysis Problem Financial Analysis on the Web	• Recall your "page pictures." • Draw diagrams where appropriate. • Practice turning your visuals back into words.	**Visual** **V**
Insight and Accounting Across the Organization boxes Review It/Do It/Action Plan Using the Decision Toolkit Summary of Study Objectives Glossary Demonstration Problem/Action Plan Self-Study Questions Questions/Exercises/Problems Financial Reporting Problem Comparative Analysis Problem Financial Analysis on the Web Decision Making case Communication Activity Ethics Case	• Talk with the instructor. • Spend time in quiet places recalling the ideas. • Practice writing answers to old exam questions. • Say your answers out loud.	**Aural** **A**
The Navigator/Feature Story/Study Objectives Review It/Do It/Action Plan Using the Decision Toolkit Summary of Study Objectives Glossary/Self-Study Questions Questions/Exercises/Problems Writing Problems Financial Reporting Problem Comparative Analysis Problem Decision Making case Communication Activity Research and Ethics cases	• Write exam answers. • Practice with multiple-choice questions. • Write paragraphs, beginnings and endings. • Write your lists in outline form. • Arrange your words into hierarchies and points.	**Reading/ Writing** **R**
The Navigator/Feature Story/Preview Infographics/Illustrations Review It/Do It/Action Plan Accounting Equation Analyses Demonstration Problem/Action Plan Using the Decision Toolkits Self-Study Questions Questions/Exercises/Problems Financial Reporting Problem Comparative Analysis Problem Financial Analysis on the Web Group Decision Caser ebook content at WileyPLUS	• Write practice answers. • Role-play the exam situation.	**Kinesthetic** **K**

For all learning styles: Be sure to use the book's website to enhance your understanding of the concepts and procedures of the text.

CONTENTS

CHAPTER 8

Reporting and Analyzing Receivables *370*

CHAPTER 9

Reporting and Analyzing Long-Lived Assets *418*

CHAPTER 10

Reporting and Analyzing Liabilities *472*

CHAPTER 17

Activity-based Costing   *844*

CHAPTER 18

Cost-volume-profit   *892*

CHAPTER 19

Variable Costing: A Decision-Making Perspective   *930*

CHAPTER 20

Budgetary planning   *970*

Accounting

Tools for Business Decision Making
2nd Edition

CHAPTER **1**

Introduction to Financial Statements

STUDY OBJECTIVES

After studying this chapter,
you should be able to:

1 Describe the primary forms of business organization.

2 Identify the users and uses of accounting information.

3 Explain the three principal types of business activity.

4 Describe the content and purpose of each of the financial statements.

5 Explain the meaning of assets, liabilities, and stockholders' equity, and state the basic accounting equation.

6 Describe the components that supplement the financial statements in an annual report.

 THE NAVIGATOR

✔ THE NAVIGATOR

- Scan *Study Objectives* ⬭
- Read *Feature Story* ⬭
- Read *Preview* ⬭
- Read text and answer *Before You Go On*
  p. 11 ⬭   p. 17 ⬭   p. 24 ⬭
- Work *Using the Decision Toolkit* ⬭
- Review *Summary of Study Objectives* ⬭
- Work *Demonstration Problem* ⬭
- Answer *Self-Study Questions* ⬭
- Complete *Assignments* ⬭

The Navigator is a learning system designed to prompt you to use the learning aids in the chapter and to set priorities as you study.

FEATURE STORY

Knowing the Numbers

M any students who take this course do not plan to be accountants. If you are in that group, you might be thinking, "If I'm not going to be an accountant, why do I need to know accounting?" In response, consider this quote from Harold Geneen, the former chairman of IT&T: "To be good at your business, you have to know the numbers—cold." Success in any business comes back to the numbers. You will rely on them to make decisions, and managers will use them to evaluate your performance. That is true whether your job involves marketing, production, management, or information systems.

In business, accounting and financial statements are the means for communicating the numbers. If you don't know how to read financial statements, you can't really know your business.

Many companies spend significant resources teaching their employees basic accounting so that they can read financial statements and understand how their actions affect the company's financial results. One such company is Springfield ReManufacturing Corporation (SRC). When Jack Stack and 11 other managers purchased SRC for 10 cents a share, it was a failing division of International Harvester. Jack had 119 employees who were counting on him for their livelihood, and he knew that the new company was on the verge of financial failure. He decided that the only chance of survival was to encourage every employee to think like a businessperson and to act like an owner. To accomplish this, all employees at SRC took basic accounting courses and participated in weekly reviews of the company's financial statements. SRC survived, and eventually thrived. To this day, every employee (now numbering more than 1,000) undergoes this same training.

Many other companies have adopted this approach, which is called "open-book management." Even in companies that do not practice open-book management, employers generally assume that managers in all areas of the company are "financially literate."

Taking this course will go a long way to making you financially literate. In this book you will learn how to read and prepare financial statements, and how to use basic tools to evaluate financial results. In this first chapter we will introduce you to the financial statements of a real company whose products you are probably familiar with—Tootsie Roll. Tootsie Roll's presentation of its financial results is complete, yet also relatively easy to understand.

Tootsie Roll started off humbly in 1896 in a small New York City candy shop owned by an Austrian immigrant, Leo Hirshfield. The candy's name came from his five-year-old daughter's nickname—"Tootsie." Today the Chicago-based company produces more than 49 million Tootsie Rolls and 16 million Tootsie Pops *each day*. In fact, Tootsie Pops are at the center of one of science's most challenging questions: How many licks does it take to get to the Tootsie Roll center of a Tootsie Pop? The answer varies: Licking machines created at Purdue University and the University of Michigan report an average of 364 and 411 licks, respectively. In studies using human lickers, the answer ranges from 144 to 252. We recommend that you take a few minutes today away from your studies to determine your own results.

Source: Tootsie Roll information adapted from www.tootsie.com.

On the World Wide Web
Springfield ReManufacturing Corporation:
www.srcreman.com
Tootsie Roll Industries:
www.tootsie.com

✔ THE NAVIGATOR

PREVIEW OF CHAPTER 1

How do you start a business? How do you make it grow into a widely recognized brand name like Tootsie Roll? How do you determine whether your business is making or losing money? When you need to expand your operations, where do you get money to finance expansion—should you borrow, should you issue stock, should you use your own funds? How do you convince lenders to lend you money or investors to buy your stock? Success in business requires making countless decisions, and decisions require financial information.

The purpose of this chapter is to show you what role accounting plays in providing financial information. The content and organization of the chapter are as follows.

INTRODUCTION TO FINANCIAL STATEMENTS

Forms of Business Organization	Users and Uses of Financial Information	Business Activities	Communicating with Users	A Quick Look at Tootsie Roll's Financial Statements
• Sole proprietorship • Partnership • Corporation	• Internal users • External users • Ethics in financial reporting	• Financing • Investing • Operating	• Income statement • Retained earnings statement • Balance sheet • Statement of cash flows • Interrelationships of statements	• Income statement • Retained earnings statement • Balance sheet • Statement of cash flows • Other elements of an annual report

THE NAVIGATOR

Forms of Business Organization

STUDY OBJECTIVE

1

Describe the primary forms of business organization.

Terms that represent essential concepts are printed in blue. They are listed and defined again in the **glossary** at the end of the chapter.

Suppose you graduate with a marketing degree and open your own marketing agency. One of your initial decisions is what organizational form your business will have. You have three choices—sole proprietorship, partnership, or corporation. A business owned by one person is a **sole proprietorship**. A business owned by two or more persons associated as partners is a **partnership**. A business organized as a separate legal entity owned by stockholders is a **corporation.**

You will probably choose the sole proprietorship form for your marketing agency. It is **simple to set up** and **gives you control** over the business. Small owner-operated businesses such as barber shops, law offices, and auto repair shops are often sole proprietorships, as are farms and small retail stores.

Another possibility is for you to join forces with other individuals to form a partnership. Partnerships often are formed because one individual does not have **enough economic resources** to initiate or expand the business. Sometimes **partners bring unique skills or resources** to the partnership. You and your partners should formalize your duties and contributions in a written partnership agreement. Retail and service-type businesses, including professional practices (lawyers, doctors, architects, and certified public accountants), often organize as partnerships.

As a third alternative, you might organize as a corporation. As an investor in a corporation you receive shares of stock to indicate your ownership claim. Buying stock in a corporation is often more attractive than investing in a partnership because shares of stock are **easy to sell** (transfer ownership). Selling a proprietorship or partnership interest is much more involved. Also, individuals can become **stockholders** by investing relatively small amounts of money. Therefore, it is **easier for corporations to raise funds**. Successful corporations often have thousands of stockholders, and their stock is traded on organized stock exchanges like the New York Stock Exchange. Many businesses start as sole proprietorships or partnerships and eventually incorporate. For example, in 1896 Leo Hirshfield started Tootsie Roll as a sole proprietorship, and by 1919 the company had incorporated.

Other factors to consider in deciding which organizational form to choose are **taxes and legal liability**. If you choose a sole proprietorship or partnership, you generally receive more favorable tax treatment than a corporation. However, proprietors and partners are personally liable for all debts of the business; corporate stockholders are not. In other words, corporate stockholders generally pay higher taxes but have no personal liability. We will discuss these issues in more depth in a later chapter. Illustration 1-1 highlights the three types of organizations and the advantages of each.

Alternative Terminology notes present synonymous terms that you may come across in practice.

Alternative Terminology
Stockholders are sometimes called *shareholders*.

Illustrations like this one convey information in pictorial form to help you visualize and apply the ideas as you study.

Illustration 1-1   Forms of business organization

Sole Proprietorship	**Partnership**	**Corporation**
-Simple to establish -Owner controlled -Tax advantages	-Simple to establish -Shared control -Broader skills and resources -Tax advantages	-Easier to transfer ownership -Easier to raise funds -No personal liability

The combined number of proprietorships and partnerships in the United States is more than five times the number of corporations. However, the revenue produced by corporations is eight times greater. Most of the largest enterprises in the United States—for example, Coca-Cola, ExxonMobil, General Motors, Citigroup, and Microsoft—are corporations. Because the majority of U.S. business is transacted by corporations, the emphasis in this book is on the corporate form of organization.

Users and Uses of Financial Information

The purpose of financial information is to provide inputs for decision making. **Accounting** is the information system that identifies, records, and communicates the economic events of an organization to interested users. Many people have an interest in knowing about the ongoing activities of the business. These people are **users** of accounting information. Users can be divided broadly into two groups: internal users and external users.

INTERNAL USERS

Internal users of accounting information are managers who plan, organize, and run a business. These include **marketing managers**, **production supervisors**, **finance directors**, **and company officers**. In running a business, managers must answer many important questions, as shown in Illustration 1-2.

Illustration 1-2

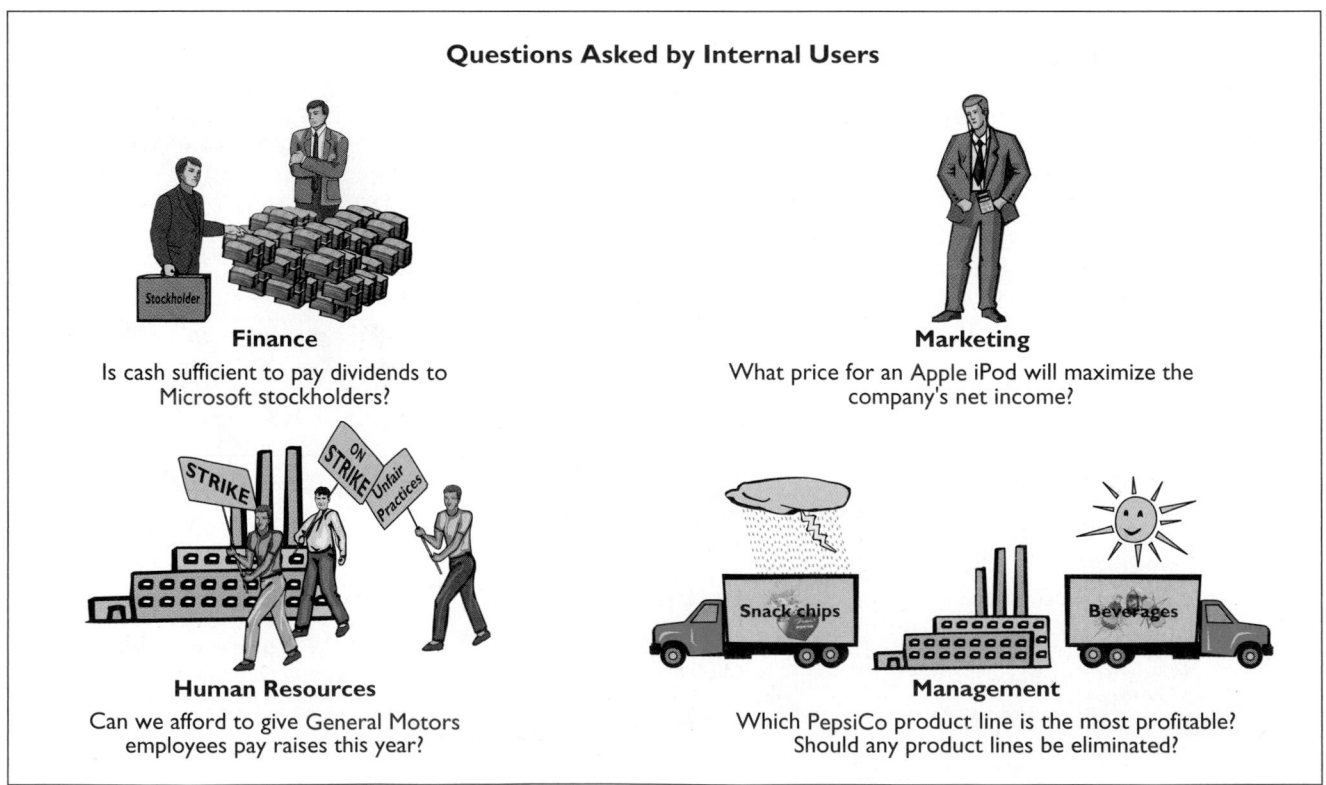

Questions Asked by Internal Users

Finance
Is cash sufficient to pay dividends to Microsoft stockholders?

Marketing
What price for an Apple iPod will maximize the company's net income?

Human Resources
Can we afford to give General Motors employees pay raises this year?

Management
Which PepsiCo product line is the most profitable? Should any product lines be eliminated?

To answer these and other questions, you need detailed information on a timely basis. For internal users, accounting provides internal reports, such as financial comparisons of operating alternatives, projections of income from new sales campaigns, and forecasts of cash needs for the next year. In addition, companies present summarized financial information in the form of financial statements.

Accounting across the Organization

Accounting can even serve as a useful recruiting tool for the human resources department. Rhino Foods, located in Burlington, VT, is a manufacturer of specialty ice cream novelties and ice cream ingredients. Its corporate website includes the following paragraphs:

> "Wouldn't it be great to work where you were part of a team? Where your input and hard work made a difference? Where you weren't kept in the dark about what management was thinking?
>
> Well—it's not a dream! It's the way we do business at Rhino Foods on Industrial Parkway in Burlington. Rhino Foods believes in family, honesty and open communication—we really care about and appreciate our employees—and it shows. Operating results are posted and monthly group meetings inform all employees about what's happening in the Company. Employees also share in the Company's profits, in addition to having an excellent comprehensive *benefits* package."

Source: www.rhinofoods.com/workforus/workforus.html.

 What are the benefits to the company and to the employees of making the financial statements available to all employees?

Accounting across the Organization stories demonstrate applications of accounting information in various business functions.

EXTERNAL USERS

There are several types of **external users** of accounting information. **Investors** (owners) use accounting information to make decisions to buy, hold, or sell stock. **Creditors** such as suppliers and bankers use accounting information to evaluate the risks of granting credit or lending money. Some questions that investors and creditors may ask about a company are shown in Illustration 1-3.

The information needs and questions of other external users vary considerably. **Taxing authorities**, such as the Internal Revenue Service, want to know whether the company complies with the tax laws. **Customers** are interested in whether a

Illustration 1-3

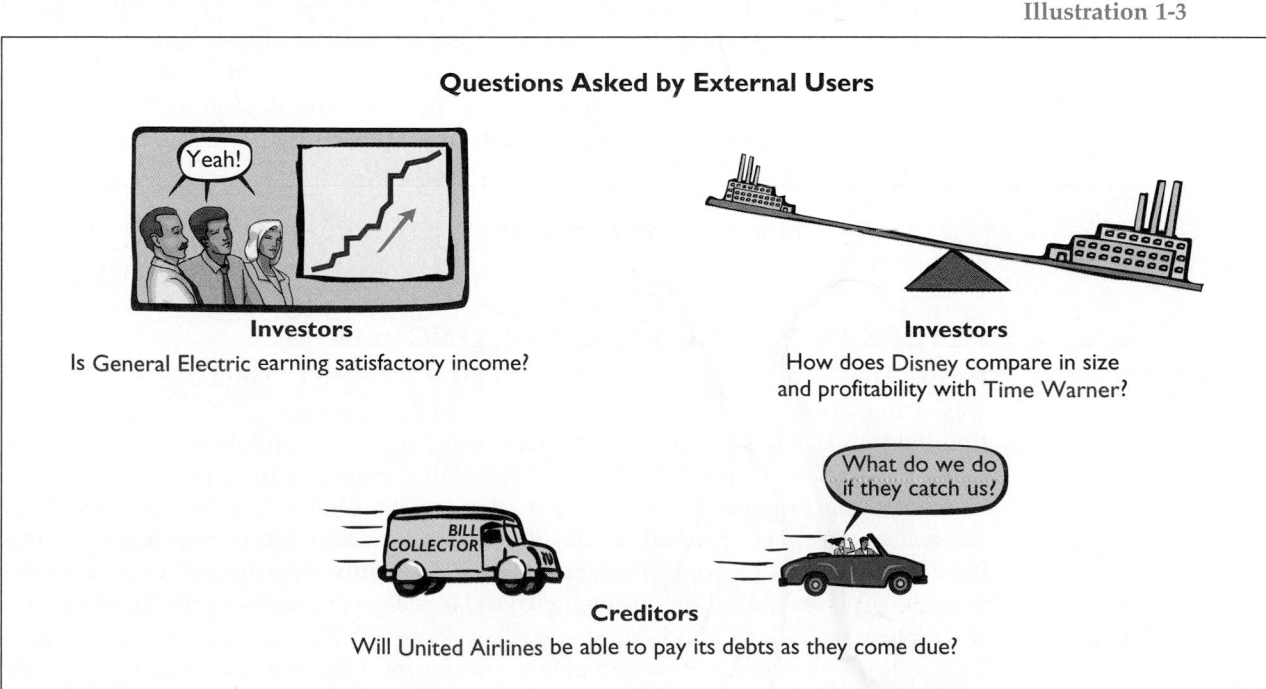

Questions Asked by External Users

Investors
Is General Electric earning satisfactory income?

Investors
How does Disney compare in size and profitability with Time Warner?

Creditors
Will United Airlines be able to pay its debts as they come due?

company like General Motors will continue to honor product warranties and otherwise support its product lines. **Labor unions** such as the Major League Baseball Players Association want to know whether the owners have the ability to pay increased wages and benefits. **Regulatory agencies**, such as the Securities and Exchange Commission or the Federal Trade Commission, want to know whether the company is operating within prescribed rules. For example, Enron, Dynegy, Duke Energy, and other big energy-trading companies reported record profits at the same time as California was paying extremely high prices for energy and suffering from blackouts. This disparity caused regulators to investigate the energy traders to make sure that the profits were earned by legitimate and fair practices.

Accounting across the Organization

One question that students of accounting frequently ask is, "How will the study of accounting help me?" It should help you a great deal, because a working knowledge of accounting is desirable for virtually every field of endeavor. Some examples of how accounting is used in other careers include:

General management: Imagine running Ford Motors, Massachusetts General Hospital, California State University–Fullerton, a McDonald's franchise, a Trek bike shop. All general managers need to understand accounting data in order to make wise business decisions.

Marketing: A marketing specialist at a company like Procter & Gamble develops strategies to help the sales force be successful. But making a sale is meaningless unless it is a profitable sale. Marketing people must be sensitive to costs and benefits, which accounting helps them quantify and understand.

Finance: Do you want to be a banker for Citicorp, an investment analyst for Goldman Sachs, a stock broker for Merrill Lynch? These fields rely heavily on accounting. In all of them you will regularly examine and analyze financial statements. In fact, it is difficult to get a good job in a finance function without two or three courses in accounting.

Real estate: Are you interested in being a real estate broker for Prudential Real Estate? Because a third party—the bank—is almost always involved in financing a real estate transaction, brokers must understand the numbers involved: Can the buyer afford to make the payments to the bank? Does the cash flow from an industrial property justify the purchase price? What are the tax benefits of the purchase?

 How might accounting help you?

ETHICS IN FINANCIAL REPORTING

People won't gamble in a casino if they think it is "rigged." Similarly, people won't "play" the stock market if they think stock prices are rigged. In recent years the financial press has been full of articles about financial scandals at Enron, WorldCom, HealthSouth, and AIG. As more scandals came to light, a mistrust of financial reporting in general seemed to be developing. One article in the *Wall Street Journal* noted that "repeated disclosures about questionable accounting practices have bruised investors' faith in the reliability of earnings reports, which in turn has sent stock prices tumbling."[1] Imagine trying to carry on a business or invest money

---

[1]"U.S. Share Prices Slump," *Wall Street Journal* (February 21, 2002).

if you could not depend on the financial statements to be honestly prepared. Information would have no credibility. There is no doubt that a sound, well-functioning economy depends on accurate and dependable financial reporting.

United States regulators and lawmakers were very concerned that the economy would suffer if investors lost confidence in corporate accounting because of unethical financial reporting. In 2002 Congress passed the **Sarbanes-Oxley Act (SOX)** to try to reduce unethical corporate behavior and consequently decrease the likelihood of future corporate scandals. As a result of SOX, top management must now certify the accuracy of financial information. In addition, penalties for fraudulent financial activity by top management are now much more severe. Also, SOX calls for increased independence of the outside auditors who review the accuracy of corporate financial statements, and increased responsibility of boards of directors in their oversight role.

Effective financial reporting depends on sound ethical behavior. To sensitize you to ethical situations and to give you practice at solving ethical dilemmas, we address ethics in a number of ways in this book: (1) A number of the *Feature Stories* and other parts of the text discuss the central importance of ethical behavior to financial reporting. (2) *Business Insight boxes* with an ethics perspective highlight ethics situations and issues in actual business settings. (3) At the end of the chapter, an *Ethics Case* simulates a business situation and asks you to put yourself in the position of a decision maker in that case. (4) The *CD* that accompanies this book has video segments on critical accounting issues.

When analyzing these various ethics cases and your own ethical experiences, you should apply the three steps outlined in Illustration 1-4.

Illustration 1-4 Steps in analyzing ethics cases

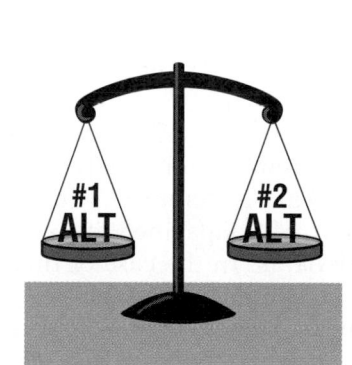

Solving an Ethical Dilemma

1. Recognize an ethical situation and the ethical issues involved.	**2. Identify and analyze the principal elements in the situation.**	**3. Identify the alternatives, and weigh the impact of each alternative on various stakeholders.**
Use your personal ethics to identify ethical situations and issues. Some businesses and professional organizations provide written codes of ethics for guidance in some business situations.	Identify the *stakeholders*— persons or groups who may be harmed or benefited. Ask the question: What are the responsibilities and obligations of the parties involved?	Select the most ethical alternative, considering all the consequences. Sometimes there will be one right answer. Other situations involve more than one right solution; these situations require you to evaluate each alternative and select the best one.

Business Insight
International Perspective

Concern over the quality and integrity of financial reporting is not limited to the United States. Recently the Chinese Ministry of Finance reprimanded a large accounting firm for preparing fraudulent financial reports for a number of its publicly traded companies. Afterward, the state-run news agency noted that investors and analysts actually felt that the punishment of the firm was not adequate. In fact, a recent survey of investors in China found that less than 10 percent had full confidence in companies' annual reports. As a result of these concerns the Chinese Institute of Certified Public Accountants vowed to strengthen its policing of its members.

Business Insights provide examples of business situations from various perspectives— ethics, investor, and international.

 What has been done in the United States to improve the quality and integrity of financial reporting and to build investor confidence in financial reports?

Business Activities

All businesses are involved in three types of activity—financing, investing, and operating. For example, Leo Hirshfield the founder of Tootsie Roll, needed financing to start and grow his business. Some of this **financing** came from personal savings, and some likely came from outside sources like banks. Hirshfield then **invested** the cash he had obtained by buying equipment necessary to run the business, such as mixing equipment and delivery vehicles. Once this equipment was in place, he could begin the **operating** activities of making and selling candy.

The **accounting information system** keeps track of the results of each of the various business activities—financing, investing, and operating. Let's look in more detail at each type of business activity.

FINANCING ACTIVITIES

Financing

It takes money to make money. The two primary sources of outside funds for corporations are borrowing money and issuing (selling) shares of stock in exchange for cash.

Tootsie Roll Industries may borrow money in a variety of ways. For example, it can take out a loan at a bank or borrow directly from investors by issuing debt securities called bonds. Persons or entities to whom Tootsie Roll owes money are its **creditors**. Amounts owed to creditors—in the form of debt and other obligations—are called liabilities. Specific names are given to different types of liabilities, depending on their source. Tootsie Roll may have a **note payable** to a bank for the money borrowed to purchase delivery trucks. Debt securities sold to investors that must be repaid at a particular date some years in the future are **bonds payable**.

A corporation may also obtain funds by selling shares of stock to investors. Common stock is the term used to describe the total amount paid in by stockholders for the shares they purchase.

The claims of creditors differ from those of stockholders. If you loan money to a company, you are one of its creditors. In lending money, you specify a payment schedule (e.g., payment at the end of three months). As a creditor, you have a legal right to be paid at the agreed time. In the event of nonpayment, you may legally force the company to sell property to pay its debts. In the case of financial difficulty, creditor claims must be paid before stockholders' claims.

Stockholders, on the other hand, have no claim to corporate resources until the claims of creditors are satisfied. If you buy a company's stock instead of loaning it money, you have no legal right to expect any payments until all of its creditors are paid. However, many corporations make payments to stockholders on a regular basis as long as there is sufficient cash to cover required payments to creditors. These payments to stockholders are called dividends.

INVESTING ACTIVITIES

Investing

Once the company has raised money through financing activities, it will then use that money in investing activities. Investing activities involve the purchase of those resources a company needs in order to operate. During the early stages of the company's life it must purchase many resources. For example, it obtains resources such as computers, delivery trucks, furniture, and buildings from investing activities. Resources owned by a business are called assets. Different types of assets are given different names. Tootsie Roll's mixing equipment is a type of asset referred to as **property**, **plant**, **and equipment**.

Cash is one of the more important assets owned by Tootsie Roll or any other business. If a company has excess cash that it does not need for a while, it might choose to invest it in debt or equity securities of other corporations. **Investments** are another example of an investing activity.

OPERATING ACTIVITIES

Once a business has the assets it needs to get started, it can begin its operations. Tootsie Roll is in the business of selling all things that taste, look, or smell like candy. It sells Tootsie Rolls, Tootsie Pops, Blow Pops, Caramel Apple Pops, Mason Dots, Mason Crows, Sugar Daddy, and Sugar Babies. In short, if it has anything to do with candy, Tootsie Roll sells it. We call amounts earned on the sale of these products *revenues*. **Revenue** is the increase in assets resulting from the sale of a product or service in the normal course of business. For example, Tootsie Roll records revenue when it sells a candy product.

Operating

Revenues arise from different sources and are identified by various names depending on the nature of the business. For instance, Tootsie Roll's primary source of revenue is the sale of candy products. However, it also generates interest revenue on debt securities held as investments. Sources of revenue common to many businesses are **sales revenue**, **service revenue**, and **interest revenue**.

The company purchases most of its longer-lived assets through investing activities as described earlier. Other assets with shorter lives, however, result from operating activities. For example, goods available for future sales to customers are assets called **inventory**. Also, if Tootsie Roll sells goods to a customer and does not receive cash immediately, then the company has a right to expect payment from that customer in the near future. This right to receive money in the future is called an **account receivable**.

Before Tootsie Roll can sell a single Tootsie Roll, Tootsie Pop, or Blow Pop, it must purchase sugar, corn syrup, and other ingredients, mix these ingredients, process the mix, and wrap and ship the finished product. It also incurs costs like salaries, rents, and utilities. All of these costs, referred to as *expenses*, are necessary to produce and sell the product. In accounting language, **expenses** are the cost of assets consumed or services used in the process of generating revenues.

Expenses take many forms and are identified by various names depending on the type of asset consumed or service used. For example, Tootsie Roll keeps track of these types of expenses: **cost of goods sold** (such as the cost of ingredients); **selling expenses** (such as the cost of salespersons' salaries); **marketing expenses** (such as the cost of advertising); **administrative expenses** (such as the salaries of administrative staff, and telephone and heat costs incurred at the corporate office); **interest expense** (amounts of interest paid on various debts); and **income taxes** (corporate taxes paid to government).

Tootsie Roll may also have liabilities arising from these expenses. For example, it may purchase goods on credit from suppliers; the obligations to pay for these goods are called **accounts payable**. Additionally, Tootsie Roll may have **interest payable** on the outstanding amounts owed to the bank. It may also have **wages payable** to its employees and **sales taxes payable**, **property taxes payable**, and **income taxes payable** to the government.

Tootsie Roll compares the revenues of a period with the expenses of that period to determine whether it earned a profit. When revenues exceed expenses, **net income** results. When expenses exceed revenues, a **net loss** results.

BEFORE YOU GO ON . . .

▶Review It

1. What are the three forms of business organization and the advantages of each?
2. What are the two primary categories of users of financial information? Give examples of each.
3. What are the three types of business activity?
4. What are assets, liabilities, common stock, revenues, expenses, and net income?

Before You Go On questions prompt you to stop and review the key points you have just studied.

▶Do It

Classify each item as an asset, liability, common stock, revenue, or expense.

Cost of renting property   Issuance of ownership shares
Truck purchased   Amount earned from providing service
Notes payable   Amounts owed to suppliers

Action Plan

- Classify each item based on its economic characteristics. Proper classification of items is critical if accounting is to provide useful information.

Solution

Cost of renting property is classified as expense.
Truck purchased is classified as an asset.
Notes payable are classified as liabilities.
Issuance of ownership shares is classified as common stock.
Amount earned from providing service is classified as revenue.
Amounts owed to suppliers are classified as liabilities.

Communicating with Users

STUDY OBJECTIVE
4
Describe the content and purpose of each of the financial statements.

Assets, liabilities, expenses, and revenues are of interest to users of accounting information. For business purposes, it is customary to arrange this information in the format of four different **financial statements**, which form the backbone of financial accounting:

- To present a picture at a point in time of what your business owns (its assets) and what it owes (its liabilities), you would present a **balance sheet**.
- To show how successfully your business performed during a period of time, you would report its revenues and expenses in an **income statement**.
- To indicate how much of previous income was distributed to you and the other owners of your business in the form of dividends, and how much was retained in the business to allow for future growth, you would present a **retained earnings statement**.
- To show from what sources your business obtained cash during a period of time and how that cash was used, you would present a **statement of cash flows**.

To introduce you to these statements, we have prepared the financial statements for a marketing agency, Sierra Corporation.

INCOME STATEMENT

The purpose of the income statement is to report the success or failure of the company's operations for a period of time. To indicate that its income statement reports the results of operations for a **period of time**, Sierra dates the income statement "For the Month Ended October 31, 2007." The income statement lists the company's revenues followed by its expenses. Finally, Sierra determines the net income (or net loss) by deducting expenses from revenues. Sierra Corporation's income statement is shown in Illustration 1-5.

Why are financial statement users interested in net income? Investors are interested in Sierra's past net income because it provides information about future net income. Investors buy and sell stock based on their beliefs about Sierra's future performance. If you believe that Sierra will be even more successful in the future and that this success will translate into a higher stock price, you should buy its stock. Creditors also use the income statement to predict the future. When

SIERRA CORPORATION Income Statement For the Month Ended October 31, 2007		
Revenues		
Service revenue		$10,600
Expenses		
Salaries expense	$5,200	
Supplies expense	1,500	
Rent expense	900	
Insurance expense	50	
Interest expense	50	
Depreciation expense	40	
Total expenses		7,740
Net income		$ 2,860

Illustration 1-5 Sierra Corporation's income statement

Helpful Hint The heading identifies the company, the type of statement, and the time period covered. Sometimes another line indicates the unit of measure — e.g., "in thousands" or "in millions."

a bank loans money to a company, it does so with the belief that it will be repaid in the future. If it didn't think it would be repaid, it wouldn't loan the money. Therefore, prior to making the loan the bank loan officer will use the income statement as a source of information to predict whether the company will be profitable enough to repay its loan.

Amounts received from issuing stock are not revenues, and amounts paid out as dividends are not expenses. As a result, they are not reported on the income statement. For example, Sierra Corporation did not treat as revenue the $10,000 of cash received from issuing new stock, nor did it regard as a business expense the $500 of dividends paid.

Decision Toolkit

Decision Toolkits summarize the financial decision-making process.

Decision Checkpoints	Info Needed for Decision	Tool to Use for Decision	How to Evaluate Results
Are the company's operations profitable?	Income statement	The income statement reports on the success or failure of the company's operations by reporting its revenues and expenses.	If the company's revenue exceeds its expenses, it will report net income; otherwise it will report a net loss.

RETAINED EARNINGS STATEMENT

If Sierra is profitable, at the end of each period it must decide what portion of profits to pay to shareholders in dividends. In theory it could pay all of its current-period profits, but few companies choose to do this. Why? Because they want to retain part of the profits to allow for further expansion. High-growth companies, such as Google and Cisco Systems, often choose to pay no dividends. **Retained earnings** is the net income retained in the corporation.

The **retained earnings statement** shows the amounts and causes of changes in retained earnings during the period. The time period is the same as that covered by the income statement. The beginning retained earnings amount appears on the first line of the statement. Then the company adds net income and deducts dividends to determine the retained earnings at the end of the period. If a company has a net loss, it deducts (rather than adds) that amount in the retained earnings statement. Illustration 1-6 presents Sierra Corporation's retained earnings statement.

Illustration 1-6 Sierra Corporation's retained earnings statement

SIERRA CORPORATION Retained Earnings Statement For the Month Ended October 31, 2007		
Retained earnings, October 1	$ 0
Add: Net income	2,860
	2,860
Less: Dividends	500
Retained earnings, October 31	$2,360

Helpful Hint The heading of this statement identifies the company, the type of statement, and the time period covered by the statement.

By monitoring the retained earnings statement, financial statement users can evaluate dividend payment practices. Some investors seek companies, such as Dow Chemical, that have a history of paying high dividends. Other investors seek companies, such as Amazon.com, that instead of paying dividends, reinvest earnings to increase the company's growth. Lenders monitor their corporate customers' dividend payments because any money paid in dividends reduces a company's ability to repay its debts.

Decision Toolkit

Decision Checkpoints	Info Needed for Decision	Tool to Use for Decision	How to Evaluate Results
What is the company's policy toward dividends and growth?	Retained earnings statement	How much of this year's income did the company pay out in dividends to shareholders?	A company striving for rapid growth will pay a low (or no) dividend.

BALANCE SHEET

STUDY OBJECTIVE
5

Explain the meaning of assets, liabilities, and stockholders' equity, and state the basic accounting equation.

The **balance sheet** reports assets and claims to those assets at a specific **point in time**. These claims are subdivided into two categories: claims of creditors and claims of owners. As noted earlier, claims of creditors are called **liabilities**. Claims of owners are called **stockholders' equity**.

The relationship among the categories on the balance sheet is shown in equation form in Illustration 1-7. This equation is referred to as the **basic accounting equation**.

Illustration 1-7 Basic accounting equation

Assets = Liabilities + Stockholders' Equity

This relationship is where the name "balance sheet" comes from. Assets must be in balance with the claims to the assets.

As you can see from looking at Sierra's balance sheet in Illustration 1-8, the balance sheet presents the company's financial position as of a specific date—in this case, October 31, 2007. It lists assets first, followed by liabilities and stockholders' equity. Stockholders' equity is comprised of two parts: (1) common stock and (2) retained earnings. As noted earlier, common stock results when the company sells new shares of stock; retained earnings is the net income retained in the corporation. Sierra has common stock of $10,000 and retained earnings of $2,360, for total stockholders' equity of $12,360.

Illustration 1-8 Sierra Corporation's balance sheet

SIERRA CORPORATION
Balance Sheet
October 31, 2007

Assets

Cash	$15,200
Accounts receivable	200
Advertising supplies	1,000
Prepaid insurance	550
Office equipment, net	4,960
Total assets	$21,910

Liabilities and Stockholders' Equity

Liabilities		
Notes payable	$ 5,000	
Accounts payable	2,500	
Interest payable	50	
Unearned revenue	800	
Salaries payable	1,200	
Total liabilities		$ 9,550
Stockholders' equity		
Common stock	10,000	
Retained earnings	2,360	
Total stockholders' equity		12,360
Total liabilities and stockholders' equity		$21,910

Helpful Hint The heading of a balance sheet must identify the company, the statement, and the date.

Creditors analyze a company's balance sheet to determine the likelihood that they will be repaid. They carefully evaluate the nature of the company's assets and liabilities. For example, does Sierra have assets that could be easily sold to repay its debts? Sierra's managers use the balance sheet to determine whether cash on hand is sufficient for immediate cash needs. They also look at the relationship between debt and stockholders' equity to determine whether the company has a satisfactory proportion of debt and common stock financing.

Decision Toolkit

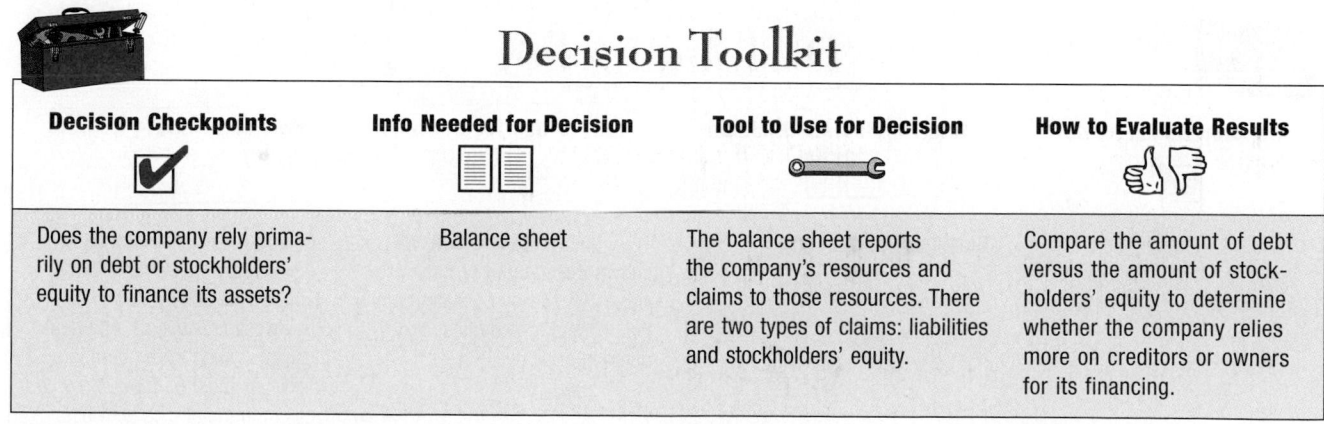

Decision Checkpoints	Info Needed for Decision	Tool to Use for Decision	How to Evaluate Results
Does the company rely primarily on debt or stockholders' equity to finance its assets?	Balance sheet	The balance sheet reports the company's resources and claims to those resources. There are two types of claims: liabilities and stockholders' equity.	Compare the amount of debt versus the amount of stockholders' equity to determine whether the company relies more on creditors or owners for its financing.

Business Insight
Ethics Perspective

What topic has performers such as Tom Waits, Clint Black, Sheryl Crow, and Madonna so concerned that they are pushing for new laws regarding its use? Accounting. Recording-company accounting to be more precise. Musicians receive royalty payments based on the accounting records kept by their recording companies. Many performers say that the recording companies—either intentionally or unintentionally—have very poor accounting systems, which, the performers say, has resulted in many inaccurate royalty payments. They would like to see laws created that would hit the recording companies with stiff fines for accounting errors.

 What is one way that some of these disputes might be resolved?

STATEMENT OF CASH FLOWS

The primary purpose of a **statement of cash flows** is to provide financial information about the cash receipts and cash payments of a business for a specific period of time. To help investors, creditors, and others in their analysis of a company's cash position, the statement of cash flows reports the cash effects of a company's **operating**, **investing**, and **financing** activities. In addition, the statement shows the net increase or decrease in cash during the period, and the amount of cash at the end of the period.

Users are interested in the statement of cash flows because they want to know what is happening to a company's most important resource. The statement of cash flows provides answers to these simple but important questions:

- Where did cash come from during the period?
- How was cash used during the period?
- What was the change in the cash balance during the period?

The statement of cash flows for Sierra, in Illustration 1-9, shows that cash increased $15,200 during the month. This increase resulted because operating activities (services to clients) increased cash $5,700, and financing activities increased cash $14,500. Investing activities used $5,000 of cash for the purchase of equipment.

Decision Toolkit

Decision Checkpoints	Info Needed for Decision	Tool to Use for Decision	How to Evaluate Results
Does the company generate sufficient cash from operations to fund its investing activities?	Statement of cash flows	The statement of cash flows shows the amount of cash provided or used by operating activities, investing activities, and financing activities.	Compare the amount of cash provided by operating activities with the amount of cash used by investing activities. Any deficiency in cash from operating activities must be made up with cash from financing activities.

SIERRA CORPORATION Statement of Cash Flows For the Month Ended October 31, 2007		
Cash flows from **operating** activities		
Cash receipts from operating activities	$11,200	
Cash payments for operating activities	(5,500)	
Net cash provided by operating activities		$ 5,700
Cash flows from **investing** activities		
Purchased office equipment	(5,000)	
Net cash used by investing activities		(5,000)
Cash flows from **financing** activities		
Issuance of common stock	10,000	
Issued note payable	5,000	
Payment of dividend	(500)	
Net cash provided by financing activities		14,500
Net increase in cash		15,200
Cash at beginning of period		0
Cash at end of period		$15,200

Illustration 1-9   Sierra Corporation's statement of cash flows

Helpful Hint The heading of this statement identifies the company, the type of statement, and the time period covered by the statement. Negative numbers are shown in parentheses.

INTERRELATIONSHIPS OF STATEMENTS

Because the results on some statements become inputs to other statements, the statements are interrelated. Illustration 1-10 (page 18) shows the interrelationships for Sierra's statements, which we describe below.

1. The retained earnings statement depends on the results of the income statement. Sierra reported net income of $2,860 for the period. It adds the net income amount to the beginning amount of retained earnings in order to determine ending retained earnings.
2. The balance sheet and retained earnings statement also are interrelated: Sierra reports the ending amount of $2,360 on the retained earnings statement as the retained earnings amount on the balance sheet.
3. Finally, the statement of cash flows relates to information on the balance sheet. The statement of cash flows shows how the cash account changed during the period. It shows the amount of cash at the beginning of the period, the sources and uses of cash during the period, and the $15,200 of cash at the end of the period. The ending amount of cash shown on the statement of cash flows must agree with the amount of cash on the balance sheet.

Study these interrelationships carefully. To prepare financial statements you must understand the sequence in which these amounts are determined, and how each statement impacts the next.

BEFORE YOU GO ON . . .

►Review It

1. What questions might each of the following decision makers ask that could be answered by financial information: marketing manager, production manager, bank loan officer, stock investor, labor union president, and federal bank regulator?
2. What are the content and purpose of each statement: income statement, balance sheet, retained earnings statement, and statement of cash flows?
3. The accounting equation is: Assets = Liabilities + Stockholders' Equity. Appendix A, at the end of this book, reproduces Tootsie Roll's financial statements. Replacing words in the equation with dollar amounts, what is

Review It questions marked with this **Tootsie Roll icon** require that you use Tootsie Roll's 2004 Annual Report in Appendix A at the back of the book.

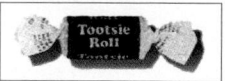

Illustration 1-10   Sierra Corporation's financial statements

SIERRA CORPORATION
Income Statement
For the Month Ended October 31, 2007

Revenues		
Service revenue		$10,600
Expenses		
Salaries expense	$5,200	
Supplies expense	1,500	
Rent expense	900	
Insurance expense	50	
Interest expense	50	
Depreciation expense	40	
Total expenses		7,740
Net income		$ 2,860

①

SIERRA CORPORATION
Retained Earnings Statement
For the Month Ended October 31, 2007

Retained earnings, October 1	$ 0
Add: Net income	2,860
	2,860
Less: Dividends	500
Retained earnings, October 31	$ 2,360

SIERRA CORPORATION
Balance Sheet
October 31, 2007

Assets

Cash	$15,200
Accounts receivable	200
Advertising supplies	1,000
Prepaid insurance	550
Office equipment, net	4,960
Total assets	$21,910

Liabilities and Stockholders' Equity

Liabilities		
Notes payable	$5,000	
Accounts payable	2,500	
Interest payable	50	
Unearned revenue	800	
Salaries payable	1,200	
Total liabilities		$ 9,550
Stockholders' equity		
Common stock	10,000	
Retained earnings	2,360	
Total stockholders' equity		12,360
Total liabilities and stockholders' equity		$21,910

②

③

SIERRA CORPORATION
Statement of Cash Flows
For the Month Ended October 31, 2007

Cash flows from operating activities		
Cash receipts from operating activities	$11,200	
Cash payments for operating activities	(5,500)	
Net cash provided by operating activities		$ 5,700
Cash flows from investing activities		
Purchased office equipment	(5,000)	
Net cash used by investing activities		(5,000)
Cash flows from financing activities		
Issuance of common stock	10,000	
Issued note payable	5,000	
Payment of dividend	(500)	
Net cash provided by financing activities		14,500
Net increase in cash		15,200
Cash at beginning of period		0
Cash at end of period		$15,200

Tootsie Roll's accounting equation at December 31, 2004? (The answer to this question appears on page 45.)

▶Do It

CSU Corporation began operations on January 1, 2007. The following information is available for CSU Corporation on December 31, 2007: service revenue $17,000; accounts receivable $4,000; accounts payable $2,000; building rental expense $9,000; notes payable $5,000; common stock $10,000; retained earnings $?; equipment $16,000; insurance expense $1,000; supplies $1,800; supplies expense $200; cash $1,400; dividends $600.

Prepare an income statement, a retained earnings statement, and a balance sheet using this information.

Action Plan

- Report the revenues and expenses for a period of time in an income statement.
- Show the amounts and causes (net income and dividends) of changes in retained earnings during the period in the retained earnings statement.
- Present the assets and claims to those assets at a specific point in time in the balance sheet.

Solution

CSU CORPORATION
Income Statement
For the Year Ended December 31, 2007

Revenues		
Service revenue		$17,000
Expenses		
Rent expense	$9,000	
Insurance expense	1,000	
Supplies expense	200	
Total expenses		10,200
Net income		$ 6,800

CSU CORPORATION
Retained Earnings Statement
For the Year Ended December 31, 2007

Retained earnings, January 1	$ 0
Add: Net income	6,800
	6,800
Less: Dividends	600
Retained earnings, December 31	$6,200

CSU CORPORATION
Balance Sheet
December 31, 2007

Assets

Cash		$ 1,400
Accounts receivable		4,000
Supplies		1,800
Equipment		16,000
Total assets		$23,200

Liabilities and Stockholders' Equity

Liabilities		
Notes payable	$ 5,000	
Accounts payable	2,000	
Total liabilities		$ 7,000
Stockholders' equity		
Common stock	10,000	
Retained earnings	6,200	
Total stockholders' equity		16,200
Total liabilities and stockholders' equity		$23,200

THE NAVIGATOR

A Quick Look at Tootsie Roll's Financial Statements

Tootsie Roll Annual Report Walkthrough

The same relationships that you observed among the financial statements of Sierra Corporation are evident in the 2004 financial statements of Tootsie Roll Industries, Inc., which are presented in Illustrations 1-11 through 1-14. We have simplified the financial statements to assist your learning—but they may look complicated to you anyway. Do not be alarmed by their seeming complexity. (If you could already read and understand them, there would be little reason to take this course, except possibly to add a high grade to your transcript—which we hope you'll do anyway.) By the end of the book, you'll have a great deal of experience in reading and understanding financial statements such as these. Tootsie Roll's **actual financial statements** are presented in **Appendix A** at the end of the book.

Before we dive in, we need to explain two points:

1. Note that numbers are reported in thousands on Tootsie Roll's financial statements—that is, the last three 000s are omitted. Thus, Tootsie Roll's net income in 2004 is $64,174,000, not $64,174.

2. Tootsie Roll, like most companies, presents its financial statements for more than one year. Financial statements that report information for more than one period are called comparative statements. Comparative statements allow users to compare the financial position of the business at the end of an accounting period with that of previous periods.

Helpful Hint The percentage change in any amount from one year to the next is calculated as follows:

$$\frac{\text{Change during period}}{\text{Previous value}}$$

Thus, the percentage change in income is:

$$\frac{\text{Change in income}}{\text{Previous year's income}}$$

INCOME STATEMENT

Tootsie Roll's income statement is presented in Illustration 1-11. It reports total revenues in 2004 of $424,894,000. It then subtracts three types of expenses—cost of goods sold; selling, marketing, and administrative expenses; and income tax expense—to arrive at net income of $64,174,000. This is a 1.3% decrease from income for the previous year.

Illustration 1-11
Tootsie Roll's income statement

TOOTSIE ROLL INDUSTRIES, INC.
Income Statements
For the Years Ended December 31, 2004, and December 31, 2003
(in thousands)

	2004	2003
Revenues		
Sales revenue	$420,110	$392,656
Other revenues	4,784	5,594
Total revenues	424,894	398,250
Expenses		
Cost of goods sold	244,501	222,547
Selling, marketing, and administrative expenses	85,705	77,756
Income tax expense	30,514	32,933
Total expenses	360,720	333,236
Net income	$ 64,174	$ 65,014

Illustration 1-12   Tootsie Roll's retained earnings statement

TOOTSIE ROLL INDUSTRIES, INC.
Retained Earnings Statements
For the Years Ended December 31, 2004, and December 31, 2003
(in thousands)

Retained earnings, December 31, 2002	$148,705
Add: Net income	65,014
	213,719
Less: Dividends	56,933
Retained earnings, December 31, 2003	156,786
Add: Net income	64,174
	220,960
Less: Dividends	71,905
Retained earnings, December 31, 2004	$149,055

RETAINED EARNINGS STATEMENT

Tootsie Roll presents information about its retained earnings in the retained earnings statement in Illustration 1-12. (Many companies present changes in retained earnings in a broader report called the Statement of Stockholders' Equity.) Find the line "Retained earnings, December 31, 2003." This number, $156,786,000, agrees with the retained earnings balance from the December 31, 2003, balance sheet.

As we proceed down the retained earnings statement, the next figure is net income of $64,174,000. Tootsie Roll distributed dividends of $71,905,000. The ending balance of retained earnings is $149,055,000 on December 31, 2004. Find this amount of retained earnings near the bottom of Tootsie Roll's balance sheet for December 31, 2004 (Illustration 1-13 on page 22).

BALANCE SHEET

As shown in its balance sheet in Illustration 1-13, Tootsie Roll's assets include the kinds previously mentioned in our discussion of Sierra Corporation. These are cash, inventories, and property, plant, and equipment, plus other types of assets that we will discuss in later chapters, such as prepaid expenses. Tootsie Roll's total assets increased from $665,297,000 on December 31, 2003, to $811,753,000 on December 31, 2004. Its liabilities include accounts payable as well as items not yet discussed, such as employee benefits payable.

You can see that Tootsie Roll relies far more on equity financing than on debt—it has more than twice as much stockholders' equity as it has liabilities. As you learn more about financial statements we will discuss how to interpret the relationships and changes in financial statement items.

STATEMENT OF CASH FLOWS

Tootsie Roll's cash decreased $27,095,000 during 2004. Tootsie Roll's balance sheet shows that cash was $84,084,000 at December 31, 2003, and $56,989,000 at December 31, 2004. The reasons for this decrease can be determined by examining the statement of cash flows in Illustration 1-14 (page 23). Tootsie Roll generated $76,228,000 from its operating activities during 2004. Its investing activities included capital expenditures (purchases of property, plant, and equipment) as well as purchases and sales of investment securities. The net effect of its investment activities was an outflow of cash of $164,039,000. Its financing activities involved the repurchase of its own common stock and the payment of

Illustration 1-13 Tootsie Roll's balance sheet

TOOTSIE ROLL INDUSTRIES, INC.
Balance Sheets
December 31, 2004, and December 31, 2003
(in thousands)

Assets	2004	2003
Cash	$ 56,989	$ 84,084
Investments	32,369	86,961
Accounts receivable	37,457	21,207
Inventories	58,777	46,086
Prepaid expenses	7,101	5,367
Property, plant, and equipment, net	178,750	129,163
Other assets	440,310	292,429
Total assets	$811,753	$665,297

Liabilities and Stockholders' Equity		
Liabilities		
Accounts payable	$ 19,315	$ 11,947
Dividends payable	3,659	3,589
Accrued liabilities	44,722	38,834
Income taxes payable	8,288	8,517
Bank loan	92,000	—
Employee benefits payable	10,075	9,302
Other liabilities	63,515	56,527
Total liabilities	241,574	128,716
Stockholders' equity		
Common stock	421,124	379,795
Retained earnings	149,055	156,786
Total stockholders' equity	570,179	536,581
Total liabilities and stockholders' equity	$811,753	$665,297

cash dividends. In all, the net effect of the cash generated from its operating and financing activities, less the cash used in its investing activities, was a decrease in cash of $27,095,000.

OTHER ELEMENTS OF AN ANNUAL REPORT

U.S. companies that are publicly traded must provide shareholders with an **annual report**. The annual report always includes the financial statements introduced in this chapter. The annual report also includes other important information such as a management discussion and analysis section, notes to the financial statements, and an independent auditor's report. No analysis of a company's financial situation and prospects is complete without a review of these items.

STUDY OBJECTIVE
6
Describe the components that supplement the financial statements in an annual report.

Management Discussion and Analysis

The **management discussion and analysis (MD&A)** section covers various financial aspects of a company, including **its ability to pay near-term obligations, its ability to fund operations and expansion, and its results of operations**. Management must highlight favorable or unfavorable trends and identify significant events and uncertainties that affect these three factors. This discussion obviously involves a number of subjective estimates and opinions.

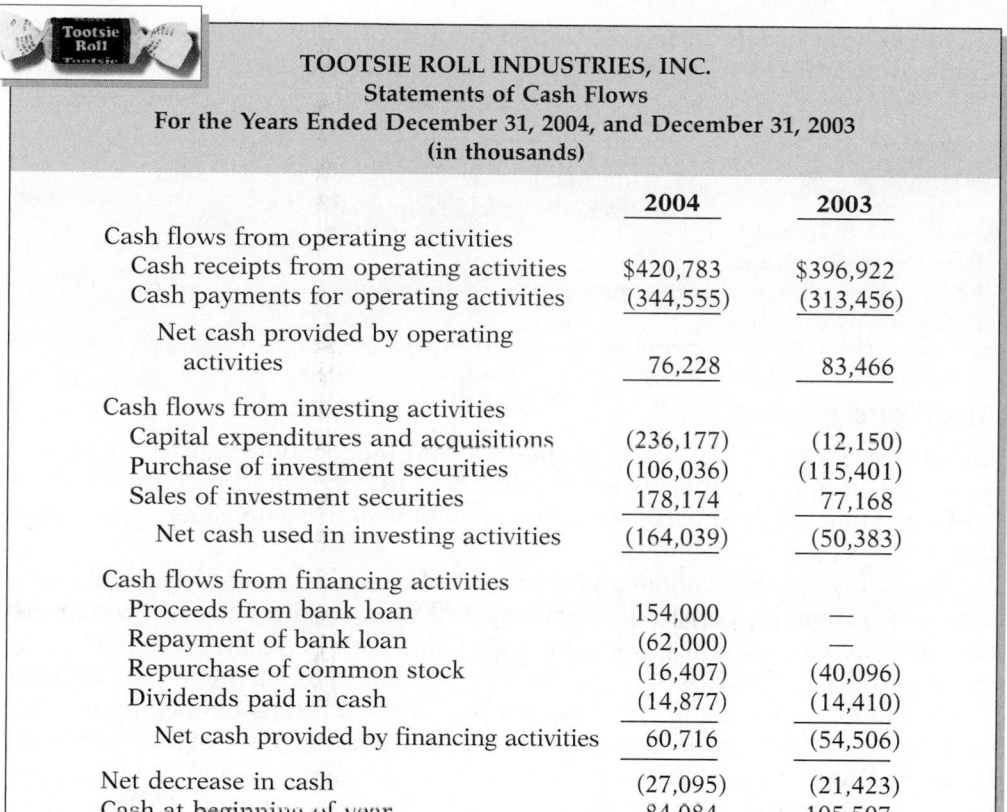

TOOTSIE ROLL INDUSTRIES, INC.
Statements of Cash Flows
For the Years Ended December 31, 2004, and December 31, 2003
(in thousands)

	2004	2003
Cash flows from operating activities		
Cash receipts from operating activities	$420,783	$396,922
Cash payments for operating activities	(344,555)	(313,456)
Net cash provided by operating activities	76,228	83,466
Cash flows from investing activities		
Capital expenditures and acquisitions	(236,177)	(12,150)
Purchase of investment securities	(106,036)	(115,401)
Sales of investment securities	178,174	77,168
Net cash used in investing activities	(164,039)	(50,383)
Cash flows from financing activities		
Proceeds from bank loan	154,000	—
Repayment of bank loan	(62,000)	—
Repurchase of common stock	(16,407)	(40,096)
Dividends paid in cash	(14,877)	(14,410)
Net cash provided by financing activities	60,716	(54,506)
Net decrease in cash	(27,095)	(21,423)
Cash at beginning of year	84,084	105,507
Cash at end of year	$ 56,989	$ 84,084

Illustration 1-14   Tootsie Roll's statement of cash flows

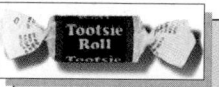

TOOTSIE ROLL INDUSTRIES, INC.
Management's Discussion and Analysis of
Financial Condition and Results of Operations

The company has a simple financial structure, and aside from an immaterial amount of operating leases, the company has no "off-balance sheet" financing arrangements. We maintain a conservative financial posture and funds generated from operations plus maturities of short term investments are expected to be adequate to meet the company's financing needs over the coming year.

Illustration 1-15   Tootsie Roll's management discussion and analysis

A brief excerpt from the MD&A section of Tootsie Roll's annual report (above) is presented in Illustration 1-15.

Notes to the Financial Statements

Explanatory notes and supporting schedules accompany every set of financial statements and are an integral part of the statements. The **notes to the financial statements** clarify information presented in the financial statements, as well as expand upon it where additional detail is needed. Information in the notes does not have to be quantifiable (numeric). Examples of notes are descriptions of the significant accounting policies and methods used in preparing the statements, explanations of uncertainties and contingencies, and various statistics and details too voluminous to be included in the statements. The notes are essential to understanding a company's operating performance and financial position.

Illustration 1-16 is an excerpt from the notes to Tootsie Roll's financial statements. It describes the methods that Tootsie Roll uses to account for revenues.

Illustration 1-16 Notes to Tootsie Roll's financial statements

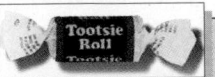

TOOTSIE ROLL INDUSTRIES, INC.
Notes to Financial Statements

Revenue recognition
Revenues are recognized when products are delivered to customers and collectibility is reasonably assured.

Auditor's Report

An **auditor's report** is a report prepared by an independent outside auditor. It states the auditor's opinion as to the fairness of the presentation of the financial position and results of operations and their conformance with generally accepted accounting standards.

An **auditor** is an accounting professional who conducts an independent examination of a company's financial statements. Only accountants who meet certain criteria and thereby attain the designation **Certified Public Accountant (CPA)** may perform audits. If the auditor is satisfied that the financial statements provide a fair representation of the company's financial position and results of operations in accordance with generally accepted accounting principles, then the auditor expresses an **unqualified opinion**. If the auditor expresses anything other than an unqualified opinion, then readers should only use the financial statements with caution. That is, without an unqualified opinion, we cannot have complete confidence that the financial statements give an accurate picture of the company's financial health.

Illustration 1-17 is an excerpt from the auditor's report from Tootsie Roll's 2004 annual report. Tootsie Roll received an unqualified opinion from its auditor, PricewaterhouseCoopers.

Illustration 1-17 Excerpt from auditor's report on Tootsie Roll's financial statements

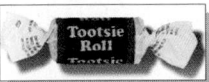

TOOTSIE ROLL INDUSTRIES, INC.
Excerpt from Auditor's Report

To the Board of Directors and Shareholders of Tootsie Roll Industries, Inc.

In our opinion, the accompanying consolidated balance sheets and the related consolidated statements of earnings, comprehensive earnings, retained earnings, and cash flows present fairly, in all material respects, the financial position of Tootsie Roll Industries, Inc. and its subsidiaries at December 31, 2004 and 2003, and the results of their operations and their cash flows for each of the three years in the period ended December 31, 2004, in conformity with accounting principles generally accepted in the United States of America.

BEFORE YOU GO ON . . .

▶Review It

1. What is the intent of the management discussion and analysis section in the annual report?
2. Why are notes to the financial statements necessary? What kinds of items are included in these notes?
3. What is the purpose of the auditor's report?

THE NAVIGATOR

Using the Decision Toolkit

Hershey Foods Corporation, located in Hershey, Pennsylvania, is the leading North American manufacturer of chocolate—for example, Hershey's Kisses, Reese's Peanut Butter Cups, Kit Kat, and Take 5 bars. Imagine that you are considering the purchase of shares of Hershey's common stock.

Using the Decision Toolkit exercises ask you to use information from financial statements to make financial decisions.

Instructions

Answer these questions related to your decision whether to invest.

(a) What financial statements should you request from the company?
(b) What should these financial statements tell you?
(c) Should you request audited financial statements? Explain.
(d) Illustrations 1-18 through 1-21 show simplified financial statements for Hershey Foods. What comparisons can you make between Tootsie Roll and Hershey in terms of their respective results from operations and financial position?

HERSHEY FOODS CORPORATION
Income Statements
For the Years Ended December 31, 2004, and
December 31, 2003 (in thousands)

	2004	2003
Revenues		
Sales revenue	$4,429,248	$4,172,551
Expenses		
Cost of goods sold	2,679,531	2,544,726
Selling, marketing, and administrative expenses	847,540	816,442
Other	—	22,395
Interest expense	66,533	63,529
Income tax expense	244,765	267,875
Total expenses	3,838,369	3,714,967
Net income	$ 590,879	$ 457,584

Illustration 1-18
Hershey Foods' income statement

HERSHEY FOODS CORPORATION
Retained Earnings Statements
For the Years Ended December 31, 2004, and
December 31, 2003 (in thousands)

Retained earnings December 31, 2002	$1,191,160
Add: Net income	457,584
	1,648,744
Less: Dividends	184,686
Other adjustments*	368,176
Retained earnings December 31, 2003	1,095,882
Add: Net income	590,879
	1,686,761
Less: Dividends	205,747
Other adjustments*	780,227
Retained earnings December 31, 2004	$ 700,787

Illustration 1-19
Hershey Foods' retained earnings statement

*Primarily the repurchase of common stock.

Illustration 1-20
Hershey Foods' balance
sheet

HERSHEY FOODS CORPORATION
Balance Sheets
December 31, 2004, and December 31, 2003
(in thousands)

Assets	2004	2003
Cash	$ 54,837	$ 114,793
Accounts receivable	408,930	407,612
Inventories	557,180	492,859
Prepaid expenses and other	161,494	116,305
Property, plant, and equipment, net	1,682,698	1,661,939
Other assets	932,392	789,032
Total assets	$3,797,531	$3,582,540

Liabilities and Stockholders' Equity

Liabilities		
Accounts payable	$ 148,686	$ 132,222
Accrued liabilities	472,096	416,181
Income taxes payable	42,280	24,898
Short-term debt and other	622,320	12,509
Long-term debt and liabilities	1,093,958	1,339,275
Other liabilities	328,889	377,589
Total liabilities	2,708,229	2,302,674
Stockholders' equity		
Common stock	388,515	183,984
Retained earnings	700,787	1,095,882
Total stockholders' equity	1,089,302	1,279,866
Total liabilities and stockholders' equity	$3,797,531	$3,582,540

Illustration 1-21
Hershey Foods' statement
of cash flows

HERSHEY FOODS CORPORATION
Statements of Cash Flows
For the Years Ended December 31, 2004, and
December 31, 2003 (in thousands)

	2004	2003
Cash flows from operating activities		
Cash receipts from operating activities	$4,446,567	$4,135,915
Cash payments for operating activities	(3,649,117)	(3,542,972)
Net cash provided by operating activities	797,450	592,943
Cash flows from investing activities		
Capital expenditures	(362,745)	(237,054)
Proceeds from divestitures	—	20,049
Net cash used in investing activities	(362,745)	(217,005)
Cash flows from financing activities		
Issuance of debt	331,245	4,091
Repayment of long-term debt	(883)	(18,633)
Dividends paid in cash	(205,747)	(184,686)
Issuance of common stock	79,634	55,120
Repurchase of common stock	(616,977)	(329,433)
Other	(81,933)	(85,347)
Net cash used in financing activities	(494,661)	(558,888)
Net decrease in cash	(59,956)	(182,950)
Cash at beginning of year	114,793	297,743
Cash at end of year	$ 54,837	$ 114,793

Solution

(a) Before you invest, you should investigate the income statement, retained earnings statement, statement of cash flows, and balance sheet.

(b) You would probably be most interested in the income statement because it tells about past performance and thus gives an indication of future performance. The retained earnings statement provides a record of the company's dividend history. The statement of cash flows reveals where the company is getting and spending its cash. This is especially important for a company that wants to grow. Finally, the balance sheet reveals the relationship between assets and liabilities.

(c) You would want audited financial statements. These statements indicate that a CPA (certified public accountant) has examined and expressed an opinion that the statements present fairly the financial position and results of operations of the company. Investors and creditors should not make decisions without studying audited financial statements.

(d) Many interesting comparisons can be made between the two companies. Tootsie Roll is smaller, with total assets of $811,753,000 versus $3,797,531,000 for Hershey, and it has lower sales revenue—$420,110,000 versus $4,429,248,000 for Hershey. In addition, Tootsie Roll's cash provided by operating activities of $76,228,000 is less than Hershey's $797,450,000.

While useful, these basic measures are not enough to determine whether one company is a better investment than the other. In later chapters you will learn of tools that will allow you to compare the relative profitability and financial health of these and other companies.

Summary of Study Objectives

1 *Describe the primary forms of business organization.* A sole proprietorship is a business owned by one person. A partnership is a business owned by two or more people associated as partners. A corporation is a separate legal entity for which evidence of ownership is provided by shares of stock.

2 *Identify the users and uses of accounting information.* Internal users are managers who need accounting information to plan, organize, and run business operations. The primary external users are investors and creditors. Investors (stockholders) use accounting information to help them decide whether to buy, hold, or sell shares of a company's stock. Creditors (suppliers and bankers) use accounting information to assess the risk of granting credit or loaning money to a business. Other groups who have an indirect interest in a business are taxing authorities, customers, labor unions, and regulatory agencies.

3 *Explain the three principal types of business activity.* Financing activities involve collecting the necessary funds to support the business. Investing activities involve acquiring the resources necessary to run the business. Operating activities involve putting the resources of the business into action to generate a profit.

4 *Describe the content and purpose of each of the financial statements.* An income statement presents the revenues and expenses of a company for a specific period of time. A retained earnings statement summarizes the changes in retained earnings that have occurred for a specific period of time. A balance sheet reports the assets, liabilities, and stockholders' equity of a business at a specific date. A statement of cash flows summarizes information concerning the cash inflows (receipts) and outflows (payments) for a specific period of time.

5 *Explain the meaning of assets, liabilities, and stockholders' equity, and state the basic accounting equation.* Assets are resources owned by a business. Liabilities are the debts and obligations of the business. Liabilities represent claims of creditors on the assets of the business. Stockholders' equity represents the claims of owners on the assets of the business. Stockholders' equity is subdivided into two parts: common stock and retained earnings. The basic accounting equation is: Assets = Liabilities + Stockholders' Equity.

6 *Describe the components that supplement the financial statements in an annual report.* The management discussion and analysis provides management's interpretation of the company's results and financial position as well as a discussion of plans for the future. Notes to the financial statements provide additional explanation or detail to make the financial statements more informative. The auditor's report expresses an opinion as to whether the financial statements present fairly the company's results of operations and financial position.

Decision Toolkit—A Summary

Decision Checkpoints	Info Needed for Decision	Tool to Use for Decision	How to Evaluate Results
Are the company's operations profitable?	Income statement	The income statement reports on the success or failure of the company's operations by reporting its revenues and expenses.	If the company's revenue exceeds its expenses, it will report net income; otherwise it will report a net loss.
What is the company's policy toward dividends and growth?	Retained earnings statement	How much of this year's income did the company pay out in dividends to shareholders?	A company striving for rapid growth will pay a low (or no) dividend.
Does the company rely primarily on debt or stockholders' equity to finance its assets?	Balance sheet	The balance sheet reports the company's resources and claims to those resources. There are two types of claims: liabilities and stockholders' equity.	Compare the amount of debt versus the amount of stockholders' equity to determine whether the company relies more on creditors or owners for its financing.
Does the company generate sufficient cash from operations to fund its investing activities?	Statement of cash flows	The statement of cash flows shows the amount of cash provided or used by operating activities, investing activities, and financing activities.	Compare the amount of cash provided by operating activities with the amount of cash used by investing activities. Any deficiency in cash from operating activities must be made up with

Glossary

Accounting The information system that identifies, records, and communicates the economic events of an organization to interested users. (p. 6)

Annual report A report prepared by corporate management that presents financial information including financial statements, notes, a management discussion and analysis section, and an independent auditor's report. (p. 22)

Assets Resources owned by a business. (p. 10)

Auditor's report A report prepared by an independent outside auditor stating the auditor's opinion as to the fairness of the presentation of the financial position and results of operations and their conformance with generally accepted accounting standards. (p. 24)

Balance sheet A financial statement that reports the assets and claims to those assets at a specific point in time. (p. 14)

Basic accounting equation Assets = Liabilities + Stockholders' Equity. (p. 14)

Certified Public Accountant (CPA) An individual who has met certain criteria and is thus allowed to perform audits of corporations. (p. 24)

Common stock Term used to describe the total amount paid in by stockholders for the shares they purchase. (p. 10)

Comparative statements A presentation of the financial statements of a company for more than one year. (p. 20)

Corporation A business organized as a separate legal entity having ownership divided into transferable shares of stock. (p. 4)

Dividends Payments of cash from a corporation to its stockholders. (p. 10)

Expenses The cost of assets consumed or services used in the process of generating revenues. (p. 11)

Income statement A financial statement that presents the revenues and expenses and resulting net income or net loss of a company for a specific period of time. (p. 12)

Liabilities The debts and obligations of a business. Liabilities represent the amounts owed to creditors. (p. 10)

Management discussion and analysis (MD&A) A section of the annual report that presents management's views on the company's ability to pay near-term obligations, its ability to fund operations and expansion, and its results of operations. (p. 22)

Net income The amount by which revenues exceed expenses. (p. 11)

Net loss The amount by which expenses exceed revenues. (p. 11)

Notes to the financial statements Notes that clarify information presented in the financial statements, as well as expand upon it where additional detail is needed. (p. 23)

Partnership A business owned by two or more persons associated as partners. (p. 4)

Retained earnings The amount of net income retained in the corporation. (p. 13)

Retained earnings statement A financial statement that summarizes the amounts and causes of changes in retained earnings for a specific period of time. (p. 13)

Revenues The increase in assets that result from the sale of a product or service in the normal course of business. (p. 11)

Sarbanes-Oxley Act Regulations passed by Congress in 2002 to try to reduce unethical corporate behavior. (p. 9)

Sole proprietorship A business owned by one person. (p. 4)

Statement of cash flows A financial statement that provides financial information about the cash receipts and cash payments of a business for a specific period of time. (p. 16)

Stockholders' equity The stockholders' claim on total assets. (p. 14)

Demonstration Problem

Jeff Andringa, a former college hockey player, quit his job and started Ice Camp, a hockey camp for kids ages 8 to 18. Eventually he would like to open hockey camps nationwide. Jeff has asked you to help him prepare financial statements at the end of his first year of operations. He relates the following facts about his business activities.

In order to get the business off the ground, he decided to incorporate. He sold shares of common stock to a few close friends, as well as buying some of the shares himself. He initially raised $25,000 through the sale of these shares. In addition, the company took out a $10,000 loan at a local bank.

Ice Camp purchased, for $12,000 cash, a bus for transporting kids. The company also bought hockey goals and other miscellaneous equipment with $1,500 cash. The company earned camp tuition during the year of $100,000 but had collected only $80,000 of this amount. Thus, at the end of the year its customers still owed $20,000. The company rents time at a local rink for $50 per hour. Total rink rental costs during the year were $8,000, insurance was $10,000, salary expense was $20,000, and administrative expenses totaled $9,000, all of which were paid in cash. The company incurred $800 in interest expense on the bank loan, which it still owed at the end of the year.

The company paid dividends during the year of $5,000 cash. The balance in the corporate bank account at December 31, 2007, was $49,500.

Instructions

Using the format of the Sierra Corporation statements in this chapter, prepare an income statement, retained earnings statement, balance sheet, and statement of cash flows. (*Hint:* Prepare the statements in the order stated to take advantage of the flow of information from one statement to the next, as shown in Illustration 1-10 on page 18.)

Demonstration Problems are a final review before you begin homework. **Action Plans** that appear in the margins give you tips about how to approach the problem.

Action Plan
- On the income statement: Show revenues and expenses for a period of time.
- On the retained earnings statement: Show the changes in retained earnings for a period of time.
- On the balance sheet: Report assets, liabilities, and stockholders' equity at a specific date.
- On the statement of cash flows: Report sources and uses of cash from operating, investing, and financing activities for a period of time.

Solution to Demonstration Problem

ICE CAMP
Income Statement
For the Year Ended December 31, 2007

Revenues		
Camp tuition revenue		$100,000
Expenses		
Salaries expense	$20,000	
Insurance expense	10,000	
Administrative expense	9,000	
Rink rental expense	8,000	
Interest expense	800	
Total expenses		47,800
Net income		$ 52,200

ICE CAMP
Retained Earnings Statement
For the Year Ended December 31, 2007

Retained earnings, January 1, 2007	$ 0
Add: Net income	52,200
	52,200
Less: Dividends	5,000
Retained earnings, December 31, 2007	$47,200

ICE CAMP
Balance Sheet
December 31, 2007

Assets

Cash	$49,500
Accounts receivable	20,000
Bus	12,000
Equipment	1,500
Total assets	$83,000

Liabilities and Stockholders' Equity

Liabilities		
Bank loan payable	$10,000	
Interest payable	800	
Total liabilities		$10,800
Stockholders' equity		
Common stock	25,000	
Retained earnings	47,200	
Total stockholders' equity		72,200
Total liabilities and stockholders' equity		$83,000

ICE CAMP
Statement of Cash Flows
For the Year Ended December 31, 2007

Cash flows from operating activities		
Cash receipts from operating activities	$80,000	
Cash payments for operating activities	(47,000)	
Net cash provided by operating activities		$33,000
Cash flows from investing activities		
Purchase of bus	(12,000)	
Purchase of equipment	(1,500)	
Net cash used by investing activities		(13,500)
Cash flows from financing activities		
Issuance of bank loan payable	10,000	
Issuance of common stock	25,000	
Dividends paid	(5,000)	
Net cash provided by financing activities		30,000
Net increase in cash		49,500
Cash at beginning of period		0
Cash at end of period		$49,500

This would be a good time to look at the **Student Owner's Manual** at the beginning of the book. Knowing the purpose of the different types of homework will help you understand what each contributes to your accounting skills and competencies.

The tool icon ⬤━━━━G indicates that an activity employs one of the decision tools presented in the chapter. The ➡ indicates that an activity relates to a business function beyond accounting. The pencil icon ▭▭▭▭➤ indicates that an activity requires written communication.

Self-Study Questions

Answers are at the end of the chapter.

(SO 1) **1.** Which is *not* one of the three forms of business organization?
(a) Sole proprietorship.   (c) Partnership.
(b) Creditorship.   (d) Corporation.

(SO 1) **2.** Which is an advantage of corporations relative to partnerships and sole proprietorships?
(a) Lower taxes.
(b) Harder to transfer ownership.
(c) Reduced legal liability for investors.
(d) Most common form of organization.

(SO 2) **3.** Which statement about users of accounting information is *incorrect*?
(a) Management is considered an internal user.
(b) Taxing authorities are considered external users.
(c) Present creditors are considered external users.
(d) Regulatory authorities are considered internal users.

(SO 3) **4.** Which is *not* one of the three primary business activities?
(a) Financing.   (c) Advertising.
(b) Operating.   (d) Investing.

(SO 3, 4) **5.** Net income will result during a time period when:
(a) assets exceed liabilities.
(b) assets exceed revenues.
(c) expenses exceed revenues.
(d) revenues exceed expenses.

(SO 4, 5) **6.** What section of a cash flow statement indicates the cash spent on new equipment during the past accounting period?
(a) The investing section.
(b) The operating section.

(c) The financing section.
(d) The cash flow statement does not give this information.

7. Which financial statement reports assets, liabilities, and stockholders' equity? (SO 5)
(a) Income statement.
(b) Retained earnings statement.
(c) Balance sheet.
(d) Statement of cash flows.

8. Stockholders' equity represents: (SO 5)
(a) claims of creditors.
(b) claims of employees.
(c) the difference between revenues and expenses.
(d) claims of owners.

9. As of December 31, 2007, Stoneland Corporation has assets of $3,500 and stockholders' equity of $2,000. What are the liabilities for Stoneland Corporation as of December 31, 2007? (SO 5)
(a) $1,500.   (c) $2,500.
(b) $1,000.   (d) $2,000.

10. The segment of a corporation's annual report that describes the corporation's accounting methods is the: (SO 6)
(a) notes to the financial statements.
(b) management discussion and analysis.
(c) auditor's report.
(d) income statement.

Go to the book's website, **www.wiley.com/college/kimmel**, to access additional Self-Study Questions.

Questions

1. What are the three basic forms of business organizations?

2. What are the advantages to a business of being formed as a corporation? What are the disadvantages?

3. What are the advantages to a business of being formed as a partnership or sole proprietorship? What are the disadvantages?

4. "Accounting is ingrained in our society and is vital to our economic system." Do you agree? Explain.

5. Who are the internal users of accounting data? How does accounting provide relevant data to the internal users?

6. Who are the external users of accounting data? Give examples.

7. What are the three main types of business activity? Give examples of each activity.

8. Listed here are some items found in the financial statements of Ellyn Toth, Inc. Indicate in which financial statement(s) each item would appear.
(a) Service revenue.   (d) Accounts receivable.
(b) Equipment.   (e) Common stock.
(c) Advertising expense.   (f) Wages payable.

9. Why would a bank want to monitor the dividend payment practices of the corporations it lends money to?

10. "A company's net income appears directly on the income statement and the retained earnings statement, and it is included indirectly in the company's balance sheet." Do you agree? Explain.

11. ○▬▬C What is the primary purpose of the statement of cash flows?

12. What are the three main categories of the statement of cash flows? Why do you think these categories were chosen?

13. What is retained earnings? What items increase the balance in retained earnings? What items decrease the balance in retained earnings?

14. What is the basic accounting equation?

15. (a) Define the terms *assets*, *liabilities*, and *stockholders'* equity.
    (b) What items affect stockholders' equity?

16. Which of these items are liabilities of White Glove Cleaning Service?
    (a) Cash.   (f) Equipment.
    (b) Accounts payable.   (g) Salaries payable.
    (c) Dividends.   (h) Service revenue.
    (d) Accounts receivable.   (i) Rent expense.
    (e) Supplies.

17. How are each of the following financial statements interrelated? (a) Retained earnings statement and income statement. (b) Retained earnings statement and balance sheet. (c) Balance sheet and statement of cash flows.

18. ○▬▬C What is the purpose of the management discussion and analysis section (MD&A)?

19. ○▬▬C Why is it important for financial statements to receive an unqualified auditor's opinion?

20. ○▬▬C What types of information are presented in the notes to the financial statements?

Brief Exercises

Describe forms of business organization.
(SO 1)

BE1-1 Match each of the following forms of business organization with a set of characteristics: sole proprietorship (SP), partnership (P), corporation (C).
(a) _____ Shared control, tax advantages, increased skills and resources.
(b) _____ Simple to set up and maintains control with founder.
(c) _____ Easier to transfer ownership and raise funds, no personal liability.

Identify users of accounting information.
(SO 2)

BE1-2 Match each of the following types of evaluation with one of the listed users of accounting information.
1. Trying to determine whether the company complied with tax laws.
2. Trying to determine whether the company can pay its obligations.
3. Trying to determine whether a marketing proposal will be cost effective.
4. Trying to determine whether the company's net income will result in a stock price increase.
5. Trying to determine whether the company should employ debt or equity financing.
(a) _____ Investors in common stock.   (d) _____ Chief Financial Officer.
(b) _____ Marketing managers.   (e) _____ Internal Revenue Service.
(c) _____ Creditors.

Classify items by activity.
(SO 4, 5)

BE1-3 Indicate in which part of the statement of cash flows each item would appear: operating activities (O), investing activities (I), or financing activities (F).
(a) _____ Cash received from customers.
(b) _____ Cash paid to stockholders (dividends).
(c) _____ Cash received from issuing new common stock.
(d) _____ Cash paid to suppliers.
(e) _____ Cash paid to purchase a new office building.

Determine effect of transactions on stockholders' equity.
(SO 4)

BE1-4 Presented below are a number of transactions. Determine whether each transaction affects common stock (C), dividends (D), revenue (R), expense (E), or does not affect stockholders' equity (NSE). Provide titles for the revenues and expenses.
(a) Costs incurred for advertising.
(b) Assets received for services performed.
(c) Costs incurred for insurance.
(d) Amounts paid to employees.
(e) Cash distributed to stockholders.
(f) Assets received in exchange for allowing the use of the company's building.
(g) Costs incurred for utilities used.
(h) Paid cash to purchase equipment.
(i) Received cash from investors in exchange for common stock.

BE1-5 In alphabetical order below are balance sheet items for Gidget Company at December 31, 2007. Prepare a balance sheet following the format of Illustration 1-8.

Prepare a balance sheet.
(SO 4, 5)

Accounts payable	$85,000
Accounts receivable	81,000
Cash	32,000
Common stock	28,000

BE1-6 Eskimo Pie Corporation markets a broad range of frozen treats, including its famous Eskimo Pie ice cream bars. The following items were taken from a recent income statement and balance sheet. In each case identify whether the item would appear on the balance sheet (BS) or income statement (IS).

Determine where items appear on financial statements.
(SO 4, 5)

(a) ___ Income tax expense.
(b) ___ Inventories.
(c) ___ Accounts payable.
(d) ___ Retained earnings.
(e) ___ Property, plant, and equipment.
(f) ___ Net sales.
(g) ___ Cost of goods sold.
(h) ___ Common stock.
(i) ___ Receivables.
(j) ___ Interest expense.

BE1-7 Indicate which statement you would examine to find each of the following items: income statement (I), balance sheet (B), retained earnings statement (R), or statement of cash flows (C).

Determine proper financial statement.
(SO 4)

(a) Revenue during the period.
(b) Supplies on hand at the end of the year.
(c) Cash received from issuing new bonds during the period.
(d) Total debts outstanding at the end of the period.

BE1-8 Use the basic accounting equation to answer these questions.

Use basic accounting equation.
(SO 5)

(a) The liabilities of Bergmann Company are $90,000 and the stockholders' equity is $230,000. What is the amount of Bergmann Company's total assets?
(b) The total assets of Buchanan Company are $170,000 and its stockholders' equity is $90,000. What is the amount of its total liabilities?
(c) The total assets of Lily Co. are $700,000 and its liabilities are equal to half of its total assets. What is the amount of Lily Co.'s stockholders' equity?

BE1-9 At the beginning of the year, Megan Company had total assets of $900,000 and total liabilities of $500,000.

Use basic accounting equation.
(SO 5)

(a) If total assets increased $150,000 during the year and total liabilities decreased $80,000, what is the amount of stockholders' equity at the end of the year?
(b) During the year, total liabilities increased $100,000 and stockholders' equity decreased $70,000. What is the amount of total assets at the end of the year?
(c) If total assets decreased $90,000 and stockholders' equity increased $110,000 during the year, what is the amount of total liabilities at the end of the year?

BE1-10 Indicate whether each of these items is an asset (A), a liability (L), or part of stockholders' equity (SE).

Identify assets, liabilities, and stockholders' equity.
(SO 5)

(a) Accounts receivable.
(b) Salaries payable.
(c) Equipment.
(d) Office supplies.
(e) Common stock.
(f) Notes payable.

BE1-11 Which is *not* a required part of an annual report of a publicly traded company?

Determine required parts of annual report.
(SO 6)

(a) Statement of cash flows.
(b) Notes to the financial statements.
(c) Management discussion and analysis.
(d) All of these are required.

Exercises

WILEY
PLUS

E1-1 Here is a list of words or phrases discussed in this chapter:

Match items with descriptions.
(SO 1, 2, 4, 6)

1. Corporation
2. Creditor
3. Accounts receivable
4. Partnership
5. Stockholder
6. Common stock
7. Accounts payable
8. Auditor's opinion

Instructions

Match each word or phrase with the best description of it.

____ (a) An expression about whether financial statements are presented in a reasonable fashion.

____ (b) A business enterprise that raises money by issuing shares of stock.

____ (c) The portion of stockholders' equity that results from receiving cash from investors.

____ (d) Obligations to suppliers of goods.

____ (e) Amounts due from customers.

____ (f) A party to whom a business owes money.

____ (g) A party that invests in common stock.

____ (h) A business that is owned jointly by two or more individuals but that does not issue stock.

Identify business activities.
(SO 3)

E1-2 All business are involved in three types of activities—financing, investing, and operating. Listed below are the names and descriptions of companies in several different industries.

Abitibi Consolidated Inc.—manufacturer and marketer of newsprint
Cal State–Northridge Stdt Union—university student union
Oracle Corporation—computer software developer and retailer
Sportsco Investments—owner of the Vancouver Canucks hockey club
Grant Thornton LLP—professional accounting and business advisory firm
Southwest Airlines—discount airline

Instructions

(a) For each of the above companies, provide examples of (1) a financing activity, (2) an investing activity, and (3) an operating activity that the company likely engages in.

(b) Which of the activities that you identified in (a) are common to most businesses? Which activities are not?

Classify accounts.
(SO 3, 4)

E1-3 The Mill Run Golf & Country Club details the following accounts in its financial statements.

	(a)	(b)
Accounts payable and accrued liabilities	____	____
Accounts receivable	____	____
Property, plant, and equipment	____	____
Food and beverage operations revenue	____	____
Golf course operations revenue	____	____
Inventory	____	____
Long-term debt	____	____
Office and general expense	____	____
Professional fees expense	____	____
Wages and benefits expense	____	____

Instructions

(a) Classify each of the above accounts as an asset (A), liability (L), stockholders' equity (SE), revenue (R), or expense (E) item.

(b) Classify each of the above accounts as a financing activity (F), investing activity (I), or operating activity (O). If you believe a particular account doesn't fit in any of these activities, explain why.

Prepare income statement and retained earnings statement.
(SO 4)

E1-4 This information relates to Connor Co. for the year 2007.

Retained earnings, January 1, 2007	$64,000
Advertising expense	1,800
Dividends paid during 2007	6,000
Rent expense	10,400
Service revenue	58,000
Utilities expense	2,400
Salaries expense	30,000

Instructions

After analyzing the data, prepare an income statement and a retained earnings statement for the year ending December 31, 2007.

E1-5 The following information was taken from the 2004 financial statements of pharmaceutical giant Merck and Co. All dollar amounts are in millions.

Prepare income statement and retained earnings statement.
(SO 4)

Retained earnings, January 1, 2004	$34,142.0
Materials and production expense	4,959.8
Marketing and administrative expense	7,346.3
Dividends	3,329.1
Sales revenue	22,938.6
Research and development expense	4,010.2
Tax expense	2,161.1
Other revenue	1,352.2

Instructions
(a) After analyzing the data, prepare an income statement and a retained earnings statement for the year ending December 31, 2004.
(b) Suppose that Merck decided to reduce its research and development expense by 50%. What would be the short-term implications? What would be the long-term implications? How do you think the stock market would react?

E1-6 Presented here is information for Anne Charlotte Inc. for 2007.

Prepare a retained earnings statement.
(SO 4)

Retained earnings, January 1	$130,000
Revenue from legal services	410,000
Total expenses	170,000
Dividends	82,000

Instructions
Prepare the 2007 retained earnings statement for Anne Charlotte Inc.

E1-7 Consider each of the following independent situations.
(a) The retained earnings statement of Motzek Corporation shows dividends of $68,000, while net income for the year was $75,000.
(b) The statement of cash flows for Cheung Corporation shows that cash provided by operating activities was $10,000, cash used in investing activities was $110,000, and cash provided by financing activities was $130,000.

Interpret financial facts.
(SO 4)

Instructions
For each company provide a brief discussion interpreting these financial facts. For example, you might discuss the company's financial health or its apparent growth philosophy.

E1-8 Here are incomplete financial statements for Brandon, Inc.

Calculate missing amounts.
(SO 4, 5)

BRANDON, INC.
Balance Sheet

Assets		Liabilities and Stockholders' Equity	
Cash	$ 5,000	Liabilities	
Inventory	10,000	Accounts payable	$ 5,000
Building	45,000	Stockholders' equity	
Total assets	$60,000	Common stock	(a)
		Retained earnings	(b)
		Total liabilities and stockholders' equity	$60,000

Income Statement

Revenues	$80,000
Cost of goods sold	(c)
Administrative expenses	10,000
Net income	$ (d)

Retained Earnings Statement

Beginning retained earnings	$10,000
Net income	(e)
Dividends	5,000
Ending retained earnings	$29,000

Compute net income and prepare a balance sheet.
(SO 4, 5)

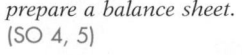

Instructions
Calculate the missing amounts.

E1-9 Sleep Cheap is a private camping ground near the Lathom Peak Recreation Area. It has compiled the following financial information as of December 31, 2007.

Revenues during 2007: camping fees	$137,000	Dividends	$ 9,000
Revenues during 2007: general store	25,000	Notes payable	50,000
Accounts payable	11,000	Expenses during 2007	129,000
Cash	8,500	Supplies	2,500
Equipment	119,000	Common stock	40,000
		Retained earnings (1/1/2007)	5,000

Instructions
(a) Determine net income from Sleep Cheap for 2007.
(b) Prepare a retained earnings statement and a balance sheet for Sleep Cheap as of December 31, 2007.
(c) Upon seeing this income statement, Terry Stevens, the campground manager immediately concluded, "The general store is more trouble than it is worth—let's get rid of it." The marketing director isn't so sure this is a good idea. What do you think?

Identify financial statement components and prepare an income statement.
(SO 4, 5)

E1-10 Kellogg Company is the world's leading producer of ready-to-eat cereal and a leading producer of grain-based convenience foods such as frozen waffles and cereal bars. The following items were taken from its 2004 income statement and balance sheet. All dollars are in millions.

____	Retained earnings	$2,701.3	____	Long-term debt	$3,892.6
____	Cost of goods sold	5,298.7	____	Inventories	681.0
____	Selling and		____	Net sales	9,613.9
	administrative expenses	2,634.1	____	Accounts payable	767.2
____	Cash	417.4	____	Common stock	103.8
____	Notes payable	709.7	____	Income tax expense	475.3
____	Interest expense	308.6	____	Other expense	6.6

Instructions
Perform each of the following.
(a) In each case identify whether the item is an asset (A), liability (L), stockholders' equity (SE), revenue (R), or expense (E).
(b) Prepare an income statement for Kellogg Company for the year ended December 31, 2004.

E1-11 This information is for Campo Corporation for the year ended December 31, 2007.

Cash received from lenders	$20,000
Cash received from customers	65,000
Cash paid for new equipment	35,000
Cash dividends paid	6,000
Cash paid to suppliers	18,000
Cash balance 1/1/07	12,000

Prepare a statement of cash flows.
(SO 5)

Instructions
(a) Prepare the 2007 statement of cash flows for Campo Corporation.
(b) Suppose you are one of Campo's creditors. Referring to the statement of cash flows, evaluate Campo's ability to repay its creditors.

Prepare a statement of cash flows.
(SO 5)

E1-12 The following data are derived from the 2004 financial statements of Southwest Airlines. All dollars are in millions. Southwest has a December 31 year-end.

Cash balance, January 1, 2004	$1,865
Cash paid for repayment of debt	207
Cash received from issuance of common stock	88
Cash received from issuance of long-term debt	512
Cash received from customers	6,455
Cash paid for property and equipment	1,850
Cash paid for dividends	14
Cash paid for repurchase of common stock	246
Cash paid for goods and services	5,298

Instructions

(a) After analyzing the data, prepare a statement of cash flows for Southwest Airlines for the year ended December 31, 2004.

(b) Discuss whether the company's cash from operations was sufficient to finance its investing activities. If it was not, how did the company finance its investing activities?

E1-13 John Paul is the bookkeeper for Gabelli Company. John has been trying to get the balance sheet of Gabelli Company to balance. It finally balanced, but now he's not sure it is correct.

Correct an incorrectly prepared balance sheet.
(SO 5)

GABELLI COMPANY
Balance Sheet
December 31, 2007

Assets		Liabilities and Stockholders' Equity	
Cash	$18,500	Accounts payable	$16,000
Supplies	9,500	Accounts receivable	(12,000)
Equipment	40,000	Common stock	40,000
Dividends	10,000	Retained earnings	34,000
Total assets	$78,000	Total liabilities and stockholders' equity	$78,000

Instructions
Prepare a correct balance sheet.

E1-14 The following items were taken from the balance sheet of Nike, Inc.

1. Cash	$ 828.0	7. Inventories	$1,633.6
2. Accounts receivable	2,120.2	8. Income taxes payable	118.2
3. Common stock	890.6	9. Property, plant, and equipment	1,586.9
4. Notes payable	146.0	10. Retained earnings	3,891.1
5. Other assets	1,722.9	11. Accounts payable	763.8
6. Other liabilities	2,081.9		

Classify items as assets, liabilities, and stockholders' equity and prepare accounting equation.
(SO 5)

Instructions
Perform each of the following.

(a) Classify each of these items as an asset, liability, or stockholders' equity. (All dollars are in millions.)

(b) Determine Nike's accounting equation by calculating the value of total assets, total liabilities, and total stockholders' equity.

(c) To what extent does Nike rely on debt versus equity financing?

E1-15 The summaries of data from the balance sheet, income statement, and retained earnings statement for two corporations, Bates Corporation and Wilson Enterprises, are presented below for 2007.

Use financial statement relationships to determine missing amounts.
(SO 5)

	Bates Corporation	Wilson Enterprises
Beginning of year		
Total assets	$110,000	$130,000
Total liabilities	80,000	(d)
Total stockholders' equity	(a)	90,000
End of year		
Total assets	(b)	180,000
Total liabilities	120,000	55,000
Total stockholders' equity	50,000	(e)
Changes during year in retained earnings		
Dividends	(c)	5,000
Total revenues	215,000	(f)
Total expenses	165,000	80,000

Instructions
Determine the missing amounts. Assume all changes in stockholders' equity are due to changes in retained earnings.

Classify various items in an annual report.
(SO 6)

E1-16 The annual report provides financial information in a variety of formats including the following.

> Management discussion and analysis (MD&A)
> Financial statements
> Notes to the financial statements
> Auditor's opinion

Instructions
For each of the following, state in what area of the annual report the item would be presented. If the item would probably not be found in an annual report, state "Not disclosed."
(a) The total cumulative amount received from stockholders in exchange for common stock.
(b) An independent assessment concerning whether the financial statements present a fair depiction of the company's results and financial position.
(c) The interest rate that the company is being charged on all outstanding debts.
(d) Total revenue from operating activities.
(e) Management's assessment of the company's results.
(f) The names and positions of all employees hired in the last year.

Problems: Set A

Determine forms of business organization.
(SO 1)

P1-1A Presented below are five independent situations.
(a) Three physics professors at MIT have formed a business to improve the speed of information transfer over the Internet for stock exchange transactions. Each has contributed an equal amount of cash and knowledge to the venture. Although their approach looks promising, they are concerned about the legal liabilities that their business might confront.
(b) Andrew Carpenter, a college student looking for summer employment, opened a bait shop in a small shed at a local marina.
(c) Dennis Lee and Paul Rowe each owned separate shoe manufacturing businesses. They have decided to combine their businesses. They expect that within the coming year they will need significant funds to expand their operations.
(d) Elaine, Jerry, and George recently graduated with marketing degrees. They have been friends since childhood. They have decided to start a consulting business focused on marketing sporting goods over the Internet.
(e) Liam O'Brien wants to rent CD players and CDs in airports across the country. His idea is that customers will be able to rent equipment and CDs at one airport, listen to the CDs on their flights, and return the equipment and CDs at their destination airport. Of course, this will require a substantial investment in equipment and CDs, as well as employees and locations in each airport. Liam has no savings or personal assets. He wants to maintain control over the business.

Instructions
In each case explain what form of organization the business is likely to take—sole proprietorship, partnership, or corporation. Give reasons for your choice.

Identify users and uses of financial statements.
(SO 2, 4, 5)

P1-2A Financial decisions often place heavier emphasis on one type of financial statement over the others. Consider each of the following hypothetical situations independently.
(a) The North Face, Inc. is considering extending credit to a new customer. The terms of the credit would require the customer to pay within 30 days of receipt of goods.
(b) An investor is considering purchasing common stock of Amazon.com. The investor plans to hold the investment for at least 5 years.
(c) Chase Manhattan is considering extending a loan to a small company. The company would be required to make interest payments at the end of each year for 5 years, and to repay the loan at the end of the fifth year.
(d) The president of Campbell Soup is trying to determine whether the company is generating enough cash to increase the amount of dividends paid to investors in this and future years, and still have enough cash to buy equipment as it is needed.

Instructions

In each situation, state whether the decision maker would be most likely to place primary emphasis on information provided by the income statement, balance sheet, or statement of cash flows. In each case provide a brief justification for your choice. Choose only one financial statement in each case.

P1-3A   On June 1 Fix-It-Up Service Co. was started with an initial investment in the company of $26,200 cash. Here are the assets and liabilities of the company at June 30, and the revenues and expenses for the month of June, its first month of operations:

Cash	$ 4,600	Notes payable	$14,000
Accounts receivable	4,000	Accounts payable	500
Revenue	8,000	Supplies expense	1,000
Supplies	2,400	Gas and oil expense	600
Advertising expense	400	Utilities expense	300
Equipment	32,000	Wage expense	1,400

In June, the company issued no additional stock, but paid dividends of $2,000.

Instructions
(a) Prepare an income statement and a retained earnings statement for the month of June and a balance sheet at June 30, 2007.
(b) Briefly discuss whether the company's first month of operations was a success.
(c) Discuss the company's decision to distribute a dividend.

P1-4A   Presented below is selected financial information for Linus Corporation for December 31, 2007.

Inventory	$ 25,000	Cash paid to purchase equipment	$ 10,000
Cash paid to suppliers	108,000	Equipment	40,000
Building	200,000	Revenues	100,000
Common stock	50,000	Cash received from customers	137,000
Cash dividends paid	7,000	Cash received from issuing	
		common stock	22,000

Instructions
(a) Determine which items should be included in a statement of cash flows and then prepare the statement for Linus Corporation.
(b) Comment on the adequacy of net cash provided by operating activities to fund the company's investing activities and dividend payments.

P1-5A   Silberman Corporation was formed on January 1, 2007. At December 31, 2007, Scott Brantner, the president and sole stockholder, decided to prepare a balance sheet, which appeared as follows.

Prepare an income statement, retained earnings statement, and balance sheet, and discuss results.
(SO 4, 5)

Marginal **check figures** (in blue) provide a key number to let you know you're on the right track.

(a) Net income $4,300
   Ret. earnings $2,300
   Tot. assets $43,000

Determine items included in a statement of cash flows, prepare the statement, and comment.
(SO 4, 5)

(a) Net increase $34,000

Comment on proper accounting treatment and prepare a corrected balance sheet.
(SO 4, 5)

SILBERMAN CORPORATION
Balance Sheet
December 31, 2007

Assets		**Liabilities and Stockholders' Equity**	
Cash	$20,000	Accounts payable	$40,000
Accounts receivable	55,000	Notes payable	15,000
Inventory	33,000	Boat loan	18,000
Boat	24,000	Stockholders' equity	55,000

Scott willingly admits that he is not an accountant by training. He is concerned that his balance sheet might not be correct. He has provided you with the following additional information.
1. The boat actually belongs to Brantner, not to Silberman Corporation. However, because he thinks he might take customers out on the boat occasionally, he decided to list it as an asset of the company. To be consistent he also listed as a liability of the corporation his personal loan that he took out at the bank to buy the boat.
2. The inventory was originally purchased for $21,000, but due to a surge in demand Scott now thinks he could sell it for $33,000. He thought it would be best to record it at $33,000.

3. Included in the accounts receivable balance is $12,000 that Scott loaned to his brother 5 years ago. Scott included this in the receivables of Silberman Corporation so he wouldn't forget that his brother owes him money.

Instructions

Tot.assets $84,000

(a) Comment on the proper accounting treatment of the three items above.
(b) Provide a corrected balance sheet for Silberman Corporation. (*Hint:* To get the balance sheet to balance, adjust stockholders' equity.)

Problems: Set B

Determine forms of business organization.
(SO 1)

P1-1B   Presented below are five independent situations.

(a) Joyce Packee, a college student looking for summer employment, opened a vegetable stand along a busy local highway. Each morning she buys produce from local farmers, then sells it in the afternoon as people return home from work.

(b) Alex Rice and Peter Gould each owned separate swing-set manufacturing businesses. They have decided to combine their businesses and try to expand their reach beyond their local market. They expect that within the coming year they will need significant funds to expand their operations.

(c) Three chemistry professors at FIU have formed a business to employ bacteria to clean up toxic waste sites. Each has contributed an equal amount of cash and knowledge to the venture. The use of bacteria in this situation is experimental, and legal obligations could result.

(d) Emma Peale has run a successful, but small cooperative health food store for over 20 years. The increased sales of her store have made her believe that the time is right to open a national chain of health food stores across the country. Of course, this will require a substantial investment in stores, inventory, and employees in each store. Emma has no savings or personal assets. She wants to maintain control over the business.

(e) Tammy Laven and Ted Peterman recently graduated with masters degrees in economics. They have decided to start a consulting business focused on teaching the basics of international economics to small business owners interested in international trade.

Instructions

In each case explain what form of organization the business is likely to take—sole proprietorship, partnership, or corporation. Give reasons for your choice.

Identify users and uses of financial statements.
(SO 2, 4, 5)

P1-2B   Financial decisions often place heavier emphasis on one type of financial statement over the others. Consider each of the following hypothetical situations independently.

(a) An investor is considering purchasing common stock of the Bally Total Fitness company. The investor plans to hold the investment for at least 3 years.

(b) Boeing is considering extending credit to a new customer. The terms of the credit would require the customer to pay within 60 days of receipt of goods.

(c) The president of Northwest Airlines is trying to determine whether the company is generating enough cash to increase the amount of dividends paid to investors in this and future years, and still have enough cash to buy new flight equipment as it is needed.

(d) Bank of America is considering extending a loan to a small company. The company would be required to make interest payments at the end of each year for 5 years, and to repay the loan at the end of the fifth year.

Instructions

In each of the situations above, state whether the decision maker would be most likely to place primary emphasis on information provided by the income statement, balance sheet, or statement of cash flows. In each case provide a brief justification for your choice. Choose only one financial statement in each case.

Prepare an income statement, retained earnings statement, and balance sheet, and discuss results.
(SO 4, 5)

P1-3B   Special Delivery was started on May 1 with an investment of $45,000 cash. To "jump start" its sales, the company spent significant money on advertising. Following are the assets and liabilities of the company on May 31, 2007, and the revenues and expenses for the month of May, its first month of operations.

Accounts receivable	$ 6,200	Notes payable	$30,000
Service revenue	10,800	Wage expense	2,200
Advertising expense	800	Equipment	60,300
Accounts payable	2,400	Repair expense	500
Cash	13,700	Fuel expense	2,400
		Insurance expense	400

(a) Net income $4,500
Ret. earnings $2,800
Tot. assets $80,200

No additional common stock was issued in May, but a dividend of $1,700 in cash was paid.

Instructions

(a) Prepare an income statement and a retained earnings statement for the month of May and a balance sheet at May 31, 2007.

(b) Briefly discuss whether the company's first month of operations was a success.

(c) Discuss the company's decision to distribute a dividend.

P1-4B Presented below are selected financial statement items for Daley Corporation for December 31, 2007.

Determine items included in a statement of cash flows, prepare the statement, and comment.
(SO 4, 5)

Inventory	$ 55,000	Cash paid to purchase equipment	$ 34,000
Cash paid to suppliers	154,000	Equipment	40,000
Building	400,000	Revenues	200,000
Common stock	20,000	Cash received from customers	173,000
Cash dividends paid	9,000	Cash received from issuing bonds payable	30,000

Instructions

(a) Determine which items should be included in a statement of cash flows, and then prepare the statement for Daley Corporation.

(b) Comment on the adequacy of net cash provided by operating activities to fund the company's investing activities and dividend payments.

(a) Net increase $6,000

P1-5B Wyoming Corporation was formed during 2006 by Sandra Lee. Sandra is the president and sole stockholder. At December 31, 2007, Sandra prepared an income statement for Wyoming Corporation. Sandra is not an accountant, but she thinks she did a reasonable job preparing the income statement by looking at the financial statements of other companies. She has asked you for advice. Sandra's income statement appears as follows.

Comment on proper accounting treatment and prepare a corrected income statement.
(SO 4, 5)

WYOMING CORPORATION
Income Statement
For the Year Ended December 31, 2007

Accounts receivable	$17,000
Revenue	60,000
Rent expense	12,000
Insurance expense	5,000
Vacation expense	2,000
Net income	58,000

Sandra has also provided you with these facts.

1. Included in the revenue account is $3,000 of revenue that the company earned and received payment for in 2006. She forgot to include it in the 2006 income statement, so she put it in this year's statement.

2. Sandra operates her business out of the basement of her parents' home. They do not charge her anything, but she thinks that if she paid rent it would cost her about $12,000 per year. She therefore included $12,000 of rent expense in the income statement.

3. To reward herself for a year of hard work, Sandra went to Greece. She did not use company funds to pay for the trip, but she reported it as an expense on the income statement since it was her job that made her need the vacation.

Instructions

(a) Comment on the proper accounting treatment of the three items above.

(b) Prepare a corrected income statement for Wyoming Corporation.

(a) Net income $52,000

Problems: Set C

Visit the book's website at **www.wiley.com/college/kimmel** and choose the Student Companion site to access Problem Set C.

Continuing Cookie Chronicle

CCC1 Natalie Koebel spent much of her childhood learning the art of cookie-making from her grandmother. They spent many happy hours mastering every type of cookie imaginable and later devised new recipes that were both healthy and delicious. Now at the start of her second year in college, Natalie is investigating possibilities for starting her own business as part of the entrepreneurship program in which she is enrolled.

A long-time friend insists that Natalie has to include cookies in her business plan. After a series of brainstorming sessions, Natalie settles on the idea of operating a cookie-making school. She will start on a part-time basis and offer her services in people's homes. Now that she has started thinking about it, the possibilities seem endless. During the fall, she will concentrate on holiday cookies. She will offer group sessions (which will probably be more entertainment than education) and individual lessons. Natalie also decides to include children in her target market. The first difficult decision is coming up with the perfect name for her business. She settles on "Cookie Creations," and then moves on to more important issues.

Instructions
(a) What form of business organization—proprietorship, partnership, or corporation—do you recommend that Natalie use for her business? Discuss the benefits and weaknesses of each form that Natalie might consider.
(b) Will Natalie need accounting information? If yes, what information will she need and why? How often will she need this information?
(c) Identify specific asset, liability, revenue, and expense accounts that Cookie Creations will likely use to record its business transactions.
(d) Should Natalie open a separate bank account for the business? Why or why not?
(e) Natalie expects she will have to use her car to drive to people's homes and to pick up supplies, but she also needs to use her car for personal reasons. She recalls from her first-year accounting course something about keeping business and personal assets separate. She wonders what she should do for accounting purposes. What do you recommend?

▶ BROADENING YOUR PERSPECTIVE

Financial Reporting and Analysis

FINANCIAL REPORTING PROBLEM: *Tootsie Roll Industries, Inc.*

BYP1-1 Simplified 2004 financial statements of Tootsie Roll Industries, Inc. are given in Illustrations 1-11 through 1-14.

Instructions
Refer to Tootsie Roll's financial statements to answer the following questions.
(a) What were Tootsie Roll's total assets at December 31, 2004? At December 31, 2003?
(b) How much cash did Tootsie Roll have on December 31, 2004?
(c) What amount of accounts payable did Tootsie Roll report on December 31, 2004? On December 31, 2003?
(d) What were Tootsie Roll's sales revenue in 2004? In 2003?
(e) What is the amount of the change in Tootsie Roll's net income from 2003 to 2004?
(f) The accounting equation is: Assets = Liabilities + Stockholders' Equity. Replacing the words in that equation with dollar amounts, give Tootsie Roll's accounting equation at December 31, 2004.

COMPARATIVE ANALYSIS PROBLEM: *Tootsie Roll vs. Hershey Foods*

BYP1-2 Simplified financial statements of Hershey Foods Corporation are presented in Illustrations 1-18 through 1-21, and Tootsie Roll's simplified financial statements are presented in Illustrations 1-11 through 1-14.

Instructions

(a) Based on the information in these financial statements, determine the following for each company.
  (1) Total assets at December 31, 2004.
  (2) Accounts receivable at December 31, 2004.
  (3) Sales revenue for 2004.
  (4) Net income for 2004.

(b) What conclusions concerning the two companies can you draw from these data?

RESEARCH CASE

BYP1-3 The newsletter *Rural Roots*, published by The Rural School and Community Trust, includes an article titled "Student-Run Grocery Store Up and Running." The article is available at **www.ruraledu.org/roots/rr201d.htm**.

Instructions
Read the article and answer the following questions.
(a) List the various ways that accounting would be critical to the successful formation and operation of Wolf Den Market.
(b) Identify various accounts that would be used by Wolf Den Market. First list balance sheet accounts; then list income statement accounts.

INTERPRETING FINANCIAL STATEMENTS

BYP1-4 The year 2000 was not a particularly pleasant year for the managers of Xerox Corporation, or its shareholders. The company's stock price had already fallen in the previous year from $60 per share to $30. Just when it seemed things couldn't get worse, Xerox's stock fell to $4 per share. The data below were taken from the December 31, 2000, statement of cash flows of Xerox. All dollars are in millions.

Cash used in operating activities		$ (663)
Cash used in investing activities		(644)
Financing activities		
Dividends paid	$ (587)	
Net cash received from issuing debt	3,498	
Cash provided by financing activities		2,911

Instructions
Analyze the information above, and then answer the following questions.
(a) If you were a creditor of Xerox, what reaction might you have to the above information?
(b) If you were an investor in Xerox, what reaction might you have to the above information?
(c) If you were evaluating the company as either a creditor or a stockholder, what other information would you be interested in seeing?
(d) Xerox decided to pay a cash dividend in 2000. This dividend was approximately equal to the amount paid in 1999. Discuss the issues that were probably considered in making this decision.

FINANCIAL ANALYSIS ON THE WEB

BYP1-5 *Purpose:* Identify summary information about companies. This information includes basic descriptions of the company's location, activities, industry, financial health, and financial performance.

Address: **http://biz.yahoo.com/i** (or go to **www.wiley.com/college/kimmel**)

Steps
1. Type in a company name, or use the index to find company name.
2. Choose **Quote**, then choose **Profile**, then choose **Income Statement**. Perform instructions (a) and (b) below.
3. Choose **Industry** to identify others in this industry. Perform instructions (c)–(e) below.

Instr.uctions
Answer the following questions.
(a) What was the company's net income? Over what period was this measured?
(b) What was the company's total sales? Over what period was this measured?
(c) What is the company's industry?

(d) What are the names of four companies in this industry?
(e) Choose one of the competitors. What is this competitor's name? What were its sales? What was its net income?

Critical Thinking

DECISION MAKING ACROSS THE ORGANIZATION

BYP1-6   Kim Perkins recently accepted a job in the production department at Tootsie Roll. Before she starts work, she decides to review the company's annual report to better understand its operations.

Instructions
Use the annual report provided in Appendix A to answer the following questions.
(a) What CPA firm performed the audit of Tootsie Roll's financial statements?
(b) What was the amount of Tootsie Roll's earnings per share in 2004?
(c) What are the company's net sales in foreign countries?
(d) What did management suggest as the cause of the increase in the sales in 2004?
(e) What were net sales in 2000?
(f) How many shares of Class B common stock have been authorized?
(g) How much cash was spent on capital expenditures in 2004?
(h) Over what life does the company depreciate its buildings?
(i) What was the value of raw material inventories in 2003?

COMMUNICATION ACTIVITY

BYP1-7   Carol Young is the bookkeeper for Evans Company, Inc. Carol has been trying to get the company's balance sheet to balance. She finally got it to balance, but she still isn't sure that it is correct.

EVANS COMPANY, INC.
Balance Sheet
For the Month Ended December 31, 2007

Assets		Liabilities and Stockholders' Equity	
Equipment	$20,500	Common stock	$11,000
Cash	10,500	Accounts receivable	(3,000)
Supplies	2,000	Dividends	(2,000)
Accounts payable	(5,000)	Notes payable	12,000
Total assets	$28,000	Retained earnings	10,000
		Total liabilities and stockholders' equity	$28,000

Instructions
Explain to Carol Young in a memo (a) the purpose of a balance sheet, and (b) why this balance sheet is incorrect and what she should do to correct it.

ETHICS CASE

BYP1-8   Rules governing the investment practices of individual certified public accountants prohibit them from investing in the stock of a company that their firm audits. The Securities and Exchange Commission became concerned that some accountants were violating this rule. In response to an SEC investigation, PricewaterhouseCoopers fired 10 people and spent $25 million educating employees about the investment rules and installing an investment tracking system.

Instructions
Answer the following questions.
(a) Why do you think rules exist that restrict auditors from investing in companies that are audited by their firms?
(b) Some accountants argue that they should be allowed to invest in a company's stock as long as they themselves aren't involved in working on the company's audit or consulting. What do you think of this idea?

(c) Today a very high percentage of publicly traded companies are audited by only four very large public accounting firms. These firms also do a high percentage of the consulting work that is done for publicly traded companies. How does this fact complicate the decision regarding whether CPAs should be allowed to invest in companies audited by their firm?

(d) Suppose you were a CPA and you had invested in IBM when IBM was not one of your firm's clients. Two years later, after IBM's stock price had fallen considerably, your firm won the IBM audit contract. You will not in any way be involved in working with the IBM audit, which will be done by one of your firm's other offices in a different state. You know that your firm's rules, as well as U.S. law, require that you sell your shares immediately. If you do sell immediately, you will sustain a large loss. Do you think this is fair? What would you do?

(e) Why do you think PricewaterhouseCoopers took such extreme steps in response to the SEC investigation?

Answers to Business Insight and Accounting across the Organization Questions

p. 7

Q: What are the benefits to the company and to the employees of making the financial statements available to all employees?

A: If employees can read and use financial reports, a company will benefit in the following ways. The *marketing department* will make better decisions about products to offer and prices to charge. The *finance department* will make better decisions about debt and equity financing and how much to distribute in dividends. The *production department* will make better decisions about when to buy new equipment and how much inventory to produce. The *human resources department* will be better able to determine whether employees can be given raises. Finally, *all employees* will be better informed about the basis on which they are evaluated, which will increase employee morale.

p. 8

Q: How might accounting help you?

A: You will need to understand financial reports in any enterprise with which you are associated. Whether you become a manager, a doctor, a lawyer, a social worker, a teacher, an engineer, an architect, or an entrepreneur, a working knowledge of accounting is relevant.

p. 9

Q: What has been done in the United States to improve the quality and integrity of financial reporting and to build investor confidence in financial reports?

A: Congress passed new laws to legislate fair business behavior and accounting and auditing practices. The *Sarbanes-Oxley Act* increases the resources for the government to combat fraud and to curb poor reporting practices. It introduces sweeping changes to the structure and practices of the accounting and auditing professions and increases the responsibility of corporate boards and officers.

p. 16

Q: What is one way that some of these disputes might be resolved?

A: Frequently, when contractual payments depend on accounting-based financial results, interested parties employ outside auditors to evaluate whether the financial information has been prepared fairly and accurately. The musicians would like auditors to have easy access to inventory and manufacturing information of the recording companies.

Answer to Tootsie Roll Review It Question 3, p. 17

Using dollar amounts, Tootsie Roll's accounting equation is:

Assets   =   Liabilities   + Stockholders' Equity
$811,753,000 = $241,574,000 + $570,179,000

Answers to Self-Study Questions

1. b   2. c   3. d   4. c   5. d   6. a   7. c   8. d   9. a   10. a

 REMEMBER TO GO BACK TO THE NAVIGATOR BOX ON THE CHAPTER-OPENING PAGE AND CHECK OFF YOUR COMPLETED WORK.

CHAPTER 2

A Further Look at Financial Statements

STUDY OBJECTIVES

After studying this chapter,
you should be able to:

1 Identify the sections of a classified balance sheet.

2 Identify and compute ratios for analyzing a company's profitability.

3 Explain the relationship between a retained earnings statement and a statement of stockholders' equity.

4 Identify and compute ratios for analyzing a company's liquidity and solvency using a balance sheet.

5 Use the statement of cash flows to evaluate solvency.

6 Explain the meaning of generally accepted accounting principles.

7 Discuss financial reporting concepts.

THE NAVIGATOR

✓ THE NAVIGATOR

- Scan *Study Objectives* ⬭
- Read *Feature Story* ⬭
- Read *Preview* ⬭
- Read text and answer *Before You Go On*
  p. 53 ⬭ p. 58 ⬭ p. 62 ⬭ p. 64 ⬭ p. 70 ⬭
- Work *Using the Decision Toolkit* ⬭
- Review *Summary of Study Objectives* ⬭
- Work *Demonstration Problem* ⬭
- Answer *Self-Study Questions* ⬭
- Complete *Assignments* ⬭

Just Fooling Around?

Few people could have predicted how dramatically the Internet would change the investment world. One of the most interesting results is how it has changed the way ordinary people invest their savings. More and more people are striking out on their own, making their own investment decisions.

Two early pioneers in providing investment information to the masses were Tom and David Gardner, brothers who created an online investor bulletin board called the Motley Fool. The name comes from Shakespeare's *As You Like It*. The fool in Shakespeare's plays was the only one who could speak unpleasant truths to kings and queens without being killed. Tom and David view themselves as 21st-century "fools," revealing the "truths" of Wall Street to the small investor, who they feel has been taken advantage of by Wall Street insiders. Their online bulletin board enables investors to exchange information and insights about companies.

Critics of these bulletin boards contend that they are high-tech rumor mills. They suggest that the fervor created by bulletin board chatter causes investors to bid up stock prices to unreasonable levels. Because bulletin board participants typically use aliases, there is little to stop people from putting misinformation on the board to influence a stock's price. For example, the stock of PairGain

Technologies jumped 32 percent in a single day as a result of a bogus takeover rumor on an investment bulletin board. Some observers are concerned that small investors—ironically, the very people the Gardner brothers are trying to help—will be hurt the most by misinformation and intentional scams.

To show how these bulletin boards work, suppose that in a recent year you had $10,000 to invest. You were considering Best Buy Company, the largest seller of electronics equipment in the United States. You scanned the Internet investment bulletin boards and found messages posted by two different investors. Here are excerpts from actual postings during the same recent year.

From: "TMPVenus": "Where are the prospects for positive movement for this company? Poor margins, poor management, astronomical P/E!"

From "broachman": "I believe that this is a LONG TERM winner, and presently at a good price."

One says sell, and one says buy. Whom should you believe? If you had taken "broachman's"

advice and purchased the stock, the $10,000 you invested would have been worth over $300,000 five years later. Best Buy was one of America's best-performing stocks during that period of time.

Deciding what information to rely on is becoming increasingly complex. For example, shortly before its share price completely collapsed, nearly every professional analyst who followed Enron was recommending its stock as a "buy."

Rather than getting swept away by rumors, investors must sort out the good information from the bad. One thing is certain—as information services such as the Motley Fool increase in number, gathering information will become even easier. Evaluating it will be the harder task.

On the World Wide Web
Motley Fool: www.fool.com.
Best Buy Company: www.bestbuy.com

PREVIEW OF CHAPTER 2

If you are thinking of purchasing Best Buy stock, or any stock, how can you decide what the stock is worth? If you manage J. Crew's credit department, how should you determine whether to extend credit to a new customer? If you are a financial executive of IBM, how do you decide whether your company is generating adequate cash to expand operations without borrowing? Your decision in each of these situations will be influenced by a variety of considerations. One of them should be your careful analysis of a company's financial statements. The reason: Financial statements offer relevant and reliable information, which will help you in your decision making.

In this chapter we take a closer look at the balance sheet and introduce some useful ways for evaluating the information provided by the financial statements. We also examine the financial reporting concepts underlying the financial statements.

A FURTHER LOOK AT FINANCIAL STATEMENTS

The Financial Statements Revisited	Financial Reporting Concepts
• Classified balance sheet	• The standard-setting environment
• Using the financial statements	• Characteristics of useful information
	• Assumptions and principles
	• Constraints

THE NAVIGATOR

SECTION ONE
THE FINANCIAL STATEMENTS REVISITED

Tootsie Roll Annual Report Walkthrough

In Chapter 1 we introduced the four financial statements. In this section we review the financial statements and present tools that are useful for evaluating them. We begin by introducing the classified balance sheet.

The Classified Balance Sheet

STUDY OBJECTIVE
1
Identify the sections of a classified balance sheet.

The balance sheet presents a snapshot of a company's financial position at a point in time. To improve users' understanding of a company's financial position, companies often group similar assets and similar liabilities together. This is useful because it tells you that items within a group have similar economic characteristics. A **classified balance sheet** generally contains the standard classifications listed in Illustration 2-1.

Illustration 2-1
Standard balance sheet classifications

Assets	Liabilities and Stockholders' Equity
Current assets	Current liabilities
Long-term investments	Long-term liabilities
Property, plant, and equipment	Stockholders' equity
Intangible assets	

These groupings help readers determine such things as (1) whether the company has enough assets to pay its debts as they come due, and (2) the claims of short- and long-term creditors on the company's total assets. Many of these groupings can be seen in the balance sheet of Franklin Corporation shown in Illustration 2-2. In the sections that follow, we explain each of these groupings.

CURRENT ASSETS

Current assets are assets that a company expects to convert to cash or use up within one year. In Illustration 2-2, Franklin Corporation had current assets of $22,100. For most businesses the cutoff for classification as current assets is one

Illustration 2-2   Classified balance sheet

FRANKLIN CORPORATION
Balance Sheet
October 31, 2007

Assets

Current assets		
Cash	$ 6,600	
Short-term investments	2,000	
Accounts receivable	7,000	
Notes receivable	1,000	
Inventories	3,000	
Supplies	2,100	
Prepaid insurance	400	
Total current assets		$22,100
Long-term investments		
Investment in stock of Walters Corp.	5,200	
Investment in real estate	2,000	7,200
Property, plant, and equipment		
Land	10,000	
Office equipment	$24,000	
Less: Accumulated depreciation	5,000	19,000	29,000
Intangible assets		
Patents		3,100
Total assets		$61,400

Liabilities and Stockholders' Equity

Current liabilities		
Notes payable	$11,000	
Accounts payable	2,100	
Salaries payable	1,600	
Unearned revenue	900	
Interest payable	450	
Total current liabilities		$16,050
Long-term liabilities		
Mortgage payable	10,000	
Notes payable	1,300	
Total long-term liabilities		11,300
Total liabilities		27,350
Stockholders' equity		
Common stock	14,000	
Retained earnings	20,050	
Total stockholders' equity		34,050
Total liabilities and stockholders' equity		$61,400

Helpful Hint Recall that the accounting equation is Assets = Liabilities + Stockholders' Equity.

year from the balance sheet date. For example, accounts receivable are current assets because the company will collect them and convert them to cash within one year. Supplies is a current asset because the company expects to use it up in operations within one year.

Some companies use a period longer than one year to classify assets and liabilities as current because they have an operating cycle longer than one year. The **operating cycle** of a company is the average time that it takes to purchase inventory, sell it on account, and then collect cash from customers. For most businesses this cycle takes less than a year, so they use a one-year cutoff. But, for some businesses, such as vineyards or airplane manufacturers, this period may be longer than a year. **Except where noted, we will assume that companies use one year to determine whether an asset or liability is current or long-term.**

Common types of current assets are (1) cash, (2) short-term investments (such as short-term U.S. government securities), (3) receivables (notes receivable, accounts receivable, and interest receivable), (4) inventories, and (5) prepaid expenses (insurance and supplies). **On the balance sheet, companies usually list these items in the order in which they expect to convert them into cash** (order of liquidity).

Illustration 2-3 presents the current assets of The Coca-Cola Company.

Illustration 2-3   Current assets section

THE COCA-COLA COMPANY
Balance Sheet (partial)
(in millions)

Current assets	
Cash and cash equivalents	$ 6,707
Short-term investments	61
Trade accounts receivable	2,171
Inventories	1,420
Prepaid expenses and other assets	1,735
Total current assets	$12,094

As explained later in the chapter, a company's current assets are important in assessing its short-term debt-paying ability.

LONG-TERM INVESTMENTS

Alternative Terminology
Long-term investments are often referred to simply as *investments*.

Long-term investments are generally investments in stocks and bonds of other corporations that are normally held for many years. This category also includes investments in long-term assets such as land or buildings that a company is not currently using in its operating activities. In Illustration 2-2 Franklin Corporation reported total long-term investments of $7,200 on its balance sheet.

Yahoo! Inc. reported long-term investments in its balance sheet as shown in Illustration 2-4.

Illustration 2-4   Long-term investments section

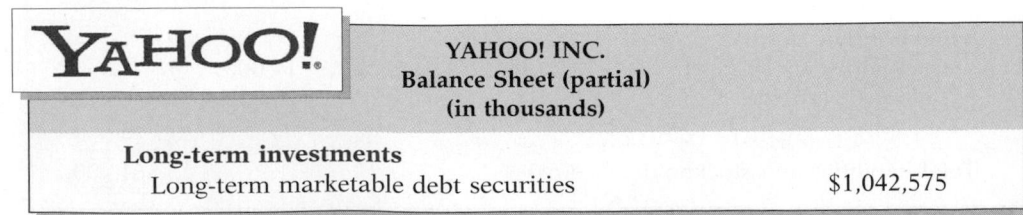

YAHOO! INC.
Balance Sheet (partial)
(in thousands)

Long-term investments	
Long-term marketable debt securities	$1,042,575

PROPERTY, PLANT, AND EQUIPMENT

Property, plant, and equipment are assets with relatively long useful lives that a company is currently using in operating the business. This category includes land, buildings, machinery and equipment, delivery equipment, and furniture. In Illustration 2-2 Franklin Corporation reported property, plant, and equipment of $29,000.

Depreciation is the practice of allocating the cost of assets to a number of years. Companies do this by systematically assigning a portion of an asset's cost as an expense each year (rather than expensing the full purchase price in the year of purchase). The assets that the company depreciates are reported on the balance sheet at cost less accumulated depreciation. The **accumulated depreciation** account shows the total amount of depreciation that the company has expensed thus far in the asset's life. In Illustration 2-2 Franklin Corporation reported accumulated depreciation of $5,000.

Illustration 2-5 presents the property, plant, and equipment of ski and sporting goods manufacturer K2, Inc.

Alternative Terminology
Property, plant, and equipment is sometimes called *fixed assets.*

K2, INC. Balance Sheet (partial) (in thousands)		
Property, plant, and equipment		
Land and land improvements	$ 6,794	
Buildings and leasehold improvements	55,900	
Machinery and equipment	204,651	
Construction in process	5,614	$272,959
Less: Accumulated depreciation		131,995
		$140,964

Illustration 2-5 Property, plant, and equipment section

INTANGIBLE ASSETS

Many companies have assets that do not have physical substance yet often are very valuable. We call these assets **intangible assets.** They include patents, copyrights, and trademarks or trade names that give the company **exclusive right** of use for a specified period of time. Franklin Corporation reported intangible assets of $3,100.

Illustration 2-6 shows how media giant Time Warner, Inc. reported its intangible assets.

Helpful Hint Sometimes intangible assets are reported under a broader heading called *"Other assets."*

TIME WARNER, INC. Balance Sheet (partial) (in millions)	
Intangible assets	
Film library	$ 3,361
Customer lists	868
Cable television franchises	29,751
Sports franchises	262
Brands, trademarks, and other intangible assets	9,643
	$43,885

Illustration 2-6 Intangible assets section

CURRENT LIABILITIES

In the liabilities and stockholders' equity section of the balance sheet, the first grouping is current liabilities. **Current liabilities** are obligations that the company is to pay within the coming year. Common examples are accounts payable, wages payable, bank loans payable, interest payable, and taxes payable. Also included as current liabilities are current maturities of long-term obligations—payments to be made within the next year on long-term obligations. In Illustration 2-2 Franklin Corporation reported five different types of current liabilities, for a total of $16,050.

Within the current liabilities section, companies usually list notes payable first, followed by accounts payable. Other items then follow in the order of their magnitude. In your homework, you should present notes payable first, followed by accounts payable, and then other liabilities in order of magnitude.

Illustration 2-7 shows the current liabilities section adapted from the balance sheet of Marcus Corporation.

Illustration 2-7 Current liabilities section

MARCUS CORPORATION Balance Sheet (partial) (in thousands)	
Current liabilities	
Notes payable	$ 2,066
Accounts payable	17,516
Current maturities of long-term debt	26,321
Taxes payable	14,889
Other current liabilities	14,809
Accrued compensation payable	8,614
Total current liabilities	$84,215

LONG-TERM LIABILITIES

Long-term liabilities are obligations that a company expects to pay **after** one year. Liabilities in this category include bonds payable, mortgages payable, long-term notes payable, lease liabilities, and pension liabilities. Many companies report long-term debt maturing after one year as a single amount in the balance sheet and show the details of the debt in notes that accompany the financial statements. Others list the various types of long-term liabilities. In Illustration 2-2 Franklin Corporation reported long-term liabilities of $11,300. In your homework, list long-term liabilities in the order of their magnitude.

Illustration 2-8 shows the long-term liabilities that Northwest Airlines Corporation reported in its balance sheet.

Illustration 2-8 Long-term liabilities section

NORTHWEST AIRLINES CORPORATION Balance Sheet (partial) (in millions)	
Long-term liabilities	
Long-term debt	$ 7,715
Other liabilities	4,346
Long-term obligations under capital leases	308
Total long-term liabilities	$12,369

STOCKHOLDERS' EQUITY

Stockholders' equity consists of two parts: common stock and retained earnings. Companies record as **common stock** the investments of assets into the business by the stockholders. They record as **retained earnings** the income retained for use in the business. These two parts, combined, make up **stockholders' equity** on the balance sheet. In Illustration 2-2 Franklin reported common stock of $14,000 and retained earnings of $20,050.

Alternative Terminology
Common stock is sometimes called *capital stock*.

BEFORE YOU GO ON . . .

▶Review It

1. What are the major sections in a classified balance sheet?
2. What is the primary determining factor to distinguish current assets from long-term assets?
3. What was Tootsie Roll's largest current asset at December 31, 2004? (The answer to this question appears on page 97.)
4. Where on the balance sheet do companies report accumulated depreciation?

▶Do It

Baxter Hoffman recently received the following information related to Hoffman Corporation's December 31, 2007, balance sheet.

Prepaid expenses	$ 2,300	Inventory	$3,400
Cash	800	Accumulated depreciation	2,700
Property, plant, and equipment	10,700	Accounts receivable	1,100

Prepare the assets section of Hoffman Corporation's balance sheet.

Action Plan

• Present current assets first. Current assets are cash and other resources that the company reasonably expects to consume in one year.
• Present current assets in the order in which the company expects to convert them into cash.
• Subtract accumulated depreciation from property, plant, and equipment to determine net property, plant, and equipment.

Solution

HOFFMAN CORPORATION		
Balance Sheet (partial)		
December 31, 2007		
Assets		
Current assets		
Cash	$ 800	
Accounts receivable	1,100	
Inventory	3,400	
Prepaid expenses	2,300	
Total current assets		$ 7,600
Property, plant, and equipment	10,700	
Less: Accumulated depreciation	2,700	8,000
Total assets		$15,600

THE NAVIGATOR

Using the Financial Statements

In Chapter 1 we introduced the four financial statements. We discussed how these statements provide information about a company's performance and financial position. In this chapter we extend this discussion by showing you specific tools that you can use to analyze financial statements in order to make a more meaningful evaluation of a company.

RATIO ANALYSIS

Ratio analysis expresses the relationship among selected items of financial statement data. A **ratio** expresses the mathematical relationship between one quantity and another. The relationship is expressed in terms of either a percentage, a rate, or a simple proportion.

To illustrate, Best Buy has current assets of $5,724 million and current liabilities of $4,501 million. We can determine a relationship between these accounts by dividing current assets by current liabilities, to get 1.27. The alternative means of expression are:

Percentage: Current assets are 127% of current liabilities.

Rate: Current assets are 1.27 times as great as current liabilities.

Proportion: The relationship of current assets to current liabilities is 1.27:1.

For analysis of the primary financial statements, we classify ratios as follows.

Illustration 2-9 Financial ratio classifications

Profitability Ratios

Measure the income or operating success of a company for a given period of time

Liquidity Ratios

Measure short-term ability of the company to pay its maturing obligations and to meet unexpected needs for cash

Solvency Ratios

Measure the ability of the company to survive over a long period of time

Ratios can provide clues to underlying conditions that may not be apparent from examination of the individual items on the financial statements. However, a single ratio by itself is not very meaningful. Accordingly, in this and the following chapters we will use various comparisons to shed light on company performance:

1. **Intracompany comparisons** covering two years for the same company.
2. **Industry-average comparisons** based on average ratios for particular industries.
3. **Intercompany comparisons** based on comparisons with a competitor in the same industry.

USING THE INCOME STATEMENT

Best Buy Company generates profits for its shareholders by selling electronics goods. The income statement reports how successful it is at generating a profit from its sales. The income statement reports the amount earned during the period (revenues) and the costs incurred during the period (expenses). Illustration 2-10 shows a simplified income statement for Best Buy.

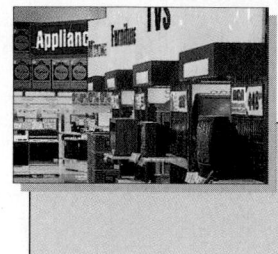

BEST BUY CO., INC. Income Statements For the Years Ended February 28, 2004, and March 1, 2003 (in millions)		
	2004	**2003**
Revenues		
Net sales and other revenue	$24,547	$20,946
Expenses		
Cost of goods sold	18,350	15,710
Selling, general, and administrative expenses	4,901	4,222
Income tax expense	496	392
Total expenses	23,747	20,324
Net income	$ 800	$ 622

Illustration 2-10   Best Buy's income statement

From this income statement we can see that Best Buy's sales and net income both increased during the year. Net income increased from $622,000,000 to $800,000,000. Best Buy's primary competitor is Circuit City. Circuit City reported a net loss of $787,000 for the year ended February 29, 2004.

To evaluate the profitability of Best Buy, we will use ratio analysis. **Profitability ratios** measure the operating success of a company for a given period of time.

EARNINGS PER SHARE.   **Earnings per share (EPS)** measures the net income earned on each share of common stock. We compute EPS by dividing **net income** by the **average number of common shares outstanding during the year**. Stockholders usually think in terms of the number of shares they own or plan to buy or sell, so stating net income earned as a per share amount provides a useful perspective for determining the investment return. Advanced accounting courses present more refined techniques for calculating earnings per share.

For now, a basic approach for calculating earnings per share is to divide earnings available to common stockholders by average common shares outstanding during the year. What is "earnings available to common stockholders"? It is an earnings amount calculated as net income less dividends paid on another type of stock, called preferred stock (Net income − Preferred stock dividends).

By comparing earnings per share of **a single company over time**, one can evaluate its relative earnings performance from the perspective of a shareholder— that is, on a per share basis. It is very important to note that comparisons of earnings per share across companies are **not meaningful** because of the wide variations in the numbers of shares of outstanding stock among companies.

Illustration 2-11 shows the earnings per share calculation for Best Buy in 2004 and 2003, based on the information presented below. (Note that to simplify our calculations, we assumed that any change in shares for Best Buy occurred in the middle of the year.)

(in millions)	2004	2003
Net income	$800	$622
Preferred stock dividends	–0–	–0–
Shares outstanding at beginning of year	322	319
Shares outstanding at end of year	325	322

Illustration 2-11 Best Buy earnings per share

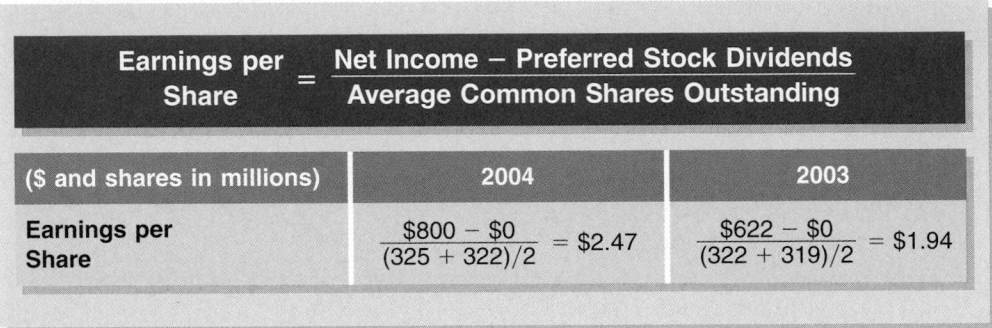

$$\text{Earnings per Share} = \frac{\text{Net Income} - \text{Preferred Stock Dividends}}{\text{Average Common Shares Outstanding}}$$

($ and shares in millions)	2004	2003
Earnings per Share	$\frac{\$800 - \$0}{(325 + 322)/2} = \$2.47$	$\frac{\$622 - \$0}{(322 + 319)/2} = \$1.94$

Decision Toolkit

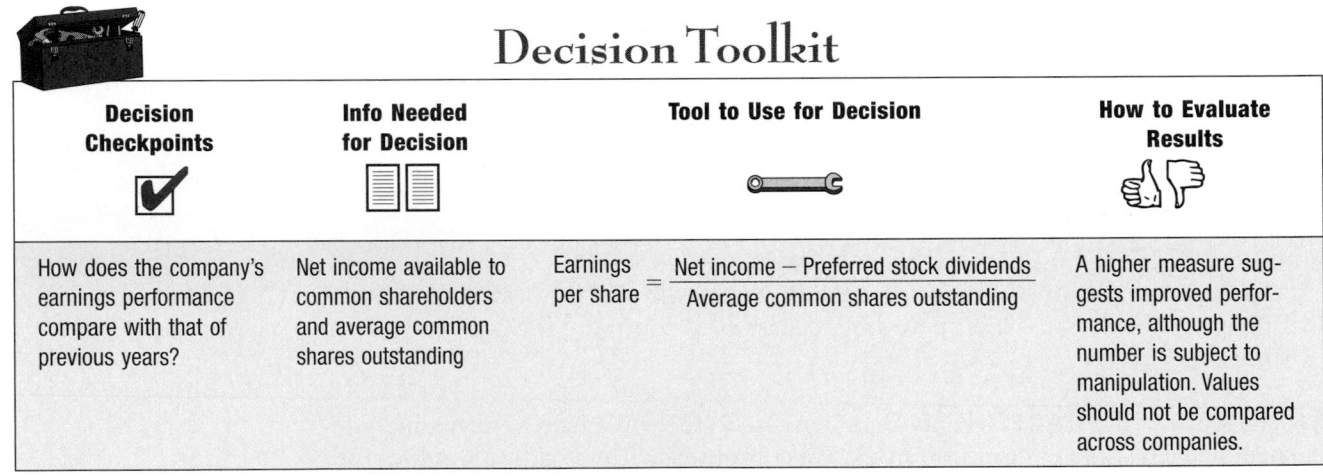

Decision Checkpoints	Info Needed for Decision	Tool to Use for Decision	How to Evaluate Results
How does the company's earnings performance compare with that of previous years?	Net income available to common shareholders and average common shares outstanding	$\text{Earnings per share} = \frac{\text{Net income} - \text{Preferred stock dividends}}{\text{Average common shares outstanding}}$	A higher measure suggests improved performance, although the number is subject to manipulation. Values should not be compared across companies.

USING THE STATEMENT OF STOCKHOLDERS' EQUITY

As discussed in Chapter 1, the retained earnings statement describes the changes in retained earnings during the year. This statement adds net income and then subtracts dividends from the beginning retained earnings to arrive at ending retained earnings.

Recall, however, that stockholders' equity is comprised of two parts: retained earnings and common stock. Therefore, the stockholders' equity of most companies is affected by factors other than just changes in retained earnings. For example, the company may issue or retire shares of common stock. Most companies, therefore, use what is called a **statement of stockholders' equity**, rather than a retained earnings statement, so that they can report **all changes** in stockholders' equity accounts. Illustration 2-12 is a simplified statement of stockholders' equity for Best Buy.

BEST BUY CO., INC. Statement of Stockholders' Equity (in millions)		
	Common Stock	**Retained Earnings**
Balances at March 3, 2001	$598	$1,224
Issuance of common stock	135	
Net income		564
Balances at March 2, 2002	733	1,788
Issuance of common stock	77	
Net income		622
Other adjustments		(490)
Balances at March 1, 2003	810	1,920
Issuance of common stock	58	
Net income		800
Dividends		(130)
Other adjustments		(36)
Balances at February 28, 2004	$868	$2,554

Illustration 2-12   Best Buy's statement of stockholders' equity

We can observe from this financial statement that Best Buy's common stock increased as the result of issuance of common stock in each of the three years. Another observation from this financial statement is that Best Buy paid no dividends until the most recent year. You might wonder why Best Buy paid no dividends during prior years when it was profitable. In fact, in a prior year, two Best Buy shareholders discussed this question about the company's dividend policy on an investor bulletin board. Here are excerpts:

From "Katwoman": "Best Buy has a nice price increase. Earnings are on the way up. But why no dividends?"

From "AngryCandy": "I guess they feel they can make better use of the money by investing back in the business. They still view Best Buy as a rapidly growing company and would prefer to invest in expanding the infrastructure (building new stores, advertising, etc.) than in paying out dividends. . . . If Best Buy gets to the stage of 'stable, big company' with little room for expansion, then I'm sure you'll see them elect to pay out a dividend."

AngryCandy's response is an excellent explanation of the thought process that management goes through in deciding whether to pay a dividend. Management must evaluate what its cash needs are. If it has uses for cash that will increase the value of the company (for example, building a new, centralized warehouse), then it should retain cash in the company. However, if it has more cash than it has valuable opportunities, it should distribute its excess cash as a dividend.

BEFORE YOU GO ON . . .

▶Review It

1. What are the three ways that ratios can be expressed?
2. What is the purpose of profitability ratios? Explain earnings per share.
3. What does a statement of stockholders' equity show?

USING A CLASSIFIED BALANCE SHEET

You can learn a lot about a company's financial health by also evaluating the relationship between its various assets and liabilities. Illustration 2-13 provides a simplified balance sheet for Best Buy.

Illustration 2-13   Best Buy's balance sheet

BEST BUY CO., INC. Balance Sheets (in millions)		
Assets	**February 28, 2004**	**March 1, 2003**
Current assets		
Cash and cash equivalents	$2,600	$1,914
Receivables	343	312
Merchandise inventories	2,607	2,077
Other current assets	174	595
Total current assets	5,724	4,898
Property and equipment	3,574	3,089
Less: Accumulated depreciation	1,330	1,027
Net property and equipment	2,244	2,062
Other assets	684	734
Total assets	$8,652	$7,694
Liabilities and Stockholders' Equity		
Current liabilities		
Accounts payable	$2,535	$2,195
Accrued liabilities	949	760
Accrued income taxes	380	374
Other current liabilities	368	321
Accrued compensation payable	269	174
Total current liabilities	4,501	3,824
Long-term liabilities		
Long-term debt	482	828
Other long-term liabilities	247	312
Total long-term liabilities	729	1,140
Total liabilities	5,230	4,964
Stockholders' equity		
Common stock	868	810
Retained earnings	2,554	1,920
Total stockholders' equity	3,422	2,730
Total liabilities and stockholders' equity	$8,652	$7,694

Liquidity

Suppose you are a banker at CitiGroup considering lending money to Best Buy, or you are a sales manager at Hewlett-Packard interested in selling computers to Best Buy on credit. You would be concerned about Best Buy's **liquidity**—its ability to pay obligations expected to become due within the next year or operating cycle. You would look closely at the relationship of its current assets to current liabilities.

STUDY OBJECTIVE

4

Identify and compute ratios for analyzing a company's liquidity and solvency using a balance sheet.

WORKING CAPITAL.   One measure of liquidity is **working capital**, which is the difference between the amounts of current assets and current liabilities:

Illustration 2-14   Working capital

$$\text{Working Capital} = \text{Current Assets} - \text{Current Liabilities}$$

When working capital is positive, current assets exceed current liabilities. When this occurs, there is greater likelihood that the company will pay its liabilities. When working capital is negative, a company might not be able to pay short-term creditors, and the company might ultimately be forced into bankruptcy. Best Buy had working capital in 2004 of $1,223,000,000 ($5,724,000,000 − $4,501,000,000).

CURRENT RATIO.   **Liquidity ratios** measure the short-term ability of the enterprise to pay its maturing obligations and to meet unexpected needs for cash. One liquidity ratio is the **current ratio**, computed as current assets divided by current liabilities.

The current ratio is a more dependable indicator of liquidity than working capital. Two companies with the same amount of working capital may have significantly different current ratios. Illustration 2-15 shows the 2004 and 2003 current ratios for Best Buy and for Circuit City, along with the 2004 industry average.

Illustration 2-15   Current ratio

$$\text{Current Ratio} = \frac{\text{Current Assets}}{\text{Current Liabilities}}$$

	2004	2003
Best Buy ($ in millions)	$\frac{\$5,724}{\$4,501} = 1.27\!:\!1$	$\frac{\$4,898}{\$3,824} = 1.28\!:\!1$
Circuit City	2.48:1	2.42:1
Industry average	1.40:1	

What does the ratio actually mean? Best Buy's 2004 current ratio of 1.27:1 means that for every dollar of current liabilities, Best Buy has $1.27 of current assets. Best Buy's current ratio decreased slightly in 2004. When compared to the industry average of 1.40:1, and Circuit City's 2.48:1 current ratio, Best Buy's liquidity needs further investigation.

The current ratio is only one measure of liquidity. It does not take into account the **composition** of the current assets. For example, a satisfactory current ratio does not disclose whether a portion of the current assets is tied up in slow-moving inventory. The composition of the assets matters because a dollar of cash is more readily available to pay the bills than is a dollar of inventory. For example, suppose a company's cash balance declined while its merchandise inventory increased substantially. If inventory increased because the company is having difficulty selling its products, then the current ratio might not fully reflect the reduction in the company's liquidity.

Accounting across the Organization

There actually is a point where a company can be too liquid—that is, it can have too much working capital. While it is important to be liquid enough to be able to pay short-term bills as they come due, a company does not want to tie up its cash in extra inventory or receivables that are not earning the company money.

By one estimate from the REL Consultancy Group, U.S. companies have on their books cumulative excess working capital of nearly $600 billion (K. Richardson, "Ignored Money Waiting to Be Spent," *Wall Street Journal*, August 30, 2004, p. C3). Based on this figure, companies could have reduced debt by 36 percent or increased net income by 9 percent. Given that managers throughout a company are interested in improving profitability, it is clear that they should have an eye toward managing working capital. They need to aim for a "Goldilocks solution"—not too much, not too little, but just right.

 What can various company managers do to ensure that working capital is managed efficiently (so as to maximize net income)?

Solvency

Now suppose that instead of being a short-term creditor, you are interested in either buying Best Buy's stock or extending the company a long-term loan. Long-term creditors and stockholders are interested in a company's long-run **solvency**—its ability to pay interest as it comes due and to repay the balance of a debt due at its maturity. **Solvency ratios** measure the ability of the enterprise to survive over a long period of time.

DEBT TO TOTAL ASSETS RATIO. The **debt to total assets ratio** is one source of information about long-term debt-paying ability. It measures the percentage of assets financed by creditors rather than stockholders. Debt financing is more risky than equity financing because debt must be repaid at specific points in time, whether the company is performing well or not. Thus, the higher the percentage of debt financing, the riskier the company.

Helpful Hint Some users evaluate solvency using a ratio of liabilities divided by stockholders' equity. The higher this "debt to equity" ratio, the lower is a company's solvency.

We compute the debt to total assets ratio as total debt (both current and long-term liabilities) divided by total assets. The higher the percentage of total liabilities (debt) to total assets, the greater the risk that the company may be unable to pay its debts as they come due. Illustration 2-16 (page 61) shows the debt to total assets ratios for Best Buy and Circuit City, along with the 2004 industry average.

The 2004 ratio of 60% means that Best Buy's creditors provided $0.60 of every dollar invested in assets by Best Buy. Best Buy's ratio exceeds the industry average of 15% and Circuit City's ratio of 39%. The higher the ratio, the lower the equity "buffer" available to creditors if the company becomes insolvent. Thus, from the creditors' point of view, a high ratio of debt to total assets is undesirable. Best Buy's solvency appears lower than that of Circuit City and lower than the average company in the industry.

Illustration 2-16   Debt to total assets ratio

	2004	2003
Best Buy **($ in millions)**	$\frac{\$5{,}230}{\$8{,}652} = 60\%$	$\frac{\$4{,}964}{\$7{,}694} = 65\%$
Circuit City	39%	38%
Industry average	15%	

$$\text{Debt to Total Assets Ratio} = \frac{\text{Total Liabilities}}{\text{Total Assets}}$$

The adequacy of this ratio is often judged in the light of the company's earnings. Generally, companies with relatively stable earnings, such as public utilities, can support higher debt to total assets ratios than can cyclical companies with widely fluctuating earnings, such as many high-tech companies. In later chapters you will learn additional ways to evaluate solvency.

Business Insight
INVESTOR PERSPECTIVE

Debt financing differs greatly across industries and companies. Here are some debt to total assets ratios for selected companies:

	Debt to Total Assets Ratio
American Pharmaceutical Partners	19%
Callaway Golf Company	20%
Microsoft	21%
Sears Holdings Corporation	73%
Eastman Kodak Company	78%
General Motors Corporation	94%

 Discuss the difference in the debt to total assets ratio of Microsoft and General Motors.

Decision Toolkit

Decision Checkpoints	Info Needed for Decision	Tool to Use for Decision	How to Evaluate Results
Can the company meet its near-term obligations?	Current assets and current liabilities	$\text{Current ratio} = \dfrac{\text{Current assets}}{\text{Current liabilities}}$	Higher ratio suggests favorable liquidity.
Can the company meet its long-term obligations?	Total debt and total assets	$\text{Debt to total assets ratio} = \dfrac{\text{Total liabilities}}{\text{Total assets}}$	Lower value suggests favorable solvency.

BEFORE YOU GO ON . . .

▶Review It

1. What is liquidity? How can it be measured using a classified balance sheet?
2. What is solvency? How can it be measured using a classified balance sheet?

▶Do It

Selected financial data for Drummond Company at December 31, 2007, are as follows: cash $60,000; receivables (net) $80,000; inventory $70,000; total assets $540,000; current liabilities $140,000; and total liabilities $270,000. Compute the current ratio and debt to total assets ratio.

Action Plan

• Use the formula for the current ratio: Current assets ÷ Current liabilities.
• Use the formula for the debt to total assets ratio: Total liabilities ÷ Total assets.

Solution

The current ratio is 1.5 : 1 ($210,000 ÷ $140,000). The debt to total assets ratio is 50% ($270,000 ÷ $540,000).

THE NAVIGATOR

STUDY OBJECTIVE
5

Use the statement of cash flows to evaluate solvency.

USING THE STATEMENT OF CASH FLOWS

As you learned in Chapter 1, the statement of cash flows provides financial information about the sources and uses of a company's cash. Investors, creditors, and others want to know what is happening to a company's most liquid resource— its cash. In fact, people often say that "cash is king" because if a company cannot generate cash, it will not survive. To aid in the analysis of cash, the statement of cash flows reports the cash effects of (1) a company's **operating activities**, (2) its **investing activities**, and (3) its **financing activities**.

Sources of cash matter. For example, you would feel much better about a company's health if you knew that the company generates its cash from the operations of the business rather than borrows it. A cash flow statement provides this information. Similarly, net income does not tell you *how much* cash the company generated from operations. The statement of cash flows can tell you that. In summary, neither the income statement nor the balance sheet directly answers most of the important questions about cash, but the statement of cash flows does. Illustration 2-17 (page 63) shows a simplified statement of cash flows for Best Buy.

Different users have different reasons for being interested in the statement of cash flows. If you were a creditor of Best Buy (either short term or long term), you would be interested to know the source of its cash in recent years. This information would give you some indication of where it might get cash to pay you. If you have a long-term interest in Best Buy as a stockholder, you would look to the statement of cash flows for information regarding the company's ability to generate cash over the long run to meet its cash needs for growth.

Companies get cash from two sources: operating activities and financing activities. In the early years of a company's life it typically will not generate enough cash from operating activities to meet its investing needs, so it will have to issue stock or borrow money. An established company, however, will often be able to meet most of its cash needs with cash from operations. Best Buy's cash provided by operating activities during these two years was sufficient to meet its needs for acquisitions of property, plant, and equipment. For example, in 2004 cash provided by operating activities was $1,414,000,000, whereas cash spent on property, plant, and equipment was $545,000,000.

Illustration 2-17 Best Buy's statement of cash flows

BEST BUY CO., INC.
Statement of Cash Flows
(in millions)

	For fiscal year ending	
	February 28, 2004	**March 1, 2003**
Cash flows provided by operating activities		
Cash receipts from operating activities	$24,520	$20,857
Cash payments for operating activities	23,106	20,111
Net cash provided (used) by operations	1,414	746
Cash flows provided by investing activities		
(Increase) decrease in property and plant	(545)	(725)
Other cash inflow (outflow)	(50)	(13)
Net cash provided (used) by investing	(595)	(738)
Cash flows provided by financing activities		
Issue of equity securities	114	40
Increase (decrease) in borrowing	(17)	5
Dividends	(130)	0
Repurchase of common stock	(100)	0
Net cash provided (used) by financing	(133)	45
Net increase (decrease) in cash and equivalents	686	53
Cash and equivalents at start of year	1,914	1,861
Cash and equivalents at year-end	$ 2,600	$ 1,914

FREE CASH FLOW. In the statement of cash flows, cash provided by operating activities is intended to indicate the cash-generating capability of the company. Analysts have noted, however, that **cash provided by operating activities fails to take into account that a company must invest in new property, plant, and equipment** (capital expenditures) just to maintain its current level of operations. Companies also must at least **maintain dividends at current levels** to satisfy investors. A measurement to provide additional insight regarding a company's cash-generating ability is free cash flow. **Free cash flow** describes the cash remaining from operations after adjusting for capital expenditures and dividends.

Consider the following example: Suppose that MPC produced and sold 10,000 personal computers this year. It reported $100,000 cash provided by operating activities. In order to maintain production at 10,000 computers, MPC invested $15,000 in equipment. It chose to pay $5,000 in dividends. Its free cash flow was $80,000 ($100,000 − $15,000 − $5,000). The company could use this $80,000 to purchase new assets to expand the business, to pay off debts, or to increase its dividend distribution. In practice, analysts often calculate free cash flow with the formula in Illustration 2-18. Alternative definitions also exist.

Illustration 2-18 Free cash flow

Free Cash Flow	=	Cash Provided by Operations	−	Capital Expenditures	−	Cash Dividends

Illustration 2-19 shows calculation of Best Buy's free cash flow.

Illustration 2-19
Calculation of Best Buy's
free cash flow ($ in
millions)

Cash provided by operating activities	$1,414
Less: Expenditures on property, plant, and equipment	545
Dividends paid	130
Free cash flow	$ 739

Best Buy generated free cash flow of $739 million which is available for the acquisition of new assets, the retirement of stock or debt, or the payment of additional dividends. Long-term creditors consider a high free cash flow amount an indication of solvency. Circuit City's free cash flow for 2004 is a negative $322 million. This lack of free cash flow calls into question Circuit City's ability to repay its long-term obligations as they come due.

Decision Toolkit

Decision Checkpoints	Info Needed for Decision	Tool to Use for Decision	How to Evaluate Results
How much cash did the company generate to expand operations, pay off debts, or distribute dividends?	Cash provided by operating activities, cash spent on fixed assets, and cash dividends	$$\text{Free cash flow} = \text{Cash provided by operations} - \text{Capital expenditures} - \text{Cash dividends}$$	Significant free cash flow indicates greater potential to finance new investment and pay additional dividends.

BEFORE YOU GO ON . . .

▶Review It

1. What information does the statement of cash flows provide that is not available in an income statement or a balance sheet?
2. What does free cash flow measure?

SECTION TWO
FINANCIAL REPORTING CONCEPTS

In Chapter 1 you learned about the four financial statements, and in this chapter we introduced you to some basic ways to interpret those statements. In this last section we will discuss concepts that underly these financial statements. It would be unwise to make business decisions based on financial statements without understanding the implications of these concepts.

STUDY OBJECTIVE
6

Explain the meaning of
generally accepted
accounting principles.

The Standard-Setting Environment

How does a company like Best Buy decide on the amount and type of financial information to disclose? What format should it use? How should it measure assets, liabilities, revenues, and expenses? The answers to these questions are found in accounting guidelines referred to as **generally accepted accounting principles (GAAP)**. Various standard-setting bodies, in consultation with the accounting profession and the business community, determine these guidelines.

The **Securities and Exchange Commission (SEC)** is the agency of the U.S. government that oversees U.S. financial markets and accounting standard-setting bodies. The primary accounting standard-setting body in the United States is the **Financial Accounting Standards Board (FASB)**. Many countries outside of the United States have adopted the accounting standards issued by the **International Accounting Standards Board (IASB)**. In recent years the FASB and IASB have worked closely to try to minimize the differences in their standards.

CHARACTERISTICS OF USEFUL INFORMATION

In establishing guidelines for reporting financial information, the FASB believes that the overriding consideration should be the generation of financial information useful for making business decisions. To be useful, information should possess these characteristics: relevance, reliability, comparability, and consistency.

Relevance

Accounting information is **relevant** if it would make a difference in a business decision. For example, the information in Best Buy's financial statements is considered relevant because it provides a basis for forecasting Best Buy's future earnings. Accounting information is also relevant to business decisions because it confirms or corrects prior expectations. Financial statements provide relevant information that helps **predict** future events and **provide feedback** about prior expectations for the financial health of the company.

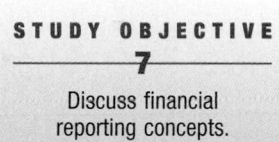

STUDY OBJECTIVE
7
Discuss financial
reporting concepts.

For accounting information to be relevant it must be **timely**. That is, it must be available to decision makers before it loses its capacity to influence decisions. The SEC requires that public companies provide their annual reports to investors within 60 days of their year-end.

Reliability

Reliability of information means that the information can be depended on. To be reliable, accounting information must be **verifiable**—we must be able to prove that it is free of error. Also, the information must be a **faithful representation** of what it purports to be—it must be factual. If Best Buy's income statement reports sales of $20 billion when it actually had sales of $10 billion, then the statement is not a faithful representation of Best Buy's financial performance. Finally, accounting information must be **neutral**—it cannot be selected, prepared, or presented to favor one set of interested users over another. As noted in Chapter 1, to ensure reliability, certified public accountants audit financial statements.

Comparability

In accounting, comparability results when different companies use the same accounting principles. U.S. accounting standards are relatively comparable because they are based on certain basic principles and assumptions. However, these principles and assumptions allow for some variation in methods. For example, there are a variety of ways to report inventory. Often these different methods result in different amounts of net income. To make comparison across companies easier, each company **must disclose** the accounting methods used.

Accounting across the Organization

Another issue related to comparability is the accounting time period. An accounting period that is one-year long is called a **fiscal year**. But a fiscal year need not match the calendar year. For example, a company could end its fiscal year on April 30, rather than December 31.

Why do companies choose the particular year-ends that they do? For example, why doesn't every company use December 31 as the accounting year-end? Many companies choose to end their accounting year when inventory or operations are at a low. This is advantageous because compiling accounting information requires much time and effort by managers, so they would rather do it when they aren't as busy operating the business. Also, inventory is easier and less costly to count when its volume is low.

Some companies whose year-ends differ from December 31 are Delta Air Lines, June 30; Walt Disney Productions, September 30; and Dunkin' Donuts, Inc., October 31. In the notes to its financial statements, Best Buy states that its accounting year-end is the Saturday nearest the end of February.

 What problems might Best Buy's year-end create for analysts?

Consistency

To compare Best Buy's net income over several years, you would need to know that it used the same accounting principles from year to year. **Consistency** means that a company uses the same accounting principles and methods from year to year. Thus, if a company selects one inventory accounting method in the first year of operations, it is expected to continue to use that same method in succeeding years.

A company *can* change to a new method of accounting if management can justify that the new method produces more useful financial information. In the year in which the change occurs, the change must be disclosed in the notes to the financial statements so that users of the statements are aware of the lack of consistency.

Illustration 2-20 summarizes the characteristics that make accounting information useful.

Illustration 2-20
Characteristics of useful information

Relevance	**Reliability**	**Comparability**	**Consistency**
1. Provides a basis for forecasts	1. Is verifiable	Different companies use similar accounting principles	Company uses same accounting methods from year to year
2. Confirms or corrects prior expectations	2. Is a faithful representation		
3. Is timely	3. Is neutral		

ASSUMPTIONS AND PRINCIPLES IN FINANCIAL REPORTING

To develop accounting standards, the FASB relies on some key assumptions and principles.

Monetary Unit Assumption

The monetary unit assumption requires that only those things that can be expressed in money are included in the accounting records. Because the exchange of money is fundamental to business transactions, it makes sense that we measure a business in terms of money.

However, the monetary unit assumption also means that certain important information needed by investors, creditors, and managers is not reported in the financial statements. For example, customer satisfaction is important to every business, but it is not easily quantified in dollar terms; thus it is not reported in the financial statements.

Economic Entity Assumption

The economic entity assumption states that every economic entity can be separately identified and accounted for. For example, suppose you are a stockholder of Best Buy. The amount of cash you have in your personal bank account and the balance owed on your personal car loan are not reported in Best Buy's balance sheet. In order to accurately assess Best Buy's performance and financial position, it is important that we not blur it with your personal transactions, or the transactions of any other person (especially its managers) or company.

Time Period Assumption

Next, notice that the income statement, retained earnings statement, and statement of cash flows all cover periods of one year, and the balance sheet is prepared at the end of each year. The time period assumption states that the life of a business can be divided into artificial time periods and that useful reports covering those periods can be prepared for the business. All companies report financial results at least annually. Many also report every three months (quarterly) to stockholders, and many prepare monthly statements for internal purposes.

Going Concern Assumption

The going concern assumption states that the business will remain in operation for the foreseeable future. Of course many businesses do fail, but in general, it is reasonable to assume that the business will continue operating. If going concern is not assumed, then the company should state plant assets at their liquidation value (selling price less cost of disposal), rather than at their cost. Only when liquidation of the business appears likely is the going concern assumption inappropriate.

Illustration 2-21 (page 68) shows these four accounting assumptions graphically.

Cost Principle

The cost principle dictates that assets be recorded at their cost. This is true not only at the time the asset is purchased, but also over the time the asset is held. For example, if Best Buy were to purchase some land for $30,000, the company would initially report it on the balance sheet at $30,000. But what would Best Buy do if, by the end of the next year, the land had increased in value to $40,000?

Illustration 2-21
Accounting assumptions

Under the cost principle the company would continue to report the land at $30,000.

The cost principle is often criticized as being irrelevant. Critics contend that market value would be more useful to financial decision makers. Proponents of the cost principle counter that cost is the best measure because it can be easily verified from transactions between two parties, whereas market value is often subjective. Recently, the FASB has changed some accounting rules requiring that certain investment securities be recorded at their market value. In choosing between cost and market value, the FASB weighed the reliability of cost figures versus the relevance of market value.

Full Disclosure Principle

The **full disclosure principle** requires that companies disclose all circumstances and events that would make a difference to financial statement users. Some important financial information is not easily reported on the face of the statements. For example, Best Buy has debt outstanding. Investors and creditors would like to know the terms of the debt; that is, when does it mature, what is its interest rate, and is it renewable? Or Best Buy might be sued by one of its customers. Investors and creditors might not know about this lawsuit. If an important item cannot reasonably be reported directly in one of the four types of financial statements, then it should be discussed in notes that accompany the statements. Some investors who lost money in Enron, WorldCom, and Global Crossing complained that the lack of full disclosure regarding some of the companies' transactions caused the financial statements to be misleading.

Illustration 2-22 depicts these two accounting principles.

Illustration 2-22
Accounting principles

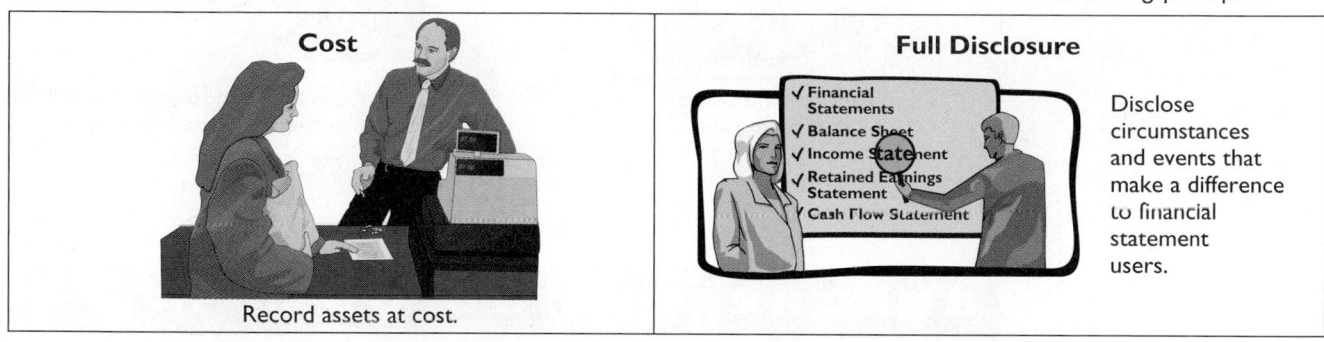

CONSTRAINTS IN ACCOUNTING

Taken to the extreme, efforts to provide useful financial information could be far too costly to a company. Therefore, the profession has agreed upon **constraints** to ensure that companies apply accounting rules in a reasonable fashion, from the perspectives of both the company and the user. The constraints are materiality and conservatism.

Materiality

Materiality relates to a financial statement item's impact on a company's overall financial condition and operations. An item is **material** when its **size** makes it likely to influence the decision of an investor or creditor. It is **immaterial** if it is too small to impact a decision maker. In short, if the item does not make a difference, the company does not have to follow GAAP in reporting it. To determine the materiality of an amount—that is, to determine its financial significance—the company compares the item with such items as total assets, sales revenue, and net income.

To illustrate, assume that Best Buy made a $100 error in recording revenue. Best Buy's total revenue is $24.5 billion; thus a $100 error is not material.

Conservatism

Conservatism in accounting means that when preparing financial statements, a company should choose the accounting method that will be least likely to overstate assets or income. It **does not mean, however, that a company should intentionally understate assets or income**.

A common application of the conservatism constraint is in valuing inventories. Companies normally record inventories at their cost. Conservatism, however, requires that companies write down inventories to market value if market value is below cost. Conservatism also requires that when the market value of inventory exceeds cost, the company should not increase the value of the inventory on the books, but instead keep it at cost. This practice results in lower net income on the income statement and a lower amount reported for inventory on the balance sheet.

Illustration 2-23 (page 70) graphically depicts the two constraints.

Illustration 2-23
Accounting constraints

Materiality	Conservatism
Companies do not have to follow GAAP for small amounts.	When in doubt, choose the solution that will be least likely to overstate assets and income.

BEFORE YOU GO ON . . .

▶Review It

1. What are generally accepted accounting principles?
2. What is the basic objective of financial information?
3. What qualitative characteristics make accounting information useful?
4. What are the materiality constraint and the conservatism constraint?

☑ THE NAVIGATOR

Using the Decision Toolkit

In this chapter we have evaluated a home electronics giant, Best Buy. Tweeter Home Entertainment sells consumer electronics products from 154 stores on the East Coast under various names. It specializes in products with high-end features. Illustrations 2-24 and 2-25 show a simplified balance sheet and income statement for Tweeter Home Entertainment. Additional information: Tweeter's cash provided by operating activities was $41,508,000 in 2004 and $10,307,000 in 2003. Its capital expenditures were $19,485,000 in 2004 and $24,188,000 in 2003. The company paid no dividends in either year. Assume that average shares outstanding during all of fiscal 2004 were 24.2 million and were 23.7 million during all of fiscal 2003. There was no preferred stock outstanding.

Instructions
Using these statements, answer the following questions.

1. Calculate the current ratio for Tweeter for 2004 and 2003 and discuss its liquidity position.
2. Calculate the debt to total assets ratio and free cash flow for Tweeter for 2004 and 2003 and discuss its solvency.
3. Calculate the earnings per share for Tweeter for 2004 and 2003, and discuss its change in profitability.
4. Best Buy's accounting year-end was February 28, 2004; Tweeter's was September 30, 2004. How does this difference affect your ability to compare their profitability?

Tweeter

TWEETER HOME ENTERTAINMENT GROUP
Balance Sheets
(in millions)

	September 30 2004	2003
Assets		
Current assets		
Cash and cash equivalents	$ 2.8	$ 1.9
Receivables	25.6	24.2
Inventories	106.6	117.6
Other current assets	17.0	26.9
Total current assets	152.0	170.6
Property, plant, and equipment, net	124.9	126.2
Other assets	24.3	11.6
Total assets	$301.2	$308.4
Liabilities and Stockholders' Equity		
Current liabilities		
Note payable	$ 3.2	$ 7.4
Accounts payable	70.0	55.2
Other current liabilities	22.5	21.4
Total current liabilities	95.7	84.0
Long-term debt	35.0	48.3
Other liabilities	14.1	11.1
Total liabilities	144.8	143.4
Stockholders' equity	156.4	165.0
Total liabilities and stockholders' equity	$301.2	$308.4

Illustration 2-24 Tweeter Home Entertainment's balance sheet

Tweeter

TWEETER HOME ENTERTAINMENT GROUP
Income Statements
(in millions)

	Years ended September 30 2004	2003
Sales	$778.2	$787.0
Cost of sales	476.2	516.9
Operating expenses	324.3	286.8
Interest expense	3.3	2.8
Other expense/(income)	(1.2)	(0.7)
Income tax expense (benefit)	(9.3)	(7.1)
Total expenses	793.3	798.7
Net loss	$ (15.1)	$ (11.7)

Illustration 2-25 Tweeter Home Entertainment's income statement

Solution

1. Current ratio:

$$2004\,(\$152.0/\$95.7) = 1.59 \qquad 2003\,(\$170.6/\$84.0) = 2.03$$

   Tweeter's liquidity declined from 2003 to 2004. In 2003 there was $2.03 of current assets available for every dollar of current liabilities. In 2004 there was $1.59. Analysts probably would consider Tweeter's 2004 current ratio acceptable, but not strong. It is higher than that of Best Buy, but Tweeter is a much smaller company than Best Buy. Often, larger companies can get by with a lower current ratio.

2. Debt to total assets ratio:

$$2004\,(\$144.8/\$301.2) = 48\% \qquad 2003\,(\$143.4/\$308.4) = 46\%$$

   Based on the change in its ratio of debt to total assets, Tweeter's reliance on debt financing increased slightly from 2003 to 2004. The increase in the value of this ratio suggests the company's solvency declined.

   Free cash flow:

$$2004 \quad \$41,508,000 - \$19,485,000 - 0 = \$22,023,000$$

$$2003 \quad \$10,307,000 - \$24,188,000 - 0 = -\$13,881,000$$

   Tweeter's free cash flow improved from a negative $13.9 million in 2003 to positive $22 million in 2004. Thus, although the debt to total assets ratio increased, the company's improved free cash flow suggests an improved ability to repay its long-term debt.

3. Loss per share:

$$2004\,(\$15.1/24.2) = \$0.62 \text{ per share} \qquad 2003\,(\$11.7/23.7) = \$0.49 \text{ per share}$$

   Tweeter's loss per share increased from $0.49 to $0.62.

4. Tweeter's income statement covers seven months not covered by Best Buy's. Suppose that the economy changed dramatically during this seven-month period, either improving or declining. This change in the economy would be reflected in Tweeter's income statement but would not be reflected in Best Buy's income statement until the following March, thus reducing the usefulness of a comparison of the income statements of the two companies.

Summary of Study Objectives

1 *Identify the sections of a classified balance sheet.* In a classified balance sheet, companies classify assets as current assets; long-term investments; property, plant, and equipment; and intangibles. They classify liabilities as either current or long-term. A stockholders' equity section shows common stock and retained earnings.

2 *Identify and compute ratios for analyzing a company's profitability.* Profitability ratios, such as earnings per share (EPS), measure aspects of the operating success of a company for a given period of time.

3 *Explain the relationship between a retained earnings statement and a statement of stockholders' equity.* The retained earnings statement presents the factors that

changed the retained earnings balance during the period. A statement of stockholders' equity presents the factors that changed stockholders' equity during the period, including those that changed retained earnings. Thus, a statement of stockholders' equity is more inclusive.

4 *Identify and compute ratios for analyzing a company's liquidity and solvency using a balance sheet.* Liquidity ratios, such as the current ratio, measure the short-term ability of a company to pay its maturing obligations and to meet unexpected needs for cash. Solvency ratios, such as the debt to total assets ratio, measure the ability of an enterprise to survive over a long period.

5 *Use the statement of cash flows to evaluate solvency.* Free cash flow indicates a company's ability to generate cash from operations that is sufficient to pay debts, acquire assets, and distribute dividends.

6 *Explain the meaning of generally accepted accounting principles.* Generally accepted accounting principles are a set of rules and practices recognized as a general guide for financial reporting purposes. The basic objective of financial reporting is to provide information that is useful for decision making.

7 *Discuss financial reporting concepts.* To be judged useful, information should have relevance, reliability, comparability, and consistency.

The *monetary unit assumption* requires that companies include in the accounting records only transaction data that can be expressed in terms of money. The *economic entity assumption* states that economic events can be identified with a particular unit of accountability. The *time period assumption* states that the economic life of a business can be divided into artificial time periods and that meaningful accounting reports can be prepared for each period. The *going concern assumption* states that the enterprise will continue in operation long enough to carry out its existing objectives and commitments.

The *cost principle* states that companies should record assets at their cost. The *full disclosure principle* dictates that companies disclose circumstances and events that matter to financial statement users.

The major constraints are materiality and conservatism.

Decision Toolkit—A Summary

Decision Checkpoints	Info Needed for Decision	Tool to Use for Decision	How to Evaluate Results
How does the company's earnings performance compare with that of previous years?	Net income available to common shareholders and average common shares outstanding	$\text{Earnings per share} = \dfrac{\text{Net income} - \text{Preferred stock dividends}}{\text{Average common shares outstanding}}$	A higher measure suggests improved performance, although the number is subject to manipulation. Values should not be compared across companies.
Can the company meet its near-term obligations?	Current assets and current liabilities	$\text{Current ratio} = \dfrac{\text{Current assets}}{\text{Current liabilities}}$	Higher ratio suggests favorable liquidity.
Can the company meet its long-term obligations?	Total debt and total assets	$\text{Debt to total assets ratio} = \dfrac{\text{Total liabilities}}{\text{Total assets}}$	Lower value suggests favorable solvency.
How much cash did the company generate to expand operations, pay off debts, or distribute dividends?	Cash provided by operating activities, cash spent on fixed assets, and cash dividends	$\text{Free cash flow} = \text{Cash provided by operations} - \text{Capital expenditures} - \text{Cash dividends}$	Significant free cash flow indicates greater potential to finance new investment and pay additional dividends.

Glossary

Classified balance sheet A balance sheet that contains a number of standard classifications or sections. (p. 48)

Comparability Ability to compare the accounting information of different companies because they use the same accounting principles. (p. 65)

Conservatism The approach of choosing an accounting method, when in doubt, that will least likely overstate assets and net income. (p. 69)

Consistency Use of the same accounting principles and methods from year to year within a company. (p. 66)

Cost principle An accounting principle that states that companies should record assets at their cost. (p. 67)

Current assets Cash and other resources that companies reasonably expect to convert to cash or use up within one year or the operating cycle, whichever is longer. (p. 49)

Current liabilities Obligations that companies reasonably expect to pay within the next year or operating cycle, whichever is longer. (p. 52)

Current ratio A measure used to evaluate a company's liquidity and short-term debt-paying ability; computed as current assets divided by current liabilities. (p. 59)

Debt to total assets ratio   Measures the percentage of total financing provided by creditors; computed as total debt divided by total assets. (p. 60)

Earnings per share (EPS)   A measure of the net income earned on each share of common stock; computed as net income minus preferred stock dividends divided by the average number of common shares outstanding during the year. (p. 55)

Economic entity assumption   An assumption that economic events can be identified with a particular unit of accountability. (p. 67).

Financial Accounting Standards Board (FASB)   The primary accounting standard-setting body in the United States. (p. 65)

Free cash flow   Cash provided by operating activities adjusted for capital expenditures and dividends paid. (p. 63)

Full disclosure principle   Accounting principle that dictates that companies disclose circumstances and events that make a difference to financial statements users. (p. 68)

Generally accepted accounting principles (GAAP)   A set of rules and practices, having substantial authoritative support, that the accounting profession recognizes as a general guide for financial reporting purposes. (p. 65)

Going concern assumption   The assumption that the enterprise will continue in operation for the foreseeable future. (p. 67).

Intangible assets   Assets that do not have physical substance. (p. 51)

International Accounting Standards Board (IASB)   An accounting standard-setting body that issues standards adopted by many countries outside of the United States. (p. 65)

Liquidity   The ability of a company to pay obligations that are expected to become due within the next year or operating cycle. (p. 59)

Liquidity ratios   Measures of the short-term ability of the company to pay its maturing obligations and to meet unexpected needs for cash. (p. 59)

Long-term investments   Generally, investments in stocks and bonds of other companies that companies normally hold for many years. Also includes long-term assets, such as land and buildings, not currently being used in the company's operations. (p. 50)

Long-term liabilities (Long-term debt)   Obligations that companies do not expect to pay within one year or the operating cycle. (p. 52)

Materiality   The constraint of determining whether an item is large enough to likely influence the decision of an investor or creditor. (p. 69)

Monetary unit assumption   An assumption that requires that only those things that can be expressed in money are included in the accounting records. (p. 67)

Operating cycle   The average time required to go from cash to cash in producing revenues. (p. 50)

Profitability ratios   Measures of the income or operating success of a company for a given period of time. (p. 55)

Property, plant, and equipment   Assets of a relatively permanent nature that companies use in the business and are not intended for resale. (p. 51)

Ratio   An expression of the mathematical relationship between one quantity and another; may be expressed as a percentage, a rate, or a proportion. (p. 54)

Ratio analysis   A technique for evaluating financial statements that expresses the relationship among selected financial statement data. (p. 54)

Relevance   The quality of information that indicates the information makes a difference in a decision. (p. 65)

Reliability   The quality of information that gives assurance that it is free of error and bias. (p. 65)

Securities and Exchange Commission (SEC)   The agency of the U.S. government that oversees U.S. financial markets and accounting standard-setting bodies. (p. 65)

Solvency   The ability of a company to pay interest as it comes due and to repay the face value of debt at maturity. (p. 60)

Solvency ratios   Measures of the ability of the company to survive over a long period of time. (p. 60)

Statement of stockholders' equity   A financial statement that presents the factors that caused stockholders' equity to change during the period, including those that caused retained earnings to change. (p. 56)

Time period assumption   An assumption that the life of a business can be divided into artificial time periods and that useful reports covering those periods can be prepared for the business. (p. 67)

Working capital   The difference between the amounts of current assets and current liabilities. (p. 59)

Demonstration Problem

Listed here are items taken from the income statement and balance sheet of Circuit City Stores, Inc. for the year ended February 29, 2004. Certain items have been combined for simplification. Amounts are given in millions.

Long-term debt, excluding current installments	$ 22.7
Cash and cash equivalents	783.5
Selling, general, and administrative expenses	2,259.5
Common stock	1,024.6

Accounts payable	$ 879.6
Prepaid expenses and other current assets	464.3
Property and equipment, net	585.9
Cost of goods sold	7,518.1
Current portion of long-term debt	1.1
Income taxes payable	161.4
Interest expense	1.8
Other long-term liabilities	209.6
Retained earnings	1,199.4
Merchandise inventory	1,517.3
Net sales and operating revenues	9,778.1
Accounts and notes receivable, net	154.0
Income tax (benefit)	(0.5)
Other assets	128.0
Accrued expenses and other current liabilities	134.6

Instructions

Prepare an income statement and a classified balance sheet using the items listed. Do not use any item more than once.

Solution

Action Plan
- In preparing the income statement, list revenues, then expenses.
- In preparing a classified balance sheet, list current assets in order of liquidity.

CIRCUIT CITY STORES, INC.
Income Statement
For the Year Ended February 29, 2004
(in millions)

Net sales and operating revenues		$9,778.1
Cost of goods sold	$7,518.1	
Selling, general, and administrative expenses	2,259.5	
Interest expense	1.8	
Income tax (benefit)	(0.5)	
Total expenses		9,778.9
Net loss		$ (0.8)

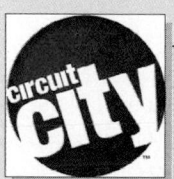

CIRCUIT CITY STORES, INC.
Balance Sheet
February 29, 2004
(in millions)

Assets

Current assets		
Cash and cash equivalents	$ 783.5	
Accounts and notes receivable, net	154.0	
Merchandise inventory	1,517.3	
Prepaid expenses and other current assets	464.3	
Total current assets		$2,919.1
Property and equipment, net		585.9
Other assets		128.0
Total assets		$3,633.0

CIRCUIT CITY STORES, INC.
Balance Sheet
February 29, 2004
(in millions)

Liabilities and Stockholders' Equity

Current liabilities		
Accounts payable	$ 879.6	
Income taxes payable	161.4	
Accrued expenses and other current liabilities	134.6	
Current portion of long-term debt	1.1	
Total current liabilities		$1,176.7
Long-term liabilities		
Long-term debt, excluding current installments	22.7	
Other long-term liabilities	209.6	232.3
Total liabilities		1,409.0
Stockholders' equity		
Common stock	1,024.6	
Retained earnings	1,199.4	
Total stockholders' equity		2,224.0
Total liabilities and stockholders' equity		$3,633.0

THE NAVIGATOR

Self-Study Questions

Answers are at the end of the chapter.

(SO 1) **1.** In a classified balance sheet, assets are usually classified as:
(a) current assets; long-term assets; property, plant, and equipment; and intangible assets.
(b) current assets; long-term investments; property, plant, and equipment; and common stock.
(c) current assets; long-term investments; tangible assets; and intangible assets.
(d) current assets; long-term investments; property, plant, and equipment; and intangible assets.

(SO 1) **2.** Current assets are listed:
(a) by liquidity.
(b) by importance.
(c) by longevity.
(d) alphabetically.

(SO 2) **3.** Which is an indicator of profitability?
(a) Current ratio.
(b) Earnings per share.
(c) Debt to total assets ratio.
(d) Free cash flow.

(SO 2) **4.** For 2007 Stoneland Corporation reported net income $24,000; net sales $400,000; and average shares outstanding 6,000. There

were no preferred stock dividends. What was the 2007 earnings per share?
(a) $4.00   (c) $16.67
(b) $0.06   (d) $66.67

5. The balance in retained earnings is *not* affected   (SO 3)
by:
(a) net income.
(b) net loss.
(c) issuance of common stock.
(d) dividends.

6. Which of these measures is an eval-   (SO 4)
uation of a company's ability to pay current liabilities?
(a) Earnings per share.
(b) Current ratio.
(c) Both (a) and (b).
(d) None of the above.

7. Companies can use free cash flow to: (SO 5)
(a) pay additional dividends.
(b) acquire property, plant, and equipment.
(c) pay off debts.
(d) All of the above.

8. Generally accepted accounting principles are: (SO 6)
(a) a set of standards and rules that are recognized as a general guide for financial reporting.

(b) usually established by the Internal Revenue Service.

(c) the guidelines used to resolve ethical dilemmas.

(d) fundamental truths that can be derived from the laws of nature.

(SO 6) **9.** What organization issues U.S. accounting standards?

(a) Financial Accounting Standards Board.

(b) International Accounting Standards Committee.

(c) International Auditing Standards Committee.

(d) None of the above.

(SO 7) **10.** What is the primary criterion by which accounting information can be judged?

(a) Consistency.

(b) Predictive value.

(c) Usefulness for decision making.

(d) Comparability.

11. Verifiability is an ingredient of: (SO 7)

	Reliability	Relevance
(a)	Yes	Yes
(b)	No	No
(c)	Yes	No
(d)	No	Yes

12. What accounting constraint refers to the tendency (SO 7) of accountants to resolve uncertainty in a way least likely to overstate assets and net income?

(a) Comparability.   (c) Conservatism.

(b) Materiality.   (d) Consistency.

Go to the book's website, **www.wiley.com/college/kimmel**, to access additional Self-Study Questions.

Questions

1. What is meant by the term *operating cycle?*

2. Define current assets. What basis is used for ordering individual items within the current assets section?

3. Distinguish between long-term investments and property, plant, and equipment.

4. How do current liabilities differ from long-term liabilities?

5. Identify the two parts of stockholders' equity in a corporation and indicate the purpose of each.

6.

(a) Brenda Starr believes that the analysis of financial statements is directed at two characteristics of a company: liquidity and profitability. Is Brenda correct? Explain.

(b) Are short-term creditors, long-term creditors, and stockholders primarily interested in the same characteristics of a company? Explain.

7. Name ratios useful in assessing (a) liquidity, (b) solvency, and (c) profitability.

8. Dave Rose, the founder of Water-boots Inc., needs to raise $500,000 to expand his company's operations. He has been told that raising the money through debt will increase the riskiness of his company much more than issuing stock. He doesn't understand why this is true. Explain it to him.

9. What do these classes of ratios measure?

(a) Liquidity ratios.

(b) Profitability ratios.

(c) Solvency ratios.

10. Holding all other factors constant, indicate whether each of the following signals generally good or bad news about a company.

(a) Increase in earnings per share.

(b) Increase in the current ratio.

(c) Increase in the debt to total assets ratio.

(d) Decrease in free cash flow.

11. Which ratio or ratios from this chapter do you think should be of greatest interest to:

(a) a pension fund considering investing in a corporation's 20-year bonds?

(b) a bank contemplating a short-term loan?

(c) an investor in common stock?

12. (a) What are generally accepted accounting principles (GAAP)?

(b) What body provides authoritative support for GAAP?

13. (a) What is the basic objective of financial reporting?

(b) Identify the characteristics of useful accounting information.

14. Sue Leonard, the president of Leon Company, is pleased. Leon substantially increased its net income in 2007 while keeping its unit inventory relatively the same. Dan Noonan, chief accountant, cautions Sue, however. Noonan says that since Leon changed its method of inventory valuation, there is a consistency problem and it is difficult to determine whether Leon is better off. Is Noonan correct? Why or why not?

15. What is the distinction between comparability and consistency?

16. Describe the two constraints inherent in the presentation of accounting information.

17. Your roommate believes that international accounting standards are uniform throughout the world. Is your roommate correct? Explain.

18. What purpose does the going concern assumption serve?

19. Tamara Swan is president of Better Books. She has no accounting background. Swan cannot understand why market value is not used as the basis for accounting measurement and reporting. Explain what basis is used and why.

20. What is the economic entity assumption? Give an example of its violation.

Brief Exercises

Classify accounts on balance sheet.
(SO 1)

BE2-1   The following are the major balance sheet classifications:

Current assets (CA)	Current liabilities (CL)
Long-term investments (LTI)	Long-term liabilities (LTL)
Property, plant, and equipment (PPE)	Common stock (CS)
Intangible assets (IA)	Retained earnings (RE)

Match each of the following accounts to its proper balance sheet classification.

_____ Accounts payable	_____ Income tax payable
_____ Accounts receivable	_____ Investment in long-term bonds
_____ Accumulated depreciation	_____ Land
_____ Building	_____ Merchandise inventory
_____ Cash	_____ Patent
_____ Goodwill	_____ Supplies

Prepare the current assets section of a balance sheet.
(SO 1)

BE2-2   A list of financial statement items for Schweitz Company includes the following: accounts receivable $14,000; prepaid insurance $3,300; cash $12,400; supplies $3,800, and short-term investments $8,200. Prepare the current assets section of the balance sheet listing the items in the proper sequence.

Compute earnings per share.
(SO 2)

BE2-3   The following information (in millions of dollars) is available for The Limited for 2005: Sales revenue $9,408; net income $705; preferred stock dividend $0; average shares outstanding 470 million. Compute the earnings per share for The Limited for 2005.

Identify items affecting stockholders' equity.
(SO 3)

BE2-4   For each of the following events affecting the stockholders' equity of Haulmarke, indicate whether the event would: increase retained earnings (IRE), decrease retained earnings (DRE), increase common stock (ICS), or decrease common stock (DCS).

_____ (a) Issued new shares of common stock.
_____ (b) Paid a cash dividend.
_____ (c) Reported net income of $75,000.
_____ (d) Reported a net loss of $20,000.

Calculate liquidity ratios.
(SO 4)

BE2-5   These selected condensed data are taken from a recent balance sheet of Bob Evans Farms (in millions of dollars).

Cash	$ 4.0
Accounts receivable	22.3
Inventories	19.5
Other current assets	1.7
Total current assets	$ 47.5
Total current liabilities	$145.8

Compute working capital and the current ratio.

Calculate liquidity and solvency ratios.
(SO 4, 5)

BE2-6   Randy's Books & Music Inc. reported the following selected information at March 30.

	2007
Total current assets	$252,787
Total assets	439,832
Total current liabilities	293,625
Total liabilities	376,002
Cash provided by operating activities	55,472

Calculate (a) the current ratio, (b) the debt to total assets ratio, and (c) free cash flow for March 30, 2007. The company paid dividends of $11,000 and spent $24,787 on capital expenditures.

BE2-7 Indicate whether each statement is *true* or *false*.

(a) GAAP is a set of rules and practices established by accounting standard-setting bodies to serve as a general guide for financial reporting purposes.

(b) Substantial authoritative support for GAAP usually comes from two standards-setting bodies: the FASB and the IRS.

Recognize generally accepted accounting principles. (SO 6)

BE2-8 The accompanying chart shows the qualitative characteristics of accounting information. Fill in the blanks.

Identify characteristics of useful information. (SO 7)

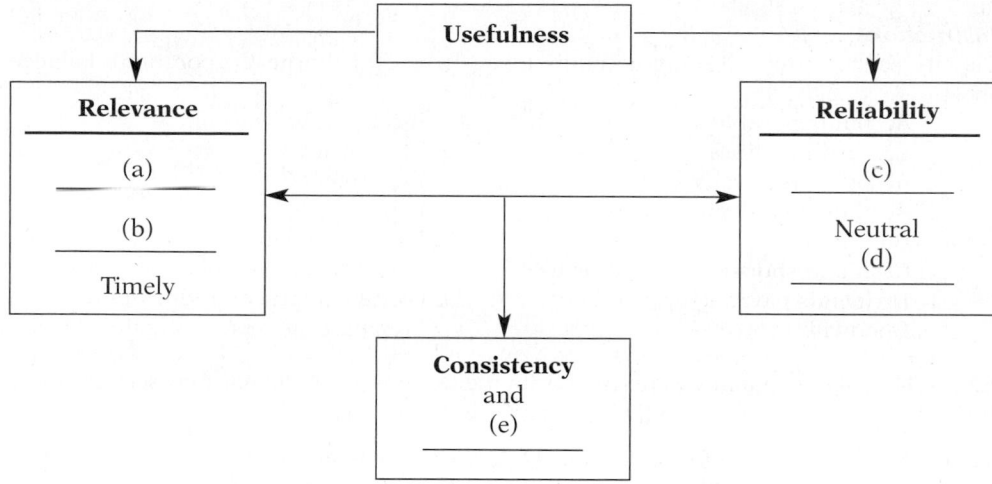

BE2-9 Given the *characteristics* of useful accounting information, complete each of the following statements.

(a) For information to be ____, it should have predictive or feedback value, and it must be presented on a timely basis.

(b) ____ is the quality of information that gives assurance that it is free of error and bias; it can be depended on.

(c) ____ means using the same accounting principles and methods from year to year within a company.

Identify characteristics of useful information. (SO 7)

BE2-10 Here are some qualitative characteristics of accounting information:

1. Predictive value   3. Verifiable
2. Neutral   4. Timely

Match each qualitative characteristic to one of the following statements.

____ (a) Accounting information should help users make predictions about the outcome of past, present, and future events.

____ (b) Accounting information cannot be selected, prepared, or presented to favor one set of interested users over another.

____ (c) Accounting information must be proved to be free of error.

____ (d) Accounting information must be available to decision makers before it loses its capacity to influence their decisions.

Identify characteristics of useful information. (SO 7)

BE2-11 The full disclosure principle dictates that:

(a) financial statements should disclose all assets at their cost.

(b) financial statements should disclose only those events that can be measured in dollars.

(c) financial statements should disclose all events and circumstances that would matter to users of financial statements.

(d) financial statements should not be relied on unless an auditor has expressed an unqualified opinion on them.

Define full disclosure principle (SO 7)

BE2-12 Herbert Company uses these accounting practices:

(a) Inventory is reported at cost when market value is lower.

(b) Small tools are recorded as plant assets and depreciated.

(c) The income statement shows paper clips expense of $10.

Indicate the accounting constraint, if any, that each practice has violated.

Identify constraints that have been violated. (SO 7)

Exercises

Classify accounts on balance sheet.
(SO 1)

E2-1 The following are the major balance sheet classifications.

Current assets (CA)	Current liabilities (CL)
Long-term investments (LTI)	Long-term liabilities (LTL)
Property, plant, and equipment (PPE)	Common stock (CS)
Intangible assets (IA)	Retained earnings (RE)

Instructions

Classify each of the following accounts taken from Hawthorne Corporation's balance sheet.

____ Accounts payable and accrued liabilities
____ Accounts receivable
____ Accumulated depreciation
____ Buildings
____ Cash and short-term investments
____ Dividends payable
____ Goodwill

____ Income taxes payable
____ Inventories
____ Investments
____ Land
____ Long-term debt
____ Materials and supplies
____ Office equipment and furniture
____ Prepaid expenses

Classify items as current or noncurrent, and prepare assets section of balance sheet.
(SO 1)

E2-2 The following items were taken from the December 31, 2004, assets section of the Boeing Company balance sheet. (All dollars are in millions.)

Inventories	$ 4,247	Other current assets	$ 2,061
Notes receivable—due after December 31, 2005	13,435	Property, plant, and equipment	21,405
Notes receivable—due before December 31, 2005	616	Cash and cash equivalents	3,204
		Accounts receivable	4,653
Accumulated depreciation	12,962	Other noncurrent assets	14,082
Intangible assets	2,903	Short-term investments	319

Instructions

Prepare the assets section of a classified balance sheet, listing the current assets in order of their liquidity.

Prepare assets section of a classified balance sheet.
(SO 1)

E2-3 The following information (in thousands of dollars) is available for H.J. Heinz Company—famous for ketchup and other fine food products—for the year ended April 28, 2004.

Prepaid expenses	$ 165,177	Inventories	$1,156,932
Land	65,836	Buildings and equipment	3,661,388
Other current assets	15,493	Cash and cash equivalents	1,180,039
Intangible assets	2,753,735	Accounts receivable	1,093,155
Other noncurrent assets	1,455,372	Accumulated depreciation	1,669,938

Instructions

Prepare the assets section of a classified balance sheet, listing the items in proper sequence and including a statement heading.

Prepare a classified balance sheet.
(SO 1)

E2-4 These items are taken from the financial statements of Donovan Co. at December 31, 2007.

Building	$105,800
Accounts receivable	12,600
Prepaid insurance	4,680
Cash	16,840
Equipment	82,400
Land	61,200
Insurance expense	780
Depreciation expense	5,300
Interest expense	2,600
Common stock	62,000

Retained earnings (January 1, 2007)	40,000
Accumulated depreciation—building	45,600
Accounts payable	9,500
Mortgage payable	93,600
Accumulated depreciation—equipment	18,720
Interest payable	3,600
Bowling revenues	19,180

Instructions

Prepare a classified balance sheet. Assume that $13,600 of the mortgage payable will be paid in 2008.

E2-5   The following items were taken from the 2004 financial statements of Texas Instruments, Inc. (All dollars are in millions.)

Prepare a classified balance sheet.
(SO 1)

Long-term debt	$ 368	Cash	$ 2,668
Common stock	2,488	Accumulated depreciation	5,655
Prepaid expenses	326	Accounts payable	1,444
Property, plant, and equipment	9,573	Other noncurrent assets	1,927
Other current assets	554	Other noncurrent liabilities	943
Other current liabilities	470	Retained earnings	10,575
Long-term investments	264	Accounts receivable	1,696
Short-term investments	3,690	Inventories	1,256
Loans payable in 2005	11		

Instructions

Prepare a classified balance sheet in good form as of December 31, 2004.

E2-6   The following information is available for Callaway Golf Company for the years 2004 and 2003. (Dollars are in thousands, except share information.)

Compute and interpret profitability ratio.
(SO 2)

	2004	**2003**
Net sales	$934,564	$814,032
Net income (loss)	(10,103)	45,523
Total assets	735,737	748,566
Share information		
Shares outstanding at year-end	69,111,349	66,862,850
Preferred dividends	–0–	–0–

There were 65,676,326 shares outstanding at the end of 2002.

Instructions

(a) What was the company's earnings per share for each year?
(b) Based on your findings above, how did the company's profitability change from 2003 to 2004?

E2-7   These financial statement items are for Snyder Corporation at year-end, July 31, 2007.

Prepare financial statements.
(SO 1, 3, 4)

Salaries payable	$ 2,080
Salaries expense	51,700
Utilities expense	22,600
Equipment	18,500
Accounts payable	4,100
Commission revenue	61,100
Rent revenue	8,500
Long-term note payable	1,800
Common stock	16,000
Cash	24,200
Accounts receivable	9,780
Accumulated depreciation	6,000
Dividends	4,000
Depreciation expense	4,000
Retained earnings (beginning of the year)	35,200

Instructions

(a) Prepare an income statement and a retained earnings statement for the year. Snyder Corporation did not issue any new stock during the year.
(b) Prepare a classified balance sheet at July 31.
(c) Compute the current ratio and debt to total assets ratio.
(d) Suppose that you are the president of Allied Equipment. Your sales manager has approached you with a proposal to sell $20,000 of equipment to Snyder. He would like to provide a loan to Snyder in the form of a 10%, 5-year note payable. Evaluate how this loan would change Snyder's current ratio and debt to total assets ratio, and discuss whether you would make the sale.

Compute liquidity ratios and compare results.
(SO 4)

E2-8 Nordstrom, Inc. operates department stores in numerous states. Selected financial statement data (in millions of dollars) for the year ended January 31, 2004, are as follows.

	End of Year	Beginning of Year
Cash and cash equivalents	$ 361	$ 340
Receivables (net)	646	667
Merchandise inventory	917	902
Other current assets	648	616
Total current assets	$2,572	$2,525
Total current liabilities	$1,341	$1,123

For the year, net sales were $7,131,000 and cost of goods sold was $4,559,000.

Instructions

(a) Compute working capital and the current ratio at the beginning of the year and at the end of the current year.
(b) Did Nordstrom's liquidity improve or worsen during the year?
(c) Using the data in the chapter, compare Nordstrom's liquidity with Best Buy's.

Compute liquidity measures and discuss findings.
(SO 4)

E2-9 The chief financial officer (CFO) of SuperClean Corporation requested that the accounting department prepare a preliminary balance sheet on December 30, 2007, so that the CFO could get an idea of how the company stood. He knows that certain debt agreements with its creditors require the company to maintain a current ratio of at least 2:1. The preliminary balance sheet is as follows.

SUPERCLEAN CORP.
Balance Sheet
December 30, 2007

Current assets			Current liabilities		
Cash	$30,000		Accounts payable	$ 25,000	
Accounts receivable	20,000		Salaries payable	15,000	$ 40,000
Prepaid insurance	10,000	$ 60,000	Long-term liabilities		
			Notes payable		80,000
			Total liabilities		120,000
Property, plant, and equipment (net)		200,000	Stockholders' equity		
Total assets		$260,000	Common stock	100,000	
			Retained earnings	40,000	140,000
			Total liabilities and stockholders equity		$260,000

Instructions

(a) Calculate the current ratio and working capital based on the preliminary balance sheet.
(b) Based on the results in (a), the CFO requested that $25,000 of cash be used to pay off the balance of the accounts payable account on December 31, 2007. Calculate the new current ratio and working capital after the company takes these actions.

(c) Discuss the pros and cons of the current ratio and working capital as measures of liquidity.

(d) Was it unethical for the CFO to take these steps?

E2-10 The following data were taken from the 2004 and 2003 financial statements of American Eagle Outfitters. (All dollars are in thousands.)

Compute and interpret solvency ratios.
(SO 4, 5)

	2004	2003
Current assets	$525,623	$427,878
Total assets	865,071	741,339
Current liabilities	189,035	141,586
Total liabilities	221,401	163,857
Total stockholders' equity	643,670	577,482
Cash provided by operating activities	189,469	104,548
Capital expenditures	64,173	61,407
Dividends paid	–0–	–0–

Instructions
Perform each of the following.
(a) Calculate the debt to total assets ratio for each year.
(b) Calculate the free cash flow for each year.
(c) Discuss American Eagle's solvency in 2004 versus 2003.
(d) Discuss American Eagle's ability to finance its investment activities with cash provided by operating activities, and how any deficiency would be met.

E2-11 Presented below are the assumptions and principles discussed in this chapter.

Identify accounting assumptions and principles.
(SO 7)

1. Full disclosure principle.
2. Going concern assumption.
3. Monetary unit assumption.
4. Time period assumption.
5. Cost principle.
6. Economic entity assumption.

Instructions
Identify by number the accounting assumption or principle that is described below. Do not use a number more than once.
(a) Is the rationale for why plant assets are not reported at liquidation value. (*Note:* Do not use the cost principle.)
(b) Indicates that personal and business record-keeping should be separately maintained.
(c) Assumes that the dollar is the "measuring stick" used to report on financial performance.
(d) Separates financial information into time periods for reporting purpose.
(e) Indicates that companies should not record in the accounts market value changes subsequent to purchase.
(f) Dictates that companies should disclose all circumstances and events that make a difference to financial statement users.

E2-12 Mere Co. had three major business transactions during 2007.
(a) Reported at its market value of $260,000 merchandise inventory with a cost of $208,000.
(b) The president of Mere Co., Issam Mere, purchased a truck for personal use and charged it to his expense account.
(c) Mere Co. wanted to make its 2007 income look better, so it added 2 more weeks to the year (a 54-week year). Previous years were 52 weeks.

Identify the assumption or principle that has been violated.
(SO 7)

Instructions
In each situation, identify the assumption or principle that has been violated, if any, and discuss what the company should have done.

Problems: Set A

Prepare a classified balance sheet.
(SO 1)

P2-1A   The following items are taken from the 2004 balance sheet of **Yahoo!, Inc.** (All dollars are in thousands.)

Intangible assets	$3,031,623
Common stock	5,684,300
Property and equipment, net	531,696
Accounts payable	48,205
Other assets	481,832
Long-term investments	1,042,575
Accounts receivable	483,951
Prepaid expenses and other current assets	94,549
Short-term investments	2,688,252
Retained earnings	1,417,146
Cash and cash equivalents	823,723
Long-term debt	750,000
Accrued expenses and other current liabilities	853,115
Unearned revenue—current	279,387
Other long-term liabilities	146,048

Instructions

Tot. current assets $4,090,475
Tot. assets $9,178,201

Prepare a classified balance sheet for Yahoo! Inc. as of December 31, 2004.

Prepare financial statements.
(SO 1, 3)

P2-2A   These items are taken from the financial statements of Drew Corporation for 2007.

Retained earnings (beginning of year)	$31,000
Utilities expense	2,000
Equipment	66,000
Accounts payable	13,300
Cash	17,900
Salaries payable	3,000
Common stock	13,000
Dividends	12,000
Service revenue	82,000
Prepaid insurance	3,500
Repair expense	1,800
Depreciation expense	3,300
Accounts receivable	14,200
Insurance expense	2,200
Salaries expense	37,000
Accumulated depreciation	17,600

Instructions

Net income $35,700
Tot. assets $84,000

Prepare an income statement, a retained earnings statement, and a classified balance sheet as of December 31, 2007.

Prepare financial statements.
(SO 1, 3)

P2-3A   You are provided with the following information for Maxim Enterprises, effective as of its April 30, 2007, year-end.

Accounts. payable	$ 834
Accounts receivable	810
Building, net of accumulated depreciation	1,537
Cash	770
Common stock	900
Cost of goods sold	990
Current portion of long-term debt	450
Depreciation expense	335
Dividends paid during the year	325

Equipment, net of accumulated depreciation	1,220
Income tax expense	165
Income taxes payable	135
Interest expense	400
Inventories	967
Land	1,600
Long-term debt	3,500
Prepaid expenses	12
Retained earnings, beginning	1,600
Revenues	3,600
Selling expenses	210
Short-term investments	1,200
Wages expense	700
Wages payable	222

Instructions

(a) Prepare an income statement and a retained earnings statement for Maxim Enterprises for the year ended April 30, 2007.

(b) Prepare a classified balance sheet for Maxim Enterprises as of April 30, 2007.

Net income	$800
Tot. current assets	$3,759
Tot. assets	$8,116

P2-4A Comparative financial statement data for Arthur Corporation and Lancelot Corporation, two competitors, appear below. All balance sheet data are as of December 31, 2007.

Compute ratios; comment on relative profitability, liquidity, and solvency.
(SO 2, 4, 5)

	Arthur Corporation	**Lancelot Corporation**
	2007	**2007**
Net sales	$1,950,000	$620,000
Cost of goods sold	1,175,000	340,000
Operating expenses	303,000	98,000
Interest expense	9,000	3,800
Income tax expense	85,000	36,000
Current assets	427,200	190,336
Plant assets (net)	532,000	139,728
Current liabilities	66,325	35,348
Long-term liabilities	108,500	29,620

Additional information:

Cash from operating activities	$148,000	$36,000
Capital expenditures	$90,000	$20,000
Dividends paid	$36,000	$15,000
Average number of shares outstanding	100,000	50,000

Instructions

(a) Comment on the relative profitability of the companies by computing the net income and earnings per share for each company for 2007.

(b) Comment on the relative liquidity of the companies by computing working capital and the current ratios for each company for 2007.

(c) Comment on the relative solvency of the companies by computing the debt to total assets ratio and the free cash flow for each company for 2007.

P2-5A Here and on page 86 are financial statements of Chiasson Company.

Compute liquidity, solvency, and profitability ratios.
(SO 2, 4, 5)

CHIASSON COMPANY
Income Statement
For the Year Ended December 31

	2007
Net sales	$2,218,500
Cost of goods sold	1,012,400
Selling and administrative expenses	906,000
Interest expense	98,000
Income tax expense	69,000
Net income	$ 133,100

CHIASSON COMPANY
Balance Sheet
December 31

Assets	2007
Current assets	
Cash	$ 60,100
Short-term investments	54,000
Accounts receivable (net)	169,800
Inventory	125,000
Total current assets	408,900
Plant assets (net)	625,300
Total assets	$1,034,200

Liabilities and Stockholders' Equity	
Current liabilities	
Accounts payable	$ 180,000
Income taxes payable	35,500
Total current liabilities	215,500
Bonds payable	200,000
Total liabilities	415,500
Stockholders' equity	
Common stock	330,000
Retained earnings	288,700
Total stockholders' equity	618,700
Total liabilities and stockholders' equity	$1,034,200

Additional information: The cash provided by operating activities for 2007 was $190,800. The cash used for capital expenditures was $92,000. The cash used for dividends was $26,000. The average number of shares outstanding during the year was 50,000.

Instructions

Compute the following values and ratios for 2007.
(a) Working capital.
(b) Current ratio.
(c) Free cash flow.
(d) Debt to total assets ratio.
(e) Earnings per share.

Compute and interpret liquidity, solvency, and profitability ratios.
(SO 2, 4, 5)

P2-6A   Condensed balance sheet and income statement data for Mere Corporation are presented here.

MERE CORPORATION
Balance Sheets
December 31

Assets	2007	2006
Cash	$ 25,000	$ 20,000
Receivables (net)	70,000	62,000
Other current assets	80,000	73,000
Long-term investments	75,000	60,000
Plant and equipment (net)	510,000	470,000
Total assets	$760,000	$685,000

Liabilities and Stockholders' Equity	2007	2006
Current liabilities	$ 85,000	$ 70,000
Long-term debt	80,000	90,000
Common stock	320,000	300,000
Retained earnings	275,000	225,000
Total liabilities and stockholders' equity	$760,000	$685,000

MERE CORPORATION
Income Statements
For the Years Ended December 31

	2007	2006
Sales	$750,000	$670,000
Cost of goods sold	440,000	400,000
Operating expenses (including income taxes)	240,000	220,000
Net income	$ 70,000	$ 50,000

Additional information:

Cash from operating activities	$87,000	$60,000
Cash used for capital expenditures	$45,000	$38,000
Dividends paid	$20,000	$15,000
Average number of shares outstanding	32,000	30,000

Instructions
Compute these values and ratios for 2006 and 2007.
(a) Earnings per share.
(b) Working capital.
(c) Current ratio.
(d) Debt to total assets ratio.
(e) Free cash flow.
(f) Based on the ratios calculated, discuss briefly the improvement or lack thereof in financial position and operating results from 2006 to 2007 of Mere Corporation.

P2-7A Selected financial data of two competitors, Target and Wal-Mart, are presented here. (All dollars are in millions.)

Compute ratios and compare liquidity, solvency, and profitability for two companies.
(SO 2, 4, 5)

	Target (2/3/04)	Wal-Mart (1/31/04)
	Income Statement Data for Year	
Net sales	$46,781	$256,329
Cost of goods sold	31,790	198,747
Selling and administrative expenses	10,696	44,909
Interest expense	559	832
Other income (loss)	(776)	2,331
Income taxes	1,119	5,118
Net income	$ 1,841	$ 9,054

	Target	Wal-Mart
	Balance Sheet Data (End of Year)	
Current assets	$12,928	$ 34,421
Noncurrent assets	18,464	70,491
Total assets	$31,392	$104,912
Current liabilities	$ 8,314	$ 37,418
Long-term debt	12,013	23,871
Total stockholders' equity	11,065	43,623
Total liabilities and stockholders' equity	$31,392	$104,912
Cash from operating activities	$ 3,160	$ 15,996
Cash paid for capital expenditures	$ 3,004	$ 10,308
Dividends paid	$ 237	$ 1,569
Average shares outstanding	911	4,373

Instructions

For each company, compute these values and ratios.

(a) Working capital.

(b) Current ratio.

(c) Debt to total assets ratio.

(d) Free cash flow.

(e) Earnings per share.

(f) Compare the liquidity, solvency, and profitability of the two companies.

Comment on the objectives and qualitative characteristics of financial reporting.
(SO 6, 7)

P2-8A   A friend of yours, Diana Maher, recently completed an undergraduate degree in science and has just started working with a biotechnology company. Diana tells you that the owners of the business are trying to secure new sources of financing which are needed in order for the company to proceed with development of a new health care product. Diana said that her boss told her that the company must put together a report to present to potential investors.

Diana thought that the company should include in this package the detailed scientific findings related to the Phase I clinical trials for this product. She said, "I know that the biotech industry sometimes has only a 10% success rate with new products, but if we report all the scientific findings, everyone will see what a sure success this is going to be! The president was talking about the importance of following some set of accounting principles. Why do we need to look at some accounting rules? What they need to realize is that we have scientific results that are quite encouraging, some of the most talented employees around, and the start of some really great customer relationships. We haven't made any sales yet, but we will. We just need the funds to get through all the clinical testing and get government approval for our product. Then these investors will be quite happy that they bought in to our company early!"

Instructions

(a) What is financial reporting? Explain to Diana what is meant by generally accepted accounting principles.

(b) Comment on how Diana's suggestions for what should be reported to prospective investors conforms to the qualitative characteristics of accounting information. Do you think that the things that Diana wants to include in the information for investors will conform to financial reporting guidelines?

Problems: Set B

Prepare a classified balance sheet.
(SO 1)

P2-1B   The following items are from the 2004 balance sheet of Kellogg Company. (All dollars are in millions.)

Common stock	$ 103.8
Other assets	5,953.5
Notes payable—current	709.7
Other current assets	247.0
Current maturities of long-term debt	278.6
Cash and cash equivalents	417.4
Other long-term liabilities	1,794.6
Retained earnings	2,153.4
Accounts payable	767.2
Other current liabilities	1,090.5
Accounts receivable, net	776.4
Property, net	2,715.1
Inventories	681.0
Long-term debt	3,892.6

Instructions

Prepare a classified balance sheet for Kellogg Company as of December 31, 2004.

Tot. current assets $ 2,121.8
Tot. assets $10,790.4

P2-2B   These items are taken from the financial statements of Stasik, Inc.

Prepare financial statements.
(SO 1, 3)

Prepaid insurance	$ 1,800
Equipment	34,000
Salaries expense	36,000
Utilities expense	2,100
Accumulated depreciation	8,600
Accounts payable	10,200
Cash	5,300
Accounts receivable	7,500
Salaries payable	2,000
Common stock	5,900
Depreciation expense	4,300
Retained earnings (beginning)	14,000
Dividends	3,600
Service revenue	58,000
Repair expense	2,900
Insurance expense	1,200

Instructions

Prepare an income statement, a retained earnings statement, and a classified balance sheet as of December 31, 2007.

Net income $11,500
Tot. assets $40,000

P2-3B   You are provided with the following information for Kiltie Corporation, effective as of its April 30, 2007, year-end.

Prepare financial statements.
(SO 1, 3)

Accounts payable	$ 2,400
Accounts receivable	4,150
Accumulated depreciation	6,600
Depreciation expense	2,200
Cash	21,955
Common stock	20,000
Dividends	2,800
Equipment	23,050
Sales revenue	14,450
Income tax expense	1,100
Income taxes payable	300
Interest expense	350
Interest payable	175
Long-term notes payable	5,700
Prepaid rent	380
Rent expense	760
Retained earnings, beginning	13,960
Salaries expense	6,840

Instructions

(a) Prepare an income statement and a retained earnings statement for Kiltie Corporation for the year ended April 30, 2007.
(b) Prepare a classified balance sheet for Kiltie as of April 30, 2007.
(c) Explain how each financial statement interrelates with the others.

Net income $ 3,200
Tot. current assets $26,485
Tot. assets $42,935
Compute ratios; comment on relative profitability, liquidity, and solvency.
(SO 2, 4, 5)

P2-4B   Comparative statement data for Oscar Company and Felix Company, two competitors, are presented on page 90. All balance sheet data are as of December 31, 2007.

	Oscar Company	Felix Company
	2007	**2007**
Net sales	$450,000	$918,000
Cost of goods sold	260,000	620,000
Operating expenses	134,000	55,000
Interest expense	6,000	10,000
Income tax expense	10,000	65,000
Current assets	180,000	700,000
Plant assets (net)	600,000	800,000
Current liabilities	60,000	250,000
Long-term liabilities	190,000	200,000

Additional information:

Cash from operating activities	$ 26,000	$180,000
Capital expenditures	$ 20,000	$ 50,000
Dividends paid	$ 4,000	$ 15,000
Average number of shares outstanding	200,000	400,000

Instructions
(a) Comment on the relative profitability of the companies by computing the net income and earnings per share for each company for 2007.
(b) Comment on the relative liquidity of the companies by computing working capital and the current ratios for each company for 2007.
(c) Comment on the relative solvency of the companies by computing the debt to total assets ratio and the free cash flow for each company for 2007.

Compute and interpret liquidity, solvency, and profitability ratios.
(SO 2, 4, 5)

P2-5B The financial statements of Jackson Company are presented here.

JACKSON COMPANY
Income Statement
For the Year Ended December 31

	2007
Net sales	$700,000
Cost of goods sold	400,000
Selling and administrative expenses	150,000
Interest expense	7,800
Income tax expense	43,000
Net income	$ 99,200

JACKSON COMPANY
Balance Sheet
December 31

Assets	**2007**
Current assets	
Cash	$ 23,100
Short-term investments	34,800
Accounts receivable (net)	106,200
Inventory	155,000
Total current assets	319,100
Plant assets (net)	465,300
Total assets	$784,400

Liabilities and Stockholders' Equity

Current liabilities	
Accounts payable	$120,200
Income taxes payable	24,000
Total current liabilities	144,200
Bonds payable	130,000
Total liabilities	274,200
Stockholders' equity	
Common stock	170,000
Retained earnings	340,200
Total stockholders' equity	510,200
Total liabilities and stockholders' equity	$784,400
Cash from operating activities	$ 71,300
Capital expenditures	$ 42,000
Dividends paid	$ 10,000
Average number of shares outstanding	70,000

Instructions

(a) Compute the following values and ratios for 2007. (We have provided the results from 2006 for comparative purposes.)
 (i) Current ratio. (2006:   2.4:1)
 (ii) Working capital. (2006: $178,000)
 (iii) Debt to total assets ratio. (2006:   31%)
 (iv) Free cash flow. (2006: $13,000)
 (v) Earnings per share. (2006: $1.35)

(b) Using your calculations from part (a), discuss changes from 2006 in liquidity, solvency, and profitability.

P2-6B   Condensed balance sheet and income statement data for Swann Corporation are presented below.

Compute and interpret liquidity, solvency, and profitability ratios.
(SO 2, 4, 5)

SWANN CORPORATION
Balance Sheets
December 31

Assets	2007	2006
Cash	$ 40,000	$ 24,000
Receivables (net)	90,000	55,000
Other current assets	74,000	73,000
Long-term investments	78,000	70,000
Plant and equipment (net)	525,000	427,000
Total assets	$807,000	$649,000

Liabilities and Stockholders' Equity	2007	2006
Current liabilities	$ 98,000	$ 75,000
Long-term debt	90,000	70,000
Common stock	370,000	340,000
Retained earnings	249,000	164,000
Total liabilities and stockholders' equity	$807,000	$649,000

SWANN CORPORATION
Income Statements
For the Years Ended December 31

	2007	2006
Sales	$760,000	$800,000
Cost of goods sold	420,000	400,000
Operating expenses (including income taxes)	200,000	237,000
Net income	$140,000	$163,000

Additional information:

Cash from operating activities	$165,000	$178,000
Capital expenditures	$ 85,000	$ 45,000
Dividends paid	$ 15,000	$ 13,000
Average number of shares outstanding	370,000	320,000

Instructions

Compute the following values and ratios for 2006 and 2007.

(a) Earnings per share.

(b) Working capital.

(c) Current ratio.

(d) Debt to total assets ratio.

(e) Free cash flow.

 (f) Based on the ratios calculated, discuss briefly the improvement or lack thereof in the financial position and operating results of Swann from 2006 to 2007.

Compute ratios and compare liquidity, solvency, and profitability for two companies.
(SO 2, 4, 5)

P2-7B Selected financial data of two competitors, Blockbuster Inc. and Hollywood Entertainment Corp., in 2004 are presented here. (All dollars are in millions.)

	Blockbuster Inc.	Hollywood Entertainment Corp.
	Income Statement Data for Year	
Net sales	$ 6,053	$1,782
Cost of goods sold	2,441	717
Selling and administrative expenses	3,111	917
Interest expense	38	30
Other expense	1,749	2
Income tax expense (refund)	(37)	45
Net income	$(1,249)	$ 71

	Blockbuster Inc.	Hollywood Entertainment Corp.
	Balance Sheet Data (End of Year)	
Current assets	$1,218	$ 403
Property, plant, and equipment (net)	854	228
Intangible assets	1,630	69
Other assets	161	420
Total assets	$3,863	$1,120
Current liabilities	$1,424	$ 351
Long-term debt	1,376	395
Total stockholders' equity	1,063	374
Total liabilities and stockholders' equity	$3,863	$1,120
Average shares outstanding	180.9	60.5
Cash from operating activities	$1,215	$401
Cash used for capital expenditures	$289	$272
Dividends paid	$920	$–0–

Instructions

For each company, compute these values and ratios.

(a) Working capital.

(b) Current ratio. (Round to two decimal places.)

(c) Debt to total assets ratio.

(d) Free cash flow.

(e) Earnings per share.

 (f) Compare the liquidity, profitability, and solvency of the two companies.

P2-8B Net Nanny Software International Inc., headquartered in Vancouver, specializes in Internet safety and computer security products for both the home and commercial markets. In a recent balance sheet, it reported a deficit (negative retained earnings) of US $5,678,288. It has reported only net losses since its inception. In spite of these losses, Net Nanny's common shares have traded anywhere from a high of $3.70 to a low of $0.32 on the Canadian Venture Exchange.

Comment on the objectives and qualitative characteristics of accounting information. (SO 6, 7)

Net Nanny's financial statements have historically been prepared in Canadian dollars. Recently, the company adopted the U.S. dollar as its reporting currency.

Instructions
(a) What is the objective of financial reporting? How does this objective meet or not meet Net Nanny's investor's needs?
(b) Why would investors want to buy Net Nanny's shares if the company has consistently reported losses over the last few years? Include in your answer an assessment of the relevance of the information reported on Net Nanny's financial statements.
(c) Comment on how the change in reporting information from Canadian dollars to U.S. dollars likely affected the readers of Net Nanny's financial statements. Include in your answer an assessment of the comparability of the information.

Problems: Set C

Visit the book's website at **www.wiley.com/college/kimmel** and choose the Student Companion site to access Problem Set C.

Continuing Cookie Chronicle

(*Note:* This is a continuation of the Cookie Chronicle from Chapter 1.)

CCC2 After investigating the different forms of business organization, Natalie Koebel decides to operate her business as a corporation, Cookie Creations Inc., and she begins the process of getting her business running.

While at a trade show, Natalie is introduced to Gerry Richards, operations manager of "Biscuits," a national food retailer. After much discussion, Gerry asks Natalie to consider being Biscuits' major supplier of oatmeal chocolate chip cookies. He provides Natalie with the most recent copy of the financial statements of Biscuits. He expects that Natalie will need to supply Biscuits' Watertown warehouse with approximately 1,500 dozen cookies a week. Natalie is to send Biscuits a monthly invoice, and she will be paid approximately 30 days from the date the invoice is received in Biscuits' Chicago office.

Natalie is thrilled with the offer. However, she has recently read in the newspaper that Biscuits has a reputation for selling cookies and donuts with high amounts of sugar and fat, and as a result, consumer demand for the company's products has decreased.

Instructions
Natalie has several questions. Answer the following questions for Natalie.
(a) What type of information does each financial statement provide?
(b) How can Natalie evaluate whether Biscuits will be able to pay her invoices? What type of information can financial statements give that will reassure her that Biscuits will pay her invoices?
(c) Will Biscuits have enough cash to meet its current liabilities? Where can she find this information?
(d) Will Biscuits be able to survive over a long period of time? Where can she find this information?
(e) Is Biscuits profitable? Where can she find this information?
(f) Does Biscuits have any debt? Is Biscuits able to pay off both its debt and the interest on it? Where can she find this information?
(g) Does Biscuits pay any dividends? Where can she find this information?
(h) In deciding whether to go ahead with this opportunity, are there other areas of concern that she should be aware of?

▶ BROADENING YOUR PERSPECTIVE

FINANCIAL REPORTING PROBLEM: *Tootsie Roll Industries, Inc.*

BYP2-1 The financial statements of Tootsie Roll Industries, Inc., are presented in Appendix A at the end of this book.

Instructions
Answer the following questions using the Consolidated Balance Sheet and the Notes to Consolidated Financial Statements section.
(a) What were Tootsie Roll's total current assets at December 31, 2004, and December 31, 2003?
(b) Are the assets included in current assets listed in the proper order? Explain.
(c) How are Tootsie Roll's assets classified?
(d) What were Tootsie Roll's current liabilities at December 31, 2004, and December 31, 2003?

COMPARATIVE ANALYSIS PROBLEM: *Tootsie Roll vs. Hershey Foods*

BYP2-2 The financial statements of Hershey Foods are presented in Appendix B, following the financial statements for Tootsie Roll in Appendix A. Hershey's average number of shares outstanding was 253,881,000, and Tootsie Roll's was 52,366,000.

Instructions
(a) For each company calculate the following values for 2004.
   (1) Working capital.   (4) Free cash flow.
   (2) Current ratio.   (5) Earnings per share.
   (3) Debt to total assets ratio

   (*Hint:* When calculating free cash flow, consider business acquisitions to be part of capital expenditures.)

(b) Based on your findings above, discuss the relative liquidity, solvency, and profitability of the two companies.

RESEARCH CASE

BYP2-3 The March 2, 2004, issue of the *Wall Street Journal* includes an article by Mitchell Pacelle and Matthew Karnitschnig titled "Spiegel's European Owner Gets a Hard Lesson in U.S. Business."

Instructions
Read the article and answer the following.
(a) Mr. Otto controls 89 companies. What was unique about Spiegel, and how did this get him into trouble?
(b) Mr. Otto is German and is accustomed to the regulatory environment in Germany. How does the German regulatory environment differ from that of the U.S.? According to the article, how is the German regulatory environment changing?
(c) Briefly explain what is meant by the "going concern assumption."
(d) Explain why Spiegel's violation of its loan agreements caused its auditor to say that it would most likely issue an audit opinion that questioned the company's ability to continue as a going concern.
(e) How would the company's creditors react to the news that the auditor questioned the company's ability to continue as a going concern?
(f) Briefly explain the "full disclosure principle" and discuss whether Spiegel appears to have violated this principle.

INTERPRETING FINANCIAL STATEMENTS

BYP2-4 The following information was reported by Gap, Inc. in its 2004 annual report.

	2004	2003	2002	2001	2000
Total assets (millions)	$10,048	$10,713	$10,283	$8,096	$7,387
Working capital	$4,062	$4,156	$2,972	$1,018	$(153)
Current ratio	2.81:1	2.63:1	2.08:1	1.48:1	0.95:1
Debt to total assets ratio	.51:1	.57:1	.66:1	.64:1	.62:1
Earnings per share	$1.29	$1.15	$0.55	$(0.03)	$0.99

(a) Determine the overall percentage increase in Gap's total assets from 2000 to 2004. What was the average increase per year?
(b) Comment on the change in Gap's liquidity. Does working capital or the current ratio appear to provide a better indication of Gap's liquidity? What might explain the change in Gap's liquidity during this period?
(c) Comment on the change in Gap's solvency during this period.
(d) Comment on the change in Gap's profitability during this period. How might this affect your prediction about Gap's future profitability?

FINANCIAL ANALYSIS ON THE WEB

BYP2-5   *Purpose:* Identify summary liquidity, solvency, and profitability information about companies, and compare this information across companies in the same industry.

Address: **http://biz.yahoo.com/i** (or go to **www.wiley.com/college/kimmel**)

Steps
  1. Type in a company name, or use the index to find a company name. Choose **Profile**. Choose **Key Statistics**. Perform instructions (a) and (b) below.
  2. Go back to **Profile**. Click on the company's particular industry behind the heading "Industry." Perform instructions (c) and (d).

Instructions
Answer the following questions.
(a) What is the company's name? What was the company's current ratio and debt to equity ratio (a variation of the debt to total assets ratio)?
(b) What is the company's industry?
(c) What is the name of a competitor? What is the competitor's current ratio and its debt to equity ratio?
(d) Based on these measures: Which company is more liquid? Which company is more solvent?

BYP2-6   The opening story described the dramatic effect that investment bulletin boards are having on the investment world. This exercise will allow you to evaluate a bulletin board discussing a company of your choice.

Address: **http://biz.yahoo.com/i** (or go to **www.wiley.com/college/kimmel**)

Steps
  1. Type in a company name, or use the index to find a company name.
  2. Choose **Msgs** or **Message Board** (for messages).
  3. Read the ten most recent messages.

Instructions
Answer the following questions.
(a) State the nature of each of these messages (e.g., offering advice, criticizing company, predicting future results, ridiculing other people who have posted messages).
(b) For those messages that expressed an opinion about the company, was evidence provided to support the opinion?
(c) What effect do you think it would have on bulletin board discussions if the participants provided their actual names? Do you think this would be a good policy?

Critical Thinking

DECISION MAKING ACROSS THE ORGANIZATION

BYP2-7   As a financial analyst in the planning department for Pre-Mold Industries, Inc., you have been requested to develop some key ratios from the comparative financial statements. This information is to be used to convince creditors that Pre-Mold Industries, Inc. is liquid, solvent, and profitable, and that it deserves their continued support. Lenders are particularly concerned about the company's ability to continue as a going concern.
    Presented on page 96 are the data requested and the computations developed from the financial statements:

	2007	**2006**
Current ratio	3.1	2.1
Working capital	Up 22%	Down 7%
Free cash flow	Up 25%	Up 18%
Debt to total assets ratio	0.60	0.70
Net income	Up 32%	Down 8%
Earnings per share	$2.40	$1.15

Instructions
Pre-Mold Industries, Inc. asks you to prepare brief comments stating how each of these items supports the argument that its financial health is improving. The company wishes to use these comments to support presentation of data to its creditors. With the class divided into groups, prepare the comments as requested, giving the implications and the limitations of each item separately, and then the collective inference that may be drawn from them about Pre-Mold's financial well-being.

COMMUNICATION ACTIVITY

BYP2-8 P. J. Thews is the chief executive officer of Tomorrow's Products. Thews is an expert engineer but a novice in accounting.

Instructions
Write a letter to P. J. Thews that explains (a) the three main types of ratios; (b) examples of each, how they are calculated, and what they measure; and (c) the bases for comparison in analyzing Tomorrow's Products' financial statements.

ETHICS CASE

BYP2-9 A May 20, 2002, *Business Week* story by Stanley Holmes and Mike France entitled "Boeing's Secret" discusses issues surrounding the timing of the disclosure of information at the giant airplane manufacturer. To summarize, on December 11, 1996, Boeing closed a giant deal to acquire another manufacturer, McDonnell Douglas. Boeing paid for the acquisition by issuing shares of its own stock to the stockholders of McDonnell Douglas. In order for the deal not to be revoked, the value of Boeing's stock could not decline below a certain level for a number of months after the deal.

The article suggests that during the first half of 1997 Boeing suffered significant cost overruns because of severe inefficiencies in its production methods. Had these problems been disclosed in the quarterly financial statements during the first and second quarter of 1997, the company's stock most likely would have plummeted, and the deal would have been revoked. Company managers spent considerable time debating when the bad news should be disclosed. One public relations manager suggested that the company's problems be revealed on the date of either Princess Diana's or Mother Teresa's funeral, in the hope that it would be lost among those big stories that day. Instead, the company waited until October 22 of that year to announce a $2.6 billion write-off due to cost overruns. Within one week the company's stock price had fallen 20%, but by this time the McDonnell Douglas deal could not be reversed.

Instructions
Answer the following questions. Although it is not required in order to answer the questions, you may want to read the *Business Week* article.
(a) Who are the stakeholders in this situation?
(b) What are the ethical issues?
(c) What assumptions or principles of accounting are relevant to this case?
(d) Do you think it is ethical to try to "time" the release of a story so as to diminish its effect?
(e) What would you have done if you were the chief executive officer of Boeing?
(f) Boeing's top management maintains that it did not have an obligation to reveal its problems during the first half of 1997, and that it wouldn't do anything differently today. What implications does this have for investors and analysts who follow Boeing's stock?

Answers to Business Insight and Accounting across the Organization Questions

p. 60

Q. What can various company managers do to ensure that working capital is managed efficiently (so as to maximize net income)?

A. Marketing and sales managers must understand that by extending generous repayment terms they are expanding the company's receivables balance and slowing the company's cash flow. Production managers must strive to minimize the amount of excess inventory on hand. Managers must coordinate efforts to speed up the collection of receivables, while also ensuring that the company pays its payables on time, but never too early.

p. 61

Q. Discuss the difference in the debt to total assets ratio of Microsoft and General Motors.

A. Microsoft has a very low debt to total assets ratio. The company is in a rapidly changing industry and thus should try to minimize the risk associated with increased debt. Also, because Microsoft generates significant amounts of cash and has minimal needs for large investments in plant assets, it does not need to borrow a lot of cash. General Motors needs to make huge investments in plant assets, and it has a very large credit operation. Thus it has large borrowing needs.

p. 66

Q. What problems might Best Buy's year-end create for analysts?

A. First, if Best Buy's competitors use a different year-end, then when you compare their financial results, you are not comparing performance over the same period of time or financial position at the same point in time. Also, by not picking a particular date, the number of weeks in Best Buy's fiscal year will change. For example, fiscal years 2002, 2003, and 2004 had 52 weeks, but fisal year 2001 had 53 weeks.

Answer to Tootsie Roll Review It Question 3, p. 53

Tootsie Roll's largest current asset at December 31, 2004, was cash and cash equivalents, at $56,989,000.

Answers to Self-Study Questions

1. d   2. a   3. b   4. a   5. c   6. b   7. d   8. a   9. a   10. c   11. c
12. c

The Accounting Information System

THE NAVIGATOR

- Scan *Study Objectives*
- Read *Feature Story*
- Read *Preview*
- Read text and answer *Before You Go On*
  p. 107 ⬭ p. 113 ⬭ p. 117 ⬭ p. 126 ⬭
  p. 128 ⬭
- Work *Using the Decision Toolkit*
- Review *Summary of Study Objectives*
- Work *Demonstration Problem*
- Answer *Self-Study Questions*
- Complete *Assignments*

FEATURE STORY

Accidents Happen

How organized are you financially? Take a short quiz. Answer *yes* or *no* to each question:

• Does your wallet contain so many cash machine receipts that you've been declared a walking fire hazard?

• Is your wallet such a mess that it is often faster to fish for money in the crack of your car seat than to dig around in your wallet?

• Was Shaquille O'Neal playing high school basketball the last time you balanced your checkbook?

• Have you ever been tempted to burn down your house so you don't have to try to find all of the receipts and records that you need to fill out your tax returns?

If you think it is hard to keep track of the many transactions that make up *your* life, imagine what it is like for a major corporation like Fidelity Investments. Fidelity is one of the largest mutual fund management firms in the world. If you had your life savings invested at Fidelity Investments, you might be just slightly displeased if, when you called to find out your balance, the representative said, "You know, I kind of remember someone with a name like yours sending us some money—now what did we do with that?"

To ensure the accuracy of your balance and the security of your funds, Fidelity Investments, like all other companies large and small, relies on a sophisticated accounting information system. That's not to say that Fidelity or any other company is error-free. In fact, if you've ever really messed up your checkbook register, you may take some comfort from one accountant's mistake at Fidelity Investments. The accountant failed to include a minus sign while doing a calculation, making what was actually a $1.3 billion loss look like a $1.3 billion gain—yes, *billion!* Fortunately, like most accounting errors, it was detected before any real harm was done.

No one expects that kind of mistake at a company like Fidelity, which has sophisticated computer systems and top investment managers.

In explaining the mistake to shareholders, a spokesperson wrote, "Some people have asked how, in this age of technology, such a mistake could be made. While many of our processes are computerized, accounting systems are complex and dictate that some steps must be handled manually by our managers and accountants, and people can make mistakes."

THE NAVIGATOR

On the World Wide Web
Fidelity Investments: www.fidelity.com

As indicated in the Feature Story, a reliable information system is a necessity for any company. The purpose of this chapter is to explain and illustrate the features of an accounting information system. The organization and content of the chapter are as follows.

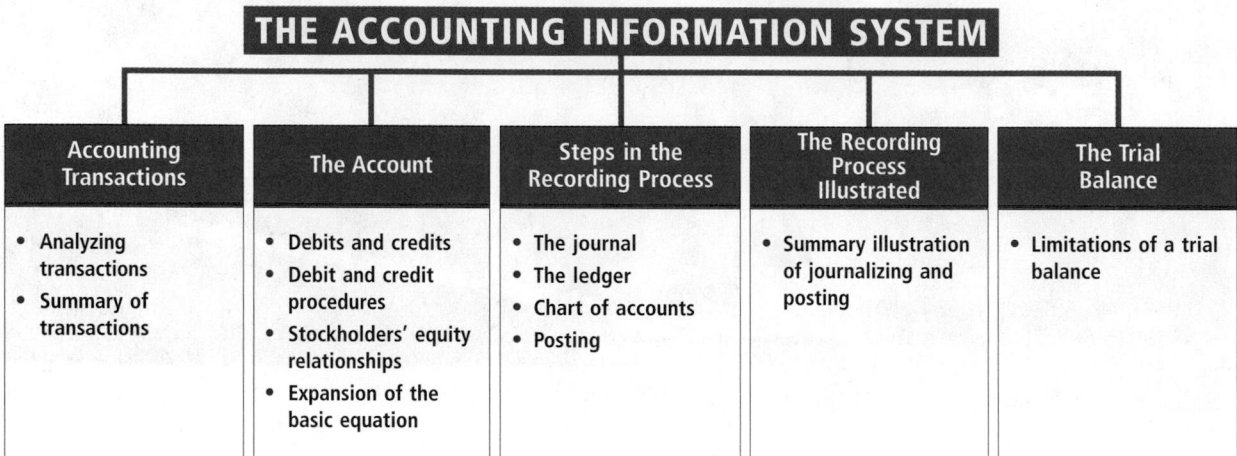

THE ACCOUNTING INFORMATION SYSTEM				
Accounting Transactions	**The Account**	**Steps in the Recording Process**	**The Recording Process Illustrated**	**The Trial Balance**
• Analyzing transactions • Summary of transactions	• Debits and credits • Debit and credit procedures • Stockholders' equity relationships • Expansion of the basic equation	• The journal • The ledger • Chart of accounts • Posting	• Summary illustration of journalizing and posting	• Limitations of a trial balance

THE NAVIGATOR

The Accounting Information System

The system of collecting and processing transaction data and communicating financial information to decision makers is known as the **accounting information system**. Factors that shape these systems include: the nature of the company's business, the types of transactions, the size of the company, the volume of data, and the information demands of management and others.

Most businesses use computerized accounting systems—sometimes referred to as electronic data processing (EDP) systems. These systems handle all the steps involved in the recording process, from initial data entry to preparation of the financial statements. In order to remain competitive, companies continually improve their accounting systems to provide accurate and timely data for decision making. For example, in a recent annual report, Tootsie Roll states, "We also invested in additional processing and data storage hardware during the year. We view information technology as a key strategic tool, and are committed to deploying leading edge technology in this area." In addition, many companies have upgraded their accounting information systems in response to the requirements of Sarbanes-Oxley.

In this chapter we focus on a manual accounting system because the accounting concepts and principles do not change whether a system is computerized or manual, and manual systems are easier to illustrate. However, many of the problems in this and subsequent chapters can also be done using the computerized general ledger package that supplements this text.

Accounting Transactions

To use an accounting information system, you need to know which economic events to recognize (record). Not all events are recorded and reported in the financial statements. For example, suppose General Motors hired a new employee or purchased a new computer. Are these events entered in its accounting records? The first event would not be recorded, but the second event would. We call economic events that require recording in the financial statements **accounting transactions**.

An accounting transaction occurs when assets, liabilities, or stockholders' equity items change as a result of some economic event. The purchase of a computer by General Motors, the payment of rent by Microsoft, and the sale of advertising space by Sierra Corporation are examples of events that change a company's assets, liabilities, or stockholders' equity. Illustration 3-1 summarizes the decision process companies use to decide whether or not to record economic events.

Illustration 3-1
Transaction identification process

ANALYZING TRANSACTIONS

In Chapter 1 you learned the basic accounting equation:

> **Assets = Liabilities + Stockholders' Equity**

STUDY OBJECTIVE
1
Analyze the effect of business transactions on the basic accounting equation.

In this chapter you will learn how to analyze transactions in terms of their effect on assets, liabilities, and stockholders' equity. **Transaction analysis** is the process of identifying the specific effects of economic events on the accounting equation.

The accounting equation must always balance. Each transaction has a dual (double-sided) effect on the equation. For example, if an individual asset is increased, there must be a corresponding:

Decrease in another asset, *or*
Increase in a specific liability, *or*
Increase in stockholders' equity.

Two or more items could be affected when an asset is increased. For example, if a company purchases a computer for $10,000 by paying $6,000 in cash and signing a note for $4,000, one asset (computer) increases $10,000, another asset (cash) decreases $6,000, and a liability (notes payable) increases $4,000. The result is that the accounting equation remains in balance—assets increased by a net $4,000 and liabilities increased by $4,000, as shown below.

Assets	=	Liabilities	+	Stockholders' Equity
+$10,000		+$4,000		
− 6,000				
$ 4,000	=	$4,000		

Chapter 1 presented the financial statements for Sierra Corporation for its first month. You should review those financial statements (on pp. 13–17) at this time. To illustrate how economic events affect the accounting equation, we will examine events affecting Sierra Corporation during its first month. If you are tempted to skip ahead after you've read a few of these, don't do it. Each has something unique to teach, something you'll need later. (We assure you that we've kept them to the minimum needed!)

EVENT (1). INVESTMENT OF CASH BY STOCKHOLDERS. On October 1 cash of $10,000 is invested in the business by investors in exchange for $10,000 of common stock. This event is an accounting transaction because it results in an increase in both assets and stockholders' equity. There is an increase of $10,000 in the asset Cash and an increase of $10,000 in Common Stock on the books of Sierra Corporation. The effect of this transaction on the basic equation is:

	Assets	=	Liabilities	+	Stockholders' Equity	
	Cash	=			Common Stock	
(1)	+$10,000	=			+$10,000	Issued stock

The equation is in balance. **The source of each change to stockholders' equity is noted to the right of the transaction.** In this case it was an issuance of common stock. Keeping track of the source of each change in stockholders' equity is essential for later accounting activities—in particular, for the calculation of net income.

EVENT (2). NOTE ISSUED IN EXCHANGE FOR CASH. On October 1 Sierra borrowed $5,000 on a 3-month, 12%, $5,000 note payable to Castle Bank. This transaction results in an equal increase in assets and liabilities: Cash (an asset) increases $5,000, and Notes Payable (a liability) increases $5,000. The specific effect of this transaction and the cumulative effect of the first two transactions are:

		Assets	=	Liabilities	+	Stockholders' Equity
		Cash	=	Notes Payable	+	Common Stock
Old Balance		$10,000				$10,000
(2)		**+5,000**		**+$5,000**		
New Balance		$15,000	=	$ 5,000	+	$10,000
				$15,000		

Total assets are now $15,000, and stockholders' equity plus the new liability also total $15,000.

EVENT (3). PURCHASE OF OFFICE EQUIPMENT FOR CASH. On October 2 Sierra purchased office equipment by paying $5,000 cash to Superior Equipment Sales Co. This event is a transaction because an equal increase and decrease in Sierra's assets occur: Office Equipment (an asset) increases $5,000, and Cash (an asset) decreases $5,000.

		Assets			=	Liabilities	+	Stockholders' Equity
		Cash	+	Office Equipment	=	Notes Payable	+	Common Stock
	Old Balance	$15,000				$5,000		$10,000
(3)		**−5,000**		**+$5,000**				
	New Balance	$10,000	+	$ 5,000	=	$5,000	+	$10,000
			$15,000			$15,000		

The total assets are now $15,000, and stockholders' equity plus the liability also total $15,000.

EVENT (4). RECEIPT OF CASH IN ADVANCE FROM CUSTOMER. On October 2 Sierra received a $1,200 cash advance from R. Knox, a client. This event is a transaction because Sierra received cash (an asset) for advertising services that are expected to be completed by Sierra in the future. Although Sierra received cash, **it does not record revenue until it has performed the work**. In some industries, such as the magazine and airline industries, customers are expected to prepay. These companies have a liability to the customer until they deliver the magazines or provide the flight. As soon as the company provides the product or service, it records the revenue.

Since Sierra received cash prior to performance of the service, Sierra has a liability for the work due. Cash increases by $1,200, and a liability, Unearned Service Revenue (abbreviated as Unearned Revenue), increases by an equal amount.

		Assets			=	Liabilities			+	Stockholders' Equity
		Cash	+	Office Equipment	=	Notes Payable	+	Unearned Revenue	+	Common Stock
	Old Balance	$10,000		$5,000		$5,000				$10,000
(4)		**+1,200**						**+$1,200**		
	New Balance	$11,200	+	$5,000	=	$5,000	+	$ 1,200	+	$10,000
			$16,200				$16,200			

EVENT (5). SERVICES PROVIDED FOR CASH. On October 3 Sierra received $10,000 in cash from Copa Company for advertising services performed. This event is a transaction because Sierra received an asset (cash) in exchange for services.

Advertising service is the principal revenue-producing activity of Sierra. **Revenue increases stockholders' equity.** This transaction, then, increases both assets and stockholders' equity. Cash is increased $10,000, and Retained Earnings is increased $10,000. The new balances in the equation are:

		Assets		=	Liabilities		+	Stockholders' Equity		
		Cash	+ Office Equipment	=	Notes Payable	+ Unearned Revenue	+	Common Stock	+ Retained Earnings	
Old Balance		$11,200	$5,000		$5,000	$1,200		$10,000		
(5)		+10,000							+$10,000	Service Revenue
New Balance		$21,200 +	$5,000	=	$5,000 +	$1,200	+	$10,000 +	$10,000	
			$26,200				$26,200			

Often companies provide services "on account." That is, they provide service for which they are paid at a later date. Revenue, however, is earned when services are performed. Therefore, stockholders' equity would increase when services are performed, even though cash has not been received. Instead of receiving cash, the company receives a different type of asset, an **account receivable**. Accounts receivable represent the right to receive payment at a later date. Suppose that Sierra had provided these services on account rather than for cash. This event would be reported using the accounting equation as:

Assets	=	Liabilities	+	Stockholders' Equity
Accounts Receivable	=			Retained Earnings
+$10,000				+$10,000 Service Revenue

Later, when Sierra collects the $10,000 from the customer, Accounts Receivable would decline by $10,000, and Cash would increase by $10,000.

Assets		=	Liabilities	+	Stockholders' Equity
Cash	Accounts Receivable				
+$10,000	−$10,000				

Note that in this case, stockholders' equity is not affected by the collection of cash. Instead we record an exchange of one asset (Accounts Receivable) for a different asset (Cash).

EVENT (6). PAYMENT OF RENT. On October 3 Sierra Corporation paid its office rent for the month of October in cash, $900. This rent payment is a transaction because it results in a decrease in an asset, cash.

Rent is an expense incurred by Sierra Corporation in its effort to generate revenues. **Expenses decrease stockholders' equity.** Sierra records the rent payment by decreasing cash and decreasing stockholders' equity (specifically, Retained Earnings) to maintain the balance of the accounting equation. To record this transaction, Sierra decreases Cash $900, and decreases Retained Earnings $900. The effect of these payments on the accounting equation is:

		Assets	=	Liabilities	+	Stockholders' Equity	
	Cash +	Office Equipment	= Notes Payable +	Unearned Revenue +	Common Stock +	Retained Earnings	
Old Balance	$21,200	$5,000	$5,000	$1,200	$10,000	$10,000	
(6)	−900					−900	Rent Expense
New Balance	$20,300 +	$5,000	= $5,000 +	$1,200 +	$10,000 +	$ 9,100	
		$25,300			$25,300		

EVENT (7). PURCHASE OF INSURANCE POLICY IN CASH.

On October 4 Sierra paid $600 for a one-year insurance policy that will expire next year on September 30. In this transaction the asset Cash is decreased $600. Payments of expenses that will benefit more than one accounting period are identified as assets called prepaid expenses or prepayments. Therefore the asset Prepaid Insurance is increased $600. The balance in total assets did not change; one asset account decreased by the same amount that another increased.

			Assets		=	Liabilities	+	Stockholders' Equity	
	Cash +	Prepaid Insurance +	Office Equipment	=	Notes Payable +	Unearned Revenue +	Common Stock +	Retained Earnings	
Old Balance	$20,300		$5,000		$5,000	$1,200	$10,000	$9,100	
(7)	−600	+$600							
New Balance	$19,700 +	$ 600 +	$5,000	=	$5,000 +	$1,200 +	$10,000 +	$9,100	
		$25,300				$25,300			

EVENT (8). PURCHASE OF SUPPLIES ON ACCOUNT.

On October 5 Sierra purchased a three-month supply of advertising materials on account from Aero Supply for $2,500. In this case, "on account" means that the company receives goods or services that it will pay for at a later date. Supplies, an asset, increases $2,500 by this transaction. Accounts Payable, a liability, increases $2,500, to indicate the amount due to Aero Supply. The effect on the equation is:

				Assets		=	Liabilities			+ Stockholders' Equity	
	Cash +	Supplies +	Prepaid Insurance +	Office Equipment	=	Notes Payable +	Accounts Payable +	Unearned Revenue +	Common Stock +	Retained Earnings	
Old Balance	$19,700		$600	$5,000		$5,000		$1,200	$10,000	$9,100	
(8)		+$2,500					+$2,500				
New Balance	$19,700 +	$ 2,500 +	$600 +	$5,000	=	$5,000 +	$ 2,500 +	$1,200 +	$10,000 +	$9,100	
			$27,800					$27,800			

EVENT (9). HIRING OF NEW EMPLOYEES.

On October 9 Sierra hired four new employees to begin work on October 15. Each employee will receive a weekly salary of $500 for a five-day work week, payable every two weeks. Employees will receive their first paychecks on October 26. On the date Sierra hires the employees, there is no effect on the accounting equation because the assets, liabilities, and stockholders' equity of the company have not changed. **An accounting transaction has not occurred.** At this point there is only an agreement that the employees will begin work on October 15. [See Event (11) for the first payment.]

EVENT (10). PAYMENT OF DIVIDEND. On October 20 Sierra paid a $500 dividend. **Dividends** are a distribution of net income and not an expense. A dividend transaction affects assets and stockholders' equity: Cash and Retained Earnings are decreased $500.

		Assets				=	Liabilities			+	Stockholders' Equity		
		Cash	+ Supplies +	Prepaid Insurance +	Office Equipment	=	Notes Payable +	Accounts Payable +	Unearned Revenue +		Common Stock +	Retained Earnings	
	Old Balance	$19,700	$2,500	$600	$5,000		$5,000	$2,500	$1,200		$10,000	$9,100	
(10)		−500										−500	Dividends
	New Balance	$19,200 +	$2,500 +	$600 +	$5,000	=	$5,000 +	$2,500 +	$1,200 +		$10,000 +	$8,600	
			$27,300						$27,300				

EVENT (11). PAYMENT OF CASH FOR EMPLOYEE SALARIES. Employees have worked two weeks, earning $4,000 in salaries, which were paid on October 26. Salaries are an expense which reduce stockholders' equity. This event is a transaction because assets and stockholders' equity are affected. Thus, Cash and Retained Earnings are each decreased $4,000.

		Assets				=	Liabilities			+	Stockholders' Equity		
		Cash	+ Supplies +	Prepaid Insurance +	Office Equipment	=	Notes Payable +	Accounts Payable +	Unearned Revenue +		Common Stock +	Retained Earnings	
	Old Balance	$19,200	$2,500	$600	$5,000		$5,000	$2,500	$1,200		$10,000	$8,600	
(11)		−4,000										−4,000	Salaries
	New Balance	$15,200 +	$2,500 +	$600 +	$5,000	=	$5,000 +	$2,500 +	$1,200 +		$10,000 +	$4,600	Expense
			$23,300						$23,300				

Business Insight
Investor Perspective

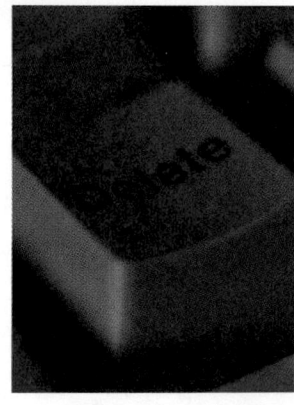

While most companies record transactions very carefully, the reality is that mistakes still happen. For example, bank regulators fined Bank One Corporation (now Chase) $1.8 million because they felt that the unreliability of the bank's accounting system caused it to violate regulatory requirements.

Also, in recent years Fannie Mae, the government-chartered mortgage association, announced a series of large accounting errors. These announcements caused alarm among investors, regulators, and politicians because they fear that the errors may suggest larger, undetected problems. This is important because the home-mortgage market depends on Fannie Mae to buy hundreds of billions of dollars of mortgages each year from banks, thus enabling the banks to issue new mortgages.

Finally, before a major overhaul of its accounting system, the financial records of Waste Management Company were in such disarray that of the company's 57,000 employees, 10,000 were receiving pay slips that were in error.

The Sarbanes-Oxley Act of 2002 was created to minimize the occurrence of errors like these by increasing every employee's responsibility for accurate financial reporting.

 In order for these companies to prepare and issue financial statements, their accounting equations (debits and credits) must have been in balance at year-end. How could these errors or misstatements have occurred?

SUMMARY OF TRANSACTIONS

Illustration 3-2 summarizes the transactions of Sierra Corporation to show their cumulative effect on the basic accounting equation. It includes the transaction number in the first column on the left. The right-most column shows the specific effect of any transaction that affects stockholders' equity. Remember that Event (9) did not result in a transaction, so no entry is included for that event. The illustration demonstrates three important points:

1. Each transaction is analyzed in terms of its effect on assets, liabilities, and stockholders' equity.
2. The two sides of the equation must always be equal.
3. The cause of each change in stockholders' equity must be indicated.

Illustration 3-2
Summary of transactions

	Cash	+ Supplies +	Prepaid Insurance +	Office Equipment =	Notes Payable +	Accounts Payable +	Unearned Revenue +	Common Stock +	Retained Earnings	
	Assets			=	**Liabilities**			+	**Stockholders' Equity**	
(1)	+$10,000			=				+$10,000		Issued stock
(2)	+5,000				+$5,000					
(3)	−5,000			+$5,000						
(4)	+1,200						+$1,200			
(5)	+10,000								+$10,000	Service Revenue
(6)	−900								−900	Rent Expense
(7)	−600		+$600							
(8)		+$2,500				+$2,500				
(10)	−500								−500	Dividends
(11)	−4,000								−4,000	Salaries Expense
	$15,200 +	$2,500 +	$600 +	$5,000 =	$5,000 +	$2,500 +	$1,200 +	$10,000 +	$ 4,600	
			$23,300				$23,300			

Decision Toolkit

Decision Checkpoints	Info Needed for Decision	Tool to Use for Decision	How to Evaluate Results
Has an accounting transaction occurred?	Details of the event	Accounting equation	If the event affected assets, liabilities, or stockholders' equity, then record as a transaction.

BEFORE YOU GO ON . . .

►Review It

1. What are the criteria that must be met for an event to be recorded in the financial statements? What is the name for events that require recording?
2. What is transaction analysis?
3. Why isn't the purchase of equipment treated as an expense at the time of purchase?
4. Why isn't an advance received from customers treated as revenue at the time of receipt?

▶**Do It**

A tabular analysis of the transactions made by Roberta Mendez & Co., a certified public accounting firm, for the month of August is shown below. Each increase and decrease in stockholders' equity is explained.

Assets		=	Liabilities +	Stockholders' Equity		
Cash	+ Office Equipment	=	Accounts Payable	+ Common Stock	+ Retained Earnings	
1. +25,000				+25,000		Issued Stock
2.	+7,000		+7,000			
3. +8,000					+8,000	Service Revenue
4. −850					−850	Rent Expense

Describe each transaction that occurred for the month.

Action Plan

• Analyze the tabular analysis to determine the nature and effect of each transaction.
• Keep the accounting equation always in balance.
• Remember that a change in an asset will require a change in another asset, a liability, or in stockholders' equity.

Solution

1. The company issued shares of stock to stockholders for $25,000 cash.
2. The company purchased $7,000 of office equipment on account.
3. The company received $8,000 of cash in exchange for services performed.
4. The company paid $850 for this month's rent.

THE NAVIGATOR

The Account

STUDY OBJECTIVE
2

Explain what an account is and how it helps in the recording process.

Rather than using a tabular summary like the one in Illustration 3-2 for Sierra Corporation, an accounting information system uses accounts. An **account** is an individual accounting record of increases and decreases in a specific asset, liability, or stockholders' equity item. For example, Sierra Corporation has separate accounts for Cash, Accounts Receivable, Accounts Payable, Service Revenue, Salaries Expense, and so on. (Note that whenever we are referring to a specific account, we capitalize the name.)

In its simplest form, an account consists of three parts: (1) the title of the account, (2) a left or debit side, and (3) a right or credit side. Because the alignment of these parts of an account resembles the letter T, it is referred to as a **T account**. The basic form of an account is shown in Illustration 3-3.

Illustration 3-3 Basic form of account

Title of Account	
Left or debit side	Right or credit side
Debit balance	Credit balance

We use this form of account often throughout this book to explain basic accounting relationships.

DEBITS AND CREDITS

The term **debit** indicates left, and **credit** indicates right. They are commonly abbreviated as **Dr.** for debit and **Cr.** for credit. They **do not** mean increase or decrease, as is commonly thought. We use the terms *debit* and *credit* repeatedly in the recording process to describe **where** entries are made in accounts. For example, the act of entering an amount on the left side of an account is called **debiting** the account. Making an entry on the right side is **crediting** the account.

When comparing the totals of the two sides, an account shows a **debit balance** if the total of the debit amounts exceeds the credits. An account shows a **credit balance** if the credit amounts exceed the debits. Note the position of the debit or credit balances in Illustration 3-3.

The procedure of recording debits and credits in an account is shown in Illustration 3-4 for the transactions affecting the Cash account of Sierra Corporation. The data are taken from the Cash column of the tabular summary in Illustration 3-2.

Tabular Summary	Account Form			
Cash		**Cash**		
$10,000	(Debits)	10,000	(Credits)	5,000
5,000		5,000		900
−5,000		1,200		600
1,200		10,000		500
10,000				4,000
−900				
−600	Balance	15,200		
−500	(Debit)			
−4,000				
$15,200				

Illustration 3-4 Tabular summary and account form for Sierra Corporation's Cash account

Every positive item in the tabular summary represents a receipt of cash; every negative amount represents a payment of cash. **Notice that in the account form we record the increases in cash as debits, and the decreases in cash as credits.** For example, the $10,000 receipt of cash (in red) is debited to Cash, and the −$5,000 payment of cash (in blue) is credited to Cash.

Having increases on one side and decreases on the other reduces recording errors and helps in determining the totals of each side of the account as well as the balance in the account. The account balance, a debit of $15,200, indicates that Sierra Corporation had $15,200 more increases than decreases in cash. That is, since it started with a balance of zero, it has $15,200 in its Cash account.

DEBIT AND CREDIT PROCEDURES

Each transaction must affect two or more accounts to keep the basic accounting equation in balance. In other words, for each transaction, debits must equal credits. The equality of debits and credits provides the basis for the double-entry accounting system.

Under the **double-entry system**, the two-sided effect of each transaction is recorded in appropriate accounts. This system provides a logical method for recording transactions. The double-entry system also helps to ensure the accuracy of the recorded amounts and helps to detect errors such as those at Fidelity Investments as discussed in the Feature Story. If every transaction is recorded with equal debits and credits, then the sum of all the debits to the accounts must equal the sum of all the credits. The double-entry system for determining the equality of the accounting equation is much more efficient than the plus/minus procedure used earlier.

Dr./Cr. Procedures for Assets and Liabilities

In Illustration 3-4 for Sierra Corporation, increases in Cash—an asset—were entered on the left side, and decreases in Cash were entered on the right side. We know that both sides of the basic equation (Assets = Liabilities + Stockholders' Equity) must be equal. It therefore follows that increases and decreases in liabilities will have to be recorded *opposite from* increases and decreases in assets. Thus, increases in liabilities must be entered on the right or credit side, and decreases in liabilities must be entered on the left or debit side. The effects that debits and credits have on assets and liabilities are summarized in Illustration 3-5.

Illustration 3-5 Debit and credit effects—assets and liabilities

Debits	Credits
Increase assets	Decrease assets
Decrease liabilities	Increase liabilities

Asset accounts normally show debit balances. That is, debits to a specific asset account should exceed credits to that account. Likewise, **liability accounts normally show credit balances**. That is, credits to a liability account should exceed debits to that account. The **normal balances** may be diagrammed as in Illustration 3-6.

Illustration 3-6 Normal balances—assets and liabilities

Knowing which is the normal balance in an account may help when you are trying to identify errors. For example, a credit balance in an asset account such as Land or a debit balance in a liability account such as Wages Payable usually indicates errors in recording. Occasionally, however, an abnormal balance may be correct. The Cash account, for example, will have a credit balance when a company has overdrawn its bank balance (written a check that "bounced"). In automated accounting systems, the computer is programmed to flag violations of the normal balance and to print out error or exception reports. In manual systems, careful visual inspection of the accounts is required to detect normal balance problems.

Dr./Cr. Procedures for Stockholders' Equity

In Chapter 1 we indicated that stockholders' equity is comprised of two parts: common stock and retained earnings. In the transaction events earlier in this chapter, you saw that revenues, expenses, and the payment of dividends affect retained earnings. We are now at the point where we can expand the subdivision of stockholders' equity. The subdivisions of stockholders' equity are: common stock, retained earnings, dividends, revenues, and expenses.

COMMON STOCK. Common stock is issued to investors in exchange for the stockholders' investment. The Common Stock account is increased by credits and decreased by debits. For example, when cash is invested in the business, Cash is debited and Common Stock is credited. The effects of debits and credits on the Common Stock account are shown in Illustration 3-7.

Debits	Credits
Decrease Common Stock	Increase Common Stock

Illustration 3-7   Debit and credit effects— Common Stock

The normal balance in the Common Stock account may be diagrammed as in Illustration 3-8.

Common Stock

Debit for decrease	Credit for increase
	Normal balance

Illustration 3-8   Normal balance—Common Stock

RETAINED EARNINGS.   Retained earnings is net income that is retained in the business. It represents the portion of stockholders' equity that has been accumulated through the profitable operation of the company. Retained Earnings is increased by credits (for example, by net income) and decreased by debits (for example, by a net loss), as shown in Illustration 3-9.

Debits	Credits
Decrease Retained Earnings	Increase Retained Earnings

Illustration 3-9   Debit and credit effects— Retained Earnings

The normal balance for Retained Earnings may be diagrammed as in Illustration 3-10.

Retained Earnings

Debit for decrease	Credit for increase
	Normal balance

Illustration 3-10   Normal balance—Retained Earnings

DIVIDENDS.   A dividend is a distribution by a corporation to its stockholders. The most common form of distribution is a cash dividend. Dividends result in a reduction of the stockholders' claims on retained earnings. Because dividends reduce stockholders' equity, increases in the Dividends account are recorded with debits. As shown in Illustration 3-11, the Dividends account normally has a debit balance.

Dividends

Debit for increase	Credit for decrease
Normal balance	

Illustration 3-11   Normal balance—Dividends

REVENUES AND EXPENSES. When a company earns revenues, stockholders' equity is increased. Revenue accounts are increased by credits and decreased by debits.

Expenses decrease stockholders' equity. Thus, expense accounts are increased by debits and decreased by credits. The effects of debits and credits on revenues and expenses are shown in Illustration 3-12.

Illustration 3-12   Debit and credit effects—revenues and expenses

Debits	Credits
Decrease revenues	Increase revenues
Increase expenses	Decrease expenses

Credits to revenue accounts should exceed debits; debits to expense accounts should exceed credits. Thus, **revenue accounts normally show credit balances, and expense accounts normally show debit balances**. The normal balances may be diagrammed as in Illustration 3-13.

Illustration 3-13   Normal balances—revenues and expenses

Expenses

Debit for increase	Credit for decrease
Normal balance	

Revenues

Debit for decrease	Credit for increase
	Normal balance

Business Insight
Investor Perspective

The Chicago Cubs baseball team has these major revenue and expense accounts:

Revenues	Expenses
Admissions (ticket sales)	Players' salaries
Concessions	Administrative salaries
Television and radio	Travel
Advertising	Ballpark maintenance

 Do you think that the Chicago Bears football team would be likely to have the same major revenue and expense accounts as the Cubs?

STOCKHOLDERS' EQUITY RELATIONSHIPS

Companies report the subdivisions of stockholders' equity in various places in the financial statements:

• Common stock and retained earnings: in the stockholders' equity section of the balance sheet.
• Dividends: on the retained earnings statement.
• Revenues and expenses: on the income statement.

Dividends, revenues, and expenses are eventually transferred to retained earnings at the end of the period. As a result, a change in any one of these three items affects stockholders' equity. Illustration 3-14 shows the relationships of the accounts affecting stockholders' equity.

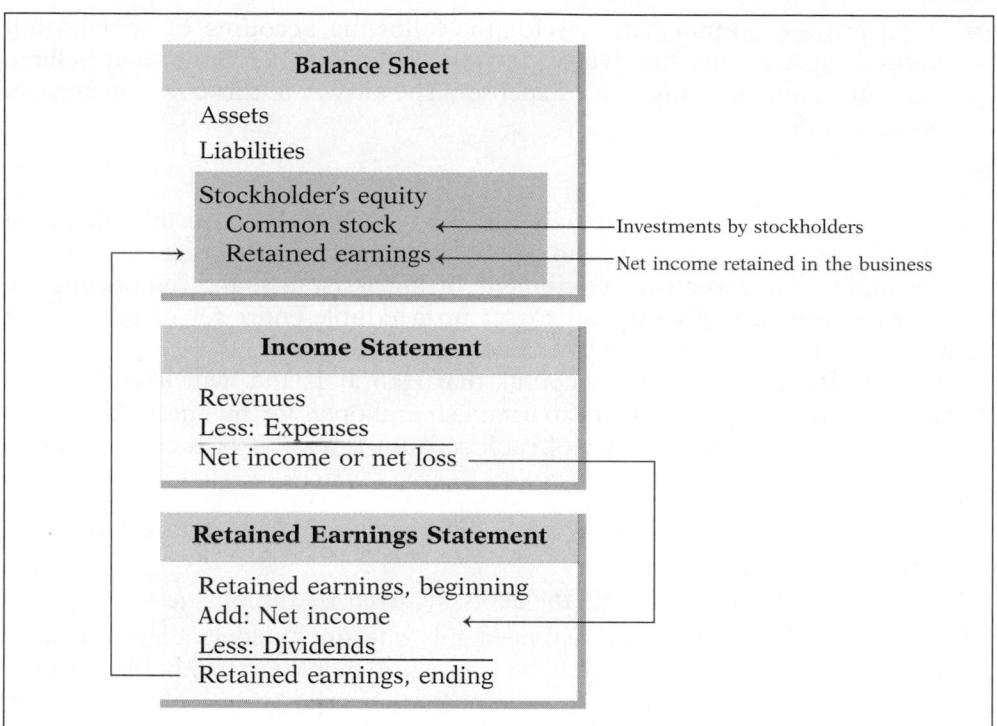

Illustration 3-14
Stockholders' equity relationships

EXPANSION OF THE BASIC EQUATION

You have already learned the basic accounting equation. Illustration 3-15 expands this equation to show the accounts that make up stockholders' equity. In addition, it illustrates the debit/credit rules and effects on each type of account. **Study this diagram carefully.** It will help you understand the fundamentals of the double-entry system. Like the basic equation, the expanded basic equation must be in balance: Total debits must equal total credits.

Illustration 3-15
Expansion of the basic accounting equation

BEFORE YOU GO ON . . .

▶Review It

1. What do the terms *debit* and *credit* indicate?
2. What are the debit and credit effects on assets, liabilities, and stockholders' equity?
3. What are the debit and credit effects on revenues, expenses, and dividends?

4. What are the normal balances for the following accounts of Tootsie Roll Industries: Accounts Receivable; Income Taxes Payable; Sales; and Selling, Marketing, and Administrative Expense? (The answer to this question appears on page 155.)

▶Do It

Kate Browne, president of Hair It Is Inc., has just rented space in a shopping mall for the purpose of opening and operating a beauty salon. Long before opening day and before purchasing equipment, hiring assistants, and remodeling the space, Kate was strongly advised to set up a double-entry set of accounting records in which to record all of her business transactions.

Identify the balance sheet accounts that Hair It Is Inc. will likely need to record the transactions necessary to establish and open for business. Also, indicate whether the normal balance of each account is a debit or a credit.

Action Plan

• First identify asset accounts for each different type of asset invested in the business.

• Then identify liability accounts for debts incurred by the business.

• Remember that Hair It Is Inc. will need only one stockholders' equity account for common stock when it begins the business. The other stockholders' equity accounts will be needed only after the business is operating.

Solution

Hair It Is Inc. would likely need the following accounts in which to record the transactions necessary to establish and ready the beauty salon for opening day: Cash (debit balance); Equipment (debit balance); Supplies (debit balance); Accounts Payable (credit balance); Notes Payable (credit balance), if the business borrows money; and Common Stock (credit balance).

✓ THE NAVIGATOR

Steps in the Recording Process

STUDY OBJECTIVE
4
Identify the basic steps in the recording process.

Although it is possible to enter transaction information directly into the accounts, few businesses do so. Practically every business uses these basic steps in the recording process:

1. Analyze each transaction in terms of its effect on the accounts.
2. Enter the transaction information in a journal.
3. Transfer the journal information to the appropriate accounts in the ledger (book of accounts).

The actual sequence of events begins with the transaction. Evidence of the transaction comes in the form of a **source document**, such as a sales slip, a check, a bill, or a cash register tape. This evidence is analyzed to determine the effect of the transaction on specific accounts. The transaction is then entered in the **journal**. Finally, the journal entry is transferred to the designated accounts in the **ledger**. The sequence of events in the recording process is shown in Illustration 3-16.

THE JOURNAL

STUDY OBJECTIVE
5
Explain what a journal is and how it helps in the recording process.

Transactions are initially recorded in chronological order in journals before they are transferred to the accounts. For each transaction the journal shows the debit and credit effects on specific accounts. (In a computerized system, journals are kept as files, and accounts are recorded in computer databases.)

Companies may use various kinds of journals, but every company has at least the most basic form of journal, a **general journal**. **The journal makes three significant contributions to the recording process:**

The Recording Process

Invoice

JOURNAL

JOURNAL
LEDGER
ASSETS   LIABILITIES
Stockholders' Equity

Analyze each transaction

Enter transaction in a journal

Transfer journal information to ledger accounts

Illustration 3-16 The recording process

1. It discloses in one place the **complete effect of a transaction**.
2. It provides a **chronological record** of transactions.
3. It **helps to prevent or locate errors** because the debit and credit amounts for each entry can be readily compared.

Entering transaction data in the journal is known as **journalizing**. To illustrate the technique of journalizing, let's look at the first three transactions of Sierra Corporation in equation form.

On October 1, Sierra issued common stock in exchange for $10,000 cash:

Assets	=	Liabilities	+	Stockholders' Equity	
Cash	=			Common Stock	
+$10,000				+$10,000	Issued stock

On October 1, Sierra borrowed $5,000 by signing a note:

Assets	=	Liabilities	+	Stockholders' Equity
Cash	=	Notes Payable		
+$5,000		+$5,000		

On October 2, Sierra purchased office equipment for $5,000:

Assets		=	Liabilities	+	Stockholders' Equity
Cash	Office Equipment				
−$5,000	+$5,000				

Sierra makes separate journal entries for each transaction. A complete entry consists of: (1) the date of the transaction, (2) the accounts and amounts to be debited and credited, and (3) a brief explanation of the transaction. These transactions are journalized in Illustration 3-17 (on page 116).

Note the following features of the journal entries.

1. The date of the transaction is entered in the Date column.
2. The account to be debited is entered first at the left. The account to be credited is then entered on the next line, indented under the line above. The indentation differentiates debits from credits and decreases the possibility of switching the debit and credit amounts.

Illustration 3-17
Recording transactions in
journal form

GENERAL JOURNAL			
Date	Account Titles and Explanation	Debit	Credit
2007 Oct. 1	Cash	10,000	
	Common Stock		10,000
	(Issued stock for cash)		
1	Cash	5,000	
	Notes Payable		5,000
	(Issued 3-month, 12% note payable for cash)		
2	Office Equipment	5,000	
	Cash		5,000
	(Purchased office equipment for cash)		

3. The amounts for the debits are recorded in the Debit (left) column, and the amounts for the credits are recorded in the Credit (right) column.

4. A brief explanation of the transaction is given.

It is important to use correct and specific account titles in journalizing. Erroneous account titles lead to incorrect financial statements. Some flexibility exists initially in selecting account titles. The main criterion is that each title must appropriately describe the content of the account. For example, a company could use any of these account titles for recording the cost of delivery trucks: Delivery Equipment, Delivery Trucks, or Trucks. Once the company chooses the specific title to use, however, it should record under that account title all subsequent transactions involving the account.

Accounting across the Organization

Bryan Lee is head of finance at Microsoft's Home and Entertainment Division. In recent years the division has lost over $4 billion, mostly due to losses on the original Xbox videogame player. With the new Xbox 360 videogame player, Mr. Lee hopes the division will become profitable. He has set strict goals for sales, revenue, and profit. "A manager seeking to spend more on a feature such as a disk drive has to find allies in the group to cut spending elsewhere, or identify new revenue to offset the increase," he explains.

For example, Microsoft originally designed the new Xbox to have 256 megabytes of memory. But the design department said that amount of memory wouldn't support the best special effects. The purchasing department said that adding more memory would cost $30—which is 10% of the estimated selling price of $300. But the marketing department "determined that adding the memory would let Microsoft reduce marketing costs and attract more game developers, boosting royalty revenue. It would also extend the life of the console, generating more sales." Microsoft doubled the memory to 512 megabytes.

Source: Robert A. Guth, "New Xbox Aim for Microsoft: Profitability," *Wall Street Journal*, May 24, 2005, p. C1.

 In what ways is this Microsoft division using accounting to assist in its effort to become more profitable?

BEFORE YOU GO ON . . .

▶**Review It**

1. What is the correct sequence of steps in the recording process?
2. What contribution does the journal make to the recording process?
3. What are the standard form and content of a journal entry made in the general journal?

▶**Do It**

The following events occurred during the first month of business of Hair It Is Inc., Kate Browne's beauty salon:

1. Issued common stock to shareholders in exchange for $20,000 cash.
2. Purchased $4,800 of equipment on account (to be paid in 30 days).
3. Interviewed three people for the position of beautician.

In what form (type of record) should the company record these three activities? Prepare the entries to record the transactions.

Action Plan

- Record the transactions in a journal, which is a chronological record of the transactions.
- Make sure to provide a complete and accurate representation of the transactions' effects on the assets, liabilities, and stockholders' equity of the business.

Solution

Each transaction that is recorded is entered in the general journal. The three activities are recorded as follows.

1. Cash	20,000	
Common Stock		20,000
(Issued stock for cash)		
2. Equipment	4,800	
Accounts Payable		4,800
(Purchased equipment on account)		
3. No entry because no transaction occurred.		

 THE NAVIGATOR

THE LEDGER

The entire group of accounts maintained by a company is referred to collectively as the **ledger**. The ledger keeps in one place all the information about changes in specific account balances.

Companies may use various kinds of ledgers, but every company has a general ledger. A **general ledger** contains all the assets, liabilities, and stockholders' equity accounts, as shown in Illustration 3-18 (page 118). Whenever we use the term *ledger* in this textbook without additional specification, it will mean the general ledger.

STUDY OBJECTIVE

6

Explain what a ledger is and how it helps in the recording process.

CHART OF ACCOUNTS

The number and type of accounts used differ for each company, depending on the size, complexity, and type of business. For example, the number of accounts depends on the amount of detail desired by management. The management of one company may want one single account for all types of utility expense. Another may keep separate expense accounts for each type of utility expenditure, such as gas, electricity, and water. A small corporation like Sierra Corporation will not have many accounts compared with a corporate giant like Ford Motor Company. Sierra may be able to manage and report its activities in 20 to 30 accounts, whereas Ford requires thousands of accounts to keep track of its worldwide activities.

Illustration 3-18 The general ledger

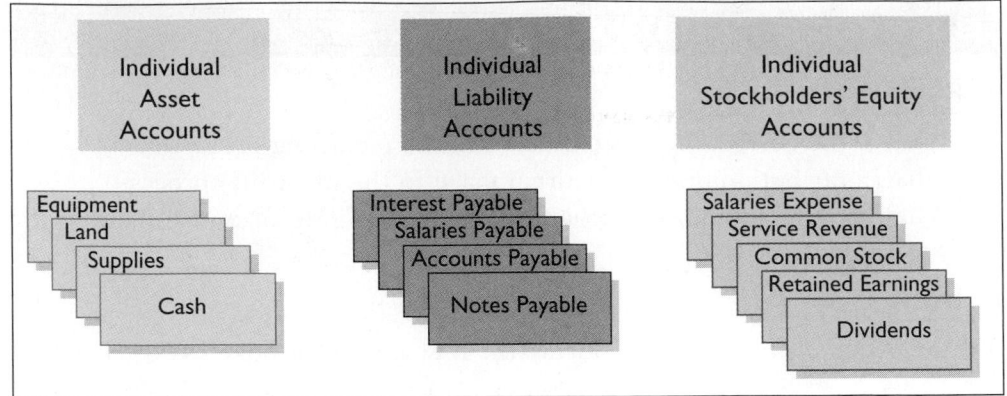

Most companies list the accounts in a **chart of accounts**. They may create new accounts as needed during the life of the business. Illustration 3-19 shows the chart of accounts for Sierra Corporation. **Accounts shown in red are used in this chapter**; accounts shown in black are explained in later chapters.

Illustration 3-19 Chart of accounts for Sierra Corporation

SIERRA CORPORATION—Chart of Accounts				
Assets	**Liabilities**	**Stockholders' Equity**	**Revenues**	**Expenses**
Cash	Notes Payable	Common Stock	Service Revenue	Salaries Expense
Accounts Receivable	Accounts Payable	Retained Earnings		Supplies Expense
Advertising Supplies	Interest Payable	Dividends		Rent Expense
Prepaid Insurance	Unearned	Income Summary		Insurance Expense
Office Equipment	Service Revenue			Interest Expense
Accumulated Depreciation—	Salaries Payable			Depreciation Expense
Office Equipment				

POSTING

STUDY OBJECTIVE

7

Explain what posting is and how it helps in the recording process.

The procedure of transferring journal entries to ledger accounts is called **posting**. **This phase of the recording process accumulates the effects of journalized transactions in the individual accounts.** Posting involves these steps:

1. In the ledger, enter in the appropriate columns of the debited account(s) the date and debit amount shown in the journal.
2. In the ledger, enter in the appropriate columns of the credited account(s) the date and credit amount shown in the journal.

The Recording Process Illustrated

Illustrations 3-20 through 3-30 on the following pages show the basic steps in the recording process using the October transactions of Sierra Corporation. Sierra's accounting period is a month. A basic analysis and a debit–credit analysis precede the journalizing and posting of each transaction. Study these transaction analyses carefully. **The purpose of transaction analysis is first to identify the type of account involved and then to determine whether a debit or a credit to the account is required.** You should always perform this type of analysis before preparing a journal entry. Doing so will help you understand the journal entries discussed in this chapter as well as more complex journal entries to be described in later chapters.

In addition, an Accounting Cycle Tutorial at the book's website, **www.wiley.com/college/kimmel**, provides an interactive presentation of the steps in the accounting cycle, using the examples in the illustrations on the following pages. The illustration at the top of the next page is a shot of the tutorial's opening screen.

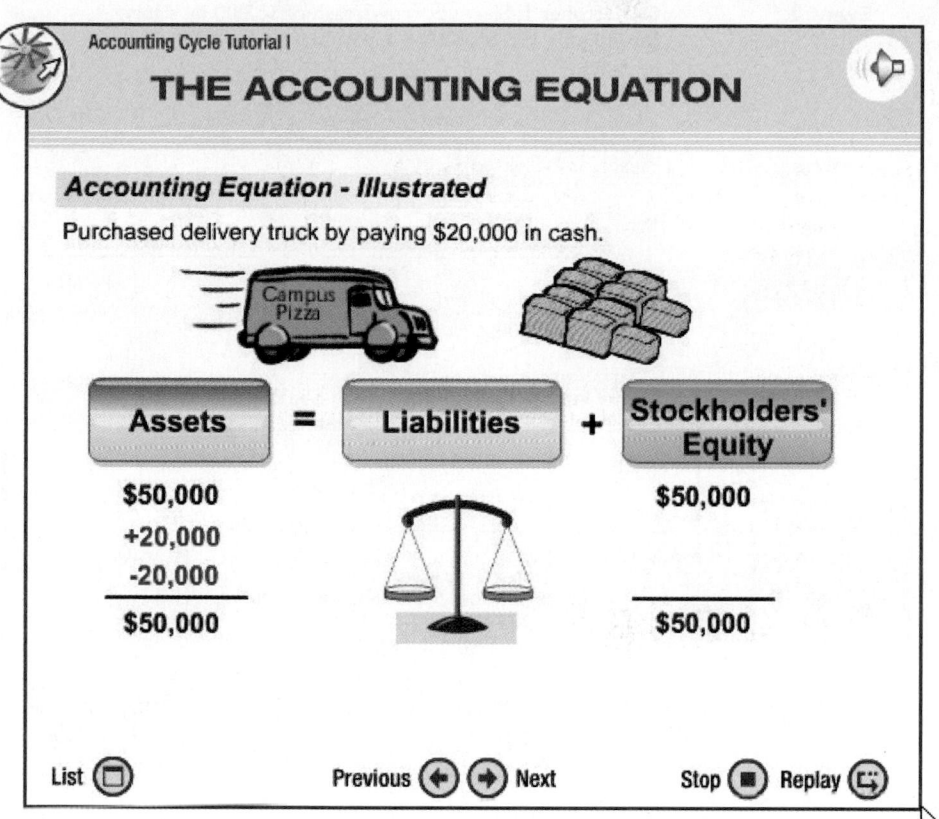

The Accounting Cycle Tutorial is available at **www.wiley.com/college/kimmel.**

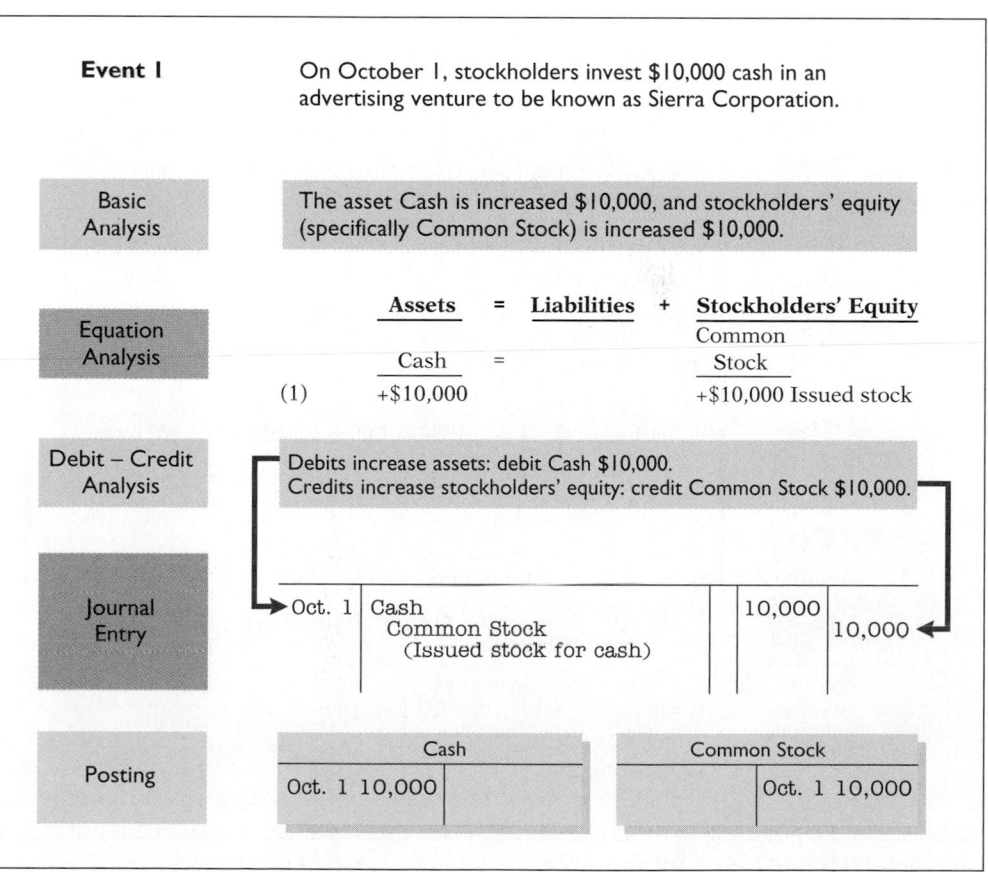

Illustration 3-20
Investment of cash by stockholders

Illustration 3-21   Issue of note payable

Illustration 3-22
Purchase of office
equipment

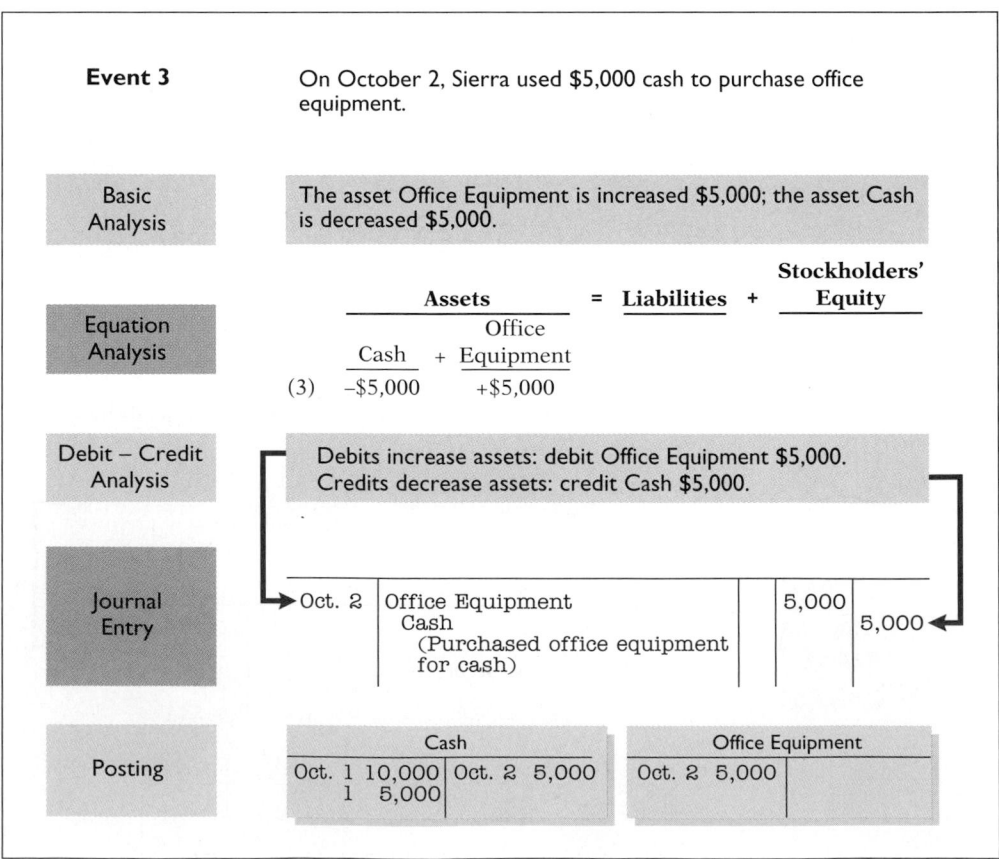

Illustration 3-23   Receipt of cash in advance from customer

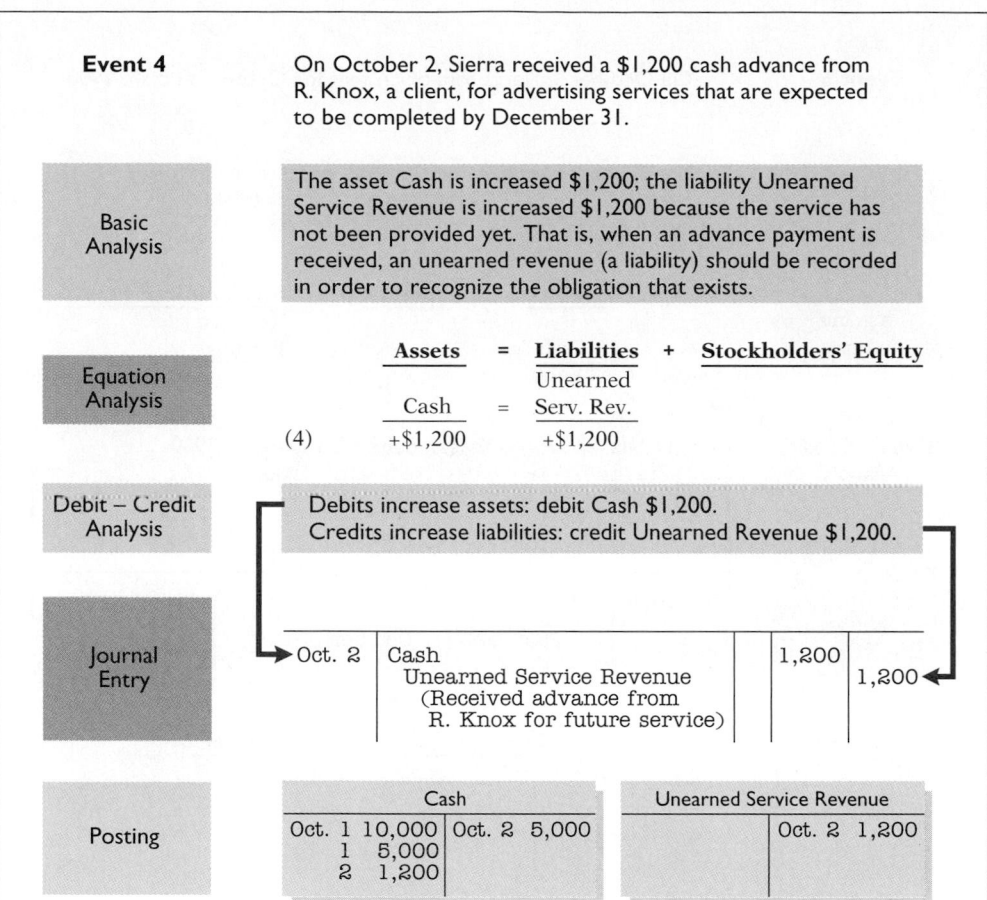

Event 4

On October 2, Sierra received a $1,200 cash advance from R. Knox, a client, for advertising services that are expected to be completed by December 31.

Basic Analysis

The asset Cash is increased $1,200; the liability Unearned Service Revenue is increased $1,200 because the service has not been provided yet. That is, when an advance payment is received, an unearned revenue (a liability) should be recorded in order to recognize the obligation that exists.

Equation Analysis

	Assets	=	Liabilities	+	Stockholders' Equity
			Unearned		
	Cash	=	Serv. Rev.		
(4)	+$1,200		+$1,200		

Debit – Credit Analysis

Debits increase assets: debit Cash $1,200.
Credits increase liabilities: credit Unearned Revenue $1,200.

Journal Entry

Oct. 2	Cash	1,200	
	Unearned Service Revenue		1,200
	(Received advance from		
	R. Knox for future service)		

Posting

Cash				Unearned Service Revenue	
Oct. 1	10,000	Oct. 2	5,000		Oct. 2 1,200
1	5,000				
2	1,200				

Illustration 3-24
Services provided for cash

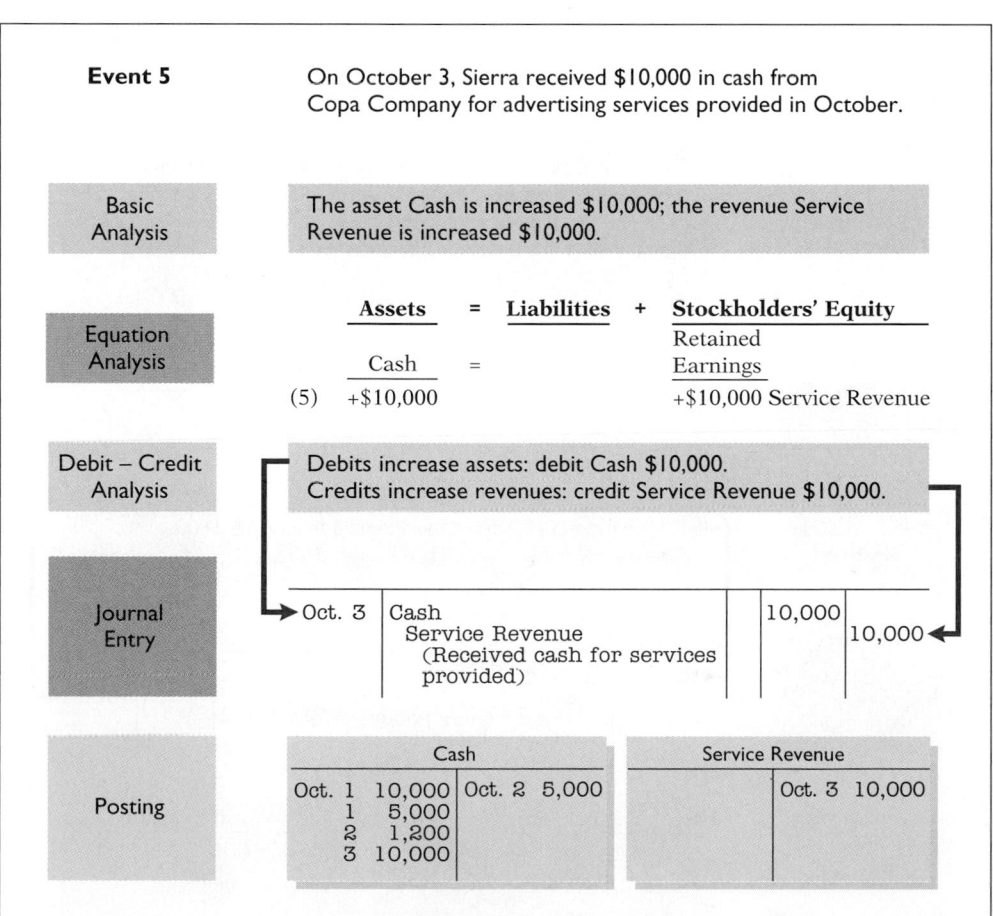

Event 5

On October 3, Sierra received $10,000 in cash from Copa Company for advertising services provided in October.

Basic Analysis

The asset Cash is increased $10,000; the revenue Service Revenue is increased $10,000.

Equation Analysis

	Assets	=	Liabilities	+	Stockholders' Equity
					Retained
	Cash	=			Earnings
(5)	+$10,000				+$10,000 Service Revenue

Debit – Credit Analysis

Debits increase assets: debit Cash $10,000.
Credits increase revenues: credit Service Revenue $10,000.

Journal Entry

Oct. 3	Cash	10,000	
	Service Revenue		10,000
	(Received cash for services		
	provided)		

Posting

Cash				Service Revenue	
Oct. 1	10,000	Oct. 2	5,000		Oct. 3 10,000
1	5,000				
2	1,200				
3	10,000				

121

Illustration 3-25
Payment of rent in cash

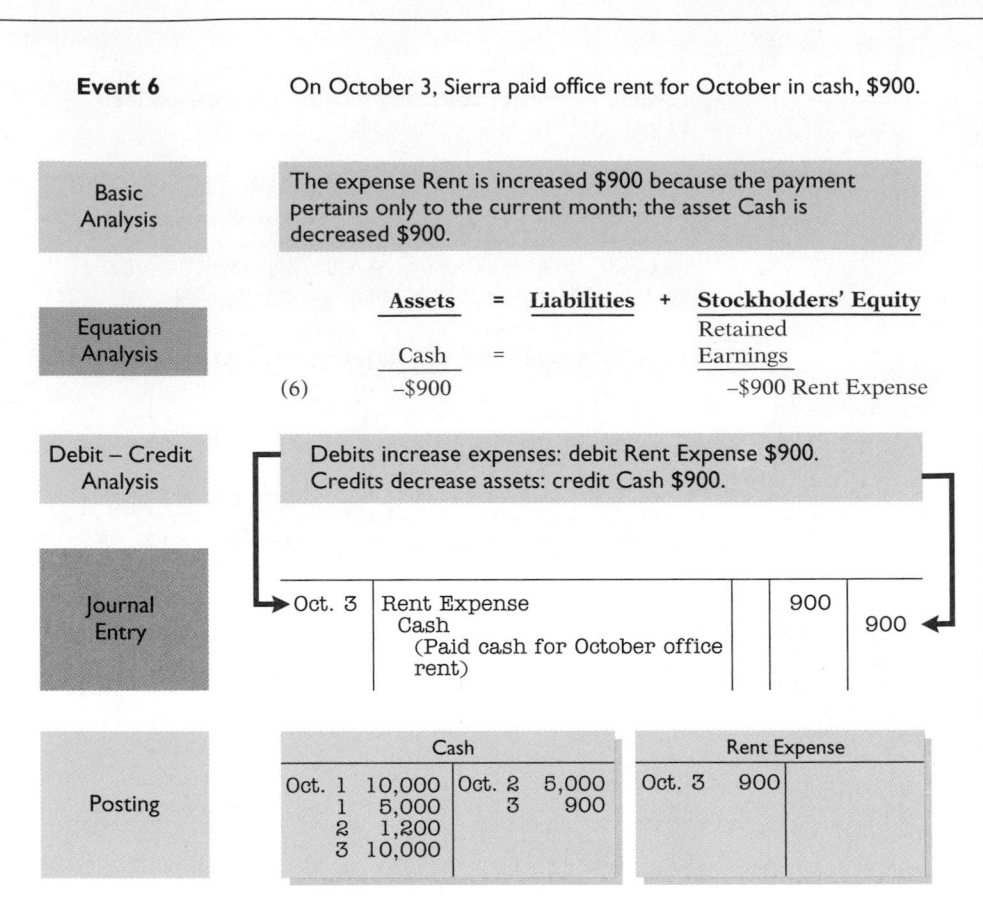

Event 6   On October 3, Sierra paid office rent for October in cash, $900.

Basic Analysis   The expense Rent is increased $900 because the payment pertains only to the current month; the asset Cash is decreased $900.

Equation Analysis

Assets	=	Liabilities	+	Stockholders' Equity
				Retained
Cash	=			Earnings
(6) −$900				−$900 Rent Expense

Debit – Credit Analysis   Debits increase expenses: debit Rent Expense $900.
Credits decrease assets: credit Cash $900.

Journal Entry

Oct. 3	Rent Expense	900	
	Cash		900
	(Paid cash for October office rent)		

Posting

Cash				Rent Expense	
Oct. 1	10,000	Oct. 2	5,000	Oct. 3	900
1	5,000	3	900		
2	1,200				
3	10,000				

Illustration 3-26
Purchase of insurance
policy in cash

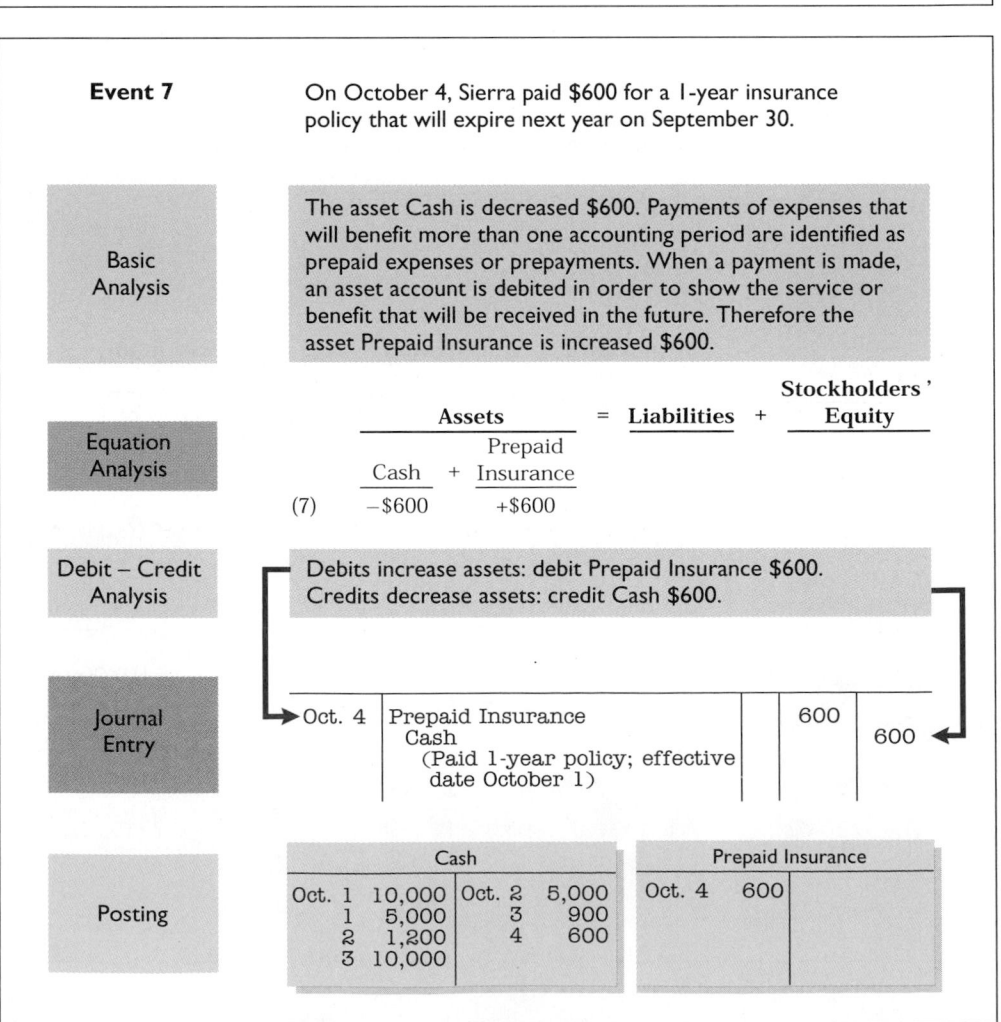

Event 7   On October 4, Sierra paid $600 for a 1-year insurance policy that will expire next year on September 30.

Basic Analysis   The asset Cash is decreased $600. Payments of expenses that will benefit more than one accounting period are identified as prepaid expenses or prepayments. When a payment is made, an asset account is debited in order to show the service or benefit that will be received in the future. Therefore the asset Prepaid Insurance is increased $600.

Equation Analysis

	Assets		=	Liabilities	+	Stockholders' Equity
		Prepaid				
	Cash +	Insurance				
(7)	−$600	+$600				

Debit – Credit Analysis   Debits increase assets: debit Prepaid Insurance $600.
Credits decrease assets: credit Cash $600.

Journal Entry

Oct. 4	Prepaid Insurance	600	
	Cash		600
	(Paid 1-year policy; effective date October 1)		

Posting

Cash				Prepaid Insurance	
Oct. 1	10,000	Oct. 2	5,000	Oct. 4	600
1	5,000	3	900		
2	1,200	4	600		
3	10,000				

Illustration 3-27
Purchase of supplies on account

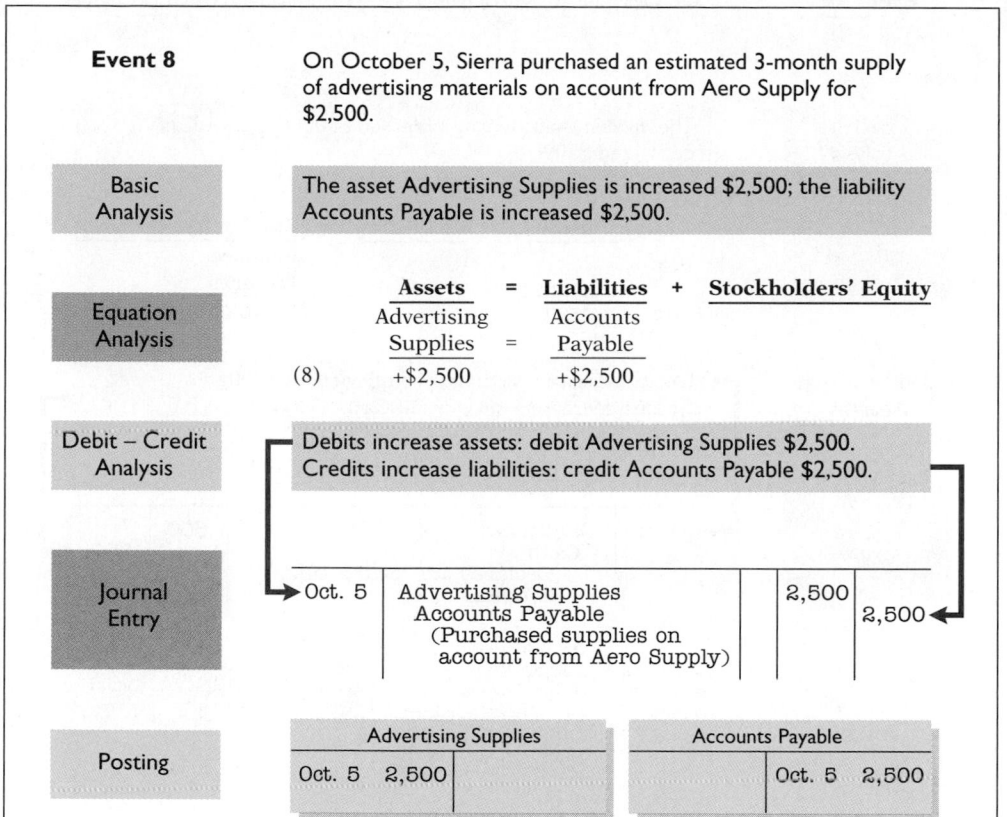

Event 8

On October 5, Sierra purchased an estimated 3-month supply of advertising materials on account from Aero Supply for $2,500.

Basic Analysis

The asset Advertising Supplies is increased $2,500; the liability Accounts Payable is increased $2,500.

Equation Analysis

	Assets	=	**Liabilities**	+	**Stockholders' Equity**
	Advertising Supplies	=	Accounts Payable		
(8)	+$2,500		+$2,500		

Debit – Credit Analysis

Debits increase assets: debit Advertising Supplies $2,500.
Credits increase liabilities: credit Accounts Payable $2,500.

Journal Entry

Oct. 5	Advertising Supplies	2,500	
	Accounts Payable		2,500
	(Purchased supplies on account from Aero Supply)		

Posting

Advertising Supplies		Accounts Payable	
Oct. 5 2,500			Oct. 5 2,500

Illustration 3-28 Hiring of new employees

Event 9

On October 9, Sierra hired four employees to begin work on October 15. Each employee is to receive a weekly salary of $500 for a 5-day work week, payable every 2 weeks — first payment made on October 26.

Basic Analysis

An accounting transaction has not occurred. There is only an agreement that the employees will begin work on October 15. Thus, a debit–credit analysis is not needed because there is no accounting entry. (See transaction of October 26 for first entry.)

Illustration 3-29
Payment of dividend

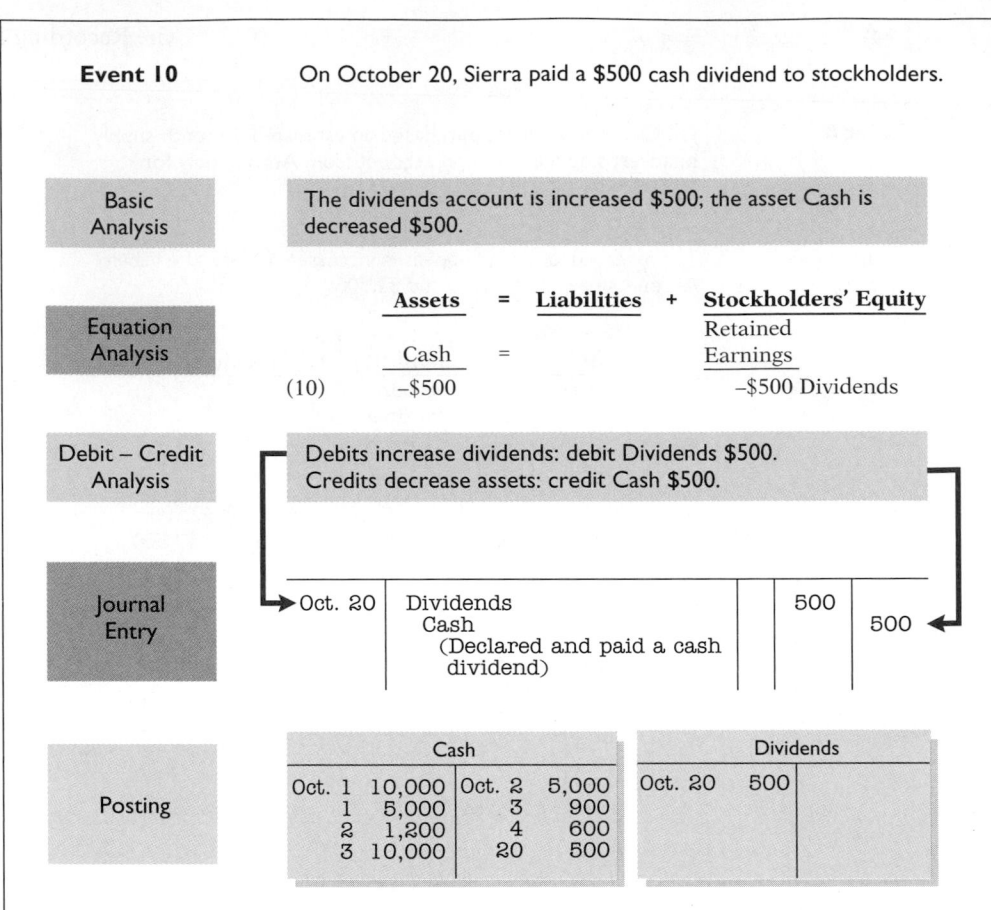

Event 10 — On October 20, Sierra paid a $500 cash dividend to stockholders.

Basic Analysis
The dividends account is increased $500; the asset Cash is decreased $500.

Equation Analysis

	Assets	=	Liabilities	+	Stockholders' Equity
					Retained
	Cash	=			Earnings
(10)	−$500				−$500 Dividends

Debit – Credit Analysis
Debits increase dividends: debit Dividends $500.
Credits decrease assets: credit Cash $500.

Journal Entry

Oct. 20	Dividends	500	
	Cash		500
	(Declared and paid a cash dividend)		

Posting

Cash						Dividends		
Oct. 1	10,000	Oct. 2	5,000		Oct. 20	500		
1	5,000	3	900					
2	1,200	4	600					
3	10,000	20	500					

Illustration 3-30
Payment of cash for
employee salaries

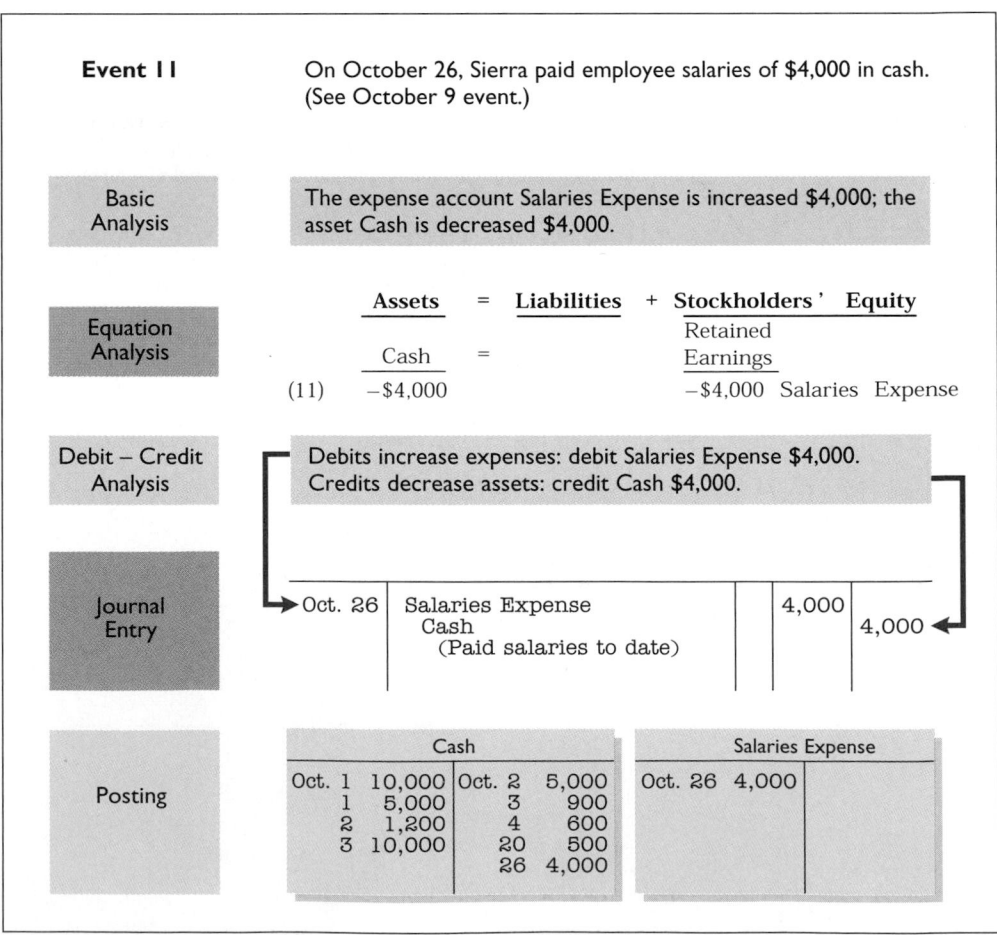

Event 11 — On October 26, Sierra paid employee salaries of $4,000 in cash. (See October 9 event.)

Basic Analysis
The expense account Salaries Expense is increased $4,000; the asset Cash is decreased $4,000.

Equation Analysis

	Assets	=	Liabilities	+	Stockholders' Equity
					Retained
	Cash	=			Earnings
(11)	−$4,000				−$4,000 Salaries Expense

Debit – Credit Analysis
Debits increase expenses: debit Salaries Expense $4,000.
Credits decrease assets: credit Cash $4,000.

Journal Entry

Oct. 26	Salaries Expense	4,000	
	Cash		4,000
	(Paid salaries to date)		

Posting

Cash						Salaries Expense		
Oct. 1	10,000	Oct. 2	5,000		Oct. 26	4,000		
1	5,000	3	900					
2	1,200	4	600					
3	10,000	20	500					
		26	4,000					

SUMMARY ILLUSTRATION OF JOURNALIZING AND POSTING

The journal for Sierra Corporation for the month of October is summarized in Illustration 3-31. The ledger is shown in Illustration 3-32 with all balances highlighted in red.

GENERAL JOURNAL

Date		Account Titles and Explanation	Debit	Credit
2007				
Oct.	1	Cash	10,000	
		Common Stock		10,000
		(Issued stock for cash)		
	1	Cash	5,000	
		Notes Payable		5,000
		(Issued 3-month, 12% note payable for cash)		
	2	Office Equipment	5,000	
		Cash		5,000
		(Purchased office equipment for cash)		
	2	Cash	1,200	
		Unearned Service Revenue		1,200
		(Received advance from R. Knox for future service)		
	3	Cash	10,000	
		Service Revenue		10,000
		(Received cash for services provided)		
	3	Rent Expense	900	
		Cash		900
		(Paid cash for October office rent)		
	4	Prepaid Insurance	600	
		Cash		600
		(Paid 1-year policy; effective date October 1)		
	5	Advertising Supplies	2,500	
		Accounts Payable		2,500
		(Purchased supplies on account from Aero Supply)		
	20	Dividends	500	
		Cash		500
		(Declared and paid a cash dividend)		
	26	Salaries Expense	4,000	
		Cash		4,000
		(Paid salaries to date)		

Illustration 3-31 General journal for Sierra Corporation

GENERAL LEDGER

Cash

Oct. 1	10,000	Oct. 2	5,000
1	5,000	3	900
2	1,200	4	600
3	10,000	20	500
		26	4,000
Bal.	**15,200**		

Unearned Service Revenue

		Oct. 2	1,200
		Bal.	**1,200**

Illustration 3-32 General ledger for Sierra Corporation

Illustration 3-32
(continued) General
ledger for Sierra
Corporation

GENERAL LEDGER

Advertising Supplies				Common Stock		
Oct. 5	2,500				Oct. 1	10,000
Bal.	**2,500**				Bal.	**10,000**

Prepaid Insurance				Dividends		
Oct. 4	600			Oct. 20	500	
Bal.	**600**			Bal.	**500**	

Office Equipment				Service Revenue		
Oct. 2	5,000				Oct. 3	10,000
Bal.	**5,000**				Bal.	**10,000**

Notes Payable				Salaries Expense		
		Oct. 1	5,000	Oct. 26	4,000	
		Bal.	**5,000**	Bal.	**4,000**	

Accounts Payable				Rent Expense		
		Oct. 5	2,500	Oct. 3	900	
		Bal.	**2,500**	Bal.	**900**	

BEFORE YOU GO ON . . .

▶ Review It

1. How does journalizing differ from posting?
2. What is the purpose of (a) the ledger and (b) a chart of accounts?

▶ Do It

Selected transactions from the journal of Faital Inc. during its first month of operations are presented below. Post these transactions to T accounts.

Date		Account Titles	Debit	Credit
July	1	Cash	30,000	
		Common Stock		30,000
	9	Accounts Receivable	6,000	
		Service Revenue		6,000
	24	Cash	4,000	
		Accounts Receivable		4,000

Action Plan

• Journalize transactions to keep track of financial activities (receipts, payments, receivables, payables, etc.).

• To make entries useful, classify and summarize them by posting the entries to specific ledger accounts.

Solution

Cash				Accounts Receivable		
July 1	30,000			July 9	6,000	July 24 4,000
24	4,000					

Common Stock			Service Revenue		
	July 1	30,000		July 9	6,000

The Trial Balance

A **trial balance** lists accounts and their balances at a given time. A company usually prepares a trial balance at the end of an accounting period. The accounts are listed in the order in which they appear in the ledger. Debit balances are listed in the left column and credit balances in the right column. The totals of the two columns must be equal.

STUDY OBJECTIVE
8
Explain the purposes of a trial balance.

The trial balance proves the mathematical equality of debits and credits after posting. Under the double-entry system this equality occurs when the sum of the debit account balances equals the sum of the credit account balances. **A trial balance may also uncover errors in journalizing and posting.** For example, a trial balance may well have detected the error at Fidelity Investments discussed in the Feature Story. **In addition, a trial balance is useful in the preparation of financial statements.**

These are the procedures for preparing a trial balance:

1. List the account titles and their balances.
2. Total the debit column and total the credit column.
3. Verify the equality of the two columns.

Illustration 3-33 presents the trial balance prepared from the ledger of Sierra Corporation. Note that the total debits, $28,700, equal the total credits, $28,700.

SIERRA CORPORATION Trial Balance October 31, 2007		
	Debit	**Credit**
Cash	$ 15,200	
Advertising Supplies	2,500	
Prepaid Insurance	600	
Office Equipment	5,000	
Notes Payable		$ 5,000
Accounts Payable		2,500
Unearned Service Revenue		1,200
Common Stock		10,000
Dividends	500	
Service Revenue		10,000
Salaries Expense	4,000	
Rent Expense	900	
	$28,700	$28,700

Illustration 3-33 Sierra Corporation trial balance

LIMITATIONS OF A TRIAL BALANCE

A trial balance does not prove that all transactions have been recorded or that the ledger is correct. Numerous errors may exist even though the trial balance columns agree. For example, the trial balance may balance even when any of the following occurs: (1) a transaction is not journalized, (2) a correct journal entry is not posted, (3) a journal entry is posted twice, (4) incorrect accounts are used in journalizing or posting, or (5) offsetting errors are made in recording the amount of a transaction. In other words, as long as equal debits and credits are posted, even to the wrong account or in the wrong amount, the total debits will equal the total credits. Nevertheless, despite these limitations, the trial balance is a useful screen for finding errors and is frequently used in practice.

BEFORE YOU GO ON . . .

►**Review It**

1. What is a trial balance, and how is it prepared?
2. What is the primary purpose of a trial balance?
3. What are the limitations of a trial balance?

Decision Toolkit

Decision Checkpoints	Info Needed for Decision	Tool to Use for Decision	How to Evaluate Results
How do you determine that debits equal credits?	All account balances	Trial balance	List the account titles and their balances; total the debit and credit columns; verify equality.

Using the Decision Toolkit

The Kansas Farmers' Vertically Integrated Cooperative, Inc. (K-VIC), was formed by over 200 northeast Kansas farmers in the late 1980s. Its purpose is to use raw materials, primarily grain and meat products grown by K-VIC's members, to process this material into end-user food products, and to distribute the products nationally. Profits not needed for expansion or investment are returned to the members annually, on a pro-rata basis, according to the market value of the grain and meat products received from each farmer.

Assume that the following information was prepared for K-VIC's trial balance.

KANSAS FARMERS' VERTICALLY INTEGRATED COOPERATIVE, INC.
Trial Balance
December 31, 2007
(in thousands)

	Debit	Credit
Accounts Receivable	$ 712,000	
Accounts Payable		$ 37,000
Advertising and Promotion Payable		141,000
Buildings	365,000	
Cash	32,000	
Cost of Goods Sold	2,384,000	
Current Maturity of Long-Term Debt		12,000
Inventories	1,291,000	
Land	110,000	
Long-Term Debt		873,000
Machinery and Equipment	63,000	
Notes Payable to Members		495,000
Retained Earnings		822,000
Sales Revenue		3,741,000
Salaries and Wages Payable		62,000
Selling and Administrative Expense	651,000	
Trucking Expense	500,000	
	$6,108,000	$6,183,000

Because the trial balance is not in balance, you have checked with various people responsible for entering accounting data and have discovered the following.

1. The purchase of 35 new trucks, costing $7 million and paid for with cash, was not recorded.
2. A data entry clerk accidentally deleted the account name for an account with a credit balance of $472 million, so the amount was added to the Long-Term Debt account in the trial balance.
3. December cash sales revenue of $75 million was credited to the Sales Revenue account, but the other half of the entry was not made.
4. $50 million of selling expenses were mistakenly charged to Trucking Expense.

Instructions
Answer these questions.
(a) Which mistake(s) have caused the trial balance to be out of balance?
(b) Should all of the items be corrected? Explain.
(c) What is the name of the account the data entry clerk deleted?
(d) Make the necessary corrections and balance the trial balance.
(e) On your trial balance, write BAL beside the accounts that go on the balance sheet and INC beside those that go on the income statement.

Solution
(a) Only mistake #3 has caused the trial balance to be out of balance.
(b) All of the items should be corrected. The misclassification error (mistake #4) on the selling expense would not affect bottom-line net income, but it does affect the amounts reported in the two expense accounts.
(c) There is no Common Stock account, so that must be the account that was deleted by the data entry clerk.
(d) and (e):

KANSAS FARMERS' VERTICALLY INTEGRATED COOPERATIVE, INC.
Trial Balance
December 31, 2007
(in thousands)

	Debit	Credit	
Accounts Receivable	$ 712,000		BAL
Accounts Payable		$ 37,000	BAL
Advertising and Promotion Payable		141,000	BAL
Buildings	365,000		BAL
Cash ($32,000 − $7,000 + $75,000)	100,000		BAL
Common Stock		472,000	BAL
Cost of Goods Sold	2,384,000		INC
Current Maturity of Long-Term Debt		12,000	BAL
Inventories	1,291,000		BAL
Land	110,000		BAL
Long-Term Debt		401,000	BAL
Machinery and Equipment	70,000		BAL
Notes Payable to Members		495,000	BAL
Retained Earnings		822,000	BAL
Sales Revenue		3,741,000	INC
Salaries and Wages Payable		62,000	BAL
Selling and Administrative Expense	701,000		INC
Trucking Expense	450,000		INC
	$6,183,000	$6,183,000	

THE NAVIGATOR

Summary of Study Objectives

1 *Analyze the effect of business transactions on the basic accounting equation.* Each business transaction must have a dual effect on the accounting equation. For example, if an individual asset is increased, there must be a corresponding (a) decrease in another asset, or (b) increase in a specific liability, or (c) increase in stockholders' equity.

2 *Explain what an account is and how it helps in the recording process.* An account is an individual accounting record of increases and decreases in specific asset, liability, and stockholders' equity items.

3 *Define debits and credits and explain how they are used to record business transactions.* The terms *debit* and *credit* are synonymous with *left* and *right*. Assets, dividends, and expenses are increased by debits and decreased by credits. Liabilities, common stock, retained earnings, and revenues are increased by credits and decreased by debits.

4 *Identify the basic steps in the recording process.* The basic steps in the recording process are: (a) analyze each transaction in terms of its effect on the accounts, (b) enter the transaction information in a journal, and (c) transfer the journal information to the appropriate accounts in the ledger.

5 *Explain what a journal is and how it helps in the recording process.* The initial accounting record of a transaction is entered in a journal before the data are entered in the accounts. A journal (a) discloses in one place the complete effect of a transaction, (b) provides a chronological record of transactions, and (c) prevents or locates errors because the debit and credit amounts for each entry can be readily compared.

6 *Explain what a ledger is and how it helps in the recording process.* The entire group of accounts maintained by a company is referred to collectively as a ledger. The ledger keeps in one place all the information about changes in specific account balances.

7 *Explain what posting is and how it helps in the recording process.* Posting is the procedure of transferring journal entries to the ledger accounts. This phase of the recording process accumulates the effects of journalized transactions in the individual accounts.

8 *Explain the purposes of a trial balance.* A trial balance is a list of accounts and their balances at a given time. The primary purpose of the trial balance is to prove the mathematical equality of debits and credits after posting. A trial balance also uncovers errors in journalizing and posting and is useful in preparing financial statements.

THE NAVIGATOR

Decision Toolkit—A Summary

Decision Checkpoints	Info Needed for Decision	Tool to Use for Decision	How to Evaluate Results
Has an accounting transaction occurred?	Details of the event	Accounting equation	If the event affected assets, liabilities, or stockholders' equity, then record as a transaction.
How do you determine that debits equal credits?	All account balances	Trial balance	List the account titles and their balances; total the debit and credit colums; verify equality.

Glossary

Account An individual accounting record of increases and decreases in specific asset, liability, or stockholders' equity items. (p. 108)

Accounting information system The system of collecting and processing transaction data and communicating financial information to interested parties. (p. 100)

Accounting transactions Events that require recording in the financial statements because they affect assets, liabilities, or stockholders' equity. (p. 101)

Chart of accounts A list of a company's accounts. (p. 118)

Credit The right side of an account. (p. 109)

Debit The left side of an account. (p. 109)

Double-entry system A system that records the dual effect of each transaction in appropriate accounts. (p. 109)

General journal The most basic form of journal. (p. 114)

General ledger A ledger that contains all asset, liability, and stockholders' equity accounts. (p. 117)

Journal An accounting record in which transactions are initially recorded in chronological order. (p. 114)

Journalizing The procedure of entering transaction data in the journal. (p. 115)

Ledger The group of accounts maintained by a company. (p. 117)

Posting The procedure of transferring journal entries to the ledger accounts. (p. 118)

T account The basic form of an account. (p. 108)

Trial balance A list of accounts and their balances at a given time. (p. 127)

Demonstration Problem

Bob Sample and other student investors opened Campus Carpet Cleaning, Inc. on September 1, 2007. During the first month of operations the following transactions occurred.

Sept. 1 Stockholders invested $20,000 cash in the business.
2 Paid $1,000 cash for store rent for the month of September.
3 Purchased industrial carpet-cleaning equipment for $25,000, paying $10,000 in cash and signing a $15,000 6-month, 12% note payable.
4 Paid $1,200 for 1-year accident insurance policy.
10 Received bill from the *Daily News* for advertising the opening of the cleaning service, $200.
15 Performed services on account for $6,200.
20 Declared and paid a $700 cash dividend to stockholders.
30 Received $5,000 from customers billed on September 15.

The chart of accounts for the company is the same as for Sierra Corporation except for the following additional accounts: Cleaning Equipment and Advertising Expense.

Instructions
(a) Journalize the September transactions.
(b) Open ledger accounts and post the September transactions.
(c) Prepare a trial balance at September 30, 2007.

Solution to Demonstration Problem

(a)

GENERAL JOURNAL

Date	Account Titles and Explanation	Debit	Credit
2007			
Sept. 1	Cash	20,000	
	Common Stock		20,000
	(Issued stock for cash)		
2	Rent Expense	1,000	
	Cash		1,000
	(Paid September rent)		
3	Cleaning Equipment	25,000	
	Cash		10,000
	Notes Payable		15,000
	(Purchased cleaning equipment for cash and 6-month, 12% note payable)		
4	Prepaid Insurance	1,200	
	Cash		1,200
	(Paid 1-year insurance policy)		
10	Advertising Expense	200	
	Accounts Payable		200
	(Received bill from *Daily News* for advertising)		
15	Accounts Receivable	6,200	
	Service Revenue		6,200
	(Services performed on account)		

Action Plan
- Proceed through the accounting cycle in the following sequence:

1. Make separate journal entries for each transaction.

2. Note that all debits precede all credit entries.

3. In journalizing, make sure debits equal credits.

4. In journalizing, use specific account titles taken from the chart of accounts.

5. Provide an appropriate explanation of each journal entry.

6. Arrange ledger in statement order, beginning with the balance sheet accounts.

7. Post in chronological order.

8. Prepare a trial balance, which lists accounts in the order in which they appear in the ledger.

9. List debit balances in the left column and credit balances in the right column.

20	Dividends		700	
	Cash			700
	(Declared and paid a cash dividend)			
30	Cash		5,000	
	Accounts Receivable			5,000
	(Collection of accounts receivable)			

(b)   **GENERAL LEDGER**

Cash

Sept.	1	20,000	Sept.	2	1,000
	30	5,000		3	10,000
				4	1,200
				20	700
Bal.		12,100			

Common Stock

			Sept.	1	20,000
			Bal.		20,000

Accounts Receivable

Sept.	15	6,200	Sept.	30	5,000
Bal.		1,200			

Dividends

Sept.	20	700		
Bal.		700		

Prepaid Insurance

Sept.	4	1,200		
Bal.		1,200		

Service Revenue

			Sept.	15	6,200
			Bal.		6,200

Cleaning Equipment

Sept.	3	25,000		
Bal.		25,000		

Advertising Expense

Sept.	10	200		
Bal.		200		

Notes Payable

			Sept.	3	15,000
			Bal.		15,000

Rent Expense

Sept.	2	1,000		
Bal.		1,000		

Accounts Payable

			Sept.	10	200
			Bal.		200

(c)   **CAMPUS CARPET CLEANING, INC.**
Trial Balance
September 30, 2007

	Debit	Credit
Cash	$12,100	
Accounts Receivable	1,200	
Prepaid Insurance	1,200	
Cleaning Equipment	25,000	
Notes Payable		$15,000
Accounts Payable		200
Common Stock		20,000
Dividends	700	
Service Revenue		6,200
Advertising Expense	200	
Rent Expense	1,000	
	$41,400	$41,400

THE NAVIGATOR

Self-Study Questions

Answers are at the end of the chapter.

(SO 1) **1.** The effects on the basic accounting equation of performing services for cash are to:
    (a) increase assets and decrease stockholders' equity.
    (b) increase assets and increase stockholders' equity.
    (c) increase assets and increase liabilities.
    (d) increase liabilities and increase stockholders' equity.

(SO 1) **2.** Genesis Company buys a $900 machine on credit. This transaction will affect the:
    (a) income statement only.
    (b) balance sheet only.
    (c) income statement and retained earnings statement only.
    (d) income statement, retained earnings statement, and balance sheet.

(SO 2) **3.** Which statement about an account is *true*?
    (a) In its simplest form, an account consists of two parts.
    (b) An account is an individual accounting record of increases and decreases in specific asset, liability, and stockholders' equity items.
    (c) There are separate accounts for specific assets and liabilities but only one account for stockholders' equity items.
    (d) The left side of an account is the credit or decrease side.

(SO 3) **4.** Debits:
    (a) increase both assets and liabilities.
    (b) decrease both assets and liabilities.
    (c) increase assets and decrease liabilities.
    (d) decrease assets and increase liabilities.

(SO 3) **5.** A revenue account:
    (a) is increased by debits.
    (b) is decreased by credits.
    (c) has a normal balance of a debit.
    (d) is increased by credits.

(SO 3) **6.** Which accounts normally have debit balances?
    (a) Assets, expenses, and revenues.
    (b) Assets, expenses, and retained earnings.
    (c) Assets, liabilities, and dividends.
    (d) Assets, dividends, and expenses.

(SO 4) **7.** Which is *not* part of the recording process?
    (a) Analyzing transactions.
    (b) Preparing a trial balance.
    (c) Entering transactions in a journal.
    (d) Posting transactions.

(SO 5) **8.** Which of these statements about a journal is *false*?
    (a) It contains only revenue and expense accounts.
    (b) It provides a chronological record of transactions.
    (c) It helps to locate errors because the debit and credit amounts for each entry can be readily compared.
    (d) It discloses in one place the complete effect of a transaction.

(SO 6) **9.** A ledger:
    (a) contains only asset and liability accounts.
    (b) should show accounts in alphabetical order.
    (c) is a collection of the entire group of accounts maintained by a company.
    (d) provides a chronological record of transactions.

(SO 7) **10.** Posting:
    (a) normally occurs before journalizing.
    (b) transfers ledger transaction data to the journal.
    (c) is an optional step in the recording process.
    (d) transfers journal entries to ledger accounts.

(SO 8) **11.** A trial balance:
    (a) is a list of accounts with their balances at a given time.
    (b) proves the mathematical accuracy of journalized transactions.
    (c) will not balance if a correct journal entry is posted twice.
    (d) proves that all transactions have been recorded.

(SO 8) **12.** A trial balance will *not* balance if:
    (a) a correct journal entry is posted twice.
    (b) the purchase of supplies on account is debited to Supplies and credited to Cash.
    (c) a $100 cash dividend is debited to Dividends for $1,000 and credited to Cash for $100.
    (d) a $450 payment on account is debited to Accounts Payable for $45 and credited to Cash for $45.

Go to the book's website, **www.wiley.com/college/kimmel**, to access additional Self-Study Questions.

✓ THE NAVIGATOR

Questions

1. Describe the accounting information system and the steps in the recording process.

2. Can a business enter into a transaction that affects only the left side of the basic accounting equation? If so, give an example.

(a) Purchased supplies on account.
(b) Received cash for providing a service.
(c) Expenses paid in cash.

*Determine effect of
transactions on basic
accounting equation.*
(SO 1)

BE3-2   During 2007, Walters Corp. entered into the following transactions.
1. Borrowed $80,000 by issuing bonds.
2. Paid $9,000 cash dividend to stockholders.
3. Received $17,000 cash from a customer who had previously been billed for services provided.
4. Purchased supplies on account for $3,100.

Using the following tabular analysis, show the effect of each transaction on the accounting equation. Put explanations for changes to Stockholders' Equity in the right-hand margin. Use Illustration 3-2 (page 107) as a model.

Assets			=	Liabilities		+	Stockholders' Equity	
Cash +	Accounts Receivable	+ Supplies =		Accounts Payable	+ Bonds Payable	+	Common Stock	+ Retained Earnings

*Determine effect of
transactions on basic
accounting equation.*
(SO 1)

BE3-3   During 2004, Starbucks entered into the following transactions.
1. Purchased property, plant, and equipment for $386,176,000 cash.
2. Issued common stock to investors for $137,590,000 cash.
3. Purchased inventory of $77,662,000 on account.

Using the following tabular analysis, show the effect of each transaction on the accounting equation. Put explanations for changes to Stockholders' Equity in the right-hand margin. Use Illustration 3-2 (page 107) as a model.

Assets			=	Liabilities +	Stockholders' Equity	
Cash	+ Inventory +	Property, Plant, and Equipment =		Accounts Payable	+ Common Stock	+ Retained Earnings

*Indicate debit and credit
effects.*
(SO 3)

BE3-4   For each of the following accounts indicate the effect of a debit or a credit on the account and the normal balance.
(a) Accounts Payable.   (d) Accounts Receivable.
(b) Advertising Expense.   (e) Retained Earnings.
(c) Service Revenue.   (f) Dividends.

*Identify accounts to be
debited and credited.*
(SO 3)

BE3-5   Transactions for Alvarez Company for the month of June are presented next. Identify the accounts to be debited and credited for each transaction.

June 1   Issues common stock to investors in exchange for $2,500 cash.
      2   Buys equipment on account for $1,100.
      3   Pays $500 to landlord for June rent.
     12   Bills Chas. Thon $700 for welding work done.

Journalize transactions.
(SO 5)
*Identify steps in the
recording process.*
(SO 4)

BE3-6   Use the data in BE3-5 and journalize the transactions. (You may omit explanations.)

BE3-7   Jeremy Oslo, a fellow student, is unclear about the basic steps in the recording process. Identify and briefly explain the steps in the order in which they occur.

*Indicate basic debit–credit
analysis.*
(SO 4)

BE3-8   Norris Corporation has the following transactions during August of the current year. Indicate (a) the basic analysis and (b) the debit–credit analysis illustrated on pages 119–124.

Aug. 1   Issues shares of common stock to investors in exchange for $5,000.
      4   Pays insurance in advance for 3 months, $1,500.
     16   Receives $900 from clients for services rendered.
     27   Pays the secretary $500 salary.

Journalize transactions.
(SO 5)
*Post journal entries to
T accounts.*
(SO 7)

BE3-9   Use the data in BE3-8 and journalize the transactions. (You may omit explanations.)

BE3-10 Selected transactions for Gonzales Company are presented in journal form (without explanations). Post the transactions to T accounts.

Date	Account Title	Debit	Credit
May 5	Accounts Receivable	2,800	
	Service Revenue		2,800
12	Cash	1,900	
	Accounts Receivable		1,900
15	Cash	2,000	
	Service Revenue		2,000

Prepare a trial balance.
(SO 8)

BE3-11   From the ledger balances below, prepare a trial balance for Shumway Company at June 30, 2007. All account balances are normal.

Accounts Payable	$ 3,000	Service Revenue	$6,600
Cash	3,400	Accounts Receivable	3,000
Common Stock	18,000	Salaries Expense	4,000
Dividends	1,200	Rent Expense	1,000
Equipment	15,000		

Prepare a corrected trial balance.
(SO 8)

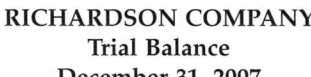

BE3-12   An inexperienced bookkeeper prepared the following trial balance that does not balance. Prepare a correct trial balance, assuming all account balances are normal.

RICHARDSON COMPANY
Trial Balance
December 31, 2007

	Debit	Credit
Cash	$18,800	
Prepaid Insurance		$ 3,500
Accounts Payable		2,500
Unearned Revenue	1,800	
Common Stock		10,000
Retained Earnings		6,400
Dividends		5,000
Service Revenue		25,600
Salaries Expense	16,600	
Rent Expense		2,400
	$37,200	$55,400

Exercises

Analyze the effect of transactions.
(SO 1)

E3-1   Selected transactions for Sidhu Advertising Company, Inc., are listed here.
1. Issued common stock to investors in exchange for cash received from investors.
2. Paid monthly rent.
3. Received cash from customers when service was rendered.
4. Billed customers for services performed.
5. Paid dividend to stockholders.
6. Incurred advertising expense on account.
7. Received cash from customers billed in (4).
8. Purchased additional equipment for cash.
9. Purchased equipment on account.

Instructions
Describe the effect of each transaction on assets, liabilities, and stockholders' equity. For example, the first answer is: (1) Increase in assets and increase in stockholders' equity.

Analyze the effect of transactions on assets, liabilities, and stockholders' equity.
(SO 1)

E3-2   Downtown Company entered into these transactions during May 2007.
1. Purchased computers for office use for $35,000 from Dell on account.
2. Paid $4,000 cash for May rent on storage space.

3. Received $12,000 cash from customers for contracts billed in April.
4. Provided computer services to Brieske Construction Company for $5,000 cash.
5. Paid Southern States Power Co. $11,000 cash for energy usage in May.
6. Stockholders invested an additional $30,000 in the business in exchange for common stock of the company.
7. Paid Dell for the computers purchased in (1).
8. Incurred advertising expense for May of $1,000 on account.

Instructions
Using the following tabular analysis, show the effect of each transaction on the accounting equation. Put explanations for changes to Stockholders' Equity in the right-hand margin. Use Illustration 3-2 (page 107) as a model.

	Assets		=	Liabilities	+	Stockholders' Equity	
Cash +	Accounts Receivable	+ Office Equipment	=	Accounts Payable	+ Common Stock	+	Retained Earnings

E3-3 During 2007, its first year of operations as a delivery service, Cheng Corp. entered into the following transactions. *Determine effect of transactions on basic accounting equation. (SO 1)*

1. Issued shares of common stock to investors in exchange for $110,000 in cash.
2. Borrowed $45,000 by issuing bonds.
3. Purchased delivery trucks for $60,000 cash.
4. Received $16,000 from customers for services provided.
5. Purchased supplies for $4,200 on account.
6. Paid rent of $5,600.
7. Performed services on account for $8,000.
8. Paid salaries of $28,000.
9. Paid a dividend of $11,000 to shareholders.

Instructions
Using the following tabular analysis, show the effect of each transaction on the accounting equation. Put explanations for changes to Stockholders' Equity in the right-hand margin. Use Illustration 3-2 (page 107) as a model.

	Assets			=	Liabilities		+	Stockholders' Equity	
Cash +	Accounts Receivable	+ Supplies +	Property, Plant, and Equipment	=	Accounts Payable	+ Bonds Payable	+	Common Stock	+ Retained Earnings

E3-4 A tabular analysis of the transactions made during August 2007 by Verbos Company during its first month of operations is shown below. Each increase and decrease in stockholders' equity is explained. *Analyze transactions and compute net income. (SO 1)*

		Assets			= Liabilities +		Stockholders' Equity	
	Cash	+ Accounts Receivable	+ Supplies +	Office Equipment	= Accounts Payable	+ Common Stock	+ Retained Earnings	
1.	+$15,000					+$15,000		Issued Common Stock
2.	−1,000			+$5,000	+$4,000			
3.	−750		+$750					
4.	+4,400	+$3,400					+$7,800	Service Revenue
5.	−1,500				−1,500			
6.	−2,000						−2,000	Dividends
7.	−800						−800	Rent Expense
8.	+450	−450						
9.	−3,000						−3,000	Salaries Expense
10.					+500		−500	Utilities Expense

Prepare an income statement, retained earnings statement, and balance sheet.
(SO 1)

Identify debits, credits, and normal balances and journalize transactions.
(SO 3, 5)

Instructions
(a) Describe each transaction.
(b) Determine how much stockholders' equity increased for the month.
(c) Compute the net income for the month.

E3-5 The tabular analysis of transactions for Verbos Company is presented in E3-4.

Instructions
Prepare an income statement and a retained earnings statement for August and a classified balance sheet at August 31, 2007.

E3-6 Selected transactions for Welcome Home, an interior decorator corporation, in its first month of business, are as follows.

1. Issued stock to investors for $12,000 in cash.
2. Purchased used car for $8,000 cash for use in business.
3. Purchased supplies on account for $300.
4. Billed customers $2,600 for services performed.
5. Paid $200 cash for advertising start of the business.
6. Received $1,100 cash from customers billed in transaction (4).
7. Paid creditor $300 cash on account.
8. Paid dividends of $400 cash to stockholders.

Instructions
(a) For each transaction indicate (a) the basic type of account debited and credited (asset, liability, stockholders' equity); (b) the specific account debited and credited (Cash, Rent Expense, Service Revenue, etc.); (c) whether the specific account is increased or decreased; and (d) the normal balance of the specific account. Use the following format, in which transaction 1 is given as an example.

	Account Debited				Account Credited			
	(a)	**(b)**	**(c)**	**(d)**	**(a)**	**(b)**	**(c)**	**(d)**
Trans-action	**Basic Type**	**Specific Account**	**Effect**	**Normal Balance**	**Basic Type**	**Specific Account**	**Effect**	**Normal Balance**
1	Asset	Cash	Increase	Debit	Stock-holders' equity	Common Stock	Increase	Credit

(b) Journalize the transactions. Do not provide explanations.

Analyze transactions and determine their effect on accounts.
(SO 3)

E3-7 This information relates to Matthews Real Estate Agency Corporation.

Oct. 1   Stockholders invested $25,000 in exchange for common stock of the corporation.
   2   Hires an administrative assistant at an annual salary of $42,000.
   3   Buys office furniture for $3,600, on account.
   6   Sells a house and lot for M.E. Mills; commissions due from Mills, $10,800 (not paid by Mills at this time).
   10   Receives cash of $140 as commission for acting as rental agent renting an apartment.
   27   Pays $700 on account for the office furniture purchased on October 3.
   30   Pays the administrative assistant $3,500 in salary for October.

Instructions
Prepare the debit–credit analysis for each transaction as illustrated on pages 119–124.

Journalize transactions.
(SO 5)

E3-8 Transaction data for Matthews Real Estate Agency are presented in E3-7.

Instructions
Journalize the transactions. Do not provide explanations.

Post journal entries and prepare a trial balance.
(SO 7, 8)

E3-9 Transaction data and journal entries for Matthews Real Estate Agency are presented in E3-7 and E3-8.

Instructions
(a) Post the transactions to T accounts.
(b) Prepare a trial balance at October 31, 2007.

E3-10 Selected transactions for P.F. Quick Corporation during its first month in business are presented below.

Analyze transactions, prepare journal entries, and post transactions to T accounts.
(SO 1, 5, 7)

Sept. 1 Issued common stock in exchange for $15,000 cash received from investors.
  5 Purchased equipment for $12,000, paying $2,000 in cash and the balance on account.
  25 Paid $5,000 cash on balance owed for equipment.
  30 Paid $500 cash dividend.

P. F. Quick's chart of accounts shows: Cash, Equipment, Accounts Payable, Common Stock, and Dividends.

Instructions
(a) Prepare a tabular analysis of the September transactions. The column headings should be: Cash + Equipment = Accounts Payable + Stockholders' Equity. For transactions affecting stockholders' equity, provide explanations in the right margin, as shown on page 107.
(b) Journalize the transactions. Do not provide explanations.
(c) Post the transactions to T accounts.

E3-11 These T accounts summarize the ledger of Hayley's Gardening Company Inc. at the end of the first month of operations.

Journalize transactions from T accounts and prepare a trial balance.
(SO 5, 8)

Cash				Unearned Revenue	
Apr. 1	12,000	Apr. 15	900	Apr. 30	600
12	700	25	3,500		
29	800				
30	600				

Accounts Receivable				Common Stock	
Apr. 7	2,400	Apr. 29	800	Apr. 1	12,000

Supplies		Service Revenue	
Apr. 4	5,200	Apr. 7	2,400
		12	700

Accounts Payable				Salaries Expense	
Apr. 25	3,500	Apr. 4	5,200	Apr. 15	900

Instructions
(a) Prepare in the order they occurred the journal entries (including explanations) that resulted in the amounts posted to the accounts.
(b) Prepare a trial balance at April 30, 2007. (*Hint:* Compute ending balances of T accounts first.)

E3-12 Selected transactions from the journal of Dewitt Inc. during its first month of operations are presented here.

Post journal entries and prepare a trial balance.
(SO 7, 8)

Date	Account Titles	Debit	Credit
Aug. 1	Cash	3,000	
	Common Stock		3,000
10	Cash	1,700	
	Service Revenue		1,700
12	Office Equipment	6,200	
	Cash		1,200
	Notes Payable		5,000
25	Accounts Receivable	3,100	
	Service Revenue		3,100
31	Cash	600	
	Accounts Receivable		600

Instructions
(a) Post the transactions to T accounts.
(b) Prepare a trial balance at August 31, 2007.

Journalize transactions from T accounts and prepare a trial balance.
(SO 5, 8)

E3-13 Here is the ledger for Arseneault Co.

Cash					Common Stock	
Oct. 1	4,800	Oct. 4	400		Oct. 1	4,800
10	750	12	1,500		25	2,000
10	8,000	15	250			
20	800	30	300			
25	2,000	31	500			

Accounts Receivable					Dividends	
Oct. 6	800	Oct. 20	800	Oct. 30	300	
20	920					

Supplies					Service Revenue	
Oct. 4	400	Oct. 31	180		Oct. 6	800
					10	750
					20	920

Furniture			Store Wages Expense	
Oct. 3	3,000		Oct. 31	500

Notes Payable			Supplies Expense	
	Oct. 10	8,000	Oct. 31	180

Accounts Payable			Rent Expense	
Oct. 12	1,500	Oct. 3	3,000	Oct. 15	250

Instructions
(a) Reproduce the journal entries for only the transactions that **occurred on October 1, 10, and 20**, and provide explanations for each.
(b) Prepare a trial balance at October 31, 2007. (*Hint:* Compute ending balances of T accounts first.)

Analyze errors and their effects on trial balance.
(SO 8)

E3-14 The bookkeeper for Beylea Corporation made these errors in journalizing and posting.

1. A credit posting of $400 to Accounts Receivable was omitted.
2. A debit posting of $750 for Prepaid Insurance was debited to Insurance Expense.
3. A collection on account of $100 was journalized and posted as a debit to Cash $100 and a credit to Accounts Payable $100.
4. A credit posting of $300 to Property Taxes Payable was made twice.
5. A cash purchase of supplies for $250 was journalized and posted as a debit to Supplies $25 and a credit to Cash $25.
6. A debit of $375 to Advertising Expense was posted as $357.

Instructions
For each error, indicate (a) whether the trial balance will balance; if the trial balance will not balance, indicate (b) the amount of the difference, and (c) the trial balance column that will have the larger total. Consider each error separately. Use the following form, in which error 1 is given as an example.

Error	(a) In Balance	(b) Difference	(c) Larger Column
1	No	$400	Debit

E3-15   The accounts in the ledger of Dependable Delivery Service contain the following balances on July 31, 2007.

Prepare a trial balance.
(SO 8)

Accounts Receivable	$13,400	Prepaid Insurance	$ 1,800
Accounts Payable	7,400	Repair Expense	1,200
Cash	?	Service Revenue	15,500
Delivery Equipment	59,360	Dividends	700
Gas and Oil Expense	758	Common Stock	40,000
Insurance Expense	600	Salaries Expense	4,428
Notes Payable, due 2010	28,450	Salaries Payable	900
		Retained Earnings	5,200
		(July 1, 2007)	

Instructions
(a) Prepare a trial balance with the accounts arranged as illustrated in the chapter, and fill in the missing amount for Cash.
(b) Prepare an income statement, a retained earnings statement, and a classified balance sheet for the month of July 2007.

E3-16   The following accounts, in alphabetical order, were selected from the 2004 financial statements of Krispy Kreme Doughnuts, Inc.

Identify normal account balance and corresponding financial statement.
(SO 3)

Accounts payable	Interest income
Accounts receivable	Inventories
Common stock	Prepaid expenses
Depreciation expense	Property and equipment
Interest expense	Revenues

Instructions
For each account, indicate (a) whether the normal balance is a debit or a credit, and (b) the financial statement—balance sheet or income statement—where the account should be presented.

Problems: Set A

P3-1A   On April 1 Far and Wide Travel Agency Inc. was established. These transactions were completed during the month.

Analyze transactions and compute net income.
(SO 1)

1. Stockholders invested $20,000 cash in the company in exchange for common stock.
2. Paid $900 cash for April office rent.
3. Purchased office equipment for $2,800 cash.
4. Purchased $200 of advertising in the *Chicago Tribune,* on account.
5. Paid $500 cash for office supplies.
6. Earned $9,000 for services provided: Cash of $1,000 is received from customers, and the balance of $8,000 is billed to customers on account.
7. Paid $400 cash dividends.
8. Paid *Chicago Tribune* amount due in transaction (4).
9. Paid employees' salaries $1,200.
10. Received $8,000 in cash from customers who have previously been billed in transaction (6).

Instructions
(a) Prepare a tabular analysis of the transactions using these column headings: Cash, Accounts Receivable, Supplies, Office Equipment, Accounts Payable, Common Stock, and Retained Earnings. Include margin explanations for any changes in Retained Earnings.
(b) From an analysis of the column Retained Earnings, compute the net income or net loss for April.

(a) Cash $23,000
Ret. earnings $ 6,300

Analyze transactions and prepare financial statements.
(SO 1)

P3-2A   Marie Blaesing started her own consulting firm, Blaesing Consulting Inc., on May 1, 2007. The following transactions occurred during the month of May.

May 1 Stockholders invested $12,000 cash in the business in exchange for common stock.
2 Paid $700 for office rent for the month.
3 Purchased $500 of supplies on account.
5 Paid $150 to advertise in the *County News*.
9 Received $1,000 cash for services provided.
12 Paid $200 cash dividend.
15 Performed $3,200 of services on account.
17 Paid $2,500 for employee salaries.
20 Paid for the supplies purchased on account on May 3.
23 Received a cash payment of $1,500 for services provided on account on May 15.
26 Borrowed $5,000 from the bank on a note payable.
29 Purchased office equipment for $2,400 paying $200 in cash and the balance on account.
30 Paid $150 for utilities.

Instructions

(a) Cash $15,100
Ret. earnings $ 500

(a) Show the effects of the previous transactions on the accounting equation using the following format. Assume the note payable is to be repaid within the year.

	Assets			=	Liabilities		+	Stockholders' Equity	
Date	Cash +	Accounts Receivable	+ Supplies +	Office Equipment =	Notes Payable	+ Accounts Payable	+	Common Stock	+ Retained Earnings

Include margin explanations for any changes in Retained Earnings.

(b) Net income $700

(b) Prepare an income statement for the month of May.
(c) Prepare a classified balance sheet at May 31, 2007.

Analyze transactions and prepare an income statement, retained earnings statement, and balance sheet.
(SO 1)

P3-3A Mark Mader created a corporation providing legal services, Mark Mader Inc., on July 1, 2007. On July 31 the balance sheet showed: Cash $4,000; Accounts Receivable $2,500; Supplies $500; Office Equipment $5,000; Accounts Payable $4,200; Common Stock $6,200; and Retained Earnings $1,600. During August the following transactions occurred.

1. Collected $1,500 of accounts receivable due from customers.
2. Paid $2,700 cash for accounts payable due.
3. Earned revenue of $6,400, of which $3,000 is collected in cash and the balance is due in September.
4. Purchased additional office equipment for $2,000, paying $400 in cash and the balance on account.
5. Paid salaries $1,400, rent for August $900, and advertising expenses $350.
6. Declared and paid a cash dividend of $700.
7. Received $2,000 from Standard Federal Bank; the money was borrowed on a 4-month note payable.
8. Incurred utility expenses for the month on account $450.

(a) Cash $4,050
Ret. earnings $4,200

Instructions

(a) Prepare a tabular analysis of the August transactions beginning with July 31 balances. The column heading should be: Cash + Accounts Receivable + Supplies + Office Equipment = Notes Payable + Accounts Payable + Common Stock + Retained Earnings. Include margin explanations for any changes in Retained Earnings.

(b) Net income $3,300

(b) Prepare an income statement for August, a retained earnings statement for August, and a classified balance sheet at August 31.

Journalize a series of transactions.
(SO 3, 5)

GLS

P3-4A Hometown Miniature Golf and Driving Range Inc. was opened on March 1 by Happy Gilmore. These selected events and transactions occurred during March.

Mar. 1 Stockholders invested $60,000 cash in the business in exchange for common stock of the corporation.
3 Purchased Arnie's Golf Land for $38,000 cash. The price consists of land $23,000, building $9,000, and equipment $6,000. (Record this in a single entry.)

5   Advertised the opening of the driving range and miniature golf course, paying advertising expenses of $1,600 cash.

6   Paid cash $2,400 for a 1-year insurance policy.

10   Purchased golf clubs and other equipment for $3,700 from Golden Bear Company, payable in 30 days.

18   Received golf fees of $1,200 in cash from customers for golf fees earned.

19   Sold 100 coupon books for $20 each in cash. Each book contains ten coupons that enable the holder to play one round of miniature golf or to hit one bucket of golf balls. (*Hint*: The revenue is not earned until the customers use the coupons.)

25   Declared and paid a $500 cash dividend.

30   Paid salaries of $700.

30   Paid Golden Bear Company in full for equipment purchased on March 10.

31   Received $800 of fees in cash from customers for golf fees earned.

The company uses these accounts: Cash, Prepaid Insurance, Land, Buildings, Equipment, Accounts Payable, Unearned Golf Revenue, Common Stock, Retained Earnings, Dividends, Golf Revenue, Advertising Expense, and Salaries Expense.

Instructions
Journalize the March transactions, including explanations.

P3-5A   F.L. Wright Architects incorporated as licensed architects on April 1, 2007. During the first month of the operation of the business, these events and transactions occurred:

Apr. 1   Stockholders invested $14,000 cash in exchange for common stock of the corporation.

1   Hired a secretary-receptionist at a salary of $375 per week, payable monthly.

2   Paid office rent for the month $900.

3   Purchased architectural supplies on account from Spring Green Company $1,000.

10   Completed blueprints on a carport and billed client $1,100 for services.

11   Received $500 cash advance from J. Madison to design a new home.

20   Received $2,300 cash for services completed and delivered to M. Svetlana.

30   Paid secretary-receptionist for the month $1,500.

30   Paid $100 to Spring Green Company for accounts payable due.

The company uses these accounts: Cash, Accounts Receivable, Supplies, Accounts Payable, Unearned Revenue, Common Stock, Service Revenue, Salaries Expense, and Rent Expense.

Instructions
(a) Journalize the transactions, including explanations.
(b) Post to the ledger T accounts.
(c) Prepare a trial balance on April 30, 2007.

P3-6A   This is the trial balance of Aladdin Company on September 30.

Journalize transactions, post, and prepare a trial balance.
(SO 3, 5, 6, 7, 8)

Journalize transactions, post, and prepare a trial balance.
(SO 3, 5, 6, 7, 8)

(c) Cash $14,300
    Tot. trial
      balance $18,800

ALADDIN COMPANY
Trial Balance
September 30, 2007

	Debit	Credit
Cash	$ 8,300	
Accounts Receivable	2,600	
Supplies	2,100	
Equipment	8,000	
Accounts Payable		$ 5,100
Unearned Revenue		900
Common Stock		15,000
	$21,000	$21,000

The October transactions were as follows.

Oct. 5 Received $1,300 in cash from customers for accounts receivable due.
10 Billed customers for services performed $4,100.
15 Paid employee salaries $1,400.
17 Performed $600 of services for customers who paid in advance in August.
20 Paid $1,100 to creditors for accounts payable due.
29 Paid a $300 cash dividend.
31 Paid utilities $700.

Instructions
(a) Prepare a general ledger using T accounts. Enter the opening balances in the ledger accounts as of October 1. Provision should be made for these additional accounts: Dividends, Service Revenue, Salaries Expense, and Utilities Expense.

(d) Cash $ 6,100
Tot. trial
balance $24,000

(b) Journalize the transactions, including explanations.
(c) Post to the ledger accounts.
(d) Prepare a trial balance on October 31, 2007.

Prepare a correct trial balance.
(SO 8)

P3-7A This trial balance of Izo Co. does not balance.

IZO CO.
Trial Balance
June 30, 2007

	Debit	Credit
Cash		$ 2,180
Accounts Receivable	$ 3,370	
Supplies	800	
Equipment	3,000	
Accounts Payable		2,666
Unearned Revenue	1,200	
Common Stock		9,000
Dividends	800	
Service Revenue		3,480
Salaries Expense	3,600	
Office Expense	910	
	$13,680	$17,326

Each of the listed accounts has a normal balance per the general ledger. An examination of the ledger and journal reveals the following errors:

1. Cash received from a customer on account was debited for $690, and Accounts Receivable was credited for the same amount. The actual collection was for $960.
2. The purchase of a printer on account for $340 was recorded as a debit to Supplies for $340 and a credit to Accounts Payable for $340.
3. Services were performed on account for a client for $800. Accounts Receivable was debited for $80 and Service Revenue was credited for $800.
4. A debit posting to Salaries Expense of $500 was omitted.
5. A payment on account for $206 was credited to Cash for $206 and credited to Accounts Payable for $260.
6. Payment of a $600 cash dividend to Izo's stockholders was debited to Salaries Expense for $600 and credited to Cash for $600.

Tot. trial balance $15,880

Instructions
Prepare the correct trial balance. (*Hint:* All accounts have normal balances.)

Journalize transactions, post, and prepare a trial balance.
(SO 3, 5, 6, 7, 8)
GLS

P3-8A The Three-Peat Theater Inc. was recently formed. It began operations in March 2007. The Three-Peat is unique in that it will show only triple features of sequential theme movies. On March 1, the ledger of The Three-Peat showed: Cash $16,000; Land $38,000; Buildings (concession stand, projection room, ticket booth, and screen) $22,000; Equipment $16,000; Accounts Payable $12,000; and Common Stock $80,000. During the month of March the following events and transactions occurred.

Mar.	2	Rented the three *Star Wars* movies (*Star Wars®, The Empire Strikes Back,* and *The Return of the Jedi*) to be shown for the first three weeks of March. The film rental was $12,000; $2,000 was paid in cash and $10,000 will be paid on March 10.
	3	Ordered the first three *Star Trek* movies to be shown the last 10 days of March. It will cost $400 per night.
	9	Received $9,200 cash from admissions.
	10	Paid balance due on *Star Wars* movies rental and $2,600 on March 1 accounts payable.
	11	Hired J. Bybee to operate the concession stand. Bybee agrees to pay The Three-Peat Theater 15% of gross receipts, payable monthly.
	12	Paid advertising expenses $900.
	20	Received $7,100 cash from customers for admissions.
	20	Received the *Star Trek* movies and paid rental fee of $4,000.
	31	Paid salaries of $3,800.
	31	Received statement from J. Bybee showing gross receipts from concessions of $9,000 and the balance due to The Three-Peat of $1,350 for March. Bybee paid half the balance due and will remit the remainder on April 5.
	31	Received $20,000 cash from customers for admissions.

In addition to the accounts identified above, the chart of accounts includes: Accounts Receivable, Admission Revenue, Concession Revenue, Advertising Expense, Film Rental Expense, and Salaries Expense.

Instructions
(a) Using T accounts, enter the beginning balances to the ledger.
(b) Journalize the March transactions, including explanations.
(c) Post the March journal entries to the ledger.
(d) Prepare a trial balance on March 31, 2007.

(d) Cash $ 29,675
Tot. trial
balance $127,050

P3-9A The bookkeeper for Shirley Temple's dance studio made the following errors in journalizing and posting.

Analyze errors and their effects on the trial balance. (SO 8)

1. A credit to Supplies of $600 was omitted.
2. A debit posting of $300 to Accounts Payable was inadvertently debited to Accounts Receivable.
3. A purchase of supplies on account of $450 was debited to Supplies for $540 and credited to Accounts Payable for $540.
4. A credit posting of $250 to Wages Payable was posted twice.
5. A debit posting to Wages Payable for $250 and a credit posting to Cash for $250 were made twice.
6. A debit posting for $1,200 of Dividends was inadvertently posted to Travel Expense instead.
7. A credit to Service Revenue for $350 was inadvertently posted as a debit to Service Revenue.
8. A credit to Accounts Receivable of $250 was credited to Accounts Payable.

Instructions
For each error, indicate (a) whether the trial balance will balance; (b) the amount of the difference if the trial balance will not balance; and (c) the trial balance column that will have the larger total. Consider each error separately. Use the following form, in which error 1 is given as an example.

	(a)	(b)	(c)
Error	**In Balance**	**Difference**	**Larger Column**
1.	No	$600	Debit

Problems: Set B

Analyze transactions and compute net income. (SO 1)

GLS

P3-1B Blue Sky Window Washing Inc. was started on May 1. Here is a summary of the May transactions.

1. Stockholders invested $16,000 cash in the company in exchange for common stock.
2. Purchased equipment for $7,000 cash.
3. Paid $700 cash for May office rent.
4. Paid $400 cash for supplies.
5. Purchased $550 of advertising in the *Beacon News* on account.
6. Received $5,800 in cash from customers for service.
7. Declared and paid a $500 cash dividend.
8. Paid part-time employee salaries $1,700.
9. Paid utility bills $140.
10. Provided service on account to customers $500.
11. Collected cash of $240 for services billed in transaction (10).

Instructions

(a) Prepare a tabular analysis of the transactions using these column headings: Cash, Accounts Receivable, Supplies, Equipment, Accounts Payable, Common Stock, and Retained Earnings. Revenue is called Service Revenue. Include margin explanations for any changes in Retained Earnings.

(b) Net income $3,210

(b) From an analysis of the column Retained Earnings, compute the net income or net loss for May.

Analyze transactions and prepare financial statements.
(SO 1)

GLS

P3-2B Patrick Coleman started his own delivery service, At Your Service Inc., on June 1, 2007. The following transactions occurred during the month of June.

June 1 Stockholders invested $16,000 cash in the business in exchange for common stock.
2 Purchased a used van for deliveries for $10,000. Patrick paid $2,000 cash and signed a note payable for the remaining balance.
3 Paid $500 for office rent for the month.
5 Performed $1,900 of services on account.
9 Paid $300 in cash dividends.
12 Purchased supplies for $150 on account.
15 Received a cash payment of $750 for services provided on June 5.
17 Purchased gasoline for $200 on account.
20 Received a cash payment of $1,500 for services provided.
23 Made a cash payment of $800 on the note payable.
26 Paid $250 for utilities.
29 Paid for the supplies purchased on account on June 12.
30 Paid $750 for employee salaries.

Instructions

(a) Cash $13,500

(a) Show the effects of the previous transactions on the accounting equation using the following format. Assume the note payable is to be repaid within the year.

		Assets			=	Liabilities		+	Stockholders' Equity	
Date	Cash +	Accounts Receivable	+ Supplies +	Delivery Van	=	Notes Payable	+ Accounts Payable	+	Common Stock	+ Retained Earnings

Include margin explanations for any changes in Retained Earnings.

(b) Net income $1,700

(b) Prepare an income statement for the month of June.
(c) Prepare a classified balance sheet at June 30, 2007.

Analyze transactions and prepare an income statement, retained earnings statement, and balance sheet.
(SO 1)

GLS

P3-3B Janna Reed opened Reed Company, a veterinary business in Neosho, Wisconsin, on August 1, 2007. On August 31 the balance sheet showed: Cash $9,000; Accounts Receivable $1,700; Supplies $600; Office Equipment $5,000; Accounts Payable $3,600; Common Stock $12,000; and Retained Earnings $700. During September the following transactions occurred.

1. Paid $3,400 cash for accounts payable due.
2. Received $1,600 from customers in payment of accounts receivable.
3. Purchased additional office equipment for $4,100, paying $1,000 in cash and the balance on account.

4. Earned revenue of $8,500, of which $2,300 is paid in cash and the balance is due in October.
5. Declared and paid a $600 cash dividend.
6. Paid salaries $900, rent for September $800, and advertising expense $250.
7. Incurred utility expenses for the month on account $170.
8. Received $7,000 from Hilldale Bank; the money was borrowed on a 6-month note payable.

Instructions
(a) Prepare a tabular analysis of the September transactions beginning with August 31 balances. The column headings should be: Cash + Accounts Receivable + Supplies + Office Equipment = Notes Payable + Accounts Payable + Common Stock + Retained Earnings. Include margin explanations for any changes in Retained Earnings.
(b) Prepare an income statement for September, a retained earnings statement for September, and a classified balance sheet at September 30, 2007.

(a) Cash $12,950
Ret. earnings $ 6,480

P3-4B RV Haven was started on April 1 by Don Patter. These selected events and transactions occurred during April.

Journalize a series of transactions.
(SO 3, 5)
GLS

Apr.	1	Stockholders invested $75,000 cash in the business in exchange for common stock.
	4	Purchased land costing $50,000 for cash.
	8	Purchased advertising in local newspaper for $1,200 on account.
	11	Paid salaries to employees $1,700.
	12	Hired park manager at a salary of $3,000 per month, effective May 1.
	13	Paid $6,000 for a 1-year insurance policy.
	17	Paid $600 cash dividends.
	20	Received $5,000 in cash from customers for admission fees.
	25	Sold 100 coupon books for $70 each. Each book contains ten coupons that entitle the holder to one admission to the park. (*Hint*: The revenue is not earned until the coupons are used.)
	30	Received $7,900 in cash from customers for admission fees.
	30	Paid $500 of the balance owed for the advertising purchased on account on April 8.

The company uses the following accounts: Cash, Prepaid Insurance, Land, Accounts Payable, Unearned Admissions, Common Stock, Dividends, Admission Revenue, Advertising Expense, and Salaries Expense.

Instructions
Journalize the April transactions, including explanations.

P3-5B Ricki Knapp incorporated Knapp Consulting, an accounting practice, on May 1, 2007. During the first month of operations, these events and transactions occurred.

Journalize transactions, post, and prepare a trial balance.
(SO 3, 5, 6, 7, 8)
GLS

May	1	Stockholders invested $52,000 cash in exchange for common stock of the corporation.
	2	Hired a secretary-receptionist at a salary of $2,000 per month.
	3	Purchased $800 of supplies on account from Keating Supply Company.
	7	Paid office rent of $1,100 for the month.
	11	Completed a tax assignment and billed client $1,500 for services provided.
	12	Received $4,200 advance on a management consulting engagement.
	17	Received cash of $3,600 for services completed for Goodman Co.
	31	Paid secretary-receptionist $2,000 salary for the month.
	31	Paid 40% of balance due Keating Supply Company.

The company uses the following chart of accounts: Cash, Accounts Receivable, Supplies, Accounts Payable, Unearned Revenue, Common Stock, Service Revenue, Salaries Expense, and Rent Expense.

Instructions
(a) Journalize the transactions, including explanations.
(b) Post to the ledger T accounts.
(c) Prepare a trial balance on May 31, 2007.

(c) Cash $56,380
Tot. trial
*   balance $61,780*

Journalize transactions, post, and prepare a trial balance.
(SO 3, 5, 6, 7, 8)

P3-6B The trial balance of Artistic Dry Cleaners on June 30 is given here.

ARTISTIC DRY CLEANERS
Trial Balance
June 30, 2007

	Debit	Credit
Cash	$12,532	
Accounts Receivable	10,536	
Supplies	3,512	
Equipment	25,950	
Accounts Payable		$15,800
Unearned Revenue		1,730
Common Stock		35,000
	$52,530	$52,530

The July transactions were as follows.

July 8   Received $5,189 in cash on June 30 accounts receivable.
       9   Paid employee salaries $2,100.
    11   Received $5,100 in cash for services provided.
    14   Paid creditors $10,750 of accounts payable.
    17   Purchased supplies on account $520.
    22   Billed customers for services provided $4,700.
    30   Paid employee salaries $3,114, utilities $1,467, and repairs $492.
    31   Paid $400 cash dividend.

Instructions
(a) Prepare a general ledger using T accounts. Enter the opening balances in the ledger accounts as of July 1. Provision should be made for the following additional accounts: Dividends, Dry Cleaning Revenue, Repair Expense, Salaries Expense, and Utilities Expense.

(d) Cash $ 4,498
    Tot. trial
       balance $52,100

(b) Journalize the transactions, including explanations.
(c) Post to the ledger accounts.
(d) Prepare a trial balance on July 31, 2007.

Prepare a correct trial balance.
(SO 8)

P3-7B This trial balance of Rosenberger Company does not balance.

ROSENBERGER COMPANY
Trial Balance
May 31, 2007

	Debit	Credit
Cash	$ 5,340	
Accounts Receivable		$ 2,750
Prepaid Insurance	700	
Equipment	8,000	
Accounts Payable		4,100
Property Taxes Payable	750	
Common Stock		5,700
Retained Earnings		6,000
Service Revenue	6,690	
Salaries Expense	4,200	
Advertising Expense		1,100
Property Tax Expense	900	
	$26,580	$19,650

Your review of the ledger reveals that each account has a normal balance. You also discover the following errors.

1. The totals of the debit sides of Prepaid Insurance, Accounts Payable, and Property Tax Expense were each understated $100.
2. Transposition errors were made in Accounts Receivable and Service Revenue. Based on postings made, the correct balances were $2,570 and $6,960, respectively.
3. A debit posting to Salaries Expense of $400 was omitted.
4. An $800 cash dividend was debited to Common Stock for $800 and credited to Cash for $800.
5. A $350 purchase of supplies on account was debited to Equipment for $350 and credited to Cash for $350.
6. A cash payment of $250 for advertising was debited to Advertising Expense for $25 and credited to Cash for $25.
7. A collection from a customer for $240 was debited to Cash for $240 and credited to Accounts Payable for $240.

Instructions
Prepare the correct trial balance, assuming all accounts have normal balances. (*Note:* The chart of accounts also includes the following: Dividends and Supplies.)

Cash $ 5,465
Tot. trial balance $24,320

P3-8B   Classic Theater Inc. was recently formed. All facilities were completed on March 31. On April 1, the ledger showed: Cash $6,300; Land $10,000; Buildings (concession stand, projection room, ticket booth, and screen) $8,000; Equipment $6,000; Accounts Payable $2,300; Mortgage Payable $8,000; and Common Stock $20,000. During April, the following events and transactions occurred.

Journalize transactions, post, and prepare a trial balance.
(SO 3, 5, 6, 7, 8)

 GLS

Apr.	2	Paid film rental fee of $800 on first movie.
	3	Ordered two additional films at $900 each.
	9	Received $3,900 cash from admissions.
	10	Paid $2,000 of mortgage payable and $1,000 of accounts payable.
	11	Hired M. Norby to operate the concession stand. Norby agrees to pay Classic Theater 17% of gross receipts, payable monthly.
	12	Paid advertising expenses $460.
	20	Received one of the films ordered on April 3 and was billed $900. The film will be shown in April.
	25	Received $3,000 cash from customers for admissions.
	29	Paid salaries $1,900.
	30	Received statement from M. Norby showing gross receipts of $1,000 and the balance due to Classic Theater of $170 for April. Norby paid half of the balance due and will remit the remainder on May 5.
	30	Prepaid $1,000 rental fee on special film to be run in May.

In addition to the accounts identified above, the chart of accounts shows: Accounts Receivable, Prepaid Rentals, Admission Revenue, Concession Revenue, Advertising Expense, Film Rental Expense, Salaries Expense.

Instructions
(a) Enter the beginning balances in the ledger T accounts as of April 1.
(b) Journalize the April transactions, including explanations.
(c) Post the April journal entries to the ledger T accounts.
(d) Prepare a trial balance on April 30, 2007.

(d) Cash $ 6,125
Tot. trial
     balance $35,270

P3-9B   A first year co-op student working for UR Here.com recorded the transactions for the month. He wasn't exactly sure how to journalize and post, but he did the best he could. He had a few questions, however, about the following transactions.

Analyze errors and their effects on the trial balance.
(SO 8)

1. Cash received from a customer on account was recorded as a debit to Cash of $560 and a credit to Accounts Receivable of $650, instead of $560.
2. A service provided for cash was posted as a debit to Cash of $2,000 and a credit to Service Revenue of $2,000.
3. A debit of $880 for services provided on account was neither recorded nor posted. The credit was recorded correctly.
4. The debit to record $1,000 of cash dividends was posted to the Salary Expense account.
5. The purchase, on account, of a computer that cost $2,500 was recorded as a debit to Supplies and a credit to Accounts Payable.
6. A cash payment of $495 for salaries was recorded as a debit to Dividends and a credit to Cash.

7. Payment of month's rent was debited to Rent Expense and credited to Cash, $850.
8. Issue of $7,000 of common shares was credited to the Common Stock account, but no debit was recorded.

Instructions
(a) Indicate which of the above transactions are correct, and which are incorrect.
(b) For each error identified in (a), indicate (1) whether the trial balance will balance; (2) the amount of the difference if the trial balance will not balance; and (3) the trial balance column that will have the larger total. Consider each error separately. Use the following form, in which transaction 1 is given as an example.

Error	(1) In Balance	(2) Difference	(3) Larger Column
1.	No	$90	Credit

Problems: Set C

Visit the book's website at **www.wiley.com/college/kimmel** and choose the Student Companion site to access Problem Set C.

Continuing Cookie Chronicle

(*Note*: This is a continuation of the Cookie Chronicle from Chapters 1 and 2.)

CCC3 In November 2006 after having incorporated Cookie Creations Inc., Natalie begins operations. She has decided to not pursue the offer to supply cookies to Biscuits. Instead she will focus on offering cooking classes. The following events occur.

Nov. 8 Natalie cashes in her U.S. Savings Bonds and receives $520, which she deposits in her personal bank account.
    8 Natalie opens a bank account for Cookie Creations Inc.
    8 Natalie purchases $500 of Cookie Creations' common stock.
   11 Natalie designs a brochure and a poster to advertise the company and the services available.
   11 The brochures and posters are printed, at a cost of $95. They will be distributed as the opportunity arises.
   14 Cookie Creations purchases baking supplies, such as flour, sugar, butter, and chocolate chips, for $125.
   15 Natalie starts to gather some baking equipment to take with her when teaching the cookie classes. She has an excellent top-of-the-line food processor and mixer that originally cost her $550. Natalie decides to start using it only in her new business. She estimates that the equipment is currently worth $300, and she transfers the equipment into the business in exchange for additional common stock.
   16 The company needs more cash to sustain its operations. Natalie's grandmother lends the company $2,000 cash, in exchange for a two-year, 6% note payable. Interest and the principal are repayable at maturity.
   17 Cookie Creations purchases more baking equipment for $900.
   18 Natalie books her first class for November 29 for $100.
   25 Natalie books a second class for December 5 for $125. She receives a $50 cash down payment, in advance.
   29 Natalie teaches her first class, booked on November 18, and collects the $100 cash.
   30 Natalie's brother develops a website for Cookie Creations Inc. that the company will use for advertising. He charges the company $600 for his work, payable at the end of December. (Because the website is expected to have a useful life of two years before upgrades are needed, it should be treated as an asset.)
   30 Cookie Creations purchases a one-year insurance policy for $1,200.
   30 Natalie teaches a group of elementary school students how to make Santa Claus cookies. At the end of the class, Natalie leaves an invoice for $250

with the school principal. The principal says that he will pass it along to the business office and it will be paid some time in December.

30   Natalie receives a $50 invoice for use of her cell phone. She uses the cell phone exclusively for Cookie Creations Inc. business. The invoice is for services provided in November, and payment is due on December 15.

Instructions
(a) Prepare journal entries to record the November transactions.
(b) Post the journal entries to the general ledger accounts.
(c) Prepare a trial balance at November 30, 2006.

(c) Trial balance total $3,850

▶ BROADENING YOUR PERSPECTIVE

Financial Reporting and Analysis

FINANCIAL REPORTING PROBLEM: *Tootsie Roll Industries*

BYP3-1   The financial statements of Tootsie Roll in Appendix A at the back of this book contain the following selected accounts, all in thousands of dollars.

Common Stock	$24,139
Accounts Payable	19,315
Accounts Receivable	28,456
Selling, Marketing, and Administrative Expenses	85,705s
Prepaid Expenses	5,719
Property, Plant, and Equipment	321,054
Net Sales	420,110

Instructions
(a) What is the increase and decrease side for each account? What is the normal balance for each account?
(b) Identify the probable other account in the transaction and the effect on that account when:
   (1) Accounts Receivable is decreased.
   (2) Accounts Payable is decreased.
   (3) Prepaid Expenses is increased.
(c) Identify the other account(s) that ordinarily would be involved when:
   (1) Interest Expense is increased.
   (2) Property, Plant, and Equipment is increased.

COMPARATIVE ANALYSIS PROBLEM: *Tootsie Roll vs. Hershey Foods*

BYP3-2   The financial statements of Hershey Foods are presented in Appendix B, following the financial statements for Tootsie Roll in Appendix A.

Instructions
(a) Based on the information contained in these financial statements, determine the normal balance for:

Tootsie Roll Industries	**Hershey Foods**
(1) Accounts Receivable	(1) Inventories
(2) Property, Plant, and Equipment	(2) Provision for Income Taxes
(3) Accounts Payable	(3) Accrued Liabilities
(4) Retained Earnings	(4) Common Stock
(5) Net Sales	(5) Interest Expense

(b) Identify the other account ordinarily involved when:
   (1) Accounts Receivable is increased.
   (2) Notes Payable is decreased.

(3) Machinery is increased.

(4) Interest Income is increased.

RESEARCH CASE

BYP3-3   The October 13, 2003, issue of *Business Week* includes an article by Stephanie Anderson titled "Is This Any Way To Run a Bank?"

Instructions

Read the article and answer the following questions.

(a) Describe Sherry Colby's account of her experiences with the mortgage company Washington Mutual.

(b) What other types of complaints has Washington Mutual received?

(c) What might be contributing to Washington Mutual's accounting troubles?

(d) What are the potential implications of the company's apparent poor accounting practices for the success of its business?

INTERPRETING FINANCIAL STATEMENTS

BYP3-4   Chieftain International, Inc., is an oil and natural gas exploration and production company. A recent balance sheet reported $208 million in assets with only $4.6 million in liabilities, all of which were short-term accounts payable.

During the year, Chieftain expanded its holdings of oil and gas rights, drilled 37 new wells, and invested in expensive 3-D seismic technology. The company generated $19 million cash from operating activities and paid no dividends. It had a cash balance of $102 million at the end of the year.

Instructions

(a) Name at least two advantages to Chieftain from having no long-term debt. Can you think of disadvantages?

(b) What are some of the advantages to Chieftain from having this large a cash balance? What is a disadvantage?

(c) Why do you suppose Chieftain has the $4.6 million balance in accounts payable, since it appears that it could have made all its purchases for cash?

BYP3-5   Doman Industries Ltd., whose products are sold in 30 countries worldwide, is an integrated Canadian forest products company.

Doman sells the majority of its lumber products in the United States, and a significant amount of its pulp products in Asia. Doman also has loans from other countries. For example, the Company borrowed US$160 million at an annual interest rate of 12%. Doman must repay this loan, and interest, in U.S. dollars.

One of the challenges global companies face is to make themselves attractive to investors from other countries. This is difficult to do when different accounting rules in different countries blur the real impact of earnings. For example, in a recent year Doman reported a loss of $2.3 million, using Canadian accounting rules. Had it reported under U.S. accounting rules, its loss would have been $12.1 million.

Many companies that want to be more easily compared with U.S. and other global competitors have switched to U.S. accounting principles. Canadian National Railway, Corel, Cott, Inco, and Thomson Corporation are but a few examples of large Canadian companies whose financial statements are now presented in U.S. dollars, adhere to U.S. GAAP, or are reconciled to U.S. GAAP.

Instructions

(a) Identify advantages and disadvantages that companies should consider when switching to U.S. reporting standards.

(b) Suppose you compare Doman Industries to a U.S.-based competitor. Do you believe the use of country-specific accounting policies would hinder your ability to compare the companies? If so, explain how.

(c) Suppose you compare Doman Industries to a Canadian-based competitor. If the companies apply generally acceptable Canadian accounting policies differently, how could this affect your ability to compare their financial results?

(d) Do you see any significant distinction between comparing statements prepared using generally accepted accounting principles of different countries and comparing statements prepared using generally accepted accounting principles of the same country (e.g. U.S.) but that apply the principles differently?

FINANCIAL ANALYSIS ON THE WEB

BYP3-6 *Purpose:* This activity provides information about career opportunities for CPAs.

Address: **www.futurecpa.org** (or go to **www.wiley.com/college/kimmel**)

Careers in Accounting

Steps
1. Go to the address shown above.
2. Click on CPA101.

Instructions
Answer the following questions.
(a) What does CPA stand for? Where do CPAs work?
(b) What is meant by "public accounting"?
(c) What skills does a CPA need?
(d) What is the salary range for a CPA at a large firm during the first three years? What is the salary range for chief financial officers and treasurers at large corporations?

Critical Thinking

DECISION MAKING ACROSS THE ORGANIZATION

BYP3-7 Katie Kim operates Double K Riding Academy, Inc. The academy's primary sources of revenue are riding fees and lesson fees, which are provided on a cash basis. Katie also boards horses for owners, who are billed monthly for boarding fees. In a few cases, boarders pay in advance of expected use. For its revenue transactions, the academy maintains these accounts: Cash, Accounts Receivable, Unearned Revenue, Riding Revenue, Lesson Revenue, and Boarding Revenue.

The academy owns 10 horses, a stable, a riding corral, riding equipment, and office equipment. These assets are accounted for in the following accounts: Horses, Building, Riding Corral, Riding Equipment, and Office Equipment.

The academy employs stable helpers and an office employee, who receive weekly salaries. At the end of each month, the mail usually brings bills for advertising, utilities, and veterinary service. Other expenses include feed for the horses and insurance. For its expenses, the academy maintains the following accounts: Hay and Feed Supplies, Prepaid Insurance, Accounts Payable, Salaries Expense, Advertising Expense, Utilities Expense, Veterinary Expense, Hay and Feed Expense, and Insurance Expense.

Katie Kim's sole source of personal income is dividends from the academy. Thus, the corporation declares and pays periodic dividends. To record stockholders' equity in the business and dividends, two accounts are maintained: Common Stock and Dividends.

During the first month of operations an inexperienced bookkeeper was employed. Katie Kim asks you to review the following eight entries of the 50 entries made during the month. In each case, the explanation for the entry is correct.

May	1	Cash	15,000	
		Unearned Revenue		15,000
		(Issued common stock in exchange for $15,000 cash)		
	5	Cash	250	
		Lesson Revenue		250
		(Received $250 cash for lesson fees)		
	7	Cash	500	
		Boarding Revenue		500
		(Received $500 for boarding of horses beginning June 1)		
	9	Hay and Feed Expense	1,700	
		Cash		1,700
		(Purchased estimated 5 months' supply of feed and hay for $1,700 on account)		

May 14	Riding Equipment	80	
	Cash		800
	(Purchased desk and other office equipment for		
	$800 cash)		
15	Salaries Expense	400	
	Cash		400
	(Issued check to Katie Kim for personal use)		
20	Cash	145	
	Riding Revenue		154
	(Received $154 cash for riding fees)		
31	Veterinary Expense	75	
	Accounts Receivable		75
	(Received bill of $75 from veterinarian for		
	services provided)		

Instructions

With the class divided into groups, answer the following.

(a) For each journal entry that is correct, so state. For each journal entry that is incorrect, prepare the entry that should have been made by the bookkeeper.

(b) Which of the incorrect entries would prevent the trial balance from balancing?

(c) What was the correct net income for May, assuming the bookkeeper originally reported net income of $4,500 after posting all 50 entries?

(d) What was the correct cash balance at May 31, assuming the bookkeeper reported a balance of $12,475 after posting all 50 entries?

COMMUNICATION ACTIVITY

BYP3-8   Clean Sweep Company offers home cleaning service. Two recurring transactions for the company are billing customers for services provided and paying employee salaries. For example, on March 15 bills totaling $6,000 were sent to customers, and $2,000 was paid in salaries to employees.

Instructions

Write a memorandum to your instructor that explains and illustrates the steps in the recording process for each of the March 15 transactions. Use the format illustrated in the text under the heading "The Recording Process Illustrated" (pp. 118–124).

ETHICS CASE

BYP3-9   Rachel McGaver is the assistant chief accountant at A2Z Company, a manufacturer of computer chips and cellular phones. The company presently has total sales of $20 million. It is the end of the first quarter and Rachel is hurriedly trying to prepare a general ledger trial balance so that quarterly financial statements can be prepared and released to management and the regulatory agencies. The total credits on the trial balance exceed the debits by $1,000.

In order to meet the 4 P.M. deadline, Rachel decides to force the debits and credits into balance by adding the amount of the difference to the Equipment account. She chose Equipment because it is one of the larger account balances; percentage-wise it will be the least misstated. Rachel plugs the difference! She believes that the difference is quite small and will not affect anyone's decisions. She wishes that she had another few days to find the error but realizes that the financial statements are already late.

Instructions

(a) Who are the stakeholders in this situation?

(b) What ethical issues are involved?

(c) What are Rachel's alternatives?

Answers to Business Insight and Accounting across the Organization Questions

p. 106

Q: In order for these companies to prepare and issue financial statements, their accounting equations (debit and credits) must have been in balance at year-end. How could these errors or misstatements have occurred?

A: A company's accounting equation (its books) can be in balance yet its financial statements have errors or misstatements because of the following: entire transactions were not recorded; transactions were recorded at wrong amounts; transactions were recorded in the wrong accounts; transactions were recorded in the wrong accounting period. Audits of financial statements uncover some, but obviously not all, errors or misstatements.

   p. 112

Q: Do you think that the Chicago Bears football team would be likely to have the same major revenue and expense accounts as the Cubs?

A: Because their businesses are similar—professional sports—many of the revenue and expense accounts for the baseball and football teams might be similar.

   p. 116

Q: In what ways is this Microsoft division using accounting to assist in its effort to become more profitable?

A: The division has used accounting to set very strict sales, revenue, and profit goals. In addition, the managers in this division use accounting to keep a tight reign on product costs. Also, accounting serves as the basis of communication so that the marketing managers and product designers can work with production managers, engineers, and accountants to achieve an exciting product within specified cost constraints.

Answer to Tootsie Roll Review It Question 4, p. 114

Normal balances for accounts in Tootsie Roll's financial statements: Accounts Receivable—debit; Income Taxes Payable—credit; Sales—credit; Selling, Marketing, and Administrative Expense—debit.

Answers to Self-Study Questions

1. b   2. b   3. b   4. c   5. d   6. d   7. b   8. a   9. c   10. d
11. a   12. c

CHAPTER 4

Accrual Accounting Concepts

STUDY OBJECTIVES

After studying this chapter,
you should be able to:

1 Explain the revenue recognition principle and the matching principle.

2 Differentiate between the cash basis and the accrual basis of accounting.

3 Explain why adjusting entries are needed, and identify the major types of adjusting entries.

4 Prepare adjusting entries for prepayments.

5 Prepare adjusting entries for accruals.

6 Describe the nature and purpose of the adjusted trial balance.

7 Explain the purpose of closing entries.

8 Describe the required steps in the accounting cycle.

THE
NAVIGATOR

THE NAVIGATOR

- Scan *Study Objectives*
- Read *Feature Story*
- Read *Preview*
- Read text and answer *Before You Go On*
  p. 161 ◯   p. 169 ◯   p. 174 ◯   p. 183 ◯
- Work *Using the Decision Toolkit*
- Review *Summary of Study Objectives*
- Work *Demonstration Problem*
- Answer *Self-Study Questions*
- Complete *Assignments*

FEATURE STORY

What Was Your Profit?

The accuracy of the financial reporting system depends on answers to a few fundamental questions. At what point has revenue been earned? At what point is the earnings process complete? When have expenses really been incurred?

During the 1990s' boom in the stock prices of dot-com companies, many dot-com companies earned most of their revenue from selling advertising space on their Web sites. To boost reported revenue, some dot-coms began swapping website ad space. Company A would put an ad for its website on company B's website, and company B would put an ad for its website on company A's website. No money ever changed hands, but each company recorded revenue (for the value of the space that it gave up on its site). This practice did little to boost net income and resulted in no additional cash flow—but it did boost *reported revenue*. Regulators eventually put an end to the practice.

Another type of transgression results from companies recording revenue or expenses in the wrong year. In fact, shifting revenues and expenses is one of the most common abuses of financial accounting. Xerox recently admitted reporting billions of dollars of lease revenue in periods earlier than it should have been reported. And WorldCom stunned the financial markets with its admission that it had boosted net income by billions of dollars

by delaying the recognition of expenses until later years.

Unfortunately, revelations such as these have become all too common in the corporate world. It is no wonder that recently the U.S. Trust Survey of affluent Americans reported that 85 percent of its respondents believed that there should be tighter regulation of financial disclosures, and 66 percent said they did not trust the management of publicly traded companies.

Why did so many companies violate basic financial reporting rules and sound ethics? Many speculate that as stock prices climbed, executives were under increasing pressure to meet higher and higher earnings expectations. If actual results weren't as good as hoped for, some gave in to temptation and "adjusted" their numbers to meet market expectations.

✓ THE NAVIGATOR

On the World Wide Web
Xerox: www.xerox.com

PREVIEW OF CHAPTER 4

As indicated in the Feature Story, making adjustments is necessary to avoid misstatement of revenues and expenses such as those at Xerox and WorldCom. In this chapter we introduce you to the accrual accounting concepts that make such adjustments possible.

The organization and content of the chapter are as follows.

THE NAVIGATOR

Helpful Hint An accounting time period that is one year long is called a **fiscal year**.

Revenue Recognition

Service performed

Customer requests service   At time cash received

Revenue should be recognized in the accounting period in which it is earned (generally when service is performed).

Timing Issues

Most businesses need immediate feedback about how well they are doing. For example, management usually wants monthly reports on financial results, most large corporations are required to present quarterly and annual financial statements to stockholders, and the Internal Revenue Service requires all businesses to file annual tax returns. **Accounting divides the economic life of a business into artificial time periods.** As indicated in Chapter 2, this is the time period assumption. **Accounting time periods are generally a month, a quarter, or a year.**

Many business transactions affect more than one of these arbitrary time periods. For example, a new building purchased by Citigroup or a new airplane purchased by Delta Air Lines will be used for many years. It doesn't make sense to expense the full cost of the building or the airplane at the time of purchase because each will be used for many subsequent periods. Instead, we determine the impact of each transaction on specific accounting periods.

Determining the amount of revenues and expenses to report in a given accounting period can be difficult. Proper reporting requires an understanding of the nature of the company's business. Two principles are used as guidelines: the revenue recognition principle and the matching principle.

THE REVENUE RECOGNITION PRINCIPLE

The **revenue recognition principle** requires that companies recognize revenue in the accounting period **in which it is earned**. In a service company, revenue is considered to be earned at the time the service is performed. To illustrate, assume Conrad Dry Cleaners cleans clothing on June 30, but customers do not claim and pay for their clothes until the first week of July. Under the revenue recognition principle, Conrad earns revenue in June when it performs the service, not in July when it receives the cash. At June 30 Conrad would report a receivable on its balance sheet and revenue in its income statement for the service performed.

Decision Toolkit

Decision Checkpoints	Info Needed for Decision	Tool to Use for Decision	How to Evaluate Results
At what point should the company record revenue?	Need to understand the nature of the company's business	Record revenue when earned. A service business earns revenue when it performs a service.	Recognizing revenue too early overstates current period revenue; recognizing it too late understates current period revenue.

THE MATCHING PRINCIPLE

In recognizing expenses, a simple rule is followed: "Let the expenses follow the revenues." Thus, expense recognition is tied to revenue recognition. Applied to the preceding example, this means that the salary expense Conrad incurred in performing the cleaning service on June 30 should be reported in the same period in which it recognizes the service revenue. The critical issue in expense recognition is determining when the expense makes its contribution to revenue. This may or may not be the same period in which the expense is paid. If Conrad does not pay the salary incurred on June 30 until July, it would report salaries payable on its June 30 balance sheet.

The practice of expense recognition is referred to as the **matching principle** because it dictates that efforts (expenses) be matched with accomplishments (revenues). Illustration 4-1 shows these relationships.

Illustration 4-1   GAAP relationships in revenue and expense recognition

Decision Toolkit

Decision Checkpoints	Info Needed for Decision	Tool to Use for Decision	How to Evaluate Results
At what point should the company record expenses?	Need to understand the nature of the company's business	Expenses should "follow" revenues—that is, match the effort (expense) with the result (revenue).	Recognizing expenses too early overstates current period expense; recognizing them too late understates current period expense.

ACCRUAL VERSUS CASH BASIS OF ACCOUNTING

 International Note

Although different accounting standards are often used by companies in other countries, the accrual basis of accounting is central to all of these standards.

Accrual-basis accounting means that transactions that change a company's financial statements are recorded **in the periods in which the events occur**. For example, using the accrual basis means that companies recognize revenues **when earned** (the revenue recognition principle) **rather than when they receive cash.** **Likewise, under the accrual basis, companies recognize expenses when incurred** (the matching principle) **rather than when paid.**

An alternative to the accrual basis is the cash basis. Under **cash-basis accounting, companies record revenue only when cash is received. They record expense only when cash is paid. The cash basis of accounting is prohibited under generally accepted accounting principles.** Why? Because it does not record revenue when earned, thus violating the revenue recognition principle. Similarly, it does not record expenses when incurred, which violates the matching principle.

Illustration 4-2 compares accrual-based numbers and cash-based numbers. Suppose that Fresh Colors paints a large building in 2006. In 2006 it incurs and pays total expenses (salaries and paint costs) of $50,000. It bills the customer $80,000, but does not receive payment until 2007. On an accrual basis, Fresh

Illustration 4-2 Accrual versus cash basis accounting

	2006	2007
Activity	Purchased paint, painted building, paid employees	Received payment for work done in 2006
Accrual basis	Revenue $80,000 Expense 50,000 Net income $30,000	Revenue $ 0 Expense 0 Net income $ 0
Cash basis	Revenue $ 0 Expense 50,000 Net loss $(50,000)	Revenue $80,000 Expense 0 Net income $80,000

Colors reports $80,000 of revenue during 2006 because that is when it is earned. The company matches expenses of $50,000 to the $80,000 of revenue. Thus, 2006 net income is $30,000 ($80,000 − $50,000). The $30,000 of net income reported for 2006 indicates the profitability of Fresh Colors' efforts during that period.

If, instead, Fresh Paint were to use cash-basis accounting, it would report $50,000 of expenses in 2006 and $80,000 of revenues during 2007. As shown in Illustration 4-2, it would report a loss of $50,000 in 2006 and would report net income of $80,000 in 2007. Clearly, the cash-basis measures are misleading because the financial performance of the company would be misstated for both 2006 and 2007.

Business Insight
Ethics Perspective

Allegations of abuse of the revenue recognition principle have become all too common in recent years. For example, it was alleged that Krispy Kreme sometimes doubled the number of doughnuts shipped to wholesale customers at the end of a quarter to boost quarterly results. The customers shipped the unsold doughnuts back after the beginning of the next quarter for a refund. Conversely, Computer Associates International was accused of backdating sales—that is, saying that a sale that occurred at the beginning of one quarter occurred at the end of the previous quarter in order to achieve the previous quarter's sales targets.

 What motivates sales executives and finance and accounting executives to participate in activities that result in inaccurate reporting of revenues?

BEFORE YOU GO ON . . .

▶ Review It

1. What are the revenue recognition and matching principles?
2. What are the differences between the cash and accrual bases of accounting?

The Basics of Adjusting Entries

In order for revenues to be recorded in the period in which they are earned, and for expenses to be recognized in the period in which they are incurred, companies make adjusting entries. **Adjusting entries ensure that the revenue recognition and matching principles are followed**.

Adjusting entries are necessary because the **trial balance**—the first pulling together of the transaction data—may not contain up-to-date and complete data. This is true for several reasons:

1. Some events are not recorded daily because it is not efficient to do so. Examples are the use of supplies and the earning of wages by employees.
2. Some costs are not recorded during the accounting period because these costs expire with the passage of time rather than as a result of recurring

STUDY OBJECTIVE
3
Explain why adjusting entries are needed, and identify the major types of adjusting entries.

daily transactions. Examples are charges related to the use of buildings and equipment, rent, and insurance.

3. Some items may be unrecorded. An example is a utility service bill that will not be received until the next accounting period.

Adjusting entries are required every time a company prepares financial statements. The company analyzes each account in the trial balance to determine whether it is complete and up to date for financial statement purposes.

TYPES OF ADJUSTING ENTRIES

Adjusting entries are classified as either prepayments or accruals. As Illustration 4-3 shows, each of these classes has two subcategories.

Illustration 4-3
Categories of adjusting entries

Prepayments:

1. **Prepaid expenses**: Expenses paid in cash and recorded as assets before they are used or consumed.
2. **Unearned revenues**: Cash received and recorded as liabilities before revenue is earned.

Accruals:

1. **Accrued revenues**: Revenues earned but not yet received in cash or recorded.
2. **Accrued expenses**: Expenses incurred but not yet paid in cash or recorded.

Subsequent sections give specific examples and explanations of each type of adjustment. Each example is based on the October 31 trial balance of Sierra Corporation, from Chapter 3, reproduced below in Illustration 4-4. Note that Retained Earnings, with a zero balance, has been added to this trial balance. We will explain its use later.

Illustration 4-4   Trial balance

SIERRA CORPORATION Trial Balance October 31, 2007		
	Debit	**Credit**
Cash	$15,200	
Advertising Supplies	2,500	
Prepaid Insurance	600	
Office Equipment	5,000	
Notes Payable		$ 5,000
Accounts Payable		2,500
Unearned Service Revenue		1,200
Common Stock		10,000
Retained Earnings		0
Dividends	500	
Service Revenue		10,000
Salaries Expense	4,000	
Rent Expense	900	
	$28,700	$28,700

We assume that Sierra Corporation uses an accounting period of one month. Thus, monthly adjusting entries are made. The entries are dated October 31.

ADJUSTING ENTRIES FOR PREPAYMENTS

Prepayments are either prepaid expenses or unearned revenues. Companies must make adjusting entries for prepayments at the statement date to record the portion of the prepayment that represents the expense incurred or the revenue earned in the current accounting period.

Prepaid Expenses

Companies record payments of expenses that will benefit more than one accounting period as assets called prepaid expenses or prepayments. When expenses are prepaid, an asset account is increased (debited) to show the service or benefit that the company will receive in the future. Examples of common prepayments are insurance, supplies, advertising, and rent. In addition, companies make prepayments when they purchase buildings and equipment.

Prepaid expenses are costs that expire either with the passage of time (e.g., rent and insurance) **or through use** (e.g., supplies). The expiration of these costs does not require daily entries, which would be impractical and unnecessary. Accordingly, companies postpone the recognition of such cost expirations until they prepare financial statements. At each statement date, they then make adjusting entries to record the expenses applicable to the current accounting period and to show the remaining amounts in the asset accounts.

Prior to adjustment, assets are overstated and expenses are understated. Therefore, as shown in Illustration 4-5, **an adjusting entry for prepaid expenses results in an increase (a debit) to an expense account and a decrease (a credit) to an asset account**.

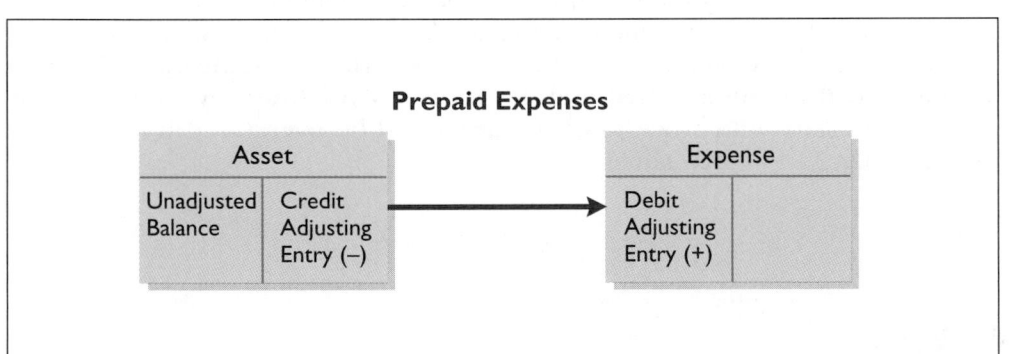

Illustration 4-5
Adjusting entries for prepaid expenses

Let's look in more detail at some specific types of prepaid expenses, beginning with supplies.

SUPPLIES. The purchase of supplies, such as paper and envelopes, results in an increase (a debit) to an asset account. During the accounting period, the company uses supplies. Rather than record supplies expense as the supplies are used, companies recognize supplies expense at the **end** of the accounting period. At the end of the accounting period the company must count the remaining supplies. The difference between the unadjusted balance in the Supplies (asset) account and the actual cost of supplies on hand represents the supplies used (an expense) for that period.

Recall from Chapter 3 that Sierra Corporation purchased advertising supplies costing $2,500 on October 5. Sierra recorded the payment by increasing (debiting) the asset Advertising Supplies. This account shows a balance of $2,500 in the October 31 trial balance. An inventory count at the close of business on October 31 reveals that $1,000 of supplies are still on hand. Thus, the cost of

Supplies

Oct.5

Supplies purchased;
record asset

Oct.31
Supplies used;
record supplies expense

supplies used is $1,500 ($2,500 − $1,000). This use of supplies decreases an asset, Advertising Supplies. It also decreases stockholders' equity by increasing an expense account, Advertising Supplies Expense. The use of supplies affects the accounting equation in the following way.

Assets	=	Liabilities	+	Stockholders' Equity
−$1,500				−$1,500

Thus, Sierra makes the following adjusting entry:

Oct. 31	Advertising Supplies Expense	1,500	
	Advertising Supplies		1,500
	(To record supplies used)		

After the adjusting entry is posted, the accounts, in T account form, appear as in Illustration 4-6.

Illustration 4-6 Supplies accounts after adjustment

Advertising Supplies				Advertising Supplies Expense	
Oct. 5	2,500	Oct.31 **Adj. 1,500**	Oct. 31 **Adj. 1,500**	
Oct. 31 Bal. 1,000			Oct. 31 Bal. 1,500	

The asset account Advertising Supplies now shows a balance of $1,000, which is equal to the cost of supplies on hand at the statement date. In addition, Advertising Supplies Expense shows a balance of $1,500, which equals the cost of supplies used in October. **If Sierra does not make the adjusting entry, October expenses will be understated and net income overstated by $1,500. Moreover, both assets and stockholders' equity will be overstated by $1,500 on the October 31 balance sheet.**

Accounting across the Organization

The method of accounting for advertising costs affects sales and marketing executives. In the past, companies sometimes recorded as assets the costs of media advertising for burgers, bleaches, athletic shoes, and such products and expensed those costs in subsequent periods as sales took place. The reasoning behind this treatment was that long ad campaigns provided benefits over multiple accounting periods. Today the accounting profession no longer allows this treatment because it was decided that the benefits were too difficult to measure.

Instead, companies now must expense advertising costs when the advertising takes place. The issue is important because the outlays for advertising can be substantial. Recent (2004) big spenders: Coca-Cola spent $2.2 billion, PepsiCo., Inc. $1.7 billion, Nike, Inc. $1,378 million, and Limited Brands $484 million.

 Why might the new accounting method cause companies sometimes to spend less on advertising?

INSURANCE.   Companies purchase insurance to protect themselves from losses due to fire, theft, and unforeseen events. Insurance must be paid in advance, often for more than one year. The cost of insurance (premiums) paid in advance is recorded as an increase (debit) in the asset account Prepaid Insurance. At the financial statement date companies increase (debit) Insurance Expense and decrease (credit) Prepaid Insurance for the cost of insurance that has expired during the period.

On October 4 Sierra Corporation paid $600 for a one-year fire insurance policy. Coverage began on October 1. Sierra recorded the payment by increasing (debiting) Prepaid Insurance. This account shows a balance of $600 in the October 31 trial balance. Insurance of $50 ($600 ÷ 12) expires each month. The expiration of Prepaid Insurance decreases an asset, Prepaid Insurance. It also decreases stockholders' equity by increasing an expense account, Insurance Expense. The expiration of Prepaid Insurance affects the accounting equation in October (and in each of the next 11 months) in the following way.

Assets	=	Liabilities	+	Stockholders' Equity
−$50				−$50

Thus, the following adjusting entry is made.

Oct. 31	Insurance Expense	50	
	Prepaid Insurance		50
	(To record insurance expired)		

After Sierra posts the adjusting entry, the accounts appear as in Illustration 4-7.

Prepaid Insurance				**Insurance Expense**		
Oct. 4	600	Oct. 31	**Adj. 50**	Oct. 31	**Adj. 50**	
Oct. 31	Bal. 550			Oct. 31	Bal. 50	

Illustration 4-7
Insurance accounts after adjustment

The asset Prepaid Insurance shows a balance of $550, which represents the unexpired cost for the remaining 11 months of coverage. At the same time the balance in Insurance Expense equals the insurance cost that expired in October. If Sierra does not make this adjustment, October expenses are understated by $50 and net income is overstated by $50. Moreover, as the accounting equation shows, both assets and stockholders' equity will be overstated by $50 on the October 31 balance sheet.

DEPRECIATION.   A company typically owns a variety of assets that have long lives, such as buildings, equipment, and motor vehicles. The period of service is referred to as the **useful life** of the asset. Because a building is expected to provide service for many years, it is recorded as an asset, rather than an expense, on the date it is acquired. As explained in Chapter 2, companies record such assets **at cost**, as required by the cost principle. According to the matching principle, companies then report a portion of this cost as an expense during each period of the asset's useful life. **Depreciation** is the process of allocating the cost of an asset to expense over its useful life.

Need for Adjustment.   The acquisition of long-lived assets is essentially a long-term prepayment for services. An adjusting entry for depreciation is

Insurance

Oct. 4

Insurance purchased; record asset

Insurance Policy			
Oct $50	Nov $50	Dec $50	Jan $50
Feb $50	March $50	April $50	May $50
June $50	July $50	Aug $50	Sept $50
I YEAR $600			

Oct. 31

Insurance expired; record insurance expense

Depreciation

Oct.2

Office equipment purchased; record asset

Office Equipment			
Oct $40	Nov $40	Dec $40	Jan $40
Feb $40	March $40	April $40	May $40
June $40	July $40	Aug $40	Sept $40
Depreciation = $480/year			

Oct.31

Depreciation recognized; record depreciation expense

needed to recognize the cost that has been used (an expense) during the period and to report the unused cost (an asset) at the end of the period. One very important point to understand: **Depreciation is an allocation concept, not a valuation concept.** That is, depreciation **allocates an asset's cost to the periods in which it is used. Depreciation does not attempt to report the actual change in the value of the asset.**

For Sierra Corporation, assume that depreciation on the office equipment is $480 a year, or $40 per month. Depreciation decreases an asset (in this example, Office Equipment). It also decreases stockholders' equity by increasing an expense account, Depreciation Expense. Depreciation affects the accounting equation in the following way.

Assets	=	**Liabilities**	+	**Stockholders' Equity**
−$40				−$40

Sierra recognizes depreciation for October by this adjusting entry.

Oct. 31	Depreciation Expense	40	
	Accumulated Depreciation—Office Equipment		40
	(To record monthly depreciation)		

After the company posts the adjusting entry, the accounts appear as in Illustration 4-8.

Illustration 4-8
Accounts after adjustment for depreciation

Office Equipment

Oct. 2   5,000

Oct. 31 Bal. 5,000

Accumulated Depreciation— Office Equipment

| | Oct. 31 **Adj. 40** |
| | Oct. 31 Bal. 40 |

Depreciation Expense

| Oct. 31 **Adj. 40** | |
| Oct. 31 Bal. 40 | |

The balance in the Accumulated Depreciation account will increase $40 each month, and the balance in Office Equipment remains $5,000.

Helpful Hint All contra accounts have increases, decreases, and normal balances **opposite to** the account to which they relate.

Statement Presentation. Accumulated Depreciation—Office Equipment is a **contra asset account.** That means that the account is offset against an asset account (Office Equipment) on the balance sheet. The normal balance of a contra asset account is a credit. A theoretical alternative to using a contra asset account would be to decrease (credit) the asset account by the amount of depreciation each period. But using the contra account is preferable for a simple reason: it discloses *both* the original cost of the equipment *and* the total cost that has expired to date. Thus, in the balance sheet, Sierra deducts Accumulated Depreciation—Office Equipment from the related asset account as shown in Illustration 4-9.

Illustration 4-9 Balance sheet presentation of accumulated depreciation

Office equipment	$ 5,000
Less: Accumulated depreciation—office equipment	40
	$4,960

Book value is the difference between the cost of any depreciable asset and its related accumulated depreciation. In Illustration 4-9, the book value of the equipment at the balance sheet date is $4,960. The book value and the market value of the asset are generally two different values. As noted earlier, **the purpose of depreciation is not valuation, but a means of cost allocation.**

Depreciation expense identifies the portion of an asset's cost that expired during the period (in this case, in October). The accounting equation shows that without this adjusting entry, total assets, total stockholders' equity, and net income are overstated by $40 and depreciation expense is understated by $40.

Unearned Revenues

Companies record cash received before revenue is earned by increasing (crediting) a liability account called **unearned revenues**. Items like rent, magazine subscriptions, and customer deposits for future service may result in unearned revenues. Airlines such as United, American, and Delta, for instance, treat receipts from the sale of tickets as unearned revenue until the flight service is provided.

Unearned revenues are the opposite of prepaid expenses. Indeed, unearned revenue on the books of one company is likely to be a prepayment on the books of the company that has made the advance payment. For example, if identical accounting periods are assumed, a landlord will have unearned rent revenue when a tenant has prepaid rent.

When a company receives payment for services to be provided in a future accounting period, it increases (credits) an unearned revenue (a liability) account to recognize the liability that exists. The company subsequently earns revenues by providing service. During the accounting period it is not practical to make daily entries as the company earns the revenue. Instead, we delay recognition of earned revenue until the adjustment process. Then the company makes an adjusting entry to record the revenue earned during the period and to show the liability that remains at the end of the accounting period. Typically, prior to adjustment, liabilities are overstated and revenues are understated. Therefore, as shown in Illustration 4-10, **the adjusting entry for unearned revenues results in a decrease (a debit) to a liability account and an increase (a credit) to a revenue account.**

Alternative Terminology
Book value is also referred to as *carrying value*.

Unearned Revenues

Oct.2 — Thank you in advance for your work / I will finish by Dec. 31 / ~ $1,200

Cash is received in advance; liability is recorded

Oct.31
Some service has been provided; some revenue is recorded

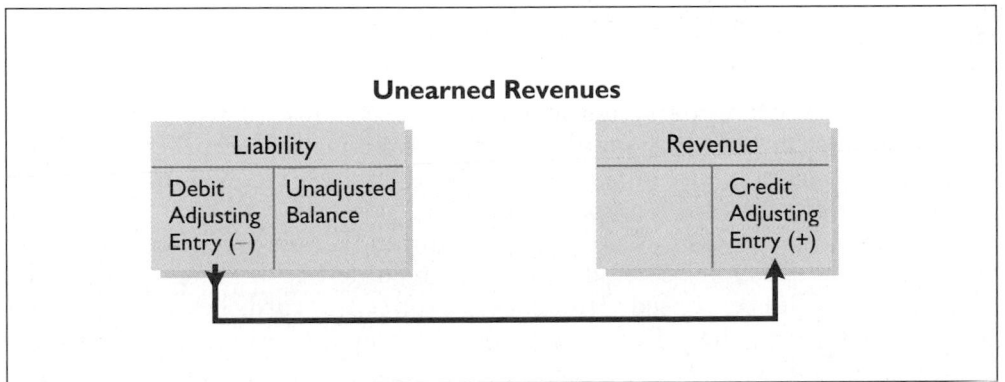

Unearned Revenues

Liability		Revenue	
Debit Adjusting Entry (−)	Unadjusted Balance		Credit Adjusting Entry (+)

Illustration 4-10
Adjusting entries for unearned revenues

Sierra Corporation received $1,200 on October 2 from R. Knox for advertising services expected to be completed by December 31. Sierra credited the payment to Unearned Service Revenue, and this liability account shows a balance of $1,200 in the October 31 trial balance. From an evaluation of the work Sierra performed for Knox during October, the company determines that it has earned $400 in October. The liability (Unearned Service Revenue) is therefore decreased, and stockholders' equity (Service Revenue) is increased. The accounting equation is affected in the following way.

Assets	=	Liabilities	+	Stockholders' Equity
		−$400		+$400

Thus, Sierra makes the following adjusting entry.

Oct. 31	Unearned Service Revenue	400	
	Service Revenue		400
	(To record revenue earned)		

After the company posts the adjusting entry, the accounts appear as in Illustration 4-11.

Illustration 4-11 Service revenue accounts after adjustment

Unearned Service Revenue				Service Revenue		
Oct. 31 **Adj. 400**	Oct. 2	1,200			Oct. 3	10,000
					31 **Adj.**	**400**
	Oct. 31	Bal. 800			Oct. 31	Bal. 10,400

The liability Unearned Service Revenue now shows a balance of $800. That amount represents the remaining advertising services expected to be performed in the future. At the same time, Service Revenue shows total revenue earned in October of $10,400. **Without this adjustment, revenues and net income are understated by $400 in the income statement. Moreover, liabilities are overstated and stockholders' equity is understated by $400 on the October 31 balance sheet.**

Accounting across the Organization

Those of you who are marketing majors (and even most of you who are not) know that gift cards are among the hottest marketing tools in merchandising today. Customers purchase gift cards and give them to someone for later use. In a recent year gift-card sales topped $95 billion.

Although these programs are popular with marketing executives, they create accounting questions. Should revenue be recorded at the time the gift card is sold, or when it is exercised? How should expired gift cards be accounted for? In its 2004 balance sheet Best Buy reported unearned revenue related to gift cards of $300 million.

Source: Robert Berner, "Gift Cards: No Gift to Investors," *Business Week* (March 14, 2005), p. 86.

 Suppose that Robert Jones purchases a $100 gift card at Best Buy on December 24, 2006, and gives it to his wife, Mary Jones, on December 25, 2006. On January 3, 2007, Mary uses the card to purchase $100 worth of CDs. When do you think Best Buy should recognize revenue and why?

BEFORE YOU GO ON . . .

▶Review It

1. What are the four types of adjusting entries?
2. What is the effect on assets, stockholders' equity, expenses, and net income if a prepaid expense adjusting entry is not made?
3. What is the effect on liabilities, stockholders' equity, revenues, and net income if an unearned revenue adjusting entry is not made?

▶ Do It

The ledger of Hammond, Inc., on March 31, 2007, includes these selected accounts before adjusting entries are prepared.

	Debit	Credit
Prepaid Insurance	$ 3,600	
Office Supplies	2,800	
Office Equipment	25,000	
Accumulated Depreciation—Office Equipment		$5,000
Unearned Service Revenue		9,200

An analysis of the accounts shows the following.

1. Insurance expires at the rate of $100 per month.
2. Supplies on hand total $800.
3. The office equipment depreciates $200 a month.
4. One-half of the unearned service revenue was earned in March.

Prepare the adjusting entries for the month of March.

Action Plan

• Make adjusting entries at the end of the period for revenues earned and expenses incurred in the period.
• Don't forget to make adjusting entries for prepayments. Failure to adjust for prepayments leads to overstatement of the asset or liability and understatement of the related expense or revenue.

Solution

		Debit	Credit
1.	Insurance Expense	100	
	Prepaid Insurance		100
	(To record insurance expired)		
2.	Office Supplies Expense	2,000	
	Office Supplies		2,000
	(To record supplies used)		
3.	Depreciation Expense	200	
	Accumulated Depreciation—Office Equipment		200
	(To record monthly depreciation)		
4.	Unearned Service Revenue	4,600	
	Service Revenue		4,600
	(To record revenue earned)		

ADJUSTING ENTRIES FOR ACCRUALS

The second category of adjusting entries is **accruals**. Prior to an accrual adjustment, the revenue account (and the related asset account) or the expense

STUDY OBJECTIVE
5
Prepare adjusting entries for accruals.

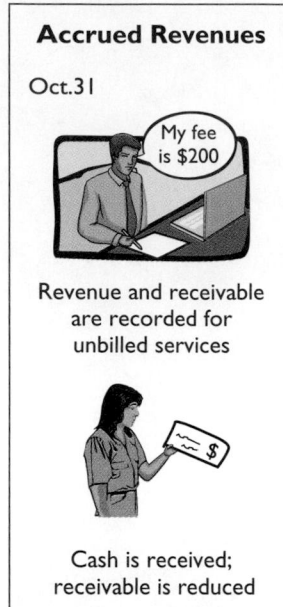

Accrued Revenues

Oct. 31

Revenue and receivable are recorded for unbilled services

Cash is received; receivable is reduced

account (and the related liability account) are understated. Thus, the adjusting entry for accruals will **increase both a balance sheet and an income statement account**.

Accrued Revenues

Revenues earned but not yet recorded at the statement date are **accrued revenues**. Accrued revenues may accumulate (accrue) with the passing of time, as in the case of interest revenue. These are unrecorded because the earning of interest does not involve daily transactions. Companies do not record interest revenue on a daily basis because it is often impractical to do so. Accrued revenues also may result from services that have been performed but not yet billed nor collected, as in the case of commissions and fees. These may be unrecorded because only a portion of the total service has been provided and the clients won't be billed until the service has been completed.

An adjusting entry records the receivable that exists at the balance sheet date and the revenue earned during the period. Prior to adjustment both assets and revenues are understated. As shown in Illustration 4-12, **an adjusting entry for accrued revenues results in an increase (a debit) to an asset account and an increase (a credit) to a revenue account**.

Illustration 4-12
Adjusting entries for accrued revenues

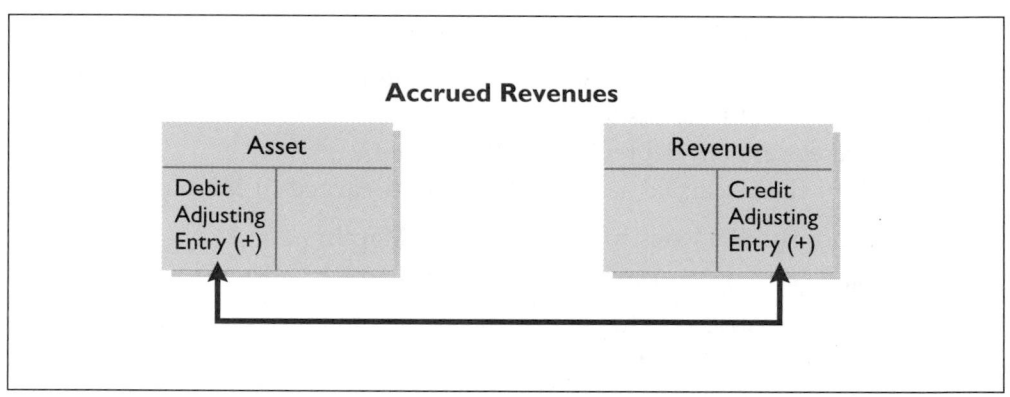

Helpful Hint For accruals, there may have been no prior entry, and the accounts requiring adjustment may both have zero balances prior to adjustment.

In October Sierra Corporation earned $200 for advertising services that were not billed to clients before October 31. Because these services are not billed, they are not recorded. The accrual of unrecorded service revenue increases an asset account, Accounts Receivable. It also increases stockholders' equity by increasing a revenue account, Service Revenue. The accrual of unrecorded service revenue affects the accounting equation in the following way.

Assets	=	Liabilities	+	Stockholders' Equity
+$200				+$200

Thus, Sierra makes the following adjusting entry.

Oct. 31	Accounts Receivable	200	
	Service Revenue		200
	(To record revenue earned)		

After the company posts the adjusting entry, the accounts appear as in Illustration 4-13.

Accounts Receivable		Service Revenue	
Oct. 31 **Adj. 200**		Oct. 3 10,000	
		31 400	
		31 **Adj. 200**	
Oct. 31 Bal. 200		Oct. 31 Bal. 10,600	

The asset Accounts Receivable shows that clients owe Sierra $200 at the balance sheet date. The balance of $10,600 in Service Revenue represents the total revenue Sierra earned during the month ($10,000 + $400 + $200). **Without the adjusting entry, assets and stockholders' equity on the balance sheet and revenues and net income on the income statement are understated.**

On November 10, Sierra receives cash of $200 for the services performed in October and makes the following entry.

Equation analyses summarize the effects of transactions on the three elements of the accounting equation, as well as the effect on cash flows.

Nov. 10	Cash	200	
	Accounts Receivable		200
	(To record cash collected on account)		

A	=	L	+	SE
+200				
−200				

Cash Flows
+200

The company records the collection of the receivables by a debit (increase) to Cash and a credit (decrease) to Accounts Receivable.

Accrued Expenses

Expenses incurred but not yet paid or recorded at the statement date are called accrued expenses. Interest, taxes, and salaries are common examples of accrued expenses.

Companies make adjustments for accrued expenses to record the obligations that exist at the balance sheet date and to recognize the expenses that apply to the current accounting period. Prior to adjustment, both liabilities and expenses are understated. Therefore, **an adjusting entry for accrued expenses results in an increase (a debit) to an expense account and an increase (a credit) to a liability account.**

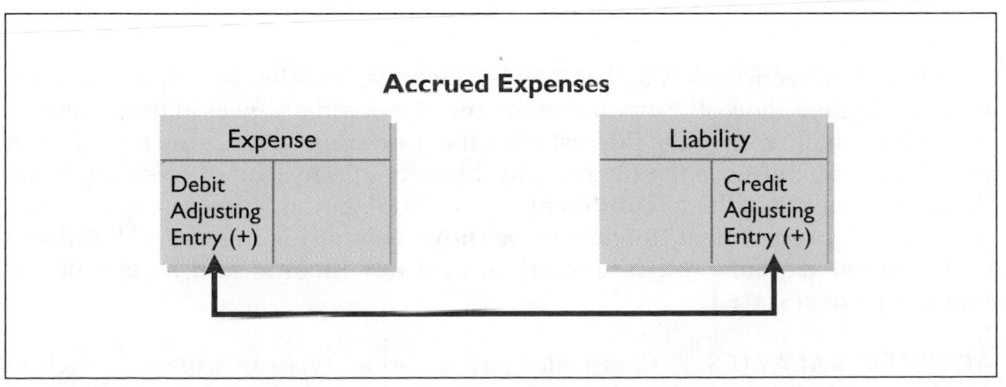

Accrued Expenses

Expense		Liability	
Debit Adjusting Entry (+)			Credit Adjusting Entry (+)

Let's look in more detail at some specific types of accrued expenses, beginning with accrued interest.

ACCRUED INTEREST. Sierra Corporation signed a three-month note payable in the amount of $5,000 on October 1. The note requires Sierra to pay interest at an annual rate of 12%.

The amount of the interest recorded is determined by three factors: (1) the face value of the note, (2) the interest rate, which is always expressed as an annual rate, and (3) the length of time the note is outstanding. For Sierra, the total interest due on the $5,000 note at its maturity date three months in the future is $150 ($5,000 $\times$ 12% $\times \frac{3}{12}$), or $50 for one month. Illustration 4-15 shows the formula for computing interest and its application to Sierra Corporation for the month of October.

Illustration 4-15
Formula for computing
interest

$$\begin{array}{ccccccc} \textbf{Face Value} & & \textbf{Annual} & & \textbf{Time} & & \\ \textbf{of Note} & \times & \textbf{Interest} & \times & \textbf{in Terms of} & = & \textbf{Interest} \\ & & \textbf{Rate} & & \textbf{One Year} & & \\ \$5{,}000 & \times & 12\% & \times & \frac{1}{12} & = & \$50 \end{array}$$

Helpful Hint In computing interest, we express the time period as a fraction of a year.

The accrual of interest at October 31 increases a liability account, Interest Payable. It also decreases stockholders' equity by increasing an expense account, Interest Expense. The accrual of interest at October 31 affects the accounting equation in the following way.

$$\underline{\textbf{Assets}} = \underline{\textbf{Liabilities}} + \underline{\textbf{Stockholders' Equity}}$$
$$+\$50 \qquad -\$50$$

Thus, Sierra makes an accrued expense adjusting entry at October 31 as follows.

Oct. 31	Interest Expense	50	
	Interest Payable		50
	(To record interest on notes payable)		

After the company posts this adjusting entry, the accounts appear as in Illustration 4-16.

Illustration 4-16 Interest accounts after adjustment

Interest Expense			Interest Payable	
Oct. 31 Adj. 50			Oct. 31	Adj. 50
Oct. 31 Bal. 50			Oct. 31	Bal. 50

Interest Expense shows the interest charges for the month of October. Interest Payable shows the amount of interest the company owes at the statement date. Sierra will not pay the interest until the note comes due at the end of three months. Companies use the Interest Payable account, instead of crediting Notes Payable, to disclose the two different types of obligations—interest and principal—in the accounts and statements. **Without this adjusting entry, liabilities and interest expense are understated, and net income and stockholders' equity are overstated.**

ACCRUED SALARIES. Companies pay for some types of expenses, such as employee salaries and commissions, after the services have been performed. Sierra Corporation last paid salaries on October 26; the next payment of salaries will not occur until November 9. As the calendar in Illustration 4-17 shows, three working days remain in October (October 29–31).

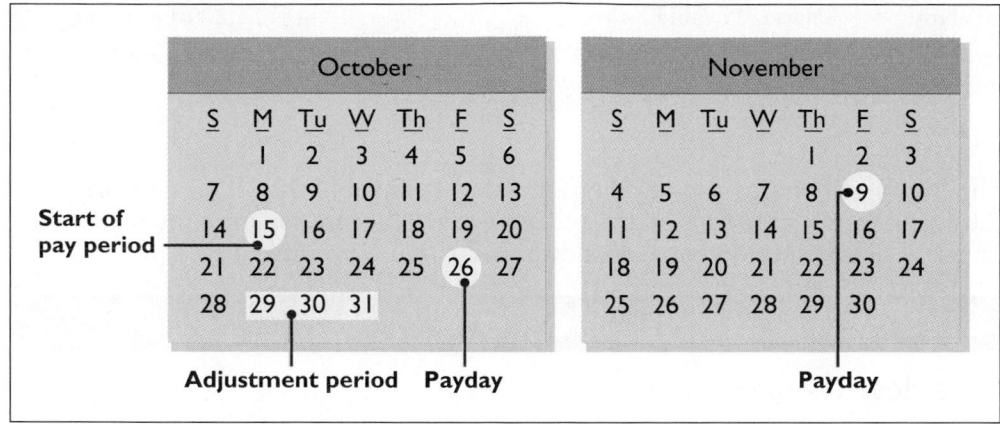

Illustration 4-17
Calendar showing Sierra
Corporation's pay periods

At October 31 the salaries for these three days represent an accrued expense and a related liability to Sierra. The employees receive total salaries of $2,000 for a five-day work week, or $400 per day. Thus, accrued salaries at October 31 are $1,200 ($400 × 3). This accrual increases a liability, Salaries Payable. It also decreases stockholders' equity by increasing an expense account, Salaries Expense. The accrual of salaries affects the accounting equation in the following way.

Assets	=	**Liabilities**	+	**Stockholders' Equity**
		+$1,200		−$1,200

Thus, Sierra makes the following adjusting entry:

Oct. 31	Salaries Expense	1,200	
	Salaries Payable		1,200
	(To record accrued salaries)		

After the company posts this adjusting entry, the accounts are as shown in Illustration 4-18.

Salaries Expense		Salaries Payable	
Oct. 26 4,000			Oct. 31 **Adj. 1,200**
31 **Adj. 1,200**			
Oct. 31 Bal. 5,200			Oct. 31 Bal. 1,200

Illustration 4-18 Salary accounts after adjustment

After this adjustment, the balance in Salaries Expense of $5,200 (13 days × $400) is the actual salary expense for October. The balance in Salaries Payable of $1,200 is the amount of the liability for salaries Sierra owes as of October 31. **Without the $1,200 adjustment for salaries, Sierra's expenses are understated $1,200 and its liabilities are understated $1,200.**

Sierra Corporation pays salaries every two weeks. Consequently, the next payday is November 9, when the company will again pay total salaries of $4,000. The payment consists of $1,200 of salaries payable at October 31 plus $2,800 of salaries expense for November (7 working days, as shown in the November calendar × $400). Therefore, Sierra makes the following entry on November 9.

Nov. 9	Salaries Payable	1,200	
	Salaries Expense	2,800	
	Cash		4,000
	(To record November 9 payroll)		

This entry eliminates the liability for Salaries Payable that Sierra recorded in the October 31 adjusting entry, and it records the proper amount of Salaries Expense for the period between November 1 and November 9.

BEFORE YOU GO ON . . .

▶Review It

1. What is the effect on assets, stockholders' equity, revenues, and net income if an accrued revenue adjusting entry is not made?
2. What is the effect on liabilities, stockholders' equity, expenses, and net income if an accrued expense adjusting entry is not made?
3. What was the amount of Tootsie Roll's 2004 depreciation expense? (*Hint:* Look in the notes to the financial statements.) The answer to this question appears on page 215.

▶ Do It

Micro Computer Services Inc. began operations on August 1, 2007. At the end of August 2007, management attempted to prepare monthly financial statements. The following information relates to August.

1. At August 31 the company owed its employees $800 in salaries that will be paid on September 1.
2. On August 1 the company borrowed $30,000 from a local bank on a 15-year mortgage. The annual interest rate is 10%.
3. Revenue earned but unrecorded for August totaled $1,100.

Prepare the adjusting entries needed at August 31, 2007.

Action Plan

• Make adjusting entries at the end of the period for revenues earned and expenses incurred in the period.
• Don't forget to make adjusting entries for accruals. Adjusting entries for accruals will increase both a balance sheet and an income statement account.

Solution

1. Salaries Expense	800	
Salaries Payable		800
(To record accrued salaries)		
2. Interest Expense	250	
Interest Payable		250
(To record accrued interest: $30,000 \times 10\% \times \frac{1}{12} = \$250$)		
3. Accounts Receivable	1,100	
Service Revenue		1,100
(To record revenue earned)		

THE NAVIGATOR

SUMMARY OF BASIC RELATIONSHIPS

Illustration 4-19 summarizes the four basic types of adjusting entries. Take some time to study and analyze the adjusting entries. Be sure to note that **each adjusting entry affects one balance sheet account and one income statement account.**

Type of Adjustment	Accounts Before Adjustment	Adjusting Entry
Prepaid expenses	Assets overstated Expenses understated	Dr. Expenses Cr. Assets
Unearned revenues	Liabilities overstated Revenues understated	Dr. Liabilities Cr. Revenues
Accrued revenues	Assets understated Revenues understated	Dr. Assets Cr. Revenues
Accrued expenses	Expenses understated Liabilities understated	Dr. Expenses Cr. Liabilities

Illustration 4-19
Summary of adjusting entries

Illustrations 4-20 and 4-21 (page 176) show the journalizing and posting of adjusting entries for Sierra Corporation on October 31. When reviewing the general ledger in Illustration 4-21, note that the adjustments are highlighted in color.

GENERAL JOURNAL

Date	Account Titles and Explanation	Debit	Credit
2007	Adjusting Entries		
Oct. 31	Advertising Supplies Expense 　Advertising Supplies 　(To record supplies used)	1,500	1,500
31	Insurance Expense 　Prepaid Insurance 　(To record insurance expired)	50	50
31	Depreciation Expense 　Accumulated Depreciation—Office Equipment 　(To record monthly depreciation)	40	40
31	Unearned Service Revenue 　Service Revenue 　(To record revenue earned)	400	400
31	Accounts Receivable 　Service Revenue 　(To record revenue earned)	200	200
31	Interest Expense 　Interest Payable 　(To record interest on notes payable)	50	50
31	Salaries Expense 　Salaries Payable 　(To record accrued salaries)	1,200	1,200

Illustration 4-20 General journal showing adjusting entries

Illustration 4-21 General ledger after adjustments

GENERAL LEDGER

Cash

Oct.	1	10,000	Oct.	2	5,000
	1	5,000		3	900
	2	1,200		4	600
	3	10,000		20	500
				26	4,000

Oct. 31	Bal. 15,200	

Accounts Receivable

Oct. 31	**200**	
Oct. 31	Bal. 200	

Advertising Supplies

Oct. 5	2,500	Oct. 31	**1,500**
Oct. 31	Bal. 1,000		

Prepaid Insurance

Oct. 4	600	Oct. 31	**50**
Oct. 31	Bal. 550		

Office Equipment

Oct. 2	5,000	
Oct. 31	Bal. 5,000	

Accumulated Depreciation— Office Equipment

	Oct. 31	**40**
	Oct. 31	Bal. 40

Notes Payable

	Oct. 1	5,000
	Oct. 31	Bal. 5,000

Accounts Payable

	Oct. 5	2,500
	Oct. 31	Bal. 2,500

Interest Payable

	Oct. 31	**50**
	Oct. 31	Bal. 50

Unearned Service Revenue

Oct. 31	**400**	Oct. 2	1,200
		Oct. 31	Bal. 800

Salaries Payable

	Oct. 31	**1,200**
	Oct. 31	Bal. 1,200

Common Stock

	Oct. 1	10,000
	Oct. 31	Bal. 10,000

Retained Earnings

	Oct. 31	Bal. 0

Dividends

Oct. 20	500	
Oct. 31	Bal. 500	

Service Revenue

	Oct. 3	10,000
	31	**400**
	31	**200**
	Oct. 31	Bal. 10,600

Salaries Expense

Oct. 26	4,000	
31	**1,200**	
Oct. 31	Bal. 5,200	

Advertising Supplies Expense

Oct. 31	**1,500**	
Oct. 31	Bal. 1,500	

Rent Expense

Oct. 3	900	
Oct. 31	Bal. 900	

Insurance Expense

Oct. 31	**50**	
Oct. 31	Bal. 50	

Interest Expense

Oct. 31	**50**	
Oct. 31	Bal. 50	

Depreciation Expense

Oct. 31	**40**	
Oct. 31	Bal. 40	

The Adjusted Trial Balance and Financial Statements

After a company has journalized and posted all adjusting entries, it prepares another trial balance from the ledger accounts. This trial balance is called an **adjusted trial balance**. It shows the balances of all accounts, including those adjusted, at the end of the accounting period. The purpose of an adjusted trial balance is to **prove the equality** of the total debit balances and the total credit balances in the ledger after all adjustments. Because the accounts contain all data needed for financial statements, the adjusted trial balance is the **primary basis for the preparation of financial statements**.

> **STUDY OBJECTIVE**
> **6**
> Describe the nature and purpose of the adjusted trial balance.

PREPARING THE ADJUSTED TRIAL BALANCE

Illustration 4-22 presents the adjusted trial balance for Sierra Corporation prepared from the ledger accounts in Illustration 4-21. The amounts affected by the adjusting entries are highlighted in color.

SIERRA CORPORATION Adjusted Trial Balance October 31, 2007	Dr.	Cr.
Cash	$15,200	
Accounts Receivable	200	
Advertising Supplies	1,000 ·	
Prepaid Insurance	550	
Office Equipment	5,000	
Accumulated Depreciation—Office Equipment		$ 40
Notes Payable		5,000
Accounts Payable		2,500
Interest Payable		50
Unearned Service Revenue		800
Salaries Payable		1,200
Common Stock		10,000
Retained Earnings		0
Dividends	500	
Service Revenue		10,600
Salaries Expense	5,200	
Advertising Supplies Expense	1,500	
Rent Expense	900	
Insurance Expense	50	
Interest Expense	50	
Depreciation Expense	40	
	$30,190	$30,190

Illustration 4-22
Adjusted trial balance

PREPARING FINANCIAL STATEMENTS

Companies can prepare financial statements directly from an adjusted trial balance. Illustrations 4-23 (page 178) and 4-24 (page 179) present the interrelationships of data in the adjusted trial balance of Sierra Corporation. As Illustration 4-23 shows, companies prepare the income statement from the revenue and expense accounts. Similarly, they derive the retained earnings statement from the retained earnings account, dividends account, and the net income (or net loss) shown in the income statement. As Illustration 4-24 shows, companies then prepare the balance sheet from the asset, liability, and stockholders' equity accounts. They obtain the amount reported for retained earnings on the balance sheet from the ending balance in the retained earnings statement.

Illustration 4-23
Preparation of the income statement and retained earnings statement from the adjusted trial balance

SIERRA CORPORATION
Adjusted Trial Balance
October 31, 2007

Account	Debit	Credit
Cash	$15,200	
Accounts Receivable	200	
Advertising Supplies	1,000	
Prepaid Insurance	550	
Office Equipment	5,000	
Accumulated Depreciation—		
Office Equipment		$ 40
Notes Payable		5,000
Accounts Payable		2,500
Interest Payable		50
Unearned Service Revenue		800
Salaries Payable		1,200
Common Stock		10,000
Retained Earnings		0
Dividends	500	
Service Revenue		10,600
Salaries Expense	5,200	
Advertising Supplies Expense	1,500	
Rent Expense	900	
Insurance Expense	50	
Interest Expense	50	
Depreciation Expense	40	
	$30,190	$30,190

SIERRA CORPORATION
Income Statement
For the Month Ended October 31, 2007

Revenues		
Service revenue		$10,600
Expenses		
Salaries expense	$5,200	
Advertising supplies expense	1,500	
Rent expense	900	
Insurance expense	50	
Interest expense	50	
Depreciation expense	40	
Total expenses		7,740
Net income		$ 2,860

SIERRA CORPORATION
Retained Earnings Statement
For the Month Ended October 31, 2007

Retained earnings, October 1		$ 0
Add: Net income		2,860
		2,860
Less: Dividends		500
Retained earnings, October 31		$ 2,360

To balance sheet

Closing the Books

Alternative Terminology
Temporary accounts are sometimes called *nominal accounts*, and permanent accounts are sometimes called *real accounts*.

In previous chapters you learned that revenue and expense accounts and the dividends account are subdivisions of retained earnings, which is reported in the stockholders' equity section of the balance sheet. Because revenues, expenses, and dividends relate to only a given accounting period, they are considered **temporary accounts**. In contrast, all balance sheet accounts are considered **permanent accounts** because their balances are carried forward into future accounting periods. Illustration 4-25 identifies the accounts in each category.

PREPARING CLOSING ENTRIES

STUDY OBJECTIVE
7
Explain the purpose of closing entries.

At the end of the accounting period, companies transfer the temporary account balances to the permanent stockholders' equity account—Retained Earnings— through the preparation of closing entries. **Closing entries** transfer net income (or net loss) and dividends to Retained Earnings, so the balance in Retained

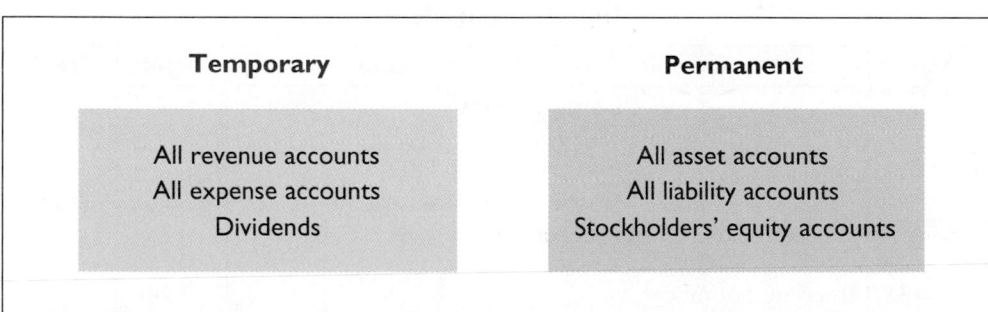

SIERRA CORPORATION Adjusted Trial Balance October 31, 2007		
Account	Debit	Credit
Cash	$15,200	
Accounts Receivable	200	
Advertising Supplies	1,000	
Prepaid Insurance	550	
Office Equipment	5,000	
Accumulated Depreciation—Office Equipment		$ 40
Notes Payable		5,000
Accounts Payable		2,500
Salaries Payable		1,200
Unearned Service Revenue		800
Interest Payable		50
Common Stock		10,000
Retained Earnings		0
Dividends	500	
Service Revenue		10,600
Salaries Expense	5,200	
Advertising Supplies Expense	1,500	
Rent Expense	900	
Insurance Expense	50	
Interest Expense	50	
Depreciation Expense	40	
	$30,190	$30,190

SIERRA CORPORATION
Balance Sheet
October 31, 2007

Assets

Cash		$15,200
Accounts receivable		200
Advertising supplies		1,000
Prepaid insurance		550
Office equipment	$5,000	
Less: Accumulated depreciation	40	4,960
Total assets		$21,910

Liabilities and Stockholders' Equity

Liabilities		
Notes payable	$ 5,000	
Accounts payable	2,500	
Salaries payable	1,200	
Unearned service revenue	800	
Interest payable	50	
Total liabilities		$ 9,550
Stockholders' equity		
Common stock	10,000	
Retained earnings	2,360	
Total stockholders' equity		12,360
Total liabilities and stockholders' equity		$21,910

Balance at Oct. 31 from Retained Earnings Statement in Illustration 4-23

Illustration 4-25
Temporary versus permanent accounts

Temporary	Permanent
All revenue accounts	All asset accounts
All expense accounts	All liability accounts
Dividends	Stockholders' equity accounts

Earnings agrees with the retained earnings statement. For example, notice that in the adjusted trial balance in Illustration 4-24, Retained Earnings has a balance of zero. Prior to the closing entries, the balance in Retained Earnings will be its beginning-of-the-period balance. For Sierra this is zero because it is Sierra's first month of operations.

In addition to updating Retained Earnings to its correct ending balance, closing entries produce a **zero balance in each temporary account**. As a result, these accounts are ready to accumulate data about revenues, expenses, and dividends in the next accounting period separate from the data in the prior periods. **Permanent accounts are not closed.**

When companies prepare closing entries, they could close each income statement account directly to Retained Earnings. However, to do so would result in excessive detail in the retained earnings account. Accordingly, companies close the revenue and expense accounts to another temporary account, **Income Summary**, and they transfer only the resulting net income or net loss from this account to Retained Earnings. Illustration 4-26 depicts the closing process. While it still takes the average large company seven days to close, some companies such as Cisco employ technology that allows them to do a so-called "virtual close" almost instantaneously any time during the year. Besides dramatically reducing the cost of closing, the virtual close provides companies with accurate data for decision making whenever they desire it.

Illustration 4-26 The closing process

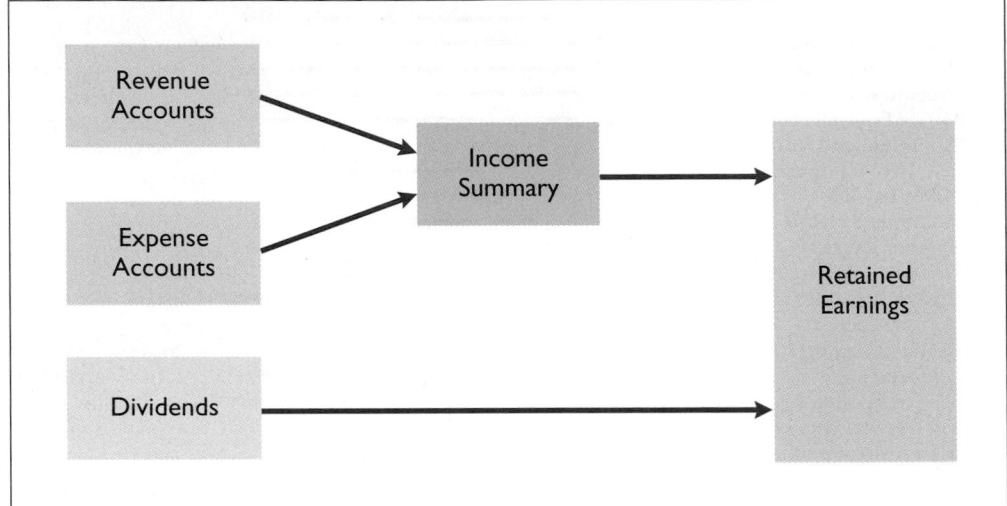

Illustration 4-27 shows the closing entries for Sierra Corporation. Illustration 4-28 (page 181) diagrams the posting process for Sierra Corporation's closing entries.

Illustration 4-27 Closing entries journalized

Helpful Hint Income Summary is a very descriptive title: Companies close total revenues to Income Summary and total expenses to Income Summary. The balance in the Income Summary is a net income or net loss.

GENERAL JOURNAL

Date		Account Titles and Explanation	Debit	Credit
		Closing Entries		
2007		(1)		
Oct.	31	Service Revenue	10,600	
		Income Summary		10,600
		(To close revenue account)		
		(2)		
	31	Income Summary	7,740	
		Salaries Expense		5,200
		Advertising Supplies Expense		1,500
		Rent Expense		900
		Insurance Expense		50
		Interest Expense		50
		Depreciation Expense		40
		(To close expense accounts)		
		(3)		
	31	Income Summary	2,860	
		Retained Earnings		2,860
		(To close net income to retained earnings)		
		(4)		
	31	Retained Earnings	500	
		Dividends		500
		(To close dividends to retained earnings)		

Illustration 4-28   Posting of closing entries

Salaries Expense			
4,000	(2)	5,200	
1,200			
5,200		5,200	

Service Revenue			
(1)	10,600	10,000	
		400	
		200	
	10,600	10,600	

Advertising Supplies Expense		
1,500	(2)	1,500

Rent Expense		
900	(2)	900

Income Summary			
(2)	7,740	(1)	10,600
(3)	2,860		
	10,600		10,600

Insurance Expense		
50	(2)	50

Interest Expense		
50	(2)	50

Retained Earnings			
(4)	500		–0–
		(3)	2,860
		Bal.	2,360

Depreciation Expense		
40	(2)	40

Dividends		
500	(4)	500

PREPARING A POST-CLOSING TRIAL BALANCE

After a company journalizes and posts all closing entries, it prepares another trial balance, called a **post-closing trial balance**, from the ledger. A post-closing trial balance is a list of all permanent accounts and their balances after closing entries are journalized and posted. **The purpose of this trial balance is to prove the equality of the permanent account balances that the company carries forward into the next accounting period.** Since all temporary accounts will have zero balances, **the post-closing trial balance will contain only permanent—balance sheet—accounts**.

SUMMARY OF THE ACCOUNTING CYCLE

Illustration 4-29 (page 182) shows the required steps in the accounting cycle. You can see that the cycle begins with the analysis of business transactions and ends with the preparation of a post-closing trial balance. Companies perform the steps in the cycle in sequence and repeat them in each accounting period.

STUDY OBJECTIVE
8

Describe the required steps in the accounting cycle.

Illustration 4-29
Required steps in the accounting cycle

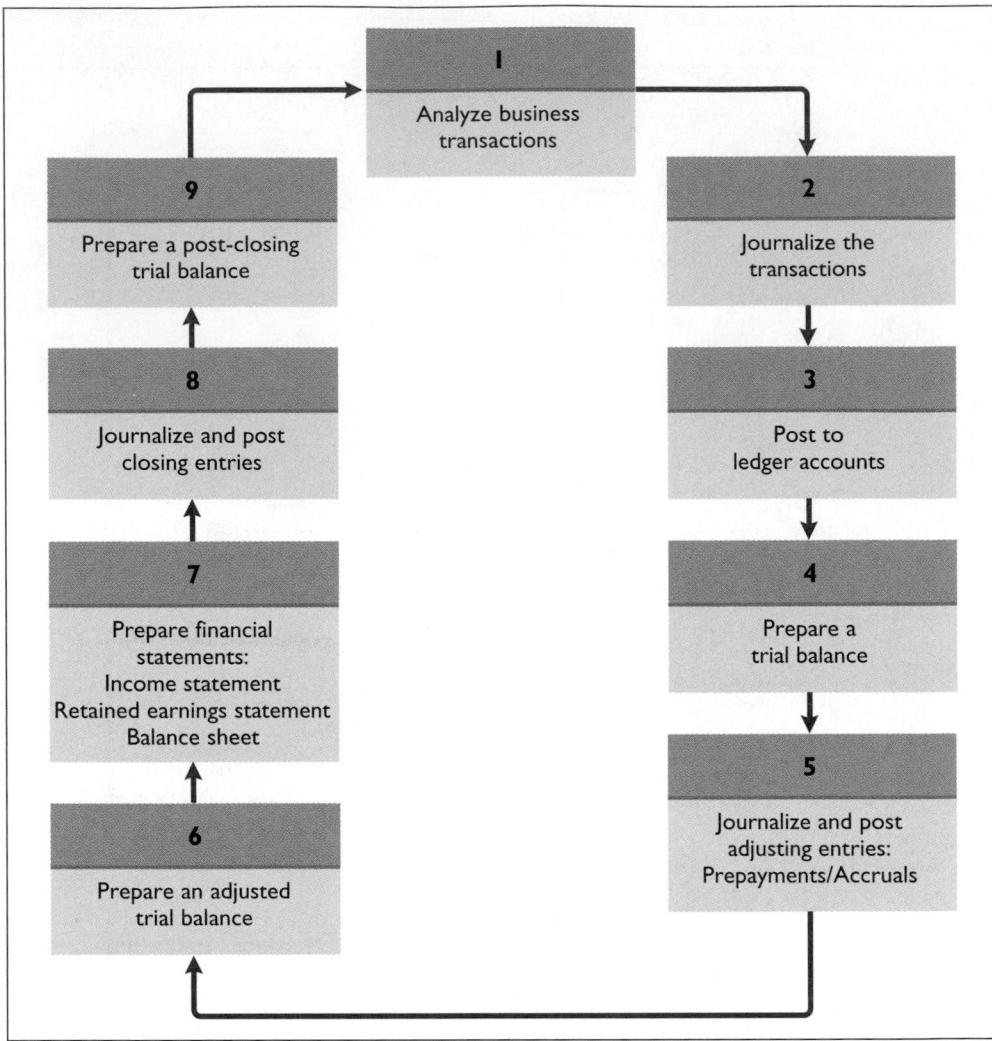

Helpful Hint Some companies prefer to reverse certain adjusting entries at the beginning of a new accounting period. The company makes a **reversing entry** at the beginning of the next accounting period; this entry is the exact opposite of the adjusting entry made in the previous period.

Steps 1–3 may occur daily during the accounting period, as explained in Chapter 3. Companies perform Steps 4–7 on a periodic basis, such as monthly, quarterly, or annually. Steps 8 and 9, closing entries and a post-closing trial balance, usually take place only at the end of a company's **annual** accounting period.

Quality of Earnings

"Did you make your numbers today?" is a question asked often in both large and small businesses. Companies and employees are continually under pressure to "make the numbers"—that is, to have earnings that are in line with expectations. As a consequence it is not surprising that many companies practice earnings management. **Earnings management** is the planned timing of revenues, expenses, gains, and losses to smooth out bumps in net income. The quality of earnings is greatly affected when a company manages earnings up or down to meet some targeted earnings number. A company that has a high **quality of earnings** provides full and transparent information that will not confuse or mislead users of the financial statements. A company with questionable quality of earnings may mislead investors and creditors, who believe they are relying on relevant and reliable information. As a consequence, investors and creditors lose confidence in financial reporting, and it becomes difficult for our capital markets to work efficiently.

Companies manage earnings in a variety of ways. One way is through the use of **one-time items** to prop up earnings numbers. For example, ConAgra Foods recorded a nonrecurring gain from the sale of Pilgrim's Pride stock for $186 million to help meet an earnings projection for the quarter.

Another way is to **inflate revenue** numbers in the short-run to the detriment of the long-run. For example, Bristol-Myers Squibb provided sales incentives to its wholesalers to encourage them to buy products at the end of the quarter. As a result Bristol-Myers was able to meet its sales projections. The problem was that the wholesalers could not sell that amount of merchandise and ended up returning it to Bristol-Myers. The result was that Bristol-Myers had to restate its income numbers.

Companies also manage earnings through **improper adjusting entries**. Regulators investigated Xerox for accusations that it was booking too much revenue up-front on multi-year contract sales. Financial executives at Office Max resigned amid accusations that the company was recognizing rebates from its vendors too early and therefore overstating revenue. Finally, WorldCom's abuse of adjusting entries to meet its net income targets is unsurpassed: It used adjusting entries to increase net income by reclassifying liabilities as revenue and reclassifying expenses as assets. Investigations of the company's books after it went bankrupt revealed adjusting entries of more than a billion dollars that had no supporting documentation.

The good news is that, as a result of investor pressure as well as the **Sarbanes-Oxley Act**, many companies are trying to improve the quality of their financial reporting. For example, hotel operator Marriott is now providing detailed information on the write-offs it has on loan guarantees it gives hotels. General Electric has decided to provide more detail on its revenues and operating profits for individual businesses it owns. IBM is attempting to provide a better breakdown of its earnings. At the same time, regulators are taking a tough stand on the issue of quality of earnings. For example, one regulator noted that companies may be required to restate their financials every single time that they account for any transaction that had no legitimate purpose but was done solely for an accounting purpose, such as to smooth net income.

BEFORE YOU GO ON . . .

▶ **Review It**

1. How do permanent accounts differ from temporary accounts?
2. What four different types of entries are required in closing the books?
3. What are the content and purpose of a post-closing trial balance?
4. What are the required steps in the accounting cycle?
5. Explain the term earnings management and describe the actions that companies take to manage earnings.

✓ THE NAVIGATOR

Using the Decision Toolkit

Humana Corporation provides managed health care services to approximately 7 million people. Headquartered in Louisville, Kentucky, it has over 13,700 employees in 15 states and Puerto Rico. A simplified version of Humana's December 31, 2004, adjusted trial balance is shown at the top of the next page.

Instructions

From the trial balance, prepare an income statement, retained earnings statement, and classified balance sheet. **Be sure to prepare them in that order, since each statement depends on information determined in the preceding statement.**

HUMANA.

HUMANA CORPORATION
Adjusted Trial Balance
December 31, 2004
(in millions)

Account	Dr.	Cr.
Cash	$ 580	
Short-Term Investments	2,146	
Receivables	580	
Other Current Assets	290	
Property and Equipment, Net	400	
Long-Term Investments	348	
Other Long-Term Assets	1,314	
Medical Costs Payable		$ 1,422
Accounts Payable		680
Other Current Liabilities		225
Long-Term Debt		1,241
Common Stock		1,046
Dividends	0	
Retained Earnings		764
Revenues		13,104
Medical Cost Expense	10,669	
Selling, General, and Administrative Expense	1,878	
Depreciation Expense	118	
Interest Expense	23	
Income Tax Expense	136	
	$18,482	$18,482

Solution

HUMANA.

HUMANA CORPORATION
Income Statement
For the Year Ended December 31, 2004
(in millions)

Revenues		$13,104
Medical cost expense	$10,669	
Selling, general, and administrative expense	1,878	
Depreciation expense	118	
Interest expense	23	
Income tax expense	136	12,824
Net income		$ 280

HUMANA.

HUMANA CORPORATION
Retained Earnings Statement
For the Year Ended December 31, 2004
(in millions)

Beginning retained earnings	$ 764
Add: Net income	280
Less: Dividends	0
Ending retained earnings	$1,044

HUMANA.

HUMANA CORPORATION
Balance Sheet
December 31, 2004
(in millions)

Assets

Current assets		
Cash	$ 580	
Short-term investments	2,146	
Receivables	580	
Other current assets	290	
Total current assets		$3,596
Long-term investments		348
Property and equipment, net		400
Other long-term assets		1,314
Total assets		$5,658

Liabilities and Stockholders' Equity

Liabilities		
Current liabilities		
Medical costs payable	$1,422	
Accounts payable	680	
Other current liabilities	225	
Total current liabilities		$2,327
Long-term debt		1,241
Total liabilities		3,568
Stockholders' equity		
Common stock	1,046	
Retained earnings	1,044	
Total stockholders' equity		2,090
Total liabilities and stockholders' equity		$5,658

Summary of Study Objectives

1 *Explain the revenue recognition principle and the matching principle.* The revenue recognition principle dictates that companies recognize revenue in the accounting period in which it is earned. The matching principle dictates that companies recognize expenses when expenses make their contribution to revenues.

2 *Differentiate between the cash basis and the accrual basis of accounting.* Accrual-based accounting means that companies record, in the periods in which the events occur, events that change a company's financial statements. Under the cash basis, companies record events only in the periods in which the company receives or pays cash.

3 *Explain why adjusting entries are needed, and identify the major types of adjusting entries.* Companies make adjusting entries at the end of an accounting period. These entries ensure that companies record revenues in the period in which they are earned and that companies recognize expenses in the period in which they are incurred. The major types of adjusting entries are prepaid expenses, unearned revenues, accrued revenues, and accrued expenses.

4 *Prepare adjusting entries for prepayments.* Prepayments are either prepaid expenses or unearned revenues. Companies make adjusting entries for prepayments at the statement date to record the portion of the prepayment that represents the expense incurred or the revenue earned in the current accounting period.

5 *Prepare adjusting entries for accruals.* Accruals are either accrued revenues or accrued expenses. Adjusting entries for accruals record revenues earned and expenses incurred in the current accounting period that have not been recognized through daily entries.

6 *Describe the nature and purpose of the adjusted trial balance.* An adjusted trial balance is a trial balance that shows the balances of all accounts, including those that have been adjusted, at the end of an accounting period. The purpose of an adjusted trial balance is to show the effects of all financial events that have occurred during the accounting period.

7 *Explain the purpose of closing entries.* One purpose of closing entries is to transfer the results of operations for the period to Retained Earnings. A second purpose is to "zero-out" all temporary accounts (revenue accounts, expense accounts, and dividends) so that they start each new period with a zero balance. To accomplish this, companies "close" all temporary accounts at the end of an accounting period. They make separate entries to close revenues and expenses to Income Summary, Income Summary to Retained Earnings, and Dividends to Retained Earnings. Only temporary accounts are closed.

8 *Describe the required steps in the accounting cycle.* The required steps in the accounting cycle are: (a) analyze business transactions, (b) journalize the transactions, (c) post to ledger accounts, (d) prepare a trial balance, (e) journalize and post adjusting entries, (f) prepare an adjusted trial balance, (g) prepare financial statements, (h) journalize and post closing entries, and (i) prepare a post-closing trial balance.

Decision Toolkit—A Summary

Decision Checkpoints	Info Needed for Decision	Tool to Use for Decision	How to Evaluate Results
At what point should the company record revenue?	Need to understand the nature of the company's business	Revenue should be recorded when earned. A service business earns revenue when it performs a service.	Recognizing revenue too early overstates current period revenue; recognizing it too late understates current period revenue.
At what point should the company record expenses?	Need to understand the nature of the company's business	Expenses should "follow" revenues—that is, match the effort (expense) with the result (revenue).	Recognizing expenses too early overstates current period expense; recognizing them too late understates current period expense.

APPENDIX
ADJUSTING ENTRIES IN AN AUTOMATED WORLD—USING A WORK SHEET

STUDY OBJECTIVE
9
Describe the purpose and the basic form of a work sheet.

In the previous discussion we used T accounts and trial balances to arrive at the amounts used to prepare financial statements. Accountants frequently use a device known as a work sheet to determine these amounts. A **work sheet** is a multiple-column form that may be used in the adjustment process and in preparing financial statements. Accountants can prepare work sheets manually, but today most use computer spreadsheets.

As its name suggests, the work sheet is a working tool for the accountant. **A work sheet is not a permanent accounting record**; it is neither a journal nor a part of the general ledger. The work sheet is merely a supplemental device used to make it easier to prepare adjusting entries and the financial statements. Small companies that have relatively few accounts and adjustments may not need a work sheet. In large companies with numerous accounts and many adjustments, a work sheet is almost indispensable.

Illustration 4A-1 shows the basic form of a work sheet. Note the headings: The work sheet starts with two columns for the Trial Balance. The next two columns record all Adjustments. Next is the Adjusted Trial Balance. The last two sets of columns correspond to the Income Statement and the Balance Sheet. All items listed in the Adjusted Trial Balance columns are included in either the Income Statement or the Balance Sheet columns.

Illustration 4A-1   Form and procedure for a work sheet

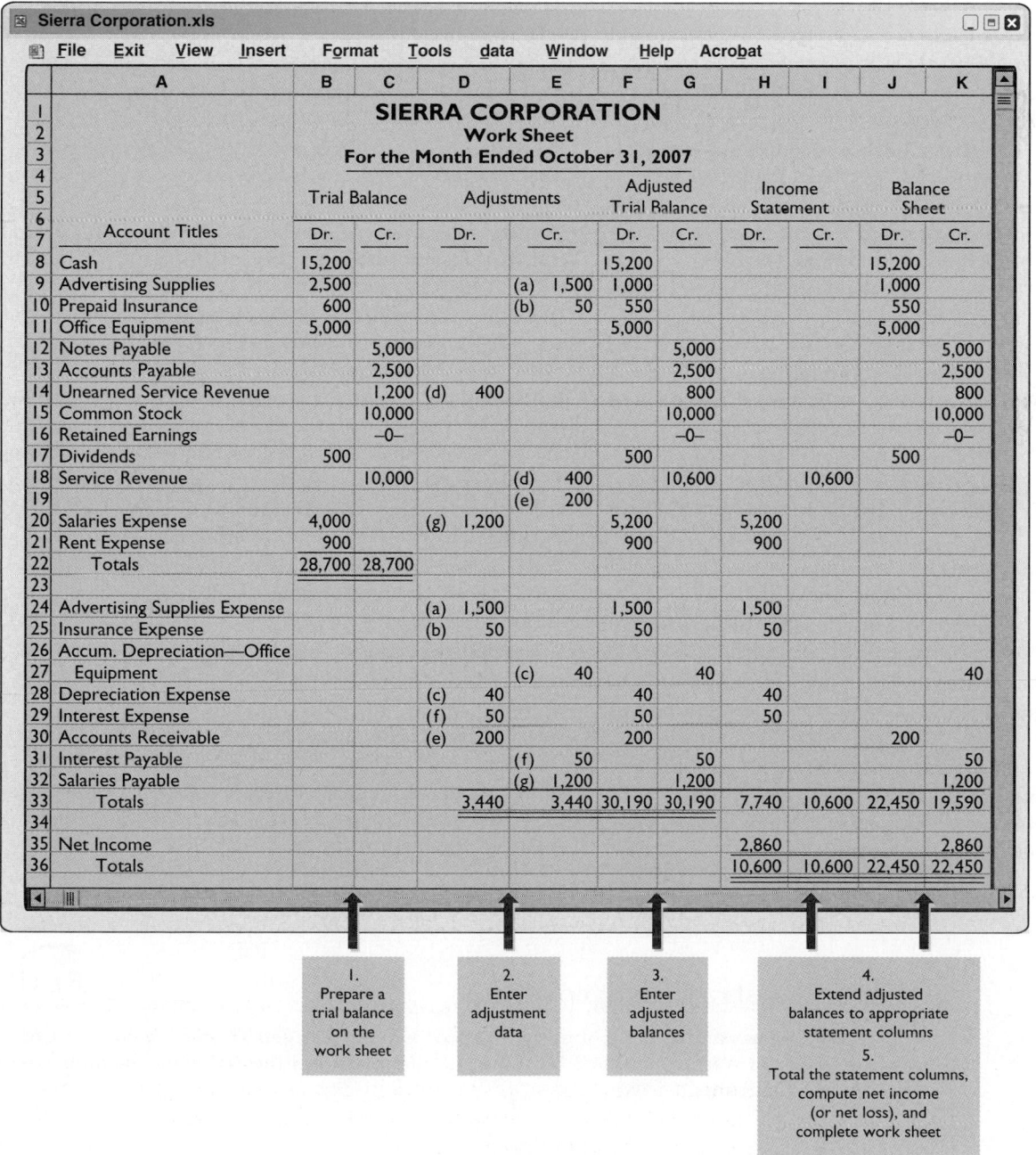

Summary of Study Objective for Appendix

9 *Describe the purpose and the basic form of a work sheet.* The work sheet is a device to make it easier to prepare adjusting entries and the financial statements. Companies often prepare a work sheet on a computer spreadsheet. The sets of columns of the work sheet are, from left to right, the unadjusted trial balance, adjustments, adjusted trial balance, income statement, and balance sheet.

Glossary

Accrual-basis accounting Accounting basis in which companies record, in the periods in which the events occur, transactions that change a company's financial statements, rather than in the periods in which the company receives or pays cash. (p. 160)

Accrued expenses Expenses incurred but not yet paid in cash or recorded. (p. 171)

Accrued revenues Revenues earned but not yet received in cash or recorded. (p. 170)

Adjusted trial balance A list of accounts and their balances after all adjustments have been made. (p. 177)

Adjusting entries Entries made at the end of an accounting period to ensure that the revenue recognition and matching principles are followed. (p. 161)

Book value The difference between the cost of a depreciable asset and its related accumulated depreciation. (p. 167)

Cash-basis accounting Accounting basis in which a company records revenue only when it receives cash, and an expense only when it pays out cash. (p. 160)

Closing entries Entries at the end of an accounting period to transfer the balances of temporary accounts to a permanent stockholders' equity account, Retained Earnings. (p. 178)

Contra asset account An account that is offset against an asset account on the balance sheet. (p. 166)

Depreciation The process of allocating the cost of an asset to expense over its useful life. (p. 165)

Earnings management The planned timing of revenues, expenses, gains, and losses to smooth out bumps in net income. (p. 182)

Fiscal year An accounting period that is one year long. (p. 158, in margin)

Income Summary A temporary account used in closing revenue and expense accounts. (p. 180)

Matching principle The principle that dictates that companies match efforts (expenses) with accomplishments (revenues). (p. 159)

Permanent accounts Balance sheet accounts whose balances are carried forward to the next accounting period. (p. 178)

Post-closing trial balance A list of permanent accounts and their balances after a company has journalized and posted closing entries. (p. 181)

Prepaid expenses (Prepayments) Expenses paid in cash and recorded as assets before they are used or consumed. (p. 163)

Quality of earnings Indicates the level of full and transparent information that a company provides to users of its financial statements. (p. 182)

Revenue recognition principle The principle that companies recognize revenue in the accounting period in which it is earned. (p. 158)

Reversing entry An entry made at the beginning of the next accounting period; the exact opposite of the adjusting entry made in the previous period. (p. 182, in margin)

Temporary accounts Revenue, expense, and dividend accounts whose balances a company transfers to Retained Earnings at the end of an accounting period. (p. 178)

Time period assumption An assumption that the economic life of a business can be divided into artificial time periods. (p. 158)

Unearned revenues Cash received before a company earns revenues and recorded as a liability until earned. (p. 167)

Useful life The length of service of a productive asset. (p. 165)

Work sheet A multiple-column form that companies may use in the adjustment process and in preparing financial statements. (p. 186)

Demonstration Problem

Terry Thomas and a group of investors incorporate the Green Thumb Lawn Care Corporation on April 1. At April 30 the trial balance shows the following balances for selected accounts.

Prepaid Insurance	$ 3,600
Equipment	28,000
Notes Payable	20,000
Unearned Service Revenue	4,200
Service Revenue	1,800

Analysis reveals the following additional data pertaining to these accounts.

1. Prepaid insurance is the cost of a 2-year insurance policy, effective April 1.
2. Depreciation on the equipment is $500 per month.
3. The note payable is dated April 1. It is a 6-month, 12% note.
4. Seven customers paid for the company's 6-month lawn service package of $600 beginning in April. These customers received the first month of services in April.
5. Lawn services performed for other customers but not billed at April 30 totaled $1,500.

Instructions

Prepare the adjusting entries for the month of April. Show computations.

Solution to Demonstration Problem

GENERAL JOURNAL

Date	Account Titles and Explanation	Debit	Credit
	Adjusting Entries		
Apr. 30	Insurance Expense	150	
	Prepaid Insurance		150
	(To record insurance expired:		
	$3,600 ÷ 24 = $150 per month)		
30	Depreciation Expense	500	
	Accumulated Depreciation—Equipment		500
	(To record monthly depreciation)		
30	Interest Expense	200	
	Interest Payable		200
	(To accrue interest on notes payable:		
	$20,000 × 12% × $\frac{1}{12}$ = $200)		
30	Unearned Service Revenue	700	
	Service Revenue		700
	(To record revenue earned: $600 ÷ 6 = $100;		
	$100 per month × 7 = $700)		
30	Accounts Receivable	1,500	
	Service Revenue		1,500
	(To accrue revenue earned but not billed		
	or collected)		

Action Plan

- Note that adjustments are being made for one month.
- Make computations carefully.
- Select account titles carefully.
- Make sure debits are made first and credits are indented.
- Check that debits equal credits for each entry.

Self-Study Questions

WILEY
PLUS

Answers are at the end of this chapter.

(SO 1) 1. What is the time period assumption?

(a) Companies should recognize revenue in the accounting period in which it is earned.

(b) Companies should match expenses with revenues.

(c) The economic life of a business can be divided into artificial time periods.

(d) The fiscal year should correspond with the calendar year.

(SO 1) **2.** Which principle dictates that efforts (expenses) be recorded with accomplishments (revenues)?
(a) Matching principle.
(b) Cost principle.
(c) Periodicity principle.
(d) Revenue recognition principle.

(SO 3) **3.** Adjusting entries are made to ensure that:
(a) expenses are recognized in the period in which they are incurred.
(b) revenues are recorded in the period in which they are earned.
(c) balance sheet and income statement accounts have correct balances at the end of an accounting period.
(d) All of the above.

(SO 4, 5) **4.** Each of the following is a major type (or category) of adjusting entry *except:*
(a) prepaid expenses.
(b) accrued revenues.
(c) accrued expenses.
(d) earned expenses.

(SO 4) **5.** The trial balance shows Supplies $1,350 and Supplies Expense $0. If $600 of supplies are on hand at the end of the period, the adjusting entry is:

(a) Supplies	600	
Supplies Expense		600
(b) Supplies	750	
Supplies Expense		750
(c) Supplies Expense	750	
Supplies		750
(d) Supplies Expense	600	
Supplies		600

(SO 4) **6.** Adjustments for unearned revenues:
(a) decrease liabilities and increase revenues.
(b) increase liabilities and increase revenues.
(c) increase assets and increase revenues.
(d) decrease revenues and decrease assets.

(SO 5) **7.** Adjustments for accrued revenues:
(a) increase assets and increase liabilities.
(b) increase assets and increase revenues.
(c) decrease assets and decrease revenues.
(d) decrease liabilities and increase revenues.

(SO 5) **8.** Colleen Mooney earned a salary of $400 for the last week of September. She will be paid on October 1. The adjusting entry for Colleen's employer at September 30 is:

(a) No entry is required.		
(b) Salaries Expense	400	
Salaries Payable		400
(c) Salaries Expense	400	
Cash		400
(d) Salaries Payable	400	
Cash		400

(SO 6) **9.** Which statement is *incorrect* concerning the adjusted trial balance?
(a) An adjusted trial balance proves the equality of the total debit balances and the total credit balances in the ledger after all adjustments are made.
(b) The adjusted trial balance provides the primary basis for the preparation of financial statements.
(c) The adjusted trial balance lists the account balances segregated by assets and liabilities.
(d) The company prepares the adjusted trial balance after it has journalized and posted the adjusting entries.

(SO 2) **10.** Which one of these statements about the accrual basis of accounting is *false?*
(a) Companies record in the periods in which the events occur events that change a company's financial statements.
(b) Companies recognize revenue in the period in which it is earned.
(c) This basis is in accord with generally accepted accounting principles.
(d) Companies record revenue only when they receive cash, and record expense only when they pay out cash.

(SO 7) **11.** Which account will have a zero balance after a company has journalized and posted closing entries?
(a) Service Revenue.
(b) Advertising Supplies.
(c) Prepaid Insurance.
(d) Accumulated Depreciation.

(SO 7) **12.** Which types of accounts will appear in the post-closing trial balance?
(a) Permanent accounts.
(b) Temporary accounts.
(c) Accounts shown in the income statement columns of a work sheet.
(d) None of the above.

(SO 8) **13.** All of the following are required steps in the accounting cycle *except:*
(a) journalizing and posting closing entries.
(b) preparing an adjusted trial balance.
(c) preparing a post-closing trial balance.
(d) preparing a work sheet.

Go to the book's website, **www.wiley.com/college/kimmel,** to access additional Self-Study Questions.

THE NAVIGATOR

Note: All asterisked Questions, Exercises, and Problems relate to material in the appendix to the chapter.

Questions

1. (a) How does the time period assumption affect an accountant's analysis of accounting transactions?
(b) Explain the term *fiscal year*.

2. Identify and state two generally accepted accounting principles that relate to adjusting the accounts.

3. Tony Galego, a lawyer, accepts a legal engagement in March, performs the work in April, and is paid in May. If Galego's law firm prepares monthly financial statements, when should it recognize revenue from this engagement? Why?

4. In completing the engagement in question 3, Galego pays no costs in March, $2,500 in April, and $2,500 in May (incurred in April). How much expense should the firm deduct from revenues in the month when it recognizes the revenue? Why?

5. "The cost principle of accounting requires adjusting entries." Do you agree? Explain.

6. Why may the financial information in a trial balance not be up-to-date and complete?

7. Distinguish between the two categories of adjusting entries, and identify the types of adjustments applicable to each category.

8. What accounts does a company debit and credit in a prepaid expense adjusting entry?

9. "Depreciation is a process of valuation that results in the reporting of the fair market value of the asset." Do you agree? Explain.

10. Explain the differences between depreciation expense and accumulated depreciation.

11. Genesis Company purchased equipment for $15,000. By the current balance sheet date, the company had depreciated $7,000. Indicate the balance sheet presentation of the data.

12. What accounts are debited and credited in an unearned revenue adjusting entry?

13. Computer Technologies provides maintenance service for computers and office equipment for companies throughout the Northeast. The sales managers is elated because she closed a $300,000 three-year maintenance contract on December 29, 2007, two days before the company's year-end. "Now we will hit this year's net income target for sure," she crowed. The customer is required to pay $100,000 on December 29 (the day the deal was closed). Two more payments of $100,000 each are also required on December 29, 2008 and 2009. Discuss the effect that this event will have on the company's financial statements.

14. SquareDeal, a large national retail chain, is nearing its fiscal year-end. It appears that the company is not going to hit its revenue and net income targets. The company's marketing manager, Randal Fox, suggests running a promotion selling $50 gift cards for $40.

He believes that this would be very popular and would enable the company to meet its targets for revenue and net income. What do you think of this idea?

15. A company fails to recognize revenue earned but not yet received. Which of the following accounts are involved in the adjusting entry: (a) asset, (b) liability, (c) revenue, or (d) expense? For the accounts selected, indicate whether they would be debited or credited in the entry.

16. A company fails to recognize an expense incurred but not paid. Indicate which of the following accounts is debited and which is credited in the adjusting entry: (a) asset, (b) liability, (c) revenue, or (d) expense.

17. A company makes an accrued revenue adjusting entry for $800 and an accrued expense adjusting entry for $300. How much was net income understated prior to these entries? Explain.

18. On January 9 a company pays $5,000 for salaries, of which $1,100 was reported as Salaries Payable on December 31. Give the entry to record the payment.

19. For each of the following items before adjustment, indicate the type of adjusting entry—prepaid expense, unearned revenue, accrued revenue, and accrued expense—that is needed to correct the misstatement. If an item could result in more than one type of adjusting entry, indicate each of the types.
(a) Assets are understated.
(b) Liabilities are overstated.
(c) Liabilities are understated.
(d) Expenses are understated.
(e) Assets are overstated.
(f) Revenue is understated

20. One-half of the adjusting entry is given below. Indicate the account title for the other half of the entry.
(a) Salaries Expense is debited.
(b) Depreciation Expense is debited.
(c) Interest Payable is credited.
(d) Supplies is credited.
(e) Accounts Receivable is debited.
(f) Unearned Service Revenue is debited.

21. "An adjusting entry may affect more than one balance sheet or income statement account." Do you agree? Why or why not?

22. Why is it possible to prepare financial statements directly from an adjusted trial balance?

23.
(a) What information do accrual basis financial statements provide that cash basis statements do not?
(b) What information do cash basis financial statements provide that accrual basis statements do not?

24. What is the relationship, if any, between the amount shown in the adjusted trial balance column for an account and that account's ledger balance?

25. Identify the account(s) debited and credited in each of the four closing entries, assuming the company has net income for the year.

26. ➡ Some companies employ technologies that allow them to do a so-called "virtual close." This enables them to close their books nearly instantaneously any time during the year. What advantages does a "virtual close" provide?

27. Describe the nature of the Income Summary account, and identify the types of summary data that may be posted to this account.

28. What items are disclosed on a post-closing trial balance, and what is its purpose?

29. Which of these accounts would not appear in the post-closing trial balance? Interest Payable, Equipment, Depreciation Expense, Dividends, Unearned Service Revenue, Accumulated Depreciation—Equipment, and Service Revenue.

30. Indicate, in the sequence in which they are made, the three required steps in the accounting cycle that involve journalizing.

31. Identify, in the sequence in which they are prepared, the three trial balances that are required in the accounting cycle.

32. ➡ Explain the terms earnings management and quality of earnings.

33. ➡ Give examples of how companies manage earnings.

* 34. What is the purpose of a work sheet?

* 35. What is the basic form of a work sheet?

Brief Exercises

Identify impact of transactions on cash and net income.
(SO 2)

BE4-1 Transactions that affect earnings do not necessarily affect cash.

Instructions
Identify the effect, if any, that each of the following transactions would have upon cash and net income. The first transaction has been completed as an example.

	Cash	Net Income
(a) Purchased $100 of supplies for cash.	−$100	$ 0
(b) Recorded an adjusting entry to record use of $30 of the above supplies.		
(c) Made sales of $1,300, all on account.		
(d) Received $800 from customers in payment of their accounts.		
(e) Purchased capital asset for cash, $2,500.		
(f) Recorded depreciation of building for period used, $600.		

Indicate why adjusting entries are needed.
(SO 3)

BE4-2 The ledger of T. J. Bahr Company includes the following accounts. Explain why each account may require adjustment.
(a) Prepaid Insurance.
(b) Depreciation Expense.
(c) Unearned Service Revenue.
(d) Interest Payable.

Identify the major types of adjusting entries.
(SO 3)

BE4-3 Lena Company accumulates the following adjustment data at December 31. Indicate (1) the type of adjustment (prepaid expense, accrued revenue, and so on) and (2) the status of the accounts before adjustment (overstated or understated).
(a) Supplies of $400 are on hand. Supplies account shows $1,900 balance.
(b) Service Revenue earned but unbilled total $700.
(c) Interest of $300 has accumulated on a note payable.
(d) Rent collected in advance totaling $1,100 has been earned.

Prepare adjusting entry for supplies.
(SO 4)

BE4-4 Adler Advertising Company's trial balance at December 31 shows Advertising Supplies $8,800 and Advertising Supplies Expense $0. On December 31 there are $1,700 of supplies on hand. Prepare the adjusting entry at December 31 and, using T accounts, enter the balances in the accounts, post the adjusting entry, and indicate the adjusted balance in each account.

BE4-5 At the end of its first year, the trial balance of Riko Company shows Equipment $22,000 and zero balances in Accumulated Depreciation—Equipment and Depreciation Expense. Depreciation for the year is estimated to be $2,700. Prepare the adjusting entry for depreciation at December 31, post the adjustments to T accounts, and indicate the balance sheet presentation of the equipment at December 31.

Prepare adjusting entry for depreciation.
(SO 4)

BE4-6 On July 1, 2007, Lumas Co. pays $14,800 to Patel Insurance Co. for a 2-year insurance contract. Both companies have fiscal years ending December 31. For Lumas Co. journalize and post the entry on July 1 and the adjusting entry on December 31.

Prepare adjusting entry for prepaid expense.
(SO 4)

BE4-7 Using the data in BE4-6, journalize and post the entry on July 1 and the adjusting entry on December 31 for Patel Insurance Co. Patel uses the accounts Unearned Insurance Revenue and Insurance Revenue.

Prepare adjusting entry for unearned revenue.
(SO 4)

BE4-8 The bookkeeper for Ahlet Company asks you to prepare the following accrual adjusting entries at December 31.
(a) Interest on notes payable of $400 is accrued.
(b) Service revenue earned but unbilled totals $1,400.
(c) Salaries of $780 earned by employees have not been recorded.
Use these account titles: Service Revenue, Accounts Receivable, Interest Expense, Interest Payable, Salaries Expense, and Salaries Payable.

Prepare adjusting entries for accruals.
(SO 5)

BE4-9 The trial balance of Cher Company includes the following balance sheet accounts. Identify the accounts that might require adjustment. For each account that requires adjustment, indicate (1) the type of adjusting entry (prepaid expenses, unearned revenues, accrued revenues, and accrued expenses) and (2) the related account in the adjusting entry.
(a) Accounts Receivable.
(b) Prepaid Insurance.
(c) Equipment.
(d) Accumulated Depreciation—Equipment.
(e) Notes Payable.
(f) Interest Payable.
(g) Unearned Service Revenue.

Analyze accounts in an adjusted trial balance.
(SO 6)

BE4-10 The adjusted trial balance of Sain Corporation at December 31, 2007, includes the following accounts: Retained Earnings $17,200; Dividends $6,000; Service Revenue $37,000; Salaries Expense $13,000; Insurance Expense $1,800; Rent Expense $3,500; Supplies Expense $1,200; and Depreciation Expense $1,000. Prepare an income statement for the year.

Prepare an income statement from an adjusted trial balance.
(SO 6)

BE4-11 Partial adjusted trial balance data for Sain Corporation are presented in BE4-10. The balance in Retained Earnings is the balance as of January 1. Prepare a retained earnings statement for the year assuming net income is $14,000.

Prepare a retained earnings statement from an adjusted trial balance.
(SO 6)

BE4-12 The following selected accounts appear in the adjusted trial balance for Shah Company. Indicate the financial statement on which each account would be reported.
(a) Accumulated Depreciation.
(b) Depreciation Expense.
(c) Retained Earnings.
(d) Dividends.
(e) Service Revenue.
(f) Supplies.
(g) Accounts Payable.

Identify financial statement for selected accounts.
(SO 6)

BE4-13 Using the data in BE4-12, identify the accounts that would be included in a post-closing trial balance.

Identify post-closing trial balance accounts.
(SO 7)

BE4-14 The required steps in the accounting cycle are listed in random order below. List the steps in proper sequence.
(a) Prepare a post-closing trial balance.
(b) Prepare an adjusted trial balance.
(c) Analyze business transactions.
(d) Prepare a trial balance.
(e) Journalize the transactions.
(f) Journalize and post closing entries.
(g) Prepare financial statements.
(h) Journalize and post adjusting entries.
(i) Post to ledger accounts.

List required steps in the accounting cycle sequence.
(SO 8)

Exercises

Identify point of revenue recognition.
(SO 1)

E4-1   The following independent situations require professional judgement for determining when to recognize revenue from the transactions.

(a) Southwest Airlines sells you an advance-purchase airline ticket in September for your flight home at Christmas.

(b) Ultimate Electronics sells you a home theatre on a "no money down, no interest, and no payments for one year" promotional deal.

(c) The Toronto Blue Jays sell season tickets online to games in the Skydome. Fans can purchase the tickets at any time, although the season doesn't officially begin until April. The major league baseball season runs from April through October.

(d) You borrow money in August from RBC Financial Group. The loan and the interest are repayable in full in November.

(e) In August, you order a sweater from Sears using its online catalog. The sweater arrives in September, and you charge it to your Sears credit card. You receive and pay the Sears bill in October.

Instructions

Identify when revenue should be recognized in each of the above situations.

Identify accounting assumptions, principles, and constraints.
(SO 1)

E4-2   These are the assumptions, principles, and constraints discussed in this and previous chapters.

1. Economic entity assumption.
2. Matching principle.
3. Monetary unit assumption.
4. Time period assumption.
5. Cost principle.
6. Materiality.
7. Full disclosure principle.
8. Going concern assumption.
9. Revenue recognition principle.
10. Conservatism.

Instructions

Identify by number the accounting assumption, principle, or constraint that describes each situation below. Do not use a number more than once.

____ (a) Is the rationale for why plant assets are not reported at liquidation value. (Do not use the cost principle.)

____ (b) Indicates that personal and business record-keeping should be separately maintained.

____ (c) Ensures that all relevant financial information is reported.

____ (d) Assumes that the dollar is the "measuring stick" used to report on financial performance.

____ (e) Requires that accounting standards be followed for all *significant* items.

____ (f) Separates financial information into time periods for reporting purposes.

____ (g) Requires recognition of expenses in the same period as related revenues.

____ (h) Indicates that market value changes subsequent to purchase are not recorded in the accounts.

Identify the violated assumption, principle, or constraint.
(SO 1)

E4-3   Here are some accounting reporting situations.

(a) Flanner Company recognizes revenue at the end of the production cycle but before sale. The price of the product, as well as the amount that can be sold, is not certain.

(b) Falk Company is in its fifth year of operation and has yet to issue financial statements. (Do not use the full disclosure principle.)

(c) Schleis, Inc. is carrying inventory at its original cost of $100,000. Inventory has a market value of $110,000.

(d) Forgetta Hospital Supply Corporation reports only current assets and current liabilities on its balance sheet. Property, plant, and equipment and bonds payable are reported as current assets and current liabilities, respectively. Liquidation of the company is unlikely.

(e) Judd Company has inventory on hand that cost $400,000. Judd reports inventory on its balance sheet at its current market value of $425,000.

(f) Kim Decker, president of Classic Music Company, bought a computer for her personal use. She paid for the computer by using company funds and debited the "Computers" account.

Instructions

For each situation, list the assumption, principle, or constraint that has been violated, if any. Some of these assumptions, principles, and constraints were presented in earlier chapters. List only one answer for each situation.

E4-4 Your examination of the records of a company that follows the cash basis of accounting tells you that the company's reported cash basis earnings in 2007 are $33,640. If this firm had followed accrual basis accounting practices, it would have reported the following year-end balances.

Convert earnings from cash to accrual basis.
(SO 2, 4, 5)

	2007	2006
Accounts receivable	$3,400	$2,300
Supplies on hand	1,300	1,160
Unpaid wages owed	1,500	2,400
Other unpaid amounts	1,400	1,600

Instructions

Determine the company's net earnings on an accrual basis for 2007. Show all your calculations in an orderly fashion.

E4-5 In its first year of operations Bere Company earned $28,000 in service revenue, $6,000 of which was on account and still outstanding at year-end. The remaining $22,000 was received in cash from customers.

Determine cash basis and accrual basis earnings.
(SO 2)

The company incurred operating expenses of $14,500. Of these expenses $13,000 were paid in cash; $1,500 was still owed on account at year-end. In addition, Bere prepaid $3,600 for insurance coverage that would not be used until the second year of operations.

Instructions

(a) Calculate the first year's net earnings under the cash basis of accounting, and calculate the first year's net earnings under the accrual basis of accounting.

(b) Which basis of accounting (cash or accrual) provides more useful information for decision makers?

E4-6 The Radical Edge, a ski tuning and repair shop, opened in November 2006. The company carefully kept track of all its cash receipts and cash payments. The following information is available at the end of the ski season, April 30, 2007.

Convert earnings from cash to accrual basis; prepare accrual-based financial statements.
(SO 2, 4, 5)

	Cash Receipts	Cash Payments
Issue of common shares	$20,000	
Payment for repair equipment		$ 9,200
Rent payments		1,225
Newspaper advertising payment		375
Utility bills payments		970
Part-time helper's wages payments		2,600
Income tax payment		10,000
Cash receipts from ski and snowboard repair services	32,150	
Subtotals	52,150	24,370
Cash balance		27,780
Totals	$52,150	$52,150

You learn that the repair equipment has an estimated useful life of 5 years. The company rents space at a cost of $175 per month on a one-year lease. The lease contract requires payment of the first and last months' rent in advance, which was done. The part-timer helper is owed $220 at April 30, 2007, for unpaid wages. At April 30, 2007, customers owe The Radical Edge $650 for services they have received but have not yet paid for.

Instructions

(a) Prepare an accrual-basis income statement for the 6 months ended April 30, 2007.

(b) Prepare the April 30, 2007, classified balance sheet.

Identify differences between cash and accrual accounting.
(SO 2, 3)

E4-7 MaxPlay, a maker of electronic games for kids, has just completed its first year of operations. The company's sales growth was explosive. To encourage large national stores to carry its products MaxPlay offered 180-day financing—meaning its largest customers do not pay for nearly 6 months. Because MaxPlay is a new company, its components suppliers insist on being paid cash on delivery. Also, it had to pay up front for 2 years of insurance. At the end of the year MaxPlay owed employees for one full month of salaries, but due to a cash shortfall, it promised to pay them the first week of next year.

Instructions

(a) Explain how cash and accrual accounting would differ for each of the events listed above and describe the proper accrual accounting.

(b) Assume that at the end of the year MaxPlay reported a favorable net income, yet the company's management is concerned because the company is very short of cash. Explain how MaxPlay could have positive net income and yet run out of cash.

Identify types of adjustments and accounts before adjustment.
(SO 3, 4, 5)

E4-8 Rollins Company accumulates the following adjustment data at December 31.

(a) Service Revenue earned but unbilled totals $600.

(b) Store supplies of $300 are on hand. Supplies account shows $1,900 balance.

(c) Utility expenses of $275 are unpaid.

(d) Service revenue of $490 collected in advance has been earned.

(e) Salaries of $800 are unpaid.

(f) Prepaid insurance totaling $400 has expired.

Instructions

For each item indicate (1) the type of adjustment (prepaid expense, unearned revenue, accrued revenue, or accrued expense) and (2) the status of the accounts before adjustment (overstated or understated).

Prepare adjusting entries from selected account data.
(SO 4, 5)

E4-9 The ledger of Reliable Rental Agency on March 31 of the current year includes these selected accounts before adjusting entries have been prepared.

	Debits	Credits
Prepaid Insurance	$ 3,600	
Supplies	3,000	
Equipment	25,000	
Accumulated Depreciation—Equipment		$ 8,400
Notes Payable		20,000
Unearned Rent Revenue		10,200
Rent Revenue		60,000
Interest Expense	0	
Wage Expense	14,000	

An analysis of the accounts shows the following.

1. The equipment depreciates $250 per month.

2. Half of the unearned rent revenue was earned during the quarter.

3. Interest of $440 is accrued on the notes payable.

4. Supplies on hand total $850.

5. Insurance expires at the rate of $300 per month.

Instructions

Prepare the adjusting entries at March 31, assuming that adjusting entries are made quarterly. Additional accounts are: Depreciation Expense, Insurance Expense, Interest Payable, and Supplies Expense.

Prepare adjusting entries.
(SO 4, 5)

E4-10 Gene Hoffman, D.D.S., opened an incorporated dental practice on January 1, 2007. During the first month of operations the following transactions occurred:

1. Performed services for patients who had dental plan insurance. At January 31, $680 of such services was earned but not yet billed to the insurance companies.

2. Utility expenses incurred but not paid prior to January 31 totaled $520.

3. Purchased dental equipment on January 1 for $80,000, paying $20,000 in cash and signing a $60,000, 3-year note payable (Interest is paid each December 31). The equipment depreciates $400 per month. Interest is $500 per month.

4. Purchased a 1-year malpractice insurance policy on January 1 for $18,000.

5. Purchased $1,750 of dental supplies. On January 31 determined that $350 of supplies were on hand.

Instructions
Prepare the adjusting entries on January 31. Account titles are: Accumulated Depreciation—Dental Equipment, Depreciation Expense, Service Revenue, Accounts Receivable, Insurance Expense, Interest Expense, Interest Payable, Prepaid Insurance, Supplies, Supplies Expense, Utilities Expense, and Utilities Payable.

E4-11 The unadjusted trial balance for Sierra Corp. is shown in Illustration 4-4 (page 162). In lieu of the adjusting entries shown in the text at October 31, assume the following adjustment data.

Prepare adjusting entries.
(SO 4, 5)

1. Advertising supplies on hand at October 31 total $700.

2. Expired insurance for the month is $100.

3. Depreciation for the month is $50.

4. As of October 31, $800 of the previously recorded unearned revenue had been earned.

5. Services provided but unbilled (and no receivable has been recorded) at October 31 are $300.

6. Interest expense accrued at October 31 is $70.

7. Accrued salaries at October 31 are $1,400.

Instructions
Prepare the adjusting entries for the items above.

E4-12 The income statement of Leno Co. for the month of July shows net income of $1,500 based on Service Revenue $5,500; Wages Expense $2,300; Supplies Expense $900, and Utilities Expense $800. In reviewing the statement, you discover the following:

Prepare a correct income statement.
(SO 1, 4, 5, 6)

1. Insurance expired during July of $350 was omitted.

2. Supplies expense includes $400 of supplies that are still on hand at July 31.

3. Depreciation on equipment of $150 was omitted.

4. Accrued but unpaid wages at July 31 of $300 were not included.

5. Revenue earned but unrecorded totaled $900.

Instructions
Prepare a correct income statement for July 2007.

E4-13 This is a partial adjusted trial balance of Marliss Company.

Analyze adjusted data.
(SO 1, 4, 5, 6)

MARLISS COMPANY
Adjusted Trial Balance
January 31, 2007

	Debit	Credit
Supplies	$ 700	
Prepaid Insurance	1,560	
Salaries Payable		$1,200
Unearned Service Revenue		750
Supplies Expense	950	
Insurance Expense	520	
Salaries Expense	1,800	
Service Revenue		2,000

Instructions
Answer these questions, assuming the year begins January 1.
(a) If the amount in Supplies Expense is the January 31 adjusting entry, and $850 of supplies was purchased in January, what was the balance in Supplies on January 1?

(b) If the amount in Insurance Expense is the January 31 adjusting entry, and the original insurance premium was for 1 year, what was the total premium and when was the policy purchased?

(c) If $2,500 of salaries was paid in January, what was the balance in Salaries Payable at December 31, 2006?

(d) If $1,600 was received in January for services performed in January, what was the balance in Unearned Service Revenue at December 31, 2006?

Journalize basic transactions and adjusting entries.
(SO 4, 5, 6)

E4-14 Selected accounts of Atlantis Company are shown here.

Supplies Expense				Salaries Payable		
July 31	850				July 31	1,200

Salaries Expense				Accounts Receivable		
July 15	1,200			July 31	500	
31	1,200					

Service Revenue				Unearned Service Revenue		
		July 14	4,100	July 31	900	July 1 Bal. 1,500
		31	900			20 700
		31	500			

Supplies			
July 1 Bal. 1,100		July 31	850
10 200			

Instructions

After analyzing the accounts, journalize (a) the July transactions and (b) the adjusting entries that were made on July 31. (*Hint:* July transactions were for cash.)

Prepare adjusting entries from analysis of trial balance.
(SO 4, 5, 6)

E4-15 The trial balances shown below are before and after adjustment for Hoi Company at the end of its fiscal year.

HOI COMPANY
Trial Balance
August 31, 2007

	Before Adjustment		After Adjustment	
	Dr.	Cr.	Dr.	Cr.
Cash	$10,900		$10,900	
Accounts Receivable	8,800		9,400	
Office Supplies	2,500		700	
Prepaid Insurance	4,000		2,500	
Office Equipment	16,000		16,000	
Accumulated Depreciation—Office Equipment		$ 3,600		$ 4,800
Accounts Payable		5,800		5,800
Salaries Payable		0		1,100
Unearned Rent Revenue		1,800		600
Common Stock		10,000		10,000
Retained Earnings		5,600		5,600
Dividends	2,800		2,800	
Service Revenue		34,000		34,600
Rent Revenue		13,200		14,400
Salaries Expense	17,000		18,100	
Office Supplies Expense	0		1,800	
Rent Expense	12,000		12,000	
Insurance Expense	0		1,500	
Depreciation Expense	0		1,200	
	$74,000	$74,000	$76,900	$76,900

Instructions
Prepare the adjusting entries that were made.

E4-16   The adjusted trial balance for Hoi Company is given in E4-15.

Prepare financial statements from adjusted trial balance.
(SO 6)

Instructions
Prepare the income and retained earnings statements for the year and the classified balance sheet at August 31.

E4-17   The adjusted trial balance for Hoi Company is given in E4-15.

Prepare closing entries.
(SO 7)

Instructions
Prepare the closing entries for the temporary accounts at August 31.

Problems: Set A

P4-1A   The following selected data are taken from the comparative financial statements of Alpine Curling Club. The Club prepares its financial statements using the accrual basis of accounting.

Record transactions on accrual basis; convert revenue to cash receipts.
(SO 2, 4)

September 30	2007	2006
Accounts receivable for member dues	$ 18,000	$ 11,000
Unearned ticket revenue	20,000	26,000
Dues revenue	148,000	135,000

Dues are billed to members based upon their use of the Club's facilities. Unearned ticket revenues arise from the sale of tickets to events such as the Skins Game.

Instructions
(*Hint:* You will find it helpful to use T accounts to analyze the following data. You must analyze these data sequentially, as missing information must first be deduced before moving on. Post your journal entries as you progress, rather than waiting until the end.)
(a) Prepare journal entries for each of the following events that took place during 2007.
  1. Dues receivable from members from 2006 were all collected during 2007.
  2. Unearned ticket revenue at the end of 2006 was all earned during 2007.
  3. Additional tickets were sold for $39,000 cash during 2007; a portion of these were used by the purchasers during the year. The entire balance remaining relates to the upcoming Skins Game in 2007.
  4. Dues for the 2006–2007 fiscal year were billed to members.
  5. Dues receivable for 2007 (i.e., those billed in item (4) above) were partially collected.
(b) Determine the amount of cash received by the Club from the above transactions during the year ended September 30, 2007.

(b) Cash received $180,000

P4-2A   Josh Stein started his own consulting firm, Astromech Consulting, on June 1, 2007. The trial balance at June 30 is as follows.

Prepare adjusting entries, post to ledger accounts, and prepare adjusted trial balance.
(SO 4, 5, 6)

ASTROMECH CONSULTING
Trial Balance
June 30, 2007

	Debit	Credit
Cash	$ 6,850	
Accounts Receivable	7,000	
Prepaid Insurance	2,640	
Supplies	2,000	
Office Equipment	15,000	
Accounts Payable		$ 4,540
Unearned Service Revenue		5,200
Common Stock		21,750
Service Revenue		8,000
Salaries Expense	4,000	
Rent Expense	2,000	
	$39,490	$39,490

In addition to those accounts listed on the trial balance, the chart of accounts for Astromech also contains the following accounts: Accumulated Depreciation—Office Equipment, Utilities Payable, Salaries Payable, Depreciation Expense, Insurance Expense, Utilities Expense, and Supplies Expense.

Other data:

1. Supplies on hand at June 30 total $980.
2. A utility bill for $180 has not been recorded and will not be paid until next month.
3. The insurance policy is for a year.
4. $2,900 of unearned service revenue has been earned at the end of the month.
5. Salaries of $1,250 are accrued at June 30.
6. The office equipment has a 5-year life with no salvage value and is being depreciated at $250 per month for 60 months.
7. Invoices representing $3,000 of services performed during the month have not been recorded as of June 30.

Instructions
(a) Prepare the adjusting entries for the month of June.
(b) Post the adjusting entries to the ledger accounts. Enter the totals from the trial balance as beginning account balances. Use T accounts.
(c) Prepare an adjusted trial balance at June 30, 2007.

(b) Service rev. $13,900
(c) Tot. trial balance $44,170

Prepare adjusting entries, adjusted trial balance, and financial statements.
(SO 4, 5, 6, 7)

GLS

P4-3A   The Julien Hotel opened for business on May 1, 2007. Here is its trial balance before adjustment on May 31.

JULIEN HOTEL
Trial Balance
May 31, 2007

	Debit	Credit
Cash	$ 2,500	
Prepaid Insurance	1,800	
Supplies	2,600	
Land	15,000	
Lodge	70,000	
Furniture	16,800	
Accounts Payable		$ 4,700
Unearned Rent Revenue		3,300
Mortgage Payable		36,000
Common Stock		60,000
Rent Revenue		9,000
Salaries Expense	3,000	
Utilities Expense	800	
Advertising Expense	500	
	$113,000	$113,000

Other data:

1. Insurance expires at the rate of $300 per month.
2. An inventory of supplies shows $1,350 of unused supplies on May 31.
3. Annual depreciation is $3,600 on the lodge and $3,000 on furniture.
4. The mortgage interest rate is 9%. (The mortgage was taken out on May 1.)
5. Unearned rent of $1,500 has been earned.
6. Salaries of $750 are accrued and unpaid at May 31.

Instructions
(a) Journalize the adjusting entries on May 31.
(b) Prepare a ledger using T accounts. Enter the trial balance amounts and post the adjusting entries.
(c) Prepare an adjusted trial balance on May 31.

(c) Rent revenue $ 10,500
Tot. trial
balance $114,570

(d) Prepare an income statement and a retained earnings statement for the month of May and a classified balance sheet at May 31.

(d) Net income $ 3,080

(e) Identify which accounts should be closed on May 31.

P4-4A Highlands Golf Inc. was organized on July 1, 2007. Quarterly financial statements are prepared. The trial balance and adjusted trial balance on September 30 are shown here.

Prepare adjusting entries and financial statements; identify accounts to be closed.
(SO 4, 5, 6, 7)

HIGHLANDS GOLF INC.
Trial Balance
September 30, 2007

	Unadjusted Dr.	Unadjusted Cr.	Adjusted Dr.	Adjusted Cr.
Cash	$ 6,700		$ 6,700	
Accounts Receivable	400		1,000	
Prepaid Rent	1,800		900	
Supplies	1,200		860	
Equipment	15,000		15,000	
Accumulated Depreciation—Equipment				$ 350
Notes Payable		$ 5,000		5,000
Accounts Payable		1,710		1,710
Salaries Payable				600
Interest Payable				50
Unearned Rent Revenue		1,000		600
Common Stock		14,000		14,000
Retained Earnings		0		0
Dividends	600		600	
Dues Revenue		13,800		14,400
Rent Revenue		400		800
Salaries Expense	8,800		9,400	
Rent Expense	900		1,800	
Depreciation Expense			350	
Supplies Expense			340	
Utilities Expense	510		510	
Interest Expense			50	
	$35,910	$35,910	$37,510	$37,510

Instructions

(a) Journalize the adjusting entries that were made.

(b) Prepare an income statement and a retained earnings statement for the 3 months ending September 30 and a classified balance sheet at September 30.

(b) Net income $ 2,750
Tot. assets $24,110

(c) Identify which accounts should be closed on September 30.

(d) If the note bears interest at 12%, how many months has it been outstanding?

P4-5A A review of the ledger of Kaffen Company at December 31, 2007, produces these data pertaining to the preparation of annual adjusting entries.

Prepare adjusting entries.
(SO 4, 5)

1. Prepaid Insurance $15,950. The company has separate insurance policies on its buildings and its motor vehicles. Policy B4564 on the building was purchased on July 1, 2006, for $10,500. The policy has a term of 3 years. Policy A2958 on the vehicles was purchased on January 1, 2007, for $7,200. This policy has a term of 2 years.

2. Unearned Subscription Revenue $29,400: The company began selling magazine subscriptions on October 1, 2007 on an annual basis. The selling price of a subscription is $30. A review of subscription contracts reveals the following.

Subscription Start Date	Number of Subscriptions
October 1	280
November 1	300
December 1	400
	980

3. Notes Payable, $40,000: This balance consists of a note for 6 months at an annual interest rate of 8%, dated October 1.

4. Salaries Payable $0: There are eight salaried employees. Salaries are paid every Friday for the current week. Five employees receive a salary of $600 each per week, and three employees earn $700 each per week. December 31 is a Wednesday. Employees do not work weekends. All employees worked the last 3 days of December.

Instructions
Prepare the adjusting entries at December 31, 2007.

Prepare adjusting entries and a corrected income statement.
(SO 4, 5)

P4-6A Happy Camper Travel Court was organized on July 1, 2006, by Brianna Brunn. Brianna is a good manager but a poor accountant. From the trial balance prepared by a part-time bookkeeper, Brianna prepared the following income statement for her fourth quarter, which ended June 30, 2007.

HAPPY CAMPER TRAVEL COURT
Income Statement
For the Quarter ended June 30, 2007

Revenues		
Travel court rental revenues		$216,000
Operating expenses		
Advertising	$ 3,800	
Wages	80,500	
Utilities	900	
Depreciation	2,700	
Repairs	4,000	
Total operating expenses		91,900
Net income		$124,100

Brianna suspected that something was wrong with the statement because net income had never exceeded $30,000 in any one quarter. Knowing that you are an experienced accountant, she asks you to review the income statement and other data.

You first look at the trial balance. In addition to the account balances reported above in the income statement, the ledger contains the following additional selected balances at June 30, 2007.

Supplies	$ 8,200
Prepaid Insurance	14,400
Note Payable	12,000

You then make inquiries and discover the following.

1. Travel court rental revenues include advanced rental payments received for summer occupancy, in the amount of $60,000.

2. There were $1,300 of supplies on hand at June 30.

3. Prepaid insurance resulted from the payment of a one-year policy on April 1, 2007.

4. The mail in July 2007 brought the following bills: advertising for the week of June 24, $110; repairs made June 18, $4,450; and utilities for the month of June, $215.

5. There are three employees who receive wages that total $250 per day. At June 30, two days' wages have been incurred but not paid.

6. The note payable is a 8% note dated May 1, 2007, and due on July 31, 2007.

7. Income tax of $13,400 for the quarter is due in July but has not yet been recorded.

Instructions
(a) Prepare any adjusting journal entries required as at June 30, 2007.
(b) Prepare a correct income statement for the quarter ended June 30, 2007.
(c) Explain to Brianna the generally accepted accounting principles that she did not recognize in preparing her income statement and their effect on her results.

(b) Net income $34,765

P4-7A On November 1, 2007, the following were the account balances of Coleman Equipment Repair.

Journalize transactions and follow through accounting cycle to preparation of financial statements.
(SO 4, 5, 6)

	Debits		**Credits**
Cash	$ 2,790	Accumulated Depreciation	$ 500
Accounts Receivable	2,910	Accounts Payable	2,300
Supplies	1,120	Unearned Service Revenue	400
Store Equipment	10,000	Salaries Payable	620
		Common Stock	10,000
		Retained Earnings	3,000
	$16,820		$16,820

During November the following summary transactions were completed.

Nov. 8 Paid $1,220 for salaries due employees, of which $600 is for November and $620 is for October salaries payable.
  10 Received $1,200 cash from customers in payment of account.
  12 Received $1,700 cash for services performed in November.
  15 Purchased store equipment on account $3,000.
  17 Purchased supplies on account $1,300.
  20 Paid creditors $2,500 of accounts payable due.
  22 Paid November rent $450.
  25 Paid salaries $1,000.
  27 Performed services on account and billed customers for services provided $900.
  29 Received $550 from customers for services to be provided in the future.

Adjustment data:

1. Supplies on hand are valued at $1,600.
2. Accrued salaries payable are $480.
3. Depreciation for the month is $250.
4. Unearned service revenue of $300 is earned.

Instructions
(a) Enter the November 1 balances in the ledger accounts. (Use T accounts.)
(b) Journalize the November transactions.
(c) Post to the ledger accounts. Use Service Revenue, Depreciation Expense, Supplies Expense, Salaries Expense, and Rent Expense.
(d) Prepare a trial balance at November 30.
(e) Journalize and post adjusting entries.
(f) Prepare an adjusted trial balance.
(g) Prepare an income statement and a retained earnings statement for November and a classified balance sheet at November 30.

(f) Cash $ 1,070
Tot. trial balance $21,880
(g) Net loss $ 700

P4-8A Katie Gage opened New View Window Washing Inc. on July 1, 2007. During July the following transactions were completed.

Complete all steps in accounting cycle.
(SO 4, 5, 6, 7, 8)

July 1 Issued 11,000 shares of common stock for $11,000 cash.
   1 Purchased used truck for $9,000, paying $3,000 cash and the balance on account.
   3 Purchased cleaning supplies for $800 on account.
   5 Paid $1,440 cash on 1-year insurance policy effective July 1.
  12 Billed customers $3,200 for cleaning services.
  18 Paid $1,000 cash on amount owed on truck and $500 on amount owed on cleaning supplies.
  20 Paid $2,000 cash for employee salaries.
  21 Collected $1,400 cash from customers billed on July 12.
  25 Billed customers $2,000 for cleaning services.
  31 Paid $260 for gas and oil used in the truck during month.
  31 Declared and paid $600 cash dividend.

The chart of accounts for New View Window Washing contains the following accounts: Cash, Accounts Receivable, Cleaning Supplies, Prepaid Insurance, Equipment, Accumulated

Depreciation—Equipment, Accounts Payable, Salaries Payable, Common Stock, Retained Earnings, Dividends, Income Summary, Service Revenue, Gas & Oil Expense, Cleaning Supplies Expense, Depreciation Expense, Insurance Expense, Salaries Expense.

Instructions
(a) Journalize the July transactions.
(b) Post to the ledger accounts. (Use T accounts.)
(c) Prepare a trial balance at July 31.
(d) Journalize the following adjustments.
    (1) Services provided but unbilled and uncollected at July 31 were $1,700.
    (2) Depreciation on equipment for the month was $250.
    (3) One-twelfth of the insurance expired.
    (4) An inventory count shows $360 of cleaning supplies on hand at July 31.
    (5) Accrued but unpaid employee salaries were $400.

(f) Cash $ 3,600
(g) Tot. assets $19,530

(e) Post adjusting entries to the T accounts.
(f) Prepare an adjusted trial balance.
(g) Prepare the income statement and a retained earnings statement for July and a classified balance sheet at July 31.
(h) Journalize and post closing entries and complete the closing process.
(i) Prepare a post-closing trial balance at July 31.

Problems: Set B

Record transactions on accrual basis; convert revenue to cash receipts.
(SO 2, 4)

P4-1B The following data are taken from the comparative balance sheets of EverGreen Club, which prepares its financial statements using the accrual basis of accounting.

December 31	2007	2006
Accounts receivable for member fees	$20,000	$ 6,000
Unearned fees revenue	17,000	18,000

Fees are billed to members based upon their use of the club's facilities. Unearned fees arise from the sale of gift certificates, which members can apply to their future use of club facilities. The 2007 income statement for the club showed that fee revenue of $157,000 was earned during the year.

Instructions
(*Hint:* You will find it helpful to use T accounts to analyze these data.)
(a) Prepare journal entries for each of the following events that took place during 2007.

    1. Fees receivable from 2006 were all collected during 2007.

    2. Gift certificates outstanding at the end of 2006 were all redeemed during 2007.

    3. An additional $30,000 worth of gift certificates were sold during 2007; a portion of these were used by the recipients during the year; the remainder were still outstanding at the end of 2007.

(b) Cash received $142,000

Prepare adjusting entries, post to ledger accounts, and prepare an adjusted trial balance.
(SO 4, 5, 6)

    4. Fees for 2007 were billed to members.

    5. Fees receivable for 2007 (i.e., those billed in item (4) above) were partially collected.

(b) Determine the amount of cash received by the club with respect to fees during 2007.

P4-2B Jessica Naboo started her own consulting firm, Naboo Consulting, on May 1, 2007. The trial balance at May 31 is as shown on page 205.

NABOO CONSULTING
Trial Balance
May 31, 2007

	Debit	Credit
Cash	$ 7,500	
Accounts Receivable	3,000	
Prepaid Insurance	3,600	
Supplies	2,500	
Office Furniture	12,000	
Accounts Payable		$ 3,500
Unearned Service Revenue		4,000
Common Stock		19,100
Service Revenue		7,500
Salaries Expense	4,000	
Rent Expense	1,500	
	$34,100	$34,100

In addition to those accounts listed on the trial balance, the chart of accounts for Naboo Consulting also contains the following accounts: Accumulated Depreciation—Office Furniture, Travel Payable, Salaries Payable, Depreciation Expense, Insurance Expense, Travel Expense, and Supplies Expense.

Other data:

1. $500 of supplies have been used during the month.

2. Travel costs incurred but not paid are $260.

3. The insurance policy is for 2 years.

4. $1,000 of the balance in the Unearned Service Revenue account remains unearned at the end of the month.

5. May 31 is a Wednesday and employees are paid on Fridays. Naboo Consulting has two employees that are paid $600 each for a 5-day work week.

6. The office furniture has a 5-year life with no salvage value and is being depreciated at $200 per month for 60 months.

7. Invoices representing $1,400 of services performed during the month have not been recorded as of May 31.

Instructions
(a) Prepare the adjusting entries for the month of May.
(b) Post the adjusting entries to the ledger accounts. Enter the totals from the trial balance as beginning account balances. Use T accounts.
(c) Prepare an adjusted trial balance at May 31, 2007.

(c) Tot. trial
     balance $36,680

P4-3B   Happy Trails Resort opened for business on June 1 with eight air-conditioned units. Its trial balance before adjustment on August 31 is presented here.

Prepare adjusting entries, adjusted trial balance, and financial statements.
(SO 4, 5, 6, 7)

HAPPY TRAILS RESORT
Trial Balance
August 31, 2007

	Debit	Credit
Cash	$ 24,600	
Prepaid Insurance	5,400	
Supplies	4,300	
Land	40,000	
Cottages	132,000	
Furniture	36,000	
Accounts Payable		$ 6,500
Unearned Rent Revenue		6,800

	Debit	Credit
Mortgage Payable		120,000
Common Stock		100,000
Dividends	5,000	
Rent Revenue		80,000
Salaries Expense	53,000	
Utilities Expense	9,400	
Repair Expense	3,600	
	$313,300	$313,300

Other data:

1. Insurance expires at the rate of $450 per month.
2. An inventory count on August 31 shows $1,200 of supplies on hand.
3. Annual depreciation is $4,800 on cottages and $4,000 on furniture.
4. Unearned rent of $5,000 was earned prior to August 31.
5. Salaries of $600 were unpaid at August 31.
6. Rentals of $1,200 were due from tenants at August 31. (Use Accounts Receivable.)
7. The mortgage interest rate is 7% per year. (The mortgage was taken out August 1.)

Instructions
(a) Journalize the adjusting entries on August 31 for the 3-month period June 1–August 31.
(b) Prepare a ledger using T accounts. Enter the trial balance amounts and post the adjusting entries.

(c) Tot. trial
    balance $318,000
(d) Net income $ 12,250

(c) Prepare an adjusted trial balance on August 31.
(d) Prepare an income statement and a retained earnings statement for the 3 months ended August 31 and a classified balance sheet as of August 31.
(e) Identify which accounts should be closed on August 31.

Prepare adjusting entries and financial statements; identify accounts to be closed.
(SO 4, 5, 6, 7)

P4-4B Khanna Advertising Agency was founded by Matt Khanna in January 2002. Presented here are both the adjusted and unadjusted trial balances as of December 31, 2007.

KHANNA ADVERTISING AGENCY
Trial Balance
December 31, 2007

	Unadjusted Dr.	Unadjusted Cr.	Adjusted Dr.	Adjusted Cr.
Cash	$ 11,000		$ 11,000	
Accounts Receivable	16,000		19,500	
Art Supplies	8,400		6,000	
Prepaid Insurance	3,350		1,790	
Printing Equipment	60,000		60,000	
Accumulated Depreciation		$ 25,000		$ 30,000
Accounts Payable		2,000		2,000
Interest Payable		0		320
Notes Payable		8,000		8,000
Unearned Advertising Revenue		4,000		3,600
Salaries Payable		0		1,300
Common Stock		20,000		20,000
Retained Earnings		5,500		5,500
Dividends	10,000		10,000	
Advertising Revenue		57,600		61,500
Salaries Expense	9,000		10,300	
Insurance Expense			1,560	
Interest Expense			320	

	Unadjusted		Adjusted	
	Dr.	**Cr.**	**Dr.**	**Cr.**
Depreciation Expense			5,000	
Art Supplies Expense			2,400	
Rent Expense	4,350		4,350	
	$122,100	$122,100	$132,220	$132,220

Instructions
(a) Journalize the annual adjusting entries that were made.
(b) Prepare an income statement and a retained earnings statement for the year ended December 31, and a classified balance sheet at December 31.
(c) Identify which accounts should be closed on December 31.
(d) If the note has been outstanding 6 months, what is the annual interest rate on that note?
(e) If the company paid $10,500 in salaries in 2007, what was the balance in Salaries Payable on December 31, 2006?

(b) Net income $37,570
Tot. assets $68,290

P4-5B A review of the ledger of Ordman Company at December 31, 2007, produces the following data pertaining to the preparation of annual adjusting entries.

Prepare adjusting entries.
(SO 4, 5)

1. Salaries Payable $0: There are eight salaried employees. Salaries are paid every Friday for the current week. Six employees receive a salary of $800 each per week, and two employees earn $600 each per week. December 31 is a Wednesday. Employees do not work weekends. All employees worked the last 3 days of December.

2. Unearned Rent Revenue $369,000: The company began subleasing office space in its new building on November 1. Each tenant is required to make a $5,000 security deposit that is not refundable until occupancy is terminated. At December 31 the company had the following rental contracts that are paid in full for the entire term of the lease.

Date	Term (in months)	Monthly Rent	Number of Leases
Nov. 1	6	$4,000	5
Dec. 1	6	8,500	4

3. Prepaid Advertising $13,200: This balance consists of payments on two advertising contracts. The contracts provide for monthly advertising in two trade magazines. The terms of the contracts are as follows.

Contract	Date	Amount	Number of Magazine Issues
A650	May 1	$6,000	12
B974	Sept. 1	7,200	18

The first advertisement runs in the month in which the contract is signed.

4. Notes Payable $80,000: This balance consists of a note for 1 year at an annual interest rate of 7%, dated October 1, 2007.

Instructions
Prepare the adjusting entries at December 31, 2007. Show all computations.

P4-6B The Fly Right Travel Agency was organized on January 1, 2005, by Sam Cheney. Sam is a good manager but a poor accountant. From the trial balance prepared by a part-time bookkeeper, Sam prepared the income statement on page 208 for the quarter that ended March 31, 2007.

Prepare adjusting entries and a corrected income statement.
(SO 4, 5)

FLY RIGHT TRAVEL AGENCY
Income Statement
For the Quarter Ended March 31, 2007

Revenues		
Travel service revenue		$50,000
Operating expenses		
Advertising	$2,600	
Depreciation	400	
Income tax	1,500	
Salaries	6,000	
Utilities	400	10,900
Net income		$39,100

Sam knew that something was wrong with the statement because net income had never exceeded $5,000 in any one quarter. Knowing that you are an experienced accountant, he asks you to review the income statement and other data.

You first look at the trial balance. In addition to the account balances reported above in the income statement, the trial balance contains the following additional selected balances at March 31, 2007.

Supplies	$ 2,900
Prepaid insurance	1,200
Note payable	10,000

You then make inquiries and discover the following:

1. Travel service revenue includes advance payments for cruises, $30,000.
2. There were $800 of supplies on hand at March 31.
3. Prepaid insurance resulted from the payment of a one-year policy on March 1, 2007.
4. The mail on April 1, 2007, brought the utility bill for the month of March's heat, light, and power, $210.
5. There are three employees who receive salaries of $75 each per day. At March 31, three days' salaries have been incurred but not paid.
6. The note payable is a 6-month, 8% note dated January 1, 2007.

Instructions

(b) Net income $5,815

(a) Prepare any adjusting journal entries required as at March 31, 2007.
(b) Prepare a correct income statement for the quarter ended March 31, 2007.
(c) Explain to Sam the generally accepted accounting principles that he did not recognize in preparing his income statement and their effect on his results.

Journalize transactions and follow through accounting cycle to preparation of financial statements.
(SO 4, 5, 6)

P4-7B On September 1, 2007, the following were the account balances of Tech Know Equipment Repair.

	Debits		**Credits**
Cash	$ 4,880	Accumulated Depreciation	$ 1,600
Accounts Receivable	3,820	Accounts Payable	3,100
Supplies	800	Unearned Service Revenue	400
Store Equipment	15,000	Salaries Payable	700
	$24,500	Common Stock	10,000
		Retained Earnings	8,700
			$24,500

During September the following summary transactions were completed.

Sept.	8	Paid $1,100 for salaries due employees, of which $400 is for September and $700 is for August salaries payable.
	10	Received $1,500 cash from customers in payment of account.
	12	Received $3,400 cash for services performed in September.
	15	Purchased store equipment on account $3,000.

Sept. 17   Purchased supplies on account $1,500.
    20   Paid creditors $4,500 of accounts payable due.
    22   Paid September rent $400.
    25   Paid salaries $1,200.
    27   Performed services on account and billed customers for services provided $850.
    29   Received $650 from customers for services to be provided in the future.

Adjustment data:

1. Supplies on hand $1,800.

2. Accrued salaries payable $400.

3. Depreciation $200 per month.

4. Unearned service revenue of $350 earned.

Instructions
(a) Enter the September 1 balances in the ledger T accounts.
(b) Journalize the September transactions.
(c) Post to the ledger T accounts. Use Service Revenue, Depreciation Expense, Supplies Expense, Salaries Expense, and Rent Expense.
(d) Prepare a trial balance at September 30.
(e) Journalize and post adjusting entries.
(f) Prepare an adjusted trial balance.
(g) Prepare an income statement and a retained earnings statement for September and a classified balance sheet at September 30.

(f) Tot. trial balance $29,300
(g) Tot. assets $24,400

P4-8B   Julie Molony opened Valet Cleaners on March 1, 2007. During March, the following transactions were completed.

Complete all steps in accounting cycle.
(SO 4, 5, 6, 7, 8)

Mar. 1   Issued 10,000 shares of common stock for $15,000 cash.
    1   Purchased used truck for $8,000, paying $5,000 cash and the balance on account.
    3   Purchased cleaning supplies for $1,200 on account.
    5   Paid $1,800 cash on 1-year insurance policy effective March 1.
    14   Billed customers $3,200 for cleaning services.
    18   Paid $1,500 cash on amount owed on truck and $500 on amount owed on cleaning supplies.
    20   Paid $1,750 cash for employee salaries.
    21   Collected $1,600 cash from customers billed on March 14.
    28   Billed customers $4,200 for cleaning services.
    31   Paid $350 for gas and oil used in truck during month.
    31   Declared and paid a $900 cash dividend.

GLS

The chart of accounts for Valet Cleaners contains the following accounts: Cash, Accounts Receivable, Cleaning Supplies, Prepaid Insurance, Equipment, Accumulated Depreciation—Equipment, Accounts Payable, Salaries Payable, Common Stock, Retained Earnings, Dividends, Income Summary, Service Revenue, Gas & Oil Expense, Cleaning Supplies Expense, Depreciation Expense, Insurance Expense, Salaries Expense.

Instructions
(a) Journalize the March transactions.
(b) Post to the ledger accounts. (Use T accounts.)
(c) Prepare a trial balance at March 31.
(d) Journalize the following adjustments.
    1. Earned but unbilled revenue at March 31 was $600.
    2. Depreciation on equipment for the month was $250.
    3. One-twelfth of the insurance expired.
    4. An inventory count shows $280 of cleaning supplies on hand at March 31.
    5. Accrued but unpaid employee salaries were $830.
(e) Post adjusting entries to the T accounts.
(f) Prepare an adjusted trial balance.
(g) Prepare the income statement and a retained earnings statement for March and a classified balance sheet at March 31.
(h) Journalize and post closing entries and complete the closing process.
(i) Prepare a post-closing trial balance at March 31.

(f) Tot. adj. trial
*   balance $26,280*
(g) Tot. assets $20,880

Problems: Set C

Visit the book's website at **www.wiley.com/college/kimmel** and choose the Student Companion site to access Problem Set C.

Continuing Cookie Chronicle

(*Note:* This is a continuation of the Cookie Chronicle from Chapters 1 through 3.)

CCC4   Cookie Creations is gearing up for the winter holiday season. During the month of December 2006, the following transactions occur.

Dec. 1 Natalie hires an assistant at an hourly wage of $8 to help with cookie making and some administrative duties.

    5 Natalie teaches the class that was booked on November 25. The balance outstanding is received.

    8 Cookie Creations receives a check for the amount due from the neighborhood school for the class given on November 30.

    9 Cookie Creations receives $625 in advance from the local school board for five classes that the company will give during December and January.

   15 Pays the cell phone invoice outstanding at November 30.

   16 Issues a check to Natalie's brother for the amount owed for the design of the website.

   19 Receives a deposit of $50 on a cookie class scheduled for early January.

   23 Additional revenue earned during the month for cookie-making classes amounts to $3,500. (Natalie has not had time to account for each class individually.) $3,000 in cash has been collected and $500 is still outstanding. (This is in addition to the December 5 and December 9 transactions.)

   23 Additional supplies purchased during the month for sugar, flour, and chocolate chips amount to $1,250 cash.

   23 Issues a check to Natalie's assistant for $800. Her assistant worked approximately 100 hours from the time in which she was hired until December 23.

   28 Pays a dividend of $500 to the common shareholder (Natalie).

As of December 31, Cookie Creations' year-end, the following adjusting entry data are provided.

1. A count reveals that $50 of brochures and posters remain at the end of December.
2. Depreciation is recorded on the baking equipment purchased in November. The baking equipment has a useful life of 5 years. Assume that 2 months' worth of depreciation is required.
3. Amortization (which is similar to depreciation) is recorded on the website. (Credit the Website account directly for the amount of the amortization.) The website is amortized over a useful life of 2 years and was available for use on December 1.
4. Interest on the note payable is accrued. (Assume that 1.5 months of interest accrued during November and December.)
5. One month's worth of insurance has expired.
6. Natalie is unexpectedly telephoned on December 28 to give a cookie class at the neighborhood community center. In early January Cookie Creations sends an invoice for $375 to the community center.
7. A count reveals that $1,025 of baking supplies were used.
8. A cell phone invoice is received for $75. The invoice is for services provided during the month of December and is due on January 15.
9. Because the cookie-making class occurred unexpectedly on December 28 and is for such a large group of children, Natalie's assistant helps out. Her assistant worked 7 hours at a rate of $8 per hour.
10. An analysis of the unearned revenue account reveals that two of the five classes paid for by the local school board on December 9 still have not been taught by the end of December. The $50 deposit received on December 19 for another class also remains unearned.

Instructions

Using the information that you have gathered and the general ledger accounts that you have prepared through Chapter 3, plus the new information on page 210, do the following.

(a) Journalize the above transactions.

(b) Post the December transactions. (Use the general ledger accounts prepared in Chapter 3.)

(c) Prepare a trial balance at December 31, 2006.

(d) Prepare and post adjusting journal entries for the month of December.

(e) Prepare an adjusted trial balance as of December 31, 2006.

(f) Prepare an income statement and a retained earnings statement for the 2-month period ending December 31, 2006, and a classified balance sheet as of December 31, 2006.

(g) Prepare and post closing entries as of December 31, 2006.

(h) Prepare a post-closing trial balance.

▷ BROADENING YOUR PERSPECTIVE

Financial Reporting and Analysis

FINANCIAL REPORTING PROBLEM: *Tootsie Roll Industries, Inc.*

BYP4-1 The financial statements of Tootsie Roll are presented in Appendix A at the end of this book.

Instructions

(a) Using the consolidated income statement and balance sheet, identify items that may result in adjusting entries for prepayments.

(b) Using the consolidated income statement, identify two items that may result in adjusting entries for accruals.

(c) What was the amount of depreciation expense for 2004 and 2003? (You will need to examine the notes to the financial statements or the statement of cash flows.) Where was accumulated depreciation reported?

(d) What was the cash paid for income taxes during 2004, reported at the bottom of the consolidated statement of cash flows? What was income tax expense (provision for income taxes) for 2004? Where is the remainder presumably reported in the balance sheet?

COMPARATIVE ANALYSIS PROBLEM: *Tootsie Roll vs. Hershey Foods*

BYP4-2 The financial statements of Hershey Foods are presented in Appendix B, following the financial statements for Tootsie Roll in Appendix A.

Instructions

(a) Identify two accounts on Hershey Foods' balance sheet that provide evidence that Hershey uses accrual accounting. In each case, identify the income statement account that would be affected by the adjustment process.

(b) Identify two accounts on Tootsie Roll's balance sheet that provide evidence that Tootsie Roll uses accrual accounting (different from the two you listed for Hershey). In each case, identify the income statement account that would be affected by the adjustment process.

RESEARCH CASE

BYP4-3 The July 2, 2004, issue of the *Wall Street Journal* includes an article by Gene Colter titled "Accrual Accounting Can Be Costly."

Instructions

Read the article and answer the following.

(a) How does the article define accrual accounting?

(b) What does the article say happens to companies in the "highest accrual category," and why does it happen?

(c) What high-accrual group companies does the article mention that experienced shareholder lawsuits?

(d) What was General Motors spokesperson's response to being included in the high-accrual group?

INTERPRETING FINANCIAL STATEMENTS

BYP4-4 Laser Recording Systems, founded in 1981, produces disks for use in the home market. The following is an excerpt from Laser Recording Systems' financial statements (all dollars in thousands).

LASER RECORDING SYSTEMS
Management Discussion

Accrued liabilities increased to $1,642 at January 31, from $138 at the end of the previous fiscal year. Compensation and related accruals increased $195 due primarily to increases in accruals for severance, vacation, commissions, and relocation expenses. Accrued professional services increased by $137 primarily as a result of legal expenses related to several outstanding contractual disputes. Other expenses increased $35, of which $18 was for interest payable.

Instructions

(a) Can you tell from the discussion whether Laser Recording Systems has prepaid its legal expenses and is now making an adjustment to the asset account Prepaid Legal Expenses, or whether the company is handling the legal expense via an accrued expense adjustment?

(b) Identify each of the adjustments Laser Recording Systems is discussing as one of the four types of possible adjustments discussed in the chapter. How is net income ultimately affected by each of the adjustments?

(c) What journal entry did Laser Recording make to record the accrued interest?

FINANCIAL ANALYSIS ON THE WEB

BYP4-5 *Purpose:* To learn about the functions of the Securities and Exchange Commission (SEC).

Address: **www.sec.gov/about/whatwedo.shtml** (or go to **www.wiley.com/college/kimmel**)

Instructions

Use the information in this site to answer the following questions.

(a) What event spurred the creation of the SEC? Why was the SEC created?

(b) What are the four divisions of the SEC? Briefly describe the purpose of each.

(c) What are the responsibilities of the chief accountant?

Critical Thinking

DECISION MAKING ACROSS THE ORGANIZATION

BYP4-6 Swiss Valley Park was organized on April 1, 2006, by Erika Barnes. Erika is a good manager but a poor accountant. From the trial balance prepared by a part-time bookkeeper, Erika prepared the income statement shown at the top of page 213 for the quarter that ended March 31, 2007.

SWISS VALLEY PARK
Income Statement
For the Quarter Ended March 31, 2007

Revenues		
Rental revenues		$89,000
Operating expenses		
Advertising	$ 4,200	
Wages	27,600	
Utilities	900	
Depreciation	800	
Repairs	2,800	
Total operating expenses		36,300
Net income		$52,700

Erika knew that something was wrong with the statement because net income had never exceeded $20,000 in any one quarter. Knowing that you are an experienced accountant, she asks you to review the income statement and other data.

You first look at the trial balance. In addition to the account balances reported in the income statement, the ledger contains these selected balances at March 31, 2007.

Supplies	$ 5,200
Prepaid Insurance	7,200
Notes Payable	14,000

You then make inquiries and discover the following.

1. Rental revenues include advanced rentals for summer-month occupancy, $26,000.
2. There were $1,300 of supplies on hand at March 31.
3. Prepaid insurance resulted from the payment of a 1-year policy on January 1, 2007.
4. The mail on April 1, 2007, brought the following bills: advertising for week of March 24, $110; repairs made March 10, $380; and utilities $240.
5. There are four employees who receive wages totaling $290 per day. At March 31, 3 days' wages have been incurred but not paid.
6. The note payable is a 3-month, 8% note dated January 1, 2007.

Instructions
With the class divided into groups, answer the following.
(a) Prepare a correct income statement for the quarter ended March 31, 2007.
(b) Explain to Erika the generally accepted accounting principles that she did not follow in preparing her income statement and their effect on her results.

COMMUNICATION ACTIVITY

BYP4-7 On numerous occasions proposals have surfaced to put the federal government on the accrual basis of accounting. This is no small issue because if this basis were used, it would mean that billions in unrecorded liabilities would have to be booked and the federal deficit would increase substantially.

Instructions
(a) What is the difference between accrual basis accounting and cash basis accounting?
(b) Comment on why politicians prefer a cash basis accounting system over an accrual basis system.
(c) Write a letter to your senators explaining why you think the federal government should adopt the accrual basis of accounting.

ETHICS CASE

BYP4-8 Beegone Company is a pesticide manufacturer. Its sales declined greatly this year due to the passage of legislation outlawing the sale of several of Beegone's chemical pesticides. During the coming year, Beegone will have environmentally safe and competitive replacement chemicals to replace these discontinued products. Sales in the next year are expected to greatly exceed those of any prior year. Therefore, the decline in this year's sales and profits appears to be a one-year aberration.

Even so, the company president believes that a large dip in the current year's profits could cause a significant drop in the market price of Beegone's stock and make it a takeover target. To avoid this possibility, he urges Clare Bolton, controller, in making this period's year-end adjusting entries to accrue every possible revenue and to defer as many expenses as possible. The president says to Clare, "We need the revenues this year, and next year we can easily absorb expenses deferred from this year. We can't let our stock price be hammered down!" Clare didn't get around to recording the adjusting entries until January 17, but she dated the entries December 31 as if they were recorded then. Clare also made every effort to comply with the president's request.

Instructions
(a) Who are the stakeholders in this situation?
(b) What are the ethical considerations of the president's request and Clare's dating the adjusting entries December 31?
(c) Can Clare accrue revenues and defer expenses and still be ethical?

Answers to Business Insight and Accounting across the Organization Questions

p. 161

Q. What motivates sales executives and finance and accounting executives to participate in activities that result in inaccurate reporting of revenues?

A. Sales executives typically receive bonuses based on their ability to meet quarterly sales targets. In addition, they often face the possibility of losing their jobs if they miss those targets. Executives in accounting and finance are very aware of the earnings targets of Wall Street analysts and investors. If they fail to meet these targets, the company's stock price will fall. As a result of these pressures, executives sometimes knowingly engage in unethical efforts to misstate revenues. As a result of the Sarbanes-Oxley Act of 2002, the penalties for such behavior are now much more severe.

p. 164

Q. Why might the new accounting method cause companies sometimes to spend less on advertising?

A. Under the old approach companies could delay to future periods the expensing of advertising costs. Under that approach, money spent this period did not necessarily immediately reduce income. Under the new approach, a dollar spent on advertising immediately reduces this year's income. If the company is concerned that it might not hit this year's earnings target, it might decide to reduce its advertising spending.

p. 168

Q. Suppose that Robert Jones purchases a $100 gift card at Best Buy on December 24, 2006, and gives it to his wife Mary Jones on December 25, 2006. On January 3, 2007, Mary uses the card to purchase $100 worth of CDs. When do you think Best Buy should recognize revenue and why?

A. According to the revenue recognition principle, companies should recognize revenue when earned. In this case revenue is not earned until Best Buy provides the goods. Thus, when Best Buy receives cash in exchange for the gift card on December 24, 2006, it should recognize a liability, Unearned Revenue, for $100. On January 3, 2007, when Mary Jones exchanges the card for merchandise, Best Buy should recognize revenue and eliminate $100 from the balance in the Unearned Revenue account.

Answer to Tootsie Roll Review It Question 3, p. 174

Under the heading "Property, plant, and equipment" in Note 1, Tootsie Roll reports 2004 depreciation expense of $11,680,000.

Answers to Self-Study Questions

1. c	2. a	3. d	4. d	5. c	6. a	7. b	8. b	9. c
10. d	11. a	12. a	13. d					

REMEMBER TO GO BACK TO THE NAVIGATOR BOX ON THE CHAPTER-OPENING PAGE AND CHECK OFF YOUR COMPLETED WORK.

CHAPTER 5

Merchandising Operations and the Multiple-Step Income Statement

STUDY OBJECTIVES

After studying this chapter,
you should be able to:

1 Identify the differences between a service enterprise and a merchandising company.

2 Explain the recording of purchases under a perpetual inventory system.

3 Explain the recording of sales revenues under a perpetual inventory system.

4 Distinguish between a single-step and a multiple-step income statement.

5 Determine cost of goods sold under a periodic system.

6 Explain the factors affecting profitability.

THE NAVIGATOR

THE NAVIGATOR

● Scan *Study Objectives*

● Read *Feature Story*

● Read *Preview*

● Read text and answer *Before You Go On*
   p. 224   p. 227   p. 232
   p. 233   p. 237

● Work *Using the Decision Toolkit*

● Review *Summary of Study Objectives*

● Work *Demonstration Problem*

● Answer *Self-Study Questions*

● Complete *Assignments*

FEATURE STORY

Who Doesn't Shop at Wal-Mart?

In his book *The End of Work*, Jeremy Rifkin notes that until the 20th century the word *consumption* evoked negative images; to be labeled a "consumer" was an insult. (In fact, one of the deadliest diseases in history, tuberculosis, was often referred to as "consumption.") Twentieth-century merchants realized, however, that in order to prosper, they had to convince people of the need for things not previously needed. For example, General Motors made annual changes in its cars so that people would be discontented with the cars they already owned. Thus began consumerism.

Today consumption describes the U.S. lifestyle in a nutshell. We consume twice as much today per person as we did at the end of World War II. The amount of U.S. retail space per person is vastly greater than that of any other country. It appears that we live to shop.

The first great retail giant was Sears, Roebuck. It started as a catalog company enabling people in rural areas to buy things by mail. For decades it was the uncontested merchandising leader.

Today Wal-Mart is the undisputed champion provider of basic (and perhaps not-so-basic) human needs. Wal-Mart opened its first store in 1962, and it now has more than 5,000 stores, serving more than 100 million customers every week. A key

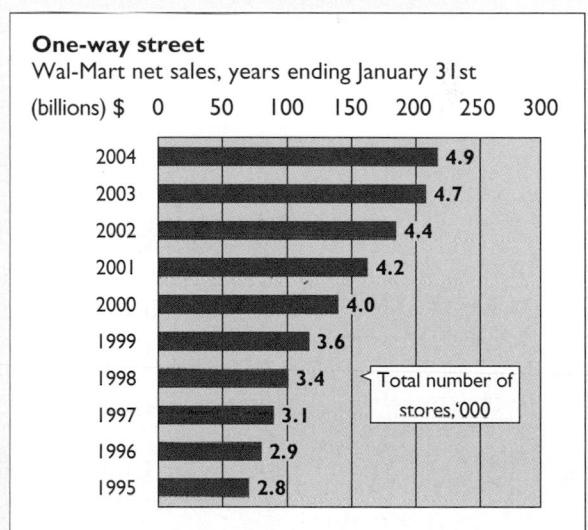

cause of Wal-Mart's incredible growth is its amazing system of inventory control and distribution. Wal-Mart has a management information system that employs six satellite channels, from which company computers receive 8.4 million updates every minute on what items customers buy and the relationship among items sold to each person.

Measured by sales revenues, Wal-Mart is the largest company in the world. In six years it went from selling almost no groceries to being America's largest grocery retailer.

It would appear that things have never looked better at Wal-Mart. On the other hand, a *Wall Street Journal* article entitled "How to Sell More to Those Who Think It's Cool to Be Frugal" suggests that consumerism as a way of life might be dying. Don't bet your wide-screen TV on it, though.

One-way street
Wal-Mart net sales, years ending January 31st

(billions) $ 0   50   100   150   200   250   300

Year	
2004	4.9
2003	4.7
2002	4.4
2001	4.2
2000	4.0
1999	3.6
1998	3.4
1997	3.1
1996	2.9
1995	2.8

Total number of stores,'000

Source: "How Big Can It Grow?" *The Economist* (April 17, 2004), pp. 67–69.

On the World Wide Web
Wal-Mart: www.wal-mart.com

217

PREVIEW OF CHAPTER 5

Merchandising is one of the largest and most influential industries in the United States. It is likely that a number of you will work for a merchandiser. Therefore, understanding the financial statements of merchandising companies is important. In this chapter you will learn the basics about reporting merchandising transactions. In addition, you will learn how to prepare and analyze a commonly used form of the income statement—the multiple-step income statement. The content and organization of the chapter are as follows.

MERCHANDISING OPERATIONS

Merchandising Operations	Recording Purchases of Merchandise	Recording Sales of Merchandise	Income Statement Presentation	Evaluating Profitability
• Operating cycles • Inventory systems—perpetual and periodic	• Freight costs • Purchase returns and allowances • Purchase discounts • Summary of purchasing transactions	• Sales returns and allowances • Sales discounts	• Sales revenues • Gross profit • Operating expenses • Nonoperating activities • Determining cost of goods sold—periodic system	• Gross profit rate • Profit margin ratio

Merchandising Operations

STUDY OBJECTIVE

1

Identify the differences between a service enterprise and a merchandising company.

Wal-Mart, Kmart, and Target are called merchandising companies because they buy and sell merchandise rather than perform services as their primary source of revenue. Merchandising companies that purchase and sell directly to consumers are called **retailers**. Merchandising companies that sell to retailers are known as **wholesalers**. For example, retailer Walgreens might buy goods from wholesaler McKesson; retailer Office Depot might buy office supplies from wholesaler United Stationers. The primary source of revenues for merchandising companies is the sale of merchandise, often referred to simply as **sales revenue** or **sales**. A merchandising company has two categories of expenses: the cost of goods sold and operating expenses.

The **cost of goods sold** is the total cost of merchandise sold during the period. This expense is directly related to the revenue recognized from the sale of goods. Illustration 5-1 shows the income measurement process for a merchandising company. The items in the two blue boxes are unique to a merchandising company; they are not used by a service company.

OPERATING CYCLES

The operating cycle of a merchandising company ordinarily is longer than that of a service company. The purchase of merchandise inventory and its eventual

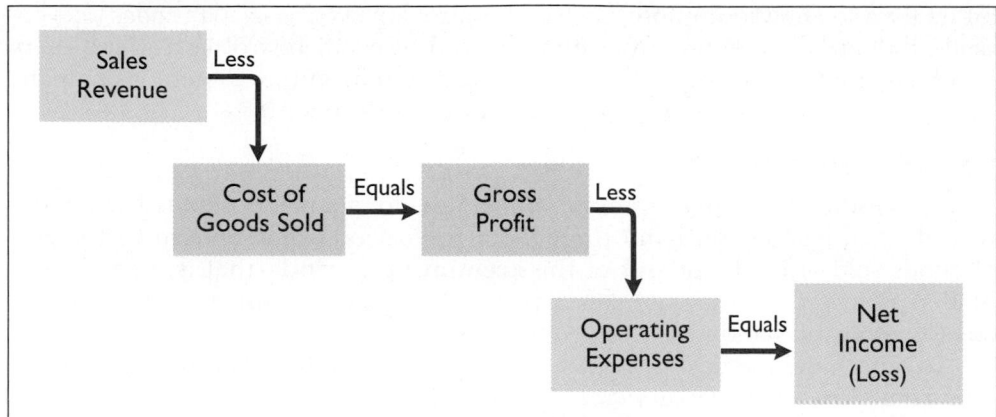

Illustration 5-1 Income measurement process for a merchandising company

sale lengthen the cycle. Illustration 5-2 contrasts the operating cycles of service and merchandising companies. Note that the added asset account for a merchandising company is the Merchandise Inventory account.

INVENTORY SYSTEMS

A merchandising company keeps track of its inventory to determine what is available for sale and what has been sold. Companies use one of two systems to account for inventory: a **perpetual inventory system** or a **periodic inventory system**.

Perpetual System

In a **perpetual inventory system**, companies maintain detailed records of the cost of each inventory purchase and sale. These records continuously—perpetually— show the inventory that should be on hand for every item. For example, a Ford dealership has separate inventory records for each automobile, truck, and van on its lot and showroom floor. Similarly, a grocery store uses bar codes and optical scanners to keep a daily running record of every box of cereal and every jar of jelly that it buys and sells. Under a perpetual inventory system, a company determines the cost of goods sold **each time a sale occurs**.

Periodic System

In a **periodic inventory system**, companies do not keep detailed inventory records of the goods on hand throughout the period. They determine the cost of goods sold **only at the end of the accounting period**—that is, periodically. At that point, the company takes a physical inventory count to determine the cost of goods on hand.

To determine the cost of goods sold under a periodic inventory system, the following steps are necessary:

1. Determine the cost of goods on hand at the beginning of the accounting period.
2. Add to it the cost of goods purchased.
3. Subtract the cost of goods on hand at the end of the accounting period.

Illustration 5-3 graphically compares the sequence of activities and the timing of the cost of goods sold computation under the two inventory systems.

Illustration 5-3
Comparing perpetual and periodic inventory systems

Additional Considerations

Companies that sell merchandise with high unit values, such as automobiles, furniture, and major home appliances, have traditionally used perpetual systems. The growing use of computers and electronic scanners has enabled many more companies to install perpetual inventory systems. The perpetual inventory system is so named because the accounting records continuously—perpetually—show the quantity and cost of the inventory that should be on hand at any time.

A perpetual inventory system provides better control over inventories than a periodic system. Since the inventory records show the quantities that should be on hand, the company can count the goods at any time to see whether the amount of goods actually on hand agrees with the inventory records. If shortages are uncovered, the company can investigate immediately. Although a perpetual inventory system requires additional clerical work and additional cost to maintain the subsidiary records, a computerized system can minimize this cost.

As noted in the Feature Story, much of Wal-Mart's success is attributed to its sophisticated inventory system.

Some businesses find it either unnecessary or uneconomical to invest in a computerized perpetual inventory system. Many small merchandising businesses, in particular, find that a perpetual inventory system costs more than it is worth. Managers of these businesses can control their merchandise and manage day-to-day operations using a periodic inventory system.

Because the perpetual inventory system is growing in popularity and use, we illustrate it in this chapter. An appendix to this chapter describes the journal entries for the periodic system.

Business Insight
Investor Perspective

Investors are often eager to invest in a company that has a hot new product. However, when snowboard maker Morrow Snowboards, Inc., issued shares of stock to the public for the first time, some investors expressed reluctance to invest in Morrow because of a number of accounting control problems. To reduce investor concerns, Morrow implemented a perpetual inventory system to improve its control over inventory. In addition, it stated that it would perform a physical inventory count every quarter until it felt that the perpetual inventory system was reliable.

 If a perpetual system keeps track of inventory on a daily basis, why do companies ever need to do a physical count?

Recording Purchases of Merchandise

Companies may purchase inventory for cash or on account (credit). They normally record purchases when they receive the goods from the seller. Every purchase should be supported by business documents that provide written evidence of the transaction. Each cash purchase should be supported by a canceled check or a cash register receipt indicating the items purchased and amounts paid. Companies record cash purchases by an increase in Merchandise Inventory and a decrease in Cash.

Each credit purchase should be supported by a **purchase invoice**, which indicates the total purchase price and other relevant information. However, the purchaser does not prepare a separate purchase invoice. Instead, the purchaser uses as a purchase invoice the copy of the sales invoice sent by the seller. In Illustration 5-4 (page 222), for example, Sauk Stereo (the buyer) uses as a purchase invoice the sales invoice prepared by PW Audio Supply, Inc. (the seller).

The associated entry for Sauk Stereo for the invoice from PW Audio Supply increases Merchandise Inventory and increases Accounts Payable.

STUDY OBJECTIVE
2
Explain the recording of purchases under a perpetual inventory system.

May	4	Merchandise Inventory	3,800	
		Accounts Payable		3,800
		(To record goods purchased on account from PW Audio Supply)		

A	=	L	+	SE
+3,800				
		+3,800		

Cash Flows
no effect

Under the perpetual inventory system, companies record purchases of merchandise for sale in the Merchandise Inventory account. Thus, Wal-Mart would increase (debit) Merchandise Inventory for clothing, sporting goods, and anything else purchased for resale to customers. Not all purchases are debited to Merchandise Inventory, however. Companies record purchases of assets acquired

Illustration 5-4 Sales invoice used as purchase invoice by Sauk Stereo

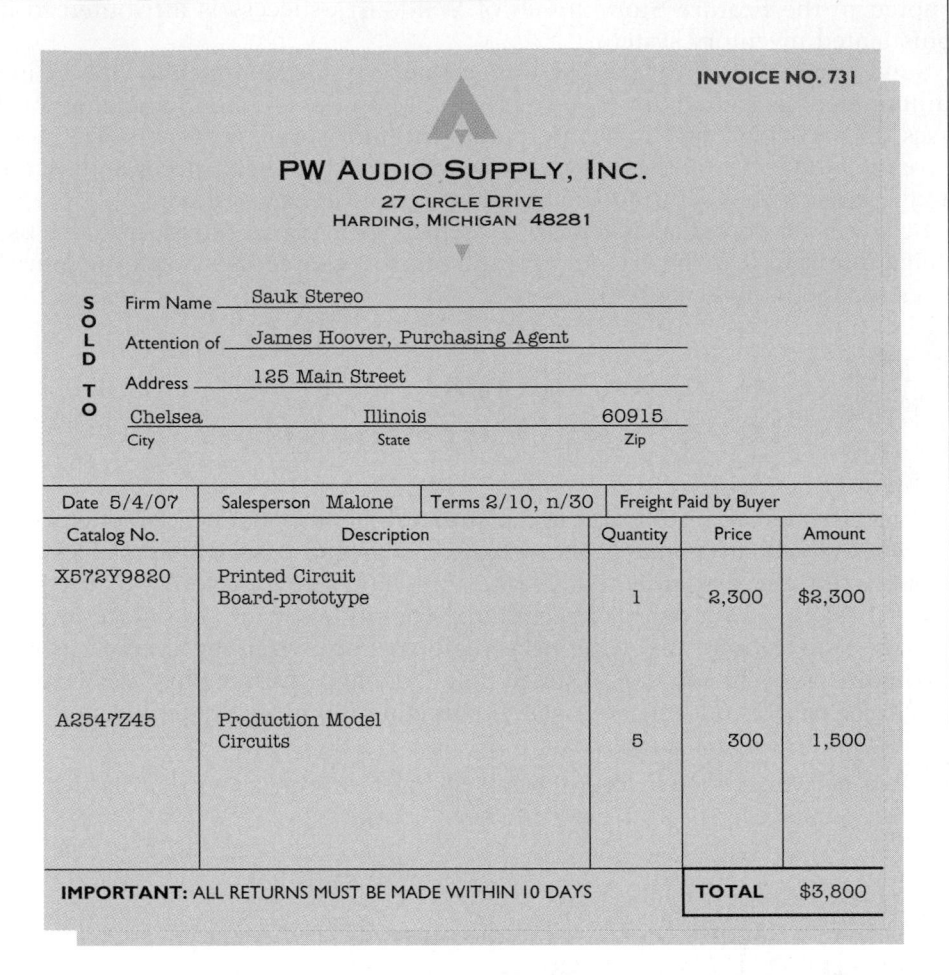

Helpful Hint To better understand the contents of this invoice, identify these items:
1. Seller
2. Invoice date
3. Purchaser
4. Salesperson
5. Credit terms
6. Freight terms
7. Goods sold: catalog number, description, quantity, price per unit
8. Total invoice amount

for use and not for resale, such as supplies, equipment, and similar items, as increases to specific asset accounts rather than to Merchandise Inventory. For example, to record the purchase of materials used to make shelf signs or for cash register receipt paper, Wal-Mart would increase Supplies.

FREIGHT COSTS

Freight Costs Incurred by Buyer

The sales invoice indicates whether the seller or the buyer pays the cost of transporting the goods to the buyer's place of business. When the buyer pays the transportation costs, these costs are considered part of the cost of purchasing inventory. As a result, the account **Merchandise Inventory is increased**. For example, if Sauk Stereo (the buyer) pays Haul-It Freight Company $150 for freight charges on May 6, the entry on Sauk's books is:

A	=	L	+	SE
+150				
−150				

Cash Flows
−150

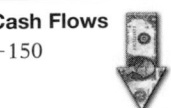

May	6	Merchandise Inventory		150	
		Cash			150
		(To record payment of freight on goods purchased)			

Freight Costs Incurred by Seller

In contrast, **freight costs incurred by the seller on outgoing merchandise are an operating expense to the seller**. These costs increase an expense account titled Freight-out or Delivery Expense. For example, if the freight terms on the invoice in Illustration 5-4 had required that PW Audio Supply (the seller) pay the $150 freight charges, the entry by PW Audio would be:

May 4	Freight-out	150	
	Cash		150
	(To record payment of freight on goods sold)		

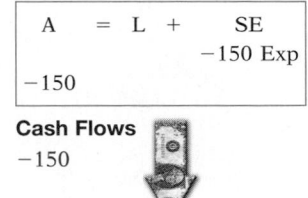

A	=	L	+	SE
				−150 Exp
−150				

Cash Flows
−150

When the seller pays the freight charges, the seller will usually establish a higher invoice price for the goods, to cover the expense of shipping.

PURCHASE RETURNS AND ALLOWANCES

A purchaser may be dissatisfied with the merchandise received because the goods are damaged or defective, of inferior quality, or do not meet the purchaser's specifications. In such cases, the purchaser may return the goods to the seller for credit if the sale was made on credit, or for a cash refund if the purchase was for cash. This transaction is known as a **purchase return**. Alternatively, the purchaser may choose to keep the merchandise if the seller is willing to grant an allowance (deduction) from the purchase price. This transaction is known as a **purchase allowance**.

Assume that Sauk Stereo returned goods costing $300 to PW Audio Supply on May 8. The following entry by Sauk Stereo for the returned merchandise decreases Accounts Payable and decreases Merchandise Inventory.

May 8	Accounts Payable	300	
	Merchandise Inventory		300
	(To record return of goods purchased from PW Audio Supply)		

A	=	L	+	SE
		−300		
−300				

Cash Flows
no effect

Because Sauk Stereo increased Merchandise Inventory when the goods were received, Merchandise Inventory is decreased when Sauk returns the goods.

PURCHASE DISCOUNTS

The credit terms of a purchase on account may permit the buyer to claim a cash discount for prompt payment. The buyer calls this cash discount a **purchase discount**. This incentive offers advantages to both parties: The purchaser saves money, and the seller is able to shorten the operating cycle by converting the accounts receivable into cash earlier.

The **credit terms** specify the amount of the cash discount and time period during which it is offered. They also indicate the length of time in which the purchaser is expected to pay the full invoice price. In the sales invoice in Illustration 5-4, credit terms are 2/10, n/30, which is read "two-ten, net thirty." This means that a 2% cash discount may be taken on the invoice price less ("net of") any returns or allowances, if payment is made within 10 days of the invoice date (the **discount period**). Otherwise, the invoice price, less any returns or allowances, is due 30 days from the invoice date. Alternatively, the discount period may extend to a specified number of days following the month in which the sale occurs. For example, 1/10 EOM (end of month) means that a 1% discount is available if the invoice is paid within the first 10 days of the next month.

When the seller elects not to offer a cash discount for prompt payment, credit terms will specify only the maximum time period for paying the balance due. For example, the credit terms may state the time period as n/30, n/60, or n/10 EOM. This means, respectively, that the buyer must pay the net amount in 30 days, 60 days, or within the first 10 days of the next month.

Helpful Hint The term *net* in "net 30" means the remaining amount due after subtracting any sales returns and allowances and partial payments.

When an invoice is paid within the discount period, the amount of the discount decreases Merchandise Inventory. Why? Because the merchandiser records inventory at its cost and, by paying within the discount period, it has reduced that cost. To illustrate, assume Sauk Stereo pays the balance due of $3,500 (gross invoice price of $3,800 less purchase returns and allowances of $300) on May 14, the last day of the discount period. The cash discount is $70 ($3,500 × 2%), and the amount of cash Sauk Stereo paid is $3,430 ($3,500 − $70). The entry Sauk makes to record its May 14 payment decreases Accounts Payable by the amount of the gross invoice price, reduces Merchandise Inventory by the $70 discount, and reduces Cash by the net amount owed.

```
A   =   L   +   SE
       -3,500
-3,430
 -70
```

Cash Flows
−3,430

May 14	Accounts Payable	3,500	
	Cash		3,430
	Merchandise Inventory		70
	(To record payment within discount period)		

If Sauk Stereo failed to take the discount and instead made full payment of $3,500 on June 3, Sauk would debit Accounts Payable and credit Cash for $3,500 each.

```
A   =   L   +   SE
       -3,500
-3,500
```

Cash Flows
−3,500

June 3	Accounts Payable	3,500	
	Cash		3,500
	(To record payment with no discount taken)		

A merchandising company usually should take all available discounts. Passing up the discount may be viewed as **paying interest** for use of the money. For example, passing up the discount offered by PW Audio would be like Sauk Stereo paying an interest rate of 2% for the use of $3,500 for 20 days. This is the equivalent of an annual interest rate of approximately 36.5% (2% × 365/20). Obviously, it would be better for Sauk Stereo to borrow at prevailing bank interest rates of 6% to 10% than to lose the discount.

SUMMARY OF PURCHASING TRANSACTIONS

The following T account (with transaction descriptions in blue) provides a summary of the effect of the previous transactions on Merchandise Inventory. Sauk originally purchased $3,800 worth of inventory for resale. It then returned $300 of goods. It paid $150 in freight charges, and finally, it received a $70 discount off the balance owed because it paid within the discount period. This results in a balance in Merchandise Inventory of $3,580.

Merchandise Inventory

Purchase	May 4	3,800	May 8	300	Purchase return
Freight-in	6	150	14	70	Purchase discount
Balance		3,580			

BEFORE YOU GO ON . . .

▶ **Review It**

1. How does a merchandising company measure net income differently from a service enterprise?
2. In what ways is a perpetual inventory system different from a periodic system?

3. Under the perpetual inventory system, what entries do companies make to record purchases, purchase returns and allowances, purchase discounts, and freight costs?

THE NAVIGATOR

Recording Sales of Merchandise

Companies record sales revenues, like service revenues, when earned, in compliance with the revenue recognition principle. Typically, companies earn sales revenues when the goods are transferred from the seller to the buyer. At this point the sales transaction is completed and the sales price is established.

Sales may be made on credit or for cash. Every sales transaction should be supported by a **business document** that provides written evidence of the sale. **Cash register tapes** provide evidence of cash sales. A sales invoice, like the one that was shown in Illustration 5-4 (page 222), provides support for a credit sale. The original copy of the invoice goes to the customer, and the seller keeps a copy for use in recording the sale. The invoice shows the date of sale, customer name, total sales price, and other relevant information.

The seller makes two entries for each sale: (1) It increases Accounts Receivable or Cash, as well as the Sales account. (2) It increases Cost of Goods Sold and decreases Merchandise Inventory. As a result, the Merchandise Inventory account will show at all times the amount of inventory that should be on hand.

To illustrate a credit sales transaction, PW Audio Supply records the sale of $3,800 on May 4 to Sauk Stereo (see Illustration 5-4) as follows (assume the merchandise cost PW Audio Supply $2,400).

> **STUDY OBJECTIVE**
> **3**
> Explain the recording of sales revenues under a perpetual inventory system.

May	4	Accounts Receivable	3,800	
		Sales		3,800
		(To record credit sale to Sauk Stereo per invoice #731)		
	4	Cost of Goods Sold	2,400	
		Merchandise Inventory		2,400
		(To record cost of merchandise sold on invoice #731 to Sauk Stereo)		

$$A = L + SE$$
$$+3,800$$
$$+3,800 \text{ Rev}$$

Cash Flows
no effect

$$A = L + SE$$
$$-2,400 \text{ Exp}$$
$$-2,400$$

Cash Flows
no effect

Helpful Hint The merchandiser credits the Sales account only for sales of goods held for resale. Sales of assets not held for resale, such as equipment or land, are credited directly to the asset account.

For internal decision-making purposes, merchandising companies may use more than one sales account. For example, PW Audio Supply may decide to keep separate sales accounts for its sales of TV sets, videocassette recorders, and microwave ovens. Wal-Mart might use separate accounts for sporting goods, children's clothing, and hardware—or it might have even more narrowly defined accounts. By using separate sales accounts for major product lines, rather than a single combined sales account, company management can monitor sales trends more closely and respond more strategically to changes in sales patterns. For example, if TV sales are increasing while microwave oven sales are decreasing, the company might reevaluate both its advertising and pricing policies on each of these items to ensure they are optimal.

On its income statement presented to outside investors a merchandising company would normally provide only a single sales figure—the sum of all of its individual sales accounts. This is done for two reasons. First, providing detail on all of its individual sales accounts would add considerable length to its income statement. Second, companies do not want their competitors to know the details of their operating results. However, Microsoft recently expanded its disclosure of revenue from three to five types. The reason: The additional categories will better enable financial statement users to evaluate the growth of the company's consumer and Internet businesses.

SALES RETURNS AND ALLOWANCES

We now look at the "flipside" of purchase returns and allowances, which the seller records as **sales returns and allowances**. PW Audio Supply's entries to record credit for returned goods involve (1) an increase in Sales Returns and Allowances and a decrease in Accounts Receivable at the $300 selling price, and (2) an increase in Merchandise Inventory (assume a $140 cost) and a decrease in Cost of Goods Sold as shown below. (We have assumed that the goods were not defective. If they were defective, PW Audio would make an adjustment to the inventory account to reflect their decline in value.)

A	=	L	+	SE
				−300 Rev
−300				

Cash Flows
no effect

A	=	L	+	SE
+140				
				+140 Exp

Cash Flows
no effect

May	8	Sales Returns and Allowances	300	
		Accounts Receivable		300
		(To record credit granted to Sauk Stereo for returned goods)		
	8	Merchandise Inventory	140	
		Cost of Goods Sold		140
		(To record cost of goods returned)		

Sales Returns and Allowances is a **contra revenue account** to Sales. The normal balance of Sales Returns and Allowances is a debit. Companies use a contra account, instead of debiting Sales, to disclose in the accounts and in the income statement the amount of sales returns and allowances. Disclosure of this information is important to management. Excessive returns and allowances suggest problems—inferior merchandise, inefficiencies in filling orders, errors in billing customers, or mistakes in delivery or shipment of goods. Moreover, a decrease (debit) recorded directly to Sales would obscure the relative importance of sales returns and allowances as a percentage of sales. It also could distort comparisons between total sales in different accounting periods.

Accounting across the Organization

In most industries sales returns are relatively minor. In the publishing industry, however, bookstores are allowed to return unsold hardcover books to the publisher. Marketing managers at the publishing companies argue that these generous return policies are necessary to encourage bookstores to buy a broader range of books, instead of focusing just on "sure things."

But with returns of hardcover books now exceeding 34% of sales, this generous return policy is taking its toll on net income. Production and inventory managers are quick to point out the many costs of excess returns. Publishers must pay to have the books shipped back to their warehouse, sorted, and then shipped to discounters. If the discounters don't sell them, the books are repackaged again, shipped back to the publisher, and destroyed. Some bookstores and publishers have proposed adopting a "no returns" policy, but no company wants to be the first one to implement it.

Source: Jeffrey A Trachtenberg, "Quest for Best Seller Creates a Pileup of Returned Books," *Wall Street Journal* (June 3, 2005), p. A1.

 If a company expects significant returns, what are the implications for revenue recognition?

SALES DISCOUNTS

As mentioned in our discussion of purchase transactions, the seller may offer the customer a cash discount—called by the seller a *sales discount*—for the prompt payment of the balance due. Like a purchase discount, a sales discount is based on the invoice price less returns and allowances, if any. The seller increases (debits) the Sales Discounts account for discounts that are taken. The entry by PW Audio Supply to record the cash receipt on May 14 from Sauk Stereo within the discount period is:

May 14	Cash	3,430	
	Sales Discounts	70	
	Accounts Receivable		3,500
	(To record collection within 2/10, n/30		
	discount period from Sauk Stereo)		

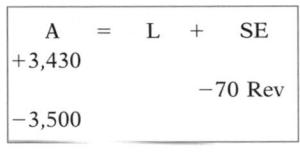

A	=	L	+	SE
+3,430				
				−70 Rev
−3,500				

Cash Flows
+3,430

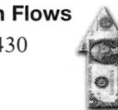

Like Sales Returns and Allowances, Sales Discounts is a **contra revenue account** to Sales. Its normal balance is a debit. Sellers use this account, instead of debiting sales, to disclose the amount of cash discounts taken by customers. If the customer does not take the discount, PW Audio Supply increases Cash for $3,500 and decreases Accounts Receivable for the same amount at the date of collection.

BEFORE YOU GO ON . . .

▶ Review It

1. Under a perpetual inventory system, what are the two entries that a selling company must record at the time of each sale?
2. Why is it important to use the Sales Returns and Allowances account, rather than simply reducing the Sales account, when purchasers return goods?

▶ Do It

On September 5, De La Hoya Company buys merchandise on account from Junot Diaz Company. The selling price of the goods is $1,500, and the cost to Diaz Company was $800. On September 8, purchasers return goods with a selling price of $200 and a cost of $105. Record the transactions on the books of both companies.

Action Plan

- Purchaser records goods at cost.
- Seller records both the sale and the cost of goods sold at the time of the sale.
- When goods are returned, purchaser reduces Merchandise Inventory, but seller records the return in a contra account, Sales Returns and Allowances.

Solution

De La Hoya Company

Sept. 5	Merchandise Inventory	1,500	
	Accounts Payable		1,500
	(To record goods purchased on account)		
Sept. 8	Accounts Payable	200	
	Merchandise Inventory		200
	(To record return of defective goods)		

Junot Diaz Company

Sept.	5	Accounts Receivable	1,500	
		Sales		1,500
		(To record credit sale)		
	5	Cost of Goods Sold	800	
		Merchandise Inventory		800
		(To record cost of goods sold on account)		
Sept.	8	Sales Returns and Allowances	200	
		Accounts Receivable		200
		(To record credit granted for receipt of returned goods)		
	8	Merchandise Inventory	105	
		Cost of Goods Sold		105
		(To record cost of goods returned)		

THE NAVIGATOR

Income Statement Presentation

STUDY OBJECTIVE

4

Distinguish between a single-step and a multiple-step income statement.

Companies widely use two forms of the income statement. One is the **single-step income statement**. The statement is so named because only one step, subtracting total expenses from total revenues, is required in determining net income (or net loss).

In a single-step statement, all data are classified into two categories: (1) **revenues**, which include both operating revenues and nonoperating revenues and gains (for example, interest revenue and gain on sale of equipment); and (2) **expenses**, which include cost of goods sold, operating expenses, and nonoperating expenses and losses (for example, interest expense, loss on sale of equipment, or income tax expense). The single-step income statement is the form we have used thus far in the text. Illustration 5-5 shows a single-step statement for Wal-Mart.

Illustration 5-5
Single-step income statements

WAL★MART ALWAYS LOW PRICES. *Always*

WAL-MART STORES, INC.
Income Statements
(in millions)

	For the years ended January 31	
	2004	**2003**
Revenues		
Net sales	$256,329	$229,616
Other revenues, net	2,352	1,961
	258,681	231,577
Expenses		
Cost of goods sold	198,747	178,299
Selling, general, and administrative expenses	44,909	39,983
Interest expense	832	927
Other expense	21	56
Income taxes	5,118	4,357
	249,627	223,622
Net income	$ 9,054	$ 7,955

There are two primary reasons for using the single-step form: (1) A company does not realize any type of profit or income until total revenues exceed total expenses, so it makes sense to divide the statement into these two categories. (2) The form is simple and easy to read.

A second form of the income statement is the **multiple-step income statement**. The multiple-step income statement is often considered more useful because it highlights the components of net income. The Wal-Mart income statement in Illustration 5-6 is an example.

WAL★MART
ALWAYS LOW PRICES.
Always

WAL-MART STORES, INC.
Income Statements
(in millions)

	2004	2003
For the years ended January 31		
Net sales	$256,329	$229,616
Cost of goods sold	198,747	178,299
Gross profit	57,582	51,317
Operating expenses		
Selling, general, and administrative expenses	44,909	39,983
Income from operations	12,673	11,334
Other revenues and gains		
Other revenues, net	2,352	1,961
Other expenses and losses		
Interest expense	832	927
Other expense	21	56
Income before income taxes	14,172	12,312
Income tax expense	5,118	4,357
Net income	$ 9,054	$ 7,955

Illustration 5-6 Multiple-step income statements

The multiple-step income statement has three important line items: gross profit, income from operations, and net income. They are determined as follows.

1. Subtract cost of goods sold from sales to determine **gross profit**.
2. Deduct operating expenses from gross profit to determine **income from operations**.
3. Add or subtract the results of activities not related to operations to determine **net income**.

You should note that companies report income tax expense in a separate section of the income statement before net income. The following discussion provides additional information about the components of a multiple-step income statement.

SALES REVENUES

The income statement for a merchandising company typically presents gross sales revenues for the period. The company deducts sales returns and allowances and sales discounts (both contra accounts) from sales in the income statement to arrive at net sales. Illustration 5-7 (page 230) shows the sales revenues section of the income statement for PW Audio Supply.

Illustration 5-7
Statement presentation of
sales revenues section

PW AUDIO SUPPLY, INC.		
Income Statement (partial)		
Sales revenues		
Sales		$480,000
Less: Sales returns and allowances	$12,000	
Sales discounts	8,000	20,000
Net sales		**$460,000**

GROSS PROFIT

Alternative Terminology
Gross profit is sometimes
referred to as *gross margin*.

Companies deduct **cost of goods sold** from sales revenue to determine **gross profit**. As shown in Illustration 5-6, for example, Wal-Mart had a gross profit of $57.6 billion in fiscal year 2004. Sales revenue used for this computation is **net sales**, which takes into account sales returns and allowances and sales discounts.

On the basis of the PW Audio Supply sales data presented in Illustration 5-7 (net sales of $460,000) and the cost of goods sold (assume a balance of $316,000), PW Audio Supply's gross profit is $144,000, computed as follows.

GNet sales	$460,000
Cost of goods sold	316,000
Gross profit	**$144,000**

It is important to understand what gross profit is—and what it is not. Gross profit represents the **merchandising profit** of a company. Because operating expenses have not been deducted, it is *not* a measure of the overall profit of a company. Nevertheless, management and other interested parties closely watch the amount and trend of gross profit. Comparisons of current gross profit with past amounts and rates and with those in the industry indicate the effectiveness of a company's purchasing and pricing policies.

OPERATING EXPENSES

Operating expenses are the next component in measuring net income for a merchandising company. At Wal-Mart, for example, operating expenses were $44.9 billion in fiscal year 2004. These expenses are similar in merchandising and service enterprises.

At PW Audio Supply, operating expenses were $114,000. The firm determines its income from operations by subtracting operating expenses from gross profit. Thus, income from operations is $30,000, as shown below.

Gross profit	$144,000
Operating expenses	**114,000**
Income from operations	$ 30,000

NONOPERATING ACTIVITIES

Nonoperating activities consist of various revenues and expenses and gains and losses that are unrelated to the company's main line of operations. When nonoperating items are included, the label "**Income from operations**" (or "Operating income") precedes them. This label clearly identifies the results of the company's normal operations, an amount determined by subtracting cost of goods sold and operating expenses from net sales. The results of nonoperating activities are shown in the categories "**Other revenues and gains**" and "**Other expenses and losses**." Illustration 5-8 lists examples of each.

Illustration 5-8   Other items of nonoperating activities

Other Revenues and Gains
Interest revenue from notes receivable and marketable securities.
Dividend revenue from investments in capital stock.
Rent revenue from subleasing a portion of the store.
Gain from the sale of property, plant, and equipment.

Other Expenses and Losses
Interest expense on notes and loans payable.
Casualty losses from recurring causes, such as vandalism and accidents.
Loss from the sale or abandonment of property, plant, and equipment.
Loss from strikes by employees and suppliers.

The distinction between operating and nonoperating activities is crucial to many external users of financial data. These users view operating income as sustainable and many nonoperating activities as nonrecurring. Therefore, when forecasting next year's income, analysts put the most weight on this year's operating income, and less weight on this year's nonoperating activities.

Business Insight
Ethics Perspective

After Enron, increased investor criticism and regulator scrutiny forced many companies to improve the clarity of their financial disclosures. For example, IBM announced that it would begin providing more detail regarding its "Other gains and losses." It had previously included these items in its selling, general, and administrative expenses, with little disclosure.

Disclosing other gains and losses in a separate line item on the income statement will not have any effect on bottom-line income. However, analysts complained that burying these details in the selling, general, and administrative expense line reduced their ability to fully understand how well IBM was performing. For example, previously if IBM sold off one of its buildings at a gain, it would include this gain in the selling, general, and administrative expense line item, thus reducing that expense. This made it appear that the company had done a better job of controlling operating expenses than it actually had.

Other companies that also recently announced changes to increase the informativeness of their income statements included PepsiCo and General Electric.

 Why have investors and analysts demanded more accuracy in isolating "Other gains and losses" from operating items?

The nonoperating activities are reported in the income statement immediately after the operating activities. Included among these activities in Illustration 5-6 for Wal-Mart is net interest expense of $0.8 billion for fiscal year 2004. The amount remaining, after adding the operating and nonoperating sections together, is Wal-Mart's net income of $9.1 billion. Note that the net incomes in Illustrations 5-5 and 5-6 (pages 228 and 229) are the same. The difference in the two income statements is the amount of detail displayed and the order presented.

In Illustration 5-9 (on page 232) we have provided the multiple-step income statement of a hypothetical company. This statement provides more detail than that of Wal-Mart.

Illustration 5-9 Multiple-step income statement

PW AUDIO SUPPLY, INC.
Income Statement
For the Year Ended December 31, 2007

Calculation of gross profit

Sales revenues		
Sales		$480,000
Less: Sales returns and allowances	$12,000	
Sales discounts	8,000	20,000
Net sales		460,000
Cost of goods sold		316,000
Gross profit		144,000

Calculation of income from operations

Operating expenses		
Store salaries expense	45,000	
Administrative salaries expense	19,000	
Utilities expense	17,000	
Advertising expense	16,000	
Depreciation expense—store equipment	8,000	
Freight-out	7,000	
Insurance expense	2,000	
Total operating expenses		114,000
Income from operations		30,000

Results of activities not related to operations

Other revenues and gains		
Interest revenue	3,000	
Gain on sale of equipment	600	
	3,600	
Other expenses and losses		
Interest expense	1,800	
Casualty loss from vandalism	200	
	2,000	
		1,600
Income before income taxes		31,600
Income tax expense		10,100
Net income		$ 21,500

For homework problems, use the multiple-step form of the income statement unless the requirements state otherwise.

BEFORE YOU GO ON . . .

▶ Review It

1. How are sales and contra revenue accounts reported in the income statement?
2. What is the significance of gross profit?
3. What title does Tootsie Roll use for gross profit? By what percentage did its gross profit change, and in what direction, in 2004? The answer to this question appears on p. 265.

The answer to this question appears on p. 265.

☑ THE NAVIGATOR

STUDY OBJECTIVE
5
Determine cost of goods sold under a periodic system.

DETERMINING COST OF GOODS SOLD UNDER A PERIODIC SYSTEM

Determining cost of goods sold is different under the periodic system than under the perpetual system. When a company uses a perpetual inventory system, it records all transactions affecting inventory (such as freight costs, returns, and discounts) directly to the Merchandise Inventory account. In addition, at the time of each sale the perpetual system requires a reduction in Merchandise Inventory and an increase in Cost of Goods Sold. But under a periodic system a company uses separate accounts to record freight costs, returns, and discounts. It does not maintain a running account of changes in inventory. Instead, it calculates the balance in ending inventory, as well as the cost of goods sold for the period, at the end of the period. Illustration 5-10 shows the determination of cost of goods sold for PW Audio Supply, using a periodic inventory system.

Illustration 5-10
Cost of goods sold for a merchandiser using a periodic inventory system

PW AUDIO SUPPLY, INC.
Cost of Goods Sold
For the Year Ended December 31, 2007

Cost of goods sold			
Inventory, January 1			$ 36,000
Purchases		$325,000	
Less: Purchase returns and allowances	$10,400		
Purchase discounts	6,800	17,200	
Net purchases		307,800	
Add: Freight-in		12,200	
Cost of goods purchased			320,000
Cost of goods available for sale			356,000
Inventory, December 31			40,000
Cost of goods sold			**$316,000**

Helpful Hint The far right column identifies the primary items that make up cost of goods sold of $316,000. The middle column explains cost of goods purchased of $320,000. The left column reports contra purchase items of $17,200.

The use of the periodic inventory system does not affect the content of the balance sheet. As under the perpetual system, a company reports merchandise inventory at the same amount in the current assets section.

The appendix to this chapter provides further detail on the use of the periodic system.

BEFORE YOU GO ON . . .

▶ Review It

1. Discuss the steps used to determine cost of goods sold in a periodic inventory system.
2. What accounts do companies use in determining the cost of goods purchased?
3. In what ways is a perpetual inventory system different from a periodic inventory system?

▶ Do It

Aerosmith Company's accounting records show the following at the year-end December 31, 2007: Purchase Discounts $3,400; Freight-in $6,100; Purchases $162,500; Beginning Inventory $18,000; Ending Inventory $20,000; and Purchase Returns $5,200. Compute these amounts for Aerosmith Company using the periodic approach:
(a) Cost of goods purchased.
(b) Cost of goods sold.

Action Plan

• To determine cost of goods purchased, adjust purchases for returns, discounts, and freight-in.

• To determine cost of goods sold, add cost of goods purchased to beginning inventory, and subtract ending inventory.

Solution

(a) Cost of goods purchased:
   Purchases − Purchase returns − Purchase discounts + Freight-in
   $162,500 − $5,200 − $3,400 + $6,100 = $160,000

(b) Cost of goods sold:
   Beginning inventory + Cost of goods purchased −
   Ending inventory
   $18,000 + $160,000 − $20,000 = $158,000

Evaluating Profitability

GROSS PROFIT RATE

STUDY OBJECTIVE
6
Explain the factors affecting profitability.

A company's gross profit may be expressed as a **percentage** by dividing the amount of gross profit by net sales. This is referred to as the **gross profit rate**. For PW Audio Supply the gross profit rate is 31.3% ($144,000 ÷ $460,000).

Analysts generally consider the gross profit *rate* to be more informative than the gross profit *amount* because it expresses a more meaningful (qualitative) relationship between gross profit and net sales. For example, a gross profit amount of $1,000,000 may sound impressive. But if it was the result of sales of $100,000,000, the company's gross profit rate was only 1%. A 1% gross profit rate is acceptable in only a few industries. Illustration 5-11 presents gross profit rates of a variety of industries.

Illustration 5-11 Gross profit rate by industry

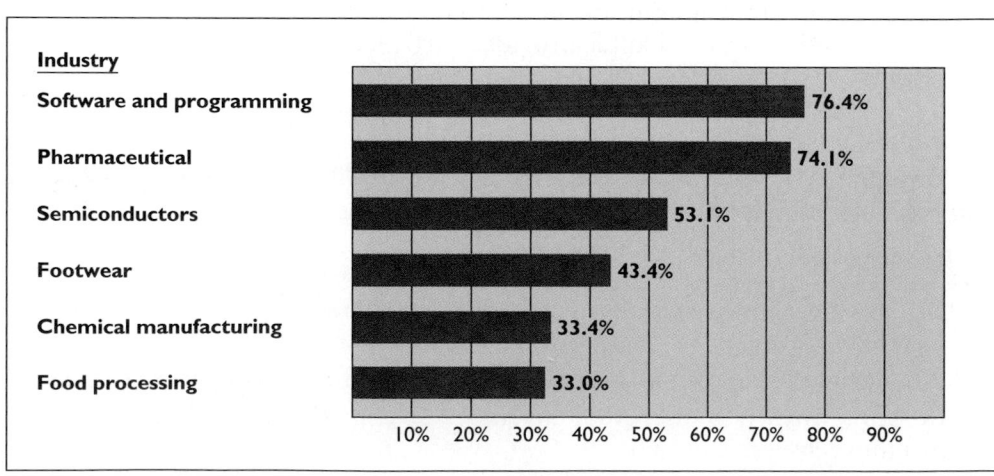

A decline in a company's gross profit rate might have several causes. The company may have begun to sell products with a lower "markup"—for example, budget blue jeans versus designer blue jeans. Increased competition may have resulted in a lower selling price. Or, the company may be forced to pay higher prices to its suppliers without being able to pass these costs on to its customers. The gross profit rates for Wal-Mart and Target, and the industry average, are presented in Illustration 5-12 on page 235.

Illustration 5-12 Gross profit rate

	2004	2003
Wal-Mart ($ in millions)	$\frac{\$57,582}{\$256,329} = 22.5\%$	$\frac{\$51,317}{\$229,616} = 22.3\%$
Target	32.0%	31.5%
Industry average	26.9%	

$$\text{Gross Profit Rate} = \frac{\text{Gross Profit}}{\text{Net Sales}}$$

Wal-Mart's gross profit rate increased from 22.3% in 2003 to 22.5% in 2004. In its Management Discussion and Analysis (MD&A), Wal-Mart explained, "This increase in gross margin occurred primarily due to a favorable shift in mix of products sold and our global sourcing efforts (which resulted in lower cost of merchandise sold), offset by increased apparel markdowns (price reductions) in the second half of the year."

At first glance it might be surprising that Wal-Mart has a lower gross profit rate than Target and the industry average. It is likely, however, that this can be explained by the fact that grocery products are becoming an increasingly large component of Wal-Mart's sales. In fact, in its MD&A, Wal-Mart says, "Because food items carry a lower gross margin than our other merchandise, increasing food sales tends to have an unfavorable impact on our total gross margin." Also, Wal-Mart has substantial warehouse-style sales in its Sam's Club stores, which are a low-margin, high-volume operation. In later chapters we will provide further discussion of the trade-off between sales volume and gross profit.

Decision Toolkit

Decision Checkpoints	Info Needed for Decision	Tool to Use for Decision	How to Evaluate Results
Is the price of goods keeping pace with changes in the cost of inventory?	Gross profit and net sales	$\text{Gross profit rate} = \frac{\text{Gross profit}}{\text{Net sales}}$	Higher ratio suggests the average margin between selling price and inventory cost is increasing. Too high a margin may result in lost sales.

PROFIT MARGIN RATIO

The **profit margin ratio** measures the percentage of each dollar of sales that results in net income. We compute this ratio by dividing net income by net sales (revenue) for the period.

How do the gross profit rate and profit margin ratio differ? The gross profit rate measures the margin by which selling price exceeds cost of goods sold. **The profit margin ratio measures the extent by which selling price covers all expenses** (including cost of goods sold). A company can improve its profit margin ratio by either increasing its gross profit rate and/or by controlling its operating expenses and other costs.

Profit margins vary across industries. Businesses with high turnover, such as grocery stores (Safeway and Kroger) and discount stores (Target and Wal-Mart), generally experience low profit margins. Low-turnover businesses, such as high-end jewelry stores (Tiffany and Co.) or major drug manufacturers (Merck), have high profit margins. Illustration 5-13 shows profit margin ratios from a variety of industries.

Illustration 5-13 Profit margin ratio by industry

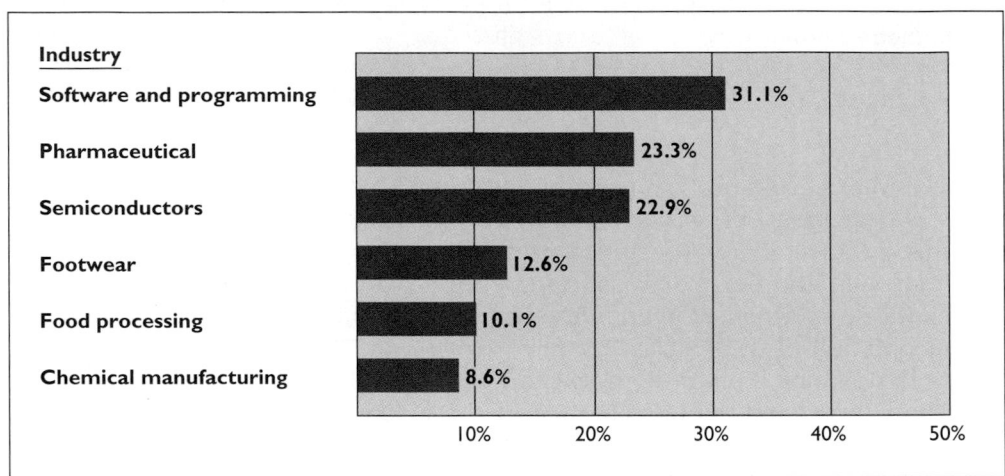

Profit margins for Wal-Mart and Target and the industry average are presented in Illustration 5-14.

Illustration 5-14 Profit margin ratio

$$\text{Profit Margin Ratio} = \frac{\text{Net Income}}{\text{Net Sales}}$$

	2004	2003
Wal-Mart ($ in millions)	$\dfrac{\$9,054}{\$256,329} = 3.5\%$	$\dfrac{\$7,955}{\$229,616} = 3.5\%$
Target	3.9%	3.9%
Industry average	6.3%	

Wal-Mart's profit margin remained constant at 3.5% in 2003 and 2004. This means that the company generated 3.5 cents on each dollar of sales. How does Wal-Mart compare to its competitors? Its profit margin ratio was lower than Target's in both 2003 and 2004 and was less than the industry average. Thus, its profit margin ratio does not suggest exceptional profitability. However, we must again keep in mind that an increasing percentage of Wal-Mart's sales is from groceries. The average profit margin ratio for the grocery industry is only 3.1%.

Accounting across the Organization

In its death spiral toward bankruptcy, Kmart appeared to make two very costly strategic errors. First, in an effort to attract customers, it decided to reduce selling prices on over 30,000 items. The problem was that this reduced its gross profit rate—and didn't even have the intended effect of increasing sales because Wal-Mart quickly matched these price cuts. Since Wal-Mart operates much more efficiently than Kmart, Wal-Mart could afford to absorb these price cuts and still operate at a profit. Kmart could not. Its second error was to try to reduce operating costs by cutting its advertising expenditures. This resulted in a reduction in customers—and sales revenue.

 Explain how Wal-Mart's profitability gave it a strategic advantage over Kmart.

BEFORE YOU GO ON . . .

▶ Review It

1. How is the gross profit rate calculated? What might cause it to decline?
2. What effect does improved efficiency of operations have on the profit margin ratio?

THE NAVIGATOR

Decision Toolkit

Decision Checkpoints	Info Needed for Decision	Tool to Use for Decision	How to Evaluate Results
Is the company maintaining an adequate margin between sales and expenses?	Net income and net sales	Profit margin ratio $= \dfrac{\text{Net income}}{\text{Net sales}}$	Higher value suggests favorable return on each dollar of sales.

Using the Decision Toolkit

After having once been as dominant as Wal-Mart, in recent years Sears has struggled to survive. It has enacted many changes trying to turn itself around. In the 1990s, it shocked and disappointed many loyal customers by closing its catalog business. It also closed 113 stores and eliminated 50,000 jobs. None of these changes was enough to make Sears truly competitive, so in March 2005 Sears merged with Kmart to form the third largest U.S. retailer. The following are pre-merger data for Sears.

($ in millions)	Year ended 01/03/04	12/28/02
Net income	$ 3,397	$ 1,376
Sales	36,372	35,698
Cost of goods sold	26,231	25,646

Instructions

Using the basic facts in the table, evaluate the following components of Sears's profitability for the years ended January 3, 2004 and December 28, 2002.

    Profit margin ratio
    Gross profit rate

How do Sears's profit margin ratio and gross profit rate compare to those of Wal-Mart and Target for 2004?

Solution

	Year ended	
($ in millions)	**01/03/04**	**12/28/02**
Profit margin ratio	$\dfrac{\$3,397}{\$36,372} = 9.3\%$	$\dfrac{\$1,376}{\$35,698} = 3.9\%$
Gross profit rate	$\dfrac{\$36,372 - \$26,231}{\$36,372} = 27.9\%$	$\dfrac{\$35,698 - \$25,646}{\$35,698} = 28.2\%$

Sears's profit margin ratio (income per dollar of sales) increased from 3.9% to 9.3%. This increase was due to the one-time sale of all of the assets and liabilities of its credit card and financial-products business, a nonoperating item. If we instead calculate the profit margin ratio using income from operations (see discussion on pages 235–236), Sears's profit margin ratio declined to 2.1%. This is well below both Wal-Mart's (3.5%) and Target's (3.9%). Thus, Sears is not as effective at turning its sales into net income as these two competitors.

    Sears's gross profit rate declined from 28.2% to 27.9%. This suggests that its ability to maintain its mark-up above its cost of goods sold eroded during this period. Sears's gross profit rate of 27.9% is lower than Target's (32%) but higher than Wal-Mart's (22.5%). As discussed in the chapter, Wal-Mart's gross profit is depressed by the fact that it sells many grocery products, which are very low-margin. Target is superior to Sears both in its ability to maintain its mark-up above its costs of goods sold (its gross profit rate) and in its ability to control operating costs (its profit margin ratio).

Summary of Study Objectives

WILEY PLUS

1 *Identify the differences between a service enterprise and a merchandising company.* Because of the presence of inventory, a merchandising company has sales revenue, cost of goods sold, and gross profit. To account for inventory, a merchandising company must choose between a perpetual inventory system and a periodic inventory system.

2 *Explain the recording of purchases under a perpetual inventory system.* The Merchandise Inventory account is debited for all purchases of merchandise and for freight costs, and it is credited for purchase discounts and purchase returns and allowances.

3 *Explain the recording of sales revenues under a perpetual inventory system.* When inventory is sold, Accounts Receivable (or Cash) is debited and Sales is credited for the selling price of the merchandise. At the same time, Cost of Goods Sold is debited and Merchandise Inventory is credited for the cost of inventory items sold. Subsequent entries are required for (a) sales returns and allowances and (b) sales discounts.

4 *Distinguish between a single-step and a multiple-step income statement.* In a single-step income statement, companies classify all data under two categories, revenues or expenses, and net income is determined in one step. A multiple-step income statement shows numerous steps in determining net income, including results of nonoperating activities.

5 *Determine cost of goods sold under a periodic system.* The periodic system uses multiple accounts to keep track of transactions that affect inventory. To determine cost of goods sold, first calculate cost of goods purchased by adjusting purchases for returns, allowances, discounts, and freight-in. Then calculate cost of goods sold by adding cost of goods purchased to beginning inventory and subtracting ending inventory.

6 *Explain the factors affecting profitability.* Profitability is affected by gross profit, as measured by the gross profit rate, and by management's ability to control costs, as measured by the profit margin ratio.

THE NAVIGATOR

Decision Toolkit—A Summary

Decision Checkpoints	Info Needed for Decision	Tool to Use for Decision	How to Evaluate Results
Is the price of goods keeping pace with changes in the cost of inventory?	Gross profit and net sales	Gross profit rate $=\dfrac{\text{Gross profit}}{\text{Net sales}}$	Higher ratio suggests the average margin between selling price and inventory cost is increasing. Too high a margin may result in lost sales.
Is the company maintaining an adequate margin between sales and expenses?	Net income and net sales	Profit margin ratio $=\dfrac{\text{Net income}}{\text{Net sales}}$	Higher value suggests favorable return on each dollar of sales.

APPENDIX
PERIODIC INVENTORY SYSTEM

As described in this chapter, companies may use one of two basic systems of accounting for inventories: (1) the perpetual inventory system or (2) the periodic inventory system. In the chapter we focused on the characteristics of the perpetual inventory system. In this appendix we discuss and illustrate the **periodic inventory system**. One key difference between the two systems is the point at which the company computes cost of goods sold. For a visual reminder of this difference, you may want to refer back to Illustration 5-3 on page 220.

Recording Merchandise Transactions

In a **periodic inventory system**, companies record revenues from the sale of merchandise when sales are made, just as in a perpetual system. Unlike the perpetual system, however, companies **do not attempt on the date of sale to record the cost of the merchandise sold**. Instead, they take a physical inventory count at the **end of the period** to determine (1) the cost of the merchandise then on hand and (2) the cost of the goods sold during the period. And, **under a periodic system, companies record purchases of merchandise in the Purchases account rather than the Merchandise Inventory account**. Also, in a periodic system, purchase returns and allowances, purchase discounts, and freight costs on purchases are recorded in separate accounts.

To illustrate the recording of merchandise transactions under a periodic inventory system, we will use purchase/sale transactions between PW Audio Supply, Inc. and Sauk Stereo, as illustrated for the perpetual inventory system in this chapter.

> **STUDY OBJECTIVE**
> **7**
> Explain the recording of purchases and sales of inventory under a periodic inventory system.

Recording Purchases of Merchandise

On the basis of the sales invoice (Illustration 5-4, shown on page 222) and receipt of the merchandise ordered from PW Audio Supply, Sauk Stereo records the $3,800 purchase as follows.

May	4	Purchases	3,800	
		Accounts Payable		3,800
		(To record goods purchased on account		
		from PW Audio Supply)		

Purchases is a temporary account whose normal balance is a debit.

FREIGHT COSTS

When the purchaser directly incurs the freight costs, it debits the account Freight-in (or Transportation-in). For example, if Sauk pays Haul-It Freight Company $150 for freight charges on its purchase from PW Audio Supply on May 6, the entry on Sauk's books is:

May	6	Freight-in (Transportation-in)	150	
		Cash		150
		(To record payment of freight on goods		
		purchased)		

Like Purchases, Freight-in is a temporary account whose normal balance is a debit. **Freight-in is part of cost of goods purchased.** The reason is that cost of goods purchased should include any freight charges necessary to bring the goods to the purchaser. Freight costs are not subject to a purchase discount. Purchase discounts apply on the invoice cost of the merchandise.

PURCHASE RETURNS AND ALLOWANCES

Because $300 of merchandise received from PW Audio Supply is inoperable, Sauk Stereo returns the goods and prepares the following entry to recognize the return.

May	8	Accounts Payable	300	
		Purchase Returns and Allowances		300
		(To record return of goods		
		purchased from PW Audio Supply)		

Purchase Returns and Allowances is a temporary account whose normal balance is a credit.

PURCHASE DISCOUNTS

On May 14 Sauk Stereo pays the balance due on account to PW Audio Supply, taking the 2% cash discount allowed by PW Audio for payment within 10 days. Sauk Stereo records the payment and discount as follows.

May	14	Accounts Payable ($3,800 − $300)	3,500	
		Purchase Discounts ($3,500 × .02)		70
		Cash		3,430
		(To record payment within the		
		discount period)		

Purchase Discounts is a temporary account whose normal balance is a credit.

Recording Sales of Merchandise

The seller, PW Audio Supply, records the sale of $3,800 of merchandise to Sauk Stereo on May 4 (sales invoice No. 731, Illustration 5-4) as follows.

May 4	Accounts Receivable	3,800	
	Sales		3,800
	(To record credit sales per invoice #731 to Sauk Stereo)		

SALES RETURNS AND ALLOWANCES

To record the returned goods received from Sauk Stereo on May 8, PW Audio Supply records the $300 sales return as follows.

May 8	Sales Returns and Allowances	300	
	Accounts Receivable		300
	(To record credit granted to Sauk Stereo for returned goods)		

SALES DISCOUNTS

On May 14, PW Audio Supply receives payment of $3,430 on account from Sauk Stereo. PW Audio honors the 2% cash discount and records the payment of Sauk's account receivable in full as follows.

May 14	Cash	3,430	
	Sales Discounts ($3,500 × .02)	70	
	Accounts Receivable ($3,800 − $300)		3,500
	(To record collection within 2/10, n/30 discount period from Sauk Stereo)		

COMPARISON OF ENTRIES— PERPETUAL vs. PERIODIC

ENTRIES ON SAUK STEREO'S BOOKS		
Transaction	**Perpetual Inventory System**	**Periodic Inventory System**

May 4 Purchase of merchandise on credit.	Merchandise Inventory 3,800
	  Accounts Payable 3,800
		Purchases 3,800
		  Accounts Payable 3,800

May 6 Freight costs on purchases.	Merchandise Inventory 150
	  Cash 150
		Freight-in 150
		  Cash 150

May 8 Purchase returns and allowances.	Accounts Payable 300
	  Merchandise Inventory 300
		Accounts Payable 300
		  Purchase Returns and Allowances 300

May 14 Payment on account with a discount.	Accounts Payable 3,500
	  Cash 3,430
	  Merchandise Inventory 70
		Accounts Payable 3,500
		  Cash 3,430
		  Purchase Discounts 70

ENTRIES ON PW AUDIO SUPPLY'S BOOKS		
Transaction	**Perpetual Inventory System**	**Periodic Inventory System**

May 4 Sale of merchandise on credit.	Accounts Receivable 3,800
	  Sales Revenue 3,800
	Cost of Goods Sold 2,400
	  Merchandise Inventory 2,400
		Accounts Receivable 3,800
		  Sales Revenue 3,800
		No entry for cost of goods sold

May 8 Return of merchandise sold.	Sales Returns and Allowances 300
	  Accounts Receivable 300
	Merchandise Inventory 140
	  Cost of Goods Sold 140
		Sales Returns and Allowances 300
		  Accounts Receivable 300
		No entry

May 14 Cash received on account with a discount.	Cash 3,430
	Sales Discounts 70
	  Accounts Receivable 3,500
		Cash 3,430
		Sales Discounts 70
		  Accounts Receivable 3,500

Summary of Study Objective for Appendix

7 *Explain the recording of purchases and sales of inventory under a periodic inventory system.* To record purchases, entries are required for (a) cash and credit purchases, (b) purchase returns and allowances, (c) purchase discounts, and (d) freight costs. To record sales, entries are required for (a) cash and credit sales, (b) sales returns and allowances, and (c) sales discounts.

Glossary

Contra revenue account An account that is offset against a revenue account on the income statement. (p. 226)

Cost of goods sold The total cost of merchandise sold during the period. (p. 218)

Gross profit The excess of net sales over the cost of goods sold. (p. 230)

Gross profit rate Gross profit expressed as a percentage by dividing the amount of gross profit by net sales. (p. 234)

Net sales Sales less sales returns and allowances and sales discounts. (p. 229)

Periodic inventory system An inventory system in which a company does not maintain detailed records of goods on hand and determines the cost of goods sold only at the end of an accounting period. (p. 220)

Perpetual inventory system A detailed inventory system in which a company maintains the cost of each inventory item and the records continuously show the inventory that should be on hand. (p. 219)

Profit margin ratio Measures the percentage of each dollar of sales that results in net income, computed by dividing net income by net sales. (p. 235)

Purchase allowance A deduction made to the selling price of merchandise, granted by the seller so that the buyer will keep the merchandise. (p. 223)

Purchase discount A cash discount claimed by a buyer for prompt payment of a balance due. (p. 223)

Purchase invoice A document that supports each credit purchase. (p. 221)

Purchase return A return of goods from the buyer to the seller for cash or credit. (p. 223)

Sales discount A reduction given by a seller for prompt payment of a credit sale. (p. 227)

Sales invoice A document that provides support for credit sales. (p. 225)

Sales returns and allowances Purchase returns and allowances from the seller's perspective. See definitions for purchase returns and purchase allowances. (p. 226)

Sales revenue Primary source of revenue in a merchandising company. (p. 218)

Demonstration Problem

The adjusted trial balance for the year ended December 31, 2007, for Dykstra Company is shown below.

DYKSTRA COMPANY
Adjusted Trial Balance
For the Year Ended December 31, 2007

	Dr.	Cr.
Cash	$ 14,500	
Accounts Receivable	11,100	
Merchandise Inventory	29,000	
Prepaid Insurance	2,500	
Store Equipment	95,000	
Accumulated Depreciation		$ 18,000
Notes Payable		25,000
Accounts Payable		10,600
Common Stock		70,000
Retained Earnings		11,000
Dividends	12,000	

	Dr.	Cr.
Sales		536,800
Sales Returns and Allowances	6,700	
Sales Discounts	5,000	
Cost of Goods Sold	363,400	
Freight-out	7,600	
Advertising Expense	12,000	
Store Salaries Expense	56,000	
Utilities Expense	18,000	
Rent Expense	24,000	
Depreciation Expense	9,000	
Insurance Expense	4,500	
Interest Expense	3,600	
Interest Revenue		2,500
	$673,900	$673,900

Instructions

Prepare a multiple-step income statement for Dykstra Company.

Solution to Demonstration Problem

DYKSTRA COMPANY
Income Statement
For the Year Ended December 31, 2007

Sales revenues		
Sales		$536,800
Less: Sales returns and allowances	$ 6,700	
Sales discounts	5,000	11,700
Net sales		525,100
Cost of goods sold		363,400
Gross profit		161,700
Operating expenses		
Store salaries expense	56,000	
Rent expense	24,000	
Utilities expense	18,000	
Advertising expense	12,000	
Depreciation expense	9,000	
Freight-out	7,600	
Insurance expense	4,500	
Total operating expenses		131,100
Income from operations		30,600
Other revenues and gains		
Interest revenue	2,500	
Other expenses and losses		
Interest expense	3,600	1,100
Net income		$ 29,500

Action Plan

• In preparing the income statement, remember that the key components are net sales, cost of goods sold, gross profit, total operating expenses, and net income (loss). These components are reported in the right-hand column of the income statement.

• Present nonoperating items after income from operations.

THE NAVIGATOR

Note: All Questions, Exercises, and Problems marked with an asterisk relate to material in the appendix to the chapter.

Self-Study Questions

Answers are at the end of the chapter.

(SO 1) **1.** Which of the following statements about a periodic inventory system is true?
  (a) Companies determine cost of goods sold only at the end of the accounting period.
  (b) Companies continuously maintain detailed records of the cost of each inventory purchase and sale.
  (c) The periodic system provides better control over inventories than a perpetual system.
  (d) The increased use of computerized systems has increased the use of the periodic system.

(SO 2) **2.** Which of the following items does *not* result in an adjustment in the merchandise inventory account under a perpetual system?
  (a) A purchase of merchandise.
  (b) A return of merchandise inventory to the supplier.
  (c) Payment of freight costs for goods shipped to a customer.
  (d) Payment of freight costs for goods received from a supplier.

(SO 3) **3.** Which sales accounts normally have a debit balance?
  (a) Sales discounts.
  (b) Sales returns and allowances.
  (c) Both (a) and (b).
  (d) Neither (a) nor (b).

(SO 3) **4.** A company makes a credit sale of $750 on June 13, terms 2/10, n/30, on which it grants a return of $50 on June 16. What amount is received as payment in full on June 23?
  (a) $700.   (c) $685.
  (b) $686.   (d) $650.

(SO 4) **5.** Gross profit will result if:
  (a) operating expenses are less than net income.
  (b) sales revenues are greater than operating expenses.
  (c) sales revenues are greater than cost of goods sold.
  (d) operating expenses are greater than cost of goods sold.

(SO 4) **6.** If sales revenues are $400,000, cost of goods sold is $310,000, and operating expenses are $60,000, what is the gross profit?
  (a) $30,000.   (c) $340,000.
  (b) $90,000.   (d) $400,000.

(SO 4) **7.** The income statement for a merchandising company shows each of these features *except:*
  (a) gross profit.
  (b) cost of goods sold.
  (c) a sales revenue section.
  (d) All of these are present.

(SO 5) **8.** If beginning inventory is $60,000, cost of goods purchased is $380,000, and ending inventory is $50,000, what is cost of goods sold under a periodic system?
  (a) $390,000.   (c) $330,000.
  (b) $370,000.   (d) $420,000.

(SO 6) **9.** Which of the following would affect the gross profit rate? (Assume sales remains constant.)
  (a) An increase in advertising expense.
  (b) A decrease in depreciation expense.
  (c) An increase in cost of goods sold.
  (d) A decrease in insurance expense.

(SO 6) **10.** The gross profit *rate* is equal to:
  (a) net income divided by sales.
  (b) cost of goods sold divided by sales.
  (c) net sales minus cost of goods sold, divided by net sales.
  (d) sales minus cost of goods sold, divided by cost of goods sold.

(SO 6) **11.** Which factor would *not* affect the gross profit rate?
  (a) An increase in the cost of heating the store.
  (b) An increase in the sale of luxury items.
  (c) An increase in the use of "discount pricing" to sell merchandise.
  (d) An increase in the price of inventory items.

(SO 7) ***12.** When goods are purchased for resale by a company using a periodic inventory system:
  (a) purchases on account are debited to Merchandise Inventory.
  (b) purchases on account are debited to Purchases.
  (c) purchase returns are debited to Purchase Returns and Allowances.
  (d) freight costs are debited to Purchases.

Go to the book's website, **www.wiley.com/college/kimmel**, to access additional Self-Study Questions.

Questions

1. (a) "The steps in the accounting cycle for a merchandising company differ from the steps in the accounting cycle for a service enterprise." Do you agree or disagree?
   (b) Is the measurement of net income in a merchandising company conceptually the same as in a service enterprise? Explain.

2. How do the components of revenues and expenses differ between a merchandising company and a service enterprise?

3. Jennifer Hopkins, CEO of Pay-A-Lot Discount Stores, is considering a recommendation made by both the company's purchasing manager and director of finance that the company should invest in a sophisticated new perpetual inventory system to replace its periodic system. Explain the primary difference between the two systems, and discuss the potential benefits of a perpetual inventory system.

4. (a) Explain the income measurement process in a merchandising company.
   (b) How does income measurement differ between a merchandising company and a service company?

5. Nick Bickler Co. has sales revenue of $100,000, cost of goods sold of $68,000, and operating expenses of $20,000. What is its gross profit?

6. Sheri Lynn believes revenues from credit sales may be earned before they are collected in cash. Do you agree? Explain.

7. (a) What is the primary source document for recording (1) cash sales and (2) credit sales?
   (b) Using XXs for amounts, give the journal entry for each of the transactions in part (a).

8. A credit sale is made on July 10 for $800, terms 2/10, n/30. On July 12, the purchaser returns $100 of goods for credit. Give the journal entry on July 19 to record the receipt of the balance due within the discount period.

9. As the end of Ray Company's fiscal year-end approached, it became clear that the company had considerable excess inventory. Alexander McBain, the head of marketing and sales, ordered salespeople to "add 20% more units to each order that you ship. The customers can always ship the extra back next period if they decide they don't want it. We've got to do it to meet this year's sales goal." Discuss the accounting implications of Alexander's action.

10. To encourage bookstores to buy a broader range of book titles, and to discourage price discounting, the publishing industry allows bookstores to return unsold books to the publisher. This results in very significant returns each year. To ensure proper recognition of revenues, how should publishing companies account for these returns?

11. Goods costing $1,600 are purchased on account on July 15 with credit terms of 2/10, n/30. On July 18 the purchaser receives a $200 credit memo from the supplier for damaged goods. Give the journal entry on July 24 to record payment of the balance due within the discount period.

12. Rosena Company reports net sales of $800,000, gross profit of $580,000, and net income of $260,000. What are its operating expenses?

13. DeGroot Company has always provided its customers with payment terms of 1/10, n/30. Members of its sale force have commented that competitors are offering customers 2/10, n/45. Explain what these terms mean, and discuss the implications to DeGroot of switching its payment terms to those of its competitors.

14. In its year-end earnings announcement press release, Optimistic Corp. announced that its earnings increased by $15 million relative to the previous year. This represented a 20% increase. Inspection of its income statement reveals that the company reported a $20 million gain under "Other revenues and gains" from the sale of one of its factories. Discuss the implications of this gain from the perspective of a potential investor.

15. Identify the distinguishing features of an income statement for a merchandising company.

16. Why is the normal operating cycle for a merchandising company likely to be longer than for a service company?

17. What merchandising account(s) will appear in the post-closing trial balance?

18. What types of businesses are most likely to use a perpetual inventory system?

19. Identify the accounts that are added to or deducted from purchases to determine the cost of goods purchased under a periodic system. For each account, indicate (a) whether it is added or deducted and (b) its normal balance.

20. In the following cases, use a periodic inventory system to identify the item(s) designated by the letters X and Y.
    (a) Purchases $- X - Y =$ Net purchases.
    (b) Cost of goods purchased $-$ Net purchases $= X$.
    (c) Beginning inventory $+ X =$ Cost of goods available for sale.
    (d) Cost of goods available for sale $-$ Cost of goods sold $= X$.

21. What two ratios measure factors that affect profitability?

22. What factors affect a company's gross profit rate—that is, what can cause the gross profit rate to increase and what can cause it to decrease?

23. Walter Lee, director of marketing, wants to reduce the selling price of his company's products by 15% to increase market share. He says, "I know this will reduce our gross profit rate, but the increased number of units sold will make up for the lost margin."

Before this action is taken, what other factors does the company need to consider?

*24. On July 15 a company purchases on account goods costing $1,600, with credit terms of 2/10, n/30. On July 18 the company receives a $200 credit memo

from the supplier for damaged goods. Give the journal entry on July 24 to record payment of the balance due within the discount period assuming a periodic inventory system.

Brief Exercises

Compute missing amounts in determining net income.
(SO 1, 4)

BE5-1 Presented here are the components in Michelle Wilson Company's income statement. Determine the missing amounts.

Sales	Cost of Goods Sold	Gross Profit	Operating Expenses	Net Income
$ 71,200	(b)	$ 39,000	(d)	$10,800
$108,000	$65,000	(c)	(e)	$29,500
(a)	$71,900	$109,600	$46,200	(f)

Journalize perpetual inventory entries.
(SO 2, 3)

BE5-2 Clare Company buys merchandise on account from Muni Company. The selling price of the goods is $900 and the cost of the goods sold is $660. Both companies use perpetual inventory systems. Journalize the transactions on the books of both companies.

Journalize sales transactions.
(SO 3)

BE5-3 Prepare the journal entries to record the following transactions on Panther Company's books using a perpetual inventory system.
(a) On March 2 Panther Company sold $900,000 of merchandise to Eagle Company, terms 2/10, n/30. The cost of the merchandise sold was $540,000.
(b) On March 6 Eagle Company returned $110,000 of the merchandise purchased on March 2. The cost of the merchandise returned was $65,000.
(c) On March 12 Panther Company received the balance due from Eagle Company.

Journalize purchase transactions.
(SO 2)

BE5-4 From the information in BE5-3, prepare the journal entries to record these transactions on Eagle Company's books under a perpetual inventory system.

Prepare sales revenue section of income statement.
(SO 4)

BE5-5 Marquette Company provides this information for the month ended October 31, 2007: sales on credit $300,000; cash sales $130,000; sales discounts $5,000; and sales returns and allowances $22,000. Prepare the sales revenues section of the income statement based on this information.

Identify placement of items on a multiple-step income statement.
(SO 4)

BE5-6 Explain where each of these items would appear on a multiple-step income statement: gain on sale of equipment, cost of goods sold, depreciation expense, and sales returns and allowances.

Compute net purchases and cost of goods purchased.
(SO 5)

BE5-7 Assume that Roshek Company uses a periodic inventory system and has these account balances: Purchases $424,000; Purchase Returns and Allowances $11,000; Purchase Discounts $7,000; and Freight-in $16,000. Determine net purchases and cost of goods purchased.

Compute cost of goods sold and gross profit.
(SO 5)

BE5-8 Assume the same information as in BE5-7 and also that Roshek Company has beginning inventory of $60,000, ending inventory of $90,000, and net sales of $650,000. Determine the amounts to be reported for cost of goods sold and gross profit.

Calculate profitability ratios.
(SO 6)

BE5-9 Red Wall Corporation reported net sales of $250,000, cost of goods sold of $100,000, operating expenses of $50,000, net income of $87,500, beginning total assets of $500,000, and ending total assets of $600,000. Calculate each of the following values and explain what they mean.
(a) Profit margin ratio. (b) Gross profit rate.

Calculate profitability ratios.
(SO 6)

BE5-10 Beardsley Corporation reported net sales $580,000; cost of goods sold $300,000; operating expenses $210,000; and net income $70,000. Calculate the following values and explain what they mean.
(a) Profit margin ratio. (b) Gross profit rate.

*BE5-11 Prepare the journal entries to record these transactions on Powell Company's books using a periodic inventory system.

(a) On March 2, Powell Company purchased $900,000 of merchandise from Rice Company, terms 2/10, n/30.

(b) On March 6 Powell Company returned $110,000 of the merchandise purchased on March 2 because it was defective.

(c) On March 12 Powell Company paid the balance due to Rice Company.

Journalize purchase transactions.
(SO 7)

Exercises

E5-1 The following transactions are for Kale Company.

1. On December 3 Kale Company sold $480,000 of merchandise to Thomson Co., terms 1/10, n/30. The cost of the merchandise sold was $320,000.
2. On December 8 Thomson Co. was granted an allowance of $28,000 for merchandise purchased on December 3.
3. On December 13 Kale Company received the balance due from Thomson Co.

Journalize sales transactions.
(SO 3)

Instructions

(a) Prepare the journal entries to record these transactions on the books of Kale Company. Kale uses a perpetual inventory system.

(b) Assume that Kale Company received the balance due from Thomson Co. on January 2 of the following year instead of December 13. Prepare the journal entry to record the receipt of payment on January 2.

E5-2 Assume that on September 1 Office Depot had an inventory that included a variety of calculators. The company uses a perpetual inventory system. During September these transactions occurred.

Journalize perpetual inventory entries.
(SO 2, 3)

Sept. 6 Purchased calculators from Black Box Co. at a total cost of $1,620, terms n/30.

9 Paid freight of $50 on calculators purchased from Black Box Co.

10 Returned calculators to Black Box Co. for $38 credit because they did not meet specifications.

12 Sold calculators costing $520 for $780 to University Book Store, terms n/30.

14 Granted credit of $45 to University Book Store for the return of one calculator that was not ordered. The calculator cost $28.

20 Sold calculators costing $570 for $900 to Campus Card Shop, terms n/30.

Instructions
Journalize the September transactions.

E5-3 This information relates to Sherper Co.

1. On April 5 purchased merchandise from Newport Company for $22,000, terms 2/10, n/30.
2. On April 6 paid freight costs of $900 on merchandise purchased from Newport.
3. On April 7 purchased equipment on account for $26,000.
4. On April 8 returned some of April 5 merchandise to Newport Company which cost $3,600.
5. On April 15 paid the amount due to Newport Company in full.

Journalize purchase transactions.
(SO 2)

Instructions

(a) Prepare the journal entries to record the transactions listed above on the books of Sherper Co. Sherper Co. uses a perpetual inventory system.

(b) Assume that Sherper Co. paid the balance due to Newport Company on May 4 instead of April 15. Prepare the journal entry to record this payment.

E5-4 On June 10 Mawmey Company purchased $6,000 of merchandise from Lima Company, terms 3/10, n/30. Mawmey pays the freight costs of $400 on June 11. Damaged

Journalize perpetual inventory entries.
(SO 2, 3)

goods totaling $500 are returned to Lima for credit on June 12. On June 19 Mawmey Company pays Lima Company in full, less the purchase discount. Both companies use a perpetual inventory system.

Instructions
(a) Prepare separate entries for each transaction on the books of Mawmey Company.
(b) Prepare separate entries for each transaction for Lima Company. The merchandise purchased by Mawmey on June 10 cost Lima $3,000, and the goods returned cost Lima $240.

Prepare sales revenues section of income statement.
(SO 4)

E5-5 The adjusted trial balance of Brighton Company shows these data pertaining to sales at the end of its fiscal year, October 31, 2007: Sales $900,000; Freight-out $12,000; Sales Returns and Allowances $15,000; and Sales Discounts $13,500.

Instructions
Prepare the sales revenues section of the income statement.

Prepare an income statement and calculate profitability ratios.
(SO 4, 6)

E5-6 Presented below is information for Zales Co. for the month of January 2007.

Cost of goods sold	$212,000	Rent expense	$ 32,000
Freight-out	7,000	Sales discounts	8,000
Insurance expense	12,000	Sales returns and allowances	13,000
Salary expense	58,000	Sales	370,000

Instructions
(a) Prepare an income statement using the format presented on page 232.
(b) Calculate the profit margin ratio and the gross profit rate.

Compute missing amounts and calculate profitability ratios.
(SO 4, 6)

E5-7 Financial information is presented here for two companies.

	King Company	Queen Company
Sales	$90,000	?
Sales returns	?	$ 5,000
Net sales	81,000	100,000
Cost of goods sold	56,700	?
Gross profit	?	38,000
Operating expenses	14,580	?
Net income	?	18,000

Instructions
(a) Fill in the missing amounts. Show all computations.
(b) Calculate the profit margin ratio and the gross profit rate for each company.
(c) Discuss your findings in part (b).

Prepare multiple-step income statement and calculate profitability ratios.
(SO 4, 6)

E5-8 In its income statement for the year ended December 31, 2007, Knitz Company reported the following condensed data.

Administrative expenses	$435,000	Selling expenses	$ 690,000
Cost of goods sold	987,000	Loss on sale of equipment	83,500
Interest expense	68,000	Net sales	2,350,000
Interest revenue	45,000		

Instructions
(a) Prepare a multiple-step income statement.
(b) Calculate the profit margin ratio and gross profit rate.
(c) In 2006 Knitz had a profit margin ratio of 9%. Is the decline in 2007 a cause for concern?

E5-9 In its income statement for the year ended June 30, 2004, The Clorox Company reported the following condensed data (dollars in millions).

Prepare multiple-step income statement and calculate profitability ratios.
(SO 4, 6)

Selling and		Research and	
administrative expenses	$ 552	development expense	$ 84
Net sales	4,324	Income tax expense	294
Interest expense	30	Other income	1
Advertising expense	429	Cost of goods sold	2,387

Instructions
(a) Prepare a multiple-step income statement.
(b) Calculate the gross profit rate and the profit margin ratio and explain what each means.
(c) Assume the marketing department has presented a plan to increase advertising expenses by $300 million. It expects this plan to result in an increase in both net sales and cost of goods sold of 25%. Redo parts (a) and (b) and discuss whether this plan has merit. (Assume a tax rate of 35%, and round all amounts to whole dollars.)

E5-10 The trial balance of Rachel Company at the end of its fiscal year, August 31, 2007, includes these accounts: Merchandise Inventory $19,200; Purchases $144,000; Sales $190,000; Freight-in $8,000; Sales Returns and Allowances $3,000; Freight-out $1,000; and Purchase Returns and Allowances $5,000. The ending merchandise inventory is $25,000.

Prepare cost of goods sold section.
(SO 5)

Instructions
Prepare a cost of goods sold section for the year ending August 31.

E5-11 Below is a series of cost of goods sold sections for companies X, F, L, and S.

Prepare cost of goods sold section.
(SO 5)

	X	F	L	S
Beginning inventory	$ 250	$ 120	$1,000	$ (j)
Purchases	1,500	1,080	(g)	43,590
Purchase returns and allowances	40	(d)	290	(k)
Net purchases	(a)	1,030	7,210	42,090
Freight-in	130	(e)	(h)	2,240
Cost of goods purchased	(b)	1,230	8,050	(l)
Cost of goods available for sale	1,840	1,350	(i)	49,530
Ending inventory	310	(f)	1,450	6,230
Cost of goods sold	(c)	1,230	7,600	43,300

Instructions
Fill in the lettered blanks to complete the cost of goods sold sections.

*E5-12 This information relates to Tandi Co.
1. On April 5 purchased merchandise from Buehler Company for $22,000, terms 2/10, net/30.
2. On April 6 paid freight costs of $900 on merchandise purchased from Buehler Company.
3. On April 7 purchased equipment on account for $26,000.
4. On April 8 returned some of the April 5 merchandise to Buehler Company which cost $3,600.
5. On April 15 paid the amount due to Buehler Company in full.

Journalize purchase transactions.
(SO 7)

Instructions
(a) Prepare the journal entries to record these transactions on the books of Tandi Co. using a periodic inventory system.
(b) Assume that Tandi Co. paid the balance due to Buehler Company on May 4 instead of April 15. Prepare the journal entry to record this payment.

Problems: Set A

Journalize, post, prepare partial income statement, and calculate ratios.
(SO 2, 3, 4, 6)

GLS

P5-1A   Banff Hardware Store completed the following merchandising transactions in the month of May. At the beginning of May, Banff's ledger showed Cash of $5,000 and Common Stock of $5,000.

May	1	Purchased merchandise on account from Jasper Wholesale Supply for $6,000, terms 2/10, n/30.
	2	Sold merchandise on account for $5,200, terms 3/10, n/30. The cost of the merchandise sold was $3,300.
	5	Received credit from Jasper Wholesale Supply for merchandise returned $200.
	9	Received collections in full, less discounts, from customers billed on sales of $5,200 on May 2.
	10	Paid Jasper Wholesale Supply in full, less discount.
	11	Purchased supplies for cash $900.
	12	Purchased merchandise for cash $2,700.
	15	Received $230 refund for return of poor-quality merchandise from supplier on cash purchase.
	17	Purchased merchandise from Northern Distributors for $1,900, terms 2/10, n/30.
	19	Paid freight on May 17 purchase $250.
	24	Sold merchandise for cash $6,200. The cost of the merchandise sold was $4,020.
	25	Purchased merchandise from Toolware Inc. for $800, terms 3/10, n/30.
	27	Paid Northern Distributors in full, less discount.
	29	Made refunds to cash customers for returned merchandise $124. The returned merchandise had cost $90.
	31	Sold merchandise on account for $1,280, terms n/30. The cost of the merchandise sold was $830.

Banff Hardware's chart of accounts includes Cash, Accounts Receivable, Merchandise Inventory, Supplies, Accounts Payable, Common Stock, Sales, Sales Returns and Allowances, Sales Discounts, and Cost of Goods Sold.

Instructions
(a) Journalize the transactions using a perpetual inventory system.
(b) Post the transactions to T accounts. Be sure to enter the beginning cash and common stock balances.
(c) Prepare an income statement through gross profit for the month of May 2007.
(d) Calculate the profit margin ratio and the gross profit rate. (Assume operating expenses were $2,400.)

(c) Gross profit $4,340

Journalize purchase and sale transactions under a perpetual inventory system.
(SO 2, 3)

P5-2A   Between the Lines Warehouse distributes hardback books to retail stores and extends credit terms of 2/10, n/30 to all of its customers. During the month of June the following merchandising transactions occurred.

June	1	Purchased 160 books on account for $5 each (including freight) from El Libro Publishers, terms 2/10, n/30.
	3	Sold 120 books on account to the Booked for Murder bookstore for $10 each.
	6	Received $50 credit for 10 books returned to El Libro Publishers.
	9	Paid El Libro Publishers in full.
	15	Received payment in full from the Booked for Murder bookstore.
	17	Sold 140 books on account to Curl Up N Read Bookstore for $10 each.
	20	Purchased 120 books on account for $5 each from Good Book Publishers, terms 1/15, n/30.
	24	Received payment in full from Curl Up N Read Bookstore.
	26	Paid Good Book Publishers in full.
	28	Sold 130 books on account to HomeTown Bookstore for $10 each.
	30	Granted HomeTown Bookstore $150 credit for 15 books returned costing $75.

Instructions

Journalize the transactions for the month of June for Between the Lines Warehouse, using a perpetual inventory system. Assume the cost of each book sold was $5.

P5-3A   At the beginning of the current season on April 1, the ledger of Fairway Pro Shop showed Cash $2,500; Merchandise Inventory $3,500; and Common Stock $6,000. The following transactions were completed during April 2007.

Journalize, post, and prepare trial balance and partial income statement.
(SO 2, 3, 4)

Apr. 5   Purchased golf bags, clubs, and balls on account from Kokott Co. $1,800, terms 3/10, n/60.
7   Paid freight on Kokott purchase $80.
9   Received credit from Kokott Co. for merchandise returned $200.
10   Sold merchandise on account to members $910, terms n/30. The merchandise sold had a cost of $620.
12   Purchased golf shoes, sweaters, and other accessories on account from Eagle Sportswear $730, terms 1/10, n/30.
14   Paid Kokott Co. in full.
17   Received credit from Eagle Sportswear for merchandise returned $30.
20   Made sales on account to members $840, terms n/30. The cost of the merchandise sold was $550.
21   Paid Eagle Sportswear in full.
27   Granted an allowance to members for clothing that did not fit properly $60.
30   Received payments on account from members $1,100.

The chart of accounts for the pro shop includes Cash, Accounts Receivable, Merchandise Inventory, Accounts Payable, Common Stock, Sales, Sales Returns and Allowances, and Cost of Goods Sold.

Instructions
(a) Journalize the April transactions using a perpetual inventory system.
(b) Using T accounts, enter the beginning balances in the ledger accounts and post the April transactions.
(c) Prepare a trial balance on April 30, 2007.
(d) Prepare an income statement through gross profit.

(c) Tot. trial
      balance $7,750
(d) Gross profit $ 520

P5-4A   Zwick Department Store is located in midtown Metropolis. During the past several years, net income has been declining because suburban shopping centers have been attracting business away from city areas. At the end of the company's fiscal year on November 30, 2007, these accounts appeared in its adjusted trial balance.

Prepare financial statements and calculate profitability ratios.
(SO 4, 6)

Accounts Payable	$ 18,300
Accounts Receivable	17,200
Accumulated Depreciation—Delivery Equipment	20,000
Accumulated Depreciation—Store Equipment	38,000
Cash	8,000
Common Stock	35,000
Cost of Goods Sold	633,300
Delivery Expense	6,200
Delivery Equipment	57,000
Depreciation Expense—Delivery Equipment	4,000
Depreciation Expense—Store Equipment	9,500
Dividends	12,000
Gain on sale of equipment	2,000
Insurance Expense	9,000
Interest Expense	5,000
Merchandise Inventory	36,200
Notes Payable	47,500
Prepaid Insurance	6,000
Property Tax Expense	3,500
Property Taxes Payable	3,500
Rent Expense	29,000
Retained Earnings	14,200
Salaries Expense	110,000

Sales	914,000
Sales Commissions Expense	17,000
Sales Commissions Payable	6,000
Sales Returns and Allowances	20,000
Store Equipment	105,000
Utilities Expense	10,600

Additional data: Notes payable are due in 2011.

Instructions

(a) Net income $ 58,900

Tot. assets $171,400

(a) Prepare a multiple-step income statement, a retained earnings statement, and a classified balance sheet.

(b) Calculate the profit margin ratio and the gross profit rate.

(c) The vice-president of marketing and the director of human resources have developed a proposal whereby the company would compensate the sales force on a strictly commission basis using 20% of net sales. Given the increased incentive, they expect net sales to increase by 15%. As a result, they estimate that gross profit will increase by $39,105 and operating expenses by $75,595. Compute the expected new net income. (*Hint:* You do not need to prepare an income statement). Then compute the revised profit margin ratio and gross profit rate. Comment on the effect that this plan would have on net income and on the ratios, and evaluate the merit of this proposal.

Prepare a correct multiple-step income statement.
(SO 4)

P5-5A An inexperienced accountant prepared this condensed income statement for Lahti Company, a retail firm that has been in business for a number of years.

LAHTI COMPANY
Income Statement
For the Year Ended December 31, 2007

Revenues		
Net sales	$850,000	
Other revenues	22,000	
		872,000
Cost of goods sold		555,000
Gross profit		317,000
Operating expenses		
Selling expenses	104,000	
Administrative expenses	93,000	
		197,000
Net earnings		$120,000

As an experienced, knowledgeable accountant, you review the statement and determine the following facts.

1. Net sales consist of sales $906,000, less delivery expense on merchandise sold $26,000, and sales returns and allowances $30,000.
2. Other revenues consist of sales discounts $14,000 and rent revenue $8,000.
3. Selling expenses consist of salespersons' salaries $80,000; depreciation on accounting equipment $8,000; advertising $10,000; and sales commissions $6,000. The commissions represent commissions paid. At December 31, $3,000 of commissions have been earned by salespersons but have not been paid.

Net income $111,000

Journalize, post, and prepare adjusted trial balance and financial statements.
(SO 4)

4. Administrative expenses consist of office salaries $37,000; dividends $18,000; utilities $12,000; interest expense $2,000; and rent expense $24,000, which includes prepayments totaling $4,000 for the first quarter of 2008.

Instructions

Prepare a correct detailed multiple-step income statement.

P5-6A The trial balance of Save-More Wholesale Company contained the accounts shown at December 31, the end of the company's fiscal year.

SAVE-MORE WHOLESALE COMPANY
Trial Balance
December 31, 2007

	Debit	Credit
Cash	$ 33,400	
Accounts Receivable	37,600	
Merchandise Inventory	70,000	
Land	92,000	
Buildings	200,000	
Accumulated Depreciation—Buildings		$ 60,000
Equipment	83,500	
Accumulated Depreciation—Equipment		40,500
Notes Payable		54,700
Accounts Payable		37,500
Common Stock		160,000
Retained Earnings		68,200
Dividends	10,000	
Sales		922,100
Sales Discounts	5,000	
Cost of Goods Sold	709,900	
Salaries Expense	71,300	
Utilities Expense	9,400	
Repair Expense	8,900	
Gas and Oil Expense	7,200	
Insurance Expense	4,800	
	$1,343,000	$1,343,000

Adjustment data:
1. Depreciation is $10,000 on buildings and $9,000 on equipment. (Both are operating expenses.)
2. Interest of $5,500 is due and unpaid on notes payable at December 31.

Other data: $15,000 of the notes payable are payable next year.

Instructions
(a) Journalize the adjusting entries.
(b) Create T accounts for all accounts used in part (a). Enter the trial balance amounts into the T accounts and post the adjusting entries.
(c) Prepare an adjusted trial balance.
(d) Prepare a multiple-step income statement and a retained earnings statement for the year, and a classified balance sheet at December 31, 2007.

(c) Tot. trial balance
$1,367,500
(d) Net income $ 81,100
Tot. assets $ 397,000

P5-7A   At the end of Jaxx Department Store's fiscal year on November 30, 2007, these accounts appeared in its adjusted trial balance.

Determine cost of goods sold and gross profit under periodic approach.
(SO 4, 5)

Freight-in	$ 5,060
Merchandise Inventory (beginning)	42,200
Purchases	636,000
Purchase Discounts	7,000
Purchase Returns and Allowances	6,760
Sales	914,000
Sales Returns and Allowances	20,000

Additional facts:
1. Merchandise inventory on November 30, 2007, is $36,200.
2. Note that Jaxx Department Store uses a periodic system.

Instructions
Prepare an income statement through gross profit for the year ended November 30, 2007.

Gross profit $260,700
Calculate missing amounts and assess profitability.
(SO 4, 5, 6)

P5-8A   Yuan Li Inc. operates a retail operation that purchases and sells snowmobiles, amongst other outdoor products. The company purchases all merchandise inventory on credit and uses a perpetual inventory system. The accounts payable account is used for recording inventory purchases only; all other current liabilities are accrued in separate accounts. You are provided with the following selected information for the fiscal years 2005 through 2008, inclusive.

	2005	2006	2007	2008
Income Statement Data				
Sales		$96,850	$ (e)	$82,220
Cost of goods sold		(a)	25,140	25,490
Gross profit		69,260	61,540	(i)
Operating expenses		63,640	(f)	52,870
Net income		$ (b)	$ 4,570	$ (j)
Balance Sheet Data				
Merchandise inventory	$13,000	$ (c)	$14,700	$ (k)
Accounts payable	5,800	6,500	4,600	(l)
Additional Information				
Purchases of merchandise inventory on account		$25,890	$ (g)	$24,050
Cash payments to suppliers		(d)	(h)	24,650

Instructions
(a) Calculate the missing amounts.
(b) The vice-presidents of sales, marketing, production, and finance are discussing the company's results with the CEO. They note that sales declined over the 3-year fiscal period, 2006–2008. Does that mean that profitability necessarily also declined? Explain, computing the gross profit rate and the profit margin ratio for each fiscal year to help support your answer.

Journalize, post, and prepare trial balance and partial income statement using periodic approach.
(SO 5, 7)

*P5-9A At the beginning of the current season on April 1, the ledger of Fairway Pro Shop showed Cash $2,500; Merchandise Inventory $3,500; and Common Stock $6,000. These transactions occured during April 2007.

Apr. 5 Purchased golf bags, clubs, and balls on account from Kokott Co. $1,800, terms 3/10, n/60.
7 Paid freight on Kokott Co. purchases $80.
9 Received credit from Kokott Co. for merchandise returned $200.
10 Sold merchandise on account to members $910, terms n/30.
12 Purchased golf shoes, sweaters, and other accessories on account from Eagle Sportswear $730, terms 1/10, n/30.
14 Paid Kokott Co. in full.
17 Received credit from Eagle Sportswear for merchandise returned $30.
20 Made sales on account to members $840, terms n/30.
21 Paid Eagle Sportswear in full.
27 Granted credit to members for clothing that did not fit properly $60.
30 Received payments on account from members $1,100.

The chart of accounts for the pro shop includes Cash, Accounts Receivable, Merchandise Inventory, Accounts Payable, Common Stock, Sales, Sales Returns and Allowances, Purchases, Purchase Returns and Allowances, Purchase Discounts, and Freight-in.

Instructions
(a) Journalize the April transactions using a periodic inventory system.
(b) Using T accounts, enter the beginning balances in the ledger accounts and post the April transactions.
(c) Prepare a trial balance on April 30, 2007.
(d) Prepare an income statement through Gross Profit, assuming merchandise inventory on hand at April 30 is $4,655.

(c) Tot. trial
balance $8,035
Gross profit $ 520

Problems: Set B

P5-1B Midwest Distributing Company completed these merchandising transactions in the month of April. At the beginning of April, the ledger of Midwest showed Cash of $9,000 and Common Stock of $9,000.

Journalize, post, prepare partial income statement, and calculate ratios.
(SO 2, 3, 4, 6)

GLS

Apr.	2	Purchased merchandise on account from Kane Supply Co. $6,300, terms 2/10, n/30.
	4	Sold merchandise on account $5,000, terms 2/10, n/30. The cost of the merchandise sold was $3,700.
	5	Paid $200 freight on April 4 sale.
	6	Received credit from Kane Supply Co. for merchandise returned $300.
	11	Paid Kane Supply Co. in full, less discount.
	13	Received collections in full, less discounts, from customers billed on April 4.
	14	Purchased merchandise for cash $4,700.
	16	Received refund from supplier for returned merchandise on cash purchase of April 14, $500.
	18	Purchased merchandise from Great Plains Distributors $4,500, terms 2/10, n/30.
	20	Paid freight on April 18 purchase $100.
	23	Sold merchandise for cash $8,300. The cost of the merchandise sold was $5,820.
	26	Purchased merchandise for cash $2,300.
	27	Paid Great Plains Distributors in full, less discount.
	29	Made refunds to cash customers for returned merchandise $180. The returned merchandise had a cost of $120.
	30	Sold merchandise on account $3,980, terms n/30. The cost of the merchandise sold was $2,500.

Midwest Distributing Company's chart of accounts includes Cash, Accounts Receivable, Merchandise Inventory, Accounts Payable, Common Stock, Sales, Sales Returns and Allowances, Sales Discounts, Cost of Goods Sold, and Freight-out.

Instructions
(a) Journalize the transactions.
(b) Post the transactions to T accounts. Be sure to enter the beginning cash and common stock balances.
(c) Prepare the income statement through gross profit for the month of April 2007.
(d) Calculate the profit margin ratio and the gross profit rate. (Assume operating expenses were $2,050.)

(c) Gross profit $5,100

P5-2B Good to Go Warehouse distributes suitcases to retail stores and extends credit terms of 1/10, n/30 to all of its customers. During the month of July the following merchandising transactions occurred.

Journalize purchase and sale transactions under a perpetual inventory system.
(SO 2, 3)

July	1	Purchased 70 suitcases on account for $30 each from Valise Manufacturers, terms 2/15, n/30.
	3	Sold 40 suitcases on account to Globe Trotters for $50 each.
	9	Paid Valise Manufacturers in full.
	12	Received payment in full from Globe Trotters.
	17	Sold 34 suitcases on account to Bon Voyage for $50 each.
	18	Purchased 60 suitcases on account for $30 (including freight) each from Pak-N-Go Manufacturers, terms 1/10, n/30.
	20	Received $300 credit for 10 suitcases returned to Pak-N-Go Manufacturers.
	21	Received payment in full from Bon Voyage.
	22	Sold 48 suitcases on account to Run Around for $52 each.
	30	Paid Pak-N-Go Manufacturers in full.
	31	Granted Run Around $260 credit for 5 suitcases returned costing $150.

Instructions
Journalize the transactions for the month of July for Good to Go Warehouse, using a perpetual inventory system. Assume the cost of each suitcase sold was $30.

Journalize, post, and prepare trial balance and partial income statement.
(SO 2, 3, 4)

P5-3B At the beginning of the current season, the ledger of Love All Tennis Shop showed Cash $2,500; Merchandise Inventory $1,700; and Common Stock $4,200. The following transactions were completed during April.

Apr.	4	Purchased racquets and balls from Connors Co. $880, terms 2/10, n/30.
	6	Paid freight on Connors Co. purchase $60.
	8	Sold merchandise to members $900, terms n/30. The merchandise sold cost $600.
	10	Received credit of $130 from Connors Co. for damaged racquets that were returned.
	11	Purchased tennis shoes from No Fault for cash $300.
	13	Paid Connors Co. in full.
	14	Purchased tennis shirts and shorts from Serena Sportswear $700, terms 3/10, n/60.
	15	Received cash refund of $50 from No Fault for damaged merchandise that was returned.
	17	Paid freight on Serena Sportswear purchase $30.
	18	Sold merchandise to members $860, terms n/30. The cost of the merchandise sold was $440.
	20	Received $500 in cash from members in settlement of their accounts.
	21	Paid Serena Sportswear in full.
	27	Granted an allowance of $30 to members for tennis clothing that did not fit properly.
	30	Received cash payments on account from members $350.

The chart of accounts for the tennis shop includes Cash, Accounts Receivable, Merchandise Inventory, Accounts Payable, Common Stock, Sales, Sales Returns and Allowances, and Cost of Goods Sold.

Instructions
(a) Journalize the April transactions.
(b) Using T accounts, enter the beginning balances in the ledger accounts and post the April transactions.

(c) Tot. trial
      balance $5,960
(d) Gross profit $ 690

(c) Prepare a trial balance on April 30, 2007.
(d) Prepare an income statement through gross profit.

Prepare financial statements and calculate profitability ratios.
(SO 4, 6)

P5-4B Danielle Department Store is located near the Crystal Shopping Mall. At the end of the company's fiscal year on December 31, 2007, the following accounts appeared in its adjusted trial balance.

Accounts Payable	$ 68,300
Accounts Receivable	50,300
Accumulated Depreciation—Building	52,500
Accumulated Depreciation—Equipment	42,600
Building	190,000
Cash	28,000
Common Stock	140,000
Cost of Goods Sold	418,000
Depreciation Expense—Building	10,400
Depreciation Expense—Equipment	13,000
Dividends	15,000
Equipment	100,000
Gain on sale of equipment	4,300
Insurance Expense	8,400
Interest Expense	7,000
Interest Payable	2,000
Merchandise Inventory	63,000
Mortgage Payable	80,000
Office Salaries Expense	32,000
Prepaid Insurance	2,400
Property Taxes Payable	4,800
Property Taxes Expense	6,200
Retained Earnings	19,200
Sales Salaries Expense	76,000

Sales	636,000
Sales Commissions Expense	14,500
Sales Commissions Payable	3,500
Sales Returns and Allowances	8,000
Utilities Expense	11,000

Additional data: $20,000 of the mortgage payable is due for payment next year.

Instructions
(a) Prepare a multiple-step income statement, a retained earnings statement, and a classified balance sheet.
(b) Calculate the profit margin ratio and the gross profit rate.
(c) The vice-president of marketing and the director of human resources have developed a proposal whereby the company would compensate the sales force on a strictly commission basis using 15% of net sales. Given the increased incentive, they expect net sales to increase by 25%. As a result, they estimate that gross profit will increase by $52,500 and operating expenses by $28,800. Compute the expected new net income. (*Hint*: You do not need to prepare an income statement.) Then compute the revised profit margin ratio and gross profit rate. Comment on the effect that this plan would have on net income and the ratios, and evaluate the merit of this proposal.

(a) Net income $ 35,800
Tot. assets $338,600

P5-5B   A part-time bookkeeper prepared this income statement for Maquoketa Company for the year ending December 31, 2007.

Prepare a correct multiple-step income statement.
(SO 4)

MAQUOKETA COMPANY
Income Statement
December 31, 2007

Revenues		
Sales		$715,000
Less: Freight-out	$14,000	
Sales discounts	11,300	25,300
Net sales		689,700
Other revenues (net)		1,300
Total revenues		688,000
Expenses		
Cost of goods sold		450,000
Selling expenses		103,000
Administrative expenses		50,000
Dividends		12,000
Total expenses		615,000
Net income		$ 73,000

As an experienced, knowledgeable accountant, you review the statement and determine the following facts.
1. Sales include $16,000 of deposits from customers for future sales orders.
2. Other revenues contain two items: interest expense $4,000 and interest revenue $5,300.
3. Selling expenses consist of sales salaries $76,000, advertising $13,000, depreciation on store equipment $7,500, and sales commissions expense $6,500.
4. Administrative expenses consist of office salaries $19,000; utilities expense $9,500; rent expense $14,500; and insurance expense $7,000. Insurance expense includes $800 of insurance applicable to 2008.

Operating
expenses $166,200
Net income $ 72,800

Instructions
Prepare a correct detailed multiple-step income statement.

Journalize, post, and prepare adjusted trial balance and financial statements.
(SO 4)

P5-6B   The trial balance of Stylynn Fashion Center contained the following accounts at November 30, the end of the company's fiscal year.

STYLYNN FASHION CENTER
Trial Balance
November 30, 2007

	Debit	Credit
Cash	$ 35,700	
Accounts Receivable	33,700	
Merchandise Inventory	43,000	
Store Supplies	8,800	
Store Equipment	105,000	
Accumulated Depreciation—Store Equipment		$ 35,000
Delivery Equipment	38,000	
Accumulated Depreciation—Delivery Equipment		6,000
Notes Payable		65,000
Accounts Payable		39,800
Common Stock		80,000
Retained Earnings		30,000
Dividends	12,000	
Sales		757,200
Sales Returns and Allowances	6,200	
Cost of Goods Sold	507,400	
Salaries Expense	130,000	
Advertising Expense	26,400	
Utilities Expense	14,000	
Repair Expense	12,100	
Delivery Expense	16,700	
Rent Expense	24,000	
	$1,013,000	$1,013,000

Adjustment data:
1. Store supplies on hand total $3,500.
2. Depreciation is $15,000 on the store equipment and $6,000 on the delivery equipment.
3. Interest of $8,000 is accrued on notes payable at November 30.

Other data: $30,000 of notes payable are due for payment next year.

Instructions
(a) Journalize the adjusting entries.
(b) Prepare T accounts for all accounts used in part (a). Enter the trial balance amounts into the T accounts and post the adjusting entries.
(c) Prepare an adjusted trial balance.
(d) Prepare a multiple-step income statement and a retained earnings statement for the year, and a classified balance sheet at November 30, 2007.

(c) Tot. trial
balance $1,042,000
(d) Net loss $(13,900)
Tot. assets $196,900

Determine cost of goods sold and gross profit under periodic approach.
(SO 4, 5)

P5-7B At the end of Neiman Fields Department Store's fiscal year on December 31, 2007, these accounts appeared in its adjusted trial balance.

Freight-in	$ 5,600
Merchandise Inventory (beginning)	40,500
Purchases	446,000
Purchase Discounts	12,000
Purchase Returns and Allowances	6,400
Sales	727,000
Sales Returns and Allowances	8,000

Additional facts:
1. Merchandise inventory on December 31, 2007, is $71,000.
2. Note that Neiman Fields Department Store uses a periodic system.

Instructions
Prepare an income statement through gross profit for the year ended December 31, 2007.

Gross profit $316,300
Calculate missing amounts and assess profitability.
(SO 4, 5, 6)

P5-8B Yelena Zhivago operates a clothing retail operation. She purchases all merchandise inventory on credit and uses a perpetual inventory system. The accounts payable account is used for recording inventory purchases only; all other current liabilities are accrued in separate accounts. You are provided with the following selected information for the fiscal years 2005, 2006, 2007, and 2008.

	2005	**2006**	**2007**	**2008**
Inventory (ending)	$13,000	$ 11,300	$ 16,400	$ 12,200
Accounts payable (ending)	17,000			
Sales		225,700	227,600	224,000
Purchases of merchandise				
inventory on account		141,000	150,700	136,000
Cash payments to suppliers		135,000	159,000	127,000

Instructions

(a) Calculate cost of goods sold for each of the 2006, 2007, and 2008 fiscal years.
(b) Calculate the gross profit for each of the 2006, 2007, and 2008 fiscal years.
(c) Calculate the ending balance of accounts payable for each of the 2006, 2007, and 2008 fiscal years.
(d) The vice-presidents of sales, marketing, production, and finance are discussing the company's results with the CEO. They note that sales declined in fiscal 2008. They wonder whether that means that profitability, as measured by the gross profit rate, necessarily also declined. Explain, calculating the gross profit rate for each fiscal year to help support your answer.

(a) 2007 $145,600
(c) 2007 $14,700

*P5-9B   At the beginning of the current season, the ledger of Love All Tennis Shop showed Cash $2,500; Merchandise Inventory $1,700; and Common Stock $4,200. The following transactions were completed during April.

Journalize, post, and prepare trial balance and partial income statement using periodic approach.
(SO 5, 7)

Apr.	4	Purchased racquets and balls from Connors Co. $880, terms 2/10, n/30.
	6	Paid freight on Connors Co. purchase $60.
	8	Sold merchandise to members $900, terms n/30.
	10	Received credit of $130 from Connors Co. for damaged racquets that were returned.
	11	Purchased tennis shoes from No Fault for cash $300.
	13	Paid Connors Co. in full.
	14	Purchased tennis shirts and shorts from Serena Sportswear $700, terms 3/10, n/60.
	15	Received cash refund of $50 from No Fault for damaged merchandise that was returned.
	17	Paid freight on Serena Sportswear purchase $30.
	18	Sold merchandise to members $860, terms n/30.
	20	Received $500 in cash from members in settlement of their accounts.
	21	Paid Serena Sportswear in full.
	27	Granted an allowance of $30 to members for tennis clothing that did not fit properly.
	30	Received cash payments on account from members $350.

The chart of accounts for the tennis shop includes Cash, Accounts Receivable, Merchandise Inventory, Accounts Payable, Common Stock, Sales, Sales Returns and Allowances, Purchases, Purchase Returns and Allowances, Purchase Discounts, and Freight-in.

Instructions

(a) Journalize the April transactions using a periodic inventory system.
(b) Using T accounts, enter the beginning balances in the ledger accounts and post the April transactions.
(c) Prepare a trial balance on April 30, 2007.
(d) Prepare an income statement through Gross Profit, assuming merchandise inventory on hand at April 30 is $2,414.

(c) Tot. trial
balance $6,176
(d) Gross profit $ 690

Problems: Set C

Comprehensive Problem

CP5 On December 1, 2007, Wheeler Distributing Company had the following account balances.

	Debits		**Credits**
Cash	$ 7,300	Accumulated Depreciation	$ 2,200
Accounts Receivable	5,600	Accounts Payable	4,600
Merchandise Inventory	12,000	Salaries Payable	1,000
Supplies	1,200	Common stock	15,000
Equipment	22,000	Retained Earnings	25,300
	$48,100		$48,100

During December the company completed the following summary transactions.

Dec. 6   Paid $1,600 for salaries due employees, of which $600 is for December and $1,000 is for November salaries payable.

8   Received $1,800 cash from customers in payment of account (no discount allowed).

10   Sold merchandise for cash $6,000. The cost of the merchandise sold was $4,000.

13   Purchased merchandise on account from King Co. $8,000, terms 2/10, n/30.

15   Purchased supplies for cash $2,000.

18   Sold merchandise on account $9,000, terms 1/10, n/30. The cost of the merchandise sold was $6,000.

20   Paid salaries $1,800.

23   Paid King Co. in full, less discount.

27   Received collections in full, less discounts, from customers billed on December 18.

Adjustment data:

1. Accrued salaries payable $600.
2. Depreciation $300 per month.
3. Supplies on hand $2,200.

Instructions

(a) Journalize the December transactions.
(b) Enter the December 1 balances in the ledger T accounts and post the December transactions. Use Cost of Goods Sold, Depreciation Expense, Salaries Expense, Sales, Sales Discounts, and Supplies Expense.
(c) Journalize and post adjusting entries.
(d) Totals $63,000   (d) Prepare an adjusted trial balance.
(e) Net income $ 610   (e) Prepare an income statement and a retained earnings statement for December and a classified balance sheet at December 31.

Continuing Cookie Chronicle

(*Note:* This is a continuation of the Cookie Chronicle from Chapters 1 through 4.)

CCC5 Because Natalie has had such a successful first few months, she is considering other opportunities to develop her business. One opportunity is the sale of fine European mixers. The owner of Mixer Deluxe has approached Natalie to become the exclusive distributor of these fine mixers. The current cost of a mixer is approximately $525, and Natalie would sell each one for $1,050. Natalie comes to you for advice on how to account for these mixers. Each appliance has a serial number and can be easily identified.
     Natalie asks you the following questions.

1. "Would you consider these mixers to be inventory? Or, should they be classified as supplies or equipment?"
2. "I've learned a little about keeping track of inventory using both the perpetual and the periodic systems of accounting for inventory. Which system do you think is better? Which one would you recommend for the type of inventory that I want to sell?"

3. "How often do I need to count inventory if I maintain it using the perpetual system? Do I need to count inventory at all?"

In the end, Natalie decides to use the perpetual method of accounting for inventory, and the following transactions happen during the month of January.

Jan. 4   She buys five deluxe mixers on account from Kzinski Supply Co. for $2,625, terms n/30.

6   She pays $100 freight on the January 4 purchase.

7   Natalie returns one of the mixers to Kzinski because it was damaged during shipping. Kzinski issues Cookie Creations credit for the cost of the mixer plus $20 for the cost of freight that was paid on January 6 for one mixer.

8   She collects the amount due from the neighborhood community center that was accrued at the end of December 2006.

12   She sells three deluxe mixers on account for $3,150, FOB destination, terms n/30.

13   Natalie pays her cell phone bill previously accrued in the December adjusting journal entries.

14   She pays $75 of delivery charges for the three mixers that were sold on January 12.

14   She buys four deluxe mixers on account from Kzinski Supply Co. for $2,100, terms n/30.

17   Natalie is concerned that there is not enough cash available to pay for all of the mixers purchased. She issues additional common stock for $1,000.

18   She pays $80 freight on the January 14 purchase.

20   She sells two deluxe mixers for $2,100 cash.

28   Natalie issues a check to her assistant. Her assistant worked 20 hours in January and is also paid for amounts owing at December 31, 2006. Recall that Natalie's assistant earns $8 an hour.

28   Natalie collects amounts due from customers in the January 12 transaction.

31   She pays Kzinski all amounts due.

31   Cash dividends of $750 are paid.

As of January 31, the following adjusting entry data are available.

1. A count of brochures and posters reveals that none were used in January.
2. A count of baking supplies reveals that none were used in January.
3. Another month's worth of depreciation needs to be recorded on the baking equipment bought in November. (Recall that the baking equipment has a useful life of 5 years or 60 months.)
4. One month's worth of amortization (write-off) needs to be recorded on the website. (Recall that the website has a useful life of 2 years or 24 months.)
5. An additional month's worth of interest on her grandmother's loan needs to be accrued. (The interest rate is 6%.)
6. One month's worth of insurance has expired.
7. Natalie receives her cell phone bill, $75. The bill is for services provided in January and is due February 15. (Recall that the cell phone is used only for business purposes.)
8. An analysis of the unearned revenue account reveals that Natalie has not had time to teach any of these lessons this month because she has been so busy selling mixers. As a result there is no change to the unearned revenue account. Natalie hopes to book the outstanding lessons in February.
9. An inventory count of mixers at the end of January reveals that Natalie has three mixers remaining.

Instructions

Using the information that you have gathered and the general ledger accounts that you have prepared through Chapter 4, plus the new information above, do the following.

(a) Answer Natalie's questions.

(b) Prepare and post the January 2007 transactions.

(c) Prepare a trial balance.   (c) Totals $11,399

(d) Prepare and post the adjusting journal entries required.

(e) Prepare an adjusted trial balance.

(f) Prepare a multiple-step income statement and retained earnings statement for the month ended January 31, 2007.   (f) Net income $ 2,060

(g) Prepare a classified balance sheet as of January 31, 2007.   (g) Total assets $ 7,504

BROADENING YOUR PERSPECTIVE

Financial Reporting and Analysis

FINANCIAL REPORTING PROBLEM: *Tootsie Roll Industries, Inc.*

BYP5-1 The financial statements for Tootsie Roll Industries are presented in Appendix A at the end of this book.

Instructions
Answer these questions using the Consolidated Income Statement.
(a) What was the percentage change in sales and in net income from 2003 to 2004?
(b) What was the profit margin ratio in each of the 3 years? Comment on the trend.
(c) What was Tootsie Roll's gross profit rate in each of the 3 years? Comment on the trend.

COMPARATIVE ANALYSIS PROBLEM: *Tootsie Roll vs. Hershey Foods*

BYP5-2 The financial statements of Hershey Foods are presented in Appendix B, following the financial statements for Tootsie Roll in Appendix A.

Instructions
(a) Based on the information contained in these financial statements, determine the following values for each company.
  (1) Profit margin ratio for 2004.
  (2) Gross profit for 2004.
  (3) Gross profit rate for 2004.
  (4) Operating income for 2004.
  (5) Percentage change in operating income from 2003 to 2004.
(b) What conclusions concerning the relative profitability of the two companies can be drawn from these data?

RESEARCH CASE

BYP5-3 The January 30, 2004, issue of the *Wall Street Journal* includes an article by Chad Terhune titled "Probe of Coke's Sales Leads to Japan."

Instructions
Read the article and answer the following questions.
(a) Describe the practice that Coke has been accused of.
(b) Explain why this practice is of concern to accountants and investors.
(c) What was suggested as the possible motivation for the alleged practice?

INTERPRETING FINANCIAL STATEMENTS

BYP5-4 Recently it was announced that two giant French retailers, Carrefour SA and Promodes SA, would merge. A headline in the *Wall Street Journal* blared, "French Retailers Create New Wal-Mart Rival." While Wal-Mart's total sales would still exceed those of the combined company, Wal-Mart's international sales are far less than those of the combined company. This is a serious concern for Wal-Mart, since its primary opportunity for future growth lies outside of the United States.

Below are basic financial data for the combined corporation (in euros) and Wal-Mart (in U.S. dollars). Even though their results are presented in different currencies, by employing ratios we can make some basic comparisons.

	Carrefour (in millions)	Wal-Mart (in millions)
Sales	euros 70,486	$256,329
Cost of goods sold	54,630	198,747
Net income	1,738	9,054
Total assets	39,063	104,912
Current assets	14,521	34,421
Current liabilities	13,660	37,418
Total liabilities	29,434	61,289

Instructions

Compare the two companies by answering the following.

(a) Calculate the gross profit rate for each of the companies, and discuss their relative abilities to control cost of goods sold.

(b) Calculate the profit margin ratio, and discuss the companies' relative profitability.

(c) Calculate the current ratio and debt to total assets ratios for the two companies, and discuss their relative liquidity and solvency.

(d) What concerns might you have in relying on this comparison?

FINANCIAL ANALYSIS ON THE WEB

BYP5-5 *Purpose:* No financial decision maker should ever rely solely on the financial information reported in the annual report to make decisions. It is important to keep abreast of financial news. This activity demonstrates how to search for financial news on the Web.

Address: **http://biz.yahoo.com/i** (or go to **www.wiley.com/college/kimmel**)

Steps

1. Type in either Wal-Mart, Target Corp., or Kmart.
2. Choose **News**.
3. Select an article that sounds interesting to you and that would be relevant to an investor in these companies.

Instructions

(a) What was the source of the article? (For example, Reuters, Businesswire, Prnewswire.)

(b) Assume that you are a personal financial planner and that one of your clients owns stock in the company. Write a brief memo to your client summarizing the article and explaining the implications of the article for their investment.

Critical Thinking

DECISION MAKING ACROSS THE ORGANIZATION

BYP5-6 Three years ago Zoe Biersack and her brother-in-law Tom Angsten opened Mallmart Department Store. For the first 2 years, business was good, but the following condensed income statement sresults for 2007 were disappointing.

MALLMART DEPARTMENT STORE
Income Statement
For the Year Ended December 31, 2007

Net sales		$700,000
Cost of goods sold		560,000
Gross profit		140,000
Operating expenses		
Selling expenses	$100,000	
Administrative expenses	15,000	
		115,000
Net income		$ 25,000

Zoe believes the problem lies in the relatively low gross profit rate of 20%. Tom believes the problem is that operating expenses are too high. Zoe thinks the gross profit rate can be improved by making two changes: (1) Increase average selling prices by 15%; this increase is expected to lower sales volume so that total sales dollars will increase only 5%. (2) Buy merchandise in larger quantities and take all purchase discounts; these changes are expected to increase the gross profit rate by 4%. Zoe does not anticipate that these changes will have any effect on operating expenses.

Tom thinks expenses can be cut by making these two changes: (1) Cut 2007 sales salaries of $60,000 in half and give sales personnel a commission of 2% of net sales. (2) Reduce store deliveries to one day per week rather than twice a week; this change will reduce 2007 delivery expenses of $30,000 by 40%. Tom feels that these changes will not have any effect on net sales.

Zoe and Tom come to you for help in deciding the best way to improve net income.

Instructions

With the class divided into groups, answer the following.

(a) Prepare a condensed income statement for 2008 assuming (1) Zoe's changes are implemented and (2) Tom's ideas are adopted.

(b) What is your recommendation to Zoe and Tom?

(c) Prepare a condensed income statement for 2008 assuming both sets of proposed changes are made.

(d) Discuss the impact that other factors might have. For example, would increasing the quantity of inventory increase costs? Would a salary cut affect employee morale? Would decreased morale affect sales? Would decreased store deliveries decrease customer satisfaction? What other suggestions might be considered?

COMMUNICATION ACTIVITY

BYP5-7 The following situation is presented in chronological order.
1. Dexter decides to buy a surfboard.
2. He calls Surfing USA Co. to inquire about their surfboards.
3. Two days later he requests Surfing USA Co. to make him a surfboard.
4. Three days later Surfing USA Co. sends him a purchase order to fill out.
5. He sends back the purchase order.
6. Surfing USA Co. receives the completed purchase order.
7. Surfing USA Co. completes the surfboard.
8. Dexter picks up the surfboard.
9. Surfing USA Co. bills Dexter.
10. Surfing USA Co. receives payment from Dexter.

Instructions

In a memo to the president of Surfing USA Co., answer the following questions.

(a) When should Surfing USA Co. record the sale?

(b) Suppose that with his purchase order, Dexter is required to make a down payment. Would that change your answer to part (a)?

ETHICS CASE

BYP5-8 Kalia Vang was just hired as the assistant treasurer of Yorkshire Stores, a specialty chain store company that has nine retail stores concentrated in one metropolitan area. Among other things, the payment of all invoices is centralized in one of the departments Kalia will manage. Her primary responsibility is to maintain the company's high credit rating by paying all bills when due and to take advantage of all cash discounts.

Dennis Hirt, the former assistant treasurer, who has been promoted to treasurer, is training Kalia in her new duties. He instructs Kalia that she is to continue the practice of preparing all checks "net of discount" and dating the checks the last day of the discount period. "But," Dennis Hirt continues, "we always hold the checks at least 4 days beyond the discount period before mailing them. That way we get another 4 days of interest on our money. Most of our creditors need our business and don't complain. And, if they scream about our missing the discount period, we blame it on the mail room or the post office. We've only lost one discount out of every hundred we take that way. I think everybody does it. By the way, welcome to our team!"

Instructions

(a) What are the ethical considerations in this case?

(b) What stakeholders are harmed or benefited?

(c) Should Kalia continue the practice started by Dennis? Does she have any choice?

Answers to Business Insight and Accounting across the Organization Questions

p. 221

Q: If a perpetual system keeps track of inventory on a daily basis, why do companies ever need to do a physical count?

A: A perpetual system keeps track of all sales and purchases on a continuous basic. This provides a constant record of the number of units in the inventory. However, if employees make errors in recording sales or purchases, the inventory value will not be correct. As a consequence, all companies do a physical count of inventory at least once a year.

p. 226

Q: If a company expects significant returns, what are the implications for revenue recognition?

A: If a company expects significant returns, it should make an adjusting entry at the end of the year reducing sales by the estimated amount of sales returns. This is necessary so as not to overstate the amount of revenue recognized in the period.

p. 231

Q: Why have investors and analysts demanded more accuracy in isolating "Other gains and losses" from operating items?

A: Greater accuracy in the classification of operating versus nonoperating ("Other gains and losses") items permit investors and analysts to judge the real operating margin, the results of continuing operations, and management's ability to control operating expenses.

p. 237

Q: Explain how Wal-Mart's profitability gave it a strategic advantage over Kmart.

A: If two competitors get into a "price war," the company with the higher profitability can reduce prices further (thus eroding its gross profit rate), but still operate at a profit. Thus, Wal-Mart's success at minimizing its operating costs has enabled it to drive many competitors out of business.

Answer to Tootsie Roll Review It Question 3, p. 232

Tootsie Roll's title for gross profit is "gross margin." Its gross profit (gross margin) increased 3.2% in 2004 ($175,609 − $170,109) ÷ $170,109.

Answers to Self-Study Questions

1. a   2. c   3. c   4. b   5. c   6. b   7. d   8. a   9. c

10. c   11. a   *12. b

CHAPTER 6

Reporting and Analyzing Inventory

STUDY OBJECTIVES

After studying this chapter,
you should be able to:

1 Describe the steps in determining inventory quantities.

2 Explain the basis of accounting for inventories and apply the inventory cost flow methods under a periodic inventory system.

3 Explain the financial statement and tax effects of each of the inventory cost flow assumptions.

4 Explain the lower of cost or market basis of accounting for inventories.

5 Compute and interpret the inventory turnover ratio.

6 Describe the LIFO reserve and explain its importance for comparing results of different companies.

THE NAVIGATOR

✓ THE NAVIGATOR

- Scan *Study Objectives* ⬭
- Read *Feature Story* ⬭
- Read *Preview* ⬭
- Read text and answer *Before You Go On*
  p. 271 ⬭ p. 280 ⬭ p. 284 ⬭
- Work *Using the Decision Toolkit* ⬭
- Review *Summary of Study Objectives* ⬭
- Work *Demonstration Problem* ⬭
- Answer *Self-Study Questions* ⬭
- Complete *Assignments* ⬭

FEATURE STORY

Where Is That Spare Bulldozer Blade?

Let's talk inventory—big, bulldozer-size inventory. Caterpillar Inc. is the world's largest manufacturer of construction and mining equipment, diesel and natural gas engines, and industrial gas turbines. It sells its products in over 200 countries, making it one of the most successful U.S. exporters. More than 70% of its productive assets are located domestically, and nearly 50% of its sales are foreign.

During the 1980s Caterpillar's profitability suffered, but today it is very successful. A big part of this turnaround can be attributed to effective management of its inventory. Imagine what a bulldozer costs. Now imagine what it costs Caterpillar to have too many bulldozers sitting around in inventory—a situation the company definitely wants to avoid. Conversely, Caterpillar must make sure it has enough inventory to meet demand.

During a recent 7-year period, Caterpillar's sales increased by 100%, while its inventory increased by only 50%. To achieve this dramatic reduction in the amount of resources tied up in inventory, while continuing to meet customers' needs, Caterpillar used a two-pronged approach. First, it completed a factory modernization program, which dramatically increased its production efficiency. The program reduced by 60% the amount of inventory the company processed at any one time. It also reduced by an incredible 75% the time it takes to manufacture a part.

Second, Caterpillar dramatically improved its parts distribution system. It ships more than 100,000 items daily from its 23 distribution centers strategically located around the world (10 *million* square feet of warehouse space—remember, we're talking bulldozers). The company can virtually guarantee that it can get any part to anywhere in the world within 24 hours. Although this network services 550,000 part numbers, Caterpillar is able to ship 99.7% of its orders within hours. In fact, Caterpillar's distribution system is so advanced that it created a subsidiary, Caterpillar Logistics Services, Inc., that warehouses and distributes other companies' products. This subsidiary distributes products as diverse as running shoes, computer software, and auto parts all around the world.

In short, how Caterpillar manages and accounts for its inventory goes a long way in explaining how profitable it is.

THE NAVIGATOR

On the World Wide Web
Caterpillar Inc.:
www.cat.com

In the previous chapter, we discussed the accounting for merchandise inventory using a perpetual inventory system. In this chapter, we explain the methods used to calculate the cost of inventory on hand at the balance sheet date and the cost of goods sold. We conclude by illustrating methods for analyzing inventory.

The content and organization of this chapter are as follows.

Classifying Inventory

How a company classifies its inventory depends on whether the firm is a merchandiser or a manufacturer. In a **merchandising** company, such as those described in Chapter 5, inventory consists of many different items. For example, in a grocery store, canned goods, dairy products, meats, and produce are just a few of the inventory items on hand. These items have two common characteristics: (1) They are owned by the company, and (2) they are in a form ready for sale to customers in the ordinary course of business. Thus, merchandisers need only one inventory classification, **merchandise inventory**, to describe the many different items that make up the total inventory.

In a **manufacturing** company, some inventory may not yet be ready for sale. As a result, manufacturers usually classify inventory into three categories: finished goods, work in process, and raw materials. **Finished goods inventory** is manufactured items that are completed and ready for sale. **Work in process** is that portion of manufactured inventory that has been placed into the production process but is not yet complete. **Raw materials** are the basic goods that will be used in production but have not yet been placed into production.

For example, Caterpillar classifies earth-moving tractors completed and ready for sale as **finished goods**. It classifies the tractors on the assembly line in various stages of production as **work in process**. The steel, glass, tires, and other components that are on hand waiting to be used in the production of tractors are identified as **raw materials**.

The accounting concepts discussed in this chapter apply to the inventory classifications of both merchandising and manufacturing companies. Our focus here is on merchandise inventory.

Helpful Hint Regardless of the classification, companies report all inventories under Current Assets on the balance sheet.

By observing the levels and changes in the levels of these three inventory types, financial statement users can gain insight into management's production plans. For example, low levels of raw materials and high levels of finished goods suggest that management believes it has enough inventory on hand, and production will be slowing down—perhaps in anticipation of a recession. On the other hand, high levels of raw materials and low levels of finished goods probably indicate that management is planning to step up production.

Many companies have significantly lowered inventory levels and costs using **just-in-time (JIT) inventory** methods. Under a just-in-time method, companies manufacture or purchase goods just in time for use. Dell is famous for having developed a system for making computers in response to individual customer requests. Even though it makes each computer to meet each customer's particular specifications, Dell is able to assemble the computer and put it on a truck in less than 48 hours. By integrating its information systems with those of its suppliers, Dell reduced its inventories to nearly zero. This is a huge advantage in an industry where products become obsolete nearly overnight.

Accounting across the Organization

Wal-Mart improved on its inventory control in 2004 with the introduction of electronic product codes (EPCs). Much like bar codes, which tell a retailer the number of boxes of a specific product it has, EPCs go a step farther, helping to distinguish one box of a specific product from another. EPCs use radio frequency identification (RFID) technology, the same technology behind keyless remotes used to unlock car doors.

Companies currently use EPCs to track shipments from supplier to distribution center to store. Other potential uses include help with monitoring product expiration dates and acting quickly on product recalls. Wal-Mart also anticipates faster returns and warranty processing using EPCs. This technology will further assist Wal-Mart managers in their efforts to ensure that their store has just the right type of inventory, in just the right amount, in just the right place.

 Why is inventory control important to managers such as those at Wal-Mart?

Determining Inventory Quantities

No matter whether they are using a periodic or perpetual inventory system, all companies need to determine inventory quantities at the end of the accounting period. If using a perpetual system, companies take a physical inventory for two purposes: The first purpose is to check the accuracy of their perpetual inventory records. The second is to determine the amount of inventory lost due to wasted raw materials, shoplifting, or employee theft.

Companies using a periodic inventory system must take a physical inventory for two *different* purposes: to determine the inventory on hand at the balance sheet date, and to determine the cost of goods sold for the period.

Determining inventory quantities involves two steps: (1) taking a physical inventory of goods on hand and (2) determining the ownership of goods.

STUDY OBJECTIVE **1**

Describe the steps in determining inventory quantities.

TAKING A PHYSICAL INVENTORY

Taking a physical inventory involves actually counting, weighing, or measuring each kind of inventory on hand. In many companies, taking an inventory is a formidable task. Retailers such as Target, True Value Hardware, or Home Depot have thousands of different inventory items. An inventory count is generally more accurate when goods are not being sold or received during the counting. Consequently, companies often "take inventory" when the business is closed or when business is slow. Many retailers close early on a chosen day in January—after the holiday sales and returns, when inventories are at their lowest level—to count inventory. Recall from Chapter 5 that Wal-Mart had a year-end of January 31. Companies take the physical inventory at the end of the accounting period.

Business Insight
Ethics Perspective

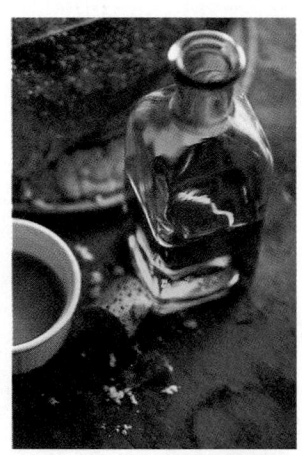

Over the years inventory has played a role in many fraud cases. A classic case involved salad oil. Management of the salad-oil company filled storage tanks mostly with water. Since oil rises to the top, the auditors thought the tanks were full of oil. In addition, management said they had more tanks than they really did—they repainted numbers on the tanks to confuse auditors.

More recently, managers at women's apparel maker Leslie Fay were convicted of falsifying inventory records to boost net income—and consequently to boost management bonuses. In another case, executives at Craig Consumer Electronics were accused of defrauding lenders by manipulating inventory records. The indictment said the company classified "defective goods as new or refurbished" and claimed that it owned certain shipments "from overseas suppliers when, in fact, Craig either did not own the shipments or the shipments did not exist."

 What effect does an overstatement of inventory have on a company's financial statements?

DETERMINING OWNERSHIP OF GOODS

One challenge in determining inventory quantities is making sure a company owns the inventory. To determine ownership of goods, two questions must be answered: Do all of the goods included in the count belong to the company? Does the company own any goods that were not included in the count?

Goods in Transit

A complication in determining ownership is **goods in transit** (on board a truck, train, ship, or plane) at the end of the period. The company may have purchased goods that have not yet been received, or it may have sold goods that have not yet been delivered. To arrive at an accurate count, the company must determine ownership of these goods.

Goods in transit should be included in the inventory of the company that has legal title to the goods. Legal title is determined by the terms of the sale, as shown in Illustration 6-1 and described below.

1. When the terms are **FOB (free on board) shipping point**, ownership of the goods passes to the buyer when the public carrier accepts the goods from the seller.

Illustration 6-1
Terms of sale

2. When the terms are **FOB destination**, ownership of the goods remains with the seller until the goods reach the buyer.

Consigned Goods

In some lines of business, it is common to hold the goods of other parties and try to sell the goods for them for a fee, but without taking ownership of the goods. These are called **consigned goods**.

For example, you might have a used car that you would like to sell. If you take the item to a dealer, the dealer might be willing to put the car on its lot and charge you a commission if it is sold. Under this agreement the dealer **would not take ownership** of the car, which would still belong to you. Therefore, if an inventory count were taken, the car would not be included in the dealer's inventory.

Many car, boat, and antique dealers sell goods on consignment to keep their inventory costs down and to avoid the risk of purchasing an item that they won't be able to sell. Today even some manufacturers are making consignment agreements with their suppliers in order to keep their inventory levels low.

BEFORE YOU GO ON . . .

►Review It

1. What are the three inventory categories a manufacturing company would be likely to use? Why should financial statement users be aware of these categories?
2. What steps are involved in determining inventory quantities?
3. How is ownership determined for goods in transit?
4. Who has title to consigned goods?

Inventory Costing

After a company has determined the quantity of units of inventory, it applies unit costs to the quantities to determine the total cost of the inventory and the cost of goods sold. This process can be complicated if a company has purchased inventory items at different times and at different prices.

For example, assume that Crivitz TV Company purchases three identical 46-inch TVs on different dates at costs of $700, $750, and $800. During the year Crivitz sold two sets at $1,200 each. These facts are summarized in Illustration 6-2.

STUDY OBJECTIVE
2

Explain the basis of accounting for inventories and apply the inventory cost flow methods under a periodic inventory system.

Illustration 6-2   Data for inventory costing example

Purchases			
February 3	1 TV	at	$700
March 5	1 TV	at	$750
May 22	1 TV	at	$800
Sales			
June 1	2 TVs	for	$2,400 ($1,200 × 2)

Cost of goods sold will differ depending on which two TVs the company sold. For example, it might be $1,450 ($700 + $750), or $1,500 ($700 + $800), or $1,550 ($750 + $800). In this section we discuss alternative costing methods available to Crivitz.

SPECIFIC IDENTIFICATION

If Crivitz sold the TVs it purchased on February 3 and May 22, then its cost of goods sold is $1,500 ($700 + $800), and its ending inventory is $750. If Crivitz can positively identify which particular units it sold and which are still in ending inventory, it can use the **specific identification method** of inventory costing (see Illustration 6-3). Using this method, companies can accurately determine ending inventory and cost of goods sold.

Illustration 6-3   Specific identification method

Cost of goods sold = $700 + $800 = $1,500
Ending inventory = $750

Ethics Note A major disadvantage of the specific identification method is that management may be able to manipulate net income. For example, it can boost net income by selling units purchased at a low cost, or reduce net income by selling units purchased at a high cost.

Specific identification requires that companies keep records of the original cost of each individual inventory item. Historically, specific identification was possible only when a company sold a limited variety of high-unit-cost items that could be identified clearly from the time of purchase through the time of sale. Examples of such products are cars, pianos, or expensive antiques.

Today, with bar coding, electronic product codes, and radio frequency identification, it is theoretically possible to do specific identification with nearly any type of product. The reality is, however, that this practice is still relatively rare. Instead, rather than keep track of the cost of each particular item sold, most companies make assumptions, called **cost flow assumptions**, about which units were sold.

COST FLOW ASSUMPTIONS

Because specific identification is often impractical, other cost flow methods are permitted. These differ from specific identification in that they **assume** flows of costs that may be unrelated to the physical flow of goods. There are three assumed cost flow methods:

1. First-in, first-out (FIFO)

2. Last-in, first-out (LIFO)

3. Average cost

There is no accounting requirement that the cost flow assumption be consistent with the physical movement of the goods. Company management selects the appropriate cost flow method.

To illustrate these three inventory cost flow methods, we will assume that Houston Electronics uses a periodic inventory system and has the information shown in Illustration 6-4 for its Astro condenser.[1] (An appendix to this chapter presents the use of these methods under a perpetual system.)

Illustration 6-4 Cost of goods available for sale

	HOUSTON ELECTRONICS — Astro Condensers			
Date	Explanation	Units	Unit Cost	Total Cost
Jan. 1	Beginning inventory	100	$10	$ 1,000
Apr. 15	Purchase	200	11	2,200
Aug. 24	Purchase	300	12	3,600
Nov. 27	Purchase	400	13	5,200
	Total	1,000		$12,000

The company had a total of 1,000 units available that it could have sold during the period. The total cost of these units was $12,000. A physical inventory at the end of the year determined that during the year Houston sold 550 units and had 450 units in inventory at December 31. The question then is how to determine what prices to use to value the goods sold and the ending inventory. The sum of the cost allocated to the units sold plus the cost of the units in inventory must add up to $12,000, the total cost of all goods available for sale.

First-In, First-Out (FIFO)

The **FIFO (first-in, first-out) method** assumes that the **earliest goods** purchased are the first to be sold. FIFO often parallels the actual physical flow of merchandise because it generally is good business practice to sell the oldest units first. Under the FIFO method, therefore, the **costs** of the earliest goods purchased are the first to be recognized in determining cost of goods sold. (Note that this does not necessarily mean that the oldest units *are* sold first, but that the costs of the oldest units are *recognized* first. In a bin of picture hangers at the hardware store, for example, no one really knows, nor would it matter, which hangers are sold first.) Illustration 6-5 (page 274) shows the allocation of the cost of goods available for sale at Houston Electronics under FIFO.

Under FIFO, since it is assumed that the first goods purchased were the first goods sold, ending inventory is based on the prices of the most recent units purchased. That is, **under FIFO, companies obtain the cost of the ending inventory by taking the unit cost of the most recent purchase and working backward until all units of inventory have been costed.** In this example, Houston Electronics prices the 450 units of ending inventory using the *most recent* prices. The last purchase was 400 units at $13 on November 27. The remaining 50 units are priced using the unit cost of the second most recent purchase, $12, on August 24. Next, Houston Electronics calculates cost of goods sold by subtracting the cost of the units **not sold** (ending inventory) from the cost of all goods available for sale.

---

[1]We have chosen to use the periodic approach for a number of reasons. First, many companies that use a perpetual inventory system use it to keep track of units on hand, but then determine cost of goods sold at the end of the period using one of the three cost flow approaches applied under essentially a periodic approach. In addition, because of the complexity, few companies use average cost on a perpetual basis. Also, most companies that use perpetual LIFO employ dollar-value LIFO, which is presented in more advanced texts. Furthermore, FIFO gives the same results under either perpetual or periodic. And finally, it is easier to demonstrate the cost flow assumptions under the periodic system, which makes it more pedagogically appropriate.

Illustration 6-5
Allocation of costs—FIFO
method

Helpful Hint Note the sequenc-
ing of the allocation: (1) Compute ending inventory, and
(2) determine cost of goods
sold.

Helpful Hint Another way of
thinking about the calculation
of FIFO **ending inventory** is
the *LISH assumption*—last in
still here.

COST OF GOODS AVAILABLE FOR SALE

Date	Explanation	Units	Unit Cost	Total Cost
Jan. 1	Beginning inventory	100	$10	$ 1,000
Apr. 15	Purchase	200	11	2,200
Aug. 24	Purchase	300	12	3,600
Nov. 27	Purchase	400	13	5,200
	Total	1,000		$12,000

STEP 1: ENDING INVENTORY   STEP 2: COST OF GOODS SOLD

Date	Units	Unit Cost	Total Cost		
Nov. 27	400	$13	$ 5,200	Cost of goods available for sale	$12,000
Aug. 24	50	12	600	Less: Ending inventory	5,800
Total	450		$5,800	Cost of goods sold	$ 6,200

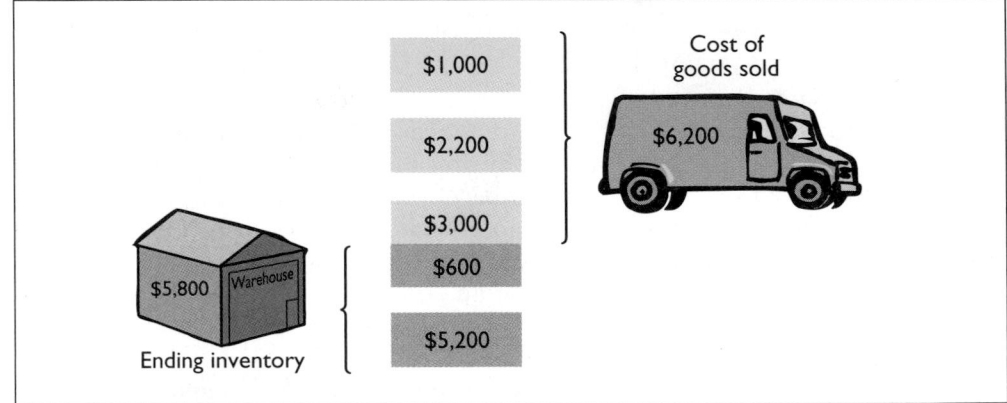

Illustration 6-6 demonstrates that companies also can calculate cost of goods sold by pricing the 550 units sold using the prices of the first 550 units acquired. Note that of the 300 units purchased on August 24, only 250 units are assumed sold. This agrees with our calculation of the cost of ending inventory, where 50 of these units were assumed unsold and thus included in ending inventory.

Illustration 6-6   Proof of
cost of goods sold

Date	Units	Unit Cost	Total Cost
Jan. 1	100	$10	$ 1,000
Apr. 15	200	11	2,200
Aug. 24	250	12	3,000
Total	550		$6,200

Last-In, First-Out (LIFO)

The **LIFO (last-in, first-out) method** assumes that the **latest goods** purchased are the first to be sold. LIFO seldom coincides with the actual physical flow of inventory. (Exceptions include goods stored in piles, such as coal or hay, where goods are removed from the top of the pile as they are sold.) Under the LIFO method, the **costs** of the latest goods purchased are the first to be recognized in determining cost of goods sold. Illustration 6-7 (page 275) shows the allocation of the cost of goods available for sale at Houston Electronics under LIFO.

Illustration 6-7
Allocation of costs—LIFO
method

COST OF GOODS AVAILABLE FOR SALE

Date	Explanation	Units	Unit Cost	Total Cost
Jan. 1	Beginning inventory	100	$10	$ 1,000
Apr. 15	Purchase	200	11	2,200
Aug. 24	Purchase	300	12	3,600
Nov. 27	Purchase	400	13	5,200
	Total	1,000		$12,000

STEP 1: ENDING INVENTORY   STEP 2: COST OF GOODS SOLD

Date	Units	Unit Cost	Total Cost		
Jan. 1	100	$10	$ 1,000	Cost of goods available for sale	$12,000
Apr. 15	200	11	2,200	Less: Ending inventory	5,000
Aug. 24	150	12	1,800	Cost of goods sold	$ 7,000
Total	450		$5,000		

Helpful Hint Another way of
thinking about the calculation
of LIFO **ending inventory** is
the *FISH assumption*—first in
still here.

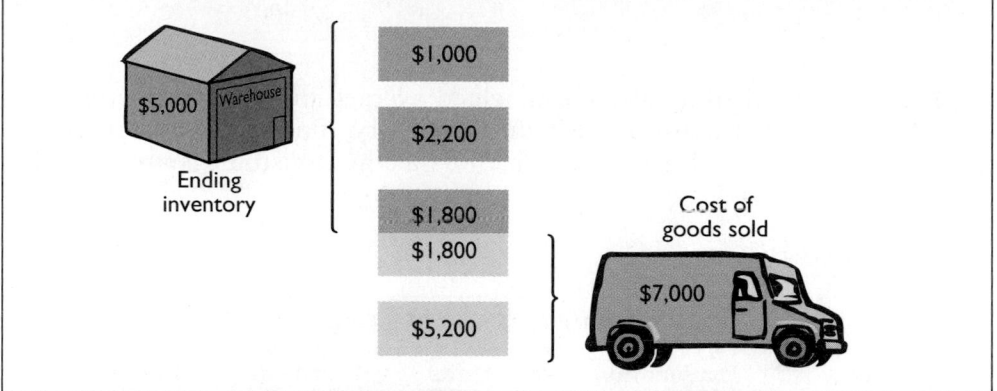

Under LIFO, since it is assumed that the first goods sold were those that were most recently purchased, ending inventory is based on the prices of the oldest units purchased. That is, **under LIFO, companies obtain the cost of the ending inventory by taking the unit cost of the earliest goods available for sale and working forward until all units of inventory have been costed**. In this example, Houston Electronics prices the 450 units of ending inventory using the *earliest* prices. The first purchase was 100 units at $10 in the January 1 beginning inventory. Then 200 units were purchased at $11. The remaining 150 units needed are priced at $12 per unit (August 24 purchase). Next, Houston Electronics calculates cost of goods sold by subtracting the cost of the units **not sold** (ending inventory) from the cost of all goods available for sale.

Illustration 6-8 demonstrates that companies also can calculate cost of goods sold by pricing the 550 units sold using the prices of the last 550 units acquired. Note that of the 300 units purchased on August 24, only 150 units are assumed sold. This agrees with our calculation of the cost of ending inventory, where 150 of these units were assumed unsold and thus included in ending inventory.

Illustration 6-8 Proof of cost of goods sold

Date	Units	Unit Cost	Total Cost
Nov. 27	400	$13	$ 5,200
Aug. 24	150	12	1,800
Total	550		$7,000

Under a periodic inventory system, which we are using here, **all goods purchased during the period are assumed to be available for the first sale, regardless of the date of purchase**.

Average Cost

The **average-cost method** allocates the cost of goods available for sale on the basis of the **weighted average unit cost** incurred. The average-cost method assumes that goods are similar in nature. Illustration 6-9 presents the formula and a sample computation of the weighted-average unit cost.

Illustration 6-9 Formula for weighted average unit cost

Cost of Goods Available for Sale	÷	Total Units Available for Sale	=	Weighted Average Unit Cost
$12,000	÷	1,000	=	$12.00

The company then applies the weighted average unit cost to the units on hand to determine the cost of the ending inventory. Illustration 6-10 shows the allocation of the cost of goods available for sale at Houston Electronics using average cost.

Illustration 6-10 Allocation of costs— average-cost method

COST OF GOODS AVAILABLE FOR SALE

Date	Explanation	Units	Unit Cost	Total Cost
Jan. 1	Beginning inventory	100	$10	$ 1,000
Apr. 15	Purchase	200	11	2,200
Aug. 24	Purchase	300	12	3,600
Nov. 27	Purchase	400	13	5,200
	Total	1,000		$12,000

STEP 1: ENDING INVENTORY

$12,000 ÷ 1,000 = $12.00

Units	Unit Cost	Total Cost
450	$12.00	$5,400

STEP 2: COST OF GOODS SOLD

Cost of goods available for sale	$12,000
Less: Ending inventory	5,400
Cost of goods sold	$ 6,600

$$\frac{\$12,000}{1,000 \text{ units}} = \$12 \text{ per unit}$$

Cost per unit

450 units × $12 = $5,400   Warehouse

Ending inventory

$12,000 − $5,400 = $6,600

Cost of goods sold

We can verify the cost of goods sold under this method by multiplying the units sold times the weighted average unit cost (550 × $12 = $6,600). Note that this method does not use the average of the unit costs. That average is $11.50 ($10 + $11 + $12 + $13 = $46; $46 ÷ 4). The average cost method instead uses the average **weighted by** the quantities purchased at each unit cost.

FINANCIAL STATEMENT AND TAX EFFECTS OF COST FLOW METHODS

Each of the three assumed cost flow methods is acceptable for use. For example, Reebok International Ltd. and Wendy's International currently use the FIFO method of inventory costing. Campbell Soup Company, Krogers, and Walgreen Drugs use LIFO for part or all of their inventory. Bristol-Myers Squibb, Starbucks, and Motorola use the average cost method. In fact, a company may also use more than one cost flow method at the same time. Black & Decker Manufacturing Company, for example, uses LIFO for domestic inventories and FIFO for foreign inventories. Illustration 6-11 shows the use of the three cost flow methods in the 600 largest U.S. companies.

The reasons companies adopt different inventory cost flow methods are varied, but they usually involve one of three factors:

1. Income statement effects
2. Balance sheet effects
3. Tax effects

Income Statement Effects

To understand why companies might choose a particular cost flow method, let's examine the effects of the different cost flow assumptions on the financial statements of Houston Electronics. The condensed income statements in Illustration 6-12 assume that Houston sold its 550 units for $11,500, had operating expenses of $2,000, and is subject to an income tax rate of 30%.

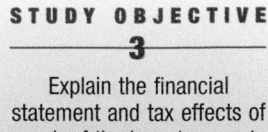

STUDY OBJECTIVE
3
Explain the financial statement and tax effects of each of the inventory cost flow assumptions.

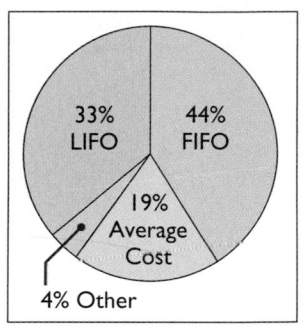

Illustration 6-11   Use of cost flow methods in major U.S. companies

HOUSTON ELECTRONICS Condensed Income Statements			
	FIFO	**LIFO**	**Average Cost**
Sales	$11,500	$11,500	$11,500
Beginning inventory	1,000	1,000	1,000
Purchases	11,000	11,000	11,000
Cost of goods available for sale	12,000	12,000	12,000
Ending inventory	**5,800**	**5,000**	**5,400**
Cost of goods sold	6,200	7,000	6,600
Gross profit	5,300	4,500	4,900
Operating expenses	2,000	2,000	2,000
Income before income taxes	3,300	2,500	2,900
Income tax expense (30%)	990	750	870
Net income	**$ 2,310**	**$ 1,750**	**$ 2,030**

Illustration 6-12
Comparative effects of cost flow methods

Note the cost of goods available for sale ($12,000) is the same under each of the three inventory cost flow methods. However, the ending inventories and the costs of goods sold are different. This difference is due to the unit costs that the company allocated to cost of goods sold and to ending inventory. Each dollar of difference in ending inventory results in a corresponding dollar difference in income before income taxes. For Houston, an $800 difference exists between FIFO and LIFO cost of goods sold.

In periods of changing prices, the cost flow assumption can have a significant impact on income and on evaluations based on income. In most instances, prices are rising (inflation). In a period of inflation, FIFO produces a higher net income because the lower unit costs of the first units purchased are matched against revenues. In a period of rising prices (as is the case in the Houston example), FIFO reports the highest net income ($2,310) and LIFO the lowest ($1,750); average cost falls in the middle ($2,030). If prices are falling, the results from the use of FIFO and LIFO are reversed: FIFO will report the lowest net income and LIFO the highest.

To management, higher net income is an advantage: It causes external users to view the company more favorably. In addition, management bonuses, if based on net income, will be higher. Therefore, when prices are rising (which is usually the case), companies tend to prefer FIFO because it results in higher net income.

Some argue that the use of LIFO in a period of inflation enables the company to avoid reporting **paper** (or **phantom**) **profit** as economic gain. To illustrate, assume that Kralik Company buys 200 units of a product at $20 per unit on January 10 and 200 more on December 31 at $24 each. During the year, Kralik sells 200 units at $30 each. Illustration 6-13 shows the results under FIFO and LIFO.

Illustration 6-13 Income statement effects compared

	FIFO	LIFO
Sales (200 × $30)	$6,000	$6,000
Cost of goods sold	**4,000** (200 × $20)	**4,800** (200 × $24)
Gross profit	$2,000	$1,200

Under LIFO, Kralik Company has recovered the current replacement cost ($4,800) of the units sold. Thus, the gross profit in economic terms is real. However, under FIFO, the company has recovered only the January 10 cost ($4,000). To replace the units sold, it must reinvest $800 (200 × $4) of the gross profit. Thus, $800 of the gross profit is said to be phantom or illusory. As a result, reported net income is also overstated in real terms.

Balance Sheet Effects

A major advantage of the FIFO method is that in a period of inflation, the costs allocated to ending inventory will approximate their current cost. For example, for Houston Electronics, 400 of the 450 units in the ending inventory are costed under FIFO at the higher November 27 unit cost of $13.

Conversely, a major shortcoming of the LIFO method is that in a period of inflation, the costs allocated to ending inventory may be significantly understated in terms of current cost. The understatement becomes greater over prolonged periods of inflation if the inventory includes goods purchased in one or more prior accounting periods. For example, Caterpillar has used LIFO for 50 years. Its balance sheet shows ending inventory of $4,675 million. But the inventory's actual current cost if FIFO had been used is $6,799 million.

Helpful Hint A tax rule, often referred to as the *LIFO conformity rule*, requires that if companies use LIFO for tax purposes they must also use it for financial reporting purposes. This means that if a company uses the LIFO method to ... its tax bills, it will also ... ort lower net ... financial

Tax Effects

We have seen that both inventory on the balance sheet and net income on the income statement are higher when companies use FIFO in a period of inflation. Yet, many companies have switched to LIFO. Why? The reason is that LIFO results in the lowest income taxes (because of lower net income) during times of rising prices. For example, at Houston Electronics, income taxes are $750 under LIFO, compared to $990 under FIFO. The tax savings of $240 makes more cash available for use in the business.

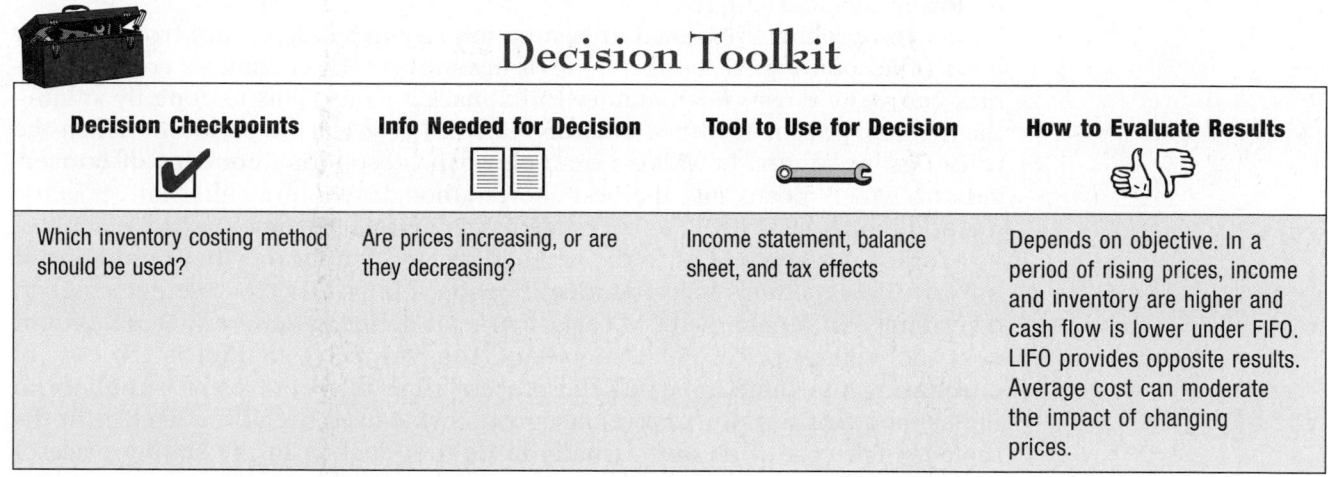

Decision Toolkit

Decision Checkpoints	Info Needed for Decision	Tool to Use for Decision	How to Evaluate Results
Which inventory costing method should be used?	Are prices increasing, or are they decreasing?	Income statement, balance sheet, and tax effects	Depends on objective. In a period of rising prices, income and inventory are higher and cash flow is lower under FIFO. LIFO provides opposite results. Average cost can moderate the impact of changing prices.

USING INVENTORY COST FLOW METHODS CONSISTENTLY

Whatever cost flow method a company chooses, it should use that method consistently from one accounting period to another. Consistent application enhances the comparability of financial statements over successive time periods. In contrast, using the FIFO method one year and the LIFO method the next year would make it difficult to compare the net incomes of the two years.

Although consistent application is preferred, it does not mean that a company may *never* change its method of inventory costing. When a company adopts a different method, it should disclose in the financial statements the change and its effects on net income. A typical disclosure is shown in Illustration 6-14, using information from recent financial statements of the Quaker Oats Company.

Helpful Hint As you learned in Chapter 2, consistency and comparability are important characteristics of accounting information.

Illustration 6-14
Disclosure of change in cost flow method

QUAKER OATS COMPANY
Notes to the Financial Statements

Note 1: Effective July 1, the Company adopted the LIFO cost flow assumption for valuing the majority of U.S. Grocery Products inventories. The Company believes that the use of the LIFO method better matches current costs with current revenues. The effect of this change on the current year was to decrease net income by $16.0 million.

LOWER OF COST OR MARKET

The value of inventory for companies selling high-technology or fashion goods can drop very quickly due to changes in technology or changes in fashions. These circumstances sometimes call for inventory valuation methods other than those presented so far. For example, in a recent year purchasing managers at Ford decided to make a large purchase of palladium, a precious metal used in vehicle emission devices. They made this large purchase because they

STUDY OBJECTIVE
4

Explain the lower of cost or market basis of accounting for inventories.

feared a future shortage. The shortage did not materialize, and by the end of the year the price of palladium had plummeted. Ford's inventory was then worth $1 billion less than its original cost. Do you think Ford's inventory should have been stated at cost, in accordance with the cost principle, or at its lower replacement cost?

As you probably reasoned, this situation requires a departure from the cost basis of accounting. When the value of inventory is lower than its cost, companies can write down the inventory to its market value. This is done by valuing the inventory at the **lower of cost or market (LCM)** in the period in which the price decline occurs. LCM is an example of the accounting **concept of conservatism**, which means that the best choice among accounting alternatives is the method that is least likely to overstate assets and net income.

Companies apply LCM to the items in inventory after they have used one of the cost flow methods (specific identification, FIFO, LIFO, or average cost) to determine cost. Under the LCM basis, market is defined as **current replacement cost**, not selling price. For a merchandising company, market is the cost of purchasing the same goods at the present time from the usual suppliers in the usual quantities. Current replacement cost is used because a decline in the replacement cost of an item usually leads to a decline in the selling price of the item.

To illustrate the application of LCM, assume that Ken Tuckie TV has the following lines of merchandise with costs and market values as indicated. LCM produces the results shown in Illustration 6-15. Note that the amounts shown in the final column are the lower of cost or market amounts for each item.

Illustration 6-15
Computation of lower of cost or market

	Cost	Market	Lower of Cost or Market
Console TVs	$ 60,000	$ 55,000	$ 55,000
Portable TVs	45,000	52,000	45,000
Video recorders	48,000	45,000	45,000
Movies	15,000	14,000	14,000
Total inventory	$168,000	$166,000	**$159,000**

BEFORE YOU GO ON . . .

▶Review It

1. What factors should management consider in selecting an inventory cost flow method?
2. What inventory cost flow method does Tootsie Roll Industries use for U.S. inventories? What method does it use for foreign inventories? (*Hint:* You will need to examine the notes for Tootsie Roll's financial statements.) The answers to these questions appear on page 313.
3. Which inventory cost flow method produces the highest net income in a period of rising prices? Which results in the lowest income taxes?
4. When should inventory be reported at a value other than cost?

▶ Do It

The accounting records of Shumway Ag Implement show the following data.

Beginning inventory	4,000 units at $ 3
Purchases	6,000 units at $ 4
Sales	5,000 units at $12

Determine the cost of goods sold during the period under a periodic inventory system using (a) the FIFO method, (b) the LIFO method, and (c) the average-cost method.

Action Plan

- Understand the periodic inventory system.
- Allocate costs between goods sold and goods on hand (ending inventory) for each cost flow method,
- Compute cost of goods sold for each cost flow method.

Solution

(a) FIFO: (4,000 @ \$3) + (1,000 @ \$4) = \$12,000 + \$4,000 = \$16,000
(b) LIFO: 5,000 @ \$4 = \$20,000
(c) Average-cost: [(4,000 @ \$3) + (6,000 @ \$4)] ÷ 10,000
= (\$12,000 + \$24,000) ÷ 10,000
= \$3.60 per unit; 5,000 @ \$3.60 = \$18,000

Analysis of Inventory

For companies that sell goods, managing inventory levels can be one of the most critical tasks. Having too much inventory on hand costs the company money in storage costs, interest cost (on funds tied up in inventory), and costs associated with the obsolescence of technical goods (e.g., computer chips) or shifts in fashion (e.g., clothes). But having too little inventory on hand results in lost sales. In this section we discuss some issues related to evaluating inventory levels.

INVENTORY TURNOVER RATIO

The **inventory turnover ratio** is calculated as cost of goods sold divided by average inventory. It indicates how quickly a company sells its goods—how many times the inventory "turns over" (is sold) during the year. Inventory turnover can be divided into 365 days to compute **days in inventory**, which indicates the average age of the inventory.

High inventory turnover (low days in inventory) indicates the company is tying up little of its funds in inventory—that it has a minimal amount of inventory on hand at any one time. Although minimizing the funds tied up in inventory is efficient, too high an inventory turnover ratio may indicate that the company is losing sales opportunities because of inventory shortages. For example, investment analysts at one time suggested that Office Depot had gone too far in reducing its inventory—they said they were seeing too many empty shelves. Thus, management should closely monitor this ratio to achieve the best balance between too much and too little inventory.

In Chapter 5 we discussed the increasingly competitive environment of retailers like Wal-Mart and Target. Wal-Mart has implemented **just-in-time inventory procedures** as well as many technological innovations to improve the efficiency of its inventory management. The following data are available for Wal-Mart.

> **STUDY OBJECTIVE**
> **5**
> Compute and interpret the inventory turnover ratio.

(in millions)	2004	2003	2002
Ending inventory	\$ 26,612	\$ 24,401	\$22,053
Cost of goods sold	198,747	178,299	

Illustration 6-16 (page 282) presents the inventory turnover ratios and days in inventory for Wal-Mart and Target, using data from the financial statements of those corporations for 2004 and 2003.

The calculations in Illustration 6-16 show that Wal-Mart turns its inventory more frequently than Target (7.8 times for Wal-Mart versus 6.3 times for Target). Consequently, the average time an item spends on a Wal-Mart shelf is shorter (46.8 days for Wal-Mart versus 57.9 days for Target). This suggests that Wal-Mart is more efficient than Target in its inventory management.

Illustration 6-16
Inventory turnover ratio and days in inventory

$$\text{Inventory Turnover Ratio} = \frac{\text{Cost of Goods Sold}}{\text{Average Inventory}}$$

$$\text{Days in Inventory} = \frac{365}{\text{Inventory Turnover Ratio}}$$

		2004	2003
Wal-Mart ($ in millions)	Inventory turnover ratio	$\frac{\$198,747}{(\$26,612 + \$24,401)/2} = 7.8$ times	$\frac{\$178,299}{(\$24,401 + \$22,053)/2} = 7.7$ times
	Days in inventory	$\frac{365 \text{ days}}{7.8} = 46.8$ days	$\frac{365 \text{ days}}{7.7} = 47.4$ days
Target	Inventory turnover ratio	6.3 times	6.4 times
	Days in inventory	57.9 days	57.0 days

Note also that Wal-Mart's inventory turnover, which was already better than Target's in 2003, improved slightly in 2004. Wal-Mart's sophisticated inventory tracking and distribution system allows it to keep minimum amounts of inventory on hand, while still keeping the shelves full of what customers are looking for.

Accounting across the Organization

Demand for cell phones typically falls during the first quarter of each year. It is a widely held principle that a company should cut back its production and inventory levels when it anticipates that demand will decrease. Thus many industry observers were surprised when Samsung Electronics Co. chose to increase production during the first quarter of the year, for the third year in a row.

Why did Samsung do this? Its executives felt that this approach would enable it to stand out against competitors by putting "a slew of new cell phones on shelves next to graying models from its rivals." It is clear that even with just-in-time inventory techniques and highly efficient inventory systems, management still must make many critical strategic decisions regarding inventory.

Source: Evan Ramstad, "Samsung to Report Whether Counterintuitive Move Paid Off," *Wall Street Journal* (April 24, 2005), p. B3.

 If Samsung isn't successful in selling the units, what steps will it have to take, and how will this show up in its financial statements?

Decision Toolkit

Decision Checkpoints	Info Needed for Decision	Tool to Use for Decision	How to Evaluate Results
How long is an item in inventory?	Cost of goods sold; beginning and ending inventory	$\text{Inventory turnover ratio} = \dfrac{\text{Cost of goods sold}}{\text{Average inventory}}$ $\text{Days in inventory} = \dfrac{365 \text{ days}}{\text{Inventory turnover ratio}}$	A higher inventory turnover ratio or lower average days in inventory suggests that management is reducing the amount of inventory on hand, relative to sales.

ANALYSTS' ADJUSTMENTS FOR LIFO RESERVE

Earlier we noted that using LIFO rather than FIFO can result in significant differences in the results reported in the balance sheet and the income statement. With increasing prices, FIFO will result in higher income than LIFO. On the balance sheet, FIFO will result in higher reported inventory. The financial statement differences of using LIFO normally increase the longer a company uses LIFO.

Use of different inventory cost flow assumptions complicates analysts' attempts to compare companies' results. Fortunately, companies using LIFO are required to report the amount that inventory would increase (or occasionally decrease) if the company had instead been using FIFO. This amount is referred to as the **LIFO reserve**. Reporting the LIFO reserve enables analysts to make adjustments to compare companies that use different cost flow methods.

Illustration 6-17 presents an excerpt from the notes to Caterpillar's 2004 financial statements that discloses and discusses Caterpillar's LIFO reserve.

STUDY OBJECTIVE
6
Describe the LIFO reserve and explain its importance for comparing results of different companies.

CATERPILLAR INC.
Notes to the Financial Statements

Inventories: Inventories are stated at the lower of cost or market. Cost is principally determined using the last-in, first-out (LIFO) method. If the FIFO (first-in, first-out) method had been in use, inventories would have been $2,124, $1,863, and $1,977 million higher than reported at December 31, 2004, 2003, and 2002, respectively.

Illustration 6-17
Caterpillar LIFO reserve

Caterpillar has used LIFO for over 50 years. Thus, the cumulative difference between LIFO and FIFO reflected in the inventory account is very large. In fact, the 2004 LIFO reserve of $2,124 million is 45 percent of the 2004 LIFO inventory of $4,675 million. Such a huge difference would clearly distort any comparisons you might try to make with one of Caterpillar's competitors that used FIFO.

To adjust Caterpillar's inventory balance we add the LIFO reserve to reported inventory, as shown in Illustration 6-18. That is, if Caterpillar had used FIFO all along, its inventory would be $6,799 million, rather than $4,675 million.

	(in millions)
2004 inventory using LIFO	$ 4,675
2004 LIFO reserve	2,124
2004 inventory assuming FIFO	**$6,799**

Illustration 6-18
Conversion of inventory from LIFO to FIFO

The LIFO reserve can have a significant effect on ratios analysts commonly use. Using the LIFO reserve adjustment, Illustration 6-19 calculates the value of the current ratio (current assets ÷ current liabilities) for Caterpillar under both the LIFO and FIFO cost flow assumptions.

Illustration 6-19   Impact of LIFO reserve on ratios

($ in millions)	LIFO	FIFO
Current ratio	$\dfrac{\$20{,}856}{\$16{,}210} = 1.3 : 1$	$\dfrac{\$20{,}856 + \$2{,}124}{\$16{,}210} = 1.4 : 1$

As Illustration 6-19 shows, if Caterpillar used FIFO, its current ratio would be 1.4:1 rather than 1.3:1 under LIFO. Thus, Caterpillar's liquidity appears stronger if a FIFO assumption were used in valuing inventories. If a similar adjustment is made for the inventory turnover ratio, Caterpillar's inventory turnover actually would look worse under FIFO than under LIFO, dropping from 5.8 times for LIFO to 3.8 times for FIFO.[2] The reason: LIFO reports low inventory amounts, which cause inventory turnover to be overstated.

CNH Global, a competitor of Caterpillar, uses FIFO to account for its inventory. Comparing Caterpillar to CNH without converting Caterpillar's inventory to FIFO would lead to distortions and potentially erroneous decisions.

BEFORE YOU GO ON . . .

▶Review It

1. What is the purpose of the inventory turnover ratio? What is the relationship between the inventory turnover ratio and average days in inventory?
2. What is the LIFO reserve? What does it tell a financial statement user?

Decision Toolkit

Decision Checkpoints	Info Needed for Decision	Tool to Use for Decision	How to Evaluate Results
What is the impact of LIFO on the company's reported inventory?	LIFO reserve, cost of goods sold, ending inventory, current assets, current liabilities	$\text{LIFO inventory} + \text{LIFO reserve} = \text{FIFO inventory}$	If these adjustments are material, they can significantly affect such measures as the current ratio and the inventory turnover ratio.

---

[2]The LIFO reserve also affects cost of goods sold, although typically by a much less material amount. The cost of goods sold adjustment is discussed in more advanced financial statement analysis texts.

Using the Decision Toolkit

The Manitowoc Company is located in Manitowoc, Wisconsin. In recent years it has made a series of strategic acquisitions to grow and enhance its market-leading positions in each of its three business segments. These include: cranes and related products (crawler cranes, tower cranes, and boom trucks); food service equipment (commercial ice-cube machines, ice-beverage dispensers, and commercial refrigeration equipment); and marine operations (shipbuilding and ship-repair services). The company reported inventory of $287,036,000 for 2004 and of $232,877,000 for 2003. Here is the inventory note taken from the 2004 financial statements.

THE MANITOWOC COMPANY
Notes to the Financial Statements

Inventories: The components of inventories are summarized at December 31 as follows (in thousands).

Components	2004	2003
Raw materials	$111,400	$ 89,851
Work in process	87,825	81,378
Finished goods*	106,348	80,266
Net inventories at FIFO cost	305,573	251,495
Excess of FIFO cost over LIFO value	(18,537)	(18,618)
Inventories—net	$287,036	$232,877

*The finished goods inventories have been reduced to reflect the company's reserve for excess and obsolete inventory.

Manitowoc carries inventory at the lower of cost or market using the first-in, first-out (FIFO) method for 90% and 88% of total inventory for 2004 and 2003, respectively. The remainder of the inventory is costed using the last-in, first-out (LIFO) method.

Additional facts:

2004 Current liabilities	$ 652,680
2004 Current assets (as reported)	$ 845,961
2004 Cost of goods sold	$1,582,131

Instructions

Answer the following questions.

1. Why does the company report its inventory in three components?
2. Why might the company use two methods (LIFO and FIFO) to account for its inventory?
3. Perform each of the following.
   (a) Calculate the inventory turnover ratio and days in inventory using the LIFO inventory.
   (b) Show the conversion of the 2004 and 2003 LIFO inventory values to FIFO values.
   (c) Calculate the 2004 current ratio using LIFO and the current ratio using FIFO. Discuss the difference.

Solution

1. The Manitowoc Company is a manufacturer, so it purchases raw materials and makes them into finished products. At the end of each period, it has some goods that have been started but are not yet complete (work in process).

   By reporting all three components of inventory, a company reveals important information about its inventory position. For example, if amounts of raw materials have increased significantly compared to the previous year, we might assume the company is planning to step up production. On the other hand, if levels of finished goods have increased relative to last year and raw materials have declined, we might conclude that sales are slowing down—that the company has too much inventory on hand and is cutting back production.

2. Companies are free to choose different cost flow assumptions for different types of inventory. A company might choose to use FIFO for a product that is expected to decrease in price over time. One common reason for choosing a method other than LIFO is that many foreign countries do not allow LIFO; thus, the company cannot use LIFO for its foreign operations.

3. (a) $$\frac{\text{Inventory turnover}}{\text{ratio}} = \frac{\text{Cost of goods sold}}{\text{Average inventory}} = \frac{\$1,582,131}{(\$287,036 + \$232,877)/2} = 6.1$$

   $$\frac{\text{Days in}}{\text{inventory}} = \frac{365}{\text{Inventory turnover ratio}} = \frac{365}{6.1} = 59.8 \text{ days}$$

   (b) Conversion from LIFO to FIFO values

	2004	2003
LIFO inventory	$287,036	$232,877
LIFO reserve	18,537	18,618
FIFO inventory	$305,573	$251,495

   (c) Current ratio

LIFO	FIFO
$\dfrac{\text{Current assets}}{\text{Current liabilities}} = \dfrac{\$845,961}{\$652,680} = 1.30:1$	$\dfrac{\$845,961 + \$18,537}{\$652,680} = 1.32:1$

This represents a 1.5% increase in the current ratio $(1.32 - 1.30)/1.30$.

Summary of Study Objectives

1 *Describe the steps in determining inventory quantities.* The steps are (1) taking a physical inventory of goods on hand and (2) determining the ownership of goods in transit or on consignment.

2 *Explain the basis of accounting for inventories and apply the inventory cost flow methods under a periodic inventory system.* The primary basis of accounting for inventories is cost. Cost includes all expenditures necessary to acquire goods and place them in condition ready for sale. Cost of goods available for sale includes (a) cost of beginning inventory and (b) cost of goods purchased. The inventory cost flow methods are: specific identification and three assumed cost flow methods—FIFO, LIFO, and average cost.

3 *Explain the financial statement and tax effects of each of the inventory cost flow assumptions.* The cost of goods available for sale may be allocated to cost of goods sold and ending inventory by specific identification or by a method based on an assumed cost flow. When prices are rising, the first-in, first-out (FIFO) method results in lower cost of goods sold and higher net income than the average cost and the last-in, first-out (LIFO) methods. The reverse is true when prices are falling. In the balance sheet, FIFO results in an ending inventory that is closest to current value, whereas the inventory under LIFO is the farthest from current value. LIFO results in the lowest income taxes (because of lower taxable income).

4 *Explain the lower of cost or market basis of accounting for inventories.* Companies may use the lower of cost or market (LCM) basis when the current replacement cost (market) is less than cost. Under LCM, companies recognize the loss in the period in which the price decline occurs.

5 *Compute and interpret the inventory turnover ratio.* The inventory turnover ratio is calculated as cost of goods sold divided by average inventory. It can be converted to average days in inventory by dividing 365 days by the inventory turnover ratio. A higher turnover ratio or lower average days in inventory suggests that management is trying to keep inventory levels low relative to its sales level.

6 *Describe the LIFO reserve and explain its importance for comparing results of different companies.* The LIFO

reserve represents the difference between ending inventory using LIFO and ending inventory if FIFO were employed instead. For some companies this difference can be significant, and ignoring it can lead to inappropriate conclusions when using the current ratio or inventory turnover ratio.

Decision Toolkit—A Summary

Decision Checkpoints	Info Needed for Decision	Tool to Use for Decision	How to Evaluate Results
Which inventory costing method should be used?	Are prices increasing, or are they decreasing?	Income statement, balance sheet, and tax effects	Depends on objective. In a period of rising prices, income and inventory are higher and cash flow is lower under FIFO. LIFO provides opposite results. Average cost can moderate the impact of changing prices.
How long is an item in inventory?	Cost of goods sold; beginning and ending inventory	$\text{Inventory turnover ratio} = \dfrac{\text{Cost of goods sold}}{\text{Average inventory}}$ $\text{Days in inventory} = \dfrac{365\ \text{days}}{\text{Inventory turnover ratio}}$	A higher inventory turnover ratio or lower average days in inventory suggests that management is reducing the amount of inventory on hand, relative to sales.
What is the impact of LIFO on the company's reported inventory?	LIFO reserve, cost of goods sold, ending inventory, current assets, current liabilities	$\dfrac{\text{LIFO}}{\text{inventory}} + \dfrac{\text{LIFO}}{\text{reserve}} = \dfrac{\text{FIFO}}{\text{inventory}}$	If these adjustments are material, they can significantly affect such measures as the current ratio and the inventory turnover ratio.

APPENDIX 6A
INVENTORY COST FLOW METHODS IN PERPETUAL INVENTORY SYSTEMS

Each of the inventory cost flow methods described in the chapter for a periodic inventory system may be used in a perpetual inventory system. To illustrate the application of the three assumed cost flow methods (FIFO, LIFO, and average cost), we will use the data shown in Illustration 6A-1 (next page) and in this chapter for Houston Electronic's Astro Condenser.

STUDY OBJECTIVE

7

Apply the inventory cost flow methods to perpetual inventory records.

Illustration 6A-1
Inventoriable units and
costs

	HOUSTON ELECTRONICS Astro Condensers				
Date	**Explanation**	**Units**	**Unit Cost**	**Total Cost**	**Balance in Units**
1/1	Beginning inventory	100	$10	$ 1,000	100
4/15	Purchases	200	11	2,200	300
8/24	Purchases	300	12	3,600	600
9/10	Sale	550			50
11/27	Purchases	400	13	5,200	450
				$12,000	

First-In, First-Out (FIFO)

Under FIFO, the cost of the earliest goods on hand **prior to each sale** is charged to cost of goods sold. Therefore, the cost of goods sold on September 10 consists of the units on hand January 1 and the units purchased April 15 and August 24. Illustration 6A-2 shows the inventory under a FIFO method perpetual system.

Illustration 6A-2
Perpetual system—FIFO

Date	Purchases	Cost of Goods Sold	Balance
January 1			(100 @ $10) $ 1,000
April 15	(200 @ $11) $2,200		(100 @ $10)⎫ (200 @ $11)⎭ $ 3,200
August 24	(300 @ $12) $3,600		(100 @ $10)⎫ (200 @ $11)⎬ $ 6,800 (300 @ $12)⎭
September 10		(100 @ $10) (200 @ $11) (250 @ $12) _____ **$6,200**	(50 @ $12) $ 600
November 27	(400 @ $13) $5,200		(50 @ $12)⎫ (400 @ $13)⎭ **$5,800**

The ending inventory in this situation is $5,800, and the cost of goods sold is $6,200 [(100 @ $10) + (200 @ $11) + (250 @ $12)].

The results under FIFO in a perpetual system are the **same as in a periodic system**. (See Illustration 6-5 on page 274 where, similarly, the ending inventory is $5,800 and cost of goods sold is $6,200.) Regardless of the system, the first costs in are the costs assigned to cost of goods sold.

Last-In, First-Out (LIFO)

Under the LIFO method using a perpetual system, the cost of the most recent purchase prior to sale is allocated to the units sold. Therefore, the cost of the goods sold on September 10 consists of all the units from the August 24 and April 15 purchases plus 50 of the units in beginning inventory. The ending inventory under the LIFO method is computed in Illustration 6A-3.

The use of LIFO in a perpetual system will usually produce cost allocations that differ from use of LIFO in a periodic system. In a perpetual system, the latest units purchased *prior to each sale* are allocated to cost of goods sold. In contrast, in a periodic system, the latest units purchased *during the period* are allocated to cost of goods sold. Thus, when a purchase is made after the last sale, the LIFO periodic system will apply this purchase to the previous sale. See

Date	Purchases	Cost of Goods Sold	Balance
January 1			(100 @ $10) $ 1,000
April 15	(200 @ $11) $2,200		(100 @ $10)] $ 3,200 (200 @ $11)]
August 24	(300 @ $12) $3,600		(100 @ $10)] (200 @ $11)} $ 6,800 (300 @ $12)]
September 10		(300 @ $12) (200 @ $11) (50 @ $10) **$6,300**	(50 @ $10) $ 500
November 27	(400 @ $13) $5,200		(50 @ $10)] **$5,700** (400 @ $13)]

Illustration 6-8 (on page 275) where the proof shows the 400 units at $13 purchased on November 27 applied to the sale of 550 units on September 10.

As shown above, under the LIFO perpetual system the 400 units at $13 purchased on November 27 are all applied to the ending inventory.

The ending inventory in this LIFO perpetual illustration is $5,700 and cost of goods sold is $6,300, as compared to the LIFO periodic illustration (on page 275) where the ending inventory is $5,000 and cost of goods sold is $7,000.

Average Cost

The average-cost method in a perpetual inventory system is called the **moving-average method**. Under this method the company computes a new average **after each purchase**. The average cost is computed by dividing the cost of goods available for sale by the units on hand. The average cost is then applied to: (1) the units sold, to determine the cost of goods sold, and (2) the remaining units on hand, to determine the ending inventory amount. Illustration 6A-4 shows the application of the average-cost method by Houston Electronics.

Date	Purchases	Cost of Goods Sold	Balance
January 1			(100 @ $10) $ 1,000
April 15	(200 @ $11) $2,200		(300 @ $10.667) $ 3,200
August 24	(300 @ $12) $3,600		(600 @ $11.333) $ 6,800
September 10		(550 @ $11.333) **$6,233**	(50 @ $11.333) $ 567
November 27	(400 @ $13) $5,200		(450 @ $12.816) **$5,767**

As indicated above, the company computes **a new average each time it makes a purchase**. On April 15, after 200 units are purchased for $2,200, a total of 300 units costing $3,200 ($1,000 + $2,200) are on hand. The average unit cost is $10.667 ($3,200 ÷ 300). On August 24, after 300 units are purchased for $3,600, a total of 600 units costing $6,800 ($1,000 + $2,200 + $3,600) are on hand at an average cost per unit of $11.333 ($6,800 ÷ 600). Houston Electronics uses this unit cost of $11.333 in costing sales until another purchase is made, when the company computes a new unit cost. Accordingly, the unit cost of the 550 units sold on September 10 is $11.333, and the total cost of goods sold is $6,233. On November 27, following the purchase of 400 units for $5,200, there are 450 units on hand costing $5,767 ($567 + $5,200) with a new average cost of $12.816 ($5,767 ÷ 450).

Compare this moving-average cost under the perpetual inventory system to Illustration 6-10 (on page 276) showing the weighted-average method under a periodic inventory system.

Summary of Study Objective for Appendix 6A

7 *Apply the inventory cost flow methods to perpetual inventory records.* Under FIFO, the cost of the earliest goods on hand prior to each sale is charged to cost of goods sold. Under LIFO, the cost of the most re-cent purchase prior to sale is charged to cost of goods sold. Under the average-cost method, a new average cost is computed after each purchase.

APPENDIX 6B
INVENTORY ERRORS

STUDY OBJECTIVE
8
Indicate the effects of inventory errors on the financial statements.

Unfortunately, errors occasionally occur in accounting for inventory. In some cases, errors are caused by failure to count or price the inventory correctly. In other cases, errors occur because companies do not properly recognize the transfer of legal title to goods that are in transit. When errors occur, they affect both the income statement and the balance sheet.

Income Statement Effects

As you know, both the beginning and ending inventories appear in the income statement. The ending inventory of one period automatically becomes the beginning inventory of the next period. Thus, inventory errors affect the computation of cost of goods sold and net income in two periods.

The effects on cost of goods sold can be computed by entering incorrect data in the formula in Illustration 6B-1 and then substituting the correct data.

Illustration 6B-1
Formula for cost of goods sold

$$\text{Beginning Inventory} + \text{Cost of Goods Purchased} - \text{Ending Inventory} = \text{Cost of Goods Sold}$$

If *beginning* inventory is understated, cost of goods sold will be understated. If *ending* inventory is understated, cost of goods sold will be overstated. Illustration 6B-2 shows the effects of inventory errors on the current year's income statement.

Illustration 6B-2 Effects of inventory errors on current year's income statement

Inventory Error	Cost of Goods Sold	Net Income
Understate beginning inventory	Understated	Overstated
Overstate beginning inventory	Overstated	Understated
Understate ending inventory	Overstated	Understated
Overstate ending inventory	Understated	Overstated

An error in the ending inventory of the current period will have a **reverse effect on net income of the next accounting period**. This is shown in Illustration 6B-3. Note that the understatement of ending inventory in 2006 results in an understatement of beginning inventory in 2007 and an overstatement of net income in 2007.

Over the two years, total net income is correct because the errors offset each other. Notice that total income using incorrect data is $35,000 ($22,000 + $13,000), which is the same as the total income of $35,000 ($25,000 + $10,000) using correct data. Also note in this example that an error in the beginning inventory does not result in a corresponding error in the ending inventory for that period. The correctness of the ending inventory depends entirely on the accuracy of taking and costing the inventory at the balance sheet date under the periodic inventory system.

Illustration 6B-3 Effects of inventory errors on two years' income statements

SAMPLE COMPANY Condensed Income Statements							
	2006				**2007**		
	Incorrect		**Correct**		**Incorrect**		**Correct**
Sales		$80,000		$80,000		$90,000		$90,000
Beginning inventory	$20,000		$20,000		**$12,000**		**$15,000**	
Cost of goods purchased	40,000		40,000		68,000		68,000	
Cost of goods available for sale	60,000		60,000		80,000		83,000	
Ending inventory	**12,000**		**15,000**		23,000		23,000	
Cost of goods sold		48,000		45,000		57,000		60,000
Gross profit		32,000		35,000		33,000		30,000
Operating expenses		10,000		10,000		20,000		20,000
Net income		$22,000		$25,000		$13,000		$10,000

$(3,000)
Net income
understated

$3,000
Net income
overstated

**The errors cancel. Thus the combined total
income for the 2-year period is correct.**

Business Insight
INVESTOR PERSPECTIVE

Inventory fraud increases during recessions. Such fraud includes pricing inventory at amounts in excess of its actual value, or claiming to have inventory when no inventory exists. Inventory fraud is usually done to overstate ending inventory, thereby understating cost of goods sold and creating higher income.

Balance Sheet Effects

The effect of ending inventory errors on the balance sheet can be determined by using the basic accounting equation: Assets = Liabilities + Stockholders' equity. Errors in the ending inventory have the effects shown in Illustration 6B-4.

Illustration 6B-4 Effects of ending inventory errors on balance sheet

Ending Inventory Error	Assets	Liabilities	Stockholders' Equity
Overstated	Overstated	No effect	Overstated
Understated	Understated	No effect	Understated

The effect of an error in ending inventory on the subsequent period was shown in Illustration 6B-3. Recall that if the error is not corrected, the combined total net income for the two periods would be correct. Thus, total stockholders' equity reported on the balance sheet at the end of 2007 will also be correct.

Summary of Study Objective for Appendix 6B

8 *Indicate the effects of inventory errors on the financial statements. In the income statement of the current year:* (a) An error in beginning inventory will have a reverse effect on net income (e.g., overstatement of inventory results in understatement of net income, and vice versa). (b) An error in ending inventory will have a similar effect on net income (e.g., overstatement of inventory results in overstatement of net in-

come). If ending inventory errors are not corrected in the following period, their effect on net income for that period is reversed, and total net income for the two years will be correct.

In the balance sheet: Ending inventory errors will have the same effect on total assets and total stockholders' equity and no effect on liabilities.

Glossary

Average-cost method An inventory costing method that uses the weighted average unit cost to allocate the cost of goods available for sale to ending inventory and cost of goods sold. (p. 276)

Consigned goods Goods held for sale by one party (the consignee) although ownership of the goods is retained by another party (the consignor). (p. 271)

Current replacement cost The current cost to replace an inventory item. (p. 280)

Days in inventory Measure of the average number of days inventory is held; calculated as 365 divided by inventory turnover ratio. (p. 281)

Finished goods inventory Manufactured items that are completed and ready for sale. (p. 268)

First-in, first-out (FIFO) method An inventory costing method that assumes that the costs of the earliest goods purchased are the first to be recognized as cost of goods sold. (p. 273)

FOB destination Freight terms indicating that the goods are placed free on board at the buyer's place of business, and the seller pays the freight cost; goods belong to the seller while in transit. (p. 271)

FOB shipping point Freight terms indicating that the goods are placed free on board the carrier by the seller, and the buyer pays the freight cost; goods belong to the buyer while in transit. (p. 270)

Inventory turnover ratio A ratio that measures the number of times on average the inventory sold during

the period; computed by dividing cost of goods sold by the average inventory during the period. (p. 281)

Just-in-time (JIT) inventory Inventory system in which companies manufacture or purchase goods just in time for use. (p. 269)

Last-in, first-out (LIFO) method An inventory costing method that assumes that the costs of the latest units purchased are the first to be allocated to cost of goods sold. (p. 274)

LIFO reserve For a company using LIFO, the difference between inventory reported using LIFO and inventory using FIFO. (p. 283)

Lower of cost or market (LCM) basis (inventories) A basis whereby inventory is stated at the lower of either its cost or its market cost as determined by current replacement cost. (p. 280)

Raw materials Basic goods that will be used in production but have not yet been placed in production. (p. 268)

Specific identification method An actual physical flow costing method in which items still in inventory are specifically costed to arrive at the total cost of the ending inventory. (p. 272)

Weighted average unit cost Average cost that is weighted by the number of units purchased at each unit cost. (p. 276)

Work in process That portion of manufactured inventory that has begun the production process but is not yet complete. (p. 268)

Demonstration Problem

Englehart Company has the following inventory, purchases, and sales data for the month of March.

Inventory, March 1	200 units @ $4.00	$ 800
Purchases		
March 10	500 units @ $4.50	2,250
March 20	400 units @ $4.75	1,900
March 30	300 units @ $5.00	1,500
Sales		
March 15	500 units	
March 25	400 units	

The physical inventory count on March 31 shows 500 units on hand.

Instructions

Under a **periodic inventory system**, determine the cost of inventory on hand at March 31 and the cost of goods sold for March under (a) the first-in, first-out (FIFO) method; (b) the last-in, first-out (LIFO) method; and (c) the average-cost method. (For average cost, carry cost per unit to three decimal places.)

Solution to Demonstration Problem

The cost of goods available for sale is $6,450:

Inventory	200 units @ $4.00	$ 800
Purchases		
March 10	500 units @ $4.50	2,250
March 20	400 units @ $4.75	1,900
March 30	300 units @ $5.00	1,500
Total cost of goods available for sale		$6,450

(a)   FIFO Method

Ending inventory:

Date	Units	Unit Cost	Total Cost	
Mar. 30	300	$5.00	$1,500	
Mar. 20	200	4.75	950	$2,450

Cost of goods sold: $6,450 − $2,450 = $4,000

(b)   LIFO Method

Ending inventory:

Date	Units	Unit Cost	Total Cost	
Mar. 1	200	$4.00	$ 800	
Mar. 10	300	4.50	1,350	$2,150

Cost of goods sold: $6,450 − $2,150 = $4,300

(c)   Weighted Average-Cost Method

Weighted average unit cost: $6,450 ÷ 1,400 = $4.607
Ending inventory: 500 × $4.607 = $2,303.50

Cost of goods sold: $6,450 − $2,303.50 = $4,146.50

Action Plan

- For FIFO, allocate the latest costs to inventory.
- For LIFO, allocate the earliest costs to inventory.
- For average cost, use a weighted average.
- Remember, the costs allocated to cost of goods sold can be proved.
- Total purchases are the same under all three cost flow assumptions.

THE NAVIGATOR

Note: All Questions, Exercises, and Problems marked with an asterisk relate to material in the appendixes to the chapter.

Self-Study Questions

Answers are at the end of the chapter.

(SO 1)   **1.** When is a physical inventory usually taken?
   (a) When the company has its greatest amount of inventory.
   (b) When goods are not being sold or received.
   (c) At the end of the company's fiscal year.
   (d) Both (b) and (c).

2. Which of the following should *not* be included   (SO 1) in the physical inventory of a company?
   (a) Goods held on consignment from another company.
   (b) Goods shipped on consignment to another company.
   (c) Goods in transit from another company shipped FOB shipping point.
   (d) All of the above should be included.

(SO 2) **3.** Kam Company has the following units and costs.

	Units	Unit Cost
Inventory, Jan. 1	8,000	$11
Purchase, June 19	13,000	12
Purchase, Nov. 8	5,000	13

If 9,000 units are on hand at December 31, what is the cost of the ending inventory under FIFO?
(a) $99,000. (c) $113,000.
(b) $108,000. (d) $117,000.

(SO 2) **4.** From the data in question 3, what is the cost of the ending inventory under LIFO?
(a) $113,000. (c) $99,000.
(b) $108,000. (d) $100,000.

(SO 3) **5.** In periods of rising prices, LIFO will produce:
(a) higher net income than FIFO.
(b) the same net income as FIFO.
(c) lower net income than FIFO.
(d) higher net income than average costing.

(SO 3) **6.** Considerations that affect the selection of an inventory costing method do *not* include:
(a) tax effects.
(b) balance sheet effects.
(c) income statement effects.
(d) perpetual versus periodic inventory system.

(SO 4) **7.** The lower of cost or market rule for inventory is an example of the application of:
(a) the conservatism constraint.
(b) the historical cost principle.
(c) the materiality constraint.
(d) the economic entity assumption.

(SO 5) **8.** Which of these would cause the inventory turnover ratio to increase the most?
(a) Increasing the amount of inventory on hand.
(b) Keeping the amount of inventory on hand constant but increasing sales.

(c) Keeping the amount of inventory on hand constant but decreasing sales.
(d) Decreasing the amount of inventory on hand and increasing sales.

(SO 6) **9.** The LIFO reserve is:
(a) the difference between the value of the inventory under LIFO and the value under FIFO.
(b) an amount used to adjust inventory to the lower of cost or market.
(c) the difference between the value of the inventory under LIFO and the value under average cost.
(d) an amount used to adjust inventory to historical cost.

(SO 7) ***10.** In a perpetual inventory system,
(a) LIFO cost of goods sold will be the same as in a periodic inventory system.
(b) average costs are based entirely on unit-cost simple averages.
(c) a new average is computed under the average cost method after each sale.
(d) FIFO cost of goods sold will be the same as in a periodic inventory system.

(SO 8) ***11.** Fran Company's ending inventory is understated by $4,000. The effects of this error on the current year's cost of goods sold and net income, respectively, are:
(a) understated and overstated.
(b) overstated and understated.
(c) overstated and overstated.
(d) understated and understated.

Go to the book's website, **www.wiley.com/college/kimmel**, to access additional Self-Study Questions.

Questions

1. "The key to successful business operations is effective inventory management." Do you agree? Explain.

2. An item must possess two characteristics to be classified as inventory. What are these two characteristics?

3. What is just-in-time inventory management? What are its potential advantages?

4. Your friend Carol Brandon has been hired to help take the physical inventory in Mozena's Hardware Store. Explain to Carol what this job will entail.

5. (a) Michelle Company ships merchandise to Matthew Corporation on December 30. The merchandise reaches the buyer on January 5. Indicate the terms of sale that will result in the goods being included in (1) Michelle's December 31 inventory and (2) Matthew's December 31 inventory.

(b) Under what circumstances should Michelle Company include consigned goods in its inventory?

6. Topp Hat Shop received a shipment of hats for which it paid the wholesaler $2,940. The price of the hats was $3,000, but Topp was given a $60 cash discount and required to pay freight charges of $95. In addition, Topp paid $100 to cover the travel expenses of an employee who negotiated the purchase of the hats. What amount should Topp include in inventory? Why?

7. What is the primary basis of accounting for inventories? What is the major objective in accounting for inventories?

8. Jon Compton believes that the allocation of cost of goods available for sale should be based on the actual physical flow of the goods. Explain to Jon why this may be both impractical and inappropriate.

9. What are the major advantage and major disadvantage of the specific identification method of inventory costing?

10. ➡ "The selection of an inventory cost flow method is a decision made by accountants." Do you agree? Explain. Once a method has been selected, what accounting requirement applies?

11. Which assumed inventory cost flow method:
(a) usually parallels the actual physical flow of merchandise?
(b) assumes that goods available for sale during an accounting period are similar in nature?
(c) assumes that the latest units purchased are the first to be sold?

12. In a period of rising prices, the inventory reported in Alpha Company's balance sheet is close to the current cost of the inventory, whereas Omega Company's inventory is considerably below its current cost. Identify the inventory cost flow method used by each company. Which company probably has been reporting the higher gross profit?

13. Millott Corporation has been using the FIFO cost flow method during a prolonged period of inflation. During the same time period, Millott has been paying out all of its net income as dividends. What adverse effects may result from this policy?

14. ➡ Brian Birdsong, a mid-level product manager for Stella's Shoes, thinks his company should switch from LIFO to FIFO. He says, "My bonus is based on net income. If we switch it will increase net income and increase my bonus. The company would be better off and so would I." Is he correct? Explain.

15. Hayley Carter is studying for the next accounting midterm examination. What should Hayley know about (a) departing from the cost basis of accounting for inventories and (b) the meaning of "market" in the lower of cost or market method?

16. Moondog Music Center has five CD players on hand at the balance sheet date that cost $400 each. The current replacement cost is $320 per unit. Under the lower of cost or market basis of accounting for inventories, what value should Moondog report for the CD players on the balance sheet? Why?

17. ⚿ What cost flow assumption may be used under the lower of cost or market basis of accounting for inventories?

18. Why is it inappropriate for a company to include freight-out expense in the Cost of Goods Sold account?

19. Dawn & Ken Company's balance sheet shows Inventories $162,800. What additional disclosures should be made?

20. ➡ ⚿ Under what circumstances might the inventory turnover ratio be too high—that is, what possible negative consequences might occur?

21. ⚿ What is the LIFO reserve? What are the consequences of ignoring a large LIFO reserve when analyzing a company?

*22. "When perpetual inventory records are kept, the results under the FIFO and LIFO methods are the same as they would be in a periodic inventory system." Do you agree? Explain.

*23. How does the average method of inventory costing differ between a perpetual inventory system and a periodic inventory system?

*24. Linx Company discovers in 2007 that its ending inventory at December 31, 2006, was $5,000 understated. What effect will this error have on (a) 2006 net income, (b) 2007 net income, and (c) the combined net income for the 2 years?

Brief Exercises

BE6-1 Mark Mader Company identifies the following items for possible inclusion in the physical inventory. Indicate whether each item should be included or excluded from the inventory taking.
(a) Goods shipped on consignment by Mader to another company.
(b) Goods in transit from a supplier shipped FOB destination.
(c) Goods sold but being held for customer pickup.
(d) Goods held on consignment from another company.

Identify items to be included in taking a physical inventory.
(SO 1)

BE6-2 In its first month of operations, Minh Lo Company made three purchases of merchandise in the following sequence: (1) 300 units at $6, (2) 400 units at $8, and (3) 500 units at $9. Assuming there are 400 units on hand, compute the cost of the ending inventory under (a) the FIFO method and (b) the LIFO method. Minh Lo uses a periodic inventory system.

Compute ending inventory using FIFO and LIFO.
(SO 2)

Compute the ending inventory using average costs.
(SO 2)

BE6-3 Data for Minh Lo Company are presented in BE6-2. Compute the cost of the ending inventory under the average cost method, assuming there are 400 units on hand. (Round the cost per unit to three decimal places.)

Explain the financial statement effect of inventory cost flow assumptions.
(SO 3)

BE6-4 The management of Laura Corp. is considering the effects of various inventory-costing methods on its financial statements and its income tax expense. Assuming that the price the company pays for inventory is increasing, which method will:
(a) provide the highest net income?
(b) provide the highest ending inventory?
(c) result in the lowest income tax expense?
(d) result in the most stable earnings over a number of years?

Explain the financial statement effect of inventory cost flow assumptions.
(SO 3)

BE6-5 In its first month of operation, Wier Company purchased 100 units of inventory for $6, then 200 units for $7, and finally 150 units for $8. At the end of the month, 160 units remained. Compute the amount of phantom profit that would result if the company used FIFO rather than LIFO. Explain why this amount is referred to as phantom profit. The company uses the periodic method.

Determine the LCM valuation.
(SO 4)

BE6-6 Sunshine Video Center accumulates the following cost and market data at December 31.

Inventory Categories	Cost Data	Market Data
Cameras	$12,000	$13,400
Camcorders	9,000	9,500
DVDs	13,000	12,800

Compute the lower of cost or market valuation for Sunshine's inventory.

Compute inventory turnover ratio and days in inventory.
(SO 5)

BE6-7 At December 31, 2004, the following information (in thousands) was available for sunglasses manufacturer Oakley, Inc.: ending inventory $115,061; beginning inventory $98,691; cost of goods sold $265,104; and sales revenue $585,468. Calculate the inventory turnover ratio and days in inventory for Oakley, Inc.

Determine ending inventory and cost of goods sold using LIFO reserve.
(SO 6)

BE6-8 Winnebago Industries, Inc. is a leading manufacturer of motor homes. Winnebago reported ending inventory at August 28, 2004, of $130,733,000 under the LIFO inventory method. In the notes to its financial statements, Winnebago reported a LIFO reserve of $27,192,000 at August 28, 2004. What would Winnebago Industries' ending inventory have been if it had used FIFO?

Apply cost flow methods to perpetual inventory records.
(SO 7)

*BE6-9 Bruno's Department Store uses a perpetual inventory system. Data for product E2-D2 include the following purchases.

Date	Number of Units	Unit Price
May 7	50	$12
July 28	30	15

On June 1 Bruno sold 35 units, and on August 27, 33 more units. Compute the cost of goods sold using (1) FIFO, (2) LIFO, and (3) average cost.

Determine correct financial statement amount.
(SO 8)

*BE6-10 Shaunna Company reports net income of $84,000 in 2007. However, ending inventory was understated by $7,000. What is the correct net income for 2007? What effect, if any, will this error have on total assets as reported in the balance sheet at December 31, 2007?

Exercises

E6-1 Springfield Bank and Trust is considering giving Homer Company a loan. Before doing so, they decide that further discussions with Homer's accountant may be desirable. One area of particular concern is the inventory account, which has a year-end balance of $295,000. Discussions with the accountant reveal the following.

Determine the correct inventory amount.
(SO 1)

1. Homer sold goods costing $55,000 to Moe Company FOB shipping point on December 28. The goods are not expected to reach Moe until January 12. The goods were not included in the physical inventory because they were not in the warehouse.
2. The physical count of the inventory did not include goods costing $95,000 that were shipped to Homer FOB destination on December 27 and were still in transit at year-end.
3. Homer received goods costing $25,000 on January 2. The goods were shipped FOB shipping point on December 26 by Lenny Co. The goods were not included in the physical count.
4. Homer sold goods costing $51,000 to Flanders of Canada FOB destination on December 30. The goods were received in Canada on January 8. They were not included in Homer's physical inventory.
5. Homer received goods costing $37,000 on January 2 that were shipped FOB destination on December 29. The shipment was a rush order that was supposed to arrive December 31. This purchase was included in the ending inventory of $295,000.

Instructions
Determine the correct inventory amount on December 31.

E6-2 Dennis Lee, an auditor with Knapp CPAs, is performing a review of Nathan Company's inventory account. Nathan did not have a good year, and top management is under pressure to boost reported income. According to its records, the inventory balance at year-end was $740,000. However, the following information was not considered when determining that amount.

Determine the correct inventory amount.
(SO 1)

1. Included in the company's count were goods with a cost of $250,000 that the company is holding on consignment. The goods belong to Anya Corporation.
2. The physical count did not include goods purchased by Nathan with a cost of $40,000 that were shipped FOB shipping point on December 28 and did not arrive at Nathan's warehouse until January 3.
3. Included in the inventory account was $17,000 of office supplies that were stored in the warehouse and were to be used by the company's supervisors and managers during the coming year.
4. The company received an order on December 29 that was boxed and was sitting on the loading dock awaiting pick-up on December 31. The shipper picked up the goods on January 1 and delivered them on January 6. The shipping terms were FOB shipping point. The goods had a selling price of $40,000 and a cost of $30,000. The goods were not included in the count because they were sitting on the dock.
5. On December 29 Nathan shipped goods with a selling price of $80,000 and a cost of $60,000 to Central Sales Corporation FOB shipping point. The goods arrived on January 3. Central Sales had only ordered goods with a selling price of $10,000 and a cost of $8,000. However, a sales manager at Nathan had authorized the shipment and said that if Central wanted to ship the goods back next week, it could.
6. Included in the count was $50,000 of goods that were parts for a machine that the company no longer made. Given the high-tech nature of Nathan's products, it was unlikely that these obsolete parts had any other use. However, management would prefer to keep them on the books at cost, "since that is what we paid for them, after all."

Instructions
Prepare a schedule to determine the correct inventory amount. Provide explanations for each item above, saying why you did or did not make an adjustment for each item.

E6-3 Shippers Inc. had the following inventory situations to consider at January 31, its year end.

Identify items in inventory.
(SO 1)

(a) Goods held on consignment for MailBoxes Corp. since December 12.
(b) Goods shipped on consignment to Rinehart Holdings Inc. on January 5.
(c) Goods shipped to a customer, FOB destination, on January 29 that are still in transit.

(d) Goods shipped to a customer, FOB shipping point, on January 29 that are still in transit.

(e) Goods purchased FOB destination from a supplier on January 25, that are still in transit.

(f) Goods purchased FOB shipping point from a supplier on January 25, that are still in transit.

(g) Office supplies on hand at January 31.

Instructions

Identify which of the preceding items should be included in inventory. If the item should not be included in inventory, state where it should be recorded.

Compute inventory and cost of goods sold using periodic FIFO and LIFO.
(SO 2)

E6-4 Boarders sells a snowboard, Xpert, that is popular with snowboard enthusiasts. Below is information relating to Boarders's purchases of Xpert snowboards during September. During the same month, 118 Xpert snowboards were sold. Boarders uses a periodic inventory system.

Date	Explanation	Units	Unit Cost	Total Cost
Sept. 1	Inventory	14	$ 97	$ 1,358
Sept. 12	Purchases	45	102	4,590
Sept. 19	Purchases	20	104	2,080
Sept. 26	Purchases	50	105	5,250
	Totals	129		$13,278

Instructions

(a) Compute the ending inventory at September 30 using the FIFO and LIFO methods. Prove the amount allocated to cost of goods sold under each method.

(b) For both FIFO and LIFO, calculate the sum of ending inventory and cost of goods sold. What do you notice about the answers you found for each method?

Calculate inventory and cost of goods sold using FIFO, average, and LIFO in a periodic inventory system.
(SO 2)

E6-5 Lois Inc. uses a periodic inventory system. Its records show the following for the month of May, in which 78 units were sold.

Date	Explanation	Units	Unit Cost	Total Cost
May 1	Inventory	30	$ 8	$240
15	Purchase	25	10	250
24	Purchase	40	11	440
	Total	95		$930

Instructions

Calculate the ending inventory at May 31 using the (a) FIFO, (b) average-cost, and (c) LIFO methods. (For average cost, round the average unit cost to three decimal places.) Prove the amount allocated to cost of goods sold under each method.

Calculate cost of goods sold using specific identification and FIFO periodic.
(SO 2, 3)

E6-6 On December 1, Bargain Electronics has three DVD players left in stock. All are identical, all are priced to sell at $85. One of the three DVD players left in stock, with serial #1012, was purchased on June 1 at a cost of $52. Another, with serial #1045, was purchased on November 1 for $45. The last player, serial #1056, was purchased on November 30 for $43.

Instructions

(a) Calculate the cost of goods sold using the FIFO periodic inventory method assuming that two of the three players were sold by the end of December, Bargain Electronic's year-end.

(b) If Bargain Electronics used the specific identification method instead of the FIFO method, how might it alter its earnings by "selectively choosing" which particular players to sell to the two customers? What would Bargain's cost of goods sold be if the company wished to minimize earnings? Maximize earnings?

(c) Which inventory method, FIFO or specific identification, do you recommend that Bargain use? Explain why.

E6-7   Plato Company reports the following for the month of June.

Instructions

Compute inventory and cost of goods sold using periodic FIFO, LIFO, and average cost.
(SO 2, 3)

Date	Explanation	Units	Unit Cost	Total Cost
June 1	Inventory	225	$5	$1,125
12	Purchase	375	6	2,250
23	Purchase	500	7	3,500
30	Inventory	180		

(a) Compute the cost of the ending inventory and the cost of goods sold under (1) FIFO, (2) LIFO, and (3) average cost.
(b) Which costing method gives the highest ending inventory? The highest cost of goods sold? Why?
(c) How do the average-cost values for ending inventory and cost of goods sold relate to ending inventory and cost of goods sold for FIFO and LIFO?
(d) Explain why the average cost is not $6.

E6-8   This information is available for PepsiCo, Inc. for 2002, 2003, and 2004.

Compute inventory turnover ratio, days in inventory, and gross profit rate.
(SO 5)

(in millions)	2002	2003	2004
Beginning inventory	$ 1,310	$ 1,342	$ 1,412
Ending inventory	1,342	1,412	1,541
Cost of goods sold	11,497	12,379	13,406
Sales	25,112	26,971	29,261

Instructions
Calculate the inventory turnover ratio, days in inventory, and gross profit rate for PepsiCo., Inc. for 2002, 2003, and 2004. Comment on any trends.

E6-9   Cody Camera Shop Inc. uses the lower of cost or market basis for its inventory. The following data are available at December 31.

Determine LCM valuation.
(SO 4)

	Units	Cost/Unit	Market Value/Unit
Cameras			
Minolta	5	$175	$160
Canon	7	150	152
Light Meters			
Vivitar	12	125	119
Kodak	10	115	135

Instructions
What amount should be reported on Cody Camera Shop's financial statements, assuming the lower of cost or market rule is applied?

E6-10   Deere & Company is a global manufacturer and distributor of agricultural, construction, and forestry equipment. It reported the following information in its 2004 annual report.

Determine the effect of the LIFO reserve on current ratio.
(SO 5, 6)

(in millions)	2004	2003
Inventories (LIFO)	$ 1,999	1,366
Current assets	21,844	
Current liabilities	7,889	
LIFO reserve	1,002	
Cost of goods sold	13,568	

Instructions
(a) Compute Deere's inventory turnover ratio and days in inventory for 2004.
(b) Compute Deere's current ratio using the 2004 data as presented, and then again after adjusting for the LIFO reserve.
(c) Comment on how ignoring the LIFO reserve might affect your evaluation of Deere's liquidity.

Calculate inventory and cost of goods sold using three cost flow methods in a perpetual inventory system.
(SO 7)

*E6-11 Inventory data for Plato Company are presented in E6-7.

Instructions
(a) Calculate the cost of the ending inventory and the cost of goods sold for each cost flow assumption, using a perpetual inventory system. Assume a sale of 430 units occurred on June 15 for a selling price of $8 and a sale of 490 units on June 27 for $9. (*Note:* For the average-cost method, round unit cost to three decimal places.)
(b) How do the results differ from E6-7?
(c) Why is the average unit cost not $6 [($5 + $6 + $7) ÷ 3 = $6]?

Apply cost flow methods to perpetual records.
(SO 7)

*E6-12 Information about Boarders is presented in E6-4. Additional data regarding the company's sales of Xpert snowboards are provided below. Assume that Boarders uses a perpetual inventory system.

Date		Units
Sept. 5	Sale	8
Sept. 16	Sale	48
Sept. 29	Sale	62
	Totals	118

Instructions
(a) Compute ending inventory at September 30 using FIFO, LIFO, and average cost. (*Note:* For average cost, round unit cost to three decimal places.)
(b) Compare ending inventory for FIFO and LIFO using a perpetual inventory system to ending inventory using a periodic inventory system (from E6-4).
(c) Which inventory cost flow method (FIFO, LIFO) gives the same ending inventory value under both periodic and perpetual? Which method gives different ending inventory values?

Determine effects of inventory errors.
(SO 8)

*E6-13 Disch Hardware reported cost of goods sold as follows.

	2008	2007
Beginning inventory	$ 30,000	$ 20,000
Cost of goods purchased	175,000	164,000
Cost of goods available for sale	205,000	184,000
Ending inventory	37,000	30,000
Cost of goods sold	$168,000	$154,000

Disch made two errors:
1. 2007 ending inventory was overstated by $4,000.
2. 2008 ending inventory was understated by $2,000.

Instructions
Compute the correct cost of goods sold for each year.

Prepare correct income statements.
(SO 8)

*E6-14 Miller Company reported these income statement data for a 2-year period.

	2008	2007
Sales	$250,000	$210,000
Beginning inventory	40,000	34,000
Cost of goods purchased	202,000	173,000
Cost of goods available for sale	242,000	207,000
Ending inventory	55,000	40,000
Cost of goods sold	187,000	167,000
Gross profit	$ 63,000	$ 43,000

Miller Company uses a periodic inventory system. The inventories at January 1, 2007, and December 31, 2008, are correct. However, the ending inventory at December 31, 2007, is overstated by $5,000.

Instructions
(a) Prepare correct income statement data for the 2 years.
(b) What is the cumulative effect of the inventory error on total gross profit for the 2 years?
(c) Explain in a letter to the president of Miller Company what has happened—that is, the nature of the error and its effect on the financial statements.

Problems: Set A

P6-1A Schilling Limited is trying to determine the value of its ending inventory as of February 28, 2007, the company's year-end. The accountant counted everything that was in the warehouse, as of February 28, which resulted in an ending inventory valuation of $48,000. However, she didn't know how to treat the following transactions so she didn't record them.

Determine items and amounts to be recorded in inventory.
(SO 1)

(a) On February 26, Schilling shipped to a customer goods costing $800. The goods were shipped FOB shipping point, and the receiving report indicates that the customer received the goods on March 2.
(b) On February 26, Seller Inc. shipped goods to Schilling FOB destination. The invoice price was $350 plus $25 for freight. The receiving report indicates that the goods were received by Schilling on March 2.
(c) Schilling had $500 of inventory at a customer's warehouse "on approval." The customer was going to let Schilling know whether it wanted the merchandise by the end of the week, March 4.
(d) Schilling also had $400 of inventory at a Balena craft shop, on consignment from Schilling.
(e) On February 26, Schilling ordered goods costing $750. The goods were shipped FOB shipping point on February 27. Schilling received the goods on March 1.
(f) On February 28, Schilling packaged goods and had them ready for shipping to a customer FOB destination. The invoice price was $350 plus $25 for freight; the cost of the items was $280. The receiving report indicates that the goods were received by the customer on March 2.
(g) Schilling had damaged goods set aside in the warehouse because they are no longer saleable. These goods originally cost $400 and, originally, Schilling expected to sell these items for $600.

Instructions
For each of the above transactions, specify whether the item in question should be included in ending inventory, and if so, at what amount. For each item that is not included in ending inventory, indicate who owns it and what account, if any, it should have been recorded in.

P6-2A Classic Distribution markets CDs of numerous performing artists. At the beginning of March, Classic had in beginning inventory 1,500 CDs with a unit cost of $7. During March Classic made the following purchases of CDs.

Determine cost of goods sold and ending inventory using FIFO, LIFO, and average cost, with analysis.
(SO 2, 3)

| March 5 | 2,000 @ $8 | March 21 | 6,000 @ $10 |
| March 13 | 5,500 @ $9 | March 26 | 2,000 @ $11 |

During March 13,000 units were sold. Classic uses a periodic inventory system.

Instructions
(a) Determine the cost of goods available for sale.
(b) Determine (1) the ending inventory and (2) the cost of goods sold under each of the assumed cost flow methods (FIFO, LIFO, and average cost). Prove the accuracy of the cost of goods sold under the FIFO and LIFO methods. (*Note:* For average cost, round cost per unit to three decimal places.)
(c) Which cost flow method results in (1) the highest inventory amount for the balance sheet and (2) the highest cost of goods sold for the income statement?

Cost of goods sold:
FIFO $116,000
LIFO $127,000
Average $120,824

Cost of goods sold:
  FIFO $17,000
  LIFO $18,200
  Average $17,591

*Compute ending inventory,
prepare income statements,
and answer questions using
FIFO and LIFO.*
(SO 2, 3)

Gross profit:
  FIFO $351,000
  LIFO $324,000

*Calculate ending inventory,
cost of goods sold, gross
profit, and gross profit rate
under periodic method;
compare results.*
(SO 2, 3)

Gross profit:
  LIFO $2,890
  FIFO $3,150
  Average $3,036

P6-3A McLean Company Inc. had a beginning inventory of 300 units of Product MLN at a cost of $8 per unit. During the year, purchases were:

Feb. 20	700 units at $ 9	Aug. 12	600 units at $11
May 5	500 units at $10	Dec. 8	100 units at $12

McLean Company uses a periodic inventory system. Sales totalled 1,800 units.

Instructions
(a) Determine the cost of goods available for sale.
(b) Determine the ending inventory and the cost of goods sold under each of the assumed cost flow methods (FIFO, LIFO, and average cost). Prove the accuracy of the cost of goods sold under the FIFO and LIFO methods. (Round average unit cost to three decimal places.)
(c) Which cost flow method results in the lowest inventory amount for the balance sheet? The lowest cost of goods sold for the income statement?

P6-4A The management of Stampfer Inc. asks your help in determining the comparative effects of the FIFO and LIFO inventory cost flow methods. For 2007 the accounting

Inventory, January 1 (10,000 units)	$ 35,000
Cost of 120,000 units purchased	480,000
Selling price of 100,000 units sold	730,000
Operating expenses	120,000

records show these data.
Units purchased consisted of 35,000 units at $3.70 on May 10; 60,000 units at $3.90 on August 15; and 25,000 units at $4.66 on November 20. Income taxes are 28%.

Instructions
(a) Prepare comparative condensed income statements for 2007 under FIFO and LIFO. (Show computations of ending inventory.)
(b) Answer the following questions for management in the form of a business letter.
  (1) Which inventory cost flow method produces the most meaningful inventory amount for the balance sheet? Why?
  (2) Which inventory cost flow method produces the most meaningful net income? Why?
  (3) Which inventory cost flow method is most likely to approximate the actual physical flow of the goods? Why?
  (4) How much more cash will be available under LIFO than under FIFO? Why?
  (5) How much of the gross profit under FIFO is illusionary in comparison with the gross profit under LIFO?

P6-5A You have the following information for Benton Inc. for the month ended October 31, 2007. Benton uses a periodic method for inventory.

Date	Description	Units	Unit Cost or Selling Price
October 1	Beginning inventory	60	$25
October 9	Purchase	120	27
October 11	Sale	100	35
October 17	Purchase	90	28
October 22	Sale	60	40
October 25	Purchase	80	29
October 29	Sale	120	40

Instructions
(a) Calculate (i) ending inventory, (ii) cost of goods sold, (iii) gross profit, and (iv) gross profit rate under each of the following methods.
  (1) LIFO.
  (2) FIFO.
  (3) Average cost. (Round cost per unit to three decimal places.)
(b) Compare results for the three cost flow assumptions.

P6-6A You have the following information for Rock Bottom Rocks. Rock Bottom uses the periodic method of accounting for its inventory transactions. Rock Bottom only carries one brand and size of diamonds—all are identical. Each batch of diamonds purchased is carefully coded and marked with its purchase cost.

March 1 Beginning inventory 200 diamonds at a cost of $300 per diamond.
March 3 Purchased 200 diamonds at a cost of $360 each.
March 5 Sold 180 diamonds for $600 each.
March 10 Purchased 330 diamonds at a cost of $375 each.
March 25 Sold 500 diamonds for $650 each.

Instructions
(a) Assume that Rock Bottom Rocks uses the specific identification cost flow method.
  (1) Demonstrate how Rock Bottom could maximize its gross profit for the month by specifically selecting which diamonds to sell on March 5 and March 25.
  (2) Demonstrate how Rock Bottom could minimize its gross profit for the month by selecting which diamonds to sell on March 5 and March 25.
(b) Assume that Rock Bottom uses the FIFO cost flow assumption. Calculate cost of goods sold. How much gross profit would Rock Bottom report under this cost flow assumption?
(c) Assume that Rock Bottom uses the LIFO cost flow assumption. Calculate cost of goods sold. How much gross profit would the company report under this cost flow assumption?
(d) Which cost flow method should Rock Bottom Rocks select? Explain.

Gross profit:
  Maximum $196,000
  Minimum $192,250

P6-7A This information is available for the Automotive and Other Operations Divisions of General Motors Corporation for 2004. General Motors uses the LIFO inventory method.

(in millions)	**2004**
Beginning inventory	$ 10,960
Ending inventory	11,717
LIFO reserve	1,442
Current assets	55,515
Current liabilities	74,892
Cost of goods sold	150,053
Sales	161,545

Instructions
(a) Calculate the inventory turnover ratio and days in inventory.
(b) Calculate the current ratio based on inventory as reported using LIFO.
(c) Calculate the current ratio after adjusting for the LIFO reserve.
(d) Comment on any difference between parts (b) and (c).

*P6-8A Psang Inc. is a retailer operating in Edmonton, Alberta. Psang uses the perpetual inventory method. All sales returns from customers result in the goods being returned to inventory. (Assume that the inventory is not damaged.) Assume that there are no credit transactions; all amounts are settled in cash. You are provided with the following information for Psang Inc. for the month of January 2007.

Date	Description	Quantity	Unit Cost or Selling Price
December 31	Ending inventory	160	$18
January 2	Purchase	100	20
January 6	Sale	180	40
January 9	Sale return	10	40
January 9	Purchase	75	24
January 10	Purchase return	15	24
January 10	Sale	50	45
January 23	Purchase	100	28
January 30	Sale	140	50

Instructions
(a) For each of the following cost flow assumptions, calculate (i) cost of goods sold, (ii) ending inventory, and (iii) gross profit.
 (1) LIFO. (Assume sales returns had a cost of $18 and purchase returns had a cost of $24.)
 (2) FIFO. (Assume sales returns had a cost of $18 and purchase returns had a cost of $24.)
 (3) Moving-average. (Round cost per unit to three decimal places.)
(b) Compare results for the three cost flow assumptions.

Determine ending inventory under a perpetual inventory system.
(SO 3, 7)

*P6-9A   Savings Center began operations on July 1. It uses a perpetual inventory system. During July the company had the following purchases and sales.

Date	Purchases Units	Purchases Unit Cost	Sales Units
July 1	7	$ 93	
July 6			3
July 11	4	$ 99	
July 14			3
July 21	3	$106	
July 27			5

Instructions
(a) Determine the ending inventory under a perpetual inventory system using (1) FIFO, (2) average cost (round unit cost to three decimal places), and (3) LIFO.
(b) Which costing method produces the highest ending inventory valuation?

Problems: Set B

Determine items and amounts to be recorded in inventory.
(SO 1)

P6-1B   Norby Limited is trying to determine the value of its ending inventory as of February 28, 2007, the company's year-end. The following transactions occurred, and the accountant asked your help in determining whether they should be recorded or not.
(a) On February 26, Norby shipped goods costing $800 to a customer and charged the customer $1,000. The goods were shipped with terms FOB destination and the receiving report indicates that the customer received the goods on March 2.
(b) On February 26, Seller Inc. shipped goods to Norby under terms FOB shipping point. The invoice price was $350 plus $25 for freight. The receiving report indicates that the goods were received by Norby on March 2.
(c) Norby had $500 of inventory isolated in the warehouse. The inventory is designated for a customer who has requested that the goods be shipped on March 10.
(d) Also included in Norby's warehouse is $400 of inventory that Meredith Producers shipped to Norby on consignment.
(e) On February 26, Norby issued a purchase order to acquire goods costing $750. The goods were shipped with terms FOB destination on February 27. Norby received the goods on March 2.
(f) On February 26, Norby shipped goods to a customer under terms FOB shipping point. The invoice price was $350 plus $25 for freight; the cost of the items was $280. The receiving report indicates that the goods were received by the customer on March 2.

Instructions
For each of the above transactions, specify whether the item in question should be included in ending inventory, and if so, at what amount.

Determine cost of goods sold and ending inventory using FIFO, LIFO, and average cost with analysis.
(SO 2, 3)

P6-2B   Tween Distribution markets CDs of the performing artist Little Sister. At the beginning of October, Tween had in beginning inventory 1,000 Sister's CDs with a unit cost of $5. During October Tween made the following purchases of Sister's CDs.

Oct. 3	4,000 @ $6	Oct. 19	2,000 @ $8
Oct. 9	3,000 @ $7	Oct. 25	2,500 @ $9

During October 9,500 units were sold. Tween uses a periodic inventory system.

Gross profit:
 LIFO $8,010
 FIFO $8,610
 Average $8,396

FIFO $318
Average $300
LIFO $279

Instructions

(a) Determine the cost of goods available for sale.

(b) Determine (1) the ending inventory and (2) the cost of goods sold under each of the assumed cost flow methods (FIFO, LIFO, and average cost). Prove the accuracy of the cost of goods sold under the FIFO and LIFO methods.

(c) Which cost flow method results in (1) the highest inventory amount for the balance sheet and (2) the highest cost of goods sold for the income statement?

Cost of goods sold:
FIFO $62,000
LIFO $71,500
Average $67,260

P6-3B   Prairie Company had a beginning inventory on January 1 of 100 units of Product SXL at a cost of $20 per unit. During the year, purchases were:

| Mar. 15 | 300 units at $22 | Sept. 4 | 350 units at $27 |
| July 20 | 250 units at $25 | Dec. 2 | 100 units at $30 |

Prairie Company sold 850 units, and it uses a periodic inventory system.

Determine cost of goods sold and ending inventory using FIFO, LIFO, and average cost in a periodic inventory system and assess financial statement effects.
(SO 2, 3)

Instructions

(a) Determine the cost of goods available for sale.

(b) Determine the ending inventory and the cost of goods sold under each of the assumed cost flow methods (FIFO, LIFO, and average cost). Prove the accuracy of the cost of goods sold under each method. (Round cost per unit to three decimal places.)

(c) Which cost flow method results in the highest inventory amount for the balance sheet? The highest cost of goods sold for the income statement?

Cost of goods sold:
FIFO $20,250
LIFO $22,000
Average $21,095

P6-4B   The management of Caradeo is reevaluating the appropriateness of using its present inventory cost flow method, which is average cost. The company requests your help in determining the results of operations for 2007 if either the FIFO or the LIFO method had been used. For 2007 the accounting records show these data:

Compute ending inventory, prepare income statements, and answer questions using FIFO and LIFO.
(SO 2, 3)

Inventories		**Purchases and Sales**	
Beginning (10,000 units)	$22,800	Total net sales (222,000 units)	$862,000
Ending (18,000 units)		Total cost of goods purchased	
		(230,000 units)	571,000

Purchases were made quarterly as follows.

Quarter	Units	Unit Cost	Total Cost
1	60,000	$2.30	$138,000
2	50,000	2.40	120,000
3	50,000	2.55	127,500
4	70,000	2.65	185,500
	230,000		$571,000

Operating expenses were $147,000, and the company's income tax rate is 32%.

Instructions

(a) Prepare comparative condensed income statements for 2007 under FIFO and LIFO. (Show computations of ending inventory.)

(b) Answer the following questions for management in business-letter form.

(1) Which cost flow method (FIFO or LIFO) produces the more meaningful inventory amount for the balance sheet? Why?

(2) Which cost flow method (FIFO or LIFO) produces the more meaningful net income? Why?

(3) Which cost flow method (FIFO or LIFO) is more likely to approximate the actual physical flow of goods? Why?

(4) How much more cash will be available for management under LIFO than under FIFO? Why?

(5) Will gross profit under the average cost method be higher or lower than FIFO? Than LIFO? (*Note:* It is not necessary to quantify your answer.)

Gross profit:
FIFO $315,900
LIFO $309,400

Calculate ending inventory, cost of goods sold, gross profit, and gross profit rate under periodic method; compare results.
(SO 2, 3)

P6-5B You have the following information for Venus Inc. for the month ended June 30, 2007. Venus uses the periodic method for inventory.

Date	Description	Quantity	Unit Cost or Selling Price
June 1	Beginning inventory	25	$60
June 4	Purchase	85	64
June 10	Sale	70	90
June 11	Sale return	5	90
June 18	Purchase	40	68
June 18	Purchase return	15	68
June 25	Sale	50	95
June 28	Purchase	20	75

Gross profit:
 LIFO $2,920
 FIFO $3,320
 Average $3,077

Instructions
(a) Calculate (i) ending inventory, (ii) cost of goods sold, (iii) gross profit, and (iv) gross profit rate under each of the following methods.
  (1) LIFO.
  (2) FIFO.
  (3) Average cost. (Round cost per unit to three decimal places.)
(b) Compare results for the three cost flow assumptions.

Compare specific identification, FIFO, and LIFO under periodic method; use cost flow assumption to justify price increase.
(SO 2, 3)

P6-6B You have the following information for Petrol Plus. Petrol Plus uses the periodic method of accounting for its inventory transactions.

March	1	Beginning inventory 1,200 litres at a cost of 40¢ per litre.
March	3	Purchased 2,000 litres at a cost of 45¢ per litre.
March	5	Sold 1,500 litres for 60¢ per litre.
March	10	Purchased 3,700 litres at a cost of 49¢ per litre.
March	20	Purchased 2,000 litres at a cost of 55¢ per litre.
March	30	Sold 5,000 litres for 70¢ per litre.

Instructions

Gross profit:
 Specific
 identification $1,276
 FIFO $1,403
 LIFO $1,127

(a) Prepare partial income statements through gross profit, and calculate the value of ending inventory that would be reported on the balance sheet, under each of the following cost flow assumptions.
  (1) Specific identification method assuming:
    (i) the March 5 sale consisted of 700 litres from the March 1 beginning inventory and 800 litres from the March 3 purchase; and
    (ii) the March 30 sale consisted of the following number of units sold from each purchase: 400 litres from March 1; 500 litres from March 3; 2,600 litres from March 10; 1,500 litres from March 20.
  (2) FIFO.
  (3) LIFO.
(b) How can companies use a cost flow method to justify price increases? Which cost flow method would best support an argument to increase prices?

Compute inventory turnover ratio, days in inventory, and current ratio based on LIFO and after adjusting for LIFO reserve.
(SO 5, 6)

P6-7B Gehl Company manufactures a full line of construction and agriculture equipment. The following information is available for Gehl for 2004. The company uses the LIFO inventory method.

(in thousands)	2004
Beginning inventory	$ 31,598
Ending inventory	38,925
LIFO reserve	27,810
Current assets	252,007
Current liabilities	89,159
Cost of goods sold	289,910
Sales	361,598

Instructions

(a) Calculate the inventory turnover ratio and days in inventory.
(b) Calculate the current ratio based on LIFO inventory.
(c) After adjusting for the LIFO reserve, calculate the current ratio.
(d) Comment on any difference between parts (b) and (c).

*P6-8B Skogmo Inc. is a retail company that uses the perpetual inventory method. All sales returns from customers result in the goods being returned to inventory. (Assume that the inventory is not damaged.) Assume that there are no credit transactions; all amounts are settled in cash. You have the following information for Skogmo Inc. for the month of January 2007.

Calculate cost of goods sold, ending inventory, and gross profit under LIFO, FIFO, and average cost under the perpetual system; compare results.

(SO 3, 7)

Date	Description	Quantity	Unit Cost or Selling Price
January 1	Beginning inventory	40	$12
January 5	Purchase	100	14
January 8	Sale	75	25
January 10	Sale return	10	25
January 15	Purchase	30	18
January 16	Purchase return	5	18
January 20	Sale	90	25
January 25	Purchase	20	20

Gross profit:
LIFO $1,665
FIFO $1,725
Average $1,691

Instructions

(a) For each of the following cost flow assumptions, calculate (i) cost of goods sold, (ii) ending inventory, and (iii) gross profit.
   (1) LIFO. (Assume sales returns had a cost of $14 and purchase returns had a cost of $18.)
   (2) FIFO. (Assume sales returns had a cost of $14 and purchase returns had a cost of $18.)
   (3) Moving-average cost. (Round cost per unit to three decimal places.)
(b) Compare results for the three cost flow assumptions.

*P6-9B Save-U-More Center began operations on July 1. It uses a perpetual inventory system. During July the company had the following purchases and sales.

Determine ending inventory under a perpetual inventory system.

(SO 3, 7)

Date	Purchases Units	Purchases Unit Cost	Sales Units
July 1	6	$31	
July 6			4
July 11	5	$34	
July 14			3
July 21	3	$36	
July 27			2

Instructions

(a) Determine the ending inventory under a perpetual inventory system using (1) FIFO, (2) average cost, and (3) LIFO. (*Note:* For average cost, round cost per unit to three decimal places.)
(b) Which costing method produces the highest ending inventory valuation?

FIFO $176
Average $172
LIFO $166

Problems: Set C

Visit the book's website at **www.wiley.com/college/kimmel** and choose the Student Companion site to access Problem Set C.

Comprehensive Problem

CP6 On December 1, 2007, Rodriquez Company had the account balances shown on page 308.

	Debits		**Credits**
Cash	$ 4,800	Accumulated Depreciation—	$ 1,500
Accounts Receivable	3,900	Equipment	
Merchandise Inventory	1,800*	Accounts Payable	3,000
Equipment	21,000	Common Stock	10,000
	$31,500	Retained Earnings	17,000
			$31,500

*(3,000 × $0.60)

The following transactions occurred during December.

Dec. 3 Purchased 4,000 units on account at a cost of $0.70 per unit.
    5 Sold 4,500 units on account for $0.90 per unit. (It sold 3,000 of the $0.60 units and 1,500 of the $0.70)
    7 Granted the December 5 customer $180 credit for 200 units returned costing $140. These units were returned to inventory.
    17 Purchased 2,400 units for cash at $0.75 each.
    22 Sold 2,000 units on account for $0.95 per unit. (It sold 2,000 of the $0.70 units).

Adjustment data:

1. Accrued salaries payable $400.
2. Depreciation $200 per month.

Instructions
(a) Journalize the December transactions and adjusting entries assuming Rodriguez uses the perpetual inventory method.
(b) Enter the December 1 balances in the ledger T accounts and post the December transactions. In addition to the accounts mentioned above use the following additional accounts: Cost of Goods Sold, Depreciation Expense, Salaries Expense, Salaries Payable, Sales, and Sales Returns and Allowances.
(c) Prepare an adjusted trial balance as of December 31, 2007.
(d) Prepare an income statement for December 2007 and a classified balance sheet at December 31, 2007.
(e) Compute ending inventory and cost of goods sold under FIFO assuming Rodriquez Company uses the periodic inventory system.
(f) Compute ending inventory and cost of goods sold under LIFO assuming Rodriquez Company uses the periodic inventory system.

Continuing Cookie Chronicle

(*Note:* This is a continuation of the Cookie Chronicle from Chapters 1 through 5.)

CCC6 Natalie is busy establishing both divisions of her business (cookie classes and mixer sales) and completing her business degree. Her goals for the next 11 months are to sell one mixer per month and to give two to three classes per week.

The cost of the fine European mixers is expected to increase. Natalie has just negotiated new terms with Kzinski that include shipping costs in the negotiated purchase price (mixers will be shipped FOB destination), but the supplier cannot guarantee the invoice price. Natalie has decided to use a periodic inventory system and now must choose a cost flow assumption for her mixer inventory.

The following transactions occur in February to May 2007.

Feb. 2 Natalie buys two deluxe mixers on account from Kzinski Supply Co. for $1,100 ($550 each), FOB destination, terms n/30.
    16 She sells one deluxe mixer for $1,050 cash.
    25 She pays the amount owed to Kzinski.
Mar. 2 She buys one deluxe mixer on account from Kzinski Supply Co. for $567, FOB destination, terms n/30.
    30 Natalie sells two deluxe mixers for a total of $2,100 cash.

	31	She pays the amount owed to Kzinski.
Apr.	1	She buys two deluxe mixers on account from Kzinski Supply Co. for $1,122 ($561 each), FOB destination, terms n/30.
	13	She sells three deluxe mixers for a total of $3,150 cash.
	30	Natalie pays the amount owed to Kzinski.
May	4	She buys three deluxe mixers on account from Kzinski Supply Co. for $1,720 ($573.33 each), FOB destination, terms n/30.
	27	She sells one deluxe mixer for $1,050 cash.

Instructions

(a) Prepare journal entries for each of the transactions.

(b) Determine the cost of goods available for sale. Recall from Chapter 5 that at the end of January, Cookie Creations had three mixers on hand at a cost of $545 each.

(c) Calculate (i) ending inventory, (ii) cost of goods sold, (iii) gross profit, and (iv) gross profit rate under each of the following methods: LIFO, FIFO, and average cost. (Round average unit cost to three decimal places.)

(d) Natalie is thinking of getting a bank loan. If this is the only factor Natalie has to consider in choosing an inventory cost flow assumption, which cost flow assumption would you recommend that Natalie use? Why?

▶ BROADENING YOUR PERSPECTIVE

Financial Reporting and Analysis

FINANCIAL REPORTING PROBLEM: *Tootsie Roll Industries, Inc.*

BYP6-1   The notes that accompany a company's financial statements provide informative details that would clutter the amounts and descriptions presented in the statements. Refer to the financial statements of Tootsie Roll and the accompanying Notes to Consolidated Financial Statements in Appendix A.

Instructions
Answer the following questions. (Give the amounts in thousands of dollars, as shown in Tootsie Roll's annual report.)

(a) What did Tootsie Roll report for the amount of inventories in its Consolidated Balance Sheet at December 31, 2004? At December 31, 2003?

(b) Compute the dollar amount of change and the percentage change in inventories between 2003 and 2004. Compute inventory as a percentage of current assets for 2004.

(c) What are the cost of goods sold reported by Tootsie Roll for 2004, 2003, and 2002? Compute the ratio of cost of goods sold to net sales in 2004.

COMPARATIVE ANALYSIS PROBLEM: *Tootsie Roll vs. Hershey Foods*

BYP6-2   The financial statements of Hershey Foods are presented in Appendix B, following the financial statements for Tootsie Roll in Appendix A.

Instructions
(a) Based on the information in the financial statements, compute these 2004 values for each company. (Do not adjust for the LIFO reserve.)

   (1) Inventory turnover ratio.

   (2) Days in inventory.

(b) What conclusions concerning the management of the inventory can you draw from these data?

RESEARCH CASE

BYP6-3 The April 16, 2005, issue of *The Washington Post* contains an article by David Brown titled, "Pediatric Vaccine Stockpile at Risk."

Instructions
Access the article on MSNBC.com at *www.msnbc.msn.com/id/7529480/print/1/display mode/1098/*. Then read the article and answer the following questions.
(a) What does the article suggest as the apparent cause of the decline of the vaccine stockpile?
(b) Describe the procedures that have been followed in the past in managing the stockpile, and how it was accounted for in the past.
(c) What was the motivation behind the SEC's decision to issue a new revenue recognition bulletin?

INTERPRETING FINANCIAL STATEMENTS

BYP6-4 The following information is from the 2005 annual report of American Greetings Corporation (all dollars in thousands).

	Feb. 28, 2005	Feb. 29, 2004
Inventories		
Finished goods	$228,088	$212,252
Work in process	19,719	30,047
Raw materials and supplies	50,957	69,526
	298,764	311,825
Less: LIFO reserve	75,890	73,213
Total (as reported)	$222,874	$238,612
Cost of goods sold	$905,201	$912,705
Current assets (as reported)	$1,281,639	$1,199,045
Current liabilities	$487,667	$424,579

The following information comes from the notes to the company's financial statements.

> Finished products, work in process, and raw material inventories are carried at the lower-of-cost-or-market. The last-in, first-out (LIFO) cost method is used for approximately 65% of the domestic inventories in 2005 and approximately 50% in 2004. The foreign subsidiaries principally use the first-in, first-out method. Display material and factory supplies are carried at average cost.

Instructions
(a) Define each of the following: finished goods, work in process, and raw materials.
(b) The company experienced an increase in finished goods inventory and a decline in raw materials. Discuss the likely cause of this.
(c) What might be a possible explanation for why the company uses FIFO for its non-domestic inventories?
(d) Calculate the company's inventory turnover ratio and days in inventory for 2004 and 2005. (2003 inventory was $278,807.) Discuss the implications of any change in the ratios.
(e) What percentage of total inventory does the 2005 LIFO reserve represent? If the company used FIFO in 2005, what would be the value of its inventory? Do you consider this difference a "material" amount from the perspective of an analyst? Which value accurately represents the value of the company's inventory?
(f) Calculate the company's 2005 current ratio with the numbers as reported, then re-calculate after adjusting for the LIFO reserve.

FINANCIAL ANALYSIS ON THE WEB

BYP6-5 *Purpose:* Use SEC filings to learn about a company's inventory accounting practices.

Address: **http://biz.yahoo.com/p/_capgds-bldmch.html**
            (or go to **www.wiley.com/college/kimmel**)

Steps

1. Go to this site and click on the name of an equipment manufacturer other than those discussed in the chapter.
2. Click on **SEC filings**.
3. Under "Recent filings" choose **Form 10K** (annual report) and click on **Full Filing at Edgar Online**.
4. Choose option "3," **Online HTML Version**.

If the 10K is not listed among the recent filings then click on **View All Filings on EDGAR Online**.

Instructions
Review the 10K to answer the following questions.

(a) What is the name of the company?
(b) How has its inventory changed from the previous year?
(c) What is the amount of raw materials, work in process, and finished goods inventory?
(d) What inventory method does the company use?
(e) Calculate the inventory turnover ratio and days in inventory for the current year.
(f) If the company uses LIFO, what was the amount of its LIFO reserve?

Critical Thinking

DECISION MAKING ACROSS THE ORGANIZATION

BYP6-6 Hector Electronics has enjoyed tremendous sales growth during the last 10 years. However, even though sales have steadily increased, the company's CEO, Karen Stevens, is concerned about certain aspects of its performance. She has called a meeting with the corporate controller and the vice presidents of finance, operations, sales, and marketing to discuss the company's performance. Karen begins the meeting by making the following observations:

> "We have been forced to take significant write-downs on inventory during each of the last three years because of obsolescence. In addition, inventory storage costs have soared. We rent four additional warehouses to store our increasingly diverse inventory. Five years ago inventory represented only 20% of the value of our total assets. It now exceeds 35%. Yet, even with all of this inventory, "stock-outs" (measured by complaints by customers that the desired product is not available) have increased by 40% during the last three years. And worse yet, it seems that we constantly must discount merchandise that we have too much of."

Karen asks the group to review the following data and make suggestions as to how the company's performance might be improved.

(in millions)	2007	2006	2005	2004
Inventory				
Raw materials	$242	$198	$155	$128
Work in process	116	77	49	33
Finished goods	567	482	398	257
Total inventory	$925	$757	$602	$418
Current assets	$1,800	$1,623	$1,183	$841
Total assets	$2,643	$2,523	$2,408	$2,090
Current liabilities	$600	$590	$525	$420
Sales	$9,428	$8,974	$7,536	$6,840
Cost of goods sold	$6,128	$5,474	$4,145	$3,557
Net income	$754	$987	$979	$958

Instructions

Using the information provided, answer the following questions.

(a) Compute the current ratio, gross profit rate, profit margin ratio, inventory turnover ratio, and days in inventory for 2005, 2006, and 2007.

(b) Discuss the trends and potential causes of the changes in the ratios in part (a).

(c) Discuss potential remedies to any problems discussed in part (b).

(d) What concerns might be raised by some members of management with regard to your suggestions in part (c)?

COMMUNICATION ACTIVITIES

BYP6-7 In a discussion of dramatic increases in coffee bean prices, a *Wall Street Journal* article noted the following fact about Starbucks.

> Before this year's bean-price hike, Starbucks added several defenses that analysts say could help it maintain earnings and revenue. The company last year began accounting for its coffee-bean purchases by taking the average price of all beans in inventory.
>
> *Source:* Aaron Lucchetti, "Crowded Coffee Market May Keep a Lid on Starbucks After Price Rise Hurt Stock," *Wall Street Journal* (June 4, 1997), p. C1.

Prior to this change the company was using FIFO.

Instructions

Your client, the CEO of Hot Cup Coffee, Inc., read this article and sent you an e-mail message requesting that you explain why Starbucks might have taken this action. Your response should explain what impact this change in accounting method has on earnings, why the company might want to do this, and any possible disadvantages of such a change.

*****BYP6-8** You are the controller of Blue Jays Inc. B. J. Dell, the president, recently mentioned to you that she found an error in the 2006 financial statements which she believes has corrected itself. She determined, in discussions with the purchasing department, that 2006 ending inventory was overstated by $1 million. B. J. says that the 2007 ending inventory is correct, and she assumes that 2007 income is correct. B. J. says to you, "What happened has happened—there's no point in worrying about it anymore."

Instructions

You conclude that B. J. is incorrect. Write a brief, tactful memo to her, clarifying the situation.

ETHICS CASE

BYP6-9 Becker Wholesale Corp. uses the LIFO cost flow method. In the current year, profit at Becker is running unusually high. The corporate tax rate is also high this year, but it is scheduled to decline significantly next year. In an effort to lower the current year's net income and to take advantage of the changing income tax rate, the president of Becker Wholesale instructs the plant accountant to recommend to the purchasing department a large purchase of inventory for delivery 3 days before the end of the year. The price of the inventory to be purchased has doubled during the year, and the purchase will represent a major portion of the ending inventory value.

Instructions

(a) What is the effect of this transaction on this year's and next year's income statement and income tax expense? Why?

(b) If Becker Wholesale had been using the FIFO method of inventory costing, would the president give the same directive?

(c) Should the plant accountant order the inventory purchase to lower income? What are the ethical implications of this order?

Answers to Business Insight and Accounting across the Organization Questions

p. 269

Q: Why is inventory control important to managers such as those at Wal-Mart?

A: In the very competitive environment of discount retailing, where Wal-Mart is the major player, small differences in price matter to the customer. Wal-Mart sells a high volume of inventory at a low gross profit rate. When operating in a high-volume, low-margin environment, small cost savings can mean the difference between being profitable or going out of business.

p. 270

Q: What effect does an overstatement of inventory have on a company's financial statements?

A: The balance sheet looks stronger because inventory and retained earnings are overstated. The income statement looks better because cost of goods sold is understated and income is overstated.

p. 282

Q. If Samsung isn't successful in selling the units, what steps will it have to take, and how will this show up in its financial statements?

A. If Samsung increases production, but then can't sell the units, its finished goods inventory will increase. Because cell phones are constantly changing, Samsung would want to take steps to sell off the inventory before it becomes obsolete. Thus, it would need to offer big discounts. Such a strategy would get its inventory down to desirable levels, but would severely depress the company's gross profit.

Answer to Tootsie Roll Review It Question 2, p. 280

Tootsie Roll uses LIFO for U.S. inventories and FIFO for foreign inventories.

Answers to Self-Study Questions

1. d   2. a   3. c   4. d   5. c   6. d   7. a   8. d   9. a
*10. d   *11. b

REMEMBER TO GO BACK TO THE NAVIGATOR BOX ON THE CHAPTER-OPENING PAGE
AND CHECK OFF YOUR COMPLETED WORK.

CHAPTER **7**

Internal Control and Cash

STUDY OBJECTIVES

After studying this chapter, you should be able to:

1 Identify the principles of internal control.

2 Explain the applications of internal control to cash receipts.

3 Explain the applications of internal control to cash disbursements.

4 Prepare a bank reconciliation.

5 Explain the reporting of cash.

6 Discuss the basic principles of cash management.

7 Identify the primary elements of a cash budget.

 THE NAVIGATOR

☑ THE NAVIGATOR

- Scan *Study Objectives* ⬭
- Read *Feature Story* ⬭
- Read *Preview* ⬭
- Read text and answer *Before You Go On*
  p. 324 ⬭   p. 327 ⬭   p. 333 ⬭   p. 339 ⬭
- Work *Using the Decision Toolkit* ⬭
- Review *Summary of Study Objectives* ⬭
- Work *Demonstration Problem* ⬭
- Answer *Self-Study Questions* ⬭
- Complete *Assignments* ⬭

FEATURE STORY

Is There a Thief in the Next Cubicle?

According to some estimates, up to one-third of U.S. employees have stolen from their employers. Some of these thefts have a relatively minor impact on the business—such as high-school-age employees consuming cheese and sausage while making pizza at the local pizzeria. Other thefts, however, can be very serious. In the case of small businesses, employee theft can result in the failure of the business. About 90 percent of employee thefts involve cash. Consider the following examples.

A movie-theater manager printed out a ticket, but if he didn't think anyone was watching, he then allowed the customer to walk into the movie without giving the customer the ticket. The manager pocketed the cash. Later he sold the ticket to a different customer, so that the number of tickets issued matched the amount of cash in the register. Total take: $30,000.

A government employee stole taxpayer refund checks that the post office had returned due to incorrect addresses. The employee then forged the signatures and deposited the checks. Total take: $2,000,000.

A purchasing agent set up a vendor file using his wife's maiden name, and then made payments to her for consulting services that she never provided. Total take: $1,000,000.

Most disconcerting is that employee thieves often are people whom you would least expect. Kay Lemon, a grandmother, was a long-time employee of a small lighting store. She handled all aspects of the store's accounting and banking, including making bank deposits, signing checks, and reconciling the store's bank account. For more than a decade she didn't steal, even though the situation created many opportunities for theft. But once she started, she couldn't stop. Ultimately she stole $416,000. Here's how.

Lemon made out company checks to herself and deposited them in her own account. To cover the theft she wrote "void" on the check stub. Then, the next time she bought inventory she added the stolen amount to the check stub when she paid for the inventory. For example, if she stole $5,000 and was paying $10,000 for inventory, she would write $15,000 on the check stub for the inventory payment. This kept the cash account in balance. Then, when the check for the stolen amount was returned to the company with the bank statement, Lemon tore up the check.

How did she get caught? Actually she didn't. The pressure of all of those years of covering up the theft became too much for her to handle. She turned herself in. The company narrowly escaped financial ruin.

Companies design internal control systems to reduce the likelihood of thefts such as those listed above. In recent years a number of extremely large business failures resulting from employees acting in their own interest caused Congress to pass the Sarbanes-Oxley Act of 2002. The new law puts considerable emphasis on corporate internal control systems.

Source: Joseph T. Wells, "Enemies Within," *Journal of Accountancy* (December 2001), pp. 31–35.

THE NAVIGATOR

PREVIEW OF CHAPTER 7

Cash is the lifeblood of any company. Large and small companies alike must guard it carefully. Even companies that are in every other way successful can go bankrupt if they fail to manage cash. Managers must know both how to use cash efficiently and how to protect it. Due to its liquid nature, cash is the easiest asset to steal. As the Feature Story suggests, a particularly difficult problem arises when a company has a dishonest employee.

In this chapter you will learn ways to reduce the risk of theft of cash and other assets, how to report cash in the financial statements, and how to manage cash. The content and organization of the chapter are as follows.

Internal Control

A recent publication sponsored by the Association of Certified Fraud Examiners estimated that fraud costs U.S. organizations more than $600 billion annually. Findings such as these, as well as situations like those in the Feature Story, emphasize the need for a good system of internal control.

Internal control consists of all the related methods and measures adopted within a business to:

1. **Safeguard its assets** from employee theft, robbery, and unauthorized use; and
2. **Enhance the accuracy and reliability of its accounting records** by reducing the risk of errors (unintentional mistakes) and irregularities (intentional mistakes and misrepresentations) in the accounting process.

Under the Sarbanes-Oxley Act, all publicly traded U.S. corporations are required to maintain an adequate system of internal control. Companies that fail to comply are subject to fines, and company officers may be imprisoned.

THE SARBANES-OXLEY ACT

"Better get those controls under control" was a comment often made after the numerous corporate scandals of recent years. As a result, Congress passed the

Sarbanes-Oxley Act of 2002 (SOX). One of the most important laws to be passed in decades, SOX forces companies to pay more attention to internal controls.

SOX imposes more responsibilities on corporate executives and boards of directors to ensure that companies' internal controls are reliable and effective. Under one part of the law, companies must develop sound principles of control over financial reporting, and continually assess that these controls are working. In addition, independent outside auditors must attest to the level of internal control. SOX also created the Public Company Accounting Oversight Board (PCAOB), which now establishes auditing standards and regulates auditor activity.

One poll found that about 60% of investors believe that SOX will help safeguard their stock investments. Many say they would be unlikely to invest in a company that fails to follow SOX requirements. Although some corporate executives have criticized the time and expense involved in following the requirements of the law, SOX appears to be working well. For example, the chief accounting officer of Eli Lily noted that SOX triggered a comprehensive review of how the company documents its controls. This review uncovered redundancies and also pointed out controls that needed to be added. In short, it added up to time and money well spent. And the finance chief at General Electric noted, "We have seen value in SOX. It helps build investors' trust and gives them more confidence."[1]

PRINCIPLES OF INTERNAL CONTROL

To safeguard assets and enhance the accuracy and reliability of accounting records, companies follow internal control principles. The specific control measures used vary with the size and nature of the business and with management's control philosophy. The six principles listed in Illustration 7-1 apply to most enterprises. They are explained on the following pages.

STUDY OBJECTIVE
1
Identify the principles of internal control.

Illustration 7-1
Principles of internal control

---

[1] "Corporate Regulation Must Be Working—There's a Backlash," *Wall Street Journal* (June 16, 2004), p. C1, and Judith Burns, "Is Sarbanes-Oxley Working?" *Wall Street Journal* (June 21, 2004), pp. R8–R9.

It's your shift now. I'm turning in my cash drawer and heading home.

Transfer of cash drawers

Establishment of Responsibility

An essential characteristic of internal control is the assignment of responsibility to specific individuals. **Control is most effective when only one person is responsible for a given task.**

To illustrate, assume that the cash on hand at the end of the day in a Safeway supermarket is $10 short of the cash rung up on the cash register. If only one person has operated the register, the shift manager can quickly assess responsibility for the shortage. If two or more individuals have worked the register, it may be impossible to determine who is responsible for the error unless each person has a separate cash drawer and register key.

Establishing responsibility includes the authorization and approval of transactions. The vice-president of sales should have the authority to establish policies for making credit sales. These policies ordinarily will require written credit department approval of credit sales.

Segregation of Duties

Segregation of duties is indispensable in a system of internal control. The rationale for segregation of duties is that **the work of one employee should, without a duplication of effort, provide a reliable basis for evaluating the work of another employee**. There are two common applications of this principle:

1. The responsibility for related activities should be assigned to different individuals.
2. The responsibility for record keeping for an asset should be separate from the physical custody of that asset.

RELATED ACTIVITIES. Companies should assign related activities to different individuals in both the purchasing and selling areas. **Making one individual responsible for all of the related activities,** as was the case in the Feature Story, **increases the potential for errors and irregularities.**

Related purchasing activities include ordering merchandise, receiving goods, and paying (or authorizing payment) for merchandise. In purchasing, for example, orders could be placed with friends or with suppliers who give kickbacks. In addition, a careless or dishonest employee might authorize payment without a careful review of the invoice, or, even worse, might approve fictitious invoices for payment. When a company assigns the responsibilities for ordering, receiving, and paying to different individuals, it minimizes the risk of such abuses.

Companies also should assign *related sales activities* to different individuals. Related sales activities include making a sale, shipping (or delivering) the goods to the customer, and billing the customer. Various frauds are possible when one person is responsible for these related sales transactions: A salesperson could make sales at unauthorized prices to increase sales commissions: A shipping clerk could ship goods to himself. A billing clerk could understate the amount billed for sales made to friends and relatives. These abuses are less likely to occur when salespersons make the sale, shipping department employees ship the goods on the basis of the sales order, and billing department employees prepare the sales invoice after comparing the sales order with the report of goods shipped.

RECORD KEEPING SEPARATE FROM PHYSICAL CUSTODY. If accounting is to provide a valid basis of accountability for an asset, the accountant, as record keeper, should have neither physical custody of the asset nor access to it.

Moreover, the custodian of the asset should not maintain or have access to the accounting records. **The custodian of the asset is not likely to convert the asset to personal use if one employee maintains the record of the asset that should be on hand and a different employee has physical custody of the asset.** The separation of accounting responsibility from the custody of assets is especially important for cash and inventories because these assets are very vulnerable to unauthorized use or misappropriation.

Illustration 7-2 shows the segregation of duties concept.

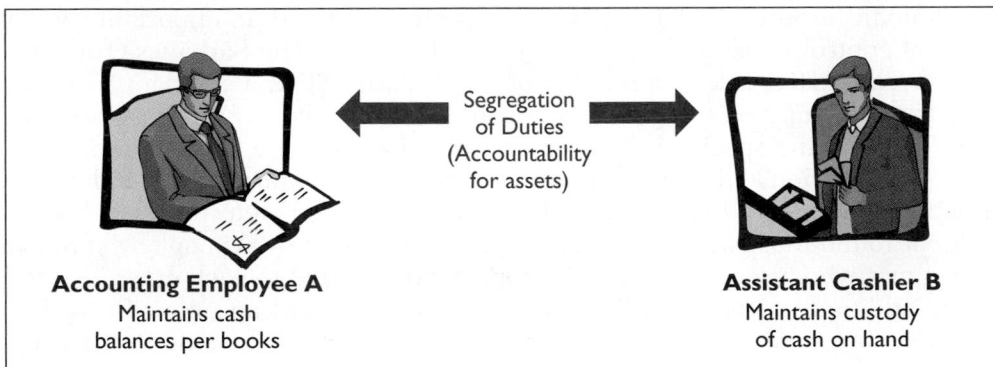

Accounting Employee A
Maintains cash
balances per books

Segregation
of Duties
(Accountability
for assets)

Assistant Cashier B
Maintains custody
of cash on hand

Illustration 7-2   The segregation of duties (accountability for assets) principle

Accounting across the Organization

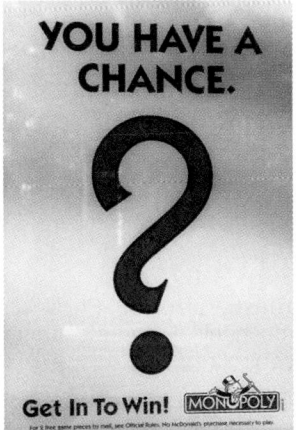

YOU HAVE A CHANCE.

Get In To Win! MONOPOLY

Employee theft comes in a wide variety of flavors, affecting nearly every type of business. Consider the case of Simon WorldWide, which ran a number of promotional games for McDonald's. Customers searched newspapers and McDonald's products for winning pieces that in some cases were worth $1 million. The problem was that a Simon employee made sure that many of the winning pieces—more than $13 million worth of prizes—ended up in the hands of his friends. The friends then gave part of the winnings back to the employee.

 What controls would have reduced the likelihood of this type of theft?

Documentation Procedures

Documents provide evidence that transactions and events have occurred. For example, the shipping document indicates that the goods have been shipped, and the sales invoice indicates that the customer has been billed for the goods. By requiring signatures (or initials) on the documents, the company can identify the individual(s) responsible for the transaction or event.

Companies should establish procedures for documents. First, whenever possible, companies should use **prenumbered documents, and all documents should be accounted for**. Prenumbering helps to prevent an employee from recording a transaction more than once or, conversely, not recording the transactions at all. Second, **the control system should require that employees promptly forward source documents for accounting entries to the accounting department to help ensure timely recording of the transaction**

Helpful Hint An important corollary to prenumbering is keeping voided documents until all documents are accounted for.

and event. This control measure contributes directly to the accuracy and reliability of the accounting records.

Accounting across the Organization

The human resources (HR) department has always played an important role in internal control by carefully screening potential hires. The Sarbanes-Oxley Act has increased HR's role in a number of ways. Under SOX, a company needs to keep track of employees' degrees and certifications to ensure that employees continue to meet the specified requirements of a job. Also, to ensure proper employee supervision and proper separation of duties, companies must develop and monitor an organizational chart. When one corporation went through this exercise it found that out of 17,000 employees, there were "400 people who didn't report to anybody, and they had 35 people who reported to each other."

In addition, under SOX, if an employee complains of an unfair firing and mentions financial issues at the company, HR must refer the case to the company audit committee and possibly to its legal counsel.

 Why would unsupervised employees or employees who report to each other represent potential internal control threats?

Physical, Mechanical, and Electronic Controls

Use of physical, mechanical, and electronic controls is essential. Physical controls relate primarily to the safeguarding of assets. Mechanical and electronic controls safeguard assets and enhance the accuracy and reliability of the accounting records. Examples of these controls are shown in Illustration 7-3.

Illustration 7-3 Physical, mechanical, and electronic controls

Physical Controls

Safes, vaults, and safety deposit boxes for cash and business papers

Locked warehouses and storage cabinets for inventories and records

Computer facilities with pass key access or fingerprint or eyeball scans

Mechanical and Electronic Controls

Alarms to prevent break-ins

Television monitors and garment sensors to deter theft

Time clocks for recording time worked

A crucial consideration in programming computerized systems is building in controls that limit unauthorized or unintentional tampering. Entire books and movies have used computer system tampering as a major theme. Most programmers would agree that tamper-proofing and debugging programs are the most difficult and time-consuming phases of their jobs.

Program controls built into the computer prevent intentional or unintentional errors or unauthorized access. To prevent unauthorized access, the computer system may require that users enter passwords or correctly answer random personal questions. Or, some systems authenticate users by means of fingerprint or retinal (eyeball) scans. Once access has been allowed, other program controls identify data having a value higher or lower than a predetermined amount (limit checks), validate computations (math checks), and detect improper processing order (sequence checks).

Independent Internal Verification

Most systems of internal control provide for **independent internal verification**. This principle involves the review, comparison, and reconciliation of data prepared by employees. Three measures are recommended to obtain maximum benefit from independent internal verification:

1. Companies should verify records periodically or on a surprise basis.
2. An employee who is independent of the personnel responsible for the information should make the verification.
3. Discrepancies and exceptions should be reported to a management level that can take appropriate corrective action.

Independent internal verification is especially useful in comparing recorded accountability with existing assets. The reconciliation of the cash register tape with the cash in the register is an example. Another common example is the reconciliation by an independent person of the cash balance per books with the cash balance per bank. Illustration 7-4 shows the relationship between this principle and the segregation of duties principle.

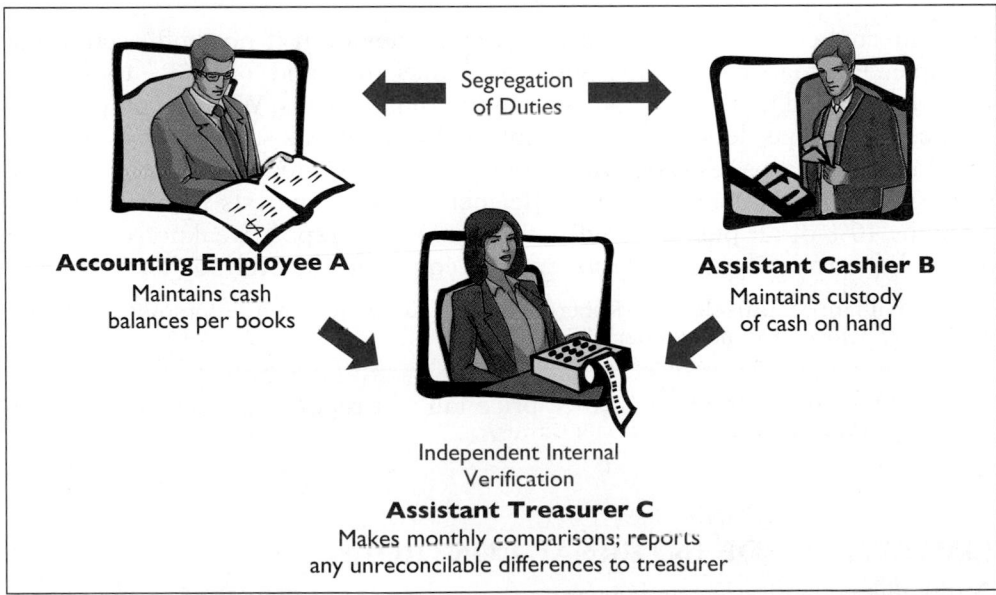

Illustration 7-4
Comparison of
segregation of duties
principle with independent
internal verification
principle

Large companies often assign independent internal verification to internal auditors. **Internal auditors** are company employees who evaluate on a continuous basis the effectiveness of the company's system of internal control. They periodically review the activities of departments and individuals to determine whether prescribed internal controls are being followed.

Companies discover most fraud through internal mechanisms, such as internal controls and internal audits. That fact illustrates the importance of independent internal verification. The fraud at WorldCom involving billions of dollars, for example, was uncovered by an internal auditor.

Other Controls

Here are three other control measures:

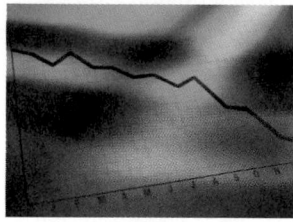

1. **Bond employees who handle cash.** Bonding involves obtaining insurance protection against misappropriation of assets by dishonest employees. This measure contributes to the safeguarding of cash in two ways: First, the insurance company carefully screens all individuals before adding them to the policy and may reject risky applicants. Second, bonded employees know that the insurance company will vigorously prosecute all offenders.
2. **Rotate employees' duties and require employees to take vacations.** These measures deter employees from attempting any thefts, since they will not be able to permanently conceal their improper actions. Many banks, for example, have discovered embezzlements when the perpetrator has been on vacation or assigned to a new position.
3. **Conduct thorough background checks.** Many believe that the most important and inexpensive measure any business can take to reduce employee theft and fraud is for the human resources department to conduct thorough background checks. Two tips: (1) Check to see whether job applicants actually graduated from the schools they list. (2) Never use the telephone numbers for previous employers given on the reference sheet; always look them up yourself.

Poor internal controls can cost a company money even if no theft occurs. For example, Eastman Kodak Co., SunTrust Banks Inc., and Toys "R" Us Inc. all recently reported material weaknesses in internal controls. When a company announces that it has deficiencies in its internal controls, its stock price often falls.

Under the Sarbanes-Oxley Act companies must evaluate their internal controls systems and report on any deficiencies. Some analysts estimate that as many as 10% of all publicly traded companies will report weaknesses in their internal controls. The estimate for smaller companies is even higher.

Source: William M. Bulkeley and Robert Tomsho, "Kodak to Get Auditors Adverse View," *Wall Street Journal Online* (January 27, 2005).

 Why would a company's stock price fall if it reports deficiencies in its internal controls?

LIMITATIONS OF INTERNAL CONTROL

Companies generally design their systems of internal control to provide **reasonable assurance** of proper safeguarding of assets and reliability of accounting records. **The concept of reasonable assurance rests on the premise that the costs of establishing control procedures should not exceed their expected benefit.**

To illustrate, consider shoplifting losses in retail stores. Stores could completely eliminate such losses by having a security guard search customers as they leave the store. Store managers have concluded, however, that the negative effects of this procedure cannot be justified. Instead, stores have attempted to "control" shoplifting losses by less costly procedures: They post signs saying, "We reserve the right to inspect all packages" and "All shoplifters will be prosecuted." They also use hidden TV cameras and store detectives to monitor customer activity and put sensor equipment at exits.

The **human element** is an important factor in every system of internal control. A good system can become ineffective as a result of employee fatigue, carelessness, or indifference. For example, a receiving clerk may not bother to count goods received or may just "fudge" the counts. Occasionally, two or more individuals may work together to get around prescribed controls. Such **collusion** can significantly impair the effectiveness of a system because it eliminates the protection anticipated from segregation of duties. If a supervisor and a cashier collaborate to understate cash receipts, they may subvert the system of internal control (at least in the short run). No system of internal control is perfect.

The size of the business may impose limitations on internal control. A small company, for example, may find it difficult to apply the principles of segregation of duties and independent internal verification because it has few employees.

As indicated earlier, the Sarbanes-Oxley Act has a good system of checks and balances that will help enhance internal control. But SOX will not eliminate fraud. No matter how effective internal control is, ethical behavior cannot be imposed by law. Unfortunately some individuals will do illegal things. The "tone at the top" of a company is what counts. We need managers and executives with high moral standards to ensure that fraudulent and deceptive practices will not be tolerated.

 International Note

Other countries also have control problems. For example, a judge in France issued a 36-page book detailing many widespread scams, such as kickbacks in public-works contracts, the skimming of development aid money to Africa, and bribes on arms sales.

Business Insight
Ethics Perspective

A study by the Association of Certified Fraud Examiners indicates that businesses with fewer than 100 employees are most at risk for employee theft. Nearly 46% of frauds occurred at companies with fewer than 100 employees. The average loss at small companies was $98,000, which was only slightly less than the average fraud at companies with more than 10,000 employees. A $100,000 loss can threaten the very existence of a small company.

Source: 2004 Report to the Nation on Occupational Fraud and Abuse, Association of Certified Fraud Examiners, *http://www.cfenet.com/pdfs/2004RttN.pdf*, p. 6.

 Why are small companies more susceptible to employee theft?

Decision Toolkit

Decision Checkpoints	Info Needed for Decision	Tool to Use for Decision	How to Evaluate Results
Are the company's financial statements supported by adequate internal controls?	Auditor's report, management discussion and analysis, articles in financial press	The required measures of internal control are to (1) establish responsibility, (2) segregate duties, (3) document procedures, (4) employ physical or automated controls, and (5) use independent internal verification.	If any indication is given that these or other controls are lacking, use the financial statements with caution.

B E F O R E   Y O U   G O   O N . . .

▶ **Review It**

1. What are the two primary objectives of internal control?
2. Identify and describe the principles of internal control.
3. What are the limitations of internal control?

▶ **Do It**

Li Song owns a small retail store. Li wants to establish good internal control procedures but is confused about the difference between segregation of duties and independent internal verification. Explain the differences to Li.

Action Plan

• Understand and explain the differences between (1) segregation of duties and (2) independent internal verification.

Solution

Segregation of duties relates to the assignment of responsibility so that (1) the work of one employee will check the work of another employee and (2) physical control of assets is separated from the records that keep track of the assets. Segregation of duties occurs daily in using assets and in executing and recording transactions.

In contrast, independent internal verification involves reviewing, comparing, and reconciling data prepared by one or several employees. Independent internal verification occurs after the fact, as in reconciling cash register totals at the end of the day with cash on hand.

THE NAVIGATOR

Cash Controls

Just as cash is the beginning of a company's operating cycle, it is usually the starting point for a company's system of internal control. Cash is the one asset that is readily convertible into any other type of asset; it is easily concealed and transported; and it is highly desired. Because of these characteristics, cash is the asset most susceptible to improper diversion and use. Moreover, because of the large volume of cash transactions, numerous errors may occur in executing and recording cash transactions. To safeguard cash and to ensure the accuracy of the accounting records for cash, effective internal control over cash is imperative.

Cash consists of coins, currency (paper money), checks, money orders, and money on hand or on deposit in a bank or similar depository. The general rule is that cash is whatever the bank will accept for deposit.

In the next sections we explain the application of internal control principles to cash receipts and cash disbursements.

INTERNAL CONTROL OVER CASH RECEIPTS

STUDY OBJECTIVE

2

Explain the applications of internal control to cash receipts.

Cash receipts result from a variety of sources: cash sales; collections on account from customers; the receipt of interest, rents, and dividends; investments by owners; bank loans; and proceeds from the sale of noncurrent assets. The internal control principles explained earlier apply to cash receipts transactions as shown in Illustration 7-5. As you might expect, companies vary considerably in how they apply these principles.

Illustration 7-5
Application of internal
control principles to cash
receipts

Internal Control over Cash Receipts

Establishment of Responsibility

Only designated personnel are authorized to handle cash receipts (cashiers)

Physical, Mechanical, and Electronic Controls

Store cash in safes and bank vaults; limit access to storage areas; use cash registers

Segregation of Duties

Different individuals receive cash, record cash receipts, and hold the cash

Independent Internal Verification

Supervisors count cash receipts daily; treasurer compares total receipts to bank deposits daily

Documentation Procedures

Use remittance advice (mail receipts), cash register tapes, and deposit slips

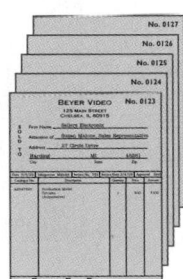

Other Controls

Bond personnel who handle cash; require employees to take vacations; deposit all cash in bank daily

INTERNAL CONTROL OVER CASH DISBURSEMENTS

Companies disburse cash for a variety of reasons, such as to pay expenses and liabilities or to purchase assets. **Generally, internal control over cash disbursements is more effective when companies pay by check, rather than by cash, except for incidental amounts that are paid out of petty cash.** Companies generally issue checks only after following specified control procedures. In addition, the "paid" check provides proof of payment. The principles of internal control apply to cash disbursements as shown in Illustration 7-6 (page 326).

STUDY OBJECTIVE
3

Explain the applications of internal control to cash disbursements.

Electronic Funds Transfer (EFT) System

Accounting for and controlling cash is an expensive and time-consuming process. The cost to process a check through a bank system is about $1 per check and is increasing. But it costs only 35¢ if the customer pays by credit card over the telephone and 1¢ if the customer pays via a computer.

Illustration 7-6
Application of internal
control principles to cash
disbursements

**Internal Control
over Cash Disbursements**

**Establishment of
Responsibility**

Only designated
personnel are
authorized to
sign checks
(treasurer)

**Physical,
Mechanical, and
Electronic Controls**

Store blank checks
in safes, with limited
access; print check
amounts by machine
in indelible ink

**Segregation
of Duties**

Different individuals
approve and make
payments; check
signers do not
record
disbursements

**Independent
Internal
Verification**

Compare checks to
invoices; reconcile
bank statement
monthly

**Documentation
Procedures**

Use prenumbered
checks and account
for them in
sequence; each
check must have
approved invoice

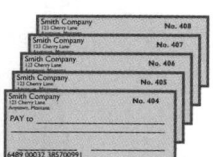

Other Controls

Stamp invoices
PAID

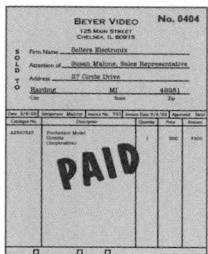

It is not surprising, therefore, that banking institutions have developed approaches to transfer funds among parties without the use of paper (deposit tickets, checks, etc.). Such procedures, called **electronic funds transfers (EFT)**, are disbursement systems that use wire, telephone, or computer to transfer cash from one location to another. Use of EFT is quite common. For example, many employees receive no formal payroll checks from their employers. Instead, the employers send magnetic tapes to the appropriate banks for deposit. In addition, individuals now frequently make regular payments such as those for house, car, or utilities by EFT.

Petty Cash Fund

As you learned earlier in the chapter, better internal control over cash disbursements is possible when companies make payments by check. However, using checks to pay such small amounts as those for postage due, employee working lunches, and taxi fares is both impractical and a nuisance. A common way of handling such

payments, while maintaining satisfactory control, is to use a petty cash fund. A
petty cash fund is a cash fund used to pay relatively small amounts. We explain
the operation of a petty cash fund in the appendix at the end of this chapter.

Business Insight
Ethics Perspective

A recent study by the Association of Certified Fraud Examiners found that two-
thirds of all employee thefts involved a fraudulent disbursement by an employee.
The most common form (52% of cases) was fraudulent billing schemes. In these,
the employee causes the company to issue a payment to the employee by submitting a bill for nonexistent goods or services, purchases of personal goods by
the employee, or inflated invoices. The following graph shows the incidence of
various types of fraudulent disbursements and the median loss from each.

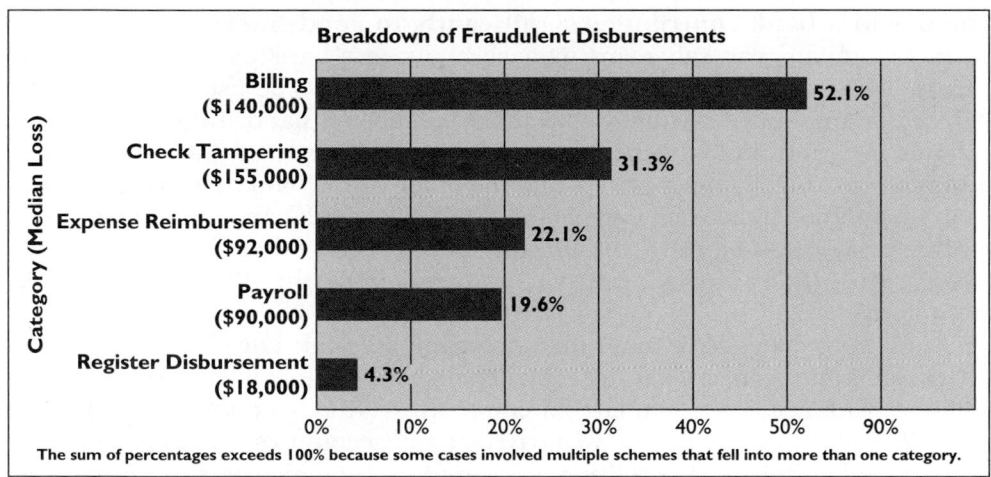

Source: 2004 Report to the Nation on Occupational Fraud and Abuse, Association of
Certified Fraud Examiners, *http://www.cfenet.com/pdfs/2004RttN.pdf,* p. 14.

 How can companies reduce the likelihood of fraudulent disbursements?

BEFORE YOU GO ON . . .

▶Review It

1. How do the principles of internal control apply to cash receipts?
2. How do the principles of internal control apply to cash disbursements?
3. What is the purpose of a petty cash fund?

▶Do It

L. R. Cortez is concerned about control over cash receipts in his fast-food restaurant, Big Cheese. The restaurant has two cash registers. At no time do more than
two employees take customer orders and ring up sales. Work shifts for employees

range from 4 to 8 hours. Cortez asks your help in installing a good system of internal control over cash receipts.

Action Plan

- Differentiate among the internal control principles of (1) establishing responsibility, (2) using electronic controls, and (3) independent internal verification.
- Design an effective system of internal control over cash receipts.

Solution

Cortez should assign a cash register to each employee at the start of each work shift, with register totals set at zero. Each employee should use only the assigned register and should ring up all sales. At the end of each work shift, Cortez or a supervisor/manager should total the register and make a cash count to see whether all cash is accounted for.

THE NAVIGATOR

USE OF A BANK

The use of a bank contributes significantly to good internal control over cash. A company can safeguard its cash by using a bank as a depository and clearinghouse for checks received and checks written. The use of a bank minimizes the amount of currency that must be kept on hand. In addition, it facilitates the control of cash because a double record is maintained of all bank transactions—one by the business and the other by the bank. The asset account Cash maintained by the company is the "flip-side" of the bank's liability account for that company. A **bank reconciliation** is the process of comparing the bank's balance with the company's balance, and explaining the differences to make them agree.

Many companies have more than one bank account. For efficiency of operations and better control, national retailers like Wal-Mart and Target often have regional bank accounts. Similarly, a company such as ExxonMobil with more than 100,000 employees may have a payroll bank account as well as one or more general bank accounts. In addition, a company may maintain several bank accounts in order to have more than one source for obtaining short-term loans when needed.

Bank Statements

Each month, the company receives from the bank a **bank statement** showing its bank transactions and balances.[2] For example, the statement for Laird Company in Illustration 7-7 (on page 329) shows the following: (1) checks paid and other debits that reduce the balance in the depositor's account, (2) deposits and other credits that increase the balance in the depositor's account, and (3) the account balance after each day's transactions.

Remember that bank statements are prepared from the *bank's* perspective. For example, every deposit the bank receives is an increase in the bank's liabilities (an account payable to the depositor). Therefore, in Illustration 7-7, National Bank and Trust *credits* to Laird Company every deposit it received from Laird. The reverse occurs when the bank "pays" a check issued by Laird Company on its checking account balance: Payment reduces the bank's liability and is therefore *debited* to Laird's account with the bank.

---

[2]Our presentation assumes that a company makes all adjustments at the end of the month. In practice, a company may also make journal entries during the month as it receives information from the bank regarding its account.

The bank statement lists in numerical sequence all paid checks along with the date the check was paid and its amount. Upon paying a check, the bank stamps the check "paid"; a paid check is sometimes referred to as a **canceled** check. In addition, the bank includes with the bank statement memoranda explaining other debits and credits it made to the depositor's account.

The bank uses a debit memorandum when a previously deposited customer's check "bounces" because of insufficient funds. In such a case, the customer's bank marks the check **NSF** (not sufficient funds) and returns it to the depositor's bank. The bank then debits (decreases) the depositor's account, as shown by the symbol NSF on the bank statement in Illustration 7-7, and sends the NSF check and debit memorandum to the depositor as notification of the charge. The NSF check creates an account receivable for the depositor and reduces cash in the bank account.

Helpful Hint Essentially, the bank statement is a copy of the bank's records sent to the customer for periodic review.

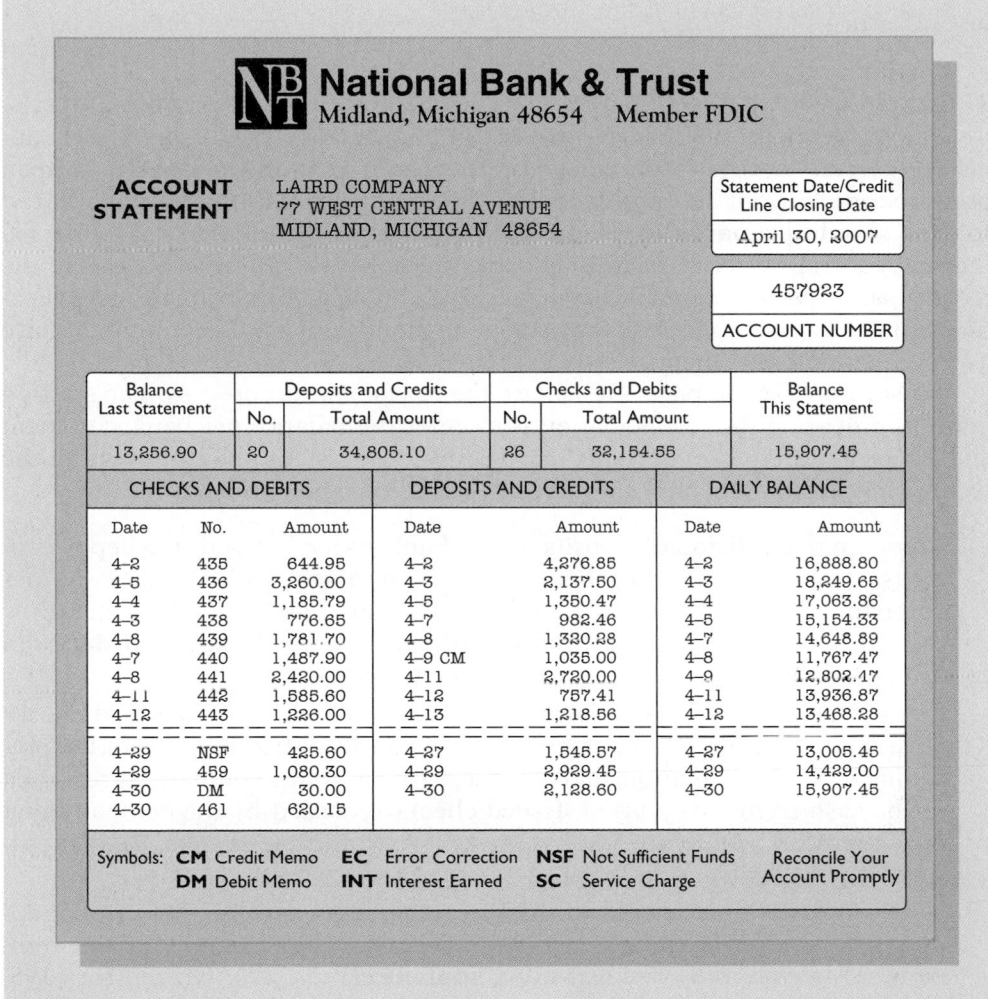

Illustration 7-7   Bank statement

Reconciling the Bank Account

Because the bank and the company maintain independent records of the company's checking account, you might assume that the respective balances will always agree. In fact, the two balances are seldom the same at any given time. Therefore it is necessary to make the balance per books agree with the balance

STUDY OBJECTIVE
4
Prepare a bank reconciliation.

per bank—a process called **reconciling the bank account**. The lack of agreement between the balances has two causes:

1. **Time lags** that prevent one of the parties from recording the transaction in the same period.
2. **Errors** by either party in recording transactions.

Time lags occur frequently. For example, several days may elapse between the time a company pays by check and the date the bank pays the check. Similarly, when a company uses the bank's night depository to make its deposits, there will be a difference of one day between the time the company records the receipts and the time the bank does so. A time lag also occurs whenever the bank mails a debit or credit memorandum to the company.

The incidence of errors depends on the effectiveness of the internal controls maintained by the company and the bank. Bank errors are infrequent. However, either party could accidentally record a $450 check as $45 or $540. In addition, the bank might mistakenly charge a check drawn by C. D. Berg to the account of C. D. Burg.

RECONCILIATION PROCEDURE.   In reconciling the bank account, it is customary to reconcile the balance per books and balance per bank to their adjusted (correct or true) cash balances. **To obtain maximum benefit from a bank reconciliation, an employee who has no other responsibilities related to cash should prepare the reconciliation.** When companies do not follow the internal control principle of independent internal verification in preparing the reconciliation, cash embezzlements may escape unnoticed. For example, in the Feature Story, a bank reconciliation by someone other than Kay Lemon might have exposed her embezzlement.

Illustration 7-8 (on page 331) shows the reconciliation process. The starting point in preparing the reconciliation is to enter the balance per bank statement and balance per books on a schedule. The following steps should reveal all the reconciling items that cause the difference between the two balances.

> **Helpful Hint** Deposits in transit and outstanding checks are reconciling items because of time lags.

1. Compare the individual deposits on the bank statement with the deposits in transit from the preceding bank reconciliation and with the deposits per company records or copies of duplicate deposit slips. Deposits recorded by the depositor that have not been recorded by the bank represent **deposits in transit**. Add these deposits to the balance per bank.
2. Compare the paid checks shown on the bank statement or the paid checks returned with the bank statement with (a) checks outstanding from the preceding bank reconciliation, and (b) checks issued by the company as recorded in the cash payments journal. Issued checks recorded by the company that have not been paid by the bank represent **outstanding checks**. Deduct outstanding checks from the balance per the bank.
3. Note any **errors** discovered in the foregoing steps and list them in the appropriate section of the reconciliation schedule. For example, if the company mistakenly recorded as $159 a paid check correctly written for $195, the company would deduct the error of $36 from the balance per books. All errors made by the depositor are reconciling items in determining the adjusted cash balance per books. In contrast, all errors made by the bank are reconciling items in determining the adjusted cash balance per the bank.
4. Trace **bank memoranda** to the depositor's records. The company lists in the appropriate section of the reconciliation schedule any unrecorded memoranda. For example, the company would deduct from the balance per books a $5 debit memorandum for bank service charges. Similarly, it would add to the balance per books a $32 credit memorandum for interest earned.

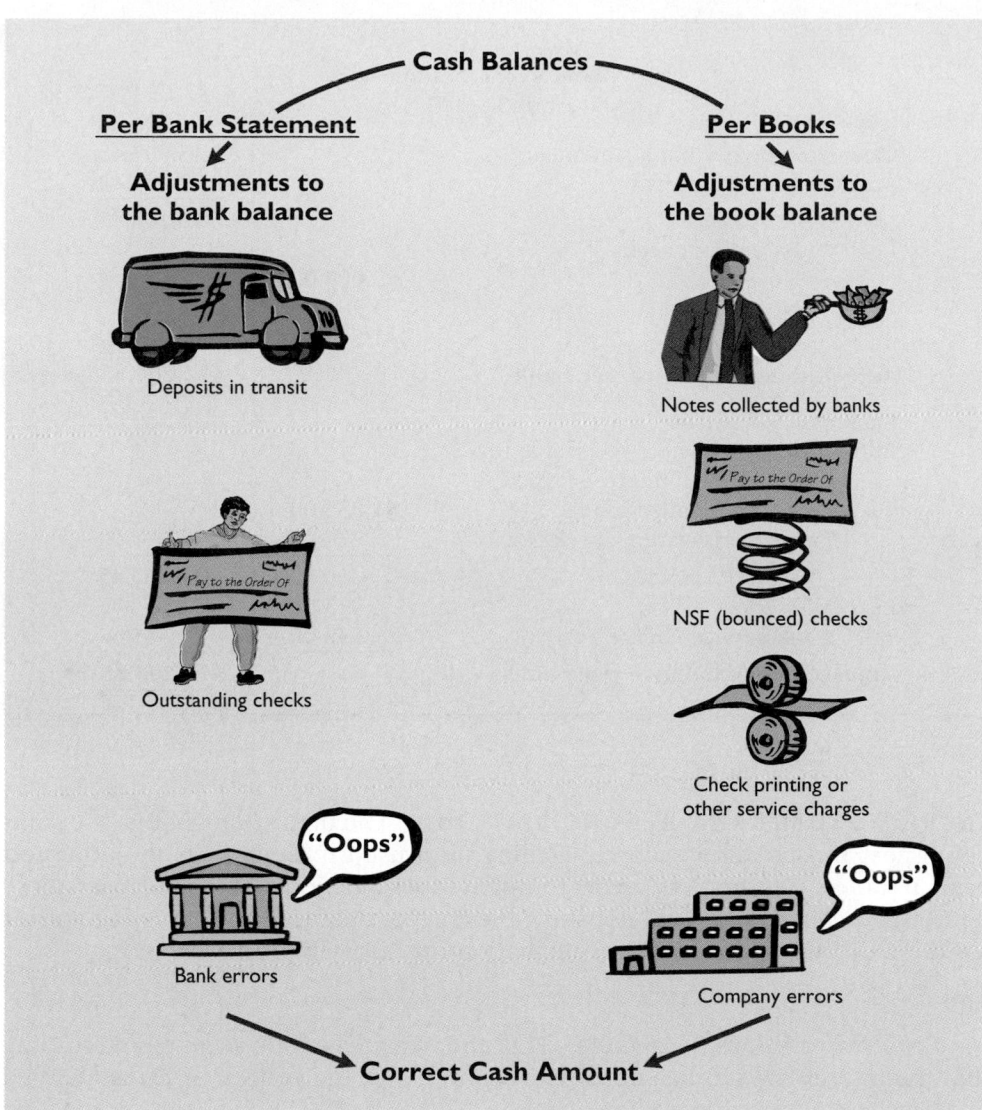

Cash Balances

Per Bank Statement

Adjustments to
the bank balance

Deposits in transit

Outstanding checks

"Oops"

Bank errors

Per Books

Adjustments to
the book balance

Notes collected by banks

NSF (bounced) checks

Check printing or
other service charges

"Oops"

Company errors

Correct Cash Amount

BANK RECONCILIATION ILLUSTRATED. Illustration 7-7 presented the bank statement for Laird Company. It shows a balance per bank of $15,907.45 on April 30, 2007. On this date the balance of cash per books is $11,589.45. From the foregoing steps, Laird determines the following reconciling items.

1. **Deposits in transit:** April 30 deposit (received by bank on May 1). $2,201.40

2. **Outstanding checks:** No. 453, $3,000.00; No. 457, $1,401.30; No. 460, $1,502.70. 5,904.00

3. **Errors:** Check No. 443 was correctly written by Laird for $1,226.00 and was correctly paid by the bank. However, Laird recorded the check as $1,262.00. 36.00

4. **Bank memoranda:**
   (a) Debit—NSF check from J. R. Baron for $425.60 425.60
   (b) Debit—Printing company checks charge, $30 30.00
   (c) Credit—Collection of note receivable for $1,000 plus interest earned $50, less bank collection fee $15 1,035.00

The bank reconciliation is shown in Illustration 7-9 (page 332).

Helpful Hint Note in the bank statement that the bank has paid checks No. 459 and 461, but check No. 460 is not listed. Thus, this check is outstanding. If a complete bank statement were provided, checks No. 453 and 457 also would not be listed. Laird obtains the amounts for these three checks from its cash payments records.

Illustration 7-9 Bank reconciliation

Alternative Terminology
The terms *adjusted cash balance*, *true cash balance*, and *correct cash balance* are used interchangeably.

LAIRD COMPANY Bank Reconciliation April 30, 2007		
Cash balance per bank statement		$ 15,907.45
Add: Deposits in transit		2,201.40
		18,108.85
Less: Outstanding checks		
No. 453	$3,000.00	
No. 457	1,401.30	
No. 460	1,502.70	5,904.00
Adjusted cash balance per bank		**$12,204.85**
Cash balance per books		$ 11,589.45
Add: Collection of note receivable for $1,000 plus interest earned $50, less collection fee $15	$1,035.00	
Error in recording check No. 443	36.00	1,071.00
		12,660.45
Less: NSF check	425.60	
Bank service charge	30.00	455.60
Adjusted cash balance per books		**$12,204.85**

Helpful Hint These entries are adjusting entries. In prior chapters, we considered Cash an account that did not require adjustment because we had not yet explained a bank reconciliation.

ENTRIES FROM BANK RECONCILIATION. The depositor (that is, the company) next must record each reconciling item used to determine the **adjusted cash balance per books**. If the company does not journalize and post these items, the Cash account will not show the correct balance. The adjusting entries for the Laird Company bank reconciliation on April 30 are as follows.

Collection of Note Receivable. This entry involves four accounts. Assuming that the interest of $50 has not been recorded and the collection fee is charged to Miscellaneous Expense, the entry is:

A	=	L	+	SE
+1,035				
				−15 Exp
−1,000				
				+50 Rev

Cash Flows
+1,035

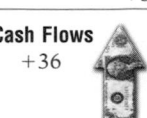

Apr. 30	Cash	1,035	
	Miscellaneous Expense	15	
	Notes Receivable		1,000
	Interest Revenue		50
	(To record collection of note receivable by bank)		

Book Error. An examination of the cash disbursements journal shows that check No. 443 was a payment on account to Andrea Company, a supplier. The correcting entry is:

A	=	L	+	SE
+36				
		+36		

Cash Flows
+36

Apr. 30	Cash	36	
	Accounts Payable—Andrea Company		36
	(To correct error in recording check No. 443)		

NSF Check. As indicated earlier, an NSF check becomes an accounts receivable to the depositor. The entry is:

Apr. 30	Accounts Receivable—J. R. Baron	425.60	
	Cash		425.60
	(To record NSF check)		

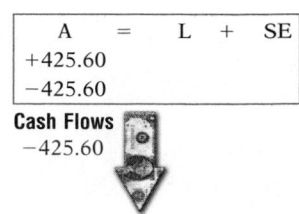

A = L + SE
+425.60
−425.60

Cash Flows
−425.60

Bank Service Charges. Companies typically debit to Miscellaneous Expense the check printing charges (DM) and other bank service charges (SC) because they are usually nominal in amount. Laird's entry is:

Apr. 30	Miscellaneous Expense	30	
	Cash		30
	(To record charge for printing company checks)		

A = L + SE
−30 Exp
−30

Cash Flows
−30

The foregoing entries could also be combined into one compound entry.

After Laird posts the entries, the Cash account will appear as in Illustration 7-10. The adjusted cash balance in the ledger should agree with the adjusted cash balance per books in the bank reconciliation in Illustration 7-9.

Cash

Apr. 30	Bal.	11,589.45	Apr. 30	425.60	
30		1,035.00	30	30.00	
30		36.00			
Apr. 30	Bal.	**12,204.85**			

Illustration 7-10
Adjusted balance in cash account

What entries does the bank make? If the company discovers any bank errors in preparing the reconciliation, it should notify the bank so the bank can make the necessary corrections on its records. The bank does not make any entries for deposits in transit or outstanding checks. Only when these items reach the bank will the bank record these items.

BEFORE YOU GO ON . . .

▶ Review It

1. Why is it necessary to reconcile a bank account?
2. What steps are involved in the reconciliation procedure?
3. What information is included in a bank reconciliation?

▶ Do It

Sally Kist owns Linen Kist Fabrics. Sally asks you to explain how Linen Kist should treat the following items in reconciling the bank account at December 31: (1) a debit memorandum for an NSF check, (2) a credit memorandum for a note collected by the bank, (3) outstanding checks, and (4) a deposit in transit.

Action Plan

• Understand the purpose of a bank reconciliation.
• Identify time lags and explain how they cause reconciling items.

Solution

In reconciling the bank account, Linen Kist should treat the reconciling items as follows.

NSF check: Deduct from balance per books.
Collection of note: Add to balance per books.
Outstanding checks: Deduct from balance per bank.
Deposit in transit: Add to balance per bank.

Reporting Cash

Companies report cash in two different statements: the balance sheet and the statement of cash flows. The balance sheet reports the amount of cash available at a given point in time. The statement of cash flows shows the sources and uses of cash during a period of time. The cash flow statement was introduced in Chapters 1 and 2 and will be discussed in much detail in Chapter 12. In this section we discuss some important points regarding the presentation of cash in the balance sheet.

When presented in a balance sheet, cash on hand, cash in banks, and petty cash are often combined and reported simply as **Cash**. Because it is the most liquid asset owned by the company, cash is listed first in the current assets section of the balance sheet.

CASH EQUIVALENTS

Many companies use the designation "Cash and cash equivalents" in reporting cash. (See Illustration 7-11 for an example.) **Cash equivalents** are short-term, highly liquid investments that are both:

1. Readily convertible to known amounts of cash, and
2. So near their maturity that their market value is relatively insensitive to changes in interest rates.

Examples of cash equivalents are Treasury bills, commercial paper (short-term corporate notes), and money market funds. All typically are purchased with cash that is in excess of immediate needs.

Illustration 7-11
Balance sheet presentation of cash

▲Delta

DELTA AIR LINES, INC.
Balance Sheet (partial)
December 31, 2004
(in millions)

Assets	
Current assets	
Cash and cash equivalents	**$1,463**
Short-term investments	336
Restricted cash	**348**
Accounts receivable, net	696
Parts inventories	203
Prepaid expenses and other	560
Total current assets	$3,606

Occasionally a company will have a net negative balance in its bank account. In this case, the company should report the negative balance among current liabilities. For example, farm equipment manufacturer Ag-Chem recently reported "Checks outstanding in excess of cash balances" of $2,145,000 among its current liabilities.

RESTRICTED CASH

A company may have cash that is not available for general use but, rather, is restricted for a special purpose. For example, landfill companies are often required to maintain a fund of restricted cash to ensure they will have adequate resources to cover closing and clean-up costs at the end of a landfill site's useful life.

Cash restricted in use should be reported separately on the balance sheet as **restricted cash**. If the company expects to use the restricted cash within the next year, it reports the amount as a current asset. When this is not the case, it reports the restricted funds as a noncurrent asset.

Illustration 7-11 shows restricted cash reported in the financial statements of **Delta Air Lines**. The company is required to maintain restricted cash as collateral to support insurance obligations related to workers' compensation claims. Delta does not have access to these funds for general use, and so it must report them separately, rather than as part of cash and cash equivalents.

Decision Toolkit

Decision Checkpoints	Info Needed for Decision	Tool to Use for Decision	How to Evaluate Results
Is all of the company's cash available for general use?	Balance sheet and notes to financial statements	Does the company report any cash as being restricted?	A restriction on the use of cash limits management's ability to use those resources for general obligations. This might be considered when assessing liquidity.

Managing and Monitoring Cash

Many companies struggle, not because they fail to generate sales, but because they can't manage their cash. A real-life example of this is a clothing manufacturing company owned by Sharon McCollick. McCollick gave up a stable, high-paying marketing job with Intel Corporation to start her own company. Soon she had more orders from stores such as JCPenney and Dayton Hudson (now Target) than she could fill. Yet she found herself on the brink of financial disaster, owing three mortgage payments on her house and $2,000 to the IRS. Her company could generate sales, but it was not collecting cash fast enough to support its operations. The bottom line is that a business must have cash.[3]

A merchandising company's operating cycle is generally shorter than that of a manufacturing company. Illustration 7-12 (page 336) shows the cash to cash operating cycle of a merchandising operation.

To understand cash management, consider the operating cycle of Sharon McCollick's clothing manufacturing company. First, it purchases cloth. Let's

---

[3]Adapted from T. Petzinger, Jr., "The Front Lines—Sharon McCollick Got Mad and Tore Down a Bank's Barriers," *Wall Street Journal* (May 19, 1995), p. B1.

Illustration 7-12
Operating cycle of a
merchandising company

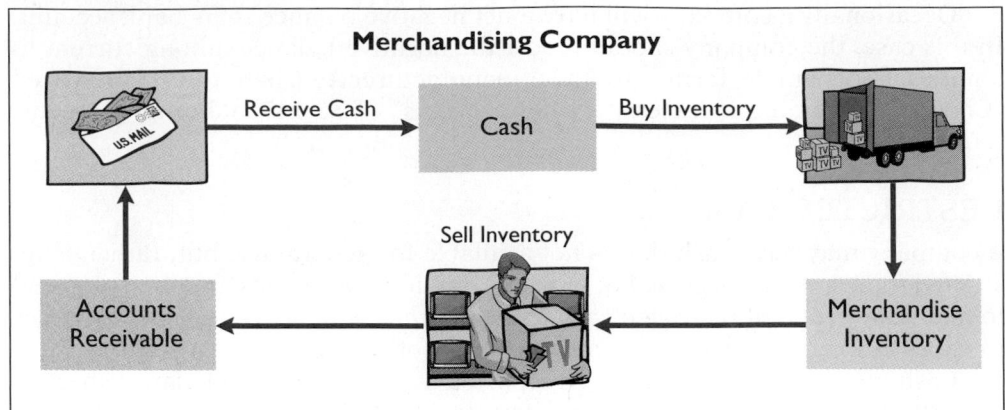

assume that it purchases the cloth on credit provided by the supplier, so the company owes its supplier money. Next, employees convert the cloth to clothing. Now the company also owes its employees money. Next, it sells the clothing to retailers, on credit. McCollick's company will have no money to repay suppliers or employees until its customers pay it. In a manufacturing operation there may be a significant lag between the original purchase of raw materials and the ultimate receipt of cash from customers.

Managing the often-precarious balance created by the ebb and flow of cash during the operating cycle is one of a company's greatest challenges. The objective is to ensure that a company has sufficient cash to meet payments as they come due, yet minimize the amount of non-revenue-generating cash on hand.

BASIC PRINCIPLES OF CASH MANAGEMENT

STUDY OBJECTIVE
6

Discuss the basic principles of cash management.

Management of cash is the responsibility of the company **treasurer**. Any company can improve its chances of having adequate cash by following five basic principles of cash management.

1. **Increase the speed of receivables collection.** Money owed Sharon McCollick by her customers is money that she can't use. The more quickly customers pay her, the more quickly she can use those funds. Thus, rather than have an average collection period of 30 days, she may want an average collection period of 15 days. However, she must carefully weigh any attempt to force her customers to pay earlier against the possibility that she may anger or alienate customers. Perhaps her competitors are willing to provide a 30-day grace period. As noted in Chapter 5, one common way to encourage customers to pay more quickly is to offer cash discounts for early payment under such terms as 2/10, n/30.

2. **Keep inventory levels low.** Maintaining a large inventory of cloth and finished clothing is costly. It ties up large amounts of cash, as well as warehouse space. Increasingly, companies are using techniques to reduce the inventory on hand, thus conserving their cash. Of course, if Sharon McCollick has inadequate inventory, she will lose sales. The proper level of inventory is an important decision.

3. **Delay payment of liabilities.** By keeping track of when her bills are due, Sharon McCollick's company can avoid paying bills too early. Let's say her supplier allows 30 days for payment. If she pays in 10 days, she has lost the use of that cash for 20 days. Therefore, she should use the full payment period. But she should not "stretch" payment past the point that could damage

her credit rating (and future borrowing ability). Sharon McCollick's company also should conserve cash by taking cash discounts offered by suppliers, when possible.

4. **Plan the timing of major expenditures.** To maintain operations or to grow, all companies must make major expenditures, which normally require some form of outside financing. In order to increase the likelihood of obtaining outside financing, McCollick should carefully consider the timing of major expenditures in light of her company's operating cycle. If at all possible, she should make any major expenditure when the company normally has excess cash—usually during the off-season.

5. **Invest idle cash.** Cash on hand earns nothing. An important part of the treasurer's job is to ensure that the company invests any excess cash, even if it is only overnight. Many businesses, such as Sharon McCollick's clothing company, are seasonal. During her slow season, when she has excess cash, she should invest it.

To avoid a cash crisis, however, it is very important that investments of idle cash be highly liquid and risk-free. A *liquid investment* is one with a market in which someone is always willing to buy or sell the investment. A *risk-free investment* means there is no concern that the party will default on its promise to pay its principal and interest. For example, using excess cash to purchase stock in a small company because you heard that it was probably going to increase in value in the near term is totally inappropriate. First, the stock of small companies is often illiquid. Second, if the stock suddenly decreases in value, you might be forced to sell the stock at a loss in order to pay your bills as they come due. The most common form of liquid investments is interest-paying U.S. government securities.

> ⊕ **International Note**
>
> International sales complicate cash management. For example, if Nike must repay a Japanese supplier 30 days from today in Japanese yen, Nike will be concerned about how the exchange rate of U.S. dollars for yen might change during those 30 days. Often corporate treasurers make investments known as *hedges* to lock in an exchange rate to reduce the company's exposure to exchange-rate fluctuation.

Illustration 7-13 summarizes these five principles of cash management.

Illustration 7-13 Five principles of sound cash management

CASH BUDGETING

Because cash is so vital to a company, **planning the company's cash needs** is a key business activity. It enables the company to plan ahead to cover possible cash shortfalls and to make investments of idle funds. The **cash budget** shows anticipated cash flows, usually over a one- to two-year period. In this

> **STUDY OBJECTIVE**
> **7**
> Identify the primary elements of a cash budget.

section we introduce the basics of cash budgeting. More advanced discussion of cash budgets and budgets in general is provided in managerial accounting texts.

As shown in Illustration 7-14, the cash budget contains three sections—cash receipts, cash disbursements, and financing—and the beginning and ending cash balances.

Illustration 7-14 Basic form of a cash budget

ANY COMPANY Cash Budget	
Beginning cash balance	$X,XXX
Add: **Cash receipts** (itemized)	X,XXX
Total available cash	X,XXX
Less: **Cash disbursements** (itemized)	X,XXX
Excess (deficiency) of available cash over cash disbursements	X,XXX
Financing needed	X,XXX
Ending cash balance	$X,XXX

The **Cash receipts** section includes expected receipts from the company's principal source(s) of cash, such as cash sales and collections from customers on credit sales. This section also shows anticipated receipts of interest and dividends, and proceeds from planned sales of investments, plant assets, and the company's capital stock.

The **Cash disbursements** section shows expected payments for direct materials, direct labor, manufacturing overhead, and selling and administrative expenses. This section also includes projected payments for income taxes, dividends, investments, and plant assets.

The **Financing** section shows expected borrowings and the repayment of the borrowed funds plus interest. The financing entry is needed when there is a cash deficiency or when the cash balance is less than management's minimum required balance.

Companies must prepare the data in the cash budget in sequence because the ending cash balance of one period becomes the beginning cash balance for the next period. They obtain data for preparing the cash budget from other budgets and from information provided by management. In practice, companies often prepare cash budgets for the next 12 months on a monthly basis.

To minimize detail, we will assume that Hayes Company prepares an annual cash budget by quarters. Preparing a cash budget requires making some assumptions. For example, Hayes makes assumptions regarding collection of accounts receivable, sales of securities, payments for materials and salaries, and purchases of property, plant, and equipment. The accuracy of the cash budget is very dependent on the accuracy of these assumptions.

Illustration 7–15 presents the cash budget for Hayes Company. The budget indicates that the company will need $3,000 of financing in the second quarter to maintain a minimum cash balance of $15,000. Since there is an excess of available cash over disbursements of $22,500 at the end of the third quarter, Hayes will repay the borrowing, plus $100 interest, in that quarter.

A cash budget contributes to more effective cash management. For example, it can show when a company will need additional financing, well before the actual need arises. Conversely, it can indicate when the company will have excess cash available for investments or other purposes.

Illustration 7-15   Cash budget

HAYES COMPANY
Cash Budget
For the Year Ending December 31, 2007

	Quarter			
	1	2	3	4
Beginning cash balance	$ 38,000	$ 25,500	$ 15,000	$ 19,400
Add: **Cash receipts**				
Collections from customers	168,000	198,000	228,000	258,000
Sale of securities	2,000	0	0	0
Total receipts	170,000	198,000	228,000	258,000
Total available cash	208,000	223,500	243,000	277,400
Less: **Cash disbursements**				
Materials	23,200	27,200	31,200	35,200
Salaries	62,000	72,000	82,000	92,000
Selling and administrative expenses (excluding depreciation)	94,300	99,300	104,300	109,300
Purchase of truck	0	10,000	0	0
Income tax expense	3,000	3,000	3,000	3,000
Total disbursements	182,500	211,500	220,500	239,500
Excess (deficiency) of available cash over disbursements	25,500	12,000	22,500	37,900
Financing				
Borrowings	0	3,000	0	0
Repayments—plus $100 interest	0	0	3,100	0
Ending cash balance	$ 25,500	$ 15,000	$ 19,400	$ 37,900

Decision Toolkit

Decision Checkpoints	Info Needed for Decision	Tool to Use for Decision	How to Evaluate Results
Will the company be able to meet its projected cash needs?	Cash budget (typically available only to management)	The cash budget shows projected sources and uses of cash. If cash uses exceed internal cash sources, then the company must look for outside sources.	Two issues: (1) Are management's projections reasonable? (2) If outside sources are needed, are they available?

BEFORE YOU GO ON . . .

▶ **Review It**

1. What are the five principal elements of sound cash management?
2. What are the three sections of the cash budget?
3. What was Tootsie Roll's balance in cash and cash equivalents at December 31, 2004? Did it report any restricted cash? How did Tootsie Roll define cash equivalents? The answers to these questions appear on p. 369.

▶Do It

Martian Company's management wants to maintain a minimum monthly cash balance of $15,000. At the beginning of March the cash balance is $16,500; expected cash receipts for March are $210,000; and cash disbursements are expected to be $220,000. How much cash, if any, must Martian borrow to maintain the desired minimum monthly balance?

Action Plan

• Insert the dollar data into the basic form of the cash budget.

Solution

Beginning cash balance	$ 16,500
Add: Cash receipts for March	210,000
Total available cash	226,500
Less: Cash disbursements for March	220,000
Excess of available cash over cash disbursements	6,500
Financing	**8,500**
Ending cash balance	$ 15,000

To maintain the desired minimum cash balance of $15,000, Martian Company must borrow $8,500 of cash.

Using the Decision Toolkit

Presented below is hypothetical financial information for Mattel Corporation. Included in this information is financial statement data from the year ended December 31, 2006, which should be used to evaluate Mattel's cash position.

Selected Financial Information
Year Ended December 31, 2006
(in millions)

Net cash provided by operations	$325
Capital expenditures	162
Dividends paid	80
Total expenses	680
Depreciation expense	40
Cash balance	206

Also provided are projected data which are management's best estimate of its sources and uses of cash during 2007. This information should be used to prepare a cash budget for 2007.

Projected Sources and Uses of Cash
(in millions)

Beginning cash balance	$206
Cash receipts from sales	355
Cash receipts from sale of short-term investments	20
Cash payments for inventory	357
Cash payments for selling and administrative expense	201
Cash payments for property, plant, and equipment	45
Cash payments for taxes	17

Mattel Corporation's management believes it should maintain a balance of $200 million cash.

Instructions

(a) Using the hypothetical projected sources and uses of cash information presented above, prepare a cash budget for 2007 for Mattel Corporation.

(b) Comment on the company's cash adequacy, and discuss steps that might be taken to improve its cash position.

Solution

(a)

MATTEL CORPORATION
Cash Budget
For the Year 2007
(in millions)

Beginning cash balance		$206
Add: Cash receipts		
From sales of product	$355	
From sale of short-term investments	20	375
Total available cash		581
Less: Cash disbursements		
Payments for inventory	357	
Payments for selling and administrative costs	201	
Payments for property, plant, and equipment	45	
Payments for taxes	17	
Total disbursements		620
Excess (deficiency) of available cash over disbursements		(39)
Financing needed		**239**
Ending cash balance		$200

(b) Using these hypothetical data, Mattel's cash position appears adequate. For 2007 Mattel is projecting a cash shortfall. This is not necessarily of concern, but it should be investigated. Given that its primary line of business is toys, and that most toys are sold during December, we would expect Mattel's cash position to vary significantly during the course of the year. After the holiday season it probably has a lot of excess cash. Earlier in the year, when it is making and selling its product but has not yet been paid, it may need to borrow to meet any temporary cash shortfalls.

If Mattel's management is concerned with its cash position, it could take the following steps: (1) Offer its customers cash discounts for early payment, such as 2/10, n/30. (2) Implement inventory management techniques to reduce the need for large inventories of such things as the plastics used to make its toys. (3) Carefully time payments to suppliers by keeping track of when payments are due, so as not to pay too early. (4) If it has plans for major expenditures, time those expenditures to coincide with its seasonal period of excess cash.

Summary of Study Objectives

1 *Identify the principles of internal control.* The principles of internal control are establishment of responsibility; segregation of duties; documentation procedures; physical, mechanical, and electronic controls; independent internal verification; and other controls.

2 *Explain the applications of internal control to cash receipts.* Internal controls over cash receipts include: (a) designating only personnel such as cashiers to handle cash; (b) assigning the duties of receiving cash, recording cash, and having custody of cash to different individuals; (c) obtaining remittance advices for mail receipts, cash register tapes for over-the-counter receipts, and deposit slips for bank deposits; (d) using company safes and bank vaults to store cash with access limited to authorized personnel, and using cash registers in executing over-the-counter receipts; (e) making independent daily counts of register receipts and daily comparisons of total receipts with total deposits; and (f) bonding personnel who handle cash and requiring them to take vacations.

3 *Explain the applications of internal control to cash disbursements.* Internal controls over cash disbursements include: (a) having only specified individuals such as the treasurer authorized to sign checks; (b) assigning the duties of approving items for payment, paying the items, and recording the payment to different individuals; (c) using prenumbered checks and accounting for all checks, with each check supported by an approved invoice; (d) storing blank checks in a safe or vault with access restricted to authorized personnel, and using a machine with indelible ink to imprint amounts on checks; (e) comparing each check with the approved invoice before issuing the check, and making monthly reconciliations of bank and book balances; and (f) after payment, stamping each approved invoice "paid."

4 *Prepare a bank reconciliation.* In reconciling the bank account, it is customary to reconcile the balance per books and the balance per bank to their adjusted balance. The steps in determining the reconciling items are to ascertain deposits in transit, outstanding checks, errors by the depositor or the bank, and unrecorded bank memoranda.

5 *Explain the reporting of cash.* Cash is listed first in the current assets section of the balance sheet. In some cases, companies report cash together with cash equivalents. Cash restricted for a special purpose is reported separately as a current asset or as a non-current asset, depending on when the company expects to use the cash.

6 *Discuss the basic principles of cash management.* The basic principles of cash management include: (a) increase the speed of receivables collection, (b) keep inventory levels low, (c) delay payment of liabilities, (d) plan timing of major expenditures, and (e) invest idle cash.

7 *Identify the primary elements of a cash budget.* The three main elements of a cash budget are the cash receipts section, cash disbursements section, and financing section.

THE NAVIGATOR

Decision Toolkit—A Summary

Decision Checkpoints	Info Needed for Decision	Tool to Use for Decision	How to Evaluate Results
Are the company's financial statements supported by adequate internal controls?	Auditor's report, management discussion and analysis, articles in financial press	The required measures of internal control are to (1) establish responsibility, (2) segregate duties, (3) document procedures, (4) employ physical or automated controls, and (5) use independent internal verification.	If any indication is given that these or other controls are lacking, use the financial statements with caution.
Is all of the company's cash available for general use?	Balance sheet and notes to financial statements	Does the company report any cash as being restricted?	A restriction on the use of cash limits management's ability to use those resources for general obligations. This might be considered when assessing liquidity.
Will the company be able to meet its projected cash needs?	Cash budget (typically available only to management)	The cash budget shows projected sources and uses of cash. If cash uses exceed internal cash sources, then the company must look for outside sources.	Two issues: (1) Are management's projections reasonable? (2) If outside sources are needed, are they available?

APPENDIX
OPERATION OF THE PETTY CASH FUND

The operation of a petty cash fund involves (1) establishing the fund, (2) making payments from the fund, and (3) replenishing the fund.

STUDY OBJECTIVE
8
Explain the operation of a petty cash fund.

Establishing the Petty Cash Fund

Two essential steps in establishing a petty cash fund are: (1) appointing a petty cash custodian who will be responsible for the fund, and (2) determining the size of the fund. Ordinarily, a company expects the amount in the fund to cover anticipated disbursements for a three- to four-week period.

When the company establishes the petty cash fund, it issues a check payable to the petty cash custodian for the stipulated amount. If Laird Company decides to establish a $100 fund on March 1, the entry in general journal form is:

Mar. 1	Petty Cash	100	
	Cash		100
	(To establish a petty cash fund)		

A	=	L	+	SE
+100				
−100				

Cash Flows
no effect

The fund custodian cashes the check and places the proceeds in a locked petty cash box or drawer. Most petty cash funds are established on a fixed-amount basis. Moreover, the company will make no additional entries to the Petty Cash account unless the stipulated amount of the fund is changed. For example, if Laird Company decides on July 1 to increase the size of the fund to $250, it would debit Petty Cash $150 and credit Cash $150.

Helpful Hint Petty cash funds are authorized and legitimate. In contrast, "slush" funds are unauthorized and hidden (under the table).

Making Payments from Petty Cash

The custodian of the petty cash fund has the authority to make payments from the fund that conform to prescribed management policies. Usually management limits the size of expenditures that come from petty cash and does not permit use of the fund for certain types of transactions (such as making short-term loans to employees).

Each payment from the fund must be documented on a prenumbered petty cash receipt (or petty cash voucher). The signatures of both the custodian and the individual receiving payment are required on the receipt. If other supporting documents such as a freight bill or invoice are available, they should be attached to the petty cash receipt.

The custodian keeps the receipts in the petty cash box until the fund is replenished. As a result, the sum of the petty cash receipts and money in the fund should equal the established total at all times. This means that management can make surprise counts at any time by an independent person, such as an internal auditor, to determine the correctness of the fund.

The company does not make an accounting entry to record a payment at the time it is taken from petty cash. It is considered both inexpedient and unnecessary to do so. Instead, the company recognizes the accounting effects of each payment when the fund is replenished.

Helpful Hint From the standpoint of internal control, the receipt satisfies two principles: (1) establishing responsibility (signature of custodian), and (2) documentation procedures.

Replenishing the Petty Cash Fund

When the money in the petty cash fund reaches a minimum level, the company replenishes the fund. The petty cash custodian initiates a request for reimbursement. This individual prepares a schedule (or summary) of the payments that have been made and sends the schedule, supported by petty cash receipts and other documentation, to the treasurer's office. The receipts and supporting documents are examined in the treasurer's office to verify that they were proper payments from the fund. The treasurer then approves the request, and a check is prepared to restore the fund to its established amount. At the same time, all supporting documentation is stamped "paid" so that it cannot be submitted again for payment.

To illustrate, assume that on March 15 the petty cash custodian requests a check for $87. The fund contains $13 cash and petty cash receipts for postage $44, supplies $38, and miscellaneous expenses $5. The entry, in general journal form, to record the check is:

Helpful Hint Replenishing involves three internal control procedures: segregation of duties, documentation procedures, and independent internal verification.

A	=	L	+	SE
				−44 Exp
+38				
				−5 Exp
−87				

Cash Flows
−87

Mar. 15	Postage Expense		44	
	Supplies		38	
	Miscellaneous Expense		5	
	Cash			87
	(To replenish petty cash fund)			

Note that the reimbursement entry does not affect the Petty Cash account. Replenishment changes the composition of the fund by replacing the petty cash receipts with cash, but it does not change the balance in the fund.

Occasionally, in replenishing a petty cash fund the company may need to recognize a cash shortage or overage. To illustrate, assume in the preceding example that the custodian had only $12 in cash in the fund plus the receipts as listed. The request for reimbursement would therefore be for $88, and the following entry would be made.

A	=	L	+	SE
				−44 Exp
+38				
				−5 Exp
				−1 Exp
−88				

Cash Flows
−88

Mar. 15	Postage Expense		44	
	Supplies		38	
	Miscellaneous Expense		5	
	Cash Over and Short		1	
	Cash			88
	(To replenish petty cash fund)			

Conversely, if the custodian had $14 in cash, the reimbursement request would be for $86, and Cash Over and Short would be credited for $1. A debit balance in Cash Over and Short is reported in the income statement as miscellaneous expense; a credit balance is reported as miscellaneous revenue. The company closes Cash Over and Short to Income Summary at the end of the year.

Companies should replenish a petty cash fund **at the end of the accounting period**, **regardless of the cash in the fund**. Replenishment at this time is necessary in order to recognize the effects of the petty cash payments on the financial statements.

Internal control over a petty cash fund is strengthened by (1) having a supervisor make surprise counts of the fund to ascertain whether the paid vouchers and fund cash equal the designated amount, and (2) canceling or mutilating the paid vouchers so they cannot be resubmitted for reimbursement.

Summary of Study Objective for Appendix

8 *Explain the operation of a petty cash fund.* In operating a petty cash fund, a company establishes the fund by appointing a custodian and determining the size of the fund. The custodian makes payments from the fund for documented expenditures. The company replenishes the fund as needed, and at least at the end of each accounting period. Accounting entries to record payments are made at that time.

Glossary

Bank reconciliation   The process of comparing the bank's account balance with the company's balance, and explaining the differences to make them agree. (p. 328)

Bank statement   A statement received monthly from the bank that shows the depositor's bank transactions and balances. (p. 328)

Cash   Resources that consist of coins, currency, checks, money orders, and money on hand or on deposit in a bank or similar depository. (p. 324)

Cash budget   A projection of anticipated cash flows, usually over a one- to two-year period. (p. 337)

Cash equivalents   Short-term, highly liquid investments that can be converted to a specific amount of cash. (p. 334)

Deposits in transit   Deposits recorded by the depositor that have not been recorded by the bank. (p. 330)

Electronic funds transfer (EFT)   A disbursement system that uses wire, telephone, telegraph, or computer to transfer cash from one location to another. (p. 326)

Internal auditors   Company employees who evaluate on a continuous basis the effectiveness of the company's system of internal control. (p. 321)

Internal control   The plan of organization and all the related methods and measures adopted within a business to safeguard its assets and enhance the accuracy and reliability of its accounting records. (p. 316)

NSF check   A check that is not paid by a bank because of insufficient funds in a customer's bank account. (p. 329)

Outstanding checks   Checks issued and recorded by a company that have not been paid by the bank. (p. 330)

Petty cash fund   A cash fund used to pay relatively small amounts. (p. 327)

Restricted cash   Cash that is not available for general use, but instead is restricted for a particular purpose. (p. 335)

Sarbanes-Oxley Act of 2002 (SOX)   Law that forces companies to pay more attention to internal control. (p. 317)

Treasurer   Employee responsible for the management of a company's cash. (p. 336)

Demonstration Problem

Trillo Company's bank statement for May 2007 shows these data.

Balance May 1	$12,650	Balance May 31	$14,280
Debit memorandum:		Credit memorandum:	
NSF check	175	Collection of note receivable	505

The cash balance per books at May 31 is $13,319. Your review of the data reveals the following.

1. The NSF check was from Hup Co., a customer.
2. The note collected by the bank was a $500, 3-month, 12% note. The bank charged a $10 collection fee. No interest has been accrued.
3. Outstanding checks at May 31 total $2,410.
4. Deposits in transit at May 31 total $1,752.
5. A Trillo Company check for $352 dated May 10 cleared the bank on May 25. This check, which was a payment on account, was journalized for $325.

Instructions
(a) Prepare a bank reconciliation at May 31.
(b) Journalize the entries required by the reconciliation.

Action Plan

- Follow the four steps used in reconciling items (p. 330).
- Work carefully to minimize mathematical errors in the reconciliation.
- Prepare entries based on reconciling items per books.
- Make sure the cash ledger balance after posting the reconciling entries agrees with the adjusted cash balance per books.

Solution to Demonstration Problem

(a)

Cash balance per bank statement		$14,280
Add: Deposits in transit		1,752
		16,032
Less: Outstanding checks		2,410
Adjusted cash balance per bank		$13,622
Cash balance per books		$13,319
Add: Collection of note receivable $500, plus $15 interest less collection fee $10		505
		13,824
Less: NSF check	$175	
Error in recording check	27	202
Adjusted cash balance per books		$13,622

(b)

May	31	Cash	505	
		Miscellaneous Expense	10	
		Notes Receivable		500
		Interest Revenue		15
		(To record collection of note by bank)		
	31	Accounts Receivable—Hup Co.	175	
		Cash		175
		(To record NSF check from Hup Co.)		
	31	Accounts Payable	27	
		Cash		27
		(To correct error in recording check)		

Note: All Questions, Exercises, and Problems marked with an asterisk relate to material in the appendix to the chapter.

Self-Study Questions

Answers are at the end of the chapter.

(SO 1) **1.** Internal control is used in a business to enhance the accuracy and reliability of its accounting records and to:
   (a) safeguard its assets.
   (b) prevent fraud.
   (c) produce correct financial statements.
   (d) deter employee dishonesty.

(SO 1) **2.** The principles of internal control do *not* include:
   (a) establishment of responsibility.
   (b) documentation procedures.
   (c) financial performance measures.
   (d) independent internal verification.

(SO 1) **3.** Physical controls do *not* include:
   (a) safes and vaults to store cash.
   (b) independent bank reconciliations.
   (c) locked warehouses for inventories.
   (d) bank safety deposit boxes for important papers.

(SO 2) **4.** Permitting only designated personnel such as cashiers to handle cash receipts is an application of the principle of:
   (a) documentation procedures.
   (b) establishment of responsibility.
   (c) independent internal verification.
   (d) other controls.

(SO 3) **5.** The use of prenumbered checks in disbursing cash is an application of the principle of:
   (a) establishment of responsibility.
   (b) segregation of duties.
   (c) physical, mechanical, and electronic controls.
   (d) documentation procedures.

(SO 3) **6.** The control features of a bank account do *not* include:
   (a) having bank auditors verify the correctness of the bank balance per books.
   (b) minimizing the amount of cash that must be kept on hand.

(c) providing a double record of all bank transactions.

(d) safeguarding cash by using a bank as a depository.

(SO 4) **7.** In a bank reconciliation, deposits in transit are:
(a) deducted from the book balance.
(b) added to the book balance.
(c) added to the bank balance.
(d) deducted from the bank balance.

(SO 5) **8.** Which of the following items in a cash drawer at November 30 is *not* cash?
(a) Money orders.
(b) Coins and currency.
(c) A customer check dated December 1.
(d) A customer check dated November 28.

(SO 7) **9.** Which of the following is *not* one of the sections of a cash budget?
(a) Cash receipts section.
(b) Cash disbursements section.
(c) Financing section.
(d) Cash from operations section.

10. Which statement correctly describes (SO 5) the reporting of cash?
(a) Cash cannot be combined with cash equivalents.
(b) Restricted cash funds may be combined with Cash.
(c) Cash is listed first in the current assets section.
(d) Restricted cash funds cannot be reported as a current asset.

*****11.** A check is written to replenish a $100 petty cash (SO 8) fund when the fund contains receipts of $94 and $3 in cash. In recording the check:
(a) Cash Over and Short should be debited for $3.
(b) Petty Cash should be debited for $94.
(c) Cash should be credited for $94.
(d) Petty Cash should be credited for $3.

Go to the book's website, **www.wiley.com/college/kimmel**, to access additional Self-Study Questions.

Questions

1. "Internal control is concerned only with enhancing the accuracy of the accounting records." Do you agree? Explain.

2. Discuss how the Sarbanes-Oxley Act has increased the importance of internal control to all employees in a company.

3. What principles of internal control apply to most business enterprises?

4. In the corner grocery store, all sales clerks make change out of one cash register drawer. Is this a violation of internal control? Why?

5. Melody Wilson is reviewing the principle of segregation of duties. What are the two common applications of this principle?

6. How do documentation procedures contribute to good internal control?

7. What internal control objectives are met by physical, mechanical, and electronic controls?

8. (a) Explain the control principle of independent internal verification.
(b) What practices are important in applying this principle?

9. As the company accountant, explain the following ideas to the management of Jason Company.
(a) The concept of reasonable assurance in internal control.
(b) The importance of the human factor in internal control.

10. Discuss the human resources department's involvement in internal controls.

11. Fitzgerald Inc. owns the following assets at the balance sheet date.

Cash in bank—savings account	$ 5,000
Cash on hand	1,100
Cash refund due from the IRS	1,000
Checking account balance	12,000
Postdated checks	500

What amount should be reported as Cash in the balance sheet?

12. What principle(s) of internal control is (are) involved in making daily cash counts of over-the-counter receipts?

13. Assume that Kohl's Department Stores installed new electronic cash registers in its stores. How do cash registers improve internal control over cash receipts?

14. At Wells Wholesale Company two mail clerks open all mail receipts. How does this strengthen internal control?

15. "To have maximum effective internal control over cash disbursements, all payments should be made by check." Is this true? Explain.

16. Swendson Company's internal controls over cash disbursements provide for the treasurer to sign checks imprinted by a checkwriter after comparing the check with the approved invoice. Identify the internal control principles that are present in these controls.

17. How do these principles apply to cash disbursements:
(a) Physical, mechanical, and electronic controls?
(b) Other controls?

18. What is the essential feature of an electronic funds transfer (EFT) procedure?

19. "The use of a bank contributes significantly to good internal control over cash." Is this true? Why?

20. Raymond Bright is confused about the lack of agreement between the cash balance per books and the balance per bank. Explain the causes for the lack of agreement to Raymond, and give an example of each cause.

21. Describe the basic principles of cash management.

22. Kelly Mills asks your help concerning an NSF check. Explain to Kelly (a) what an NSF check is, (b) how

it is treated in a bank reconciliation, and (c) whether it will require an adjusting entry on the company's books.

23.
   (a) "Cash equivalents are the same as cash." Do you agree? Explain.
   (b) How should restricted cash funds be reported on the balance sheet?

*24. (a) Identify the three activities that pertain to a petty cash fund, and indicate an internal control principle that is applicable to each activity.
   (b) When are journal entries required in the operation of a petty cash fund?

Brief Exercises

Explain the importance of internal control.
(SO 1)

BE7-1 Jo Duma is the new owner of JoJo Co. She has heard about internal control but is not clear about its importance for her business. Explain to Jo the two purposes of internal control, and give her one application of each purpose for JoJo Co.

Identify internal control principles.
(SO 1)

BE7-2 The internal control procedures in Barton Company make the following provisions. Identify the principles of internal control that are being followed in each case.
(a) Employees who have physical custody of assets do not have access to the accounting records.
(b) Each month the assets on hand are compared to the accounting records by an internal auditor.
(c) A prenumbered shipping document is prepared for each shipment of goods to customers.

Identify the internal control principles applicable to cash receipts.
(SO 2)

BE7-3 Allen Company has the following internal control procedures over cash receipts. Identify the internal control principle that is applicable to each procedure.
(a) All over-the-counter receipts are registered on cash registers.
(b) All cashiers are bonded.
(c) Daily cash counts are made by cashier department supervisors.
(d) The duties of receiving cash, recording cash, and having custody of cash are assigned to different individuals.
(e) Only cashiers may operate cash registers.

Identify the internal control principles applicable to cash disbursements.
(SO 3)

BE7-4 Pascal Company has the following internal control procedures over cash disbursements. Identify the internal control principle that is applicable to each procedure.
(a) Company checks are prenumbered.
(b) The bank statement is reconciled monthly by an internal auditor.
(c) Blank checks are stored in a safe in the treasurer's office.
(d) Only the treasurer or assistant treasurer may sign checks.
(e) Check signers are not allowed to record cash disbursement transactions.

Identify the control features of a bank account.
(SO 3)

BE7-5 Colton Amon is uncertain about the control features of a bank account. Explain the control benefits of (a) a check and (b) a bank statement.

Indicate location of reconciling items in a bank reconciliation.
(SO 4)

BE7-6 The following reconciling items are applicable to the bank reconciliation for Pileggi Co. Indicate how each item should be shown on a bank reconciliation.
(a) Outstanding checks.
(b) Bank debit memorandum for service charge.
(c) Bank credit memorandum for collecting a note for the depositor.
(d) Deposit in transit.

Identify reconciling items that require adjusting entries.
(SO 4)

BE7-7 Using the data in BE7-6, indicate (a) the items that will result in an adjustment to the depositor's records and (b) why the other items do not require adjustment.

BE7-8 At July 31 Ballah Company has this bank information: cash balance per bank $7,800; outstanding checks $762; deposits in transit $1,350; and a bank service charge $40. Determine the adjusted cash balance per bank at July 31.

Prepare partial bank reconciliation.
(SO 4)

BE7-9 In the month of November, Drajna Company Inc. wrote checks in the amount of $9,250. In December, checks in the amount of $11,880 were written. In November, $8,800 of these checks were presented to the bank for payment, and $10,889 in December. What is the amount of outstanding checks at the end of November? At the end of December?

Analyze outstanding checks.
(SO 4)

BE7-10 Elizondo Company has these cash balances: cash in bank $12,742; payroll bank account $6,000; and plant expansion fund cash $25,000. Explain how each balance should be reported on the balance sheet.

Explain the statement presentation of cash balances.
(SO 5)

BE7-11 The following information is available for Gurek Company for the month of January: expected cash receipts $60,000; expected cash disbursements $67,000; cash balance on January 1, $12,000. Management wishes to maintain a minimum cash balance of $8,000. Prepare a basic cash budget for the month of January.

Prepare a cash budget.
(SO 7)

*****BE7-12** On March 20 Slater's petty cash fund of $100 is replenished when the fund contains $21 in cash and receipts for postage $40, supplies $26, and travel expense $13. Prepare the journal entry to record the replenishment of the petty cash fund.

Prepare entry to replenish a petty cash fund.
(SO 8)

Exercises

E7-1 Bank employees use a system known as the "maker-checker" system. An employee will record an entry in the appropriate journal, and then a supervisor will verify and approve the entry. These days, as all of a bank's accounts are computerized, the employee first enters a batch of entries into the computer, and then the entries are posted automatically to the general ledger account after the supervisor approves them on the system.

Identify the principles of internal control.
(SO 1)

Access to the computer system is password-protected and task-specific, which means that the computer system will not allow the employee to approve a transaction or the supervisor to record a transaction.

Instructions
Identify the principles of internal control inherent in the "maker-checker" procedure used by banks.

E7-2 Culotti's Pizza operates strictly on a carryout basis. Customers pick up their orders at a counter where a clerk exchanges the pizza for cash. While at the counter, the customer can see other employees making the pizzas and the large ovens in which the pizzas are baked.

Identify the principles of internal control.
(SO 1)

Instructions
Identify the six principles of internal control and give an example of each principle that you might observe when picking up your pizza. (*Note:* It may not be possible to observe all the principles.)

E7-3 The following control procedures are used in Elke Company for over-the-counter cash receipts.

List internal control weaknesses over cash receipts and suggest improvements.
(SO 1, 2)

1. Cashiers are experienced; thus, they are not bonded.

2. All over-the-counter receipts are registered by three clerks who share a cash register with a single cash drawer.

3. To minimize the risk of robbery, cash in excess of $100 is stored in an unlocked attaché case in the stock room until it is deposited in the bank.

4. At the end of each day the total receipts are counted by the cashier on duty and reconciled to the cash register total.

5. The company accountant makes the bank deposit and then records the day's receipts.

Instructions
(a) For each procedure, explain the weakness in internal control and identify the control principle that is violated.

(b) For each weakness, suggest a change in the procedure that will result in good internal control.

List internal control weaknesses for cash disbursements and suggest improvements.
(SO 1, 3)

E7-4 The following control procedures are used in Albina's Boutique Shoppe for cash disbursements.

1. Each week Albina leaves 100 company checks in an unmarked envelope on a shelf behind the cash register.
2. The store manager personally approves all payments before signing and issuing checks.
3. The company checks are unnumbered.
4. After payment, bills are "filed" in a paid invoice folder.
5. The company accountant prepares the bank reconciliation and reports any discrepancies to the owner.

Instructions
(a) For each procedure, explain the weakness in internal control and identify the internal control principle that is violated.
(b) For each weakness, suggest a change in the procedure that will result in good internal control.

Identify internal control weaknesses for cash disbursements and suggest improvements.
(SO 1, 3)

E7-5 At Nystrom Company checks are not prenumbered because both the purchasing agent and the treasurer are authorized to issue checks. Each signer has access to unissued checks kept in an unlocked file cabinet. The purchasing agent pays all bills pertaining to goods purchased for resale. Prior to payment, the purchasing agent determines that the goods have been received and verifies the mathematical accuracy of the vendor's invoice. After payment, the invoice is filed by vendor and the purchasing agent records the payment in the cash disbursements journal. The treasurer pays all other bills following approval by authorized employees. After payment, the treasurer stamps all bills "paid," files them by payment date, and records the checks in the cash disbursements journal. Nystrom Company maintains one checking account that is reconciled by the treasurer.

Instructions
(a) List the weaknesses in internal control over cash disbursements.
(b) Identify improvements for correcting these weaknesses.

Prepare bank reconciliation and adjusting entries.
(SO 4)

E7-6 Leng Xiong is unable to reconcile the bank balance at January 31. Leng's reconciliation is shown here.

Cash balance per bank	$3,660.20
Add: NSF check	370.00
Less: Bank service charge	25.00
Adjusted balance per bank	$4,005.20
Cash balance per books	$3,975.20
Less: Deposits in transit	590.00
Add: Outstanding checks	670.00
Adjusted balance per books	$4,055.20

Instructions
(a) What is the proper adjusted cash balance per bank?
(b) What is the proper adjusted cash balance per books?
(c) Prepare the adjusting journal entries necessary to determine the adjusted cash balance per books.

Determine outstanding checks.
(SO 4)

E7-7 At April 30 the bank reconciliation of Engstrom Company shows three outstanding checks: No. 254 $650, No. 255 $800, and No. 257 $410. The May bank statement and the May cash payments journal are given here.

Bank Statement Checks Paid			Cash Payments Journal Checks Issued		
Date	Check No.	Amount	Date	Check No.	Amount
5-4	254	$650	5-2	258	$159
5-2	257	410	5-5	259	275
5-17	258	159	5-10	260	925
5-12	259	275	5-15	261	500
5-20	261	500	5-22	262	750
5-29	264	360	5-24	263	480
5-30	262	750	5-29	264	360

Instructions
Using step 2 in the reconciliation procedure (see page 330), list the outstanding checks at May 31.

Prepare bank reconciliation and adjusting entries.
(SO 4)

E7-8   The following information pertains to DeVries Company.

1. Cash balance per bank, July 31, $7,328.

2. July bank service charge not recorded by the depositor $40.

3. Cash balance per books, July 31, $7,280.

4. Deposits in transit, July 31, $1,700.

5. Note for $1,000 collected for DeVries in July by the bank, plus interest $36 less fee $20. The collection has not been recorded by Allied, and no interest has been accrued.

6. Outstanding checks, July 31, $772.

Instructions
(a) Prepare a bank reconciliation at July 31, 2007.
(b) Journalize the adjusting entries at July 31 on the books of DeVries Company.

E7-9   This information relates to the Cash account in the ledger of Espejel Company.

Prepare bank reconciliation and adjusting entries.
(SO 4)

Balance September 1—$16,400; Cash deposited—$64,000
Balance September 30—$17,600; Checks written—$62,800

The September bank statement shows a balance of $16,422 at September 30 and the following memoranda.

Credits		Debits	
Collection of $1,800 note plus interest $30	$1,830	NSF check: J. Hower	$360
Interest earned on checking account	45	Safety deposit box rent	50

At September 30 deposits in transit were $5,026 and outstanding checks totaled $2,383.

Instructions
(a) Prepare the bank reconciliation at September 30, 2007.
(b) Prepare the adjusting entries at September 30, assuming (1) the NSF check was from a customer on account, and (2) no interest had been accrued on the note.

E7-10   The cash records of Dana Company show the following.

For July:

Compute deposits in transit and outstanding checks for two bank reconciliations.
(SO 4)

1. The June 30 bank reconciliation indicated that deposits in transit total $750. During July the general ledger account Cash shows deposits of $16,200, but the bank statement indicates that only $15,600 in deposits were received during the month.

2. The June 30 bank reconciliation also reported outstanding checks of $990. During the month of July, Dana Company books show that $17,500 of checks were issued, yet the bank statement showed that $16,400 of checks cleared the bank in July.

For September:

3. In September deposits per bank statement totaled $25,900, deposits per books were $25,400, and deposits in transit at September 30 were $2,200.

4. In September cash disbursements per books were $23,700, checks clearing the bank were $24,000, and outstanding checks at September 30 were $2,100.

There were no bank debit or credit memoranda, and no errors were made by either the bank or Dana Company.

Instructions
Answer the following questions.
(a) In situation 1, what were the deposits in transit at July 31?
(b) In situation 2, what were the outstanding checks at July 31?
(c) In situation 3, what were the deposits in transit at August 31?
(d) In situation 4, what were the outstanding checks at August 31?

Prepare bank reconciliation and adjusting entries.
(SO 4)

E7-11   Mayo Inc.'s bank statement from Western Bank at August 31, 2007, gives the following information.

Balance, August 1	$16,400	Bank debit memorandum:	
August deposits	73,000	Safety deposit box fee	$ 25
Checks cleared in August	68,660	Service charge	50
Bank credit memorandum:		Balance, August 31	20,710
Interest earned	45		

A summary of the Cash account in the ledger for August shows the following: balance, August 1, $16,900; receipts $77,000; disbursements $73,570; and balance, August 31, $20,330. Analysis reveals that the only reconciling items on the July 31 bank reconciliation were a deposit in transit for $5,000 and outstanding checks of $4,500. In addition, you determine that there were two errors involving company checks drawn in August: (1) A check for $400 to a creditor on account that cleared the bank in August was journalized and posted for $40. (2) A salary check to an employee for $275 was recorded by the bank as $257.

Instructions
(a) Prepare a bank reconciliation at August 31.
(b) Journalize the adjusting entry(ies) to be made by Mayo Inc. at August 31.

Identify reporting of cash.
(SO 5)

E7-12   A new accountant at La Maison Inc. is trying to identify which of the following amounts should be reported as the current asset "Cash and cash equivalents" in the year-end balance sheet, as of April 30, 2007.

1. $60 of currency and coin in a locked box used for incidental cash transactions.

2. A $10,000 U.S. Treasury bill, due May 31, 2007.

3. $300 of April-dated checks that La Maison has received from customers but not yet deposited.

4. An $85 check received from a customer in payment of its April account, but postdated to May 1.

5. $2,500 in the company's checking account.

6. $4,000 in its savings account.

7. $75 of prepaid postage in its postage meter.

8. A $25 IOU from the company receptionist.

Instructions
(a) What balance should La Maison report as its "Cash and cash equivalents" balance at April 30, 2007?
(b) In what account(s) and in what financial statement(s) should the items not included in "Cash and cash equivalents" be reported?

Review cash management practices.
(SO 6)

E7-13   Adams, Hadzic, and Tene, three law students who have joined together to open a law practice, are struggling to manage their cash flow. They haven't yet built up sufficient clientele and revenues to support their legal practice's ongoing costs. Initial costs, such as advertising, renovations to their premises, and the like, all result in outgoing cash flow at a time when little is coming in. Adams, Hadzic, and Tene haven't had time to establish a billing system since most of their clients' cases haven't yet reached the courts, and the lawyers didn't think it would be right to bill them until "results were achieved."

Unfortunately, Adams, Hadzic, and Tene suppliers don't feel the same way. Their suppliers expect them to pay their accounts payable within a few days of receiving their bills.

So far, there hasn't even been enough money to pay the three lawyers, and they are not sure how long they can keep practicing law without getting some money into their pockets.

Instructions
Can you provide any suggestions for Adams, Hadzic, and Tene to improve their cash management practices?

E7-14 Schaefer Company expects to have a cash balance of $46,000 on January 1, 2007. These are the relevant monthly budget data for the first two months of 2007.

Prepare a cash budget for two months.
(SO 7)

1. Collections from customers: January $70,000, February $146,000
2. Payments to suppliers: January $40,000, February $75,000
3. Wages: January $30,000, February $40,000. Wages are paid in the month they are incurred.
4. Administrative expenses: January $21,000, February $28,000. These costs include depreciation of $1,000 per month. All other costs are paid as incurred.
5. Selling expenses: January $15,000, February $20,000. These costs are exclusive of depreciation. They are paid as incurred.
6. Sales of short-term investments in January are expected to realize $12,000 in cash. Schaefer has a line of credit at a local bank that enables it to borrow up to $25,000. The company wants to maintain a minimum monthly cash balance of $20,000.

Instructions
Prepare a cash budget for January and February.

*E7-15 During October, Guiding Light Company experiences the following transactions in establishing a petty cash fund.

Prepare journal entries for a petty cash fund.
(SO 8)

Oct. 1 A petty cash fund is established with a check for $100 issued to the petty cash custodian.

   31 A count of the petty cash fund disclosed the following items:

Currency	$5.00
Coins	0.40
Expenditure receipts (vouchers):	

Office supplies	$28.10
Telephone, Internet, and fax	16.40
Postage	42.00
Freight-out	6.80

   31 A check was written to reimburse the fund and increase the fund to $200.

Instructions
Journalize the entries in October that pertain to the petty cash fund.

*E7-16 Mora Company maintains a petty cash fund for small expenditures. These transactions occurred during the month of August.

Journalize and post petty cash fund transactions.
(SO 8)

Aug. 1 Established the petty cash fund by writing a check on Central Bank for $200.

   15 Replenished the petty cash fund by writing a check for $170. On this date, the fund consisted of $30 in cash and these petty cash receipts: freight-out $74.40, entertainment expense $36, postage expense $33.70 and miscellaneous expense $27.50.

   16 Increased the amount of the petty cash fund to $400 by writing a check for $200.

   31 Replenished the petty cash fund by writing a check for $283. On this date, the fund consisted of $117 in cash and these petty cash receipts: postage expense $145, entertainment expense $90.60, and freight-out $46.40.

Instructions
(a) Journalize the petty cash transactions.
(b) Post to the Petty Cash account.
(c) What internal control features exist in a petty cash fund?

Problems: Set A

Identify internal control weaknesses for cash receipts.
(SO 1, 2)

P7-1A Saratoga Theater is in the Federal Mall. A cashier's booth is located near the entrance to the theater. Two cashiers are employed. One works from 1:00 to 5:00 P.M., the other from 5:00 to 9:00 P.M. Each cashier is bonded. The cashiers receive cash from customers and operate a machine that ejects serially numbered tickets. The rolls of tickets are inserted and locked into the machine by the theater manager at the beginning of each cashier's shift.

After purchasing a ticket, the customer takes the ticket to a doorperson stationed at the entrance of the theater lobby some 60 feet from the cashier's booth. The doorperson tears the ticket in half, admits the customer, and returns the ticket stub to the customer. The other half of the ticket is dropped into a locked box by the doorperson.

At the end of each cashier's shift, the theater manager removes the ticket rolls from the machine and makes a cash count. The cash count sheet is initialed by the cashier. At the end of the day, the manager deposits the receipts in total in a bank night deposit vault located in the mall. In addition, the manager sends copies of the deposit slip and the initialed cash count sheets to the theater company treasurer for verification and to the company's accounting department. Receipts from the first shift are stored in a safe located in the manager's office.

Instructions
(a) Identify the internal control principles and their application to the cash receipts transactions of Saratoga Theater.
(b) If the doorperson and cashier decided to collaborate to misappropriate cash, what actions might they take?

Identify internal control weaknesses in cash receipts and cash disbursements.
(SO 1, 2, 3)

P7-2A Della Valle Middle School wants to raise money for a new sound system for its auditorium. The primary fund-raising event is a dance at which the famous disc jockey Jay Dee will play classic and not-so-classic dance tunes. Frank Cerra, the music and theater instructor, has been given the responsibility for coordinating the fund-raising efforts. This is Frank's first experience with fund-raising. He decides to put the eighth-grade choir in charge of the event; he will be a relatively passive observer.

Frank had 500 unnumbered tickets printed for the dance. He left the tickets in a box on his desk and told the choir students to take as many tickets as they thought they could sell for $5 each. In order to ensure that no extra tickets would be floating around, he told them to dispose of any unsold tickets. When the students received payment for the tickets, they were to bring the cash back to Frank, and he would put it in a locked box in his desk drawer.

Some of the students were responsible for decorating the gymnasium for the dance. Frank gave each of them a key to the money box and told them that if they took money out to purchase materials, they should put a note in the box saying how much they took and what it was used for. After two weeks the money box appeared to be getting full, so Frank asked Blair Norris to count the money, prepare a deposit slip, and deposit the money in a bank account Frank had opened.

The day of the dance, Frank wrote a check from the account to pay Jay Dee. The DJ said, however, that he accepted only cash and did not give receipts. So Frank took $200 out of the cash box and gave it to Jay. At the dance Frank had Sara Billings working at the entrance to the gymnasium, collecting tickets from students and selling tickets to those who had not pre-purchased them. Frank estimated that 400 students attended the dance.

The following day Frank closed out the bank account, which had $250 in it, and gave that amount plus the $180 in the cash box to Principal Skinner. Principal Skinner seemed surprised that, after generating roughly $2,000 in sales, the dance netted only $430 in cash. Frank did not know how to respond.

Instructions
Identify as many internal control weaknesses as you can in this scenario, and suggest how each could be addressed.

Prepare a bank reconciliation and adjusting entries.
(SO 4)

P7-3A On July 31, 2007, Hanlon Company had a cash balance per books of $6,140. The statement from Jackson State Bank on that date showed a balance of $7,695.80. A comparison of the bank statement with the cash account revealed the facts on page 355.

1. The bank service charge for July was $25.

2. The bank collected a note receivable of $1,800 for Hanlon Company on July 15, plus $30 of interest. The bank made a $10 charge for the collection. Hanlon has not accrued any interest on the note.

3. The July 31 receipts of $1,193.30 were not included in the bank deposits for July. These receipts were deposited by the company in a night deposit vault on July 31.

4. Company check No. 2480 issued to H. Coby, a creditor, for $384 that cleared the bank in July was incorrectly entered in the cash payments journal on July 10 for $348.

5. Checks outstanding on July 31 totaled $1,480.10.

6. On July 31 the bank statement showed an NSF charge of $490 for a check received by the company from P. Figura, a customer, on account.

Instructions
(a) Prepare the bank reconciliation as of July 31.
(b) Prepare the necessary adjusting entries at July 31.

(a) Cash bal. $7,409.00

P7-4A The bank portion of the bank reconciliation for Kingston Company at October 31, 2007, is shown here.

Prepare a bank reconciliation and adjusting entries from detailed data.
(SO 4)

KINGSTON COMPANY
Bank Reconciliation
October 31, 2007

Cash balance per bank		$12,367.90
Add: Deposits in transit		1,530.20
		13,898.10

Less: Outstanding checks

Check Number	Check Amount	
2451	$ 1,260.40	
2470	720.10	
2471	844.50	
2472	426.80	
2474	1,050.00	4,301.80
Adjusted cash balance per bank		$ 9,596.30

The adjusted cash balance per bank agreed with the cash balance per books at October 31. The November bank statement showed the following checks and deposits.

Bank Statement

Checks			Deposits	
Date	Number	Amount	Date	Amount
11-1	2470	$ 720.10	11-1	$ 1,530.20
11-2	2471	844.50	11-4	1,211.60
11-5	2474	1,050.00	11-8	990.10
11-4	2475	1,640.70	11-13	2,575.00
11-8	2476	2,830.00	11-18	1,472.70
11-10	2477	600.00	11-21	2,945.00
11-15	2479	1,750.00	11-25	2,567.30
11-18	2480	1,330.00	11-28	1,650.00
11-27	2481	695.40	11-30	1,186.00
11-30	2483	575.50	Total	$16,127.90
11-29	2487	398.00		
	Total	$12,434.20		

The cash records per books for November showed the following.

Cash Payments Journal						Cash Receipts Journal	
Date	Number	Amount	Date	Number	Amount	Date	Amount
11-1	2475	$1,640.70	11-20	2483	$ 575.50	11-3	$ 1,211.60
11-2	2476	2,830.00	11-22	2484	829.50	11-7	990.10
11-2	2477	600.00	11-23	2485	974.80	11-12	2,575.00
11-4	2478	538.20	11-24	2486	900.00	11-17	1,472.70
11-8	2479	1,570.00	11-29	2487	398.00	11-20	2,954.00
11-10	2480	1,330.00	11-30	2488	800.00	11-24	2,567.30
11-15	2481	695.40	Total		$14,294.10	11-27	1,650.00
11-18	2482	612.00				11-29	1,186.00
						11-30	1,218.00
						Total	$15,824.70

The bank statement contained two bank memoranda:

1. A credit of $1,875 for the collection of an $1,800 note for Kingston Company plus interest of $90 and less a collection fee of $15. Kingston Company has not accrued any interest on the note.

2. A debit for the printing of additional company checks $85.

At November 30 the cash balance per books was $11,126.90 and the cash balance per bank statement was $17,851.60. The bank did not make any errors, but **two errors were made by Kingston Company**.

Instructions

(a) Cash bal. $12,727.90

(a) Using the four steps in the reconciliation procedure described on page 330, prepare a bank reconciliation at November 30, 2007.

(b) Prepare the adjusting entries based on the reconciliation. (*Note:* The correction of any errors pertaining to recording checks should be made to Accounts Payable. The correction of any errors relating to recording cash receipts should be made to Accounts Receivable.)

Prepare a bank reconciliation and adjusting entries.
(SO 4)

P7-5A   Green Acres Company of Canton, Iowa, spreads herbicides and applies liquid fertilizer for local farmers. On May 31, 2007, the company's cash account per its general ledger showed a balance of $6,738.90.

The bank statement from Canton State Bank on that date showed the following balance.

CANTON STATE BANK

Checks and Debits	Deposits and Credits	Daily Balance
XXX	XXX	5-31 7,112.00

A comparison of the details on the bank statement with the details in the cash account revealed the following facts.

1. The statement included a debit memo of $40 for the printing of additional company checks.

2. Cash sales of $833.15 on May 12 were deposited in the bank. The cash receipts journal entry and the deposit slip were incorrectly made for $839.15. The bank credited Green Acres Company for the correct amount.

3. Outstanding checks at May 31 totaled $276.25, and deposits in transit were $1,180.15.

4. On May 18, the company issued check No. 1181 for $685 to R. Delzer, on account. The check, which cleared the bank in May, was incorrectly journalized and posted by Green Acres Company for $658.

5. A $2,200 note receivable was collected by the bank for Green Acres Company on May 31 plus $110 interest. The bank charged a collection fee of $20. No interest has been accrued on the note.

6. Included with the cancelled checks was a check issued by Green Day Company to P. Jonet for $360 that was incorrectly charged to Green Acres Company by the bank.

7. On May 31, the bank statement showed an NSF charge of $580 for a check issued by Natalie Fong, a customer, to Green Acres Company on account.

Instructions
(a) Prepare the bank reconciliation at May 31, 2007.
(b) Prepare the necessary adjusting entries for Green Acres Company at May 31, 2007.

(a) Cash bal. $8,375.90

P7-6A You are provided with the following information taken from Burlington Inc.'s March 31, 2007, balance sheet.

Prepare a cash budget.
(SO 7)

Cash	$ 8,000
Accounts receivable	20,000
Inventory	36,000
Property, plant, and equipment, net of depreciation	120,000
Accounts payable	22,400
Common stock	150,000
Retained earnings	11,600

Additional information concerning Burlington Inc. is as follows.

1. Gross profit is 25% of sales.

2. Actual and budgeted sales data:

March (actual)	$50,000
April (budgeted)	65,000

3. Sales are 60% for cash and 40% on credit. There are no sales discounts, and credit sales are collected in the month following the sale.

4. Half of a month's purchases are paid for in the month of purchase and half in the following month. Purchases of inventory totalled $44,800 for the month of March and are anticipated to total $52,200 for the month of April. Ending inventory is expected to be $39,450 at the end of April.

5. Cash operating costs are anticipated to be $12,700 for the month of April.

6. Equipment costing $2,500 will be purchased for cash in April.

7. The company wishes to maintain a minimum cash balance of $8,000. An open line of credit is available at the bank. All borrowing is done at the beginning of the month, and all repayments are made at the end of the month. The interest rate is 12% per year, and interest expense is accrued at the end of the month and paid in the following month.

Instructions
(a) Calculate cash collections in April for March and April sales.
(b) Calculate the cash disbursements in April related to March and April purchases.
(c) Prepare a cash budget for the month of April. Determine how much cash Burlington Inc. must borrow, or can repay, in April.

(a) Apr. customer
*   collections $59,000*
(c) Apr.
*   borrowings $ 4,700*

P7-7A BossaNova Corporation prepares monthly cash budgets. Here are relevant data from operating budgets for 2007.

Prepare a cash budget.
(SO 7)

	January	February
Sales	$350,000	$400,000
Purchases	110,000	130,000
Salaries	84,000	95,000
Administrative expenses	70,000	75,000
Selling expenses	79,000	88,000

All sales are on account. Collections are expected to be 60% in the month of sale, 30% in the first month following the sale, and 10% in the second month following the sale. Fifty percent (50%) of purchases are paid in cash in the month of purchase, and the balance due is paid in the month following the purchase. All other expenses are paid in the month incurred except for administrative expenses, which include $1,000 of depreciation per month.

Other data.

1. Credit sales — November 2006, $260,000; December 2006, $300,000

2. Purchases — December 2006, $100,000

3. Other receipts — January: collection of December 31, 2006, notes receivable $15,000; February: proceeds from sale of securities $6,000

4. Other disbursements—February: $12,000 cash dividend

The company's cash balance on January 1, 2007, is expected to be $52,000. The company wants to maintain a minimum cash balance of $50,000.

(a) Jan. customer
collections $326,000
(b) Jan. 31
cash bal. $ 56,000

Instructions

(a) Prepare schedules for (1) expected collections from customers and (2) expected payments for purchases for January and February.

(b) Prepare a cash budget for January and February.

Prepare a comprehensive
bank reconciliation with
thieft and internal control
deficiencies.
(SO 1, 2, 3, 4)

P7-8A Dusk 'til Dawn Company is a very profitable small business. It has not, however, given much consideration to internal control. For example, in an attempt to keep clerical and office expenses to a minimum, the company has combined the jobs of cashier and bookkeeper. As a result, Scott Dillon handles all cash receipts, keeps the accounting records, and prepares the monthly bank reconciliations.

The balance per the bank statement on October 31, 2007, was $18,415. Outstanding checks were: No. 62 for $126.75, No. 183 for $180, No. 284 for $253.25, No. 862 for $190.71, No. 863 for $226.80, and No. 864 for $165.28. Included with the statement was a credit memorandum of $265 indicating the collection of a note receivable for Dusk 'til Dawn Company by the bank on October 25. This memorandum has not been recorded by Dusk 'til Dawn.

The company's ledger showed one cash account with a balance of $21,992.72. The balance included undeposited cash on hand. Because of the lack of internal controls, Scott took for personal use all of the undeposited receipts in excess of $3,795.51. He then prepared the following bank reconciliation in an effort to conceal his theft of cash.

Cash balance per books, October 31		$21,992.72
Add: Outstanding checks		
No. 862	$190.71	
No. 863	226.80	
No. 864	165.28	482.79
		22,475.51
Less: Undeposited receipts		3,795.51
Unadjusted balance per bank, October 31		18,680.00
Less: Bank credit memorandum		265.00
Cash balance per bank statement, October 31		$18,415.00

Instructions

(a) Cash bal. $21,067.72

(a) Prepare a correct bank reconciliation. (*Hint:* Deduct the amount of the theft from the adjusted balance per books.)

(b) Indicate the three ways that Scott attempted to conceal the theft and the dollar amount involved in each method.

(c) What principles of internal control were violated in this case?

Problems: Set B

P7-1B Marais Company recently changed its system of internal control over cash disbursements. The system includes the following features.

1. Instead of being unnumbered and manually prepared, all checks must now be prenumbered and written by using the new checkwriter purchased by the company.
2. Before a check can be issued, each invoice must have the approval of Jane Bell, the purchasing agent, and Vorn Lor, the receiving department supervisor.
3. Checks must be signed by either Derek Madsen, the treasurer, or Sara Goss, the assistant treasurer. Before signing a check, the signer is expected to compare the amounts of the check with the amounts on the invoice.
4. After signing a check, the signer stamps the invoice "paid" and inserts within the stamp, the date, check number, and amount of the check. The "paid" invoice is then sent to the accounting department for recording.
5. Blank checks are stored in a safe in the treasurer's office. The combination to the safe is known by only the treasurer and assistant treasurer.
6. Each month the bank statement is reconciled with the bank balance per books by the assistant chief accountant.

Identify internal control principles for cash disbursements.
(SO 1, 3)

Instructions
Identify the internal control principles and their application to cash disbursements of Marais Company.

P7-2B The board of trustees of a local church is concerned about the internal accounting controls pertaining to the offering collections made at weekly services. They ask you to serve on a three-person audit team with the internal auditor of the university and a CPA who has just joined the church. At a meeting of the audit team and the board of trustees you learn the following.

Identify internal control weaknesses in cash receipts.
(SO 1, 2)

1. The church's board of trustees has delegated responsibility for the financial management and audit of the financial records to the finance committee. This group prepares the annual budget and approves major disbursements but is not involved in collections or recordkeeping. No audit has been made in recent years because the same trusted employee has kept church records and served as financial secretary for 15 years. The church does not carry any fidelity insurance.

2. The collection at the weekly service is taken by a team of ushers who volunteer to serve for 1 month. The ushers take the collection plates to a basement office at the rear of the church. They hand their plates to the head usher and return to the church service. After all plates have been turned in, the head usher counts the cash received. The head usher then places the cash in the church safe along with a notation of the amount counted. The head usher volunteers to serve for 3 months.

3. The next morning the financial secretary opens the safe and recounts the collection. The secretary withholds $150 – $200 in cash, depending on the cash expenditures expected for the week, and deposits the remainder of the collections in the bank. To facilitate the deposit, church members who contribute by check are asked to make their checks payable to "Cash."

4. Each month the financial secretary reconciles the bank statement and submits a copy of the reconciliation to the board of trustees. The reconciliations have rarely contained any bank errors and have never shown any errors per books.

Instructions
(a) Indicate the weaknesses in internal accounting control in the handling of collections.
(b) List the improvements in internal control procedures that you plan to make at the next meeting of the audit team for (1) the ushers, (2) the head usher, (3) the financial secretary, and (4) the finance committee.
(c) What church policies should be changed to improve internal control?

P7-3B On May 31, 2007, Galenti Company had a cash balance per books of $5,681.50. The bank statement from Community Bank on that date showed a balance of $7,964.60. A comparison of the statement with the cash account revealed the following facts.

Prepare a bank reconciliation and adjusting entries.
(SO 4)

1. The statement included a debit memo of $70 for the printing of additional company checks.

2. Cash sales of $786.15 on May 12 were deposited in the bank. The cash receipts journal entry and the deposit slip were incorrectly made for $796.15. The bank credited Galenti Company for the correct amount.

3. Outstanding checks at May 31 totaled $806.25, and deposits in transit were $836.15.

4. On May 18 the company issued check No. 1181 for $685 to N. Habben, on account. The check, which cleared the bank in May, was incorrectly journalized and posted by Galenti Company for $658.

5. A $3,000 note receivable was collected by the bank for Galenti Company on May 31 plus $80 interest. The bank charged a collection fee of $30. No interest has been accrued on the note.

6. Included with the cancelled checks was a check issued by Gallen Company to C. Young for $290 that was incorrectly charged to Galenti Company by the bank.

7. On May 31 the bank statement showed an NSF charge of $340 for a check issued by K. Uzong, a customer, to Galenti Company on account.

Instructions

(a) Cash bal. $8,284.50

(a) Prepare the bank reconciliation as of May 31, 2007.
(b) Prepare the necessary adjusting entries at May 31, 2007.

Prepare a bank reconciliation and adjusting entries from detailed data.
(SO 4)

P7-4B The bank portion of the bank reconciliation for Blue Diamond Company at November 30, 2007, is shown here.

BLUE DIAMOND COMPANY
Bank Reconciliation
November 30, 2007

Cash balance per bank		$14,367.90
Add: Deposits in transit		2,530.20
		16,898.10
Less: Outstanding checks		

Check Number	Check Amount	
3451	$2,260.40	
3470	1,100.10	
3471	844.50	
3472	1,426.80	
3474	1,050.00	6,681.80
Adjusted cash balance per bank		$10,216.30

The adjusted cash balance per bank agreed with the cash balance per books at November 30. The December bank statement showed the following checks and deposits.

Bank Statement

Checks			Deposits	
Date	Number	Amount	Date	Amount
12-1	3451	$ 2,260.40	12-1	$ 2,530.20
12-2	3470	1,100.10	12-4	1,211.60
12-7	3472	1,426.80	12-8	2,365.10
12-4	3475	1,640.70	12-16	2,672.70
12-8	3476	1,300.00	12-21	2,945.00
12-10	3477	2,130.00	12-26	2,567.30
12-15	3479	3,080.00	12-29	2,836.00
12-27	3480	600.00	12-30	1,025.00
12-30	3482	475.50	Total	$18,152.90
12-29	3483	1,140.00		
12-31	3485	540.80		
	Total	$15,694.30		

The cash records per books for December showed the following.

	Cash Payments Journal						Cash Receipts Journal	
Date	**Number**	**Amount**	**Date**	**Number**	**Amount**		**Date**	**Amount**
12-1	3475	$1,640.70	12-20	3482	$ 475.50		12-3	$ 1,211.60
12-2	3476	1,300.00	12-22	3483	1,140.00		12-7	2,365.10
12-2	3477	2,130.00	12-23	3484	764.00		12-15	2,672.70
12-4	3478	538.20	12-24	3485	450.80		12-20	2,954.00
12-8	3479	3,080.00	12-30	3486	1,389.50		12-25	2,567.30
12-10	3480	600.00	Total		$14,316.10		12-28	2,836.00
12-17	3481	807.40					12-30	1,025.00
							12-31	1,190.40
							Total	$16,822.10

The bank statement contained two memoranda.

1. A credit of $3,145 for the collection of a $3,000 note for Blue Diamond Company plus interest of $160 and less a collection fee of $15. Blue Diamond Company has not accrued any interest on the note.
2. A debit of $943.10 for an NSF check written by J. Waller, a customer. At December 31 the check had not been redeposited in the bank.

At December 31 the cash balance per books was $12,722.30, and the cash balance per bank statement was $19,028.40. The bank did not make any errors, **but two errors were made by Blue Diamond Company**.

Instructions
(a) Using the four steps in the reconciliation procedure described on page 330, prepare a bank reconciliation at December 31, 2007.
(b) Prepare the adjusting entries based on the reconciliation. [*Note:* The correction of any errors pertaining to recording checks should be made to Accounts Payable. The correction of any errors relating to recording cash receipts should be made to Accounts Receivable.]

(a) Cash bal. $14,825.20

P7-5B   Fertile Crescent Company of Omaha, Nebraska, provides liquid fertilizer and herbicides to regional farmers. On July 31, 2007, the company's cash account per its general ledger showed a balance of $5,909.70.

Prepare a bank reconciliation and adjusting entries. (SO 4)

The bank statement from Tri-County Bank on that date showed the following balance.

TRI-COUNTY BANK

Checks and Debits	Deposits and Credits	Daily Balance
XXX	XXX	7-31 7,075.80

A comparison of the details on the bank statement with the details in the cash account revealed the following facts.

1. The bank service charge for July was $32.
2. The bank collected a note receivable of $1,200 for Fertile Crescent Company on July 15, plus $48 of interest. The bank made a $10 charge for the collection. Fertile Crescent has not accrued any interest on the note.
3. The July 31 receipts of $1,839 were not included in the bank deposits for July. These receipts were deposited by the company in a night deposit vault on July 31.
4. Company check No. 2480 issued to N. Teig, a creditor, for $492 that cleared the bank in July was incorrectly entered in the cash payments journal on July 10 for $429.
5. Checks outstanding on July 31 totaled $2,480.10.

6. On July 31, the bank statement showed an NSF charge of $618 for a check received by the company from N. O. Doe, a customer, on account.

Instructions

(a) Cash bal. $6,434.70

(a) Prepare the bank reconciliation as of July 31, 2007.

(b) Prepare the necessary adjusting entries at July 31, 2007.

Prepare a cash budget.
(SO 7)

P7-6B Tran Co. expects to have a cash balance of $26,000 on January 1, 2007. Relevant monthly budget data for the first two months of 2007 are as follows.

Collections from customers: January $70,000; February $160,000

Payments to suppliers: January $48,000; February $75,000

Salaries: January $35,000; February $40,000. Salaries are paid in the month they are incurred.

Selling and administrative expenses: January $27,000; February $39,000. These costs are exclusive of depreciation and are paid as incurred.

Sales of short-term investments in January are expected to realize $9,000 in cash.

Tran has a line of credit at a local bank that enables it to borrow up to $45,000. The company wants to maintain a minimum monthly cash balance of $25,000. Any excess cash above the $25,000 minimum is used to pay off the line of credit.

Instructions

(a) Jan. cash bal. $25,000

(a) Prepare a cash budget for January and February.

(b) Explain how a cash budget contributes to effective management.

Prepare a cash budget.
(SO 7)

P7-7B Zurich Inc. prepares monthly cash budgets. Here are relevant data from operating budgets for 2007.

	January	February
Sales	$340,000	$400,000
Purchases	100,000	130,000
Salaries	80,000	95,000
Selling and administrative expenses	135,000	160,000

All sales are on account. Collections are expected to be 50% in the month of sale, 30% in the first month following the sale, and 20% in the second month following the sale. Forty percent (40%) of purchases are paid in cash in the month of purchase, and the balance due is paid in the month following the purchase. All other items above are paid in the month incurred. Depreciation has been excluded from selling and administrative expenses.

Other data.

1. Credit sales — November 2006, $240,000; December 2006, $280,000

2. Purchases — December 2006, $90,000

3. Other receipts — January: collection of December 31, 2006, interest receivable $2,000; February: proceeds from sale of short-term investments $8,000

4. Other disbursements—February: payment of $20,000 for land

The company's cash balance on January 1, 2007, is expected to be $60,000. The company wants to maintain a minimum cash balance of $50,000.

Instructions

(a) Jan. customer
    collections $302,000
(b) Jan. 31 cash bal. $ 55,000

(a) Prepare schedules for (1) expected collections from customers and (2) expected payments for purchases for January and February.

(b) Prepare a cash budget for January and February.

Prepare a comprehensive bank reconciliation with theft and internal control deficiencies.
(SO 1, 2, 3, 4)

P7-8B Emporia Company is a very profitable small business. It has not, however, given much consideration to internal control. For example, in an attempt to keep clerical and office expenses to a minimum, the company has combined the jobs of cashier and bookkeeper. As a result, M. Kohnert handles all cash receipts, keeps the accounting records, and prepares the monthly bank reconciliations.

The balance per the bank statement on October 31, 2007, was $12,800. Outstanding checks were: No. 62 for $126.75, No. 183 for $180, No. 284 for $253.25, No. 862 for $190.71, No. 863 for $226.80, and No. 864 for $165.28. Included with the statement was a credit memorandum of $790 indicating the collection of a note receivable for Emporia Company by the bank on October 25. This memorandum has not been recorded by Emporia Company.

The company's ledger showed one cash account with a balance of $15,847.21. The balance included undeposited cash on hand. Because of the lack of internal controls, Kohnert took for personal use all of the undeposited receipts in excess of $2,740. He then prepared the following bank reconciliation in an effort to conceal his theft of cash.

Cash balance per books, October 31		$15,847.21
Add: Outstanding checks		
No. 862	$190.71	
No. 863	226.80	
No. 864	165.28	482.79
		16,330.00
Less: Undeposited receipts		2,740.00
Unadjusted balance per bank, October 31		13,590.00
Less: Bank credit memorandum		790.00
Cash balance per bank statement, October 31		$12,800.00

Instructions

(a) Prepare a correct bank reconciliation. (*Hint:* Deduct the amount of the theft from the adjusted balance per books.)

(b) Indicate the three ways that Kohnert attempted to conceal the theft and the dollar amount pertaining to each method.

(c) What principles of internal control were violated in this case?

(a) Cash bal. $14,397.21

Problems: Set C

Visit the book's website at **www.wiley.com/college/kimmel** and choose the Student Companion site to access Problem Set C.

Comprehensive Problem

CP7 On December 1, 2007, Stephens Company had the following account balances.

	Debits		Credits
Cash	$18,000	Accumulated Depreciation	$ 3,000
Notes Receivable	2,700	Accounts Payable	6,100
Accounts Receivable	7,500	Common Stock	20,000
Merchandise Inventory	16,000	Retained Earnings	44,700
Prepaid Insurance	1,600		$73,800
Equipment	28,000		
	$73,800		

During December the company completed the following transactions.

Dec. 7 Received $3,200 cash from customers in payment of account (no discount allowed).

12 Purchased merchandise on account from King Co. $10,000, terms 2/10, n/30.

17 Sold merchandise on account $12,000, terms 1/10, n/30. The cost of the merchandise sold was $8,000.

19 Paid salaries $2,500.

22 Paid King Co. in full, less discount.

26 Received collections in full, less discounts, from customers billed on December 17.

Adjustment data:
1. Depreciation $200 per month.
2. Insurance expired $400.

Instructions
(a) Journalize the December transactions.
(b) Enter the December 1 balances in the ledger T accounts and post the December transactions. Use Cost of Goods Sold, Depreciation Expense, Insurance Expense, Salaries Expense, Sales, and Sales Discounts.
(c) The statement from Lyon County Bank on December 31 showed a balance of $22,164. A comparison of the bank statement with the cash account revealed the following facts.
  1. The bank collected a note receivable of $2,700 for Stephens Company on December 15.
  2. The December 31 receipts of $2,736 were not included in the bank deposits for December. The company deposited these receipts in a night deposit vault on December 31.
  3. Checks outstanding on December 31 totaled $2,220.
  4. On December 31 the bank statement showed a NSF charge of $800 for a check received by the company from C. Park, a customer, on account.

Prepare a bank reconciliation as of December 31 based on the available information. (*Hint:* The cash balance per books is $20,780. This can be proven by finding the balance in the Cash account from parts (a) and (b).)
(d) Journalize the adjusting entries resulting from the bank reconciliation and adjustment data.
(e) Post the adjusting entries to the ledger T accounts.

(f) Totals $76,000   (f) Prepare an adjusted trial balance.
(g) Net income $ 780   (g) Prepare an income statement for December and a classified balance sheet at
Total assets $61,580   December 31.

Continuing Cookie Chronicle

(Note: This is a continuation of the Cookie Chronicle from Chapters 1 through 6.)

CCC7 Part 1 Natalie is struggling to keep up with the recording of her accounting transactions. She is spending a lot of time marketing and selling mixers and giving her cookie classes. Her friend John is an accounting student who runs his own accounting service. He has asked Natalie if she would like to have him do her accounting.

John and Natalie meet and discuss her business. John suggests that he do the following for Natalie.

1. Hold onto cash until there is enough to be deposited. (He would keep the cash locked up in his vehicle). He would also take all of the deposits to the bank at least twice a month.
2. Write and sign all of the checks.
3. Record all of the deposits in the accounting records.
4. Record all of the checks in the accounting records.
5. Prepare the monthly bank reconciliation.
6. Transfer all of Natalie's manual accounting records to his computer accounting program. John maintains all of the accounting information that he keeps for his clients on his laptop computer.
7. Prepare monthly financial statements for Natalie to review.
8. Write himself a check every month for the work he has done for Natalie.

Instructions
Identify the weaknesses in internal control that you see in the system that John is recommending. (Consider the principles of internal control identified in the chapter.) Can you suggest any improvements if John is hired to do Natalie's accounting?

Part 2   Natalie decides that she cannot afford to hire John to do her accounting. One way that she can ensure that her cash account does not have any errors and is accurate and up-to-date is to prepare a bank reconciliation at the end of each month.

Natalie would like you to help her. She asks you to prepare a bank reconciliation for June 2007 using the following information.

GENERAL LEDGER—COOKIE CREATIONS

Cash

Date	Explanation	Ref.	Debit	Credit	Balance
2007					
June 1	Balance				2,657
1			750		3,407
3	Check #600			625	2,782
3	Check #601			95	2,687
8	Check #602			56	2,631
9			1,050		3,681
13	Check #603			425	3,256
20			155		3,411
28	Check #604			247	3,164
28			110		3,274

PREMIER BANK
Statement of Account—Cookie Creations
June 30, 2007

Date	Explanation	Checks and Other Debits	Deposits	Balance
May 31	Balance			3,256
June 1	Deposit		750	4,006
6	Check #600	625		3,381
6	Check #601	95		3,286
8	Check #602	56		3,230
9	Deposit		1,050	4,280
10	NSF check	100		4,180
10	NSF–fee	35		4,145
14	Check #603	452		3,693
20	Deposit		125	3,818
23	EFT–Telus	85		3,733
28	Check #599	361		3,372
30	Bank charges	13		3,359

Additional information:

1. On May 31, there were two outstanding checks: #595 for $238 and #599 for $361.
2. Premier Bank made a posting error to the bank statement: check #603 was issued for $425, not $452.
3. The deposit made on June 20 was for $125 that Natalie received for teaching a class. Natalie made an error in recording this transaction.
4. The electronic funds transfer (EFT) was for Natalie's cell phone use. Remember that she uses this phone only for business.
5. The NSF check was from Ron Black. Natalie received this check for teaching a class to Ron's children. Natalie contacted Ron and he assured her that she will receive a check in the mail for the outstanding amount of the invoice and the NSF bank charge.

Instructions
(a) Prepare Cookie Creations' bank reconciliation for June 2007.
(b) Prepare any necessary general journal entries.
(c) If a balance sheet is prepared for Cookie Creations at June 30, 2007, what balance will be reported as cash in the current assets section?

▶ BROADENING YOUR PERSPECTIVE

Financial Reporting and Analysis

FINANCIAL REPORTING PROBLEM: *Tootsie Roll Industries, Inc.*

BYP7-1 The financial statements of Tootsie Roll are presented in Appendix A of this book, together with an auditor's report—Report of Independent Auditors.

Instructions
Using the financial statements and reports, answer these questions about Tootsie Roll's internal controls and cash.
(a) What comments, if any, are made about cash in the report of the independent auditors?
(b) What data about cash and cash equivalents are shown in the consolidated balance sheet (statement of financial condition)?
(c) What activities are identified in the consolidated statement of cash flows as being responsible for the changes in cash during 2004?
(d) How are cash equivalents defined in the Notes to Consolidated Financial Statements?
(e) Read the section of the report titled "Management's Report on Internal Control Over Financial Reporting." Summarize the statements made in that section of the report.

COMPARATIVE ANALYSIS PROBLEM: *Tootsie Roll vs. Hershey Foods*

BYP7-2 The financial statements of Hershey Foods are presented in Appendix B, following the financial statements for Tootsie Roll in Appendix A.

Instructions
Answer the following questions for each company.
(a) What is the balance in cash and cash equivalents at December 31, 2004?
(b) What percentage of total assets does cash represent for each company over the last two years? Has it changed significantly for either company?
(c) How much cash was provided by operating activities during 2004?
(d) Comment on your findings in parts (a) through (c).

RESEARCH CASE

BYP7-3 The January 27, 2005, issue of the *Wall Street Journal* contains an article by William M. Bulkeley and Robert Tomsho titled "Kodak to Get Auditors' Adverse View."

Instructions
Read the article and answer the following questions.
(a) How does the article define a "material weakness" in internal financial controls? Does the existence of a material weakness mean that a misstatement of the company's results has occurred?
(b) What other well-known companies received similar opinions from their auditors, and what percentage of U.S. companies are expected to report problems in their internal controls?
(c) What type of company is expected to be particularly affected by this problem?

INTERPRETING FINANCIAL STATEMENTS

BYP7-4 The international accounting firm Ernst and Young recently performed a global survey. The results of that survey are summarized in a report titled "Fraud: The Unmanaged Risk."

You can find this report at **www.ey.com/global/download.nsf/Belgium_E/8th_ Global_Fraud_Survey/$file/EY_8th_Global_Fraud_Survey.pdf** (or go to **www. wiley.com/ college/kimmel**).

Instructions
Read the Key Findings section, and then skim the remainder of the report to answer the following questions.
(a) Examining the graphs presented under the heading "General Fraud Experience," what percentage of respondents experienced a significant fraud during the year? Do the findings differ by geographic region?

(b) What percentage of frauds does the report estimate are actually both detected and made public by companies?

(c) How did respondents rank various factors in terms of their ability to detect fraud and prevent fraud?

(d) What percentage of employees committing fraud are part of management? Are new managers more or less likely to commit fraud?

FINANCIAL ANALYSIS ON THE WEB

BYP7-5 The Financial Accounting Standards Board (FASB) is a private organization established to improve accounting standards and financial reporting. The FASB conducts extensive research before issuing a "Statement of Financial Accounting Standards," which represents an authoritative expression of generally accepted accounting principles.

Address: **www.fasb.org**
        (or go to **www.wiley.com/college/kimmel**)

Steps:

Choose **Facts about FASB**.

Instructions
Answer the following questions.
(a) What is the mission of the FASB?
(b) How are topics added to the FASB technical agenda?
(c) What characteristics make the FASB's procedures an "open" decision-making process?

BYP7-6 The Public Company Accounting Oversight Board (PCAOB) was created as a result of the Sarbanes-Oxley Act. It has oversight and enforcement responsibilities over accounting firms in the U.S.

Address: **http://www.pcaobus.org/**
        (or go to **www.wiley.com/college/kimmel**)

Instructions
Answer the following questions.
(a) What is the mission of the PCAOB?
(b) Briefly summarize its responsibilities related to inspections.
(c) Briefly summarize its responsibilities related to enforcement.

Critical Thinking

DECISION MAKING ACROSS THE ORGANIZATION

BYP7-7 Alternative Distributor Corp., a distributor of groceries and related products, is headquartered in Medford, Massachusetts.

During a recent audit, Alternative Distributor Corp. was advised that existing internal controls necessary for the company to develop reliable financial statements were inadequate. The audit report stated that the current system of accounting for sales, receivables, and cash receipts constituted a material weakness. Among other items, the report focused on nontimely deposit of cash receipts, exposing Alternative Distributor to potential loss or misappropriation, excessive past due accounts receivable due to lack of collection efforts, disregard of advantages offered by vendors for prompt payment of invoices, absence of appropriate segregation of duties by personnel consistent with appropriate control objectives, inadequate procedures for applying accounting principles, lack of qualified management personnel, lack of supervision by an outside board of directors, and overall poor recordkeeping.

Instructions
(a) Identify the principles of internal control violated by Alternative Distributor Corporation.
(b) Explain why managers of various functional areas in the company should be concerned about internal controls.

COMMUNICATION ACTIVITY

BYP7-8 As a new auditor for the CPA firm of Ticke and Tie, you have been assigned to review the internal controls over mail cash receipts of Rangel Company. Your review reveals that checks are promptly endorsed "For Deposit Only," but no list of the checks is prepared by the person opening the mail. The mail is opened either by the cashier or by the employee who maintains the accounts receivable records. Mail receipts are deposited in the bank weekly by the cashier.

Instructions
Write a letter to S.A. Forness, owner of the Rangel Company, explaining the weaknesses in internal control and your recommendations for improving the system.

ETHICS CASE

BYP7-9 As noted in the chapter, banks charge fees of up to $30 for "bounced" checks—that is, checks that exceed the balance in the account. It has been estimated that processing bounced checks costs a bank roughly $1.50 per check. Thus, the profit margin on bounced checks is very high. Recognizing this, some banks have started to process checks from largest to smallest. By doing this, they maximize the number of checks that bounce if a customer overdraws an account. For example, NationsBank (now Bank of America) projected a $14 million increase in fee revenue as a result of processing largest checks first. In response to criticism, banks have responded that their customers prefer to have large checks processed first, because those tend to be the most important. At the other extreme, some banks will cover their customers' bounced checks, effectively extending them an interest-free loan while their account is overdrawn.

Instructions
Answer each of the following questions.
(a) Antonio Freeman had a balance of $1,500 in his checking account at First National Bank on a day when the bank received the following five checks for processing against his account.

Check Number	Amount	Check Number	Amount
3150	$ 35	3165	$ 550
3162	400	3166	1,510
		3169	180

Assuming a $30 fee assessed by the bank for each bounced check, how much fee revenue would the bank generate if it processed checks (1) from largest to smallest, (2) from smallest to largest, and (3) in order of check number?
(b) Do you think that processing checks from largest to smallest is an ethical business practice?
(c) In addition to ethical issues, what other issues must a bank consider in deciding whether to process checks from largest to smallest?
(d) If you were managing a bank, what policy would you adopt on bounced checks?

BYP7-10 Fraud Bureau is a free service, established to alert consumers and investors about prior complaints relating to online vendors, including sellers at online auctions, and to provide consumers, investors, and users with information and news. One of the services it provides is a collection of online educational articles related to fraud.

Address: **www.fraudbureau.com/articles/** (or go to **www.wiley.com/college/kimmel**)

Instructions
Go to this site and choose an article of interest to you. Write a short summary of your findings.

Answers to Business Insight and Accounting across the Organization Questions
p. 319
Q: What controls would have reduced the likelihood of this type of theft?
A: One step would have been segregation of duties. The same employee who determined the winning number should not also have had physical control of that ticket.

p. 320

Q: Why would unsupervised employees or employees who report to each other represent potential internal control threats?

A. An unsupervised employee may have a fraudulent job (or may even be a fictitious person)—e.g., a person drawing a paycheck without working. Or, if two employees supervise each other, there is no real separation of duties, and they can conspire to defraud the company.

p. 322

Q. Why would a company's stock price fall if it reports deficiencies in its internal controls?

A. Internal controls protect against employee theft, but they also provide protection against manipulation of accounting numbers. If a company has poor internal controls, investors will have less confidence that its financial statements are accurate. As a consequence, its stock price will suffer.

p. 323

Q. Why are small companies more susceptible to employee theft?

A. The high degree of trust often found in small companies makes them more vulnerable. Also, small companies tend to have less sophisticated systems of internal control, and they usually lack internal auditors. In addition, it is very hard to achieve some internal control features, such as segregation of duties, when you have very few employees.

p. 327

Q. How can companies reduce the likelihood of fraudulent disbursements?

A. To reduce the occurrence of fraudulent disbursements a company should follow the procedures discussed in this chapter. These include having only designated personnel sign checks; having different personnel approve payments and make payments; ensuring that check signers do not record disbursements; using prenumbered checks and matching each check to an approved invoice; storing blank checks securely; reconciling the bank statement; and stamping invoices PAID.

Answer to Tootsie Roll Review It Question 3, p. 339

At December 31, 2004, Tootsie Roll reported cash and cash equivalents of $56,989,000. It reported no restricted cash. In Note 1 to its financial statements it defines cash equivalents as "temporary cash investments with an original maturity of three months or less."

Answers to Self-Study Questions

1. a   2. c   3. b   4. b   5. d   6. a   7. c   8. c   9. d   10. c
*11. a

REMEMBER TO GO BACK TO THE NAVIGATOR BOX ON THE CHAPTER-OPENING PAGE AND CHECK OFF YOUR COMPLETED WORK.

CHAPTER 8

Reporting and Analyzing Receivables

STUDY OBJECTIVES

After studying this chapter,
you should be able to:

1 Identify the different types of receivables.

2 Explain how accounts receivable are recognized in the accounts.

3 Describe the methods used to account for bad debts.

4 Compute the interest on notes receivable.

5 Describe the entries to record the disposition of notes receivable.

6 Explain the statement presentation of receivables.

7 Describe the principles of sound accounts receivable management.

8 Identify ratios to analyze a company's receivables.

9 Describe methods to accelerate the receipt of cash from receivables.

THE NAVIGATOR

✓ THE NAVIGATOR

- Scan *Study Objectives* ⬭
- Read *Feature Story* ⬭
- Read *Preview* ⬭
- Read text and answer *Before You Go On*
  p. 379 ⬭   p. 384 ⬭   p. 385 ⬭   p. 393 ⬭
- Work *Using the Decision Toolkit* ⬭
- Review *Summary of Study Objectives* ⬭
- Work *Demonstration Problem* ⬭
- Answer *Self-Study Questions* ⬭
- Complete *Assignments* ⬭

FEATURE STORY

A Dose of Careful Management Keeps Receivables Healthy

"Sometimes you have to know when to be very tough, and sometimes you can give them a bit of a break," says Vivi Su. She's not talking about her children, but about the customers of a subsidiary of pharmaceutical company Whitehall-Robins, where she works as supervisor of credit and collections.

For example, while the company's regular terms are 1/15, n/30 (1% discount if paid within 15 days), a customer might ask for and receive a few days of grace and still get the discount. Or a customer might place orders above its credit limit, in which case, depending on its payment history and the circumstances, Ms. Su might authorize shipment of the goods anyway.

"It's not about drawing a line in the sand, and that's all," she explains. "You want a good relationship with your customers—but you also need to bring in the money."

"The money," in Whitehall-Robins's case amounts to some $170 million in sales a year. Nearly all of it comes in through the credit accounts Ms. Su manages. The process starts with the decision to grant a customer an account in the first place, Ms. Su explains. The sales rep gives the customer a credit application. "My department reviews this application very carefully; a customer needs to supply three good references, and we also run a check with a credit firm like Equifax. If we accept them, then based on their size and history, we assign a credit limit."

Once accounts are established, the company supervises them very carefully. "I get an aging report every single day," says Ms. Su.

"The rule of thumb is that we should always have at least 85% of receivables current—meaning they were billed less than 30 days ago," she continues. "But we try to do even better than that—I like to see 90%." Similarly, her guideline is never to have more than 5% of receivables at over 90 days. But long before that figure is reached, "we jump on it," she says firmly.

At 15 days overdue, Whitehall-Robins phones the client. Often there's a reasonable explanation for the delay—an invoice may have gone astray, or the payables clerk is away. "But if a customer keeps on delaying, and tells us several times that it'll only be a few more days, we know there's a problem," says Ms. Su. After 45 days, "I send a letter. Then a second notice is sent in writing.

After the third and final notice, the client has 10 days to pay, and then I hand it over to a collection agency, and it's out of my hands."

Ms. Su's boss, Terry Norton, records an estimate for bad debts every year, based on a percentage of receivables. What percentage depends on the current aging history. He also calculates and monitors the company's receivables turnover ratio, which the company reports in its financial statements. "I think of it in terms of collection period of DSO—days of sales outstanding," he explains.

Ms. Su knows that she and Mr. Norton are crucial to the profitability of Whitehall-Robins. "Receivables are generally the second-largest asset of any company (after its capital assets)," she points out. "So it's no wonder we keep a very close eye on them."

PREVIEW OF CHAPTER 8

In this chapter we discuss some of the decisions related to reporting and analyzing receivables. As indicated in the Feature Story, receivables are a significant asset on the books of pharmaceutical company Whitehall-Robins. Receivables are significant to companies in other industries as well, because a significant portion of sales are made on credit in the United States. As a consequence, companies must pay close attention to their receivables balances and manage them carefully.

The organization and content of the chapter are as follows.

REPORTING AND ANALYZING RECEIVABLES

Types of Receivables	Accounts Receivable	Notes Receivable	Statement Presentation of Receivables	Managing Receivables
• Accounts receivable • Notes receivable • Other receivables	• Recognizing accounts receivable • Valuing accounts receivable	• Computing interest • Recognizing notes receivable • Valuing notes receivable • Disposing of notes receivable	• Balance sheet or notes • Income statement	• Extending credit • Establishing a payment period • Monitoring collections • Evaluating liquidity of receivables • Accelerating cash receipts

THE NAVIGATOR

Types of Receivables

STUDY OBJECTIVE

1

Identify the different types of receivables.

The term **receivables** refers to amounts due from individuals and companies. Receivables are claims that are expected to be collected in cash. The management of receivables is a very important activity for any company that sells goods or services on credit.

Receivables are important because they represent one of a company's most liquid assets. For many companies, receivables are also one of the largest assets. For example, receivables represented 11% of the current assets of pharmacy giant Rite Aid in 2004. Illustration 8-1 lists receivables as a percentage of total assets for five other well-known companies in a recent year.

Illustration 8-1
Receivables as a percentage of assets

Company	Receivables as a Percentage of Total Assets
General Electric	44%
Ford Motor Company	40%
Minnesota Mining and Manufacturing Company (3M)	13%
Krispy Kreme	11%
Intel Corporation	6%

The relative significance of a company's receivables as a percentage of its assets depends on various factors: its industry, the time of year, whether it extends long-term financing, and its credit policies. To reflect important differences among receivables, they are frequently classified as (1) accounts receivable, (2) notes receivable, and (3) other receivables.

Accounts receivable are amounts customers owe on account. They result from the sale of goods and services. Companies generally expect to collect accounts receivable within 30 to 60 days. They are usually the most significant type of claim held by a company.

Notes receivable represent claims for which formal instruments of credit are issued as evidence of the debt. The credit instrument normally requires the debtor to pay interest and extends for time periods of 60–90 days or longer. Notes and accounts receivable that result from sales transactions are often called trade receivables.

Other receivables include non-trade receivables such as interest receivable, loans to company officers, advances to employees, and income taxes refundable. These do not generally result from the operations of the business. Therefore, they are generally classified and reported as separate items in the balance sheet.

Accounts Receivable

Two accounting problems associated with accounts receivable are:

1. Recognizing accounts receivable.
2. Valuing accounts receivable.

A third issue, accelerating cash receipts from receivables, is discussed later in the chapter.

RECOGNIZING ACCOUNTS RECEIVABLE

Initial recognition of accounts receivable is relatively straightforward. A service organization records a receivable when it provides service on account. A merchandiser records accounts receivable at the point of sale of merchandise on account. When a merchandiser sells goods, it increases both the Accounts Receivable and Sales accounts.

Sales discounts reduce receivables. The seller may offer terms that encourage early payment by providing a discount. For example, terms of 2/10, n/30 provide the buyer with a 2% discount if it pays within 10 days. If the buyer chooses to pay within the discount period, the seller reduces its accounts receivable.

Sales returns also reduce receivables. The buyer might find some of the goods unacceptable and choose to return the unwanted goods. For example, if the buyer returns merchandise with a selling price of $100, the seller reduces Accounts Receivable by $100 upon receipt of the returned merchandise.

STUDY OBJECTIVE
2
Explain how accounts receivable are recognized in the accounts.

VALUING ACCOUNTS RECEIVABLE

Once companies record receivables in the accounts, the next question is: How should they report receivables in the financial statements? Companies report accounts receivable on the balance sheet as an asset. Determining the **amount** to report is sometimes difficult because some receivables will become uncollectible.

Although each customer must satisfy the credit requirements of the seller before the credit sale is approved, inevitably some accounts receivable become uncollectible. For example, a corporate customer may not be able to pay because it experienced a sales decline due to an economic downturn. Similarly, individuals may be laid off from their jobs or be faced with unexpected hospital bills. The seller debits such credit losses to **Bad Debts Expense** (or Uncollectible Accounts Expense). Such losses are a normal and necessary risk of doing business on a credit basis.

STUDY OBJECTIVE
3
Describe the methods used to account for bad debts.

The accounting profession uses two methods for uncollectible accounts: (1) the direct write-off method, and (2) the allowance method. We explain each of these methods in the following sections.

Direct Write-off Method for Uncollectible Accounts

Under the **direct write-off method**, when a company determines a particular account to be uncollectible, it charges the loss to Bad Debts Expense. Assume, for example, that Warden Co. writes off M. E. Doran's $200 balance as uncollectible on December 12. Warden's entry is:

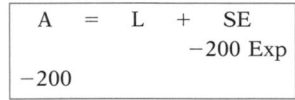

A	=	L	+	SE
				−200 Exp
−200				

Cash Flows
no effect

Dec.	12	Bad Debts Expense	200	
		Accounts Receivable—M. E. Doran		200
		(To record write-off of M. E. Doran account)		

Under this method, bad debts expense will show only **actual losses** from uncollectibles. The company will report accounts receivable at its gross amount.

Use of the direct write-off method can reduce the usefulness of both the income statement and balance sheet. Consider the following example. In 2007, Quick Buck Computer Company decided it could increase its revenues by offering computers to college students without requiring any money down, and with no credit-approval process. It went on campuses across the country and sold one million computers at a selling price of $800 each. This promotion increased Quick Buck's revenues and receivables by $800,000,000. It was a huge success: The 2007 balance sheet and income statement looked wonderful. Unfortunately, during 2008, nearly 40% of the college student customers defaulted on their loans. The 2008 income statement and balance sheet looked terrible. Illustration 8-2 shows the effect of these events on the financial statements using the direct write-off method.

Illustration 8-2 Effects of direct write-off method

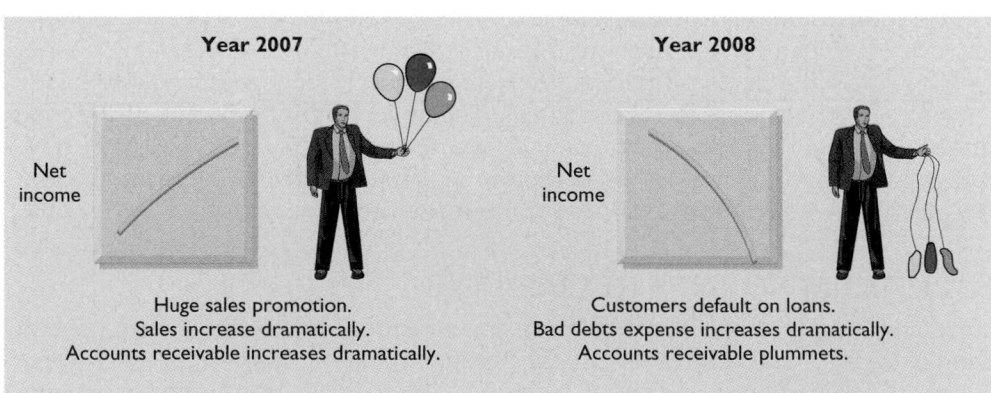

Under the direct write-off method, companies often record bad debts expense in a period different from the period in which they recorded the revenue. Thus, no attempt is made to match bad debts expense to sales revenues in the income statement. Nor does the company try to show accounts receivable in the balance sheet at the amount actually expected to be received. **Consequently, unless a company expects bad debts losses to be insignificant, the direct write-off method is not acceptable for financial reporting purposes.**

Allowance Method for Uncollectible Accounts

The **allowance method** of accounting for bad debts involves estimating uncollectible accounts at the end of each period. This provides better matching of expenses with revenues on the income statement. It also ensures that receivables are stated at their cash (net) realizable value on the balance sheet. **Cash (net) realizable value** is the net amount a company expects to receive in cash. It excludes amounts that the company estimates it will not collect. Estimated uncollectible receivables therefore reduce receivables on the balance sheet through use of the allowance method.

Companies must use the allowance method for financial reporting purposes when bad debts are material in amount. It has three essential features:

1. Companies **estimate** uncollectible accounts receivable and **match them against revenues** in the same accounting period in which the revenues are recorded.
2. Companies record estimated uncollectibles as an increase (a debit) to Bad Debts Expense and an increase (a credit) to Allowance for Doubtful Accounts (a contra asset account) through an adjusting entry at the end of each period.
3. Companies debit actual uncollectibles to Allowance for Doubtful Accounts and credit them to Accounts Receivable at the time the specific account is written off as uncollectible.

RECORDING ESTIMATED UNCOLLECTIBLES. To illustrate the allowance method, assume that Hampson Furniture has credit sales of $1,200,000 in 2007, of which $200,000 remains uncollected at December 31. The credit manager estimates that $12,000 of these sales will prove uncollectible. The adjusting entry to record the estimated uncollectibles is:

Dec. 31	Bad Debts Expense	12,000	
	Allowance for Doubtful Accounts		12,000
	(To record estimate of uncollectible accounts)		

A	=	L	+	SE
				−12,000 Exp
−12,000				

Cash Flows
no effect

Companies report Bad Debts Expense in the income statement as an operating expense (usually as a selling expense). Thus, Hampson matches the estimated uncollectibles with sales in 2007 because the expense is recorded in the same year the company makes the sales.

Allowance for Doubtful Accounts shows the estimated amount of claims on customers that companies expect will become uncollectible in the future. Companies use a contra account instead of a direct credit to Accounts Receivable because they do not know *which* customers will not pay. The credit balance in the allowance account will absorb the specific write-offs when they occur. The company deducts the allowance account from Accounts Receivable in the current assets section of the balance sheet as shown in Illustration 8-3.

HAMPSON FURNITURE Balance Sheet (partial)		
Current assets		
Cash		$ 14,800
Accounts receivable	$200,000	
Less: Allowance for doubtful accounts	12,000	188,000
Merchandise inventory		310,000
Prepaid expense		25,000
Total current assets		$537,800

Illustration 8-3
Presentation of allowance for doubtful accounts

The amount of $188,000 in Illustration 8-3 represents the expected **cash realizable value** of the accounts receivable at the statement date. **Companies do not close Allowance for Doubtful Accounts at the end of the fiscal year.**

RECORDING THE WRITE-OFF OF AN UNCOLLECTIBLE ACCOUNT. Companies use various methods of collecting past-due accounts, as discussed in the Feature Story. When a company has exhausted all means of collecting a past-due account and collection appears unlikely, the company should write off the account. In the credit card industry it is standard practice to write off accounts that are 210 days past due. To prevent premature or unauthorized write-offs, authorized management personnel should formally approve each write-off. To maintain good internal control, companies should not authorize someone to write off accounts who also has daily responsibilities related to cash or receivables.

To illustrate a receivables write-off, assume that the vice-president of finance of Hampson Furniture on March 1, 2008, authorizes a write-off of the $500 balance owed by R. A. Ware. The entry to record the write-off is:

A	=	L	+	SE
+500				
−500				

Cash Flows
no effect

Mar. 1	Allowance for Doubtful Accounts	500	
	Accounts Receivable—R. A. Ware		500
	(Write-off of R. A. Ware account)		

The company does not increase Bad Debts Expense when the write-off occurs. **Under the allowance method, a company debits every bad debt write-off to the allowance account and not to Bad Debts Expense.** A debit to Bad Debts Expense would be incorrect because the company has already recognized the expense, when it made the adjusting entry for estimated bad debts. Instead, the entry to record the write-off of an uncollectible account reduces both Accounts Receivable and the Allowance for Doubtful Accounts. After posting, the general ledger accounts will appear as in Illustration 8-4.

Illustration 8-4 General ledger balances after write-off

Accounts Receivable		Allowance for Doubtful Accounts	
Jan. 1 Bal. 200,000	Mar. 1 **500**	Mar. 1 **500**	Jan. 1 Bal. 12,000
Mar. 1 Bal. 199,500			Mar. 1 Bal. 11,500

A write-off affects only balance sheet accounts. Cash realizable value in the balance sheet, therefore, remains the same, as shown in Illustration 8-5.

Illustration 8-5 Cash realizable value comparison

	Before Write-off	After Write-off
Accounts receivable	$ 200,000	$ 199,500
Allowance for doubtful accounts	12,000	11,500
Cash realizable value	**$188,000**	**$188,000**

RECOVERY OF AN UNCOLLECTIBLE ACCOUNT. Occasionally, a company collects from a customer after the account has been written off as uncollectible. The company must make two entries to record the recovery of a bad debt: (1) It reverses the entry made in writing off the account. This reinstates the customer's account. (2) It journalizes the collection in the usual manner.

To illustrate, assume that on July 1, R. A. Ware pays the $500 amount that Hampson Furniture had written off on March 1. Hampson makes these entries:

			(1)		
July	1	Accounts Receivable—R. A. Ware		500	
		Allowance for Doubtful Accounts			500
		(To reverse write-off of R. A. Ware account)			

			(2)		
	1	Cash		500	
		Accounts Receivable—R. A. Ware			500
		(To record collection from R. A. Ware)			

A	=	L	+	SE
+500				
−500				

Cash Flows
no effect

A	=	L	+	SE
+500				
−500				

Cash Flows
+500

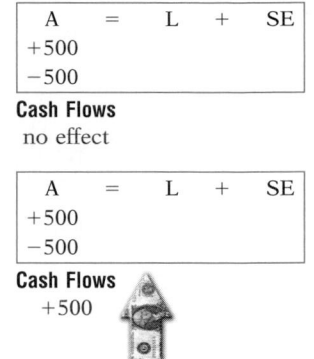

Note that the recovery of a bad debt, like the write-off of a bad debt, affects only balance sheet accounts. The net effect of the two entries is an increase in Cash and an increase in Allowance for Doubtful Accounts for $500. Accounts Receivable and the Allowance for Doubtful Accounts both increase in entry (1) for two reasons: First, the company made an error in judgment when it wrote off the account receivable. Second, R. A. Ware did pay, and therefore the Accounts Receivable account should show this collection for possible future credit purposes.

Helpful Hint Like the write-off, a recovery does not involve the income statement.

ESTIMATING THE ALLOWANCE. For Hampson Furniture in Illustration 8-3, the amount of the expected uncollectibles was given. However, in "real life," companies must estimate the amount of expected uncollectible accounts if they use the allowance method. Frequently they estimate the allowance as a percentage of the outstanding receivables.

Under the **percentage of receivables basis**, management establishes a percentage relationship between the amount of receivables and expected losses from uncollectible accounts. The company prepares a schedule in which it classifies customer balances by the length of time they have been unpaid. Because of its emphasis on time, this schedule is often called an **aging schedule**, and the analysis of it is often called **aging the accounts receivable**.

After the company arranges the accounts by age, it determines the expected bad debt losses by applying percentages, based on past experience, to the totals of each category. The longer a receivable is past due, the less likely it is to be collected. As a result, the estimated percentage of uncollectible debts increases as the number of days past due increases. Illustration 8-6 shows an aging schedule for Dart Company. Note the increasing uncollectible percentages from 2% to 40%.

Customer	Total	Not Yet Due	Number of Days Past Due			
			1–30	31–60	61–90	Over 90
T. E. Adert	$ 600		$ 300		$ 200	$ 100
R. C. Bortz	300	$ 300				
B. A. Carl	450		200	$ 250		
O. L. Diker	700	500			200	
T. O. Ebbet	600			300		300
Others	36,950	26,200	5,200	2,450	1,600	1,500
	$39,600	$27,000	$5,700	$3,000	$2,000	$1,900
Estimated percentage uncollectible		2%	4%	10%	20%	40%
Total estimated uncollectible accounts	$ 2,228	$ 540	$ 228	$ 300	$ 400	$ 760

Illustration 8-6 Aging schedule

Total estimated uncollectible accounts for Dart Company ($2,228) represent the existing customer claims expected to become uncollectible in the future. Thus, this amount represents the **required balance** in Allowance for Doubtful Accounts at the balance sheet date. Accordingly, **the amount of the bad debts expense adjusting entry is the difference between the required balance and the existing balance in the allowance account**.

For example, if the trial balance shows Allowance for Doubtful Accounts with a credit balance of $528, then an adjusting entry for $1,700 ($2,228 − $528) is necessary:

```
A  =  L  +  SE
            −1,700 Exp
−1,700
```
Cash Flows
no effect

Dec.	31	Bad Debts Expense	1,700	
		Allowance for Doubtful Accounts		1,700
		(To adjust allowance account to total estimated uncollectibles)		

After Dart posts the adjusting entry, its accounts will appear as in Illustration 8-7.

Illustration 8-7 Bad debts accounts after posting

Bad Debts Expense

Dec. 31 Adj. **1,700**

Allowance for Doubtful Accounts

Jan. 1 Bal. 528
Dec. 31 Adj. **1,700**

Dec. 31 Bal. 2,228

An important aspect of accounts receivable management is simply maintaining a close watch on the accounts. Studies have shown that accounts more than 60 days past due lose approximately 50% of their value if no payment activity occurs within the next 30 days. For each additional 30 days that pass, the collectible value halves once again. As noted in our Feature Story, Vivi Su of Whitehall-Robins monitors accounts receivable closely, using an aging schedule to set the percentage of bad debts and computing the company's receivables turnover.

Occasionally the allowance account will have a **debit balance** prior to adjustment because write-offs during the year have **exceeded** previous estimates for bad debts. In such a case, the company **adds the debit balance to the required balance** when it makes the adjusting entry. Thus, if there had been a $500 debit balance in the allowance account before adjustment, the adjusting entry would have been for $2,728 ($2,228 + $500) in order to arrive at a credit balance of $2,228.

The percentage of receivables basis provides an estimate of the cash realizable value of the receivables. It also provides a reasonable matching of expense to revenue.

Decision Toolkit

Decision Checkpoints	Info Needed for Decision	Tool to Use for Decision	How to Evaluate Results
Is the amount of past due accounts increasing? Which accounts require management's attention?	List of outstanding receivables and their due dates	Prepare an aging schedule showing the receivables in various stages: outstanding 0–30 days, 31–60 days, 61–90 days, and over 90 days.	Accounts in the older categories require follow-up: letters, phone calls, and possible renegotiation of terms.

The following note regarding accounts receivable comes from the annual report of healthcare company McKesson Corp.

McKESSON CORP. Notes to the Financial Statements		

Receivables, net

	March 31,	
(In millions)	2004	2003
Customer accounts	$4,986.1	$4,305.9
Other	609.5	574.2
Total	5,595.6	4,880.1
Allowances	(176.8)	(285.4)
Net	$5,418.8	$4,594.7

The allowances are for uncollectible accounts, discounts, returns, refunds, customer settlements and other adjustments. Allowances declined in 2004 primarily due to a $66.4 million reversal of accrued customer settlements into operating expenses and a $44.1 million write-off of a previously reserved note receivable.

Illustration 8-8 Note disclosure of accounts receivable

Business Insight
Investor Perspective

Recently Nortel Networks announced that half of its previous year's earnings were "fake." Should investors have seen this coming? Well, there were issues in its annual report that should have caused investors to ask questions. The company had cut its allowance for doubtful accounts on all receivables from $1,253 million to $544 million, even though its total balance of receivables remained relatively unchanged.

This reduction in bad debt expense was responsible for a very large part of the company's earnings that year. At the time it was unclear whether Nortel might have set the reserves too high originally and needed to reduce them, or whether it slashed the allowance to artificially boost earnings. But one thing is certain—when a company makes an accounting change of this magnitude, investors need to ask questions.

Source: Jonathan Weil, "Outside Audit: At Nortel, Warning Signs Existed Months Ago," *Wall Street Journal* (May, 18, 2004), p. C3.

 When would it be appropriate for a company to lower its allowance for doubtful accounts as a percentage of its receivables?

BEFORE YOU GO ON . . .

▶ Review It

1. What types of receivables does Tootsie Roll report on its balance sheet? Does it use the allowance method or the direct write-off method to account for uncollectibles? The answer to these questions appears on page 417.

2. To maintain adequate internal controls over receivables, who should authorize receivables write-offs?

3. What are the essential features of the allowance method?

4. What is the primary criticism of the direct write-off method?

▶ Do It

Brule Corporation has been in business for 5 years. The ledger at the end of the current year shows: Accounts Receivable $30,000; Sales $180,000; and Allowance for Doubtful Accounts with a debit balance of $2,000. Brule estimates bad debts to be 10% of accounts receivable. Prepare the entry necessary to adjust the Allowance for Doubtful Accounts.

Action Plan

Helpful Hint The debit to Bad Debts Expense is calculated as follows:

Allowance for Doubtful Accounts

2,000	**5,000**
	3,000

• Report receivables at their cash (net) realizable value—that is, the amount the company expects to collect in cash.

• Estimate the amount the company does not expect to collect.

• Consider the existing balance in the allowance account when using the percentage of receivables basis.

Solution

Brule should make the following entry to bring the balance in the Allowance for Doubtful Accounts up to a balance of $3,000 (.1 × $30,000):

Bad Debts Expense	5,000	
Allowance for Doubtful Accounts		5,000
(To record estimate of		
uncollectible accounts)		

THE NAVIGATOR

Notes Receivable

Companies also may grant credit in exchange for a formal credit instrument known as a promissory note. A **promissory note** is a written promise to pay a specified amount of money on demand or at a definite time. Promissory notes may be used (1) when individuals and companies lend or borrow money, (2) when the amount of the transaction and the credit period exceed normal limits, and (3) in settlement of accounts receivable.

In a promissory note, the party making the promise to pay is called the **maker**. The party to whom payment is to be made is called the **payee**. The promissory note may specifically identify the payee by name or may designate the payee simply as the bearer of the note.

In the note shown in Illustration 8-9 (page 381), Brent Company is the maker, and Wilma Company is the payee. To Wilma Company, the promissory note is a note receivable; to Brent Company, the note is a note payable.

Notes receivable give the holder a stronger legal claim to assets than do accounts receivable. Like accounts receivable, notes receivable can be readily sold to another party. Promissory notes are negotiable instruments (as are checks), which means that, when sold, the seller can transfer them to another party by endorsement.

Companies frequently accept notes receivable from customers who need to extend the payment of an outstanding account receivable, and they often require them from high-risk customers. In some industries (e.g., the pleasure and sport boat industry) all credit sales are supported by notes. The majority of notes, however, originate from lending transactions.

Illustration 8-9
Promissory note

Helpful Hint Who are the two key parties to a note? What entry does each party make when the note is issued?
Answer:
1. The maker, Brent Company, credits Notes Payable.
2. The payee, Wilma Company, debits Notes Receivable.

There are three basic issues in accounting for notes receivable:

1. **Recognizing** notes receivable.
2. **Valuing** notes receivable.
3. **Disposing** of notes receivable.

We will look at each of these issues, but first we need to consider an issue that did not apply to accounts receivable: computing interest.

COMPUTING INTEREST

Illustration 8-10 gives the basic formula for computing interest on an interest-bearing note.

STUDY OBJECTIVE
4
Compute the interest on notes receivable.

Illustration 8-10 Formula for computing interest

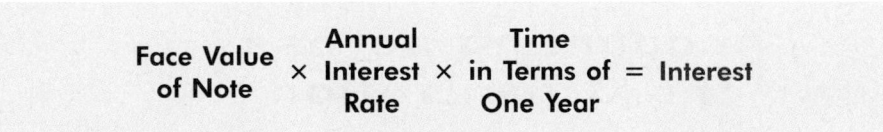

The interest rate specified on the note is an **annual** rate of interest. The time factor in the computation expresses the fraction of a year that the note is outstanding. When the maturity date is stated in days, the time factor is frequently the number of days divided by 360. When the due date is stated in months, the time factor is the number of months divided by 12. Illustration 8-11 shows computation of interest for various time periods.

Helpful Hint The maturity date of a 60-day note dated July 17 is determined as follows:

Term of note		60 days
July (31 − 17)	14	
August	31	45
September		**15**
(Maturity date)		

Illustration 8-11
Computation of interest

Terms of Note	Interest Computation				
	Face	× Rate ×	Time	=	Interest
$ 730, 12%, 120 days	$ 730 ×	12% ×	120/360	=	$ 29.20
$1,000, 9%, 6 months	$1,000 ×	9% ×	6/12	=	$ 45.00
$2,000, 6%, 1 year	$2,000 ×	6% ×	1/1	=	$120.00

There are different ways to calculate interest. For example, the computation in Illustration 8-11 assumed 360 days for the year. Most financial institutions use 365 days to compute interest. (*For homework problems, assume 360 days to simplify computations.*)

RECOGNIZING NOTES RECEIVABLE

To illustrate the basic entry for notes receivable, we will use Brent Company's $1,000, two-month, 8% promissory note dated May 1. Assuming that Brent

Company wrote the note to settle an open account, Wilma Company makes the following entry for the receipt of the note.

A	=	L	+	SE
+1,000				
−1,000				

Cash Flows
no effect

	May	1	Notes Receivable	1,000	
			Accounts Receivable—Brent Company		1,000
			(To record acceptance of Brent Company note)		

The company records the note receivable at its **face value**, the value shown on the face of the note. No interest revenue is reported when the company accepts the note because the revenue recognition principle does not recognize revenue until earned. Interest is earned (accrued) as time passes.

If a company exchanges a note for cash, the entry is a debit to Notes Receivable and a credit to Cash in the amount of the loan.

VALUING NOTES RECEIVABLE

Like accounts receivable, companies report short-term notes receivable at their **cash (net) realizable value**. The notes receivable allowance account is Allowance for Doubtful Accounts. Valuing short-term notes receivable is the same as valuing accounts receivable. The computations and estimations involved in determining cash realizable value and in recording the proper amount of bad debts expense and related allowance are similar.

Long-term notes receivable, however, pose additional estimation problems. As an example, we need only look at the problems large U.S. banks sometimes have in collecting their receivables. Loans to less-developed countries are particularly worrisome. Developing countries need loans for development but often

Accounting across the Organization

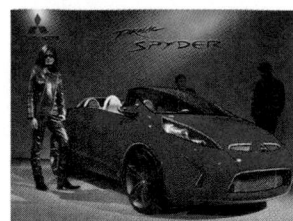

Management must decide to whom it will grant credit. This is one of the hardest, and most critical, decisions that it makes. Consider the case of Mitsubishi Motors. It had been floundering, reporting large losses for a number of years in a row. Then management came up with what appeared to be a great plan. It began a marketing campaign aimed at giving Mitsubishi a hip image (think flashy ads with loud music), thus making its vehicles attractive to single people in their early twenties. The company combined this campaign with easy credit-terms—so called "zero-zero-zero" deals. This meant no down-payment, no payments for the first six months, and 0% financing.

The plan worked great—sort of. Sales took off. But then the twenty-somethings started defaulting on their loans. Soon Mitsubishi's losses were even bigger than before. It has since refocused its ads and credit terms. It now focuses on people who are "young at heart" (as opposed to just young)—and "economically safer."

Source: Todd Zaun, "Bad Loans Bump Mitsubishi Motors Off Road to Recovery," *Wall Street Journal Online* (November 12, 2003).

 How would reported net income likely differ during the first year of this promotion if Mitsubishi used the direct write-off method versus the allowance method?

find repayment difficult. U.S. loans (notes) to less-developed countries at one time totaled approximately $135 billion. In Brazil alone, Citigroup at one time had loans equivalent to 80% of its stockholders' equity. In some cases, developed nations have intervened to provide financial assistance to the financially troubled borrowers so as to minimize the political and economic turmoil to the borrower and to ensure the survival of the lender.

DISPOSING OF NOTES RECEIVABLE

Notes may be held to their maturity date, at which time the face value plus accrued interest is due. In some situations, the maker of the note defaults, and the payee must make appropriate adjustment. In other situations, similar to accounts receivable, the holder of the note speeds up the conversion to cash by selling the receivables.

> **STUDY OBJECTIVE**
> **5**
> Describe the entries to record the disposition of notes receivable.

Honor of Notes Receivable

A note is **honored** when its maker pays in full at its maturity date. For each interest-bearing note, the **amount due at maturity** is the face value of the note plus interest for the length of time specified on the note.

To illustrate, assume that Wolder Co. lends Higley Inc. $10,000 on June 1, accepting a five-month, 9% interest note. In this situation, interest is $375 ($10,000 $\times$ 9% $\times$ $\frac{5}{12}$). The amount due, the maturity value, is $10,375 ($10,000 + $375). To obtain payment, Wolder (the payee) must present the note either to Higley Inc. (the maker) or to the maker's agent, such as a bank. If Wolder presents the note to Higley Inc. on November 1, the maturity date, Wolder's entry to record the collection is:

> **Helpful Hint** How many days of interest should be accrued at September 30 for a 90-day note issued on August 16? *Answer:* 45 days (15 days in August plus 30 days in September).

Nov. 1	Cash	10,375	
	Notes Receivable		10,000
	Interest Revenue ($10,000 $\times$ 9% $\times$ $\frac{5}{12}$)		375
	(To record collection of Higley Inc. note and interest)		

A = L + SE
+10,375
−10,000
   +375 Rev

Cash Flows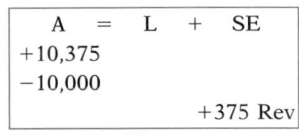
+10,375

Accrual of Interest Receivable

If Wolder Co. prepares financial statements as of September 30, it must accrue interest. In this case, the adjusting entry by Wolder is for four months, or $300, as shown below.

Sept. 30	Interest Receivable ($10,000 $\times$ 9% $\times$ $\frac{4}{12}$)	300	
	Interest Revenue		300
	(To accrue 4 months' interest on Higley note)		

A = L + SE
+300
   +300 Rev

Cash Flows
no effect

When interest has been accrued, the company must credit Interest Receivable at maturity. Also, since an additional month has passed, the company records one month of interest revenue. Wolder's entry to record the honoring of the Higley note on November 1 is:

Nov. 1	Cash	10,375	
	Notes Receivable		10,000
	Interest Receivable		300
	Interest Revenue ($10,000 $\times$ 9% $\times$ $\frac{1}{12}$)		75
	(To record collection of Higley Inc. note and interest)		

A = L + SE
+10,375
−10,000
−300
   +75 Rev

Cash Flows
+10,375

In this case, Wolder credits Interest Receivable because the receivable was established in the adjusting entry on September 30.

Dishonor of Notes Receivable

A **dishonored note** is a note that is not paid in full at maturity. A dishonored note receivable is no longer negotiable; however, the payee still has a claim against the maker of the note for both the note and the interest. If the lender expects that it eventually will be able to collect, the Notes Receivable account is transferred to an Account Receivable for both the face value of the note and the interest due. Sometimes the two parties negotiate new terms to make it easier for the borrower to repay the debt. If there is no hope of collection, the payee should write off the face value of the note.

BEFORE YOU GO ON . . .

▶ Review It

1. What is the basic formula for computing interest?
2. At what value do companies report notes receivable on the balance sheet?
3. Explain the difference between honoring and dishonoring a note receivable.

▶ Do It

Gambit Stores accepts from Leonard Co. a $3,400, 90-day, 6% note dated May 10 in settlement of Leonard's overdue open account. The note matures on August 8. What entry does Gambit make at the maturity date, assuming Leonard pays the note and interest in full at that time?

Action Plan

• Determine whether interest was accrued.
• Compute the accrued interest.
• Prepare the entry for payment of the note and the interest. The entry to record interest at maturity in this solution assumes that no interest has been previously accrued on this note.

Solution

The interest payable at maturity date is $51, computed as follows.

$$\text{Face} \times \text{Rate} \times \text{Time} = \text{Interest}$$

$$\$3,400 \times 6\% \times \frac{90}{360} = \$51$$

Gambit Stores records this entry at the maturity date:

Cash	3,451	
Notes Receivable		3,400
Interest Revenue		51
(To record collection of Leonard note and interest)		

THE
NAVIGATOR

Financial Statement Presentation of Receivables

Companies should identify in the balance sheet or in the notes to the financial statements each of the major types of receivables. Short-term receivables are reported in the current assets section of the balance sheet, below short-term investments. Short-term investments appear before short-term receivables because these investments are nearer to cash. Companies report both the gross amount of receivables and the allowance for doubtful accounts.

Illustration 8-12 shows a presentation of receivables for Deere & Company from its 2004 balance sheet and notes.

STUDY OBJECTIVE 6

Explain the statement presentation of receivables.

DEERE & COMPANY Balance Sheet (partial) (in millions)	
Receivables	
Receivables from unconsolidated subsidiaries	$ 17.6
Trade accounts and notes receivable	3,262.9
Financing receivables	11,377.6
Other receivables	663.0
Total receivables	15,321.1
Less: Allowance for doubtful trade receivables	201.0
Net receivables	$15,120.1

Illustration 8-12 Balance sheet presentation of receivables

In the income statement, companies report bad debts expense under "Selling expenses" in the operating expenses section. They show interest revenue under "Other revenues and gains" in the nonoperating section of the income statement.

If a company has significant risk of uncollectible accounts or other problems with its receivables, it is required to discuss this possibility in the notes to the financial statements.

BEFORE YOU GO ON . . .

▶ **Review It**

1. Explain where companies report receivables on the balance sheet and in what order.
2. Where do companies report bad debts expense and interest revenue on the income statement?

Managing Receivables

Managing accounts receivable involves five steps:

1. Determine to whom to extend credit.
2. Establish a payment period.
3. Monitor collections.
4. Evaluate the liquidity of receivables.
5. Accelerate cash receipts from receivables when necessary.

STUDY OBJECTIVE 7

Describe the principles of sound accounts receivable management.

EXTENDING CREDIT

A critical part of managing receivables is determining who should be extended credit and who should not. Many companies increase sales by being generous with their credit policy, but, like Mitsubishi in the *Accounting across the Organization* story, they may end up extending credit to risky customers who do not pay. If the credit policy is too tight, you will lose sales. If it is too loose, you may sell to "deadbeats" who will pay either very late or not at all. One CEO noted that prior to getting his credit and collection department in order, his salespeople had 300 square feet of office space **per person**, while the people in credit and collections had six people crammed into a single 300-square-foot space. Although this arrangement boosted sales, it had very expensive consequences in bad debts expense.

Companies can take certain steps to help minimize losses as they relax credit standards. They might require risky customers to provide letters of credit or bank guarantees. Then if the customer does not pay, the bank that provided the guarantee will do so. Particularly risky customers might be required to pay cash on delivery.

In addition, companies should ask potential customers for references from banks and suppliers, to determine their payment history. It is important to check these references on potential new customers as well as periodically to check the financial health of continuing customers. Many resources are available for investigating customers. For example, *The Dun & Bradstreet Reference Book of American Business* (*www.dnb.com*) lists millions of companies and provides credit ratings for many of them.

Accounting across the Organization

In the weeks prior to Kmart's decision to file for Chapter 11 bankruptcy protection, many of its suppliers were taking concrete steps to protect themselves. For example, the garden supply company The Scotts Company, which in the previous year sold Kmart $175 million in goods, decided to quit shipping to Kmart until its survival plans were more clear. This was a big decision for Scotts, since Kmart represented 10% of its sales in the previous year.

One consultant said that in an informal survey of Kmart suppliers, one-third weren't shipping to Kmart, one-third were holding back shipments until they learned more, and one-third were doing business as usual. The result: Kmart had a lot of empty shelves, at a time when it was hard pressed for cash.

Source: Amy Merrick, "Kmart Suppliers Limit Risk in Case of Chapter 11 Filing," *Wall Street Journal Online* (January 21, 2002).

 Rather than refusing to ship to Kmart, what could suppliers have done to protect their interests?

ESTABLISHING A PAYMENT PERIOD

Companies that extend credit should determine a required payment period and communicate that policy to their customers. It is important to make sure that your company's payment period is consistent with that of your competitors. For example, if you decide to require payment within 15 days, but your competitors require payment within 45 days, you may lose sales to your competitors. However, to match competitors' terms yet still encourage prompt payment of accounts, you might allow up to 45 days to pay but offer a sales discount for people paying within 15 days.

MONITORING COLLECTIONS

We discussed preparation of the accounts receivable aging schedule earlier in the chapter (page 377). Companies should prepare an accounts receivable aging schedule at least monthly. In addition to estimating the allowance for doubtful accounts, the aging schedule has other uses: It helps managers estimate the timing of future cash inflows, which is very important to the treasurer's efforts to prepare a cash budget. It provides information about the overall collection experience of the company and identifies problem accounts. For example, management would compute and compare the percentage of receivables that are over 90 days past due.

The aging schedule identifies problem accounts that the company needs to pursue with phone calls, letters, and occasionally legal action. Sometimes special arrangements must be made with problem accounts. For example, it was reported that Intel Corporation (a major manufacturer of computer chips) required that Packard Bell (at one time one of the largest U.S. sellers of personal computers) give Intel an interest-bearing note receivable in exchange for a past-due account receivable. This caused concern within the investment community, first because it suggested that Packard Bell was in trouble, and second because of the impact on Intel's accounts receivable, since Packard Bell was one of its largest customers.

Decision Toolkit

Decision Checkpoints	Info Needed for Decision	Tool to Use for Decision	How to Evaluate Results
Is the company's credit risk increasing?	Customer account balances and due dates	Accounts receivable aging schedule	Compute and compare the percentage of receivables over 90 days old.

If a company has significant concentrations of credit risk, it must discuss this risk in the notes to its financial statements. A **concentration of credit risk** is a threat of nonpayment from a single customer or class of customers that could adversely affect the financial health of the company. Illustration 8-13 shows an excerpt from the credit risk note from the 2004 annual report of McKesson Corp. McKesson reports that its ten largest customers account for 50% of its total revenues and receivables.

McKESSON CORP.
Notes to the Financial Statements

Concentrations of Credit Risk: Trade receivables subject us to a concentration of credit risk with customers primarily in our Pharmaceutical Solutions segment. A significant proportion of our revenue growth has been with a limited number of large customers and as a result, our credit concentration has increased. Accordingly, any defaults in payment by or a reduction in purchases from these large customers could have a significant negative impact on our financial condition, results of operations and liquidity. At March 31, 2004, revenues and accounts receivable from our ten largest customers accounted for approximately 50% of total consolidated revenues and accounts receivable. Fiscal 2004 revenues and March 31, 2004 receivables from our largest customer, Rite Aid Corporation, represented approximately 11% of total consolidated revenues and 8% of accounts receivable. We have also provided financing arrangements to certain of our customers within our Pharmaceutical Solutions segment, some of which are on a revolving basis. At March 31, 2004, these arrangements totaled $196.1 million and we have a security interest in the customers' assets.

Illustration 8-13
Excerpt from note on concentration of credit risk

This note to McKesson Corp.'s financial statements indicates it has a high level of credit concentration. A default by any of these large customers could have a significant negative impact on its financial performance.

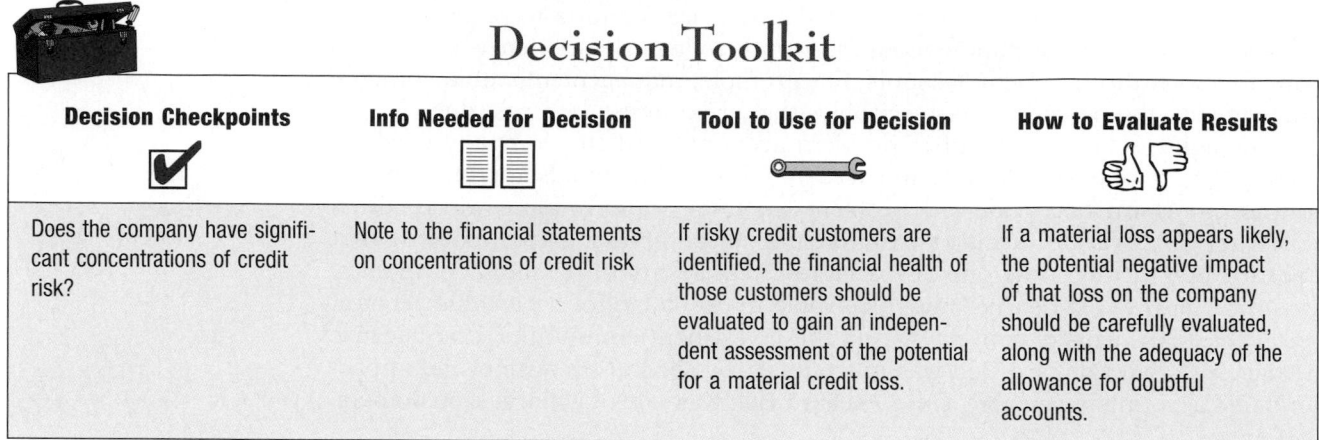

Decision Toolkit

Decision Checkpoints	Info Needed for Decision	Tool to Use for Decision	How to Evaluate Results
Does the company have significant concentrations of credit risk?	Note to the financial statements on concentrations of credit risk	If risky credit customers are identified, the financial health of those customers should be evaluated to gain an independent assessment of the potential for a material credit loss.	If a material loss appears likely, the potential negative impact of that loss on the company should be carefully evaluated, along with the adequacy of the allowance for doubtful accounts.

STUDY OBJECTIVE
8

Identify ratios to analyze a company's receivables.

EVALUATING LIQUIDITY OF RECEIVABLES

Investors and managers keep a watchful eye on the relationship among sales, accounts receivable, and cash collections. If sales increase, then accounts receivable are also expected to increase. But a disproportionate increase in accounts receivable might signal trouble. Perhaps the company increased its sales by loosening its credit policy, and these receivables may be difficult or impossible to collect. Such receivables are considered less liquid. Recall that liquidity is measured by how quickly certain assets can be converted to cash.

The ratio analysts use to assess the liquidity of the receivables is the **receivables turnover ratio**. This ratio measures the number of times, on average, a company collects receivables during the period. The receivables turnover ratio is computed by dividing net credit sales (net sales less cash sales) by the average net accounts receivables during the year. Unless seasonal factors are significant, **average** accounts receivable outstanding can be computed from the beginning and ending balances of the net receivables.[1]

A popular variant of the receivables turnover ratio is to convert it into an **average collection period** in terms of days. This is done by dividing the receivables turnover ratio into 365 days. Companies frequently use the average collection period to assess the effectiveness of a company's credit and collection policies. The general rule is that the average collection period should not greatly exceed the credit term period (i.e., the time allowed for payment).

The following data (in millions) are available for McKesson Corp.

	For the year ended March 31,	
	2004	**2003**
Sales	$69,506.1	$57,120.8
Accounts receivable (net)	$ 5,418.8	$ 4,594.7

---

[1]If seasonal factors are significant, the company might determine the average accounts receivable balance by using monthly amounts.

Illustration 8-14 shows the receivables turnover ratio and average collection period for McKesson Corp., along with comparative industry data. These calculations assume that all sales were credit sales.

Illustration 8-14
Receivables turnover and average collection period

$$\text{Receivables Turnover Ratio} = \frac{\text{Net Credit Sales}}{\text{Average Net Receivables}}$$

$$\text{Average Collection Period} = \frac{365}{\text{Receivables Turnover Ratio}}$$

($ in millions)		2004	2003
McKesson	Receivables turnover	$\frac{\$69,506.1}{(\$5,418.8 + \$4,594.7)/2} = 13.9$ times	$\frac{\$57,120.8}{(\$4,594.7 + \$3,998.1)/2^*} = 13.3$ times
	Average collection period	$\frac{365}{13.9} = 26.3$ days	$\frac{365}{13.3} = 27.4$ days
Industry average	Receivables turnover	10.4 times	
	Average collection period	35.1 days	

*The receivables balance at March 31, 2002, was $3,998.1 million.

McKesson's receivables turnover was 13.9 times in 2004, with a corresponding average collection period of 26.3 days. This was slightly better than its 2003 collection period of 27.4 days. It compares favorably with the industry average collection period of 35.1 days. What this means is that McKesson is able to turn its receivables into cash more quickly than most of its competitors. Therefore, it has a better likelihood of paying its current obligations than a company with a slower receivables turnover.

Decision Toolkit

Decision Checkpoints	Info Needed for Decision	Tool to Use for Decision	How to Evaluate Results
Are collections being made in a timely fashion?	Net credit sales and average receivables balance	Receivables turnover ratio = $\frac{\text{Net credit sales}}{\text{Average net receivables}}$ Average collection period = $\frac{365 \text{ days}}{\text{Receivables turnover ratio}}$	Average collection period should be consistent with corporate credit policy. An increase may suggest a decline in financial health of customers.

In some cases, receivables turnover may be misleading. Some companies, especially large retail chains, encourage credit and revolving charge sales, and they slow collections in order to earn a healthy return on the outstanding receivables in the form of interest at rates of 18% to 22%. On the other hand, companies that sell their receivables on a consistent basis will have a faster turnover than those that do not. Thus, to interpret receivables turnover, you must know how a company manages its receivables. In general, the faster the turnover, the greater the reliability of the current ratio for assessing liquidity.

ACCELERATING CASH RECEIPTS

In the normal course of events, companies collect accounts receivable in cash and remove them from the books. However, as credit sales and receivables have grown in size and significance, the "normal course of events" has changed. Two common expressions apply to the collection of receivables: (1) "Time is money"—that is, waiting for the normal collection process costs money. (2) "A bird in the hand is worth two in the bush"—that is, getting the cash now is better than getting it later or not at all. Therefore, in order to accelerate the receipt of cash from receivables, companies frequently sell their receivables to another company for cash, thereby shortening the cash-to-cash operating cycle.

There are three reasons for the sale of receivables. The first is their **size**. In recent years, for competitive reasons, sellers (retailers, wholesalers, and manufacturers) often have provided financing to purchasers of their goods. For example, many major companies in the automobile, truck, industrial and farm equipment, computer, and appliance industries have created companies that accept responsibility for accounts receivable financing. General Motors has General Motors Acceptance Corp. (GMAC), General Electric has GE Capital, and Ford has Ford Motor Credit Corp. (FMCC). These companies are referred to as **captive finance companies** because they are wholly owned by the company selling the product. The purpose of captive finance companies is to encourage the sale of the company's products by assuring financing to buyers. However, the parent companies involved do not necessarily want to hold large amounts of receivables, so they may sell them.

Second, **companies may sell receivables because they may be the only reasonable source of cash**. When credit is tight, companies may not be able to borrow money in the usual credit markets. Even if credit is available, the cost of borrowing may be prohibitive.

A final reason for selling receivables is that **billing and collection are often time-consuming and costly**. As a result, it is often easier for a retailer to sell the receivables to another party that has expertise in billing and collection matters. Credit card companies such as MasterCard, Visa, American Express, and Discover specialize in billing and collecting accounts receivable.

National Credit Card Sales

Approximately one billion credit cards were in use recently—more than three credit cards for every man, woman, and child in this country. A common type of credit card is a national credit card such as Visa and MasterCard. Three parties are involved when national credit cards are used in making retail sales: (1) the credit card issuer, who is independent of the retailer, (2) the retailer, and (3) the customer. **A retailer's acceptance of a national credit card is another form of selling—factoring—the receivable by the retailer.**

The use of national credit cards translates to more sales and zero bad debts for the retailer. Both are powerful reasons for a retailer to accept such cards. Illustration 8-15 shows the major advantages of national credit cards to the

Illustration 8-15
Advantages of credit
cards to the retailer

Issuer does credit investigation of customer

Issuer maintains customer accounts

Credit card issuer   Customer   Retailer

Issuer undertakes collection process and absorbs any losses

Retailer receives cash more quickly from credit card issuer

retailer. In exchange for these advantages, the retailer pays the credit card issuer a fee of 2% to 4% of the invoice price for its services.

The retailer considers sales resulting from the use of Visa and MasterCard as **cash sales**. Upon notification of a credit card charge from a retailer, the bank that issued the card immediately adds the amount to the seller's bank balance. Companies therefore record these credit card charges in the same manner as checks deposited from a cash sale. The banks that issue national credit cards generally charge retailers a fee of 2% to 4% of the credit card sales slips for this service.

To illustrate, Morgan Marie purchases $1,000 of compact discs for her restaurant from Sondgeroth Music Co., and she charges this amount on her Visa First Bank Card. The service fee that First Bank charges Sondgeroth Music is 3%. Sondgeroth Music's entry to record this transaction is:

Cash	970	
Service Charge Expense	30	
Sales		1,000
(To record Visa credit card sales)		

A	=	L	+	SE
+970				
				−30 Exp
				+1,000 Rev

Cash Flows
+970

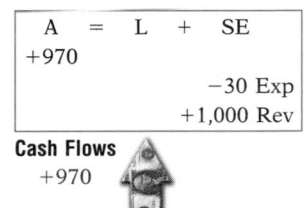

Sale of Receivables to a Factor

A common way to accelerate receivables collection is a sale to a factor. A **factor** is a finance company or bank that buys receivables from businesses for a fee and then collects the payments directly from the customers.

Factoring was traditionally associated with the textiles, apparel, footwear, furniture, and home furnishing industries. It has now spread to other types of businesses and is a multibillion dollar industry. For example, Sears, Roebuck & Co. (now Sears Holdings) once sold $14.8 billion of customer accounts receivable.

McKesson has a pre-arranged agreement allowing it to sell up to $850 million of its receivables. McKesson's sale of receivables may explain why its receivables turnover ratio exceeds the industry average.

Factoring arrangements vary widely, but typically the factor charges a commission. It ranges from 1% to 3% of the amount of receivables purchased. To illustrate, assume that Hendredon Furniture factors $600,000 of receivables to Federal Factors, Inc. Federal Factors assesses a service charge of 2% of the amount of receivables sold. The following journal entry records Hendredon's sale of receivables.

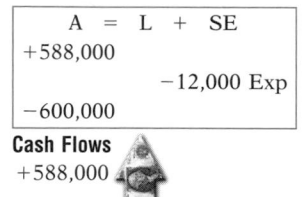

A = L + SE
+588,000
           −12,000 Exp
−600,000

Cash Flows
+588,000

Cash	588,000	
Service Charge Expense (2% × $600,000)	12,000	
Accounts Receivable		600,000
(To record the sale of accounts		
receivable)		

If the company usually sells its receivables, it records the service charge expense as a selling expense. If the company sells receivables infrequently, it may report this amount under "Other expenses and losses" in the income statement.

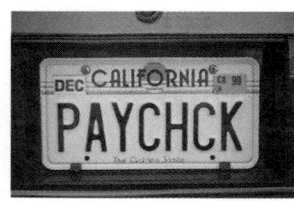

Accounting across the Organization

In the past, smaller companies primarily factored receivables. Today, businesses of all sizes and types factor their receivables. For example, Wal-Mart's suppliers, many of them large companies, need their cash more quickly than Wal-Mart wants to pay, so many of them factor their receivables. Also, some businesses have found it economical to outsource their whole billing and collection function to factors. One factor, CDS Capital, will provide all billing and collecting, as well as a record of clients' daily cash position, cash received, bills paid, and receivables still outstanding.

Source: Martin Mayer, "Taking the Fear Out of Factoring," *Inc. Magazine* (December 2003), pp. 90–97.

? What factors should management consider in deciding whether to factor its receivables?

Illustration 8-16 summarizes the basic principles of managing accounts receivable.

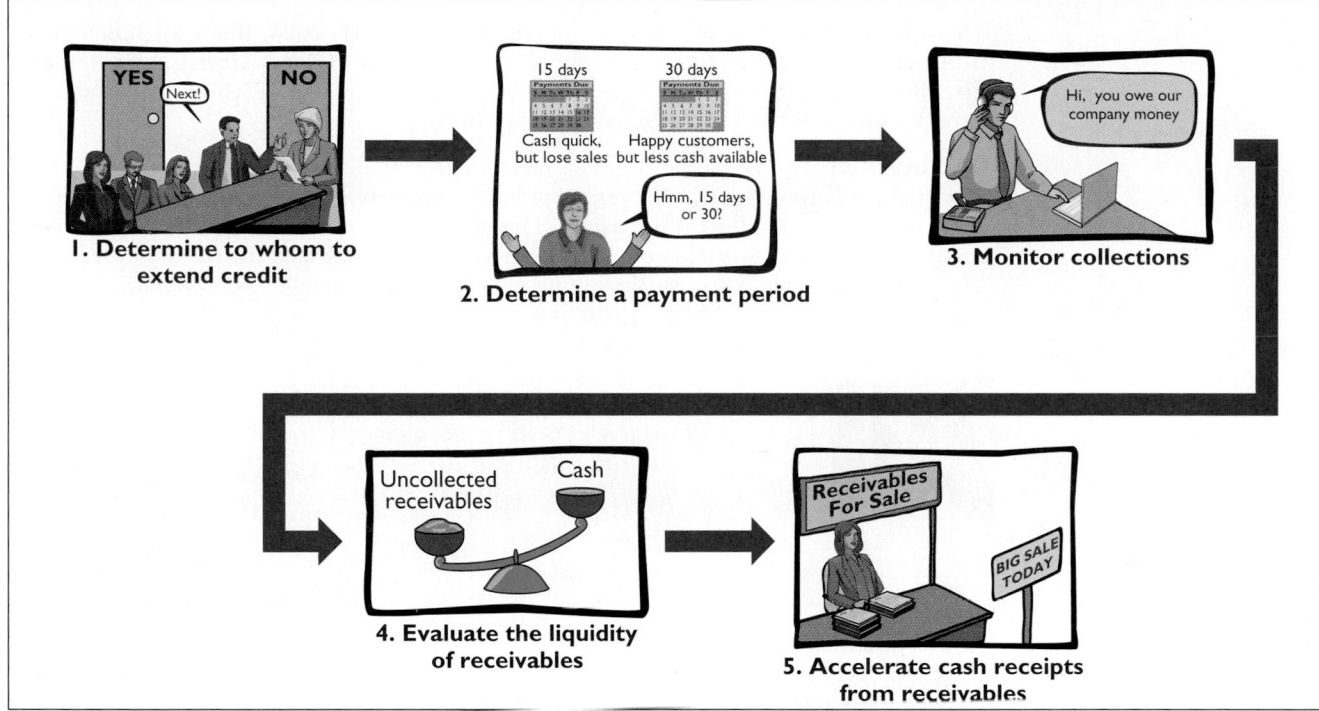

BEFORE YOU GO ON . . .

▶ Review It

1. What is meant by a concentration of credit risk?
2. What is the interpretation of the receivables turnover ratio and the average collection period?
3. For whom is the service charge on a credit card sale an expense?
4. Why do companies sell their receivables?

▶ Do It

Peter M. Kell Wholesalers Co. needs to raise $120,000 in cash to safely cover next Friday's employee payroll. Kell has reached its debt ceiling. Kell's present balance of outstanding receivables totals $750,000. What might Kell do to alleviate this cash crunch? Record the entry that Kell would make when it raises the needed cash. (Assume a 1% service charge.)

Action Plan

• Consider sale of receivables to a factor.
• Weigh cost of factoring against benefit of having cash in hand.

Solution

If Kell Co. factors $125,000 of its accounts receivable at a 1% service charge, it would make this entry:

Cash	123,750	
Service Charge Expense	1,250	
Accounts Receivable		125,000
(To record sale of receivables to factor)		

THE NAVIGATOR

Using the Decision Toolkit

The information below was taken from the December 31, 2004, financial statements of Amerisource Bergen Corp., Inc. Similar to McKesson Corp., Amerisource Bergen distributes drugs and related services to pharmaceutical manufacturers and health-care providers in the United States and Puerto Rico.

Instructions

Comment on Amerisource Bergen's accounts receivable management and liquidity relative to that of McKesson, using (1) the current ratio and (2) the receivables turnover ratio and average collection period. McKesson's current ratio was 1.38:1. The other ratio values for McKesson were calculated earlier in the chapter.

AMERISOURCE BERGEN CORP., INC.
Selected Financial Information
(in millions)

	2004		2003	
Sales		$53,179		$49,657
Current assets				
Cash and cash equivalents		$ 871		$ 800
Accounts receivable	$2,725		$2,488	
Allowance for doubtful accounts	464		192	
Net accounts receivable		2,261		2,296
Inventories		5,136		5,734
Other current assets		27		29
Total current assets		$ 8,295		$ 8,859
Total current liabilities		$ 6,104		$ 6,256

Solution

1. Here is the current ratio (Current assets ÷ Current liabilities) for each company.

McKesson	Amerisource Bergen
1.38:1	$\dfrac{\$8,295}{\$6,104} = 1.36:1$

This suggests that McKesson and Amerisource Bergen have similar liquidity.

2. The receivables turnover ratio and average collection period for each company are:

	McKesson	Amerisource Bergen
Receivables turnover ratio	13.9 times	$\dfrac{\$53,179}{(\$2,261 + \$2,296)/2} = 23.3$ times
Average collection period	26.3 days	$\dfrac{365}{23.3} = 15.7$ days

Amerisource Bergen's receivables turnover ratio of 23.3 compared to McKesson's 13.9, and its average collection days of 15.7 days versus McKesson's 26.3 days, suggest that Amerisource Bergen is able to collect from its customers much more rapidly.

THE NAVIGATOR

Summary of Study Objectives

1 *Identify the different types of receivables.* Receivables are frequently classified as accounts, notes, and other. Accounts receivable are amounts customers owe on account. Notes receivable represent claims that are evidenced by formal instruments of credit. Other receivables include nontrade receivables such as interest receivable, loans to company officers, advances to employees, and income taxes refundable.

2 *Explain how accounts receivable are recognized in the accounts.* Accounts receivable are recorded at invoice price. They are reduced by sales returns and allowances. Cash discounts reduce the amount received on accounts receivable.

3 *Describe the methods used to account for bad debts.* The two methods of accounting for uncollectible accounts are the allowance method and the direct write-off method. Under the allowance method, companies estimate uncollectible accounts as a percentage of receivables. It emphasizes the cash realizable value of the accounts receivable. An aging schedule is frequently used with this approach.

4 *Compute the interest on notes receivable.* The formula for computing interest is: Face value × Interest rate × Time.

5 *Describe the entries to record the disposition of notes receivable.* Notes can be held to maturity, at which time the borrower (maker) pays the face value plus accrued interest and the payee removes the note from the accounts. In many cases, however, similar to accounts receivable, the holder of the note speeds up the conversion by selling the receivable to another party. In some situations, the maker of the note dishonors the note (defaults), and the note is written off.

6 *Explain the statement presentation of receivables.* Companies should identify each major type of receivable in the balance sheet or in the notes to the financial statements. Short-term receivables are considered current assets. Companies report the gross amount of receivables and allowance for doubtful accounts. They report bad debts and service charge expenses in the income statement as operating (selling) expenses, and interest revenue as other revenues and gains in the nonoperating section of the statement.

Decision Toolkit—A Summary

Decision Checkpoints	Info Needed for Decision	Tool to Use for Decision	How to Evaluate Results
Is the amount of past due accounts increasing? Which accounts require management's attention?	List of outstanding receivables and their due dates	Prepare an aging schedule showing the receivables in various stages: outstanding 0–30 days, 31–60 days, 61–90 days, and over 90 days.	Accounts in the older categories require follow-up: letters, phone calls, and possible renegotiation of terms.
Is the company's credit risk increasing?	Customer account balances and due dates	Accounts receivable aging schedule	Compute and compare the percentage of receivables over 90 days old.
Does the company have significant concentrations of credit risk?	Note to the financial statements on concentrations of credit risk	If risky credit customers are identified, the financial health of those customers should be evaluated to gain an independent assessment of the potential for a material credit loss.	If a material loss appears likely, the potential negative impact of that loss on the company should be carefully evaluated, along with the adequacy of the allowance for doubtful accounts.
Are collections being made in a timely fashion?	Net credit sales and average receivables balance	$$\text{Receivables turnover ratio} = \frac{\text{Net credit sales}}{\text{Average net receivables}}$$ $$\text{Average collection period} = \frac{365 \text{ days}}{\text{Receivables turnover ratio}}$$	Average collection period should be consistent with corporate credit policy. An increase may suggest a decline in financial health of customers.

7 *Describe the principles of sound accounts receivable management.* To properly manage receivables, management must (a) determine to whom to extend credit, (b) establish a payment period, (c) monitor collections, (d) evaluate the liquidity of receivables, and (e) accelerate cash receipts from receivables when necessary.

8 *Identify ratios to analyze a company's receivables.* The receivables turnover ratio and the average collection period both are useful in analyzing management's

effectiveness in managing receivables. The accounts receivable aging schedule also provides useful information.

9 *Describe methods to accelerate the receipt of cash from receivables.* If the company needs additional cash, management can accelerate the collection of cash from receivables by selling (factoring) its receivables or by allowing customers to pay with bank credit cards.

THE NAVIGATOR

Glossary

Accounts receivable Amounts customers owe on account. (p. 373)

Aging the accounts receivable The analysis of customer balances by the length of time they have been unpaid. (p. 377)

Allowance method A method of accounting for bad debts that involves estimating uncollectible accounts at the end of each period. (p. 375)

Average collection period The average amount of time that a receivable is outstanding, calculated by dividing 365 days by the receivables turnover ratio. (p. 388)

Bad debts expense An expense account to record credit losses. (p. 373)

Cash (net) realizable value The net amount a company expects to receive in cash. (p. 375)

Concentration of credit risk The threat of nonpayment from a single customer or class of customers that could adversely affect the financial health of the company. (p. 387)

Direct write-off method A method of accounting for bad debts that involves expensing accounts at the time they are determined to be uncollectible. (p. 374)

Dishonored note A note that is not paid in full at maturity. (p. 384)

Factor A finance company or bank that buys receivables from businesses for a fee and then collects the payments directly from the customers. (p. 391)

Maker The party in a promissory note who is making the promise to pay. (p. 380)

Notes receivable Claims for which formal instruments of credit are issued as evidence of the debt. (p. 373)

Payee The party to whom payment of a promissory note is to be made. (p. 380)

Percentage of receivables basis Management establishes a percentage relationship between the amount of receivables and the expected losses from uncollectible accounts. (p. 377)

Promissory note A written promise to pay a specified amount of money on demand or at a definite time. (p. 380)

Receivables Amounts due from individuals and companies that are expected to be collected in cash. (p. 372)

Receivables turnover ratio A measure of the liquidity of receivables, computed by dividing net credit sales by average net receivables. (p. 388)

Trade receivables Notes and accounts receivable that result from sales transactions. (p. 373)

Demonstration Problem

WILEY PLUS

Presented here are selected transactions related to B. Dylan Corp.

Mar.	1	Sold $20,000 of merchandise to Potter Company, terms 2/10, n/30.
	11	Received payment in full from Potter Company for balance due.
	12	Accepted Juno Company's $20,000, 6-month, 12% note for balance due on outstanding account receivable.
	13	Made B. Dylan Corp. credit card sales for $13,200.
	15	Made Visa credit sales totaling $6,700. A 5% service fee is charged by Visa.
Apr.	11	Sold accounts receivable of $8,000 to Harcot Factor. Harcot Factor assesses a service charge of 2% of the amount of receivables sold.
	13	Received collections of $8,200 on B. Dylan Corp. credit card sales.
May	10	Wrote off as uncollectible $16,000 of accounts receivable. (B. Dylan Corp. uses the percentage of receivables basis to estimate bad debts.)
June	30	The balance in accounts receivable at the end of the first 6 months is $200,000 and the bad debt percentage is 10%. At June 30 the credit balance in the allowance account prior to adjustment is $3,500. Recorded bad debt expense.

July   16   One of the accounts receivable written off in May pays the amount due, $4,000, in full.

Instructions
Prepare the journal entries for the transactions.

Solution to Demonstration Problem

Mar.	1	Accounts Receivable—Potter Company	20,000	
		Sales		20,000
		(To record sales on account)		
	11	Cash	19,600	
		Sales Discounts (2% × $20,000)	400	
		Accounts Receivable—Potter Company		20,000
		(To record collection of accounts receivable)		
	12	Notes Receivable	20,000	
		Accounts Receivable—Juno Company		20,000
		(To record acceptance of Juno Company note)		
	13	Accounts Receivable	13,200	
		Sales		13,200
		(To record company credit card sales)		
	15	Cash	6,365	
		Service Charge Expense (5% × $6,700)	335	
		Sales		6,700
		(To record credit card sales)		
Apr.	11	Cash	7,840	
		Service Charge Expense (2% × $8,000)	160	
		Accounts Receivable		8,000
		(To record sale of receivables to factor)		
	13	Cash	8,200	
		Accounts Receivable		8,200
		(To record collection of accounts receivable)		
May	10	Allowance for Doubtful Accounts	16,000	
		Accounts Receivable		16,000
		(To record write-off of accounts receivable)		
June	30	Bad Debts Expense	16,500	
		Allowance for Doubtful Accounts		16,500
		[($200,000 × 10%) − $3,500]		
		(To record estimate of uncollectible accounts)		
July	16	Accounts Receivable	4,000	
		Allowance for Doubtful Accounts		4,000
		(To reverse write-off of accounts receivable)		
		Cash	4,000	
		Accounts Receivable		4,000
		(To record collection of accounts receivable)		

Action Plan
- Generally, record accounts receivable at invoice price.
- Recognize that sales returns and allowances and cash discounts reduce the amount received on accounts receivable.
- Record a service charge expense on the seller's books when accounts receivable are sold.
- Prepare an adjusting entry for bad debts expense.
- Recognize the balance in the allowance account under the percentage of receivables basis.
- Record write-offs of accounts receivable only in balance sheet accounts.

Self-Study Questions

WILEY
PLUS

Answers are at the end of the chapter.

(SO 2) **1.** Kersee Company on June 15 sells merchandise on account to Soo Eng Co. for $1,000, terms 2/10, n/30. On June 20 Eng Co. returns merchandise worth $300 to Kersee Company. On June 24 payment is received from Eng Co. for the balance due. What is the amount of cash received?
(a) $700. (c) $686.
(b) $680. (d) None of the above.

(SO 3) **2.** Net credit sales for the month are $800,000. The accounts receivable balance is $160,000. The allowance is calculated as 7.5% of the receivables balance using the percentage of receivables basis. If the Allowance for Doubtful Accounts has a credit balance of $5,000 before adjustment, what is the balance after adjustment?
(a) $12,000. (c) $17,000.
(b) $7,000. (d) $31,000.

(SO 3) **3.** In 2007 Patterson Wholesale Company had net credit sales of $750,000. On January 1, 2007, Allowance for Doubtful Accounts had a credit balance of $18,000. During 2007, $30,000 of uncollectible accounts receivable were written off. Past experience indicates that the allowance should be 10% of the balance in receivables (percentage of receivables basis). If the accounts receivable balance at December 31 was $200,000, what is the required adjustment to the Allowance for Doubtful Accounts at December 31, 2007?
(a) $20,000. (c) $32,000.
(b) $75,000. (d) $30,000.

(SO 3) **4.** An analysis and aging of the accounts receivable of Raja Company at December 31 reveal these data:

Accounts receivable	$800,000
Allowance for doubtful accounts per books before adjustment (credit)	50,000
Amounts expected to become uncollectible	65,000

What is the cash realizable value of the accounts receivable at December 31, after adjustment?
(a) $685,000. (c) $800,000.
(b) $750,000. (d) $735,000.

(SO 4) **5.** Which of these statements about promissory notes is *incorrect*?
(a) The party making the promise to pay is called the maker.
(b) The party to whom payment is to be made is called the payee.
(c) A promissory note is not a negotiable instrument.
(d) A promissory note is more liquid than an account receivable.

(SO 4) **6.** Michael Co. accepts a $1,000, 3-month, 12% promissory note in settlement of an account with Tani Co. The entry to record this transaction is:

(a) Notes Receivable	1,030	
Accounts Receivable		1,030
(b) Notes Receivable	1,000	
Accounts Receivable		1,000
(c) Notes Receivable	1,000	
Sales		1,000
(d) Notes Receivable	1,020	
Accounts Receivable		1,020

(SO 5) **7.** Schleis Co. holds Murphy Inc.'s $10,000, 120-day, 9% note. The entry made by Schleis Co. when the note is collected, assuming no interest has previously been accrued, is:

(a) Cash	10,300	
Notes Receivable		10,300
(b) Cash	10,000	
Notes Receivable		10,000
(c) Accounts Receivable	10,300	
Notes Receivable		10,000
Interest Revenue		300
(d) Cash	10,300	
Notes Receivable		10,000
Interest Revenue		300

(SO 8) **8.** Eddy Corporation had net credit sales during the year of $800,000 and cost of goods sold of $500,000. The balance in receivables at the beginning of the year was $100,000 and at the end of the year was $150,000. What was the receivables turnover ratio?
(a) 6.4 (b) 8.0 (c) 5.3 (d) 4.0

(SO 8) **9.** Prall Corporation sells its goods on terms of 2/10, n/30. It has a receivables turnover ratio of 7. What is its average collection period (days)?
(a) 2,555 (b) 30 (c) 52 (d) 210

(SO 9) **10.** Which of these statements about **Visa** credit card sales is *incorrect*?
(a) The credit card issuer conducts the credit investigation of the customer.
(b) The retailer is not involved in the collection process.
(c) The retailer must wait to receive payment from the issuer.
(d) The retailer receives cash more quickly than it would from individual customers.

(SO 9) **11.** Good Stuff Retailers accepted $50,000 of Citibank Visa credit card charges for merchandise sold on July 1. Citibank charges 4% for its credit card use. The entry to record this transaction by Good Stuff Retailers will include a credit to Sales of $50,000 and a debit(s) to:

(a) Cash $48,000 and Service Charge Expense $2,000.

(b) Accounts Receivable $48,000 and Service Charge Expense $2,000.

(c) Cash $50,000.

(d) Accounts Receivable $50,000.

Go to the book's website, **www.wiley.com/college/kimmel**, to access additional Self-Study Questions.

Questions

1. What is the difference between an account receivable and a note receivable?

2. What are some common types of receivables other than accounts receivable or notes receivable?

3. What are the essential features of the allowance method of accounting for bad debts?

4. Lauren Anderson cannot understand why the cash realizable value does not decrease when an uncollectible account is written off under the allowance method. Clarify this point for Lauren.

5. Essex Company has a credit balance of $3,200 in Allowance for Doubtful Accounts before adjustment. The estimated uncollectibles under the percentage of receivables basis is $5,800. Prepare the adjusting entry.

6. How are bad debts accounted for under the direct write-off method? What are the disadvantages of this method?

7. ➡ Susan Lowe, the vice president of sales for Holiday Pools and Spas, wants the company's credit department to be less restrictive in granting credit. "How can we sell anything when you guys won't approve anybody?" she asks. Discuss the pros and cons of "easy credit." What are the accounting implications?

8. Your roommate is uncertain about the advantages of a promissory note. Compare the advantages of a note receivable with those of an account receivable.

9. How may the maturity date of a promissory note be stated?

10. Compute the missing amounts for each of the following notes.

Principal	Annual Interest Rate	Time	Total Interest
(a)	9%	60 days	$ 270
$30,000	8%	3 years	(d)
$60,000	(b)	5 months	$2,500
$50,000	11%	(c)	$1,375

11. Searcy Company dishonors a note at maturity. What are the options available to the lender?

12. General Motors Company has accounts receivable and notes receivable. How should the receivables be reported on the balance sheet?

13. ➡ ⚙ What are the steps to good receivables management?

14. ⚙ How might a company monitor the risk related to its accounts receivable?

15. ⚙ What is meant by a concentration of credit risk?

16. ⚙ The President of Hutley Inc. proudly announces her company's improved liquidity since its current ratio has increased substantially from one year to the next. Does an increase in the current ratio always indicate improved liquidity? What other ratio or ratios might you review to determine whether or not the increase in the current ratio is an improvement in financial health?

17. ➡ Since hiring a new sales director, Steps Inc. has enjoyed a 50% increase in sales. The CEO has also noticed, however, that the company's average collection period has increased from 17 days to 38 days. What might be the cause of this increase? What are the implications to management of this increase?

18. ⚙ The Coca-Cola Company's receivables turnover ratio was 10.31 in 2004, and its average amount of net receivables during the period was $2,131 million. What is the amount of its net credit sales for the period? What is the average collection period in days?

19. ➡ ⚙ JCPenney Company accepts both its own credit cards and national credit cards. What are the advantages of accepting both types of cards?

20. ➡ ⚙ An article in the *Wall Street Journal* indicated that companies are selling their receivables at a record rate. Why do companies sell their receivables?

21. Calico Corners decides to sell $630,000 of its accounts receivable to First Central Factors Inc. First Central Factors assesses a service charge of 3% of the amount of receivables sold. Prepare the journal entry that Calico Corners makes to record this sale.

Brief Exercises

BE8-1 Presented on page 400 are three receivables transactions. Indicate whether these receivables are reported as accounts receivable, notes receivable, or other receivables on a balance sheet.

Identify different types of receivables.
(SO 1)

(a) Advanced $10,000 to an employee.
(b) Received a promissory note of $34,000 for services performed.
(c) Sold merchandise on account for $60,000 to a customer.

*Record basic accounts
receivable transactions.*
(SO 2)

BE8-2 Record the following transactions on the books of Massey Co.
(a) On July 1 Massey Co. sold merchandise on account to Opal Inc. for $17,000, terms 2/10, n/30.
(b) On July 8 Opal Inc. returned merchandise worth $2,400 to Massey Co.
(c) On July 11 Opal Inc. paid for the merchandise.

*Prepare entry for write-off,
and determine cash realizable
value.*
(SO 3)

BE8-3 At the end of 2007, Wendy Co. has accounts receivable of $700,000 and an allowance for doubtful accounts of $28,000. On January 24, 2008, it is learned that the company's receivable from Mayfield Inc. is not collectible and therefore management authorizes a write-off of $3,000.
(a) Prepare the journal entry to record the write-off.
(b) What is the cash realizable value of the accounts receivable (1) before the write-off and (2) after the write-off?

*Prepare entries for collection
of bad debt write-off.*
(SO 3)

BE8-4 Assume the same information as BE8-3 and that on March 4, 2008, Wendy Co. receives payment of $3,000 in full from Mayfield Inc. Prepare the journal entries to record this transaction.

*Prepare entry using percent-
age of receivables method.*
(SO 3)

BE8-5 Jaya Co. uses the percentage of receivables basis to record bad debts expense and concludes that 2% of accounts receivable will become uncollectible. Accounts receivable are $500,000 at the end of the year, and the allowance for doubtful accounts has a credit balance of $1,500.
(a) Prepare the adjusting journal entry to record bad debts expense for the year.
(b) If the allowance for doubtful accounts had a debit balance of $600 instead of a credit balance of $1,500, prepare the adjusting journal entry for bad debts expense.

*Compute interest rate and
interest on note.*
(SO 4)

BE8-6 Presented below are three promissory notes. Determine the missing amounts.

Date of Note	Terms	Principal	Annual Interest Rate	Total Interest
April 1	2 years	$900,000	8%	(a)
July 2	30 days	79,000	(b)	$592.50
March 7	6 months	56,000	11%	(c)

*Prepare entry for note receiv-
able exchanged for accounts
receivable.*
(SO 4)

BE8-7 On January 10, 2007, Santiago Co. sold merchandise on account to Croix for $8,000, terms n/30. On February 9 Croix gave Santiago Co. a 7% promissory note in settlement of this account. Prepare the journal entry to record the sale and the settlement of the accounts receivable.

*Prepare entry for estimated
uncollectibles and classifications, and compute ratios.*
(SO 3, 6, 7, 8)

BE8-8 During its first year of operations, Salizar Company had credit sales of $3,000,000, of which $600,000 remained uncollected at year-end. The credit manager estimates that $24,000 of these receivables will become uncollectible.
(a) Prepare the journal entry to record the estimated uncollectibles. (Assume an unadjusted balance of zero.)
(b) Prepare the current assets section of the balance sheet for Salizar Company, assuming that in addition to the receivables it has cash of $90,000, merchandise inventory of $180,000, and prepaid expenses of $13,000.
(c) Calculate the receivables turnover ratio and average collection period. Assume that average net receivables were $300,000. Explain what these measures tell us.

Analyze accounts receivable.
(SO 8)

BE8-9 The 2004 financial statements of 3M Company report net sales of $20.0 billion. Accounts receivable (net) are $2.7 billion at the beginning of the year and $2.8 billion at the end of the year. Compute 3M's receivables turnover ratio. Compute 3M's average collection period for accounts receivable in days.

*Prepare entries for credit card
sale and sale of accounts
receivable.*
(SO 9)

BE8-10 Consider these transactions:
(a) Albanese Restaurant accepted a Visa card in payment of a $100 lunch bill. The bank charges a 3% fee. What entry should Albanese make?
(b) Beverly Company sold its accounts receivable of $68,000. What entry should Beverly make, given a service charge of 3% on the amount of receivables sold?

Exercises

E8-1 On January 6 Trisha Co. sells merchandise on account to Alma Inc. for $6,000, terms 1/10, n/30. On January 16 Alma pays the amount due.

Prepare entries for recognizing accounts receivable.
(SO 2)

Instructions

Prepare the entries on Trisha Co.'s books to record the sale and related collection.

E8-2 On January 10 Alana Davis uses her Idaho Co. credit card to purchase merchandise from Idaho Co. for $1,400. On February 10 Davis is billed for the amount due of $1,400. On February 12 Davis pays $1,000 on the balance due. On March 10 Davis is billed for the amount due, including interest at 1% per month on the unpaid balance as of February 12.

Prepare entries for recognizing accounts receivable.
(SO 2)

Instructions

Prepare the entries on Idaho Co.'s books related to the transactions that occurred on January 10, February 12, and March 10.

E8-3 At the beginning of the current period, Huang Corp. had balances in Accounts Receivable of $200,000 and in Allowance for Doubtful Accounts of $9,000 (credit). During the period, it had net credit sales of $800,000 and collections of $743,000. It wrote off as uncollectible accounts receivable of $7,000. However, a $4,000 account previously written off as uncollectible was recovered before the end of the current period. Uncollectible accounts are estimated to total $25,000 at the end of the period.

Journalize receivables transactions.
(SO 2, 3)

Instructions

(a) Prepare the entries to record sales and collections during the period.
(b) Prepare the entry to record the write-off of uncollectible accounts during the period.
(c) Prepare the entries to record the recovery of the uncollectible account during the period.
(d) Prepare the entry to record bad debts expense for the period.
(e) Determine the ending balances in Accounts Receivable and Allowance for Doubtful Accounts.
(f) What is the net realizable value of the receivables at the end of the period?

E8-4 The ledger of Garcia Company at the end of the current year shows Accounts Receivable $96,000; Credit Sales $780,000; and Sales Returns and Allowances $40,000.

Prepare entries to record allowance for doubtful accounts.
(SO 3)

Instructions

(a) If Garcia uses the direct write-off method to account for uncollectible accounts, journalize the adjusting entry at December 31, assuming Garcia determines that Allied's $900 balance is uncollectible.
(b) If Allowance for Doubtful Accounts has a credit balance of $1,100 in the trial balance, journalize the adjusting entry at December 31, assuming bad debts are expected to be 10% of accounts receivable.
(c) If Allowance for Doubtful Accounts has a debit balance of $500 in the trial balance, journalize the adjusting entry at December 31, assuming bad debts are expected to be 8% of accounts receivable.

E8-5 Hachey Company has accounts receivable of $95,100 at March 31, 2007. An analysis of the accounts shows these amounts.

Determine bad debt expense, and prepare the adjusting entry.
(SO 3)

	Balance, March 31	
Month of Sale	**2007**	**2006**
March	$65,000	$75,000
February	12,600	8,000
December and January	10,100	2,400
November and October	7,400	1,100
	$95,100	$86,500

Credit terms are 2/10, n/30. At March 31, 2007, there is a $2,200 credit balance in Allowance for Doubtful Accounts prior to adjustment. The company uses the percentage of receivables basis for estimating uncollectible accounts. The company's estimates of bad debts are as shown on page 402.

Age of Accounts	Estimated Percentage Uncollectible
Current	2%
1–30 days past due	7
31–90 days past due	30
Over 90 days	50

Instructions
(a) Determine the total estimated uncollectibles.
(b) Prepare the adjusting entry at March 31, 2007, to record bad debts expense.
(c) Discuss the implications of the changes in the aging schedule from 2006 to 2007.

Prepare entry for estimated uncollectibles, write-off, and recovery.
(SO 3)

E8-6 On December 31, 2007, when its Allowance for Doubtful Accounts had a debit balance of $1,000, North Star Co. estimates that 9% of its accounts receivable balance of $70,000 will become uncollectible and records the necessary adjustment to the Allowance for Doubtful Accounts. On May 11, 2008, North Star Co. determined that J. Tory's account was uncollectible and wrote off $1,200. On June 12, 2008, Tory paid the amount previously written off.

Instructions
Prepare the journal entries on December 31, 2007, May 11, 2008, and June 12, 2008.

Prepare entries for notes receivable transactions.
(SO 4, 5)

E8-7 Great Plains Supply Co. has the following transactions related to notes receivable during the last 2 months of the year.

Nov. 1 Loaned $30,000 cash to B. Wedunn on a 1-year, 8% note.
Dec. 11 Sold goods to R. P. Meier, Inc., receiving a $3,600, 90-day, 7% note.
16 Received an $8,000, 6-month, 9% note to settle an open account from M. Fong.
31 Accrued interest revenue on all notes receivable.

Instructions
Journalize the transactions for Great Plains Supply Co.

Journalize notes receivable transactions.
(SO 4, 5)

E8-8 These transactions took place for Pautsch Co.

2006

May 1 Received a $4,000, 1-year, 9% note in exchange for an outstanding account receivable from S. Bajwa.
Dec. 31 Accrued interest revenue on the S. Bajwa note.

2007

May 1 Received principal plus interest on the S. Bajwa note. (No interest has been accrued since December 31, 2006.)

Instructions
Record the transactions in the general journal.

Prepare a balance sheet presentation of receivables.
(SO 6)

E8-9 Milne Corp. had the following balances in receivable accounts at October 31, 2007 (in thousands): Allowance for Doubtful Accounts $56; Accounts Receivable $2,870; Other Receivables $189; Notes Receivable $853.

Instructions
Prepare the balance sheet presentation of Milne Corp.'s receivables in good form.

Identify the principles of receivables management.
(SO 7)

E8-10 The following is a list of activities that companies perform in relation to their receivables.
1. Selling receivables to a factor.
2. Reviewing company ratings in *The Dun and Bradstreet Reference Book of American Business.*
3. Collecting information on competitors' payment period policies.
4. Preparing monthly accounts receivable aging schedule and investigating problem accounts.
5. Calculating the receivables turnover ratio and average collection period.

Instructions
Match each of the activities listed above with a purpose of the activity listed below.
(a) Determine to whom to extend credit.
(b) Establish a payment period.
(c) Monitor collections.
(d) Evaluate the liquidity of receivables.
(e) Accelerate cash receipts from receivables when necessary.

E8-11 The following information was taken from the 2004 financial statements of FedEx Corporation, a major global transportation/delivery company.

Compute ratios to evaluate a company's receivables balance.
(SO 7, 8)

(in millions)	2004	2003
Accounts receivable (gross)	$ 3,178	$ 2,776
Accounts receivable (net)	$ 3,027	$ 2,627
Allowance for doubtful accounts	151	149
Sales	24,710	22,487
Total current assets	4,970	3,941

Instructions
Answer each of the following questions.
(a) Calculate the receivables turnover ratio and the average collection period for 2004 for FedEx.
(b) Is accounts receivable a material component of the company's total current assets?
(c) Evaluate the balance in FedEx's allowance for uncollectible accounts.

E8-12 The following ratios are available for Tianjin Inc.

Evaluate liquidity.
(SO 7, 8, 9)

	2004	2003
Current ratio	1.3:1	1.5:1
Receivables turnover	12 times	10 times
Inventory turnover	11 times	9 times

Instructions
(a) Is Tianjin's short-term liquidity improving or deteriorating in 2004? Be specific in your answer, referring to relevant ratios.
(b) Do changes in turnover ratios affect profitability? Explain.
(c) Identify any steps Tianjin might have taken, or might wish to take, to improve its management of its receivables and inventory turnover.

E8-13 On March 3 Metro Appliances sells $760,000 of its receivables to Universal Factors Inc. Universal Factors Inc. assesses a finance charge of 5% of the amount of receivables sold.

Prepare entry for sale of accounts receivable.
(SO 9)

Instructions
Prepare the entry on Metro Appliances' books to record the sale of the receivables.

E8-14 In a recent annual report, Office Depot, Inc. notes that the company entered into an agreement to sell all of its credit card program receivables to financial service companies.

Identify reason for sale of receivables.
(SO 9)

Instructions
Explain why Office Depot, a financially stable company with positive cash flow, would choose to sell its receivables.

E8-15 On May 10 Oman Company sold merchandise for $4,000 and accepted the customer's First Business Bank MasterCard. At the end of the day, the First Business Bank MasterCard receipts were deposited in the company's bank account. First Business Bank charges a 3.5% service charge for credit card sales.

Prepare entry for credit card sale.
(SO 9)

Instructions
Prepare the entry on Oman Company's books to record the sale of merchandise.

Prepare entry for credit card sale.
(SO 9)

E8-16   On July 4 Alice's Restaurant accepts a Visa card for a $300 dinner bill. Visa charges a 3% service fee.

Instructions
Prepare the entry on Alice's books related to the transaction.

Problems: Set A

Journalize transactions related to bad debts.
(SO 2, 3)

P8-1A   Donedeal.com uses the allowance method to estimate uncollectible accounts receivable. The company produced the following aging of the accounts receivable at year end.

| | Total | Number of Days Outstanding | | | | |
		0–30	31–60	61–90	91–120	Over 120
Accounts receivable	$378,000	$222,000	$90,000	$38,000	$10,000	$18,000
% uncollectible		1%	4%	5%	6%	10%
Estimated bad debts						

Instructions

(a) Tot. est.
* bad debts $10,120*

(a) Calculate the total estimated bad debts based on the above information.
(b) Prepare the year-end adjusting journal entry to record the bad debts using the aged uncollectible accounts receivable determined in (a). Assume the unadjusted balance in Allowance for Doubtful Accounts is a $4,000 debit.
(c) Of the above accounts, $5,000 is determined to be specifically uncollectible. Prepare the journal entry to write off the uncollectible account.
(d) The company collects $5,000 subsequently on a specific account that had previously been determined to be uncollectible in (c). Prepare the journal entry(ies) necessary to restore the account and record the cash collection.
(e) Comment on how your answers to (a)–(d) would change if Donedeal.com used 3% of *total* accounts receivable, rather than aging the accounts receivable. What are the advantages to the company of aging the accounts receivable rather than applying a percentage to total accounts receivable?

Prepare journal entries related to bad debt expense, and compute ratios.
(SO 2, 3, 8)

P8-2A   At December 31, 2007, Curtis Imports reported this information on its balance sheet.

Accounts receivable	$600,000
Less: Allowance for doubtful accounts	40,000

During 2008 the company had the following transactions related to receivables.

1. Sales on account	$2,600,000
2. Sales returns and allowances	40,000
3. Collections of accounts receivable	2,200,000
4. Write-offs of accounts receivable deemed uncollectible	45,000
5. Recovery of bad debts previously written off as uncollectible	18,000

Instructions

(a) Prepare the journal entries to record each of these five transactions. Assume that no cash discounts were taken on the collections of accounts receivable.

(b) A/R bal. $915,000

(b) Enter the January 1, 2008, balances in Accounts Receivable and Allowance for Doubtful Accounts, post the entries to the two accounts (use T accounts), and determine the balances.
(c) Prepare the journal entry to record bad debts expense for 2008, assuming that aging the accounts receivable indicates that estimated bad debts are $46,000.
(d) Compute the receivables turnover ratio and average collection period.

P8-3A Presented below is an aging schedule for Joplin Company.

Journalize transactions related to bad debts.
(SO 2, 3)

Customer	Total	Not Yet Due	Number of Days Past Due			
			1–30	31–60	61–90	Over 90
Adisy	$ 20,000		$ 9,000	$11,000		
Bloom	30,000	$ 30,000				
Cai	50,000	5,000	5,000		$40,000	
Dahl	38,000					$38,000
Others	120,000	72,000	35,000	13,000		
	$258,000	$107,000	$49,000	$24,000	$40,000	$38,000
Estimated percentage uncollectible		3%	5%	12%	24%	50%
Total estimated bad debts	$ 37,140	$ 3,210	$ 2,450	$ 2,880	$ 9,600	$19,000

At December 31, 2007, the unadjusted balance in Allowance for Doubtful Accounts is a credit of $8,000.

Instructions
(a) Journalize and post the adjusting entry for bad debts at December 31, 2007. (Use T accounts.)
(b) Journalize and post to the allowance account these 2008 events and transactions:
   1. March 1, a $600 customer balance originating in 2007 is judged uncollectible.
   2. May 1, a check for $600 is received from the customer whose account was written off as uncollectible on March 1.
(c) Journalize the adjusting entry for bad debts at December 31, 2008, assuming that the unadjusted balance in Allowance for Doubtful Accounts is a debit of $1,100 and the aging schedule indicates that total estimated bad debts will be $32,700.

P8-4A Here is information related to Kettle Moraine Company for 2007.

Compute bad debt amounts.
(SO 3)

Total credit sales	$1,500,000
Accounts receivable at December 31	440,000
Bad debts written off	31,000

Instructions
(a) What amount of bad debts expense will Kettle Moraine Company report if it uses the direct write-off method of accounting for bad debts?
(b) Assume that Kettle Moraine Company decides to estimate its bad debts expense based on 3% of accounts receivable. What amount of bad debts expense will the company record if Allowance for Doubtful Accounts has a credit balance of $3,000?
(c) Assume the same facts as in part (b), except that there is a $1,000 debit balance in Allowance for Doubtful Accounts. What amount of bad debts expense will Kettle Moraine record?
(d) ■■■▶ What is a weakness of the direct write-off method of reporting bad debts expense?

P8-5A At December 31, 2007, the trial balance of Nora Company contained the following amounts before adjustment.

Journalize entries to record transactions related to bad debts.
(SO 2, 3)

	Debits	Credits
Accounts Receivable	$250,000	
Allowance for Doubtful Accounts		$ 1,500
Sales		875,000

Instructions
(a) Prepare the adjusting entry at December 31, 2007, to record bad debts expense assuming that the aging schedule indicates that $11,800 of accounts receivable will be uncollectible.

(b) Repeat part (a) assuming that instead of a credit balance there is a $1,500 debit balance in the Allowance for Doubtful Accounts.

(c) During the next month, January 2008, a $2,200 account receivable is written off as uncollectible. Prepare the journal entry to record the write-off.

(d) Repeat part (c) assuming that Nora Company uses the direct write-off method instead of the allowance method in accounting for uncollectible accounts receivable.

(e) What are the advantages of using an aging schedule and the allowance method in accounting for uncollectible accounts as compared to the direct write-off method?

Journalize various receivables transactions.
(SO 1, 2, 4, 5)

P8-6A   On January 1, 2007, Paris Company had Accounts Receivable of $54,200 and Allowance for Doubtful Accounts of $3,700. Paris Company prepares financial statements annually and uses a perpetual inventory system. During the year the following selected transactions occurred.

Jan.	5	Sold $6,000 of merchandise to London Company, terms n/30. Cost of the merchandise sold was $4,000.
Feb.	2	Accepted a $6,000, 4-month, 9% promissory note from London Company for balance due.
	12	Sold $8,100 of merchandise costing $5,000 to Dublin Company and accepted Dublin's $8,100, 2-month, 10% note for the balance due.
	26	Sold $5,200 of merchandise costing $3,300 to Florence Co., terms n/10.
Apr.	5	Accepted a $5,200, 3-month, 8% note from Florence Co. for balance due.
	12	Collected Dublin Company note in full.
June	2	Collected London Company note in full.
	15	Sold $2,000 of merchandise costing $1,500 to Madrid Inc. and accepted a $2,000, 6-month, 12% note for the amount due.

Instructions
Journalize the transactions.

Explain the impact of transactions on ratios.
(SO 8)

P8-7A   The president of Starz Enterprises asks if you could indicate the impact certain transactions have on the following ratios.

Transaction	Current Ratio (2:1)	Receivables Turnover (10X)	Average Collection Period (36.5 days)
1. Recorded $2,500 sales on account. The cost of the goods sold was $1,500.			
2. Recorded bad debts expense of $500 using allowance method.			
3. Wrote off a $100 account receivable as uncollectible.			
4. Received $3,000 on cash sale. The cost of the goods sold was $1,800.			

Instructions
Complete the table, indicating whether each transaction will increase (I), decrease (D), or have no effect (NE) on the specific ratios provided for Starz Enterprises.

Prepare entries for various credit card and notes receivable transactions.
(SO 2, 4, 5, 6, 9)

P8-8A   NewBay Company closes its books on July 31. On June 30 the Notes Receivable account balance is $23,800. Notes Receivable include the following.

Date	Maker	Face Value	Term	Maturity Date	Interest Rate
May 21	Emery Inc.	$ 9,000	60 days	July 20	8%
May 25	Tulane Co.	4,800	60 days	July 24	10%
June 30	LSU Corp.	10,000	6 months	December 31	9%

During July the following transactions were completed.

July 5   Made sales of $7,100 on NewBay credit cards.
    14   Made sales of $600 on Visa credit cards. The credit card service charge is 3%.
    20   Received payment in full from Emery Inc. on the amount due.
    25   Received payment in full from Tulane Co. on the amount due.

Instructions
(a) Journalize the July transactions and the July 31 adjusting entry for accrued interest receivable. (Interest is computed using 360 days.)
(b) Enter the balances at July 1 in the receivable accounts and post the entries to all of the receivable accounts. (Use T accounts.)
(c) Show the balance sheet presentation of the receivable accounts at July 31.

(b) A/R bal. $ 7,100
(c) Tot.
     receivables $17,175

P8-9A Presented here is basic financial information (in millions) from the 2004 annual reports of Nike and Reebok.

Calculate and interpret various ratios.
(SO 7, 8)

	Nike	Reebok
Sales	$12,253.1	$3,785.3
Allowance for doubtful accounts, Jan. 1	81.9	70.8
Allowance for doubtful accounts, Dec. 31	95.3	81.3
Accounts receivable balance (gross), Jan. 1	2,165.8	532.3
Accounts receivable balance (gross), Dec. 31	2,215.5	660.6

Instructions
Calculate the receivables turnover ratio and average collection period for both companies. Comment on the difference in their collection experiences.

Problems: Set B

P8-1B The following represents selected information taken from a company's aging schedule to estimate uncollectible accounts receivable at year end.

Journalize transactions related to bad debts.
(SO 2, 3)

		Number of Days Outstanding				
	Total	0–30	31–60	61–90	91–120	Over 120
Accounts receivable	$280,000	$107,000	$60,000	$50,000	$38,000	$25,000
% uncollectible		1%	5%	7.5%	10%	12%
Estimated bad debts						

Instructions
(a) Calculate the total estimated bad debts based on the above information.
(b) Prepare the year-end adjusting journal entry to record the bad debts using the allowance method and the aged uncollectible accounts receivable determined in (a). Assume the unadjusted balance in the Allowance for Doubtful Accounts account is a $10,000 credit.
(c) Of the above accounts, $2,600 is determined to be specifically uncollectible. Prepare the journal entry to write off the uncollectible accounts.
(d) The company subsequently collects $1,000 on a specific account that had previously been determined to be uncollectible in (c). Prepare the journal entry(ies) necessary to restore the account and record the cash collection.
(e) Explain how establishing an allowance account satisfies the matching principle.

(a) Tot. est.
    bad debts $14,620

*Prepare journal entries
related to bad debt expense,
and compute ratios.*
(SO 2, 3, 8)

P8-2B At December 31, 2007, Guardian Company reported this information on its balance sheet.

Accounts receivable	$960,000
Less: Allowance for doubtful accounts	84,000

During 2008 the company had the following transactions related to receivables.

1. Sales on account	$3,800,000
2. Sales returns and allowances	50,000
3. Collections of accounts receivable	3,000,000
4. Write-offs of accounts receivable deemed uncollectible	92,000
5. Recovery of bad debts previously written off as uncollectible	40,000

Instructions
(a) Prepare the journal entries to record each of these five transactions. Assume that no cash discounts were taken on the collections of accounts receivable.

(b) A/R bal. $1,618,000

(b) Enter the January 1, 2008, balances in Accounts Receivable and Allowance for Doubtful Accounts, post the entries to the two accounts (use T accounts), and determine the balances.
(c) Prepare the journal entry to record bad debts expense for 2008, assuming that aging the accounts receivable indicates that expected bad debts are $113,000.
(d) Compute the receivables turnover ratio and average collection period.

*Journalize transactions
related to bad debts.*
(SO 2, 3)

P8-3B Presented here is an aging schedule for West Beach Company.

Customer	Total	Not Yet Due	Number of Days Past Due			
			1–30	31–60	61–90	Over 90
Aaron	$ 22,000		$12,000	$10,000		
Brett	40,000	$ 40,000				
Cara	60,000	16,000	6,000		$38,000	
Dustin	28,000					$28,000
Others	126,000	96,000	16,000	14,000		
	$276,000	$152,000	$34,000	$24,000	$38,000	$28,000
Estimated percentage uncollectible		4%	9%	15%	25%	50%
Total estimated bad debts	$ 36,240	$ 6,080	$ 3,060	$ 3,600	$ 9,500	$14,000

At December 31, 2007, the unadjusted balance in Allowance for Doubtful Accounts is a credit of $11,700.

Instructions
(a) Journalize and post the adjusting entry for bad debts at December 31, 2007. (Use T accounts.)
(b) Journalize and post to the allowance account these 2008 events and transactions:
1. March 31, a $500 customer balance originating in 2007 is judged uncollectible.
2. May 31, a check for $500 is received from the customer whose account was written off as uncollectible on March 31.
(c) Journalize the adjusting entry for bad debts on December 31, 2008, assuming that the unadjusted balance in Allowance for Doubtful Accounts is a debit of $800 and the aging schedule indicates that total estimated bad debts will be $33,300.

Compute bad debt amounts.
(SO 3)

P8-4B Here is information related to Virtual Company for 2007.

Total credit sales	$2,000,000
Accounts receivable at December 31	500,000
Bad debts written off	19,000

Instructions
(a) What amount of bad debts expense will Virtual Company report if it uses the direct write-off method of accounting for bad debts?
(b) Assume that Virtual Company decides to estimate its bad debts expense based on 4% of accounts receivable. What amount of bad debts expense will the company record if it has an Allowance for Doubtful Accounts credit balance of $4,000?
(c) Assume the same facts as in part (b), except that there is a $2,000 debit balance in Allowance for Doubtful Accounts. What amount of bad debts expense will Virtual record?
(d) What is the weakness of the direct write-off method of reporting bad debts expense?

P8-5B At December 31, 2007, the trial balance of Thews Company contained the following amounts before adjustment.

Journalize entries to record transactions related to bad debts.
(SO 2, 3)

	Debits	**Credits**
Accounts Receivable	$400,000	
Allowance for Doubtful Accounts		$ 4,800
Sales		2,200,000

Instructions
(a) Based on the information given, which method of accounting for bad debts is Thews Company using—the direct write-off method or the allowance method? How can you tell?
(b) Prepare the adjusting entry at December 31, 2007, for bad debts expense assuming that the aging schedule indicates that $17,500 of accounts receivable will be uncollectible.
(c) Repeat part (b) assuming that instead of a credit balance there is a $4,800 debit balance in the Allowance for Doubtful Accounts.
(d) During the next month, January 2008, a $5,000 account receivable is written off as uncollectible. Prepare the journal entry to record the write-off.
(e) Repeat part (d) assuming that Thews uses the direct write-off method instead of the allowance method in accounting for uncollectible accounts receivable.
(f) What type of account is the allowance for doubtful accounts? How does it affect how accounts receivable is reported on the balance sheet at the end of the accounting period?

P8-6B On January 1, 2007, Kenyan Company had Accounts Receivable $154,000; Notes Receivable of $11,000; and Allowance for Doubtful Accounts of $13,200. The note receivable is from Brennan Company. It is a 4-month, 9% note dated December 31, 2006. Kenyan Company prepares financial statements annually. During the year the following selected transactions occurred. (Kenyan Company uses a periodic inventory system.)

Journalize various receivables transactions.
(SO 1, 2, 4, 5)

Jan.   5   Sold $12,000 of merchandise to Dorfner Company, terms n/15.
       20   Accepted Dorfner Company's $12,000, 3-month, 9% note for balance due.
Feb. 18   Sold $5,000 of merchandise to Cheng Company and accepted Cheng's $5,000, 6-month, 10% note for the amount due.
Apr. 20   Collected Dorfner Company note in full.
       30   Received payment in full from Brennan Company on the amount due.
May 25   Accepted Ardan Inc.'s $9,000, 6-month, 8% note in settlement of a past-due balance on account.
Aug. 18   Received payment in full from Cheng Company on note due.
Sept. 1   Sold $8,000 of merchandise to Charles Company and accepted an $8,000, 6-month, 10% note for the amount due.

Instructions
Journalize the transactions.

Explain the impact of transactions on ratios: discuss acceleration of receipt of cash from receivables.
(SO 8, 9)

P8-7B The president of Castle Enterprises Ltd., Nicole Castle, is considering the impact that certain transactions have on its receivables turnover and average collection period ratios. Prior to the following transactions, Castle's receivables turnover was 6 times, and its average collection period was 61 days.

Transaction	Receivables Turnover (6×)	Average Collection Period (61 days)
1. Recorded sales on account $100,000.		
2. Collected $25,000 owing from customers.		
3. Recorded bad debts expense for the year $7,500, using the allowance method.		
4. Recorded sales returns of $1,500 and credited the customers' accounts.		
5. Wrote off a $2,500 account from a customer as uncollectible.		

Instructions
(a) Complete the table, indicating whether each transaction will increase (I), decrease (D), or have no effect (NE) on the ratios.
(b) Nicole was reading through the financial statements for some publicly traded companies and noticed that they had recorded a loss on sale of receivables. She would like you to explain why companies sell their receivables.

Prepare entries for various credit card and notes receivable transactions.
(SO 2, 4, 5, 6, 9)

GLS

P8-8B Haley Company closes its books on October 31. On September 30 the Notes Receivable account balance is $24,700. Notes Receivable include the following.

Date	Maker	Face Value	Term	Maturity Date	Interest Rate
Aug. 16	Vinje Inc.	$ 8,500	60 days	Oct. 15	9%
Aug. 25	Rath Co.	6,000	2 months	Oct. 25	7%
Sept. 30	Flagg Corp.	10,200	6 months	Mar. 30	8%

Interest is computed using a 360-day year. During October the following transactions were completed.

Oct. 7 Made sales of $5,600 on Haley credit cards.
12 Made sales of $600 on Visa credit cards. The credit card service charge is 3%.
15 Received payment in full from Vinje Inc. on the amount due.
25 Received payment in full from Rath Co. on amount due.

Instructions
(a) Journalize the October transactions and the October 31 adjusting entry for accrued interest receivable.

(b) A/R bal. $ 5,600
(c) Tot. receivables $15,868

(b) Enter the balances at October 1 in the receivable accounts and post the entries to all of the receivable accounts. (Use T accounts.)
(c) Show the balance sheet presentation of the receivable accounts at October 31.

Calculate and interpret various ratios.
(SO 7, 8)

P8-9B Presented here is basic financial information from the 2004 annual reports of Intel and Advanced Micro Devices (AMD), the two primary manufacturers of silicon chips for personal computers.

(in millions)	Intel	AMD
Sales	$34,209	$3,924.3
Allowance for doubtful accounts, Jan. 1	55	20.7
Allowance for doubtful accounts, Dec. 31	43	17.8
Accounts receivable balance (gross), Jan. 1	3,015	585.5
Accounts receivable balance (gross), Dec. 31	3,042	737.4

Instructions

Calculate the receivables turnover ratio and average collection period for both companies. Comment on the difference in their collection experiences.

Problems: Set C

Visit the book's website at **www.wiley.com/college/kimmel** and choose the Student Companion site to access Problem Set C.

Comprehensive Problem

CP8 Mulder Corporation's balance sheet at December 31, 2006, is presented below.

MULDER CORPORATION
Balance Sheet
December 31, 2006

Cash	$13,100	Accounts payable	$ 8,750
Accounts receivable	19,780	Common stock	20,000
Allowance for doubtful accounts	(1,000)	Retained earnings	12,530
Merchandise inventory	9,400		$41,280
	$41,280		

During January 2007, the following transactions occurred. Mulder uses the perpetual inventory method.

Jan. 1 Mulder accepted a 4-month, 12% note from Alien Company in payment of Alien's $1,000 account.
   3 Mulder wrote off as uncollectible the accounts of Ex Corporation ($450) and Files Company ($230).
   8 Mulder purchased $17,200 of inventory on account.
   11 Mulder sold for $25,000 on account inventory that cost $15,000.
   15 Mulder sold inventory that cost $600 to Ben Borke for $1,000. Borke charged this amount on his Visa First Bank card. The service fee charged Mulder by First Bank is 3%.
   17 Mulder collected $21,900 from customers on account.
   21 Mulder paid $16,300 on accounts payable.
   24 Mulder received payment in full ($230) from Files Company on the account written off on January 3.
   27 Mulder purchased advertising supplies for $1,400 cash.
   31 Mulder paid other operating expenses, $4,218.

Adjustment data:

1. Interest is recorded for the month on the note from January 1.
2. Bad debts are expected to be 6% of the January 31, 2007, accounts receivable.
3. A count of advertising supplies on January 31, 2007, reveals that $560 remains unused.
4. The income tax rate is 30%. (*Hint:* Prepare the income statement up to "Income before taxes" and multiply by 30% to compute the amount.)

Instructions

(You may want to set up T accounts to determine ending balances.)
(a) Prepare journal entries for the transactions listed above and adjusting entries.

(b) Prepare an adjusted trial balance at January 31, 2007.

(c) Prepare an income statement and a retained earnings statement for the month ending January 31, 2007, and a classified balance sheet as of January 31, 2007.

Continuing Cookie Chronicle

(*Note:* This is a Continuation of the Cookie Chronicle from Chapters 1 through 7.)

CCC8   One of Natalie's friends, Curtis Lesperance, runs a coffee shop where he sells specialty coffees and prepares and sells muffins and cookies. He is eager to buy one of Natalie's fine European mixers, which would enable him to make larger batches of muffins and cookies. However, Curtis cannot afford to pay for the mixer for at least 30 days. He asks Natalie if she would be willing to sell him the mixer on credit.

Natalie comes to you for advice and asks the following questions.

1. "Curtis has provided me with a set of his most recent financial statements. What calculations should I do with the data from these statements, and what questions should I ask him after I have analyzed the statements? How will this information help me decide if I should extend credit to Curtis?"
2. "Is there an alternative other than extending credit to Curtis for 30 days?"
3. "I am thinking seriously about permitting my customers to use credit cards. What are some of the advantages and disadvantages of letting my customers pay by credit card?"

The following transactions occurred in June through August.

June 1		After much thought, Natalie sells a mixer to Curtis on credit, terms n/30, for $1,025 (cost of mixer $566).
	2	Natalie meets with the bank manager and arranges to get access to a credit card account. The terms of credit card transactions are 3% of the sales transactions and a monthly equipment rental charge of $75.
	30	Natalie teaches 12 classes in June. Seven classes were paid for in cash, $875; the other five classes were paid for by credit card, $750.
	30	Natalie receives and reconciles her bank statement. She makes sure that the bank has correctly processed the monthly $75 charge for the rental of the credit card equipment and the 3% fee on the credit card transactions.
	30	Curtis calls Natalie. He is unable to pay the amount outstanding for another month, so he signs a one-month, 8.25% note receivable.
July 15		Natalie sells a mixer to a friend of Curtis's. The friend pays $1,025 for the mixer by credit card (cost of mixer $566).
	30	Natalie teaches 15 classes in July. Eight classes are paid for in cash, $1,000; seven classes are paid for by credit card, $1,050.
	31	Natalie reconciles her bank statement and makes sure the bank has recorded the correct amounts for the rental of the credit card equipment and the credit card sales.
	31	Curtis calls Natalie. He cannot pay today but hopes to have a check for her at the end of the week. Natalie prepares the appropriate journal entry.
Aug. 10		Curtis calls again and promises to pay at the end of August, including interest for 2 months.
	31	Natalie receives a check from Curtis in payment of his balance plus interest outstanding.

Instructions

(a) Answer Natalie's questions.

(b) Prepare journal entries for the transactions that occurred in June, July, and August.

BROADENING YOUR PERSPECTIVE

Financial Reporting and Analysis

FINANCIAL REPORTING PROBLEM: *Tootsie Roll Industries*

BYP8-1   Refer to the financial statements of Tootsie Roll Industries and the accompanying notes to its financial statements in Appendix A.

Instructions
(a) Calculate the receivables turnover ratio and average collection period for 2004.
(b) Did Tootsie Roll have any potentially significant credit risks in 2004? (*Hint:* Review Note 9 to the financial statements.)
(c) What conclusions can you draw from the information in parts (a) and (b)?

COMPARATIVE ANALYSIS PROBLEM: *Tootsie Roll vs. Hershey Foods*

BYP8-2   The financial statements of Hershey Foods are presented in Appendix B, following the financial statements for Tootsie Roll in Appendix A.

Instructions
(a) Based on the information contained in these financial statements, compute the following 2004 values for each company.
   (1) Receivables turnover ratio. (Assume all sales were credit sales.)
   (2) Average collection period for receivables.
(b) What conclusions concerning the management of accounts receivable can be drawn from these data?

RESEARCH CASE

BYP8-3   The February 21, 2005, issue of *Business Week* includes an article by Amey Stone titled "How Banks Pretty up the Profit Picture."

Instructions
Read the article and answer the following questions.
(a) According to the article, what was one way that banks increased their net income in 2004? Why does the author think that this is a problem?
(b) What evidence did banks provide to justify their actions?
(c) According to the author, what problems do the banks' actions pose for investors?

INTERPRETING FINANCIAL STATEMENTS

BYP8-4   The information below and the notes on page 414 are from the 2004 financial statements and accompanying notes of The Scotts Company, a major manufacturer of lawn-care products.

(in millions)	2004	2003
Accounts receivable	$ 321.4	$ 319.5
Allowance for uncollectible accounts	29.0	29.0
Sales	2,037.9	1,887.7
Total current assets	830.3	812.6

Instructions
Answer each of the following questions.
(a) Calculate the receivables turnover ratio and average collection period for 2004 for the company.
(b) Is accounts receivable a material component of the company's total current assets?
(c) Scotts sells seasonal products. How might this affect the accuracy of your answer to part (a)?

THE SCOTTS COMPANY
Notes to the Financial Statements

Note 17. Concentrations of Credit Risk

Financial instruments which potentially subject the Company to concentration of credit risk consist principally of trade accounts receivable. The Company sells its consumer products to a wide variety of retailers, including mass merchandisers, home centers, independent hardware stores, nurseries, garden outlets, warehouse clubs and local and regional chains. Professional products are sold to commercial nurseries, greenhouses, landscape services, and growers of specialty agriculture crops.

At September 30, 2004, 71% of the Company's accounts receivable was due in North America, with 6% related to on-going litigation documented in Note 16 to the Consolidated Financial Statements. Approximately 84% of the North American accounts receivable was generated from the Company's consumer business. The most significant concentration of receivables within the North American consumer business was from our top 3 customers, which accounted for 68% of the total.

The remaining 16% of North American accounts receivable was generated from customers of Scotts LawnService and North American Professional businesses. Nearly all of the accounts receivable for the North America Professional business at September 30, 2004 were due from distributors.

The 29% of accounts receivable generated outside of North America was due from retailers, distributors, nurseries and growers. No concentrations of customers or individual customers within this group account for more than 10% of the Company's accounts receivable balance at September 30, 2004.

At September 30, 2004, the Company's concentrations of credit risk were similar to those existing at September 30, 2003.

The Company's two largest customers accounted for the following percentage of net sales in each respective period:

	Largest Customer	2nd Largest Customer
2004	25.9%	13.3%
2003	24.8%	13.9%
2002	25.8%	13.2%

Sales to the Company's two largest customers are reported within Scotts' North America segment. No other customers accounted for more that 10% of fiscal 2004, 2003 or 2002 net sales.

(d) Evaluate the credit risk of Scotts' concentrated receivables.
(e) Comment on the informational value of Scotts' Note 17 on concentrations of credit risk.

BYP8-5 Art World Industries, Inc., was incorporated in 1986 in Delaware, although it is located in Los Angeles. The company prints, publishes, and sells limited-edition graphics and reproductive prints in the wholesale market.

The company's balance sheet at the end of a recent year showed an allowance for doubtful accounts of $175,477. The allowance was set up against certain Japanese accounts receivable that average more than one year in age. The Japanese acknowledge the amount due, but with the slow economy in Japan, they lack the resources to pay at this time.

Instructions
(a) Which method of accounting for uncollectible accounts does Art World Industries use?
(b) Explain the difference between the direct write-off and percentage of receivables methods. Based on Art World's disclosure above, what important factor would you have

to consider in arriving at appropriate percentages to apply for the percentage of receivables method?
(c) What are the implications for a company's receivables management of selling its products internationally?

FINANCIAL ANALYSIS ON THE WEB

BYP8-6 *Purpose:* To learn more about factoring from a website that provides factoring services.

Address: **www.invoicefinancial.com** (or go to **www.wiley.com/college/kimmel**)

Instructions
Go to the website and answer the following questions.
(a) What are some of the benefits of factoring?
(b) What amount of accounts receivable are factored each year?
(c) What is the range of the percentages of the typical discount rate?
(d) If a company factors its receivables, what percentage of the value of the receivables can it expect to receive from the factor in the form of cash, and how quickly will it receive the cash?

Critical Thinking

DECISION MAKING ACROSS THE ORGANIZATION

BYP8-7 Rae and Rob Tillman own Glad Rags. From its inception Glad Rags has sold merchandise on either a cash or credit basis, but no credit cards have been accepted. During the past several months, the Tillmans have begun to question their credit-sales policies. First, they have lost some sales because of their refusal to accept credit cards. Second, representatives of two metropolitan banks have convinced them to accept their national credit cards. One bank, City National Bank, has stated that (1) its credit card fee is 4% and (2) it pays the retailer 96 cents on each $1 of sales within 3 days of receiving the credit card billings.

The Tillmans decide that they should determine the cost of carrying their own credit sales. From the accounting records of the past 3 years they accumulate these data:

	2007	2006	2005
Net credit sales	$520,000	$580,000	$430,000
Collection agency fees for slow-paying customers	2,900	2,600	1,600
Salary of part-time accounts receivable clerk	4,400	4,400	4,400

Credit and collection expenses as a percentage of net credit sales are as follows: uncollectible accounts 1.6%, billing and mailing costs .5%, and credit investigation fee on new customers .2%.

Rae and Rob also determine that the average accounts receivable balance outstanding during the year is 5% of net credit sales. The Tillmans estimate that they could earn an average of 10% annually on cash invested in other business opportunities.

Instructions
With the class divided into groups, answer the following.
(a) Prepare a tabulation for each year showing total credit and collection expenses in dollars and as a percentage of net credit sales.
(b) Determine the net credit and collection expenses in dollars and as a percentage of sales after considering the revenue not earned from other investment opportunities. (*Note:* The income lost on the cash held by the bank for 3 days is considered to be immaterial.)
(c) Discuss both the financial and nonfinancial factors that are relevant to the decision.

COMMUNICATION ACTIVITY

BYP8-8 Home Fibers Corporation is a recently formed business selling the "World's Best Doormat." The corporation is selling doormats faster than Home Fibers can make them. It has been selling the product on a credit basis, telling customers to "pay when they can." Oddly, even though sales are tremendous, the company is having trouble paying its bills.

Instructions
Write a memo to the president of Home Fibers Corporation discussing these questions:
(a) What steps should be taken to improve the company's ability to pay its bills?
(b) What accounting steps should be taken to measure its success in improving collections and in recording its collection success?
(c) If the corporation is still unable to pay its bills, what additional steps can be taken with its receivables to ease its liquidity problems?

ETHICS CASE

BYP8-9 The controller of Rojas Corporation believes that the company's yearly allowance for doubtful accounts should be 2% of net credit sales. The president of Rojas Corporation, nervous that the stockholders might expect the company to sustain its 10% growth rate, suggests that the controller increase the allowance for doubtful accounts to 4%. The president thinks that the lower net income, which reflects a 6% growth rate, will be a more sustainable rate for Rojas Corporation.

Instructions
(a) Who are the stakeholders in this case?
(b) Does the president's request pose an ethical dilemma for the controller?
(c) Should the controller be concerned with Rojas Corporation's growth rate in estimating the allowance? Explain your answer.

Answers to Business Insight and Accounting across the Organization Questions

p. 379
Q: When would it be appropriate for a company to lower its allowance for doubtful accounts as a percentage of its receivables?
A: It would be appropriate for a company to lower its allowance for doubtful accounts as a percentage of receivables if the company's collection experience had improved, or was expected to improve, and therefore the company expected lower defaults as a percentage of receivables.

p. 382
Q: How would reported net income likely differ during the first year of this promotion if Mitsubishi used the direct write-off method versus the allowance method?
A: Under the direct write-off method, Mitsubishi would not record bad debt expense until a customer actually defaulted on a loan. Under the allowance method, Mitsubishi would estimate how many of its loans would default rather than waiting until they actually default. For Mitsubishi, the direct write-off method would have resulted in higher net income during the first year of the promotion.

p. 386
Q: Rather than refusing to ship to Kmart, what could suppliers have done to protect their interests?
A: Suppliers could have demanded cash payment upon delivery, no longer offering Kmart the option of purchasing on credit.

p. 392
Q: What factors should management consider in deciding whether to factor its receivables?
A: Management must prepare a cash budget and evaluate its projected cash needs. If it projects a cash deficiency, it should first pursue more traditional bank financing, since it tends to be less expensive than factoring. If traditional bank financing is not

available, management could pursue factoring. If carefully structured, a factoring arrangement can be quite cost-effective since it can enable the company to outsource much of its billing and collection activities.

Answer to Tootsie Roll Review It Question 1, p. 379

Tootsie Roll reports two types of receivables on its balance sheet: Accounts receivable trade, and Other receivables. Since Tootsie Roll's balance sheet reports allowance amounts for receivables, we know that Tootsie Roll uses the allowance method rather than the direct write-off method.

Answers to Self-Study Questions

1. c   2. a   3. c   4. d   5. c   6. b   7. d   8. a   9. c
10. c   11. a

REMEMBER TO GO BACK TO THE NAVIGATOR BOX ON THE CHAPTER-OPENING PAGE
AND CHECK OFF YOUR COMPLETED WORK.

CHAPTER 9

Reporting and Analyzing Long-Lived Assets

STUDY OBJECTIVES

After studying this chapter,
you should be able to:

1 Describe how the cost principle applies to plant assets.

2 Explain the concept of depreciation.

3 Compute periodic depreciation using the straight-line method, and contrast its expense pattern with those of other methods.

4 Describe the procedure for revising periodic depreciation.

5 Explain how to account for the disposal of plant assets.

6 Describe methods for evaluating the use of plant assets.

7 Identify the basic issues related to reporting intangible assets.

8 Indicate how long-lived assets are reported on the balance sheet.

 THE NAVIGATOR

✓ THE NAVIGATOR

- Scan *Study Objectives* ⬭
- Read *Feature Story* ⬭
- Read *Preview* ⬭
- Read text and answer *Before You Go On* ⬭
  - p. 425 ⬭   p. 428 ⬭   p. 433 ⬭
  - p. 436 ⬭   p. 440 ⬭   p. 446 ⬭
- Work *Using the Decision Toolkit* ⬭
- Review *Summary of Study Objectives* ⬭
- Work *Demonstration Problems* ⬭
- Answer *Self-Study Questions* ⬭
- Complete *Assignments* ⬭

FEATURE STORY

A Tale of Two Airlines

So, you're interested in starting a new business. Have you thought about the airline industry? Your only experience with airlines is as a passenger? Don't let that stop you. Today the most profitable airlines in the industry are not well-known majors like American Airlines and United. In fact, most giant, old airlines are either bankrupt or on the verge of bankruptcy. During 2004, five major airlines representing 24% of total U.S. capacity were operating under bankruptcy protection.

Not all airlines are hurting. The growth and profitability in the airline industry today is found at relative newcomers like Southwest Airlines and JetBlue. These and other new airlines compete primarily on ticket prices. During the most recent five years the low-fare airline market share has increased by 47%; the low-fare airlines now have over 22% of U.S. airline capacity.

Southwest was the first upstart to make it big. It did so by taking a different approach. It bought small, new, fuel-efficient planes. Also, instead of the "hub-and-spoke" approach used by the majors, it opted for direct, short hop, no frills flights. It was all about controlling costs—getting the most out of its efficient new planes.

Other upstarts, such as Valujet, chose a different approach. They bought planes that were 20 to 30 years old (known in the industry as *zombies*). By buying used planes Valujet was able to add one or two planes a month to its fleet—an unheard of expansion. Valujet started with a $3.4 million investment and grew to be worth $630 million in its first three years.

But a terrible crash of a Valujet aircraft focused the spotlight on its strategy of using old planes. Although the cause of the crash appears to have been unrelated to the age of its planes, in the aftermath of the crash Valujet struggled to survive under the weight of government scrutiny and lack of customer confidence. In the face of continuing financial problems and customer skepticism, Valujet merged with AirWays Corp. and took the name of its airline, AirTran Airways. Today AirTran is one of the most profitable airlines in the industry.

But with fuel costs at record high levels, AirTran is no longer in the market for old planes. Nobody is. In fact, the old Boeing 727, which until very recently was a mainstay of nearly every airline, is no longer used for passenger flights because it couldn't be operated efficiently. Today success in the airline business comes from owning the newest and most efficient equipment, and knowing how to get the most out of it.

✈ THE NAVIGATOR

On the World Wide Web
Southwest Airlines: www.southwest.com
AirTran Airways: www.airtran.com
JetBlue Airways: www.jetblue.com

Was Valujet's approach to buying equipment really the "right formula," or was it a recipe for disaster? For airlines and many other companies, making the right decisions regarding long-lived assets is critical because these assets represent huge investments. Management must make many ongoing decisions about long-lived assets—what assets to acquire and when, how to finance them, how to account for them, and when to dispose of them.

In this chapter we address these and other issues surrounding long-lived assets. The discussion is in two parts: plant assets and intangible assets. *Plant assets* are the property, plant, and equipment (physical assets) that commonly come to mind when we think of what a company owns. Companies also have many important *intangible assets*. These assets, such as copyrights and patents, lack physical substance but can be extremely valuable and vital to a company's success.

The content and organization of this chapter are as follows.

REPORTING AND ANALYZING LONG-LIVED ASSETS

Plant Assets

- Determining the cost of plant assets
- Accounting for plant assets
- Analyzing plant assets

Intangible Assets

- Accounting for intangible assets
- Types of intangible assets
- Financial statement presentation of long-lived assets

THE NAVIGATOR

SECTION ONE
PLANT ASSETS

Plant assets are resources that have physical substance (a definite size and shape), are used in the operations of a business, and are not intended for sale to customers. They are called various names—*property, plant, and equipment; plant and equipment;* and *fixed assets.* By whatever name, these assets are expected to provide services to the company for a number of years. Except for land, plant assets decline in service potential (value) over their useful lives.

Plant assets are critical to a company's success because they determine the company's capacity and therefore its ability to satisfy customers. With too few planes, for example, AirTran and Southwest Airlines would lose customers to their competitors. But with too many planes, they would be flying with empty seats. Management must constantly monitor its needs and acquire assets accordingly. Failure to do so results in lost business opportunities or inefficient use of existing assets and is likely to show up eventually in poor financial results.

It is important for a company to (1) keep assets in good operating condition, (2) replace worn-out or outdated assets, and (3) expand its productive assets as needed. The decline of rail travel in the United States can be traced in part to the failure of railroad companies to maintain and update their assets. Conversely, the growth of air travel in this country can be attributed in part to the general willingness of airline companies to follow these essential guidelines.

For many companies, investments in plant assets are substantial. Illustration 9-1 shows the percentages of plant assets in relation to total assets in various companies.

Illustration 9-1
Percentages of plant assets in relation to total assets

Determining the Cost of Plant Assets

The **cost principle** requires that companies record plant assets at cost. Thus, AirTran and Southwest Airlines record their planes at cost. **Cost consists of all expenditures necessary to acquire an asset and make it ready for its intended use.** For example, the purchase price, freight costs paid by the purchaser, and installation costs are all part of the cost of factory machinery.

Determining which costs to include in a plant asset account and which costs not to include is very important. If a cost is not included in a plant asset account, then it must be expensed immediately. Such costs are referred to as **revenue expenditures**. On the other hand, costs that are not expensed immediately but are instead included in a plant asset account are referred to as **capital expenditures**.

This distinction is important; it has immediate, and often material, implications for the income statement. Some companies, in order to boost current income, have improperly capitalized expenditures that they should have expensed. For example, suppose that a company improperly capitalizes to a building account $1,000 of maintenance costs incurred at the end of the year. (That is, the costs are included in the asset account Buildings rather than being expensed immediately.) If the company is allocating the cost of the building as an expense (depreciating it) over a 40-year life, then the maintenance cost of $1,000 will be incorrectly spread across 40 years instead of being expensed in the current year. As a result, the company will understate current-year expenses by $1,000, and will overstate current-year income by $1,000. Thus, determining which costs to capitalize and which to expense is very important.

STUDY OBJECTIVE
1

Describe how the cost principle applies to plant assets.

🌐 **International Note**

The United Kingdom is flexible regarding asset valuation. Companies revalue to fair value when they believe this information is more relevant. Switzerland and the Netherlands also permit revaluations.

Cost is measured by the cash paid in a cash transaction or by the **cash equivalent price** paid when companies use noncash assets in payment. **The cash equivalent price is equal to the fair market value of the asset given up or the fair market value of the asset received, whichever is more clearly determinable.** Once cost is established, it becomes the basis of accounting for the plant asset over its useful life. Current market value is not used to increase the recorded cost after acquisition. We explain the application of the cost principle to each of the major classes of plant assets in the following sections.

Business Insight
Ethics Perspective

In what has been one of the largest accounting frauds in history, WorldCom announced the discovery of $7 billion in expenses improperly booked as capital expenditures, a gimmick that boosted profit over a five-quarter period. If these expenses had been booked properly, WorldCom, at one time one of the biggest stock market stars, would have reported losses. Instead, WorldCom reported billions of dollars of profit. As a result of these problems, WorldCom declared bankruptcy, to the dismay of its investors and creditors.

 How did the capitalization of expenses increase WorldCom's income?

LAND

Companies often use land as a building site for a manufacturing plant or office site. The cost of land includes (1) the cash purchase price, (2) closing costs such as title and attorney's fees, (3) real estate brokers' commissions, and (4) accrued property taxes and other liens on the land assumed by the purchaser. For example, if the cash price is $50,000 and the purchaser agrees to pay accrued taxes of $5,000, the cost of the land is $55,000.

All necessary costs incurred in making land **ready for its intended use** increase (debit) the Land account. When a company acquires vacant land, its cost includes expenditures for clearing, draining, filling, and grading. If the land has a building on it that must be removed to make the site suitable for construction of a new building, the company includes all demolition and removal costs, less any proceeds from salvaged materials, in the Land account.

To illustrate, assume that Hayes Manufacturing Company acquires real estate at a cash cost of $100,000. The property contains an old warehouse that is razed at a net cost of $6,000 ($7,500 in costs less $1,500 proceeds from salvaged materials). Additional expenditures are for the attorney's fee $1,000 and the real estate broker's commission $8,000. Given these factors, the cost of the land is $115,000, computed as shown in Illustration 9-2.

Illustration 9-2
Computation of cost of land

Land	
Cash price of property	$ 100,000
Net removal cost of warehouse	6,000
Attorney's fee	1,000
Real estate broker's commission	8,000
Cost of land	**$115,000**

When Hayes records the acquisition, it debits Land for $115,000 and credits Cash for $115,000.

LAND IMPROVEMENTS

Land improvements are structural additions made to land, such as driveways, parking lots, fences, landscaping, and underground sprinklers. The cost of land improvements includes all expenditures necessary to make the improvements ready for their intended use. For example, the cost of a new company parking lot includes the amount paid for paving, fencing, and lighting. Thus the company would debit the total of all of these costs to Land Improvements.

Land improvements have limited useful lives, and their maintenance and replacement are the responsibility of the company. Because of their limited useful life, companies expense (depreciate) the cost of land improvements over their useful lives.

BUILDINGS

Buildings are facilities used in operations, such as stores, offices, factories, warehouses, and airplane hangers. Companies charge to the Buildings account all necessary expenditures relating to the purchase or construction of a building. When a building is **purchased**, such costs include the purchase price, closing costs (attorney's fees, title insurance, etc.), and real estate broker's commission. Costs to make the building ready for its intended use consist of expenditures for remodeling rooms and offices and replacing or repairing the roof, floors, electrical wiring, and plumbing. When a new building is **constructed**, its cost consists of the contract price plus payments made by the owner for architects' fees, building permits, and excavation costs.

In addition, companies charge certain interest costs to the cost of a building: Interest costs incurred to finance a construction project are included in the cost of the asset when a significant period of time is required to get the asset ready for use. In these circumstances, interest costs are considered as necessary as materials and labor. However, the inclusion of interest costs in the cost of a constructed building is **limited to interest costs incurred during the construction period**. When construction has been completed, subsequent interest payments on funds borrowed to finance the construction are recorded as increases (debits) to Interest Expense.

EQUIPMENT

Equipment includes assets used in operations, such as store check-out counters, office furniture, factory machinery, delivery trucks, and airplanes. The cost of equipment consists of the cash purchase price, sales taxes, freight charges, and insurance during transit paid by the purchaser. It also includes expenditures required in assembling, installing, and testing the unit. However, companies treat as expenses the costs of motor vehicle licenses and accident insurance on company trucks and cars. Such items are annual recurring expenditures and do not benefit future periods. Two criteria apply in determining the cost of equipment: (1) the frequency of the cost—one time or recurring, and (2) the benefit period—the life of the asset or one year.

To illustrate, assume that Lenard Company purchases a delivery truck at a cash price of $22,000. Related expenditures are sales taxes $1,320, painting and lettering $500, motor vehicle license $80, and a three-year accident insurance policy $1,600. The cost of the delivery truck is $23,820, computed as shown in Illustration 9-3 on the next page.

Illustration 9-3
Computation of cost of delivery truck

Delivery Truck	
Cash price	$ 22,000
Sales taxes	1,320
Painting and lettering	500
Cost of delivery truck	**$23,820**

Lenard treats the cost of a motor vehicle license as an expense and the cost of an insurance policy as a prepaid asset. Thus, the company records the purchase of the truck and related expenditures as follows.

A	=	L	+	SE
+23,820				
				−80 Exp
+1,600				
−25,500				

Cash Flows
−25,500

Delivery Truck		23,820	
License Expense		80	
Prepaid Insurance		1,600	
Cash			25,500
(To record purchase of delivery truck and related expenditures)			

For another example, assume Merten Company purchases factory machinery at a cash price of $50,000. Related expenditures are sales taxes $3,000, insurance during shipping $500, and installation and testing $1,000. The cost of the factory machinery is $54,500, computed as in Illustration 9-4.

Illustration 9-4
Computation of cost of factory machinery

Factory Machinery	
Cash price	$ 50,000
Sales taxes	3,000
Insurance during shipping	500
Installation and testing	1,000
Cost of factory machinery	**$54,500**

Thus, Merten records the purchase and related expenditures as follows.

A	=	L	+	SE
+54,500				
−54,500				

Cash Flows
−54,500

Factory Machinery		54,500	
Cash			54,500
(To record purchase of factory machinery and related expenditures)			

TO BUY OR LEASE?

In this chapter we focus on purchased assets, but we want to expose you briefly to an alternative—leasing. In a lease, a party that owns an asset (the **lessor**) agrees to allow another party (the **lessee**) to use the asset for an agreed period of time at an agreed price. In many industries leasing is quite common. For example, one-third of heavy-duty commercial trucks are leased.

Some advantages of leasing an asset versus purchasing it are:

1. **Reduced risk of obsolescence.** Frequently, lease terms allow the party using the asset (the lessee) to exchange the asset for a more modern one if it becomes outdated. This is much easier than trying to sell an obsolete asset.

2. **Little or no down payment.**   To purchase an asset, most companies must borrow money, which usually requires a down payment of at least 20%. Leasing an asset requires little or no down payment.

3. **Shared tax advantages.**   Startup companies typically do not make much money in their early years, and so they have little need for the tax deductions available from owning an asset. In a lease, the lessor gets the tax advantage because it owns the asset. It often will pass these tax savings on to the lessee in the form of lower lease payments.

4. **Assets and liabilities not reported.**   Many companies prefer to keep assets and especially liabilities off their books. Certain types of leases, called **operating leases**, allow the lessee to account for the transaction as a rental, with neither an asset nor a liability recorded.

Airlines often choose to lease many of their airplanes in long-term lease agreements. In its 2004 financial statements, Southwest Airlines stated that it leased 88 of its 417 planes under operating leases. Because operating leases are accounted for as a rental, these 88 planes did not show up on its balance sheet.

Under another type of lease, a **capital lease**, companies show both the asset and the liability on the balance sheet. The lessee under a capital lease, accounts for long-term lease agreements in a way that is very similar to purchases: The lessee shows the leased item as an asset on its balance sheet, and the obligation owed to the lessor as a liability. The lessee depreciates the leased asset in a manner similar to purchased assets. Southwest Airlines' balance sheet accounts for about 0.5% of the company's property, plant, and equipment as capital leases. We discuss leasing further in Chapter 10 on liabilities.

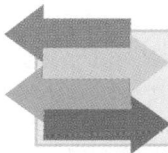

Accounting across the Organization

Leasing is big business for U.S. companies. For example, business investment in equipment in 2004 totaled $709 billion. Leasing accounted for about 31% of all business investment ($218 billion).

Who does the most leasing? Interestingly major banks, such as Continental Bank, J.P. Morgan Leasing, and US Bancorp Equipment Finance, are the major lessors. Also, many companies have established separate leasing companies, such as Boeing Capital Corporation, Dell Financial Services, and John Deere Capital Corporation. And, as an excellent example of the magnitude of leasing, leased planes account for nearly 40% of the U.S. fleet of commercial airlines. In addition, leasing is becoming increasingly common in the hotel industry. Marriott, Hilton, and InterContinental are increasingly choosing to lease hotels that are owned by someone else.

 Why might airline managers choose to lease rather than purchase their planes?

BEFORE YOU GO ON . . .

▶ Review It

1. What are plant assets? What are the major classes of plant assets? At what value should companies record plant assets?

2. What are revenue expenditures? What are capital expenditures?

3. What are the primary advantages of leasing?

▶ Do It

Assume that a company purchases a delivery truck for $15,000 cash plus sales taxes of $900 and delivery costs of $500. The buyer also pays $200 for painting and lettering, $600 for an annual insurance policy, and $80 for a motor vehicle license. Explain how the company should account for each of these costs.

Action Plan

• Identify expenditures made in order to get delivery equipment ready for its intended use.

• Expense operating costs incurred during the useful life of the equipment.

Solution

The first four payments ($15,000, $900, $500, and $200) are expenditures necessary to make the truck ready for its intended use. Thus, the cost of the truck is $16,600. The payments for insurance and the license are operating expenses incurred during the useful life of the asset.

THE NAVIGATOR

Accounting for Plant Assets

DEPRECIATION

As explained in Chapter 4, **depreciation is the process of allocating to expense the cost of a plant asset over its useful (service) life in a rational and systematic manner.** Such cost allocation is designed to properly match expenses with revenues. (See Illustration 9-5.)

Illustration 9-5
Depreciation as an allocation concept

Depreciation Tutorial

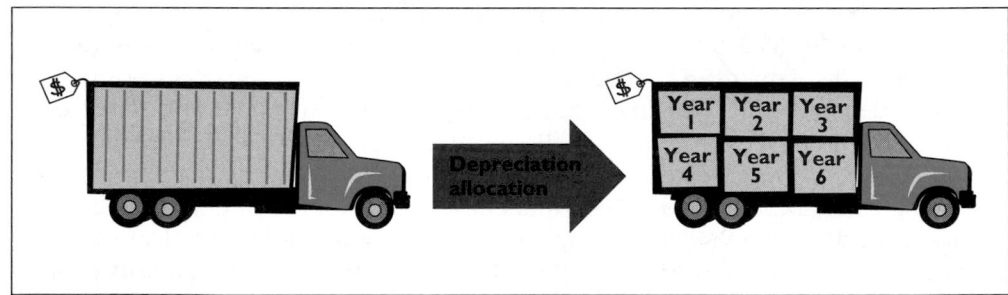

Depreciation affects the balance sheet through accumulated depreciation, which companies report as a deduction from plant assets. It affects the income statement through depreciation expense.

It is important to understand that **depreciation is a cost allocation process, not an asset valuation process**. No attempt is made to measure the change in an asset's market value during ownership. Thus, the **book value**—cost less accumulated depreciation—of a plant asset may differ significantly from its **market value**. In fact, if an asset is fully depreciated, it can have zero book value but still have a significant market value.

Depreciation applies to **three classes of plant assets**: land improvements, buildings, and equipment. Each of these classes is considered to be a **depreciable asset** because the usefulness to the company and the revenue-producing ability of each class decline over the asset's useful life. Depreciation **does not**

Helpful Hint Remember that depreciation is the process of *allocating cost* over the useful life of an asset. It is not a measure of value.

apply to land because its usefulness and revenue-producing ability generally remain intact as long as the land is owned. In fact, in many cases, the usefulness of land increases over time because of the scarcity of good sites. Thus, **land is not a depreciable asset**.

Helpful Hint Land does not depreciate because it does not wear out.

During a depreciable asset's useful life its revenue-producing ability declines because of wear and tear. A delivery truck that has been driven 100,000 miles will be less useful to a company than one driven only 800 miles.

A decline in revenue-producing ability may also occur because of obsolescence. **Obsolescence** is the process by which an asset becomes out of date before it physically wears out. The rerouting of major airlines from Chicago's Midway Airport to Chicago-O'Hare International Airport because Midway's runways were too short for giant jets is an example. Similarly, many companies replace their computers long before they originally planned to do so because improvements in new computers make their old computers obsolete.

Recognizing depreciation for an asset does not result in the accumulation of cash for replacement of the asset. The balance in Accumulated Depreciation represents the total amount of the asset's cost that the company has charged to expense to date; **it is not a cash fund**.

Factors in Computing Depreciation

Three factors affect the computation of depreciation, as shown in Illustration 9-6.

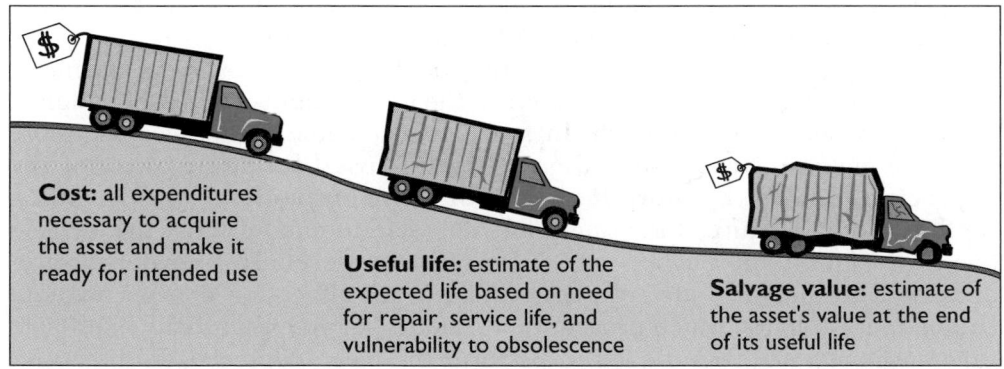

Illustration 9-6 Three factors in computing depreciation

1. **Cost.** Earlier in the chapter we explained the considerations that affect the cost of a depreciable asset. Remember that companies record plant assets at cost, in accordance with the cost principle.
2. **Useful life.** Useful life is an estimate of the expected productive life, also called *service life*, of the asset for its owner. Useful life may be expressed in terms of time, units of activity (such as machine hours), or units of output. Useful life is an estimate. In making the estimate, management considers such factors as the intended use of the asset, repair and maintenance policies, and vulnerability of the asset to obsolescence. The company's past experience with similar assets is often helpful in deciding on expected useful life.
3. **Salvage value.** Salvage value is an estimate of the asset's value at the end of its useful life for its owner. Companies may base the value on the asset's worth as scrap or on its expected trade-in value. Like useful life, salvage value is an estimate. In making the estimate, management considers how it plans to dispose of the asset and its experience with similar assets.

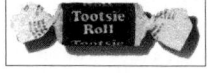

BEFORE YOU GO ON . . .

▶ Review It

1. What is the relationship, if any, of depreciation to (a) cost allocation, (b) asset valuation, and (c) cash accumulation?
2. Explain the factors that affect the computation of depreciation.
3. What does Tootsie Roll use as the estimated useful life on its buildings? On its machinery and equipment? The answer to this question appears on page 471.

Depreciation Methods

STUDY OBJECTIVE

3

Compute periodic depreciation using the straight-line method, and contrast its expense pattern with those of other methods.

Although a number of methods exist, depreciation is generally computed using one of three methods:

1. Straight-line
2. Declining-balance
3. Units-of-activity

Like the alternative inventory methods discussed in Chapter 6, each of these depreciation methods is acceptable under generally accepted accounting principles. Management selects the method it believes best measures an asset's contribution to revenue over its useful life. Once a company chooses a method, it should apply that method consistently over the useful life of the asset. Consistency enhances the comparability of financial statements.

Illustration 9-7 shows the distribution of the *primary* depreciation methods in 600 of the largest U.S. companies. Clearly, straight-line depreciation is the most widely used approach. In fact, because some companies use more than one method, **straight-line depreciation is used for some or all of the depreciation taken by more than 95% of U.S. companies.** For this reason, we illustrate procedures for straight-line depreciation and discuss the alternative depreciation approaches only at a conceptual level. This coverage introduces you to the basic idea of depreciation as an allocation concept without entangling you in too much procedural detail. (Also, note that many hand-held calculators are preprogrammed to perform the basic depreciation methods.) Details on the alternative approaches are presented in the appendix to this chapter (pages 449–451).

Illustration 9-7 Use of depreciation methods in major U.S. companies

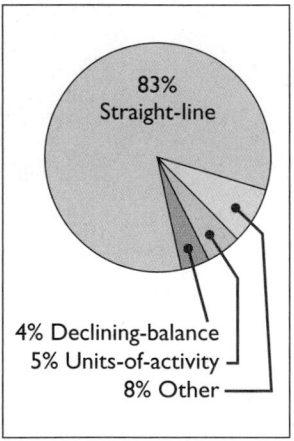

Our illustration of depreciation methods, both here and in the appendix, is based on the following data relating to a small delivery truck purchased by Bill's Pizzas on January 1, 2007.

Cost	$13,000
Expected salvage value	$1,000
Estimated useful life (in years)	5
Estimated useful life (in miles)	100,000

STRAIGHT-LINE. Under the **straight-line method**, companies expense an equal amount of depreciation each year of the asset's useful life. Management must choose the useful life of an asset based on its own expectations and experience.

To compute the annual depreciation expense, we divide depreciable cost by the estimated useful life. **Depreciable cost** represents the total amount subject to depreciation; it is calculated as the cost of the asset less its salvage value. Illustration 9-8 shows the computation of depreciation expense in the first year for Bill's Pizzas' delivery truck.

Illustration 9-8 Formula for straight-line method

$$\underset{\$13{,}000}{\underset{\text{Cost}}{}} \quad - \quad \underset{\$1{,}000}{\underset{\substack{\text{Salvage}\\ \text{Value}}}{}} \quad = \quad \underset{\$12{,}000}{\underset{\substack{\text{Depreciable}\\ \text{Cost}}}{}}$$

$$\underset{\$12{,}000}{\underset{\substack{\text{Depreciable}\\ \text{Cost}}}{}} \quad \div \quad \underset{5}{\underset{\substack{\text{Useful Life}\\ \text{(in years)}}}{}} \quad = \quad \underset{\mathbf{\$2{,}400}}{\underset{\substack{\text{Depreciation}\\ \text{Expense}}}{}}$$

Alternatively, we can compute an annual *rate* at which the company depreciates the delivery truck. In this case, the rate is 20% (100% ÷ 5 years). When an annual rate is used under the straight-line method, the company applies the percentage rate to the depreciable cost of the asset, as shown in the **depreciation schedule** in Illustration 9-9.

BILL'S PIZZAS

	Computation			Annual	End of Year	
Year	Depreciable Cost	×	Depreciation Rate	= Depreciation Expense	Accumulated Depreciation	Book Value
2007	$12,000		20%	**$ 2,400**	$ 2,400	$10,600*
2008	12,000		20	**2,400**	4,800	8,200
2009	12,000		20	**2,400**	7,200	5,800
2010	12,000		20	**2,400**	9,600	3,400
2011	12,000		20	**2,400**	12,000	**1,000**
			Total	**$12,000**		

*$13,000 − $2,400

Illustration 9-9
Straight-line depreciation schedule

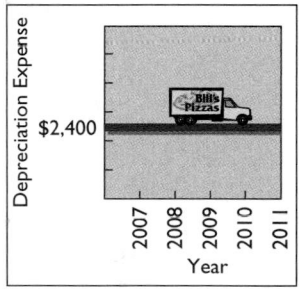

Note that the depreciation expense of $2,400 is the same each year. The book value at the end of the useful life is equal to the estimated $1,000 salvage value.

What happens when an asset is purchased **during** the year, rather than on January 1 as in our example? In that case, it is necessary to **prorate the annual depreciation** for the portion of a year used. If Bill's Pizzas had purchased the delivery truck on April 1, 2007, the company would use the truck for 9 months in 2007. The depreciation for 2007 would be $1,800 ($12,000 × 20% × $\frac{9}{12}$ of a year).

As indicated earlier, the straight-line method predominates in practice. For example, such large companies as Campbell Soup, Marriott, and General Mills use the straight-line method. It is simple to apply, and it matches expenses with revenues appropriately when the use of the asset is reasonably uniform throughout the service life. The types of assets that give equal benefits over useful life generally are those for which daily use does not affect productivity. Examples are office furniture and fixtures, buildings, warehouses, and garages for motor vehicles.

DECLINING-BALANCE. The **declining-balance method** computes periodic depreciation using a declining book value. This method is called an **accelerated-depreciation method** because it results in more depreciation in the early years of an asset's life than does the straight-line approach. However, because the total amount of depreciation (the depreciable cost) taken over an asset's life is the same **no matter what approach** is used, the declining-balance method produces a decreasing annual depreciation expense over the asset's useful life. In early years declining-balance depreciation expense will exceed straight-line, but in later years it will be less than straight-line. Managers might choose an accelerated approach if they think that an asset's utility will decline quickly.

Companies can apply the declining-balance approach at different rates, which result in varying speeds of depreciation. A common declining-balance rate is double the straight-line rate. Using that rate, the method is referred to as the **double-declining-balance method**.

If we apply the double-declining-balance method to Bill's Pizzas' delivery truck, assuming a five-year life, we get the pattern of depreciation shown in Illustration 9-10. **The chapter's appendix, page 449, presents the computations behind these numbers.** Again, note that total depreciation over the life of the truck is $12,000, the depreciable cost.

Illustration 9-10
Declining-balance depreciation schedule

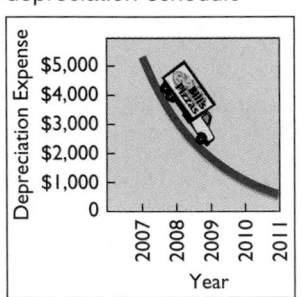

		BILL'S PIZZAS		
		Annual	End of Year	
		Depreciation	Accumulated	Book
Year		Expense	Depreciation	Value
2007		$ 5,200	$ 5,200	$ 7,800
2008		3,120	8,320	4,680
2009		1,872	10,192	2,808
2010		1,123	11,315	1,685
2011		685	12,000	1,000
	Total	$12,000		

UNITS-OF-ACTIVITY.   As indicated earlier, useful life can be expressed in ways other than a time period. Under the **units-of-activity method**, useful life is expressed in terms of the total units of production or the use expected from the asset. The units-of-activity method is ideally suited to factory machinery: Companies can measure production in terms of units of output or in terms of machine hours used in operating the machinery. It is also possible to use the method for such items as delivery equipment (miles driven) and airplanes (hours in use). The units-of-activity method is generally not suitable for such assets as buildings or furniture because activity levels are difficult to measure for these assets.

Applying the units-of-activity method to the delivery truck owned by Bill's Pizzas, we first must know some basic information. Bill's expects to be able to drive the truck a total of 100,000 miles. Illustration 9-11 shows depreciation over the five-year life based on an assumed mileage pattern. **The chapter's appendix, pages 450–451, presents the computations used to arrive at these results.**

Illustration 9-11
Units-of-activity depreciation schedule

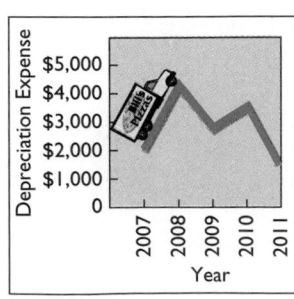

			BILL'S PIZZAS		
	Units of	Annual	End of Year		
	Activity	Depreciation	Accumulated	Book
Year	(miles)	Expense	Depreciation	Value
2007	15,000	$ 1,800	$ 1,800	$11,200
2008	30,000	3,600	5,400	7,600
2009	20,000	2,400	7,800	5,200
2010	25,000	3,000	10,800	2,200
2011	10,000	1,200	12,000	1,000
Total	100,000	$12,000		

As the name implies, under units-of-activity depreciation, the amount of depreciation is proportional to the activity that took place during that period. For example, the delivery truck was driven twice as many miles in 2008 as in 2007, and depreciation was exactly twice as much in 2008 as it was in 2007.

Management's Choice: Comparison of Methods

Illustration 9-12 compares annual and total depreciation expense for Bill's Pizzas under the three methods.

Year	Straight-Line	Declining-Balance	Units-of-Activity
2007	$ 2,400	$ 5,200	$ 1,800
2008	2,400	3,120	3,600
2009	2,400	1,872	2,400
2010	2,400	1,123	3,000
2011	2,400	685	1,200
	$12,000	$12,000	$12,000

Illustration 9-12
Comparison of depreciation methods

Periodic depreciation varies considerably among the methods, but **total depreciation is the same for the five-year period**. Each method is acceptable in accounting because each recognizes the decline in service potential of the asset in a rational and systematic manner. Illustration 9-13 graphs the depreciation expense pattern under each method.

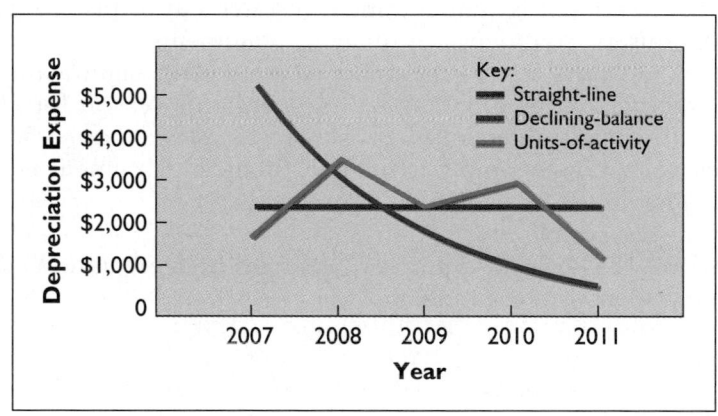

Illustration 9-13
Patterns of depreciation

Depreciation and Income Taxes

The Internal Revenue Service (IRS) allows corporate taxpayers to deduct depreciation expense when computing taxable income. However, the tax regulations of the IRS do not require the taxpayer to use the same depreciation method on the tax return that it uses in preparing financial statements.

Consequently, many large corporations use straight-line depreciation in their financial statements in order to maximize net income; at the same time they use a special accelerated-depreciation method on their tax returns in order to minimize their income taxes. For tax purposes, taxpayers must use on their tax returns either the straight-line method or a special accelerated-depreciation method called the **Modified Accelerated Cost Recovery System** (MACRS).

Helpful Hint Depreciation per GAAP is usually different from depreciation per IRS rules.

Depreciation Disclosure in the Notes

Companies must disclose the choice of depreciation method in their financial statements or in related notes that accompany the statements. Illustration 9-14 shows the "Property and equipment" notes from the financial statements of Southwest Airlines.

Illustration 9-14
Disclosure of depreciation policies

SOUTHWEST AIRLINES
Notes to the Financial Statements

Property and equipment Depreciation is provided by the straight-line method to estimated residual values over periods ranging from 20 to 25 years for flight equipment and 5 to 30 years for ground property and equipment once the asset is placed in service. Amortization of property under capital leases is on a straight-line basis over the lease term and is included in depreciation expense.

From this note we learn that Southwest Airlines uses the straight-line method to depreciate its planes over periods of 20 to 25 years.

Revising Periodic Depreciation

STUDY OBJECTIVE
4

Describe the procedure for revising periodic depreciation.

Management should periodically review annual depreciation expense. If wear and tear or obsolescence indicates that annual depreciation is either inadequate or excessive, the company should change the depreciation expense amount.

When a change in an estimate is required, the company makes the change in **current and future years but not to prior periods**. Thus, when making the change, the company (1) does not correct previously recorded depreciation expense, but (2) revises depreciation expense for current and future years. The rationale for this treatment is that continual restatement of prior periods would adversely affect users' confidence in financial statements.

Companies must disclose in the financial statements significant changes in estimates. Although a company may have a legitimate reason for changing an estimated life, financial statement users should be aware that some companies might change an estimate simply to achieve financial statement goals. For example, extending an asset's estimated life reduces depreciation expense and increases current period income.

Illustration 9-15 shows an example of changes in depreciation estimates for AirTran Airways that increased income.

Illustration 9-15
Disclosure of changes in depreciation estimates

AIR TRAN AIRWAYS
Notes to the Financial Statements

Note 1. Property and equipment Property and equipment is stated on the basis of cost. Flight equipment is depreciated to its salvage values using the straight-line method.
    The estimated salvage values and depreciable lives are periodically reviewed for reasonableness, and revised if necessary. The Boeing 717 (B717) fleet has a salvage value of 10 percent. At July 1, 2001, we revised the useful lives on our B717 fleet, as outlined below, in order to more accurately reflect the estimated useful life of the aircraft:

	2001 Useful Life	2000 Useful Life
Airframes	30 years	25 years
Engines	30 years	25 years
Aircraft parts	30 years	5 years

The effect of this change for the year ended December 31, 2001, was to decrease our net loss by approximately $0.6 million, or $0.01 per share.

AirTran was operating at a loss at the time of these changes. Whether these changes are reasonable depends on the accuracy of the assumptions regarding these planes. Our Feature Story suggests that although many planes last a long time, safety concerns might ground many older planes.

BEFORE YOU GO ON . . .

▶ Review It

1. Why is depreciation an allocation concept rather than a valuation concept?
2. What is the formula for computing annual depreciation under the straight-line method?
3. How do the depreciation methods differ in their effects on annual depreciation over the useful life of an asset?
4. Are revisions of periodic depreciation made to prior periods? Explain.

▶ Do It

On January 1, 2007, Iron Mountain Ski Corporation purchased a new snow grooming machine for $50,000. The machine is estimated to have a 10-year life with a $2,000 salvage value. What journal entry would Iron Mountain Ski Corporation make at December 31, 2007, if it uses the straight-line method of depreciation?

Action Plan

• Calculate depreciable cost (Cost − Salvage value).
• Divide the depreciable cost by the asset's estimated useful life.

Solution

$$\text{Depreciation expense} = \frac{\text{Cost} - \text{Salvage value}}{\text{Useful life}} = \frac{\$50,000 - \$2,000}{10} = \$4,800$$

Iron Mountain would record the first year's depreciation as follows:

Dec. 31	Depreciation Expense	4,800	
	Accumulated Depreciation—Machinery		4,800
	(To record annual depreciation on snow		
	grooming machine)		

✓ THE NAVIGATOR

EXPENDITURES DURING USEFUL LIFE

During the useful life of a plant asset, a company may incur costs for ordinary repairs, additions, and improvements. **Ordinary repairs** are expenditures to maintain the operating efficiency and expected productive life of the unit. They usually are fairly small amounts that occur frequently throughout the service life. Examples are motor tune-ups and oil changes, the painting of buildings, and the replacing of worn-out gears on factory machinery. Ordinary repairs are debited to Repair (or Maintenance) Expense as incurred. Because they are immediately charged against revenues as an expense, these costs are **revenue expenditures**.

Additions and improvements are costs incurred to **increase** the operating efficiency, productive capacity, or expected useful life of the plant asset. These expenditures are usually material in amount and occur infrequently during the period of ownership. Expenditures for additions and improvements increase the company's investment in productive facilities and are generally debited to the plant asset affected. Thus, they are **capital expenditures**. The accounting for capital expenditures varies depending on the nature of the expenditure.

Northwest Airlines at one time spent $120 million to spruce up 40 DC9-30 jets. The improvements were designed to extend the lives of the planes, meet stricter government noise limits, and save money. The capital expenditure was expected to extend the life of the jets by 10 to 15 years and save about $560 million compared to the cost of buying new planes. The DC9 jets were, on average, 24 years old.

IMPAIRMENTS

As noted earlier, the book value of plant assets is rarely the same as the market value. In instances where the value of a plant asset declines substantially, its market value might fall materially below book value. This may happen because a machine has become obsolete, or the market for the product made by the machine has dried up or has become very competitive. A **permanent decline** in the market value of an asset is referred to as an impairment. So as not to overstate the asset on the books, the company writes the asset down to its new market value during the year in which the decline in value occurs. For example, AirTran recently announced a $28 million impairment loss on its DC9s and a $10.8 million impairment loss on its B737s. AirTran used appraisals and considered recent transactions and market trends involving similar aircraft in determining the fair market values.

In the past, some companies delayed recording losses on impairments until a year when it was "convenient" to do so—when the impact on the company's reported results was minimized. For example, if a company has record profits in one year, it can then afford to write down some of its bad assets without hurting its reported results too much. As discussed in Chapter 4, the practice of timing the recognition of gains and losses to achieve certain income results is known as **earnings management**. Earnings management reduces earnings quality. Immediate recognition of these write-downs is now required.

Write-downs can create problems for users of financial statements. Critics of write-downs note that after a company writes down assets, its depreciation expense will be lower in all subsequent periods. Some companies intentionally write down assets in bad years, when they are going to report poor results anyway. Then in subsequent years, when the company recovers, its results will look even better because of lower depreciation expense.

PLANT ASSET DISPOSALS

STUDY OBJECTIVE
5
Explain how to account for the disposal of plant assets.

Companies dispose of plant assets that are no longer useful to them. Illustration 9-16 shows the three ways in which companies make plant asset disposals.

Whatever the disposal method, the company must determine the book value of the plant asset at the time of disposal in order to determine the gain or loss. Recall that the book value is the difference between the cost of the plant asset

Sale	**Retirement**	**Exchange**
Equipment is sold to another party.	Equipment is scrapped or discarded.	Existing equipment is traded for new equipment.

Illustration 9-16
Methods of plant asset disposal

and the accumulated depreciation to date. If the disposal occurs at any time during the year, the company must record depreciation for the fraction of the year to the date of disposal. The company then eliminates the book value by reducing (debiting) Accumulated Depreciation for the total depreciation associated with that asset to the date of disposal and reducing (crediting) the asset account for the cost of the asset.

Sale of Plant Assets

In a disposal by sale, the company compares the book value of the asset with the proceeds received from the sale. If the proceeds from the sale **exceed** the book value of the plant asset, a **gain on disposal** occurs. If the proceeds from the sale **are less than** the book value of the plant asset sold, a **loss on disposal** occurs.

Only by coincidence will the book value and the fair market value of the asset be the same at the time the asset is sold. Gains and losses on sales of plant assets are therefore quite common. As an example, Delta Air Lines reported a $94,343,000 gain on the sale of five Boeing B-727-200 aircraft and five Lockheed L-1011-1 aircraft.

GAIN ON SALE. To illustrate a gain on sale of plant assets, assume that on July 1, 2007, Wright Company sells office furniture for $16,000 cash. The office furniture originally cost $60,000 and as of January 1, 2007, had accumulated depreciation of $41,000. Depreciation for the first six months of 2007 is $8,000. Wright records depreciation expense and updates accumulated depreciation to July 1 as follows.

July 1	Depreciation Expense	8,000	
	Accumulated Depreciation—Office Furniture		8,000
	(To record depreciation expense for the first 6 months of 2007)		

A	=	L	+	SE
				−8,000 Exp
−8,000				

Cash Flows
no effect

After the accumulated depreciation balance is updated, the company computes the gain or loss as the difference between the proceeds from sale and the book value at the date of disposal. Wright Company has a gain on disposal of $5,000, as computed in Illustration 9-17.

Cost of office furniture	$60,000
Less: Accumulated depreciation ($41,000 + $8,000)	49,000
Book value at date of disposal	11,000
Proceeds from sale	16,000
Gain on disposal of plant asset	**$ 5,000**

Illustration 9-17
Computation of gain on disposal

Wright records the sale and the gain on sale of the plant asset as follows.

July 1	Cash	16,000	
	Accumulated Depreciation—Office Furniture	49,000	
	Office Furniture		60,000
	Gain on Disposal		5,000
	(To record sale of office furniture at a gain)		

A	=	L	+	SE
+16,000				
+49,000				
−60,000				
				+5,000 Rev

Cash Flows
+16,000

Companies report a gain on disposal of the plant asset in the "Other revenues and gains" section of the income statement.

LOSS ON SALE. Assume that instead of selling the office furniture for $16,000, Wright sells it for $9,000. In this case, Wright experiences a loss of $2,000, as computed in Illustration 9-18.

Illustration 9-18
Computation of loss on disposal

Cost of office furniture	$60,000
Less: Accumulated depreciation	49,000
Book value at date of disposal	11,000
Proceeds from sale	9,000
Loss on disposal of plant asset	**$ 2,000**

Wright records the sale and the loss on sale of the plant asset as follows.

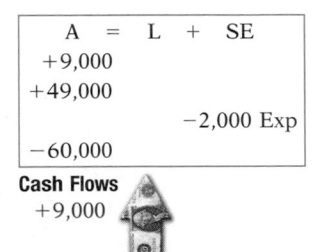

A	=	L +	SE
+9,000			
+49,000			
			−2,000 Exp
−60,000			

Cash Flows
+9,000

July 1	Cash	9,000	
	Accumulated Depreciation—Office Furniture	49,000	
	Loss on Disposal	2,000	
	Office Furniture		60,000
	(To record sale of office furniture at a loss)		

Companies report a loss on disposal of the plant asset in the "Other expenses and losses" section of the income statement.

Retirement of Plant Assets

Companies simply retire, rather than sell, some assets at the end of their useful life. For example, some productive assets used in manufacturing may have very specific uses, and they consequently have no ready market when the company no longer needs them. In such a case the asset is simply retired.

Companies record retirement of an asset as a special case of a disposal where no cash is received. They decrease (debit) Accumulated Depreciation for the full amount of depreciation taken over the life of the asset and decrease (credit) the asset account for the original cost of the asset. The loss (a gain is not possible on a retirement) is equal to the asset's book value on the date of retirement.[1]

BEFORE YOU GO ON . . .

▶**Review It**

1. What is the difference between an ordinary repair and an addition or improvement? Why is this distinction important to financial reporting?
2. What is an impairment? In what way do critics suggest that companies manage their earnings through the write-downs associated with impairments?
3. What is the proper accounting for sales and retirements of plant assets?

▶**Do It**

Overland Trucking has an old truck that cost $30,000 and has accumulated depreciation of $16,000. Assume two different situations:

1. The company sells the old truck for $17,000 cash.
2. The truck is worthless, so the company simply retires it.

What entry should Overland use to record each scenario?

---

[1]More advanced courses discuss the accounting for exchanges, the third method of plant asset disposal.

Action Plan

- Compare the asset's book value and its fair value to determine whether a gain or loss has occurred.
- Make sure that both the Truck account and Accumulated Depreciation—Truck are reduced upon disposal.

Solution

1. Sale of truck for cash:

Cash	17,000	
Accumulated Depreciation—Truck	16,000	
Truck		30,000
Gain on Disposal [$17,000 − ($30,000 − $16,000)]		3,000
(To record sale of truck at a gain)		

2. Retirement of truck:

Accumulated Depreciation—Truck	16,000	
Loss on Disposal	14,000	
Truck		30,000
(To record retirement of truck at a loss)		

☑ **THE NAVIGATOR**

Analyzing Plant Assets

The presentation of financial statement information about plant assets enables decision makers to analyze the company's use of its plant assets. We will use two measures to analyze plant assets: return on assets ratio, and asset turnover ratio.

STUDY OBJECTIVE
6

Describe methods for evaluating the use of plant assets.

RETURN ON ASSETS RATIO

An overall measure of profitability is the **return on assets ratio**. This ratio is computed by dividing net income by average assets. (Average assets are commonly calculated by adding the beginning and ending values of assets and dividing by 2.) The return on assets ratio indicates the amount of net income generated by each dollar invested in assets. Thus, the higher the return on assets, the more profitable the company.

Information is provided below related to AirTran and Southwest Airlines.

	AirTran (in millions)	Southwest Airlines (in millions)
Net income, 2004	$ 12	$ 313
Net income,* 2003	63	171
Total assets, 12/31/04	906	11,337
Total assets, 12/31/03	808	9,878
Total assets, 12/31/02	473	8,954
Net sales, 2004	1,041	6,530
Net sales, 2003	918	5,937

*In 2003, AirTran received $38 million and Southwest received $271 million in federal grants resulting from the Emergency Wartime Supplemental Appropriations Act. We have excluded these "one-time" sources of income from the net income reported here, to make the amounts more comparable to 2004's reported net income.

Illustration 9-19 (page 438) presents the 2004 and 2003 return on assets of AirTran, Southwest Airlines, and industry averages.

Illustration 9-19 Return on assets ratio

Return on Assets Ratio = $\dfrac{\text{Net Income}}{\text{Average Total Assets}}$		
	2004	**2003**
AirTran ($ in millions)	$\dfrac{\$12}{(\$906 + \$808)/2^*} = 1.4\%$	$\dfrac{\$63}{(\$808 + \$473)/2} = 9.8\%$
Southwest Airlines ($ in millions)	$\dfrac{\$313}{(\$11,337 + \$9,878)/2} = 3.0\%$	$\dfrac{\$171}{(\$9,878 + \$8,954)/2} = 1.8\%$
Industry average	0.65%	

*Amounts in the ratio calculations have been rounded.

Southwest Airline's 2004 return on assets was better than that of AirTran and the airline industry, but its 2003 return was less than AirTran's. The airline industry has experienced financial difficulties in recent years as it attempted to cover high labor, fuel, and security costs while offering fares low enough to attract customers. Such difficulties are reflected in the very low industry average for return on assets and in the volatility of this ratio between years for a single airline.

Accounting across the Organization

Marketing executives now are using the basic finance concept underlying return on assets to determine "marketing return on investment (ROI)." They calculate *marketing ROI* as the profit generated by a marketing initiative divided by the investment in that initiative.

It can be tricky to determine what to include in the "investment" amount and how to attribute profit to a particular marketing initiative. However, many firms feel that measuring marketing ROI is worth the effort because it allows managers to evaluate the relative effectiveness of various programs. In addition, it helps quantify the benefits that marketing provides to the organization. In periods of tight budgets, the marketing ROI number can provide particularly valuable evidence to help a marketing manager avoid budget cuts.

Source: James O. Mitchel, "Marketing ROI," *LIMRA's MarketFacts Quarterly* (Summer 2004), p. 15.

How does measuring marketing ROI support the overall efforts of the organization?

Decision Toolkit

Decision Checkpoints	Info Needed for Decision	Tool to Use for Decision	How to Evaluate Results
Is the company using its assets effectively?	Net income and average assets	Return on assets ratio $= \dfrac{\text{Net income}}{\text{Average total assets}}$	Higher value suggests favorable efficiency (use of assets).

ASSET TURNOVER RATIO

The **asset turnover ratio** indicates how efficiently a company uses its assets— that is, how many dollars of sales a company generates for each dollar invested in assets. It is calculated by dividing net sales by average total assets. When we compare two companies in the same industry, the one with the higher asset turnover ratio is operating more *efficiently:* It is generating more sales per dollar invested in assets.

Illustration 9-20 presents the asset turnover ratios for AirTran and Southwest Airlines for 2004.

Asset Turnover Ratio = $\dfrac{\text{Net Sales}}{\text{Average Total Assets}}$	
AirTran ($ in millions)	**Southwest Airlines** ($ in millions)
$\dfrac{\$1,041}{(\$906 + \$808)/2} = 1.21$ times	$\dfrac{\$6,530}{(\$11,337 + \$9,878)/2} = .62$ times

Illustration 9-20   Asset turnover ratio for 2004

These asset turnover ratios tell us that for each dollar invested in assets, AirTran generates sales of $1.21 and Southwest $0.62. AirTran is more successful in generating sales per dollar invested in assets, perhaps due in part to its decision to purchase older planes. The average asset turnover ratio for the airline industry is .75 times, more in line with Southwest's asset turnover.

Asset turnover ratios vary considerably across industries. The average asset turnover for electric utility companies is .34; the grocery industry has an average asset turnover of 2.89. Asset turnover ratios, therefore, are only comparable within—not between—industries.

PROFIT MARGIN RATIO REVISTED

In Chapter 5 you learned about the profit margin ratio. The profit margin ratio is calculated by dividing net income by net sales. It tells how effective a company is in turning its sales into income—that is, how much income each dollar of sales provides. Illustration 9-21 shows that the return on assets ratio can be computed from the profit margin ratio and the asset turnover ratio.

Illustration 9-21
Composition of return on assets ratio

This relationship has very important strategic implications for management. From Illustration 9-21 we can see that if a company wants to increase its return on assets, it can do so in two ways: (1) by increasing the margin it generates from each dollar of goods that it sells (the profit margin ratio), or (2) by increasing the volume of goods that it sells (the asset turnover). For example, most grocery stores have very low profit margins, often in the range of 1 or 2 cents for every dollar of goods sold. Grocery stores, therefore, focus on asset turnover: They rely on high turnover to increase their return on assets. Alternatively, a store selling luxury goods, such as expensive jewelry, doesn't generally have a high turnover. Consequently, a seller of luxury goods focuses on having a high profit margin. Recently Apple decided to offer a less expensive version of its popular iPod. This new product would provide a lower margin, but higher volume, than Apple's more expensive version.

Let's evaluate the return on assets ratio of Southwest Airlines for 2004 by evaluating its components—the profit margin ratio and the asset turnover ratio. See Illustration 9-22.

Illustration 9-22
Components of Southwest Airlines' rate of return

	Profit Margin	×	Asset Turnover	=	Return on Assets
Southwest Airlines	4.8%	×	.62 times	=	3.0%

Southwest Airlines has a profit margin ratio of 4.8% ($313 ÷ $6,530). Compared to the industry average of 1.72%, this suggests that Southwest has better control of its costs than most in the industry. As noted previously, Southwest's asset turnover is about equal to the industry average. Therefore, it would appear that if Southwest can increase its asset turnover by increasing the amount of sales it generates per dollar invested in planes, it will increase its reputation even further as one of the most profitable companies in the industry.

Decision Toolkit

Decision Checkpoints	Info Needed for Decision	Tool to Use for Decision	How to Evaluate Results
How effective is the company at generating sales from its assets?	Net sales and average total assets	Asset turnover ratio = $\dfrac{\text{Net sales}}{\text{Average total assets}}$	Indicates the sales dollars generated per dollar of assets. A high value suggests the company is effective in using its resources to generate sales.

BEFORE YOU GO ON . . .

▶Review It

1. What is the purpose of the return on assets ratio? How is it calculated?
2. What is the purpose of the asset turnover ratio? How is it computed?
3. What are the two key components that explain the return on assets ratio?

THE NAVIGATOR

SECTION TWO
INTANGIBLE ASSETS

Intangible assets are rights, privileges, and competitive advantages that result from ownership of long-lived assets that do not possess physical substance. Many companies' most valuable assets are intangible. Some widely known intangibles are Microsoft's patents, McDonald's franchises, the trade name iPod, and Nike's trademark "swoosh."

Analysts estimated that in the early 1980s the market value of intangible assets to total assets was close to 40%. By 2000, the percentage was over 80%—quite a difference. What has happened is that research and development (e.g., hi-tech and bio-tech) has grown substantially. At the same time, many companies (e.g., Nike and Gatorade) have developed brand power which enables them to maintain their market position.

As you will learn in this section, financial statements do report numerous intangibles. Yet, many other financially significant intangibles are not reported. To give an example, according to its 2004 financial statements, Microsoft had a net book value of $64.9 billion. But its *market* value—the total market price of all its shares on that same date—was roughly $306 billion. Thus, its actual market value was about $241 billion greater than what its balance sheet said the company was worth. It is not uncommon for a company's reported book value to differ from its market value, because balance sheets are reported at historical cost. But such an extreme difference seriously diminishes the usefulness of the balance sheet to decision makers. In the case of Microsoft, the difference is due to unrecorded intangibles. For many high-tech or so-called intellectual-property companies, most of their value is from intangibles, many of which are not reported under current accounting rules.

Intangibles may be evidenced by contracts, licenses, and other documents. Intangibles may arise from the following sources:

1. Government grants such as patents, copyrights, franchises, trademarks, and trade names.
2. Acquisition of another business in which the purchase price includes a payment for goodwill.
3. Private monopolistic arrangements arising from contractual agreements, such as franchises and leases.

Accounting for Intangible Assets

Companies record intangible assets at cost. Intangibles are categorized as having either a limited life or an indefinite life. If an intangible has a **limited life**, the company allocates its cost over the asset's useful life using a process similar to depreciation. The process of allocating the cost of intangibles is referred to as **amortization**. The cost of intangible assets with **indefinite lives should not be amortized**.

To record amortization of an intangible asset, a company increases (debits) Amortization Expense, and decreases (credits) the specific intangible asset. (Unlike depreciation, no contra account, such as Accumulated Amortization, is usually used.)

Intangible assets are typically amortized on a straight-line basis. For example, the legal life of a patent is 20 years. Companies **amortize the cost of a patent over its 20-year life or its useful life, whichever is shorter.** To illustrate the computation of patent amortization, assume that National Labs purchases a

STUDY OBJECTIVE

7

Identify the basic issues related to reporting intangible assets.

patent at a cost of $60,000. If National estimates the useful life of the patent to be eight years, the annual amortization expense is $7,500 ($60,000 ÷ 8). National records the annual amortization as follows.

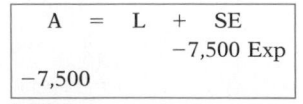

A	=	L	+	SE
				−7,500 Exp
−7,500				

Cash Flows
no effect

Dec. 31	Amortization Expense—Patent	7,500	
	Patent		7,500
	(To record patent amortization)		

When a company has significant intangibles, analysts should evaluate the reasonableness of the useful life estimates. In determining useful life, the company should consider obsolescence, inadequacy, and other factors. These may cause a patent or other intangible to become economically ineffective before the end of its legal life.

For example, suppose Intel obtained a patent on a new computer chip it had developed. The legal life of the patent is 20 years. From experience, however, we know that the useful life of a computer chip patent is rarely more than five years. Because new superior chips are developed so rapidly, existing chips become obsolete. Consequently, we would question the amortization expense of Intel if it amortized its patent on a computer chip for a life significantly longer than a five-year period. Amortizing an intangible over a period that is too long will understate amortization expense, overstate Intel's net income, and overstate its assets.

Decision Toolkit

Decision Checkpoints	Info Needed for Decision	Tool to Use for Decision	How to Evaluate Results
Is the company's amortization of intangibles reasonable?	Estimated useful life of intangibles from notes to financial statements of this company and its competitors	If the company's estimated useful life significantly exceeds that of competitors or does not seem reasonable in light of the circumstances, the reason for the difference should be investigated.	Too high an estimated useful life will result in understating amortization expense and overstating net income.

Types of Intangible Assets

PATENTS

A **patent** is an exclusive right issued by the United States Patent Office that enables the recipient to manufacture, sell, or otherwise control an invention for a period of 20 years from the date of the grant. **The initial cost of a patent is the cash or cash equivalent price paid to acquire the patent.**

The saying "A patent is only as good as the money you're prepared to spend defending it" is very true. Most patents are subject to some type of litigation by competitors. A well-known example is the patent infringement suit brought by Amazon.com against Barnes & Noble.com regarding its online shopping software. If the owner incurs legal costs in successfully defending the patent in an infringement suit, such costs are considered necessary to establish the validity of the patent. Thus, **the owner adds those costs to the Patent account and amortizes them over the remaining life of the patent**.

RESEARCH AND DEVELOPMENT COSTS

Research and development costs are expenditures that may lead to patents, copyrights, new processes, and new products. Many companies spend considerable sums of money on research and development (R&D) in an ongoing effort to develop new products or processes. For example, in a recent year IBM spent over $5.1 billion on research and development. There are uncertainties in identifying the extent and timing of the future benefits of these expenditures. As a result, companies usually record research and development costs **as an expense when incurred**, whether the R&D is successful or not.

To illustrate, assume that Laser Scanner Company spent $3 million on research and development that resulted in two highly successful patents. It spent $20,000 on legal fees for the patents. It can include the legal fees in the cost of the patents, but cannot include the R&D costs in the cost of the patents. Instead, Laser Scanner records the R&D costs as an expense when incurred.

Many disagree with this accounting approach. They argue that to expense these costs leads to understated assets and net income. Others argue that capitalizing these costs would lead to highly speculative assets on the balance sheet. Who is right is difficult to determine.

> **Helpful Hint** Research and development costs are not intangible costs, but because these expenditures may lead to patents and copyrights, we discuss them in this section.

> **International Note**
>
> Many factors, including differences in accounting treatment of R&D, contribute to differences in R&D expenditures across nations.

COPYRIGHTS

The federal government grants **copyrights**, which give the owner the exclusive right to reproduce and sell an artistic or published work. Copyrights last for the life of the creator plus 70 years. The cost of the copyright consists of the **cost of acquiring and defending it**. The cost may be only the $10 fee paid to the U.S. Copyright Office, or it may amount to a great deal more if a copyright infringement suit is involved. The useful life of a copyright generally is significantly shorter than its legal life.

TRADEMARKS AND TRADE NAMES

A **trademark** or **trade name** is a word, phrase, jingle, or symbol that distinguishes or identifies a particular enterprise or product. Trade names like Wheaties, Monopoly, Sunkist, Kleenex, Coca-Cola, Big Mac, and Jeep create immediate product identification and generally enhance the sale of the product. The creator or original user may obtain the exclusive legal right to the trademark or trade name by registering it with the U.S. Patent Office. Such registration provides 20 years' protection and may be renewed indefinitely as long as the trademark or trade name is in use.

If a company purchases the trademark or trade name, the cost is the purchase price. If the company develops the trademark or trade name itself, the cost includes attorney's fees, registration fees, design costs, successful legal defense costs, and other expenditures directly related to securing it. Because trademarks and trade names have indefinite lives, they are not amortized.

FRANCHISES AND LICENSES

When you drive down the street in your RAV4 purchased from a Toyota dealer, fill up your tank at the corner Shell station, eat lunch at Wendy's, or make plans to vacation at a Marriott resort, you are dealing with franchises. A **franchise** is a contractual arrangement under which the franchisor grants the franchisee the right to sell certain products, to provide specific services, or to use certain trademarks or trade names, usually within a designated geographic area.

Another type of franchise, granted by a governmental body, permits the enterprise to use public property in performing its services. Examples are the use of city streets for a bus line or taxi service; the use of public land for telephone, electric, and cable television lines; and the use of airwaves for radio or TV broadcasting. Such operating rights are referred to as **licenses**.

Franchises and licenses may be granted for a definite period of time, an indefinite period, or perpetual. **When a company can identify costs with the acquisition of the franchise or license, it should recognize an intangible asset.** Companies record as **operating expenses** annual payments made under a franchise agreement in the period in which they are incurred. In the case of a limited life, a company amortizes the cost of a franchise (or license) as operating expense over the useful life. If the life is indefinite or perpetual, the cost is not amortized.

Accounting across the Organization

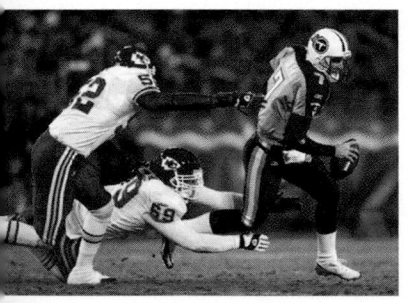

What is a well-known franchise worth? Recently ESPN outbid its rivals for the right to broadcast Monday Night Football. At a price of $1.1 billion per year—nearly twice what rival ABC paid in previous years—it isn't clear who won and who lost.

When bidding for a unique franchise like Monday Night Football, management must consider many factors to determine a price. As part of the deal, ESPN also got wireless rights and Spanish-language telecasts. By its estimation, ESPN will generate a profit of $200 million per year from Monday Night Football. ABC was losing $150 million per year.

Another factor in the decision was ESPN management's concern that if ESPN didn't win the bid, a buyer would emerge that would use Monday Night Football as a launching pad for a new sports network. ESPN doesn't want any more competitors than it already has. It is hard to put a price tag on the value of keeping the competition to a minimum.

Source: Ronald Grover and Tom Lowry, "A Ball ESPN Couldn't Afford to Drop," *BusinessWeek* (May 2, 2005), p. 42.

 How should ESPN account for the $1.1 billion per year franchise fee?

GOODWILL

Usually the largest intangible asset that appears on a company's balance sheet is goodwill. **Goodwill** represents the value of all favorable attributes that relate to a business enterprise. These include exceptional management, desirable location, good customer relations, skilled employees, high-quality products, fair pricing policies, and harmonious relations with labor unions. Goodwill is unique because unlike other assets such as investments, plant assets, and even other intangibles, which can be sold *individually* in the marketplace, goodwill can be identified only with the business *as a whole*.

If goodwill can be identified only with the business as a whole, how can it be determined? Certainly, many business enterprises have many of the factors cited above (exceptional management, desirable location, and so on). However, to determine the amount of goodwill in these situations would be difficult and very subjective. In other words, to recognize goodwill without an exchange transaction that puts a value on the goodwill would lead to subjective valuations that do not contribute to the reliability of financial statements. **Therefore, companies record goodwill only when there is an exchange transaction that involves the purchase of an entire business. When an entire business is purchased, goodwill is the excess of cost over the fair market value of the net assets (assets less liabilities) acquired.**

In recording the purchase of a business, a company debits the net assets at their fair market values, credits cash for the purchase price, and records the difference as the cost of goodwill. Goodwill is not amortized because it is considered to have an indefinite life. However, it must be written down if a company determines the value of goodwill has been permanently impaired.

Financial Statement Presentation of Long-Lived Assets

BALANCE SHEET PRESENTATION

Usually companies show plant assets in the financial statements under "Property, plant, and equipment," and they show intangibles separately under "Intangible assets." Illustration 9-23 shows a typical balance sheet presentation of long-lived assets, adapted from The Coca-Cola Company's 2004 balance sheet.

Intangibles do not usually use a contra asset account like the contra asset account Accumulated Depreciation used for plant assets. Instead, companies record amortization of intangibles as a direct decrease (credit) to the asset account.

STUDY OBJECTIVE
8
Indicate how long-lived assets are reported on the balance sheet.

The Coca-Cola Company

THE COCA-COLA COMPANY	
Balance Sheet (partial)	
(in millions)	
Property, plant, and equipment	
Land	$ 479
Buildings and improvements	2,853
Machinery and equipment	6,337
Containers	480
	10,149
Less: Accumulated depreciation	4,058
	6,091
Trademarks and other intangible assets	3,836
Total	$ 9,927

Illustration 9-23
Presentation of property, plant, and equipment and intangible assets

Either within the balance sheet or in the notes, companies should disclose the balances of the major classes of assets, such as land, buildings, and equipment, and of accumulated depreciation by major classes or in total. In addition, they should describe the depreciation and amortization methods used and disclose the amount of depreciation and amortization expense for the period.

STATEMENT OF CASH FLOWS PRESENTATION

It is also interesting to examine the statement of cash flows to determine the amount of property, plant, and equipment a company purchased and the cash it received from property, plant, and equipment sold in a given year. For example, the investing activities section of Coca-Cola reports the following.

Illustration 9-24
Purchases and dispositions of property, plant, and equipment

The Coca-Cola Company

THE COCA-COLA COMPANY
Statement of Cash Flows (partial)
(in millions)

Cash flow from investing activities	
Purchases of property, plant, and equipment	$(755)
Proceeds from disposals of property, plant, and equipment	341

As indicated, Coca-Cola made significant investments in property, plant, and equipment which should be viewed positively given the company's overall profitability. The level of investment suggests that Coca-Cola believes that it can earn a reasonable rate of return on these assets.

BEFORE YOU GO ON . . .

▶Review It

1. Identify the major types of intangible assets and the proper accounting for them.
2. Explain the accounting for research and development costs.
3. How are intangible assets presented on the balance sheet?

✓ THE NAVIGATOR

Using the Decision Toolkit

JetBlue Airways Corporation is a low-cost airline operating primarily out of New York. It operates 280 flights to 30 destinations daily. Although it has operated for only five years, it is now the tenth largest U.S. airline based on total passenger miles. It currently operates 70 planes, and expects to add more than 350 planes over the next 11 years. While the major airlines suffer, JetBlue appears to have found a formula for success.

Instructions

Review the excerpts from the company's 2004 annual report that follow and then answer the following questions.

1. What method does the company use to depreciate its aircraft? Over what period is the company depreciating these aircraft?

2. What type of intangible assets does the company have, and how are they being accounted for?

3. Compute the company's return on assets ratio, asset turnover ratio, and profit margin ratio for 2003 and 2004. Comment on your results.

(in thousands)	2004	2003
Net income	$47	$104
Net sales	$1,266	$998
Beginning total assets	$2,186	$1,379
Ending total assets	$2,799	$2,186

JETBLUE AIRWAYS CORPORATION
Notes to the Financial Statements

Property and Equipment: We record our property and equipment at cost and depreciate these assets on a straight-line basis to their estimated residual values over their estimated useful lives. Additions, modifications that enhance the operating performance of our assets, and interest related to predelivery deposits to acquire new aircraft and for the construction of facilities are capitalized.

Estimated useful lives and residual values for our property and equipment are as follows:

	Estimated Useful Life	**Residual Value**
Aircraft	25 years	20%
In-flight entertainment systems	12 years	0%
Aircraft parts	Fleet life	10%
Flight equipment leasehold improvements	Lease term	0%
Ground property and equipment	3–10 years	0%
Leasehold improvements	15 years or lease term	0%

We record impairment losses on long-lived assets used in operations when events and circumstances indicate that the assets may be impaired and the undiscounted future cash flows estimated to be generated by these assets are less than the assets' net book value. If impairment occurs, the loss is measured by comparing the fair value of the asset to its carrying amount.

Note 5—LiveTV Purchased technology, which is an intangible asset related to our September 2002 acquisition of the membership interests of LiveTV, is being amortized over six years based on the average number of aircraft expected to be in service as of the date of acquisition. Projected amortization expense is $10.9 million in 2005, $13.1 million in 2006, $15.5 million in 2007 and $14.7 million in 2008.

Solution

1. The company depreciates property and equipment using the straight-line approach. It depreciates aircraft over a 25-year life.
2. The company has an intangible asset called "purchased technology" related to its purchase of membership interests in "LiveTV." It amortizes this intangible asset based on the company's estimate of the average number of aircraft expected to be in service over a six-year period from 2003 through 2008.
3.

	2004	**2003**
Return on assets	$\dfrac{\$47}{(\$2,799 + \$2,186)/2} = 1.9\%$	$\dfrac{\$104}{(\$2,186 + \$1,379)/2} = 5.8\%$
Asset turnover	$\dfrac{\$1,266}{(\$2,799 + \$2,186)/2} = .51$ times	$\dfrac{\$998}{(\$2,186 + \$1,379)/2} = .56$ times
Profit margin	$\dfrac{\$47}{\$1,266} = 3.7\%$	$\dfrac{\$104}{\$998} = 10.4\%$

JetBlue's return on assets ratio declined from 5.8% in 2003 to 1.9% in 2004. This means that the company was earning less net income per dollar of assets in 2004 than it did in 2003. This decline was the result of two factors. First, as shown by the asset turnover ratio, the company was not generating as many sales per dollar of assets. Its asset turnover ratio declined from .56 times to .51 times. Second, the company's ability to generate net income from its sales declined, as evidenced by its profit margin decline from 10.4% to 3.7%.

Summary of Study Objectives

1 *Describe how the cost principle applies to plant assets.* The cost of plant assets includes all expenditures necessary to acquire the asset and make it ready for its intended use. Cost is measured by the cash or cash equivalent price paid.

2 *Explain the concept of depreciation.* Depreciation is the process of allocating to expense the cost of a plant asset over its useful (service) life in a rational and systematic manner. Depreciation is not a process of valuation, and it is not a process that results in an accumulation of cash. Depreciation reflects an asset's decreasing usefulness and revenue-producing ability, resulting from wear and tear and from obsolescence.

3 *Compute periodic depreciation using the straight-line method, and contrast its expense pattern with those of other methods.* The formula for straight-line depreciation is:

$$\frac{\text{Cost} - \text{Salvage value}}{\text{Useful life (in years)}}$$

The expense patterns of the three depreciation methods are as follows.

Method	Annual Depreciation Pattern
Straight-line	Constant amount
Declining-balance	Decreasing amount
Units-of-activity	Varying amount

4 *Describe the procedure for revising periodic depreciation.* Companies make revisions of periodic depreciation in present and future periods, not retroactively.

5 *Explain how to account for the disposal of plant assets.* The procedure for accounting for the disposal of a plant asset through sale or retirement is: (a) Eliminate the book value of the plant asset at the date of disposal. (b) Record cash proceeds, if any. (c) Account for the difference between the book value and the cash proceeds as a gain or a loss on disposal.

6 *Describe methods for evaluating the use of plant assets.* Plant assets may be analyzed using the return on assets ratio and the asset turnover ratio. The return on assets ratio consists of two components: the asset turnover ratio and the profit margin ratio.

7 *Identify the basic issues related to reporting intangible assets.* Companies report intangible assets at their cost less any amounts amortized. If an intangible asset has a limited life, its cost should be allocated over its useful life. Intangible assets with indefinite lives should not be amortized.

8 *Indicate how long-lived assets are reported on the balance sheet.* Companies usually show plant assets under "Property, plant, and equipment"; they show intangibles separately under "Intangible assets." Either within the balance sheet or in the notes, companies disclose the balances of the major classes of assets, such as land, buildings, and equipment, and accumulated depreciation by major classes or in total. They describe the depreciation and amortization methods used, and disclose the amount of depreciation and amortization expense for the period.

THE NAVIGATOR

Decision Toolkit—A Summary

Decision Checkpoints	Info Needed for Decision	Tool to Use for Decision	How to Evaluate Results
Is the company using its assets effectively?	Net income and average assets	$\text{Return on assets ratio} = \dfrac{\text{Net income}}{\text{Average total assets}}$	Higher value suggests favorable efficiency (use of assets).
How effective is the company at generating sales from its assets?	Net sales and average total assets	$\text{Asset turnover ratio} = \dfrac{\text{Net sales}}{\text{Average total assets}}$	Indicates the sales dollars generated per dollar of assets. A high value suggests the company is effective in using its resources to generate sales.
Is the company's amortization of intangibles reasonable?	Estimated useful life of intangibles from notes to financial statements of this company and its competitors	If the company's estimated useful life significantly exceeds that of competitors or does not seem reasonable in light of the circumstances, the reason for the difference should be investigated.	Too high an estimated useful life will result in understating amortization expense and overstating net income.

APPENDIX
CALCULATION OF DEPRECIATION USING OTHER METHODS

In this appendix we show the calculations of the depreciation expense amounts that we used in the chapter for the declining-balance and units-of-activity methods.

STUDY OBJECTIVE
9
Compute periodic depreciation using the declining-balance method and the units-of-activity method.

Declining-Balance

The **declining-balance method** produces a decreasing annual depreciation expense over the useful life of the asset. The method is so named because the computation of periodic depreciation is based on a **declining book value** (cost less accumulated depreciation) of the asset. Annual depreciation expense is computed by multiplying the book value at the beginning of the year by the declining-balance depreciation rate. **The depreciation rate remains constant from year to year, but the book value to which the rate is applied declines each year.**

Book value for the first year is the cost of the asset because the balance in accumulated depreciation at the beginning of the asset's useful life is zero. In subsequent years, book value is the difference between cost and accumulated depreciation at the beginning of the year. **Unlike other depreciation methods, the declining-balance method ignores salvage value in determining the amount to which the declining-balance rate is applied.** Salvage value, however, does limit the total depreciation that can be taken. Depreciation stops when the asset's book value equals its expected salvage value.

As noted in the chapter, a common declining-balance rate is double the straight-line rate—the **double-declining-balance method**. If Bill's Pizzas uses the double-declining-balance method, the depreciation rate is 40% (2 × the straight-line rate of 20%). Illustration 9A-1 presents the formula and computation of depreciation for the first year on the delivery truck.

Helpful Hint The straight-line rate is approximated as 1 ÷ Estimated life. In this case it is 1 ÷ 5 = 20%.

Book Value at Beginning of Year	×	Declining-Balance Rate	=	Depreciation Expense
$13,000	×	40%	=	$5,200

Illustration 9A-1 Formula for declining-balance method

Illustration 9A-2 presents the depreciation schedule under this method.

BILL'S PIZZAS

Year	Book Value Beginning of Year	×	Depreciation Rate	=	Annual Depreciation Expense	Accumulated Depreciation	Book Value
2007	$13,000		40%		**$5,200**	$ 5,200	$ 7,800*
2008	7,800		40		**3,120**	8,320	4,680
2009	4,680		40		**1,872**	10,192	2,808
2010	2,808		40		**1,123**	11,315	1,685
2011	1,685		40		**685****	12,000	**1,000**

*$13,000 − $5,200
**Computation of $674 ($1,685 × 40%) is adjusted to $685 in order for book value to equal salvage value.

Illustration 9A-2 Double-declining-balance depreciation schedule

Helpful Hint Depreciation stops when the asset's book value equals its expected salvage value.

The delivery equipment is 69% depreciated ($8,320 ÷ $12,000) at the end of the second year. Under the straight-line method it would be depreciated 40% ($4,800 ÷ $12,000) at that time. Because the declining-balance method produces higher depreciation expense in the early years than in the later years, it is considered an **accelerated-depreciation method**.

The declining-balance method is compatible with the matching principle. It matches the higher depreciation expense in early years with the higher benefits received in these years. Conversely, it recognizes lower depreciation expense in later years when the asset's contribution to revenue is less. Also, some assets lose their usefulness rapidly because of obsolescence. In these cases, the declining-balance method provides a more appropriate depreciation amount.

When an asset is purchased during the year, it is necessary to prorate the declining-balance depreciation in the first year on a time basis. For example, if Bill's Pizzas had purchased the delivery equipment on April 1, 2007, depreciation for 2007 would be $3,900 ($13,000 × 40% × $\frac{9}{12}$). The book value for computing depreciation in 2008 then becomes $9,100 ($13,000 − $3,900), and the 2008 depreciation is $3,640 ($9,100 × 40%).

Units-of-Activity

Alternative Terminology
Another term often used is the *units-of-production method.*

Under the **units-of-activity method**, useful life is expressed in terms of the total units of production or use expected from the asset. The units-of-activity method is ideally suited to equipment whose activity can be measured in units of output, miles driven, or hours in use. The units-of-activity method is generally not suitable for assets for which depreciation is a function more of time than of use.

To use this method, a company estimates the total units of activity for the entire useful life and divides that amount into the depreciable cost to determine the depreciation cost per unit. It then multiplies the depreciation cost per unit by the units of activity during the year to find the annual depreciation for that year.

To illustrate, assume that Bill's Pizzas estimates it will drive its new delivery truck 15,000 miles in the first year. Illustration 9A-3 presents the formula and computation of depreciation expense in the first year.

Illustration 9A-3
Formula for units-of-activity method

Depreciable Cost	÷	Total Units of Activity	=	Depreciation Cost per Unit
$12,000	÷	100,000 miles	=	$0.12

Depreciation Cost per Unit	×	Units of Activity during the Year	=	Depreciation Expense
$0.12	×	15,000 miles	=	$1,800

Illustration 9A-4 shows the depreciation schedule, using assumed mileage data.

BILL'S PIZZAS					
	Computation		Annual	End of Year	
Year	Units of Activity ×	Depreciation Cost/Unit =	Depreciation Expense	Accumulated Depreciation	Book Value
2007	15,000	$0.12	$1,800	$ 1,800	$11,200*
2008	30,000	0.12	3,600	5,400	7,600
2009	20,000	0.12	2,400	7,800	5,200
2010	25,000	0.12	3,000	10,800	2,200
2011	10,000	0.12	1,200	12,000	1,000
*$13,000 − $1,800					

Illustration 9A-4
Units-of-activity depreciation schedule

Helpful Hint Depreciation stops when the asset's book value equals its expected salvage value.

The units-of-activity method is not nearly as popular as the straight-line method, primarily because it is often difficult to make a reasonable estimate of total activity. However, this method is used by some very large companies, such as Standard Oil Company of California and Boise Cascade Corporation. When the productivity of the asset varies significantly from one period to another, the units-of-activity method results in the best matching of expenses with revenues.

This method is easy to apply when assets are purchased during the year. In such a case, companies use the productivity of the asset for the partial year in computing the depreciation.

Summary of Study Objective for Appendix

9 *Compute periodic depreciation using the declining-balance method and the units-of-activity method.* The depreciation expense calculation for each of these methods is:

Declining-balance:

$$\text{Book value at beginning of year} \times \text{Declining-balance rate} = \text{Depreciation expense}$$

Units-of-activity:

$$\text{Depreciable cost} \div \text{Total units of activity} = \text{Depreciation cost per unit}$$

$$\text{Depreciation cost per unit} \times \text{Units of activity during year} = \text{Depreciation expense}$$

Glossary

Accelerated-depreciation method A depreciation method that produces higher depreciation expense in the early years than the straight-line approach. (p. 429)

Additions and improvements Costs incurred to increase the operating efficiency, productive capacity, or expected useful life of a plant asset. (p. 433)

Amortization The process of allocating to expense the cost of an intangible asset. (p. 441)

Asset turnover ratio Indicates how efficiently a company uses its assets; calculated as net sales divided by average total assets. (p. 439)

Capital expenditures Expenditures that increase the company's investment in plant assets. (p. 421)

Capital lease A long-term agreement allowing one party (the lessee) to use another party's asset (the lessor); accounted for like a purchase. (p. 425)

Cash equivalent price An amount equal to the fair market value of the asset given up or the fair market value of the asset received, whichever is more clearly determinable. (p. 422)

Copyright An exclusive right granted by the federal government allowing the owner to reproduce and sell an artistic or published work. (p. 443)

Declining-balance method A depreciation method that applies a constant rate to the declining book value of the asset and produces a decreasing annual depreciation expense over the useful life of the asset. (pp. 429, 449)

Depreciable cost   The cost of a plant asset less its salvage value. (p. 428)

Depreciation   The process of allocating to expense the cost of a plant asset over its useful life in a rational and systematic manner. (p. 426)

Franchise   A contractual arrangement under which the franchisor grants the franchisee the right to sell certain products, to render specific services, or to use certain trademarks or trade names, usually within a designated geographic area. (p. 443)

Goodwill   The value of all favorable attributes that relate to a business enterprise. (p. 444)

Impairment   A permanent decline in the market value of an asset. (p. 434)

Intangible assets   Rights, privileges, and competitive advantages that result from the ownership of long-lived assets that do not possess physical substance. (p. 441)

Lessee   A party that has made contractual arrangements to use another party's asset without purchasing it. (p. 424)

Lessor   A party that has agreed contractually to let another party use its asset. (p. 424)

Licenses   Operating rights to use public property, granted by a governmental agency to a business enterprise. (p. 444)

Operating lease   An arrangement allowing one party (the lessee) to use the asset of another party (the lessor); accounted for as a rental. (p. 425)

Ordinary repairs   Expenditures to maintain the operating efficiency and expected productive life of the asset. (p. 433)

Patent   An exclusive right issued by the U.S. Patent Office that enables the recipient to manufacture, sell, or otherwise control an invention for a period of 20 years from the date of the grant. (p. 442)

Plant assets   Tangible resources that have physical substance, are used in the operations of the business, and are not intended for sale to customers. (p. 420)

Research and development costs   Expenditures that may lead to patents, copyrights, new processes, and new products. (p. 443)

Return on assets ratio   A profitability measure that indicates the amount of net income generated by each dollar invested in assets; computed as net income divided by average assets. (p. 437)

Revenue expenditures   Expenditures that are immediately charged against revenues as an expense. (p. 421)

Straight-line method   A method in which periodic depreciation is the same for each year of the asset's useful life. (p. 428)

Trademark (trade name)   A word, phrase, jingle, or symbol that distinguishes or identifies a particular enterprise or product. (p. 443)

Units-of-activity method   A depreciation method in which useful life is expressed in terms of the total units of production or use expected from the asset. (pp. 430, 450)

Demonstration Problem 1

DuPage Company purchased a factory machine at a cost of $18,000 on January 1, 2007. DuPage expected the machine to have a salvage value of $2,000 at the end of its 4-year useful life.

Instructions
Prepare a depreciation schedule using the straight-line method.

Action Plan
- Under the straight-line method, apply the depreciation rate to depreciable cost.

Solution to Demonstration Problem

DUPAGE COMPANY
Depreciation Schedule—Straight-Line Method

| | Computation | | | Annual | End of Year | |
| | Depreciable | | Depreciation | Depreciation | Accumulated | Book |
Year	Cost (a)	×	Rate (b) =	Expense	Depreciation	Value (c)
2007	$16,000		25%	$4,000	$ 4,000	$14,000
2008	16,000		25	4,000	8,000	10,000
2009	16,000		25	4,000	12,000	6,000
2010	16,000		25	4,000	16,000	2,000

(a) $18,000 − $2,000   (b) $\frac{1}{4} = 25\%$ (c) Cost less accumulated depreciation.

Demonstration Problem 2

On January 1, 2004, Skyline Limousine Co. purchased a limousine at an acquisition cost of $28,000. Skyline depreciated the vehicle by the straight-line method using a 4-year service life and a $4,000 salvage value. The company's fiscal year ends on December 31.

Instructions
Prepare the journal entry or entries to record the disposal of the limousine assuming that it was:
(a) Retired and scrapped with no salvage value on January 1, 2008.
(b) Sold for $5,000 on July 1, 2007.

Solution to Demonstration Problem

(a) Jan. 1, 2008	Accumulated Depreciation—Limousine	24,000	
	Loss on Disposal	4,000	
	Limousine		28,000
	(To record retirement of limousine)		
(b) July 1, 2007	Depreciation Expense	3,000	
	Accumulated Depreciation—Limousine		3,000
	(To record depreciation to date of disposal)		
	Cash	5,000	
	Accumulated Depreciation—Limousine	21,000	
	Loss on Disposal	2,000	
	Limousine		28,000
	(To record sale of limousine)		

Action Plan
• Calculate accumulated depreciation (depreciation expense per year × years in use).
• At the time of disposal, determine the book value of the asset.
• Recognize any gain or loss from disposal of the asset.

Note: All Questions, Exercises, and Problems marked with an asterisk relate to material in the appendix to the chapter.

Self-Study Questions

Answers are at the end of the chapter.

(SO 1) **1.** Corrieten Company purchased equipment and incurred these costs:

Cash price	$24,000
Sales taxes	1,200
Insurance during transit	200
Installation and testing	400
Total costs	$25,800

What amount should be recorded as the cost of the equipment?
(a) $24,000.   (c) $25,400.
(b) $25,200.   (d) $25,800.

(SO 1) **2.** 🔧 Harrington Corporation recently leased a number of trucks from Andre Corporation. In inspecting the books of Harrington Corporation, you notice that the trucks have not been recorded as assets on its balance sheet. From this you can conclude that Harrington is accounting for this transaction as a/an:
(a) operating lease.   (c) purchase.
(b) capital lease.   (d) None of the above.

3. Depreciation is a process of: (SO 2)
(a) valuation.   (c) cash accumulation.
(b) cost allocation.   (d) appraisal.

4. Cuso Company purchased equipment on January   (SO 3)
1, 2006, at a total invoice cost of $400,000. The equipment has an estimated salvage value of $10,000 and an estimated useful life of 5 years. What is the amount of accumulated depreciation at December 31, 2007, if the straight-line method of depreciation is used?
(a) $80,000.   (c) $78,000.
(b) $160,000.   (d) $156,000.

5. 🔧 A company would minimize its de-   (SO 3)
preciation expense in the first year of owning an asset if it used:
(a) a high estimated life, a high salvage value, and declining-balance depreciation.
(b) a low estimated life, a high salvage value, and straight-line depreciation.
(c) a high estimated life, a high salvage value, and straight-line depreciation.
(d) a low estimated life, a low salvage value, and declining-balance depreciation.

(SO 4)   **6.** When there is a change in estimated depreciation:
  (a) previous depreciation should be corrected.
  (b) current and future years' depreciation should be revised.
  (c) only future years' depreciation should be revised.
  (d) None of the above.

(SO 5)   **7.** Additions to plant assets:
  (a) are revenue expenditures.
  (b) increase a Repair Expense account.
  (c) increase a Purchases account.
  (d) are capital expenditures.

(SO 6)   **8.** Which of the following measures provides an indication of how efficient a company is in employing its assets?
  (a) Current ratio.
  (b) Profit margin ratio.
  (c) Debt to total assets ratio.
  (d) Asset turnover ratio.

(SO 7)   **9.** Pierce Company incurred $150,000 of research and development costs in its laboratory to develop a new product. It spent $20,000 in legal fees for a patent granted on January 2, 2007. On July 31, 2007, Pierce paid $15,000 for legal fees in a successful defense of the patent. What is the total amount that should be debited to Patents through July 31, 2007?
  (a) $150,000.   (c) $185,000.
  (b) $35,000.   (d) Some other amount.

(SO 7, 8)   **10.** Indicate which one of these statements is *true*.
  (a) Since intangible assets lack physical substance, they need to be disclosed only in the notes to the financial statements.
  (b) Goodwill should be reported as a contra account in the stockholders' equity section.
  (c) Totals of major classes of assets can be shown in the balance sheet, with asset

details disclosed in the notes to the financial statements.
  (d) Intangible assets are typically combined with plant assets and natural resources and then shown in the property, plant, and equipment section.

(SO 7)   **11.** If a company reports goodwill as an intangible asset on its books, what is the one thing you know with certainty?
  (a) The company is a valuable company worth investing in.
  (b) The company has a well-established brand name.
  (c) The company purchased another company.
  (d) The goodwill will generate a lot of positive business for the company for many years to come.

(SO 9)   ***12.** Kant Enterprises purchased a truck for $11,000 on January 1, 2006. The truck will have an estimated salvage value of $1,000 at the end of 5 years. If you use the units-of-activity method, the balance in accumulated depreciation at December 31, 2007, can be computed by the following formula:
  (a) ($11,000 ÷ Total estimated activity) × Units of activity for 2007.
  (b) ($10,000 ÷ Total estimated activity) × Units of activity for 2007.
  (c) ($11,000 ÷ Total estimated activity) × Units of activity for 2006 and 2007.
  (d) ($10,000 ÷ Total estimated activity) × Units of activity for 2006 and 2007.

Go to the book's website, **www.wiley.com/college/kimmel**, to access additional Self-Study Questions.

Questions

1. Mrs. Whistler is uncertain about how the cost principle applies to plant assets. Explain the principle to Mrs. Whistler.

2. How is the cost for a plant asset measured in a cash transaction? In a noncash transaction?

3. What are the primary advantages of leasing?

4. HaiFat Company acquires the land and building owned by Benz Company. What types of costs may be incurred to make the asset ready for its intended use if HaiFat Company wants to use only the land? If it wants to use both the land and the building?

5. ➡   Stellar Inc. needs to upgrade its diagnostic equipment. At the time of purchase, Stellar had expected the equipment to last 8 years. Unfortunately, it was

obsolete after only 4 years. Randy Waters, CFO of Stellar Inc., is considering leasing new equipment rather than buying it. What are the potential benefits of leasing?

6. In a recent newspaper release, the president of Heller Company asserted that something has to be done about depreciation. The president said, "Depreciation does not come close to accumulating the cash needed to replace the asset at the end of its useful life." What is your response to the president?

7. Daria is studying for the next accounting examination. She asks your help on two questions: (a) What is salvage value? (b) How is salvage value used in determining depreciable cost under the straight-line method? Answer Daria's questions.

8. Contrast the straight-line method and the units-of-activity method in relation to (a) useful life and (b) the pattern of periodic depreciation over useful life.

9. Contrast the effects of the three depreciation methods on annual depreciation expense.

10. In the fourth year of an asset's 5-year useful life, the company decides that the asset will have a 6-year service life. How should the revision of depreciation be recorded? Why?

11. Distinguish between revenue expenditures and capital expenditures during an asset's useful life.

12. How is a gain or a loss on the sale of a plant asset computed?

13. LaBelle Corporation owns a machine that is fully depreciated but is still being used. How should LaBelle account for this asset and report it in the financial statements?

14. What are the similarities and differences between depreciation and amortization?

15. During a recent management meeting, Roger Bees, director of marketing, proposed that the company should begin capitalizing its marketing expenditures as goodwill. In his words, "Marketing expenditures create goodwill for the company which benefits the company for multiple periods. Therefore it doesn't make good sense to have to expense it as it is incurred. Besides, if we capitalize it as goodwill we won't have to amortize it, and this will boost reported income." Discuss the merits of Roger's proposal.

16. Omega Company hires an accounting intern who says that intangible assets should always be amortized over their legal lives. Is the intern correct? Explain.

17. Goodwill has been defined as the value of all favorable attributes that relate to a business enterprise. What types of attributes could result in goodwill?

18. Susan Day, a business major, is working on a case problem for one of her classes. In this case problem, the company needs to raise cash to market a new product it developed. Anthony Capp, an engineering major, takes one look at the company's balance sheet and says, "This company has an awful lot of goodwill. Why don't you recommend that they sell some of it to raise cash?" How should Susan respond to Anthony?

19. Under what conditions is goodwill recorded? What is the proper accounting treatment for amortizing goodwill?

20. Often research and development costs provide companies with benefits that last a number of years. (For example, these costs can lead to the development of a patent that will increase the company's income for many years.) However, generally accepted accounting principles require that such costs be recorded as an expense when incurred. Why?

21. In 2004 Campbell Soup Company reported average total assets of $6,440 million, net sales of $7,109 million, and net income of $647 million. What was Campbell Soup's return on assets ratio?

22. Stacy Simmons, a marketing executive for Fresh Views Inc., has proposed expanding its product line of framed graphic art by producing a line of lower-quality products. These would require less processing by the company and would provide a lower profit margin. Terry Concord, the company's CFO, is concerned that this new product line would reduce the company's return on assets. Discuss the potential effect on return on assets that this product might have.

23. Give an example of an industry that would be characterized by (a) a high asset turnover ratio and a low profit margin ratio, and (b) a low asset turnover ratio and a high profit margin ratio.

24. Caitlin Corporation and Samantha Corporation both operate in the same industry. Caitlin uses the straight-line method to account for depreciation, whereas Samantha uses an accelerated method. Explain what complications might arise in trying to compare the results of these two companies.

25. Rocky Corporation uses straight-line depreciation for financial reporting purposes but an accelerated method for tax purposes. Is it acceptable to use different methods for the two purposes? What is Rocky Corporation's motivation for doing this?

26. You are comparing two companies in the same industry. You have determined that Leno Corp. depreciates its plant assets over a 40-year life, whereas Letterman Corp. depreciates its plant assets over a 20-year life. Discuss the implications this has for comparing the results of the two companies.

Brief Exercises

BE9-1   These expenditures were incurred by Gerald Ford Company in purchasing land: cash price $50,000; accrued taxes $5,000; attorney's fees $2,100; real estate broker's commission $2,800; and clearing and grading $3,500. What is the cost of the land?

Determine the cost of land.
(SO 1)

BE9-2   HeFlin Company incurs these expenditures in purchasing a truck: cash price $18,000; accident insurance (during use) $2,000; sales taxes $1,080; motor vehicle license $300; and painting and lettering $1,200. What is the cost of the truck?

Determine the cost of a truck.
(SO 1)

Compute straight-line depreciation.
(SO 3)

BE9-3 Apex Chemicals Company acquires a delivery truck at a cost of $26,000 on January 1, 2007. The truck is expected to have a salvage value of $4,000 at the end of its 5-year useful life. Compute annual depreciation for the first and second years using the straight-line method.

Compute revised depreciation.
(SO 4)

BE9-4 On January 1, 2007, the Ewing Company ledger shows Equipment $32,000 and Accumulated Depreciation $14,000. The depreciation resulted from using the straight-line method with a useful life of 10 years and a salvage value of $2,000. On this date the company concludes that the equipment has a remaining useful life of only 2 years with the same salvage value. Compute the revised annual depreciation.

Journalize entries for disposal of plant assets.
(SO 5)

BE9-5 Prepare journal entries to record these transactions: (a) Blaska Company retires its delivery equipment, which cost $41,000. Accumulated depreciation is also $41,000 on this delivery equipment. No salvage value is received. (b) Assume the same information as in part (a), except that accumulated depreciation for Blaska Company is $36,800 instead of $41,000.

Journalize entries for sale of plant assets.
(SO 5)

BE9-6 Carlton Company sells office equipment on September 30, 2007, for $21,000 cash. The office equipment originally cost $72,000 and as of January 1, 2007, had accumulated depreciation of $42,000. Depreciation for the first 9 months of 2007 is $7,500. Prepare the journal entries to (a) update depreciation to September 30, 2007, and (b) record the sale of the equipment.

Account for intangibles— patents.
(SO 7)

BE9-7 Jazz Company purchases a patent for $180,000 on January 2, 2007. Its estimated useful life is 5 years.
(a) Prepare the journal entry to record amortization expense for the first year.
(b) Show how this patent is reported on the balance sheet at the end of the first year.

Compute return on assets ratio and asset turnover ratio.
(SO 6)

BE9-8 In its 2004 annual report, McDonald's Corporation reports beginning total assets of $25.5 billion; ending total assets of $27.8 billion; net sales of $19.1 billion, and net income of $2.3 billion.
(a) Compute McDonald's return on assets ratio.
(b) Compute McDonald's asset turnover ratio.

Classification of long-lived assets on balance sheet.
(SO 8)

BE9-9 Nike, Inc. reported the following plant assets and intangible assets for the year ended May 31, 2004 (in millions): other plant assets $530.6; land $179.5; patents and trademarks (at cost) $400.5; machinery and equipment $1,608.6; buildings $813.6; goodwill (at cost) $135.4; accumulated amortization $34.2; accumulated depreciation $1,545.4. Prepare a partial balance sheet for Nike for these items.

Compute declining-balance depreciation.
(SO 9)

*BE9-10 Depreciation information for Apex Chemicals Company is given in BE9-3. Assuming the declining-balance depreciation rate is double the straight-line rate, compute annual depreciation for the first and second years under the declining-balance method.

Compute depreciation using units-of-activity method.
(SO 9)

*BE9-11 Pack in Taxi Service uses the units-of-activity method in computing depreciation on its taxicabs. Each cab is expected to be driven 150,000 miles. Taxi 10 cost $24,500 and is expected to have a salvage value of $500. Taxi 10 was driven 28,000 miles in 2006 and 30,000 miles in 2007. Compute the depreciation for each year.

Exercises

WILEY
PLUS

Determine cost of plant acquisitions.
(SO 1)

E9-1 The following expenditures relating to plant assets were made by Bel Air Company during the first 2 months of 2007.
1. Paid $7,000 of accrued taxes at the time the plant site was acquired.
2. Paid $200 insurance to cover a possible accident loss on new factory machinery while the machinery was in transit.
3. Paid $850 sales taxes on a new delivery truck.
4. Paid $21,000 for parking lots and driveways on the new plant site.
5. Paid $250 to have the company name and slogan painted on the new delivery truck.
6. Paid $8,000 for installation of new factory machinery.
7. Paid $900 for a 1-year accident insurance policy on the new delivery truck.
8. Paid $75 motor vehicle license fee on the new truck.

Instructions
(a) Explain the application of the cost principle in determining the acquisition cost of plant assets.
(b) List the numbers of the transactions, and opposite each indicate the account title to which each expenditure should be debited.

E9-2 On March 1, 2007, Geoffrey Company acquired real estate, on which it planned to construct a small office building, by paying $90,000 in cash. An old warehouse on the property was demolished at a cost of $8,200; the salvaged materials were sold for $1,700. Additional expenditures before construction began included $1,500 attorney's fee for work concerning the land purchase, $5,000 real estate broker's fee, $9,100 architect's fee, and $14,000 to put in driveways and a parking lot.

Determine acquisition costs of land.
(SO 1)

Instructions
(a) Determine the amount to be reported as the cost of the land.
(b) For each cost not used in part (a), indicate the account to be debited.

E9-3 Hillary Company purchased a new machine on September 1, 2007, at a cost of $96,000. The company estimated that the machine has a salvage value of $6,000. The machine is expected to be used for 70,000 working hours during its 8-year life.

Determine straight-line depreciation for partial period.
(SO 3)

Instructions
Compute the depreciation expense under the straight-line method for 2007 and 2008, assuming a December 31 year-end.

E9-4 Will Smith, the new controller of Fresh Prince Company, has reviewed the expected useful lives and salvage values of selected depreciable assets at the beginning of 2007. Here are his findings:

Compute revised annual depreciation.
(SO 3,4)

Type of Asset	Date Acquired	Cost	Accumulated Depreciation, Jan. 1, 2007	Useful Life (in years)		Salvage Value	
				Old	Proposed	Old	Proposed
Building	Jan. 1, 1999	$900,000	$172,000	40	50	$40,000	$47,600
Warehouse	Jan. 1, 2001	120,000	27,600	25	20	5,000	3,600

All assets are depreciated by the straight-line method. Fresh Prince Company uses a calendar year in preparing annual financial statements. After discussion, management has agreed to accept Will's proposed changes. (The "Proposed" useful life is total life, not remaining life.)

Instructions
(a) Compute the revised annual depreciation on each asset in 2007. (Show computations.)
(b) Prepare the entry (or entries) to record depreciation on the building in 2007.

E9-5 Phill Co. has delivery equipment that cost $54,000 and has been depreciated $20,000.

Journalize transactions related to disposals of plant assets.
(SO 5)

Instructions
Record entries for the disposal under the following assumptions.
(a) It was scrapped as having no value.
(b) It was sold for $37,000.
(c) It was sold for $18,000.

E9-6 Here are selected 2007 transactions of Beck Corporation.

Record disposal of equipment.
(SO 5)

Jan. 1   Retired a piece of machinery that was purchased on January 1, 1997. The machine cost $62,000 and had a useful life of 10 years with no salvage value.

June 30   Sold a computer that was purchased on January 1, 2005. The computer cost $33,000 and had a useful life of 3 years with no salvage value. The computer was sold for $5,000 cash.

Dec. 31   Sold a delivery truck for $9,000 cash. The truck cost $27,000 when it was purchased on January 1, 2004, and was depreciated based on a 5-year useful life with a $3,000 salvage value.

Instructions

Journalize all entries required on the above dates, including entries to update depreciation on assets disposed of, where applicable. Beck Corporation uses straight-line depreciation.

Apply accounting concepts.
(SO 1, 6, 7)

E9-7 The following situations are independent of one another:

1. An accounting student can't understand why the company is only depreciating its buildings and equipment, but not its land. The student prepared journal entries to depreciate all the company's property, plant, and equipment for the current year-end.
2. The same student also thinks the company's amortization policy on its intangible assets is wrong. The company is currently amortizing its patents but not its goodwill. The student fixed that for the current year-end by adding goodwill to her adjusting entry for amortization. She told a fellow student that she felt she had improved the consistency of the company's accounting policies by making these changes.
3. The same company has a building still in use that has a zero book value but a substantial market value. The student felt that this practice didn't benefit the company's users—especially the bank—and wrote the building up to its market value. After all, she reasoned, you can write down assets if market values are lower. Writing them up if market value is higher is yet another example of the improved consistency that her employment has brought to the company's accounting practices.

Instructions

Explain whether or not the accounting treatment in each of the above situations is in accordance with generally accepted accounting principles. Explain what accounting principle or assumption, if any, has been violated and what the appropriate accounting treatment should be.

Calculate asset turnover ratio and return on assets ratio.
(SO 6)

E9-8 During 2004 Federal Express reported the following information (in millions): net sales of $24,710 and net income of $838. Its balance sheet also showed total assets at the beginning of the year of $15,385 and total assets at the end of the year of $19,134.

Instructions

Calculate the (a) asset turnover ratio and (b) return on assets ratio.

Calculate and interpret ratios.
(SO 6)

E9-9 Optix International is considering a significant expansion to its product line. The sales force is excited about the opportunities that the new products will bring. The new products are a significant step up in quality above the company's current offerings, but offer a complementary fit to its existing product line. Frank Renolds, senior production department manager, is very excited about the high-tech new equipment that will have to be acquired to produce the new products. Carol Fischer, the company's CFO, has provided the following projections based on results with and without the new products.

	Without New Products	**With New Products**
Sales	$10,000,000	$18,000,000
Net income	$800,000	$1,800,000
Average total assets	$5,000,000	$15,000,000

Instructions

(a) Compute the company's return on assets ratio, profit margin ratio, and asset turnover ratio, both with and without the new product line.
(b) Discuss the implications that your findings in part (a) have for the company's decision.

Calculate and interpret ratios.
(SO 6)

E9-10 Empire Company reports the following information (in millions) during a recent year: net sales, $9,926.5; net earnings, $195.9; total assets, ending, $4,312.6; and total assets, beginning, $4,254.3.

Instructions

(a) Calculate the (1) return on assets, (2) asset turnover, and (3) profit margin ratios.
(b) Prove mathematically how the profit margin and asset turnover ratios work together to explain return on assets, by showing the appropriate calculation.
(c) Empire Company owns Sobeys (grocery), Empire Theaters, Lawton Drugstores, and Wajax (heavy equipment), and manages commercial real estate, among other activities. Does this diversity of activities affect your ability to interpret the ratios you calculated in (a)? Explain.

E9-11 These are selected 2007 transactions for Neuman Corporation:

Jan. 1 Purchased a copyright for $140,000. The copyright has a useful life of 8 years and a remaining legal life of 30 years.

May 1 Purchased a patent with an estimated useful life of 4 years and a legal life of 20 years for $36,000.

Prepare adjusting entries for amortization.
(SO 7)

Instructions

Prepare all adjusting entries at December 31 to record amortization required by the events.

E9-12 Keshan Company, organized in 2007, has these transactions related to intangible assets in that year:

Jan. 2 Purchased a patent (5-year life) $330,000.

Apr. 1 Goodwill purchased (indefinite life) $360,000.

July 1 Acquired a 9-year franchise; expiration date July 1, 2016, $450,000.

Sept. 1 Research and development costs $185,000.

Prepare entries to set up appropriate accounts for different intangibles; calculate amortization.
(SO 7)

Instructions

(a) Prepare the necessary entries to record these intangibles. All costs incurred were for cash.

(b) Make the entries as of December 31, 2007, recording any necessary amortization.

(c) Indicate what the balances should be on December 31, 2007.

E9-13 Alliance Atlantis Communications Inc. changed its accounting policy to amortize broadcast rights over the contracted exhibition period, which is based on the estimated useful life of the program. Previously, the company amortized broadcast rights over the lesser of 2 years or the contracted exhibition period.

Discuss implications of amortization period.
(SO 7)

Instructions

 Write a short memo to your client explaining the implications this has for the analysis of Alliance Atlantis's results. Also, discuss whether this change in amortization period appears reasonable.

E9-14 The questions listed below are independent of one another.

Answer questions on depreciation and intangibles.
(SO 2, 7)

Instructions

Provide a brief answer to each question.

(a) Why should a company depreciate its buildings?

(b) How can a company have a building that has a zero reported book value but substantial market value?

(c) What are some examples of intangibles that you might find on your college campus?

(d) Give some examples of company or product trademarks or trade names. Are trade names and trademarks reported on a company's balance sheet?

*E9-15 Blue Highway Bus Lines uses the units-of-activity method in depreciating its buses. One bus was purchased on January 1, 2007, at a cost of $120,000. Over its 4-year useful life, the bus is expected to be driven 160,000 miles. Salvage value is expected to be $8,000.

Compute depreciation under units-of-activity method.
(SO 9)

Instructions

(a) Compute the depreciation cost per unit.

(b) Prepare a depreciation schedule assuming actual mileage was: 2007, 40,000; 2008, 52,000; 2009, 41,000; and 2010, 27,000.

*E9-16 Basic information relating to a new machine purchased by Hillary Company is presented in E9-3.

Compute declining-balance and units-of-activity depreciation.
(SO 9)

Instructions

Using the facts presented in E9-3, compute depreciation using the following methods in the year indicated.

(a) Declining-balance using double the straight-line rate for 2007 and 2008.

(b) Units-of-activity for 2007, assuming machine usage was 2,900 hours. (Round depreciation per unit to the nearest cent.)

Problems: Set A

P9-1A Basler Company was organized on January 1. During the first year of operations, the following plant asset expenditures and receipts were recorded in random order.

Determine acquisition costs of land and building.
(SO 1)

Debits

1. Cost of real estate purchased as a plant site (land $255,000 and building $25,000)	$280,000
2. Installation cost of fences around property	6,800
3. Cost of demolishing building to make land suitable for construction of new building	19,000
4. Excavation costs for new building	23,000
5. Accrued real estate taxes paid at time of purchase of real estate	2,179
6. Cost of parking lots and driveways	29,000
7. Architect's fees on building plans	38,000
8. Real estate taxes paid for the current year on land	5,800
9. Full payment to building contractor	640,000
	$1,043,779

Credits

10. Proceeds from salvage of demolished building	$8,000

Instructions

Analyze the transactions using the following table column headings. Enter the number of each transaction in the Item column, and enter the amounts in the appropriate columns. For amounts in the Other Accounts column, also indicate the account title.

Land $293,179

Item	**Land**	**Building**	**Other Accounts**

Journalize equipment transactions related to purchase, sale, retirement, and depreciation.
(SO 5, 8)

P9-2A   At December 31, 2007, Ruiz Corporation reported the following plant assets.

Land		$ 3,000,000
Buildings	$26,500,000	
Less: Accumulated depreciation—buildings	12,100,000	14,400,000
Equipment	40,000,000	
Less: Accumulated depreciation—equipment	5,000,000	35,000,000
Total plant assets		$52,400,000

During 2008, the following selected cash transactions occurred.

Apr.	1	Purchased land for $2,200,000.
May	1	Sold equipment that cost $660,000 when purchased on January 1, 2001. The equipment was sold for $200,000.
June	1	Sold land for $1,800,000. The land cost $700,000.
July	1	Purchased equipment for $1,300,000.
Dec.	31	Retired equipment that cost $500,000 when purchased on December 31, 1998. No salvage value was received.

Instructions

(a) Journalize the transactions. (*Hint:* You may wish to set up T accounts, post beginning balances, and then post 2008 transactions.) Ruiz uses straight-line depreciation for buildings and equipment. The buildings are estimated to have a 40-year useful life and no salvage value; the equipment is estimated to have a 10-year useful life and no salvage value. Update depreciation on assets disposed of at the time of sale or retirement.

(c) Tot. plant assets
$50,340,500

(b) Record adjusting entries for depreciation for 2008.

(c) Prepare the plant assets section of Ruiz's balance sheet at December 31, 2008.

Journalize entries for disposal of plant assets.
(SO 5)

P9-3A   Presented here are selected transactions for Riley Company for 2007.

Jan.	1	Retired a piece of machinery that was purchased on January 1, 1997. The machine cost $71,000 on that date and had a useful life of 10 years with no salvage value.

June 30 Sold a computer that was purchased on January 1, 2004. The computer cost $32,000 and had a useful life of 5 years with no salvage value. The computer was sold for $10,000.

Dec. 31 Discarded a delivery truck that was purchased on January 1, 2002. The truck cost $27,000 and was depreciated based on an 8-year useful life with a $3,000 salvage value.

Instructions

Journalize all entries required on the above dates, including entries to update depreciation, where applicable, on assets disposed of. Riley Company uses straight-line depreciation. (Assume depreciation is up to date as of December 31, 2006.)

P9-4A The intangible assets section of El-Gazzar Corporation's balance sheet at December 31, 2007, is presented here.

Prepare entries to record transactions related to acquisition and amortization of intangibles; prepare the intangible assets section and note.
(SO 7, 8)

Patents ($60,000 cost less $6,000 amortization)	$54,000
Copyrights ($36,000 cost less $25,200 amortization)	10,800
Total	$64,800

The patent was acquired in January 2007 and has a useful life of 10 years. The copyright was acquired in January 2001 and also has a useful life of 10 years. The following cash transactions may have affected intangible assets during 2008.

Jan. 2 Paid $36,000 legal costs to successfully defend the patent against infringement by another company.

Jan.–June Developed a new product, incurring $210,000 in research and development costs. A patent was granted for the product on July 1, and its useful life is equal to its legal life. Legal and other costs for the patent were $9,000.

Sept. 1 Paid $40,000 to a quarterback to appear in commercials advertising the company's products. The commercials will air in September and October.

Oct. 1 Acquired a copyright for $180,000. The copyright has a useful life and legal life of 50 years.

Instructions

(a) Prepare journal entries to record the transactions.
(b) Prepare journal entries to record the 2008 amortization expense for intangible assets.
(c) Prepare the intangible assets section of the balance sheet at December 31, 2008.
(d) Prepare the note to the financial statements on El-Gazzar Corporation's intangible assets as of December 31, 2008.

(c) Tot. intangibles $275,075

P9-5A Due to rapid employee turnover in the accounting department, the following transactions involving intangible assets were improperly recorded by Dische Corporation in 2007.

Prepare entries to correct errors in recording and amortizing intangible assets.
(SO 7)

1. Dische developed a new manufacturing process, incurring research and development costs of $150,000. The company also purchased a patent for $37,400. In early January Dische capitalized $187,400 as the cost of the patents. Patent amortization expense of $9,370 was recorded based on a 20-year useful life.

2. On July 1, 2007, Dische purchased a small company and as a result acquired goodwill of $60,000. Dische recorded a half-year's amortization in 2007, based on a 40-year life ($750 amortization). The goodwill has an indefinite life.

Instructions

Prepare all journal entries necessary to correct any errors made during 2007. Assume the books have not yet been closed for 2007.

P9-6A Roger Corporation and Sean Corporation, two companies of roughly the same size, are both involved in the manufacture of shoe-tracing devices. Each company depreciates its plant assets using the straight-line approach. An investigation of their financial statements reveals the information shown on page 462.

Calculate and comment on return on assets, profit margin, and asset turnover ratio.
(SO 6)

	Roger Corp.	Sean Corp.
Net income	$ 400,000	$ 500,000
Sales	1,300,000	1,200,000
Total assets (average)	3,300,000	2,900,000
Plant assets (average)	2,400,000	1,800,000
Intangible assets (goodwill)	300,000	0

Instructions
(a) For each company, calculate these values:
   (1) Return on assets ratio.
   (2) Profit margin.
   (3) Asset turnover ratio.
(b) Based on your calculations in part (a), comment on the relative effectiveness of the two companies in using their assets to generate sales. What factors complicate your ability to compare the two companies?

Compute depreciation under different methods.
(SO 3, 9)

*P9-7A In recent years Ping Company has purchased three machines. Because of frequent employee turnover in the accounting department, a different accountant was in charge of selecting the depreciation method for each machine, and various methods have been used. Information concerning the machines is summarized in the table below.

Machine	Acquired	Cost	Salvage Value	Useful Life (in years)	Depreciation Method
1	Jan. 1, 2004	$96,000	$ 6,000	6	Straight-line
2	July 1, 2005	80,000	10,000	5	Declining-balance
3	Nov. 1, 2005	78,000	6,000	6	Units-of-activity

For the declining-balance method, Ping Company uses the double-declining rate. For the units-of-activity method, total machine hours are expected to be 24,000. Actual hours of use in the first 3 years were: 2005, 400; 2006, 4,500; and 2007, 5,000.

Instructions

(a) Machine 2 $56,960

(a) Compute the amount of accumulated depreciation on each machine at December 31, 2007.
(b) If machine 2 was purchased on October 1 instead of July 1, what would be the depreciation expense for this machine in 2005? In 2006?

Compute depreciation under different methods.
(SO 3, 9)

*P9-8A Tabesh Corporation purchased machinery on January 1, 2007, at a cost of $210,000. The estimated useful life of the machinery is 4 years, with an estimated residual value at the end of that period of $10,000. The company is considering different depreciation methods that could be used for financial reporting purposes.

Instructions

(a) Double-declining-balance expense 2009 $26,250

(a) Prepare separate depreciation schedules for the machinery using the straight-line method, and the declining-balance method using double the straight-line rate. Round to the nearest dollar.
(b) Which method would result in the higher reported 2007 income? In the highest total reported income over the 4-year period?
(c) Which method would result in the lower reported 2007 income? In the lowest total reported income over the 4-year period?

Determine acquisition costs of land and building.
(SO 1)

Problems: Set B

P9-1B Cairo Company was organized on January 1. During the first year of operations, the following plant asset expenditures and receipts were recorded in random order.

Debits

1. Cost of real estate purchased as a plant site (land $180,000 and
   building $70,000) · $ 250,000
2. Accrued real estate taxes paid at time of purchase of real estate   6,000
3. Cost of demolishing building to make land suitable for
   construction of new building   27,000
4. Cost of filling and grading the land   7,100
5. Excavation costs for new building   21,900
6. Architect's fees on building plans   45,000
7. Full payment to building contractor   629,500
8. Cost of parking lots and driveways   36,000
9. Real estate taxes paid for the current year on land   7,300

                                                                        $1,029,800

Credits

10. Proceeds for salvage of demolished building $ 12,700

Instructions

Analyze the transactions using the table column headings provided here. Enter the number of each transaction in the Item column, and enter the amounts in the appropriate columns. For amounts in the Other Accounts column, also indicate the account titles.

Item	Land	Building	Other Accounts

Land $277,400

P9-2B At December 31, 2007, Harrington Corporation reported these plant assets.

Journalize equipment transactions related to purchase, sale, retirement, and depreciation.
(SO 5, 8)

Land		$ 4,000,000
Buildings	$28,500,000	
Less: Accumulated depreciation—buildings	12,100,000	16,400,000
Equipment	48,000,000	
Less: Accumulated depreciation—equipment	5,000,000	43,000,000
Total plant assets		$63,400,000

During 2008, the following selected cash transactions occurred.

Apr. 1   Purchased land for $2,630,000.
May 1   Sold equipment that cost $600,000 when purchased on January 1, 2003.
         The equipment was sold for $350,000.
June 1   Sold land purchased on June 1, 1995, for $1,800,000. The land cost
         $500,000.
July 1   Purchased equipment for $800,000.
Dec. 31 Retired fully depreciated equipment that cost $470,000 when purchased
         on December 31, 1998. No salvage value was received.

Instructions

(a) Journalize the transactions. (*Hint:* You may wish to set up T accounts, post beginning balances, and then post 2008 transactions.) Harrington uses straight-line depreciation for buildings and equipment. The buildings are estimated to have a 40-year life and no salvage value; the equipment is estimated to have a 10-year useful life and no salvage value. Update depreciation on assets disposed of at the time of sale or retirement.
(b) Record adjusting entries for depreciation for 2008. (*Note:* The only assets that are fully depreciated are those that were retired on December 31.)
(c) Prepare the plant assets section of Harrington's balance sheet at December 31, 2008.

(c) Tot. plant assets
                    $60,537,500

P9-3B Here are selected transactions for Andre Corporation for 2007.

Journalize entries for disposal of plant assets.
(SO 5)

Jan. 1   Retired a piece of machinery that was purchased on January 1, 1997.
         The machine cost $52,000 and had a useful life of 10 years with no
         salvage value.

June 30 Sold a computer that was purchased on January 1, 2004. The computer cost $35,000 and had a useful life of 7 years with no salvage value. The computer was sold for $23,000.

Dec. 31 Discarded a delivery truck that was purchased on January 1, 2003. The truck cost $30,000 and was depreciated based on a 6-year useful life with a $3,000 salvage value.

Instructions
Journalize all entries required on the above dates, including entries to update depreciation on assets disposed of, where applicable. Andre Corporation uses straight-line depreciation.

Prepare entries to record transactions related to acquisition and amortization of intangibles; prepare the intangible assets section and notes.
(SO 7, 8)

P9-4B The intangible assets section of the balance sheet for Cuso Company at December 31, 2007, is presented here.

Patents ($70,000 cost less $7,000 amortization)	$63,000
Copyrights ($48,000 cost less $18,000 amortization)	30,000
Total	$93,000

The patent was acquired in January 2007 and has a useful life of 10 years. The copyright was acquired in January 2005 and also has a useful life of 8 years. The following cash transactions may have affected intangible assets during 2008.

Jan. 2 Paid $22,500 legal costs to successfully defend the patent against infringement by another company.

Jan.–June Developed a new product, incurring $220,000 in research and development costs. A patent was granted for the product on July 1, and its useful life is equal to its legal life. Legal and other costs for the patent were $14,000.

Sept. 1 Paid $110,000 to an extremely large defensive lineman to appear in commercials advertising the company's products. The commercials will air in September and October.

Oct. 1 Acquired a copyright for $150,000. The copyright has a useful life and legal life of 50 years.

Instructions
(a) Prepare journal entries to record the transactions.
(b) Prepare journal entries to record the 2008 amortization expense.
(c) Tot. intangibles $262,900
(c) Prepare the intangible assets section of the balance sheet at December 31, 2008.
(d) Prepare the notes to the financial statements on Cuso Company's intangible assets as of December 31, 2008.

Prepare entries to correct errors in recording and amortizing intangible assets.
(SO 7)

P9-5B Due to rapid employee turnover in the accounting department, the following transactions involving intangible assets were improperly recorded by the Mooney Company in 2007.
1. Mooney developed a new manufacturing process, incurring research and development costs of $120,000. The company also purchased a patent for $72,000. In early January Mooney capitalized $192,000 as the cost of the patents. Patent amortization expense of $16,000 was recorded based on a 12-year useful life.
2. On July 1, 2007, Mooney purchased a small company and as a result acquired goodwill of $80,000. Mooney recorded a half-year's amortization in 2007 based on a 40-year life ($1,000 amortization). The goodwill has an indefinite life.

Instructions
Prepare all journal entries necessary to correct any errors made during 2007. Assume the books have not yet been closed for 2007.

Calculate and comment on return on assets, profit margin, and asset turnover ratio.
(SO 6)

P9-6B Montreal Corporation and Quebec Corporation, two corporations of roughly the same size, are both involved in the manufacture of umbrellas. Each company depreciates its plant assets using the straight-line approach. An investigation of their financial statements reveals the following information.

	Montreal Corp.	Quebec Corp.
Net income	$ 800,000	$ 900,000
Sales	1,400,000	1,500,000
Total assets (average)	2,000,000	1,800,000
Plant assets (average)	1,400,000	1,200,000
Intangible assets (goodwill)	400,000	0

Instructions
(a) For each company, calculate these values:
   (1) Return on assets ratio.
   (2) Profit margin.
   (3) Asset turnover ratio.
(b) Based on your calculations in part (a), comment on the relative effectiveness of the two companies in using their assets to generate sales. What factors complicate your ability to compare the two companies?

*P9-7B   In recent years Brian Transportation purchased three used buses. Because of frequent employee turnover in the accounting department, a different accountant selected the depreciation method for each bus, and various methods have been used. Information concerning the buses is summarized in the table below.

Compute depreciation under different methods.
(SO 3, 9)

Bus	Acquired	Cost	Salvage Value	Useful Life (in years)	Depreciation Method
1	Jan. 1, 2005	$ 86,000	$ 6,000	4	Straight-line
2	Jan. 1, 2005	150,000	10,000	4	Declining-balance
3	Jan. 1, 2005	100,000	9,000	5	Units-of-activity

For the declining-balance method, Brian Transportation uses the double-declining rate. For the units-of-activity method, total miles are expected to be 130,000. Actual miles of use in the first 3 years were: 2005, 26,000; 2006, 34,000; and 2007, 30,000.

Instructions
(a) Compute the amount of accumulated depreciation on each bus at December 31, 2007.
(b) If Bus 2 was purchased on March 1 instead of January 1, what would be the depreciation expense for this bus in 2005? In 2006?

(a) Bus 1 $60,000

*P9-8B   Shumway Corporation purchased machinery on January 1, 2007, at a cost of $290,000. The estimated useful life of the machinery is 5 years, with an estimated salvage value at the end of that period of $30,000. The company is considering different depreciation methods that could be used for financial reporting purposes.

Compute depreciation under different methods.
(SO 3, 9)

Instructions
(a) Prepare separate depreciation schedules for the machinery using the straight-line method, and the declining-balance method using double the straight-line rate.
(b) Which method would result in the higher reported 2007 income? In the higher total reported income over the 5-year period?
(c) Which method would result in the lower reported 2007 income? In the lower total reported income over the 5-year period?

(a) Double-declining-balance exp. 2008 $69,600

Problems: Set C

Visit the book's website at **www.wiley.com/college/kimmel** and choose the Student Companion site to access Problem Set C.

Comprehensive Problem

CP9   Squarepants Corporation's trial balance at December 31, 2007, is presented on page 466. All 2007 transactions have been recorded except for the items described after the trial balance.

	Debit	Credit
Cash	$ 28,000	
Accounts Receivable	36,800	
Notes Receivable	10,000	
Interest Receivable	–0–	
Merchandise Inventory	36,200	
Prepaid Insurance	3,600	
Land	20,000	
Building	150,000	
Equipment	60,000	
Patent	9,000	
Allowance for Doubtful Accounts		$ 500
Accumulated Depreciation—Building		50,000
Accumulated Depreciation—Equipment		24,000
Accounts Payable		27,300
Salaries Payable		–0–
Unearned Rent		6,000
Notes Payable (short-term)		11,000
Interest Payable		–0–
Notes Payable (long-term)		35,000
Common Stock		50,000
Retained Earnings		63,600
Dividends	12,000	
Sales		900,000
Interest Revenue		–0–
Rent Revenue		–0–
Gain on Disposal		–0–
Bad Debts Expense	–0–	
Cost of Goods Sold	630,000	
Depreciation Expense—Buildings	–0–	
Depreciation Expense—Equipment	–0–	
Insurance Expense	–0–	
Interest Expense	–0–	
Other Operating Expenses	61,800	
Amortization Expense—Patents	–0–	
Salaries Expense	110,000	
Total	$1,167,400	$1,167,400

Unrecorded transactions

1. On May 1, 2007, Squarepants purchased equipment for $12,000 plus sales taxes of $600 (all paid in cash).
2. On July 1, 2007, Squarepants sold for $3,500 equipment which originally cost $5,000. Accumulated depreciation on this equipment at January 1, 2007, was $1,800; 2007 depreciation prior to the sale of equipment was $450.
3. On December 31, 2007, Squarepants sold for $3,000 on account inventory that cost $2,100.
4. Squarepants estimates that uncollectible accounts receivable at year-end are $4,000.
5. The note receivable is a one-year, 12% note dated April 1, 2007. No interest has been recorded.
6. The balance in prepaid insurance represents payment of a $3,600, 6-month premium on September 1, 2007.
7. The building is being depreciated using the straight-line method over 30 years. The salvage value is $30,000.
8. The equipment owned prior to this year is being depreciated using the straight-line method over 5 years. The salvage value is 10% of cost.
9. The equipment purchased on May 1, 2007, is being depreciated using the straight-line method over 5 years, with a salvage value of $1,800.
10. The patent was acquired on January 1, 2007, and has a useful life of 10 years from that date.
11. Unpaid salaries at December 31, 2007, total $2,200.
12. The unearned rent of $6,000 was received on December 1, 2007, for 3 months rent.
13. Both the short-term and long-term notes payable are dated January 1, 2007, and carry a 12% interest rate. All interest is payable in the next 12 months.

Instructions
(a) Prepare journal entries for the transactions listed above.
(b) Prepare an updated December 31, 2007, trial balance.
(c) Prepare a 2007 income statement and a 2007 retained earnings statement.
(d) Prepare a December 31, 2007, balance sheet.

(b) Totals $1,196,810
(c) Net income $72,440
(d) Total assets $259,060

Continuing Cookie Chronicle

(*Note:* This is a continuation of the Cookie Chronicle from Chapters 1 through 8.)

CCC9

Part 1 Now that she is selling mixers and her customers can use credit cards to pay for them, Natalie is thinking of upgrading her website to include the online sale of mixers and payment by credit card. This would enable her to sell these mixers to a wider range of customers using the Internet.

Natalie contacts her brother who originally prepared the website for her. He agrees to upgrade the site so it can handle credit card security issues as well as direct order entry. The cost of the upgrade is $1,800. This cost would be incurred and paid for during the month of August 2007, and the upgrade would be operational September 1, 2007. Recall that Natalie's website had an original cost of $600 and is being amortized using the straight-line method over 24 months, starting December 1, 2006, with zero residual value. Additional costs for website maintenance and insurance are estimated to be $1,200 per year.

If Natalie decides to upgrade the website, its useful life will not change and there will be no change in residual value.

Instructions
(a) Prepare the journal entry to record the upgrade.
(b) Calculate the monthly amortization expense before the upgrade and the accumulated amortization and book value on August 31, 2007.
(c) Calculate the revised monthly amortization expense as of September 1, 2007.
(d) Calculate the accumulated amortization and book value on December 31, 2007.
(e) Explain to Natalie the difference in accounting for the website upgrade costs and accounting for the costs incurred for website maintenance and insurance. In your explanation, comment on the generally accepted accounting principles that affect the accounting for these transactions.

Part 2 Natalie is also thinking of buying a van that will be used only for business. The cost of the van is estimated at $32,500. Natalie would spend an additional $2,500 to have the van painted. In addition, she wants the back seat of the van removed so that she will have lots of room to transport her mixer inventory as well as her baking supplies. The cost of taking out the back seat and installing shelving units is estimated at $1,500. She expects the van to last her about 5 years, and she expects to drive it for 100,000 miles. The annual cost of vehicle insurance will be $2,400. Natalie estimates that at the end of the 5-year useful life the van will sell for $6,500. Assume that she will buy the van on August 15, 2007, and it will be ready for use on September 1, 2007.

Natalie is concerned about the impact of the van's cost on her income statement and balance sheet. She has come to you for advice on calculating the van's depreciation.

Instructions
(a) Determine the cost of the van.
(b) Prepare a depreciation table for straight-line depreciation (similar to the one in Illustration 9-9). Recall that Cookie Creations has a December 31 fiscal year-end.
(c) What method should Natalie use for tax purposes? Provide a justification for your choice. Is she required to use the same approach for financial reporting and tax reporting?

BROADENING YOUR PERSPECTIVE

Financial Reporting and Analysis

FINANCIAL REPORTING PROBLEM: *Tootsie Roll Industries, Inc.*

BYP9-1 Refer to the financial statements and the Notes to Consolidated Financial Statements of Tootsie Roll Industries in Appendix A.

Instructions

Answer the following questions.

(a) What were the total cost and book value of property, plant, and equipment at December 31, 2004?

(b) What method or methods of depreciation are used by Tootsie Roll for financial reporting purposes?

(c) What was the amount of depreciation and amortization expense for each of the 3 years 2002–2004? (*Hint:* Use statement of cash flows.)

(d) Using the statement of cash flows, what are the amounts of property, plant, and equipment purchased (capital expenditures) in 2004 and 2003?

(e) Explain how Tootsie Roll accounted for its intangible assets in 2004.

(f) Read Tootsie Roll's note 8 on commitments. Does the company primarily engage in capital leases or operating leases? What are the implications for analysis of its financial statements?

COMPARATIVE ANALYSIS PROBLEM: *Tootsie Roll vs. Hershey Foods*

BYP9-2 The financial statements of Hershey Foods are presented in Appendix B, following the financial statements for Tootsie Roll Industries in Appendix A.

Instructions

(a) Based on the information in these financial statements and the accompanying notes and schedules, compute the following values for each company in 2004.

   (1) Return on assets ratio.

   (2) Profit margin.

   (3) Asset turnover ratio.

(b) What conclusions concerning the management of plant assets can be drawn from these data?

RESEARCH CASE

BYP9-3 The May 16, 2005, issue of the *Wall Street Journal* includes an article by Pui-Wing Tam titled "Will H-P's Hurd Wipe the Slate Clean?"

Instructions

Read the article and answer the following questions.

(a) What are some of the reasons given for expecting that Hewlett-Packard will make a significant write-down against its goodwill? What would this charge relate to?

(b) According to accounting standards, how is goodwill to be accounted for?

(c) What is one possible reason given for why Mr. Hurd's predecessor CEO at Hewlett-Packard did not take a large write-off on goodwill?

(d) What other examples of large goodwill write-offs are given in the article?

INTERPRETING FINANCIAL STATEMENTS

BYP9-4 Bob Evans Farms, Inc. operates 568 restaurants in 22 states and produces fresh and fully cooked sausage products, fresh salads, and related products distributed to grocery stores in the Midwest, Southwest, and Southeast. For a recent 3-year period Bob Evans Farms reported the following selected income statement data (in millions of dollars).

	2004	**2003**	**2002**
Sales	$1,198.0	$1,091.3	$1,061.8
Cost of goods sold	340.8	287.0	298.3
Net income	72.0	75.1	67.7
Total assets	868.2	784.6	722.0

In his letters to stockholders, the chief executive officer (CEO) explained the decline in earnings. An excerpt from that letter is shown on page 469.

BOB EVANS FARMS, INC.
Letter to Stockholders (partial)

During fiscal 2004, we continued building long-term value for Bob Evans stockholders by pursuing our time-tested strategies for steady, complementary growth of our family-casual restaurants and food products. However, financial results for the year were affected primarily by increased commodity costs, which resulted in a slight decline in earnings per share from fiscal 2003's record level.

Instructions

(a) Compute the percentage change in sales and in net income from 2002 to 2004.
(b) What contribution, if any, did the company's gross profit rate make to the decline in earnings?
(c) What was Bob Evans's profit margin ratio in each of the 3 years? Comment on any trend in this percentage.
(d) The CEO's letter also stated that the company continued to invest prudently in restaurants, opening 37 new restaurants in 2004, compared to 29 openings in 2003. What effect would you expect this change to have on return on assets? Calculate the company's return on assets for 2003 and 2004 to see if it reflects the increase in number of stores.
(e) Based on the trends in these ratios, does the CEO's explanation seem appropriate?

BYP9-5 The accounting for goodwill differs in countries around the world. The discussion of a change in goodwill accounting practices shown below was taken from the notes to the financial statements of J Sainsbury Plc, one of the world's leading retailers. Headquartered in the United Kingdom, it serves 11 million customers a week.

J SAINSBURY PLC
Notes to the Financial Statements

Accounting Policies Goodwill arising in connection with the acquisition of shares in subsidiaries and associated undertakings is calculated as the excess of the purchase price over the fair value of the net tangible assets acquired. In prior years goodwill has been deducted from reserves in the period of acquisition. FRS 10 is applicable in the current financial year, and in accordance with the standard acquired goodwill is now shown as an asset on the Group's Balance Sheet. As permitted by FRS 10, goodwill written off to reserves in prior periods has not been restated as an asset.

Goodwill is treated as having an indefinite economic life where it is considered that the acquired business has strong customer loyalty built up over a long period of time, based on advantageous store locations and a commitment to maintain the marketing advantage of the retail brand. The carrying value of the goodwill will be reviewed annually for impairment and adjusted to its recoverable amount if required. Where goodwill is considered to have a finite life, amortisation will be applied over that period.

For amounts stated as goodwill which are considered to have indefinite life, no amortisation is charged to the Profit and Loss Account.

Instructions

Answer the following questions.

(a) How does the initial determination and recording of goodwill compare with that in the United States? That is, is goodwill initially recorded in the same circumstances, and is the calculation of the amount the same in both the United Kingdom and the United States?
(b) Prior to adoption of the new accounting standard (*FRS 10*), how did the company account for goodwill? What were the implications for the income statement?
(c) Under the new accounting standard, how does the company account for its goodwill? Is it possible, under the new standard, for a company to avoid charging goodwill amortization to net income?
(d) In what ways is the new standard similar to U.S. standards, and in what ways is it different?

FINANCIAL ANALYSIS ON THE WEB

BYP9-6 *Purpose:* Use an annual report to identify a company's plant assets and the depreciation method used.

Address: **www.reportgallery.com** (or go to **www.wiley.com/college/kimmel**)

Steps
1. From Report Gallery Homepage, choose **View the Library of Annual Reports**.
2. Select a particular company.
3. Choose **Annual Report**.
4. Follow instructions below.

Instructions
Answer the following questions.
(a) What is the name of the company?
(b) What is the Internet address of the annual report?
(c) At fiscal year-end, what is the net amount of its plant assets?
(d) What is the accumulated depreciation?
(e) Which method of depreciation does the company use?

Critical Thinking

DECISION MAKING ACROSS THE ORGANIZATION

BYP9-7 Kreugers Furniture Corp. is nationally recognized for making high-quality products. Management is concerned that it is not fully exploiting its brand power. Kreugers' production managers are also concerned because their plants are not operating at anywhere near full capacity. Management is currently considering a proposal to offer a new line of affordable furniture.

Those in favor of the proposal (including the vice president of production) believe that, by offering these new products, the company could attract a clientele that it is not currently servicing. Also, it could operate its plants at full capacity, thus taking better advantage of its assets.

The vice president of marketing, however, believes that the lower-priced (and lower-margin) product would have a negative impact on the sales of existing products. The vice president believes that $10,000,000 of the sales of the new product will be from customers that would have purchased the more expensive product, but switched to the lower-margin product because it was available. (This is often referred to as *cannibalization* of existing sales). Top management feels, however, that even with cannibalization, the company's sales will increase and the company will be better off.

The following data are available.

(in thousands)	Current results	Proposed results without cannibalization	Proposed results with cannibalization
Sales	$40,000	$60,000	$50,000
Net income	$10,000	$12,500	$10,000
Average total assets	$100,000	$100,000	$100,000

Instructions
(a) Compute Kreugers' return on assets ratio, profit margin ratio, and asset turnover ratio, both with and without the new product line.
(b) Discuss the implications that your findings in part (a) have for Kreugers' decision.
(c) Are there any other options that Kreugers should consider? What impact would each of these have on the above ratios?

COMMUNICATION ACTIVITY

BYP9-8 The chapter presented some concerns regarding the current accounting standards for research and development expenditures.

Instructions
Assume that you are either (a) the president of a company that is very dependent on ongoing research and development, writing a memo to the FASB complaining about the current accounting standards regarding research and development, or (b) the FASB member defending the current standards regarding research and development. Your memo should address the questions shown on page 471.

1. By requiring expensing of R&D, do you think companies will spend less on R&D? Why or why not? What are the possible implications for the competitiveness of U.S. companies?
2. If a company makes a commitment to spend money for R&D, it must believe it has future benefits. Shouldn't these costs therefore be capitalized just like the purchase of any long-lived asset that you believe will have future benefits?

ETHICS CASE

BYP9-9 Green Line Anti-Pollution Company is suffering declining sales of its principal product, nonbiodegradable plastic cartons. The president, Peter Wall, instructs his controller, Chuck Meitz, to lengthen asset lives to reduce depreciation expense. A processing line of automated plastic extruding equipment, purchased for $2.5 million in January 2006, was originally estimated to have a useful life of 8 years and a salvage value of $400,000. Depreciation has been recorded for 2 years on that basis. Peter wants the estimated life changed to 12 years total and the straight-line method continued. Chuck is hesitant to make the change, believing it is unethical to increase net income in this manner. Peter says, "Hey, the life is only an estimate, and I've heard that our competition uses a 12-year life on their production equipment."

Instructions
(a) Who are the stakeholders in this situation?
(b) Is the proposed change in asset life unethical, or is it simply a good business practice by an astute president?
(c) What is the effect of Peter's proposed change on income before taxes in the year of change?

Answers to Business Insight and Accounting across the Organization Questions

p. 422
Q: How did the capitalization of expenses increase WorldCom's income?
A: By capitalizing these expenditures, WorldCom spread expenses over multiple future years, rather than expensing it fully in the current year.

p. 425
Q: Why might airline managers choose to lease rather than purchase their planes?
A: The reasons for leasing include favorable tax treatment, better financing options, increased flexibility, reduced risk of obsolescence, and low airline income.

p. 438
Q: How does measuring marketing ROI support the overall efforts of the organization?
A: Top management is ultimately concerned about maximizing the company's return on assets. Holding marketing managers accountable for the marketing ROI will contribute to the company's overall goal of maximizing return on assets.

p. 444
Q: How should ESPN account for the $1.1 billion per year franchise fee?
A: Since this is an annual franchise fee, ESPN should expense it each year, rather than capitalizing and amortizing it.

Answer to Tootsie Roll Review It Question 3, p. 428

Tootsie Roll depreciates its buildings over 20 to 35 years and its machinery and equipment over 5 to 20 years.

Answers to Self-Study Questions

1. d   2. a   3. b   4. d   5. c   6. b   7. d   8. d   9. b   10. c
11. c   *12. d

REMEMBER TO GO BACK TO THE NAVIGATOR BOX ON THE CHAPTER-OPENING PAGE AND CHECK OFF YOUR COMPLETED WORK.

10

Reporting and Analyzing Liabilities

STUDY OBJECTIVES

After studying this chapter,
you should be able to:

1 Explain a current liability and identify the major types
of current liabilities.

2 Describe the accounting for notes payable.

3 Explain the accounting for other current liabilities.

4 Identify the types of bonds.

5 Prepare the entries for the issuance of bonds and
interest expense.

6 Describe the entries when bonds are redeemed.

7 Identify the requirements for the financial statement presentation and analysis
of liabilities.

THE
NAVIGATOR

THE NAVIGATOR

- Scan *Study Objectives*
- Read *Feature Story*
- Read *Preview*
- Read text and answer *Before You Go On*
  p. 479   p. 483   p. 489
  p. 496
- Work *Using the Decision Toolkit*
- Review *Summary of Study Objectives*
- Work *Demonstration Problem*
- Answer *Self-Study Questions*
- Complete *Assignments*

FEATURE STORY

And Then There Were Two

Debt can help a company acquire the things it needs to grow, but it is often the very thing that kills a company. A brief history of Maxwell Car Company illustrates the role of debt in the U.S. auto industry. In 1920 Maxwell Car Company was on the brink of financial ruin. Because it was axle-deep in debt and unable to pay its bills, its creditors stepped in and took over. They hired a former General Motors executive named Walter Chrysler to reorganize the company. By 1925 he had taken over the company and renamed it Chrysler. By 1933 Chrysler was booming, with sales surpassing even those of Ford.

But the next few decades saw Chrysler make a series of blunders. During the 1940s, while its competitors were making yearly design changes to boost customer interest, Chrysler made no changes. During the 1960s, when customers wanted large cars, Chrysler produced small cars. During the 1970s, when customers wanted small cars, Chrysler offered big "boats." By 1980, with its creditors pounding at the gates, Chrysler was again on the brink of financial ruin.

At that point Chrysler brought in a former Ford executive named Lee Iacocca to save the company. Iacocca, considered by many as good a politician as a businessman, argued that the United States could not afford to let Chrysler fail because of the loss of jobs.

He convinced the federal government to grant loan guarantees—promises that if Chrysler failed to pay its creditors, the government would pay them. Iacocca then streamlined operations and brought out some profitable products. Chrysler repaid all of its government-guaranteed loans by 1983, seven years ahead of the scheduled final payment.

What has happened since? In the 1990s Chrysler knew both feast and famine: In 1991 it operated in the red, with Iacocca leaving the company under pressure in 1992. By 1995 Chrysler was the most profitable U.S.-based car manufacturer and the envy of the entire industry.

But to compete in today's global vehicle market, you must be big—really big. So in 1998 Chrysler merged with German automaker Daimler-Benz, to form DaimlerChrysler. This left just two U.S.-based auto manufacturers—General Motors and Ford.

These companies are giants. General Motors and Ford typically rank among the top five U.S. firms in total assets. But General Motors and Ford have accumulated a truckload of debt on their way to getting this big. Combined, they have approximately $600 billion in total outstanding liabilities. Although debt has made it possible to get so big, the Chrysler story makes it clear that debt can also threaten a company's survival.

THE NAVIGATOR

On the World Wide Web
DaimlerChrysler:
   www.daimlerchrysler.com
Ford: www.ford.com
General Motors: www.gm.com

PREVIEW OF CHAPTER 10

The Feature Story suggests that General Motors and Ford have tremendous amounts of debt. It is unlikely that they could have grown so large without this debt, but at times the debt threatens their very existence. Given this risk, why do companies borrow money? Why do they sometimes borrow short-term and other times long-term? Besides bank borrowings, what other kinds of debts do companies incur? In this chapter we address these issues.

The content and organization of the chapter are as follows.

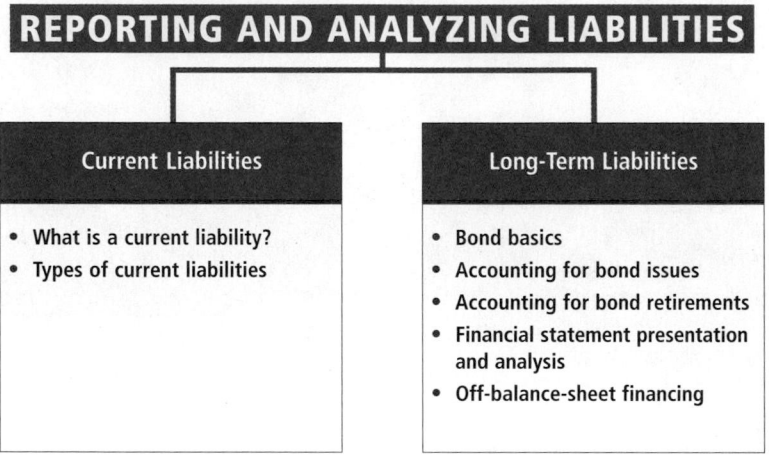

REPORTING AND ANALYZING LIABILITIES

Current Liabilities	Long-Term Liabilities
• What is a current liability? • Types of current liabilities	• Bond basics • Accounting for bond issues • Accounting for bond retirements • Financial statement presentation and analysis • Off-balance-sheet financing

THE NAVIGATOR

SECTION ONE
CURRENT LIABILITIES

What Is a Current Liability?

STUDY OBJECTIVE

1

Explain a current liability and identify the major types of current liabilities.

You have learned that liabilities are defined as "creditors' claims on total assets" and as "existing debts and obligations." Companies must settle or pay these claims, debts, and obligations at some time in the future by transferring assets or services. The future date on which they are due or payable (the maturity date) is a significant feature of liabilities.

As explained in Chapter 2, a **current liability** is a debt that a company reasonably expects to pay (1) from existing current assets or through the creation of other current liabilities, and (2) within one year or the operating cycle, whichever is longer. Debts that do not meet both criteria are **long-term liabilities**.

Financial statement users want to know whether a company's obligations are current or long-term. A company that has more current liabilities than current assets often lacks liquidity, or short-term debt-paying ability. In addition, users want to know the types of liabilities a company has. If a company declares bankruptcy, a specific, predetermined order of payment to creditors exists. Thus, the amount and type of liabilities are of critical importance.

Types of Current Liabilities

The different types of current liabilities include notes payable, accounts payable, unearned revenues, and accrued liabilities such as taxes, salaries and wages, and interest. In this section we discuss a few of the common and more important types of current liabilities.

Helpful Hint In previous chapters we explained the entries for accounts payable and the adjusting entries for some current liabilities.

NOTES PAYABLE

Companies record obligations in the form of written notes as **notes payable**. They often use notes payable instead of accounts payable because notes payable give the lender written documentation of the obligation in case legal remedies are needed to collect the debt. Companies frequently issue notes payable to meet short-term financing needs. Notes payable usually require the borrower to pay interest.

Notes are issued for varying periods of time. **Those due for payment within one year of the balance sheet date are usually classified as current liabilities.** Most notes are interest-bearing.

To illustrate the accounting for notes payable, assume that First National Bank agrees to lend $100,000 on September 1, 2007, if Cole Williams Co. signs a $100,000, 12%, four-month note maturing on January 1. When a company issues an interest-bearing note, the amount of assets it receives generally equals the note's face value. Cole Williams Co. therefore will receive $100,000 cash and will make the following journal entry.

STUDY OBJECTIVE 2

Describe the accounting for notes payable.

Sept. 1	Cash	100,000	
	Notes Payable		100,000
	(To record issuance of 12%, 4-month note to First National Bank)		

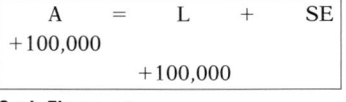

Interest accrues over the life of the note, and the issuer must periodically record that accrual. If Cole Williams Co. prepares financial statements annually, it makes an adjusting entry at December 31 to recognize interest expense and interest payable of $4,000 ($100,000 × 12% × $\frac{4}{12}$):

Dec. 31	Interest Expense	4,000	
	Interest Payable		4,000
	(To accrue interest for 4 months on First National Bank note)		

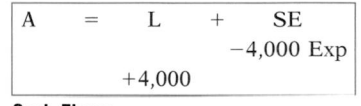

In the December 31 financial statements, the current liabilities section of the balance sheet will show notes payable $100,000 and interest payable $4,000. In addition, the company will report interest expense of $4,000 under "Other expenses and losses" in the income statement.

At maturity (January 1), Cole Williams Co. must pay the face value of the note ($100,000) plus $4,000 interest ($100,000 × 12% × $\frac{4}{12}$). It records payment of the note and accrued interest as follows.

Jan. 1	Notes Payable	100,000	
	Interest Payable	4,000	
	Cash		104,000
	(To record payment of First National Bank interest-bearing note and accrued interest at maturity)		

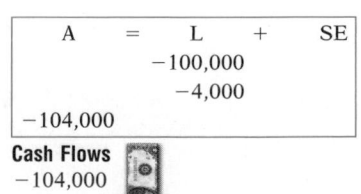

Appendix 10C at the end of this chapter discusses the accounting for long-term installment notes payable.

SALES TAXES PAYABLE

Helpful Hint Watch how sales are rung up at local retailers to see whether the sales tax is computed separately.

Many of the products we purchase at retail stores are subject to sales taxes. Many states are now implementing sales taxes on purchases made on the Internet as well. Sales taxes are expressed as a percentage of the sales price. The retailer (or selling company) collects the tax from the customer when the sale occurs and periodically (usually monthly) remits the collections to the state's department of revenue.

Under most state laws, the selling company must ring up separately on the cash register the amount of the sale and the amount of the sales tax collected. (Gasoline sales are a major exception.) The company then uses the cash register readings to credit Sales and Sales Taxes Payable. For example, if the March 25 cash register readings for Cooley Grocery show sales of $10,000 and sales taxes of $600 (sales tax rate of 6%), the journal entry is:

A	=	L	+	SE
+10,600				
				+10,000 Rev
		+600		

Cash Flows
+10,600

Mar. 25	Cash	10,600	
	Sales		10,000
	Sales Taxes Payable		600
	(To record daily sales and sales taxes)		

When the company remits the taxes to the taxing agency, it decreases (debits) Sales Taxes Payable and decreases (credits) Cash. The company does not report sales taxes as an expense; it simply forwards to the government the amount paid by the customer. Thus, Cooley Grocery serves only as a **collection agent** for the taxing authority.

Sometimes companies do not ring up sales taxes separately on the cash register. To determine the amount of sales in such cases, divide total receipts by 100% plus the sales tax percentage. For example, assume that Cooley Grocery rings up total receipts of $10,600. Because the amount received from the sale is equal to the sales price 100% plus 6% of sales, or 1.06 times the sales total, we can compute sales as follows: $10,600 ÷ 1.06 = $10,000. Thus, we can find the sales tax amount of $600 by either (1) subtracting sales from total receipts ($10,600 − $10,000) or (2) multiplying sales by the sales tax rate ($10,000 × 6%).

PAYROLL AND PAYROLL TAXES PAYABLE

Assume that Susan Alena works 40 hours this week for Pepitone Inc., earning a wage of $10 per hour. Will Susan receive a $400 check at the end of the week? Not likely. The reason: Pepitone is required to withhold amounts from her wages to pay various governmental authorities. For example, Pepitone will withhold amounts for Social Security taxes and for federal and state income taxes. If these withholdings total $100, Susan will receive a check for only $300. Illustration 10-1 summarizes the types of payroll deductions that normally occur for most companies.

As a result of these deductions, companies withhold from employee paychecks amounts that must be paid to other parties. Pepitone therefore has incurred a liability to pay these third parties, and must report this liability in its balance sheet.

As a second illustration, assume that Cargo Corporation records its payroll for the week of March 7 with the journal entry shown on page 477.

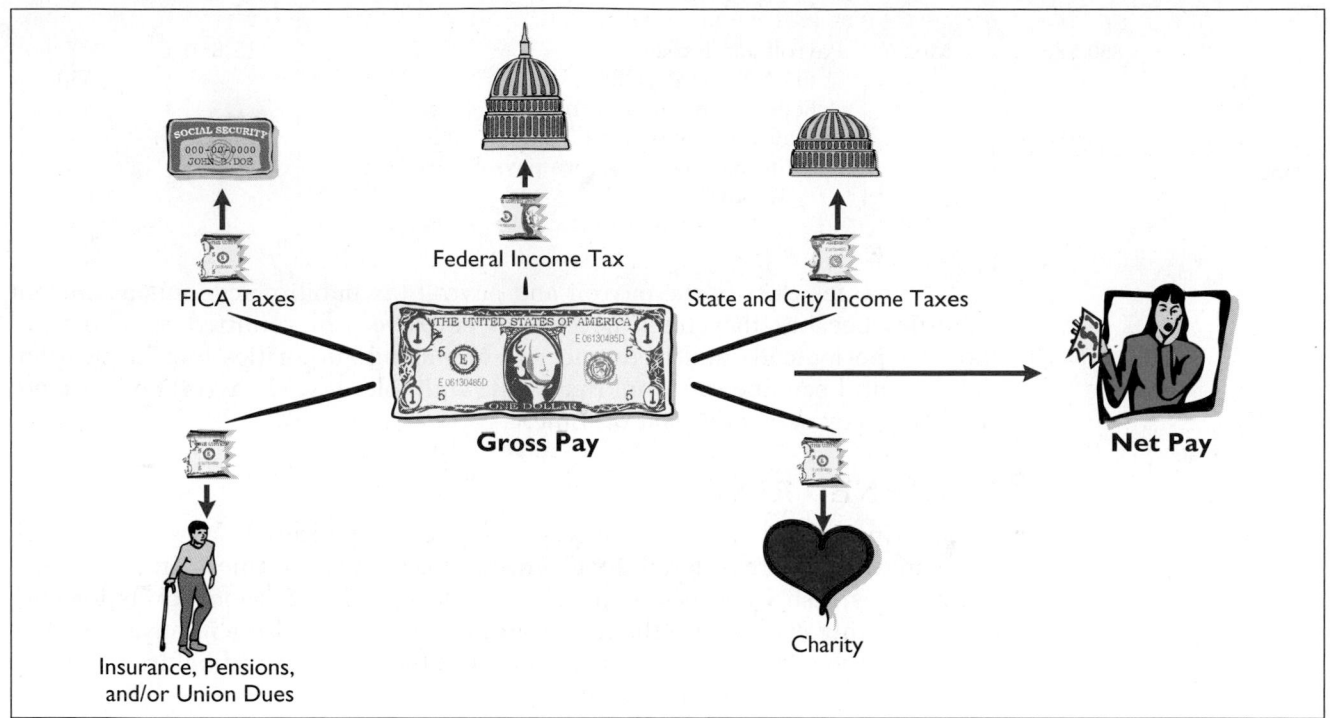

Illustration 10-1
Payroll deductions

Mar. 7	Salaries and Wages Expense	100,000			
	FICA Taxes Payable[1]		7,650		
	Federal Income Taxes Payable		21,864		
	State Income Taxes Payable		2,922		
	Salaries and Wages Payable		67,564		
	(To record payroll and withholding taxes for the week ending March 7)				

A	=	L	+	SE
				−100,000 Exp
		+7,650		
		+21,864		
		+2,922		
		+67,564		

Cash Flows
no effect

Cargo then records payment of this payroll on March 7 as follows.

Mar. 7	Salaries and Wages Payable	67,564	
	Cash		67,564
	(To record payment of the March 7 payroll)		

A	=	L	+	SE
		−67,564		
−67,564				

Cash Flows
−67,564

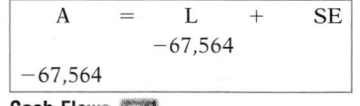

In this case Cargo reports $100,000 in wages and salaries expense. In addition, it reports liabilities for the wages payable as well as liabilities to governmental agencies. Rather than pay the employees $100,000, Cargo instead must withhold the taxes and make the tax payments directly. In summary, Cargo is essentially serving as a tax collector.

In addition to the liabilities incurred as a result of withholdings, employers also incur a second type of payroll-related liability. With every payroll, the employer incurs liabilities to pay various **payroll taxes** levied upon the employer. These payroll taxes include the *employer's share* of Social Security (FICA) taxes and state and federal unemployment taxes. Based on Cargo Corp.'s $100,000 payroll, the company would record the employer's expense and liability for these payroll taxes as follows.

---

[1]Social Security taxes are commonly called FICA taxes. In 1937 Congress enacted the Federal Insurance Contribution Act (FICA). As can be seen in this journal entry and the payroll tax journal entry, the employee and employer must make equal contributions to Social Security. The Social Security rate in 2005 was 7.65% for each.

A	=	L	+	SE
				−13,850 Exp
+7,650				
+800				
+5,400				

Cash Flows
no effect

Mar. 7	Payroll Tax Expense		13,850	
	FICA Taxes Payable			7,650
	Federal Unemployment Taxes Payable			800
	State Unemployment Taxes Payable			5,400
	(To record employer's payroll taxes on March 7 payroll)			

Companies classify the payroll and payroll tax liability accounts as current liabilities because they must be paid to employees or remitted to taxing authorities periodically and in the near term. Taxing authorities impose substantial fines and penalties on employers if the withholding and payroll taxes are not computed correctly and paid on time.

UNEARNED REVENUES

A magazine publisher such as Sports Illustrated may receive a customer's check when magazines are ordered. An airline company such as American Airlines often receives cash when it sells tickets for future flights. Season tickets for concerts, sporting events, and theatre programs are also paid for in advance. How do companies account for unearned revenues that are received before goods are delivered or services are provided?

1. When the company receives an advance, it increases (debits) Cash and also increases (credits) a current liability account identifying the source of the unearned revenue.
2. When the company earns the revenue, it decreases (debits) the unearned revenue account and increases (credits) an earned revenue account.

To illustrate, assume that Superior University sells 10,000 season football tickets at $50 each for its five-game home schedule. The entry for the sales of season tickets is:

A	=	L	+	SE
+500,000				
		+500,000		

Cash Flows
+500,000

Aug. 6	Cash		500,000	
	Unearned Football Ticket Revenue			500,000
	(To record sale of 10,000 season tickets)			

As each game is completed, Superior records the earning of revenue with the following entry.

A	=	L	+	SE
		−100,000		
				+100,000 Rev

Cash Flows
no effect

Sept. 7	Unearned Football Ticket Revenue		100,000	
	Football Ticket Revenue			100,000
	(To record football ticket revenues earned)			

The account Unearned Football Ticket Revenue represents unearned revenue, and the university would report it as a current liability. As the school earns the revenue, it reclassifies the amount from unearned revenue to earned revenue. Unearned revenue is material for some companies: In the airline industry, tickets sold for future flights represent almost 50% of total current liabilities. At United Airlines, unearned ticket revenue recently was the largest current liability, amounting to more than $1 billion.

Illustration 10-2 shows specific unearned and earned revenue accounts used in selected types of businesses.

Type of Business	Account Title	
	Unearned Revenue	**Earned Revenue**
Airline	Unearned Passenger Ticket Revenue	Passenger Ticket Revenue
Magazine publisher	Unearned Subscription Revenue	Subscription Revenue
Hotel	Unearned Rental Revenue	Rental Revenue

Illustration 10-2
Unearned and earned
revenue accounts

CURRENT MATURITIES OF LONG-TERM DEBT

Companies often have a portion of long-term debt that comes due in the current year. As an example, assume that Wendy Construction issues a five-year, interest-bearing $25,000 note on January 1, 2006. This note specifies that each January 1, starting January 1, 2007, Wendy should pay $5,000 of the note. When the company prepares financial statements on December 31, 2006, it should report $5,000 as a current liability and $20,000 as a long-term liability. Companies often identify current maturities of long-term debt on the balance sheet as **long-term debt due within one year**. At December 31, 2003, the Automotive Division of General Motors had $1,090 million of such debt.

It is not necessary to prepare an adjusting entry to recognize the current maturity of long-term debt. At the balance sheet date, all obligations due within one year are classified as current, and all other obligations are classified as long-term.

Accounting across the Organization

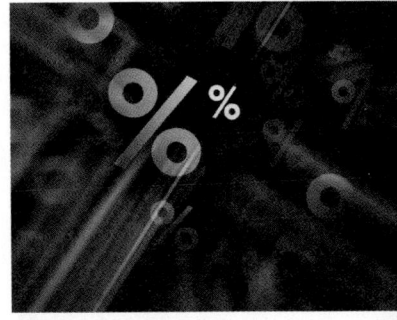

A decision that all companies must make is to what extent to rely on short-term versus long-term financing. The critical nature of this decision was highlighted in the fall of 2001, after the World Trade Center disaster. Prior to September 11, short-term interest rates had been extremely low relative to long-term rates. In order to minimize interest costs, many companies were relying very heavily on short-term financing to purchase things they normally would have used long-term debt for. The problem with short-term financing is that it requires companies to continually find new financing as each loan comes due. This makes them vulnerable to sudden changes in the economy.

After September 11, lenders and short-term investors became very reluctant to loan money. This put the squeeze on many companies: as short-term loans came due, they were unable to refinance. Some were able to get other financing, but at extremely high rates (for example, 12% as compared to 3%). Others were unable to get loans and instead had to sell assets to generate cash for their immediate needs.

Source: Henny Sender, "Firms Feel Consequences of Short-Term Borrowing," *Wall Street Journal Online* (October 12, 2001).

 Based on this story, what is a good general rule to use in choosing between short-term and long-term financing?

BEFORE YOU GO ON . . .

▶ Review It

1. What are the two criteria for classifying a debt as a current liability?
2. What are some examples of current liabilities?
3. What are three items generally withheld from employees' wages or salaries?

4. List three examples of unearned revenues.

5. Identify the liabilities classified as current by Tootsie Roll. The answer to this question appears on page 531.

▶ Do It

During the month of September, Lake Corporation's employees earned wages of $60,000. Withholdings related to these wages were $3,500 for Social Security (FICA), $6,500 for federal income tax, and $2,000 for state income tax. Costs incurred for unemployment taxes were $90 for federal and $150 for state.

Prepare the September 30 journal entries for (a) wages expense and wages payable assuming that all September wages will be paid in October and (b) the company's payroll tax expense.

Action Plan

• Remember that wages earned are an expense to the company, but withholdings reduce the amount due to be paid to the employee.

• Payroll taxes are taxes the company incurs related to its employees.

Solution

(a) To determine wages payable, reduce wages expense by the withholdings for FICA, federal income tax, and state income tax.

Sept. 30	Wages Expense	60,000	
	FICA Taxes Payable		3,500
	Federal Income Taxes Payable		6,500
	State Income Taxes Payable		2,000
	Wages Payable		48,000

(b) Payroll taxes would be for the company's share of FICA, as well as for federal and state unemployment tax.

Sept. 30	Payroll Tax Expense	3,740	
	FICA Taxes Payable		3,500
	Federal Unemployment Taxes Payable		90
	State Unemployment Taxes Payable		150

SECTION TWO
LONG-TERM LIABILITIES

Long-term liabilities are obligations that a company expects to pay after one year. In this section we explain the accounting for the principal types of obligations reported in the long-term liabilities section of the balance sheet. These obligations often are in the form of bonds or long-term notes.

STUDY OBJECTIVE
———4———
Identify the types of bonds.

Bond Basics

Bonds are a form of interest-bearing note payable issued by corporations, universities, and governmental agencies. Bonds, like common stock, are sold in small denominations (usually $1,000 or multiples of $1,000). As a result, bonds attract many investors.

TYPES OF BONDS

Bonds may have different features. In the following sections we describe some commonly issued types of bonds.

Secured and Unsecured Bonds

Secured bonds have specific assets of the issuer pledged as collateral for the bonds. **Unsecured bonds** are issued against the general credit of the borrower. Large corporations with good credit ratings use unsecured bonds extensively. For example, in a recent annual report, Dupont reported more than $2 billion of unsecured bonds outstanding.

Convertible and Callable Bonds

Bonds that can be converted into common stock at the bondholder's option are **convertible bonds**. Bonds that the issuing company can retire at a stated dollar amount prior to maturity are **callable bonds**. Convertible bonds have features that are attractive both to bondholders and to the issuer. The conversion often gives bondholders an opportunity to benefit if the market price of the common stock increases substantially. Furthermore, until conversion, the bondholder receives interest on the bond. For the issuer, the bonds sell at a higher price and pay a lower rate of interest than comparable debt securities that do not have a conversion option. Many corporations, such as USAir, United States Steel Corp., and General Motors Corporation, have convertible bonds outstanding.

Convertible Bonds

"Hey Harv, call in those bonds"

Bond

Bond

Bond

Callable Bonds

Accounting across the Organization

During the boom times of the late 1990s, many rapidly growing companies issued large quantities of convertible bonds. Investors found the convertible bonds attractive because they paid regular interest but also had the upside potential of being converted to stock if the stock price increased. At the time, stock prices were increasing rapidly, so many investors viewed convertible bonds as a cheap and safe way to buy stock.

As a consequence, companies were able to pay much lower interest rates on convertible bonds than on standard bonds. When the bonds were issued, company managers assumed that the bonds would be converted. Thus the company would never have to repay the debt with cash. It seemed too good to be true—and it was.

When stock prices plummeted in the early 2000s, investors no longer had an incentive to convert, since the market price was below the conversion price. Now many of these massive bonds are coming due, and companies are being forced either to pay them off or to issue new debt at much higher rates.

 The drop in stock prices did not change the debt to total assets ratios of these companies. Discuss how the perception of a high debt to total assets ratio changed before and after the fall in stock prices.

ISSUING PROCEDURES

A **bond certificate** is issued to the investor to provide evidence of the investor's claim against the company. As Illustration 10-3 (page 482) shows, the bond certificate provides information such as the name of the company that issued the bonds, the face value of the bonds, the maturity date of the bonds, and the contractual interest rate. The **face value** is the amount due at the maturity date. The **maturity date** is the date that the final payment is due to the investor from the issuing company. The **contractual interest rate** is the rate used to determine the amount of cash interest the borrower pays and the investor receives. Usually the contractual rate is stated as an annual rate, and interest is generally paid semiannually.

Alternative Terminology
The contractual rate is often referred to as the *stated rate*.

Illustration 10-3
Bond certificate

DETERMINING THE MARKET VALUE OF BONDS

If you were an investor wanting to purchase a bond, how would you determine how much to pay? To be more specific, assume that Coronet, Inc. issues a zero-interest (pays no interest) bond with a face value of $1,000,000 due in 20 years. For this bond, the only cash you receive is $1 million at the end of 20 years. Would you pay $1 million for this bond?

We hope not, because $1 million received 20 years from now is not the same as $1 million received today. The term **time value of money** is used to indicate the relationship between time and money—that a dollar received today is worth more than a dollar promised at some time in the future. If you had $1 million today, you would invest it and earn interest so that at the end of 20 years, your investment would be worth much more than $1 million. Thus, if someone is going to pay you $1 million 20 years from now, you would want to find its equivalent today, or its **present value**. In other words, you would want to determine how much must be invested today at current interest rates to have $1 million in 20 years.

The current market value (present value) of a bond is therefore a function of three factors: (1) the dollar amounts to be received, (2) the length of time until the amounts are received, and (3) the market interest rate. The **market interest**

Same dollars at different times are not equal.

rate is the rate investors demand for loaning funds. The process of finding the present value is referred to as **discounting** the future amounts.

To illustrate, assume that Acropolis Company on January 1, 2007, issues $100,000 of 9% bonds, due in five years, with interest payable annually at year-end. The purchaser of the bonds would receive the following two types of cash payments: (1) **principal** of $100,000 to be paid at maturity, and (2) five $9,000 **interest payments** ($100,000 × 9%) over the term of the bonds. Illustration 10-4 shows a time diagram depicting both cash flows.

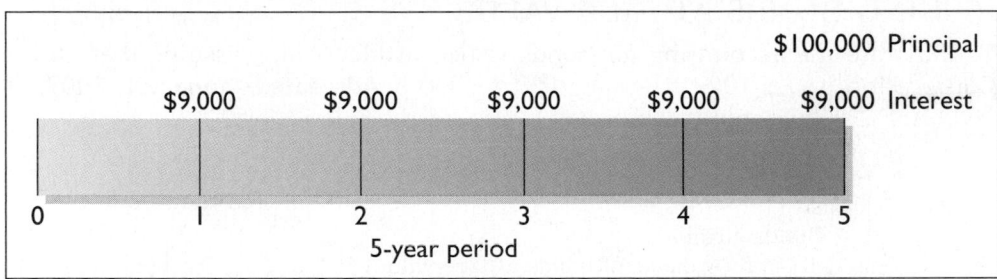

Illustration 10-4
Time diagram depicting cash flows

The current market value of a bond is equal to the present value of all the future cash payments promised by the bond. Illustration 10-5 lists and totals the present values of these amounts, assuming the market rate of interest is 9%.

Present value of $100,000 received in 5 years	$ 64,993
Present value of $9,000 received annually for 5 years	35,007
Market price of bonds	**$100,000**

Illustration 10-5
Computing the market price of bonds

Tables are available to provide the present value numbers to be used, or these values can be determined mathematically.[2] Appendix C, near the end of the book, provides further discussion of the concepts and the mechanics of the time value of money computations.

BEFORE YOU GO ON . . .

▶ **Review It**

1. What are bonds?
2. What are secured versus unsecured bonds and callable versus convertible bonds?
3. Explain the terms *face value* and *contractual interest rate*.
4. Explain why you would prefer to receive $1 million today rather than five years from now.

Accounting for Bond Issues

A corporation records bond transactions when it issues or retires (buys back) bonds and when bondholders convert bonds into common stock. If bondholders sell their bond investments to other investors, the issuing firm receives no

---

[2]For those knowledgable in the use of present value tables, the computations in this example are: $100,000 × .64993 = $64,993 and $9,000 × 3.88965 = $35,007 (rounded).

further money on the transaction, **nor does the issuing corporation journalize the transaction** (although it does keep records of the names of bondholders in some cases).

Bonds may be issued at face value, below face value (discount), or above face value (premium). Bond prices for both new issues and existing bonds are quoted as **a percentage of the face value of the bond. Face value is usually $1,000.** Thus, a $1,000 bond with a quoted price of 97 means that the selling price of the bond is 97% of face value, or $970.

STUDY OBJECTIVE

5

Prepare the entries for the issuance of bonds and interest expense.

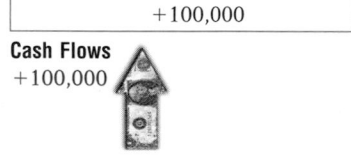

ISSUING BONDS AT FACE VALUE

To illustrate the accounting for bonds issued at face value, assume that Devor Corporation issues 100, five-year, 10%, $1,000 bonds dated January 1, 2007, at 100 (100% of face value). The entry to record the sale is:

Jan. 1	Cash	100,000	
	Bonds Payable		100,000
	(To record sale of bonds at face value)		

Devor reports bonds payable in the long-term liabilities section of the balance sheet because the maturity date is January 1, 2012 (more than one year away).

Over the term (life) of the bonds, companies make entries to record bond interest. Interest on bonds payable is computed in the same manner as interest on notes payable, as explained earlier. If we assume that interest is payable annually on January 1 on the bonds described above, Devor accrues interest of $10,000 ($100,000 × 10% × $\frac{12}{12}$) on December 31.

At December 31 Devor recognizes the $10,000 of interest expense incurred with the following adjusting entry.

Helpful Hint Interest Expense = Principal × Rate × Time

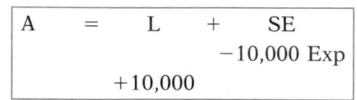

Dec. 31	Bond Interest Expense	10,000	
	Bond Interest Payable		10,000
	(To accrue bond interest)		

The company classifies **bond interest payable as a current liability** because it is scheduled for payment within the next year. When Devor pays the interest on January 1, 2008, it decreases (debits) Bond Interest Payable and decreases (credits) Cash for $10,000.

Devor records the payment on January 1 as follows.

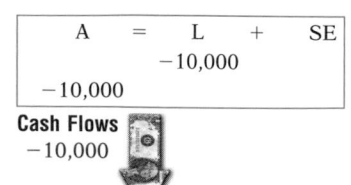

Jan. 1	Bond Interest Payable	10,000	
	Cash		10,000
	(To record payment of bond interest)		

DISCOUNT OR PREMIUM ON BONDS

The previous illustrations assumed that the contractual (stated) interest rate and the market (effective) interest rate paid on bonds were the same. Recall that the **contractual interest rate** is the rate applied to the face (par) value to arrive at the interest paid in a year. The **market interest rate** is the rate investors demand for loaning funds to the corporation. When the contractual interest rate and the market interest rate are the same, **bonds sell at face value.**

However, market interest rates change daily. The type of bond issued, the state of the economy, current industry conditions, and the company's individual performance all affect market interest rates. As a result, the contractual and market interest rates often differ. To make bonds salable when the two rates differ, bonds sell below or above face value.

To illustrate, suppose that a company issues 10% bonds at a time when other bonds of similar risk are paying 12%. Investors will not be interested in buying the 10% bonds, so their value will fall below their face value. In this case, we say the 10% bonds are **selling at a** discount. As a result of the decline in the bonds' selling price, the actual interest rate incurred by the company increases to the level of the current market interest rate.

Conversely, if the market rate of interest is **lower than** the contractual interest rate, investors will have to pay more than face value for the bonds. That is, if the market rate of interest is 8% but the contractual interest rate on the bonds is 10%, the issuer will require more funds from the investor. In these cases, **bonds sell at a** premium. Illustration 10-6 shows these relationships graphically.

Helpful Hint Bond prices *vary inversely* with changes in the market interest rate: As market interest rates decline, bond prices will increase. When a bond is issued, if the market interest rate is below the contractual rate, the price will be higher than the face value.

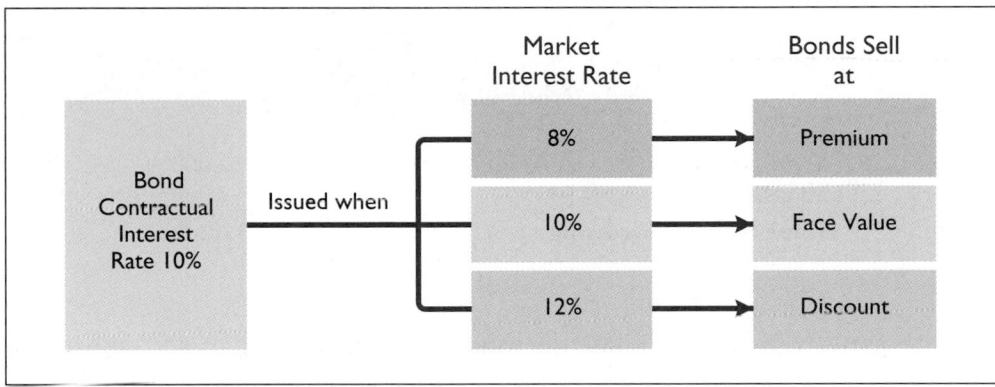

Illustration 10-6 Interest rates and bond prices

Issuance of bonds at an amount different from face value is quite common. By the time a company prints the bond certificates and markets the bonds, it will be a coincidence if the market rate and the contractual rate are the same. Thus, the issuance of bonds at a discount does not mean that the financial strength of the issuer is suspect. Conversely, the sale of bonds at a premium does not indicate that the financial strength of the issuer is exceptional.

Helpful Hint Some bonds are sold at a discount by design. "Zero-coupon" bonds, which pay no interest, sell at a deep discount to face value.

ISSUING BONDS AT A DISCOUNT

To illustrate the issuance of bonds at a discount, assume that on January 1, 2007, Candlestick Inc. sells $100,000, five-year, 10% bonds at 98 (98% of face value) with interest payable on January 1. The entry to record the issuance is:

Jan. 1	Cash	98,000	
	Discount on Bonds Payable	2,000	
	Bonds Payable		100,000
	(To record sale of bonds at a discount)		

A	=	L	+	SE
+98,000				
				−2,000
				+100,000

Cash Flows
+98,000

Although Discount on Bonds Payable has a debit balance, **it is not an asset**. Rather it is a **contra account**, which is **deducted from bonds payable** on the balance sheet as shown in Illustration 10-7 (page 486).

Illustration 10-7
Statement presentation of discount on bonds payable

CANDLESTICK INC. Balance Sheet (partial)		
Long-term liabilities		
Bonds payable	$100,000	
Less: Discount on bonds payable	2,000	$98,000

Helpful Hint The carrying value (book value) of bonds issued at a discount is determined by subtracting the balance of the discount account from the balance of the Bonds Payable account.

The $98,000 represents the **carrying (or book) value** of the bonds. On the date of issue this amount equals the market price of the bonds.

The issuance of bonds below face value causes the total cost of borrowing to differ from the bond interest paid. That is, the issuing corporation not only must pay the contractual interest rate over the term of the bonds but also must pay the face value (rather than the issuance price) at maturity. Therefore, the difference between the issuance price and the face value of the bonds—the discount—is an **additional cost of borrowing**. The company records this cost as **bond interest expense** over the life of the bonds. The total cost of borrowing $98,000 for Candlestick Inc. is $52,000, computed as shown in Illustration 10-8.

Illustration 10-8
Computation of total cost of borrowing—bonds issued at discount

Bonds Issued at a Discount	
Annual interest payments	
($100,000 × 10% = $10,000; $10,000 × 5)	$ 50,000
Add: Bond discount ($100,000 − $98,000)	2,000
Total cost of borrowing	**$52,000**

Alternatively, we can compute the total cost of borrowing as shown in Illustration 10-9.

Illustration 10-9
Alternative computation of total cost of borrowing—bonds issued at discount

Bonds Issued at a Discount	
Principal at maturity	$100,000
Annual interest payments ($10,000 × 5)	50,000
Cash to be paid to bondholders	150,000
Cash received from bondholders	98,000
Total cost of borrowing	**$ 52,000**

To follow the matching principle, companies allocate bond discount to expense in each period in which the bonds are outstanding. This is referred to as **amortizing the discount**. Amortization of the discount **increases** the amount of interest expense reported each period. That is, after the company amortizes the discount, the amount of interest expense it reports in a period will exceed the contractual amount. As shown in Illustration 10-8, for the bonds issued by Candlestick Inc., total interest expense will exceed the contractual interest by $2,000 over the life of the bonds.

As the discount is amortized, its balance declines. As a consequence, the carrying value of the bonds will increase, until at maturity the carrying value of the bonds equals their face amount. This is shown in Illustration 10-10. Appendix 10A and Appendix 10B at the end of this chapter discuss procedures for amortizing bond discount.

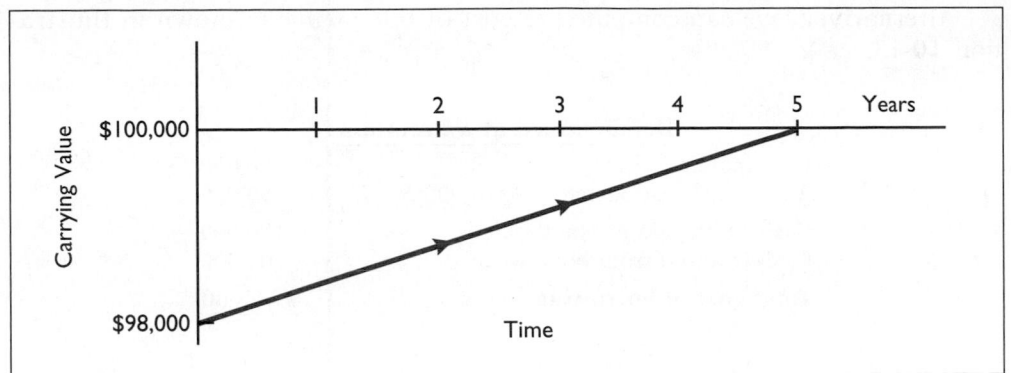

Illustration 10-10
Amortization of bond discount

ISSUING BONDS AT A PREMIUM

We can illustrate the issuance of bonds at a premium by now assuming the Candlestick Inc. bonds described above sell at 102 (102% of face value) rather than at 98. The entry to record the sale is:

Helpful Hint Both a discount and a premium account are valuation accounts. A *valuation account* is one that is needed to value properly the item to which it relates.

Jan. 1	Cash	102,000	
	Bonds Payable		100,000
	Premium on Bonds Payable		2,000
	(To record sale of bonds at a premium)		

A	=	L	+	SE
+102,000				
		+100,000		
		+2,000		

Cash Flows
+102,000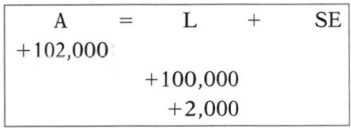

Candlestick adds the premium on bonds payable **to the bonds payable** amount on the balance sheet, as shown in Illustration 10-11.

Illustration 10-11
Statement presentation of bond premium

CANDLESTICK INC.		
Balance Sheet (partial)		
Long-term liabilities		
Bonds payable	$100,000	
Add: Premium on bonds payable	**2,000**	$102,000

The sale of bonds above face value causes the total cost of borrowing to be **less than the bond interest paid** because the borrower is not required to pay the bond premium at the maturity date of the bonds. Thus, the premium is considered to be **a reduction in the cost of borrowing** that reduces bond interest expense over the life of the bonds. The total cost of borrowing $102,000 for Candlestick Inc. is $48,000, computed as in Illustration 10-12.

Illustration 10-12
Computation of total cost of borrowing—bonds issued at a premium

Bonds Issued at a Premium	
Annual interest payments	
($100,000 × 10% = $10,000; $10,000 × 5)	$ 50,000
Less: Bond premium ($102,000 − $100,000)	2,000
Total cost of borrowing	**$48,000**

Alternatively, we can compute the cost of borrowing as shown in Illustration 10-13.

Bonds Issued at a Premium	
Principal at maturity	$100,000
Annual interest payments ($10,000 × 5)	50,000
Cash to be paid to bondholders	150,000
Cash received from bondholders	102,000
Total cost of borrowing	**$ 48,000**

Similar to bond discount, companies allocate bond premium to expense in each period in which the bonds are outstanding. This is referred to as **amortizing the premium**. Amortization of the premium **decreases** the amount of interest expense reported each period. That is, after the company amortizes the premium, the amount of interest expense it reports in a period will be less than the contractual amount. As shown in Illustration 10-12, for the bonds issued by Candlestick Inc., contractual interest will exceed the interest expense by $2,000 over the life of the bonds.

As the premium is amortized, its balance declines. As a consequence, the carrying value of the bonds will decrease, until at maturity the carrying value of the bonds equals their face amount. This is shown in Illustration 10-14. Appendix 10A and Appendix 10B at the end of this chapter discuss procedures for amortizing bond premium.

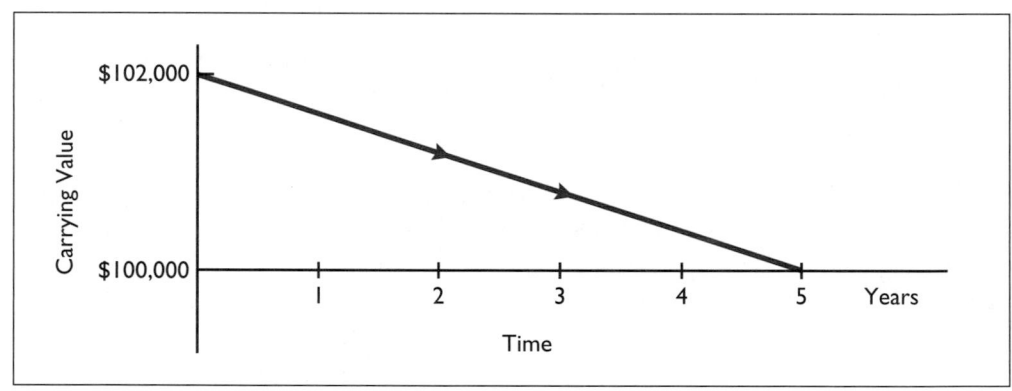

Accounting for Bond Retirements

Bonds are retired when the issuing corporation purchases (redeems) them. The appropriate entries for these transactions are explained next.

REDEEMING BONDS AT MATURITY

Regardless of the issue price of bonds, the book value of the bonds at maturity will equal their face value. Assuming that the company pays and records separately the interest for the last interest period, Candlestick records the redemption of its bonds at maturity as:

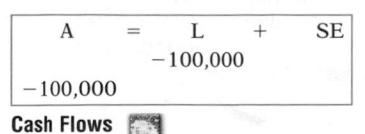

Bonds Payable	100,000	
Cash		100,000
(To record redemption of bonds at maturity)		

REDEEMING BONDS BEFORE MATURITY

Bonds may be redeemed before maturity. A company may decide to retire bonds before maturity in order to reduce interest cost and remove debt from its balance sheet. A company should retire debt early only if it has sufficient cash resources.

When bonds are retired before maturity, it is necessary to: (1) eliminate the carrying value of the bonds at the redemption date, (2) record the cash paid, and (3) recognize the gain or loss on redemption. The **carrying value** of the bonds is the face value of the bonds less unamortized bond discount or plus unamortized bond premium at the redemption date.

To illustrate, assume at the end of the fourth period, Candlestick Inc., having sold its bonds at a premium, retires the bonds at 103 after paying the annual interest. Assume that the carrying value of the bonds at the redemption date is $100,400. Candlestick records the redemption at the end of the fourth interest period (January 1, 2011) as:

Jan. 1	Bonds Payable	100,000	
	Premium on Bonds Payable	400	
	Loss on Bond Redemption	2,600	
	Cash		103,000
	(To record redemption of bonds at 103)		

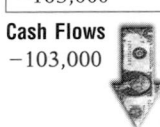

Cash Flows
−103,000

Note that the loss of $2,600 is the difference between the $103,000 cash paid and the $100,400 carrying value of the bonds.

BEFORE YOU GO ON . . .

▶ Review It

1. What entry is made to record the issuance of bonds payable of $1 million at 100? At 96? At 102?
2. Why do bonds sell at a discount? At a premium? At face value?
3. Explain the accounting for redemption of bonds at maturity and before maturity by payment in cash.

▶ Do It

Assume a company issued bonds with the following characteristics: (a) interest to be paid $50,000, (b) interest expense to be recorded $52,000, and (c) amortization $2,000. Answer these questions: (1) Were the bonds sold at a premium or a discount? (2) After recording the interest expense, will the bond carrying value increase or decrease?

Action Plan

• Know the effects that the amortization of bond discount and bond premium have on bond interest expense and on the carrying value of the bonds.
• Remember bond discount amortization increases both bond interest expense and the carrying value of the bonds. Bond premium amortization has the reverse effects.

Solution

(1) Interest expense is $2,000 greater than the interest paid. This difference is equal to the amortization amount. Thus, the bonds were sold at a discount. (2) The interest entry will decrease Discount on Bonds Payable and increase the carrying value of the bonds.

THE NAVIGATOR

STUDY OBJECTIVE
7

Identify the requirements for the financial statement presentation and analysis of liabilities.

Financial Statement Presentation and Analysis

BALANCE SHEET PRESENTATION

Current liabilities are the first category under Liabilities on the balance sheet. Companies list each of the principal types of current liabilities separately within the category.

Within the current liabilities section, companies usually list notes payable first, followed by accounts payable. Other items sometimes are listed in the order of their magnitude. *In your homework, you should present notes payable first, followed by accounts payable, and then other liabilities in order of magnitude.*

Companies report long-term liabilities in a separate section of the balance sheet immediately following "Current liabilities." An example is shown in Illustration 10-15.

Illustration 10-15
Balance sheet presentation of liabilities

MARAIS COMPANY Balance Sheet (partial)		
Liabilities		
Current liabilities		
Notes payable	$ 250,000	
Accounts payable	125,000	
Current maturities of long-term debt	300,000	
Accrued liabilities	75,000	
Total current liabilities		$ 750,000
Long-term liabilities		
Bonds payable	1,000,000	
Less: Discount on bonds payable	80,000	920,000
Notes payable, secured by plant assets		540,000
Lease liability		500,000
Total long-term liabilities		1,960,000
Total liabilities		$2,710,000

Disclosure of debt is very important. Failures at Enron, WorldCom, and Global Crossing, have made investors very concerned about companies' debt obligations. Summary data regarding debts may be presented in the balance sheet with detailed data (such as interest rates, maturity dates, conversion privileges, and assets pledged as collateral) shown in a supporting schedule in the notes. Companies should report current maturities of long-term debt as a current liability.

STATEMENT OF CASH FLOWS PRESENTATION

The balance sheet presents the balances of a company's debts at a point in time. The statement of cash flows also presents information about a company's debts. Information regarding cash inflows and outflows during the year that resulted from the principal portion of debt transactions appears in the "Financing activities" section of the statement of cash flows. Interest expense is reported in the "Operating activities" section, even though it resulted from debt transactions.

Illustration 10-16 presents the cash flows from financing activities from the statement of cash flows for the Automotive Division of General Motors. From this we learn that the division issued new long-term debt of $758 million and repaid long-term debt of $79 million.

**GENERAL MOTORS CORPORATION—
AUTOMOTIVE DIVISION**
Statement of Cash Flows (partial)
2004
(in millions)

Cash flows from financing activities	
Net increase (decrease) in loans payable	$ (803)
Long-term debt—borrowings	**758**
Long-term debt—repayments	**(79)**
Cash dividends paid to stockholders	(1,129)
Net cash (used in) provided by financing activities	$ (1,253)

Illustration 10-16
Financing activities
section of statement of
cash flows

ANALYSIS

Careful examination of debt obligations helps you assess a company's ability to pay its current and long-term obligations. It also helps you determine whether a company can obtain debt financing in order to grow. We will use the following information from the financial statements of General Motors to illustrate the analysis of a company's liquidity and solvency.

**GENERAL MOTORS CORPORATION—
AUTOMOTIVE DIVISION**
Balance Sheets
December 31, 2004 and 2003
(in millions)

Assets	2004	2003
Total current assets	$ 55,515	$ 57,855
Noncurrent assets	103,788	103,930
Total assets	$159,303	$161,785
Liabilities and Stockholders' Equity		
Total current liabilities	$ 74,892	$ 71,264
Noncurrent liabilities	78,894	85,397
Total liabilities	153,786	156,661
Total stockholders' equity	5,517	5,124
Total liabilities and stockholders' equity	$159,303	$161,785

Illustration 10-17
Simplified balance sheets
for General Motors
Corporation

Liquidity

Liquidity ratios measure the short-term ability of a company to pay its maturing obligations and to meet unexpected needs for cash. A commonly used measure of liquidity is the current ratio (presented in Chapter 2). The current ratio is calculated as current assets divided by current liabilities. Illustration 10-18 presents the current ratio for General Motors along with the industry average.

Illustration 10-18
Current ratio

($ in millions)	General Motors		Industry Average
	2004	**2003**	**2004**
Current Ratio	$\dfrac{\$55,515}{\$74,892} = .74{:}1$	$\dfrac{\$57,855}{\$71,264} = .81{:}1$	1.59:1

General Motors' current assets are less than its current liabilities. Therefore its current ratio is less than 1 in both 2003 and 2004. The industry average current ratio for manufacturers of autos and trucks is 1.59:1.[3] Thus, General Motors appears to lack liquidity.

Many companies today minimize their liquid assets (such as cash, accounts receivable, and inventory) in order to improve profitability measures, such as return on assets. This is particularly true of large companies such as GM. Companies that keep fewer liquid assets on hand must rely on other sources of liquidity. One such source is a **bank line of credit**. A line of credit is a prearranged agreement between a company and a lender that permits the company, should it be necessary, to borrow up to an agreed-upon amount. The disclosure regarding debt in General Motors' financial statements states that it has $8.3 billion of unused lines of credit. This represents a substantial amount of available cash. In addition, the Management Discussion and Analysis section of GM's annual report provides an extensive discussion of the company's liquidity. In it, GM notes that even though its credit rating was downgraded during the year, its "access to the capital markets remained sufficient to meet the Corporation's capital needs." Thus, even though General Motors has a low current ratio, its available lines of credit as well as other sources of financing appear adequate to meet any short-term cash deficiency it might experience.

Decision Toolkit

Decision Checkpoints	Info Needed for Decision	Tool to Use for Decision	How to Evaluate Results
Can the company obtain short-term financing when necessary?	Available lines of credit, from notes to the financial statements.	Compare available lines of credit to current liabilities. Also, evaluate liquidity ratios.	If liquidity ratios are low, then lines of credit should be high to compensate.

Solvency

Solvency ratios measure the ability of a company to survive over a long period of time. The Feature Story in this chapter mentioned that although there once were many U.S. automobile manufacturers, only two U.S.-based companies remain today. Many of the others went bankrupt. This highlights the fact that when making a long-term loan or purchasing a company's stock, you must give consideration to a company's solvency.

To reduce the risks associated with having a large amount of debt during an economic downturn, U.S. automobile manufacturers have taken two precautionary steps. First, they have built up large balances of cash and cash equivalents to avoid a cash crisis. Second, recently they have been reluctant to build new plants or hire new workers to meet their production needs. Instead, they have asked existing workers to put in overtime, or they "outsource" work to other companies. In this way, if an economic downturn occurs, they avoid having to make debt payments on idle production plants, and they minimize layoffs.

In Chapter 2 you learned that one measure of a company's solvency is the debt to total assets ratio. This is calculated as total liabilities divided by total assets. This ratio indicates the extent to which a company's assets are financed with debt.

---

[3]Market Guide based this and subsequent industry ratios used in this chapter on a group of 29 companies that manufacture cars and trucks (see *multex.com*).

Other measures can also be useful in assessing solvency. One such measure is the **times interest earned ratio**, which provides an indication of a company's ability to meet interest payments as they come due. It is computed by dividing income before interest expense and income taxes by interest expense. It uses income before interest expense and taxes because this number best represents the amount available to pay interest.

We can use the balance sheet information presented on page 491 and the additional information below to calculate solvency ratios for the Automotive Division of General Motors.

($ in millions)	2004	2003
Net income (loss)	$(89)	$995
Interest expense	2,480	1,780
Tax expense (refund)	(2,325)	(869)

The debt to total assets ratios and times interest earned ratios for General Motors and averages for the industry are shown in Illustration 10-19.

Illustration 10-19
Solvency ratios

$$\text{Debt to Total Assets Ratio} = \frac{\text{Total Liabilities}}{\text{Total Assets}}$$

$$\frac{\text{Times Interest Earned}}{\text{Ratio}} = \frac{\text{Net Income} + \text{Interest Expense} + \text{Tax Expense}}{\text{Interest Expense}}$$

($ in millions)	General Motors 2004	General Motors 2003	Industry Average 2004
Debt to Total Assets Ratio	$\dfrac{\$153,786}{\$159,303} = 97\%$	$\dfrac{\$156,661}{\$161,785} = 97\%$	84.6%
Times Interest Earned Ratio	$\dfrac{\$(89) + \$2,480 - \$2,325}{\$2,480}$ = .03 times	$\dfrac{\$995 + \$1,780 - \$869}{\$1,780}$ = 1.07 times	6.38 times

General Motors' debt to total assets ratio remained constant at 97%. The industry average for manufacturers of autos and trucks is 84.6%. Thus, General Motors' ratio is very high, especially considering that we are looking only at the automotive division and have excluded the financing division of the company, which traditionally has a very high debt to total assets ratio.

General Motors' times interest earned ratio declined from 1.07 times in 2003 to .03 in 2004. The industry average for manufacturers of autos and trucks is much higher at 6.38 times. In 2004, General Motors' income before interest expense and taxes—that is, income after adding back interest expense and in this case, deducting a tax refund—was only $66 million. The company's high debt to total assets ratio, combined with its interest coverage ratio of .03, should be of obvious concern to the company's creditors and investors. This concern was reflected in a downgrade to GM's credit rating by debt-rating services.

Business Insight
Investor Perspective

The Williams Companies recently faced the prospect of a credit-rating downgrade by Moody's Investors Service Inc. Lenders are heavily influenced by these ratings, so a downgrade would make it harder for the company to borrow funds, as well as make borrowing more expensive. The company quickly announced plans to improve its liquidity and solvency. It said it would sell assets of $1.5 to $3.0 billion, issue common stock of $1 to $1.5 billion, and cut annual costs by $100 million. It also said it would continue to evaluate the size of its dividend payment on common stock. It said it would use the funds generated by these actions to pay down existing debt and to increase its liquidity.

Source: "Williams Unveils Measures to Bolster its Balance Sheet," *Wall Street Journal Online* (May 28, 2002).

 Explain how the sale of plant assets could improve the company's solvency.

Decision Toolkit

Decision Checkpoints	Info Needed for Decision	Tool to Use for Decision	How to Evaluate Results
Can the company meet its obligations in the long term?	Interest expense and net income before interest and taxes	Times interest earned ratio $= \dfrac{\text{Net income} + \text{Interest expense} + \text{Tax expense}}{\text{Interest expense}}$	High ratio indicates ability to meet interest payments as scheduled.

Off-Balance-Sheet Financing

A concern for analysts when they evaluate a company's liquidity and solvency is whether that company has properly recorded all of its obligations. The bankruptcy of Enron Corporation, one of the largest bankruptcies in U.S. history, demonstrated how much damage can result when a company does not properly record or disclose all of its debts. Many would say Enron was practicing off-balance-sheet financing. **Off-balance-sheet financing** is an attempt to borrow funds in such a way that the obligations are not recorded. Two common types of off-balance-sheet financing result from contingencies and lease transactions.

CONTINGENCIES

One reason a company's balance sheet might not fully reflect its potential obligations is due to contingencies. **Contingencies** are events with uncertain outcomes. A common type of contingency is lawsuits. Suppose, for example, that you were analyzing the financial statements of a cigarette manufacturer and did not consider the possible negative implications of existing unsettled lawsuits. Your analysis of the company's financial position would certainly be misleading. Other common types of contingencies are product warranties and environmental cleanup obligations. For example, in 2004 Novartis AG began offering a money-back guarantee on its blood-pressure medications The creation of this guarantee will necessitate an accrual for the estimated claims that will result from returns.

Accounting rules require that companies disclose contingencies in the notes; in some cases they must accrue them as liabilities. For example, suppose that Waterbury Inc. is sued by a customer for $1 million due to an injury sustained by a defective product. If at the company's year-end, the lawsuit had not yet been resolved, how should Waterbury account for this event? If the company can determine **a reasonable estimate** of the expected loss and if it is **probable** it will lose the suit, then the company should accrue for the loss. It records the loss by increasing (debiting) a loss account and increasing (crediting) a liability such as Lawsuit Liability. If *both* of these conditions are not met, then the company discloses the basic facts regarding this suit in the notes to its financial statements.

LEASING

One common type of off-balance-sheet financing results from leasing. Most lessees do not like to report leases on their balance sheets because the lease increases the company's total liabilities. Recall from Chapter 9 that operating leases are treated like rentals—no asset or liabilities show on the books. Capital leases are treated like a purchase—increasing both assets and liabilities. **As a result, many companies structure their lease agreements to avoid meeting the criteria of a capital lease.**

Recall from Chapter 9 that many U.S. airlines lease a large portion of their planes without showing any debt related to them on their balance sheets. For example, the total increase in assets and liabilities that would result if Southwest Airlines recorded on the balance sheet its off-balance-sheet **"operating" leases** would be approximately $2.7 billion. Illustration 10-20 presents Southwest Airlines' debt to total assets ratio using the numbers presented in its balance sheet and also shows the ratio after adjusting for the off-balance-sheet leases. After those adjustments, Southwest has a ratio of 61% versus 51% before. This means that of every dollar of assets, 61 cents was funded by debt. This would be of interest to analysts evaluating Southwest's solvency.

	Using numbers as presented on balance sheet	Adjusted for off-balance-sheet leases
Debt to total assets ratio	$\dfrac{\$5,813}{\$11,337} = 51\%$	$\dfrac{\$5,813 + \$2,677}{\$11,337 + \$2,677} = 61\%$

Illustration 10-20
Debt to total assets ratio adjusted for leases

Critics of off-balance-sheet financing contend that many leases represent unavoidable obligations that meet the definition of a liability, and therefore companies should report them as liabilities on the balance sheet. To reduce these concerns, companies are required to report in a note their operating lease obligations for subsequent years. This allows analysts and other financial statement users to adjust a company's financial statements by adding leased assets and lease liabilities if they feel that this treatment is more appropriate.

Decision Toolkit

Decision Checkpoints	Info Needed for Decision	Tool to Use for Decision	How to Evaluate Results
Does the company have any contingent liabilities?	Knowledge of events with uncertain negative outcomes	Notes to financial statements and financial statements	If negative outcomes are possible, determine the probability, the amount of loss, and the potential impact on financial statements.
Does the company have significant off-balance-sheet financing, such as unrecorded lease obligations?	Information on unrecorded obligations, such as a schedule of minimum lease payments from the lease note	Compare liquidity and solvency ratios with and without unrecorded obligations included.	If ratios differ significantly after including unrecorded obligations, these obligations should not be ignored in analysis.

BEFORE YOU GO ON . . .

▶ Review It

1. What is meant by solvency?
2. What information does the times interest earned ratio provide, and how is the ratio calculated?
3. What is meant by "off-balance-sheet financing"? What is a common example of off-balance-sheet financing?
4. What are contingent liabilities?

 THE NAVIGATOR

Using the Decision Toolkit

Ford Motor Company has enjoyed some tremendous successes, including its popular Taurus and Explorer vehicles. Yet observers are looking for the next big hit. Development of a new vehicle costs billions. A flop is financially devastating, and the financial effect is magnified if the company has large amounts of outstanding debt.

The balance sheets below provide financial information for the Automotive Division of Ford Motor Company as of December 31, 2004 and 2003. We have chosen to analyze only the Automotive Division rather than the total corporation, which includes Ford's giant financing division. In an actual analysis you would want to analyze the major divisions individually as well as the combined corporation as a whole.

Instructions

1. Evaluate Ford's liquidity using appropriate ratios, and compare to those of General Motors and to industry averages.
2. Evaluate Ford's solvency using appropriate ratios, and compare to those of General Motors and to industry averages.
3. Comment on Ford's available lines of credit.

FORD MOTOR COMPANY—AUTOMOTIVE DIVISION
Balance Sheets
December 31, 2004 and 2003
(in millions)

Assets	2004	2003
Current assets	$ 44,703	$ 43,742
Noncurrent assets	71,719	71,702
Total assets	$116,422	$115,444
Liabilities and Shareholders' Equity		
Current liabilities	$ 55,027	$ 52,292
Noncurrent liabilities	57,612	64,612
Total liabilities	112,639	116,904
Total shareholders' equity	3,783	(1,460)
Total liabilities and shareholders' equity	$116,422	$115,444
Other Information		
Net income (loss)	$ (155)	$ (1,908)
Tax expense (refund)	(30)	(175)
Interest expense	1,221	1,323
Available lines of credit (Automotive Division)	7,100	

Solution

1. Ford's liquidity can be measured using the current ratio:

	2004	**2003**
Current ratio	$\dfrac{\$44,703}{\$55,027} = .81{:}1$	$\dfrac{\$43,742}{\$52,292} = .84{:}1$

Like that of General Motors, Ford's current ratio is well below the industry average of 1.59:1 and below 1—indicating that its current assets are less than its current liabilities. These are increasingly common levels for large companies that have reduced the amount of cash, inventory, and receivables they hold. As noted earlier, these low current ratios are not necessarily cause for concern, but they do require more careful monitoring. Ford must also make sure to have other short-term financing options available, such as lines of credit.

2. Ford's solvency can be measured with the debt to total assets ratio and the times interest earned ratio:

	2004	**2003**
Debt to total assets ratio	$\dfrac{\$112,639}{\$116,422} = 97\%$	$\dfrac{\$116,904}{\$115,444} = 101\%$
Times interest earned ratio	$\dfrac{\$(155) + \$1,221 - \$30}{\$1,221}$	$\dfrac{\$(1,908) + \$1,323 - \$175}{\$1,323}$
	$= .85$ times	$= 0$ times

The debt to total assets ratio suggests that Ford, like General Motors, relies very heavily on debt financing. The ratio decreased from 2003 to 2004, indicating that the company's solvency improved slightly. In 2003 its ratio exceeds 1. This is possible because we have calculated the ratio for the Automotive Division only, rather than the whole company. The debt to total assets ratio for the entire company is 94.5%. This is extremely high.

  The times interest earned ratio increased from a zero in 2003 to .85 in 2004. The 2003 ratio is zero because, even after adding back interest and taxes, the company's income was negative. This is well below the industry average of 6.38 times. It is likely that the company's solvency was a concern to investors and creditors and would be closely monitored.

3. Ford has available lines of credit of $7.1 billion. These financing sources significantly improve its liquidity.

Summary of Study Objectives

1 *Explain a current liability and identify the major types of current liabilities.* A current liability is a debt that a company can reasonably expect to pay (a) from existing current assets or through the creation of other current liabilities, and (b) within one year or the operating cycle, whichever is longer. The major types of current liabilities are notes payable, accounts payable, sales taxes payable, unearned revenues, and accrued liabilities such as taxes, salaries and wages, and interest payable.

2 *Describe the accounting for notes payable.* When a promissory note is interest-bearing, the amount of assets received upon the issuance of the note is generally equal to the face value of the note, and interest expense is accrued over the life of the note. At maturity, the amount paid is equal to the face value of the note plus accrued interest.

3 *Explain the accounting for other current liabilities.* Companies record sales taxes payable at the time the related sales occur. The company serves as a collection agent for the taxing authority. Sales taxes are not an expense to the company. Companies hold employee withholding taxes, and credit them to appropriate liability accounts, until they remit these taxes to the governmental taxing authorities. Unearned revenues are initially recorded in an unearned revenue account.

As the company earns the revenue, a transfer from unearned revenue to earned revenue occurs. Companies should report the current maturities of long-term debt as a current liability in the balance sheet.

4 *Identify the types of bonds.* The following different types of bonds may be issued: secured and unsecured bonds, and convertible and callable bonds.

5 *Prepare the entries for the issuance of bonds and interest expense.* When companies issue bonds, they debit Cash for the cash proceeds and credit Bonds Payable for the face value of the bonds. In addition, they use the accounts Premium on Bonds Payable and Discount on Bonds Payable to show the bond premium and bond discount, respectively. Bond discount and bond premium are amortized over the life of the bond.

6 *Describe the entries when bonds are redeemed.* When companies redeem bonds at maturity, they credit Cash and debit Bonds Payable for the face value of the bonds. When companies redeem bonds before maturity, they (a) eliminate the carrying value of the bonds at the redemption date, (b) record the cash paid, and (c) recognize the gain or loss on redemption.

7 *Identify the requirements for the financial statement presentation and analysis of liabilities.* Current liabilities appear first on the balance sheet, followed by long-term liabilities. Companies should report the nature and amount of each liability in the balance sheet or in schedules in the notes accompanying the statements. They report inflows and outflows of cash related to the principal portion of long-term debt in the financing section of the statement of cash flows.

The liquidity of a company may be analyzed by computing the current ratio. The long-run solvency of a company may be analyzed by computing the debt to total assets ratio and the times interest earned ratio. Other factors to consider are contingent liabilities and lease obligations.

Decision Toolkit—A Summary

Decision Checkpoints	Info Needed for Decision	Tool to Use for Decision	How to Evaluate Results
Can the company obtain short-term financing when necessary?	Available lines of credit, from notes to the financial statements	Compare available lines of credit to current liabilities. Also, evaluate liquidity ratios.	If liquidity ratios are low, then lines of credit should be high to compensate.
Can the company meet its obligations in the long term?	Interest expense and net income before interest and taxes	$$\text{Times interest earned ratio} = \frac{\text{Net income} + \text{Interest expense} + \text{Tax expense}}{\text{Interest expense}}$$	High ratio indicates ability to meet interest payments as scheduled.
Does the company have any contingent liabilities?	Knowledge of events with uncertain negative outcomes	Notes to financial statements and financial statements	If negative outcomes are possible, determine the probability, the amount of loss, and the potential impact on financial statements.
Does the company have significant off-balance-sheet financing, such as unrecorded lease obligations?	Information on unrecorded obligations, such as a schedule of minimum lease payments from the lease note	Compare liquidity and solvency ratios with and without unrecorded obligations included.	If ratios differ significantly after including unrecorded obligations, these obligations should not be ignored in analysis.

APPENDIX 10A
STRAIGHT-LINE AMORTIZATION

STUDY OBJECTIVE

8

Apply the straight-line method of amortizing bond discount and bond premium.

Amortizing Bond Discount

To follow the matching principle, companies allocate bond discount to expense in each period in which the bonds are outstanding. The **straight-line method of amortization** allocates the same amount to interest expense in each interest period. The calculation is presented in Illustration 10A-1.

Illustration 10A-1
Formula for straight-line
method of bond discount
amortization

Bond Discount	÷	Number of Interest Periods	=	Bond Discount Amortization

In the Candlestick Inc. example (page 485), the company sold $100,000, five-year, 10% bonds on January 1, 2007, for $98,000. This resulted in a $2,000 bond discount ($100,000 − $98,000). The bond discount amortization is $400 ($2,000 ÷ 5) for each of the five amortization periods. Candlestick records the first accrual of bond interest and the amortization of bond discount on December 31 as follows.

Dec. 31	Bond Interest Expense	10,400	
	Discount on Bonds Payable		400
	Bond Interest Payable		10,000
	(To record accrued bond interest and amortization of bond discount)		

A	=	L	+	SE	
					−10,400 Exp
		+400			
		+10,000			

Cash Flows
no effect

Over the term of the bonds, the balance in Discount on Bonds Payable will decrease annually by the same amount until it has a zero balance at the maturity date of the bonds. Thus, the carrying value of the bonds at maturity will be equal to the face value of the bonds.

Alternative Terminology The amount in the Discount on Bonds Payable account is often referred to as *Unamortized Discount on Bonds Payable*.

Preparing a bond discount amortization schedule, as shown in Illustration 10A-2, is useful to determine interest expense, discount amortization, and the carrying value of the bond. As indicated, the interest expense recorded each period is $10,400. Also note that the carrying value of the bond increases $400 each period until it reaches its face value of $100,000 at the end of period 5.

Illustration 10A-2
Bond discount amortization schedule

BOND DISCOUNT AMORTIZATION SCHEDULE
Straight-Line Method—Annual Interest Payments
$100,000 of 10%, 5-Year Bonds

Interest Periods	(A) Interest To Be Paid (10% × $100,000)	(B) Interest Expense To Be Recorded (A) + (C)	(C) Discount Amortization ($2,000 ÷ 5)	(D) Unamortized Discount (D) − (C)	(E) Bond Carrying Value ($100,000 − D)
Issue date				$2,000	$ 98,000
1	$10,000	$10,400	$ 400	1,600	98,400
2	10,000	10,400	400	1,200	98,800
3	10,000	10,400	400	800	99,200
4	10,000	10,400	400	400	99,600
5	10,000	10,400	400	0	100,000
	$50,000	$52,000	$2,000		

Column **(A)** remains constant because the face value of the bonds ($100,000) is multiplied by the annual contractual interest rate (10%) each period.
Column **(B)** is computed as the interest paid (Column A) plus the discount amortization (Column C).
Column **(C)** indicates the discount amortization each period.
Column **(D)** decreases each period by the same amount until it reaches zero at maturity.
Column **(E)** increases each period by the amount of discount amortization until it equals the face value at maturity.

Amortizing Bond Premium

The amortization of bond premium parallels that of bond discount. Illustration 10A-3 presents the formula for determining bond premium amortization under the straight-line method.

Illustration 10A-3
Formula for straight-line
method of bond premium
amortization

Bond Premium	÷	Number of Interest Periods	=	Bond Premium Amortization

Continuing our example, assume Candlestick Inc., sells the bonds described above for $102,000, rather than $98,000. This results in a bond premium of $2,000 ($102,000 − $100,000). The premium amortization for each interest period is $400 ($2,000 ÷ 5). Candlestick records the first accrual of interest on December 31 as follows.

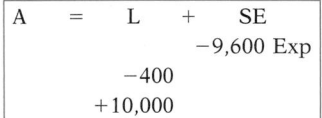

A = L + SE
−9,600 Exp
−400
+10,000

Cash Flows
no effect

Dec. 31	Bond Interest Expense	9,600	
	Premium on Bonds Payable	400	
	Bond Interest Payable		10,000
	(To record accrued bond interest and amortization of bond premium)		

Over the term of the bonds, the balance in Premium on Bonds Payable will decrease annually by the same amount until it has a zero balance at maturity.

A bond premium amortization schedule, as shown in Illustration 10A-4, is useful to determine interest expense, premium amortization, and the carrying value of the bond. As indicated, the interest expense Candlestick records each period is $9,600. Note that the carrying value of the bond decreases $400 each period until it reaches its face value of $100,000 at the end of period 5.

Illustration 10A-4 Bond premium amortization schedule

BOND PREMIUM AMORTIZATION SCHEDULE
Straight-Line Method—Annual Interest Payments
$100,000 of 10%, 5-Year Bonds

Interest Periods	(A) Interest To Be Paid (10% × $100,000)	(B) Interest Expense To Be Recorded (A) − (C)	(C) Premium Amortization ($2,000 ÷ 5)	(D) Unamortized Premium (D) − (C)	(E) Bond Carrying Value ($100,000 + D)
Issue date				$2,000	$102,000
1	$10,000	$ 9,600	$ 400	1,600	101,600
2	10,000	9,600	400	1,200	101,200
3	10,000	9,600	400	800	100,800
4	10,000	9,600	400	400	100,400
5	10,000	9,600	400	0	100,000
	$50,000	$48,000	$2,000		

Column **(A)** remains constant because the face value of the bonds ($100,000) is multiplied by the annual contractual interest rate (10%) each period.
Column **(B)** is computed as the interest paid (Column A) less the premium amortization (Column C).
Column **(C)** indicates the premium amortization each period.
Column **(D)** decreases each period by the same amount until it reaches zero at maturity.
Column **(E)** decreases each period by the amount of premium amortization until it equals the face value at maturity.

Summary of Study Objective for Appendix 10A

8 *Apply the straight-line method of amortizing bond discount and bond premium.* The straight-line method of amortization results in a constant amount of amortization and interest expense per period.

APPENDIX 10B
EFFECTIVE-INTEREST AMORTIZATION

To follow the matching principle, companies allocate bond discount to expense in each period in which the bonds are outstanding. However, to completely comply with the matching principle, interest expense as a percentage of carrying value should not change over the life of the bonds. This percentage, referred to as the **effective-interest rate**, is established when the bonds are issued and remains constant in each interest period. Unlike the straight-line method, the effective-interest method of amortization accomplishes this result.

Under the **effective-interest method**, the amortization of bond discount or bond premium results in periodic interest expense equal to a constant percentage of the carrying value of the bonds. The effective-interest method results in **varying amounts** of amortization and interest expense per period but a **constant percentage rate.** In contrast, the straight-line method results in constant amounts of amortization and interest expense per period but a varying percentage rate.

Companies follow three steps under the effective-interest method:

1. Compute the **bond interest expense** by multiplying the carrying value of the bonds at the beginning of the interest period by the effective-interest rate.

2. Compute the **bond interest paid** (or accrued) by multiplying the face value of the bonds by the contractual interest rate.

3. Compute the **amortization amount** by determining the difference between the amounts computed in steps (1) and (2).

Illustration 10B-1 depicts these steps.

> **STUDY OBJECTIVE**
> **9**
> Apply the effective-interest method of amortizing bond discount and bond premium.

(1) Bond Interest Expense		(2) Bond Interest Paid		(3)
Carrying Value of Bonds at Beginning of Period	× Effective Interest Rate	− Face Amount × of Bonds	Contractual Interest Rate	= **Amortization Amount**

Illustration 10B-1
Computation of amortization using effective-interest method

Both the straight-line and effective-interest methods of amortization result in the same total amount of interest expense over the term of the bonds. Furthermore, interest expense each interest period is generally comparable in amount. However, **when the amounts are materially different, generally accepted accounting principles (GAAP) require use of the effective-interest method.**

Helpful Hint Note that the amount of periodic interest expense increases over the life of the bonds when the effective-interest method is used for bonds issued at a discount. The reason is that a constant percentage is applied to an increasing bond carrying value to compute interest expense. The carrying value is increasing because of the amortization of the discount.

Amortizing Bond Discount

To illustrate the effective-interest method of bond discount amortization, assume that Wrightway Corporation issues $100,000 of 10%, five-year bonds on January 1, 2007, with interest payable each January 1. The bonds sell for $92,790 (92.79% of face value), which results in bond discount of $7,210 ($100,000 − $92,790) and an effective-interest rate of 12%. (Note that the $92,790 can be proven as shown in Appendix C at the end of this book.)

Preparing a bond discount amortization schedule as shown in Illustration 10B-2 facilitates the recording of interest expense and the discount amortization. Note that interest expense as a percentage of carrying value remains constant at 12%.

Illustration 10B-2
Bond discount amortization schedule

WRIGHTWAY CORPORATION
Bond Discount Amortization
Effective-Interest Method—Annual Interest Payments
10% Bonds Issued at 12%

Interest Periods	(A) Interest to Be Paid (10% × $100,000)	(B) Interest Expense to Be Recorded (12% × Preceding Bond Carrying Value)		(C) Discount Amortization (B) − (A)	(D) Unamortized Discount (D) − (C)	(E) Bond Carrying Value ($100,000 − D)
Issue date					$7,210	$ 92,790
1	$10,000	$11,135	(12% × $92,790)	$1,135	6,075	93,925
2	10,000	11,271	(12% × $ 93,925)	1,271	4,804	95,196
3	10,000	11,424	(12% × $ 95,196)	1,424	3,380	96,620
4	10,000	11,594	(12% × $ 96,620)	1,594	1,786	98,214
5	10,000	11,786	(12% × $ 98,214)	1,786	−0−	100,000
	$ 50,000	$ 57,210		$ 7,210		

Column **(A)** remains constant because the face value of the bonds ($100,000) is multiplied by the annual contractual interest rate (10%) each period.
Column **(B)** is computed as the preceding bond carrying value times the annual effective-interest rate (12%).
Column **(C)** indicates the discount amortization each period.
Column **(D)** decreases each period until it reaches zero at maturity.
Column **(E)** increases each period until it equals face value at maturity.

For the first interest period, the computations of bond interest expense and the bond discount amortization are as follows.

Illustration 10B-3
Computation of bond discount amortization

Bond interest expense ($92,790 × 12%)	$11,135
Bond interest paid ($100,000 × 10%)	10,000
Bond discount amortization	**$ 1,135**

As a result, Wrightway Corporation records the accrual of interest and amortization of bond discount on December 31, as follows.

A	=	L	+	SE
				−11,135 Exp
		+1,135		
		+10,000		

Cash Flows
no effect

Dec. 31	Bond Interest Expense	11,135	
	Discount on Bonds Payable		1,135
	Bond Interest Payable		10,000
	(To record accrued interest and amortization of bond discount)		

For the second interest period, bond interest expense will be $11,271 ($93,925 × 12%), and the discount amortization will be $1,271. At December 31, Wrightway makes the following adjusting entry.

Dec. 31	Bond Interest Expense	11,271	
	Discount on Bonds Payable		1,271
	Bond Interest Payable		10,000
	(To record accrued interest and		
	amortization of bond discount)		

```
A    =    L    +    SE
                    −11,271 Exp
         +1,271
         +10,000
```
Cash Flows
no effect

Amortizing Bond Premium

The amortization of bond premium by the effective-interest method is similar to the procedures described for bond discount. As an example, assume that Wrightway Corporation issues $100,000, 10%, five-year bonds on January 1, with interest payable on January 1. In this case, the bonds sell for $107,985, which results in bond premium of $7,985 and an effective-interest rate of 8%. Illustration 10B-4 shows the bond premium amortization schedule.

Helpful Hint When a bond sells for $107,985 it is quoted at 107.985% of face value. Note that $107,985 can be proven as shown in Appendix C.

Illustration 10B-4
Bond premium amortization schedule

Interest Periods	(A) Interest to Be Paid (10% × $100,000)	(B) Interest Expense to Be Recorded (8% × Preceding Bond Carrying Value)	(C) Premium Amortization (A) − (B)	(D) Unamortized Premium (D) − (C)	(E) Bond Carrying Value ($100,000 + D)
Issue date				$7,985	$107,985
1	$10,000	$ 8,639 (8% × $107,985)	$1,361	6,624	106,624
2	10,000	8,530 (8% × $ 106,624)	1,470	5,154	105,154
3	10,000	8,412 (8% × $ 105,154)	1,588	3,566	103,566
4	10,000	8,285 (8% × $ 103,566)	1,715	1,851	101,851
5	10,000	8,149* (8% × $ 101,851)	1,851	–0–	100,000
	$50,000	$ 42,015	$7,985		

WRIGHTWAY CORPORATION
Bond Premium Amortization
Effective-Interest Method—Annual Interest Payments
10% Bonds Issued at 8%

Column **(A)** remains constant because the face value of the bonds ($100,000) is multiplied by the contractual interest rate (10%) each period.
Column **(B)** is computed as the carrying value of the bonds times the annual effective-interest rate (8%).
Column **(C)** indicates the premium amortization each period.
Column **(D)** decreases each period until it reaches zero at maturity.
Column **(E)** decreases each period until it equals face value at maturity.

*$1 difference due to rounding.

For the first interest period, the computations of bond interest expense and the bond premium amortization are:

Illustration 10B-5
Computation of bond premium amortization

Bond interest paid ($100,000 × 10%)	$10,000
Bond interest expense ($107,985 × 8%)	8,639
Bond premium amortization	**$ 1,361**

The entry Wrightway makes on December 31 is:

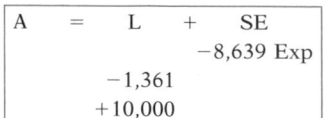

Cash Flows
no effect

Dec. 31	Bond Interest Expense	8,639	
	Premium on Bonds Payable	1,361	
	Bond Interest Payable		10,000
	(To record accrued interest and		
	amortization of bond premium)		

For the second interest period, interest expense will be $8,530, and the premium amortization will be $1,470. Note that the amount of periodic interest expense decreases over the life of the bond when companies apply the effective-interest method to bonds issued at a premium. The reason is that a constant percentage is applied to a decreasing bond carrying value to compute interest expense. The carrying value is decreasing because of the amortization of the premium.

Summary of Study Objective for Appendix 10B

9   *Apply the effective-interest method of amortizing bond discount and bond premium.* The effective-interest method results in varying amounts of amortization and interest expense per period but a constant percentage rate of interest. When the difference between the straight-line and effective-interest method is material, GAAP requires use of the effective-interest method.

APPENDIX 10C
ACCOUNTING FOR
LONG-TERM NOTES PAYABLE

STUDY OBJECTIVE
10
Describe the accounting for long-term notes payable.

The use of notes payable in long-term debt financing is quite common. Long-term notes payable are similar to short-term interest-bearing notes payable except that the terms of the notes exceed one year. In periods of unstable interest rates, lenders may tie the interest rate on long-term notes to changes in the market rate for comparable loans. Examples are the 8.03% adjustable rate notes issued by General Motors and the floating-rate notes issued by American Express Company.

A long-term note may be secured by a document called a **mortgage** that pledges title to specific assets as security for a loan. Individuals widely use **mortgage notes payable** to purchase homes, as do many small and some large companies to acquire plant assets. For example, at one time approximately 18% of McDonalds' long-term debt related to mortgage notes on land, buildings, and improvements.

Like other long-term notes payable, the mortgage loan terms may stipulate either a fixed or an adjustable interest rate. Typically, the terms require the borrower to make equal installment payments over the term of the loan. Each payment consists of (1) interest on the unpaid balance of the loan and (2) a reduction of loan principal. The interest decreases each period, while the portion applied to the loan principal increases.

Companies initially record mortgage notes payable at face value, and subsequently make entries for each installment payment. To illustrate, assume that Porter Technology Inc. issues a $500,000, 12%, 20-year mortgage note on December 31, 2007, to obtain needed financing for the construction of a new research laboratory.

Helpful Hint Electronic spreadsheet programs can create a schedule of installment loan payments. This allows you to put in the data for your own mortgage loan and get an illustration that really hits home.

The terms provide for semiannual installment payments of $33,231 (not including real estate taxes and insurance). The installment payment schedule for the first two years is as follows.

Semiannual Interest Period	(A) Cash Payment	(B) Interest Expense (D) × 6%	(C) Reduction of Principal (A) − (B)	(D) Principal Balance (D) − (C)
Issue date				$500,000
1	$33,231	$30,000	$3,231	496,769
2	33,231	29,806	3,425	493,344
3	33,231	29,601	3,630	489,714
4	33,231	29,383	3,848	485,866

Illustration 10C-1
Mortgage installment payment schedule

Porter Technology records the mortgage loan and first installment payment as follows.

Dec. 31	Cash	500,000	
	Mortgage Notes Payable		500,000
	(To record mortgage loan)		

```
A    =    L    +    SE
+500,000
              +500,000
Cash Flows
+500,000
```

June 30	Interest Expense	30,000	
	Mortgage Notes Payable	3,231	
	Cash		33,231
	(To record semiannual payment on		
	mortgage)		

```
A    =    L    +    SE
                       −30,000 Exp
           −3,231
−33,231
Cash Flows
−33,231
```

In the balance sheet, the company reports the reduction in principal for the next year as a current liability, and classifies the remaining unpaid principal balance as a long-term liability. At December 31, 2008, the total liability is $493,344, of which $7,478 ($3,630 + $3,848) is current and $485,866 ($493,344 − $7,478) is long-term.

Summary of Study Objective for Appendix 10C

10 *Describe the accounting for long-term notes payable.* Each payment consists of (1) interest on the unpaid balance of the loan, and (2) a reduction of loan principal. The interest decreases each period, while the portion applied to the loan principal increases each period.

Glossary

Bond certificate A legal document that indicates the name of the issuer, the face value of the bonds, and such other data as the contractual interest rate and the maturity date of the bonds. (p. 481)

Bonds A form of interest-bearing notes payable issued by corporations, universities, and governmental entities. (p. 480)

Callable bonds Bonds that are the issuing company can retire at a stated dollar amount prior to maturity. (p. 481)

Capital lease A type of lease whose characteristics make it similar to a debt-financed purchase and that is consequently accounted for in that fashion. (p. 495)

Contingencies Events with uncertain outcomes, such as a potential liability that may become an actual liability sometime in the future. (p. 494)

Contractual (stated) interest rate Rate used to determine the amount of interest the borrower pays and the investor receives. (p. 481)

Convertible bonds Bonds that permit bondholders to convert them into common stock at their option. (p. 481)

Current liability A debt that a company reasonably expects to pay (1) from existing current assets or through the creation of other current liabilities, and (2) within one year or the operating cycle, whichever is longer. (p. 474)

Discount (on a bond) The difference between the face value of a bond and its selling price, when a bond is sold for less than its face value. (p. 485)

Effective-interest method of amortization A method of amortizing bond discount or bond premium that results in periodic interest expense equal to a constant percentage of the carrying value of the bonds. (p. 501)

Effective-interest rate Rate established when bonds are issued that remains constant in each interest period. (p. 501)

Face value Amount of principal due at the maturity date of the bond. (p. 481)

Long-term liabilities Obligations that a company expects to pay more than one year in the future. (p. 480)

Market interest rate The rate investors demand for loaning funds to the corporation. (p. 482)

Maturity date The date on which the final payment on a bond is due from the bond issuer to the investor. (p. 481)

Mortgage note payable A long-term note secured by a mortgage that pledges title to specific units of property as security for the loan. (p. 504)

Notes payable An obligation in the form of a written promissory note. (p. 475)

Off-balance-sheet financing The intentional effort by a company to structure its financing arrangements so as to avoid showing liabilities on its books. (p. 494)

Operating lease A contractual arrangement giving the lessee temporary use of the property with continued ownership of the property by the lessor. Accounted for as a rental. (p. 495)

Premium (on a bond) The difference between the selling price and the face value of a bond when a bond is sold for more than its face value. (p. 485)

Present value The value today of an amount to be received at some date in the future after taking into account current interest rates. (p. 482)

Secured bonds Bonds that have specific assets of the issuer pledged as collateral. (p. 481)

Straight-line method of amortization A method of amortizing bond discount or bond premium that allocates the same amount to interest expense in each interest period. (p. 498)

Time value of money The relationship between time and money. A dollar received today is worth more than a dollar promised at some time in the future. (p. 482)

Times interest earned ratio A measure of a company's solvency, calculated by dividing income before interest expense and taxes by interest expense. (p. 493)

Unsecured bonds Bonds issued against the general credit of the borrower. (p. 481)

Demonstration Problem

Snyder Software Inc. successfully developed a new spreadsheet program. However, to produce and market the program, the company needed $2.0 million of additional financing. On January 1, 2007, Snyder borrowed money as follows.

1. Snyder issued $500,000, 11%, 10-year bonds. The bonds sold at face value and pay interest on January 1.

2. Snyder issued $1.0 million, 10%, 10-year bonds for $886,996. Interest is payable on January 1. Snyder uses the straight-line method of amortization.

Instructions

(a) For the 11% bonds, prepare journal entries for the following items.
    (1) The issuance of the bonds on January 1, 2007.
    (2) Accrue interest expense on December 31, 2007.
    (3) The payment of interest on January 1, 2008.
(b) For the 10-year, 10% bonds:
    (1) Journalize the issuance of the bonds on January 1, 2007.
    (2) Prepare the entry for the redemption of the bonds at 101 on January 1, 2010, after paying the interest due on this date. The carrying value of the bonds at the redemption date was $920,897.

Solution to Demonstration Problem

(a) (1) 2007

Jan. 1	Cash	500,000	
	Bonds Payable		500,000
	(To record issue of 11%, 10-year		
	bonds at face value)		

(2) 2007

Dec. 31	Bond Interest Expense	55,000	
	Bond Interest Payable		55,000
	(To record accrual of bond interest)		

(3) 2008

Jan. 1	Bond Interest Payable	55,000	
	Cash		55,000
	(To record payment of accrued		
	interest)		

(b) (1) 2007

Jan. 1	Cash	886,996	
	Discount on Bonds Payable	113,004	
	Bonds Payable		1,000,000
	(To record issuance of bonds at a		
	discount)		

(2) 2008

Jan. 1	Bonds Payable	1,000,000	
	Loss on Bond Redemption	89,103*	
	Discount on Bonds Payable		79,103
	Cash		1,010,000
	(To record redemption of bonds at		
	101)		
	*($1,010,000 − $920,897)		

Action Plan

• Record the discount on bonds issued as a contra liability account.

• Compute the loss on bond redemption as the excess of the cash paid over the carrying value of the redeemed bonds.

Note: All Questions, Exercises, and Problems marked with an asterisk relate to material in the appendixes to the chapter.

Self-Study Questions

WILEY PLUS

Answers are at the end of the chapter.

(SO 1)   **1.** The time period for classifying a liability as current is one year or the operating cycle, whichever is:
(a) longer.   (c) probable.
(b) shorter.   (d) possible.

(SO 1)   **2.** To be classified as a current liability, a debt must be expected to be paid:
(a) out of existing current assets.
(b) by creating other current liabilities.
(c) within 2 years.
(d) Either (a) or (b)

(SO 2)   **3.** Corricten Company borrows $88,500 on September 1, 2007, from Harrington State Bank by signing an $88,500, 12%, one-year note. What is the accrued interest at December 31, 2007?

(a) $2,655.   (c) $4,425.
(b) $3,540.   (d) $10,620.

(SO 3)   **4.** Andre Company has total proceeds from sales of $4,515. If the proceeds include sales taxes of 5%, what is the amount to be credited to Sales?
(a) $4,000.
(b) $4,300.
(c) $4,289.25.
(d) The correct answer is not given.

(SO 7)   **5.** Which of the following is *not* a measure of liquidity?
(a) Debt to total assets ratio.
(b) Working capital.
(c) Current ratio.
(d) Current cash debt coverage.

(SO 4)   **6.** What term is used for bonds that have specific assets pledged as collateral?
  (a) Callable bonds.
  (b) Convertible bonds.
  (c) Secured bonds.
  (d) Discount bonds.

(SO 5)   **7.** Cuso Inc. issues 10-year bonds with a maturity value of $200,000. If the bonds are issued at a premium, this indicates that:
  (a) the contractual interest rate exceeds the market interest rate.
  (b) the market interest rate exceeds the contractual interest rate.
  (c) the contractual interest rate and the market interest rate are the same.
  (d) no relationship exists between the two rates.

(SO 5)   **8.** On January 1, 2007, Scissors Corp. issues $200,000, 5-year, 7% bonds at face value. The entry to record the issuance of the bonds would include a:
  (a) debit to cash for $14,000.
  (b) debit to bonds payable for $200,000.
  (c) credit to bonds payable for $200,000.
  (d) credit to bond interest expense of $14,000.

(SO 6)   **9.** Kant Corporation retires its $100,000 face value bonds at 105 on January 1, following the payment of interest. The carrying value of the bonds at the redemption date is $103,745. The entry to record the redemption will include a:
  (a) credit of $3,745 to Loss on Bond Redemption.
  (b) debit of $3,745 to Premium on Bonds Payable.
  (c) credit of $1,255 to Gain on Bond Redemption.
  (d) debit of $5,000 to Premium on Bonds Payable.

(SO 7)   **10.** 🔧 In a recent year Day Corporation had net income of $150,000, interest expense of $30,000, and tax expense of $20,000. What was Day Corporation's times interest earned ratio for the year?
  (a) 5.00.   (c) 6.67.
  (b) 4.00.   (d) 7.50.

*11. On January 1 Pierce Corporation issues   (SO 8)
  $500,000, 5-year, 12% bonds at 96 with interest payable on January 1. The entry on December 31 to record accrued bond interest and the amortization of bond discount using the straight-line method will include a:
  (a) debit to Interest Expense, $57,600.
  (b) debit to Interest Expense, $60,000.
  (c) credit to Discount on Bonds Payable, $4,000.
  (d) credit to Discount on Bonds Payable, $2,000.

*12. For the bonds issued in question 11, what is the   (SO 8)
  carrying value of the bonds at the end of the third interest period?
  (a) $492,000.   (c) $472,000.
  (b) $488,000.   (d) $464,000.

*13. On January 1, Daisey Duke Inc. issued   (SO 9)
  $1,000,000, 9% bonds for $939,000. The market rate of interest for these bonds is 10%. Interest is payable annually on December 31. Daisey Duke uses the effective-interest method of amortizing bond discount. At the end of the first year, Daisey Duke should report unamortized bond discount of:
  (a) $54,900.   (c) $51,610.
  (b) $57,100.   (d) $51,000.

*14. On January 1, Anthony Corporation issued   (SO 9)
  $1,000,000, 14%, 5-year bonds with interest payable on December 31. The bonds sold for $1,072,096. The market rate of interest for these bonds was 12%. On the first interest date, using the effective-interest method, the debit entry to Bond Interest Expense is for:
  (a) $120,000.
  (b) $125,581.
  (c) $128,652.
  (d) $140,000.

Go to the book's website, **www.wiley.com/college/kimmel**, to access additional Self-Study Questions.

Questions

1. Georgia Lazenby believes a current liability is a debt that can be expected to be paid in one year. Is Georgia correct? Explain.

2. Travelyan Company obtains $25,000 in cash by signing a 9%, 6-month, $25,000 note payable to First Bank on July 1. Travelyan's fiscal year ends on September 30. What information should be reported for the note payable in the annual financial statements?

3. (a) Your roommate says, "Sales taxes are reported as an expense in the income statement." Do you agree? Explain.

(b) Hard Wok Cafe has cash proceeds from sales of $10,550. This amount includes $550 of sales taxes. Give the entry to record the proceeds.

4. Holt University sold 8,000 season football tickets at $90 each for its five-game home schedule. What entries should be made (a) when the tickets are sold and (b) after each game?

5. Identify three taxes commonly withheld by the employer from an employee's gross pay.

6. (a) Identify three taxes commonly paid by employers on employees' salaries and wages.
(b) Where in the financial statements does the employer report taxes withheld from employees' pay?

7. (a) What are long-term liabilities? Give two examples.
(b) What is a bond?

8. Contrast these types of bonds:
(a) Secured and unsecured.
(b) Convertible and callable.

9. Explain each of these important terms in issuing bonds:
(a) Face value.
(b) Contractual interest rate.
(c) Bond certificate.

10. (a) What is a convertible bond?
(b) Discuss the advantages of a convertible bond from the standpoint of the bondholders and of the issuing corporation.

11. Describe the two major obligations incurred by a company when bonds are issued.

12. Assume that Mimi Inc. sold bonds with a face value of $100,000 for $104,000. Was the market interest rate equal to, less than, or greater than the bonds' contractual interest rate? Explain.

13. Magda and Helga are discussing how the market price of a bond is determined. Magda believes that the market price of a bond is solely a function of the amount of the principal payment at the end of the term of a bond. Is she right? Discuss.

14. If a 6%, 10-year, $600,000 bond is issued at face and interest is paid annually, what is the amount of the interest payment at the end of the first period?

15. If the Bonds Payable account has a balance of $900,000 and the Discount on Bonds Payable account has a balance of $36,000, what is the carrying value of the bonds?

16. Which accounts are debited and which are credited if a bond issue originally sold at a premium is redeemed before maturity at 97 immediately following the payment of interest?

17. Stephanie Wolcott, the chief financial officer of Hangers Inc., is considering the options available to her for financing the company's new plant. Short-term interest rates right now are 6%, and long-term rates are 8%. The company's current ratio is 2.2:1. If she finances the new plant with short-term debt, the current ratio will fall to 1.5:1. Briefly discuss the issues that Stephanie should consider.

18. (a) In general, what are the requirements for the financial statement presentation of long-term liabilities?
(b) What ratios may be computed to evaluate a company's liquidity and solvency?

19. Valentin Zukovsky says that liquidity and solvency are the same thing. Is he correct? If not, how do they differ?

20. The management of Ultra Vehicle Corporation is concerned because survey data suggest that many potential customers do not buy vehicles due to quality concerns. It is considering taking the bold step of increasing the length of its warranty from the industry standard of 3 years up to an unprecedented 10 years in an effort to increase confidence in its quality. Discuss the business as well as accounting implications of this move.

21. Hector Gonzales needs a few new trucks for his business. He is considering buying the trucks but is concerned that the additional debt he will need to borrow will make his liquidity and solvency ratios look bad. What options does he have other than purchasing the trucks, and how will these options affect his financial statements?

22. Empire Corporation has a current ratio of 1.1. Tom has always been told that a corporation's current ratio should exceed 2.0. Empire argues that its ratio is low because it has a minimal amount of inventory on hand so as to reduce operating costs. Empire also points out that it has significant available lines of credit. Is Tom still correct? What do some companies do to compensate for having fewer liquid assets?

23. What are the implications for analysis if a company has significant operating leases?

24. What criteria must be met before a contingency must be recorded as a liability? How should the contingency be disclosed if the criteria are not met?

*25. Explain the straight-line method of amortizing discount and premium on bonds payable.

*26. Osato Corporation issues $200,000 of 6%, 5-year bonds on January 1, 2007, at 104. Assuming that the straight-line method is used to amortize the premium, what is the total amount of interest expense for 2007?

*27. Maria Lopez is discussing the advantages of the effective-interest method of bond amortization with her accounting staff. What do you think Maria is saying?

*28. Snooper Corporation issues $400,000 of 9%, 5-year bonds on January 1, 2007, at 104. If Snooper uses the effective-interest method in amortizing the premium, will the annual interest expense increase or decrease over the life of the bonds? Explain.

Brief Exercises

Identify whether obligations are current liabilities.
(SO 1)

BE10-1 Kananga Company has these obligations at December 31: (a) a note payable for $100,000 due in 2 years, (b) a 10-year mortgage payable of $200,000 payable in ten $20,000 annual payments, (c) interest payable of $15,000 on the mortgage, and (d) accounts payable of $60,000. For each obligation, indicate whether it should be classified as a current liability.

Prepare entries for an interest-bearing note payable.
(SO 2)

BE10-2 Popp Company borrows $70,000 on July 1 from the bank by signing a $70,000, 8%, 1-year note payable. Prepare the journal entries to record (a) the proceeds of the note and (b) accrued interest at December 31, assuming adjusting entries are made only at the end of the year.

Compute and record sales taxes payable.
(SO 3)

BE10-3 Gold Supply does not segregate sales and sales taxes at the time of sale. The register total for March 16 is $10,388. All sales are subject to a 6% sales tax. Compute sales taxes payable and make the entry to record sales taxes payable and sales.

Prepare entries for unearned revenues.
(SO 3)

BE10-4 Denton University sells 3,800 season basketball tickets at $60 each for its 10-game home schedule. Give the entry to record (a) the sale of the season tickets and (b) the revenue earned by playing the first home game.

Compare bond financing to stock financing.
(SO 4)

BE10-5 Domino Inc. is considering these two alternatives to finance its construction of a new $2 million plant:
  (a) Issuance of 200,000 shares of common stock at the market price of $10 per share.
  (b) Issuance of $2 million, 6% bonds at face value.

Complete the table and indicate which alternative is preferable.

	Issue Stock	Issue Bond
Income before interest and taxes	$1,000,000	$1,000,000
Interest expense from bonds	_____	_____
Income before income taxes		
Income tax expense (30%)	_____	_____
Net income	$_____	$_____
Outstanding shares	_____	700,000
Earnings per share	$_____	$_____

Prepare journal entries for bonds issued at face value.
(SO 5)

BE10-6 Lazar Corporation issued 1,000 7%, 5-year, $1,000 bonds dated January 1, 2007, at face value. Interest is paid each January 1.
  (a) Prepare the journal entry to record the sale of these bonds on January 1, 2007.
  (b) Prepare the adjusting journal entry on December 31, 2007, to record interest expense.
  (c) Prepare the journal entry on January 1, 2008, to record interest paid.

Prepare journal entry for redemption of bonds.
(SO 6)

BE10-7 The balance sheet for Tiffany Company reports the following information on July 1, 2007.

TIFFANY COMPANY
Balance Sheet (partial)

Long-term liabilities		
Bonds payable	$1,000,000	
Less: Discount on bonds payable	30,000	$970,000

Tiffany decides to redeem these bonds at 102 after paying annual interest. Prepare the journal entry to record the redemption on July 1, 2007.

Prepare statement presentation of long-term liabilities.
(SO 7)

BE10-8 Presented here are long-term liability items for Carlton Inc. at December 31, 2007. Prepare the long-term liabilities section of the balance sheet for Carlton Inc.

Bonds payable, due 2011	$900,000
Notes payable, due 2009	80,000
Discount on bonds payable	21,000

BE10-9 Presented here are liability items for Warner Inc. at December 31, 2007. Prepare the liabilities section of Warner's balance sheet.

Prepare liabilities section of balance sheet.
(SO 7)

Accounts payable	$135,000	Employee benefits payable	$ 7,800
Bank note payable			
(due May 1, 2008)	20,000	Interest payable	40,000
Bonds payable, due 2011	900,000	Notes payable, due 2009	80,000
Current portion of			
long-term debt	240,000	Property tax payable	3,500
Discount on bonds payable	45,000	Sales taxes payable	1,400

BE10-10 The 2004 Reebok financial statements contain the following selected data (in millions).

Analyze solvency.
(SO 7)

Current assets	$1,858	Interest expense	$ 26
Total assets	2,441	Income taxes	68
Current liabilities	806	Net income	192
Total liabilities	1,221		
Cash	565		

Compute the following values and provide a brief interpretation of each.
(a) Working capital.   (c) Debt to total assets ratio.
(b) Current ratio.   (d) Times interest earned ratio.

BE10-11 The Canadian National Railway Company's (CN) total assets in a recent year were $18,924 million and its total liabilities were $12,297 million. That year, CN reported operating lease commitments for its locomotives, freight cars, and equipment totalling $1,154 million. If these assets had been recorded as capital leases, assume that assets and liabilities would have risen by approximately $1,154 million.

Analyze solvency.
(SO 7)

(a) Calculate CN's debt to total assets ratio, first using the figures reported, and then after increasing assets and liabilities for the unrecorded operating leases.
(b) Discuss the potential effect of these operating leases on your assessment of CN's solvency.

*BE10-12** Vijay Company issues $2 million, 10-year, 6% bonds at 99, with interest payable on December 31. The straight-line method is used to amortize bond discount.

Prepare journal entries for bonds issued at a discount.
(SO 8)

(a) Prepare the journal entry to record the sale of these bonds on January 1, 2007.
(b) Prepare the journal entry to record interest expense and bond discount amortization on December 31, 2007, assuming no previous accrual of interest.

*BE10-13** Sydor Inc. issues $5 million, 5-year, 8% bonds at 103, with interest payable on January 1. The straight-line method is used to amortize bond premium.

Prepare journal entries for bonds issued at a premium.
(SO 8)

(a) Prepare the journal entry to record the sale of these bonds on January 1, 2007.
(b) Prepare the journal entry to record interest expense and bond premium amortization on December 31, 2007, assuming no previous accrual of interest.

*BE10-14** Presented below is the partial bond discount amortization schedule for Nuong Tu Corp., which uses the effective-interest method of amortization.

Use effective-interest method of bond amortization.
(SO 9)

Interest Periods	Interest to Be Paid	Interest Expense to Be Recorded	Discount Amortization	Unamortized Discount	Bond Carrying Value
Issue date				$62,311	$937,689
1	$45,000	$46,884	$1,884	60,427	939,573
2	45,000	46,979	1,979	58,448	941,552

Instructions
(a) Prepare the journal entry to record the payment of interest and the discount amortization at the end of period 1.
(b) Explain why interest expense is greater than interest paid.
(c) Explain why interest expense will increase each period.

Exercises

Prepare entries for interest-bearing notes.
(SO 2)

E10-1   Rebecca Fleming and Carrie Platt borrowed $12,000 on a 7-month, 9% note from Gopher State Bank to open their business, RC's Coffee House. The money was borrowed on June 1, 2007, and the note matures January 1, 2008.

Instructions
(a) Prepare the entry to record the receipt of the funds from the loan.
(b) Prepare the entry to accrue the interest on June 30.
(c) Assuming adjusting entries are made at the end of each month, determine the balance in the interest payable account at December 31, 2007.
(d) Prepare the entry required on January 1, 2008, when the loan is paid back.

Prepare entries for interest-bearing notes.
(SO 2)

E10-2   On May 15, Kiwi's Outback Clothiers borrowed some money on a 4-month note to provide cash during the slow season of the year. The interest rate on the note was 8%. At the time the note was due, the amount of interest owed was $320.

Instructions
(a) Determine the amount borrowed by Kiwi's.
(b) Assume the amount borrowed was $18,500. What was the interest rate if the amount of interest owed was $740?
(c) Prepare the entry for the initial borrowing and the repayment for the facts in part (a).

Prepare entries for interest-bearing notes.
(SO 2)

E10-3   On June 1, Avery Company Ltd. borrows $50,000 from First Bank on a 6-month, $50,000, 9% note. The note matures on December 1.

Instructions
(a) Prepare the entry on June 1.
(b) Prepare the adjusting entry on June 30.
(c) Prepare the entry at maturity (December 1), assuming monthly adjusting entries have been made through November 30.
(d) What was the total financing cost (interest expense)?

Journalize sales and related taxes.
(SO 3)

E10-4   In providing accounting services to small businesses, you encounter the following situations pertaining to cash sales.
1. Mariella Company rings up sales and sales taxes separately on its cash register. On April 10 the register totals are sales $25,000 and sales taxes $1,250.
2. Brent Company does not segregate sales and sales taxes. Its register total for April 15 is $11,660, which includes a 6% sales tax.

Instructions
Prepare the entries to record the sales transactions and related taxes for (a) Mariella Company and (b) Brent Company.

Journalize payroll entries.
(SO 3)

E10-5   During the month of March, Pouncer Company's employees earned wages of $70,000. Withholdings related to these wages were $5,355 for Social Security (FICA), $7,500 for federal income tax, $3,100 for state income tax, and $400 for union dues. The company incurred no cost related to these earnings for federal unemployment tax, but incurred $700 for state unemployment tax.

Instructions
(a) Prepare the necessary March 31 journal entry to record wages expense and wages payable. Assume that wages earned during March will be paid during April.
(b) Prepare the entry to record the company's payroll tax expense.

Journalize unearned revenue transactions.
(SO 3)

E10-6   Season tickets for the Lame Ducks are priced at $230 and include 20 games. Revenue is recognized after each game is played. When the season began, the amount credited to Unearned Season Ticket Revenue was $1,104,000. By the end of October, $772,800 of the Unearned Season Ticket Revenue had been recorded as earned.

Instructions
(a) How many season tickets did the Lame Ducks sell?
(b) How many home games had the Lame Ducks played by the end of October?

(c) Prepare the entry for the initial recording of the Unearned Season Ticket Revenue.

(d) Prepare the entry to recognize the revenue after the first home game had been played.

E10-7 Walter Company Ltd. publishes a monthly sports magazine, *Fishing Preview*. Subscriptions to the magazine cost $22 per year. During November 2007, Walter sells 6,000 subscriptions for cash, beginning with the December issue. Walter prepares financial statements quarterly and recognizes subscription revenue earned at the end of the quarter. The company uses the accounts Unearned Subscription Revenue and Subscription Revenue. The company has a December 31 year-end.

Journalize unearned subscription revenue. (SO 3)

Instructions

(a) Prepare the entry in November for the receipt of the subscriptions.

(b) Prepare the adjusting entry at December 31, 2007, to record subscription revenue earned in December 2007.

(c) Prepare the adjusting entry at March 31, 2008, to record subscription revenue earned in the first quarter of 2008.

E10-8 On September 1, 2007, Chardin Corporation issued $300,000, 8%, 10-year bonds at face value. Interest is payable annually on September 1. Chardin's year-end is December 31.

Prepare journal entries for issuance of bonds and payment of accrual of interest. (SO 5)

Instructions

Prepare journal entries to record the following events.

(a) The issuance of the bonds.

(b) The accrual of interest on December 31, 2007.

(c) The payment of interest on September 1, 2008.

E10-9 On January 1 Stanhope Company issued $100,000, 7%, 10-year bonds at face value. Interest is payable annually on January 1.

Prepare journal entries for issuance of bonds and payment and accrual of interest. (SO 5)

Instructions

Prepare journal entries to record the following events.

(a) The issuance of the bonds.

(b) The accrual of interest on December 31.

(c) The payment of interest on January 1.

E10-10 Assume that the following are independent situations recently reported in the *Wall Street Journal*.

1. General Electric (GE) 7% bonds, maturing January 28, 2010, were issued at 111.12.

2. Boeing 7% bonds, maturing September 24, 2027, were issued at 99.08.

Prepare entries for issue of bonds. (SO 5)

Instructions

(a) Were GE and Boeing bonds issued at a premium or a discount?

(b) Explain how bonds, both paying the same contractual interest rate, could be issued at different prices.

(c) Prepare the journal entry to record the issue of each of these two bonds, assuming each company issued $500,000 of bonds in total.

E10-11 Boone Company issued $240,000 of 8%, 20-year bonds on January 1, 2007, at face value. Interest is payable annually on January 1.

Prepare journal entries to record issuance of bonds, payment of interest, and redemption at maturity. (SO 5, 6)

Instructions

Prepare the journal entries to record the following events.

(a) The issuance of the bonds

(b) The accrual of interest on December 31, 2007.

(c) The payment of interest on January 1, 2008.

(d) The redemption of the bonds at maturity, assuming interest for the last interest period has been paid and recorded.

E10-12 The situations presented here are independent of each other.

Prepare journal entries for redemption of bonds. (SO 6)

Instructions

For each situation prepare the appropriate journal entry for the redemption of the bonds.

(a) Thunder Corporation retired $130,000 face value, 12% bonds on June 30, 2007, at 102. The carrying value of the bonds at the redemption date was $122,500. The bonds pay annual interest, and the interest payment due on June 30, 2007, has been made and recorded.

(b) Lightning, Inc., retired $180,000 face value, 12.5% bonds on June 30, 2007, at 98. The carrying value of the bonds at the redemption date was $184,000. The bonds pay annual interest, and the interest payment due on June 30, 2007, has been made and recorded.

Prepare liabilities section of balance sheet.
(SO 7)

E10-13 Cyclone, Inc. reports the following liabilities (in thousands) on its January 31, 2007, balance sheet and notes to the financial statements.

Accounts payable	$3,263.9	Notes payable—long-term	$5,746.7
Accrued pension liability	1,215.2	Operating leases	1,641.7
Accrued liabilities	1,258.1	Loans payable—long-term	335.6
Bonds payable	1,961.2	Payroll-related liabilities	558.1
Current portion of		Short-term borrowings	2,563.6
long-term debt	1,992.2	Unused operating line of credit	3,337.6
Income taxes payable	235.2	Warranty liability—current	1,417.3

Instructions
(a) Identify which of the above liabilities are likely current and which are likely long-term. Say if an item fits in neither category. Explain the reasoning for your selection.
(b) Prepare the liabilities section of Cyclone's balance sheet as at January 31, 2007.

Calculate liquidity and solvency ratios; discuss impact of unrecorded obligations on liquidity and solvency.
(SO 7)

E10-14 McDonald's 2004 financial statements contain the following selected data (in millions).

Current assets	$ 2,857.8	Interest expense	$ 358.4
Total assets	27,837.5	Income taxes	923.9
Current liabilities	3,520.5	Net income	2,278.5
Total liabilities	13,636		

Instructions
(a) Compute the following values and provide a brief interpretation of each.
  (1) Working capital. (3) Debt to total assets ratio.
  (2) Current ratio.   (4) Times interest earned ratio.
(b) The notes to McDonald's financial statements show that subsequent to 2004 the company will have future minimum lease payments under operating leases of $11,442.6 million. If these assets had been purchased with debt, assets and liabilities would rise by approximately $10,500 million. Recompute the debt to total assets ratio after adjusting for this. Discuss your result.

Calculate current ratio before and after paying accounts payable.
(SO 7)

E10-15 3M Company reported the following financial data for 2004 and 2003 ($ in millions).

3M COMPANY
Balance Sheet (partial)

	2004	2003
Current assets		
Cash and cash equivalents	$2,757	$1,836
Accounts receivable, net	2,792	2,714
Inventories	1,897	1,816
Other current assets	1,274	1,354
Total current assets	$8,720	$7,720
Current liabilities	$6,071	$5,082

Instructions
(a) Calculate the current ratio for 3M for 2004 and 2003.
(b) Suppose that at the end of 2004 3M management used $300 million cash to pay off $300 million of accounts payable. How would its current ratio change?

E10-16 Unique Boutique reported the following financial data for 2007 and 2006.

Calculate current ratio before and after paying accounts payable.
(SO 7)

UNIQUE BOUTIQUE
Balance Sheet (partial)
September 30 (in thousands)

	2007	2006
Current assets		
Cash and short-term deposits	$2,574	$1,021
Accounts receivable	2,347	1,575
Inventories	1,201	1,010
Other current assets	322	192
Total current assets	$6,444	$3,798
Current liabilities	$5,303	$4,008

Instructions
(a) Calculate the current ratio for Unique Boutique for 2007 and 2006.
(b) Suppose that at the end of 2007, the Unique Boutique used $1.5 million cash to pay off $1.5 million of accounts payable. How would its current ratio change?
(c) At September 30, the Unique Boutique has an undrawn operating line of credit of $12.5 million. Would this affect any assessment that you might make of the Unique Boutique's short-term liquidity? Explain.

E10-17 Wal-Mart was sued nearly 5,000 times in a recent year—about once every two hours every day of the year. Wal-Mart has been sued for everything imaginable—ranging from falls on icy parking lots to injuries sustained in shoppers' stampedes to a murder with a rifle purchased at Wal-Mart.

Discuss contingent liabilities.
(SO 7)

Wal-Mart does not adhere to the legal strategy many businesses use of "Settle quickly and cut your losses." Instead, Wal-Mart aggressively fights lawsuits, even when it would be cheaper to settle. The company reported the following in the notes to its financial statements:

The Company and its subsidiaries are involved from time to time in claims, proceedings, and litigation arising from the operation of its business. The Company does not believe that any such claim, proceeding, or litigation, either alone or in the aggregate, will have a material adverse effect on the Company's financial position or results of its operations.

Instructions
(a) Explain why Wal-Mart does not have to record these contingent liabilities.
(b) Comment on any implications for analysis of the financial statements.

*E10-18 Columbo Company issued $300,000, 7%, 20-year bonds on January 1, 2007, at 103. Interest is payable annually on January 1. Columbo uses straight-line amortization for bond premium or discount.

Prepare journal entries to record issuance of bonds, payment of interest, amortization of premium using straight-line, and redemption at maturity.
(SO 5, 6, 8)

Instructions
Prepare the journal entries to record the following events.
(a) The issuance of the bonds.
(b) The accrual of interest and the premium amortization on December 31, 2007.
(c) The payment of interest on January 1, 2008.
(d) The redemption of the bonds at maturity, assuming interest for the last interest period has been paid and recorded.

*E10-19 Pierce Company issued $220,000, 8%, 10-year bonds on December 31, 2006, for $215,000. Interest is payable annually on December 31. Pierce uses the straight-line method to amortize bond premium or discount.

Prepare journal entries to record issuance of bonds, payment of interest, amortization of discount using straight-line, and redemption at maturity.
(SO 5, 6, 8)

Instructions
Prepare the journal entries to record the following events.
(a) The issuance of the bonds.
(b) The payment of interest and the discount amortization on December 31, 2007.
(c) The redemption of the bonds at maturity, assuming interest for the last interest period has been paid and recorded.

Prepare journal entries for issuance of bonds, payment of interest, and amortization of discount using effective-interest method.
(SO 5, 9)

*E10-20   Midas Corporation issued $260,000, 7%, 10-year bonds on January 1, 2007, for $242,554. This price resulted in an effective interest rate of 8% on the bonds. Interest is payable annually on January 1. Midas uses the effective-interest method to amortize bond premium or discount.

Instructions
Prepare the journal entries to record (round to the nearest dollar):
(a) The issuance of the bonds.
(b) The accrual of interest and the discount amortization on December 31, 2007.
(c) The payment of interest on January 1, 2008.

Prepare journal entries for issuance of bonds, payment of interest, and amortization of premium using effective-interest method.
(SO 5, 9)

*E10-21   Melina Company issued $180,000, 7%, 10-year bonds on January 1, 2007, for $193,248. This price resulted in an effective interest rate of 6% on the bonds. Interest is payable annually on January 1. Melina uses the effective-interest method to amortize bond premium or discount.

Instructions
Prepare the journal entries (rounded to the nearest dollar) to record:
(a) The issuance of the bonds.
(b) The accrual of interest and the premium amortization on December 31, 2007.
(c) The payment of interest on January 1, 2008.

Prepare journal entries to record mortgage note and installment payments.
(SO 10)

*E10-22   Moore Co. receives $110,000 when it issues a $110,000, 8%, mortgage note payable to finance the construction of a building at December 31, 2007. The terms provide for semiannual installment payments of $7,041 on June 30 and December 31.

Instructions
Prepare the journal entries to record the mortgage loan and the first two installment payments.

Problems: Set A

Prepare current liability entries, adjusting entries, and current liabilities section.
(SO 1, 2, 3, 7)

GLS

P10-1A   On January 1, 2007, the ledger of Daniels Company contained these liability accounts.

Accounts Payable	$42,500
Sales Taxes Payable	6,600
Unearned Service Revenue	19,000

During January the following selected transactions occurred.

Jan. 1   Borrowed $12,000 in cash from Midland Bank on a 4-month, 8%, $12,000 note.
    5   Sold merchandise for cash totaling $6,510, which includes 5% sales taxes.
    12   Provided services for customers who had made advance payments of $10,000. (Credit Service Revenue.)
    14   Paid state treasurer's department for sales taxes collected in December 2006, $6,600.
    20   Sold 500 units of a new product on credit at $48 per unit, plus 5% sales tax.

During January the company's employees earned wages of $60,000. Withholdings related to these wages were $4,590 for Social Security (FICA), $5,000 for federal income tax, and $1,500 for state income tax. The company owed no money related to these earnings for federal or state unemployment tax. Assume that wages earned during January will be paid during February. No entry had been recorded for wages or payroll tax expense as of January 31.

Instructions
(a) Journalize the January transactions.
(b) Journalize the adjusting entries at January 31 for the outstanding note payable and for wages expense and payroll tax expense.

(c) Tot. current liabilities $129,680

(c) Prepare the current liabilities section of the balance sheet at January 31, 2007. Assume no change in Accounts Payable.

P10-2A   On the Edge Corporation sells rock-climbing products and also operates an indoor climbing facility for climbing enthusiasts. During the last part of 2007, On the Edge had the following transactions related to notes payable.

Sept. 1		Issued a $9,000 note to Gibraltar to purchase inventory. The 3-month note payable bears interest of 8% and is due December 1.
Sept. 30		Recorded accrued interest for the Gibraltar note.
Oct. 1		Issued a $18,000, 9%, 4-month note to Apex Bank to finance the purchase of a new climbing wall for advanced climbers. The note is due February 1.
Oct. 31		Recorded accrued interest for the Gibraltar note and the Apex Bank note.
Nov. 1		Issued a $20,000 note and paid $8,000 cash to purchase a vehicle to transport clients to nearby climbing sites as part of a new series of climbing classes. This note bears interest of 6% and matures in 12 months.
Nov. 30		Recorded accrued interest for the Gibraltar note, the Apex Bank note, and the vehicle note.
Dec. 1		Paid principal and interest on the Gibraltar note.
Dec. 31		Recorded accrued interest for the Apex Bank note and the vehicle note.

Instructions
(a) Prepare journal entries for the transactions noted above.
(b) Post the above entries to the Notes Payable, Interest Payable, and Interest Expense accounts. (Use T accounts.)
(c) Show the balance sheet presentation of notes payable and interest payable at December 31.
(d) How much interest expense relating to notes payable did On the Edge incur during the year?

P10-3A   The following section is taken from Majestic's balance sheet at December 31, 2006.

Current liabilities	
Bond interest payable	$ 24,000
Long-term liabilities	
Bonds payable, 8%, due January 1, 2013	300,000

Interest is payable annually on January 1. The bonds are callable on any annual interest date.

Instructions
(a) Journalize the payment of the bond interest on January 1, 2007.
(b) Assume that on January 1, 2007, after paying interest, Majestic calls bonds having a face value of $50,000. The call price is 104. Record the redemption of the bonds.
(c) Prepare the adjusting entry on December 31, 2007, to accrue the interest on the remaining bonds.

P10-4A   On October 1, 2006, Ferdinand Corp. issued $500,000, 7%, 10-year bonds at face value. The bonds were dated October 1, 2006, and pay interest annually on October 1. Financial statements are prepared annually on December 31.

Instructions
(a) Prepare the journal entry to record the issuance of the bonds.
(b) Prepare the adjusting entry to record the accrual of interest on December 31, 2006.
(c) Show the balance sheet presentation of bonds payable and bond interest payable on December 31, 2006.
(d) Prepare the journal entry to record the payment of interest on October 1, 2007.
(e) Prepare the adjusting entry to record the accrual of interest on December 31, 2007.
(f) Assume that on January 1, 2008, Ferdinand pays the accrued bond interest and calls the bonds. The call price is 102. Record the payment of interest and redemption of the bonds.

P10-5A   Margaret Rose Company sold $4,000,000, 8%, 20-year bonds on January 1, 2007. The bonds were dated January 1, 2007, and pay interest on December 31. The bonds were sold at 98.

Instructions
(a) Prepare the journal entry to record the issuance of the bonds on January 1, 2007.
(b) At December 31, 2007, $4,000 of the bond discount had been amortized. Show the balance sheet presentation of the bond liability at December 31, 2007. (Assume that interest has been paid.)

(c) Loss $152,000

(c) At December 31, 2008, when the carrying value of the bonds was $3,928,000, the company redeemed the bonds at 102. Record the redemption of the bonds assuming that interest for the year had already been paid.

Calculate and comment on ratios.
(SO 7)

P10-6A You have been presented with the following selected information taken from the financial statements of Southwest Airlines Co.

SOUTHWEST AIRLINES CO.
Balance Sheet (partial)
December 31
(in millions)

	2004	2003
Total current assets	$2,172	$2,313
Noncurrent assets	9,165	7,565
Total assets	$11,337	$9,878
Current liabilities	$2,142	$1,723
Long-term liabilities	3,671	3,103
Total liabilities	5,813	4,826
Shareholders' equity	5,524	5,052
Total liabilities and shareholders' equity	$11,337	$9,878

Other information:

	2004	2003
Net income (loss)	$ 313	$ 442
Income tax expense	176	266
Interest expense	88	91
Cash provided by operations	1,157	1,336
Capital expenditures	1,775	1,238
Cash dividends	14	14

Note 8. Leases
The majority of the Company's terminal operations space, as well as 88 aircraft, were under operating leases at December 31, 2004. Future minimum lease payments under noncancelable operating leases are as follows: 2005, $343,000; 2006, $279,000; 2007, $256,000; 2008, $226,000; 2009, $204,000; after 2009, $1,369,000.

Instructions
(a) Calculate each of the following ratios for 2004 and 2003.
   (1) Current ratio.
   (2) Free cash flow.
   (3) Debt to total assets.
   (4) Times interest earned ratio.
(b) Comment on the trend in ratios.
(c) Read the company's note on leases. If the operating leases had instead been accounted for like a purchase, assets and liabilities would increase by approximately $1,500 million. Recalculate the debt to total assets ratio for 2004 in light of this information, and discuss the implictions for analysis.

Prepare journal entries to record interest payments, straight-line discount amortization, and redemption of bonds.
(SO 5, 6, 8)

*P10-7A** The information on page 519 is taken from Simon Corp.'s balance sheet at December 31, 2007.

Current liabilities		
Bond interest payable		$ 192,000
Long-term liabilities		
Bonds payable, 8%, due January 1, 2018	$2,400,000	
Less: Discount on bonds payable	42,000	2,358,000

Interest is payable annually on January 1. The bonds are callable on any annual interest date. Simon uses straight-line amortization for any bond premium or discount. From December 31, 2007, the bonds will be outstanding for an additional 10 years (120 months).

Instructions

(Round all computations to the nearest dollar.)

(a) Journalize the payment of bond interest on January 1, 2008.

(b) Prepare the entry to amortize bond discount and to accrue the interest on December 31, 2008.

(c) Assume on January 1, 2009, after paying interest, that Simon Corp. calls bonds having a face value of $300,000. The call price is 103. Record the redemption of the bonds.

(c) Loss $13,725

(d) Prepare the adjusting entry at December 31, 2009, to amortize bond discount and to accrue interest on the remaining bonds.

*P10-8A   Peru Corporation sold $1,500,000, 6%, 10-year bonds on January 1, 2007. The bonds were dated January 1, 2007, and pay interest on January 1. Peru Corporation uses the straight-line method to amortize bond premium or discount.

Prepare journal entries to record issuance of bonds, interest, and straight-line amortization, and balance sheet presentation.
(SO 5, 7, 8)

Instructions

(a) Prepare all the necessary journal entries to record the issuance of the bonds and bond interest expense for 2007, assuming that the bonds sold at 103.

(b) Prepare journal entries as in part (a) assuming that the bonds sold at 98.

(c) Show the balance sheet presentation for the bond issue at December 31, 2007, using (1) the 103 selling price, and then (2) the 98 selling price.

*P10-9A   McGraw Co. sold $4,000,000, 9%, 5-year bonds on January 1, 2007. The bonds were dated January 1, 2007, and pay interest on January 1. The company uses straight-line amortization on bond premiums and discounts. Financial statements are prepared annually.

Prepare journal entries to record issuance of bonds, interest, and straight-line amortization, and balance sheet presentation.
(SO 5, 6, 8)

Instructions

(a) Prepare the journal entries to record the issuance of the bonds assuming they sold at:
(1) 101.
(2) 97.

(b) Prepare amortization tables for both assumed sales for the first three interest payments.

(c) Prepare the journal entries to record interest expense for 2007 under both assumed sales.

(d) Show the balance sheet presentation for both assumed sales at December 31, 2007.

*P10-10A   On January 1, 2007, Lucy Corporation issued $1,200,000 face value, 7%, 10-year bonds at $1,119,479. This price resulted in an effective-interest rate of 8% on the bonds. Lucy uses the effective-interest method to amortize bond premium or discount. The bonds pay annual interest January 1.

Prepare journal entries to record issuance of bonds, payment of interest, and amortization of bond discount using effective-interest method.
(SO 9)

Instructions

(Round all computations to the nearest dollar.)

(a) Prepare the journal entry to record the issuance of the bonds on January 1, 2007.

(b) Prepare an amortization table through December 31, 2009 (three interest periods) for this bond issue.

(c) Prepare the journal entry to record the accrual of interest and the amortization of the discount on December 31, 2007.

(c) Interest
     Expense $89,558

(d) Prepare the journal entry to record the payment of interest on January 1, 2008.

(e) Prepare the journal entry to record the accrual of interest and the amortization of the discount on December 31, 2008.

Prepare journal entries to record issuance of bonds, payment of interest, and effective-interest amortization, and balance sheet presentation.
(SO 5, 7, 9)
(a) (4) Interest
Expense $136,324

*P10-11A On January 1, 2007, HiLo Company issued $2,000,000 face value, 8%, 10-year bonds at $2,294,403. This price resulted in a 6% effective-interest rate on the bonds. HiLo uses the effective-interest method to amortize bond premium or discount. The bonds pay annual interest on each January 1.

Instructions
(a) Prepare the journal entries to record the following transactions.
  (1) The issuance of the bonds on January 1, 2007.
  (2) Accrual of interest and amortization of the premium on December 31, 2007.
  (3) The payment of interest on January 1, 2008.
  (4) Accrual of interest and amortization of the premium on December 31, 2008.
(b) Show the proper balance sheet presentation for the liability for bonds payable on the December 31, 2008, balance sheet.
(c) Provide the answers to the following questions in narrative form.
  (1) What amount of interest expense is reported for 2008?
  (2) Would the bond interest expense reported in 2008 be the same as, greater than, or less than the amount that would be reported if the straight-line method of amortization were used?

Prepare installment payments schedule, journal entries, and balance sheet presentation for a mortgage note payable.
(SO 7, 10)

*P10-12A Fowler purchased a new piece of equipment to be used in its new facility. The $550,000 piece of equipment was purchased with a $50,000 down payment and with cash received through the issuance of a $500,000, 8%, 4-year mortgage note payable issued on October 1, 2007. The terms provide for quarterly installment payments of $36,825 on December 31, March 31, June 30, and September 30.

Instructions
(Round all computations to the nearest dollar.)
(a) Prepare an installment payments schedule for the first five payments of the notes payable.
(b) Prepare all journal entries related to the notes payable for December 31, 2007.

(c) Current portion $112,773

(c) Show the balance sheet presentation for this obligation for December 31, 2007. (*Hint:* Be sure to distinguish between the current and long-term portions of the note.)

Prepare journal entries to record payments for long-term note payable, and balance sheet presentation.
(SO 7, 10)

*P10-13A Cindy Davito has just approached a venture capitalist for financing for her new business venture, the development of a local ski hill. On July 1, 2007, Cindy was loaned $100,000 at an annual interest rate of 7%. The loan is repayable over 5 years in annual installments of $24,389, principal and interest, due each June 30. The first payment is due June 30, 2008. Cindy uses the effective-interest method for amortizing debt. Her ski hill company's year-end will be June 30.

Instructions
(a) Prepare an amortization schedule for the 5 years, 2007–2012. Round all calculations to the nearest dollar.

(b) 6/30/08 Interest
Expense $7,000

(b) Prepare all journal entries for Cindy Davito for the first 2 fiscal years ended June 30, 2008, and June 30, 2009. Round all calculations to the nearest dollar.
(c) Show the balance sheet presentation of the note payable as of June 30, 2009. (*Hint:* Be sure to distinguish between the current and long-term portions of the note.)

Problems: Set B

Prepare current liability entries, adjusting entries, and current liabilities section.
(SO 1, 2, 3, 7)
GLS

P10-1B On January 1, 2007, the ledger of Cramer Company contained the following liability accounts.

Accounts Payable	$52,000
Sales Taxes Payable	8,500
Unearned Service Revenue	11,000

During January the following selected transactions occurred.

Jan. 1 Borrowed $18,000 from TriCounty Bank on a 3-month, 6%, $18,000 note.
  5 Sold merchandise for cash totaling $17,172, which includes 6% sales taxes.
  12 Provided services for customers who had made advance payments of $8,000. (Credit Service Revenue.)

14 Paid state revenue department for sales taxes collected in December 2006 ($8,500).

20 Sold 500 units of a new product on credit at $50 per unit, plus 6% sales tax.

During January the company's employees earned wages of $40,000. Withholdings related to these wages were $3,060 for Social Security (FICA), $3,800 for federal income tax, and $1,100 for state income tax. The company owed no money related to these earnings for federal or state unemployment tax. Assume that wages earned during January will be paid during February. No entry had been recorded for wages or payroll tax expense as of January 31.

Instructions
(a) Journalize the January transactions.
(b) Journalize the adjusting entries at January 31 for the outstanding notes payable and for wages expense and payroll tax expense.
(c) Prepare the current liabilities section of the balance sheet at January 31, 2007. Assume no change in accounts payable.

(c) Tot. current liabilities $118,622

P10-2B Cougar Mountain Bikes markets mountain-bike tours to clients vacationing in various locations in the mountains of Colorado. In preparation for the upcoming summer biking season, Cougar entered into the following transactions related to notes payable.

Journalize and post note transactions; show balance sheet presentation.
(SO 2, 7)

Mar. 1 Purchased Puma bikes for use as rentals by issuing an $8,000, 3-month, 6% note payable that is due June 1.
Mar. 31 Recorded accrued interest for the Puma note.
Apr. 1 Issued a $24,000 9-month note for the purchase of mountain property on which to build bike trails. The note bears 8% interest and is due January 1.
Apr. 30 Recorded accrued interest for the Puma note and the land note.
May 1 Issued a 4-month note to Rocky National Bank for $20,000 at 6%. The funds will be used for working capital for the beginning of the season; the note is due September 1.
May 31 Recorded accrued interest for all three notes.
June 1 Paid principal and interest on the Puma note.
June 30 Recorded accrued interest for the land note and the Rocky Bank note.

Instructions
(a) Prepare journal entries for the transactions noted above.
(b) Post the above entries to the Notes Payable, Interest Payable, and Interest Expense accounts. (Use T accounts.)
(c) Assuming that Cougar's year-end is June 30, show the balance sheet presentation of notes payable and interest payable at that date.
(d) How much interest expense relating to notes payable did Cougar incur during the year?

(b) Interest Payable $680

P10-3B The following section is taken from Barnaby Corp.'s balance sheet at December 31, 2006.

Prepare journal entries to record interest payments and redemption of bonds.
(SO 5, 6)

Current liabilities
  Bond interest payable $ 128,000
Long-term liabilities
  Bonds payable, 8%, due January 1, 2011   1,600,000

Interest is payable annually on January 1. The bonds are callable on any annual interest date.

Instructions
(a) Journalize the payment of the bond interest on January 1, 2007.
(b) Assume that on January 1, 2007, after paying interest, Barnaby Corp. calls bonds having a face value of $400,000. The call price is 105. Record the redemption of the bonds.
(c) Prepare the adjusting entry on December 31, 2007, to accrue the interest on the remaining bonds.

(b) Loss $20,000

Prepare journal entries to record issuance of bonds, interest, balance sheet presentation, and bond redemption.
(SO 5, 6, 7)

(f) Loss 16,000

P10-4B On April 1, 2006, ERV Corp. issued $800,000, 7%, 5-year bonds at face value. The bonds were dated April 1, 2006, and pay interest annually on April 1. Financial statements are prepared annually on December 31.

Instructions
(a) Prepare the journal entry to record the issuance of the bonds.
(b) Prepare the adjusting entry to record the accrual of interest on December 31, 2006.
(c) Show the balance sheet presentation of bonds payable and bond interest payable on December 31, 2006.
(d) Prepare the journal entry to record the payment of interest on April 1, 2007.
(e) Prepare the adjusting entry to record the accrual of interest on December 31, 2007.
(f) Assume that on January 1, 2008, ERV pays the accrued bond interest and calls the bonds. The call price is 102. Record the payment of interest and redemption of the bonds.

Prepare journal entries to record issuance of bonds, show balance sheet presentation, and record bond redemption.
(SO 5, 6, 7)

(c) Loss $39,000

P10-5B Buzz Electric sold $3,000,000, 9%, 20-year bonds on January 1, 2007. The bonds were dated January 1 and pay interest on January 1. The bonds were sold at 103.

Instructions
(a) Prepare the journal entry to record the issuance of the bonds on January 1, 2007.
(b) At December 31, 2007, $4,500 of the bond premium had been amortized. Show the balance sheet presentation of the bond liability at December 31, 2007. (Assume that interest has been paid.)
(c) At December 31, 2008, when the carrying value of the bonds was $3,081,000, the company redeemed the bonds at 104. Record the redemption of the bonds assuming that interest for the year had already been paid.

Calculate and comment on ratios.
(SO 7)

P10-6B The following selected information was taken from the financial statements of Krispy Kreme Doughnuts, Inc.

KRISPY KREME DOUGHNUTS, INC.
Balance Sheet (partial)

(in thousands)

	Feb. 1, 2004	Feb. 2, 2003
Total current assets	$138,644	$141,128
Capital assets and other long-term assets	522,020	269,359
	$660,664	$410,487
Current liabilities	$ 53,493	$ 59,687
Long-term liabilities	154,964	77,448
Total liabilities	208,457	137,135
Shareholders' equity	452,207	273,352
Total liabilities and shareholders' equity	$660,664	$410,487

Other information:

	2004	2003
Interest expense	$ 4,409	$ 1,781
Tax expense	37,590	21,295
Net income	33,478	57,087
Cash provided by operations	95,553	51,036
Capital expenditures	79,649	83,196
Cash dividends	-0-	-0-

Note 8. Lease Commitments
The Company conducts some of its operations from leased facilities and, additionally, leases certain equipment under operating leases. Generally, these have initial terms of 3 to 20 years and contain provisions for renewal options of 5 to 10 years.

At February 1, 2004, future minimum annual rental commitments, gross, under noncancelable operating leases, including lease commitments on consolidated joint ventures, are as follows:

Fiscal Year Ending in	Amount (in thousands)
2005	$ 21,119
2006	18,560
2007	15,657
2008	13,099
2009	11,692
Thereafter	75,599
	$155,726

Rental expense, net of rental income, totaled $10,576,000 in fiscal 2002, $13,169,000 in fiscal 2003 and $19,574,000 in fiscal 2004.

Instructions
(a) Calculate each of the following ratios for 2004 and 2003.
   (1) Current ratio.
   (2) Free cash flow.
   (3) Debt to total assets ratio.
   (4) Times interest earned ratio.
(b) Comment on Krispy Kreme's liquidity and solvency.
(c) Read the company's note on leases (Note 8). If the operating leases had instead been accounted for like a purchase, assets and liabilities would have increased by approximately $110,000,000. Recalculate the debt to total assets ratio for 2004 and discuss the implications for analysis.

*P10-7B   The following section is taken from Clampette Oil Company's balance sheet at December 31, 2007.

Prepare journal entries to record interest payments, straight-line premium amortization, and redemption of bonds (SO 5, 6, 8)

Current liabilities		
Bond interest payable		$ 342,000
Long-term liabilities		
Bonds payable, 9% due January 1, 2018	$3,800,000	
Add: Premium on bonds payable	200,000	4,000,000

Interest is payable annually on January 1. The bonds are callable on any annual interest date. Clampette uses straight-line amortization for any bond premium or discount. From December 31, 2007, the bonds will be outstanding for an additional 10 years (120 months).

Instructions
(Round all computations to the nearest dollar.)
(a) Journalize the payment of bond interest on January 1, 2008.
(b) Prepare the entry to amortize bond premium and to accrue interest due on December 31, 2008.
(c) Assume on January 1, 2009, after paying interest, that Clampette Company calls bonds having a face value of $1,900,000. The call price is 102. Record the redemption of the bonds.
(d) Prepare the adjusting entry at December 31, 2009, to amortize bond premium and to accrue interest on the remaining bonds.

(c) Gain $52,000

Prepare journal entries to record issuance of bonds, interest, and straight-line amortization, and balance sheet presentation. (SO 5, 7, 8)

*P10-8B   Smudge Company sold $1,500,000, 10%, 10-year bonds on January 1, 2007. The bonds were dated January 1, 2007, and pay interest on January 1. Smudge Company uses the straight-line method to amortize bond premium or discount.

Instructions

(a) Prepare all the necessary journal entries to record the issuance of the bonds and bond interest expense for 2007, assuming that the bonds sold at 102.
(b) Prepare journal entries as in part (a) assuming that the bonds sold at 96.
(c) Show the balance sheet presentation for the bond issue at December 31, 2007, using (1) the 102 selling price, and then (2) the 96 selling price.

Prepare journal entries to record issuance of bonds, interest, and straight-line amortization, and balance sheet presentation.
(SO 5, 7, 8)

*P10-9B Zorin Corporation sold $3,500,000, 7%, 20-year bonds on December 31, 2006. The bonds were dated December 31, 2006, and pay interest on December 31. The company uses straight-line amortization for premiums and discounts. Financial statements are prepared annually.

Instructions

(a) Prepare the journal entry to record the issuance of the bonds assuming they sold at:
    (1) 97½.
    (2) 104.

(b) Prepare amortization tables for both of the assumed sales for the first three interest payments.

(c) (2) 12/31/07 Interest Expense $238,000

(c) Prepare the journal entries to record interest expense for the first two interest payments under both assumed sales.
(d) Show the balance sheet presentation for both assumed sales at December 31, 2007.

Prepare journal entries to record issuance of bonds, payment of interest, and amortization of bond premium using effective-interest method.
(SO 5, 9)

*P10-10B On January 1, 2007, Stavlund Corporation issued $1,400,000 face value, 12%, 10-year bonds at $1,572,048. This price resulted in an effective-interest rate of 10% on the bonds. Stavlund uses the effective-interest method to amortize bond premium or discount. The bonds pay annual interest January 1.

Instructions

(Round all computations to the nearest dollar.)

(a) Prepare the journal entry to record the issuance of the bonds on January 1, 2007.
(b) Prepare an amortization table through December 31, 2009 (three interest periods) for this bond issue.

(c) Interest Expense $157,205

(c) Prepare the journal entry to record the accrual of interest and the amortization of the premium on December 31, 2007.
(d) Prepare the journal entry to record the payment of interest on January 1, 2008.
(e) Prepare the journal entry to record the accrual of interest and the amortization of the premium on December 31, 2008.

Prepare journal entries to record issuance of bonds, payment of interest, and effective-interest amortization, and balance sheet presentation.
(SO 5, 7, 9)

*P10-11B On January 1, 2007, Gelber Company issued $2,200,000 face value, 10%, 15-year bonds at $1,900,322. This price resulted in an effective interest rate of 12% on the bonds. Gelber uses the effective-interest method to amortize bond premium or discount. The bonds pay annual interest January 1.

Instructions

(a) Prepare the journal entries to record the following transactions.
    (1) The issuance of the bonds on January 1, 2007.
    (2) The accrual of interest and the amortization of the discount on December 31, 2007.
    (3) The payment of interest on January 1, 2008.
    (4) The accrual of interest and the amortization of the discount on December 31, 2008.

(b) Show the proper balance sheet presentation for the liability for bonds payable on the December 31, 2008, balance sheet.

(c) (1) $229,003

(c) Provide the answers to the following questions in narrative form.
    (1) What amount of interest expense is reported for 2008?
    (2) Would the bond interest expense reported in 2008 be the same as, greater than, or less than the amount that would be reported if the straight-line method of amortization were used?
    (3) Determine the total cost of borrowing over the life of the bond.
    (4) Would the total bond interest expense be greater than, the same as, or less than the total interest expense that would be reported if the straight-line method of amortization were used?

Prepare installment payments schedule, journal entries for a mortgage note payable, and balance sheet presentation.
(SO 7, 10)

*P10-12B Angela Corporation purchased a new piece of equipment to be used in its new facility. The $750,000 piece of equipment was purchased with a $50,000 down payment and with cash received through the issuance of a $700,000, 8%, 4-year mortgage note payable issued on October 1, 2007. The terms provide for quarterly installment payments of $51,555 on December 31, March 31, June 30, and September 30.

Instructions
(Round all computations to the nearest dollar.)
(a) Prepare an installment payments schedule for the first five payments of the notes payable.
(b) Prepare all necessary journal entries related to the notes payable for December 31, 2007.
(c) Show the balance sheet presentation for these obligations for December 31, 2007. (*Hint:* Be sure to distinguish between the current and long-term portions of the note.)

(b) Interest Expense $14,000

P10-13B James Clark has just approached a venture capitalist for financing for his sailing school. The venture capitalist is willing to loan James $70,000 at a high-risk annual interest rate of 24%. The loan is payable over 3 years in monthly installments of $2,746. Each payment includes principal and interest, calculated using the effective-interest method for amortizing debt. James receives the loan on May 1, 2007, which is the first day of his fiscal year. James makes the first payment on May 31, 2007.

Prepare journal entries to record payments for long-term note payable.
(SO 10)

Instructions
(a) Prepare an amortization schedule for the period from May 1, 2007, to August 31, 2007. Round all calculations to the nearest dollar.
(b) Prepare all journal entries for James Clark for the period beginning May 1, 2007, and ending July 31, 2007. Round all calculations to the nearest dollar.

(b) 6/30 Interest
     Expense $1,373

Problems: Set C

Visit the book's website at **www.wiley.com/college/kimmel** and choose the Student Companion site to access Problem Set C.

Comprehensive Problem

CP10 Crow Corporation's balance sheet at December 31, 2006, is presented below.

CROW CORPORATION
Balance Sheet
December 31, 2006

Cash	$30,500	Accounts payable	$13,750
Inventory	25,750	Bond interest payable	3,000
Prepaid insurance	5,600	Bonds payable	50,000
Equipment	38,000	Common stock	20,000
	$99,850	Retained earnings	$13,100
			$99,850

During 2007, the following transactions occurred.
1. Crow paid $3,000 interest on the bonds on January 1, 2007.
2. Crow purchased $241,100 of inventory on account.
3. Crow sold for $400,000 cash inventory which cost $240,000. Crow also collected $24,000 sales taxes.
4. Crow paid $230,000 on accounts payable.
5. Crow paid $3,000 interest on the bonds on July 1, 2007.
6. The prepaid insurance ($5,600) expired on July 31.
7. On August 1, Crow paid $10,800 for insurance coverage from August 1, 2007, through July 31, 2008.
8. Crow paid $17,000 sales taxes to the state.
9. Paid other operating expenses, $91,000.
10. Retired the bonds on December 31, 2007, by paying $48,000 plus $3,000 interest.
11. Issued $70,000 of 8% bonds on December 31, 2007, at 104. The bonds pay interest every June 30 and December 31.

Adjustment data:
1. Recorded the insurance expired from item 7.
2. The equipment was acquired on December 31, 2006, and will be depreciated on a straight-line basis over 5 years with a $3,000 salvage value.
3. The income tax rate is 30%. (*Hint*: Prepare the income statement up to income before taxes and multiply by 30% to compute the amount.)

Instructions
(You may want to set up T accounts to determine ending balances.)
(a) Prepare journal entries for the transactions listed above and adjusting entries.
(b) Prepare an adjusted trial balance at December 31, 2007.
(c) Prepare an income statement and a retained earnings statement for the year ending December 31, 2007, and a classified balance sheet as of December 31, 2007.

Continuing Cookie Chronicle

(*Note:* This is a continuation of the Cookie Chronicle from Chapters 1 through 9.)

CCC10   Natalie is thinking of repaying all amounts outstanding to her grandmother. Recall that Cookie Creations borrowed $2,000 on November 16, 2006, from Natalie's grandmother. Interest on the note is 6% per year, and the note plus interest was to be repaid in 24 months. Recall that a monthly adjusting journal entry was prepared for the months of November 2006 (1/2 month), December 2006, and January 2007.

Instructions
(a) Calculate the interest payable that was accrued and recorded to January 31, 2007.
(b) Calculate the total interest expense and interest payable to August 31, 2007. Prepare the journal entry at August 31, 2007, to bring the accounting records up to date.
(c) Natalie repays her grandmother on September 15, 2007—10 months after her grandmother extended the loan to Cookie Creations. Prepare the journal entry for the loan repayment.

► BROADENING YOUR PERSPECTIVE

Financial Reporting and Analysis

FINANCIAL REPORTING PROBLEM: *Tootsie Roll Industries*

BYP10-1   Refer to the financial statements of Tootsie Roll Industries and the Notes to Consolidated Financial Statements in Appendix A.

Instructions
Answer the following questions.
(a) What were Tootsie Roll's total current liabilities at December 31, 2004? What was the increase/decrease in Tootsie Roll's total current liabilities from the prior year?
(b) How much were the accounts payable at December 31, 2004?
(c) What were the components of total current liabilities on December 31, 2004 (other than accounts payable already discussed above)?

COMPARATIVE ANALYSIS PROBLEM: *Tootsie Roll vs. Hershey Foods*

BYP10-2   The financial statements of Hershey Foods are presented in Appendix B, following the financial statements for Tootsie Roll Industries in Appendix A.

Instructions
(a) Based on the information contained in these financial statements, compute the current ratio for 2004 for each company.

What conclusions concerning the companies' liquidity can be drawn from these ratios?

(b) Based on the information contained in these financial statements, compute the following 2004 ratios for each company.

   (1) Debt to total assets.
   (2) Times interest earned. (Hershey's total interest expense for 2004 was $67,919,000.)

What conclusions about the companies' long-run solvency can be drawn from the ratios?

RESEARCH CASE

BYP10-3 The July 2, 2004, edition of the *Wall Street Journal* contains an article by Ken Brown and Mark Heinzl titled "Nortel Board Finds Accounting Tricks Behind '03 Profits."

Instructions

Read the article and answer the following questions.

(a) Describe the process of "cookie jar" accounting. Include the example used in the article.

(b) What motivation did Nortel's executives have to engage in the practice of "cookie jar" accounting?

(c) What actions did Nortel's board of directors take once the improper accounting was revealed?

INTERPRETING FINANCIAL STATEMENTS

BYP10-4 Hechinger Co. and Home Depot are two home improvement retailers. Compared to Hechinger, founded in the early 1900s, Home Depot is a relative newcomer. But, in recent years, while Home Depot was reporting large increases in net income, Hechinger was reporting increasingly large net losses. Finally, largely due to competition from Home Depot, Hechinger was forced to file for bankruptcy. Here are financial data for both companies (in millions).

	Hechinger	Home Depot
Cash	$ 21	$ 62
Receivables	0	469
Total current assets	1,153	4,933
Beginning total assets	1,668	11,229
Ending total assets	1,577	13,465
Beginning current liabilities	935	2,456
Ending current liabilities	938	2,857
Beginning total liabilities	1,392	4,015
Ending total liabilities	1,339	4,716
Interest expense	67	37
Income tax expense	3	1,040
Cash provided (used) by operations	(257)	1,917
Net income	(93)	1,614
Net sales	3,444	30,219

Instructions

Using the data, perform the following analysis.

(a) Calculate working capital and the current ratio for each company. Discuss their relative liquidity.

(b) Calculate the debt to total assets ratio and times interest earned for each company. Discuss their relative solvency.

(c) Calculate the return on assets ratio and profit margin ratio for each company. Comment on their relative profitability.

(d) The notes to Home Depot's financial statements indicate that it leases many of its facilities using operating leases. If these assets had instead been purchased with debt, assets and liabilities would have increased by approximately $2,347 million. Calculate the company's debt to total assets ratio employing this adjustment. Discuss the implications.

BYP10-5 Many multinational companies find it beneficial to have their shares listed on stock exchanges in foreign countries. In order to do this, they must comply with the securities laws of those countries. Some of these laws relate to the form of financial disclosure the company must provide, including disclosures related to contingent liabilities. This exercise investigates the Tokyo Stock Exchange, the largest stock exchange in Japan.

Address: **www.tse.or.jp/english/index.shtml** (or go to **www.wiley.com/college/kimmel**)

Steps

1. Choose **About TSE**.
2. Choose **History**. Answer questions (a) and (b).
3. Choose **Listed Companies**.
4. Choose **Disclosure**. Answer questions (c) and (d).

Instructions

Answer the following questions.

(a) When was the first stock exchange opened in Japan? How many exchanges does Japan have today?

(b) What event caused trading to stop for a period of time in Japan?

(c) What are four examples of decisions by corporations that must be disclosed at the time of their occurrence?

(d) What are four examples of "occurrence of material fact" that must be disclosed at the time of their occurrence?

FINANCIAL ANALYSIS ON THE WEB

BYP10-6 *Purpose:* Bond or debt securities pay a stated rate of interest. This rate of interest is dependent on the risk associated with the investment. Moody's Investment Service provides ratings for companies that issue debt securities.

Address: **www.moodys.com/** (or go to **www.wiley.com/college/kimmel**)

Steps: From Moody's homepage, choose **About Moody's**.

Instructions

Answer the following questions.

(a) In what year did Moody's introduce the first bond rating? (See **Moody's History.**)

(b) What is the total amount of debt securities that Moody's analysts "track"? (See **An Introduction.**)

(c) What characteristics must debt ratings have in order to be useful to the capital markets? (See **Understand Risk: The Truth About Credit Ratings.**)

BYP10-7 *Purpose:* To illustrate the usefulness of financial calculators on the Web.

Address: **www.centura.com/tools** (or go to **www.wiley.com/college/kimmel**)

Steps: Go to the site shown above.

Instructions

Choose one of the many financial decisions listed at the site. Fill in inputs based on two different sets of assumptions. Print out your results, and then write up a short description of the decision model for your instructor. Describe the inputs and assumptions the model uses. Also try to identify the strengths and weaknesses of the site.

Critical Thinking

DECISION MAKING ACROSS THE ORGANIZATION

BYP10-8   On January 1, 2005, Troy Corporation issued $1,200,000 of 5-year, 8% bonds at 97. The bonds pay interest annually on January 1. By January 1, 2007, the market rate of interest for bonds of risk similar to those of Troy Corporation had risen. As a result the market value of these bonds was $1,000,000 on January 1, 2007—below their carrying value of $1,178,400.

Troy Athens, president of the company, suggests repurchasing all of these bonds in the open market at the $1,000,000 price. But to do so the company will have to issue $1,000,000 (face value) of new 10-year, 12% bonds at par. The president asks you, as controller, "What is the feasibility of my proposed repurchase plan?"

Instructions

With the class divided into groups, answer the following.
(a) Prepare the journal entry to retire the 5-year bonds on January 1, 2007. Prepare the journal entry to issue the new 10-year bonds.
(b) Prepare a short memo to the president in response to his request for advice. List the economic factors that you believe should be considered for his repurchase proposal.

COMMUNICATION ACTIVITY

BYP10-9   Adam Merritt, president of Good to Go, is considering the issuance of bonds to finance an expansion of his business. He has asked you to do the following: (1) discuss the advantages of bonds over common stock financing, (2) indicate the types of bonds he might issue, and (3) explain the issuing procedures used in bond transactions.

Instructions

Write a memorandum to the president, answering his request.

ETHICS CASE

BYP10-10   The July 1998 issue of *Inc.* magazine includes an article by Jeffrey L. Seglin entitled "Would You Lie to Save Your Company?" It recounts the following true situation:

"A Chief Executive Officer (CEO) of a $20-million company that repairs aircraft engines received notice from a number of its customers that engines that it had recently repaired had failed, and that the company's parts were to blame. The CEO had not yet determined whether his company's parts were, in fact, the cause of the problem. The Federal Aviation Administration (FAA) had been notified and was investigating the matter.

What complicated the situation was that the company was in the midst of its year-end audit. As part of the audit, the CEO was required to sign a letter saying that he was not aware of any significant outstanding circumstances that could negatively impact the company—in accounting terms, of any contingent liabilities. The auditor was not aware of the customer complaints or the FAA investigation.

The company relied heavily on short-term loans from eight banks. The CEO feared that if these lenders learned of the situation, they would pull their loans. The loss of these loans would force the company into bankruptcy, leaving hundreds of people without jobs. Prior to this problem, the company had a stellar performance record."

Instructions

Answer the following questions.
(a) Who are the stakeholders in this situation?
(b) What are the CEO's possible courses of action? What are the potential results of each course of action? (Take into account the two alternative outcomes: the FAA determines the company (1) was not at fault, and (2) was at fault.)
(c) What would you do, and why?

(d) Suppose the CEO decides to conceal the situation, and that during the next year the company is found to be at fault and is forced into bankruptcy. What losses are incurred by the stakeholders in this situation? Do you think the CEO should suffer legal consequences if he decides to conceal the situation?

BYP10-11 During the summer of 2002 the financial press reported that Citigroup was being investigated for allegations that it had arranged transactions for Enron so as to intentionally misrepresent the nature of the transactions and consequently achieve favorable balance sheet treatment. Essentially, the deals were structured to make it appear that money was coming into Enron from trading activities, rather than from loans.

A July 23, 2002, *New York Times* article by Richard Oppel and Kurt Eichenwald entitled "Citigroup Said to Mold Deal to Help Enron Skirt Rules" suggested that Citigroup intentionally kept certain parts of a secret oral agreement out of the written record for fear that it would change the accounting treatment. Critics contend that this had the effect of significantly understating Enron's liabilities, thus misleading investors and creditors. Citigroup maintains that, as a lender, it has no obligation to ensure that its clients account for transactions properly. The proper accounting, Citigroup insists, is the responsibility of the client and its auditor.

Instructions
Answer the following questions.
  (a) Who are the stakeholders in this situation?
  (b) Do you think that a lender, in general, in arranging so called "structured financing" has a responsibility to ensure that its clients account for the financing in an appropriate fashion, or is this the responsibility of the client and its auditor?
  (c) What effect did the fact that the written record did not disclose all characteristics of the transaction probably have on the auditor's ability to evaluate the accounting treatment of this transaction?
  (d) The *New York Times* article noted that in one presentation made to sell this kind of deal to Enron and other energy companies, Citigroup stated that using such an arrangement "eliminates the need for capital markets disclosure, keeping structure mechanics private." Why might a company wish to conceal the terms of a financing arrangement from the capital markets (investors and creditors)? Is this appropriate? Do you think it is ethical for a lender to market deals in this way?
  (e) Why was this deal more potentially harmful to shareholders than other off-balance-sheet transactions (for example, lease financing)?

Answers to Business Insight and Accounting across the Organization Questions

p. 479
Q: Based on this story, what is a good general rule to use in choosing between short-term and long-term financing?
A: In general, it is best to finance short-term assets with short-term liabilities and long-term assets with long-term liabilities in order to reduce the likelihood of a liquidity crunch such as this.

p. 481
Q: The drop in stock prices did not change the debt to total assets ratios of these companies. Discuss how the perception of a high debt to total assets ratio changed before and after the fall in stock prices.
A: When stock prices fell, the debt to total assets of these companies was unchanged: The debt was outstanding before the fall, and it was outstanding after the fall. However, before the fall, many investors did not worry if a company had a high debt to total assets ratio; they assumed that the debt would be converted to stock and so would never have to be repaid with cash. After the fall it became clear that the debt would not be converted to stock; suddenly, a high debt to total assets ratio was a real concern.

p. 494

Q: Explain how the sale of plant assets could improve the company's solvency.

A: A common measure of solvency is the debt to total assets ratio. By selling some of its fixed assets and using the cash to pay off debt, the company would reduce its reliance on debt financing and improve its debt to assets ratio.

Answer to Tootsie Roll Review It Question 5, p. 480

The liabilities that Tootsie Roll has identified as current are: Bank loan, Accounts payable, Dividends payable, Accrued liabilities, and Income taxes payable.

Answers to Self-Study Questions

1. a   2. d   3. b   4. b   5. a   6. c   7. a   8. c   9. b   10. c
11. c   12. a   13. b   14. c

CHAPTER 11

Reporting and Analyzing Stockholders' Equity

STUDY OBJECTIVES

After studying this chapter,
you should be able to:

1 Identify and discuss the major characteristics of a corporation.

2 Record the issuance of common stock.

3 Explain the accounting for the purchase of treasury stock.

4 Differentiate preferred stock from common stock.

5 Prepare the entries for cash dividends and understand the effect of stock dividends and stock splits.

6 Identify the items that affect retained earnings.

7 Prepare a comprehensive stockholders' equity section.

8 Evaluate a corporation's dividend and earnings performance from a stock-holder's perspective.

 THE NAVIGATOR

THE NAVIGATOR

- Scan *Study Objectives*
- Read *Feature Story*
- Read *Preview*
- Read text and answer *Before You Go On*
  p. 539   p. 543   p. 545
  p. 552   p. 556   p. 560
- Work *Using the Decision Toolkit*
- Review *Summary of Study Objectives*
- Work *Demonstration Problem*
- Answer *Self-Study Questions*
- Complete *Assignments*

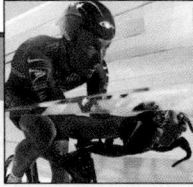

FEATURE STORY

What's Cooking?

What major U.S. corporation got its start 35 years ago with a waffle iron? Hint: It doesn't sell food. Another hint: Swoosh. Another hint: "Just do it." That's right, Nike. In 1971 Nike co-founder Bill Bowerman put a piece of rubber into a kitchen waffle iron, and the trademark waffle sole was born. It seems fair to say that at Nike, "They don't make 'em like they used to."

Nike was co-founded by Bowerman and Phil Knight, a member of Bowerman's University of Oregon track team. Each began in the shoe business independently during the early 1960s. Bowerman got his start by making hand-crafted running shoes for his University of Oregon track team. Knight, after completing graduate school, started a small business importing low-cost, high-quality shoes from Japan. In 1964 the two joined forces, each contributing $500, and formed Blue Ribbon Sports, a partnership, marketing Japanese shoes.

It wasn't until 1971 that the company began manufacturing its own line of shoes. With the new shoes came a new corporate name—Nike—the Greek goddess of victory. It is hard to imagine that the company that now boasts a stable full of world-class athletes as promoters at one time had part-time employees selling shoes out of car trunks at track meets. Nike has achieved its success through relentless innovation combined with unbridled promotion.

By 1980 Nike was sufficiently established that it was able to issue its first stock to the public. In that same year it also created a stock ownership program for its employees, allowing them to share in the company's success. Since then Nike has enjoyed phenomenal growth, with 2004 sales reaching $12.3 billion and total dividends paid of $179 million.

Nike is not alone in its quest for the top of the sport shoe world. Competitor Reebok pushes Nike every step of the way. However, Nike's recent success has resulted in sales that are three times those of Reebok.

Is the race over? Probably not. The shoe market is fickle, with new styles becoming popular almost daily and vast international markets still lying untapped. Whether one of these two giants does eventually take control of the planet remains to be seen. Meanwhile the shareholders sit anxiously in the stands as this Olympic-size drama unfolds.

On the World Wide Web
Nike: www.nike.com
Reebok: www.reebok.com

Corporations like Nike and Reebok have substantial resources at their disposal. In fact, the corporation is the dominant form of business organization in the United States in terms of sales, earnings, and number of employees. All of the 500 largest U.S. companies are corporations. In this chapter we look at the essential features of a corporation and explain the accounting for a corporation's capital stock transactions.

The content and organization of the chapter are as follows.

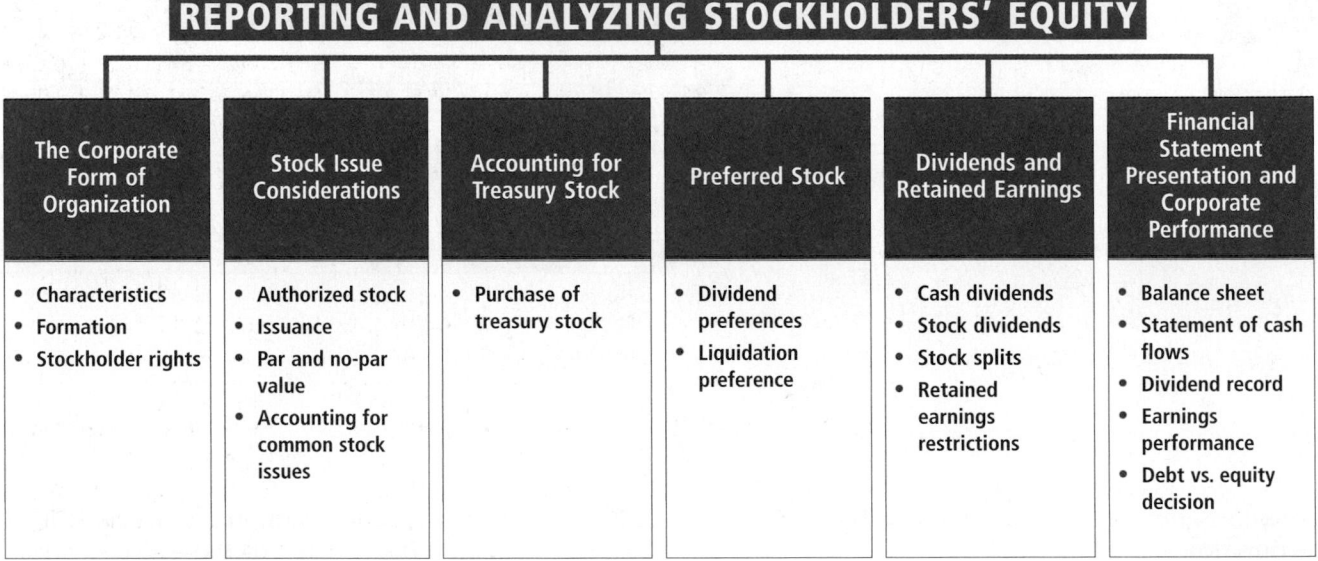

The Corporate Form of Organization

A corporation is created by law. As a legal entity, a **corporation** has most of the rights and privileges of a person. The major exceptions relate to privileges that can be exercised only by a living person, such as the right to vote or to hold public office. Similarly, a corporation is subject to the same duties and responsibilities as a person. For example, it must abide by the law and it must pay taxes.

We can classify corporations in a variety of ways. Two common classifications are **by purpose** and **by ownership**. A corporation may be organized for the purpose of making a profit (such as Nike or General Motors), or it may be a nonprofit charitable, medical, or educational corporation (such as Salvation Army or the American Cancer Society).

Classification by ownership differentiates publicly held and privately held corporations. A **publicly held corporation** may have thousands of stockholders, and its stock is regularly traded on a national securities market such as the New York Stock Exchange. Examples are IBM, Caterpillar, and General Electric. In contrast, a **privately held corporation**, often referred to as a closely held corporation, usually has only a few stockholders and does not offer its stock for sale to the general public. Privately held companies are generally much smaller than publicly held companies, although some notable exceptions exist. Cargill Inc., a private corporation that trades in grain and other commodities, is one of the largest companies in the United States. This chapter deals primarily with issues related to publicly held companies.

STUDY OBJECTIVE
1
Identify and discuss the major characteristics of a corporation.

CHARACTERISTICS OF A CORPORATION

In 1964, when Nike's founders, Knight and Bowerman, were just getting started in the running shoe business, they formed their original organization as a partnership. In 1968 they reorganized the company as a corporation. A number of characteristics distinguish a corporation from sole proprietorships and partnerships. The most important of these characteristics are explained below.

Separate Legal Existence

As an entity separate and distinct from its owners, the corporation acts under its own name rather than in the name of its stockholders. Nike, for example, may buy, own, and sell property, borrow money, and enter into legally binding contracts in its own name. It may also sue or be sued. It pays taxes as a separate entity.

In contrast to a partnership, in which the acts of the owners (partners) bind the partnership, the acts of the owners (stockholders) do not bind the corporation unless such owners are agents of the corporation. For example, if you owned shares of Nike stock, you would not have the right to purchase inventory for the company unless you were designated as an agent of the corporation.

Stockholders
Legal existence separate from owners

Limited Liability of Stockholders

Since a corporation is a separate legal entity, creditors ordinarily have recourse only to corporate assets to satisfy their claims. The liability of stockholders is normally limited to their investment in the corporation. Creditors have no legal claim on the personal assets of the stockholders unless fraud has occurred. Thus, even in the event of bankruptcy of the corporation, stockholders' losses are generally limited to the amount of capital they have invested in the corporation.

Stockholders
Limited liability of stockholders

Transferable Ownership Rights

Ownership of a corporation is held in shares of capital stock, which are transferable units. Stockholders may dispose of part or all of their interest in a corporation simply by selling their stock. The transfer of an ownership interest in a partnership requires the consent of each partner. In contrast, the transfer of stock is entirely at the discretion of the stockholder. It does not require the approval of either the corporation or other stockholders.

The transfer of ownership rights among stockholders normally has no effect on the operating activities of the corporation. Nor does it affect the corporation's assets, liabilities, and total stockholders' equity. The transfer of ownership rights is a transaction between individual owners. The company does not participate in the transfer of these ownership rights after the original sale of the capital stock.

Transferable ownership rights

Ability to Acquire Capital

It is relatively easy for a corporation to obtain capital through the issuance of stock. Buying stock in a corporation is often attractive to an investor because a stockholder has limited liability and shares of stock are readily transferable. Also, numerous individuals can become stockholders by investing small amounts of money.

Ability to acquire capital

Continuous Life

The life of a corporation is stated in its charter. The life may be perpetual or it may be limited to a specific number of years. If it is limited, the company can extend the period of existence through renewal of the charter. Since a corporation is a separate legal entity, its continuance as a going concern is not affected by

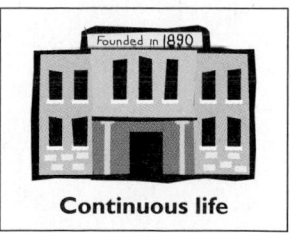

Continuous life

the withdrawal, death, or incapacity of a stockholder, employee, or officer. As a result, a successful corporation can have a continuous and perpetual life.

Corporation Management

Although stockholders legally own the corporation, they manage it indirectly through a board of directors they elect. Philip Knight is the chairman of Nike's board of directors. The board, in turn, formulates the operating policies for the company. The board also selects officers, such as a president and one or more vice-presidents, to execute policy and to perform daily management functions. As a result of the Sarbanes-Oxley Act, the board is now required to monitor management's actions more closely. Many feel that the failures at Enron and WorldCom could have been avoided by more diligent boards.

Illustration 11-1 depicts a typical organization chart showing the delegation of responsibility.

Illustration 11-1
Corporation organization chart

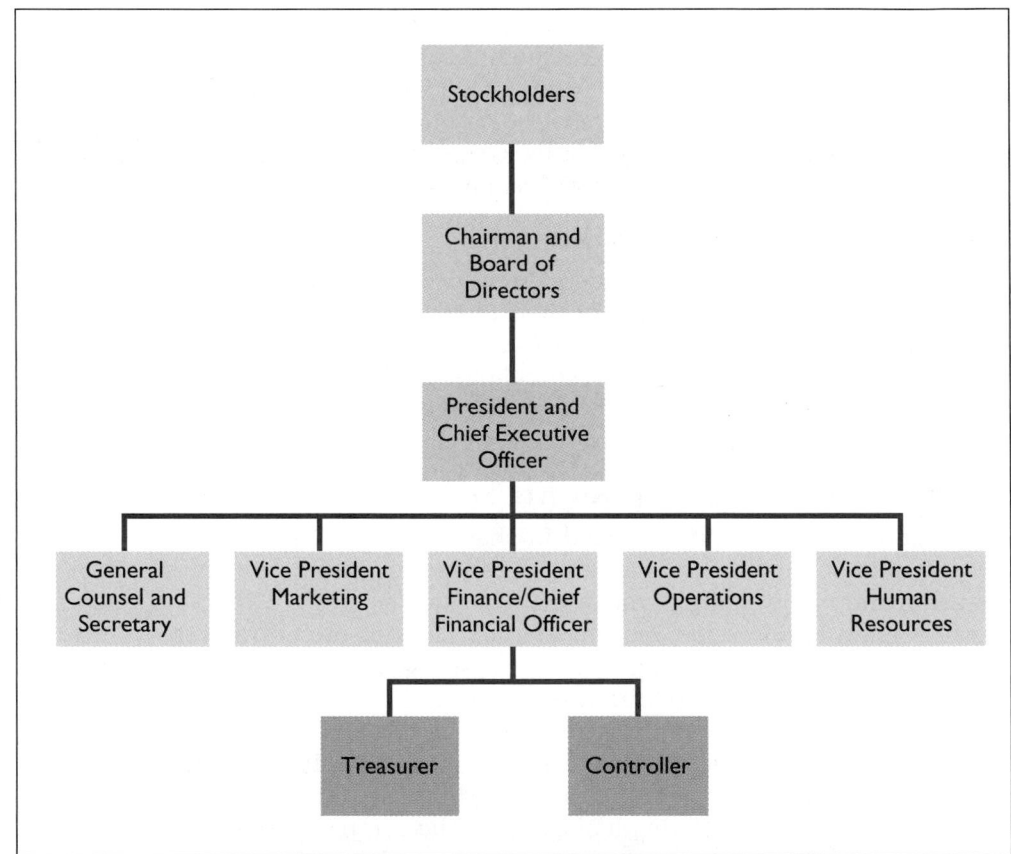

The chief executive officer (CEO) has overall responsibility for managing the business. As the organization chart shows, the CEO delegates responsibility to other officers. The chief accounting officer is the **controller**. The controller's responsibilities are to (1) maintain the accounting records, (2) maintain an adequate system of internal control and (3) prepare financial statements, tax returns, and internal reports. The **treasurer** has custody of the corporation's funds and is responsible for maintaining the company's cash position.

The organizational structure of a corporation enables a company to hire professional managers to run the business. On the other hand, the separation of ownership and management often reduces an owner's ability to actively manage the company.

Government Regulations

A corporation is subject to numerous state and federal regulations. For example, state laws usually prescribe the requirements for issuing stock, the distributions of earnings permitted to stockholders, and acceptable methods for retiring stock. Federal securities laws govern the sale of capital stock to the general public. Also, most publicly held corporations are required to make extensive disclosure of their financial affairs to the Securities and Exchange Commission (SEC) through quarterly and annual reports. The Sarbanes-Oxley Act increased the company's responsibility for the accuracy of these reports. In addition, when a corporate stock is listed and traded on organized securities exchanges, the corporation must comply with the reporting requirements of these exchanges.

Government regulations

Accounting across the Organization

During the hot stock market of the late 1990s, the dream of nearly every entrepreneur was to "take the company public." But times have changed, and now top managers at small- to medium-sized companies are reevaluating the costs versus the benefits of being a publicly traded company.

In 2004 and 2005 a record number of publicly traded companies repurchased all of their shares and took their companies private. Most cited the increased regulatory costs associated with Sarbanes-Oxley as the reason for going private. Estimates of these costs were about $2.3 million per year—roughly ten times what they were a few years earlier. In about two-thirds of the deals it was the managers themselves who bought the company's shares.

Source: Emily Thorton, "A Little Privacy Please," *Business Week* (May 24, 2004), pp. 74–75.

 In addition to regulatory cost, what is another reason why some owners choose not to take their companies public?

Additional Taxes

Owners of proprietorships and partnerships report their share of earnings on their personal income tax returns. The individual owner then pays taxes on this amount. Corporations, on the other hand, must pay federal and state income taxes as a separate legal entity. These taxes are substantial: They can amount to as much as 40% of taxable income.

In addition, stockholders are required to pay taxes on cash dividends. Thus, many argue that corporate income is **taxed twice (double taxation)**—once at the corporate level and again at the individual level.

Illustration 11-2 shows the advantages and disadvantages of a corporation compared to a sole proprietorship and partnership.

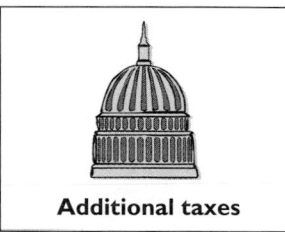

Additional taxes

Advantages	Disadvantages
• Separate legal existence • Limited liability of stockholders • Transferable ownership rights • Ability to acquire capital • Continuous life • Corporation management—professional managers	• Corporation management—separation of ownership and management • Government regulations • Additional taxes

Illustration 11-2
Advantages and disadvantages of a corporation

Other Forms of Business Organization

A variety of "hybrid" organizational forms—forms that combine different attributes of partnerships and corporations—now exist. For example, one type of corporate form, called an **S corporation**, allows for legal treatment as a corporation but tax treatment as a partnership—that is, no double taxation. Because of changes to the S corporation's rules, more small- and medium-sized businesses now may choose S corporation treatment. One of the primary criteria is that the company cannot have more than 75 shareholders. Other forms of organization include limited partnerships, limited liability partnerships (LLPs), and limited liability corporations (LLCs).

Decision Toolkit

Decision Checkpoints	Info Needed for Decision	Tool to Use for Decision	How to Evaluate Results
Should the company incorporate?	Capital needs, growth expectations, type of business, tax status	Corporations have limited liability, easier capital raising ability, and professional managers; but they suffer from additional taxes, government regulations, and separation of ownership from management.	Must carefully weigh the costs and benefits in light of the particular circumstances.

FORMING A CORPORATION

A corporation is formed by grant of a state **charter**. Regardless of the number of states in which a corporation has operating divisions, it is incorporated in only one state. It is to the company's advantage to incorporate in a state whose laws are favorable to the corporate form of business organization. For example, although General Motors has its headquarters in Michigan, it is incorporated in New Jersey. In fact, more and more corporations have been incorporating in states with rules that favor existing management. For example, Gulf Oil changed its state of incorporation to Delaware to thwart possible unfriendly takeovers. There, certain defensive tactics against takeovers can be approved by the board of directors alone, without a vote by shareholders.

Upon receipt of its charter from the state of incorporation, the corporation establishes **by-laws**. The by-laws establish the internal rules and procedures for conducting the affairs of the corporation. Corporations engaged in interstate commerce must also obtain a **license** from each state in which they do business. The license subjects the corporation's operating activities to the general corporation laws of the state.

STOCKHOLDER RIGHTS

When chartered, the corporation may begin selling shares of stock. When a corporation has only one class of stock, it is identified as **common stock**. Each share of common stock gives the stockholder the ownership rights pictured in Illustration 11-3 (page 539). The articles of incorporation or the by-laws state the ownership rights of a share of stock.

Illustration 11-3
Ownership rights of stockholders

Stockholders have the right to:

1. Vote in election of board of directors at annual meeting and vote on actions that require stockholder approval.

2. Share the corporate earnings through receipt of dividends.

dividends

3. Keep the same percentage ownership when new shares of stock are issued (**preemptive right**[1]).

Before

14%

New shares issued

After

14%

4. Share in assets upon liquidation in proportion to their holdings. This is called a **residual claim** because owners are paid with assets that remain after all claims have been paid.

GON Corp.

Going out of business

Lenders

Creditors

Stockholders

Proof of stock ownership is evidenced by a printed or engraved form known as a **stock certificate**. As shown in Illustration 11-4 (page 540), the face of the certificate shows the name of the corporation, the stockholder's name, the class and special features of the stock, the number of shares owned, and the signatures of authorized corporate officials. Certificates are prenumbered to ensure proper control over their use; they may be issued for any quantity of shares.

BEFORE YOU GO ON . . .

▶ Review It

1. What are the advantages and disadvantages of a corporation compared to a proprietorship and a partnership?
2. Identify the principal steps in forming a corporation.
3. What are the ownership rights of owning a share of stock in a corporation?

---

[1]A number of companies have eliminated the preemptive right because they believe it places an unnecessary and cumbersome demand on management. For example, IBM, by stockholder approval, has dropped its preemptive right for stockholders.

Illustration 11-4
A stock certificate

Stock Issue Considerations

Although Nike incorporated in 1968, it did not sell stock to the public until 1980. At that time Nike evidently decided it would benefit from the infusion of cash that a public sale of its shares would bring. When a corporation decides to issue stock, it must resolve a number of basic questions: How many shares should it authorize for sale? How should it issue the stock? What value should it assign to the stock? We address these questions in the following sections.

AUTHORIZED STOCK

The amount of stock that a corporation is authorized to sell is indicated in its charter. If the corporation has sold all of its **authorized stock**, then it must obtain consent of the state to amend its charter before it can issue additional shares.

The authorization of common stock does not result in a formal accounting entry. The reason is that the event has no immediate effect on either corporate assets or stockholders' equity. However, the corporation must disclose in the stockholders' equity section of the balance sheet the number of shares authorized.

ISSUANCE OF STOCK

A corporation can issue common stock **directly** to investors. Alternatively, it can issue common stock **indirectly** through an investment banking firm that specializes in bringing securities to the attention of prospective investors. Direct issue is typical in closely held companies. Indirect issue is customary for a publicly held corporation.

New issues of stock may be offered for sale to the public through various organized U.S. securities exchanges: the New York Stock Exchange, the American Stock Exchange, and 13 regional exchanges. Stock may also be traded on the NASDAQ national market.

⊕ **International Note**

U.S. and U.K. corporations raise most of their capital through millions of outside shareholders and bondholders. In contrast, companies in Germany, France, and Japan acquire financing mostly from large banks or other financial institutions. Consequently, in the latter environment, shareholders are less important, and external reporting and auditing receive less emphasis.

PAR AND NO-PAR VALUE STOCKS

Par value stock is capital stock that has been assigned a value per share in the corporate charter. Years ago, par value was used to determine the **legal capital** per share that must be retained in the business for the protection of corporate creditors. That amount is not available for withdrawal by stockholders. Thus, in the past, most states required the corporation to sell its shares at par or above.

However, the usefulness of par value as a protective device to creditors was questionable because par value was often immaterial relative to the value of the company's stock in the securities markets—even at the time of issue. For example, Reebok's par value is $0.01 per share, yet a new issue in 2004 would have sold at a **market value** in the $38 per share range. Thus, par has no relationship with market value and in the vast majority of cases is an immaterial amount. As a consequence, today many states do not require a par value. Instead, they use other means to determine legal capital to protect creditors.

No-par value stock is capital stock that has not been assigned a value in the corporate charter. No-par value stock is quite common today. For example, Nike, Procter & Gamble, and North American Van Lines all have no-par stock. In many states the board of directors assigns a **stated value** to the no-par shares.

ACCOUNTING FOR COMMON STOCK ISSUES

The stockholders' equity section of a corporation's balance sheet includes: (1) **paid-in (contributed) capital** and (2) **retained earnings (earned capital)**. The distinction between paid-in capital and retained earnings is important from both a legal and an economic point of view. **Paid-in capital** is the amount stockholders paid to the corporation in exchange for shares of ownership. **Retained earnings** is earned capital held for future use in the business. In this section we discuss the accounting for paid-in capital. In a later section we discuss retained earnings.

Let's now look at how to account for new issues of common stock. The primary objectives in accounting for the issuance of common stock are: (1) to identify the specific sources of paid-in capital and (2) to maintain the distinction between paid-in capital and retained earnings. As shown below, **the issuance of common stock affects only paid-in capital accounts**.

As discussed earlier, par value does not indicate a stock's market value. The cash proceeds from issuing par value stock may be equal to, greater than, or less than par value. When a company records the issuance of common stock for cash, it credits the par value of the shares to Common Stock, and records in a separate paid-in capital account the portion of the proceeds that is above or below par value.

To illustrate, assume that Hydro-Slide, Inc. issues 1,000 shares of $1 par value common stock at par for cash. The entry to record this transaction is:

STUDY OBJECTIVE 2

Record the issuance of common stock.

Helpful Hint Stock is sometimes issued in exchange for services (payment to attorneys or consultants, for example) or other noncash assets (land or buildings). The value recorded for the shares issued is determined by either the market value of the shares, or the value of the good or service received depending upon which value the company can more readily determine.

Cash	1,000	
Common Stock		1,000
(To record issuance of 1,000 shares of $1 par common stock at par)		

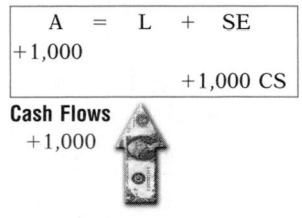

A	=	L	+	SE
+1,000				
				+1,000 CS

Cash Flows
+1,000

If Hydro-Slide, Inc. issues an additional 1,000 shares of the $1 par value common stock for cash at $5 per share, the entry is:

Cash	5,000	
Common Stock		1,000
Paid-in Capital in Excess of Par Value		4,000
(To record issuance of 1,000 shares of common stock in excess of par)		

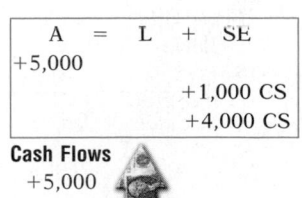

A	=	L	+	SE
+5,000				
				+1,000 CS
				+4,000 CS

Cash Flows
+5,000

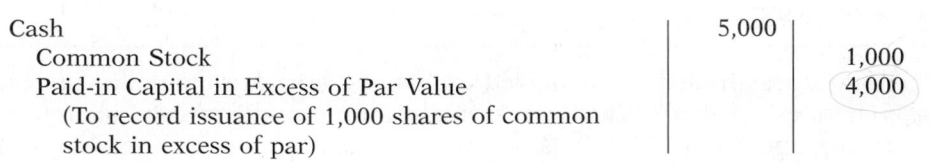

The total paid-in capital from these two transactions is $6,000. If Hydro-Slide, Inc. has retained earnings of $27,000, the stockholders' equity section of the balance sheet is as shown in Illustration 11-5.

Illustration 11-5
Stockholders' equity—
paid-in capital in excess of
par value

HYDRO-SLIDE, INC. Balance Sheet (partial)	
Stockholders' equity	
Paid-in capital	
Common stock	$ 2,000
Paid-in capital in excess of par value	**4,000**
Total paid-in capital	6,000
Retained earnings	27,000
Total stockholders' equity	$33,000

Some companies issue no-par stock with a stated value. For accounting purposes, companies treat the stated value in the same way as the par value. For example, if in our Hydro-Slide example the stock was no-par stock with a stated value of $1, the entries would be the same as those presented for the par stock except the term "Par Value" would be replaced with "Stated Value." If a company issues no-par stock that does not have a stated value, then it credits to the Common Stock account the full amount received. In such a case, there is no need for the Paid-in Capital in Excess of Stated Value account.

Business Insight
Investor Perspective

Organized exchanges trade the stock of publicly held companies at dollar prices per share established by the interaction between buyers and sellers. For each listed security the financial press reports the high and low prices of the stock during the year, the total volume of stock traded on a given day, the high and low prices for the day, and the closing market price, with the net change for the day. Nike is listed on the New York Stock Exchange. Here is a recent listing for Nike:

	52 Weeks						
Stock	**High**	**Low**	**Volume**	**High**	**Low**	**Close**	**Net Change**
Nike	92.43	68.61	263,000	87.49	86.80	87.03	+.09

These numbers indicate the following: The high and low market prices for the last 52 weeks have been $92.43 and $68.61. The trading volume for the previous day was 263,000 shares. The high, low, and closing prices for that date were $87.49, $86.80, and $87.03, respectively. The net change for the day was an increase of $0.09 per share.

 For stocks traded on organized exchanges, how are the dollar prices per share established? What factors might influence the price of shares in the marketplace?

BEFORE YOU GO ON . . .

▶ Review It

1. Of what significance to a corporation is the amount of authorized stock?
2. What alternative approaches may a corporation use to sell new shares to investors?
3. Distinguish between par value and market value.
4. Explain the accounting for par and no-par common stock issued for cash.

▶ Do It

Cayman Corporation begins operations on March 1 by issuing 100,000 shares of $10 par value common stock for cash at $12 per share. Journalize the issuance of the shares.

Action Plan

• In issuing shares for cash, credit Common Stock for par value per share.
• Credit any additional proceeds in excess of par value to a separate paid-in capital account.

Solution

Mar. 1	Cash	1,200,000	
	Common Stock		1,000,000
	Paid-in Capital in Excess of Par Value		200,000
	(To record issuance of 100,000 shares at $12 per share)		

Accounting for Treasury Stock

Treasury stock is a corporation's own stock that has been issued, fully paid for, and reacquired by the corporation and is being held in its treasury for future use. A corporation may acquire treasury stock for various reasons:

STUDY OBJECTIVE
3
Explain the accounting for the purchase of treasury stock.

1. To reissue the shares to officers and employees under bonus and stock compensation plans.
2. To increase trading of the company's stock in the securities market. Companies expect that buying their own stock will signal that management believes the stock is underpriced, which they hope will enhance its market value.
3. To have additional shares available for use in acquiring other companies.
4. To reduce the number of shares outstanding and thereby increase earnings per share.

Another infrequent reason for purchasing treasury shares is that management may want to eliminate hostile shareholders by buying them out.

Many corporations have treasury stock. For example, in the United States approximately 68% of companies have treasury stock.[2] Specifically, in 2004 Nike purchased 6.4 million treasury shares, IBM, 78.6 million, and Limited Brands, 125 million shares. Stock repurchases have been so substantial that a recent study by two Federal Reserve economists suggested that a sharp reduction in

---

[2]*Accounting Trends & Techniques—2004* (New York: American Institute of Certified Public Accountants).

corporate purchases of treasury shares might result in a sharp drop in the value of the U.S. stock market.

PURCHASE OF TREASURY STOCK

The purchase of treasury stock is generally accounted for by the **cost method**. This method derives its name from the fact that the Treasury Stock account is maintained at the cost of shares purchased. Under the cost method, **companies increase (debit) Treasury Stock by the price paid to reacquire the shares. Treasury Stock decreases by the same amount when the company later sells the shares.**

To illustrate, assume that on January 1, 2007, the stockholders' equity section for Mead, Inc. has 100,000 shares of $5 par value common stock outstanding (all issued at par value) and Retained Earnings of $200,000. Illustration 11-6 shows the stockholders' equity section of the balance sheet before purchase of treasury stock.

Illustration 11-6
Stockholders' equity with no treasury stock

MEAD, INC. Balance Sheet (partial)	
Stockholders' equity	
Paid-in capital	
Common stock, $5 par value, 100,000 shares issued and outstanding	$500,000
Retained earnings	200,000
Total stockholders' equity	$700,000

On February 1, 2007, Mead acquires 4,000 shares of its stock at $8 per share. The entry is:

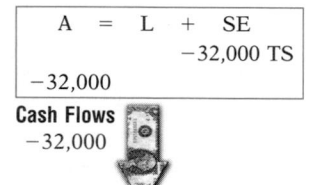

A	=	L	+	SE
				−32,000 TS
−32,000				

Cash Flows
−32,000

Feb. 1	Treasury Stock	32,000	
	Cash		32,000
	(To record purchase of 4,000 shares of treasury stock at $8 per share)		

The Treasury Stock account would increase by the cost of the shares purchased ($32,000). The original paid-in capital account, Common Stock, would not be affected because **the number of issued shares does not change**.

Companies show treasury stock as a deduction from total paid-in capital and retained earnings in the stockholders' equity section of the balance sheet. Illustration 11-7 shows this presentation for Mead, Inc. Thus, the acquisition of treasury stock reduces stockholders' equity.

Helpful Hint Treasury Stock is a contra stockholders' equity account.

Illustration 11-7
Stockholders' equity with treasury stock

MEAD, INC. Balance Sheet (partial)	
Stockholders' equity	
Paid-in capital	
Common stock, $5 par value, 100,000 shares issued and 96,000 shares outstanding	$500,000
Retained earnings	200,000
Total paid-in capital and retained earnings	700,000
Less: Treasury stock (4,000 shares)	**32,000**
Total stockholders' equity	$668,000

Companies disclose in the balance sheet both the number of shares issued (100,000) and the number in the treasury (4,000). The difference is the number of shares of stock outstanding (96,000). The term **outstanding stock** means the number of shares of issued stock that are being held by stockholders.

Accounting across the Organization

In a bold (and some would say risky) move, Reebok at one time bought back nearly a *third* of its shares. This repurchase of shares dramatically reduced Reebok's available cash. In fact, the company borrowed significant funds to accomplish the repurchase. In a press release, management stated that it was repurchasing the shares because it believed that the stock was severely underpriced. The repurchase of so many shares was meant to signal management's belief in good future earnings.

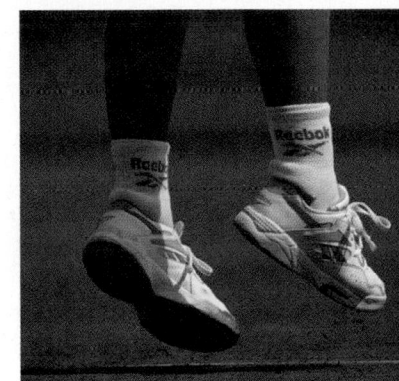

Skeptics, however, suggested that Reebok's management was repurchasing shares to make it less likely that the company would be acquired by another company (in which case Reebok's top managers would likely lose their jobs). Acquiring companies like to purchase companies with large cash reserves so they can pay off debt used in the acquisition. By depleting its cash, Reebok became a less likely acquisition target.

 What signal might a large stock repurchase send to investors regarding management's belief about the company's growth opportunities?

BEFORE YOU GO ON . . .

▶ Review It

1. What is treasury stock, and why do companies acquire it?
2. How do companies record treasury stock?
3. Where in the financial statements do companies report treasury stock?

▶ Do It

Santa Anita Inc. purchases 3,000 shares of its $50 par value common stock for $180,000 cash on July 1. It expects to hold the shares in the treasury until resold. Journalize the treasury stock transaction.

Action Plan
• Record the purchase of treasury stock at cost.
• Report treasury stock as a deduction from stockholders' equity (contra account) at the bottom of the stockholders' equity section.

Solution

July 1	Treasury Stock	180,000	
	Cash		180,000
	(To record the purchase of 3,000 shares at $60 per share)		

Preferred Stock

To appeal to a larger segment of potential investors, a corporation may issue an additional class of stock, called preferred stock. **Preferred stock** has contractual provisions that give it preference or priority over common stock in certain areas. Typically, preferred stockholders have a priority in relation to (1) dividends and (2) assets in the event of liquidation. However, they sometimes do not have voting rights. Reebok has no outstanding preferred stock, whereas Nike has a very minor amount outstanding. Approximately 15% of U.S. companies have one or more classes of preferred stock.[3]

Like common stock, companies may issue preferred stock for cash or for noncash consideration. The entries for these transactions are similar to the entries for common stock. When a corporation has more than one class of stock, each paid-in capital account title should identify the stock to which it relates (e.g., Preferred Stock, Common Stock, Paid-in Capital in Excess of Par Value—Preferred Stock, and Paid-in Capital in Excess of Par Value—Common Stock).

Assume that Stine Corporation issues 10,000 shares of $10 par value preferred stock for $12 cash per share. The entry to record the issuance is:

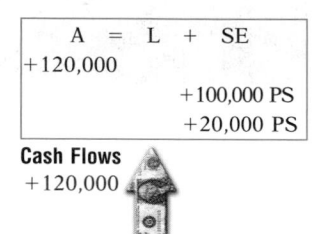

A = L + SE
+120,000
　　　　+100,000 PS
　　　　+20,000 PS

Cash Flows
+120,000

Cash	120,000	
Preferred Stock		100,000
Paid-in Capital in Excess of Par Value—Preferred Stock		20,000
(To record the issuance of 10,000 shares of $10 par value preferred stock)		

Preferred stock may have either a par value or no-par value. In the stockholders' equity section of the balance sheet, companies show preferred stock first because of its dividend and liquidation preferences over common stock.

DIVIDEND PREFERENCES

As indicated above, **preferred stockholders have the right to share in the distribution of corporate income before common stockholders**. For example, if the dividend rate on preferred stock is $5 per share, common shareholders will not receive any dividends in the current year until preferred stockholders have received $5 per share. The first claim to dividends does not, however, **guarantee** dividends. Dividends depend on many factors, such as adequate retained earnings and availability of cash.

For preferred stock, companies state the per share dividend amount as a percentage of the par value of the stock or as a specified amount. For example, EarthLink specifies a 3% dividend, whereas Nike pays 10 cents per share on its $1 par preferred stock.

Cumulative Dividend

Preferred stock contracts often contain a **cumulative dividend** feature. This right means that preferred stockholders must be paid both current-year dividends and any unpaid prior-year dividends before common stockholders receive dividends. When preferred stock is cumulative, preferred dividends not declared in a given period are called **dividends in arrears**.

---

[3]*Accounting Trends & Techniques—2004* (New York: American Institute of Certified Public Accountants).

To illustrate, assume that Scientific Leasing has 5,000 shares of 7%, $100 par value cumulative preferred stock outstanding. Each $100 share pays a $7 dividend (.07 × $100). The annual dividend is $35,000 (5,000 × $7 per share). If dividends are two years in arrears, preferred stockholders are entitled to receive in the current year the dividends as shown in Illustration 11-8.

Dividends in arrears ($35,000 × 2)	$ 70,000
Current-year dividends	35,000
Total preferred dividends	**$105,000**

Illustration 11-8
Computation of total dividends to preferred stock

No distribution can be made to common stockholders until Scientific Leasing pays this entire preferred dividend. In other words, companies cannot pay dividends to common stockholders while any preferred stock dividend is in arrears.

Dividends in arrears are not considered a liability. No obligation exists until the board of directors formally "declares" that the corporation will pay a dividend. However, companies should disclose in the notes to the financial statements the amount of dividends in arrears. Doing so enables investors to assess the potential impact of this commitment on the corporation's financial position.

The investment community does not look favorably upon companies that are unable to meet their dividend obligations. As a financial officer noted in discussing one company's failure to pay its cumulative preferred dividend for a period of time, "Not meeting your obligations on something like that is a major black mark on your record."

LIQUIDATION PREFERENCE

Most preferred stocks have a preference on corporate assets if the corporation fails. This feature provides security for the preferred stockholder. The preference to assets may be for the par value of the shares or for a specified liquidating value. For example, Commonwealth Edison issued preferred stock that entitles the holders to receive $31.80 per share, plus accrued and unpaid dividends, in the event of involuntary liquidation. The liquidation preference is used in litigation pertaining to bankruptcy lawsuits involving the respective claims of creditors and preferred stockholders.

Dividends

As noted earlier, a **dividend is a distribution by a corporation to its stockholders on a pro rata basis.** *Pro rata* means that if you own, say, 10% of the common shares, you will receive 10% of the dividend. Dividends can take four forms: cash, property, script (promissory note to pay cash), or stock. Cash dividends, which predominate in practice, and stock dividends, which are declared with some frequency, are the focus of our discussion.

Investors are very interested in a company's dividend practices. In the financial press, **dividends are generally reported quarterly as a dollar amount per share.** (Sometimes they are reported on an annual basis.) For example, Nike's **quarterly** dividend rate in the fourth quarter of 2004 was 20 cents per share; the dividend rate for that quarter for Target was 7 cents, and for PepsiCo it was 23 cents.

STUDY OBJECTIVE 5

Prepare the entries for cash dividends and understand the effect of stock dividends and stock splits.

CASH DIVIDENDS

A **cash dividend** is a pro rata distribution of cash to stockholders. For a corporation to pay a cash dividend, it must have the following.

1. **Retained earnings.** Many states prohibit payment of dividends from legal capital. However, payment of dividends from paid-in capital in excess of par is legal in some states. **Payment of dividends from retained earnings is legal in all states.** In addition, loan agreements frequently constrain companies to pay dividends only from retained earnings.

2. **Adequate cash.** Recently Nike had a balance in retained earnings of $3,983 million but a cash balance of only $828 million. If it had wanted to pay a dividend equal to its retained earnings, Nike would have had to raise $3,155 million more in cash. It would have been unlikely to do this because it would not be able to pay this much in dividends in future years. In addition, such a dividend would completely deplete Nike's balance in retained earnings, so it would not be able to pay a dividend in the next year unless it had positive net income.

3. **Declared dividends.** The board of directors has full authority to determine the amount of income to distribute in the form of dividends and the amount to retain in the business. Dividends do not accrue like interest on a note payable, and they are not a liability until they are declared.

   In order to remain in business, companies must honor their interest payments to creditors, bankers, and bondholders. But the payment of dividends to stockholders is another matter. Many companies can survive, and even thrive, without such payouts. "Why give money to those strangers?" was the response of one company president.

The amount and timing of a dividend are important issues for management to consider. The payment of a large cash dividend could lead to liquidity problems for the company. Conversely, a small dividend or a missed dividend may cause unhappiness among stockholders who expect to receive a reasonable cash payment from the company on a periodic basis. Many companies declare and pay cash dividends quarterly. On the other hand, a number of high-growth companies pay no dividends, preferring to retain earnings and use them to finance capital expenditures.

Investors must keep an eye on the company's dividend policy and understand what it may mean. For most companies, for example, regular dividend boosts in the face of irregular earnings can be a warning signal. Companies with high dividends and rising debt may be borrowing money to pay shareholders. On the other hand, low dividends may not be a negative sign because they may mean the company is reinvesting in itself, which may result in high returns through increases in the stock price. Presumably, investors for whom regular dividends are important tend to buy stock in companies that pay periodic dividends, and those for whom growth in the stock price (capital gains) is more important tend to buy stock in companies that retain their earnings.

Entries for Cash Dividends

Three dates are important in connection with dividends: (1) the declaration date, (2) the record date, and (3) the payment date. Companies make accounting entries on the declaration date and the payment date.

On the **declaration date**, the board of directors formally authorizes the cash dividend and announces it to stockholders. The declaration of a cash dividend **commits the corporation to a binding legal obligation**. Thus, the company must make an entry to recognize the decrease in retained earnings and the increase in the liability Dividends Payable.

To illustrate, assume that on December 1, 2007, the directors of Media General declare a $0.50 per share cash dividend on 100,000 shares of $10 par value common stock. The dividend is $50,000 (100,000 × $0.50). The entry to record the declaration is:

Declaration Date

Dec. 1	Retained Earnings (or Cash Dividends)	50,000	
	Dividends Payable		50,000
	(To record declaration of cash dividend)		

A	=	L	+	SE
				−50,000 Div
		+50,000		

Cash Flows
no effect

Dividends Payable is a current liability: It will normally be paid within the next several months.

You may recall that in Chapter 3, instead of decreasing Retained Earnings, we used the account Dividends. The Dividends account provides additional information in the ledger. For example, a company may have separate dividend accounts for each class of stock or each type of dividend. When a company uses a separate dividend account, it transfers the account's balance to Retained Earnings at the end of the year by a closing entry. Whichever account is used for the dividend declaration, the effect is the same: The company decreases retained earnings and increases a current liability. To avoid additional detail in the textbook, we have chosen to use the Retained Earnings account. *For homework problems, you should use the Retained Earnings account for recording dividend declarations.*

At the **record date**, the company determines ownership of the outstanding shares for dividend purposes. The stockholders' records maintained by the corporation supply this information.

For Media General, the record date is December 22. No entry is required on the record date.

Helpful Hint The record date is important in determining the dividend to be paid to each stockholder but not the total dividend.

Record Date

| Dec. 22 | | | |
| | No entry necessary | | |

On the **payment date**, the company mails dividend checks to the stockholders on record as of December 22, and it also records the payment of the dividend. If January 20 is the payment date for Media General, the entry on that date is:

Payment Date

Jan. 20	Dividends Payable	50,000	
	Cash		50,000
	(To record payment of cash dividend)		

A	=	L	+	SE
		−50,000		
−50,000				

Cash Flows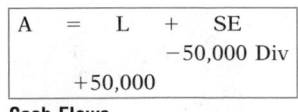
−50,000

Note that payment of the dividend reduces both current assets and current liabilities, but it has no effect on stockholders' equity. The cumulative effect of the **declaration and payment** of a cash dividend on a company's financial statements is to **decrease both stockholders' equity and total assets**.

Accounting across the Organization

The decision whether to pay a cash dividend, and how much, is a very important management decision. During 2004 cash dividend payments were a record $181 billion—not including a one-time $32.6 billion dividend by Microsoft. The $181 billion does include a 44% dividend increase by Wal-Mart and a doubling of the dividend payment by Intel.

One explanation for the increase is that Congress lowered, from 39% to 15%, the tax rate paid by investors on dividends received, making dividends more attractive to investors. Another driving force for the dividend increases was that companies were sitting on record amounts of cash. Because they did not see a lot of good expansion opportunities, companies decided to return the cash to shareholders.

Bigger dividends are still possible in the future. Large companies paid out 34% of their earnings as dividends in 2004—well below the historical average payout of 54% of earnings.

Source: Alan Levinsohn, "Divine Dividends," *Strategic Finance* (May 2005), pp. 59–60.

 What factors must management consider in deciding how large a dividend to pay?

STOCK DIVIDENDS

A **stock dividend** is a pro rata distribution of the corporation's own stock to stockholders. Whereas a cash dividend is paid in cash, a stock dividend is paid in stock. **A stock dividend results in a decrease in retained earnings and an increase in paid-in capital.** Unlike a cash dividend, a stock dividend does not decrease total stockholders' equity or total assets.

Because a stock dividend does not result in a distribution of assets, many view it as nothing more than a publicity gesture. Stock dividends are often issued by companies that do not have adequate cash to issue a cash dividend. These companies may not want to announce that they are not going to be issuing a cash dividend at their normal time to do so. By issuing a stock dividend they "save face" by giving the appearance of distributing a dividend. Note that since a stock dividend neither increases nor decreases the assets in the company, investors are not receiving anything they didn't already own. In a sense it is like asking for two pieces of pie and having your host take one piece of pie and cut it into two smaller pieces. You are not better off, but you got your two pieces of pie.

To illustrate a stock dividend, assume that you have a 2% ownership interest in Cetus Inc.; you own 20 of its 1,000 shares of common stock. If Cetus declares a 10% stock dividend, it would issue 100 shares (1,000 × 10%) of stock. You would receive two shares (2% × 100), but your ownership interest would remain at 2% (22 ÷ 1,100). **You now own more shares of stock, but your ownership interest has not changed.** Moreover, the company disburses no cash, and assumes no liabilities.

What, then, are the purposes and benefits of a stock dividend? Corporations generally issue stock dividends for one of the following reasons.

Helpful Hint Because of its effects, a stock dividend is also referred to as *capitalizing retained earnings.*

1. To satisfy stockholders' dividend expectations without spending cash.
2. To increase the marketability of the stock by increasing the number of shares outstanding and thereby decreasing the market price per share. Decreasing

the market price of the stock makes it easier for smaller investors to purchase the shares.

3. To emphasize that the company has permanently reinvested in the business a portion of stockholders' equity, which therefore is unavailable for cash dividends.

When the dividend is declared, the board of directors determines the size of the stock dividend and the value to be assigned to each dividend share. In order to meet legal requirements, the per share amount must be at least equal to the par or stated value.

The accounting profession distinguishes between a **small stock dividend** (less than 20%–25% of the corporation's issued stock) and a **large stock dividend** (greater than 20%–25%). It recommends that the directors assign the **fair market value per share** for small stock dividends. The recommendation is based on the assumption that a small stock dividend will have little effect on the market price of the shares previously outstanding. Thus, many stockholders consider small stock dividends to be distributions of earnings equal to the fair market value of the shares distributed. The accounting profession does not specify the amount to be assigned for a large stock dividend. However, companies normally assign **par or stated value per share**. Small stock dividends predominate in practice. In the appendix at the end of the chapter, we illustrate the journal entries for small stock dividends.

Effects of Stock Dividends

How do stock dividends affect stockholders' equity? They **change the composition of stockholders' equity** because they result in a transfer of a portion of retained earnings to paid-in capital. However, **total stockholders' equity remains the same**. Stock dividends also have no effect on the par or stated value per share, but the number of shares outstanding increases.

To illustrate, assume that Medland Corp. declares a 10% stock dividend on its $10 par common stock when 50,000 shares were outstanding. The market price was $15 per share.

	Before Dividend	After Dividend
Stockholders' equity		
Paid-in capital		
Common stock, $10 par	$ 500,000	$ 550,000
Paid-in capital in excess of par value	—	25,000
Total paid-in capital	500,000	575,000
Retained earnings	300,000	225,000
Total stockholders' equity	$800,000	$800,000
Outstanding shares	50,000	55,000

Illustration 11-9
Stock dividend effects

In this example, total paid-in capital increased by $75,000 (50,000 shares × 10% × $15), and retained earnings is decreased by the same amount. Note also that total stockholders' equity remains unchanged at $800,000.

STOCK SPLITS

A **stock split**, like a stock dividend, involves the issuance of additional shares of stock to stockholders according to their percentage ownership. However, **a stock split results in a reduction in the par or stated value per share**. The purpose of a stock split is to increase the marketability of the stock by lowering

Helpful Hint A stock split changes the par value per share but does not affect any balances in stockholders' equity.

its market value per share. This, in turn, makes it easier for the corporation to issue additional stock.

The effect of a split on market value is generally **inversely proportional** to the size of the split. For example, after a recent 2-for-1 stock split, the market value of Nike's stock fell from $111 to approximately $55.

In a stock split, the company increases the number of shares in the same proportion that it decreases the par or stated value per share. For example, in a 2-for-1 split, the company exchanges one share of $10 par value stock for two shares of $5 par value stock. **A stock split does not have any effect on paid-in capital, retained earnings, and total stockholders' equity.** However, the number of shares outstanding increases. These effects are shown in Illustration 11-10, assuming that instead of issuing a 10% stock dividend, Medland splits its 50,000 shares of common stock on a 2-for-1 basis.

Illustration 11-10 Stock split effects

	Before Stock Split	After Stock Split
Stockholders' equity		
Paid-in capital		
Common stock (Before: 50,000 $10 par shares; after: 100,000 $5 par shares)	$ 500,000	$ 500,000
Paid-in capital in excess of par value	0	0
Total paid-in capital	500,000	500,000
Retained earnings	300,000	300,000
Total stockholders' equity	$800,000	$800,000
Outstanding shares	50,000	100,000

Because a stock split does not affect the balances in any stockholders' equity accounts, a company **does not need to journalize a stock split**. However, a memorandum entry explaining the effect of the split is typically made.

The differences between the effects of stock dividends and stock splits are shown in Illustration 11-11.

Illustration 11-11 Effects of stock splits and stock dividends differentiated

Item	Stock Dividend	Stock Split
Total paid-in capital	Increase	No change
Total retained earnings	Decrease	No change
Total par value (common stock)	Increase	No change
Par value per share	No change	Decrease

BEFORE YOU GO ON . . .

▶ **Review It**

1. What factors affect the size of a company's cash dividend?
2. Why do companies issue stock dividends? Why do companies declare stock splits?
3. Distinguish between a small and a large stock dividend and indicate the basis for valuing each kind of dividend.
4. Contrast the effects of a small stock dividend and a 2-for-1 stock split on (a) stockholders' equity and (b) outstanding shares.

▶ Do It

Due to five years of record earnings at Sing CD Corporation, the market price of its 500,000 shares of $2 par value common stock tripled from $15 per share to $45. During this period, paid-in capital remained the same at $2,000,000. Retained earnings increased from $1,500,000 to $10,000,000. President Joan Elbert is considering either a 10% stock dividend or a 2-for-1 stock split. She asks you to show the before and after effects of each option on retained earnings.

Action Plan

• Calculate the stock dividend's effect on retained earnings by multiplying the number of new shares times the market price of the stock (or par value for a large stock dividend).

• Recall that a stock dividend increases the number of shares without affecting total equity.

• Recall that a stock split only increases the number of shares outstanding and decreases the par value per share without affecting total equity.

Solution

The stock dividend amount is $2,250,000 [(500,000 × 10%) × $45]. The new balance in retained earnings is $7,750,000 ($10,000,000 − $2,250,000). The retained earnings balance after the stock split is the same as it was before the split: $10,000,000. The effects on the stockholders' equity accounts are as follows.

	Original Balances	After Dividend	After Split
Paid-in capital	$ 2,000,000	$ 4,250,000	$ 2,000,000
Retained earnings	10,000,000	7,750,000	10,000,000
Total stockholders' equity	$12,000,000	$12,000,000	$12,000,000
Shares outstanding	500,000	550,000	1,000,000

Retained Earnings

Retained earnings is net income that a company retains in the business. The balance in retained earnings is part of the stockholders' claim on the total assets of the corporation. It does not, however, represent a claim on any specific asset. Nor can the amount of retained earnings be associated with the balance of any asset account. For example, a $100,000 balance in retained earnings does not mean that there should be $100,000 in cash. The reason is that the company may have used the cash resulting from the excess of revenues over expenses to purchase buildings, equipment, and other assets. Illustration 11-12 shows recent amounts of retained earnings and cash in selected companies.

STUDY OBJECTIVE
6

Identify the items that affect retained earnings.

	(in millions)	
Company	Retained Earnings	Cash
Circuit City Stores, Inc.	$1,199	$783
Nike, Inc.	3,983	828
Starbucks Coffee Company	1,449	299
Amazon.com	(2,386)	1,303

Illustration 11-12
Retained earnings and cash balances

When expenses exceed revenues, a **net loss** results. In contrast to net income, a net loss decreases retained earnings. In closing entries a company debits a net loss to the Retained Earnings account. **It does not debit net losses to**

paid-in capital accounts. To do so would destroy the distinction between paid-in and earned capital. If cumulative losses exceed cumulative income over a company's life, a debit balance in Retained Earnings results. A debit balance in retained earnings, such as that of Amazon.com in 2004, is a **deficit**. A company reports a deficit as a deduction in the stockholders' equity section of the balance sheet, as shown in Illustration 11-13.

Illustration 11-13
Stockholders' equity with deficit

AMAZON.COM Balance Sheet (partial) December 31, 2004 (in thousands)		
Stockholders' equity		
Paid-in capital		
Common stock	$	4,097
Paid-in capital in excess of par value		2,154,669
Total paid-in capital		2,158,766
Accumulated deficit		**(2,385,977)**
Total stockholders' equity (deficit)	$	(227,211)

RETAINED EARNINGS RESTRICTIONS

The balance in retained earnings is generally available for dividend declarations. Some companies state this fact. In some cases, however, there may be **retained earnings restrictions**. These make a portion of the balance currently unavailable for dividends. Restrictions result from one or more of these causes: legal, contractual, or voluntary.

Companies generally disclose retained earnings restrictions in the notes to the financial statements. For example, Tektronix Inc., a manufacturer of electronic measurement devices, recently had total retained earnings of $774 million, but the unrestricted portion was only $223.8 million.

Illustration 11-14
Disclosure of unrestricted retained earnings

Tektronix	**TEKTRONIX INC.** **Notes to the Financial Statements**

Certain of the Company's debt agreements require compliance with debt covenants. Management believes that the Company is in compliance with such requirements for the fiscal year ended May 26, 2001. The Company had unrestricted retained earnings of $223.8 million after meeting those requirements.

Financial Statement Presentation of Stockholders' Equity

BALANCE SHEET PRESENTATION

STUDY OBJECTIVE
7
Prepare a comprehensive stockholders' equity section.

In the stockholders' equity section of the balance sheet, companies report paid-in capital and retained earnings and identify the specific sources of paid-in capital. Within paid-in capital, two classifications are recognized:

1. **Capital stock**, which consists of preferred and common stock. Companies show preferred stock before common stock because of its preferential rights. They report information about the par value, shares authorized, shares issued, and shares outstanding for each class of stock.

2. **Additional paid-in capital**, which includes the excess of amounts paid in over par or stated value.

Illustration 11-15 presents the stockholders' equity section of the balance sheet of Graber Inc. The company discloses a retained earnings restriction in the notes.

GRABER INC.
Balance Sheet (partial)

Stockholders' equity		
Paid-in capital		
Capital stock		
9% preferred stock, $100 par value, cumulative,		
10,000 shares authorized, 6,000 shares issued		
and outstanding		$ 600,000
Common stock, no par, $5 stated value,		
500,000 shares authorized, 400,000 shares		
issued, and 390,000 outstanding		2,000,000
Total capital stock		2,600,000
Additional paid-in capital		
In excess of par value—preferred stock	$ 30,000	
In excess of stated value—common stock	1,050,000	
Total additional paid-in capital		1,080,000
Total paid-in capital		3,680,000
Retained earnings **(see Note R)**		1,160,000
Total paid-in capital and retained earnings		4,840,000
Less: Treasury stock—common (10,000 shares)		(80,000)
Total stockholders' equity		$4,760,000

Note R: Retained earnings is restricted for the cost of treasury stock, $80,000.

Illustration 11-15
Comprehensive stockholders' equity section

⊕ International Note

In Switzerland, there are no specific disclosure requirements for stockholders' equity. However, companies typically disclose separate categories of capital on the balance sheet.

The stockholders' equity section for Graber Inc. includes most of the accounts discussed in this chapter. The disclosures pertaining to Graber's common stock indicate that 400,000 shares are issued; 100,000 shares are unissued (500,000 authorized less 400,000 issued); and 390,000 shares are outstanding (400,000 issued less 10,000 shares in treasury).

In published annual reports, companies seldom present subclassifications within the stockholders' equity section. Moreover, they often combine and report as a single amount the individual sources of additional paid-in capital. Notes often provide additional detail. Illustration 11-16 is an excerpt from Columbia Sportswear Company's 2004 balance sheet.

Columbia Sportswear Company
Balance Sheet (partial)
December 31, 2004
(in thousands)

Shareholders' equity	
Preferred stock; 10,000 shares authorized;	
none issued and outstanding	$ —
Common stock; 125,000 shares authorized; 40,126 and	
40,253 issued and outstanding (Note 9)	164,317
Retained earnings	573,988
Accumulated other comprehensive income (Note 15)	41,945
Total shareholders' equity	$780,250

Illustration 11-16
Stockholders' equity section

STATEMENT OF CASH FLOWS PRESENTATION

The balance sheet presents the balances of a company's stockholders' equity accounts at a point in time. Companies report in the "Financing Activities" section of the statement of cash flows information regarding cash inflows and outflows during the year that resulted from equity transactions. Illustration 11-17 presents the cash flows from financing activities from the statement of cash flows of Sara Lee Corporation. From this information we learn that the company's purchases of treasury stock during the period far exceeded its issuances of new common stock, and its financing activities resulted in a net reduction in its cash balance.

Illustration 11-17
Financing activities of statement of cash flows

SARA LEE CORPORATION
Statement of Cash Flows (partial)
For the Year Ended June 30, 2004
(in millions)

Cash Flows from Financing Activities	
Issuances of common stock	$ 139
Purchases of common stock	(350)
Payments of dividends	(714)
Borrowings of long-term debt	1
Repayments of long-term debt	(1,288)
Short-term (repayments) borrowings, net	15
Net cash used in financing activities	$(2,197)

BEFORE YOU GO ON . . .

▶ **Review It**

1. Identify the classifications within the paid-in capital section and the totals that are stated in the stockholders' equity section of a balance sheet.
2. What is a retained earnings restriction?
3. What was the total cost of Tootsie Roll's treasury stock in 2004? What was the total value of the 2004 cash dividend? What was the total charge to retained earnings of the 2004 stock dividend? The answer to these questions appears on p. 583.

THE NAVIGATOR

Measuring Corporate Performance

Investors are interested in both a company's dividend record and its earnings performance. Although those two measures are often parallel, that is not always the case. Thus, investors should investigate each one separately.

DIVIDEND RECORD

One way that companies reward stock investors for their investment is to pay them dividends. The **payout ratio** measures the percentage of earnings a company distributes in the form of cash dividends to common stockholders. It is computed by **dividing total cash dividends declared to common shareholders by**

net income. Using the information shown below, the payout ratio for Nike in 2004 and 2003 is calculated in Illustration 11-18.

	2004	**2003**
Dividends (in millions)	$194.9	$142.7
Net income (in millions)	945.6	740.1*

Illustration 11-18 Nike's payout ratio

$$\text{Payout Ratio} = \frac{\text{Cash Dividends Declared on Common Stock}}{\text{Net Income}}$$

($ in millions)	2004	2003
Payout Ratio	$\dfrac{\$194.9}{\$945.6} = 21\%$	$\dfrac{\$142.7}{\$740.1^*} = 19\%$

*Nike's reported net income for 2003 included a one-time charge of $266.1 due to an accounting change. Net income of $740.1 was used to make 2003 more comparable to 2004. Using reported net income of $474.0 produces a payout ratio of 30%.

Companies that have high growth rates are characterized by low payout ratios because they reinvest most of their net income in the business. Thus, a low payout ratio is not necessarily bad news. Companies that believe they have many good opportunities for growth, such as Nike and Reebok, will reinvest those funds in the company rather than pay high dividends. In fact, dividend payout ratios for the 500 largest U.S. companies currently are very low relative to historical rates. However, low dividend payments, or a cut in dividend payments, might signal that a company has liquidity or solvency problems and is trying to free up cash by not paying dividends. Thus, investors and analysts should investigate the reason for low dividend payments.

Illustration 11-19 lists recent payout ratios of four well-known companies.

Company	**Payout Ratio**
Microsoft	312.7%
Kellogg	45.0%
Johnson & Johnson	37.9%
Sears Holdings Corp.	0%

Illustration 11-19 Variability of payout ratios among companies

Decision Toolkit

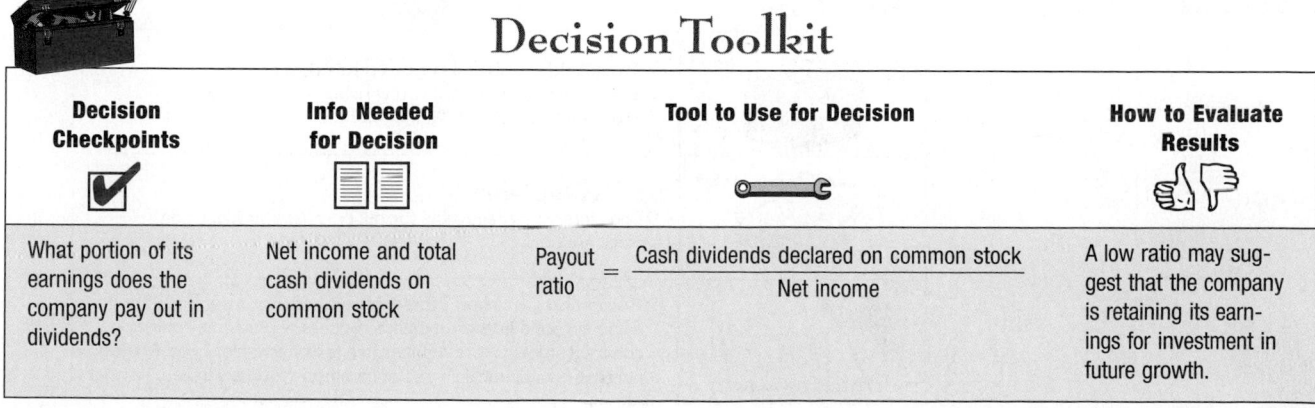

Decision Checkpoints	Info Needed for Decision	Tool to Use for Decision	How to Evaluate Results
What portion of its earnings does the company pay out in dividends?	Net income and total cash dividends on common stock	$\text{Payout ratio} = \dfrac{\text{Cash dividends declared on common stock}}{\text{Net income}}$	A low ratio may suggest that the company is retaining its earnings for investment in future growth.

EARNINGS PERFORMANCE

Another way to measure corporate performance is through profitability. A widely used ratio that measures profitability from the common stockholders' viewpoint is **return on common stockholders' equity**. This ratio shows how many dollars of net income a company earned for each dollar invested by common stockholders. It is computed by dividing net income available to common stockholders (Net income − Preferred stock dividends) by average common stockholders' equity.

Using the additional information presented below, Illustration 11-20 shows Nike's return on common stockholders' equity ratios, calculated for 2004 and 2003.

(in thousands)	2004	2003	2002
Net income	$ 945,600	$ 740,100	$ 668,300
Preferred stock dividends	30	30	30
Common stockholders' equity	4,781,400	3,990,400	3,838,700

Illustration 11-20 Nike's return on common stockholders' equity

$$\text{Return on Common Stockholders' Equity Ratio} = \frac{\text{Net Income} - \text{Preferred Stock Dividends}}{\text{Average Common Stockholders' Equity}}$$

($ in thousands)	2004	2003
Return on Common Stockholders' Equity Ratio	$\frac{\$945,600 - \$30}{(\$4,781,400 + \$3,990,400)/2} = 21.6\%$	$\frac{\$740,100 - \$30}{(\$3,990,400 + \$3,838,700)/2} = 18.9\%$

From 2003 to 2004, Nike's return on common shareholders' equity increased more than 14%. As a company grows larger, it becomes increasingly hard to sustain a high return. In Nike's case, since many believe the U.S. market for expensive sports shoes is saturated, it will need to grow either along new product lines, such as hiking shoes and golf equipment, or in new markets, such as Europe and Asia.

DEBT VERSUS EQUITY DECISION

To obtain large amounts of long-term capital, corporate managers must decide whether to issue bonds or to sell common stock. Bonds have three primary advantages relative to common stock, as shown in Illustration 11-21.

Illustration 11-21 Advantages of bond financing over common stock

Bond Financing	Advantages
	1. **Stockholder control is not affected.** Bondholders do not have voting rights, so current owners (stockholders) retain full control of the company.
	2. **Tax savings result.** Bond interest is deductible for tax purposes; dividends on stock are not.
	3. **Return on common stockholders' equity may be higher.** Although bond interest expense reduces net income, return on common stockholders' equity often is higher under bond financing because no additional shares of common stock are issued.

How does the debt versus equity decision affect the return on common stockholders' equity ratio? Illustration 11-22 shows that the return on common stockholders' equity is affected by the return on assets ratio and the amount of leverage a company uses—that is, by the company's reliance on debt (often measured by the debt to total assets ratio). If a company wants to increase its return on common stockholders' equity, it can either increase its return on assets or increase its reliance on debt financing.

Illustration 11-22
Components of the return on common stockholders' equity

To illustrate the potential effect of debt financing on the return on common stockholders' equity, assume that Microsystems Inc. is considering two plans for financing the construction of a new $5 million plant: Plan A involves issuing 200,000 shares of common stock at the current market price of $25 per share. Plan B involves issuing $5 million of 12% bonds at face value. Income before interest and taxes on the new plant will be $1.5 million; income taxes are expected to be 30%. Microsystems currently has 100,000 shares of common stock outstanding issued at $25 per share. The alternative effects on the return on common stockholders' equity are shown in Illustration 11-23.

	Plan A: Issue stock	Plan B: Issue bonds
Income before interest and taxes	$1,500,000	$1,500,000
Interest (12% × $5,000,000)	—	600,000
Income before income taxes	1,500,000	900,000
Income tax expense (30%)	450,000	270,000
Net income	$1,050,000	$ 630,000
Common stockholders' equity	$7,500,000	$2,500,000
Return on common stockholders' equity	14%	25.2%

Illustration 11-23
Effects on return on common stockholders' equity of issuing debt

Note that with long-term debt financing (bonds), net income is $420,000 ($1,050,000 − $630,000) less. However, the return on common stockholders' equity increases from 14% to 25.2% with the use of debt financing because there is less common stockholders' equity to spread the income across. **In general, as long as the return on assets rate exceeds the rate paid on debt, a company will increase the return on common stockholders' equity by the use of debt.**

After seeing this illustration, one might ask, why don't companies rely almost exclusively on debt financing, rather than equity? Debt has one major disadvantage: **The company locks in fixed payments that it must make in good times and bad. The company must pay interest on a periodic basis,**

and must pay the principal (face value) of the bonds at maturity. A company with fluctuating earnings and a relatively weak cash position may experience great difficulty in meeting interest requirements in periods of low earnings. In the extreme, this can result in bankruptcy. With common stock financing, on the other hand, the company can decide to pay low (or no) dividends if earnings are low.

Decision Toolkit

Decision Checkpoints	Info Needed for Decision	Tool to Use for Decision	How to Evaluate Results
What is the company's return on common stockholders' investment?	Earnings available to common stockholders and average common stockholders' equity	Return on common stockholders' equity ratio $=$ $\dfrac{\text{Net income} - \text{Preferred stock dividends}}{\text{Average common stockholders' equity}}$	A high measure suggests strong earnings performance from common stockholders' perspective.

BEFORE YOU GO ON . . .

▶ Review It

1. What measure can be used to evaluate a company's dividend record, and how is it calculated?
2. What factors affect the return on common stockholders' equity ratio?
3. What are the advantages and disadvantages of debt and equity financing?

Using the Decision Toolkit

Reebok remains one of Nike's fiercest competitors. In such a competitive and rapidly changing environment, one wrong step can spell financial disaster. After bottoming out at the end of 1999, Reebok's stock has rebounded.

Instructions
The following facts are available for Reebok. Using this information, evaluate its (1) dividend record and (2) earnings performance, and contrast them with those for Nike for 2003 and 2004. Nike's earnings per share were $3.59 in 2004 and $2.80 in 2003.

(in thousands except per share data)	2004	2003	2002
Dividends declared	$ 17,839	$ 8,847	0
Net income	$ 192,425	$ 157,254	$126,458
Preferred stock dividends	0	0	0
Shares outstanding at end of year	101,827	101,081	99,235
Common stockholders' equity	$1,219,956	$1,033,710	$884,570

Solution

1. *Dividend record:* A measure to evaluate dividend record is the payout ratio. For Reebok, this measure in 2004 and 2003 is calculated as shown below.

	2004	2003
Payout ratio	$\dfrac{\$17,839}{\$192,425} = 9.3\%$	$\dfrac{\$8,847}{\$157,254} = 5.6\%$

Nike's payout ratio remained nearly constant at 21%. Reebok's payout ratio increased significantly from 2003 to 2004 but was still less than half Nike's ratio.

2. *Earnings performance:* There are many measures of earnings performance. Some of those presented thus far in the book were earnings per share (page 55) and the return on common stockholders' equity ratio (this chapter). These measures for Reebok in 2004 and 2003 are calculated as shown here.

	2004	2003
Earnings per share	$\dfrac{\$192,425 - 0}{(101,827 + 101,081)/2} = \$1.90$	$\dfrac{\$157,254 - 0}{(101,081 + 99,235)/2} = \$1.57$
Return on common stockholders' equity ratio	$\dfrac{\$192,425 - 0}{(\$1,219,956 + \$1,033,710)/2} = 17.1\%$	$\dfrac{\$157,254 - 0}{(\$1,033,710 + \$884,570)/2} = 16.4\%$

From 2003 to 2004, Reebok's net income improved 22% and its earnings per share increased 21%. During the same time period Nike's earnings per share increased 28%.

Reebok's return on common stockholders' equity increased from 16.4% to 17.1%. While this represents a healthy increase, it is still less than Nike's 21.6%.

Summary of Study Objectives

1 *Identify and discuss the major characteristics of a corporation.* The major characteristics of a corporation are separate legal existence, limited liability of stockholders, transferable ownership rights, ability to acquire capital, continuous life, corporation management, government regulations, and additional taxes.

2 *Record the issuance of common stock.* When a company records issuance of common stock for cash, it credits the par value of the shares to Common Stock; it records in a separate paid-in capital account the portion of the proceeds that is above par value. When no-par common stock has a stated value, the entries are similar to those for par value stock. When no-par common stock does not have a stated value, the entire proceeds from the issue are credited to Common Stock.

3 *Explain the accounting for the purchase of treasury stock.* Companies generally use the cost method in accounting for treasury stock. Under this approach, a company debits Treasury Stock at the price paid to reacquire the shares.

4 *Differentiate preferred stock from common stock.* Preferred stock has contractual provisions that give it priority over common stock in certain areas. Typically, preferred stockholders have a preference as to (1) dividends and (2) assets in the event of liquidation. However, they often do not have voting rights.

5 *Prepare the entries for cash dividends and understand the effect of stock dividends and stock splits.* Companies make entries for dividends at the declaration date and the payment date. At the declaration date the entries for a cash dividend are: debit Retained Earnings and credit Dividends Payable. The effects of stock dividends and splits: Small *stock dividends* transfer an amount equal to the fair market value of the shares issued from retained earnings to the paid-in capital accounts. *Stock splits* reduce the par value per share of the common stock while increasing the number of shares so that total par value remains the same.

6 *Identify the items that affect retained earnings.* Additions to retained earnings consist of net income. Deductions consist of net loss and cash and stock dividends. In some instances, portions of retained earnings are restricted, making that portion un-available for the payment of dividends.

7 *Prepare a comprehensive stockholders' equity section.* In the stockholders' equity section of the balance sheet, companies report paid-in capital and retained earnings and identify specific sources of paid-in capital. Within paid-in capital, companies show two classifications: capital stock and additional paid-in capital. If a corporation has treasury stock, it deducts the cost of treasury stock from total paid-in capital and retained earnings to determine total stockholders' equity.

8 *Evaluate a corporation's dividend and earnings performance from a stockholder's perspective.* A company's dividend record can be evaluated by looking at what percentage of net income it chooses to pay out in dividends, as measured by the dividend payout ratio (dividends divided by net income). Earnings performance is measured with the return on common stockholders' equity ratio (income available to common shareholders divided by average common shareholders' equity).

THE NAVIGATOR

Decision Toolkit—A Summary

Decision Checkpoints	Info Needed for Decision	Tool to Use for Decision	How to Evaluate Results
Should the company incorporate?	Capital needs, growth expectations, type of business, tax status	Corporations have limited liability, easier capital raising ability, and professional managers; but they suffer from additional taxes, government regulations, and separation of ownership from management.	Must carefully weigh the costs and benefits in light of the particular circumstances.
What portion of its earnings does the company pay out in dividends?	Net income and total cash dividends on common stock	$$\text{Payout ratio} = \frac{\text{Cash dividends declared on common stock}}{\text{Net income}}$$	A low ratio may suggest that the company is retaining its earnings for investment in future growth.
What is the company's return on common stockholders' investment?	Earnings available to common stockholders and average common stockholders' equity	$$\text{Return on common stockholders' equity ratio} = \frac{\text{Net income} - \text{Preferred stock dividends}}{\text{Average common stockholders' equity}}$$	A high measure suggests strong earnings performance from common stockholders' perspective.

APPENDIX
ENTRIES FOR STOCK DIVIDENDS

STUDY OBJECTIVE

9

Prepare entries for stock dividends.

To illustrate the accounting for stock dividends, assume that Medland Corporation has a balance of $300,000 in retained earnings and declares a 10% stock dividend on its 50,000 shares of $10 par value common stock. The current fair market value of its stock is $15 per share. The number of shares to be issued is 5,000 (10% × 50,000), and the total amount to be debited to Retained Earnings is $75,000 (5,000 × $15). The entry to record this transaction at the declaration date is:

A	=	L	+	SE
				−75,000 Div
				+50,000 CS
				+25,000 CS

Cash Flows
no effect

Retained Earnings (or Stock Dividends)	75,000	
Common Stock Dividends Distributable		50,000
Paid-in Capital in Excess of Par Value		25,000
(To record declaration of 10% stock dividend)		

At the declaration date Medland decreases (debits) Retained Earnings for the fair market value of the stock issued; increases (credits) Common Stock Dividends Distributable for the par value of the dividend shares (5,000 × $10); and credits the excess over par (5,000 × $5) to an additional paid-in capital account.

Common Stock Dividends Distributable is a stockholders' equity account; it is not a liability because assets will not be used to pay the dividend. If Medland prepares a balance sheet before it issues the dividend shares, it reports the distributable account in paid-in capital as an addition to common stock issued, as shown in Illustration 11A-1.

MEDLAND CORPORATION Balance Sheet (partial)		
Paid-in capital		
Common stock	$500,000	
Common stock dividends distributable	**50,000**	**$550,000**

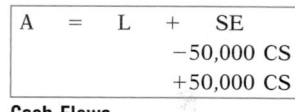

Illustration 11A-1
Statement presentation of common stock dividends distributable

When Medland issues the dividend shares, it decreases Common Stock Dividends Distributable and increases Common Stock as follows.

Helpful Hint Note that the dividend account title is *distributable*, not *payable*.

Common Stock Dividends Distributable	50,000	
Common Stock		50,000
(To record issuance of 5,000 shares in a stock dividend)		

A = L + SE
    −50,000 CS
    +50,000 CS

Cash Flows
no effect

Summary of Study Objective for Appendix

9 *Prepare entries for stock dividends.* To record the declaration of a small stock dividend (less than 20%), reduce Retained Earnings for an amount equal to the fair value of the shares issued. Record a credit to a temporary stockholders' equity account—Common Stock Dividends Distributable—for the par value of the shares, and credit the balance to Paid-in Capital in Excess of Par Value. When the shares are issued, debit Common Stock Dividends Distributable and credit Common Stock.

Glossary

Authorized stock The amount of stock that a corporation is authorized to sell as indicated in its charter. (p. 540)

Cash dividend A pro rata distribution of cash to stockholders. (p. 548)

Corporation A company organized as a separate legal entity, with most of the rights and privileges of a person. (p. 534)

Cumulative dividend A feature of preferred stock entitling the stockholder to receive current and unpaid prior-year dividends before common stockholders receive any dividends. (p. 546)

Declaration date The date the board of directors formally authorizes the dividend and announces it to stockholders. (p. 548)

Deficit A debit balance in retained earnings. (p. 554)

Dividend A distribution by a corporation to its stockholders on a pro rata (proportional) basis. (p. 547)

Dividends in arrears Preferred dividends that were supposed to be declared but were not declared during a given period. (p. 546)

Legal capital The amount per share of stock that must be retained in the business for the protection of corporate creditors. (p. 541)

No-par value stock Capital stock that has not been assigned a value in the corporate charter. (p. 541)

Outstanding stock Capital stock that has been issued and is being held by stockholders. (p. 545)

Paid-in capital The amount stockholders paid in to the corporation in exchange for shares of ownership. (p. 541)

Par value stock Capital stock that has been assigned a value per share in the corporate charter. (p. 541)

Payment date The date dividend checks are mailed to stockholders. (p. 549)

Payout ratio A measure of the percentage of earnings a company distributes in the form of cash dividends to common stockholders. (p. 556)

Preferred stock Capital stock that has contractual preferences over common stock in certain areas. (p. 546)

Privately held corporation A corporation that has only a few stockholders and whose stock is not available for sale to the general public. (p. 534)

Publicly held corporation   A corporation that may have thousands of stockholders and whose stock is regularly traded on a national securities market. (p. 534)

Record date   The date when the company determines ownership of outstanding shares for dividend purposes. (p. 549)

Retained earnings   Net income that a company retains in the business. (p. 553)

Retained earnings restrictions   Circumstances that make a portion of retained earnings currently unavailable for dividends. (p. 554)

Return on common stockholders' equity ratio   A measure of profitability from the stockholders' point of view; computed by dividing net income minus preferred stock dividends by average common stockholders' equity. (p. 558)

Stated value   The amount per share assigned by the board of directors to no-par stock. (p. 541)

Stock dividend   A pro rata distribution of the corporation's own stock to stockholders. (p. 550)

Stock split   The issuance of additional shares of stock to stockholders accompanied by a reduction in the par or stated value per share. (p. 551)

Treasury stock   A corporation's own stock that has been issued, fully paid for, and reacquired by the corporation and is being held in the treasury for future use. (p. 543)

Demonstration Problem

Rolman Corporation is authorized to issue 1,000,000 shares of $5 par value common stock. In its first year the company has the following stock transactions.

Jan. 10   Issued 400,000 shares of stock at $8 per share.
Sept. 1   Purchased 10,000 shares of common stock for the treasury at $9 per share.
Dec. 24   Declared a cash dividend of 10 cents per share on common stock outstanding.

Instructions
(a) Journalize the transactions.
(b) Prepare the stockholders' equity section of the balance sheet assuming the company had retained earnings of $150,600 at December 31.

Action Plan
- When common stock has a par value, credit Common Stock for par value and Paid-in Capital in Excess of Par Value for the amount above par value.
- Debit the Treasury Stock account at cost.

Solution to Demonstration Problem

(a)

Date	Account	Debit	Credit
Jan. 10	Cash	3,200,000	
	Common Stock		2,000,000
	Paid-in Capital in Excess of Par Value		1,200,000
	(To record issuance of 400,000 shares of $5 par value stock)		
Sept. 1	Treasury Stock	90,000	
	Cash		90,000
	(To record purchase of 10,000 shares of treasury stock at cost)		
Dec. 24	Retained Earnings	39,000	
	Dividends Payable		39,000
	(To record declaration of 10 cents per share cash dividend)		

(b)

ROLMAN CORPORATION
Balance Sheet (partial)

Stockholders' equity		
Paid-in capital		
Capital stock		
Common stock, $5 par value, 1,000,000 shares authorized, 400,000 shares issued, 390,000 outstanding	$2,000,000	
Additional paid-in capital		
In excess of par value—common stock	1,200,000	
Total paid-in capital	3,200,000	
Retained earnings	150,600	
Total paid-in capital and retained earnings	3,350,600	
Less: Treasury stock (10,000 shares)	90,000	
Total stockholders' equity	$3,260,600	

Note: All Questions, Exercises, and Problems marked with an asterisk relate to material in the appendix to the chapter.

Self-Study Questions

Answers are at the end of the chapter.

(SO 1) **1.** Which of these is *not* a major advantage of a corporation?
(a) Separate legal existence.
(b) Continuous life.
(c) Government regulations.
(d) Transferable ownership rights.

(SO 1) **2.** A major disadvantage of a corporation is:
(a) limited liability of stockholders.
(b) additional taxes.
(c) transferable ownership rights.
(d) None of the above.

(SO 1) **3.** Which of these statements is *false?*
(a) Ownership of common stock gives the owner a voting right.
(b) The stockholders' equity section begins with paid-in capital.
(c) The authorization of capital stock does not result in a formal accounting entry.
(d) Legal capital is intended to protect stockholders.

(SO 2) **4.** ABC Corp. issues 1,000 shares of $10 par value common stock at $12 per share. When the transaction is recorded, credits are made to:
(a) Common Stock $10,000 and Paid-in Capital in Excess of Stated Value $2,000.
(b) Common Stock $12,000.
(c) Common Stock $10,000 and Paid-in Capital in Excess of Par Value $2,000.
(d) Common Stock $10,000 and Retained Earnings $2,000.

(SO 4) **5.** Preferred stock may have which of the following features?
(a) dividend preference.
(b) preference to assets in the event of liquidation.
(c) cumulative dividends.
(d) all of the above.

(SO 5) **6.** Entries for cash dividends are required on the:
(a) declaration date and the record date.
(b) record date and the payment date.

(c) declaration date, record date, and payment date.
(d) declaration date and the payment date.

7. Which of these statements about stock dividends is *true?*   (SO 5)
(a) Stock dividends reduce a company's cash balance.
(b) A stock dividend has no effect on total stockholders' equity.
(c) A stock dividend decreases total stockholders' equity.
(d) A stock dividend ordinarily will increase total stockholders' equity.

8. In the stockholders' equity section, the cost of   (SO 7) treasury stock is deducted from:
(a) total paid-in capital and retained earnings.
(b) retained earnings.
(c) total stockholders' equity.
(d) common stock in paid-in capital.

9. The return on stockholders' equity   (SO 8) is increased by all of the following, *except*:
(a) an increase in the return on assets ratio.
(b) an increase in the use of debt financing.
(c) an increase in the company's stock price.
(d) an increase in the company's net income.

10. Roger is nearing retirement and   (SO 8) would like to invest in a stock that will provide a good steady income supply. Roger should choose a stock with a:
(a) high current ratio.
(b) high dividend payout.
(c) high earnings per share.
(d) high price-earnings ratio.

Go to the book's website, **www.wiley.com/ college/kimmel**, to access additional Self-Study Questions.

Questions

1. Warren, a student, asks your help in understanding some characteristics of a corporation. Explain each of these to Warren.
(a) Separate legal existence.
(b) Limited liability of stockholders.
(c) Transferable ownership rights.

2. (a) Your friend R. L. Duran cannot understand how the characteristic of corporate management is both an advantage and a disadvantage. Clarify this problem for R. L.

(b) Identify and explain two other disadvantages of a corporation.

3. Ann Adler believes a corporation must be incorporated in the state in which its headquarters office is located. Is Ann correct? Explain.

4. What are the basic ownership rights of common stockholders in the absence of restrictive provisions?

5. A corporation has been defined as an entity separate and distinct from its owners. In what ways is a corporation a separate legal entity?

6. What are the two principal components of stockholders' equity?

7. The corporate charter of Clio Corporation allows the issuance of a maximum of 100,000 shares of common stock. During its first 2 years of operation, Clio sold 60,000 shares to shareholders and reacquired 4,000 of these shares. After these transactions, how many shares are authorized, issued, and outstanding?

8. Which is the better investment—common stock with a par value of $5 per share or common stock with a par value of $20 per share?

9. For what reasons might a company like **IBM** repurchase some of its stock (treasury stock)?

10. Malon, Inc. purchases 1,000 shares of its own previously issued $5 par common stock for $11,000. Assuming the shares are held in the treasury, what effect does this transaction have on (a) net income, (b) total assets, (c) total paid-in capital, and (d) total stockholders' equity?

11. (a) What are the principal differences between common stock and preferred stock?
    (b) Preferred stock may be cumulative. Discuss this feature.
    (c) How are dividends in arrears presented in the financial statements?

12. Identify the events that result in credits and debits to retained earnings.

13. Indicate how each of these accounts should be classified in the stockholders' equity section of the balance sheet.
    (a) Common Stock.
    (b) Paid-in Capital in Excess of Par Value.
    (c) Retained Earnings.
    (d) Treasury Stock.
    (e) Paid-in Capital in Excess of Stated Value.
    (f) Preferred Stock.

14. What three conditions must be met before a cash dividend is paid?

15. Three dates associated with Mega Company's cash dividend are May 1, May 15, and May 31. Discuss the significance of each date and give the entry at each date.

16. Contrast the effects of a cash dividend and a stock dividend on a corporation's balance sheet.

17. Wendy Naylor asks, "Since stock dividends don't change anything, why declare them?" What is your answer to Wendy?

18. Flynn Corporation has 10,000 shares of $15 par value common stock outstanding when it announces a 2-for-1 split. Before the split, the stock had a market price of $120 per share. After the split, how many shares of stock will be outstanding, and what will be the approximate market price per share?

19. The board of directors is considering a stock split or a stock dividend. They understand that total stockholders' equity will remain the same under either action. However, they are not sure of the different effects of the two actions on other aspects of stockholders' equity. Explain the differences to the directors.

20. (a) What is the purpose of a retained earnings restriction?
    (b) Identify the possible causes of retained earnings restrictions.

21. Reo Inc.'s common stock has a par value of $1 and a current market value of $15. Explain why these amounts are different.

22. What is the formula for the payout ratio? What does it indicate?

23. Explain the circumstances under which debt financing will increase the return on stockholders' equity ratio.

24. Under what circumstances will the return on assets ratio and the return on common stockholders' equity ratio be equal?

25. Kirk Corp. has a return on assets ratio of 12%. It plans to issue bonds at 8% and use the cash to retire debt. What effect will this have on its debt to total assets ratio and on its return on common stockholders' equity?

Brief Exercises

Cite advantages and disadvantages of a corporation.
(SO 1)

BE11-1 Jeni Phelps is planning to start a business. Identify for Jeni the advantages and disadvantages of the corporate form of business organization.

Journalize issuance of par value common stock.
(SO 2)

BE11-2 On May 10 McLain Corporation issues 1,000 shares of $5 par value common stock for cash at $13 per share. Journalize the issuance of the stock.

Journalize issuance of no-par common stock.
(SO 2)

BE11-3 On June 1 Harmon Inc. issues 2,000 shares of no-par common stock at a cash price of $6 per share. Journalize the issuance of the shares.

Journalize issuance of preferred stock.
(SO 4)

BE11-4 Duggen Inc. issues 5,000 shares of $100 par value preferred stock for cash at $108 per share. Journalize the issuance of the preferred stock.

Prepare entries for a cash dividend.
(SO 5)

BE11-5 Michelle Corporation has 7,000 shares of common stock outstanding. It declares a $1 per share cash dividend on November 1 to stockholders of record on December

1. The dividend is paid on December 31. Prepare the entries on the appropriate dates to record the declaration and payment of the cash dividend.

BE11-6 The stockholders' equity section of Saber Corporation's balance sheet consists of common stock ($10 par) $1,000,000 and retained earnings $400,000. A 10% stock dividend (10,000 shares) is declared when the market value per share is $19. Show the before and after effects of the dividend on (a) the components of stockholders' equity and (b) the shares outstanding.

Show before and after effects of a stock dividend.
(SO 5)

BE11-7 Indicate whether each of the following transactions would increase (+), decrease (−), or not affect (N/A) total assets, total liabilities, and total stockholders' equity.

Compare impact of cash dividend, stock dividend, and stock split.
(SO 5)

Transaction	Assets	Liabilities	Stockholders' Equity
(a) Declared cash dividend.			
(b) Paid cash dividend declared in (a).			
(c) Declared stock dividend.			
(d) Distributed stock dividend declared in (c).			
(e) Split stock 3-for-1.			

BE11-8 Duffy Corporation has these accounts at December 31: Common Stock, $10 par, 5,000 shares issued, $50,000; Paid-in Capital in Excess of Par Value $18,000; Retained Earnings $32,000; and Treasury Stock—Common, 500 shares, $12,000. Prepare the stockholders' equity section of the balance sheet.

Prepare a stockholders' equity section.
(SO 7)

BE11-9 Nick Gross, president of Gross Corporation, believes that it is a good practice for a company to maintain a constant payout of dividends relative to its earnings. Last year net income was $600,000, and the corporation paid $150,000 in dividends. This year, due to some unusual circumstances, the corporation had income of $1,500,000. Nick expects next year's net income to be about $700,000. What was Gross Corporation's payout ratio last year? If it is to maintain the same payout ratio, what amount of dividends would it pay this year? Is this necessarily a good idea—that is, what are the pros and cons of maintaining a constant payout ratio in this scenario?

Evaluate a company's dividend record.
(SO 8)

BE11-10 SUPERVALU, one of the largest grocery retailers in the United States, is headquartered in Minneapolis. The following financial information (in millions) was taken from the company's 2005 annual report. Net sales $19,543.2; net income $385.8; beginning stockholders' equity $2,209.6; ending stockholders' equity $2,510.6. Compute the return on stockholders' equity ratio. Provide a brief interpretation of your findings.

Calculate the return on stockholders' equity.
(SO 8)

*BE11-11** Howell Corporation has 100,000 shares of $10 par value common stock outstanding. It declares a 10% stock dividend on December 1 when the market value per share is $17. The dividend shares are issued on December 31. Prepare the entries for the declaration and distribution of the stock dividend.

Prepare entries for a stock dividend.
(SO 9)

Exercises

E11-1 During its first year of operations, Ritter Corporation had these transactions pertaining to its common stock.

Journalize issuance of common stock.
(SO 2)

Jan. 10 Issued 90,000 shares for cash at $5 per share.
July 1 Issued 50,000 shares for cash at $7 per share.

Instructions
(a) Journalize the transactions, assuming that the common stock has a par value of $5 per share.
(b) Journalize the transactions, assuming that the common stock is no-par with a stated value of $1 per share.

E11-2 Somer Co. had these transactions during the current period.

Journalize issuance of common stock and preferred stock and purchase of treasury stock.
(SO 2, 3, 4)

June 12 Issued 60,000 shares of $1 par value common stock for cash of $300,000.
July 11 Issued 1,000 shares of $100 par value preferred stock for cash at $104 per share.
Nov. 28 Purchased 2,000 shares of treasury stock for $11,000.

Instructions
Prepare the journal entries for the transactions shown on page 567.

Journalize preferred stock transactions and indicate statement presentation.
(SO 4, 7)

E11-3   Oritz Corporation is authorized to issue both preferred and common stock. The par value of the preferred is $50. During the first year of operations, the company had the following events and transactions pertaining to its preferred stock.

Feb. 1   Issued 40,000 shares for cash at $51 per share.
July 1   Issued 20,000 shares for cash at $56 per share.

Instructions
(a) Journalize the transactions.
(b) Post to the stockholders' equity accounts. (Use T accounts.)
(c) Discuss the statement presentation of the accounts.

Answer questions about stockholders' equity section.
(SO 2, 3, 4, 7)

E11-4   The stockholders' equity section of MaiStyle Corporation's balance sheet at December 31 is presented here.

MAISTYLE CORPORATION
Balance Sheet (partial)

Stockholders' equity	
Paid-in capital	
Preferred stock, cumulative, 10,000 shares authorized,	
6,000 shares issued and outstanding	$ 900,000
Common stock, no par, 750,000 shares authorized,	
600,000 shares issued	1,800,000
Total paid-in capital	2,700,000
Retained earnings	1,158,000
Total paid-in capital and retained earnings	3,858,000
Less: Treasury stock (8,000 common shares)	(32,000)
Total stockholders' equity	$3,826,000

Instructions
From a review of the stockholders' equity section, answer the following questions.
(a) How many shares of common stock are outstanding?
(b) Assuming there is a stated value, what is the stated value of the common stock?
(c) What is the par value of the preferred stock?
(d) If the annual dividend on preferred stock is $36,000, what is the dividend rate on preferred stock?
(e) If dividends of $72,000 were in arrears on preferred stock, what would be the balance reported for retained earnings?

Prepare correct entries for capital stock transactions.
(SO 2, 3, 4)

E11-5   Yanik Corporation recently hired a new accountant with extensive experience in accounting for partnerships. Because of the pressure of the new job, the accountant was unable to review what he had learned earlier about corporation accounting. During the first month, he made the following entries for the corporation's capital stock.

May 2	Cash	120,000	
	Capital Stock		120,000
	(Issued 10,000 shares of $5 par value		
	common stock at $12 per share)		
10	Cash	530,000	
	Capital Stock		530,000
	(Issued 10,000 shares of $50 par value		
	preferred stock at $53 per share)		
15	Capital Stock	7,200	
	Cash		7,200
	(Purchased 600 shares of common		
	stock for the treasury at $12 per share)		

Instructions
On the basis of the explanation for each entry, prepare the entries that should have been made for the capital stock transactions.

E11-6 On January 1 Weiss Corporation had 75,000 shares of no-par common stock issued and outstanding. The stock has a stated value of $5 per share. During the year, the following transactions occurred.

Journalize cash dividends and indicate statement presentation.
(SO 5)

Apr.	1	Issued 8,000 additional shares of common stock for $11 per share.
June	15	Declared a cash dividend of $1.50 per share to stockholders of record on June 30.
July	10	Paid the $1.50 cash dividend.
Dec.	1	Issued 4,000 additional shares of common stock for $12 per share.
	15	Declared a cash dividend on outstanding shares of $1.70 per share to stockholders of record on December 31.

Instructions
(a) Prepare the entries, if any, on each of the three dates that involved dividends.
(b) How are dividends and dividends payable reported in the financial statements prepared at December 31?

E11-7 On October 31 the stockholders' equity section of Davis Company's balance sheet consists of common stock $648,000 and retained earnings $400,000. Davis is considering the following two courses of action: (1) declaring a 5% stock dividend on the 54,000 $12 par value shares outstanding or (2) effecting a 3-for-1 stock split that will reduce par value to $4 per share. The current market price is $15 per share.

Compare effects of a stock dividend and a stock split.
(SO 5)

Instructions
Prepare a tabular summary of the effects of the alternative actions on the company's stockholders' equity and outstanding shares. Use these column headings: **Before Action**, **After Stock Dividend**, and **After Stock Split**.

E11-8 Wells Fargo & Company, headquartered in San Francisco, is one of the nation's largest financial institutions. It reported the following selected accounts (in millions) as of December 31, 2004.

Prepare a stockholders' equity section.
(SO 7)

Retained earnings	$27,143
Preferred stock	270
Common stock—$1⅔ par value, authorized 6,000,000,000 shares;	
issued 1,736,381,025 shares	2,894
Treasury stock—41,789,388 shares	(2,247)
Additional paid-in capital—common stock	9,806

Instructions
Prepare the stockholders' equity section of the balance sheet for Wells Fargo as of December 31, 2004.

E11-9 The following stockholders' equity accounts, arranged alphabetically, are in the ledger of Marvel Corporation at December 31, 2007.

Prepare a stockholders' equity section.
(SO 7)

Common Stock ($5 stated value)	$1,500,000
Paid-in Capital in Excess of Par Value—Preferred Stock	45,000
Paid-in Capital in Excess of Stated Value—Common Stock	1,050,000
Preferred Stock (8%, $100 par, noncumulative)	500,000
Retained Earnings	1,134,000
Treasury Stock—Common (8,000 shares)	78,000

Instructions
Prepare the stockholders' equity section of the balance sheet at December 31, 2007.

E11-10 The following accounts appear in the ledger of Sycamore Inc. after the books are closed at December 31, 2007.

Prepare a stockholders' equity section.
(SO 7)

Common Stock (no-par, $1 stated value, 400,000 shares authorized, 200,000 shares issued)	$ 200,000
Paid-in Capital in Excess of Stated Value—Common Stock	1,200,000
Preferred Stock ($50 par value, 8%, 40,000 shares authorized, 12,000 shares issued)	600,000
Retained Earnings	900,000
Treasury Stock (10,000 common shares)	64,000
Paid-in Capital in Excess of Par Value—Preferred Stock	24,000

Instructions
Prepare the stockholders' equity section at December 31, assuming $100,000 of retained earnings is restricted for plant expansion. (Use Note R.)

Calculate ratios to evaluate dividend and earnings performance.
(SO 8)

E11-11   The following financial information is available for Sara Lee Corporation.

(in millions)	2004	2003
Average common stockholders' equity	$2,500	$1,897
Dividends declared for common stockholders	594	497
Dividends declared for preferred stockholders	0	10
Net income	1,272	1,221

Instructions
Calculate the payout ratio and return on common stockholders' equity ratio for 2004 and 2003. Comment on your findings.

Calculate ratios to evaluate dividend and earnings performance.
(SO 8)

E11-12   The following financial information is available for Walgreen Company.

(in millions)	2004	2003
Average common stockholders' equity	$7,628.8	$6,640.4
Dividends declared for common stockholders	186.4	159.6
Dividends declared for preferred stockholders	0	0
Net income	1,349.8	1,165.1

Instructions
Calculate the payout ratio and return on common stockholders' equity ratio for 2004 and 2003. Comment on your findings.

Calculate ratios to evaluate profitability and solvency.
(SO 8)

E11-13   Mann Corporation decided to issue common stock and used the $400,000 proceeds to retire all of its outstanding bonds on January 1, 2007. The following information is available for the company for 2006 and 2007.

	2007	2006
Net income	$ 182,000	$ 150,000
Average stockholders' equity	1,100,000	700,000
Total assets	1,200,000	1,200,000
Current liabilities	100,000	100,000
Total liabilities	100,000	500,000

Instructions
(a) Compute the return on stockholder's equity ratio for both years.
(b) Explain how it is possible that net income increased, but the return on common stockholders' equity decreased.
(c) Compute the debt to total assets ratio for both years, and comment on the implications of this change in the company's solvency.

Journalize stock dividends.
(SO 5, 9)

*E11-14   On January 1, 2007, Kern Corporation had $1,500,000 of common stock outstanding that was issued at par and retained earnings of $750,000. The company issued 30,000 shares of common stock at par on July 1 and earned net income of $400,000 for the year.

Instructions
Journalize the declaration of a 15% stock dividend on December 10, 2007, for the following two independent assumptions.
(a) Par value is $10 and market value is $12.
(b) Par value is $5 and market value is $9.

Problems: Set A

P11-1A Norris Corporation was organized on January 1, 2007. It is authorized to issue 20,000 shares of 6%, $50 par value preferred stock and 500,000 shares of no-par common stock with a stated value of $1 per share. The following stock transactions were completed during the first year.

Jan.	10	Issued 60,000 shares of common stock for cash at $4 per share.
Mar.	1	Issued 12,000 shares of preferred stock for cash at $54 per share.
May	1	Issued 100,000 shares of common stock for cash at $5 per share.
Sept.	1	Issued 5,000 shares of common stock for cash at $6 per share.
Nov.	1	Issued 2,000 shares of preferred stock for cash at $56 per share.

Journalize stock transactions, post, and prepare paid-in capital section.
(SO 2, 4, 7)

Instructions
(a) Journalize the transactions.
(b) Post to the stockholders' equity accounts. (Use T accounts.)
(c) Prepare the paid-in capital portion of the stockholders' equity section at December 31, 2007.

(c) Tot. paid-in capital
$1,530,000

P11-2A The stockholders' equity accounts of Alpha Corporation on January 1, 2007, were as follows.

Preferred Stock (8%, $100 par noncumulative, 5,000 shares authorized)	$ 400,000
Common Stock ($5 stated value, 300,000 shares authorized)	1,000,000
Paid-in Capital in Excess of Par Value—Preferred Stock	15,000
Paid-in Capital in Excess of Stated Value—Common Stock	480,000
Retained Earnings	688,000
Treasury Stock—Common (5,000 shares)	40,000

Journalize transactions, post, and prepare a stockholders' equity section; calculate ratios.
(SO 2, 3, 5, 7, 8)

During 2007 the corporation had the following transactions and events pertaining to its stockholders' equity.

Feb.	1	Issued 3,000 shares of common stock for $18,600.
Mar.	20	Purchased 1,000 additional shares of common treasury stock at $7 per share.
Oct.	1	Declared an 8% cash dividend on preferred stock, payable November 1.
Nov.	1	Paid the dividend declared on October 1.
Dec.	1	Declared a $0.50 per share cash dividend to common stockholders of record on December 15, payable December 31, 2007.
	31	Determined that net income for the year was $280,000. Paid the dividend declared on December 1.

Instructions
(a) Journalize the transactions. (Include entries to close net income to Retained Earnings.)
(b) Enter the beginning balances in the accounts and post the journal entries to the stockholders' equity accounts. (Use T accounts.)
(c) Prepare the stockholders' equity section of the balance sheet at December 31, 2007.
(d) Calculate the payout ratio, earnings per share, and return on common stockholders' equity ratio. (*Note:* Use the common shares outstanding on January 1 and December 31 to determine the average shares outstanding.)

(c) Tot. paid-in capital
$1,913,600

P11-3A On December 31, 2006, Pepp Company had 1,300,000 shares of $5 par common stock issued and outstanding. The stockholders' equity accounts at December 31, 2006, had the balances listed here.

Common Stock	$6,500,000
Additional Paid-in Capital	1,800,000
Retained Earnings	1,200,000

Prepare a stockholders' equity section.
(SO 7)

Transactions during 2007 and other information related to stockholders' equity accounts were as follows.

1. On January 10, 2007, issued at $109 per share 100,000 shares of $100 par value, 8% cumulative preferred stock.

2. On February 8, 2007, reacquired 15,000 shares of its common stock for $11 per share.
3. On June 8, 2007, declared a cash dividend of $1.20 per share on the common stock outstanding, payable on July 10, 2007, to stockholders of record on July 1, 2007.
4. On December 9, 2007, declared the yearly cash dividend on preferred stock, payable January 10, 2008, to stockholders of record on December 15, 2007.
5. Net income for the year was $3,600,000.

Tot. stockholders' equity
$21,493,000

Instructions
Prepare the stockholders' equity section of Pepp's balance sheet at December 31, 2007.

Reproduce retained earnings account, and prepare a stockholders' equity section.
(SO 5, 6, 7)

P11-4A The ledger of Omega Corporation at December 31, 2007, after the books have been closed, contains the following stockholders' equity accounts.

Preferred Stock (10,000 shares issued)	$1,000,000
Common Stock (450,000 shares issued)	2,250,000
Paid-in Capital in Excess of Par Value—Preferred Stock	200,000
Paid-in Capital in Excess of Stated Value—Common Stock	1,600,000
Retained Earnings	3,060,000

A review of the accounting records reveals this information:

1. Preferred stock is 7%, $100 par value, noncumulative. Since January 1, 2006, 10,000 shares have been outstanding; 20,000 shares are authorized.
2. Common stock is no-par with a stated value of $5 per share; 600,000 shares are authorized.
3. The January 1, 2007, balance in Retained Earnings was $2,580,000.
4. On October 1, 60,000 shares of common stock were sold for cash at $8 per share.
5. A cash dividend of $400,000 was declared and properly allocated to preferred and common stock on November 1. No dividends were paid to preferred stockholders in 2006.
6. Net income for the year was $880,000.
7. On December 31, 2007, the directors authorized disclosure of a $130,000 restriction of retained earnings for plant expansion. (Use Note A.)

Instructions

(b) Tot. paid-in capital
$5,050,000

(a) Reproduce the retained earnings account (T account) for the year.
(b) Prepare the stockholders' equity section of the balance sheet at December 31.

Prepare entries for stock transactions, and prepare a stockholders' equity section.
(SO 2, 3, 4, 7)

P11-5A Milner Corporation has been authorized to issue 20,000 shares of $100 par value, 10%, noncumulative preferred stock and 1,000,000 shares of no-par common stock. The corporation assigned a $5 stated value to the common stock. At December 31, 2007, the ledger contained the following balances pertaining to stockholders' equity.

Preferred Stock	$ 130,000
Paid-in Capital in Excess of Par Value—Preferred Stock	20,000
Common Stock	2,000,000
Paid-in Capital in Excess of Stated Value—Common Stock	1,850,000
Treasury Stock—Common (5,000 shares)	55,000
Retained Earnings	82,000

The preferred stock was issued for $150,000 cash. All common stock issued was for cash. In November 5,000 shares of common stock were purchased for the treasury at a per share cost of $11. No dividends were declared in 2007.

Instructions
(a) Prepare the journal entries for the following.
    (1) Issuance of preferred stock for cash.
    (2) Issuance of common stock for cash.
    (3) Purchase of common treasury stock for cash.

(b) Tot. stockholders' equity
$4,027,000

(b) Prepare the stockholders' equity section of the balance sheet at December 31, 2007.

Prepare a stockholders' equity section.
(SO 7)

P11-6A On January 1, 2007, Rothchild Inc. had these stockholders' equity balances.

Common Stock, $1 par (2,000,000 shares authorized, 800,000 shares issued and outstanding)	$800,000
Paid-in Capital in Excess of Par Value	1,500,000
Retained Earnings	600,000

During 2007, the following transactions and events occurred.

1. Issued 50,000 shares of $1 par value common stock for $3 per share.
2. Issued 40,000 shares of common stock for cash at $4 per share.
3. Purchased 15,000 shares of common stock for the treasury at $3.50 per share.
4. Declared and paid a cash dividend of $115,000.
5. Earned net income of $300,000.

Instructions
Prepare the stockholders' equity section of the balance sheet at December 31, 2007.

Tot. stockholders' equity
$3,342,500

P11-7A Stuffitt Company manufactures backpacks. During 2007 Stuffitt issued bonds at 10% interest and used the cash proceeds to purchase treasury stock. The following financial information is available for Stuffitt Company for the years 2007 and 2006.

Evaluate a company's profitability and solvency.
(SO 8)

	2007	2006
Sales	$ 9,000,000	$ 9,000,000
Net income	2,340,000	2,700,000
Interest expense	500,000	140,000
Tax expense	670,000	780,000
Dividends paid	890,000	1,026,000
Total assets (year-end)	14,500,000	16,875,000
Average total assets	14,937,500	17,647,000
Total liabilities (year-end)	6,000,000	3,000,000
Average total stockholders' equity	9,400,000	14,100,000

Instructions
(a) Use the information above to calculate the following ratios for both years: (i) return on assets ratio, (ii) return on common stockholders' equity ratio, (iii) payout ratio, (iv) debt to total assets ratio, (v) times interest earned ratio.
(b) Referring to your findings in part (a), discuss the changes in the company's profitability from 2006 to 2007.
(c) Referring to your findings in part (a), discuss the changes in the company's solvency from 2006 to 2007.
(d) Based on your findings in (b), was the decision to issue debt to purchase common stock a wise one?

*P11-8A On January 1, 2007, Aglar Corporation had these stockholders' equity accounts.

Prepare dividend entries, prepare a stockholders' equity section, and calculate ratios.
(SO 5, 7, 8, 9)

GLS

Common Stock ($10 par value, 60,000 shares issued and outstanding)	$600,000
Paid-in Capital in Excess of Par Value	500,000
Retained Earnings	620,000

During the year, the following transactions occurred.

Jan. 15 Declared a $0.50 cash dividend per share to stockholders of record on January 31, payable February 15.
Feb. 15 Paid the dividend declared in January.
Apr. 15 Declared a 10% stock dividend to stockholders of record on April 30, distributable May 15. On April 15 the market price of the stock was $14 per share.
May 15 Issued the shares for the stock dividend.
Dec. 1 Declared a $0.55 per share cash dividend to stockholders of record on December 15, payable January 10, 2006.
    31 Determined that net income for the year was $370,000.

Instructions
(a) Journalize the transactions. (Include entries to close net income to Retained Earnings.)
(b) Enter the beginning balances and post the entries to the stockholders' equity T accounts. (*Note:* Open additional stockholders' equity accounts as needed.)
(c) Prepare the stockholders' equity section of the balance sheet at December 31.
(d) Calculate the payout ratio and return on common stockholders' equity ratio.

(c) Tot. stockholders' equity
$2,023,700

Problems: Set B

Journalize stock transactions, post, and prepare paid-in capital section.
(SO 2, 4, 7)

P11-1B   Hawes Corporation was organized on January 1, 2007. It is authorized to issue 10,000 shares of 8%, $100 par value preferred stock and 500,000 shares of no-par common stock with a stated value of $2 per share. The following stock transactions were completed during the first year.

Jan.	10	Issued 80,000 shares of common stock for cash at $3.50 per share.
Mar.	1	Issued 5,000 shares of preferred stock for cash at $102 per share.
May	1	Issued 60,000 shares of common stock for cash at $4 per share.
Sept.	1	Issued 10,000 shares of common stock for cash at $5 per share.
Nov.	1	Issued 2,000 shares of preferred stock for cash at $104 per share.

Instructions
(a) Journalize the transactions.

(c) Tot. paid-in capital
$1,288,000

(b) Post to the stockholders' equity accounts. (Use T accounts.)
(c) Prepare the paid-in capital section of stockholders' equity at December 31, 2007.

Journalize transactions, post, and prepare a stockholders' equity section; calculate ratios.
(SO 2, 3, 5, 7, 8)

P11-2B   The stockholders' equity accounts of Sosa Corporation on January 1, 2007, were as follows.

Preferred Stock (7%, $50 par cumulative, 10,000 shares authorized)	$ 400,000
Common Stock ($1 stated value, 2,000,000 shares authorized)	1,000,000
Paid-in Capital in Excess of Par Value—Preferred Stock	80,000
Paid-in Capital in Excess of Stated Value—Common Stock	1,400,000
Retained Earnings	1,716,000
Treasury Stock—Common (10,000 shares)	30,000

During 2007 the corporation had these transactions and events pertaining to its stockholders' equity.

Feb.	1	Issued 15,000 shares of common stock for $60,000.
Nov.	10	Purchased 4,000 shares of common stock for the treasury at a cost of $18,000.
Nov.	15	Declared a 7% cash dividend on preferred stock, payable December 15.
Dec.	1	Declared a $0.30 per share cash dividend to stockholders of record on December 15, payable December 31, 2007.
	15	Paid the dividend declared on November 15.
	31	Determined that net income for the year was $408,000. The market price of the common stock on this date was $5 per share. Paid the dividend declared on December 1.

Instructions
(a) Journalize the transactions. (Include entries to close net income to Retained Earnings.)

(c) Tot. paid-in capital
$2,940,000

(b) Enter the beginning balances in the accounts, and post the journal entries to the stockholders' equity accounts. (Use T accounts.)
(c) Prepare the stockholders' equity section of the balance sheet at December 31, 2007.
(d) Calculate the payout ratio, earnings per share, and return on common stockholders' equity ratio. (*Hint:* Use the common shares outstanding on January 1 and December 31 to determine average shares outstanding.)

Prepare a stockholders' equity section.
(SO 7)

P11-3B   On December 31, 2006, Klein Company had 1,000,000 shares of $1 par common stock issued and outstanding. The stockholders' equity accounts at December 31, 2006, had the balances listed here.

Common Stock	$1,000,000
Additional Paid-in Capital	100,000
Retained Earnings	800,000

Transactions during 2007 and other information related to stockholders' equity accounts were as follows.

1. On January 9, 2007, issued at $8 per share 100,000 shares of $5 par value, 9% cumulative preferred stock.

2. On February 8, 2007, reacquired 12,000 shares of its common stock for $9 per share.
3. On June 10, 2007, declared a cash dividend of $1 per share on the common stock out-standing, payable on July 10, 2007, to stockholders of record on July 1, 2007.
4. On December 15, 2007, declared the yearly cash dividend on preferred stock, payable December 28, 2007, to stockholders of record on December 15, 2007.
5. Net income for the year is $2,400,000. At December 31, 2007, the market price of the common stock was $12 per share.

Instructions
Prepare the stockholders' equity section of Klein Company's balance sheet at December 31, 2007.

Tot. stockholders' equity
$3,959,000

P11-4B   The post-closing trial balance of Mantelle Corporation at December 31, 2007, contains these stockholders' equity accounts.

Reproduce retained earnings account, and prepare a stockholders' equity section. (SO 5, 6, 7)

Preferred Stock (8,000 shares issued)	$ 400,000
Common Stock (250,000 shares issued)	2,500,000
Paid-in Capital in Excess of Par Value—Preferred Stock	250,000
Paid-in Capital in Excess of Par Value—Common Stock	700,000
Retained Earnings	1,215,000

A review of the accounting records reveals this information:

1. Preferred stock is $50 par, 10%, and cumulative; 8,000 shares have been outstanding since January 1, 2006.
2. Authorized stock is 20,000 shares of preferred and 500,000 shares of common with a $10 par value.
3. The January 1, 2007, balance in Retained Earnings was $960,000.
4. On July 1, 20,000 shares of common stock were sold for cash at $16 per share.
5. A cash dividend of $220,000 was declared and properly allocated to preferred and common stock on October 1. No dividends were paid to preferred stockholders in 2006.
6. Net income for the year was $475,000.
7. On December 31, 2007, the directors authorized disclosure of a $150,000 restriction of retained earnings for plant expansion. (Use Note X.)

Instructions
(a) Reproduce the retained earnings account for the year.
(b) Prepare the stockholders' equity section of the balance sheet at December 31.

(b) Tot. paid-in capital
$3,850,000

P11-5B   The following stockholders' equity accounts, arranged alphabetically, are in the ledger of Aaron Corporation at December 31, 2007.

Prepare a stockholders' equity section. (SO 7)

Common Stock ($5 stated value, 800,000 shares authorized)	$2,600,000
Paid-in Capital in Excess of Par Value—Preferred Stock	108,000
Paid-in Capital in Excess of Stated Value— Common Stock	1,500,000
Preferred Stock (8%, $50 par, noncumulative, 50,000 shares	
authorized)	900,000
Retained Earnings	1,958,000
Treasury Stock—Common (20,000 shares)	150,000

Instructions
Prepare the stockholders' equity section of the balance sheet at December 31, 2007.

Tot. stockholders' equity
$6,916,000

P11-6B   On January 1, 2007, Willow Inc. had these stockholder equity balances.

Prepare a stockholders' equity section. (SO 7)

Common Stock, $1 par (1,000,000 shares authorized;	
500,000 shares issued and outstanding)	$ 500,000
Paid-in Capital in Excess of Par Value	1,000,000
Retained Earnings	600,000

During 2007, the following transactions and events occurred.

1. Issued 50,000 shares of $1 par common stock for $125,000.
2. Issued 30,000 common shares for cash at $4 per share.
3. Purchased 10,000 shares of common stock for the treasury at $4 per share.
4. Declared and paid a cash dividend of $160,000.
5. Reported net income of $400,000.

Tot. stockholders' equity
$2,545,000

Instructions
Prepare the stockholders' equity section of the balance sheet at December 31, 2007.

*Evaluate a company's
profitability and solvency.*
(SO 8)

P11-7B Gene Kelly Company manufactures raingear. During 2007 Gene Kelly Company decided to issue bonds at 8% interest and then used the cash to purchase a significant amount of treasury stock. The following information is available for Gene Kelly Company.

	2007	2006
Sales	$3,000,000	$3,000,000
Net income	830,000	900,000
Interest expense	120,000	50,000
Tax expense	166,000	200,000
Total assets	5,000,000	5,625,000
Average total assets	5,312,500	6,250,000
Total liabilities	2,000,000	1,000,000
Average total stockholders' equity	3,312,500	5,250,000
Dividends	270,000	300,000

Instructions
(a) Use the information above to calculate the following ratios for both years: (i) return on assets ratio, (ii) return on common stockholders' equity ratio, (iii) payout ratio, (iv) debt to total assets ratio, (v) times interest earned ratio.
(b) Referring to your findings in part (a), discuss the changes in the company's profitability from 2006 to 2007.
(c) Referring to your findings in part (a), discuss the changes in the company's solvency from 2006 to 2007.
(d) Based on your findings in (b), was the decision to issue debt to purchase common stock a wise one?

*Prepare dividend entries,
prepare a stockholders' equity
section, and calculate ratios.*
(SO 5, 7, 8, 9)

GLS

*P11-8B On January 1, 2007, Frenz Corporation had these stockholders' equity accounts.

Common Stock ($20 par value, 60,000 shares issued and outstanding)	$1,200,000
Paid-in Capital in Excess of Par Value	240,000
Retained Earnings	750,000

During the year, the following transactions occurred.

Feb.	1	Declared a $0.50 cash dividend per share to stockholders of record on February 15, payable March 1.
Mar.	1	Paid the dividend declared in February.
July	1	Declared a 10% stock dividend to stockholders of record on July 15, distributable July 31. On July 1 the market price of the stock was $26 per share.
	31	Issued the shares for the stock dividend.
Dec.	1	Declared a $1 per share dividend to stockholders of record on December 15, payable January 5, 2008.
	31	Determined that net income for the year was $440,000. The market price of the common stock on this date was $32.

Instructions
(a) Journalize the transactions. (Include entries to close net income to Retained Earnings.)
(b) Enter the beginning balances and post the entries to the stockholders' equity T accounts. (*Note:* Open additional stockholders' equity accounts as needed.)

(c) Tot. stockholders' equity
$2,534,000

(c) Prepare the stockholders' equity section of the balance sheet at December 31.
(d) Calculate the payout ratio and return on common stockholders' equity ratio.

Problems: Set C

Visit the book's website at **www.wiley.com/college/kimmel** and choose the Student Companion site to access Problem Set C.

Comprehensive Problem

CP11 Servo Corporation's balance sheet at December 31, 2006, is presented below.

SERVO CORPORATION
Balance Sheet
December 31, 2006

Cash	$ 24,600	Accounts payable	$ 25,600
Accounts receivable	45,500	Common stock ($10 par)	80,000
Allowance for doubtful		Retained earnings	127,400
accounts	(1,500)		$233,000
Supplies	4,400		
Land	40,000		
Building	142,000		
Accumulated depreciation-			
building	(22,000)		
	$233,000		

During 2007, the following transactions occurred.

1. On January 1, 2007, Servo issued 1,500 shares of $20 par, 7% preferred stock for $33,000.
2. On January 1, 2007, Servo also issued 600 shares of the $10 par value common stock for $21,000.
3. Servo performed services for $280,000 on account.
4. On April 1, 2007, Servo collected fees of $48,000 in advance for services to be performed from April 1, 2007, to March 31, 2008.
5. Servo collected $267,000 from customers on account.
6. Servo bought $30,100 of supplies on account.
7. Servo paid $32,200 on accounts payable.
8. Servo reacquired 400 shares of its common stock on June 1, 2007, for $38 per share.
9. Paid other operating expenses of $188,200.
10. On December 31, 2007, Servo declared the annual preferred stock dividend and a $1.20 per share dividend on the outstanding common stock, all payable on January 15, 2008.
11. An account receivable of $1,300 which originated in 2006 is written off as uncollectible.

Adjustment data:

1. A count of supplies indicates that $5,900 of supplies remain unused at year-end.
2. Recorded revenue earned from item 4 above.
3. The allowance for doubtful accounts should have a balance of $3,500 at year end.
4. Depreciation is recorded on the building on a straight-line basis based on a 30-year life and a salvage value of $10,000.
5. The income tax rate is 30%. (*Hint:* Prepare the income statement up to income before taxes and multiply by 30% to compute the amount.)

Instructions
(You may want to set up T accounts to determine ending balances.)

(a) Prepare journal entries for the transactions listed above and adjusting entries.
(b) Prepare an adjusted trial balance at December 31, 2007.
(c) Prepare an income statement and a retained earnings statement for the year ending December 31, 2007, and a classified balance sheet as of December 31, 2007.

(b) Totals $670,250

(c) Net income $64,050
Tot. assets $373,200

Continuing Cookie Chronicle

(*Note:* This is a continuation of the Cookie Chronicle from Chapters 1 through 10.)

CCC11

Part 1   Because Natalie has been so successful with Cookie Creations and Curtis has been just as successful with his coffee shop, they both conclude that they could benefit from each other's business expertise. Curtis and Natalie next evaluate the different types of business organization, and because of the advantage of limited personal liability, decide to form a new corporation.

Curtis has operated his coffee shop for 2 years. He buys coffee, muffins, and cookies from a local supplier. Natalie's business consists of giving cookie-making classes and selling fine European mixers. The plan is for Natalie to use the premises Curtis currently rents as a location for her cookie-making classes and demonstrations of the mixers that she sells. Natalie will also hire, train, and supervise staff hired to bake cookies and muffins sold in the coffee shop. By offering her classes on the premises, Natalie will save on travel, and the coffee shop will provide one central location for selling the mixers. Combining forces will also allow Natalie and Curtis to pool their resources and buy a few more assets to run their new business venture.

The current market values of the assets of both businesses are as follows.

Description	Curtis' Coffee	Cookie Creations
Cash	$ 7,500	$10,000
Accounts receivable	100	500
Merchandise inventory	450	1,130
Equipment	2,500	1,000
	$10,550	$12,630

Curtis and Natalie meet with a lawyer and form their corporation, called Cookie & Coffee Creations Inc., on November 1, 2007. The new corporation is authorized to issue 50,000 shares of $1 par common stock and 10,000 shares of no par, $6 cumulative preferred stock.

The assets held by each business will be transferred into the corporation at current market value of $1 per share. Curtis will receive 10,550 common shares, and Natalie will receive 12,630 common shares in the corporation.

Natalie and Curtis are very excited about this new business venture. They come to you with the following questions.

1. Curtis' Dad and Natalie's grandmother are interested in investing $5,000 each in the new business venture. Curtis and Natalie are considering issuing them preferred shares. What would be the advantage of issuing them preferred stock instead of common?
2. What would be the advantages and disadvantages of issuing cumulative preferred?
3. "Our lawyer sent us a bill for $750. When we talked the bill over with her, she said she would be willing to receive common stock in our corporation instead of cash. We would be happy to issue her stock, but we're worried about accounting for this transaction. Can we do this? If so, how do we determine how many shares to give her?"

Instructions
(a) Answer Natalie and Curtis' questions.
(b) Prepare the journal entries required on November 1, 2007, the date when Natalie and Curtis transfer the assets of their respective businesses into Cookie & Coffee Creations Inc.
(c) Assume that Cookie & Coffee Creations Inc. issues 1,000 $6 cumulative preferred shares to Curtis' Dad and the same number to Natalie's grandmother, in both cases for $5,000. Also assume that Cookie & Coffee Creations Inc. issues 750 common shares to its lawyer. Prepare the journal entries required for each of these transactions that also occurred on November 1.
(d) Prepare the opening balance sheet for Cookie & Coffee Creations Inc. as of November 1, 2007, including the journal entries in (b) and (c) above.

Part 2   After establishing their company's fiscal year-end to be October 31, Natalie and Curtis began operating Cookie & Coffee Creations Inc. on November 1, 2007. The company had the following selected transactions during its first year of operations, 2008.

Jan.   1   Issued an additional 500 preferred shares to Natalie's brother for $2,500 cash.

June 30   Repurchased 750 shares issued to the lawyer, for $500 cash. The lawyer had decided to retire and wanted to liquidate all of her assets.

Oct. 15   The company had a very successful first year of operations and as a result declared dividends of $25,000, payable November 15, 2008. (Indicate the amounts payable to the preferred stockholders and to the common stockholders.)

Oct. 31   The company earned revenues of $462,500 and incurred expenses of $406,500 (including the $750 legal expense from November 1 but excluding income tax). Record income tax expense, assuming the company has a 20% income tax rate.

Instructions
(a) Prepare the journal entries to record each of the above transactions.
(b) Prepare all of the closing entries required on October 31, 2008.
(c) Prepare the retained earnings statement for the year ended October 31, 2008.
(d) Prepare the stockholders' equity section of the balance sheet as of October 31, 2008.

(d) Tot. stockholders' equity
$55,730

BROADENING YOUR PERSPECTIVE

Financial Reporting and Analysis

FINANCIAL REPORTING PROBLEM: *Tootsie Roll Industries, Inc.*

BYP11-1   The stockholders' equity section of Tootsie Roll Industries' balance sheet is shown in the Consolidated Statement of Financial Position in Appendix A. You will also find data relative to this problem on other pages of Appendix A. (Note that Tootsie Roll has two classes of common stock. To answer the following questions, add the two classes of stock together.)

Instructions
Answer the following questions.
(a) What is the par or stated value per share of Tootsie Roll's common stock?
(b) What percentage of Tootsie Roll's authorized common stock was issued at December 31, 2004? (Round to the nearest full percent.)
(c) How many shares of common stock were outstanding at December 31, 2003, and at December 31, 2004?
(d) Calculate the payout ratio, earnings per share, and return on common stockholders' equity ratio for 2004.

COMPARATIVE ANALYSIS PROBLEM: *Tootsie Roll vs. Hershey Foods*

BYP11-2   The financial statements of Hershey Foods are presented in Appendix B, following the financial statements for Tootsie Roll in Appendix A.

Instructions
(a) Based on the information in these financial statements, compute the 2004 return on common stockholders' equity, debt to total assets ratio, and return on assets ratio for each company.
(b) What conclusions concerning the companies' profitability can be drawn from these ratios? Which company relies more on debt to boost its return to common shareholders?
(c) Compute the payout ratio for each company. Which pays out a higher percentage of its earnings?

RESEARCH CASE

BYP11-3 The May 2003 edition of *Strategic Finance* has an article by Alan Levinsohn titled "Does it Make Sense to Pay Dividends?"

Instructions
Read the article and answer the following questions.
(a) According to the author of the article, what are some potential benefits of paying dividends?
(b) What are some potential disadvantages of paying dividends?
(c) If a company has excess cash that it would like to distribute, what alternative exists to paying a dividend? Why might this alternative be preferred by some investors?
(d) What is meant by "double taxation of dividends," and what implications does this have for the choice that companies make between debt and equity financing?

INTERPRETING FINANCIAL STATEMENTS

BYP11-4 Marriott Corporation split into two companies: Host Marriott Corporation and Marriott International. Host Marriott retained ownership of the corporation's vast hotel and other properties, while Marriott International, rather than owning hotels, managed them. The purpose of this split was to free Marriott International from the "baggage" associated with Host Marriott, thus allowing it to be more aggressive in its pursuit of growth. The following information (in millions) is provided for each corporation for their first full year operating as independent companies.

	Host Marriott	Marriott International
Sales	$1,501	$8,415
Net income	(25)	200
Total assets	3,822	3,207
Total liabilities	3,112	2,440
Stockholders' equity	710	767

Instructions
(a) The two companies were split by the issuance of shares of Marriott International to all shareholders of the previous combined company. Discuss the nature of this transaction.
(b) Calculate the debt to total assets ratio for each company.
(c) Calculate the return on assets and return on common stockholders' equity ratios for each company.
(d) The company's debtholders were fiercely opposed to the original plan to split the two companies because the original plan had Host Marriott absorbing the majority of the company's debt. They relented only when Marriott International agreed to absorb a larger share of the debt. Discuss the possible reasons the debtholders were opposed to the plan to split the company.

BYP11-5 The January 25, 2005, edition of the *Wall Street Journal* has an article by Mary Kissel (on p. C1) titled "Known for Growth, Asian Firms Answer Call of the Dividend."

Instructions
Read the article and answer the following questions.
(a) What is the "dividend yield"? How does the dividend yield of Asian companies compare to that of companies in other regions?
(b) What has happened to Asian company debt levels in recent years? What implications has this had for return on equity? Explain why this would be the case.
(c) What measure is used to determine whether a company is paying out a high percentage of its earnings in the form of dividends? What percentage of their earnings are Asian firms paying out? According to the article, how have the stock prices of dividend-paying companies performed relative to non-dividend-paying companies? What explanations are given for this?

FINANCIAL ANALYSIS ON THE WEB

BYP11-6 *Purpose:* Use the stockholders' equity section of an annual report and identify the major components.

Address: **www.reportgallery.com** (or go to **www.wiley.com/college/kimmel**)

Steps
1. From Report Gallery Homepage, choose **Viewing Library**.
2. Select a particular company.
3. Choose **Annual Report**.
4. Follow instructions below.

Instructions
Answer the following questions.
(a) What is the company's name?
(b) What classes of capital stock has the company issued?
(c) For each class of stock:
    (1) How many shares are authorized, issued, and/or outstanding?
    (2) What is the par value?
(d) What are the company's retained earnings?
(e) Has the company acquired treasury stock? How many shares?

Critical Thinking

DECISION MAKING ACROSS THE ORGANIZATION

BYP11-7 In recent years the fast-food chain Wendy's International has purchased many treasury shares. From January 3, 1999, to December 30, 2001, the number of shares outstanding has fallen from 124 million to 105 million. The following information was drawn from the company's financial statements (in millions).

	Year ended	
	Dec. 30, 2001	**Jan. 3, 1999**
Net income	$ 193.6	$ 123.4
Total assets	2,076.0	1,837.9
Average total assets	2,016.9	1,889.8
Total common stockholders' equity	1,029.8	1,068.1
Average common stockholders' equity	1,078.0	1,126.2
Total liabilities	1,046.3	769.9
Average total liabilities	939.0	763.7
Interest expense	30.2	19.8
Income taxes	113.7	84.3
Cash provided by operations	305.2	233.8
Cash dividends paid on common stock	26.8	31.0
Preferred stock dividends	0	0
Average number of common shares outstanding	109.7	119.9

Instructions
Use the information provided to answer the following questions.
(a) Compute earnings per share, return on common stockholders' equity, and return on assets for both years. Discuss the change in the company's profitability over this period.
(b) Compute the dividend payout ratio. Also compute the average cash dividend paid per share of common stock (dividends paid divided by the average number of common shares outstanding). Discuss any change in these ratios during this period and the implications for the company's dividend policy.
(c) Compute the debt to total assets ratio and interest coverage ratio. Discuss the change in the company's solvency.
(d) Based on your findings in (a) and (c), discuss to what extent any change in the return on common stockholders' equity was the result of increased reliance on debt.
(e) Do the purchase of treasury stock and the shift toward more reliance on debt appear to have been wise strategic moves?

COMMUNICATION ACTIVITY

BYP11-8 Scott Kreiter, your uncle, is an inventor who has decided to incorporate. Uncle Scott knows that you are an accounting major at U.N.O. In a recent letter to you, he ends with the question, "I'm filling out a state incorporation application. Can you tell me the difference among the following terms: (1) authorized stock, (2) issued stock, (3) outstanding stock, and (4) preferred stock?"

Instructions

In a brief note, differentiate for Uncle Scott the four different stock terms. Write the letter to be friendly, yet professional.

ETHICS CASES

BYP11-9 The R&D division of Renew Corp. has just developed a chemical for sterilizing the vicious Brazilian "killer bees" which are invading Mexico and the southern United States. The president of Renew is anxious to get the chemical on the market because Renew profits need a boost—and his job is in jeopardy because of decreasing sales and profits. Renew has an opportunity to sell this chemical in Central American countries, where the laws are much more relaxed than in the United States.

The director of Renew's R&D division strongly recommends further research in the laboratory to test the side effects of this chemical on other insects, birds, animals, plants, and even humans. He cautions the president, "We could be sued from all sides if the chemical has tragic side effects that we didn't even test for in the lab." The president answers, "We can't wait an additional year for your lab tests. We can avoid losses from such lawsuits by establishing a separate wholly owned corporation to shield Renew Corp. from such lawsuits. We can't lose any more than our investment in the new corporation, and we'll invest just the patent covering this chemical. We'll reap the benefits if the chemical works and is safe, and avoid the losses from lawsuits if it's a disaster." The following week Renew creates a new wholly owned corporation called Offspring Inc., sells the chemical patent to it for $10, and watches the spraying begin.

Instructions
(a) Who are the stakeholders in this situation?
(b) Are the president's motives and actions ethical?
(c) Can Renew shield itself against losses of Offspring Inc.?

BYP11-10 Greenwood Corporation has paid 60 consecutive quarterly cash dividends (15 years). The last 6 months have been a real cash drain on the company, however, as profit margins have been greatly narrowed by increasing competition. With a cash balance sufficient to meet only day-to-day operating needs, the president, Gil Mailor, has decided that a stock dividend instead of a cash dividend should be declared. He tells Greenwood's financial vice-president, Vicki Lemke, to issue a press release stating that the company is extending its consecutive dividend record with the issuance of a 5% stock dividend. "Write the press release convincing the stockholders that the stock dividend is just as good as a cash dividend," he orders. "Just watch our stock rise when we announce the stock dividend; it must be a good thing if that happens."

Instructions
(a) Who are the stakeholders in this situation?
(b) Is there anything unethical about president Mailor's intentions or actions?
(c) What is the effect of a stock dividend on a corporation's stockholders' equity accounts? Which would you rather receive as a stockholder—a cash dividend or a stock dividend? Why?

Answers to Business Insight and Accounting across the Organization Questions
p. 537
Q: In addition to regulatory cost, what is another reason why some owners choose not to take their companies public?
A: One reason for being a private company is that managers then have more control over the company's future. For example, they can make decisions that they feel might be best for the company over the long-term, and not have to worry about the short-term stock price implications.

p. 542

Q: For stocks traded on organized stock exchanges, how are the dollar prices per share established? What factors might influence the price of shares in the marketplace?

A: The dollar prices per share are established by the interaction between buyers and sellers of the shares. The prices of shares are influenced by a company's earnings and dividends as well as by factors beyond a company's control, such as changes in interest rates, labor strikes, scarcity of supplies or resources, and politics. The number of willing buyers and sellers (demand and supply) also plays a part in the price of shares.

p. 545

Q: What signal might a large stock repurchase send to investors regarding management's belief about the company's growth opportunities?

A: When a company has many growth opportunities it will normally conserve its cash in order to be better able to fund expansion. A large use of cash to buy back stock (and essentially shrink the company) would suggest that management was not optimistic about its growth opportunities.

p. 550

Q: What factors must management consider in deciding how large a dividend to pay?

A: Management must consider the size of its retained earnings balance, the amount of available cash, its expected near-term cash needs, its growth opportunities, and what level of dividend it will be able to sustain based upon its expected future earnings.

Answer to Tootsie Roll Review It Question 3, p. 556

The cost of Tootsie Roll's treasury stock in 2004 was $1,992,000. It declared cash dividends of $14,547,000. The stock dividend reduced retained earnings by $57,358,000.

Answers to Self-Study Questions

1. c   2. b   3. d   4. c   5. d   6. d   7. b   8. a   9. c   10. b

CHAPTER **12**

Statement of Cash Flows

STUDY OBJECTIVES

After studying this chapter,
you should be able to:

1 Indicate the usefulness of the statement of cash flows.

2 Distinguish among operating, investing, and financing activities.

3 Explain the impact of the product life cycle on a company's cash flows.

4 Prepare a statement of cash flows using the indirect method.

5 Use the statement of cash flows to evaluate a company.

THE NAVIGATOR

THE NAVIGATOR

- Scan *Study Objectives*
- Read *Feature Story*
- Read *Preview*
- Read text and answer *Before You Go On*
  p. 590   p. 594   p. 602
  p. 609
- Work *Using the Decision Toolkit*
- Review *Summary of Study Objectives*
- Work *Demonstration Problem*
- Answer *Self-Study Questions*
- Complete *Assignments*

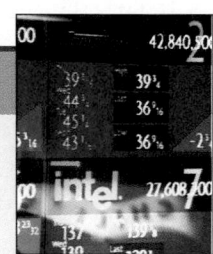

FEATURE STORY

Got Cash?

In today's environment, companies must be ready to respond to changes quickly in order to survive and thrive. They need to produce new products and expand into new markets continually. To do this takes cash—lots and lots of cash. Keeping lots of cash available is a real challenge for a young company. It requires careful cash management and attention to cash flow.

One company that managed cash successfully in its early years was Microsoft. During those years the company paid much of its payroll with stock options (rights to purchase company stock in the future at a given price) instead of cash. This strategy conserved cash, and turned more than a thousand of its employees into millionaires during the company's first 20 years of business.

In recent years Microsoft has had a different kind of cash problem. Now that it has reached a more "mature" stage in life, it generates so much cash—roughly $1 billion per month—that it cannot always figure out what to do with it. By 2004 Microsoft had accumulated $60 billion.

The company said it was accumulating cash to invest in new opportunities, buy other companies, and pay off pending lawsuits. But for years, the federal government has blocked attempts by Microsoft to buy anything other than small firms because it feared that purchase of a large firm would only increase Microsoft's monopolistic position. In addition, even the largest estimates of Microsoft's legal obligations related to pending lawsuits would use up only about $6 billion in cash.

Microsoft's stockholders have complained for years that holding all this cash was putting a drag on the company's profitability. Why? Because Microsoft had the cash invested in very low-yielding government securities. Stockholders felt that the company either should find new investment projects that would bring higher returns, or return some of the cash to stockholders.

Finally, in July 2004 Microsoft announced a plan to return cash to stockholders, by paying a special one-time $32 billion dividend in December 2004. This special dividend was so large that, according to the U.S. Commerce Department, it caused total personal income in the United States to rise by 3.7% in one month—the largest increase ever recorded by the agency. (It also made the holiday season brighter, especially for retailers in the Seattle area.) Microsoft also doubled its regular annual dividend to $3.50 per share. Further, it announced that it would spend another $30 billion over the next four years buying treasury stock. These actions will help to deplete some of its massive cash horde, but as you will see in this chapter, for a cash-generating machine like Microsoft, the company will be anything but cash-starved.

Source: "Business: An End to Growth? Microsoft's Cash Bonanza," *The Economist* (July 23, 2005), p. 61.

THE NAVIGATOR

On the World Wide Web
Microsoft: www.microsoft.com

PREVIEW OF CHAPTER 12

The balance sheet, income statement, and retained earnings statement do not always show the whole picture of the financial condition of a company or institution. In fact, looking at the financial statements of some well-known companies, a thoughtful investor might ask questions like these: How did Eastman Kodak finance cash dividends of $649 million in a year in which it earned only $17 million? How could United Airlines purchase new planes that cost $1.9 billion in a year in which it reported a net loss of over $2 billion? How did the companies that spent a combined fantastic $3.4 trillion on mergers and acquisitions in a recent year finance those deals? Answers to these and similar questions can be found in this chapter, which presents the statement of cash flows.

The content and organization of this chapter are as follows.

The Statement of Cash Flows: Usefulness and Format

The balance sheet, income statement, and retained earnings statement provide only limited information about a company's cash flows (cash receipts and cash payments). For example, comparative balance sheets show the increase in property, plant, and equipment during the year. But they do not show how the additions were financed or paid for. The income statement shows net income. But it does not indicate the amount of cash generated by operating activities. The retained earnings statement shows cash dividends declared but not the cash dividends paid during the year. None of these statements presents a detailed summary of where cash came from and how it was used.

USEFULNESS OF THE STATEMENT OF CASH FLOWS

The **statement of cash flows** reports the cash receipts, cash payments, and net change in cash resulting from operating, investing, and financing activities during a period. The information in a statement of cash flows should help investors, creditors, and others assess:

STUDY OBJECTIVE

1

Indicate the usefulness of the statement of cash flows.

1. **The entity's ability to generate future cash flows.** By examining relationships between items in the statement of cash flows, investors can make predictions of the amounts, timing, and uncertainty of future cash flows better than they can from accrual basis data.

2. **The entity's ability to pay dividends and meet obligations.** If a company does not have adequate cash, it cannot pay employees, settle debts, or pay dividends. Employees, creditors, and stockholders should be particularly interested in this statement, because it alone shows the flows of cash in a business.

3. **The reasons for the difference between net income and net cash provided (used) by operating activities.** Net income provides information on the success or failure of a business enterprise. However, some financial statement users are critical of accrual-basis net income because it requires many estimates. As a result, users often challenge the reliability of the number. Such is not the case with cash. Many readers of the statement of cash flows want to know the reasons for the difference between net income and net cash provided by operating activities. Then they can assess for themselves the reliability of the income number.

4. **The cash investing and financing transactions during the period.** By examining a company's investing and financing transactions, a financial statement reader can better understand why assets and liabilities changed during the period.

_E_THICS NOTE

Though we would discourage reliance on cash flows to the exclusion of accrual accounting, comparing cash from operations to net income can reveal important information about the "quality" of reported net income. Such a comparison can reveal the extent to which net income provides a good measure of actual performance.

CLASSIFICATION OF CASH FLOWS

The statement of cash flows classifies cash receipts and cash payments as operating, investing, and financing activities. Transactions and other events characteristic of each kind of activity are as follows.

STUDY OBJECTIVE

2

Distinguish among operating, investing, and financing activities.

1. **Operating activities** include the cash effects of transactions that create revenues and expenses. They thus enter into the determination of net income.

2. **Investing activities** include (a) acquiring and disposing of investments and property, plant, and equipment, and (b) lending money and collecting the loans.

3. **Financing activities** include (a) obtaining cash from issuing debt and repaying the amounts borrowed, and (b) obtaining cash from stockholders, repurchasing shares, and paying dividends.

The operating activities category is the most important. It shows the cash provided by company operations. This source of cash is generally considered to be the best measure of a company's ability to generate sufficient cash to continue as a going concern.

Illustration 12-1 (next page) lists typical cash receipts and cash payments within each of the three classifications. **Study the list carefully.** It will prove very useful in solving homework exercises and problems.

Illustration 12-1
Typical receipt and
payment classifications

**Operating
activities**

Investing activities

**Financing
activities**

Types of Cash Inflows and Outflows

Operating activities—Income statement items

Cash inflows:

From sale of goods or services.

From interest received and dividends received.

Cash outflows:

To suppliers for inventory.

To employees for services.

To government for taxes.

To lenders for interest.

To others for expenses.

Investing activities—Changes in investments and long-term assets

Cash inflows:

From sale of property, plant, and equipment.

From sale of investments in debt or equity securities of other entities.

From collection of principal on loans to other entities.

Cash outflows:

To purchase property, plant, and equipment.

To purchase investments in debt or equity securities of other entities.

To make loans to other entities.

**Financing activities—Changes in long-term liabilities and stockholders'
equity**

Cash inflows:

From sale of common stock.

From issuance of debt (bonds and notes).

Cash outflows:

To stockholders as dividends.

To redeem long-term debt or reacquire capital stock (treasury stock).

Note the following general guidelines:

1. Operating activities involve income statement items.
2. Investing activities involve cash flows resulting from changes in investments and long-term asset items.
3. Financing activities involve cash flows resulting from changes in long-term liability and stockholders' equity items.

Companies classify as operating activities some cash flows related to investing or financing activities. For example, receipts of investment revenue (interest and dividends) are classified as operating activities. So are payments of interest to lenders. Why are these considered operating activities? **Because companies report these items in the income statement, where results of operations are shown.**

SIGNIFICANT NONCASH ACTIVITIES

Not all of a company's significant activities involve cash. Examples of significant noncash activities are:

1. Direct issuance of common stock to purchase assets.
2. Conversion of bonds into common stock.
3. Direct issuance of debt to purchase assets.
4. Exchanges of plant assets.

Companies do not report in the body of the statement of cash flows significant financing and investing activities that do not affect cash. Instead, they report these activities in either a **separate schedule** at the bottom of the statement of cash flows or in a **separate note or supplementary schedule** to the financial statements. The reporting of these noncash activities in a separate schedule satisfies the **full disclosure principle**.

In solving homework assignments you should present significant noncash investing and financing activities in a separate schedule at the bottom of the statement of cash flows. (See the last entry in Illustration 12-2, at the bottom of this page, for an example.)

Helpful Hint Do not include **noncash** investing and financing activities in the body of the statement of cash flows. Report this information in a separate schedule.

Accounting across the Organization

Net income is not the same as net cash provided by operations. The differences are illustrated by the following results from annual reports for 2004 ($ in millions). Note the wide disparity among these companies that all engaged in retail merchandising.

Company	Net Income	Net Cash Provided by Operations
Kohl's Corporation	$ 730	$ 948
Wal-Mart Stores, Inc.	10,267	15,044
JCPenney Company, Inc.	524	61
Costco Wholesale Corp.	882	2,099
Target Corporation	3,198	3,195

 In general, why do differences exist between net income and net cash provided by operating activities?

FORMAT OF THE STATEMENT OF CASH FLOWS

The general format of the statement of cash flows presents the results of the three activities discussed previously—operating, investing, and financing—plus the significant noncash investing and financing activities. Illustration 12–2 shows a widely used form of the statement of cash flows.

Illustration 12-2
Format of statement of cash flows

COMPANY NAME		
Statement of Cash Flows		
Period Covered		
Cash flows from operating activities		
(List of individual items)	XX	
Net cash provided (used) by operating activities		XXX
Cash flows from investing activities		
(List of individual inflows and outflows)	XX	
Net cash provided (used) by investing activities		XXX
Cash flows from financing activities		
(List of individual inflows and outflows)	XX	
Net cash provided (used) by financing activities		XXX
Net increase (decrease) in cash		XXX
Cash at beginning of period		XXX
Cash at end of period		XXX
Noncash investing and financing activities		
(List of individual noncash transactions)		XXX

The cash flows from operating activities section always appears first, followed by the investing activities section and then the financing activities section.

BEFORE YOU GO ON . . .

▶ Review It

1. Why is the statement of cash flows useful?
2. What are the major classifications of cash flows on the statement of cash flows?
3. What are some examples of significant noncash activities?
4. What is the general format of the statement of cash flows? In what sequence are the three types of business activities presented?

▶ Do It

During its first week, Duffy & Stevenson Company had these transactions.
1. Issued 100,000 shares of $5 par value common stock for $800,000 cash.
2. Borrowed $200,000 from Castle Bank, signing a 5-year note bearing 8% interest.
3. Purchased two semi-trailer trucks for $170,000 cash.
4. Paid employees $12,000 for salaries and wages.
5. Collected $20,000 cash for services provided.

Classify each of these transactions by type of cash flow activity.

Action Plan

• Identify the three types of activities used to report all cash inflows and outflows.
• Report as operating activities the cash effects of transactions that create revenues and expenses and enter into the determination of net income.
• Report as investing activities transactions that (a) acquire and dispose of investments and productive long-lived assets and (b) lend money and collect loans.
• Report as financing activities transactions that (a) obtain cash from issuing debt and repay the amounts borrowed and (b) obtain cash from stockholders and pay them dividends.

Solution

1. Financing activity   4. Operating activity
2. Financing activity   5. Operating activity
3. Investing activity

THE CORPORATE LIFE CYCLE

STUDY OBJECTIVE

——— 3 ———

Explain the impact of the product life cycle on a company's cash flows.

All products go through a series of phases called the **product life cycle**. The phases (in order of their occurrence) are: **introductory phase**, **growth phase**, **maturity phase**, and **decline phase**. The introductory phase occurs at the beginning of a company's life, when it is purchasing fixed assets and beginning to produce and sell products. During the growth phase, the company is striving to expand its production and sales. In the maturity phase, sales and production level off. During the decline phase, sales of the product fall due to a weakening in consumer demand.

If a company had only one product and that product was nearing the end of its salable life, we could easily say that the company was in the decline phase. Companies generally have more than one product, however, and not all of a company's products are in the same phase of the product life cycle at the same time. Still, we can characterize a company as being in one of the four phases, because the majority of its products are in a particular phase.

Illustration 12-3 shows that the phase a company is in affects its cash flows. In the **introductory phase**, we expect that the company will not be generating positive cash from operations. That is, cash used in operations will exceed cash generated by operations in the introductory phase. Also, the company will be spending considerable amounts to purchase productive assets such as buildings and equipment. To support its asset purchases the company will have to issue stock or debt. Thus, during the introductory phase we expect cash from operations to be negative, cash from investing to be negative, and cash from financing to be positive.

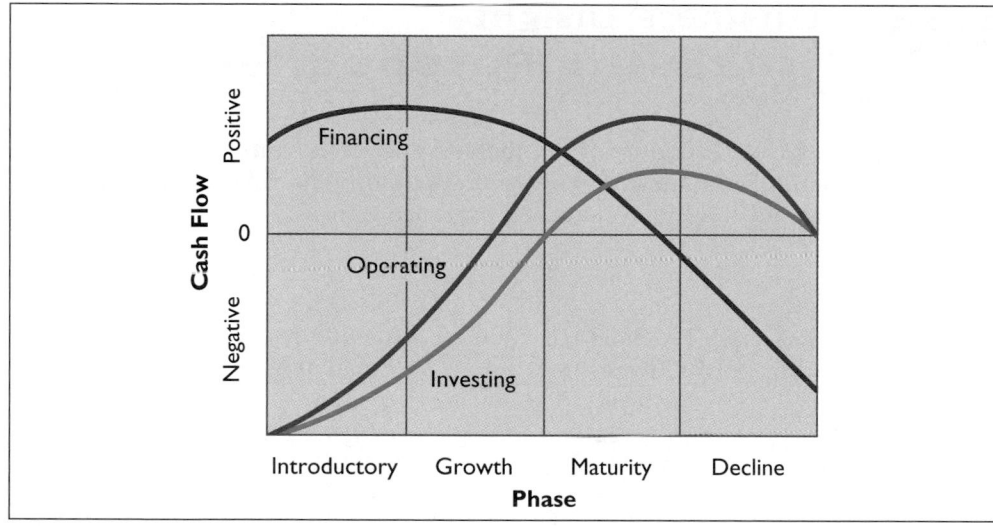

Illustration 12-3
Impact of product life cycle on cash flows

During the **growth phase**, we expect to see the company start to generate small amounts of cash from operations. During this phase, cash from operations on the statement of cash flows will be less than net income on the income statement. One reason income will exceed cash flow from operations during this period is explained by the difference between the cash paid for inventory and the amount expensed as cost of goods sold. Since the company projects increasing sales, the size of inventory purchases must increase. Thus, in the growth phase the company will expense less inventory on an accrual basis than it purchases on a cash basis. Also, collections on accounts receivable will lag behind sales, and accrual sales during a period will exceed cash collections during that period. Cash needed for asset acquisitions will continue to exceed cash provided by operations, requiring that the company make up the deficiency by issuing new stock or debt. Thus, in the growth phase, the company continues to show negative cash from investing and positive cash from financing.

During the **maturity phase**, cash from operations and net income are approximately the same. Cash generated from operations exceeds investing needs. Thus, in the maturity phase the company can actually start to pay dividends, retire debt, or buy back stock.

Finally, during the **decline phase**, cash from operations decreases. Cash from investing might actually become positive as the company sells off excess assets. Cash from financing may be negative as the company buys back stock and retires debt.

Consider Microsoft: During its early years it had significant product development costs and little revenue. Microsoft was lucky in that its agreement with IBM to provide the operating system for IBM PCs gave it an early steady source of cash to support growth. As noted in the Feature Story, one way Microsoft conserved cash was to pay employees with stock options rather than cash. Today Microsoft could best be characterized as being in the maturity phase. It continues to spend considerable amounts on research and development and investment in new assets. For the last three years, though its cash from operations has exceeded its net income. Also, cash from operations over this period exceeded cash used for investing, and common stock repurchased exceeded common stock issued. For Microsoft, as for any large company, the challenge is to maintain its growth. In the software industry, where products become obsolete very quickly, the challenge is particularly great.

Business Insight
Investor Perspective

Listed here are recent amounts of net income and cash from operations, investing, and financing for some well-known companies. The final column suggests their likely phase in the life cycle based on these figures.

Company ($ in millions)	Net Income	Cash Provided by Operations	Cash Provided (Used) by Investing	Cash Provided (Used) by Financing	Likely Phase in Life Cycle
Amazon.com	$ 588	$ 567	$ (318)	$ (97)	Growth
Real Networks Inc.	(21)	(9)	(22)	107	Introductory
United States Steel	1,091	1,400	(484)	(203)	Early decline
Kellogg	891	1,229	(270)	(716)	Early decline
Southwest Airlines	313	1,157	(1,850)	133	Early maturity
Starbucks	391	820	(659)	(67)	Late growth

 Why do companies have negative cash from operations during the introductory phase?

PREPARING THE STATEMENT OF CASH FLOWS

Companies prepare the statement of cash flows differently from the three other basic financial statements. First, it is not prepared from an adjusted trial balance. It requires detailed information concerning the changes in account balances that occurred between two points in time. An adjusted trial balance will not provide the necessary data. Second, the statement of cash flows deals with cash receipts and payments. As a result, the company **must adjust** the effects of the use of accrual accounting **to determine cash flows**.

The information to prepare this statement usually comes from three sources:

- **Comparative balance sheets.** Information in the comparative balance sheets indicates the amount of the changes in assets, liabilities, and stockholders' equities from the beginning to the end of the period.
- **Current income statement.** Information in this statement helps determine the amount of cash provided or used by operations during the period.

- **Additional information.** Such information includes transaction data that are needed to determine how cash was provided or used during the period.

Preparing the statement of cash flows from these data sources involves three major steps, explained in Illustration 12-4 below.

Step 1: Determine net cash provided/used by operating activities by converting net income from an accrual basis to a cash basis.

This step involves analyzing not only the current year's income statement but also comparative balance sheets and selected additional data.

Step 2: Analyze changes in noncurrent asset and liability accounts and record as investing and financing activities, or disclose as noncash transactions.

This step involves analyzing comparative balance sheet data and selected additional information for their effects on cash.

Step 3: Compare the net change in cash on the statement of cash flows with the change in the cash account reported on the balance sheet to make sure the amounts agree.

The difference between the beginning and ending cash balances can be easily computed from comparative balance sheets.

Illustration 12-4
Three major steps in preparing the statement of cash flows

INDIRECT AND DIRECT METHODS

In order to perform step 1, a company **must convert net income from an accrual basis to a cash basis**. This conversion may be done by either of two methods: (1) the indirect method or (2) the direct method. **Both methods arrive at the same total amount** for "Net cash provided by operating activities." They differ in **how** they arrive at the amount.

The **indirect method** adjusts net income for items that do not affect cash. A great majority of companies (98.8%) use this method, as shown in the nearby chart.[1] Companies favor the indirect method for two reasons: (1) It is easier and less costly to prepare, and (2) it focuses on the differences between net income and net cash flow from operating activities.

The **direct method** shows operating cash receipts and payments, making it more consistent with the objective of a statement of cash flows. The FASB has expressed a preference for the direct method, but allows the use of either method.

The next section illustrates the more popular indirect method. The appendix to this chapter illustrates the direct method.

Usage of Methods

98.8% Indirect Method

1.2% Direct Method

---

[1]*Accounting Trends and Techniques—2004* (New York: American Institute of Certified Public Accountants, 2004).

Business Insight
Investor Perspective

Analysts increasingly use cash-flow-based measures of income, such as cash flow provided by operations, instead of or in addition to net income. As more investors focus on cash flow from operations, and as some compensation contracts now have bonuses tied to cash-flow numbers, some managers have taken actions that artificially increase cash flow from operations. They do this by moving negative amounts out of the operating section and into the investing or financing section. For example, WorldCom, Inc. disclosed that it had improperly capitalized expenses: It had moved $3.8 billion of cash outflows from the "Cash from operating activities" section of the cash flow statement to the "Investing activities" section, thereby greatly enhancing cash provided by operating activities. Similarly, Dynegy, Inc. restated its cash flow statement because it had improperly included in operating activities, instead of in financing activities, $300 million from natural gas trading. The restatement resulted in a drop of 37% in cash flow from operations.

Source: Henny Sender, "Sadly, These Days Even Cash Flow Isn't Always What It Seems To Be," *Wall Street Journal Online* (May 8, 2002).

For what reasons might managers at WorldCom and at Dynegy take the actions noted above?

BEFORE YOU GO ON . . .

▶ Review It

1. What are the phases of the product life cycle, and how do they affect the statement of cash flows?
2. Based on its statement of cash flows, in what stage of the product life cycle is Tootsie Roll Industries? The answer to this question appears on page 643.
3. What are the three major steps in preparing a statement of cash flows?
4. What is the primary difference between the indirect and direct approaches to the statement of cash flows? Which method is more commonly used in practice?

THE NAVIGATOR

Preparation of the Statement of Cash Flows—Indirect Method

STUDY OBJECTIVE
4

Prepare a statement of cash flows using the indirect method.

To explain how to prepare a statement of cash flows using the indirect method, we use financial information from Computer Services Company. Illustration 12-5 (page 595) presents Computer Services' current and previous-year balance sheets, its current-year income statement, and related financial information.

COMPUTER SERVICES COMPANY
Comparative Balance Sheets
December 31

Assets	2007	2006	Change in Account Balance Increase/Decrease
Current assets			
Cash	$ 55,000	$ 33,000	$ 22,000 Increase
Accounts receivable	20,000	30,000	10,000 Decrease
Merchandise inventory	15,000	10,000	5,000 Increase
Prepaid expenses	5,000	1,000	4,000 Increase
Property, plant, and equipment			
Land	130,000	20,000	110,000 Increase
Building	160,000	40,000	120,000 Increase
Accumulated depreciation—building	(11,000)	(5,000)	6,000 Increase
Equipment	27,000	10,000	17,000 Increase
Accumulated depreciation—equipment	(3,000)	(1,000)	2,000 Increase
Total assets	$398,000	$138,000	
Liabilities and Stockholders' Equity			
Current liabilities			
Accounts payable	$ 28,000	$ 12,000	$ 16,000 Increase
Income tax payable	6,000	8,000	2,000 Decrease
Long-term liabilities			
Bonds payable	130,000	20,000	110,000 Increase
Stockholders' equity			
Common stock	70,000	50,000	20,000 Increase
Retained earnings	164,000	48,000	116,000 Increase
Total liabilities and stockholders' equity	$398,000	$138,000	

Illustration 12-5
Comparative balance sheets, income statement, and additional information for Computer Services Company

COMPUTER SERVICES COMPANY
Income Statement
For the Year Ended December 31, 2007

Revenues		$507,000
Cost of goods sold	$150,000	
Operating expenses (excluding depreciation)	111,000	
Depreciation expense	9,000	
Loss on sale of equipment	3,000	
Interest expense	42,000	315,000
Income before income tax		192,000
Income tax expense		47,000
Net income		$145,000

Additional information for 2007:
1. The company declared and paid a $29,000 cash dividend.
2. Issued $110,000 of long-term bonds in direct exchange for land.
3. A building costing $120,000 was purchased for cash. Equipment costing $25,000 was also purchased for cash.
4. The company sold equipment with a book value of $7,000 (cost $8,000, less accumulated depreciation $1,000) for $4,000 cash.
5. Issued common stock for $20,000 cash.
6. Depreciation expense was comprised of $6,000 for building and $3,000 for equipment.

We will now apply the three steps to the information provided for Computer Services Company.

STEP 1: OPERATING ACTIVITIES

DETERMINE NET CASH PROVIDED/USED BY OPERATING ACTIVITIES BY CONVERTING NET INCOME FROM AN ACCRUAL BASIS TO A CASH BASIS

To determine net cash provided by operating activities under the indirect method, companies **adjust net income in numerous ways**. A useful starting point is to understand **why** net income must be converted to net cash provided by operating activities.

Under generally accepted accounting principles, most companies use the accrual basis of accounting. As you have learned, this basis requires that companies record revenue when earned and record expenses when incurred. Earned revenues may include credit sales for which the company has not yet collected cash. Expenses incurred may include some items that it has not yet paid in cash. Thus, under the accrual basis of accounting, net income is not the same as net cash provided by operating activities.

Therefore, under the **indirect method**, companies must adjust net income to convert certain items to the cash basis. The indirect method (or reconciliation method) starts with net income and converts it to net cash provided by operating activities. Illustration 12-6 lists the three types of adjustments.

Illustration 12-6
Three types of adjustments to convert net income to net cash provided by operating activities

Net Income	+/−	Adjustments	=	Net Cash Provided/ Used by Operating Activities
		• **Add back noncash expenses**, such as depreciation expense, amortization, or depletion.		
		• **Deduct gains and add losses** that resulted from investing and financing activities.		
		• **Analyze changes** to noncash current asset and current liability accounts.		

We explain the three types of adjustments in the next three sections.

Depreciation Expense

Helpful Hint Depreciation is similar to any other expense in that it reduces net income. It differs in that it does not involve a current cash outflow; that is why it must be *added back* to net income to arrive at cash provided by operations.

Computer Services' income statement reports depreciation expense of $9,000. Although depreciation expense reduces net income, it does not reduce cash. In other words, depreciation expense is a noncash charge. The company must add it back to net income to arrive at net cash provided by operating activities. Computer Services reports depreciation expense as follows in the statement of cash flows.

Illustration 12-7
Adjustment for depreciation

Cash flows from operating activities	
Net income	$145,000
Adjustments to reconcile net income to net cash provided by operating activities:	
Depreciation expense	**9,000**
Net cash provided by operating activities	$154,000

As the first adjustment to net income in the statement of cash flows, companies frequently list depreciation and similar noncash charges such as amortization of intangible assets, depletion expense, and bad debt expense.

Loss on Sale of Equipment

Illustration 12-1 states that the investing activities section should report cash received from the sale of plant assets. Because of this, **companies must eliminate from net income all gains and losses, to arrive at cash provided by operating activities**.

In our example, Computer Services' income statement reports a $3,000 loss on the sale of equipment (book value $7,000, less cash received from sale of equipment $4,000). The company's loss of $3,000 should not be included in the operating activities section of the statement of cash flows. Illustration 12-8 shows that the $3,000 loss is eliminated by adding $3,000 back to net income to arrive at net cash provided by operating activities.

Cash flows from operating activities		
Net income		$145,000
Adjustments to reconcile net income to net cash provided by operating activities:		
Depreciation expense	$9,000	
Loss on sale of equipment	**3,000**	12,000
Net cash provided by operating activities		$157,000

Illustration 12-8
Adjustment for loss on sale of equipment

If a gain on sale occurs, the company deducts the gain from its net income in order to determine net cash provided by operating activities. **In the case of either a gain or a loss, companies report as a source of cash in the investing activities section of the statement of cash flows the actual amount of cash received from the sale.**

Changes to Noncash Current Asset and Current Liability Accounts

A final adjustment in reconciling net income to net cash provided by operating activities involves examining all changes in current asset and current liability accounts. The accrual accounting process records revenues in the period earned and expenses in the period incurred. For example, companies use Accounts Receivable to record amounts owed to the company for sales that have been made but for which cash collections have not yet been received. They use the Prepaid Insurance account to reflect insurance that has been paid for, but which has not yet expired, and therefore has not been expensed. Similarly, the Salaries Payable account reflects salaries expense that has been incurred by the company but has not been paid.

As a result, we need to adjust net income for these accruals and prepayments to determine net cash provided by operating activities. Thus we must analyze the change in each current asset and current liability account to determine its impact on net income and cash.

CHANGES IN NONCASH CURRENT ASSETS.   The adjustments required for changes in noncash current asset accounts are as follows: **Deduct from net income increases in current asset accounts, and add to net income decreases in current asset accounts, to arrive at net cash provided by operating activities.** We can observe these relationships by analyzing the accounts of Computer Services Company.

DECREASE IN ACCOUNTS RECEIVABLE. Computer Services Company's accounts receivable decreased by $10,000 (from $30,000 to $20,000) during the period. For Computer Services this means that cash receipts were $10,000 higher than revenues. The Accounts Receivable account in Illustration 12-9 shows that Computer Services Company had $507,000 in revenues (as reported on the income statement), but it collected $517,000 in cash. As shown in Illustration 12-10, to adjust net income to net cash provided by operating activities, the company adds to net income the decrease of $10,000 in accounts receivable.

Illustration 12-9
Analysis of accounts receivable

Accounts Receivable				
1/1/07	Balance	30,000	**Receipts from customers**	**517,000**
	Revenues	**507,000**		
12/31/07	Balance	20,000		

When the Accounts Receivable balance increases, cash receipts are lower than revenue earned under the accrual basis. Therefore, the company deducts from net income the amount of the increase in accounts receivable, to arrive at net cash provided by operating activities.

INCREASE IN MERCHANDISE INVENTORY. Computer Services' Company's Merchandise Inventory balance increased $5,000 (from $10,000 to $15,000) during the period. The change in the Merchandise Inventory account reflects the difference between the amount of inventory purchased and the amount sold. For Computer Services this means that the cost of merchandise purchased exceeded the cost of goods sold by $5,000. As a result, cost of goods sold does not reflect $5,000 of cash payments made for merchandise. The company deducts from net income this inventory increase of $5,000 during the period, to arrive at net cash provided by operating activities (see Illustration 12-10). If inventory decreases, the company adds to net income the amount of the change, to arrive at net cash provided by operating activities.

INCREASE IN PREPAID EXPENSES. Computer Services' prepaid expenses increased during the period by $4,000. This means that cash paid for expenses is higher than expenses reported on an accrual basis. In other words, the company has made cash payments in the current period, but will not charge expenses to income until future periods (as charges to the income statement). To adjust net income to net cash provided by operating activities, the company deducts from net income the $4,000 increase in prepaid expenses (see Illustration 12-10).

Illustration 12-10
Adjustments for changes in current asset accounts

Cash flows from operating activities		
Net income		$145,000
Adjustments to reconcile net income to net cash provided by operating activities:		
Depreciation expense	$ 9,000	
Loss on sale of equipment	3,000	
Decrease in accounts receivable	**10,000**	
Increase in merchandise inventory	**(5,000)**	
Increase in prepaid expenses	**(4,000)**	13,000
Net cash provided by operating activities		$158,000

If prepaid expenses decrease, reported expenses are higher than the expenses paid. Therefore, the company adds to net income the decrease in prepaid expense, to arrive at net cash provided by operating activities.

CHANGES IN CURRENT LIABILITIES. The adjustments required for changes in current liability accounts are as follows: **Add to net income increases in current liability accounts, and deduct from net income decreases in current liability accounts, to arrive at net cash provided by operating activities.**

INCREASE IN ACCOUNTS PAYABLE. For Computer Services Company, Accounts Payable increased by $16,000 (from $12,000 to $28,000) during the period. That means the company received $16,000 more in goods than it actually paid for. As shown in Illustration 12-11 (below), to adjust net income to determine net cash provided by operating activities, the company adds to net income the $16,000 increase in Accounts Payable.

DECREASE IN INCOME TAXES PAYABLE. When a company incurs income tax expense but has not yet paid its taxes, it records income tax payable. A change in the Income Tax Payable account reflects the difference between income tax expense incurred and income tax actually paid. Computer Services' Income Tax Payable account decreased by $2,000. That means the $47,000 of income tax expense reported on the income statement was $2,000 less than the amount of taxes paid during the period of $49,000. As shown in Illustration 12-11, to adjust net income to a cash basis, the company must reduce net income by $2,000.

Cash flows from operating activities		
Net income		$145,000
Adjustments to reconcile net income to net cash provided by operating activities:		
Depreciation expense	$ 9,000	
Loss on sale of equipment	3,000	
Decrease in accounts receivable	10,000	
Increase in merchandise inventory	(5,000)	
Increase in prepaid expenses	(4,000)	
Increase in accounts payable	**16,000**	
Decrease in income tax payable	**(2,000)**	27,000
Net cash provided by operating activities		$172,000

Illustration 12-11
Adjustments for changes in current liability accounts

Illustration 12-11 shows that, after starting with net income of $145,000, the sum of all of the adjustments to net income was $27,000. This resulted in net cash provided by operating activities of $172,000.

SUMMARY OF CONVERSION TO NET CASH PROVIDED BY OPERATING ACTIVITIES—INDIRECT METHOD

As shown in the previous illustrations, the statement of cash flows prepared by the indirect method starts with net income. It then adds or deducts items to arrive at net cash provided by operating activities. The required adjustments are of three types:

1. Noncash charges such as depreciation, amortization, and depletion.
2. Gains and losses on the sale of plant assets.
3. Changes in noncash current asset and current liability accounts.

Illustration 12-12 (page 600) provides a summary of these changes.

Illustration 12-12
Adjustments required to
convert net income to net
cash provided by
operating activities

		Adjustment Required to Convert Net Income to Net Cash Provided by Operating Activities
Noncash charges	Depreciation expense	Add
	Patent amortization expense	Add
	Depletion expense	Add
Gains and losses	Loss on sale of plant asset	Add
	Gain on sale of plant asset	Deduct
Changes in current assets and current liabilities	Increase in current asset account	Deduct
	Decrease in current asset account	Add
	Increase in current liability account	Add
	Decrease in current liability account	Deduct

Accounting across the Organization

Market share matters—and it shows up in the accounting numbers. Just ask General Motors (GM). In recent years GM has seen its market share erode until, at 25.6% of the market, the company reached the point where it actually consumes more cash than it generates. It isn't time to panic yet—GM has about $20 billion in cash on hand—but it is time to come up with a plan.

To address immediate cash needs, GM management may be forced to quit paying its $1.1 billion annual dividend, and it may sell off some assets and businesses. But in the long term, GM must either increase its market share or shrink its operations to fit its sales figures. The following table shows net income and cash provided by operating activities at various market-share levels.

Data: Merrill Lynch & Co.

**Net income and cash flow figures in billions of dollars, including GMAC.

* Assumes overall North American car sales hold steady at a 16.9 million vehicle annual rate.

Source: David Welch and Dan Beucke, "Why GM's Plan Won't Work," *Business Week* (May 9, 2005), pp. 85–93.

 Why does GM's cash provided by operating activities drop so precipitously when the company's sales figures decline?

STEP 2: INVESTING AND FINANCING ACTIVITIES

ANALYZE CHANGES IN NONCURRENT ASSET AND LIABILITY ACCOUNTS AND RECORD AS INVESTING AND FINANCING ACTIVITIES, OR AS NONCASH INVESTING AND FINANCING ACTIVITIES

INCREASE IN LAND. As indicated from the change in the Land account and the additional information, the company purchased land of $110,000 through the issuance of long-term bonds. The issuance of bonds payable for land has no effect on cash. But it is a significant noncash investing and financing activity that merits disclosure in a separate schedule. (See Illustration 12–14 on next page.)

INCREASE IN BUILDING. As the additional data indicate, Computer Services Company acquired an office building for $120,000 cash. This is a cash outflow reported in the investing section. (See Illustration 12–14 on next page.)

INCREASE IN EQUIPMENT. The Equipment account increased $17,000. The additional information explains that this was a net increase that resulted from two transactions: (1) a purchase of equipment of $25,000, and (2) the sale for $4,000 of equipment costing $8,000. These transactions are investing activities. The company should report each transaction separately. Thus it reports the purchase of equipment as an outflow of cash for $25,000. It reports the sale as an inflow of cash for $4,000. The T account below shows the reasons for the change in this account during the year.

Helpful Hint The investing and financing activities are measured and reported the same under both the direct and indirect methods.

Illustration 12-13
Analysis of equipment

Equipment		
1/1/07 Balance	10,000	Cost of equipment sold 8,000
Purchase of equipment 25,000		
12/31/07 Balance	27,000	

Cash Flows
+4,000

The following entry shows the details of the equipment sale transaction.

Cash	4,000	
Accumulated Depreciation	1,000	
Loss on Sale of Equipment	3,000	
Equipment		8,000

A	=	L	+	SE
+4,000				
+1,000				
				−3,000 Exp
−8,000				

INCREASE IN BONDS PAYABLE. The Bonds Payable account increased $110,000. As indicated in the additional information, the company acquired land from the issuance of these bonds. It reports this noncash transaction in a separate schedule at the bottom of the statement.

Helpful Hint When companies issue stocks or bonds for cash, the actual proceeds will appear in the statement of cash flows as a financing inflow (rather than the par value of the stocks or face value of bonds).

INCREASE IN COMMON STOCK. The balance sheet reports an increase in Common Stock of $20,000. The additional information section notes that this increase resulted from the issuance of new shares of stock. This is a cash inflow reported in the financing section.

INCREASE IN RETAINED EARNINGS. Retained earnings increased $116,000 during the year. This increase can be explained by two factors: (1) Net income of $145,000 increased retained earnings. (2) Dividends of $29,000 decreased retained earnings. The company adjusts net income to net cash provided by operating activities in the operating activities section. Payment of the dividends (not the declaration) is a **cash outflow that the company reports as a financing activity**.

Statement of Cash Flows—2007

Using the previous information, we can now prepare a statement of cash flows for 2007 for Computer Services Company as shown in Illustration 12-14.

Illustration 12-14
Statement of cash flows, 2007—indirect method

Helpful Hint Note that in the investing and financing activities sections, positive numbers indicate cash inflows (receipts), and negative numbers indicate cash outflows (payments).

COMPUTER SERVICES COMPANY Statement of Cash Flows—Indirect Method For the Year Ended December 31, 2007		
Cash flows from operating activities		
Net income		$ 145,000
Adjustments to reconcile net income to net cash		
provided by operating activities:		
Depreciation expense	$ 9,000	
Loss on sale of equipment	3,000	
Decrease in accounts receivable	10,000	
Increase in merchandise inventory	(5,000)	
Increase in prepaid expenses	(4,000)	
Increase in accounts payable	16,000	
Decrease in income tax payable	(2,000)	27,000
Net cash provided by operating activities		172,000
Cash flows from investing activities		
Purchase of building	(120,000)	
Purchase of equipment	(25,000)	
Sale of equipment	4,000	
Net cash used by investing activities		(141,000)
Cash flows from financing activities		
Issuance of common stock	20,000	
Payment of cash dividends	(29,000)	
Net cash used by financing activities		(9,000)
Net increase in cash		22,000
Cash at beginning of period		33,000
Cash at end of period		$ 55,000
Noncash investing and financing activities		
Issuance of bonds payable to purchase land		$ 110,000

STEP 3: NET CHANGE IN CASH

COMPARE THE NET CHANGE IN CASH ON THE STATEMENT OF CASH FLOWS WITH THE CHANGE IN THE CASH ACCOUNT REPORTED ON THE BALANCE SHEET TO MAKE SURE THE AMOUNTS AGREE

Illustration 12-14 indicates that the net change in cash during the period was an increase of $22,000. This agrees with the change in Cash account reported on the balance sheet in Illustration 12-5 (page 595).

BEFORE YOU GO ON . . .

▶ **Review It**

1. What is the format of the operating activities section of the statement of cash flows using the indirect method?
2. Where is depreciation expense shown on a statement of cash flows using the indirect method?
3. Where are significant noncash investing and financing activities shown in a statement of cash flows? Give some examples.

▶ Do It

Presented below is information related to Reynolds Company. Use it to prepare a statement of cash flows using the indirect method.

REYNOLDS COMPANY
Comparative Balance Sheets
December 31

Assets	2007	2006	Change Increase/Decrease
Cash	$ 54,000	$ 37,000	$ 17,000 Increase
Accounts receivable	68,000	26,000	42,000 Increase
Inventories	54,000	–0–	54,000 Increase
Prepaid expenses	4,000	6,000	2,000 Decrease
Land	45,000	70,000	25,000 Decrease
Buildings	200,000	200,000	–0–
Accumulated depreciation—buildings	(21,000)	(11,000)	10,000 Increase
Equipment	193,000	68,000	125,000 Increase
Accumulated depreciation—equipment	(28,000)	(10,000)	18,000 Increase
Totals	$569,000	$386,000	

Liabilities and Stockholders' Equity			
Accounts payable	$ 23,000	$ 40,000	$ 17,000 Decrease
Accrued expenses payable	10,000	–0–	10,000 Increase
Bonds payable	110,000	150,000	40,000 Decrease
Common stock ($1 par)	220,000	60,000	160,000 Increase
Retained earnings	206,000	136,000	70,000 Increase
Totals	$569,000	$386,000	

REYNOLDS COMPANY
Income Statement
For the Year Ended December 31, 2007

Revenues		$890,000
Cost of goods sold	$465,000	
Operating expenses	221,000	
Interest expense	12,000	
Loss on sale of equipment	2,000	700,000
Income before income taxes		190,000
Income tax expense		65,000
Net income		$125,000

Additional information:
1. Operating expenses include depreciation expense of $33,000 and charges from prepaid expenses of $2,000.
2. Land was sold at its book value for cash.
3. Cash dividends of $55,000 were declared and paid in 2007.
4. Interest expense of $12,000 was paid in cash.
5. Equipment with a cost of $166,000 was purchased for cash. Equipment with a cost of $41,000 and a book value of $36,000 was sold for $34,000 cash.
6. Bonds of $10,000 were redeemed at their book value for cash. Bonds of $30,000 were converted into common stock.
7. Common stock ($1 par) of $130,000 was issued for cash.
8. Accounts payable pertain to merchandise suppliers.

Action Plan

- Determine net cash provided/used by operating activities by adjusting net income for items that did not affect cash.
- Determine net cash provided/used by investing activities and financing activities.
- Determine the net increase/decrease in cash.

Solution

REYNOLDS COMPANY Statement of Cash Flows—Indirect Method For the Year Ended December 31, 2007		
Cash flows from operating activities		
Net income		$ 125,000
Adjustments to reconcile net income to net cash provided by operating activities:		
Depreciation expense	$ 33,000	
Loss on sale of equipment	2,000	
Increase in accounts receivable	(42,000)	
Increase in inventories	(54,000)	
Decrease in prepaid expenses	2,000	
Decrease in accounts payable	(17,000)	
Increase in accrued expenses payable	10,000	(66,000)
Net cash provided by operating activities		59,000
Cash flows from investing activities		
Sale of land	25,000	
Sale of equipment	34,000	
Purchase of equipment	(166,000)	
Net cash used by investing activities		(107,000)
Cash flows from financing activities		
Redemption of bonds	(10,000)	
Sale of common stock	130,000	
Payment of dividends	(55,000)	
Net cash provided by financing activities		65,000
Net increase in cash		17,000
Cash at beginning of period		37,000
Cash at end of period		$ 54,000
Noncash investing and financing activities		
Conversion of bonds into common stock		$ 30,000

Using Cash Flows to Evaluate a Company

Traditionally, investors and creditors have most commonly used ratios based on accrual accounting. These days, cash-based ratios are gaining increased acceptance among analysts. In this section we review free cash flow and introduce two new measures.

FREE CASH FLOW

In the statement of cash flows, cash provided by operating activities is intended to indicate the cash-generating capability of the company. Analysts have noted, however, that **cash provided by operating activities fails to take into account that a company must invest in new fixed assets** just to maintain its current level of operations. Companies also must at least **maintain dividends at current**

levels to satisfy investors. As we discussed in Chapter 2, the measurement of free cash flow provides additional insight regarding a company's cash-generating ability. **Free cash flow** describes the cash remaining from operations after adjustment for capital expenditures and dividends.

Consider the following example: Suppose that MPC produced and sold 10,000 personal computers this year. It reported $100,000 cash provided by operating activities. In order to maintain production at 10,000 computers, MPC invested $15,000 in equipment. It chose to pay $5,000 in dividends. Its free cash flow was $80,000 ($100,000 − $15,000 − $5,000). The company could use this $80,000 either to purchase new assets to expand the business or to pay an $80,000 dividend and continue to produce 10,000 computers. In practice, free cash flow is often calculated with the formula in Illustration 12-15. Alternative definitions also exist.

$$\text{Free Cash Flow} = \text{Cash Provided by Operations} - \text{Capital Expenditures} - \text{Cash Dividends}$$

Illustration 12-15 Free cash flow

Illustration 12-16 provides basic information excerpted from the 2004 statement of cash flows of Microsoft Corporation.

MICROSOFT CORPORATION
Statement of Cash Flows (partial)
2004

Cash provided by operations		$14,626
Cash flows from investing activities		
Additions to property and equipment	$ (1,109)	
Purchases of investments	(92,495)	
Sales of investments	85,302	
Acquisitions of companies	(4)	
Maturities of investments	5,561	
Cash used by investing activities		(2,745)
Cash paid for dividends		(1,729)

Illustration 12-16 Microsoft cash flow information ($ in millions)

Microsoft's free cash flow is calculated as shown in Illustration 12-17.

Cash provided by operating activities	$14,626
Less: Expenditures on property, plant, and equipment	1,109
Dividends paid	1,729
Free cash flow	$11,788

Illustration 12-17 Calculation of Microsoft's free cash flow ($ in millions)

This is a tremendous amount of cash generated in a single year. It is available for the acquisition of new assets, the retirement of stock or debt, or the payment of dividends. Also note that this amount far exceeds Microsoft's 2004 net income of $8,168 million. This lends additional credibility to Microsoft's income number as an indicator of potential future performance. If anything, Microsoft's net income might understate its actual performance.

Oracle Corporation is one of the world's largest sellers of database software and information management services. Like Microsoft, its success depends on continuing to improve its existing products while developing new products to keep pace with rapid changes in technology. Oracle's free cash flow for 2004 was $2,988 million. This is impressive, but significantly less than Microsoft's amazing ability to generate cash.

Decision Toolkit

Decision Checkpoints	Info Needed for Decision	Tool to Use for Decision	How to Evaluate Results
How much cash did the company generate to either expand operations or pay dividends?	Cash provided by operating activities, cash spent on fixed assets, and cash dividends	Free cash flow = Cash provided by operations − Capital expenditures − Cash dividends	Significant free cash flow indicates greater potential to finance new investment and pay additional dividends.

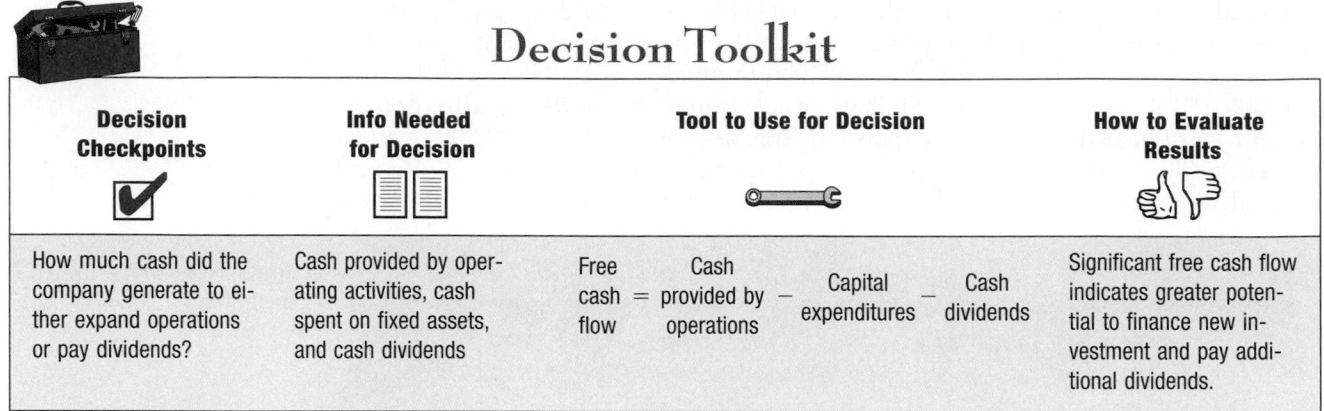

Business Insight
Investor Perspective

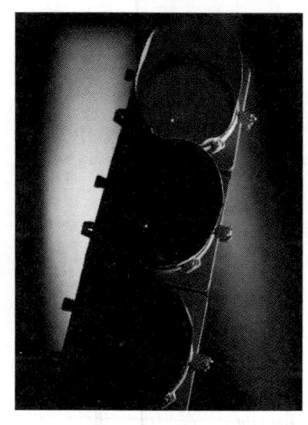

Investors and analysts are placing increasing emphasis on the statement of cash flows. As one person put it, "If you really want to put the quality of a company's earnings to the test, you need to examine the cash flow statement, too."

Here are some tips from the pros. David Zion, a Bear Stearns accounting analyst, says that you should compare net income with net cash flow from operating activities: "Generally, the closer a ratio of these numbers is to one, the higher-quality the earnings." Howard Schilit, of the Center for Financial Research and Analysis, says to compare the growth rate of net income with the growth rate of cash from operating activities. He says that if the two normally increase at similar rates, but now cash suddenly lags, "it's a terrific early warning sign."

Source: Anne Tergesen, "The Ins and Outs of Cash Flow," *Business Week* (January 22, 2001), pp. 102–103.

 If the ratio of net income to cash from operations differs significantly from 1, does that always mean that a company has poor-quality earnings?

ASSESSING LIQUIDITY AND SOLVENCY USING CASH FLOWS

Previous chapters have presented ratios used to analyze a company's liquidity and solvency. Many of those ratios used accrual-based numbers from the income statement and balance sheet. In this section we focus on ratios that are *cash-based* rather than accrual-based. That is, instead of using numbers from the income statement, these ratios use numbers from the statement of cash flows.

As discussed earlier, many analysts are critical of accrual-based numbers because they feel that the adjustment process allows too much management discretion. These analysts like to supplement accrual-based analysis with measures that use the cash flow statement. One disadvantage of these cash-based measures is that, unlike the more commonly employed accrual-based measures, there are no readily available industry averages for comparison. In the following discussion we use cash flow-based ratios to analyze Microsoft. In addition to the cash flow information provided in Illustration 12-16, we need the following information related to Microsoft.

($ in millions)	2004	2003
Current liabilities	$14,969	$13,974
Total liabilities	17,564	16,820

Liquidity

Liquidity is the ability of a business to meet its immediate obligations. You learned (in Chapter 2) that one measure of liquidity is the *current ratio*: current assets divided by current liabilities. A disadvantage of the current ratio is that it uses year-end balances of current asset and current liability accounts. These year-end balances may not be representative of the company's position during most of the year.

A ratio that partially corrects this problem is the **current cash debt coverage ratio**. It is computed as cash provided by operating activities divided by average current liabilities. Because cash provided by operating activities involves the entire year rather than a balance at one point in time, this ratio is often considered a better representation of liquidity on the average day. In general, a value below .40 times is cause for additional investigation of a company's liquidity.

Illustration 12-18 shows the current cash debt coverage ratio for Microsoft, with comparative numbers for Oracle. For comparative purposes, we have also provided each company's current ratio.

Illustration 12-18 Current cash debt coverage ratio

$$\text{Current Cash Debt Coverage Ratio} = \frac{\text{Cash Provided by Operations}}{\text{Average Current Liabilities}}$$

	Current cash debt coverage ratio	Current ratio
Microsoft ($ in millions)	$\dfrac{\$14,626}{(\$14,969 + \$13,974)/2} = 1.01$ times	4.71:1
Oracle	.75 times	2.65:1

Microsoft's net cash provided by operating activities is approximately equal to its average current liabilities. Oracle's ratio of .75 times, though not a cause for concern, is 26% lower than that of Microsoft. Keep in mind that Microsoft's cash position is extraordinary. For example, many large companies now have current ratios in the range of 1.0. By this standard, Oracle's current ratio of 2.65:1 and Microsoft's current ratio of 4.71:1 are both very strong.

Decision Toolkit

Decision Checkpoints	Info Needed for Decision	Tool to Use for Decision	How to Evaluate Results
Is the company generating sufficient cash provided by operating activities to meet its current obligations?	Cash provided by operating activities and average current liabilities	Current cash debt coverage ratio $= \dfrac{\text{Cash provided by operations}}{\text{Average current liabilities}}$	A high value suggests good liquidity. Since the numerator contains a "flow" measure, it provides a good supplement to the current ratio.

Solvency

Solvency is the ability of a company to survive over the long term. A measure of solvency that uses cash figures is the **cash debt coverage ratio**. It is computed as the ratio of cash provided by operating activities to total debt as represented by average total liabilities. This ratio indicates a company's ability to repay its liabilities from cash generated from operations—that is, without having to liquidate productive assets such as property, plant, and equipment. A general rule of thumb is that a cash debt coverage ratio below .20 times is cause for additional investigation.

Illustration 12-19 shows the cash debt coverage ratios for Microsoft and Oracle for 2004. For comparative purposes, we have also provided the debt to total assets ratios for each company.

Illustration 12-19 Cash debt coverage ratio

$$\text{Cash Debt Coverage Ratio} = \frac{\text{Cash Provided by Operations}}{\text{Average Total Liabilities}}$$

	Cash debt coverage ratio	Debt to total assets ratio
Microsoft ($ in millions)	$\dfrac{\$14,626}{(\$17,564 + \$16,820)/2} = .85$ times	19%
Oracle	.66 times	38%

Microsoft has few long-term obligations. Thus, its cash debt coverage ratio is similar to its current cash debt coverage ratio. Obviously, Microsoft is very solvent. Oracle has some long-term debt with a debt to total assets ratio of 38%. Its cash debt coverage ratio of .66 times is three-fourths as strong as Microsoft's. Neither the cash nor accrual measures suggest any cause for concern for either company.

Decision Toolkit

Decision Checkpoints	Info Needed for Decision	Tool to Use for Decision	How to Evaluate Results
✔️			
Is the company generating sufficient cash provided by operating activities to meet its long-term obligations?	Cash provided by operating activities and average total liabilities	Cash debt coverage ratio $= \dfrac{\text{Cash provided by operations}}{\text{Average total liabilities}}$	A high value suggests the company is solvent; that is, it will meet its obligations in the long term.

BEFORE YOU GO ON . . .

▶ Review It

1. What is the difference between cash from operations and free cash flow?
2. What does it mean if a company has negative free cash flow?
3. Why might an analyst want to supplement accrual-based ratios with cash-based ratios? What are some cash-based ratios?

✓ THE NAVIGATOR

Using the Decision Toolkit

Intel Corporation is the leading producer of computer chips for personal computers. It makes the hugely successful Pentium chip. Its primary competitor is AMD (formerly Advanced Micro Devices). The two are vicious competitors, with frequent lawsuits filed between them. Financial statement data for Intel are provided below.

Instructions
Calculate the following cash-based measures for Intel, and compare them with the data for AMD provided on page 610.

1. Free cash flow.
2. Current cash debt coverage ratio.
3. Cash debt coverage ratio.

INTEL CORPORATION Balance Sheets December 31, 2004 and 2003 (in millions)		
Assets	**2004**	**2003**
Current assets	$24,058	$22,882
Noncurrent assets	24,085	24,261
Total assets	$48,143	$47,143
Liabilities and Stockholders' Equity		
Current liabilities	$ 8,006	$ 6,879
Long-term liabilities	1,558	2,418
Total liabilities	9,564	9,297
Stockholders' equity	38,579	37,846
Total liabilities and stockholders' equity	$48,143	$47,143

INTEL CORPORATION Income Statements For the Years Ended December 31, 2004 and 2003 (in millions)		
	2004	**2003**
Net revenues	$34,209	$ 30,141
Expenses	26,693	24,500
Net income	$ 7,516	$ 5,641

INTEL CORPORATION Statements of Cash Flows For the Years Ended December 31, 2004 and 2003 (in millions)		
	2004	**2003**
Net cash provided by operating activities	$ 13,119	$ 11,515
Net cash used for investing activities	(5,032)	(7,090)
Net cash used for financing activities	(7,651)	(3,858)
Net increase (decrease) in cash and cash equivalents	$ 436	$ 567

Note.   Cash spent on property, plant, and equipment in 2004 was $3,843. Cash paid for dividends was $1,022.

Comparative data for AMD:

1. Free cash flow   −$354 million
2. Current cash debt coverage ratio   .67 times
3. Cash debt coverage ratio   .23 times

Solution

1. Intel's free cash flow is $8,254 million ($13,119 − $3,843 − $1,022). AMD's is actually a negative $354 million. This gives Intel a huge advantage in the ability to move quickly to invest in new projects.
2. The current cash debt coverage ratio for Intel is calculated as follows.

$$\frac{\$13,119}{(\$8,006 + \$6,879)/2} = 1.76 \text{ times}$$

Compared to AMD's value of .67 times, Intel appears to be significantly more liquid.
3. The cash debt coverage ratio for Intel is calculated as follows.

$$\frac{\$13,119}{(\$9,564 + \$9,297)/2} = 1.39 \text{ times}$$

Compared to AMD's value of .23 times, Intel appears to be significantly more solvent.

THE
NAVIGATOR

WILEY
PLUS

Summary of Study Objectives

1 *Indicate the usefulness of the statement of cash flows.* The statement of cash flows provides information about the cash receipts, cash payments, and net change in cash resulting from the operating, investing, and financing activities of a company during the period.

2 *Distinguish among operating, investing, and financing activities.* Operating activities include the cash effects of transactions that enter into the determination of net income. Investing activities involve cash flows resulting from changes in investments and long-term asset items. Financing activities involve cash flows resulting from changes in long-term liability and stockholders' equity items.

3 *Explain the impact of the product life cycle on a company's cash flows.* During the introductory stage, cash provided by operating activities and cash from investing are negative, and cash from financing is positive. During the growth stage, cash provided by operating activities becomes positive. During the maturity stage, cash provided by operating activities exceeds investing needs, so the company begins to retire debt. During the decline stage, cash provided by operating activities is reduced, cash from investing becomes positive, and cash from financing becomes more negative.

4 *Prepare a statement of cash flows using the indirect method.* The preparation of a statement of cash flows

involves three major steps: (1) Determine net cash provided/used by operating activities by converting net income from an accrual basis to a cash basis. (2) Analyze changes in noncurrent asset and liability accounts and record as investing and financing activities, or disclose as noncash transactions. (3) Compare the net change in cash on the statement of cash flows with the change in the cash account reported on the balance sheet to make sure the amounts agree.

5 *Use the statement of cash flows to evaluate a company.* A number of measures can be derived by using information from the statement of cash flows as well as the other required financial statements. Free cash flow indicates the amount of cash a company generated during the current year that is available for the payment of dividends or for expansion. Liquidity can be measured with the current cash debt coverage ratio (cash provided by operating activities divided by average current liabilities). Solvency can be measured by the cash debt coverage ratio (cash provided by operating activities divided by average total liabilities).

THE NAVIGATOR

Decision Toolkit—A Summary

Decision Checkpoints	Info Needed for Decision	Tool to Use for Decision	How to Evaluate Results
How much cash did the company generate to either expand operations or pay dividends?	Cash provided by operating activities, cash spent on fixed assets, and cash dividends	$\text{Free cash flow} = \text{Cash provided by operations} - \text{Capital expenditures} - \text{Cash dividends}$	Significant free cash flow indicates greater potential to finance new investment and pay additional dividends.
Is the company generating sufficient cash provided by operating activities to meet its current obligations?	Cash provided by operating activities and average current liabilities	$\text{Current cash debt coverage ratio} = \dfrac{\text{Cash provided by operations}}{\text{Average current liabilities}}$	A high value suggests good liquidity. Since the numerator contains a "flow" measure, it provides a good supplement to the current ratio.
Is the company generating sufficient cash provided by operating activities to meet its long-term obligations?	Cash provided by operating activities and average total liabilities	$\text{Cash debt coverage ratio} = \dfrac{\text{Cash provided by operations}}{\text{Average total liabilities}}$	A high value suggests the company is solvent; that is, it will meet its obligations in the long term.

APPENDIX
STATEMENT OF CASH FLOWS—DIRECT METHOD

STUDY OBJECTIVE

6

Prepare a statement of cash flows using the direct method.

To explain and illustrate the direct method, we will use the transactions of Juarez Company for 2007, to prepare a statement of cash flows. Illustration 12A-1 (page 612) presents information related to 2007 for Juarez Company.

Illustration 12A-1
Comparative balance
sheets, income statement,
and additional information
for Juarez Company

JUAREZ COMPANY
Comparative Balance Sheets
December 31

Assets	2007	2006	Change Increase/Decrease
Cash	$191,000	$159,000	$ 32,000 Increase
Accounts receivable	12,000	15,000	3,000 Decrease
Inventory	170,000	160,000	10,000 Increase
Prepaid expenses	6,000	8,000	2,000 Decrease
Land	140,000	80,000	60,000 Increase
Equipment	160,000	–0–	160,000 Increase
Accumulated depreciation—equipment	(16,000)	–0–	16,000 Increase
Total	$663,000	$422,000	
Liabilities and Stockholders' Equity			
Accounts payable	$ 52,000	$ 60,000	$ 8,000 Decrease
Accrued expenses payable	15,000	20,000	5,000 Decrease
Income taxes payable	12,000	–0–	12,000 Increase
Bonds payable	130,000	–0–	130,000 Increase
Common stock	360,000	300,000	60,000 Increase
Retained earnings	94,000	42,000	52,000 Increase
Total	$663,000	$422,000	

JUAREZ COMPANY
Income Statement
For the Year Ended December 31, 2007

Revenues		$975,000
Cost of goods sold	$660,000	
Operating expenses (excluding depreciation)	176,000	
Depreciation expense	18,000	
Loss on sale of store equipment	1,000	855,000
Income before income taxes		120,000
Income tax expense		36,000
Net income		$ 84,000

Additional information:
1. In 2007, the company declared and paid a $32,000 cash dividend.
2. Bonds were issued at face value for $130,000 in cash.
3. Equipment costing $180,000 was purchased for cash.
4. Equipment costing $20,000 was sold for $17,000 cash when the book value of the equipment was $18,000.
5. Common stock of $60,000 was issued to acquire land.

Preparation of the Statement of Cash Flows—Direct Method

To prepare a statement of cash flows under the direct approach, we will apply the three steps outlined in Illustration 12-4 (page 593).

STEP 1: OPERATING ACTIVITIES

DETERMINE NET CASH PROVIDED/USED BY OPERATING ACTIVITIES BY CONVERTING NET INCOME FROM AN ACCRUAL BASIS TO A CASH BASIS

Under the **direct method**, companies compute net cash provided by operating activities by **adjusting each item in the income statement** from the accrual basis to the cash basis. To simplify and condense the operating activities section, companies **report only major classes of operating cash receipts and cash payments**. For these major classes, the difference between cash receipts and cash payments is the net cash provided by operating activities. These relationships are as shown in Illustration 12A-2.

Illustration 12A-2 Major classes of cash receipts and payments

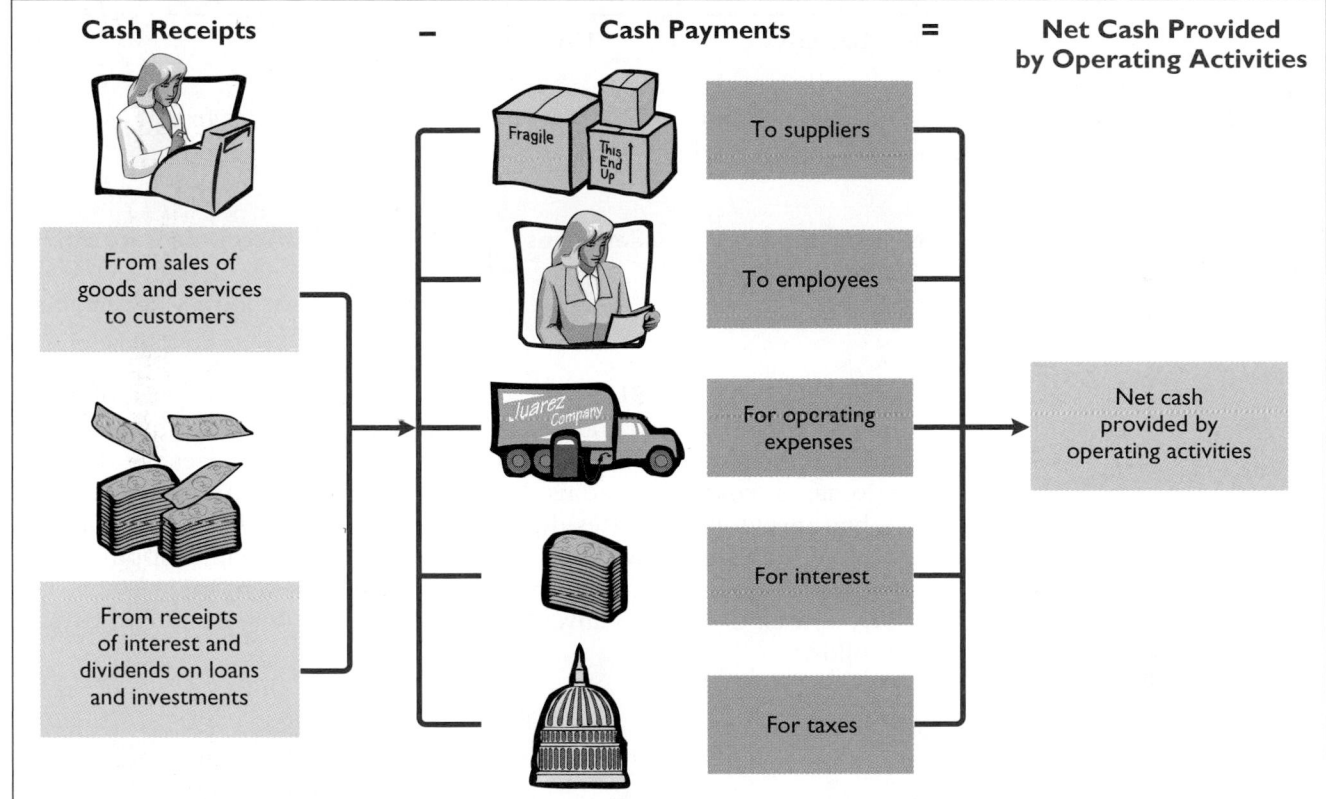

An efficient way to apply the direct method is to analyze the items reported in the income statement in the order in which they are listed. We then determine cash receipts and cash payments related to these revenues and expenses. The following pages present the adjustments required to prepare a statement of cash flows for Juarez Company using the direct approach.

CASH RECEIPTS FROM CUSTOMERS. The income statement for Juarez Company reported revenues from customers of $975,000. How much of that was cash receipts? To answer that, companies need to consider the change in accounts receivable during the year. When accounts receivable increase during the year, revenues on an accrual basis are higher than cash receipts from customers. Operations led to revenues, but not all of these revenues resulted in cash receipts.

To determine the amount of cash receipts, the company deducts from sales revenues the increase in accounts receivable. On the other hand, there may be a decrease in accounts receivable. That would occur if cash receipts from customers exceeded sales revenues. In that case, the company adds to sales revenues the decrease in accounts receivable.

For Juarez Company, accounts receivable decreased $3,000. Thus, cash receipts from customers were $978,000, computed as shown in Illustration 12A-3 (page 614).

Illustration 12A-3
Computation of cash
receipts from customers

Revenues from sales	$ 975,000
Add: Decrease in accounts receivable	3,000
Cash receipts from customers	**$ 978,000**

Juarez can also determine cash receipts from customers from an analysis of the Accounts Receivable account, as shown in Illustration 12A-4.

Illustration 12A-4
Analysis of accounts
receivable

Accounts Receivable

1/1/07 Balance	15,000	**Receipts from customers**	**978,000**
Revenues from sales	975,000		
12/31/07 Balance	12,000		

Helpful Hint The T account shows that revenue plus decrease in receivables equals cash receipts.

Illustration 12A-5 shows the relationships among cash receipts from customers, revenues from sales, and changes in accounts receivable.

Illustration 12A-5
Formula to compute cash
receipts from customers—
direct method

Cash Receipts from Customers	=	**Revenues from Sales**	**+ Decrease in Accounts Receivable** or **− Increase in Accounts Receivable**

CASH PAYMENTS TO SUPPLIERS. Juarez Company reported cost of goods sold of $660,000 on its income statement. How much of that was cash payments to suppliers? To answer that, it is first necessary to find purchases for the year. To find purchases, companies adjust cost of goods sold for the change in inventory. When inventory increases during the year, purchases for the year have exceeded cost of goods sold. As a result, to determine the amount of purchases, the company adds to cost of goods sold the increase in inventory.

In 2007, Juarez Company's inventory increased $10,000. It computes purchases as follows.

Illustration 12A-6
Computation of purchases

Cost of goods sold	$ 660,000
Add: Increase in inventory	10,000
Purchases	**$670,000**

After computing purchases, a company can determine cash payments to suppliers. This is done by adjusting purchases for the change in accounts payable. When accounts payable increase during the year, purchases on an accrual basis are higher than they are on a cash basis. As a result, to determine cash payments to suppliers, a company deducts from purchases the increase in accounts payable. On the other hand, if cash payments to suppliers exceed purchases, there may be a decrease in accounts payable. In that case, a company adds to purchases the decrease in accounts payable.

For Juarez Company, cash payments to suppliers were $678,000, computed as follows.

Illustration 12A-7
Computation of cash
payments to suppliers

Purchases	$ 670,000
Add: Decrease in accounts payable	8,000
Cash payments to suppliers	**$678,000**

Juarez also can determine cash payments to suppliers from an analysis of the Accounts Payable account, as shown in Illustration 12A-8.

Illustration 12A-8
Analysis of accounts payable

Accounts Payable

Payments to suppliers	678,000	1/1/07	Balance	60,000
			Purchases	670,000
		12/31/07	Balance	52,000

Illustration 12A-9 shows the relationships among cash payments to suppliers, cost of goods sold, changes in inventory, and changes in accounts payable.

Helpful Hint The T account shows that purchases plus decrease in accounts payable equals payments to suppliers.

Illustration 12A-9
Formula to compute cash payments to suppliers—direct method

$$\begin{array}{l}\text{Cash Payments to Suppliers} = \text{Cost of Goods Sold} \left\{\begin{array}{l}+\text{ Increase in Inventory}\\ \text{or}\\ -\text{ Decrease in Inventory}\end{array}\right. \left\{\begin{array}{l}+\text{ Decrease in Accounts Payable}\\ \text{or}\\ -\text{ Increase in Accounts Payable}\end{array}\right.\end{array}$$

CASH PAYMENTS FOR OPERATING EXPENSES. Juarez reported on its income statement operating expenses of $176,000. How much of that amount was cash paid for operating expenses? To answer that, we need to adjust this amount for any changes in prepaid expenses and accrued expenses payable. For example, if prepaid expenses increased during the year, cash paid for operating expenses is higher than operating expenses reported on the income statement. To convert operating expenses to cash payments for operating expenses, a company adds the increase to operating expenses. On the other hand, if prepaid expenses decrease during the year, it deducts the decrease from operating expenses.

Companies must also adjust operating expenses for changes in accrued expenses payable. When accrued expenses payable increase during the year, operating expenses on an accrual basis are higher than they are in a cash basis. As a result, to determine cash payments for operating expenses, a company deducts from operating expenses an increase in accrued expenses payable. On the other hand, a company adds to operating expenses a decrease in accrued expenses payable because cash payments exceed operating expenses.

Juarez Company's cash payments for operating expenses were $179,000, computed as follows.

Illustration 12A-10
Computation of cash payments for operating expenses

Operating expenses	$ 176,000
Deduct: Decrease in prepaid expenses	(2,000)
Add: Decrease in accrued expenses payable	5,000
Cash payments for operating expenses	**$ 179,000**

Illustration 12A-11 shows the relationships among cash payments for operating expenses, changes in prepaid expenses, and changes in accrued expenses payable.

Illustration 12A-11
Formula to compute cash payments for operating expenses—direct method

$$\begin{array}{l}\text{Cash Payments for Operating Expenses} = \text{Operating Expenses} \left\{\begin{array}{l}+\text{ Increase in Prepaid Expense}\\ \text{or}\\ -\text{ Decrease in Prepaid Expense}\end{array}\right. \left\{\begin{array}{l}+\text{ Decrease in Accrued Expenses Payable}\\ \text{or}\\ -\text{ Increase in Accrued Expenses Payable}\end{array}\right.\end{array}$$

DEPRECIATION EXPENSE AND LOSS ON SALE OF EQUIPMENT. Companies show operating expenses exclusive of depreciation. Juarez's depreciation expense in 2007 was

$18,000. Depreciation expense is not shown on a statement of cash flows because it is a noncash charge. If the amount for operating expenses includes depreciation expense, the company must reduce operating expenses by the amount of depreciation to determine cash payments for operating expenses.

The loss on sale of equipment of $1,000 is also a noncash charge. The loss on sale of equipment reduces net income, but it does not reduce cash. Thus, companies do not report on a statement of cash flows the loss on sale of equipment.

Other charges to expense that do not require the use of cash, such as the amortization of intangible assets, depletion expense, and bad debt expense, are treated in the same manner as depreciation.

CASH PAYMENTS FOR INCOME TAXES. Juarez reported income tax expense of $36,000 on the income statement. Income taxes payable, however, increased $12,000. This increase means that the company has not yet paid $12,000 of the income taxes. As a result, income taxes paid were less than income taxes reported in the income statement. Cash payments for income taxes were, therefore, $24,000 as shown below.

Illustration 12A-12
Computation of cash payments for income taxes

Income tax expense	$ 36,000
Deduct: Increase in income taxes payable	12,000
Cash payments for income taxes	**$ 24,000**

Illustration 12A-13 shows the relationships among cash payments for income taxes, income tax expense, and changes in income taxes payable.

Illustration 12A-13
Formula to compute cash payments for income taxes—direct method

Cash Payments for Income Taxes =	**Income Tax Expense**	**+ Decrease in Income Taxes Payable** or **− Increase in Income Taxes Payable**

The operating activities section of the statement of cash flows of Juarez Company is shown in Illustration 12A-14.

Illustration 12A-14
Operating activities section of the statement of cash flows

Cash flows from operating activities		
Cash receipts from customers		$978,000
Less: Cash payments:		
To suppliers	$678,000	
For operating expenses	179,000	
For income taxes	24,000	881,000
Net cash provided by operating activities		$ 97,000

When a company uses the direct method, it must also provide in a **separate schedule** (not shown here) the net cash flows from operating activities as computed under the indirect method.

STEP 2: INVESTING AND FINANCING ACTIVITIES

ANALYZE CHANGES IN NONCURRENT ASSET AND LIABILITY ACCOUNTS AND RECORD AS INVESTING AND FINANCING ACTIVITIES, OR AS SIGNIFICANT NONCASH TRANSACTIONS

INCREASE IN LAND. Juarez's land increased $60,000. The additional information section indicates that the company issued common stock to purchase the land.

The issuance of common stock for land has no effect on cash. But it is a **significant noncash investing and financing transaction**. This transaction requires disclosure in a separate schedule at the bottom of the statement of cash flows.

INCREASE IN EQUIPMENT. The comparative balance sheets show that equipment increased $160,000 in 2007. The additional information in Illustration 12A-1 indicates that the increase resulted from two investing transactions: (1) Juarez purchased for cash equipment costing $180,000. And (2) it sold for $17,000 cash equipment costing $20,000, whose book value was $18,000. The relevant data for the statement of cash flows is the cash paid for the purchase and the cash proceeds from the sale. For Juarez Company, the investing activities section will show the following: The $180,000 purchase of equipment as an outflow of cash, and the $17,000 sale of equipment also as an inflow of cash. The company **should not net** the two amounts. **Both individual outflows and inflows of cash should be shown.**

The analysis of the changes in equipment should include the related Accumulated Depreciation account. These two accounts for Juarez Company are shown in Illustration 12A-15.

Illustration 12A-15
Analysis of equipment and related accumulated depreciation

Equipment

1/1/07	Balance	–0–	Cost of equipment sold	20,000
	Cash purchase	180,000		
12/31/07	Balance	160,000		

Accumulated Depreciation—Equipment

Sale of equipment	2,000	1/1/07	Balance	–0–
			Depreciation expense	18,000
		12/31/07	Balance	16,000

INCREASE IN BONDS PAYABLE. Bonds Payable increased $130,000. The additional information in Illustration 12A-1 (page 612) indicated that Juarez issued, for $130,000 cash, bonds with a face value of $130,000. The issuance of bonds is a financing activity. For Juarez Company, there is an inflow of cash of $130,000 from the issuance of bonds.

INCREASE IN COMMON STOCK. The Common Stock account increased $60,000. The additional information indicated that Juarez acquired land from the issuance of common stock. This transaction is a **significant noncash investing and financing transaction** which the company should report separately at the bottom of the statement.

INCREASE IN RETAINED EARNINGS. The $52,000 net increase in Retained Earnings resulted from net income of $84,000 and the declaration and payment of a cash dividend of $32,000. Companies **do not report net income in the statement of cash flows under the direct method**. Cash dividends paid of $32,000 are reported in the financing activities section as an outflow of cash.

Statement of Cash Flows—2007

Illustration 12A-16 (page 618) shows the statement of cash flows for Juarez.

Illustration 12A-16
Statement of cash flows,
2007—direct method

JUAREZ COMPANY		
Statement of Cash Flows—Direct Method		
For the Year Ended December 31, 2007		
Cash flows from operating activities		
Cash receipts from customers		$ 978,000
Less: Cash payments:		
To suppliers	$ 678,000	
For operating expenses	179,000	
For income taxes	24,000	881,000
Net cash provided by operating activities		97,000
Cash flows from investing activities		
Purchase of equipment	(180,000)	
Sale of equipment	17,000	
Net cash used by investing activities		(163,000)
Cash flows from financing activities		
Issuance of bonds payable	130,000	
Payment of cash dividends	(32,000)	
Net cash provided by financing activities		98,000
Net increase in cash		32,000
Cash at beginning of period		159,000
Cash at end of period		$ 191,000
Noncash investing and financing activities		
Issuance of common stock to purchase land		$ 60,000

STEP 3: NET CHANGE IN CASH

COMPARE THE NET CHANGE IN CASH ON THE STATEMENT OF CASH FLOWS WITH THE CHANGE IN THE CASH ACCOUNT REPORTED ON THE BALANCE SHEET TO MAKE SURE THE AMOUNTS AGREE

Illustration 12A-16 indicates that the net change in cash during the period was an increase of $32,000. This agrees with the change in balances in the cash account reported on the balance sheets in Illustration 12A-1 (page 612).

Summary of Study Objective for Appendix

6 *Prepare a statement of cash flows using the direct method.* The preparation of the statement of cash flows involves three major steps: (1) Determine net cash provided/used by operating activities by converting net income from an accrual basis to a cash basis. (2) Analyze changes in noncurrent asset and liability accounts and record as investing and financing activities, or disclose as noncash transactions. (3) Compare the net change in cash on the statement of cash flows with the change in the cash account reported on the balance sheet to make sure the amounts agree. The direct method reports cash receipts less cash payments to arrive at net cash provided by operating activities.

Glossary

Cash debt coverage ratio A cash-basis ratio used to evaluate solvency, calculated as cash provided by operating activities divided by average total liabilities. (p. 608)

Current cash debt coverage ratio A cash-basis ratio used to evaluate liquidity, calculated as cash provided by operations divided by average current liabilities. (p. 607)

Direct method A method of determining net cash provided by operating activities by adjusting each item in the income statement from the accrual basis to the cash basis. (pp. 593, 613)

Financing activities Cash flow activities that include (a) obtaining cash from issuing debt and repaying the amounts borrowed and (b) obtaining cash from stockholders, repurchasing shares, and paying dividends. (p. 587)

Free cash flow Cash provided by operating activities adjusted for capital expenditures and dividends paid. (p. 605)

Indirect method A method of preparing a statement of cash flows in which net income is adjusted for items that do not affect cash, to determine net cash provided by operating activities. (pp. 593, 596)

Investing activities   Cash flow activities that include (a) purchasing and disposing of investments and property, plant, and equipment using cash and (b) lending money and collecting the loans. (p. 587)

Operating activities   Cash flow activities that include the cash effects of transactions that create revenues and expenses and thus enter into the determination of net income. (p. 587)

Product life cycle   A series of phases in a product's sales and cash flows over time; these phases, in order of occurrence, are introductory, growth, maturity, and decline. (p. 590)

Statement of cash flows   A basic financial statement that provides information about the cash receipts and cash payments of an entity during a period, classified as operating, investing, and financing activities, in a format that reconciles the beginning and ending cash balances. (p. 587)

Demonstration Problem

The income statement for Kosinski Manufacturing Company contains the following condensed information.

KOSINSKI MANUFACTURING COMPANY
Income Statement
For the Year Ended December 31, 2007

Revenues		$6,583,000
Operating expenses, excluding depreciation	$4,920,000	
Depreciation expense	880,000	5,800,000
Income before income taxes		783,000
Income tax expense		353,000
Net income		$ 430,000

Included in operating expenses is a $24,000 loss resulting from the sale of machinery for $270,000 cash. Machinery was purchased at a cost of $750,000. The following balances are reported on Kosinski's comparative balance sheet at December 31.

	2007	2006
Cash	$672,000	$130,000
Accounts receivable	775,000	610,000
Inventories	834,000	867,000
Accounts payable	521,000	501,000

Income tax expense of $353,000 represents the amount paid in 2007. Dividends declared and paid in 2007 totaled $200,000.

Instructions

(a) Prepare the statement of cash flows using the indirect method.
*(b) Prepare the statement of cash flows using the direct method.

Solution to Demonstration Problem

(a)
KOSINSKI MANUFACTURING COMPANY
Statement of Cash Flows—Indirect Method
For the Year Ended December 31, 2007

Cash flows from operating activities		
Net income		$ 430,000
Adjustments to reconcile net income to net cash		
provided by operating activities:		
Depreciation expense	$ 880,000	
Loss on sale of machinery	24,000	
Increase in accounts receivable	(165,000)	
Decrease in inventories	33,000	
Increase in accounts payable	20,000	792,000
Net cash provided by operating activities		1,222,000

Action Plan

• Apply the same data to the preparation of a statement of cash flows under both the indirect and direct methods.

• Note the similarities of the two methods: Both methods report the same information in the investing and financing sections.

• Note the differences between the two methods: The cash flows from operating activities sections report different information, but the amount of net cash provided by operating activities is the same for both methods.

Cash flows from investing activities
    Sale of machinery   270,000
    Purchase of machinery   (750,000)

      Net cash used by investing activities   (480,000)

Cash flows from financing activities
    Payment of cash dividends   (200,000)

      Net cash used by financing activities   (200,000)

Net increase in cash   542,000
Cash at beginning of period   130,000

Cash at end of period $ 672,000

*(b)   **KOSINSKI MANUFACTURING COMPANY**
           Statement of Cash Flows—Direct Method
             For the Year Ended December 31, 2007

Cash flows from operating activities
    Cash collections from customers $6,418,000*
    Cash payments:
      For operating expenses $4,843,000**
      For income taxes   353,000   5,196,000
        Net cash provided by operating activities   1,222,000

Cash flows from investing activities
    Sale of machinery   270,000
    Purchase of machinery   (750,000)

      Net cash used by investing activities   (480,000)

Cash flows from financing activities
    Payment of cash dividends   (200,000)

      Net cash used by financing activities   (200,000)

Net increase in cash   542,000
Cash at beginning of period   130,000

Cash at end of period $ 672,000

Direct-Method Computations:

*Computation of cash collections from customers:
    Revenues per the income statement $6,583,000
    Deduct: Increase in accounts receivable   (165,000)

    Cash collections from customers $6,418,000
**Computation of cash payments for operating
    expenses:
    Operating expenses per the income statement $4,920,000
    Deduct: Loss from sale of machinery   (24,000)
    Deduct: Decrease in inventories   (33,000)
    Deduct: Increase in accounts payable   (20,000)
    Cash payments for operating expenses $4,843,000

Note: All Questions, Exercises, and Problems marked with an asterisk relate to material in the appendix to the chapter.

Self-Study Questions

Answers are at the end of the chapter.

(SO 1)   **1.** Which of the following is *incorrect* about the statement of cash flows?
    (a) It is a fourth basic financial statement.
    (b) It provides information about cash

receipts and cash payments of an entity during a period.
    (c) It reconciles the ending cash account balance to the balance per the bank statement.

(d) It provides information about the operating, investing, and financing activities of the business.

(SO 2)   **2.** The statement of cash flows classifies cash receipts and cash payments by these activities:
(a) operating and nonoperating.
(b) investing, financing, and operating.
(c) financing, operating, and nonoperating.
(d) investing, financing, and nonoperating.

(SO 2)   **3.** Which is an example of a cash flow from an operating activity?
(a) Payment of cash to lenders for interest.
(b) Receipt of cash from the sale of capital stock.
(c) Payment of cash dividends to the company's stockholders.
(d) None of the above.

(SO 2)   **4.** Which is an example of a cash flow from an investing activity?
(a) Receipt of cash from the issuance of bonds payable.
(b) Payment of cash to repurchase outstanding capital stock.
(c) Receipt of cash from the sale of equipment.
(d) Payment of cash to suppliers for inventory.

(SO 2)   **5.** Cash dividends paid to stockholders are classified on the statement of cash flows as:
(a) operating activities.
(b) investing activities.
(c) a combination of (a) and (b).
(d) financing activities.

(SO 2)   **6.** Which is an example of a cash flow from a financing activity?
(a) Receipt of cash from sale of land.
(b) Issuance of debt for cash.
(c) Purchase of equipment for cash.
(d) None of the above

(SO 2)   **7.** Which of the following is *incorrect* about the statement of cash flows?
(a) The direct method may be used to report cash provided by operations.
(b) The statement shows the cash provided (used) for three categories of activity.
(c) The operating section is the last section of the statement.
(d) The indirect method may be used to report cash provided by operations.

(SO 3)   **8.** During the introductory phase of a company's life cycle, one would normally expect to see:
(a) negative cash from operations, negative cash from investing, and positive cash from financing.
(b) negative cash from operations, positive cash from investing, and positive cash from financing.
(c) positive cash from operations, negative cash from investing, and negative cash from financing.

(d) positive cash from operations, negative cash from investing, and positive cash from financing.

Questions 9 and 10 apply only to the indirect method.

9. Net income is $132,000, accounts payable increased $10,000 during the year, inventory decreased $6,000 during the year, and accounts receivable increased $12,000 during the year. Under the indirect method, what is net cash provided by operations?   (SO 4)
(a) $102,000.   (c) $124,000.
(b) $112,000.   (d) $136,000.

10. Items that are added back to net income in determining cash provided by operations under the indirect method do *not* include: (SO 4)
(a) depreciation expense.
(b) an increase in inventory.
(c) amortization expense.
(d) loss on sale of equipment.

11. The statement of cash flows should *not* be used to evaluate an entity's ability to: (SO 5)
(a) earn net income.
(b) generate future cash flows.
(c) pay dividends.
(d) meet obligations.

12. Free cash flow provides an indication of a company's ability to: (SO 5)
(a) generate net income.
(b) generate cash to pay dividends.
(c) generate cash to invest in new capital expenditures.
(d) both (b) and (c).

Questions 13 and 14 apply only to the direct method.

*13. The beginning balance in accounts receivable is $44,000, the ending balance is $42,000, and sales during the period are $129,000. What are cash receipts from customers?   (SO 6)
(a) $127,000.   (c) $131,000.
(b) $129,000.   (d) $141,000.

*14. Which of the following items is reported on a cash flow statement prepared by the direct method?   (SO 6)
(a) Loss on sale of building.
(b) Increase in accounts receivable.
(c) Depreciation expense.
(d) Cash payments to suppliers.

Go to the book's website, **www.wiley.com/college/kimmel**, to access additional Self-Study Questions.

Questions

1. (a) What is a statement of cash flows?
   (b) John Norris maintains that the statement of cash flows is an optional financial statement. Do you agree? Explain.

2. What questions about cash are answered by the statement of cash flows?

3. Distinguish among the three activities reported in the statement of cash flows.

4. (a) What are the major sources (inflows) of cash in a statement of cash flows?
   (b) What are the major uses (outflows) of cash?

5. Why is it important to disclose certain noncash transactions? How should they be disclosed?

6. Wilma Flintstone and Barny Rublestone were discussing the format of the statement of cash flows of Hart Candy Co. At the bottom of Hart Candy's statement of cash flows was a separate section entitled "Noncash investing and financing activities." Give three examples of significant noncash transactions that would be reported in this section.

7. Why is it necessary to use comparative balance sheets, a current income statement, and certain transaction data in preparing a statement of cash flows?

8.
   (a) What are the phases of the corporate life cycle?
   (b) What effect does each phase have on the numbers reported in a statement of cash flows?

9. Contrast the advantages and disadvantages of the direct and indirect methods of preparing the statement of cash flows. Are both methods acceptable? Which method is preferred by the FASB? Which method is more popular?

10. When the total cash inflows exceed the total cash outflows in the statement of cash flows, how and where is this excess identified?

11. Describe the indirect method for determining net cash provided (used) by operating activities.

12. Why is it necessary to convert accrual-based net income to cash-basis income when preparing a statement of cash flows?

13. The president of Ferneti Company is puzzled. During the last year, the company experienced a net loss of $800,000, yet its cash increased $300,000 during the same period of time. Explain to the president how this could occur.

14. Identify five items that are adjustments to convert net income to net cash provided by operating activities under the indirect method.

15. Why and how is depreciation expense reported in a statement prepared using the indirect method?

16. Why is the statement of cash flows useful?

17. During 2007 Doubleday Company converted $1,700,000 of its total $2,000,000 of bonds payable into common stock. Indicate how the transaction would be reported on a statement of cash flows, if at all.

18. Give examples of accrual-based and cash-based ratios to measure each of these characteristics of a company:
    (a) Liquidity.
    (b) Solvency.

*19. Describe the direct method for determining net cash provided by operating activities.

*20. Give the formulas under the direct method for computing (a) cash receipts from customers and (b) cash payments to suppliers.

*21. Garcia Inc. reported sales of $2 million for 2007. Accounts receivable decreased $200,000 and accounts payable increased $300,000. Compute cash receipts from customers, assuming that the receivable and payable transactions related to operations.

*22. In the direct method, why is depreciation expense not reported in the cash flows from operating activities section?

Brief Exercises

Indicate statement presentation of selected transactions.
(SO 2)

BE12-1   Each of these items must be considered in preparing a statement of cash flows for Kiner Co. for the year ended December 31, 2007. For each item, state how it should be shown in the statement of cash flows for 2007.
  (a) Issued bonds for $200,000 cash.
  (b) Purchased equipment for $150,000 cash.
  (c) Sold land costing $20,000 for $20,000 cash.
  (d) Declared and paid a $50,000 cash dividend.

Classify items by activities.
(SO 2)

BE12-2   Classify each item as an operating, investing, or financing activity. Assume all items involve cash unless there is information to the contrary.
  (a) Purchase of equipment.   (d) Depreciation.
  (b) Sale of building.   (e) Payment of dividends.
  (c) Redemption of bonds.   (f) Issuance of capital stock.

BE12-3 The following T account is a summary of the cash account of Edmonds Company.

Identify financing activity transactions.
(SO 2)

Cash (Summary Form)

Balance, Jan. 1	8,000		
Receipts from customers	364,000	Payments for goods	200,000
Dividends on stock investments	6,000	Payments for operating expenses	140,000
Proceeds from sale of equipment	36,000	Interest paid	10,000
Proceeds from issuance of		Taxes paid	8,000
bonds payable	300,000	Dividends paid	50,000
Balance, Dec. 31	306,000		

What amount of net cash provided (used) by financing activities should be reported in the statement of cash flows?

BE12-4

(a) Why is cash from operations likely to be lower than reported net income during the growth phase?

(b) Why is cash from investing often positive during the late maturity phase and during the decline phase?

Answer questions related to the phases of product life cycle.
(SO 3)

BE12-5 Martinez, Inc. reported net income of $2.5 million in 2007. Depreciation for the year was $160,000, accounts receivable decreased $350,000, and accounts payable decreased $280,000. Compute net cash provided by operating activities using the indirect approach.

Compute cash provided by operating activities—indirect method.
(SO 4)

BE12-6 The net income for Adcock Co. for 2007 was $280,000. For 2007 depreciation on plant assets was $70,000, and the company incurred a loss on sale of plant assets of $12,000. Compute net cash provided by operating activities under the indirect method.

Compute cash provided by operating activities—indirect method.
(SO 4)

BE12-7 The comparative balance sheets for Goltra Company show these changes in noncash current asset accounts: accounts receivable decrease $80,000, prepaid expenses increase $28,000, and inventories increase $30,000. Compute net cash provided by operating activities using the indirect method assuming that net income is $200,000.

Compute net cash provided by operating activities—indirect method.
(SO 4)

BE12-8 The T accounts for Equipment and the related Accumulated Depreciation for Pettengill Company at the end of 2007 are shown here.

Determine cash received from sale of equipment.
(SO 4)

Equipment

Beg. bal.	80,000	Disposals	22,000
Acquisitions	41,600		
End. bal.	99,600		

Accumulated Depreciation

Disposals	5,500	Beg. bal.	44,500
		Depr. exp.	12,000
		End. bal.	51,000

In addition, Pettengill Company's income statement reported a loss on the sale of equipment of $5,500. What amount was reported on the statement of cash flows as "cash flow from sale of equipment"?

BE12-9 During 2004 Cypress Semiconductor Corporation reported cash provided by operations of $155,793,000 cash used in investing of $207,826,000, and cash used in financing of $33,372,000. In addition, cash spent for fixed assets during the period was $132,280,000. Average current liabilities were $226,238,500, and average total liabilities were $959,567,000. No dividends were paid. Calculate these values:

(a) Free cash flow.

(b) Current cash debt coverage ratio.

(c) Cash debt coverage ratio.

Calculate cash-based ratios.
(SO 5)

BE12-10 Lott Corporation reported cash provided by operating activities of $360,000, cash used by investing activities of $250,000, and cash provided by financing activities of $70,000. In addition, cash spent for capital assets during the period was $200,000.

Calculate cash-based ratios.
(SO 5)

Average current liabilities were $150,000, and average total liabilities were $225,000. No dividends were paid. Calculate these values:
(a) Free cash flow.
(b) Current cash debt coverage ratio.
(c) Cash debt coverage ratio.

Calculate cash-based ratios.
(SO 5)

BE12-11 Alliance Atlantis Communications Inc. reported a $35.8 million increase in operating cash flow for its first quarter of 2005. Alliance reported cash provided by operating activities of $45,600,000 and revenues of $264,800,000. Cash spent on plant asset additions during the quarter was $1,600,000. Calculate free cash flow.

Calculate and analyze free cash flow.
(SO 5)

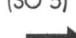

BE12-12 The management of Radar Inc. is trying to decide whether it can increase its dividend. During the current year it reported net income of $875,000. It had cash provided by operating activities of $734,000, paid cash dividends of $70,000, and had capital expenditures of $280,000. Compute the company's free cash flow, and discuss whether an increase in the dividend appears warranted. What other factors should be considered?

Compute receipts from customers—direct method.
(SO 6)

***BE12-13** Columbia Sportswear Company had accounts receivable of $206,024,000 at January 1, 2004, and $267,653,000 at December 31, 2004. Sales revenues were $1,095,307,000 for the year 2004. What is the amount of cash receipts from customers in 2004?

Compute cash payments for income taxes—direct method.
(SO 6)

***BE12-14** Young Corporation reported income taxes of $340,000,000 on its 2007 income statement and income taxes payable of $277,000,000 at December 31, 2006, and $522,000,000 at December 31, 2006. What amount of cash payments were made for income taxes during 2006?

Compute cash payments for operating expenses—direct method.
(SO 6)

***BE12-15** Flynn Corporation reports operating expenses of $80,000 excluding depreciation expense of $15,000 for 2007. During the year prepaid expenses decreased $6,600 and accrued expenses payable increased $4,400. Compute the cash payments for operating expenses in 2007.

Exercises

Classify transactions by type of activity.
(SO 2)

E12-1 Pioneer Corporation had these transactions during 2007.
(a) Issued $50,000 par value common stock for cash.
(b) Purchased a machine for $30,000, giving a long-term note in exchange.
(c) Issued $200,000 par value common stock upon conversion of bonds having a face value of $200,000.
(d) Declared and paid a cash dividend of $18,000.
(e) Sold a long-term investment with a cost of $15,000 for $15,000 cash.
(f) Collected $16,000 of accounts receivable.
(g) Paid $18,000 on accounts payable.

Instructions
Analyze the transactions and indicate whether each transaction resulted in a cash flow from operating activities, investing activities, financing activities, or noncash investing and financing activities.

Classify transactions by type of activity.
(SO 2)

E12-2 An analysis of comparative balance sheets, the current year's income statement, and the general ledger accounts of Gagliano Corp. uncovered the following items. Assume all items involve cash unless there is information to the contrary.

(a) Payment of interest on notes payable.
(b) Exchange of land for patent.
(c) Sale of building at book value.
(d) Payment of dividends.
(e) Depreciation.
(f) Receipt of dividends on investment in stock.
(g) Receipt of interest on notes receivable.
(h) Issuance of capital stock.
(i) Amortization of patent.
(j) Issuance of bonds for land.
(k) Purchase of land.
(l) Conversion of bonds into common stock.
(m) Loss on sale of land.
(n) Retirement of bonds.

Instructions
Indicate how each item should be classified in the statement of cash flows using these four major classifications: operating activity (indirect method), investing activity, financing activity, and significant noncash investing and financing activity.

E12-3   The information in the table is from the statement of cash flows for a company at four different points in time (A, B, C, and D). Negative values are presented in parentheses.

Identify phases of product life cycle.
(SO 3)

	Point in Time			
	A	**B**	**C**	**D**
Cash provided by operations	$ (60,000)	$ 30,000	$120,000	$(10,000)
Cash provided by investing	(100,000)	25,000	30,000	(40,000)
Cash provided by financing	70,000	(110,000)	(50,000)	120,000
Net income	(40,000)	10,000	100,000	(5,000)

Instructions
For each point in time, state whether the company is most likely in the introductory phase, growth phase, maturity phase, or decline phase. In each case explain your choice.

E12-4   Villa Company reported net income of $195,000 for 2007. Villa also reported depreciation expense of $45,000 and a loss of $5,000 on the sale of equipment. The comparative balance sheet shows a decrease in accounts receivable of $15,000 for the year, a $17,000 increase in accounts payable, and a $4,000 decrease in prepaid expenses.

Prepare the operating activities section—indirect method.
(SO 4)

Instructions
Prepare the operating activities section of the statement of cash flows for 2007. Use the indirect method.

E12-5   The current sections of Bellinham Inc.'s balance sheets at December 31, 2006 and 2007, are presented here.
Bellinham's net income for 2007 was $153,000. Depreciation expense was $24,000.

Prepare the operating activities section—indirect method.
(SO 4)

	2007	**2006**
Current assets		
Cash	$105,000	$ 99,000
Accounts receivable	110,000	89,000
Inventory	158,000	172,000
Prepaid expenses	27,000	22,000
Total current assets	$400,000	$382,000
Current liabilities		
Accrued expenses payable	$ 15,000	$ 5,000
Accounts payable	85,000	92,000
Total current liabilities	$100,000	$ 97,000

Instructions
Prepare the net cash provided by operating activities section of the company's statement of cash flows for the year ended December 31, 2007, using the indirect method.

E12-6   The three accounts shown below and on page 626 appear in the general ledger of Cesar Corp. during 2007.

Prepare partial statement of cash flows—indirect method.
(SO 4)

Equipment

Date		Debit	Credit	Balance
Jan. 1	Balance			160,000
July 31	Purchase of equipment	70,000		230,000
Sept. 2	Cost of equipment constructed	53,000		283,000
Nov. 10	Cost of equipment sold		49,000	234,000

Accumulated Depreciation—Equipment

Date		Debit	Credit	Balance
Jan. 1	Balance			71,000
Nov. 10	Accumulated depreciation on equipment sold	30,000		41,000
Dec. 31	Depreciation for year		28,000	69,000

Retained Earnings

Date		Debit	Credit	Balance
Jan. 1	Balance			105,000
Aug. 23	Dividends (cash)	14,000		91,000
Dec. 31	Net income		67,000	158,000

Instructions

From the postings in the accounts, indicate how the information is reported on a statement of cash flows using the indirect method. The loss on sale of equipment was $5,000. (*Hint:* Cost of equipment constructed is reported in the investing activities section as a decrease in cash of $53,000.)

Prepare a statement of cash flows—indirect method, and compute cash-based ratios.
(SO 4, 5)

E12-7   Here are comparative balance sheets for Taguchi Company.

TAGUCHI COMPANY
Comparative Balance Sheets
December 31

Assets	2007	2006
Cash	$ 73,000	$ 22,000
Accounts receivable	85,000	76,000
Inventories	170,000	189,000
Land	75,000	100,000
Equipment	260,000	200,000
Accumulated depreciation	(66,000)	(32,000)
Total	$597,000	$555,000

Liabilities and Stockholders' Equity	2007	2006
Accounts payable	$ 39,000	$ 47,000
Bonds payable	150,000	200,000
Common stock ($1 par)	216,000	174,000
Retained earnings	192,000	134,000
Total	$597,000	$555,000

Additional information:
1. Net income for 2007 was $103,000.
2. Cash dividends of $45,000 were declared and paid.
3. Bonds payable amounting to $50,000 were redeemed for cash $50,000.
4. Common stock was issued for $42,000 cash.
5. No equipment was sold during 2007.

Instructions
(a) Prepare a statement of cash flows for 2007 using the indirect method.
(b) Compute these cash-basis ratios:

   (1) Current cash debt coverage.
   (2) Cash debt coverage.

Compare two companies by using cash-based ratios.
(SO 5)

E12-8   Presented on page 627 is 2004 information for PepsiCo, Inc. and The Coca-Cola Company.

($ in millions)	PepsiCo	Coca-Cola
Cash provided by operations	$ 5,054	$ 5,968
Average current liabilities	6,584	9,429
Average total liabilities	13,959	14,322
Net income	4,212	4,847
Sales	29,261	21,962
Capital expenditures	1,387	755
Dividends paid	1,329	2,429

Instructions

Using the cash-based measures presented in this chapter, compare the (a) liquidity and (b) solvency of the two companies.

E12-9 Information for two companies in the same industry, Linn Corporation and Nye Corporation, is presented here.

Compare two companies by using cash-based ratios.
(SO 5)

	Linn Corporation	Nye Corporation
Cash provided by operating activities	$150,000	$150,000
Average current liabilities	50,000	100,000
Average total liabilities	200,000	250,000
Net earnings	200,000	200,000
Capital expenditures	40,000	70,000
Dividends paid	5,000	10,000

Instructions

Using the cash-based measures presented in this chapter, compare the (a) liquidity and (b) solvency of the two companies.

*E12-10 Hairston Company completed its first year of operations on December 31, 2007. Its initial income statement showed that Hairston had revenues of $192,000 and operating expenses of $78,000. Accounts receivable and accounts payable at year-end were $60,000 and $23,000, respectively. Assume that accounts payable related to operating expenses. Ignore income taxes.

Compute cash provided by operating activities—direct method.
(SO 6)

Instructions

Compute net cash provided by operating activities using the direct method.

*E12-11 The 2004 income statement for McDonald's Corporation shows cost of goods sold $4,852.7 million and operating expenses (including depreciation expense of $1,201 million) $10,671.5 million. The comparative balance sheet for the year shows that inventory increased $18.1 million, prepaid expenses increased $56.3 million, accounts payable (merchandise suppliers) increased $136.9 million, and accrued expenses payable increased $160.9 million.

Compute cash payments—direct method.
(SO 6)

Instructions

Using the direct method, compute (a) cash payments to suppliers and (b) cash payments for operating expenses.

*E12-12 The 2007 accounting records of Verlander Transport reveal these transactions and events.

Compute cash flow from operating activities—direct method.
(SO 6)

Payment of interest	$ 10,000	Collection of accounts receivable	$182,000
Cash sales	48,000	Payment of salaries and wages	53,000
Receipt of dividend revenue	18,000	Depreciation expense	16,000
Payment of income taxes	12,000	Proceeds from sale of vehicles	812,000
Net income	38,000	Purchase of equipment for cash	22,000
Payment of accounts payable		Loss on sale of vehicles	3,000
for merchandise	115,000	Payment of dividends	14,000
Payment for land	74,000	Payment of operating expenses	28,000

Instructions

Prepare the cash flows from operating activities section using the direct method. (Not all of the items will be used.)

Calculate cash flows—direct method.
(SO 6)

*E12-13 The following information is taken from the 2007 general ledger of Pierzynski Company.

Rent	Rent expense	$ 40,000
	Prepaid rent, January 1	5,900
	Prepaid rent, December 31	9,000
Salaries	Salaries expense	$ 54,000
	Salaries payable, January 1	10,000
	Salaries payable, December 31	8,000
Sales	Revenue from sales	$170,000
	Accounts receivable, January 1	16,000
	Accounts receivable, December 31	7,000

Instructions
In each case, compute the amount that should be reported in the operating activities section of the statement of cash flows under the direct method.

Problems: Set A

Distinguish among operating, investing, and financing activities.
(SO 6)

P12-1A You are provided with the following transactions that took place during a recent fiscal year.

Transaction	Where Reported on Statement	Cash Inflow, Outflow, or No Effect?
(a) Recorded depreciation expense on the plant assets.		
(b) Recorded and paid interest expense.		
(c) Recorded cash proceeds from a sale of plant assets.		
(d) Acquired land by issuing common stock.		
(e) Paid a cash dividend to preferred stockholders.		
(f) Distributed a stock dividend to common stockholders.		
(g) Recorded cash sales.		
(h) Recorded sales on account.		
(i) Purchased inventory for cash.		
(j) Purchased inventory on account.		

Instructions
Complete the table indicating whether each item (1) should be reported as an operating (O) activity, investing (I) activity, financing (F) activity, or as a noncash (NC) transaction reported in a separate schedule, and (2) represents a cash inflow or cash outflow or has no cash flow effect. Assume use of the indirect approach.

Determine cash flow effects of changes in equity accounts.
(SO 4)

P12-2A The following account balances relate to the stockholders' equity accounts of Gore Corp. at year-end.

	2007	2006
Common stock, 10,500 and 10,000 shares, respectively, for 2007 and 2006	$160,000	$140,000
Preferred stock, 5,000 shares	125,000	125,000
Retained earnings	300,000	260,000

A small stock dividend was declared and issued in 2007. The market value of the shares was $10,500. Cash dividends were $15,000 in both 2007 and 2006. The common stock has no par or stated value.

Instructions

(a) What was the amount of net income reported by Gore Corp. in 2007?

(b) Determine the amounts of any cash inflows or outflows related to the common stock and dividend accounts in 2007.

(c) Indicate where each of the cash inflows or outflows identified in (b) would be classified on the statement of cash flows.

(a) Net income $65,500

P12-3A   The income statement of Elbert Company is presented here.

Prepare the operating activities section—indirect method.
(SO 4)

ELBERT COMPANY
Income Statement
For the Year Ended November 30, 2007

Sales		$7,700,000
Cost of goods sold		
Beginning inventory	$1,900,000	
Purchases	4,400,000	
Goods available for sale	6,300,000	
Ending inventory	1,400,000	
Total cost of goods sold		4,900,000
Gross profit		2,800,000
Operating expenses		
Selling expenses	450,000	
Administrative expenses	700,000	1,150,000
Net income		$1,650,000

Additional information:

1. Accounts receivable increased $250,000 during the year, and inventory decreased $500,000.
2. Prepaid expenses increased $150,000 during the year.
3. Accounts payable to suppliers of merchandise decreased $340,000 during the year.
4. Accrued expenses payable decreased $100,000 during the year.
5. Administrative expenses include depreciation expense of $90,000.

Instructions

Prepare the operating activities section of the statement of cash flows for the year ended November 30, 2007, for Elbert Company, using the indirect method.

Cash from operations
$1,400,000

*P12-4A   Data for Elbert Company are presented in P12-3A.

Prepare the operating activities section—direct method.
(SO 6)

Instructions

Prepare the operating activities section of the statement of cash flows using the direct method.

Cash from operations
$1,400,000

P12-5A   Grania Company's income statement contained the condensed information below.

Prepare the operating activities section—indirect method.
(SO 4)

GRANIA COMPANY
Income Statement
For the Year Ended December 31, 2007

Revenues		$970,000
Operating expenses, excluding depreciation	$624,000	
Depreciation expense	60,000	
Loss on sale of equipment	16,000	700,000
Income before income taxes		270,000
Income tax expense		40,000
Net income		$230,000

Grania's balance sheet contained the comparative data at December 31, shown on page 630.

	2007	2006
Accounts receivable	$75,000	$60,000
Accounts payable	41,000	28,000
Income taxes payable	11,000	7,000

Accounts payable pertain to operating expenses.

Cash from operations $308,000

Instructions
Prepare the operating activities section of the statement of cash flows using the indirect method.

Prepare the operating activities section—direct method.
(SO 6) Cash from operations $308,000

*P12-6A Data for Grania Company are presented in P12-5A.

Instructions
Prepare the operating activities section of the statement of cash flows using the direct method.

Prepare a statement of cash flows—indirect method, and compute cash-based ratios.
(SO 4, 5)

P12-7A Presented below are the financial statements of Weller Company.

WELLER COMPANY
Comparative Balance Sheets
December 31

Assets	2007	2006
Cash	$ 35,000	$ 20,000
Accounts receivable	33,000	14,000
Merchandise inventory	27,000	20,000
Property, plant, and equipment	60,000	78,000
Accumulated depreciation	(29,000)	(24,000)
Total	$126,000	$108,000

Liabilities and Stockholders' Equity	2007	2006
Accounts payable	$ 29,000	$ 15,000
Income taxes payable	7,000	8,000
Bonds payable	27,000	33,000
Common stock	18,000	14,000
Retained earnings	45,000	38,000
Total	$126,000	$108,000

WELLER COMPANY
Income Statement
For the Year Ended December 31, 2007

Sales		$242,000
Cost of goods sold		175,000
Gross profit		67,000
Selling expenses	$18,000	
Administrative expenses	6,000	24,000
Income from operations		43,000
Interest expense		3,000
Income before income taxes		40,000
Income tax expense		8,000
Net income		$ 32,000

Additional data:
1. Dividends declared and paid were $25,000.
2. During the year equipment was sold for $8,500 cash. This equipment cost $18,000 originally and had a book value of $8,500 at the time of sale.

3. All depreciation expense is in the selling expense category.
4. All sales and purchases are on account.

Instructions
(a) Prepare a statement of cash flows using the indirect method.
(b) Compute these cash-basis measures:
   (1) Current cash debt coverage ratio.
   (2) Cash debt coverage ratio.
   (3) Free cash flow.

(a) Cash from operations
$33,500

*P12-8A Data for Weller Company are presented in P12-7A. Further analysis reveals the following.

1. Accounts payable pertain to merchandise suppliers.
2. All operating expenses except for depreciation were paid in cash.

Prepare a statement of cash flows—direct method, and compute cash-based ratios.
(SO 5, 6)

Instructions
(a) Prepare a statement of cash flows for Weller Company using the direct method.
(b) Compute these cash-basis measures:
   (1) Current cash debt coverage ratio.
   (2) Cash debt coverage ratio.
   (3) Free cash flow.

(a) Cash from operations
$33,500

P12-9A Condensed financial data of Arma Inc. follow.

Prepare a statement of cash flows—indirect method.
(SO 4)

ARMA INC.
Comparative Balance Sheets
December 31

Assets	2007	2006
Cash	$ 90,800	$ 48,400
Accounts receivable	92,800	33,000
Inventories	112,500	102,850
Prepaid expenses	28,400	26,000
Investments	138,000	114,000
Plant assets	270,000	242,500
Accumulated depreciation	(50,000)	(52,000)
Total	$682,500	$514,750

Liabilities and Stockholders' Equity		
Accounts payable	$112,000	$ 67,300
Accrued expenses payable	16,500	17,000
Bonds payable	110,000	150,000
Common stock	220,000	175,000
Retained earnings	224,000	105,450
Total	$682,500	$514,750

ARMA INC.
Income Statement Data
For the Year Ended December 31, 2007

Sales		$392,780
Less:		
Cost of goods sold	$135,460	
Operating expenses, excluding depreciation	12,410	
Depreciation expense	46,500	
Income taxes	27,280	
Interest expense	4,730	
Loss on sale of plant assets	7,500	233,880
Net income		$158,900

Additional information:

1. New plant assets costing $85,000 were purchased for cash during the year.
2. Old plant assets having an original cost of $57,500 were sold for $1,500 cash.
3. Bonds matured and were paid off at face value for cash.
4. A cash dividend of $40,350 was declared and paid during the year.

Cash from operations
$185,250

Instructions

Prepare a statement of cash flows using the indirect method.

Prepare a statement of cash flows—direct method.
(SO 6)

*P12-10A   Data for Arma Inc. are presented in P12-9A. Further analysis reveals that accounts payable pertain to merchandise creditors.

Cash from operations
$185,250

Instructions

Prepare a statement of cash flows for Arma Inc. using the direct method.

Prepare a statement of cash flows—indirect method.
(SO 4)

P12-11A   The comparative balance sheets for Ramirez Company as of December 31 are presented below.

RAMIREZ COMPANY
Comparative Balance Sheets
December 31

Assets	2007	2006
Cash	$ 71,000	$ 45,000
Accounts receivable	44,000	62,000
Inventory	151,450	142,000
Prepaid expenses	15,280	21,000
Land	105,000	130,000
Equipment	228,000	155,000
Accumulated depreciation—equipment	(45,000)	(35,000)
Building	200,000	200,000
Accumulated depreciation—building	(60,000)	(40,000)
Total	$709,730	$680,000

Liabilities and Stockholders' Equity		
Accounts payable	$ 47,730	$ 40,000
Bonds payable	260,000	300,000
Common stock, $1 par	200,000	160,000
Retained earnings	202,000	180,000
Total	$709,730	$680,000

Additional information:

1. Operating expenses include depreciation expense of $42,000 and charges from prepaid expenses of $5,720.
2. Land was sold for cash at book value.
3. Cash dividends of $15,000 were paid.
4. Net income for 2007 was $37,000.
5. Equipment was purchased for $95,000 cash. In addition, equipment costing $22,000 with a book value of $10,000 was sold for $6,000 cash.
6. Bonds were converted at face value by issuing 40,000 shares of $1 par value common stock.

Cash from operations
$105,000

Instructions

Prepare a statement of cash flows for the year ended December 31, 2007, using the indirect method.

P12-12A You are provided with the following transactions that took place during the year. *Identify the impact of transactions on ratios.* (SO 5)

Transactions	Free Cash Flow ($125,000)	Current Cash Debt Coverage Ratio (0.5 times)	Cash Debt Coverage Ratio (0.3 times)
(a) Recorded credit sales $2,500.			
(b) Collected $1,500 owing from customers.			
(c) Paid amount owing to suppliers $2,750.			
(d) Recorded sales returns of $500 and credited the customer's account.			
(e) Purchased new equipment $5,000; signed a long-term note payable for the cost of the equipment.			
(f) Purchased a patent and paid $15,000 cash for the asset.			

Instructions
For each transaction listed above, indicate whether it will increase (I), decrease (D), or have no effect (NE) on the ratios.

Problems: Set B

P12-1B You are provided with the following transactions that took place during a recent fiscal year. *Distinguish among operating, investing, and financing activities.* (SO 2)

Transaction	Where Reported on Statement	Cash Inflow, Outflow, or No Effect?
(a) Recorded depreciation expense on the plant assets.		
(b) Incurred a loss on disposal of plant assets.		
(c) Acquired a building by paying cash.		
(d) Made principal repayments on a mortgage.		
(e) Issued common stock.		
(f) Purchased shares of another company to be held as a long-term equity investment.		
(g) Paid dividends to common stockholders.		
(h) Sold inventory on credit. The company uses a perpetual inventory system.		
(i) Purchased inventory on credit.		
(j) Paid wages to employees.		

Instructions
Complete the table indicating whether each item (1) should be reported as an operating (O) activity, investing (I) activity, financing (F) activity, or as a noncash (NC) transaction reported in a separate schedule, and (2) represents a cash inflow or cash outflow or has no cash flow effect. Assume use of the indirect approach.

Determine cash flow effects of changes in plant asset accounts.
(SO 4)

P12-2B The following selected account balances relate to the plant asset accounts of Zambia Inc. at year-end.

	2007	2006
Accumulated depreciation—buildings	$337,500	$300,000
Accumulated depreciation—equipment	144,000	96,000
Buildings	750,000	750,000
Depreciation expense	101,500	85,500
Equipment	300,000	240,000
Land	100,000	70,000
Loss on sale of equipment	3,000	0

Additional information:

1. Zambia purchased $85,000 of equipment and $30,000 of land for cash in 2007.
2. Zambia also sold equipment in 2007.
3. Depreciation expense in 2007 was $37,500 on building and $64,000 on equipment.

Instructions

(a) Cash proceeds $6,000

(a) Determine the amounts of any cash inflows or outflows related to the plant asset accounts in 2007.
(b) Indicate where each of the cash inflows or outflows identified in (a) would be classified on the statement of cash flows.

Prepare the operating activities section—indirect method.
(SO 4)

P12-3B The income statement of Marquette Company is presented below.

Additional information:

1. Accounts receivable decreased $520,000 during the year, and inventory increased $140,000.
2. Prepaid expenses increased $175,000 during the year.
3. Accounts payable to merchandise suppliers increased $50,000 during the year.
4. Accrued expenses payable increased $165,000 during the year.

MARQUETTE COMPANY
Income Statement
For the Year Ended December 31, 2007

Sales		$5,400,000
Cost of goods sold		
Beginning inventory	$1,780,000	
Purchases	3,430,000	
Goods available for sale	5,210,000	
Ending inventory	1,920,000	
Total cost of goods sold		3,290,000
Gross profit		2,110,000
Operating expenses		
Selling expenses	420,000	
Administrative expense	525,000	
Depreciation expense	105,000	
Amortization expense	20,000	1,070,000
Net income		$1,040,000

Cash from operations $1,585,000

Instructions
Prepare the operating activities section of the statement of cash flows for the year ended December 31, 2007, for Marquette Company, using the indirect method.

Prepare the operating activities section—direct method.
(SO 6)
Cash from operations $1,585,000

P12-4B Data for Marquette Company are presented in P12-3B.

Instructions
Prepare the operating activities section of the statement of cash flows using the direct method.

P12-5B The income statement of Shapiro Inc. reported the following condensed information.

Prepare the operating activities section—indirect method.
(SO 4)

SHAPIRO INC.
Income Statement
For the Year Ended December 31, 2007

Revenues	$545,000
Operating expenses	400,000
Income from operations	145,000
Income tax expense	47,000
Net income	$ 98,000

Shapiro's balance sheet contained these comparative data at December 31.

	2007	2006
Accounts receivable	$50,000	$75,000
Accounts payable	30,000	51,000
Income taxes payable	10,000	4,000

Shapiro has no depreciable assets. Accounts payable pertain to operating expenses.

Instructions
Prepare the operating activities section of the statement of cash flows using the indirect method.

Cash from operations
$108,000

*P12-6B Data for Shapiro Inc. are presented in P12-5B.

Prepare the operating activities section—direct method.
(SO 6)

Instructions
Prepare the operating activities section of the statement of cash flows using the direct method.

Cash from operations
$108,000

P12-7B Here and on page 636 are the financial statements of Molina Company.

Prepare a statement of cash flows—indirect method, and compute cash-based ratios.
(SO 4, 5)

MOLINA COMPANY
Comparative Balance Sheets
December 31

Assets		2007		2006
Cash		$ 28,000		$ 33,000
Accounts receivable		23,000		14,000
Merchandise inventory		41,000		25,000
Property, plant, and equipment	$ 70,000		$ 78,000	
Less: Accumulated depreciation	(27,000)	43,000	(24,000)	54,000
Total		$135,000		$126,000

Liabilities and Stockholders' Equity	2007	2006
Accounts payable	$ 31,000	$ 43,000
Income taxes payable	26,000	20,000
Bonds payable	20,000	10,000
Common stock	25,000	25,000
Retained earnings	33,000	28,000
Total	$135,000	$126,000

MOLINA COMPANY
Income Statement
For the Year Ended December 31, 2007

Sales		$286,000
Cost of goods sold		194,000
Gross profit		92,000
Selling expenses	$28,000	
Administrative expenses	9,000	37,000
Income from operations		55,000
Interest expense		7,000
Income before income taxes		48,000
Income tax expense		10,000
Net income		$ 38,000

Additional data:

1. Dividends of $33,000 were declared and paid.
2. During the year equipment was sold for $10,000 cash. This equipment cost $13,000 originally and had a book value of $10,000 at the time of sale.
3. All depreciation expense, $6,000, is in the selling expense category.
4. All sales and purchases are on account.
5. Additional equipment was purchased for $5,000 cash.

Instructions

(a) Cash from operations $13,000

(a) Prepare a statement of cash flows using the indirect method.
(b) Compute these cash-basis measures:
  (1) Current cash debt coverage ratio.
  (2) Cash debt coverage ratio.
  (3) Free cash flow.

Prepare a statement of cash flows—direct method, and compute cash-based ratios. (SO 5, 6)

*P12-8B Data for Molina Company are presented in P12-7B. Further analysis reveals the following.

1. Accounts payable pertains to merchandise creditors.
2. All operating expenses except for depreciation are paid in cash.

Instructions

(a) Cash from operations $13,000

(a) Prepare a statement of cash flows using the direct method.
(b) Compute these cash-basis measures:
  (1) Current cash debt coverage ratio.
  (2) Cash debt coverage ratio.
  (3) Free cash flow.

Prepare a statement of cash flows—indirect method. (SO 4)

P12-9B Condensed financial data of Yaeger Company are shown below and on page 637.

YAEGER COMPANY
Comparative Balance Sheets
December 31

Assets	2007	2006
Cash	$ 97,700	$ 33,400
Accounts receivable	70,800	37,000
Inventories	121,900	102,650
Investments	89,500	107,000
Plant assets	310,000	205,000
Accumulated depreciation	(49,500)	(40,000)
Total	$640,400	$445,050

Liabilities and Stockholders' Equity

Accounts payable	$ 62,700	$ 48,280
Accrued expenses payable	15,100	18,830
Bonds payable	140,000	70,000
Common stock	250,000	200,000
Retained earnings	172,600	107,940
Total	$640,400	$445,050

YAEGER COMPANY
Income Statement Data
For the Year Ended December 31, 2007

Sales		$297,500
Gain on sale of plant assets		5,000
		302,500
Less:		
Cost of goods sold	$99,460	
Operating expenses, excluding depreciation expense	14,670	
Depreciation expense	35,500	
Income taxes	27,270	
Interest expense	2,940	179,840
Net income		$122,660

Additional information:

1. New plant assets costing $141,000 were purchased for cash during the year.
2. Investments were sold at cost.
3. Plant assets costing $36,000 were sold for $15,000, resulting in a gain of $5,000.
4. A cash dividend of $58,000 was declared and paid during the year.

Instructions
Prepare a statement of cash flows using the indirect method.

Cash from operations
$110,800

*P12-10B Data for Yaeger Company are presented in P12-9B. Further analysis reveals that accounts payable pertain to merchandise creditors.

Prepare a statement of cash flows—direct method.
(SO 6)

Instructions
Prepare a statement of cash flows for Yaeger Company using the direct method.

Cash from operations
$110,800

P12-11B Presented below and on the next page are the comparative balance sheets for Lewis Company at December 31.

Prepare a statement of cash flows—indirect method.
(SO 4)

LEWIS COMPANY
Comparative Balance Sheets
December 31

Assets	2007	2006
Cash	$ 31,000	$ 57,000
Accounts receivable	77,000	64,000
Inventory	192,000	140,000
Prepaid expenses	12,140	16,540
Land	100,000	150,000
Equipment	215,000	175,000
Accumulated depreciation—equipment	(70,000)	(42,000)
Building	250,000	250,000
Accumulated depreciation—building	(70,000)	(50,000)
Total	$737,140	$760,540

Liabilities and Stockholders' Equity

Accounts payable	$ 58,000	$ 45,000
Bonds payable	235,000	265,000
Common stock, $1 par	280,000	250,000
Retained earnings	164,140	200,540
Total	$737,140	$760,540

Additional information:

1. Operating expenses include depreciation expense $65,000 and charges from prepaid expenses of $4,400.
2. Land was sold for cash at cost.
3. Cash dividends of $69,290 were paid.
4. Net income for 2007 was $32,890.
5. Equipment was purchased for $80,000 cash. In addition, equipment costing $40,000 with a book value of $23,000 was sold for $25,000 cash.
6. Bonds were converted at face value by issuing 30,000 shares of $1 par value common stock.

Instructions

Prepare a statement of cash flows for 2007 using the indirect method.

Cash from operations
$48,290

Problems: Set C

Visit the book's website at **www.wiley.com/college/kimmel** and choose the Student Companion site to access Problem Set C.

Continuing Cookie Chronicle

(*Note:* This is a continuation of the Cookie Chronicle from Chapters 1 through 11.)

CCC12 Natalie is preparing the balance sheet and income statement of Cookie & Coffee Creations Inc. and would like you to prepare the cash flow statement. The comparative balance sheet of Cookie & Coffee Creations Inc. at October 31, 2009 for the years 2009 and 2008 and the income statement for the year ended October 31, 2009, are presented on page 639.

Additional information:

1. All of the computer equipment was disposed of at the beginning of the year for $500 cash. New computer equipment was then bought for $4,000 cash.
2. Additional kitchen equipment was bought for $14,000 on November 1, 2008. A $9,000 note payable was signed. The terms provide for equal semi-annual installment payments of $1,500 on May 1 and November 1 of each year, plus interest of 5% on the outstanding principal balance.
3. Additional furniture was bought for $7,500 cash.
4. Dividends were declared on the preferred and common stock on October 15, 2009, to be paid on November 15, 2009.
5. Accounts payable relate only to merchandise creditors.
6. Prepaid expenses relate only to other operating expenses.

Instructions

(a) Prepare a statement of cash flows for Cookie & Coffee Creations Inc. for the year ended October 31, 2009, using the indirect method.
*(b) Prepare a statement of cash flows for Cookie & Coffee Creations Inc. for the year ended October 31, 2009, using the direct method.

COOKIE & COFFEE CREATIONS INC.
Balance Sheet
October 31, 2009

Assets	2009	2008
Cash	$ 34,324	$13,050
Accounts receivable	3,250	2,710
Inventory	7,897	7,450
Prepaid expenses	6,300	6,050
Furniture and fixtures	12,500	5,000
Accumulated depreciation—furniture and fixtures	(2,000)	(1,000)
Computer equipment	4,000	4,500
Accumulated depreciation—computer equipment	(600)	(1,500)
Kitchen equipment	80,000	66,000
Accumulated depreciation—kitchen equipment	(22,600)	(6,600)
Total assets	$123,071	$95,660

Liabilities and Stockholders' Equity		
Accounts payable	$ 3,650	$ 2,450
Income taxes payable	10,251	11,200
Dividends payable	28,000	25,000
Salaries payable	2,250	1,280
Interest payable	188	0
Note payable	7,500	0
Preferred stock, no par, $6 cumulative, 3,000 and 2,500 shares issued, respectively	15,000	12,500
Common stock, $1 par—23,180 shares issued and outstanding	23,180	23,180
Additional paid-in capital—Treasury stock	250	250
Retained earnings	32,802	19,800
Total liabilities and stockholders' equity	$123,071	$95,660

COOKIE & COFFEE CREATIONS INC.
Income Statement
Year Ended October 31, 2009

Sales		$485,625
Cost of goods sold		222,694
Gross profit		262,931
Operating expenses		
Depreciation expense	$ 17,600	
Salaries and wages expense	147,979	
Other operating expenses	43,186	208,765
Income from operations		54,166
Other expenses		
Interest expense	$ 413	
Loss on sale of computer equipment	2,500	2,913
Income before income tax		51,253
Income tax expense		10,251
Net income		$ 41,002

▶ BROADENING YOUR PERSPECTIVE

Financial Reporting and Analysis

FINANCIAL REPORTING PROBLEM: *Tootsie Roll Industries, Inc.*

BYP12-1 The financial statements of Tootsie Roll Industries are presented in Appendix A.

Instructions
Answer the following questions.
(a) What was the amount of net cash provided by operating activities for 2004? For 2003? What were some causes of any significant changes in cash from operations between 2003 and 2004?
(b) What was the amount of increase or decrease in cash and cash equivalents for the year ended December 31, 2004?
(c) Which method of computing net cash provided by operating activities does Tootsie Roll use?
(d) From your analysis of the 2004 statement of cash flows, was the change in accounts receivable a decrease or an increase? Was the change in inventories a decrease or an increase? Was the change in accounts payable a decrease or an increase?
(e) What was the net cash used by investing activities for 2004?
(f) What was the amount of interest paid in 2004? What was the amount of income taxes paid in 2004?

COMPARATIVE ANALYSIS PROBLEM: *Tootsie Roll vs. Hershey Foods*

BYP12-2 The financial statements of Hershey Foods are presented in Appendix B, following the financial statements for Tootsie Roll Industries in Appendix A.

Instructions
(a) Based on the information in these financial statements, compute these 2004 ratios for each company:
  (1) Current cash debt coverage.
  (2) Cash debt coverage.
(b) What conclusions about the management of cash can you draw from these data?

RESEARCH CASE

BYP12-3 The April 16, 2004, edition of the *Wall Street Journal* contains an article by Jonathan Weil titled, "Outside Audit: 'Cash Flow Never Lies'—Or Does It?"

Instructions
Read the article and answer the following questions.
(a) According to the article, why do investors pay close attention to the statement of cash flows?
(b) In what section of the statement of cash flows are customer-related cash flows usually reported? In what section of the statement of cash flows are loans to other entities usually reported?
(c) In what section of the statement of cash flows does Ford Motor Co. report loans to customers? In what section of the statement of cash flows does Navistar report loans to customers? What implication does this have for cash flows from operations?

INTERPRETING FINANCIAL STATEMENTS

BYP12-4 The incredible growth of Amazon.com has put fear into the hearts of traditional retailers. Its stock price has soared to amazing levels. However, in 2001 many investors were very concerned about whether Amazon would survive since it had never earned a profit, and it was burning through cash. Some investors sold, but others decided to hold on to their investment in the company's stock. The following information is taken from the 2001 and 2004 financial statements of Amazon.com.

($ in millions)	2001	2004
Current assets	$1,207.9	$2,539.4
Total assets	1,637.5	3,248.5
Current liabilities	921.4	1,620.4
Total liabilities	3,077.5	5,096.1
Cash provided by operations	(119.8)	566.6
Capital expenditures	50.3	89.1
Dividends paid	0	0
Net income (loss)	(567.3)	588.5
Average current liabilities	948.2	1,436.6
Average total liabilities	3,090.0	4,773.4

Instructions
(a) Calculate the current ratio and current cash debt coverage ratio for Amazon.com for 2001 and 2004, and discuss its comparative liquidity.
(b) Calculate the cash debt coverage ratio and the debt to total assets ratio for Amazon.com for 2001 and 2004, and discuss its comparative solvency.
(c) Amazon.com has avoided purchasing large warehouses. Instead, it has used those of others. In order to increase customer satisfaction Amazon may have to build its own warehouses. Calculate free cash flow for Amazon.com for 2001 and 2004, and discuss its ability to purchase warehouses and to finance expansion from internally generated cash.
(d) Based on your findings in parts (a) through (d), can you conclude whether or not Amazon.com's amazing stock price is justified?

FINANCIAL ANALYSIS ON THE WEB

BYP12-5 *Purpose:* Use the Internet to view SEC filings.

Address: **biz.yahoo.com/i** (or go to **www.wiley.com/college/kimmel**)

Steps
1. Enter a company's name.
2. Choose **Quote**. Answer questions (a) and (b).
3. Choose **Profile;** then choose **SEC**. Answer questions (c) and (d).

Instructions
Answer the following questions.
(a) What company did you select?
(b) What is its stock symbol? What is its selling price?
(c) What recent SEC filings are available for your viewing?
(d) Which filing is the most recent? What is the date?

Critical Thinking

DECISION MAKING ACROSS THE ORGANIZATION

BYP12-6 Ron Nord and Lisa Smith are examining the following statement of cash flows for Carpino Company for the year ended January 31, 2007.

CARPINO COMPANY
Statement of Cash Flows
For the Year Ended January 31, 2007

Sources of cash	
From sales of merchandise	$380,000
From sale of capital stock	420,000
From sale of investment (purchased below)	80,000
From depreciation	55,000
From issuance of note for truck	20,000
From interest on investments	6,000
Total sources of cash	961,000

(continues on next page)

Uses of cash		
For purchase of fixtures and equipment	330,000	
For merchandise purchased for resale	258,000	
For operating expenses (including depreciation)	160,000	
For purchase of investment	75,000	
For purchase of truck by issuance of note	20,000	
For purchase of treasury stock	10,000	
For interest on note payable	3,000	
Total uses of cash		856,000
Net increase in cash		$ 105,000

Ron claims that Carpino's statement of cash flows is an excellent portrayal of a superb first year with cash increasing $105,000. Lisa replies that it was not a superb first year. Rather, she says, the year was an operating failure, that the statement is presented incorrectly, and that $105,000 is not the actual increase in cash. The cash balance at the beginning of the year was $140,000.

Instructions
With the class divided into groups, answer the following.
(a) Using the data provided, prepare a statement of cash flows in proper form using the indirect method. The only noncash items in the income statement are depreciation and the gain from the sale of the investment.
(b) With whom do you agree, Ron or Lisa? Explain your position.

COMMUNICATION ACTIVITY

BYP12-7 Kyle Benson, the owner-president of Iris Co., is unfamiliar with the statement of cash flows that you, as his accountant, prepared. He asks for further explanation.

Instructions
Write him a brief memo explaining the form and content of the statement of cash flows as shown in Illustration 12-14 (page 602).

ETHICS CASE

BYP12-8 On The Road Again Corp. is a medium-sized wholesaler of automotive parts. It has 10 stockholders who have been paid a total of $1 million in cash dividends for 8 consecutive years. The board's policy requires that, for this dividend to be declared, net cash provided by operating activities as reported in On The Road Again's current year's statement of cash flows must exceed $1 million. President and CEO Willie Morton's job is secure so long as he produces annual operating cash flows to support the usual dividend.

At the end of the current year, controller Robert Jennings presents president Willie Morton with some disappointing news: The net cash provided by operating activities is calculated by the indirect method to be only $970,000. The president says to Robert, "We must get that amount above $1 million. Isn't there some way to increase operating cash flow by another $30,000?" Robert answers, "These figures were prepared by my assistant. I'll go back to my office and see what I can do." The president replies, "I know you won't let me down, Robert."

Upon close scrutiny of the statement of cash flows, Robert concludes that he can get the operating cash flows above $1 million by reclassifying a $60,000, 2-year note payable listed in the financing activities section as "Proceeds from bank loan—$60,000." He will report the note instead as "Increase in payables—$60,000" and treat it as an adjustment of net income in the operating activities section. He returns to the president, saying, "You can tell the board to declare their usual dividend. Our net cash flow provided by operating activities is $1,030,000." "Good man, Robert! I knew I could count on you," exults the president.

Instructions
(a) Who are the stakeholders in this situation?
(b) Was there anything unethical about the president's actions? Was there anything unethical about the controller's actions?
(c) Are the board members or anyone else likely to discover the misclassification?

Answers to Business Insight and Accounting across the Organization Questions

p. 589

Q: In general, why do differences exist between net income and net cash provided by operating activities?

A: The differences are explained by differences in the timing of the reporting of revenues and expenses under accrual accounting versus cash. Under accrual accounting, companies report revenues when earned, even if cash hasn't been received, and they report expenses when incurred, even if cash hasn't been paid.

p. 592

Q: Why do companies have negative cash from operations during the introductory phase?

A: During the introductory phase companies usually spend more on inventory than the amount expensed for cost of goods sold because they are building up inventory, and their cash collections frequently lag the amount reported for sales. Therefore, even if they are reporting positive net income, they frequently report negative cash from operations.

p. 594

Q: For what reasons might managers at WorldCom and at Dynegy take the actions noted above?

A: Analysts increasingly use cash-flow-based measures of income, such as cash flow provided by operations, in addition to net income. More investors now focus on cash flow from operations, and some compensation contracts now have bonuses tied to cash-flow numbers. Thus, some managers have taken actions that artificially increase cash flow from operations.

p. 600

Q: Why does GM's cash provided by operating activities drop so precipitously when the company's sales figures decline?

A: GM's cash inflow is directly related to how many cars it sells. But many of its cash outflows are not tied to sales—they are "fixed." For example, many of its employee payroll costs are very rigid due to labor contracts. Therefore, even though sales (and therefore cash inflows) fall, these cash outflows don't decline.

p. 606

Q: If the ratio of net income to cash from operations differs significantly from 1, does that always mean that a company has poor-quality earnings?

A: When the ratio of net income to cash from operations differs significantly from 1, it means that an investor should closely examine the reasons why net income and cash from operations differ. However, as discussed in this chapter, at various stages in a company's life cycle, there can be legitimate reasons why net income and cash flow differ.

Answer to Tootsie Roll Review It Question 2, p. 594

Tootsie Roll has positive cash from operations that exceeds its net income. Its cash from operations exceeded its dividends paid and its capital expenditures. Tootsie Roll appears to be in the middle to late maturity phase.

Answers to Self-Study Questions

1. c   2. b   3. a   4. c   5. d   6. b   7. c   8. a   9. d   10. b
11. a   12. d   *13. c   *14. d

 REMEMBER TO GO BACK TO THE NAVIGATOR BOX ON THE CHAPTER-OPENING PAGE AND CHECK OFF YOUR COMPLETED WORK.

CHAPTER 13

Financial Analysis: The Big Picture

STUDY OBJECTIVES

After studying this chapter,
you should be able to:

1 Understand the concept of sustainable income.

2 Indicate how irregular items are presented.

3 Explain the concept of comprehensive income.

4 Describe and apply horizontal analysis.

5 Describe and apply vertical analysis.

6 Identify and compute ratios used in analyzing a company's liquidity, solvency, and profitability.

7 Understand the concept of quality of earnings.

THE NAVIGATOR

✓ THE NAVIGATOR

- Scan *Study Objectives* ⬭
- Read *Feature Story* ⬭
- Read *Preview* ⬭
- Read text and answer *Before You Go On*
  p. 653 ⬭   p. 661 ⬭   p. 663 ⬭
- Work *Using the Decision Toolkit* ⬭
- Review *Summary of Study Objectives* ⬭
- Work *Demonstration Problem* ⬭
- Answer *Self-Study Questions* ⬭
- Complete *Assignments* ⬭

FEATURE STORY

Making the Numbers

There it is again, perched near the top of *Fortune*'s "Most Admired Companies" list. But when the people who run General Electric go out in public these days, they don't exactly get to bask in adulation. Instead, they have to explain how their company is *not* like Enron, or Global Crossing, or Tyco.

At one level, that's a pretty easy argument to make. GE is not about to collapse or to break up. It has tons of cash, and its businesses generate upwards of a billion dollars every month. It is one of only a handful of companies with a triple-A credit rating. It makes real things like turbines and refrigerators that people spend real money to buy.

GE also has an enviable record of pleasing Wall Street. Quarter after quarter, year after year, GE's earnings come gushing in, usually at least 10% higher than the year before, and almost invariably in line with analysts' estimates.

This used to be seen as a good thing. "Making the numbers" became the most watched measure of corporate performance. By missing only once during a 10-year period (by a penny, in the fourth quarter of 1997), GE ensured itself a hallowed place in the corporate hall of fame.

But as one analyst noted, "Smoking used to be chic and fashionable and cool; now it's not. The companies that reliably deliver 15% earnings growth year after year are the new smokers." All of which means that GE's chief executive, Jeffrey Immelt, now finds himself having to tell interviewer after interviewer that no, he's not an earnings cheat.

"Would a miss be more honest?" Immelt asks, with exasperation in his voice. "I think that's terrible. That's where the world has gotten totally turned on its head, where somewhere I'd walk up to a podium and get a Nobel Peace Prize for saying 'I missed my numbers—aren't you proud of me?' "

Source: Adapted from Justin Fox, "What's So Great About GE?" *Fortune* (March 4, 2002), pp. 65–66.

THE NAVIGATOR

On the World Wide Web
General Electric: www.ge.com

P R E V I E W   O F   C H A P T E R   1 3

As indicated in our Feature Story, even the most admired companies in the United States are under attack for their earnings and disclosure practices. A climate of skepticism has caused many companies to lose billions of dollars in market value if there is even the slightest hint that the company is involved in some form of creative accounting. The purpose of this chapter is to explain the importance of **performance measurement** and to highlight the difficulties of developing **high-quality earnings numbers**, given the complexities of modern business transactions.

The content and organization of this chapter are as follows.

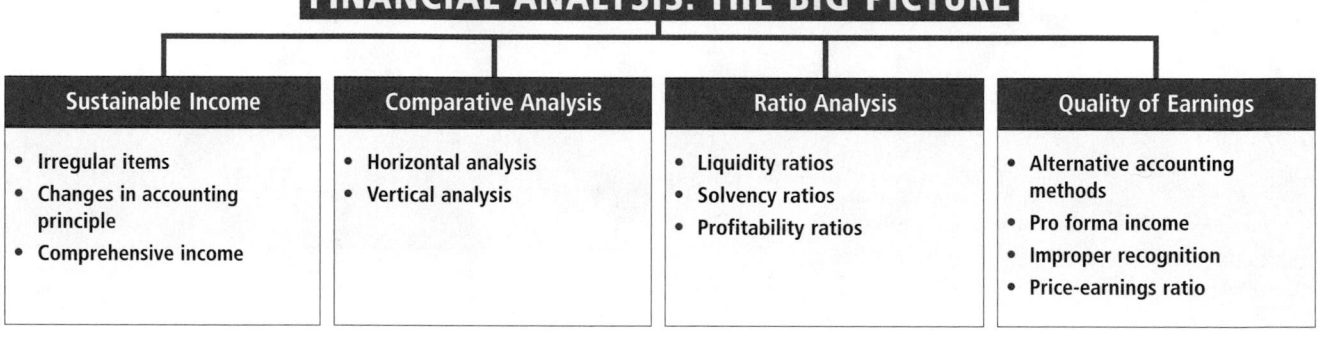

FINANCIAL ANALYSIS: THE BIG PICTURE

Sustainable Income	Comparative Analysis	Ratio Analysis	Quality of Earnings
• Irregular items • Changes in accounting principle • Comprehensive income	• Horizontal analysis • Vertical analysis	• Liquidity ratios • Solvency ratios • Profitability ratios	• Alternative accounting methods • Pro forma income • Improper recognition • Price-earnings ratio

Sustainable Income

STUDY OBJECTIVE

1

Understand the concept of sustainable income.

Ultimately, the value of a company is a function of its future cash flows. When analysts use this year's net income to estimate future cash flows, they must make sure that this year's net income does not include irregular (i.e., out of the ordinary) revenues, expenses, gains, or losses. Net income adjusted for irregular items is referred to as **sustainable income**. **Sustainable income is the most likely level of income to be obtained in the future.** Sustainable income differs from actual net income by the amount of irregular revenues, expenses, gains, and losses included in this year's net income.

Users are interested in sustainable income because it helps them derive an estimate of future earnings without the "noise" of irregular items. For example, suppose Rye Corporation reports that this year's net income is $500,000 but included in that amount is a once-in-a-lifetime gain of $400,000. In estimating next year's net income for Rye Corporation, we would likely ignore this $400,000 gain and estimate that next year's net income will be in the neighborhood of $100,000. That is, based on this year's results, the company's sustainable income is roughly $100,000. Therefore, identifying irregular items is important if you are going to use reported earnings to estimate a company's value.

In earlier chapters you learned how to prepare and use a basic multiple-step income statement. In this chapter we will explain additional components of the income statement as well as a broader measure of performance called *comprehensive income*. Illustration 13-1 (page 647) presents the components of the income statement and comprehensive income; new items are presented in red. When estimating future cash flows, analysts must consider the implications that each of these components has for future cash flows.

Income Statement

Sales	$XX
Cost of goods sold	XX
Gross profit	XX
Operating expenses	XX
Income from operations	XX
Other revenues (expenses) and gains (losses)	XX
Income before income taxes	XX
Income tax expense	XX
Income before irregular items	XX
Irregular items (net of tax)	XX
Net income	XX
Other comprehensive income items (net of tax)	XX
Comprehensive income	$XX

IRREGULAR ITEMS

As an aid in determining sustainable income, we identify irregular items by type on the income statement. There, companies report two types of irregular items:

1. Discontinued operations
2. Extraordinary items

Irregular items are reported net of income taxes. That is, a company first calculates income tax expense for the income before irregular items. Then it calculates income tax expense for each individual irregular item. The general concept is, "Let the tax follow the income or loss."

Discontinued Operations

To downsize its operations, General Dynamics Corp. sold its missile business to Hughes Aircraft Co. for $450 million. In its income statement, General Dynamics reported the sale in a separate section entitled "Discontinued operations." **Discontinued operations** refers to the disposal of a significant component of a business, such as the elimination of a major class of customers or an entire activity. When the disposal of a significant component occurs, the income statement should report the gain (or loss) from discontinued operations, net of tax.

To illustrate, assume that Rozek Inc. has revenues of $2.5 million and expenses of $1.7 million from continuing operations in 2007. The company therefore has income before income taxes of $800,000. During 2007 the company discontinued and sold its unprofitable chemical division. The loss on disposal of the chemical division (net of $90,000 taxes) was $210,000. Illustration 13-2 shows the income statement presentation, assuming a 30% tax rate on income before income taxes.

ROZEK INC.
Income Statement (partial)
For the Year Ended December 31, 2007

Income before income taxes	$ 800,000
Income tax expense	240,000
Income before irregular items	560,000
Discontinued operations	
Loss from disposal of chemical division, net of $90,000 income tax savings	(210,000)
Net income	$ 350,000

This presentation clearly indicates the separate effects of continuing operations and discontinued operations on net income.

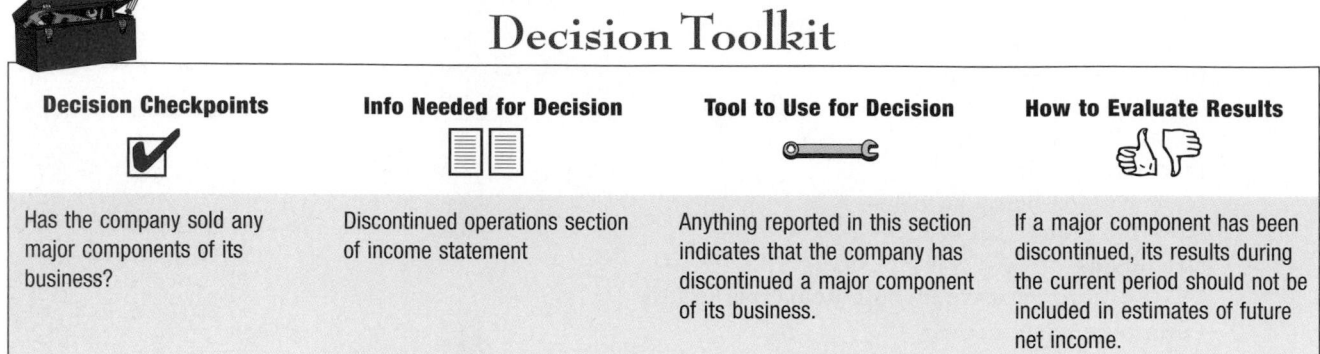

Decision Toolkit

Decision Checkpoints	Info Needed for Decision	Tool to Use for Decision	How to Evaluate Results
Has the company sold any major components of its business?	Discontinued operations section of income statement	Anything reported in this section indicates that the company has discontinued a major component of its business.	If a major component has been discontinued, its results during the current period should not be included in estimates of future net income.

Extraordinary Items

Extraordinary items are events and transactions that meet two conditions: They are **unusual in nature** and **infrequent in occurrence**. To be considered *unusual*, the item should be abnormal and only incidentally related to the customary activities of the entity. To be regarded as *infrequent*, the event or transaction should not be reasonably expected to recur in the foreseeable future.

A company must evaluate both criteria in terms of the environment in which it operates. Thus, Weyerhaeuser Co. reported the $36 million in damages to its timberland caused by the eruption of Mount St. Helens as an extraordinary item because the event was both unusual and infrequent. In contrast, Florida Citrus Company does not report frost damage to its citrus crop as an extraordinary item because frost damage is not viewed as infrequent.

Companies report extraordinary items net of taxes in a separate section of the income statement, immediately below discontinued operations. To illustrate, assume that in 2007 a revolutionary foreign government expropriated property held as an investment by Rozek Inc. If the loss is $70,000 before applicable income taxes of $21,000, the income statement presentation will show a deduction of $49,000, as in Illustration 13-3.

Helpful Hint Ordinary gains and losses are reported at pretax amounts in arriving at income before income taxes.

Illustration 13-3
Statement presentation of extraordinary items

ROZEK INC. Income Statement (partial) For the Year Ended December 31, 2007	
Income before income taxes	$ 800,000
Income tax expense	240,000
Income before irregular items	560,000
Discontinued operations: Loss from disposal of chemical division, net of $90,000 income tax savings	(210,000)
Extraordinary item: Expropriation of investment, net of $21,000 income tax savings	**(49,000)**
Net income	$ 301,000

If a transaction or event meets one but not both of the criteria for an extraordinary item, a company should report it in a separate line item in the upper half of the income statement, rather than in the bottom half as an extraordinary item. Usually companies report these items under either "Other revenues and gains" or "Other expenses and losses" at their gross amount (not net of tax). This is true, for example, of gains (losses) resulting from the sale of property, plant, and equipment, as explained in Chapter 9. Illustration 13-4 shows the appropriate classification of extraordinary and ordinary items.

Illustration 13-4
Classification of extraordinary and ordinary items

Extraordinary items	**Ordinary items**

Extraordinary items

1. Effects of major natural casualties, if rare in the area.

2. Expropriation (takeover) of property by a foreign government.

3. Effects of a newly enacted law or regulation, such as a condemnation action.

Ordinary items

1. Effects of major natural casualties, not uncommon in the area.

2. Write-down of inventories or write-off of receivables.

3. Losses attributable to labor strikes.

4. Gains or losses from sales of property, plant, or equipment.

In summary, in evaluating a company, it generally makes sense to eliminate all irregular items in estimating future sustainable income.

Business Insight
Investor Perspective

Many companies these days are incurring restructuring charges as a result of attempting to reduce costs. Are these costs ordinary or extraordinary? Some companies report "one-time" restructuring charges over and over. Case in point: Toothpaste and diapers giant Procter & Gamble Co. reported a restructuring charge in 12 consecutive quarters, and Motorola had "special" charges 14 quarters in a row. On the other hand, some companies take a restructuring charge only once in five years. The one-size-fits-all classification therefore will not work. There appears to be no substitute for a careful analysis of the numbers that comprise net income.

 If a company takes a large restructuring charge, what is the effect on the company's current income statements versus future ones?

Decision Toolkit

Decision Checkpoints	Info Needed for Decision	Tool to Use for Decision	How to Evaluate Results
✔			
Has the company experienced any extraordinary events or transactions?	Extraordinary item section of income statement	Anything reported in this section indicates that the company experienced an event that was both unusual and infrequent.	These items should usually be ignored in estimating future net income.

CHANGES IN ACCOUNTING PRINCIPLE

For ease of comparison, users of financial statements expect companies to prepare such statements on a basis **consistent** with the preceding period. A **change in accounting principle** occurs when the principle used in the current year is different from the one used in the preceding year. Accounting rules permit a change when management can show that the new principle is preferable to the old principle. An example is a change in inventory costing methods (such as FIFO to average cost).

Companies report most changes in accounting principle retroactively.[1] That is, they report both the current period and previous periods using the new principle. As a result the same principle applies in all periods. This treatment improves the ability to compare results across years.

Decision Toolkit

Decision Checkpoints	Info Needed for Decision	Tool to Use for Decision	How to Evaluate Results
✔			
Has the company changed any of its accounting principles?	Effect of change in accounting principle on current and prior periods.	Management indicates that the new principle is preferable to the old principle.	Examine current and prior years reported, using new-principle basis to assess trends for estimating future income.

COMPREHENSIVE INCOME

Most revenues, expenses, gains, and losses are included in net income. However, certain gains and losses bypass net income. Instead, companies record these items as direct adjustments to stockholders' equity. Many analysts have expressed concern about this practice because they believe it reduces the usefulness of the income statement. To address this concern, the FASB requires companies to report not only net income, but also comprehensive income. **Comprehensive income** includes all changes in stockholders' equity during a period except those

---

[1] An exception to the general rule is a change in depreciation methods. The effects of this change are reported in current and future periods. Discussion of this approach in left for more advanced courses.

changes resulting from investments by stockholders and distributions (dividends) to stockholders.

Illustration of Comprehensive Income

Accounting standards require that companies adjust most investments in stocks and bonds up or down to their market value at the end of each accounting period. For example, assume that during 2007 Stassi Company purchased IBM stock for $10,000 as an investment. At the end of 2007 Stassi was still holding the investment, but the stock's market value was now $8,000. In this case, Stassi is required to reduce the recorded value of its IBM investment by $2,000. The $2,000 difference is an unrealized loss.

Should Stassi include this $2,000 unrealized loss in net income? It depends on whether Stassi classifies the IBM stock as a trading security or an available-for-sale security. A **trading security** is bought and held primarily for sale in the near term to generate income on short-term price differences. Companies report unrealized losses on trading securities in the "Other expenses and losses" section of the income statement. The rationale: It is likely that the company will realize the unrealized loss (or an unrealized gain), so the company should report the loss (gain) as part of net income.

If Stassi did not purchase the investment for trading purposes, it is classified as available-for-sale. **Available-for-sale securities** are held with the intent of selling them sometime in the future. Companies do not include unrealized gains or losses on available-for-sale securities in net income. Instead, they report them as part of "Other comprehensive income." For example, if Stassi does not intend to sell its IBM stock in the near term, it may not ever have to realize the loss. By the time Stassi sells the IBM stock, its value may have recovered, and Stassi may actually end up with a gain.

Format

One format for reporting comprehensive income is to report a combined statement of income and comprehensive income.[2] For example, assuming that Stassi Company has a net income of $300,000, the unrealized loss would adjust net income as follows.

STASSI CORPORATION Combined Statement of Income and Comprehensive Income (partial)	
Net income	$300,000
Unrealized loss on available-for-sale securities	2,000
Comprehensive income	$298,000

Illustration 13-5 Lower portion of combined statement of income and comprehensive income

Companies also report the unrealized loss on available-for-sale securities as a separate component of stockholders' equity. To illustrate, assume Stassi Corporation has common stock of $3,000,000, retained earnings of $1,500,000, and an unrealized loss on available-for-sale securities of $2,000. Illustration 13-6 (page 652) shows the balance sheet presentation of the unrealized loss.

---

[2]Computation of comprehensive income is sometimes shown in a separate statement of comprehensive income or as a section in the stockholders' equity statement.

Illustration 13-6
Unrealized loss in
stockholders' equity
section

STASSI CORPORATION Balance Sheet (partial)	
Stockholders' equity	
Common stock	$3,000,000
Retained earnings	1,500,000
Total paid-in capital and retained earnings	4,500,000
Less: **Unrealized loss on available-for-sale securities**	**(2,000)**
Total stockholders' equity	$4,498,000

Note that the presentation of the loss is similar to the presentation of the cost of treasury stock in the stockholders' equity section. (An unrealized gain would be added in this section of the balance sheet.) Reporting the unrealized gain or loss in the stockholders' equity section serves two important purposes: (1) It reduces the volatility of net income due to fluctuations in fair value, and (2) it informs the financial statement user of the gain or loss that would occur if the company sold the securities at fair value.

Complete Income Statement

The income statement for Pace Corporation in Illustration 13-7 presents the types of items found on this statement, such as net sales, cost of goods sold, operating expenses, and income taxes. In addition, it shows how companies report irregular items and comprehensive income (highlighted in red).

Illustration 13-7
Complete income
statement

PACE CORPORATION Income Statement and Statement of Comprehensive Income For the Year Ended December 31, 2007		
Net sales		$440,000
Cost of goods sold		260,000
Gross profit		180,000
Operating expenses		110,000
Income from operations		70,000
Other revenues and gains	$ 5,600	
Other expenses and losses	(9,600)	(4,000)
Income before income taxes		66,000
Income tax expense ($66,000 × 30%)		19,800
Income before irregular items		46,200
Discontinued operations: Gain on disposal of Plastics Division, net of $15,000 income taxes ($50,000 × 30%)		**35,000**
Extraordinary item: Tornado loss, net of income tax savings $18,000 ($60,000 × 30%)		**(42,000)**
Net income		**39,200**
Add: Unrealized gain on available-for-sale securities		**10,000**
Comprehensive income		**$ 49,200**

CONCLUDING REMARKS

We have shown that the computation of the correct net income number can be elusive. In assessing the future prospects of a company, some investors focus on income from operations and therefore ignore all irregular and other items.

Others use measures such as net income, comprehensive income, or some modified version of one of these amounts.

BEFORE YOU GO ON . . .

▶ **Review It**

1. What is sustainable income?
2. What are irregular items, and what effect might they have on the estimation of future earnings and future cash flows?
3. What amount did Tootsie Roll Industries report as "Other comprehensive earnings" in 2004? By what percentage did Tootsie Roll's "Comprehensive earnings" differ from its "Net earnings"? The answer to this question appears on page 703.

Comparative Analysis

As indicated, in assessing the financial performance of a company, investors are interested in the core or sustainable earnings of a company. In addition, investors are interested in making comparisons from period to period. Throughout this book, we have relied on three types of comparisons to improve the decision usefulness of financial information.

1. **Intracompany basis.** Comparisons within a company are often useful to detect changes in financial relationships and significant trends. For example, a comparison of Kellogg's current year's cash amount with the prior year's cash amount shows either an increase or a decrease. Likewise, a comparison of Kellogg's year-end cash amount with the amount of its total assets at year-end shows the proportion of total assets in the form of cash.
2. **Intercompany basis.** Comparisons with other companies provide insight into a company's competitive position. For example, investors can compare Kellogg's total sales for the year with the total sales of its competitors in the breakfast cereal area, such as Quaker Oats and General Mills.
3. **Industry averages.** Comparisons with industry averages provide information about a company's relative position within the industry. For example, financial statement readers can compare Kellogg's financial data with the averages for its industry compiled by financial ratings organizations such as Dun & Bradstreet, Moody's, and Standard & Poor's, or with information provided on the Internet by organizations such as Yahoo! on its financial site.

We use three basic tools in financial statement analysis to highlight the significance of financial statement data:

1. Horizontal analysis
2. Vertical analysis
3. Ratio analysis

In previous chapters we relied primarily on ratio analysis, supplemented with some basic horizontal and vertical analysis. In the remainder of this section, we introduce more formal forms of horizontal and vertical analysis. In the next section we review ratio analysis in some detail.

HORIZONTAL ANALYSIS

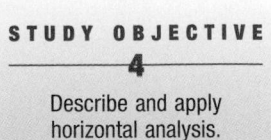

Horizontal analysis, also known as trend analysis, is a technique for evaluating a series of financial statement data over a period of time. Its purpose is to determine the increase or decrease that has taken place, expressed as either an amount or a percentage. For example, here are recent net sales figures (in millions) of Kellogg Company:

2004	2003	2002	2001	2000
$9,613.9	$8,811.5	$8,304.1	$7,548.4	$6,086.7

Alternative Terminology
Horizontal analysis is also often referred to as *trend analysis*.

If we assume that 2000 is the base year, we can measure all percentage increases or decreases relative to this base-period amount with the formula shown in Illustration 13-8.

Illustration 13-8
Horizontal analysis—
Computation of changes since base period

$$\text{Change Since Base Period} = \frac{\text{Current-Year Amount} - \text{Base-Year Amount}}{\text{Base-Year Amount}}$$

For example, we can determine that net sales for Kellogg Company increased approximately 24.0% [($7,548.4 − $6,086.7) ÷ $6,086.7] from 2000 to 2001. Similarly, we can also determine that net sales increased by 57.9% [($9,613.9 − $6,086.7) ÷ $6,086.7] from 2000 to 2004.

Alternatively, we can express current-year sales as a percentage of the base period. To do so, we would divide the current-year amount by the base-year amount, as shown in Illustration 13-9.

Illustration 13-9
Horizontal analysis—
Computation of current
year in relation to base
year

$$\text{Current Results in Relation to Base Period} = \frac{\text{Current-Year Amount}}{\text{Base-Year Amount}}$$

Current-period sales expressed as a percentage of the base period for each of the five years, using 2000 as the base period, are shown in Illustration 13-10.

Illustration 13-10
Horizontal analysis of net
sales

		KELLOGG COMPANY		
		Net Sales (in millions)		
		Base Period 2000		
2004	**2003**	**2002**	**2001**	**2000**
$9,613.9	$8,811.5	$8,304.1	$7,548.4	$6,086.7
157.95%	144.77%	136.43%	124.01%	100%

The large increase in net sales during 2001 would raise questions regarding possible reasons for such a significant change. Kellogg's 2001 notes to the financial statements explain that "the Company completed its acquisition of Keebler Foods Company" during 2001. This major acquisition would help explain the increase in sales highlighted by horizontal analysis.

To further illustrate horizontal analysis, we use the financial statements of Kellogg Company. Its two-year condensed balance sheets for 2004 and 2003, showing dollar and percentage changes, are presented in Illustration 13-11.

			Increase (Decrease) during 2004	
Assets	**2004**	**2003**	**Amount**	**Percent**
Current assets	$ 2,121.8	$ 1,787.9	$333.9	18.7
Property assets (net)	2,715.1	2,780.2	(65.1)	(2.3)
Other assets	5,953.5	5,574.6	378.9	6.8
Total assets	$10,790.4	$10,142.7	$647.7	6.4
Liabilities and Stockholders' Equity				
Current liabilities	$ 2,846.0	$ 2,766.0	$ 80.0	2.9
Long-term liabilities	5,687.2	5,933.5	(246.3)	(4.2)
Total liabilities	8,533.2	8,699.5	(166.3)	(1.9)
Stockholders' equity				
Common stock	103.8	128.3	(24.5)	(19.1)
Retained earnings	2,261.4	1,518.5	742.9	48.9
Treasury stock (cost)	(108.0)	(203.6)	(95.6)	(47.0)
Total stockholders' equity	2,257.2	1,443.2	814.0	56.4
Total liabilities and stockholders' equity	$10,790.4	$10,142.7	$647.7	6.4

KELLOGG COMPANY, INC.
Condensed Balance Sheets
December 31
(in millions)

Illustration 13-11
Horizontal analysis of a balance sheet

Helpful Hint When using horizontal analysis, be sure to examine both dollar amount changes and percentage changes. It is not necessarily bad if a company's earnings are growing at a declining rate. The **amount** of increase may be the same as or more than the base year, but the **percentage** change may be less because the base is greater each year.

The comparative balance sheet shows that a number of changes occurred in Kellogg's financial position from 2003 to 2004. In the assets section, current assets increased $333.9 million, or 18.7% ($333.9 ÷ $1,787.9), and property assets (net) decreased $65.1 million, or 2.3%. Other assets increased $378.9, or 6.8%. In the liabilities section, current liabilities increased $80.0 million, or 2.9%, while long-term liabilities decreased $246.3 million, or 4.2%. In the stockholders' equity section, we find that retained earnings increased $742.9 million, or 48.9%.

Illustration 13-12 presents a two-year comparative income statement of Kellogg Company for 2004 and 2003, showing dollar and percentage changes.

KELLOGG COMPANY, INC.
Condensed Income Statements
For the Years Ended December 31
(in millions)

Illustration 13-12
Horizontal analysis of an income statement

			Increase (Decrease) during 2004	
	2004	**2003**	**Amount**	**Percent**
Net sales	$9,613.9	$8,811.5	$802.4	9.1
Cost of goods sold	5,298.7	4,898.9	399.8	8.2
Gross profit	4,315.2	3,912.6	402.6	10.3
Selling and administrative expenses	2,634.1	2,368.5	265.6	11.2
Income from operations	1,681.1	1,544.1	137.0	8.9
Interest expense	308.6	371.4	(62.8)	(16.9)
Other income (expense), net	(6.6)	(3.2)	3.4	106.3
Income before income taxes	1,365.9	1,169.5	196.4	16.8
Income tax expense	475.3	382.4	92.9	24.3
Net income	$ 890.6	$ 787.1	$103.5	13.1

Helpful Hint Note that, in a horizontal analysis, while the amount column is additive (the total is $103.5 million), the percentage column is not additive (13.1% is **not a total**).

Horizontal analysis of the income statements shows the following changes: Net sales increased $802.4 million, or 9.1% ($802.4 ÷ $8,811.5). Cost of goods sold increased $399.8 million, or 8.2% ($399.8 ÷ $4,898.9). Selling and administrative expenses increased $265.6 million, or 11.2% ($265.6 ÷ $2,368.5). Overall, gross profit increased 10.3% and net income increased 13.1%. The increase in net income can be attributed to the increase in net sales and a decrease in interest expense.

The measurement of changes from period to period in percentages is relatively straightforward and quite useful. However, complications can result in making the computations. If an item has no value in a base year or preceding year and a value in the next year, no percentage change can be computed. Likewise, no percentage change can be computed if a negative amount appears in the base or preceding period and a positive amount exists the following year.

Decision Toolkit

Decision Checkpoints	Info Needed for Decision	Tool to Use for Decision	How to Evaluate Results
How do the company's financial position and operating results compare with those of the previous period?	Income statement and balance sheet	Comparative financial statements should be prepared over at least two years, with the first year reported being the base year. Changes in each line item relative to the base year should be presented both by amount and by percentage. This is called horizontal analysis.	Significant changes should be investigated to determine the reason for the change.

VERTICAL ANALYSIS

STUDY OBJECTIVE
5
Describe and apply vertical analysis.

Alternative Terminology
Vertical analysis is sometimes referred to as *common-size analysis.*

Vertical analysis, also called common-size analysis, is a technique for evaluating financial statement data that expresses each item in a financial statement as a **percent of a base amount**. For example, on a balance sheet we might say that current assets are 22% of total assets (total assets being the base amount). Or on an income statement we might say that selling expenses are 16% of net sales (net sales being the base amount).

Presented in Illustration 13-13 (page 657) is the comparative balance sheet of Kellogg for 2004 and 2003, analyzed vertically. The base for the asset items is **total assets**, and the base for the liability and stockholders' equity items is **total liabilities and stockholders' equity**.

In addition to showing the relative size of each category on the balance sheet, vertical analysis may show the percentage change in the individual asset, liability, and stockholders' equity items. In this case, current assets increased $333.9 million from 2003 to 2004, and they increased from 17.6% to 19.7% of total assets. Property assets (net) decreased from 27.4% to 25.1% of total assets. Other assets increased from 55% to 55.2% of total assets. Also, retained earnings increased by $742.9 million from 2003 to 2004, and total stockholders' equity increased from 14.2% to 20.9% of total liabilities and stockholders' equity. This switch to a higher percentage of equity financing has two causes: First, total liabilities decreased by $166.3 million, going from 85.8% to 79.1% of total liabilities and stockholders' equity. Second, retained earnings increased by $742.9 million, going from 15.0% to 20.9% of total liabilities and stockholders' equity. Thus, the

KELLOGG COMPANY, INC. Condensed Balance Sheets December 31 (in millions)				
	2004		**2003**	
Assets	**Amount**	**Percent***	**Amount**	**Percent***
Current assets	$ 2,121.8	19.7	$ 1,787.9	17.6
Property assets (net)	2,715.1	25.1	2,780.2	27.4
Other assets	5,953.5	55.2	5,574.6	55.0
Total assets	$10,790.4	100.0	$10,142.7	100.0
Liabilities and Stockholders' Equity				
Current liabilities	$ 2,846.0	26.4	$ 2,766.0	27.3
Long-term liabilities	5,687.2	52.7	5,933.5	58.5
Total liabilities	8,533.2	79.1	8,699.5	85.8
Stockholders' equity				
Common stock	103.8	1.0	128.3	1.2
Retained earnings	2,261.4	20.9	1,518.5	15.0
Treasury stock (cost)	(108.0)	(1.0)	(203.6)	(2.0)
Total stockholders' equity	2,257.2	20.9	1,443.2	14.2
Total liabilities and stockholders' equity	$10,790.4	100.0	$10,142.7	100.0

*Numbers have been rounded to total 100%.

Illustration 13-13
Vertical analysis of a
balance sheet

company shifted toward a heavier reliance on equity financing both by using less long-term debt and by increasing the amount of retained earnings.

Vertical analysis of the comparative income statements of Kellogg, shown in Illustration 13-14, reveals that cost of goods sold **as a percentage of net sales** decreased from 55.6% to 55.1%, and selling and administrative expenses increased from 26.9% to 27.4%. Net income as a percent of net sales increased from 8.9% to 9.3%. Kellogg's increase in net income as a percentage of sales is due primarily to the decrease in interest expense as a percent of sales.

KELLOGG COMPANY, INC. Condensed Income Statements For the Years Ended December 31 (in millions)				
	2004		**2003**	
	Amount	**Percent***	**Amount**	**Percent***
Net sales	$9,613.9	100.0	$8,811.5	100.0
Cost of goods sold	5,298.7	55.1	4,898.9	55.6
Gross profit	4,315.2	44.9	3,912.6	44.4
Selling and administrative expenses	2,634.1	27.4	2,368.5	26.9
Income from operations	1,681.1	17.5	1,544.1	17.5
Interest expense	308.6	3.2	371.4	4.2
Other income (expense), net	(6.6)	.1	(3.2)	.1
Income before income taxes	1,365.9	14.2	1,169.5	13.2
Income tax expense	475.3	4.9	382.4	4.3
Net income	$ 890.6	9.3	$ 787.1	8.9

*Numbers have been rounded to total 100%.

Illustration 13-14
Vertical analysis of an
income statement

Vertical analysis also enables you to compare companies of different sizes. For example, one of Kellogg's main competitors is General Mills. Using vertical analysis, we can more meaningfully compare the condensed income statements of Kellogg and General Mills, as shown in Illustration 13-15.

Illustration 13-15
Intercompany comparison by vertical analysis

CONDENSED INCOME STATEMENTS For the Year Ended December 31, 2004 (in millions)				
	Kellogg Company, Inc.		General Mills, Inc.	
	Amount	**Percent***	**Amount**	**Percent***
Net sales	$9,613.9	**100.0**	$11,070.0	**100.0**
Cost of goods sold	5,298.7	**55.1**	6,584.0	**59.5**
Gross profit	4,315.2	**44.9**	4,486.0	**40.5**
Selling and administrative expenses	2,634.1	**27.4**	2,443.0	**22.1**
Nonrecurring charges	0.0	**—**	26.0	**.2**
Income from operations	1,681.1	**17.5**	2,017.0	**18.2**
Other expenses and revenues (including income taxes)	790.5	**8.2**	962.0	**8.7**
Net income	$ 890.6	**9.3**	$ 1,055.0	**9.5**

*Numbers have been rounded to total 100%.

Although Kellogg's net sales are 13% less than those of General Mills, vertical analysis eliminates the impact of this size difference for our analysis. Kellogg has a higher gross profit, 44.9%, compared to 40.5% for General Mills, but Kellogg's selling and administrative expenses are 27.4% of net sales, while those of General Mills are 22.1% of net sales. Looking at net income, we see that the companies report similar percentages: Kellogg's net income as a percentage of net sales is 9.3%, compared to 9.5% for General Mills.

Decision Toolkit

Decision Checkpoints	Info Needed for Decision	Tool to Use for Decision	How to Evaluate Results
How do the relationships between items in this year's financial statements compare with those of last year or those of competitors?	Income statement and balance sheet	Each line item on the income statement should be presented as a percentage of net sales, and each line item on the balance sheet should be presented as a percentage of total assets or total liabilities and stockholders' equity. These percentages should be investigated for differences either across years in the same company or in the same year across different companies. This is called vertical analysis.	Any differences either across years or between companies should be investigated to determine the cause.

Ratio Analysis

In previous chapters we presented many ratios used for evaluating the financial health and performance of a company. Here we provide a summary listing of those ratios. (Page references to prior discussions are provided if you feel you need to review any individual ratios.) The appendix to this chapter provides an example of a comprehensive financial analysis employing these ratios.

> **STUDY OBJECTIVE**
> **6**
> Identify and compute ratios used in analyzing a company's liquidity, solvency, and profitability.

LIQUIDITY RATIOS

Liquidity ratios (Illustration 13-16) measure the short-term ability of the enterprise to pay its maturing obligations and to meet unexpected needs for cash. Short-term creditors such as bankers and suppliers are particularly interested in assessing liquidity.

Illustration 13-16
Summary of liquidity ratios

Liquidity Ratios		
Working capital	Current assets − Current liabilities	p. 59
Current ratio	$\dfrac{\text{Current assets}}{\text{Current liabilities}}$	p. 59
Current cash debt coverage ratio	$\dfrac{\text{Cash provided by operations}}{\text{Average current liabilities}}$	p. 607
Inventory turnover ratio	$\dfrac{\text{Cost of goods sold}}{\text{Average inventory}}$	p. 281
Days in inventory	$\dfrac{365 \text{ days}}{\text{Inventory turnover ratio}}$	p. 281
Receivables turnover ratio	$\dfrac{\text{Net credit sales}}{\text{Average net receivables}}$	p. 388
Average collection period	$\dfrac{365 \text{ days}}{\text{Receivables turnover ratio}}$	p. 388

SOLVENCY RATIOS

Solvency ratios (Illustration 13-17) measure the ability of the enterprise to survive over a long period of time. Long-term creditors and stockholders are interested in a company's long-run solvency, particularly its ability to pay interest as it comes due and to repay the face value of debt at maturity.

Illustration 13-17
Summary of solvency ratios

Solvency Ratios		
Debt to total assets ratio	$\dfrac{\text{Total liabilities}}{\text{Total assets}}$	p. 60
Cash debt coverage ratio	$\dfrac{\text{Cash provided by operations}}{\text{Average total liabilities}}$	p. 608
Times interest earned ratio	$\dfrac{\text{Net income} + \text{Interest expense} + \text{Tax expense}}{\text{Interest expense}}$	p. 493
Free cash flow	$\begin{array}{c}\text{Cash provided by} \\ \text{operations}\end{array} - \begin{array}{c}\text{Capital} \\ \text{expenditures}\end{array} - \begin{array}{c}\text{Cash} \\ \text{dividends}\end{array}$	p. 63

PROFITABILITY RATIOS

Profitability ratios (Illustration 13-18) measure the income or operating success of an enterprise for a given period of time. A company's income, or lack of it, affects its ability to obtain debt and equity financing, its liquidity position, and its ability to grow. As a consequence, creditors and investors alike are interested in evaluating profitability. Profitability is frequently used as the ultimate test of management's operating effectiveness.

Illustration 13-18
Summary of profitability ratios

Profitability Ratios		
Earnings per share	$\dfrac{\text{Net income} - \text{Preferred stock dividends}}{\text{Average common shares outstanding}}$	p. 55
Price-earnings ratio	$\dfrac{\text{Stock price per share}}{\text{Earnings per share}}$	p. 662
Gross profit rate	$\dfrac{\text{Gross profit}}{\text{Net sales}}$	p. 234
Profit margin ratio	$\dfrac{\text{Net income}}{\text{Net sales}}$	p. 235
Return on assets ratio	$\dfrac{\text{Net income}}{\text{Average total assets}}$	p. 437
Asset turnover ratio	$\dfrac{\text{Net sales}}{\text{Average total assets}}$	p. 439
Payout ratio	$\dfrac{\text{Cash dividends declared on common stock}}{\text{Net income}}$	p. 556
Return on common stockholders' equity ratio	$\dfrac{\text{Net income} - \text{Preferred stock dividends}}{\text{Average common stockholders' equity}}$	p. 558

Business Insight
Investor Perspective

The apparent simplicity of the current ratio can have real-world limitations because adding equal amounts to both the numerator and the denominator causes the ratio to decrease.

Assume, for example, that a company has $2,000,000 of current assets and $1,000,000 of current liabilities; its current ratio is 2 : 1. If it purchases $1,000,000 of inventory on account, it will have $3,000,000 of current assets and $2,000,000 of current liabilities; its current ratio decreases to 1.5 : 1. If, instead, the company pays off $500,000 of its current liabilities, it will have $1,500,000 of current assets and $500,000 of current liabilities; its current ratio increases to 3 : 1. Thus, any trend analysis should be done with care because the ratio is susceptible to quick changes and is easily influenced by management.

 How might management influence a company's current ratio?

BEFORE YOU GO ON . . .

► **Review It**

1. What different bases can be used to compare financial information?
2. What is horizontal analysis?
3. What is vertical analysis?
4. Describe ratios that measure liquidity, solvency, and profitability.

Quality of Earnings

In evaluating the financial performance of a company, the quality of a company's earnings is of extreme importance to analysts. A company that has a high **quality of earnings** provides full and transparent information that will not confuse or mislead users of the financial statements.

The issue of quality of earnings has taken on increasing importance because recent accounting scandals suggest that some companies are spending too much time managing their income and not enough time managing their business. Here are some of the factors affecting quality of earnings.

STUDY OBJECTIVE

7

Understand the concept of quality of earnings.

ALTERNATIVE ACCOUNTING METHODS

Variations among companies in the application of generally accepted accounting principles may hamper comparability and reduce quality of earnings. For example, one company may use the FIFO method of inventory costing, while another company in the same industry may use LIFO. If inventory is a significant asset to both companies, it is unlikely that their current ratios are comparable. For example, if General Motors Corporation had used FIFO instead of LIFO for inventory valuation, its inventories in a recent year would have been 26% higher, which significantly affects the current ratio (and other ratios as well).

In addition to differences in inventory costing methods, differences also exist in reporting such items as depreciation, depletion, and amortization. Although these differences in accounting methods might be detectable from reading the notes to the financial statements, adjusting the financial data to compensate for the different methods is often difficult, if not impossible.

PRO FORMA INCOME

Companies whose stock is publicly traded are required to present their income statement following generally accepted accounting principles (GAAP). In recent years, many companies have been also reporting a second measure of income, called pro forma income. **Pro forma income** usually excludes items that the company thinks are unusual or nonrecurring. For example, in a recent year, Cisco Systems (a high-tech company) reported a quarterly net loss under GAAP of $2.7 billion. Cisco reported pro forma income for the same quarter as a profit of $230 million. This large difference in profits between GAAP income numbers and pro forma income is not unusual these days. For example, during one recent 9-month period the 100 largest firms on the Nasdaq stock exchange reported a total pro forma income of $19.1 billion, but a total loss as measured by GAAP of $82.3 billion—a difference of about $100 billion!

To compute pro forma income, companies generally can exclude any items they deem inappropriate for measuring their performance. Many analysts and investors are critical of the practice of using pro forma income because these numbers often make companies look better than they really are. As the financial press noted, pro forma numbers might be called EBS, which stands for "earnings before bad stuff." Companies, on the other hand, argue that pro forma numbers more clearly indicate sustainable income because they exclude unusual and non-recurring expenses. "Cisco's technique gives readers of financial statements a clear picture of Cisco's normal business activities," the company said in a statement issued in response to questions about its pro forma income accounting.

Recently, the SEC provided some guidance on how companies should present pro forma information. Stay tuned: Everyone seems to agree that pro forma numbers can be useful if they provide insights into determining a company's sustainable income. However, many companies have abused the flexibility that pro forma numbers allow and have used the measure as a way to put their companies in a good light.

IMPROPER RECOGNITION

Because some managers have felt pressure from Wall Street to continually increase earnings, they have manipulated the earnings numbers to meet these expectations. The most common abuse is the improper recognition of revenue. One practice that companies are using is *channel stuffing*: Offering deep discounts on their products to customers, companies encourage their customers to buy early (stuff the channel) rather than later. This lets the company report good earnings in the current period, but it often leads to a disaster in subsequent periods because customers have no need for additional goods. To illustrate, Bristol-Myers Squibb recently indicated that it used sales incentives to encourage wholesalers to buy more drugs than needed to meet patients' demands. As a result, the company had to issue revised financial statements showing corrected revenues and income.

Another practice is the improper capitalization of operating expenses. The classic case is WorldCom. It capitalized over $7 billion dollars of operating expenses so that it would report positive net income. In other situations, companies fail to report all their liabilities. Enron had promised to make payments on certain contracts if financial difficulty developed, but these guarantees were not reported as liabilities. In addition, disclosure was so lacking in transparency that it was impossible to understand what was happening at the company.

PRICE-EARNINGS RATIO

Earnings per share is net income available to common stockholders divided by the average number of common shares outstanding. The market value of a company's stock changes based on investors' expectations about a company's future earnings per share. In order to make a meaningful comparison of market values and earnings across firms, investors calculate the **price-earnings (P-E) ratio**. The P-E ratio divides the market price of a share of common stock by earnings per share.

Illustration 13-19
Formula for price-earnings (P-E) ratio

$$\text{Price-Earnings (P-E) Ratio} = \frac{\text{Stock Price per Share}}{\text{Earnings per Share}}$$

The P-E ratio reflects investors' assessment of a company's future earnings. The ratio of price to earnings will be higher if investors think that earnings will increase substantially in the future and therefore are willing to pay more per share of stock. A low price-earnings ratio often signifies that investors think the company's future earnings will not be strong. In addition, sometimes a low P-E ratio reflects the market's belief that a company has poor-quality earnings.

To illustrate, assume that two identical firms each have earnings per share of $5, but that one of the companies manipulated its accounting numbers to achieve the $5 figure. If investors perceive that one firm has lower-quality earnings, this perception will be reflected in a lower stock price, and consequently, a lower P-E.

Illustration 13-20 shows earnings per share and P-E ratios for five companies for 2004. Note the extreme difference in the P-E ratio of United States Steel versus Google Inc.

Company	Earnings Per Share	Price-Earnings Ratio
Kellogg Company	$ 2.22	20.5
Google Inc.	3.41	86.6
United States Steel	11.40	3.9
eBay Inc.	0.68	62.4
Nike	19.50	4.3

Illustration 13-20
Earnings per share and P-E ratios of various companies

Accounting across the Organization

Many company managers preparing their annual reports are piling on the paper in order to ease Enron-type worries on the part of investors. Natural-gas producer Williams Companies, Inc. turned out an eye-glazing annual report 1,234 pages in length. Nortel Networks Corporation added an extra two dozen pages to its annual report. Other companies have followed suit.

The trend to fuller disclosure has been a long time coming, observers say. But they caution that more paper does not necessarily mean more information that the average investor will understand. In addition, it is important to remember that annual reports are just one piece of the puzzle as to how companies present information to decision-makers.

Source: Elizabeth Church, "No Item Too Small as Firms Cave to Enron Disclosure Craze," *The (Toronto) Globe and Mail* (April 1, 2002), p. B1.

 Why might adding extra pages to the annual report not be beneficial to investors and analysts? What should be management's overriding objective in financial reporting?

BEFORE YOU GO ON . . .

▶ Review It

1. Explain what is meant by pro forma income.
2. Describe factors that reduce the quality of earnings.
3. Give an example of improper recognition.
4. What is the purpose of the P-E ratio?

THE NAVIGATOR

Using the Decision Toolkit

In analyzing a company, you should always investigate an extended period of time in order to determine whether the condition and performance of the company are changing. The condensed financial statements of Kellogg Company for 2002 and 2001 are presented here. (The appendix to this chapter provides a complete analysis of Kellogg's 2004 and 2003 financial statements.)

KELLOGG COMPANY, INC.
Balance Sheets
December 31
(in millions)

Assets	2002	2001
Current assets		
Cash and short-term investments	$ 100.6	$ 231.8
Accounts receivable (net)	741.0	762.3
Inventories	603.2	574.5
Prepaid expenses and other current assets	318.6	333.4
Total current assets	1,763.4	1,902.0
Property assets (net)	2,840.2	2,952.8
Intangibles and other assets	5,615.7	5,513.8
Total assets	$10,219.3	$10,368.6
Liabilities and Stockholders' Equity		
Current liabilities	$ 3,014.9	$ 2,207.6
Long-term liabilities	6,309.3	7,289.5
Stockholders' equity—common	895.1	871.5
Total liabilities and stockholders' equity	$10,219.3	$10,368.6

KELLOGG COMPANY, INC.
Condensed Income Statements
For the Years Ended December 31
(in millions)

	2002	2001
Net sales	$8,304.1	$7,548.4
Cost of goods sold	4,569.0	4,211.4
Gross profit	3,735.1	3,337.0
Selling and administrative expenses	2,227.0	2,135.8
Nonrecurring charges	0	33.3
Income from operations	1,508.1	1,167.9
Interest expense	391.2	351.5
Other income (expense), net	27.4	(24.9)
Income before income taxes	1,144.3	791.5
Income tax expense	423.4	317.9
Net income	$ 720.9	$ 473.6

Instructions

Compute the following ratios for Kellogg for 2002 and 2001 and discuss your findings.

1. Liquidity:
   (a) Current ratio.
   (b) Inventory turnover ratio. (Inventory on December 31, 2000, was $443.8 million.)

2. Solvency:
   (a) Debt to total assets ratio.
   (b) Times interest earned ratio.
3. Profitability:
   (a) Return on common stockholders' equity ratio. (Stockholders' equity on December 31, 2000, was $897.5 million.)
   (b) Return on assets ratio. (Assets on December 31, 2000, were $4,886 million.)
   (c) Profit margin ratio.

Solution

1. Liquidity
   (a) Current ratio:

   2002: $\dfrac{\$1,763.4}{\$3,014.9} = .58:1$

   2001: $\dfrac{\$1,902.0}{\$2,207.6} = .86:1$

   (b) Inventory turnover ratio:

   2002: $\dfrac{\$4,569.0}{(\$603.2 + \$574.5)/2} = 7.8$ times

   2001: $\dfrac{\$4,211.4}{(\$574.5 + \$443.8)/2} = 8.3$ times

We see that between 2001 and 2002 the current ratio decreased. The inventory turnover ratio also decreased. Both measures indicate that the company was less liquid in 2002.

2. Solvency
   (a) Debt to total assets ratio:

   2002: $\dfrac{\$9,324.2}{\$10,219.3} = 91\%$

   2001: $\dfrac{\$9,497.1}{\$10,368.6} = 92\%$

   (b) Times interest earned ratio:

   2002: $\dfrac{\$720.9 + \$423.4 + \$391.2}{\$391.2} = 3.9$ times

   2001: $\dfrac{\$473.6 + \$317.9 + \$351.5}{\$351.5} = 3.3$ times

Kellogg's solvency as measured by the debt to total assets ratio improved slightly in 2002. We also can see that the times interest earned ratio increased.

3. Profitability
   (a) Return on common stockholders' equity ratio:

   2002: $\dfrac{\$720.9}{(\$895.1 + \$871.5)/2} = 82\%$

   2001: $\dfrac{\$473.6}{(\$871.5 + \$897.5)/2} = 54\%$

   (b) Return on assets ratio:

   2002: $\dfrac{\$720.9}{(\$10,219.3 + \$10,368.6)/2} = 7\%$

   2001: $\dfrac{\$473.6}{(\$10,368.6 + \$4,886.0)/2} = 6\%$

(c) Profit margin ratio:

$$2002: \quad \frac{\$720.9}{\$8,304.1} = 9\%$$

$$2001: \quad \frac{\$473.6}{\$7,548.4} = 6\%$$

Kellogg's return on common stockholders' equity ratio increased sharply. This increase was the result of increases in both its return on assets and its profit margin ratios.

Summary of Study Objectives

1 *Understand the concept of sustainable income.* Sustainable income refers to a company's ability to sustain its profits from operations.

2 *Indicate how irregular items are presented.* Irregular items—discontinued operations and extraordinary items—are presented on the income statement net of tax below "Income before irregular items" to highlight their unusual nature. Changes in accounting principle are reported retroactively.

3 *Explain the concept of comprehensive income.* Comprehensive income includes all changes in stockholders' equity during a period except those resulting from investments by stockholders and distributions to stockholders. "Other comprehensive income" is added to net income to arrive at comprehensive income.

4 *Describe and apply horizontal analysis.* Horizontal analysis is a technique for evaluating a series of data over a period of time to determine the increase or decrease that has taken place, expressed as either an amount or a percentage.

5 *Describe and apply vertical analysis.* Vertical analysis is a technique that expresses each item in a financial statement as a percentage of a relevant total or a base amount.

6 *Identify and compute ratios used in analyzing a company's liquidity, solvency, and profitability.* Financial ratios are provided in Illustration 13-16 (liquidity), Illustration 13-17 (solvency), and Illustration 13-18 (profitability).

7 *Understand the concept of quality of earnings.* A high quality of earnings provides full and transparent information that will not confuse or mislead users of the financial statements. Issues related to quality of earnings are (1) alternative accounting methods, (2) pro forma income, and (3) improper recognition. The price-earnings (P-E) ratio reflects investors' assessment of a company's future earnings potential.

Decision Toolkit—A Summary

Decision Checkpoints	Info Needed for Decision	Tool to Use for Decision	How to Evaluate Results
Has the company sold any major components of its business?	Discontinued operations section of income statement	Anything reported in this section indicates that the company has discontinued a major component of its business.	If a major component has been discontinued, its results during the current period should not be included in estimates of future net income.
Has the company experienced any extraordinary events or transactions?	Extraordinary item section of income statement	Anything reported in this section indicates that the company experienced an event that was both unusual and infrequent.	These items should usually be ignored in estimating future net income.
Has the company changed any of its accounting principles?	Effect of change in accounting principle on current and prior periods.	Management indicates that the new principle is preferable to the old principle.	Examine current and prior years reported, using new-principle basis to assess trends for estimating future income.
How do the company's financial position and operating results compare with those of the previous period?	Income statement and balance sheet	Comparative financial statements should be prepared over at least two years, with the first year reported being the base year. Changes in each line item relative to the base year should be presented both by amount and by percentage. This is called horizontal analysis.	Significant changes should be investigated to determine the reason for the change.
How do the relationships between items in this year's financial statements compare with those of last year or those of competitors?	Income statement and balance sheet	Each line item on the income statement should be presented as a percentage of net sales, and each line item on the balance sheet should be presented as a percentage of total assets or total liabilities and stockholders' equity. These percentages should be investigated for differences either across years in the same company or in the same year across different companies. This is called vertical analysis.	Any differences either across years or between companies should be investigated to determine the cause.

APPENDIX
COMPREHENSIVE ILLUSTRATION
OF RATIO ANALYSIS

In previous chapters we presented many ratios used for evaluating the financial health and performance of a company. In this appendix we provide a comprehensive review of those ratios and discuss some important relationships among them. Since earlier chapters demonstrated the calculation of each of these ratios, in this chapter we instead focus on their interpretation. Page references to prior discussions point you to any individual ratios you feel you need to review.

We used the financial information in Illustrations 13A-1 through 13A-4 to calculate Kellogg's 2004 ratios. You can use these data to review the computations.

Illustration 13A-1
Kellogg Company's
balance sheet

Kellogg's

KELLOGG COMPANY, INC.
Balance Sheets
December 31
(in millions)

Assets	2004	2003
Current assets		
Cash and short-term investments	$ 417.4	$ 141.2
Accounts receivable	776.4	754.8
Inventories	681.0	649.8
Prepaid expenses and other current assets	247.0	242.1
Total current assets	2,121.8	1,787.9
Property assets (net)	2,715.1	2,780.2
Intangibles and other assets	5,953.5	5,574.6
Total assets	$10,790.4	$10,142.7
Liabilities and Stockholders' Equity		
Current liabilities	$ 2,846.0	$ 2,766.0
Long-term liabilities	5,687.2	5,933.5
Stockholders' equity—common	2,257.2	1,443.2
Total liabilities and stockholders' equity	$10,790.4	$10,142.7

As indicated in the chapter, we can classify ratios into three types for analysis of the primary financial statements.

1. **Liquidity ratios:** Measures of the short-term ability of the enterprise to pay its maturing obligations and to meet unexpected needs for cash.
2. **Solvency ratios:** Measures of the ability of the enterprise to survive over a long period of time.
3. **Profitability ratios:** Measures of the income or operating success of an enterprise for a given period of time.

As a tool of analysis, ratios can provide clues to underlying conditions that may not be apparent from an inspection of the individual components of a particular ratio. But a single ratio by itself is not very meaningful. Accordingly, in this discussion we use the three comparisons listed on the top of page 670.

KELLOGG COMPANY, INC.
Condensed Income Statements
For the Years Ended December 31
(in millions)

	2004	2003
Net sales	$9,613.9	$8,811.5
Cost of goods sold	5,298.7	4,898.9
Gross profit	4,315.2	3,912.6
Selling and administrative expenses	2,634.1	2,368.5
Income from operations	1,681.1	1,544.1
Interest expense	308.6	371.4
Other income (expense), net	(6.6)	(3.2)
Income before income taxes	1,365.9	1,169.5
Income tax expense	475.3	382.4
Net income	$ 890.6	$ 787.1

Illustration 13A-2 Kellogg Company's income statement

KELLOGG COMPANY, INC.
Condensed Statements of Cash Flows
For the Years Ended December 31
(in millions)

	2004	2003
Cash flows from operating activities		
Cash receipts from operating activities	$ 9,592.3	$8,797.7
Cash payments for operating activities	8,363.3	7,626.7
Net cash provided by operating activities	1,229.0	1,171.0
Cash flows from investing activities		
Purchases of property, plant, and equipment	(278.6)	(247.2)
Other investing activities	8.2	28.2
Net cash used in investing activities	(270.4)	(219.0)
Cash flows from financing activities		
Issuance of common stock	291.8	121.6
Issuance of debt	537.6	773.6
Reductions of debt	(823.9)	(1,331.6)
Payment of dividends	(417.6)	(412.4)
Repurchase of common stock and other items	(304.2)	(90.6)
Net cash provided by (used in) financing activities	(716.3)	(939.4)
Other	33.9	28.0
Increase (decrease) in cash and cash equivalents	276.2	40.6
Cash and cash equivalents at beginning of year	141.2	100.6
Cash and cash equivalents at end of year	$ 417.4	$ 141.2

Illustration 13A-3 Kellogg Company's statement of cash flows

Additional information	2004	2003
Average number of shares (millions)	412	407.9
Stock price at year-end	$44.66	$38.80

Illustration 13A-4
Additional information for Kellogg Company

1. **Intracompany comparisons** covering two years for Kellogg Company (using comparative financial information from Illustrations 13A-1, 13A-2, and 13A-3).

2. **Intercompany comparisons** using General Mills as one of Kellogg's principal competitors.

3. **Industry average comparisons** based on Reuters.com's median ratios for manufacturers of flour and other grain mill products and comparisons with other sources. For some of the ratios that we use, industry comparisons are not available. (These are denoted "na.")

Liquidity Ratios

Liquidity ratios measure the short-term ability of the enterprise to pay its maturing obligations and to meet unexpected needs for cash. Short-term creditors such as bankers and suppliers are particularly interested in assessing liquidity. The measures used to determine the enterprise's short-term debt-paying ability are the current ratio, the current cash debt coverage ratio, the receivables turnover ratio, the average collection period, the inventory turnover ratio, and average days in inventory.

1. **Current ratio.** The current ratio expresses the relationship of current assets to current liabilities, computed by dividing current assets by current liabilities. It is widely used for evaluating a company's liquidity and short-term debt-paying ability. The 2004 and 2003 current ratios for Kellogg and comparative data are shown in Illustration 13A-5.

Illustration 13A-5
Current ratio

Ratio	Formula	Indicates:	Kellogg 2004	Kellogg 2003	General Mills 2004	Industry 2004	Page in book
Current ratio	Current assets / Current liabilities	Short-term debt-paying ability	.75	.65	1.17	1.41	59

What do the measures tell us? Kellogg's 2004 current ratio of .75 means that for every dollar of current liabilities, Kellogg has $0.75 of current assets. We sometimes state such ratios as .75:1 to reinforce this interpretation. Kellogg's current ratio—and therefore its liquidity—increased significantly in 2004. It is well below the industry average and that of General Mills.

2. **Current cash debt coverage ratio.** A disadvantage of the current ratio is that it uses year-end balances of current asset and current liability accounts. These year-end balances may not represent the company's current position during most of the year. The current cash debt coverage ratio partially corrects for this problem. It is the ratio of cash provided by operating activities to average current liabilities. Because it uses cash provided by operating activities rather than a balance at one point in time, it may provide a better representation of liquidity. Kellogg's current cash debt coverage ratio is shown in Illustration 13A-6.

Illustration 13A-6
Current cash debt coverage ratio

Ratio	Formula	Indicates:	Kellogg 2004	Kellogg 2003	General Mills 2004	Industry 2004	Page in book
Current cash debt coverage ratio	Cash provided by operations / Average current liabilities	Short-term debt-paying ability (cash basis)	.44	.41	.47	na	607

Like the current ratio, this ratio increased in 2004 for Kellogg. Is the coverage adequate? Probably so. Kellogg's operating cash flow coverage of average current liabilities is similar to that of General Mills, and it exceeds a commonly accepted threshold of .40. No industry comparison is available.

3. **Receivables turnover ratio.** Analysts can measure liquidity by how quickly a company converts certain assets to cash. Low values of the previous ratios can sometimes be compensated for if some of the company's current assets are highly liquid.

How liquid, for example, are the receivables? The ratio used to assess the liquidity of the receivables is the **receivables turnover ratio**, which measures the number of times, on average, a company collects receivables during the period. The receivables turnover ratio is computed by dividing net credit sales (net sales less cash sales) by average net receivables during the year. The receivables turnover ratio for Kellogg is shown in Illustration 13A-7.

Illustration 13A-7
Receivables turnover ratio

Ratio	Formula	Indicates:	Kellogg 2004	Kellogg 2003	General Mills 2004	Industry 2004	Page in book
Receivables turnover ratio	Net credit sales / Average net receivables	Liquidity of receivables	12.6	11.8	11.1	11.5	388

We have assumed that all Kellogg's sales are credit sales. The receivables turnover ratio for Kellogg rose in 2004. The turnover of 12.6 times compares favorably with the industry median of 11.5 times, and is much higher than General Mills's turnover of 11.1 times.

4. **Average collection period.** A popular variant of the receivables turnover ratio converts it into an **average collection period** in days. This is done by dividing the receivables turnover ratio into 365 days. The average collection period for Kellogg is shown in Illustration 13A-8.

Illustration 13A-8
Average collection period

Ratio	Formula	Indicates:	Kellogg 2004	Kellogg 2003	General Mills 2004	Industry 2004	Page in book
Average collection period	365 days / Receivables turnover ratio	Liquidity of receivables and collection success	29.0	30.9	32.9	31.7	388

Kellogg's 2004 receivables turnover of 12.6 times is divided into 365 days to obtain approximately 29 days. This means that the average collection period for receivables is about 29 days.

Analysts frequently use the average collection period to assess the effectiveness of a company's credit and collection policies. The general rule is that the collection period should not greatly exceed the credit term period (i.e., the time allowed for payment). Kellogg's average collection period is similar to those of General Mills and the industry.

5. **Inventory turnover ratio.** The **inventory turnover ratio** measures the number of times on average a company sells the inventory during the period. Its purpose is to measure the liquidity of the inventory. The inventory turnover ratio is computed by dividing the cost of goods sold by the average inventory during the period. Unless seasonal factors are significant, average inventory can be computed from the beginning and ending inventory balances. Kellogg's inventory turnover ratio is shown in Illustration 13A-9.

Ratio	Formula	Indicates:	Kellogg 2004	Kellogg 2003	General Mills 2004	Industry 2004	Page in book
Inventory turnover ratio	Cost of goods sold / Average inventory	Liquidity of inventory	8.0	7.8	6.1	6.6	281

Illustration 13A-9
Inventory turnover ratio

Kellogg's inventory turnover ratio increased slightly in 2004. The turnover ratio of 8 times is higher than the industry average of 6.6 times and significantly better than General Mills's 6.1 times. Generally, the faster the inventory turnover, the less cash is tied up in inventory and the less the chance of inventory becoming obsolete. Of course, a downside of high inventory turnover is that the company can run out of inventory when it is needed.

6. **Days in inventory.** A variant of the inventory turnover ratio is the **days in inventory**, which measures the average number of days it takes to sell the inventory. The days in inventory for Kellogg is shown in Illustration 13A-10.

Illustration 13A-10
Days in inventory

Ratio	Formula	Indicates:	Kellogg 2004	Kellogg 2003	General Mills 2004	Industry 2004	Page in book
Days in inventory	365 days / Inventory turnover ratio	Liquidity of inventory and inventory management	45.6	46.8	59.8	55.3	281

Kellogg's 2004 inventory turnover ratio of 8 divided into 365 is approximately 45.6 days. An average selling time of 45 days is faster than the industry average and significantly faster than that of General Mills. Some of this difference might be explained by differences in product lines across the two companies, although in many ways the types of products of these two companies are quite similar.

Inventory turnover ratios vary considerably among industries. For example, grocery store chains have a turnover of 10 times and an average selling period of 37 days. In contrast, jewelry stores have an average turnover of 1.3 times and an average selling period of 281 days. Within a company there may even be significant differences in inventory turnover among different types of products. Thus, in a grocery store the turnover of perishable items such as produce, meats, and dairy products is faster than the turnover of soaps and detergents.

To conclude, nearly all of these liquidity measures suggest that Kellogg's liquidity increased slightly during 2004. Its liquidity appears acceptable when compared to the industry as a whole and better than that of General Mills.

Solvency Ratios

Solvency ratios measure the ability of the enterprise to survive over a long period of time. Long-term creditors and stockholders are interested in a company's long-run solvency, particularly its ability to pay interest as it comes due and to repay the face value of debt at maturity. The debt to total assets ratio, the times interest earned ratio, and the cash debt coverage ratio provide information about debt-paying ability. In addition, free cash flow provides information about the company's solvency and its ability to pay additional dividends or invest in new projects.

7. **Debt to total assets ratio.** The debt to total assets ratio measures the percentage of the total assets provided by creditors. It is computed by dividing total liabilities (both current and long-term) by total assets. This ratio indicates the degree of financial leveraging. It also provides some indication of the company's ability to withstand losses without impairing the interests of its creditors. The higher the percentage of debt to total assets, the greater the risk that the company may be unable to meet its maturing obligations. The lower the ratio, the more equity "buffer" is available to creditors if the company becomes insolvent. Thus, from the creditors' point of view, a low ratio of debt to total assets is desirable. Kellogg's debt to total assets ratio is shown in Illustration 13A-11.

Illustration 13A-11
Debt to total assets ratio

Ratio	Formula	Indicates:	Kellogg 2004	Kellogg 2003	General Mills 2004	Industry 2004	Page in book
Debt to total assets ratio	Total liabilities / Total assets	Percentage of total assets provided by creditors	79%	86%	72%	48%	60

Kellogg's 2004 ratio of 79% means that creditors have provided financing sufficient to cover 79% of the company's total assets. Alternatively, it says that Kellogg would have to liquidate 79% of its assets at their book value in order to pay off all of its debts. Kellogg's 79% is above the industry average of 48% as well as the 72% ratio of General Mills. Kellogg's solvency improved during the year. In that time, Kellogg's use of debt financing changed in two ways: First, Kellogg decreased its use of long-term debt slightly, and second, increased its equity by 56%. Both of these factors improved its solvency.

The adequacy of this ratio is often judged in light of the company's earnings. Generally, companies with relatively stable earnings, such as public utilities, have higher debt to total assets ratios than cyclical companies with widely fluctuating earnings, such as many high-tech companies.

Another ratio with a similar meaning is the **debt to equity ratio**. It shows the relative use of borrowed funds (total liabilities) compared with resources invested by the owners. Because this ratio can be computed in several ways, be careful when making comparisons with it. Debt may be defined to include only the noncurrent portion of liabilities, and intangible assets may be excluded from stockholders' equity (which would equal tangible net worth). If debt and assets are defined as above (all liabilities and all assets), then when the debt to total assets ratio equals 50%, the debt to equity ratio is 1:1.

8. **Times interest earned ratio.** The times interest earned ratio (also called interest coverage) indicates the company's ability to meet interest payments as they come due. It is computed by dividing income before interest expense and income taxes by interest expense. Note that this ratio uses income before interest expense and income taxes because this amount represents what is available to cover interest. Kellogg's times interest earned ratio is shown in Illustration 13A-12.

Illustration 13A-12
Times interest earned ratio

Ratio	Formula	Indicates:	Kellogg 2004	Kellogg 2003	General Mills 2004	Industry 2004	Page in book
Times interest earned ratio	(Net Income + Interest expense + Tax expense) / Interest expense	Ability to meet interest payments as they come due	5.4	4.1	4.1	5.9	493

For Kellogg the 2004 interest coverage was 5.4, which indicates that income before interest and taxes was 5.4 times the amount needed for interest expense. This exceeds the rate for General Mills, but it is less than the average rate for the industry. The debt to total assets ratio decreased for Kellogg during 2004, and its times interest earned ratio increased. These ratios indicate that Kellogg is better able to service its debt.

9. **Cash debt coverage ratio.** The ratio of cash provided by operating activities to average total liabilities, called the **cash debt coverage ratio**, is a cash-basis measure of solvency. This ratio indicates a company's ability to repay its liabilities from cash generated from operating activities without having to liquidate the assets used in its operations. Illustration 13A-13 shows Kellogg's cash debt coverage ratio.

Illustration 13A-13
Cash debt coverage ratio

Ratio	Formula	Indicates:	Kellogg 2004	Kellogg 2003	General Mills 2004	Industry 2004	Page in book
Cash debt coverage ratio	Cash provided by operations / Average total liabilities	Long-term debt-paying ability (cash basis)	.14	.13	.11	na	608

An industry average for this measure is not available. Kellogg's .14 is higher than General Mills's .11, and it increased from .13 in 2003. One way of interpreting this ratio is to say that net cash generated from one year of operations would be sufficient to pay off 14% of Kellogg's total liabilities. If 14% of this year's liabilities were retired each year, it would take approximately seven years to retire all of its debt. It would take General Mills approximately nine years to do so. A general rule of thumb is that a measure above .20 is acceptable.

10. **Free cash flow.** One indication of a company's solvency, as well as of its ability to pay dividends or expand operations, is the amount of excess cash it generated after investing to maintain its current productive capacity and paying dividends. This amount is referred to as **free cash flow**. For example, if you generate $100,000 of cash from operations but you spend $30,000 to maintain and replace your productive facilities at their current levels and pay $10,000 in dividends, you have $60,000 ($100,000 − $30,000 − $10,000) to use either to expand operations or to pay additional dividends. Kellogg's free cash flow is shown in Illustration 13A-14.

Illustration 13A-14
Free cash flow

Ratio	Formula	Indicates:	Kellogg 2004	Kellogg 2003	General Mills 2004	Industry 2004	Page in book
Free cash flow	Cash provided by operations − Capital expenditures − Cash dividends	Cash available for paying dividends or expanding operations	$532.8 (in millions)	$511.4 (in millions)	$421.0 (in millions)	na	63

Kellogg's free cash flow increased slightly from 2003 to 2004. During both years, the cash provided by operations was more than enough to allow Kellogg to acquire additional productive assets and maintain dividend payments. Kellogg could have used the remaining cash to reduce debt if necessary.

Profitability Ratios

Profitability ratios measure the income or operating success of an enterprise for a given period of time. A company's income, or the lack of it, affects its ability to obtain debt and equity financing, its liquidity position, and its ability to grow. As a consequence, creditors and investors alike are interested in evaluating profitability. Analysts frequently use profitability as the ultimate test of management's operating effectiveness.

Throughout this book we have introduced numerous measures of profitability. The relationships among measures of profitability are very important. Understanding them can help management determine where to focus its efforts to improve profitability. Illustration 13A-15 diagrams these relationships. Our discussion of Kellogg's profitability is structured around this diagram.

Illustration 13A-15
Relationships among profitability measures

11. **Return on common stockholders' equity ratio.**   A widely used measure of profitability from the common stockholder's viewpoint is the **return on common stockholders' equity ratio**. This ratio shows how many dollars of net income the company earned for each dollar invested by the owners. It is computed by dividing net income minus any preferred stock dividends—that is, income available to common stockholders—by average common stockholders' equity. The return on common stockholders' equity for Kellogg is shown in Illustration 13A-16.

Illustration 13A-16
Return on common stockholders' equity ratio

| | | | Kellogg | | General Mills | Industry | Page in |
Ratio	Formula	Indicates:	2004	2003	2004	2004	book
Return on common stockholders' equity ratio	$\dfrac{\text{Net income} - \text{Preferred stock dividends}}{\text{Average common stockholders' equity}}$	Profitability of common stockholders' investment	48%	67%	22%	23%	558

Kellogg's 2004 rate of return on common stockholders' equity is unusually high at 48%, considering an industry average of 23% and General Mills's return of 22%. In the subsequent sections we investigate the causes of this high return.

12. **Return on assets ratio.** The return on common stockholders' equity ratio is affected by two factors: the **return on assets ratio** and the degree of leverage. The return on assets ratio measures the overall profitability of assets in terms of the income earned on each dollar invested in assets. It is computed by dividing net income by average total assets. Kellogg's return on assets ratio is shown in Illustration 13A-17.

Illustration 13A-17
Return on assets ratio

Ratio	Formula	Indicates:	Kellogg 2004	Kellogg 2003	General Mills 2004	Industry 2004	Page in book
Return on assets ratio	$\dfrac{\text{Net income}}{\text{Average total assets}}$	Overall profitability of assets	8.5%	7.7%	6%	7%	437

Kellogg had an 8.5% return on assets in 2004. This rate is higher than that of General Mills and the industry average.

Note that Kellogg's rate of return on stockholders' equity (48%) is substantially higher than its rate of return on assets (9%). The reason is that Kellogg has made effective use of **leverage**. **Leveraging** or **trading on the equity** at a gain means that the company has borrowed money at a lower rate of interest than the rate of return it earns on the assets it purchased with the borrowed funds. Leverage enables management to use money supplied by nonowners to increase the return to owners.

A comparison of the rate of return on assets with the rate of interest paid for borrowed money indicates the profitability of trading on the equity. If you borrow money at 8% and your rate of return on assets is 11%, you are trading on the equity at a gain. Note, however, that trading on the equity is a two-way street: For example, if you borrow money at 11% and earn only 8% on it, you are trading on the equity at a loss.

Kellogg earns more on its borrowed funds than it has to pay in interest. Thus, the return to stockholders exceeds the return on the assets because of the positive benefit of leverage. Recall from our earlier discussion that Kellogg's percentage of debt financing as measured by the ratio of debt to total assets (or debt to equity) was higher than General Mills's and the industry average. It appears that Kellogg's high return on stockholders' equity is due in part to its use of leverage.

13. **Profit margin ratio.** The return on assets ratio is affected by two factors, the first of which is the profit margin ratio. The **profit margin ratio**, or rate of return on sales, is a measure of the percentage of each dollar of sales that results in net income. It is computed by dividing net income by net sales for the period. Kellogg's profit margin ratio is shown in Illustration 13A-18.

Illustration 13A-18
Profit margin ratio

Ratio	Formula	Indicates:	Kellogg 2004	Kellogg 2003	General Mills 2004	Industry 2004	Page in book
Profit margin ratio	$\dfrac{\text{Net income}}{\text{Net sales}}$	Net income generated by each dollar of sales	9.3%	8.9%	10%	7%	235

Kellogg experienced a slight increase in its profit margin ratio from 2003 to 2004 of 8.9% to 9.3%. Its profit margin ratio was greater than the industry average of 7% but less than General Mills's 10%.

High-volume (high inventory turnover) enterprises such as grocery stores and pharmacy chains generally have low profit margins. Low-volume enterprises such as jewelry stores and airplane manufacturers have high profit margins.

14. **Asset turnover ratio.** The other factor that affects the return on assets ratio is the asset turnover ratio. The **asset turnover ratio** measures how efficiently a company uses its assets to generate sales. It is determined by dividing net sales by average total assets for the period. The resulting number shows the dollars of sales produced by each dollar invested in assets. Illustration 13A-19 shows the asset turnover ratio for Kellogg.

Illustration 13A-19
Asset turnover ratio

Ratio	Formula	Indicates:	Kellogg 2004	Kellogg 2003	General Mills 2004	Industry 2004	Page in book
Asset turnover ratio	Net sales / Average total assets	How efficiently assets are used to generate sales	.92	.87	.60	1.17	439

The asset turnover ratio shows that in 2004 Kellogg generated sales of $0.92 for each dollar it had invested in assets. The ratio rose from 2003 to 2004. Kellogg's asset turnover ratio is below the industry average of 1.17 times but well above General Mills's ratio of .60.

Asset turnover ratios vary considerably among industries. The average asset turnover for utility companies is .45, for example, while the grocery store industry has an average asset turnover of 3.49.

In summary, Kellogg's return on assets ratio increased from 7.7% in 2003 to 8.5% in 2004. Underlying this increase was an increased profitability on each dollar of sales (as measured by the profit margin ratio) and a rise in the sales-generating efficiency of its assets (as measured by the asset turnover ratio). We can analyze the combined effects of profit margin and asset turnover on return on assets for Kellogg as shown in Illustration 13A-20.

Ratios:	Profit Margin	×	Asset Turnover	=	Return on Assets
	Net Income / Net Sales	×	Net Sales / Average Total Assets	=	Net Income / Average Total Assets
Kellogg					
2004	9.3%	×	.92 times	=	8.5%
2003	8.9%	×	.87 times	=	7.7%

Illustration 13A-20
Composition of return on assets ratio

15. **Gross profit rate.** Two factors strongly influence the profit margin ratio. One is the gross profit rate. The **gross profit rate** is determined by dividing gross profit (net sales less cost of goods sold) by net sales. This rate indicates a company's ability to maintain an adequate selling price above its cost of goods sold.

As an industry becomes more competitive, this ratio declines. For example, in the early years of the personal computer industry, gross profit rates were quite high. Today, because of increased competition and a belief that most brands of personal computers are similar in quality, gross profit rates have become thin. Analysts should closely monitor gross profit rates over time. Illustration 13A-21 (page 678) shows Kellogg's gross profit rate.

Ratio	Formula	Indicates:	Kellogg 2004	Kellogg 2003	General Mills 2004	Industry 2004	Page in book
Gross profit rate	Gross profit / Net sales	Margin between selling price and cost of goods sold	45%	44%	41%	32%	234

Illustration 13A-21
Gross profit rate

Kellogg's gross profit rate increased slightly from 2003 to 2004.

16. **Earnings per share (EPS).** Stockholders usually think in terms of the number of shares they own or plan to buy or sell. Expressing net income earned on a per share basis provides a useful perspective for determining profitability. **Earnings per share** is a measure of the net income earned on each share of common stock. It is computed by dividing net income by the average number of common shares outstanding during the year.

The terms "net income per share" or "earnings per share" refer to the amount of net income applicable to each share of *common stock*. Therefore, when we compute earnings per share, if there are preferred dividends declared for the period, we must deduct them from net income to arrive at income available to the common stockholders. Kellogg's earnings per share is shown in Illustration 13A-22.

Illustration 13A-22
Earnings per share

Ratio	Formula	Indicates:	Kellogg 2004	Kellogg 2003	General Mills 2004	Industry 2004	Page in book
Earnings per share (EPS)	(Net income − Preferred stock dividends) / Average common shares outstanding	Net income earned on each share of common stock	$2.16	$1.93	$2.82	na	55

Note that no industry average is presented in Illustration 13A-22. Industry data for earnings per share are not reported, and in fact the Kellogg and General Mills ratios should not be compared. Such comparisons are not meaningful because of the wide variations in the number of shares of outstanding stock among companies. Kellogg's earnings per share increased 23 cents per share in 2004. This represents an 11.9% increase from the 2003 EPS of $1.93.

17. **Price-earnings ratio.** The **price-earnings ratio** is an oft-quoted statistic that measures the ratio of the market price of each share of common stock to the earnings per share. The price-earnings (P-E) ratio reflects investors' assessments of a company's future earnings. It is computed by dividing the market price per share of the stock by earnings per share. Kellogg's price-earnings ratio is shown in Illustration 13A-23.

Illustration 13A-23
Price-earnings ratio

Ratio	Formula	Indicates:	Kellogg 2004	Kellogg 2003	General Mills 2004	Industry 2004	Page in book
Price-earnings ratio	Stock price per share / Earnings per share	Relationship between market price per share and earnings per share	20.7	20.1	16.3	19.9	662

At the end of 2004 and 2003 the market price of Kellogg's stock was $44.66 and $38.80, respectively. General Mills's stock was selling for $46.05 at the end of 2004.

In 2004 each share of Kellogg's stock sold for 20.7 times the amount that was earned on each share. Kellogg's price-earnings ratio is higher than General Mills's ratio of 16.3 and the industry average of 19.9 times. Its higher P-E ratio suggests that the market is more optimistic about Kellogg than about General Mills and the other companies in the industry. However, it might also signal that its stock is overpriced.

18. **Payout ratio.** The payout ratio measures the percentage of earnings distributed in the form of cash dividends. It is computed by dividing cash dividends declared on common stock by net income. Companies that have high growth rates are characterized by low payout ratios because they reinvest most of their net income in the business. The payout ratio for Kellogg is shown in Illustration 13A-24.

Illustration 13A-24
Payout ratio

Ratio	Formula	Indicates:	Kellogg 2004	Kellogg 2003	General Mills 2004	Industry 2004	Page in book
Payout ratio	Cash dividends declared on common stock / Net income	Percentage of earnings distributed in the form of cash dividends	47%	52%	39%	37%	556

The 2004 and 2003 payout ratios for Kellogg are comparatively high in relation to that of General Mills (39%) and the industry average (37%).

Management has some control over the amount of dividends paid each year, and companies are generally reluctant to reduce a dividend below the amount paid in a previous year. Therefore, the payout ratio will actually increase if a company's net income declines but the company keeps its total dividend payment the same. Of course, unless the company returns to its previous level of profitability, maintaining this higher dividend payout ratio is probably not possible over the long run.

Before drawing any conclusions regarding Kellogg's dividend payout ratio, we should calculate this ratio over a longer period of time to evaluate any trends, and also try to find out whether management's philosophy regarding dividends has changed recently. The "Selected Financial Data" section of Kellogg's Management Discussion and Analysis shows that over a 5-year period earnings per share rose 49%, while dividends per share grew only 1.5%.

In terms of the types of financial information available and the ratios used by various industries, what can be practically covered in this textbook gives you only the "Titanic approach": That is, you are seeing only the tip of the iceberg compared to the vast databases and types of ratio analysis that are available on computers. The availability of information is not a problem. The real trick is to be discriminating enough to perform relevant analysis and select pertinent comparative data.

Glossary

Asset turnover ratio A measure of how efficiently a company uses its assets to generate sales, computed as net sales divided by average total assets. (p. 677)

Available-for-sale securities Securities that are held with the intent of selling them sometime in the future. (p. 651)

Average collection period The average number of days that receivables are outstanding, calculated as receivables turnover divided into 365 days. (p. 671)

Cash debt coverage ratio A cash-basis measure used to evaluate solvency, computed as cash from operations divided by average total liabilities. (p. 674)

Change in accounting principle Use of an accounting principle in the current year different from the one used in the preceding year. (p. 650)

Comprehensive income A measure of income that includes all changes in stockholders' equity during a period except those resulting from investments by stockholders and distributions to stockholders. (p. 650)

Current cash debt coverage ratio A cash-basis measure of short-term debt-paying ability, computed as cash provided by operations divided by average current liabilities. (p. 670)

Current ratio A measure that expresses the relationship of current assets to current liabilities, calculated as current assets divided by current liabilities. (p. 670)

Days in inventory A measure of the average number of days it takes to sell the inventory, computed as inventory turnover divided into 365 days. (p. 672)

Debt to total assets ratio A measure of the percentage of total assets provided by creditors, computed as total debt divided by total assets. (p. 673)

Discontinued operations The disposal of a significant component of a business. (p. 647)

Earnings per share The net income earned by each share of common stock, computed as net income less dividends on preferred stock divided by the average common shares outstanding. (p. 678)

Extraordinary items Events and transactions that meet two conditions: (1) unusual in nature and (2) infrequent in occurrence. (p. 648)

Free cash flow A measure of solvency, calculated as cash from operations less capital expenditures and cash dividends. (p. 674)

Gross profit rate An indicator of a company's ability to maintain an adequate selling price above its cost of goods sold, computed as gross profit divided by net sales. (p. 677)

Horizontal analysis A technique for evaluating a series of financial statement data over a period of time to determine the increase (decrease) that has taken place, expressed as either an amount or a percentage. (p. 654)

Inventory turnover ratio A measure of the liquidity of inventory, computed as cost of goods sold divided by average inventory. (p. 671)

Leveraging Borrowing money at a lower rate of interest than can be earned by using the borrowed money; also referred to as trading on the equity. (p. 676)

Liquidity ratios Measures of the short-term ability of the enterprise to pay its maturing obligations and to meet unexpected needs for cash. (p. 659)

Payout ratio A measure of the percentage of earnings distributed in the form of cash dividends, calculated as cash dividends declared on common stock divided by net income. (p. 679)

Price-earnings (P-E) ratio A comparison of the market price of each share of common stock to the earnings per share, computed as the market price of the stock divided by earnings per share. (pp. 662, 678)

Pro forma income A measure of income that usually excludes items that a company thinks are unusual or nonrecurring. (p. 661)

Profit margin ratio A measure of the net income generated by each dollar of sales, computed as net income divided by net sales. (p. 676)

Profitability ratios Measures of the income or operating success of an enterprise for a given period of time. (p. 660)

Quality of earnings Indicates the level of full and transparent information that is provided to users of the financial statements. (p. 661)

Receivables turnover ratio A measure of the liquidity of receivables, computed as net credit sales divided by average net receivables. (p. 671)

Return on assets ratio An overall measure of profitability, calculated as net income divided by average total assets. (p. 676)

Return on common stockholders' equity ratio A measure of the dollars of net income earned for each dollar invested by the owners, computed as income available to common stockholders divided by average common stockholders' equity. (p. 675)

Solvency ratios Measures of the ability of the enterprise to survive over a long period of time. (p. 659)

Sustainable income The most likely level of income to be obtained in the future; calculated as net income adjusted for irregular items. (p. 646)

Times interest earned ratio A measure of a company's ability to meet interest payments as they come due, calculated as income before interest expense and income taxes divided by interest expense. (p. 673)

Trading on the equity Same as leveraging. (p. 676)

Trading securities Securities bought and held primarily for sale in the near term to generate income on short-term price differences. (p. 651)

Vertical analysis A technique for evaluating financial statement data that expresses each item in a financial statement as a percent of a base amount. (p. 656)

Demonstration Problem

The events and transactions of Dever Corporation for the year ending December 31, 2007, resulted in these data.

Cost of goods sold	$2,600,000
Net sales	4,400,000
Other expenses and losses	9,600
Other revenues and gains	5,600
Selling and administrative expenses	1,100,000

Gain from discontinued division	570,000
Loss from tornado disaster (extraordinary loss)	600,000

Analysis reveals the following.

1. All items are before the applicable income tax rate of 30%.
2. The plastics division was sold on July 1.
3. All operating data for the plastics division have been segregated.

Instructions

Prepare an income statement for the year, excluding the presentation of earnings per share.

Solution to Demonstration Problem

Action Plan

- Remember that material items not typical of operations are reported in separate sections net of taxes.
- Associate income taxes with the item that affects the taxes.
- On a corporation income statement, report income tax expense when there is income before income tax.

DEVER CORPORATION
Income Statement
For the Year Ended December 31, 2007

Net sales		$4,400,000
Cost of goods sold		2,600,000
Gross profit		1,800,000
Selling and administrative expenses		1,100,000
Income from operations		700,000
Other revenues and gains	$ 5,600	
Other expenses and losses	(9,600)	(4,000)
Income before income taxes		696,000
Income tax expense ($696,000 × 30%)		208,800
Income before irregular items		487,200
Discontinued operations: Gain from discontinued division, net of taxes of $171,000 ($570,000 × 30%)		399,000
Extraordinary item: Tornado loss, net of income tax savings $180,000 ($600,000 × 30%)		(420,000)
Net income		$ 466,200

Self-Study Questions

Answers are at the end of the chapter.

All of the Self-Study Questions in this chapter employ decision tools.

(SO 2) **1.** In reporting discontinued operations, the income statement should show in a special section:
   (a) gains on the disposal of the discontinued component.
   (b) losses on the disposal of the discontinued component.
   (c) Neither (a) nor (b).
   (d) Both (a) and (b).

(SO 2) **2.** Cool Stools Corporation has income before taxes of $400,000 and an extraordinary loss of $100,000. If the income tax rate is 25% on all

items, the income statement should show income before irregular items and an extraordinary loss, respectively, of
   (a) $325,000 and $100,000.
   (b) $325,000 and $75,000.
   (c) $300,000 and $100,000.
   (d) $300,000 and $75,000.

3. Which of the following would be considered an (SO 3) "Other comprehensive income" item?
   (a) gain on disposal of discontinued operations.
   (b) unrealized loss on available-for-sale securities.
   (c) extraordinary loss related to flood.
   (d) net income.

(SO 4)   **4.** In horizontal analysis, each item is expressed as a percentage of the:
(a) net income amount.
(b) stockholders' equity amount.
(c) total assets amount.
(d) base-year amount.

(SO 4)   **5.** Adams Corporation reported net sales of $300,000, $330,000, and $360,000 in the years 2005, 2006, and 2007, respectively. If 2005 is the base year, what percentage do 2007 sales represent of the base?
(a) 77%.   (c) 120%.
(b) 108%.   (d) 130%.

(SO 5)   **6.** The following schedule is a display of what type of analysis?

	Amount	Percent
Current assets	$200,000	25%
Property, plant, and equipment	600,000	75%
Total assets	$800,000	

(a) Horizontal analysis.
(b) Differential analysis.
(c) Vertical analysis.
(d) Ratio analysis.

(SO 5)   **7.** In vertical analysis, the base amount for depreciation expense is generally:
(a) net sales.
(b) depreciation expense in a previous year.
(c) gross profit.
(d) fixed assets.

(SO 6)   **8.** Which measure is an evaluation of a company's ability to pay current liabilities?
(a) Current cash debt coverage ratio.
(b) Current ratio.

(c) Both (a) and (b).
(d) None of the above.

(SO 6)   **9.** Which measure is useful in evaluating the efficiency in managing inventories?
(a) Inventory turnover ratio.
(b) Days in inventory.
(c) Both (a) and (b).
(d) None of the above.

(SO 6)   **10.** Which of these is *not* a liquidity ratio?
(a) Current ratio.
(b) Asset turnover ratio.
(c) Inventory turnover ratio.
(d) Receivables turnover ratio.

(SO 6)   **11.** Plano Corporation reported net income $24,000; net sales $400,000; and average assets $600,000 for 2007. What is the 2007 profit margin ratio?
(a) 6%.
(b) 12%.
(c) 40%.
(d) 200%.

(SO 7)   **12.** Which situation below might indicate a company has a low quality of earnings?
(a) The same accounting principles are used each year.
(b) Revenue is recognized when earned.
(c) Maintenance costs are capitalized and then depreciated.
(d) The company's P-E ratio is high relative to competitors.

Go to the book's website, **www.wiley.com/college/ kimmel**, to access additional Self-Study Questions.

Questions

All of the Questions in this chapter employ decision tools.

1. Explain sustainable income. What relationship does this concept have to the treatment of irregular items on the income statement?

2. Indicate which of the following items would be reported as an extraordinary item on Food Feast Corporation's income statement.
(a) Loss from damages caused by a volcano eruption.
(b) Loss from the sale of short-term investments.
(c) Loss attributable to a labor strike.
(d) Loss caused when the Food and Drug Administration prohibited the manufacture and sale of a product line.
(e) Loss of inventory from flood damage because a warehouse is located on a flood plain that floods every 5 to 10 years.

(f) Loss on the write-down of outdated inventory.
(g) Loss from a foreign government's expropriation of a production facility.
(h) Loss from damage to a warehouse in southern California from a minor earthquake.

3. Top Drawer Inc. reported 2006 earnings per share of $3.26 and had no extraordinary items. In 2007 earnings per share on income before extraordinary items was $2.99, and earnings per share on net income was $3.49. Do you consider this trend to be favorable? Why or why not?

4. Caradco Inc. has been in operation for 3 years. and uses the FIFO method of pricing inventory. During the fourth year, Caradco changes to the average cost method for all its inventory. How will Caradco report this change?

5. (a) Sharon Weber believes that the analysis of financial statements is directed at two characteristics of a company: liquidity and profitability. Is Sharon correct? Explain.
   (b) Are short-term creditors, long-term creditors, and stockholders interested in primarily the same characteristics of a company? Explain.

6. (a) Distinguish among the following bases of comparison: intracompany, industry averages, and intercompany.
   (b) Give the principal value of using each of the three bases of comparison.

7. Two popular methods of financial statement analysis are horizontal analysis and vertical analysis. Explain the difference between these two methods.

8. (a) If Simon Company had net income of $350,000 in 2006 and it experienced a 24.5% increase in net income for 2007, what is its net income for 2007?
   (b) If 6 cents of every dollar of Simon's revenue is net income in 2006, what is the dollar amount of 2006 revenue?

9. Name the major ratios useful in assessing (a) liquidity and (b) solvency.

10. James Slater is puzzled. His company had a profit margin of 10% in 2007. He feels that this is an indication that the company is doing well. Jill Farvell, his accountant, says that more information is needed to determine the company's financial well-being. Who is correct? Why?

11. What does each type of ratio measure?
    (a) Liquidity ratios.
    (b) Solvency ratios.
    (c) Profitability ratios.

12. What is the difference between the current ratio and working capital?

13. Fast Buck, a retail store, has a receivables turnover ratio of 4.5 times. The industry average is 12.5 times. Does Fast Buck have a collection problem with its receivables?

14. Which ratios should be used to help answer each of these questions?
    (a) How efficient is a company in using its assets to produce sales?
    (b) How near to sale is the inventory on hand?
    (c) How many dollars of net income were earned for each dollar invested by the owners?
    (d) How able is a company to meet interest charges as they fall due?

15. In September 2004 the price-earnings ratio of General Motors was 11.3, and the price-earnings ratio of Microsoft was 28.14. Which company did the stock market favor? Explain.

16. What is the formula for computing the payout ratio? Do you expect this ratio to be high or low for a growth company?

17. Holding all other factors constant, indicate whether each of the following changes generally signals good or bad news about a company.
    (a) Increase in profit margin ratio.
    (b) Decrease in inventory turnover ratio.
    (c) Increase in current ratio.
    (d) Decrease in earnings per share.
    (e) Increase in price-earnings ratio.
    (f) Increase in debt to total assets ratio.
    (g) Decrease in times interest earned ratio.

18. The return on assets for Elverum Corporation is 7.6%. During the same year Elverum's return on common stockholders' equity is 12.8%. What is the explanation for the difference in the two rates?

19. Which two ratios do you think should be of greatest interest in each of the following cases?
    (a) A pension fund considering the purchase of 20-year bonds.
    (b) A bank contemplating a short-term loan.
    (c) A common stockholder.

20. Happy Daze Inc. has net income of $300,000, average shares of common stock outstanding of 50,000, and preferred dividends for the period of $20,000. What is Happy Daze earnings per share of common stock? Art Fonz, the president of Happy Daze, believes that the computed EPS of the company is high. Comment.

21. Identify and explain factors that affect quality of earnings.

22. Explain how the choice of one of the following accounting methods over the other raises or lowers a company's net income during a period of continuing inflation.
    (a) Use of FIFO instead of LIFO for inventory costing.
    (b) Use of a 6-year life for machinery instead of a 9-year life.
    (c) Use of straight-line depreciation instead of accelerated declining-balance depreciation.

Brief Exercises

All of the Brief Exercises in this chapter employ decision tools.

BE13-1 On June 30 Rojas Corporation discontinued its operations in Mexico. On September 1 Rojas disposed of the Mexico facility at a pretax loss of $480,000. The applicable tax rate is 25%. Show the discontinued operations section of Rojas's income statement.

Prepare a discontinued operations section of an income statement.
(SO 2)

Prepare a corrected income statement with an extraordinary item.
(SO 2)

BE13-2   An inexperienced accountant for Barlay Corporation showed the following in Barlay's 2007 income statement: Income before income taxes $300,000; Income tax expense $48,000; Extraordinary loss from flood (before taxes) $60,000; and Net income $192,000. The extraordinary loss and taxable income are both subject to a 20% tax rate. Prepare a corrected income statement beginning with "Income before income taxes."

Indicate how a change in accounting principles is reported.
(SO 2)

BE13-3   On January 1, 2007, Cannon Inc. changed from the LIFO method of inventory pricing to the FIFO method. Explain how this change in accounting principle should be treated in the company's financial statements.

Prepare horizontal analysis.
(SO 4)

BE13-4   Using these data from the comparative balance sheet of De Rosa Company, perform horizontal analysis.

	December 31, 2007	December 31, 2006
Accounts receivable	$ 520,000	$ 400,000
Inventory	780,000	600,000
Total assets	3,220,000	2,800,000

Prepare vertical analysis.
(SO 5)

BE13-5   Using the data presented in BE13-4 for De Rosa Company, perform vertical analysis.

Calculate percentage of change.
(SO 4)

BE13-6   Net income was $500,000 in 2005, $480,000 in 2006, and $537,600 in 2007. What is the percentage of change from (a) 2005 to 2006, and (b) from 2006 to 2007? Is the change an increase or a decrease?

Calculate net income.
(SO 4)

BE13-7   If Parthenon Company had net income of $672,300 in 2007 and it experienced a 17% increase in net income over 2006, what was its 2006 net income?

Analyze change in net income.
(SO 5)

BE13-8   Vertical analysis (common-size) percentages for Bellamy Company's sales, cost of goods sold, and expenses are listed here.

Vertical Analysis	2007	2006	2005
Sales	100.0%	100.0%	100.0%
Cost of goods sold	59.2	62.4	64.5
Expenses	26.0	26.6	28.5

Did Bellamy's net income as a percent of sales increase, decrease, or remain unchanged over the 3-year period? Provide numerical support for your answer.

Analyze change in net income.
(SO 4)

BE13-9   Horizontal analysis (trend analysis) percentages for Kirvida Company's sales, cost of goods sold, and expenses are listed here.

Horizontal Analysis	2007	2006	2005
Sales	96.2%	104.8%	100.0%
Cost of goods sold	102.0	97.0	100.0
Expenses	108.6	95.4	100.0

Explain whether Kirvida's net income increased, decreased, or remained unchanged over the 3-year period.

Calculate current ratio.
(SO 6)

BE13-10   These selected condensed data are taken from recent balance sheets of Bob Evans Farms (in thousands).

	2005	2004
Cash	$ 5,267	$ 3,986
Accounts receivable	25,330	22,282
Inventories	24,416	19,540
Other current assets	2,226	1,664
Total current assets	$ 57,239	$ 47,472
Total current liabilities	$188,628	$145,847

Compute the current ratio for each year and comment on your results.

BE13-11 The following data are taken from the financial statements of Tall Tail Company.

Evaluate collection of accounts receivable.
(SO 6)

	2007	2006
Accounts receivable (net), end of year	$ 560,000	$ 540,000
Net sales on account	4,700,000	4,000,000
Terms for all sales are 1/10, n/45.		

Compute for each year (a) the receivables turnover ratio and (b) the average collection period. What conclusions about the management of accounts receivable can be drawn from these data? At the end of 2005, accounts receivable was $500,000.

BE13-12 The following data were taken from the income statements of Long Haul Company.

Evaluate management of inventory.
(SO 6)

	2007	2006
Sales revenue	$6,420,000	$6,240,000
Beginning inventory	970,000	837,000
Purchases	4,640,000	4,661,000
Ending inventory	1,020,000	970,000

Compute for each year (a) the inventory turnover ratio and (b) days in inventory. What conclusions concerning the management of the inventory can be drawn from these data?

BE13-13 Staples, Inc. is one of the largest suppliers of office products in the United States. It had net income of $708.4 million and net revenue of $14,448.4 million in 2004. Its total assets were $6,503.0 million at the beginning of the year and $7,071.4 million at the end of the year. What is Staples, Inc.'s (a) asset turnover ratio and (b) profit margin ratio? (Round to two decimals.) Provide a brief interpretation of your results.

Calculate profitability ratios.
(SO 6)

BE13-14 Royal Ware Company has stockholders' equity of $400,000 and net income of $60,000. It has a payout ratio of 25% and a return on assets ratio of 16%. How much did Royal Ware pay in cash dividends, and what were its average total assets?

Calculate profitability ratios.
(SO 6)

BE13-15 Selected data taken from the 2004 financial statements of trading card company Topps Company, Inc. are as follows (in millions).

Calculate cash-basis liquidity and solvency ratios.
(SO 6)

	2004
Net sales for 2004	$295.9
Current liabilities, February 28, 2004	39.5
Current liabilities, February 26, 2005	47.5
Net cash provided by operating activities	22.9
Total liabilities, February 28, 2004	64.2
Total liabilities, February 26, 2005	71.2
Capital expenditures	2.6
Cash dividends	6.5

Compute these ratios at February 26, 2005: (a) current cash debt coverage ratio (b) cash debt coverage ratio, and (c) free cash flow. Provide a brief interpretation of your results.

Exercises

All of the Exercises in this chapter employ decision tools.

E13-1 Prentiss Company has income before irregular items of $270,000 for the year ended December 31, 2007. It also has the following items (before considering income taxes): (1) an extraordinary fire loss of $50,000 and (2) a gain of $40,000 from the disposal of a division. Assume all items are subject to income taxes at a 30% tax rate.

Prepare irregular items portion of an income statement.
(SO 2)

Instructions

Prepare Prentiss Company's income statement for 2007, beginning with "Income before irregular items."

Evaluate the effects of unusual or irregular items.
(SO 1, 2, 6)

E13-2 The *Wall Street Journal* routinely publishes summaries of corporate quarterly and annual earnings reports in a feature called the "Earnings Digest." A typical "digest" report takes the following form.

ENERGY ENTERPRISES (A)

Quarter ending July 31

	2007	2006
Revenues	$2,049,000,000	$1,754,000,000
Net income	97,000,000	(a) 68,750,000
EPS: Net income	1.31	0.93

9 months ending July 31

	2007	2006
Revenues	$5,578,500,000	$5,065,300,000
Extraordinary item	(b) 1,900,000	
Net income	102,700,000	(a) 33,250,000
EPS: Net income	1.36	0.53

(a) Includes a net charge of $26,000,000 from loss on the sale of electrical equipment
(b) Extraordinary gain on Middle East property expropriation

The letter in parentheses following the company name indicates the exchange on which Energy Enterprises' stock is traded—in this case, the American Stock Exchange.

Instructions

Answer the following questions.

(a) How was the loss on the electrical equipment reported on the income statement? Was it reported in the third quarter of 2006? How can you tell?
(b) Why did the *Wall Street Journal* list the extraordinary item separately?
(c) What is the extraordinary item? Was it included in income for the third quarter? How can you tell?
(d) Did Energy Enterprises have an operating loss in any quarter of 2006? Of 2007? How do you know?
(e) Approximately how many shares of stock were outstanding in 2007? Did the number of outstanding shares change from July 31, 2006 to July 31, 2007?
(f) As an investor, what numbers should you use to determine Energy Enterprises' profit margin ratio? Calculate the 9-month profit margin ratio for 2006 and 2007 that you consider most useful. Explain your decision.

Prepare horizontal analysis.
(SO 4)

E13-3 Here is financial information for Ride Away Inc.

	December 31, 2007	December 31, 2006
Current assets	$128,000	$ 80,000
Plant assets (net)	400,000	360,000
Current liabilities	91,000	65,000
Long-term liabilities	144,000	90,000
Common stock, $1 par	138,000	115,000
Retained earnings	155,000	170,000

Prepare vertical analysis.
(SO 5)

Instructions

Prepare a schedule showing a horizontal analysis for 2007 using 2006 as the base year.

E13-4 Operating data for Poseidon Corporation are presented on page 687.

	2007	2006
Sales	$800,000	$600,000
Cost of goods sold	500,000	408,000
Selling expenses	120,000	72,000
Administrative expenses	72,000	48,000
Income tax expense	32,000	21,600
Net income	76,000	50,400

Instructions
Prepare a schedule showing a vertical analysis for 2007 and 2006.

E13-5 The comparative balance sheets of Philip Morris Companies, Inc. are presented here.

Prepare horizontal and vertical analyses.
(SO 4, 5)

PHILIP MORRIS COMPANIES, INC.
Comparative Balance Sheets
December 31
($ in millions)

Assets	2004	2003
Current assets	$ 25,901	$21,382
Property, plant, and equipment (net)	16,305	16,067
Other assets	59,442	58,726
Total assets	$101,648	$96,175
Liabilities and Stockholders' Equity		
Current liabilities	$ 23,574	$21,393
Long-term liabilities	47,360	49,705
Stockholders' equity	30,714	25,077
Total liabilities and stockholders' equity	$101,648	$96,175

Instructions
(a) Prepare a horizontal analysis of the balance sheet data for Philip Morris using 2003 as a base. (Show the amount of increase or decrease as well.)
(b) Prepare a vertical analysis of the balance sheet data for Philip Morris for 2004.

E13-6 Here are the comparative income statements of Erik Corporation.

Prepare horizontal and vertical analyses.
(SO 4, 5)

ERIK CORPORATION
Comparative Income Statements
For the Years Ended December 31

	2007	2006
Net sales	$572,000	$520,000
Cost of goods sold	477,000	450,000
Gross profit	$ 95,000	$ 70,000
Operating expenses	60,000	45,000
Net income	$ 35,000	$ 25,000

Instructions
(a) Prepare a horizontal analysis of the income statement data for Erik Corporation using 2006 as a base. (Show the amounts of increase or decrease.)
(b) Prepare a vertical analysis of the income statement data for Erik Corporation for both years.

E13-7 Nordstrom, Inc. operates department stores in numerous states. Selected financial statement data (in millions) for 2005 are presented on page 688.

Compute liquidity ratios.
(SO 6)

	End of Year	Beginning of Year
Cash and cash equivalents	$ 360.3	$ 340.3
Receivables (net)	645.7	666.8
Merchandise inventory	917.2	901.6
Other current assets	649.2	616.1
Total current assets	$2,572.4	$2,524.8
Total current liabilities	$1,341.2	$1,122.6

For the year, net credit sales were $7,131.4 million, cost of goods sold was $4,559.4 million, and cash from operations was $660.3 million.

Instructions
Compute the current ratio, current cash debt coverage ratio, receivables turnover ratio, average collection period, inventory turnover ratio, and days in inventory at the end of the current year.

Perform current ratio analysis.
(SO 6)

E13-8 Trolls Incorporated had the following transactions involving current assets and current liabilities during February 2007.

Feb.	3	Collected accounts receivable of $15,000.
	7	Purchased equipment for $20,000 cash.
	11	Paid $3,000 for a 3-year insurance policy.
	14	Paid accounts payable of $14,000.
	18	Declared cash dividends, $6,000.

Additional information:
As of February 1, 2007, current assets were $100,000 and current liabilities were $40,000.

Instructions
Compute the current ratio as of the beginning of the month and after each transaction.

Compute selected ratios.
(SO 6)

E13-9 Maury Company has these comparative balance sheet data:

MAURY COMPANY
Balance Sheets
December 31

	2007	2006
Cash	$ 25,000	$ 30,000
Receivables (net)	65,000	60,000
Inventories	60,000	50,000
Plant assets (net)	200,000	180,000
	$350,000	$320,000
Accounts payable	$ 55,000	$ 60,000
Mortgage payable (15%)	100,000	100,000
Common stock, $10 par	135,000	120,000
Retained earnings	60,000	40,000
	$350,000	$320,000

Additional information for 2007:
1. Net income was $25,000.
2. Sales on account were $400,000. Sales returns and allowances amounted to $25,000.
3. Cost of goods sold was $198,000.
4. Net cash provided by operating activities was $48,000.
5. Capital expenditures were $25,000, and cash dividends were $18,000.

Instructions
Compute the following ratios at December 31, 2007.
(a) Current.
(b) Receivables turnover.
(c) Average collection period.
(d) Inventory turnover.
(e) Days in inventory.
(f) Cash debt coverage.
(g) Current cash debt coverage.
(h) Free cash flow.

E13-10 Selected comparative statement data for the giant bookseller Barnes & Noble are presented here. All balance sheet data are as of December 31 (in millions). *Compute selected ratios.* (SO 6)

	2004	2003
Net sales	$4,873.6	$5,951.0
Cost of goods sold	3,386.6	4,323.8
Net income	143.3	151.9
Accounts receivable	74.6	60.5
Inventory	1,274.6	1,526.1
Total assets	3,301.5	3,507.3
Total common stockholders' equity	1,165.9	1,259.7

Instructions
Compute the following ratios for 2004:
(a) Profit margin.
(b) Asset turnover.
(c) Return on assets.
(d) Return on common stockholders' equity.
(e) Gross profit rate.

E13-11 Here is the income statement for New Do, Inc. *Compute selected ratios.* (SO 6)

NEW DO, INC.
Income Statement
For the Year Ended December 31, 2007

Sales	$400,000
Cost of goods sold	230,000
Gross profit	170,000
Expenses (including $14,000 interest and $24,000 income taxes)	88,000
Net income	$ 82,000

Additional information:
1. Common stock outstanding January 1, 2007, was 30,000 shares, and 40,000 shares were outstanding at December 31, 2007.
2. The market price of New Do, Inc., stock was $17.60 in 2007.
3. Cash dividends of $21,000 were paid, $5,000 of which were to preferred stockholders.

Instructions
Compute the following measures for 2007.
(a) Earnings per share.
(b) Price-earnings ratio.
(c) Payout ratio.
(d) Times interest earned ratio.

E13-12 Zubick Corporation experienced a fire on December 31, 2007, in which its financial records were partially destroyed. It has been able to salvage some of the records and has ascertained the following balances. *Compute amounts from ratios.* (SO 6)

	December 31, 2007	December 31, 2006
Cash	$ 30,000	$ 10,000
Receivables (net)	72,500	126,000
Inventory	200,000	180,000
Accounts payable	50,000	10,000
Notes payable	30,000	20,000
Common stock, $100 par	400,000	400,000
Retained earnings	113,500	101,000

Additional information:
1. The inventory turnover is 4.0 times.
2. The return on common stockholders' equity is 20%. The company had no additional paid-in capital.
3. The receivables turnover is 11.2 times.
4. The return on assets is 16%.
5. Total assets at December 31, 2006, were $605,000.

Instructions
Compute the following for Zubick Corporation.
(a) Cost of goods sold for 2007.
(b) Net credit sales for 2007.
(c) Net income for 2007.
(d) Total assets at December 31, 2007.

Problems: Set A

Prepare vertical analysis and comment on profitability.
(SO 5, 6)

P13-1A Here are comparative statement data for East Company and West Company, two competitors. All balance sheet data are as of December 31, 2007, and December 31, 2006.

	East Company 2007	East Company 2006	West Company 2007	West Company 2006
Net sales	$1,849,035		$546,000	
Cost of goods sold	1,080,490		238,000	
Operating expenses	230,000		82,000	
Interest expense	6,800		1,600	
Income tax expense	62,030		31,000	
Current assets	325,975	$312,410	83,336	$ 79,467
Plant assets (net)	526,800	500,000	139,728	125,812
Current liabilities	66,325	75,815	35,348	30,281
Long-term liabilities	113,990	90,000	29,620	25,000
Common stock, $10 par	500,000	500,000	120,000	120,000
Retained earnings	172,460	146,595	38,096	29,998

Instructions
(a) Prepare a vertical analysis of the 2007 income statement data for East Company and West Company.
(b) Comment on the relative profitability of the companies by computing the 2007 return on assets and the return on common stockholders' equity ratios for both companies.

Compute ratios from balance sheet and income statement.
(SO 6)

P13-2A The comparative statements of Jack Frost Company are presented here.

JACK FROST COMPANY
Income Statements
For the Years Ended December 31

	2007	2006
Net sales	$1,890,540	$1,750,500
Cost of goods sold	1,058,540	996,000
Gross profit	832,000	754,500
Selling and administrative expenses	506,000	479,000
Income from operations	326,000	275,500
Other expenses and losses		
Interest expense	25,000	19,000
Income before income taxes	301,000	256,500
Income tax expense	86,000	77,000
Net income	$ 215,000	$ 179,500

JACK FROST COMPANY
Balance Sheets
December 31

Assets	2007	2006
Current assets		
Cash	$ 60,100	$ 64,200
Short-term investments	74,000	50,000
Accounts receivable	107,800	102,800
Inventory	133,000	115,500
Total current assets	374,900	332,500
Plant assets (net)	615,300	520,300
Total assets	$990,200	$852,800

Liabilities and Stockholders' Equity		
Current liabilities		
Accounts payable	$160,000	$145,400
Income taxes payable	43,500	42,000
Total current liabilities	203,500	187,400
Bonds payable	210,000	200,000
Total liabilities	413,500	387,400
Stockholders' equity		
Common stock ($5 par)	290,000	300,000
Retained earnings	286,700	165,400
Total stockholders' equity	576,700	465,400
Total liabilities and stockholders' equity	$990,200	$852,800

All sales were on account. Net cash provided by operating activities for 2007 was $240,000. Capital expenditures were $120,000, and cash dividends were $80,000.

Instructions
Compute the following ratios for 2007.
(a) Earnings per share.
(b) Return on common stockholders' equity.
(c) Return on assets.
(d) Current ratio.
(e) Receivables turnover.
(f) Average collection period.
(g) Inventory turnover.
(h) Days in inventory.
(i) Times interest earned.
(j) Asset turnover.
(k) Debt to total assets.
(l) Current cash debt coverage.
(m) Cash debt coverage.
(n) Free cash flow.

P13-3A Condensed balance sheet and income statement data for Here and There Corporation are presented here.

Perform ratio analysis, and discuss change in financial position and operating results.
(SO 6)

HERE AND THERE CORPORATION
Balance Sheets
December 31

	2007	2006	2005
Cash	$ 30,000	$ 20,000	$ 18,000
Receivables (net)	50,000	45,000	48,000
Other current assets	90,000	85,000	64,000
Investments	55,000	70,000	45,000
Plant and equipment (net)	500,000	370,000	258,000
	$725,000	$590,000	$433,000
Current liabilities	$ 85,000	$ 80,000	$ 30,000
Long-term debt	185,000	85,000	20,000
Common stock, $10 par	320,000	300,000	300,000
Retained earnings	135,000	125,000	83,000
	$725,000	$590,000	$433,000

HERE AND THERE CORPORATION
Income Statements
For the Years Ended December 31

	2007	2006
Sales	$640,000	$500,000
Less: Sales returns and allowances	40,000	30,000
Net sales	600,000	470,000
Cost of goods sold	425,000	300,000
Gross profit	175,000	170,000
Operating expenses (including income taxes)	117,000	94,000
Net income	$ 58,000	$ 76,000

Additional information:

1. The market price of Here and There's common stock was $6.00, $9.00, and $7.00 for 2005, 2006, and 2007, respectively.
2. You must compute dividends paid. All dividends were paid in cash.

Instructions
(a) Compute the following ratios for 2006 and 2007.
   (1) Profit margin.
   (2) Gross profit.
   (3) Asset turnover.
   (4) Earnings per share.
   (5) Price-earnings.
   (6) Payout.
   (7) Debt to total assets.

(b) Based on the ratios calculated, discuss briefly the improvement or lack thereof in the financial position and operating results from 2006 to 2007 of Here and There Corporation.

Compute ratios; comment on overall liquidity and profitability.
(SO 6)

P13-4A The following financial information is for Inca Company.

INCA COMPANY
Balance Sheets
December 31

Assets	2007	2006
Cash	$ 70,000	$ 65,000
Short-term investments	55,000	40,000
Receivables	104,000	90,000
Inventories	230,000	125,000
Prepaid expenses	25,000	23,000
Land	130,000	130,000
Building and equipment (net)	260,000	175,000
Total assets	$874,000	$648,000

Liabilities and Stockholders' Equity	2007	2006
Notes payable	$170,000	$100,000
Accounts payable	65,000	42,000
Accrued liabilities	40,000	40,000
Bonds payable, due 2009	250,000	150,000
Common stock, $10 par	200,000	200,000
Retained earnings	149,000	116,000
Total liabilities and stockholders' equity	$874,000	$648,000

INCA COMPANY
Income Statements
For the Years Ended December 31

	2007	2006
Sales	$880,000	$790,000
Cost of goods sold	640,000	575,000
Gross profit	240,000	215,000
Operating expenses	192,000	170,000
Net income	$ 48,000	$ 45,000

Additional information:

1. Inventory at the beginning of 2006 was $115,000.
2. Receivables (net) at the beginning of 2006 were $88,000.
3. Total assets at the beginning of 2006 were $630,000.
4. No common stock transactions occurred during 2006 or 2007.
5. All sales were on account.

Instructions
(a) Indicate, by using ratios, the change in liquidity and profitability of Inca Company from 2006 to 2007. (*Note:* Not all profitability ratios can be computed nor can cash-basis ratios be computed.)
(b) Given below are three independent situations and a ratio that may be affected. For each situation, compute the affected ratio (1) as of December 31, 2007, and (2) as of December 31, 2008, after giving effect to the situation. Net income for 2008 was $40,000. Total assets on December 31, 2008, were $900,000.

Situation	Ratio
1. 18,000 shares of common stock were sold at par on July 1, 2008.	Return on common stockholders' equity
2. All of the notes payable were paid in 2008.	Debt to total assets
3. The market price of common stock was $9 and $12 on December 31, 2007 and 2008, respectively.	Price-earnings

P13-5A Selected financial data of Target and Wal-Mart for 2004 are presented here (in millions).

Compute selected ratios, and compare liquidity, profitability, and solvency for two companies.
(SO 6)

	Target Corporation	Wal-Mart Stores, Inc.
	Income Statement Data for Year	
Net sales	$48,163	$258,681
Cost of goods sold	31,790	198,747
Selling and administrative expenses	10,696	44,909
Interest expense	559	996
Other income (expense)	(2,158)	143
Income tax expense	1,119	5,118
Net income	$ 1,841	$ 9,054
	Balance Sheet Data (End of Year)	
Current assets	$12,928	$ 34,421
Noncurrent assets	18,464	70,491
Total assets	$31,392	$104,912
Current liabilities	$ 8,314	$ 37,418
Long-term debt	12,013	23,871
Total stockholders' equity	11,065	43,623
Total liabilities and stockholders' equity	$31,392	$104,912

	Beginning-of-Year Balances	
Total assets	$28,603	$ 94,808
Total stockholders' equity	9,443	39,461
Current liabilities	7,523	32,519
Total liabilities	11,637	55,347

	Other Data	
Average net receivables	$ 5,670.5	$ 1,411.5
Average inventory	5,051.5	25,506.5
Net cash provided by operating activities	3,160	15,996
Capital expenditures	3,004	9,245
Dividends	237	1,328

Instructions

(a) For each company, compute the following ratios.

(1) Current.	(8) Return on assets.
(2) Receivables turnover.	(9) Return on common stockholders' equity.
(3) Average collection period.	(10) Debt to total assets.
(4) Inventory turnover.	(11) Times interest earned.
(5) Days in inventory.	(12) Current cash debt coverage.
(6) Profit margin.	(13) Cash debt coverage.
(7) Asset turnover.	(14) Free cash flow.

(b) Compare the liquidity, solvency, and profitability of the two companies.

Problems: Set B

▢━━━◖ All of the Problems in this chapter employ decision tools.

Prepare vertical analysis and comment on profitability.
(SO 5, 6)

P13-1B Here are comparative statement data for Night Company and Day Company, two competitors. All balance sheet data are as of December 31, 2007, and December 31, 2006.

	Night Company		Day Company	
	2007	**2006**	**2007**	**2006**
Net sales	$350,000		$1,200,000	
Cost of goods sold	180,000		624,000	
Operating expenses	51,000		278,000	
Interest expense	3,000		10,000	
Income tax expense	17,000		54,000	
Current assets	130,000	$100,000	700,000	$650,000
Plant assets (net)	400,000	270,000	1,000,000	750,000
Current liabilities	60,000	52,000	250,000	275,000
Long-term liabilities	50,000	68,000	200,000	150,000
Common stock	360,000	210,000	950,000	700,000
Retained earnings	60,000	40,000	300,000	275,000

Instructions

(a) Prepare a vertical analysis of the 2007 income statement data for Night Company and Day Company.

(b) Comment on the relative profitability of the companies by computing the return on assets and the return on common stockholders' equity ratios for both companies.

Compute ratios from balance sheet and income statement.
(SO 6)

P13-2B The comparative statements of Fraggle Rock Company are shown on page 695.

FRAGGLE ROCK COMPANY
Income Statements
For the Years Ended December 31

	2007	2006
Net sales	$780,000	$624,000
Cost of goods sold	440,000	405,600
Gross profit	340,000	218,400
Selling and administrative expense	146,880	149,760
Income from operations	193,120	68,640
Other expenses and losses		
Interest expense	9,920	7,200
Income before income taxes	183,200	61,440
Income tax expense	35,000	14,000
Net income	$148,200	$ 47,440

FRAGGLE ROCK COMPANY
Balance Sheets
December 31

Assets	2007	2006
Current assets		
Cash	$ 23,100	$ 21,600
Short-term investments	44,800	33,000
Accounts receivable	106,200	93,800
Inventory	116,400	64,000
Total current assets	290,500	212,400
Plant assets (net)	485,300	439,600
Total assets	$775,800	$652,000
Liabilities and Stockholders' Equity		
Current liabilities		
Accounts payable	$148,200	$132,000
Income taxes payable	25,300	24,000
Total current liabilities	173,500	156,000
Bonds payable	132,000	120,000
Total liabilities	305,500	276,000
Stockholders' equity		
Common stock ($10 par)	140,000	130,000
Retained earnings	330,300	246,000
Total stockholders' equity	470,300	376,000
Total liabilities and stockholders' equity	$775,800	$652,000

All sales were on account. Net cash provided by operating activities was $94,000. Capital expenditures were $47,000, and cash dividends were $55,000.

Instructions
Compute the following ratios for 2007.
(a) Earnings per share.
(b) Return on common stockholders' equity.
(c) Return on assets.
(d) Current.
(e) Receivables turnover.
(f) Average collection period.
(g) Inventory turnover.
(h) Days in inventory.
(i) Times interest earned.
(j) Asset turnover.
(k) Debt to total assets.
(l) Current cash debt coverage.
(m) Cash debt coverage.
(n) Free cash flow.

P13-3B The condensed balance sheet and income statement data for Whitcomb Corporation are presented on page 696.

Perform ratio analysis, and discuss change in financial position and operating results.
(SO 6)

WHITCOMB CORPORATION
Balance Sheets
December 31

	2007	2006	2005
Cash	$ 30,000	$ 24,000	$ 20,000
Receivables (net)	110,000	48,000	48,000
Other current assets	80,000	78,000	62,000
Investments	90,000	70,000	50,000
Plant and equipment (net)	603,000	400,000	360,000
	$913,000	$620,000	$540,000
Current liabilities	$ 98,000	$ 75,000	$ 70,000
Long-term debt	230,000	75,000	65,000
Common stock, $10 par	400,000	340,000	300,000
Retained earnings	185,000	130,000	105,000
	$913,000	$620,000	$540,000

WHITCOMB CORPORATION
Income Statements
For the Years Ended December 31

	2007	2006
Sales	$800,000	$750,000
Less: Sales returns and allowances	40,000	50,000
Net sales	760,000	700,000
Cost of goods sold	420,000	400,000
Gross profit	340,000	300,000
Operating expenses (including income taxes)	200,000	215,000
Net income	$140,000	$ 85,000

Additional information:
1. The market price of Whitcomb common stock was $5.00, $3.50, and $2.30 for 2005, 2006, and 2007, respectively.
2. You must compute dividends paid. All dividends were paid in cash.

Instructions
(a) Compute the following ratios for 2006 and 2007.

    (1) Profit margin.   (5) Price-earnings.
    (2) Gross profit rate.   (6) Payout.
    (3) Asset turnover.   (7) Debt to total assets.
    (4) Earnings per share.

 (b) Based on the ratios calculated, discuss briefly the improvement or lack thereof in the financial position and operating results from 2006 to 2007 of Whitcomb Corporation.

Compute ratios; comment on overall liquidity and profitability.
(SO 6)

P13-4B Financial information for Yazbeck Company is presented here.

YAZBECK COMPANY
Balance Sheets
December 31

Assets	2007	2006
Cash	$ 50,000	$ 42,000
Short-term investments	80,000	50,000
Receivables	100,000	87,000
Inventories	410,000	300,000
Prepaid expenses	30,000	31,000
Land	75,000	75,000
Building and equipment (net)	570,000	400,000
Total assets	$1,315,000	$985,000

Liabilities and Stockholders' Equity

Notes payable	$ 120,000	$ 25,000
Accounts payable	160,000	90,000
Accrued liabilities	50,000	50,000
Bonds payable, due 2009	180,000	100,000
Common stock, $5 par	500,000	500,000
Retained earnings	305,000	220,000
Total liabilities and stockholders' equity	$1,315,000	$985,000

YAZBECK COMPANY
Income Statements
For the Years Ended December 31

	2007	2006
Sales	$1,000,000	$940,000
Cost of goods sold	655,000	635,000
Gross profit	345,000	305,000
Operating expenses	235,000	225,000
Net income	$ 110,000	$ 80,000

Additional information:
1. Inventory at the beginning of 2006 was $350,000.
2. Receivables at the beginning of 2006 were $80,000.
3. Total assets at the beginning of 2006 were $1,175,000.
4. No common stock transactions occurred during 2006 or 2007.
5. All sales were on account.

Instructions
(a) Indicate, by using ratios, the change in liquidity and profitability of the company from 2006 to 2007. (*Note:* Not all profitability ratios can be computed nor can cash-basis ratios be computed.)
(b) Given below are three independent situations and a ratio that may be affected. For each situation, compute the affected ratio (1) as of December 31, 2007, and (2) as of December 31, 2008, after giving effect to the situation. Net income for 2008 was $125,000. Total assets on December 31, 2008, were $1,450,000.

Situation	Ratio
1. 50,000 shares of common stock were sold at par on July 1, 2008.	Return on common stockholders' equity
2. All of the notes payable were paid in 2008.	Debt to total assets
3. The market price of common stock on December 31, 2008, was $6.25. The market price on December 31, 2007, was $5.	Price-earnings

P13-5B Selected financial data for Black & Decker and Snap-On Tools for 2004 are presented here (in millions).

Compute selected ratios, and compare liquidity, profitability, and solvency for two companies. (SO 6)

	Black & Decker	Snap-On Tools
	Income Statement Data for Year	
Net sales	$5,398.4	$2,407.2
Cost of goods sold	3,432.9	1,319.8
Selling and administrative expenses	1,336.3	945.1
Interest expense	57.9	23.0
Other income	(33.0)	(1.1)
Income tax expense	163.2	38.7
Net income (before irregular items)	$ 441.1	$ 81.7

	Balance Sheet Data (End of Year)	
Current assets	$2,927.2	$1,192.6
Property, plant, and equipment (net)	754.6	313.6
Other assets	1,849.0	783.9
Total assets	$5,530.8	$2,290.1
Current liabilities	$1,792.6	$ 674.2
Long-term debt	2,179.5	505.2
Total stockholders' equity	1,558.7	1,110.7
Total liabilities and stockholders' equity	$5,530.8	$2,290.1

	Beginning-of-Year Balances	
Total assets	$4,222.5	$2,138.5
Total stockholders' equity	846.5	1,010.9
Current liabilities	1,312.1	567.2
Total liabilities	3,376.0	1,127.6

	Other Data	
Average receivables (net)	$ 927.6	$ 618.7
Average inventory	845.9	346.5
Net cash provided by operating activities	619.1	146.8
Capital expenditures	117.8	38.7
Cash dividends	67.5	57.7

Instructions
(a) For each company, compute the following ratios.
   (1) Current ratio.
   (2) Receivables turnover.
   (3) Average collection period.
   (4) Inventory turnover.
   (5) Days in inventory.
   (6) Profit margin.
   (7) Asset turnover.
   (8) Return on assets.
   (9) Return on common stockholders' equity.
   (10) Debt to total assets.
   (11) Times interest earned.
   (12) Current cash debt coverage.
   (13) Cash debt coverage.
   (14) Free cash flow.
(b) Compare the liquidity, solvency, and profitability of the two companies.

Problems: Set C

Visit the book's website at **www.wiley.com/college/kimmel** and choose the Student Companion site to access Problem Set C.

Continuing Cookie Chronicle

(*Note:* This is a continuation of the Cookie Chronicle from Chapters 1 through 12.)

CCC13 The comparative balance sheet of Cookie & Coffee Creations Inc. at October 31, 2009 for the years 2009 and 2008, and the income statements for the years ended October 31, 2008 and 2009, are presented on the following page.

COOKIE & COFFEE CREATIONS INC.
Balance Sheet
October 31

Assets	2009	2008
Cash	$ 34,324	$13,050
Accounts receivable	3,250	2,710
Inventory	7,897	7,450
Prepaid expenses	6,300	6,050
Equipment	96,500	75,500
Accumulated depreciation	(25,200)	(9,100)
Total assets	$123,071	$95,660

Liabilities and Stockholders' Equity		
Accounts payable	$ 3,650	$ 2,450
Income taxes payable	10,251	11,200
Dividends payable (on common stock)	28,000	25,000
Salaries payable	2,250	1,280
Interest payable	188	0
Note payable—current portion	3,000	0
Note payable—long-term portion	4,500	0
Preferred stock, no par, $6 cumulative— 3,000 and 2,500 shares issued, respectively	15,000	12,500
Common stock, $1 par—23,180 shares issued	23,180	23,180
Additional paid in capital—treasury stock	250	250
Retained earnings	32,802	19,800
Total liabilities and stockholders' equity	$123,071	$95,660

COOKIE & COFFEE CREATIONS INC.
Income Statement
Year Ended October 31

	2009	2008
Sales	$485,625	$462,500
Cost of goods sold	222,694	208,125
Gross profit	262,931	254,375
Operating expenses		
Depreciation expense	17,850	9,100
Salaries and wages expense	147,979	146,350
Other operating expenses	43,186	42,925
Total operating expenses	209,015	198,375
Income from operations	53,916	56,000
Other expenses		
Interest expense	413	0
Loss on sale of computer equipment	2,250	0
Total other expenses	2,663	0
Income before income tax	51,253	56,000
Income tax expense	10,251	11,200
Net income	$ 41,002	$ 44,800

Additional information:
Natalie and Curtis are thinking about borrowing an additional $20,000 to buy more kitchen equipment. The loan would be repaid over a 4-year period. The terms of the loan provide for equal semi-annual payments of $2,500 on May 1 and November 1 of each year, plus interest of 5% on the outstanding balance.

Instructions

(a) Calculate the following ratios for 2008 and 2009.
1. Current ratio
2. Debt to total assets
3. Gross profit rate
4. Profit margin
5. Return on assets (Total assets at November 1, 2007, were $33,180.)
6. Return on common stockholders' equity (Total common stockholders' equity at November 1, 2007, was $23,180.)
7. Payout ratio

(b) Prepare a horizontal analysis of the income statement for Cookie & Coffee Creations Inc. using 2008 as a base year.

(c) Prepare a vertical analysis of the income statement for Cookie & Coffee Creations Inc. for 2009 and 2008.

(d) Comment on your findings from parts (a) to (c).

(e) What impact would borrowing an additional $20,000 to buy more equipment have on each of the ratios in (a) above, assuming that no changes are expected on the income statement and balance sheet? Comment on your findings.

(f) What would justify a decision by Cookie & Coffee Creations Inc. to buy the additional equipment? What alternatives are there instead of bank financing?

BROADENING YOUR PERSPECTIVE

Financial Reporting and Analysis

FINANCIAL REPORTING PROBLEM: *Tootsie Roll Industries, Inc.*

BYP13-1 Your parents are considering investing in Tootsie Roll Industries common stock. They ask you, as an accounting expert, to make an analysis of the company for them. Fortunately, excerpts from a recent annual report of Tootsie Roll are presented in Appendix A of this textbook.

Instructions

(a) Make a 5-year trend analysis, using 2000 as the base year, of (1) net sales and (2) net earnings. Comment on the significance of the trend results.

(b) Compute for 2004 and 2003 the (1) debt to total assets ratio and (2) times interest earned ratio. (See note 6 for interest expense.) How would you evaluate Tootsie Roll's long-term solvency?

(c) Compute for 2004 and 2003 the (1) profit margin ratio, (2) asset turnover ratio, (3) return on assets ratio, and (4) return on common stockholders' equity ratio. How would you evaluate Tootsie Roll's profitability? Total assets at December 31, 2002, were $646,080,000, and total stockholders' equity at December 31, 2002, was $526,740,000.

(d) What information outside the annual report may also be useful to your parents in making a decision about Tootsie Roll?

COMPARATIVE ANALYSIS PROBLEM: *Tootsie Roll vs. Hershey Foods*

BYP13-2 The financial statements of Hershey Foods are presented in Appendix B, following the financial statements for Tootsie Roll Industries in Appendix A.

Instructions

(a) Based on the information in the financial statements, determine each of the following for each company:
(1) The percentage increase (i) in net sales and (ii) in net income from 2003 to 2004.
(2) The percentage increase (i) in total assets and (ii) in total stockholders' equity from 2003 to 2004.
(3) The earnings per share for 2004.

(b) What conclusions concerning the two companies can be drawn from these data?

RESEARCH CASE

BYP13-3 The October 15, 2002, issue of the *Wall Street Journal* included an article by Jesse Drucker titled "Motorola's Profit: 'Special' Again?"

Instructions
Read the article and answer the following questions.
(a) For how many consecutive quarters, including the quarter anticipated in the article, has Motorola reported a "special" item on its income statement? What is the total amount of these special charges over this period?
(b) What justification does Motorola give for reporting these charges as special items on its income statement, rather than reporting them as ordinary expenses?
(c) In the second quarter of 2002, what was Motorola's pro forma income, and what was its net income according to generally accepted accounting principles (GAAP)?
(d) According to the article, do Wall Street analysts give more attention to GAAP income or pro forma income? Do analysts agree on how to treat special charges, such as those of Motorola?

INTERPRETING FINANCIAL STATEMENTS

BYP13-4 The Coca-Cola Company and PepsiCo, Inc. provide refreshments to every corner of the world. Selected data from the 2004 consolidated financial statements for The Coca-Cola Company and for PepsiCo, Inc., are presented here (in millions).

	Coca-Cola	PepsiCo
Total current assets	$ 12,094	$ 8,639
Total current liabilities	10,971	6,752
Net sales	21,962	29,261
Cost of goods sold	7,638	13,406
Net income	4,847	4,212
Average (net) receivables for the year	2,131	2,915
Average inventories for the year	1,336	1,477
Average total assets	29,335	26,657
Average common stockholders' equity	15,013	12,734
Average current liabilities	9,429	6,584
Average total liabilities	14,322	27,917
Total assets	31,327	27,987
Total liabilities	15,392	14,464
Income taxes	1,375	1,372
Interest expense	196	167
Cash provided by operating activities	5,968	5,054
Capital expenditures	755	1,387
Cash dividends	2,429	1,329

Instructions
(a) Compute the following liquidity ratios for 2004 for Coca-Cola and for PepsiCo and comment on the relative liquidity of the two competitors.
    (1) Current ratio.   (4) Inventory turnover.
    (2) Receivables turnover.   (5) Days in inventory.
    (3) Average collection period. (6) Current cash debt coverage.

(b) Compute the following solvency ratios for the two companies and comment on the relative solvency of the two competitors.
    (1) Debt to total assets ratio.
    (2) Times interest earned.
    (3) Cash debt coverage ratio.
    (4) Free cash flow.

(c) Compute the following profitability ratios for the two companies and comment on the relative profitability of the two competitors.
    (1) Profit margin.
    (2) Asset turnover.
    (3) Return on assets.
    (4) Return on common stockholders' equity.

FINANCIAL ANALYSIS ON THE WEB

BYP13-5 *Purpose:* To employ comparative data and industry data to evaluate a company's performance and financial position.

Address: **http://www.investor.reuters.com** (or go to **www.wiley.com/college/kimmel**)

Steps
(1) Identify two competing companies.
(2) Go to the above address.
(3) Type in the first company's name.
(4) Choose **Ratios**.
(5) Print out the results.
(6) Repeat steps 3–5 for the competitor.

Instructions
(a) Evaluate the company's liquidity relative to the industry averages and to the competitor that you chose.
(b) Evaluate the company's solvency relative to the industry averages and to the competitor that you chose.
(c) Evaluate the company's profitability relative to the industry averages and to the competitor that you chose.

Critical Thinking

DECISION MAKING ACROSS THE ORGANIZATION

BYP13-6 You are a loan officer for Lakeland Bank of Port Washington. Edmund Jeffries, president of E. Jeffries Corporation, has just left your office. He is interested in an 8-year loan to expand the company's operations. The borrowed funds would be used to purchase new equipment. As evidence of the company's debt-worthiness, Jeffries provided you with the following facts.

	2007	2006
Current ratio	3.1	2.1
Asset turnover ratio	2.8	2.2
Cash debt coverage ratio	.1	.2
Net income	Up 32%	Down 8%
Earnings per share	$3.30	$2.50

Jeffries is a very insistent (some would say pushy) man. When you told him that you would need additional information before making your decision, he acted offended, and said, "What more could you possibly want to know?" You responded that, at a minimum, you would need complete, audited financial statements.

Instructions
With the class divided into groups, answer the following.
(a) Explain why you would want the financial statements to be audited.
(b) Discuss the implications of the ratios provided for the lending decision you are to make. That is, does the information paint a favorable picture? Are these ratios relevant to the decision?
(c) List three other ratios that you would want to calculate for this company, and explain why you would use each.

COMMUNICATION ACTIVITY

BYP13-7 R.J. Falk is the chief executive officer of Ventura Electronics. Falk is an expert engineer but a novice in accounting. Falk asks you, as an accounting major, to explain (a) the bases for comparison in analyzing Ventura financial statements and (b) the limitations, if any, in financial statement analysis.

Instructions

Write a memo to R.J. Falk that explains the basis for comparison and the factors affecting quality of earnings.

ETHICS CASE

BYP13-8 Sandra Maxwell, president of XL Industries, wishes to issue a press release to bolster her company's image and maybe even its stock price, which has been gradually falling. As controller, you have been asked to provide a list of 20 financial ratios and other operating statistics for XL Industries' first-quarter financials and operations.

Two days after you provide the data requested, Chinda Khuon, the public relations director of XL, asks you to prove the accuracy of the financial and operating data contained in the press release written by the president and edited by Chinda. In the news release, the president highlights the sales increase of 25% over last year's first quarter and the positive change in the current ratio from 1.5:1 last year to 3:1 this year. She also emphasizes that production was up 50% over the prior year's first quarter.

You note that the release contains only positive or improved ratios and none of the negative or deteriorated ratios. For instance, no mention is made that the debt to total assets ratio has increased from 35% to 55%, that inventories are up 89%, and that although the current ratio improved, the current cash debt coverage ratio fell from .15 to .05. Nor is there any mention that the reported profit for the quarter would have been a loss had not the estimated lives of XL plant and machinery been increased by 30%. Chinda emphasized, "The Pres wants this release by early this afternoon."

Instructions
(a) Who are the stakeholders in this situation?
(b) Is there anything unethical in the president's actions?
(c) Should you as controller remain silent? Does Chinda have any responsibility?

Answers to Business Insight and Accounting across the Organization Questions

p. 649

Q: If a company takes a large restructuring charge, what is the effect on the company's current income statements versus future ones?

A: The current period's net income can be greatly diminished by a large restructuring charge. The net incomes in future periods can be enhanced because they are relieved of costs (i.e., depreciation and labor expenses) that would have been charged to them.

p. 660

Q: How might management influence a company's current ratio?

A: Management can affect the current ratio by speeding up or withholding payments on accounts payable just before the balance sheet date. Management can alter the cash balance by increasing or decreasing long-term assets or long-term debt, or by issuing or purchasing common stock.

p. 663

Q: Why might adding extra pages to the annual report not be beneficial to investors and analysts? What should be management's overriding objective in financial reporting?

A: When given too much information, investors may suffer from "information overload"—they may have a hard time sorting out what is important from what is not. Management's overriding financial reporting objective should be to provide an accurate depiction of the company's financial position and operating results in a clear and concise fashion. It should provide as much detail as is necessary to accomplish that.

Answer to Tootsie Roll Review It Question 3, p. 653

Tootsie Roll reported "Other comprehensive earnings" of $778,000 in 2004. "Comprehensive earnings" exceeded "Net earnings" by 1.2% [($64,952 − $64,174) ÷ $64,174].

Answers to Self-Study Questions

1. d   2. d   3. b   4. d   5. c   6. c   7. a   8. c   9. c   10. b
11. a   12. c

REMEMBER TO GO BACK TO THE NAVIGATOR BOX ON THE CHAPTER-OPENING PAGE AND CHECK OFF YOUR COMPLETED WORK.

CHAPTER 14

Managerial Accounting

STUDY OBJECTIVES

After studying this chapter,
you should be able to:

1 Explain the distinguishing features of managerial accounting.

2 Identify the three broad functions of management.

3 Define the three classes of manufacturing costs.

4 Distinguish between product and period costs.

5 Explain the difference between a merchandising and a manufacturing income statement.

6 Indicate how cost of goods manufactured is determined.

7 Explain the difference between a merchandising and a manufacturing balance sheet.

8 Identify trends in managerial accounting.

THE NAVIGATOR

✓ THE NAVIGATOR

- Scan *Study Objectives* ⬭
- Read *Feature Story* ⬭
- Read *Preview* ⬭
- Read text and answer *Before You Go On*
  p. 712 ⬭   p. 714 ⬭   p. 720 ⬭
  p. 725 ⬭
- Work *Using the Decision Toolkit* ⬭
- Review *Summary of Study Objectives* ⬭
- Work *Demonstration Problem* ⬭
- Answer *Self-Study Questions* ⬭
- Complete *Assignments* ⬭

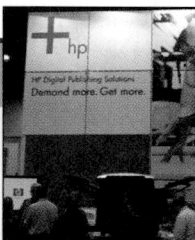

FEATURE STORY

What a Difference a Day Makes

In January 1998 Compaq Computer had just become the largest seller of personal computers, and it was *Forbes* magazine's "company of the year." Its chief executive, Eckhard Pfeiffer, was riding high. But during the next two years Compaq lost $2 billion. The company was in chaos, and Mr. Pfeiffer was out of a job. What happened?

First, Dell happened. Dell Computer pioneered a new way of making and selling personal computers. Its customers "custom design" their computer over the Internet or phone. Dell reengineered its "supply chain": It coordinated its efforts with its suppliers and streamlined its order-taking and production process. It can ship a computer within two days of taking an order. Personal computers lose 1 percent of their value every week they sit on a shelf. Thus, having virtually no inventory is a great advantage to Dell. Compaq tried to adopt Dell's approach, but with limited success.

The second shock to Compaq came when it acquired a company even larger than itself—Digital Equipment. Digital was famous as much for its technical service as it was for its products. Mr. Pfeiffer believed that the purchase of Digital, with its huge and respected technical sales force, opened new opportunities for Compaq as a global service company. Now it could sell to and service high-end corporate customers. But combining the two companies proved to be hugely expensive and extremely complicated. Ultimately Compaq decided to merge with Hewlett-Packard in order to survive.

But now Hewlett-Packard is looking over its shoulder for Dell. Why? Because in 2003 Dell moved into the computer printer business—a segment that Hewlett-Packard has long dominated. Dell currently sells only 2 million printers per year, compared to Hewlett-Packard's 42 million. But many analysts predict that by employing the same techniques that it used in its PC business, Dell will soon take a major share of the printer business—and in the process drive down prices and force some less-nimble competitors out of business.

THE NAVIGATOR

On the World Wide Web
www.compaq.com
www.dell.com
www.hp.com

This book focuses on issues illustrated in the Feature Story about Compaq Computer and Dell. These include determining and controlling the costs of material, labor, and overhead and the relationship between costs and profits. In the previous financial accounting chapters, you learned about the form and content of **financial statements for external users** of financial information, such as stockholders and creditors. These financial statements represent the principal product of financial accounting. Managerial accounting focuses primarily on the preparation of **reports for internal users** of financial information, such as the managers and officers of a company. Managers are evaluated on the results of their decisions. In today's rapidly changing global environment, managers often make decisions that determine their company's fate—and their own fate. Managerial accounting provides tools for assisting management in making decisions and for evaluating the effectiveness of those decisions.

The content and organization of this chapter are as follows.

Managerial Accounting Basics

Managerial accounting, also called **management accounting**, is a field of accounting that provides economic and financial information for managers and other internal users. The activities that are part of managerial accounting (and the chapters in which they are discussed in this textbook) are as follows.

1. Explaining manufacturing and nonmanufacturing costs and how they are reported in the financial statements (Chapter 14).

2. Computing the cost of providing a service or manufacturing a product (Chapters 15, 16, and 17).

3. Determining the behavior of costs and expenses as activity levels change and analyzing cost–volume–profit relationships within a company (Chapter 18).

4. Evaluating the impact on decision making of alternative approaches for costing inventory (Chapter 19).

5. Assisting management in profit planning and formalizing these plans in the form of budgets (Chapter 20).
6. Providing a basis for controlling costs and expenses by comparing actual results with planned objectives and standard costs (Chapters 21 and 22).
7. Accumulating and presenting data for capital expenditure decisions (Chapter 23).

Managerial accounting applies to all types of businesses—service, merchandising, and manufacturing. It also applies to all forms of business organizations—proprietorships, partnerships, and corporations. Managerial accounting is needed in not-for-profit entities as well as in profit-oriented enterprises.

In the past, managerial accountants were primarily engaged in cost accounting—collecting and reporting costs to management. Recently that role changed significantly. First as the business environment has become more automated, methods to determine the amount and type of cost in a product have changed. Second, managerial accountants are now more responsible for strategic cost management; that is, assisting in evaluating how well the company is employing its resources. As a result, managerial accountants now serve as team members alongside personnel from production, marketing, and engineering when critical strategic decisions are being made.

Opportunities for managerial accountants to advance within the company are considerable. Financial executives must have a background that includes an understanding of managerial accounting concepts. Whatever your position in the company—marketing, sales, or production, knowledge of managerial accounting greatly improves your opportunities for advancement. As the CEO of Microsoft noted: "If you're supposed to be making money in business and supposed to be satisfying customers and building market share, there are numbers that characterize those things. And if somebody can't sort of speak to me quantitatively about it, then I'm nervous."

Helpful Hint According to the U.S. Department of Labor's Bureau of Labor Statistics (BLS) more than one million accountants and auditors currently work for accounting firms, companies, governmental agencies, and other employers. The BLS projects that employment in the profession will increase 10 to 20 percent by 2008, ensuring that accountants will continue to play a vital role in business.

COMPARING MANAGERIAL AND FINANCIAL ACCOUNTING

STUDY OBJECTIVE

1

Explain the distinguishing features of managerial accounting.

There are both similarities and differences between managerial and financial accounting. First, each field of accounting deals with the economic events of a business. Thus, their interests overlap. For example, determining the unit cost of manufacturing a product is part of managerial accounting. Reporting the total cost of goods manufactured and sold is part of financial accounting. In addition, both managerial and financial accounting require that a company's economic events be quantified and communicated to interested parties.

The principal differences between financial accounting and managerial accounting are summarized in Illustration 14-1 (page 708). The need for various types of economic data is responsible for many of the differences.

MANAGEMENT FUNCTIONS

STUDY OBJECTIVE

2

Identify the three broad functions of management.

Management's activities and responsibilities can be classified into three broad functions. They are:

1. Planning.
2. Directing.
3. Controlling.

In performing these functions, managers make decisions that have a significant impact on the organization.

Financial Accounting		Managerial Accounting
• External users: stockholders, creditors, and regulators.	**Primary Users of Reports**	• Internal users: officers and managers.
• Financial statements. • Quarterly and annually.	**Types and Frequency of Reports**	• Internal reports. • As frequently as needed.
• General-purpose.	**Purpose of Reports**	• Special-purpose for specific decisions.
• Pertains to business as a whole. • Highly aggregated (condensed). • Limited to double-entry accounting and cost data. • Generally accepted accounting principles.	**Content of Reports**	• Pertains to subunits of the business. • Very detailed. • Extends beyond double-entry accounting to any relevant data. • Standard is relevance to decisions.
• Audit by CPA.	**Verification Process**	• No independent audits.

Illustration 14-1 Differences between financial and managerial accounting

Planning requires management to look ahead and to establish objectives. These objectives are often diverse: maximizing short-term profits and market share, maintaining a commitment to environmental protection, and contributing to social programs. For example, Hewlett-Packard in an attempt to gain a stronger foothold in the computer industry has greatly reduced its prices to compete with Dell. A key objective of management is to add **value** to the business under its control. Value is usually measured by the trading price of the company's stock and by the potential selling price of the company.

Directing involves coordinating a company's diverse activities and human resources to produce a smooth-running operation. This function relates to implementing planned objectives and providing necessary incentives to motivate employees. For example, manufacturers such as Campbell Soup Company, General Motors, and Dell must coordinate purchasing, manufacturing, warehousing, and selling. Service corporations such as American Airlines, Federal Express, and AT&T must coordinate scheduling, sales, service, and acquisitions of equipment and supplies. Directing also involves selecting executives, appointing managers and supervisors, and hiring and training employees.

The third management function, **controlling**, is the process of keeping the company's activities on track. In controlling operations, managers determine whether planned goals are being met. When there are deviations from targeted objectives, they must decide what changes are needed to get back on track. Recent scandals at companies like Enron, Lucent, and Xerox attest to the fact that companies must have adequate controls to ensure that accurate information is developed.

How do managers achieve control? A smart manager in a small operation can make personal observations, ask good questions, and know how to evaluate the answers. But using this approach in a large organization would result in chaos. Imagine the president of Dell attempting to determine whether planned objectives are being met without some record of what has happened and what is expected to occur. Thus, a formal system of evaluation is typically used in large businesses. These systems include such features as budgets, responsibility centers, and performance evaluation reports.

The trend toward more automated and computerized factories has changed the way managers and employees interact. For one thing, managers have fewer direct labor employees to supervise because fewer are needed on the line. Instead of standing in one spot all day, employees and managers have become more mobile, monitoring the computers that control production, and involving themselves in a variety of jobs.

Recently, two technology giants, General Electric and Cisco Systems, joined forces to build computerized infrastructures for manufacturers. Their goal is to improve productivity by making better use of data generated by factory-automation equipment. Ultimately their systems should provide a closer link between the factory and corporate offices.

Decision making is not a separate management function. Rather, it is the outcome of the exercise of good judgment in planning, directing, and controlling.

ORGANIZATIONAL STRUCTURE

In order to assist in carrying out management functions, most companies prepare **organization charts** to show the interrelationships of activities and the delegation of authority and responsibility within the company. A typical organization chart showing the delegation of responsibility is shown in Illustration 14-2.

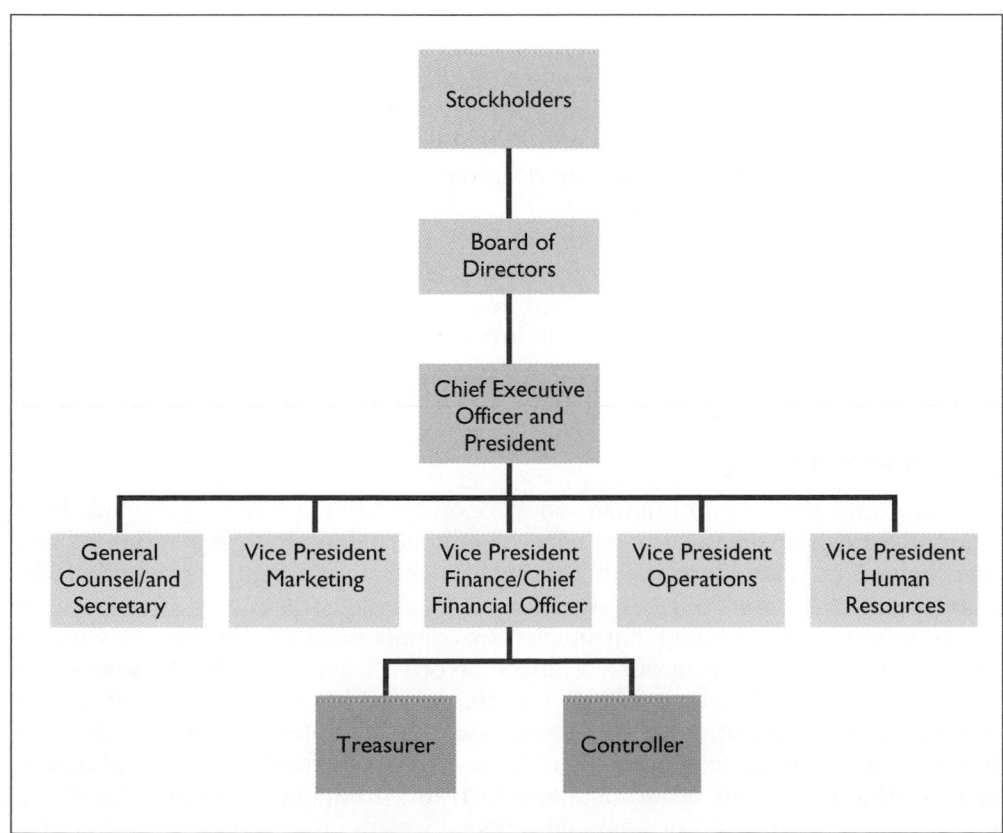

Illustration 14-2 Corporation's organization chart

Stockholders own the corporation, but they manage it indirectly through a **board of directors** they elect. Even not-for-profit organizations have a board of directors. The board formulates the operating policies for the company. The board also selects officers, such as a president and one or more vice presidents, to execute policy and to perform daily management functions.

The **chief executive officer (CEO)** has overall responsibility for managing the business. Obviously, even in a small business, in order to accomplish organizational objectives, the company relies on delegation of responsibilities. As the organization chart on page 6 shows, the CEO delegates responsibility to other officers. Each member of the organization has a clearly defined role to play.

Responsibilities within the company are frequently classified as either line or staff positions. Employees with **line positions** are directly involved in the company's primary revenue-generating operating activities. Examples of line positions include the vice president of operations, vice president of marketing, plant managers, supervisors, and production personnel. Employees with **staff positions** are involved in activities that support the efforts of the line employees. In a firm like General Electric or ExxonMobil, employees in finance, legal, purchasing, and human resources have staff positions. While activities of staff employees are vital to the company, these employees are nonetheless there to serve the line employees that engage in the company's primary operations.

The **chief financial officer (CFO)** is responsible for all of the accounting and finance issues the company faces. The CFO is supported by the **controller** and the **treasurer**. The controller's responsibilities include (1) maintaining the accounting records, (2) maintaining an adequate system of internal control, and (3) preparing financial statements, tax returns, and internal reports. The treasurer has custody of the corporation's funds and is responsible for maintaining the company's cash position.

Also serving the CFO would be the **internal audit staff**. The staff's responsibilities include reviewing the reliability and integrity of financial information provided by the controller and treasurer. Staff members also ensure that internal control systems are functioning properly to safeguard corporate assets. In addition, they investigate compliance with policies and regulations, and in many companies they determine whether resources are being used in the most economical and efficient fashion.

The vice president of operations oversees employees with line positions. For example, the company might have multiple plant managers, each of whom would report to the vice president of operations. Each plant would also have department managers, such as fabricating, painting, and shipping, each of whom would report to the plant manager.

BUSINESS ETHICS

All employees within an organization are expected to act ethically in their business activities. Given the importance of ethical behavior to corporations and their owners (stockholders), an increasing number of organizations provide codes of business ethics for their employees.

Despite these efforts, recent business scandals have resulted in massive investment losses and numerous employee layoffs. A 2003 survey of fraud by international accounting firm KPMG reported a 13 percent increase in instances of corporate fraud compared to five years earlier. It noted that while employee fraud (such things as expense-account abuse, payroll fraud, and theft of assets) represented 60 percent of all instances of fraud, financial reporting fraud (the intentional misstatement of financial reports) was the most costly to companies. That should not be surprising given the long list of companies such as Enron,

Global Crossing, WorldCom, and others that engaged in massive financial frauds, which have led to huge financial losses and thousands of lost jobs.

Creating Proper Incentives

Complex systems within companies like Motorola, IBM, and Nike are used to control and evaluate the actions of managers. Substantial resources are dedicated to ensure that the actions of employees are monitored and effectively evaluated. Unfortunately, these systems and controls sometimes unwittingly create incentives for managers to take unethical actions. For example, budgets (plans of actions) are prepared by companies to provide future direction. Because the budget is also used as an evaluation tool, some managers try to "game" the budgeting process by underestimating their division's predicted performance so that it will be easier to meet their performance targets. On the other hand, if the budget is set at unattainable levels, managers sometimes take unethical actions to meet the targets in order to receive higher compensation or in some cases to keep their jobs.

For example, in recent years, airline manufacturer Boeing has been plagued by a series of scandals including charges of over-billing, corporate espionage, and illegal conflicts of interest. Some long-time employees of Boeing blame the decline in ethics on a change in the corporate culture that took place after Boeing merged with McDonnell Douglas. They suggest that evaluation systems implemented after the merger to monitor results and evaluate employee performance made employees believe they needed to succeed no matter what.

As another example, manufacturing companies need to establish production goals for their processes. Again, if controls are not effective and realistic, problems develop. To illustrate, Schering-Plough, a pharmaceutical manufacturer, found that employees were so concerned with meeting production standards that they failed to monitor the quality of the product, and as a result the dosages were often wrong.

New Legislation

As a result of the breakdown of controls at a number of large companies, the U.S. Congress enacted legislation to help prevent lapses in internal control from occurring. This legislation, referred to as the Sarbanes-Oxley Act of 2002 (SOX) has important implications for the financial community. One result of SOX was to clarify top management's responsibility for the company's financial statements. CEOs and CFOs must now certify that financial statements give a fair presentation of the company's operating results and its financial condition. In addition, top management must certify that the company maintains an adequate system of internal controls to safeguard the company's assets and ensure accurate financial reports.

Another result of SOX is that more attention is now paid to the composition of the company's board of directors. In particular, the audit committee of the board of directors must be comprised entirely of independent members (that is, non-employees) and must contain at least one financial expert.

Finally, to increase the likelihood of compliance with these and other new rules that are part of the new legislation, the penalties for misconduct were substantially increased.

To provide guidance for managerial accountants, the Institute of Management Accountants (IMA) has developed a code of ethical standards, entitled *Standards of Ethical Conduct for Practitioners of Management Accounting and Financial Management*. The code states that management accountants should not commit acts in violation of these standards. Nor should they condone such acts by others within their organizations. The IMA code of ethical standards can be accessed at *www.imanet.org/pdf/981.pdf*. Throughout the managerial accounting chapters we will address various ethical issues faced by managers.

BEFORE YOU GO ON . . .

▶**Review It**

1. Compare financial accounting and managerial accounting, identifying the principal differences.
2. Identify and discuss the three broad functions of management.
3. What are staff positions? What are line positions? Give examples.
4. What were some of the regulatory changes enacted under the Sarbanes-Oxley Act?

THE NAVIGATOR

Managerial Cost Concepts

For managers at companies like Dell or Hewlett-Packard to plan, direct, and control operations effectively, good information is needed. One very important type of information is related to costs. Questions such as the following should be asked.

1. What costs are involved in making a product or providing a service?
2. If production volume is decreased, will costs decrease?
3. What impact will automation have on total costs?
4. How can costs best be controlled?

To answer these questions, management needs reliable and relevant cost information. We now explain and illustrate the various cost categories that management uses.

STUDY OBJECTIVE
3
Define the three classes of manufacturing costs.

MANUFACTURING COSTS

Manufacturing consists of activities and processes that convert raw materials into finished goods. Contrast this type of operation with merchandising, which sells merchandise in the form in which it is purchased. Manufacturing costs are typically classified as shown in Illustration 14-3.

Illustration 14-3 Classifications of manufacturing costs

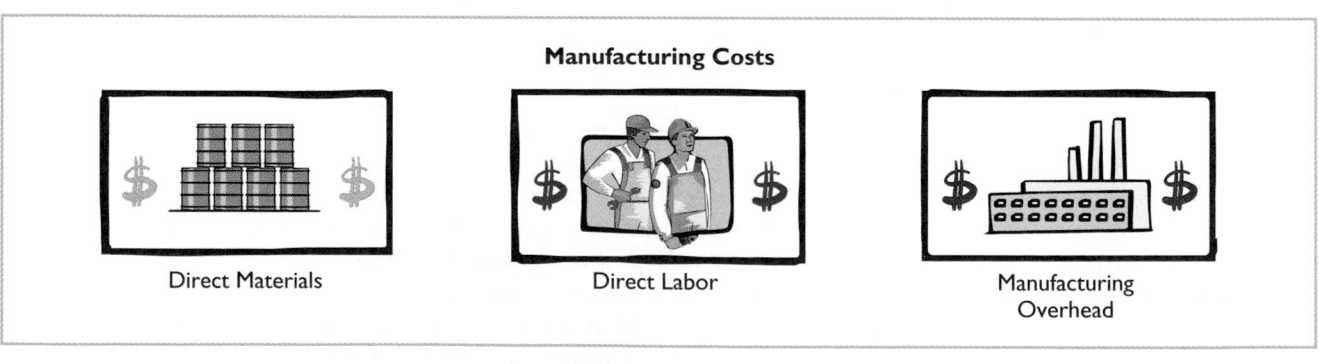

Manufacturing Costs

Direct Materials   Direct Labor   Manufacturing Overhead

Direct Materials

To obtain the materials that will be converted into the finished product, the manufacturer purchases raw materials. **Raw materials** are the basic materials and parts used in the manufacturing process. For example, auto manufacturers such as General Motors, Ford, and DaimlerChrysler use steel, plastics, and tires as raw materials in making cars.

Raw materials that can be physically and directly associated with the finished product during the manufacturing process are called **direct materials**.

Examples include flour in the baking of bread, syrup in the bottling of soft drinks, and steel in the making of automobiles. In the Feature Story, direct materials for Hewlett-Packard and Dell Computer include plastic, glass, hard drives, and processing chips.

But some raw materials cannot be easily associated with the finished product. These are called indirect materials. **Indirect materials** have one of two characteristics. Either (1) they do not physically become part of the finished product, such as lubricants and polishing compounds. Or (2) they cannot be traced because their physical association with the finished product is too small in terms of cost, such as cotter pins and lock washers. Indirect materials are accounted for as part of **manufacturing overhead**.

Direct Labor

The work of factory employees that can be physically and directly associated with converting raw materials into finished goods is called **direct labor**. Bottlers at Coca-Cola, bakers at Sara Lee, and typesetters at TechBooks are employees whose activities are usually classified as direct labor. **Indirect labor** refers to the work of factory employees that has no physical association with the finished product, or for which it is impractical to trace costs to the goods produced. Examples include wages of maintenance people, time-keepers, and supervisors. Like indirect materials, indirect labor is classified as **manufacturing overhead**.

Direct Labor

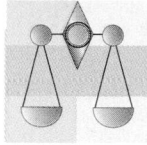

Business Insight
Management Perspective

Recently a closely watched study of productivity in the automobile industry reported some encouraging improvements for U.S. auto manufacturers. For example, the U.S. unit of DaimlerChrysler improved its overall productivity 8.3 percent. But a Nissan Motor plant in Tennessee set the standard for least amount of labor hours per vehicle. It produced Altima automobiles using only 15.74 labor hours per vehicle. Chrysler assembly plants required 28 hours per vehicle, and Ford took 26 hours.

SOURCE: Ann Keeton, "Chrysler Leads Big Three in Productivity Gains," *Wall Street Journal Online* (June 18, 2003).

Manufacturing Overhead

Manufacturing overhead consists of costs that are indirectly associated with the manufacture of the finished product. These costs may also be manufacturing costs that cannot be classified as direct materials or direct labor. Manufacturing overhead includes indirect materials, indirect labor, depreciation on factory buildings and machines, and insurance, taxes, and maintenance on factory facilities.

One study found the following magnitudes of the three different product costs as a percentage of the total product cost: direct materials 54 percent, direct labor 13 percent, and manufacturing overhead 33 percent. Note that the direct labor component is the smallest. This component of product cost is dropping substantially because of automation. In some companies, direct labor has become as little as 5 percent of the total cost.

Allocating materials and labor costs to specific products is fairly straightforward. Good record keeping can tell a company how much plastic is used in making each type of gear, or how many hours of factory labor were used to assemble a part. But allocating overhead costs to specific products presents problems. How much of the purchasing agent's salary is attributable to the hun-

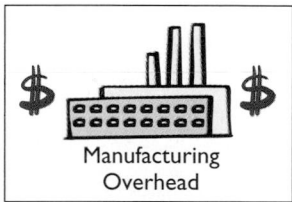
Manufacturing
Overhead

Alternative Terminology
Terms such as *factory overhead*, *indirect manufacturing costs*, and *burden* are sometimes used instead of manufacturing overhead.

dreds of different products made in the same plant? What about the grease that keeps the machines humming, or the computers that make sure paychecks come out on time? Boiled down to its simplest form, the question becomes: Which products cause the incurrence of which costs? In subsequent chapters we show various methods of allocating overhead to products.

PRODUCT VERSUS PERIOD COSTS

STUDY OBJECTIVE
4
Distinguish between product and period costs.

Each of the manufacturing cost components (direct materials, direct labor, and manufacturing overhead) are product costs. As the term suggests, **product costs** are costs that are a necessary and integral part of producing the finished product. Product costs are recorded as inventory when incurred. Under the matching principle, these costs do not become expenses until the finished goods inventory is sold. The expense is cost of goods sold.

Alternative Terminology
Product costs are also called *inventoriable costs.*

Period costs are costs that are matched with the revenue of a specific time period rather than included as part of the cost of a salable product. These are nonmanufacturing costs. Period costs include selling and administrative expenses. They are deducted from revenues in the period in which they are incurred in order to determine net income.

The foregoing relationships and cost terms are summarized in Illustration 14-4. Our main concern in this chapter is with product costs.

Illustration 14-4 Product versus period costs

BEFORE YOU GO ON . . .

►Review It

1. What are the major cost classifications involved in manufacturing a product?
2. What are product and period costs, and what is their relationship to the manufacturing process?

►Do It

A bicycle company has these costs: tires, salaries of employees who put tires on the wheels, factory building depreciation, wheel nuts, spokes, salary of factory manager, handle bars, and salaries of factory maintenance employees. Classify each cost as direct materials, direct labor, or overhead.

Action Plan

- Classify as direct materials any raw materials that can be physically and directly associated with the finished product.
- Classify as direct labor the work of factory employees that can be physically and directly associated with the finished product.
- Classify as manufacturing overhead any costs that are indirectly associated with the finished product.

Solution

Tires, spokes, and handle bars are direct materials. Salaries of employees who put tires on the wheels are direct labor. All of the other costs are manufacturing overhead.

Related exercise material: BE14-4, BE14-5, BE14-7, E14-2, E14-3, and E14-4.

Manufacturing Costs in Financial Statements

The financial statements of a manufacturer are very similar to those of a merchandiser. The principal differences pertain to the cost of goods sold section in the income statement and the current assets section in the balance sheet.

INCOME STATEMENT

Under a periodic inventory system, the income statements of a merchandiser and a manufacturer differ in the cost of goods sold section. For a merchandiser, cost of goods sold is computed by adding the beginning merchandise inventory to the **cost of goods purchased** and subtracting the ending merchandise inventory. For a manufacturer, cost of goods sold is computed by adding the beginning finished goods inventory to the **cost of goods manufactured** and subtracting the ending finished goods inventory. (See Illustration 14-5.)

STUDY OBJECTIVE
5

Explain the difference between a merchandising and a manufacturing income statement.

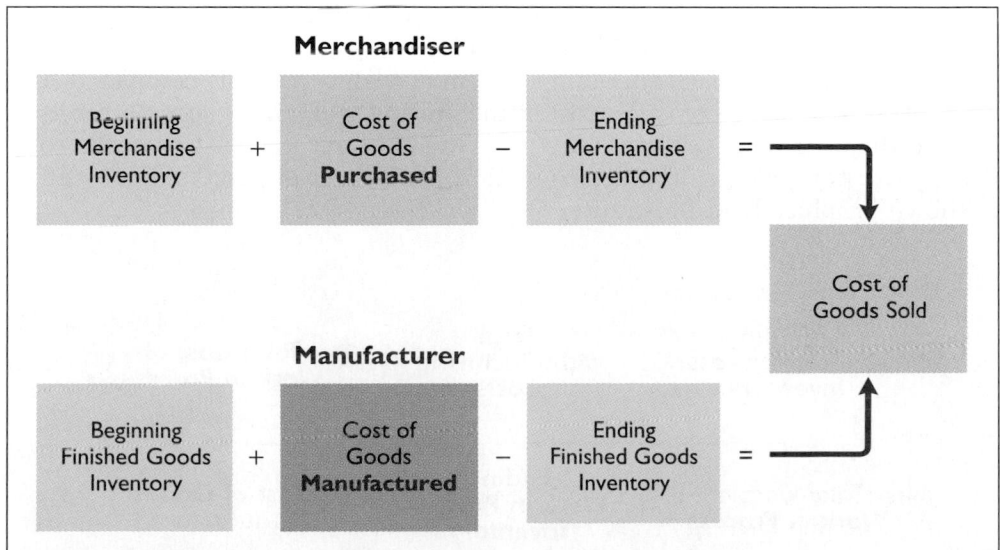

Illustration 14-5 Cost of goods sold components

Helpful Hint A periodic inventory system is assumed here.

The cost of goods sold sections for merchandising and manufacturing companies in Illustration 14-6 show the different presentations. The other sections of an income statement are similar for merchandisers and manufacturers.

MERCHANDISING COMPANY Income Statement (partial) For the Year Ended December 31, 2007		MANUFACTURING COMPANY Income Statement (partial) For the Year Ended December 31, 2007	
Cost of goods sold		Cost of goods sold	
Merchandise inventory, January 1	$ 70,000	**Finished goods inventory, January 1**	$ 90,000
Cost of goods purchased	650,000	**Cost of goods manufactured** (see Illustration 14-8)	370,000
Cost of goods available for sale	720,000	Cost of goods available for sale	460,000
Merchandise inventory, December 31	400,000	**Finished goods inventory, December 31**	80,000
Cost of goods sold	$320,000	Cost of goods sold	$380,000

A number of accounts are involved in determining the cost of goods manufactured. To eliminate excessive detail, income statements typically show only the total cost of goods manufactured. The details are presented in a Cost of Goods Manufactured Schedule. The form and content of this schedule are shown in Illustration 14-8 (page 717).

Determining the Cost of Goods Manufactured

An example may help show how the cost of goods manufactured is determined. Assume that Dell has a number of computers in various stages of production on January 1. In total, these partially completed units are called **beginning work in process inventory**. The costs assigned to beginning work in process inventory are based on the **manufacturing costs incurred in the prior period**.

The manufacturing costs incurred in the current year are used first to complete the work in process on January 1. They then are used to start the production of other computers. The sum of the direct materials costs, direct labor costs, and manufacturing overhead incurred in the current year is the total manufacturing costs for the current period.

We now have two cost amounts: (1) the cost of the beginning work in process and (2) the total manufacturing costs for the current period. The sum of these costs is the total cost of work in process for the year.

At the end of the year, some computers may be only partially completed. The costs of these units become the cost of the **ending work in process inventory**. To find the cost of goods manufactured, we subtract this cost from the total cost of work in process. The determination of the cost of goods manufactured is shown graphically in Illustration 14-7.

Illustration 14-7 Cost of goods manufactured formula

Cost of Goods Manufactured Schedule

An internal report shows each of the cost elements presented in Illustration 14-7. This report is called the **cost of goods manufactured schedule**. The schedule for Olsen Manufacturing Company (using assumed data) is shown in Illustration 14-8. Note that the schedule presents detailed data for direct materials and for manufacturing overhead.

Review Illustration 14-7 and then examine the cost of goods manufactured schedule in Illustration 14-8. You should be able to distinguish between "Total manufacturing costs" and "Cost of goods manufactured." The difference is the effect of the change in work in process during the period.

Illustration 14-8 Cost of goods manufactured schedule

OLSEN MANUFACTURING COMPANY
Cost of Goods Manufactured Schedule
For the Year Ended December 31, 2007

Work in process, January 1			$ 18,400
Direct materials			
Raw materials inventory, January 1	$ 16,700		
Raw materials purchases	152,500		
Total raw materials available for use	169,200		
Less: Raw materials inventory, December 31	22,800		
Direct materials used		$146,400	
Direct labor		175,600	
Manufacturing overhead			
Indirect labor	14,300		
Factory repairs	12,600		
Factory utilities	10,100		
Factory depreciation	9,440		
Factory insurance	8,360		
Total manufacturing overhead		54,800	
Total manufacturing costs			376,800
Total cost of work in process			395,200
Less: Work in process, December 31			25,200
Cost of goods manufactured			$370,000

Decision Toolkit

Decision Checkpoints	Info Needed for Decision	Tool to Use for Decision	How to Evaluate Results
Is the company maintaining control over the costs of production?	Cost of material, labor, and overhead	Cost of goods manufactured schedule	Compare the cost of goods manufactured to revenue expected from product sales.

BALANCE SHEET

The balance sheet for a merchandising company shows just one category of inventory. In contrast, the balance sheet for a manufacturer may have three inventory accounts. They are shown in Illustration 14-9 (next page).

Illustration 14-9
Inventory accounts for a manufacturer

Raw Materials Inventory

Shows the cost of raw materials on hand.

Work in Process Inventory

Shows the cost applicable to units that have been started into production but are only partially completed.

Finished Goods Inventory

Shows the cost of completed goods on hand.

STUDY OBJECTIVE

7

Explain the difference between a merchandising and a manufacturing balance sheet.

Finished Goods Inventory is to a manufacturer what Merchandise Inventory is to a merchandiser. It represents the goods that are available for sale.

The current assets sections presented in Illustration 14-10 contrast the presentations of inventories for merchandising and manufacturing companies. Manufacturing inventories are generally listed in the order of their liquidity—the order in which they are expected to be realized in cash. Thus, finished goods inventory is listed first. The remainder of the balance sheet is similar for the two types of companies.

Illustration 14-10
Current assets sections of merchandising and manufacturing balance sheets

MERCHANDISING COMPANY Balance Sheet December 31, 2007		MANUFACTURING COMPANY Balance Sheet December 31, 2007		
Current assets		Current assets		
Cash	$100,000	Cash		$180,000
Receivables (net)	210,000	Receivables (net)		210,000
Merchandise inventory	**400,000**	**Inventories**		
Prepaid expenses	22,000	**Finished goods**	**$80,000**	
Total current assets	$732,000	**Work in process**	25,200	
		Raw materials	22,800	128,000
		Prepaid expenses		18,000
		Total current assets		$536,000

Each step in the accounting cycle for a merchandiser applies to a manufacturer. For example, prior to preparing financial statements, adjusting entries are required. The adjusting entries are essentially the same as those of a merchandiser. The closing entries are also similar for manufacturers and merchandisers. (For more detail, see the appendix at the end of the chapter.)

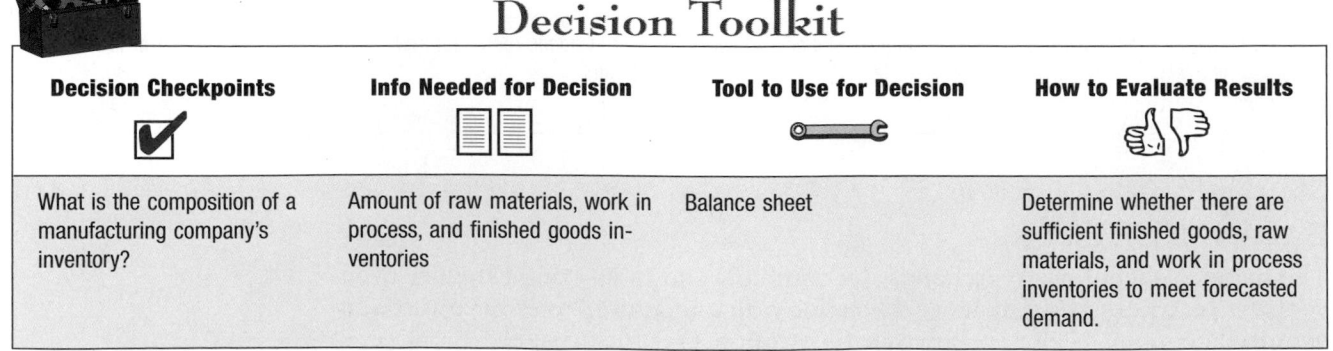

Decision Toolkit

Decision Checkpoints	Info Needed for Decision	Tool to Use for Decision	How to Evaluate Results
What is the composition of a manufacturing company's inventory?	Amount of raw materials, work in process, and finished goods inventories	Balance sheet	Determine whether there are sufficient finished goods, raw materials, and work in process inventories to meet forecasted demand.

COST CONCEPTS—A REVIEW

You have learned a number of cost concepts in this chapter. Because many of these concepts are new, here we provide an extended example for review.

Assume that Northridge Company manufactures and sells pre-hung metal doors. Recently, it also has decided to start selling pre-hung wood doors. An old warehouse that the company owns will be used to manufacture the new product. Northridge identifies the following costs associated with manufacturing and selling the pre-hung wood doors.

1. The material cost (wood) for each door is $10.
2. Labor costs required to construct a wood door are $8 per door.
3. Depreciation on the factory equipment used to make the wood doors is $25,000 per year.
4. Property taxes on the factory building used to make the wood doors are $6,000 per year.
5. Advertising costs for the pre-hung wood doors total $2,500 per month or $30,000 per year.
6. Sales commissions related to pre-hung wood doors sold are $4 per door.
7. Salaries for employees who maintain the factory facilities are $28,000.
8. The salary of the plant manager in charge of pre-hung wood doors is $70,000.
9. The cost of shipping pre-hung wood doors is $12 per door sold.

These manufacturing and selling costs can be assigned to the various categories shown in Illustration 14-11.

	Product Costs			
Cost Item	Direct Materials	Direct Labor	Manufacturing Overhead	Period Costs
1. Material cost ($10) per door	X			
2. Labor costs ($8) per door		X		
3. Depreciation on factory equipment ($25,000 per year)			X	
4. Property taxes on factory building ($6,000 per year)			X	
5. Advertising costs ($30,000 per year)				X
6. Sales commissions ($4 per door)				X
7. Maintenance salaries (factory facilities) ($28,000 per year)			X	
8. Salary of plant manager ($70,000)			X	
9. Cost of shipping pre-hung doors ($12 per door)				X

Illustration 14-11
Assignment of costs to cost categories

Remember that total manufacturing costs are the sum of the **product costs—** direct materials, direct labor, and manufacturing overhead. If Northridge Company produces 10,000 pre-hung wood doors the first year, the total manufacturing costs would be $309,000 as shown in Illustration 14-12.

Illustration 14-12
Computation of total
manufacturing costs

Cost Number and Item	Manufacturing Cost
1. Material cost ($10 × 10,000)	$100,000
2. Labor cost ($8 × 10,000)	80,000
3. Depreciation on factory equipment	25,000
4. Property taxes on factory building	6,000
7. Maintenance salaries (factory facilities)	28,000
8. Salary of plant manager	70,000
Total manufacturing costs	**$309,000**

Knowing the total manufacturing costs, Northridge can compute the manufacturing cost per unit. Assuming 10,000 units, the cost to produce one pre-hung wood door is $30.90 ($309,000 ÷ 10,000 units).

The cost concepts discussed in this chapter will be used extensively in subsequent chapters. Study Illustration 14-11 carefully. If you do not understand any of these classifications, go back and reread the appropriate section in this chapter.

BEFORE YOU GO ON . . .

▶**Review It**

1. How does the content of an income statement for a merchandiser differ from that for a manufacturer?
2. How are the work in process inventories reported in the cost of goods manufactured schedule?
3. How does the content of the balance sheet for a merchandiser differ from that for a manufacturer?

✓ THE NAVIGATOR

Managerial Accounting Today

In recent years, the competitive environment for U.S. business has changed significantly. For example, the airline, financial services, and telecommunications industries have been deregulated. Global competition has intensified. The world economy now has the European Union, NAFTA, and ASEAN. Countries like China and India are becoming economic powerhouses. As indicated earlier, managerial accountants must be forward-looking, acting as advisors and information providers to different parts of the organization. Some of the issues they face are discussed below.

SERVICE INDUSTRY TRENDS

The Feature Story notes that at the peak of its success as a personal computer manufacturer, Compaq purchased Digital Equipment. Its management believed that the future of computing was in providing computer services, rather than in manufacturing computer hardware. In fact, during the most recent decade, the U.S. economy in general shifted toward an emphasis on providing services, rather than goods. Today over 50 percent of U.S. workers are employed by service companies, and that percentage is projected to increase in coming years. Much of this chapter focused on manufacturers. But most of the techniques that you will learn in this course are equally applicable to service entities.

Managers of service companies look to managerial accounting to answer many questions. Illustration 14-13 presents examples of such questions. In some instances the managerial accountant may need to develop new systems for measuring the cost of serving individual customers. In others, companies may need new operating controls to improve the quality and efficiency of specific services. Many of the examples we present in subsequent chapters will be based on service companies.

Illustration 14-13
Service industries and companies and the managerial accounting questions they face

	Industry/Company	Questions Faced by Service-Company Managers
	Transportation (American Airlines, Amtrak)	Whether to buy new or used planes? Whether to service a new route?
	Package delivery services (FedEx, UPS)	What fee structure to use? What mode of transportation to use?
	Telecommunications (AT&T, Time Warner)	What fee structure to use? Whether to service a new community? How many households will it take to break even? Whether to invest in a new satellite or lay new cable?
	Professional services (attorneys, accountants, physicians)	How much to charge for particular services? How much office overhead to allocate to particular jobs? How efficient and productive are individual staff members?
	Financial institutions (Wells Fargo, Merrill Lynch)	Which services to charge for, and which to provide for free? Whether to build a new branch office or to install a new ATM? Should fees vary depending on the size of the customers' accounts?
	Health care (Blue Cross-Blue Shield, HMOs)	Whether to invest in new equipment? How much to charge for various services? How to measure the quality of services provided?

MANAGERIAL ACCOUNTING PRACTICES

As discussed earlier, the practice of managerial accounting has changed significantly in recent years to better address the needs of managers. The following sections explain some recent managerial accounting practices.

The Value Chain

The **value chain** refers to all activities associated with providing a product or service. For a manufacturer these include research and development, product design, acquisition of raw materials, production, sales and marketing, delivery, customer relations, and subsequent service. Illustration 14-14 depicts the value chain for a manufacturer. In recent years, companies have made huge strides in analyzing all stages of the value chain in an effort to improve productivity and eliminate waste. Japanese automobile manufacturer Toyota pioneered many of these innovations.

Illustration 14-14 A manufacturer's value chain

| Research & development and product design | Acquisition of raw materials | Production | Sales & marketing | Delivery | Customer relations and subsequent services |

In the 1980s many companies purchased giant machines to replace humans in the manufacturing process. These machines were designed to produce large batches of products. In recent years these large-batch manufacturing processes have been recognized as very wasteful. They require vast amounts of inventory storage capacity and considerable movement of materials. Consequently, many companies have reengineered their manufacturing processes. As one example, the manufacturing company Pratt and Whitney has replaced many large machines with smaller, more flexible ones and has begun reorganizing its plants for more efficient flow of goods. Pratt and Whitney was able to reduce the time that its turbine engine blades spend in the grinding section of its factory from 10 days down to 2 hours. It cut the total amount of time spent making a blade from 22 days to 7 days. The improvements that have resulted from analysis of the value chain have made companies far more responsive to customer needs and have improved profitability.

Technological Change

Technology has played a large role in affecting the value chain. The computerization and automation that have occurred have permitted companies to be much more effective in streamlining production and thus enhancing the value chain. For example, many companies now employ **enterprise resource planning (ERP)** software systems to manage their value chain. ERP systems provide a comprehensive, centralized, integrated source of information used to manage all major business processes, from purchasing to manufacturing to recording human resources.

In large companies, an ERP system might replace as many as 200 individual software packages. For example, an ERP system can eliminate the need for individual software packages for personnel, inventory management, receivables, and payroll. Because the value chain extends beyond the walls of the company, ERP systems both collect from and provide information to the company's major suppliers, customers, and business partners. The largest ERP provider, German corporation SAP, has more than 22,000 customers worldwide.

Another example of technological change is **computer-integrated manufacturing (CIM)**. Using CIM, many companies can now manufacture products that are untouched by human hands. An example is the use of robotic equipment in the steel and automobile industries. Automation significantly reduces direct labor costs in many cases. The worker simply monitors the manufacturing process by watching instrument panels.

Also, the widespread use of computers has greatly reduced the cost of accumulating, storing, and reporting managerial accounting information. Computers now make it possible to do more detailed costing of products, processes, and services than was possible under manual processing.

Technology is also affecting the value chain through business-to-business (B2B) e-commerce on the Internet. The Internet has dramatically changed the way corporations do business with one another. Interorganizational information systems connected over the Internet enable customers and suppliers to share information nearly instantaneously. In addition, the Internet has changed the marketplace, often having the effect of cutting out intermediaries (the "middle man"). Industries such as the automobile, airline, hotel, and electronics industries have made commitments to purchase some or all of their supplies and raw materials in the huge B2B electronic marketplaces. For example, Hilton Hotels recently committed to purchase as much as $1.5 billion of bed sheets, pest control services, and other items from an online supplier, PurchasePro.com.

Just-in-Time Inventory Methods

Many companies have significantly lowered inventory levels and costs using **just-in-time (JIT) inventory** methods. Under a just-in-time method, goods are manufactured or purchased just in time for use. As noted in the Feature Story, Dell is famous for having developed a system for making computers in response to individual customer requests. Even though each computer is custom-made to meet each customer's particular specifications, it takes Dell less than 48 hours to assemble the computer and put it on a truck. By integrating its information systems with those of its suppliers, Dell reduced its inventories to nearly zero. This is a huge advantage in an industry where products become obsolete nearly overnight. JIT is discussed further in the appendix to Chapter 17.

Quality

JIT inventory systems require an increased emphasis on product quality. If products are produced only as they are needed, it is very costly for the company to have to stop production because of defects or machine breakdowns. Many companies have installed **total quality management (TQM)** systems to reduce defects in finished products. The goal is to achieve zero defects. These systems require timely data on defective products, rework costs, and the cost of honoring warranty contracts. Often this information is used to help redesign the product in a way that makes it less prone to defect. Or it may be used to reengineer the production process to reduce setup time and decrease the potential for error. TQM systems also provide information on nonfinancial measures such as customer satisfaction, number of service calls, and time to generate reports. Attention to these measures, which employees can control, leads to increased profitability.

Activity-Based Costing

As discussed earlier, overhead costs have become an increasingly large component of product and service costs. By definition, overhead costs cannot be directly traced to individual products. But to determine each product's cost, overhead must be **allocated** to the various products. In order to obtain more accurate product costs, many companies now allocate overhead using **activity-based costing (ABC)**. Under ABC, overhead is allocated based on each product's use of activities in making the product. For example, the company can keep track of the cost of setting up machines for each batch of a production process. Then a particular product can be allocated part of the total set-up cost based on the number of set-ups that product required.

Activity-based costing is beneficial because it results in more accurate product costing and in more careful scrutiny of all activities in the value chain. For example, if a product's cost is high because it requires a high number of set-ups, management will be motivated to determine how to produce the product using the optimal number of machine set-ups. ABC is now widely used by both manufacturing and service companies. Allied Signal and Coca-Cola have both enjoyed improved results from ABC. Fidelity Investments uses ABC to identify which customers are actually costing it money. Chapter 17 discusses ABC further.

Business Insight
Management Perspective

When it comes to total quality management, few companies can compare with Chiquita Brands International. Grocery store customers are very picky about bananas—bad bananas are consistently the number one grocery store complaint. Because bananas often account for up to 3 percent of a grocery store's sales, Chiquita goes to great lengths to protect the popular fruit. While bananas are in transit from Central America, "black box" recording devices attached to shipping crates ensure that they are kept in an environment of 90 percent humidity and an unvarying 55-degree temperature. Upon arrival in the U.S., bananas are ripened in airtight warehouses that use carefully monitored levels of ethylene gas. Regular checks are made of each warehouse using ultrasonic detectors that can detect leaks the size of a pinhole. Says one grocery store executive, "No other item in the store has this type of attention and resources devoted to it."

SOURCE: Devon Spurgeon, "When Grocers in U.S. Go Bananas Over Bad Fruit, They Call Laubenthal," *Wall Street Journal* (August 14, 2000), p. A1.

Theory of Constraints

All companies have certain aspects of their business that create "bottlenecks"—constraints that limit the company's potential profitability. An important aspect of managing the value chain is identifying these constraints. The **theory of constraints** is a specific approach used to identify and manage constraints in order to achieve the company goals. Automobile manufacturer General Motors has implemented the theory of constraints in all of its North American plants. GM has found that it is most profitable when it focuses on fixing bottlenecks, rather than worrying about whether all aspects of the company are functioning at full capacity. It has greatly improved the company's ability to effectively use overtime labor while meeting customer demand.

Balanced Scorecard

As various business practice innovations have been implemented, managers sometimes focus too enthusiastically on the latest innovation, to the detriment of other areas of the business. For example, in focusing on improving quality, companies sometimes lost sight of cost/benefit considerations. Similarly, in focusing on reducing inventory levels through just-in-time, companies sometimes lost sales due to inventory shortages. The **balanced scorecard** is a performance-measurement approach that uses both financial and nonfinancial measures to evaluate all aspects of a company's operations in an **integrated** fashion. The performance measures are linked in a cause-and-effect fashion to ensure that they all tie to the company's overall objectives.

For example, the company may desire to increase its return on assets, a common financial performance measure (calculated as net income divided by average total assets). It will then identify a series of linked goals that, if each is accomplished, will ultimately result in an increase in return on assets. For example, in order to increase return on assets, sales must increase. In order to increase sales, customer satisfaction must be increased. In order to increase customer satisfaction, product defects must be reduced. In order to reduce product defects, employee training must be increased. Note the linkage, which starts with employee training and ends with return on assets. Each objective will have associated performance measures.

The use of the balanced scorecard is widespread among well-known and respected companies. For example, Hilton Hotels Corporation uses the balanced scorecard to evaluate the performance of employees at all of its hotel chains. Wal-Mart employs the balanced scorecard, and actually extends its use to evaluation of its suppliers. For example, Wal-Mart recently awarded Welch Company the "Dry Grocery Division Supplier of the Year Award" for its balanced scorecard results. The balanced scorecard is discussed further in Chapter 22.

BEFORE YOU GO ON . . .

►Review It

1. Describe, in sequence, the main components of a manufacturer's value chain.
2. What is an enterprise resource planning (ERP) system? What are its primary benefits?
3. Why is product quality important for companies that implement a just-in-time inventory system?
4. Explain what is meant by "balanced" in the balanced scorecard approach.

✓ THE NAVIGATOR

Using the Decision Toolkit

Giant Manufacturing Co. Ltd. specializes in manufacturing many different models of bicycles. Assume that a new model, the Jaguar, has been well accepted. As a result, the company has established a separate manufacturing facility to produce these bicycles. The company produces 1,000 bicycles per month. Giant's monthly manufacturing cost and other expenses data related to these bicycles are as follows.

1. Rent on manufacturing equipment (lease cost) $2,000/month
2. Insurance on manufacturing building $750/month
3. Raw materials (frames, tires, etc.) $80/bicycle
4. Utility costs for manufacturing facility $1,000/month
5. Supplies for administrative office $800/month
6. Wages for assembly line workers in manufacturing facility $30/bicycle
7. Depreciation on office equipment $650/month
8. Miscellaneous materials (lubricants, solders, etc.) $1.20/bicycle
9. Property taxes on manufacturing building $2,400/year
10. Manufacturing supervisor's salary $3,000/month
11. Advertising for bicycles $30,000/year
12. Sales commissions $10/bicycle
13. Depreciation on manufacturing building $1,500/month

Instructions
(a) Prepare an answer sheet with the following column headings.

	Product Costs			
Cost Item	Direct Materials	Direct Labor	Manufacturing Overhead	Period Costs

Enter each cost item on your answer sheet, placing an "X" mark under the appropriate headings.
(b) Compute total manufacturing costs for the month.

Solution

(a)

Cost Item	Direct Materials	Direct Labor	Manufacturing Overhead	Period Costs
	Product Costs			
1. Rent on manufacturing equipment ($2,000/month)			X	
2. Insurance on manufacturing building ($750/month)			X	
3. Raw materials ($80/bicycle)	X			
4. Manufacturing utilities ($1,000/month)			X	
5. Office supplies ($800/month)				X
6. Wages for workers ($30/bicycle)		X		
7. Depreciation on office equipment ($650/month)				X
8. Miscellaneous materials ($1.20/bicycle)			X	
9. Property taxes on manufacturing building ($2,400/year)			X	
10. Manufacturing supervisor's salary ($3,000/month)			X	
11. Advertising cost ($30,000/year)				X
12. Sales commissions ($10/bicycle)				X
13. Depreciation on manufacturing building ($1,500/month)			X	

(b)

Cost Item	Manufacturing Cost
Rent on manufacturing equipment	$ 2,000
Insurance on manufacturing building	750
Raw materials ($80 × 1,000)	80,000
Manufacturing utilities	1,000
Labor ($30 × 1,000)	30,000
Miscellaneous materials ($1.20 × 1,000)	1,200
Property taxes on manufacturing building ($2,400 ÷ 12)	200
Manufacturing supervisor's salary	3,000
Depreciation on manufacturing building	1,500
Total manufacturing costs	$119,650

Summary of Study Objectives

1 *Explain the distinguishing features of managerial accounting.* The distinguishing features of managerial accounting are:

Primary users of reports—internal users, who are officers, department heads, managers, and supervisors in the company.

Type and frequency of reports—internal reports that are issued as frequently as the need arises.

Purpose of reports—to provide special-purpose information for a particular user for a specific decision.

Content of reports—pertains to subunits of the business and may be very detailed; may extend beyond double-entry accounting system; the reporting standard is relevance to the decision being made.

Verification of reports—no independent audits.

2 *Identify the three broad functions of management.* The three functions are planning, directing, and controlling. Planning requires management to look ahead and to establish objectives. Directing involves coordinating the diverse activities and human resources of a company to produce a smooth-running operation. Controlling is the process of keeping the activities on track.

3 *Define the three classes of manufacturing costs.* Manufacturing costs are typically classified as either (1) direct materials, (2) direct labor, or (3) manufacturing overhead. Raw materials that can be physically and directly associated with the finished product during the manufacturing process are called direct materials. The work of factory employees that can be physically and directly associated with converting raw materials into finished goods is considered direct labor. Manufacturing overhead consists of costs that are indirectly associated with the manufacture of the finished product.

4 *Distinguish between product and period costs.* Product costs are costs that are a necessary and integral part of producing the finished product. Product costs are also called inventoriable costs. Under the matching principle, these costs do not become expenses un-

til the inventory to which they attach is sold. Period costs are costs that are identified with a specific time period rather than with a salable product. These costs relate to nonmanufacturing costs and therefore are not inventoriable costs.

5 *Explain the difference between a merchandising and a manufacturing income statement.* The difference between a merchandising and a manufacturing income statement is in the cost of goods sold section. A manufacturing cost of goods sold section shows beginning and ending finished goods inventories and the cost of goods manufactured.

6 *Indicate how cost of goods manufactured is determined.* The cost of the beginning work in process is added to the total manufacturing costs for the current year to arrive at the total cost of work in process for the year. The ending work in process is then subtracted from the total cost of work in process to arrive at the cost of goods manufactured.

7 *Explain the difference between a merchandising and a manufacturing balance sheet.* The difference between a merchandising and a manufacturing balance sheet is in the current assets section. In the current assets section of a manufacturing company's balance sheet, three inventory accounts are presented: finished goods inventory, work in process inventory, and raw materials inventory.

8 *Identify trends in managerial accounting.* Managerial accounting has experienced many changes in recent years. Among these are a shift toward addressing the needs of service companies and improving practices to better meet the needs of managers. Improved practices include a focus on managing the value chain through techniques such as just-in-time inventory, and technological applications such as enterprise resource planning (ERP). In addition, techniques have been developed to improve decision making, such as the theory of constraints and activity-based costing (ABC). Finally, the balanced scorecard is now used by many companies in order to attain a more comprehensive view of the company's operations.

Decision Toolkit—A Summary

Decision Checkpoints	Info Needed for Decision	Tool to Use for Decision	How to Evaluate Results
Is the company maintaining control over the costs of production?	Cost of material, labor, and overhead	Cost of goods manufactured schedule	Compare the cost of goods manufactured to revenue expected from product sales.
What is the composition of a manufacturing company's inventory?	Amount of raw materials, work in process, and finished goods inventories	Balance sheet	Determine whether there are sufficient finished goods, raw materials, and work in process inventories to meet forecasted demand.

APPENDIX
ACCOUNTING CYCLE FOR A MANUFACTURING COMPANY

STUDY OBJECTIVE
9

Prepare a work sheet and closing entries for a manufacturing company.

The accounting cycle for a manufacturing company is the same as for a merchandising company when a periodic inventory system is used. The journalizing and posting of transactions is the same, except for the additional manufacturing inventories and manufacturing cost accounts. Similarly, the preparation of a trial balance and the journalizing and posting of adjusting entries are the same. Some changes, however, occur in the use of a work sheet and in preparing closing entries.

To illustrate the changes in the work sheet, we will use the cost of goods manufactured schedule for Olsen Manufacturing presented in Illustration 14-8, along with other assumed data. For convenience, the cost of goods manufactured schedule is reproduced in Illustration 14A-1.

Illustration 14A-1 Cost of goods manufactured schedule

OLSEN MANUFACTURING COMPANY
Cost of Goods Manufactured Schedule
For the Year Ended December 31, 2007

Work in process, January 1			$ 18,400
Direct materials			
Raw materials inventory, January 1	$ 16,700		
Raw materials purchases	152,500		
Total raw materials available for use	169,200		
Less: Raw materials inventory, December 31	22,800		
Direct materials used		$146,400	
Direct labor		175,600	
Manufacturing overhead			
Indirect labor	14,300		
Factory repairs	12,600		
Factory utilities	10,100		
Factory depreciation	9,440		
Factory insurance	8,360		
Total manufacturing overhead		54,800	
Total manufacturing costs			376,800
Total cost of work in process			395,200
Less: Work in process, December 31			25,200
Cost of goods manufactured			$370,000

Work Sheet

When a work sheet is used in preparing financial statements, two additional columns are needed for the cost of goods manufactured schedule. As illustrated in the work sheet in Illustration 14A-2, debit and credit columns for this schedule are inserted before the income statement columns.

Illustration 14A-2 Partial work sheet

	Adjusted Trial Balance Dr.	Adjusted Trial Balance Cr.	Cost of Goods Manufactured Dr.	Cost of Goods Manufactured Cr.	Income Statement Dr.	Income Statement Cr.	Balance Sheet Dr.	Balance Sheet Cr.
6 Cash	42,500						42,500	
7 Accounts Receivable (Net)	71,900						71,900	
8 Finished Goods Inv.	24,600				24,600	19,500	19,500	
9 Work in Process Inv.	18,400		18,400	25,200			25,200	
10 Raw Material Inv.	16,700		16,700	22,800			22,800	
11 Plant Assets	724,000						724,000	
12 Accumulated Depr.		278,400						278,400
13 Notes Payable		100,000						100,000
14 Accounts Payable		40,000						40,000
15 Income Taxes Payable		5,000						5,000
16 Common Stock		200,000						200,000
17 Retained Earnings		205,100						205,100
18 Sales		680,000				680,000		
19 Raw Materials Purchases	152,500		152,500					
20 Direct Labor	175,600		175,600					
21 Indirect Labor	14,300		14,300					
22 Factory Repairs	12,600		12,600					
23 Factory Utilities	10,100		10,100					
24 Factory Depreciation	9,440		9,440					
25 Factory Insurance	8,360		8,360					
26 Selling Expenses	114,900				114,900			
27 Administrative Exp.	92,600				92,600			
28 Income Tax Exp.	20,000				20,000			
29 Totals	1,508,500	1,508,500	418,000	48,000				
30 Cost of Goods Manufactured				370,000	370,000			
31 Totals			418,000	418,000	622,100	699,500	905,900	828,500
32 Net Income					77,400			77,400
33 Totals					699,500	699,500	905,900	905,900

In the cost of goods manufactured columns, the beginning inventories of raw materials and work in process are entered as debits. In addition, all of the manufacturing costs are entered as debits. The reason is that each of these amounts increases cost of goods manufactured. Ending inventories for raw materials and work in process are entered as credits in the cost of goods manufactured columns because they have the opposite effect—they decrease cost of goods manufactured. The balancing amount for these columns is the cost of goods manufactured. Note that the amount ($370,000) agrees with the amount reported for cost of goods manufactured in Illustration 14A-1. This amount is also entered in the income statement debit column.

The income statement and balance sheet columns for a manufacturing company are basically the same as for a merchandising company. For example, the treatment of the finished goods inventories is identical with the treatment of merchandise inventory. That is, the beginning inventory is entered in the debit column of the income statement, and the ending finished goods inventory is entered in the income statement credit column as well as in the balance sheet debit column.

As in the case of a merchandising company, financial statements for a manufacturing company can be prepared from the statement columns of the work sheet. In addition, the cost of goods manufactured schedule can also be prepared directly from the work sheet.

Closing Entries

The closing entries are different for manufacturing and merchandising companies. **A Manufacturing Summary account is used to close all accounts that appear in the cost of goods manufactured schedule.** The balance of the Manufacturing Summary account is the Cost of Goods Manufactured for the period. Manufacturing Summary is then closed to Income Summary.

The closing entries can be prepared from the work sheet. As illustrated below, the closing entries for the manufacturing accounts are prepared first. The closing entries for Olsen Manufacturing are as follows.

Dec. 31	Work in Process Inventory (Dec. 31)		25,200	
	Raw Materials Inventory (Dec. 31)		22,800	
	Manufacturing Summary			**48,000**
	(To record ending raw materials and work in process inventories)			
31	**Manufacturing Summary**		**418,000**	
	Work in Process Inventory (Jan. 1)			18,400
	Raw Materials Inventory (Jan. 1)			16,700
	Raw Materials Purchases			152,500
	Direct Labor			175,600
	Indirect Labor			14,300
	Factory Repairs			12,600
	Factory Utilities			10,100
	Factory Depreciation			9,440
	Factory Insurance			8,360
	(To close beginning raw materials and work in process inventories and manufacturing cost accounts)			
31	Finished Goods Inventory (Dec. 31)		19,500	
	Sales		680,000	
	Income Summary			699,500
	(To record ending finished goods inventory and close sales account)			
31	Income Summary		622,100	
	Finished Goods Inventory (Jan. 1)			24,600
	Manufacturing Summary			**370,000**
	Selling Expenses			114,900
	Administrative Expenses			92,600
	Income Tax Expense			20,000
	(To close beginning finished goods inventory, manufacturing summary, and expense accounts)			

(The closing entries continue on the next page.)

31	Income Summary	77,400	
	Retained Earnings		77,400
	(To close net income to retained earnings)		

After posting, the summary accounts will show the following.

Manufacturing Summary

Dec. 31	Close	418,000	Dec. 31	Close	48,000
			31	Close	370,000

Income Summary

Dec. 31	Close	622,100	Dec. 31	Close	699,500
31	Close	77,400			

Illustration 14A-3 Summary accounts for a manufacturing company, after posting

It also would be possible to post each account balance to the Manufacturing Summary account.

Summary of Study Objective for Appendix

9 *Prepare a work sheet and closing entries for a manufacturing company.* Two additional columns are needed in the work sheet for the cost of goods manufactured. In these columns, the beginning inventories of raw materials and work in process are entered as debits, and the ending inventories are entered as credits. All manufacturing costs are entered as debits. To close all of the accounts that appear in the cost of goods manufactured schedule, a Manufacturing Summary account is used.

Glossary

Activity-based costing (ABC) A method of allocating overhead based on each product's use of activities in making the product. (p. 723)

Balanced scorecard A performance-measurement approach that uses both financial and nonfinancial measures, tied to company objectives, to evaluate a company's operations in an integrated fashion. (p. 724)

Board of directors The group of officials elected by the stockholders of a corporation to formulate operating policies, select officers, and otherwise manage the company. (p. 710)

Chief executive officer (CEO) Corporate officer who has overall responsibility for managing the business and delegates that responsibility to other corporate officers. (p. 710)

Chief financial officer (CFO) Corporate officer who is responsible for all of the accounting and finance issues of the company. (p. 710)

Controller Financial officer responsible for a company's accounting records, system of internal control, and preparation of financial statements, tax returns, and internal reports. (p. 710)

Cost of goods manufactured Total cost of work in process less the cost of the ending work in process inventory. (p. 716)

Direct labor The work of factory employees that can be physically and directly associated with converting raw materials into finished goods. (p. 713)

Direct materials Raw materials that can be physically and directly associated with manufacturing the finished product. (p. 712)

Enterprise resource planning (ERP) system Software that provides a comprehensive, centralized, integrated source of information used to manage all major business processes. (p. 722)

Indirect labor   Work of factory employees that has no physical association with the finished product, or for which it is impractical to trace the costs to the goods produced. (p. 713)

Indirect materials   Raw materials that do not physically become part of the finished product or cannot be traced because their physical association with the finished product is too small. (p. 713)

Just-in-time (JIT) inventory   Inventory system in which goods are manufactured or purchased just in time for use. (p. 723)

Line positions   Jobs that are directly involved in a company's primary revenue-generating operating activities. (p. 710)

Managerial accounting   A field of accounting that provides economic and financial information for managers and other internal users. (p. 706)

Manufacturing overhead   Manufacturing costs that are indirectly associated with the manufacture of the finished product. (p. 713)

Period costs   Costs that are matched with the revenue of a specific time period and charged to expense as incurred. (p. 714)

Product costs   Costs that are a necessary and integral part of producing the finished product. (p. 714)

Staff positions   Jobs that support the efforts of line employees. (p. 710)

Theory of constraints   A specific approach used to identify and manage constraints in order to achieve the company's goals. (p. 724)

Total cost of work in process   Cost of the beginning work in process plus total manufacturing costs for the current period. (p. 716)

Total manufacturing costs   The sum of direct materials, direct labor, and manufacturing overhead incurred in the current period. (p. 716)

Total quality management (TQM)   Systems implemented to reduce defects in finished products with the goal of achieving zero defects. (p. 723)

Treasurer   Financial officer responsible for custody of a company's funds and for maintaining its cash position. (p. 710)

Value chain   All activities associated with providing a product or service. (p. 722)

Demonstration Problem

Superior Manufacturing Company has the following cost and expense data for the year ending December 31, 2007.

Raw materials, 1/1/07	$ 30,000	Insurance, factory	$ 14,000
Raw materials, 12/31/07	20,000	Property taxes, factory building	6,000
Raw materials purchases	205,000	Sales (net)	1,500,000
Indirect materials	15,000	Delivery expenses	100,000
Work in process, 1/1/07	80,000	Sales commissions	150,000
Work in process, 12/31/07	50,000	Indirect labor	90,000
Finished goods, 1/1/07	110,000	Factory machinery rent	40,000
Finished goods, 12/31/07	120,000	Factory utilities	65,000
Direct labor	350,000	Depreciation, factory building	24,000
Factory manager's salary	35,000	Administrative expenses	300,000

Instructions

(a) Prepare a cost of goods manufactured schedule for Superior Company for 2007.

(b) Prepare an income statement for Superior Company for 2007.

(c) Assume that Superior Company's ledgers show the balances of the following current asset accounts: Cash $17,000, Accounts Receivable (net) $120,000, Prepaid Expenses $13,000, and Short-term Investments $26,000. Prepare the current assets section of the balance sheet for Superior Company as of December 31, 2007.

Solution to Demonstration Problem

(a)   SUPERIOR MANUFACTURING COMPANY
                    Cost of Goods Manufactured Schedule
                     For the Year Ended December 31, 2007

Work in process, 1/1			$ 80,000
Direct materials			
Raw materials inventory, 1/1	$ 30,000		
Raw materials purchases	205,000		
Total raw materials available for use	235,000		
Less: Raw materials inventory, 12/31	20,000		
Direct materials used		$215,000	
Direct labor		350,000	
Manufacturing overhead			
Indirect labor	90,000		
Factory utilities	65,000		
Factory machinery rent	40,000		
Factory manager's salary	35,000		
Depreciation on building	24,000		
Indirect materials	15,000		
Factory insurance	14,000		
Property taxes	6,000		
Total manufacturing overhead		289,000	
Total manufacturing costs			854,000
Total cost of work in process			934,000
Less: Work in process, 12/31			50,000
Cost of goods manufactured			$884,000

(b)   SUPERIOR MANUFACTURING COMPANY
                              Income Statement
                     For the Year Ended December 31, 2007

Sales (net)		$1,500,000
Cost of goods sold		
Finished goods inventory, January 1	$110,000	
Cost of goods manufactured	884,000	
Cost of goods available for sale	994,000	
Less: Finished goods inventory, December 31	120,000	
Cost of goods sold		874,000
Gross profit		626,000
Operating expenses		
Administrative expenses	300,000	
Sales commissions	150,000	
Delivery expenses	100,000	
Total operating expenses		550,000
Net income		$ 76,000

Action Plan

- Start with beginning work in process as the first item in the cost of goods manufactured schedule.
- Sum direct materials used, direct labor, and total manufacturing overhead to determine total manufacturing costs.
- Sum beginning work in process and total manufacturing costs to determine total cost of work in process.
- Cost of goods manufactured is the total cost of work in process less ending work in process.
- In the cost of goods sold section of the income statement, show beginning and ending finished goods inventory and cost of goods manufactured.
- In the balance sheet, list manufacturing inventories in the order of their expected realization in cash, with finished goods first.

(c)

SUPERIOR MANUFACTURING COMPANY
Balance Sheet (partial)
December 31, 2007

Current assets		
Cash		$ 17,000
Short-term investments		26,000
Accounts receivable (net)		120,000
Inventories		
Finished goods	$120,000	
Work in process	50,000	
Raw materials	20,000	190,000
Prepaid expenses		13,000
Total current assets		$366,000

THE NAVIGATOR

Note: All asterisked Questions, Exercises, and Problems relate to material in the appendix to the chapter.

Self-Study Questions

WILEY
PLUS

(SO 1)   Answers are at the end of the chapter.
   1. Managerial accounting:
      (a) is governed by generally accepted accounting principles.
      (b) places emphasis on special-purpose information.
      (c) pertains to the entity as a whole and is highly aggregated.
      (d) is limited to cost data.

(SO 2)   **2.** The management of an organization performs several broad functions. They are:
      (a) planning, directing, and selling.
      (b) planning, directing, and controlling.
      (c) planning, manufacturing, and controlling.
      (d) directing, manufacturing, and controlling.

(SO 3)   **3.** Direct materials are a:

	Product Cost	Manufacturing Overhead	Period Cost
(a)	Yes	Yes	No
(b)	Yes	No	No
(c)	Yes	Yes	Yes
(d)	No	No	No

(SO 4)   **4.** Indirect labor is a:
      (a) nonmanufacturing cost.
      (b) raw material cost.
      (c) product cost.
      (d) period cost.

(SO 3)   **5.** Which of the following costs would be included in manufacturing overhead of a computer manufacturer?

      (a) The cost of the disk drives.
      (b) The wages earned by computer assemblers.
      (c) The cost of the memory chips.
      (d) Depreciation on testing equipment.

(SO 3)   **6.** Which of the following is *not* an element of manufacturing overhead?
      (a) Sales manager's salary.
      (b) Plant manager's salary.
      (c) Factory repairman's wages.
      (d) Product inspector's salary.

(SO 5)   **7.** For the year, Redder Company has cost of goods manufactured of $600,000, beginning finished goods inventory of $200,000, and ending finished goods inventory of $250,000. The cost of goods sold is:
      (a) $450,000.
      (b) $500,000.
      (c) $550,000.
      (d) $600,000.

(SO 6)   **8.** A cost of goods manufactured schedule shows beginning and ending inventories for:
      (a) raw materials and work in process only.
      (b) work in process only.
      (c) raw materials only.
      (d) raw materials, work in process, and finished goods.

(SO 7)   **9.** In a manufacturer's balance sheet, three inventories may be reported: (1) raw materials, (2) work in process, and (3) finished goods. Indicate

in what sequence these inventories generally appear on a balance sheet.
(a) (1), (2), (3)
(b) (2), (3), (1)
(c) (3), (1), (2)
(d) (3), (2), (1)

10. Which of the following managerial accounting (SO 8) techniques attempts to allocate manufacturing overhead in a more meaningful fashion?
(a) Just-in-time inventory.
(b) Total-quality management.
(c) Theory of constraints.
(d) Activity-based costing.

Questions

1. (a) "Managerial accounting is a field of accounting that provides economic information for all interested parties." Do you agree? Explain.
(b) Tina Turner believes that managerial accounting serves only manufacturing firms. Is Tina correct? Explain.

2. Distinguish between managerial and financial accounting as to (a) primary users of reports, (b) types and frequency of reports, and (c) purpose of reports.

3. How does the content of reports and the verification of reports differ between managerial and financial accounting?

4. In what ways can the budgeting process create incentives for unethical behavior?

5. Kent Krause is studying for the next accounting midterm examination. Summarize for Kent what he should know about management functions.

6. "Decision making is management's most important function." Do you agree? Why or why not?

7. Explain the primary difference between line positions and staff positions, and give examples of each.

8. What new rules were enacted under the Sarbanes-Oxley Act to address unethical accounting practices?

9. Alan Bruski is studying for his next accounting examination. Explain to Alan what he should know about the differences between the income statements for a manufacturing and for a merchandising company.

10. Sandy Cesska is unclear as to the difference between the balance sheets of a merchandising company and a manufacturing company. Explain the difference to Sandy.

11. How are manufacturing costs classified?

12. Tony Siebers claims that the distinction between direct and indirect materials is based entirely on physical association with the product. Is Tony correct? Why?

13. Trenton Hipp is confused about the differences between a product cost and a period cost. Explain the differences to Trenton.

14. Identify the differences in the cost of goods sold section of an income statement between a merchandising company and a manufacturing company.

15. The determination of the cost of goods manufactured involves the following factors: (A) beginning work in process inventory, (B) total manufacturing costs, and (C) ending work in process inventory. Identify the meaning of x in the following formulas:
(a) $A + B = x$
(b) $A + B - C = x$

16. Gruber Manufacturing has beginning raw materials inventory $12,000, ending raw materials inventory $15,000, and raw materials purchases $180,000. What is the cost of direct materials used?

17. Jelk Manufacturing Inc. has beginning work in process $26,000, direct materials used $240,000, direct labor $200,000, total manufacturing overhead $150,000, and ending work in process $32,000. What are total manufacturing costs?

18. Using the data in Q17, what are (a) the total cost of work in process and (b) the cost of goods manufactured?

19. In what order should manufacturing inventories be listed in a balance sheet?

20. What is the value chain? Describe, in sequence, the main components of a manufacturer's value chain.

21. What is an enterprise resource planning (ERP) system? What are its primary benefits?

22. Why is product quality important for companies that implement a just-in-time inventory system?

23. Explain what is meant by "balanced" in the balanced scorecard approach.

24. What is activity-based costing, and what are its potential benefits?

*25. How, if at all, does the accounting cycle differ between a manufacturing company and a merchandising company?

*26. What typical account balances are carried into the cost of goods manufactured columns of the manufacturing work sheet?

*27. Prepare the closing entries for (a) ending work in process and raw materials inventories and (b) manufacturing summary. Use XXXs for amounts.

Brief Exercises

Distinguish between managerial and financial accounting.
(SO 1)

BE14-1 Complete the following comparison table between managerial and financial accounting.

	Financial Accounting	Managerial Accounting
Primary users		
Types of reports		
Frequency of reports		
Purpose of reports		
Content of reports		
Verification		

Identify important regulatory changes.
(SO 2)

BE14-2 The Sarbanes Oxley Act of 2002 (SOX) has important implications for the financial community. Explain two implications of SOX.

Identify the three management functions.
(SO 2)

BE14-3 Listed below are the three functions of the management of an organization.

1. Planning   2. Directing   3. Controlling

Identify which of the following statements best describes each of the above functions.
(a) ____ require(s) management to look ahead and to establish objectives. A key objective of management is to add value to the business.
(b) ____ involve(s) coordinating the diverse activities and human resources of a company to produce a smooth-running operation. This function relates to the implementation of planned objectives.
(c) ____ is the process of keeping the activities on track. Management must determine whether goals are being met and what changes are necessary when there are deviations.

Classify manufacturing costs.
(SO 3)

BE14-4 Determine whether each of the following costs should be classified as direct materials (DM), direct labor (DL), or manufacturing overhead (MO).
(a) ____Frames and tires used in manufacturing bicycles.
(b) ____Wages paid to production workers.
(c) ____Insurance on factory equipment and machinery.
(d) ____Depreciation on factory equipment.

Classify manufacturing costs.
(SO 3)

BE14-5 Indicate whether each of the following costs of an automobile manufacturer would be classified as direct materials, direct labor, or manufacturing overhead.
(a) ____Windshield.
(b) ____Engine.
(c) ____Wages of assembly line worker.
(d) ____Depreciation of factory machinery.
(e) ____Factory machinery lubricants.
(f) ____Tires.
(g) ____Steering wheel.
(h) ____Salary of painting supervisor.

Identify product and period costs.
(SO 4)

BE14-6 Identify whether each of the following costs should be classified as product costs or period costs.
(a) ____Manufacturing overhead.
(b) ____Selling expenses.
(c) ____Administrative expenses.
(d) ____Advertising expenses.
(e) ____Direct labor.
(f) ____Direct material.

Classify manufacturing costs.
(SO 3)

BE14-7 Presented below are Apex Company's monthly manufacturing cost data related to its personal computer products.
(a) Utilities for manufacturing equipment $116,000
(b) Raw material (CPU, chips, etc.) $85,000
(c) Depreciation on manufacturing building $880,000
(d) Wages for production workers $191,000

Enter each cost item in the following table, placing an "X" under the appropriate headings.

	Product Costs		
	Direct Materials	**Direct Labor**	**Factory Overhead**
(a)			
(b)			
(c)			
(d)			

BE14-8   Sielert Manufacturing Company has the following data: direct labor $249,000, direct materials used $180,000, total manufacturing overhead $208,000, and beginning work in process $25,000. Compute (a) total manufacturing costs and (b) total cost of work in process.

Compute total manufacturing costs and total cost of work in process.
(SO 6)

BE14-9   In alphabetical order below are current asset items for Osgood Company's balance sheet at December 31, 2007. Prepare the current assets section (including a complete heading).

Prepare current assets section.
(SO 7)

Accounts receivable	$200,000
Cash	62,000
Finished goods	71,000
Prepaid expenses	38,000
Raw materials	68,000
Work in process	87,000

BE14-10   Presented below are incomplete manufacturing cost data. Determine the missing amounts for three different situations.

Determine missing amounts in computing total manufacturing costs.
(SO 6)

	Direct Materials Used	Direct Labor Used	Factory Overhead	Total Manufacturing Costs
(1)	$35,000	$61,000	$ 50,000	?
(2)	?	$75,000	$140,000	$296,000
(3)	$55,000	?	$111,000	$300,000

BE14-11   Use the same data from BE14–10 above and the data below. Determine the missing amounts.

Determine missing amounts in computing cost of goods manufactured.
(SO 6)

	Total Manufacturing Costs	Work in Process (1/1)	Work in Process (12/31)	Cost of Goods Manufactured
(1)	?	$120,000	$82,000	?
(2)	$296,000	?	$98,000	$321,000
(3)	$300,000	$463,000	?	$715,000

*BE14-12   A work sheet is used in preparing financial statements for Table Manufacturing Company. The following accounts are included in the adjusted trial balance: Finished Goods Inventory $28,000, Work in Process Inventory $21,600, Raw Materials Purchases $175,000, and Direct Labor $140,000. Indicate the work sheet column(s) to which each account should be extended.

Identify work sheet columns for selected accounts.
(SO 8)

Exercises

E14-1   The following is a list of terms related to a company's organizational structure.

Identify positions within organizational structure.
(SO 2)

1. Board of directors.
2. Chief financial officer.
3. Treasurer.
4. Controller.
5. Line position.
6. Chief executive officer.
7. Staff position.

Instructions
Match each of the above terms with the statement below that best describes the term.

(a) ____ Employee who has overall responsibility for managing the business.
(b) ____ Employees who are directly involved in the company's primary revenue-generating activities.
(c) ____ Employee with overall responsibility for all accounting and finance issues.

(d) _____ Group of people elected by the shareholders that selects and oversees company officers and formulates operating policies.

(e) _____ Employees who provide support services to those employees who are directly involved in the company's primary revenue-generating activities.

(f) _____ Employee who maintains accounting records and system of internal controls and prepares financial statements, tax returns, and internal reports.

(g) _____ Employee who has custody of the company's funds and maintains company's cash position.

Classify costs into three classes of manufacturing costs.
(SO 3)

E14-2   Presented below is a list of costs and expenses usually incurred by Burrand Corporation, a manufacturer of furniture, in its factory.

1. Salaries for assembly line inspectors.
2. Insurance on factory machines.
3. Property taxes on the factory building.
4. Factory repairs.
5. Upholstery used in manufacturing furniture.
6. Wages paid to assembly line workers.
7. Factory machinery depreciation.
8. Glue, nails, paint, and other small parts used in production.
9. Factory supervisors' salaries.
10. Wood used in manufacturing furniture.

Instructions
Classify the above items into the following categories: (a) direct materials, (b) direct labor, and (c) manufacturing overhead.

Determine the total amount of various types of costs.
(SO 3, 4)

E14-3   Caroline Company reports the following costs and expenses in May.

Factory utilities	$ 8,500	Direct labor	$69,100
Depreciation on factory		Sales salaries	49,400
equipment	12,650	Property taxes on factory	
Depreciation on delivery trucks	3,800	building	2,500
Indirect factory labor	48,900	Repairs to office equipment	1,300
Indirect materials	80,800	Factory repairs	2,000
Direct materials used	137,600	Advertising	18,000
Factory manager's salary	8,000	Office supplies used	2,640

Instructions
From the information, determine the total amount of:
(a) Manufacturing overhead.
(b) Product costs.
(c) Period costs.

Classify various costs into different cost categories.
(SO 3, 4)

E14-4   Sota Company is a manufacturer of personal computers. Various costs and expenses associated with its operations are as follows.

1. Property taxes on the factory building.
2. Production superintendents' salaries.
3. Memory boards and chips used in assembling computers.
4. Depreciation on the factory equipment.
5. Salaries for assembly line quality control inspectors.
6. Sales commissions paid to sell personal computers.
7. Electrical components used in assembling computers.
8. Wages of workers assembling personal computers.
9. Soldering materials used on factory assembly lines.
10. Salaries for the night security guards for the factory building.

The company intends to classify these costs and expenses into the following categories:
(a) direct materials, (b) direct labor, (c) manufacturing overhead, and (d) period costs.

Instructions
List the items (1) through (10). For each item, indicate the cost category to which it belongs.

E14-5   The administrators of San Diego County's Memorial Hospital are interested in identifying the various costs and expenses that are incurred in producing a patient's X-ray. A list of such costs and expenses in presented below.

1. Salaries for the X-ray machine technicians.
2. Wages for the hospital janitorial personnel.
3. Film costs for the X-ray machines.
4. Property taxes on the hospital building.
5. Salary of the X-ray technicians' supervisor.
6. Electricity costs for the X-ray department.
7. Maintenance and repairs on the X-ray machines.
8. X-ray department supplies.
9. Depreciation on the X-ray department equipment.
10. Depreciation on the hospital building.

Classify various costs into different cost categories.
(SO 3)

Homework materials related to **service companies** are indicated by this icon.

The administrators want these costs and expenses classified as: (a) direct materials, (b) direct labor, or (c) service overhead.

Instructions
List the items (1) through (10). For each item, indicate the cost category to which the item belongs.

E14-6   Rapid Delivery Service reports the following costs and expenses in June 2007.

Indirect materials	$ 5,400	Drivers' salaries	$ 8,000
Depreciation on delivery		Advertising	1,600
equipment	11,200	Delivery equipment	
Dispatcher's salary	5,000	repairs	300
Property taxes on office		Office supplies	650
building	870	Office utilities	990
CEO's salary	10,000	Repairs on office	
Gas and oil for delivery trucks	2,200	equipment	180

Classify various costs into different cost categories.
(SO 4)

Instructions
Determine the total amount of (a) delivery service (product) costs and (b) period costs.

E14-7   An incomplete cost of goods manufactured schedule is presented below.

Determine missing amounts in cost of goods manufactured schedule.
(SO 6)

MADLOCK MANUFACTURING COMPANY
Cost of Goods Manufactured Schedule
For the Year Ended December 31, 2007

Work in process (1/1)			$210,000
Direct materials			
Raw materials inventory (1/1)	$?		
Add: Raw materials purchases	158,000		
Total raw materials available for use	?		
Less: Raw materials inventory (12/31)	7,500		
Direct materials used		$190,000	
Direct labor		?	
Manufacturing overhead			
Indirect labor	$ 18,000		
Factory depreciation	36,000		
Factory utilities	68,000		
Total overhead		122,000	
Total manufacturing costs			?
Total cost of work in process			?
Less: Work in process (12/31)			81,000
Cost of goods manufactured			$530,000

Instructions
Complete the cost of goods manufactured schedule for Madlock Manufacturing Company.

Determine the missing amount of different cost items.
(SO 6)

E14-8 Manufacturing cost data for Darlinda Company are presented below.

	Case A	Case B	Case C
Direct materials used	(a)	$68,400	$130,000
Direct labor	$ 57,000	86,000	(g)
Manufacturing overhead	46,500	81,600	102,000
Total manufacturing costs	180,650	(d)	253,700
Work in process 1/1/07	(b)	16,500	(h)
Total cost of work in process	221,500	(e)	327,000
Work in process 12/31/07	(c)	11,000	70,000
Cost of goods manufactured	185,275	(f)	(i)

Instructions

Indicate the missing amount for each letter (a) through (i).

Determine the missing amount of different cost items, and prepare a condensed cost of goods manufactured schedule.
(SO 6)

E14-9 Incomplete manufacturing cost data for Motta Company for 2007 are presented as follows for four different situations.

	Direct Materials Used	Direct Labor Used	Manufacturing Overhead	Total Manufacturing Costs	Work in Process 1/1	Work in Process 12/31	Cost of Goods Manufactured
(1)	$117,000	$140,000	$ 77,000	(a)	$33,000	(b)	$360,000
(2)	(c)	200,000	132,000	$440,000	(d)	$40,000	470,000
(3)	80,000	100,000	(e)	255,000	60,000	80,000	(f)
(4)	70,000	(g)	75,000	288,000	45,000	(h)	270,000

Instructions

(a) Indicate the missing amount for each letter.

(b) Prepare a condensed cost of goods manufactured schedule for situation (1) for the year ended December 31, 2007.

Prepare a cost of goods manufactured schedule and a partial income statement.
(SO 5, 6)

E14-10 Berger Corporation has the following cost records for June 2007.

Indirect factory labor	$ 4,500	Factory utilities	$ 400
Direct materials used	20,000	Depreciation, factory equipment	1,400
Work in process, 6/1/07	3,000	Direct labor	25,000
Work in process, 6/30/07	3,800	Maintenance, factory equipment	1,800
Finished goods, 6/1/07	5,000	Indirect materials	2,200
Finished goods, 6/30/07	7,500	Factory manager's salary	3,000

Instructions

(a) Prepare a cost of goods manufactured schedule for June 2007.

(b) Prepare an income statement through gross profit for June 2007 assuming net sales are $97,100.

Classify various costs into different categories and prepare cost of services provided schedule.
(SO 4, 5, 6)

E14-11 Jill Blinton, the bookkeeper for Dewey, Cheatum, and Howe, a political consulting firm, has recently completed a managerial accounting course at her local college. One of the topics covered in the course was the cost of goods manufactured schedule. Jill wondered if such a schedule could be prepared for her firm. She realized that, as a service-oriented company, it would have no Work-in-Process inventory to consider.

Listed below are the costs her firm incurred for the month ended August 31, 2007.

Supplies used on consulting contracts	$ 1,200
Supplies used in the administrative offices	1,500
Depreciation on equipment used for contract work	900
Depreciation used on administrative office equipment	1,050
Salaries of professionals working on contracts	12,600
Salaries of administrative office personnel	7,700
Janitorial services for professional offices	400
Janitorial services for administrative offices	500
Insurance on contract operations	800
Insurance on administrative operations	900
Utilities for contract operations	1,100
Utilities for administrative offices	1,300

Instructions
(a) Prepare a schedule of cost of contract services provided (similar to a cost of goods manufactured schedule) for the month.
(b) For those costs not included in (a), explain how they would be classified and reported in the financial statements.

E14-12 Marla Manufacturing Company produces blankets. From its accounting records it prepares the following schedule and financial statements on a yearly basis.
(a) Cost of goods manufactured schedule.
(b) Income statement.
(c) Balance sheet.

Indicate in which schedule or financial statement(s) different cost items will appear.
(SO 5, 6, 7)

The following items are found in its ledger and accompanying data.

1. Direct labor
2. Raw materials inventory, 1/1
3. Work in process inventory, 12/31
4. Finished goods inventory, 1/1
5. Indirect labor
6. Depreciation on factory machinery
7. Work in process, 1/1
8. Finished goods inventory, 12/31
9. Factory maintenance salaries
10. Cost of goods manufactured
11. Depreciation on delivery equipment
12. Cost of goods available for sale
13. Direct materials used
14. Heat and electricity for factory
15. Repairs to roof of factory building
16. Cost of raw materials purchases

Instructions
List the items (1)–(16). For each item, indicate by using the appropriate letter or letters, the schedule and/or financial statement(s) in which the item will appear.

E14-13 An analysis of the accounts of Yellowknife Manufacturing reveals the following manufacturing cost data for the month ended June 30, 2007.

Prepare a cost of goods manufactured schedule, and present the ending inventories of the balance sheet.
(SO 6, 7)

Inventories	Beginning	Ending
Raw materials	$9,000	$13,100
Work in process	5,000	8,000
Finished goods	9,000	6,000

Costs incurred: Raw materials purchases $64,000, direct labor $57,000, manufacturing overhead $19,900. The specific overhead costs were: indirect labor $5,500, factory insurance $4,000, machinery depreciation $4,000, machinery repairs $1,800, factory utilities $3,100, miscellaneous factory costs $1,500. Assume that all raw materials used were direct materials.

Instructions
(a) Prepare the cost of goods manufactured schedule for the month ended June 30, 2007.
(b) Show the presentation of the ending inventories on the June 30, 2007, balance sheet.

E14-14 Kam Motor Company manufactures automobiles. During September 2007 the company purchased 5,000 head lamps at a cost of $9 per lamp. Kam withdrew 4,650 lamps from the warehouse during the month. Fifty of these lamps were used to replace the head lamps in autos used by traveling sales staff. The remaining 4,600 lamps were put in autos manufactured during the month.

Determine the amount of cost to appear in various accounts, and indicate in which financial statements these accounts would appear.
(SO 5, 6, 7)

Of the autos put into production during September 2007, 90% were completed and transferred to the company's storage lot. Of the cars completed during the month, 75% were sold by September 30.

Instructions
(a) Determine the cost of head lamps that would appear in each of the following accounts at September 30, 2007: Raw Materials, Work in Process, Finished Goods, Cost of Goods Sold, and Selling Expenses.
(b) ▐▐▐⇒ Write a short memo to the chief accountant, indicating whether and where each of the accounts in (a) would appear on the income statement or on the balance sheet at September 30, 2007.

E14-15 The following is a list of terms related to managerial accounting practices.

Identify various managerial accounting practices.
(SO 8)

1. Theory of constraints.
2. Activity-based costing.
3. Just-in-time inventory.

4. Balanced scorecard.
5. Value chain.
6. Enterprise resource planning (ERP).

Instructions
Match each of the terms with the statement below that best describes the term.

(a) ____ A system that provides a comprehensive, centralized, integrated source of information used to manage all major business processes.
(b) ____ The group of activities associated with providing a product or service.
(c) ____ An approach used to reduce the cost associated with handling and holding inventory by reducing the amount of inventory on hand.
(d) ____ A method used to allocate overhead to products based on each product's use of the activities that cause the incurrence of the overhead cost.
(e) ____ An approach used to identify those factors that limit a company's productive capacity and to address those limitations so as to maximize profitability.
(f) ____ A performance-measurement technique that attempts to consider and evaluate all aspects of performance using financial and nonfinancial measures in an integrated fashion.

Prepare a partial worksheet for a manufacturing firm.
(SO 9)

*E14-16 Data for Yellowknife Manufacturing are presented in E14-13.

Instructions
Beginning with the adjusted trial balance, prepare a partial work sheet for Yellowknife Manufacturing using the format shown in Illustration 14A-2.

Problems: Set A

Classify manufacturing costs into different categories and compute the unit cost.
(SO 3, 4)

P14-1A Lair Company specializes in manufacturing motorcycle helmets. The company has enough orders to keep the factory production at 1,000 motorcycle helmets per month. Lair's monthly manufacturing cost and other expense data are as follows.

Maintenance costs on factory building	$ 300
Factory manager's salary	4,000
Advertising for helmets	10,000
Sales commissions	3,000
Depreciation on factory building	700
Rent on factory equipment	6,000
Insurance on factory building	3,000
Raw materials (plastic, polystyrene, etc.)	20,000
Utility costs for factory	800
Supplies for general office	200
Wages for assembly line workers	44,000
Depreciation on office equipment	500
Miscellaneous materials (glue, thread, etc.)	2,000

Instructions

(a) Prepare an answer sheet with the following column headings.

(a) DM $20,000
    DL $44,000
    MO $16,800
    PC $13,700

	Product Costs			
Cost Item	**Direct Materials**	**Direct Labor**	**Manufacturing Overhead**	**Period Costs**

Enter each cost item on your answer sheet, placing the dollar amount under the appropriate headings. Total the dollar amounts in each of the columns.
(b) Compute the cost to produce one motorcycle helmet.

Classify manufacturing costs into different categories and compute the unit cost.
(SO 3, 4)

P14-2A Tomlin Company, a manufacturer of tennis rackets, started production in November 2007. For the preceding 5 years Tomlin had been a retailer of sports equipment. After a thorough survey of tennis racket markets, Tomlin decided to turn its retail store into a tennis racket factory.

Raw materials cost for a tennis racket will total $23 per racket. Workers on the production lines are paid on average $13 per hour. A racket usually takes 2 hours to complete. In addition, the rent on the equipment used to produce rackets amounts to $1,300 per month. Indirect materials cost $3 per racket. A supervisor was hired to oversee production; her monthly salary is $3,500.

Janitorial costs are $1,400 monthly. Advertising costs for the rackets will be $6,000 per month. The factory building depreciation expense is $8,400 per year. Property taxes on the factory building will be $4,320 per year.

Instructions
(a) Prepare an answer sheet with the following column headings.

(a) DM $46,000
DL $52,000
MO $13,260
PC $ 6,000

Cost Item	Product Costs			Period Costs
	Direct Materials	Direct Labor	Manufacturing Overhead	

Assuming that Tomlin manufactures, on average, 2,000 tennis rackets per month, enter each cost item on your answer sheet, placing the dollar amount per month under the appropriate headings. Total the dollar amounts in each of the columns.
(b) Compute the cost to produce one racket.

P14-3A Incomplete manufacturing costs, expenses, and selling data for two different cases are as follows.

Indicate the missing amount of different cost items, and prepare a condensed cost of goods manufactured schedule, an income statement, and a partial balance sheet.
(SO 5, 6, 7)

	Case	
	1	2
Direct Materials Used	$ 8,300	$ (g)
Direct Labor	3,000	4,000
Manufacturing Overhead	6,000	5,000
Total Manufacturing Costs	(a)	20,000
Beginning Work in Process Inventory	1,000	(h)
Ending Work in Process Inventory	(b)	2,000
Sales	22,500	(i)
Sales Discounts	1,500	1,200
Cost of Goods Manufactured	15,800	21,000
Beginning Finished Goods Inventory	(c)	4,000
Goods Available for Sale	17,300	(j)
Cost of Goods Sold	(d)	(k)
Ending Finished Goods Inventory	1,200	2,500
Gross Profit	(e)	6,000
Operating Expenses	2,700	(l)
Net Income	(f)	3,200

Instructions
(a) Indicate the missing amount for each letter.
(b) Prepare a condensed cost of goods manufactured schedule for Case 1.
(c) Prepare an income statement and the current assets section of the balance sheet for Case 1. Assume that in Case 1 the other items in the current assets section are as follows: Cash $3,000, Receivables (net) $10,000, Raw Materials $700, and Prepaid Expenses $200.

(c) Current assets $17,600

P14-4A The following data were taken from the records of Cruz Manufacturing Company for the year ended December 31, 2007.

Prepare a cost of goods manufactured schedule, a partial income statement, and a partial balance sheet.
(SO 5, 6, 7)

Raw Materials		Factory Insurance	$ 7,400
Inventory 1/1/07	$ 47,000	Factory Machinery	
Raw Materials		Depreciation	7,700
Inventory 12/31/07	44,200	Factory Utilities	12,900
Finished Goods		Office Utilities Expense	8,600
Inventory 1/1/07	85,000	Sales	475,000
Finished Goods			
Inventory 12/31/07	77,800		

Work in Process		Sales Discounts	2,500
Inventory 1/1/07	9,500	Plant Manager's Salary	30,000
Work in Process		Factory Property Taxes	6,100
Inventory 12/31/07	8,000	Factory Repairs	800
Direct Labor	145,100	Raw Materials Purchases	67,500
Indirect Labor	18,100	Cash	28,000
Accounts Receivable	27,000		

Instructions

(a) CGM $299,900
(b) Gross profit $165,400
(c) Current assets $185,000

(a) Prepare a cost of goods manufactured schedule. (Assume all raw materials used were direct materials.)
(b) Prepare an income statement through gross profit.
(c) Prepare the current assets section of the balance sheet at December 31.

Prepare a cost of goods manufactured schedule and a correct income statement. (SO 5, 6)

P14-5A   Agler Company is a manufacturer of toys. Its controller, Joyce Rotzen, resigned in August 2007. An inexperienced assistant accountant has prepared the following income statement for the month of August 2007.

AGLER COMPANY
Income Statement
For the Month Ended August 31, 2007

Sales (net)		$675,000
Less: Operating expenses		
Raw materials purchases	$200,000	
Direct labor cost	160,000	
Advertising expense	75,000	
Selling and administrative salaries	70,000	
Rent on factory facilities	60,000	
Depreciation on sales equipment	50,000	
Depreciation on factory equipment	35,000	
Indirect labor cost	20,000	
Utilities expense	10,000	
Insurance expense	5,000	685,000
Net loss		$ (10,000)

Prior to August 2007 the company had been profitable every month. The company's president is concerned about the accuracy of the income statement. As her friend, you have been asked to review the income statement and make necessary corrections. After examining other manufacturing cost data, you have acquired additional information as follows.

1. Inventory balances at the beginning and end of August were:

	August 1	**August 31**
Raw materials	$19,500	$30,000
Work in process	25,000	21,000
Finished goods	40,000	64,000

2. Only 60% of the utilities expense and 70% of the insurance expense apply to factory operations; the remaining amounts should be charged to selling and administrative activities.

Instructions

(a) CGM $478,000
(b) NI $ 20,500

(a) Prepare a cost of goods manufactured schedule for August 2007.
(b) Prepare a correct income statement for August 2007.

*P14-6A**   Medina Manufacturing Company uses a simple manufacturing accounting system. At the end of its fiscal year on August 31, 2007, the adjusted trial balance contains the following accounts.

Complete a work sheet;
prepare a cost of goods
manufactured schedule, an
income statement, and a
balance sheet; journalize and
post the closing entries.
(SO 9)

Debits			Credits	
Cash	$ 16,700		Accumulated Depreciation	$353,000
Accounts Receivable (net)	62,900		Notes Payable	45,000
Finished Goods Inventory	56,000		Accounts Payable	36,200
Work in Process Inventory	27,800		Income Taxes Payable	9,000
Raw Materials Inventory	37,200		Common Stock	352,000
Plant Assets	890,000		Retained Earnings	205,300
Raw Materials Purchases	236,500		Sales	998,000
Direct Labor	283,900			
Indirect Labor	27,400			$1,998,500
Factory Repairs	17,200			
Factory Depreciation	16,000			
Factory Manager's Salary	40,000			
Factory Insurance	11,000			
Factory Property Taxes	14,900			
Factory Utilities	13,300			
Selling Expenses	96,500			
Administrative Expenses	115,200			
Income Tax Expense	36,000			
	$1,998,500			

Physical inventory accounts on August 31, 2007, show the following inventory amounts:
Finished Goods $50,600, Work in Process $23,400, and Raw Materials $44,500.

Instructions
(a) Enter the adjusted trial balance data on a work sheet in financial statement order
and complete the work sheet.
(b) Prepare a cost of goods manufactured schedule for the year.
(c) Prepare an income statement for the year and a balance sheet at August 31, 2007.
(d) Journalize the closing entries.
(e) Post the closing entries to Manufacturing Summary and to Income Summary.

(b) CGM $657,300
(c) NI $ 87,600

Problems: Set B

P14-1B   Bjerg Company specializes in manufacturing a unique model of bicycle
helmet. The model is well accepted by consumers, and the company has enough orders to keep the factory production at 10,000 helmets per month (80% of its full capacity). Bjerg's monthly manufacturing cost and other expense data are as follows.

Classify manufacturing costs
into different categories and
compute the unit cost.
(SO 3, 4)

Rent on factory equipment	$ 7,000
Insurance on factory building	1,500
Raw materials (plastics, polystyrene, etc.)	75,000
Utility costs for factory	900
Supplies for general office	300
Wages for assembly line workers	43,000
Depreciation on office equipment	800
Miscellaneous materials (glue, thread, etc.)	1,100
Factory manager's salary	5,700
Property taxes on factory building	400
Advertising for helmets	14,000
Sales commissions	7,000
Depreciation on factory building	1,500

Instructions
(a) Prepare an answer sheet with the following column headings.

(a) DM $75,000
DL $43,000
MO $18,100
PC $22,100

	Product Costs			
Cost Item	Direct Materials	Direct Labor	Manufacturing Overhead	Period Costs

Enter each cost item on your answer sheet, placing the dollar amount under the appropriate headings. Total the dollar amounts in each of the columns.

(b) Compute the cost to produce one helmet

Classify manufacturing costs into different categories and compute the unit cost.
(SO 3, 4)

P14-2B Copa Company, a manufacturer of stereo systems, started its production in October 2007. For the preceding 3 years Copa had been a retailer of stereo systems. After a thorough survey of stereo system markets, Copa decided to turn its retail store into a stereo equipment factory.

Raw materials cost for a stereo system will total $74 per unit. Workers on the production lines are on average paid $12 per hour. A stereo system usually takes 5 hours to complete. In addition, the rent on the equipment used to assemble stereo systems amounts to $4,900 per month. Indirect materials cost $5 per system. A supervisor was hired to oversee production; her monthly salary is $3,000.

Janitorial costs are $1,300 monthly. Advertising costs for the stereo system will be $8,500 per month. The factory building depreciation expense is $7,200 per year. Property taxes on the factory building will be $9,000 per year.

Instructions

(a) DM $96,200
DL $78,000
MO $17,050
PC $ 8,500

(a) Prepare an answer sheet with the following column headings.

	Product Costs			
Cost Item	Direct Materials	Direct Labor	Manufacturing Overhead	Period Costs

Assuming that Copa manufactures, on average, 1,300 stereo systems per month, enter each cost item on your answer sheet, placing the dollar amount per month under the appropriate headings. Total the dollar amounts in each of the columns.

(b) Compute the cost to produce one stereo system.

Indicate the missing amount of different cost items, and prepare a condensed cost of goods manufactured schedule, an income statement, and a partial balance sheet.
(SO 5, 6, 7)

P14-3B Incomplete manufacturing costs, expenses, and selling data for two different cases are as follows.

	Case	
	1	2
Direct Materials Used	$ 7,600	$ (g)
Direct Labor	5,000	8,000
Manufacturing Overhead	8,000	4,000
Total Manufacturing Costs	(a)	18,000
Beginning Work in Process Inventory	1,000	(h)
Ending Work in Process Inventory	(b)	3,000
Sales	24,500	(i)
Sales Discounts	2,500	1,400
Cost of Goods Manufactured	17,000	22,000
Beginning Finished Goods Inventory	(c)	3,300
Goods Available for Sale	18,000	(j)
Cost of Goods Sold	(d)	(k)
Ending Finished Goods Inventory	3,400	2,500
Gross Profit	(e)	7,000
Operating Expenses	2,500	(l)
Net Income	(f)	5,000

Instructions

(a) Indicate the missing amount for each letter.

(b) Prepare a condensed cost of goods manufactured schedule for Case 1.

(c) Current assets $28,000

(c) Prepare an income statement and the current assets section of the balance sheet for Case 1. Assume that in Case 1 the other items in the current assets section are as follows: Cash $4,000, Receivables (net) $15,000, Raw Materials $600, and Prepaid Expenses $400.

P14-4B The following data were taken from the records of Stellar Manufacturing Company for the fiscal year ended June 30, 2007.

Raw Materials		Factory Insurance	$ 4,600	
Inventory 7/1/06	$ 48,000	Factory Machinery		
Raw Materials		Depreciation	16,000	
Inventory 6/30/07	39,600	Factory Utilities	27,600	
Finished Goods		Office Utilities Expense	8,650	
Inventory 7/1/06	96,000	Sales	554,000	
Finished Goods		Sales Discounts	4,200	
Inventory 6/30/07	95,900	Plant Manager's Salary	29,000	
Work in Process		Factory Property Taxes	9,600	
Inventory 7/1/06	19,800	Factory Repairs	1,400	
Work in Process		Raw Materials Purchases	96,400	
Inventory 6/30/07	18,600	Cash	32,000	
Direct Labor	149,250			
Indirect Labor	24,460			
Accounts Receivable	27,000			

Prepare a cost of goods manufactured schedule, a partial income statement, and a partial balance sheet.
(SO 5, 6, 7)

Instructions

(a) Prepare a cost of goods manufactured schedule. (Assume all raw materials used were direct materials.)

(b) Prepare an income statement through gross profit.

(c) Prepare the current assets section of the balance sheet at June 30, 2007.

(a) CGM $367,910

(b) Gross profit $181,790
(c) Current assets $213,100

P14-5B Tombert Company is a manufacturer of computers. Its controller resigned in October 2007. An inexperienced assistant accountant has prepared the following income statement for the month of October 2007.

Prepare a cost of goods manufactured schedule and a correct income statement.
(SO 5, 6)

TOMBERT COMPANY
Income Statement
For the Month Ended October 31, 2007

Sales (net)		$780,000
Less: Operating expenses		
Raw materials purchases	$264,000	
Direct labor cost	190,000	
Advertising expense	90,000	
Selling and administrative salaries	75,000	
Rent on factory facilities	60,000	
Depreciation on sales equipment	45,000	
Depreciation on factory equipment	31,000	
Indirect labor cost	28,000	
Utilities expense	12,000	
Insurance expense	8,000	803,000
Net loss		$(23,000)

Prior to October 2007 the company had been profitable every month. The company's president is concerned about the accuracy of the income statement. As his friend, you have been asked to review the income statement and make necessary corrections. After examining other manufacturing cost data, you have acquired additional information as follows.

1. Inventory balances at the beginning and end of October were:

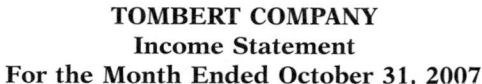

	October 1	October 31
Raw materials	$18,000	$34,000
Work in process	16,000	14,000
Finished goods	30,000	48,000

2. Only 70% of the utilities expense and 60% of the insurance expense apply to factory operations. The remaining amounts should be charged to selling and administrative activities.

Instructions

(a) Prepare a schedule of cost of goods manufactured for October 2007.

(b) Prepare a correct income statement for October 2007.

(a) CGM $572,200
(b) NI $ 9,000

Problems: Set C

Visit the book's website at **www.wiley.com/college/kimmel** and choose the Student Companion site to access Problem Set C.

▶ BROADENING YOUR PERSPECTIVE

Group Decision Case

BYP14-1   Mismatch Manufacturing Company specializes in producing fashion outfits. On July 31, 2007, a tornado touched down at its factory and general office. The inventories in the warehouse and the factory were completely destroyed as was the general office nearby. Next morning, through a careful search of the disaster site, however, Ross Clarkson, the company's controller, and Catherine Harper, the cost accountant, were able to recover a small part of manufacturing cost data for the current month.

"What a horrible experience," sighed Ross. "And the worst part is that we may not have enough records to use in filing an insurance claim."

"It was terrible," replied Catherine. "However, I managed to recover some of the manufacturing cost data that I was working on yesterday afternoon. The data indicate that our direct labor cost in July totaled $240,000 and that we had purchased $345,000 of raw materials. Also, I recall that the amount of raw materials used for July was $350,000. But I'm not sure this information will help. The rest of our records are blown away."

"Well, not exactly," said Ross. "I was working on the year-to-date income statement when the tornado warning was announced. My recollection is that our sales in July were $1,260,000 and our gross profit ratio has been 40% of sales. Also, I can remember that our cost of goods available for sale was $770,000 for July."

"Maybe we can work something out from this information!" exclaimed Catherine. "My experience tells me that our manufacturing overhead is usually 60% of direct labor."

"Hey, look what I just found," cried Catherine. "It's a copy of this June's balance sheet, and it shows that our inventories as of June 30 are Finished goods $38,000, Work in process $25,000, and Raw materials $19,000."

"Super," yelled Ross. "Let's go work something out."

In order to file an insurance claim, Mismatch Company must determine the amount of its inventories as of July 31, 2007, the date of the tornado touchdown.

Instructions
With the class divided into groups, determine the amount of cost in the Raw Materials, Work in Process, and Finished Goods inventory accounts as of the date of the tornado touchdown.

Managerial Analysis

BYP14-2   Love All is a fairly large manufacturing company located in the southern United States. The company manufactures tennis rackets, tennis balls, tennis clothing, and tennis shoes, all bearing the company's distinctive logo, a large green question mark on a white flocked tennis ball. The company's sales have been increasing over the past 10 years.

The tennis racket division has recently implemented several advanced manufacturing techniques. Robot arms hold the tennis rackets in place while glue dries, and machine vision systems check for defects. The engineering and design team uses computerized drafting and testing of new products. The following managers work in the tennis racket division.

Andre Agassi, Sales Manager (supervises all sales representatives).
Serena Williams, technical specialist (supervises computer programmers).
Pete Sampras, cost accounting manager (supervises cost accountants).
Andy Roddick, production supervisor (supervises all manufacturing employees).
Venus Williams, engineer (supervises all new-product design teams).

Instructions
(a) What are the primary information needs of each manager?
(b) Which, if any, financial accounting report(s) is each likely to use?
(c) Name one special-purpose management accounting report that could be designed for each manager. Include the name of the report, the information it would contain, and how frequently it should be issued.

Real-World Focus

BYP14-3 Anchor Glass Container Corporation, the third largest manufacturer of glass containers in the U.S., supplies beverage and food producers and consumer products manufacturers nationwide. Parent company Consumers Packaging Inc. *(Toronto Stock Exchange:* CGC) is a leading international designer and manufacturer of glass containers.

The following management discussion appeared in a recent annual report of Anchor Glass.

ANCHOR GLASS CONTAINER CORPORATION
Management Discussion

Cost of Products Sold Cost of products sold as a percentage of net sales was 89.3% in the current year compared to 87.6% in the prior year. The increase in cost of products sold as a percentage of net sales principally reflected the impact of operational problems during the second quarter of the current year at a major furnace at one of the Company's plants, higher downtime, and costs and expenses associated with an increased number of scheduled capital improvement projects, increases in labor, and certain other manufacturing costs (with no corresponding selling price increases in the current year). Reduced fixed costs from the closing of the Streator, Illinois, plant in June of the current year and productivity and efficiency gains partially offset these cost increases.

Instructions
What factors affect the costs of products sold at Anchor Glass Container Corporation?

Exploring the Web

BYP14-4 The Institute of Management Accountants (IMA) is an organization dedicated to excellence in the practice of management accounting and financial management.

Address: **www.imanet.org** (or go to **www.wiley.com/college/kimmel**)

Instructions
At the IMA's home page, locate the answers to the following questions.
(a) How many members does the IMA have, and what are their job titles?
(b) What are some of the benefits of joining the IMA as a student?
(c) Use the chapter locator function to locate the IMA chapter nearest you, and find the name of the chapter president.

Communication Activity

BYP14-5 Refer to Problem 14–5A and add the following requirement.
Prepare a letter to the president of the company, Sue Agler, describing the changes you made. Explain clearly why net income is different after the changes. Keep the following points in mind as you compose your letter.

1. This is a letter to the president of a company, who is your friend. The style should be generally formal, but you may relax some requirements. For example, you may call the president by her first name.

2. Executives are very busy. Your letter should tell the president your main results first (for example, the amount of net income).

3. You should include brief explanations so that the president can understand the changes you made in the calculations.

Research Assignment

BYP14-6 The March 26, 2004, issue of the *Wall Street Journal* includes an article by Gabriel Kahn titled "Tiger's New Threads." The article discusses a unique approach employed by a company in the textile industry.

Instructions
Read the article and answer the following questions.
(a) Why is Esquel Group able to produce a new product faster than its competitors?
(b) Why did Esquel's client list change as it adopted this new approach?
(c) Are there any risks associated with this approach?

Ethics Case

BYP14-7 Wayne Terrago, controller for Robbin Industries, was reviewing production cost reports for the year. One amount in these reports continued to bother him—advertising. During the year, the company had instituted an expensive advertising campaign to sell some of its slower-moving products. It was still too early to tell whether the advertising campaign was successful.

There had been much internal debate as how to report advertising cost. The vice president of finance argued that advertising costs should be reported as a cost of production, just like direct materials and direct labor. He therefore recommended that this cost be identified as manufacturing overhead and reported as part of inventory costs until sold. Others disagreed. Terrago believed that this cost should be reported as an expense of the current period, based on the conservatism principle. Others argued that it should be reported as Prepaid Advertising and reported as a current asset.

The president finally had to decide the issue. He argued that these costs should be reported as inventory. His arguments were practical ones. He noted that the company was experiencing financial difficulty and expensing this amount in the current period might jeopardize a planned bond offering. Also, by reporting the advertising costs as inventory rather than as prepaid advertising, less attention would be directed to it by the financial community.

Instructions
(a) Who are the stakeholders in this situation?
(b) What are the ethical issues involved in this situation?
(c) What would you do if you were Wayne Terrago?

Answers to Self-Study Questions

1. b   2. b   3. b   4. c   5. d   6. a   7. c   8. a   9. d   10. d

CHAPTER 15

Job Order Costing

STUDY OBJECTIVES

After studying this chapter,
you should be able to:

1 Explain the characteristics and purposes of cost accounting.

2 Describe the flow of costs in a job order cost accounting system.

3 Explain the nature and importance of a job cost sheet.

4 Indicate how the predetermined overhead rate is determined and used.

5 Prepare entries for jobs completed and sold.

6 Distinguish between under- and over-applied manufacturing overhead.

 THE NAVIGATOR

✓ THE NAVIGATOR

- Scan *Study Objectives* ⬭
- Read *Feature Story* ⬭
- Read *Preview* ⬭
- Read text and answer *Before You Go On*
  p. 756 ⬭ p. 767 ⬭ p. 773 ⬭
- Work *Using the Decision Toolkit* ⬭
- Review *Summary of Study Objectives* ⬭
- Work *Demonstration Problem* ⬭
- Answer *Self-Study Questions* ⬭
- Complete *Assignments* ⬭

FEATURE STORY

" . . . And We'd Like It in Red"

Western States Fire Apparatus, Inc., of Cornelius, Oregon, is one of the few U.S. companies that makes fire trucks. The company builds about 25 trucks per year. Founded in 1941, the company is run by the children and grandchildren of the original founder.

"We buy the chassis, which is the cab and the frame," says Susan Scott, the company's bookkeeper. "In our computer, we set up an account into which all of the direct material that is purchased for that particular job is charged." Other direct materials include the water pump—which can cost $10,000—the lights, the siren, ladders, and hoses.

As for direct labor, the production workers fill out time tickets that tell what jobs they worked on. Usually, the company is building four trucks at any one time. On payday, the controller allocates the payroll to the appropriate job record.

Indirect materials, such as nuts and bolts, wiring, lubricants, and abrasives, are allocated to each job in proportion to direct material dollars. Other costs, such as insurance and supervisors' salaries, are allocated based on direct labor hours. "We need to allocate overhead in order to know what kind of price we have to charge when we submit our bids," she says.

Western gets orders through a "blind-bidding" process. That is, Western submits its bid without knowing the bid prices made by its competitors. "If we bid too low, we won't make a profit. If we bid too high, we don't get the job."

Regardless of the final price for the truck, the quality had better be first-rate. "The fire departments let you know if they don't like what you did, and you usually end up fixing it."

The Feature Story about Western States Fire Apparatus described the manufacturing costs used in making a fire truck. It demonstrated that accurate costing is critical to the company's success. For example, in order to submit accurate bids on new jobs and to know whether it profited from past jobs, the company needs a good costing system. This chapter illustrates how these manufacturing costs would be assigned to specific jobs, such as the manufacture of individual fire trucks. We begin the discussion in this chapter with an overview of the flow of costs in a job order cost accounting system. We then use a case study to explain and illustrate the documents, entries, and accounts in this type of cost accounting system.

The content and organization of Chapter 15 are as follows.

Cost Accounting Systems

STUDY OBJECTIVE

1

Explain the characteristics and purposes of cost accounting.

Cost accounting involves the measuring, recording, and reporting of product costs. From the data accumulated, both the total cost and the unit cost of each product are determined. The accuracy of the product cost information produced by the cost accounting system is critical to the success of the company. As you will see in later chapters, this information is used to determine which products to produce, what price to charge, and the amounts to produce. Accurate product cost information is also vital for effective evaluation of employee performance.

A **cost accounting system** consists of accounts for the various manufacturing costs. These accounts are fully integrated into the general ledger of a company. **An important feature of a cost accounting system is the use of a perpetual inventory system.** Such a system **provides immediate, up-to-date information on the cost of a product**. There are two basic types of cost accounting systems: (1) a job order cost system and (2) a process cost system. Although cost accounting systems differ widely from company to company, most are based on one of these two traditional product costing systems.

JOB ORDER COST SYSTEM

Under a **job order cost system**, costs are assigned to each **job** or to each **batch** of goods. An example of a job would be the manufacture of a mainframe computer by IBM, the production of a movie by Disney, or the making of a fire truck by Western States. An example of a batch would be the printing of 225 wedding invitations by a local print shop, or the printing of a weekly issue of *Fortune* magazine by a hi-tech printer such as Quad Graphics. Jobs or batches may be completed to fill a specific customer order or to replenish inventory.

An important feature of job order costing is that each job (or batch) has its own distinguishing characteristics. For example, each house is custom built, each consulting engagement by a CPA firm is unique, and each printing job is different. **The objective is to compute the cost per job.** At each point in the manufacturing of a product or the providing of a service, the job and its associated costs can be identified. A job order cost system measures costs for each completed job, rather than for set time periods. The recording of costs in a job order cost system is shown in Illustration 15-1.

Illustration 15-1   Job order cost system

Job Order Cost System
Two jobs: Wedding Invitations and Menus

Black ink $ — Typesetting $ — 225 Invitations $ — 225 Envelopes $ — Vellum stock, pure white $

Job # 9501

Typesetting $ — Lamination $ — MENU — Colored ink $ — Yellow stock $ — 50 Copies $

Job # 9502

Each job has distinguishing characteristics and related costs.

PROCESS COST SYSTEM

A **process cost system** is used when a large volume of similar products are manufactured. Production is continuous to ensure that adequate inventories of the finished product(s) are on hand. A process cost system is used in the manufacture of cereal by Kellogg, the refining of petroleum by ExxonMobil, and the production of automobiles by General Motors. Process costing accumulates product-related costs **for a period of time** (such as a week or a month) instead of assigning costs to specific products or job orders. In process costing, the costs are assigned to departments or processes for a set period of time. The recording of costs in a process cost system is shown in Illustration 15-2. The process cost system will be discussed further in Chapter 16.

Illustration 15-2   Process cost system

Process Cost System
Compact Disc Production

1. Oil is pumped.   2. Benzene is removed.   3. The benzene is made into pellets...   4. ...from which compact discs are produced.

Similar products are produced over a specified time period.

A company may use both types of cost systems. For example, General Motors uses process cost accounting for its standard model cars, such as Saturns and Corvettes, and job order cost accounting for a custom-made limousine for the President of the United States. The objective of both systems is to provide unit cost information for product pricing, cost control, inventory valuation, and financial statement presentation. End-of-period inventory values are computed by using unit cost data.

Business Insight
Management Perspective

Many companies suffer from poor cost accounting. As a result, they sometimes make products they ought not to be selling at all and buy others that they could more profitably make themselves. Also, inaccurate cost data lead companies to misallocate capital and frustrate efforts by plant managers to improve efficiency.

For example, consider the case of a diversified company in the business of rebuilding diesel locomotives. The managers thought they were making money, but a consulting firm found that costs had been seriously underestimated. The company bailed out of the business, and not a moment too soon. Says the consultant who advised the company, "The more contracts it won, the more money it lost." Given that situation, a company cannot stay in business very long!

BEFORE YOU GO ON . . .

▶Review It

1. What is cost accounting?
2. What does a cost accounting system consist of?
3. How does a job order cost system differ from a process cost system?

Job Order Cost Flow

STUDY OBJECTIVE
2

Describe the flow of costs in a job order cost accounting system.

The flow of costs (direct materials, direct labor, and manufacturing overhead) in job order cost accounting parallels the physical flow of the materials as they are converted into finished goods. As shown in Illustration 15-3 (page 757), manufacturing costs are assigned to the Work in Process Inventory account. When a job is completed, the cost of the job is transferred to Finished Goods Inventory. Later when the goods are sold, their cost is transferred to Cost of Goods Sold.

Illustration 15-3 provides a basic overview of the flow of costs in a manufacturing setting. A more detailed presentation of the flow of costs is shown in Illustration 15-4 (page 757). It indicates that there are two major steps in the flow of costs: (1) *accumulating* the manufacturing costs incurred and (2) *assigning* the accumulated costs to the work done. As shown, manufacturing costs incurred are accumulated in entries 1–3 by debits to Raw Materials Inventory, Factory Labor, and Manufacturing Overhead. When these costs are incurred, no attempt is made to associate the costs with specific jobs. The remaining entries (entries 4–8) assign manufacturing costs incurred. In the remainder of this chapter (pages 758–773), we will use a case study to explain how a job order system operates.

Illustration 15-3 Flow of costs in job order cost accounting

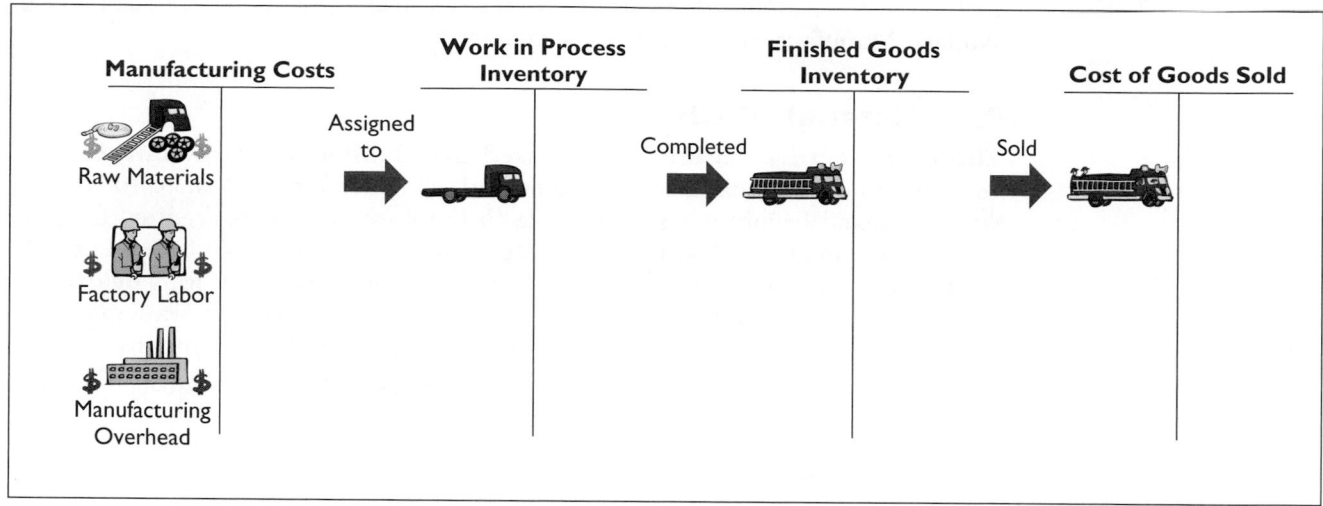

Illustration 15-4 Job order cost accounting system

Job Order Cost Accounting

Raw Materials Inventory

(1) Purchases	(4) Materials used

Factory Labor

(2) Factory labor incurred	(5) Factory labor used

Manufacturing Overhead

Actual overhead incurred:	(6) Overhead applied
(3) Depreciation Insurance Repairs	
(4) Indirect materials used	
(5) Indirect labor used	

Work in Process Inventory

(4) Direct materials used	(7) Cost of completed jobs
(5) Direct labor used	
(6) Overhead applied	

Finished Goods Inventory

(7) Cost of completed jobs	(8) Cost of goods sold

Cost of Goods Sold

(8) Cost of goods sold	

Key to Entries:

Accumulation	Assignment
1. Purchase raw materials	4. Raw materials are used
2. Incur factory labor	5. Factory labor is used
3. Incur manufacturing overhead	6. Overhead is applied
	7. Completed goods are recognized
	8. Cost of goods sold is recognized

ACCUMULATING MANUFACTURING COSTS

In a job order cost system, manufacturing costs are recorded in the period in which they are incurred. To illustrate, we will use the January transactions of Wallace Manufacturing Company, which makes machine tools.

Raw Materials Costs

The costs of raw materials purchased are debited to Raw Materials Inventory when the materials are received. This account is debited for the invoice cost and freight costs chargeable to the purchaser. It is credited for purchase discounts taken and purchase returns and allowances. **No effort is made at this point to associate the cost of materials with specific jobs or orders.** The procedures for ordering, receiving, recording, and paying for raw materials are similar to the purchasing procedures of a merchandising company.

To illustrate, assume that Wallace Manufacturing purchases 2,000 handles (Stock No. AA2746) at $5 per unit ($10,000) and 800 modules (Stock No. AA2850) at $40 per unit ($32,000) for a total cost of $42,000 ($10,000 + $32,000). The entry to record this purchase on January 4 is:

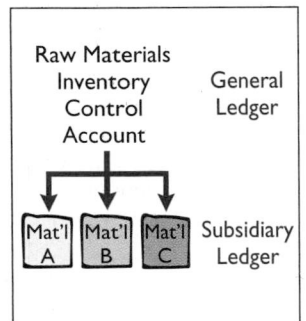

Raw Materials Inventory Control Account — General Ledger
Mat'l A, Mat'l B, Mat'l C — Subsidiary Ledger

(1)

Jan. 4	Raw Materials Inventory	42,000	
	Accounts Payable		42,000
	(Purchase of raw materials on account)		

Raw Materials Inventory is a general ledger account. It is also referred to as a **control account** because it summarizes the detailed data regarding specific inventory accounts in the subsidiary ledger. The subsidiary ledger consists of individual records for each item of raw materials. The records may take the form of accounts (or cards) that are manually or mechanically prepared. Or the records may be kept as computer data files. The records are referred to as **materials inventory records** (or **stores ledger cards**). The card for Stock No. AA2746 following the purchase is shown in Illustration 15-5.

Illustration 15-5 Materials inventory card

Item: Handles							Part No: AA2746		
	Receipts			**Issues**			**Balance**		
Date	Units	Cost	Total	Units	Cost	Total	Units	Cost	Total
1/4	2,000	$5	$10,000				2,000	$5	$10,000

Postings are made daily to the subsidiary ledger. After all postings have been completed, the sum of the balances in the raw materials subsidiary ledger should equal the balance in the Raw Materials Inventory control account.

Factory Labor Costs

The procedures for accumulating factory labor costs are similar to those for computing the payroll for a merchandising company. Time clocks and time cards are used to determine total hours worked; gross and net earnings for each employee are listed in a payroll register; and individual employee earnings records are maintained. To help ensure the accuracy of data, a company should follow the principles of internal control.

In a manufacturing company, the cost of factory labor consists of (1) gross earnings of factory workers, (2) employer payroll taxes on these earnings, and (3) fringe benefits (such as sick pay, pensions, and vacation pay) incurred by the employer. **Labor costs are debited to Factory Labor when they are incurred.**

To illustrate, assume that Wallace Manufacturing incurs $32,000 of factory labor costs. Of that amount, $27,000 relates to wages payable and $5,000 relates to payroll taxes payable in January. The entry is:

	(2)		
Jan. 31	Factory Labor	32,000	
	Factory Wages Payable		27,000
	Employer Payroll Taxes Payable		5,000
	(To record factory labor costs)		

Factory labor is subsequently assigned to work in process and manufacturing overhead, as explained later in the chapter.

Manufacturing Overhead Costs

A company may have many types of overhead costs. These costs may be recognized **daily**, as in the case of machinery repairs and the use of indirect materials and indirect labor. Or overhead costs may be recorded **periodically** through adjusting entries. Property taxes, depreciation, and insurance are recorded periodically, for example. This is done using a summary entry, which summarizes the totals from multiple transactions. Using assumed data, the summary entry for manufacturing overhead in Wallace Manufacturing Company is:

	(3)		
Jan. 31	Manufacturing Overhead	13,800	
	Utilities Payable		4,800
	Prepaid Insurance		2,000
	Accounts Payable (for repairs)		2,600
	Accumulated Depreciation		3,000
	Property Taxes Payable		1,400
	(To record overhead costs)		

Manufacturing Overhead is a control account. The subsidiary ledger consists of individual accounts for each type of cost, such as Factory Utilities, Factory Insurance, and Factory Repairs.

ASSIGNING MANUFACTURING COSTS TO WORK IN PROCESS

As shown in Illustration 15-4, assigning manufacturing costs to work in process results in the following entries:

1. **Debits** are made to Work in Process Inventory.
2. **Credits** are made to Raw Materials Inventory, Factory Labor, and Manufacturing Overhead.

Journal entries to assign costs to work in process are usually made and posted **monthly**.

An essential accounting record in assigning costs to jobs is a **job cost sheet** shown in Illustration 15-6. A job cost sheet is a form used to record the costs chargeable to a specific job and to determine the total and unit costs of the completed job.

STUDY OBJECTIVE
3
Explain the nature and importance of a job cost sheet.

Illustration 15-6 Job cost sheet

Job Cost Sheet

Job No. _____ Quantity _____

Item _____ Date Requested _____

For _____ Date Completed _____

Date	Direct Materials	Direct Labor	Manufacturing Overhead

Cost of completed job
 Direct materials $ _____
 Direct labor   _____
 Manufacturing overhead   _____
Total cost $ _____
Unit cost (total dollars ÷ quantity) $ _____

Helpful Hint In today's electronic environment, job cost sheets are maintained as computer files.

Postings to job cost sheets are made daily, directly from supporting documents.

A separate job cost sheet is kept for each job. The job cost sheets constitute the subsidiary ledger for the Work in Process Inventory account. **Each entry to Work in Process Inventory must be accompanied by a corresponding posting to one or more job cost sheets.**

Business Insight
e-Business Perspective

General Motors recently launched a new Internet-based ordering system intended to deliver custom vehicles in 15 to 20 days instead of the 55 to 60 days it previously took. Customers interested in a GM car can search online to see if any dealers have a car with the options they want. If not, the customer uses an online program to configure a car with the desired options and then places the order. While this online approach could potentially provide savings for automakers by reducing inventory costs, some people are skeptical. One auto analyst stated, "I don't think it's going to lead to a massive change in the way vehicles are built and sold in the next 10 years."

SOURCE: Karen Lundegaard, "GM Tests Web-Based Ordering System, Seeking to Slash Custom-Delivery Time," *Wall Street Journal* (November 17, 2000).

Raw Materials Costs

Helpful Hint Approvals are an important part of a materials requisition slip because they help to establish individual accountability over inventory.

Raw materials costs are assigned when the materials are issued by the storeroom. To achieve effective internal control over the issuance of materials, the storeroom worker should receive a written authorization before materials are released to production. Such authorization for issuing raw materials is made on a prenumbered **materials requisition slip**. This form is signed by an authorized employee such as a department supervisor. The materials issued may be used directly on a job, or they may be considered indirect materials. As shown in Illustration 15-7, the requisition should indicate the quantity and type of materials withdrawn and the account to be charged. Direct materials will be charged to Work in Process Inventory, and indirect materials to Manufacturing Overhead.

Illustration 15-7 Materials requisition slip

Wallace Manufacturing Company
Materials Requisition Slip

| Deliver to: | Assembly Department | | Req. No. | R247 |
| Charge to: | Work in Process—Job No. 101 | | Date: | 1/6/07 |

Quantity	Description	Stock No.	Cost per Unit	Total
200	Handles	AA2746	$5.00	$1,000

Requested by *Bruce Howart*   Received by *Herb Crowley*

Approved by *Kap Shin*   Costed by *Heather Remmers*

Helpful Hint The internal control principle of documentation includes prenumbering to enhance accountability.

The requisition is prepared in duplicate. A copy is retained in the storeroom as evidence of the materials released. The original is sent to Accounting, where the cost per unit and total cost of the materials used are determined. Any of the inventory costing methods (FIFO, LIFO, or average cost) may be used in costing the requisitions. After the requisition slips have been costed, they are posted daily to the materials inventory records. Also, **requisitions for direct materials are posted daily to the individual job cost sheets**.

Periodically, the requisitions are sorted, totaled, and journalized. For example, if $24,000 of direct materials and $6,000 of indirect materials are used in Wallace Manufacturing in January, the entry is:

	(4)		
Jan. 31	Work in Process Inventory	24,000	
	Manufacturing Overhead	6,000	
	Raw Materials Inventory		30,000
	(To assign materials to jobs and overhead)		

The requisition slips show total direct materials costs of $12,000 for Job No. 101, $7,000 for Job No. 102, and $5,000 for Job No. 103. The posting of requisition slip R247 and other assumed postings to the job cost sheets for materials are shown in Illustration 15-8. After all postings have been completed, the sum of the direct materials columns of the job cost sheets should equal the direct materials debited to Work in Process Inventory.

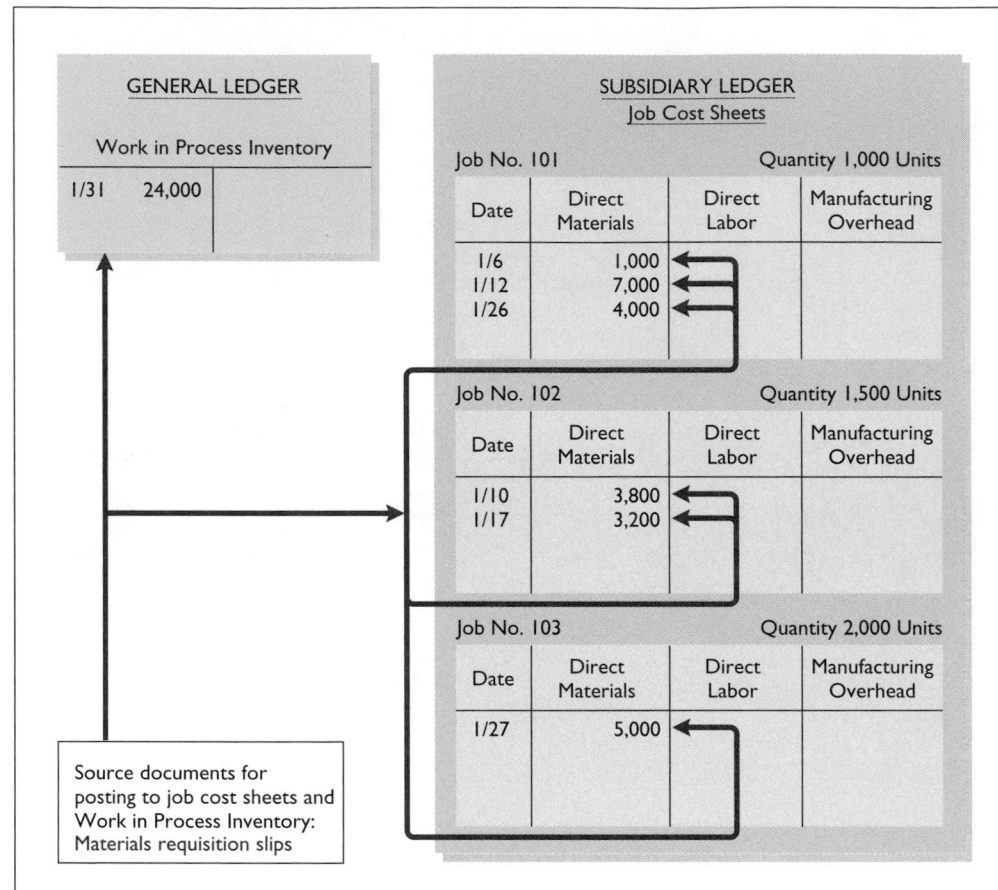

Illustration 15-8 Job cost sheets—direct materials

Helpful Hint Postings to control accounts are made monthly, and postings to job cost sheets are made daily.

The materials inventory record for Part No. AA2746 is shown in Illustration 15-9. It shows the posting of requisition slip R247 for 200 handles and an assumed requisition slip for 760 handles costing $3,800 on January 10 for Job 102.

Illustration 15-9 Materials inventory card following issuances

Item: Handles										Part No: AA2746
	Receipts			Issues			Balance			
Date	Units	Cost	Total	Units	Cost	Total	Units	Cost	Total	
1/4	2,000	$5	$10,000				2,000	$5	$10,000	
1/6				200	$5	$1,000	1,800	$5	9,000	
1/10				760	$5	3,800	1,040	$5	5,200	

Factory Labor Costs

Factory labor costs are assigned to jobs on the basis of time tickets prepared when the work is performed. The time ticket indicates the employee, the hours worked, the account and job to be charged, and the total labor cost. In many companies these data are accumulated through the use of bar coding and scanning devices. When they start and end work, employees scan bar codes on their identification badges and bar codes associated with each job they work on. When direct labor is involved, the job number must be indicated, as shown in Illustration 15-10. All time tickets should be approved by the employee's supervisor.

Illustration 15-10   Time ticket

Helpful Hint In some companies, different colored time tickets are used for direct and indirect labor.

The time tickets are later sent to the payroll department. There, the total time reported for an employee for a pay period is reconciled with total hours worked, as shown on the employee's time card. Then the employee's hourly wage rate is applied, and the total labor cost is computed. Finally, the time tickets are sorted, totaled, and journalized. The account Work in Process Inventory is debited for direct labor, and Manufacturing Overhead is debited for indirect labor. For example, if the $32,000 total factory labor cost consists of $28,000 of direct labor and $4,000 of indirect labor, the entry is:

	(5)		
Jan. 31	Work in Process Inventory	28,000	
	Manufacturing Overhead	4,000	
	Factory Labor		32,000
	(To assign labor to jobs and overhead)		

As a result of this entry, Factory Labor is left with a zero balance, and gross earnings are assigned to the appropriate manufacturing accounts.

Let's assume that the labor costs chargeable to Wallace's three jobs are $15,000, $9,000, and $4,000. The Work in Process Inventory and job cost sheets after posting are shown in Illustration 15-11. As in the case of direct materials, the postings to the direct labor columns of the job cost sheets should equal the posting of direct labor to Work in Process Inventory.

Illustration 15-11 Job cost sheets—direct labor

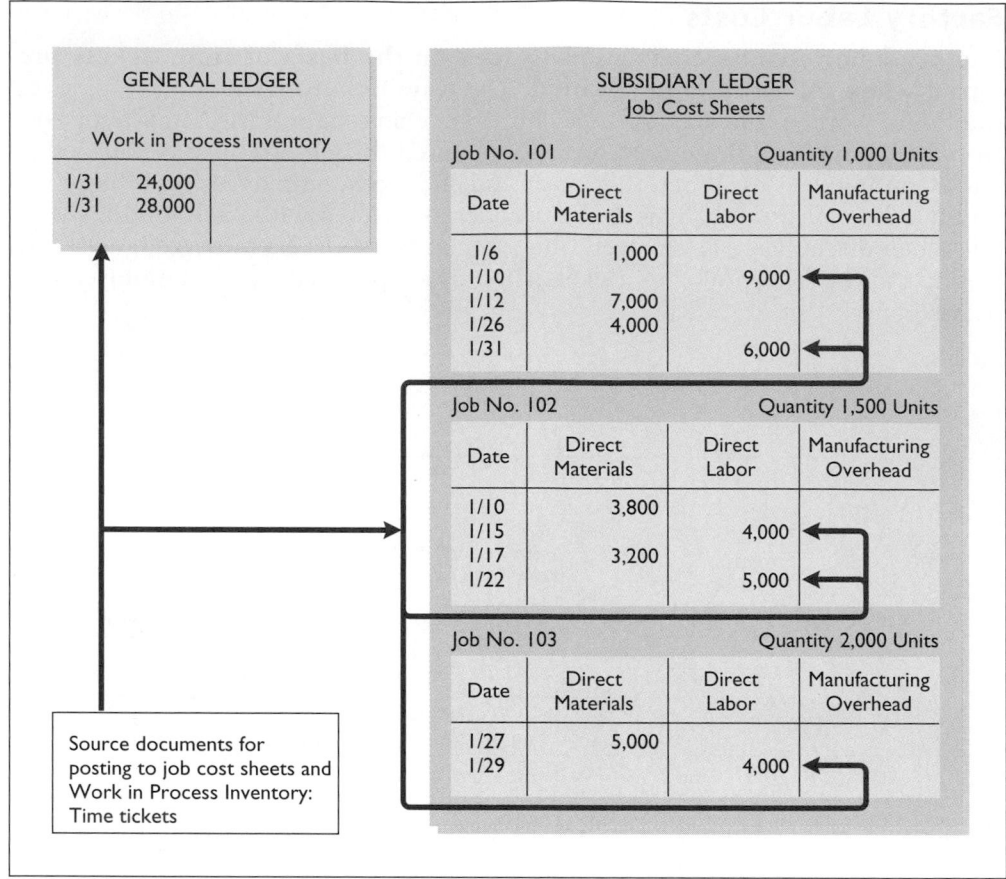

Helpful Hint Prove the $28,000 by totaling the charges by jobs:

101	$15,000
102	9,000
103	4,000
	$28,000

Manufacturing Overhead Costs

STUDY OBJECTIVE

4

Indicate how the predetermined overhead rate is determined and used.

We've seen that the actual costs of direct materials and direct labor can be charged to specific jobs. In contrast, manufacturing overhead relates to production operations **as a whole**. As a result, overhead costs cannot be assigned to specific jobs on the basis of actual costs incurred. Instead, manufacturing overhead is assigned to work in process and to specific jobs **on an estimated basis through the use of a predetermined overhead rate**.

Accounting across the Organization

What do companies like Noratek Solutions, Business Systems of America, Foundation Software, Inc., and R.C. Systems, Inc. have in common? All of them provide software to help in recording job order costing information. For example, Noratek Solutions software analyzes every job from every angle, and it supports reporting of estimated and actual costs and revenues for any number of jobs. The system is integrated with purchasing, accounts payable, payroll, and receivables so that a complete cross-reference into all transactions can be easily developed. Users have a complete audit trail so that they can examine the details of any job.

A manual system is provided in this chapter so that the major concepts related to a job order cost system are understood. In practice, sophisticated job order cost software packages frequently are used.

The **predetermined overhead rate** is based on the relationship between estimated annual overhead costs and expected annual operating activity. This relationship is expressed in terms of a common **activity base**. The activity may be stated in terms of direct labor costs, direct labor hours, machine hours, or any other measure that will provide an equitable basis for applying overhead costs to jobs. The predetermined overhead rate is established at the beginning of the year. Small companies often will have a single, company-wide predetermined overhead rate. Large companies, however, often have rates that vary from department to department. The formula for a predetermined overhead rate is as follows.

Estimated Annual Overhead Costs	÷	Expected Annual Operating Activity	=	Predetermined Overhead Rate

Illustration 15-12 Formula for predetermined overhead rate

We indicated earlier that overhead relates to production operations as a whole. In order to know what "the whole" is, the logical thing would be to wait until the end of the year's operations, when all costs for the period would be available. But as a practical matter, that wouldn't work: Managers could not wait that long before having information about product costs of specific jobs completed during the year in order to price products accurately. Instead, using a predetermined overhead rate enables a cost to be determined for the job immediately. Illustration 15-13 indicates how manufacturing overhead is assigned to work in process.

Helpful Hint In contrast to overhead, actual costs for direct materials and direct labor are used to assign costs to Work in Process.

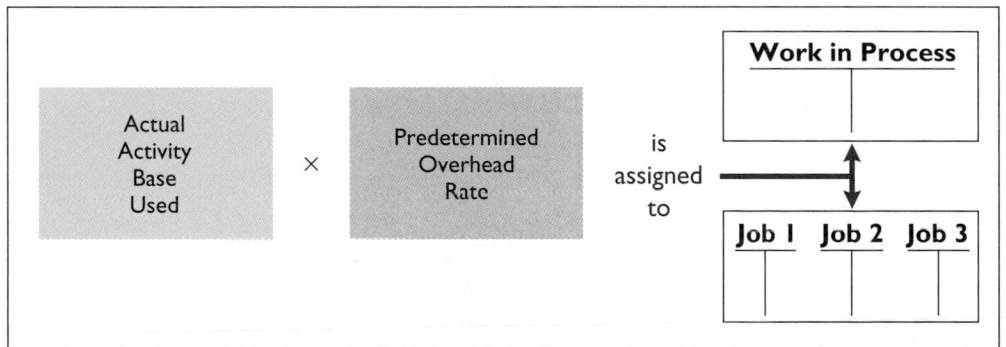

Illustration 15-13 Using predetermined overhead rates

Wallace Manufacturing uses direct labor cost as the activity base. Assuming that annual overhead costs are expected to be $280,000 and that $350,000 of direct labor costs are anticipated for the year, the overhead rate is 80 percent, computed as follows:

$$\$280,000 \div \$350,000 = 80\%$$

This means that for every dollar of direct labor, 80 cents of manufacturing overhead will be assigned to a job. The use of a predetermined overhead rate enables the company to determine the approximate total cost of each job **when the job is completed**.

Historically, direct labor costs or direct labor hours have often been used as the activity base. The reason was the relatively high correlation between direct labor and manufacturing overhead. In recent years, **there has been a trend toward use of machine hours as the activity base, due to increased reliance on automation in manufacturing operations**. Or, as mentioned in Chapter 14, many companies have implemented activity-based costing in an attempt to more accurately allocate overhead costs based on the activities that give rise to the costs.

A company may use more than one activity base. For example, if a job order is manufactured in more than one factory department, each department may have its own overhead rate. In the Feature Story about fire trucks, two bases were used in assigning overhead to jobs: direct materials dollars for indirect materials, and direct labor hours for such costs as insurance and supervisors' salaries.

Manufacturing overhead is applied to work in process when direct labor costs are assigned. It also is applied to specific jobs at the same time. For Wallace Manufacturing, overhead applied for January is $22,400 ($28,000 × 80%). This application is recorded through the following entry.

	(6)		
Jan. 31	Work in Process Inventory	22,400	
	Manufacturing Overhead		22,400
	(To assign overhead to jobs)		

The overhead applied to each job will be 80 percent of the direct labor cost of the job for the month. After posting, the Work in Process Inventory account and the job cost sheets will appear as shown in Illustration 15-14. Note that the debit

Illustration 15-14 Job cost sheets—manufacturing overhead applied

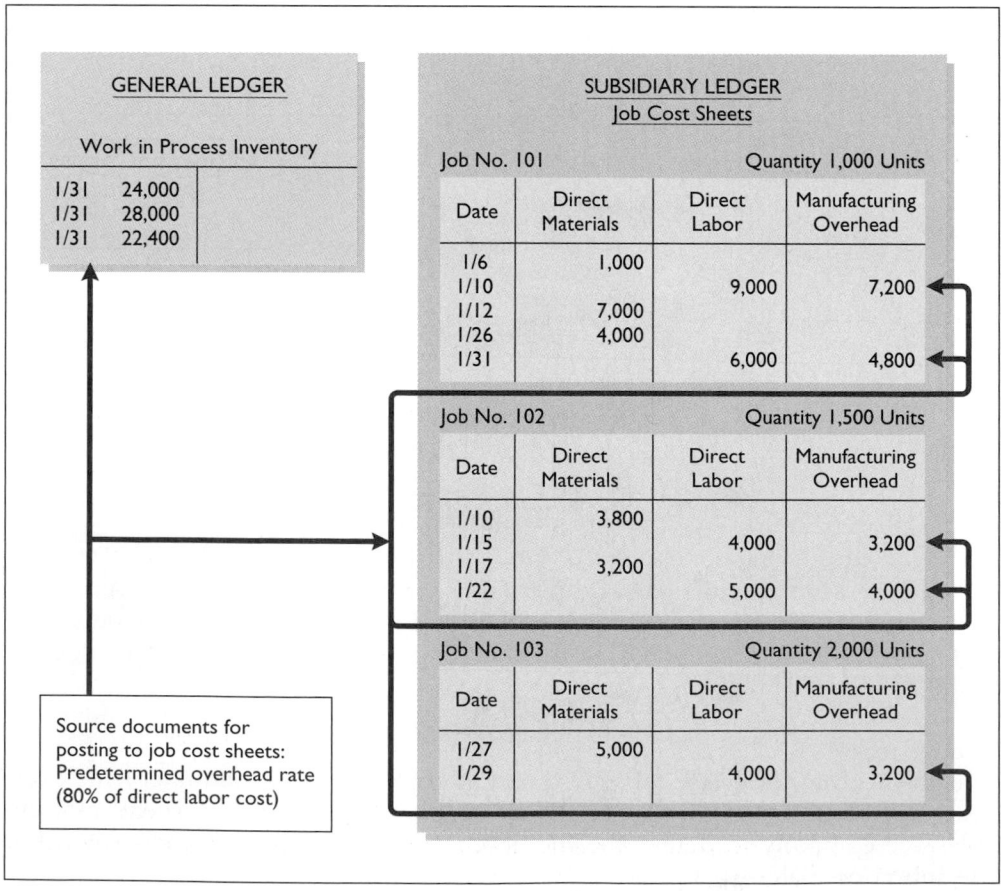

of $22,400 to Work in Process Inventory equals the sum of the overhead applied to jobs: Job 101 $12,000 + Job 102 $7,200 + Job 103 $3,200.

At the end of each month, **the balance in Work in Process Inventory should equal the sum of the costs shown on the job cost sheets of unfinished jobs**. Assuming that all jobs are unfinished, proof of the agreement of the control and subsidiary accounts in Wallace Manufacturing is shown below.

Work in Process Inventory		Job Cost Sheets	
Jan. 31	24,000	No. 101	$39,000
31	28,000	102	23,200
31	22,400	103	12,200
	74,400 ←	————	**$74,400**

Illustration 15-15 Proof of job cost sheets to work in process inventory

DECISION TOOLKIT

Decision Checkpoints	Info Needed for Decision	Tool to Use for Decision	How to Evaluate Results
What is the cost of a job?	Cost of material, labor, and overhead assigned to a specific job	Job cost sheet	Compare costs to those of previous periods and to those of competitors to ensure that costs are in line. Compare costs to expected selling price or service fees charged to determine overall profitability.

BEFORE YOU GO ON . . .

▶Review It

1. What source documents are used in assigning manufacturing costs to Work in Process Inventory?
2. What is a job cost sheet, and what is its primary purpose?
3. What is the formula for computing a predetermined overhead rate?

▶Do It

Danielle Company is working on two job orders. The job cost sheets show the following:

    Direct materials — Job 120 $6,000, Job 121 $3,600
    Direct labor — Job 120 $4,000, Job 121 $2,000
    Manufacturing overhead — Job 120 $5,000, Job 121 $2,500

Prepare the three summary entries to record the assignment of costs to Work in Process from the data on the job cost sheets.

Action Plan
• Recognize that Work in Process Inventory is the control account for all unfinished job cost sheets.
• Debit Work in Process Inventory for the materials, labor, and overhead charged to the job cost sheets.
• Credit the accounts that were debited when the manufacturing costs were accumulated.

Solution
The three summary entries are:

Work in Process Inventory ($6,000 + $3,600)	9,600	
Raw Materials Inventory		9,600
(To assign materials to jobs)		
Work in Process Inventory ($4,000 + $2,000)	6,000	
Factory Labor		6,000
(To assign labor to jobs)		
Work in Process Inventory ($5,000 + $2,500)	7,500	
Manufacturing Overhead		7,500
(To assign overhead to jobs)		

Related exercise material: BE15-3, BE15-4, BE15-7, E15-2, E15-3, E15-7, and E15-8.

 THE NAVIGATOR

ASSIGNING COSTS TO FINISHED GOODS

STUDY OBJECTIVE
5

Prepare entries for jobs completed and sold.

When a job is completed, the costs are summarized and the lower portion of the applicable job cost sheet is completed. For example, if we assume that Job No. 101 is completed on January 31, the job cost sheet will show the following.

Illustration 15-16 Completed job cost sheet

Job Cost Sheet

Job No. _____101_____   Quantity _____1,000_____
Item _____Magnetic Sensors_____   Date Requested _____February 5_____
For _____Tanner Company_____   Date Completed _____January 31_____

Date	Direct Materials	Direct Labor	Manufacturing Overhead
1/6	$ 1,000		
1/10		$ 9,000	$ 7,200
1/12	7,000		
1/26	4,000		
1/31		6,000	4,800
	$12,000	$15,000	$12,000

Cost of completed job
  Direct materials $ 12,000
  Direct labor   15,000
  Manufacturing overhead   12,000
Total cost $ 39,000
Unit cost ($39,000 ÷ 1,000) $ 39.00

When a job is finished, an entry is made to transfer its total cost to finished goods inventory. The entry for Wallace Manufacturing is:

	(7)		
Jan. 31	Finished Goods Inventory	39,000	
	Work in Process Inventory		39,000
	(To record completion of Job No. 101)		

Finished Goods Inventory is a control account. It controls individual finished goods records in a finished goods subsidiary ledger. Postings to the receipts columns are made directly from completed job cost sheets. The finished goods inventory record for Job No. 101 is shown in Illustration 15-17 below.

ASSIGNING COSTS TO COST OF GOODS SOLD

Cost of goods sold is recognized when each sale occurs. To illustrate the entries when a completed job is sold, assume that on January 31 Wallace Manufacturing sells on account Job 101, costing $39,000, for $50,000. The entries to record the sale and recognize cost of goods sold are:

	(8)		
Jan. 31	Accounts Receivable	50,000	
	Sales		50,000
	(To record sale of Job No. 101)		
31	Cost of Goods Sold	39,000	
	Finished Goods Inventory		39,000
	(To record cost of Job No. 101)		

The units sold, the cost per unit, and the total cost of goods sold for each job sold are recorded in the issues section of the finished goods record, as shown in Illustration 15-17.

Illustration 15-17
Finished goods record

Item: Magnetic Sensors									Job No: 101	
	Receipts			Issues			Balance			
Date	Units	Cost	Total	Units	Cost	Total	Units	Cost	Total	
1/31	1,000	$39	$39,000				1,000	$39	$39,000	
1/31				1,000	$39	$39,000			–0–	

SUMMARY OF JOB ORDER COST FLOWS

A completed flow chart for a job order cost accounting system is shown in Illustration 15-18 (page 770). All postings are keyed to entries 1–8 in Wallace Manufacturing's accounts presented in the cost flow graphic in Illustration 15-4. Illustration 15-19 (page 770) provides a summary of the flow of documents in a job order cost system.

Illustration 15-18 Flow of costs in a job order cost system

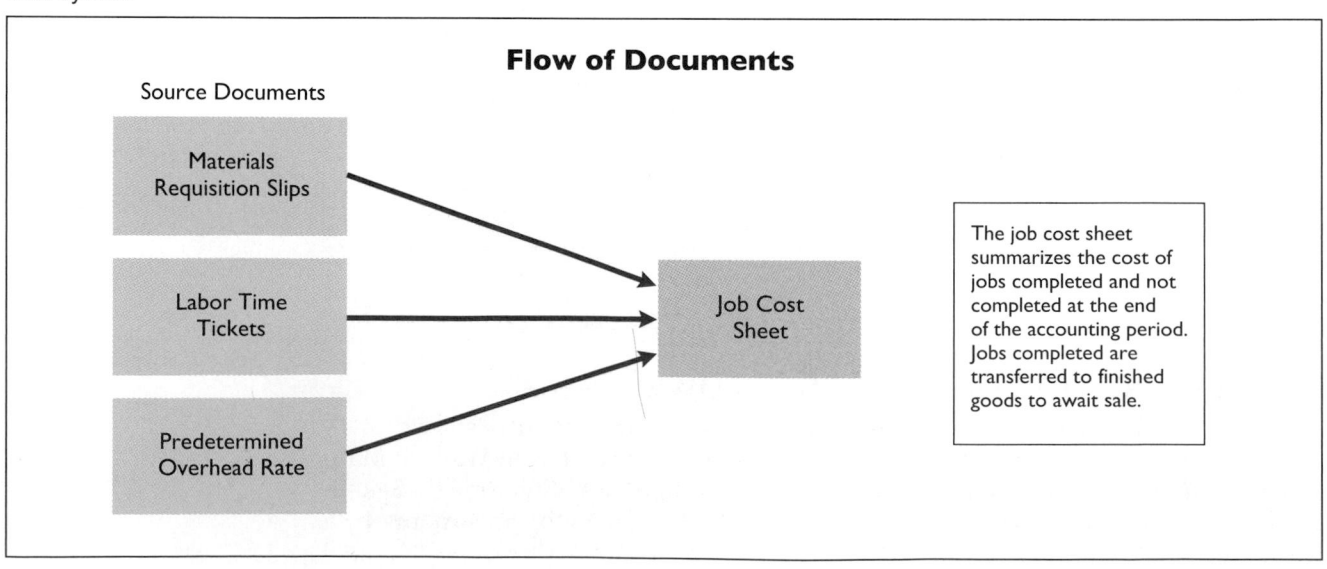

Flow of Costs

Raw Materials Inventory		
(1) 42,000	(4)	30,000
Bal. 12,000		

Work in Process Inventory		
(4) 24,000	(7)	39,000
(5) 28,000		
(6) 22,400		
Bal. 35,400		

Finished Goods Inventory		
(7) 39,000	(8)	39,000

Factory Labor		
(2) 32,000	(5)	32,000

Cost of Goods Sold	
(8) 39,000	

Manufacturing Overhead		
(3) 13,800	(6)	22,400
(4) 6,000		
(5) 4,000		
Bal. 1,400		

Key to Entries:

Accumulation	Assignment
1. Purchase raw materials	4. Raw materials are used
2. Incur factory labor	5. Factory labor is used
3. Incur manufacturing overhead	6. Overhead is applied
	7. Completed goods are recognized
	8. Cost of goods sold is recognized

Illustration 15-19 Flow of documents in a job order cost system

Flow of Documents

Source Documents

- Materials Requisition Slips
- Labor Time Tickets
- Predetermined Overhead Rate

→ Job Cost Sheet

The job cost sheet summarizes the cost of jobs completed and not completed at the end of the accounting period. Jobs completed are transferred to finished goods to await sale.

Accounting across the Organization

Service companies like the Mayo Clinic (health care), PriceWaterhouse-Coopers (accounting firm), and Merrill Lynch (financial services firm) also use job order costing systems. The major difference in a job order costing system between a manufacturing company such as Coca-Cola and a service company such as Massachusetts General Hospital involves inventory. Service companies do not have raw materials nor finished goods inventory. However, similar to manufacturing companies, many service companies have substantial overhead costs, which must be allocated.

Because job order costing systems are used extensively in service industries, exercises are provided in the end-of-chapter material to help you understand how to cost various types of services.

Reporting Job Cost Data

At the end of a period, financial statements are prepared that present aggregate data on all jobs manufactured and sold. The cost of goods manufactured schedule in job order costing is the same as in Chapter 14 with one exception: **The schedule shows manufacturing overhead applied, rather than actual overhead costs. This amount is added to direct materials and direct labor to determine total manufacturing costs.** The schedule is prepared directly from the Work in Process Inventory account. A condensed schedule for Wallace Manufacturing Company for January is as follows.

Helpful Hint Monthly financial statements are usually prepared for management use only.

Illustration 15-20 Cost of goods manufactured schedule

WALLACE MANUFACTURING COMPANY Cost of Goods Manufactured Schedule For the Month Ended January 31, 2007		
Work in process, January 1		$ –0–
Direct materials used	$24,000	
Direct labor	28,000	
Manufacturing overhead applied	**22,400**	
Total manufacturing costs		74,400
Total cost of work in process		74,400
Less: Work in process, January 31		35,400
Cost of goods manufactured		$39,000

Note that the cost of goods manufactured ($39,000) agrees with the amount transferred from Work in Process Inventory to Finished Goods Inventory in journal entry no. 7 in Illustration 15-18.

The income statement and balance sheet are the same as those illustrated in Chapter 14. For example, the partial income statement for Wallace Manufacturing for the month of January is shown in Illustration 15-21.

Illustration 15-21   Partial income statement

WALLACE MANUFACTURING COMPANY
Income Statement (partial)
For the Month Ending January 31, 2007

Sales		$50,000
Cost of goods sold		
Finished goods inventory, January 1	$ –0–	
Cost of goods manufactured (See Illustration 15-20)	**39,000**	
Cost of goods available for sale	39,000	
Less: Finished goods inventory, January 31	–0–	
Cost of goods sold		39,000
Gross profit		$11,000

Under- or Overapplied Manufacturing Overhead

STUDY OBJECTIVE
6

Distinguish between under- and overapplied manufacturing overhead.

When Manufacturing Overhead has a **debit balance**, overhead is said to be underapplied. **Underapplied overhead** means that the overhead assigned to work in process is less than the overhead incurred. Conversely, when manufacturing overhead has a **credit balance**, overhead is overapplied. **Overapplied overhead** means that the overhead assigned to work in process is greater than the overhead incurred. These concepts are shown in Illustration 15-22.

Illustration 15-22   Under- and overapplied overhead

Manufacturing Overhead	
Actual (Costs incurred)	Applied (Costs assigned)

If actual is *greater* than applied, manufacturing overhead is underapplied.

If actual is *less* than applied, manufacturing overhead is overapplied.

YEAR-END BALANCE

At the end of the year, all manufacturing overhead transactions are complete. There is no further opportunity for offsetting events to occur. Accordingly, any balance in Manufacturing Overhead is eliminated by an adjusting entry. Usually, under- or overapplied overhead is considered to be an **adjustment to cost of goods sold**. Thus, **underapplied overhead is debited to Cost of Goods Sold. Overapplied overhead is credited to Cost of Goods Sold.** To illustrate, assume that Wallace Manufacturing has a $2,500 credit balance in Manufacturing Overhead at December 31. The adjusting entry for the overapplied overhead is:

Dec. 31	Manufacturing Overhead	2,500	
	Cost of Goods Sold		2,500
	(To transfer overapplied overhead to cost of goods sold)		

After this entry is posted, Manufacturing Overhead will have a zero balance. In preparing an income statement for the year, the amount reported for cost of goods sold will be the account balance **after the adjustment** for either under- or overapplied overhead.

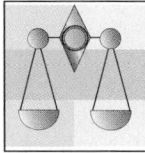

Business Insight
Management Perspective

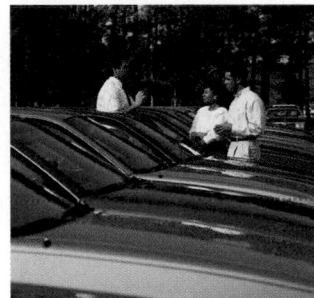

Overhead also applies in nonmanufacturing companies. The State of Michigan found that auto dealers were charging documentary and service fees ranging from $18 to $445 per automobile and inspection fees from $88 to $360. These fees often were charged auto buyers after a base sales price for the car had been negotiated. The Attorney General of the State of Michigan ruled that auto dealers cannot charge customers additional fees for routine overhead costs. The attorney general said: "Overhead is part of the sales price of a motor vehicle. Processing paper work, dealer incurred costs, and inspection fees to qualify cars for extended warranty plans are ordinary overhead expenses."

Conceptually, it can be argued that under- or overapplied overhead at the end of the year should be allocated among ending work in process, finished goods, and cost of goods sold. The discussion of this possible allocation approach is left to more advanced courses.

DECISION TOOLKIT

Decision Checkpoints	Info Needed for Decision	Tool to Use for Decision	How to Evaluate Results
Has the company over- or underapplied overhead for the period?	Actual overhead costs and overhead applied	Manufacturing overhead account	If the account balance is a credit, overhead applied exceeded actual overhead costs. If the account balance is a debit, overhead applied was less than actual overhead costs.

BEFORE YOU GO ON . . .

▶Review It

1. When are entries made to record the completion and sale of a job?
2. What costs are included in total manufacturing costs in the cost of goods manufactured schedule?

THE NAVIGATOR

Using the Decision Toolkit

Martinez Building Products Company is one of the largest manufacturers and marketers of unique, custom-made residential garage doors in the U.S. as well as a major supplier of industrial and commercial doors, grills, and counter shutters for the new construction, repair, and remodel markets. Martinez has developed plans for continued expansion of a network of service operations that sell, install, and service manufactured fireplaces, garage doors, and related products.

Martinez uses a job cost system and applies overhead to production on the basis of direct labor cost. In computing a predetermined overhead rate for the year 2007, the company estimated manufacturing overhead to be $24 million and direct labor costs to be $20 million. In addition the following information is provided.

Actual costs incurred during 2007

Direct materials used	$30,000,000
Direct labor cost incurred	21,000,000
Insurance, factory	500,000
Indirect labor	7,500,000
Maintenance	1,000,000
Rent on building	11,000,000
Depreciation on equipment	2,000,000

Instructions
Answer each of the following.
(a) Why is Martinez Building Products Company using a job order costing system?
(b) On what basis does Martinez allocate its manufacturing overhead? Compute the predetermined overhead rate for the current year.
(c) Compute the amount of the under- or overapplied overhead for 2007.
(d) Martinez had balances in the beginning and ending work in process and finished goods accounts as follows.

	1/1/07	12/31/07
Work in process	$ 5,000,000	$ 4,000,000
Finished goods	13,000,000	11,000,000

Determine the (1) cost of goods manufactured and (2) cost of goods sold for Martinez during 2007. Assume that any under- or overapplied overhead should be included in the cost of goods sold.
(e) During 2007, Job G408 was started and completed. Its cost sheet showed a total cost of $100,000, and the company prices its product at 50% above its cost. What is the price to the customer if the company follows this pricing strategy?

Solution

(a) The company is using a job order system because each job (or batch) must have its own distinguishing characteristics. For example, each type of garage door would be different, and therefore a different cost per garage door should be assigned.

(b) The company allocates its overhead on the basis of direct labor cost. The predetermined overhead rate is 120%, computed as follows.

$$\$24,000,000 \div \$20,000,000 = 120\%$$

(c)		
	Actual manufacturing overhead	$22,000,000
	Applied overhead cost ($21,000,000 × 120%)	25,200,000
	Overapplied overhead	$ 3,200,000

(d) (1)	Work in process, 1/1/07		$ 5,000,000
	Direct materials used	$30,000,000	
	Direct labor	21,000,000	
	Manufacturing overhead applied	25,200,000	
	Total manufacturing costs		76,200,000
	Total cost of work in process		81,200,000
	Less: Work in process, 12/31/07		4,000,000
	Cost of goods manufactured		$77,200,000
(2)	Finished goods inventory, 1/1/07	$13,000,000	
	Cost of goods manufactured (see above)	77,200,000	
	Cost of goods available for sale	90,200,000	
	Finished goods inventory, 12/31/07	11,000,000	
	Cost of goods sold (unadjusted)	79,200,000	
	Less: Overapplied overhead	3,200,000	
	Cost of goods sold	$76,000,000	
(e)	G408 cost	$ 100,000	
	Markup percentage	× 50%	
	Profit	$ 50,000	

Price to customer: $150,000 ($100,000 + $50,000)

Summary of Study Objectives

1 *Explain the characteristics and purposes of cost accounting.* Cost accounting involves the procedures for measuring, recording, and reporting product costs. From the data accumulated, the total cost and the unit cost of each product is determined. The two basic types of cost accounting systems are job order cost and process cost.

2 *Describe the flow of costs in a job order cost accounting system.* In job order cost accounting, manufacturing costs are first accumulated in three accounts: Raw Materials Inventory, Factory Labor, and Manufacturing Overhead. The accumulated costs are then assigned to Work in Process Inventory and eventually to Finished Goods Inventory and Cost of Goods Sold.

3 *Explain the nature and importance of a job cost sheet.* A job cost sheet is a form used to record the costs chargeable to a specific job and to determine the total and unit costs of the completed job. Job cost sheets constitute the subsidiary ledger for the Work in Process Inventory control account.

4 *Indicate how the predetermined overhead rate is determined and used.* The predetermined overhead rate is based on the relationship between estimated annual overhead costs and expected annual operating activity. This is expressed in terms of a common activity base, such as direct labor cost. The rate is used in assigning overhead costs to work in process and to specific jobs.

5 *Prepare entries for jobs completed and sold.* When jobs are completed, the cost is debited to Finished Goods Inventory and credited to Work in Process Inventory. When a job is sold the entries are: (a) Debit Cash or Accounts Receivable and credit Sales for the selling price. And (b) debit Cost of Goods Sold and credit Finished Goods Inventory for the cost of the goods.

6 *Distinguish between under- and overapplied manufacturing overhead.* Underapplied manufacturing overhead means that the overhead assigned to work in process is less than the overhead incurred. Overapplied overhead means that the overhead assigned to work in process is greater than the overhead incurred.

DECISION TOOLKIT—A SUMMARY

Decision Checkpoints	Info Needed for Decision	Tool to Use for Decision	How to Evaluate Results
What is the cost of a job?	Cost of material, labor, and overhead assigned to a specific job	Job cost sheet	Compare costs to those of previous periods and to those of competitors to ensure that costs are in line. Compare costs to expected selling price or service fees charged to determine overall profitability.
Has the company over- or underapplied overhead for the period?	Actual overhead costs and overhead applied	Manufacturing overhead account	If the account balance is a credit, overhead applied exceeded actual overhead costs. If the account balance is a debit, overhead applied was less than actual overhead costs.

Glossary

Cost accounting An area of accounting that involves measuring, recording, and reporting product costs. (p. 754)

Cost accounting system Manufacturing cost accounts that are fully integrated into the general ledger of a company. (p. 754)

Job cost sheet A form used to record the costs chargeable to a job and to determine the total and unit costs of the completed job. (p. 759)

Job order cost system A cost accounting system in which costs are assigned to each job or batch. (p. 755)

Materials requisition slip A document authorizing the issuance of raw materials from the storeroom to production. (p. 760)

Overapplied overhead A situation in which overhead assigned to work in process is greater than the overhead incurred. (p. 772)

Predetermined overhead rate A rate based on the relationship between estimated annual overhead costs and expected annual operating activity, expressed in terms of a common activity base. (p. 765)

Process cost system A system of accounting used when a large volume of similar products are manufactured. (p. 755)

Summary entry A journal entry that summarizes the totals from multiple transactions. (p. 759)

Time ticket A document that indicates the employee, the hours worked, the account and job to be charged, and the total labor cost. (p. 763)

Underapplied overhead A situation in which overhead assigned to work in process is less than the overhead incurred. (p. 772)

Demonstration Problem

During February, Cardella Manufacturing works on two jobs: A16 and B17. Summary data concerning these jobs are as follows.

Manufacturing Costs Incurred

Purchased $54,000 of raw materials on account.
Factory labor $76,000, plus $4,000 employer payroll taxes.
Manufacturing overhead exclusive of indirect materials and indirect labor $59,800.

Assignment of Costs

Direct materials: Job A16 $27,000, Job B17 $21,000
Indirect materials: $3,000
Direct labor: Job A16 $52,000, Job B17 $26,000
Indirect labor: $2,000
Manufacturing overhead rate: 80% of direct labor costs.

Job A16 was completed and sold on account for $150,000. Job B17 was only partially completed.

Instructions

(a) Journalize the February transactions in the sequence followed in the chapter.
(b) What was the amount of under- or overapplied manufacturing overhead?

Solution to Demonstration Problem

(a)

1.

Feb. 28	Raw Materials Inventory	54,000	
	Accounts Payable		54,000
	(Purchase of raw materials on account)		

2.

28	Factory Labor	80,000	
	Factory Wages Payable		76,000
	Employer Payroll Taxes Payable		4,000
	(To record factory labor costs)		

3.

28	Manufacturing Overhead	59,800	
	Accounts Payable, Accumulated		
	Depreciation, and Prepaid Insurance		59,800
	(To record overhead costs)		

4.

28	Work in Process Inventory	48,000	
	Manufacturing Overhead	3,000	
	Raw Materials Inventory		51,000
	(To assign raw materials to production)		

5.

28	Work in Process Inventory	78,000	
	Manufacturing Overhead	2,000	
	Factory Labor		80,000
	(To assign factory labor to production)		

6.

28	Work in Process Inventory	62,400	
	Manufacturing Overhead		62,400
	(To assign overhead to jobs—		
	80% × $78,000)		

7.

28	Finished Goods Inventory	120,600	
	Work in Process Inventory		120,600
	(To record completion of Job A16: direct		
	materials $27,000, direct labor $52,000,		
	and manufacturing overhead $41,600)		

Action Plan

- In accumulating costs, debit three accounts: Raw Materials Inventory, Factory Labor, and Manufacturing Overhead.
- When Work in Process Inventory is debited, credit one of the three accounts listed above.
- Debit Finished Goods Inventory for the cost of completed jobs. Debit Cost of Goods Sold for the cost of jobs sold.
- Overhead is underapplied when Manufacturing Overhead has a debit balance.

8.

Feb 28	Accounts Receivable	150,000	
	Sales		150,000
	(To record sale of Job A16)		
28	Cost of Goods Sold	120,600	
	Finished Goods Inventory		120,600
	(To record cost of sale for Job A16)		

(b) Manufacturing Overhead has a debit balance of $2,400 as shown below.

Manufacturing Overhead

(3)	59,800	(6)	62,400
(4)	3,000		
(5)	2,000		
Bal.	2,400		

Thus, manufacturing overhead is underapplied for the month.

Self-Study Questions

Answers are at the end of the chapter.

(SO 1) **1.** Cost accounting involves the measuring, recording, and reporting of:
(a) product costs.
(b) future costs.
(c) manufacturing processes.
(d) managerial accounting decisions.

(SO 2) **2.** In accumulating raw materials costs, the cost of raw materials purchased in a perpetual system is debited to:
(a) Raw Materials Purchases.
(b) Raw Materials Inventory.
(c) Purchases.
(d) Work in Process.

(SO 2) **3.** When incurred, factory labor costs are debited to:
(a) Work in Process.
(b) Factory Wages Expense.
(c) Factory Labor.
(d) Factory Wages Payable.

(SO 3) **4.** The source documents for assigning costs to job cost sheets are:
(a) invoices, time tickets, and the predetermined overhead rate.
(b) materials requisition slips, time tickets, and the actual overhead costs.
(c) materials requisition slips, payroll register, and the predetermined overhead rate.
(d) materials requisition slips, time tickets, and the predetermined overhead rate.

(SO 3) **5.** In recording the issuance of raw materials in a job order cost system, it would be *incorrect* to:
(a) debit Work in Process Inventory.
(b) debit Finished Goods Inventory.
(c) debit Manufacturing Overhead.
(d) credit Raw Materials Inventory.

(SO 3) **6.** The entry when direct factory labor is assigned to jobs is a debit to:
(a) Work in Process Inventory and a credit to Factory Labor.
(b) Manufacturing Overhead and a credit to Factory Labor.
(c) Factory Labor and a credit to Manufacturing Overhead.
(d) Factory Labor and a credit to Work in Process Inventory.

(SO 4) **7.** The formula for computing the predetermined manufacturing overhead rate is estimated annual overhead costs divided by an expected annual operating activity, expressed as:
(a) direct labor cost.
(b) direct labor hours.
(c) machine hours.
(d) any of the above.

(SO 4) **8.** In Crawford Company, the predetermined overhead rate is 80% of direct labor cost. During the month, $210,000 of factory labor costs are incurred, of which $180,000 is direct labor and $30,000 is indirect labor. Actual overhead

incurred was $200,000. The amount of overhead debited to Work in Process Inventory should be:
(a) $120,000.
(b) $144,000.
(c) $168,000.
(d) $160,000.

(SO 5) **9.** In Mynex Company, Job No. 26 is completed at a cost of $4,500 and later sold for $7,000 cash. A correct entry is:
(a) Debit Finished Goods Inventory $7,000 and credit Work in Process Inventory $7,000.
(b) Debit Cost of Goods Sold $7,000 and credit Finished Goods Inventory $7,000.

(c) Debit Finished Goods Inventory $4,500 and credit Work in Process Inventory $4,500.
(d) Debit Accounts Receivable $7,000 and credit Sales $7,000.

10. Manufacturing overhead is underapplied if: (SO 6)
(a) actual overhead is less than applied.
(b) actual overhead is greater than applied.
(c) the predetermined rate equals the actual rate.
(d) actual overhead equals applied overhead.

Questions

1. (a) Kent Krause is not sure about the difference between cost accounting and a cost accounting system. Explain the difference to Kent. (b) What is an important feature of a cost accounting system?

2. (a) Distinguish between the two types of cost accounting systems. (b) May a company use both types of cost accounting systems?

3. What type of industry is likely to use a job order cost system? Give some examples.

4. What type of industry is likely to use a process cost system? Give some examples.

5. Your roommate asks your help in understanding the major steps in the flow of costs in a job order cost system. Identify the steps for your roommate.

6. There are three inventory control accounts in a job order system. Identify the control accounts and their subsidiary ledgers.

7. What source documents are used in accumulating direct labor costs?

8. "Entries to Manufacturing Overhead normally are only made daily." Do you agree? Explain.

9. Alan Bruski is confused about the source documents used in assigning materials and labor costs. Identify the documents and give the entry for each document.

10. What is the purpose of a job cost sheet?

11. Indicate the source documents that are used in charging costs to specific jobs.

12. Differentiate between a "materials inventory record" and a "materials requisition slip" as used in a job order cost system.

13. Joe Gruber believes actual manufacturing overhead should be charged to jobs. Do you agree? Why or why not?

14. What relationships are involved in computing a predetermined overhead rate?

15. How can the agreement of Work in Process Inventory and job cost sheets be verified?

16. Jane Jelk believes that the cost of goods manufactured schedule in job order cost accounting is the same as shown in Chapter 14. Is Jane correct? Explain.

17. Alex Cesska is confused about under- and overapplied manufacturing overhead. Define the terms for Alex, and indicate the balance in the manufacturing overhead account applicable to each term.

18. "At the end of the year, under- or overapplied overhead is closed to Income Summary." Is this correct? If not, indicate the customary treatment of this amount.

Brief Exercises

BE15-1 Sandy Tool & Die begins operations on January 1. Because all work is done to customer specifications, the company decides to use a job order cost accounting system. Prepare a flow chart of a typical job order system with arrows showing the flow of costs. Identify the eight transactions.

Prepare a flowchart of a job order cost accounting system, and identify transactions.
(SO 2)

BE15-2 During the first month of operations, Sandy Tool & Die accumulated the following manufacturing costs: raw materials $3,000 on account, factory labor $5,000 of which $4,500 relates to factory wages payable and $500 relates to payroll taxes payable, and utilities payable $2,000. Prepare separate journal entries for each type of manufacturing cost.

Prepare entries in accumulating manufacturing costs.
(SO 2)

Prepare entry for the assignment of raw materials costs.
(SO 2)

BE15-3   In January, Sandy Tool & Die requisitions raw materials for production as follows: Job 1 $900, Job 2 $1,200, Job 3 $500, and general factory use $600. Prepare a summary journal entry to record raw materials used.

Prepare entry for the assignment of factory labor costs.
(SO 2)

BE15-4   Factory labor data for Sandy Tool & Die is given in BE15-2. During January, time tickets show that the factory labor of $5,000 was used as follows: Job 1 $1,200, Job 2 $1,600 Job 3 $1,700, and general factory use $500. Prepare a summary journal entry to record factory labor used.

Prepare job cost sheets.
(SO 3)

BE15-5   Data pertaining to job cost sheets for Sandy Tool & Die are given in BE15-3 and BE15-4. Prepare the job cost sheets for each of the three jobs. (*Note:* You may omit the column for Manufacturing Overhead.)

Compute predetermined overhead rates.
(SO 4)

BE15-6   Burrand Company estimates that annual manufacturing overhead costs will be $600,000. Estimated annual operating activity bases are: direct labor cost $500,000, direct labor hours 50,000, and machine hours 100,000. Compute the predetermined overhead rate for each activity base.

Assign manufacturing overhead to production.
(SO 4)

BE15-7   During the first quarter, Sota Company incurs the following direct labor costs: January $40,000, February $30,000, and March $50,000. For each month, prepare the entry to assign overhead to production using a predetermined rate of 120% of direct labor cost.

Prepare entries for completion and sale of completed jobs.

BE15-8   In March, Caroline Company completes Jobs 10 and 11. Job 10 cost $25,000 and Job 11 $32,000. On March 31, Job 10 is sold to the customer for $35,000 in cash. Journalize the entries for the completion of the two jobs and the sale of Job 10.

Prepare adjusting entries for under- and overapplied overhead.
(SO 6)

BE15-9   At December 31, balances in Manufacturing Overhead are: Apex Company—debit $1,200, Lopez Company—credit $900. Prepare the adjusting entry for each company at December 31, assuming the adjustment is made to cost of goods sold.

Exercises

Prepare entries for factory labor.
(SO 2)

E15-1   The gross earnings of the factory workers for Darlinda Company during the month of January are $80,000. The employer's payroll taxes for the factory payroll are $8,000. The fringe benefits to be paid by the employer on this payroll are $4,000. Of the total accumulated cost of factory labor, 85% is related to direct labor and 15% is attributable to indirect labor.

Instructions
(a) Prepare the entry to record the factory labor costs for the month of January.
(b) Prepare the entry to assign factory labor to production.

Prepare journal entries for manufacturing costs.
(SO 2, 3, 4, 5)

E15-2   Dooley Manufacturing uses a job order cost accounting system. On May 1, the company has a balance in Work in Process Inventory of $3,200 and two jobs in process: Job No. 429 $2,000, and Job No. 430 $1,200. During May, a summary of source documents reveals the following.

Job Number	Materials Requisition Slips		Labor Time Tickets	
429	$2,500		$2,400	
430	3,500		3,000	
431	4,400	$10,400	7,600	$13,000
General use		800		1,200
		$11,200		$14,200

Dooley Manufacturing applies manufacturing overhead to jobs at an overhead rate of 90% of direct labor cost. Job No. 429 is completed during the month.

Instructions

(a) Prepare summary journal entries to record: (i) the requisition slips, (ii) the time tickets, (iii) the assignment of manufacturing overhead to jobs, and (iv) the completion of Job No. 429.

(b) Post the entries to Work in Process Inventory, and prove the agreement of the control account with the job cost sheets.

E15-3 A job order cost sheet for Bjerg Company is shown below.

Analyze a job cost sheet and prepare entries for manufacturing costs.
(SO 2, 3, 4, 5)

Job No. 92			For 2,000 Units
Date	Direct Materials	Direct Labor	Manufacturing Overhead
Beg. bal. Jan. 1	5,000	6,000	4,200
8	6,000		
12		8,000	6,400
25	2,000		
27		4,000	3,200
	13,000	18,000	13,800

Cost of completed job:	
Direct materials	$13,000
Direct labor	18,000
Manufacturing overhead	13,800
Total cost	$44,800
Unit cost ($44,800 ÷ 2,000)	$22.40

Instructions

(a) ▭▭▭▷ On the basis of the foregoing data answer the following questions.

(1) What was the balance in Work in Process Inventory on January 1 if this was the only unfinished job?

(2) If manufacturing overhead is applied on the basis of direct labor cost, what overhead rate was used in each year?

(b) Prepare summary entries at January 31 to record the current year's transactions pertaining to Job No. 92.

E15-4 Manufacturing cost data for Copa Company, which uses a job order cost system, are presented below.

Analyze costs of manufacturing and determine missing amounts.
(SO 2, 5)

	Case A	Case B	Case C
Direct materials used	$ (a)	$ 83,000	$ 63,150
Direct labor	50,000	100,000	(h)
Manufacturing overhead applied	42,500	(d)	(i)
Total manufacturing costs	165,650	(e)	250,000
Work in process 1/1/07	(b)	15,500	18,000
Total cost of work in process	201,500	(f)	(j)
Work in process 12/31/07	(c)	11,800	(k)
Cost of goods manufactured	192,300	(g)	262,000

Instructions

Indicate the missing amount for each letter. Assume that in all cases manufacturing overhead is applied on the basis of direct labor cost and the rate is the same.

Compute the manufacturing overhead rate and under- or overapplied overhead.
(SO 4, 6)

E15-5 Rodriquez Company applies manufacturing overhead to jobs on the basis of machine hours used. Overhead costs are expected to total $300,000 for the year, and machine usage is estimated at 125,000 hours.

For the year, $322,000 of overhead costs are incurred and 130,000 hours are used.

Analyze job cost sheet and prepare entry for completed job.
(SO 2, 3, 4, 5)

Instructions
(a) Compute the manufacturing overhead rate for the year.
(b) What is the amount of under- or overapplied overhead at December 31?
(c) Assuming the under- or overapplied overhead for the year is not allocated to inventory accounts, prepare the adjusting entry to assign the amount to cost of goods sold.

E15-6 A job cost sheet of Battle Company is given below.

Job Cost Sheet

JOB NO. 469   Quantity 2,000

ITEM   White Lion Cages   Date Requested   7/2

FOR   Tesla Company   Date Completed   7/31

Date	Direct Materials	Direct Labor	Manufacturing Overhead
7/10	828		
12	900		
15		440	528
22		380	456
24	1,600		
27	1,500		
31		540	648

Cost of completed job:
Direct materials   ———
Direct labor   ———
Manufacturing overhead   ———
Total cost   ═══
Unit cost   ═══

Instructions
(a) ▭▭▭▷ Answer the following questions.
  (1) What are the source documents for direct materials, direct labor, and manufacturing overhead costs assigned to this job?
  (2) What is the predetermined manufacturing overhead rate?
  (3) What are the total cost and the unit cost of the completed job?
(b) Prepare the entry to record the completion of the job.

Prepare entries for manufacturing costs.
(SO 2, 4, 5)

E15-7 Laird Corporation incurred the following transactions.

1. Purchased raw materials on account $46,300.
2. Raw Materials of $36,000 were requisitioned to the factory. An analysis of the materials requisition slips indicated that $8,800 was classified as indirect materials.
3. Factory labor costs incurred were $53,900, of which $49,000 pertained to factory wages payable and $4,900 pertained to employer payroll taxes payable.
4. Time tickets indicated that $50,000 was direct labor and $3,900 was indirect labor.
5. Overhead costs incurred on account were $80,500.
6. Manufacturing overhead was applied at the rate of 150% of direct labor cost.
7. Goods costing $88,000 were completed and transferred to finished goods.
8. Finished goods costing $75,000 to manufacture were sold on account for $103,000.

Instructions
Journalize the transactions. (Omit explanations.)

Prepare entries for manufacturing costs.
(SO 2, 3, 4, 5)

E15-8 Tombert Printing Corp. uses a job order cost system. The following data summarize the operations related to the first quarter's production.

1. Materials purchased on account $192,000, and factory wages incurred $87,300.
2. Materials requisitioned and factory labor used by job:

		Factory
Job Number	Materials	Labor
A20	$ 32,240	$18,000
A21	42,920	22,000
A22	36,100	15,000
A23	39,270	25,000
General factory use	4,470	7,300
	$155,000	$87,300

3. Manufacturing overhead costs incurred on account $39,500.
4. Depreciation on machinery and equipment $14,550.
5. Manufacturing overhead rate is 70% of direct labor cost.
6. Jobs completed during the quarter: A20, A21, and A23.

Instructions
Prepare entries to record the operations summarized above. (Prepare a schedule showing the individual cost elements and total cost for each job in item 6.)

E15-9 At May 31, 2007, the accounts of Yellow Knife Manufacturing Company show the following.

Prepare a cost of goods manufactured schedule and partial financial statements.
(SO 2, 5)

1. May 1 inventories—finished goods $12,600, work in process $14,700, and raw materials $8,200.
2. May 31 inventories—finished goods $11,500, work in process $17,900, and raw materials $7,100.
3. Debit postings to work in process were: direct materials $62,400, direct labor $32,000, and manufacturing overhead applied $48,000.
4. Sales totaled $200,000.

Instructions
(a) Prepare a condensed cost of goods manufactured schedule.
(b) Prepare an income statement for May through gross profit.
(c) Indicate the balance sheet presentation of the manufacturing inventories at May 31, 2007.

E15-10 Tomlin Company begins operations on April 1. Information from job cost sheets shows the following.

Compute work in process and finished goods from job cost sheets.
(SO 3, 5)

Job	Manufacturing Costs Assigned			Month
Number	April	May	June	Completed
10	$5,200	$4,400		May
11	6,100	3,900	$3,000	June
12	1,200			April
13		4,700	4,500	June
14		3,900	3,600	Not complete

Job 12 was completed in April. Job 10 was completed in May. Jobs 11 and 13 were completed in June. Each job was sold for 50% above its cost in the month following completion.

Instructions
(a) What is the balance in Work in Process Inventory at the end of each month?
(b) What is the balance in Finished Goods Inventory at the end of each month?
(c) What is the gross profit for May, June, and July?

E15-11 Shown at the top of the next page are the job cost related accounts for the law firm of Chan, King, and Lou and their manufacturing equivalents:

Prepare entries for costs of services provided.
(SO 2, 4, 5)

Law Firm Accounts	Manufacturing Firm Accounts
Supplies	Raw Materials
Direct Attorney Cost	Direct Labor
Operating Overhead	Manufacturing Overhead
Work in Process	Work in Process
Cost of Completed Work	Cost of Goods Sold

Cost data for the month of March follow.

1. Purchased supplies on account $1,500.
2. Issued supplies $1,200 (60% direct and 40% indirect).
3. Time cards for the month indicated labor costs of $75,000 (80% direct and 20% indirect).
4. Operating overhead costs incurred for cash totaled $40,000.
5. Operating overhead is applied at a rate of 90% of direct attorney cost.
6. Work completed totaled $100,000.

Instructions
(a) Journalize the transactions for March. Omit explanations.
(b) Determine the balance of the Work in Process account. Use a T account.

Determine cost of jobs and ending balance in work in process and overhead accounts.
(SO 3, 4, 6)

E15-12 Armando Ortiz and Associates, a C.P.A. firm, uses job order costing to capture the costs of its audit jobs. There were no audit jobs in process at the beginning of November. Listed below are data concerning the three audit jobs conducted during November.

	Hernandez	Navarro	Vallejo
Direct materials	$600	$400	$200
Auditor labor costs	$5,400	$6,600	$3,375
Auditor hours	72	88	45

Overhead costs are applied to jobs on the basis of auditor hours, and the predetermined overhead rate is $50 per auditor hour. The Hernandez job is the only incomplete job at the end of November. Actual overhead for the month was $11,000.

Instructions
(a) Determine the cost of each job.
(b) Indicate the balance of the Work in Process account at the end of November.
(c) Calculate the ending balance of the Manufacturing Overhead account for November.

Determine predetermined overhead rate, apply overhead and determine whether balance under- or overapplied.
(SO 4, 6)

E15-13 Deco Decorating uses a job order costing system to collect the costs of its interior decorating business. Each client's consultation is treated as a separate job. Overhead is applied to each job based on the number of decorator hours incurred. Listed below are data for the current year.

Budgeted overhead	$960,000
Actual overhead	$982,800
Budgeted decorator hours	38,400
Actual decorator hours	39,000

The company uses Operating Overhead in place of Manufacturing Overhead.

Instructions
(a) Compute the predetermined overhead rate.
(b) Prepare the entry to apply the overhead for the year.
(c) Determine whether the overhead was under- or overapplied and by how much.

Problems: Set A

Prepare entries in a job cost system and job cost sheets.
(SO 2, 3, 4, 5, 6)

P15-1A Elite Manufacturing uses a job order cost system and applies overhead to production on the basis of direct labor hours. On January 1, 2007, Job No. 25 was the only job in process. The costs incurred prior to January 1 on this job were as follows: direct materials $10,000; direct labor $6,000; and manufacturing overhead $9,000. Job No. 23 had been completed at a cost of $45,000 and was part of finished goods inventory. There was a $5,000 balance in the Raw Materials Inventory account.

During the month of January, the company began production on Jobs 26 and 27, and completed Jobs 25 and 26. Jobs 23 and 25 were sold on account during the month for $67,000 and $74,000, respectively. The following additional events occurred during the month.

1. Purchased additional raw materials of $45,000 on account.
2. Incurred factory labor costs of $35,500. Of this amount $6,500 related to employer payroll taxes.
3. Incurred manufacturing overhead costs as follows: indirect materials $10,000; indirect labor $7,500; depreciation expense $12,000; and various other manufacturing overhead costs on account $6,000.
4. Assigned direct materials and direct labor to jobs as follows.

Job No.	Direct Materials	Direct Labor
25	$ 5,000	$ 3,000
26	20,000	12,000
27	15,000	9,000

5. The company uses direct labor hours as the activity base to assign overhead. Direct labor hours incurred on each job were as follows: Job No. 25, 200; Job No. 26, 800; and Job No. 27, 600.

Instructions
(a) Calculate the predetermined overhead rate for the year 2007, assuming Elite Manufacturing estimates total manufacturing overhead costs of $400,000, direct labor costs of $300,000, and direct labor hours of 20,000 for the year.
(b) Open job cost sheets for Jobs 25, 26, and 27. Enter the January 1 balances on the job cost sheet for Job No. 25.
(c) Prepare the journal entries to record the purchase of raw materials, the factory labor costs incurred, and the manufacturing overhead costs incurred during the month of January.
(d) Prepare the journal entries to record the assignment of direct materials, direct labor, and manufacturing overhead costs to production. In assigning manufacturing overhead costs, use the overhead rate calculated in (a). Post all costs to the job cost sheets as necessary.
(e) Total the job cost sheets for any job(s) completed during the month. Prepare the journal entry (or entries) to record the completion of any job(s) during the month.

(e) Job 25, $37,000
Job 26, $48,000

(f) Prepare the journal entry (or entries) to record the sale of any job(s) during the month.
(g) What is the balance in the Work in Process Inventory account at the end of the month? What does this balance consist of?
(h) What is the amount of over- or underapplied overhead?

P15-2A   For the year ended December 31, 2007, the job cost sheets of Sprague Company contained the following data.

Prepare entries in a job cost system and partial income statement.
(SO 2, 3, 4, 5, 6)

Job Number	Explanation	Direct Materials	Direct Labor	Manufacturing Overhead	Total Costs
7650	Balance 1/1	$18,000	$20,000	$25,000	$ 63,000
	Current year's costs	27,000	30,000	37,500	94,500
7651	Balance 1/1	12,000	18,000	22,500	52,500
	Current year's costs	28,000	40,000	50,000	118,000
7652	Current year's costs	40,000	64,000	80,000	184,000

Other data:

1. Raw materials inventory totaled $20,000 on January 1. During the year, $100,000 of raw materials were purchased on account.
2. Finished goods on January 1 consisted of Job No. 7648 for $98,000 and Job No. 7649 for $62,000.

3. Job No. 7650 and Job No. 7651 were completed during the year.
4. Job Nos. 7648, 7649, and 7650 were sold on account for $490,000.
5. Manufacturing overhead incurred on account totaled $120,000.
6. Other manufacturing overhead consisted of indirect materials $12,000, indirect labor $18,000 and depreciation on factory machinery $19,500.

Instructions

(a) (1) $115,500
    (4) $167,500
    Unfinished job 7652,
        $184,000

(b) Amount = $2,000

(c) $170,500

(a) Prove the agreement of Work in Process Inventory with job cost sheets pertaining to unfinished work. (*Hint*: Use a single T account for Work in Process Inventory.) Calculate each of the following, then post each to the T account: (1) beginning balance, (2) direct materials, (3) direct labor, (4) manufacturing overhead, and (5) completed jobs.
(b) Prepare the adjusting entry for manufacturing overhead, assuming the balance is allocated entirely to cost of goods sold.
(c) Determine the gross profit to be reported for 2007.

Prepare entries in a job cost system and cost of goods manufactured schedule.
(SO 2, 3, 4, 5)

P15-3A Steve Taylor is a contractor specializing in custom-built jacuzzis. On May 1, 2007, his ledger contains the following data.

Raw Materials Inventory	$30,000
Work in Process Inventory	12,600
Manufacturing Overhead	2,500 (dr.)

The Manufacturing Overhead account has debit totals of $12,500 and credit totals of $10,000. Subsidiary data for Work in Process Inventory on May 1 include:

Job Cost Sheets

Job by Customer	Direct Materials	Direct Labor	Manufacturing Overhead
Farley	$2,500	$2,000	$1,600
Hendricks	2,000	1,200	960
Minor	900	800	640
	$5,400	$4,000	$3,200

During May, the following costs were incurred: (a) raw materials purchased on account $5,000, (b) labor paid $8,000, (c) manufacturing overhead paid $1,400.

A summary of materials requisition slips and time tickets for the month of May reveals the following.

Job by Customer	Materials Requisition Slips	Time Tickets
Farley	$ 500	$ 400
Hendricks	600	1,000
Minor	2,300	1,300
Bennett	2,400	3,300
	5,800	6,000
General use	1,500	2,000
	$7,300	$8,000

Overhead was charged to jobs on the basis of $0.80 per dollar of direct labor cost.
The jacuzzis for customers Farley, Hendricks, and Minor were completed during May. Each jacuzzi was sold for $12,500 cash.

Instructions

(a) Prepare journal entries for the May transactions: (i) for purchase of raw materials, factory labor costs incurred, and manufacturing overhead costs incurred; (ii) assignment of direct materials, labor, and overhead to production; and (iii) completion of jobs and sale of goods.
(b) Post the entries to Work in Process Inventory.

(d) Cost of goods manufactured
    $20,860

(c) Reconcile the balance in Work in Process Inventory with the costs of unfinished jobs.
(d) Prepare a cost of goods manufactured schedule for May.

P15-4A   Acquatic Manufacturing uses a job order cost system in each of its three man- *Compute predetermined over-*
ufacturing departments. Manufacturing overhead is applied to jobs on the basis of direct *head rates, apply overhead,*
labor cost in Department A, direct labor hours in Department B, and machine hours in *and calculate under- or over-*
Department C. *applied overhead.*

In establishing the predetermined overhead rates for 2007 the following estimates *(SO 4, 6)*
were made for the year.

	Department		
	A	**B**	**C**
Manufacturing overhead	$930,000	$800,000	$750,000
Direct labor cost	$600,000	$100,000	$600,000
Direct labor hours	50,000	40,000	40,000
Machine hours	100,000	120,000	150,000

During January, the job cost sheets showed the following costs and production data.

	Department		
	A	**B**	**C**
Direct materials used	$92,000	$86,000	$64,000
Direct labor cost	$48,000	$35,000	$50,400
Manufacturing overhead incurred	$76,000	$74,000	$61,500
Direct labor hours	4,000	3,500	4,200
Machine hours	8,000	10,500	12,600

Instructions
(a) Compute the predetermined overhead rate for each department.   *(a)* 155%, $20, $5
(b) Compute the total manufacturing costs assigned to jobs in January in each depart-   *(b)* $214,400, $191,000
   ment. $177,400
(c) Compute the under- or overapplied overhead for each department at January 31.   *(c)* $1,600, $4,000, $(1,500)

P15-5A   Freedo Company's fiscal year ends on June 30. The following accounts are found *Analyze manufacturing*
in its job order cost accounting system for the first month of the new fiscal year. *accounts and determine*
missing amounts.

Raw Materials Inventory

July	1	Beginning balance	19,000	July 31	Requisitions	(a)
	31	Purchases	90,400			
July 31		Ending balance	(b)			

Work in Process Inventory

July	1	Beginning balance	(c)	July 31	Jobs completed	(f)
	31	Direct materials	80,000			
	31	Direct labor	(d)			
	31	Overhead	(e)			
July 31		Ending balance	(g)			

Finished Goods Inventory

July	1	Beginning balance	(h)	July 31	Cost of goods sold	(j)
	31	Completed jobs	(i)			
July 31		Ending balance	(k)			

Factory Labor

July 31	Factory wages	(l)	July 31	Wages assigned	(m)

Manufacturing Overhead

July 31	Indirect materials	8,900	July 31	Overhead applied	117,000
31	Indirect labor	16,000			
31	Other overhead	(n)			

Other data:

1. On July 1, two jobs were in process: Job No. 4085 and Job No. 4086, with costs of
   $19,000 and $8,200, respectively.

2. During July, Job Nos. 4087, 4088, and 4089 were started. On July 31, only Job No. 4089 was unfinished. This job had charges for direct materials $2,000 and direct labor $1,000, plus manufacturing overhead. Manufacturing overhead was applied at the rate of 130% of direct labor cost.
3. On July 1, Job No. 4084, costing $135,000, was in the finished goods warehouse. On July 31, Job No. 4088, costing $143,000, was in finished goods.
4. Overhead was $3,000 underapplied in July.

Instructions
List the letters (a) through (n) and indicate the amount pertaining to each letter. Show computations.

Problems: Set B

P15-1B Medina Manufacturing uses a job order cost system and applies overhead to production on the basis of direct labor costs. On January 1, 2007, Job No. 50 was the only job in process. The costs incurred prior to January 1 on this job were as follows: direct materials $20,000, direct labor $12,000, and manufacturing overhead $16,000. As of January 1, Job No. 49 had been completed at a cost of $90,000 and was part of finished goods inventory. There was a $15,000 balance in the Raw Materials Inventory account.

During the month of January, Medina Manufacturing began production on Jobs 51 and 52, and completed Jobs 50 and 51. Jobs 49 and 50 were also sold on account during the month for $122,000 and $158,000, respectively. The following additional events occurred during the month.

1. Purchased additional raw materials of $90,000 on account.
2. Incurred factory labor costs of $65,000. Of this amount $13,000 related to employer payroll taxes.
3. Incurred manufacturing overhead costs as follows: indirect materials $14,000; indirect labor $15,000; depreciation expense $19,000, and various other manufacturing overhead costs on account $20,000.
4. Assigned direct materials and direct labor to jobs as follows.

Job No.	Direct Materials	Direct Labor
50	$10,000	$ 5,000
51	39,000	25,000
52	30,000	20,000

Instructions
(a) Calculate the predetermined overhead rate for 2007, assuming Medina Manufacturing estimates total manufacturing overhead costs of $980,000, direct labor costs of $700,000, and direct labor hours of 20,000 for the year.
(b) Open job cost sheets for Jobs 50, 51, and 52. Enter the January 1 balances on the job cost sheet for Job No. 50.
(c) Prepare the journal entries to record the purchase of raw materials, the factory labor costs incurred, and the manufacturing overhead costs incurred during the month of January.
(d) Prepare the journal entries to record the assignment of direct materials, direct labor, and manufacturing overhead costs to production. In assigning manufacturing overhead costs, use the overhead rate calculated in (a). Post all costs to the job cost sheets as necessary.

(e) Total the job cost sheets for any job(s) completed during the month. Prepare the journal entry (or entries) to record the completion of any job(s) during the month.
(f) Prepare the journal entry (or entries) to record the sale of any job(s) during the month.
(g) What is the balance in the Finished Goods Inventory account at the end of the month? What does this balance consist of?
(h) What is the amount of over- or underapplied overhead?

P15-2B   For the year ended December 31, 2007, the job cost sheets of Amend Company contained the following data.

Prepare entries in a job cost system and partial income statement.
(SO 2, 3, 4, 5, 6)

Job Number	Explanation	Direct Materials	Direct Labor	Manufacturing Overhead	Total Costs
7640	Balance 1/1	$25,000	$24,000	$28,800	$ 77,800
	Current year's costs	30,000	36,000	43,200	109,200
7641	Balance 1/1	11,000	18,000	21,600	50,600
	Current year's costs	40,000	48,000	57,600	145,600
7642	Current year's costs	48,000	50,000	60,000	158,000

Other data:

1. Raw materials inventory totaled $15,000 on January 1. During the year, $140,000 of raw materials were purchased on account.
2. Finished goods on January 1 consisted of Job No. 7638 for $87,000 and Job No. 7639 for $92,000.
3. Job No. 7640 and Job No. 7641 were completed during the year.
4. Job Nos. 7638, 7639, and 7641 were sold on account for $530,000.
5. Manufacturing overhead incurred on account totaled $115,000.
6. Other manufacturing overhead consisted of indirect materials $14,000, indirect labor $20,000, and depreciation on factory machinery $8,000.

Instructions
(a) Prove the agreement of Work in Process Inventory with job cost sheets pertaining to unfinished work. *Hint:* Use a single T account for Work in Process Inventory. Calculate each of the following, then post each to the T account: (1) beginning balance, (2) direct materials, (3) direct labor, (4) manufacturing overhead, and (5) completed jobs.
(b) Prepare the adjusting entry for manufacturing overhead, assuming the balance is allocated entirely to Cost of Goods Sold.
(c) Determine the gross profit to be reported for 2007.

(a) $158,000; Job 7642: $158,000

(b) Amount = $3,800

(c) $158,600

P15-3B   Zion Inc. is a construction company specializing in custom patios. The patios are constructed of concrete, brick, fiberglass, and lumber, depending upon customer preference. On June 1, 2007, the general ledger for Zion Inc. contains the following data.

Prepare entries in a job cost system and cost of goods manufactured schedule.
(SO 2, 3, 4, 5)

Raw Materials Inventory	$4,200	Manufacturing Overhead Applied	$32,640
Work in Process Inventory	$5,540	Manufacturing Overhead Incurred	$31,650

Subsidiary data for Work in Process Inventory on June 1 are as follows.

Job Cost Sheets

	Customer Job		
Cost Element	Powell	Aurora	Hayden
Direct materials	$ 600	$ 800	$ 900
Direct labor	320	540	580
Manufacturing overhead	400	675	725
	$1,320	$2,015	$2,205

During June, raw materials purchased on account were $3,900, and all wages were paid. Additional overhead costs consisted of depreciation on equipment $700 and miscellaneous costs of $400 incurred on account.

A summary of materials requisition slips and time tickets for June shows the following.

Customer Job	Materials Requisition Slips	Time Tickets
Powell	$ 800	$ 450
Elgin	2,000	800
Aurora	500	360
Hayden	1,300	800
Powell	300	390
	4,900	2,800
General use	1,500	1,200
	$6,400	$4,000

Overhead was charged to jobs at the same rate of $1.25 per dollar of direct labor cost. The patios for customers Powell, Aurora, and Hayden were completed during June and sold for a total of $18,900. Each customer paid in full.

Instructions
(a) Journalize the June transactions: (i) for purchase of raw materials, factory labor costs incurred, and manufacturing overhead costs incurred; (ii) assignment of direct materials, labor, and overhead to production; and (iii) completion of jobs and sale of goods.
(b) Post the entries to Work in Process Inventory.

(d) Cost of goods manufactured   (c) Reconcile the balance in Work in Process Inventory with the costs of unfinished jobs.
$12,940   (d) Prepare a cost of goods manufactured schedule for June.

Compute predetermined overhead rates, apply overhead and calculate under- or over-applied overhead.
(SO 4, 6)

P15-4B   Stein Manufacturing Company uses a job order cost system in each of its three manufacturing departments. Manufacturing overhead is applied to jobs on the basis of direct labor cost in Department D, direct labor hours in Department E, and machine hours in Department K.

In establishing the predetermined overhead rates for 2008 the following estimates were made for the year.

	Department		
	D	**E**	**K**
Manufacturing overhead	$1,200,000	$1,500,000	$900,000
Direct labor costs	$1,500,000	$1,250,000	$450,000
Direct labor hours	100,000	125,000	40,000
Machine hours	400,000	500,000	120,000

During January, the job cost sheets showed the following costs and production data.

	Department		
	D	**E**	**K**
Direct materials used	$140,000	$126,000	$78,000
Direct labor costs	$120,000	$110,000	$37,500
Manufacturing overhead incurred	$ 98,000	$129,000	$74,000
Direct labor hours	8,000	11,000	3,500
Machine hours	34,000	45,000	10,400

(a) 80%, $12, $7.50
(b) $356,000, $368,000
   $193,500
(c) $2,000, $(3,000), $(4,000)

Analyze manufacturing accounts and determine missing amounts.
(SO 2, 3, 4, 5, 6)

Instructions
(a) Compute the predetermined overhead rate for each department.
(b) Compute the total manufacturing costs assigned to jobs in January in each department.
(c) Compute the under- or overapplied overhead for each department at January 31.

P15-5B   Vargas Corporation's fiscal year ends on November 30. The following accounts are found in its job order cost accounting system for the first month of the new fiscal year.

Raw Materials Inventory

Dec. 1	Beginning balance	(a)	Dec. 31	Requisitions	16,850
31	Purchases	19,225			
Dec. 31	Ending balance	7,975			

Work in Process Inventory

Dec. 1	Beginning balance	(b)	Dec. 31	Jobs completed	(f)
31	Direct materials	(c)			
31	Direct labor	8,800			
31	Overhead	(d)			
Dec. 31	Ending balance	(e)			

Finished Goods Inventory

Dec. 1	Beginning balance	(g)	Dec. 31	Cost of goods sold	(i)
31	Completed jobs	(h)			
Dec. 31	Ending balance	(j)			

Factory Labor

Dec. 31	Factory wages	12,025	Dec. 31	Wages assigned	(k)

Manufacturing Overhead

Dec. 31	Indirect materials	1,900	Dec. 31	Overhead applied	(m)
31	Indirect labor	(l)			
31	Other overhead	1,245			

Other data:

1. On December 1, two jobs were in process: Job No. 154 and Job No. 155. These jobs had combined direct materials costs of $9,750 and direct labor costs of $15,000. Overhead was applied at a rate that was 75% of direct labor cost.
2. During December, Job Nos. 156, 157, and 158 were started. On December 31, Job No. 158 was unfinished. This job had charges for direct materials $3,800 and direct labor $4,800, plus manufacturing overhead. All jobs, except for Job No. 158, were completed in December.
3. On December 1, Job No. 153 was in the finished goods warehouse. It had a total cost of $5,000. On December 31, Job No. 157 was the only job finished that was not sold. It had a cost of $4,000.
4. Manufacturing overhead was $230 overapplied in December.

Instructions
List the letters (a) through (m) and indicate the amount pertaining to each letter.

(c) $14,950
(f) $54,150
(i) $55,150

Problems: Set C

Visit the book's website at **www.wiley.com/college/kimmel** and choose the Student Companion site to access Problem Set C.

BROADENING YOUR PERSPECTIVE

Group Decision Case

BYP15-1 Wang Products Company uses a job order cost system. For a number of months there has been an ongoing rift between the sales department and the production department concerning a special-order product, TC-1. TC-1 is a seasonal product that is manufactured in batches of 1,000 units. TC-1 is sold at cost plus a markup of 40% of cost.

The sales department is unhappy because fluctuating unit production costs significantly affect selling prices. Sales personnel complain that this has caused excessive customer complaints and the loss of considerable orders for TC-1.

The production department maintains that each job order must be fully costed on the basis of the costs incurred during the period in which the goods are produced. Production personnel maintain that the only real solution to the problem is for the sales department to increase sales in the slack periods.

Sandra Devona, president of the company, asks you as the company accountant to collect quarterly data for the past year on TC-1. From the cost accounting system, you accumulate the following production quantity and cost data.

	Quarter			
Costs	**1**	**2**	**3**	**4**
Direct materials	$100,000	$220,000	$ 80,000	$200,000
Direct labor	60,000	132,000	48,000	120,000
Manufacturing overhead	105,000	153,000	97,000	125,000
Total	$265,000	$505,000	$225,000	$445,000
Production in batches	5	11	4	10
Unit cost (per batch)	$ 53,000	$ 45,909	$ 56,250	$ 44,500

Instructions

With the class divided into groups, answer the following questions.

(a) What manufacturing cost element is responsible for the fluctuating unit costs? Why?
(b) What is your recommended solution to the problem of fluctuating unit cost?
(c) Restate the quarterly data on the basis of your recommended solution.

Managerial Analysis

BYP15-2 In the course of routine checking of all journal entries prior to preparing year-end reports, Sally Yount discovered several strange entries. She recalled that the president's son Ken had come in to help out during an especially busy time and that he had recorded some journal entries. She was relieved that there were only a few of his entries, and even more relieved that he had included rather lengthy explanations. The entries Ken made were:

1.

Work in Process Inventory	25,000	
Cash		25,000

(This is for materials put into process. I don't find the record that we paid for these, so I'm crediting Cash, because I know we'll have to pay for them sooner or later.)

2.

Manufacturing Overhead	12,000	
Cash		12,000

(This is for bonuses paid to salespeople. I know they're part of overhead, and I can't find an account called "Non-factory Overhead" or "Other Overhead" so I'm putting it in Manufacturing Overhead. I have the check stubs, so I know we paid these.)

3.

Wages Expense	120,000	
Cash		120,000

(This is for the factory workers' wages. I have a note that payroll taxes are $12,000. I still think that's part of wages expense, and that we'll have to pay it all in cash sooner or later, so I credited Cash for the wages and the taxes.)

4.

Work in Process Inventory	3,000	
Raw Materials Inventory		3,000

(This is for the glue used in the factory. I know we used this to make the products, even though we didn't use very much on any one of the products. I got it out of inventory, so I credited an inventory account.)

Instructions

(a) How should Ken have recorded each of the four events?

(b) If the entry was not corrected, which financial statements (income statement or balance sheet) would be affected? What balances would be overstated or understated?

Real-World Focus

BYP15-3 Founded in 1970, Parlex Corporation is a world leader in the design and manufacture of flexible interconnect products. Utilizing proprietary and patented technologies, Parlex produces custom flexible interconnects including flexible circuits, polymer thick film, laminated cables, and value-added assemblies for sophisticated electronics used in automotive, telecommunications, computer, diversified electronics, and aerospace applications. In addition to manufacturing sites in Methuen, Massachusetts; Salem, New Hampshire; Cranston, Rhode Island; San Jose, California; Shanghai, China; Isle of Wight, UK; and Empalme, Mexico, Parlex has logistic support centers and strategic alliances throughout North America, Asia, and Europe.

    The following information was provided in the company's annual report.

PARLEX COMPANY
Notes to the Financial Statements

The Company's products are manufactured on a job order basis to customers' specifications. Customers submit requests for quotations on each job, and the Company prepares bids based on its own cost estimates. The Company attempts to reflect the impact of changing costs when establishing prices. However, during the past several years, the market conditions for flexible circuits and the resulting price sensitivity haven't always allowed this to transpire. Although still not satisfactory, the Company was able to reduce the cost of products sold as a percentage of sales to 85% this year versus 87% that was experienced in the two immediately preceding years. Management continues to focus on improving operational efficiency and further reducing costs.

Instructions

(a) Parlex management discusses the job order cost system employed by their company. What are several advantages of using the job order approach to costing?

(b) Contrast the products produced in a job order environment, like Parlex, to those produced when process cost systems are used.

Exploring the Web

BYP15-4 The Institute of Management Accountants sponsors a certification for management accountants, allowing them to obtain the title of Certified Management Accountant.

Address: **www.imanet.org** (or go to **www.wiley.com/college/kimmel**)

Steps

1. Go to the site shown above.
2. Choose **Certification**, and then, **Become Certified**.

Instructions

(a) What are the objectives of the certification program?

(b) What is the "experience requirement"?

(c) How many hours of continuing education are required, and what types of courses qualify?

Communication Activity

BYP15-5 You are the management accountant for Clemente Manufacturing. Your company does custom carpentry work and uses a job order cost accounting system. Clemente sends detailed job cost sheets to its customers, along with an invoice. The job cost sheets show the date materials were used, the dollar cost of materials, and the hours and cost of labor. A predetermined overhead application rate is used, and the total overhead applied is also listed.

Cindy Stein is a customer who recently had custom cabinets installed. Along with her check in payment for the work done, she included a letter. She thanked the company for including the detailed cost information but questioned why overhead was estimated. She stated that she would be interested in knowing exactly what costs were included in overhead, and she thought that other customers would, too.

Instructions
Prepare a letter to Ms. Stein (address: 123 Cedar Lane, Altoona, Kansas 66651) and tell her why you did not send her information on exact costs of overhead included in her job. Respond to her suggestion that you provide this information.

Research Assignment

BYP15-6   The April 19, 2004, edition of the *Wall Street Journal* contains an article by Andy Pasztor and Jonathan Karp titled "Northrop Papers Indicate Coverup."

Instructions
Read the article and answer the following questions.

(a) What type of costing system would Northrop use for these government contracts? Explain your answer.
(b) These contracts were billed on a "cost-plus" basis, meaning that the contract allowed the company simply to keep track of its costs and then bill the government for the costs it incurred, plus a profit. In what ways did Northrop abuse this arrangement?
(c) What systems were in place to try to ensure that the company did not violate the terms of the contract?

Ethics Case

BYP15-7   ESU Printing provides printing services to many different corporate clients. Although ESU bids most jobs, some jobs, particularly new ones, are negotiated on a "cost-plus" basis. Cost-plus means that the buyer is willing to pay the actual cost plus a return (profit) on these costs to ESU.

Clara Biggio, controller for ESU, has recently returned from a meeting where ESU's president stated that he wanted her to find a way to charge most costs to any project that was on a cost-plus basis. The president noted that the company needed more profits to meet its stated goals this period. By charging more costs to the cost-plus projects and therefore fewer costs to the jobs that were bid, the company should be able to increase its profit for the current year.

Clara knew why the president wanted to take this action. Rumors were that he was looking for a new position and if the company reported strong profit, the president's opportunities would be enhanced. Clara also recognized that she could probably increase the cost of certain jobs by changing the basis used to allocate manufacturing overhead.

Instructions
(a) Who are the stakeholders in this situation?
(b) What are the ethical issues in this situation?
(c) What would you do if you were Clara Biggio?

Answers to Self-Study Questions
1. a   **2.** b   **3.** c   **4.** d   **5.** b   **6.** a   **7.** d   **8.** b   **9.** c   **10.** b

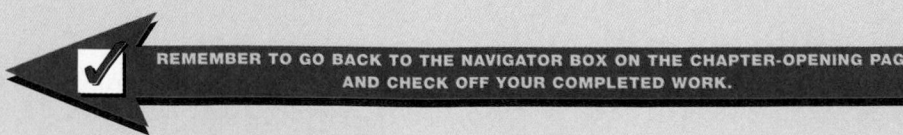
REMEMBER TO GO BACK TO THE NAVIGATOR BOX ON THE CHAPTER-OPENING PAGE AND CHECK OFF YOUR COMPLETED WORK.

16

Process Costing

FEATURE STORY

Ben & Jerry's Tracks Its Mix-Ups

At one time, one of the fastest growing companies in the nation was Ben & Jerry's Homemade, Inc., based in Waterbury, Vermont. The ice cream company that started out of a garage in 1978 is now a public company.

Making ice cream is a process—a movement of product from a mixing department to a prepping department to a pint department. The mixing department is where the ice cream is created. The prep area is where extras such as cherries and walnuts are added to make plain ice cream into "Cherry Garcia." And the pint department is where the ice cream is actually put into containers. As the product is processed from one department to the next, the appropriate materials, labor, and overhead are added to it.

"The incoming ingredients from the shipping and receiving departments are stored in certain locations, either in a freezer or dry warehouse," says Beecher Eurich, staff accountant. "As ingredients get added, so do the costs associated with them." How much ice cream is actually produced? Running the plants around the clock, 18 million gallons are produced each year.

Using a process costing system, Eurich can tell you how much a certain batch of ice cream costs to make—its materials, labor, and overhead in each of the production departments. She generates reports for the production department heads, but makes sure not to overdo it. "You can get bogged down in numbers," says Eurich. "If you're generating a report that no one can use, then that's a waste of time." More likely, though, Ben & Jerry's production people want to know how efficient they are. Why? Many own stock in the company.

On the World Wide Web
www.benjerry.com

THE
NAVIGATOR

PREVIEW OF CHAPTER 16

The cost accounting system used by companies such as Ben & Jerry's is called a **process cost accounting** system. In contrast to job order cost accounting, which focuses on the individual job, process cost accounting focuses on the processes involved in mass-producing products that are identical or very similar in nature. The primary objective of the chapter is to explain and illustrate process cost accounting.

The content and organization of this chapter are as follows.

PROCESS COSTING		
Nature of Process Cost Systems	**Equivalent Units**	**Comprehensive Example of Process Costing**
• Uses • Similarities and differences • Process cost flow • Assignment of manufacturing costs	• Weighted-average method • Refinements • Production cost report	• Physical units • Equivalent units of production • Unit production costs • Cost reconciliation schedule • Production cost report • Costing systems—Final comments

THE NAVIGATOR

The Nature of Process Cost Systems

USES OF PROCESS COST SYSTEMS

Process cost systems are used to apply costs to similar products that are mass-produced in a continuous fashion. Ben & Jerry's uses a process cost system: Production of the ice cream, once it begins, continues until the ice cream emerges, and the processing is the same for the entire run—with precisely the same amount of materials, labor, and overhead. Each finished pint of ice cream is indistinguishable from another.

A company such as USX uses process costing in the manufacturing of steel. Kellogg and General Mills use process costing for cereal production; Exxon-Mobil uses process costing for its oil refining. And Sherwin Williams uses process costing for its paint products. At a bottling company like Coca-Cola, the manufacturing process begins with the blending of ingredients. Next the beverage is dispensed into bottles that are moved into position by automated machinery. The bottles are then capped, packaged, and forwarded to the finished goods warehouse. This process is shown in Illustration 16-1.

Illustration 16-1   Manufacturing processes

Manufacturing Processes — Blending → Filling → Packaging

For Coca-Cola, as well as the other companies just mentioned, once the production begins, it continues until the finished product emerges, and each unit of finished product is like every other unit.

In comparison, costs in a job order cost system are assigned to a *specific job*. Examples are the construction of a customized home, the making of a motion picture, or the manufacturing of a specialized machine. Illustration 16-2 provides examples of companies that primarily use either a process cost system or a job order cost system.

Illustration 16-2   Process cost and job order cost companies and products

Process Cost System Company	Product	Job Order Cost System Company	Product
Coca-Cola, PepsiCo	Soft drinks	Young & Rubicam, J. Walter Thompson	Advertising
ExxonMobil, Royal Dutch Shell	Oil	Walt Disney, Warner Brothers	Motion pictures
Intel, Advanced Micro Devices	Computer chips	Center Ice Consultants, Ice Pro	Ice rinks
Dow Chemical, DuPont	Chemicals	Kaiser, Mayo Clinic	Patient health care

SIMILARITIES AND DIFFERENCES BETWEEN JOB ORDER COST AND PROCESS COST SYSTEMS

STUDY OBJECTIVE

2

Explain the similarities and differences between job order cost and process cost systems.

In a job order cost system, costs are assigned to each job. In a process cost system, costs are tracked through a series of connected manufacturing processes or departments, rather than by individual jobs. Thus, process cost systems are used when a large volume of uniform or relatively homogeneous products is produced. The basic flow of costs in these two systems is shown in Illustration 16-3.

Illustration 16-3   Job order cost and process cost flow

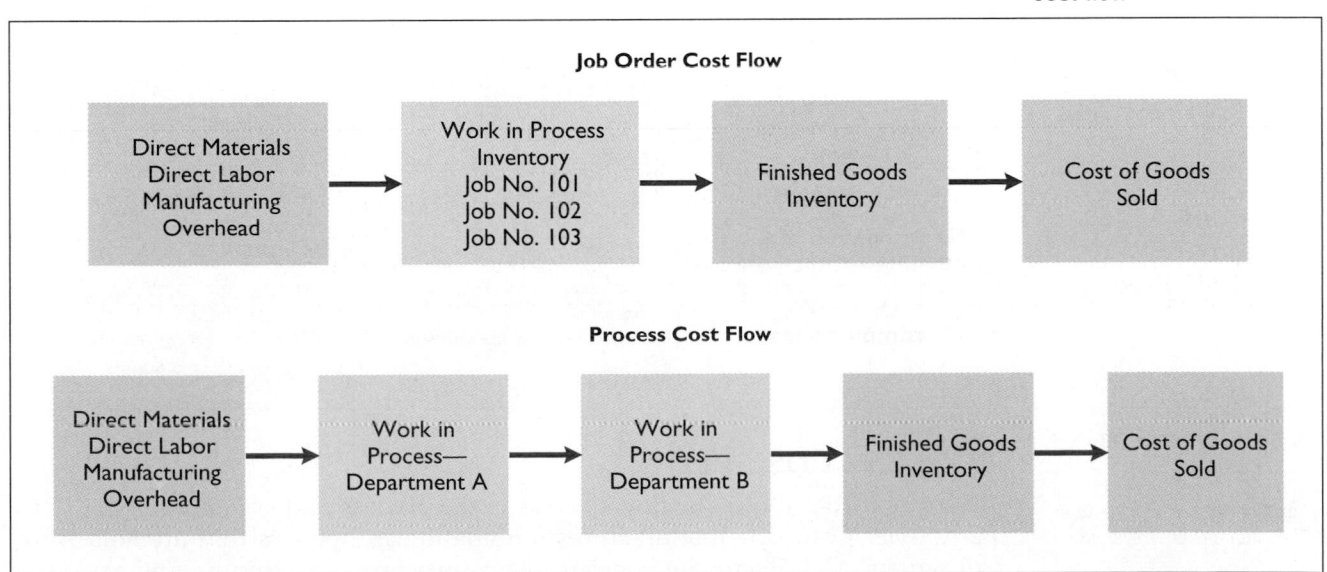

Job Order Cost Flow

Direct Materials Direct Labor Manufacturing Overhead → Work in Process Inventory Job No. 101 Job No. 102 Job No. 103 → Finished Goods Inventory → Cost of Goods Sold

Process Cost Flow

Direct Materials Direct Labor Manufacturing Overhead → Work in Process— Department A → Work in Process— Department B → Finished Goods Inventory → Cost of Goods Sold

The basic similarities and differences between these two systems are highlighted in the following analysis.

Similarities

Job order cost and process cost systems are similar in three ways:

1. **The manufacturing cost elements.** Both costing systems track three manufacturing cost elements—direct materials, direct labor, and manufacturing overhead.
2. **The accumulation of the costs of materials, labor, and overhead.** In both costing systems, raw materials are debited to Raw Materials Inventory; factory labor is debited to Factory Labor; and manufacturing overhead costs are debited to Manufacturing Overhead.
3. **The flow of costs.** As noted above, all manufacturing costs are accumulated by debits to Raw Materials Inventory, Factory Labor, and Manufacturing Overhead. These costs are then assigned to the same accounts in both costing systems—Work in Process, Finished Goods Inventory, and Cost of Goods Sold. **The methods of assigning costs, however, differ significantly.** These differences are explained and illustrated later in the chapter.

Differences

The differences between a job order cost and a process cost system are as follows.

1. **The number of work in process accounts used.** In a job order cost system, only one work in process account is used. In a process cost system, multiple work in process accounts are used.
2. **Documents used to track costs.** In a job order cost system, costs are charged to individual jobs and summarized in a job cost sheet. In a process cost system, costs are summarized in a production cost report for each department.
3. **The point at which costs are totaled.** In a job order cost system, total costs are determined when the job is completed. In a process cost system, total costs are determined at the end of a period of time.
4. **Unit cost computations.** In a job order cost system, the unit cost is the total cost per job divided by the units produced. In a process cost system, the unit cost is total manufacturing costs for the period divided by the units produced during the period.

The major differences between a job order cost and a process cost system are summarized in Illustration 16-4.

Illustration 16-4 Job order versus process cost systems

Features	Job Order Cost System	Process Cost System
Work in process accounts	• One work in process account	• Multiple work in process accounts
Documents used	• Job cost sheets	• Production cost reports
Determination of total manufacturing costs	• Each job	• Each period
Unit-cost computations	• Cost of each job ÷ Units produced for the job	• Total manufacturing costs ÷ Units produced during the period

STUDY OBJECTIVE
3
Explain the flow of costs in a process cost system.

PROCESS COST FLOW

Illustration 16-5 shows the flow of costs in the process cost system for Tyler Company. Tyler Company manufactures automatic can openers that are sold to retail outlets. Manufacturing consists of two processes: machining and assembly.

In the Machining Department, the raw materials are shaped, honed, and drilled. In the Assembly Department, the parts are assembled and packaged.

Illustration 16-5   Flow of costs in process cost system

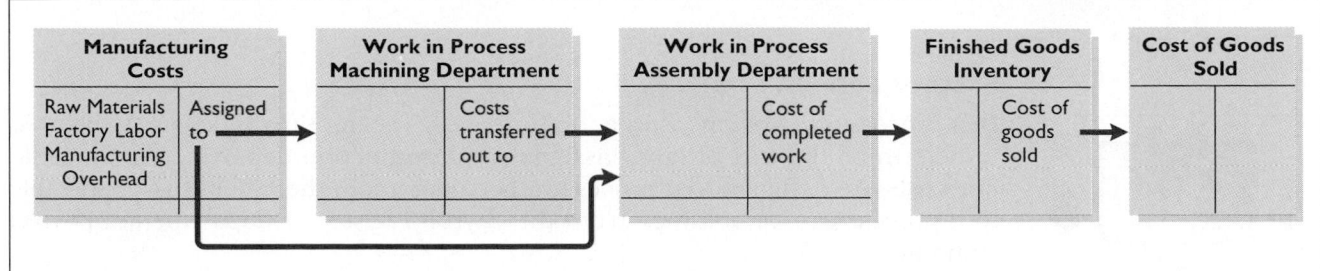

As the flow of costs indicates, materials, labor, and manufacturing overhead can be added in both the Machining and Assembly Departments. When the Machining Department finishes its work, the partially completed units are transferred to the Assembly Department. In the Assembly Department, the goods are finished and are then transferred to the finished goods inventory. Upon sale, the goods are removed from the finished goods inventory. Within each department, a similar set of activities is performed on each unit processed.

ASSIGNMENT OF MANUFACTURING COSTS— JOURNAL ENTRIES

As indicated earlier, the accumulation of the costs of materials, labor, and manufacturing overhead is the same in a process cost system as in a job order cost system. All raw materials are debited to Raw Materials Inventory when the materials are purchased. All factory labor is debited to Factory Labor when the labor costs are incurred. And overhead costs are debited to Manufacturing Overhead as they are incurred. However, the assignment of the three manufacturing cost elements to Work in Process in a process cost system is different from a job order cost system. Here we'll look at how these manufacturing cost elements are assigned in a process cost system.

STUDY OBJECTIVE

4

Make the journal entries to assign manufacturing costs in a process cost system.

Materials Costs

All raw materials issued for production are a materials cost to the producing department. Materials requisition slips may be used in a process cost system, but **fewer requisitions are generally required than in a job order cost system, because the materials are used for processes rather than for specific jobs**. Requisitions are issued less frequently in a process cost system because the requisitions are for larger quantities.

Materials

Materials are usually added to production at the beginning of the first process. However, in subsequent processes, other materials may be added at various points. For example, in the manufacture of Hershey candy bars, the chocolate and other ingredients are added at the beginning of the first process, and the wrappers and cartons are added at the end of the packaging process. At Tyler Company, materials are entered at the beginning of each process. The entry to record the materials used is:

Work in Process—Machining	XXXX	
Work in Process—Assembly	XXXX	
Raw Materials Inventory		XXXX
(To record materials used)		

At ice cream maker Ben & Jerry's, materials are added in three departments: milk and flavoring in the mixing department; extras such as cherries and walnuts in the prepping department; and cardboard containers in the pinting (packaging) department.

Factory Labor Costs

Factory Labor

In a process cost system, as in a job order cost system, time tickets may be used to determine the cost of labor assignable to production departments. Since labor costs are assigned to a process rather than a job, the labor cost chargeable to a process can be obtained from the payroll register or departmental payroll summaries.

Labor costs for the Machining Department will include the wages of employees who shape, hone, and drill the raw materials. The entry to assign these costs for Tyler Company is:

Work in Process—Machining	XXXX	
Work in Process—Assembly	XXXX	
Factory Labor		XXXX
(To assign factory labor to production)		

Manufacturing Overhead Costs

Manufacturing Overhead

The objective in assigning overhead in a process cost system is to allocate the overhead costs to the production departments on an objective and equitable basis. That basis is the activity that "drives" or causes the costs. A primary driver of overhead costs in continuous manufacturing operations is **machine time used**, not direct labor. Thus, **machine hours are widely used** in allocating manufacturing overhead costs. The entry to allocate overhead to the two processes is:

Work in Process—Machining	XXXX	
Work in Process—Assembly	XXXX	
Manufacturing Overhead		XXXX
(To assign overhead to production)		

Business Insight
Management Perspective

In one of Caterpillar's automated cost centers, work is fed into the cost center, processed by robotic machines, and transferred to the next cost center without human intervention. One person tends all of the machines and spends more time maintaining machines than operating them. In such cases, overhead rates based on direct labor hours may be misleading. Surprisingly, some companies continue to assign manufacturing overhead on the basis of direct labor despite the fact that there is no cause-and-effect relationship between labor and overhead.

Transfer to Next Department

At the end of the month, an entry is needed to record the cost of the goods transferred out of the department. In this case, the transfer is to the Assembly Department, and the following entry is made.

Work in Process—Assembly	XXXXX	
Work in Process—Machining		XXXXX
(To record transfer of units to the Assembly		
Department)		

Transfer to Finished Goods

The units completed in the Assembly Department are transferred to the finished goods warehouse. The entry for this transfer is as follows.

Finished Goods Inventory	XXXXX	
Work in Process—Assembly		XXXXX
(To record transfer of units to finished goods)		

Transfer to Cost of Goods Sold

When finished goods are sold, the entry to record the cost of goods sold is as follows.

Cost of Goods Sold	XXXXX	
Finished Goods Inventory		XXXXX
(To record cost of units sold)		

BEFORE YOU GO ON . . .

▶Review It

1. What type of manufacturing companies might use a process cost accounting system?
2. What are the principal similarities and differences between a job order cost system and a process cost system?

▶Do It

Ruth Company manufactures ZEBO through two processes: Blending and Bottling. In June, raw materials used were Blending $18,000 and Bottling $4,000; factory labor costs were Blending $12,000 and Bottling $5,000; manufacturing overhead costs were Blending $6,000 and Bottling $2,500. Units completed at a cost of $19,000 in the Blending Department are transferred to the Bottling Department. Units completed at a cost of $11,000 in the Bottling Department are transferred to Finished Goods. Journalize the assignment of these costs to the two processes and the transfer of units as appropriate.

Action Plan

• In process cost accounting, keep separate work in process accounts for each process.
• When the costs are assigned to production, debit the separate work in process accounts.
• Transfer cost of completed units to the next process or to Finished Goods.

Solution The entries are:

Work in Process—Blending	18,000	
Work in Process—Bottling	4,000	
Raw Materials Inventory		22,000
(To record materials used)		
Work in Process—Blending	12,000	
Work in Process—Bottling	5,000	
Factory Labor		17,000
(To assign factory labor to production)		
Work in Process—Blending	6,000	
Work in Process—Bottling	2,500	
Manufacturing Overhead		8,500
(To assign overhead to production)		
Work in Process—Bottling	19,000	
Work in Process—Blending		19,000
(To record transfer of units to the Bottling Department)		
Finished Goods Inventory	11,000	
Work in Process—Bottling		11,000
(To record transfer of units to finished goods)		

Related exercise material: BE16-1, BE16-2, BE16-3, E16-1, and E16-2.

THE NAVIGATOR

STUDY OBJECTIVE
5
Compute equivalent units.

Equivalent Units

Suppose you were asked to compute the cost of instruction per full-time equivalent student at your college. You are provided the following information.

Illustration 16-6
Information for full-time student example

Costs:	
Total cost of instruction	$9,000,000
Student population:	
Full-time students	900
Part-time students	1,000

Part-time students take 60 percent of the classes of a full-time student during the year. To compute the number of full-time equivalent students per year, you would make the following computation.

Illustration 16-7 Full-time equivalent unit computation

Full-time Students	+	Equivalent Units of Part-time Students	=	Full-time Equivalent Students
900	+	(60% × 1,000)	=	1,500

The cost of instruction per full-time equivalent student is therefore the total cost of instruction ($9,000,000) divided by the number of full-time equivalent students (1,500), which is $6,000 ($9,000,000 ÷ 1,500).

In a process cost system, the same idea, called equivalent units of production, is used. **Equivalent units of production** measure the work done during the period, expressed in fully completed units. This concept is used to determine the cost per unit of completed product.

WEIGHTED-AVERAGE METHOD
The formula to compute equivalent units of production is as follows.

Units Completed and Transferred Out	+	Equivalent Units of Ending Work in Process	=	Equivalent Units of Production

Illustration 16-8   Equivalent units of production formula

To better understand this concept of equivalent units, consider the following two separate examples.

Example 1: The Blending Department's entire output during the period consists of ending work in process of 4,000 units which are 60 percent complete as to materials, labor, and overhead. The equivalent units of production for the Blending Department are therefore 2,400 units (4,000 × 60%).

Example 2: The Packaging Department's output during the period consists of 10,000 units completed and transferred out, and 5,000 units in ending work in process which are 70 percent completed. The equivalent units of production are therefore 13,500 [10,000 + (5,000 × 70%)].

This method of computing equivalent units is referred to as the **weighted-average method**. It considers the degree of completion (weighting) of the units completed and transferred out and the ending work in process. An alternative method, called the FIFO method, is discussed in the appendix to this chapter.

REFINEMENTS ON THE WEIGHTED-AVERAGE METHOD
Kellogg Company has produced Eggo® Waffles since 1970. Three departments are used to produce these waffles: Mixing, Baking, and Freezing/Packaging. In the Mixing Department dry ingredients, including flour, salt, and baking powder, are mixed with liquid ingredients, including eggs and vegetable oil, to make waffle batter. Information related to the Mixing Department at the end of June is provided in Illustration 16-9.

Illustration 16-9
Information for Mixing Department

MIXING DEPARTMENT		Percentage Complete	
	Physical Units	Materials	Conversion Costs
Work in process, June 1	100,000	100%	70%
Started into production	800,000		
Total units	900,000		
Units transferred out	700,000		
Work in process, June 30	200,000	100%	60%
Total units	900,000		

Illustration 16-9 indicates that the beginning work in process is 100 percent complete as to materials cost and 70 percent complete as to conversion costs. **Conversion costs** refers to the sum of labor costs and overhead costs. In other words, both the dry and liquid ingredients (materials) are added at the beginning of the process to make Eggo® Waffles. The conversion costs (labor and overhead) related to the mixing of these ingredients were incurred uniformly and are 70 percent complete. The ending work in process is 100 percent complete as to materials cost and 60 percent complete as to conversion costs.

We then use the Mixing Department information to determine equivalent units. **In computing equivalent units, the beginning work in process is not part of the equivalent units of production formula.** The units transferred out to the Baking Department are fully complete as to both materials and conversion costs. The ending work in process is fully complete as to materials, but only 60 percent complete as to conversion costs. **Two equivalent unit computations are therefore necessary:** one for materials and the other for conversion costs. Illustration 16-10 shows these computations.

Illustration 16-10
Computation of equivalent units—Mixing Department

	Equivalent Units	
	Materials	**Conversion Costs**
Units transferred out	700,000	700,000
Work in process, June 30		
200,000 × 100%	200,000	
200,000 × 60%		120,000
Total equivalent units	900,000	820,000

The earlier formula used to compute equivalent units of production can be refined to show the computations for materials and for conversion costs, as follows.

Illustration 16-11
Refined equivalent units of production formula

Units Completed and Transferred Out— Materials	+	Equivalent Units of Ending Work in Process—Materials	=	Equivalent Units of Production— Materials
Units Completed and Transferred Out— Conversion Costs	+	Equivalent Units of Ending Work in Process—Conversion Costs	=	Equivalent Units of Production— Conversion Costs

PRODUCTION COST REPORT

As mentioned earlier, a production cost report is prepared for each department in a process cost system. A **production cost report** is the key document used by management to understand the activities in a department; it shows the production quantity and cost data related to that department. For example, in producing Eggo® Waffles, Kellogg Company would have three production cost reports: Mixing, Baking, and Freezing/Packaging. Illustration 16-12 shows the flow of costs to make an Eggo® Waffle and the related production cost reports for each department.

In order to complete a production cost report, the company must perform four steps, which as a whole, make up the process costing system.

1. Compute the physical unit flow.
2. Compute the equivalent units of production.
3. Compute unit production costs.
4. Prepare a cost reconciliation schedule.

The next section explores these steps in an extended example.

Comprehensive Example of Process Costing

Assumed data for the Mixing Department at Kellogg Company for the month of June are shown in Illustration 16-13. We will use this information to complete a production cost report for the Mixing Department.

MIXING DEPARTMENT	
Units	
Work in process, June 1	100,000
Direct materials: 100% complete	
Conversion costs: 70% complete	
Units started into production during June	800,000
Units completed and transferred out to Baking Department	700,000
Work in process, June 30	200,000
Direct materials: 100% complete	
Conversion costs: 60% complete	
Costs	
Work in process, June 1	
Direct materials: 100% complete	$ 50,000
Conversion costs: 70% complete	35,000
Cost of work in process, June 1	$ 85,000
Costs incurred during production in June	
Direct materials	$400,000
Conversion costs	170,000
Costs incurred in June	$570,000

COMPUTE THE PHYSICAL UNIT FLOW
(STEP 1)

Physical units are the actual units to be accounted for during a period, irrespective of any work performed. To keep track of these units, it is necessary to add the units started (or transferred) into production during the period to the units in process at the beginning of the period. This amount is referred to as the **total units to be accounted for.**

The total units then are accounted for by the output of the period. The output consists of units transferred out during the period and any units in process at the end of the period. This amount is referred to as the **total units accounted for.** Illustration 16-14 shows the flow of physical units for Kellogg Company for the month of June for the Mixing Department.

Illustration 16-14
Physical unit flow—Mixing
Department

MIXING DEPARTMENT	
	Physical Units
Units to be accounted for	
Work in process, June 1	100,000
Started (transferred) into production	800,000
Total units	**900,000**
Units accounted for	
Completed and transferred out	700,000
Work in process, June 30	200,000
Total units	**900,000**

The records indicate that 900,000 units must be accounted for in the Mixing Department. Of this sum, 700,000 units were transferred to the Baking Department and 200,000 units were still in process.

COMPUTE EQUIVALENT UNITS OF
PRODUCTION (STEP 2)

Helpful Hint Materials are not always added at the beginning of the process. For example, materials are sometimes added uniformly during the process.

Once the physical flow of the units is established, it is necessary to measure the Mixing Department's productivity in terms of equivalent units of production. In the Mixing Department, materials are added at the beginning of the process, and conversion costs are incurred uniformly during the process. Thus, two computations of equivalent units are required: one for materials, and one for conversion costs. The equivalent unit computation is as follows.

Illustration 16-15   Computation of equivalent units—Mixing Department

Helpful Hint Remember that the beginning work in process is ignored in this computation.

	Equivalent Units	
	Materials	**Conversion Costs**
Units transferred out	700,000	700,000
Work in process, June 30		
200,000 × 100%	200,000	
200,000 × 60%		120,000
Total equivalent units	**900,000**	**820,000**

COMPUTE UNIT PRODUCTION COSTS (STEP 3)

Armed with the knowledge of the equivalent units of production, we can now compute the unit production costs. **Unit production costs** are costs expressed in terms of equivalent units of production. When equivalent units of production are different for materials and conversion costs, three unit costs are computed: (1) materials, (2) conversion, and (3) total manufacturing.

The computation of total materials cost related to Eggo® Waffles is as follows.

Work in process, June 1		
Direct materials cost		$ 50,000
Costs added to production during June		
Direct materials cost		400,000
Total materials cost		**$450,000**

Illustration 16-16 Total materials cost computation

The computation of unit materials cost is as follows.

Total Materials Cost	÷	Equivalent Units of Materials	=	Unit Materials Cost
$450,000	÷	900,000	=	$0.50

Illustration 16-17 Unit materials cost computation

The computation of total conversion costs is shown in Illustration 16-18.

Work in process, June 1		
Conversion costs		$ 35,000
Costs added to production during June		
Conversion costs		170,000
Total conversion costs		**$205,000**

Illustration 16-18 Total conversion costs computation

The computation of unit conversion cost is as follows.

Total Conversion Costs	÷	Equivalent Units of Conversion Costs	=	Unit Conversion Cost
$205,000	÷	820,000	=	$0.25

Illustration 16-19 Unit conversion cost computation

Total manufacturing cost per unit is therefore computed as shown in Illustration 16-20 (next page).

Illustration 16-20 Total manufacturing cost per unit

Unit Materials Cost	+	Unit Conversion Cost	=	Total Manufacturing Cost per Unit
$0.50	+	$0.25	=	$0.75

PREPARE A COST RECONCILIATION SCHEDULE (STEP 4)

We are now ready to determine the cost of goods transferred out of the Mixing Department to the Baking Department and the costs in ending work in process. The total costs that were charged to the Mixing Department in June are as follows.

Illustration 16-21 Costs charged to Mixing Department

Costs to be accounted for	
Work in process, June 1	$ 85,000
Started into production	570,000
Total costs	**$655,000**

The total costs charged to the Mixing Department in June are therefore $655,000.

A cost reconciliation schedule is then prepared to assign these costs to (1) units transferred out to the Baking Department and (2) ending work in process.

Illustration 16-22 Cost reconciliation schedule— Mixing Department

MIXING DEPARTMENT
Cost Reconciliation Schedule

Costs accounted for		
Transferred out (700,000 × $0.75)		$ 525,000
Work in process, June 30		
Materials (200,000 × $0.50)	$100,000	
Conversion costs (120,000 × $0.25)	30,000	130,000
Total costs		**$655,000**

The total manufacturing cost per unit, $0.75, is used in costing the units completed and transferred to the Baking Department. In contrast, the unit cost of materials and the unit cost of conversion are needed in costing units in process. The **cost reconciliation schedule** shows that the **total costs accounted for** (Illustration 16-22) equal the **total costs to be accounted for** (see Illustration 16-21).

PREPARING THE PRODUCTION COST REPORT

At this point, we are ready to prepare the production cost report for the Mixing Department. As indicated earlier, this report is an internal document for management that shows production quantity and cost data for a production department.

There are four steps in preparing a production cost report. They are: (1) Prepare a physical unit schedule. (2) Compute equivalent units. (3) Compute unit costs. (4) Prepare a cost reconciliation schedule. The production cost report for the Mixing Department is shown in Illustration 16-23. The four steps are identified in the report.

Illustration 16-23
Production cost report

Mixing Department.xls

File Edit View Insert Format Tools Data Window Help Acrobat   Type a question for help

	A	B	C	D	E	F
1			**Mixing Department**			
2			Production Cost Report			
3			For the Month Ended June 30, 2007			
4				Equivalent Units		
5			Physical Units	Materials	Conversion Costs	
6	QUANTITIES		Step 1	Step 2		
7	Units to be accounted for					
8	Work in process, June 1		100,000			
9	Started into production		800,000			
10	Total units		900,000			
11	Units accounted for					
12	Transferred out		700,000	700,000	700,000	
13	Work in process, June 30		200,000	200,000	120,000	(200,000 × 60%)
14	Total units		900,000	900,000	820,000	
15	COSTS Unit costs		Step 3	Materials	Conversion Costs	Total
16	Costs in June			$450,000	$205,000	$655,000
17	Equivalent units		(a)	900,000	820,000	
18	Unit costs [(a) ÷ (b)]		(b)	$0.50	$0.25	$0.75
19	Costs to be accounted for					
20	Work in process, June 1					$85,000
21	Started into production					570,000
22	Total costs					$655,000
23	**Cost Reconciliation Schedule**		Step 4			
24	Costs accounted for					
25	Transferred out (700,000 × $0.75)					$525,000
26	Work in process, June 30					
27	Materials (200,000 × $0.50)				$100,000	
28	Conversion costs (120,000 × $0.25)				30,000	130,000
29	Total costs					$655,000

Ill 16 -23

Production cost reports provide a basis for evaluating the productivity of a department. In addition, the cost data can be used to assess whether unit costs and total costs are reasonable. By comparing the quantity and cost data with predetermined goals, top management can also judge whether current performance is meeting planned objectives.

Decision Toolkit

Decision Checkpoints	Info Needed for Decision	Tool to Use for Decision	How to Evaluate Results
What is the cost of a product?	Costs of materials, labor, and overhead assigned to processes used to make the product	Production cost report	Compare costs to previous periods, to competitors, and to expected selling price to evaluate overall profitability.

BEFORE YOU GO ON . . .

▶**Review It**

1. How do physical units differ from equivalent units of production?
2. What are the formulas for computing unit costs of production?
3. How are costs assigned to units transferred out and in process?
4. What are the four steps in preparing a production cost report?

▶**Do It**

In March, Rodayo Manufacturing had the following unit production costs: materials $6 and conversion costs $9. On March 1, it had zero work in process. During March, 12,000 units were transferred out, and 800 units that were 25 percent completed as to conversion costs and 100 percent complete as to materials were in ending work in process at March 31. Assign the costs to the units transferred out and in process.

Action Plan

• Assign the total manufacturing cost of $15 per unit to the 12,000 units transferred out.

• Assign the materials cost and conversion costs based on equivalent units of production to units in process.

Solution The assignment of costs is as follows.

Costs accounted for		
Transferred out (12,000 × $15)		$180,000
Work in process, March 31		
Materials (800 × $6)	$4,800	
Conversion costs (200ᵃ × $9)	1,800	6,600
Total costs		$186,600

ᵃ800 × 25%

Related exercise material: BE16-4, BE16-5, BE16-6, BE16-7, BE16-8, BE16-10, E16-3, E16-4, E16-6, E16-8, E16-11, and E16-12.

✓ THE NAVIGATOR

COSTING SYSTEMS—FINAL COMMENTS

Companies often use a combination of a process cost and a job order cost system, called **operations costing**. Operations costing is similar to process costing in that standardized methods are used to manufacture the product. At the same time, the product may have some customized, individual features that require the use of a job order cost system.

Consider, for example, the automobile manufacturer Ford Motor Company. Each vehicle at a given plant goes through the same assembly line, but different materials (such as seat coverings, paint, and tinted glass) may be used for different vehicles. Similarly, Kellogg's Pop-Tarts Toaster Pastries® go through numerous processes—mixing, filling, baking, frosting, and packaging. The pastry dough, though, comes in three flavors—plain, chocolate, and graham—and fillings include Smucker's® real fruit, chocolate fudge, vanilla creme, brown sugar cinnamon, and S'mores.

A cost-benefit tradeoff occurs as a company decides which costing system to use. A job order system, for example, provides detailed information related to the cost of the product. Because each job has its own distinguishing characteristics, an accurate cost per job can be provided. This information is useful in controlling costs and pricing products. However, the cost of implementing a job order cost system is often expensive because of the accounting costs involved.

On the other hand, for a company like Intel, which makes computer chips, is there a benefit in knowing whether the cost of the one hundredth chip produced is different from the one thousandth chip produced? Probably not. An average cost of the product will suffice for control and pricing purposes. In summary, when deciding to use one of these systems, or a combination system, a company must weigh the costs of implementing the system against the benefits from the additional information provided.

Accounting across the Organization

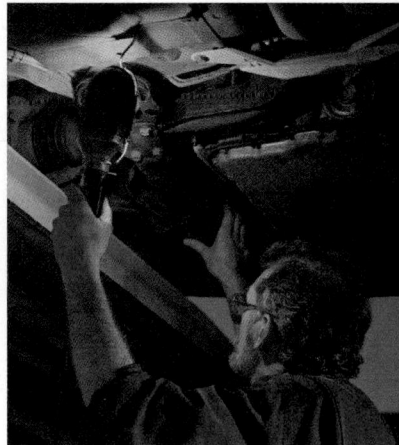

Frequently when we think of service companies we think of specific, nonroutine tasks, such as rebuilding an automobile engine, providing consulting services on a business acquisition, or working on a major lawsuit. Clearly, such nonroutine situations would call for job order costing.

However, many service companies specialize in performing repetitive, routine aspects of a particular business. For example, auto-care vendors such as Jiffy Lube focus on the routine aspects of car care. H&R Block focuses on the routine aspects of basic tax practice, and many large law firms focus on routine legal services, such as uncomplicated divorces. For service companies that perform routine, repetitive services, process costing provides a simple solution to their accounting needs. In fact, since in many instances there is little or no work in process at the end of the period, applying process costing in this setting can be even easier than for a manufacturer.

BEFORE YOU GO ON . . .

▶Review It

1. In what circumstances would a manufacturer use operations costing instead of process costing?
2. Describe the cost-benefit tradeoff in deciding what costing system to use.

Decision Toolkit

Decision Checkpoints	Info Needed for Decision	Tool to Use for Decision	How to Evaluate Results
✔	📄📄	🔧	👍👎
What costing method should be used?	Type of product produced	Cost of accounting system; benefits of additional information	The benefits of providing the additional information should exceed the costs of the accounting system needed to develop the information.

Using the Decision Toolkit

Essence Company manufactures a high-end after-shave lotion, called Eternity, which is sold in 10-ounce shaped glass bottles. Because the market for after-shave lotion is highly competitive, the company is very concerned about keeping its costs under control. Eternity is manufactured through three processes: mixing, filling, and corking. Materials are added at the beginning of the process, and labor and overhead are incurred uniformly throughout each process. The company uses a weighted-average method to cost its product.

A partially completed production cost report for the month of May for the Mixing Department is shown below.

ESSENCE COMPANY
Mixing Department
Production Cost Report
For the Month Ended May 31, 2007

	Physical Units	Equivalent Units Materials	Conversion Costs
Quantities	Step 1	Step 2	
Units to be accounted for			
Work in process, May 1	1,000		
Started into production	2,000		
Total units	3,000		
Units accounted for			
Transferred out	2,200	?	?
Work in process, May 31	800	?	?
Total units	3,000	?	?

Costs	Materials	Conversion Costs	Total
Unit costs Step 3			
Costs in May (a)	?	?	?
Equivalent units (b)	?	?	
Unit costs [(a) ÷ (b)]	?	?	?
Costs to be accounted for			
Work in process, May 1			$ 56,300
Started into production			119,320
Total costs			$175,620

Cost Reconciliation Schedule Step 4

Costs accounted for		
Transferred out		?
Work in process, May 31		
Materials	?	
Conversion costs	?	?
Total costs		?

Additional information:
Work in process, May 1, 1000 units
Materials cost, 1,000 units (100% complete) $49,100
Conversion costs, 1,000 units (70% complete) 7,200 $ 56,300
Materials cost for May, 2,000 units $100,000
Conversion costs for May $ 19,320

Work in process, May 31, 800 units, 100% complete as to materials and 50% complete as to conversion costs.

Instructions

(a) Prepare a production cost report for the Mixing Department for the month of May.

(b) Prepare the journal entry to record the transfer of goods from the Mixing Department to the Filling Department.

(c) Explain why Essence Company is using a process cost system to account for its costs.

Solution

(a) A completed production cost report for the Mixing Department is shown below. Computations to support the amounts reported follow the report.

ESSENCE COMPANY
Mixing Department
Production Cost Report
For the Month Ended May 31, 2007

	Physical Units	Equivalent Units	
		Materials	Conversion Costs
Quantities	Step 1		Step 2
Units to be accounted for			
Work in process, May 1	1,000		
Started into production	2,000		
Total units	3,000		
Units accounted for			
Transferred out	2,200	2,200	2,200
Work in process, May 31	800	800	400 (800 × 50%)
Total units	3,000	3,000	2,600

Costs		Materials	Conversion Costs	Total
Unit costs Step 3				
Costs in May	(a)	$149,100	$26,520	$175,620
Equivalent units	(b)	3,000	2,600	
Unit costs [(a) ÷ (b)]		$49.70	$10.20	$59.90
Costs to be accounted for				
Work in process, May 1				$ 56,300
Started into production				119,320
Total costs				$175,620

Cost Reconciliation Schedule Step 4

Costs accounted for		
Transferred out (2,200 × $59.90)		$131,780
Work in process, May 31		
Materials (800 × $49.70)	$39,760	
Conversion costs (400 × $10.20)	4,080	43,840
Total costs		$175,620

Additional computations to support production cost report data:
Materials cost—$49,100 + $100,000
Conversion costs—$7,200 + $19,320

(b) Work in Process—Filling		131,780	
Work in Process—Mixing			131,780

(c) Process cost systems are used to apply costs to similar products that are mass-produced in a continuous fashion. Essence Company uses a process cost system: production of the after-shave lotion, once it begins, continues until the after-shave lotion emerges. The processing is the same for the entire run—with precisely the same amount of materials, labor, and overhead. Each bottle of Eternity after-shave lotion is indistinguishable from another.

Summary of Study Objectives

1 *Understand who uses process cost systems.* Process cost systems are used by companies that mass-produce similar products in a continuous fashion. Once production begins, it continues until the finished product emerges. Each unit of finished product is indistinguishable from every other unit.

2 *Explain the similarities and differences between job order cost and process cost systems.* Job order cost systems are similar to process cost systems in three ways: (1) Both systems track the same cost elements—direct materials, direct labor, and manufacturing overhead. (2) Costs are accumulated in the same accounts—Raw Materials Inventory, Factory Labor, and Manufacturing Overhead. (3) Accumulated costs are assigned to the same accounts—Work in Process, Finished Goods Inventory, and Cost of Goods Sold. However, the method of assigning costs differs significantly.

There are four main differences between the two cost systems: (1) A process cost system uses separate accounts for each production department or manufacturing process, rather than only one work in process account used in a job order cost system. (2) In a process cost system, costs are summarized in a production cost report for each department; in a job cost system, costs are charged to individual jobs and summarized in a job cost sheet. (3) Costs are totaled at the end of a time period in a process cost system and at the completion of a job in a job cost system. (4) In a process cost system, unit cost is calculated as: Total manufacturing costs for the period ÷ Units produced during the period. Unit cost in a job cost system is: Total cost per job ÷ Units produced.

3 *Explain the flow of costs in a process cost system.* Manufacturing costs for raw materials, labor, and overhead are assigned to work in process accounts for various departments or manufacturing processes, and the costs of units completed in a department are transferred from one department to another as those units move through the manufacturing process. The costs of completed work are transferred to Finished Goods Inventory. When inventory is sold, costs are transferred to Cost of Goods Sold.

4 *Make the journal entries to assign manufacturing costs in a process cost system.* Entries to assign the costs of raw materials, labor, and overhead consist of a credit to Raw Materials Inventory, Factory Labor, and Manufacturing Overhead, and a debit to Work in Process for each of the departments doing the processing.

Entries to record the cost of goods transferred to another department are a credit to Work in Process for the department whose work is finished and a debit to the department to which the goods are transferred.

The entry to record units completed and transferred to the warehouse is a credit for the department whose work is finished and a debit to Finished Goods Inventory.

Finally, the entry to record the sale of goods is a credit to Finished Goods Inventory and a debit to Cost of Goods Sold.

5 *Compute equivalent units.* Equivalent units of production measure work done during a period, expressed in fully completed units. This concept is used to determine the cost per unit of completed product. Equivalent units are the sum of units completed and transferred out plus equivalent units of ending work in process.

6 *Explain the four steps necessary to prepare a production cost report.* The four steps to complete a production cost report are: (1) Compute the physical unit flow—that is, the total units to be accounted for. (2) Compute the equivalent units of production. (3) Compute the unit production costs, expressed in terms of equivalent units of production. (4) Prepare a cost reconciliation schedule, which shows that the total costs accounted for equal the total costs to be accounted for.

7 *Prepare a production cost report.* The production cost report contains both quantity and cost data for a production department. There are four sections in the report: (1) number of physical units, (2) equivalent units determination, (3) unit costs, and (4) cost reconciliation schedule.

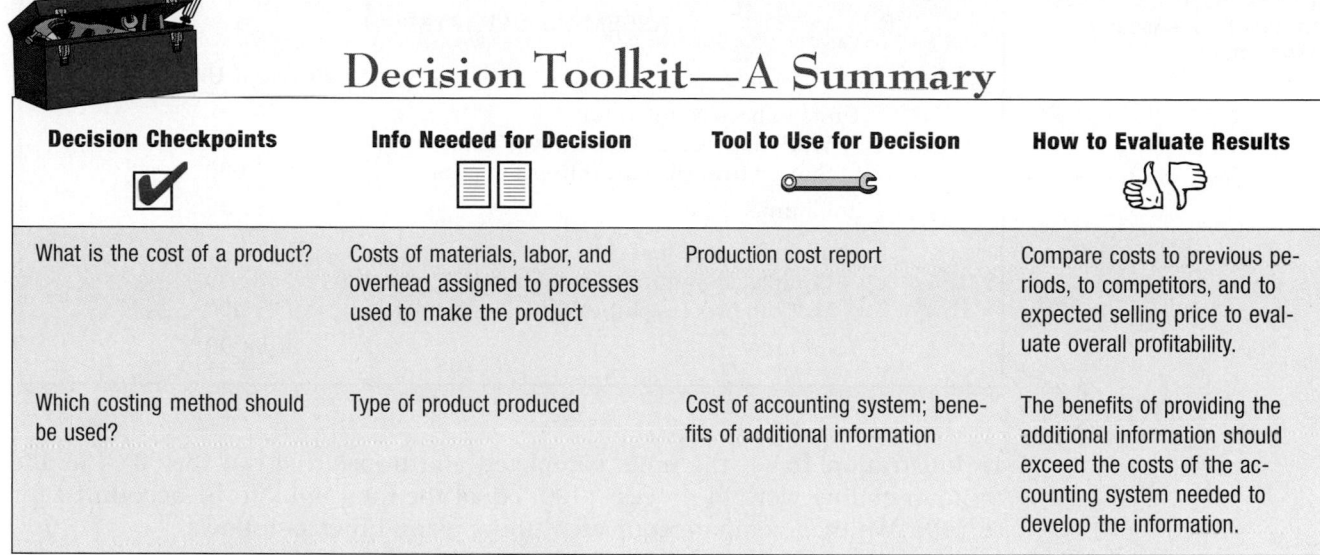

Decision Toolkit—A Summary

Decision Checkpoints	Info Needed for Decision	Tool to Use for Decision	How to Evaluate Results
What is the cost of a product?	Costs of materials, labor, and overhead assigned to processes used to make the product	Production cost report	Compare costs to previous periods, to competitors, and to expected selling price to evaluate overall profitability.
Which costing method should be used?	Type of product produced	Cost of accounting system; benefits of additional information	The benefits of providing the additional information should exceed the costs of the accounting system needed to develop the information.

APPENDIX
FIFO METHOD

In this chapter, we demonstrated the weighted-average method of computing equivalent units. Some companies use a different method to compute equivalent units, which is referred to as the **first-in, first-out (FIFO) method**. The purpose of this appendix is to illustrate how the FIFO method is used in practice.

Equivalent Units Under FIFO

Under the FIFO method, the computation of equivalent units is done on a first-in, first-out basis. Some companies favor the FIFO method because the FIFO cost assumption usually corresponds to the actual physical flow of the goods. Under the FIFO method, it is assumed therefore that the beginning work in process is completed before new work is started.

> **STUDY OBJECTIVE**
> **8**
> Compute equivalent units using the FIFO method.

Using the FIFO method, equivalent units are the sum of the work performed to:

1. Finish the units of beginning work in process inventory.
2. Complete the units started into production during the period (referred to as the **units started and completed**).
3. Start, but only partially complete, the units in ending work in process inventory.

Normally, in a process costing system, some units will always be in process at both the beginning and end of the period.

> **Helpful Hint** The computation of unit production costs and the assignment of costs to units transferred out and in process also are done on the same basis.

ILLUSTRATION

Illustration 16A-1 (page 818) shows the physical flow of units for the Assembly Department of Shutters Inc. In addition, the illustration indicates the degree of completion of the work in process accounts in regard to conversion costs.

ASSEMBLY DEPARTMENT	
	Physical Units
Units to be accounted for	
Work in process, June 1 (40% complete)	500
Started (transferred) into production	8,000
Total units	**8,500**
Units accounted for	
Completed and transferred out	8,100
Work in process, June 30 (75% complete)	400
Total units	**8,500**

In Illustration 16A-1, the units completed and transferred out (8,100) plus the units in ending work in process (400) equal the total units to be accounted for (8,500). We then compute equivalent units using FIFO as follows.

1. The 500 units of beginning work in process were 40 percent complete. Thus, 300 equivalent units (60% × 500 units) were required to complete the beginning inventory.
2. The units started and completed during the current month are the units transferred out minus the units in beginning work in process. For the Assembly Department, units started and completed are 7,600 (8,100 − 500).
3. The 400 units of ending work in process were 75 percent complete. Thus, equivalent units were 300 (400 × 75%).

Thus, equivalent units for the Assembly Department are 8,200, computed as follows.

Illustration 16A-2 Computation of equivalent units—FIFO method

ASSEMBLY DEPARTMENT			
Production Data	**Physical Units**	**Work Added This Period**	**Equivalent Units**
Work in process, June 1	500	60%	**300**
Started and completed	7,600	100%	**7,600**
Work in process, June 30	400	75%	**300**
Total	8,500		**8,200**

Comprehensive Example

To provide a complete illustration of the FIFO method, we will use the data for the Mixing Department at Kellogg Company for the month of June, as shown in Illustration 16A-3 (page 819).

COMPUTE THE PHYSICAL UNIT FLOW (STEP 1)

Illustration 16A-4 (page 819) shows the physical flow of units for Kellogg Company for the month of June for the Mixing Department.

Under the FIFO method, the physical units schedule is often expanded (as shown in Illustration 16A-5, page 819) to explain the transferred-out section. As a result, in this section the beginning work in process and the units started and completed are reported. These two items further explain the completed and transferred out section.

MIXING DEPARTMENT

Units

Work in process, June 1	100,000
Direct materials: 100% complete	
Conversion costs: 70% complete	
Units started into production during June	800,000
Units completed and transferred out to Baking Department	700,000
Work in process, June 30	200,000
Direct materials: 100% complete	
Conversion costs: 60% complete	

Costs

Work in process, June 1	
Direct materials: 100% complete	$ 50,000
Conversion costs: 70% complete	35,000
Cost of work in process, June 1	$ 85,000
Costs incurred during production in June	
Direct materials	$400,000
Conversion costs	170,000
Costs incurred in June	$570,000

Illustration 16A-3 Unit and cost data—Mixing Department

MIXING DEPARTMENT

	Physical Units
Units to be accounted for	
Work in process, June 1	100,000
Started (transferred) into production	800,000
Total units	**900,000**
Units accounted for	
Completed and transferred out	700,000
Work in process, June 30	200,000
Total units	**900,000**

Illustration 16A-4 Physical unit flow—Mixing Department

MIXING DEPARTMENT

	Physical Units
Units to be accounted for	
Work in process, June 1	100,000
Started (transferred) into production	800,000
Total units	**900,000**
Units accounted for	
Completed and transferred out	
Work in process, June 1	**100,000**
Started and completed	**600,000**
	700,000
Work in process, June 30	200,000
Total units	**900,000**

Illustration 16A-5 Physical unit flow (FIFO)—Mixing Department

The records indicate that 900,000 units must be accounted for in the Mixing Department. Of this sum, 700,000 units were transferred to the Baking Department and 200,000 units were still in process.

COMPUTE EQUIVALENT UNITS OF PRODUCTION (STEP 2)

As with the method presented in the chapter, once the physical flow of the units is established, it is necessary to determine equivalent units of production. In the Mixing Department, materials are added at the beginning of the process, and conversion costs are incurred uniformly during the process. Thus, two computations of equivalent units are required: one for materials and one for conversion costs.

Equivalent Units for Materials

Since materials are entered at the beginning of the process, no additional materials costs are required to complete the beginning work in process. In addition, 100 percent of the materials costs has been incurred on the ending work in process. Thus, the computation of equivalent units for materials is as follows.

Illustration 16A-6 Computation of equivalent units—materials

MIXING DEPARTMENT—MATERIALS			
Production Data	Physical Units	Materials Added This Period	Equivalent Units
Work in process, June 1	100,000	–0–	–0–
Started and finished	600,000	100%	600,000
Work in process, June 30	200,000	100%	200,000
Total	900,000		800,000

Equivalent Units for Conversion Costs

The 100,000 units of beginning work in process were 70 percent complete in terms of conversion costs. Thus, 30,000 equivalent units (30% × 100,000 units) of conversion costs were required to complete the beginning inventory. In addition, the 200,000 units of ending work in process were 60 percent complete in terms of conversion costs. Thus, the equivalent units for conversion costs is 750,000, computed as follows.

Illustration 16A-7 Computation of equivalent units—conversion costs

MIXING DEPARTMENT—CONVERSION COSTS			
Production Data	Physical Units	Work Added This Period	Equivalent Units
Work in process, June 1	100,000	30%	30,000
Started and finished	600,000	100%	600,000
Work in process, June 30	200,000	60%	120,000
Total	900,000		750,000

COMPUTE UNIT PRODUCTION COSTS (STEP 3)

Armed with the knowledge of the equivalent units of production, we can now compute the unit production costs. Unit production costs are costs expressed in terms of equivalent units of production. When equivalent units of production are different for materials and conversion costs, three unit costs are computed: (1) materials, (2) conversion, and (3) total manufacturing.

Under the FIFO method, the unit costs of production are based entirely on the production costs incurred during the month. Thus, the costs in the beginning work in process are not relevant, because they were incurred on work done in the preceding month. As indicated from Illustration 16A-3, the costs incurred during production in June were:

Direct materials	$400,000
Conversion costs	170,000
Total costs	$570,000

Illustration 16A-8   Costs incurred during production in June

The computation of unit materials cost, unit conversion costs, and total unit cost related to Eggo® Waffles is as follows.

Illustration 16A-9   Unit cost formulas and computations—Mixing Department

(1)	Total Materials Cost	÷	Equivalent Units of Materials	=	Unit Materials Cost
	$400,000	÷	800,000	=	$0.50

(2)	Total Conversion Costs	÷	Equivalent Units of Conversion Costs	=	Unit Conversion Cost
	$170,000	÷	750,000	=	$0.227 (rounded)*

(3)	Unit Materials Cost	+	Unit Conversion Cost	=	Total Manufacturing Cost per Unit
	$0.50	+	$0.227	=	$0.727

***For homework problems, round unit costs to three decimal places.**

As shown, the unit costs are $0.50 for materials, $0.227 for conversion costs, and $0.727 for total manufacturing costs.

PREPARE A COST RECONCILIATION SCHEDULE (STEP 4)

We are now ready to determine the cost of goods transferred out of the Mixing Department to the Baking Department and the costs in ending work in process. The total costs that were charged to the Mixing Department in June are as follows.

Illustration 16A-10 Costs charged to Mixing Department

Costs to be accounted for	
Work in process, June 1	$ 85,000
Started into production	570,000
Total costs	$655,000

The total costs charged to the Mixing Department in June are $655,000. A cost reconciliation is then prepared to assign these costs to (1) units transferred out to the Baking Department and (2) ending work in process. Under the FIFO method, the first goods to be completed during the period are the units in beginning work in process. Thus, the cost of the beginning work in process is always assigned to the goods transferred to finished goods (or the next department). The FIFO method also means that ending work in process will be assigned only production costs that are incurred in the current period. Illustration 16A-11 shows a cost reconciliation schedule for the Mixing Department.

MIXING DEPARTMENT Cost Reconciliation Schedule		
Costs accounted for		
Transferred out		
Work in process, June 1		$ 85,000
Costs to complete beginning work in process		
Conversion costs (30,000 × $0.227)		6,810
Total costs		91,810
Units started and completed (600,000 × $0.727)		435,950*
Total costs transferred out		527,760
Work in process, June 30		
Materials (200,000 × $0.50)	$100,000	
Conversion costs (120,000 × $0.227)	27,240	127,240
Total costs		$655,000

*Any rounding errors should be adjusted in the "Units started and completed" calculation.

As you can see, the total costs accounted for ($655,000 from Illustration 16A-11) equal the total costs to be accounted for ($655,000 from Illustration 16A-10).

PREPARING THE PRODUCTION COST REPORT

At this point, we are ready to prepare the production cost report for the Mixing Department. This report is an internal document for management that shows production quantity and cost data for a production department.

There are four steps in preparing a production cost report. They are: (1) Prepare a physical unit schedule. (2) Compute equivalent units. (3) Compute unit costs. (4) Prepare a cost reconciliation schedule. The production cost report for the Mixing Department is shown in Illustration 16A-12 (page 823), with the four steps identified in the report.

As indicated in the chapter, production cost reports provide a basis for evaluating the productivity of a department. In addition, the cost data can be used to assess whether unit costs and total costs are reasonable. By comparing the quantity and cost data with predetermined goals, top management can also judge whether current performance is meeting planned objectives.

FIFO and Weighted Average

The weighted-average method of computing equivalent units has **one major advantage:** It is simple to understand and apply. In cases where prices do not fluctuate significantly from period to period, the weighted-average method will be very similar to the FIFO method. In addition, companies that have been using just-in-time procedures effectively for inventory control purposes will have minimal inventory balances, and therefore differences between the weighted-average and the FIFO methods will not be material.

Conceptually, the FIFO method is superior to the weighted-average method because **current performance is measured** using only costs incurred in the

Illustration 16A-12   Production cost report

Mixing Department.xls

File Edit View Insert Format Tools Data Window Help Acrobat

	A	B	C	D	E	F	G
1	**Mixing Department**						
2	Production Cost Report						
3	For the Month Ended June 30, 2007						
4			**Equivalent Units**				
5		Physical Units	Materials	Conversion Costs			
6	**QUANTITIES**	Step 1	Step 2				
7	Units to be accounted for						
8	Work in process, June 1	100,000					
9	Started into production	800,000					
10	Total units	900,000					
11							
12	Units accounted for						
13	Completed and transferred out						
14	Work in process, June 1	100,000	0	30,000			
15	Started and completed	600,000	600,000	600,000			
16	Work in process, June 30	200,000	200,000	120,000			
17	Total units	900,000	800,000	750,000			
18							
19	**COSTS**						
20	Unit costs **Step 3**	Materials	Conversion Costs	Total			
21	Costs in June (excluding beginning WIP) (a)	$400,000	$170,000	$570,000	(WIP - Work in Process)		
22	Equivalent units (b)	800,000	750,000				
23	Unit costs [(a) ÷ (b)]	$0.50	$0.227	$0.727			
24							
25	Costs to be accounted for						
26	Work in process, June 1			$85,000			
27	Started into production			570,000			
28	Total costs			$655,000			
29							
30	**Cost Reconciliation Schedule** **Step 4**						
31	Costs accounted for						
32	Transferred out						
33	Work in process, June 1			$85,000			
34	Costs to complete beginning work in process						
35	Conversion costs (30,000 × $0.227)			6,810			
36	Total costs			91,810			
37	Units started and completed (600,000 × $0.727)**			435,950	** Any rounding errors		
38	Total costs transferred out			527,760	should be adjusted in the		
39	Work in process, June 30				"Units started and		
40	Materials (200,000 × $0.50)		$100,000		completed"		
41	Conversion costs (120,000 × $0.227)		27,240	127,240			
42	Total costs			$655,000			
43							

current period. Managers are, therefore, not held responsible for costs from prior periods over which they may not have any control. In addition, the FIFO method **provides current cost information**, which can be used to establish **more accurate pricing strategies** for goods manufactured and sold in the current period.

Helpful Hint What are the two self-checks in the report? Answer: (1) Total physical units accounted for must equal the total units to be accounted for. (2) Total costs accounted for must equal the total costs to be accounted for.

Summary of Study Objective for Appendix

8 *Compute equivalent units using the FIFO method.* Equivalent units under the FIFO method are the sum of the work performed to: (1) Finish the units of beginning work in process inventory, if any; (2) com-plete the units started into production during the period; and (3) start, but only partially complete, the units in ending work in process inventory.

Glossary

Conversion costs The sum of labor costs and overhead costs. (p. 806)

Cost reconciliation schedule A schedule that shows that the total costs accounted for equal the total costs to be accounted for. (p. 810)

Equivalent units of production A measure of the work done during the period, expressed in fully completed units. (p. 805)

Operations costing A combination of a process cost and a job order cost system, in which products are manufactured primarily by standardized methods, with some customization. (p. 812)

Physical units Actual units to be accounted for during a period, irrespective of any work performed. (p. 808)

Process cost system An accounting system used to apply costs to similar products that are mass-produced in a continuous fashion. (p. 798)

Production cost report An internal report for management that shows both production quantity and cost data for a production department. (p. 806)

Total units (costs) accounted for The sum of the units (costs) transferred out during the period plus the units (costs) in process at the end of the period. (pp. 808, 810)

Total units (costs) to be accounted for The sum of the units (costs) started (or transferred) into production during the period plus the units (costs) in process at the beginning of the period. (pp. 808, 810)

Unit production costs Costs expressed in terms of equivalent units of production. (p. 809)

Weighted-average method Method used to compute equivalent units of production which considers the degree of completion (weighting) of the units completed and transferred out and the ending work in process. (p. 805)

Demonstration Problem

Karlene Industries produces plastic ice cube trays in two processes: heating and stamping. All materials are added at the beginning of the Heating Department. Karlene uses the weighted-average method to compute equivalent units.

On November 1, 1,000 trays that were 70% complete were in process in the Heating Department. During November 12,000 trays were started into production. On November 30, 2007, 2,000 trays that were 60% complete were in process.

The following cost information for the Heating Department was also available.

Work in process, November 1:		Costs incurred in November:	
Materials	$ 640	Material	$3,000
Conversion costs	360	Labor	2,300
Cost of work in process, Nov. 1	$1,000	Overhead	4,050

Instructions

(a) Prepare a production cost report for the Heating Department for the month of November 2007, using the weighted-average method.

(b) Journalize the transfer of costs to the Stamping Department.

Solution to Demonstration Problem

(a)

KARLENE INDUSTRIES
Heating Department
Production Cost Report
For the Month Ended November 30, 2007

	Physical Units	Equivalent Units	
		Materials	Conversion Costs
Quantities	Step 1		Step 2
Units to be accounted for			
Work in process, November 1	1,000		
Started into production	12,000		
Total units	13,000		
Units accounted for			
Transferred out	11,000	11,000	11,000
Work in process, November 30	2,000	2,000	1,200
Total units	13,000	13,000	12,200

Costs		Materials	Conversion Costs	Total
Unit costs Step 3				
Costs in November	(a)	$ 3,640	$ 6,710	$10,350
Equivalent units	(b)	13,000	12,200	
Unit costs [(a) ÷ (b)]		$0.28	$0.55	$0.83
Costs to be accounted for				
Work in process, November 1				$ 1,000
Started into production				9,350
Total costs				$10,350

Cost Reconciliation Schedule Step 4

Costs accounted for		
Transferred out (11,000 × $0.83)		$ 9,130
Work in process, November 30		
Materials (2,000 × $0.28)	$ 560	
Conversion costs (1,200 × $0.55)	660	1,220
Total costs		$10,350

(b) Work in Process—Stamping	9,130	
Work in Process—Heating		9,130
(To record transfer of units to the Stamping Department)		

 THE NAVIGATOR

Action Plan
- Compute the physical unit flow— that is, the total units to be accounted for.
- Compute the equivalent units of production.
- Compute the unit production costs, expressed in terms of equivalent units of production.
- Prepare a cost reconciliation schedule, which shows that the total costs accounted for equal the total costs to be accounted for.

Note: All asterisked Questions, Exercises, and Problems relate to material in the appendix to the chapter.

Self-Study Questions

WILEY PLUS

Answers are at the end of the chapter.

(SO 1) **1.** Which of the following items is *not* a characteristic of a process cost system?

(a) Once production begins, it continues until the finished product emerges.

(b) The products produced are heterogeneous in nature.

(c) The focus is on continually producing homogeneous products.

(d) When the finished product emerges, all units have precisely the same amount of materials, labor, and overhead.

(SO 2) **2.** Indicate which of the following statements is *not* correct.

(a) Both a job order and a process cost system track the same three manufacturing cost elements—direct materials, direct labor, and manufacturing overhead.

(b) In a job order cost system, only one work in process account is used, whereas in a process cost system, multiple work in process accounts are used.

(c) Manufacturing costs are accumulated the same way in a job order and in a process cost system.

(d) Manufacturing costs are assigned the same way in a job order and in a process cost system.

(SO 3) **3.** In a process cost system, the flow of costs is:

(a) work in process, cost of goods sold, finished goods.

(b) finished goods, work in process, cost of goods sold.

(c) finished goods, cost of goods sold, work in process.

(d) work in process, finished goods, cost of goods sold.

(SO 4) **4.** In making the journal entry to assign raw materials costs:

(a) the debit is to Finished Goods Inventory.

(b) the debit is often to two or more work in process accounts.

(c) the credit is generally to two or more work in process accounts.

(d) the credit is to Finished Goods Inventory.

(SO 5) **5.** The Mixing Department's output during the period consists of 20,000 units completed and transferred out, and 5,000 units in ending work in process 60% complete as to materials and conversion costs. Beginning inventory is 1,000 units, 40% complete as to materials and conversion costs. The equivalent units of production are:

(a) 22,600. (c) 24,000.
(b) 23,000. (d) 25,000.

(SO 6) **6.** In the RYZ Company, there are zero units in beginning work in process, 7,000 units started into production, and 500 units in ending work in process 20% completed. The physical units to be accounted for are:

(a) 7,000. (c) 7,500.
(b) 7,360. (d) 7,340.

(SO 6) **7.** Mora Company has 2,000 units in beginning work in process, 20% complete as to conversion costs, 23,000 units transferred out to finished goods, and 3,000 units in endiing work in process $33\frac{1}{3}\%$ complete as to conversion costs.

The beginning and ending inventory is fully complete as to materials costs. Equivalent units for materials and conversion costs are, respectively:

(a) 22,000, 24,000.
(b) 24,000, 26,000.
(c) 26,000, 24,000.
(d) 26,000, 26,000.

(SO 6) **8.** Fortner Company has no beginning work in process; 9,000 units are transferred out and 3,000 units in ending work in process are one-third finished as to conversion costs and fully complete as to materials cost. If total materials cost is $60,000, the unit materials cost is:

(a) $5.00.
(b) $5.45 rounded.
(c) $6.00.
(d) No correct answer is given.

(SO 6) **9.** Largo Company has unit costs of $10 for materials and $30 for conversion costs. If there are 2,500 units in ending work in process, 40% complete as to conversion costs, and fully complete as to materials cost, the total cost assignable to the ending work in process inventory is:

(a) $45,000.
(b) $55,000.
(c) $75,000.
(d) $100,000.

10. A production cost report

(a) is an external report.

(b) shows both the production quantity and cost data related to a department.

(c) shows equivalent units of production but not physical units.

(d) contains six steps.

(SO 7)

*(SO 8) ***11.** Hollins Company uses the FIFO method to compute equivalent units. It has 2,000 units in beginning work in process, 20% complete as to conversion costs, 25,000 units started and completed, and 3,000 units in ending work in process, 30% complete as to conversion costs. All units are 100% complete as to materials. Equivalent units for materials and conversion costs are, respectively:

(a) 28,000 and 26,600.
(b) 28,000 and 27,500.
(c) 27,000 and 26,200.
(d) 27,000 and 29,600.

*(SO 8) ***12.** KLM Company uses the FIFO method to compute equivalent units. It has no beginning work in process; 9,000 units are started and completed and 3,000 units in ending work in process are one-third completed. All material is added at the beginning of the process. If total materials cost is $60,000, the unit materials cost is:

(a) $5.00.
(b) $6.00.
(c) $6.67 (rounded).
(d) No correct answer given.

(SO 8)*13. Toney Company uses the FIFO method to compute equivalent units. It has unit costs of $10 for materials and $30 for conversion costs. If there are 2,500 units in ending work in process,

100% complete as to materials and 40% complete as to conversion costs, the total cost assignable to the ending work in process inventory is:
(a) $45,000.   (c) $75,000.
(b) $55,000.   (d) $100,000.

Questions

1. Identify which costing system—job order or process cost—the following companies would use: (a) Quaker Oats, (b) Ford Motor Company, (c) Kinko's Print Shop, and (d) Warner Bros. Motion Pictures.

2. Contrast the primary focus of job order cost accounting and of process cost accounting.

3. What are the similarities between a job order and a process cost system?

4. Your roommate is confused about the features of process cost accounting. Identify and explain the distinctive features for your roommate.

5. Tina Turner believes there are no significant differences in the flow of costs between job order cost accounting and process cost accounting. Is Turner correct? Explain.

6. (a) What source documents are used in assigning (1) materials and (2) labor to production?
   (b) What criterion and basis are commonly used in allocating overhead to processes?

7. At Cale Company, overhead is assigned to production departments at the rate of $15 per machine hour. In July, machine hours were 3,000 in the Machining Department and 2,400 in the Assembly Department. Prepare the entry to assign overhead to production.

8. Ben Bratt is uncertain about the steps used to prepare a production cost report. State the procedures that are required, in the sequence in which they are performed.

9. Aaron Carter is confused about computing physical units. Explain to Aaron how physical units to be accounted for and physical units accounted for are determined.

10. What is meant by the term "equivalent units of production"?

11. How are equivalent units of production computed?

12. Clay Company had zero units of beginning work in process. During the period, 9,000 units were completed, and there were 600 units of ending work in process. What were the units started into production?

13. Gia Co. has zero units of beginning work in process. During the period 12,000 units were completed, and there were 600 units of ending work in process 20% complete as to conversion cost and 100% complete as to materials cost. What were the equivalent units

of production for (a) materials and (b) conversion costs?

14. Hall Co. started 3,000 units during the period. Its beginning inventory is 800 units 25% complete as to conversion costs and 100% complete as to materials costs. Its ending inventory is 400 units 20% complete as to conversion costs and 100% complete as to materials costs. How many units were transferred out this period?

15. Grael Company transfers out 14,000 units and has 2,000 units of ending work in process that are 25% complete. Materials are entered at the beginning of the process and there is no beginning work in process. Assuming unit materials costs of $3 and unit conversion costs of $9, what are the costs to be assigned to units (a) transferred out and (b) in ending work in process?

16. (a) Jim Jain believes the production cost report is an external report for stockholders. Is Jim correct? Explain.
    (b) Identify the sections in a production cost report.

17. What purposes are served by a production cost report?

18. At Adan Company, there are 800 units of ending work in process that are 100% complete as to materials and 40% complete as to conversion costs. If the unit cost of materials is $4 and the costs assigned to the 800 units is $6,600, what is the per-unit conversion cost?

19. What is the difference between operations costing and a process costing system?

20. How does a company decide whether to use a job order or a process cost system?

*21. Silva Co. started and completed 2,000 units for the period. Its beginning inventory is 600 units 25% complete and its ending inventory is 400 units 20% complete. Silva uses the FIFO method to compute equivalent units. How many units were transferred out this period?

*22. Ortiz Company transfers out 12,000 units and has 2,000 units of ending work in process that are 25% complete. Materials are entered at the beginning of the process and there is no beginning work in process. Ortiz uses the FIFO method to compute equivalent units. Assuming unit materials costs of $3 and unit conversion costs of $9, what are the costs to be assigned to units (a) transferred out and (b) in ending work in process?

Brief Exercises

Journalize entries for accumulating costs.
(SO 4)

BE16-1   Turner Manufacturing purchases $60,000 of raw materials on account, and it incurs $40,000 of factory labor costs. Journalize the two transactions on May 31 assuming the labor costs are not paid until June.

Journalize the assignment of materials and labor costs.
(SO 4)

BE16-2   Data for Turner Manufacturing are given in BE16-1. Supporting records show that (a) the Assembly Department used $29,000 of raw materials and $28,000 of the factory labor, and (b) the Finishing Department used the remainder. Journalize the assignment of the costs to the processing departments on May 31.

Journalize the assignment of overhead costs.
(SO 4)

BE16-3   Factory labor data for Turner Manufacturing are given in BE16-2. Manufacturing overhead is assigned to departments on the basis of 150% of labor costs. Journalize the assignment of overhead to the Assembly and Finishing Departments.

Compute physical units of production.
(SO 6)

BE16-4   Barclay Manufacturing Company has the following production data for selected months.

Month	Beginning Work in Process	Units Transferred Out	Ending Work in Process	
			Units	% Complete as to Conversion Cost
January	–0–	20,000	5,000	40%
March	–0–	30,000	4,000	75
July	–0–	50,000	10,000	25

Compute the physical unit flow for each month.

Compute equivalent units of production.
(SO 5)

BE16-5   Using the data in BE16-4, compute equivalent units of production for materials and conversion costs, assuming materials are entered at the beginning of the process.

Compute unit costs of production.
(SO 6)

BE16-6   In Georgia Company, total material costs are $52,000, and total conversion costs are $60,000. Equivalent units of production are materials 10,000 and conversion costs 12,000. Compute the unit costs for materials, conversion costs, and total manufacturing costs.

Assign costs to units transferred out and in process.
(SO 6)

BE16-7   Sosa Company has the following production data for March: units transferred out 40,000, and ending work in process 5,000 units that are 100% complete for materials and 40% complete for conversion costs. If unit materials cost is $8 and unit conversion cost is $15, determine the costs to be assigned to the units transferred out and the units in ending work in process.

Compute unit costs.
(SO 6)

BE16-8   Production costs chargeable to the Finishing Department in July in Murdock Company are materials $9,000, labor $23,800, overhead $18,000. Equivalent units of production are materials 20,000 and conversion costs 19,000. Compute the unit costs for materials and conversion costs.

Prepare cost reconciliation schedule.
(SO 6)

BE16-9   Data for Murdock Company are given in BE16-8. Production records indicate that 18,000 units were transferred out, and 2,000 units in ending work in process were 50% complete as to conversion cost and 100% complete as to materials. Prepare a cost reconciliation schedule.

Compute equivalent units of production.
(SO 5)

BE16-10   The Smelting Department of Dewey Manufacturing Company has the following production and cost data for October.

Production: Beginning work in process 2,000 units that are 100% complete as to materials and 20% complete as to conversion costs; units transferred out 8,000 units; and ending work in process 3,000 units that are 100% complete as to materials and 40% complete as to conversion costs.

Compute the equivalent units of production for (a) materials and (b) conversion costs for the month of October.

Assign costs to units transferred out and in process.
(SO 8)

*BE16-11   Mora Company has the following production data for March: no beginning work in process, units started and completed 30,000, and ending work in process 5,000 units that are 100% complete for materials and 40% complete for conversion costs. Mora uses the FIFO method to compute equivalent units. If unit materials cost is $8 and unit conversion cost is $12, determine the costs to be assigned to the units transferred out and the units in ending work in process. The total costs to be assigned are $664,000.

*BE16-12   Using the data in BE16-11, prepare the cost section of the production cost report for Mora Company.

*BE16-13   Production costs chargeable to the Finishing Department in May at Bell Company are materials $8,000, labor $20,000, overhead $18,000, and transferred-in costs $62,000. Equivalent units of production are materials 20,000 and conversion costs 19,000. Bell uses the FIFO method to compute equivalent units. Compute the unit costs for materials and conversion costs. Transferred-in costs are considered materials costs.

Prepare a partial production cost report.
(SO 7, 8)
Compute unit costs.
(SO 8)

Exercises

E16-1   Sally May Company manufactures pizza sauce through two production departments: Cooking and Canning. In each process, materials and conversion costs are incurred evenly throughout the process. For the month of March, the work in process accounts show the following debits.

Journalize transactions.
(SO 3, 4)

	Cooking	Canning
Beginning work in process	$ –0–	$ 4,000
Materials	14,000	6,000
Labor	8,500	7,000
Overhead	29,500	22,000
Costs transferred in		45,000

Instructions
Journalize the March transactions.

E16-2   Greenleaf Manufacturing Company has two production departments: Cutting and Assembly. August 1 inventories are Raw Materials $4,200, Work in Process—Cutting $3,900, Work in Process—Assembly $10,600, and Finished Goods $31,900. During August, the following transactions occurred.

Journalize transactions for two processes.
(SO 4)

1. Purchased $56,300 of raw materials on account.
2. Incurred $55,000 of factory labor. (Credit Wages Payable.)
3. Incurred $70,000 of manufacturing overhead; $36,000 was paid and the remainder is unpaid.
4. Requisitioned materials for Cutting $15,700 and Assembly $8,900.
5. Used factory labor for Cutting $28,000 and Assembly $27,000.
6. Applied overhead at the rate of $20 per machine hour. Machine hours were Cutting 1,640 and Assembly 1,720.
7. Transferred goods costing $77,600 from the Cutting Department to the Assembly Department.
8. Transferred goods costing $135,000 from Assembly to Finished Goods.
9. Sold goods costing $130,000 for $200,000 on account.

Instructions
Journalize the transactions. (Omit explanations.)

E16-3   In Bing Company, materials are entered at the beginning of each process. Work in process inventories, with the percentage of work done on conversion costs, and production data for its Sterilizing Department in selected months during 2007 are as follows.

Compute physical units and equivalent units of production.
(SO 5, 6)

Month	Beginning Work in Process Units	Beginning Work in Process Conversion Cost %	Units Transferred Out	Ending Work in Process Units	Ending Work in Process Conversion Cost %
January	–0–	—	7,000	2,000	70
March	–0–	—	12,000	3,000	30
May	–0–	—	16,000	5,000	80
July	–0–	—	10,000	1,500	40

Instructions

(a) Compute the physical unit flow for January and May.

(b) Compute the equivalent units of production for (1) materials and (2) conversion costs for each month.

Determine equivalent units, unit costs, and assignment of costs.
(SO 5, 6)

E16-4 The Cutting Department of Behan Manufacturing has the following production and cost data for July.

Production	Costs	
1. Transferred out 9,000 units.	Beginning work in process	$ –0–
2. Started 1,000 units that are 40% complete as to conversion costs and 100% complete as to materials at July 31.	Materials	45,000
	Labor	14,940
	Manufacturing overhead	18,900

Materials are entered at the beginning of the process. Conversion costs are incurred uniformly during the process.

Instructions

(a) Determine the equivalent units of production for (1) materials and (2) conversion costs.

(b) Compute unit costs and prepare a cost reconciliation schedule.

Prepare a production cost report.
(SO 5, 6, 7)

E16-5 The Sanding Department of Han Furniture Company has the following production and manufacturing cost data for April 2007.

Production: 12,000 units finished and transferred out; 3,000 units started that are 100% complete as to materials and 40% complete as to conversion costs.

Manufacturing costs: Materials $36,000; labor $30,000; overhead $37,320.

Instructions

Prepare a production cost report. There is no beginning work in process.

Determine equivalent units, unit costs, and assignment of costs.
(SO 5, 6)

E16-6 The Blending Department of Ceja Company has the following cost and production data for the month of May.

Work in process, May 1	
Direct materials: 100% complete	$100,000
Conversion costs: 20% complete	75,000
Cost of work in process, May 1	$175,000
Costs incurred during production in May	
Direct materials	$ 800,000
Conversion costs	350,000
Costs incurred in May	$1,150,000

Units transferred out totaled 8,000. Ending work in process was 2,000 units that are 100% complete as to materials and 25% complete as to conversion costs.

Instructions

(a) Compute the equivalent units of production for (1) materials and (2) conversion costs for the month of May.

(b) Compute the unit costs for the month.

(c) Determine the costs to be assigned to the units transferred out and in ending work in process.

Answer questions on costs and production.
(SO 3, 5, 6)

E16-7 The ledger of Liu Company has the following work in process account.

Work in Process—Painting

7/1	Balance	4,450	7/31	Transferred out	?
7/31	Materials	6,100			
7/31	Labor	2,500			
7/31	Overhead	1,650			
7/31	Balance	?			

Production records show that there were 700 units in the beginning inventory, 30% complete, 1,100 units started, and 1,300 units transferred out. The beginning work in process had materials cost of $2,900 and conversion costs of $1,550. The units in ending inventory were 40% complete. Materials are entered at the beginning of the painting process.

Instructions
(a) How many units are in process at July 31?
(b) What is the unit materials cost for July?
(c) What is the unit conversion cost for July?
(d) What is the total cost of units transferred out in July?
(e) What is the cost of the July 31 inventory?

E16-8 The Polishing Department of Dimetry Manufacturing Company has the following production and manufacturing cost data for October. Materials are entered at the beginning of the process.

Compute equivalent units, unit costs, and costs assigned.
(SO 5, 6)

Production: Beginning inventory 1,600 units that are 100% complete as to materials and 30% complete as to conversion costs; units started during the period are 11,000; ending inventory of 2,000 units 10% complete as to conversion costs.

Manufacturing costs: Beginning inventory costs, comprised of $20,000 of materials and $43,180 of conversion costs; materials costs added in Polishing during the month, $162,700; labor and overhead applied in Polishing during the month, $100,080 and $250,940, respectively.

Instructions
(a) Compute the equivalent units of production for materials and conversion costs for the month of October.
(b) Compute the unit costs for materials and conversion costs for the month.
(c) Determine the costs to be assigned to the units transferred out and in process.

E16-9 Mary Mahr has recently been promoted to production manager, and so she has just started to receive various managerial reports. One of the reports she has received is the production cost report that you prepared. It showed that her department had 1,000 equivalent units in ending inventory. Her department has had a history of not keeping enough inventory on hand to meet demand. She has come to you, very angry, and wants to know why you credited her with only 1,000 units when she knows she had at least twice that many on hand.

Explain the production cost report.
(SO 7)

Instructions
⬛⬛➤ Explain to her why her production cost report showed only 1,000 equivalent units in ending inventory. Write an informal memo. Be kind and explain very clearly why she is mistaken.

E16-10 The Welding Department of Marlin Manufacturing Company has the following production and manufacturing cost data for February 2007. All materials are added at the beginning of the process.

Prepare a production cost report.
(SO 5, 6, 7)

Manufacturing Costs			Production Data	
Beginning work in process			Beginning work in process	15,000 units,
Materials	$15,000			10% complete
Conversion costs	30,435	$ 45,435	Units transferred out	49,000
Materials		180,000	Units started	60,000
Labor		35,100	Ending work in process	26,000,
Overhead		64,545		20% complete

Instructions
Prepare a production cost report for the Welding Department for the month of February.

E16-11 Container Shipping, Inc. is contemplating the use of process costing to track the costs of its operations. The operation consists of three segments (departments): receiving, shipping, and delivery. Containers are received at Container's docks and sorted according to the ship they will be carried on. The containers are loaded onto a ship, which carries them to the appropriate port of destination. The containers are then off-loaded and delivered to the receiving company.

Compute physical units and equivalent units of production.
(SO 5, 6)

Container Shipping wants to begin using process costing in the shipping department. Direct materials represent the fuel costs to run the ship, and "Containers in transit" represents work in process. Listed below is information about the shipping department's first month's activity.

Containers in transit, April 1	0
Containers loaded	800
Containers in transit, April 30	350, 40% of direct materials and 30% of conversion costs

Instructions
(a) Determine the physical flow of containers for the month.
(b) Calculate the equivalent units for direct materials and conversion costs.

Determine equivalent units, unit costs, and assignment of costs.
(SO 5, 6)

E16-12   Hi-Tech Mortgage Company uses a process costing system to accumulate costs in its loan application department. When an application is completed it is forwarded to the loan department for final processing. The following processing and cost data pertain to September.

1. Applications in process on September 1, 100	**Beginning WIP:**	
	Direct materials	$ 1,000
2. Applications started in September, 900	Conversion costs	4,000
	September costs:	
3. Completed applications during September, 800	Direct materials	$ 4,000
	Direct labor	12,000
4. Applications still in process at September 30 were 100% complete as to materials (forms) and 60% complete as to conversion costs.	Overhead	9,400

Materials are the forms used in the application process, and these costs are incurred at the beginning of the process. Conversion costs are incurred uniformly during the process.

Instructions
(a) Determine the equivalent units of service (production) for materials and conversion costs.
(b) Compute the unit costs and prepare a cost reconciliation schedule.

Compute equivalent units, unit costs, and costs assigned.
(SO 4, 5, 6, 8)

*E16-13**   Using the data in E16-12, assume Hi-Tech Mortgage Company uses the FIFO method. Also assume that the applications in process on September 1 were 100% complete as to materials (forms) and 40% complete as to conversion costs.

Instructions
(a) Determine the equivalent units of service (production) for materials and conversion costs.
(b) Compute the unit costs and prepare a cost reconciliation schedule.

Determine equivalent units, unit costs, and assignment of costs.
(SO 4, 5, 6, 8)

* **E16-14**   The Cutting Department of Chan Manufacturing has the following production and cost data for August.

Production	Costs	
1. Started and completed 8,000 units.	Beginning work in process	$ –0–
2. Started 1,000 units that are 40% completed at August 31.	Materials	45,000
	Labor	14,700
	Manufacturing overhead	18,900

Materials are entered at the beginning of the process. Conversion costs are incurred uniformly during the process. Chan Manufacturing uses the FIFO method to compute equivalent units.

Instructions
(a) Determine the equivalent units of production for (1) materials and (2) conversion costs.
(b) Compute unit costs and show the assignment of manufacturing costs to units transferred out and in work in process.

*E16-15 The Smelting Department of Amber Manufacturing Company has the following production and cost data for September.

Compute equivalent units, unit costs, and costs assigned.
(SO 4, 5, 6, 8)

Production: Beginning work in process 2,000 units that are 100% complete as to materials and 20% complete as to conversion costs; units started and finished 11,000 units; and ending work in process 1,000 units that are 100% complete as to materials and 40% complete as to conversion costs.

Manufacturing costs: Work in process, September 1, $15,200; materials added $60,000; labor and overhead $143,000.

Amber uses the FIFO method to compute equivalent units.

Instructions
(a) Compute the equivalent units of production for (1) materials and (2) conversion costs for the month of September.
(b) Compute the unit costs for the month.
(c) Determine the costs to be assigned to the units transferred out and in process.

*E16-16 The ledger of Platt Company has the following work in process account.

Answer questions on costs and production.
(SO 3, 4, 5, 6, 8)

Work in Process—Painting

3/1	Balance	3,680	3/31	Transferred out	?
3/31	Materials	6,600			
3/31	Labor	2,500			
3/31	Overhead	1,280			
3/31	Balance	?			

Production records show that there were 800 units in the beginning inventory, 30% complete, 1,000 units started, and 1,300 units transferred out. The units in ending inventory were 40% complete. Materials are entered at the beginning of the painting process. Platt uses the FIFO method to compute equivalent units.

Instructions
Answer the following questions.
(a) How many units are in process at March 31?
(b) What is the unit materials cost for March?
(c) What is the unit conversion cost for March?
(d) What is the total cost of units started in February and completed in March?
(e) What is the total cost of units started and finished in March?
(f) What is the cost of the March 31 inventory?

*E16-17 The Welding Department of Hirohama Manufacturing Company has the following production and manufacturing cost data for February 2007. All materials are added at the beginning of the process. Hirohama uses the FIFO method to compute equivalent units.

Prepare a production cost report for a second process.
(SO 8)

Manufacturing Costs		Production Data	
Beginning work in process	$ 32,175	Beginning work in process	15,000 units, 10% complete
Costs transferred in	135,000		
Materials	57,000	Units transferred out	50,000
Labor	35,100	Units transferred in	60,000
Overhead	71,900	Ending work in process	25,000, 20% complete

Instructions
Prepare a production cost report for the Welding Department for the month of February. Transferred-in costs are considered materials costs.

Problems: Set A

P16-1A Vargas Company manufactures a nutrient, Everlife, through two manufacturing processes: Blending and Packaging. All materials are entered at the beginning of each process. On August 1, 2007, inventories consisted of Raw Materials $5,000, Work in Process—Blending $0, Work in Process—Packaging $3,945, and Finished Goods $7,500. The beginning inventory for Packaging consisted of 500 units, two-fifths complete as to

Journalize transactions.
(SO 3, 4)

conversion costs and fully complete as to materials. During August, 9,000 units were started into production in Blending, and the following transactions were completed.

1. Purchased $25,000 of raw materials on account.
2. Issued raw materials for production: Blending $16,800 and Packaging $7,200.
3. Incurred labor costs of $18,770.
4. Used factory labor: Blending $12,230 and Packaging $6,540.
5. Incurred $41,300 of manufacturing overhead on account.
6. Applied manufacturing overhead at the rate of $35 per machine hour. Machine hours were Blending 900 and Packaging 300.
7. Transferred 8,200 units from Blending to Packaging at a cost of $54,940.
8. Transferred 8,600 units from Packaging to Finished Goods at a cost of $74,490.
9. Sold goods costing $62,000 for $85,000 on account.

Instructions
Journalize the August transactions.

Complete four steps necessary to prepare a production cost report.
(SO 5, 6, 7)

P16-2A Zion Corporation manufactures water skis through two processes: Molding and Packaging. In the Molding Department fiberglass is heated and shaped into the form of a ski. In the Packaging Department, the skis are placed in cartons and sent to the finished goods warehouse. Materials are entered at the beginning of both processes. Labor and manufacturing overhead are incurred uniformly throughout each process. Production and cost data for the Molding Department for January 2007 are presented below.

Production Data	January
Beginning work in process units	–0–
Units started into production	43,000
Ending work in process units	3,000
Percent complete—ending inventory	40%

Cost Data	
Materials	$550,400
Labor	126,640
Overhead	170,000
Total	$847,040

Instructions
(a) Compute the physical unit flow.
(b) Determine the equivalent units of production for materials and conversion costs.
(c) Compute the unit costs of production.
(d) Determine the costs to be assigned to the units transferred out and in process.
(e) Prepare a production cost report for the Molding Department for the month of January.

(c) Materials $12.80
(d) Transferred out $800,000
    WIP $47,040

Complete four steps necessary to prepare a production cost report.
(SO 5, 6, 7)

P16-3A Stein Corporation manufactures in separate processes refrigerators and freezers for homes. In each process, materials are entered at the beginning and conversion costs are incurred uniformly. Production and cost data for the first process in making two products in two different manufacturing plants are as follows.

(a) Plant A:
(1) Transferred out   18,000
    WIP   2,000
(2) Materials   20,000
    CC   19,400
(3) Materials $42
    CC $32
(4) Transferred out $1,332,000
    WIP $128,800

| Production Data—June | Stamping Department | |
	Plant A R12 Refrigerators	Plant B F24 Freezers
Work in process units, June 1	–0–	–0–
Units started into production	20,000	20,000
Work in process units, June 30	2,000	3,000
Work in process percent complete	70%	50%

Cost Data—June		
Work in process, June 1	$ –0–	$ –0–
Materials	840,000	700,000
Labor	200,800	236,000
Overhead	420,000	319,000
Total	$1,460,800	$1,255,000

Instructions
(a) For each plant:
    (1) Compute the physical unit flow.
    (2) Compute equivalent units of production for materials and for conversion costs.
    (3) Determine the unit costs of production.
    (4) Show the assignment of costs to units transferred out and in process.
(b) Prepare the production cost report for Plant A for June 2007.

P16-4A Elite Company has several processing departments. Costs charged to the Assembly Department for October 2007 totaled $1,328,400 as follows.

Assign costs and prepare production cost report.
(SO 5, 6, 7)

Work in process, October 1		
Materials	$ 9,000	
Conversion costs	27,400	$ 36,400
Materials added		1,071,000
Labor		90,000
Overhead		131,000

Production records show that 35,000 units were in beginning work in process 40% complete as to conversion cost, 415,000 units were started into production, and 45,000 units were in ending work in process 20% complete as to conversion costs. Materials are entered at the beginning of each process.

Instructions
(a) Determine the equivalent units of production and the unit costs for the Assembly Department.
(b) Determine the assignment of costs to goods transferred out and in process.
(c) Prepare a production cost report for the Assembly Department.

(b) Transferred out $1,215,000
WIP $113,400

P16-5A Sprague Company manufactures bicycles and tricycles. For bicycles, materials are added at the beginning of the production process, and conversion costs are incurred uniformly. Production and cost data for the month of July are as follows.

Determine equivalent units and unit costs and assign costs.
(SO 5, 6, 7)

Production Data—Bicycles	Units	Percent Complete
Work in process units, July 1	400	80%
Units started in production	1,100	
Work in process units, July 31	500	10%

Cost Data—Bicycles		
Work in process, July 1		
Materials	$10,000	
Conversion costs	9,300	$19,300
Direct materials		50,000
Direct labor		23,700
Manufacturing overhead		30,000

Instructions
(a) Calculate the following.
    (1) The equivalent units of production for materials and conversion.
    (2) The unit costs of production for materials and conversion costs.
    (3) The assignment of costs to units transferred out and in process at the end of the accounting period.
(b) Prepare a production cost report for the month of July.

(a) (1) Materials   1,500
*   (2) Materials $40*
*   (3) Transferred*
*   out $100,000*
*   WIP $23,000*

P16-6A Taylor Cleaner Company uses a weighted-average process cost system and manufactures a single product—an all-purpose liquid cleaner. The manufacturing activity for the month of May has just been completed. A partially completed production cost report for the month of May for the Mixing and Blending Department is shown on the next page.

Compute equivalent units and complete production cost report.
(SO 5, 7)

TAYLOR CLEANER COMPANY
Mixing and Blending Department
Production Cost Report
For the Month Ended May 31

| | | Equivalent Units | |
| | Physical | | Conversion |
Quantities	Units	Materials	Costs
Units to be accounted for			
Work in process, May 1			
(40% materials, 20%			
conversion costs)	7,000		
Started into production	100,000		
Total units	107,000		
Units accounted for			
Transferred out	95,000	?	?
Work in process, May 31			
(3/4 materials, 1/4			
conversion costs)	12,000	?	?
Total units accounted for	107,000	?	?

| | | Conversion | |
| Costs | | | |
Unit costs	Materials	Costs	Total
Costs in May	$166,400	$98,000	$264,400
Equivalent units	?	?	
Unit costs	$? +	$? =	$?
Costs to be accounted for			
Work in process, May 1			$ 12,000
Started into production			252,400
Total costs			$264,400

Cost Reconciliation Schedule

Costs accounted for			
Transferred out			$?
Work in process, May 31			
Materials		$?	
Conversion costs		?	$?
Total costs			$?

(a) Materials   104,000
(b) Materials $1.60
(c) Transferred
    out $247,000
    WIP $17,400

Instructions

(a) Prepare a schedule that shows how the equivalent units were computed so that you can complete the "Quantities: Units accounted for" equivalent units section shown in the production cost report above.
(b) Compute May unit costs.
(c) Complete the "Cost Reconciliation Schedule" part of the production cost report above.

Determine equivalent units and unit costs and assign costs for processes; prepare production cost report.
(SO 8)

* P16-7A   Nicholas Company manufactures bicycles and tricycles. For both products, materials are added at the beginning of the production process, and conversion costs are incurred uniformly. Nicholas Company uses the FIFO method to compute equivalent units. Production and cost data for the month of March are as follows.

Production Data—Bicycles	Units	Percent Complete
Work in process units, March 1	200	80%
Units started into production	1,000	
Work in process units, March 31	200	40%

Cost Data—Bicycles	Units	Percent Complete
Work in process, March 1	$19,280	
Direct materials	50,000	
Direct labor	25,200	
Manufacturing overhead	30,000	

Production Data—Tricycles	Units	Percent Complete
Work in process units, March 1	100	75%
Units started into production	800	
Work in process units, March 31	60	25%

Cost Data—Tricycles	
Work in process, March 1	$ 6,125
Direct materials	38,400
Direct labor	15,100
Manufacturing overhead	20,000

Instructions

(a) Calculate the following for both the bicycles and the tricycles.
  (1) The equivalent units of production for materials and conversion.
  (2) The unit costs of production for materials and conversion costs.
  (3) The assignment of costs to units transferred out and in process at the end of the accounting period.

(b) Prepare a production cost report for the month of March for the bicycles only.

(a) Bicycles:
(1) Materials   1,000
(2) Materials $50
(3) Transferred out $109,680
    WIP $14,800

Problems: Set B

P16-1B Pepi Company manufactures its product, Vitadrink, through two manufacturing processes: Mixing and Packaging. All materials are entered at the beginning of each process. On October 1, 2007, inventories consisted of Raw Materials $26,000, Work in Process—Mixing $0, Work in Process—Packaging $250,000, and Finished Goods $89,000. The beginning inventory for Packaging consisted of 10,000 units that were 50% complete as to conversion costs and fully complete as to materials. During October, 50,000 units were started into production in the Mixing Department and the following transactions were completed.

Journalize transactions.
(SO 3, 4)

1. Purchased $500,000 of raw materials on account.
2. Issued raw materials for production: Mixing $210,000 and Packaging $45,000.
3. Incurred labor costs of $238,900.
4. Used factory labor: Mixing $182,000 and Packaging $56,900.
5. Incurred $800,000 of manufacturing overhead on account.
6. Applied manufacturing overhead on the basis of $24 per machine hour. Machine hours were 28,000 in Mixing and 7,000 in Packaging.
7. Transferred 45,000 units from Mixing to Packaging at a cost of $999,000.
8. Transferred 53,000 units from Packaging to Finished Goods at a cost of $1,455,000.
9. Sold goods costing $1,500,000 for $2,500,000 on account.

Instructions
Journalize the October transactions.

P16-2B Aquatic Company manufactures bowling balls through two processes: Molding and Packaging. In the Molding Department, the urethane, rubber, plastics, and other materials are molded into bowling balls. In the Packaging Department, the balls are placed in cartons and sent to the finished goods warehouse. All materials are entered at the beginning of each process. Labor and manufacturing overhead are incurred uniformly throughout each process. Production and cost data for the Molding Department during June 2007 are presented below.

Complete four steps necessary to prepare a production cost report.
(SO 5, 6, 7)

Production Data	June
Beginning work in process units	–0–
Units started into production	20,000
Ending work in process units	5,000
Percent complete—ending inventory	40%

Cost Data	
Materials	$286,000
Labor	114,000
Overhead	101,900
Total	$501,900

Instructions

(a) Prepare a schedule showing physical unit flow.

(b) Determine the equivalent units of production for materials and conversion costs.

(c) Compute the unit costs of production.

(d) Determine the costs to be assigned to the units transferred and in process for June.

(e) Prepare a production cost report for the Molding Department for the month of June.

(c) Materials $14.30
CC $12.70
(d) Transferred out $405,000
WIP $96,900

Complete four steps necessary to prepare a production cost report.
(SO 5, 6, 7)

P16-3B   Freedo Industries Inc. manufactures in separate processes furniture for homes. In each process, materials are entered at the beginning, and conversion costs are incurred uniformly. Production and cost data for the first process in making two products in two different manufacturing plants are as follows.

	Cutting Department	
Production Data—August	**Plant 1** **T12-Tables**	**Plant 2** **C10-Chairs**
Work in process units, August 1	–0–	–0–
Units started into production	20,000	15,000
Work in process units, August 31	2,000	500
Work in process percent complete	50%	80%

Cost Data—August		
Work in process, August 1	$ –0–	$ –0–
Materials	380,000	225,000
Labor	190,000	118,100
Overhead	76,000	60,700
Total	$646,000	$403,800

(a) Plant 1:
(1) Transferred out 18,000
WIP 2,000
(2) Materials 20,000
CC 19,000
(3) Materials $19
CC $14
(4) Transferred out $594,000
WIP $52,000

Instructions

(a) For each plant:

    (1) Compute the physical unit flow.

    (2) Compute equivalent units of production for materials and for conversion costs.

    (3) Determine the unit costs of production.

    (4) Show the assignment of costs of units transferred out and in process.

(b) Prepare the production cost report for Plant 1 for August 2007.

Assign costs and prepare production cost report.
(SO 5, 6, 7)

P16-4B   Wang Company has several processing departments. Costs charged to the Assembly Department for November 2007 totaled $2,126,000 as follows.

Work in process, November 1		
Materials	$70,000	
Conversion costs	48,000	$ 118,000
Materials added		1,270,000
Labor		358,000
Overhead		380,000

Production records show that 30,000 units were in beginning work in process 30% complete as to conversion costs, 640,000 units were started into production, and 25,000 units were in ending work in process 40% complete as to conversion costs. Materials are entered at the beginning of each process.

Instructions
(a) Determine the equivalent units of production and the unit costs for the Assembly Department.
(b) Determine the assignment of costs to goods transferred out and in process.
(c) Prepare a production cost report for the Assembly Department.

(b) Transferred out $2,064,000
WIP $62,000

P16-5B   Clemente Company manufactures basketballs. Materials are added at the beginning of the production process and conversion costs are incurred uniformly. Production and cost data for the month of July 2007 are as follows.

Determine equivalent units and unit costs and assign costs.
(SO 5, 6, 7)

Production Data—Basketballs	Units	Percent Complete
Work in process units, July 1	500	60%
Units started into production	1,600	
Work in process units, July 31	600	40%

Cost Data—Basketballs		
Work in process, July 1		
Materials	$540	
Conversion costs	500	$1,040
Direct materials		2,400
Direct labor		1,600
Manufacturing overhead		1,380

Instructions
(a) Calculate the following.
   (1) The equivalent units of production for materials and conversion costs.
   (2) The unit costs of production for materials and conversion costs.
   (3) The assignment of costs to units transferred out and in process at the end of the accounting period.
(b) Prepare a production cost report for the month of July for the basketballs.

(a) (1) Materials   2,100
    (2) Materials $1.40
    (3) Transferred
        out $5,100
        WIP $1,320

P16-6B   Magic Processing Company uses a weighted-average process cost system and manufactures a single product—a premium rug shampoo and cleaner. The manufacturing activity for the month of November has just been completed. A partially completed production cost report for the month of November for the Mixing and Cooking Department is shown below and on the next page.

Compute equivalent units and complete production cost report.
(SO 5, 7)

MAGIC PROCESSING COMPANY
Mixing and Cooking Department
Production Cost Report
For the Month Ended November 30

Quantities	Physical Units	Equivalent Units	
		Materials	Conversion Costs
Units to be accounted for			
Work in process, November 1 (all materials, 70% conversion costs)	10,000		
Started into production	160,000		
Total units	170,000		
Units accounted for			
Transferred out	130,000	?	?
Work in process, November 30 (50% materials, 25% conversion costs)	40,000	?	?
Total units accounted for	170,000	?	?

Costs

Unit costs	Materials	Conversion Costs	Total
Costs in November	$240,000	$98,000	$338,000
Equivalent units	?	?	
Unit costs	$? +	$? =	$?

Costs to be accounted for		
Work in process, November 1		$ 38,000
Started into production		300,000
Total costs		$338,000

Cost Reconciliation Schedule

Costs accounted for			
Transferred out			$?
Work in process, November 30			
Materials		$?	
Conversion costs		?	?
Total costs			$?

Instructions

(a) Prepare a schedule that shows how the equivalent units were computed so that you can complete the "Quantities: Units accounted for" equivalent units section shown in the production cost report above.

(b) Compute November unit costs.

(c) Complete the "Cost Reconciliation Schedule" part of the production cost report above.

(a) Materials 150,000
(b) Materials $1.60
(c) Transferred out $299,000
*   WIP $39,000*

Determine equivalent units and unit costs and assign costs for processes; prepare production cost report.
(SO 8)

*P16-7B Jessica Company manufactures basketballs and soccer balls. For both products, materials are added at the beginning of the production process and conversion costs are incurred uniformly. Jessica uses the FIFO method to compute equivalent units. Production and cost data for the month of August are as follows.

Production Data—Basketballs	Units	Percent Complete
Work in process units, August 1	500	60%
Units started into production	1,600	
Work in process units, August 31	600	50%

Cost Data—Basketballs	
Work in process, August 1	$1,125
Direct materials	1,600
Direct labor	1,175
Manufacturing overhead	1,000

Production Data—Soccer Balls	Units	Percent Complete
Work in process units, August 1	200	80%
Units started into production	2,000	
Work in process units, August 31	150	70%

Cost Data—Soccer Balls	
Work in process, August 1	$ 450
Direct materials	2,600
Direct labor	1,000
Manufacturing overhead	995

Instructions

(a) Calculate the following for both the basketballs and the soccer balls.

(1) The equivalent units of production for materials and conversion.

(2) The unit costs of production for materials and conversion costs.

(3) The assignment of costs to units transferred out and in process at the end of the accounting period.

(b) Prepare a production cost report for the month of August for the basketballs only.

(a) Basketballs:
(1) Materials 1,600
(2) Materials $1
(3) Transferred out $3,865
*   WIP $1,035*

Problems: Set C

Visit the book's website at **www.wiley.com/college/kimmel** and choose the Student Companion site to access Problem Set C.

BROADENING YOUR PERSPECTIVE

Group Decision Case

BYP16-1 British Beach Company manufactures suntan lotion, called Surtan, which is sold in 11-ounce plastic bottles. Surtan is sold in a competitive market. As a result, management is very cost-conscious. Surtan is manufactured through two processes: mixing and filling. Materials are entered at the beginning of each process, and labor and manufacturing overhead occur uniformly throughout each process. Unit costs are based on the cost per gallon of Surtan using the weighted-average costing approach.

On June 30, 2007, Sara Simmons, the chief accountant for the past 20 years, opted to take early retirement. Her replacement, Joe Jacobs, had extensive accounting experience with motels in the area but only limited contact with manufacturing accounting.

During July, Joe correctly accumulated the following production quantity and cost data for the Mixing Department.

> Production quantities: Work in process, July 1, 8,000 gallons 75% complete; started into production 100,000 gallons; work in process, July 31, 5,000 gallons 20% complete. Materials are added at the beginning of the process.
>
> Production costs: Beginning work in process $88,000, comprised of $21,000 of materials costs and $67,000 of conversion costs; incurred in July: materials $600,000, conversion costs $785,800.

Joe then prepared a production cost report on the basis of physical units started into production. His report showed a production cost of $14.738 per gallon of Surtan. The management of British Beach was surprised at the high unit cost. The president comes to you, as Sara's top assistant, to review Joe's report and prepare a correct report if necessary.

Instructions

With the class divided into groups, answer the following questions.

(a) Show how Joe arrived at the unit cost of $14.738 per gallon of Surtan.
(b) What error(s) did Joe make in preparing his production cost report?
(c) Prepare a correct production cost report for July.

Managerial Analysis

BYP16-2 Harris Furniture Company manufactures living room furniture through two departments: Framing and Upholstering. Materials are entered at the beginning of each process. Costs transferred in should be treated as materials cost. For May, the following cost data are obtained from the two work in process accounts.

	Framing	Upholstering
Work in process, May 1	$ –0–	$?
Materials	420,000	?
Conversion costs	210,000	330,000
Costs transferred in	–0–	550,000
Costs transferred out	550,000	?
Work in process, May 31	80,000	?

Instructions

Answer the following questions.

(a) If 3,000 sofas were started into production on May 1 and 2,500 sofas were transferred to Upholstering, what was the unit cost of materials for May in the Framing Department?

(b) Using the data in (a), what was the per unit conversion cost of the sofas transferred to Upholstering?

(c) Continuing the assumptions in (a), what is the percentage of completion of the units in process at May 31 in the Framing Department?

Real-World Focus

BYP16-3 General Microwave Corp. is engaged primarily in the design, development, manufacture, and marketing of microwave, electronic, and fiber-optic test equipment, components, and subsystems. A substantial portion of the company's microwave product is sold to manufacturers and users of microwave systems and equipment for applications in the defense electronics industry.

General Microwave Corp. reports the following information in one of the notes to its financial statements.

GENERAL MICROWAVE CORPORATION
Notes to the Financial Statements

Work in process inventory reflects all accumulated production costs, which are comprised of direct production costs and overhead, reduced by amounts attributable to units delivered. Work in process inventory is reduced to its estimated net realizable value by a charge to cost of sales in the period [in which] excess costs are identified. Raw materials and finished goods inventories are reflected at the lower of cost or market.

Instructions

(a) What types of manufacturing costs are accumulated in the work in process inventory account?

(b) What types of information must General Microwave have to be able to compute equivalent units of production?

(c) How does General Microwave assign costs to the completed units transferred out of work in process?

Exploring the Web

BYP16-4 Search the Internet and find the Web sites of two manufacturers that you think are likely to use process costing. Are there any specifics included in their Web sites that confirm the use of process costing for each of these companies?

Communication Activity

BYP16-5 Jenna Haines was a good friend of yours in high school and is from your home town. While you chose to major in accounting when you both went away to college, she majored in marketing and management. You have recently been promoted to accounting manager for the Snack Foods Division of Clark Enterprises, and your friend was promoted to regional sales manager for the same division of Clark. Jenna recently telephoned you. She explained that she was familiar with job cost sheets, which had been used by the Special Projects division where she had formerly worked. She was, however, very uncomfortable with the production cost reports prepared by your division. She faxed you a list of her particular questions. These included the following.

1. Since Clark occasionally prepares snack foods for special orders in the Snack Foods Division, why don't we track costs of the orders separately?

2. What is an equivalent unit?

3. Why am I getting four production cost reports? Isn't there only one Work in Process account?

Instructions

Prepare a memo to Jenna. Answer her questions, and include any additional information you think would be helpful. You may write informally, but be careful to use proper grammar and punctuation.

Research Assignment

BYP16-6   The May 10, 2004, edition of the *Wall Street Journal* includes an article by Evan Ramstad titled "A Tight Squeeze" (p. R9).

Instructions

Read the article and answer the following questions.

(a) What is Proview's profit margin on computer monitors? Why is the profit margin so thin on computer monitors?
(b) What are some of the steps that Proview International has taken to control costs?
(c) Why does the company continue to build tube-based monitors even as many consumers are moving away from them?
(d) Mr. Wang's final comment is, "Every aspect of the business is important, but the most important is cost." Why does he feel this way?

Ethics Case

BYP16-7   C. C. Daibo Company manufactures a high-tech component that passes through two production processing departments, Molding and Assembly. Department managers are partially compensated on the basis of units of products completed and transferred out relative to units of product put into production. This was intended as encouragement to be efficient and to minimize waste.

Barb Crusmer is the department head in the Molding Department, and Wayne Terrago is her quality control inspector. During the month of June, Barb had three new employees who were not yet technically skilled. As a result, many of the units produced in June had minor molding defects. In order to maintain the department's normal high rate of completion, Barb told Wayne to pass through inspection and on to the Assembly Department all units that had defects nondetectable to the human eye. "Company and industry tolerances on this product are too high anyway," says Barb. "Less than 2% of the units we produce are subjected in the market to the stress tolerance we've designed into them. The odds of those 2% being any of this month's units are even less. Anyway, we're saving the company money."

Instructions

(a) Who are the potential stakeholders involved in this situation?
(b) What alternatives does Wayne have in this situation? What might the company do to prevent this situation from occurring?

Answers to Self-Study Questions

1. b   2. d   3. d   4. b   5. b   6. a   7. c   8. a   9. b   10. b
*11. b   *12. a   *13. b

CHAPTER 17

Activity-Based Costing

STUDY OBJECTIVES

After studying this chapter,
you should be able to:

1 Recognize the difference between traditional costing and activity-based costing.
2 Identify the steps in the development of an activity-based costing system.
3 Know how companies identify the activity cost pools used in activity-based costing.
4 Know how companies identify and use cost drivers in activity-based costing.
5 Understand the benefits and limitations of activity-based costing.
6 Differentiate between value-added and non-value-added activities.
7 Understand the value of using activity levels in activity-based costing.
8 Apply activity-based costing to service industries.

THE NAVIGATOR

- Scan *Study Objectives*
- Read *Feature Story*
- Read *Preview*
- Read text and answer *Before You Go On*
  p. 853 ◯ p. 861 ◯ p. 864 ◯
- Work *Using the Decision Toolkit*
- Review *Summary of Study Objectives*
- Work *Demonstration Problem*
- Answer *Self-Study Questions*
- Complete *Assignments*

FEATURE STORY

The ABCs of Donut Making—Virtual-Reality Style

Super Bakery, Inc., created in 1990 by former Pittsburgh Steelers' running back Franco Harris, is a nationwide supplier of mineral-, vitamin-, and protein-enriched donuts and other baked goods to the institutional food market, primarily school systems. Super Bakery is a *virtual corporation*, in which only the core, strategic functions of the business are performed inside the company. The remaining activities—selling, manufacturing, warehousing, and shipping—are outsourced to a network of external companies.

Super Bakery draws these cooperating companies together and organizes the work flow. The goal is to add maximum value to the company while making the minimum investment in permanent staff, fixed assets, and working capital. The results are notable: Super Bakery's sales have grown at an average annual rate of approximately 20 percent during most of its existence.

One of Super Bakery's challenges has been to control the cost of the outsourced activities. Management suspected a wide variation in the cost of serving customers in different parts of the country. Yet its traditional costing methods were spreading costs over the entire customer base. Each customer's order *appeared* to cost the same amount to complete. In actuality, orders with high profit margins were subsidizing orders with low profit margins. Super Bakery desired a system that would more accurately assign the costs of each order. With such a system, pricing could be improved.

The company looked at and eventually changed to a system that could identify the costs associated with the *activities* performed in the business—manufacturing, sales, warehousing, and shipping. The new activity-based costing system showed that the costs and profit margins on each sale vary significantly. Super Bakery is now able to track the profitability of each customer's account and the performance of outsourced activities. This donut maker, as a result, even knows the cost of the donut holes!

Source: Tom R.V. Davis and Bruce L. Darling, "ABC in a Virtual Corporation," *Management Accounting* (October 1996), pp. 18–26.

PREVIEW OF CHAPTER 17

As indicated in our Feature Story about Super Bakery, Inc., the traditional costing systems described in earlier chapters are not the best answer for every company. Because Super Bakery suspected that the traditional system was masking significant differences in its real cost structure, it sought a new method of assigning costs. Similar searches by other companies for ways to improve operations and gather more accurate data for decision-making have resulted in the development of powerful new management tools, including **activity-based costing (ABC)**. The primary objective of this chapter is to explain and illustrate this concept.

The content and organization of this chapter are as follows.

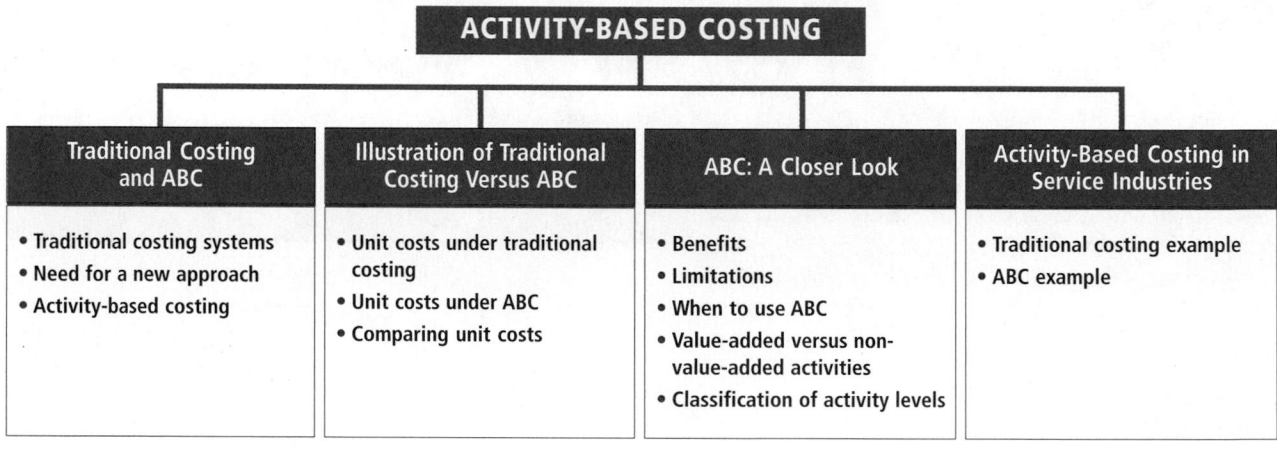

ACTIVITY-BASED COSTING			
Traditional Costing and ABC	**Illustration of Traditional Costing Versus ABC**	**ABC: A Closer Look**	**Activity-Based Costing in Service Industries**
• Traditional costing systems • Need for a new approach • Activity-based costing	• Unit costs under traditional costing • Unit costs under ABC • Comparing unit costs	• Benefits • Limitations • When to use ABC • Value-added versus non-value-added activities • Classification of activity levels	• Traditional costing example • ABC example

Traditional Costing and Activity-Based Costing

TRADITIONAL COSTING SYSTEMS

STUDY OBJECTIVE
1

Recognize the difference between traditional costing and activity-based costing.

It is probably impossible to determine the **exact** cost of a product or service. However, in order to achieve improved management decisions, every effort to provide decision makers with the most accurate cost estimates must be made. The most accurate estimate of product cost occurs when the costs are traceable directly to the product produced or the service provided. Direct material and direct labor costs are the easiest to trace directly to the product through the use of material requisition forms and payroll time sheets. Overhead costs, on the other hand, are an indirect or common cost that generally cannot be easily or directly traced to individual products or services. Instead, we use estimates to assign overhead costs to products and services.

Often the most difficult part of computing accurate unit costs is determining the proper amount of **overhead cost** to assign to each product, service, or job. In our coverage of job order costing in Chapter 15 and of process costing in Chapter 16, we used a single or plantwide overhead rate throughout the year for the entire factory operation. That rate was called the **predetermined overhead rate**. For job order costing we assumed that **direct labor cost** was the relevant activity base for assigning all overhead costs to jobs. For process costing, we assumed that **machine hours** was the relevant activity base for assigning all overhead to the process or department.

The use of direct labor as the activity base made sense when overhead cost allocation systems were first developed. At that time, direct labor made up a large portion of total manufacturing cost. Therefore, it was widely accepted that there was a high correlation between direct labor and the incurrence of overhead cost. As a result, direct labor became the most popular basis for allocating overhead.

Even in today's increasingly automated environment, direct labor is sometimes the appropriate basis for assigning overhead cost to products. It is appropriate to use direct labor when (a) direct labor constitutes a significant part of total product cost, and (b) a high correlation exists between direct labor and changes in the amount of overhead costs. A simplified (one-stage) traditional costing system relying on direct labor to assign overhead is displayed in Illustration 17-1.

THE NEED FOR A NEW APPROACH

In recent years manufacturers and service providers have experienced tremendous change. Advances in computerized systems, technological innovation, global competition, and automation have changed the manufacturing environment drastically. As a result, the amount of direct labor used in many industries has greatly decreased, and total overhead costs resulting from depreciation on expensive equipment and machinery, utilities, repairs, and maintenance have significantly increased. When there is not a correlation between direct labor and overhead, it is inappropriate to use plantwide predetermined overhead rates based on direct labor. Companies that use overhead rates based on direct labor, when this correlation does not exist, experience significant product cost distortions.

To avoid such distortions, many companies now use machine hours as the basis on which to allocate overhead in an automated manufacturing environment. But even machine hours may not suffice as the only plantwide basis for allocating all overhead. If the manufacturing process is complex, then only multiple allocation bases can result in more accurate product-cost computations. In such situations, managers need to consider an overhead cost allocation method that uses multiple bases. That method is **activity-based costing**.

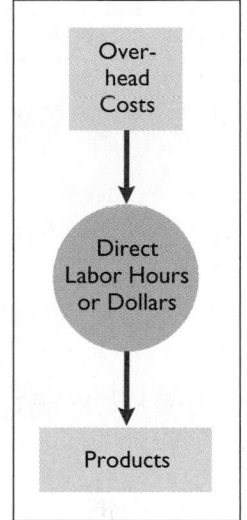

Illustration 17-1 Traditional one-stage costing system

ACTIVITY-BASED COSTING

Broadly, **activity-based costing (ABC)** is an approach for allocating overhead costs. More specifically, ABC allocates overhead to multiple activity cost pools, and it then assigns the activity cost pools to products and services by means of cost drivers. To understand more clearly what that means, you need to apply some new meanings to the rather common-sounding words that make up the definition. In activity-based costing, an **activity** is any event, action, transaction, or work sequence that incurs cost when producing a product or providing a service. An **activity cost pool** is a distinct type of activity (e.g., ordering materials or setting up machines). A **cost driver** is any factor or activity that has a direct cause-effect relationship with the resources consumed. The reasoning behind ABC cost allocation is simple: **Products consume activities, and activities consume resources**.

These definitions of terms will become clearer as we look more closely at how ABC works. ABC allocates overhead in a two-stage process. In the first stage, overhead costs are allocated to activity cost pools. (In traditional costing systems, in contrast, these costs are allocated to departments or to jobs.) Examples of overhead cost pools are ordering materials, setting up machines, assembling products, inspecting products.

In the second stage, the overhead allocated to the activity cost pools is assigned to products using cost drivers. The cost drivers measure the number of individual activities undertaken or performed to produce products or provide services. Examples are number of purchase orders, number of setups, labor hours, or number of inspections. Illustration 17-2 shows examples of activities, and possible cost drivers to measure them, for a company that manufactures two products—axles and steering wheels.

Illustration 17-2   Activities and related cost drivers

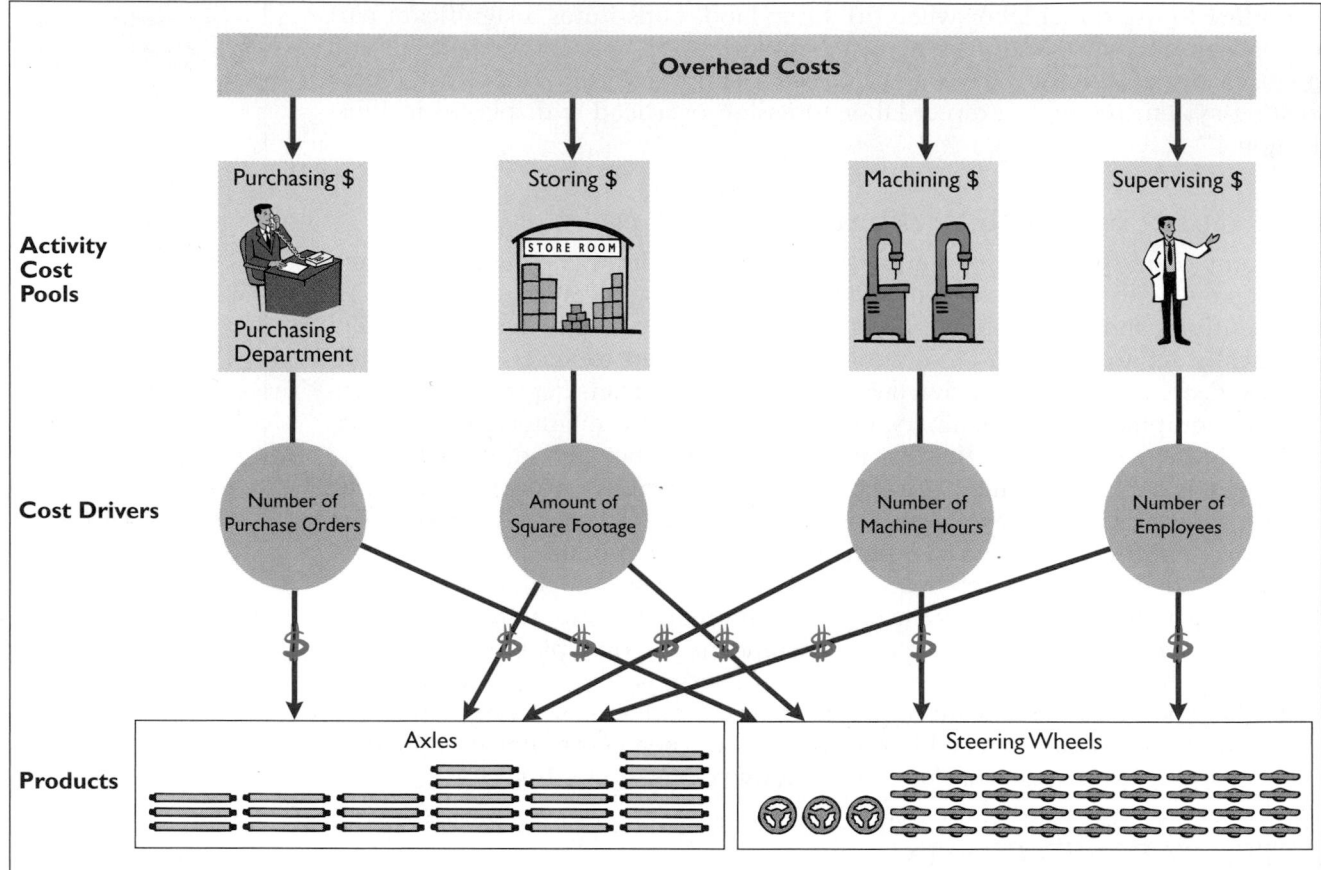

In the first step (as shown at the top of Illustration 17-2), the company's overhead costs are allocated to activity cost pools. In this simplified example, four activity cost pools have been identified: purchasing, storing, machining, and supervising. After the costs are allocated to the activity cost pools, the company uses cost drivers to determine the costs to be assigned to the individual products (either axles or steering wheels) based on each product's use of each activity. For example, if axles require more activity by the purchasing department, as measured by the number of required purchase orders, then more of the overhead cost from the purchasing pool will be allocated to the axles.

The more complex a product's manufacturing operation, the more activities and cost drivers it is likely to have. If there is little or no correlation between changes in the cost driver and consumption of the overhead cost, inaccurate product costs are inevitable.

The design of a more complex activity-based costing system with seven activity cost pools is graphically shown in Illustration 17-3 for Lift Jack Company. Lift Jack Company manufactures two automotive jacks—an automobile scissors jack and a truck hydraulic jack.

Illustration 17-3   ABC system design—Lift Jack Company

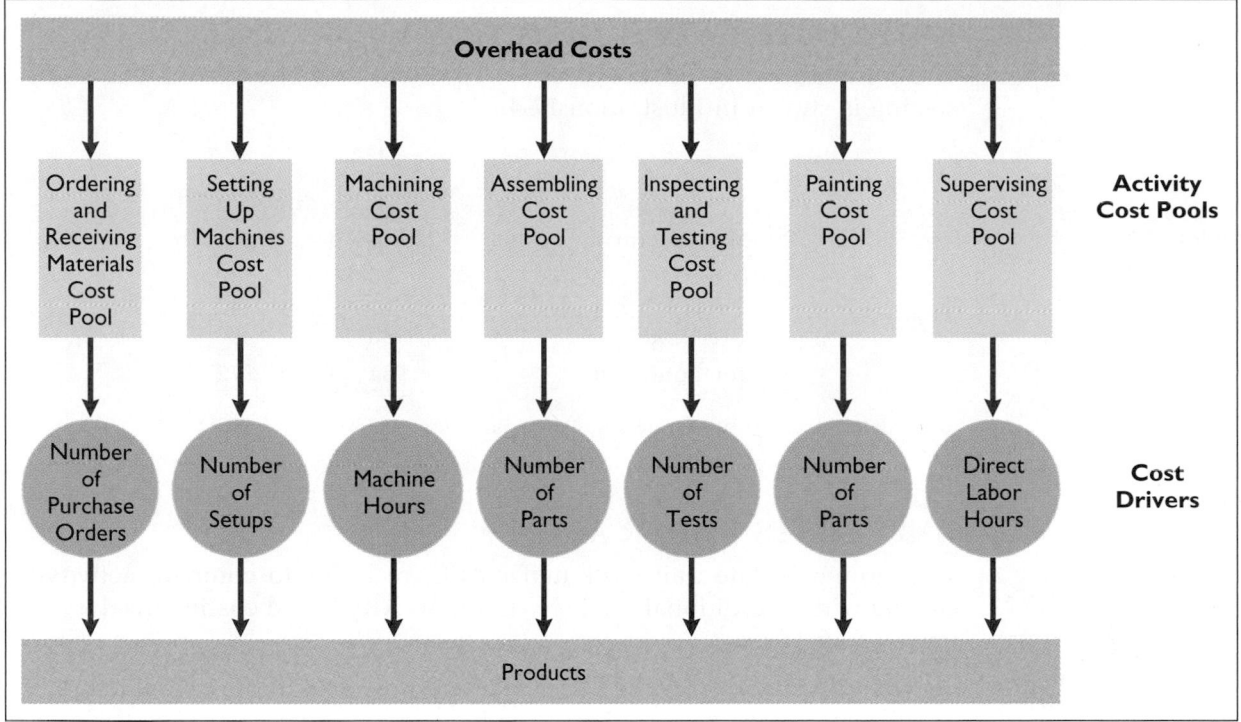

The Lift Jack Company illustration contains seven activity cost pools. In some companies the number of activities related to a cost pool can be substantial. For example, at Clark-Hurth (a division of Clark Equipment Company), a manufacturer of axles and transmissions, over 170 activities were identified. At Compumotor (a division of Parker Hannifin) over 80 activities were identified in just the procurement function of its Material Control Department.

Illustration of Traditional Costing versus ABC

In this section we present a simple case example that compares traditional costing and activity-based costing. It illustrates how ABC eliminates the distortion that can occur in traditional overhead cost allocation. You should understand that ABC does not replace an existing job order or process costing system. What ABC does is to segregate overhead into various cost pools in an effort to provide more accurate cost information. As a result, ABC supplements—not replaces—the traditional cost systems.

Assume that Atlas Company produces two automobile antitheft devices, The Boot and The Club. The Boot is a high-volume item totaling 25,000 units annually. The Club is a low-volume item totaling only 5,000 units per year. Each product requires one hour of direct labor for completion. Therefore, total annual direct labor hours are 30,000 (25,000 + 5,000). Expected annual manufacturing overhead costs are $900,000. Thus, the predetermined overhead rate is $30 ($900,000 ÷ 30,000) per direct labor hour.

The direct materials cost per unit is $40 for The Boot and $30 for The Club. The direct labor cost is $12 per unit for each product.

UNIT COSTS UNDER TRADITIONAL COSTING

The computation of the unit cost for The Boot and The Club under traditional costing is shown in Illustration 17-4.

Illustration 17-4   Computation of unit costs—traditional costing

	Products	
Manufacturing Costs	**The Boot**	**The Club**
Direct materials	$0	$30
Direct labor	12	12
Overhead	30*	30*
Total unit cost	$82	$72

*Predetermined overhead rate times direct labor hours ($30 × 1 hr. = $30).

UNIT COSTS UNDER ABC

STUDY OBJECTIVE
2

Identify the steps in the development of an activity-based costing system.

Let's now calculate unit costs under ABC, in order to compare activity-based costing with a traditional costing system. Activity-based costing involves the following four steps.

1. Identify and classify the major activities involved in the manufacture of specific products, and allocate manufacturing overhead costs to the appropriate cost pools.
2. Identify the cost driver that has a strong correlation to the costs accumulated in the cost pool.
3. Compute the overhead rate for each cost driver.
4. Assign manufacturing overhead costs for each cost pool to products, using the overhead rates (cost per driver).

Identify and Classify Activities and Allocate Overhead to Cost Pools (Step 1)

STUDY OBJECTIVE
3

Know how companies identify the activity cost pools used in activity-based costing.

A well-designed activity-based costing system starts with an analysis of the activities performed to manufacture a product or provide a service. This analysis should identify all resource-consuming activities. It requires a detailed, step-by-step walk-through of each operation, documenting every activity undertaken to accomplish a task. Atlas Company identified three activity-cost pools: setting up machines, machining, and inspecting.

Next, overhead costs are assigned directly to the appropriate activity cost pool. For example, all overhead costs directly associated with Atlas Company's machine setups (such as salaries, supplies, and depreciation) would be assigned to the machine setup cost pool. The three cost pools, along with the estimated overhead allocated to each cost pool, are shown in Illustration 17-5.

Illustration 17-5   Activity cost pools and estimated overhead

Activity Cost Pools	Estimated Overhead
Setting up machines	$300,000
Machining	500,000
Inspecting	100,000
Total	$ 900,000

Identify Cost Drivers (Step 2)

After costs are allocated to the activity cost pools, the cost drivers for each cost pool must be identified. The cost driver must accurately measure the actual consumption of the activity by the various products. To achieve accurate costing, a **high degree of correlation** must exist between the cost driver and the actual consumption of the overhead costs in the cost pool.

The cost drivers identified by Atlas and their total expected use per activity cost pool are shown in Illustration 17-6.

STUDY OBJECTIVE

4

Know how companies identify and use cost drivers in activity-based costing.

Activity Cost Pools	Cost Drivers	Expected Use of Cost Drivers per Activity
Setting up machines	Number of setups	**1,500** setups
Machining	Machine hours	**50,000** machine hours
Inspecting	Number of inspections	**2,000** inspections

Illustration 17-6   Cost drivers and their expected use

Availability and ease of obtaining data relating to the cost driver is an important factor that must be considered in its selection.

Compute Overhead Rates (Step 3)

Next, an **activity-based overhead rate** per cost driver is computed by dividing the estimated overhead per activity by the number of cost drivers expected to be used per activity. The formula for this computation is shown in Illustration 17-7.

$$\frac{\text{Estimated Overhead Per Activity}}{\text{Expected Use of Cost Drivers Per Activity}} = \text{Activity-Based Overhead Rate}$$

Illustration 17-7   Formula for computing activity-based overhead rate

Atlas Company computes its activity-based overhead rates by using estimated overhead per activity cost pool, shown in Illustration 17-5, and the expected use of cost drivers per activity, shown in Illustration 17-6. The computations are presented in Illustration 17-8.

Activity Cost Pools	Estimated Overhead	÷ Expected Use of Cost Drivers per Activity	= Activity-Based Overhead Rates
Setting up machines	$300,000	1,500 setups	$200 per setup
Machining	500,000	50,000 machine hours	$10 per machine hour
Inspecting	100,000	2,000 inspections	$50 per inspection
Total	$900,000		

Illustration 17-8   Computation of activity-based overhead rates

Assign Overhead Costs to Products (Step 4)

In assigning overhead costs, it is necessary to know the expected use of cost drivers **for each product**. Because of its low volume, The Club requires more setups and inspections than The Boot. The expected use of cost drivers per product for each of Atlas's products is shown in Illustration 17-9 (page 852).

Activity Cost Pools	Cost Drivers	Expected Use of Cost Drivers per Activity	Expected Use of Cost Drivers per Product	
			The Boot	The Club
Setting up machines	Number of setups	1,500 setups	500	1,000
Machining	Machine hours	50,000 machine hours	30,000	20,000
Inspecting	Number of inspections	2,000 inspections	500	1,500

To assign overhead costs to each product, the activity-based overhead rates per cost driver (Illustration 17-8) are multiplied by the number of cost drivers expected to be used per product (Illustration 17-9). The amount of overhead cost assigned to each product for Atlas Company is shown in Illustration 17-10.

Atlas Company.xls — ATLAS COMPANY

Activity Cost Pools	The Boot					The Club			
	Expected Use of Cost Drivers per Product	×	Activity-Based Overhead Rates	=	Cost Assigned	Expected Use of Cost Drivers per Product	×	Activity-Based Overhead Rates	= Cost Assigned
Setting up machines	500		$200		$100,000	1,000		$200	$200,000
Machining	30,000		10		300,000	20,000		10	200,000
Inspecting	500		50		25,000	1,500		50	75,000
Total costs assigned [(a)]					$425,000				$475,000
Units produced [(b)]					25,000				5,000
Overhead cost per unit [(a) ÷ (b)]					$17				$95

These data show that under ABC, overhead costs are shifted from the high-volume product (The Boot) to the low-volume product (The Club). This shift results in more accurate costing for two reasons:

1. Low-volume products often require more special handling, such as more machine setups and inspections, than high-volume products. This is true for Atlas Company. Thus, the low-volume product frequently is responsible for more overhead costs per unit than is a high-volume product.[1]

2. Assigning overhead using ABC will usually increase the cost per unit for low-volume products as compared to a traditional overhead allocation. Therefore, traditional cost drivers such as direct labor hours are usually not appropriate for assigning overhead costs to low-volume products.

COMPARING UNIT COSTS

A comparison of unit manufacturing costs under traditional costing and ABC shows the following significant differences.

---

[1]Robin Cooper and Robert S. Kaplan, "How Cost Accounting Distorts Product Costs," *Management Accounting* 69, No. 10 (April 1988), pp. 20–27.

Illustration 17-11   Comparison of unit product costs

| | The Boot | | The Club | |
Manufacturing Costs	Traditional Costing	ABC	Traditional Costing	ABC
Direct materials	$40	$40	$30	$30
Direct labor	12	12	12	12
Overhead	30	17	30	95
Total cost per unit	$82	$69	$72	$137

Overstated $13

Understated $65

The comparison shows that unit costs under traditional costing are significantly distorted. The cost of producing The Boot is overstated $13 per unit ($82 − $69), and the cost of producing The Club is understated $65 per unit ($137 − $72). These differences are attributable entirely to how manufacturing overhead is assigned. A likely consequence of the differences in assigning overhead is that Atlas Company has been overpricing The Boot and possibly losing market share to competitors. Moreover, it has been sacrificing profitability by underpricing The Club.

Business Insight
International Perspective

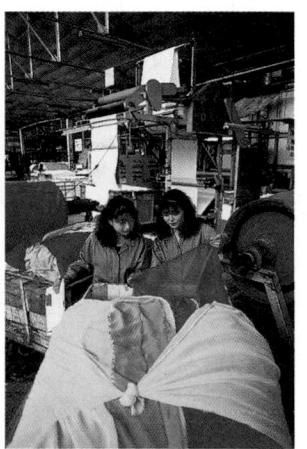

Activity-based costing was pioneered in the United States: John Deere Company coined the term less than 25 years ago. ABC has been adopted by numerous well-known U.S. companies including IBM, AT&T, Hewlett-Packard, Procter and Gamble, Tektronix, Hughes Aircraft, Caterpillar, and American Express. Its use outside the United States is limited. The cost of implementation may discourage some foreign companies.

In Japan, where activity-based costing is less used, companies prefer volume measures such as direct labor hours to assign overhead cost to products. Japanese managers are convinced that reducing direct labor is essential to continuous cost reduction. And, using direct labor as the basis for overhead allocation forces Japanese companies to watch direct labor more closely. Possibly, labor cost reduction is more of a priority than developing more accurate product costs.

BEFORE YOU GO ON . . .

►Review It

1. Historically, why has direct labor hours been the most popular basis for allocating overhead costs to products?
2. What changes have occurred in the industrial environment to diminish the appeal of traditional volume-based overhead allocation systems?
3. What four steps are involved in developing an ABC system?

▶**Do It**

Lift Jack Company, as shown in Illustration 17-3, page 849, has seven activity cost pools and two products. It expects to produce 200,000 units of its automobile scissors jack, and 80,000 units of its truck hydraulic jack. Having identified its activity cost pools and the cost drivers for each cost pool, Lift Jack Company accumulated the following data relative to those activity cost pools and cost drivers.

Annual Overhead Data				Expected Use of Cost Drivers per Product	
Activity Cost Pools	Cost Drivers	Estimated Overhead	Expected Use of Cost Drivers per Activity	Scissors Jacks	Hydraulic Jacks
Ordering and receiving	Purchase orders	$ 200,000	2,500 orders	1,000	1,500
Machine setup	Setups	600,000	1,200 setups	500	700
Machining	Machine hours	2,000,000	800,000 hours	300,000	500,000
Assembling	Parts	1,800,000	3,000,000 parts	1,800,000	1,200,000
Inspecting and testing	Tests	700,000	35,000 tests	20,000	15,000
Painting	Parts	300,000	3,000,000 parts	1,800,000	1,200,000
Supervising	Direct labor hours	1,200,000	200,000 hours	130,000	70,000
		$6,800,000			

Using the above data, do the following:
(a) Prepare a schedule showing the computations of the activity-based overhead rates per cost driver.
(b) Prepare a schedule assigning each activity's overhead cost to the two products.
(c) Compute the overhead cost per unit for each product.
(d) Comment on the comparative overhead cost per unit.

Action Plan

• Determine the activity-based overhead rate by dividing the estimated overhead per activity by the expected use of cost drivers per activity.

• Assign the overhead of each activity cost pool to the individual products by multiplying the expected use of cost driver per product times the activity-based overhead rate.

• Determine overhead cost per unit by dividing the overhead assigned to each product by the number of units of that product.

Solution

(a) Computations of activity-based overhead rates per cost driver:

Activity Cost Pools	Estimated Overhead	÷	Expected Use of Cost Drivers per Activity	=	Activity-Based Overhead Rates
Ordering and receiving	$ 200,000		2,500 purchase orders		$80 per order
Machine setup	600,000		1,200 setups		$500 per setup
Machining	2,000,000		800,000 machine hours		$2.50 per machine hour
Assembling	1,800,000		3,000,000 parts		$0.60 per part
Inspecting and testing	700,000		35,000 tests		$20 per test
Painting	300,000		3,000,000 parts		$0.10 per part
Supervising	1,200,000		200,000 direct labor hours		$6 per direct labor hour
	$6,800,000				

(b) Assignment of each activity's overhead cost to products using ABC:

	Scissors Jacks			Hydraulic Jacks		
Activity Cost Pools	**Expected Use of Cost Drivers per Product** ×	**Activity-Based Overhead Rates**	**Cost = Assigned**	**Expected Use of Cost Drivers per Product** ×	**Activity-Based Overhead Rates**	**Cost = Assigned**
Ordering and receiving	1,000	$80	$ 80,000	1,500	$80	$ 120,000
Machine setup	500	$500	250,000	700	$500	350,000
Machining	300,000	$2.50	750,000	500,000	$2.50	1,250,000
Assembling	1,800,000	$0.60	1,080,000	1,200,000	$0.60	720,000
Inspecting and testing	20,000	$20	400,000	15,000	$20	300,000
Painting	1,800,000	$0.10	180,000	1,200,000	$0.10	120,000
Supervising	130,000	$6	780,000	70,000	$6	420,000
Total assigned costs			$3,520,000			$3,280,000

(c) Computation of overhead cost per unit:

	Scissors Jack	**Hydraulic Jack**
Total costs assigned	$3,520,000	$3,280,000
Total units produced	200,000	80,000
Overhead cost per unit	$17.60	$41.00

(d) These data show that the total overhead assigned to 80,000 hydraulic jacks is nearly as great as the overhead assigned to 200,000 scissors jacks. However, the overhead cost per hydraulic jack is $41.00. It is only $17.60 per scissors jack.

Related exercise material: BE17-1, BE17-2, BE17-3, BE17-4, BE17-5, BE17-6, BE17-7, E17-1, E17-2, E17-3, E17-4, E17-5, E17-6, E17-7, E17-8, E17-9, E17-10, and E17-11.

THE NAVIGATOR

Activity-Based Costing: A Closer Look

As the use of activity-based costing has grown, both its practical benefits and its limitations have become apparent.

BENEFITS OF ABC

The primary benefit of ABC is **more accurate product costing**. Here's why:

1. **ABC leads to more cost pools** used to assign overhead costs to products. Instead of one plantwide pool (or even departmental pools) and a single cost driver, numerous activity cost pools with more relevant cost drivers are utilized. Costs are assigned more directly on the basis of the number of cost drivers used to produce each product.

2. **ABC leads to enhanced control over overhead costs.** Under ABC, many overhead costs can be traced directly to activities—allowing some indirect costs to be identified as direct costs. Thus, managers have become more aware of their responsibility to control the activities that generate those costs.

STUDY OBJECTIVE

5

Understand the benefits and limitations of activity-based costing.

3. **ABC leads to better management decisions.** More accurate product costing should contribute to setting selling prices that can help achieve desired product profitability levels. In addition, more accurate cost data could be helpful in deciding whether to make or buy a product part or component, and sometimes even whether to eliminate a product.

In fact, identification of what activities drive costs can result in some indirect costs being accounted for as direct costs. This is because, under ABC, these costs are traceable to specific activities.

Activity-based costing does not change the amount of overhead costs. What it does do is to allocate those overhead costs in a more accurate manner. Furthermore, if the score-keeping is more realistic and more accurate, managers should be able to better understand cost behavior and overall profitability.

LIMITATIONS OF ABC

Although ABC systems often provide better product cost data than traditional volume-based systems, there are limitations:

1. **ABC can be expensive to use.** Many companies are discouraged from using ABC by the increased cost of identifying multiple activities and applying numerous cost drivers. Activity-based costing systems are more complex than traditional costing systems—sometimes significantly more complex. So companies must ask, is the cost of implementation greater than the benefits of greater accuracy? Sometimes it may be. For some companies there may be no need to consider ABC at all because their existing system is sufficient. If the costs of ABC outweigh the benefits, then the company should not implement ABC.

2. **Some arbitrary allocations continue.** Even though more overhead costs can be assigned directly to products through ABC's multiple activity cost pools, certain overhead costs remain to be allocated by means of some arbitrary volume-based cost driver such as labor or machine hours.

Accounting across the Organization

Although most publicized ABC applications are in manufacturing companies or large service firms, ABC can be applied in a very small service business. Mahany Welding Supply, a small family-run welding service business in Rochester, N.Y., applied ABC to determine the cost of servicing customers and to identify feasible cost reduction opportunities.

Application of ABC at Mahany Welding's operations provided information about the five employees who were involved in different activities of revenue generation—i.e., delivery of supplies (rural versus city), welding services, repairs, telephone sales, field or door-to-door sales, repeat business sales, and cold-call sales. Activity cost pools were assigned to the five revenue-producing employees using relevant cost drivers. ABC revealed annual net income (loss) by employee as follows: Employee #1, $65,431; Employee #2, $35,154; Employee #3, $13,731; Employee #4, ($10,957); Employee #5, ($46,180). This comparative information was an eye-opener to the owner of Mahany Welding— who was Employee #5!

Source: Michael Krupnicki and Thomas Tyson, "Using ABC to Determine the Cost of Servicing Customers," *Management Accounting* (December 31, 1997), pp. 40–46.

WHEN TO USE ABC

How does a company know when to use ABC? The presence of one or more of the following factors would point to possibly using ABC:

1. Product lines differ greatly in volume and manufacturing complexity.
2. Product lines are numerous, diverse, and require differing degrees of support services.
3. Overhead costs constitute a significant portion of total costs.
4. The manufacturing process or the number of products has changed significantly—for example, from labor-intensive to capital-intensive due to automation.
5. Production or marketing managers are ignoring data provided by the existing system and are instead using "bootleg" costing data or other alternative data when pricing or making other product decisions.

The redesign and installation of a product-costing system is a significant decision that requires considerable cost and a major effort to accomplish. Therefore, financial managers need to be very cautious and deliberate when initiating changes in costing systems. A key factor in implementing a successful ABC system is the support of top management.

Decision Toolkit

Decision Checkpoints	Info Needed for Decision	Tool to Use for Decision	How to Evaluate Results
When should we use ABC?	Knowledge of the products or product lines, the manufacturing process, and overhead costs.	A detailed and accurate cost accounting system; cooperation between accountants and operating managers	Compare the results under both costing systems. If managers are better able to understand and control their operations using ABC, and the costs are not prohibitive, use of ABC would be beneficial.

VALUE-ADDED VERSUS NON-VALUE-ADDED ACTIVITIES

Some companies that have experienced the benefits of activity-based costing have applied it to a broader range of management activities. **Activity-based management (ABM)** extends the use of ABC from product costing to a comprehensive management tool that focuses on reducing costs and improving processes and decision making. A refinement of activity-based costing used in ABM is the classification of activities as either value-added or non-value-added.

Value-added activities increase the worth of a product or service to customers; they involve resource usage and related costs that customers are willing to pay for. Value-added activities are the activities of actually manufacturing a product or performing a service—they increase the worth of the product or service. Examples of value-added activities in a manufacturing operation are engineering design, machining, assembly, painting, and packaging. Examples of value-added activities in a service company would be performing surgery, providing legal research for legal services, or delivering packages by a delivery service.

> **STUDY OBJECTIVE**
> **6**
> Differentiate between value-added and non-value-added activities.

Non-value-added activities are production- or service-related activities that simply **add cost to, or increase the time spent on, a product or service without increasing its market value**. Examples of non-value-added activities in a manufacturing operation include the repair of machines; the storage of inventory; the moving of raw materials, assemblies, and finished product within the factory; building maintenance; inspections; and inventory control. Examples of non-value-added activities in service enterprises might include taking appointments, reception, bookkeeping, billing, traveling, ordering supplies, advertising, cleaning, and computer repair.

Activity flowcharts are often used to help identify the activities that will be used in ABC costing. Illustration 17-12 shows an activity flowchart.

Illustration 17-12 Flowchart showing value-added and non-value-added activities

| | | | | **HEARTLAND MANUFACTURING COMPANY** | | | | | | | | |
| | | | | **Activity Flowchart** | | | | | | | | |

Activities

NVA	NVA	NVA	NVA	VA		NVA	NVA	VA	NVA	NVA	NVA	VA
Receive and Inspect Materials	Move and Store Materials	Move Materials to Production and Wait	Set up Machines	Machining: Drill	Lathe	Inspect	Move and Wait	Assembly	Inspect and Test	Move to Storage	Store Finished Goods	Package and Ship
Current Days 1	12	2.5	1.5	2	1	0.2	6	2	0.3	0.5	14	1

◄─────────────── *Total Current Average Time* $= 44\ days$ ───────────────►

| Proposed Days 1 | 4 | 1.5 | 1.5 | 2 | 1 | 0.2 | 2 | 2 | 0.3 | 0.5 | 10 | 1 |

◄─────────────── *Total Proposed Average Time* $= 27\ days$ ───────────────►

Proposed reduction in nonvalue-added time = 17 days

VA = Value-added   NVA = Non-value-added

In the top part of this flowchart, activities are identified as value-added or non-value-added. The value-added activities are highlighted in red. In the lower part of the flowchart are two rows showing the number of days spent on each activity. The first row shows the number of days spent on each activity under the current manufacturing process. The second row shows the number of days expected to be spent on each activity under management's proposed reengineered manufacturing process.

The proposed changes would reduce time spent on non-value-added activities by 17 days. This 17-day improvement would be due entirely to moving inventory more quickly through the non-value-added processes—that is, by reducing inventory time in moving, storage, and waiting. The appendix at the end of this chapter discusses a just-in-time inventory system, which is used to eliminate non-value-added activities related to inventory.

Not all activities labeled non-value-added are totally wasteful, nor can they be totally eliminated. For example, although inspection time is a non-value-added activity from a customer's perspective, few companies would eliminate their quality control functions. Similarly, moving and waiting time is non-value-added, but it would be impossible to completely eliminate. Nevertheless, when managers recognize the non-value-added characteristic of these activities, they are motivated to minimize them as much as possible. Attention to such matters is part of the growing practice of activity-based management which helps managers concentrate on **continuous improvement** of operations and activities.

Business Insight
Management Perspective

Often the best way to improve a process is to learn from observing a different process. At the giant food producer General Mills, production line technicians were flown to North Carolina to observe first-hand how race-car pit crews operate. In a NASCAR car race, the value-added activity is driving toward the finish-line; any time spent in the pit is non-value-added. Every split second saved in the pit increases the chances of winning. From what the General Mills technicians learned at the car race, as well as other efforts, they were able to reduce set-up time from 5 hours to just 20 minutes.

Decision Toolkit

Decision Checkpoints	Info Needed for Decision	Tool to Use for Decision	How to Evaluate Results
How can activity-based-management help managers manage the business?	Activities classified as value-added and non-value-added	The activity analysis flowchart extended to identify each activity as value-added or non-value-added	The flowchart should motivate managers to minimize non-value-added activities. Managers should better understand the relationship between activities and the resources they consume.

CLASSIFICATION OF ACTIVITY LEVELS

As mentioned earlier, traditional costing systems are volume-driven—driven by unit-based cost drivers such as direct labor or machine hours. Some activity costs are strictly variable and are caused by the production or acquisition of a single unit of product or the performance of a single unit of service. However, the recognition that other activity costs are not driven by unit-based cost drivers has led to the development of a classification of ABC activities, consisting of four levels. The four levels of activities are classified and defined as follows.

STUDY OBJECTIVE
7
Understand the value of using activity levels in activity-based costing.

1. **Unit-level activities.** Activities performed for each unit of production.
2. **Batch-level activities.** Activities performed for each batch of products rather than each unit.
3. **Product-level activities.** Activities performed in support of an entire product line, but not always performed every time a new unit or batch of products is produced.
4. **Facility-level activities.** Activities required to support or sustain an entire production process.

Greater accuracy in overhead cost allocation may be achieved by recognizing these four different levels of activities and, from them, developing specific activity cost pools and their related cost drivers. Illustration 17-13 graphically displays this four-level activity hierarchy, along with the types of activities and examples of cost drivers for those activities at each level.

Illustration 17-13 Hierarchy of activity levels

Illustration 17-13 Hierarchy of activity levels

Four Levels	Types of Activities	Examples of Cost Drivers
Unit-Level Activities	Machine-related Drilling, cutting, milling, trimming, pressing	Machine hours
	Labor-related Assembling, painting, sanding, sewing	Direct labor hours or cost
Batch-Level Activities	Equipment setups	Number of setups or setup time
	Purchase ordering	Number of purchase orders
	Inspection	Number of inspections or inspection time
	Material handling	Number of material moves
Product-Level Activities	Product design	Number of product designs
	Engineering changes	Number of changes
Facility-Level Activities	Plant management salaries	Number of employees managed
	Plant depreciation	Square footage
	Property taxes	Square footage
	Utilities	Square footage

This classification provides managers a structured way of thinking about the relationships between activities and the resources they consume. In contrast, traditional volume-based costing recognizes only unit-level costs. **Failure to recognize this classification of activities is one of the reasons that volume-based cost allocation causes distortions in product costing.**

As indicated earlier, allocating all overhead costs by unit-based cost drivers can send false signals to managers: Dividing batch-, product-, or facility-level costs by the number of units produced gives the mistaken impression that these costs vary with the number of units. **The resources consumed by batch-, product-, and facility-level supporting activities do not vary at the unit level**, nor can they be controlled at the unit level. The number of activities performed at the batch level goes up as the number of batches rises—not as the number of units within the batches changes. Similarly, the number of product-level activities performed depends on the number of different products—not on how many units or batches are produced. Furthermore, facility-sustaining activity costs are not dependent upon the number of products, batches, or units produced. Batch-, product-, and facility-level costs can be controlled only by modifying batch-, product-, and facility-level activities.

BEFORE YOU GO ON . . .

▶**Review It**

1. What are the benefits of activity-based costing?
2. What are the limitations of activity-based costing?
3. What company factors would indicate ABC as the superior costing system?
4. What is the benefit of classifying activities as value-added and non-value-added?
5. How is the classification of activities into unit-level, batch-level, product-level, and facility-level important to managers?

▶**Do It**

Morgan Toy Company manufactures six primary product lines in its Morganville plant. As a result of an activity analysis, the accounting department has identified eight activity cost pools. Each of the toy products is produced in large batches, with the whole plant devoted to one product at a time. Classify each of the following activities as either unit-level, batch-level, product-level, or facility-level: (a) engineering design, (b) machine setup, (c) inventory management, (d) plant cafeteria, (e) inspections after each setup, (f) polishing parts, (g) assembling parts, (h) health and safety.

Action Plan

• Recall that:
  Unit-level activities are performed for each individual unit of product.
  Batch-level activities are performed each time a batch of a product is produced.
  Product-level activities are performed to support an entire product line.
  Facility-level activities support the production process across the entire range of products.

Solution (a) Product-level, (b) batch-level, (c) product-level, (d) facility-level, (e) batch-level, (f) unit-level, (g) unit-level, (h) facility-level.

Related exercise material: BE17-10, BE17-11, BE17-12, E17-17, and E17-18.

✓ THE NAVIGATOR

Activity-Based Costing in Service Industries

Although initially developed and implemented by manufacturers, activity-based costing has been widely adopted in service industries as well. ABC has been a useful tool in such diverse industries as airlines, railroads, hotels, hospitals, banks, insurance companies, telephone companies, and financial services firms. The overall objective of ABC in service firms is no different than it is in a manufacturing company. That objective is to identify the key activities that generate costs and to keep track of how many of those activities are performed for each service provided (by job, service, contract, or customer).

The general approach to identifying activities, activity cost pools, and cost drivers is the same for service companies and for manufacturers. Also, the labeling of activities as value-added and non-value-added, and the attempt to reduce or eliminate non-value-added activities as much as possible, is just as valid in service industries as in manufacturing operations. What sometimes makes implementation of activity-based costing difficult in service industries is that **a larger proportion of overhead costs are company-wide costs** that cannot be directly traced to specific services provided by the company.

STUDY OBJECTIVE 8

Apply activity-based costing to service industries.

To illustrate the application of activity-based costing to a service enterprise, contrasted to traditional costing, we use a public accounting firm. This illustration is equally applicable to a law firm, consulting firm, architect, or any service firm that performs numerous services for a client as part of a job.

TRADITIONAL COSTING EXAMPLE

Assume that the public accounting firm of Check and Doublecheck prepares the following condensed annual budget (see Illustration 17-14).

Illustration 17-14 Condensed annual budget of a service firm under traditional costing

CHECK AND DOUBLECHECK, CPAs
Annual Budget

Revenue		$2,000,000
Direct labor	$ 600,000	
Overhead (expected)	1,200,000	
Total costs		1,800,000
Operating income		$ 200,000

$$\frac{\text{Estimated overhead}}{\text{Direct labor cost}} = \text{Predetermined overhead rate}$$

$$\frac{\$1,200,000}{\$600,000} = 200\%$$

Under traditional costing, direct labor is the professional service performed, and it is the basis for overhead application to each audit job. To determine the operating income earned on any job, Check and Doublecheck applies overhead at the rate of 200 percent of actual direct professional labor costs incurred. For example, assume that Check and Doublecheck records $70,000 of actual direct professional labor cost during its audit of Plano Molding Company, which was billed an audit fee of $260,000. Under traditional costing, using 200 percent as the rate for applying overhead to the job, applied overhead and operating income related to the Plano Molding Company audit would be computed as shown in Illustration 17-15.

Illustration 17-15 Overhead applied under traditional costing system

CHECK AND DOUBLECHECK, CPAs
Plano Molding Company Audit

Revenue		$260,000
Less: Direct professional labor	$ 70,000	
Applied overhead (200% × $70,000)	140,000	210,000
Operating income		$ 50,000

In this example, only one direct cost item and one overhead application rate are used under traditional costing.

ACTIVITY-BASED COSTING EXAMPLE

Under activity-based costing, Check and Doublecheck's estimated annual overhead costs of $1,200,000 are distributed to several activity cost pools. Activity-based overhead rates per cost driver are computed by dividing each activity overhead cost pool by the expected number of cost drivers used per activity. Illustration 17-16 shows an annual overhead budget using an ABC system.

CHECK AND DOUBLECHECK, CPAs
Annual Overhead Budget

Activity Cost Pools	Cost Drivers	Estimated Overhead	÷ Expected Use of Cost Drivers per Activity	= Activity-Based Overhead Rates
Secretarial support	Direct professional hours	$ 210,000	30,000	$7 per hour
Direct labor fringe benefits	Direct labor cost	240,000	$ 600,000	$0.40 per $1 labor cost
Printing and photocopying	Working paper pages	20,000	20,000	$1 per page
Computer support	CPU minutes	200,000	50,000	$4 per minute
Telephone and postage	None (Traced directly)	71,000	N/A	Based on usage
Legal support	Hours used	129,000	860	$150 per hour
Insurance (professional liability, etc.)	Revenue billed	120,000	$2,000,000	$0.06 per $1 revenue
Recruiting and training	Direct professional hours	210,000	30,000	$7 per hour
		$1,200,000		

Note that some of the overhead costs can be directly assigned (see telephone and postage).

The assignment of the individual overhead activity rates to the actual number of activities used in the performance of the Plano Molding audit results in total overhead assigned of $165,100 as shown in Illustration 17-17.

Illustration 17-17
Assigning overhead in a service company

	A	B	C	D	E
1	**Check and DoubleCheck CPAS**				
2	Plano Molding Company Audit				
3	Activity Cost Pools	Cost Drivers	Actual Use of Drivers	Activity-Based Overhead Rates	Cost Assigned
4	Secretarial support	Direct professional hours	3,800	$7.00	$26,600
5	Direct labor fringe benefits	Direct labor cost	$70,000	$0.40	28,000
6	Printing and photocopying	Working paper pages	1,800	$1.00	1,800
7	Computer support	CPU minutes	8,600	$4.00	34,400
8	Telephone and postage	None (Traced directly)			8,700
9	Legal support	Hours used	156	$150.00	23,400
10	Insurance (professional liability, etc.)	Revenue billed	$260,000	$0.06	15,600
11	Recruiting and training	Direct professional hours	3,800	$7.00	26,600
12					$165,100

Under activity-based costing, overhead costs of $165,100 are assigned to the Plano Molding Company audit, as compared to $140,000 under traditional costing. A comparison of total costs and operating margins is shown in Illustration 17-18 (page 864).

Illustration 17-18 Comparison of traditional costing with ABC in a service company

CHECK AND DOUBLECHECK, CPAs Plano Molding Company Audit				
	Traditional Costing		ABC	
Revenue		$260,000		$260,000
Expenses				
Direct professional labor	$ 70,000		$ 70,000	
Applied overhead	140,000		165,100	
Total expenses		210,000		235,100
Operating income		**$ 50,000**		**$ 24,900**
Profit margin		19.2%		9.6%

The comparison shows that the assignment of overhead costs under traditional costing is distorted. The total cost assigned to performing the audit of Plano Molding Company is greater under activity-based costing by $25,100, or 12 percent higher, and the profit margin is only half as great. Traditional costing gives the false impression of an operating profit of $50,000. This is more than double the operating income of $24,900 using ABC.

BEFORE YOU GO ON . . .

▶**Review It**

1. What is the primary barrier to effectively implementing ABC in a service-company environment?
2. What is the main advantage to be gained by using ABC in a service-company environment?

THE NAVIGATOR

Using the Decision Toolkit

Precor Company manufactures a line of high-end exercise equipment of commercial quality. Assume that the chief accountant has proposed changing from a traditional costing system to an activity-based costing system. The financial vice-president is not convinced, so she requests that the next large order for equipment be costed under both systems for purposes of comparison and analysis. An order from Slim-Way Salons, Inc., for 150 low-impact treadmills is received and is identified as the order to be subjected to dual costing. The following cost data relate to the Slim-Way order.

Data relevant to both costing systems

Direct materials	$55,500
Direct labor hours	820
Direct labor rate per hour	$18.00

Data relevant to the traditional costing system

Predetermined overhead rate is 300% of direct labor cost.

Data relevant to the activity-based costing system

Activity Cost Pools	Cost Drivers	Activity-Based Overhead Rate	Expected Use of Cost Drivers per Treadmill
Engineering design	Engineering hours	$30 per hour	330
Machine setup	Setups	$200 per setup	22
Machining	Machine hours	$25 per hour	732
Assembly	Number of subassemblies	$8 per subassembly	1,450
Packaging and shipping	Packaging/shipping hours	$15 per hour	152
Building occupancy	Machine hours	$6 per hour	732

Instructions

Compute the total cost of the Slim-Way Salons, Inc. order under (a) the traditional costing system and (b) the activity-based costing system. (c) As a result of this comparison, which costing system is Precor likely to adopt? Why?

Solution

(a) Traditional costing system:

Direct materials	$ 55,500
Direct labor (820 × $18)	14,760
Overhead assigned ($14,760 × 300%)	44,280
Total costs assigned to Slim-Way order	$114,540
Number of low-impact treadmills	150
Cost per unit	$763.60

(b) Activity-based costing system:

Direct materials		$ 55,500
Direct labor (820 × $18)		14,760
Overhead activities costs:		
Engineering design (330 hours @ $30)	$ 9,900	
Machine setup (22 setups @ $200)	4,400	
Machining (732 machine hours @ $25)	18,300	
Assembly (1,450 subassemblies @ $8)	11,600	
Packaging and shipping (152 hours @ $15)	2,280	
Building occupancy (732 hours @ $6)	4,392	50,872
Total costs assigned to Slim-Way order		$121,132
Number of low-impact treadmills		150
Cost per unit		$807.55

(c) Precor Company will likely adopt ABC because of the difference in the cost per unit (which ABC found to be higher). More importantly, ABC provides greater insight into the sources and causes of the cost per unit. Managers are given greater insight into which activities to control in order to reduce costs. ABC will provide better product costing and greater profitability for the company.

Summary of Study Objectives

1 *Recognize the difference between traditional costing and activity-based costing.* A traditional costing system allocates overhead to products on the basis of predetermined plantwide or departmentwide volume of unit-based output rates such as direct labor or machine hours. An ABC system allocates overhead to identified activity cost pools, and costs are then assigned to products using related cost drivers that measure the activities (resources) consumed.

2 *Identify the steps in the development of an activity-based costing system.* The development of an activity-based costing system involves four steps: (1) Identify and classify the major activities involved in the manufacture of specific products, and allocate manufacturing overhead costs to the appropriate cost pools. (2) Identify the cost driver that has a strong correlation to the costs accumulated in the cost pool. (3) Compute the overhead rate per cost driver. (4) Assign manufacturing overhead costs for each cost pool to products or services using the overhead rates.

3 *Know how companies identify the activity cost pools used in activity-based costing.* To identify activity cost pools, a company must perform an analysis of each operation or process, documenting and timing every task, action, or transaction.

4 *Know how companies identify and use cost drivers in activity-based costing.* Cost drivers identified for assigning activity cost pools must (a) accurately measure the actual consumption of the activity by the various products, and (b) have related data easily available.

5 *Understand the benefits and limitations of activity-based costing.* Features of ABC that make it a more accurate product costing system include: (1) the increased number of cost pools used to assign overhead, (2) the enhanced control over overhead costs,

and (3) the better management decisions it makes possible. The limitations of ABC are: (1) the higher analysis and measurement costs that accompany multiple activity centers and cost drivers, and (2) the necessity still to allocate some costs arbitrarily.

6 *Differentiate between value-added and non-value-added activities.* Value-added activities increase the worth of a product or service. Non-value-added activities simply add cost to, or increase the time spent on, a product or service without increasing its market value. Awareness of these classifications encourages managers to reduce or eliminate the time spent on the non-value-added activities.

7 *Understand the value of using activity levels in activity-based costing.* Activities may be classified as unit-level, batch-level, product-level, and facility-level. Overhead costs at unit-, batch-, product-, and facility-levels are controlled by modifying unit-, batch-, product-, and facility-level activities, respectively. Failure to recognize this classification of levels can result in distorted product costing.

8 *Apply activity-based costing to service industries.* The overall objective of using ABC in service industries is no different than for manufacturing industries, that is, improved costing of services provided (by job, service, contract, or customer). The general approach to costing is the same: analyze operations, identify activities, accumulate overhead costs by activity cost pools, and identify and use cost drivers to assign the cost pools to the services.

THE NAVIGATOR

Decision Toolkit—A Summary

Decision Checkpoints	Info Needed for Decision	Tool to Use for Decision	How to Evaluate Results
When should we use ABC?	Knowledge of the products or product lines, the manufacturing process, and overhead costs.	A detailed and accurate cost accounting system; cooperation between accountants and operating managers	Compare the results under both costing systems. If managers are better able to understand and control their operations using ABC, and the costs are not prohibitive, the use of ABC would be beneficial.
How can activity-based management help managers manage the business?	Activities classified as value-added and non-value-added	The activity analysis flowchart extended to identify each activity as value-added or non-value-added	The flowchart should motivate managers to minimize non-value-added activities. Managers should better understand the relationship between activities and the resources they consume.

APPENDIX
JUST-IN-TIME PROCESSING

Traditionally, continuous process manufacturing has been based on a **just-in-case** philosophy: Inventories of raw materials are maintained *just in case* some items are of poor quality or a key supplier is shut down by a strike. Similarly, subassembly parts are manufactured and stored *just in case* they are needed later in the manufacturing process. Finished goods are completed and stored *just in case* unexpected and rush customer orders are received. This philosophy often results in a **push approach**, in which raw materials and subassembly parts are pushed through each process. Traditional processing often results in the buildup of extensive manufacturing inventories.

Primarily in response to foreign competition, many U.S. firms have switched to **just-in-time (JIT) processing**. JIT manufacturing is dedicated to having the right amount of materials, parts, or products at the time they are needed. Under JIT processing, raw materials are received **just in time** for use in production, subassembly parts are completed **just in time** for use in finished goods, and finished goods are completed **just in time** to be sold. Illustration 17A-1 shows the sequence of activities in just-in-time processing.

STUDY OBJECTIVE
9
Explain just-in-time (JIT) processing.

Illustration 17A-1   Just-in-time processing

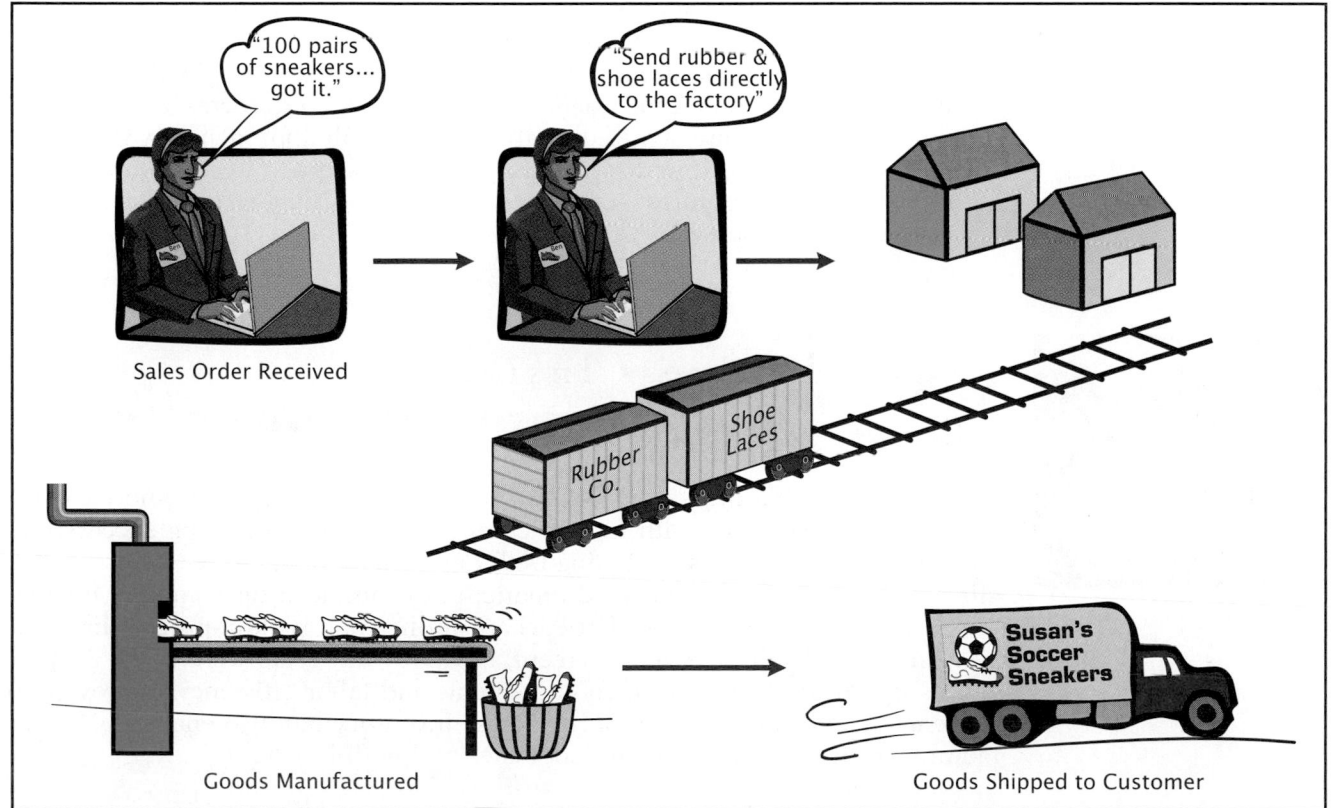

Objective of JIT Processing

The primary objective of JIT is to eliminate all manufacturing inventories. Inventories are considered to have an adverse effect on net income because they tie up funds and storage space that could be made available for more productive purposes. JIT strives to eliminate inventories by using a **demand-pull approach** in manufacturing. This approach begins with the customer placing an order with the company. This order, which indicates product demand, starts the process of pulling the product through the manufacturing process. A signal is sent via a computer to the next preceding work station indicating the exact materials (parts and subassemblies) needed for a time period, such as an eight-hour shift, to complete the production of a specified product. The preceding process, in turn, sends its signal to other preceding processes. The goal is a smooth continuous flow in the manufacturing process, with no buildup of inventories at any point.

Elements of JIT Processing

There are three important elements in JIT processing:

1. A company must have **dependable suppliers** who are willing to deliver on short notice exact quantities of raw materials according to precise quality specifications. (This may even include multiple deliveries within the same day.) Suppliers must also be willing to deliver the raw materials at specified work stations rather than at a central receiving department. This type of purchasing requires constant and direct communication with suppliers, which is facilitated by an online computer linkage between the company and its suppliers.
2. A **multiskilled work force** must be developed. Under JIT, machines are often strategically grouped into work cells or centers and much of the work is automated. As a result, one worker may have the responsibility to operate and maintain several different types of machines.
3. A **total quality control system** must be established throughout the manufacturing operations. Total quality control means **no defects**. Since only required quantities are signaled by the demand-pull approach, any defects at a work station will shut down operations at subsequent work stations. Total quality control requires continuous monitoring by both employees and supervisors at each work station.

Business Insight
Management Perspective

JIT first hit the USA in the early 1980s when it was adopted by automobile companies to help compete with foreign competition. It is now being successfully used in many companies, including Dell, Caterpillar, and Harley-Davidson. The effects in many cases have been dramatic. For example, after using JIT for two years, a major division of Hewlett-Packard found that work-in-process inventories (in dollars) were down 82 percent, scrap/rework costs were down 30 percent, space utilization was down 40 percent, and labor efficiency improved 50 percent. As indicated, JIT not only reduces inventory but also enables a manufacturer to produce a better product faster and with less waste.

Benefits of JIT Processing

The major benefits of implementing JIT processing are:

1. Manufacturing inventories are significantly reduced or eliminated.
2. Product quality is enhanced.

3. Rework costs and inventory storage costs are reduced or eliminated.
4. Production cost savings are realized from the improved flow of goods through the processes.

> **Helpful Hint** JIT is easier said than done. JIT requires a total commitment by management and employees, a complete change in philosophy, and significant changes in the way production is organized. JIT takes time to implement.

One of the major accounting benefits of JIT is the elimination of separate raw materials and work-in-process inventory accounts. These accounts are replaced by one account called Raw and In-Process Inventory. All materials and conversion costs are charged to this account. Due to the reduction (or elimination) of in-process inventories, the computation of equivalent units of production is simplified.

BEFORE YOU GO ON . . .

►Review It

1. What is the difference between the push approach and the demand-pull approach to handling inventories in a manufacturing operation?
2. What are the major benefits of implementing JIT?
3. What are the principal accounting effects of just-in-time processing?

Summary of Study Objective for Appendix

9 *Explain just-in-time (JIT) processing.* JIT is a processing system that is dedicated to having on hand the right materials and products at the time they are needed, thereby reducing the amount of inventory and the time inventory is held. One of the principal accounting effects is that one account, Raw and In-Process Inventory, replaces both the raw materials and work-in-process inventory accounts.

Glossary

Activity Any event, action, transaction, or work sequence that causes a cost to be incurred in producing a product or providing a service. (p. 847)

Activity-based costing (ABC) An overhead cost allocation system that allocates overhead to multiple activity cost pools and assigns the activity cost pools to products or services by means of cost drivers that represent the activities used. (p. 847)

Activity-based management (ABM) Extends ABC from product costing to a comprehensive management tool that focuses on reducing costs and improving processes and decision making. (p. 857)

Activity cost pool The overhead cost attributed to a distinct type of activity or related activities. (p. 847)

Batch-level activities Activities performed for each batch of products. (p. 859)

Cost driver Any factor or activity that has a direct cause–effect relationship with the resources consumed. In ABC cost drivers are used to assign activity cost pools to products or services. (p. 847)

Facility-level activities Activities required to support or sustain an entire production process and not dependent on number of products, batches, or units produced. (p. 859)

Just-in-time (JIT) processing A processing system dedicated to having the right amount of materials, parts, or products arrive as they are needed, thereby reducing the amount of inventory. (p. 867)

Non-value-added activity An activity that adds cost to, or increases the time spent on, a product or service without increasing its market value. (p. 858)

Product-level activities Activities performed for and identifiable with an entire product line. (p. 859)

Unit-level activities Activities performed for each unit of production. (p. 859)

Value-added activity An activity that increases the worth of a product or service. (p. 857)

Demonstration Problem

Spreadwell Paint Company manufactures two high-quality base paints: an **oil-based** paint and a **latex** paint. Both paints are housepaints and are manufactured in neutral white color only. The white base paints are sold to franchised retail paint and decorating stores where pigments are added to tint (color) the paint as desired by the customer. The oil-based paint is made from, thinned, and cleaned with organic solvents (petroleum products) such as mineral spirits or turpentine. The latex paint is made from, thinned, and cleaned with water; synthetic resin particles are suspended in the water and dry and harden when exposed to the air.

Spreadwell uses the same processing equipment to produce both paints in different production runs. Between batches, the vats and other processing equipment must be washed and cleaned.

After analyzing the company's entire operations, Spreadwell's accountants and production managers have identified activity cost pools and accumulated annual budgeted overhead costs by pool as follows.

Activity Cost Pools	Estimated Overhead
Purchasing	$ 240,000
Processing (weighing and mixing, grinding, thinning and drying, straining)	1,400,000
Packaging (quarts, gallons, and 5-gallons)	580,000
Testing	240,000
Storage and inventory control	180,000
Washing and cleaning equipment	560,000
Total annual budgeted overhead	$3,200,000

Following further analysis, activity cost drivers were identified and their expected use by product and activity were scheduled as follows.

Activity Cost Pools	Cost Drivers	Expected Cost Drivers per Activity	Expected Use of Drivers per Product	
			Oil-based	Latex
Purchasing	Purchase orders	1,500 orders	800	700
Processing	Gallons processed	1,000,000 gals.	400,000	600,000
Packaging	Containers filled	400,000 containers	180,000	220,000
Testing	Number of tests	4,000 tests	2,100	1,900
Storing	Avg. gals. on hand	18,000 gals.	10,400	7,600
Washing	Number of batches	800 batches	350	450

Spreadwell has budgeted 400,000 gallons of oil-based paint and 600,000 gallons of latex paint for processing during the year.

Instructions
(a) Prepare a schedule showing the computations of the activity-based overhead rates.
(b) Prepare a schedule assigning each activity's overhead cost pool to each product.
(c) Compute the overhead cost per unit for each product.
(d) Classify each activity cost pool as value-added or non-value-added.

Solution to Demonstration Problem

(a) Computations of activity-based overhead rates:

Activity Cost Pools	Estimated Overhead	÷	Expected Use of Cost Drivers	=	Activity-Based Overhead Rates
Purchasing	$ 240,000		1,500 orders		$160 per order
Processing	1,400,000		1,000,000 gallons		$1.40 per gallon
Packaging	580,000		400,000 containers		$1.45 per container
Testing	240,000		4,000 tests		$60 per test
Storing	180,000		18,000 gallons		$10 per gallon
Washing	560,000		800 batches		$700 per batch
	$3,200,000				

(b) Assignment of activity cost pools to products:

Activity Cost Pools	Oil-Based Paint Expected Use of Drivers	Overhead Rates	Cost Assigned	Latex Paint Expected Use of Drivers	Overhead Rates	Cost Assigned
Purchasing	800	$160	$ 128,000	700	$160	$ 112,000
Processing	400,000	$1.40	560,000	600,000	$1.40	840,000
Packaging	180,000	$1.45	261,000	220,000	$1.45	319,000
Testing	2,100	$60	126,000	1,900	$60	114,000
Storing	10,400	$10	104,000	7,600	$10	76,000
Washing	350	$700	245,000	450	$700	315,000
Total overhead assigned			$1,424,000			$1,776,000

(c) Computation of overhead cost assigned per unit:

	Oil-Based Paint	Latex Paint
Total overhead cost assigned	$1,424,000	$1,776,000
Total gallons produced	400,000	600,000
Overhead cost per gallon	$3.56	$2.96

(d) Value-added activities: processing and packaging.
Non-value-added activities: purchasing, testing, storing, and washing.

Action Plan
- Identify the major activities that pertain to the manufacture of specific products and allocate manufacturing overhead costs to activity cost pools.
- Identify the cost drivers that accurately measure each activity's contribution to the finished product.
- Compute the activity-based overhead rates.
- Assign manufacturing overhead costs for each activity cost pool to products, using the activity-based overhead rates.

Note: All asterisked Questions, Exercises, and Problems relate to material in the appendix to the chapter.

Self-Study Questions

Answers are at the end of the chapter.

(SO 1) **1.** Activity-based costing (ABC):
(a) can be used only in a process cost system.
(b) focuses on units of production.
(c) focuses on activities performed to produce a product.
(d) uses only a single basis of allocation.

(SO 1) **2.** Activity-based costing:
(a) is the initial phase of converting to a just-in-time operating environment.
(b) can be used only in a job order costing system.

(c) is a two-stage overhead cost allocation system that identifies activity cost pools and cost drivers.
(d) uses direct labor as its primary cost driver.

(SO 1, 4) **3.** Any activity that causes resources to be consumed is called a:
(a) just-in-time activity.
(b) facility-level activity.
(c) cost driver.
(d) non-value-added activity.

(SO 4) **4.** The overhead rate for Machine Setups is $100 per setup. Products A and B have 80 and 60

setups, respectively. The overhead assigned to each product is:
(a) Product A $8,000, Product B $8,000.
(b) Product A $8,000, Product B $6,000.
(c) Product A $6,000, Product B $6,000.
(d) Product A $6,000, Product B $8,000.

(SO 4) **5.** Donna Crawford Co. has identified an activity cost pool to which it has allocated estimated overhead of $1,920,000. It has determined the expected use of cost drivers per that activity to be 160,000 inspections. Widgets require 40,000 inspections, Gadgets 30,000 inspections, and Targets, 90,000 inspections. The overhead assigned to each product is:
(a) Widgets $40,000, Gadgets $30,000, Targets $90,000.
(b) Widgets $480,000, Gadgets $360,000, Targets $108,000.
(c) Widgets $360,000, Gadgets $480,000, Targets $1,080,000.
(d) Widgets $480,000, Gadgets $360,000, Targets $1,080,000.

(SO 6) **6.** An activity that adds costs to the product but does not increase its market value is a:
(a) value-added activity.
(b) cost driver.
(c) cost–benefit activity.
(d) non-value-added activity.

7. The following activity is value-added: (SO 6)
(a) Storage of raw materials.
(b) Moving parts from machine to machine.
(c) Shaping a piece of metal on a lathe.
(d) All of the above.

8. A relevant facility-level cost driver for heating costs is: (SO 7)
(a) machine hours.
(b) direct material.
(c) floor space.
(d) direct labor cost.

*9. Under just-in-time processing: (SO 9)
(a) raw materials are received just in time for use in production.
(b) subassembly parts are completed just in time for use in assembling finished goods.
(c) finished goods are completed just in time to be sold.
(d) All of the above.

*10. The primary objective of just-in-time processing is to: (SO 9)
(a) accumulate overhead in activity cost pools.
(b) eliminate or reduce all manufacturing inventories.
(c) identify relevant activity cost drivers.
(d) identify value-added activities.

Questions

1. Under what conditions is direct labor a valid basis for allocating overhead?

2. What has happened in recent industrial history to reduce the usefulness of direct labor as the primary basis for allocating overhead to products?

3. In an automated manufacturing environment, what basis of overhead allocation is frequently more relevant than direct labor hours?

4. What is generally true about overhead allocation to high-volume products versus low-volume products under a traditional costing system?

5. (a) What are the principal differences between activity-based costing (ABC) and traditional product costing?
(b) What assumptions must be met for ABC costing to be useful?

6. What is the formula for computing activity-based overhead rates?

7. What steps are involved in developing an activity-based costing system?

8. Explain the preparation and use of a value-added/non-value-added activity flowchart in an ABC system.

9. What is an activity cost pool?

10. What is a cost driver?

11. What makes a cost driver accurate and appropriate?

12. What is the formula for assigning activity cost pools to products?

13. What are the benefits of activity-based costing?

14. What are the limitations of activity-based costing?

15. Under what conditions is ABC generally the superior overhead costing system?

16. What refinement has been made to enhance the efficiency and effectiveness of ABC for use in managing costs?

17. Of what benefit is classifying activities as value-added and non-value-added?

18. In what ways is the application of ABC to service industries the same as its application to manufacturing companies?

19. What is the relevance of the classification of levels of activity to ABC?

*20. (a) Describe the philosophy and approach of just-in-time processing.
(b) Identify the major elements of JIT processing.

Brief Exercises

BE17-1 Infotrac Inc. sells a high-speed retrieval system for mining information. It provides the following information for the year.

	Budgeted	Actual
Overhead cost	$1,000,000	$950,000
Machine hours	50,000	45,000
Direct labor hours	100,000	90,000

Identify differences between costing systems.
(SO 1)

Overhead is applied on the basis of direct labor hours. (a) Compute the predetermined overhead rate. (b) Determine the amount of overhead applied for the year. (c) Explain how an activity-based costing system might differ in terms of computing a predetermined overhead rate.

BE17-2 Sassafras Inc. has conducted an analysis of overhead costs related to one of its product lines using a traditional costing system (volume-based) and an activity-based costing system. Here are its results.

Identify differences between costing systems.
(SO 1)

	Traditional Costing	ABC
Sales revenues	$600,000	$600,000
Overhead costs:		
Product RX3	$ 34,000	$ 50,000
Product Y12	36,000	20,000
	$ 70,000	$ 70,000

Explain how a difference in the overhead costs between the two systems may have occurred.

BE17-3 Altex Co. identifies the following activities that pertain to manufacturing overhead: Materials Handling, Machine Setups, Factory Machine Maintenance, Factory Supervision, and Quality Control. For each activity, identify an appropriate cost driver.

Identify cost drivers.
(SO 4)

BE17-4 Ayala Company manufactures four products in a single production facility. The company uses activity-based costing. The following activities have been identified through the company's activity analysis: (a) inventory control, (b) machine setups, (c) employee training, (d) quality inspections, (e) material ordering, (f) drilling operations, and (g) building maintenance.

For each activity, name a cost driver that might be used to assign overhead costs to products.

Identify cost drivers.
(SO 4)

BE17-5 Gomez Company identifies three activities in its manufacturing process: machine setups, machining, and inspections. Estimated annual overhead cost for each activity is $180,000, $325,000, and $87,500, respectively. The cost driver for each activity and the expected annual usage are: number of setups 2,500, machine hours 25,000, and number of inspections 1,750. Compute the overhead rate for each activity.

Compute activity-based overhead rates.
(SO 4)

BE17-6 Coats Galore, Inc. uses activity-based costing as the basis for information to set prices for its six lines of seasonal coats. Compute the activity-based overhead rates using the following budgeted data for each of the activity cost pools.

Compute activity-based overhead rates.
(SO 4)

Activity Cost Pools	Estimated Overhead	Expected Use of Cost Drivers per Activity
Designing	$ 450,000	12,000 designer hours
Sizing and cutting	4,000,000	160,000 machine hours
Stitching and trimming	1,440,000	80,000 labor hours
Wrapping and packing	336,000	32,000 finished units

BE17-7 Computer Parts, Inc., a manufacturer of computer chips, employs activity-based costing. The following budgeted data for each of the activity cost pools is provided below for the year 2007.

Compute activity-based overhead rates.
(SO 4)

Activity Cost Pools	Estimated Overhead	Expected Use of Cost Drivers per Activity
Ordering and receiving	$ 90,000	15,000 orders
Etching	480,000	60,000 machine hours
Soldering	1,760,000	440,000 labor hours

For 2007, the company had 11,000 orders and used 50,000 machine hours, and labor hours totaled 500,000. What is the total overhead applied?

Classify activities as value- or non-value-added.
(SO 6)

BE17-8   Jerry Lewis Novelty Company identified the following activities in its production and support operations. Classify each of these activities as either value-added or non-value-added.

(a) Purchasing.   (e) Cost accounting.
(b) Receiving.   (f) Moving work-in-process.
(c) Design engineering.   (g) Inspecting and testing.
(d) Storing inventory.   (h) Painting and packing.

Classify service company activities as value- or non-value-added.
(SO 6, 8)

BE17-9   Rowan and Martin is an architectural firm that is contemplating the installation of activity-based costing. The following activities are performed daily by staff architects. Classify these activities as value-added or non-value-added: (1) designing and drafting, 3 hours; (2) staff meetings, 1 hour; (3) on-site supervision, 2 hours; (4) lunch, 1 hour; (5) consultation with client on specifications, 1.5 hours; (6) entertaining a prospective client for dinner, 2 hours.

Classify activities according to level.
(SO 7, 8)

BE17-10   Quick Pix is a large film developing and processing center that serves 130 outlets in grocery stores, service stations, camera and photo shops, and drug stores in 16 nearby towns. Quick Pix operates 24 hours a day, 6 days a week. Classify each of the following activity costs of Quick Pix as either unit-level, batch-level, product-level, or facility-level.

(a) Developing fluids.   (f) Ordering materials.
(b) Photocopy paper.   (g) Pickup and delivery.
(c) Depreciation of machinery.   (h) Commission to dealers.
(d) Setups for enlargements.   (i) Insurance on building.
(e) Supervisor's salary.   (j) Loading developing machines.

Classify activities according to level.
(SO 7)

BE17-11   Tool Time, Inc. operates 20 injection molding machines in the production of tool boxes of four different sizes, named the Apprentice, the Handyman, the Journeyman, and the Professional. Classify each of the following costs as unit-level, batch-level, product-level, or facility-level.

(a) First-shift supervisor's salary.
(b) Powdered raw plastic.
(c) Dies for casting plastic components.
(d) Depreciation on injection molding machines.
(e) Changing dies on machines.
(f) Moving components to assembly department.
(g) Engineering design.
(h) Employee health and medical insurance coverage.

Compute rates and activity levels.
(SO 4, 7)

BE17-12   Trek Cycle Company uses three activity pools to apply overhead to its products. Each activity has a cost driver used to allocate the overhead costs to the product. The activities and related overhead costs are as follows: Product design $50,000; Machining $300,000; and Material handling $100,000. The cost drivers and expected use are as follows.

Activities	Cost Drivers	Expected Use of Cost Drivers per Activity
Product design	Number of product changes	10
Machining	Machine hours	150,000
Material handling	Number of set ups	100

(a) Compute the predetermined overhead rate for each activity. (b) Classify each of these activities as unit-level, batch-level, product-level, or facility-level.

Exercises

Assign overhead using traditional costing and ABC.
(SO 1, 4)

E17-1   Elle Inc. has two types of handbags: standard and custom. The controller has decided to use a plantwide overhead rate based on direct labor costs. The president has heard of activity-based costing and wants to see how the results would differ if this system were used. Two activity cost pools were developed: machining and machine setup. Presented below is information related to the company's operations.

	Standard	Custom
Direct labor costs	$50,000	$100,000
Machine hours	1,000	1,000
Setup hours	100	400

Total estimated overhead costs are $300,000. Overhead cost allocated to the machining activity cost pool is $200,000, and $100,000 is allocated to the machine setup activity cost pool.

Instructions
(a) Compute the overhead rate using the traditional (plantwide) approach.
(b) Compute the overhead rates using the activity based costing approach.
(c) Determine the difference in allocation between the two approaches.

E17-2 Perdon Inc. has conducted the following analysis related to its product lines, using a traditional costing system (volume-based) and an activity-based costing system. Both the traditional and the activity-based costing systems include direct materials and direct labor costs.

Explain difference between traditional and activity-based costing.
(SO 1)

		Total Costs	
Products	**Sales Revenue**	**Traditional**	**ABC**
Product 540X	$200,000	$55,000	$50,000
Product 137Y	160,000	50,000	35,000
Product 249S	80,000	15,000	35,000

Instructions
(a) For each product line, compute operating income using the traditional costing system.
(b) For each product line, compute operating income using the activity-based costing system.
(c) Using the following formula, compute the percentage difference in operating income for each of the product lines of Perdon: Operating Income (ABC) − Operating Income (traditional cost) ÷ Operating Income (traditional cost). (Round the percentage to two decimals.)
(d) Provide a rationale as to why the costs for Product 540X are approximately the same using either the traditional or activity-based costing system.

E17-3 International Fabrics has budgeted overhead costs of $900,000. It has allocated overhead on a plantwide basis to its two products (wool and cotton) using direct labor hours which are estimated to be 450,000 for the current year. The company has decided to experiment with activity-based costing and has created two activity cost pools and related activity cost drivers. These two cost pools are: Cutting (cost driver is machine hours) and Design (cost driver is number of setups). Overhead allocated to the Cutting cost pool is $300,000 and $600,000 is allocated to the Design cost pool. Additional information related to these pools is as follows.

Assign overhead using traditional costing and ABC.
(SO 1, 4)

	Wool	Cotton	Total
Machine hours	100,000	100,000	200,000
Number of setups	1,000	500	1,500

Instructions
(a) Determine the amount of overhead allocated to the wool product line and the cotton product line using activity-based costing.
(b) What is the difference between the allocation of overhead to the wool and cotton product lines using activity-based costing versus the traditional approach, assuming direct labor hours were incurred evenly between the cutting and design activities?

E17-4 Alonzo Inc. manufactures two products: car and truck wheels. To determine the amount of overhead to assign to each product line, the controller, YuYu Ortega, has developed the following information.

Assign overhead using traditional costing and ABC.
(SO 1, 4)

	Car	Truck
Estimated wheels produced	40,000	10,000
Direct labor hours per wheel	1	3

Total estimated overhead costs for the two product lines are $700,000.

Instructions

(a) Compute the overhead cost assigned to the car and truck wheels, assuming that direct labor hours is used to allocate overhead costs.

(b) Ortega is not satisfied with the traditional method of allocating overhead because he believes that most of the overhead costs relate to the truck wheel product line because of its complexity. He therefore develops the following three activity cost pools and related cost drivers to better understand these costs.

Activity Cost Pools	Expected Use of Cost Drivers	Estimated Overhead Costs
Setting up machines	1,000 setups	$180,000
Assembling	70,000 labor hours	280,000
Inspection	1,200 inspections	240,000

Compute the activity-based overhead rates for these three cost pools.

(c) Compute the cost that is assigned to the car and truck product lines using an activity-based costing system, given the following information.

Expected Use of Cost Drivers per Product

	Car	Truck
Number of setups	200	800
Direct labor hours	40,000	30,000
Number of inspections	100	1,100

(d) What do you believe Ortega should do?

Assign overhead using traditional costing and ABC.
(SO 1, 4)

E17-5 Shady Lady sells window coverings to both commercial and residential customers. The following information relates to its budgeted operations for the current year.

	Commercial		Residential	
Revenues		$300,000		$480,000
Direct material costs	$ 30,000		$ 50,000	
Direct labor costs	100,000		300,000	
Overhead costs	50,000	180,000	150,000	500,000
Operating income (loss)		$120,000		($ 20,000)

The controller, Wanda Lewis, is concerned about the residential product line. She cannot understand why this line is not more profitable given that the installations of window coverings are less complex to install for residential customers. In addition, the residential client base resides in close proximity to the company office, so travel costs are not as expensive on a per client visit for residential customers. As a result, she has decided to take a closer look at the overhead costs assigned to the two product lines to determine whether a more accurate product costing model can be developed. Here are the three activity cost pools and related information she developed:

Activity Cost Pools	Estimated Overhead	Cost Drivers
Scheduling and travel	$90,000	Hours of travel
Setup time	70,000	Number of setups
Supervision	40,000	Direct labor cost

Expected Use of Cost Drivers per Product

	Commercial	Residential
Scheduling and travel	1,000	500
Setup time	450	250

Instructions

(a) Compute the activity-based overhead rates for each of the three cost pools, and determine the overhead cost assigned to each product line.

(b) Compute the operating income for the each product line, using the activity-based overhead rates.

(c) What do you believe Wanda Lewis should do?

E17-6 Wilkins Corporation manufactures safes—large mobile safes, and large walk-in stationary bank safes. As part of its annual budgeting process, Wilkins is analyzing the profitability of its two products. Part of this analysis involves estimating the amount of overhead to be allocated to each product line. The following information relates to overhead.

Assign overhead using traditional costing and ABC.
(SO 1, 4)

	Mobile Safes	Walk-in Safes
Units planned for production	200	50
Material moves per product line	300	200
Purchase orders per product line	450	350
Direct labor hours per product line	800	1,700

Instructions

(a) The total estimated manufacturing overhead was $235,000. Under traditional costing (which assigns overhead on the basis of direct-labor hours), what amount of manufacturing overhead costs are assigned to:
  (1) One mobile safe?
  (2) One walk-in safe?

(b) The total estimated manufacturing overhead of $235,000 was comprised of $150,000 for material-handling costs and $85,000 for purchasing activity costs. Under activity-based costing (ABC):
  (1) What amount of material handling costs are assigned to:
    (a) One mobile safe?
    (b) One walk-in safe?
  (2) What amount of purchasing activity costs are assigned to:
    (a) One mobile safe?
    (b) One walk-in safe?

(c) Compare the amount of overhead allocated to one mobile safe and to one walk-in safe under the traditional costing approach versus under ABC.

E17-7 Quik Prints Company is a small printing and copying firm with three high-speed offset printing presses, five copiers (two color and three black and white), one collator, one cutting and folding machine, and one fax machine. To improve its pricing practices, owner-manager Damon Hastings is installing activity-based accounting. Additionally, Damon employs five employees: two printers/designers, one receptionist/bookkeeper, one sales and copy-machine operator, and one janitor/delivery clerk. Damon can operate any of the machines and, in addition to managing the entire operation, he performs the training, designing, selling, and marketing functions.

Identify activity cost pools.
(SO 3)

Instructions

As Quik Prints' independent accountant who prepares tax forms and quarterly financial statements, you have been asked to identify the activities that would be used to accumulate overhead costs for assignment to jobs and customers. Using your knowledge of a small printing and copying firm (and some imagination), identify at least twelve activity cost pools as the start of an activity-based costing system for Quik Prints Company.

E17-8 Galavic Corporation manufactures snowmobiles in its Blue Mountain, Wisconsin plant. The following costs are budgeted for the first quarter's operations.

Identify activity cost pools and cost drivers.
(SO 3, 4)

Machine setup, indirect materials	$ 4,000
Inspections	16,000
Tests	4,000
Insurance, plant	110,000
Engineering design	140,000
Depreciation, machinery	520,000
Machine setup, indirect labor	20,000
Property taxes	29,000
Oil, heating	19,000
Electricity, plant lighting	21,000
Engineering prototypes	60,000
Depreciation, plant	210,000
Electricity, machinery	36,000
Custodial (machine maintenance) wages	19,000

Instructions

Classify the above costs of Galavic Corporation into activity cost pools using the following: engineering, machinery, machine setup, quality control, factory utilities, maintenance. Next, identify a cost driver that may be used to assign each cost pool to each line of snowmobiles.

Identify activity cost drivers.
(SO 4)

E17-9   Peter Catalano's Verde Vineyards in Oakville, California produces three varieties of wine: Merlot, Viognier, and Pinot Noir. His winemaster, Kyle Ward, has identified the following activities as cost pools for accumulating overhead and assigning it to products.

1. Culling and replanting. Dead or overcrowded vines are culled, and new vines are planted or relocated. (Separate vineyards by variety.)
2. Tying. The posts and wires are reset, and vines are tied to the wires for the dormant season.
3. Trimming. At the end of the harvest the vines are cut and trimmed back in preparation for the next season.
4. Spraying. The vines are sprayed with chemicals for protection against insects and fungi.
5. Harvesting. The grapes are hand-picked, placed in carts, and transported to the crushers.
6. Stemming and crushing. Cartfuls of bunches of grapes of each variety are separately loaded into machines which remove stems and gently crush the grapes.
7. Pressing and filtering. The crushed grapes are transferred to presses which mechanically remove the juices and filter out bulk and impurities.
8. Fermentation. The grape juice, by variety, is fermented in either stainless-steel tanks or oak barrels.
9. Aging. The wines are aged in either stainless-steel tanks or oak barrels for one to three years depending on variety.
10. Bottling and corking. Bottles are machine-filled and corked.
11. Labeling and boxing. Each bottle is labeled, as is each nine-bottle case, with the name of the vintner, vintage, and variety.
12. Storing. Packaged and boxed bottles are stored awaiting shipment.
13. Shipping. The wine is shipped to distributors and private retailers.
14. Heating and air-conditioning of plant and offices.
15. Maintenance of buildings and equipment. Printing, repairs, replacements, and general maintenance are performed in the off-season.

Instructions

For each of Verde's fifteen activity cost pools, identify a probable cost driver that might be used to assign overhead costs to its three wine varieties.

Identify activity cost drivers.
(SO 4)

E17-10   Anna Bellatorre, Inc. manufactures five models of kitchen appliances at its Mesa plant. The company is installing activity-based costing and has identified the following activities performed at its Mesa plant.

1. Designing new models.
2. Purchasing raw materials and parts.
3. Storing and managing inventory.
4. Receiving and inspecting raw materials and parts.
5. Interviewing and hiring new personnel.
6. Machine forming sheet steel into appliance parts.
7. Manually assembling parts into appliances.
8. Training all employees of the company.
9. Insuring all tangible fixed assets.
10. Supervising production.
11. Maintaining and repairing machinery and equipment.
12. Painting and packaging finished appliances.

Having analyzed its Mesa plant operations for purposes of installing activity-based costing, Anna Bellatorre, Inc. identified its activity cost centers. It now needs to identify relevant activity cost drivers in order to assign overhead costs to its products.

Instructions

Using the activities listed above, identify for each activity one or more cost drivers that might be used to assign overhead to Anna Bellatorre's five products.

Compute overhead rates and
assign overhead using ABC.
(SO 4, 5)

E17-11   Fontillas Instrument, Inc. manufactures two products: missile range instruments and space pressure gauges. During April, 50 range instruments and 300 pressure gauges were produced, and overhead costs of $89,500 were estimated. An analysis of estimated overhead costs reveals the following activities.

Activities	Cost Drivers	Total Cost
1. Materials handling	Number of requisitions	$35,000
2. Machine setups	Number of setups	27,500
3. Quality inspections	Number of inspections	27,000

The cost driver volume for each product was as follows.

Cost Drivers	Instruments	Gauges	Total
Number of requisitions	400	600	1,000
Number of setups	200	300	500
Number of inspections	200	400	600

Instructions
(a) Determine the overhead rate for each activity.
(b) Assign the manufacturing overhead costs for April to the two products using activity-based costing.
(c) [icon] Write a memorandum to the president of Fontillas Instrument explaining the benefits of activity-based costing.

E17-12 Lim Clothing Company manufactures its own designed and labeled sports attire and sells its products through catalog sales and retail outlets. While Lim has for years used activity-based costing in its manufacturing activities, it has always used traditional costing in assigning its selling costs to its product lines. Selling costs have traditionally been assigned to Lim's product lines at a rate of 70% of direct material costs. Its direct material costs for the month of March for Lim's "high intensity" line of attire are $400,000. The company has decided to extend activity-based costing to its selling costs. Data relating to the "high intensity" line of products for the month of March are as follows.

Assign overhead using traditional costing and ABC; classify activities as value- or non-value-added.
(SO 1, 4, 6)

Activity Cost Pools	Cost Drivers	Overhead Rate	Number of Cost Drivers Used per Activity
Sales commissions	Dollar sales	$0.05 per dollar sales	$930,000
Advertising—TV/Radio	Minutes	$300 per minute	250
Advertising—Newspaper	Column inches	$10 per column inch	2,000
Catalogs	Catalogs mailed	$2.50 per catalog	60,000
Cost of catalog sales	Catalog orders	$1 per catalog order	9,000
Credit and collection	Dollar sales	$0.03 per dollar sales	$930,000

Instructions
(a) Compute the selling costs to be assigned to the "high-intensity" line of attire for the month of March: (1) using the traditional product costing system (direct material cost is the cost driver), and (2) using activity-based costing.
(b) By what amount does the traditional product costing system undercost or overcost the "high-intensity" product line?
(c) Classify each of the activities as value-added or non-value-added.

E17-13 Healthy Products, Inc., uses a traditional product costing system to assign overhead costs uniformly to all products. To meet Food and Drug Administration requirements and to assure its customers of safe, sanitary, and nutritious food, Healthy engages in a high level of quality control. Healthy assigns its quality-control overhead costs to all products at a rate of 17% of direct-labor costs. Its direct-labor cost for the month of June for its low-calorie dessert line is $55,000. In response to repeated requests from its financial vice president, Healthy's management agrees to adopt activity-based costing. Data relating to the low-calorie dessert line for the month of June are as follows.

Assign overhead using traditional costing and ABC; classify activities as value- or non-value-added.
(SO 1, 4, 6)

Activity Cost Pools	Cost Drivers	Overhead Rate	Number of Cost Drivers Used per Activity
Inspections of material received	Number of pounds	$0.60 per pound	6,000 pounds
In-process inspections	Number of servings	$0.33 per serving	10,000 servings
FDA certification	Customer orders	$12.00 per order	420 orders

Instructions

(a) Compute the quality-control overhead cost to be assigned to the low-calorie dessert product line for the month of June: (1) using the traditional product costing system (direct labor cost is the cost driver), and (2) using activity-based costing.

(b) By what amount does the traditional product costing system undercost or overcost the low-calorie dessert line?

(c) Classify each of the activities as value-added or non-value-added.

Classify activities as value-added or non-value-added.
(SO 6)

E17-14 In an effort to expand the usefulness of its activity-based costing system, Peter Catalano's Verde Vineyards decides to adopt activity-based management techniques. One of these ABM techniques is qualifying its activities as either value-added or non-value-added.

Instructions

Using Verde's list of fifteen activity cost pools in Exercise 17-9, classify each of the activities as either value-added or non-value-added.

Classify activities as value-added or non-value-added.
(SO 6)

E17-15 Anna Bellatorre, Inc. is interested in using its activity-based costing system to improve its operating efficiency and its profit margins by applying activity-based management techniques. As part of this undertaking, you have been asked to classify its Mesa plant activities as value-added or non-value-added.

Instructions

Using the list of activities identified in Exercise 17-10, classify each activity as either value-added or non-value-added.

Classify service company activities as value-added or non-value-added.
(SO 6, 8)

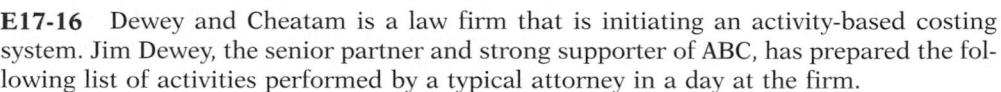

E17-16 Dewey and Cheatam is a law firm that is initiating an activity-based costing system. Jim Dewey, the senior partner and strong supporter of ABC, has prepared the following list of activities performed by a typical attorney in a day at the firm.

Activities	Hours
Writing contracts and letters	1.0
Attending staff meetings	0.5
Taking depositions	1.0
Doing research	1.0
Traveling to/from court	1.0
Contemplating legal strategy	1.0
Eating lunch	1.0
Litigating a case in court	2.5
Entertaining a prospective client	2.0

Instructions

Classify each of the activities listed by Jim Dewey as value-added or non-value-added and defend your classification. How much was value-added time and how much was non-value-added?

Classify activities by level.
(SO 7)

E17-17 Having itemized its costs for the first quarter of next year's budget, Galavic Corporation desires to install an activity-based costing system. First it identified the activity cost pools in which to accumulate factory overhead; second, it identified the relevant cost drivers. (This was done in Exercise 17-8.)

Instructions

Using the activity cost pools identified in Exercise 17-8, classify each of those cost pools as either unit-level, batch-level, product-level, or facility-level.

Classify activities by level.
(SO 7)

E17-18 Otto Dieffenbach & Sons, Inc. is a small manufacturing company in La Jolla that uses activity-based costing. Dieffenbach & Sons accumulates overhead in the following activity cost pools.

1. Hiring personnel.
2. Managing parts inventory.
3. Purchasing.
4. Testing prototypes.
5. Designing products.
6. Setting up equipment.
7. Training employees.
8. Inspecting machined parts.
9. Machining.
10. Assembling.

Instructions

For each activity cost pool, indicate whether the activity cost pool would be unit-level, batch-level, product-level, or facility-level.

Problems: Set A

P17-1A FireOut, Inc. manufactures steel cylinders and nozzles for two models of fire extinguishers: (1) a home fire extinguisher and (2) a commercial fire extinguisher. The **home model** is a high-volume (54,000 units), half-gallon cylinder that holds $2\frac{1}{2}$ pounds of multipurpose dry chemical at 480 PSI. The **commercial model** is a low-volume (10,200 units), two-gallon cylinder that holds 10 pounds of multi-purpose dry chemical at 390 PSI. Both products require 1.5 hours of direct labor for completion. Therefore, total annual direct labor hours are 96,300 or [1.5 hrs. × (54,000 + 10,200)]. Expected annual manufacturing overhead is $1,502,280. Thus, the predetermined overhead rate is $15.60 or ($1,502,280 ÷ 96,300) per direct labor hour. The direct materials cost per unit is $18.50 for the home model and $26.50 for the commercial model. The direct labor cost is $19 per unit for both the home and the commercial models.

The company's managers identified six activity cost pools and related cost drivers and accumulated overhead by cost pool as follows.

Assign overhead using traditional costing and ABC; compute unit costs; classify activities as value- or non-value-added.
(SO 1, 4, 6)

Activity Cost Pools	Cost Drivers	Estimated Overhead	Expected Use of Cost Drivers	Expected Use of Drivers by Product	
				Home	Commercial
Receiving	Pounds	$ 70,350	335,000	215,000	120,000
Forming	Machine hours	150,500	35,000	27,000	8,000
Assembling	Number of parts	390,600	217,000	165,000	52,000
Testing	Number of tests	51,000	25,500	15,500	10,000
Painting	Gallons	52,580	5,258	3,680	1,578
Packing and shipping	Pounds	787,250	335,000	215,000	120,000
		$1,502,280			

Instructions

(a) Under traditional product costing, compute the total unit cost of each product. Prepare a simple comparative schedule of the individual costs by product (similar to Illustration 17-4).

(b) Under ABC, prepare a schedule showing the computations of the activity-based overhead rates (per cost driver).

(c) Prepare a schedule assigning each activity's overhead cost pool to each product based on the use of cost drivers. (Include a computation of overhead cost per unit, rounding to the nearest cent.)

(d) Compute the total cost per unit for each product under ABC.

(e) Classify each of the activities as a value-added activity or a non-value-added activity.

(f) Comment on (1) the comparative overhead cost per unit for the two products under ABC, and (2) the comparative total costs per unit under traditional costing and ABC.

(a) Unit cost—H.M. $60.90

(c) Cost assigned—H.M. $1,031,300

(d) Cost/unit—H.M. $56.60

P17-2A Jacobson Electronics manufactures two large-screen television models: the Royale which sells for $1,600, and a new model, the Majestic, which sells for $1,300. The production cost computed per unit under traditional costing for each model in 2007 was as follows.

Assign overhead to products using ABC and evaluate decision.
(SO 4)

Traditional Costing	Royale	Majestic
Direct materials	$ 700	$420
Direct labor ($20 per hour)	120	100
Manufacturing overhead ($38 per DLH)	228	190
Total per unit cost	$1,048	$710

In 2007, Jacobson manufactured 25,000 units of the Royale and 10,000 units of the Majestic. The overhead rate of $38 per direct labor hour was determined by dividing total expected manufacturing overhead of $7,600,000 by the total direct labor hours (200,000) for the two models.

Under traditional costing, the gross profit on the models was: Royale $552 or ($1,600 − $1,048), and Majestic $590 or ($1,300 − $710). Because of this difference, management is considering phasing out the Royale model and increasing the production of the Majestic model.

Before finalizing its decision, management asks Jacobson's controller to prepare an analysis using activity-based costing (ABC). The controller accumulates the following information about overhead for the year ended December 31, 2007.

Activities	Cost Drivers	Estimated Overhead	Expected Use of Cost Drivers	Activity-Based Overhead Rate
Purchasing	Number of orders	$1,200,000	40,000	$30
Machine setups	Number of setups	900,000	18,000	50
Machining	Machine hours	4,800,000	120,000	40
Quality control	Number of inspections	700,000	28,000	25

The cost drivers used for each product were:

Cost Drivers	Royale	Majestic	Total
Purchase orders	15,000	25,000	40,000
Machine setups	5,000	13,000	18,000
Machine hours	75,000	45,000	120,000
Inspections	9,000	19,000	28,000

Instructions

(a) Royale $3,925,000

(a) Assign the total 2007 manufacturing overhead costs to the two products using activity-based costing (ABC).

(b) Cost/unit—Royale $977

(b) What was the cost per unit and gross profit of each model using ABC costing?

(c) ▭▭▭▭▷ Are management's future plans for the two models sound? Explain.

Assign overhead costs using traditional costing and ABC; compare results.
(SO 1, 4)

P17-3A Stellar Stairs Co. of Poway designs and builds factory-made premium wooden stairs for homes. The manufactured stair components (spindles, risers, hangers, hand rails) permit installation of stairs of varying lengths and widths. All are of white oak wood. Its budgeted manufacturing overhead costs for the year 2008 are as follows.

Overhead Cost Pools	Amount
Purchasing	$ 57,000
Handling materials	82,000
Production (cutting, milling, finishing)	210,000
Setting up machines	85,000
Inspecting	90,000
Inventory control (raw materials and finished goods)	126,000
Utilities	180,000
Total budget overhead costs	$830,000

For the last 4 years, Stellar Stairs Co. has been charging overhead to products on the basis of machine hours. For the year 2008, 100,000 machine hours are budgeted.

Heather Fujar, owner-manager of Stellar Stairs Co., recently directed her accountant, Lindsay Baker, to implement the activity-based costing system that she has repeatedly proposed. At Heather Fujar's request, Lindsay and the production foreman identify the following cost drivers and their usage for the previously budgeted overhead cost pools.

Activity Cost Pools	Cost Drivers	Expected Use of Cost Drivers
Purchasing	Number of orders	600
Handling materials	Number of moves	8,000
Production (cutting, milling, finishing)	Direct labor hours	100,000
Setting up machines	Number of setups	1,250
Inspecting	Number of inspections	6,000
Inventory control (raw materials and finished goods)	Number of components	168,000
Utilities	Square feet occupied	90,000

Jason Dion, sales manager, has received an order for 280 stairs from Community Builders, Inc., a large housing development contractor. At Jason's request, Lindsay prepares cost estimates for producing components for 280 stairs so Jason can submit a contract price per stair to Community Builders. She accumulates the following data for the production of 280 stairways.

Direct materials	$103,600
Direct labor	$112,000
Machine hours	14,500
Direct labor hours	5,000
Number of purchase orders	60
Number of material moves	800
Number of machine setups	100
Number of inspections	450
Number of components	16,000
Number of square feet occupied	8,000

Instructions

(a) Compute the predetermined overhead rate using traditional costing with machine hours as the basis.

(b) What is the manufacturing cost per stairway under traditional costing?

(c) What is the manufacturing cost per stairway under the proposed activity-based costing? (Prepare all of the necessary schedules.)

(d) ▭▭▭▶ Which of the two costing systems is preferable in pricing decisions and why?

(b) Cost/stair $1,199.82
(c) Cost/stair $1,055.54

P17-4A   Mendocino Corporation produces two grades of wine from grapes that it buys from California growers. It produces and sells roughly 3,000,000 liters per year of a low-cost, high-volume product called CoolDay. It sells this in 600,000 5-liter jugs. Mendocino also produces and sells roughly 300,000 liters per year of a low-volume, high-cost product called LiteMist. LiteMist is sold in 1-liter bottles. Based on recent data, the CoolDay product has not been as profitable as LiteMist. Management is considering dropping the inexpensive CoolDay line so it can focus more attention on the LiteMist product. The LiteMist product already demands considerably more attention than the CoolDay line.

Tyler Silva, president and founder of Mendocino, is skeptical about this idea. He points out that for many decades the company produced only the CoolDay line, and that it was always quite profitable. It wasn't until the company started producing the more complicated LiteMist wine that the profitability of CoolDay declined. Prior to the introduction of LiteMist, the company had simple equipment, simple growing and production procedures, and virtually no need for quality control. Because LiteMist is bottled in 1-liter bottles, it requires considerably more time and effort, both to bottle and to label and box than does CoolDay. The company must bottle and handle 5 times as many bottles of LiteMist to sell the same quantity as CoolDay. CoolDay requires 1 month of aging; LiteMist requires 1 year. CoolDay requires cleaning and inspection of equipment every 10,000 liters; LiteMist requires such maintenance every 600 liters.

Tyler has asked the accounting department to prepare an analysis of the cost per liter using the traditional costing approach and using activity-based costing. The following information was collected.

Assign overhead costs using traditional costing and ABC; compare results.
(SO 1, 4)

	CoolDay	LiteMist
Direct materials per liter	$0.40	$1.20
Direct labor cost per liter	$0.25	$0.50
Direct labor hours per liter	0.05	0.09
Total direct labor hours	120,000	25,000

Activity Cost Pools	Cost Drivers	Estimated Overhead	Expected Use of Cost Drivers	Expected Use of Cost Drivers per Product	
				CoolDay	LiteMist
Grape processing	Cart of grapes	$ 145,860	6,600	6,000	600
Aging	Total months	396,000	6,600,000	3,000,000	3,600,000
Bottling and corking	Number of bottles	270,000	900,000	600,000	300,000
Labeling and boxing	Number of bottles	189,000	900,000	600,000	300,000
Maintain and inspect equipment	Number of inspections	240,800	800	350	450
		$1,241,660			

Instructions

Answer each of the following questions. (Round all calculations to three decimal places.)

(a) Cost/liter—C.D. $1.078

(a) Under traditional product costing using direct labor hours, compute the total manufacturing cost per **liter** of both products.

(b) Under ABC, prepare a schedule showing the computation of the activity-based overhead rates (per cost driver).

(c) Cost/liter—C.D. $.241

(c) Prepare a schedule assigning each activity's overhead cost pool to each product, based on the use of cost drivers. Include a computation of overhead cost per liter.

(d) Compute the total manufacturing cost per liter for both products under ABC.

(e) ▰▰▰▶ Write a memo to Tyler Silva discussing the implications of your analysis for the company's plans. In this memo provide a brief description of ABC, as well as an explanation of how the traditional approach can result in distortions.

Assign overhead costs to services using traditional costing and ABC; compute overhead rates and unit costs; compare results.
(SO 1, 4, 6, 8)

P17-5A Hy and Lowe is a public accounting firm that offers two primary services, auditing and tax return preparation. A controversy has developed between the partners of the two service lines as to who is contributing the greater amount to the bottom line. The area of contention is the assignment of overhead. The tax partners argue for assigning overhead on the basis of 40% of direct labor dollars, while the audit partners argue for implementing activity-based costing. The partners agree to use next year's budgeted data for purposes of analysis and comparison. The following overhead data are collected to develop the comparison.

Activity Cost Pools	Cost Drivers	Estimated Overhead	Expected Use of Cost Drivers	Expected Use of Cost Drivers per Service	
				Audit	Tax
Employee training	Direct labor dollars	$216,000	$1,800,000	$1,000,000	$800,000
Typing and secretarial	Number of reports/forms	76,200	2,500	600	1,900
Computing	Number of minutes	204,000	60,000	25,000	35,000
Facility rental	Number of employees	142,500	40	22	18
Travel	Per expense reports	81,300	Direct	56,000	25,300
		$720,000			

Instructions

(a) Using traditional product costing as proposed by the tax partners, compute the total overhead cost assigned to both services (audit and tax) of Hy and Lowe.

(b) (2) Cost assigned—Tax $362,337

(b) (1) Using activity-based costing, prepare a schedule showing the computations of the activity-based overhead rates (per cost driver).

(2) Prepare a schedule assigning each activity's overhead cost pool to each service based on the use of the cost drivers.

(c) Classify each of the activities as a value-added activity or a non-value-added activity.

(d) Difference—Audit $42,337

(d) ▰▰▰▶ Comment on the comparative overhead cost per unit for the two products under both traditional costing and ABC.

Problems: Set B

Assign overhead using traditional costing and ABC; compute unit costs; classify activities as value- or non-value-added.
(SO 1, 4, 6)

P17-1B Waves Galore, Inc. manufactures hair curlers and blow-dryers. The handheld hair curler is Waves Galore's high volume product (80,000 units annually). It is a "large barrel," 20-watt, triple-heat appliance designed to appeal to the teenage market segment with its glow-in-the-dark handle. The handheld blow-dryer is Waves Galore's lower-volume product (40,000 units annually). It is a three-speed, 2,000 watt appliance with a "cool setting" and a removable filter. It also is designed for the teen market.

Both products require one hour of direct labor for completion. Therefore, total annual direct labor hours are 120,000, (80,000 + 40,000). Expected annual manufacturing overhead is $438,000. Thus, the predetermined overhead rate is $3.65 per direct labor hour. The direct materials cost per unit is $5.25 for the hair curler and $9.75 for the blow-dryer. The direct labor cost is $8.00 per unit for the hair curler and the blow-dryer.

Waves Galore purchases most of the parts from suppliers and assembles the finished product at its Fargo, North Dakota plant. It recently adopted activity-based costing, which after this year-end will totally replace its traditional direct labor-based cost accounting system. Waves Galore has identified the following six activity cost pools and related cost drivers and has assembled the following information.

Activity Cost Pools	Cost Drivers	Estimated Overhead	Expected Use of Cost Drivers	Expected Use of Cost Drivers per Product	
				Curlers	Dryers
Purchasing	Orders	$ 57,500	500	170	330
Receiving	Pounds	42,000	140,000	58,000	82,000
Assembling	Parts	166,000	830,000	415,000	415,000
Testing	Tests	52,000	130,000	82,000	48,000
Finishing	Units	60,000	120,000	80,000	40,000
Packing and shipping	Cartons	60,500	12,100	8,040	4,060
		$438,000			

Instructions

(a) Under traditional product costing, compute the total unit cost of each product. Prepare a simple comparative schedule of the individual costs by product (similar to Illustration 17-4).

(b) Under ABC, prepare a schedule showing the computations of the activity-based overhead rates (per cost driver).

(c) Prepare a schedule assigning each activity's overhead cost pool to each product based on the use of cost drivers. (Include a computation of overhead cost per unit, rounding to the nearest cent.)

(d) Compute the total cost per unit for each product under ABC.

(e) Classify each of the activities as a value-added activity or a non-value-added activity.

(f) Comment on (1) the comparative overhead cost per unit for the two products under ABC, and (2) the comparative total costs per unit under traditional costing and ABC.

(a) Unit cost—Dryer $21.40

(c) Cost assigned—Dryer $205,050

(d) Cost/unit—Dryer $22.88

Assign overhead to products using ABC and evaluate decision.
(SO 4)

P17-2B Tough Thermos, Inc. manufactures two plastic thermos containers at its plastic molding facility in Bend, Oregon. Its large container, called the Ice House, has a volume of 5 gallons, side carrying handles, a snap-down lid, and a side drain and plug. Its smaller container, called the Cool Chest, has a volume of 2 gallons, an over-the-top carrying handle which is part of a tilting lid, and a removable shelf. Both containers and their parts are made entirely of hard-molded plastic. The Ice House sells for $35 and the Cool Chest sells for $24. The production costs computed per unit under traditional costing for each model in 2007 were as follows.

Traditional Costing	Ice House	Cool Chest
Direct materials	$ 9.50	$ 6.00
Direct labor ($10 per hour)	8.00	5.00
Manufacturing overhead ($17.08 per DLH)	13.66	8.54
Total per unit cost	$31.16	$19.54

In 2007, Tough Thermos manufactured 50,000 units of the Ice House and 20,000 units of the Cool Chest. The overhead rate of $17.08 per direct labor hour was determined by dividing total expected manufacturing overhead of $854,000 by the total direct labor hours (50,000) for the 2 models.

Under traditional costing, the gross profit on the two containers was: Ice House $3.84 or ($35 − $31.16), and Cool Chest $4.46 or ($24 − $19.54). The gross margin rates on cost are: Ice House 12% or ($3.84 ÷ $31.16), and Cool Chest 23% or ($4.46 ÷ $19.54). Because Tough Thermos can earn a gross margin rate on the Cool Chest that is nearly twice as great as that earned on the Ice House, with less investment in inventory and labor costs, its management is urging its sales staff to put its efforts into selling the Cool Chest over the Ice House.

Before finalizing its decision, management asks the controller Sven Meza to prepare a product costing analysis using activity-based costing (ABC). Meza accumulates the following information about overhead for the year ended December 31, 2007.

Activities	Cost Drivers	Estimated Overhead	Expected Use of Cost Drivers	Activity-Based Overhead Rate
Purchasing	Number of orders	$179,000	4,475	$40 per order
Machine setups	Number of setups	195,000	780	$250 per setup
Extruding	Machine hours	320,000	80,000	$4 per machine hour
Quality control	Tests and inspections	160,000	8,000	$20 per test

The cost drivers used for each product were:

Cost Drivers	Ice House	Cool Chest	Total
Purchase orders	2,500	1,975	4,475
Machine setups	480	300	780
Machine hours	60,000	20,000	80,000
Tests and inspections	5,000	3,000	8,000

Instructions

(a) Ice House $560,000

(b) Cost/unit—Ice $28.70

(a) Assign the total 2007 manufacturing overhead costs to the two products using activity-based costing (ABC).
(b) What was the cost per unit and gross profit of each model using ABC costing?
(c) ▭▭▭▷ Are management's future plans for the two models sound?

Assign overhead costs using traditional costing and ABC; compare results.
(SO 1, 4)

P17-3B Kitchen Kabinets Company designs and builds upscale kitchen cabinets for luxury homes. Many of the kitchen cabinet and counter arrangements are custom made, but occasionally the company does mass production on order. Its budgeted manufacturing overhead costs for the year 2008 are as follows.

Overhead Cost Pools	Amount
Purchasing	$ 114,400
Handling materials	164,320
Production (cutting, milling, finishing)	500,000
Setting up machines	174,480
Inspecting	184,800
Inventory control (raw materials and finished goods)	252,000
Utilities	360,000
Total budget overhead costs	$1,750,000

For the last 3 years, Kitchen Kabinets Company has been charging overhead to products on the basis of machine hours. For the year 2008, 100,000 machine hours are budgeted.

Ben Chen, the owner-manager, recently directed his accountant, John Kandy, to implement the activity-based costing system he has repeatedly proposed. At Ben's request, John and the production foreman identify the following cost drivers and their usage for the previously budgeted overhead cost pools.

Activity Cost Pools	Activity Cost Drivers	Expected Use of Cost Drivers
Purchasing	Number of orders	650
Handling materials	Numbers of moves	8,000
Production (cutting, milling, finishing)	Direct labor hours	100,000
Setting up machines	Number of setups	1,200
Inspecting	Number of inspections	6,000
Inventory control (raw materials and finished goods)	Number of components	36,000
Utilities	Square feet occupied	90,000

Sara Sosa, sales manager, has received an order for 50 kitchen cabinet arrangements from Bitty Builders, a housing development contractor. At Sara's request, John prepares cost estimates for producing components for 50 cabinet arrangements so Sara can submit a contract price per kitchen arrangement to Bitty Builders. He accumulates the following data for the production of 50 kitchen cabinet arrangements.

Direct materials	$180,000
Direct labor	$200,000
Machine hours	15,000
Direct labor hours	12,000
Number of purchase orders	50
Number of material moves	800
Number of machine setups	100
Number of inspections	450
Number of components (cabinets and accessories)	3,000
Number of square feet occupied	8,000

Instructions

(a) Compute the predetermined overhead rate using traditional costing with machine hours as the basis. (Round to the nearest cent.)

(b) What is the manufacturing cost per complete kitchen arrangement under traditional costing?

(b) Cost/Kitchen $12,850

(c) What is the manufacturing cost per kitchen arrangement under the proposed activity-based costing? (Prepare all of the necessary schedules.)

(c) Cost/Kitchen $10,932.64

(d) ▭▭▭▭▷ Which of the two costing systems is preferable in pricing decisions and why?

P17-4B Vino Verite Corporation produces two grades of wine from grapes that it buys from California growers. It produces and sells, in 1-gallon jugs, roughly 800,000 gallons per year of a low-cost, high-volume product called StarDew. It also produces and sells roughly 200,000 gallons per year of a low-volume, high-cost product called VineRose. VineRose is sold in 1-liter bottles; thus 200,000 gallons results in roughly 800,000 bottles. Based on recent data, the StarDew product has not been as profitable as VineRose. Management is considering dropping the inexpensive StarDew so it can focus more attention on the VineRose line product. VineRose already demands considerably more attention than StarDew.

Jorge Rojo, president and founder of Vino Verite, is skeptical about this idea. He points out that for many decades the company produced only the StarDew line, and that it was always quite profitable. It wasn't until the company started producing the more complicated VineRose wine that the profitability of StarDew declined. Prior to the introduction of VineRose the company had simple equipment, simple growing and production procedures, and virtually no need for quality control. Because VineRose is bottled in 1-liter bottles it requires considerably more time and effort, both to bottle and to label and box, than does StarDew. (There are roughly 4 liters in a gallon; thus the company must bottle and handle 4 bottles of VineRose to sell the same amount of wine as StarDew.) StarDew requires 1 month of aging; VineRose requires 1 year. StarDew requires cleaning and inspection of equipment every 5,000 gallons; VineRose requires such maintenance every 500 gallons.

Jorge has asked the accounting department to prepare an analysis of the cost per gallon using the traditional costing approach and using activity-based costing. The following information was collected.

Assign overhead costs using traditional costing and ABC; compare results.
(SO 1, 4)

	StarDew	VineRose
Direct materials per gallon	$1.10	$2.40
Direct labor cost per gallon	$0.50	$1.00
Direct labor hours per gallon	0.075	0.15
Total direct labor hours	60,000	30,000

Activity Cost Pools	Cost Drivers	Estimated Overhead	Expected Use of Cost Drivers	Expected Use of Cost Drivers per Product	
				StarDew	VineRose
Grape processing	Cart of grapes	$ 189,000	10,000	8,000	2,000
Aging	Total months	416,000	10,400,000	800,000	9,600,000
Bottling and corking	Number of bottles	360,000	1,600,000	800,000	800,000
Labeling and boxing	Number of bottles	240,000	1,600,000	800,000	800,000
Maintain and in-spect equipment	Number of inspections	280,000	560	160	400
		$1,485,000			

Instructions

Answer each of the following questions. (Round all calculations to three decimal places.)

(a) Cost/gal.—S.D. $2.838

(a) Under traditional product costing using direct labor hours, compute the total manufacturing cost per **gallon** of both products.

(b) Under ABC, prepare a schedule showing the computation of the activity-based overhead rates (per cost driver).

(c) Cost/gal.—S.D. $0.704

(c) Prepare a schedule assigning each activity's overhead cost pool to each product, based on the use of cost drivers. Include a computation of overhead cost per unit.

(d) Compute the total manufacturing cost per gallon for both products under ABC.

(e) ✏️ Write a memo to Jorge Rojo discussing the implications of your analysis for the company's plans. In this memo provide a brief description of ABC, as well as an explanation of how the traditional approach can result in distortions.

Assign overhead costs to services using traditional costing and ABC; compute overhead rates and unit costs; compare results.
(SO 1, 4, 6, 8)

P17-5B Farm and Home Veterinary Clinic is a small-town partnership that offers two primary services, farm animal services and pet care services. Providing veterinary care to farm animals requires travel to the farm animal (house calls), while veterinary care to pets generally requires that the pet be brought into the clinic. As part of an investigation to determine the contribution that each of these two types of services makes to overall profit, one partner argues for allocating overhead using activity-based costing while the other partner argues for a more simple overhead cost allocation on the basis of direct labor hours. The partners agree to use next year's budgeted data, as prepared by their public accountant, for analysis and comparison purposes. The following overhead data are collected to develop the comparison.

Activity Cost Pools	Cost Drivers	Estimated Overhead	Expected Use of Cost Drivers	Expected Use of Cost Drivers by Service	
				Farm Animals	Pets
Drug treatment	Treatments	$ 64,000	4,000	1,700	2,300
Surgery	Operations	70,000	800	200	600
Travel	Mileage	28,000	28,000	26,000	2,000
Consultation	Appointment/Calls	33,000	3,000	600	2,400
Accounting/office	Direct labor hours	30,000	5,000	2,000	3,000
Boarding and grooming	100% pets	40,000			
		$265,000			

Instructions

(a) Using traditional product costing as proposed by the one partner, compute the total overhead cost assigned to both services of Farm and Home Veterinary Clinic.

(b) Cost assigned—Farm Animals $89,300

(b) (1) Using activity-based costing, prepare a schedule showing the computations of the activity-based overhead rates (per cost driver).

(2) Prepare a schedule assigning each activity's overhead cost pool to each service based on the use of the cost drivers.

(c) Classify each of the activities as a value-added activity or a non-value-added activity.

(d)   Comment on the comparative overhead cost assigned to the two services under both traditional costing and ABC.

(d) ABC—Pets 66%

Problems: Set C

Visit the book's website at **www.wiley.com/college/kimmel** and choose the Student Companion site to access Problem Set C.

BROADENING YOUR PERSPECTIVE

Group Decision Case

BYP17-1 East Valley Hospital is a primary medical health care facility and trauma center that serves 11 small, rural midwestern communities within a 40-mile radius. The hospital offers all the medical/surgical services of a typical small hospital. It has a staff of 18 full-time doctors and 20 part-time visiting specialists. East Valley has a payroll of 150 employees consisting of technicians, nurses, therapists, managers, directors, administrators, dieticians, secretaries, data processors, and janitors.

Instructions

With the class divided into groups, discuss and answer the following.

(a) Using your (limited, moderate, or in-depth) knowledge of a hospital's operations, identify as many **activities** as you can that would serve as the basis for implementing an activity-based costing system.

(b) For each of the activities listed in (a), identify a **cost driver** that would serve as a valid measure of the resources consumed by the activity.

Managerial Analysis

BYP17-2 Ideal Manufacturing Company of Sycamore, Illinois has supported a research and development (R&D) department that has for many years been the sole contributor to the company's new farm machinery products. The R&D activity is an overhead cost center that provides services only to in-house manufacturing departments (four different product lines), all of which produce agricultural/farm/ranch related machinery products.

The department has never sold its services outside, but because of its long history of success, larger manufacturers of agricultural products have approached Ideal to hire its R&D department for special projects. Because the costs of operating the R&D department have been spiraling uncontrollably, Ideal's management is considering entertaining these outside approaches to absorb the increasing costs. But, (1) management doesn't have any cost basis for charging R&D services to outsiders, and (2) it needs to gain control of its R&D costs. Management decides to implement an activity-based costing system in order to determine the charges for both outsiders and the in-house users of the department's services.

R&D activities fall into four pools with the following annual costs.

Market analysis	$1,050,000
Product design	2,280,000
Product development	3,600,000
Prototype testing	1,400,000

Activity analysis determines that the appropriate cost drivers and their usage for the four activities are:

Activities	Cost Drivers	Total Estimated Drivers
Market analysis	Hours of analysis	15,000 hours
Product design	Number of designs	2,500 designs
Product development	Number of products	90 products
Prototype testing	Number of tests	700 tests

Instructions
(a) Compute the activity-based overhead rate for each activity cost pool.
(b) How much cost would be charged to an in-house manufacturing department that consumed 1,800 hours of market analysis time, was provided 280 designs relating to 10 products, and requested 92 engineering tests?
(c) How much cost would serve as the basis for pricing an R&D bid with an outside company on a contract that would consume 800 hours of analysis time, require 178 designs relating to 3 products, and result in 70 engineering tests?
(d) What is the benefit to Ideal Manufacturing of applying activity-based costing to its R&D activity for both in-house and outside charging purposes?

Real-World Focus

BYP17-3 Hewlett-Packard (H-P) is considered one of the most innovative companies in the world. It continually has shown an ability to adapt to global competitive challenges through technical innovation and continual reassessment of its management and control mechanisms. Most applications of activity-based costing by Hewlett-Packard have been successful.

But, over the period August 1988 to August 1989, the Colorado Springs Division of Hewlett-Packard designed an activity-based costing system with the goal of providing for better product costing and inventory valuation. It began implementation in November 1989 but halted the process in the summer of 1992. Since then, the Colorado Springs Division has made no further attempts to re-implement a more expansive ABC approach.

Instructions
The March 1997 issue of *Management Accounting* contains an article by Steven P. Landry, Larry M. Wood, and Tim M. Linquist about the Colorado Springs Division titled "Can ABC Bring Mixed Results?" Read the article and answer the following questions.
(a) What went wrong at H-P's Colorado Springs Division in the design, development, and implementation of its activity-based costing system?
(b) What conclusions were drawn from H-P's Colorado Springs Division experience? What does successful ABC implementation require?

Exploring the Web

BYP17-4 Cost Technology describes itself as a "global consulting company specializing in profit management." The company helps manufacturing, service, and government organizations implement methods, such as activity-based costing and activity-based management, that will improve corporate profitability. The home page of Cost Technology includes information about the company, its markets, and products. The following exercise investigates the company in more depth.

Address: **http://costechnology.com**
           (*or go to* **www.wiley.com/college/kimmel**)

Instructions
Answer the following questions.
(a) Under the "services" section of Cost Technology's Web page, the company provides a definition of activity-based costing. What is this definition, and how does it differ from the one provided in the textbook?
(b) Under the "knowledgebase" section of its Web page, Cost Technology identifies a number of seminars related to activity-based costing. Explain the contents of these two seminars: (1) "The ABC Assessment: Obtaining the Highest Value from Your Implementation" and (2) "The Drivers of Successful ABC Implementation."

Communication Activity

BYP17-5 In our Feature Story about Super Bakery, Inc., we described a virtual corporation as one that consists of a core unit that is supported by a network of outsourced activities. A virtual corporation minimizes investment in human resources, fixed assets, and working capital. The application of ABC to Super Bakery, Inc. is described in an article titled "ABC in a Virtual Corporation" by Tom Davis and Bruce Darling, in the October 1996 issue of *Management Accounting*.

Instructions

Assume you are the controller of a virtual corporation. Using the article as a basis for your communication, write a summary that answers the following questions.

(a) What unique strategies and tactics did Super Bakery's management implement that caused sales to take off and continue to grow at an average rate of 20%?

(b) Why did Super Bakery's management feel that it was necessary to install an ABC system?

(c) What is the main difference between Super Bakery's ABC system and other manufacturers' ABC systems?

Research Assignment

BYP17-6   The April 1998 issue of *Management Accounting* includes an article by Kip R. Krumwiede titled "ABC: Why It's Tried and How It Succeeds."

Instructions

Read the article and answer the following questions.

(a) What is the adoption and implementation status of ABC according to the survey conducted in 1996 by the Cost Management Group of the Institute of Management Accountants?

(b) What did Krumwiede's survey attempt to determine?

(c) In Krumwiede's survey, what factors appeared to separate those companies that adopted ABC from those that did not adopt ABC?

(d) Identify at least five "Basic ABC Implementation Tips" recommended in the article.

Ethics Case

BYP17-7   Marcus Lim, the cost accountant for Hi-Power Mower Company, recently installed activity-based costing at Hi-Power's St. Louis lawn tractor (riding mower) plant where three models—the 8-horsepower Bladerunner, the 12-horsepower Quickcut, and the 18-horsepower Supercut—are manufactured. Marcus's new product costs for these three models show that the company's traditional costing system had been significantly undercosting the 18-horsepower Supercut. This was due primarily to the lower sales volume of the Supercut compared to the Bladerunner and the Quickcut.

Before completing his analysis and reporting these results to management, Marcus is approached by his friend Ray Pon, who is the production manager for the 18-horsepower Supercut model. Ray has heard from one of Marcus's staff about the new product costs and is upset and worried for his job because the new costs show the Supercut to be losing, rather than making, money.

At first Ray condemns the new cost system, whereupon Marcus explains the practice of activity-based costing and why it is more accurate than the company's present system. Even more worried now, Ray begs Marcus, "Massage the figures just enough to save the line from being discontinued. You don't want me to lose my job do you? Anyway, nobody will know."

Marcus holds firm but agrees to recompute all his calculations for accuracy before submitting his costs to management.

Instructions

(a) Who are the stakeholders in this situation?

(b) What, if any, are the ethical considerations in this situation?

(c) What are Marcus's ethical obligations to the company? To his friend?

Answers to Self-Study Questions

1. c   2. c   3. c   4. b   5. d   6. d   7. c   8. c   *9. d   *10. b

CHAPTER 18

Cost-Volume-Profit

STUDY OBJECTIVES

After studying this chapter,
you should be able to:

1 Distinguish between variable and fixed costs.

2 Explain the significance of the relevant range.

3 Explain the concept of mixed costs.

4 List the five components of cost-volume-profit analysis.

5 Indicate what contribution margin is and how it can be expressed.

6 Identify the three ways to determine the break-even point.

7 Give the formulas for determining sales required to earn target net income.

8 Define margin of safety, and give the formulas for computing it.

THE NAVIGATOR

- Scan *Study Objectives*
- Read *Feature Story*
- Read *Preview*
- Read text and answer *Before You Go On*
  p. 901 ⬭ p. 908 ⬭ p. 913 ⬭
- Work *Using the Decision Toolkit*
- Review *Summary of Study Objectives*
- Work *Demonstration Problem*
- Answer *Self-Study Questions*
- Complete *Assignments*

FEATURE STORY

Growing by Leaps and Leotards

When the last of her three children went off to school, Amy began looking for a job. At this same time, her daughter asked to take dance classes. The nearest dance studio was over 20 miles away, and Amy didn't know how she would balance a new job and drive her daughter to dance class. Suddenly it hit her—why not start her own dance studio?

Amy sketched out a business plan: A local church would rent its basement for $6 per hour. The size of the basement limited the number of students she could teach, but the rent was low. Insurance for a small studio was $50 per month. Initially she would teach classes only for young kids since that was all she felt qualified to do. She thought she could charge $2.50 for a one-hour class. There was room for 8 students per class. She wouldn't get rich—but at least it would be fun, and she didn't have much at risk.

Amy soon realized that the demand for dance classes far exceeded her capacity. She considered renting a bigger space that could serve 15 students per class. But her rent would also increase significantly. Also, rather than paying rent by the hour, she would have to pay $600 per month, even during the summer months when demand for dance classes was low. She also would have to pay utilities—roughly $70 per month.

However, with a bigger space Amy could offer classes for teens and adults. Teens and adults would pay a higher fee—$5 per hour—though the number of students per class would have to be smaller, probably only 8 per class. She could hire a part-time instructor at about $18 per hour to teach advanced classes. Insurance costs could increase to $100 per month. In addition, she would need a part-time administrator at $100 per month to keep records. Amy also realized she could increase her income by selling dance supplies such as shoes, towels, and leotards.

Amy laid out a new business plan based on these estimates. If she failed, she stood to lose real money. Convinced she could make a go of it, she made the big plunge.

Her planning paid off: Within 10 years of starting her business in a church basement Amy had over 800 students, seven instructors, two administrators, and a facility with three separate studios.

THE NAVIGATOR

As the Feature Story indicates, to manage any size business you must understand how costs respond to changes in sales volume and the effect of costs and revenues on profits. A prerequisite to understanding cost-volume-profit (CVP) relationships is knowledge of how costs behave. In this chapter, we first explain the considerations involved in cost behavior analysis. Then we discuss and illustrate CVP analysis.

The content and organization of Chapter 18 are as follows.

COST-VOLUME-PROFIT

Cost Behavior Analysis	**Cost-Volume-Profit Analysis**
• Variable costs • Fixed costs • Relevant range • Mixed costs • Identifying variable and fixed costs	• Basic components • CVP income statement • Break-even analysis • Target net income • Margin of safety • Changes in business environment

THE NAVIGATOR

Cost Behavior Analysis

Cost behavior analysis is the study of how specific costs respond to changes in the level of business activity. As you might expect, some costs change, and others remain the same. For example, for an airline company such as Southwest or United, the longer the flight the higher the fuel costs. On the other hand, Massachusetts General Hospital's employee costs to run the emergency room on any given night are relatively constant regardless of the number of patients serviced. A knowledge of cost behavior helps management plan operations and decide between alternative courses of action. Cost behavior analysis applies to all types of entities, as the Feature Story about Amy's dance studio indicates.

The starting point in cost behavior analysis is measuring the key business activities. Activity levels may be expressed in terms of sales dollars (in a retail company), miles driven (in a trucking company), room occupancy (in a hotel), or dance classes taught (by a dance studio). Many companies use more than one measurement base. A manufacturer, for example, may use direct labor hours or units of output for manufacturing costs and sales revenue or units sold for selling expenses.

For an activity level to be useful in cost behavior analysis, changes in the level or volume of activity should be correlated with changes in costs. The activity level selected is referred to as the activity (or volume) index. The **activity index** identifies the activity that causes changes in the behavior of costs.

With an appropriate activity index, it is possible to classify the behavior of costs in response to changes in activity levels into three categories: variable, fixed, or mixed.

VARIABLE COSTS

Variable costs are costs that vary **in total** directly and proportionately with changes in the activity level. If the level increases 10 percent, total variable costs will increase 10 percent. If the level of activity decreases by 25 percent, variable costs will decrease 25 percent. Examples of variable costs include direct materials and direct labor for a manufacturer; cost of goods sold, sales commissions, and freight-out for a merchandiser; and gasoline in airline and trucking companies. A variable cost may also be defined as a cost that **remains the same *per unit* at every level of activity**.

STUDY OBJECTIVE
1
Distinguish between variable and fixed costs.

To illustrate the behavior of a variable cost, assume that Damon Company manufactures radios that contain a $10 digital clock. The activity index is the number of radios produced. As each radio is manufactured, the total cost of the clocks increases by $10. As shown in part (a) of Illustration 18-1, total cost of the clocks will be $20,000 if 2,000 radios are produced, and $100,000 when 10,000 radios are produced. We also can see that a variable cost remains the same per unit as the level of activity changes. As shown in part (b) of Illustration 18-1, the unit cost of $10 for the clocks is the same whether 2,000 or 10,000 radios are produced.

Illustration 18-1 Behavior of total and unit variable costs

Helpful Hint True or false: Variable cost per unit changes directly and proportionately with changes in activity. Answer: False. Per unit cost remains constant at all levels of activity.

Companies that rely heavily on labor to manufacture a product, such as Nike or Reebok, or to provide a service, such as Hilton or Marriott, are likely to have many variable costs. In contrast, companies that use a high proportion of machinery and equipment in producing revenue, such as AT&T or Duke Energy Co., may have few variable costs.

FIXED COSTS

Fixed costs are costs that **remain the same in total** regardless of changes in the activity level. Examples include property taxes, insurance, rent, supervisory salaries, and depreciation on buildings and equipment. Because total fixed costs remain constant as activity changes, it follows that **fixed costs *per unit* vary inversely with activity: As volume increases, unit cost declines, and vice versa**.

To illustrate the behavior of fixed costs, assume that Damon Company leases its productive facilities at a cost of $10,000 per month. Total fixed costs of the facilities will remain constant at every level of activity, as shown in part (a) of Illustration 18-2. But, on a per unit basis, the cost of rent will decline as activity increases, as shown in part (b) of Illustration 18-2. At 2,000 units, the unit cost is $5 ($10,000 ÷ 2,000). When 10,000 radios are produced, the unit cost is only $1 ($10,000 ÷ 10,000).

Illustration 18-2 Behavior of total and unit fixed costs

The trend for many manufacturers is to have more fixed costs and fewer variable costs. This trend is the result of increased use of automation and less use of employee labor. As a result, depreciation and lease charges (fixed costs) increase, whereas direct labor costs (variable costs) decrease.

Business Insight
Management Perspective

When Thomas Moser quit teaching communications at Bates College 25 years ago, he turned to what he loved doing—furniture woodworking. Today he has over 120 employees. In a business where profit margins are seldom thicker than wood shavings, cost control is everything. Moser keeps no inventory; a 50 percent deposit buys the wood. Because computer-driven machines cut most of the standardized parts and joints, "we're free to be inefficient in assembly and finishing work, where the craft is most obviously expressed," says Moser. Direct labor costs are a manageable 30 percent of revenues. By keeping a tight lid on costs and running an efficient operation, Moser is free to spend most of his time doing what he enjoys most—designing furniture.

Source: Excerpts from "Out of the Woods," *Forbes* (April 5, 1999), p. 74.

RELEVANT RANGE

In Illustration 18-1, a straight line was drawn throughout the entire range of the activity index for total variable costs. In essence, the assumption was made that the costs were **linear**. If a relationship is linear (that is straight-line), then changes in the activity index will result in a direct, proportional change in the variable cost. For example, if the activity level doubles, the cost will double.

It is now necessary to ask: Is the straight-line relationship realistic? Does the linear assumption produce useful data for CVP analysis?

In most business situations, a straight-line relationship **does not exist** for variable costs throughout the entire range of possible activity. At abnormally low levels of activity, it may be impossible to be cost-efficient. Small-scale operations may not allow the company to obtain quantity discounts for raw materials or to use specialized labor. In contrast, at abnormally high levels of activity, labor costs may increase sharply because of overtime pay. Also at high activity levels, materials costs may jump significantly because of excess spoilage caused by worker fatigue. As a result, in the real world, the relationship between the behavior of a variable cost and changes in the activity level is often **curvilinear**, as shown in part (a) of Illustration 18-3. In the curved sections of the line, a change in the activity index will not result in a direct, proportional change in the variable cost. That is, a doubling of the activity index will not result in an exact doubling of the variable cost. The variable cost may more than double, or it may be less than double.

Illustration 18-3
Nonlinear behavior of variable and fixed costs

Total fixed costs also do not have a straight-line relationship over the entire range of activity. Some fixed costs will not change. But it is possible for management to change other fixed costs. For example, in the Feature Story the dance studio's rent was originally variable and then became fixed at a certain amount. It then increased to a new fixed amount when the size of the studio increased beyond a certain point. An example of the behavior of total fixed costs through all potential levels of activity is shown in part (b) of Illustration 18-3.

Helpful Hint Fixed costs that may be changeable include research, such as new product development, and management training programs.

For most companies, operating at almost zero or at 100 percent capacity is the exception rather than the rule. Instead, companies often operate over a somewhat narrower range, such as 40–80 percent of capacity. The range over which a company expects to operate during a year is called the **relevant range** of the activity index. Within the relevant range, as shown in both diagrams in Illustration 18-4 (page 898), a straight-line relationship generally exists for both variable and fixed costs.

Alternative Terminology The relevant range is also called the *normal* or *practical range*.

Illustration 18-4 Linear behavior within relevant range

As you can see, although the linear (straight-line) relationship may not be completely realistic, **the linear assumption produces useful data for CVP analysis as long as the level of activity remains within the relevant range**.

MIXED COSTS

Mixed costs are costs that contain both a variable element and a fixed element. Sometimes called **semivariable costs, mixed costs change in total but not proportionately with changes in the activity level**.

The rental of a U-Haul truck is a good example of a mixed cost. Assume that local rental terms for a 17-foot truck, including insurance, are $50 per day plus 50 cents per mile. When determining the cost of a one-day rental, the per day charge is a fixed cost (with respect to miles driven), whereas the mileage charge is a variable cost. The graphic presentation of the rental cost for a one-day rental is as follows.

Illustration 18-5 Behavior of a mixed cost

In this case, the fixed cost element is the cost of having the service available. The variable cost element is the cost of actually using the service. Another example of a mixed cost is utility costs (electric, telephone, and so on), where there is a flat service fee plus a usage charge.

For purposes of CVP analysis, **mixed costs must be classified into their fixed and variable elements**. How does management make the classification? One possibility is to determine the variable and fixed components each time a mixed cost is incurred. But because of time and cost constraints, this approach is rarely followed. Instead, the usual approach is to collect data on the behavior of the mixed costs at various levels of activity. An analysis is then performed to identify the fixed and variable cost components. Various types of analysis can be used. One type of analysis, called the **high-low method**, is discussed below. Other methods, such as the scatter diagram method and least squares regression analysis, are more appropriately explained in cost accounting courses.

High-Low Method

The high-low method uses the total costs incurred at the high and low levels of activity to classify mixed costs into fixed and variable components. The difference in costs between the high and low levels represents variable costs, since only the variable cost element can change as activity levels change. The steps in computing fixed and variable costs under this method are as follows.

1. **Determine variable cost per unit from the following formula.**

Change in Total Costs	÷	High minus Low Activity Level	=	Variable Cost per Unit

Illustration 18-6 Formula for variable cost per unit using high-low method

To illustrate, assume that Metro Transit Company has the following maintenance costs and mileage data for its fleet of buses over a 4-month period.

Month	Miles Driven	Total Cost	Month	Miles Driven	Total Cost
January	20,000	$30,000	March	35,000	$49,000
February	40,000	48,000	April	50,000	63,000

Illustration 18-7 Assumed maintenance costs and mileage data

The high and low levels of activity are 50,000 miles in April and 20,000 miles in January. The maintenance costs at these two levels are $63,000 and $30,000, respectively. The difference in maintenance costs is $33,000 ($63,000 − $30,000) and the difference in miles is 30,000 (50,000 − 20,000). Therefore, for Metro Transit, variable cost per unit is $1.10, computed as follows.

$$\$33,000 \div 30,000 = \$1.10$$

2. **Determine the fixed cost by subtracting the total variable cost at either the high or the low activity level from the total cost at that activity level.**

For Metro Transit, the computations are shown in Illustration 18-8.

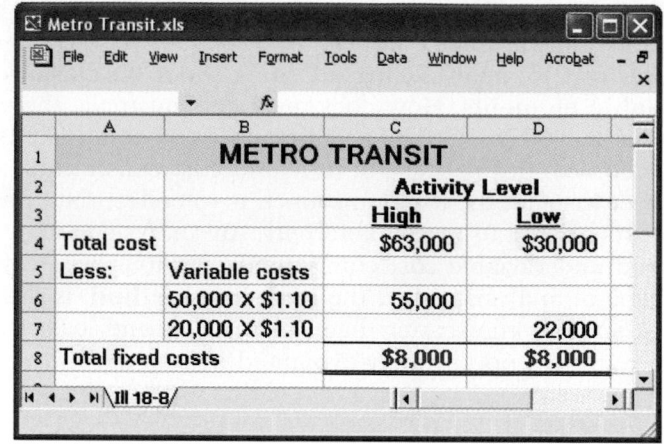

		Activity Level	
		High	Low
Total cost		$63,000	$30,000
Less:	Variable costs		
	50,000 X $1.10	55,000	
	20,000 X $1.10		22,000
Total fixed costs		$8,000	$8,000

METRO TRANSIT

Maintenance costs are therefore $8,000 per month plus $1.10 per mile. This is represented by the following formula:

Maintenance costs = Fixed costs + ($1.10 × miles driven)

For example, at 45,000 miles, estimated maintenance costs would be $8,000 fixed and $49,500 variable ($1.10 × 45,000) for a total of $57,500.

The high-low method generally produces a reasonable estimate for analysis. However, it does not produce a precise measurement of the fixed and variable elements in a mixed cost because other activity levels are ignored in the computation.

IMPORTANCE OF IDENTIFYING VARIABLE AND FIXED COSTS

Why is it important to segregate costs into variable and fixed elements? The answer may become apparent if we look at the following four business decisions.

1. If American Airlines is to make a profit when it reduces all domestic fares by 30 percent, what reduction in costs or increase in passengers will be required? **Answer**: To make a profit when it cuts domestic fares by 30 percent, American Airlines will have to increase the number of passengers or cut its variable costs for those flights. Its fixed costs will not change.

2. If Ford Motor Company meets the United Auto Workers' demands for higher wages, what increase in sales revenue will be needed to maintain current profit levels? **Answer**: Higher wages to UAW members at Ford Motor Company will increase the variable costs of manufacturing automobiles. To maintain present profit levels, Ford will have to cut other variable costs or increase the price of its automobiles.

3. If USX Corp.'s program to modernize plant facilities through significant equipment purchases reduces the work force by 50 percent, what will be the effect on the cost of producing one ton of steel? **Answer**: The modernizing of plant facilities at USX Corp. changes the proportion of fixed and variable costs of producing one ton of steel. Fixed costs increase because of higher depreciation charges, whereas variable costs decrease due to the reduction in the number of steelworkers.

4. What happens if Kellogg Company increases its advertising expenses but cannot increase prices because of competitive pressure? **Answer**: Sales volume must be increased to cover the increase in fixed advertising costs.

BEFORE YOU GO ON . . .

▶Review It

1. What are the effects on (a) a variable cost and (b) a fixed cost due to a change in activity?
2. What is the relevant range, and how do costs behave within this range?
3. What are the steps in applying the high-low method to mixed costs?

▶Do It

Helena Company reports the following total costs at two levels of production.

	10,000 units	20,000 units
Direct materials	$20,000	$40,000
Maintenance	8,000	10,000
Depreciation	4,000	4,000

Classify each cost as either variable, fixed, or mixed.

Action Plan

• Recall that a variable cost varies in total directly and proportionately with each change.
• Recall that a fixed cost remains the same in total with each change.
• Recall that a mixed cost changes in total but not proportionately with each change.

Solution Direct materials is a variable cost. Maintenance is a mixed cost. Depreciation is a fixed cost.

Related exercise material: BE18-1, BE18-2, BE18-3, E18-1, E18-2, and E18-3.

THE NAVIGATOR

Cost-Volume-Profit Analysis

Cost-volume-profit (CVP) analysis is the study of the effects of changes in costs and volume on a company's profits. CVP analysis is important in profit planning. It also is a critical factor in such management decisions as setting selling prices, determining product mix, and maximizing use of production facilities.

STUDY OBJECTIVE
4
List the five components of cost-volume-profit analysis.

BASIC COMPONENTS

CVP analysis considers the interrelationships among the components shown in Illustration 18-9.

Illustration 18-9   Components of CVP analysis

| Volume or level of activity | Unit selling prices | Variable cost per unit | Total fixed costs | Sales mix |

The following assumptions underlie each CVP analysis.

1. The behavior of both costs and revenues is linear throughout the relevant range of the activity index.
2. Costs can be classified accurately as either variable or fixed.
3. Changes in activity are the only factors that affect costs.
4. All units produced are sold.
5. When more than one type of product is sold, the sales mix will remain constant. That is, the percentage that each product represents of total sales will stay the same. Sales mix complicates CVP analysis because different products will have different cost relationships. In this chapter we assume a single product. Sales mix issues are addressed in Chapter 19.

When these assumptions are not valid, the CVP analysis may be inaccurate.

CVP INCOME STATEMENT

STUDY OBJECTIVE

5

Indicate what contribution margin is and how it can be expressed.

Because CVP is so important for decision making, management often wants this information reported in a **CVP income statement** format. The CVP income statement classifies costs as variable or fixed and computes a contribution margin. **Contribution margin** is the amount of revenue remaining after deducting variable costs. It is often stated both as a total amount and on a per unit basis.

We will use Vargo Video Company to illustrate a CVP income statement. Vargo Video produces a high-end, progressive-scan DVD player/recorder with up to 160-hour recording capacity and MP3 playback capability. Relevant data for the DVD players sold by this company in June 2007 are as follows.

Illustration 18-10
Assumed selling and cost data for Vargo Video

Unit selling price of DVD player	$500
Unit variable costs	$300
Total monthly fixed costs	$200,000
Units sold	1,600

The CVP income statement for Vargo Video therefore would be reported as follows.

Illustration 18-11   CVP income statement, with net income

VARGO VIDEO COMPANY
CVP Income Statement
For the Month Ended June 30, 2007

	Total	Per Unit
Sales (1,600 DVD players)	$ 800,000	$ 500
Variable costs	480,000	300
Contribution margin	**320,000**	**$200**
Fixed costs	200,000	
Net income	**$120,000**	

A traditional income statement and a CVP income statement both report the same bottom-line net income of $120,000. However a traditional income statement does not classify costs as variable or fixed, and therefore a contribution margin would not be reported. In addition, both a total and a per unit amount are often shown on a CVP income statement to facilitate CVP analysis.

In the applications of CVP analysis that follow, we will assume that the term "cost" includes all costs and expenses pertaining to production and sale of the product. That is, cost includes manufacturing costs plus selling and administrative expenses. An expanded format for the CVP income statement is discussed in Chapter 19.

Contribution Margin Per Unit

Vargo Video's CVP income statement shows a contribution margin of $320,000, and a contribution margin per unit of $200 ($500 − $300). The formula for **contribution margin per unit** and the computation for Vargo Video are:

Unit Selling Price	−	Unit Variable Costs	=	Contribution Margin per Unit
$500	−	$300	=	$200

Contribution margin per unit indicates that for every DVD player sold, Vargo will have $200 to cover fixed costs and contribute to net income. Because Vargo Video has fixed costs of $200,000, it must sell 1,000 DVD players ($200,000 ÷ $200) before it earns any net income. Vargo's CVP income statement, assuming a zero net income, would report the following.

VARGO VIDEO COMPANY
CVP Income Statement
For the Month Ended June 30, 2007

	Total	Per Unit
Sales (1,000 DVD players)	$500,000	$500
Variable costs	300,000	300
Contribution margin	**200,000**	**$200**
Fixed costs	200,000	
Net income	**$ –0–**	

Illustration 18-13   CVP income statement, with zero net income

It follows that for every DVD player sold above 1,000 units, net income is increased $200. For example, assume that Vargo sold one more DVD player, for a total of 1,001 DVD players sold. In this case it would report net income of $200 as shown in Illustration 18-14.

VARGO VIDEO COMPANY
CVP Income Statement
For the Month Ended June 30, 2007

	Total	Per Unit
Sales (1,001 DVD players)	$500,500	$500
Variable costs	300,300	300
Contribution margin	**200,200**	**$200**
Fixed costs	200,000	
Net income	**$ 200**	

Illustration 18-14   CVP income statement, with net income

Contribution Margin Ratio

Some managers prefer to use a contribution margin ratio in CVP analysis. The **contribution margin ratio** is the contribution margin per unit divided by the unit selling price. For Vargo Video, the ratio is as follows.

Illustration 18-15 Formula for contribution margin ratio

Contribution Margin per Unit	÷	Unit Selling Price	=	Contribution Margin Ratio
$200	÷	$500	=	40%

The contribution margin ratio of 40 percent means that $0.40 of each sales dollar ($1 × 40%) is available to apply to fixed costs and to contribute to net income.

This expression of contribution margin is very helpful in determining the effect of changes in sales on net income. For example, if sales increase $100,000, net income will increase $40,000 (40% × $100,000). Thus, by using the contribution margin ratio, managers can quickly determine increases in net income from any change in sales.

We can also see this effect through a CVP income statement. Assume that Vargo Video's current sales are $500,000 and it wants to know the effect of a $100,000 increase in sales. It could prepare a comparative CVP income statement analysis as follows.

Illustration 18-16 Comparative CVP income statements

VARGO VIDEO COMPANY
CVP Income Statements
For the Month Ended June 30, 2007

	No Change		With Change	
	Total	Per Unit	Total	Per Unit
Sales	$500,000	$ 500	$600,000	$ 500
Variable costs	300,000	300	360,000	300
Contribution margin	**200,000**	**$200**	**240,000**	**$200**
Fixed costs	200,000		200,000	
Net income	**$ –0–**		**$ 40,000**	

Study these CVP income statements carefully. The concepts presented in these statements will be used extensively in this and later chapters.

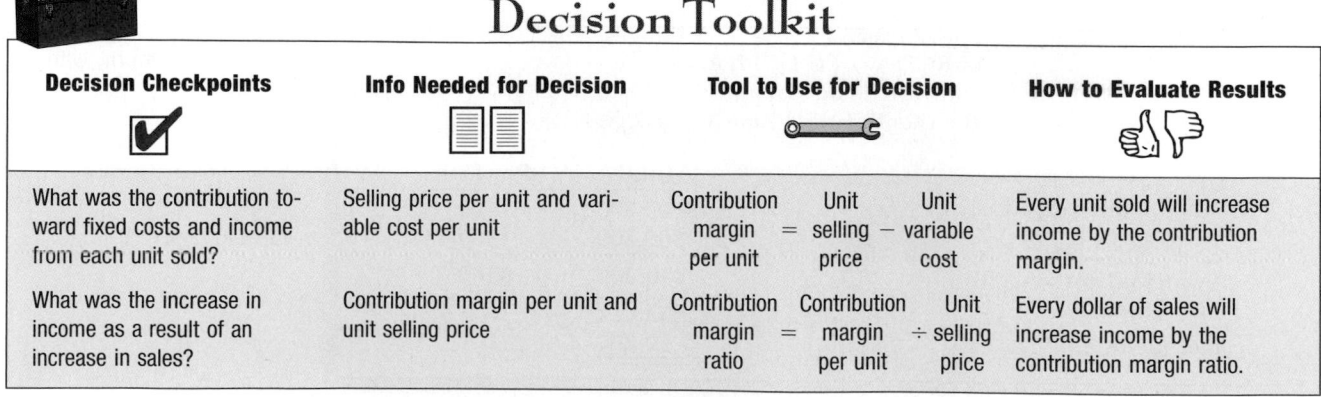

Decision Toolkit

Decision Checkpoints	Info Needed for Decision	Tool to Use for Decision	How to Evaluate Results
What was the contribution toward fixed costs and income from each unit sold?	Selling price per unit and variable cost per unit	Contribution margin per unit = Unit selling price − Unit variable cost	Every unit sold will increase income by the contribution margin.
What was the increase in income as a result of an increase in sales?	Contribution margin per unit and unit selling price	Contribution margin ratio = Contribution margin per unit ÷ Unit selling price	Every dollar of sales will increase income by the contribution margin ratio.

BREAK-EVEN ANALYSIS

A key relationship in CVP analysis is the level of activity at which total revenues equal total costs (both fixed and variable). This level of activity is called the **break-even point**. At this volume of sales, the company will realize no income and will suffer no loss. The process of finding the break-even point is called **break-even analysis**. Knowledge of the break-even point is useful to management when it decides whether to introduce new product lines, change sales prices on established products, or enter new market areas.

The break-even point can be:

1. Computed from a mathematical equation.
2. Computed by using contribution margin.
3. Derived from a cost-volume-profit (CVP) graph.

The break-even point can be expressed **either in sales units or sales dollars**.

Mathematical Equation

A common equation used for CVP analysis is shown in Illustration 18-17.

$$\text{Sales} = \text{Variable Costs} + \text{Fixed Costs} + \text{Net Income}$$

Illustration 18-17 Basic CVP equation

Identifying the break-even point is a special case of CVP analysis. Because at the break-even point net income is zero, **break-even occurs where total sales equal variable costs plus fixed costs**.

The break-even point **in units** can be computed directly from the equation by **using unit selling prices** and **unit variable costs**. The computation for Vargo Video is:

$$\text{Sales} = \text{Variable Costs} + \text{Fixed Costs} + \text{Net Income}$$
$$\$500Q = \$300Q + \$200,000 + \$0$$
$$\$200Q = \$200,000$$
$$Q = 1,000 \text{ units}$$

where

$$Q = \text{sales volume in units}$$
$$\$500 = \text{selling price}$$
$$\$300 = \text{variable cost per unit}$$
$$\$200,000 = \text{total fixed costs}$$

Illustration 18-18 Computation of break-even point in units

Thus, Vargo Video must sell 1,000 units to break even.

To find **sales dollars** required to break even, we multiply the units sold at the break-even point times the selling price per unit, as shown below.

$$1,000 \times \$500 = \$500,000 \text{ (break-even sales dollars)}$$

Contribution Margin Technique

We know that contribution margin equals total revenues less variable costs. It follows that at the break-even point, **contribution margin must equal total fixed costs**. On the basis of this relationship, we can compute the break-even point using either the contribution margin per unit or the contribution margin ratio.

When the contribution margin per unit is used, the formula to compute break-even point in units is fixed costs divided by contribution margin per unit. For Vargo Video the computation is as follows.

Illustration 18-19 Formula for break-even point in units using contribution margin

Fixed Costs	÷	Contribution Margin per Unit	=	Break-even Point in Units
$200,000	÷	$200	=	1,000 units

One way to interpret this formula is that Vargo Video generates $200 of contribution margin with each unit that it sells. This $200 is used to pay off fixed costs. Therefore, the company must sell 1,000 units to pay off $200,000 in fixed costs.

When the contribution margin ratio is used, the formula to compute break-even point in dollars is fixed costs divided by the contribution margin ratio. We know that the contribution margin ratio for Vargo Video is 40 percent ($200 ÷ $500), which means that every dollar of sales generates 40¢ to pay off fixed costs. Thus, the break-even point in dollars is:

Illustration 18-20 Formula for break-even point in dollars using contribution margin ratio

Fixed Costs	÷	Contribution Margin Ratio	=	Break-even Point in Dollars
$200,000	÷	40%	=	$500,000

Accounting across the Organization

The Internet is wringing inefficiencies out of nearly every industry. While commercial aircraft spend roughly 4,000 hours a year in the air, chartered aircraft spend only 500 hours flying. That means that they are sitting on the ground—not making any money—nearly 90 percent of the time. Enter Flightserve.com. For about the same cost as a first-class ticket, Flightserve.com matched up executives with charter flights in small "private jets." The executive got a more comfortable ride and avoided the hassle of big airports. Flightserve.com noted that the average charter jet has eight seats. When all eight seats are full, the company would have an 80 percent profit margin. It would break even at an average of 3.3 full seats per flight.

Source: "Jet Set Go," The Economist (March 18, 2000), p. 68.

Graphic Presentation

An effective way to find the break-even point is to prepare a break-even graph. Because this graph also shows costs, volume, and profits, it is referred to as a **cost-volume-profit (CVP) graph.**

As shown in the CVP graph in Illustration 18-21, sales volume is recorded along the horizontal axis. This axis should extend to the maximum level of expected sales. Both total revenues (sales) and total costs (fixed plus variable) are recorded on the vertical axis.

Illustration 18-21 CVP graph

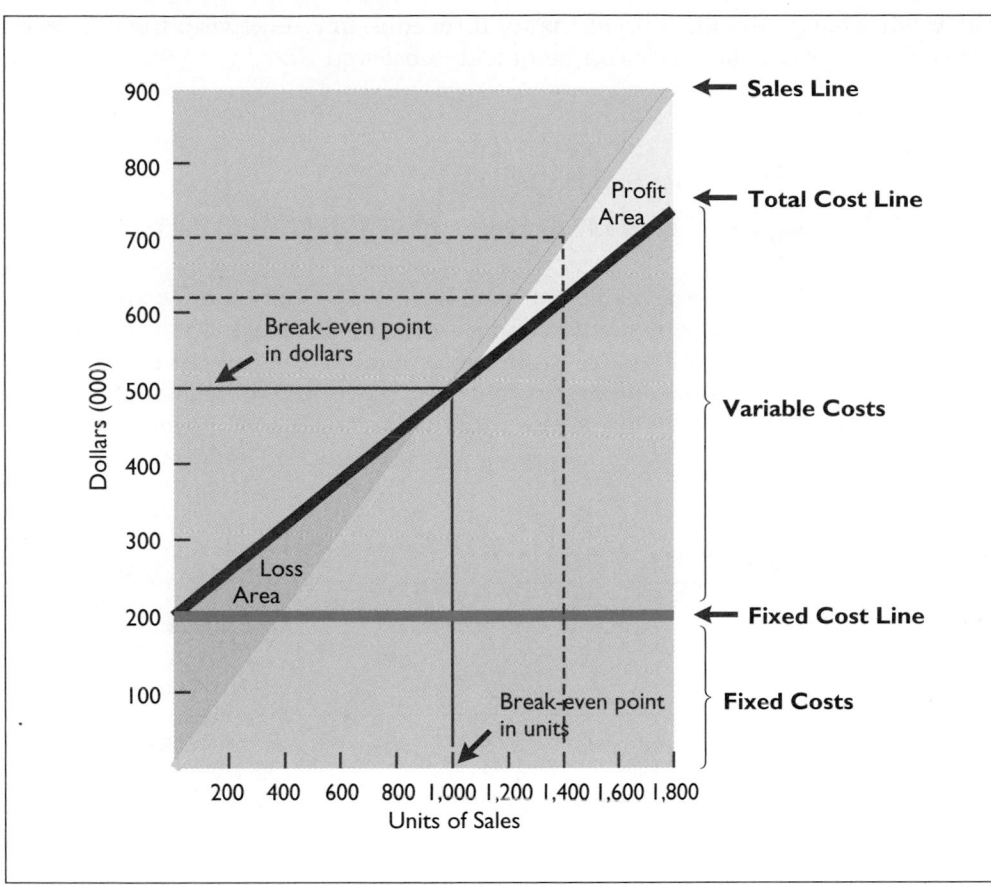

The construction of the graph, using the data for Vargo Video, is as follows.

1. Plot the total-sales line, starting at the zero activity level. For every DVD player sold, total revenue increases by $500. For example, at 200 units, sales are $100,000. At the upper level of activity (1,800 units), sales are $900,000. The revenue line is assumed to be linear through the full range of activity.

2. Plot the total fixed cost using a horizontal line. For the DVD players, this line is plotted at $200,000. The fixed cost is the same at every level of activity.

3. Plot the total cost line. This starts at the fixed-cost line at zero activity. It increases by the variable cost at each level of activity. For each DVD player, variable costs are $300. Thus, at 200 units, total variable cost is $60,000, and the total cost is $260,000. At 1,800 units total variable cost is $540,000, and total cost is $740,000. On the graph, the amount of the variable cost can be derived from the difference between the total cost and fixed cost lines at each level of activity.

4. Determine the break-even point from the intersection of the total cost line and the total revenue line. The break-even point in dollars is found by drawing a horizontal line from the break-even point to the vertical axis. The break-even point in units is found by drawing a vertical line from the break-even point to the horizontal axis. For the DVD players, the break-even point is $500,000 of sales, or 1,000 units. At this sales level, Vargo Video will cover costs but make no profit.

The CVP graph also shows both the net income and net loss areas. Thus, the amount of income or loss at each level of sales can be derived from the total sales and total cost lines.

A CVP graph is useful because the effects of a change in any element in the CVP analysis can be quickly seen. For example, a 10 percent increase in selling price will change the location of the total revenue line. Likewise, the effects on total costs of wage increases can be quickly observed.

Business Insight
℮-Business Perspective

Computer graphics are a valuable companion to many computer software packages. Color graphs can be instantly changed to provide visual "what if" analysis.

Current technology allows for stunning graphs in a variety of different formats (pie charts, bar, stacked bar, two-dimensional, three-dimensional, etc.). In the appropriate situation, a graph can literally be worth a thousand words.

Decision Toolkit

Decision Checkpoints	Info Needed for Decision	Tool to Use for Decision	How to Evaluate Results
At what amount of sales does a company cover its costs?	Unit selling price, unit variable cost, and total fixed costs	Break-even point analysis *In units:* $$\text{Break-even point} = \frac{\text{Fixed costs}}{\text{Unit contribution margin}}$$ *In dollars:* $$\text{Break-even point} = \frac{\text{Fixed costs}}{\text{Contribution margin ratio}}$$	Below the break-even point, the company is unprofitable.

BEFORE YOU GO ON . . .

▶Review It

1. What are the assumptions that underlie each CVP application?
2. What is contribution margin, and how can it be expressed?
3. How can the break-even point be determined?

▶Do It

Lombardi Company has a unit selling price of $400, variable costs per unit of $240, and fixed costs of $180,000. Compute the break-even point in units using (a) a mathematical equation and (b) contribution margin per unit.

Action Plan

• Apply the formula: Sales = Variable costs + Fixed costs + Net income.

• Apply the formula: Fixed costs ÷ Contribution margin per unit = Break-even point in units.

Solution (a) The formula is $400Q = $240Q + $180,000. The break-even point in units is 1,125 ($180,000 ÷ $160). (b) The contribution margin per unit is $160 ($400 − $240). The formula therefore is $180,000 ÷ $160, and the break-even point in units is 1,125.

Related exercise material: BE18-6, BE18-8, BE18-9, E18-4, E18-5, E18-6, E18-9, and E18-10.

THE NAVIGATOR

TARGET NET INCOME

Rather than simply "breaking even," management usually sets an income objective for individual product lines. This objective is called **target net income**. It indicates the sales necessary to achieve a specified level of income. The sales necessary to achieve target net income can be determined from each of the approaches used to determine break-even sales.

STUDY OBJECTIVE

7

Give the formulas for determining sales required to earn target net income.

Mathematical Equation

We know that at the break-even point no profit or loss results for the company. By adding an amount for target net income to the same basic equation, we obtain the following formula for determining required sales.

Required Sales	=	Variable Costs	+	Fixed Costs	+	Target Net Income

Illustration 18-22 Formula for required sales to meet target net income

Required sales may be expressed in **either sales units or sales dollars**. Assuming that target net income is $120,000 for Vargo Video, the computation of required sales in units is as follows.

Required Sales	=	Variable Costs	+	Fixed Costs	+	Target Net Income
$500Q	=	$300Q	+	$200,000	+	$120,000

$$\$200Q = \$320,000$$
$$Q = 1,600$$

where

$$Q = \text{sales volume}$$
$$\$500 = \text{selling price}$$
$$\$300 = \text{variable costs per unit}$$
$$\$200,000 = \text{total fixed costs}$$
$$\$120,000 = \text{target net income}$$

Illustration 18-23 Computation of required sales

The sales dollars required to achieve the target net income is found by multiplying the units sold by the unit selling price [$(1,600 \times \$500) = \$800,000$].

Contribution Margin Technique

As in the case of break-even sales, the sales required to meet a target net income can be computed in either units or dollars. The formula to compute required sales in units for Vargo Video using the contribution margin per unit is as follows.

Fixed Costs + Target Net Income	÷	Contribution Margin Per Unit	=	Required Sales in Units
($200,000 + $120,000)	÷	$200	=	1,600 units

Illustration 18-24 Formula for required sales in units using contribution margin per unit

This computation tells Vargo that to achieve its desired target net income of $120,000, it must sell 1,600 DVD players.

The formula to compute the required sales in dollars for Vargo Video using the contribution margin ratio is as follows.

Illustration 18-25 Formula for required sales in dollars using contribution margin ratio

Fixed Costs + Target Net Income	÷	Contribution Margin Ratio	=	Required Sales in Dollars
($200,000 + $120,000)	÷	40%	=	$800,000

This computation tells Vargo that to achieve its desired target net income of $120,000, it must generate sales of $800,000.

Graphic Presentation

The CVP graph in Illustration 18-21 (on page 907) can also be used to find the sales required to meet target net income. In the profit area of the graph, the distance between the sales line and the total cost line at any point equals net income. Required sales are found by analyzing the differences between the two lines until the desired net income is found.

For example, suppose Vargo Video sells 1,400 DVD players. Illustration 18-21 shows that a vertical line drawn at 1,400 units intersects the sales line at $700,000 and the total cost line at $620,000. The difference between the two amounts represents the net income (profit) of $80,000.

MARGIN OF SAFETY

STUDY OBJECTIVE

8

Define margin of safety, and give the formulas for computing it.

The margin of safety is another relationship that may be calculated in CVP analysis. **Margin of safety** is the difference between actual or expected sales and sales at the break-even point. This relationship measures the "cushion" that management has, allowing it to still break even if expected sales fail to materialize. The margin of safety may be expressed in dollars or as a ratio.

The formula for stating the **margin of safety in dollars** is actual (or expected) sales minus break-even sales. Assuming that actual (expected) sales for Vargo Video are $750,000, the computation is:

Illustration 18-26 Formula for margin of safety in dollars

Actual (Expected) Sales	−	Break-even Sales	=	Margin of Safety in Dollars
$750,000	−	$500,000	=	$250,000

This means that the company's sales could fall by $250,000 before it would be operating at a loss.

The **margin of safety ratio** is computed by dividing the margin of safety in dollars by actual (or expected) sales. The formula and computation for determining the margin of safety ratio are:

Illustration 18-27 Formula for margin of safety ratio

Margin of Safety in Dollars	÷	Actual (Expected) Sales	=	Margin of Safety Ratio
$250,000	÷	$750,000	=	33%

This means that the company's sales could fall by 33 percent before it would be operating at a loss.

The higher the dollars or the percentage, the greater the margin of safety. Management should evaluate the adequacy of the margin of safety in terms of such factors as the vulnerability of the product to competitive pressures and to downturns in the economy.

Business Insight
Service Company Perspective

Computation of break-even and margin of safety is important for service companies as well. Consider how the promoter for the Rolling Stones' tour used the break-even point and margin of safety. For example, one outdoor show should bring 70,000 individuals for a gross of $2.45 million. The promoter guarantees $1.2 million to the Rolling Stones. In addition, 20 percent of gross, or approximately $500,000, goes to the stadium in which the performance is staged. Add another $400,000 for other expenses such as ticket takers, parking attendants, advertising, and so on. This leaves $350,000 to the promoter per show, if it sells out. At 75 percent, the promoter breaks about even. At 50 percent, the promoter loses hundreds of thousands of dollars. However, the promoter also shares in sales of T-shirts and memorabilia for which the promoter will net over $7 million during the tour. From a successful Rolling Stones' tour, the promoter could make $35 million!

CVP AND CHANGES IN
THE BUSINESS ENVIRONMENT

When the IBM personal computer (PC) was introduced, it sold for $2,500. Today the same type of computer sells for much less. Recently, when oil prices rose, the break-even point for airline companies such as American, Southwest, and United rose dramatically. Because of lower prices for imported steel, the demand for domestic steel dropped significantly. The point should be clear: Business conditions change rapidly, and management must respond intelligently to these changes. CVP analysis can help.

To illustrate how CVP analysis can be used in responding to change, we will look at three independent situations that might occur at Vargo Video. Each case is based on the original DVD player sales and cost data, which were:

Unit selling price	$500
Unit variable cost	$300
Total fixed costs	$200,000
Break-even sales	$500,000 or 1,000 units

Illustration 18-28 Original DVD player sales and cost data

CASE 1. A competitor is offering a 10 percent discount on the selling price of its DVD players. Management must decide whether to offer a similar discount. **Question**: What effect will a 10 percent discount on selling price have on the break-even point for DVD players? **Answer**: A 10 percent discount on selling price reduces the selling price per unit to $450 [$500 − ($500 × 10%)]. Variable costs per unit remain unchanged at $300. Thus, the contribution margin per unit is $150. Assuming no change in fixed costs, break-even sales are 1,333 units, computed as follows.

Illustration 18-29 Computation of break-even sales in units

Fixed Costs	÷	Contribution Margin per Unit	=	Break-even Sales
$200,000	÷	$150	=	1,333 units (rounded)

For Vargo Video, this change would require monthly sales to increase by 333 units, or 33⅓ percent, in order to break even. In reaching a conclusion about offering a 10 percent discount to customers, management must determine how likely it is to achieve the increased sales. Also, management should estimate the possible loss of sales if the competitor's discount price is not matched.

CASE II. To meet the threat of foreign competition, management invests in new robotic equipment that will lower the amount of direct labor required to make DVD players. It is estimated that total fixed costs will increase 30 percent and that variable cost per unit will decrease 30 percent. **Question**: What effect will the new equipment have on the sales volume required to break even? **Answer**: Total fixed costs become $260,000 [$200,000 + (30% × $200,000)]. The variable cost per unit becomes $210 [$300 − (30% × $300)]. The new break-even point is approximately 900 units, computed as follows.

Illustration 18-30 Computation of break-even sales in units

Fixed Costs	÷	Contribution Margin per Unit	=	Break-even Sales
$260,000	÷	($500 − $210)	=	900 units (rounded)

These changes appear to be advantageous for Vargo Video. The break-even point is reduced by 10 percent, or 100 units.

CASE III. Vargo's principal supplier of raw materials has just announced a price increase. The higher cost is expected to increase the variable cost of DVD players by $25 per unit. Management would like to hold the line on the selling price of the DVD players. It plans a cost-cutting program that will save $17,500 in fixed costs per month. Vargo is currently realizing monthly net income of $80,000 on sales of 1,400 DVD players. **Question**: What increase in units sold will be needed to maintain the same level of net income? **Answer**: The variable cost per unit increases to $325 ($300 + $25). Fixed costs are reduced to $182,500 ($200,000 − $17,500). Because of the change in variable cost, the contribution margin per unit becomes $175 ($500 − $325). The required number of units sold to achieve the target net income is computed as follows.

Illustration 18-31 Computation of required sales

Fixed Costs + Target Net Income	÷	Contribution Margin per Unit	=	Required Sales in Units
($182,500 + $80,000)	÷	$175	=	1,500

To achieve the required sales, 1,500 DVD players will have to be sold, an increase of 100 units. If this does not seem to be a reasonable expectation, management will either have to make further cost reductions or accept less net income if the selling price remains unchanged.

Business Insight
e-Business Perspective

For Internet businesses, a "conversion rate" is calculated by dividing the number of people who take action at an Internet site (e.g., buy something) by the total number who visit the site. Average conversion rates are from 3 to 5 percent. A rate below 2 percent is poor, while a rate above 10 percent is great.

Conversion rates have an obvious effect on break-even point. Suppose you spend $10,000 on your site, and you attract 5,000 visitors. If you get a 2 percent conversion rate (100 purchases), your site costs $100 per purchase ($10,000 ÷ 100). A 4 percent conversion rate gets you down to a cost of $50 per transaction, and an 8 percent conversion rate gets you down to $25. Studies have shown that conversion rates increase if the site has an easy-to-use interface, fast-performing screens, a convenient ordering process, and advertising that is both clever and clear.

Source: J. William Gurley, "The One Internet Metric That Really Counts," *Fortune* (March 6, 2000), p. 392.

Decision Toolkit

Decision Checkpoints	Info Needed for Decision	Tool to Use for Decision	How to Evaluate Results
How can a company use CVP analysis to improve profitability?	Data on what effect a price change, a fixed-cost change, or a trade-off between fixed and variable costs would have on volume and costs	Measurement of income at new volume levels	If profitability increases under proposed change, adopt change.

BEFORE YOU GO ON . . .

►Review It

1. What is the formula for computing the margin of safety
   (a) in dollars and (b) as a ratio?
2. What is the equation to compute target net income?

☑ THE NAVIGATOR

Using the Decision Toolkit

B.T. Hernandez Company, maker of high-quality flashlights, has experienced steady growth over the last 6 years. However, increased competition has led Mr. Hernandez, the president, to believe that an aggressive campaign is needed next year to maintain the company's present growth. The company's accountant has presented Mr. Hernandez with the following data for the current year, 2007, for use in preparing next year's advertising campaign.

Cost Schedules

Variable costs	
Direct labor per flashlight	$ 8.00
Direct materials	4.00
Variable overhead	3.00
Variable cost per flashlight	$15.00

Fixed costs	
Manufacturing	$ 25,000
Selling	40,000
Administrative	70,000
Total fixed costs	$135,000
Selling price per flashlight	$ 25.00
Expected sales, 2007 (20,000 flashlights)	$500,000

Mr. Hernandez has set the sales target for the year 2008 at a level of $550,000 (22,000 flashlights).

Instructions
(Ignore any income tax considerations.)

(a) What is the projected operating income for 2007?
(b) What is the contribution margin per unit for 2007?
(c) What is the break-even point in units for 2007?
(d) Mr. Hernandez believes that to attain the sales target in the year 2008, the company must incur an additional selling expense of $10,000 for advertising in 2008, with all other costs remaining constant. What will be the break-even point in dollar sales for 2008 if the company spends the additional $10,000?
(e) If the company spends the additional $10,000 for advertising in 2008, what is the sales level in dollars required to equal 2007 operating income?

Solution

(a)

Expected sales		$500,000
Less:		
Variable cost (20,000 flashlights × $15)		300,000
Fixed costs		135,000
Projected operating income		$ 65,000

(b)

Selling price per flashlight	$25
Variable cost per flashlight	15
Contribution margin per unit	$10

(c) Fixed costs ÷ Contribution margin per unit = Break-even point in units
$135,000 ÷ $10 = 13,500 units

(d) Fixed costs ÷ Contribution margin ratio = Break-even point in dollars
$145,000 ÷ 40% = $362,500

Fixed costs (from 2007)	$135,000
Additional advertising expense	10,000
Fixed costs (2008)	$145,000

Contribution margin = Sales − Variable costs	
Expected sales	$550,000
Variable costs (22,000 × $15)	330,000
Contribution margin	$220,000

Contribution margin ratio = Contribution margin ÷ Sales
40% = $220,000 ÷ $550,000

(e) Required sales = (Fixed costs + Target net income) ÷ Contribution margin ratio

$525,000 = ($145,000 + $65,000) ÷ 40%

THE NAVIGATOR

Summary of Study Objectives

1 *Distinguish between variable and fixed costs.* Variable costs are costs that vary in total directly and proportionally with changes in the activity index. Fixed costs are costs that remain the same in total regardless of changes in the activity index.

2 *Explain the significance of the relevant range.* The relevant range is the range of activity in which a company expects to operate during a year. It is important in CVP analysis because the behavior of costs is assumed to be linear throughout the relevant range.

3 *Explain the concept of mixed costs.* Mixed costs increase in total but not proportionally with changes in the activity level. For purposes of CVP analysis, mixed costs must be classified into their fixed and variable elements. One method that management may use to classify these costs is the high-low method.

4 *List the five components of cost-volume-profit analysis.* The five components of CVP analysis are (a) volume or level of activity, (b) unit selling prices, (c) variable cost per unit, (d) total fixed costs, and (e) sales mix.

5 *Indicate what contribution margin is and how it can be expressed.* Contribution margin is the amount of revenue remaining after deducting variable costs. It is identified in a CVP income statement, which classifies

costs as variable or fixed. It can be expressed as a per unit amount or as a ratio.

6 *Identify the three ways to determine the break-even point.* The break-even point can be (a) computed from a mathematical equation, (b) computed by using a contribution margin technique, and (c) derived from a CVP graph.

7 *Give the formulas for determining sales required to earn target net income.* The general formula is: Required sales = Variable costs + Fixed costs + Target net income. Two other formulas are: Required sales in units = (Fixed costs + Target net income) ÷ Contribution margin per unit, and Required sales in dollars = (Fixed costs + Target net income) ÷ Contribution margin ratio.

8 *Define margin of safety, and give the formulas for computing it.* Margin of safety is the difference between actual or expected sales and sales at the break-even point. The formulas for margin of safety are: Actual (expected) sales − Break-even sales = Margin of safety in dollars; Margin of safety in dollars ÷ Actual (expected) sales = Margin of safety ratio.

Decision Toolkit—A Summary

Decision Checkpoints ✔	**Info Needed for Decision**	**Tool to Use for Decision**	**How to Evaluate Results** 👍
What was the contribution toward fixed costs and income from each unit sold?	Selling price per unit and variable cost per unit	$\dfrac{\text{Contribution}}{\text{margin per unit}} = \dfrac{\text{Unit}}{\text{selling price}} - \dfrac{\text{Unit}}{\text{variable cost}}$	Every unit sold will increase income by the contribution margin.
What was the increase in income as a result of an increase in sales?	Contribution margin per unit and unit selling price	$\dfrac{\text{Contribution}}{\text{margin ratio}} = \dfrac{\text{Contribution}}{\text{margin per unit}} \div \dfrac{\text{Unit}}{\text{selling price}}$	Every dollar of sales will increase income by the contribution margin ratio.
At what amount of sales does a company cover its costs?	Unit selling price, unit variable cost, and total fixed costs	Break-even point analysis *In units:* $\dfrac{\text{Break-even}}{\text{point}} = \dfrac{\text{Fixed costs}}{\text{Unit contribution margin}}$ *In dollars:* $\dfrac{\text{Break-even}}{\text{point}} = \dfrac{\text{Fixed costs}}{\text{Contribution margin ratio}}$	Below the break-even point, the company is unprofitable.
How can a company use CVP analysis to improve profitability?	Data on what effect a price change, a fixed-cost change, or a trade-off between fixed and variable costs would have on volume and costs	Measurement of income at new volume levels	If profitability increases under proposed change, adopt change.

Glossary

Activity index The activity that causes changes in the behavior of costs. (p. 894)

Break-even point The level of activity at which total revenues equal total costs. (p. 905)

Contribution margin (CM) The amount of revenue remaining after deducting variable costs. (p. 902)

Contribution margin per unit The amount of revenue remaining per unit after deducting variable costs; calculated as unit selling price minus unit variable cost. (p. 903)

Contribution margin ratio The percentage of each dollar of sales that is available to apply to fixed costs and to contribute to net income; calculated as contribution margin per unit divided by unit selling price. (p. 904)

Cost behavior analysis The study of how specific costs respond to changes in the level of business activity. (p. 894)

Cost-volume-profit (CVP) analysis The study of the effects of changes in costs and volume on a company's profits. (p. 901)

Cost-volume-profit (CVP) graph A graph showing the relationship between costs, volume, and profits. (p. 906)

Cost-volume-profit (CVP) income statement A statement for internal use that classifies costs as fixed or variable and reports contribution margin in the body of the statement. (p. 902)

Fixed costs Costs that remain the same in total regardless of changes in the activity level. (p. 895)

High-low method A mathematical method that uses the total costs incurred at the high and low levels of activity to classify mixed costs into fixed and variable components. (p. 899)

Margin of safety The difference between actual or expected sales and sales at the break-even point. (p. 910)

Mixed costs Costs that contain both a variable and a fixed cost element and change in total but not proportionately with changes in the activity level. (p. 898)

Relevant range The range of the activity index over which the company expects to operate during the year. (p. 897)

Target net income The income objective for individual product lines. (p. 909)

Variable costs Costs that vary in total directly and proportionately with changes in the activity level. (p. 895)

Demonstration Problem

Mabo Company makes calculators that sell for $20 each. For the coming year, management expects fixed costs to total $220,000 and variable costs to be $9 per unit.

Instructions
(a) Compute break-even point in units using the mathematical equation.
(b) Compute break-even point in dollars using the contribution margin (CM) ratio.
(c) Compute the margin of safety percentage assuming actual sales are $500,000.
(d) Compute the sales required in dollars to earn net income of $165,000 using the mathematical equation.

Action Plan
• Know the formulas.
• Recognize that variable costs change with sales volume; fixed costs do not.
• Avoid computational errors.

Solution to Demonstration Problem

(a) Sales = Variable costs + Fixed costs + Net income
$20Q = $9Q + $220,000 + $0
$11Q = $220,000
Q = 20,000 units

(b) Contribution margin per unit = Unit selling price − Unit variable costs
$11 = $20 − $9
Contribution margin ratio = Contribution margin per unit ÷ Unit selling price
55% = $11 ÷ $20
Break-even point in dollars = Fixed cost ÷ Contribution margin ratio
= $220,000 ÷ 55%
= $400,000

(c) Margin of safety $= \dfrac{\text{Actual sales} - \text{Break-even sales}}{\text{Actual sales}}$

$$= \dfrac{\$500,000 - \$400,000}{\$500,000}$$

$$= 20\%$$

(d) Required sales = Variable costs + Fixed costs + Net income
$$\$20Q = \$9Q + \$220,000 + \$165,000$$
$$\$11Q = \$385,000$$
$$Q = 35,000 \text{ units}$$
$$35,000 \text{ units} \times \$20 = \$700,000 \text{ required sales}$$

Self-Study Questions

Answers are at the end of the chapter.

(SO 1) **1.** Variable costs are costs that:
    (a) vary in total directly and proportionately with changes in the activity level.
    (b) remain the same per unit at every activity level.
    (c) Neither of the above.
    (d) Both (a) and (b) above.

(SO 2) **2.** The relevant range is:
    (a) the range of activity in which variable costs will be curvilinear.
    (b) the range of activity in which fixed costs will be curvilinear.
    (c) the range over which the company expects to operate during a year.
    (d) usually from zero to 100% of operating capacity.

(SO 3) **3.** Mixed costs consist of a:
    (a) variable cost element and a fixed cost element.
    (b) fixed cost element and a controllable cost element.
    (c) relevant cost element and a controllable cost element.
    (d) variable cost element and a relevant cost element.

(SO 3) **4.** Kendra Corporation's total utility costs during the past year were $1,200 during its highest month and $600 during its lowest month. These costs corresponded with 10,000 units of production during the high month and 2,000 units during the low month. What are the fixed and variable components of its utility costs using the high-low method?
    (a) $0.075 variable and $450 fixed.
    (b) $0.120 variable and $0 fixed.
    (c) $0.300 variable and $0 fixed.
    (d) $0.060 variable and $600 fixed.

(SO 4) **5.** One of the following is *not* involved in CVP analysis. That factor is:
    (a) sales mix.
    (b) unit selling prices.
    (c) fixed costs per unit.
    (d) volume or level of activity.

(SO 5) **6.** Contribution margin:
    (a) is revenue remaining after deducting variable costs.
    (b) may be expressed as contribution margin per unit.
    (c) is selling price less cost of goods sold.
    (d) Both (a) and (b) above.

(SO 5) **7.** Cournot Company sells 100,000 wrenches for $12 a unit. Fixed costs are $300,000, and net income is $200,000. What should be reported as variable expenses in the CVP income statement?
    (a) $700,000.   (c) $500,000.
    (b) $900,000.   (d) $1,000,000.

(SO 6) **8.** Gossen Company is planning to sell 200,000 pliers for $4 per unit. The contribution margin ratio is 25%. If Gossen will break even at this level of sales, what are the fixed costs?
    (a) $100,000.   (c) $200,000.
    (b) $160,000.   (d) $300,000.

(SO 7) **9.** Gabriel Corporation has fixed costs of $180,000 and variable costs of $8.50 per unit. It has a target income of $268,000. How many units must it sell at $12 per unit to achieve its target net income?
    (a) 51,429 units.   (c) 76,571 units.
    (b) 128,000 units.   (d) 21,176 units.

(SO 8) **10.** Marshall Company had actual sales of $600,000 when break-even sales were $420,000. What is the margin of safety ratio?
    (a) 25%.   (c) 33⅓%.
    (b) 30%.   (d) 45%.

Questions

1. (a) What is cost behavior analysis?
   (b) Why is cost behavior analysis important to management?

2. (a) Jenny Beason asks your help in understanding the term "activity index." Explain the meaning and importance of this term for Jenny.
   (b) State the two ways that variable costs may be defined.

3. Contrast the effects of changes in the activity level on total fixed costs and on unit fixed costs.

4. E.L. Dion claims that the relevant range concept is important only for variable costs.
   (a) Explain the relevant range concept.
   (b) Do you agree with E.L.'s claim? Explain.

5. "The relevant range is indispensable in cost behavior analysis." Is this true? Why or why not?

6. Shawn Grace is confused. He does not understand why rent on his apartment is a fixed cost and rent on a Hertz rental truck is a mixed cost. Explain the difference to Shawn.

7. How should mixed costs be classified in CVP analysis? What approach is used to effect the appropriate classification?

8. At the high and low levels of activity during the month, direct labor hours are 90,000 and 40,000, respectively. The related costs are $185,000 and $100,000. What are the fixed and the unit variable costs at any level of activity?

9. "Cost-volume-profit (CVP) analysis is based entirely on unit data." Do you agree? Explain.

10. Andrea Dubois defines contribution margin as the amount of profit available to cover operating expenses. Is there any truth in this definition? Discuss.

11. The traditional income statement for Rice Company shows sales $900,000, cost of goods sold $500,000, and operating expenses $200,000. Assuming all costs and expenses are 70% variable and 30% fixed, prepare a CVP income statement through contribution margin.

12. Darosa Company's Speedo pocket calculator sells for $40. Variable costs per unit are estimated to be $25. What are the contribution margin per unit and the contribution margin ratio?

13. "Break-even analysis is of limited use to management because a company cannot survive by just breaking even." Do you agree? Explain.

14. Total fixed costs are $22,000 for Forrest Inc. It has a contribution margin per unit of $15, and a contribution margin ratio of 25%. Compute the break-even sales in dollars.

15. Luz Foly asks your help in constructing a CVP graph. Explain to Luz (a) how the break-even point is plotted, and (b) how the level of activity and dollar sales at the break-even point are determined.

16. Jain Company's break-even sales are $600,000. Assuming fixed costs are $240,000, what sales volume is needed to achieve a target net income of $60,000?

17. Define the term "margin of safety." If Harold Company expects to sell 1,600 units of its product at $12 per unit, and break-even sales for the product are $13,440, what is the margin of safety ratio?

Brief Exercises

Classify costs as variable, fixed, or mixed.
(SO 1, 3)

BE18-1   Monthly production costs in Ogden Company for two levels of production are as follows.

Cost	2,000 units	4,000 units
Indirect labor	$10,000	$20,000
Supervisory salaries	5,000	5,000
Maintenance	2,500	4,000

Indicate which costs are variable, fixed, and mixed, and give the reason for each answer.

Diagram the behavior of costs within the relevant range.
(SO 2)

BE18-2   For Leahy Company, the relevant range of production is 40–80% of capacity. At 40% of capacity, a variable cost is $2,000 and a fixed cost is $5,000. Diagram the behavior of each cost within the relevant range assuming the behavior is linear.

Diagram the behavior of a mixed cost.
(SO 3)

BE18-3   For Stork Company, a mixed cost is $40,000 plus $6 per direct labor hour. Diagram the behavior of the cost using increments of 1,000 hours up to 5,000 hours on the horizontal axis and increments of $10,000 up to $70,000 on the vertical axis.

BE18-4 Spitz Company accumulates the following data concerning a mixed cost, using miles as the activity level.

	Miles Driven	Total Cost		Miles Driven	Total Cost
January	8,000	$14,100	March	8,500	$15,000
February	7,500	13,500	April	8,200	14,400

Compute the variable and fixed cost elements using the high-low method.

BE18-5 Westerville Corp. has collected the following data concerning its maintenance costs for the past 6 months.

	Units produced	Total cost
July	18,000	$32,000
August	32,000	48,000
September	36,000	55,000
October	22,000	38,000
November	40,000	65,000
December	38,000	62,000

Compute the variable and fixed cost elements using the high-low method.

BE18-6 Determine the missing amounts.

	Unit Selling Price	Unit Variable Costs	Contribution Margin per Unit	Contribution Margin Ratio
1.	$260	$160	(a)	(b)
2.	$500	(c)	$140	(d)
3.	(e)	(f)	$360	30%

BE18-7 Fontillas Manufacturing Inc. has sales of $1,800,000 for the first quarter of 2007. In making the sales, the company incurred the following costs and expenses.

	Variable	Fixed
Cost of goods sold	$750,000	$540,000
Selling expenses	95,000	60,000
Administrative expenses	79,000	70,000

Prepare a CVP income statement for the quarter ended March 31, 2007.

BE18-8 Lehi Company has a unit selling price of $400, variable costs per unit of $250, and fixed costs of $150,000. Compute the break-even point in units using (a) the mathematical equation and (b) contribution margin per unit.

BE18-9 Wesland Corp. had total variable costs of $170,000, total fixed costs of $120,000, and total revenues of $250,000. Compute the required sales in dollars to break even.

BE18-10 For Biswell Company, variable costs are 75% of sales, and fixed costs are $180,000. Management's net income goal is $60,000. Compute the required sales in dollars needed to achieve management's target net income of $60,000. (Use the contribution margin approach.)

BE18-11 For Korb Company actual sales are $1,200,000 and break-even sales are $840,000. Compute (a) the margin of safety in dollars and (b) the margin of safety ratio.

BE18-12 PCB Corporation has fixed costs of $480,000. It has a unit selling price of $6, unit variable cost of $4.50, and a target net income of $1,500,000. Compute the required sales in units to achieve its target net income.

Exercises

Define and classify variable, fixed, and mixed costs.
(SO 1, 3)

E18-1 Fowler Company manufactures a single product. Annual production costs incurred in the manufacturing process are shown below for two levels of production.

	Costs Incurred			
Production in Units	5,000		10,000	
Production Costs	Total Cost	Cost/ Unit	Total Cost	Cost/ Unit
Direct materials	$8,250	$1.65	$16,500	$1.65
Direct labor	9,400	1.88	18,800	1.88
Utilities	1,400	0.28	2,300	0.23
Rent	4,000	0.80	4,000	0.40
Maintenance	800	0.16	1,200	0.12
Supervisory salaries	1,000	0.20	1,000	0.10

Instructions
(a) Define the terms variable costs, fixed costs, and mixed costs.
(b) Classify each cost above as either variable, fixed, or mixed.

Determine fixed and variable costs using the high-low method and use cost equation.
(SO 1, 3)

E18-2 The owner/operator of Toledo Taxi Company is interested in determining the cost equation for his one-vehicle taxi service, based on the number of miles driven. To that end he has collected the following volume and cost data.

Month	Total Operating Costs	Number of Miles Driven
July	$16,000	13,000
August	17,800	14,250
September	12,400	9,750
October	15,100	12,500
November	13,250	10,500
December	11,500	9,000

Instructions
(a) Use the high-low method to calculate the variable and fixed cost components.
(b) The owner feels that the maximum level of operating costs that the company can sustain, because of cash flow concerns, is $14,500. Determine the number of miles that correspond to that level of costs.

Determine fixed and variable costs using the high-low method and prepare graph.
(SO 1, 3)

E18-3 The controller of Gutierrez Industries has collected the following monthly expense data for use in analyzing the cost behavior of maintenance costs.

Month	Total Maintenance Costs	Total Machine Hours
January	$2,800	3,000
February	3,000	4,000
March	3,600	6,000
April	4,500	7,900
May	3,200	5,000
June	5,000	8,000

Instructions
(a) Determine the fixed and variable cost components using the high-low method.
(b) Prepare a graph showing the behavior of maintenance costs, and identify the fixed and variable cost elements. Use 2,000 unit increments and $1,000 cost increments.

E18-4 The San Marcos Inn is trying to determine its break-even point. The inn has 75 rooms that are rented at $50 a night. Operating costs are as follows.

Compute break-even point and margin of safety.
(SO 5, 6, 8)

Salaries	$8,500 per month
Utilities	2,000 per month
Depreciation	1,000 per month
Maintenance	500 per month
Maid service	5 per room
Other costs	33 per room

Instructions
(a) Determine the inn's break-even point in (1) number of rented rooms per month and (2) dollars.
(b) If the inn plans on renting an average of 50 rooms per day (assuming a 30-day month), what is (1) the monthly margin of safety in dollars and (2) the margin of safety ratio?

E18-5 In 2007, Demuth Company had a break-even point of $320,000 based on a selling price of $8 per unit and fixed costs of $140,000. In 2008, the selling price and the variable cost per unit did not change, but the break-even point increased to $450,000.

Compute variable cost per unit, contribution margin ratio, and increase in fixed costs.
(SO 5)

Instructions
(a) Compute the variable cost per unit and the contribution margin ratio for 2007.
(b) Compute the increase in fixed costs for 2008.

E18-6 In the month of June, Angela's Beauty Salon gave 3,500 haircuts, shampoos, and permanents at an average price of $30. During the month, fixed costs were $16,800 and variable costs were 80% of sales.

Compute contribution margin, break-even point, and margin of safety.
(SO 5, 6, 8)

Instructions
(a) Determine the contribution margin in dollars, per unit, and as a ratio.
(b) Using the contribution margin technique, compute the break-even point in dollars and in units.
(c) Compute the margin of safety in dollars and as a ratio.

E18-7 Johansen Company had $150,000 of net income in 2007 when the selling price per unit was $150, the variable costs per unit were $100, and the fixed costs were $750,000. Management expects per unit data and total fixed costs to remain the same in 2008. The president of Johansen Company is under pressure from stockholders to increase net income by $90,000 in 2008.

Compute various components to derive target net income under different assumptions.
(SO 6, 7)

Instructions
(a) Compute the number of units sold in 2007.
(b) Compute the number of units that would have to be sold in 2008 to reach the stockholders' desired profit level.
(c) Assume that Johansen Company sells the same number of units in 2008 as it did in 2007. What would the selling price have to be in order to reach the stockholders' desired profit level?

E18-8 Ger Company reports the following operating results for the month of August: Sales $300,000 (units 5,000); variable costs $210,000; and fixed costs $70,000. Management is considering the following independent courses of action to increase net income.

Compute net income under different alternatives.
(SO 8)

1. Increase selling price by 10% with no change in total variable costs.
2. Reduce variable costs to 58% of sales.
3. Reduce fixed costs by $20,000.

Instructions
Compute the net income to be earned under each alternative. Which course of action will produce the highest net income?

E18-9 Regional Airways, Inc., a small two-plane passenger airline, has asked for your assistance in some basic analysis of its operations. Both planes seat 10 passengers each, and they fly commuters from Regional's base airport to the major city in the state, Metropolis. Each month 40 round-trip flights are made. Shown on page 922 is a recent month's activity in the form of a cost-volume-profit income statement.

Compute break-even point and prepare CVP income statement.
(SO 5, 6, 8)

Fare revenues (300 fares)		$45,000
Variable costs		
Fuel	$14,000	
Snacks and drinks	800	
Landing fees	2,000	
Supplies and forms	1,200	18,000
Contribution margin		27,000
Fixed costs		
Depreciation	3,000	
Salaries	15,000	
Advertising	500	
Airport hanger fees	1,750	20,250
Net income		$ 6,750

Instructions
(a) Calculate the break-even point in (1) dollars and (2) number of fares.
(b) Without calculations, determine the contribution margin at the break-even point.
(c) If fares were decreased by 10%, an additional 100 fares could be generated. However, variable costs would increase by 35%. Should the fare decrease be adopted?

Prepare a CVP graph and compute break-even point and margin of safety.
(SO 6, 8)

E18-10   Embleton Company estimates that variable costs will be 40% of sales, and fixed costs will total $900,000. The selling price of the product is $5.

Instructions
(a) Prepare a CVP graph, assuming maximum sales of $4,000,000. (*Note*: Use $500,000 increments for sales and costs and 100,000 increments for units.)
(b) Compute the break-even point in (1) units and (2) dollars.
(c) Compute the margin of safety in (1) dollars and (2) as a ratio, assuming actual sales are $2 million.

Prepare a CVP income statement before and after changes in business environment.
(SO 5)

E18-11   Hall Company had sales in 2007 of $1,500,000 on 60,000 units. Variable costs totaled $720,000, and fixed costs totaled $400,000.

A new raw material is available that will decrease the variable costs per unit by 25% (or $3.00). However, to process the new raw material, fixed operating costs will increase by $150,000. Management feels that one-half of the decline in the variable costs per unit should be passed on to customers in the form of a sales price reduction. The marketing department expects that this sales price reduction will result in a 5% increase in the number of units sold.

Instructions
Prepare a CVP income statement for 2007, (a) assuming the changes have not been made, and (b) assuming that changes are made as described.

Problems: Set A

Determine variable and fixed costs, compute break-even point, prepare a CVP graph, and determine net income.
(SO 1, 3, 5, 6)

(a) VC $5

P18-1A   The Peace Barber Shop employs four barbers. One barber, who also serves as the manager, is paid a salary of $1,800 per month. The other barbers are paid $1,300 per month. In addition, each barber is paid a commission of $4 per haircut. Other monthly costs are: store rent $800 plus 60 cents per haircut, depreciation on equipment $500, barber supplies 40 cents per haircut, utilities $300, and advertising $200. The price of a haircut is $11.

Instructions
(a) Determine the variable cost per haircut and the total monthly fixed costs.
(b) Compute the break-even point in (1) units and (2) dollars.
(c) Prepare a CVP graph, assuming a maximum of 1,500 haircuts in a month. Use increments of 300 haircuts on the horizontal axis and $3,300 increments on the vertical axis.

(d) NI $1,500

(d) Determine the net income, assuming 1,500 haircuts are given in a month.

P18-2A Tyson Company bottles and distributes LO-KAL, a fruit drink. The beverage is sold for 50 cents per 16-ounce bottle to retailers, who charge customers 70 cents per bottle. Management estimates the following revenues and costs.

Prepare a CVP income statement, compute break-even point, contribution margin ratio, margin of safety ratio, and sales for target net income.
(SO 5, 6, 7, 8)

Net sales	$2,500,000	Selling expenses—variable	$ 90,000
Direct materials	360,000	Selling expenses—fixed	200,000
Direct labor	650,000	Administrative expenses—	
Manufacturing overhead—		variable	30,000
variable	370,000	Administrative expenses—	
Manufacturing overhead—		fixed	140,000
fixed	260,000		

Instructions
(a) Compute (1) the contribution margin and (2) the fixed costs.
(b) Compute the break-even point in (1) units and (2) dollars.
(c) Compute the contribution margin ratio and the margin of safety ratio.
(d) Determine the sales dollars required to earn net income of $240,000.

(b) 3,000,000 units

P18-3A Cruz Manufacturing had a bad year in 2007. For the first time in its history it operated at a loss. The company's income statement showed the following results from selling 80,000 units of product: Net sales $1,600,000; total costs and expenses $1,740,000; and net loss $140,000. Costs and expenses consisted of the following.

Compute break-even point under alternative courses of action.
(SO 5, 6)

	Total	Variable	Fixed
Cost of goods sold	$1,200,000	$780,000	$420,000
Selling expenses	420,000	75,000	345,000
Administrative expenses	120,000	45,000	75,000
	$1,740,000	$900,000	$840,000

Management is considering the following independent alternatives for 2008.

1. Increase unit selling price 25% with no change in costs and expenses.
2. Change the compensation of salespersons from fixed annual salaries totaling $200,000 to total salaries of $40,000 plus a 5% commission on net sales.
3. Purchase new high-tech factory machinery that will change the proportion between variable and fixed cost of goods sold to 50:50.

Instructions
(a) Compute the break-even point in dollars for 2007.
(b) Compute the break-even point in dollars under each of the alternative courses of action. (Round to the nearest dollar.) Which course of action do you recommend?

(b) (2) $1,754,839

P18-4A Lois Baiser is the advertising manager for Value Shoe Store. She is currently working on a major promotional campaign. Her ideas include the installation of a new lighting system and increased display space that will add $27,000 in fixed costs to the $225,000 currently spent. In addition, Lois is proposing that a 6⅔% price decrease (from $30 to $28) will produce an increase in sales volume from 17,000 to 20,000 units. Variable costs will remain at $10 per pair of shoes. Management is impressed with Lois's ideas but concerned about the effects that these changes will have on the break-even point and the margin of safety.

Compute break-even point and margin of safety ratio, and prepare a CVP income statement before and after changes in business environment.
(SO 5, 6, 7, 8)

Instructions
(a) Compute the current break-even point in units, and compare it to the break-even point in units if Lois's ideas are used.
(b) Compute the margin of safety ratio for current operations and after Lois's changes are introduced. (Round to nearest full percent.)
(c) Prepare a CVP income statement for current operations and after Lois's changes are introduced. Would you make the changes suggested?

(b) current 34%
new 30%

P18-5A Poole Corporation has collected the following information after its first year of sales. Net sales were $1,600,000 on 100,000 units; selling expenses $240,000 (40% variable and 60% fixed); direct materials $511,000; direct labor $285,000; administrative expenses $280,000 (20% variable and 80% fixed); manufacturing overhead $360,000 (70% variable and 30% fixed). Top management has asked you to do a CVP analysis so that it can make plans for the coming year. It has projected that unit sales will increase by 10% next year.

Compute break-even point and margin of safety ratio, and prepare a CVP income statement before and after changes in business environment.
(SO 5, 6, 7, 8)

Instructions

(a) Compute (1) the contribution margin for the current year and the projected year, and (2) the fixed costs for the current year. (Assume that fixed costs will remain the same in the projected year.)

(b) Compute the break-even point in units and sales dollars.

(c) The company has a target net income of $310,000. What is the required sales in dollars for the company to meet its target?

(d) If the company meets its target net income number, by what percentage could its sales fall before it is operating at a loss? That is, what is its margin of safety ratio?

(e) The company is considering a purchase of equipment that would reduce its direct labor costs by $104,000 and would change its manufacturing overhead costs to 30% variable and 70% fixed (assume total manufacturing overhead cost is $360,000, as above). It is also considering switching to a pure commission basis for its sales staff. This would change selling expenses to 90% variable and 10% fixed (assume total selling expense is $240,000, as above). Compute (1) the contribution margin and (2) the contribution margin ratio, and recompute (3) the break-even point in sales dollars. Comment on the effect each of management's proposed changes has on the break-even point.

Problems: Set B

Determine variable and fixed costs, compute break-even point, prepare a CVP graph, and determine net income.
(SO 1, 3, 5, 6)

P18-1B Hung Van owns the College Barber Shop. He employs five barbers and pays each a base rate of $1,200 per month. One of the barbers serves as the manager and receives an extra $600 per month. In addition to the base rate, each barber also receives a commission of $3.50 per haircut.

Other costs are as follows.

Advertising	$200 per month
Rent	$1,000 per month
Barber supplies	$0.30 per haircut
Utilities	$175 per month plus $0.20 per haircut
Magazines	$25 per month

Hung currently charges $12 per haircut.

Instructions

(a) Determine the variable cost per haircut and the total monthly fixed costs.

(b) Compute the break-even point in (1) units and (2) dollars.

(c) Prepare a CVP graph, assuming a maximum of 2,000 haircuts in a month. Use increments of 400 haircuts on the horizontal axis and $4,000 on the vertical axis.

(d) Determine net income, assuming 1,500 haircuts are given in a month.

Prepare a CVP income statement, compute break-even point, contribution margin ratio, margin of safety ratio, and sales for target net income.
(SO 5, 6, 7, 8)

P18-2B Corbin Company bottles and distributes NO-KAL, a diet soft drink. The beverage is sold for 40 cents per 16-ounce bottle to retailers, who charge customers 60 cents per bottle. Management estimates the following revenues and costs.

Net sales	$1,500,000	Selling expenses—variable	$80,000
Direct materials	400,000	Selling expenses—fixed	65,000
Direct labor	250,000	Administrative expenses—	
Manufacturing overhead—		variable	20,000
variable	300,000	Administrative expenses—	
Manufacturing overhead—		fixed	52,000
fixed	93,000		

Instructions

(a) Compute (1) the contribution margin and (2) the fixed costs.

(b) Compute the break-even point in (1) units and (2) dollars.

(c) Compute the contribution margin ratio and the margin of safety ratio. (Round to full percents.)

(d) Determine the sales dollars required to earn net income of $120,000.

Compute break-even point under alternative courses of action.
(SO 5, 6)

P18-3B Griffey Manufacturing's sales slumped badly in 2007. For the first time in its history, it operated at a loss. The company's income statement showed the following results from selling 500,000 units of product: Net sales $2,500,000; total costs and expenses $2,600,000; and net loss $100,000. Costs and expenses consisted of the following.

	Total	Variable	Fixed
Cost of goods sold	$2,100,000	$1,440,000	$ 660,000
Selling expenses	300,000	72,000	228,000
Administrative expenses	200,000	48,000	152,000
	$2,600,000	$1,560,000	$1,040,000

Management is considering the following independent alternatives for 2008.

1. Increase unit selling price 20% with no change in costs and expenses.
2. Change the compensation of salespersons from fixed annual salaries totaling $210,000 to total salaries of $70,000 plus a 4% commission on net sales.
3. Purchase new automated equipment that will change the proportion between variable and fixed cost of goods sold to 60% variable and 40% fixed.

Instructions
(a) Compute the break-even point in dollars for 2007.
(b) Compute the break-even point in dollars under each of the alternative courses of action. (Round to the nearest dollar.) Which course of action do you recommend?

(b) (1) $2,166,667

P18-4B Barb Tsai is the advertising manager for Thrifty Shoe Store. She is currently working on a major promotional campaign. Her ideas include the installation of a new lighting system and increased display space that will add $25,000 in fixed costs to the $300,000 currently spent. In addition, Barb is proposing that a 5% price decrease ($40 to $38) will produce a 20% increase in sales volume (30,000 to 36,000). Variable costs will remain at $25 per pair of shoes. Management is impressed with Barb's ideas but concerned about the effects that these changes will have on the break-even point and the margin of safety.

Compute break-even point and margin of safety ratio, and prepare a CVP income statement before and after changes in business environment.
(SO 5, 6)

Instructions
(a) Compute the current break-even point in units, and compare it to the break-even point in units if Barb's ideas are used.
(b) Compute the margin of safety ratio for current operations and after Barb's changes are introduced. (Round to nearest full percent.)
(c) Prepare a CVP income statement for current operations and after Barb's changes are introduced. Would you make the changes suggested?

(b) current 33%
new 31%

P18-5B Washington Corporation has collected the following information after its first year of sales. Net sales were $2,400,000 on 200,000 units; selling expenses $360,000 (30% variable and 70% fixed); direct materials $626,500; direct labor $507,500; administrative expenses $420,000 (40% variable and 60% fixed); manufacturing overhead $540,000 (50% variable and 50% fixed). Top management has asked you to do a CVP analysis so that it can make plans for the coming year. It has projected that unit sales will increase by 20% next year.

Compute break-even point and margin of safety ratio, and prepare a CVP income statement before and after changes in business environment.
(SO 5, 6, 7, 8)

Instructions
(a) Compute (1) the contribution margin for the current year and the projected year, and (2) the fixed costs for the current year. (Assume that fixed costs will remain the same in the projected year.)
(b) Compute the break-even point in units and sales dollars.
(c) The company has a target net income of $620,000. What is the required sales in dollars for the company to meet its target?
(d) If the company meets its target net income number, by what percentage could its sales fall before it is operating at a loss? That is, what is its margin of safety ratio?
(e) The company is considering a purchase of equipment that would reduce its direct labor costs by $240,000 and would change its manufacturing overhead costs to 30% variable and 70% fixed (assume total manufacturing overhead cost is $540,000, as above). It is also considering switching to a pure commission basis for its sales staff. This would change selling expenses to 80% variable and 20% fixed (assume total selling expense is $360,000, as above). Compute (1) the contribution margin and (2) the contribution margin ratio, and recompute (3) the break-even point in sales dollars. Comment on the effect each of management's proposed changes has on the break-even point.

(b) 215,000 units

(e) (3) $1,897,297

Problems: Set C

Visit the book's website at **www.wiley.com/college/kimmel** and choose the Student Companion site to access Problem Set C.

BROADENING YOUR PERSPECTIVE

Group Decision Case

BYP18-1   Clay Company has decided to introduce a new product. The new product can be manufactured by either a capital-intensive method or a labor-intensive method. The manufacturing method will not affect the quality of the product. The estimated manufacturing costs by the two methods are as follows.

	Capital-Intensive	Labor-Intensive
Direct materials	$5 per unit	$5.50 per unit
Direct labor	$6 per unit	$7.20 per unit
Variable overhead	$3 per unit	$4.80 per unit
Fixed manufacturing costs	$2,440,000	$1,390,000

Clay's market research department has recommended an introductory unit sales price of $30. The incremental selling expenses are estimated to be $500,000 annually plus $2 for each unit sold, regardless of manufacturing method.

Instructions
With the class divided into groups, answer the following.
(a) Calculate the estimated break-even point in annual unit sales of the new product if Clay Company uses the:
   (1) capital-intensive manufacturing method.
   (2) labor-intensive manufacturing method.
(b) Determine the annual unit sales volume at which Clay Company would be indifferent between the two manufacturing methods.
(c) Explain the circumstance under which Clay should employ each of the two manufacturing methods.

(CMA adapted)

Managerial Analysis

BYP18-2   The condensed income statement for the Phan and Nguyen partnership for 2007 is as follows.

PHAN AND NGUYEN COMPANY
Income Statement
For the Year Ended December 31, 2007

Sales (200,000 units)		$1,200,000
Cost of goods sold		800,000
Gross profit		400,000
Operating expenses		
Selling	$320,000	
Administrative	160,000	480,000
Net loss		($80,000)

A cost behavior analysis indicates that 75% of the cost of goods sold are variable, 50% of the selling expenses are variable, and 25% of the administrative expenses are variable.

Instructions
(Round to nearest unit, dollar, and percentage, where necessary.)
(a) Compute the break-even point in units and in total sales dollars for 2007.
(b) Phan has proposed a plan to get the partnership "out of the red" and improve its profitability. She feels that the quality of the product could be substantially improved by spending $0.55 more per unit on better raw materials. The selling price per unit could be increased to only $6.50 because of competitive pressures. Phan estimates that sales volume will increase by 30%. What effect would Phan's plan have on the profits and the break-even point in dollars of the partnership?
(c) Nguyen was a marketing major in college. He believes that sales volume can be increased only by intensive advertising and promotional campaigns. He therefore proposed the following plan as an alternative to Phan's. (1) Increase variable selling expenses to $0.85 per unit, (2) lower the selling price per unit by $0.20, and (3) increase fixed selling expenses by $20,000. Nguyen quoted an old marketing research report that said that sales volume would increase by 50% if these changes were made. What effect would Nguyen's plan have on the profits and the break-even point in dollars of the partnership?
(d) Which plan should be accepted? Explain your answer.

Real-World Focus

BYP18-3 The Coca-Cola Company hardly needs an introduction. A line taken from the cover of a recent annual report says it all: If you measured time in servings of Coca-Cola, "a billion Coca-Cola's ago was yesterday morning." On average, every U.S. citizen drinks 363 8-ounce servings of Coca-Cola products each year. Coca-Cola's primary line of business is the making and selling of syrup to bottlers. These bottlers then sell the finished bottles and cans of Coca-Cola to the consumer.

In the annual report of Coca-Cola, the following information was provided.

THE COCA-COLA COMPANY
Management Discussion

Our gross margin declined to 61 percent this year from 62 percent in the prior year, primarily due to costs for materials such as sweeteners and packaging.

The increases [in selling expenses] in the last two years were primarily due to higher marketing expenditures in support of our Company's volume growth.

We measure our sales volume in two ways: (1) gallon shipments of concentrates and syrups and (2) unit cases of finished product (bottles and cans of Coke sold by bottlers).

Instructions
Answer the following questions.
(a) Are sweeteners and packaging a variable cost or a fixed cost? What is the impact on the contribution margin of an increase in the per unit cost of sweeteners or packaging? What are the implications for profitability?
(b) In your opinion, are marketing expenditures a fixed cost, variable cost, or mixed cost to The Coca-Cola Company? Give justification for your answer.
(c) Which of the two measures cited for measuring volume represents the activity index as defined in this chapter? Why might Coca-Cola use two different measures?

Exploring the Web

BYP18-4   Ganong Bros. Ltd., located in St. Stephen, New Brunswick, is Canada's oldest independent candy company. Its products are distributed worldwide. In 1885, Ganong invented the popular "chicken bone," a cinnamon flavored, pink, hard candy jacket over a chocolate center. The home page of Ganong, listed below, includes information about the company and its products.

Address: **www.ganong.com/index.cfm?section=3&page=10**
            (*or go to* **www.wiley.com/college/kimmel**)

Instructions
Read the description of "chicken bones," and answer the following.
(a) Describe the steps in making "chicken bones."
(b) Identify at least two variable and two fixed costs that are likely to affect the production of "chicken bones."

Communication Activity

BYP18-5   Your roommate asks your help on the following questions about CVP analysis formulas.
(a) How can the mathematical equation for break-even sales show both sales units and sales dollars?
(b) How do the formulas differ for contribution margin per unit and contribution margin ratio?
(c) How can contribution margin be used to determine break-even sales in units and in dollars?

Instructions
Write a memo to your roommate stating the relevant formulas and answering each question.

Research Assignment

BYP18-6   The June 2, 2003, issue of the *Wall Street Journal* includes an article by Anna Wilde Mathews and Jennifer Ordonez titled "Clear Channel Revamps Its Concert Strategy."

Instructions
Read the article and answer the following questions.
(a) The article notes that Clear Channel cut performer Peter Gabriel's upfront per concert fee in half (from $600,000 down to approximately $300,000). Discuss the impact this change would have on the company's cost structure.
(b) Clear Channel also cut the average ticket price of the Peter Gabriel shows from $91 to $43. This will increase the number of tickets the company must sell to break-even. Why might it be desirable for Clear Channel to lower its ticket price?
(c) Clear Channel owns many of the arenas and amphitheatres that it books concerts in. How does this impact its cost structure and its corporate strategy?
(d) Why did Clear Channel choose not to book some "big-name" acts in the current year that it did book in the past?

Ethics Case

BYP18-7   Ronnie Drake is an accountant for Benson Company. Early this year Ronnie made a highly favorable projection of sales and profits over the next 3 years for Benson's hot-selling computer PLEX. As a result of the projections Ronnie presented to senior management, they decided to expand production in this area. This decision led to dislocations of some plant personnel who were reassigned to one of the company's newer plants in another state. However, no one was fired, and in fact the company expanded its work force slightly.

Unfortunately, Ronnie rechecked his computations on the projections a few months later and found that he had made an error that would have reduced his projections substantially. Luckily, sales of PLEX have exceeded projections so far, and management is satisfied with its decision. Ronnie, however, is not sure what to do. Should he confess his honest mistake and jeopardize his possible promotion? He suspects that no one will catch the error because sales of PLEX have exceeded his projections, and it appears that profits will materialize close to his projections.

Instructions

(a) Who are the stakeholders in this situation?

(b) Identify the ethical issues involved in this situation.

(c) What are the possible alternative actions for Ronnie? What would you do in Ronnie's position?

Answers to Self-Study Questions

1. d   2. c   3. a   4. a   5. c   6. d   7. a   8. c   9. b   10. b

REMEMBER TO GO BACK TO THE NAVIGATOR BOX ON THE CHAPTER-OPENING PAGE AND CHECK OFF YOUR COMPLETED WORK.

CHAPTER 19

Variable Costing: A Decision-Making Perspective

STUDY OBJECTIVES

After studying this chapter,
you should be able to:

1 Explain the difference between absorption costing and variable costing.

2 Discuss the effect that changes in production level and sales level have on net income measured under absorption costing versus variable costing.

3 Discuss the relative merits of absorption costing versus variable costing for management decision making.

4 Explain the term sales mix and its effects on break-even sales.

5 Understand how operating leverage affects profitability.

 THE NAVIGATOR

☑ THE NAVIGATOR

- ● Scan *Study Objectives*
- ● Read *Feature Story*
- ● Read *Preview*
- ● Read text and answer *Before You Go On*
  p. 942 ⬭   p. 946 ⬭   p. 949 ⬭
- ● Work *Using the Decision Toolkit*
- ● Review *Summary of Study Objectives*
- ● Work *Demonstration Problem*
- ● Answer *Self-Study Questions*
- ● Complete *Assignments*

FEATURE STORY

What Goes Up (*fast*), Must Come Down (*fast*)

During the late 1990s many people marveled at the efficiency of the so-called "New Economy," which uses digital technologies to improve business processes. Some managers were actually startled by their own success. The New Economy had created a new formula for profit. For example, David Peterschmidt, chief executive at software developer Inktomi, noted that the company had incurred considerable fixed costs in developing new software, but its variable costs were minor. As a consequence, once sales had covered the fixed costs, every additional sale was basically pure profit. When sales were booming, he happily stated, "Next to the federal government, this is the only business that's allowed to print money." But that was then. When the economy lagged, the new profit formula went sour. The company's sales disappeared, but its fixed costs did not. In no time, Inktomi went from record profits to staggering losses.

Many other companies have had similar experiences. As their manufacturing plants have become more automated, their fixed costs have become increasingly high. For example, during a 5-year period, the average cost of a typical Intel semiconductor plant rose from $500 million to $2 billion as its manufacturing processes became increasingly sophisticated.

These high fixed costs have made Intel very dependent on producing a high volume of computer chips. It needs high volume so that it can spread its fixed costs across a lot of units, thereby reducing the fixed cost per unit. As one Intel employee put it, "You have high fixed costs, so you want to minimize those fixed costs and keep factories running 24 hours a day."

However, when management focuses too heavily on keeping volume high to reduce fixed costs per unit, it sometimes produces more inventory than the market wants. When this happens, companies have to cut prices sharply. High-tech firms, like Intel, whose products become rapidly obsolete, have occasionally been stuck with inventory that nobody wanted. Thus, while the huge outlays for new equipment have made these companies exceptionally efficient, such outlays have also increased their exposure to economic swings. In fact, because so many companies now have cost structures that rely heavily on fixed costs, many economists worry that swings in the entire economy will be more volatile than in the past.

Source: Greg Ip, "As Profits Swoon, Companies Blame A Marked Change in Cost Structure," *Wall Street Journal Online* (May 16, 2001).

PREVIEW OF CHAPTER 19

As the Feature Story about Inktomi and Intel suggests, the relationship between a company's fixed and variable costs can have a huge impact on its profitability. In particular, the trend toward cost structures dominated by fixed costs has significantly increased the volatility of many companies' net income. In order to better track and understand the impact of cost structure on corporate profitability, some companies use an approach called *variable costing*. The purpose of this chapter is to show how variable costing can be helpful in making sound business decisions. The content and organization of this chapter are as follows.

Absorption Costing versus Variable Costing

STUDY OBJECTIVE

1

Explain the difference between absorption costing and variable costing.

In the earlier chapters, both variable and fixed manufacturing costs were classified as product costs. In job order costing, for example, a job is assigned the costs of direct materials, direct labor, and **both** variable and fixed manufacturing overhead. This costing approach is referred to as **full** or **absorption costing**. It is so named because all manufacturing costs are charged to, or absorbed by, the product. Absorption costing is the approach used for external reporting under generally accepted accounting principles.

An alternative approach is to use variable costing. Under **variable costing**, only direct materials, direct labor, and variable manufacturing overhead costs are considered product costs. Fixed manufacturing overhead costs are recognized as period costs (expenses) when incurred. The difference between absorption costing and variable costing is graphically shown as follows.

Illustration 19-1   Difference between absorption costing and variable costing

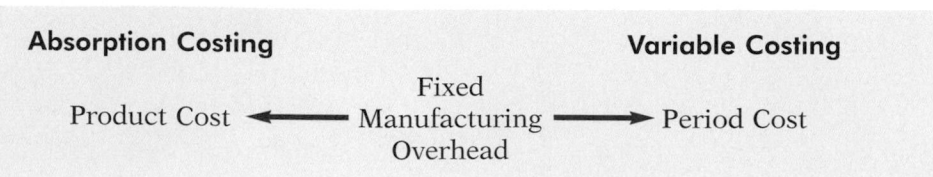

Selling and administrative expenses are period costs under both absorption and variable costing.

Variable costing may not be used for external financial reports because generally accepted accounting principles require that fixed manufacturing overhead be accounted for as a product cost.

ILLUSTRATION COMPARING ABSORPTION COSTING AND VARIABLE COSTING

To illustrate absorption and variable costing, assume that Premium Products Corporation manufactures a polyurethane sealant, called Fix-it, for car windshields. Relevant data for Fix-it in January 2007, the first month of production, are as follows.

Selling price	$20 per unit.
Units	Produced 30,000; sold 20,000; beginning inventory zero.
Variable unit costs	Manufacturing $9 (direct materials $5, direct labor $3, and variable overhead $1).
	Selling and administrative expenses $2.
Fixed costs	Manufacturing overhead $120,000.
	Selling and administrative expenses $15,000.

Illustration 19-2   Sealant sales and cost data for Premium Products Corporation

The per unit manufacturing cost under each costing approach is computed in Illustration 19-3.

Type of Cost	Absorption Costing	Variable Costing
Direct materials	$ 5	$5
Direct labor	3	3
Variable manufacturing overhead	1	1
Fixed manufacturing overhead **($120,000 ÷ 30,000 units produced)**	4	0
Manufacturing cost per unit	**$13**	**$9**

Illustration 19-3   Computation of per unit manufacturing cost

The manufacturing cost per unit is $4 ($13 − $9) higher for absorption costing. This occurs because fixed manufacturing overhead costs are a product cost under absorption costing. Under variable costing, they are, instead, a period cost, and so they are expensed. Based on these data, each unit sold and each unit remaining in inventory is costed at $13 under absorption costing and at $9 under variable costing.

Absorption Costing Illustration

The income statement for Premium Products using absorption costing is shown in Illustration 19-4 (page 934). It shows that cost of goods manufactured is $390,000, computed by multiplying the 30,000 units produced times the manufacturing cost per unit of $13 (see Illustration 19-3). Cost of goods sold is $260,000, after subtracting ending inventory of $130,000. Under absorption costing, $40,000 (10,000 units × $4) of the fixed overhead is deferred to a future period as part of the cost of ending inventory.

PREMIUM PRODUCTS CORPORATION
Income Statement
For the Month Ended January 31, 2007
Absorption Costing

Sales (20,000 units × $20)		$400,000
Cost of goods sold		
Inventory, January 1	$ –0–	
Cost of goods manufactured (30,000 units × $13)	390,000	
Cost of goods available for sale	390,000	
Inventory, January 31 (10,000 units × $13)	**130,000**	
Cost of goods sold (20,000 units × $13)		260,000
Gross profit		140,000
Variable selling and administrative expenses		
(20,000 × $2)	40,000	
Fixed selling and administrative expenses	15,000	55,000
Net income		**$ 85,000**

Variable Costing Illustration

As shown in Illustration 19-5, the cost–volume–profit format is used in preparing a variable costing income statement. The variable manufacturing cost of $270,000 is computed by multiplying the 30,000 units produced times variable manufacturing cost of $9 per unit (see Illustration 19-3). As in absorption costing, both variable and fixed selling and administrative expenses are treated as period costs.

PREMIUM PRODUCTS CORPORATION
Income Statement
For the Month Ended January 31, 2007
Variable Costing

Sales (20,000 units × $20)		$400,000
Variable cost of goods sold		
Inventory, January 1	$ –0–	
Variable cost of goods manufactured		
(30,000 units × $9)	270,000	
Variable cost of goods available for sale	270,000	
Inventory, January 31 (10,000 units × $9)	**90,000**	
Variable cost of goods sold	180,000	
Variable selling and administrative expenses		
(20,000 units × $2)	40,000	220,000
Contribution margin		180,000
Fixed manufacturing overhead	120,000	
Fixed selling and administrative expenses	15,000	135,000
Net income		**$ 45,000**

There is one primary difference between variable and absorption costing: Under variable costing, the fixed manufacturing overhead is charged as an expense in the current period. Fixed manufacturing overhead costs of the current period, therefore, are not deferred to future periods through the ending inventory. As a result, absorption costing will show a higher net income number than variable costing whenever units produced exceed units sold. This difference can be seen in the income statements in Illustrations 19-4 and 19-5. There is a $40,000 difference in the ending inventories ($130,000 under absorption costing versus $90,000 under variable costing). Under absorption costing, $40,000 of the fixed overhead costs (10,000 units × $4) has been deferred to a future period as part of inventory. In contrast, under variable costing, all fixed manufacturing costs are expensed in the current period.

As shown, when units produced exceed units sold, income under absorption costing is **higher**. When units produced are less than units sold, income under absorption costing is **lower**. When units produced and sold are the same, net income will be **equal** under the two costing approaches. In this case, there is no increase in ending inventory. So fixed overhead costs of the current period are not deferred to future periods through the ending inventory.

AN EXTENDED EXAMPLE

To further illustrate the concepts underlying absorption and variable costing, an extended example using Overbay Inc., a manufacturer of small airplane drones, is provided below. We assume that production volume stays the same each year over the three-year period, but the number of units sold varies each year.

STUDY OBJECTIVE

2

Discuss the effect that changes in production level and sales level have on net income measured under absorption costing versus variable costing.

2007 Results

As indicated in Illustration 19-6 below, the variable manufacturing cost per drone is $240,000, and the fixed manufacturing cost per drone is $60,000. Total manufacturing cost per drone is therefore $300,000 ($240,000 + $60,000). Overbay also has variable selling and administrative expenses of $5,000 per drone, or $50,000 per year ($5,000 × 10 drones sold). The fixed selling and administrative expenses are $80,000.

	2007	2008	2009
Volume information			
Drones in beginning inventory	0	0	2
Drones produced	10	10	10
Drones sold	10	8	12
Drones in ending inventory	0	2	0
Financial information			
Selling price per drone	$400,000		
Variable manufacturing cost per drone	$240,000		
Fixed manufacturing overhead for the year	$600,000		
Fixed manufacturing overhead per drone	$60,000 ($600,000 ÷ 10)		
Variable selling and administrative expenses per drone	$5,000		
Fixed selling and administrative expenses	$80,000		

Illustration 19-6   Information for Overbay Inc.

An absorption costing income statement for 2007 for Overbay Inc. is shown in Illustration 19-7.

Illustration 19-7   Absorption costing income statement—2007

OVERBAY INC.
Income Statement
For the Year Ended 2007
Absorption Costing

Sales (10 drones × $400,000)		$4,000,000
Cost of goods sold (10 drones × $300,000)		3,000,000
Gross profit		1,000,000
Variable selling and administrative expenses (10 drones × $5,000)	$50,000	
Fixed selling and administrative expenses	80,000	130,000
Net income		$ 870,000

Overbay reports net income of $870,000 under absorption costing.

Under a variable costing system the income statement follows a cost–volume–profit (CVP) format. In this case, the manufacturing cost is comprised solely of the variable manufacturing costs of $240,000 per drone. The fixed manufacturing costs of $600,000 for the year are expensed in 2007. As in absorption costing, the fixed and variable selling and administrative expenses are period costs expensed in 2007. A variable costing income statement for Overbay Inc. for 2007 is shown in Illustration 19-8.

Illustration 19-8 Variable costing income statement—2007

OVERBAY INC. Income Statement For the Year Ended 2007 Variable Costing		
Sales (10 drones × $400,000)		$4,000,000
Variable cost of goods sold (10 drones × $240,000)	$2,400,000	
Variable selling and administrative expenses (10 drones × $5,000)	50,000	2,450,000
Contribution margin		1,550,000
Fixed manufacturing overhead	600,000	
Fixed selling and administrative expenses	80,000	680,000
Net income		$ 870,000

As shown in Illustration 19-8, the variable costing net income of $870,000 is the same as the absorption costing net income computed in Illustration 19-7. **When the numbers of units produced and sold are the same, net income is equal under the two costing approaches.** Because no increase in ending inventory occurs, no fixed manufacturing overhead costs incurred in 2007 are deferred to future periods using absorption costing.

2008 Results

In 2008, Overbay produced ten drones but sold only eight drones. As a result, there are two drones in ending inventory. The absorption costing income statement for 2008 is shown in Illustration 19-9.

Illustration 19-9 Absorption costing income statement—2008

OVERBAY INC. Income Statement For the Year Ended 2008 Absorption Costing		
Sales (8 drones × $400,000)		$3,200,000
Cost of goods sold (8 drones × $300,000)		2,400,000
Gross profit		800,000
Variable selling and administrative expenses (8 drones × $5,000)	$40,000	
Fixed selling and administrative expenses	80,000	120,000
Net income		$ 680,000

Under absorption costing, the ending inventory of two drones is $600,000 ($300,000 × 2). Each unit of ending inventory includes $60,000 of fixed manufacturing overhead. Therefore, fixed manufacturing overhead costs of $120,000 ($60,000 × 2 drones) are deferred until a future period.

The variable costing income statement for 2008 is shown in Illustration 19-10.

Illustration 19-10   Variable costing income statement—2008

OVERBAY INC.
Income Statement
For the Year Ended 2008
Variable Costing

Sales (8 drones × $400,000)		$3,200,000
Variable cost of goods sold (8 drones × $240,000)	$1,920,000	
Variable selling and administrative expenses (8 drones × $5,000)	40,000	1,960,000
Contribution margin		1,240,000
Fixed manufacturing overhead	600,000	
Fixed selling and administrative expenses	80,000	680,000
Net income		$ 560,000

As shown, when units produced (10) exceeds units sold (8), net income under absorption costing ($680,000) is higher than net income under variable costing ($560,000). The reason: The cost of the ending inventory is higher under absorption costing than under variable costing. In 2008, under absorption costing, fixed manufacturing overhead of $120,000 is deferred and carried to future periods as part of inventory. Under variable costing, the $120,000 is expensed in the current period and, therefore the difference in the two net income numbers is $120,000 ($680,000 − $560,000).

2009 Results

In 2009, Overbay produced ten drones and sold twelve (10 drones from the current year's production and 2 drones from the beginning inventory). As a result, there are no drones in ending inventory. The absorption costing income statement for 2009 is shown in Illustration 19-11.

Illustration 19-11   Absorption costing income statement—2009

OVERBAY INC.
Income Statement
For the Year Ended 2009
Absorption Costing

Sales (12 drones × $400,000)		$4,800,000
Cost of goods sold (12 drones × $300,000)		3,600,000
Gross profit		1,200,000
Variable selling and administrative expenses (12 drones × $5,000)	$60,000	
Fixed selling and administrative expenses	80,000	140,000
Net income		$1,060,000

Fixed manufacturing costs of $720,000 are expensed as part of cost of goods sold in 2009. This $720,000 includes $120,000 of fixed manufacturing costs incurred during 2008 and included in beginning inventory, plus $600,000 of fixed manufacturing costs incurred during 2009. Given this result for the absorption costing statement, what would you now expect the result to be under variable costing? Let's take a look.

The variable costing income statement for 2009 is shown in Illustration 19-12.

Illustration 19-12 Variable costing income statement—2009

OVERBAY INC.
Income Statement
For the Year Ended 2009
Variable Costing

Sales (12 drones × $400,000)		$4,800,000
Variable cost of goods sold		
(12 drones × $240,000)	$2,880,000	
Variable selling and administrative expenses		
(12 drones × $5,000)	60,000	2,940,000
Contribution margin		1,860,000
Fixed manufacturing overhead	600,000	
Fixed selling and administrative expenses	80,000	680,000
Net income		$1,180,000

When Drones produced (10) are less than Drones sold (12), net income under absorption costing ($1,060,000) is less than net income under variable costing ($1,180,000). This difference of $120,000 ($1,180,000 − $1,060,000) results because $120,000 of fixed manufacturing overhead costs in beginning inventory are charged to 2009 under absorption costing. Under variable costing, there is no fixed manufacturing overhead cost in beginning inventory.

The results of the three years are summarized in Illustration 19-13.

Illustration 19-13 Comparison of net income under two costing approaches

	Net Income under Two Costing Approaches		
	2007	**2008**	**2009**
	Production = Sales	**Production > Sales**	**Production < Sales**
Absorption costing	$ 870,000	$ 680,000	$1,060,000
Variable costing	870,000	560,000	1,180,000
Difference	$ –0–	$120,000	$(120,000)

This relationship between production and sales and its effect on net income under the two costing approaches is shown graphically in Illustration 19-14.

Illustration 19-14 Summary of income effects under absorption costing and variable costing

DECISION-MAKING CONCERNS

Generally accepted accounting principles (GAAP) requires that absorption costing be used for the costing of inventory for external reporting purposes. Net income measured under GAAP (absorption costing) is often used internally to evaluate performance, justify cost reductions, or evaluate new projects. Some companies, however, have recognized that net income calculated using GAAP does not highlight differences between variable and fixed costs and may lead to poor business decisions. Consequently, these companies use variable costing for internal reporting purposes. The following discussion and example highlight a significant problem related to the use of absorption costing for decision-making purposes.

When production exceeds sales, absorption costing reports a higher net income than variable costing. The reason is that some fixed manufacturing costs are not expensed in the current period, but are deferred to future periods as part of inventory. As a result, management may be tempted to overproduce in a given period in order to increase net income. Although net income will increase, this decision to overproduce may not be in the company's best interest.

Suppose, for example, a division manager's compensation is based upon the division's net income. In such a case the manager may decide to meet the net income targets by increasing production. While this overproduction may increase the manager's compensation, the buildup of inventories in the long run will lead to additional costs to the company. This situation is avoided under variable costing, because net income under variable costing is unaffected by changes in production levels. This is shown in the following illustration.

Warren Lund, a division manager of Walker Enterprises, is under pressure to boost the performance of the Lighting Division in 2007. Unfortunately, recent profits have not met expectations. The expected sales for this year are 20,000 units. As he plans for the year, Warren has to decide whether to produce 20,000 or 30,000 units. The following facts are available for the division.

STUDY OBJECTIVE

3

Discuss the relative merits of absorption costing versus variable costing for management decision making.

Beginning inventory	0
Expected sales in units	20,000
Selling price per unit	$15
Variable manufacturing cost per unit	$6
Fixed manufacturing overhead cost (total)	$60,000
Fixed manufacturing overhead costs per unit	
Based on 20,000 units	$3 per unit ($60,000 ÷ 20,000 units)
Based on 30,000 units	$2 per unit ($60,000 ÷ 30,000 units)
Total manufacturing cost per unit	
Based on 20,000 units	$9 per unit ($6 variable + $3 fixed)
Based on 30,000 units	$8 per unit ($6 variable + $2 fixed)
Variable selling and administrative expenses per unit	$1
Fixed selling and administrative expenses	$15,000

Illustration 19-15   Facts for Lighting Division—2007

The division's results based upon the two possible levels of output are presented in Illustration 19-16 (page 940) under absorption costing.

If the Lighting Division produces 20,000 units, its net income under absorption costing is $85,000. If it produces 30,000 units, its net income is $105,000. By producing 30,000 units, the division has inventory of 10,000 units. This excess inventory causes net income to increase $20,000 because $20,000 of fixed costs (10,000 units × $2) are not charged to the current year, but are deferred to future periods. What do you think Warren Lund might do in this situation? Given his concern about the profit numbers of the Lighting Division, he may be tempted to increase production. Although this increased production will increase 2007 net income, it may be costly to the company in the long run.

Illustration 19-16 Absorption costing income statement—2007

LIGHTING DIVISION Income Statement For the Year Ended 2007 Absorption Costing	20,000 Produced	30,000 Produced
Sales (20,000 units × $15)	$300,000	$ 300,000
Cost of goods sold	180,000*	160,000**
Gross profit	120,000	140,000
Variable selling and administrative expenses (20,000 units × $1)	20,000	20,000
Fixed selling and administrative expenses	15,000	15,000
Net income	$ 85,000	$105,000

*(20,000 units × $9)
**(20,000 units × $8)

Now let's evaluate the same situation under variable costing. A variable costing income statement is shown for production at both 20,000 and 30,000 units, using the information in Illustration 19-15.

Illustration 19-17 Variable costing income statement—2007

LIGHTING DIVISION Income Statement For the Year Ended 2007 Variable Costing	20,000 Produced	30,000 Produced
Sales (20,000 units × $15)	$300,000	$300,000
Variable cost of goods sold (20,000 units × $6)	120,000	120,000
Variable selling and administrative expenses (20,000 units × $1)	20,000	20,000
Contribution margin	160,000	160,000
Fixed manufacturing overhead	60,000	60,000
Fixed selling and administrative expenses	15,000	15,000
Net income	$ 85,000	$ 85,000

From this example we see that under variable costing, net income is not affected by the number of units produced. Net income is $85,000 whether 20,000 or 30,000 units are produced. Why? Because fixed manufacturing overhead is treated as a period expense. Unlike absorption costing, no fixed manufacturing overhead is deferred through inventory buildup. Therefore, under variable costing, production does not increase income; sales do. As a result, managers like Warren Lund cannot affect profitability by increasing production if variable costing is used.

POTENTIAL ADVANTAGES OF VARIABLE COSTING

Variable costing has a number of potential advantages relative to absorption costing:

1. Net income computed under variable costing is unaffected by changes in production levels. As a result, it is much easier to understand the impact of fixed and variable costs on the computation of net income when variable costing is used.

2. The use of variable costing is consistent with the cost–volume–profit material presented in Chapter 18 and the incremental analysis material presented in Chapter 23. Later in this chapter you will see other situations where the variable costing approach would be beneficial.

3. Net income computed under variable costing is closely tied to changes in sales levels (not production levels), and therefore provides a more realistic assessment of the company's success or failure during a period.

4. The presentation of fixed and variable cost components on the face of the variable costing income statement makes it easier to identify these costs and understand their effect on the business. Under absorption costing, the allocation of fixed costs to inventory makes it difficult to evaluate the impact of fixed costs on the company's results.

Companies that use just-in-time processing techniques to minimize their inventories will not have significant differences between absorption and variable costing net income.

Accounting across the Organization

Although most service companies don't have inventory, the distinction between absorption costing and variable costing is still relevant to them. For example, many shipping companies have begun to rely more heavily on variable costing for decision making, especially for pricing decisions. For shipping companies, the problems with absorption costing become most apparent when operations are below full capacity. If they set their price based on absorption cost, they will spread their full fixed costs over their existing jobs—resulting in a high fixed cost charge per shipment. This will make their price too high relative to competitors, and they will lose business—thus operating even further below capacity, and consequently charging an even higher fixed charge per job. This cycle continues until they are out of business. If, instead, they set their prices using variable costing, they can avoid this dangerous cycle.

Decision Toolkit

Decision Checkpoints	Info Needed for Decision	Tool to Use for Decision	How to Evaluate Results
What is the company's composition of fixed versus variable costs?	Variable cost of goods sold; variable selling and administrative expenses, fixed manufacturing overhead, fixed selling and administrative expenses	**Variable costing income statement** Sales Less: Variable cost of goods sold Variable selling and administrative expenses Contribution margin Less: Fixed manufacturing overhead Fixed selling and administrative expenses Net income	Variable costing income statement provides information about variable and fixed costs that is needed for CVP analysis and incremental analysis.

BEFORE YOU GO ON . . .

►Review It

1. What is the primary distinction between absorption costing and variable costing?
2. Explain how a difference between the amount produced and amount sold creates a difference between net income under absorption costing and net income under variable costing.
3. What are the potential advantages of variable costing for decision making?

►Do It

Justin and Andrea Doll Company produces and sells tennis balls. The following costs are available for the year ended December 31, 2007. The company has no beginning inventory. In 2007, 8,000,000 units were produced, but only 7,500,000 units were sold. The unit selling price was $0.50 per ball. Costs and expenses were:

Variable costs per unit	
Direct materials	$0.10
Direct labor	0.05
Variable manufacturing overhead	0.08
Variable selling and administrative expenses	0.02
Annual fixed costs and expenses	
Manufacturing overhead	$500,000
Selling and administrative expenses	100,000

(a) Compute the manufacturing cost of one unit of product using variable costing. (b) Prepare a 2007 income statement for Justin and Andrea Doll Company using variable costing.

Action Plan

• Recall that under variable costing, only variable manufacturing costs are treated as manufacturing (product) costs.
• Subtract all fixed costs, both manufacturing overhead and selling and administrative expenses, as period costs.

Solution

(a) The cost of one unit of product under variable costing would be:

Direct materials	$0.10
Direct labor	0.05
Variable manufacturing overhead	0.08
	$0.23

(b) The variable costing income statement would be as follows.

JUSTIN AND ANDREA DOLL COMPANY
Income Statement
For the Year Ended December 31, 2007
Variable Costing

Sales (7,500,000 × $0.50)		$3,750,000
Variable cost of goods sold (7,500,000 × $0.23)	$1,725,000	
Variable selling and administrative expenses	150,000	1,875,000
Contribution margin		1,875,000
Fixed manufacturing overhead	500,000	
Fixed selling and administrative expenses	100,000	600,000
Net income		$1,275,000

Related exercise material: BE19-1, BE19-3, BE19-5, BE19-6, BE19-8, E19-1, E19-2, E19-3, and E19-4.

Sales Mix

The information provided by a variable costing income statement is very useful for management decision making. One of the most important considerations a company must face is evaluation of the mix of products that it sells. Most companies sell more than one product. **Sales mix** is the relative percentage in which each product is sold when a company sells more than one product. For example, if 75 percent of Hewlett Packard's sales are printers and if the other 25 percent are PCs, its sales mix is 75 percent to 25 percent.

STUDY OBJECTIVE

4

Explain the term sales mix and its effects on break-even sales.

Sales mix is important to managers because different products often have substantially different contribution margins. For example, Ford's SUVs and F150 pickups have higher contribution margins compared to its economy cars. Similarly, first-class tickets sold by United Airlines provide substantially higher contribution margins than coach-class tickets.

In this section we discuss how sales mix affects decision making using break-even analysis. The information needed for this analysis is readily available on variable costing income statements. This analysis is illustrated below for both sales in units and sales in dollars.

BREAK-EVEN SALES IN UNITS

Break-even sales can be computed for a mix of two or more products by determining the **weighted-average unit contribution margin of all the products**. To illustrate, we will assume that Vargo Video sells both DVD players and television sets with the per unit data shown in Illustration 19-18. It also incurs $200,000 in fixed costs.

Unit Data	DVD Players	TVs
Selling price	$500	$800
Variable costs	300	400
Contribution margin	$200	$400
Sales mix	**75%**	**25%**

Illustration 19-18   Per unit data—sales mix

The weighted-average unit contribution margin for the sales mix of 75 percent DVD players and 25 percent TVs is $250, which is computed as follows.

Illustration 19-19 Weighted-average unit contribution margin

DVD Players				TVs			
Unit Contribution Margin	×	Sales Mix Percentage	+	Unit Contribution Margin	×	Sales Mix Percentage	= Weighted-Average Unit Contribution Margin
($200	×	.75)	+	($400	×	.25)	= $250

We then use the weighted-average unit contribution margin to compute the break-even point in unit sales. The computation of break-even sales in units for Vargo Video, assuming $200,000 of fixed costs, is as follows.

Illustration 19-20   Break-even point in units

Fixed Costs	÷	Weighted-Average Unit Contribution Margin	=	Break-even Point in Units
$200,000	÷	$250	=	800 units

Note that with the sales mix of 75 percent to 25 percent, 75 percent of the units sold will be DVD players and 25 percent will be TVs. Therefore, in order to break even, Vargo Video must sell 600 DVD players (.75 × 800 units) and 200 TVs (.25 × 800 units). This can be verified by the following.

Illustration 19-21 Break-even proof—sales mix

Product	Unit Sales	×	Unit Contribution Margin	=	Total Contribution Margin
DVD players	600	×	$200	=	$ 120,000
TVs	200	×	400	=	80,000
	800				**$200,000**

Management should continually review the company's sales mix. At any level of units sold, **net income will be greater if higher contribution margin units are sold than lower contribution margin units**. For Vargo Video, the television sets produce the higher contribution margin. Consequently, if 300 TVs and 500 DVD players are sold, net income would be higher than in the current sales mix, even though total units sold has not changed.

An analysis of these relationships shows that a shift from low-margin sales to high-margin sales may increase net income, even though there is a decline in total units sold. Likewise, a shift from high- to low-margin sales may result in a decrease in net income, even though there is an increase in total units sold.

Decision Toolkit

Decision Checkpoints	Info Needed for Decision	Tool to Use for Decision	How to Evaluate Results
How many units of product A and product B do we need to sell to break even?	Fixed costs, weighted-average contribution margin, sales mix	$$\text{Break-even point in units} = \frac{\text{Fixed costs}}{\text{Weighted-average unit contribution margin}}$$	To determine number of units of product A and B, allocate total units based on sales mix.

BREAK-EVEN SALES IN DOLLARS

The calculation of the break-even point presented for Vargo Video in the previous section works well if the company has **only a small number of products**. In contrast, consider 3M, the maker of Post-it Notes, which has more than 30,000 products. In order to calculate the break-even point for 3M using a weighted-average unit contribution margin, we would need to calculate 30,000 different contribution margins. That is not realistic. For a company like 3M we calculate the break-even point using sales information for divisions or product lines, rather than for individual products.

To illustrate, suppose that Kale Garden Supply Company has two divisions—Indoor Plants and Outdoor Plants. Each division has hundreds of different types of plants and plant-care products. During the last year, 20 percent of the company's sales were from the Indoor Plant Division, and 80 percent were from the Outdoor Plant Division. The Indoor Plant Division has a contribution margin ratio of 40 percent, while the Outdoor Plant Division has a contribution margin ratio of 30 percent. Total fixed costs are $300,000.

The formula for computing the **break-even point in dollars is fixed costs divided by the weighted-average contribution margin ratio**. To compute the company's weighted-average contribution margin ratio, we multiply each division's contribution margin ratio by its sales mix percentage and then sum these amounts, as shown in Illustration 19-22.

Illustration 19-22 Calculation of weighted-average contribution margin

Indoor Plant Division				Outdoor Plant Division				Weighted-Average Contribution Margin Ratio
(Contribution Margin Ratio	×	Sales Mix Percentage)	+	(Contribution Margin Ratio	×	Sales Mix Percentage)	=	
(.40	×	.20)	+	(.30	×	.80)	=	.32

We then can use the weighted-average contribution margin ratio of 32 percent to compute the company's break-even point in dollars.

Illustration 19-23 Calculation of break-even point in dollars

Fixed Costs	÷	Weighted-Average Contribution Margin Ratio	=	Break-even Point in Dollars
$300,000	÷	.32	=	$937,500

The break-even point is based on the sales mix of 20 percent to 80 percent. Of the company's total break-even sales of $937,500, a total of $187,500 (.20 × $937,500) will come from the Indoor Plant Division and $750,000 (.80 × $937,500) will come from the Outdoor Plant Division.

This break-even point is based on the sales mix of 20 percent to 80 percent. What would be the impact on the break-even point if a higher percentage of the company's sales were to come from the Indoor Plant Division? Because the Indoor Plant Division enjoys a higher contribution margin ratio, this change in the sales mix would result in a higher weighted-average contribution margin ratio, and consequently a lower break-even point in dollars. The opposite would occur if a higher percentage of sales were expected from the Outdoor Plant Division. As you can see, the information provided under variable costing can help managers better understand the impact of sales mix on profitability.

Business Insight
Management Perspective

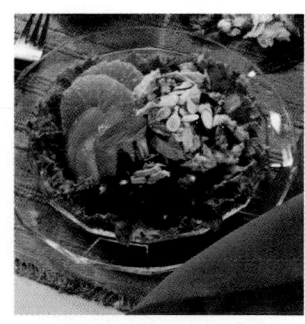

Zoom Kitchen, a chain of four restaurants in the Chicago area, is known for serving sizable portions of meat and potatoes. But the company's management is quite pleased with the fact that during the past four years salad sales have increased from 18 percent of its sales mix to 40 percent. Why are they pleased? Because the contribution margin on salads is much higher than on meat. The restaurant made a conscious effort to encourage people to buy more salads by offering an interesting assortment of salad ingredients including jicama, beets, marinated mushrooms, grilled tuna, and carved turkey. Management has to be very sensitive to contribution margin—it costs about $600,000 to open up a new Zoom Kitchen restaurant.

SOURCE: Amy Zuber, "Salad Sales 'Zoom' at Meat-and-Potatoes Specialist," *Nation's Restaurant News* (November 12, 2001), p. 26.

Decision Toolkit

Decision Checkpoints	Info Needed for Decision	Tool to Use for Decision	How to Evaluate Results
☑	📄📄	⚙	👍👎
How many dollars of sales are required from each division in order to break even?	Fixed costs, weighted-average contribution margin ratio, sales mix	$\text{Break-even point in dollars} = \dfrac{\text{Fixed costs}}{\text{Weighted-average contribution margin ratio}}$	To determine the sales dollars required from each division, allocate the total break-even sales using the sales mix.

BEFORE YOU GO ON . . .

▶Review It

1. What is meant by the term sales mix?
2. Why is sales mix important for break-even analysis?
3. How does the number of products that a company sells affect the method that is used to determine the break-even point?
4. What information is needed to compute break-even sales in units? Break-even sales in dollars?

THE NAVIGATOR

Cost Structure and Operating Leverage

Cost structure refers to the relative proportion of fixed versus variable costs that a company incurs. Cost structure can have a significant effect on profitability.

Consider the following example of two separate companies that make wooden croquet mallets. Old English Mallet Company uses a traditional, labor-intensive approach to form, sand, and apply a protective finish to the mallets. New Wave Mallet Company has invested in a completely automated system. The factory employees are involved only in setting up, adjusting, and maintaining the machinery. Variable cost income statements for each company are shown in Illustration 19-24.

Illustration 19-24 Variable costing income statements for two companies

	Old English Company	New Wave Company
Sales	$300,000	$300,000
Variable costs	255,000	120,000
Contribution margin	45,000	180,000
Fixed costs	15,000	150,000
Net income	$ 30,000	$ 30,000

Both companies have the same sales and the same net income. However, because of the differences in their cost structures, they differ greatly in the way they would be managed. Let's evaluate the impact of cost structure on the profitability of the two companies.

EFFECT ON CONTRIBUTION MARGIN RATIO

First let's look at the contribution margin ratio. Illustration 19-25 shows the computation of the contribution margin ratio for each company.

	Contribution Margin	÷	Sales	=	Contribution Margin Ratio
Old English	$45,000	÷	$300,000	=	.15
New Wave	$180,000	÷	$300,000	=	.60

Illustration 19-25 Contribution margin ratio for two companies

New Wave has a contribution margin ratio of 60 percent versus only 15 percent for Old English. That means that with every dollar of sales, New Wave generates 60 cents of contribution margin (and thus a 60 cent increase in net income), versus only 15 cents for Old English. However, it also means that for every dollar that sales decline, New Wave loses 60 cents in net income, whereas Old English will lose only 15 cents. New Wave's cost structure, which relies more heavily on fixed costs, makes it more sensitive to changes in sales revenue.

Operating leverage refers to the extent to which a company's net income reacts to a given change in sales. Companies that have higher fixed costs relative to variable costs have higher operating leverage. When a company's sales revenue is increasing, high operating leverage is a good thing because it means that profits will increase rapidly. But when sales are declining, too much operating leverage can have devastating consequences.

DEGREE OF OPERATING LEVERAGE

How can we compare operating leverage across two companies? The degree of operating leverage provides a measure of a company's earnings volatility and can be used to compare companies. Degree of operating leverage is computed by dividing total contribution margin by net income. This formula is presented in Illustration 19-26, and applied to our two mallet manufacturers.

	Contribution Margin	÷	Net Income	=	Degree of Operating Leverage
Old English	$45,000	÷	$30,000	=	1.5
New Wave	$180,000	÷	$30,000	=	6

Illustration 19-26 Computation of degree of operating leverage

New Wave's earnings would go up (or down) by 4.0 times (6 ÷ 1.5) as much as Old English Company's with an equal increase (or decrease) in sales. For example, suppose both companies experience a 5 percent decrease in sales. Old English's net income will decrease by 7.5 percent (1.5 × 5%), while New Wave's will decrease by 30 percent (6 × 5%). Thus, New Wave's higher operating leverage exposes it to greater earnings volatility risk.

EFFECT ON BREAK-EVEN POINT

The difference in operating leverage also affects the break-even point. The break-even point for each company is calculated in Illustration 19-27 (page 948).

Illustration 19-27   Computation of break-even point for two companies

	Fixed Costs	÷	Contribution Margin Ratio	=	Break-even Point in Dollars
Old English	$15,000	÷	.15	=	$100,000
New Wave	$150,000	÷	.60	=	$250,000

New Wave needs to generate $150,000 ($250,000 − $100,000) more in sales than Old English before it breaks even. This makes New Wave riskier than Old English because a company cannot survive for very long unless it at least breaks even.

EFFECT ON MARGIN OF SAFETY RATIO

We can also evaluate the relative impact that changes in sales would have on the two companies by computing the margin of safety ratio (see Chapter 18, p. 910). Illustration 19-28 shows the computation of the **margin of safety ratio** for the two companies.

Illustration 19-28   Computation of margin of safety ratio for two companies

	(Actual Sales	−	Break-even Sales)	÷	Actual Sales	=	Margin of Safety Ratio
Old English	($300,000	−	$100,000)	÷	$300,000	=	.67
New Wave	($300,000	−	$250,000)	÷	$300,000	=	.17

The difference in the margin of safety ratio also reflects the difference in risk between the two companies. Old English could sustain a 67 percent decline in sales before it would be operating at a loss. New Wave could sustain only a 17 percent decline in sales before it would be "in the red."

You should be careful not to conclude from this analysis that a cost structure that relies on higher fixed costs, and consequently has higher operating leverage, is necessarily bad. When used carefully, operating leverage can add considerably to a company's profitability. Computer equipment manufacturer Komag enjoyed a 66 percent increase in net income when its sales increased by only 8 percent. As one commentator noted, "Komag's fourth quarter illustrates the company's significant operating leverage; a small increase in sales leads to a big profit rise." However, as our illustration demonstrates, increased reliance on fixed costs increases a company's risk. In recent years, computer equipment manufacturer Cisco Systems has substantially reduced its operating leverage by choosing to outsource much of its production. While this has made the company less susceptible to economic swings, it has also reduced its ability to experience the incredible profitability that it used to have during economic booms.

The choice of cost structure must be carefully considered. There are many ways that companies can influence their cost structure. For example, by acquiring sophisticated robotic equipment, many companies have reduced their use of manual labor. Similarly, some brokerage firms, such as E*Trade, have reduced their reliance on human brokers and have instead invested heavily in computers and online technology. In so doing, they have increased their reliance on fixed costs (through depreciation on the robotic equipment or computer equipment) and reduced their reliance on variable costs (the variable employee labor cost). Alternatively, some companies such as Cisco Systems, have reduced their fixed costs and increased their variable costs by outsourcing their production. Nike, for example, does very little manufacturing, but instead outsources the manufacture of nearly all of its shoes. It has consequently converted many of its fixed costs into variable costs and therefore reduced its operating leverage.

Business Insight
Management Perspective

Cost structures vary considerably across industries, but they also vary considerably across companies within industries. For example, the airline industry is characterized by two types of companies—low-cost, low-fare airlines such as Southwest Airlines and JetBlue Airways, and the high-cost, high-fare airline giants such as United Airlines and American Airlines. One reason that airline giants have higher costs is that they are trapped in a flight system that they invented—the hub-and-spoke approach. Under this approach, passengers are flown from their city of origination to centralized hub cities and then flown to their ultimate destination. This results in high-fixed costs and high operating leverage. When air traffic was at peak volumes during the late 1990s, the large carriers enjoyed record profits. But in recent years this same cost structure has resulted in massive losses and a series of bankruptcy declarations.

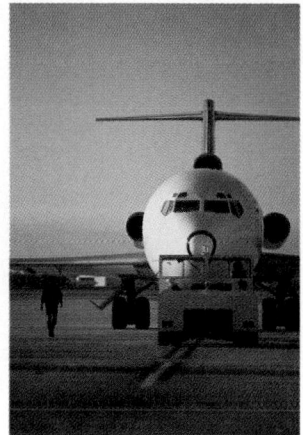

Decision Toolkit

Decision Checkpoints	Info Needed for Decision	Tool to Use for Decision	How to Evaluate Results
How sensitive is the company's net income to changes in sales?	Contribution margin and net income	$\text{Degree of operating leverage} = \dfrac{\text{Contribution margin}}{\text{Net income}}$	Reports the change in net income that will occur with a given change in sales. A high degree of operating leverage means that the company's net income is very sensitive to changes in sales.

BEFORE YOU GO ON . . .

▶Review It

1. What is operating leverage?
2. What are the benefits of operating leverage? What are the drawbacks of operating leverage?
3. How can operating leverage be measured?
4. What impact does an increase in operating leverage have on a company's break-even point? On a company's margin of safety ratio?

THE NAVIGATOR

Using the Decision Toolkit

Rexfield Corp. is contemplating a huge investment in automated mass-spectrometers for its medical laboratory testing services. Its current process relies heavily on the expertise of a high number of lab technicians. The new equipment would employ a computer expert system that integrates much of the decision process and knowledge base that is used by a skilled lab technician.

Rex Field, the company's CEO, has requested that an analysis of projected results using the old technology versus the new technology be done for the coming year. The accounting department has prepared the following variable costing income statements for use in your analysis.

	Old	**New**
Sales revenue	$2,000,000	$2,000,000
Variable costs	1,400,000	600,000
Contribution margin	600,000	1,400,000
Fixed costs	400,000	1,200,000
Net income	$ 200,000	$ 200,000

Instructions

Use the information provided above to do the following.
(a) Compute the degree of operating leverage for the company under each scenario, and discuss your results.
(b) Compute the break-even point in dollars and margin of safety ratio for the company under each scenario, and discuss your results.
(c) The company's sales, like most companies in healthcare-related fields, have been nearly unaffected by economic swings. Jason Wells, the head of the sales department, is on the verge of closing a deal with a nationwide chain of hospitals that would increase sales by $1,000,000 per year. Prepare new variable costing income statements under both the old and new approaches. Discuss your conclusions regarding what actions management should take.

Solution

(a)

	Contribution Margin	÷	Net Income	=	Degree of Operating Leverage
Old	$600,000	÷	$200,000	=	3
New	$1,400,000	÷	$200,000	=	7

The degree of operating leverage measures the company's sensitivity to changes in sales. By switching to a cost structure dominated by fixed costs, the company would significantly increase its operating leverage. As a result, with a percentage change in sales, its percentage change in net income would be 2.33 as much (7 ÷ 3) under the new structure as it would under the old.

(b) To compute the break-even point in sales dollars, we need first to compute the contribution margin ratio under each scenario. Under the old structure the contribution margin ratio would be .30 ($600,000 ÷ $2,000,000), and under the new it would be .70 ($1,400,000 ÷ $2,000,000).

	Fixed Costs	÷	Contribution Margin Ratio	=	Break-even point in dollars
Old	$400,000	÷	.30	=	$1,333,333
New	$1,200,000	÷	.70	=	$1,714,286

Because the company's fixed costs would be substantially higher under the new cost structure, its break-even point would increase significantly, from $1,333,333 to $1,714,286. A higher break-even point is riskier because it means that the company must generate higher sales to be profitable.

The margin of safety ratio tells how far sales can fall before the company is operating at a loss.

	(Actual Sales − Break-even Sales)	÷	Actual Sales	=	Margin of Safety Ratio
Old	($2,000,000 − $1,333,333)	÷	$2,000,000	=	.33
New	($2,000,000 − $1,714,286)	÷	$2,000,000	=	.14

Under the old structure, sales could fall by 33 percent before the company would be operating at a loss. Under the new structure, sales could fall by only 14 percent.

(c)

	Old	New
Sales	$3,000,000	$3,000,000
Variable costs	2,100,000*	900,000**
Contribution margin	900,000	2,100,000
Fixed costs	400,000	1,200,000
Net income	$ 500,000	$ 900,000

*$3,000,000 × ($1,400,000 ÷ $2,000,000)
**$3,000,000 × ($600,000 ÷ $2,000,000)

If sales increase by $1,000,000, net income under the old cost structure will increase to $500,000. Under the new cost structure, net income will increase to $900,000. Because of the high degree of operating leverage under the new cost structure, the company's net income would be much more sensitive to changes in sales. Given the fact that the company's sales are not very susceptible to economic swings, switching to the new cost structure would appear to make sense. It would result in a significant increase in net income compared to the amount of incremental risk that it would incur.

Summary of Study Objectives

1 *Explain the difference between absorption costing and variable costing.* Under absorption costing, fixed manufacturing costs are product costs. Under variable costing, fixed manufacturing costs are period costs.

2 *Discuss the effect that changes in production level and sales level have on net income measured under absorption costing versus variable costing.* If production volume exceeds sales volume, net income under absorption costing will exceed net income under variable costing by the amount of fixed manufacturing costs included in ending inventory that results from units produced but not sold during the period. If production volume is less than sales volume, net income under absorption costing will be less than under variable costing by the amount of fixed manufacturing costs included in the units sold during the period that were not produced during the period.

3 *Discuss the relative merits of absorption costing versus variable costing for management decision making.* The use of variable costing is consistent with cost–volume–profit analysis and incremental analysis. Net income under variable costing is unaffected by changes in production levels. Instead, it is closely tied to changes in sales. The presentation of fixed costs in the variable costing approach makes it easier

to identify fixed costs and to evaluate their impact on the company's profitability.

4 *Explain the term sales mix and its effects on break-even sales.* Sales mix is the relative proportion in which each product is sold when a company sells more than one product. For a company with a small number of products, break-even sales in units is determined by using the weighted-average unit contribution margin of all the products. If the company sells many different products, then calculating the break-even point using unit information is not practical. Instead, in a company with many products, break-even sales in dollars is calculated using the weighted-average contribution margin ratio.

5 *Understand how operating leverage affects profitability.* Operating leverage refers to the degree to which a company's net income reacts to a change in sales. Operating leverage is determined by a company's relative use of fixed versus variable costs. Companies with high fixed costs relative to variable costs have high operating leverage. A company with high operating leverage will experience a sharp increase (decrease) in net income with a given increase (decrease) in sales. The degree of operating leverage can be measured by dividing contribution margin by net income.

Decision Toolkit—A Summary

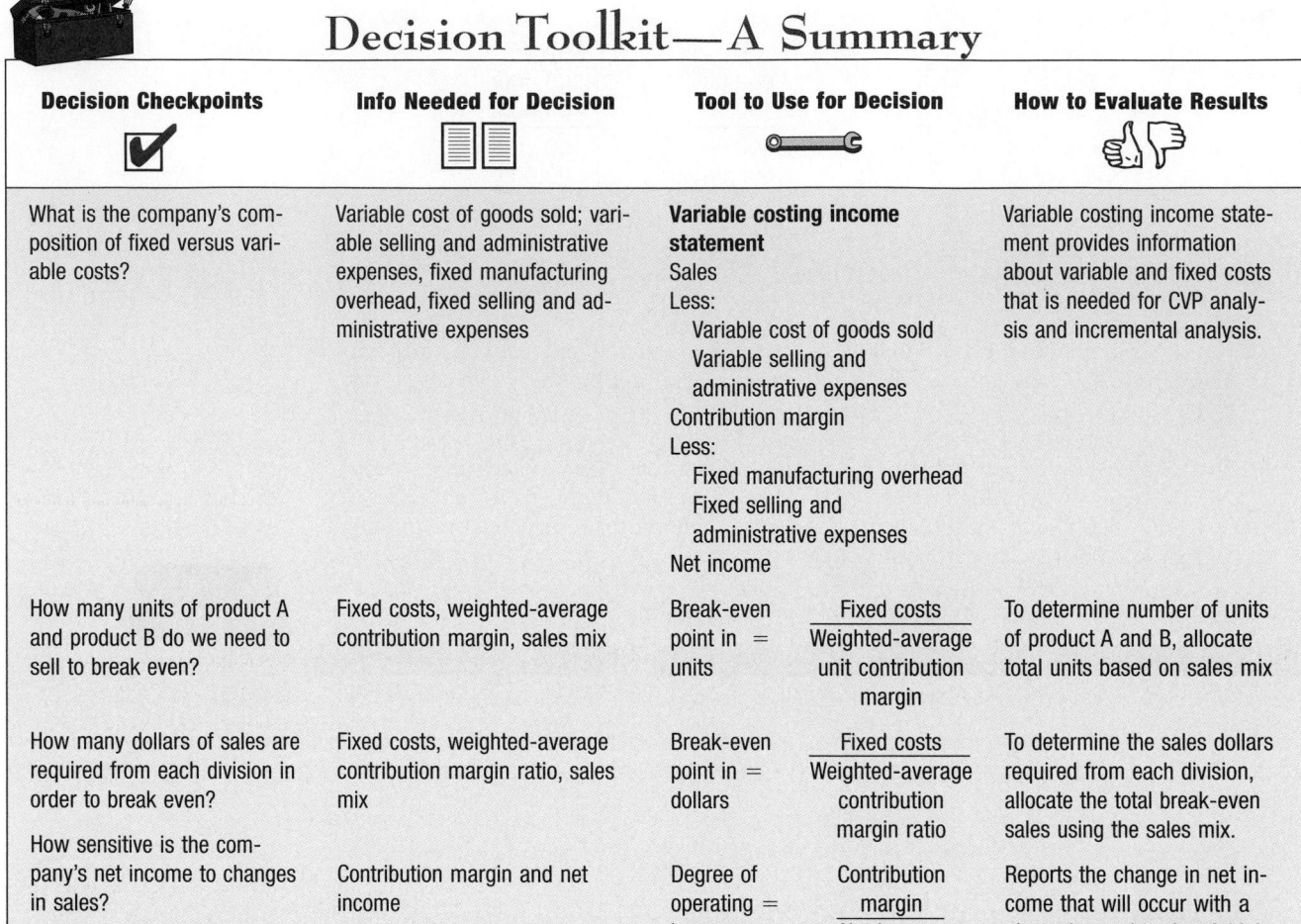

Decision Checkpoints	Info Needed for Decision	Tool to Use for Decision	How to Evaluate Results

What is the company's composition of fixed versus variable costs?	Variable cost of goods sold; variable selling and administrative expenses, fixed manufacturing overhead, fixed selling and administrative expenses	**Variable costing income statement**
		Sales
		Less:
		    Variable cost of goods sold
		    Variable selling and administrative expenses
		Contribution margin
		Less:
		    Fixed manufacturing overhead
		    Fixed selling and administrative expenses
		Net income
			Variable costing income statement provides information about variable and fixed costs that is needed for CVP analysis and incremental analysis.

How many units of product A and product B do we need to sell to break even?	Fixed costs, weighted-average contribution margin, sales mix	Break-even point in units $=\dfrac{\text{Fixed costs}}{\text{Weighted-average unit contribution margin}}$	To determine number of units of product A and B, allocate total units based on sales mix
How many dollars of sales are required from each division in order to break even?	Fixed costs, weighted-average contribution margin ratio, sales mix	Break-even point in dollars $=\dfrac{\text{Fixed costs}}{\text{Weighted-average contribution margin ratio}}$	To determine the sales dollars required from each division, allocate the total break-even sales using the sales mix.
How sensitive is the company's net income to changes in sales?	Contribution margin and net income	Degree of operating leverage $=\dfrac{\text{Contribution margin}}{\text{Net income}}$	Reports the change in net income that will occur with a given change in sales. A high degree of operating leverage means that the company's net income is very sensitive to changes in sales.

Glossary

Absorption costing A costing approach in which all manufacturing costs are charged to the product. (p. 932)

Cost structure The relative proportion of fixed versus variable costs that a company incurs. (p. 946)

Degree of operating leverage A measure of the extent to which a company's net income reacts to a change in sales. It is calculated by dividing contribution margin by net income. (p. 947)

Operating leverage The extent to which a company's net income reacts to a given change in sales. Operating leverage is determined by a company's relative use of fixed versus variable costs. (p. 947)

Sales mix The relative percentage in which each product is sold when a company sells more than one product. (p. 943)

Variable costing A costing approach in which only variable manufacturing costs are product costs, and fixed manufacturing costs are period costs (expenses). (p. 932)

Demonstration Problem

Taylor Enterprises produces birdhouses. In 2007 it began the year with no beginning inventory. During the year it produced 10,000 birdhouses and sold 8,000 for $30 per house. Variable manufacturing costs were $9 per house produced; variable selling and administrative expenses were $4 per unit sold; fixed manufacturing costs were $70,000 in total and $7 ($70,000 ÷ 10,000) per unit; fixed selling and administrative costs were $20,000.

Instructions
(a) Prepare an income statement using absorption costing.
(b) Prepare an income statement using variable costing.
(c) Show a computation that explains the difference in net income under the two costing approaches.

Action Plan
- Recall that under variable costing, only variable manufacturing costs are treated as manufacturing costs.
- For variable costing, subtract all fixed costs, both manufacturing overhead and selling and administrative expenses as period costs.
- For absorption costing, manufacturing costs include variable materials and labor and overhead, as well as an allocated per unit charge for fixed manufacturing overhead.

Solution to Demonstration Problem

(a)

TAYLOR ENTERPRISES
Income Statement
For the Year Ended 2007
Absorption Costing

Sales (8,000 units × $30)		$240,000
Cost of goods sold [8,000 units × ($9 + $7)]		128,000
Gross profit		112,000
Variable selling and administrative expenses		
(8,000 units × $4)	$32,000	
Fixed selling and administrative expenses	20,000	52,000
Net income		$ 60,000

(b)

TAYLOR ENTERPRISES
Income Statement
For the Year Ended 2007
Variable Costing

Sales (8,000 units × $30)		$240,000
Variable cost of goods sold (8,000 units × $9)	$72,000	
Variable selling and administrative expenses		
(8,000 units × $4)	32,000	104,000
Contribution margin		136,000
Fixed manufacturing overhead	70,000	
Fixed selling and administrative expenses	20,000	90,000
Net income		$ 46,000

(c) The difference in net income of $14,000 can be explained by the 2,000-unit difference between the number of *units sold* (8,000) versus the number of *units produced* (10,000). The company deferred $7 per unit of fixed manufacturing costs in the 2,000 units of ending inventory. This represents the total difference of $14,000 ($7 × 2,000 units) in net income under variable costing ($46,000) versus absorption costing ($60,000).

✓ THE NAVIGATOR

Self-Study Questions

Answers are at the end of the chapter.

(SO 1) **1.** Fixed manufacturing overhead costs are recognized as:
(a) period costs under absorption costing.
(b) product costs under absorption costs.
(c) product costs under variable costing.
(d) part of ending inventory costs under both absorption and variable costing.

(SO 1, 2) **2.** Net income computed under absorption costing will be:
(a) higher than net income under variable costing in all cases.
(b) equal to net income under variable costing in all cases.
(c) higher than net income under variable costing when units produced are greater than units sold.
(d) higher than net income under variable costing when units produced are less than units sold.

(SO 2) **3.** A company will be in compliance with GAAP when it prepares financial statements in accordance with:
(a) cost-volume-profit principles.
(b) absorption costing principles.
(c) variable costing principles.
(d) All of the above methods.

(SO 2) **4.** A manager can increase reported income by:
(a) producing more units than units sold under absorption costing.
(b) producing fewer units than sold under absorption costing.
(c) producing more units than sold under variable costing.
(d) producing fewer units than sold under variable costing.

(SO 2) **5.** Gross profit is disclosed on an income statement prepared using:
(a) CVP analysis.
(b) absorption costing.
(c) variable costing.
(d) All costing methods.

(SO 3) **6.** When preparing internal reports, service companies:
(a) cannot benefit from variable costing because they have no inventory.
(b) cannot use variable costing.
(c) can benefit from variable costing because they have both fixed and variable costs.
(d) Both (a) and (b) are correct.

(SO 3) **7.** Using variable costing rather than absorption costing is an advantage to a company because:
(a) variable costing is consistent with cost-volume-profit and incremental analysis used by managers for decision making.
(b) it agrees with the income information released to external users under GAAP.
(c) it always produces higher net income.
(d) it focuses on gross profit, which is the best indicator of a company's ability to meet income goals.

(SO 4) **8.** Sales mix is:
(a) important to sales managers but not to accountants.
(b) easier to analyze on absorption costing income statements.
(c) a measure of the relative percentage of a company's variable costs to its fixed costs.
(d) a measure of the relative percentage in which a company's products are sold.

(SO 4) **9.** Net income will be:
(a) greater if more higher-contribution margin units are sold than lower-contribution margin units.
(b) greater if more lower-contribution margin units are sold than higher-contribution margin units.
(c) equal as long as total sales remain equal, regardless of which products are sold.
(d) unaffected by changes in the mix of products sold.

(SO 5) **10.** The degree of operating leverage:
(a) can be computed by dividing total contribution margin by net income.
(b) provides a measure of the company's earnings volatility.
(c) affects a company's break-even point.
(d) All of the above.

(SO 5) **11.** A high degree of operating leverage:
(a) indicates that a company has a larger percentage of variable costs relative to its fixed costs.
(b) is computed by dividing fixed costs by contribution margin.
(c) exposes a company to greater earnings volatility risk.
(d) exposes a company to less earnings volatility risk.

✓ **THE NAVIGATOR**

Questions

1. What is variable costing? What is absorption costing?

2. What costs are considered as product costs in a variable costing system?

3. How are fixed manufacturing overhead costs treated in a variable costing system?

4. Under absorption costing, what happens to fixed manufacturing overhead costs if ending inventories increase during the period?

5. What is the main difference between absorption and variable costing approaches?

6. Flygt Corporation sells one product, its waterproof hiking boot. It began operations in the current year and had an ending inventory of 10,500 units. The company sold 20,000 units throughout the year. Fixed manufacturing overhead is $5 per unit, and total manufacturing cost per unit is $20 (including fixed manufacturing overhead costs). What is the difference in net income between absorption and variable costing?

7. If production equals sales, what, if any, is the difference between net income under absorption costing versus under variable costing?

8. If production is greater than sales, how does absorption costing net income differ from variable costing net income?

9. In the long run, will net income be higher or lower under variable costing compared to absorption costing?

10. Brunow Company uses an absorption costing system for internal reporting. If its production exceeds sales by 5,000 units, how will fixed manufacturing overhead be affected?

11. Can variable costing be used for external financial statements? Why or why not?

12. What are some of the benefits to a manager of using variable costing instead of absorption costing?

13. How might the use of just-in-time inventory techniques affect the difference in net income computed under variable costing and under absorption costing?

14. Which method, absorption or variable costing, is better for a company to use as its costing system? Explain. Why do those firms that use variable costing also maintain absorption costing systems?

15. What is meant by the term sales mix? How does sales mix affect the calculation of the break-even point?

16. Radial Company sells two types of radial tires. The lower-priced model is guaranteed for only 40,000 miles; the higher-priced model is guaranteed for 100,000 miles. The unit contribution margin on the higher-priced tire is twice as high as that of the lower-priced tire. If the sales mix shifts so that the company begins to sell more units of the lower-priced tire, explain how the company's break-even point in units will change.

17. What approach should be used to calculate the break-even point of a company that has many products?

18. What is meant by "cost structure?" Explain how a company's cost structure affects its break-even point.

19. What is operating leverage? How does a company increase its operating leverage?

20. How does the replacement of manual labor with automated equipment affect a company's cost structure? What implications does this have for its operating leverage and break-even point?

21. What is a measure of operating leverage, and how is it calculated?

22. Acorn Company has a degree of operating leverage of 8. Oak Company has a degree of operating leverage of 4. Interpret these measures.

Brief Exercises

BE19-1 Determine whether each of the following costs would be classified as product costs or period costs under a variable costing system.

Identify costs as product costs or period costs under variable costing.
(SO 1)

	Product Cost	Period Cost
Commission fees for salespersons		
Glue for wooden chairs—variable		
Fabric for T-shirts		
Labor costs for producing TVs		
Factory rent expense—fixed		
Factory utility costs—variable		
Car mileage costs for salespersons		
Administrative expenses—fixed		
Administrative Internet connection fees		
Wages—assembly line		

BE19-2 Determine whether each of the costs shown at the top of page 956 would be classified as product costs or period costs under an absorption costing system.

Identify costs as product costs or period costs under absorption costing.
(SO 1)

	Product Cost	Period Cost
Commission fees for salespersons		
Glue for wooden chairs—variable		
Fabric for T-shirts		
Labor costs for producing TVs		
Factory rent expense—fixed		
Factory utility costs—variable		
Car mileage costs for salespersons		
Administrative expenses—fixed		
Administrative Internet connection fees		
Wages—assembly line		

Compute product costs under variable costing.
(SO 1)

BE19-3   Large Orange Company produces basketballs. It incurred the following costs during the year.

Direct materials	$14,490
Direct labor	$25,530
Fixed manufacturing overhead	$10,000
Variable manufacturing overhead	$32,420
Selling costs	$21,000

What are the total product costs for the company under variable costing?

Compute product costs under absorption costing.
(SO 1)

BE19-4   Information concerning Large Orange Company is provided in BE19-3. What are the total product costs for the company under absorption costing?

Determine manufacturing cost per unit under absorption and variable costing.
(SO 1)

BE19-5   Burns Manufacturing incurred the following costs during the year: direct materials $20 per unit; direct labor $12 per unit; variable manufacturing overhead $15 per unit; variable selling and administrative costs $8 per unit; fixed manufacturing overhead $120,000; and fixed selling and administrative costs $10,000. Burns produced 12,000 units and sold 10,000 units. Determine the manufacturing cost per unit under (a) absorption costing and (b) variable costing.

Prepare a variable costing income statement.
(SO 1)

BE19-6   During 2007 Rafael Corp. produced 40,000 units and sold 30,000 units for $12 per unit. Variable manufacturing costs were $4 per unit. Annual fixed manufacturing overhead was $80,000 ($2 per unit). Variable selling and administrative costs were $1 per unit sold, and fixed selling and administrative expenses were $10,000. Prepare a variable costing income statement.

Prepare an absorption costing income statement and reconcile difference between variable costing and absorption costing net income.
(SO 1, 2)

BE19-7   Information for Rafael Corp. is given in BE19-6. (a) Prepare an absorption costing income statement. (b) Reconcile the difference between net income under variable costing and net income under absorption costing. That is, show a calculation that explains what causes the difference in net income between the two approaches.

Determine net income under variable costing.
(SO 1, 2)

BE19-8   Caspian Company produced 20,000 units and sold 18,000 units during the current year. Under absorption costing, net income was $25,000. Fixed overhead was $190,000. Determine the net income under variable costing.

Compute weighted-average unit contribution margin based on sales mix.
(SO 4)

BE19-9   Russell Corporation sells three different models of mosquito "zapper." Model A12 sells for $50 and has variable costs of $40. Model B22 sells for $100 and has variable costs of $70. Model C124 sells for $400 and has variable costs of $300. The sales mix of the three models is: A12, 60%; B22, 25%; and C124, 15%. What is the weighted-average unit contribution margin?

Compute break-even point in units for company with multiple products.
(SO 4)

BE19-10   Information for Russell Corporation is given in BE19-9. If the company has fixed costs of $199,500, how many units of each model must the company sell in order to break even?

Compute break-even point in dollars for company with multiple product lines.
(SO 4)

BE19-11   Presto Candle Supply makes candles. The sales mix (as a percent of total dollar sales) of its three product lines is: birthday candles 30%, standard tapered candles 50%, and large scented candles 20%. The contribution margin ratio of each candle type is shown on the top of page 957.

Candle Type	Contribution Margin Ratio
Birthday	10%
Standard tapered	20%
Large scented	45%

If the company's fixed costs are $440,000 per year, what is the dollar amount of each type of candle that must be sold to break even?

BE19-12 Family Furniture Co. consists of two divisions, Bedroom Division and Dining Room Division. The results of operations for the most recent quarter are:

Determine weighted-average contribution margin.
(SO 4)

	Bedroom Division	Dining Room Division
Sales	$500,000	$750,000
Variable costs	250,000	450,000
Contribution margin	$250,000	$300,000

Determine the company's weighted-average contribution margin ratio.

BE19-13 Ron's Shingle Corporation is considering the purchase of a new automated shingle-cutting machine. The new machine will reduce variable labor costs but will increase depreciation expense. Contribution margin is expected to increase from $160,000 to $240,000. Net income is expected to be the same at $40,000. Compute the degree of operating leverage before and after the purchase of the new equipment. Interpret your results.

Compute degree of operating leverage.
(SO 5)

BE19-14 Presented below are variable costing income statements for Finch Company and Sparrow Company. They are in the same industry, with the same net incomes, but different cost structures.

Compute break-even point with change in operating leverage.
(SO 5)

	Finch Co.	Sparrow Co.
Sales	$150,000	$150,000
Variable costs	60,000	15,000
Contribution margin	90,000	135,000
Fixed costs	50,000	95,000
Net income	$ 40,000	$ 40,000

Compute the break-even point in dollars for each company and comment on your findings.

BE19-15 The degree of operating leverage for Delta Corp. and Epsilon Co. are 1.4 and 5.6, respectively. Both have net incomes of $50,000. Determine their respective contribution margins.

Determine contribution margin from degree of operating leverage.
(SO 5)

Exercises

E19-1 Wu Equipment Company manufactures and distributes industrial air compressors. The following costs are available for the year ended December 31, 2007. The company has no beginning inventory. In 2007, 1,500 units are produced, but only 1,200 units are sold. The unit selling price was $4,500. Costs and expenses were as follows.

Compute total product cost, and prepare an income statement using variable costing.
(SO 1)

Variable cost per unit:	
Direct materials	$ 800
Direct labor	$1,500
Variable manufacturing overhead	$ 300
Variable selling and administrative expenses	$ 70
Annual fixed costs and expenses:	
Manufacturing overhead	$1,200,000
Selling and administrative expenses	$ 100,000

Instructions
(a) Compute the manufacturing cost of one unit of product using variable costing.
(b) Prepare a 2007 income statement for Wu Company using variable costing.

E19-2 Asian Windows manufactures a hand-painted bamboo window shade for standard-size windows. Production and sales data for 2007 are shown at the top of page 958.

Prepare income statements under absorption costing and variable costing.
(SO 1)

Variable manufacturing costs	$40 per shade
Fixed manufacturing overhead costs	$100,000
Variable selling and administrative expenses	$9 per shade
Fixed selling and administrative expenses	$250,000
Selling price	$90 per shade
Units produced	10,000 shades
Units sold	8,500 shades

Instructions

(a) Prepare an income statement using absorption costing.
(b) Prepare an income statement using variable costing.

Compute product cost and prepare an income statement under variable costing.
(SO 1)

E19-3 Bob's Company builds custom fishing lures for sporting goods stores. In its first year of operations, 2007, the company incurred the following costs.

Variable cost per unit

Direct materials	$7.50
Direct labor	$2.45
Variable manufacturing overhead	$5.75
Variable selling and administrative expenses	$3.90

Fixed costs per year

Fixed manufacturing overhead	$234,650
Fixed selling and administrative expenses	$240,100

Bob's Company sells the fishing lures for $25. During 2007, the company sold 80,000 lures and produced 95,000 lures.

Instructions

(a) Assuming the company uses variable costing, calculate Bob's manufacturing cost per unit for 2007.
(b) Prepare a variable costing income statement for 2007.

Compute product cost and prepare an income statement under absorption costing.
(SO 1)

E19-4 Information for Bob's Company is provided in E19-3.

Instructions

(a) Assuming the company uses absorption costing, calculate Bob's manufacturing cost per unit for 2007.
(b) Prepare an absorption costing income statement for 2007.

Compute product cost under absorption costing and variable costing; prepare an absorption costing income statement; compare usefulness of variable costing format versus absorption costing format.
(SO 1, 2, 3)

E19-5 Empey Manufacturing produces towels to be sold as souvenirs to sporting events throughout the world. Assume that units produced equaled units sold in 2007. Here is the company's variable costing income statement.

EMPEY MANUFACTURING
Income Statement
For the Year Ended December 31, 2007
Variable Costing

Sales (260,700 units)		$521,400
Variable cost of goods sold	$255,486	
Variable selling expenses	31,284	
Variable administrative expenses	36,498	323,268
Contribution margin		198,132
Fixed manufacturing overhead	96,459	
Fixed selling expenses	38,500	
Fixed administrative expenses	42,625	177,584
Net income		$ 20,548

Unit selling price:	$2.00
Variable costs per unit:	
Direct materials	$0.26
Direct labor	$0.34
Variable manufacturing overhead	$0.38
Variable selling	$0.12
Variable administrative	$0.14

Instructions

(a) Under variable costing, what was the manufacturing cost per unit for each towel?

(b) Under absorption costing, what was the manufacturing cost per unit for each towel?

(c) Prepare an absorption costing income statement for Empey Manufacturing.

(d) Can you explain why there is or is not a difference in net income numbers for the two types of income statements?

(e) Why might Empey Manufacturing want to prepare both an absorption costing income statement and a variable costing income statement?

E19-6 Ortiz Company produced 10,000 units during the past year, but only 9,000 of the units were sold. The following additional information is also available.

Direct materials used	$90,000
Direct labor incurred	$30,000
Variable manufacturing overhead	$24,000
Fixed manufacturing overhead	$50,000
Fixed selling and administrative expenses	$70,000
Variable selling and administrative expenses	$10,000

Determine ending inventory under variable costing and determine whether absorption or variable costing would result in higher net income.
(SO 1, 2)

There was no work-in-process inventory at the beginning of the year, nor did Ortiz have any beginning finished goods inventory.

Instructions

(a) What would be Ortiz Company's finished goods inventory cost on December 31 under variable costing?

(b) Which costing method, absorption or variable costing, would show a higher net income for the year? By what amount?

E19-7 Hardwood Inc. produces wooden crates used for shipping products by ocean liner. In 2007, Hardwood incurred the following costs.

Wood used in crate production	$54,000
Nails (considered insignificant and a variable expense)	$ 340
Direct labor	$37,000
Utilities for the plant:	
$2,000 each month,	
plus $0.45 for each kilowatt-hour used each month	
Rent expense for the plant for the year	$21,400

Compute manufacturing cost under absorption and variable costing and explain difference.
(SO 2)

Assume Hardwood used an average 500 kilowatt-hours each month over the past year.

Instructions

(a) What is Hardwood's total manufacturing cost if it uses a variable costing approach?

(b) What is Hardwood's total manufacturing cost if it uses an absorption costing approach?

(c) What accounts for the difference in manufacturing costs between these two costing approaches?

E19-8 Grass King manufactures lawnmowers, weed-trimmers, and chainsaws. Its sales mix and contribution margin per unit are as follows.

Compute break-even point in units for a company with more than one product.
(SO 4)

	Sales Mix	Contribution Margin per Unit
Lawnmowers	30%	$30
Weed-trimmers	50%	$20
Chainsaws	20%	$40

Grass King has fixed costs of $4,600,000.

Instructions

Compute the number of units of each product that Grass King must sell in order to break even under this product mix.

E19-9 Rapid Auto has over 200 auto-maintenance service outlets nationwide. It provides primarily two lines of service: oil changes and brake repair. Oil change–related services represent 65% of its sales and provide a contribution margin ratio of 20%. Brake repair represents 35% of its sales and provides a 60% contribution margin ratio. The company's fixed costs are $16,000,000 (that is, $80,000 per service outlet).

Compute service line break-even point and target net income in dollars for a company with more than one service.
(SO 4)

Instructions

(a) Calculate the dollar amount of each type of service that the company must provide in order to break even.

(b) The company has a desired net income of $60,000 per service outlet. What is the dollar amount of each type of service that must be provided by each service outlet to meet its target net income per outlet?

Compute break-even point in dollars for a company with more than one service.
(SO 4)

E19-10   Blazer Delivery is a rapidly growing delivery service. Last year 80% of its revenue came from the delivery of mailing "pouches" and small, standardized delivery boxes (which provides a 10% contribution margin). The other 20% of its revenue came from delivering non-standardized boxes (which provides a 60% contribution margin). With the rapid growth of Internet retail sales, Blazer believes that there are great opportunities for growth in the delivery of non-standardized boxes. The company has fixed costs of $12,000,000.

Instructions

(a) What is the company's break-even point in total sales dollars? At the break-even point, how much of the company's sales are provided by each type of service?

(b) The company's management would like to hold its fixed costs constant, but shift its sales mix so that 60% of its revenue comes from the delivery of non-standardized boxes and the remainder from pouches and small boxes. If this were to occur, what would be the company's break-even sales, and what amount of sales would be provided by each service type?

Compute break-even point in units for a company with multiple products.
(SO 4)

E19-11   Tiger Golf Accessories sells golf shoes, gloves, and a laser-guided range-finder that measures distance. Shown below are unit cost and sales data.

	Pairs of Shoes	Pairs of Gloves	Range-Finder
Unit sales price	$100	$30	$250
Unit variable costs	60	10	200
Unit contribution margin	$ 40	$20	$ 50
Sales mix	40%	50%	10%

Fixed costs are $620,000.

Instructions

(a) Compute the break-even point in units for the company.

(b) Determine the number of units to be sold at the break-even point for each product line.

(c) Verify that the mix of sales units determined in (b) will generate a zero net income.

Determine break-even point in dollars for two divisions.
(SO 4)

E19-12   Mega Electronix sells television sets and DVD players. The business is divided into two divisions along product lines. Variable costing income statements for a recent quarter's activity are presented below.

	TV Division	DVD Division	Total
Sales	$600,000	$400,000	$1,000,000
Variable costs	450,000	240,000	690,000
Contribution margin	$150,000	$160,000	310,000
Fixed costs			124,000
Net income			$ 186,000

Instructions

(a) Determine sales mix percentage and contribution margin ratio for each division.

(b) Calculate the company's weighted-average contribution margin ratio.

(c) Calculate the company's break-even point in dollars.

(d) Determine the sales level in dollars for each division at the break-even point.

Compute degree of operating leverage and evaluate impact of alternative cost structures on net income.
(SO 5)

E19-13   The variable costing income statements shown on page 961 are available for Billings Company and Bozeman Company.

961

	Billings Co.	Bozeman Co.
Sales revenue	$600,000	$600,000
Variable costs	280,000	80,000
Contribution margin	320,000	520,000
Fixed costs	170,000	370,000
Net income	$150,000	$150,000

Instructions
(a) Compute the degree of operating leverage for each company and interpret your results.
(b) Assuming that sales revenue increases by 10%, prepare a variable costing income statement for each company.
(c) Discuss how the cost structure of these two companies affects their operating leverage and profitability.

E19-14 Imagen Arquitectonica of Tijuana, B.C., Mexico is contemplating a major change in its cost structure. Currently, all of its drafting work is performed by skilled draftsmen. Alfredo Ayala, Imagen's owner, is considering replacing the draftsmen with a computerized drafting system. However, before making the change Alfredo would like to know the consequences of the change, since the volume of business varies significantly from year to year. Shown below are variable costing income statements for each alternative.

Compute degree of operating leverage and evaluate impact of alternative cost structures on net income and margin of safety.
(SO 5)

	Manual System	Computerized System
Sales	$1,500,000	$1,500,000
Variable costs	1,200,000	600,000
Contribution margin	300,000	900,000
Fixed costs	60,000	660,000
Net income	$ 240,000	$ 240,000

Instructions
(a) Determine the degree of operating leverage for each alternative.
(b) Which alternative would produce the higher net income if sales increased by $100,000?
(c) Using the margin of safety ratio, determine which alternative could sustain the greater decline in sales before operating at a loss.

E19-15 An investment banker is analyzing two companies that specialize in the production and sale of candied apples. Old-Fashion Apples uses a labor-intensive approach, and Mech-Apple uses a mechanized system. Variable costing income statements for the two companies are shown below.

Compute degree of operating leverage and impact on net income of alternative cost structures.
(SO 5)

	Old-Fashion Apples	Mech-Apple
Sales	$400,000	$400,000
Variable costs	320,000	160,000
Contribution margin	80,000	240,000
Fixed costs	20,000	180,000
Net income	$ 60,000	$ 60,000

The investment banker is interested in acquiring one of these companies. However, she is concerned about the impact that each company's cost structure might have on its profitability.

Instructions
(a) Calculate each company's degree of operating leverage. Determine which company's cost structure makes it more sensitive to changes in sales volume.
(b) Determine the effect on each company's net income if sales decrease by 10% and if sales increase by 5%. Do not prepare income statements.
(c) Which company should the investment banker acquire? Discuss.

Problems: Set A

Calculate product cost; prepare income statements under variable costing and absorption costing and reconcile difference.
(SO 1, 2)

P19-1A   Blue Mountain Products manufactures and sells a variety of camping products. Recently the company opened a new plant to manufacture a light-weight, self-standing tent. Cost and sales data for the first month of operations are shown below.

Manufacturing costs:	
Fixed overhead	$200,000
Variable overhead	$4 per tent
Direct labor	$16 per tent
Direct materials	$40 per tent
Beginning inventory	0 tents
Tents produced	10,000
Tents sold	9,000
Selling and administrative costs:	
Fixed	$400,000
Variable	$6 per tent sold

The tent sells for $150. Management is interested in the opening month's results and has asked for an income statement.

Instructions
(a) Assuming the company uses absorption costing, do the following.
  (i) Calculate the manufacturing cost per unit.
  (ii) Prepare an absorption costing income statement for the month of June 2007.
(b) Assuming the company uses variable costing, do the following.
  (i) Calculate the manufacturing cost per unit.
  (ii) Prepare a variable costing income statement for the month of June 2007.
(c) Reconcile the difference in net income between the two methods.

(a) (i) $80

(b) (i) $60

Prepare income statements under absorption costing and variable costing for a company with beginning inventory, and reconcile difference.
(SO 1, 2, 3)

P19-2A   AFN Company produces plastic that is used for injection-molding applications such as gears for small motors. In 2007, the first year of operations, AFN produced 4,000 tons of plastic and sold 3,000 tons. In 2008, the production and sales results were exactly reversed. In each year, the selling price per ton was $2,000, variable manufacturing costs were 15% of the sales price of units produced, variable selling expenses were 10% of the selling price of units sold, fixed manufacturing costs were $2,400,000, and fixed administrative expenses were $600,000.

Instructions
(a) Prepare income statements for each year using variable costing. (Use the format from Illustration 19-5.)
(b) Prepare income statements for each year using absorption costing. (Use the format from Illustration 19-4.)
(c) Reconcile the differences each year in net income under the two costing approaches.
(d) ▭▭▭▷ Comment on the effects of production and sales on net income under the two costing approaches.

(a) 2007 NI $1,500,000

(b) 2007 NI $2,100,000

Prepare absorption and variable costing income statements and reconcile differences between absorption and variable costing income statements when sales level and production level change. Discuss relative usefulness of absorption costing versus variable costing.
(SO 1, 2, 3)

P19-3A   Basic Electric Motors is a division of Basic Electric Products Corporation. The division manufactures and sells an electric motor used in a wide variety of applications. During the coming year it expects to sell 50,000 units for $30 per unit. Esther Madonna is the division manager. She is considering producing either 50,000 or 80,000 units during the period. Other information is presented in the schedule.

Division Information for 2007

Beginning inventory	0
Expected sales in units	50,000
Selling price per unit	$30
Variable manufacturing costs per unit	$12
Fixed manufacturing overhead costs (total)	$400,000

Fixed manufacturing overhead costs per unit:
    Based on 50,000 units $8 per unit ($400,000 ÷ 50,000)
    Based on 80,000 units $5 per unit ($400,000 ÷ 80,000)

Manufacturing cost per unit:
    Based on 50,000 units $20 per unit ($12 variable + $8 fixed)
    Based on 80,000 units $17 per unit ($12 variable + $5 fixed)
    Variable selling and administrative expenses $2
    Fixed selling and administrative expenses (total) $40,000

Instructions

(a) Prepare an absorption costing income statement, with one column showing the re-
    sults if 50,000 units are produced and one column showing the results if 80,000 units
    are produced.

(b) Prepare a variable costing income statement, with one column showing the results
    if 50,000 units are produced and one column showing the results if 80,000 units are
    produced.

(c) Reconcile the difference in net incomes under the two approaches and explain what
    accounts for this difference.

(d) ◼◼◼▶ Discuss the relative usefulness of the variable costing income statements
    versus the absorption costing income statements for decision making and for evalu-
    ating the manager's performance.

(a) 80,000 produced:
*   NI $510,000*

(b) 80,000 produced:
*   NI $360,000*

P19-4A The Creekside Inn is a restaurant in Tucson, Arizona. It specializes in southwestern style meals in a moderate price range. Terry Wilson, the manager of Creekside,
has determined that during the last 2 years the sales mix and contribution margin ratio
of its offerings are as follows.

Determine break-even sales
under alternative sales strate-
gies and evaluate results.
(SO 4)

	Percent of Total Sales	**Contribution Margin Ratio**
Appetizers	10%	60%
Main entrees	60%	30%
Desserts	10%	50%
Beverages	20%	80%

Terry is considering a variety of options to try to improve the profitability of the restaurant. Her goal is to generate a target net income of $150,000. The company has fixed
costs of $1,200,000 per year.

Instructions

(a) Calculate the total restaurant sales and the sales of each product line that would be
    necessary to achieve the desired target net income.

(b) Terry believes the restaurant could greatly improve its profitability by reducing the
    complexity and selling price of its entrees to increase the number of clients that it
    serves. It would then more heavily market its appetizers and beverages. She is pro-
    posing to drop the contribution margin ratio on the main entrees to 10% by drop-
    ping the average selling price. She envisions an expansion of the restaurant that would
    increase fixed costs by 50%. At the same time, she is proposing to change the sales
    mix to the following.

(a) Total sales $3,000,000

(b) Total sales $3,750,000

	Percent of Total Sales	**Contribution Margin Ratio**
Appetizers	20%	60%
Main entrees	30%	10%
Desserts	10%	50%
Beverages	40%	80%

Compute the total restaurant sales, and the sales of each product line that would be
necessary to achieve the desired target net income.

(c) Suppose that Terry drops the selling price on entrees and increases fixed costs as
    proposed in part (b), but customers are not swayed by the marketing efforts and the
    sales mix remains what it was in part (a). Compute the total restaurant sales and the
    sales of each product line that would be necessary to achieve the desired target net
    income. Comment on the potential risks and benefits of this strategy.

(c) Total sales $5,909,091

Compute degree of operating leverage and evaluate impact of operating leverage on financial results.
(SO 5)

P19-5A The following variable costing income statements are available for Old Company and New Company.

	Old Company	New Company
Sales	$400,000	$400,000
Variable costs	180,000	80,000
Contribution margin	220,000	320,000
Fixed costs	170,000	270,000
Net income	$ 50,000	$ 50,000

Instructions

(a) BE, Old $309,091
    BE, New $337,500

(b) DOL, Old 4.4
    DOL, New 6.4

(a) Compute the break-even point in dollars and the margin of safety ratio for each company.

(b) Compute the degree of operating leverage for each company and interpret your results.

(c) Assuming that sales revenue increases by 20%, prepare a variable costing income statement for each company.

(d) Assuming that sales revenue decreases by 20%, prepare a variable costing income statement for each company.

(e) ▭▭▭✏▶ Discuss how the cost structure of these two companies affects their operating leverage and profitability.

Problems: Set B

Calculate product cost; prepare income statements under variable costing and absorption costing and reconcile difference.
(SO 1, 2)

P19-1B Spongebob Products manufactures and sells a variety of swimming products. Recently the company opened a new plant to manufacture a light-weight, inflatable boat. Cost and sales data for the first month of operations are shown below.

Manufacturing costs:	
Fixed overhead costs	$150,000
Variable overhead	$5 per boat
Direct labor	$10 per boat
Direct materials	$10 per boat
Beginning inventory	0 boats
Boats produced	50,000
Boats sold	46,000
Selling and administrative costs:	
Fixed	$300,000
Variable	$8 per boat sold

The boat sells for $60. Management is interested in the opening month's results and has asked for an income statement.

Instructions

(a) (i) $28

(a) Assuming the company uses absorption costing, do the following.
    (i) Calculate the production cost per unit.
    (ii) Prepare an income statement for the month of July 2007.

(b) (i) $25

(b) Assuming the company uses variable costing, do the following.
    (i) Calculate the production cost per unit.
    (ii) Prepare an income statement for the month of July 2007.

(c) Reconcile the difference in net income between the two methods.

Prepare income statements under absorption costing and variable costing for a company with beginning inventory, and reconcile difference.
(SO 1, 2, 3)

P19-2B Zaki Metal Company produces the steel wire that is used for the production of paper clips. In 2007, the first year of operations, Zaki produced 40,000 miles of wire and sold 30,000 miles. In 2008, the production and sales results were exactly reversed. In each year, the selling price per mile was $80, variable manufacturing costs were 25% of the sales price of units produced, variable selling expenses were $6 per mile sold, fixed manufacturing costs were $1,200,000, and fixed administrative expenses were $200,000.

Instructions

(a) Prepare income statements for each year using variable costing. (Use the format from Illustration 19-5.)

(b) Prepare income statements for each year using absorption costing. (Use the format from Illustration 19-4.)

(c) Reconcile the differences each year in net income under the two costing approaches.

(d) ▬▬▬▶ Comment on the effects of production and sales on net income under the two costing approaches.

(a) 2007 NI $220,000

(b) 2007 NI $520,000

P19-3B Harrison Pumps is a division of Liverpool Controls Corporation. The division manufactures and sells a pump used in a wide variety of applications. During the coming year it expects to sell 60,000 units for $20 per unit. Richard Starkey manages the division. He is considering producing either 60,000 or 100,000 units during the period. Other information is presented in the following schedule.

Prepare absorption and variable costing income statements and reconcile differences between absorption and variable costing income statements when sales level and production level change. Discuss relative usefulness of absorption costing versus variable costing.
(SO 1, 2, 3)

Division Information for 2007

Beginning inventory	0
Expected sales in units	60,000
Selling price per unit	$20.00
Variable manufacturing costs per unit	$9.00
Fixed manufacturing overhead costs (total)	$240,000

Fixed manufacturing overhead costs per unit:
Based on 60,000 units	$4.00 per unit ($240,000 ÷ 60,000)
Based on 100,000 units	$2.40 per unit ($240,000 ÷ 100,000)

Manufacturing cost per unit:
Based on 60,000 units	$13.00 per unit ($9.00 variable + $4.00 fixed)
Based on 100,000 units	$11.40 per unit ($9.00 variable + $2.40 fixed)
Variable selling and administrative expenses	$1
Fixed selling and administrative expenses (total)	$30,000

Instructions

(a) Prepare an absorption costing income statement, with one column showing the results if 60,000 units are produced and one column showing the results if 100,000 units are produced.

(b) Prepare a variable costing income statement, with one column showing the results if 60,000 units are produced and one column showing the results if 100,000 units are produced.

(c) Reconcile the difference in net incomes under the two approaches and explain what accounts for this difference.

(d) ▬▬▬▶ Discuss the relative usefulness of the variable costing income statements versus the absorption costing income statements for decision making and for evaluating the manager's performance.

(a) 100,000 produced: NI $426,000

(b) 100,000 produced: NI $330,000

P19-4B The Bricktown Pub is a restaurant in Platteville, Wisconsin. It specializes in classic American fare in a moderate price range. Ben Borke, the manager of Bricktown, has determined that during the last 2 years the sales mix and contribution margin of its offerings are as follows.

Determine break-even sales under alternative sales strategies and evaluate results.
(SO 4)

	Percent of Total Sales	Contribution Margin Ratio
Appetizers	10%	50%
Main entrees	55%	30%
Desserts	10%	60%
Beverages	25%	75%

Ben is considering a variety of options to try to improve the profitability of the restaurant. His goal is to generate a target net income of $155,000. The company has fixed costs of $400,000 per year.

Instructions

(a) Calculate the total restaurant sales and the sales of each product line that would be necessary to achieve the desired target net income.

(a) Total sales $1,200,000

(b) Total sales $1,480,392

(b) Ben believes the restaurant could greatly improve its profitability by reducing the complexity and selling price of its entrees to increase the number of clients that it serves, and then more heavily marketing its appetizers and beverages. He is proposing to drop the contribution margin on the main entrees to 15% by dropping the average selling price. He envisions an expansion of the restaurant that would increase fixed costs by 50%. At the same time, he is proposing to change the sales mix to the following.

	Percent of Total Sales	Contribution Margin Ratio
Appetizers	15%	50%
Main entrees	30%	15%
Desserts	15%	60%
Beverages	40%	75%

Compute the total restaurant sales, and the sales of each product line that would be necessary to achieve the desired target net income.

(c) Total sales $1,986,842

(c) Suppose that Ben drops the selling price on entrees, and increases fixed costs as proposed in part (b), but customers are not swayed by his marketing efforts, and the sales mix remains what it was in part (a). Compute the total restaurant sales and the sales of each product line that would be necessary to achieve the desired target net income. Comment on the potential risks and benefits of this strategy.

Compute degree of operating leverage and evaluate impact of operating leverage on financial results.
(SO 5)

P19-5B The following variable costing income statements are available for Retro Company and Modern Company.

	Retro Company	Modern Company
Sales	$500,000	$500,000
Variable costs	300,000	100,000
Contribution margin	200,000	400,000
Fixed costs	140,000	340,000
Net income	$ 60,000	$ 60,000

Instructions

(a) BE, Retro $350,000

(a) Compute the break-even point in dollars and the margin of safety ratio for each company.

(b) DOL, Retro 3.3

(b) Compute the degree of operating leverage for each company and interpret your results.
(c) Assuming that sales revenue increases by 25%, prepare a variable costing income statement for each company.
(d) Assuming that sales revenue decreases by 25%, prepare a variable costing income statement for each company.
(e) ▭▭▭▭➤ Discuss how the cost structure of these two companies affects their operating leverage and profitability.

Problems: Set C

Visit the book's website at **www.wiley.com/college/kimmel** and choose the Student Companion site to access Problem Set C.

BROADENING YOUR PERSPECTIVE

Group Decision Case

BYP19-1 ComfortCraft manufactures swivel seats for customized vans. It currently manufactures 10,000 seats per year, which it sells for $480 per seat. It incurs variable costs of $180 per seat and fixed costs of $2,200,000. It is considering automating the upholstery process, which is now largely manual. It estimates that if it does so, its fixed costs will be $3,200,000, and its variable costs will decline to $80 per seat.

Instructions

With the class divided into groups, answer the following questions.

(a) Prepare a variable costing income statement based on current activity.
(b) Compute contribution margin ratio, break-even point in dollars, margin of safety ratio, and degree of operating leverage based on current activity.
(c) Prepare a variable costing income statement assuming that the company invests in the automated upholstery system.
(d) Compute contribution margin ratio, break-even point in dollars, margin of safety ratio, and degree of operating leverage assuming the new upholstery system is implemented.
(e) Discuss the implications of adopting the new system.

Managerial Analysis

BYP19-2 Big Brick Manufacturing produces basketballs used for indoor or outdoor games. The company has been having significant troubles over the past few years, as the number of competitors in the basketball market has increased dramatically. Recently, the company has been forced to cut back production, in order to decrease its rising inventory level. The following is a list of costs for the company in 2007.

Variable Cost Per Unit:	
Rubber	$2.75
Other materials—indirect	1.40
Ball makers—direct labor	5.60
Factory electricity usage	0.50
Factory water usage	0.15
Other labor—indirect	0.27
Selling and administrative expense	0.40
Fixed Costs Per Year:	
Factory property taxes	$120,000
Factory sewer usage	50,000
Factory electricity usage	40,000
Selling and administrative expense	83,000

Big Brick Manufacturing had ending inventories of 85,000 basketballs in 2006. For these units, fixed manufacturing overhead cost was $4.00 per unit, and variable manufacturing cost per unit was $9.67. In 2007, the company produced 35,000 basketballs; it sold 90,000 basketballs and had an ending inventory of 30,000 units. The basketballs sold for $18 each. Assume that Big Brick uses the FIFO method for computing cost of goods sold.

Instructions

(a) Compute Brick Manufacturing's 2007 manufacturing cost per unit under a variable costing system.
(b) Prepare a variable costing income statement for 2007. (Use the format from Illustration 19-5.)
(c) Compute Brick Manufacturing's 2007 manufacturing cost per unit under absorption costing.
(d) Prepare an absorption costing income statement for 2007. (Use the format from Illustration 19-4.)
(e) Big Brick Manufacturing's chief financial officer, Mr. Swish, is contemplating the benefits of using absorption and variable costing approaches. He has asked you to perform a variety of tasks to help him analyze the difference between the two approaches.
 (i) Reconcile the differences between the net income values of the two approaches.
 (ii) Mr. Swish has been very impressed with the variable costing techniques that he has seen so far. He has been contemplating doing away with absorption costing for the company. What do you think about this suggestion?

Real-World Focus

BYP19-3 In its 2003 annual report the Del Monte Foods Company reported three separate operating segments: consumer products (which includes a variety of canned foods including tuna, fruit, and vegetables); pet products (which includes pet food and snacks and veterinary products); and soup and infant-feeding products (which includes soup, broth, and infant feeding and pureed products).

In its annual report Del Monte uses absorption costing. As a result, information regarding the relative composition of its fixed and variable costs is not available. We have assumed that $860.3 million of its total operating expenses of $1,920.3 million are fixed and have allocated the remaining variable costs across the three divisions. Sales data, along with assumed expense data, are provided below.

	(in millions)	
	Sales	**Variable Costs**
Consumer products	$1,031.8	$ 610
Pet products	837.3	350
Soup and infant-feeding products	302.0	100
	$2,171.1	$1,060

Instructions
(a) Compute each segment's contribution margin ratio and the sales mix.
(b) Using the information computed in part (a), compute the company's break-even point in dollars, and then determine the amount of sales that would be generated by each division at the break-even point.

Exploring the Web

BYP19-4 The external financial statements published by publicly traded companies are based on absorption cost accounting. As a consequence, it is very difficult to gain an understanding of the relative composition of the companies' fixed and variable costs. It is possible, however, to learn about a company's sales mix and the relative profitability of its various divisions. This exercise looks at the financial statements of FedEx Corporation.

Address: **www.fedex.com/us/investorrelations/**
(or go to **www.wiley.com/college/kimmel**)

Steps
1. Go to the site above.
2. Choose "Annual Reports."
3. Choose "2006 Annual Report."

Instructions
(a) Read page 38 of the report under the heading "Description of Business." What are the three primary product lines of the company? What does the company identify as the key factors affecting operating results?
(b) Page 46 of the report lists the operating expenses of FedEx Ground. Assuming that rentals, depreciation, and "other" are all fixed costs, prepare a variable costing income statement for 2006, and compute the division's contribution margin ratio and the break-even point in dollars.
(c) Page 82, Note 14, ("Business segment information") provides additional information regarding the relative profitability of the three business segments.
  (i) Calculate the sales mix for 2004 and 2006. (Note: Exclude "other" among your categories, and deduct it from the total revenue.)
  (ii) The company does not provide the contribution margin for each division, but it does provide "operating margin" (operating income divided by revenues) on pages 46, 48, and 49. List these for each division for 2004 and 2006.
  (iii) Assuming that the "operating margin" (operating income divided by revenues) moves in parallel with each division's contribution margin, how has the shift in sales mix affected the company's profitability from 2004 to 2006?

Communication Activity

BYP19-5 Gigliuto Company's fixed overhead costs are $4 per unit, and its variable overhead costs are $8 per unit. In the first month of operations, 50,000 units are produced and 45,000 units are sold.

Instructions
Write a short memo to the chief financial officer explaining which costing approach will produce the higher income and what the difference will be. Also, explain what potential

benefits the company might obtain by supplementing its absorption costing system with a variable costing system. Finally, explain why the company probably needs to continue to maintain an absorption costing system, even if it decides to adopt a variable costing system.

Research Assignment

BYP19-6   The May 12, 2004, edition of the *Wall Street Journal* has an article by David Bank and Gary McWilliams titled "Squeeze Play: Picking a Big Fight With Dell, H-P Cuts PC Profits Razor-Thin" (page A1).

Instructions
Read the article and answer the following questions.

(a) How is HP using its sales mix as a strategic weapon in its battle with Dell?
(b) What are some of the reasons that Dell's PC division has higher profit margins than the PC division of HP?
(c) Why is HP willing to sell its PCs at prices that enable it to just break even, rather than to make a profit? What are some of the advantages of this approach? What are some of the disadvantages?
(d) Dell has recently entered the market for computer printers. It hopes to apply the same just-in-time techniques to the manufacture and sale of printers that it has used so successfully for PCs. HP is currently the largest seller of printers, and its printer division has a high contribution margin ratio. If Dell is successful in moving into the printer business, what implications might this have for HP's corporate break-even point and its corporate profitability?

Ethics Case

BYP19-7   Scott Bestor was hired during January 2007 to manage the home products division of Advanced Techno. As part of his employment contract, he was told that he would get $5,000 of additional bonus for every 1% increase that the division's profits exceeded those of the previous year.

Soon after coming on board, Scott met with his plant managers and explained that he wanted the plants to be run at full capacity. Previously the plant had employed just-in-time inventory practices and had consequently produced units only as they were needed. Scott stated that under previous management the company had missed out on too many sales opportunities because it didn't have enough inventory on hand. Because previous management had employed just-in-time inventory practices, when Scott came on board there was virtually no beginning inventory. The selling price and variable cost per unit remained the same from 2006 to 2007. Additional information is provided below.

	2006	2007
Net income	$ 400,000	$ 600,000
Units produced	20,000	25,000
Units sold	20,000	20,000
Fixed manufacturing overhead costs	$1,000,000	$1,000,000
Fixed manufacturing overhead costs per unit	$ 50	$ 40

Instructions
(a) Calculate Scott's bonus based upon the net income shown above.
(b) Recompute the 2006 and 2007 results using variable costing.
(c) Recompute Scott's 2007 bonus under variable costing.
(d) Were Scott's actions unethical? Do you think any actions need to be taken by the company?

Answers to Self-Study Questions
1. b   2. c   3. b   4. a   5. b   6. c   7. a   8. d   9. a   10. d   11. c

REMEMBER TO GO BACK TO THE NAVIGATOR BOX ON THE CHAPTER-OPENING PAGE AND CHECK OFF YOUR COMPLETED WORK.

CHAPTER 20

Budgetary Planning

STUDY OBJECTIVES

After studying this chapter, you should be able to:

1 Indicate the benefits of budgeting.

2 State the essentials of effective budgeting.

3 Identify the budgets that comprise the master budget.

4 Describe the sources for preparing the budgeted income statement.

5 Explain the principal sections of a cash budget.

6 Indicate the applicability of budgeting in nonmanufacturing companies.

 THE NAVIGATOR

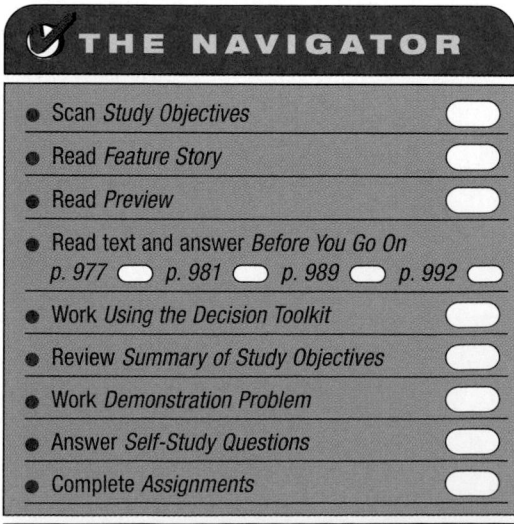

THE NAVIGATOR

- Scan *Study Objectives* ⬭
- Read *Feature Story* ⬭
- Read *Preview* ⬭
- Read text and answer *Before You Go On*
  p. 977 ⬭   p. 981 ⬭   p. 989 ⬭   p. 992 ⬭
- Work *Using the Decision Toolkit* ⬭
- Review *Summary of Study Objectives* ⬭
- Work *Demonstration Problem* ⬭
- Answer *Self-Study Questions* ⬭
- Complete *Assignments* ⬭

FEATURE STORY

The Next Amazon.com? Not Quite

The bursting of the dot-com bubble resulted in countless stories of dot-com failures. Many of these ventures were half-baked, get-rich-quick schemes, rarely based on sound business practices. Initially they saw money flowing in faster than they knew what to do with—which was precisely the problem. Without proper planning and budgeting, much of the money went to waste. In some cases, failure was actually brought on by rapid, uncontrolled growth.

One such example was online discount bookseller, www.Positively-You.com. One of the Web site's co-founders, Lyle Bowline, had never run a business. However, his experience as an assistant director of an entrepreneurial center had provided him with knowledge about the do's and don'ts of small business. To minimize costs, he started the company off small and simple. He invested $5,000 in computer equipment and ran the business out of his basement. In the early months, even though sales were only about $2,000 a month, the company actually made a profit because it kept its costs low (a feat few other dot-coms could boast of).

Things changed dramatically when the company received national publicity in the financial press. Suddenly the company's sales increased to $50,000 a month—fully 25 times the previous level. The "simple" little business suddenly needed a business plan, a strategic plan, and a budget. It needed to rent office space and to hire employees.

Initially, members of a local book club donated time to help meet the sudden demand. But quickly the number of paid employees ballooned. The sudden growth necessitated detailed planning and budgeting. The need for a proper budget was accentuated by the fact that the company's gross profit was only 16 cents on each dollar of goods sold. This meant that after paying for its inventory, the company had only 16 cents of every dollar to cover its remaining operating costs.

Unfortunately, the company never got things under control. Within a few months, sales had plummeted to $12,000 per month. At this level of sales the company could not meet the mountain of monthly expenses that it had accumulated in trying to grow. Ironically, the company's sudden success, and the turmoil it created, appears to have been what eventually caused the company to fail.

PREVIEW OF CHAPTER 20

As the Feature Story about Positively-You.com indicates, budgeting is critical to financial well-being. As a student, you budget your study time and your money. Families budget income and expenses. Governmental agencies budget revenues and expenditures. Business enterprises use budgets in planning and controlling their operations.

Our primary focus in this chapter is budgeting—specifically, how budgeting is used as a **planning tool** by management. Through budgeting, it should be possible for management to maintain enough cash to pay creditors, to have sufficient raw materials to meet production requirements, and to have adequate finished goods to meet expected sales.

The content and organization of Chapter 20 are as follows.

BUDGETARY PLANNING

Budgeting Basics	Preparing the Operating Budgets	Preparing the Financial Budgets	Budgeting in Non-manufacturing Companies
• Budgeting and accounting • Benefits • Essentials of effective budgeting • Length of budget period • Budgeting process • Budgeting and human behavior • Budgeting and long-range planning • The master budget	• Sales • Production • Direct materials • Direct labor • Manufacturing overhead • Selling and administrative expense • Budgeted income statement	• Cash • Budgeted balance sheet	• Merchandisers • Service • Not-for-profit

THE NAVIGATOR

Budgeting Basics

One of management's major responsibilities is planning. As explained in Chapter 14, **planning** is the process of establishing enterprise-wide objectives. A successful organization makes both long-term and short-term plans. These plans set forth the objectives of the company and the proposed way of accomplishing them.

A **budget** is a formal written statement of management's plans for a specified future time period, expressed in financial terms. It normally represents the primary method of communicating agreed-upon objectives throughout the organization. Once adopted, a budget becomes an important basis for evaluating performance. It promotes efficiency and serves as a deterrent to waste and inefficiency. We consider the role of budgeting as a **control device** in Chapter 21.

BUDGETING AND ACCOUNTING

Accounting information makes major contributions to the budgeting process. From the accounting records, historical data on revenues, costs, and expenses can be obtained. These data are helpful in formulating future budget goals.

Normally, accountants have the responsibility for presenting management's budgeting goals in financial terms. In this role, they translate management's plans and communicate the budget to employees throughout the company. Periodic budget reports are prepared that provide the basis for measuring performance and comparing actual results with planned objectives. The budget itself, and the administration of the budget, however, are entirely management responsibilities.

THE BENEFITS OF BUDGETING

The primary benefits of budgeting are:

1. It requires all levels of management to **plan ahead** and to formalize goals on a recurring basis.
2. It provides **definite objectives** for evaluating performance at each level of responsibility.
3. It creates an **early warning system** for potential problems so that management can make changes before things get out of hand.
4. It facilitates the **coordination of activities** within the business. It does this by correlating the goals of each segment with overall company objectives. Thus, production and sales promotion can be integrated with expected sales.
5. It results in greater **management awareness** of the entity's overall operations and the impact on operations of external factors, such as economic trends.
6. It **motivates personnel** throughout the organization to meet planned objectives.

A budget is an aid to management; it is not a substitute for management. A budget cannot operate or enforce itself. The benefits of budgeting will be realized only when budgets are carefully administered by management.

> **STUDY OBJECTIVE**
> **1**
> Indicate the benefits of budgeting.

ESSENTIALS OF EFFECTIVE BUDGETING

Effective budgeting depends on a **sound organizational structure**. In such a structure, authority and responsibility for all phases of operations are clearly defined. Budgets based on **research and analysis** should result in realistic goals that will contribute to the growth and profitability of a company. And, the effectiveness of a budget program is directly related to its **acceptance by all levels of management**.

Once the budget has been adopted, it should be an important tool for evaluating performance. Variations between actual and expected results should be systematically and periodically reviewed to determine their cause(s). However, individuals should not be held responsible for variations that are beyond their control.

> **STUDY OBJECTIVE**
> **2**
> State the essentials of effective budgeting.

LENGTH OF THE BUDGET PERIOD

The budget period is not necessarily one year in length. **A budget may be prepared for any period of time**. Various factors influence the length of the budget period. These factors include the type of budget, the nature of the organization, the need for periodic appraisal, and prevailing business conditions. For example, cash may be budgeted monthly, whereas a plant expansion budget may cover a 10-year period.

The budget period should be long enough to provide an attainable goal under normal business conditions. Ideally, the time period should minimize the impact of seasonal or cyclical fluctuations. On the other hand, the budget period should not be so long that reliable estimates are impossible.

The **most common budget period is one year**. The annual budget, in turn, is often supplemented by monthly and quarterly budgets. Many companies use **continuous 12-month budgets**. These budgets drop the month just ended and add a future month. One advantage of continuous budgeting is that it keeps management planning a full year ahead.

THE BUDGETING PROCESS

The development of the budget for the coming year generally starts several months before the end of the current year. The budgeting process usually begins with the collection of data from each organizational unit of the company. Past performance is often the starting point from which future budget goals are formulated.

The budget is developed within the framework of a **sales forecast**. This forecast shows potential sales for the industry and the company's expected share of such sales. Sales forecasting involves a consideration of various factors: (1) general economic conditions, (2) industry trends, (3) market research studies, (4) anticipated advertising and promotion, (5) previous market share, (6) changes in prices, and (7) technological developments. The input of sales personnel and top management are essential to the sales forecast.

In small companies like Positively-You.com, the budgeting process is often informal. In larger companies, responsibility for coordinating the preparation of the budget is assigned to a **budget committee**. The committee ordinarily includes the president, treasurer, chief accountant (controller), and management personnel from each of the major areas of the company, such as sales, production, and research. The budget committee serves as a review board where managers can defend their budget goals and requests. Differences are reviewed, modified if necessary, and reconciled. The budget is then put in its final form by the budget committee, approved, and distributed.

Business Insight
Management Perspective

A recent study by Willard & Shullman Group Ltd. found that fewer than 14 percent of businesses with fewer than 500 employees do an annual budget or have a written business plan. In all, nearly 60 percent of these businesses have no plans on paper at all. For many small businesses the basic assumption is that, "As long as I sell as much as I can, and keep my employees paid, I'm doing OK." A few small business owners even say that they see no need for budgeting and planning. Most small business owners, though, say that they understand that budgeting and planning are critical for survival and growth. But given the long hours that they already work addressing day-to-day challenges, they also say that they are "just too busy to plan for the future."

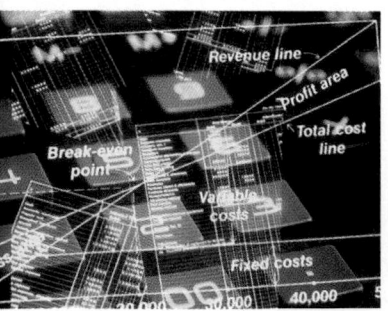

BUDGETING AND HUMAN BEHAVIOR

A budget can have a significant impact on human behavior. It may inspire a manager to higher levels of performance. Or, it may discourage additional effort and pull down the morale of a manager. Why do these diverse effects occur? The answer is found in how the budget is developed and administered.

In developing the budget, each level of management should be invited to participate. This "bottom-to-top" approach is referred to as **participative budgeting**. The advantages of participative budgeting are, first, that lower-level managers have more detailed knowledge of their specific area and thus should be able to provide more accurate budgetary estimates. Second, by inviting lower-level managers to participate in the budgeting process, they are more likely to perceive the resulting budget as fair. The overall goal is to reach agreement on a budget that the managers consider fair and achievable, but which also meets the corporate goals set by top management. When this goal is met, the budget will provide positive motivation for the managers. In contrast, if the managers view the budget as being unfair and unrealistic, they may feel discouraged and uncommitted to budget goals. The risk of having unrealistic budgets is generally greater when the budget is developed from top management down to lower management than vice versa.

Participative budgeting does, however, have potential disadvantages. First, it can be far more time-consuming (and thus more costly) than a "top-down" approach, in which the budget is simply dictated to lower-level managers. A second disadvantage of participative budgeting is that it can foster budgetary "gaming" through budgetary slack. **Budgetary slack** occurs when managers intentionally underestimate budgeted revenues or overestimate budgeted expenses in order to make it easier to achieve budgetary goals. To minimize budgetary slack, higher-level managers must carefully review and thoroughly question the budget projections provided to them by employees whom they supervise. Illustration 20-1 graphically displays the appropriate flow of budget data from bottom to top in an organization.

Illustration 20-1 Flow of budget data from lower levels of management to top levels

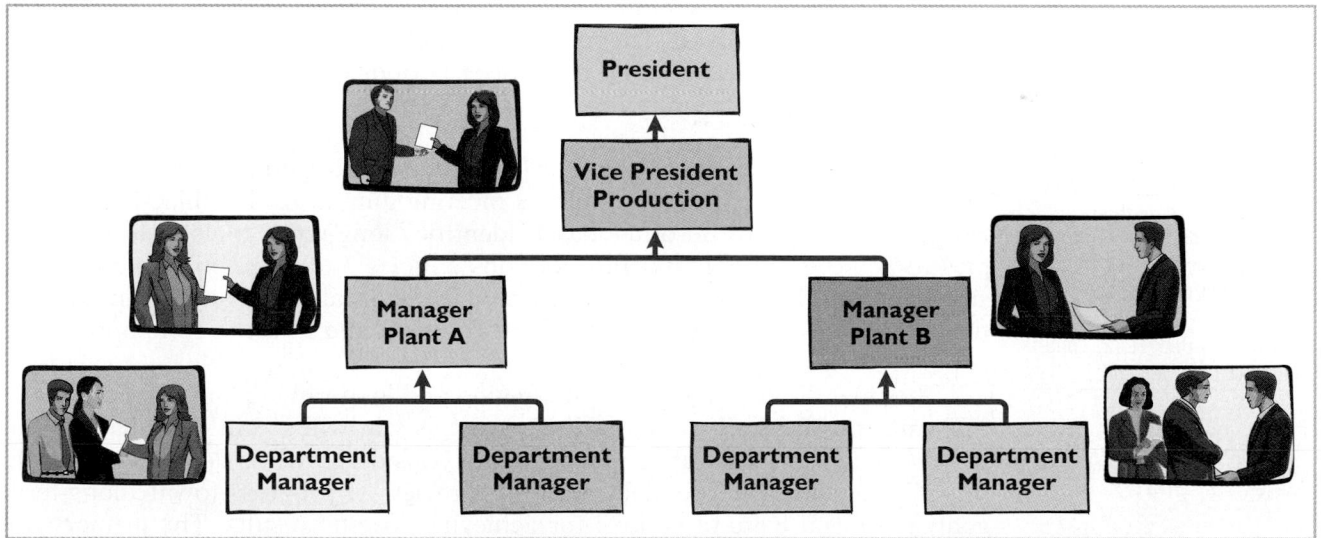

Administering the budget relates to how the budget is used by top management. As explained earlier, the budget should have the complete support of top management. The budget also should be an important basis for evaluating performance. The effect of an evaluation will be positive when top management tempers criticism with advice and assistance. In contrast, a manager is likely to respond negatively if the budget is used exclusively to assess blame.

A budget may be used improperly as a pressure device to force improved performance. Or, it can be used as a positive aid in achieving projected goals. In sum, a budget can become a manager's friend or a foe.

Helpful Hint Unrealistic budgets can lead to unethical employee behavior such as cutting corners on the job or distorting internal financial reports.

Accounting across the Organization

The merits of participative budgeting are not lost on the employees of Time Warner. In 2000, in an effort to revive its plummeting stock, the company's top management determined and publicly announced (without consulting middle managers) bold new financial goals for the coming year. The company's middle-level managers felt that the 2001 budgets were based on top management's growth aspirations, and that those budgetary goals were unattainable. At the end of the year they were proven correct.

The next year the company got a new CEO who promised in 2002, "We will not over promise, and we will deliver." The 2002 budgets were developed from the bottom up, with each operating unit setting what it felt were optimistic but attainable goals. In the words of one manager, using this approach created a sense of teamwork: "We're all going forward with our arms locked together."

Source: Carol J. Loomis, "AOL Time Warner's New Math," *Fortune* (February 4, 2002), pp. 98–102.

BUDGETING AND LONG-RANGE PLANNING

In business, you may hear talk about the need for long-range planning. Budgeting and long-range planning are not the same. One important difference is the **time period involved**. The maximum length of a budget is usually one year, and budgets are often prepared for shorter periods of time, such as a month or a quarter. In contrast, long-range planning usually encompasses a period of at least five years.

> **Helpful Hint** In comparing a budget with a long-range plan: (1) Which has more detail? (2) Which is done for a longer period of time? (3) Which is more concerned with short-term goals?
> Answers: (1) Budget. (2) Long-range plan. (3) Budget.

A second significant difference is in **emphasis**. Budgeting focuses on achieving specific short-term goals, such as meeting annual profit objectives. **Long-range planning**, on the other hand, identifies long-term goals, selects strategies to achieve those goals, and develops policies and plans to implement the strategies. In long-range planning, management also considers anticipated trends in the economic and political environment and how the company should cope with them.

The final difference between budgeting and long-range planning pertains to the **amount of detail presented**. Budgets, as you will see in this chapter, can be very detailed. Long-range plans contain considerably less detail. The data in long-range plans are intended more for a review of progress toward long-term goals than as a basis of control for achieving specific results. The primary objective of long-range planning is to develop the best strategy to maximize the company's performance over an extended future period.

THE MASTER BUDGET

> **STUDY OBJECTIVE**
> **3**
> Identify the budgets that comprise the master budget.

The term "budget" is actually a shorthand term to describe a variety of budget documents. All of these documents are combined into a master budget. The **master budget** is a set of interrelated budgets that constitutes a plan of action for a specified time period. The individual budgets included in a master budget are pictured in Illustration 20-2.

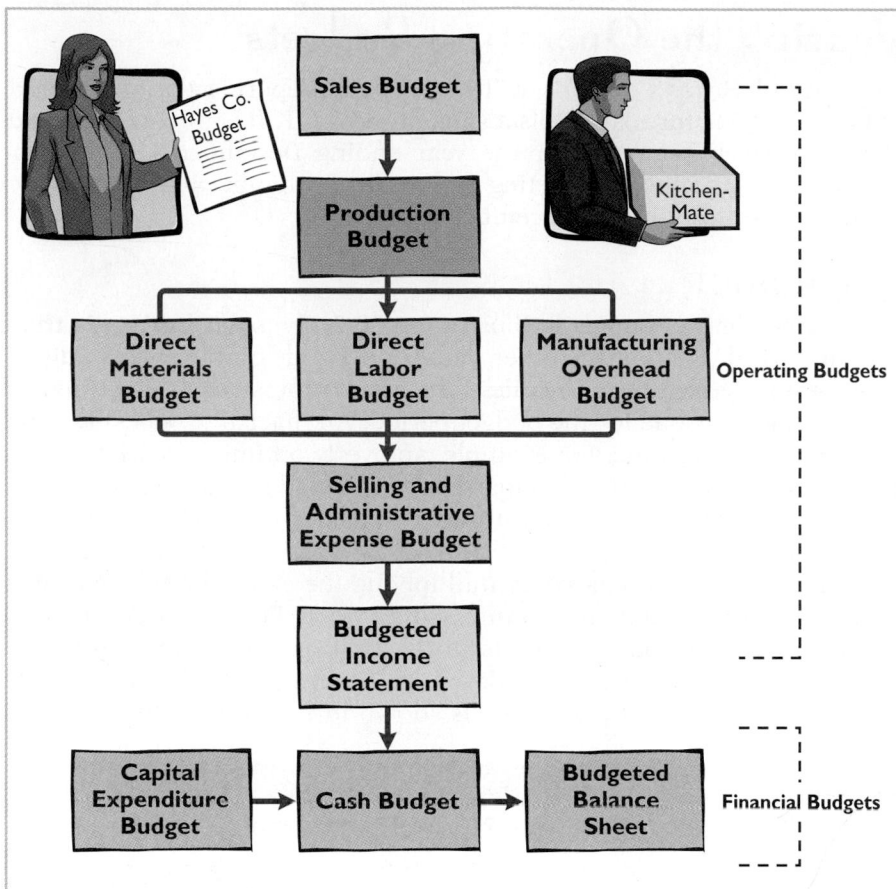

Illustration 20-2 Components of the master budget

As the illustration shows, the master budget contains two classes of budgets. **Operating budgets** are the individual budgets that result in the preparation of the budgeted income statement. These budgets establish goals for the company's sales and production personnel. In contrast, **financial budgets** are the capital expenditure budget, the cash budget, and the budgeted balance sheet. These budgets focus primarily on the cash resources needed to fund expected operations and planned capital expenditures.

The master budget is prepared in the sequence shown in Illustration 20-2. The operating budgets are developed first, beginning with the sales budget. Then the financial budgets are prepared. We will explain and illustrate each budget shown in Illustration 20-2 except the capital expenditure budget. This budget is discussed under the topic of capital budgeting in Chapter 23.

BEFORE YOU GO ON . . .

▶Review It

1. What are the benefits of budgeting?
2. What are the factors essential to effective budgeting?
3. How does the budget process work?
4. How does budgeting differ from long-range planning?
5. What is a master budget?

Preparing the Operating Budgets

A case study of Hayes Company will be used in preparing the operating budgets. Hayes manufactures and sells a single product, Kitchen-mate. The budgets will be prepared by quarters for the year ending December 31, 2007. Hayes Company begins its annual budgeting process on September 1, 2006, and it completes the budget for 2007 by December 1, 2006.

SALES BUDGET

As shown in the master budget in Illustration 20-2, **the sales budget is the first budget prepared**. Each of the other budgets depends on the sales budget. The sales budget is derived from the sales forecast. It represents management's best estimate of sales revenue for the budget period. An inaccurate sales budget may adversely affect net income. For example, an overly optimistic sales budget may result in excessive inventories that may have to be sold at reduced prices. In contrast, an unduly conservative budget may result in loss of sales revenue due to inventory shortages.

The sales budget is prepared by multiplying the expected unit sales volume for each product by its anticipated unit selling price. For Hayes Company, sales volume is expected to be 3,000 units in the first quarter, with 500-unit increments in each succeeding quarter. Based on a sales price of $60 per unit, the sales budget for the year, by quarters, is shown in Illustration 20-3.

Illustration 20-3 Sales budget

Hayes Company Sales Budget.xls

File Edit View Insert Format Tools Data Window Help Acrobat

HAYES COMPANY
Sales Budget
For the Year Ending December 31, 2007

	Quarter				
	1	2	3	4	Year
Expected unit sales	3,000	3,500	4,000	4,500	15,000
Unit selling price	× $60	× $60	× $60	× $60	× $60
Total sales	$180,000	$210,000	$240,000	$270,000	$900,000

20-3

Some companies classify the anticipated sales revenue as cash or credit sales and by geographical regions, territories, or salespersons.

PRODUCTION BUDGET

The production budget shows the units that must be produced to meet anticipated sales. Production requirements are determined from the following formula.[1]

Illustration 20-4 Production requirements formula

| Budgeted Sales Units | + | Desired Ending Finished Goods Units | − | Beginning Finished Goods Units | = | Required Production Units |

A realistic estimate of ending inventory is essential in scheduling production requirements. Excessive inventories in one quarter may lead to cutbacks in production and employee layoffs in a subsequent quarter. On the other

---

[1]This formula ignores any work in process inventories, which are assumed to be nonexistent in Hayes Company.

hand, inadequate inventories may result either in added costs for overtime work or in lost sales. Hayes Company believes it can meet future sales requirements by maintaining an ending inventory equal to 20 percent of the next quarter's budgeted sales volume. For example, the ending finished goods inventory for the first quarter is 700 units (20% × anticipated second-quarter sales of 3,500 units). The production budget is shown in Illustration 20-5.

Illustration 20-5   Production budget

Hayes Company Production Budget.xls

File   Edit   View   Insert   Format   Tools   Data   Window   Help   Acrobat   Type a question for help

	A	B	C	D	E	F	G	H	I	J
1				**HAYES COMPANY**						
2				Production Budget						
3				For the Year Ending December 31, 2007						
4				Quarter						
5		1		2		3		4		Year
6	Expected unit sales (Illustration 20-3)	3,000		3,500		4,000		4,500		
7	Add: Desired ending finished goods units a	700		800		900		1,000 b		
8	Total required units	3,700		4,300		4,900		5,500		
9	Less: Beginning finished goods units	600 c		700		800		900		
10	Required production units	3,100		3,600		4,100		4,600		15,400
11										
12	a 20% of next quarter's sales									
13	b Expected 2008 first-quarter sales, 5,000 units × 20%									
14	c 20% of estimated first-quarter 2007 sales units									

III 20-5

The production budget, in turn, provides the basis for determining the budgeted costs for each manufacturing cost element, as explained in the following pages.

Business Insight
Management Perspective

Wrong move, wrong time, poor planning. When Fruit of the Loom Inc. saw underwear and apparel sales slowing, it cut back production sharply. Too sharply, in fact: almost overnight, demand soared. Caught with its shorts down, the company hired back thousands of workers and frantically increased production. The mistimed production cuts contributed to a 43 percent fall in first-quarter profits. For the year, Fruit stood to lose $200 million in sales, and analysts expected an 11 percent drop in profits for the year.

DIRECT MATERIALS BUDGET

The **direct materials budget** shows both the quantity and cost of direct materials to be purchased. The quantities of direct materials are derived from the following formula.

Illustration 20-6 Formula for direct materials quantities

Direct Materials Units Required for Production	+	Desired Ending Direct Materials Units	−	Beginning Direct Materials Units	=	Required Direct Materials Units to be Purchased

The budgeted cost of direct materials to be purchased is then computed by multiplying the required units of direct materials by the anticipated cost per unit.

The desired ending inventory is again a key component in the budgeting process. For example, inadequate inventories could result in temporary shutdowns of production. Because of its close proximity to suppliers, Hayes Company has found that an ending inventory of raw materials equal to 10 percent of the next quarter's production requirements is sufficient. The manufacture of each Kitchen-mate requires 2 pounds of raw materials, and the expected cost per pound is $4. The direct materials budget is shown in Illustration 20-7.

Illustration 20-7 Direct materials budget

HAYES COMPANY
Direct Materials Budget
For the Year Ending December 31, 2007

	Quarter				Year
	1	2	3	4	
Units to be produced (Illustration 20-5)	3,100	3,600	4,100	4,600	
Direct materials per unit	×2	×2	×2	×2	
Total pounds needed for production	6,200	7,200	8,200	9,200	
Add: Desired ending direct materials (pounds) ᵃ	720	820	920	1,020 ᵇ	
Total materials required	6,920	8,020	9,120	10,220	
Less: Beginning direct materials (pounds)	620	720	820	920	
Direct materials purchases	6,300	7,300	8,300	9,300	
Cost per pound	×$4	×$4	×$4	×$4	
Total cost of direct materials purchases	$25,200	$29,200	$33,200	$37,200	$124,800

ᵃ 10% of next quarter's production requirements
ᵇ Estimated 2008 first-quarter pounds needed for production, 10,200 × 10%
ᶜ 10% of estimated first-quarter pounds needed for production

DIRECT LABOR BUDGET

Like the direct materials budget, the **direct labor budget** contains the quantity (hours) and cost of direct labor necessary to meet production requirements. The total direct labor cost is derived from the following formula.

Illustration 20-8 Formula for direct labor cost

Units to be Produced	×	Direct Labor Time per Unit	×	Direct Labor Cost per Hour	=	Total Direct Labor Cost

Direct labor hours are determined from the production budget. At Hayes Company, two hours of direct labor are required to produce each unit of finished goods. The anticipated hourly wage rate is $10. These data are shown in Illustration 20-9. The direct labor budget is critical in maintaining a labor force that can meet the expected levels of production.

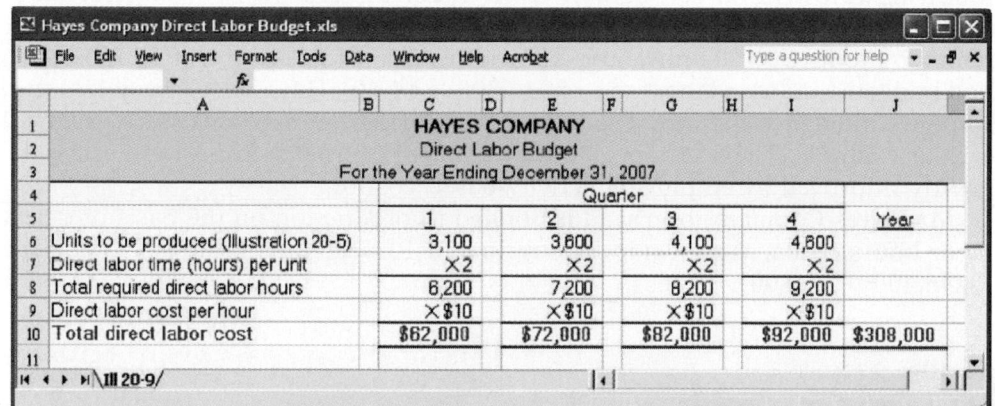

Illustration 20-9   Direct labor budget

BEFORE YOU GO ON . . .

▶**Review It**

1. What is the formula to determine required production units?
2. What are the inputs necessary to prepare the direct labor budget?
3. Which budget must be prepared before the direct materials budget?

▶**Do It**

Becker Company estimates that 2007 unit sales in quarter 1 will be 12,000, 16,000 in quarter 2, and 20,000 in quarter 3, at a unit selling price of $30. Management desires to have ending finished goods inventory equal to 15% of the next quarter's expected unit sales. Prepare a production budget by quarter for the first 6 months of 2007.

Helpful Hint An important assumption in Illustration 20-9 is that the company can add to and subtract from its work force as needed so that the $10 per hour labor cost applies to a wide range of possible production activity.

Action Plan

• Begin with budgeted sales in units.
• Add desired finished goods inventory.
• Subtract beginning finished goods inventory.

Solution

BECKER COMPANY
Production Budget
For the Six Months Ending June 30, 2007

	Quarter		Six
	1	**2**	**Months**
Expected unit sales	12,000	16,000	28,000
Add: Desired ending finished goods	2,400	3,000	3,000
Total required units	14,400	19,000	31,000
Less: Beginning finished goods inventory	1,800	2,400	1,800
Required production units	12,600	16,600	29,200

Related exercise material: BE20-3, E20-3, and E20-5.

☑ THE NAVIGATOR

MANUFACTURING OVERHEAD BUDGET

The **manufacturing overhead budget** shows the expected manufacturing overhead costs for the budget period. As shown in Illustration 20-10, **this budget distinguishes between variable and fixed overhead costs**. Hayes Company expects variable costs to fluctuate with production volume on the basis of the following rates per direct labor hour: indirect materials $1.00, indirect labor $1.40, utilities $0.40, and maintenance $0.20. Thus, for the 6,200 direct labor hours to produce 3,100 units, budgeted indirect materials are $6,200 (6,200 × $1), and budgeted indirect labor is $8,680 (6,200 × $1.40). Hayes also recognizes that some maintenance is fixed. The amounts reported for fixed costs are assumed for our example. The accuracy of budgeted fixed overhead cost estimates can be greatly improved by employing activity-based costing.

At Hayes Company, overhead is applied to production on the basis of direct labor hours. Thus, as shown in Illustration 20-10, the annual rate is $8 per hour ($246,400 ÷ 30,800).

Illustration 20-10   Manufacturing overhead budget

A	1	2	3	4	Year
HAYES COMPANY Manufacturing Overhead Budget For the Year Ending December 31, 2007			Quarter		
Variable costs					
Indirect materials ($1.00 / hour)	$6,200	$7,200	$8,200	$9,200	$30,800
Indirect labor ($1.40 / hour)	8,680	10,080	11,480	12,880	43,120
Utilities ($0.40 / hour)	2,480	2,880	3,280	3,680	12,320
Maintenance ($0.20 / hour)	1,240	1,440	1,640	1,840	6,160
Total variable costs	18,600	21,600	24,600	27,600	92,400
Fixed costs					
Supervisory salaries	20,000	20,000	20,000	20,000	80,000
Depreciation	3,800	3,800	3,800	3,800	15,200
Property taxes and insurance	9,000	9,000	9,000	9,000	36,000
Maintenance	5,700	5,700	5,700	5,700	22,800
Total fixed costs	38,500	38,500	38,500	38,500	154,000
Total manufacturing overhead	$57,100	$60,100	$63,100	$66,100	$246,400
Direct labor hours (Illustration 20-9)	6,200	7,200	8,200	9,200	30,800
Manufacturing overhead rate per direct labor hour ($246,400 ÷ 30,800)					$8

SELLING AND ADMINISTRATIVE EXPENSE BUDGET

Hayes Company combines its operating expenses into one budget, the **selling and administrative expense budget**. This budget projects anticipated selling and administrative expenses for the budget period. In this budget, as in the preceding one, expenses are classified as either variable or fixed. In this case, the variable expense rates per unit of sales are sales commissions $3 and freight-out $1. Variable expenses per quarter are based on the unit sales from the sales budget (Illustration 20-3). For example, sales in the first quarter are expected to be 3,000 units. Thus, Sales Commissions Expense is $9,000 (3,000 × $3), and Freight-out is $3,000 (3,000 × $1). Fixed expenses are based on assumed data. The selling and administrative expense budget is shown in Illustration 20-11.

Illustration 20-11   Selling and administrative expense budget

Hayes Company Manufacturing Selling and Administrative Expense Budget.xls						
File Edit View Insert Format Tools Data Window Help Acrobat				Type a question for help		
	A	B	C	D	E	F
1	HAYES COMPANY					
2	Selling and Administrative Expense Budget					
3	For the Year Ending December 31, 2007					
4		Quarter				
5		1	2	3	4	Year
6	Budgeted sales in units	3,000	3,500	4,000	4,500	15,000
7	Variable expenses					
8	Selling commissions ($3 per unit)	$9,000	$10,500	$12,000	$13,500	$45,000
9	Freight-out ($1 per unit)	3,000	3,500	4,000	4,500	15,000
10	Total variable expenses	12,000	14,000	16,000	18,000	60,000
11	Fixed expenses					
12	Advertising	5,000	5,000	5,000	5,000	20,000
13	Sales salaries	15,000	15,000	15,000	15,000	60,000
14	Office salaries	7,500	7,500	7,500	7,500	30,000
15	Depreciation	1,000	1,000	1,000	1,000	4,000
16	Property taxes and insurance	1,500	1,500	1,500	1,500	6,000
17	Total fixed expenses	30,000	30,000	30,000	30,000	120,000
18	Total selling and administrative expenses	$42,000	$44,000	$46,000	$48,000	$180,000
19						

20-11

Business Insight
e-Business Perspective

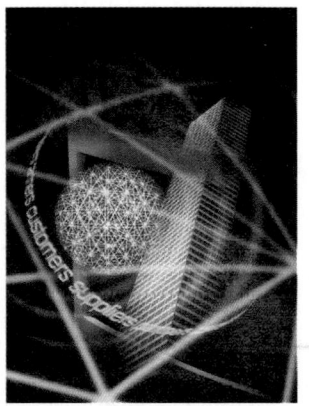

Good budgeting depends on good information. And good information is what e-business is all about. As manufacturers, suppliers, and customers become electronically linked, each benefits by being better informed. Dell Computer not only is directly linked to Solectron, one of its main suppliers, but also to Texas Instruments, one of the main suppliers of parts to Solectron. This linking takes a lot of guesswork out of planning and budgeting for all three companies.

To further improve planning and budgeting, Dell hopes that some day everyone in its industry will anonymously provide their up-to-the-minute production and sales information at a central, electronic exchange. A centralized database such as this would provide valuable information about the supply and demand of computer goods in the marketplace. This information might dramatically improve sales projections, leading to significant improvements in the budgeting process.

Source: "E-Management," *The Economist* (November 11, 2000).

BUDGETED INCOME STATEMENT

The **budgeted income statement** is the important end-product of the operating budgets. This budget indicates the expected profitability of operations for the budget period. The budgeted income statement provides the basis for evaluating company performance.

As you would expect, this budget is prepared from the various operating budgets. For example, to find the cost of goods sold, it is first necessary to determine the total unit cost of producing one Kitchen-mate, as follows.

STUDY OBJECTIVE

4

Describe the sources for preparing the budgeted income statement.

Illustration 20-12 Computation of total unit cost

Cost of One Kitchen-mate

Cost Element	Illustration	Quantity	Unit Cost	Total
Direct materials	20-7	2 pounds	$ 4.00	$ 8.00
Direct labor	20-9	2 hours	$10.00	20.00
Manufacturing overhead	20-10	2 hours	$ 8.00	16.00
Total unit cost				**$44.00**

Cost of goods sold can then be determined by multiplying the units sold by the unit cost. For Hayes Company, budgeted cost of goods sold is $660,000 (15,000 × $44). All data for the statement are obtained from the individual operating budgets except the following: (1) interest expense is expected to be $100, and (2) income taxes are estimated to be $12,000. The budgeted income statement is shown in Illustration 20-13.

Illustration 20-13
Budgeted income
statement

HAYES COMPANY
Budgeted Income Statement
For the Year Ending December 31, 2007

Sales (Illustration 20-3)	$900,000
Cost of goods sold (15,000 × $44)	660,000
Gross profit	240,000
Selling and administrative expenses (Illustration 20-11)	180,000
Income from operations	60,000
Interest expense	100
Income before income taxes	59,900
Income tax expense	12,000
Net income	$ 47,900

Decision Toolkit

Decision Checkpoints	Info Needed for Decision	Tool to Use for Decision	How to Evaluate Results
Has the company met its targets for sales, production expenses, selling and administrative expenses, and net income?	Sales forecasts, inventory levels, projected materials, labor, overhead, and selling and administrative requirements	Master budget—a set of interrelated budgets including sales, production, materials, labor, overhead, and selling and administrative budgets	Results are favorable if revenues exceed budgeted amounts, or if expenses are less than budgeted amounts.

Preparing the Financial Budgets

As shown in Illustration 20-2, the financial budgets consist of the capital expenditure budget, the cash budget, and the budgeted balance sheet. The capital expenditure budget is discussed in Chapter 23; the other budgets are explained in the following sections.

CASH BUDGET

The **cash budget** shows anticipated cash flows. Because cash is so vital, this budget is often considered to be the most important output in preparing financial budgets.

The cash budget contains three sections (cash receipts, cash disbursements, and financing) and the beginning and ending cash balances, as shown in Illustration 20-14.

STUDY OBJECTIVE
5
Explain the principal sections of a cash budget.

ANY COMPANY Cash Budget	
Beginning cash balance	$X,XXX
Add: Cash receipts (Itemized)	X,XXX
Total available cash	X,XXX
Less: Cash disbursements (Itemized)	X,XXX
Excess (deficiency) of available cash over cash disbursements	X,XXX
Financing	X,XXX
Ending cash balance	$X,XXX

Illustration 20-14 Basic form of a cash budget

The **cash receipts section** includes expected receipts from the company's principal source(s) of revenue. These are usually cash sales and collections from customers on credit sales. This section also shows anticipated receipts of interest and dividends, and proceeds from planned sales of investments, plant assets, and the company's capital stock.

The **cash disbursements section** shows expected cash payments. Such payments include direct materials, direct labor, manufacturing overhead, and selling and administrative expenses. This section also includes projected payments for income taxes, dividends, investments, and plant assets.

The **financing section** shows expected borrowings and the repayment of the borrowed funds plus interest. This section is needed when there is a cash deficiency or when the cash balance is below management's minimum required balance.

Data in the cash budget must be prepared in sequence. The ending cash balance of one period becomes the beginning cash balance for the next period. Data for preparing the cash budget are obtained from other budgets and from information provided by management. In practice, cash budgets are often prepared for the year on a monthly basis.

To minimize detail, we will assume that Hayes Company prepares an annual cash budget by quarters. The cash budget for Hayes Company is based on the following assumptions.

1. The January 1, 2007, cash balance is expected to be $38,000.
2. Sales (Illustration 20-3): 60 percent are collected in the quarter sold and 40 percent are collected in the following quarter. Accounts receivable of $60,000 at December 31, 2006, are expected to be collected in full in the first quarter of 2007.
3. Short-term investments are expected to be sold for $2,000 cash in the first quarter.
4. Direct materials (Illustration 20-7): 50 percent are paid in the quarter purchased and 50 percent are paid in the following quarter. Accounts payable

Helpful Hint Why is the cash budget prepared after the other budgets are prepared? Answer: Because the information generated by the other budgets dictates the need for inflows and outflows of cash.

of $10,600 at December 31, 2006, are expected to be paid in full in the first quarter of 2007.

5. Direct labor (Illustration 20-9): 100 percent is paid in the quarter incurred.
6. Manufacturing overhead (Illustration 20-10) and selling and administrative expenses (Illustration 20-11): All items except depreciation are paid in the quarter incurred.
7. Management plans to purchase a truck in the second quarter for $10,000 cash.
8. Hayes makes equal quarterly payments of its estimated annual income taxes.
9. Loans are repaid in the earliest quarter in which there is sufficient cash (that is, when the cash on hand exceeds the $15,000 minimum required balance).

In preparing the cash budget, it is useful to prepare schedules for collections from customers (assumption No. 2, above) and cash payments for direct materials (assumption No. 4, above). These schedules are shown in Illustrations 20-15 and 20-16.

Illustration 20-15 Collections from customers

SCHEDULE OF EXPECTED COLLECTIONS FROM CUSTOMERS

| | Quarter | | | |
	1	2	3	4
Accounts receivable, 12/31/06	$ 60,000			
First quarter ($180,000)	108,000	$ 72,000		
Second quarter ($210,000)		126,000	$ 84,000	
Third quarter ($240,000)			144,000	$ 96,000
Fourth quarter ($270,000)				162,000
Total collections	$168,000	$198,000	$228,000	$258,000

Illustration 20-16 Payments for direct materials

SCHEDULE OF EXPECTED PAYMENTS FOR DIRECT MATERIALS

| | Quarter | | | |
	1	2	3	4
Accounts payable, 12/31/06	$10,600			
First quarter ($25,200)	12,600	$12,600		
Second quarter ($29,200)		14,600	$14,600	
Third quarter ($33,200)			16,600	$16,600
Fourth quarter ($37,200)				18,600
Total payments	$23,200	$27,200	$31,200	$35,200

The cash budget for Hayes Company is shown in Illustration 20-17 (page 987). The budget indicates that $3,000 of financing will be needed in the second quarter to maintain a minimum cash balance of $15,000. Since there is an excess of available cash over disbursements of $22,500 at the end of the third quarter, the borrowing, plus $100 interest, is repaid in this quarter.

	Hayes Company Cash Budget.xls									
	File Edit View Insert Format Tools Data Window Help Acrobat					Type a question for help				
	fx									
	A	B	C	D	E	F	G	H	I	J
1			HAYES COMPANY							
2			Cash Budget							
3			For the Year Ending December 31, 2007							
4					Quarter					
5		Assumption	1		2		3		4	
6	Beginning cash balance	1	$38,000		$25,500		$15,000		$19,400	
7	Add: Receipts									
8	Collections from customers	2	168,000		198,000		228,000		258,000	
9	Sale of securities	3	2,000		0		0		0	
10	Total receipts		170,000		198,000		228,000		258,000	
11	Total available cash		208,000		223,500		243,000		277,400	
12	Less: Disbursements									
13	Direct materials	4	23,200		27,200		31,200		35,200	
14	Direct labor	5	62,000		72,000		82,000		92,000	
15	Manufacturing overhead	6	53,300 [a]		56,300		59,300		62,300	
16	Selling and administrative expenses	6	41,000 [b]		43,000		45,000		47,000	
17	Purchase of truck	7	0		10,000		0		0	
18	Income tax expense	8	3,000		3,000		3,000		3,000	
19	Total disbursements		182,500		211,500		220,500		239,500	
20	Excess (deficiency) of available cash over cash disbursements		25,500		12,000		22,500		37,900	
21	Financing									
22	Borrowings		0		3,000		0		0	
23	Repayments - plus $100 interest	9	0		0		3,100		0	
24	Ending cash balance		$25,500		$15,000		$19,400		$37,900	
25										
26	[a] $57,100 - $3,800 depreciation									
27	[b] $42,000 - $1,000 depreciation									

| | \III 20-17/ | | | |

Business Insight
Management Perspective

Douglas Roberson, president of Atlantic Network, woke up one morning to find that his company was out of cash. At that point, Roberson realized that managing cash flow is different from simply accumulating sales. He says: "If you don't do serious projections about how much cash you will need to handle sales—and how long it will take to collect on invoices—you can end up out of business no matter how fast you are growing." In fact, Roberson says, fast growth makes cash flow problems worse because the company can be spending cash on supplies and payroll at an accelerated pace while waiting 45 days or longer to collect receivables.

A cash budget contributes to more effective cash management. It can show managers when additional financing will be necessary well before the actual need arises. And, it can indicate when excess cash will be available for investments or other purposes.

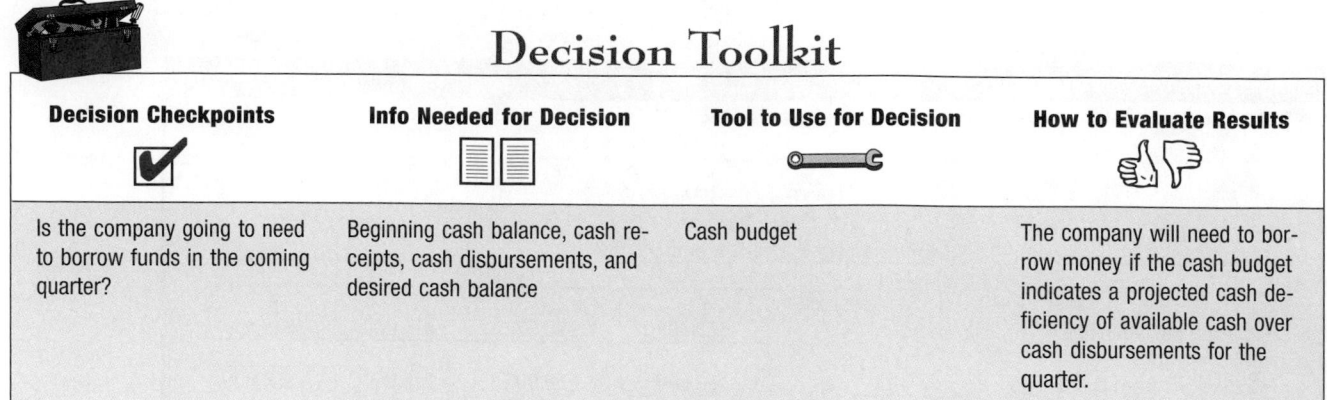

Decision Toolkit

Decision Checkpoints	Info Needed for Decision	Tool to Use for Decision	How to Evaluate Results
Is the company going to need to borrow funds in the coming quarter?	Beginning cash balance, cash receipts, cash disbursements, and desired cash balance	Cash budget	The company will need to borrow money if the cash budget indicates a projected cash deficiency of available cash over cash disbursements for the quarter.

BUDGETED BALANCE SHEET

The **budgeted balance sheet** is a projection of financial position at the end of the budget period. This budget is developed from the budgeted balance sheet for the preceding year and the budgets for the current year. Pertinent data from the budgeted balance sheet at December 31, 2006, are as follows.

Buildings and equipment	$182,000	Common stock	$225,000
Accumulated depreciation	$ 28,800	Retained earnings	$ 46,480

The budgeted balance sheet at December 31, 2007, is shown below.

Illustration 20-18 Budgeted balance sheet

HAYES COMPANY
Budgeted Balance Sheet
December 31, 2007

Assets

Cash		$ 37,900
Accounts receivable		108,000
Finished goods inventory		44,000
Raw materials inventory		4,080
Buildings and equipment	$192,000	
Less: Accumulated depreciation	48,000	144,000
Total assets		$337,980

Liabilities and Stockholders' Equity

Accounts payable	$ 18,600
Common stock	225,000
Retained earnings	94,380
Total liabilities and stockholders' equity	$337,980

The computations and sources of the amounts are explained below.

Cash: Ending cash balance $37,900, shown in the cash budget (Illustration 20-17).

Accounts receivable: 40 percent of fourth-quarter sales $270,000, shown in the schedule of expected collections from customers (Illustration 20-15).

Finished goods inventory: Desired ending inventory 1,000 units, shown in the production budget (Illustration 20-5) times the total unit cost $44 (shown in Illustration 20-12).

Raw materials inventory: Desired ending inventory 1,020 pounds, times the cost per pound $4, shown in the direct materials budget (Illustration 20-7).

Buildings and equipment: December 31, 2006, balance $182,000, plus purchase of truck for $10,000.

Accumulated depreciation: December 31, 2006, balance $28,800, plus $15,200 depreciation shown in manufacturing overhead budget (Illustration 20-10) and $4,000 depreciation shown in selling and administrative expense budget (Illustration 20-11).

Accounts payable: 50 percent of fourth-quarter purchases $37,200, shown in schedule of expected payments for direct materials (Illustration 20-16).

Common stock: Unchanged from the beginning of the year.

Retained earnings: December 31, 2006, balance $46,480, plus net income $47,900, shown in budgeted income statement (Illustration 20-13).

After the budgeting data are entered into the computer, the various budgets (sales, cash, etc.) can be prepared, as well as the budgeted financial statements. Management can also manipulate the budgets in "what if" (sensitivity) analyses based on different hypothetical assumptions. For example, suppose that sales were budgeted to be 10 percent higher in the coming quarter. What impact would the change have on the rest of the budgeting process and the financing needs of the business? The computer can quickly "play out" the impact of the various assumptions on the budgets. Armed with these analyses, management can make more informed decisions about the impact of various projects. They also can anticipate future problems and business opportunities. As seen in this chapter, budgeting is an excellent use of electronic spreadsheets.

BEFORE YOU GO ON . . .

▶Review It

1. What are the two classifications of the individual budgets in the master budget?
2. What is the sequence for preparing the budgets that comprise the operating budgets?
3. Identify some of the source documents that would be used in preparing each of the operating budgets.
4. What are the three principal sections of the cash budget?

▶Do It

Martian Company management wants to maintain a minimum monthly cash balance of $15,000. At the beginning of March, the cash balance is $16,500, expected cash receipts for March are $210,000, and cash disbursements are expected to be $220,000. How much cash, if any, must be borrowed to maintain the desired minimum monthly balance?

Action Plan

- Write down the basic form of the cash budget, starting with the beginning cash balance, adding cash receipts for the period, deducting cash disbursements, and identifying the needed financing to achieve the desired minimum ending cash balance.
- Insert the data given into the outlined form of the cash budget.

Solution

MARTIAN COMPANY
Cash Budget
For the Month Ending March 31, 2007

Beginning cash balance	$ 16,500
Add: Cash receipts for March	210,000
Total available cash	226,500
Less: Cash disbursements for March	220,000
Excess of available cash over cash disbursements	6,500
Financing	8,500
Ending cash balance	$ 15,000

To maintain the desired minimum cash balance of $15,000, Martian Company must borrow $8,500 of cash.

Related exercise material: BE20-9, E20-10, E20-11, and E20-12.

THE NAVIGATOR

Budgeting in Nonmanufacturing Companies

STUDY OBJECTIVE
6

Indicate the applicability of budgeting in nonmanufac-turing companies.

Budgeting is not limited to manufacturers. Budgets may also be used by merchandisers, service enterprises, and not-for-profit organizations.

MERCHANDISERS

As in manufacturing operations, the sales budget for a merchandiser is both the starting point and the key factor in the development of the master budget. The major differences between the master budgets of a merchandiser and a manufacturer are these: (1) A merchandiser **uses a merchandise purchases budget instead of a production budget**. (2) A merchandiser **does not use the manufacturing budgets (direct materials, direct labor, and manufacturing overhead)**. The merchandise purchases budget shows the estimated cost of goods to be purchased to meet expected sales. The formula for determining budgeted merchandise purchases is:

Illustration 20-19   Merchandise purchases formula

Budgeted Cost of Goods Sold	+	Desired Ending Merchandise Inventory	−	Beginning Merchandise Inventory	=	Required Merchandise Purchases

To illustrate, assume that the budget committee of Lima Company is preparing the merchandise purchases budget for July 2007. It estimates that budgeted sales will be $300,000 in July and $320,000 in August. Cost of goods sold is expected to be 70 percent of sales—that is, $210,000 in July (.70 × $300,000) and $224,000 in August (.70 × $320,000). The company's desired ending inventory is 30 percent of the following month's cost of goods sold. Required merchandise purchases for July are $214,200, computed as follows.

Illustration 20-20   Merchandise purchases budget

LIMA COMPANY **Merchandise Purchases Budget** **For the Month Ending July 31, 2007**	
Budgeted cost of goods sold ($300,000 × 70%)	$ 210,000
Add: Desired ending merchandise inventory ($224,000 × 30%)	67,200
Total	277,200
Less: Beginning merchandise inventory ($210,000 × 30%)	63,000
Required merchandise purchases for July	**$214,200**

When a merchandiser is departmentalized, separate budgets are prepared for each department. For example, a grocery store may start by preparing sales budgets and purchases budgets for each of its major departments, such as meats, dairy, and produce. These budgets are then combined into a master budget for the store. When a retailer has branch stores, separate master budgets are prepared for each store. Then these budgets are incorporated into master budgets for the company as a whole.

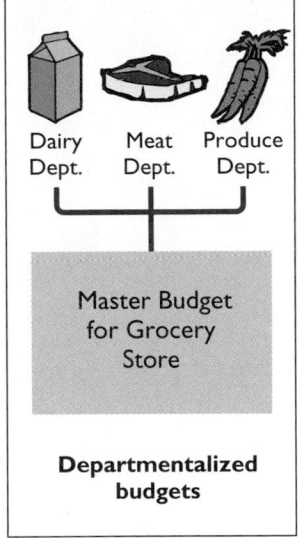

Dairy Dept.   Meat Dept.   Produce Dept.

Master Budget for Grocery Store

Departmentalized budgets

SERVICE ENTERPRISES

In a service enterprise, such as a public accounting firm, a law office, or a medical practice, the critical factor in budgeting is **coordinating professional staff needs with anticipated services**. If a firm is overstaffed, several problems may result: (1) Labor costs will be disproportionately high. (2) Profits will be lower because of the additional salaries. (3) Staff turnover may increase because of lack of challenging work. In contrast, if an enterprise is understaffed, revenue may be lost because existing and prospective client needs for service cannot be met. Also, professional staff may seek other jobs because of excessive work loads.

Budget data for service revenue may be obtained from **expected output** or **expected input**. When output is used, it is necessary to determine the expected billings of clients for services provided. In a public accounting firm, for example, output would be the sum of its billings in auditing, tax, and consulting services. When input data are used, each professional staff member is required to project his or her billable time. Billing rates are then applied to billable time to produce expected service revenue.

Business Insight
Service Company Perspective

Alstom is one of Europe's largest engineering companies. It typically receives a significant prepayment from its customers to finance the early stages of a project. This is advantageous because it means that Alstom doesn't have to borrow as much to finance its operations. However, these advances can get a company into trouble if it isn't careful about budgeting its cash inputs and needs. As one observer noted, "If the money is simply absorbed into the general business, there is a danger that ongoing projects will need large injections of cash that can be found only by borrowing or by advancing cash from new prepayments. If a company manages its contracts poorly, it can soon start to resemble a pyramid scheme, in which prepayments from new orders become vital to finance the completion of old contracts."

SOURCE: "Alstom: Nasty Numbers," *The Economist* (December 8, 2001), p. 59.

NOT-FOR-PROFIT ORGANIZATIONS

Budgeting is just as important for not-for-profit organizations as for profit-oriented enterprises. The budget process, however, is significantly different. In most cases not-for-profit entities budget **on the basis of cash flows (expenditures and receipts), rather than on a revenue and expense basis**. Further, the starting point in the process is usually expenditures, not receipts. For the not-for-profit entity, management's task generally is to find the receipts needed to support the planned expenditures. The activity index is also likely to be significantly different. For example, in a not-for-profit entity, such as a university, budgeted faculty positions may be based on full-time equivalent students or credit hours expected to be taught in a department.

For some governmental units, the budget must be approved by voters. In other cases, such as state governments and the federal government, legislative approval is required. After the budget is adopted, it must be strictly followed. Overspending is often illegal. In governmental budgets, authorizations tend to be on a line-by-line basis. That is, the budget for a municipality may have a specified authorization for police and fire protection, garbage collection, street paving, and so on. The line-item authorization of governmental budgets significantly limits the amount of discretion management can exercise. The city manager often cannot use savings from one line item, such as street paving, to cover increased spending in another line item, such as snow removal.

BEFORE YOU GO ON . . .

▶**Review It**

1. What is the formula for computing required merchandise purchases?
2. How does budgeting in service and not-for-profit organizations differ from budgeting for manufacturers and merchandisers?

✓ **THE NAVIGATOR**

Using the Decision Toolkit

The University of Wisconsin and its subunits must prepare budgets. One unique subunit of the University of Wisconsin is Babcock Ice Cream, a functioning producer of dairy products (and famous, at least on campus, for its delicious ice cream).

Assume that Babcock Ice Cream prepares monthly cash budgets. Relevant data from assumed operating budgets for 2007 are:

	January	February
Sales	$460,000	$412,000
Direct materials purchases	185,000	210,000
Direct labor	70,000	85,000
Manufacturing overhead	50,000	65,000
Selling and administrative expenses	85,000	95,000

Babcock sells 50% of its ice cream in its shops on campus, as well as selling to local stores. All sales on campus are cash sales. Collections from local stores are expected to be 75% in the month of sale, and 25% in the month following sale. Sixty percent (60%) of direct materials purchases are paid in cash in the month of purchase, and the balance due is paid in the month following the purchase. All other items above are paid in the month incurred. (Depreciation has been excluded from manufacturing overhead and selling and administrative expenses.)

Other data:

(1) Sales: December 2006, $320,000
(2) Purchases of direct materials: December 2006, $175,000
(3) Other receipts: January—Donation received, $2,000
February—Sale of used equipment, $4,000
(4) Other disbursements: February—Purchased equipment, $10,000
(5) Repaid debt: January, $30,000

The company's cash balance on January 1, 2007, is expected to be $50,000. The company wants to maintain a minimum cash balance of $45,000.

Instructions

(a) Prepare schedules for (1) expected collections from customers and (2) expected payments for direct materials purchases.

(b) Prepare a cash budget for January and February in columnar form.

Solution

(a) (1)   Expected Collections from Customers

	January	February
December ($320,000)	$ 80,000	$ 0
January ($460,000)	345,000	115,000
February ($412,000)	0	309,000
Totals	$425,000	$424,000

(2)   Expected Payments for Direct Materials

	January	February
December ($175,000)	$ 70,000	$ 0
January ($185,000)	111,000	74,000
February ($210,000)	0	126,000
Totals	$181,000	$200,000

(b)   BABCOCK ICE CREAM
Cash Budget
For the Two Months Ending February 28, 2007

	January	February
Beginning cash balance	$ 50,000	$ 61,000
Add: Receipts		
Collections from customers	425,000	424,000
Donations received	2,000	0
Sale of used equipment	0	4,000
Total receipts	427,000	428,000
Total available cash	477,000	489,000
Less: Disbursements		
Direct materials	181,000	200,000
Direct labor	70,000	85,000
Manufacturing overhead	50,000	65,000
Selling and administrative expenses	85,000	95,000
Purchase of equipment	0	10,000
Total disbursements	386,000	455,000
Excess (deficiency) of available cash over cash disbursements	91,000	34,000
Financing		
Borrowings	0	11,000
Repayments	30,000	0
Ending cash balance	$ 61,000	$ 45,000

THE NAVIGATOR

Summary of Study Objectives

1 *Indicate the benefits of budgeting.* The primary advantages of budgeting are that it (a) requires management to plan ahead, (b) provides definite objectives for evaluating performance, (c) creates an early warning system for potential problems, (d) facilitates coordination of activities, (e) results in greater management awareness, and (f) motivates personnel to meet planned objectives.

2 *State the essentials of effective budgeting.* The essentials of effective budgeting are (a) sound organizational structure, (b) research and analysis, and (c) acceptance by all levels of management.

3 *Identify the budgets that comprise the master budget.* The master budget consists of the following budgets: (a) sales, (b) production, (c) direct materials, (d) direct labor, (e) manufacturing overhead, (f) selling and administrative expense, (g) budgeted income statement, (h) capital expenditure budget, (i) cash budget, and (j) budgeted balance sheet.

4 *Describe the sources for preparing the budgeted income statement.* The budgeted income statement is prepared from (a) the sales budget, (b) the budgets for direct materials, direct labor, and manufacturing overhead, and (c) the selling and administrative expense budget.

5 *Explain the principal sections of a cash budget.* The cash budget has three sections (receipts, disbursements, and financing) and the beginning and ending cash balances.

6 *Indicate the applicability of budgeting in non-manufacturing companies.* Budgeting may be used by merchandisers for development of a master budget. In service enterprises budgeting is a critical factor in coordinating staff needs with anticipated services. In not-for-profit organizations, the starting point in budgeting is usually expenditures, not receipts.

THE NAVIGATOR

Decision Toolkit—A Summary

Decision Checkpoints	Info Needed for Decision	Tool to Use for Decision	How to Evaluate Results
Has the company met its targets for sales, production expenses, selling and administrative expenses, and net income?	Sales forecasts, inventory levels, projected materials, labor, overhead, and selling and administrative requirements	Master budget—a set of interrelated budgets including sales, production, materials, labor, overhead, and selling and administrative budgets	Results are favorable if revenues exceed budgeted amounts, or if expenses are less than budgeted amounts.
Is the company going to need to borrow funds in the coming quarter?	Beginning cash balance, cash receipts, cash disbursements, and desired cash balance	Cash budget	The company will need to borrow money if the cash budget indicates a projected cash deficiency of available cash over cash disbursements for the quarter.

Glossary

Budget A formal written statement of management's plans for a specified future time period, expressed in financial terms. (p. 972)

Budget committee A group responsible for coordinating the preparation of the budget. (p. 974)

Budgetary slack The amount by which a manager intentionally underestimates budgeted revenues or overes-

timates budgeted expenses in order to make it easier to achieve budgetary goals. (p. 975)

Budgeted balance sheet A projection of financial position at the end of the budget period. (p. 988)

Budgeted income statement An estimate of the expected profitability of operations for the budget period. (p. 983)

Cash budget A projection of anticipated cash flows. (p. 985)

Direct labor budget A projection of the quantity and cost of direct labor necessary to meet production requirements. (p. 980)

Direct materials budget An estimate of the quantity and cost of direct materials to be purchased. (p. 979)

Financial budgets Individual budgets that focus primarily on the cash resources needed to fund expected operations and planned capital expenditures. (p. 977)

Long-range planning A formalized process of selecting strategies to achieve long-term goals and developing policies and plans to implement the strategies. (p. 976)

Manufacturing overhead budget An estimate of expected manufacturing overhead costs for the budget period. (p. 982)

Master budget A set of interrelated budgets that constitutes a plan of action for a specific time period. (p. 976)

Merchandise purchases budget The estimated cost of goods to be purchased by a merchandiser to meet expected sales. (p. 990)

Operating budgets Individual budgets that result in a budgeted income statement. (p. 977)

Participative budgeting A budgetary approach that starts with input from lower-level managers and works upward so that managers at all levels participate. (p. 975)

Production budget A projection of the units that must be produced to meet anticipated sales. (p. 978)

Sales budget An estimate of expected sales for the budget period. (p. 978)

Sales forecast The projection of potential sales for the industry and the company's expected share of such sales. (p. 974)

Selling and administrative expense budget A projection of anticipated selling and administrative expenses for the budget period. (p. 982)

Demonstration Problem

Soroco Company is preparing its master budget for 2007. Relevant data pertaining to its sales and production budgets are as follows:

Sales: Sales for the year are expected to total 1,200,000 units. Quarterly sales are 20%, 25%, 30%, and 25% respectively. The sales price is expected to be $50 per unit for the first three quarters and $55 per unit beginning in the fourth quarter. Sales in the first quarter of 2008 are expected to be 10% higher than the budgeted sales volume for the first quarter of 2007.

Production: Management desires to maintain ending finished goods inventories at 25% of the next quarter's budgeted sales volume.

Instructions
Prepare the sales budget and production budget by quarters for 2007.

Solution to Demonstration Problem

SOROCO COMPANY
Sales Budget
For the Year Ending December 31, 2007

	Quarter				
	1	2	3	4	Year
Expected unit sales	240,000	300,000	360,000	300,000	1,200,000
Unit selling price	× $50	× $50	× $50	× $55	—
Total sales	$12,000,000	$15,000,000	$18,000,000	$16,500,000	$61,500,000

Action Plan
- Know the form and content of the sales budget.
- Prepare the sales budget first as the basis for the other budgets.
- Determine the units that must be produced to meet anticipated sales.
- Know how to compute the beginning and ending finished goods units.

	SOROCO COMPANY Production Budget For the Year Ending December 31, 2007				
	Quarter				
	1	**2**	**3**	**4**	**Year**
Expected unit sales	240,000	300,000	360,000	300,000	
Add: Desired ending finished goods units	75,000	90,000	75,000	66,000[1]	
Total required units	315,000	390,000	435,000	366,000	
Less: Beginning finished goods units	60,000[2]	75,000	90,000	75,000	
Required production units	255,000	315,000	345,000	291,000	1,206,000

[1]Estimated first-quarter 2008 sales volume 240,000 + (240,000 × 10%) = 264,000; 264,000 × 25%.
[2]25% of estimated first-quarter 2007 sales units (240,000 × 25%).

Self-Study Questions

Answers are at the end of the chapter.

(SO 1) **1.** Which of the following is not a benefit of budgeting?
 (a) Management can plan ahead.
 (b) An early warning system is provided for potential problems.
 (c) It enables disciplinary action to be taken at every level of responsibility.
 (d) The coordination of activities is facilitated.

(SO 2) **2.** The essentials of effective budgeting do *not* include:
 (a) top-down budgeting.
 (b) management acceptance.
 (c) research and analysis.
 (d) sound organizational structure.

(SO 2) **3.** Compared to budgeting, long-range planning generally has the:
 (a) same amount of detail.
 (b) longer time period.
 (c) same emphasis.
 (d) same time period.

(SO 3) **4.** A sales budget is:
 (a) derived from the production budget.
 (b) management's best estimate of sales revenue for the year.
 (c) not the starting point for the master budget.
 (d) prepared only for credit sales.

(SO 3) **5.** The formula for the production budget is budgeted sales in units plus:
 (a) desired ending merchandise inventory less beginning merchandise inventory.

 (b) beginning finished goods units less desired ending finished goods units.
 (c) desired ending direct materials units less beginning direct materials units.
 (d) desired ending finished goods units less beginning finished goods units.

(SO 3) **6.** Direct materials inventories are kept in pounds in Byrd Company, and the total pounds of direct materials needed for production is 9,500. If the beginning inventory is 1,000 pounds and the desired ending inventory is 2,200 pounds, the total pounds to be purchased is:
 (a) 9,400.
 (b) 9,500.
 (c) 9,700.
 (d) 10,700.

(SO 3) **7.** The formula for computing the direct labor budget is to multiply the direct labor cost per hour by the:
 (a) total required direct labor hours.
 (b) physical units to be produced.
 (c) equivalent units to be produced.
 (d) No correct answer is given.

(SO 4) **8.** Each of the following budgets is used in preparing the budgeted income statement *except* the:
 (a) sales budget.
 (b) selling and administrative budget.
 (c) capital expenditure budget.
 (d) direct labor budget.

(SO 5) **9.** Expected direct materials purchases in Read Company are $70,000 in the first quarter and

$90,000 in the second quarter. Forty percent of the purchases are paid in cash as incurred, and the balance is paid in the following quarter. The budgeted cash payments for purchases in the second quarter are:
(a) $96,000.
(b) $90,000.
(c) $78,000.
(d) $72,000.

10. The budget for a merchandiser differs from a budget for a manufacturer because: (SO 6)
(a) a merchandise purchases budget replaces the production budget.
(b) the manufacturing budgets are not applicable.
(c) None of the above.
(d) Both (a) and (b) above.

Questions

1. (a) What is a budget?
(b) How does a budget contribute to good management?

2. Donna Cox and Tony Carpino are discussing the benefits of budgeting. They ask you to identify the primary advantages of budgeting. Comply with their request.

3. Kate Coulter asks your help in understanding the essentials of effective budgeting. Identify the essentials for Kate.

4. (a) "Accounting plays a relatively unimportant role in budgeting." Do you agree? Explain.
(b) What responsibilities does management have in budgeting?

5. What criteria are helpful in determining the length of the budget period? What is the most common budget period?

6. Ann Wilkins maintains that the only difference between budgeting and long-range planning is time. Do you agree? Why or why not?

7. What is participative budgeting? What are its potential benefits? What are its potential shortcomings?

8. What is budgetary slack? What incentive do managers have to create budgetary slack?

9. Distinguish between a master budget and a sales forecast.

10. What budget is the starting point in preparing the master budget? What may result if this budget is inaccurate?

11. "The production budget shows both unit production data and unit cost data." Is this true? Explain.

12. Alov Company has 10,000 beginning finished goods units. Budgeted sales units are 160,000. If management desires 20,000 ending finished goods units, what are the required units of production?

13. In preparing the direct materials budget for Quan Company, management concludes that required purchases are 54,000 units. If 52,000 direct materials units are required in production and there are 7,000

units of beginning direct materials, what is the desired units of ending direct materials?

14. The production budget of Layden Company calls for 90,000 units to be produced. If it takes 30 minutes to make one unit and the direct labor rate is $16 per hour, what is the total budgeted direct labor cost?

15. Marrero Company's manufacturing overhead budget shows total variable costs of $168,000 and total fixed costs of $162,000. Total production in units is expected to be 160,000. It takes 15 minutes to make one unit, and the direct labor rate is $15 per hour. Express the manufacturing overhead rate as (a) a percentage of direct labor cost, and (b) an amount per direct labor hour.

16. Ankiel Company's variable selling and administrative expenses are 10% of net sales. Fixed expenses are $60,000 per quarter. The sales budget shows expected sales of $200,000 and $250,000 in the first and second quarters, respectively. What are the total budgeted selling and administrative expenses for each quarter?

17. For Tomko Company, the budgeted cost for one unit of product is direct materials $10, direct labor $20, and manufacturing overhead 80% of direct labor cost. If 25,000 units are expected to be sold at $69 each, what is the budgeted gross profit?

18. Indicate the supporting schedules used in preparing a budgeted income statement through gross profit for a manufacturer.

19. Identify the three sections of a cash budget. What balances are also shown in this budget?

20. Springer Company has credit sales of $400,000 in January. Past experience suggests that 45% is collected in the month of sale, 50% in the month following the sale, and 5% in the second month following the sale. Compute the cash collections from January sales in January, February, and March.

21. What is the formula for determining required merchandise purchases for a merchandiser?

22. How may expected revenues in a service enterprise be computed?

Brief Exercises

Prepare a diagram of a master budget.
(SO 3)

BE20-1 Russo Manufacturing Company uses the following budgets: Balance Sheet, Capital Expenditure, Cash, Direct Labor, Direct Materials, Income Statement, Manufacturing Overhead, Production, Sales, and Selling and Administrative. Prepare a diagram of the interrelationships of the budgets in the master budget. Indicate whether each budget is an operating or a financial budget.

Prepare a sales budget.
(SO 3)

BE20-2 Maltz Company estimates that unit sales will be 10,000 in quarter 1; 12,000 in quarter 2; 14,000 in quarter 3; and 18,000 in quarter 4. Using a sales price of $70 per unit, prepare the sales budget by quarters for the year ending December 31, 2007.

Prepare a production budget for 2 quarters.
(SO 3)

BE20-3 Sales budget data for Maltz Company are given in BE20-2. Management desires to have an ending finished goods inventory equal to 25% of the next quarter's expected unit sales. Prepare a production budget by quarters for the first 6 months of 2007.

Prepare a direct materials budget for 1 month.
(SO 3)

BE20-4 Gomez Company has 1,600 pounds of raw materials in its December 31, 2007, ending inventory. Required production for January and February of 2008 are 4,000 and 5,500 units, respectively. Two pounds of raw materials are needed for each unit, and the estimated cost per pound is $6. Management desires an ending inventory equal to 20% of next month's materials requirements. Prepare the direct materials budget for January.

Prepare a direct labor budget for 2 quarters.
(SO 3)

BE20-5 For Tracey Company, units to be produced are 5,000 in quarter 1 and 6,000 in quarter 2. It takes 1.8 hours to make a finished unit, and the expected hourly wage rate is $14 per hour. Prepare a direct labor budget by quarters for the 6 months ending June 30, 2007.

Prepare a manufacturing overhead budget.
(SO 3)

BE20-6 For Savage Inc. variable manufacturing overhead costs are expected to be $20,000 in the first quarter of 2007 with $2,000 increments in each of the remaining three quarters. Fixed overhead costs are estimated to be $35,000 in each quarter. Prepare the manufacturing overhead budget by quarters and in total for the year.

Prepare a selling and administrative expense budget.
(SO 3)

BE20-7 Rado Company classifies its selling and administrative expense budget into variable and fixed components. Variable expenses are expected to be $25,000 in the first quarter, and $3,000 increments are expected in the remaining quarters of 2007. Fixed expenses are expected to be $40,000 in each quarter. Prepare the selling and administrative expense budget by quarters and in total for 2007.

Prepare a budgeted income statement for the year.
(SO 4)

BE20-8 Stoker Company has completed all of its operating budgets. The sales budget for the year shows 50,000 units and total sales of $2,000,000. The total unit cost of making one unit of sales is $24. Selling and administrative expenses are expected to be $300,000. Income taxes are estimated to be $150,000. Prepare a budgeted income statement for the year ending December 31, 2007.

Prepare data for a cash budget.
(SO 5)

BE20-9 Chow Industries expects credit sales for January, February, and March to be $200,000, $260,000, and $310,000, respectively. It is expected that 70% of the sales will be collected in the month of sale, and 30% will be collected in the following month. Compute cash collections from customers for each month.

Determine required merchandise purchases for 1 month.
(SO 6)

BE20-10 Reebles Wholesalers is preparing its merchandise purchases budget. Budgeted sales are $400,000 for April and $450,000 for May. Cost of goods sold is expected to be 60% of sales. The company's desired ending inventory is 20% of the following month's cost of goods sold. Compute the required purchases for April.

Exercises

Prepare a sales budget for 2 quarters.
(SO 3)

E20-1 Vosser Electronics Inc. produces and sells two models of pocket calculators, XQ-103 and XQ-104. The calculators sell for $12 and $25, respectively. Because of the intense competition Vosser faces, management budgets sales semiannually. Its projections for the first 2 quarters of 2007 are as follows.

Product	Unit Sales	
	Quarter 1	Quarter 2
XQ-103	30,000	25,000
XQ-104	12,000	13,000

No changes in selling prices are anticipated.

Instructions

Prepare a sales budget for the 2 quarters ending June 30, 2007. List the products and show for each quarter and for the 6 months, units, selling price, and total sales by product and in total.

E20-2   Roche and Young, CPAs, are preparing their service revenue (sales) budget for the coming year (2007). The practice is divided into three departments: auditing, tax, and consulting. Billable hours for each department, by quarter, are provided below.

Prepare a sales budget for four quarters.
(SO 3, 6)

Department	Quarter 1	Quarter 2	Quarter 3	Quarter 4
Auditing	2,200	1,600	2,000	2,400
Tax	3,000	2,400	2,000	2,500
Consulting	1,500	1,500	1,500	1,500

Average hourly billing rates are: auditing $80, tax $90, and consulting $100.

Instructions

Prepare the service revenue (sales) budget for 2007 by listing the departments and showing for each quarter and the year in total, billable hours, billable rate, and total revenue.

E20-3   Wayans Company produces and sells automobile batteries, the heavy-duty HD-240. The 2007 sales budget is as follows.

Prepare quarterly production budgets.
(SO 3)

Quarter	HD-240
1	5,000
2	7,000
3	8,000
4	10,000

The January 1, 2007, inventory of HD-240 is 2,000 units. Management desires an ending inventory each quarter equal to 40% of the next quarter's sales. Sales in the first quarter of 2008 are expected to be 30% higher than sales in the same quarter in 2007.

Instructions

Prepare quarterly production budgets for each quarter and in total for 2007.

E20-4   Samano Industries has adopted the following production budget for the first 4 months of 2008.

Prepare a direct materials purchases budget.
(SO 3)

Month	Units	Month	Units
January	10,000	March	5,000
February	8,000	April	4,000

Each unit requires 5 pounds of raw materials costing $2 per pound. On December 31, 2007, the ending raw materials inventory was 15,000 pounds. Management wants to have a raw materials inventory at the end of the month equal to 30% of next month's production requirements.

Instructions

Prepare a direct materials purchases budget by month for the first quarter.

E20-5   On January 1, 2008, the Sanchez Company budget committee has reached agreement on the following data for the 6 months ending June 30, 2008.

Prepare production and direct materials budgets by quarters for 6 months.
(SO 3)

Sales units:	First quarter 5,000; second quarter 8,000; third quarter 7,000
Ending raw materials inventory:	50% of the next quarter's production requirements
Ending finished goods inventory:	30% of the next quarter's expected sales units
Third-quarter production:	7,250 units

The ending raw materials and finished goods inventories at December 31, 2007, follow the same percentage relationships to production and sales that occur in 2008. Three pounds of raw materials are required to make each unit of finished goods. Raw materials purchased are expected to cost $4 per pound.

Instructions
(a) Prepare a production budget by quarters for the 6-month period ended June 30, 2008.
(b) Prepare a direct materials budget by quarters for the 6-month period ended June 30, 2008.

Prepare a direct labor budget.
(SO 3)

E20-6   Pacer, Inc., is preparing its direct labor budget for 2007 from the following production budget based on a calendar year.

Quarter	Units	Quarter	Units
1	20,000	3	35,000
2	25,000	4	30,000

Each unit requires 1.2 hours of direct labor.

Instructions
Prepare a direct labor budget for 2007. Wage rates are expected to be $15 for the first 2 quarters and $16 for quarters 3 and 4.

Prepare a manufacturing overhead budget for the year.
(SO 3)

E20-7   Keyser Company is preparing its manufacturing overhead budget for 2007. Relevant data consist of the following.

Units to be produced (by quarters): 10,000, 12,000, 14,000, 16,000.

Direct labor: Time is 1.5 hours per unit.

Variable overhead costs per direct labor hour: Indirect materials $0.70; indirect labor $1.20; and maintenance $0.30.

Fixed overhead costs per quarter: Supervisory salaries $35,000; depreciation $16,000; and maintenance $12,000.

Instructions
Prepare the manufacturing overhead budget for the year, showing quarterly data.

Prepare a selling and administrative expense budget for 2 quarters.
(SO 3)

E20-8   Lockwood Company combines its operating expenses for budget purposes in a selling and administrative expense budget. For the first 6 months of 2007, the following data are available.
1. Sales: 20,000 units quarter 1; 24,000 units quarter 2.
2. Variable costs per dollar of sales: Sales commissions 5%, delivery expense 2%, and advertising 3%.
3. Fixed costs per quarter: Sales salaries $10,000, office salaries $6,000, depreciation $4,200, insurance $1,500, utilities $800, and repairs expense $600.
4. Unit selling price: $20.

Instructions
Prepare a selling and administrative expense budget by quarters for the first 6 months of 2007.

Prepare a budgeted income statement for the year.
(SO 3, 4)

E20-9   Haven Company has accumulated the following budget data for the year 2007.
1. Sales: 40,000 units, unit selling price $80.
2. Cost of one unit of finished goods: Direct materials 2 pounds at $5 per pound, direct labor 3 hours at $12 per hour, and manufacturing overhead $6 per direct labor hour.
3. Inventories (raw materials only): Beginning, 10,000 pounds; ending, 15,000 pounds.
4. Raw materials cost: $5 per pound.
5. Selling and administrative expenses: $200,000.
6. Income taxes: 30% of income before income taxes.

Instructions
(a) Prepare a schedule showing the computation of cost of goods sold for 2007.
(b) Prepare a budgeted income statement for 2007.

Prepare a cash budget for 2 months.
(SO 5)

E20-10   Nunez Company expects to have a cash balance of $46,000 on January 1, 2007. Relevant monthly budget data for the first 2 months of 2007 are as follows.

Collections from customers: January $75,000, February $150,000.

Payments for direct materials: January $45,000, February $70,000.

Direct labor: January $30,000, February $45,000. Wages are paid in the month they are incurred.

Manufacturing overhead: January $21,000, February $30,000. These costs include depreciation of $1,000 per month. All other overhead costs are paid as incurred.

Selling and administrative expenses: January $15,000, February $20,000. These costs are exclusive of depreciation. They are paid as incurred.

Sales of marketable securities in January are expected to realize $10,000 in cash. Nunez Company has a line of credit at a local bank that enables it to borrow up to $25,000. The company wants to maintain a minimum monthly cash balance of $20,000.

Instructions
Prepare a cash budget for January and February.

E20-11 Environmental Landscaping Inc. is preparing its budget for the first quarter of 2007. The next step in the budgeting process is to prepare a cash receipts schedule and a cash payments schedule. To that end the following information has been collected.

Prepare schedules for cash receipts and cash payments, and determine ending balances for balance sheet.
(SO 5, 6)

Clients usually pay 60% of their fee in the month that service is provided, 30% the month after, and 10% the second month after receiving service.

Actual service revenue for 2006 and expected service revenues for 2007 are: November 2006, $90,000; December 2006, $80,000; January 2007, $100,000; February 2007, $120,000; March 2007, $130,000.

Purchases on landscaping supplies (direct materials) are paid 40% in the month of purchase and 60% the following month. Actual purchases for 2006 and expected purchases for 2007 are: December 2006, $14,000; January 2007, $12,000; February 2007, $15,000; March 2007, $18,000.

Instructions
(a) Prepare the following schedules for each month in the first quarter of 2007 and for the quarter in total:
  (1) Expected collections from clients.
  (2) Expected payments for landscaping supplies.
(b) Determine the following balances at March 31, 2007:
  (1) Accounts receivable.
  (2) Accounts payable.

E20-12 Donnegal Dental Clinic is a medium-sized dental service specializing in family dental care. The clinic is currently preparing the master budget for the first 2 quarters of 2007. All that remains in this process is the cash budget. The following information has been collected from other portions of the master budget and elsewhere.

Prepare a cash budget for two quarters.
(SO 5, 6)

Beginning cash balance	$ 30,000
Required minimum cash balance	25,000
Payment of income taxes (2nd quarter)	4,000
Professional salaries:	
1st quarter	140,000
2nd quarter	140,000
Interest from investments (2nd quarter)	5,000
Overhead costs:	
1st quarter	75,000
2nd quarter	100,000
Selling and administrative costs, including	
$3,000 depreciation:	
1st quarter	50,000
2nd quarter	70,000
Purchase of equipment (2nd quarter)	50,000
Sale of equipment (1st quarter)	15,000
Collections from clients:	
1st quarter	230,000
2nd quarter	380,000
Interest payments (2nd quarter)	300

Instructions
Prepare a cash budget for each of the first two quarters of 2007.

Prepare a purchases budget and budgeted income statement for a merchandiser.
(SO 6)

E20-13 In May 2007, the budget committee of Loebs Stores assembles the following data in preparation of budgeted merchandise purchases for the month of June.

1. Expected sales: June $550,000, July $600,000.
2. Cost of goods sold is expected to be 70% of sales.
3. Desired ending merchandise inventory is 40% of the following (next) month's cost of goods sold.
4. The beginning inventory at June 1 will be the desired amount.

Instructions
(a) Compute the budgeted merchandise purchases for June.
(b) Prepare the budgeted income statement for June through gross profit.

Problems: Set A

Prepare budgeted income statement and supporting budgets.
(SO 3, 4)

P20-1A Tilger Farm Supply Company manufactures and sells a fertilizer called Basic II. The following data are available for preparing budgets for Basic II for the first 2 quarters of 2007.

1. Sales: Quarter 1, 40,000 bags; quarter 2, 55,000 bags. Selling price is $60 per bag.
2. Direct materials: Each bag of Basic II requires 6 pounds of Crup at a cost of $3 per pound and 10 pounds of Dert at $1.50 per pound.
3. Desired inventory levels:

Type of Inventory	January 1	April 1	July 1
Basic II (bags)	10,000	15,000	20,000
Crup (pounds)	9,000	12,000	15,000
Dert (pounds)	15,000	20,000	25,000

4. Direct labor: Direct labor time is 15 minutes per bag at an hourly rate of $12 per hour.
5. Selling and administrative expenses are expected to be 10% of sales plus $150,000 per quarter.
6. Income taxes are expected to be 30% of income from operations.

Your assistant has prepared two budgets: (1) The manufacturing overhead budget shows expected costs to be 100% of direct labor cost. (2) The direct materials budget which shows the cost of Dert purchases to be $682,500 in quarter 1 and $907,500 in quarter 2.

Instructions

Net income $787,500
Cost per bag $39.00

Prepare the budgeted income statement for the first 6 months of 2007 and all required supporting budgets by quarters. (*Note:* Use variable and fixed in the selling and administrative expense budget.) Do not prepare the manufacturing overhead budget or the direct materials budget for Dert.

Prepare sales, production, direct materials, direct labor, and income statement budgets.
(SO 3, 4)

P20-2A Greish Inc. is preparing its annual budgets for the year ending December 31, 2007. Accounting assistants furnish the following data.

	Product LN 35	Product LN 40
Sales budget:		
Anticipated volume in units	350,000	180,000
Unit selling price	$20	$30
Production budget:		
Desired ending finished goods units	30,000	25,000
Beginning finished goods units	20,000	15,000
Direct materials budget:		
Direct materials per unit (pounds)	2	3
Desired ending direct materials pounds	50,000	20,000
Beginning direct materials pounds	40,000	10,000
Cost per pound	$2	$3
Direct labor budget:		
Direct labor time per unit	0.5	0.75
Direct labor rate per hour	$10	$10
Budgeted income statement:		
Total unit cost	$10	$20

An accounting assistant has prepared the detailed manufacturing overhead budget and the selling and administrative expense budget. The latter shows selling expenses of $560,000 for product LN 35 and $440,000 for product LN 40, and administrative expenses of $420,000 for product LN 35 and $380,000 for product LN 40. Income taxes are expected to be 30%.

Instructions

Prepare the following budgets for the year. Show data for each product. Quarterly budgets should not be prepared.

(a) Sales   (d) Direct labor
(b) Production   (e) Income statement (*Note*: Income taxes are
(c) Direct materials   not allocated to the products.)

(a) Total sales $12,400,000
(b) Required production units:
LN 35, 360,000
(c) Total cost of direct materials purchases $3,200,000
(d) Total direct labor cost $3,225,000
(e) Net income $2,450,000

P20-3A   Hirsch Industries has sales in 2007 of $5,250,000 (750,000 units) and gross profit of $1,587,500. Management is considering two alternative budget plans to increase its gross profit in 2008.

Prepare sales and production budgets and compute cost per unit under two plans. (SO 3, 4)

Plan A would increase the selling price per unit from $7.00 to $7.60. Sales volume would decrease by 10% from its 2007 level. Plan B would decrease the selling price per unit by 5%. The marketing department expects that the sales volume would increase by 100,000 units.

At the end of 2007, Hirsch has 75,000 units on hand. If Plan A is accepted, the 2008 ending inventory should be equal to 90,000 units. If Plan B is accepted, the ending inventory should be equal to 100,000 units. Each unit produced will cost $2.00 in direct materials, $1.50 in direct labor, and $0.50 in variable overhead. The fixed overhead for 2008 should be $965,000.

Instructions

(a) Prepare a sales budget for 2008 under (1) Plan A and (2) Plan B.
(b) Prepare a production budget for 2008 under (1) Plan A and (2) Plan B.
(c) Compute the cost per unit under (1) Plan A and (2) Plan B. Explain why the cost per unit is different for each of the two plans. (Round to two decimals.)
(d) Which plan should be accepted? (*Hint*: Compute the gross profit under each plan.)

(c) Unit cost: Plan A $5.40, Plan B $5.10
(d) Gross profit:
Plan A $1,485,000
Plan B $1,317,500

P20-4A   Lorch Company prepares monthly cash budgets. Relevant data from operating budgets for 2008 are:

Prepare cash budget for 2 months. (SO 5)

	January	February
Sales	$360,000	$400,000
Direct materials purchases	100,000	110,000
Direct labor	100,000	115,000
Manufacturing overhead	60,000	75,000
Selling and administrative expenses	75,000	80,000

All sales are on account. Collections are expected to be 60% in the month of sale, 30% in the first month following the sale, and 10% in the second month following the sale. Thirty percent (30%) of direct materials purchases are paid in cash in the month of purchase, and the balance due is paid in the month following the purchase. All other items above are paid in the month incurred. Depreciation has been excluded from manufacturing overhead and selling and administrative expenses.

Other data:

1. Credit sales: November 2007, $200,000; December 2007, $280,000.
2. Purchases of direct materials: December 2007, $90,000.
3. Other receipts: January—Collection of December 31, 2007, interest receivable $3,000;
        February—Proceeds from sale of securities $5,000.
4. Other disbursements: February—payment of $20,000 for land.

The company's cash balance on January 1, 2008, is expected to be $60,000. The company wants to maintain a minimum cash balance of $50,000.

Instructions

(a) Prepare schedules for (1) expected collections from customers and (2) expected payments for direct materials purchases.
(b) Prepare a cash budget for January and February in columnar form.

(a) January:
collections $320,000
payments $93,000
(b) Ending cash balance:
January $55,000
February $50,000

Prepare purchases and
income statement budgets for
a merchandiser.
(SO 6)

P20-5A   The budget committee of Ridder Company collects the following data for its Westwood Store in preparing budgeted income statements for July and August 2007.

1. Expected sales: July $400,000, August $450,000, September $500,000.
2. Cost of goods sold is expected to be 60% of sales.
3. Company policy is to maintain ending merchandise inventory at 25% of the following month's cost of goods sold.
4. Operating expenses are estimated to be:

Sales salaries	$30,000 per month
Advertising	4% of monthly sales
Delivery expense	2% of monthly sales
Sales commissions	3% of monthly sales
Rent expense	$3,000 per month
Depreciation	$700 per month
Utilities	$500 per month
Insurance	$300 per month

5. Income taxes are estimated to be 30% of income from operations.

(a) Purchases: July $247,500
     August $277,500
(b) Net income: July $62,650
     August $73,500

Instructions
(a) Prepare the merchandise purchases budget for each month in columnar form.
(b) Prepare budgeted income statements for each month in columnar form. Show the details of cost of goods sold in the statements.

Prepare budgeted income
statement and balance sheet.
(SO 4, 5)

P20-6A   Kurian Industries' balance sheet at December 31, 2007, is presented below.

KURIAN INDUSTRIES
Balance Sheet
December 31, 2007

Assets

Current assets		
Cash		$ 7,500
Accounts receivable		82,500
Finished goods inventory (2,000 units)		30,000
Total current assets		120,000
Property, plant, and equipment		
Equipment	$40,000	
Less: Accumulated depreciation	10,000	30,000
Total assets		$150,000

Liabilities and Stockholders' Equity

Liabilities		
Notes payable		$ 25,000
Accounts payable		45,000
Total liabilities		70,000
Stockholders' equity		
Common stock	$50,000	
Retained earnings	30,000	
Total stockholders' equity		80,000
Total liabilities and stockholders' equity		$150,000

Additional information accumulated for the budgeting process is as follows.
Budgeted data for the year 2008 include the following.

	4th Qtr. of 2008	Year 2008 Total
Sales budget (8,000 units at $30)	$70,000	$240,000
Direct materials used	17,000	69,400
Direct labor	8,500	38,600
Manufacturing overhead applied	10,000	54,000
Selling and administrative expenses	18,000	76,000

To meet sales requirements and to have 3,000 units of finished goods on hand at December 31, 2008, the production budget shows 9,000 required units of output. The total unit cost of production is expected to be $18. Kurian Industries uses the first-in, first-out (FIFO) inventory costing method. Selling and administrative expenses include $4,000 for depreciation on equipment. Interest expense is expected to be $3,500 for the year. Income taxes are expected to be 30% of income before income taxes.

All sales and purchases are on account. It is expected that 60% of quarterly sales are collected in cash within the quarter and the remainder is collected in the following quarter. Direct materials purchased from suppliers are paid 50% in the quarter incurred and the remainder in the following quarter. Purchases in the fourth quarter were the same as the materials used. In 2008, the company expects to purchase additional equipment costing $14,000. It expects to pay $8,000 on notes payable plus all interest due and payable to December 31 (included in interest expense $3,500, above). Accounts payable at December 31, 2008, includes amounts due suppliers (see above) plus other accounts payable of $10,700. In 2008, the company expects to declare and pay a $5,000 cash dividend. Unpaid income taxes at December 31 will be $5,000. The company's cash budget shows an expected cash balance of $9,950 at December 31, 2008.

Instructions

Prepare a budgeted income statement for 2008 and a budgeted balance sheet at December 31, 2008. In preparing the income statement, you will need to compute cost of goods manufactured (direct materials + direct labor + manufacturing overhead) and finished goods inventory (December 31, 2008).

Net income $15,750
Total assets $131,950

Problems: Set B

P20-1B   Wahlen Farm Supply Company manufactures and sells a pesticide called Snare. The following data are available for preparing budgets for Snare for the first 2 quarters of 2008.

Prepare budgeted income statement and supporting budgets.
(SO 3, 4)

1. Sales: Quarter 1, 28,000 bags: quarter 2, 40,000 bags. Selling price is $60 per bag.
2. Direct materials: Each bag of Snare requires 4 pounds of Gumm at a cost of $3 per pound and 6 pounds of Tarr at $1.50 per pound.
3. Desired inventory levels:

Type of Inventory	January 1	April 1	July 1
Snare (bags)	8,000	12,000	18,000
Gumm (pounds)	9,000	10,000	13,000
Tarr (pounds)	14,000	20,000	25,000

4. Direct labor: Direct labor time is 15 minutes per bag at an hourly rate of $14 per hour.
5. Selling and administrative expenses are expected to be 15% of sales plus $175,000 per quarter.
6. Income taxes are expected to be 30% of income from operations.

Your assistant has prepared two budgets: (1) The manufacturing overhead budget shows expected costs to be 150% of direct labor cost. (2) The direct materials budget shows the cost of Tarr purchases to be $297,000 in quarter 1 and $421,500 in quarter 2.

Instructions

Prepare the budgeted income statement for the first 6 months and all required supporting budgets by quarters. (*Note*: Use variable and fixed in the selling and administrative expense budget). Do not prepare the manufacturing overhead budget or the direct materials budget for Tarr.

Net income $766,500
Cost per bag $29.75

Prepare sales, production, direct materials, direct labor, and income statement budgets.
(SO 3, 4)

P20-2B   Lasorda Inc. is preparing its annual budgets for the year ending December 31, 2008. Accounting assistants furnish the data shown on page 1006.

	Product JB 50	Product JB 60
Sales budget:		
Anticipated volume in units	450,000	200,000
Unit selling price	$20	$25
Production budget:		
Desired ending finished goods units	25,000	15,000
Beginning finished goods units	30,000	10,000
Direct materials budget:		
Direct materials per unit (pounds)	2	3
Desired ending direct materials pounds	30,000	15,000
Beginning direct materials pounds	40,000	10,000
Cost per pound	$3	$4
Direct labor budget:		
Direct labor time per unit	0.4	0.6
Direct labor rate per hour	$10	$10
Budgeted income statement:		
Total unit cost	$12	$20

An accounting assistant has prepared the detailed manufacturing overhead budget and the selling and administrative expense budget. The latter shows selling expenses of $660,000 for product JB 50 and $360,000 for product JB 60, and administrative expenses of $540,000 for product JB 50 and $340,000 for product JB 60. Income taxes are expected to be 30%.

Instructions

Prepare the following budgets for the year. Show data for each product. Quarterly budgets should not be prepared.

(a) Sales
(b) Production
(c) Direct materials
(d) Direct labor
(e) Income statement (*Note*: Income taxes are not allocated to the products.)

(a) Total sales $14,000,000
(b) Required production units:
JB 50, 445,000
JB 60, 205,000
(c) Total cost of direct materials purchases $5,120,000
(d) Total direct labor cost $3,010,000
(e) Net income $1,890,000

Prepare sales and production budgets and compute cost per unit under two plans.
(SO 3, 4)

P20-3B Tick Industries had sales in 2007 of $6,000,000 and gross profit of $1,500,000. Management is considering two alternative budget plans to increase its gross profit in 2008.

Plan A would increase the selling price per unit from $8.00 to $8.40. Sales volume would decrease by 5% from its 2007 level. Plan B would decrease the selling price per unit by $0.50. The marketing department expects that the sales volume would increase by 150,000 units.

At the end of 2007, Tick has 30,000 units of inventory on hand. If Plan A is accepted, the 2008 ending inventory should be equal to 4% of the 2008 sales. If Plan B is accepted, the ending inventory should be equal to 40,000 units. Each unit produced will cost $1.80 in direct labor, $2.00 in direct materials, and $1.20 in variable overhead. The fixed overhead for 2008 should be $1,800,000.

Instructions

(a) Prepare a sales budget for 2008 under each plan.
(b) Prepare a production budget for 2008 under each plan.
(c) Compute the production cost per unit under each plan. Why is the cost per unit different for each of the two plans? (Round to two decimals.)
(d) Which plan should be accepted? (*Hint*: Compute the gross profit under each plan.)

(c) Unit cost: Plan A $7.53
Plan B $6.98
(d) Gross profit:
Plan A $619,875
Plan B $468,000

Prepare cash budget for 2 months.
(SO 5)

P20-4B Nigh Company prepares monthly cash budgets. Relevant data from operating budgets for 2008 are:

	January	February
Sales	$350,000	$400,000
Direct materials purchases	120,000	130,000
Direct labor	80,000	100,000
Manufacturing overhead	70,000	75,000
Selling and administrative expenses	79,000	81,000

All sales are on account. Collections are expected to be 50% in the month of sale, 30% in the first month following the sale, and 20% in the second month following the sale. Sixty percent (60%) of direct materials purchases are paid in cash in the month of purchase, and the balance due is paid in the month following the purchase. All other items above are paid in the month incurred except for selling and administrative expenses that include $1,000 of depreciation per month.

Other data:

1. Credit sales: November 2007, $260,000; December 2007, $300,000.
2. Purchases of direct materials: December 2007, $100,000.
3. Other receipts: January—Collection of December 31, 2007, notes receivable $15,000; February—Proceeds from sale of securities $6,000.
4. Other disbursements: February—Withdrawal of $5,000 cash for personal use of owner, Dewey Yaeger.

The company's cash balance on January 1, 2008, is expected to be $60,000. The company wants to maintain a minimum cash balance of $50,000.

Instructions

(a) Prepare schedules for (1) expected collections from customers and (2) expected payments for direct materials purchases.
(b) Prepare a cash budget for January and February in columnar form.

(a) January:
collections $317,000
payments $112,000
(b) Ending cash balance:
January $52,000
February $50,000

P20-5B The budget committee of Lococo Company collects the following data for its San Miguel Store in preparing budgeted income statements for May and June 2008.

Prepare purchases and income statement budgets for a merchandiser.
(SO 6)

1. Sales for May are expected to be $600,000. Sales in June and July are expected to be 10% higher than the preceding month.
2. Cost of goods sold is expected to be 75% of sales.
3. Company policy is to maintain ending merchandise inventory at 20% of the following month's cost of goods sold.
4. Operating expenses are estimated to be:

Sales salaries	$30,000 per month
Advertising	5% of monthly sales
Delivery expense	3% of monthly sales
Sales commissions	4% of monthly sales
Rent expense	$5,000 per month
Depreciation	$800 per month
Utilities	$600 per month
Insurance	$500 per month

5. Income taxes are estimated to be 30% of income from operations.

Instructions

(a) Prepare the merchandise purchases budget for each month in columnar form.
(b) Prepare budgeted income statements for each month in columnar form. Show in the statements the details of cost of goods sold.

(a) Purchases:
May $459,000
June $504,900
(b) Net income:
May $28,770
June $34,230

Problems: Set C

Visit the book's website at **www.wiley.com/college/kimmel** and choose the Student Companion site to access Problem Set C.

BROADENING YOUR PERSPECTIVE

Group Decision Case

BYP20-1 Peters Corporation operates on a calendar-year basis. It begins the annual budgeting process in late August when the president establishes targets for the total dollar sales and net income before taxes for the next year.

The sales target is given first to the marketing department. The marketing manager formulates a sales budget by product line in both units and dollars. From this budget, sales quotas by product line in units and dollars are established for each of the corporation's sales districts. The marketing manager also estimates the cost of the marketing activities required to support the target sales volume and prepares a tentative marketing expense budget.

The executive vice president uses the sales and profit targets, the sales budget by product line, and the tentative marketing expense budget to determine the dollar amounts that can be devoted to manufacturing and corporate office expense. The executive vice president prepares the budget for corporate expenses. She then forwards to the production department the product-line sales budget in units and the total dollar amount that can be devoted to manufacturing.

The production manager meets with the factory managers to develop a manufacturing plan that will produce the required units when needed within the cost constraints set by the executive vice president. The budgeting process usually comes to a halt at this point because the production department does not consider the financial resources allocated to be adequate.

When this standstill occurs, the vice president of finance, the executive vice president, the marketing manager, and the production manager meet together to determine the final budgets for each of the areas. This normally results in a modest increase in the total amount available for manufacturing costs and cuts in the marketing expense and corporate office expense budgets. The total sales and net income figures proposed by the president are seldom changed. Although the participants are seldom pleased with the compromise, these budgets are final. Each executive then develops a new detailed budget for the operations in his or her area.

None of the areas has achieved its budget in recent years. Sales often run below the target. When budgeted sales are not achieved, each area is expected to cut costs so that the president's profit target can be met. However, the profit target is seldom met because costs are not cut enough. In fact, costs often run above the original budget in all functional areas (marketing, production, and corporate office).

The president is disturbed that Peters has not been able to meet the sales and profit targets. He hired a consultant with considerable experience with companies in Peters's industry. The consultant reviewed the budgets for the past 4 years. He concluded that the product line sales budgets were reasonable and that the cost and expense budgets were adequate for the budgeted sales and production levels.

Instructions
With the class divided into groups, answer the following.
(a) Discuss how the budgeting process employed by Peters Corporation contributes to the failure to achieve the president's sales and profit targets.
(b) Suggest how Peters Corporation's budgeting process could be revised to correct the problems.
(c) Should the functional areas be expected to cut their costs when sales volume falls below budget? Explain your answer.   (CMA adapted.)

Managerial Analysis

BYP20-2   Prasad & Green Inc. manufactures ergonomic devices for computer users. Some of their more popular products include glare screens (for computer monitors), keyboard stands with wrist rests, and carousels that allow easy access to magnetic disks. Over the past 5 years, they experienced rapid growth, with sales of all products increasing 20% to 50% each year.

Last year, some of the primary manufacturers of computers began introducing new products with some of the ergonomic designs, such as glare screens and wrist rests, already built in. As a result, sales of Prasad & Green's accessory devices have declined somewhat. The company believes that the disk carousels will probably continue to show growth, but that the other products will probably continue to decline. When the next year's budget was prepared, increases were built in to research and development so that replacement products could be developed or the company could expand into some other product line. Some product lines being considered are general-purpose ergonomic devices including back supports, foot rests, and sloped writing pads.

The most recent results have shown that sales decreased more than was expected for the glare screens. As a result, the company may have a shortage of funds. Top management has therefore asked that all expenses be reduced 10% to compensate for these reduced sales. Summary budget information is as follows.

Direct materials	$240,000
Direct labor	110,000
Insurance	50,000
Depreciation	90,000
Machine repairs	30,000
Sales salaries	50,000
Office salaries	80,000
Factory salaries (indirect labor)	50,000
Total	$700,000

Instructions

Using the information above, answer the following questions.

(a) What are the implications of reducing each of the costs? For example, if the company reduces direct materials costs, it may have to do so by purchasing lower-quality materials. This may affect sales in the long run.

(b) Based on your analysis in (a), what do you think is the best way to obtain the $70,000 in cost savings requested? Be specific. Are there any costs that cannot or should not be reduced? Why?

Real-World Focus

BYP20-3 Network Computing Devices Inc. was founded in 1988 in Mountain View, California. The company develops software products such as X-terminals, Z-mail, PC X-ware, and related hardware products. Presented below is a discussion by management in its annual report.

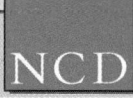

NETWORK COMPUTING DEVICES, INC.
Management Discussion

The Company's operating results have varied significantly, particularly on a quarterly basis, as a result of a number of factors, including general economic conditions affecting industry demand for computer products, the timing and market acceptance of new product introductions by the Company and its competitors, the timing of significant orders from large customers, periodic changes in product pricing and discounting due to competitive factors, and the availability of key components, such as video monitors and electronic subassemblies, some of which require substantial order lead times. The Company's operating results may fluctuate in the future as a result of these and other factors, including the Company's success in developing and introducing new products, its product and customer mix, and the level of competition which it experiences. The Company operates with a small backlog. Sales and operating results, therefore, generally depend on the volume and timing of orders received, which are difficult to forecast. The Company has experienced slowness in orders from some customers during the first quarter of each calendar year due to budgeting cycles common in the computer industry. In addition, sales in Europe typically are adversely affected in the third calendar quarter as many European customers reduce their business activities during the month of August.

Due to the Company's rapid growth rate and the effect of new product introductions on quarterly revenues, these seasonal trends have not materially impacted the Company's results of operations to date. However, as the Company's product lines mature and its rate of revenue growth declines, these seasonal factors may become more evident. Additionally, the Company's international sales are denominated in U.S. dollars, and an increase or decrease in the value of the U.S. dollar relative to foreign currencies could make the Company's products less or more competitive in those markets.

Instructions

(a) Identify the factors that affect the budgeting process at Network Computing Devices, Inc.

(b) Explain the additional budgeting concerns created by the international operations of the company.

Exploring the Web

BYP20-4 The opportunities for business consulting in the areas of corporate planning, budgeting, and strategy are almost limitless as new, more powerful software continues to be developed. This exercise takes you to the Web site of CP Corporate Planning, a European consulting firm.

Address: **www.corporate-planning.com/us/pages/sitemap/sitemap.htm** or go to **www.wiley.com/college/kimmel**

Steps: Go to the site above.

Instructions

Choose three case studies, and in each case identify the problem the company faced and how the situation was resolved.

Communication Activity

BYP20-5 In order to better serve their rural patients, Drs. Ken and Dick Ginavan (brothers) began giving safety seminars. Especially popular were their "emergency-preparedness" talks given to farmers. Many people asked whether the "kit" of materials the doctors recommended for common farm emergencies was commercially available.

After checking with several suppliers, the doctors realized that no other company offered the supplies they recommended in their seminars, packaged in the way they described. Their wives, Nancy and Sue, agreed to make a test package by ordering supplies from various medical supply companies and assembling them into a "kit" that could be sold at the seminars. When these kits proved a runaway success, the sisters-in-law decided to market them. At the advice of their accountant, they organized this venture as a separate company, called Life Protection Products (LPP), with Nancy Ginavan as CEO and Sue Ginavan as Secretary-Treasurer.

LPP soon started receiving requests for the kits from all over the country, as word spread about their availability. Even without advertising, LPP was able to sell its full inventory every month. However, the company was becoming financially strained. Nancy and Sue had about $100,000 in savings, and they invested about half that amount initially. They believed that this venture would allow them to make money. However, at the present time, only about $30,000 of the cash remains, and the company is constantly short of cash.

Nancy Ginavan has come to you for advice. She does not understand why the company is having cash flow problems. She and Sue have not even been withdrawing salaries. However, they have rented a local building and have hired two more full-time workers to help them cope with the increasing demand. They do not think they could handle the demand without this additional help.

Nancy is also worried that the cash problems mean that the company may not be able to support itself. She has prepared the cash budget shown on the next page. All seminar customers pay for their products in full at the time of purchase. In addition, several large companies have ordered the kits for use by employees who work in remote sites. They have requested credit terms and have been allowed to pay in the month following the sale. These large purchasers amount to about 25% of the sales at the present time. LPP purchases the materials for the kits about 2 months ahead of time. Nancy and Sue are considering slowing the growth of the company by simply purchasing less materials, which will mean selling fewer kits.

The workers are paid in cash weekly. Nancy and Sue need about $15,000 cash on hand at the beginning of the month to pay for purchases of raw materials. Right now they have been using cash from their savings, but as noted, only $30,000 is left.

Instructions

Write a response to Nancy Ginavan. Explain why LPP is short of cash. Will this company be able to support itself? Explain your answer. Make any recommendations you deem appropriate.

LIFE PROTECTION PRODUCTS
Cash Budget
For the Quarter Ending June 30, 2008

	April	May	June
Cash balance, beginning	$15,000	$15,000	$15,000
Cash received			
From prior month sales	5,000	7,500	12,500
From current sales	15,000	22,500	37,500
Total cash on hand	35,000	45,000	65,000
Cash payments			
To employees	3,000	3,000	3,000
For products	25,000	35,000	45,000
Miscellaneous expenses	5,000	6,000	7,000
Postage	1,000	1,000	1,000
Total cash payments	34,000	45,000	56,000
Cash balance	$ 1,000	$ 0	$ 9,000
Borrow from savings	$14,000	$15,000	$ 1,000
Borrow from bank?	$ 0	$ 0	$ 5,000

Research Assignment

BYP20-6 The October 2003 issue of *Inc.* magazine contains an article by Suzanne McGee titled "Breaking Free from Budgets."

Instructions

Read the article and answer the following questions.

(a) What are the deficiencies of a traditional budget according to the proponents of the "Beyond Budgeting Movement"?

(b) Summarize the pros and cons of budgets as perceived by Al Osborne from UCLA. What does he see as the potential benefit of Beyond Budgeting?

(c) What has remained the same and what has changed at Omgeo since it began implementing the principles of Beyond Budgeting?

Ethics Case

BYP20-7 You are an accountant in the budgetary, projections, and special projects department of National Conductor, Inc., a large manufacturing company. The president, Richard Sheen, asks you on very short notice to prepare some sales and income projections covering the next 2 years of the company's much heralded new product lines. He wants these projections for a series of speeches he is making while on a 2-week trip to eight East Coast brokerage firms. The president hopes to bolster National's stock sales and price.

You work 23 hours in 2 days to compile the projections, hand deliver them to the president, and are swiftly but graciously thanked as he departs. A week later you find time to go over some of your computations and discover a miscalculation that makes the projections grossly overstated. You quickly inquire about the president's itinerary and learn that he has made half of his speeches and has half yet to make. You are in a quandary as to what to do.

Instructions

(a) What are the consequences of telling the president of your gross miscalculations?

(b) What are the consequences of *not* telling the president of your gross miscalculations?

(c) What are the ethical considerations to you and the president in this situation?

Answers to Self-Study Questions

1. c   **2.** a   **3.** b   **4.** b   **5.** d   **6.** d   **7.** a   **8.** c   **9.** c   **10.** d

REMEMBER TO GO BACK TO THE NAVIGATOR BOX ON THE CHAPTER-OPENING PAGE AND CHECK OFF YOUR COMPLETED WORK.

Budgetary Control and Responsibility Accounting

STUDY OBJECTIVES

After studying this chapter, you should be able to:

1 Describe the concept of budgetary control.

2 Evaluate the usefulness of static budget reports.

3 Explain the development of flexible budgets and the usefulness of flexible budget reports.

4 Describe the concept of responsibility accounting.

5 Indicate the features of responsibility reports for cost centers.

6 Identify the content of responsibility reports for profit centers.

7 Explain the basis and formula used in evaluating performance in investment centers.

 THE NAVIGATOR

✓ THE NAVIGATOR

- Scan *Study Objectives*
- Read *Feature Story*
- Read *Preview*
- Read text and answer *Before You Go On*
  p. 1024 ◯   p. 1032 ◯   p. 1037 ◯
- Work *Using the Decision Toolkit*
- Review *Summary of Study Objectives*
- Work *Demonstration Problem*
- Answer *Self-Study Questions*
- Complete *Assignments*

FEATURE STORY

Trying to Avoid an Electric Shock

Budgets are critical to evaluating an organization's success. They are based on management's expectations of what is most likely to happen in the future. In order to be useful, they must be accurate. But what if management's expectations are wrong? Estimates are never exactly correct, and sometimes, especially in volatile industries, estimates can be "off by a mile."

In recent years the electric utility industry has become very volatile. Deregulation, volatile prices for natural gas, coal, and oil, changes in environmental regulations, and economic swings have all contributed to large changes in the profitability of electric utility companies. This means that for planning and budgeting purposes, utilites must plan and budget based on multiple "what if" scenarios that take into account factors beyond management's control. For example, in recent years, Duke Energy Corporation, headquartered in Charlotte, North Carolina, built budgeting and planning models based on three different scenarios of what the future might hold. One scenario assumes that the U.S. economy will slow considerably. A second scenario assumes that the company will experience "pricing pressure" as the market for energy becomes more efficient as a result of more energy being traded in Internet auctions. A third scenario assumes a continuation of the current environment of rapid growth, changing regulation, and large swings in the prices for the fuels the company uses to create energy.

Compounding this budgeting challenge is the fact that changes in many indirect costs can also significantly affect the company. For example, even a tiny change in market interest rates has a huge effect on the company because it has massive amounts of outstanding debt. And finally, as a result of the California energy crisis, there is mounting pressure for government intervention and regulation. This pressure has resulted in setting "rate caps" that limit the amount that utilities and energy companies can charge, thus lowering profits. The bottom line is that for budgeting and planning purposes, utility companies must remain alert and flexible.

THE NAVIGATOR

In contrast to Chapter 20, we now consider how budgets are used by management to control operations. In the Feature Story on Duke Energy, we saw that budgeting must take into account factors beyond management's control. This chapter focuses on two aspects of management control: (1) budgetary control and (2) responsibility accounting.

The content and organization of Chapter 21 are as follows.

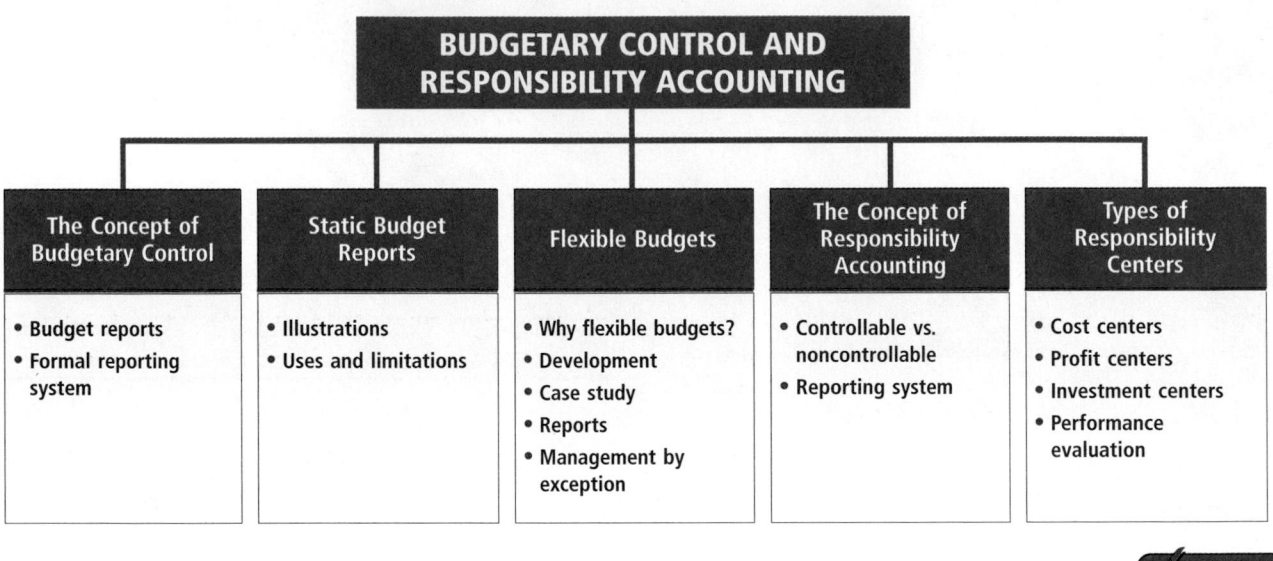

BUDGETARY CONTROL AND RESPONSIBILITY ACCOUNTING				
The Concept of Budgetary Control	**Static Budget Reports**	**Flexible Budgets**	**The Concept of Responsibility Accounting**	**Types of Responsibility Centers**
• Budget reports • Formal reporting system	• Illustrations • Uses and limitations	• Why flexible budgets? • Development • Case study • Reports • Management by exception	• Controllable vs. noncontrollable • Reporting system	• Cost centers • Profit centers • Investment centers • Performance evaluation

THE NAVIGATOR

The Concept of Budgetary Control

STUDY OBJECTIVE
1
Describe the concept of budgetary control.

One of management's major functions is to control company operations. Control consists of the steps taken by management to see that planned objectives are met. We now ask: How do budgets contribute to control of operations?

The use of budgets in controlling operations is known as **budgetary control**. Such control takes place by means of **budget reports** that compare actual results with planned objectives. The use of budget reports is based on the belief that planned objectives lose much of their potential value without some monitoring of progress along the way. Just as your professors give midterm exams to evaluate your progress, so top management requires periodic reports on the progress of department managers toward their planned objectives.

Budget reports provide management with feedback on operations. The feedback for a crucial objective, such as having enough cash on hand to pay bills, may be made daily. For other objectives, such as meeting budgeted annual sales and operating expenses, monthly budget reports may suffice. Budget reports can be prepared as frequently as needed. From these reports, management analyzes any differences between actual and planned results and determines their causes. Management then may take corrective action, or it may decide to modify future plans.

Budgetary control involves the following activities.

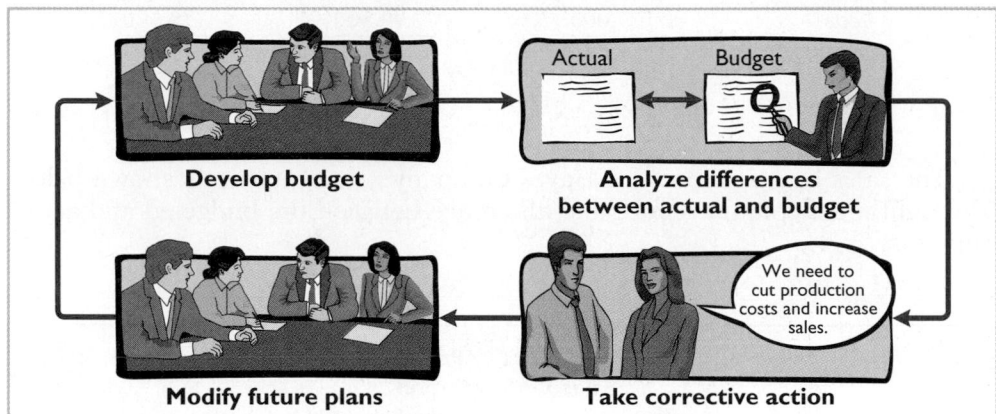

Illustration 21-1 Budgetary control

Budgetary control works best when a company has a formalized reporting system. The system should do the following: (1) Identify the name of the budget report, such as the sales budget or the manufacturing overhead budget. (2) State the frequency of the report, such as weekly or monthly. (3) Specify the purpose of the report. And (4) indicate the primary recipient(s) of the report. Illustration 21-2 provides a partial budgetary control system for a manufacturing company. Note the frequency of the reports and their emphasis on control. For example, there is a daily report on scrap and a weekly report on labor.

Illustration 21-2 Budgetary control reporting system

Name of Report	Frequency	Purpose	Primary Recipient(s)
Sales	Weekly	Determine whether sales goals are being met	Top management and sales manager
Labor	Weekly	Control direct and indirect labor costs	Vice president of production and production department managers
Scrap	Daily	Determine efficient use of materials	Production manager
Departmental overhead costs	Monthly	Control overhead costs	Department manager
Selling expenses	Monthly	Control selling expenses	Sales manager
Income statement	Monthly and quarterly	Determine whether income objectives are being met	Top management

Static Budget Reports

You learned in Chapter 20 that the master budget formalizes management's planned objectives for the coming year. When used in budgetary control, each budget included in the master budget is considered to be static. A **static budget** is a projection of budget data **at one level of activity**. Data for different levels of activity are not considered. As a result, actual results are always compared with budget data at the activity level that was used in developing the master budget.

ILLUSTRATIONS

To illustrate the role of a static budget in budgetary control, we will use selected data prepared for Hayes Company in Chapter 20. Budget and actual sales data for the Kitchen-mate product in the first and second quarters of 2007 are as follows.

Illustration 21-3 Budget and actual sales data

Sales	First Quarter	Second Quarter	Total
Budgeted	$180,000	$210,000	$390,000
Actual	179,000	199,500	378,500
Difference	$ 1,000	$ 10,500	$ 11,500

The sales budget report for Hayes Company's first quarter is shown below. The right-most column reports the difference between the budgeted and actual amounts.

Illustration 21-4 Sales budget report—first quarter

Alternative Terminology
The difference between budget and actual is sometimes called a *budget variance.*

HAYES COMPANY
Sales Budget Report
For the Quarter Ended March 31, 2007

Product Line	Budget	Actual	Difference Favorable F Unfavorable U
Kitchen-mate[a]	$180,000	$179,000	$1,000 U

[a]In practice, each product line would be included in the report.

The report shows that sales are $1,000 under budget—an unfavorable result. This difference is less than 1 percent of budgeted sales ($1,000 ÷ $180,000 = .0056). Top management's reaction to unfavorable differences is often influenced by the materiality (significance) of the difference. Since the difference of $1,000 is immaterial in this case, we will assume that Hayes Company management takes no specific corrective action.

The budget report for the second quarter is presented in Illustration 21-5. It contains one new feature: cumulative year-to-date information. This report indicates that sales for the second quarter were $10,500 below budget. This is 5 percent of budgeted sales ($10,500 ÷ $210,000). Top management may now conclude that the difference between budgeted and actual sales requires investigation.

Illustration 21-5 Sales budget report—second quarter

HAYES COMPANY
Sales Budget Report
For the Quarter Ended June 30, 2007

Product Line	Second Quarter Budget	Actual	Difference Favorable F Unfavorable U	Year-to-Date Budget	Actual	Difference Favorable F Unfavorable U
Kitchen-mate	$210,000	$199,500	$10,500 U	$390,000	$378,500	$11,500 U

Management's analysis should start by asking the sales manager the cause(s) of the shortfall. The need for corrective action should be considered. For example, management may decide to spur sales by offering sales incentives to customers or by increasing the advertising of Kitchen-mates. Or, if management concludes that a downturn in the economy is responsible for the lower sales, it may modify planned sales and profit goals for the remainder of the year.

USES AND LIMITATIONS

From these examples, you can see that a master sales budget is useful in evaluating the performance of a sales manager. It is now necessary to ask: Is the master budget appropriate for evaluating a manager's performance in controlling costs? Recall that in a static budget, data are not modified or adjusted, regardless of changes in activity. It follows, then, that a static budget is appropriate in evaluating a manager's effectiveness in controlling costs when:

1. The actual level of activity closely approximates the master budget activity level, and/or
2. The behavior of the costs in response to changes in activity is fixed.

A static budget report is, therefore, appropriate for **fixed manufacturing costs** and for **fixed selling and administrative expenses**. But, as you will see shortly, static budget reports may not be a proper basis for evaluating a manager's performance in controlling variable costs.

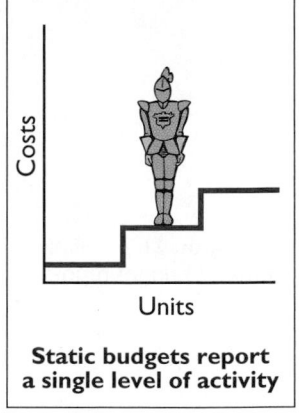

Static budgets report a single level of activity

Flexible Budgets

STUDY OBJECTIVE

3

Explain the development of flexible budgets and the usefulness of flexible budget reports.

In contrast to a static budget, which is based on one level of activity, a **flexible budget** projects budget data for various levels of activity. In essence, **the flexible budget is a series of static budgets at different levels of activity**. The flexible budget recognizes that the budgetary process is more useful if it is adaptable to changed operating conditions.

Flexible budgets can be prepared for each of the types of budgets included in the master budget. For example, Marriott Hotels can budget revenues and net income on the basis of 60 percent, 80 percent, and 100 percent of room occupancy. Similarly, American Van Lines can budget its operating expenses on the basis of various levels of truck miles driven. Likewise, in the Feature Story, Duke Energy can budget revenue and net income on the basis of estimated billions of kwh (kilowatt hours) of residential, commercial, and industrial electricity generated. In the following pages, we will illustrate a flexible budget for manufacturing overhead.

Flexible budgets are static budgets at different activity levels

WHY FLEXIBLE BUDGETS?

Assume that you are the manager in charge of manufacturing overhead in the Forging Department of Barton Steel. In preparing the manufacturing overhead budget for 2007, you prepare the following static budget based on a production volume of 10,000 units of steel ingots.

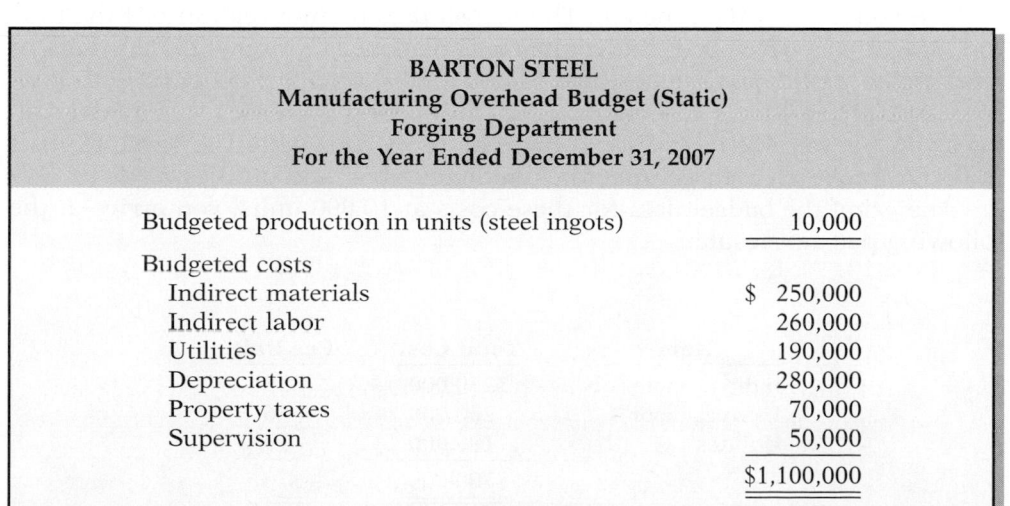

BARTON STEEL Manufacturing Overhead Budget (Static) Forging Department For the Year Ended December 31, 2007	
Budgeted production in units (steel ingots)	10,000
Budgeted costs	
Indirect materials	$ 250,000
Indirect labor	260,000
Utilities	190,000
Depreciation	280,000
Property taxes	70,000
Supervision	50,000
	$1,100,000

Illustration 21-6 Static overhead budget

Helpful Hint The static budget is the master budget described in Chapter 20.

Fortunately for the company, the demand for steel ingots has increased, and 12,000 units are produced and sold during the year, rather than 10,000. You are elated: Increased sales means increased profitability, which should mean a bonus or a raise for you and the employees in your department. Unfortunately, a comparison of Forging Department actual and budgeted costs has put you on the spot. The budget report is shown below.

Illustration 21-7 Static overhead budget report

Barton Steel
Manufacturing Overhead Budget Report (Static)
For the Year Ended December 31, 2007

	Budget	Actual	Difference Favorable - F Unfavorable - U
Production in units	10,000	12,000	
Costs			
Indirect materials	$250,000	$295,000	$45,000 U
Indirect labor	260,000	312,000	52,000 U
Utilities	190,000	225,000	35,000 U
Depreciation	280,000	280,000	0
Property taxes	70,000	70,000	0
Supervision	50,000	50,000	0
	$1,100,000	$1,232,000	$132,000 U

Helpful Hint A static budget is not useful for performance evaluation if a company has substantial variable costs.

This comparison uses budget data based on the original activity level (10,000 steel ingots). It indicates that the Forging Department is significantly **over budget** for three of the six overhead costs. And, there is a total unfavorable difference of $132,000, which is 12 percent over budget ($132,000 ÷ $1,100,000). Your supervisor is very unhappy! Instead of sharing in the company's success, you may find yourself looking for another job. What went wrong?

When you calm down and carefully examine the manufacturing overhead budget, you identify the problem: The budget data are not relevant! At the time the budget was developed, the company anticipated that only 10,000 units of steel ingots would be produced, **not** 12,000 ingots. Comparing actual with budgeted variable costs is meaningless. As production increases, the budget allowances for variable costs should increase proportionately. The variable costs in this example are indirect materials, indirect labor, and utilities.

Analyzing the budget data for these costs at 10,000 units, you arrive at the following per unit results.

Illustration 21-8 Variable costs per unit

Item	Total Cost	Per Unit
Indirect materials	$250,000	$25
Indirect labor	260,000	26
Utilities	190,000	19
	$700,000	$70

You then can calculate the budgeted variable costs at 12,000 units as follows.

Illustration 21-9 Budgeted variable costs, 12,000 units

Item	Computation	Total
Indirect materials	$25 × 12,000	$300,000
Indirect labor	26 × 12,000	312,000
Utilities	19 × 12,000	228,000
		$840,000

Because fixed costs do not change in total as activity changes, the budgeted amounts for these costs remain the same. The budget report based on the flexible budget for **12,000 units** of production is shown in Illustration 21-10. (Compare this with Illustration 21-7.)

Illustration 21-10 Flexible overhead budget report

	A	B	C	D	E
1		**Barton Steel**			
2		Manufacturing Overhead Budget Report (Flexible)			
3		For the Year Ended December 31, 2007			
4				Difference	
5		Budget	Actual	Favorable - F Unfavorable - U	
6	Production in units	12,000	12,000		
7					
8	Variable costs				
9	Indirect materials	$300,000	$295,000	$5,000	F
10	Indirect labor	312,000	312,000	0	
11	Utilities	228,000	225,000	3,000	F
12	Total variable costs	840,000	832,000	8,000	F
13					
14	Fixed costs				
15	Depreciation	280,000	280,000	0	
16	Property taxes	70,000	70,000	0	
17	Supervision	50,000	50,000	0	
18	Total fixed costs	400,000	400,000	0	
19	Total costs	$1,240,000	$1,232,000	$8,000	F

This report indicates that the Forging Department is below budget—a favorable difference. Instead of worrying about being fired, you may be in line for a bonus or a raise after all! As this analysis shows, the only appropriate comparison is between actual costs at 12,000 units of production and budgeted costs at 12,000 units. Flexible budget reports provide this comparison.

DEVELOPING THE FLEXIBLE BUDGET

The flexible budget uses the master budget as its basis. To develop the flexible budget, management should take the following steps.

1. Identify the activity index and the relevant range of activity.
2. Identify the variable costs, and determine the budgeted variable cost per unit of activity for each cost.

3. Identify the fixed costs, and determine the budgeted amount for each cost.
4. Prepare the budget for selected increments of activity within the relevant range.

The activity index chosen should be one that significantly influences the costs that are being budgeted. For manufacturing overhead costs, for example, the activity index is usually the same as the index used in developing the predetermined overhead rate—that is, direct labor hours or machine hours. For selling and administrative expenses, the activity index usually is sales or net sales.

The choice of the increment of activity is largely a matter of judgment. For example, if the relevant range is 8,000 to 12,000 direct labor hours, increments of 1,000 hours may be selected. The flexible budget is then prepared for each increment within the relevant range.

Decision Toolkit

Decision Checkpoints	Info Needed for Decision	Tool to Use for Decision	How to Evaluate Results
Are the increased costs resulting from increased production reasonable?	Variable costs projected at different levels of production	Flexible budget	After taking into account different production levels, results are favorable if expenses are less than budgeted amounts.

FLEXIBLE BUDGET—A CASE STUDY

To illustrate the flexible budget, we will use Fox Manufacturing Company. Fox's management wants to use a **flexible budget for monthly comparisons** of actual and budgeted manufacturing overhead costs of the Finishing Department. The master budget for the year ending December 31, 2007, shows expected annual operating capacity of 120,000 direct labor hours and the following overhead costs.

Illustration 21-11 Master budget data

Variable Costs		Fixed Costs	
Indirect materials	$180,000	Depreciation	$180,000
Indirect labor	240,000	Supervision	120,000
Utilities	60,000	Property taxes	60,000
Total	$480,000	Total	$360,000

The four steps for developing the flexible budget are applied as follows.

STEP 1. **Identify the activity index and the relevant range of activity.** The activity index is direct labor hours. Management concludes that the relevant range is 8,000–12,000 direct labor hours per month.

STEP 2. **Identify the variable costs, and determine the budgeted variable cost per unit of activity for each cost.** There are three variable costs. The variable cost per unit is found by dividing each total budgeted cost by the direct labor hours used in preparing the master budget (120,000 hours). For Fox Manufacturing, the computations are:

Variable Cost	Computation	Variable Cost per Direct Labor Hour
Indirect materials	$180,000 ÷ 120,000	$1.50
Indirect labor	$240,000 ÷ 120,000	2.00
Utilities	$ 60,000 ÷ 120,000	0.50
Total		$4.00

Illustration 21-12 Computation of variable costs per direct labor hour

STEP 3. **Identify the fixed costs, and determine the budgeted amount for each cost.** There are three fixed costs. Since Fox desires **monthly budget data**, the budgeted amount is found by dividing each annual budgeted cost by 12. For Fox Manufacturing, the monthly budgeted fixed costs are: depreciation $15,000, supervision $10,000, and property taxes $5,000.

STEP 4. **Prepare the budget for selected increments of activity within the relevant range.** Management decides to prepare the budget in increments of 1,000 direct labor hours.

The flexible budget is shown in Illustration 21-13.

Illustration 21-13 Flexible monthly overhead budget

Fox Manufacturing Company
Flexible Monthly Manufacturing Overhead Budget
Finishing Department
For the Year 2007

Activity level	B	C	D	E	F
Direct labor hours	8,000	9,000	10,000	11,000	12,000
Variable costs					
Indirect materials	$12,000	$13,500	$15,000	$16,500	$18,000
Indirect labor	16,000	18,000	20,000	22,000	24,000
Utilities	4,000	4,500	5,000	5,500	6,000
Total variable costs	32,000	36,000	40,000	44,000	48,000
Fixed costs					
Depreciation	15,000	15,000	15,000	15,000	15,000
Supervision	10,000	10,000	10,000	10,000	10,000
Property taxes	5,000	5,000	5,000	5,000	5,000
Total fixed costs	30,000	30,000	30,000	30,000	30,000
Total costs	$62,000	$66,000	$70,000	$74,000	$78,000

From the budget, the following formula may be used to determine total budgeted costs at any level of activity.

Illustration 21-14 Formula for total budgeted costs

$$\text{Fixed Costs} + \text{Variable Costs*} = \text{Total Budgeted Costs}$$

*Total variable cost per unit × Activity level.

For Fox Manufacturing, fixed costs are $30,000, and total variable cost per unit is $4.00. Thus, at 9,000 direct labor hours, total budgeted costs are $66,000 [$30,000 + ($4.00 × 9,000)]. Similarly, at 8,622 direct labor hours, total budgeted costs are $64,488 [$30,000 + ($4.00 × 8,622)].

Total budgeted costs can also be shown graphically, as in Illustration 21-15. In the graph, the activity index is shown on the horizontal axis, and costs are indicated on the vertical axis. The graph highlights two activity levels (10,000 and 12,000). As shown, total budgeted costs at these activity levels are $70,000 [$30,000 + ($4.00 × 10,000)] and $78,000 [$30,000 + ($4.00 × 12,000)], respectively.

Illustration 21-15
Graphic flexible budget data highlighting 10,000 and 12,000 activity levels

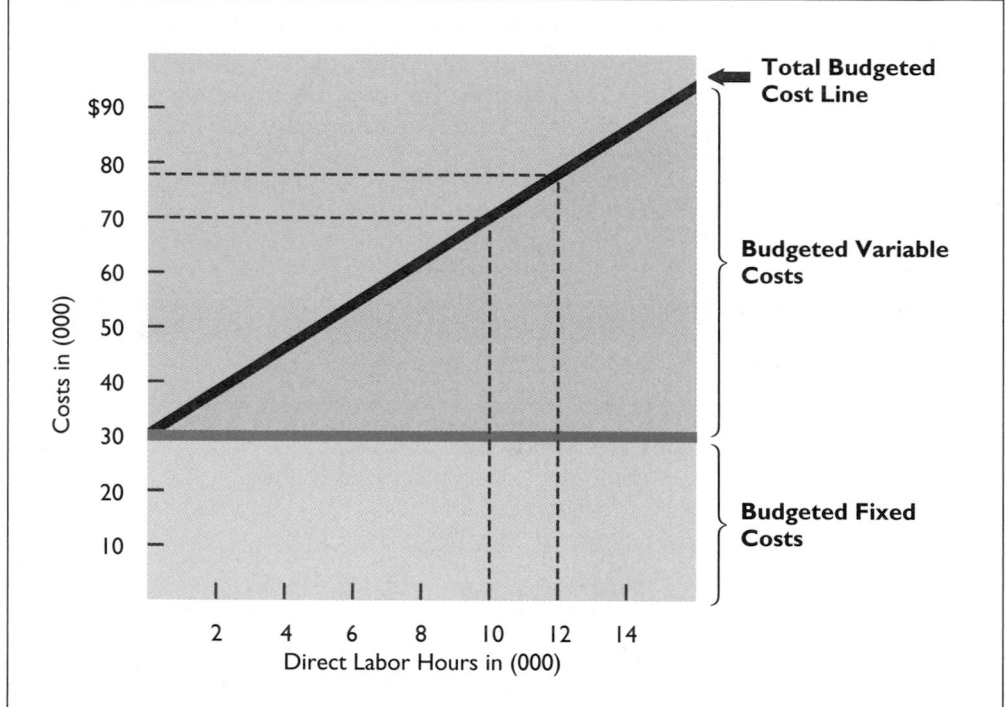

FLEXIBLE BUDGET REPORTS

Flexible budget reports are another type of internal report. The flexible budget report consists of two sections: (1) production data for a selected activity index, such as direct labor hours, and (2) cost data for variable and fixed costs. The report provides a basis for evaluating a manager's performance in two areas: production control and cost control. Flexible budget reports are widely used in production and service departments.

A budget report for the Finishing Department of Fox Company for the month of January is shown in Illustration 21-16 (on page 1023). In this month, 9,000 hours were worked. The budget data are therefore based on the flexible budget for 9,000 hours in Illustration 21-13. The actual cost data are assumed.

How appropriate is this report in evaluating the Finishing Department manager's performance in controlling overhead costs? The report clearly provides a reliable basis. Both actual and budget costs are based on the activity level worked during January. Since variable costs generally are incurred directly by the department, the difference between the budget allowance for those hours and the actual costs is the responsibility of the department manager.

Illustration 21-16 Flexible overhead budget report

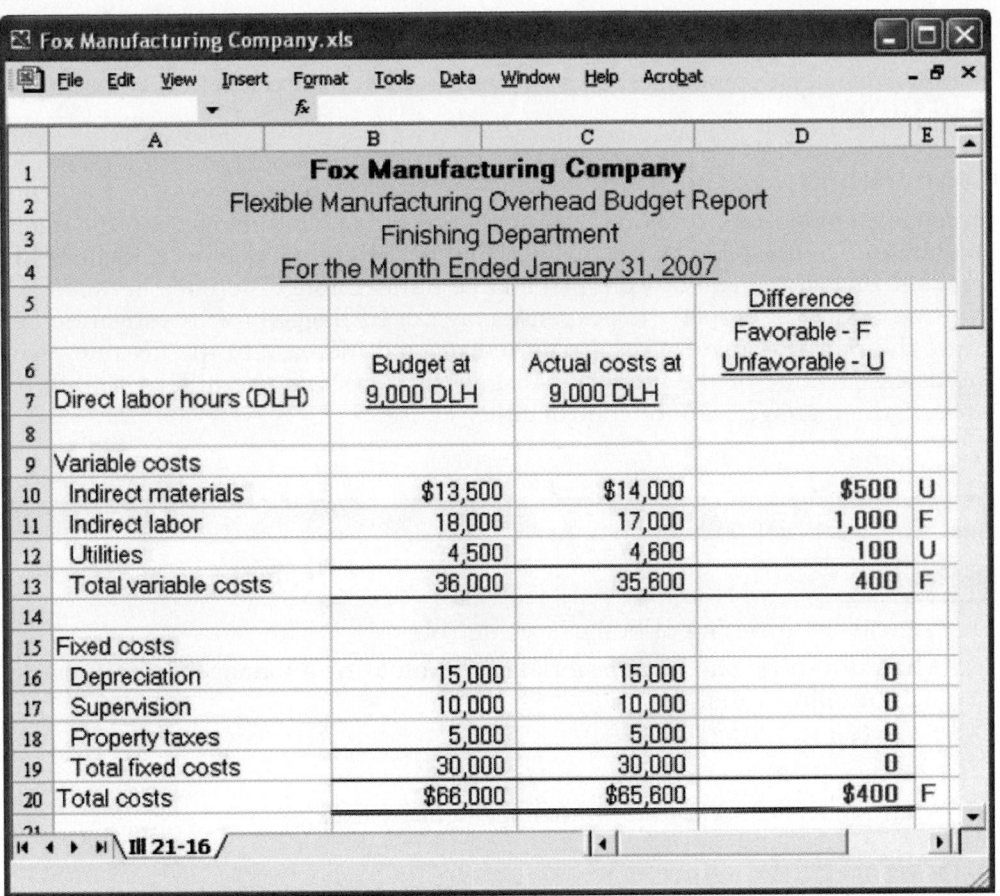

Fox Manufacturing Company				
Flexible Manufacturing Overhead Budget Report				
Finishing Department				
For the Month Ended January 31, 2007				
			Difference	
			Favorable - F	
	Budget at	Actual costs at	Unfavorable - U	
Direct labor hours (DLH)	9,000 DLH	9,000 DLH		
Variable costs				
Indirect materials	$13,500	$14,000	$500	U
Indirect labor	18,000	17,000	1,000	F
Utilities	4,500	4,600	100	U
Total variable costs	36,000	35,600	400	F
Fixed costs				
Depreciation	15,000	15,000	0	
Supervision	10,000	10,000	0	
Property taxes	5,000	5,000	0	
Total fixed costs	30,000	30,000	0	
Total costs	$66,000	$65,600	$400	F

In subsequent months, other flexible budget reports will be prepared. For each month, the budget data are based on the actual activity level attained. In February that level may be 11,000 direct labor hours, in July 10,000, and so on.

MANAGEMENT BY EXCEPTION

Management by exception means that top management's review of a budget report is focused either entirely or primarily on differences between actual results and planned objectives. This approach enables top management to focus on problem areas. Management by exception does not mean that top management will investigate every difference. For this approach to be effective, there must be guidelines for identifying an exception. The usual criteria are materiality and controllability.

Materiality

Without quantitative guidelines, management would have to investigate every budget difference regardless of the amount. Materiality is usually expressed as a percentage difference from budget. For example, management may set the percentage difference at 5 percent for important items and 10 percent for other items. All differences either over or under budget by the specified percentage will be investigated. Costs over budget warrant investigation to determine why they were not controlled. Likewise, costs under budget merit investigation to determine whether costs critical to profitability are being curtailed. For example, if maintenance costs are budgeted at $80,000 but only $40,000 is spent, major unexpected breakdowns in productive facilities may occur in the future.

Helpful Hint Note that this flexible budget is based on a single cost driver. A more accurate budget often can be developed using the activity-based costing concepts explained in Chapter 17.

Alternatively, a company may specify a single percentage difference from budget for all items and supplement this guideline with a minimum dollar limit. For example, the exception criteria may be stated at 5 percent of budget or more than $10,000.

Controllability of the Item

Exception guidelines are more restrictive for controllable items than for items that are not controllable by the manager. In fact, there may be no guidelines for noncontrollable items. For example, a large unfavorable difference between actual and budgeted property tax expense may not be flagged for investigation because the only possible causes are an unexpected increase in the tax rate or in the assessed value of the property. An investigation into the difference will be useless: the manager cannot control either cause.

BEFORE YOU GO ON . . .

▶Review It

1. What is the meaning of budgetary control?
2. When is a static budget appropriate for evaluating a manager's effectiveness in controlling costs?
3. What is a flexible budget?
4. How is a flexible budget developed?
5. What are the criteria used in management by exception?

▶Do It

Your roommate asks your help in understanding how total budgeted costs are computed at any level of activity. Compute total budgeted costs at 30,000 direct labor hours, assuming that in the flexible budget graph, the fixed cost line and the total budgeted cost line intersect the vertical axis at $36,000 and that the total budget cost line is $186,000 at an activity level of 50,000 direct labor hours.

Action Plan

• Apply the formula: Fixed costs + Variable costs (Total variable costs per unit × Activity level) = Total budgeted costs.

Solution   Using the graph, fixed costs are $36,000, and variable costs are $3 per direct labor hour [($186,000 − $36,000) ÷ 50,000]. Thus, at 30,000 direct labor hours, total budgeted costs are $126,000 [$36,000 + ($3 × 30,000)].

Related exercise material: BE21-3, BE21-4, BE21-5, E21-1, E21-2, E21-3, E21-4, E21-5, and E21-6.

The Concept of Responsibility Accounting

STUDY OBJECTIVE
———— 4 ————
Describe the concept of responsibility accounting.

Like budgeting, responsibility accounting is an important part of management accounting. **Responsibility accounting** involves accumulating and reporting costs (and revenues, where relevant) on the basis of the manager who has the authority to make the day-to-day decisions about the items. Under responsibility accounting, a manager's performance is evaluated on matters directly under that manager's control. Responsibility accounting can be used at every level of management in which the following conditions exist.

1. Costs and revenues can be directly associated with the specific level of management responsibility.
2. The costs and revenues are controllable at the level of responsibility with which they are associated.
3. Budget data can be developed for evaluating the manager's effectiveness in controlling the costs and revenues.

Levels of responsibility for controlling costs are depicted in Illustration 21-17.

Under responsibility accounting, any individual who has control and is accountable for a specified set of activities can be recognized as a responsibility center. Thus, responsibility accounting may extend from the lowest level of control to the top strata of management. Once responsibility has been established, the effectiveness of the individual's performance is first measured and reported for the specified activity. It is then reported upward throughout the organization.

Responsibility accounting is especially valuable in a decentralized company. **Decentralization** means that the control of operations is delegated to many managers throughout the organization. The term **segment** is sometimes used to identify an area of responsibility in decentralized operations. Under responsibility accounting, segment reports are prepared periodically such as monthly, quarterly, and annually, to evaluate managers' performance.

Responsibility accounting is an essential part of any effective system of budgetary control. The reporting of costs and revenues under responsibility accounting differs from budgeting in two respects.

1. A distinction is made between controllable and noncontrollable items.
2. Performance reports either emphasize or include only items controllable by the individual manager.

Responsibility accounting applies to both profit and not-for-profit entities. The former seek to maximize net income. The latter wish to minimize the cost of providing services.

Helpful Hint All companies use responsibility accounting. Without some form of responsibility accounting, there would be chaos in discharging management's control function.

Accounting across the Organization

Since devising its budgeting and control system, JKL, Inc., a large New York advertising agency, has become aware of which specific customer accounts are unprofitable and the reasons why. As a result, the agency has dropped several unprofitable accounts that otherwise would have gone unnoticed. Account managers now feel responsible for the profitability of their accounts. They carefully monitor actual hours spent on each account to make sure the account is being managed and run as efficiently as possible. For example, an account manager noticed a large amount of supervisory creative time was being spent on one account. Further investigation showed that the supervisors, rather than the creative department, were doing the actual creative work. The account manager pointed this out, and a junior creative team was appointed to the account, saving JKL a great deal of money.

CONTROLLABLE VERSUS NONCONTROLLABLE REVENUES AND COSTS

All costs and revenues are controllable at some level of responsibility within a company. This truth underscores the adage by the CEO of any organization that "the buck stops here." Under responsibility accounting, the critical issue is **whether the cost or revenue is controllable at the level of responsibility with which it is associated**.

> **Helpful Hint** Are there more or fewer controllable costs as you move to higher levels of management? Answer: More.

A cost over which a manager has control is called a **controllable cost**. From this definition, it follows that:

1. All costs are controllable by top management because of the broad range of its authority.
2. Fewer costs are controllable as one moves down to each lower level of managerial responsibility because of the manager's decreasing authority.

> **Helpful Hint** The longer the time span, the more likely that the cost becomes controllable.

In general, **costs incurred directly by a level of responsibility are controllable at that level**. In contrast, costs incurred indirectly and allocated to a responsibility level are considered to be **noncontrollable costs** at that level.

RESPONSIBILITY REPORTING SYSTEM

A **responsibility reporting system** involves the preparation of a report for each level of responsibility in the company's organization chart. To illustrate such a system, we will use the partial organization chart and production departments of Francis Chair Company in Illustration 21-18 (page 1027).

The responsibility reporting system begins with the lowest level of responsibility for controlling costs and moves upward to each higher level. The connections between levels are detailed in Illustration 21-19 (on page 1028). A brief description of the four reports for Francis Chair Company is as follows.

1. **Report D** is typical of reports that go to managers at the lowest level of responsibility shown in the organization chart—department managers. Similar reports are prepared for the managers of the Fabricating, Assembly, and Enameling Departments.
2. **Report C** is an example of reports that are sent to plant managers. It shows the costs of the Chicago plant that are controllable at the second level of

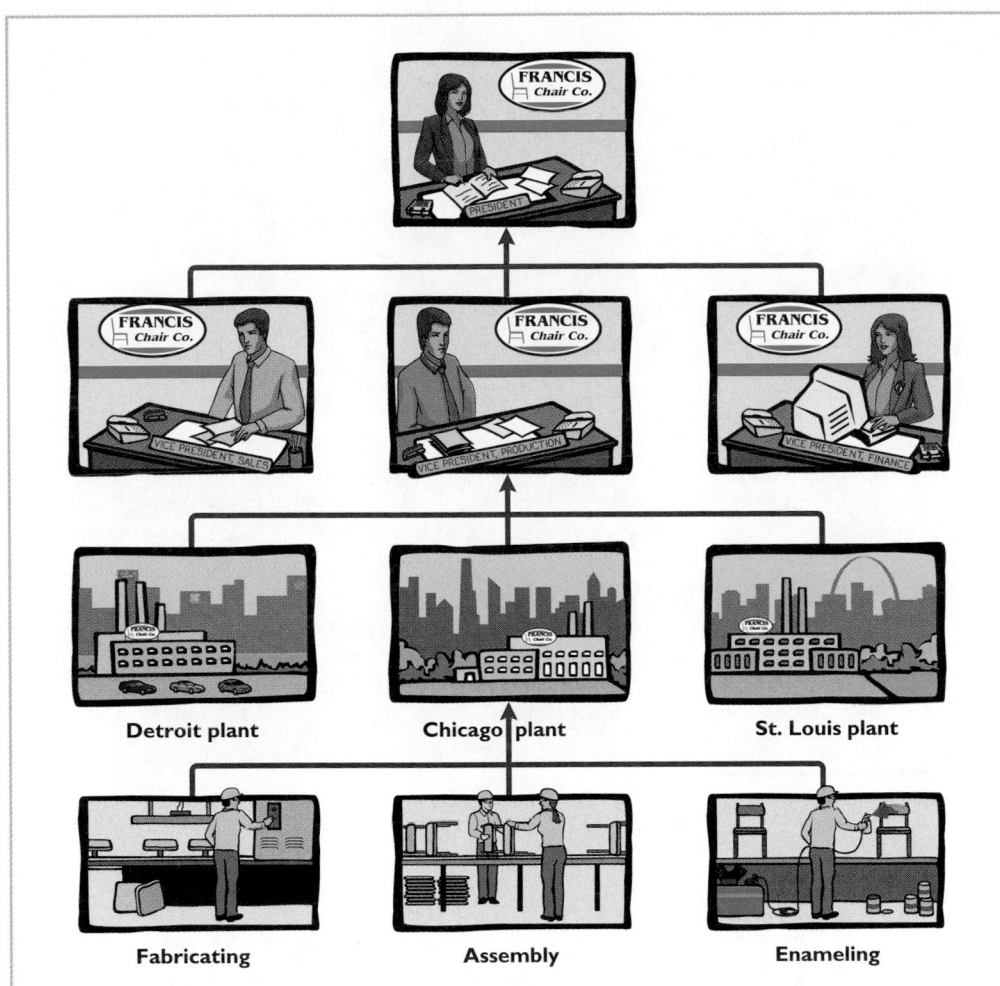

Illustration 21-18 Partial
organization chart

Report A
President sees summary
data of vice presidents.

Report B
Vice president sees sum-
mary of controllable costs
in his/her functional area.

Report C
Plant manager sees sum-
mary of controllable costs
for each department in the
plant.

Report D
Department manager
sees controllable costs of
his/her department.

Detroit plant Chicago plant St. Louis plant

Fabricating Assembly Enameling

responsibility. In addition, Report C shows summary data for each department that is controlled by the plant manager. Similar reports are prepared
for the Detroit and St. Louis plant managers.

3. **Report B** illustrates the reports at the third level of responsibility. It shows
the controllable costs of the vice president of production and summary data
on the three assembly plants for which this officer is responsible. Similar reports are prepared for the vice presidents of sales and finance.

4. **Report A** is typical of the reports that go to the top level of responsibility—the
president. This report shows the controllable costs and expenses of this office
and summary data on the vice presidents that are accountable to the president.

A responsibility reporting system permits management by exception at each
level of responsibility. And, each higher level of responsibility can obtain the detailed report for each lower level of responsibility. For example, the vice president of production in the Francis Chair Company may request the Chicago plant
manager's report because this plant is $5,300 over budget.

This type of reporting system also permits comparative evaluations. In
Illustration 21-19 (page 1028), the Chicago plant manager can easily rank the
department managers' effectiveness in controlling manufacturing costs. Comparative rankings provide further incentive for a manager to control costs. For
example, the Detroit plant manager will want to continue to be No. 1 in the report to the vice president of production. The Chicago plant manager will not
want to remain No. 3 in future reporting periods.

Illustration 21-19 Responsibility reporting system

Report A
President sees summary data of vice presidents.

Report B
Vice president sees summary of controllable costs in his/her functional area.

Report C
Plant manager sees summary of controllable costs for each department in the plant.

Report D
Department manager sees controllable costs of his/her department.

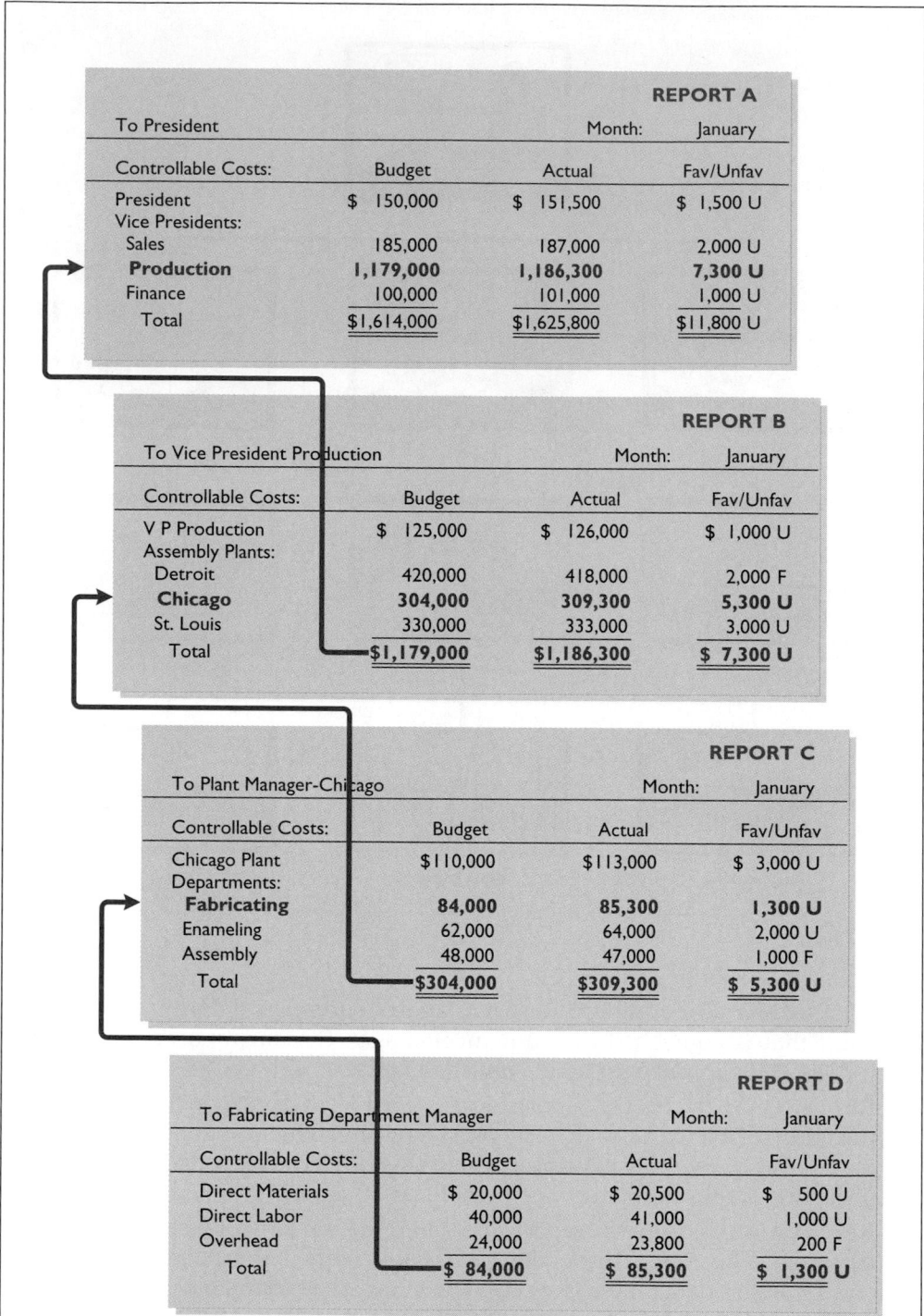

REPORT A

To President   Month: January

Controllable Costs:	Budget	Actual	Fav/Unfav
President	$ 150,000	$ 151,500	$ 1,500 U
Vice Presidents:			
Sales	185,000	187,000	2,000 U
Production	**1,179,000**	**1,186,300**	**7,300 U**
Finance	100,000	101,000	1,000 U
Total	$1,614,000	$1,625,800	$11,800 U

REPORT B

To Vice President Production   Month: January

Controllable Costs:	Budget	Actual	Fav/Unfav
V P Production	$ 125,000	$ 126,000	$ 1,000 U
Assembly Plants:			
Detroit	420,000	418,000	2,000 F
Chicago	**304,000**	**309,300**	**5,300 U**
St. Louis	330,000	333,000	3,000 U
Total	$1,179,000	$1,186,300	$ 7,300 U

REPORT C

To Plant Manager-Chicago   Month: January

Controllable Costs:	Budget	Actual	Fav/Unfav
Chicago Plant	$110,000	$113,000	$ 3,000 U
Departments:			
Fabricating	**84,000**	**85,300**	**1,300 U**
Enameling	62,000	64,000	2,000 U
Assembly	48,000	47,000	1,000 F
Total	$304,000	$309,300	$ 5,300 U

REPORT D

To Fabricating Department Manager   Month: January

Controllable Costs:	Budget	Actual	Fav/Unfav
Direct Materials	$ 20,000	$ 20,500	$ 500 U
Direct Labor	40,000	41,000	1,000 U
Overhead	24,000	23,800	200 F
Total	$ 84,000	$ 85,300	$ 1,300 U

Business Insight
e-Business Perspective

In Chapter 14 we discussed enterprise resource planning (ERP) software packages that collect all information regarding the results of the supply chain. A recent innovation is to attach enterprise application systems (EAS) to ERP systems. EAS systems are budgeting and planning tools. By attaching an EAS system called Hyperion Pillar to its ERP system, Fujitsu Computer Products of America found that it could more easily compare its budgeted amounts to its actual results. It also reduced its typical time spent on planning and budgeting from 6 to 8 weeks down to 10 to 15 days. Finally, the new system has enabled the company to respond quickly to new developments. For example, recently, the software forewarned the company of a potential oversupply problem, and provided recommendations for changes in staffing and capital needs.

SOURCE: Russ Banham, "Better Budgets," *Journal of Accountancy* (February 2000), p. 37.

Types of Responsibility Centers

There are three basic types of responsibility centers: cost centers, profit centers, and investment centers. These classifications indicate the degree of responsibility the manager has for the performance of the center.

A **cost center** incurs costs (and expenses) but does not directly generate revenues. Managers of cost centers have the authority to incur costs. They are evaluated on their ability to control costs. **Cost centers are usually either production departments or service departments.** The former participate directly in making the product. The latter provide only support services. In a Ford Motor Company automobile plant, the welding, painting, and assembling departments are production departments; the maintenance, cafeteria, and human resources departments are service departments. All of them are cost centers.

A **profit center** incurs costs (and expenses) and also generates revenues. Managers of profit centers are judged on the profitability of their centers. Examples of profit centers include the individual departments of a retail store, such as clothing, furniture, and automotive products, and branch offices of banks.

Like a profit center, an **investment center** incurs costs (and expenses) and generates revenues. In addition, an investment center has control over decisions regarding the investment funds available for use. Managers of investment centers are evaluated on both the profitability of the center and the rate of return earned on the funds invested. Investment centers are often associated with subsidiary companies. For example, General Mills's product lines include cereals, helper dinner mixes, fruit snacks, popcorn, and yogurt. Utility, Duke Energy has operating divisions such as electric utility, energy trading, and natural gas. The manager of the investment center (product line) is able to control or significantly influence investment decisions pertaining to such matters as plant expansion and entry into new market areas. These three types of responsibility centers are depicted in Illustration 21-20 (page 1030).

The evaluation of a manager's performance in each type of responsibility center is explained in the remainder of this chapter.

> **Helpful Hint** (1) Is the jewelry department of Macy's department store a profit center or a cost center? (2) Is the props department of a movie studio a profit center or a cost center? Answers: (1) Profit center. (2) Cost center.

Illustration 21-20 Types
of responsibility centers

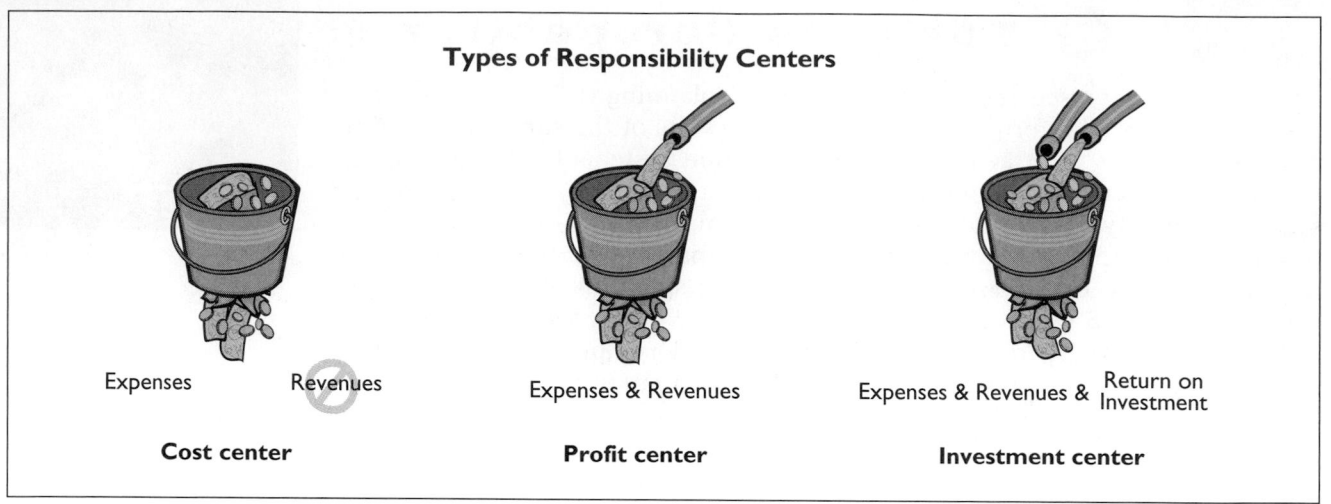

Types of Responsibility Centers

Expenses   Revenues

Cost center

Expenses & Revenues

Profit center

Expenses & Revenues & Return on Investment

Investment center

RESPONSIBILITY ACCOUNTING FOR COST CENTERS

STUDY OBJECTIVE
5
Indicate the features of responsibility reports for cost centers.

The evaluation of a manager's performance for cost centers is based on his or her ability to meet budgeted goals for controllable costs. **Responsibility reports for cost centers compare actual controllable costs with flexible budget data.**

A responsibility report is illustrated in Illustration 21-21. The report is adapted from the flexible budget report for Fox Manufacturing Company in Illustration 21-16 on page 1023. It assumes that the Finishing Department manager is able to control all manufacturing overhead costs except depreciation, property taxes, and his own monthly salary of $6,000. The remaining $4,000 ($10,000 − $6,000) of supervision costs are assumed to apply to other supervisory personnel within the Finishing Department, whose salaries are controllable by the manager.

Illustration 21-21 Responsibility report for a cost center

Fox Manufacturing Company.xls

File   Edit   View   Insert   Format   Tools   Data   Window   Help   Acrobat

	A	B	C	D	E
1	**Fox Manufacturing Company**				
2	Finishing Department				
3	Responsibility Report				
4	For the Month Ended January 31, 2007				
5				Difference	
6	Controllable Cost	Budget	Actual	Favorable - F Unfavorable - U	
7	Indirect materials	$13,500	$14,000	$500	U
8	Indirect labor	18,000	17,000	1,000	F
9	Utilities	4,500	4,600	100	U
10	Supervision	4,000	4,000	0	
11		$40,000	$39,600	$400	F

III 21-21

Only controllable costs are included in the report, and no distinction is made between variable and fixed costs. The responsibility report continues the concept of management by exception. In this case, top management may request an explanation of the $1,000 favorable difference in indirect labor and/or the $500 unfavorable difference in indirect materials.

RESPONSIBILITY ACCOUNTING FOR PROFIT CENTERS

To evaluate the performance of a manager of a profit center, detailed information is needed about both controllable revenues and controllable costs. The operating revenues earned by a profit center, such as sales, are controllable by the manager. All variable costs (and expenses) incurred by the center are also controllable by the manager because they vary with sales. However, to determine the controllability of fixed costs, it is necessary to distinguish between direct and indirect fixed costs.

STUDY OBJECTIVE

6

Identify the content of responsibility reports for profit centers.

Direct and Indirect Fixed Costs

A profit center may have both direct and indirect fixed costs. Direct fixed costs are costs that relate specifically to one center and are incurred for the sole benefit of that center. Examples of such costs include the salaries established by the profit center manager for supervisory personnel and the cost of a timekeeping department for the center's employees. Since these fixed costs can be traced directly to a center, they are also called **traceable costs**. **Most direct fixed costs are controllable by the profit center manager.**

In contrast, indirect fixed costs pertain to a company's overall operating activities and are incurred for the benefit of more than one profit center. Indirect fixed costs are allocated to profit centers on some type of equitable basis. For example, property taxes on a building occupied by more than one center may be allocated on the basis of square feet of floor space used by each center. Or, the costs of a company's human resources department may be allocated to profit centers on the basis of the number of employees in each center. Because these fixed costs apply to more than one center, they are also called **common costs**. **Most indirect fixed costs are not controllable by the profit center manager.**

Responsibility Report

The responsibility report for a profit center shows budgeted and actual **controllable revenues and costs**. The report is prepared using the cost-volume-profit income statement explained in Chapter 18. In the report:

1. Controllable fixed costs are deducted from contribution margin.
2. The excess of contribution margin over controllable fixed costs is identified as **controllable margin**.
3. Noncontrollable fixed costs are not reported.

The responsibility report for the manager of the Marine Division, a profit center of Mantle Manufacturing Company, is shown in Illustration 21-22 (page 1032). For the year, the Marine Division also had $60,000 of indirect fixed costs that were not controllable by the profit center manager.

Controllable margin is considered to be the best measure of the manager's performance **in controlling revenues and costs**. This report shows that the manager's performance was below budgeted expectations by 10 percent ($36,000 ÷ $360,000). Top management would likely investigate the causes of this unfavorable result. Note that the report does not show the Marine Division's noncontrollable fixed costs of $60,000. These costs would be included in a report on the profitability of the profit center.

Responsibility reports for profit centers may also be prepared monthly. In addition, they may include cumulative year-to-date results.

Helpful Hint Recognize that we are emphasizing financial measures of performance. These days companies are also making an effort to stress nonfinancial performance measures such as product quality, labor productivity, market growth, materials' yield, manufacturing flexibility, and technological capability.

Illustration 21-22 Responsibility report for profit center

Mantle Manufacturing Company.xls				
File Edit View Insert Format Tools Data Window Help Acrobat			Type a question for help	
	A	B	C	D	E
1		**Mantle Manufacturing Company**			
2		Marine Division			
3		Responsibility Report			
4		For the Year Ended December 31, 2007			
5				Difference	
6		Budget	Actual	Favorable - F Unfavorable - U	
7	Sales	$1,200,000	$1,150,000	$50,000	U
8	Variable costs				
9	Cost of goods sold	500,000	490,000	10,000	F
10	Selling and administrative	160,000	156,000	4,000	F
11	Total	660,000	646,000	14,000	F
12	Contribution margin	540,000	504,000	36,000	U
13	Controllable fixed costs				
14	Cost of goods sold	100,000	100,000	0	
15	Selling and administrative	80,000	80,000	0	
16	Total	180,000	180,000	0	
17	Controllable margin	$360,000	$324,000	$36,000	U
18					

Decision Toolkit

Decision Checkpoints	Info Needed for Decision	Tool to Use for Decision	How to Evaluate Results
Have the individual managers been held accountable for the costs and revenues under their control?	Relevant costs and revenues, where the individual manager has authority to make day-to-day decisions about the items	Responsibility reports focused on cost centers, profit centers, and investment centers as appropriate	Compare budget to actual costs and revenues for controllable items.

BEFORE YOU GO ON . . .

▶Review It

1. What conditions are essential for responsibility accounting?
2. What is involved in a responsibility reporting system?
3. What is the primary objective of a responsibility report for a cost center?
4. How does contribution margin differ from controllable margin in a responsibility report for a profit center?

▶Do It

Midwest Division operates as a profit center. It reports the following actual results for the year: Sales $1,700,000, variable costs $800,000, controllable fixed costs $400,000, noncontrollable fixed costs $200,000. Annual budgeted amounts were $1,500,000, $700,000, $400,000, and $200,000, respectively. Prepare a responsibility report for the Midwest Division for December 31, 2007.

Action Plan

• Deduct variable costs from sales to show contribution margin.

• Deduct controllable fixed costs from the contribution margin to show controllable margin.

• Do not report noncontrollable fixed costs.

Solution

MIDWEST DIVISION
Responsibility Report
For the Year Ended December 31, 2007

	Budget	Actual	Difference Favorable F Unfavorable U
Sales	$1,500,000	$1,700,000	$200,000 F
Variable costs	700,000	800,000	100,000 U
Contribution margin	800,000	900,000	100,000 F
Controllable fixed costs	400,000	400,000	–0–
Controllable margin	$ 400,000	$ 500,000	$100,000 F

Related exercise material: BE21-7 and E21-10.

RESPONSIBILITY ACCOUNTING FOR INVESTMENT CENTERS

As explained earlier, an investment center manager can control or significantly influence the investment funds available for use. Thus, the primary basis for evaluating the performance of a manager of an investment center is **return on investment (ROI)**. The return on investment is considered to be a useful performance measurement because it shows the **effectiveness of the manager in utilizing the assets at his or her disposal**.

STUDY OBJECTIVE

7

Explain the basis and formula used in evaluating performance in investment centers.

Return on Investment (ROI)

The formula for computing ROI for an investment center, together with assumed illustrative data, is shown in Illustration 21-23. Both factors in the formula are controllable by the investment center manager. Operating assets consist of current assets and plant assets used in operations by the center and controlled by the manager. Nonoperating assets such as idle plant assets and land held for future use are excluded. Average operating assets are usually based on the cost or book value of the assets at the beginning and end of the year.

Controllable Margin	÷	Average Operating Assets	=	Return on Investment (ROI)
$1,000,000	÷	$5,000,000	=	20%

Illustration 21-23 ROI formula

Responsibility Report

The scope of the investment center manager's responsibility significantly affects the content of the performance report. Since an investment center is an independent entity for operating purposes, **all fixed costs are controllable by its**

manager. For example, the manager is responsible for depreciation on investment center assets. Therefore, more fixed costs are identified as controllable in the performance report for an investment center manager than in a performance report for a profit center manager. The report also shows budgeted and actual ROI below controllable margin.

To illustrate this responsibility report, we will now assume that the Marine Division of Mantle Manufacturing Company is an investment center. It has budgeted and actual average operating assets of $2,000,000. The manager can control $60,000 of fixed costs that were not controllable when the division was a profit center. The responsibility report is shown in Illustration 21-24.

Illustration 21-24   Responsibility report for investment center

The report shows that the manager's performance based on ROI was 12 percent (1.8% ÷ 15%) below budget expectations. Top management would likely want an explanation of the reasons for this unfavorable result.

Judgmental Factors in ROI

The return on investment approach includes two judgmental factors:

1. **Valuation of operating assets.** Operating assets may be valued at acquisition cost, book value, appraised value, or market value. The first two bases are readily available from the accounting records.

2. **Margin (income) measure.** This measure may be controllable margin, income from operations, or net income.

Each of the alternative values for operating assets can provide a reliable basis for evaluating a manager's performance as long as it is consistently applied between reporting periods. However, the use of income measures other than controllable margin will not result in a valid basis for evaluating the performance of an investment center manager.[1]

Improving ROI

The manager of an investment center can improve ROI in two ways: (1) increase controllable margin, and/or (2) reduce average operating assets. To illustrate, we will use the following assumed data for the Laser Division of Berra Manufacturing.

Sales	$2,000,000
Variable cost	1,100,000
Contribution margin (45%)	900,000
Controllable fixed costs	300,000
Controllable margin (a)	$ 600,000
Average operating assets (b)	$5,000,000
Return on investment (a) ÷ (b)	12%

Illustration 21-25
Assumed data for Laser Division

INCREASING CONTROLLABLE MARGIN. Controllable margin can be increased by increasing sales or by reducing variable and controllable fixed costs as follows.

1. **Increase sales 10 percent.** Sales will increase $200,000 ($2,000,000 × .10). Assuming no change in the contribution margin percentage of 45 percent, contribution margin will increase $90,000 ($200,000 × .45). Controllable margin will increase by the same amount because controllable fixed costs will not change. Thus, controllable margin becomes $690,000 ($600,000 + $90,000). The new ROI is 13.8 percent, computed as follows.

$$\text{ROI} = \frac{\text{Controllable margin}}{\text{Average operating assets}} = \frac{\$690,000}{\$5,000,000} = \textbf{13.8\%}$$

Illustration 21-26 ROI computation—increase in sales

An increase in sales benefits both the investment center and the company if it results in new business. It would not benefit the company if the increase was achieved at the expense of other investment centers.

2. **Decrease variable and fixed costs 10 percent.** Total costs will decrease $140,000 [($1,100,000 + $300,000) × .10]. This reduction will result in a corresponding increase in controllable margin. Thus, controllable margin becomes $740,000 ($600,000 + $140,000). The new ROI is 14.8 percent, computed as follows.

$$\text{ROI} = \frac{\text{Controllable margin}}{\text{Average operating assets}} = \frac{\$740,000}{\$5,000,000} = \textbf{14.8\%}$$

Illustration 21-27 ROI computation—decrease in costs

---

[1]Although the ROI approach is often used in evaluating investment performance, it has some disadvantages. The appendix to this chapter illustrates a second method for evaluation referred to as the residual income approach.

This course of action is clearly beneficial when waste and inefficiencies are eliminated. But, a reduction in vital costs such as required maintenance and inspections is not likely to be acceptable to top management.

REDUCING AVERAGE OPERATING ASSETS.   Assume that average operating assets are reduced 10 percent or $500,000 ($5,000,000 × .10). Average operating assets become $4,500,000 ($5,000,000 − $500,000). Since controllable margin remains unchanged at $600,000, the new ROI is 13.3 percent, computed as follows.

Illustration 21-28   ROI computation—decrease in operating assets

$$ROI = \frac{\text{Controllable margin}}{\text{Average operating assets}} = \frac{\$600,000}{\$4,500,000} = \textbf{13.3\%}$$

Reductions in operating assets may or may not be prudent. It is beneficial to eliminate overinvestment in inventories and to dispose of excessive plant assets. However, it is unwise to reduce inventories below expected needs or to dispose of essential plant assets.

Decision Toolkit

Decision Checkpoints	Info Needed for Decision	Tool to Use for Decision	How to Evaluate Results
Has the investment center performed up to expectations?	Controllable margin (contribution margin minus controllable fixed costs), and average investment center operating assets	Return on investment	Compare actual ROI to expected ROI.

PRINCIPLES OF PERFORMANCE EVALUATION

Performance evaluation is at the center of responsibility accounting. **Performance evaluation** is a management function that compares actual results with budget goals. Performance evaluation involves both behavioral and reporting principles.

Behavioral Principles

The human factor is critical in evaluating performance. Behavioral principles include the following.

1. **Managers of responsibility centers should have direct input into the process of establishing budget goals of their area of responsibility.** Without such input, managers may view the goals as unrealistic or arbitrarily set by top management. Such views adversely affect the managers' motivation to meet the targeted objectives.
2. **The evaluation of performance should be based entirely on matters that are controllable by the manager being evaluated.** Criticism of a manager on matters outside his or her control reduces the effectiveness of the evaluation process. It leads to negative reactions by a manager and to doubts about the fairness of the company's evaluation policies.
3. **Top management should support the evaluation process.** As explained earlier, the evaluation process begins at the lowest level of responsibility and extends upward to the highest level of management. Managers quickly lose

faith in the process when top management ignores, overrules, or bypasses established procedures for evaluating a manager's performance.

4. **The evaluation process must allow managers to respond to their evaluations.** Evaluation is not a one-way street. Managers should have the opportunity to defend their performance. Evaluation without feedback is both impersonal and ineffective.

5. **The evaluation should identify both good and poor performance.** Praise for good performance is a powerful motivating factor for a manager. This is especially true when a manager's compensation includes rewards for meeting budget goals.

Reporting Principles

Performance evaluation under responsibility accounting should be based on certain reporting principles. These principles pertain primarily to the internal reports that provide the basis for evaluating performance. Performance reports should:

1. Contain only data that are controllable by the manager of the responsibility center.
2. Provide accurate and reliable budget data to measure performance.
3. Highlight significant differences between actual results and budget goals.
4. Be tailor-made for the intended evaluation.
5. Be prepared at reasonable intervals.

BEFORE YOU GO ON . . .

▶**Review It**

1. What is the formula for computing return on investment (ROI)?
2. Identify three actions a manager may take to improve ROI.

Using the Decision Toolkit

The manufacturing overhead budget for Reebles Company contains the following items.

Variable costs	
Indirect materials	$25,000
Indirect labor	12,000
Maintenance expenses	10,000
Manufacturing supplies	6,000
Total variable	$53,000
Fixed costs	
Supervision	$17,000
Inspection costs	1,000
Insurance expenses	2,000
Depreciation	15,000
Total fixed	$35,000

The budget was based on an estimated 2,000 units being produced. During November, 1,500 units were produced, and the following costs incurred.

Variable costs		
Indirect materials	$25,200	
Indirect labor	13,500	
Maintenance expenses	8,200	
Manufacturing supplies	5,100	
Total variable	$52,000	
Fixed costs		
Supervision	$19,300	
Inspection costs	1,200	
Insurance expenses	2,200	
Depreciation	14,700	
Total fixed	$37,400	

Instructions

(a) Determine which items would be controllable by Ed Lopat, the production manager. (Assume "supervision" excludes Lopat's own salary.)

(b) How much should have been spent during the month for the manufacture of the 1,500 units?

(c) Prepare a flexible manufacturing overhead budget report for Mr. Lopat.

(d) Prepare a responsibility report. Include only the costs that would have been controllable by Mr. Lopat. In an attached memo, describe clearly for Mr. Lopat the areas in which his performance needs to be improved.

Solution

(a) Ed Lopat should be able to control all the variable costs and the fixed costs of supervision and inspection. Insurance and depreciation ordinarily are not the responsibility of the department manager.

(b) The total variable cost per unit is $26.50 ($53,000 ÷ 2,000). The total budgeted cost during the month to manufacture 1,500 units is variable costs $39,750 (1,500 × $26.50) plus fixed costs ($35,000), for a total of $74,750 ($39,750 + $35,000).

(c)

REEBLES COMPANY
Production Department
Manufacturing Overhead Budget Report (Flexible)
For the Month Ended November 30, 2007

	Budget at 1,500 units	Actual at 1,500 units	Difference Favorable F Unfavorable U
Variable costs			
Indirect materials	$18,750	$25,200	$ 6,450 U
Indirect labor	9,000	13,500	4,500 U
Maintenance	7,500	8,200	700 U
Manufacturing supplies	4,500	5,100	600 U
Total variable	39,750	52,000	12,250 U
Fixed costs			
Supervision	17,000	19,300	2,300 U
Inspection	1,000	1,200	200 U
Insurance	2,000	2,200	200 U
Depreciation	15,000	14,700	300 F
Total fixed	35,000	37,400	2,400 U
Total costs	$74,750	$89,400	$14,650 U

(d) Because a production department is a cost center, the responsibility report should include only the costs that are controllable by the production manager. In this type of report, no distinction is made between variable and fixed costs. Budget data in the report should be based on the units actually produced.

REEBLES COMPANY
Production Department
Manufacturing Overhead Responsibility Report
For the Month Ended November 30, 2007

Controllable Cost	Budget	Actual	Difference Favorable F Unfavorable U
Indirect materials	$18,750	$25,200	$ 6,450 U
Indirect labor	9,000	13,500	4,500 U
Maintenance	7,500	8,200	700 U
Manufacturing supplies	4,500	5,100	600 U
Supervision	17,000	19,300	2,300 U
Inspection	1,000	1,200	200 U
Total	$57,750	$72,500	$14,750 U

To: Mr. Ed Lopat, Production Manager

From: _____, Vice-President of Production

Subject: Performance Evaluation for the Month of November
Your performance in controlling costs that are your responsibility was very disappointing in the month of November. As indicated in the accompanying responsibility report, total costs were $14,750 over budget. On a percentage basis, costs were 26% over budget. As you can see, actual costs were over budget for every cost item. In three instances, costs were significantly over budget (indirect materials 34%, indirect labor 50%, and supervision 14%).

Ed, it is imperative that you get costs under control in your department as soon as possible.

I think we need to talk about ways to implement more effective cost control measures. I would like to meet with you in my office at 9 a.m. on Wednesday to discuss possible alternatives.

Summary of Study Objectives

1 *Describe the concept of budgetary control.* Budgetary control consists of (a) preparing periodic budget reports that compare actual results with planned objectives, (b) analyzing the differences to determine their causes, (c) taking appropriate corrective action, and (d) modifying future plans, if necessary.

2 *Evaluate the usefulness of static budget reports.* Static budget reports are useful in evaluating the progress toward planned sales and profit goals. They are also appropriate in assessing a manager's effectiveness in controlling costs when (a) actual activity closely approximates the master budget activity level, and/or

(b) the behavior of the costs in response to changes in activity is fixed.

3 *Explain the development of flexible budgets and the usefulness of flexible budget reports.* To develop the flexible budget it is necessary to:
(a) Identify the activity index and the relevant range of activity.
(b) Identify the variable costs, and determine the budgeted variable cost per unit of activity for each cost.
(c) Identify the fixed costs, and determine the budgeted amount for each cost.

(d) Prepare the budget for selected increments of activity within the relevant range.

Flexible budget reports permit an evaluation of a manager's performance in controlling production and costs.

4 *Describe the concept of responsibility accounting.* Responsibility accounting involves accumulating and reporting revenues and costs on the basis of the individual manager who has the authority to make the day-to-day decisions about the items. The evaluation of a manager's performance is based on the matters directly under the manager's control. In responsibility accounting, it is necessary to distinguish between controllable and noncontrollable fixed costs and to identify three types of responsibility centers: cost, profit, and investment.

5 *Indicate the features of responsibility reports for cost centers.* Responsibility reports for cost centers compare actual costs with flexible budget data. The reports show only controllable costs, and no distinction is made between variable and fixed costs.

6 *Identify the content of responsibility reports for profit centers.* Responsibility reports show contribution margin, controllable fixed costs, and controllable margin for each profit center.

7 *Explain the basis and formula used in evaluating performance in investment centers.* The primary basis for evaluating performance in investment centers is return on investment (ROI). The formula for computing ROI for investment centers is: Controllable margin ÷ Average operating assets.

THE NAVIGATOR

Decision Toolkit—A Summary

Decision Checkpoints	Info Needed for Decision	Tool to Use for Decision	How to Evaluate Results
Are the increased costs resulting from increased production reasonable?	Variable costs projected at different levels of production	Flexible budget	After taking into account different production levels, results are favorable if expenses are less than budgeted amounts.
Have the individual managers been held accountable for the costs and revenues under their control?	Relevant costs and revenues, where the individual manager has authority to make day-to-day decisions about the items	Responsibility reports focused on cost centers, profit centers, and investment centers as appropriate	Compare budget to actual costs and revenues for controllable items.
Has the investment center performed up to expectations?	Controllable margin (contribution margin minus controllable fixed costs), and average investment center operating assets	Return on investment	Compare actual ROI to expected ROI.

APPENDIX
RESIDUAL INCOME—ANOTHER PERFORMANCE MEASUREMENT

STUDY OBJECTIVE
8
Explain the difference between ROI and residual income.

Although most companies use ROI in evaluating their investment performance, ROI has a significant disadvantage. To illustrate, let's look at the Electronics Division of Pujols Manufacturing Company. It has an ROI of 20 percent computed as follows.

Illustration 21A-1 ROI formula

Controllable Margin	÷	Average Operating Assets	=	Return on Investment (ROI)
$1,000,000	÷	$5,000,000	=	20%

The Electronics Division is considering producing a new product, a GPS satellite tracker (hereafter referred to as Tracker), for its boats. To produce Tracker, operating assets will have to increase $2,000,000. Tracker is expected to generate an additional $260,000 of controllable margin. Illustration 21A-2 shows how Tracker will effect ROI.

	Without Tracker	Tracker	With Tracker
Controllable margin (a)	$1,000,000	$ 260,000	$1,260,000
Average operating assets (b)	$5,000,000	$2,000,000	$7,000,000
Return on investment [(a) ÷ (b)]	**20%**	**13%**	**18%**

Illustration 21A-2   ROI comparison

The investment in Tracker reduces ROI from 20 percent to 18 percent.

Let's suppose that you are the manager of the Electronics Division and must make the decision to produce or not produce Tracker. If you were evaluated using ROI, you probably would not produce Tracker because your ROI would drop from 20 percent to 18 percent. The problem with this ROI analysis is that it ignores an important variable, the minimum rate of return on a company's operating assets. The **minimum rate of return** is the rate at which the Electronics Division can cover its costs and earn a profit. Assuming that the Electronics Division has a minimum rate of return of 10 percent, it should invest in Tracker because its ROI of 13 percent is greater than 10 percent.

Residual Income Compared to ROI

To evaluate performance using the minimum rate of return, companies use the residual income approach. **Residual income** is the income that remains after subtracting from the controllable margin the minimum rate of return on a company's average operating assets. The residual income for Tracker would be computed as follows.

Controllable Margin	−	Minimum Rate of Return × Average Operating Assets	=	Residual Income
$260,000	−	10% × $2,000,000	=	$60,000

Illustration 21A-3   Residual income formula

As shown, the residual income related to the Tracker investment is $60,000. Illustration 21A-4 indicates how residual income changes as the additional investment is made.

	Without Tracker	Tracker	With Tracker
Controllable margin (a)	$1,000,000	$260,000	$1,260,000
Average operating assets × 10% (b)	500,000	200,000	700,000
Residual income [(a) − (b)]	$ 500,000	$ 60,000	**$ 560,000**

Illustration 21A-4   Residual income comparison

This example illustrates how performance evaluation based on ROI can be misleading and can even cause managers to reject projects that would actually increase income for the company. As a result, many companies such as Coca-Cola, Briggs and Stratton, Eli Lilly, and Siemens AG use residual income (or a variant often referred to as economic value added) to evaluate investment alternatives and measure company performance.

Residual Income Weakness

It might appear from the above discussion that the goal of any company should be to maximize the total amount of residual income in each division. This goal, however, ignores the fact that one division might use substantially fewer assets to attain the same level of residual income as another division. For example, we know that to produce Tracker, the Electronics Division of Pujols Manufacturing used $2,000,000 of average operating assets to generate $260,000 of controllable margin. Now let's say a different division produced a product called SeaDog, which used $4,000,000 to generate $460,000 of controllable margin, as shown in Illustration 21A-5.

Illustration 21A-5   Comparison of two products

	Tracker	SeaDog
Controllable margin (a)	$260,000	$460,000
Average operating assets × 10% (b)	200,000	400,000
Residual income [(a) − (b)]	$ 60,000	$ 60,000

If the performance of these two investments were evaluated using residual income, they would be considered equal: Both products have the same total residual income. This ignores, however, the fact that SeaDog required **twice** as many operating assets to achieve the same level of residual income.

Summary of Study Objective for Appendix

8 *Explain the difference between ROI and residual income.* ROI is controllable margin divided by average operating assets. Residual income is the income that remains after subtracting the minimum rate of return on a company's average operating assets. ROI sometimes provides misleading results because profitable investments are often rejected when the investment reduces ROI but increases overall profitability.

Glossary

Budgetary control   The use of budgets to control operations. (p. 1014)

Controllable cost   A cost over which a manager has control. (p. 1026)

Controllable margin   Contribution margin less controllable fixed costs. (p. 1031)

Cost center   A responsibility center that incurs costs but does not directly generate revenues. (p. 1029)

Decentralization   Control of operations is delegated to many managers throughout the organization. (p. 1025)

Direct fixed costs   Costs that relate specifically to a responsibility center and are incurred for the sole benefit of the center. (p. 1031)

Flexible budget   A projection of budget data for various levels of activity. (p. 1017)

Indirect fixed costs Costs that are incurred for the benefit of more than one profit center. (p. 1031)

Investment center A responsibility center that incurs costs, generates revenues, and has control over decisions regarding the assets available for use. (p. 1029)

Management by exception The review of budget reports by top management focused entirely or primarily on differences between actual results and planned objectives. (p. 1023)

Noncontrollable costs Costs incurred indirectly and allocated to a responsibility center that are not controllable at that level. (p. 1026)

Profit center A responsibility center that incurs costs and also generates revenues. (p. 1029)

Residual income The income that remains after subtracting from the controllable margin the minimum rate of return on a company's operating assets. (p. 1041)

Responsibility accounting A part of management accounting that involves accumulating and reporting revenues and costs on the basis of the manager who has the authority to make the day-to-day decisions about the items. (p. 1024)

Responsibility reporting system The preparation of reports for each level of responsibility in the company's organization chart. (p. 1026)

Return on investment (ROI) A measure of management's effectiveness in utilizing assets at its disposal in an investment center. (p. 1033)

Segment An area of responsibility in decentralized operations. (p. 1025)

Static budget A projection of budget data at one level of activity. (p. 1015)

Demonstration Problem

Glenda Company uses a flexible budget for manufacturing overhead based on direct labor hours. For 2007 the master overhead budget for the Packaging Department based on 300,000 direct labor hours was as follows.

Variable Costs		Fixed Costs	
Indirect labor	$360,000	Supervision	$ 60,000
Supplies and lubricants	150,000	Depreciation	24,000
Maintenance	210,000	Property taxes	18,000
Utilities	120,000	Insurance	12,000
	$840,000		$114,000

During July, 24,000 direct labor hours were worked. The company incurred the following variable costs in July: indirect labor $30,200, supplies and lubricants $11,600, maintenance $17,500, and utilities $9,200. Actual fixed overhead costs were the same as monthly budgeted fixed costs.

Instructions

Prepare a flexible budget report for the Packaging Department for July.

Solution to Demonstration Problem

GLENDA COMPANY
Manufacturing Overhead Budget Report (Flexible)
Packaging Department
For the Month Ended July 31, 2007

	Budget	Actual Costs	Difference Favorable F Unfavorable U
Direct labor hours (DLH)	24,000 DLH	24,000 DLH	
Variable costs			
Indirect labor	$28,800	$30,200	$1,400 U
Supplies and lubricants	12,000	11,600	400 F
Maintenance	16,800	17,500	700 U
Utilities	9,600	9,200	400 F
Total variable	67,200	68,500	1,300 U

Action Plan

• Use budget data for actual direct labor hours worked.

• Classify each cost as variable or fixed.

• Determine the difference between budgeted and actual costs.

• Identify the difference as favorable or unfavorable.

• Determine the difference in total variable costs, total fixed costs, and total costs.

Direct labor hours (DLH)	Budget 24,000 DLH	Actual Costs 24,000 DLH	Difference Favorable F Unfavorable U
Fixed costs			
Supervision	$ 5,000	$ 5,000	–0–
Depreciation	2,000	2,000	–0–
Property taxes	1,500	1,500	–0–
Insurance	1,000	1,000	–0–
Total fixed	9,500	9,500	–0–
Total costs	$76,700	$78,000	$1,300 U

THE NAVIGATOR

Note: All asterisked Questions, Exercises, and Problems relate to the material contained in the appendix to the chapter.

Self-Study Questions

WILEY PLUS

Answers are at the end of the chapter.

(SO 1) **1.** Budgetary control involves all but one of the following:
   (a) modifying future plans.
   (b) analyzing differences.
   (c) using static budgets.
   (d) determining differences between actual and planned results.

(SO 2) **2.** A static budget is useful in controlling costs when cost behavior is:
   (a) mixed.   (c) variable.
   (b) fixed.   (d) linear.

(SO 3) **3.** At zero direct labor hours in a flexible budget graph, the total budgeted cost line intersects the vertical axis at $30,000. At 10,000 direct labor hours, a horizontal line drawn from the total budgeted cost line intersects the vertical axis at $90,000. Fixed and variable costs may be expressed as:
   (a) $30,000 fixed plus $6 per direct labor hour variable.
   (b) $30,000 fixed plus $9 per direct labor hour variable.
   (c) $60,000 fixed plus $3 per direct labor hour variable.
   (d) $60,000 fixed plus $6 per direct labor hour variable.

(SO 3) **4.** At 9,000 direct labor hours, the flexible budget for indirect materials is $27,000. If $28,000 of indirect materials costs are incurred at 9,200 direct labor hours, the flexible budget report should show the following difference for indirect materials:
   (a) $1,000 unfavorable.
   (b) $1,000 favorable.

   (c) $400 favorable.
   (d) $400 unfavorable.

(SO 4) **5.** Under responsibility accounting, the evaluation of a manager's performance is based on matters that the manager:
   (a) directly controls.
   (b) directly and indirectly controls.
   (c) indirectly controls.
   (d) has shared responsibility for with another manager.

(SO 4) **6.** Responsibility centers include:
   (a) cost centers.
   (b) profit centers.
   (c) investment centers.
   (d) all of the above.

(SO 5) **7.** Responsibility reports for cost centers:
   (a) distinguish between fixed and variable costs.
   (b) use static budget data.
   (c) include both controllable and noncontrollable costs.
   (d) include only controllable costs.

(SO 6) **8.** In a responsibility report for a profit center, controllable fixed costs are deducted from contribution margin to show:
   (a) profit center margin.
   (b) controllable margin.
   (c) net income.
   (d) income from operations.

(SO 7) **9.** In the formula for return on investment (ROI), the factors for controllable margin and operating assets are, respectively:
   (a) controllable margin percentage and total operating assets.

(b) controllable margin dollars and average operating assets.

(c) controllable margin dollars and total assets.

(d) controllable margin percentage and average operating assets.

(SO 7) **10.** A manager of an investment center can improve ROI by:

(a) increasing average operating assets.

(b) reducing sales.

(c) increasing variable costs.

(d) reducing variable and/or controllable fixed costs.

*11. In the formula for residual income, the factors (SO 8) for computing residual income are:

(a) contribution margin, controllable margin, and average operating assets.

(b) controllable margin, average operating assets, and ROI.

(c) controllable margin, average operating assets, and minimum rate of return.

(d) controllable margin, ROI, and minimum rate of return.

Questions

1. (a) What is budgetary control?

(b) Tony Crespino is describing budgetary control. What steps should be included in Tony's description?

2. The following purposes are part of a budgetary reporting system: (a) Determine efficient use of materials. (b) Control overhead costs. (c) Determine whether income objectives are being met. For each purpose, indicate the name of the report, the frequency of the report, and the primary recipient(s) of the report.

3. How may a budget report for the second quarter differ from a budget report for the first quarter?

4. Don Cox questions the usefulness of a master sales budget in evaluating sales performance. Is there justification for Don's concern? Explain.

5. Under what circumstances may a static budget be an appropriate basis for evaluating a manager's effectiveness in controlling costs?

6. "A flexible budget is really a series of static budgets." Is this true? Why?

7. The static manufacturing overhead budget based on 40,000 direct labor hours shows budgeted indirect labor costs of $56,000. During March, the department incurs $65,000 of indirect labor while working 45,000 direct labor hours. Is this a favorable or unfavorable performance? Why?

8. A static overhead budget based on 40,000 direct labor hours shows Factory Insurance $6,500 as a fixed cost. At the 50,000 direct labor hours worked in March, factory insurance costs were $6,200. Is this a favorable or unfavorable performance? Why?

9. Kate Coulter is confused about how a flexible budget is prepared. Identify the steps for Kate.

10. Alou Company has prepared a graph of flexible budget data. At zero direct labor hours, the total budgeted cost line intersects the vertical axis at $35,000. At 10,000 direct labor hours, the line drawn from the total budgeted cost line intersects the vertical axis at $85,000. How may the fixed and variable costs be expressed?

11. The flexible budget formula is fixed costs $40,000 plus variable costs of $3 per direct labor hour. What is the total budgeted cost at (a) 9,000 hours and (b) 12,345 hours?

12. What is management by exception? What criteria may be used in identifying exceptions?

13. What is responsibility accounting? Explain the purpose of responsibility accounting.

14. Ann Wilkins is studying for an accounting examination. Describe for Ann what conditions are necessary for responsibility accounting to be used effectively.

15. Distinguish between controllable and noncontrollable costs.

16. How do responsibility reports differ from budget reports?

17. What is the relationship, if any, between a responsibility reporting system and a company's organization chart?

18. Distinguish among the three types of responsibility centers.

19. (a) What costs are included in a performance report for a cost center? (b) In the report, are variable and fixed costs identified?

20. How do direct fixed costs differ from indirect fixed costs? Are both types of fixed costs controllable?

21. Lori Quan is confused about controllable margin reported in an income statement for a profit center. How is this margin computed, and what is its primary purpose?

22. What is the primary basis for evaluating the performance of the manager of an investment center? Indicate the formula for this basis.

23. Explain the ways that ROI can be improved.

24. Indicate two behavioral principles that pertain to (a) the manager being evaluated and (b) top management.

*25. What is a major disadvantage of using ROI to evaluate investment and company performance?

*26. What is residual income, and what is one of its major weaknesses?

Brief Exercises

Prepare static budget report.
(SO 2)

BE21-1 For the quarter ended March 31, 2007, Westphal Company accumulates the following sales data for its product, Garden-Tools: $315,000 budget; $304,000 actual. Prepare a static budget report for the quarter.

Prepare static budget report
for 2 quarters.
(SO 2)

BE21-2 Data for Westphal Company are given in BE21-1. In the second quarter, budgeted sales were $380,000, and actual sales were $386,000. Prepare a static budget report for the second quarter and for the year to date.

Show usefulness of flexible
budgets in evaluating per-
formance.
(SO 3)

BE21-3 In Hinsdale Company, direct labor is $20 per hour. The company expects to operate at 10,000 direct labor hours each month. In January 2007, direct labor totaling $205,000 is incurred in working 10,400 hours. Prepare (a) a static budget report and (b) a flexible budget report. Evaluate the usefulness of each report.

Prepare a flexible budget for
variable costs.
(SO 3)

BE21-4 Dukane Company expects to produce 1,200,000 units of Product XX in 2007. Monthly production is expected to range from 80,000 to 120,000 units. Budgeted variable manufacturing costs per unit are: direct materials $4, direct labor $6, and overhead $9. Budgeted fixed manufacturing costs per unit for depreciation are $2 and for supervision are $1. Prepare a flexible manufacturing budget for the relevant range value using 20,000 unit increments.

Prepare flexible budget
report.
(SO 3)

BE21-5 Data for Dukane Company are given in BE21-4. In March 2007, the company incurs the following costs in producing 100,000 units: direct materials $425,000, direct labor $590,000, and variable overhead $915,000. Prepare a flexible budget report for March. Were costs controlled?

Prepare a responsibility
report for a cost center.
(SO 5)

BE21-6 In the Assembly Department of Emil Company, budgeted and actual manufacturing overhead costs for the month of April 2007 were as follows.

	Budget	**Actual**
Indirect materials	$15,000	$14,300
Indirect labor	20,000	20,800
Utilities	10,000	10,750
Supervision	5,000	5,000

All costs are controllable by the department manager. Prepare a responsibility report for April for the cost center.

Prepare a responsibility
report for a profit center.
(SO 6)

BE21-7 Advent Manufacturing Company accumulates the following summary data for the year ending December 31, 2007, for its Water Division which it operates as a profit center: sales—$2,000,000 budget, $2,080,000 actual; variable costs—$1,000,000 budget, $1,030,000 actual; and controllable fixed costs—$300,000 budget, $310,000 actual. Prepare a responsibility report for the Water Division.

Prepare a responsibility
report for an investment
center.
(SO 7)

BE21-8 For the year ending December 31, 2007, Nathan Company accumulates the following data for the Plastics Division which it operates as an investment center: contribution margin—$700,000 budget, $715,000 actual; controllable fixed costs—$300,000 budget, $305,000 actual. Average operating assets for the year were $2,000,000. Prepare a responsibility report for the Plastics Division beginning with contribution margin.

Compute return on invest-
ment using the ROI formula.
(SO 7)

BE21-9 For its three investment centers, Stahl Company accumulates the following data:

	I	**II**	**III**
Sales	$2,000,000	$3,000,000	$ 4,000,000
Controllable margin	1,200,000	2,000,000	3,000,000
Average operating assets	6,000,000	8,000,000	10,000,000

Compute the return on investment (ROI) for each center.

Compute return on investment
under changed conditions.
(SO 7)

BE21-10 Data for the investment centers for Stahl Company are given in BE21-9. The centers expect the following changes in the next year: (I) increase sales 15%; (II) decrease costs $200,000; (III) decrease average operating assets $400,000. Compute the expected return on investment (ROI) for each center. Assume center I has a contribution margin percentage of 80%.

*BE21-11 Wasson, Inc. reports the following financial information.

Average operating assets	$3,000,000
Controllable margin	$ 600,000
Minimum rate of return	9%

Compute the return on investment and the residual income.

*BE21-12 Presented below is information related to the Santa Clara Division of Cut Wood, Inc.

Contribution margin	$1,200,000
Controllable margin	$ 800,000
Average operating assets	$3,200,000
Minimum rate of return	16%

Compute the Santa Clara's return on investment and residual income.

Exercises

E21-1 Twyla Company uses a flexible budget for manufacturing overhead based on direct labor hours. Variable manufacturing overhead costs per direct labor hour are as follows.

Indirect labor	$1.00
Indirect materials	0.60
Utilities	0.40

Fixed overhead costs per month are: Supervision $4,000, Depreciation $1,500, and Property Taxes $800. The company believes it will normally operate in a range of 7,000–10,000 direct labor hours per month.

Instructions
Prepare a monthly flexible manufacturing overhead budget for 2007 for the expected range of activity, using increments of 1,000 direct labor hours.

E21-2 Using the information in E21-1, assume that in July 2007, Twyla Company incurs the following manufacturing overhead costs.

Variable Costs		**Fixed Costs**	
Indirect labor	$8,700	Supervision	$4,000
Indirect materials	5,300	Depreciation	1,500
Utilities	3,200	Property taxes	800

Instructions
(a) Prepare a flexible budget performance report, assuming that the company worked 9,000 direct labor hours during the month.
(b) Prepare a flexible budget performance report, assuming that the company worked 8,500 direct labor hours during the month.
(c) ▭▭▭▭▷ Comment on your findings.

E21-3 Vincent Company uses flexible budgets to control its selling expenses. Monthly sales are expected to range from $170,000 to $200,000. Variable costs and their percentage relationship to sales are: Sales Commissions 6%, Advertising 4%, Traveling 3%, and Delivery 2%. Fixed selling expenses will consist of Sales Salaries $32,000, Depreciation on Delivery Equipment $7,000, and Insurance on Delivery Equipment $1,000.

Instructions
Prepare a monthly flexible budget for each $10,000 increment of sales within the relevant range for the year ending December 31, 2007.

Prepare flexible budget reports for selling expenses.
(SO 3)

E21-4   The actual selling expenses incurred in March 2007 by Vincent Company are as follows.

Variable Expenses		Fixed Expenses	
Sales commissions	$11,000	Sales salaries	$32,000
Advertising	7,000	Depreciation	7,000
Travel	5,100	Insurance	1,000
Delivery	3,500		

Instructions

(a) Prepare a flexible budget performance report for March using the budget data in E21-3, assuming that March sales were $170,000. Expected and actual sales are the same.

(b) Prepare a flexible budget performance report, assuming that March sales were $180,000. Expected sales and actual sales are the same.

(c) Comment on the importance of using flexible budgets in evaluating the performance of the sales manager.

Prepare flexible budget and responsibility report for manufacturing overhead.
(SO 3, 5)

E21-5   Sublette Company's manufacturing overhead budget for the first quarter of 2007 contained the following data.

Variable Costs		Fixed Costs	
Indirect materials	$12,000	Supervisory salaries	$36,000
Indirect labor	10,000	Depreciation	7,000
Utilities	8,000	Property taxes and insurance	8,000
Maintenance	5,000	Maintenance	5,000

Actual variable costs were: indirect materials $13,800, indirect labor $9,600, utilities $8,700, and maintenance $4,200. Actual fixed costs equaled budgeted costs except for property taxes and insurance, which were $8,400.

All costs are considered controllable by the production department manager except for depreciation, and property taxes and insurance.

Instructions

(a) Prepare a flexible manufacturing overhead budget report for the first quarter.

(b) Prepare a responsibility report for the first quarter.

Prepare flexible budget report, and answer question.
(SO 2, 3)

E21-6   As sales manager, Shawn Keyser was given the following static budget report for selling expenses in the Clothing Department of Dunham Company for the month of October.

DUNHAM COMPANY
Clothing Department
Budget Report
For the Month Ended October 31, 2007

	Budget	Actual	Difference Favorable F Unfavorable U
Sales in units	8,000	10,000	2,000 F
Variable expenses			
Sales commissions	$ 2,000	$ 2,600	$ 600 U
Advertising expense	800	850	50 U
Travel expense	4,400	4,900	500 U
Free samples given out	1,600	1,300	300 F
Total variable	8,800	9,650	850 U
Fixed expenses			
Rent	1,500	1,500	–0–
Sales salaries	1,200	1,200	–0–
Office salaries	800	800	–0–
Depreciation—autos (sales staff)	500	500	–0–
Total fixed	4,000	4,000	–0–
Total expenses	$12,800	$13,650	$ 850 U

As a result of this budget report, Shawn was called into the president's office and congratulated on his fine sales performance. He was reprimanded, however, for allowing his costs to get out of control. Shawn knew something was wrong with the performance report that he had been given. However, he was not sure what to do, and comes to you for advice.

Instructions
(a) Prepare a budget report based on flexible budget data to help Shawn.
(b) Should Shawn have been reprimanded? Explain.

E21-7 Pronto Plumbing Company is a newly formed company specializing in plumbing services for home and business. The owner, Paul Pronto, had divided the company into two segments: Home Plumbing Services and Business Plumbing Services. Each segment is run by its own supervisor, while basic selling and administrative services are shared by both segments.

Prepare and discuss a responsibility report.
(SO 3, 5)

Paul has asked you to help him create a performance reporting system that will allow him to measure each segment's performance in terms of its profitability. To that end, the following information has been collected on the Home Plumbing Services segment for the first quarter of 2007.

	Budgeted	Actual
Service revenue	$25,000	$26,000
Allocated portion of:		
Building depreciation	11,000	11,000
Advertising	5,000	4,200
Billing	3,500	3,000
Property taxes	1,200	1,000
Material and supplies	1,500	1,200
Supervisory salaries	9,000	9,400
Insurance	4,000	3,500
Wages	3,000	3,300
Gas and oil	2,700	3,400
Equipment depreciation	1,600	1,300

Instructions
(a) Prepare a responsibility report for the first quarter of 2007 for the Home Plumbing Services segment.
(b) ▭▭▭▷ Write a memo to Paul Pronto discussing the principles that should be used when preparing performance reports.

E21-8 Sherrer Company has two production departments, Fabricating and Assembling. At a department managers' meeting, the controller uses flexible budget graphs to explain total budgeted costs. Separate graphs based on direct labor hours are used for each department. The graphs show the following.

State total budgeted cost formulas, and prepare flexible budget graph.
(SO 3)

1. At zero direct labor hours, the total budgeted cost line and the fixed cost line intersect the vertical axis at $40,000 in the Fabricating Department and $35,000 in the Assembling Department.
2. At normal capacity of 50,000 direct labor hours, the line drawn from the total budgeted cost line intersects the vertical axis at $160,000 in the Fabricating Department, and $110,000 in the Assembling Department.

Instructions
(a) State the total budgeted cost formula for each department.
(b) Compute the total budgeted cost for each department, assuming actual direct labor hours worked were 53,000 and 47,000, in the Fabricating and Assembling Departments, respectively.
(c) Prepare the flexible budget graph for the Fabricating Department, assuming the maximum direct labor hours in the relevant range is 100,000. Use increments of 10,000 direct labor hours on the horizontal axis and increments of $50,000 on the vertical axis.

E21-9 Marcum Company's organization chart includes the president; the vice president of production; three assembly plants—Dallas, Atlanta, and Tucson; and two departments within each plant—Machining and Finishing. Budget and actual manufacturing cost data for July 2007 are shown on the next page.

Prepare reports in a responsibility reporting system.
(SO 4)

Finishing Department—Dallas: Direct materials $41,000 actual, $45,000 budget; direct labor $83,000 actual, $82,000 budget; manufacturing overhead $51,000 actual, $49,200 budget.

Machining Department—Dallas: Total manufacturing costs $220,000 actual, $214,000 budget.

Atlanta Plant: Total manufacturing costs $424,000 actual, $421,000 budget.

Tucson Plant: Total manufacturing costs $494,000 actual, $499,000 budget.

The Dallas plant manager's office costs were $95,000 actual and $92,000 budget. The vice president of production's office costs were $132,000 actual and $130,000 budget. Office costs are not allocated to departments and plants.

Instructions

Using the format on page 1028, prepare the reports in a responsibility system for:

(a) The Finishing Department—Dallas.
(b) The plant manager—Dallas.
(c) The vice president of production.

Compute missing amounts in responsibility reports for three profit centers, and prepare a report.
(SO 6)

E21-10   Longhead Manufacturing Inc. has three divisions which are operated as profit centers. Actual operating data for the divisions listed alphabetically are as follows.

Operating Data	Women's Shoes	Men's Shoes	Children's Shoes
Contribution margin	$250,000	(3)	$170,000
Controllable fixed costs	100,000	(4)	(5)
Controllable margin	(1)	$ 90,000	96,000
Sales	600,000	450,000	(6)
Variable costs	(2)	320,000	250,000

Instructions

(a) Compute the missing amounts. Show computations.
(b) Prepare a responsibility report for the Women's Shoe Division assuming (1) the data are for the month ended June 30, 2007, and (2) all data equal budget except variable costs which are $10,000 over budget.

Compute ROI for current year and for possible future changes.
(SO 7)

E21-11   The Green Division of Campana Company reported the following data for the current year.

Sales	$3,000,000
Variable costs	1,800,000
Controllable fixed costs	600,000
Average operating assets	5,000,000

Top management is unhappy with the investment center's return on investment (ROI). It asks the manager of the Green Division to submit plans to improve ROI in the next year. The manager believes it is feasible to consider the following independent courses of action.

1. Increase sales by $320,000 with no change in the contribution margin percentage.
2. Reduce variable costs by $100,000.
3. Reduce average operating assets by 4%.

Instructions

(a) Compute the return on investment (ROI) for the current year.
(b) Using the ROI formula, compute the ROI under each of the proposed courses of action. (Round to one decimal.)

Prepare a responsibility report for an investment center.
(SO 7)

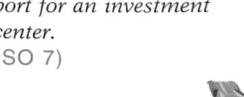

E21-12   The Medina and Ortiz Dental Clinic provides both preventive and orthodontic dental services. The two owners, Martin Medina and Olga Ortiz, operate the clinic as two separate investment centers: Preventive Services and Orthodontic Services. Each of them is in charge of one of the centers: Martin for Preventive Services and Olga for Orthodontic Services. Each month they prepare an income statement on the two centers to evaluate performance and make decisions about how to improve the operational efficiency and profitability of the clinic.

Recently they have been concerned about the profitability of the Preventive Services operations. For several months it has been reporting a loss. Shown on the next page is the responsibility report for the month of May 2007.

	Actual	Difference from Budget
Service revenue	$40,000	$1,000 F
Variable costs:		
Filling materials	5,000	100 U
Novocain	4,000	200 U
Supplies	2,000	250 F
Dental assistant wages	2,500	–0–
Utilities	500	50 U
Total variable costs	14,000	100 U
Fixed costs:		
Allocated portion of receptionist's salary	3,000	200 U
Dentist salary	10,000	500 U
Equipment depreciation	6,000	–0–
Allocated portion of building depreciation	15,000	1,000 U
Total fixed costs	34,000	1,700 U
Operating income (loss)	$(8,000)	$ 800 U

In addition, the owners know that the investment in operating assets at the beginning of the month was $82,400, and it was $77,600 at the end of the month. They have asked for your assistance in evaluating their current performance reporting system.

Instructions
(a) Prepare a responsibility report for an investment center as illustrated in the chapter.
(b) ▢▢▭▷ Write a memo to the owners discussing the deficiencies of their current reporting system.

E21-13 The Transamerica Transportation Company uses a responsibility reporting system to measure the performance of its three investment centers: Planes, Taxis, and Limos. Segment performance is measured using a system of responsibility reports and return on investment calculations. The allocation of resources within the company and the segment managers' bonuses are based in part on the results shown in these reports.

Prepare missing amounts in responsibility reports for three investment centers.
(SO 7)

Recently, the company was the victim of a computer virus that deleted portions of the company's accounting records. This was discovered when the current period's responsibility reports were being prepared. The printout of the actual operating results appeared as follows.

	Planes	Taxis	Limos
Service revenue	$?	$500,000	$?
Variable costs	5,500,000	?	320,000
Contribution margin	?	200,000	480,000
Controllable fixed costs	1,500,000	?	?
Controllable margin	?	80,000	240,000
Average operating assets	25,000,000	?	1,600,000
Return on investment	12%	10%	?

Instructions
Determine the missing pieces of information above.

*****E21-14** Presented below is selected information for three regional divisions of Yono Company.

Compare ROI and residual income.
(SO 8)

	Divisions		
	North	West	South
Contribution margin	$ 300,000	$ 500,000	$ 400,000
Controllable margin	$ 150,000	$ 400,000	$ 225,000
Average operating assets	$1,000,000	$2,000,000	$1,500,000
Minimum rate of return	13%	16%	10%

Instructions
(a) Compute the return on investment for each division.
(b) Compute the residual income for each division.
(c) Assume that each division has an investment opportunity that would provide a rate of return of 19%.
    (1) If ROI is used to measure performance, which division or divisions will probably make the additional investment?
    (2) If residual income is used to measure performance, which division or divisions will probably make the additional investment?

Fill in information related to ROI and residual income.
(SO 8)

*E21-15 Presented below is selected financial information for two divisions of Capital Brewery. You are to supply the missing information for the lettered items.

	Lager	Lite Lager
Contribution margin	$500,000	$ 300,000
Controllable margin	200,000	(c)
Average operating assets	(a)	$1,000,000
Minimum rate of return	(b)	13%
Return on investment	25%	(d)
Residual income	$ 90,000	$ 200,000

Problems: Set A

Prepare flexible budget and budget report for manufacturing overhead.
(SO 3)

P21-1A Alcore Company estimates that 240,000 direct labor hours will be worked during 2007 in the Assembly Department. On this basis, the following budgeted manufacturing overhead data are computed.

Variable Overhead Costs		Fixed Overhead Costs	
Indirect labor	$ 72,000	Supervision	$ 72,000
Indirect materials	48,000	Depreciation	36,000
Repairs	24,000	Insurance	9,600
Utilities	38,400	Rent	9,000
Lubricants	9,600	Property taxes	6,000
	$192,000		$132,600

It is estimated that direct labor hours worked each month will range from 18,000 to 24,000 hours.

During January, 20,000 direct labor hours were worked and the following overhead costs were incurred.

Variable Overhead Costs		Fixed Overhead Costs	
Indirect labor	$ 6,200	Supervision	$ 6,000
Indirect materials	3,600	Depreciation	3,000
Repairs	1,600	Insurance	800
Utilities	2,500	Rent	800
Lubricants	830	Property taxes	500
	$14,730		$11,100

Instructions

(a) Total costs: 18,000 DLH, $25,450; 24,000 DLH, $30,250
(b) Budget, $27,050 Actual, $25,830

(a) Prepare a monthly flexible manufacturing overhead budget for each increment of 2,000 direct labor hours over the relevant range for the year ending December 31, 2007.
(b) Prepare a manufacturing overhead budget report for January.
(c) ▣▬▬▶ Comment on management's efficiency in controlling manufacturing overhead costs in January.

P21-2A Borealis Manufacturing Company produces one product, Kebo. Because of wide fluctuations in demand for Kebo, the Assembly Department experiences significant variations in monthly production levels.

Prepare flexible budget, budget report, and graph for manufacturing overhead.
(SO 3)

The annual master manufacturing overhead budget is based on 300,000 direct labor hours. In July 27,500 labor hours were worked. The master manufacturing overhead budget for the year and the actual overhead costs incurred in July are as follows.

Overhead Costs	Master Budget (annual)	Actual in July
Variable		
Indirect labor	$ 300,000	$26,000
Indirect materials	210,000	17,000
Utilities	90,000	8,100
Maintenance	60,000	5,400
Fixed		
Supervision	180,000	15,000
Depreciation	120,000	10,000
Insurance and taxes	60,000	5,000
Total	$1,020,000	$86,500

Instructions
(a) Prepare a monthly flexible overhead budget for the year ending December 31, 2007, assuming monthly production levels range from 22,500 to 30,000 direct labor hours. Use increments of 2,500 direct labor hours.
(b) Prepare a budget performance report for the month of July 2007 comparing actual results with budget data based on the flexible budget.
(c) ▣▣▤▶ Were costs effectively controlled? Explain.
(d) State the formula for computing the total monthly budgeted costs in the Borealis Manufacturing Company.
(e) Prepare the flexible budget graph showing total budgeted costs at 25,000 and 27,500 direct labor hours. Use increments of 5,000 on the horizontal axis and increments of $10,000 on the vertical axis.

(a) Total costs: 22,500 DLH, $79,500; 30,000 DLH, $96,000
(b) Budget $90,500 Actual $86,500

P21-3A Chambers Company uses budgets in controlling costs. The May 2007 budget report for the company's Packaging Department is as follows.

State total budgeted cost formula, and prepare flexible budget reports for 2 time periods.
(SO 2, 3)

CHAMBERS COMPANY
Budget Report
Packaging Department
For the Month Ended May 31, 2007

Manufacturing Costs	Budget	Actual	Difference Favorable F Unfavorable U
Variable costs			
Direct materials	$ 35,000	$ 37,500	$2,500 U
Direct labor	50,000	53,000	3,000 U
Indirect materials	15,000	15,200	200 U
Indirect labor	12,500	13,000	500 U
Utilities	7,500	7,100	400 F
Maintenance	5,000	5,200	200 U
Total variable	125,000	131,000	6,000 U
Fixed costs			
Rent	8,000	8,000	–0–
Supervision	9,000	9,000	–0–
Depreciation	5,000	5,000	–0–
Total fixed	22,000	22,000	–0–
Total costs	$147,000	$153,000	$6,000 U

The monthly budget amounts in the report were based on an expected production of 50,000 units per month or 600,000 units per year.

The company president was displeased with the department manager's performance. The department manager, who thought he had done a good job, could not understand the unfavorable results. In May, 55,000 units were produced.

Instructions

(a) State the total budgeted cost formula.

(b) Budget $159,500

(b) Prepare a budget report for May using flexible budget data. Why does this report provide a better basis for evaluating performance than the report based on static budget data?

(c) Budget $122,000
Actual $126,800

(c) In June, 40,000 units were produced. Prepare the budget report using flexible budget data, assuming (1) each variable cost was 20% less in June than its actual cost in May, and (2) fixed costs were the same in the month of June as in May.

Prepare responsibility report for a profit center.
(SO 6)

P21-4A Korene Manufacturing Inc. operates the Home Appliance Division as a profit center. Operating data for this division for the year ended December 31, 2007, are shown below.

	Budget	Difference from Budget
Sales	$2,400,000	$80,000 U
Cost of goods sold		
Variable	1,200,000	47,000 U
Controllable fixed	200,000	10,000 F
Selling and administrative		
Variable	240,000	8,000 F
Controllable fixed	60,000	6,000 U
Noncontrollable fixed costs	50,000	2,000 U

In addition, Korene Manufacturing incurs $150,000 of indirect fixed costs that were budgeted at $155,000. Twenty percent (20%) of these costs are allocated to the Home Appliance Division. None of these costs are controllable by the division manager.

Instructions

(a) Contribution margin
$119,000 U
Controllable margin
$115,000 U

(a) Prepare a responsibility report for the Home Appliance Division (a profit center) for the year.

(b) ▭▭▭▷ Comment on the manager's performance in controlling revenues and costs.

(c) Identify any costs excluded from the responsibility report and explain why they were excluded.

Prepare responsibility report for an investment center, and compute ROI.
(SO 7)

P21-5A Chudzik Manufacturing Company manufactures a variety of garden and lawn equipment. The company operates through three divisions. Each division is an investment center. Operating data for the Lawnmower Division for the year ended December 31, 2007, and relevant budget data are as follows.

	Actual	Comparison with Budget
Sales	$3,000,000	$150,000 unfavorable
Variable cost of goods sold	1,400,000	100,000 unfavorable
Variable selling and administrative expenses	300,000	50,000 favorable
Controllable fixed cost of goods sold	270,000	On target
Controllable fixed selling and administrative expenses	130,000	On target

Average operating assets for the year for the Lawnmower Division were $5,000,000 which was also the budgeted amount.

Instructions

(a) Controllable margin:
Budget $1,100
Actual $900

(a) Prepare a responsibility report (in thousands of dollars) for the Lawnmower Division.

(b) Evaluate the manager's performance. Which items will likely be investigated by top management?

(c) Compute the expected ROI in 2008 for the Lawnmower Division, assuming the following independent changes.

(1) Variable cost of goods sold is decreased by 15%.

(2) Average operating assets are decreased by 20%.

(3) Sales are increased by $500,000 and this increase is expected to increase contribution margin by $200,000.

P21-6A Kojak Company uses a responsibility reporting system. It has divisions in Denver, Seattle, and San Diego. Each division has three production departments: Cutting, Shaping, and Finishing. The responsibility for each department rests with a manager who reports to the division production manager. Each division manager reports to the vice president of production. There are also vice presidents for marketing and finance. All vice presidents report to the president.

Prepare reports for cost centers under responsibility accounting, and comment on performance of managers.
(SO 4)

In January 2007, controllable actual and budget manufacturing overhead cost data for the departments and divisions were as shown below.

Manufacturing Overhead	Actual	Budget
Individual costs—Cutting Department—Seattle		
Indirect labor	$ 73,000	$ 70,000
Indirect materials	46,700	46,000
Maintenance	20,500	18,000
Utilities	20,100	17,000
Supervision	22,000	20,000
	$ 182,300	$ 171,000
Total costs		
Shaping Department—Seattle	$ 158,000	$ 148,000
Finishing Department—Seattle	210,000	208,000
Denver division	676,000	673,000
San Diego division	722,000	715,000

Additional overhead costs were incurred as follows: Seattle division production manager—actual costs $52,500, budget $51,000; vice president of production—actual costs $65,000, budget $64,000; president—actual costs $76,400, budget $74,200. These expenses are not allocated.

The vice presidents who report to the president, other than the vice president of production, had the following expenses.

Vice president	Actual	Budget
Marketing	$133,600	$130,000
Finance	108,000	105,000

Instructions
(a) Using the format on page 1028, prepare the following responsibility reports.
  (1) Manufacturing overhead—Cutting Department manager—Seattle division.
  (2) Manufacturing overhead—Seattle division manager.
  (3) Manufacturing overhead—vice president of production.
  (4) Manufacturing overhead and expenses—president.
(b) Comment on the comparative performances of:
  (1) Department managers in the Seattle division.
  (2) Division managers.
  (3) Vice presidents.

(a) (1) $11,300 U
    (2) $24,800 U
    (3) $35,800 U
    (4) $44,600 U

*P21-7A Haniwall Industries has manufactured prefabricated houses for over 20 years. The houses are constructed in sections to be assembled on customers' lots. Haniwall expanded into the precut housing market when it acquired Orlando Company, one of its suppliers. In this market, various types of lumber are precut into the appropriate lengths, banded into packages, and shipped to customers' lots for assembly. Haniwall designated the Orlando Division as an investment center.

Compare ROI and residual income.
(SO 8)

Haniwall uses return on investment (ROI) as a performance measure with investment defined as average operating assets. Management bonuses are based in part on ROI. All investments are expected to earn a minimum rate of return of 16%. Orlando's ROI has ranged from 20.1% to 23.5% since it was acquired. Orlando had an investment opportunity in 2007 that had an estimated ROI of 19%. Orlando's management decided against the investment because it believed the investment would decrease the division's overall ROI.

Selected financial information for Orlando are presented on the next page. The division's average operating assets were $12,300,000 for the year 2007.

ORLANDO DIVISION
Selected Financial Information
For the Year Ended December 31, 2007

Sales	$26,000,000
Contribution margin	9,100,000
Controllable margin	2,460,000

Instructions

(a) Calculate the following performance measures for 2007 for the Orlando Division.

(1) Return on investment (ROI).

(a) (2) $492,000

(2) Residual income.

(b) ▭▭✏▷ Would the management of Orlando Division have been more likely to accept the investment opportunity it had in 2007 if residual income were used as a performance measure instead of ROI? Explain your answer.

(CMA, adapted)

Problems: Set B

Prepare flexible budget and budget report for manufacturing overhead.
(SO 3)

P21-1B   Oakley Company estimates that 360,000 direct labor hours will be worked during the coming year, 2007, in the Packaging Department. On this basis, the following budgeted manufacturing overhead cost data are computed for the year.

Fixed Overhead Costs		Variable Overhead Costs	
Supervision	$ 90,000	Indirect labor	$144,000
Depreciation	60,000	Indirect materials	90,000
Insurance	30,000	Repairs	54,000
Rent	36,000	Utilities	72,000
Property taxes	18,000	Lubricants	18,000
	$234,000		$378,000

It is estimated that direct labor hours worked each month will range from 27,000 to 36,000 hours.

During October, 27,000 direct labor hours were worked and the following overhead costs were incurred.

Fixed overhead costs: Supervision $7,500, Depreciation $5,000, Insurance $2,470, Rent $3,000, and Property taxes $1,500.

Variable overhead costs: Indirect labor $11,760, Indirect materials, $6,400, Repairs $4,000, Utilities $5,700, and Lubricants $1,640.

Instructions

(a) Total costs: DLH 27,000, $47,850; DLH 36,000, $57,300
(b) Total $1,120 U

(a) Prepare a monthly flexible manufacturing overhead budget for each increment of 3,000 direct labor hours over the relevant range for the year ending December 31, 2007.

(b) Prepare a flexible budget report for October.

(c) ▭▭✏▷ Comment on management's efficiency in controlling manufacturing overhead costs in October.

Prepare flexible budget, budget report, and graph for manufacturing overhead.
(SO 3)

P21-2B   Hindu Company manufactures tablecloths. Sales have grown rapidly over the past 2 years. As a result, the president has installed a budgetary control system for 2007. The following data were used in developing the master manufacturing overhead budget for the Ironing Department, which is based on an activity index of direct labor hours.

Variable Costs	Rate per Direct Labor Hour	Annual Fixed Costs	
Indirect labor	$0.40	Supervision	$30,000
Indirect materials	0.60	Depreciation	18,000
Factory utilities	0.30	Insurance	12,000
Factory repairs	0.20	Rent	24,000

The master overhead budget was prepared on the expectation that 480,000 direct labor hours will be worked during the year. In June, 42,000 direct labor hours were worked. At that level of activity, actual costs were as shown on the next page.

Variable—per direct labor hour: Indirect labor $0.43, Indirect materials $0.58, Factory utilities $0.32, and Factory repairs $0.24.
Fixed: same as budgeted.

Instructions
(a) Prepare a monthly flexible manufacturing overhead budget for the year ending December 31, 2007, assuming production levels range from 35,000 to 50,000 direct labor hours. Use increments of 5,000 direct labor hours.
(b) Prepare a budget performance report for June comparing actual results with budget data based on the flexible budget.
(c) Were costs effectively controlled? Explain.
(d) State the formula for computing the total budgeted costs for Hindu Company.
(e) Prepare the flexible budget graph, showing total budgeted costs at 35,000 and 45,000 direct labor hours. Use increments of 5,000 direct labor hours on the horizontal axis and increments of $10,000 on the vertical axis.

(a) Total costs: 35,000 DLH, $59,500; 50,000 DLH, $82,000

(b) Budget $70,000 Actual $72,940

P21-3B Yaeger Company uses budgets in controlling costs. The August 2007 budget report for the company's Assembling Department is as follows.

State total budgeted cost formula, and prepare flexible budget reports for 2 time periods.
(SO 2, 3)

YAEGER COMPANY
Budget Report
Assembling Department
For the Month Ended August 31, 2007

Manufacturing Costs	Budget	Actual	Difference Favorable F Unfavorable U
Variable costs			
Direct materials	$ 48,000	$ 47,000	$1,000 F
Direct labor	66,000	62,700	3,300 F
Indirect materials	24,000	24,200	200 U
Indirect labor	18,000	17,500	500 F
Utilities	15,000	14,900	100 F
Maintenance	9,000	9,200	200 U
Total variable	180,000	175,500	4,500 F
Fixed costs			
Rent	12,000	12,000	–0–
Supervision	17,000	17,000	–0–
Depreciation	7,000	7,000	–0–
Total fixed	36,000	36,000	–0–
Total costs	$216,000	$211,500	$4,500 F

The monthly budget amounts in the report were based on an expected production of 60,000 units per month or 720,000 units per year. The Assembling Department manager is pleased with the report and expects a raise, or at least praise for a job well done. The company president, however, is unhappy with the results for August, because only 58,000 units were produced.

Instructions
(a) State the total monthly budgeted cost formula.
(b) Prepare a budget report for August using flexible budget data. Why does this report provide a better basis for evaluating performance than the report based on static budget data?
(c) In September, 64,000 units were produced. Prepare the budget report using flexible budget data, assuming (1) each variable cost was 10% higher than its actual cost in August, and (2) fixed costs were the same in September as in August.

(b) Budget $210,000

(c) Budget $228,000 Actual $229,050

P21-4B Henning Manufacturing Inc. operates the Patio Furniture Division as a profit center. Operating data for this division for the year ended December 31, 2007, are as shown on the next page.

Prepare responsibility report for a profit center.
(SO 6)

	Budget	**Difference from Budget**
Sales	$2,500,000	$70,000 F
Cost of goods sold		
Variable	1,300,000	33,000 F
Controllable fixed	200,000	5,000 U
Selling and administrative		
Variable	220,000	7,000 U
Controllable fixed	50,000	2,000 U
Noncontrollable fixed costs	70,000	4,000 U

In addition, Henning Manufacturing incurs $180,000 of indirect fixed costs that were budgeted at $175,000. Twenty percent (20%) of these costs are allocated to the Patio Furniture Division.

(a) Contribution margin
$96,000 F
Controllable margin
$89,000 F

Instructions
(a) Prepare a responsibility report for the Patio Furniture Division for the year.
(b) ▭▭▭▶ Comment on the manager's performance in controlling revenues and costs.
(c) Identify any costs excluded from the responsibility report and explain why they were excluded.

Prepare responsibility report for an investment center, and compute ROI.
(SO 7)

P21-5B Alosio Manufacturing Company manufactures a variety of tools and industrial equipment. The company operates through three divisions. Each division is an investment center. Operating data for the Home Division for the year ended December 31, 2007, and relevant budget data are as follows.

	Actual	**Comparison with Budget**
Sales	$1,550,000	$100,000 favorable
Variable cost of goods sold	700,000	70,000 unfavorable
Variable selling and administrative expenses	125,000	25,000 unfavorable
Controllable fixed cost of goods sold	170,000	On target
Controllable fixed selling and administrative expenses	100,000	On target

Average operating assets for the year for the Home Division were $2,500,000 which was also the budgeted amount.

Instructions

(a) Controllable margin:
Budget $450;
Actual $455

(a) Prepare a responsibility report (in thousands of dollars) for the Home Division.
(b) Evaluate the manager's performance. Which items will likely be investigated by top management?
(c) Compute the expected ROI in 2008 for the Home Division, assuming the following independent changes to actual data.
(1) Variable cost of goods sold is decreased by 6%.
(2) Average operating assets are decreased by 10%.
(3) Sales are increased by $200,000, and this increase is expected to increase contribution margin by $90,000.

Problems: Set C

Visit the book's website at **www.wiley.com/college/kimmel** and choose the Student Companion site to access Problem Set C.

BROADENING YOUR PERSPECTIVE

Group Decision Case

BYP21-1 Z-Bar Pastures is a 400-acre farm on the outskirts of the Kentucky Bluegrass, specializing in the boarding of broodmares and their foals. A recent economic downturn in the thoroughbred industry has led to a decline in breeding activities, and

it has made the boarding business extremely competitive. To meet the competition, Z-Bar Pastures planned in 2007 to entertain clients, advertise more extensively, and absorb expenses formerly paid by clients such as veterinary and blacksmith fees.

The budget report for 2007 is presented below. As shown, the static income statement budget for the year is based on an expected 21,900 boarding days at $25 per mare. The variable expenses per mare per day were budgeted: Feed $5, Veterinary fees $3, Blacksmith fees $0.30, and Supplies $0.70. All other budgeted expenses were either semifixed or fixed.

During the year, management decided not to replace a worker who quit in March, but it did issue a new advertising brochure and did more entertaining of clients.[2]

Z-BAR PASTURES
Static Budget Income Statement
Year Ended December 31, 2007

	Actual	Master Budget	Difference
Number of mares	52	60	8*
Number of boarding days	18,980	21,900	2,920*
Sales	$379,600	$547,500	$167,900*
Less variable expenses:			
Feed	104,390	109,500	5,110
Veterinary fees	58,838	65,700	6,862
Blacksmith fees	6,074	6,570	496
Supplies	12,954	15,330	2,376
Total variable expenses	182,256	197,100	14,844
Contribution margin	197,344	350,400	153,056*
Less fixed expenses:			
Depreciation	40,000	40,000	–0–
Insurance	11,000	11,000	–0–
Utilities	12,000	14,000	2,000
Repairs and maintenance	10,000	11,000	1,000
Labor	88,000	96,000	8,000
Advertisement	12,000	8,000	4,000*
Entertainment	7,000	5,000	2,000*
Total fixed expenses	180,000	185,000	5,000
Net income	$ 17,344	$165,400	$148,056*

*Unfavorable.

Instructions

With the class divided into groups, answer the following.

(a) Based on the static budget report:
   (1) What was the primary cause(s) of the loss in net income?
   (2) Did management do a good, average, or poor job of controlling expenses?
   (3) Were management's decisions to stay competitive sound?
(b) Prepare a flexible budget report for the year.
(c) Based on the flexible budget report, answer the three questions in part (a) above.
(d) What course of action do you recommend for the management of Z-Bar Pastures?

Managerial Analysis

BYP21-2 Castle Company manufactures expensive watch cases sold as souvenirs. Three of its sales departments are: Retail Sales, Wholesale Sales, and Outlet Sales. The

---

[2]Data for this case are based on Hans Sprohge and John Talbott, "New Applications for Variance Analysis," *Journal of Accountancy* (AICPA, New York), April 1989, pp. 137–141.

Retail Sales Department is a profit center. The Wholesale Sales Department is a cost center. Its managers merely take orders from customers who purchase through the company's wholesale catalog. The Outlet Sales Department is an investment center, because each manager is given full responsibility for an outlet store location. The manager can hire and discharge employees, purchase, maintain, and sell equipment, and in general is fairly independent of company control.

Sara Sutton is a manager in the Retail Sales Department. Gilbert Lewis manages the Wholesale Sales Department. Jose Lopez manages the Golden Gate Club outlet store in San Francisco. The following are the budget responsibility reports for each of the three departments.

Budget

	Retail Sales	Wholesale Sales	Outlet Sales
Sales	$ 750,000	$ 400,000	$200,000
Variable costs			
Cost of goods sold	150,000	100,000	25,000
Advertising	100,000	30,000	5,000
Sales salaries	75,000	15,000	3,000
Printing	10,000	20,000	5,000
Travel	20,000	30,000	2,000
Fixed costs			
Rent	50,000	30,000	10,000
Insurance	5,000	2,000	1,000
Depreciation	75,000	100,000	40,000
Investment in assets	$1,000,000	$1,200,000	$800,000

Actual Results

	Retail Sales	Wholesale Sales	Outlet Sales
Sales	$ 750,000	$ 400,000	$200,000
Variable costs			
Cost of goods sold	195,000	120,000	26,250
Advertising	100,000	30,000	5,000
Sales salaries	75,000	15,000	3,000
Printing	10,000	20,000	5,000
Travel	15,000	20,000	1,500
Fixed costs			
Rent	40,000	50,000	12,000
Insurance	5,000	2,000	1,000
Depreciation	80,000	90,000	60,000
Investment in assets	$1,000,000	$1,200,000	$800,000

Instructions

(a) Determine which of the items should be included in the responsibility report for each of the three managers.
(b) Compare the budgeted measures with the actual results. Decide which results should be called to the attention of each manager.

Real-World Focus

BYP21-3 Computer Associates International, Inc., the world's leading business software company, delivers the end-to-end infrastructure to enable e-business through innovative technology, services, and education. CA has 19,000 employees worldwide and recently had revenue of over $6 billion.

Presented below is information from the company's annual report.

COMPUTER ASSOCIATES INTERNATIONAL
Management Discussion

The Company has experienced a pattern of business whereby revenue for its third and fourth fiscal quarters reflects an increase over first- and second-quarter revenue. The Company attributes this increase to clients' increased spending at the end of their calendar year budgetary periods and the culmination of its annual sales plan. Since the Company's costs do not increase proportionately with the third- and fourth-quarters' increase in revenue, the higher revenue in these quarters results in greater profit margins and income. Fourth-quarter profitability is traditionally affected by significant new hirings, training, and education expenditures for the succeeding year.

Instructions
(a) Why don't the company's costs increase proportionately as the revenues increase in the third and fourth quarters?
(b) What type of budgeting seems appropriate for the Computer Associates situation?

Exploring the Web

BYP21-4 Genelle and Doug have recorded the story of their wedding planning. They are on a strict budget and need help in preparing what they call "a somewhat flexible budget."

Address: **www.wednet.com/inspire/wedstory/story1.htm**, or go to **www.wiley.com/college/kimmel**

Steps
1. Go to Genelle and Doug's Web site, and read about their trials and tribulations in planning a wedding.
2. Review the **Planning and Budgeting** section in "Part 1" of their story. They mention that this is a "somewhat flexible budget" for 250 guests, totalling $7,150. They would like to reduce their total costs to $7,000, if at all possible.

Instructions
Recast Genelle and Doug's budget into a truly flexible budget so that they can see the effects on their total costs of reducing the number of invited guests to 225 or 200.

Communication Activity

BYP21-5 The manufacturing overhead budget for Dillons Company contains the following items.

Variable costs	
Indirect materials	$28,000
Indirect labor	12,000
Maintenance expense	10,000
Manufacturing supplies	6,000
Total variable	$56,000
Fixed costs	
Supervision	$18,000
Inspection costs	1,000
Insurance expense	2,000
Depreciation	15,000
Total fixed	$36,000

The budget was based on an estimated 2,000 units being produced. During the past month, 1,500 units were produced, and the following costs incurred.

Variable costs	
Indirect materials	$28,200
Indirect labor	13,500
Maintenance expense	8,200
Manufacturing supplies	5,100
Total variable	$55,000
Fixed costs	
Supervision	$19,300
Inspection costs	1,200
Insurance expense	2,200
Depreciation	14,700
Total fixed	$37,400

Instructions

(a) Determine which items would be controllable by Jeff Howell, the production manager.
(b) How much should have been spent during the month for the manufacture of the 1,500 units?
(c) Prepare a flexible manufacturing overhead budget report for Mr. Howell.
(d) Prepare a responsibility report. Include only the costs that would have been controllable by Mr. Howell. Assume that the supervision cost includes Mr. Howell's salary of $10,000, both at budget and actual. In an attached memo, describe clearly for Mr. Howell the areas in which his performance needs to be improved.

Research Assignment

BYP21-6   The February 2000 issue of the *Journal of Accountancy* contains an article by Russ Banham titled "Better Budgets."

Instructions
Read the article and answer the following questions.

(a) Why have some companies decided not to do major overhauls of their budgeting systems after some initial investigations into the possibility? What percentage of companies that attempt overhauls give up before finishing?
(b) What is the "new planning paradigm"?
(c) What does the author argue is the "final link" necessary for successful budgeting and planning?

Ethics Case

BYP21-7   American Products Corporation participates in a highly competitive industry. In order to meet this competition and achieve profit goals, the company has chosen the decentralized form of organization. Each manager of a decentralized investment center is measured on the basis of profit contribution, market penetration, and return on investment. Failure to meet the objectives established by corporate management for these measures has not been acceptable and usually has resulted in demotion or dismissal of an investment center manager.

An anonymous survey of managers in the company revealed that the managers feel the pressure to compromise their personal ethical standards to achieve the corporate objectives. For example, at certain plant locations there was pressure to reduce quality control to a level which could not assure that all unsafe products would be rejected. Also, sales personnel were encouraged to use questionable sales tactics to obtain orders, including gifts and other incentives to purchasing agents.

The chief executive officer is disturbed by the survey findings. In his opinion such behavior cannot be condoned by the company. He concludes that the company should do something about this problem.

Instructions

(a) Who are the stakeholders (the affected parties) in this situation?
(b) Identify the ethical implications, conflicts, or dilemmas in the above described situation.
(c) What might the company do to reduce the pressures on managers and decrease the ethical conflicts?

(CMA adapted)

_____

Answers to Self-Study Questions

1. c   **2.** b   **3.** a   **4.** d   **5.** a   **6.** d   **7.** d   **8.** b   **9.** b   **10.** d   *11. c

Standard Costs and Balanced Scorecard

STUDY OBJECTIVES

After studying this chapter, you should be able to:

1 Distinguish between a standard and a budget.

2 Identify the advantages of standard costs.

3 Describe how standards are set.

4 State the formulas for determining direct materials and direct labor variances.

5 State the formulas for determining manufacturing overhead variances.

6 Discuss the reporting of variances.

7 Prepare an income statement for management under a standard costing system.

8 Describe the balanced scorecard approach to performance evaluation.

THE NAVIGATOR

THE NAVIGATOR

- Scan *Study Objectives*
- Read *Feature Story*
- Read *Preview*
- Read text and answer *Before You Go On*
  p. 1072 ◯ p. 1076 ◯ p. 1086 ◯
- Work *Using the Decision Toolkit*
- Review *Summary of Study Objectives*
- Work *Demonstration Problem*
- Answer *Self-Study Questions*
- Complete *Assignments*

FEATURE STORY

Highlighting Performance Efficiency

There's a very good chance that the highlighter you're holding in your hand was made by Sanford, a maker of permanent markers and other writing instruments. Sanford, headquartered in Illinois, annually sells hundreds of millions of dollars' worth of ACCENT highlighters, fine-point pens, Sharpie permanent markers, Expo dry-erase markers for overhead projectors, and other writing instruments.

Since Sanford makes literally billions of writing utensils per year, the company must keep tight control over manufacturing costs. A very important part of Sanford's manufacturing process is determining how much direct materials, labor, and overhead should cost. These costs are then compared to actual costs to assess performance efficiency. Raw materials for Sanford's markers include a barrel, plug, cap, ink reservoir, and a nib (tip). These parts are assembled by machine to produce thousands of units per hour. A major component of manufacturing overhead is machine maintenance—some fixed, some variable.

"Labor costs are associated with material handling and equipment maintenance functions. Although the assembly process is highly automated, labor is still required to move raw materials to the machine and to package the finished product. In addition, highly skilled technicians are required to service and maintain each piece of equipment," says Mike Orr, vice president, operations.

Labor rates are predictable because the hourly workers are covered by a union contract. The story is the same with the fringe benefits and some supervisory salaries. Even volume levels are fairly predictable—demand for the product is high—so fixed overhead is efficiently absorbed. Raw material standard costs are based on the previous year's actual prices plus any anticipated inflation. Lately, though, inflation has been so low

that the company is considering any price increase in raw material to be unfavorable because its standards will remain unchanged.

On the World Wide Web
www.sanfordcorp.com

PREVIEW OF CHAPTER 22

Standards are a fact of life. You met the admission standards for the school you are attending. The vehicle that you drive had to meet certain governmental emissions standards. The hamburgers and salads you eat in a restaurant have to meet certain health and nutritional standards before they can be sold. And, as described in our Feature Story, Sanford Corp. develops standards for the costs of its materials, labor, and overhead which it compares with its actual costs. The reason for standards in these cases is very simple: They help to ensure that overall product quality is high. Without standards, quality control is lost.

In this chapter we continue the study of controlling costs. You will learn how to evaluate performance using standard costs and a balanced scorecard.

The content and organization of Chapter 22 are as follows.

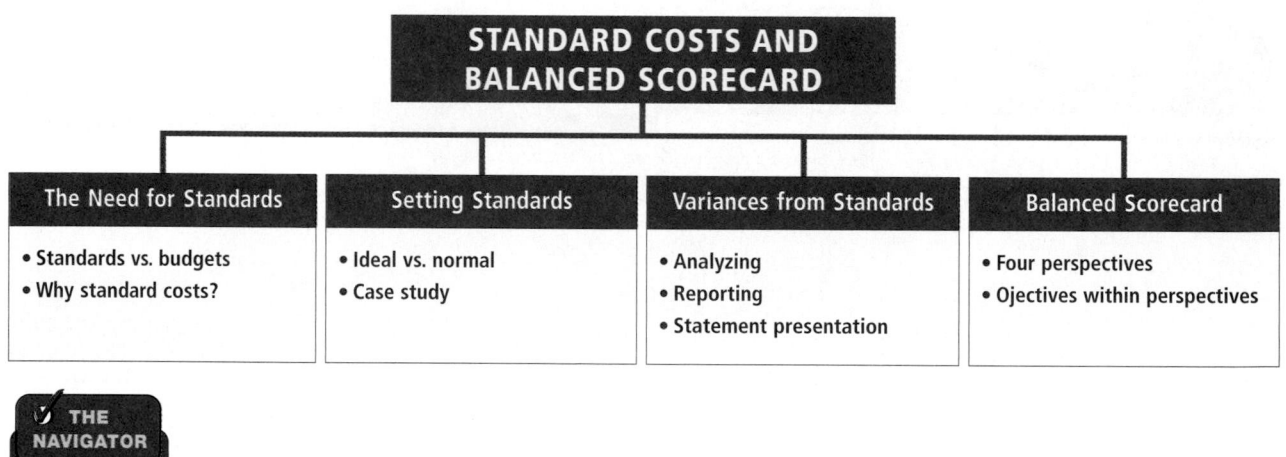

STANDARD COSTS AND BALANCED SCORECARD

The Need for Standards	Setting Standards	Variances from Standards	Balanced Scorecard
• Standards vs. budgets • Why standard costs?	• Ideal vs. normal • Case study	• Analyzing • Reporting • Statement presentation	• Four perspectives • Ojectives within perspectives

THE NAVIGATOR

The Need for Standards

Standards are common in business. Those imposed by government agencies are often called **regulations**. They include the Fair Labor Standards Act, the Equal Employment Opportunity Act, and a multitude of environmental standards. Standards established internally by a company may extend to personnel matters, such as employee absenteeism and ethical codes of conduct, quality control standards for products, and standard costs for goods and services. In managerial accounting, standard costs are predetermined unit costs, which are used as measures of performance.

We will focus on manufacturing operations in the remainder of this chapter. But you should also recognize that standard costs also apply to many types of service businesses as well. For example, a fast-food restaurant such as McDonald's knows the price it should pay for pickles, beef, buns, and other ingredients. It also knows how much time it should take an employee to flip hamburgers. If too much is paid for pickles or too much time is taken to prepare Big Macs, the deviations are noticed and corrective action is taken. Standard costs also may be used in not-for-profit enterprises such as universities, charitable organizations, and governmental agencies.

DISTINGUISHING BETWEEN STANDARDS AND BUDGETS

In concept, **standards** and **budgets** are essentially the same. Both are prede-termined costs, and both contribute to management planning and control. There is a difference, however, in the way the terms are expressed. A standard is a **unit** amount. A budget is a **total** amount. Thus, it is customary to state that the stan-dard cost of direct labor for a unit of product is $10. If 5,000 units of the prod-uct are produced, the $50,000 of direct labor is the **budgeted** labor cost. A stan-dard is the budgeted cost per unit of product. A standard is therefore concerned with each individual cost component that makes up the entire budget.

There are important accounting differences between budgets and standards. Ex-cept in the application of manufacturing overhead to jobs and processes, budget data are not journalized in cost accounting systems. In contrast, as will be illus-trated in the appendix to this chapter, standard costs may be incorporated into cost accounting systems. Also, a company may report its inventories at standard cost in its financial statements, but it would not report inventories at budgeted costs.

STUDY OBJECTIVE
1
Distinguish between a stan-dard and a budget.

WHY STANDARD COSTS?

Standard costs offer a number of advantages to an organization, as shown in Illustration 22-1. These advantages will be realized only when standard costs are carefully established and prudently used. Using standards solely as a means of placing blame can have a negative effect on managers and employees. In an ef-fort to minimize this effect, many companies offer wage incentives to those who meet their standards.

STUDY OBJECTIVE
2
Identify the advantages of standard costs.

Illustration 22-1   Advan-tages of standard costs

Advantages of standard costs

Facilitate management planning

Promote greater economy by making employees more "cost-conscious"

Useful in setting selling prices

Contribute to management control by providing basis for evaluation of cost control

Useful in highlighting variances in management by exception

Simplify costing of inventories and reduce clerical costs

Setting Standard Costs—A Difficult Task

STUDY OBJECTIVE

3

Describe how standards are set.

The setting of standard costs to produce a unit of product is a difficult task. It requires input from all persons who have responsibility for costs and quantities. To determine the standard cost of direct materials, management may have to consult purchasing agents, product managers, quality control engineers, and production supervisors. In setting the cost standard for direct labor, pay rate data are obtained from the payroll department, and the labor time requirements may be determined by industrial engineers. The managerial accountant provides important input to management into the standards-setting process by accumulating historical cost data and by knowing how costs respond to changes in activity levels.

To be effective in controlling costs, standard costs need to be current at all times. Thus, standards should be under continuous review. They should be changed whenever it is determined that the existing standard is not a good measure of performance. Circumstances that may warrant revision of a standard include changed wage rates resulting from a new union contract, a change in product specifications, or the implementation of a new manufacturing method.

IDEAL VERSUS NORMAL STANDARDS

Standards may be set at one of two levels: ideal or normal. **Ideal standards** represent optimum levels of performance under perfect operating conditions. **Normal standards** represent efficient levels of performance that are attainable under expected operating conditions.

Some managers believe ideal standards will stimulate workers to ever-increasing improvement. However, most managers believe that ideal standards lower the morale of the entire workforce because they are so difficult, if not impossible, to meet. Very few companies use ideal standards.

Helpful Hint When standards are set too high, employees sometimes feel pressure to consider unethical practices to meet these standards.

Most companies that use standards set them at a normal level. Properly set, normal standards should be **rigorous but attainable**. Normal standards allow for rest periods, machine breakdowns, and other "normal" contingencies in the production process. It will be assumed in the remainder of this chapter that standard costs are set at a normal level.

Business Insight
Management Perspective

Recently a number of organizations, including corporations, consultants, and governmental agencies, agreed to share information regarding performance standards in an effort to create a standard set of measures for thousands of business processes. Having such standards would enable companies to evaluate their performance relative to others with regard to such things as the amount of materials they waste when making a product, or how long it takes to process a purchase order. The group, referred to as the Open Standards Benchmarking Collaborative, includes IBM, Procter and Gamble, the U.S. Navy, and the World Bank. Companies that are interested in participating can go to the group's Web site and enter their information.

Source: William M. Bulkeley, "Business, Agencies to Standardize Their Benchmarks," *Wall Street Journal Online* (May 19, 2004).

A CASE STUDY

To establish the standard cost of producing a product, it is necessary to establish standards for each manufacturing cost element—direct materials, direct labor, and manufacturing overhead. The standard for each element is derived from the standard price to be paid and the standard quantity to be used. To illustrate, we will look at a case study of how standard costs are set. In this extended example, we will assume that Xonic, Inc. wishes to use standard costs to measure performance in filling an order for 1,000 gallons of Weed-O, a liquid weed killer.

Direct Materials

The **direct materials price standard** is the cost per unit of direct materials that should be incurred. This standard should be based on the purchasing department's best estimate of the **cost of raw materials**. This is frequently based on current purchase prices. The price standard should also include an amount for related costs such as receiving, storing, and handling. The materials price standard per pound of material for Xonic's weed killer is:

Item	Price
Purchase price, net of discounts	$ 2.70
Freight	0.20
Receiving and handling	0.10
Standard direct materials price per pound	**$3.00**

Illustration 22-2   Setting direct materials price standard

The **direct materials quantity standard** is the quantity of direct materials that should be used per unit of finished goods. This standard is expressed as a physical measure, such as pounds, barrels, or board feet. In setting the standard, management should consider both the quality and quantity of materials required to manufacture the product. The standard should include allowances for unavoidable waste and normal spoilage. The standard quantity per unit for Xonic, Inc. is as follows.

Item	Quantity (Pounds)
Required materials	3.5
Allowance for waste	0.4
Allowance for spoilage	0.1
Standard direct materials quantity per unit	**4.0**

Illustration 22-3   Setting direct materials quantity standard

The standard direct materials cost per unit is the standard direct materials price times the standard direct materials quantity. For Xonic, Inc., the standard direct materials cost per gallon of Weed-O is $12.00 ($3.00 × 4.0 pounds).

Direct Labor

The **direct labor price standard** is the rate per hour that should be incurred for direct labor. This standard is based on current wage rates, adjusted for anticipated changes such as cost of living adjustments (COLAs). The price standard also generally includes employer payroll taxes and fringe benefits, such as paid holidays and vacations. For Xonic, Inc., the direct labor price standard is as follows.

Alternative Terminology The direct labor price standard is also called the *direct labor rate standard.*

Illustration 22-4   Setting direct labor price standard

Item	Price
Hourly wage rate	$ 7.50
COLA	0.25
Payroll taxes	0.75
Fringe benefits	1.50
Standard direct labor rate per hour	**$10.00**

Alternative Terminology The direct labor quantity standard is also called the *direct labor efficiency standard.*

The **direct labor quantity standard** is the time that should be required to make one unit of the product. This standard is especially critical in labor-intensive companies. Allowances should be made in this standard for rest periods, cleanup, machine setup, and machine downtime. For Xonic, Inc., the direct labor quantity standard is as follows.

Illustration 22-5   Setting direct labor quantity standard

Item	Quantity (Hours)
Actual production time	1.5
Rest periods and cleanup	0.2
Setup and downtime	0.3
Standard direct labor hours per unit	**2.0**

The standard direct labor cost per unit is the standard direct labor rate times the standard direct labor hours. For Xonic, Inc., the standard direct labor cost per gallon of Weed-O is $20 ($10.00 × 2.0 hours).

Manufacturing Overhead

For manufacturing overhead, a **standard predetermined overhead rate** is used in setting the standard. This overhead rate is determined by dividing budgeted overhead costs by an expected standard activity index. For example, the index may be standard direct labor hours or standard machine hours.

As discussed in Chapter 17, many companies employ activity-based costing (ABC) to allocate overhead costs. Because ABC uses multiple activity indices to allocate overhead costs, it results in a better correlation between activities and costs incurred. As a result, the use of ABC can significantly improve the usefulness of a standard costing system for management decision making.

Xonic, Inc. uses standard direct labor hours as the activity index. The company expects to produce 13,200 gallons of Weed-O during the year at normal capacity. Since it takes 2 direct labor hours for each gallon, total standard direct labor hours are 26,400 (13,200 gallons × 2 hours). At this level of activity, overhead costs are expected to be $132,000. Of that amount, $79,200 are variable and $52,800 are fixed. The standard predetermined overhead rates are computed as shown in Illustration 22-6.

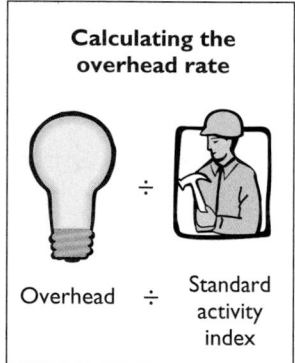

Calculating the overhead rate

Overhead ÷ Standard activity index

Illustration 22-6   Computing predetermined overhead rates

Budgeted Overhead Costs	Amount	÷	Standard Direct Labor Hours	=	Overhead Rate per Direct Labor Hour
Variable	$ 79,200		26,400		$3.00
Fixed	52,800		26,400		2.00
Total	$132,000		26,400		$5.00

The standard manufacturing overhead rate per unit is the predetermined overhead rate times the activity index quantity standard. For Xonic, Inc., which uses direct labor hours as its activity index, the standard manufacturing overhead rate per gallon of Weed-O is $10 ($5 × 2 hours).

Total Standard Cost per Unit

Now that the standard quantity and price have been established per unit of product, the total standard cost can be determined. The total standard cost per unit is the sum of the standard costs of direct materials, direct labor, and manufacturing overhead. For Xonic, Inc., the total standard cost per gallon of Weed-O is $42, as shown on the following standard cost card.

Illustration 22-7   Standard cost per gallon of Weed-O

Product: Weed-O	Unit Measure: Gallon		
Manufacturing Cost Elements	Standard Quantity ×	Standard Price =	Standard Cost
Direct materials	4 pounds	$ 3.00	$12.00
Direct labor	2 hours	$10.00	$20.00
Manufacturing overhead	2 hours	$ 5.00	$10.00
			$42.00

A standard cost card is prepared for each product. This card provides the basis for determining variances from standards.

Business Insight
Management Perspective

Setting standards can be difficult. Consider Susan's Chili Factory, which manufactures and sells chili. The cost of manufacturing Susan's chili consists of the costs of raw materials, labor to convert the basic ingredients to chili, and overhead. We will use materials cost as an example. Three standards need to be developed: (1) What should be the formula (mix) of ingredients for one gallon of chili? (2) What should be the normal wastage (or shrinkage) for the individual ingredients? (3) What should be the standard cost for the individual ingredients that go into the chili?

Susan's Chili Factory also illustrates how standard costs can be used by management in controlling costs. Suppose that summer droughts have reduced crop yields. As a result, prices have doubled for beans, onions, and peppers. In this case, actual costs will be significantly higher than standard costs, which will cause management to evaluate the situation. Management might decide to increase the price charged for a gallon of chili. It might reexamine the product mix to see if other types of ingredients can be used. Or it might curtail production until ingredients can be purchased at or near standard costs. Similarly, assume that poor maintenance caused the onion-dicing blades to become dull. As a result, usage of onions to make a gallon of chili tripled. Because this deviation is quickly highlighted through standard costs, corrective action can be promptly taken.

Source: Adapted from David R. Beran, "Cost Reduction Through Control Reporting," *Management Accounting* (April 1982), pp. 29–33.

BEFORE YOU GO ON . . .

▶Review It

1. How do standards differ from budgets?
2. What are the advantages of standard costs to an organization?
3. Distinguish between normal standards and ideal standards. Which standard is more widely used? Why?

▶Do It

The management of Arapahoe Company has decided to use standard costs. Management asks you to explain the components used in setting the standard cost per unit for direct materials, direct labor, and manufacturing overhead.

Action Plan

• Differentiate between the two components of each standard: price and quantity.

Solution The standard direct materials cost per unit is the standard direct materials price times the standard direct materials quantity. The standard direct labor cost per unit is the standard direct labor rate times the standard direct labor hours. The standard manufacturing overhead rate per unit is the standard predetermined overhead rate times the activity index quantity standard.

Related exercise material: BE22-2, BE22-3, and E22-1.

Variances from Standards

Alternative Terminology In business, the term *variance* is also used to indicate differences between total budgeted and total actual costs.

One of the major management uses of standard costs is to identify variances from standards. **Variances** are the differences between total actual costs and total standard costs. To illustrate, we will assume that in producing 1,000 gallons of Weed-O in the month of June, Xonic, Inc. incurred the following costs.

Illustration 22-8 Actual production costs

Direct materials	$13,020
Direct labor	20,580
Variable overhead	6,500
Fixed overhead	4,400
Total actual costs	$44,500

Total standard costs are determined by multiplying the units produced by the standard cost per unit. The total standard cost of Weed-O is $42,000 (1,000 gallons × $42). Thus, the total variance is $2,500, as shown below.

Illustration 22-9 Computation of total variance

Actual costs	$44,500
Less: Standard costs	42,000
Total variance	**$ 2,500**

Note that the variance is expressed in total dollars and not on a per unit basis.

When actual costs exceed standard costs, the variance is **unfavorable**. The $2,500 variance in June for Weed-O is unfavorable. An unfavorable variance has a negative connotation. It suggests that too much was paid for one or more of the manufacturing cost elements or that the elements were used inefficiently.

If actual costs are less than standard costs, the variance is **favorable**. A favorable variance has a positive connotation. It suggests efficiencies in incurring manufacturing costs and in using direct materials, direct labor, and manufacturing overhead. However, be careful: A favorable variance could be obtained by using inferior materials. In printing wedding invitations, for example, a favorable variance could result from using an inferior grade of paper. Or, a favorable variance might be achieved in installing tires on an automobile assembly line by tightening only half of the lug bolts. A variance is not favorable if quality control standards have been sacrificed.

ANALYZING VARIANCES

To interpret properly the significance of a variance, you must analyze it to determine the underlying factors. Analyzing variances begins by determining the cost elements that comprise the variance. **For each manufacturing cost element, a total dollar variance is computed. Then this variance is analyzed into a price variance and a quantity variance.** The relationships are shown graphically as follows.

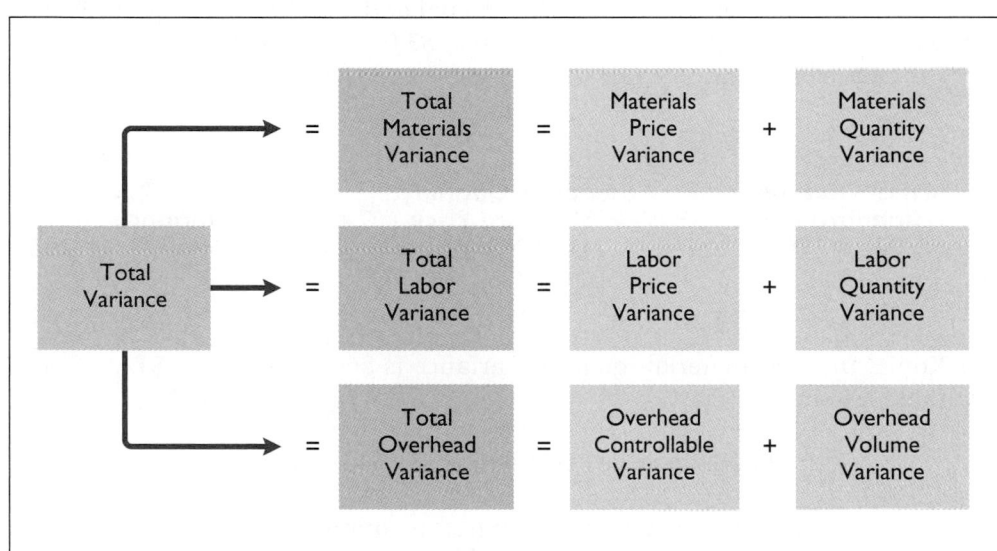

Illustration 22-10 Variance relationships

Each of the variances is explained below.

Direct Materials Variances

In completing the order for 1,000 gallons of Weed-O, Xonic used 4,200 pounds of direct materials. These were purchased at a cost of $3.10 per unit. The **total materials variance** is computed from the following formula.

STUDY OBJECTIVE

4

State the formulas for determining direct materials and direct labor variances.

Actual Quantity × Actual Price (AQ) × (AP)	−	Standard Quantity × Standard Price (SQ) × (SP)	=	Total Materials Variance (TMV)

Illustration 22-11 Formula for total materials variance

For Xonic, Inc., the total materials variance is $1,020 ($13,020 − $12,000) unfavorable as shown below.

$$(4,200 \times \$3.10) - (4,000 \times \$3.00) = \$1,020 \text{ U}$$

Next, the total variance is analyzed to determine the amount attributable to price (costs) and to quantity (use). The **materials price variance** is computed from the following formula.[1]

Illustration 22-12 Formula for materials price variance

Actual Quantity × Actual Price (AQ) × (AP)	−	Actual Quantity × Standard Price (AQ) × (SP)	=	Materials Price Variance (MPV)

For Xonic, Inc., the materials price variance is $420 ($13,020 − $12,600) unfavorable as shown below.

$$(4,200 \times \$3.10) - (4,200 \times \$3.00) = \$420 \text{ U}$$

Helpful Hint The alternative formula is:

$$\boxed{AQ} \times \boxed{AP - SP} = \boxed{MPV}$$

The price variance can also be computed by multiplying the actual quantity purchased by the difference between the actual and standard price per unit. The computation in this case is 4,200 × ($3.10 − $3.00) = $420 U.

The **materials quantity variance** is determined from the following formula.

Illustration 22-13 Formula for materials quantity variance

Actual Quantity × Standard Price (AQ) × (SP)	−	Standard Quantity × Standard Price (SQ) × (SP)	=	Materials Quantity Variance (MQV)

For Xonic, Inc., the materials quantity variance is $600 ($12,600 − $12,000) unfavorable, as shown below.

$$(4,200 \times \$3.00) - (4,000 \times \$3.00) = \$600 \text{ U}$$

Helpful Hint The alternative formula is:

$$\boxed{SP} \times \boxed{AQ - SQ} = \boxed{MQV}$$

The price variance can also be computed by applying the standard price to the difference between actual and standard quantities used. The computation in this example is $3.00 × (4,200 − 4,000) = $600 U.

The total materials variance of $1,020 U, therefore, consists of the following.

Illustration 22-14 Summary of materials variances

Materials price variance	$ 420 U
Materials quantity variance	600 U
Total materials variance	**$1,020 U**

A matrix is sometimes used to analyze a variance. **When the matrix is used, the formulas for each cost element are computed first and then the variances.**

---

[1]We will assume that all materials purchased during the period are used in production and that no units remain in inventory at the end of the period.

The completed matrix for the direct materials variance for Xonic, Inc. is shown in Illustration 22-15. The matrix provides a convenient structure for determining each variance.

Illustration 22-15 Matrix for direct materials variances

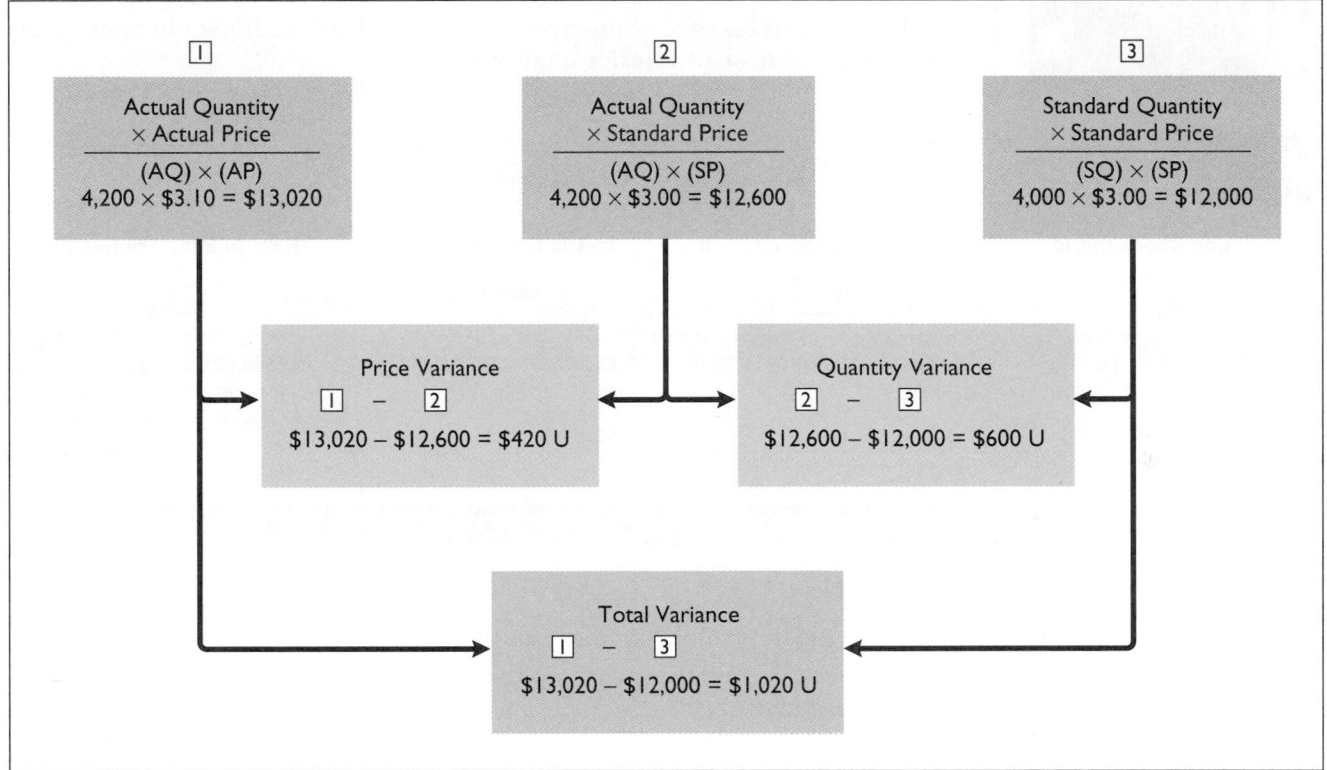

CAUSES OF MATERIALS VARIANCES. What are the causes of a variance? The causes may relate to both internal and external factors. **The investigation of a materials price variance usually begins in the purchasing department.** Many factors affect the price paid for raw materials. These include the delivery method used, availability of quantity and cash discounts, and the quality of the materials requested. To the extent that these factors have been considered in setting the price standard, the purchasing department should be responsible for any variances.

However, a variance may be beyond the control of the purchasing department. Sometimes, for example, prices may rise faster than expected. Moreover, actions by groups over which the company has no control, such as the OPEC nations' oil price increases, may cause an unfavorable variance. There are also times when a production department may be responsible for the price variance. This may occur when a rush order forces the company to pay a higher price for the materials.

The starting point for determining the cause(s) of an unfavorable **materials quantity variance** is in the **production department**. If the variances are due to inexperienced workers, faulty machinery, or carelessness, the production department would be responsible. However, if the materials obtained by the purchasing department were of inferior quality, then the purchasing department should be responsible.

Business Insight
Management Perspective

If purchase price variances are used as a basis for measuring performance, purchasing departments often will continually search for the lowest-cost item. However, this basis can become counterproductive if it leads to late deliveries of the goods or the purchase of inferior-quality goods.

Decision Toolkit

Decision Checkpoints	Info Needed for Decision	Tool to Use for Decision	How to Evaluate Results
Has management accomplished its price and quantity objectives regarding materials?	Actual cost and standard cost of materials	Materials price and materials quantity variances	Positive (favorable) variances suggest that price and quantity objectives have been met.

BEFORE YOU GO ON . . .

▶Review It

1. What are the three main components of the total variance from standard cost?
2. What are the formulas for computing the total, price, and quantity variances for direct materials?

▶Do It

The standard cost of Product XX includes two units of direct materials at $8.00 per unit. During July, 22,000 units of direct materials are purchased at $7.50 and used to produce 10,000 units. Compute the total, price, and quantity variances for materials.

Action Plan

Use the formulas for computing each of the materials variances:
- Total materials variance $= (AQ \times AP) - (SQ \times SP)$
- Materials price variance $= (AQ \times AP) - (AQ \times SP)$
- Materials quantity variance $= (AQ \times SP) - (SQ \times SP)$

Solution Substituting amounts into the formulas, the variances are:

Total materials variance $= (22{,}000 \times \$7.50) - (20{,}000 \times \$8.00) = \$5{,}000$ unfavorable.

Materials price variance $= (22{,}000 \times \$7.50) - (22{,}000 \times \$8.00) = \$11{,}000$ favorable.

Materials quantity variance $= (22{,}000 \times \$8.00) - (20{,}000 \times \$8.00) = \$16{,}000$ unfavorable.

Related exercise material: BE22-4, E22-2, E22-5, and E22-6.

THE NAVIGATOR

Direct Labor Variances

The process of determining direct labor variances is the same as for determining the direct materials variances. In completing the Weed-O order, Xonic, Inc. incurred 2,100 direct labor hours at an average hourly rate of $9.80. The standard hours allowed for the units produced were 2,000 hours (1,000 gallons × 2 hours). The standard labor rate was $10 per hour. The **total labor variance** is obtained from the following formula.

Actual Hours × Actual Rate (AH) × (AR)	−	Standard Hours × Standard Rate (SH) × (SR)	=	Total Labor Variance (TLV)

Illustration 22-16 Formula for total labor variance

The total labor variance is $580 ($20,580 − $20,000) unfavorable, as shown below.

$$(2,100 \times \$9.80) - (2,000 \times \$10.00) = \$580 \text{ U}$$

The formula for the **labor price variance** is:

Actual Hours × Actual Rate (AH) × (AR)	−	Actual Hours × Standard Rate (AH) × (SR)	=	Labor Price Variance (LPV)

Illustration 22-17 Formula for labor price variance

For Xonic, Inc., the labor price variance is $420 ($20,580 − $21,000) favorable as shown below.

$$(2,100 \times \$9.80) - (2,100 \times \$10.00) = \$420 \text{ F}$$

The labor price variance can also be computed by multiplying actual hours worked by the difference between the actual pay rate and the standard pay rate. The computation in this example is 2,100 × ($10.00 − $9.80) = $420 F.

The **labor quantity variance** is derived from the following formula.

Helpful Hint The alternative formula is:
$$\boxed{\text{AH}} \times \boxed{\text{AR} - \text{SR}} = \boxed{\text{LPV}}$$

Actual Hours × Standard Rate (AH) × (SR)	−	Standard Hours × Standard Rate (SH) × (SR)	=	Labor Quantity Variance (LQV)

Illustration 22-18 Formula for labor quantity variance

For Xonic, Inc., the labor quantity variance is $1,000 ($21,000 − $20,000) unfavorable:

$$(2,100 \times \$10.00) - (2,000 \times \$10.00) = \$1,000 \text{ U}$$

The same result can be obtained by multiplying the standard rate by the difference between actual hours worked and standard hours allowed. In this case the computation is $10.00 × (2,100 − 2,000) = $1,000 U.

Helpful Hint The alternative formula is:
$$\boxed{\text{SR}} \times \boxed{\text{AH} - \text{SH}} = \boxed{\text{LQV}}$$

The total direct labor variance of $580 U, therefore, consists of:

Illustration 22-19   Summary of labor variances

Labor price variance	$ 420 F
Labor quantity variance	1,000 U
Total direct labor variance	**$ 580 U**

Illustration 22-20   Matrix for direct labor variances

These results can also be obtained from the matrix in Illustration 22-20.

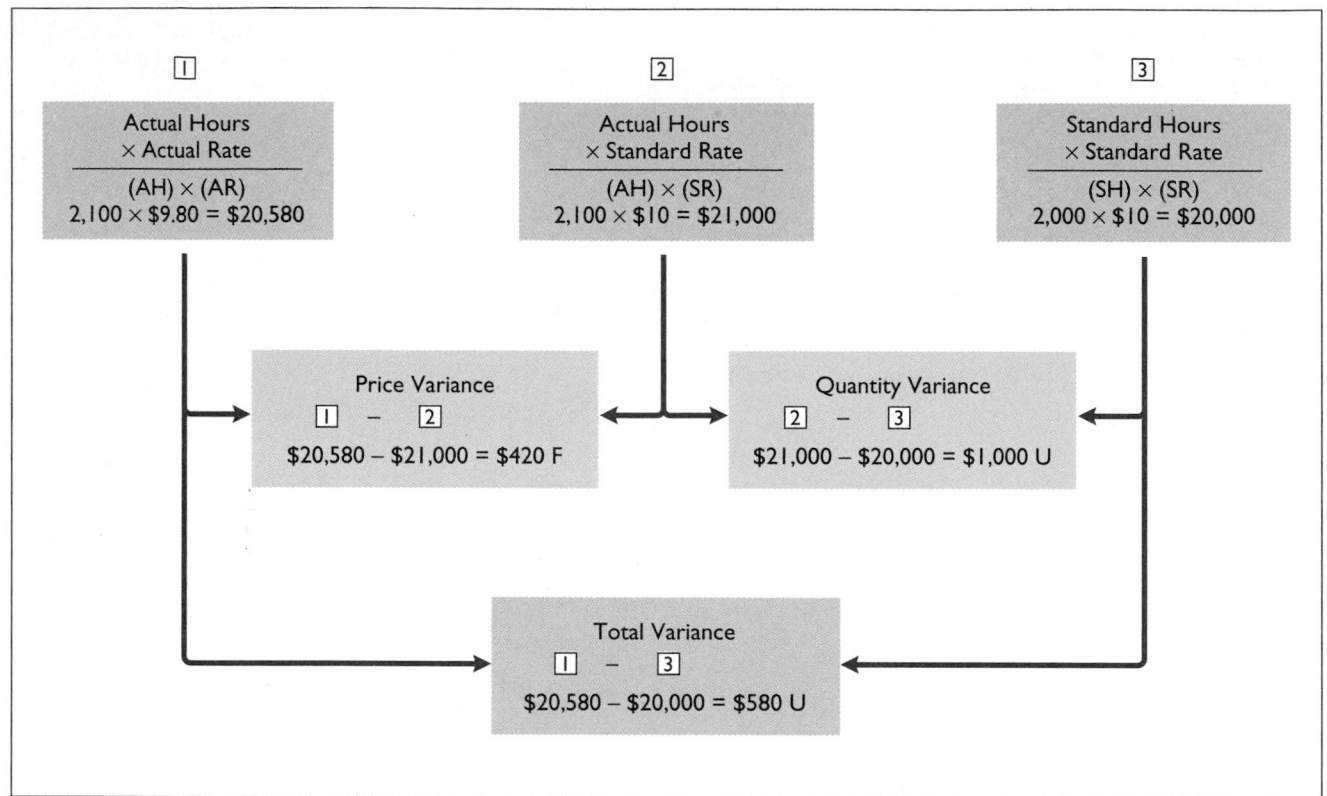

CAUSES OF LABOR VARIANCES.   **Labor price variances** usually result from two factors: (1) paying workers **higher wages than expected**, and (2) **misallocation of workers**. In companies where pay rates are determined by union contracts, labor price variances should be infrequent. When workers are not unionized, there is a much higher likelihood of such variances. The responsibility for these variances rests with the manager who authorized the wage increase.

"What caused labor price variances?"

Personnel decisions

Misallocation of the workforce refers to using skilled workers in place of unskilled workers and vice versa. The use of an inexperienced worker instead of an experienced one will result in a favorable price variance because of the lower pay rate of the unskilled worker. An unfavorable price variance would result if a skilled worker were substituted for an inexperienced one. The production department generally is responsible for labor price variances resulting from misallocation of the workforce.

"What caused labor quantity variances?"

Production Dept.

Labor quantity variances relate to the **efficiency of workers**. The cause of a quantity variance generally can be traced to the production department. The causes of an unfavorable variance may be poor training, worker fatigue, faulty machinery, or carelessness. These causes are the responsibility of the **production department**. However, if the excess time is due to inferior materials, the responsibility falls outside the production department.

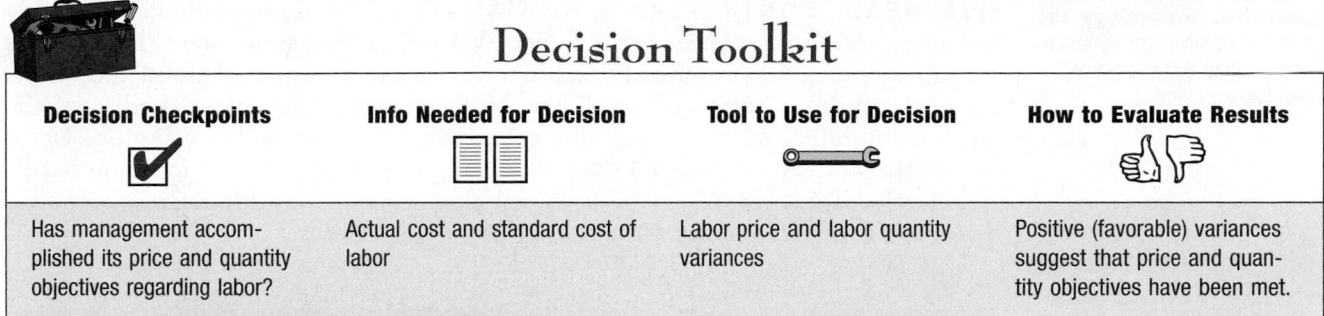

Decision Toolkit

Decision Checkpoints	Info Needed for Decision	Tool to Use for Decision	How to Evaluate Results
Has management accomplished its price and quantity objectives regarding labor?	Actual cost and standard cost of labor	Labor price and labor quantity variances	Positive (favorable) variances suggest that price and quantity objectives have been met.

Manufacturing Overhead Variances

The computation of the manufacturing overhead variances is conceptually the same as the computation of the materials and labor variances. However, the task is more challenging for manufacturing overhead because both variable and fixed overhead costs must be considered.

> **STUDY OBJECTIVE**
> **5**
> State the formulas for determining manufacturing overhead variances.

TOTAL OVERHEAD VARIANCE. The **total overhead variance** is the difference between actual overhead costs and overhead costs applied to work done. As indicated earlier, actual manufacturing overhead costs incurred by Xonic were $10,900, as follows.

Variable overhead	$ 6,500
Fixed overhead	4,400
Total actual overhead	**$10,900**

Illustration 22-21 Actual overhead costs

Under a standard costing system, manufacturing overhead costs are applied to work in process on the basis of the **standard hours allowed** for the work done. **Standard hours allowed** are the hours that should have been worked for the units produced. For the 1,000 gallon Weed-O order, the standard hours allowed are 2,000 (1,000 gallons × 2 hours). The predetermined overhead rate is $5 per direct labor hour (see Illustration 22-6 on page 1070). Thus, overhead applied is $10,000 (2,000 hours × $5). Note that actual hours of direct labor (2,100) are not used in applying manufacturing overhead.

The formula for the total overhead variance and the calculation for Xonic, Inc. are shown in Illustration 22-22.

Actual Overhead	−	Overhead Applied*	=	Total Overhead Variance
$10,900	−	$10,000	=	$900 U

*Based on standard hours allowed.

Illustration 22-22 Formula for total overhead variance

Thus, for Xonic, Inc., the total overhead variance is $900 unfavorable.

The overhead variance is generally analyzed through a price variance and a quantity variance. The name usually given to the price variance is the **overhead controllable variance**, whereas the quantity variance is referred to as the **overhead volume variance**.

Alternative Terminology The overhead controllable variance is also called the *budget* or *spending variance.*

OVERHEAD CONTROLLABLE VARIANCE. The **overhead controllable variance** shows whether overhead costs were effectively controlled. To compute this variance, actual overhead costs incurred are compared with budgeted costs for the **standard hours allowed**. The budgeted costs are determined from the flexible manufacturing overhead budget which was presented in Chapter 21. For Xonic the budget formula for manufacturing overhead is variable manufacturing overhead cost of $3 per hour of labor plus fixed manufacturing overhead costs of $4,400. The budget for Xonic, Inc. is as follows.

Illustration 22-23   Flexible budget using standard direct labor hours

XONIC, INC.
Flexible Manufacturing Overhead Budget

Activity Index				
Standard direct labor hours	1,800	2,000	2,200	2,400
Costs				
Variable costs				
Indirect materials	$1,800	$2,000	$2,200	$2,400
Indirect labor	2,700	3,000	3,300	3,600
Utilities	900	1,000	1,100	1,200
Total variable costs	5,400	6,000	6,600	7,200
Fixed costs				
Supervision	3,000	3,000	3,000	3,000
Depreciation	1,400	1,400	1,400	1,400
Total fixed costs	4,400	4,400	4,400	4,400
Total costs	$9,800	$10,400	$11,000	$11,600

As shown, the budgeted costs for 2,000 standard hours are $10,400 ($6,000 variable and $4,400 fixed).

The formula for the overhead controllable variance and the calculation for Xonic, Inc. are shown in Illustration 22-24.

Illustration 22-24   Formula for overhead controllable variance

Actual Overhead	–	Overhead Budgeted*	=	Overhead Controllable Variance
$10,900	–	$10,400	=	$500 U

*Based on standard hours allowed.

The overhead controllable variance for Xonic, Inc. is $500 unfavorable.

Most controllable variances are associated with variable costs, which are controllable costs. Fixed costs are usually known at the time the budget is prepared. At Xonic, Inc., the variance is accounted for by comparing the actual variable overhead costs ($6,500) with the budgeted variable costs ($6,000).

Management can compare actual and budgeted overhead for each manufacturing overhead cost that contributes to the controllable variance. In addition, cost and quantity variances can be developed for each overhead cost, such as indirect materials and indirect labor.

OVERHEAD VOLUME VARIANCE. The **overhead volume variance** is the difference between normal capacity hours and standard hours allowed times the fixed overhead rate. The overhead volume variance relates to whether fixed costs were under- or over-applied during the year. For example, the overhead volume variance answers the question of whether Xonic effectively used its fixed costs. If Xonic produces less Weed-O than normal capacity would allow, an unfavorable variance results. Conversely, if Xonic produces more Weed-O than what is considered normal capacity, a favorable variance results.

The formula for computing the overhead volume variance is as follows.

Fixed Overhead Rate	×	| Normal Capacity − Standard Hours Hours Allowed |	=	Overhead Volume Variance

Illustration 22-25
Formula for overhead volume variance

To illustrate the fixed overhead rate computation, recall that Xonic Inc. budgeted fixed overhead cost for the year of $52,800 (Illustration 22-6 on page 1070). At normal capacity, 26,400 standard direct labor hours are required. The fixed overhead rate is therefore $2 ($52,800 ÷ 26,400 hours).

Xonic Inc. produced 1,000 units of Weed-O in June. As indicated earlier, the standard hours allowed for the 1,000 gallons produced in June is 2,000 (1,000 gallons × 2 hours). For Xonic, standard direct labor hours for June at normal capacity is 2,200 (26,400 annual hours ÷ 12 months). The computation of the overhead volume variance in this case is as follows.

Fixed Overhead Rate	×	| Normal Capacity − Standard Hours Hours Allowed |	=	Overhead Volume Variance
$2	×	(2,200 − 2,000)	=	$400 U

Illustration 22-26 Computation of overhead volume variance for Xonic Co.

In Xonic's case, a $400 unfavorable volume variance results. The volume variance is unfavorable because Xonic produced only 1,000 gallons rather than the normal capacity of 1,100 gallons in the month of June. As a result, it underapplied fixed overhead for that period.

In computing the overhead variances, it is important to remember the following.

1. Standard hours allowed are used in each of the variances.
2. Budgeted costs for the controllable variance are derived from the flexible budget.
3. The controllable variance generally pertains to variable costs.
4. The volume variance pertains solely to fixed costs.

CAUSES OF MANUFACTURING OVERHEAD VARIANCES. Since the **controllable variance** relates to variable manufacturing costs, the responsibility for the variance rests with the **production department**. The cause of an unfavorable variance may be: (1) **higher than expected use** of indirect materials, indirect labor, and factory supplies, or (2) **increases in indirect manufacturing costs**, such as fuel and maintenance costs.

"What caused manufacturing overhead variances?"

Controllable Variance	Overhead Volume Variance
Production Dept.	**Production or Sales Dept.**

The **overhead volume variance** is the responsibility of the **production department** if the cause is inefficient use of direct labor or machine breakdowns. When the cause is a **lack of sales orders**, the responsibility rests **outside** the production department.

Decision Toolkit

Decision Checkpoints	Info Needed for Decision	Tool to Use for Decision	How to Evaluate Results
Has management accomplished its price and quantity objectives regarding overhead?	Actual cost and standard cost of overhead	Overhead controllable variance and overhead volume variance	Positive (favorable) variances suggest that price and quantity objectives have been met.

REPORTING VARIANCES

STUDY OBJECTIVE
6
Discuss the reporting of variances.

All variances should be reported to appropriate levels of management as soon as possible. The sooner management is informed, the sooner problems can be evaluated and corrective actions taken if necessary.

The form, content, and frequency of variance reports vary considerably among companies. One approach is to prepare a weekly report for each department that has primary responsibility for cost control. Under this approach, materials price variances are reported to the purchasing department, and all other variances are reported to the production department that did the work. The following report for Xonic, Inc., with the materials for the Weed-O order listed first, illustrates this approach.

Illustration 22-27
Materials price variance report

XONIC, INC.
Variance Report—Purchasing Department
For Week Ended June 8, 2007

Type of Materials	Quantity Purchased	Actual Price	Standard Price	Price Variance	Explanation
× 100	4,200 lbs.	$3.10	$3.00	$420 U	Rush order
× 142	1,200 units	2.75	2.80	60 F	Quantity discount
A 85	600 doz.	5.20	5.10	60 U	Regular supplier on strike
Total price variance				**$420 U**	

The explanation column is completed after consultation with the purchasing department manager.

Variance reports facilitate the principle of "management by exception" explained in Chapter 21. For example, the vice president of purchasing can use the report shown above to evaluate the effectiveness of the purchasing department manager. Or, the vice president of production can use production department variance reports to determine how well each production manager is controlling costs. In using variance reports, top management normally looks for **significant variances**. These may be judged on the basis of some quantitative measure, such as more than 10 percent of the standard or more than $1,000.

Business Insight
ⓔ-Business Perspective

Computerized standard cost systems represent one of the most complex ac-counting systems to develop and maintain. The standard cost system must be fully integrated into the general ledger. It must allow for the creation and timely maintenance of the database of standard usage and costs for every product. It must perform variance computations. And it must also produce variance reports by product, department, or employee. With the increased use of automation and robotics, the computerized standard cost system may even be tied directly into these systems to gather variance information.

STATEMENT PRESENTATION OF VARIANCES

In income statements **prepared for management** under a standard cost ac-counting system, **cost of goods sold is stated at standard cost and the vari-ances are separately disclosed**, as shown in Illustration 22-28. The statement shown is based entirely on the production and sale of Weed-O. It assumes sell-ing and administrative costs of $3,000. Observe that each variance is shown, as well as the total net variance. In this example, variations from standard costs reduced net income by $2,500.

STUDY OBJECTIVE
7

Prepare an income state-ment for management under a standard costing system.

Illustration 22-28
Variances in income statement for management

XONIC, INC.		
Income Statement		
For the Month Ended June 30, 2007		
Sales		$60,000
Cost of goods sold (at standard)		42,000
Gross profit (at standard)		18,000
Variances		
Materials price	$ 420	
Materials quantity	600	
Labor price	(420)	
Labor quantity	1,000	
Overhead controllable	500	
Overhead volume	400	
Total variance unfavorable		2,500
Gross profit (actual)		15,500
Selling and administrative expenses		3,000
Net income		$12,500

In financial statements prepared for stockholders and other external users, standard costs may be used. The costing of inventories at standard costs is in accordance with generally accepted accounting principles when there are no sig-nificant differences between actual costs and standard costs. Hewlett-Packard and Jostens, Inc., for example, report their inventories at standard costs. How-ever, if there are significant differences between actual and standard costs, inventories and cost of goods sold must be reported at actual costs.

It is also possible to show the variances in an income statement prepared in the variable costing (CVP) format. To do so, it is necessary to analyze the over-head variances into variable and fixed components. This type of analysis is explained in cost accounting textbooks.

Balanced Scorecard

Financial measures (measurement of dollars), such as variance analysis and return on investment (ROI), are useful tools for evaluating performance. However, many companies now supplement these financial measures with nonfinancial measures to better assess performance and anticipate future results. For example, airlines, like Delta, American, and United, use capacity utilization as an important measure to understand and predict future performance. Newspaper publishers, such as the *New York Times* and the *St. Louis Post-Dispatch*, use circulation figures as another measure by which to assess performance. Some key nonfinancial measures used in various industries are listed in Illustration 22-29.

Illustration 22-29
Nonfinancial measures used in various industries

Industry		Measure
Automobiles		Capacity utilization of plants. Average age of key assets. Impact of strikes. Brand-loyalty statistics.
Computer Systems		Market profile of customer end-products. Number of new products. Employee stock ownership percentages. Number of scientists and technicians used in R&D.
Chemicals		Customer satisfaction data. Factors affecting customer product selection. Number of patents and trademarks held. Customer brand awareness.
Regional Banks		Number of ATMs by state. Number of products used by average customer. Percentage of customer service calls handled by interactive voice response units. Personnel cost per employee. Credit card retention rates.

Source: Financial Accounting Standards Board, *Business Reporting: Insights into Enhancing Voluntary Disclosures* (Norwalk, Conn.: FASB, 2001)

Most companies recognize that both financial and nonfinancial measures can provide useful insights into what is happening in the company. As a result, many companies now use a broad-based measurement approach, called the **balanced scorecard**, to evaluate performance. The **balanced scorecard** incorporates financial and nonfinancial measures in an integrated system that links performance measurement and a company's strategic goals. The balanced scorecard concept is very popular: Nearly 50 percent of the largest companies in the United States including Unilever, Chase, and Wal-Mart, are using this approach.

The balanced scorecard evaluates company performance from a series of "perspectives." The four most commonly employed perspectives are as follows.

1. The **financial perspective** is the most traditional view of the company. It employs financial measures of performance used by most firms.
2. The **customer perspective** evaluates how well the company is performing from the viewpoint of those people who buy and use its products or services. This view measures how well the company compares to competitors in terms of price, quality, product innovation, customer service, and other dimensions.

3. The **internal process perspective** evaluates the internal operating processes critical to success. All critical aspects of the value chain—including product development, production, delivery and after-sale service—are evaluated to ensure that the company is operating effectively and efficiently.

4. The **learning and growth perspective** evaluates how well the company develops and retains its employees. This would include an evaluation of such things as employee skills, employee satisfaction, training programs, and information dissemination.

Within each perspective, the balanced scorecard identifies objectives that will contribute to attainment of strategic goals. Illustration 22-30 shows examples of objectives within each perspective.

Financial perspective
Return on assets
Net income
Credit rating
Share price
Profit per employee

Customer perspective
Percentage of customers who would recommend product to a friend
Customer retention
Response time per customer request
Brand recognition
Customer service expense per customer

Internal process perspective
Percentage of defect-free products
Stockouts
Labor utilization rates
Waste reduction
Planning accuracy

Learning and growth perspective
Percentage of employees leaving in less than one year
Number of cross-trained employees
Ethics violations
Training hours
Reportable accidents

Illustration 22-30
Examples of objectives within the four perspectives of balanced scorecard

The objectives are linked across perspectives in order to tie performance measurement to company goals. The financial objectives are normally set first, and then objectives are set in the other perspectives in order to accomplish the financial objectives.

For example, within the financial perspective, a common goal is to increase profit per dollars invested as measured by ROI. In order to increase ROI, a customer perspective objective might be to increase customer satisfaction as measured by the percentage of customers who would recommend the product to a friend. In order to increase customer satisfaction, an internal business process perspective objective might be to increase product quality as measured by the percentage of defect-free units. Finally, in order to increase the percentage of defect-free units, the learning and growth perspective objective might be to reduce factory employee turnover as measured by percentage of employees leaving in under one year.

Illustration 22-31 illustrates this linkage across perspectives.

Illustration 22-31 Linked process across balanced scorecard perspectives

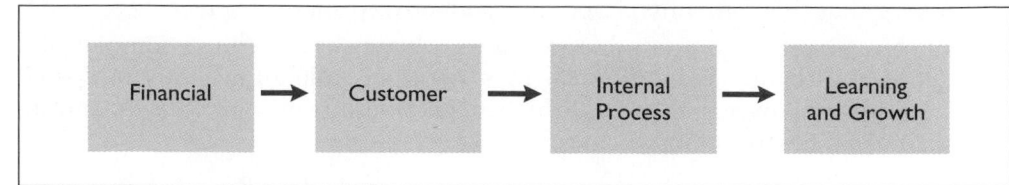

Through this linked process, the company can better understand how to achieve its goals and what measures to use to evaluate performance.

In summary, the balanced scorecard does the following:

1. Employs both financial and nonfinancial measures. (For example, ROI is a financial measure; employee turnover is a nonfinancial measure.)
2. Creates linkages so that high-level corporate goals can be communicated all the way down to the shop floor.
3. Provides measurable objectives for such nonfinancial measures as product quality, rather than vague statements such as "We would like to improve quality."
4. Integrates all of the company's goals into a single performance measurement system, so that an inappropriate amount of weight will not be placed on any single goal.

Accounting across the Organization

Many of the benefits of a balanced scorecard approach are evident in the improved operations at United Airlines. At the time it filed for bankruptcy in 2002, United had a reputation for some of the worst service in the airline business. But when Glenn Tilton took over as United's Chief Executive Officer in September 2002, he recognized that things had to change.

One thing he did was to implement an incentive program that allows all of United's 63,000 employees to earn a bonus of 2.5 percent or more of their wages if the company "exceeds its goals for on-time flight departures and for customer intent to fly United again." Since instituting this program the company's on-time departures are among the best, its customer complaints have been reduced considerably, and its number of customers who say that they would fly United again is at its highest level ever. While none of these things guarantees that United will survive, these improvements certainly increase its chances.

Source: Susan Carey, "Friendlier Skies: In Bankruptcy, United Airlines Forges a Path to Better Service," *Wall Street Journal Online* (June 15, 2004).

BEFORE YOU GO ON . . .

▶**Review It**

1. What are the formulas for computing the total, price, and quantity variances for direct labor?

2. What are the formulas for computing the total, controllable, and volume variances for manufacturing overhead?

3. How are standard costs and variances reported in income statements prepared for management?

4. What are the basic characteristics of the balanced scorecard?

Using the Decision Toolkit

Assume that during the past month Sanford produced 10,000 cartons of Liquid ACCENT® highlighters. Liquid ACCENT® offers a translucent barrel and cap with a visible ink supply for see-through color. The special fluorescent ink is fade- and water-resistant. Each carton contains 100 boxes of markers, and each box contains five markers. The markers come in boxes of one of five fluorescent colors—orange, blue, yellow, green, and pink—and in a five-color set.

Assume the following additional facts: The standard cost for one carton of 500 markers is as follows.

Manufacturing Cost Elements	Standard		
	Quantity	× Price	= Cost
Direct materials			
Tips (boxes of 500)	500	× $ 0.03 =	$ 15.00
Translucent barrels and caps (boxes of 500)	500	× $ 0.09 =	45.00
Fluorescent ink (100 oz. containers)	100 oz.	× $ 0.32 =	32.00
Total direct materials			92.00
Direct labor	0.25 hours	× $ 9.00 =	2.25
Overhead	0.25 hours	× $48.00 =	12.00
			$106.25

During the month, the following transactions occurred in manufacturing the 10,000 cartons of highlighters.

1. Purchased 10,000 boxes of tips for $148,000 ($14.80 per 500 tips); purchased 10,200 boxes of translucent barrels and caps for $453,900 ($44.50 per 500 barrels and caps); and purchased 9,900 containers of fluorescent ink for $328,185 ($33.15 per 100 ounces).

2. All materials purchased during the period were used to make markers during the period.

3. 2,300 direct labor hours were worked at a total labor cost of $20,240 (an average hourly rate of $8.80).

4. Variable manufacturing overhead incurred was $34,600, and fixed overhead incurred was $84,000.

The manufacturing overhead rate of $48.00 is based on a normal capacity of 2,600 direct labor hours. The total budget at this capacity is $83,980 fixed and $40,820 variable.

Instructions
Determine whether Sanford met its price and quantity objectives relative to materials, labor, and overhead.

Solution

To determine whether Sanford met its price and quantity objectives, compute the total variance and the variances for each of the manufacturing cost elements.

Total Variance

Actual cost incurred:		
Direct materials		
Tips	$148,000	
Translucent barrels and caps	453,900	
Fluorescent ink	328,185	
Total direct materials		$ 930,085
Direct labor		20,240
Overhead		118,600
Total actual costs		1,068,925
Standard cost (10,000 × $106.25)		1,062,500
Total variance		$ 6,425 U

Direct Materials Variances

Total	=	$930,085	−	$920,000 (10,000 × $92)	=	$10,085 U
Price (Tips)	=	$148,000 (10,000 × $14.80)	−	$150,000 (10,000 × $15.00)	=	$ 2,000 F
Price (Barrels and caps)	=	$453,900 (10,200 × $44.50)	−	$459,000 (10,200 × $45.00)	=	$ 5,100 F
Price (Ink)	=	$328,185 (9,900 × $33.15)	−	$316,800 (9,900 × $32.00)	=	$11,385 U
Quantity (Tips)	=	$150,000 (10,000 × $15.00)	−	$150,000 (10,000 × $15.00)	=	$ 0
Quantity (Barrels and caps)	=	$459,000 (10,200 × $45.00)	−	$450,000 (10,000 × $45.00)	=	$ 9,000 U
Quantity (Ink)	=	$316,800 (9,900 × $32.00)	−	$320,000 (10,000 × $32.00)	=	$ 3,200 F

Direct Labor Variances

Total	=	$20,240 (2,300 × $8.80)	−	$22,500 (2,500 × $9.00)	=	$ 2,260 F
Price	=	$20,240 (2,300 × $8.80)	−	$20,700 (2,300 × $9.00)	=	$ 460 F
Quantity	=	$20,700 (2,300 × $9.00)	−	$22,500 (2,500 × $9.00)	=	$ 1,800 F

Overhead Variances

Total	=	$118,600 ($84,000 + $34,600)	−	$120,000 (2,500 × $48)	= $ 1,400 F
Controllable	=	$118,600 ($84,000 + $34,600) *$40,820 ÷ 2,600	−	$123,230 [(2,500 × $15.70)* + $83,980] = $15.70 per direct labor hour	= $ 4,630 F
Volume	=	$32.30** **$83,980 ÷ 2,600		× (2,600 − 2,500) = $ 32.30	= $ 3,230 U

Sanford's total variance was an unfavorable $6,425. The unfavorable materials variance outweighed the favorable labor and overhead variances. The primary determinants were an unfavorable price variance for ink and an unfavorable quantity variance for barrels and caps.

Summary of Study Objectives

1 *Distinguish between a standard and a budget.* Both standards and budgets are predetermined costs. The primary difference is that a standard is a unit amount, whereas a budget is a total amount. A standard may be regarded as the budgeted cost per unit of product.

2 *Identify the advantages of standard costs.* Standard costs offer a number of advantages. They (a) facilitate management planning, (b) promote greater economy, (c) are useful in setting selling prices, (d) contribute to management control, (e) permit "management by exception," and (f) simplify the costing of inventories and reduce clerical costs.

3 *Describe how standards are set.* The direct materials price standard should be based on the delivered cost of raw materials plus an allowance for receiving and handling. The direct materials quantity standard should establish the required quantity plus an allowance for waste and spoilage.

The direct labor price standard should be based on current wage rates and anticipated adjustments such as COLAs. It also generally includes payroll taxes and fringe benefits. Direct labor quantity standards should be based on required production time plus an allowance for rest periods, cleanup, machine setup, and machine downtime.

For manufacturing overhead, a standard predetermined overhead rate is used. It is based on an expected standard activity index such as standard direct labor hours or standard machine hours.

4 *State the formulas for determining direct materials and direct labor variances.* The formulas for the direct materials variances are:

$$\begin{pmatrix} \text{Actual quantity} \\ \times \text{ Actual price} \end{pmatrix} - \begin{pmatrix} \text{Standard quantity} \\ \times \text{ Standard price} \end{pmatrix} = \begin{matrix} \text{Total} \\ \text{materials} \\ \text{variance} \end{matrix}$$

$$\begin{pmatrix} \text{Actual quantity} \\ \times \text{ Actual price} \end{pmatrix} - \begin{pmatrix} \text{Actual quantity} \\ \times \text{ Standard price} \end{pmatrix} = \begin{matrix} \text{Materials} \\ \text{price} \\ \text{variance} \end{matrix}$$

$$\begin{pmatrix} \text{Actual quantity} \\ \times \text{ Standard price} \end{pmatrix} - \begin{pmatrix} \text{Standard quantity} \\ \times \text{ Standard price} \end{pmatrix} = \begin{matrix} \text{Materials} \\ \text{quantity} \\ \text{variance} \end{matrix}$$

The formulas for the direct labor variances are:

$$\begin{pmatrix} \text{Actual hours} \\ \times \text{ Actual rate} \end{pmatrix} - \begin{pmatrix} \text{Standard hours} \\ \times \text{ Standard rate} \end{pmatrix} = \begin{matrix} \text{Total} \\ \text{labor} \\ \text{variance} \end{matrix}$$

$$\begin{pmatrix} \text{Actual hours} \\ \times \text{ Actual rate} \end{pmatrix} - \begin{pmatrix} \text{Actual hours} \\ \times \text{ Standard rate} \end{pmatrix} = \begin{matrix} \text{Labor} \\ \text{price} \\ \text{variance} \end{matrix}$$

$$\begin{pmatrix} \text{Actual hours} \\ \times \text{ Standard rate} \end{pmatrix} - \begin{pmatrix} \text{Standard hours} \\ \times \text{ Standard rate} \end{pmatrix} = \begin{matrix} \text{Labor} \\ \text{quantity} \\ \text{variance} \end{matrix}$$

5 *State the formulas for determining manufacturing overhead variances.* The formulas for the manufacturing overhead variances are:

$$\begin{pmatrix} \text{Actual} \\ \text{overhead} \end{pmatrix} - \begin{pmatrix} \text{Overhead} \\ \text{applied} \end{pmatrix} = \begin{matrix} \text{Total overhead} \\ \text{variance} \end{matrix}$$

$$\begin{pmatrix} \text{Actual} \\ \text{overhead} \end{pmatrix} - \begin{pmatrix} \text{Overhead} \\ \text{budgeted} \end{pmatrix} = \begin{matrix} \text{Overhead control-} \\ \text{lable variance} \end{matrix}$$

$$\begin{pmatrix} \text{Fixed} \\ \text{overhead} \\ \text{rate} \end{pmatrix} \times \begin{pmatrix} \text{Normal} & \text{Standard} \\ \text{capacity} - \text{hours} \\ \text{hours} & \text{allowed} \end{pmatrix} = \begin{matrix} \text{Overhead} \\ \text{volume} \\ \text{variance} \end{matrix}$$

6 *Discuss the reporting of variances.* Variances are reported to management in variance reports. The reports facilitate management by exception by highlighting significant differences.

7 *Prepare an income statement for management under a standard costing system.* Under a standard costing system, an income statement prepared for management will report cost of goods sold at standard cost and then disclose each variance separately.

8 *Describe the balanced scorecard approach to performance evaluation.* The balanced scorecard incorporates financial and nonfinancial measures in an integrated system that links performance measurement and a company's strategic goals. It employs four perspectives: financial; customer; internal processes; and learning and growth. Objectives are set within each of these perspectives that link to objectives within the other perspectives.

THE NAVIGATOR

Decision Toolkit—A Summary

Decision Checkpoints	Info Needed for Decision	Tool to Use for Decision	How to Evaluate Results
Has management accomplished its price and quantity objectives regarding materials?	Actual cost and standard cost of materials	Materials price and materials quantity variances	Positive (favorable) variances suggest that price and quantity objectives have been met.
Has management accomplished its price and quantity objectives regarding labor?	Actual cost and standard cost of labor	Labor price and labor quantity variances	Positive (favorable) variances suggest that price and quantity objectives have been met.
Has management accomplished its price and quantity objectives regarding overhead?	Actual cost and standard cost of overhead	Overhead controllable variance and overhead volume variance	Positive (favorable) variances suggest that price and quantity objectives have been met.

APPENDIX
STANDARD COST ACCOUNTING SYSTEM

STUDY OBJECTIVE
9

Identify the featres of a standard cost accounting system

A **standard cost accounting system** is a double-entry system of accounting. In this system, standard costs are used in making entries, and variances are formally recognized in the accounts. A standard cost system may be used with either job order or process costing. At this point, we will explain and illustrate a **standard cost, job order cost accounting system**. The system is based on two important assumptions: (1) Variances from standards are recognized at the earliest opportunity. (2) The Work in Process account is maintained exclusively on the basis of standard costs. In practice, there are many variations among standard cost systems. The system described here should prepare you for systems you see in the "real world."

Journal Entries

We will use the transactions of Xonic, Inc. to illustrate the journal entries. Note as you study the entries that the major difference between the entries here and those for the job order cost accounting system in Chapter 15 is the **variance accounts**.

1. Purchase raw materials on account for $13,020 when the standard cost is $12,600.

Raw Materials Inventory	12,600	
Materials Price Variance	420	
Accounts Payable		13,020
(To record purchase of materials)		

The inventory account is debited for actual quantities at standard cost. This enables the perpetual materials records to show actual quantities. The price variance, which is unfavorable, is debited to Materials Price Variance.

2. Incur direct labor costs of $20,580 when the standard labor cost is $21,000.

Factory Labor	21,000	
Labor Price Variance		420
Wages Payable		20,580
(To record direct labor costs)		

Like the raw materials inventory account, Factory Labor is debited for actual hours worked at the standard hourly rate of pay. In this case, the labor variance is favorable. Thus, Labor Price Variance is credited.

3. Incur actual manufacturing overhead costs of $10,900.

Manufacturing Overhead	10,900	
Accounts Payable/Cash/Acc. Depreciation		10,900
(To record overhead incurred)		

The controllable overhead variance is not recorded at this time. It depends on standard hours applied to work in process. This amount is not known at the time overhead is incurred.

4. Issue raw materials for production at a cost of $12,600 when the standard cost is $12,000.

Work in Process Inventory	12,000	
Materials Quantity Variance	600	
Raw Materials Inventory		12,600
(To record issuance of raw materials)		

Work in Process Inventory is debited for standard materials quantities used at standard prices. The variance account is debited because the variance is unfavorable. Raw Materials Inventory is credited for actual quantities at standard prices.

5. Assign factory labor to production at a cost of $21,000 when standard cost is $20,000.

Work in Process Inventory	20,000	
Labor Quantity Variance	1,000	
Factory Labor		21,000
(To assign factory labor to jobs)		

Work in Process Inventory is debited for standard labor hours at standard rates. The unfavorable variance is debited to Labor Quantity Variance. The credit to Factory Labor produces a zero balance in this account.

6. Applying manufacturing overhead to production $10,000.

Work in Process Inventory	10,000	
Manufacturing Overhead		10,000
(To assign overhead to jobs)		

Work in Process Inventory is debited for standard hours allowed multiplied by the standard overhead rate.

7. Transfer completed work to finished goods $42,000.

Finished Goods Inventory	42,000	
Work in Process Inventory		42,000
(To record transfer of completed work to		
finished goods)		

In this example, both inventory accounts are at standard cost.

8. The 1,000 gallons of Weed-O are sold for $60,000.

Accounts Receivable	60,000	
Cost of Goods Sold	42,000	
Sales		60,000
Finished Goods Inventory		42,000
(To record sale of finished goods and the		
cost of goods sold)		

Cost of Goods Sold is debited at standard cost. Gross profit, in turn, is the difference between sales and the standard cost of goods sold.

9. Recognize unfavorable overhead variances: controllable, $500; volume, $400.

Overhead Controllable Variance	500	
Overhead Volume Variance	400	
Manufacturing Overhead		900
(To recognize overhead variances)		

Prior to this entry, a debit balance of $900 existed in Manufacturing Overhead. This entry therefore produces a zero balance in the Manufacturing Overhead account. The information needed for this entry is often not available until the end of the accounting period.

Ledger Accounts

The cost accounts for Xonic, Inc., after posting the entries, are shown in Illustration 22A-1. Note that six variance accounts are included in the ledger. The remaining accounts are the same as those illustrated for a job order cost system in Chapter 15, in which only actual costs were used.

Illustration 22A-1 Cost accounts with variances

Helpful Hint All debit balances in variance accounts indicate unfavorable variances; all credit balances indicate favorable variances.

Summary of Study Objective for Appendix

9 *Identify the features of a standard cost accounting system.* In a standard cost accounting system, standard costs are journalized and posted, and separate variance accounts are maintained in the ledger.

Glossary

Balanced scorecard An approach that incorporates financial and nonfinancial measures in an integrated system that links performance measurement and a company's strategic goals. (p. 1084)

Customer perspective A viewpoint employed in the balanced scorecard to evaluate the company from the perspective of those people who buy and use its products or services. (p. 1084)

Direct labor price standard The rate per hour that should be incurred for direct labor. (p. 1069)

Direct labor quantity standard The time that should be required to make one unit of product. (p. 1070)

Direct materials price standard The cost per unit of direct materials that should be incurred. (p. 1069)

Direct materials quantity standard The quantity of direct materials that should be used per unit of finished goods. (p. 1069)

Financial perspective A viewpoint employed in the balanced scorecard to evaluate a company's performance using financial measures. (p. 1084)

Ideal standards Standards based on the optimum level of performance under perfect operating conditions. (p. 1068)

Internal process perspective A viewpoint employed in the balanced scorecard to evaluate the effectiveness and efficiency of a company's value chain, including product development, production, delivery, and after-sale service. (p. 1085)

Labor price variance The difference between the actual hours times the actual rate and the actual hours times the standard rate for labor. (p. 1077)

Labor quantity variance The difference between actual hours times the standard rate and standard hours times the standard rate for labor. (p. 1077)

Learning and growth perspective A viewpoint employed in the balanced scorecard to evaluate how well a company develops and retains its employees. (p. 1085)

Materials price variance The difference between the actual quantity times the actual price and the actual quantity times the standard price for materials. (p. 1074)

Materials quantity variance The difference between the actual quantity times the standard price and the standard quantity times the standard price for materials. (p. 1074)

Normal standards Standards based on an efficient level of performance that are attainable under expected operating conditions. (p. 1068)

Overhead controllable variance The difference between actual overhead incurred and overhead budgeted for the standard hours allowed. (p. 1080)

Overhead volume variance The difference between normal capacity hours and standard hours allowed times the fixed overhead rate. (p. 1081)

Standard cost accounting system A double-entry system of accounting in which standard costs are used in making entries and variances are recognized in the accounts. (p. 1090)

Standard costs Predetermined unit costs which are used as measures of performance. (p. 1066)

Standard hours allowed The hours that should have been worked for the units produced. (p. 1079)

Standard predetermined overhead rate An overhead rate determined by dividing budgeted overhead costs by an expected standard activity index. (p. 1070)

Total labor variance The difference between actual hours times the actual rate and standard hours times the standard rate for labor. (p. 1077)

Total materials variance The difference between the actual quantity times the actual price and the standard quantity times the standard price of materials. (p. 1073)

Total overhead variance The difference between actual overhead costs and overhead costs applied to work done. (p. 1079)

Variances The difference between total actual costs and total standard costs. (p. 1072)

Demonstration Problem

Manlow Company makes a cologne called Allure. The standard cost for one bottle of Allure is as follows.

Manufacturing Cost Elements	Standard Quantity	×	Price	=	Cost
Direct materials	6 oz.	×	$ 0.90	=	$ 5.40
Direct labor	0.5 hrs.	×	$12.00	=	6.00
Manufacturing overhead	0.5 hrs.	×	$ 4.80	=	2.40
					$13.80

During the month, the following transactions occurred in manufacturing 10,000 bottles of Allure.

1. 58,000 ounces of materials were purchased at $1.00 per ounce.
2. All the materials purchased were used to produce the 10,000 bottles of Allure.
3. 4,900 direct labor hours were worked at a total labor cost of $56,350.
4. Variable manufacturing overhead incurred was $15,000 and fixed overhead incurred was $10,400.

The manufacturing overhead rate of $4.80 is based on a normal capacity of 5,200 direct labor hours. The total budget at this capacity is $10,400 fixed and $14,560 variable.

Instructions

Compute the total variance and the variances for each of the manufacturing cost elements.

Action Plan

- Check to make sure the total variance and the sum of the individual variances are equal.
- Find the price variance first, then the quantity variance.
- Base budgeted overhead costs on flexible budget data.
- Base overhead applied on standard hours allowed.
- Ignore actual hours worked in computing overhead variances.
- Relate the overhead volume variance solely to fixed costs.

Solution to Demonstration Problem

Total Variance

Actual costs incurred		
Direct materials	$ 58,000	
Direct labor	56,350	
Manufacturing overhead	25,400	
	139,750	
Standard cost (10,000 × $13.80)	138,000	
Total variance	$ 1,750 U	

Direct Materials Variances

Total	=	$58,000 (58,000 × $1.00)	−	$54,000 (60,000 × $0.90)	=	$4,000 U
Price	=	$58,000 (58,000 × $1.00)	−	$52,200 (58,000 × $0.90)	=	$5,800 U
Quantity	=	$52,200 (58,000 × $0.90)	−	$54,000 (60,000 × $0.90)	=	$1,800 F

Direct Labor Variances

Total	=	$56,350 (4,900 × $11.50)	−	$60,000 (5,000 × $12.00)	=	$3,650 F
Price	=	$56,350 (4,900 × $11.50)	−	$58,800 (4,900 × $12.00)	=	$2,450 F
Quantity	=	$58,800 (4,900 × $12.00)	−	$60,000 (5,000 × $12.00)	=	$1,200 F

Overhead Variances

Total	=	$25,400	−	$24,000	=	$ 1,400 U
		($15,000 + $10,400)		(5,000 × $4.80)		
Controllable	=	$25,400	−	$24,400	=	$ 1,000 U
		($15,000 + $10,400)		($14,000* + $10,400)		
		*$14,560 ÷ 5,200	=	$2.80; $2.80 × 5,000	=	$14,000
Volume	=	$2.00**	×	(5,200 − 5,000)	=	$ 400 U
		**$10,400 ÷ 5,200	=	$2.00		

Note: All asterisked Questions, Exercises, and Problems relate to material in the appendix to the chapter.

Self-Study Questions

Answers are at the end of the chapter.

(SO 1)   **1.** Standards differ from budgets in that:
(a) budgets but not standards may be used in valuing inventories.
(b) budgets but not standards may be journalized and posted.
(c) budgets are a total amount and standards are a unit amount.
(d) only budgets contribute to management planning and control.

(SO 2)   **2.** The advantages of standard costs include all of the following *except:*
(a) management by exception may be used.
(b) management planning is facilitated.
(c) they may simplify the costing of inventories.
(d) management must use a static budget.

(SO 3)   **3.** The setting of standards is:
(a) a managerial accounting decision.
(b) a management decision.
(c) a worker decision.
(d) preferably set at the ideal level of performance.

(SO 4)   **4.** Each of the following formulas is correct except:
(a) Labor price variance = (Actual hours × Actual rate) − (Actual hours × Standard rate).
(b) Overhead controllable variance = Actual overhead − Overhead budgeted.
(c) Materials price variance = (Actual quantity × Actual cost) − (Standard quantity × Standard cost).
(d) Overhead volume variance = Fixed overhead rate × (Normal capacity hours − Standard capacity hours).

(SO 4)   **5.** In producing product AA, 6,300 pounds of direct materials were used at a cost of $1.10 per pound. The standard was 6,000 pounds at $1.00 per pound. The direct materials quantity variance is:
(a) $330 unfavorable.
(b) $300 unfavorable.
(c) $600 unfavorable.
(d) $630 unfavorable.

(SO 4)   **6.** In producing product ZZ, 14,800 direct labor hours were used at a rate of $8.20 per hour. The standard was 15,000 hours at $8.00 per hour. Based on these data, the direct labor:

(a) quantity variance is $1,600 favorable.
(b) quantity variance is $1,600 unfavorable.
(c) price variance is $2,960 favorable.
(d) price variance is $3,000 unfavorable.

(SO 5)   **7.** Which of the following is *correct* about overhead variances?
(a) The controllable variance generally pertains to fixed overhead costs.
(b) The volume variance pertains solely to variable overhead costs.
(c) Standard hours actually worked are used in each variance.
(d) Budgeted overhead costs are based on the flexible overhead budget.

(SO 5)   **8.** The formula for computing the total overhead variance is:
(a) actual overhead less overhead applied.
(b) overhead budgeted less overhead applied.
(c) actual overhead less overhead budgeted.
(d) No correct answer given.

(SO 6)   **9.** Which of the following is *incorrect* about variance reports?
(a) They facilitate "management by exception."
(b) They should only be sent to the top level of management.
(c) They should be prepared as soon as possible.
(d) They may vary in form, content, and frequency among companies.

(SO 8)   **10.** Which of the following would *not* be an objective used in the customer perspective of the balanced scorecard approach?
(a) Percentage of customers who would recommend product to a friend.
(b) Customer retention.
(c) Brand recognition.
(d) Earnings per share.

(SO 9)   *****11.** Which of the following is *incorrect* about a standard cost accounting system?
(a) It is applicable to job order costing.
(b) It is applicable to process costing.
(c) It is a single-entry system.
(d) It keeps separate accounts for each variance.

Questions

1. (a) "Standard costs are the expected total cost of completing a job." Is this correct? Explain.
(b) "A standard imposed by a governmental agency is known as a regulation." Do you agree? Explain.

2. (a) Explain the similarities and differences between standards and budgets.
(b) Contrast the accounting for standards and budgets.

3. Standard costs facilitate management planning. What are the other advantages of standard costs?

4. Contrast the roles of the management accountant and management in setting standard costs.

5. Distinguish between an ideal standard and a normal standard.

6. What factors should be considered in setting (a) the direct materials price standard and (b) the direct materials quantity standard?

7. "The objective in setting the direct labor quantity standard is to determine the aggregate time required to make one unit of product." Do you agree? What allowances should be made in setting this standard?

8. How is the predetermined overhead rate determined when standard costs are used?

9. What is the difference between a favorable cost variance and an unfavorable cost variance?

10. In each of the following formulas, supply the words that should be inserted for each number in parentheses.
(a) (Actual quantity × (1)) − (Standard quantity × (2)) = Total materials variance
(b) ((3) × Actual price) − (Actual quantity × (4)) = Materials price variance
(c) (Actual quantity × (5)) − ((6) × Standard price) = Materials quantity variance

11. In the direct labor variance matrix, there are three factors: (1) Actual hours × Actual rate, (2) Actual hours × Standard rate, and (3) Standard hours × Standard rate. Using the numbers, indicate the formulas for each of the direct labor variances.

12. Keene Company's standard predetermined overhead rate is $8 per direct labor hour. For the month of June, 26,000 actual hours were worked, and 27,500 standard hours were allowed. Normal capacity hours were 28,000. How much overhead was applied?

13. If the $8 per hour overhead rate in question 12 includes $5 variable, and actual overhead costs were $218,000, what is the overhead controllable variance for June? Is the variance favorable or unfavorable?

14. Using the data in questions 12 and 13, what is the overhead volume variance for June? Is the variance favorable or unfavorable?

15. What is the purpose of computing the overhead volume variance? What is the basic formula for this variance?

16. Nancy Morgan does not understand why the overhead volume variance indicates that fixed overhead costs are under- or overapplied. Clarify this matter for Nancy.

17. Mike Darby is attempting to outline the important points about overhead variances on a class examination. List four points that Mike should include in his outline.

18. How often should variances be reported to management? What principle may be used with variance reports?

19. What circumstances may cause the purchasing department to be responsible for both an unfavorable materials price variance and an unfavorable materials quantity variance?

20. What are the four perspectives used in the balanced scorecard? Discuss the nature of each, and how the perspectives are linked.

21. Tom Jones says that the balanced scorecard was created to replace financial measures as the primary mechanism for performance evaluation. He says that it uses only nonfinancial measures. Is this true?

22. What are some examples of nonfinancial measures used by companies to evaluate performance?

23. (a) How are variances reported in income statements prepared for management? (b) May standard costs be used in preparing financial statements for stockholders? Explain.

***24.** (a) Explain the basic features of a standard cost accounting system. (b) What type of balance will exist in the variance account when (1) the materials price variance is unfavorable and (2) the labor quantity variance is favorable?

Brief Exercises

Distinguish between a standard and a budget.
(SO 1)

BE22-1 Valdez Company uses both standards and budgets. For the year, estimated production of Product X is 500,000 units. Total estimated cost for materials and labor are $1,000,000 and $1,600,000. Compute the estimates for (a) a standard cost and (b) a budgeted cost.

Set direct materials standard.
(SO 3)

BE22-2 Hideo Company accumulates the following data concerning raw materials in making one gallon of finished product: (1) Price—net purchase price $3.20, freight-in

$0.20 and receiving and handling $0.10. (2) Quantity—required materials 2.6 pounds, allowance for waste and spoilage 0.4 pounds. Compute the following.
(a) Standard direct materials price per gallon.
(b) Standard direct materials quantity per gallon.
(c) Total standard materials cost per gallon.

BE22-3 Labor data for making one gallon of finished product in Hideo Company are as follows: (1) Price—hourly wage rate $10.00, payroll taxes $0.80, and fringe benefits $1.20. (2) Quantity—actual production time 1.2 hours, rest periods and clean up 0.25 hours, and setup and downtime 0.15 hours. Compute the following.
(a) Standard direct labor rate per hour.
(b) Standard direct labor hours per gallon.
(c) Standard labor cost per gallon.

Set direct labor standard.
(SO 3)

BE22-4 Sprague Company's standard materials cost per unit of output is $10 (2 pounds × $5). During July, the company purchases and uses 3,300 pounds of materials costing $16,731 in making 1,500 units of finished product. Compute the total, price, and quantity materials variances.

Compute direct materials variances.
(SO 4)

BE22-5 Talbot Company's standard labor cost per unit of output is $20 (2 hours × $10 per hour). During August, the company incurs 1,900 hours of direct labor at an hourly cost of $9.60 per hour in making 1,000 units of finished product. Compute the total, price, and quantity labor variances.

Compute direct labor variances.
(SO 4)

BE22-6 In October, Russo Company reports 21,000 actual direct labor hours, and it incurs $96,000 of manufacturing overhead costs. Standard hours allowed for the work done is 20,000 hours. The predetermined overhead rate is $5 per direct labor hour. Compute the total overhead variance.

Compute total overhead variance.
(SO 5)

BE22-7 Some overhead data for Russo Company are given in BE22-6. In addition, the flexible manufacturing overhead budget shows that budgeted costs are $4 variable per direct labor hour and $25,000 fixed. Compute the overhead controllable variance.

Compute the overhead controllable variance.
(SO 5)

BE22-8 Using the data in BE22-6 and BE22-7, compute the overhead volume variance. Normal capacity was 25,000 direct labor hours.

Compute overhead volume variance.
(SO 5)

BE22-9 The four perspectives in the balanced scorecard are (1) financial, (2) customer, (3) internal process, and (4) learning and growth. Match each of the following objectives with the perspective it is most likely associated with: (a) Plant capacity utilization. (b) Employee work days missed due to injury. (c) Return on assets. (d) Brand recognition.

Match balanced scorecard perspectives.
(SO 8)

*BE22-10 Journalize the following transactions for McBee Manufacturing.
(a) Purchased 6,000 units of raw materials on account for $11,500. The standard cost was $12,000.
(b) Issued 5,600 units of raw materials for production. The standard units were 5,800.

Journalize materials variances.
(SO 9)

*BE22-11 Journalize the following transactions for Worrel Manufacturing.
(a) Incurred direct labor costs of $24,000 for 3,000 hours. The standard labor cost was $24,600.
(b) Assigned 3,000 direct labor hours costing $24,000 to production. Standard hours were 3,100.

Journalize labor variances.
(SO 9)

Exercises

E22-1 Raul Mondesi manufactures and sells homemade wine, and he wants to develop a standard cost per gallon. The following are required for production of a 50-gallon batch.

Compute standard materials costs.
(SO 3)

  3,000 ounces of grape concentrate at $0.04 per ounce
  54 pounds of granulated sugar at $0.30 per pound
  60 lemons at $0.60 each
  50 yeast tablets at $0.25 each
  50 nutrient tablets at $0.20 each
  2,500 ounces of water at $0.003 per ounce

Raul estimates that 4% of the grape concentrate is wasted, 10% of the sugar is lost, and 20% of the lemons cannot be used.

Instructions

Compute the standard cost of the ingredients for one gallon of wine. (Carry computations to two decimal places.)

Compute materials price and quantity variances.
(SO 4)

E22-2 The standard cost of Product B manufactured by Gomez Company includes three units of direct materials at $5.00 per unit. During June, 27,600 units of direct materials are purchased at a cost of $4.70 per unit, and 27,600 units of direct materials are used to produce 9,000 units of Product B.

Instructions

(a) Compute the materials variance and the price and quantity variances.
(b) Repeat (a), assuming the purchase price is $5.20 and the quantity purchased and used is 26,400 units.

Compute labor price and quantity variances.
(SO 4)

E22-3 Pagley Company's standard labor cost of producing one unit of Product DD is 4 hours at the rate of $12.00 per hour. During August, 40,500 hours of labor are incurred at a cost of $12.10 per hour to produce 10,000 units of Product DD.

Instructions

(a) Compute the total labor variance.
(b) Compute the labor price and quantity variances.
(c) Repeat (b), assuming the standard is 4.2 hours of direct labor at $12.20 per hour.

Compute labor quantity variance.
(SO 3, 4)

E22-4 Rapid Repair Services, Inc. is trying to establish the standard labor cost of a typical oil change. The following data have been collected from time and motion studies conducted over the past month.

Actual time spent on the oil change	1.0 hour
Hourly wage rate	$10
Payroll taxes	10% of wage rate
Setup and downtime	10% of actual labor time
Cleanup and rest periods	30% of actual labor time
Fringe benefits	25% of wage rate

Instructions

(a) Determine the standard direct labor hours per oil change.
(b) Determine the standard direct labor hourly rate.
(c) Determine the standard direct labor cost per oil change.
(d) If an oil change took 1.5 hours at the standard hourly rate, what was the direct labor quantity variance?

Compute materials and labor variances.
(SO 4)

E22-5 Kopecky Inc., which produces a single product, has prepared the following standard cost sheet for one unit of the product.

Direct materials (8 pounds at $2.50 per pound)	$20
Direct labor (3 hours at $12.00 per hour)	$36

During the month of April, the company manufactures 240 units and incurs the following actual costs.

Direct materials purchased and used (1,900 pounds)	$4,940
Direct labor (700 hours)	$8,120

Instructions

Compute the total, price, and quantity variances for materials and labor.

Compute the materials and labor variances and list reasons for unfavorable variances.
(SO 4, 6)

E22-6 The following direct materials and direct labor data pertain to the operations of Batista Manufacturing Company for the month of August.

Costs		**Quantities**	
Actual labor rate	$13 per hour	Actual hours incurred and used	4,250 hours
Actual materials price	$128 per ton	Actual quantity of materials purchased and used	1,250 tons
Standard labor rate	$12 per hour	Standard hours used	4,300 hours
Standard materials price	$130 per ton	Standard quantity of materials used	1,200 tons

Instructions
(a) Compute the total, price, and quantity variances for materials and labor.
(b) ▉▉▊➤ Provide two possible explanations for each of the unfavorable variances calculated above, and suggest where responsibility for the unfavorable result might be placed.

E22-7   The following information was taken from the annual manufacturing overhead cost budget of Fernetti Company.

Compute manufacturing overhead variances and interpret findings.
(SO 5)

Variable manufacturing overhead costs	$33,000
Fixed manufacturing overhead costs	$21,450
Normal production level in labor hours	16,500
Normal production level in units	4,125
Standard labor hours per unit	4

During the year, 4,000 units were produced, 16,100 hours were worked, and the actual manufacturing overhead was $54,000. Actual fixed manufacturing overhead costs equaled budgeted fixed manufacturing overhead costs. Overhead is applied on the basis of direct labor hours.

Instructions
(a) Compute the total, fixed, and variable predetermined manufacturing overhead rates.
(b) Compute the total, controllable, and volume overhead variances.
(c) ▉▉▊➤ Briefly interpret the overhead controllable and volume variances computed in (b).

E22-8   The loan department of Local Bank uses standard costs to determine the overhead cost of processing loan applications. During the current month a fire occurred, and the accounting records for the department were mostly destroyed. The following data were salvaged from the ashes.

Compute overhead variances.
(SO 5)

Standard variable overhead rate per hour	$9
Standard hours per application	2
Standard hours allowed	2,000
Standard fixed overhead rate per hour	$6
Actual fixed overhead cost	$13,200
Variable overhead budget based on standard hours allowed	$18,000
Fixed overhead budget	$13,200
Overhead controllable variance	$ 1,500 U

Instructions
(a) Determine the following.
   (1) Total actual overhead cost.
   (2) Actual variable overhead cost.
   (3) Variable overhead cost applied.
   (4) Fixed overhead cost applied.
   (5) Overhead volume variance.
(b) Determine how many loans were processed.

E22-9   Manufacturing overhead data for the production of Product H by Rondell Company are as follows.

Compute overhead variances.
(SO 5)

Overhead incurred for 52,000 actual direct labor hours worked	$213,000
Overhead rate (variable $3; fixed $1) at normal capacity of 54,000 direct labor hours	$4
Standard hours allowed for work done	52,000

Instructions
Compute the total, controllable, and volume overhead variances.

E22-10   During March 2007, Garner Tool & Die Company worked on four jobs. A review of direct labor costs reveals the following summary data.

Prepare a variance report for direct labor.
(SO 4, 6)

Job	Actual		Standard		Total
Number	Hours	Costs	Hours	Costs	Variance
A257	220	$ 4,400	225	$4,500	$ 100 F
A258	450	10,350	430	8,600	1,750 U
A259	300	6,150	300	6,000	150 U
A260	115	2,070	110	2,200	130 F
Total variance					$1,670 U

Analysis reveals that Job A257 was a repeat job. Job A258 was a rush order that required overtime work at premium rates of pay. Job A259 required a more experienced replacement worker on one shift. Work on Job A260 was done for one day by a new trainee when a regular worker was absent.

Instructions

Prepare a report for the plant supervisor on direct labor cost variances for March. The report should have columns for (1) Job No., (2) Actual Hours, (3) Standard Hours, (4) Quantity Variance, (5) Actual Rate, (6) Standard Rate, (7) Price Variance, and (8) Explanation.

Prepare a variance report.
(SO 6)

E22-11 Imperial Landscaping plants grass seed as the basic landscaping for business campuses. During a recent month the company worked on three projects (Ames, Korman, and Stilles). The company is interested in controlling the material costs, namely the grass seed, for these plantings projects.

   In order to provide management with useful cost control information, the company uses standard costs and prepares monthly variance reports. Analysis reveals that the purchasing agent mistakenly purchased poor-quality seed for the Ames project. The Korman project, however, received higher-than-standard-quality seed that was on sale. The Stilles project received standard-quality seed; however, the price had increased and a new employee was used to spread the seed.

   Shown below are quantity and cost data for each project.

	Actual		Standard		Total
Project	Quantity	Costs	Quantity	Costs	Variance
Ames	500 lbs.	$1,175	460 lbs.	$1,150	$ 25 U
Korman	400	960	410	1,025	65 F
Stilles	500	1,300	480	1,200	100 U
Total variance					$ 60 U

Instructions

(a) Prepare a variance report for the purchasing department with the following columns: (1) Project, (2) Actual pounds purchased, (3) Actual price, (4) Standard price, (5) Price variance, and (6) Explanation.

(b) Prepare a variance report for the production department with the following columns: (1) Project, (2) Actual pounds, (3) Standard pounds, (4) Standard price, (5) Quantity variance, and (6) Explanation.

Prepare income statement for management.
(SO 7)

E22-12 Carlos Company uses a standard cost accounting system. During January, the company reported the following manufacturing variances.

Materials price variance	$1,250 U	Labor quantity variance	$ 725 U
Materials quantity variance	700 F	Overhead controllable	200 F
Labor price variance	525 U	Overhead volume	1,000 U

In addition, 6,000 units of product were sold at $8.00 per unit. Each unit sold had a standard cost of $6.00. Selling and administrative expenses were $6,000 for the month.

Instructions

Prepare an income statement for management for the month ended January 31, 2007.

Identify performance evaluation terminology.
(SO 8)

E22-13 The following is a list of terms related to performance evaluation.
   (1) Balanced scorecard
   (2) Variance
   (3) Learning and growth perspective
   (4) Nonfinancial measures
   (5) Customer perspective
   (6) Internal process perspective
   (7) Ideal standards
   (8) Normal standards

Instructions

Match each of the following descriptions with one of the terms above.
(a) The difference between total actual costs and total standard costs.
(b) An efficient level of performance that is attainable under expected operating conditions.

(c) An approach that incorporates financial and nonfinancial measures in an integrated system that links performance measurement and a company's strategic goals.

(d) A viewpoint employed in the balanced scorecard to evaluate how well a company develops and retains its employees.

(e) An evaluation tool that is not based on dollars.

(f) A viewpoint employed in the balanced scorecard to evaluate the company from the perspective of those people who buy and use its products or services.

(g) An optimum level of performance under perfect operating conditions.

(h) A viewpoint employed in the balanced scorecard to evaluate the efficiency and effectiveness of the company's value chain.

*E22-14 Marley Company installed a standard cost system on January 1. Selected transactions for the month of January are as follows.

1. Purchased 18,000 units of raw materials on account at a cost of $4.50 per unit. Standard cost was $4.25 per unit.
2. Issued 18,000 units of raw materials for jobs that required 17,600 standard units of raw materials.
3. Incurred 15,200 actual hours of direct labor at an actual rate of $4.80 per hour. The standard rate is $5.25 per hour. (Credit Wages Payable)
4. Performed 15,200 hours of direct labor on jobs when standard hours were 15,400.
5. Applied overhead to jobs at the rate of 100% of direct labor cost for standard hours allowed.

Journalize entries in a standard cost accounting system.
(SO 9)

Instructions
Journalize the January transactions.

*E22-15 Tovar Company uses a standard cost accounting system. Some of the ledger accounts have been destroyed in a fire. The controller asks your help in reconstructing some missing entries and balances.

Answer questions concerning missing entries and balances.
(SO 4, 5, 9)

Instructions
Answer the following questions.

(a) Materials Price Variance shows a $3,000 favorable balance. Accounts Payable shows $128,000 of raw materials purchases. What was the amount debited to Raw Materials Inventory for raw materials purchased?

(b) Materials Quantity Variance shows a $3,000 unfavorable balance. Raw Materials Inventory shows a zero balance. What was the amount debited to Work in Process Inventory for direct materials used?

(c) Labor Price Variance shows a $1,500 unfavorable balance. Factory Labor shows a debit of $150,000 for wages incurred. What was the amount credited to Wages Payable?

(d) Factory Labor shows a credit of $150,000 for direct labor used. Labor Quantity Variance shows a $900 unfavorable balance. What was the amount debited to Work in Process for direct labor used?

(e) Overhead applied to Work in Process totaled $165,000. If the total overhead variance was $1,000 unfavorable, what was the amount of overhead costs debited to Manufacturing Overhead?

(f) Overhead Controllable Variance shows a debit balance of $1,500. What was the amount and type of balance (debit or credit) in Overhead Volume Variance?

*E22-16 Data for Kopecky Inc. are given in E22-5.

Journalize entries for materials and labor variances.
(SO 9)

Instructions
Journalize the entries to record the materials and labor variances.

*E22-17 Data for Rondell Company are given in E22-9.

Journalize overhead variances.
(SO 9)

Instructions

(a) Journalize the incurrence of the overhead costs and the application of overhead to the job, assuming a standard cost accounting system is used.

(b) Prepare the adjusting entry for the overhead variances.

Problems: Set A

Compute variances.
(SO 4, 5)

P22-1A   Inman Corporation manufactures a single product. The standard cost per unit of product is as follows.

Direct materials—2 pounds of plastic at $5 per pound	$10
Direct labor—2 hours at $12 per hour	24
Variable manufacturing overhead	12
Fixed manufacturing overhead	6
Total standard cost per unit	$52

The master manufacturing overhead budget for the month based on normal productive capacity of 15,000 direct labor hours (7,500 units) shows total variable costs of $90,000 ($6 per labor hour) and total fixed costs of $45,000 ($3 per labor hour). Normal productive capacity is 15,000 direct labor hours. Overhead is applied on the basis of direct labor hours. Actual costs for November in producing 7,600 units were as follows.

Direct materials (15,000 pounds)	$ 73,500
Direct labor (14,900 hours)	181,780
Variable overhead	88,990
Fixed overhead	44,000
Total manufacturing costs	$388,270

The purchasing department normally buys the quantities of raw materials that are expected to be used in production each month. Raw materials inventories, therefore, can be ignored.

MPV $1,500 F
LQV $3,600 F
OVV $600 F

Instructions
Compute all of the materials, labor, and overhead variances.

Compute variances, and prepare income statement.
(SO 4, 5, 7)

P22-2A   Soriano Manufacturing Company uses a standard cost accounting system to account for the manufacture of exhaust fans. In July 2007, it accumulates the following data relative to 1,500 units started and finished.

Cost and Production Data	Actual	Standard
Raw materials		
Units purchased	17,400	
Units used	17,400	18,000
Unit cost	$3.40	$3.00
Direct labor		
Hours worked	2,900	3,000
Hourly rate	$11.80	$12.20
Manufacturing overhead		
Incurred	$87,500	
Applied		$93,750

Manufacturing overhead was applied on the basis of direct labor hours. Normal capacity for the month was 2,800 direct labor hours. At normal capacity, budgeted overhead costs were $20 per labor hour variable and $11.25 per labor hour fixed. Total budgeted fixed overhead costs were $31,500.

Jobs finished during the month were sold for $240,000. Selling and administrative expenses were $25,000.

Instructions

(a) MQV $1,800 F
   OCV $4,000 F
(b) NI $34,120

(a) Compute all of the variances for (1) direct materials, (2) direct labor, and (3) manufacturing overhead.
(b) Prepare an income statement for management showing variances. Ignore income taxes.

Compute and identify significant variances.
(SO 4, 5, 6)

P22-3A   Kohler Clothiers manufactures women's business suits. The company uses a standard cost accounting system. In March 2007, 11,800 suits were made. The following standard and actual cost data applied to the month of March when normal capacity was 15,000 direct labor hours. All materials purchased were used in production.

Cost Element	Standard (per unit)	Actual
Direct materials	5 yards at $7.00 per yard	$410,400 for 57,000 yards ($7.20 per yard)
Direct labor	1.0 hours at $12.00 per hour	$125,440 for 11,200 hours ($11.20 per hour)
Overhead	1.0 hours at $9.30 per hour (fixed $6.30; variable $3.00)	$90,000 fixed overhead $42,000 variable overhead

Overhead is applied on the basis of direct labor hours. At normal capacity, budgeted fixed overhead costs were $94,500, and budgeted variable overhead costs were $45,000.

Instructions
(a) Compute the total, price, and quantity variances for (1) materials and (2) labor, and (3) the total, controllable, and volume variances for manufacturing overhead.
(b) ▧▬▭▭▷ Which of the materials and labor variances should be investigated if management considers a variance of more than 6% from standard to be significant? Discuss the potential causes of this variance.

(a) MPV $11,400 U
LPV $8,960 F
OVV $20,160 U

P22-4A Crede Manufacturing Company uses a standard cost accounting system. In 2007, 33,000 units were produced. Each unit took several pounds of direct materials and 1⅓ standard hours of direct labor at a standard hourly rate of $12.00. Normal capacity was 42,000 direct labor hours. During the year, 132,000 pounds of raw materials were purchased at $0.90 per pound. All pounds purchased were used during the year.

Answer questions about variances.
(SO 4, 5)

Instructions
(a) If the materials price variance was $3,960 unfavorable, what was the standard materials price per pound?
(b) If the materials quantity variance was $2,871 favorable, what was the standard materials quantity per unit?
(c) What were the standard hours allowed for the units produced?
(d) If the labor quantity variance was $8,400 unfavorable, what were the actual direct labor hours worked?
(e) If the labor price variance was $4,470 favorable, what was the actual rate per hour?
(f) If total budgeted manufacturing overhead was $327,600 at normal capacity, what was the predetermined overhead rate per direct labor hour?
(g) What was the standard cost per unit of product?
(h) How much overhead was applied to production during the year?
(i) If the standard fixed overhead rate was $2.50, what was the overhead volume variance?
(j) If the overhead controllable variance was $3,000 favorable, what were the total variable overhead costs incurred? (Assume that the overhead controllable variance relates only to variable costs.)
(k) Using selected answers above, what were the total costs assigned to work in process?

(a) $0.87

(c) 44,000

(e) $11.90

(g) $29.967

(i) $5,000 F

(k) $988,911

P22-5A Hi-Tek Labs performs steroid testing services to high schools, colleges, and universities. Because the company deals solely with educational institutions, the price of each test is strictly regulated. Therefore, the costs incurred must be carefully monitored and controlled. Shown below are the standard costs for a typical test.

Compute variances, prepare an income statement, and explain unfavorable variances.
(SO 4, 5, 7)

Direct materials (1 petrie dish @ $2 per dish)	$ 2.00
Direct labor (0.5 hours @ $20 per hour)	10.00
Variable overhead (0.5 hours @ $8 per hour)	4.00
Fixed overhead (0.5 hours @ $3 per hour)	1.50
Total standard cost per test	$17.50

The lab does not maintain an inventory of petrie dishes. Therefore, the dishes purchased each month are used that month. Actual activity for the month of May 2007, when 2,000 tests were conducted, resulted in the following.

Direct materials (2,020 dishes)	$ 4,242
Direct labor (995 hours)	20,895
Variable overhead	8,100
Fixed overhead	3,400

Monthly budgeted fixed overhead is $3,600. Revenues for the month were $45,000, and selling and administrative expenses were $2,000.

(a) MQV $40 U
  LQV $100 F
(b) NI $6,363

Journalize and post standard cost entries, and prepare income statement.
(SO 4, 5, 7, 9)

(a) MPV $2,480 F
  LPV $925 U
(c) OCV $210 F;
  OVV $6,000 U
(d) NI $58,805

Compute variances.
(SO 4, 5)

MPV $1,530 U
LQV $2,400 F
OVV $750 U

Instructions
(a) Compute the price and quantity variances for direct materials and direct labor, and for overhead the controllable and volume variances.
(b) Prepare an income statement for management.
(c) Provide possible explanations for each unfavorable variance.

*P22-6A   Fayman Manufacturing Company uses standard costs with its job order cost accounting system. In January, an order (Job 84) was received for 3,900 units of Product D. The standard cost of 1 unit of Product D is as follows.

Direct materials—1.4 pounds at $4.00 per pound	$ 5.60
Direct labor—1 hour at $9.00 per hour	9.00
Overhead—1 hour (variable $7.40; fixed $10.00)	17.40
Standard cost per unit	$32.00

Overhead is applied on the basis of direct labor hours. Normal capacity for the month of January was 4,500 direct labor hours. During January, the following transactions applicable to Job No. 84 occurred.

1. Purchased 6,200 pounds of raw materials on account at $3.60 per pound.
2. Requisitioned 6,200 pounds of raw materials for production.
3. Incurred 3,700 hours of direct labor at $9.25 per hour.
4. Worked 3,700 hours of direct labor on Job No. 84.
5. Incurred $73,650 of manufacturing overhead on account.
6. Applied overhead to Job No. 84 on the basis of direct labor hours.
7. Transferred Job No. 84 to finished goods.
8. Billed customer for Job No. 84 at a selling price of $250,000.
9. Incurred selling and administrative expenses on account $61,000.

Instructions
(a) Journalize the transactions.
(b) Post to the job order cost accounts.
(c) Prepare the entry to recognize the overhead variances.
(d) Prepare the income statement for management for January 2007.

Problems: Set B

P22-1B   Ranier Corporation manufactures a single product. The standard cost per unit of product is shown below.

Direct materials—1 pound plastic at $7.00 per pound	$ 7.00
Direct labor—1.5 hours at $12.00 per hour	18.00
Variable manufacturing overhead	11.25
Fixed manufacturing overhead	3.75
Total standard cost per unit	$40.00

The predetermined manufacturing overhead rate is $10 per direct labor hour ($15.00 ÷ 1.5). It was computed from a master manufacturing overhead budget based on normal production of 7,500 direct labor hours (5,000 units) for the month. The master budget showed total variable costs of $56,250 ($7.50 per hour) and total fixed overhead costs of $18,750 ($2.50 per hour). Actual costs for October in producing 4,800 units were as follows.

Direct materials (5,100 pounds)	$ 37,230
Direct labor (7,000 hours)	87,500
Variable overhead	56,170
Fixed overhead	19,680
Total manufacturing costs	$200,580

The purchasing department buys the quantities of raw materials that are expected to be used in production each month. Raw materials inventories, therefore, can be ignored.

Instructions
Compute all of the materials, labor, and overhead variances.

P22-2B Finley Manufacturing Corporation accumulates the following data relative to jobs started and finished during the month of June 2007.

Compute variances, and prepare income statement.
(SO 4, 5, 7)

Costs and Production Data	Actual	Standard
Raw materials unit cost	$2.25	$2.00
Raw materials units used	10,400	10,000
Direct labor payroll	$124,100	$120,000
Direct labor hours worked	14,600	15,000
Manufacturing overhead incurred	$182,500	
Manufacturing overhead applied		$189,000
Machine hours expected to be used at normal capacity		42,500
Budgeted fixed overhead for June		$51,000
Variable overhead rate per hour		$3.00
Fixed overhead rate per hour		$1.20

Overhead is applied on the basis of standard machine hours. Three hours of machine time are required for each direct labor hour. The jobs were sold for $400,000. Selling and administrative expenses were $40,000. Assume that the amount of raw materials purchased equaled the amount used.

Instructions
(a) Compute all of the variances for (1) direct materials, (2) direct labor, and (3) manufacturing overhead.
(b) Prepare an income statement for management. Ignore income taxes.

(a) MQV $800 U
 LPV $7,300 U
 OCV $3,500 F
(b) NI $30,000

P22-3B Merando Clothiers is a small company that manufactures tall-men's suits. The company has used a standard cost accounting system. In May 2007, 11,200 suits were produced. The following standard and actual cost data applied to the month of May when normal capacity was 14,000 direct labor hours. All materials purchased were used.

Compute and identify significant variances.
(SO 4, 5, 6)

Cost Element	Standard (per unit)	Actual
Direct materials	8 yards at $4.50 per yard	$371,050 for 90,500 yards ($4.10 per yard)
Direct labor	1.2 hours at $13.00 per hour	$201,630 for 14,300 hours ($14.10 per hour)
Overhead	1.2 hours at $6.00 per hour (fixed $3.50; variable $2.50)	$49,000 fixed overhead $36,000 variable overhead

Overhead is applied on the basis of direct labor hours. At normal capacity, budgeted fixed overhead costs were $49,000, and budgeted variable overhead was $35,000.

Instructions
(a) Compute the total, price, and quantity variances for (1) materials and (2) labor, and (3) the total, controllable, and volume variances for manufacturing overhead.
(b) ▣▤▤▤▶ Which of the materials and labor variances should be investigated if management considers a variance of more than 7% from standard to be significant?

(a) MPV $36,200 F
 LPV $15,730 U
 LQV $11,180 U
 OCV $2,400 U

P22-4B Harbaugh Manufacturing Company uses a standard cost accounting system. In 2007, 30,000 units were produced. Each unit took several pounds of direct materials and 1½ standard hours of direct labor at a standard hourly rate of $12.00. Normal capacity was 50,000 direct labor hours. During the year, 133,000 pounds of raw materials were purchased at $0.92 per pound. All pounds purchased were used during the year.

Answer questions about variances.
(SO 4, 5)

Instructions
(a) If the materials price variance was $5,320 favorable, what was the standard materials price per pound?
(b) If the materials quantity variance was $3,840 unfavorable, what was the standard materials quantity per unit?
(c) What were the standard hours allowed for the units produced?
(d) If the labor quantity variance was $7,200 unfavorable, what were the actual direct labor hours worked?
(e) If the labor price variance was $9,120 favorable, what was the actual rate per hour?
(f) If total budgeted manufacturing overhead was $340,000 at normal capacity, what was the predetermined overhead rate?
(g) What was the standard cost per unit of product?
(h) How much overhead was applied to production during the year?

(a) $0.96

(b) 4.3 pounds

(f) 6.80 per DLH

(h) $306,000

(j) $219,000

(i) If the fixed overhead rate was $2.00, what was the overhead volume variance?

(j) If the overhead controllable variance is $3,000 unfavorable, what were the total variable overhead costs incurred? (Assume that the overhead controllable variance relates only to variable costs.)

(k) Using one or more answers above, what were the total costs assigned to work in process?

Compute variances, prepare an income statement, and explain unfavorable variances.
(SO 4, 5, 7)

P22-5B Farm Labs, Inc. provides mad cow disease testing for both state and federal governmental agricultural agencies. Because the company's customers are governmental agencies, prices are strictly regulated. Therefore, Farm Labs must constantly monitor and control its testing costs. Shown below are the standard costs for a typical test.

Direct materials (2 test tubes @ $1.50 per tube)	$ 3
Direct labor (1 hour @ $25 per hour)	25
Variable overhead (1 hour @ $5 per hour)	5
Fixed overhead (1 hour @ $10 per hour)	10
Total standard cost per test	$43

The lab does not maintain an inventory of test tubes. Therefore, the tubes purchased each month are used that month. Actual activity for the month of November 2007, when 1,500 tests were conducted, resulted in the following:

Direct materials (3,050 test tubes)	$ 4,270
Direct labor (1,600 hours)	36,800
Variable overhead	7,400
Fixed overhead	14,000

Monthly budgeted fixed overhead is $14,000. Revenues for the month were $75,000, and selling and administrative expenses were $4,000.

Instructions

(a) MPV $305 F
LQV $2,500 U
OCV $100 F
(b) NI $8,530

(a) Compute the price and quantity variances for direct materials and direct labor, and for overhead the controllable and volume variances.

(b) Prepare an income statement for management.

(c) Provide possible explanations for each unfavorable variance.

Journalize and post standard cost entries, and prepare income statement.
(SO 4, 5, 7, 9)

*P22-6B Berman Corporation uses standard costs with its job order cost accounting system. In January, an order (Job No. 12) for 1,950 units of Product B was received. The standard cost of one unit of Product B is as follows.

Direct materials	3 pounds at $1.00 per pound	$ 3.00
Direct labor	1 hour at $8.00 per hour	8.00
Overhead	2 hours (variable $4.00 per machine hour; fixed $2.25 per machine hour)	12.50
Standard cost per unit		$23.50

Normal capacity for the month was 4,200 machine hours. During January, the following transactions applicable to Job No. 12 occurred.

1. Purchased 6,250 pounds of raw materials on account at $1.04 per pound.
2. Requisitioned 6,250 pounds of raw materials for Job No. 12.
3. Incurred 2,200 hours of direct labor at a rate of $7.75 per hour.
4. Worked 2,200 hours of direct labor on Job No. 12.
5. Incurred manufacturing overhead on account $25,800.
6. Applied overhead to Job No. 12 on basis of standard machine hours used.
7. Completed Job No. 12.
8. Billed customer for Job No. 12 at a selling price of $70,000.
9. Incurred selling and administrative expenses on account $2,000.

Instructions

(a) MPV $250 U
LPV $550 F

(d) NI $18,650

(a) Journalize the transactions.

(b) Post to the job order cost accounts.

(c) Prepare the entry to recognize the overhead variances.

(d) Prepare the January 2007 income statement for management.

Problems: Set C

Visit the book's website at **www.wiley.com/college/kimmel** and choose the student Companion site to access Problem Set C.

Group Decision Case

BYP22-1   Agmar Professionals, a management consulting firm, specializes in strategic planning for financial institutions. Tim Agler and Jill Marlin, partners in the firm, are assembling a new strategic planning model for use by clients. The model is designed for use on most personal computers and replaces a rather lengthy manual model currently marketed by the firm. To market the new model Tim and Jill will need to provide clients with an estimate of the number of labor hours and computer time needed to operate the model. The model is currently being test marketed at five small financial institutions. These financial institutions are listed below, along with the number of combined computer/labor hours used by each institution to run the model one time.

Financial Institutions	Computer/Labor Hours Required
Midland National	25
First State	45
Financial Federal	40
Pacific America	30
Lakeview National	30
Total	170
Average	34

Any company that purchases the new model will need to purchase user manuals for the system. User manuals will be sold to clients in cases of 20, at a cost of $300 per case. One manual must be used each time the model is run because each manual includes a nonreusable computer-accessed password for operating the system. Also required are specialized computer forms that are sold only by Agmar. The specialized forms are sold in packages of 250, at a cost of $50 per package. One application of the model requires the use of 50 forms. This amount includes two forms that are generally wasted in each application due to printer alignment errors. The overall cost of the strategic planning model to clients is $12,000. Most clients will use the model four times annually.

Agmar must provide its clients with estimates of ongoing costs incurred in operating the new planning model, and would like to do so in the form of standard costs.

Instructions

With the class divided into groups, answer the following.
(a) What factors should be considered in setting a standard for computer/labor hours?
(b) What alternatives for setting a standard for computer/labor hours might be used?
(c) What standard for computer/labor hours would you select? Justify your answer.
(d) Determine the standard materials cost associated with the user manuals and computer forms for each application of the strategic planning model.

Managerial Analysis

BYP22-2   Mo Vaughn and Associates is a medium-sized company located near a large metropolitan area in the Midwest. The company manufactures cabinets of mahogany, oak, and other fine woods for use in expensive homes, restaurants, and hotels. Although some of the work is custom, many of the cabinets are a standard size.

One such non-custom model is called Luxury Base Frame. Normal production is 1,000 units. Each unit has a direct labor hour standard of 5 hours. Overhead is applied to production based on standard direct labor hours. During the most recent month, only 900 units were produced; 4,500 direct labor hours were allowed for standard production, but only 4,000 hours were used. Standard and actual overhead costs were as follows.

	Standard (1,000 units)	Actual (900 units)
Indirect materials	$ 12,000	$ 12,300
Indirect labor	48,000	51,000
(Fixed) Manufacturing supervisors salaries	22,000	22,000

	Standard (1,000 units)	Actual (900 units)
(Fixed) Manufacturing office employees salaries	13,000	11,500
(Fixed) Engineering costs	26,000	25,000
Computer costs	10,000	10,000
Electricity	2,500	2,500
(Fixed) Manufacturing building depreciation	8,000	8,000
(Fixed) Machinery depreciation	3,000	3,000
(Fixed) Trucks and forklift depreciation	1,500	1,500
Small tools	700	1,400
(Fixed) Insurance	500	500
(Fixed) Property taxes	300	300
Total	$147,500	$149,000

Instructions

(a) Determine the overhead application rate.

(b) Determine how much overhead was applied to production.

(c) Calculate the controllable overhead variance and the overhead volume variance.

(d) Decide which overhead variances should be investigated.

(e) Discuss causes of the overhead variances. What can management do to improve its performance next month?

Real-World Focus

BYP22-3 Glassmaster Co. is organized as two divisions and one subsidiary. One division focuses on the manufacture of filaments such as fishing line and sewing thread; the other division manufactures antennas and specialty fiberglass products. Its subsidiary manufactures flexible steel wire controls and molded control panels.

The annual report of Glassmaster provides the following information.

GLASSMASTER COMPANY
Management Discussion

Gross profit margins for the year improved to 20.9% of sales compared to last year's 18.5%. All operations reported improved margins due in large part to improved operating efficiencies as a result of cost reduction measures implemented during the second and third quarters of the fiscal year and increased manufacturing throughout due to higher unit volume sales. Contributing to the improved margins was a favorable materials price variance due to competitive pricing by suppliers as a result of soft demand for petrochemical-based products. This favorable variance is temporary and will begin to reverse itself as stronger worldwide demand for commodity products improves in tandem with the economy. Partially offsetting these positive effects on profit margins were competitive pressures on sales prices of certain product lines. The company responded with pricing strategies designed to maintain and/or increase market share.

Instructions

(a) Is it apparent from the information whether Glassmaster utilizes standard costs?

(b) Do you think the price variance experienced should lead to changes in standard costs for the next fiscal year?

Exploring the Web

BYP22-4   The Caelus Management System (CMS), is a real-time, fully integrated decision support, operational control, and financial management system.

Address: **www.caelus.com**
    (*or go to* **www.wiley.com/college/kimmel**)

Steps
1. Choose **CMS Product Info** and answer part (a), below.
2. Choose **Standard Cost** and answer parts (b) and (c).

Instructions
(a) List some of the modules that are familiar to you.
(b) What types of decisions does this module of the software support?
(c) Does this product distinguish between fixed and variable costs?

Communication Activity

BYP22-5 The setting of standards is critical to the effective use of standards in evaluating performance.

Instructions
Explain the following in a memo to your instructor.
(a) The comparative advantages and disadvantages of ideal versus normal standards.
(b) The factors that should be included in setting the price and quantity standards for direct materials, direct labor, and manufacturing overhead.

Research Assignment

BYP22-6 The June 14, 2004, edition of SmartPros.com contains an article titled "'7 Habits' Author Says Workers Need Four Basic Disciplines of Execution."

Instructions
Read the article at *http://www.smartpros.com/x43931.xml*; answer the following questions.
(a) What are the author's four "disciplines of execution"?
(b) What are some of the potential downfalls of having too many goals, and what are the characteristics of effective goal setting?
(c) What approach for planning does the author suggest?
(d) What are the processes of a good staff meeting?

Ethics Case

BYP22-7 At Camden Manufacturing Company, production workers in the Painting Department are paid on the basis of productivity. The labor time standard for a unit of production is established through periodic time studies conducted by the Foster Management Department. In a time study, the actual time required to complete a specific task by a worker is observed. Allowances are then made for preparation time, rest periods, and clean-up time. Dan Renfro is one of several veterans in the Painting Department.

Dan is informed by Foster Management that he will be used in the time study for the painting of a new product. The findings will be the basis for establishing the labor time standard for the next 6 months. During the test, Dan deliberately slows his normal work pace in an effort to obtain a labor time standard that will be easy to meet. Because it is a new product, the Foster Management representative who conducted the test is unaware that Dan did not give the test his best effort.

Instructions
(a) Who was benefited and who was harmed by Dan's actions?
(b) Was Dan ethical in the way he performed the time study test?
(c) What measure(s) might the company take to obtain valid data for setting the labor time standard?

Answers to Self-Study Questions
1. c   2. d   3. b   4. c   5. b   6. a   7. d   8. a   9. b   10. d   *11. c

REMEMBER TO GO BACK TO THE NAVIGATOR BOX ON THE CHAPTER-OPENING PAGE AND CHECK OFF YOUR COMPLETED WORK.

CHAPTER 23

Incremental Analysis and Capital Budgeting

After studying this chapter,
you should be able to:

1 Identify the steps in management's decision-making process.

2 Describe the concept of incremental analysis.

3 Identify the relevant costs in accepting an order at a special price.

4 Identify the relevant costs in a make-or-buy decision.

5 Give the decision rule for whether to sell or process materials further.

6 Identify the factors to consider in retaining or replacing equipment.

7 Explain the relevant factors in whether to eliminate an unprofitable segment.

8 Determine which products to make and sell when resources are limited.

9 Contrast annual rate of return and cash payback in capital budgeting.

10 Distinguish between the net present value and internal rate of return methods.

THE NAVIGATOR

FEATURE STORY

Soup Is Good Food

When you hear the word *Campbell,* what is the first thing that comes to mind? Soup. Campbell *is* soup. It sells 38 percent of all the soup—including homemade—consumed in the United States.

But can a company survive on soup alone? In an effort to expand its operations and to lessen its reliance on soup, Campbell Soup Company in 1990 began searching for an additional line of business. Campbell's management believed it saw an opportunity in convenient meals that were low in fat, nutritionally rich, and had therapeutic value for heart patients and diabetics. This venture would require a huge investment—but the rewards were potentially tremendous.

The initial investment required building food labs, hiring nutritional scientists, researching prototype products, constructing new production facilities, and marketing the new products. Management predicted that with an initial investment of roughly $55 million, the company might generate sales of $200 million per year.

By 1994 the company had created 24 meals, and an extensive field-study revealed considerable health benefits from the products. Unfortunately, initial sales of the new product line, called Intelligent Quisine, were less than stellar. In 1997 Campbell hired a consulting firm to evaluate whether to continue the project. Product development of the new line was costing $20 million per year—a sum that some managers felt could be better spent developing new products in other divisions, or expanding overseas operations. In 1998 Campbell discontinued the project.

Campbell was not giving up on growth, but simply had decided to refocus its efforts on soup. The company's annual report stated management's philosophy: "Soup will be our growth engine." Campbell has sold off many of its non-soup businesses and in a recent year introduced 20 new soup products.

Source: Vanessa O'Connell, "Food for Thought: How Campbell Saw a Breakthrough Menu Turn into Leftovers," *Wall Street Journal,* October 6, 1998.

✔ THE NAVIGATOR

- Scan *Study Objectives*
- Read *Feature Story*
- Read *Preview*
- Read text and answer *Before You Go On* p. xx
- Work *Demonstration Problem 1*
- Read text and answer *Before You Go On* p. xx
- Work *Demonstration Problem 2*
- Review *Summary of Study Objectives*
- Answer *Self-Study Questions*
- Complete *Assignments*

On the World Wide Web
www.compbellsoup.com.

PREVIEW OF CHAPTER 23

An important purpose of management accounting is to provide relevant information for decision making. Examples of these decisions include the following: (1) Campbell Soup's decision to produce "therapeutic meals" rather than some other food product. (2) Boeing's strategic decisions to spend $5 billion to build a plane for the 21st century—the B-777—and to cancel development of a larger version of the B-747. (3) The Coca-Cola Company's decision to spend $750 million to build twelve plants in Russia.

This chapter begins with an explanation of management's decision-making process. It then considers the topics of incremental analysis and capital budgeting. The content and organization of Chapter 23 are as follows.

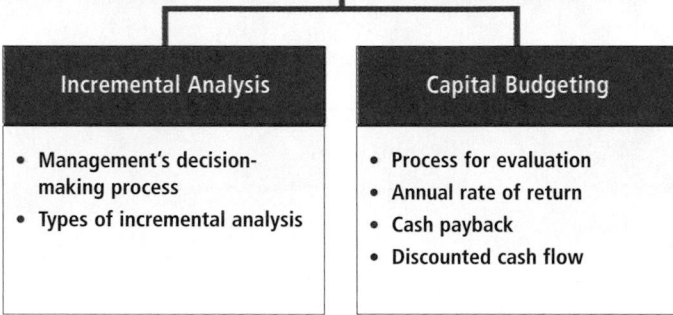

INCREMENTAL ANALYSIS AND CAPITAL BUDGETING

Incremental Analysis	Capital Budgeting
• Management's decision-making process • Types of incremental analysis	• Process for evaluation • Annual rate of return • Cash payback • Discounted cash flow

THE NAVIGATOR

SECTION ONE
INCREMENTAL ANALYSIS

STUDY OBJECTIVE

1

Identify the steps in Managements decision-making process

Management's Decision-Making Process

Making decisions is an important management function. Management's decision-making process does not always follow a set pattern, because decisions vary significantly in their scope, urgency, and importance. It is possible, though, to identify some steps that are frequently involved in the process. These steps are shown in Illustration 23-1.

Accounting's contribution to the decision-making process occurs primarily in Steps 2 and 4—evaluating possible courses of action, and reviewing the results. In

Illustration 23-1
Management's decision-making process

1. Identify the problem and assign responsibility → **2.** Determine and evaluate possible courses of action → **3.** Make a decision → **4.** Review results of the decision

Step 2, for each possible course of action, accounting provides relevant revenue and cost data. These show the expected overall effect on net income. In Step 4, accounting prepares internal reports that review the actual impact of the decision.

In making business decisions, management ordinarily considers both financial and nonfinancial information. *Financial information* is related to revenues and costs and their effect on the company's overall profitability. *Nonfinancial information* relates to such factors as the effect of the decision on employee turnover, the environment, or the overall image of the company in the community. Although the nonfinancial information can be as important as the financial information, we will focus primarily on financial information that is relevant to the decision.

THE INCREMENTAL ANALYSIS APPROACH

Decisions involve a choice among alternative courses of action. Suppose that you were deciding whether to purchase or lease a computer for use in doing your accounting homework. The financial data relate to the cost of leasing versus the cost of purchasing. For example, leasing would involve periodic lease payments; purchasing would require "up-front" payment of the purchase price. In other words, the financial data relevant to the decision are the data that would vary among the possible alternatives. The process used to identify the financial data that change under alternative courses of action is called **incremental analysis**. In some cases, you will find that when you use incremental analysis, both costs **and** revenues will change. In other cases, only costs **or** revenues will change.

Just as your decision to buy or lease a PC will affect your future, similar decisions, on a larger scale, will affect a company's future. Incremental analysis identifies the probable effects of those decisions on future earnings. Such analysis inevitably involves estimates and uncertainty. Gathering data for incremental analyses may involve market analysts, engineers, and accountants. In quantifying the data, the accountant is expected to produce the most reliable information available at the time the decision must be made.

STUDY OBJECTIVE 2
Describe the concept of incremental analysis.

Alternative Terminology
Incremental analysis is also called *differential analysis* because the analysis focuses on differences.

HOW INCREMENTAL ANALYSIS WORKS

The following example illustrates the basic approach in incremental analysis.

Illustration 23-2
Basic approach in incremental analysis

	Alternative A	Alternative B	Net Income Increase (Decrease)
Revenues	$125,000	$110,000	$ (15,000)
Costs	100,000	80,000	20,000
Net income	$ 25,000	$ 30,000	$ 5,000

This example compares alternative B with alternative A. The net income column shows the differences between the alternatives. In this case, incremental revenue will be $15,000 less under alternative B than under alternative A, but a $20,000 incremental cost saving will be realized.[1] Thus, alternative B will produce $5,000 more net income than alternative A.

Incremental analysis sometimes involves changes that at first glance might seem contrary to your intuition. For example, sometimes variable costs *do not change* under the alternative courses of action. Also, sometimes fixed costs *do*

[1] Although income taxes are sometimes important in incremental analysis, they are ignored in the chapter for simplicity's sake.

change. For example, direct labor, normally a variable cost, is not an incremental cost in deciding between two new factory machines if each asset requires the same amount of direct labor. In contrast, rent expense, normally a fixed cost, is an incremental cost in a decision to continue occupancy of a building or to purchase or lease a new building.

Types of Incremental Analysis

A number of different types of decisions involve incremental analysis. The more common types of decisions are:

1. Accept an order at a special price.
2. Make or buy.
3. Sell or process further.
4. Retain or replace equipment.
5. Eliminate an unprofitable business segment.
6. Allocate limited resources.

We will consider each of these types of analysis in the following pages.

ACCEPT AN ORDER AT A SPECIAL PRICE

STUDY OBJECTIVE

3

Identify the relevant costs in accepting an order at a special price.

Sometimes, a company may have an opportunity to obtain additional business if it is willing to make a major price concession to a specific customer. To illustrate, assume that Sunbelt Company produces 100,000 automatic blenders per month, which is 80% of plant capacity. Variable manufacturing costs are $8 per unit. Fixed manufacturing costs are $400,000, or $4 per unit. The blenders are normally sold directly to retailers at $20 each. Sunbelt has an offer from Mexico Co. (a foreign wholesaler) to purchase an additional 2,000 blenders at $11 per unit. Acceptance of the offer would not affect normal sales of the product, and the additional units can be manufactured without increasing plant capacity. What should management do?

Helpful Hint This is a good example of different costs for different purposes. In the long-run all costs are relevant, but for this decision only costs that change are relevant.

If management makes its decision on the basis of the total cost per unit of $12 ($8 + $4), the order would be rejected, because costs ($12) would exceed revenues ($11) by $1 per unit. However, since the units can be produced within existing plant capacity, the special order **will not increase fixed costs**. The relevant data for the decision, therefore, are the variable manufacturing costs per unit of $8 and the expected revenue of $11 per unit. Thus, as shown in Illustration 23-3, Sunbelt will increase its net income by $6,000 by accepting this special order.

Illustration 23-3
Incremental analysis—accepting an order at a special price

	A	B	C	D
		Reject Order	**Accept Order**	**Net Income Increase (Decrease)**
2	Revenues	$0	$22,000	**$ 22,000**
3	Costs	0	16,000	**(16,000)**
4	Net income	$0	$ 6,000	**$ 6,000**

Accepting an order at a special price.xls — File Edit View Insert Format Tools Data Window Help

Two points should be emphasized: First, we assume that sales of the product in other markets would not be affected by this special order. If other sales were affected, then Sunbelt would have to consider the lost sales in making the decision. Second, if Sunbelt is operating at full capacity, it is likely that the special order would be rejected. Under such circumstances, the company would have to expand plant capacity. In that case, the special order would have to absorb these additional fixed manufacturing costs, as well as the variable manufacturing costs.

MAKE OR BUY

When a manufacturer assembles component parts in producing a finished product, management must decide whether to make or buy the components. For example, General Motors Corporation may either make or buy the batteries, tires, and radios used in its cars. Similarly, Hewlett-Packard Corporation may make or buy the electronic circuitry, cases, and printer heads for its printers. The decision to make or buy components should be made on the basis of incremental analysis.

To illustrate the analysis, assume that Baron Company incurs the following annual costs in producing 25,000 ignition switches for motor scooters.

STUDY OBJECTIVE

4

Identify the relevant costs in a make-or-buy decision.

Direct materials	$ 50,000
Direct labor	75,000
Variable manufacturing overhead	40,000
Fixed manufacturing overhead	60,000
Total manufacturing costs	$225,000
Total cost per unit ($225,000 ÷ 25,000)	**$9.00**

Illustration 23-4
Annual product cost data

Or, instead of making its own switches, Baron Company might purchase the ignition switches from Ignition Inc. at a price of $8 per unit. The question again is, "What should management do?"

At first glance, it appears that management should purchase the ignition switches for $8, rather than make them at a cost of $9. However, a review of operations indicates that if Baron purchases the ignition switches from Ignition Inc., it will eliminate *all* of its variable costs but only $10,000 of its fixed manufacturing costs. Thus, $50,000 of the fixed manufacturing costs will remain if the ignition switches are purchased. The relevant costs for incremental analysis, therefore, are as follows.

Illustration 23-5
Incremental analysis—make or buy

```
Incremental Analysis - Make or buy.xls
  File    Edit    View    Insert    Format    Tools    Data    Window    Help
```

	A	B	C	D
1		Make	Buy	Net Income Increase (Decrease)
2	Direct materials	$ 50,000	$ 0	$ 50,000
3	Direct labor	75,000	0	75,000
4	Variable manufacturing costs	40,000	0	40,000
5	Fixed manufacturing costs	60,000	50,000	10,000
6	Purchase price (25,000 × $8)	0	200,000	(200,000)
7	Total annual cost	$225,000	$250,000	$ (25,000)
8				

This analysis indicates that Baron Company will incur $25,000 of additional costs by buying the ignition switches. Therefore, Baron should continue to make the ignition switches, even though the total manufacturing cost is $1 higher than the purchase price. The reason is that if the company purchases the ignition switches, it will still have fixed costs of $50,000 to absorb.

Opportunity Cost

The foregoing make-or-buy analysis is complete only if the productive capacity used to make the ignition switches cannot be converted to another purpose. If there is an opportunity to use this productive capacity in some other manner, then this opportunity cost must be considered. **Opportunity cost** is the potential benefit that may be obtained by following an alternative course of action.

To illustrate, assume that through buying the switches, Baron Company can use the released productive capacity to generate additional income of $28,000. This lost income is an additional cost of continuing to make the switches in the

Helpful Hint In the make-or-buy decision it is important for management to take into account the social impact of their choice. For instance, buying may be the most economically feasible solution, but such action could result in the closure of a manufacturing plant that employs many good workers.

make-or-buy decision. This opportunity cost therefore is added to the "Make" column, for comparison. As shown, it is now advantageous to buy the ignition switches.

Illustration 23-6
Incremental analysis—
make or buy, with
opportunity cost

Incremental Analysis - Make or buy with opportunity cost.xls			
File Edit View Insert Format Tools Data Window Help			
A	**B**	**C**	**D**
1	**Make**	**Buy**	**Net Income Increase (Decrease)**
2 Total annual cost	$225,000	$250,000	$(25,000)
3 **Opportunity cost**	**28,000**	0	**28,000**
4 Total cost	$253,000	$250,000	$ 3,000
5			

The qualitative factors in this decision include the possible loss of jobs for employees who produce the ignition switches. In addition, management must assess how long the supplier will be able to satisfy the company's quality control standards at the quoted price per unit.

Accounting across the Organization

Consider the make-or-buy decision faced by Superior Industries International, Inc., a big aluminum-wheel maker in Van Nuys, California. For years, president Steve Borick had ignored the possibility of Chinese manufacturing. Then Mr. Borick started getting a blunt message from General Motors and Ford, with whom Superior does 85% of its business: Match the prices of Chinese wheel suppliers. Both auto makers said separately that if Superior could not agree to the lower prices, they would go directly to Chinese manufacturers or turn to other North American wheel-makers.

Stories like this, repeated in various industries, illustrate why manufacturers engage in overseas *off-shoring* (outsourcing). For example, compare the relative labor costs in major auto-producing nations, in dollars per hour, to see why incremental analysis often leads to outsourcing production to countries like China.

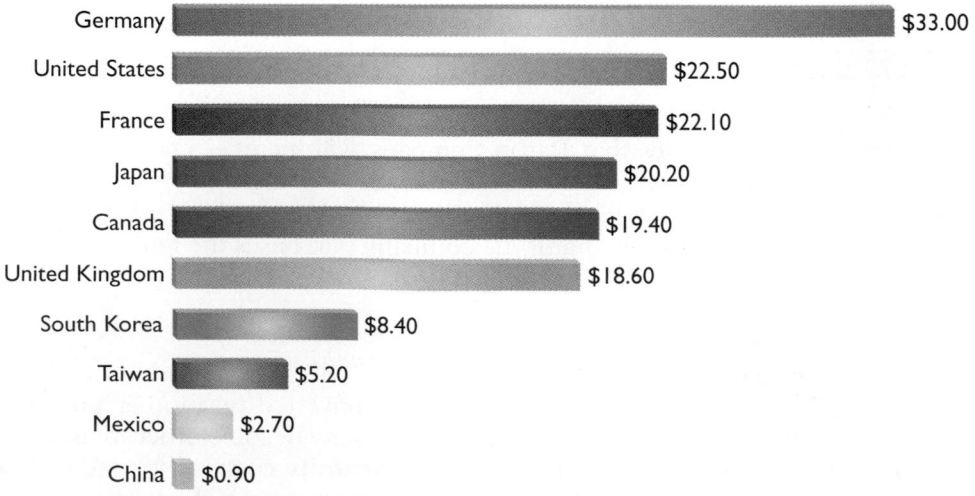

Germany	$33.00
United States	$22.50
France	$22.10
Japan	$20.20
Canada	$19.40
United Kingdom	$18.60
South Korea	$8.40
Taiwan	$5.20
Mexico	$2.70
China	$0.90

Source: Norihiko Shirouzu, "Big Three's Outsourcing Plan: Make Parts Suppliers Do It," *Wall Street Journal,* June 10, 2004, p. A1.

SELL OR PROCESS FURTHER

Many manufacturers have the option of selling products at a given point in the production cycle or continuing to process with the expectation of selling them at a higher price. For example, a bicycle manufacturer such as Schwinn could sell its 10-speed bicycles to retailers either unassembled or assembled. A furniture manufacturer such as Ethan Allen could sell its dining room sets to furniture stores either unfinished or finished. The sell-or-process-further decision should be made on the basis of incremental analysis. The basic decision rule is: **Process further as long as the incremental revenue from such processing exceeds the incremental processing costs.**

Assume, for example, that Woodmasters Inc. makes tables. The cost to manufacture an unfinished table is $35, computed as follows.

STUDY OBJECTIVE **5**

Give the decision rule for whether to sell or process materials further.

Direct material	$15
Direct labor	10
Variable manufacturing overhead	6
Fixed manufacturing overhead	4
Manufacturing cost per unit	**$35**

Illustration 23-7
Per unit cost of unfinished table

The selling price per unfinished unit is $50. Woodmasters currently has unused productive capacity that is expected to continue indefinitely. Management concludes that some of this capacity can be used to finish the tables and sell them at $60 per unit. For a finished table, direct materials will increase $2 and direct labor costs will increase $4. Variable manufacturing overhead costs will increase by $2.40 (60% of direct labor). No increase is anticipated in fixed manufacturing overhead. Illustration 23-8 shows the incremental analysis on a per unit basis.

Illustration 23-8
Incremental analysis—sell or process further

	Sell	Process Further	Net Income Increase (Decrease)
Sales per unit	$50.00	$60.00	$10.00
Cost per unit			
Direct materials	15.00	17.00	(2.00)
Direct labor	10.00	14.00	(4.00)
Variable manufacturing overhead	6.00	8.40	(2.40)
Fixed manufacturing overhead	4.00	4.00	0.00
Total	35.00	43.40	(8.40)
Net income per unit	$15.00	$16.60	$ 1.60

Helpful Hint Current net income is known. Net income from processing further is an estimate. In making its decision, management could add a "risk" factor for the estimate.

It would be advantageous for Woodmaster to process the tables further. The incremental revenue of $10.00 from the additional processing is $1.60 higher than the incremental processing costs of $8.40.

RETAIN OR REPLACE EQUIPMENT

STUDY OBJECTIVE
6
Identify the factors to
consider in retaining or
replacing equipment.

Management often has to decide whether to continue using an asset or replace it. To illustrate, assume that Jeffcoat Company has a factory machine with a book value of $40,000 and a remaining useful life of four years. A new machine is available that costs $120,000. It is expected to have zero salvage value at the end of its four-year useful life. If Jeffcoat acquires the new machine, variable manufacturing costs are expected to decrease from $160,000 to $125,000 annually, and the old unit will be scrapped. The incremental analysis for the four-year period is as follows.

Illustration 23-9
Incremental analysis—
retain or replace
equipment

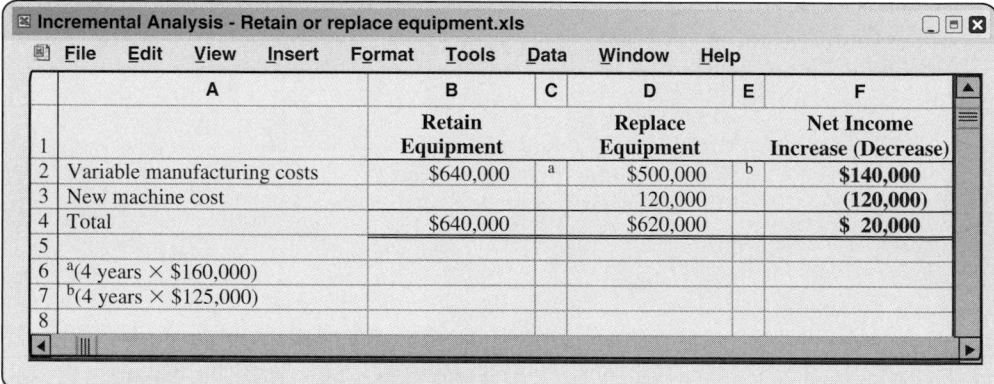

In this case, it is advantageous to replace the equipment. The lower variable manufacturing costs related to the new equipment more than offset its purchase cost.

One other point should be mentioned regarding Jeffcoat's decision: **The book value of the old machine does not affect the decision.** Book value is a **sunk cost**, which is a cost that cannot be changed by any present or future decision. Sunk costs **are not relevant in incremental analysis.** In this example, if the company retains the asset, book value will be depreciated over its remaining useful life. Or, if the company acquires the new unit, book value will be recognized as a loss of the current period. Thus, the effect of book value on current and future earnings is the same regardless of the replacement decision. However, **any trade-in allowance or cash disposal value of the existing asset is relevant** to the decision, because the company will not realize this value if the old asset is continued in use.

ELIMINATE AN UNPROFITABLE SEGMENT

STUDY OBJECTIVE
7
Explain the relevant factors
in whether to eliminate an
unprofitable segment.

Management sometimes must decide whether to eliminate an unprofitable business segment. Again, the key is to focus on the relevant amounts—the data that change under the alternative courses of action. To illustrate, assume that Martina Company manufactures tennis racquets in three models: Pro, Master, and Champ. Pro and Master are profitable lines. Champ (highlighted in color in illustration 23-10) operates at a loss. Condensed income statement data for the three segments are:

Illustration 23-10
Segment income data

	Pro	Master	Champ	Total
Sales	$800,000	$300,000	**$100,000**	$1,200,000
Variable expenses	520,000	210,000	**90,000**	820,000
Contribution margin	280,000	90,000	**10,000**	380,000
Fixed expenses	80,000	50,000	**30,000**	160,000
Net income	$200,000	$ 40,000	**$(20,000)**	$ 220,000

It might be expected that total net income will increase by $20,000 to $240,000 if Martina Company eliminates the unprofitable line of racquets. However, **net income may decrease if the Champ line is discontinued**. The reason is that the other products will have to absorb the fixed expenses allocated to the Champ racquets. To illustrate, assume that the $30,000 of fixed costs applicable to the unprofitable segment are allocated ⅔ and ⅓ to the Pro and Master product lines, respectively. Fixed expenses will increase to $100,000 ($80,000 + $20,000) in the Pro line and to $60,000 ($50,000 + $10,000) in the Master line. Illustration 23-11 shows the revised income statement.

Helpful Hint A decision to discontinue a segment based solely on the bottom line—net loss—is inappropriate.

Illustration 23-11
Income data after eliminating unprofitable product line

	Pro	Master	Total
Sales	$800,000	$300,000	$1,100,000
Variable expenses	520,000	210,000	730,000
Contribution margin	280,000	90,000	370,000
Fixed expenses	**100,000**	**60,000**	160,000
Net income	$180,000	$ 30,000	$ 210,000

Total net income has decreased $10,000 ($220,000 − $210,000). This result is also obtained in the following incremental analysis of the Champ racquets.

Illustration 23-12
Incremental analysis—eliminating an unprofitable segment

Incremental Analysis - Eliminating an unprofitable segment.xls

File   Edit   View   Insert   Format   Tools   Data   Window   Help

	A	B	C	D
		Continue	Eliminate	Net Income Increase (Decrease)
2	Sales	$100,000	$ 0	$(100,000)
3	Variable costs	90,000	0	90,000
4	Contribution margin	10,000	0	(10,000)
5	Fixed costs	30,000	30,000	0
6	Net income	$(20,000)	$(30,000)	$ (10,000)

The loss in net income is attributable to the contribution margin ($10,000) that the company will not realize if it discontinues the segment.

In deciding on the future status of an unprofitable segment, management should consider the effect of elimination on related product lines. It may be possible for continuing product lines to obtain some or all of the sales lost by the discontinued product line. In some businesses, services or products may be linked—for example, free checking accounts at a bank, or coffee at a donut shop. In addition, management should consider the effect of eliminating the product line on employees who may have to be discharged or retrained.

Accounting across the Organization

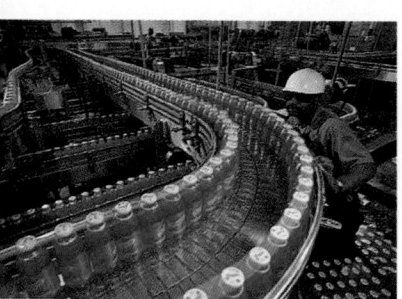

In 1994 Quaker Oats paid $1.7 billion for one of America's hottest new beverage companies. While some observers thought that Quaker Oats had overpaid, Quaker's management believed it was an exciting purchase because it would make a great strategic partner for the company's famous sport drink—Gatorade.

But, for a variety of reasons, the acquisition didn't work out. One of those reasons was that at about the same time, several other major beverage manufacturers decided to begin producing and selling competing fruit and tea drinks. Worse yet, the processing methods used by these other manufacturers appeared to allow them to produce their drinks much more inexpensively.

Only a few years after purchasing the beverage company, Quaker Oats sold it and took a $1.4 billion loss.

Decision Toolkit

Decision Checkpoints	Info Needed for Decision	Tool to Use for Decision	How to Evaluate Results
☑			
Which alternative should the company choose?	All relevant costs and opportunity costs	Compare relevant cost of each alternative.	Choose the alternative that maximizes net income.

ALLOCATE LIMITED RESOURCES

STUDY OBJECTIVE
8

Determine which products to make and sell when resources are limited.

Companies, like individuals, face limited resources. For a retail department store, the limited resource may be floor space. For a manufacturing company, the limited resource may be raw materials, direct labor hours, or machine capacity. When a company has limited resources, management must decide which products to make and sell in order to maximize net income.

To illustrate, assume that Collins Company manufactures deluxe and standard pen and pencil sets. The limiting resource is machine capacity, which is 3,600 hours per month. Relevant data consist of the following.

Illustration 23-13
Contribution margin and machine hours

	Deluxe Sets	Standard Sets
Contribution margin per unit	$8	$6
Machine hours required	0.4	0.2

Helpful Hint CM alone is not enough in this decision. The key factor is CM per limited resource.

The deluxe sets may appear to be more profitable: They have a higher contribution margin ($8) than the standard sets ($6). However, the standard sets take fewer machine hours to produce than the deluxe sets. Therefore, Collins needs to find the **contribution margin per unit of limited resource**—in this case, contribution margin per machine hour. This is obtained by dividing the contribution margin per unit of each product by the number of units of the limited resource required for each product, as shown in Illustration 23-14.

	Deluxe Sets	Standard Sets
Contribution margin per unit (**a**)	$8	$6
Machine hours required (**b**)	0.4	0.2
Contribution margin per unit of limited resource [(a) ÷ (b)]	$20	$30

Illustration 23-14
Contribution margin per unit of limited resource

The computation shows that the standard sets have a higher contribution margin per unit of limited resource. This would suggest that, given sufficient demand for standard sets, the company should shift the sales mix to standard sets or should increase machine capacity. If Collins Company is able to increase machine capacity from 3,600 hours to 4,200 hours, the additional 600 hours could be used to produce either the standard or deluxe pen and pencil sets. The total contribution margin under each alternative is found by multiplying the machine hours by the contribution margin per unit of limited resource, as shown below.

	Produce Deluxe Sets	Produce Standard Sets
Machine hours (**a**)	600	600
Contribution margin per unit of limited resource (**b**)	$20	$30
Contribution margin [(a) × (b)]	**$12,000**	**$18,000**

Illustration 23-15
Incremental analysis—computation of total contribution margin

From this analysis, we can see that to maximize net income, Collins should use all of the increased capacity to make and sell the standard sets.

Decision Toolkit

Decision Checkpoints	Info Needed for Decision	Tool to Use for Decision	How to Evaluate Results
How many units of product A and B should we produce in light of a limited resource?	Contribution margin per unit, limited resource required per unit	$$\frac{\text{Contribution margin per unit of limited resource}} {} = \frac{\text{Contribution margin per unit}}{\text{Limited resource per unit}}$$	Any additional capacity of limited resource should be applied toward the product with higher contribution margin per unit of limited resource.

BEFORE YOU GO ON . . .

►Review It

1. Give three examples of how companies might use incremental analysis.
2. What is the decision rule in deciding to sell or process products further?
3. How may the elimination of an unprofitable segment decrease the overall net income of a company?
4. What is the critical factor in allocating limited resources?

▶**Do It**

Cobb Company incurs a cost of $28 per unit, of which $18 is variable, to make a product that normally sells for $42. A foreign wholesaler offers to buy 5,000 units at $25 each. Cobb will incur shipping costs of $1 per unit. Compute the net income (loss) Cobb will realize by accepting the special order, assuming Cobb has excess operating capacity. Should Cobb Company accept the special order?

Action Plan

• Identify all revenues that will change as a result of accepting the order.
• Identify all costs that will change as a result of accepting the order, and net this amount against the change in revenues.

Solution

	Reject	**Accept**	**Net Income Increase (Decrease)**
Revenues	$–0–	$125,000	$125,000
Costs	–0–	95,000*	(95,000)
Net income	$–0–	$ 30,000	$ 30,000

*(5,000 × $18) + (5,000 × $1)

Given the result of the above analysis, Cobb Company should accept the special order.

Related exercise material: *BE23-2, BE23-3, E23-2, and E23-3.*

SECTION TWO
CAPITAL BUDGETING

Individuals make capital expenditures when they buy a new home, car, or television set. Similarly, businesses make capital expenditures when they modernize plant facilities or expand operations. Companies like Campbell Soup must constantly determine how to invest their resources. Other examples: Hollywood studios recently built 25 new sound stage projects to allow for additional filming in future years. Also, Union Pacific Resources Group Inc. announced that it would cut its capital budget by 19% in order to use the funds to reduce its outstanding debt.

In business, as for individuals, the amount of possible capital expenditures usually exceeds the funds available for such expenditures. Thus, the resources available must be allocated (budgeted) among the competing alternatives. The process of making capital expenditure decisions in business is known as **capital budgeting**. Capital budgeting involves choosing among various capital projects to find the one(s) that will maximize a company's return on its financial investment.

Process for Evaluation

Many companies follow a standard process in capital budgeting. At least once a year, top management requests proposals for projects from each department. A capital budgeting committee screens the proposals and submits its findings to the officers of the company. The officers, in turn, select the projects they believe to be most worthy of funding. They submit this list to the board of directors. Ultimately, the directors approve the capital expenditure budget for the year.

The involvement of top management and the board of directors in the process demonstrates the importance of capital budgeting decisions. These decisions often have a significant impact on a company's future profitability. In fact, poor capital budgeting decisions have led to the bankruptcy of some companies.

Accounting data are indispensable in assessing the probable effects of capital expenditures. To provide management with relevant data for capital budgeting decisions, you should be familiar with the quantitative techniques that may be used. The three most common techniques are: (1) annual rate of return, (2) cash payback, and (3) discounted cash flow. We demonstrate each of these techniques in the following sections. To illustrate the three quantitative techniques, assume that Tappan Company is considering an investment of $130,000 in new equipment. The new equipment is expected to last 10 years. It will have zero salvage value at the end of its useful life. Tappan uses the straight-line method of depreciation for accounting purposes. The expected annual revenues and costs of the new product that will be produced from the investment are:

Sales		$200,000
Less: Costs and expenses		
Manufacturing costs (exclusive of depreciation)	$145,000	
Depreciation expenses ($130,000 ÷ 10)	13,000	
Selling and administrative expenses	22,000	180,000
Income before income taxes		20,000
Income tax expense		7,000
Net income		$ 13,000

Illustration 23-16
Estimated annual net income from capital expenditure

Annual Rate of Return

The **annual rate of return technique** is based directly on accounting data. It indicates **the profitability of a capital expenditure** by dividing expected annual net income by the average investment. Illustration 23-17 shows the formula for computing annual rate of return.

STUDY OBJECTIVE
9
Contrast annual rate of return and cash payback in capital budgeting.

$$\text{Expected Annual Net Income} \div \text{Average Investment} = \text{Annual Rate of Return}$$

Illustration 23-17
Annual rate of return formula

Expected annual net income is obtained from the projected income statement. Tappan Company's expected annual net income is $13,000. Average investment is derived from the following formula.

$$\text{Average Investment} = \frac{\text{Original Investment} + \text{Value at End of Useful Life}}{2}$$

Illustration 23-18
Formula for computing average investment

The "value at the end of useful life" is the asset's salvage value, if any.

For Tappan Company, average investment is $65,000 ($130,000 + $0) ÷ 2. The expected annual rate of return for Tappan Company's investment in new equipment is therefore 20%, computed as follows:

$$\$13,000 \div \$65,000 = 20\%$$

Alternative Terminology
The minimum rate of return is also called the *hurdle rate* or *cutoff rate*.

Management then compares this annual rate of return with its required **minimum rate of return** for investments of similar risk. The minimum rate of return is generally based on the company's **cost of capital**. The cost of capital is the rate of return that management expects to pay on all borrowed and equity funds. The cost of capital is a company-wide (or sometimes a division-wide) rate; it does not relate to the cost of funding a specific project.

Helpful Hint A capital budgeting decision based on only one technique may be misleading. It is often wise to analyze the investment from a number of different perspectives.

The annual rate of return decision rule is: **A project is acceptable if its rate of return is greater than management's minimum rate of return. It is unacceptable when the reverse is true.** When the rate of return technique is used in deciding among several acceptable projects, **the higher the rate of return for a given risk, the more attractive the investment.**

The principal advantages of this technique are simplicity of calculation and management's familiarity with the accounting terms used in the computation. A major limitation of the annual rate of return approach is that it does not consider the time value of money. For example, no consideration is given as to whether cash inflows will occur early or late in the life of the investment. As explained in Appendix C at the back of the book, recognition of the time value of money can make a significant difference between the future value and the present value of an investment.

Cash Payback

The **cash payback technique** identifies the time period required to recover the cost of the capital investment from the annual cash inflow produced by the investment. Illustration 23-19 presents the formula for computing the cash payback period.

Illustration 23-19
Cash payback formula

Cost of Capital Investment	÷	Net Annual Cash Flow	=	Cash Payback Period

Helpful Hint Net annual cash flow can also be approximated by net cash provided by operating activities from the statement of cash flows.

Net annual cash flow is approximated by taking net income and adding back depreciation expense. Depreciation expense is added back because depreciation on the capital expenditure does not involve an annual outflow of cash. Accordingly, the depreciation deducted in determining net income must be added back to determine net annual cash flows.

In the Tappan Company example, net annual cash flow is $26,000, as shown below.

Illustration 23-20
Computation of net annual cash flow

Net income	$13,000
Add: Depreciation expense	13,000
Net annual cash flow	**$26,000**

The cash payback period in this example is therefore five years, computed as follows.

$$\$130,000 \div \$26,000 = 5 \text{ years}$$

Evaluation of the payback period is often related to the expected useful life of the asset. For example, assume that at Tappan Company a project is unacceptable if the payback period is longer than 60% of the asset's expected useful life. The five-year payback period in this case is 50% of the project's expected useful life. Thus, the project is acceptable.

It follows that when companies use the payback technique to decide among acceptable alternative projects, **the shorter the payback period, the more attractive the investment.** This is true for two reasons: First, the earlier the investment is recovered, the sooner the cash funds can be used for other purposes. Second, the risk of loss from obsolescence and changed economic conditions is less in a shorter payback period.

The computation of the cash payback period above assumes equal cash flows in each year of the investment's life. In many cases, this assumption is not valid. In the case of **uneven** cash flows, the cash payback period is determined when the cumulative net cash flows from the investment equal the cost of the investment.

To illustrate, assume that Chan Company proposes an investment in a new Website that is estimated to cost $300,000. Illustration 23-21 shows the proposed investment cost, annual cash net flows, cumulative net cash flows, and the cash payback period.

Year	Investment	Net Annual Cash Flow	Cumulative Net Cash Flow
0	$300,000		
1		$ 60,000	$ 60,000
2		90,000	150,000
3		90,000	240,000
4		120,000	360,000
5		100,000	460,000

Cash payback period = **3.5 years**

Illustration 23-21
Net annual cash flow schedule

As Illustration 23-21 indicates, at the end of year 3, cumulative net cash flow of $240,000 is less than the investment cost of $300,000. However, at the end of year 4 the cumulative net cash flows of $360,000 exceed the investment cost. The net cash flow needed in year 4 to equal the investment cost is $60,000 ($300,000 − $240,000). Assuming the net cash flow occurred evenly during year 4, we then divide this amount by the annual net cash flow in year 4 ($120,000) to determine the point during the year when the cash payback occurs. Thus, we get 0.50 ($60,000/$120,000), or half of the year, and the cash payback period is 3.5 years.

The cash payback technique may be useful as an initial screening tool. It also may be the most critical factor in the capital budgeting decision for a company that desires a fast turnaround of its investment because of a weak cash position. Like the annual rate of return, cash payback is relatively easy to compute and understand.

However, cash payback should not ordinarily be the only basis for the capital budgeting decision because it ignores the expected profitability of the project. To illustrate, assume that Projects X and Y have the same payback period, but Project X's useful life is double the useful life of Project Y's. Project X's earning power, therefore, is twice as long as Project Y's. A further disadvantage of this technique is that it ignores the time value of money.

Business Insight
Management Perspective

Building a new factory to produce 50-inch-plus TV screens can cost $4 billion at a time when prices for flat screens are tumbling. Now the makers of those giant liquid-crystal displays are wondering whether such investments are worth the gamble.

If LCD makers decide to hold off on new factories, price declines for widescreen TVs could slow in two or three years as production falls behind added consumer demand. But experts say a slowdown in factory building could also bring welcome relief for the industry by reducing its volatile profit swings.

Since 2000, LCD makers have been on a nonstop construction binge, building new factories to produce the latest generation of screens arriving every 18 months or so. . . .

Now, with the eighth generation of screens, the cost to build new factories is higher than ever—running between $3 billion to $4 billion each. And this generation of factories is optimized for screens measuring 50 inches or more diagonally, which so far is a much smaller potential market than that targeted by previous screen generations.

Source: Evan Ramstad, "The 50-Inch Screen Poses a Gamble," *Wall Street journal*, June 8, 2006, p. B3.

Discounted Cash Flow

The **discounted cash flow technique** is generally recognized as the best conceptual approach to making capital budgeting decisions. This technique considers both the estimated total net cash flows from the investment and the time value of money. The expected total net cash flow consists of the sum of the annual net cash flows plus the estimated liquidation proceeds when the asset is sold for salvage at the end of its useful life. But because liquidation proceeds are generally immaterial, we ignore them in subsequent discussions.

Two methods are used with the discounted cash flow technique: (1) net present value, and (2) internal rate of return. **Before we discuss the methods, we recommend that you examine Appendix C if you need a review of present value concepts.**

NET PRESENT VALUE METHOD

The **net present value method** involves discounting net cash flows to their present value and then comparing the present value with the capital outlay required by the investment. The difference between these two amounts is referred to as **net present value (NPV)**. The interest rate to be used in discounting the future net cash flows is the required minimum rate of return.

The NPV decision rule is this: **A proposal is acceptable when net present value is zero or positive.** This means that the rate of return on the investment equals or exceeds the required rate of return. When net present value is negative, the project is unacceptable. Illustration 23-22 shows the net present value decision criteria.

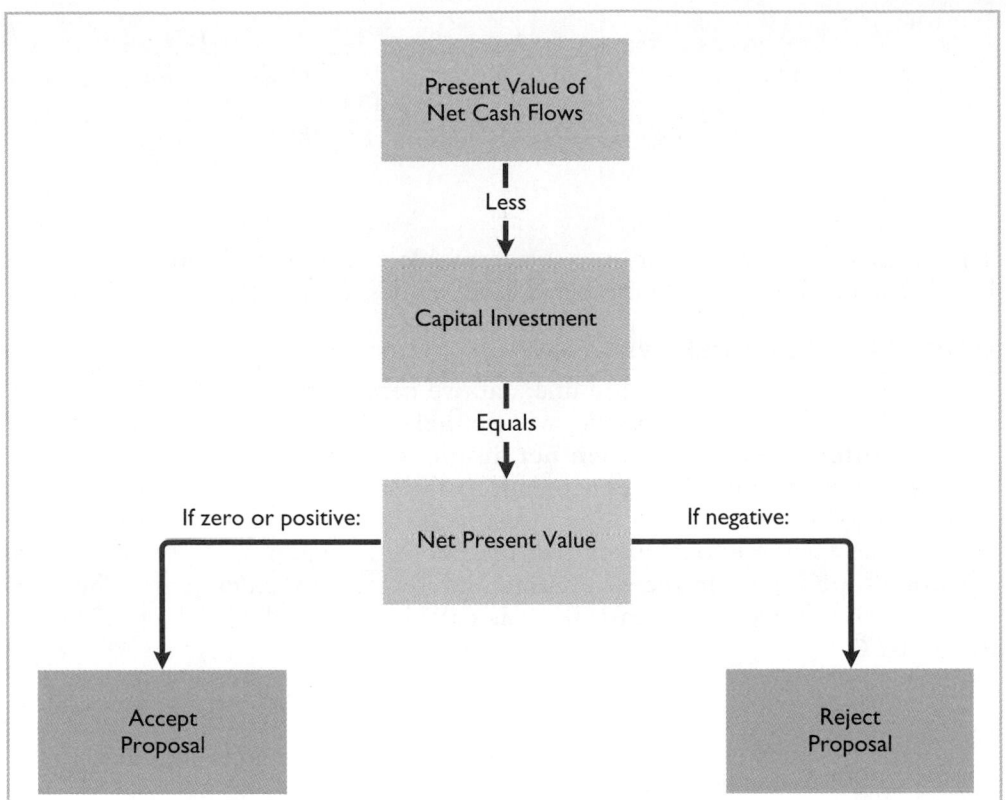

Illustration 23-22
Net present value decision criteria

When making a selection among acceptable proposals, **the higher the positive net present value, the more attractive the investment**. The next two sections demonstrate use of this method. In each case, we will assume that the investment has no salvage value.

Helpful Hint Discounted future cash flows may not take into account all of the important considerations needed to make an informed capital budgeting decision. Other issues, for example, could include worker safety, product quality, and environmental impact.

Equal Net Annual Cash Flows

Tappan Company's net annual cash flows are $26,000. If we assume this amount **is uniform over the asset's useful life**, we can compute the present value of the net annual cash flows by using the present value of an annuity of 1 for 10 periods (in Table 2, Appendix C). The computations at rates of return of 12% and 15%, respectively, are:

	Present Values at Different Discount Rates	
	12%	15%
Discount factor for 10 periods	5.65022	5.01877
Present value of net annual cash flows:		
$26,000 × 5.65022	**$146,906**	
$26,000 × 5.01877		**$130,488**

Illustration 23-23
Present value of net annual cash flows

The analysis of the proposal by the net present value method is as follows:

Illustration 23-24
Computations of net
present value

	12%	**15%**
Present value of net annual cash flows	$146,906	$130,488
Capital investment	130,000	130,000
Positive (negative) net present value	**$ 16,906**	**$ 488**

The proposed capital expenditure is acceptable at a required rate of return of both 12% and 15% because the net present values are positive.

Unequal Net Annual Cash Flows

When net annual cash flows are unequal, we cannot use annuity tables to calculate their present value. Instead, we use tables showing the **present value of a single future amount for each net annual cash flow**. To illustrate, assume that Tappan Company management expects the same aggregate net annual cash flow ($260,000) over the life of the investment. But because of a declining market demand for the new product over the life of the equipment, the net annual cash flows are higher in the early years and lower in the later years. The present value of the net annual cash flows is calculated as follows using Table 1 in Appendix C.

Illustration 23-25
Computing present value
of unequal annual cash
flows

Year	Assumed Net Annual Cash Flows	Discount Factor 12%	Discount Factor 15%	Present Value 12%	Present Value 15%
	(1)	(2)	(3)	(1) × (2)	(1) × (3)
1	$ 36,000	.89286	.86957	$ 32,143	$ 31,305
2	32,000	.79719	.75614	25,510	24,196
3	29,000	.71178	.65752	20,642	19,068
4	27,000	.63552	.57175	17,159	15,437
5	26,000	.56743	.49718	14,753	12,927
6	24,000	.50663	.43233	12,159	10,376
7	23,000	.45235	.37594	10,404	8,647
8	22,000	.40388	.32690	8,885	7,192
9	21,000	.36061	.28426	7,573	5,969
10	20,000	.32197	.24719	6,439	4,944
	$260,000			**$155,667**	**$140,061**

Therefore, the analysis of the proposal by the net present value method is as follows.

Illustration 23-26
Analysis of proposal using
net present value method

	12%	**15%**
Present value of net annual cash flows	$155,667	$140,061
Capital investment	130,000	130,000
Positive (negative) net present value	**$ 25,667**	**$ 10,061**

In this example, the present values of the net annual cash flows are greater than the $130,000 capital investment. Thus, the project is acceptable at both a 12% and 15% required rate of return. The difference between the present values using the 12% rate under equal cash flows ($146,906) and unequal net annual cash flows ($155,667) is due to the pattern of the net cash flows.

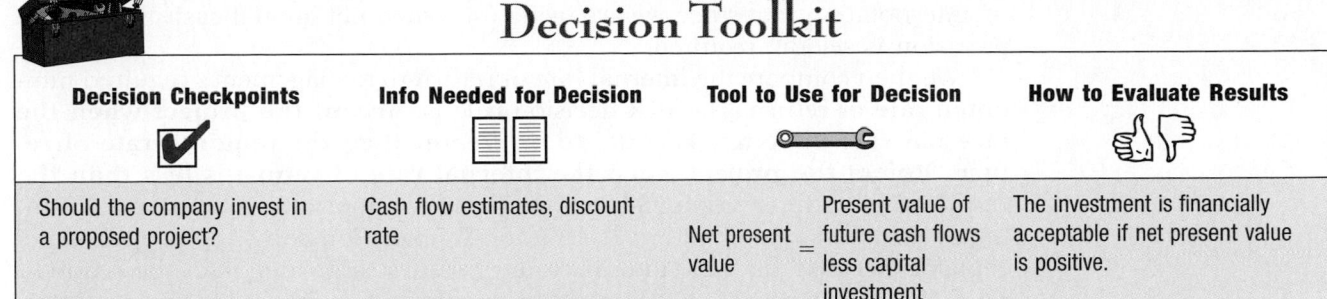

Decision Toolkit

Decision Checkpoints	Info Needed for Decision	Tool to Use for Decision	How to Evaluate Results
Should the company invest in a proposed project?	Cash flow estimates, discount rate	Net present value $=$ Present value of future cash flows less capital investment	The investment is financially acceptable if net present value is positive.

INTERNAL RATE OF RETURN METHOD

The **internal rate of return method** differs from the net present value method in that it finds the **interest yield of the potential investment**. The **internal rate of return (IRR)** is the interest rate that will cause the present value of the proposed capital expenditure to equal the present value of the expected net annual cash flows. The determination of the internal rate of return involves two steps.

Step 1. Compute the internal rate of return factor. The formula for this factor is:

$$\frac{\text{Capital}}{\text{Investment}} \div \frac{\text{Net Annual}}{\text{Cash Flows}} = \frac{\text{Internal Rate}}{\text{of Return Factor}}$$

Illustration 23-27
Formula for internal rate of return factor

The computation for the Tappan Company, assuming equal net annual cash flows,[2] is:

$$\$130,000 \div \$26,000 = 5.0$$

Step 2. Use the factor and the present value of an annuity of 1 table to find the internal rate of return. Table 2 of Appendix C is used in this step. The internal rate of return is the discount factor that is closest to the internal rate of return factor for the time period covered by the net annual cash flows.

For Tappan Company, the net annual cash flows are expected to continue for 10 years. Thus, it is necessary to read across the period-10 row in Table 2 to find the discount factor. Row 10 is reproduced below for your convenience.

TABLE 2								
PRESENT VALUE OF AN ANNUITY OF 1								
(*n*) Periods	5%	6%	8%	9%	10%	11%	12%	15%
10	7.72173	7.36009	6.71008	6.41766	6.14457	5.88923	5.65022	**5.01877**

In this case, the closest discount factor to 5.0 is 5.01877, which represents an interest rate of approximately 15%. The rate of return can be further determined

---

[2]When net annual cash flows are equal, the internal rate of return factor is the same as the cash payback period.

by interpolation, but since we are using estimated net annual cash flows, such precision is seldom required.

We then compare the internal rate of return to management's required minimum rate of return. The IRR decision rule is: **Accept the project when the internal rate of return is equal to or greater than the required rate of return. Reject the project when the internal rate of return is less than the required rate.** Illustration 23-28 shows these relationships. Assuming the minimum required rate of return is 10% for Tappan Company, the project is acceptable because the 15% internal rate of return is greater than the required rate. The IRR method is widely used in practice. Most managers find the internal rate of return easy to interpret.

Illustration 23-28
Internal rate of return
decision criteria

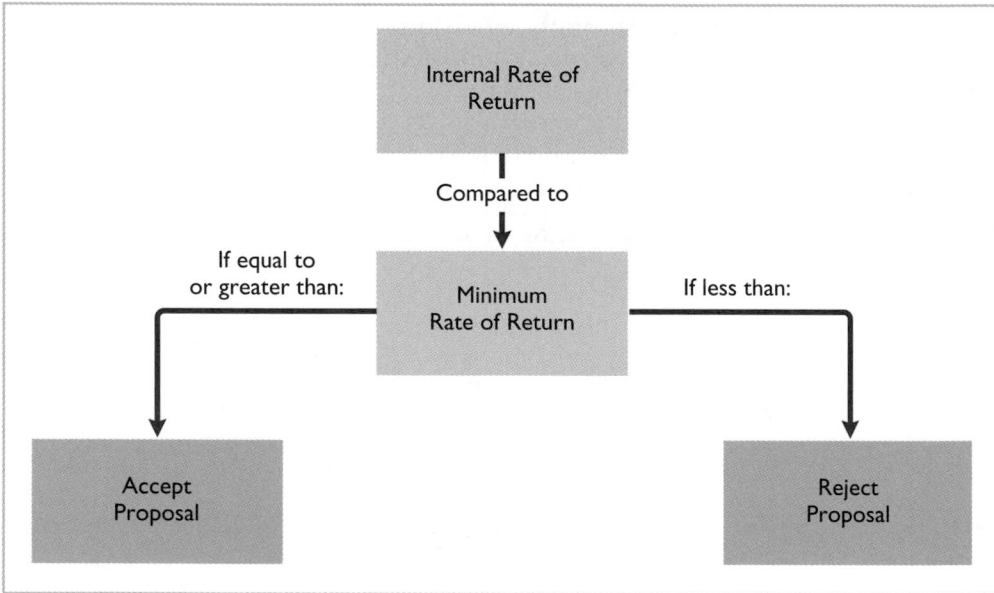

COMPARISON OF DISCOUNTED CASH FLOW METHODS

Illustration 23-29 compares the two discounted cash flow methods—net present value and internal rate of return. When properly used, either method will provide management with relevant quantitative data for making capital budgeting decisions.

Illustration 23-29
Comparison of discounted
cash flow methods

Item	Net Present Value	Internal Rate of Return
1. Objective	Compute net present value (a dollar amount).	Compute internal rate of return (a percentage).
2. Decision rule	If net present value is zero or positive, accept the proposal. If net present value is negative, reject the proposal.	If internal rate of return is equal to or greater than the minimum required rate of return, accept the proposal. If internal rate of return is less than the minimum rate, reject the proposal.

BEFORE YOU GO ON . . .

▶ **Review It**

1. What is the formula for and the decision rule in using the annual rate of return method?
2. What is the formula for the cash payback method?
3. When is a proposal acceptable under (a) the net present value method, and (b) the internal rate of return method?

THE NAVIGATOR

Using the Decision Toolkit

Suppose Hewlett-Packard Company must decide whether to make or buy some of its components from Solectron Corp. The cost of producing 50,000 electrical connectors for its printers is $110,000, broken down as follows.

| Direct materials | $60,000 | Variable overhead | $12,000 |
| Direct labor | 30,000 | Fixed overhead | 8,000 |

Instead of making the electrical connectors at an average cost per unit of $2.20 ($110,000 ÷ 50,000), the company has an opportunity to buy the connectors at $2.15 per unit. If the connectors are purchased, all variable costs and one-half of the fixed costs will be eliminated.

Instructions
(a) Prepare an incremental analysis showing whether the company should make or buy the electrical connectors.
(b) Will your answer be different if the released productive capacity resulting from the purchase of the connectors will generate additional income of $25,000?

Solution

(a)

	Make	Buy	Net Income Increase (Decrease)
Direct materials	$ 60,000	$ -0-	$ 60,000
Direct labor	30,000	-0-	30,000
Variable manufacturing costs	12,000	-0-	12,000
Fixed manufacturing costs	8,000	4,000	4,000
Purchase price	-0-	107,500	(107,500)
Total cost	$110,000	$ 111,500	$ (1,500)

This analysis indicates that Hewlett-Packard will incur $1,500 of additional costs if it buys the electrical connectors. H-P therefore would choose to make the connectors.

(b)

	Make	Buy	Net Income Increase (Decrease)
Total cost	$110,000	$111,500	$ (1,500)
Opportunity cost	25,000	–0–	25,000
Total cost	$135,000	$111,500	$ 23,500

Yes, the answer is different. The analysis shows that if additional capacity is released, net income will be increased by $23,500 if the electrical connectors are purchased. In this case, H-P would choose to purchase the connectors.

Summary of Study Objectives

1 *Identify the steps in management's decision-making process.* Management's decision-making process consists of (a) identifying the problem or opportunity, (b) assigning responsibility for the decision, (c) determining possible courses of action, (d) developing data relevant to each course of action, (e) making the decision, and (f) reviewing the results of the decision.

2 *Describe the concept of incremental analysis.* Incremental analysis identifies financial data that change under alternative courses of action. These data are relevant to the decision because they will vary in the future among the possible alternatives.

3 *Identify the relevant costs in accepting an order at a special price.* The relevant information in accepting an order at a special price is the difference between the variable manufacturing costs to produce the special order and expected revenues.

4 *Identify the relevant costs in a make-or-buy decision.* In a make-or-buy decision, the relevant costs are (a) the variable manufacturing costs that will be saved, (b) the purchase price, and (c) opportunity costs.

5 *Give the decision rule for whether to sell or process materials further.* The decision rule for whether to sell or process materials further is: Process further as long as the incremental revenue from processing exceeds the incremental processing costs.

6 *Identify the factors to consider in retaining or replacing equipment.* The factors to consider in determining whether equipment should be retained or replaced are the effects on variable costs and the cost of the new equipment. Also, any disposal value of the existing asset must be considered.

7 *Explain the relevant factors in whether to eliminate an unprofitable segment.* In deciding whether to eliminate an unprofitable segment, determine the contribution margin, if any, produced by the segment and the disposition of the segment's fixed expenses.

8 *Determine which products to make and sell when resources are limited.* When a company has limited resources, find the contribution margin per unit of limited resource. Then multiply this amount by the units of limited resource to determine which product maximizes net income.

9 *Contrast annual rate of return and cash payback in capital budgeting.* The *annual rate of return* is obtained by dividing expected annual net income by the average investment. The higher the rate of return, the more attractive the investment. The *cash payback* technique identifies the time period to recover the cost of the investment. The formula is: Cost of capital expenditure divided by estimated net annual cash flow equals cash payback period. The shorter the payback period, the more attractive the investment.

10 *Distinguish between the net present value and internal rate of return methods.* Under the *net present value* method, compare the present value of future net cash flows with the capital investment to determine net present value. The NPV decision rule is: Accept the project if net present value is zero or positive. Reject the investment if net present value is negative.

Under the *internal rate of return* method, find the interest yield of the potential investment. The IRR decision rule is: Accept the project when the internal rate of return is equal to or greater than the required rate of return. Reject the project when the internal rate of return is less than the required rate.

Decision Toolkit—A Summary

Decision Checkpoints	Info Needed for Decision	Tool to Use for Decision	How to Evaluate Results
Which alternative should the company choose?	All relevant costs and opportunity costs	Compare relevant cost of each alternative.	Choose the alternative that maximizes net income.
How many units of product A and B should we produce in light of a limited resource?	Contribution margin per unit, limited resource required per unit	$\dfrac{\text{Contribution margin per unit of limited resource}} {} = \dfrac{\text{Contribution margin per unit}}{\text{Limited resource per unit}}$	Any additional capacity of limited resource should be applied toward the product with higher contribution margin per unit of limited resource.
Should the company invest in a proposed project?	Cash flow estimates, discount rate	$\text{Net present value} = \dfrac{\text{Present value of future cash flows}}{} - \text{capital investment}$	The investment is financially acceptable if net present value is positive.
Should the company invest in a proposed project?	Estimated cash flows and the required rate of return (hurdle rate)	Internal rate of return = Interest rate that results in a net present value of zero	If the internal rate of return exceeds the specified discount rate (hurdle rate) for the project, then the project is financially acceptable.

Glossary

Annual rate of return technique Determines the profitability of a capital expenditure by dividing expected annual net income by the average investment. (p. 1123)

Capital budgeting The process of making capital expenditure decisions in business. (p. 1122)

Cash payback technique Identifies the time period required to recover the cost of a capital investment from the net annual cash flow produced by the investment. (p. 1124)

Cost of capital The rate of return that management expects to pay on all borrowed and equity funds. (p. 1124)

Discounted cash flow technique Considers both the estimated total net cash flows from the investment and the time value of money. (p. 1126)

Incremental analysis The process of identifying the financial data that change under alternative courses of action. (p. 1113)

Internal rate of return (IRR) The rate that will cause the present value of the proposed capital expenditure to equal the present value of the expected net annual cash flows. (p. 1129)

Internal rate of return method Finds the interest yield of the potential investment. (p. 1129)

Net present value (NPV) The difference that results when the original capital outlay is subtracted from the discounted net cash flows. (p. 1126)

Net present value method Discounts net cash flows to their present value and then compares that present value to the capital outlay required by the investment. (p. 1126)

Opportunity cost The potential benefit that may be obtained from following an alternative course of action. (p. 1115)

Sunk cost A cost that cannot be changed by any present or future decision. (p. 1118)

Demonstration Problem 1

Juanita Company must decide whether to make or buy some of its components. The costs of producing 50,000 electrical cords for its floor lamps are as follows.

Direct materials	$60,000	Variable overhead	$12,000
Direct labor	30,000	Fixed overhead	8,000

Instead of making the electrical cords at an average cost per unit of $2.20 ($110,000 ÷ 50,000), the company has an opportunity to buy the cords at $2.15 per unit. If the company purchases the cords, all variable costs and one-half of the fixed costs will be eliminated.

Instructions

(a) Prepare an incremental analysis showing whether the company should make or buy the electrical cords.

(b) Will your answer be different if the released productive capacity will generate additional income of $25,000?

Solution to Demonstration Problem 1

(a)

	Make	**Buy**	**Net Income Increase (Decrease)**
Direct materials	$ 60,000	$ –0–	$ 60,000
Direct labor	30,000	–0–	30,000
Variable manufacturing costs	12,000	–0–	12,000
Fixed manufacturing costs	8,000	4,000	4,000
Purchase price	–0–	107,500	(107,500)
Total cost	$110,000	$111,500	$ (1,500)

This analysis indicates that Juanita Company will incur $1,500 of additional costs if it buys the electrical cords.

(b)

	Make	**Buy**	**Net Income Increase (Decrease)**
Total cost	$110,000	$111,500	$ (1,500)
Opportunity cost	25,000		25,000
Total cost	$135,000	$111,500	$ 23,500

Yes, the answer is different because the analysis shows that net income will be increased by $23,500 if Juanita Company purchases the electrical cords.

Demonstration Problem 2

Sierra Company is considering a long-term capital investment project called ZIP. The project will require an investment of $120,000, and it will have a useful life of 4 years. Annual net income for ZIP is expected to be: Year 1 $12,000; Year 2 $10,000; Year 3 $8,000; and Year 4 $6,000. Depreciation is computed by the straight-line method with no salvage value. The company's cost of capital is 12%.

Instructions

(Round all computations to two decimal places.)

(a) Compute the annual rate of return for the project.

(b) Compute the cash payback period for the project. (Round to two decimals.)

(c) Compute the net present value for the project. (Round to nearest dollar.)

(d) Should the project be accepted? Why?

Solution to Demonstration Problem 2

(a) $9,000 ($36,000 ÷ 4) ÷ $60,000 ($120,000 ÷ 2) = 15%

(b) Depreciation expense is $120,000 ÷ 4 years = $30,000.

Net annual cash flows are:

Year 1	$12,000 + $30,000 = $42,000
Year 2	$10,000 + $30,000 = $40,000
Year 3	$8,000 + $30,000 = $38,000
Year 4	$6,000 + $30,000 = $36,000

Cumulative net cash flows would be $82,000 ($42,000 + $40,000) at the end of year 2 and $120,000 ($42,000 + $40,000 + $38,000) at the end of year 3. Since the cumulative net cash flows at the end of year 3 exactly equal the initial cash investment of $120,000, the cash payback period is 3 years.

(c)

Year	Discount Factor	Net Annual Cash Flow	Present Value
1	.89286	$42,000	$ 37,500
2	.79719	40,000	31,888
3	.71178	38,000	27,048
4	.63552	36,000	22,879
			119,315
		Capital investment	120,000
		Negative net present value	$ (685)

(d) The annual rate of return of 15% is good. However, the cash payback period is 75% of the project's useful life, and net present value is negative. The recommendation is to reject the project.

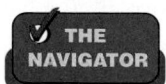
THE NAVIGATOR

Self-Study Questions

WILEY PLUS

Answers are at the end of the chapter.

(SO 1) **1.** Three of the steps in management's decision process are: (1) Review results of decision. (2) Identify the problem. (3) Make the decision. The steps are preformed in the following order.
(a) (1), (2), (3).
(b) (3), (2), (1).
(c) (2), (1), (3).
(d) (2), (3), (1).

(SO 2) **2.** Incremental analysis is the process of identifying the financial data that:
(a) do not change under alternative courses of action.
(b) change under alternative courses of action.
(c) are mixed under alternative courses of action.
(d) No correct answer is given.

(SO 3) **3.** It costs a company $14 of variable costs and $6 of fixed costs to produce product A that sells for $30. A foreign buyer offers to purchase 3,000 units at $18 each. If the special offer is accepted and produced with unused capacity, net income will:
(a) decrease $6,000.
(b) increase $6,000.
(c) increase $12,000.
(d) increase $9,000.

(SO 4) **4.** In a make-or-buy decision, relevant costs are:
(a) manufacturing costs that will be saved.
(b) the purchase price of the units.
(c) opportunity costs.
(d) all of the above.

(SO 5) **5.** The decision rule in a sell-or-process-further decision is: Process further as long as the incremental revenue from processing exceeds:
(a) incremental processing costs.
(b) variable processing costs.
(c) fixed processing costs.
(d) No correct answer is given.

6. In a decision to retain or replace equipment, the book value of the old equipment is a(n): (SO 6)
(a) opportunity cost.
(b) sunk cost.
(c) incremental cost.
(d) marginal cost.

7. If an unprofitable segment is eliminated: (SO 7)
(a) net income will always increase.
(b) variable expenses of the eliminated segment will have to be absorbed by other segments.
(c) fixed expenses allocated to the eliminated segment will have to be absorbed by other segments.
(d) net income will always decrease.

8. If the contribution margin per unit is $15 and it takes 3.0 machine hours to produce the unit, the contribution margin per unit of limited resource is: (SO 8)
(a) $25.
(b) $5.
(c) $45.
(d) No correct answer is given.

9. Which of the following is *incorrect* about the annual rate of return technique? (SO 9)
(a) The calculation is simple.
(b) The accounting terms used are familiar to management.
(c) The timing of the net cash flows is not considered.
(d) The time value of money is considered.

(SO 10) **10.** A positive net present value means that the:
  (a) project's rate of return is less than the cut-off rate.
  (b) project's rate of return exceeds the required rate of return.
  (c) project's rate of return equals the required rate of return.
  (d) project is unacceptable.

Questions

1. What steps are frequently involved in management's decision-making process?

2. Your roommate, Matt Mikan, contends that accounting contributes to most of the steps in management's decision-making process. Is your roommate correct? Explain.

3. "Incremental analysis involves the accumulation of information concerning a single course of action." Do you agree? Why?

4. Jerry Karr asks your help concerning the relevance of variable and fixed costs in incremental analysis. Help Jerry with his problem.

5. What data are relevant in deciding whether to accept an order at a special price?

6. Parney Company has an opportunity to buy parts at $7 each that currently cost $10 to make. What manufacturing costs are relevant to this make-or-buy decision?

7. Define the term "opportunity cost." How may this cost be relevant in a make-or-buy decision?

8. What is the decision rule in deciding whether to sell a product or process it further?

9. Your roommate, Betty Melton, is confused about sunk costs. Explain to your roommate the meaning of sunk costs and their relevance to a decision to retain or replace equipment.

10. Slocum Inc. has one product line that is unprofitable. What circumstances may cause overall company net income to be lower if the unprofitable product line is eliminated?

11. How is the contribution margin per unit of limited resources computed?

12. Describe the process a company may use in screening and approving the capital expenditure budget.

13. Your classmate, Laura Elder, is confused about the factors that are included in the annual rate of return technique. What is the formula for this technique?

14. Hector Ruiz is trying to understand the term "cost of capital." Define the term, and indicate its relevance to the decision rule under the annual rate of return technique.

15. Pete Hetzel claims the formula for the cash payback technique is the same as the formula for the annual rate of return technique. Is Pete correct? What is the formula for the cash payback technique?

16. What are the advantages and disadvantages of the cash payback technique?

17. Two types of present value tables may be used with the discounted cash flow technique. Identify the tables and the circumstance(s) when each table should be used.

18. What is the decision rule under the net present value method?

19. Identify the steps required in using the internal rate of return method.

20. Gillaspie Company uses the internal rate of return method. What is the decision rule for this method?

Brief Exercises

Identify the steps in management's decision-making process.
(SO 1)

BE23-1   The steps in management's decision-making process are listed in random order below. Indicate the order in which the steps should be executed.
  —Make a decision.
  —Identify the problem and assign responsibility.
  —Review results of the decision.
  —Determine and evaluate possible courses of action.

Determine incremental changes.
(SO, 2)

BE23-2   Ming Company is considering two alternatives. Alternative A will have sales of $150,000 and costs of $100,000. Alternative B will have sales of $180,000 and costs of $120,000. Compare Alternative A to Alternative B showing incremental revenues, costs, and net income.

Determine whether to accept a special order.
(SO 3)

BE23-3   In Karnes Company it costs $30 per unit ($20 variable and $10 fixed) to make a product that normally sells for $45. A foreign wholesaler offers to buy 4,000 units at $23 each. Karnes will incur special shipping costs of $1 per unit. Assuming that Karnes has excess operating capacity, indicate the net income (loss) Karnes would realize by accepting the special order.

BE23-4 Bartley Manufacturing incurs unit costs of $8 ($5 variable and $3 fixed) in making a sub-assembly part for its finished product. A supplier offers to make 10,000 of the part at $5.30 per unit. If the offer is accepted, Bartley will save all variable costs but no fixed costs. Prepare an analysis showing the total cost saving, if any, Bartley will realize by buying the part.

Determine whether to make or buy a part.
(SO 4)

BE23-5 Stanton Inc. makes unfinished bookcases that it sells for $60. Production costs are $30 variable and $10 fixed. Because it has unused capacity, Stanton is considering finishing the bookcases and selling them for $72. Variable finishing costs are expected to be $8 per unit with no increase in fixed costs. Prepare an analysis on a per unit basis showing whether Stanton should sell unfinished or finished bookcases.

Determine whether to sell or process further.
(SO 5)

BE23-6 Felton Company has a factory machine with a book value of $90,000 and a remaining useful life of 4 years. A new machine is available at a cost of $200,000. This machine will have a 4-year useful life with no salvage value. The new machine will lower annual variable manufacturing costs from $600,000 to $440,000. Prepare an analysis showing whether the old machine should be retained or replaced.

Determine whether to retain or replace equipment.
(SO 6)

BE23-7 Derby, Inc. manufactures golf clubs in three models. For the year, the Eagle line has a net loss of $20,000 from sales $200,000, variable expenses $180,000, and fixed expenses $40,000. If the Eagle line is eliminated, $34,000 of fixed costs will remain. Prepare an analysis showing whether the Eagle line should be eliminated.

Determine whether to eliminate an unprofitable segment.
(SO 7)

BE23-8 In Nevitt Company, data concerning two products are: Contribution margin per unit—Product A $11, Product B $12; machine hours required for one unit—Product A 2, Product B 2.5. Compute the contribution margin per unit of limited resource for each product.

Show allocation of limited resources.
(SO 8)

BE23-9 Adler Company is considering purchasing new equipment for $300,000. It is expected that the equipment will produce annual net income of $10,000 over its 10-year useful life. Annual depreciation will be $30,000. Compute the cash payback period.

Compute the cash payback period for a capital investment.
(SO 9)

BE23-10 Engles Oil Company is considering investing in a new oil well. It is expected that the oil well will increase annual revenues by $130,000 and will increase annual expenses by $80,000 including depreciation. The oil well will cost $490,000 and will have a $10,000 salvage value at the end of its 10-year useful life. Calculate the annual rate of return.

Compute annual rate of return.
(SO 9)

BE23-11 Harry Company is considering two different, mutually exclusive capital expenditure proposals. Project A will cost $395,000, has an expected useful life of 10 years, a salvage value of zero, and is expected to increase net annual cash flows by $70,000. Project B will cost $270,000, has an expected useful life of 10 years, a salvage value of zero, and is expected to increase net annual cash flows by $50,000. A discount rate of 9% is appropriate for both projects. Compute the net present value of each project. Which project should be accepted?

Compute net present value.
(SO 10)

BE23-12 Frost Company is evaluating the purchase of a rebuilt spot-welding machine to be used in the manufacture of a new product. The machine will cost $170,000, has an estimated useful life of 7 years, a salvage value of zero, and will increase net annual cash flows by $33,740. What is its approximate internal rate of return?

Calculate internal rate of return.
(SO 10)

BE23-13 Horak Company accumulates the following data concerning a proposed capital investment: cash cost $225,000, net annual cash flow $34,000, present value factor of cash inflows for 10 years 6.71 (rounded). Determine the net present value, and indicate whether the investment should be made.

Compute net present value of an investment.
(SO 10)

Exercises

E23-1 Pender has prepared the following list of statements about decision making and incremental analysis.

1. The first step in management's decision-making process is, "Determine and evaluate possible courses of action."
2. The final step in management's decision-making process is to actually make the decision.
3. Accounting's contribution to management's decision-making process occurs primarily in evaluating possible courses of action and in reviewing the results.

Analyze statements about decision making and incremental analysis.
(SO 1, 2, 3)

4. In making business decisions, management ordinarily considers only financial information because it is objectively determined.
5. Decisions involve a choice among alternative courses of action.
6. The process used to identify the financial data that change under alternative courses of action is called incremental analysis.
7. Costs that are the same under all alternative courses of action sometimes affect the decision.
8. When using incremental analysis, some costs will always change under alternative courses of action, but revenues will not.
9. Variable costs will change under alternative courses of action, but fixed costs will not.

Instructions
Identify each statement as true or false. If false, indicate how to correct the statement.

Make incremental analysis for special order.
(SO 3)

E23-2 Wyco Company manufactures toasters. For the first 8 months of 2007, the company reported the following operating results while operating at 75% of plant capacity.

Sales (400,000 units)	$4,000,000
Cost of goods sold	2,400,000
Gross profit	1,600,000
Operating expenses	900,000
Net income	$ 700,000

Cost of goods sold was 70% variable and 30% fixed. Operating expenses were 60% variable and 40% fixed.

In September, Wyco Company receives a special order for 40,000 toasters at $6.00 each from Salono Company of Mexico City. Acceptance of the order would result in $8,000 of shipping costs but no increase in fixed operating expenses.

Instructions
(a) Prepare an incremental analysis for the special order.
(b) ▭▭▭▷ Should Wyco Company accept the special order? Why or why not?

Make incremental analysis for special-order decision.
(SO 3)

E23-3 Innova Company produces golf discs which it normally sells to retailers for $7 each. The cost of manufacturing 20,000 golf discs is:

Materials	$ 10,000
Labor	30,000
Variable overhead	20,000
Fixed overhead	40,000
Total	$100,000

Innova also incurs 5% sales commission ($0.35) on each disc sold.

Mudd Corporation offers Innova $4.75 per disc for 5,000 discs. Mudd would sell the discs under its own brand name in foreign markets not yet served by Innova. If Innova accepts the offer, its fixed overhead will increase from $50,000 to $55,000 due to the purchase of a new imprinting machine. No sales commission will result from the special order.

Instructions
(a) Prepare an incremental analysis for the special order.
(b) Should Innova accept the special order? Why or why not?
(c) What assumptions underlie the decision made in part (b)?

Make incremental analysis for make-or-buy decision.
(SO 4)

E23-4 Shannon Inc. has been manufacturing its own shades for its table lamps. The company is currently operating at 100% of capacity. Variable manufacturing overhead is charged to production at the rate of 50% of direct labor cost. The direct materials and direct labor cost per unit to make the lamp shades are $4.00 and $6.00, respectively. Normal production is 40,000 table lamps per year.

A supplier offers to make the lamp shades at a price of $13.50 per unit. If Shannon Inc. accepts the supplier's offer, all variable manufacturing costs will be eliminated, but the $40,000 of fixed manufacturing overhead currently being charged to the lamp shades will have to be absorbed by other products.

Instructions
(a) Prepare the incremental analysis for the decision to make or buy the lamp shades.
(b) ▮▮▭▭▭▷ Should Shannon Inc. buy the lamp shades?
(c) ▮▮▭▭▭▷ Would your answer be different in (b) if the productive capacity released by not making the lamp shades could be used to produce income of $35,000?

E23-5   Stacy McGuire recently opened her own basketweaving studio. She sells finished baskets in addition to the raw materials needed by customers to weave baskets of their own. Stacy has put together a variety of raw material kits, each including materials at various stages of completion. Unfortunately, owing to space limitations, Stacy is unable to carry all varieties of kits originally assembled and must choose between two basic packages.

Make incremental analysis for further processing of materials.
(SO 5)

The basic introductory kit includes undyed, uncut reeds (with dye included) for weaving one basket. This basic package costs Stacy $12 and sells for $27. The second kit, called Stage 2, includes cut reeds that have already been dyed. With this kit the customer need only soak the reeds and weave the basket. Stacy is able to produce the second kit by using the basic materials included in the first kit and adding one hour of her own time (to produce two kits), which she values at $18 per hour. Because she is more efficient at cutting and dying reeds than her average customer, Stacy is able to make two kits of the dyed reeds, in one hour, from one kit of undyed reeds. The kit of dyed and cut reeds sells for $33.

Instructions
Determine whether Stacy's basketweaving shop should carry the basic introductory kit with undyed and uncut reeds, or the Stage 2 kit with reeds already dyed and cut. Prepare an incremental analysis to support your answer.

E23-6   Donkey Bikes could sell its bicycles to retailers either assembled or unassembled. The cost of an unassembled bike is as follows.

Make incremental analysis for sell-or-process-further decision.
(SO 5)

Direct materials	$150
Direct labor	70
Variable overhead (70% of direct labor)	49
Fixed overhead (30% of direct labor)	21
Manufacturing cost per unit	$290

The unassembled bikes are sold to retailers at $400 each.

Donkey currently has unused productive capacity that is expected to continue indefinitely; management has concluded that some of this capacity can be used to assemble the bikes and sell them at $450 each. Assembling the bikes will increase direct materials by $5 per bike, and direct labor by $20 per bike. Additional variable overhead will be incurred at the normal rates, but there will be no additional fixed overhead as a result of assembling the bikes.

Instructions
(a) Prepare an incremental analysis for the sell-or-process-further decision.
(b) Should Donkey sell or process further? Why or why not?

E23-7   Crone Enterprises uses a word processing computer to handle its sales invoices. Lately, business has been so good that it takes an extra 3 hours per night, plus every third Saturday, to keep up with the volume of sales invoices. Management is considering updating its computer with a faster model that would eliminate all of the overtime processing.

Make incremental analysis for retaining or replacing equipment.
(SO 6)

	Current Machine	**New Machine**
Original purchase cost	$15,000	$21,000
Accumulated depreciation	6,000	—
Estimated operating costs	24,000	20,000
Useful life	5 years	5 years

If sold now, the current machine would have a salvage value of $5,000. If operated for the remainder of its useful life, the current machine would have zero salvage value. The new machine is expected to have zero salvage value after 5 years.

Instructions
Should the current machine be replaced? (Ignore the time value of money.)

*Make incremental analysis
for elimination of division.
(SO 7)*

E23-8   Judy Herzog, a recent graduate of Rolling's accounting program, evaluated the operating performance of Klumpe Company's six divisions. Judy made the following presentation to Klumpe's Board of Directors and suggested the Ketchum Division be eliminated. "If the Ketchum Division is eliminated," she said, "our total profits would increase by $16,870."

	The Other Five Divisions	Ketchum Division	Total
Sales	$1,664,200	$ 98,200	$1,762,400
Cost of goods sold	978,520	76,470	1,054,990
Gross profit	685,680	21,730	707,410
Operating expenses	527,940	38,600	566,540
Net income	$ 157,740	$(16,870)	$ 140,870

In the Ketchum Division, cost of goods sold is $56,000 variable and $20,470 fixed, and operating expenses are $12,000 variable and $26,600 fixed. None of the Ketchum Division's fixed costs will be eliminated if the division is discontinued.

Instructions

▶ Is Judy right about eliminating the Ketchum Division? Prepare a schedule to support your answer.

*Make incremental analysis
for elimination of a product
line.
(SO 7) E*

E23-9   Shatner Company makes three models of phasers. Information on the three products is given below.

	Stunner	Double-Set	Mega-Power
Sales	$300,000	$500,000	$ 200,000
Variable expenses	150,000	200,000	140,000
Contribution margin	150,000	300,000	60,000
Fixed expenses	120,000	225,000	90,000
Net income	$ 30,000	$ 75,000	$(30,000)

Fixed expenses consist of $300,000 of common costs allocated to the three products based on relative sales, and additional fixed expenses of $30,000 (Stunner), $75,000 (Double-Set), and $30,000 (Mega-Power). The common costs will be incurred regardless of how many models are produced. The other fixed expenses would be eliminated if a model is phased out.

Jim Kirk, an executive with the company, feels the Mega-Power line should be discontinued to increase the company's net income.

Instructions

(a) Compute current net income for Shatner Company.

(b) Compute net income by product line and in total for Shatner Company if the company discontinues the Mega-Power product line. (*Hint:* Allocate the $300,000 common costs to the two remaining product lines based on their relative sales.)

(c) Should Shatner eliminate the Mega-Power product line? Why or why not?

*Compute contribution
margin and determine the
product to be manufactured.
(SO 8)*

E23-10   Freese Company manufactures and sells three products. Relevant per unit data concerning each product are given below.

	Product		
	A	B	C
Selling price	$11	$12	$15
Variable costs and expenses	$ 4	$ 8	$ 9
Machine hours to produce	2	1	2

Instructions

(a) Compute the contribution margin per unit of the limited resource (machine hour) for each product.

(b) Assuming 3,000 additional machine hours are available, which product should be manufactured?

(c) Prepare an analysis showing the total contribution margin if the additional hours are (1) divided equally among the products, and (2) allocated entirely to the product identified in (b) above.

E23-11 Carleton Service Center just purchased an automobile hoist for $15,000. The hoist has a 5-year life and an estimated salvage value of $1,080. Installation costs were $2,900, and freight charges were $820. Carleton uses straight-line depreciation.

The new hoist will be used to replace mufflers and tires on automobiles. Carleton estimates that the new hoist will enable his mechanics to replace four extra mufflers per week. Each muffler sells for $65 installed. The cost of a muffler is $35, and the labor cost to install a muffler is $10.

Compute cash payback period and annual rate of return.
(SO 9)

Instructions
(a) Compute the payback period for the new hoist.
(b) Compute the annual rate of return for the new hoist. (Round to one decimal.)

E23-12 Suzaki Manufacturing Company is considering three new projects, each requiring an equipment investment of $22,000. Each project will last for 3 years and produce the following cash inflows.

Compute cash payback period and net present value.
(SO 9, 10)

Year	AA	BB	CC
1	$ 7,000	$ 9,500	$13,000
2	9,000	9,500	10,000
3	15,000	9,500	9,000
Total	$31,000	$28,500	$32,000

The equipment's salvage value is zero. Suzaki uses straight-line depreciation. Suzaki will not accept any project with a payback period over 2 years. Suzaki's minimum required rate of return is 12%.

Instructions
(a) Compute each project's payback period, indicating the most desirable project and the least desirable project using this method. (Round to two decimals.)
(b) Compute the net present value of each project. Does your evaluation change? (Round to nearest dollar.)

E23-13 Rondello Company is considering a capital investment of $150,000 in additional productive facilities. The new machinery is expected to have a useful life of 5 years with no salvage value. Depreciation is by the straight-line method. During the life of the investment, annual net income and cash inflows are expected to be $18,000 and $48,000, respectively. Rondello has a 12% cost of capital rate, which is the minimum acceptable rate of return on the investment.

Compute annual rate of return, cash payback period, and net present value.
(SO 9, 10)

Instructions
(Round to two decimals.)
(a) Compute (1) the annual rate of return and (2) the cash payback period on the proposed capital expenditure.
(b) Using the discounted cash flow technique, compute the net present value.

E23-14 Omega Company is considering three capital expenditure projects. Relevant data for the projects are as follows.

Determine internal rate of return.
(SO 10)

Project	Investment	Annual Income	Life of Project
22A	$240,000	$13,300	6 years
23A	270,000	21,000	9 years
24A	288,000	20,000	8 years

Annual income is constant over the life of the project. Each project is expected to have zero salvage value at the end of the project. Omega Company uses the straight-line method of depreciation.

Instructions
(a) Determine the internal rate of return for each project. Round the internal rate of return factor to three decimals.

(b) If Omega Company's minimum required rate of return is 11%, which projects are acceptable?

E23-15 Vasquez Corporation is considering investing in two different projects. It could invest in both, neither, or just one of the projects. The forecasts for the projects are as follows.

	Project A	Project B
Capital investment	$200,000	$300,000
Net annual cash flows	$ 50,000	$ 65,000
Length of project	5 years	7 years

The minimum rate of return acceptable to Vasquez is 10%.

Instructions
(a) Compute the net present value of the two projects.
(b) What capital budgeting decision should Vasquez make?
(c) Project A could be modified. By spending $20,000 more initially, the net annual cash flows could be increased by $10,000 per year. Would this change Vasquez's decision?

Problems: Set A

P23-1A Korte Company is currently producing 16,000 units per month, which is 80% of its production capacity. Variable manufacturing costs are currently $8.00 per unit. Fixed manufacturing costs are $56,000 per month. Korte pays a 9% sales commission to its sales people, has $30,000 in fixed administrative expenses per month, and is averaging $320,000 in sales per month.

A special order received from a foreign company would enable Korte Company to operate at 100% capacity. The foreign company offered to pay 75% of Korte's current selling price per unit. If the order is accepted, Korte will have to spend an extra $2.00 per unit to package the product for overseas shipping. Also, Korte Company would need to lease a new stamping machine to imprint the foreign company's logo on the product, at a monthly cost of $2,500. The special order would require a sales commission of $3,500.

Instructions
(a) Compute the number of units involved in the special order and the foreign company's offered price per unit.
(b) What is the manufacturing cost of producing one unit of Korte's product for regular customers?

(c) Prepare an incremental analysis of the special order. Should management accept the order?
(d) What is the lowest price that Korte could accept for the special order to earn net income of $1.20 per unit?
(e) ▭▭▭▭▷ What nonfinancial factors should management consider in making its decision?

P23-2A The management of Martinez Manufacturing Company has asked for your assistance in deciding whether to continue manufacturing a part or to buy it from an outside supplier. The part, called Tropica, is a component of Martinez's finished product.

An analysis of the accounting records and the production data revealed the following information for the year ending December 31, 2007.

1. The Machinery Department produced 36,000 units of Tropica.
2. Each Tropica unit requires 10 minutes to produce. Three people in the Machinery Department work full time (2,000 hours per year) producing Tropica. Each person is paid $11.00 per hour.
3. The cost of materials per Tropica unit is $2.00.
4. Manufacturing costs directly applicable to the production of Tropica are: indirect labor, $5,500; utilities, $1,300; depreciation, $1,600; property taxes and insurance, $1,000. All of the costs will be eliminated if Tropica is purchased.
5. The lowest price for a Tropica from an outside supplier is $3.90 per unit. Freight charges will be $0.30 per unit, and a part-time receiving clerk at $8,500 per year will be required.

6. If Tropica is purchased, the excess space will be used to store Martinez's finished product. Currently, Martinez rents storage space at approximately $0.60 per unit stored per year. Approximately 6,000 units per year are stored in the rented space.

Instructions
(a) Prepare an incremental analysis for the make-or-buy decision. Should Martinez make or buy the part? Why?

(b) Prepare an incremental analysis, assuming the released facilities can be used to produce $10,000 of net income in addition to the savings on the rental of storage space. What decision should now be made?

(c) ▭▭▭▭▷ What nonfinancial factors should be considered in the decision?

P23-3A   Deskins Manufacturing Company has four operating divisions. During the first quarter of 2007 the company reported total income from operations of $61,000 and the following results for the divisions.

Compute contribution margin, and prepare incremental analysis concerning elimination of divisions.

(SO 7)

	Division			
	Denver	**Miami**	**San Diego**	**Tacoma**
Sales	$455,000	$730,000	$920,000	$515,000
Cost of goods sold	380,000	480,000	576,000	430,000
Selling and administrative expenses	120,000	207,000	246,000	120,000
Income (loss) from operations	$(45,000)	$ 43,000	$ 98,000	$(35,000)

Analysis reveals the following percentages of variable costs in each division.

	Denver	**Miami**	**San Diego**	**Tacoma**
Cost of goods sold	95%	80%	90%	90%
Selling and administrative expenses	80	60	70	60

Discontinuance of any division would save 60% of the fixed costs and expenses for that division.

Top management is deeply concerned about the unprofitable divisions (Denver and Tacoma). The consensus is that one or both of the divisions should be eliminated.

Instructions
(a) Compute the contribution margin for the two unprofitable divisions.

(b) Prepare an incremental analysis concerning the possible elimination of (1) the Denver Division and (2) the Tacoma Division. What course of action do you recommend for each division?
(c) Prepare a columnar condensed income statement using the CVP format for Deskins Manufacturing Company, assuming (1) the Denver Division is eliminated, and (2) the unavoidable fixed costs and expenses of the Denver Division are allocated 30% to Miami, 50% to San Diego, and 20% to Tacoma.

(d) Compare the total income from operations with the Denver Division ($61,000) to total income from operations without this division.

P23-4A   Timmons Corporation is considering three long-term capital investment proposals. Relevant data on each project are as follows.

Compute annual rate of return, cash payback, and net present value.

(SO 9, 10)

	Project		
	Brown	**Red**	**Yellow**
Capital investment	$190,000	$220,000	$250,000
Annual net income:			
Year 1	25,000	20,000	26,000
2	16,000	20,000	24,000
3	13,000	20,000	23,000
4	10,000	20,000	17,000
5	8,000	20,000	20,000
Total	$ 72,000	$100,000	$110,000

Salvage value is expected to be zero at the end of each project. Depreciation is computed by the straight-line method. The company's minimum rate of return is the company's cost of capital which is 12%.

Instructions
(a) Compute the annual rate of return for each project. (Round to two decimals.)
(b) Compute the cash payback period for each project. (Round to two decimals.)
(c) Compute the net present value for each project. (Round to nearest dollar.)
(d) Rank the projects on each of the foregoing bases. Which project do you recommend?

Brown	Red	Yellow
(a) 15.2%		
(b)	3.44	
(c)		$11,109

Compute annual rate of return, cash payback, and net present value.

(SO 9, 10)

P23-5A   Wendy Dobson is managing director of the Wichita Day Care Center. Wichita is currently set up as a full-time child care facility for children between the ages of 12 months and 6 years. Wendy is trying to determine whether the center should expand its facilities to incorporate a newborn care room for infants between the ages of 6 weeks and 12 months. The necessary space already exists. An investment of $25,000 would be needed, however, to purchase cribs, high chairs, etc. The equipment purchased for the room would have a 5-year useful life with zero salvage value.

The newborn nursery would be staffed to handle 12 infants on a full-time basis. The parents of each infant would be charged $200 weekly, and the facility would operate 52 weeks of the year. Staffing the nursery would require two full-time specialists and five part-time assistants at an annual cost of $103,800. Food, diapers, and other miscellaneous supplies are expected to total $14,000 annually.

Instructions
(a) Determine (1) annual net income and (2) net cash flow for the new nursery.
(b) Compute (1) the annual rate of return and (2) the cash payback period for the new nursery. (Round to two decimals.)
(c) Assuming that Wichita can borrow the money needed for expansion at 10%, compute the net present value of the new room. (Round to the nearest dollar.)
(d) ✏️ What should Wendy conclude from these computations?

(a) (1) $2,000

Compute net present value and internal rate of return.

(SO 10)

P23-6A   Aqua Tech Testing is considering investing in a new testing device. It has two options: Option A would have an initial lower cost but would require a significant expenditure for rebuilding after 5 years. Option B would require no rebuilding expenditure, but its maintenance costs would be higher. Since the option B machine is of initial higher quality, it is expected to have a salvage value at the end of its useful life. The following estimates were provided. The company's cost of capital is 9%.

	Option A	Option B
Initial cost	$ 90,000	$170,000
Net annual cash flows	$ 20,000	$ 32,000
Cost to rebuild (end of year 5)	$ 26,500	$ 0
Salvage value	$ 0	$ 27,500
Estimated useful life	8 years	8 years

Instructions
(a) Compute the (1) net present value, and (2) internal rate of return for each option. (*Hint:* To solve for internal rate of return, experiment with alternative discount rates to arrive at a net present value of zero.)
(b) Which option should be accepted?

(a) (1) NPV A $3,473
(2) IRR B 12%

Problems: Set B

Make incremental analysis for special order, and identify nonfinancial factors in decision.

(SO 3)

P23-1B   Houston Inc. manufactures basketballs for the National Basketball Association (NBA). For the first 6 months of 2007, the company reported the following operating results while operating at 90% of plant capacity.

	Amount	Per Unit
Sales	$4,500,000	$50.00
Cost of goods sold	3,600,000	40.00
Selling and administrative expenses	360,000	4.00
Net income	$ 540,000	$ 6.00

Fixed costs for the period were: Cost of goods sold $900,000, and selling and administrative expenses $225,000.

In July, normally a slack manufacturing month, Houston receives a special order for 6,000 basketballs at $35 each from the Italian Basketball Association (IBA). Acceptance of the order would increase variable selling and administrative expenses $0.50 per unit because of shipping costs but would not increase fixed costs and expenses.

Instructions
(a) Prepare an incremental analysis for the special order.
(b) Should Houston Inc. accept the special order?
(c) What is the minimum selling price on the special order to produce net income of $3.00 per ball?
(d) ▇▇▇▇▶ What nonfinancial factors should management consider in making its decision?

(a) NI increases $18,000

P23-2B   The management of Edgerton Manufacturing Company is trying to decide whether to continue manufacturing a part or to buy it from an outside supplier. The part, called WISCO, is a component of the company's finished product.

The following information was collected from the accounting records and production data for the year ending December 31, 2007.

Make incremental analysis related to make or buy; consider opportunity cost, and identify nonfinancial factors. (SO 4)

1. 9,000 units of WISCO were produced in the Machining Department.
2. Variable manufacturing costs applicable to the production of each WISCO unit were: direct materials $4.75, direct labor $4.60, indirect labor $0.45, utilities $0.35.
3. Fixed manufacturing costs applicable to the production of WISCO were:

Cost Item	Direct	Allocated
Depreciation	$1,600	$ 900
Property taxes	400	200
Insurance	900	600
	$2,900	$1,700

All variable manufacturing and direct fixed costs will be eliminated if WISCO is purchased. Allocated costs will have to be absorbed by other production departments.
4. The lowest quotation for 8,000 WISCO units from a supplier is $88,000.
5. If WISCO units are purchased, freight and inspection costs would be $0.30 per unit, and receiving costs totaling $750 per year would be incurred by the Machining Department.

Instructions
(a) Prepare an incremental analysis for WISCO. Your analysis should have columns for (1) Make WISCO, (2) Buy WISCO, and (3) Net Income Increase/Decrease.
(b) Based on your analysis, what decision should management make?
(c) Would the decision be different if Edgerton Company has the opportunity to produce $8,000 of net income with the facilities currently being used to manufacture WISCO? Show computations.
(d) ▇▇▇▇▶ What nonfinancial factors should management consider in making its decision?

(a) NI decrease $7,050

(c) NI increase $950

P23-3B   Plott Manufacturing Company has four operating divisions. During the first quarter of 2007, the company reported aggregate income from operations of $155,000 and the following divisional results.

Compute contribution margin, and prepare incremental analysis concerning elimination of divisions. (SO 7)

	Division			
	I	**II**	**III**	**IV**
Sales	$490,000	$410,000	$ 290,000	$ 200,000
Cost of goods sold	300,000	250,000	270,000	180,000
Selling and administrative expenses	60,000	80,000	35,000	60,000
Income (loss) from operations	$130,000	$ 80,000	$ (15,000)	$ (40,000)

Analysis reveals the following percentages of variable costs in each division.

	I	II	III	IV
Cost of goods sold	70%	80%	75%	90%
Selling and administrative expenses	40	50	60	70

Discontinuance of any division would save 50% of the fixed costs and expenses for that division.

Top management is very concerned about the unprofitable divisions (III and IV). Consensus is that one or both of the divisions should be discontinued.

Instructions

(a) III $66,500

(a) Compute the contribution margin for Divisions III and IV.

(b) Prepare an incremental analysis concerning the possible discontinuance of (1) Division III and (2) Division IV. What course of action do you recommend for each division?

(c) Income: III ($21,000)

(c) Prepare a columnar condensed income statement for Plott Manufacturing, assuming Division IV is eliminated. Use the CVP format. Division IV's unavoidable fixed costs are allocated equally to the continuing divisions.

(d) Reconcile the total income from operations ($155,000) with the total income from operations without Division IV.

Compute annual rate of return, cash payback, and net present value.

(SO 9, 10)

P23-4B Lapham Corporation is considering three long-term capital investment proposals. Each investment has a useful life of 5 years. Relevant data on each project are as follows.

	Project Tic	Project Tac	Project Toe
Capital investment	$160,000	$180,000	$200,000
Annual net income:			
Year 1	13,000	18,000	27,000
2	13,000	17,000	22,000
3	13,000	16,000	16,000
4	13,000	12,000	13,000
5	13,000	9,000	12,000
Total	$ 65,000	$ 72,000	$ 90,000

Depreciation is computed by the straight-line method with no salvage value. The company's cost of capital is 15%.

TIC	TAC	TOE
(a) 16.3%		
(b)		3.28
(c)		($8,960)

Instructions

(a) Compute the annual rate of return for each project. (Round to two decimals.)

(b) Compute the cash payback period for each project. (Round to two decimals.)

(c) Compute the net present value for each project. (Round to nearest dollar.)

(d) Rank the projects on each of the foregoing bases. Which project do you recommend?

Compute annual rate of return, cash payback, and net present value.

(SO, 9, 10)

P23-5B Marie Dunston is an accounting major at a midwestern state university located approximately 60 miles from a major city. Many of the students attending the university are from the metropolitan area and visit their homes regularly on the weekends. Marie, an entrepreneur at heart, realizes that few good commuting alternatives are available for students doing weekend travel. She believes that a weekend commuting service could be organized and run profitably from several suburban and downtown shopping mall locations. Marie has gathered the following investment information.

1. Six used vans would cost a total of $90,000 to purchase and would have a 3-year useful life with negligible salvage value. Marie plans to use straight-line depreciation.
2. Ten drivers would have to be employed at a total payroll expense of $70,000.
3. Other annual out of pocket expenses associated with running the commuter service would include Gasoline $20,000, Maintenance $2,800, Repairs $3,500, Insurance $3,200, Advertising $1,500. (Exclude interest expense.)
4. Marie has visited several financial institutions to discuss funding for her new venture. The best interest rate she has been able to negotiate is 10%. Use this rate for cost of capital.

5. Marie expects each van to make ten round trips weekly and carry an average of five students each trip. The service is expected to operate 30 weeks each years. Each student will be charged $15.00 for a round-trip ticket.

Instructions
(a) Determine the annual (1) net income, and (2) net cash flow for the commuter service.
(b) Compute (1) the annual rate of return, and (2) the cash payback period. (Round to two decimals.)
(c) Compute the net present value of the commuter service. (Round to the nearest dollar.)
(d) ▭▭▭▭▶ What should Marie conclude from these computations?

(a) (1) $4,000
(b) (2) 2.65 years

P23-6B Carolina Clinic is considering investing in new heart-monitoring equipment. It has two options: Option A would have an initial lower cost but would require a significant expenditure for rebuilding after 4 years. Option B would require no rebuilding expenditure, but its maintenance costs would be higher. Since the option B machine is of initial higher quality, it is expected to have a salvage value at the end of its useful life. The following estimates were made of the cash flows. The company's cost of capital is 11%.

Compute net present value, and internal rate of return.
(SO 10)

	Option A	Option B
Initial cost	$160,000	$227,000
Net annual cash flows	$ 40,000	$ 50,000
Cost to rebuild (end of year 4)	$ 60,000	$ 0
Salvage value	$ 0	$ 12,000
Estimated useful life	8 years	8 years

Instructions
(a) Compute the (1) net present value and (2) internal rate of return for each option. (*Hint:* To solve for internal rate of return, experiment with alternative discount rates to arrive at a net present value of zero.)
(b) Which option should be accepted?

(a) (1) NPV A $6,321
    (2) IRR B 15%

Problems: Set C

Visit the book's website at **www.wiley.com/college/kimmel** and choose the Student Companion site to access Problem Set C.

Comprehensive Problem: Chapters 14 to 23

You would like to start a business manufacturing a unique model of bicycle helmet. In preparation for an interview with the bank to discuss your financing needs, you develop answers to the following questions. A number of assumptions are required; clearly note all assumptions that you make.

Instructions
(a) Identify the types of costs that would likely be involved in making this product.
(b) Set up five columns as indicated.

	Product Costs			
Item	**Direct Materials**	**Direct Labor**	**Manufacturing Overhead**	**Period Costs**

Classify the costs you identified in (a) into the manufacturing cost classifications of product costs (direct materials, direct labor, and manufacturing overhead) and period costs.
(c) Assign hypothetical monthly dollar figures to the costs you identified in (a) and (b).
(d) Assume you have no raw materials or work in process beginning or ending inventories. Prepare a projected cost of goods manufactured schedule for the first month of operations.
(e) Project the number of helmets you expect to produce the first month of operations. Compute the cost to produce one bicycle helmet. Review the result to ensure it is reasonable; if not, return to part (c) and adjust the monthly dollar figures you assigned accordingly.

(f) What type of cost accounting system will you likely use—job order or process costing?

(g) Explain how you would assign costs in either the job order or process costing system you plan to use.

(h) Classify your costs as either variable or fixed costs. For simplicity, assign all costs to either variable or fixed, assuming there are no mixed costs, using the format shown.

Item	Variable Costs	Fixed Costs	Total Costs

(i) Compute the unit variable cost, using the production number you determined in (e).

(j) Project the number of helmets you anticipate selling the first month of operations. Set a unit selling price, and compute both the contribution margin per unit and the contribution margin ratio.

(k) Determine your break-even point in dollars and in units.

(l) Prepare projected operating budgets (sales, production, direct materials, direct labor, manufacturing overhead, selling and administrative expense, and income statement). You will need to make assumptions for each of the following:

Direct materials budget:	Quantity of direct materials required to produce one helmet; cost per unit of quantity; desired ending direct materials (assume none).
Direct labor budget:	Direct labor time required per helmet; direct labor cost per hour.
Budgeted income statement:	Income tax expense is 45% of income from operations.

(m)Prepare a cash budget for the month. Assume the percentage of sales that will be collected from customers is 75%, and the percentage of direct materials that will be paid in the current month is 75%.

(n) Determine a relevant range of activity, using the number of helmets produced as your activity index. Recast your manufacturing overhead budget into a flexible monthly budget for two additional activity levels.

(o) Identify one potential cause of materials, direct labor, and manufacturing overhead variances for your product.

(p) Assume that you wish to purchase production equipment that costs $720,000. Determine the cash payback period, utilizing the monthly cash flow that you computed in part (m) multiplied by 12 months (for simplicity).

(q) Identify any nonfinancial factors that should be considered before commencing your business venture.

► BROADENING YOUR PERSPECTIVE

Group Decision Case

BYP23-1 Morganstern Company is considering the purchase of a new machine. The invoice price of the machine is $170,000, freight charges are estimated to be $4,000, and installation costs are expected to be $6,000. Salvage value of the new equipment is expected to be zero after a useful life of 4 years. Existing equipment could be retained and used for an additional 4 years if the new machine is not purchased. At that time, the salvage value of the equipment would be zero. If the new machine is purchased now, the existing machine would be scrapped. Morganstern's accountant, Diane Gallup, has accumulated the following data regarding annual sales and expenses with and without the new machine.

1. Without the new machine, Morganstern can sell 10,000 units of product annually at a per unit selling price of $100. If the new unit is purchased, the number of units produced and sold would increase by 20%. The selling price would remain the same.

2. The new machine is faster than the old machine, and it is more efficient in its usage of materials. With the old machine the gross profit rate will be 25% of sales. With the new machine the rate will be 28% of sales.

3. Annual selling expenses are $135,000 with the current equipment. Because the new equipment would produce a greater number of units to be sold, annual selling expenses are expected to increase by 10% if it is purchased.

4. Annual administrative expenses are expected to be $100,000 with the old machine and $113,000 with the new machine.
5. The current book value of the existing machine is $36,000. Morganstern uses straight-line depreciation.
6. Morganstern's management wants a minimum rate of return of 15% on its investment and a payback period of no more than 3 years.

Instructions
With the class divided into groups, answer the following. (Ignore income tax effects.)
(a) Prepare an incremental analysis for the 4 years showing whether Morganstern should keep the existing machine or buy the new machine.
(b) Calculate the annual rate of return for the new machine. (Round to two decimals.)
(c) Compute the payback period for the new machine. (Round to two decimals.)
(d) Compute the net present value of the new machine. (Round to the nearest dollar.)
(e) On the basis of the foregoing data, would you recommend that Morganstern buy the machine? Why?

Managerial Analysis

BYP23-2   Barone Company manufactures private-label small electronic products, such as alarm clocks, calculators, kitchen timers, stopwatches, and automatic pencil sharpeners. Some of the products are sold as sets, and others are sold individually. Products are studied as to their sales potential, and then cost estimates are made. The Engineering Department develops production plans, and then production begins. The company has generally had very successful product introduction. Only two products introduced by the company have been discontinued.

One of the products currently sold is a multi-alarm alarm clock. The clock has four alarms that can be programmed to sound at various times and for varying lengths of time. The company has experienced a great deal of difficulty in making the circuit boards for the clocks. The production process has never operated smoothly. The product is unprofitable at the present time, primarily because of warranty repairs and product recalls. Two models of the clocks were recalled, for example, because they sometimes caused an electric shock when the alarms were being shut off. The Engineering Department is attempting to revise the manufacturing process, but the revision will take another 6 months at least.

The clocks were very popular when they were introduced, and since they are private-label, the company has not suffered much from the recalls. Presently, the company has a very large order for several items from Kmart Stores. The order includes 5,000 of the multi-alarm clocks. When the company suggested that Kmart purchase the clocks from another manufacturer, Kmart threatened to rescind the entire order unless the clocks were included.

The company has therefore investigated the possibility of having another company make the clocks for them. The clocks were bid for the Kmart order, based on an estimated $5.50 cost to manufacture, as follows.

Circuit board, 1 each @ $1.00	$1.00
Plastic case, 1 each @ $0.50	0.50
Alarms, 4 @ $0.15 each	0.60
Labor, 15 minutes @ $12/hour	3.00
Overhead, $1.60 per labor hour	0.40

Barone could purchase clocks to fill the Kmart order for $9 from Silver Star, a Korean manufacturer with a very good quality record. Silver Star has offered to reduce the price to $7.50 after Barone has been a customer for 6 months, placing an order of at least 1,000 units per month. If Barone becomes a "preferred customer" by purchasing 15,000 units per year, the price would be reduced still further to $4.50.

Sigma Products, a local manufacturer, has also offered to make clocks for Barone. They have offered to sell 5,000 clocks for $5 each. However, Sigma Products has been in business for only 6 months. They have experienced significant turnover in their labor force, and the local media have reported that the owners may soon face tax evasion charges. The owner of Sigma Products is an electronic engineer, however, and the quality of the clocks is likely to be good.

If Barone decides to purchase the clocks from either Silver Star or Sigma, all the costs to manufacturer could be avoided, except a total of $5,000 in overhead costs for machine depreciation. The machinery is fairly new, and has no alternate use.

Instructions

(a) What is the difference in profit under each of the alternatives if the clocks are to be sold for $13.00 each to Kmart?

(b) What are the most important nonfinancial factors that Barone should consider when making this decision?

(c) What should Barone do in regard to the Kmart order? What should it do in regard to continuing to manufacture the multi-alarm alarm clocks? Be prepared to defend your answer.

Real-World Focus

BYP23-3 Founded in 1983, the Beverly Hills Fan Company is located in Woodland Hills, California. With 23 employees and sales of less than $10 million, the company is relatively small. Management feels that there is potential for growth in the upscale market for ceiling fans and lighting. They are particularly optimistic about growth in Mexican and Canadian markets.

Presented below is information from the president's letter in the company's annual report.

BEVERLY HILLS FAN COMPANY
President's Letter

An aggressive product development program was initiated during the past year resulting in new ceiling fan models planned for introduction in 1993. Award winning industrial designer Ron Rezek created several new fan models for the Beverly Hills Fan and L.A. Fan lines, including a new Showroom Collection, designed specifically for the architectural and designer markets. Each of these models has received critical acclaim, and order commitments for 1993 have been outstanding. Additionally, our Custom Color and special order fans continued to enjoy increasing popularity and sales gains as more and more customers desire fans that match their specific interior decors. Currently, Beverly Hills Fan Company offers a product line of over 100 models of contemporary, traditional, and transitional ceiling fans.

Instructions

(a) What points did the company management need to consider before deciding to offer the special-order fans to customers?

(b) How would incremental analysis be employed to assist in this decision?

Exploring the Web

BYP23-4 Campbell Soup Company is an international provider of soup products. Management is very interested in continuing to grow the company in its core business, while "spinning off" those businesses that are not part of its core operation.

Address: **www.campbellsoups.com**
      (*or go to* **www.wiley.com/college/kimmel**)

Steps

1. Go to the home page of Campbell Soup Company at the address shown above.
2. Choose **Our Company** and then **Investor Center**.
3. Choose **Financial Reports**.
4. Choose the 2005 annual report, or the current annual report if 2005 is no longer available.

Instructions

Review the financial statements and management's discussion and analysis, and answer the following questions.

(a) What was the total amount reported as "Purchases of Plant Assets" in the 2005 statement of cash flows? How does this amount compare with the previous year?

(b) What range of interest rates does the company report on its long-term liabilities in the notes to its financial statements?

(c) Assume that this year's capital expenditures are expected to increase cash flows by $45 million. What is the expected internal rate of return (IRR) for these capital expenditures? (Assume a 10-year period for the cash flows.)

Communication Activity

BYP23-5   Refer back to Exercise 23-11 to address the following.

Instructions
Prepare a memo to Angie Baden, your supervisor. Show your calculations from E23-11, parts **(a)** and **(b)**. In one or two paragraphs, discuss important nonfinancial considerations. Make any assumptions you believe to be necessary. Make a recommendation, based on your analysis.

Research Assignment

BYP23-6   The April 1998 issue of *Management Accounting* includes an article by Julie Hertenstein and Marjorie Platt entitled "Why Product Development Teams Need Management Accountants."

Instructions
Read the article and answer the following questions.
(a) What percentage of a product's cost are determined at the design stage?
(b) Why do the authors say that management accountants can provide a broader perspective on costs than purchasing managers?
(c) What are some of the roles and responsibilites that managment accountants can have on a design team?
(d) What are some nonfinancial measures used to evaluate industrial design performance?

Ethics Case

BYP23-7   DeVito Company operates in a state where corporate taxes and workmen's compensation insurance rates have recently doubled. DeVito's president has assigned you the task of preparing an economic analysis and making a recommendation about whether to move the company's entire operation to Missouri. The president is slightly in favor of such a move because Missouri is his boyhood home, and he also owns a fishing lodge there.

You have just completed building your dream house, moved in, and sodded the lawn. Your children are all doing well in school and sports and, along with your spouse, want no part of a move to Missouri. If the company does move, so will you because your town is a one-industry community, and you and your spouse will have to move to have employment. Moving when everyone else does will cause you to take a big loss on the sale of your house. The same hardships will be suffered by your coworkers, and the town will be devastated.

In compiling the costs of moving versus not moving, you have latitude in the assumptions you make, the estimates you compute, and the discount rates and time periods you project. You are in a position to influence the decision singlehandedly.

Instructions
(a) Who are the stakeholders in this situation?
(b) What are the ethical issues in this situation?
(c) What would you do in this situation?

Answers to Self-Study Questions
1. d   **2.** b   **3.** c   **4.** d   **5.** a   **6.** b   **7.** c   **8.** b   **9.** d   **10.** b

REMEMBER TO GO BACK TO THE NAVIGATOR BOX ON THE CHAPTER-OPENING PAGE AND CHECK OFF YOUR COMPLETED WORK.

Specimen Financial Statements: Tootsie Roll Industries, Inc.

The Annual Report

Once each year a corporation communicates to its stockholders and other interested parties by issuing a complete set of audited financial statements. The **annual report**, as this communication is called, summarizes the financial results of the company's operations for the year and its plans for the future. Many annual reports are attractive, multicolored, glossy public relations pieces, containing pictures of corporate officers and directors as well as photos and descriptions of new products and new buildings. Yet the basic function of every annual report is to report financial information, almost all of which is a product of the corporation's accounting system.

Tootsie Roll Annual Report Walkthrough

The content and organization of corporate annual reports have become fairly standardized. Excluding the public relations part of the report (pictures, products, and propaganda), the following items are the traditional financial portions of the annual report:

Financial Highlights
Letter to the Stockholders
Management's Discussion and Analysis
Financial Statements
Notes to the Financial Statements
Management's Report on Internal Control
Management Certification of Financial Statements
Auditor's Report
Supplementary Financial Information

In this appendix we illustrate current financial reporting with a comprehensive set of corporate financial statements that are prepared in accordance with generally accepted accounting principles and audited by an international independent certified public accounting firm. We are grateful for permission to use the actual financial statements and other accompanying financial information from the annual report of a large, publicly held company, Tootsie Roll Industries, Inc.

Financial Highlights

Companies usually present the financial highlights section inside the front cover of the annual report or on its first two pages. This section generally reports the total or per share amounts for five to ten financial items for the current year and one or more previous years.

Financial items from the income statement and the balance sheet that typically are presented are sales, income from continuing operations, net income, net income per share, dividends per common share, and the amount of capital expenditures. The financial highlights section from **Tootsie Roll Industries' Annual Report** is shown on page A-2. We have also included Tootsie Roll's discussion of its corporate principles and corporate profile.

The financial information herein is reprinted with permission from the Tootsie Roll Industries, Inc. 2004 Annual Report. The complete financial statements for Tootsie Roll Industries are also available on the book's companion website.

Corporate Profile

Tootsie Roll Industries, Inc. has been engaged in the manufacture and sale of confectionery products for 108 years. Our products are primarily sold under the familiar brand names, Tootsie Roll, Tootsie Roll Pops, Caramel Apple Pops, Child's Play, Charms, Blow Pop, Blue Razz, Cella's chocolate covered cherries, Mason Dots, Mason Crows, Junior Mints, Charleston Chew, Sugar Daddy, Sugar Babies, Andes, Fluffy Stuff cotton candy, Dubble Bubble, Razzles, Cry Baby, Nik-L-Nip and El Bubble.

Corporate Principles

We believe that the differences among companies are attributable to the caliber of their people, and therefore we strive to attract and retain superior people for each job.

We believe that an open family atmosphere at work combined with professional management fosters cooperation and enables each individual to maximize his or her contribution to the company and realize the corresponding rewards.

We do not jeopardize long-term growth for immediate, short-term results.

We maintain a conservative financial posture in the deployment and management of our assets.

We run a trim operation and continually strive to eliminate waste, minimize cost and implement performance improvements.

We invest in the latest and most productive equipment to deliver the best quality product to our customers at the lowest cost.

We seek to outsource functions where appropriate and to vertically integrate operations where it is financially advantageous to do so.

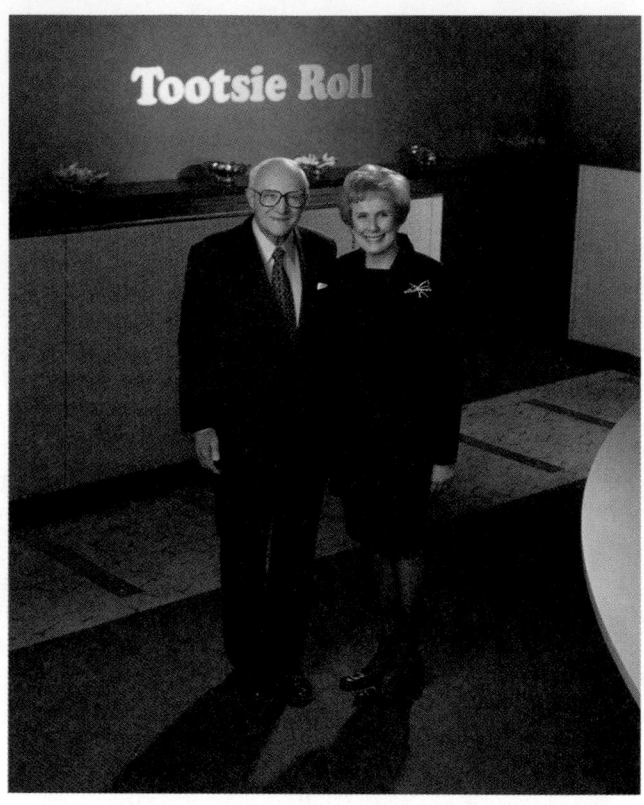

Melvin J. Gordon, Chairman and Chief Executive Officer and Ellen R. Gordon, President and Chief Operating Officer.

We view our well known brands as prized assets to be aggressively advertised and promoted to each new generation of consumers.

We conduct business with the highest ethical standards and integrity which are codified in the Company's "Code of Business Conduct and Ethics."

Letter to the Stockholders

Nearly every annual report contains a letter to the stockholders from the chairman of the board or the president, or both. This letter typically discusses the company's accomplishments during the past year and highlights significant events such as mergers and acquisitions, new products, operating achievements, business philosophy, changes in officers or directors, financing commitments, expansion plans, and future prospects. The letter to the stockholders signed by Melvin J. Gordon, Chairman of the Board and Chief Executive Officer, and Ellen R. Gordon, President and Chief Operating Officer, of Tootsie Roll Industries is shown on the next pages.

To Our Shareholders

Sales in 2004 increased to $420 million compared to 2003 sales of $392 million. This represents a new record level of sales for the company.

Net earnings in 2004 were $64 million as compared to $65 million in 2003. On a per share basis, earnings increased from $1.22 in 2003 to $1.23 in 2004. The increase in earnings per share results from fewer shares outstanding in 2004 due to stock repurchases.

Other highlights of 2004 include:

- We purchased Concord Confections, the largest acquisition in the company's history.

- Cash dividends were paid for the sixty-second consecutive year, earning us recognition as a "Dividend Aristocrat" by Standard & Poors and a "Dividend Achiever" by Mergent.

- Our fortieth consecutive annual 3% stock dividend was distributed in April.

- Again this year, capital expenditures were made for projects that will improve operating efficiencies and support growth.

Our conservative financial posture coupled with many years of profitable operations enabled us to make these significant outlays without incurring undue leverage or putting the company at financial risk. Of the $154 million borrowed in August in conjunction with the Concord purchase, approximately 40% or $62 million was paid back, and cash and investments, net of interest bearing debt, was $86 million by year end.

We remain prepared to capitalize on appropriate investment opportunities as they may arise. These may include initiatives to develop niche products, investment in strategically or economically prudent capital projects and pursuit of additional complementary business acquisitions. We remain active in our evaluation of opportunities in each of these areas.

Sales and Marketing

We have long recognized the competitive advantage of having strong brands which position us well against the continuing onslaught of low priced foreign imports, private label imitators and branded competition from other confectionery manufacturers.

In 2004 we again offered focused promotional programs such as bonus bags, shippers and combo packs to high volume classes of trade. These programs reinforce the attributes of quality and value that consumers expect and generate high-turn, profitable use of shelf and floor space that retailers demand.

We also successfully continued our sales initiatives in the growing dollar store class of trade. Consumers who frequent these outlets tend to be value oriented in their purchasing decisions, and find that our brands deliver excellent quality at an affordable price.

Halloween was once again our strongest sales period. Our bagged goods, in particular our popular mixed bags assortments such as Childs Play, continued to sell well through the mass merchandise, drug, supermarket and warehouse club venues.

Outside of Halloween, our line of "theater" products continued to receive good consumer acceptance in the drug, mass merchandise, supermarket and dollar store trade classes. This family of products presents many of our most popular candies to consumers in large "theater sized" reclosable boxes with attractive display panels.

Brands featured in this line include four varieties of Dots as well as Crows, Sugar Babies, Mini-Charleston Chews and Junior

Financial Highlights

	December 31,	
	2004	2003
	(in thousands except per share data)	
Net Sales	$420,110	$392,656
Net Earnings	64,174	65,014
Working Capital	110,376	180,818
Net Property, Plant and Equipment	178,750	129,163
Shareholders' Equity	570,179	536,581
Average Shares Outstanding*	52,366	53,305
Per Share Items*		
Net Earnings	$1.23	$1.22
Cash Dividends Paid	.28	.27

*Adjusted for stock dividends.

Mints. In 2004 we introduced a new item in the theater box format-Junior Caramels. These boxed candies put the company in a strong position in regard to sales to theaters and to home video sections of self-service outlets.

Junior Caramels

Junior Caramels consist of delicious, soft caramel centers enrobed in a shell of rich milk chocolate and polished to a beautiful shine. They were offered on a limited introductory basis in 2004, and met with enthusiastic consumer acceptance. National rollout is planned for 2005. Junior Caramels are an excellent example of the type of niche product extension we continually seek.

We also brought out two popular items from mixed assortments, and introduced them as stand-alone, "Limited Edition" goods. Packaged in foil bags to preserve freshness, Chocolate Tootsie Pops and Vanilla Tootsie Rolls gave consumers an opportunity to indulge in their personal favorite treats.

Limited Edition Tootsie Rolls and Tootsie Pops

Excitement about the Tootsie Pop brand was further stimulated by the addition of a sixth flavor to our traditional five-flavor mix. Consumers can now enjoy one of three tantalizing new "mystery" flavors, watermelon, strawberry or blue raspberry, in every package they buy.

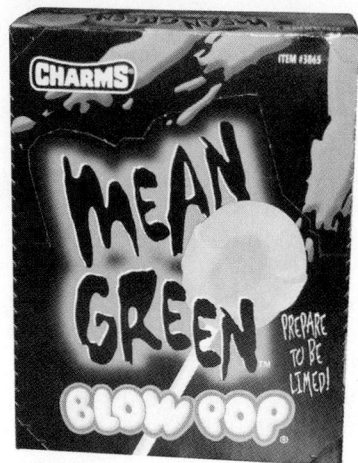

Mean Green Blow Pops

In the Blow Pop line, we updated the packaging with enhanced graphics on a brighter white, opaque background. We also introduced Mean Green, an intensely lime flavored translucent candy shell surrounding a bright green, sour lime flavored bubble gum center. Its distinctive packaging cautions consumers to "Prepare to be Limed!"

Concord Confections

In keeping with our stated goal of making complimentary business acquisitions, in August we purchased Concord Confections, maker of Dubble Bubble, to our knowledge the largest maker of bubble gum in the world. This icon brand comes in two primary formats.

Dubble Bubble

"Chunk gum" is the familiar pink colored, tutti-frutti flavored bubble gum wrapped in wax paper bearing the instantly recognizable red oval Dubble Bubble trademark. "Gum balls" are brightly colored, spherically shaped and come in many sizes and flavors, primarily for sale in gumball machines and tube packs. Dubble Bubble is the market leader in both the chunk and ball gum categories.

Many other brands were included in the acquisition. Some of these are:

Razzles—the magic dextrose candy that turns into gum while you eat it.

Cry Baby—gum so sour it can bring a tear to your eye!

Nik-L-Nip—chewable wax bottles filled with tasty juice.

Along with these and other brands, the Concord acquisition included its principal manufacturing facilities located near Toronto.

Our sales and marketing departments are integrating Concord's broad product assortment and developing appropriate promotional strategies for these new items.

Advertising and Public Relations

Our products again received extensive cable television exposure through special interest features. The Food Network's *Unwrapped* program produced new segments on Fluffy Stuff Cotton Candy, Super Blow Pops and Tootsie Fruit Rolls. These are in addition to previous *Unwrapped* shows that feature nearly all of our major brands.

Tootsie Rolls and Tootsie Pops were spotlighted in "Snack Food Tech" on *Modern Marvels*, the History Channel's signature series. That show, based on engineering accomplishments, explored the snack food industry from early discoveries to the present innovative technologies employed today.

Exposure on these highly rated shows, including periodic replays, generates positive awareness of our products.

We also utilized cable television to convey our classic "How Many Licks?" Tootsie Pops advertising message. The 2004 campaign was directed toward cartoon and family programs, and generated the inevitable letters from many consumers who succumbed to the urge to convey just how many licks it does take. Alas, the precise answer remains elusive, lending credence to Mr. Owl's wise observation: "the world may never know!"

The company has had a long history of making products for military rations. We continue to receive many gratifying letters from soldiers in Iraq and elsewhere, commenting on how Tootsie Rolls in their ration kits brightened their day or brought forth a nostalgic reminder of home.

There were also numerous articles and stories in newspapers and other publications throughout the year publicizing our products. Many of these focus on holiday themes such as "popular Halloween candies" or "what's new for the Easter season." Other articles highlight certain consumer trends such as the current popularity of nostalgic 'retro' products and feature many of our brands, which have stood the test of time and remain consumer favorites.

Manufacturing and Distribution

We continue to invest in projects that support growing product lines, keep our production facilities as efficient as possible and improve product quality.

We began new capital projects of these types during the year and completed several other major initiatives, which began in prior years. As technology evolves, we have continued to realize benefits through automation.

We have long found merit in sharing ideas among facilities. As with past acquisitions, we anticipate that the addition of Concord's operations will enhance this process. Accordingly, we have eagerly begun to share ideas and best practices between our other manufacturing and distribution centers and Concord.

Our distribution centers are physically capable of handling the volume of Concord inventory, enabling us to focus on the complex process of integrating these products into our supply chain. This effort is already well underway.

Purchasing

Prices for key raw materials and packaging were generally favorable during the year. In particular, cocoa eased substantially from recent

historically high levels. However, this saving was nearly offset by increased costs in edible oils.

We are in the process of bringing the procurement activities for Concord on line with our purchasing systems. Where possible we will leverage this additional volume in our competitive bidding, hedging and forward purchase programs to ensure that the company's purchases are sourced as economically as possible, with minimum exposure to short-term market fluctuations.

Information Technology and Internal Controls

Integrating Concord into our systems was a major operational initiative during 2004. Planning was completed, certain systems have been brought over and the remaining system areas will be converted to our platform during the first half of 2005.

Projects of this scope reinforce the wisdom of past investments of time and money toward developing state-of-the-art business systems and data management protocols. We remain convinced that information technology is a prime strategic tool to support future growth.

Also during 2004 we, as well as other large public companies, undertook the substantial task of documenting and testing our system of internal controls in order to meet the requirements of the Sarbanes-Oxley Act. Completing this process in a timely fashion required commitment and cooperation throughout our organization. We are pleased to note that our controls over financial reporting, which we always believed to be good, are now documented and tested.

International

Our international sales increased during 2004. We manufacture and sell products in Mexico under the Tutsi trademark. We also sell Tootsie, Charms and Concord products to Canada and over 30 other countries in Europe, Asia and South and Central America. Our legacy product line, coupled with newly acquired Dubble Bubble products, offer a compelling and broad assortment of items that can be extended to additional foreign markets.

In Appreciation

We believe that people have been the key ingredient in our recipe for success over the years. Excellence is required at every level of the organization to meet the growing demands in today's increasingly competitive marketplace. Accordingly, we wish to thank our many loyal employees, customers, foreign distributors, suppliers and sales brokers for their efforts on behalf of the company during 2004. We also thank our shareholders for their support through the years.

We remain committed to growing the sales and profits of the company and believe that we are well positioned in this regard as we enter 2005.

Melvin J. Gordon

Melvin J. Gordon
Chairman of the Board and
Chief Executive Officer

Ellen R. Gordon

Ellen R. Gordon
President and
Chief Operating Officer

Management Discussion and Analysis

The management discussion and analysis (MD&A) section covers three financial aspects of a company: its results of operations, its ability to pay near-term obligations, and its ability to fund operations and expansion. Management must highlight favorable or unfavorable trends and identify significant events and uncertainties that affect these three factors. This discussion obviously involves a number of subjective estimates and opinions. The MD&A section of Tootsie Roll's annual report is presented below.

Management's Discussion and Analysis of Financial Condition and Results of Operations

(in thousands except per share, percentage and ratio figures)

FINANCIAL REVIEW

This financial review discusses the company's financial condition, results of operations, liquidity and capital resources, market risks and other matters. It should be read in conjunction with the Consolidated Financial Statements and related footnotes that follow this discussion.

FINANCIAL CONDITION

The strong financial condition in which the company entered 2004,

coupled with profitable operations during the year, enabled us to make the largest acquisition in the company's history without incurring undue leverage or placing the company at financial risk. Working capital ended the year at $110,376, down from $180,818 at the beginning of the year. The decrease of $70,442 is due to lower cash and short-term investments and higher current debt used to finance the Concord acquisition, partially offset by the working capital acquired.

Interest bearing debt was $99,500 at year end, $62,000 lower than the peak of $161,500 on August 31, 2004 immediately following the acquisition. Debt was paid down through a combination of cash flow provided by operating activities and investment maturities.

Shareholders equity increased to $570,179 in 2004 from $536,581 primarily due to net earnings during the year, net of cash dividends and share repurchases. The company has paid cash dividends for sixty-two consecutive years and has distributed a stock dividend for forty consecutive years.

The company has a simple financial structure, and aside from an immaterial amount of operating leases, the company has no "off-balance sheet" financing arrangements. We maintain a conservative financial posture and funds generated from operations plus maturities of short term investments are expected to be adequate to meet the company's financing needs over the coming year. These funds may be augmented by prudent borrowing for significant investments such as was done for the Concord acquisition.

RESULTS OF OPERATIONS

2004 vs. 2003

Net sales in 2004 grew to a record $420,110, an increase of $27,454 from 2003 sales of $392,656. Sales benefited from successful marketing and promotional programs, including pre-Halloween sales programs that have traditionally made our third quarter the highest selling period of the year and did so again this year.

However, the sales increase in 2004 is attributable to sales resulting from the Concord acquisition as core brand sales were approximately even with the prior year.

Cost of goods sold increased from 56.7% to 58.2% of sales. This increase is due to lower margins on acquired brands, lower production volumes in several core product lines, approximately $1,800 in start-up costs associated with a new production line and a $600 inventory adjustment for a discontinued product line. These expenses were partially offset by somewhat lower raw material and packaging costs.

Due to the seasonal nature of our business and corresponding

variations in product mix, gross margins have historically been lower in the second half of the year, and this was the case in 2004. The impact of the factors discussed above was concentrated in the fourth quarter. As a result, fourth quarter gross margins were lower than in 2003.

Selling, marketing and administrative expense increased as a percent of sales to 20.4% in 2004 from 19.8% in 2003. The increase is due to expenses associated with Concord and approximately $1,500 higher freight costs related to fuel surcharges, as well as higher fees associated with Sarbanes-Oxley compliance and general cost increases.

Other income declined from $5,594 in 2003 to $4,784 in 2004 due to higher interest expense and lower investment earnings, both related to financing the Concord acquisition. The consolidated effective tax rate declined from 33.6% in 2003 to 32.2%. This decline generally reflects a reduction in foreign income taxes.

Consolidated net earnings were $64,174 and $65,014 and earnings per share were $1.23 and $1.22 in 2004 and 2003, respectively. Average shares outstanding declined from 53,305 to 52,366 due to share repurchases.

2003 vs. 2002

Net sales were $392,656 in 2003 compared to $393,185 in 2002, a decrease of $529 or 0.1%. Factors effecting sales growth were generally sluggish US economic conditions, higher promotional expense and lower sales in Mexico. Seasonal sales again peaked in the third quarter due to Halloween sales and promotions.

Cost of goods sold as a percentage of net sales was

NET SALES
Millions of dollars

NET EARNINGS
Per Share

56.7% and 56.5% for 2003 and 2002, respectively. Higher costs for our principal ingredients and increased plant overhead costs incurred during 2003 were generally offset by selective price increases. Gross margins were lower in the second half of the year due to seasonality and corresponding variations in product mix.

Selling, marketing and administrative expenses were $77,756 in 2003 as compared to $75,751 in 2002, an increase of 2.6%. These costs were 19.8% of sales in 2003 versus 19.3% in the prior year.

SHAREHOLDERS'
EQUITY
Millions of dollars

CASH DIVIDENDS
Per Share

Accordingly, earnings from operations were $92,353 in 2003, or $2,877 below the $95,230 attained in 2002. Other income was $5,594 in 2003 as compared to $5,458 in 2002. The increase of $136 is primarily attributable to a $541 property tax refund in 2003, partially offset by lower interest income due to lower interest rates.

The consolidated effective tax rate decreased from 34.1% in 2002 to 33.6% in 2003. This decline generally reflects a reduction in state income taxes.

Net earnings were $65,014 and $66,388 and earnings per share were $1.22 in both 2003 and 2002. Earnings per share remained constant on lower net earnings due to share repurchases. Average shares outstanding declined from 54,592 in 2002 to 53,305 in 2003.

LIQUIDITY AND CAPITAL RESOURCES

Cash flows from operating activities were $76,228 in 2004, $83,466 in 2003 and $75,473 in 2002. Both the decline in 2004 and the increase in 2003 were principally attributable to changes in accounts receivable due to the timing of sales and customer payments. Also, while inventories grew in each of 2004, 2003 and 2002, the 2004 increase was higher because of the addition of Concord items to our supply chain.

Cash flows from investing activities reflect the purchase of Concord Confections for $218,229 as well as capital expenditures of $17,948 and a $72,138 net decrease in marketable securities associated with financing the acquisition. In 2003, capital expenditures were $12,150 and marketable securities increased by a net of $38,233. In 2002, capital expenditures were $10,308 and marketable securities increased by $19,263.

Cash flows from financing activities reflect a borrowing of $154,000 for the acquisition and $62,000 of payments against this loan. Share repurchases were $16,407, $40,096 and $32,313 in 2004, 2003 and 2002, respectively. Cash dividends of $14,877, $14,410 and $14,614 were paid in 2004, 2003 and 2002, respectively. 2004 was the sixty-second consecutive year in which we have paid cash dividends.

MARKET RISKS

The company is exposed to market risks related to commodity prices, interest rates, equity prices and foreign exchange.

Commodity price risks relate to ingredients (primarily sugar, cocoa, corn syrup and vegetable oils). The company believes its competitors face similar risks, and the industry has historically adjusted prices to compensate for adverse fluctuations in commodity costs.

To mitigate the impact of commodity cost fluctuations, the company enters into commodity futures contracts to hedge anticipated purchases of certain ingredients (primarily sugar). These contracts are effective as hedges under Statement of Financial Accounting Standards (SFAS) 133, "Accounting for Derivative Instruments and Hedging Activities." The unrealized gains and losses on such contracts are deferred as a component of accumulated other comprehensive earnings (loss) and are recognized as a component of cost of goods sold when the related inventory is sold.

Interest rate risks relate to the company's investments in debt securities (primarily municipal bonds) with maturities of generally up to four years. The majority of these have historically been held to maturity, which limits the company's exposure to interest rate fluctuations. Interest rates on the company's debt obligations are reset weekly.

Equity price risk relates to the company's investments in mutual funds.

Foreign exchange risk relates to the company's foreign operations including Concord and purchase commitments.

The company has no outstanding guarantees of obligations to third parties.

Commodities

The potential change in fair value of commodity derivative instruments (primarily sugar futures contracts) held by the company, assuming a 10% change in the underlying commodity price, was $858. This analysis only includes commodity derivative instruments and, therefore, does not consider the offsetting effect of changes in the price of the underlying commodity. This amount is not significant compared with the net earnings and shareholders equity of the company.

Equity price

At December 31, 2004, the company has investments in mutual funds of $25,332. These investments primarily relate to hedging deferred compensation liabilities, and any potential change in their fair value would be offset by a corresponding change in such liabilities.

Interest rates

The accompanying chart summarizes the maturities of the company's investments in debt securities at December 31, 2004.

Less than 1 year	$ 28,701
1 - 2 years	53,014
2 - 3 years	18,293
Total.	$100,008

Foreign exchange

Prior to the acquisition of Concord, the company's operations outside of the United States represented less than 10% of its consolidated operations. Accordingly, the company did not use derivative financial instruments to hedge its foreign currency assets or liabilities or its overall investments in its foreign subsidiaries.

Certain of Concord's manufacturing expenses, including labor and a portion of its packaging, ingredients and supplies are sourced in Canadian dollars. From time to time the company may use forward foreign exchange contracts and derivative instruments to mitigate its exposure to these costs as well as those related to firm commitments to purchase equipment from foreign

vendors. As of December 31, 2004 the company had not entered into any forward foreign exchange contracts with respect to the Canadian dollar, and other outstanding foreign exchange contracts were not material.

CRITICAL ACCOUNTING POLICIES

Preparation of the company's financial statements involves judgments due to uncertainties affecting the application of accounting policies, and the likelihood that different amounts would be reported under different conditions or using different assumptions. In the opinion of management, the company does not have any individual accounting policy that is "critical." However, following is a summary of the more significant accounting policies and methods where estimates are used.

Revenue recognition

Revenue, net of applicable provisions for discounts, returns, allowances, and certain advertising and promotional costs, is recognized when products are delivered to customers and collectibility is reasonably assured. The accounting for such promotional programs is discussed below.

Provisions for bad debts are recorded as selling, marketing and administrative expense. Such provisions have not exceeded 0.2% of net sales for 2004, 2003 and 2002 and, accordingly, have not been significant to the company's financial position or results of operations.

Intangible assets

Effective January 1, 2002 the company adopted SFAS No. 142, whereby goodwill and other indefinite lived assets are not amortized, but are instead subjected to annual testing for impairment. The company's intangible assets consist

primarily of trademarks, the values of which the company has determined are not impaired.

This determination is made by comparing the carrying value of the asset with its estimated fair value, which is calculated on the basis of discounted projected future cash flows. These projected future cash flows are dependent on a number of factors including future business plans and projected operating results. Although the majority of the company's trademarks relate to well established brands with a long history of consumer acceptance, projected cash flows are inherently uncertain. A change in the assumptions underlying the impairment analysis, such as a reduction in projected cash flows or the use of a different discount rate, could cause an impairment in the future.

Customer incentive programs, advertising and marketing

Advertising and marketing costs are recorded in the period to which such costs relate. The company does not defer the recognition of any amounts on its consolidated balance sheet with respect to such costs. Customer incentives and other promotional costs are recorded at the time of sale based upon incentive program terms and historical utilization statistics, which are generally consistent from year to year.

The liabilities associated with these programs are reviewed quarterly and adjusted if utilization rates differ from management's original estimates. Such adjustments have not historically been material to the company's operating results.

Investments

The company invests in certain high-quality debt securities primarily Aa or better rated municipal bonds. The accounting for such investments is outlined in Note 1 and does not involve any significant estimates on the part of management. Due to their relatively short maturities, changes in interest rates have an immaterial effect on the principal value of these investments and no credit losses have been incurred.

Guarantees

The Financial Accounting Standards Board issued Interpretation No. 45 relating to the accounting for and disclosure of certain types of guarantees. The disclosure provisions are effective for financial statements with years ending after December 15, 2002. No disclosures were required for the company as a result of adoption of this standard, as it has no such guarantees outstanding.

Other matters

In the opinion of management, other than contracts for raw materials, including commodity hedges and outstanding purchase orders for packaging, ingredients and supplies, all entered into in the ordinary course of business, the company does not have any significant contractual obligations or future commitments. The company's outstanding contractual commitments as of December 31, 2004, all of which are normal and recurring in nature, are summarized in the accompanying chart.

The company provides split dollar life insurance benefits to certain executive officers and records an asset equal to the cumulative premiums paid on the related policies, as the company will fully recover these premiums under the terms of the plan.

The results of our operations and our financial condition are expressed in the following financial statements.

Open Contractual Commitments as of December 31, 2004

Payable in	Total	Less than 1 year	1 to 3 Years	3 to 5 Years	More than 5 Years
Commodity hedges	$8,588	$5,176	$3,412	$ —	$ —
Purchase obligations	68,919	68,919	—	—	—
Split dollar insurance	8,256	3,441	4,815	—	—
Interest bearing debt	99,500	6,333	85,667	—	7,500
Operating leases	1,350	851	499	—	—
Total	$186,613	$84,720	$94,393	$ —	$7,500

Note: the above amounts exclude deferred income tax liabilities of $25,995, post retirement health care and life insurance benefits of $10,075 and deferred compensation and other liabilities of $30,020 because the timing of payments relating to these items cannot be reasonably determined.

Financial Statements and Accompanying Notes

The standard set of financial statements consists of: (1) a comparative income statement for three years, (2) a comparative balance sheet for two years, (3) a comparative statement of cash flows for three years, (4) a statement of retained earnings (or stockholders' equity) for three years, and (5) a set of accompanying notes that are considered an integral part of the financial statements. The auditor's report, unless stated otherwise, covers the financial statements and the accompanying notes. The financial statements and accompanying notes plus some supplementary data and analyses for Tootsie Roll Industries follow.

CONSOLIDATED STATEMENT OF

Financial Position

TOOTSIE ROLL INDUSTRIES, INC. AND SUBSIDIARIES   (in thousands)

Assets

December 31,

	2004	2003
CURRENT ASSETS:		
Cash and cash equivalents	$ 56,989	$ 84,084
Investments	32,369	86,961
Accounts receivable trade, less allowances of $2,440 and $1,970	28,456	18,131
Other receivables	9,001	3,076
Inventories:		
Finished goods and work-in-process	37,384	28,969
Raw materials and supplies	21,393	17,117
Prepaid expenses	5,719	4,416
Deferred income taxes	1,382	951
Total current assets	192,693	243,705
PROPERTY, PLANT AND EQUIPMENT, at cost:		
Land	14,973	8,265
Buildings	61,714	44,960
Machinery and equipment	244,367	206,697
	321,054	259,922
Less—Accumulated depreciation	142,304	130,759
	178,750	129,163
OTHER ASSETS:		
Goodwill	74,002	38,151
Trademarks	193,342	79,348
Investments	96,640	112,431
Split dollar officer life insurance	66,094	62,499
Investement in joint venture	10,232	—
	440,310	292,429
	$811,753	$665,297

(The accompanying notes are an integral part of these statements.)

(in thousands except per share data)

Liabilities and Shareholders' Equity   December 31,

	2004	2003
CURRENT LIABILITIES:		
Bank loan	$ 6,333	$ —
Accounts payable	19,315	11,947
Dividends payable	3,659	3,589
Accrued liabilities	44,722	38,834
Income taxes payable	8,288	8,517
Total current liabilities	82,317	62,887
NONCURRENT LIABILITIES:		
Bank loan	85,667	—
Deferred income taxes	25,995	22,631
Postretirement health care and life insurance benefits	10,075	9,302
Industrial development bonds	7,500	7,500
Deferred compensation and other liabilities	30,020	26,396
Total noncurrent liabilities	159,257	65,829
SHAREHOLDERS' EQUITY:		
Common stock, $.69-4/9 par value—		
120,000 shares authorized—		
34,760 and 34,082, respectively, issued	24,139	23,668
Class B common stock, $.69-4/9 par value—		
40,000 shares authorized—		
17,515 and 17,145, respectively, issued	12,163	11,906
Capital in excess of par value	397,745	357,922
Retained earnings, per accompanying statement	149,055	156,786
Accumulated other comprehensive earnings (loss)	(10,931)	(11,709)
Treasury stock (at cost)—		
58 shares and 56 shares, respectively	(1,992)	(1,992)
	570,179	536,581
	$811,753	$665,297

CONSOLIDATED STATEMENT OF

Earnings, Comprehensive Earnings and Retained Earnings

TOOTSIE ROLL INDUSTRIES. INC. AND SUBSIDIARIES   (in thousands except per share data)

	For the year ended December 31,		
	2004	2003	2002
Net sales	$420,110	$392,656	$393,185
Cost of goods sold	244,501	222,547	222,204
Gross margin	175,609	170,109	170,981
Selling, marketing and administrative expenses	85,705	77,756	75,751
Earnings from operations	89,904	92,353	95,230
Other income, net	4,784	5,594	5,458
Earnings before income taxes	94,688	97,947	100,688
Provision for income taxes	30,514	32,933	34,300
Net earnings	$ 64,174	$ 65,014	$ 66,388
Net earnings	$ 64,174	$ 65,014	$ 66,388
Other comprehensive earnings (loss)	778	(657)	(1,139)
Comprehensive earnings	$ 64,952	$ 64,357	$ 65,249
Retained earnings at beginning of year	$156,786	$148,705	$161,345
Net earnings	64,174	65,014	66,388
Cash dividends ($.28, $.27 and $.26 per share, respectively)	(14,547)	(14,362)	(14,304)
Stock dividends	(57,358)	(42,571)	(64,724)
Retained earnings at end of year	$149,055	$156,786	$148,705
Earnings per share	$ 1.23	$ 1.22	$ 1.22
Average common and class B common shares outstanding	52,366	53,305	54,592

(The accompanying notes are an integral part of these statements.)

CONSOLIDATED STATEMENT OF

Cash Flows

TOOTSIE ROLL INDUSTRIES, INC. AND SUBSIDIARIES

(in thousands)

	For the year ended December 31,		
	2004	2003	2002
CASH FLOWS FROM OPERATING ACTIVITIES:			
Net earnings	$ 64,174	$ 65,014	$ 66,388
Adjustments to reconcile net earnings to net cash provided by operating activities:			
Depreciation and amortization	11,680	11,379	12,354
Amortization of marketable securities	1,885	2,534	1,407
Purchase of trading securities	(2,507)	(3,154)	(2,602)
Changes in operating assets and liabilities:			
Accounts receivable	673	4,266	(2,886)
Other receivables	1,574	490	619
Inventories	(4,567)	(2,579)	(2,734)
Prepaid expenses and other assets	(5,054)	(4,864)	(6,502)
Accounts payable and accrued liabilities	2,478	2,582	5,052
Income taxes payable and deferred	2,712	3,827	318
Postretirement health care and life insurance benefits	773	1,151	701
Deferred compensation and other liabilities	2,227	2,651	2,554
Other	180	169	804
Net cash provided by operating activities	76,228	83,466	75,473
CASH FLOWS FROM INVESTING ACTIVITIES:			
Acquisition of business, net of cash acquired	(218,229)	—	—
Capital expenditures	(17,948)	(12,150)	(10,308)
Purchase of held to maturity securities	(22,049)	(57,823)	(64,956)
Maturity of held to maturity securities	44,113	25,643	46,797
Purchase of available for sale securities	(83,987)	(57,578)	(34,795)
Sale and maturity of available for sale securities	134,061	51,525	33,691
Net cash used in investing activities	(164,039)	(50,383)	(29,571)
CASH FLOWS FROM FINANCING ACTIVITIES:			
Proceeds from bank loan	154,000	—	—
Repayment of bank loan	(62,000)	—	—
Shares repurchased and retired	(16,407)	(40,096)	(32,313)
Dividends paid in cash	(14,877)	(14,410)	(14,614)
Net cash provided by (used in) financing activities	60,716	(54,506)	(46,927)
Decrease in cash and cash equivalents	(27,095)	(21,423)	(1,025)
Cash and cash equivalents at beginning of year	84,084	105,507	106,532
Cash and cash equivalents at end of year	$ 56,989	$ 84,084	$105,507
Supplemental cash flow information:			
Income taxes paid	$ 28,966	$ 31,561	$ 34,099
Interest paid	$ 879	$ 172	$ 309
Stock dividend issued	$ 56,959	$ 42,513	$ 64,371

(The accompanying notes are an integral part of these statements.)

Notes to Consolidated Financial Statements

TOOTSIE ROLL INDUSTRIES, INC. AND SUBSIDIARIES

($ in thousands except per share data)

NOTE 1—SIGNIFICANT ACCOUNTING POLICIES:

Basis of consolidation:

The consolidated financial statements include the accounts of Tootsie Roll Industries, Inc. and its wholly-owned subsidiaries (the company), which are primarily engaged in the manufacture and sale of candy products. All significant intercompany transactions have been eliminated.

The preparation of financial statements in conformity with generally accepted accounting principles in the United States of America requires management to make estimates and assumptions that affect the reported amounts of assets and liabilities and disclosure of contingent assets and liabilities at the date of the financial statements and the reported amounts of revenues and expenses during the reporting period. Actual results could differ from those estimates.

Certain reclassifications have been made to the prior year financial statements to conform to the current year presentation.

Revenue recognition and other accounting pronouncements:

Products are sold to customers based on accepted purchase orders which include quantity, sales price and other relevant terms of sale. Revenues are recognized when products are delivered to customers and collectibility is reasonably assured. Shipping and handling costs of $31,795, $28,217 and $28,579 in 2004, 2003 and 2002, respectively, are included in selling, marketing and administrative expenses. Accounts receivable are unsecured. Revenues from a major customer aggregated approximately 20.8%, 20.6% and 19.6% of total net sales during the years ended December 31, 2004, 2003 and 2002, respectively.

In November 2004, the Financial Accounting Standards Board (FASB) issued Statement of Financial Accounting Standards (SFAS) No. 151, "Inventory Costs—an amendment to ARB No. 43, Chapter 4," which amends guidance in accounting for abnormal amounts of idle facility expense. The company believes that the pronouncement is generally not applicable to the company's operations and to the extent it may be applicable it is not expected to have a significant impact on the company's consolidated financial statements.

Cash and cash equivalents:

The company considers temporary cash investments with an original maturity of three months or less to be cash equivalents.

Investments:

Investments consist of various marketable securities with maturities of generally up to four years. The company classifies debt and equity securities as either held to maturity, available for sale or trading. Held to maturity securities represent those securities that the company has both the positive intent and ability to hold to maturity and are carried at amortized cost. Available for sale securities represent those securities that do not meet the classification of held to maturity, are not actively traded and are carried at fair value. Unrealized gains and losses on these securities are excluded from earnings and are reported as a separate component of shareholders' equity, net of applicable taxes, until realized. Trading securities relate to deferred compensation arrangements and are carried at fair value.

Hedging activities:

From time to time, the company enters into commodities futures contracts that are intended and effective as hedges of market price risks associated with the anticipated purchase of certain raw materials (primarily sugar). To qualify as a hedge, the company evaluates a variety of characteristics of these transactions, including the probability that the anticipated transaction will occur. If the anticipated transaction were not to occur, the gain or loss would then be recognized in current earnings. The company does not engage in trading or other speculative use of derivative instruments. The company does assume the risk that counter parties may not be able to meet the terms of their contracts. The company does not expect any losses as a result of counter party defaults.

The company's derivative instruments are being accounted for as cash flow hedges and are recorded on the balance sheet at fair value. Changes therein are recorded in other comprehensive earnings and are reclassified to earnings in the periods in which earnings are affected by the hedged item. Substantially all amounts reported in accumulated other comprehensive earnings (loss) are expected to be reclassified to cost of goods sold. During the years ended December 31, 2004, 2003 and 2002, ineffectiveness related to cash flow hedges was not material.

Inventories:

Inventories are stated at cost, not to exceed market. The cost of substantially all of the company's inventories ($54,794 and $42,735 at December 31, 2004 and 2003, respectively) has been determined by the last-in, first-out (LIFO) method. The excess of current cost over LIFO cost of inventories approximates $5,868 and $6,442 at December 31, 2004 and 2003, respectively. The cost of certain foreign inventories

($3,983 and $3,351 at December 31, 2004 and 2003, respectively) has been determined by the first-in, first-out (FIFO) method. Rebates, discounts and other cash consideration received from a vendor related to inventory purchases is reflected as a reduction in the cost of the related inventory item, and is therefore reflected in cost of sales when the related inventory item is sold.

Property, plant and equipment:

Depreciation is computed for financial reporting purposes by use of the straight-line method based on useful lives of 20 to 35 years for buildings and 5 to 20 years for machinery and equipment. Depreciation expense was $11,680, $11,379 and $12,354 in 2004, 2003 and 2002, respectively, including $744 relating to equipment disposals.

Carrying value of long-lived assets:

The company reviews long-lived assets to determine if there are events or circumstances indicating that the amount of the asset reflected in the company's balance sheet may not be recoverable. When such indicators are present, the company compares the carrying value of the long-lived asset, or asset group, to the future undiscounted cash flows of the underlying assets to determine if an impairment exists. If applicable, an impairment charge would be recorded to write down the carrying value to its fair value. The determination of fair value involves the use of estimates of future cash flows that involve considerable management judgment and are based upon assumptions about expected future operating performance. The actual cash flows could differ from management's estimates due to changes in business conditions, operating performance, and economic conditions. No impairment charges were recorded by the company during 2004, 2003 or 2002.

Postretirement health care and life insurance benefits:

The company provides certain postretirement health care and life insurance benefits. The cost of these postretirement benefits is accrued during employees' working careers. The company also provides split dollar life insurance benefits to certain executive officers. The company records an asset equal to the cumulative insurance premiums that will be recovered upon the death of a covered employee(s) or earlier under the terms of the plan. Split dollar premiums paid were $3,620, $4,237 and $6,890 in 2004, 2003 and 2002, respectively.

Intangible assets:

The company accounts for intangible assets in accordance with SFAS No. 142, "Goodwill and Other Intangible Assets," which was adopted by the company on January 1, 2002. In accordance with this statement, goodwill and intangible assets with indefinite lives are not amortized, but rather tested for impairment at least annually. All trademarks have been assessed by management to have indefinite lives because they are expected to generate cash flows indefinitely. The company

has completed its annual impairment testing of its goodwill and trademarks during the fourth quarter of each of the years presented, and no impairment was found.

Income taxes:

Deferred income taxes are recorded and recognized for future tax effects of temporary differences between financial and income tax reporting. Federal income taxes are provided on the portion of income of foreign subsidiaries that is expected to be remitted to the U.S. and become taxable, but not on the portion that is considered to be permanently invested in the foreign subsidiary.

Foreign currency translation:

The company has determined the functional currency for each foreign subsidiary. The U.S. dollar is used as the functional currency where a substantial portion of the subsidiary's business is indexed to the U.S. dollar or where its manufactured products are principally sold in the U.S. All other foreign subsidiaries use the local currency as their functional currency. Where the U.S. dollar is used as the functional currency, foreign currency translation adjustments are recorded as a charge or credit to other income in the statement of earnings. Where the foreign currency is used as the functional currency, translation adjustments are recorded as a separate component of comprehensive earnings (loss).

Joint venture:

The company's 50% interest in two Spanish companies is accounted for using the equity method. The company records an increase in its investment in the joint venture to the extent of its share of the joint venture's earnings, and reduces its investment to the extent of dividends received. No dividends were received during 2004.

Comprehensive earnings:

Comprehensive earnings includes net earnings, foreign currency translation adjustments and unrealized gains/losses on commodity hedging contracts and marketable securities.

Earnings per share:

A dual presentation of basic and diluted earnings per share is not required due to the lack of potentially dilutive securities under the company's simple capital structure. Therefore, all earnings per share amounts represent basic earnings per share.

The Class B Common Stock has essentially the same rights as Common Stock, except that each share of Class B Common Stock has ten votes per share (compared to one vote per share of Common Stock), is not traded on any exchange, is restricted as to transfer and is convertible on a share-for-share basis, at any time and at no cost to the holders, into shares of Common Stock which are traded on the New York Stock Exchange.

NOTE 2—ACCRUED LIABILITIES:

Accrued liabilities are comprised of the following:

	December 31,	
	2004	2003
Compensation	$13,839	$12,213
Other employee benefits	5,261	4,998
Taxes, other than income	2,248	2,531
Advertising and promotions	13,710	11,525
Other	9,664	7,567
	$44,722	$38,834

NOTE 3—BANK LOAN AND INDUSTRIAL DEVELOPMENT BONDS:

The bank loan is payable in quarterly installments through August of 2006. As a result of prepayments made in 2004, the next quarterly installment is due in December, 2005. The loan is collateralized by investments in marketable securities and is subject to other terms and conditions, none of which are significant. Interest is LIBOR based, and the average rate was 2.0% in 2004.

Industrial development bonds are due in 2027. The average floating interest rate was 1.3% and 1.2% in 2004 and 2003, respectively.

NOTE 4—INCOME TAXES:

The domestic and foreign components of pretax income are as follows:

	2004	2003	2002
Domestic	$89,164	$96,170	$ 98,978
Foreign........	5,524	1,777	1,710
	$94,688	$97,947	$100,688

The provision for income taxes is comprised of the following:

	2004	2003	2002
Current:			
Federal	$26,303	$27,904	$32,303
Foreign	731	485	553
State	1,070	1,202	1,523
	28,104	29,591	34,379
Deferred:			
Federal.	2,907	3,465	(286)
Foreign	(605)	(252)	176
State	108	129	31
	2,410	3,342	(79)
	$30,514	$32,933	$34,300

Significant components of the company's net deferred tax liability at year end were as follows:

	December 31,	
	2004	2003
Deferred tax assets:		
Deferred compensation	$ 9,937	$ 8,855
Post retirement benefits	3,493	3,076
Reserve for uncollectible accounts	480	480
Other accrued expenses	2,380	2,337
Foreign subsidiary tax loss carry forward	1,164	157
Foreign subsidiary tax credit carry forward	2,039	2,098
Inventory reserves	1,106	1,080
Other	1,512	1,231
	22,111	19,314
Valuation reserve	(1,183)	(1,522)
Total deferred tax assets	$20,928	$17,792
Deferred tax liabilities:		
Depreciation	$19,638	$18,333
Deductible goodwill and trademarks	15,840	12,835
Accrued export company commissions	3,087	2,825
VEBA funding	711	460
Inventory reserves	2,233	2,629
Prepaid insurance	985	—
Other	3,047	2,390
Total deferred tax liabilities	$45,541	$39,472
Net deferred tax assets	$24,613	$21,680

At December 31, 2004, the tax benefit of foreign subsidiary tax loss carry forwards expiring by year are as follows: $27 in 2005, $11 in 2009, $928 in 2011, $27 in 2012 and $171 in 2014.

Also at December 31, 2004, the amounts of the foreign subsidiary tax credit carry forwards expiring by year are as follows: $48 in 2005, $244 in 2007, $222 in 2008, $198 in 2009, $329 in 2010, $342 in 2011, $328 in 2012, $279 in 2013 and $49 in 2014. A valuation allowance has been established for these carry forward credits to reduce the future income tax benefits to amounts expected to be realized.

The effective income tax rate differs from the statutory rate as follows:

	2004	2003	2002
U.S. statutory rate	35.0%	35.0%	35.0%
State income taxes, net	0.8	0.9	1.0
Exempt municipal bond interest	(1.2)	(1.6)	(1.8)
Foreign tax rates	(1.9)	—	—
Other, net	(0.5)	(0.7)	(0.1)
Effective income tax rate	32.2%	33.6%	34.1%

The company has not provided for U.S. federal or foreign withholding taxes on $13,411 and $7,763 of foreign subsidiaries' undistributed earnings as of December 31, 2004 and December 31, 2003, respectively because such earnings are considered to be permanently reinvested. It is not practicable to determine the amount of income taxes that would be payable upon remittance of the undistributed earnings.

On October 22, 2004, the President signed the American Jobs Creation Act of 2004 (the "Act"). The Act creates a temporary incentive for U.S. corporations to repatriate accumulated income earned abroad by providing an 85% dividends received deduction for certain dividends from controlled foreign corporations. The deduction is subject to a number of limitations and, as of today uncertainty remains as to how to interpret certain provisions of the Act. As such, the Company has not yet determined whether, and to what extent, it may repatriate earnings that have not yet been remitted to the U.S. and therefore makes no estimate as to the amount of future remittances.

The Act also provides for a deduction for income from qualified domestic production activities, which will be phased in from 2005 through 2010. This provision also is subject to a number of limitations which effect the effective tax rate in 2005 and later. The company has not yet determined the extent to which its effective rate will change.

Certain Mexican tax laws were amended during 2004. These become effective primarily during 2005. The company has considered these amendments in determining the 2004 income tax provision, and will continue to monitor their impact during 2005.

NOTE 5—SHARE CAPITAL AND CAPITAL IN EXCESS OF PAR VALUE:

	Common Stock		Class B Common Stock		Treasury Stock		Capital in excess of par value
	Shares	Amount	Shares	Amount	Shares	Amount	
	(000's)		(000's)		(000's)		
Balance at January 1, 2002	34,139	$23,708	16,319	$11,332	(53)	$(1,992)	$323,981
Issuance of 3% stock dividend	1,009	700	488	339	(2)	—	63,332
Conversion of Class B common shares to common shares	48	33	(48)	(33)	—	—	—
Purchase and retirement of common shares	(948)	(658)	—	—	—	—	(31,655)
Balance at December 31, 2002	34,248	23,783	16,759	11,638	(55)	(1,992)	355,658
Issuance of 3% stock dividend	1,017	706	502	349	(1)	—	41,458
Conversion of Class B common shares to common shares	116	81	(116)	(81)	—	—	—
Purchase and retirement of common shares	(1,299)	(902)	—	—	—	—	(39,194)
Balance at December 31, 2003	34,082	23,668	17,145	11,906	(56)	(1,992)	357,922
Issuance of 3% stock dividend	1,009	701	513	356	(2)	—	55,901
Conversion of Class B common shares to common shares	143	99	(143)	(99)	—	—	—
Purchase and retirement of common shares	(474)	(329)	—	—	—	—	(16,078)
Balance at December 31, 2004	34,760	$24,139	17,515	$12,163	(58)	$(1,992)	$397,745

Average shares outstanding and all per share amounts included in the financial statements and notes thereto have been adjusted retroactively to reflect annual three percent stock dividends.

While the company does not have a formal or publicly announced stock repurchase program, the company's board of directors periodically authorizes a dollar amount for share repurchases.

Based upon this policy shares were purchased and retired as follows:

Year	Total Number Of Shares Purchased	Average Price Paid Per Share
2004	474	$34.56
2003	1,299	$30.82
2002	948	$34.03

NOTE 6—OTHER INCOME, NET:

Other income (expense) is comprised of the following:

	2004	2003	2002
Interest and dividend income	$3,784	$4,465	$5,556
Interest expense	(912)	(172)	(309)
Joint venture income	232	—	—
Foreign exchange gains (losses)	453	(78)	(206)
Royalty income	698	542	371
Capital gains (losses)	(163)	112	(35)
Rental income	413	88	2
Miscellaneous, net	279	637	79
	$4,784	$5,594	$5,458

NOTE 7—EMPLOYEE BENEFIT PLANS:

Pension plans:

The company sponsors defined contribution pension plans covering certain nonunion employees with over one year of credited service. The company's policy is to fund pension costs accrued based on compensation levels. Total pension expense for 2004, 2003 and 2002 approximated $3,135, $3,073 and $2,867, respectively. The company also maintains certain profit sharing and savings-investment plans. Company contributions in 2004, 2003 and 2002 to these plans were $806, $796 and $709, respectively.

The company also contributes to multi-employer defined benefit pension plans for its union employees. Such contributions aggregated $1,007, $1,048 and $1,055 in 2004, 2003 and 2002, respectively. The relative position of each employer associated with the multi-employer plans with respect to the actuarial present value of benefits and net plan assets is not determinable by the company.

Deferred compensation

The company sponsors three deferred compensation plans for selected executives and other employees: (i) the Excess Benefit Plan, which restores retirement benefits lost due to IRS limitations on contributions to tax-qualified plans, (ii) the Supplemental Plan, which allows eligible employees to defer the receipt of eligible compensation until designated future dates and (iii) the Career Achievement Plan, which provides a deferred annual incentive award to selected executives. Participants in these plans earn a return on amounts due them based on several investment options, which mirror returns on underlying investments (primarily mutual funds). The company hedges its obligations under the plans by investing in the actual underlying investments. These investments are classified as trading securities and are carried at fair value. At December 31, 2004 and 2003, these investments totaled $25,300 and $21,200, respectively. All gains and losses in these investments are equally offset by corresponding gains and losses in the company's deferred compensation liabilities.

Postretirement health care and life insurance benefit plans:

The company provides certain postretirement health care and life insurance benefits for corporate office and management employees. Employees become eligible for these benefits based upon their age and service and if they agree to contribute a portion of the cost. The company has the right to modify or terminate these benefits. The company does not fund postretirement health care and life insurance benefits in advance of payments for benefit claims.

The changes in the accumulated postretirement benefit obligation at December 31, 2004 and 2003 consist of the following:

	December 31,	
	2004	2003
Benefit obligation, beginning of year	$ 9,302	$8,151
Net periodic postretirement benefit cost	992	1,327
Benefits paid	(219)	(176)
Benefit obligation, end of year	$10,075	$9,302

Net periodic postretirement benefit cost included the following components:

	2004	2003	2002
Service cost—benefits attributed to service during the period	$521	$ 638	$462
Interest cost on the accumulated postretirement benefit obligation	514	604	481
Amortization of unrecognized net gain	(43)	85	(30)
Net periodic postretirement benefit cost	$992	$1,327	$913

For measurement purposes, a 9.0% annual rate of increase in the per capita cost of covered health care benefits was assumed for 2004; the rate was assumed to decrease gradually to 5.5% for 2011 and remain at that level thereafter. The health care cost trend rate assumption has a significant effect on the amounts reported. The weighted-average discount rate used in determining the accumulated postretirement benefit obligation was 5.75% and 6.0% at December 31, 2004 and 2003, respectively.

Increasing or decreasing the health care trend rates by one percentage point in each year would have the following effect on:

	1% Increase	1% Decrease
Postretirement benefit obligation	$1,315	$(1,075)
Total of service and interest cost components	$ 212	$ (170)

The company estimates future benefit payments will be $364, $355, $424, $447 and $455 in 2005 through 2009, respectively, and a total of $2,633 in 2010 through 2014. In December 2003, the FASB issued a revised SFAS No. 132, "Employers' Disclosures about Pensions and Other Postretirement Benefits," which the company adopted in 2003. In January 2004, the FASB issued Staff Position No. 106-1, "Accounting and Disclosure Requirements Related to the Medicare Prescription Drug, Improvement and Modernization Act of 2003" (FSP 106-1) which the company adopted during 2004. The company intends to integrate its retiree prescription drug benefit with the federal benefit that will become available to Medicare eligible retirees in 2006. In accordance with FSP 106-1 the company's accumulated postretirement benefit obligation has been reduced by an unrecognized gain of $864 as of December 31, 2004 related to the federal benefit.

NOTE 8—COMMITMENTS:

Rental expense aggregated $1,012, $962 and $941 in 2004, 2003 and 2002, respectively.

Future operating lease commitments are not significant.

NOTE 9—SEGMENT AND GEOGRAPHIC INFORMATION:

The company operates as a single reportable segment encompassing the manufacture and sale of confectionery products. Its principal manufacturing operations are located in the United States and Canada, and its principal market is the United States. The company also manufactures and sells confectionery products in Mexico, and exports products to Canada as well as to over 30 countries worldwide.

The following geographic data include net sales summarized on the basis of the customer location and long-lived assets based on their physical location.

	2004	2003	2002
Net Sales:			
United States	$387,280	$362,373	$361,446
Foreign	32,830	30,283	31,739
	$420,110	$392,656	$393,185

Long-lived assets:			
United States	$293,618	$283,362	$297,894
Foreign	58,098	5,013	5,738
	$351,716	$288,375	$303,632

NOTE 10—DISCLOSURES ABOUT THE FAIR VALUE AND CARRYING AMOUNT OF FINANCIAL INSTRUMENTS:

The carrying amount approximates fair value of cash and cash equivalents because of the short maturity of those instruments. The fair values of investments are estimated based on quoted market prices. The fair value of the company's bank loan and industrial development bonds approximates their carrying value because they have a floating interest rate.

During the third quarter of 2004 approximately $36,000 of held to maturity investments were liquidated in connection with financing the acquisition of Concord Confections. As a result, the $101,000 balance of held to maturity securities was reclassified to available for sale. This change in classification was not significant to the company's 2004 net earnings or comprehensive earnings.

The carrying amount and estimated fair values of the company's financial instruments are as follows [in table below]:

	2004		2003	
	Carrying Amount	Fair Value	Carrying Amount	Fair Value
Cash and cash equivalents	$ 56,989	$ 56,989	$ 84,084	$ 84,084
Investments held to maturity	—	—	136,801	137,609
Investments available for sale	103,676	103,676	41,346	41,346
Investments in trading securities	25,332	25,332	21,243	21,243
Bank loan and industrial development bonds	99,500	99,500	7,500	7,500

A summary of the aggregate fair value, gross unrealized gains, gross unrealized losses and amortized cost basis of the company's investment portfolio by major security type is as follows:

	December 31, 2004			
			Unrealized	
Available for sale:	Cost	Fair Value	Gains	Losses
Municipal bonds	$ 100,630	$ 100,008	$ —	$ (622)
Mutual funds	2,714	3,668	954	—
	$ 103,344	$ 103,676	$ 954	$ (622)

	December 31, 2003			
	Amortized		Unrealized	
Held to Maturity:	Cost	Fair Value	Gains	Losses
Municipal bonds	$ 136,356	$ 137,170	$ 814	$ —
Unit investment trusts of municipal bonds	445	439	—	(6)
	$ 136,801	$ 137,609	$ 814	$ (6)
Available for sale:				
Municipal bonds	$ 53,061	$ 53,202	$ 141	$ —
Mutual funds	2,454	3,075	621	—
	$ 55,515	$ 56,277	$ 762	$ —

Available for sale securities of $14,931 were included in cash and cash equivalents at December 31, 2003. There were no securities with maturities greater than four years and gross realized gains and losses on the sale of available for sale securities in 2004 and 2003 were not significant.

NOTE 11—COMPREHENSIVE INCOME:

The following table sets forth information with respect to accumalated other comprehensive income (loss):

	Foreign Currency Translation Adjustment	Unrealized Gain (Loss) on Investments	Unrealized Gains (Losses) on Derivatives	Accumulated Other Comprehensive Earnings (Loss)
Balance at January 1, 2002	$ (9,977)	$ 449	$ (385)	$ (9,913)
Unrealized gains (losses)	(1,533)	(798)	(65)	(2,396)
(Gains) losses reclassified to net earnings	—	60	1,429	1,489
Tax effect	—	273	(505)	(232)
Net of tax amount	(1,533)	(465)	859	(1,139)
Balance at December 31, 2002	(11,510)	(16)	474	(11,052)
Unrealized gains (losses)	(647)	784	890	1,027
(Gains) losses reclassified to net earnings	—	2	(1,690)	(1,688)
Tax effect	—	(290)	294	4
Net of tax amount	(647)	496	(506)	(657)
Balance at December 31, 2003	(12,157)	480	(32)	(11,709)
Unrealized gains (losses)	193	(585)	2,594	2,202
(Gains) losses reclassified to net earnings	—	155	(1,237)	(1,082)
Tax effect	—	159	(501)	(342)
Net of tax amount	193	(271)	856	778
Balance at December 31, 2004	$(11,964)	$ 209	$ 824	$(10,931)

NOTE 12—ACQUISITION:

On August 30, 2004, the company purchased certain assets and assumed certain liabilities from Concord Confections, Inc. and its affiliates (collectively Concord) including its 50% equity interest in a Spanish joint venture. Cash consideration paid of $218,229 was funded by the liquidation of $64,229 of marketable securities and a bank term loan of $154,000. The results of Concord's operations have been included in the company's condensed consolidated financial statements since August 30, 2004. Concord holds a strong market position in the bubble gum category and its products are sold primarily under the Dubble Bubble brand name and trademark.

The acquisition has been accounted for under SFAS 141, "Business Combinations," and accordingly the purchase method of accounting has been used. The allocation of purchase price is based on management's determination and professional valuations of the fair value of the assets acquired and liabilities to be assumed. The final allocation to goodwill could be affected by the final determination of the required minimum working capital amount that was to be provided under the terms of the Concord purchase contract. The adjusted purchase price was allocated as follows:

Calculation of adjusted purchase price:	
Cash consideration paid for net assets acquired	$218,229
Direct transactions fees and expenses	1,000
Less— Adjustment to purchase relating to minimum working capital required	(6,642)
Total adjusted purchase price	$212,587

Allocation of adjusted purchase price:	
Net working capital	$ 7,722
Step up of inventories	1,622
Investment in joint venture	10,000
Property, plant and equipment	43,399
Indefinite lived trademarks	113,994
Goodwill—deductible for income tax	35,850
Total adjusted purchase price	$212,587

The following table includes the unaudited pro forma net sales, net earnings and net earnings per share for 2004 and 2003 as if the company had acquired Concord as of January 1, 2003. Pro forma adjustments are necessary to reflect costs and expenses of financing the purchase, including additional interest expense relating to bank borrowings and the decrease in investment income reflecting the sale of marketable securities, and changes in depreciation expense resulting from fair value adjustments to net tangible assets.

The unaudited pro forma combined financial information presented does not reflect any cost savings or synergies that might be realized, including the anticipated elimination of substantially all of the Concord historical senior executive compensation and other management expenses which aggregated approximately $3,872 and $10,283 net of income taxes for the twelve months of 2004 and 2003, respectively. The pro forma results also reflect $495 and $12,007 of historical foreign exchange gains net of tax for 2004 and 2003, respectively.

UNAUDITED PRO FORMA COMBINED
INCOME STATEMENT OF TOOTSIE ROLL AND CONCORD
FOR THE TWELVE MONTHS ENDED DECEMBER 31, 2004
AND 2003

	2004 Combined Pro forma	2003 Combined Pro forma
Net sales	$479,278	$467,522
Net earnings	$ 64,673	$ 71,802
Earnings per share	$ 1.24	$ 1.35

The pro forma results are not necessarily indicative of what actually would have occurred if the acquisition had been completed as of the beginning of the presented periods, nor are they necessarily indicative of future consolidated results.

Management's Report on Internal Control and Management Certifications of Financial Statements

The Sarbanes-Oxley Act of 2002, requires managers of publicly traded companies to establish and maintain systems of internal control on the company's financial reporting processes. In addition, the Act requires the company's top management to provide certifications regarding the accuracy of the financial statements. The reports of Tootsie Roll are shown below.

Management's Report on Internal Control Over Financial Reporting

The management of Tootsie Roll Industries, Inc. is responsible for establishing and maintaining adequate internal control over financial reporting, as such term is defined in the Securities Exchange Act of 1934 (SEC) Rule 13a-15(f). Our management conducted an evaluation of the effectiveness of the company's internal control over financial reporting as of December 31, 2004 as required by SEC Rule 13a-15(c). In making this assessment, we used the criteria established in *Internal Control—Integrated Framework* issued by the Committee of Sponsoring Organizations of the Treadway Commission (the COSO criteria). Based on our evaluation under the COSO criteria, our management concluded that our internal control over financial reporting was effective as of December 31, 2004.

Management has excluded Concord Confections, Ltd. from its assessment of internal control over financial reporting as of December 31, 2004 because it was acquired by the company in a purchase business combination during 2004. Concord Confections, Ltd. is a wholly-owned subsidiary whose total assets and total revenues represent 29% and 6%, respectively, of the related consolidated financial statement amounts as of and for the year ended December 31, 2004.

Our management's assessment of the effectiveness of our internal control over financial reporting as of December 31, 2004 has been audited by PricewaterhouseCoopers, LLP an independent registered public accounting firm, as stated in their report which appears on page 19 [see pages A-23 and A-24 in this textbook].

Tootsie Roll Industries, Inc.

Chicago, Illinois
March 11, 2005

Required Certifications

In 2004, the Company's Chief Executive Officer submitted to the New York Stock Exchange the required Annual CEO Certification certifying that he was not aware of any violation by the Company of the exchange's corporate governance listing standards, other than that the certification itself was inadvertently filed later than within 30 days subsequent to the 2004 annual stockholders' meeting date as required.

The Company filed with the Securities and Exchange Commission the certifications required of the Company's Chief Executive Officer and Chief Financial Officer required under Section 302 of the Sarbanes–Oxley Act of 2002 as exhibits to the Form 10-K for the years ended December 31, 2003 and 2004.

Auditor's Report

All publicly held corporations, as well as many other enterprises and organizations (both profit and not-for-profit, large and small) engage the services of independent certified public accountants for the purpose of obtaining an objective, expert report on their financial statements. Based on a comprehensive examination of the company's accounting system, accounting records, and the financial statements, the outside CPA issues the auditor's report.

The standard auditor's report consists of three paragraphs: (1) an introductory paragraph, (2) a scope paragraph, and (3) the opinion paragraph. In the **introductory paragraph**, the auditor identifies who and what was audited and indicates the responsibilities of management and the auditor relative to the financial statements. In the **scope paragraph** the auditor states that the audit was conducted in accordance with generally accepted auditing standards and discusses the nature and limitations of the audit. In the **opinion paragraph**, the auditor expresses an informed opinion as to (1) the fairness of the financial statements and (2) their conformity with generally accepted accounting principles. The Report of PricewaterhouseCoopers LLP appearing in Tootsie Roll's Annual Report is shown here.

Report of Independent Registered Public Accounting Firm

To the Board of Directors and Shareholders of Tootsie Roll Industries, Inc.:

We have completed an integrated audit of Tootsie Roll Industries, Inc. 's 2004 consolidated financial statements and of its internal control over financial reporting as of December 31, 2004 and audits of its 2003 and 2002 consolidated financial statements in accordance with the standards of the Public Company Accounting Oversight Board (United States). Our opinions, based on our audits, are presented below.

Consolidated financial statements

In our opinion, the accompanying consolidated balance sheets and the related consolidated statements of earnings, comprehensive earnings, retained earnings, and cash flows present fairly, in all material respects, the financial position of Tootsie Roll Industries, Inc. and its subsidiaries at December 31, 2004 and 2003, and the results of their operations and their cash flows for each of the three years in the period ended December 31, 2004 in conformity with accounting principles generally accepted in the United States of America. These financial statements are the responsibility of the Company's management. Our responsibility is to express an opinion on these financial statements based on our audits. We conducted our audits of these statements in accordance with the standards of the Public Company Accounting Oversight Board (United States). Those standards require that we plan and perform the audit to obtain reasonable assurance about whether the financial statements are free of material misstatement. An audit of financial statements includes examining, on a test basis, evidence supporting the amounts and disclosures in the financial statements, assessing the accounting principles used and significant estimates made by management, and evaluating the overall financial statement presentation. We believe that our audits provide a reasonable basis for our opinion.

Internal control over financial reporting

Also, in our opinion, management's assessment, included in the accompanying Management's Report on Internal Control Over Financial Reporting, that the Company maintained effective internal control over financial reporting as of December 31, 2004 based on criteria established in *Internal Control—Integrated Framework* issued by the Committee of Sponsoring Organizations of the Treadway Commission (COSO), is fairly stated, in all material respects, based on those criteria. Furthermore, in our opinion, the Company maintained, in all material respects, effective internal control over financial reporting as of December 31, 2004, based on criteria established in *Internal Control—Integrated Framework* issued by the COSO. The Company's management is responsible for maintaining effective internal control over financial reporting and for its assessment of the effectiveness of internal control over financial reporting. Our responsibility is to express opinions on management's assessment and on the effectiveness of the Company's internal control over financial reporting based on our audit. We conducted our audit of internal control over financial reporting in accordance with the standards of the Public Company Accounting Oversight Board (United States). Those standards require that we plan and perform the audit to obtain reasonable assurance about whether effective internal control over financial reporting was maintained in all material respects. An audit of internal control over financial reporting includes obtaining an understanding of internal control over financial reporting, evaluating management's assessment, testing and evaluating the design and operating effectiveness of internal control, and performing such other procedures as we consider necessary in the circumstances. We believe that our audit provides a reasonable basis for our opinions.

A company's internal control over financial reporting is a process designed to provide reasonable assurance regarding the reliability of financial reporting and the preparation of financial statements for external purposes in accordance with generally accepted accounting principles. A company's internal control over financial reporting includes those policies and procedures that (i) pertain to the maintenance of records that, in reasonable detail, accurately and fairly reflect the transactions and dispositions of the assets of the company; (ii) provide reasonable assurance that transactions are recorded as necessary to permit preparation of financial statements in accordance with generally accepted accounting principles, and that receipts and expenditures of the company are being made only in accordance with authorizations of management and directors of the company; and (iii) provide reasonable assurance regarding prevention or timely detection of unauthorized acquisition, use, or disposition of the company's assets that could have a material effect on the financial statements.

Because of its inherent limitations, internal control over financial reporting may not prevent or detect misstatements. Also, projections of any evaluation of effectiveness to future periods are subject to the risk that controls may become inadequate because of changes in conditions, or that the degree of compliance with the policies or procedures may deteriorate.

As described in Management's Report on Internal Control Over Financial Reporting, management has excluded Concord Confections, Ltd. from its assessment of internal control over financial reporting as of December 31, 2004 because it was acquired by the Company in a purchase business combination during 2004. We have also excluded Concord Confections, Ltd. from our audit of internal control over financial reporting. Concord Confections, Ltd. is a wholly-owned subsidiary whose total assets and total revenues represent 29% and 6%, respectively, of the related consolidated financial statement amounts as of and for the year ended December 31, 2004.

PricewaterhouseCoopers LLP

Chicago, Illinois
March 11, 2005

Supplementary Financial Information

In addition to the financial statements and the accompanying notes, companies often present supplementary financial information. Tootsie Roll has provided quarterly financial data, stock performance information, and a five-year summary of earnings and financial highlights.

Quarterly Financial Data (Unaudited)

TOOTSIE ROLL INDUSTRIES, INC. AND SUBSIDIARIES

		(Thousands of dollars except per share data)			
2004	First	Second	Third	Fourth	Total
Net sales	$80,046	$77,157	$156,971	$105,936	$420,110
Gross margin	34,730	34,992	64,804	41,083	175,609
Net earnings	11,493	11,828	26,976	13,877	64,174
Net earnings per share	.22	.22	.52	.27	1.23
2003					
Net sales	$75,570	$77,725	$147,201	$ 92,160	$392,656
Gross margin	32,601	35,541	61,932	40,035	170,109
Net earnings	10,909	12,317	26,945	14,843	65,014
Net earnings per share	.20	.23	.51	.28	1.22
2002					
Net sales	$78,991	$77,131	$146,298	$ 90,765	$393,185
Gross margin	35,505	35,411	61,560	38,505	170,981
Net earnings	12,772	12,316	26,616	14,684	66,388
Net earnings per share	.23	.23	.49	.27	1.22

Net earnings per share is based upon average outstanding shares as adjusted for 3% stock dividends issued during the second quarter of each year. The sum of the per share amounts may not equal annual amounts due to rounding.

2004-2003 QUARTERLY SUMMARY OF TOOTSIE ROLL INDUSTRIES, INC. STOCK PRICE AND DIVIDENDS PER SHARE

STOCK PRICES*

	2004		2003	
	High	Low	High	Low
1st Qtr	$37.86	$35.00	$30.91	$27.30
2nd Qtr	$37.60	$32.41	$32.37	$28.75
3rd Qtr	$32.60	$29.08	$32.05	$29.60
4th Qtr	$34.63	$29.24	$36.94	$32.08

*NYSE—Composite Quotations

Estimated Number of shareholders at March 2005:
- Common Stock 18,000
- Class B Common Stock 5,000

DIVIDENDS

	2004	2003
1st Qtr	$.0681	$.0662
2nd Qtr	$.0701	$.0680
3rd Qtr	$.0700	$.0680
4th Qtr	$.0700	$.0680

NOTE: In addition to the above cash dividends, a 3% stock dividend was issued on April 14, 2004 and April 16, 2003. Cash dividends are restated to reflect 3% stock dividends.

Five Year Summary of Earnings and Financial Highlights

TOOTSIE ROLL INDUSTRIES, INC. AND SUBSIDIARIES

(Thousands of dollars except per share, percentage and ratio figures)

(See Management's Comments starting on page [A-6 of this textbook])

	2004	2003	2002	2001	2000
Sales and Earnings Data (2)					
Net sales	$420,110	$392,656	$393,185	$391,755	$396,816
Gross margin	175,609	170,109	170,981	173,858	188,585
Interest expense	912	172	309	356	866
Provision for income taxes	30,514	32,933	34,300	35,100	42,071
Net earnings	64,174	65,014	66,388	65,687	75,737
% of sales	15.3%	16.6%	16.9%	16.8%	19.1%
% of shareholders' equity	11.3%	12.1%	12.6%	12.9%	16.5%
Per Common Share Data (1)					
Net earnings	$ 1.23	$ 1.22	$ 1.22	$ 1.19	$ 1.37
Cash dividends declared	.28	.27	.26	.26	.24
Stock dividends	3%	3%	3%	3%	3%
Additional Financial Data (2)					
Working capital	$110,376	$180,818	$161,852	$188,250	$145,765
Net cash provided by operating activities	76,228	83,466	75,473	80,915	82,591
Net cash used in investing activities	164,039	50,383	29,571	19,165	64,177
Net cash provided by (used in) financing activities	60,716	(54,506)	(46,927)	(16,100)	(46,036)
Property, plant & equipment additions . . .	17,948	12,150	10,308	14,148	16,189
Net property, plant & equipment	178,750	129,163	128,869	132,575	131,118
Total assets	811,753	665,297	646,080	618,676	562,442
Long term debt	93,167	7,500	7,500	7,500	7,500
Shareholders' equity	570,179	536,581	526,740	508,461	458,696
Average shares outstanding (1)	52,366	53,305	54,592	54,985	55,432

(1) Adjusted for annual 3% stock dividends.

(2) Certain reclassifications have been made to prior year numbers to conform to current year presentation.

Specimen Financial Statements: Hershey Foods Corporation

HERSHEY FOODS CORPORATION

CONSOLIDATED STATEMENTS OF INCOME

For the years ended December 31, In thousands of dollars except per share amounts	2004	2003	2002
Net Sales	**$4,429,248**	$4,172,551	$4,120,317
Costs and Expenses:			
Cost of sales	**2,679,531**	2,544,726	2,561,052
Selling, marketing and administrative	**847,540**	816,442	833,426
Business realignment and asset impairments, net	—	23,357	27,552
Gain on sale of business	—	(8,330)	—
Total costs and expenses	**3,527,071**	3,376,195	3,422,030
Income before Interest and Income Taxes	**902,177**	796,356	698,287
Interest expense, net	**66,533**	63,529	60,722
Income before Income Taxes	**835,644**	732,827	637,565
Provision for income taxes	**244,765**	267,875	233,987
Income before Cumulative Effect of Accounting Change	**590,879**	464,952	403,578
Cumulative effect of accounting change, net of $4,933 tax benefit	—	7,368	—
Net Income	**$ 590,879**	$ 457,584	$ 403,578
Earnings Per Share—Basic—Common Stock			
Income before Cumulative Effect of Accounting Change	$ **2.38**	$ 1.81	$ 1.51
Cumulative Effect of Accounting Change, net of $.02 Tax Benefit	—	.03	—
Net Income	$ **2.38**	$ 1.78	$ 1.51
Earnings Per Share—Basic—Class B Common Stock			
Income before Cumulative Effect of Accounting Change	$ **2.17**	$ 1.64	$ 1.37
Cumulative Effect of Accounting Change, net of $.02 Tax Benefit	—	.03	—
Net Income	$ **2.17**	$ 1.61	$ 1.37
Earnings Per Share—Diluted			
Income before Cumulative Effect of Accounting Change	$ **2.30**	$ 1.76	$ 1.47
Cumulative Effect of Accounting Change, net of $.02 Tax Benefit	—	.03	—
Net Income	$ **2.30**	$ 1.73	$ 1.47
Cash Dividends Paid Per Share:			
Common Stock	$ **.8350**	$ .7226	$ .6300
Class B Common Stock	**.7576**	.6526	.5675

The notes to consolidated financial statements are an integral part of these statements.

HERSHEY FOODS CORPORATION

CONSOLIDATED BALANCE SHEETS

December 31, In thousands of dollars	2004	2003
ASSETS		
Current Assets:		
Cash and cash equivalents	$ 54,837	$ 114,793
Accounts receivable—trade	408,930	407,612
Inventories	557,180	492,859
Deferred income taxes	46,503	13,285
Prepaid expenses and other	114,991	103,020
Total current assets	1,182,441	1,131,569
Property, Plant and Equipment, Net	1,682,698	1,661,939
Goodwill	463,947	388,960
Other Intangibles	125,233	38,511
Other Assets	343,212	361,561
Total assets	$ 3,797,531	$ 3,582,540
LIABILITIES AND STOCKHOLDERS' EQUITY		
Current Liabilities:		
Accounts payable	$ 148,686	$ 132,222
Accrued liabilities	472,096	416,181
Accrued income taxes	42,280	24,898
Short-term debt	343,277	12,032
Current portion of long-term debt	279,043	477
Total current liabilities	1,285,382	585,810
Long-term Debt	690,602	968,499
Other Long-term Liabilities	403,356	370,776
Deferred Income Taxes	328,889	377,589
Total liabilities	2,708,229	2,302,674
Stockholders' Equity:		
Preferred Stock, shares issued: none in 2004 and 2003	—	—
Common Stock, shares issued: 299,060,235 in 2004 and 149,528,776 on a pre-split basis in 2003	299,060	149,528
Class B Common Stock, shares issued: 60,841,509 in 2004 and 30,422,096 on a pre-split basis in 2003	60,841	30,422
Additional paid-in capital	28,614	4,034
Unearned ESOP compensation	(6,387)	(9,580)
Retained earnings	3,469,169	3,263,988
Treasury—Common Stock shares, at cost: 113,313,827 in 2004 and 50,421,139 on a pre-split basis in 2003	(2,762,304)	(2,147,441)
Accumulated other comprehensive income (loss)	309	(11,085)
Total stockholders' equity	1,089,302	1,279,866
Total liabilities and stockholders' equity	$ 3,797,531	$ 3,582,540

The notes to consolidated financial statements are an integral part of these balance sheets.

HERSHEY FOODS CORPORATION

CONSOLIDATED STATEMENTS OF CASH FLOWS

For the years ended December 31, In thousands of dollars	2004	2003	2002
Cash Flows Provided from (Used by)			
Operating Activities			
Net income	**$ 590,879**	$ 457,584	$ 403,578
Adjustments to reconcile net income to net cash provided from operations:			
Depreciation and amortization	**189,665**	180,567	177,908
Deferred income taxes	**(81,931)**	38,895	137,817
Gain on sale of business, net of tax of $2,624	—	(5,706)	—
Business realignment initiatives, net of tax of $9,988 and $12,470, respectively	—	15,488	21,509
Cumulative effect of accounting change, net of tax of $4,933	—	7,368	—
Changes in assets and liabilities, net of effects from business acquisitions and divestitures:			
Accounts receivable—trade	**17,319**	(36,636)	(9,250)
Inventories	**(40,043)**	9,095	8,843
Accounts payable	**(11,266)**	7,715	(8,542)
Other assets and liabilities	**132,827**	(81,427)	(106,520)
Net Cash Provided from Operating Activities	**797,450**	592,943	625,343
Cash Flows Provided from (Used by)			
Investing Activities			
Capital additions	**(181,728)**	(218,650)	(132,736)
Capitalized software additions	**(14,158)**	(18,404)	(11,836)
Business acquisitions	**(166,859)**	—	—
Proceeds from divestitures	—	20,049	12,000
Net Cash (Used by) Investing Activities	**(362,745)**	(217,005)	(132,572)
Cash Flows Provided from (Used by)			
Financing Activities			
Net change in short-term borrowings	**331,245**	897	4,130
Long-term borrowings	—	3,194	304
Repayment of long-term debt	**(883)**	(18,633)	(9,578)
Cash dividends paid	**(205,747)**	(184,686)	(167,821)
Exercise of stock options	**79,634**	55,120	86,491
Incentive plan transactions	**(81,933)**	(85,347)	(158,507)
Repurchase of Common Stock	**(616,977)**	(329,433)	(84,194)
Net Cash (Used by) Financing Activities	**(494,661)**	(558,888)	(329,175)
(Decrease) Increase in Cash and Cash Equivalents	**(59,956)**	(182,950)	163,596
Cash and Cash Equivalents as of January 1	**114,793**	297,743	134,147
Cash and Cash Equivalents as of December 31	**$ 54,837**	$ 114,793	$ 297,743
Interest Paid	**$ 66,151**	$ 65,347	$ 64,343
Income Taxes Paid	**289,607**	207,672	57,495

The notes to consolidated financial statements are an integral part of these statements.

HERSHEY FOODS CORPORATION

CONSOLIDATED STATEMENTS OF STOCKHOLDERS' EQUITY

In thousands of dollars	Preferred Stock	Common Stock	Class B Common Stock	Additional Paid-in Capital	Unearned ESOP Compensation	Retained Earnings	Treasury Common Stock	Accumulated Other Comprehensive Income (Loss)	Total Stockholders' Equity
Balance as of January 1, 2002	$—	$149,516	$30,434	$ 3,263	$(15,967)	$2,755,333	$(1,689,243)	$ (86,132)	$1,147,204
Net income						403,578			403,578
Other comprehensive income								107,203	107,203
Comprehensive income									510,781
Dividends:									
Common Stock, $.63 per share						(133,285)			(133,285)
Class B Common Stock, $.5675 per share						(34,536)			(34,536)
Conversion of Class B Common Stock into Common Stock		12	(12)						—
Incentive plan transactions				(298)					(298)
Exercise of stock options				(3,517)			(34,790)		(38,307)
Employee stock ownership trust/benefits transactions				1,145	3,193				4,338
Repurchase of Common Stock							(84,194)		(84,194)
Balance as of December 31, 2002	—	149,528	30,422	593	(12,774)	2,991,090	(1,808,227)	21,071	1,371,703
Net income						457,584			457,584
Other comprehensive (loss)								(32,156)	(32,156)
Comprehensive income									425,428
Dividends:									
Common Stock, $.7226 per share						(144,985)			(144,985)
Class B Common Stock, $.6526 per share						(39,701)			(39,701)
Incentive plan transactions				455					455
Exercise of stock options				1,519			(9,781)		(8,262)
Employee stock ownership trust/benefits transactions				1,467	3,194				4,661
Repurchase of Common Stock							(329,433)		(329,433)
Balance as of December 31, 2003	—	149,528	30,422	4,034	(9,580)	3,263,988	(2,147,441)	(11,085)	1,279,866
Net income						590,879			590,879
Other comprehensive income								11,394	11,394
Comprehensive income									602,273
Dividends:									
Common Stock, $.835 per share						(159,658)			(159,658)
Class B Common Stock, $.7576 per share						(46,089)			(46,089)
Two-for-one stock split		149,529	30,422	36		(179,951)			—
Conversion of Class B Common Stock into Common Stock		3	(3)						—
Incentive plan transactions				36					36
Exercise of stock options				23,248			2,114		25,362
Employee stock ownership trust/benefits transactions				1,296	3,193				4,489
Repurchase of Common Stock							(616,977)		(616,977)
Balance as of December 31, 2004	$—	$299,060	$60,841	$28,614	$ (6,387)	$3,469,169	$(2,762,304)	$ 309	$1,089,302

The notes to consolidated financial statements are an integral part of these statements.

Time Value of Money

Would you rather receive $1,000 today or a year from now? You should prefer to receive the $1,000 today because you can invest the $1,000 and earn interest on it. As a result, you will have more than $1,000 a year from now. What this example illustrates is the concept of the **time value of money**. Everyone prefers to receive money today rather than in the future because of the interest factor.

Nature of Interest

Interest is payment for the use of another person's money. It is the difference between the amount borrowed or invested (called the **principal**) and the amount repaid or collected. The amount of interest to be paid or collected is usually stated as a rate over a specific period of time. The rate of interest is generally stated as an annual rate.

The amount of interest involved in any financing transaction is based on three elements:

1. **Principal (p):** The original amount borrowed or invested.
2. **Interest Rate (i):** An annual percentage of the principal.
3. **Time (n):** The number of years that the principal is borrowed or invested.

SIMPLE INTEREST

Simple interest is computed on the principal amount only. It is the return on the principal for one period. Simple interest is usually expressed as shown in Illustration C-1 on the next page.

STUDY OBJECTIVE
1
Distinguish between simple and compound interest.

Illustration C-1
Interest computation

| Interest | = | Principal
p | × | Rate
i | × | Time
n |

For example, if you borrowed $5,000 for 2 years at a simple interest rate of 12% annually, you would pay $1,200 in total interest computed as follows:

$$\text{Interest} = p \times i \times n$$
$$= \$5,000 \times .12 \times 2$$
$$= \$1,200$$

COMPOUND INTEREST

Compound interest is computed on principal **and** on any interest earned that has not been paid or withdrawn. It is the return on (or growth of) the principal for two or more time periods. Compounding computes interest not only on the principal but also on the interest earned to date on that principal, assuming the interest is left on deposit.

To illustrate the difference between simple and compound interest, assume that you deposit $1,000 in Bank Two, where it will earn simple interest of 9% per year, and you deposit another $1,000 in Citizens Bank, where it will earn compound interest of 9% per year compounded annually. Also assume that in both cases you will not withdraw any interest until three years from the date of deposit. Illustration C-2 shows the computation of interest to be received and the accumulated year-end balances.

Illustration C-2 Simple versus compound interest

Bank Two				Citizens Bank		
Simple Interest Calculation	Simple Interest	Accumulated Year-end Balance		Compound Interest Calculation	Compound Interest	Accumulated Year-end Balance
Year 1 $1,000.00 × 9%	$ 90.00	$1,090.00		Year 1 $1,000.00 × 9%	$ 90.00	$1,090.00
Year 2 $1,000.00 × 9%	90.00	$1,180.00		Year 2 $1,090.00 × 9%	98.10	$1,188.10
Year 3 $1,000.00 × 9%	90.00	$1,270.00		Year 3 $1,188.10 × 9%	106.93	$1,295.03
	$ 270.00		$25.03 Difference		$ 295.03	

Note in Illustration C-2 that simple interest uses the initial principal of $1,000 to compute the interest in all three years. Compound interest uses the accumulated balance (principal plus interest to date) at each year-end to compute interest in the succeeding year—which explains why your compound interest account is larger.

Obviously, if you had a choice between investing your money at simple interest or at compound interest, you would choose compound interest, all other things—especially risk—being equal. In the example, compounding provides $25.03 of additional interest income. For practical purposes, compounding assumes that unpaid interest earned becomes a part of the principal, and the accumulated balance at the end of each year becomes the new principal on which interest is earned during the next year.

Illustration C-2 indicates that you should invest your money at the bank that compounds interest annually. Most business situations use compound interest. Simple interest is generally applicable only to short-term situations of one year or less.

SECTION ONE
FUTURE VALUE CONCEPTS

Future Value of a Single Amount

The **future value of a single amount** is the value at a future date of a given amount invested, assuming compound interest. For example, in Illustration C-2, $1,295.03 is the future value of the $1,000 investment earning 9% for three years. The $1,295.03 could be determined more easily by using the following formula:

$$FV = p \times (1 + i)^n$$

Illustration C-3
Formula for future value

where:

$$FV = \text{future value of a single amount}$$
$$p = \text{principal (or present value)}$$
$$i = \text{interest rate for one period}$$
$$n = \text{number of periods}$$

The $1,295.03 is computed as follows:

$$
\begin{aligned}
FV &= p \times (1 + i)^n \\
&= \$1,000 \times (1 + .09)^3 \\
&= \$1,000 \times 1.29503 \\
&= \$1,295.03
\end{aligned}
$$

The 1.29503 is computed by multiplying (1.09 × 1.09 × 1.09). The amounts in this example can be depicted in the time diagram shown in Illustration C-4.

Illustration C-4
Time diagram

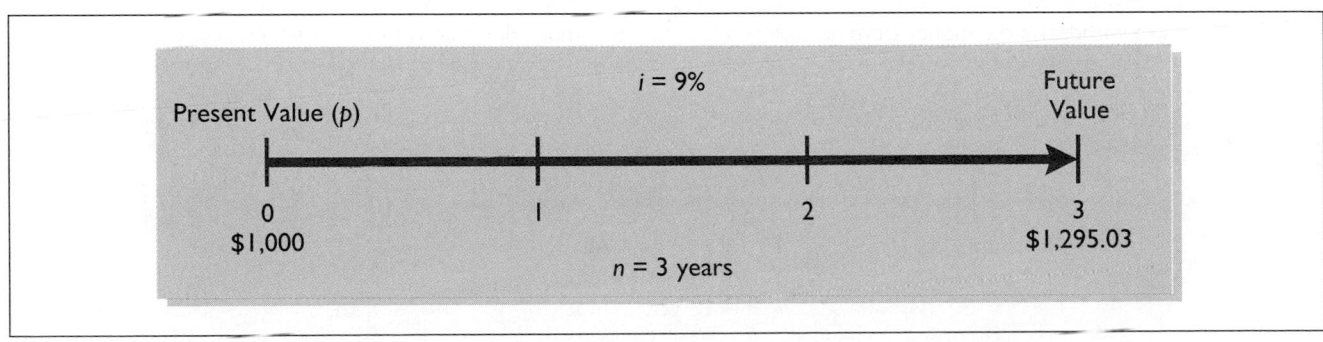

Another method used to compute the future value of a single amount involves a compound interest table. This table shows the future value of 1 for n periods. Table 1 on the next page is such a table.

TABLE 1 Future Value of 1

(n) Periods	4%	5%	6%	8%	9%	10%	11%	12%	15%
1	1.04000	1.05000	1.06000	1.08000	1.09000	1.10000	1.11000	1.12000	1.15000
2	1.08160	1.10250	1.12360	1.16640	1.18810	1.21000	1.23210	1.25440	1.32250
3	1.12486	1.15763	1.19102	1.25971	1.29503	1.33100	1.36763	1.40493	1.52088
4	1.16986	1.21551	1.26248	1.36049	1.41158	1.46410	1.51807	1.57352	1.74901
5	1.21665	1.27628	1.33823	1.46933	1.53862	1.61051	1.68506	1.76234	2.01136
6	1.26532	1.34010	1.41852	1.58687	1.67710	1.77156	1.87041	1.97382	2.31306
7	1.31593	1.40710	1.50363	1.71382	1.82804	1.94872	2.07616	2.21068	2.66002
8	1.36857	1.47746	1.59385	1.85093	1.99256	2.14359	2.30454	2.47596	3.05902
9	1.42331	1.55133	1.68948	1.99900	2.17189	2.35795	2.55803	2.77308	3.51788
10	1.48024	1.62889	1.79085	2.15892	2.36736	2.59374	2.83942	3.10585	4.04556
11	1.53945	1.71034	1.89830	2.33164	2.58043	2.85312	3.15176	3.47855	4.65239
12	1.60103	1.79586	2.01220	2.51817	2.81267	3.13843	3.49845	3.89598	5.35025
13	1.66507	1.88565	2.13293	2.71962	3.06581	3.45227	3.88328	4.36349	6.15279
14	1.73168	1.97993	2.26090	2.93719	3.34173	3.79750	4.31044	4.88711	7.07571
15	1.80094	2.07893	2.39656	3.17217	3.64248	4.17725	4.78459	5.47357	8.13706
16	1.87298	2.18287	2.54035	3.42594	3.97031	4.59497	5.31089	6.13039	9.35762
17	1.94790	2.29202	2.69277	3.70002	4.32763	5.05447	5.89509	6.86604	10.76126
18	2.02582	2.40662	2.85434	3.99602	4.71712	5.55992	6.54355	7.68997	12.37545
19	2.10685	2.52695	3.02560	4.31570	5.14166	6.11591	7.26334	8.61276	14.23177
20	2.19112	2.65330	3.20714	4.66096	5.60441	6.72750	8.06231	9.64629	16.36654

In Table 1, *n* is the number of compounding periods, the percentages are the periodic interest rates, and the 5-digit decimal numbers in the respective columns are the future value of 1 factors. In using Table 1, you would multiply the principal amount by the future value factor for the specified number of periods and interest rate. For example, the future value factor for two periods at 9% is 1.18810. Multiplying this factor by $1,000 equals $1,188.10—which is the accumulated balance at the end of year 2 in the Citizens Bank example in Illustration C-2. The $1,295.03 accumulated balance at the end of the third year can be calculated from Table 1 by multiplying the future value factor for three periods (1.29503) by the $1,000.

The demonstration problem in Illustration C-5 shows how to use Table 1.

Illustration C-5
Demonstration problem—
Using Table 1 for *FV* of 1

John and Mary Rich invested $20,000 in a savings account paying 6% interest at the time their son, Mike, was born. The money is to be used by Mike for his college education. On his 18th birthday, Mike withdraws the money from his savings account. How much did Mike withdraw from his account?

Present Value (*p*) i = 6% Future Value = ?

0 1 2 3 4 5 6 7 8 9 10 11 12 13 14 15 16 17 18
$20,000

n = 18 years

Answer: The future value factor from Table 1 is 2.85434 (18 periods at 6%). The future value of $20,000 earning 6% per year for 18 years is **$57,086.80** ($20,000 × 2.85434).

Future Value of an Annuity

The preceding discussion involved the accumulation of only a single principal sum. Individuals and businesses frequently encounter situations in which a **series** of equal dollar amounts are to be paid or received periodically, such as loans or lease (rental) contracts. Such payments or receipts of equal dollar amounts are referred to as **annuities**.

STUDY OBJECTIVE
3
Solve for future value of an annuity.

The **future value of an annuity** is the sum of all the payments (receipts) plus the accumulated compound interest on them. In computing the future value of an annuity, it is necessary to know (1) the interest rate, (2) the number of compounding periods, and (3) the amount of the periodic payments or receipts.

To illustrate the computation of the future value of an annuity, assume that you invest $2,000 at the end of each year for three years at 5% interest compounded annually. This situation is depicted in the time diagram in Illustration C-6.

Illustration C-6 Time diagram for a three-year annuity

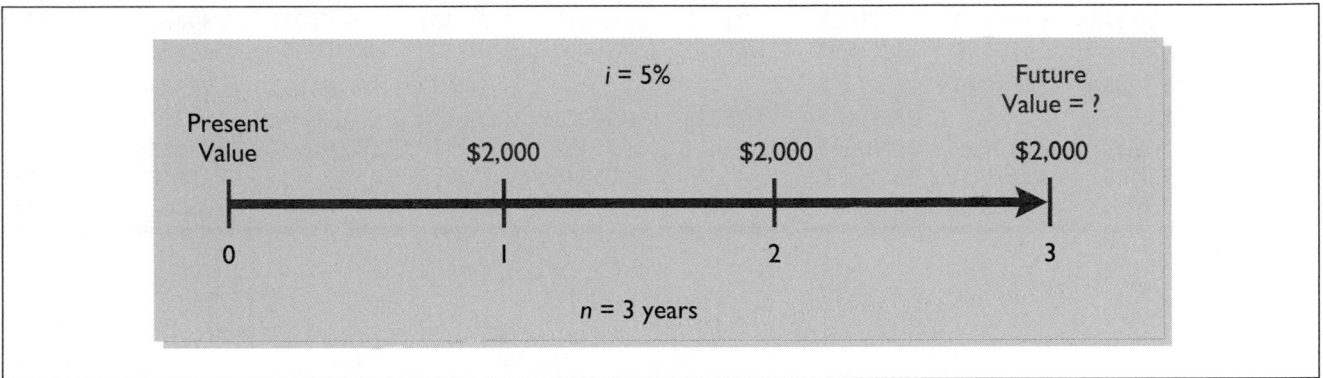

The $2,000 invested at the end of year 1 will earn interest for two years (years 2 and 3), and the $2,000 invested at the end of year 2 will earn interest for one year (year 3). However, the last $2,000 investment (made at the end of year 3) will not earn any interest. The future value of these periodic payments could be computed using the future value factors from Table 1, as shown in Illustration C-7.

Year Invested	Amount Invested	×	Future Value of 1 Factor at 5%	=	Future Value
1	$2,000	×	1.10250		$2,205
2	$2,000	×	1.05000		2,100
3	$2,000	×	1.00000		2,000
			3.15250		**$6,305**

Illustration C-7 Future value of periodic payment computation

The first $2,000 investment is multiplied by the future value factor for two periods (1.1025) because two years' interest will accumulate on it (in years 2 and 3). The second $2,000 investment will earn only one year's interest (in year 3) and therefore is multiplied by the future value factor for one year (1.0500). The final $2,000 investment is made at the end of the third year and will not earn any interest. Consequently, the future value of the last $2,000 invested is only $2,000 since it does not accumulate any interest.

Calculating the future value of each individual cash flow is required when the periodic payments or receipts are not equal in each period. However, when the periodic payments (receipts) are **the same in each period**, the future value can be computed by using a future value of an annuity of 1 table. Table 2 is such a table.

TABLE 2   **Future Value of an Annuity of 1**

(n) Periods	4%	5%	6%	8%	9%	10%	11%	12%	15%
1	1.00000	1.00000	1.00000	1.00000	1.00000	1.00000	1.00000	1.00000	1.00000
2	2.04000	2.05000	2.06000	2.08000	2.09000	2.10000	2.11000	2.12000	2.15000
3	3.12160	3.15250	3.18360	3.24640	3.27810	3.31000	3.34210	3.37440	3.47250
4	4.24646	4.31013	4.37462	4.50611	4.57313	4.64100	4.70973	4.77933	4.99338
5	5.41632	5.52563	5.63709	5.86660	5.98471	6.10510	6.22780	6.35285	6.74238
6	6.63298	6.80191	6.97532	7.33592	7.52334	7.71561	7.91286	8.11519	8.75374
7	7.89829	8.14201	8.39384	8.92280	9.20044	9.48717	9.78327	10.08901	11.06680
8	9.21423	9.54911	9.89747	10.63663	11.02847	11.43589	11.85943	12.29969	13.72682
9	10.58280	11.02656	11.49132	12.48756	13.02104	13.57948	14.16397	14.77566	16.78584
10	12.00611	12.57789	13.18079	14.48656	15.19293	15.93743	16.72201	17.54874	20.30372
11	13.48635	14.20679	14.97164	16.64549	17.56029	18.53117	19.56143	20.65458	24.34928
12	15.02581	15.91713	16.86994	18.97713	20.14072	21.38428	22.71319	24.13313	29.00167
13	16.62684	17.71298	18.88214	21.49530	22.95339	24.52271	26.21164	28.02911	34.35192
14	18.29191	19.59863	21.01507	24.21492	26.01919	27.97498	30.09492	32.39260	40.50471
15	20.02359	21.57856	23.27597	27.15211	29.36092	31.77248	34.40536	37.27972	47.58041
16	21.82453	23.65749	25.67253	30.32428	33.00340	35.94973	39.18995	42.75328	55.71747
17	23.69751	25.84037	28.21288	33.75023	36.97351	40.54470	44.50084	48.88367	65.07509
18	25.64541	28.13238	30.90565	37.45024	41.30134	45.59917	50.39593	55.74972	75.83636
19	27.67123	30.53900	33.75999	41.44626	46.01846	51.15909	56.93949	63.43968	88.21181
20	29.77808	33.06595	36.78559	45.76196	51.16012	57.27500	64.20283	72.05244	102.44358

Table 2 shows the future value of 1 to be received periodically for a given number of periods. We can see from Table 2 that the future value of an annuity of 1 factor for three periods at 5% is 3.15250. The future value factor is the total of the three individual future value factors as shown in Illustration C-7. Multiplying this amount by the annual investment of $2,000 produces a future value of $6,305.

The demonstration problem in Illustration C-8 shows how to use Table 2.

Illustration C-8
Demonstration problem—
Using Table 2 for *FV* of an annuity of 1

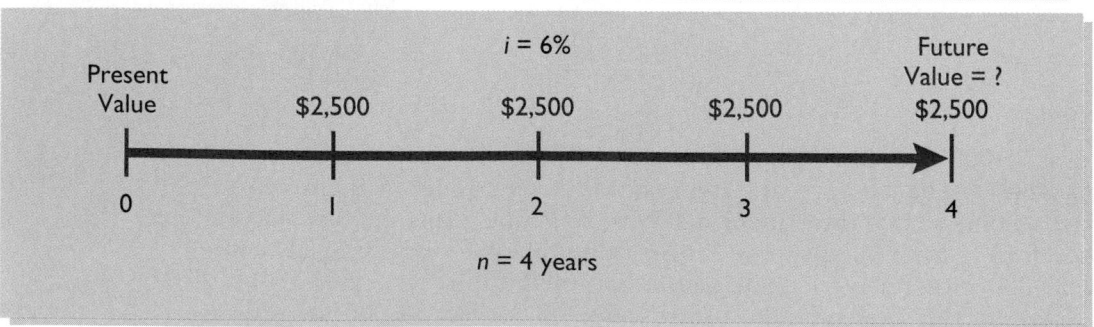

John and Char Lewis' daughter, Debra, has just started high school. They decide to start a college fund for her and will invest $2,500 in a savings account at the end of each year she is in high school (4 payments total). The account will earn 6% interest compounded annually. How much will be in the college fund at the time Debra graduates from high school?

$i = 6\%$

Present Value $2,500 $2,500 $2,500   Future Value = ? $2,500

0   1   2   3   4

$n = 4$ years

Answer: The future value factor from Table 2 is 4.37462 (4 periods at 6%). The future value of $2,500 invested each year for 4 years at 6% interest is **$10,936.55** ($2,500 × 4.37462).

SECTION TWO
PRESENT VALUE CONCEPTS

Present Value Variables

The **present value** is the value now of a given amount to be paid or received in the future, assuming compound interest. The present value, like the future value, is based on three variables: (1) the dollar amount to be received (future amount), (2) the length of time until the amount is received (number of periods), and (3) the interest rate (the discount rate). The process of determining the present value is referred to as **discounting the future amount**.

> **STUDY OBJECTIVE**
> **4**
> Identify the variables fundamental to solving present value problems.

In this textbook, we use present value computations in measuring several items. For example, Chapter 10 computed the present value of the principal and interest payments to determine the market price of a bond. In addition, determining the amount to be reported for notes payable and lease liability involves present value computations.

Present Value of a Single Amount

To illustrate present value, assume that you want to invest a sum of money that will yield $1,000 at the end of one year. What amount would you need to invest today to have $1,000 one year from now? If you want a 10% rate of return, the investment or present value is $909.09 ($1,000 ÷ 1.10). The formula for calculating present value is shown in Illustration C-9.

> **STUDY OBJECTIVE**
> **5**
> Solve for present value of a single amount.

> **Present Value = Future Value ÷ (1 + *i*)^n**

Illustration C-9 Formula for present value

The computation of $1,000 discounted at 10% for one year is as follows:

$$PV = FV \div (1 + i)^n$$
$$= \$1,000 \div (1 + .10)^1$$
$$= \$1,000 \div 1.10$$
$$= \$909.09$$

The future amount ($1,000), the discount rate (10%), and the number of periods (1) are known. The variables in this situation can be depicted in the time diagram in Illustration C-10.

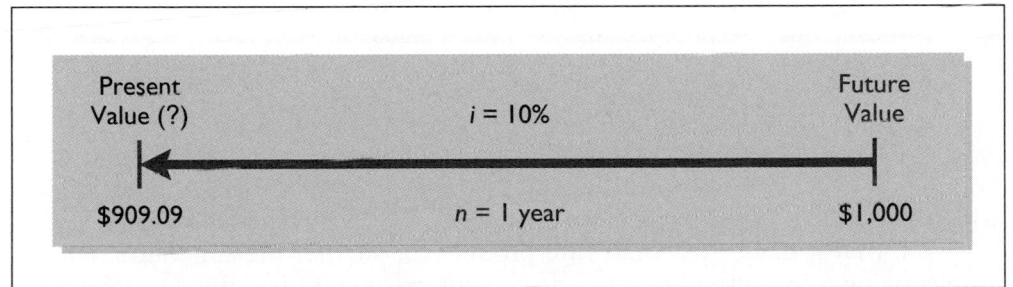

Illustration C-10
Finding present value if discounted for one period

Present Value (?)   *i* = 10%   Future Value

$909.09   *n* = 1 year $1,000

If the single amount of $1,000 is to be received **in two years** and discounted at 10% [$PV = \$1,000 \div (1 + .10)^2$], its present value is $826.45 [($1,000 ÷ 1.21), depicted as shown in Illustration C-11 on the next page.

Illustration C-11
Finding present value if
discounted for two periods

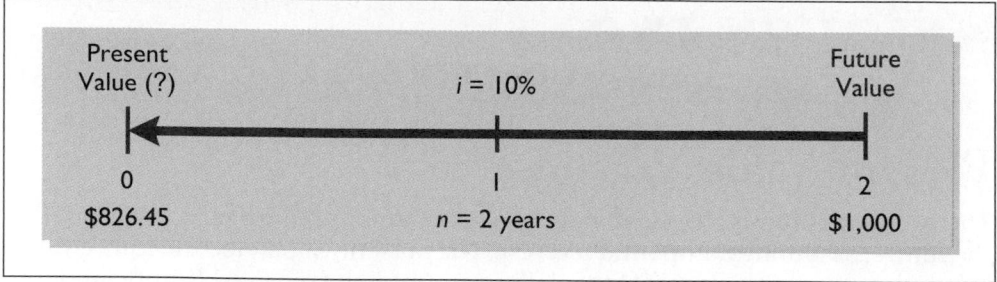

The present value of 1 may also be determined through tables that show the present value of 1 for *n* periods. In Table 3, *n* is the number of discounting periods involved. The percentages are the periodic interest rates or discount rates, and the 5-digit decimal numbers in the respective columns are the present value of 1 factors.

When using Table 3, the future value is multiplied by the present value factor specified at the intersection of the number of periods and the discount rate.

TABLE 3   Present Value of 1

(*n*) Periods	4%	5%	6%	8%	9%	10%	11%	12%	15%
1	.96154	.95238	.94340	.92593	.91743	.90909	.90090	.89286	.86957
2	.92456	.90703	.89000	.85734	.84168	.82645	.81162	.79719	.75614
3	.88900	.86384	.83962	.79383	.77218	.75132	.73119	.71178	.65752
4	.85480	.82270	.79209	.73503	.70843	.68301	.65873	.63552	.57175
5	.82193	.78353	.74726	.68058	.64993	.62092	.59345	.56743	.49718
6	.79031	.74622	.70496	.63017	.59627	.56447	.53464	.50663	.43233
7	.75992	.71068	.66506	.58349	.54703	.51316	.48166	.45235	.37594
8	.73069	.67684	.62741	.54027	.50187	.46651	.43393	.40388	.32690
9	.70259	.64461	.59190	.50025	.46043	.42410	.39092	.36061	.28426
10	.67556	.61391	.55839	.46319	.42241	.38554	.35218	.32197	.24719
11	.64958	.58468	.52679	.42888	.38753	.35049	.31728	.28748	.21494
12	.62460	.55684	.49697	.39711	.35554	.31863	.28584	.25668	.18691
13	.60057	.53032	.46884	.36770	.32618	.28966	.25751	.22917	.16253
14	.57748	.50507	.44230	.34046	.29925	.26333	.23199	.20462	.14133
15	.55526	.48102	.41727	.31524	.27454	.23939	.20900	.18270	.12289
16	.53391	.45811	.39365	.29189	.25187	.21763	.18829	.16312	.10687
17	.51337	.43630	.37136	.27027	.23107	.19785	.16963	.14564	.09293
18	.49363	.41552	.35034	.25025	.21199	.17986	.15282	.13004	.08081
19	.47464	.39573	.33051	.23171	.19449	.16351	.13768	.11611	.07027
20	.45639	.37689	.31180	.21455	.17843	.14864	.12403	.10367	.06110

For example, the present value factor for one period at a discount rate of 10% is .90909, which equals the $909.09 ($1,000 × .90909) computed in Illustration C-10. For two periods at a discount rate of 10%, the present value factor is .82645, which equals the $826.45 ($1,000 × .82645) computed previously.

Note that a higher discount rate produces a smaller present value. For example, using a 15% discount rate, the present value of $1,000 due one year from now is $869.57 versus $909.09 at 10%. Also note that the further removed from the present the future value is, the smaller the present value. For example, using the same discount rate of 10%, the present value of $1,000 due in **five years** is $620.92 versus the present value of $1,000 due in **one year**, which is $909.09.

The following two demonstration problems (Illustrations C-12, C-13) illustrate how to use Table 3.

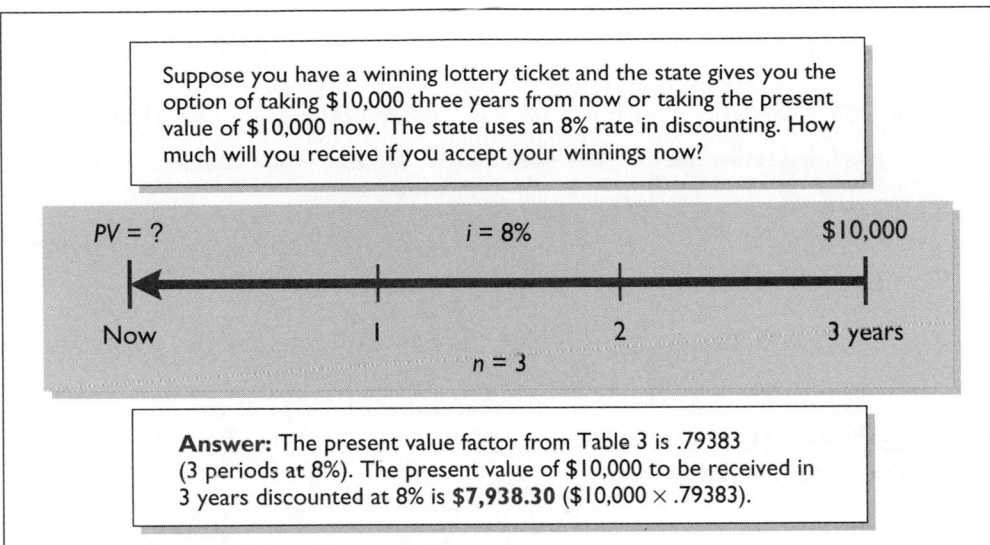

Suppose you have a winning lottery ticket and the state gives you the option of taking $10,000 three years from now or taking the present value of $10,000 now. The state uses an 8% rate in discounting. How much will you receive if you accept your winnings now?

PV = ?   i = 8% $10,000

Now   1   2   3 years

n = 3

Answer: The present value factor from Table 3 is .79383 (3 periods at 8%). The present value of $10,000 to be received in 3 years discounted at 8% is **$7,938.30** ($10,000 × .79383).

Illustration C-12
Demonstration problem—
Using Table 3 for *PV* of 1

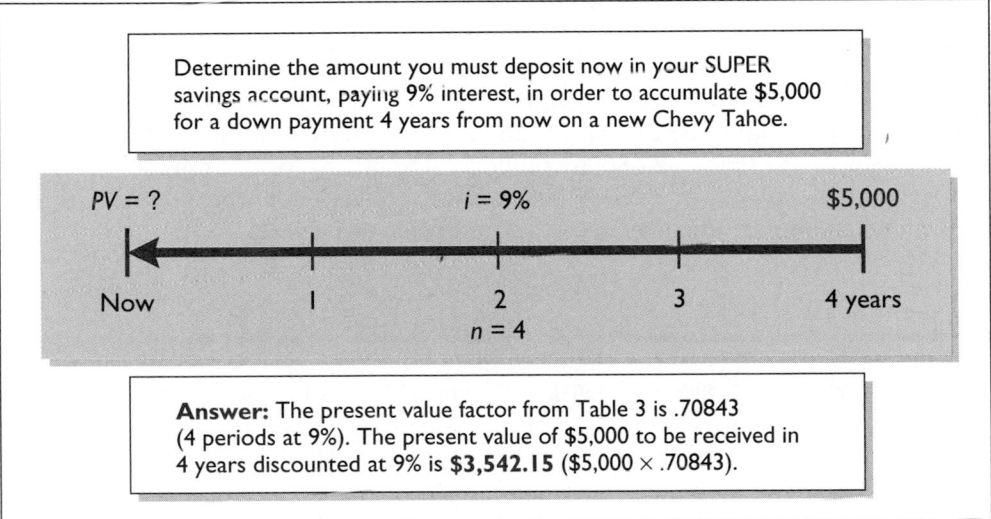

Determine the amount you must deposit now in your SUPER savings account, paying 9% interest, in order to accumulate $5,000 for a down payment 4 years from now on a new Chevy Tahoe.

PV = ?   i = 9% $5,000

Now   1   2   3   4 years

n = 4

Answer: The present value factor from Table 3 is .70843 (4 periods at 9%). The present value of $5,000 to be received in 4 years discounted at 9% is **$3,542.15** ($5,000 × .70843).

Illustration C-13
Demonstration problem—
Using Table 3 for *PV* of 1

Present Value of an Annuity

The preceding discussion involved the discounting of only a single future amount. Businesses and individuals frequently engage in transactions in which a series of equal dollar amounts are to be received or paid periodically. Examples of a series of periodic receipts or payments are loan agreements, installment sales, mortgage notes, lease (rental) contracts, and pension obligations. As discussed earlier, these periodic receipts or payments are **annuities**.

The **present value of an annuity** is the value now of a series of future receipts or payments, discounted assuming compound interest. In computing the present value of an annuity, it is necessary to know (1) the discount rate, (2) the number of discount periods, and (3) the amount of the periodic receipts or payments. To illustrate the computation of the present value of an annuity, assume that you will receive $1,000 cash annually for three years at a time when the discount rate is 10%. This situation is depicted in the time diagram in Illustration C-14. Illustration C-15 shows computation of the present value in this situation.

Illustration C-14 Time diagram for a three-year annuity

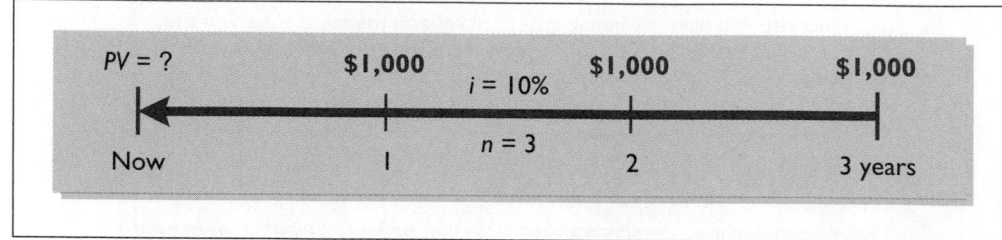

Illustration C-15 Present value of a series of future amounts computation

Future Amount	×	Present Value of 1 Factor at 10%	=	Present Value
$1,000 (one year away)		.90909		$ 909.09
1,000 (two years away)		.82645		826.45
1,000 (three years away)		.75132		751.32
		2.48686		**$2,486.86**

This method of calculation is required when the periodic cash flows are not uniform in each period. However, when the future receipts are the same in each period, there are two other ways to compute present value. First, the annual cash flow can be multiplied by the sum of the three present value factors. In the previous example, $1,000 × 2.48686 equals $2,486.86. Second, annuity tables can be used. As illustrated in Table 4 below, these tables show the present value of 1 to be received periodically for a given number of periods.

TABLE 4   Present Value of an Annuity of 1

(n) Periods	4%	5%	6%	8%	9%	10%	11%	12%	15%
1	.96154	.95238	.94340	.92593	.91743	.90909	.90090	.89286	.86957
2	1.88609	1.85941	1.83339	1.78326	1.75911	1.73554	1.71252	1.69005	1.62571
3	2.77509	2.72325	2.67301	2.57710	2.53130	2.48685	2.44371	2.40183	2.28323
4	3.62990	3.54595	3.46511	3.31213	3.23972	3.16986	3.10245	3.03735	2.85498
5	4.45182	4.32948	4.21236	3.99271	3.88965	3.79079	3.69590	3.60478	3.35216
6	5.24214	5.07569	4.91732	4.62288	4.48592	4.35526	4.23054	4.11141	3.78448
7	6.00205	5.78637	5.58238	5.20637	5.03295	4.86842	4.71220	4.56376	4.16042
8	6.73274	6.46321	6.20979	5.74664	5.53482	5.33493	5.14612	4.96764	4.48732
9	7.43533	7.10782	6.80169	6.24689	5.99525	5.75902	5.53705	5.32825	4.77158
10	8.11090	7.72173	7.36009	6.71008	6.41766	6.14457	5.88923	5.65022	5.01877
11	8.76048	8.30641	7.88687	7.13896	6.80519	6.49506	6.20652	5.93770	5.23371
12	9.38507	8.86325	8.38384	7.53608	7.16073	6.81369	6.49236	6.19437	5.42062
13	9.98565	9.39357	8.85268	7.90378	7.48690	7.10336	6.74987	6.42355	5.58315
14	10.56312	9.89864	9.29498	8.24424	7.78615	7.36669	6.98187	6.62817	5.72448
15	11.11839	10.37966	9.71225	8.55948	8.06069	7.60608	7.19087	6.81086	5.84737
16	11.65230	10.83777	10.10590	8.85137	8.31256	7.82371	7.37916	6.97399	5.95424
17	12.16567	11.27407	10.47726	9.12164	8.54363	8.02155	7.54879	7.11963	6.04716
18	12.65930	11.68959	10.82760	9.37189	8.75563	8.20141	7.70162	7.24967	6.12797
19	13.13394	12.08532	11.15812	9.60360	8.95012	8.36492	7.83929	7.36578	6.19823
20	13.59033	12.46221	11.46992	9.81815	9.12855	8.51356	7.96333	7.46944	6.25933

Table 4 shows that the present value of an annuity of 1 factor for three periods at 10% is 2.48685.[1] This present value factor is the total of the three individual present value factors, as shown in Illustration C-15. Applying this amount to the annual cash flow of $1,000 produces a present value of $2,486.85.

The following demonstration problem (Illustration C-16) illustrates how to use Table 4.

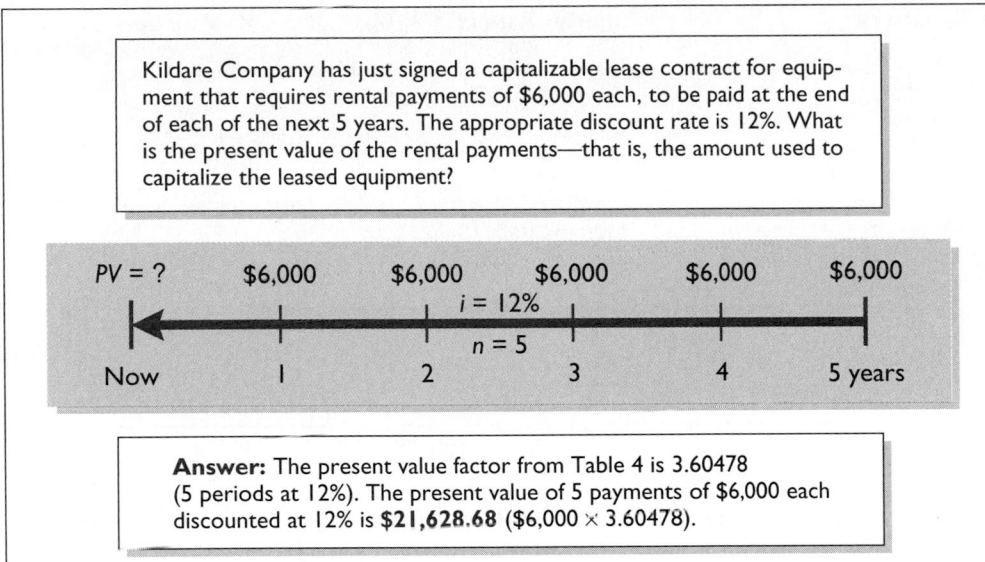

Illustration C-16
Demonstration problem—
Using Table 4 for *PV* of an annuity of 1

Time Periods and Discounting

In the preceding calculations, the discounting was done on an annual basis using an annual interest rate. Discounting may also be done over shorter periods of time such as monthly, quarterly, or semiannually.

When the time frame is less than one year, it is necessary to convert the annual interest rate to the applicable time frame. Assume, for example, that the investor in Illustration C-14 received $500 **semiannually** for three years instead of $1,000 annually. In this case, the number of periods becomes six (3 × 2), the discount rate is 5% (10% ÷ 2), the present value factor from Table 4 is 5.07569, and the present value of the future cash flows is $2,537.85 (5.07569 × $500). This amount is slightly higher than the $2,486.86 computed in Illustration C-15 because interest is computed twice during the same year; therefore interest is earned on the first half year's interest.

Computing the Present Value of a Long-Term Note or Bond

The present value (or market price) of a long-term note or bond is a function of three variables: (1) the payment amounts, (2) the length of time until the amounts are paid, and (3) the discount rate. Our illustration uses a five-year bond issue.

STUDY OBJECTIVE
7
Compute the present value of notes and bonds.

---

[1]The difference of .00001 between 2.48686 and 2.48685 is due to rounding.

The first variable (dollars to be paid) is made up of two elements: (1) a series of interest payments (an annuity) and (2) the principal amount (a single sum). To compute the present value of the bond, both the interest payments and the principal amount must be discounted—two different computations. The time diagrams for a bond due in five years are shown in Illustration C-17.

Illustration C-17 Present value of a bond time diagram

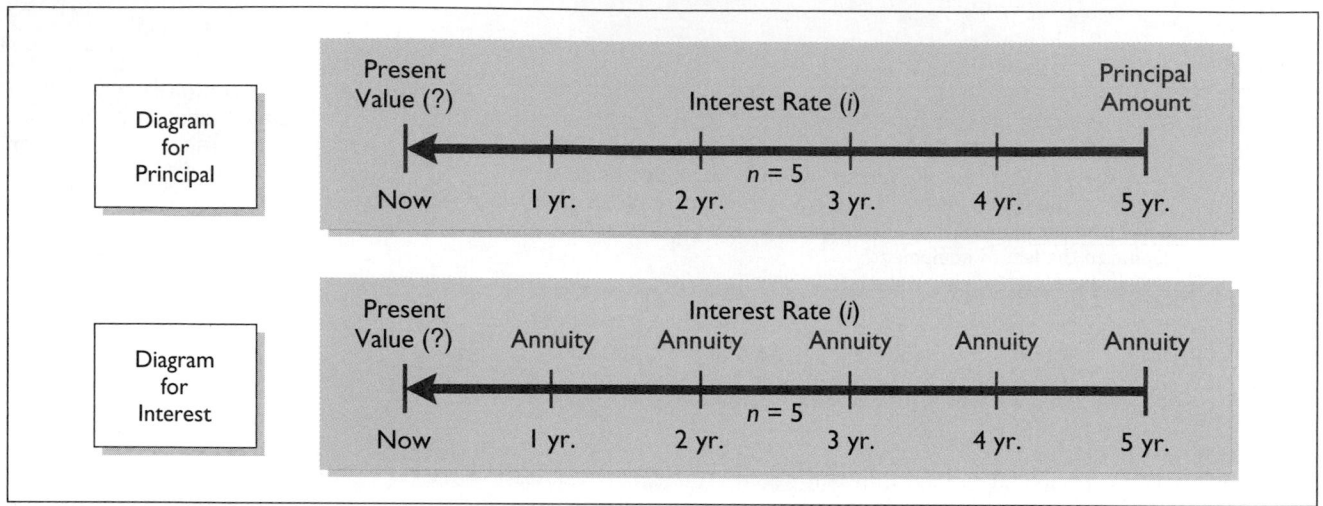

When the investor's market interest rate is equal to the bond's contractual interest rate, the present value of the bonds will equal the face value of the bonds. To illustrate, assume a bond issue of 10%, five-year bonds with a face value of $100,000 with interest payable **semiannually** on January 1 and July 1. If the discount rate is the same as the contractual rate, the bonds will sell at face value. In this case, the investor will receive (1) $100,000 at maturity and (2) a series of ten $5,000 interest payments [($100,000 × 10%) ÷ 2] over the term of the bonds. The length of time is expressed in terms of interest periods—in this case—10, and the discount rate per interest period, 5%. The following time diagram (Illustration C-18) depicts the variables involved in this discounting situation.

Illustration C-18 Time diagram for present value of a 10%, five-year bond paying interest semiannually

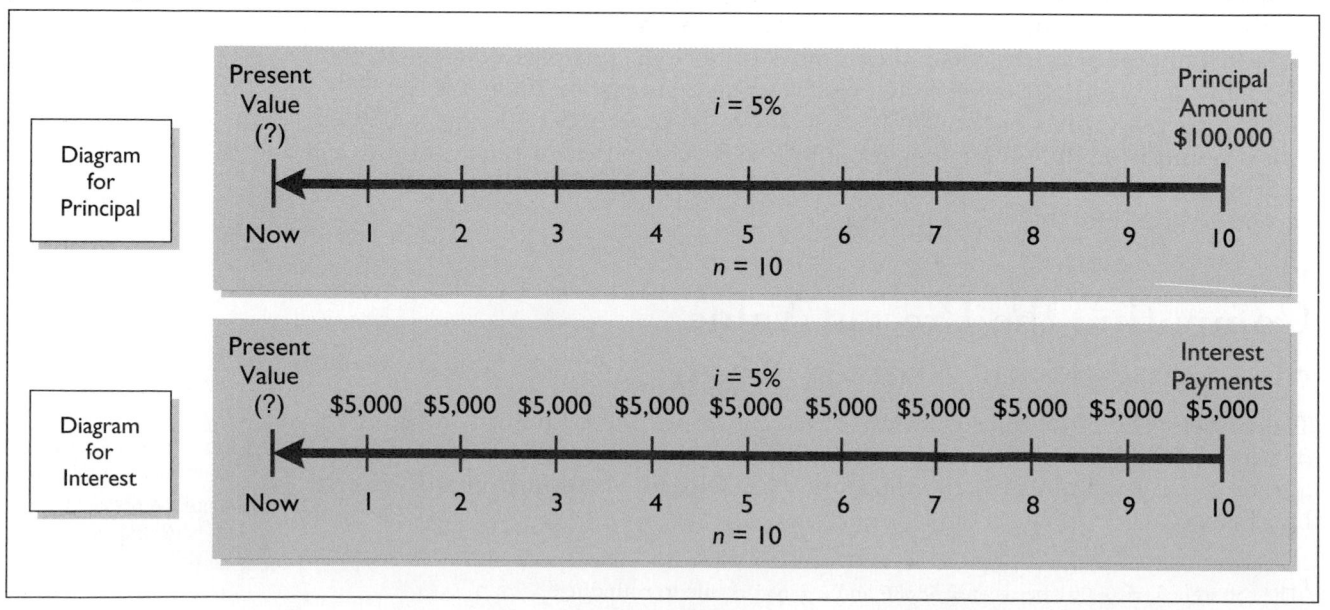

Illustration C-19 shows the computation of the present value of these bonds.

10% Contractual Rate—10% Discount Rate	
Present value of principal to be received at maturity	
$100,000 × *PV* of 1 due in 10 periods at 5%	
$100,000 × .61391 (Table 3)	$ 61,391
Present value of interest to be received periodically	
over the term of the bonds	
$5,000 × *PV* of 1 due periodically for 10 periods at 5%	
$5,000 × 7.72173 (Table 4)	38,609*
Present value of bonds	**$100,000**

*Rounded

Illustration C-19 Present value of principal and interest—face value

Now assume that the investor's required rate of return is 12%, not 10%. The future amounts are again $100,000 and $5,000, respectively, but now a discount rate of 6% (12% ÷ 2) must be used. The present value of the bonds is $92,639, as computed in Illustration C-20.

10% Contractual Rate—12% Discount Rate	
Present value of principal to be received at maturity	
$100,000 × .55839 (Table 3)	$55,839
Present value of interest to be received periodically	
over the term of the bonds	
$5,000 × 7.36009 (Table 4)	36,800
Present value of bonds	**$92,639**

Illustration C-20 Present value of principal and interest—discount

Conversely, if the discount rate is 8% and the contractual rate is 10%, the present value of the bonds is $108,111, computed as shown in Illustration C-21.

10% Contractual Rate—8% Discount Rate	
Present value of principal to be received at maturity	
$100,000 × .67556 (Table 3)	$ 67,556
Present value of interest to be received periodically	
over the term of the bonds	
$5,000 × 8.11090 (Table 4)	40,555
Present value of bonds	**$108,111**

Illustration C-21 Present value of principal and interest—premium

The above discussion relied on present value tables in solving present value problems. Electronic hand-held calculators may also be used to compute present values without the use of these tables. Many calculators, especially the "business" calculators, have present value (*PV*) functions that allow you to calculate present values by merely inputting the proper amount, discount rate, periods, and pressing the PV key.

Summary of Study Objectives

1 *Distinguish between simple and compound interest.* Simple interest is computed on the principal only, while compound interest is computed on the principal and any interest earned that has not been withdrawn.

2 *Solve for future value of a single amount.* Prepare a time diagram of the problem. Identify the principal amount, the number of compounding periods, and the interest rate. Using the future value of 1 table, multiply the principal amount by the future value factor specified at the intersection of the number of periods and the interest rate.

3 *Solve for future value of an annuity.* Prepare a time diagram of the problem. Identify the amount of the periodic payments, the number of compounding periods, and the interest rate. Using the future value of an annuity of 1 table, multiply the amount of the payments by the future value factor specified at the intersection of the number of periods and the interest rate.

4 *Identify the variables fundamental to solving present value problems.* The following three variables are fundamental to solving present value problems: (1) the future amount, (2) the number of periods, and (3) the interest rate (the discount rate).

5 *Solve for present value of a single amount.* Prepare a time diagram of the problem. Identify the future amount, the number of discounting periods, and the discount (interest) rate. Using the present value of a single amount table, multiply the future amount by the present value factor specified at the intersection of the number of periods and the discount rate.

6 *Solve for present value of an annuity.* Prepare a time diagram of the problem. Identify the future amounts (annuities), the number of discounting periods, and the discount (interest) rate. Using the present value of an annuity of 1 table, multiply the amount of the annuity by the present value factor specified at the intersection of the number of periods and the interest rate.

7 *Compute the present value of notes and bonds.* Determine the present value of the principal amount: Multiply the principal amount (a single future amount) by the present value factor (from the present value of 1 table) intersecting at the number of periods (number of interest payments) and the discount rate. Determine the present value of the series of interest payments: Multiply the amount of the interest payment by the present value factor (from the present value of an annuity of 1 table) intersecting at the number of periods (number of interest payments) and the discount rate. Add the present value of the principal amount to the present value of the interest payments to arrive at the present value of the note or bond.

Glossary

Annuity A series of equal dollar amounts to be paid or received periodically. (p. C-5)

Compound interest The interest computed on the principal and any interest earned that has not been paid or withdrawn. (p. C-2)

Discounting the future amount(s) The process of determining present value. (p. C-7)

Future value of a single amount The value at a future date of a given amount invested, assuming compound interest. (p. C-3)

Future value of an annuity The sum of all the payments or receipts plus the accumulated compound interest on them. (p. C-5)

Interest Payment for the use of another's money. (p. C-1)

Present value The value now of a given amount to be paid or received in the future assuming compound interest. (p. C-7)

Present value of an annuity The value now of a series of future receipts or payments, discounted assuming compound interest. (p. C-9)

Principal The amount borrowed or invested. (p. C-1)

Simple interest The interest computed on the principal only. (p. C-1)

Brief Exercises

(Use tables to solve exercises.)

Compute the future value of a single amount.
(SO 2)

BEC-1 Jerry Cora invested $8,000 at 5% annual interest, and left the money invested without withdrawing any of the interest for 12 years. At the end of the 12 years, Jerry withdrew the accumulated amount of money. (a) What amount did Jerry withdraw, assuming the investment earns simple interest? (b) What amount did Jerry withdraw, assuming the investment earns interest compounded annually?

BEC-2 For each of the following cases, indicate (a) to what interest rate columns and (b) to what number of periods you would refer in looking up the future value factor.

Use future value tables.
(SO 2, 3)

(1) In Table 1 (future value of 1):

	Annual Rate	Number of Years Invested	Compounded
Case A	6%	3	Annually
Case B	8%	5	Semiannually

(2) In Table 2 (future value of an annuity of 1):

	Annual Rate	Number of Years Invested	Compounded
Case A	5%	8	Annually
Case B	4%	6	Semiannually

BEC-3 Logan Company signed a lease for an office building for a period of 12 years. Under the lease agreement, a security deposit of $10,000 is made. The deposit will be returned at the expiration of the lease with interest compounded at 4% per year. What amount will Logan receive at the time the lease expires?

Compute the future value of a single amount.
(SO 2)

BEC-4 Summitt Company issued $1,000,000, 10-year bonds and agreed to make annual sinking fund deposits of $80,000. The deposits are made at the end of each year into an account paying 5% annual interest. What amount will be in the sinking fund at the end of 10 years?

Compute the future value of an annuity.
(SO 3)

BEC-5 Brad and Nancy Unruh invested $7,000 in a savings account paying 4% annual interest when their daughter, Laurel, was born. They also deposited $1,000 on each of her birthdays until she was 18 (including her 18th birthday). How much was in the savings account on her 18th birthday (after the last deposit)?

Compute the future value of a single amount and of an annuity.
(SO 2, 3)

BEC-6 Mike Snyder borrowed $25,000 on July 1, 2007. This amount plus accrued interest at 9% compounded annually is to be repaid on July 1, 2012. How much will Mike have to repay on July 1, 2012?

Compute the future value of a single amount.
(SO 2)

BEC-7 For each of the following cases, indicate (a) to what interest rate columns and (b) to what number of periods you would refer in looking up the discount rate.

Use present value tables.
(SO 5, 6)

(1) In Table 3 (present value of 1):

	Annual Rate	Number of Years Involved	Discounts per Year
Case A	12%	6	Annually
Case B	10%	11	Annually
Case C	6%	10	Semiannually

(2) In Table 4 (present value of an annuity of 1):

	Annual Rate	Number of Years Involved	Number of Payments Involved	Frequency of Payments
Case A	12%	20	20	Annually
Case B	10%	5	5	Annually
Case C	6%	4	8	Semiannually

BEC-8 **(a)** What is the present value of $20,000 due 9 periods from now, discounted at 10%?
(b) What is the present value of $20,000 to be received at the end of each of 6 periods, discounted at 9%?

Determine present values.
(SO 5, 6)

BEC-9 McCovey Company is considering an investment which will return a lump sum of $500,000 five years from now. What amount should McCovey Company pay for this investment to earn a 9% return?

Compute the present value of a single amount investment.
(SO 5)

BEC-10 Harrington Company earns 10% on an investment that will return $875,000 eight years from now. What is the amount Harrington should invest now to earn this rate of return?

Compute the present value of a single amount investment.
(SO 5)

Compute the present value of an annuity investment.
(SO 6)

BEC-11   Ritz Company is considering investing in an annuity contract that will return $30,000 annually at the end of each year for 15 years. What amount should Ritz Company pay for this investment if it earns a 5% return?

Compute the present value of an annuity investment.
(SO 6)

BEC-12   Orear Enterprises earns 8% on an investment that pays back $120,000 at the end of each of the next 6 years. What is the amount Orear Enterprises invested to earn the 8% rate of return?

Compute the present value of bonds.
(SO 5, 6, 7)

BEC-13   Santo Railroad Co. is about to issue $200,000 of 10-year bonds paying a 9% interest rate, with interest payable semiannually. The discount rate for such securities is 8%. How much can Santo expect to receive for the sale of these bonds?

Compute the present value of bonds.
(SO 5, 6, 7)

BEC-14   Assume the same information as BEC-13 except that the discount rate was 10% instead of 8%. In this case, how much can Santo expect to receive from the sale of these bonds?

Compute the present value of a note.
(SO 5, 6, 7)

BEC-15   Garcia Taco Company receives a $50,000, 6-year note bearing interest of 6% (paid annually) from a customer at a time when the discount rate is 8%. What is the present value of the note received by Garcia?

Compute the present value of bonds.
(SO 5, 6, 7)

BEC-16   Lucky Treasures Enterprises issued 9%, 8-year, $2,000,000 par value bonds that pay interest semiannually on October 1 and April 1. The bonds are dated April 1, 2007, and are issued on that date. The discount rate of interest for such bonds on April 1, 2007, is 10%. What cash proceeds did Lucky Treasures receive from issuance of the bonds?

Compute the present value of a machine for purposes of making a purchase decision.
(SO 6, 7)

BEC-17   Andrew Larson owns a garage and is contemplating purchasing a tire retreading machine for $16,100. After estimating costs and revenues, Andrew projects a net cash flow from the retreading machine of $2,690 annually for 8 years. Andrew hopes to earn a return of 10 percent on such investments. What is the present value of the retreading operation? Should Andrew purchase the retreading machine?

Compute the present value of a note.
(SO 6)

BEC-18   Harry Hart Company issues an 8%, 5-year mortgage note on January 1, 2007, to obtain financing for new equipment. Land is used as collateral for the note. The terms provide for semiannual installment payments of $112,825. What were the cash proceeds received from the issuance of the note?

Compute the maximum price to pay for a machine.
(SO 6, 7)

BEC-19   Reagan Company is considering purchasing equipment. The equipment will produce the following cash flows: Year 1, $35,000; Year 2, $45,000; Year 3, $55,000. Reagan requires a minimum rate of return of 10%. What is the maximum price Reagan should pay for this equipment?

Compute the interest rate on a single amount.
(SO 5)

BEC-20   If Shelly Remington invests $2,393.90 now and she will receive $10,000 at the end of 15 years, what annual rate of interest will Shelly earn on her investment? [*Hint:* Use Table 3.]

Compute the number of periods of a single amount.
(SO 5)

BEC-21   Elliot Dane has been offered the opportunity of investing $36,061 now. The investment will earn 12% per year and at the end of that time will return Elliot $100,000. How many years must Elliot wait to receive $100,000? [*Hint:* Use Table 3.]

Compute the interest rate on an annuity.
(SO 6)

BEC-22   Rene Barone made an investment of $9,128.55. From this investment, she will receive $1,000 annually for the next 20 years starting one year from now. What rate of interest will Rene's investment be earning for her? [*Hint:* Use Table 4.]

Compute the number of periods of an annuity.
(SO 6)

BEC-23   Cortney Eldred invests $6,710.08 now for a series of $1,000 annual returns beginning one year from now. Cortney will earn a return of 8% on the initial investment. How many annual payments of $1,000 will Cortney receive? [*Hint:* Use Table 4.]

Payroll Accounting

STUDY OBJECTIVES

After studying this appendix,
you should be able to:

1 Discuss the objectives of internal control for payroll.

2 Compute and record the payroll for a pay period.

3 Describe and record employer payroll taxes.

Payroll and related fringe benefits often make up a large percentage of current liabilities. Employee compensation is often the most significant expense that a company incurs. For example, General Motors recently reported total employees of 386,000 and labor costs of $21.6 billion. Add to labor costs such fringe benefits as health insurance, life insurance, disability insurance, and so on, and you can see why proper accounting and control of payroll are so important.

Payroll accounting involves more than paying employees' wages. Companies are required by law to maintain payroll records for each employee, file and pay payroll taxes, and comply with numerous state and federal tax laws related to employee compensation. Accounting for payroll has become much more complex due to these regulations.

Payroll Defined

The term "payroll" pertains to both salaries and wages. Managerial, administrative, and sales personnel are generally paid **salaries**. Salaries are often expressed in terms of a specified amount per month or per year rather than an hourly rate. For example, the faculty and administrative personnel at the college or university you are attending are paid salaries. In contrast, store clerks, factory employees, and manual laborers are normally paid **wages**. Wages are based on a rate per hour or on a piecework basis (such as per unit of product). Frequently, the terms "salaries" and "wages" are used interchangeably.

The term "payroll" does not apply to payments made for services of professionals such as certified public accountants, attorneys, and architects. Such professionals are independent contractors rather than salaried employees. Payments to them are called **fees**, rather than salaries or wages. This distinction is important because government regulations relating to the payment and reporting of payroll taxes apply only to employees.

Internal Control of Payroll

STUDY OBJECTIVE

1

Discuss the objectives of internal control for payroll.

Internal control was introduced in Chapter 7. As applied to payrolls, the objectives of internal control are (1) to safeguard company assets against unauthorized payments of payrolls, and (2) to ensure the accuracy and reliability of the accounting records pertaining to payrolls.

Irregularities often result if internal control is lax. Overstating hours, using unauthorized pay rates, adding fictitious employees to the payroll, continuing terminated employees on the payroll, and distributing duplicate payroll checks are all methods of stealing from a company. Moreover, inaccurate records will result in incorrect paychecks, financial statements, and payroll tax returns.

Payroll activities involve four functions: hiring employees, timekeeping, preparing the payroll, and paying the payroll. For effective internal control, these four functions should be assigned to different departments or individuals. To illustrate these functions, we will examine the case of Academy Company and one of its employees, Michael Jordan.

Hiring Employees

Human resources

Human Resources department documents and authorizes employment.

HIRING EMPLOYEES

The human resources (personnel) department is responsible for posting job openings, screening and interviewing applicants, and hiring employees. From a control standpoint, this department provides significant documentation and authorization. When an employee is hired, the human resources department prepares an authorization form. The one used by Academy Company for Michael Jordan is shown in Illustration D-1.

Illustration D-1
Authorization form prepared by the human resources department

ACADEMY COMPANY		

Employee Name __Jordan,_____ __Michael_____ ____   Starting Date __9/01/05____
                      LAST   FIRST   MI

Classification __Skilled-Level 10_____   Social Security No. __329-36-9547__

Department __Shipping_____   Division __Entertainment_____

NEW HIRE	Classification __Clerk_____ Salary Grade __Level 10__ Trans. from Temp. ☐ Rate $__10.00__ per __hour__ Bonus __N/A_____ Non-exempt ☒ Exempt ☐
RATE CHANGE	New Rate $ __12.00_____ Effective Date __9/1/07_____ Present Rate $__10.00_____ Merit ☒ Promotion ☐ Decrease ☐ Other_____ Previous Increase Date ____None____ Amount $_____ per_____ Type_____
SEPARATION	Resignation ☐ Discharge ☐ Retirement ☐ Reason_____ _____ Leave of absence ☐ From_____ to_____ Type_____ Last Day Worked_____
APPROVALS	_BEW_____ _9/1/07___ _EMW_____ _9-1-07___ BRANCH OR DEPT. MANAGER DATE DIVISION V.P. DATE *James E. Speer* PERSONNEL DEPARTMENT

The authorization form is sent to the payroll department, where it is used to place the new employee on the payroll. A chief concern of the human resources department is ensuring the accuracy of this form. The reason is quite simple: one of the most common types of payroll frauds is adding fictitious employees to the payroll.

The human resources department is also responsible for authorizing changes in employment status. Specifically, they must authorize (1) changes in pay rates and (2) terminations of employment. Every authorization should be in writing, and a copy of the change in status should be sent to the payroll department. Notice in Illustration D-1 that Jordan received a pay increase of $2 per hour.

TIMEKEEPING

Another area in which internal control is important is timekeeping. Hourly employees are usually required to record time worked by "punching" a time clock. Times of arrival and departure are automatically recorded by the employee by inserting a time card into the clock. Michael Jordan's time card is shown in Illustration D-2.

In large companies, time clock procedures are often monitored by a supervisor or security guard to make sure an employee punches only one card. At the end of the pay period, each employee's supervisor approves the hours shown by signing the time card. When overtime hours are involved, approval by a supervisor is usually mandatory. This guards against unauthorized overtime. The approved time cards are then sent to the payroll department. For salaried employees, a manually prepared weekly or monthly time report kept by a supervisor may be used to record time worked.

Timekeeping

Supervisors monitor hours worked through time cards and time reports.

	PAY PERIOD ENDING
No. 17	1/14/07

NAME Michael Jordan

EXTRA TIME			REGULAR TIME
		A.M. IN	8:58
	1st Day	NOON OUT	12:00
		NOON IN	1:00
		P.M. OUT	5:01
		A.M. IN	9:00
	2nd Day	NOON OUT	11:59
		NOON IN	12:59
		P.M. OUT	5:00
		A.M. IN	8:59
	3rd Day	NOON OUT	12:01
		NOON IN	1:01
		P.M. OUT	5:00
5:00	4th Day	A.M. IN	9:00
9:00		NOON OUT	12:00
		NOON IN	1:00
		P.M. OUT	5:00
		A.M. IN	8:57
	5th Day	NOON OUT	11:58
		NOON IN	1:00
		P.M. OUT	5:01
		A.M. IN	8:00
	6th Day	NOON OUT	1:00
		NOON IN	
		P.M. OUT	
		A.M. IN	
	7th Day	NOON OUT	
		NOON IN	
		P.M. OUT	
TOTAL 4		TOTAL	40

(Vertical side text: THIS SIDE OUT)

Illustration D-2
Time card

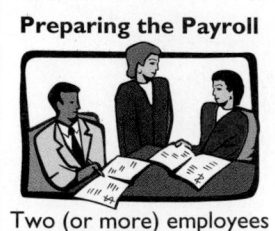

Preparing the Payroll

Two (or more) employees verify payroll amounts; supervisor approves.

PREPARING THE PAYROLL

The payroll is prepared in the payroll department on the basis of two inputs: (1) human resources department authorizations and (2) approved time cards. Numerous calculations are involved in determining gross wages and payroll deductions. Therefore, a second payroll department employee, working independently, verifies all calculated amounts, and a payroll department supervisor then approves the payroll. The payroll department is also responsible for preparing (but not signing) payroll checks, maintaining payroll records, and preparing payroll tax returns.

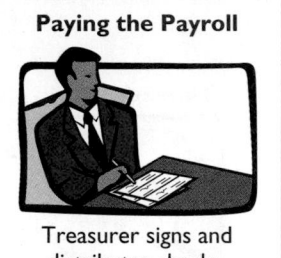

Paying the Payroll

Treasurer signs and distributes checks.

PAYING THE PAYROLL

The payroll is paid by the treasurer's department. **Payment by check minimizes the risk of loss from theft, and the endorsed check provides proof of payment.** For good internal control, payroll checks should be prenumbered, and all checks should be accounted for. All checks must be signed by the treasurer (or a designated agent). Distribution of the payroll checks to employees should be controlled by the treasurer's department. Many employees have their pay credited electronically to their bank account. To control such disbursements, receipts detailing gross pay, deductions, and net pay are provided to employees.

Occasionally the payroll is paid in currency. In such cases it is customary to have a second person count the cash in each pay envelope. The paymaster should obtain a signed receipt from the employee upon payment.

Determining the Payroll

Determining the payroll involves computing three amounts: (1) gross earnings, (2) payroll deductions, and (3) net pay.

STUDY OBJECTIVE
2
Compute and record the payroll for a pay period.

GROSS EARNINGS

Gross earnings is the total compensation earned by an employee. It consists of wages or salaries, plus any bonuses and commissions.

Total **wages** for an employee are determined by multiplying the hours worked by the hourly rate of pay. In addition to the hourly pay rate, most companies are required by law to pay hourly workers a minimum of $1\frac{1}{2}$ times the regular hourly rate for overtime work in excess of 8 hours per day or 40 hours per week. In addition, many employers pay overtime rates for work done at night, on weekends, and on holidays.

Helpful Hint The law that governs pay rates is the Federal Fair Labor Standards Act. It applies to all companies involved in interstate commerce.

Michael Jordan's time card (Illustration D-2) shows that he worked 44 hours for the weekly pay period ending January 14. The computation of his gross earnings (total wages) is shown in Illustration D-3.

Illustration D-3
Computation of total wages

Type of Pay	Hours	×	Rate	=	Gross Earnings
Regular	40	×	$12	=	$ 480
Overtime	4	×	18	=	72
Total wages					**$552**

This computation assumes that Jordan receives $1\frac{1}{2}$ times his regular hourly rate ($12 × 1.5) for his overtime hours. Union contracts often require that overtime rates be as much as twice the regular rates.

The **salary** for an employee is generally based on a monthly or yearly rate. These rates are then prorated to the payroll periods used by the company. Most executive and administrative positions are salaried. Federal law does not require overtime pay for employees in such positions.

Many companies have **bonus** agreements for management personnel and other employees. A recent survey found that over 94% of the largest U.S. manufacturing companies offer annual bonuses to their key executives. Bonus arrangements may be based on such factors as increased sales or net income. Bonuses may be paid in cash and/or by granting executives and employees the opportunity to acquire shares of company stock at favorable prices (called stock option plans).

> ***E*THICS NOTE**
> Bonuses often reward outstanding individual performance; but successful corporations also need considerable teamwork. A challenge is to motivate individuals while preventing an unethical employee from taking another's idea for his or her own advantage.

PAYROLL DEDUCTIONS

As anyone who has received a paycheck knows, gross earnings are usually very different from the amount actually received. The difference is due to **payroll deductions**. Such deductions do not result in payroll tax expense to the employer. The employer is merely a collection agent, and subsequently transfers the amounts deducted to the government and designated recipients. Payroll deductions may be mandatory or voluntary. Mandatory deductions are required by law and consist of FICA taxes and income taxes. Voluntary deductions are at the option of the employee. Illustration D-4 summarizes the types of payroll deductions.

Illustration D-4 Payroll deductions

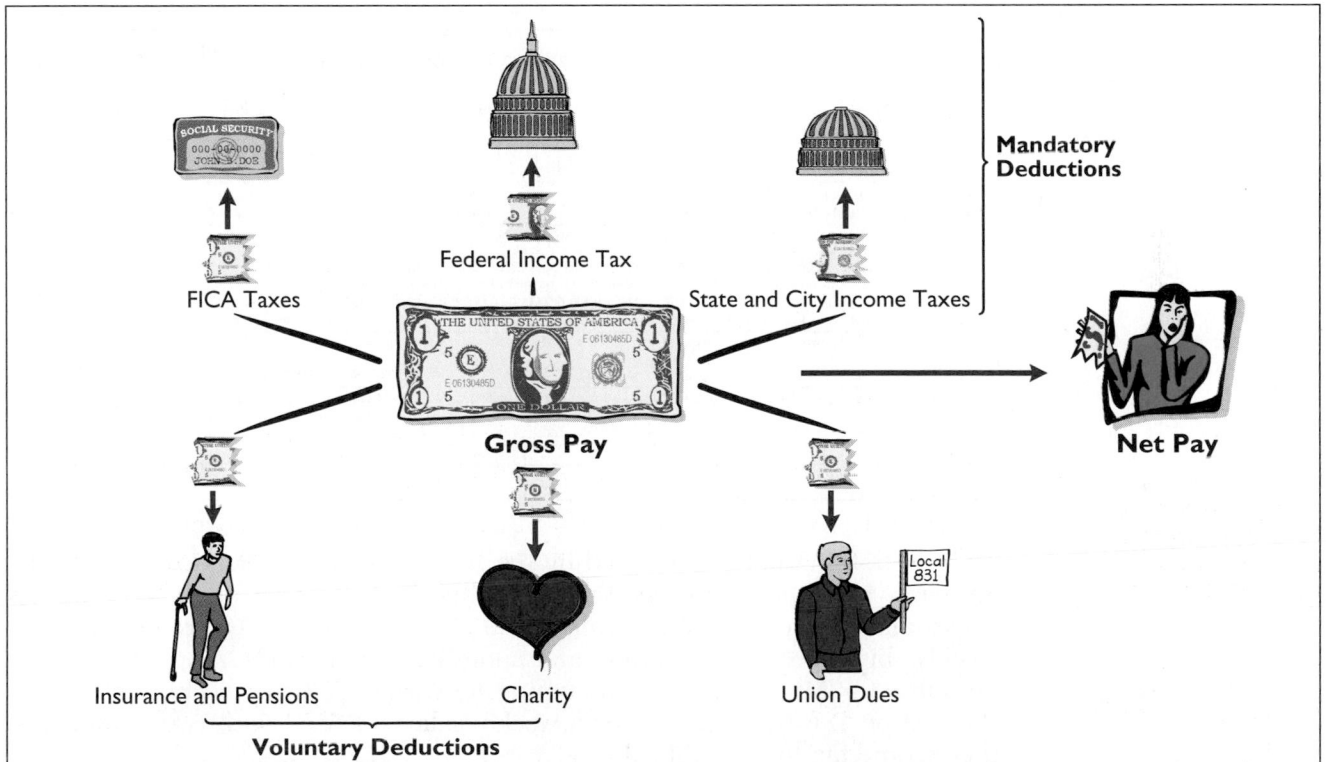

FICA Taxes

In 1937 Congress enacted the Federal Insurance Contribution Act (FICA). **FICA taxes are designed to provide workers with supplemental retirement, employment disability, and medical benefits.** In 1965, Congress extended benefits to include Medicare for individuals over 65 years of age. The benefits are financed by a tax levied on employees' earnings. FICA taxes are commonly referred to as **Social Security taxes**.

The tax rate and the tax base for FICA taxes are set by Congress. When FICA taxes were first imposed, the rate was 1% on the first $3,000 of gross earnings, or a maximum of $30 per year. The rate and base have changed dramatically since that time! In 2006, the rate was 7.65% (6.2% Social Security plus 1.45% Medicare) on the first $94,200 of gross earnings for each employee.[1] For purpose of illustration in this appendix, we will assume a rate of 8% on the first $90,000 of gross earnings, or a maximum of $7,200. Using the 8% rate, the FICA withholding for Jordan for the weekly pay period ending January 14 is $44.16 ($552 × 8%).

Income Taxes

Under the U.S. pay-as-you-go system of federal income taxes, employers are required to withhold income taxes from employees each pay period. The amount to be withheld is determined by three variables: (1) the employee's gross earnings; (2) the number of allowances claimed by the employee; and (3) the length of the pay period. The number of allowances claimed typically includes the employee, his or her spouse, and other dependents. **To indicate to the Internal Revenue Service the number of allowances claimed, the employee must complete an Employee's Withholding Allowance Certificate (Form W-4).** As shown in Illustration D-5, Michael Jordan claims two allowances on his W-4.

Illustration D-5 W-4 form

Withholding tables furnished by the Internal Revenue Service indicate the amount of income tax to be withheld. Withholding amounts are based on gross wages and the number of allowances claimed. Separate tables are provided for weekly, biweekly, semimonthly, and monthly pay periods. The withholding tax table for Michael Jordan (assuming he earns $552 per week) is shown in Illustration D-6 (next page). For a weekly salary of $552 with two allowances, the income tax to be withheld is $49.

Most states (and some cities) also require **employers** to withhold income taxes from employees' earnings. As a rule, the amounts withheld are a percentage (specified in the state revenue code) of the amount withheld for the federal

---

[1]The Medicare provision also includes a tax of 1.45% on gross earnings in excess of $94,200. In the interest of simplification, we ignore this 1.45% charge in our end-of-chapter assignment material. We assume zero FICA withholdings on gross earnings above $90,000.

MARRIED Persons — **WEEKLY** Payroll Period
(For Wages Paid in 2007)

If the wages are –		And the number of withholding allowances claimed is –										
At least	But less than	0	1	2	3	4	5	6	7	8	9	10
		The amount of income tax to be withheld is –										
490	500	56	48	40	32	24	17	9	1	0	0	0
500	510	57	49	42	34	26	18	10	3	0	0	0
510	520	59	51	43	35	27	20	12	4	0	0	0
520	530	60	52	45	37	29	21	13	6	0	0	0
530	540	62	54	46	38	30	23	15	7	0	0	0
540	550	63	55	48	40	32	24	16	9	1	0	0
550	560	65	57	49	41	33	26	18	10	2	0	0
560	570	66	58	51	43	35	27	19	12	4	0	0
570	580	68	60	52	44	36	29	21	13	5	0	0
580	590	69	61	54	46	38	30	22	15	7	0	0
590	600	71	63	55	47	39	32	24	16	8	1	0
600	610	72	64	57	49	41	33	25	18	10	2	0
610	620	74	66	58	50	42	35	27	19	11	4	0
620	630	75	67	60	52	44	36	28	21	13	5	0
630	640	77	69	61	53	45	38	30	22	14	7	0
640	650	78	70	63	55	47	39	31	24	16	8	0
650	660	80	72	64	56	48	41	33	25	17	10	2
660	670	81	73	66	58	50	42	34	27	19	11	3
670	680	83	75	67	59	51	44	36	28	20	13	5
680	690	84	76	69	61	53	45	37	30	22	14	6

income tax. Or they may be a specified percentage of the employee's earnings. For the sake of simplicity, we have assumed that Jordan's wages are subject to state income taxes of 2%, or $11.04 (2% × $552) per week.

There is no limit on the amount of gross earnings subject to income tax withholdings. In fact, the higher the earnings, the higher the amount of taxes withheld.

Other Deductions

Employees may voluntarily authorize withholdings for charitable, retirement, and other purposes. All voluntary deductions from gross earnings should be authorized in writing by the employee. The authorization(s) may be made individually or as part of a group plan. Deductions for charitable organizations, such as the United Way, or for financial arrangements, such as U.S. savings bonds and repayment of loans from company credit unions, are made individually. Deductions for union dues, health and life insurance, and pension plans are often made on a group basis. We will assume that Jordan has weekly voluntary deductions of $10 for the United Way and $5 for union dues.

NET PAY

Net pay is determined by subtracting payroll deductions from gross earnings. For Michael Jordan, net pay for the pay period is $432.80, computed as shown in Illustration D-7 (page D-8). Assuming that Michael Jordan's wages for each week during the year are $552, total wages for the year are $28,704 (52 × $552). Thus, all of Jordan's wages are subject to FICA tax during the year. Let's assume that Jordan's department head earns $1,350 per week, or $70,200 for the year. Since we are assuming that only the first $90,000 is subject to FICA taxes, the maximum FICA withholdings on the department head's earnings would be $7,200 ($90,000 × 8%).

Alternative Terminology
Net pay is also called *take-home pay.*

Illustration D-7
Computation of net pay

Gross earnings		$ 552.00
Payroll deductions:		
FICA taxes	$44.16	
Federal income taxes	49.00	
State income taxes	11.04	
United Way	10.00	
Union dues	5.00	119.20
Net pay		**$432.80**

Recording the Payroll

Recording the payroll involves maintaining payroll department records, recognizing payroll expenses and liabilities, and recording payment of the payroll.

MAINTAINING PAYROLL DEPARTMENT RECORDS

To comply with state and federal laws, an employer must keep a cumulative record of each employee's gross earnings, deductions, and net pay during the year. The record that provides this information is the **employee earnings record**. Michael Jordan's employee earnings record is shown in Illustration D-8.

Illustration D-8
Employee earnings record

ACADEMY COMPANY
Employee Earnings Record
for the Year 2007

Name	Michael Jordan	**Address**	2345 Mifflin Ave.
Social Security Number	329-36-9547		Hampton, Michigan 48292
Date of Birth	December 24, 1967	**Telephone**	555-238-9051
Date Employed	September 1, 2005	**Date Employment Ended**	
Sex	Male	**Exemptions**	2
Single ____	**Married** __X__		

2007 Period Ending	Total Hours	Gross Earnings				Deductions						Payment	
		Regular	Overtime	Total	Cumulative	FICA	Fed. Inc. Tax	State Inc. Tax	United Fund	Union Dues	Total	Net Amount	Check No.
1/7	42	480.00	36.00	516.00	516.00	41.28	43.00	10.32	10.00	5.00	109.60	406.40	974
1/14	**44**	**480.00**	**72.00**	**552.00**	1,068.00	**44.16**	**49.00**	**11.04**	**10.00**	**5.00**	**119.20**	**432.80**	**1028**
1/21	43	480.00	54.00	534.00	1,602.00	42.72	46.00	10.68	10.00	5.00	114.40	419.60	1077
1/28	42	480.00	36.00	516.00	2,118.00	41.28	43.00	10.32	10.00	5.00	109.60	406.40	1133
Jan. Total		1,920.00	198.00	2,118.00		169.44	181.00	42.36	40.00	20.00	452.80	1,665.20	

A separate earnings record is kept for each employee. It is updated after each pay period. The cumulative payroll data on the earnings record are used by the employer to: (1) determine when an employee has earned the maximum earnings subject to FICA taxes, (2) file state and federal payroll tax returns (as explained later in the appendix), and (3) provide each employee with a statement of gross earnings and tax withholdings for the year. Illustration D-12 (on page D-13) shows this statement.

In addition to employee earnings records, many companies find it useful to prepare a **payroll register**. This record accumulates the gross earnings, deductions, and net pay by employee for each pay period. It provides the documentation for preparing a paycheck for each employee. Academy Company's payroll register is presented in Illustration D-9. It shows the data for Michael Jordan in the wages section. In this example, Academy Company's total weekly payroll is $17,210, as shown in the gross earnings column.

Illustration D-9 Payroll register

ACADEMY COMPANY
Payroll Register
for the Week Ending January 14, 2007

		Earnings			Deductions						Paid		Accounts Debited	
Employee	Total Hours	Regular	Over-time	Gross	FICA	Federal Income Tax	State Income Tax	United Way	Union Dues	Total	Net Pay	Check No.	Office Salaries Expense	Wages Expense
Office Salaries														
Arnold, Patricia	40	580.00		580.00	46.40	61.00	11.60	15.00		134.00	446.00	998	580.00	
Canton, Matthew	40	590.00		590.00	47.20	63.00	11.80	20.00		142.00	448.00	999	590.00	
Mueller, William	40	530.00		530.00	42.40	54.00	10.60	11.00		118.00	412.0	1010	530.00	
Subtotal		5,200.00		5,200.00	416.00	1,090.00	104.00	120.00		1,730.00	3,470.00		5,200.00	
Wages														
Bennett, Robin	42	480.00	36.00	516.00	41.28	43.00	10.32	18.00	5.00	117.60	398.40	1025		516.00
Jordan, Michael	**44**	**480.00**	**72.00**	**552.00**	**44.16**	**49.00**	**11.04**	**10.00**	**5.00**	**119.20**	**432.80**	**1028**		**552.00**
Milroy, Lee	43	480.00	54.00	534.00	42.72	46.00	10.68	10.00	5.00	114.40	419.60	1040		534.00
Subtotal		11,000.00	1,010.00	12,010.00	960.80	2,400.00	240.20	301.50	115.00	4,017.50	7,992.50			12,010.00
Total		16,200.00	1,010.00	17,210.00	1,376.80	3,490.00	344.20	421.50	115.00	5,747.50	11,462.50		5,200.00	12,010.00

Note that this record is a listing of each employee's payroll data for the pay period. In some companies, a payroll register is a journal or book of original entry. Postings are made from it directly to ledger accounts. In other companies, the payroll register is a memorandum record that provides the data for a general journal entry and subsequent posting to the ledger accounts. At Academy Company, the latter procedure is followed.

RECOGNIZING PAYROLL EXPENSES AND LIABILITIES

From the payroll register in Illustration D-9, a journal entry is made to record the payroll. For the week ending January 14 the entry is:

Jan. 14	Office Salaries Expense	5,200.00	
	Wages Expense	12,010.00	
	FICA Taxes Payable		1,376.80
	Federal Income Taxes Payable		3,490.00
	State Income Taxes Payable		344.20
	United Fund Payable		421.50
	Union Dues Payable		115.00
	Salaries and Wages Payable		11,462.50
	(To record payroll for the week ending January 14)		

```
A   =   L    +    SE
   +1,376.80   −5,200.00 Exp
   +3,490.00  −12,010.00 Exp
   +344.20
   +421.50
   +115.00
   +11,462.50
```
Cash Flows
no effect

Specific liability accounts are credited for the mandatory and voluntary deductions made during the pay period. In the example, debits to Office Salaries and Wages Expense are used for gross earnings because office workers are on a salary and other employees are paid on an hourly rate. In other companies, there may be debits to other accounts such as Store Salaries or Sales Salaries. The amount credited to Salaries and Wages Payable is the sum of the individual checks the employees will receive.

RECORDING PAYMENT OF THE PAYROLL

Payment by check is made either from the employer's regular bank account or a payroll bank account. Each paycheck is usually accompanied by a detachable **statement of earnings** document. This shows the employee's gross earnings, payroll deductions, and net pay for the period and for the year-to-date. The Academy Company uses its regular bank account for payroll checks. The paycheck and statement of earnings for Michael Jordan are shown in Illustration D-10.

Illustration D-10
Paycheck and statement of earnings

Helpful Hint Do any of the income tax liabilities result in payroll tax expense for the employer? Answer: No. The employer is acting only as a collection agent for the government.

Following payment of the payroll, the check numbers are entered in the payroll register. The entry to record payment of the payroll for Academy Company is as follows.

A	=	L	+	SE
−11,462.50		−11,462.50		

Cash Flows
−11,462.50

Jan. 14	Salaries and Wages Payable	11,462.50	
	Cash		11,462.50
	(To record payment of payroll)		

When currency is used in payment, one check is prepared for the payroll's total amount of net pay. This check is then cashed, and the coins and currency are inserted in individual pay envelopes for disbursement to individual employees.

Employer Payroll Taxes

STUDY OBJECTIVE
3
Describe and record employer payroll taxes.

Payroll tax expense for businesses results from three taxes **levied on employers** by governmental agencies. These taxes are: (1) FICA, (2) federal unemployment tax, and (3) state unemployment tax. These taxes plus such items as paid vacations and pensions are collectively referred to as **fringe benefits**. As indicated earlier, the cost of fringe benefits in many companies is substantial.

FICA TAXES

We have seen that each employee must pay FICA taxes. An employer must match each employee's FICA contribution. The matching contribution results in **payroll tax expense** to the employer. The employer's tax is subject to the same rate and maximum earnings applicable to the employee. The account, FICA Taxes Payable, is used for both the employee's and the employer's FICA contributions. For the January 14 payroll, Academy Company's FICA tax contribution is $1,376.80 ($17,210.00 × 8%).

FEDERAL UNEMPLOYMENT TAXES

The Federal Unemployment Tax Act (FUTA) is another feature of the federal Social Security program. **Federal unemployment taxes** provide benefits for a limited period of time to employees who lose their jobs through no fault of their own. Under provisions of the Act, the employer is required to pay a tax of 6.2% on the first $7,000 of gross wages paid to each employee during a calendar year. The law allows the employer a maximum credit of 5.4% on the federal rate for contributions to state unemployment taxes. Because of this provision, state unemployment tax laws generally provide for a 5.4% rate. The effective federal unemployment tax rate thus becomes 0.8% (6.2% − 5.4%). This tax is borne **entirely by the employer**. There is no deduction or withholding from employees.

The account Federal Unemployment Taxes Payable is used to recognize this liability. The federal unemployment tax for Academy Company for the January 14 payroll is $137.68 ($17,210.00 × 0.8%).

> **Helpful Hint** FICA taxes are paid by both the employer and employee. Federal unemployment taxes and (in most states) the state unemployment taxes are borne entirely by the employer.

STATE UNEMPLOYMENT TAXES

All states have unemployment compensation programs under state unemployment tax acts (SUTA). Like federal unemployment taxes, **state unemployment taxes** provide benefits to employees who lose their jobs. These taxes are levied on employers.[2] The basic rate is usually 5.4% on the first $7,000 of wages paid to an employee during the year. The basic rate is adjusted according to the employer's experience rating: Companies with a history of unstable employment may pay more than the basic rate. Companies with a history of stable employment may pay less than 5.4%. Regardless of the rate paid, the credit on the federal unemployment tax is still 5.4%.

The account State Unemployment Taxes Payable is used for this liability. The state unemployment tax for Academy Company for the January 14 payroll is $929.34 ($17,210.00 × 5.4%).

RECORDING EMPLOYER PAYROLL TAXES

Employer payroll taxes are usually recorded at the same time the payroll is journalized. The entire amount of gross pay ($17,210.00) shown in the payroll register in Illustration D-9 is subject to each of the three taxes mentioned above. Accordingly, the entry to record the payroll tax expense associated with the January 14 payroll is:

[2]In a few states, the employee is also required to make a contribution. In this textbook, including the homework, we will assume that the tax is only on the employer.

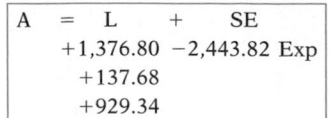

A	=	L	+	SE
		+1,376.80	−2,443.82	Exp
		+137.68		
		+929.34		

Cash Flows
no effect

Jan. 14	Payroll Tax Expense	2,443.82	
	FICA Taxes Payable		1,376.80
	Federal Unemployment Taxes Payable		137.68
	State Unemployment Taxes Payable		929.34
	(To record employer's payroll taxes on		
	January 14 payroll)		

Separate liability accounts are used instead of a single credit to Payroll Taxes Payable. Why? Because these liabilities are payable to different taxing authorities at different dates. The liability accounts are classified in the balance sheet as current liabilities since they will be paid within the next year. Payroll Tax Expense is classified on the income statement as an operating expense. Illustration D-11 summarizes the types of employer payroll taxes.

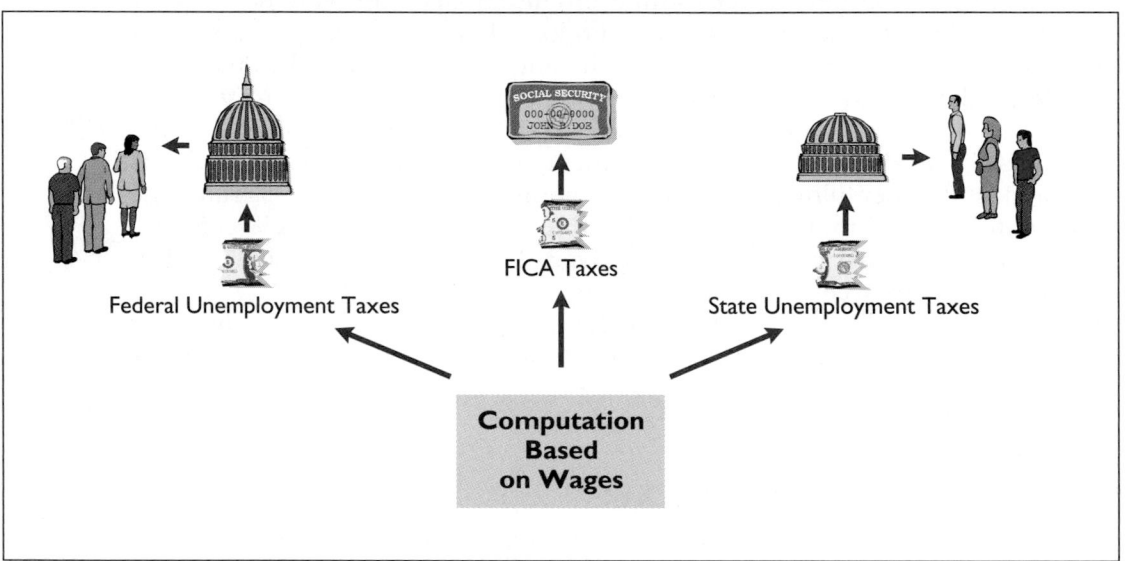

Illustration D-11
Employer payroll taxes

Filing and Remitting Payroll Taxes

Preparation of payroll tax returns is the responsibility of the payroll department. Payment of the taxes is made by the treasurer's department. Much of the information for the returns is obtained from employee earnings records.

For purposes of reporting and remitting to the IRS, FICA taxes and federal income taxes that were withheld are combined. **The taxes must be reported quarterly**, no later than one month following the close of each quarter. The remitting requirements depend on the amount of taxes withheld and the length of the pay period. Remittances are made through deposits in either a Federal Reserve bank or an authorized commercial bank.

Federal unemployment taxes are generally filed and remitted **annually** on or before January 31 of the subsequent year. Earlier payments are required when the tax exceeds a specified amount. State unemployment taxes usually must be filed and paid by the **end of the month following each quarter**. When payroll taxes are paid, payroll liability accounts are debited, and Cash is credited.

The employer is also required to provide each employee with a **Wage and Tax Statement (Form W-2)** by January 31 following the end of a calendar year. This statement shows gross earnings, FICA taxes withheld, and income taxes withheld for the year. The required W-2 form for Michael Jordan, using assumed annual data, is shown in Illustration D-12.

The employer must send a copy of each employee's Wage and Tax Statement (Form W-2) to the Social Security Administration. This agency subsequently furnishes the Internal Revenue Service with the income data required.

Form **W-2 Wage and Tax Statement**		Calendar Year **2007**

1 Control number

OMB No. 1545-0008

2 Employer's name, address and ZIP code

Academy Company
19 Center St.
Hampton, MI 48291

3 Employer's identification number

36-2167852

4 Employer's State number

5 Stat. employee ☐ Deceased ☐ Legal rep. ☐ 942 emp. ☐ Subtotal ☐ Void ☐

6 Allocated tips

7 Advance EIC payment

8 Employee's social security number

329-36-9547

9 Federal income tax withheld

$2,248.00

10 Wages, tips, other compensation

$26,300.00

11 Social security tax withheld

$2,104.00

12 Employee's name, address, and ZIP code

Michael Jordan
2345 Mifflin Ave.
Hampton, MI 48292

13 Social security wages

$26,300.00

14 Social security tips

16

17 State income tax

$526.00

18 State wages, tips, etc.

19 Name of State

Michigan

20 Local income tax

21 Local wages, tips, etc.

22 Name of locality

Summary of Study Objectives

1 *Discuss the objectives of internal control for payroll.* The objectives of internal control for payroll are (1) to safeguard company assets against unauthorized payments of payrolls, and (2) to ensure the accuracy of the accounting records pertaining to payrolls.

2 *Compute and record the payroll for a pay period.* The computation of the payroll involves gross earnings, payroll deductions, and net pay. In recording the payroll, Salaries (or Wages) Expense is debited for gross earnings, individual tax and other liability accounts are credited for payroll deductions, and Salaries (Wages) Payable is credited for net pay. When the payroll is paid, Salaries and Wages Payable is debited, and Cash is credited.

3 *Describe and record employer payroll taxes.* Employer payroll taxes consist of FICA, federal unemployment taxes, and state unemployment taxes. The taxes are usually accrued at the time the payroll is recorded by debiting Payroll Tax Expense and crediting separate liability accounts for each type of tax.

Glossary

Bonus Compensation to management personnel and other employees, based on factors such as increased sales or the amount of net income. (p. D-5)

Employee earnings record A cumulative record of each employee's gross earnings, deductions, and net pay during the year. (p. D-8)

Employee's Withholding Allowance Certificate (Form W-4) An Internal Revenue Service form on which the employee indicates the number of allowances claimed for withholding federal income taxes. (p. D-6)

Federal unemployment taxes Taxes imposed on the employer that provide benefits for a limited time period to employees who lose their jobs through no fault of their own. (p. D-11)

FICA taxes Taxes designed to provide workers with supplemental retirement, employment disability, and medical benefits. (p. D-5)

Gross earnings Total compensation earned by an employee. (p. D-4)

Net pay Gross earnings less payroll deductions. (p. D-7)

Payroll deductions Deductions from gross earnings to determine the amount of a paycheck. (p. D-5)

Payroll register A payroll record that accumulates the gross earnings, deductions, and net pay by employee for each pay period. (p. D-8)

Salaries Specified amount per month or per year paid to managers and administrative personnel. (p. D-1)

Statement of earnings   A document attached to a paycheck that indicates the employee's gross earnings, payroll deductions, and net pay. (p. D-10)

State unemployment taxes   Taxes imposed on the employer that provide benefits to employees who lose their jobs. (p. D-11)

Wage and Tax Statement (Form W-2)   A form showing gross earnings, FICA taxes withheld, and income taxes withheld which is prepared annually by an employer for each employee. (p. D-12)

Wages   Amounts paid to employees based on a rate per hour or on a piece-work basis. (p. D-1)

Questions

1. You are a newly hired accountant with Schindlebeck Company. On your first day, the controller asks you to identify the main internal control objectives related to payroll accounting. How would you respond?

2. What are the four functions associated with payroll activities?

3. What is the difference between gross pay and net pay? Which amount should a company record as wages or salaries expense?

4. Which payroll tax is levied on both employers and employees?

5. Are the federal and state income taxes withheld from employee paychecks a payroll tax expense for the employer? Explain your answer.

6. What do the following acronyms stand for: FICA, FUTA, and SUTA?

7. What information is shown on a W-4 statement? On a W-2 statement?

8. Distinguish between the two types of payroll deductions and give examples of each.

9. What are the primary uses of the employees earnings record?

10. (a) Identify the three types of employer payroll taxes.
    (b) How are tax liability accounts and Payroll Tax Expense classified in the financial statements?

Brief Exercises

Identify payroll functions.
(SO 1)

BED-1   Gutierrez Company has the following payroll procedures.
  (a) Supervisor approves overtime work.
  (b) The human resources department prepares hiring authorization forms for new hires.
  (c) A second payroll department employee verifies payroll calculations.
  (d) The treasurer's department pays employees.

Identify the payroll function to which each procedure pertains.

Compute gross earnings and net pay.
(SO 2)

BED-2   Becky Sherrick's regular hourly wage rate is $14, and she receives an hourly rate of $21 for work in excess of 40 hours. During a January pay period, Becky works 45 hours. Becky's federal income tax withholding is $95, and she has no voluntary deductions. Compute Becky Sherrick's gross earnings and net pay for the pay period.

Record a payroll and the payment of wages.
(SO 2)

BED-3   Data for Becky Sherrick are presented in BED-2. Prepare the journal entries to record (a) Becky's pay for the period and (b) the payment of Becky's wages. Use January 15 for the end of the pay period and the payment date.

Record employer payroll taxes.
(SO 3)

BED-4   In January, gross earnings in Bri Company totaled $70,000. All earnings are subject to 8% FICA taxes, 5.4% state unemployment taxes, and 0.8% federal unemployment taxes. Prepare the entry to record January payroll tax expense.

Exercises

Compute net pay and record pay for one employee.
(SO 2)

ED-1   Linda O'Neill's regular hourly wage rate is $16.00, and she receives a wage of 1½ times the regular hourly rate for work in excess of 40 hours. During a March weekly pay period Linda worked 42 hours. Her gross earnings prior to the current week were $8,000. Linda is married and claims three withholding allowances. Her only voluntary deduction is for group hospitalization insurance at $15.00 per week.

Instructions

(a) Compute the following amounts for Linda's wages for the current week.

(1) Gross earnings.
(2) FICA taxes. (Assume an 8% rate on maximum of $90,000.)
(3) Federal income taxes withheld. (Use the withholding table in the text, page D-7.)
(4) State income taxes withheld. (Assume a 2.0% rate.)
(5) Net pay.

(b) Record Linda's pay, assuming she is an office computer operator.

ED-2 Employee earnings records for Borelias Company reveal the following gross earnings for four employees through the pay period of December 15.

Compute maximum FICA deductions.
(SO 2)

C. Mull	$83,500	D. Chambers	$86,100
L. Church	$85,600	T. Olejnik	$87,000

For the pay period ending December 31, each employee's gross earnings is $3,000. The FICA tax rate is 8% on gross earnings of $90,000.

Instructions

Compute the FICA withholdings that should be made for each employee for the December 31 pay period. (Show computations.)

ED-3 Martinez Company has the following data for the weekly payroll ending January 31.

Prepare payroll register and record payroll and payroll tax expense.
(SO 2, 3)

	Hours						Hourly Rate	Federal Income Tax Withholding	Health Insurance
Employee	M	T	W	T	F	S			
M. Miller	8	8	9	8	10	3	$10	$34	$10
E. Neupert	8	8	8	8	8	2	12	37	15
K. Mann	9	10	8	8	9	0	13	58	15

Employees are paid 1½ times the regular hourly rate for all hours worked in excess of 40 hours per week. FICA taxes are 8% on the first $90,000 of gross earnings. Martinez Company is subject to 5.4% state unemployment taxes and 0.8% federal unemployment taxes on the first $7,000 of gross earnings.

Instructions

(a) Prepare the payroll register for the weekly payroll.
(b) Prepare the journal entries to record the payroll and Martinez's payroll tax expense.

ED-4 Selected data from a February payroll register for Andrew Manion Company are presented below. Some amounts are intentionally omitted.

Compute missing payroll amounts and record payroll.
(SO 2)

Gross earnings:			
Regular	$8,900	State income taxes	$ (3)
Overtime	(1)	Union dues	100
Total	(2)	Total deductions	(4)
Deductions:		Net pay	$7,660
FICA taxes	$ 800	Accounts debited:	
Federal income taxes	1,140	Warehouse wages	(5)
		Store wages	$4,000

FICA taxes are 8%. State income taxes are 3% of gross earnings.

Instructions

(a) Fill in the missing amounts.
(b) Journalize the February payroll and the payment of the payroll.

ED-5 According to a payroll register summary of Parolini Company, the amount of employees' gross pay in December was $800,000, of which $70,000 was not subject to FICA tax and $760,000 was not subject to state and federal unemployment taxes.

Determine employer's payroll taxes and record payroll tax expense.
(SO 3)

Instructions
(a) Determine the employer's payroll tax expense for the month, using the following rates: FICA 8%, state unemployment 5.4%, federal unemployment 0.8%.
(b) Prepare the journal entry to record December payroll tax expense.

Problems

Identify internal control weaknesses and make recommendations for improvement.
(SO 1)

PD-1 Selected payroll procedures of Palmcopiolet Company are described below.
1. Department managers interview applicants and on the basis of the interview either hire or reject the applicants. When an applicant is hired, the applicant fills out a W-4 form (Employer's Withholding Exemption Certificate). One copy of the form is sent to the human resources department, and one copy is sent to the payroll department as notice that the individual has been hired. On the copy of the W-4 sent to payroll, the managers manually indicate the hourly pay rate for the new hire.
2. The payroll checks are manually signed by the chief accountant and given to the department managers for distribution to employees in their department. The managers are responsible for seeing that any absent employees receive their checks.
3. There are two clerks in the payroll department. The payroll is divided alphabetically; one clerk has employees A to L and the other has employees M to Z. Each clerk computes the gross earnings, deductions, and net pay for employees in the section and posts the data to the employee earning records.

Instructions
(a) Indicate the weaknesses in internal control.
(b) For each weakness, describe the control procedures that will provide effective internal control. Use the following format for your answer:

(a) Weaknesses   **(b) Recommended Procedures**

Prepare payroll register and payroll entries.
(SO 2, 3)

PD-2 Happy Hardware has four employees who are paid on an hourly basis plus time-and-a half for all hours worked in excess of 40 a week. Payroll data for the week ended March 15, 2007, are presented below.

Employee	Hours Worked	Hourly Rate	Federal Income Tax Withholdings	United Fund
Joe McKane	40	$14.00	$?	$5.00
Mary Miller	42	13.00	?	5.00
Andy Manion	44	13.00	60	8.00
Kim Cheng	46	13.00	51	5.00

McKane and Miller are married. They claim 0 and 4 withholding allowances, respectively. The following tax rates are applicable: FICA 8%, state income taxes 3%, state unemployment taxes 5.4%, and federal unemployment 0.8%. The first three employees are sales clerks (store wages expense). The fourth employee performs administrative duties (office wages expense).

Instructions

(a) Net pay $1,862.06

(a) Prepare a payroll register for the weekly payroll. (Use the wage-bracket withholding table in the text for federal income tax withholdings.)
(b) Journalize the payroll on March 15, 2007, and the accrual of employer payroll taxes.
(c) Journalize the payment of the payroll on March 16, 2007.

(d) Cash paid $ 586.64

(d) Journalize the deposit in a Federal Reserve bank on March 31, 2007, of the FICA and federal income taxes payable to the government.

Journalize payroll transactions and adjusting entries.
(SO 2, 3)

PD-3 The payroll liability accounts shown on page D-17 are included in the ledger of Nam Viet Company on January 1, 2007.

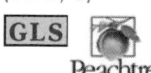

FICA Taxes Payable	$ 760.00
Federal Income Taxes Payable	1,004.60
State Income Taxes Payable	108.95
Federal Unemployment Taxes Payable	288.95
State Unemployment Taxes Payable	1,954.40
Union Dues Payable	870.00
U.S. Savings Bonds Payable	360.00

In January, the following transactions occurred.

Jan. 10 Sent check for $870.00 to union treasurer for union dues.
12 Deposited check for $1,764.60 in Federal Reserve bank for FICA taxes and federal income taxes withheld.
15 Purchased U.S. Savings Bonds for employees by writing check for $360.00.
17 Paid state income taxes withheld from employees.
20 Paid federal and state unemployment taxes.
31 Completed monthly payroll register, which shows office salaries $14,600, store wages $28,400, FICA taxes withheld $3,440, federal income taxes payable $1,684, state income taxes payable $360, union dues payable $400, United Fund contributions payable $1,888, and net pay $35,228.
31 Prepared payroll checks for the net pay and distributed checks to employees.

At January 31, the company also makes the following accrued adjustments pertaining to employee compensation.
1. Employer payroll taxes: FICA taxes 8%, federal unemployment taxes 0.8%, and state unemployment taxes 5.4%.
2. Vacation pay: 6% of gross earnings.

Instructions
(a) Journalize the January transactions.
(b) Journalize the adjustments pertaining to employee compensation at January 31.

(b) Payroll tax expense $6,106.00; vacation benefits expense $2,580

PD-4 For the year ended December 31, 2007, Malaysia Electrical Repair Company reports the following summary payroll data.

Prepare entries for payroll and payroll taxes, and prepare W-2 data. (SO 2, 3)

Gross earnings:	
Administrative salaries	$180,000
Electricians' wages	470,000
Total	$650,000

Deductions:	
FICA taxes	$ 45,200
Federal income taxes withheld	188,000
State income taxes withheld (2.6%)	16,900
United Fund contributions payable	32,500
Hospital insurance premiums	20,300
Total	$302,900

Malaysia Company's payroll taxes are: FICA 8%, state unemployment 2.5% (due to a stable employment record), and 0.8% federal unemployment. Gross earnings subject to FICA taxes total $565,000, and gross earnings subject to unemployment taxes total $145,000.

Instructions
(a) Prepare a summary journal entry at December 31 for the full year's payroll.
(b) Journalize the adjusting entry at December 31 to record the employer's payroll taxes.
(c) The W-2 Wage and Tax Statement requires the following dollar data.

(a) Wages payable $347,100
(b) Payroll tax expense $ 49,985

Wages, Tips, Other Compensation	Federal Income Tax Withheld	State Income Tax Withheld	FICA Wages	FICA Tax Withheld

Complete the required data for the following employees.

Employee	Gross Earnings	Federal Income Tax Withheld
Anna Makarov	$59,000	$28,500
Sharon Livingston	28,000	10,800

Subsidiary Ledgers and Special Journals

STUDY OBJECTIVES

After studying this appendix,
you should be able to:

1 Describe the nature and purpose of a subsidiary ledger.

2 Explain how special journals are used in journalizing.

3 Indicate how a multi-column journal is posted.

SECTION ONE
EXPANDING THE LEDGER—SUBSIDIARY LEDGERS

Nature and Purpose of Subsidiary Ledgers

Imagine a business that has several thousand charge (credit) customers and shows the transactions with these customers in only one general ledger account—Accounts Receivable. It would be virtually impossible to determine the balance owed by an individual customer at any specific time. Similarly, the amount payable to one creditor would be difficult to locate quickly from a single Accounts Payable account in the general ledger.

Instead, companies use subsidiary ledgers to keep track of individual balances. A **subsidiary ledger** is a group of accounts with a common characteristic (for example, all accounts receivable). The subsidiary ledger frees the general ledger from the details of individual balances. A subsidiary ledger is an addition to, and an expansion of, the general ledger.

Two common subsidiary ledgers are:

1. The **accounts receivable** (or **customers'**) **subsidiary ledger**, which collects transaction data of individual customers.

2. The **accounts payable** (or **creditors'**) **subsidiary ledger**, which collects transaction data of individual creditors.

> **STUDY OBJECTIVE**
> **1**
> Describe the nature and purpose of a subsidiary ledger.

In each of these subsidiary ledgers, individual accounts are usually arranged in alphabetical order.

The detailed data from a subsidiary ledger are summarized in a general ledger account. For example, the detailed data from the accounts receivable subsidiary ledger are summarized in Accounts Receivable in the general ledger. The general ledger account that summarizes subsidiary ledger data is called a **control account**. An overview of the relationship of subsidiary ledgers to the general ledger is shown in Illustration E-1. The general ledger control accounts and subsidiary ledger accounts are shown in green color. Note that cash and stockholders' equity in this illustration are not control accounts because there are no subsidiary ledger accounts related to these accounts.

Illustration E-1
Relationship of general ledger and subsidiary ledgers

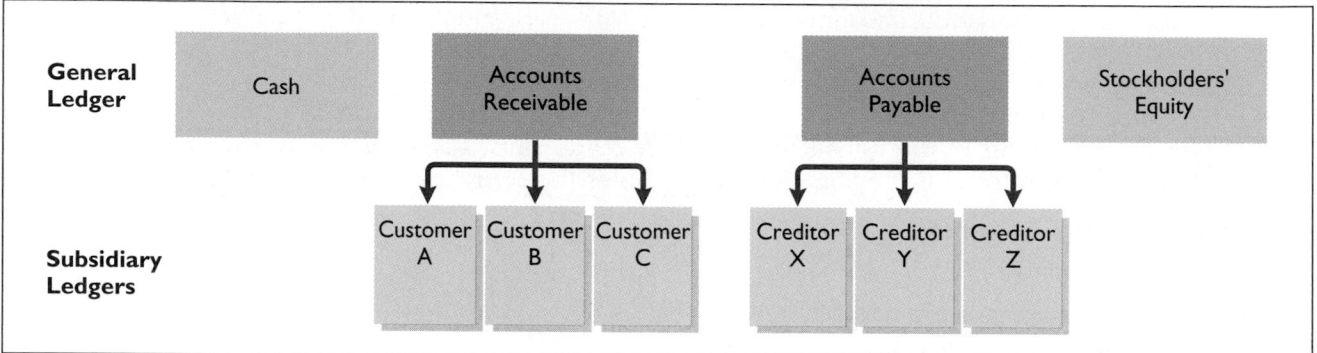

Each general ledger control account balance must equal the composite balance of the individual accounts in the related subsidiary ledger at the end of an accounting period. For example, the balance in Accounts Payable in Illustration E-1 must equal the total of the subsidiary balances of Creditors X + Y + Z.

EXAMPLE

An example of a control account and subsidiary ledger for Larson Enterprises is provided in Illustration E-2. (The explanation column in these accounts is not shown in this and subsequent illustrations due to space considerations.)

Illustration E-2
Relationship between general and subsidiary ledgers

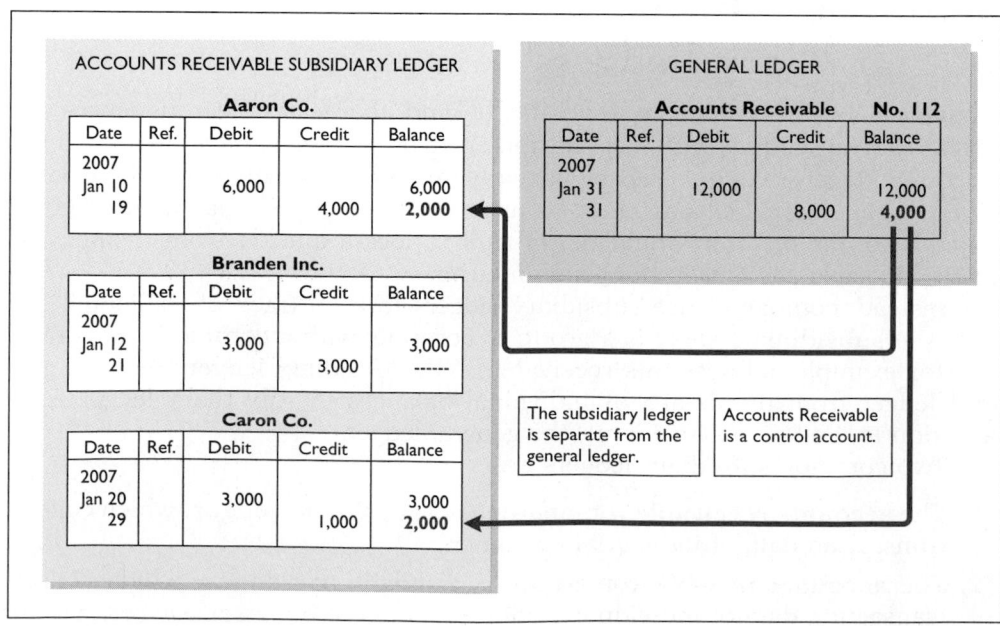

The example is based on the transactions listed below.

Illustration E-3 Sales and collection transactions

Credit Sales			Collections on Account		
Jan. 10	Aaron Co.	$ 6,000	Jan. 19	Aaron Co.	$4,000
12	Branden Inc.	3,000	21	Branden Inc.	3,000
20	Caron Co.	3,000	29	Caron Co.	1,000
		$12,000			$8,000

The total debits ($12,000) and credits ($8,000) in Accounts Receivable in the general ledger are reconcilable to the detailed debits and credits in the subsidiary accounts. Also, the balance of $4,000 in the control account agrees with the total of the balances in the individual accounts (Aaron Co. $2,000 + Branden Inc. $0 + Caron Co. $2,000) in the subsidiary ledger.

As shown, postings are made monthly to the control accounts in the general ledger. This practice allows monthly financial statements to be prepared. Postings to the individual accounts in the subsidiary ledger are made daily. Daily posting ensures that account information is current. This enables the company to monitor credit limits, bill customers, and answer inquiries from customers about their account balances.

Advantages of Subsidiary Ledgers

Subsidiary ledgers have several advantages. They:

1. **Show transactions affecting one customer or one creditor in a single account**, thus providing up-to-date information on specific account balances.
2. **Free the general ledger of excessive details.** As a result, a trial balance of the general ledger does not contain vast numbers of individual account balances.
3. **Help locate errors in individual accounts** by reducing the number of accounts in one ledger and by using control accounts.
4. **Make possible a division of labor** in posting. One employee can post to the general ledger while someone else posts to the subsidiary ledgers.

SECTION TWO
EXPANDING THE JOURNAL—SPECIAL JOURNALS

So far you have learned to journalize transactions in a two-column general journal and post each entry to the general ledger. This procedure is satisfactory in only the very smallest companies. To expedite journalizing and posting, most companies use special journals **in addition to the general journal**.

A **special journal** is used to record similar types of transactions. Examples would be all sales of merchandise on account, or all cash receipts. The special journals a company uses depends largely on the types of transactions that occur frequently. Most merchandising enterprises use the journals shown in Illustration E-4 (on the next page) to record transactions daily.

If a transaction cannot be recorded in a special journal, it is recorded in the general journal. For example, if you had special journals only for the four types of transactions shown in Illustration E-4, purchase returns and

STUDY OBJECTIVE
2
Explain how special journals are used in journalizing.

Sales Journal	Cash Receipts Journal	Purchases Journal	Cash Payments Journal	General Journal
Used for: All sales of merchandise on account	Used for: All cash received (including cash sales)	Used for: All purchases of merchandise on account	Used for: All cash paid (including cash purchases)	Used for: Transactions that cannot be entered in a special journal, including correcting, adjusting, and closing entries

Illustration E-4 Use of special journals and the general journal

allowances would be recorded in the general journal. So would sales returns and allowances. Similarly, **correcting**, **adjusting**, **and closing entries are recorded in the general journal**. Other types of special journals may sometimes be used in some situations. For example, when sales returns and allowances are frequent, special journals may be used to record these transactions.

Special journals **permit greater division of labor** because several people can record entries in different journals at the same time. For example, one employee may journalize all cash receipts, and another may journalize all credit sales. Also, the use of special journals **reduces the time needed to complete the posting process**. With special journals, some accounts may be posted monthly, instead of daily, as will be illustrated later in the chapter.

Sales Journal

The **sales journal** is used to record sales of merchandise on account. Cash sales of merchandise are entered in the cash receipts journal. Credit sales of assets other than merchandise are entered in the general journal.

JOURNALIZING CREDIT SALES

Helpful Hint Postings are also made daily to individual ledger accounts in the inventory subsidiary ledger to maintain a perpetual inventory.

Illustration E-5 Journalizing credit sales—perpetual inventory system

Karns Wholesale Supply uses a **perpetual inventory** system. Under this system, each entry in the sales journal results in one entry **at selling price**—a debit to Accounts Receivable (a control account) and a credit of equal amount to Sales—and another entry at cost. The entry **at cost** is a debit to Cost of Goods Sold and a credit of equal amount to Merchandise Inventory (a control account). The sales journal for Karns Wholesale Supply is shown in Illustration E-5. (It uses as-

KARNS WHOLESALE SUPPLY
Sales Journal   S1

Date	Account Debited	Invoice No.	Ref.	Accts. Receivable Dr. Sales Cr.	Cost of Goods Sold Dr. Merchandise Inventory Cr.
2007					
May 3	Abbot Sisters	101		10,600	6,360
7	Babson Co.	102		11,350	7,370
14	Carson Bros.	103		7,800	5,070
19	Deli Co.	104		9,300	6,510
21	Abbot Sisters	105		15,400	10,780
24	Deli Co.	106		21,210	15,900
27	Babson Co.	107		14,570	10,200
				90,230	62,190

summed credit sales transactions for sales invoices 101–107.) A sales journal with two amount columns, like that in Illustration E-5, shows a transaction at both selling price and cost on a single line. The reference (Ref.) column is not used in journalizing. It is used in posting the sales journal, as explained in the next section. Also, note that, unlike the general journal, an explanation is not required for each entry in a special journal. Finally, note that each invoice is prenumbered to ensure that all invoices are journalized.

POSTING THE SALES JOURNAL

Postings from the sales journal are made **daily to the individual accounts receivable** in the subsidiary ledger. Posting **to the general ledger** is made **monthly**. Illustration E-6 shows both the daily and monthly postings.

Illustration E-6 Posting the sales journal

¹The normal balance for Merchandise Inventory is a debit. But, because of the sequence in which we have posted the special journals, with the sales journals first, the credits to Merchandise Inventory are posted before the debits. This posting sequence explains the credit balance, in Merchandise Inventory, which exists only until the other journals are posted.

A check mark (✓) is inserted in the reference posting column to indicate that the daily posting to the customer's account has been made. A check mark (✓) is used in this illustration because the subsidiary ledger accounts are not numbered. At the end of the month, the column totals of the sales journal are posted to the general ledger. Here, the column totals are a debit of $90,230 to Accounts Receivable (account No. 112), a credit of $90,230 to Sales (account No. 401), a debit of $62,190 to Cost of Goods Sold (account No. 505), and a credit of $62,190 to Merchandise Inventory (account No. 120). Insertion of the account numbers below the column total indicates that the postings have been made. In both the general ledger and subsidiary ledger accounts, the reference **S1** indicates that the posting came from page 1 of the sales journal.

PROVING THE LEDGERS

The next step is to "prove" the ledgers. To do so, we must determine two things: (1) The total of the general ledger debit balances must equal the total of the general ledger credit balances. (2) The sum of the subsidiary ledger balances must equal the balance in the control account. The proof of the postings from the sales journal to the general and subsidiary ledger is shown in Illustration E-7.

Illustration E-7 Proving the equality of the postings from the sales journal

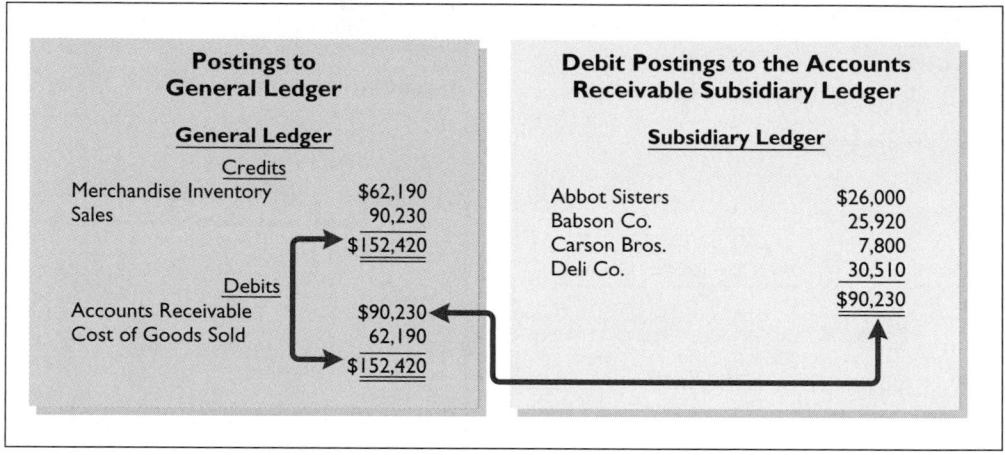

ADVANTAGES OF THE SALES JOURNAL

The use of a special journal to record sales on account has a number of advantages. First, the one-line entry for each sales transaction **saves time**. In the sales journal, it is not necessary to write out the four account titles for each transaction. Second, only totals, rather than individual entries, are posted to the general ledger. This **saves posting time and reduces the possibilities of errors in posting**. Finally, **a division of labor results**, because one individual can take responsibility for the sales journal.

Cash Receipts Journal

All receipts of cash are recorded in the **cash receipts journal**. The most common types of cash receipts are cash sales of merchandise and collections of accounts receivable. Many other possibilities exist, such as receipt of money from bank loans and cash proceeds from disposal of equipment. A one- or two-column cash receipts journal would not have space enough for all possible cash receipt transactions. Therefore, a multiple-column cash receipts journal is used.

Generally, a cash receipts journal includes the following columns: debit columns for cash and sales discounts; and credit columns for accounts receivable, sales, and "other" accounts. The Other Accounts category is used when the cash receipt does not involve a cash sale or a collection of accounts receivable. Under a perpetual inventory system, each sales entry is accompanied by another entry that debits Cost of Goods Sold and credits Merchandise Inventory for the cost of the merchandise sold. This entry may be recorded separately. A six-column cash receipts journal is shown in Illustration E-8 (on page E-8).

Additional credit columns may be used if they significantly reduce postings to a specific account. For example, a loan company, such as Household International, receives thousands of cash collections from customers. A significant saving in posting would result from using separate credit columns for Loans Receivable and Interest Revenue, rather than using the Other Accounts credit column. In contrast, a retailer that has only one interest collection a month would not find it useful to have a separate column for Interest Revenue.

JOURNALIZING CASH RECEIPTS TRANSACTIONS

To illustrate the journalizing of cash receipts transactions, we will continue with the May transactions of Karns Wholesale Supply. Collections from customers relate to the entries recorded in the sales journal in Illustration E-5. The entries in the cash receipts journal are based on the following cash receipts.

May 1 Stockholders invest $5,000 in the business in common stock.
7 Cash sales of merchandise total $1,900 (cost, $1,240).
10 A check for $10,388 is received from Abbot Sisters in payment of invoice No. 101 for $10,600 less a 2% discount.
12 Cash sales of merchandise total $2,600 (cost, $1,690).
17 A check for $11,123 is received from Babson Co. in payment of invoice No. 102 for $11,350 less a 2% discount.
22 Cash is received by signing a note for $6,000.
23 A check for $7,644 is received from Carson Bros. in full for invoice No. 103 for $7,800 less a 2% discount.
28 A check for $9,114 is received from Deli Co. in full for invoice No. 104 for $9,300 less a 2% discount.

Further information about the columns in the cash receipts journal (see Illustration E-8) is listed below.

Debit Columns:

1. **Cash.** The amount of cash actually received in each transaction is entered in this column. The column total indicates the total cash receipts for the month.

2. **Sales Discounts.** Karns includes a Sales Discounts column in its cash receipts journal. By doing so, it is not necessary to enter sales discount items in the general journal. As a result, the collection of an account receivable within the discount period is expressed on one line in the appropriate columns of the cash receipts journal.

Credit Columns:

3. **Accounts Receivable.** The Accounts Receivable column is used to record cash collections on account. The amount entered here is the amount to be credited to the individual customer's account.

4. **Sales.** The Sales column records all cash sales of merchandise. Cash sales of other assets (plant assets, for example) are not reported in this column.

5. **Other Accounts.** The Other Accounts column is used whenever the credit is other than to Accounts Receivable or Sales. For example, in the first

Helpful Hint When is an account title entered in the "Account Credited" column of the cash receipts journal? Answer: A *subsidiary ledger* title is entered whenever the entry involves a collection of accounts receivable. A *general ledger* account title is entered whenever the entry involves an account that is not the subject of a special column (and an amount must be entered in the Other Accounts column). No account title is entered there if neither of the foregoing applies.

Illustration E-8
Journalizing and posting
the cash receipts journal

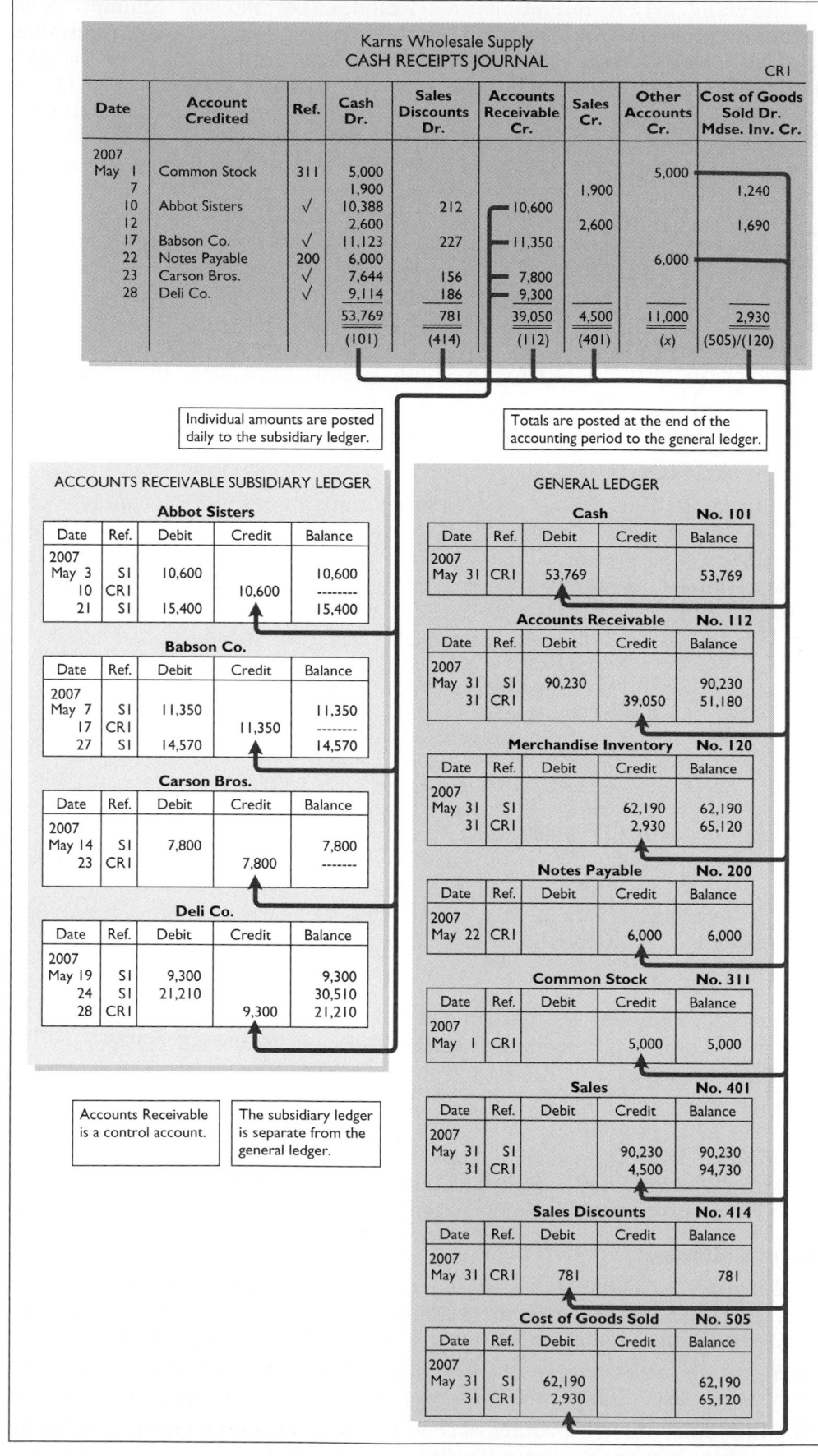

entry, $5,000 is entered as a credit to Common Stock. This column is often referred to as the **sundry accounts column**.

Debit and Credit Column:

6. **Cost of Goods Sold and Merchandise Inventory.** This column records debits to Cost of Goods Sold and credits to Merchandise Inventory.

In a multi-column journal, generally only one line is needed for each entry. Debit and credit amounts for each line must be equal. When the collection from Abbot Sisters on May 10 is journalized, for example, three amounts are indicated. Note also that the Account Credited column is used to identify both general ledger and subsidiary ledger account titles. General ledger accounts are illustrated in the May 1 and May 22 entries. A subsidiary account is illustrated in the May 10 entry for the collection from Abbot Sisters.

When the journalizing of a multi-column journal has been completed, the amount columns are totaled, and the totals are compared to prove the equality of debits and credits. The proof of the equality of Karns's cash receipts journal is shown in Illustration E-9. Totaling the columns of a journal and proving the equality of the totals is called **footing** and **cross-footing** a journal.

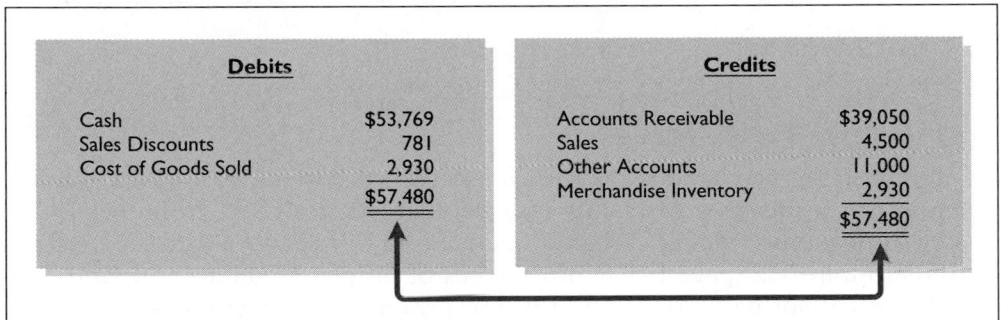

Illustration E-9 Proving the equality of the cash receipts journal

POSTING THE CASH RECEIPTS JOURNAL

Posting a multi-column journal involves the following steps.

1. All column totals except for the Other Accounts total are posted **once at the end of the month** to the account title(s) specified in the column heading (such as Cash or Accounts Receivable). Account numbers are entered below the column totals to show that they have been posted. Cash is posted to account No. 101, accounts receivable to account No. 112, merchandise inventory to account No. 120, sales to account No. 401, sales discounts to account No. 414, and cost of goods sold to account No. 505.

2. The **individual amounts comprising the Other Accounts total are posted separately** to the general ledger accounts specified in the Account Credited column. See, for example, the credit posting to Common Stock. The total amount of this column is not posted. The symbol (X) is inserted below the total to this column to indicate that the amount has not been posted.

3. The individual amounts in a column, posted in total to a control account (Accounts Receivable, in this case), are posted **daily to the subsidiary ledger** account specified in the Account Credited column. See, for example, the credit posting of $10,600 to Abbot Sisters.

STUDY OBJECTIVE
3
Indicate how a multi-column journal is posted.

The symbol **CR** is used in both the subsidiary and general ledgers to identify postings from the cash receipts journal.

PROVING THE LEDGERS

After posting of the cash receipts journal is completed, it is necessary to prove the ledgers. As shown in Illustration E-10, the general ledger totals are in agreement. Also, the sum of the subsidiary ledger balances equals the control account balance.

Illustration E-10 Proving the ledgers after posting the sales and the cash receipts journals

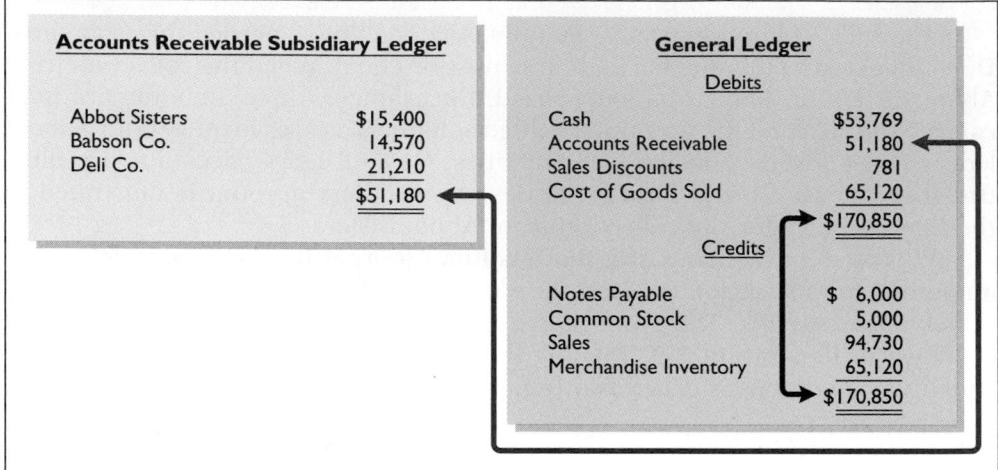

Purchases Journal

All purchases of merchandise on account are recorded in the **purchases journal**. Each entry in this journal results in a debit to Merchandise Inventory and a credit to Accounts Payable. When a one-column purchases journal is used (as in Illustration E-12, page E-11), other types of purchases on account and cash purchases cannot be journalized in it. For example, credit purchases of equipment or supplies must be recorded in the general journal. Likewise, all cash purchases are entered in the cash payments journal. As illustrated later, where credit purchases for items other than merchandise are numerous, the purchases journal is often expanded to a multi-column format.

JOURNALIZING CREDIT PURCHASES OF MERCHANDISE

Entries in the purchases journal are made from purchase invoices. The journalizing procedure is similar to that for a sales journal. In contrast to the sales journal, the purchases journal may not have an invoice number column, because invoices received from different suppliers will not be in numerical sequence. To assure that all purchase invoices are recorded, some companies consecutively number each invoice upon receipt and then use an internal document number column in the purchases journal.

Karns Wholesale Supply made the assumed credit purchases shown in Illustration E-11. The purchases journal for Karns Wholesale Supply is shown in Illustration E-12.

Illustration E-11 Credit purchases transactions

Date	Supplier	Amount
5/6	Jasper Manufacturing Inc.	$11,000
5/10	Eaton and Howe Inc.	7,200
5/14	Fabor and Son	6,900
5/19	Jasper Manufacturing Inc.	17,500
5/26	Fabor and Son	8,700
5/29	Eaton and Howe Inc.	12,600

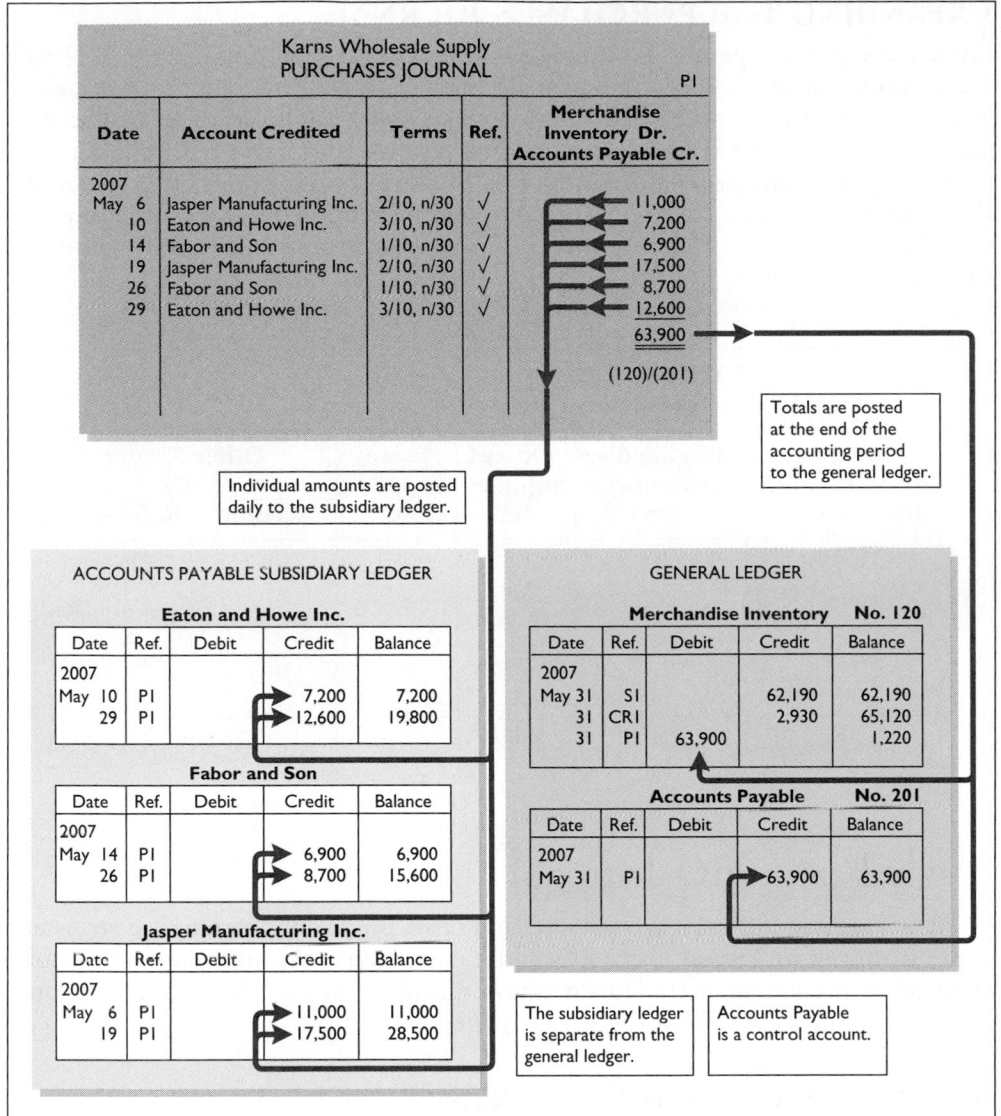

Illustration E-12
Journalizing and posting
the purchases journal

Helpful Hint A single-column
purchases journal needs only to
be footed to prove the equality
of debits and credits.

POSTING THE PURCHASES JOURNAL

The procedures for posting the purchases journal are similar to those for the sales journal. In this case, postings are made **daily** to the **accounts payable ledger** and **monthly** to Merchandise Inventory and Accounts Payable in the general ledger. In both ledgers, P1 is used in the reference column to show that the postings are from page 1 of the purchases journal. Proof of the equality of the postings from the purchases journal to both ledgers is shown as follows.

Helpful Hint Postings to subsidiary ledger accounts are done daily because it is often necessary to know a current balance for the subsidiary accounts.

Illustration E-13 Proving
the equality of the
purchases journal

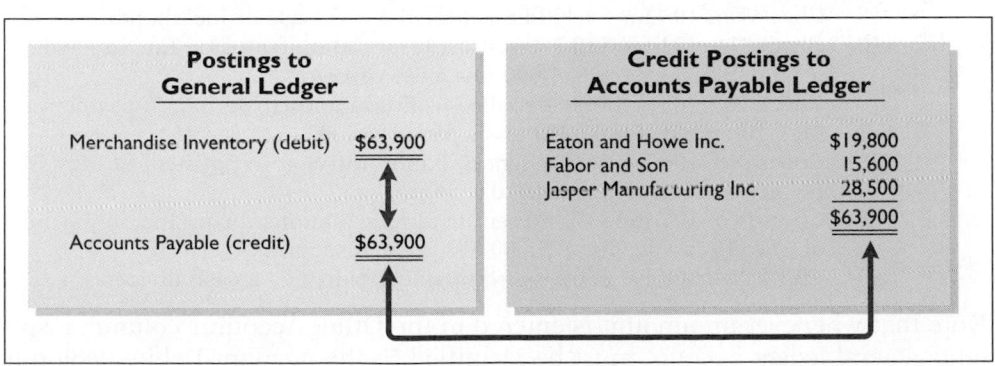

EXPANDING THE PURCHASES JOURNAL

Some companies expand the purchases journal to include all types of purchases on account. Instead of one column for merchandise inventory and accounts payable, they use a multiple-column format. The multi-column format usually includes a credit column for accounts payable and debit columns for purchases of merchandise, of office supplies, of store supplies, and other accounts. Illustration E-14 is an example of a multi-column purchases journal for Hanover Co. The posting procedures are similar to those illustrated earlier for posting the cash receipts journal.

Illustration E-14 Multi-column purchases journal

							Other Accounts Dr.		
Date	Account Credited	Ref.	Accounts Payable Cr.	Merchandise Inventory Dr.	Office Supplies Dr.	Store Supplies Dr.	Account	Ref.	Amount
2007									
June 1	Signe Audio	✓	2,000		2,000				
3	Wright Co.	✓	1,500	1,500					
5	Orange Tree Co.	✓	2,600				Equipment	157	2,600
30	Sue's Business Forms	✓	800			800			
			56,600	43,000	7,500	1,200			4,900

HANOVER CO.
Purchases Journal   P1

Cash Payments Journal

All disbursements of cash are entered in a **cash payments journal**. Entries are made from prenumbered checks. Because cash payments are made for various purposes, the cash payments journal has multiple columns. A four-column journal is shown in Illustration E-15 (next page).

JOURNALIZING CASH PAYMENTS TRANSACTIONS

The procedures for journalizing transactions in this journal are similar to those described earlier for the cash receipts journal. Each transaction is entered on one line, and for each line there must be equal debit and credit amounts. The entries in the cash payments journal in Illustration E-15 are based on the following transactions for Karns Wholesale Supply.

May 1   Check No. 101 for $1,200 issued for the annual premium on a fire insurance policy.

     3   Check No. 102 for $100 issued in payment of freight when terms were FOB shipping point.

     8   Check No. 103 for $4,400 issued for the purchase of merchandise.

   10   Check No. 104 for $10,780 sent to Jasper Manufacturing Inc. in payment of May 6 invoice for $11,000 less a 2% discount.

   19   Check No. 105 for $6,984 mailed to Eaton and Howe Inc. in payment of May 10 invoice for $7,200 less a 3% discount.

   23   Check No. 106 for $6,831 sent to Fabor and Son in payment of May 14 invoice for $6,900 less a 1% discount.

   28   Check No. 107 for $17,150 sent to Jasper Manufacturing Inc. in payment of May 19 invoice for $17,500 less a 2% discount.

   30   Check No. 108 for $500 issued to stockholders as a cash dividend.

Note that whenever an amount is entered in the Other Accounts column, a specific general ledger account must be identified in the Account Debited column.

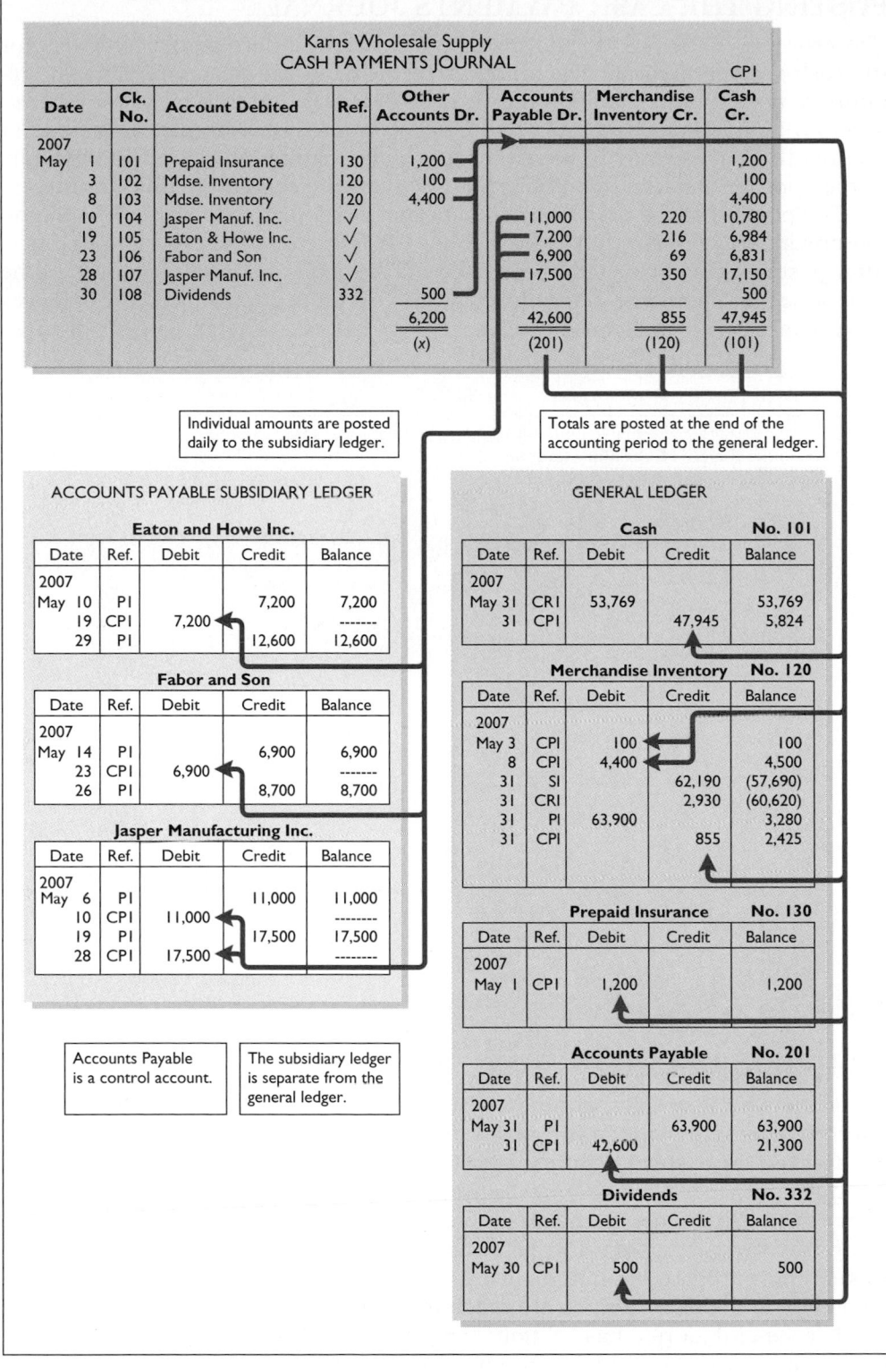

Illustration E-15
Journalizing and posting
the cash payments journal

The entries for checks No. 101, 102, and 103 illustrate this situation. Similarly, a subsidiary account must be identified in the Account Debited column whenever an amount is entered in the Accounts Payable column. See, for example, the entry for check No. 104.

After the cash payments have been journalized, the columns are totaled. The totals are then balanced to prove the equality of debits and credits.

POSTING THE CASH PAYMENTS JOURNAL

The procedures for posting the cash payments journal are similar to those for the cash receipts journal. The amounts recorded in the Accounts Payable column are posted individually to the subsidiary ledger and in total to the control account. Merchandise Inventory and Cash are posted only in total at the end of the month. Transactions in the Other Accounts column are posted individually to the appropriate account(s) affected. No totals are posted for this column.

The posting of the cash payments journal is shown in Illustration E-15 (on the previous page). Note that the symbol **CP** is used as the posting reference. After postings are completed, the equality of the debit and credit balances in the general ledger should be determined. In addition, the control account balances should agree with the subsidiary ledger total balance. The agreement of these balances is shown in Illustration E-16.

Illustration E-16 Proving the ledgers after postings from the sales, cash receipts, purchases, and cash payments journals

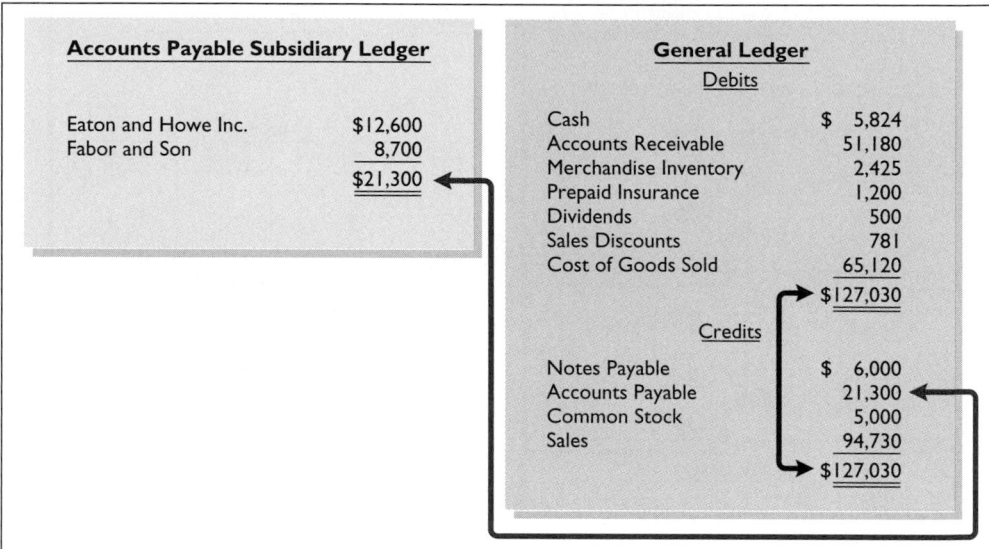

Accounts Payable Subsidiary Ledger	
Eaton and Howe Inc.	$12,600
Fabor and Son	8,700
	$21,300

General Ledger	
Debits	
Cash	$ 5,824
Accounts Receivable	51,180
Merchandise Inventory	2,425
Prepaid Insurance	1,200
Dividends	500
Sales Discounts	781
Cost of Goods Sold	65,120
	$127,030
Credits	
Notes Payable	$ 6,000
Accounts Payable	21,300
Common Stock	5,000
Sales	94,730
	$127,030

Effects of Special Journals on General Journal

Special journals for sales, purchases, and cash substantially reduce the number of entries that are made in the general journal. **Only transactions that cannot be entered in a special journal are recorded in the general journal.** For example, the general journal may be used to record such transactions as granting of credit to a customer for a sales return or allowance, granting of credit from a supplier for purchases returned, acceptance of a note receivable from a customer, and purchase of equipment by issuing a note payable. Also, correcting, adjusting, and closing entries are made in the general journal.

The general journal has columns for date, account title and explanation, reference, and debit and credit amounts. When control and subsidiary accounts are not involved, the procedures for journalizing and posting of transactions are the same as those described in earlier chapters. When control and subsidiary accounts are involved, two changes from the earlier procedures are required:

1. In **journalizing**, both the control and the subsidiary accounts must be identified.

2. In **posting**, there must be a **dual posting**: once to the control account and once to the subsidiary account.

To illustrate, assume that on May 31, Karns Wholesale Supply returns $500 of merchandise for credit to Fabor and Son. The entry in the general journal and the posting of the entry are shown in Illustration E-17. Note that if cash is received instead of credit granted on this return, then the transaction is recorded in the cash receipts journal.

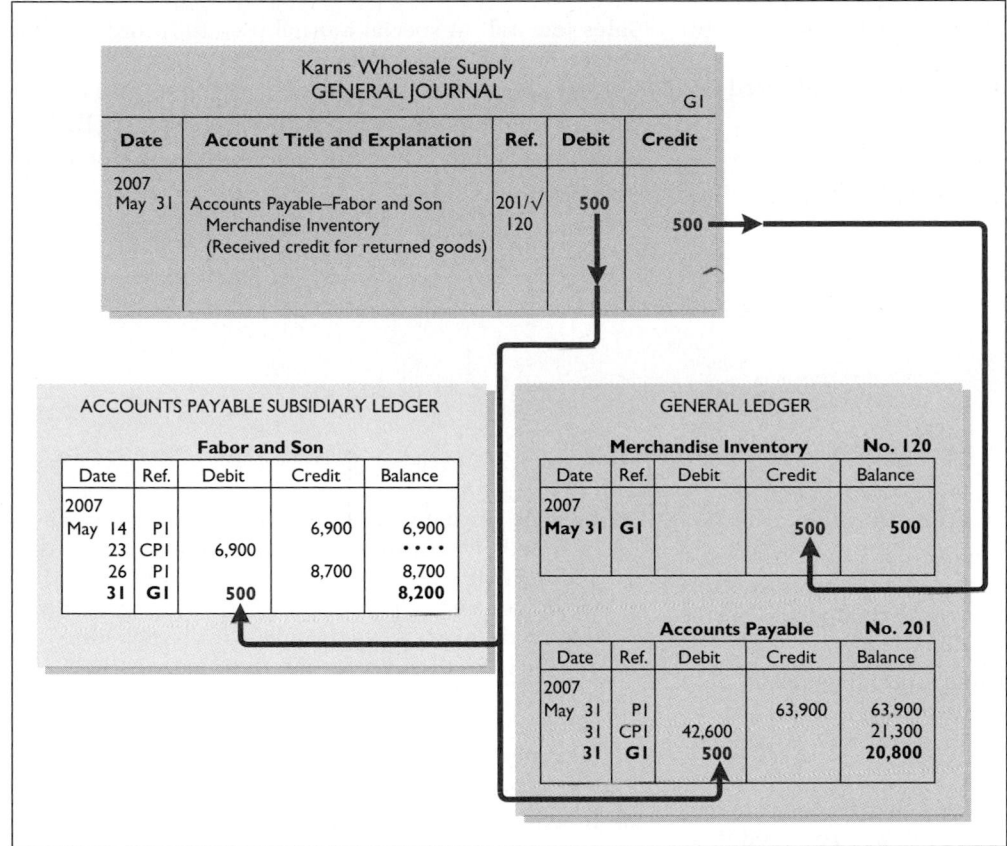

Illustration E-17
Journalizing and posting the general journal

Observe in the journal that two accounts are indicated for the debit, and two postings ("201/✓") are indicated in the reference column. One amount is posted to the control account and the other to the creditor's account in the subsidiary ledger.

Summary of Study Objectives

1 *Describe the nature and purpose of a subsidiary ledger.* A subsidiary ledger is a group of accounts with a common characteristic. It facilitates the recording process by freeing the general ledger from details of individual balances.

2 *Explain how special journals are used in journalizing.* A special journal is used to group similar types of transactions. In a special journal, generally only one line is used to record a complete transaction.

3 *Indicate how a multi-column journal is posted.* In posting a multi-column journal:
(a) All column totals except for the Other Accounts column are posted once at the end of the month

to the account title specified in the column heading.
(b) The total of the Other Accounts column is not posted. Instead, the individual amounts comprising the total are posted separately to the general ledger accounts specified in the Account Credited column.
(c) The individual amounts in a column posted in total to a control account are posted daily to the subsidiary ledger accounts specified in the Account Credited column.

Glossary

Accounts payable (creditors') subsidiary ledger A subsidiary ledger that collects transaction data of individual creditors. (p. E-1).

Accounts receivable (customers') subsidiary ledger A subsidiary ledger that collects transaction data of individual customers. (p. E-1).

Cash payments journal A special journal used to record all cash paid. (p. E-12).

Cash receipts journal A special journal used to record all cash received. (p. E-6).

Control account An account in the general ledger that summarizes a subsidiary ledger. (p. E-2).

Purchases journal A special journal used to record all purchases of merchandise on account. (p. E-10).

Sales journal A special journal used to record all sales of merchandise on account. (p. E-4).

Special journal A journal that is used to record similar types of transactions, such as all credit sales. (p. E-3).

Subsidiary ledger A group of accounts with a common characteristic. (p. E-1).

Questions

1. What are the advantages of using subsidiary ledgers?

2. (a) When are postings normally made to (1) the subsidiary accounts and (2) the general ledger control accounts? (b) Describe the relationship between a control account and a subsidiary ledger.

3. Identify and explain the four special journals discussed in the chapter. List an advantage of using each of these journals rather than using only a general journal.

4. A. Mega Company uses special journals. A sale made on account to K. Hansen for $435 was recorded in a sales journal. A few days later, K. Hansen returns $70 worth of merchandise for credit. Where should A. Mega Company record the sales return? Why?

5. A $500 purchase of merchandise on account from Julia Company was properly recorded in the purchases journal. When posted, however, the amount recorded in the subsidiary ledger was $50. How might this error be discovered?

6. Why would special journals used in different businesses not be identical in format? Can you think of a business that would maintain a cash receipts journal but not include a column for accounts receivable?

7. The cash and the accounts receivable columns in the cash receipts journal were mistakenly overadded by $4,000 at the end of the month. (a) Will the customers' ledger agree with the Accounts Receivable control account? (b) Assuming no other errors, will the trial balance totals be equal?

8. One column total of a special journal is posted at month-end to only two general ledger accounts. One of these two accounts is Accounts Receivable. What is the name of this special journal? What is the other general ledger account to which that same month-end total is posted?

9. In what journal would the following transactions be recorded? (Assume that a two-column sales journal and a single-column purchases journal are used.)
   (a) Recording of depreciation expense for the year.
   (b) Credit given to a customer for merchandise purchased on credit and returned.
   (c) Sales of merchandise for cash.
   (d) Sales of merchandise on account.
   (e) Collection of cash on account from a customer.
   (f) Purchase of office supplies on account.

10. In what journal would the following transactions be recorded? (Assume that a two-column sales journal and a single-column purchases journal are used.)
    (a) Cash received from signing a note payable.
    (b) Investment of cash by stockholders of the company.
    (c) Closing of the expense accounts at the end of the year.
    (d) Purchase of merchandise on account.
    (e) Credit received for merchandise purchased and returned to supplier.
    (f) Payment of cash on account due a supplier.

11. What transactions might be included in a multiple-column purchases journal that would not be included in a single-column purchases journal?

12. Give an example of a transaction in the general journal that causes an entry to be posted twice (i.e., to two accounts), one in the general ledger, the other in the subsidiary ledger. Does this affect the debit/credit equality of the general ledger?

13. Give some examples of appropriate general journal transactions for an organization using special journals.

Brief Exercises

BEE-1 Presented below is information related to Bradley Company for its first month of operations. Identify the balances that appear in the accounts receivable subsidiary ledger and the accounts receivable balance that appears in the general ledger at the end of January.

Identify subsidiary ledger balances.
(SO 1)

Credit Sales			Cash Collections		
Jan. 7	Avon Co.	$8,000	Jan. 17	Avon Co.	$7,000
15	Barto Co.	6,000	24	Barto Co.	5,000
23	Cecil Co.	9,000	29	Cecil Co.	9,000

BEE-2 Identify in what ledger (general or subsidiary) each of the following accounts is shown.

Identify subsidiary ledger accounts.
(SO 1)

  1. Rent Expense
  2. Accounts Receivable—Olsen
  3. Notes Payable
  4. Accounts Payable—Kerns

BEE-3 Identify the journal in which each of the following transactions is recorded.

Identify special journals.
(SO 2)

  1. Cash sales
  2. Payment of cash dividends
  3. Cash purchase of land
  4. Credit sales
  5. Purchase of merchandise on account
  6. Receipt of cash for services performed

BEE-4 Indicate whether each of the following debits and credits is included in the cash receipts journal. (Use "Yes" or "No" to answer this question.)

Identify entries to cash receipts journal.
(SO 2)

  1. Debit to Sales
  2. Credit to Merchandise Inventory
  3. Credit to Accounts Receivable
  4. Debit to Accounts Payable

BEE-5 Steering Computer Components Inc. uses a multi-column cash receipts journal. Indicate which column(s) is/are posted only in total, only daily, or both in total and daily.

Indicate postings to cash receipts journal.
(SO 3)

  1. Accounts Receivable
  2. Sales Discounts
  3. Cash
  4. Other Accounts

BEE-6 Cohen Co. uses special journals and a general journal. Identify the journal in which each of the following transactions is recorded.

Identify transactions for special journals.
(SO 2)

  (a) Purchased equipment on account.
  (b) Purchased merchandise on account.
  (c) Paid utility expense in cash.
  (d) Sold merchandise on account.

BEE-7 Identify the special journal(s) in which the following column headings appear.

Identify transactions for special journals.
(SO 2)

  1. Sales Discounts Dr.
  2. Accounts Receivable Cr.
  3. Cash Dr.
  4. Sales Cr.
  5. Merchandise Inventory Dr.

Exercises

EE-1 Yan Company uses both special journals and a general journal as described in this appendix. On June 30, after all monthly postings had been completed, the Accounts Receivable control account in the general ledger had a debit balance of $350,000; the Accounts Payable control account had a credit balance of $87,000.

Determine control account balances, and explain posting of special journals.
(SO 1, 2)

The July transactions recorded in the special journals are summarized below. No entries affecting accounts receivable and accounts payable were recorded in the general journal for July.

Sales journal	Total sales $161,400
Purchases journal	Total purchases $54,360
Cash receipts journal	Accounts receivable column total $141,000
Cash payments journal	Accounts payable column total $47,500

Instructions
  (a) What is the balance of the Accounts Receivable control account after the monthly postings on July 31?

(b) What is the balance of the Accounts Payable control account after the monthly postings on July 31?

(c) To what account(s) is the column total of $161,400 in the sales journal posted?

(d) To what account(s) is the accounts receivable column total of $141,000 in the cash receipts journal posted?

Explain postings to subsidiary ledger.
(SO 1)

EE-2 Presented below is the subsidiary accounts receivable account of Warren Moyer.

Date	Ref.	Debit	Credit	Balance
2007				
Sept. 2	S31	61,000		61,000
9	G4		14,000	47,000
27	CR8		47,000	—

Instructions

Write a memo that explains each transaction.

Post various journals to control and subsidiary accounts.
(SO 1, 2)

EE-3 On September 1 the balance of the Accounts Receivable control account in the general ledger of Odesto Company was $11,960. The customers' subsidiary ledger contained account balances as follows: Edmonds $2,440, Park $2,640, Roemer $2,060, Schulz $4,820. At the end of September the various journals contained the following information.

Sales journal: Sales to Schulz $800; to Edmonds $1,350; to Henry $1,030; to Roemer $1,100.

Cash receipts journal: Cash received from Roemer $1,310; from Schulz $2,300; from Henry $410; from Park $1,800; from Edmonds $1,240.

General journal: An allowance is granted to Schulz $220.

Instructions

(a) Set up control and subsidiary accounts and enter the beginning balances. Do not construct the journals.

(b) Post the various journals. Post the items as individual items or as totals, whichever would be the appropriate procedure. (No sales discounts given.)

(c) Prepare a list of customers and prove the agreement of the controlling account with the subsidiary ledger at September 30, 2007.

Record transactions in sales and purchases journals.
(SO 1, 2)

EE-4 Hurley Company uses special journals and a general journal. The following transactions occurred during September 2007.

Sept. 2 Sold merchandise on account to S. Rusch, invoice no. 101, $480, terms n/30. The cost of the merchandise sold was $300.

10 Purchased merchandise on account from L. Dayne $600, terms 2/10, n/30.

12 Purchased office equipment on account from B. Piazza $6,500.

21 Sold merchandise on account to L. Perez, invoice no. 102 for $800, terms 2/10, n/30. The cost of the merchandise sold was $480.

25 Purchased merchandise on account from F. Sage $900, terms n/30.

27 Sold merchandise to M. Deitrich for $700 cash. The cost of the merchandise sold was $420.

Instructions

(a) Draw a sales journal (see Illustration E-6) and a single-column purchase journal (see Illustration E-12). (Use page 1 for each journal.)

(b) Record the transaction(s) for September that should be journalized in the sales journal and the purchases journal.

Record transactions in cash receipts and cash payments journals.
(SO 1, 2)

EE-5 Pena Co. uses special journals and a general journal. The following transactions occurred during May 2007.

May 1 R. Pena invested $60,000 cash in the business in exchange for common stock.

2 Sold merchandise to J. Simon for $6,000 cash. The cost of the merchandise sold was $4,200.

3 Purchased merchandise for $9,000 from L. M. Farr using check no. 101.

14 Paid salary to S. Little $700 by issuing check no. 102.
16 Sold merchandise on account to B. Jones for $900, terms n/30. The cost of the merchandise sold was $630.
22 A check of $9,000 is received from R. Dusto in full for invoice 101; no discount given.

Instructions

(a) Draw a multiple-column cash receipts journal (see Illustration E-8) and a multiple-column cash payments journal (see Illustration E-15). (Use page 1 for each journal.)
(b) Record the transaction(s) for May that should be journalized in the cash receipts journal and cash payments journal.

EE-6 Abbott Company uses the columnar cash journals illustrated in the textbook. In April, the following selected cash transactions occurred.

Explain journalizing in cash journals.
(SO 2)

1. Made a refund to a customer for the return of damaged goods.
2. Received collection from customer within the 3% discount period.
3. Purchased merchandise for cash.
4. Paid a creditor within the 3% discount period.
5. Received collection from customer after the 3% discount period had expired.
6. Paid freight on merchandise purchased.
7. Paid cash for office equipment.
8. Received cash refund from supplier for merchandise returned.
9. Paid cash dividend to stockholders.
10. Made cash sales.

Instructions

Indicate **(a)** the journal, and **(b)** the columns in the journal that should be used in recording each transaction.

EE-7 Santiago Company has the following selected transactions during March.

Journalize transactions in general journal and post.
(SO 1, 2)

Mar. 2 Purchased equipment costing $6,000 from Briggs Company on account.
5 Received credit memorandum for $300 from Sanchez Company for merchandise damaged in shipment to Santiago.
7 Issued a credit memorandum for $400 to Sparks Company for merchandise the customer returned. The returned merchandise had a cost of $260.

Santiago Company uses a one-column purchases journal, a sales journal, the columnar cash journals used in the text, and a general journal.

Instructions

(a) Journalize the transactions in the general journal.
(b) ▭▬▭▷ In a brief memo to the president of Santiago Company, explain the postings to the control and subsidiary accounts.

EE-8 Below are some typical transactions incurred by Heide Company.

Indicate journalizing in special journals.
(SO 2)

1. Payment of creditors on account.
2. Return of merchandise sold for credit.
3. Collection on account from customers.
4. Sale of land for cash.
5. Sale of merchandise on account.
6. Sale of merchandise for cash.
7. Received credit for merchandise purchased on credit.
8. Sales discount taken on goods sold.
9. Payment of employee wages.
10. Paid a cash dividend to stockholders.
11. Depreciation on building.
12. Purchase of office supplies for cash.
13. Purchase of merchandise on account.

Instructions

For each transaction, indicate whether it would normally be recorded in a cash receipts journal, cash payments journal, sales journal, single-column purchases journal, or general journal.

Explain posting to control account and subsidiary ledger.
(SO 1, 3)

EE-9 The general ledger of Williams Company contained the following Accounts Payable control account (in T-account form). Also shown is the related subsidiary ledger.

GENERAL LEDGER

Accounts Payable

Feb. 15	General journal	1,400	Feb. 1	Balance		26,025
28	?	?	5	General journal		265
			11	General journal		550
			28	Purchases		13,900
			Feb. 28	Balance		9,840

ACCOUNTS PAYABLE LEDGER

Sealy

Feb. 28 Bal. 4,600

Wolcott

Feb. 28 Bal. ?

Gates

Feb. 28 Bal. 2,000

Instructions

(a) Indicate the missing posting reference and amount in the control account, and the missing ending balance in the subsidiary ledger.

(b) Indicate the amounts in the control account that were dual-posted (i.e., posted to the control account and the subsidiary accounts).

Prepare purchases and general journals.
(SO 1, 2)

EE-10 Selected accounts from the ledgers of Juan Perez Company at July 31 showed the following.

GENERAL LEDGER

Store Equipment No. 153

Date	Explanation	Ref.	Debit	Credit	Balance
July 1		G1	3,600		3,600

Accounts Payable No. 201

Date	Explanation	Ref.	Debit	Credit	Balance
July 1		G1		3,600	3,600
15		G1		400	4,000
18		G1	100		3,900
25		G1	200		3,700
31		P1		8,400	12,100

Merchandise Inventory No. 120

Date	Explanation	Ref.	Debit	Credit	Balance
July 15		G1	400		400
18		G1		100	300
25		G1		200	100
31		P1	8,400		8,500

ACCOUNTS PAYABLE LEDGER

Alou Equipment Co.

Date	Explanation	Ref.	Debit	Credit	Balance
July 1		G1		3,600	3,600

Benton Co.

Date	Explanation	Ref.	Debit	Credit	Balance
July 3		P1		2,000	2,000
20		P1		700	2,700

Comerica Materials

Date	Explanation	Ref.	Debit	Credit	Balance
July 17		P1		1,400	1,400
18		G1	100		1,300
29		P1		2,100	3,400

Dunlap Co.

Date	Explanation	Ref.	Debit	Credit	Balance
July 14		P1		1,100	1,100
25		G1	200		900

Emerick Co.

Date	Explanation	Ref.	Debit	Credit	Balance
July 12		P1		500	500
21		P1		600	1,100

Galant Transit

Date	Explanation	Ref.	Debit	Credit	Balance
July 15		G1		400	400

Instructions

From the data, prepare:

(a) the single-column purchases journal for July.

(b) the general journal entries for July.

EE-11 Valdez Products uses both special journals and a general journal as described in this appendix. Valdez also posts customers' accounts in the accounts receivable subsidiary ledger. The postings for the most recent month are included in the subsidiary T accounts below.

Determine correct posting amount to control account.
(SO 3)

	Ellie				Rambo	
Bal.	340	250	Bal.	150		150
	200			290		

	Panos				Tenant	
Bal.	–0–	145	Bal.	120		120
	145			190		
				170		

Instructions

Determine the correct amount of the end-of-month posting from the sales journal to the Accounts Receivable control account.

Problems

PE-1 Lemon Company's chart of accounts includes the following selected accounts.

101 Cash	401 Sales
112 Accounts Receivable	414 Sales Discounts
120 Merchandise Inventory	505 Cost of Goods Sold
311 Common Stock	

Journalize transactions in cash receipts journal; post to control account and subsidiary ledger.
(SO 1, 2, 3)

Peachtree

On April 1 the accounts receivable ledger of Lemon Company showed the following balances: Horner $1,550, Harris $1,200, Northeast Co. $2,900, and Smith $1,700. The April transactions involving the receipt of cash were as follows.

Apr. 1 Stockholders invested additional cash in the business, $6,000, for common stock.

4 Received check for payment of account from Smith less 2% cash discount.

5 Received check for $620 in payment of invoice no. 307 from Northeast Co.

8 Made cash sales of merchandise totaling $7,245. The cost of the merchandise sold was $4,347.

10 Received check for $800 in payment of invoice no. 309 from Horner.

11 Received cash refund from a supplier for damaged merchandise $550.

23 Received check for $1,500 in payment of invoice no. 310 from Northeast Co.

29 Received check for payment of account from Harris.

Instructions

(a) Journalize the transactions above in a six-column cash receipts journal with columns for Cash Dr., Sales Discounts Dr., Accounts Receivable Cr., Sales Cr., Other Accounts Cr., and Cost of Goods Sold Dr./Merchandise Inventory Cr. Foot and crossfoot the journal.

(b) Insert the beginning balances in the Accounts Receivable control and subsidiary accounts, and post the April transactions to these accounts.

(c) Prove the agreement of the control account and subsidiary account balances.

(a) Balancing totals $19,615

(c) Accounts receivable $ 1,530

Journalize transactions in cash payments journal; post to control account and subsidiary ledgers.
(SO 1, 2, 3)

PE-2 Simpson Company's chart of accounts includes the following selected accounts.

101 Cash	201 Accounts Payable
120 Merchandise Inventory	332 Dividends
130 Prepaid Insurance	505 Cost of Goods Sold
157 Equipment	

On October 1 the accounts payable ledger of Simpson Company showed the following balances: Hester Company $1,700, Milo Co. $2,500, Ontario Co. $1,400, and Pagan Company $3,700. The October transactions involving the payment of cash were as follows.

Oct. 1 Purchased merchandise, check no. 63, $700.
   3 Purchased equipment, check no. 64, $800.
   5 Paid Hester Company balance due of $1,700, less 2% discount, check no. 65, $1,666.
   10 Purchased merchandise, check no. 66, $2,250.
   15 Paid Ontario Co. balance due of $1,400, check no. 67.
   16 A cash dividend is paid in the amount of $400, check no. 68.
   19 Paid Milo Co. in full for invoice no. 610, $1,400 less 2% cash discount, check no. 69, $1,372.
   29 Paid Pagan Company in full for invoice no. 264, $2,600, check no. 70.

Instructions

(a) Balancing totals $11,250

(a) Journalize the transactions above in a four-column cash payments journal with columns for Other Accounts Dr., Accounts Payable Dr., Merchandise Inventory Cr., and Cash Cr. Foot and crossfoot the journal.

(b) Insert the beginning balances in the Accounts Payable control and subsidiary accounts, and post the October transactions to these accounts.

(c) Accounts payable $2,200

(c) Prove the agreement of the control account and the subsidiary account balances.

Journalize transactions in multi-column purchases journal; post to the general and subsidiary ledgers.
(SO 1, 2, 3)

Peachtree

PE-3 The chart of accounts of Hernandez Company includes the following selected accounts.

112 Accounts Receivable	401 Sales
120 Merchandise Inventory	412 Sales Returns and Allowances
126 Supplies	505 Cost of Goods Sold
157 Equipment	610 Advertising Expense
201 Accounts Payable	

In July the following selected transactions were completed. All purchases and sales were on account. The cost of all merchandise sold was 70% of the sales price.

July 1 Purchased merchandise from Denton Company $7,000.
   2 Received freight bill from Johnson Shipping on Denton purchase $400.
   3 Made sales to Lyons Company $1,300, and to Franklin Bros. $1,900.
   5 Purchased merchandise from Grant Company $3,200.
   8 Received credit on merchandise returned to Grant Company $300.
   13 Purchased store supplies from Brent Supply $720.
   15 Purchased merchandise from Denton Company $3,600 and from Ruiz Company $2,900.
   16 Made sales to Martin Company $3,450 and to Franklin Bros. $1,570.
   18 Received bill for advertising from Marlin Advertisements $600.
   21 Made sales to Lyons Company $310 and to Randee Company $2,300.
   22 Granted allowance to Lyons Company for merchandise damaged in shipment $40.
   24 Purchased merchandise from Grant Company $3,000.
   26 Purchased equipment from Brent Supply $600.
   28 Received freight bill from Johnson Shipping on Grant purchase of July 24, $380.
   30 Made sales to Martin Company $4,900.

Instructions

(a) Purchases journal:
   Accounts Payable $22,400
   Sales journal $15,730

(a) Journalize the transactions above in a purchases journal, a sales journal, and a general journal. The purchases journal should have the following column headings:

Date, Account Credited (Debited), Ref., Other Accounts Dr., and Merchandise Inventory Dr., Accounts Payable Cr.

(b) Post to both the general and subsidiary ledger accounts. (Assume that all accounts have zero beginning balances.)

(c) Prove the agreement of the control and subsidiary accounts.

(c) Accounts Receivable $15,690

PE-4 Selected accounts from the chart of accounts of Clark Company are shown below.

Journalize transactions in special journals.
(SO 1, 2, 3)

`GLS`

101 Cash
112 Accounts Receivable
120 Merchandise Inventory
126 Supplies
157 Equipment
201 Accounts Payable

401 Sales
412 Sales Returns and Allowances
414 Sales Discounts
505 Cost of Goods Sold
726 Salaries Expense

The cost of all merchandise sold was 60% of the sales price. During January, Clark completed the following transactions.

Jan. 3   Purchased merchandise on account from Bell Co. $10,000.
4   Purchased supplies for cash $80.
4   Sold merchandise on account to Gilbert $7,250, invoice no. 371, terms 1/10, n/30.
5   Issued a debit memorandum to Bell Co. and returned $300 worth of damaged goods.
6   Made cash sales for the week totaling $3,150.
8   Purchased merchandise on account from Law Co. $4,500.
9   Sold merchandise on account to Mays Corp. $5,800, invoice no. 372, terms 1/10, n/30.
11   Purchased merchandise on account from Hoble Co. $3,700.
13   Paid in full Bell Co. on account less a 2% discount.
13   Made cash sales for the week totaling $5,340.
15   Received payment from Mays Corp. for invoice no. 372.
15   Paid semi-monthly salaries of $14,300 to employees.
17   Received payment from Gilbert for invoice no. 371.
17   Sold merchandise on account to Amber Co. $1,200, invoice no. 373, terms 1/10, n/30.
19   Purchased equipment on account from Johnson Corp. $5,500.
20   Made cash sales for the week totaling $3,200.
20   Paid in full Law Co. on account less a 2% discount.
23   Purchased merchandise on account from Bell Co. $7,800.
24   Purchased merchandise on account from Levine Corp. $4,690.
27   Made cash sales for the week totaling $3,730.
30   Received payment from Amber Co. for invoice no. 373.
31   Paid semi-monthly salaries of $13,200 to employees.
31   Sold merchandise on account to Gilbert $9,330, invoice no. 374, terms 1/10, n/30.

Clark Company uses the following journals.
1. Sales journal.
2. Single-column purchases journal.
3. Cash receipts journal with columns for Cash Dr., Sales Discounts Dr., Accounts Receivable Cr., Sales Cr., Other Accounts Cr., and Cost of Goods Sold Dr./Merchandise Inventory Cr.
4. Cash payments journal with columns for Other Accounts Dr., Accounts Payable Dr., Merchandise Inventory Cr., and Cash Cr.
5. General journal.

Instructions
Using the selected accounts provided:
(a) Record the January transactions in the appropriate journal noted.
(b) Foot and crossfoot all special journals.
(c) Show how postings would be made by placing ledger account numbers and checkmarks as needed in the journals. (Actual posting to ledger accounts is not required.)

(a) Sales journal $23,580

Journalize in sales and cash receipts journals; post; prepare a trial balance; prove control to subsidiary; prepare adjusting entries; prepare an adjusted trial balance.
(SO 1, 2, 3)

Peachtree

PE-5 Presented below are the purchases and cash payments journals for Collins Co. for its first month of operations.

PURCHASES JOURNAL — P1

Date	Account Credited	Ref.	Merchandise Inventory Dr. Accounts Payable Cr.
July 4	J. Dixon		6,800
5	W. Engel		7,500
11	R. Gamble		3,920
13	M. Hill		15,300
20	D. Jacob		8,800
			42,320

CASH PAYMENTS JOURNAL — CP1

Date	Account Debited	Ref.	Other Accounts Dr.	Accounts Payable Dr.	Merchandise Inventory Cr.	Cash Cr.
July 4	Store Supplies		600			600
10	W. Engel			7,500	75	7,425
11	Prepaid Rent		6,000			6,000
15	J. Dixon			6,800		6,800
19	Dividends		2,500			2,500
21	M. Hill			15,300	153	15,147
			9,100	29,600	228	38,472

In addition, the following transactions have not been journalized for July. The cost of all merchandise sold was 65% of the sales price.

July 1 The founder, R. Collins, invests $80,000 in cash in exchange for common stock.
6 Sell merchandise on account to Hardy Co. $5,400 terms 1/10, n/30.
7 Make cash sales totaling $4,000.
8 Sell merchandise on account to D. Wasburn $3,600, terms 1/10, n/30.
10 Sell merchandise on account to L. Lemansky $4,900, terms 1/10, n/30.
13 Receive payment in full from D. Wasburn.
16 Receive payment in full from L. Lemansky.
20 Receive payment in full from Hardy Co.
21 Sell merchandise on account to S. Kane $4,000, terms 1/10, n/30.
29 Returned damaged goods to J. Dixon and received cash refund of $450.

Instructions

(a) Open the following accounts in the general ledger.

101 Cash	332 Dividends
112 Accounts Receivable	401 Sales
120 Merchandise Inventory	414 Sales Discounts
127 Store Supplies	505 Cost of Goods Sold
131 Prepaid Rent	631 Supplies Expense
201 Accounts Payable	729 Rent Expense
311 Common Stock	

(b) Cash receipts
     journal balancing
       totals $98,350

(b) Journalize the transactions that have not been journalized in the sales journal, the cash receipts journal (see Illustration E-8), and the general journal.

(c) Post to the accounts receivable and accounts payable subsidiary ledgers. Follow the sequence of transactions as shown in the problem.

(d) Post the individual entries and totals to the general ledger.

(e) Prepare a trial balance at July 31, 2007.

(f) Determine whether the subsidiary ledgers agree with the control accounts in the general ledger.

(g) The following adjustments at the end of July are necessary.

(1) A count of supplies indicates that $140 is still on hand.

(2) Recognize rent expense for July, $500.

Prepare the necessary entries in the general journal. Post the entries to the general ledger.

(h) Prepare an adjusted trial balance at July 31, 2007.

PE-6 The post-closing trial balance for Alomar Co. is as follows.

Journalize in special journals; post; prepare a trial balance.
(SO 1, 2, 3)

ALOMAR CO.
Post-Closing Trial Balance
December 31, 2007

	Debit	Credit
Cash	$ 41,500	
Accounts Receivable	15,000	
Notes Receivable	45,000	
Merchandise Inventory	23,000	
Equipment	6,450	
Accumulated Depreciation—Equipment		$ 1,500
Accounts Payable		43,000
Common Stock		86,450
	$130,950	$130,950

The subsidiary ledgers contain the following information: (1) accounts receivable—R. Barton $2,500, B. Cole $7,500, S. Devine $5,000; (2) accounts payable—S. Field $10,000, R. Grilson $18,000, and D. Harms $15,000. The cost of all merchandise sold was 65% of the sales price.

The transactions for January 2008 are as follows.

Jan.   3   Sell merchandise to B. Senton $4,000, terms 2/10, n/30.

5   Purchase merchandise from S. Warren $2,500, terms 2/10, n/30.

7   Receive a check from S. Devine $3,500.

11   Pay freight on merchandise purchased $300.

12   Pay rent of $1,000 for January.

13   Receive payment in full from B. Senton.

14   Post all entries to the subsidiary ledgers. Issue a credit memo to acknowledge receipt of damaged merchandise of $700 returned by R. Barton.

15   Send D. Harms a check for $14,850 in full payment of account, discount $150.

17   Purchase merchandise from D. Lapeska $1,600, terms 2/10, n/30.

18   Pay sales salaries of $2,800 and office salaries $1,500.

20   Give R. Grilson a 60-day note for $18,000 in full payment of account payable.

23   Total cash sales amount to $8,600.

24   Post all entries to the subsidiary ledgers. Sell merchandise on account to B. Cole $7,700, terms 1/10, n/30.

27   Send S. Warren a check for $950.

29   Receive payment on a note of $40,000 from S. Lava.

30   Return merchandise of $500 to D. Lapeska for credit. Post all journals to the subsidiary ledger.

Instructions

(a) Open general and subsidiary ledger accounts for the following.

101 Cash	311 Common Stock
112 Accounts Receivable	401 Sales
115 Notes Receivable	412 Sales Returns and Allowances
120 Merchandise Inventory	414 Sales Discounts
157 Equipment	505 Cost of Goods Sold
158 Accumulated Depreciation—Equipment	726 Salaries Expense
200 Notes Payable	727 Office Salaries Expense
201 Accounts Payable	729 Rent Expense

(b) Record the January transactions in a sales journal, a single-column purchases journal, a cash receipts journal (see Illustration E-8), a cash payments journal (see Illustration E-15), and a general journal.

(c) Post the appropriate amounts to the general ledger.

(d) Prepare a trial balance at January 31, 2008.

(e) Determine whether the subsidiary ledgers agree with controlling accounts in the general ledger.

Accounting for Sole Proprietorships

After studying this appendix,
you should be able to:

1 Identify the differences in equity accounts between a corporation and a sole proprietorship.

2 Understand what accounts increase and decrease owner's equity.

3 Describe the differences between a retained earnings statement and an owner's equity statement.

4 Explain the process of closing the books for a sole proprietorship.

Chapter 1 identified three forms of business organization. Two forms, the sole proprietorship and the partnership, were discussed only briefly. Emphasis was placed on the corporate form in Chapter 1 as well as in subsequent chapters.

The purpose of this appendix is to discuss and illustrate the accounting for the operations and financial condition of a sole proprietorship. **The primary difference between accounting and reporting for a sole proprietorship and a corporation involves accounting for equity transactions.** Because a sole proprietorship has a single owner rather than numerous stockholders, a sole proprietorship uses a permanent **owner's capital account**, such as "Sally Jones, Capital," instead of Common Stock and Retained Earnings. In a sole proprietorship there is no need to separate owner's investments from net income retained for dividends because the sole proprietor does not declare or receive dividends. Instead, withdrawals by the owner of cash or other assets from the business for personal use are recorded in a temporary **drawing** account. The different equity accounts are contrasted as shown in Illustration F-1.

> **STUDY OBJECTIVE**
> ——— **1** ———
> Identify the differences in equity accounts between a corporation and a sole proprietorship.

Corporation	Sole Proprietorship
Stockholders' equity	Owner's equity
Common stock	Owner's Name, Capital
Retained earnings	

Illustration F-1
Equity section of the balance sheet—corporation vs. proprietorship

For purposes of comparing the accounting for a corporation with a sole proprietorship, the illustrations in this Appendix F assume a sole proprietorship owned by R. Neal and named Sierra Company. **Except for equity transactions we use the same accounts, amounts, and transactions as those of Sierra Corporation presented in Chapters 1 through 4.**

STUDY OBJECTIVE
2
Understand what accounts
increase and decrease
owner's equity.

Owner's Equity in a Sole Proprietorship

The ownership claim on total assets is known as **owner's equity**. It is equal to total assets minus total liabilities.

INCREASES IN OWNER'S EQUITY

In a proprietorship, owner's equity is increased by owner's investments and revenues.

Investments by Owner

Investments by owner are the assets the owner puts into the business. These investments increase owner's equity.

Revenues

Revenues are the gross increase in owner's equity resulting from business activities entered into for the purpose of earning income.

DECREASES IN OWNER'S EQUITY

In a proprietorship, owner's equity is decreased by owner's drawings and expenses.

Drawings

An owner may withdraw cash or other assets for personal use. These withdrawals could be recorded as a direct decrease of owner's equity. However, it is generally considered preferable to use a separate classification called **drawings** to determine the total withdrawals for each accounting period. **Drawings decrease owner's equity**.

Expenses

Expenses are the cost of assets consumed or services used in the process of earning revenue. They are **decreases in owner's equity that result from operating the business**.

In summary, owner's equity is increased by an owner's investments and by revenues from business operations. In contrast, owner's equity is decreased by an owner's withdrawals of assets and by expenses. These relationships are shown in Illustration F-2. **Net income** results when revenues exceed expenses. A **net loss** occurs when expenses exceed revenues.

Illustration F-2
Increases and decreases
in owner's equity

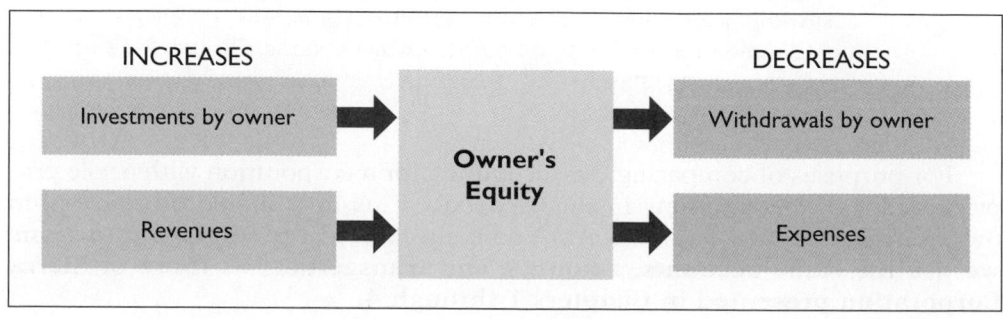

Recording Transactions of a Proprietorship

Chapter 3 described the basic steps employed in the accounting process as follows:

Analyze transactions.
Record transactions in the journal.
Post journal entries to the general ledger.
Prepare a trial balance.

These same steps apply to all forms of business. Illustration 3-2 (page 107) presented the impact of Sierra's transactions on its accounting equation. Illustration F-3 shows how the same transactions would have been recorded for a sole proprietor. The only differences are related to the accounts used to record equity transactions. Those differences are highlighted here in red.

Illustration F-3 Summary of transactions

	Assets				=	Liabilities			+	Owner's Equity	
	Cash	+ Supplies	+ Prepaid Insurance	+ Office Equipment	=	Notes Payable	+ Accounts Payable	+ Unearned Revenue	+	R. Neal, Capital	
(1)	+$10,000				=					+$10,000	**Investment by owner**
(2)	+5,000					+$5,000					
	15,000				=	5,000			+	10,000	
(3)	−5,000			+$5,000							
	10,000			5,000	=	5,000			+	10,000	
(4)	+1,200							+$1,200			
	11,200			5,000	=	5,000		1,200	+	10,000	
(5)	+10,000									+10,000	Service Revenue
	21,200			5,000	=	5,000		1,200	+	20,000	
(6)	−900									−900	Rent Expense
	20,300			5,000	=	5,000		1,200	+	19,100	
(7)	−600		+$600								
	19,700		600	5,000	=	5,000		1,200	+	19,100	
(8)		+$2,500					+$2,500				
	19,700 +	2,500 +	600	+ 5,000	=	5,000 +	2,500	+ 1,200	+	19,100	
(10)	−500		+							−500	**Drawings**
	19,200 +	2,500 +	600	+ 5,000	=	5,000 +	2,500	+ 1,200	+	18,600	
(11)	−4,000									−4,000	Salaries Expense
	$15,200 +	$2,500 +	$600	+ $5,000	=	$5,000 +	$2,500	+ $1,200	+	$14,600	

$23,300 $23,300

Financial Statements for a Proprietorship

Chapter 4 described accounting for adjusting entries. A sole proprietor makes the same types of adjustments as a corporation. After recording and posting all of the adjustments, an adjusted trial balance is prepared. Illustrations F-4 and F-5 on the following pages show how the adjusted trial balance is used to prepare a sole proprietor's financial statements.

The primary differences between these statements and those of a corporation (presented in Illustrations 4-23 and 4-24, pages 178 and 179) relate to the way equity is reported. A sole proprietor prepares an **owner's equity statement** rather than a retained earnings statement and uses different titles for the equity items shown on the balance sheet.

STUDY OBJECTIVE
3
Describe the differences between a retained earnings statement and an owner's equity statement.

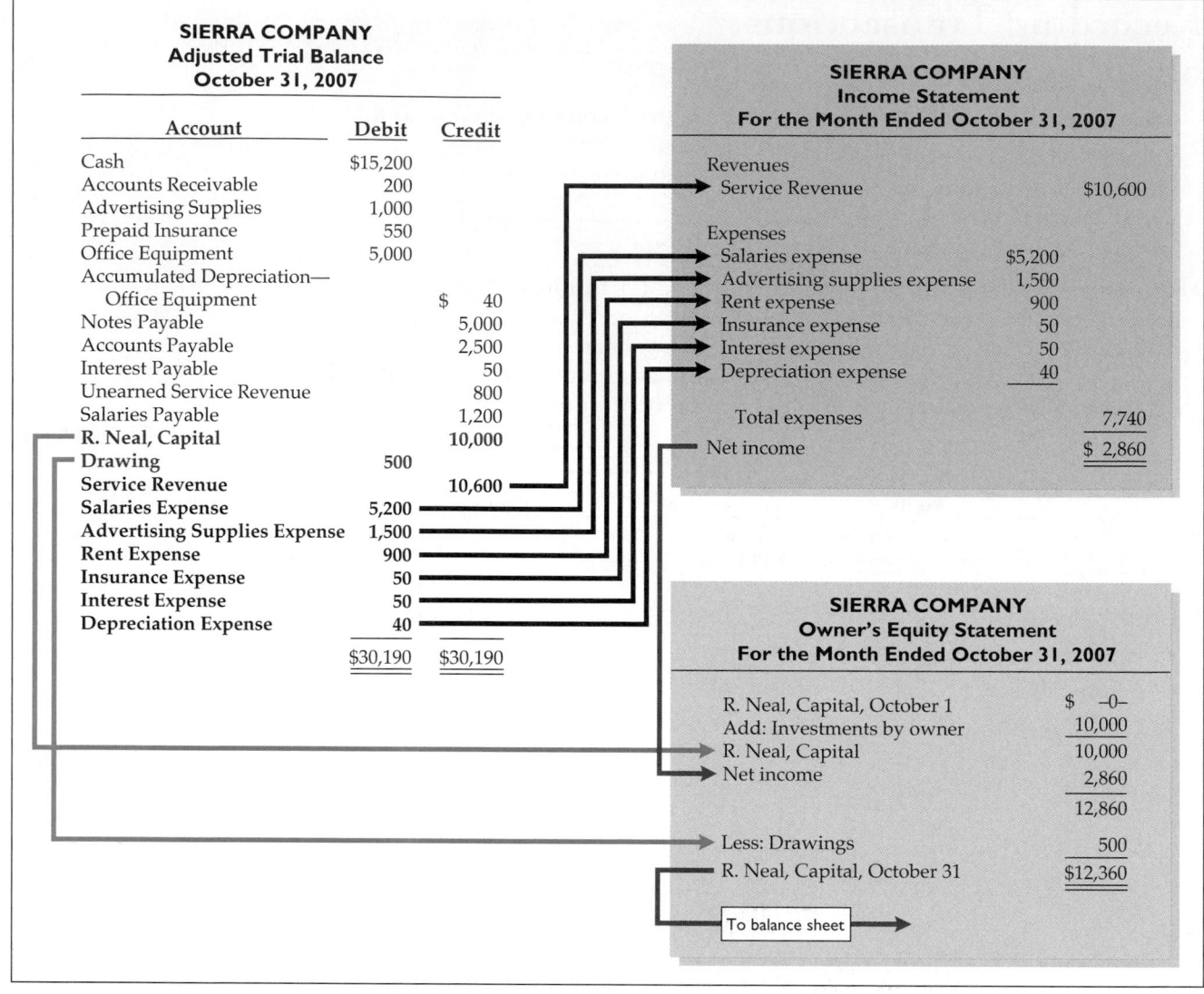

Illustration F-4
Preparation of the income
statement and owner's
equity statement from the
adjusted trial balance

Closing the Books of a Proprietorship

STUDY OBJECTIVE
4

Explain the process of
closing the books for a sole
proprietorship.

At the end of the accounting period, the temporary account balances are transferred to the permanent owner's equity account, Owner's Capital, through the preparation of closing entries. **Closing entries** for a proprietorship formally recognize in the ledger the transfer of net income (or net loss) and owner's drawing to owner's capital. The results of these entries are shown in the owner's equity statement.

Journalizing and posting closing entries is a required step in the accounting cycle. (See Illustration 4-27 on page 180 for Sierra Corporation.)

In preparing closing entries for a proprietorship, each income statement account could be closed directly to owner's capital. However, to do so would result in excessive detail in the permanent owner's capital account. Instead, the revenue and expense accounts are closed, in the same manner as for a corporation, to another temporary account, **Income Summary**. Only the net income or net loss is transferred from this account to Owner's Capital.

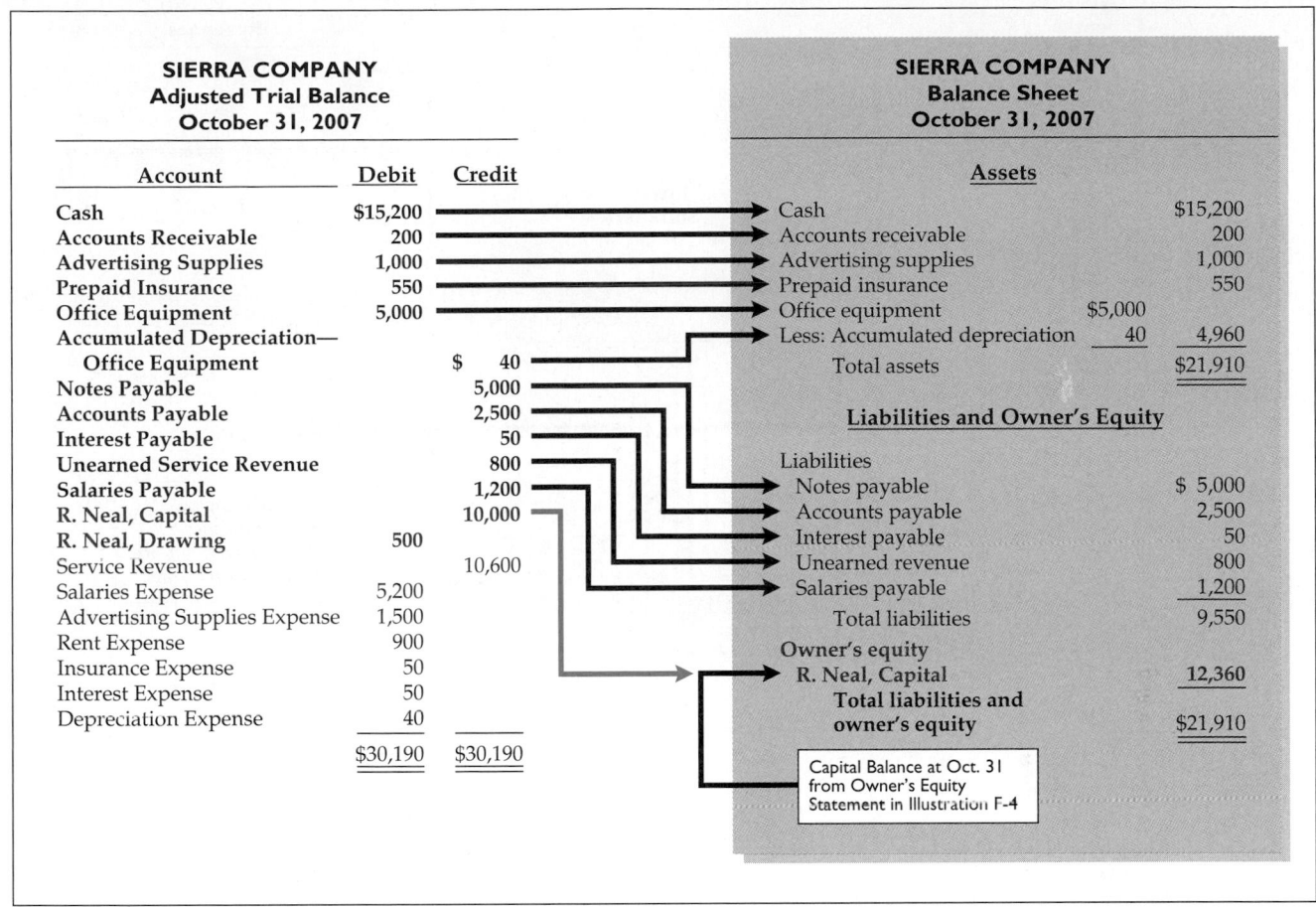

Illustration F-5
Preparation of the balance
sheet from the adjusted
trial balance

Closing entries for a proprietorship may be prepared directly from the adjusted balances in the ledger, from the income statement and balance sheet columns of the work sheet, or from the income and owner's equity statements. Separate closing entries could be prepared for each nominal account, but the following four entries accomplish the desired result more efficiently:

1. Debit each revenue account for its balance, and credit Income Summary for total revenues.

2. Debit Income Summary for total expenses, and credit each expense account for its balance.

3. Debit Income Summary and credit Owner's Capital for the amount of net income.

4. Debit Owner's Capital for the balance in the Owner's Drawing account, and credit Owner's Drawing for the same amount.

Helpful Hint Owner's Drawing is closed directly to Capital and *not* to Income Summary because Owner's Drawing is not an expense.

The four entries are referenced in the diagram of the closing process shown in Illustration F-6 and in the journal entries in Illustration F-7, both on page F-6. The posting of closing entries is shown in Illustration F-8 (page F-7).

If there were a net loss because expenses exceeded revenues, entry 3 in Illustration F-6 would be reversed: Credit Income Summary and debit Owner's Capital.

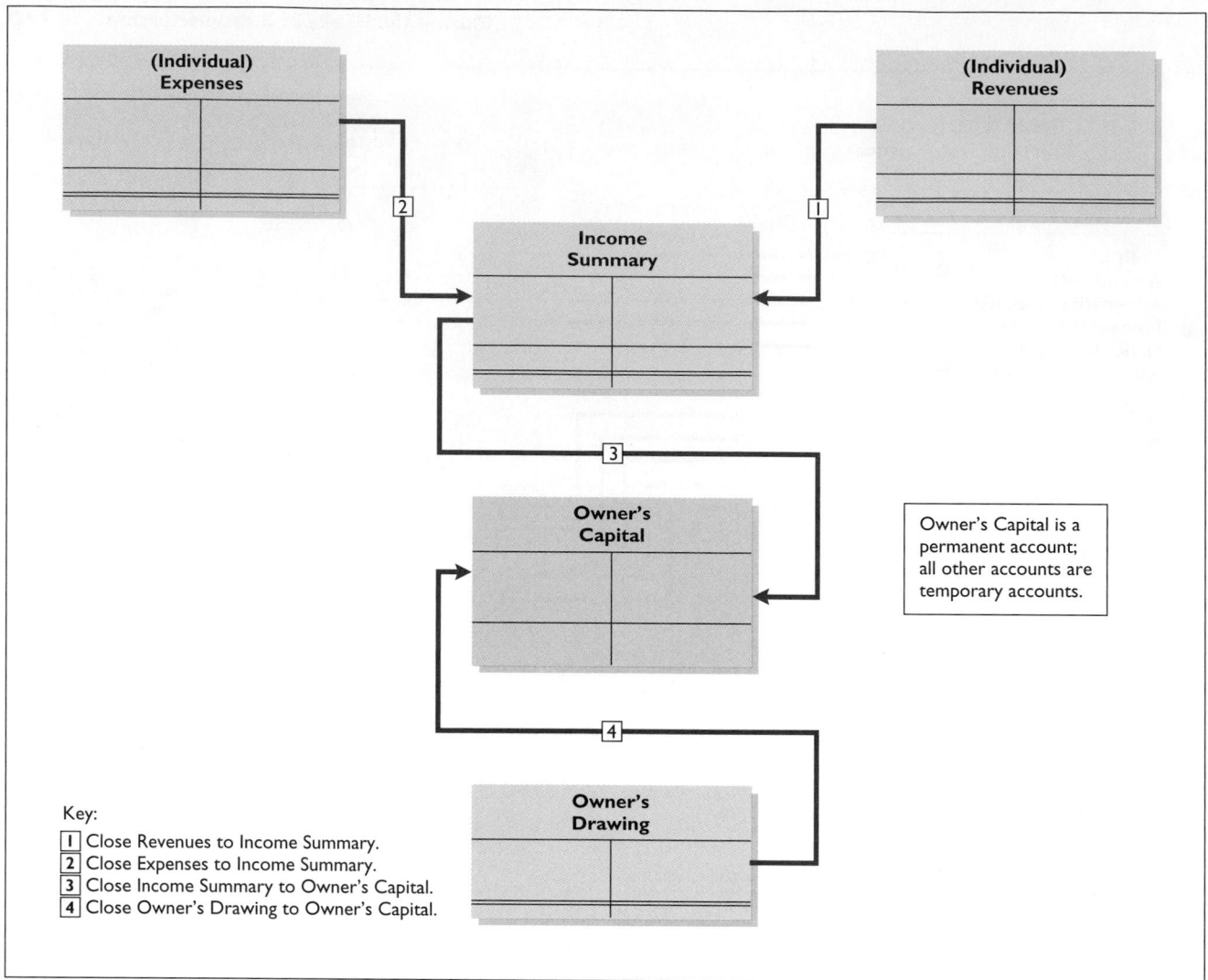

Illustration F-6
Diagram of closing process

Key:
1 Close Revenues to Income Summary.
2 Close Expenses to Income Summary.
3 Close Income Summary to Owner's Capital.
4 Close Owner's Drawing to Owner's Capital.

Owner's Capital is a permanent account; all other accounts are temporary accounts.

Illustration F-7
Closing entries journalized

Helpful Hint Income Summary is a very descriptive title: Total revenues are closed to Income Summary, total expenses are closed to Income Summary, and the balance in the Income Summary is a net income or net loss.

GENERAL JOURNAL

Date	Account Titles and Explanation	Debit	Credit
	Closing Entries		
2007	(1)		
Oct. 31	Service Revenue	10,600	
	Income Summary		10,600
	(To close revenue account)		
	(2)		
31	Income Summary	7,740	
	Salaries Expense		5,200
	Advertising Supplies Expense		1,500
	Rent Expense		900
	Insurance Expense		50
	Interest Expense		50
	Depreciation Expense		40
	(To close expense accounts)		
	(3)		
31	Income Summary	2,860	
	R. Neal, Capital		2,860
	(To close net income to owner's capital)		
	(4)		
31	**R. Neal, Capital**	500	
	R. Neal, Drawing		500
	(To close drawings to owner's capital)		

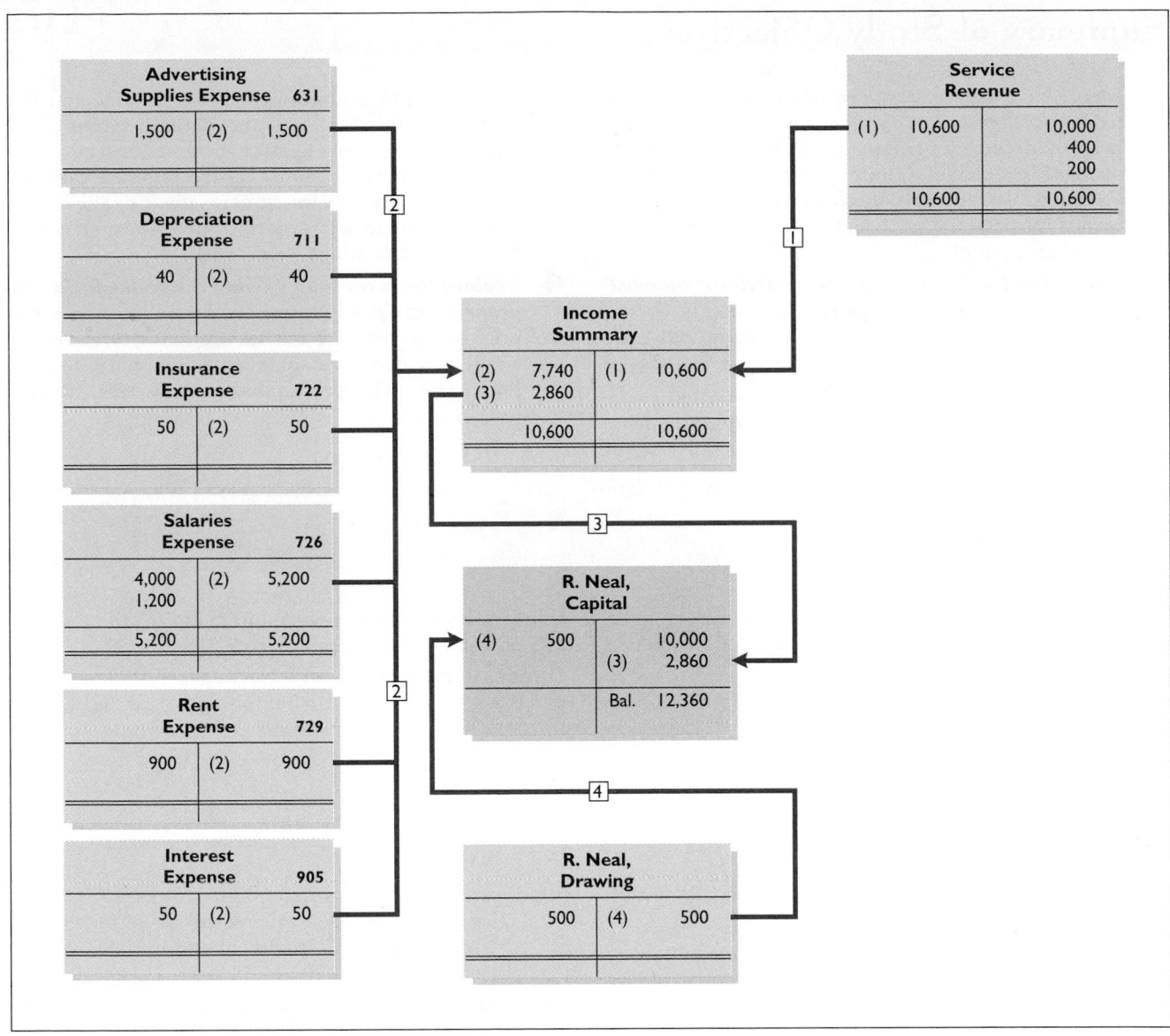

Illustration F-8
Posting of closing entries

Preparing a Post-Closing Trial Balance for a Proprietorship

After all closing entries are journalized and posted, the **post-closing trial balance** is prepared from the ledger. A post-closing trial balance is a list of all permanent accounts and their balances after closing entries are journalized and posted. As with a corporation, **the purpose of a proprietorship post-closing trial balance is to prove the equality of the permanent account balances that are carried forward into the next accounting period.** Since all temporary accounts will have zero balances, **the post-closing trial balance will contain only permanent—balance sheet—accounts.**

Summary of Study Objectives

1 *Identify the differences in equity accounts between a corporation and a sole proprietorship.* A sole proprietorship uses a permanent owner's equity Capital account instead of Common Stock and Retained Earnings. Withdrawals of cash or other assets by the owner for personal use are recorded in a temporary Drawing account.

2 *Understand what account transactions increase and decrease owner's equity.* Investments by the owner and revenue increase owner's equity. Owner's drawings and expenses decrease owner's equity.

3 *Describe the differences between a retained earnings statement and an owner's equity statement.* A sole proprietor prepares an owner's equity state-

ment rather than a retained earnings statement. The owner's equity statement shows the beginning balance in the owner's capital account (instead of retained earnings, as shown in the retained earnings statement), plus any investments made by the owner, less any drawings (in place of dividends, shown in the retained earnings statement).

4 *Explain the process of closing the books for a sole proprietorship.* In closing the books for a sole proprietorship, separate entries are made to close revenues and expenses to Income Summary, Income Summary to Owner's Capital, and Owner's Drawing to Owner's Capital.

Glossary

Drawings Withdrawal of cash or other assets from a sole proprietorship for the personal use of the owner. (p. F-2).

Investments by owner The assets put into the business by a sole proprietor. (p. F-2).

Owner's equity The ownership claim on the total assets of a sole proprietorship. (p. F-2).

Owner's equity statement The financial statement prepared for a sole proprietorship to summarize the changes in owner's equity for a specific period of time. (p. F-3).

Questions

1. What is the basic accounting equation for a sole proprietorship?

2. What are the differences in the equity accounts of a sole proprietorship versus those of a corporation?

3. What items affect owner's equity, and in what direction?

4. In February 2007, Joe Kirby invested an additional $10,000 in his business, Kirby's Pharmacy, which is

organized as a proprietorship. Kirby's accountant, Lance Jones, recorded this receipt as an increase in cash revenues. Is this treatment appropriate? Why or why not?

5. What are the steps in preparing an owner's equity statement?

6. Identify the account(s) debited and credited in each of the required closing entries for a sole proprietorship, assuming the company has net income for the year.

Brief Exercises

Determine effect of transactions on basic accounting equation.
(SO 2)

BEF-1 Presented below are three business transactions. On a sheet of paper, list the letters (a), (b), (c) with columns for assets, liabilities, and owner's equity. For each column, indicate whether the transactions increased (+), decreased (−), or had no effect (NE) on assets, liabilities, and owner's equity.
  (a) Invested cash in the business.
  (b) Withdrawal of cash by owner.
  (c) Received cash from a customer who had previously been billed for services provided.

Determine effect of transactions on owner's equity.
(SO 2)

BEF-2 Presented below are three transactions. Mark each transaction as affecting owner's investment (I), owner's drawing (D), revenue (R), expense (E), or not affecting owner's equity (NOE).
  _____ **(a)** Received cash for services performed
  _____ **(b)** Paid cash to purchase equipment
  _____ **(c)** Paid employee salaries

BEF-3 For each of the following accounts indicate the effects of (a) a debit and (b) a credit on the accounts and (c) the normal balance of the account.

    1. Accounts Payable.   **4.** Accounts Receivable.
    2. Advertising Expense.   **5.** B. C. Jardine, Capital.
    3. Service Revenue.   **6.** B. C. Jardine, Drawing.

Indicate debit and credit effects and normal balance.
(SO 2)

Exercises

EF-1 An analysis of the transactions made by Roberta Mendez & Co., a certified public accounting firm, for the month of August is shown below. Each increase and decrease in owner's equity is explained.

Analyze transactions and compute net income.
(SO 2)

	Cash	+	Accounts Receivable	+	Supplies	+	Office Equipment	=	Accounts Payable	+	Owner's Equity R. Mendez, Capital	
1.	+$12,000										+$12,000	Investment
2.	−2,000						+$5,000		+$3,000			
3.	−750				+$750							
4.	+2,600		+$3,700								+6,300	Service Revenue
5.	−1,500								−1,500			
6.	−2,000										−2,000	Drawings
7.	−650										−650	Rent Expense
8.	+450		−450									
9.	−2,900										−2,900	Salaries Expense
10.									+500		−500	Utilities Expense

Instructions
  (a) ▭▭▭▷ Describe each transaction that occurred for the month.
  (b) Determine how much owner's equity increased for the month.
  (c) Compute the amount of net income for the month.

(b) Increase in O.E. $12,250
(c) Net income $2,250

EF-2 Presented below is information related to the sole proprietorship of Mark Garland, attorney.

Prepare an owner's equity statement.
(SO 3)

Legal service revenue—2007	$360,000
Total expenses—2007	211,000
Assets, January 1, 2007	85,000
Liabilities, January 1, 2007	62,000
Assets, December 31, 2007	168,000
Liabilities, December 31, 2007	70,000
Drawings—2007	?

Instructions
Prepare the 2007 owner's equity statement for Mark Garland's legal practice.

Capital, Dec. 31 $98,000

EF-3 The adjusted trial balance of Mozart Company at the end of its fiscal year is:

Prepare income statement, owner's equity statement, and balance sheet.
(SO 1, 2, 3, 4)

MOZART COMPANY
Adjusted Trial Balance
July 31, 2007

No.	Account Titles	Debits	Credits
101	Cash	$ 14,940	
112	Accounts Receivable	8,780	
157	Equipment	15,900	
167	Accumulated Depreciation		$ 5,400
201	Accounts Payable		4,220
208	Unearned Rent Revenue		1,800
301	W.A. Mozart, Capital		45,200
306	W.A. Mozart, Drawing	14,000	
404	Commission Revenue		65,100
429	Rent Revenue		6,500
711	Depreciation Expense	4,000	
720	Salaries Expense	55,700	
732	Utilities Expense	14,900	
		$128,220	$128,220

(a) Net loss $ 3,000
(b) Total assets $34,220

Instructions
(a) Prepare an income statement and an owner's equity statement for the year. Mozart did not make any capital investments during the year.
(b) Prepare a classified balance sheet at July 31.

Problems

Prepare income statement, owner's equity statement, and balance sheet.
(SO 1, 2, 3, 4)

PF-1   On May 1, Dennis Chambers started Skyline Flying School, a company that provides flying lessons, by investing $45,000 cash in the business. Following are the assets and liabilities of the company on May 31, 2007, and the revenues and expenses for the month of May.

Cash	$ 6,500	Notes Payable	$30,000
Accounts Receivable	7,200	Rent Expense	1,200
Equipment	64,000	Repair Expense	400
Lesson Revenue	8,600	Fuel Expense	2,500
Advertising Expense	500	Insurance Expense	400
		Accounts Payable	800

Dennis Chambers made no additional investment in May, but he withdrew $1,700 in cash for personal use.

Instructions

(a) Net income $ 3,600
   Owner's equity $46,900
   Total assets $77,700
(b) Net income $ 1,200
   Owner's equity $44,500

(a) Prepare an income statement and owner's equity statement for the month of May and a balance sheet at May 31.
(b) Prepare an income statement and owner's equity statement for May assuming that the data above need to be adjusted for the following items: (1) $900 of revenue was earned and billed but not collected at May 31, and (2) $3,300 of fuel expense was incurred but not paid.

Prepare financial statements, closing entries, and post-closing trial balance.
(SO 1, 2, 3, 4)

Peachtree

PF-2   The adjusted trial balance columns of the work sheet for Shmi Skywalker Company is as follows.

SHMI SKYWALKER COMPANY
Adjusted Trial Balance
For the Year Ended December 31, 2007

Account No.	Account Titles	Adjusted Trial Balance Dr.	Cr.
101	Cash	20,800	
112	Accounts Receivable	15,400	
126	Supplies	2,300	
130	Prepaid Insurance	4,800	
151	Office Equipment	44,000	
152	Accumulated Depreciation—Office Equipment		18,000
200	Notes Payable		20,000
201	Accounts Payable		8,000
212	Salaries Payable		3,000
230	Interest Payable		1,000
301	S. Skywalker, Capital		36,000
306	S. Skywalker, Drawing	12,000	
400	Service Revenue		79,000
610	Advertising Expense	12,000	
631	Supplies Expense	3,700	
711	Depreciation Expense	6,000	
722	Insurance Expense	4,000	
726	Salaries Expense	39,000	
905	Interest Expense	1,000	
	Totals	165,000	165,000

Instructions
(a) Prepare an income statement, owner's equity statement, and a classified balance sheet. $10,000 of the notes payable become due in 2008. S. Skywalker did not make any additional investments in the business during 2007.
(b) Prepare the closing entries.
(c) Post the closing entries. Use the three-column form of account. Income summary is No. 350.
(d) Prepare a post-closing trial balance.

(a) Net income $13,300
    Current assets $43,300
    Current liabilities $22,000

(d) Post-closing trial
    balance $87,300

PF-3 The adjusted trial balance columns of the work sheet for Boss Nass Company, owned by Boss Nass, are as follows.

Prepare financial statements, closing entries, and post-closing trial balance.
(SO 1, 2, 3, 4)

BOSS NASS COMPANY
Adjusted Trial Balance
For the Year Ended December 31, 2007

Account No.	Account Titles	Adjusted Trial Balance Dr.	Cr.
101	Cash	13,600	
112	Accounts Receivable	15,400	
126	Supplies	1,500	
130	Prepaid Insurance	2,800	
151	Office Equipment	34,000	
152	Accumulated Depreciation—Office Equipment		8,000
200	Notes Payable		16,000
201	Accounts Payable		6,000
212	Salaries Payable		3,000
230	Interest Payable		500
301	Boss Nass, Capital		25,000
306	Boss Nass, Drawing	10,000	
400	Service Revenue		88,000
610	Advertising Expense	12,000	
631	Supplies Expense	5,700	
711	Depreciation Expense	4,000	
722	Insurance Expense	5,000	
726	Salaries Expense	42,000	
905	Interest Expense	500	
	Totals	146,500	146,500

Instructions
(a) Prepare an income statement, owner's equity statement, and a classified balance sheet (*Note:* $10,000 of the notes payable become due in 2008.) Boss Nass did not make any additional investments in the business during the year.
(b) Prepare the closing entries. Use J14 for the journal page.
(c) Post the closing entries. Use the three-column form of account. Income Summary is No. 350.
(d) Prepare a post-closing trial balance.

(a) Net income $18,800
    Current assets $33,300
    Current liabilities $19,500

(d) Post-closing trial
    balance $67,300

Accounting for Partnerships

STUDY OBJECTIVES

After studying this chapter,
you should be able to:

1 Identify the characteristics of the partnership form of business organization.

2 Explain the accounting entries for the formation of a partnership.

3 Identify the bases for dividing net income or net loss.

4 Describe the form and content of partnership financial statements.

5 Explain the effects of the entries to record the liquidation of a partnership.

Partnership Form of Organization

The Uniform Partnership Act provides the basic rules for the formation and operation of partnerships in most states in the United States. This act defines a **partnership** as an association of two or more persons to carry on as co-owners of a business for profit. Partnerships are common in retail establishments and in small manufacturing companies. Also, accountants, lawyers, and doctors find it desirable to form partnerships with other professionals in their field. Professional partnerships vary in size from a medical partnership of 3 to 5 doctors, to 150 to 200 partners in a large law firm, to more than 2,000 partners in an international accounting firm.

CHARACTERISTICS OF PARTNERSHIPS

Partnerships are fairly easy to form. They can be formed simply by a verbal agreement or, more formally, by putting in writing the rights and obligations of the partners. Partners who have not put their agreement in writing sometimes have found that the characteristics of partnerships can lead to later difficulties. The principal characteristics of the partnership form of business organization are shown in Illustration G-1 (page G-2) and explained in the following sections.

STUDY OBJECTIVE
1
Identify the characteristics of the partnership form of business organization.

Association of Individuals

The voluntary association of two or more individuals in a partnership may be based on as simple an act as a handshake. However, it is preferable to state

Illustration G-1
Partnership characteristics

the agreement in writing. Under the Uniform Partnership Act, a partnership is a legal entity for certain purposes. For instance, property (land, buildings, equipment) can be owned in the name of the partnership, and the firm can sue or be sued. **A partnership also is an accounting entity for financial reporting purposes.** Thus, the purely personal assets, liabilities, and transactions of the partners are excluded from the accounting records of the partnership.

The net income of a partnership is not taxed as a separate entity. But, a partnership must file an information tax return showing partnership net income and each partner's share of that net income. Each partner's share is taxable at personal tax rates, regardless of the amount of net income withdrawn from the business during the year.

Mutual Agency

Helpful Hint Because of mutual agency, an individual should be extremely cautious in selecting partners.

Mutual agency means that each partner acts on behalf of the partnership when engaging in partnership business. The act of any partner is binding on all other partners. This is true even when partners act beyond the scope of their authority, so long as the act appears to be appropriate for the partnership. For example, a partner of a grocery store who purchases a delivery truck creates a binding contract in the name of the partnership, even if the partnership agreement denies this authority. On the other hand, if a partner in a law firm purchased a snowmobile for the partnership, such an act would not be binding on the partnership. The purchase is clearly outside the scope of partnership business.

Limited Life

A partnership does not have unlimited life. It may be ended voluntarily at any time through the acceptance of a new partner or the withdrawal of a partner. A partnership may be ended involuntarily by the death or incapacity of a partner. Thus the life of a partnership is indefinite. **Partnership dissolution** occurs whenever a partner withdraws or a new partner is admitted. Dissolution of a partnership does not necessarily mean that the business ends. If the continuing partners agree, operations can continue without interruption by forming a new partnership.

Unlimited Liability

Each partner is **personally and individually liable** for all partnership liabilities. Creditors' claims attach first to partnership assets. If these are insufficient, the claims then attach to the personal resources of any partner, irrespective of that partner's equity in the partnership. Because each partner is responsible for all the debts of the partnership, each partner is said to have **unlimited liability**.

Co-Ownership of Property

Partnership assets are owned jointly by the partners. If the partnership is dissolved, the assets do not legally revert to the original contributor. Each partner has a claim on total assets equal to the balance in his or her respective capital account. This claim does not attach to specific assets that an individual partner contributed to the firm. Similarly, if a partner invests a building in the partnership valued at $100,000 and the building is later sold at a gain of $20,000, that partner does not personally receive the entire gain.

Partnership net income (or net loss) is also co-owned. **If the partnership contract does not specify to the contrary, all net income or net loss is shared equally by the partners.** As you will see later, though, partners may agree to unequal sharing of net income or net loss.

ORGANIZATIONS WITH PARTNERSHIP CHARACTERISTICS

With surprising speed, states are creating special forms of business organizations that have partnership characteristics. These new organizations are being adopted by many small companies. These special forms are: limited partnerships, limited liability partnerships, limited liability companies, and "S" corporations.

Limited Partnerships

In a limited partnership, one or more partners have **unlimited liability** and one or more partners have **limited liability** for the debts of the firm. Those with unlimited liability are called general partners. Those with limited liability are called limited partners. Limited partners are responsible for the debts of the partnership up to the limit of their investment in the firm. This organization is identified in its name with the words "Limited Partnership," or "Ltd.," or "LP." For the privilege of limited liability, the limited partner usually accepts less compensation than a general partner and exercises less influence in the affairs of the firm.

Limited Liability Partnership

Most states allow professionals such as lawyers, doctors, and accountants to form a limited liability partnership or "LLP." The LLP is designed to protect innocent partners from malpractice or negligence claims resulting from the acts of another partner. LLPs generally carry large insurance policies in case the partnership is guilty of malpractice.

Limited Liability Companies

A new, hybrid form of business organization with certain features like a corporation and others like a limited partnership is the limited liability company, or "LLC" (or "LC"). An LLC usually has a limited life. The owners, called **members**, have limited liability like owners of a corporation. Whereas limited partners do not actively participate in the management of a limited partnership (LP), the members of a limited liability company (LLC) can assume an active management role. For income tax purposes, the IRS usually classifies an LLC as a partnership.

"S" Corporations

An **"S" corporation** is a corporation that is taxed in the same way that a partnership is taxed. To qualify as an "S" corporation, the company must have 75 or fewer stockholders, all of whom must be citizens or residents of the United States. The advantage of an "S" corporation (also called a Sub-Chapter "S" corporation) is that, like a partnership and unlike a corporation, it does not pay income taxes.

ADVANTAGES AND DISADVANTAGES OF PARTNERSHIPS

Why do people choose partnerships? One major advantage of a partnership is that the **skills and resources of two or more individuals can be combined**. For example, a large public accounting firm such as Ernst & Young must have expertise in auditing, taxation, and management consulting. In addition, a partnership is **easily formed and is relatively free from governmental regulations and restrictions**. A partnership does not have to contend with the "red tape" that a corporation must face. Also, decisions can be made quickly on substantive matters affecting the firm; there is no board of directors that must be consulted.

On the other hand, partnerships also have some major disadvantages: **mutual agency**, **limited life**, and **unlimited liability**. Unlimited liability is particularly troublesome. Many individuals fear they may lose not only their initial investment but also their personal assets, if those assets are needed to pay partnership creditors. As a result, partnerships often find it difficult to obtain large amounts of investment capital. That is one reason why the largest business enterprises in the United States are corporations, not partnerships.

The advantages and disadvantages of the partnership form of business organization are summarized in Illustration G-2.

Illustration G-2
Advantages and
disadvantages of a
partnership

Advantages	Disadvantages
Combining skills and resources of two or more individuals	Mutual agency
Ease of formation	Limited life
Freedom from governmental regulations and restrictions	Unlimited liability
Ease of decision making	

THE PARTNERSHIP AGREEMENT

Ideally, the agreement of two or more individuals to form a partnership should be expressed in writing. This written contract is often called the **partnership agreement** or **articles of co-partnership**. The partnership agreement contains such basic information as the name and principal location of the firm, the purpose of the business, and date of inception. In addition, relationships among the partners should be specified, such as:

1. Names and capital contributions of partners.
2. Rights and duties of partners.
3. Basis for sharing net income or net loss.
4. Provision for withdrawals of assets.
5. Procedures for submitting disputes to arbitration.
6. Procedures for the withdrawal or addition of a partner.
7. Rights and duties of surviving partners in the event of a partner's death.

We cannot overemphasize the importance of a written contract. The agreement should be drawn with care and should attempt to anticipate all possible situations, contingencies, and disagreements. The help of a lawyer is highly desirable in preparing the agreement.

Basic Partnership Accounting

We now turn to the basic accounting for partnerships. The major accounting issues relate to forming the partnership, dividing income or loss, and preparing financial statements.

FORMING A PARTNERSHIP

Each partner's initial investment in a partnership is entered in the partnership records. These investments should be recorded at the **fair market value of the assets at the date of their transfer to the partnership**. The values assigned must be agreed to by all of the partners.

To illustrate, assume that A. Rolfe and T. Shea combine their proprietorships to start a partnership named U.S. Software. The firm will specialize in developing financial modeling software packages. Rolfe and Shea have the following assets prior to the formation of the partnership.

> **STUDY OBJECTIVE**
> ──── **2** ────
> Explain the accounting entries for the formation of a partnership.

	Book Value		Market Value	
	A. Rolfe	**T. Shea**	**A. Rolfe**	**T. Shea**
Cash	$ 8,000	$ 9,000	$ 8,000	$ 9,000
Office equipment	5,000		4,000	
Accumulated depreciation	(2,000)			
Accounts receivable		4,000		4,000
Allowance for doubtful accounts		(700)		(1,000)
	$11,000	$12,300	$12,000	$12,000

Illustration G-3 Book and market values of assets invested

The entries to record the investments are:

Investment of A. Rolfe

Cash	8,000	
Office Equipment	4,000	
A. Rolfe, Capital		12,000
(To record investment of Rolfe)		

A	=	L	+	OE
+8,000				+12,000
+4,000				

Cash Flows
+8,000

Investment of T. Shea

Cash	9,000	
Accounts Receivable	4,000	
Allowance for Doubtful Accounts		1,000
T. Shea, Capital		12,000
(To record investment of Shea)		

A	=	L	+	OE
+9,000				+12,000
+4,000				
−1,000				

Cash Flows
+9,000

Note that neither the original cost of the office equipment ($5,000) nor its book value ($5,000 − $2,000) is recorded by the partnership. The equipment is recorded at its fair market value, $4,000. Because the equipment has not been used by the partnership, there is no accumulated depreciation.

In contrast, the gross claims on customers ($4,000) are carried forward to the partnership. The allowance for doubtful accounts is adjusted to $1,000 to arrive at a cash (net) realizable value of $3,000. A partnership may start with an allowance for doubtful accounts because it will continue to collect existing accounts receivable, some of which are expected to be uncollectible. In addition, this procedure maintains the control and subsidiary relationship between Accounts Receivable and the accounts receivable subsidiary ledger.

After the partnership has been formed, the accounting for transactions is similar to any other type of business organization. For example, all transactions with outside parties, such as the purchase or sale of merchandise inventory and the payment or receipt of cash, should be recorded the same for a partnership as for a corporation.

The steps in the accounting cycle described in Chapter 4 also apply to a partnership. For example, the partnership prepares a trial balance and journalizes and posts adjusting entries. A work sheet may be used. There are minor differences in journalizing and posting closing entries and in preparing financial statements, as explained in the following sections.

DIVIDING NET INCOME OR NET LOSS

Partnership net income or net loss is shared equally unless the partnership contract indicates otherwise. The same basis of division usually applies to both net income and net loss. It is customary to refer to this basis as the **income ratio**, the **income and loss ratio**, or the **profit and loss (P&L) ratio**. Because of its wide acceptance, we will use the term income ratio to identify the basis for dividing net income and net loss. A partner's share of net income or net loss is recognized in the capital accounts through closing entries.

Closing Entries

Four entries are required in preparing closing entries for a partnership. The entries are:

1. Debit each revenue account for its balance, and credit Income Summary for total revenues.

2. Debit Income Summary for total expenses, and credit each expense account for its balance.

3. Debit Income Summary for its balance, and credit each partner's Capital account for his or her share of net income. Or, credit Income Summary, and debit each partner's Capital account for his or her share of net loss.

4. Debit each partner's Capital account for the balance in that partner's drawing account, and credit each partner's drawing account for the same amount.

The first two entries are the same as in a corporation. The last two entries are different because (1) there are two or more owners' capital and drawing accounts, and (2) it is necessary to divide net income (or net loss) among the partners.

To illustrate the last two closing entries, assume that AB Company has net income of $32,000 for 2007. The partners, L. Arbor and D. Barnett, share net income and net loss equally. Drawings for the year were Arbor $8,000 and Barnett $6,000. The last two closing entries are:

Dec. 31	Income Summary	32,000	
	L. Arbor, Capital ($32,000 × 50%)		16,000
	D. Barnett, Capital ($32,000 × 50%)		16,000
	(To transfer net income to partners' capital accounts)		
31	L. Arbor, Capital	8,000	
	D. Barnett, Capital	6,000	
	L. Arbor, Drawing		8,000
	D. Barnett, Drawing		6,000
	(To close drawing accounts to capital accounts)		

Assume that the beginning capital balance is $47,000 for Arbor and $36,000 for Barnett. The capital and drawing accounts will show the following after posting the closing entries.

L. Arbor, Capital		D. Barnett, Capital	
12/31 **Clos.** **8,000**	1/1 Bal. 47,000	12/31 **Clos.** **6,000**	1/1 Bal. 36,000
	12/31 **Clos.** **16,000**		12/31 **Clos.** **16,000**
	12/31 Bal. 55,000		12/31 Bal. 46,000

L. Arbor, Drawing		D. Barnett, Drawing	
12/31 Bal. 8,000	12/31 **Clos.** **8,000**	12/31 Bal. 6,000	12/31 **Clos.** **6,000**

The partners' capital accounts are permanent accounts; their drawing accounts are temporary accounts. Normally, the capital accounts will have credit balances and the drawing accounts will have debit balances. Drawing accounts are debited when partners withdraw cash or other assets from the partnership for personal use.

Income Ratios

As noted earlier, the partnership agreement should specify the basis for sharing net income or net loss. The following are typical income ratios.

1. A fixed ratio, expressed as a proportion (6:4), a percentage (70% and 30%), or a fraction (2/3 and 1/3).
2. A ratio based either on capital balances at the beginning of the year or on average capital balances during the year.
3. Salaries to partners and the remainder on a fixed ratio.
4. Interest on partners' capital balances and the remainder on a fixed ratio.
5. Salaries to partners, interest on partners' capital, and the remainder on a fixed ratio.

The objective is to settle on a basis that will equitably reflect the partners' capital investment and service to the partnership.

A fixed ratio is easy to apply, and it may be an equitable basis in some circumstances. Assume, for example, that Hughes and Lane are partners. Each contributes the same amount of capital, but Hughes expects to work full-time in the partnership and Lane expects to work only half-time. Accordingly, the partners agree to a fixed ratio of 2/3 to Hughes and 1/3 to Lane.

A ratio based on capital balances may be appropriate when the funds invested in the partnership are considered the critical factor. Capital ratios may also be equitable when a manager is hired to run the business and the partners do not plan to take an active role in daily operations.

The three remaining ratios (items 3, 4, and 5) give specific recognition to differences among partners. These ratios provide salary allowances for time worked and interest allowances for capital invested. Then, any remaining net income or net loss is allocated on a fixed ratio. Some caution needs to be exercised in working with these types of income ratios. These ratios pertain exclusively to **the computations that are required in dividing net income or net loss** among the partners.

Salaries to partners and interest on partners' capital are not expenses of the partnership. Therefore, these items do not enter into the matching

of expenses with revenues and the determination of net income or net loss. For a partnership, as for other entities, salaries expense pertains to the cost of services performed by employees. Likewise, interest expense relates to the cost of borrowing from creditors. But partners, as owners, are not considered either **employees** or **creditors**. Therefore, when the income ratio includes a salary allowance for partners, some partnership agreements permit the partner to make monthly withdrawals of cash based on their "salary." Such withdrawals are debited to the partner's drawing account.

Salaries, Interest, and Remainder on a Fixed Ratio

Under income ratio (5) in the list above, the provisions for salaries and interest must be applied **before** the remainder is allocated on the specified fixed ratio. **This is true even if the provisions exceed net income. It is also true even if the partnership has suffered a net loss for the year.** Detailed information concerning the division of net income or net loss should be shown below net income on the income statement.

To illustrate this income ratio, assume that Sara King and Ray Lee are co-partners in the Kingslee Company. The partnership agreement provides for: (1) salary allowances of $8,400 to King and $6,000 to Lee, (2) interest allowances of 10% on capital balances at the beginning of the year, and (3) the remainder equally. Capital balances on January 1 were King $28,000, and Lee $24,000. In 2007, partnership net income is $22,000. The division of net income is as follows.

Illustration G-5 Income statement with division of net income

KINGSLEE COMPANY
Income Statement (partial)
For the Year Ended December 31, 2007

	Sales	$200,000		
	Net income	$ 22,000		

Division of Net Income

	Sara King	Ray Lee	Total
Salary allowance	$ 8,400	$ 6,000	$ 14,400
Interest allowance on partners' capital			
Sara King ($28,000 × 10%)	2,800		
Ray Lee ($24,000 × 10%)		2,400	
Total interest allowance			5,200
Total salaries and interest	11,200	8,400	19,600
Remaining income, $2,400			
($22,000 − $19,600)			
Sara King ($2,400 × 50%)	1,200		
Ray Lee ($2,400 × 50%)		1,200	
Total remainder			2,400
Total division of net income	**$12,400**	**$9,600**	**$22,000**

The entry to record the division of net income is:

A	=	L	+	OE
				−22,000
				+12,400
				+9,600

Cash Flows
no effect

Dec. 31	Income Summary	22,000	
	Sara King, Capital		12,400
	Ray Lee, Capital		9,600
	(To close net income to partners' capital)		

Now let's look at a situation in which the salary and interest allowances exceed net income. Assume that Kingslee Company's net income is only $18,000. In this case, the salary and interest allowances will create a deficiency of $1,600 ($19,600 − $18,000). The computations of the allowances are the same as those in the preceding example. Beginning with total salaries and interest, we complete the division of net income as follows.

	Sara King	Ray Lee	Total
Total salaries and interest	$ 11,200	$ 8,400	$ 19,600
Remaining deficiency ($1,600)			
($18,000 − $19,600)			
Sara King ($1,600 × 50%)	(800)		
Ray Lee ($1,600 × 50%)		(800)	
Total remainder			(1,600)
Total division	**$10,400**	**$7,600**	**$18,000**

Illustration G-6 Division of net income—income deficiency

PARTNERSHIP FINANCIAL STATEMENTS

The financial statements of a partnership are similar to those of a corporation. The income statement for a partnership is identical to the income statement for a corporation except for the additional section that reports the division of net income, as shown earlier.

The owners' equity statement for a partnership is called the **partners' capital statement**. Its function is to explain the changes in each partner's capital account and in total partnership capital during the year. The partners' capital statement for Kingslee Company is shown below. It is based on the division of $22,000 of net income in Illustration G-5. The statement includes assumed data for the additional investment and drawings.

STUDY OBJECTIVE **4**
Describe the form and content of partnership financial statements.

KINGSLEE COMPANY
Partners' Capital Statement
For the Year Ended December 31, 2007

	Sara King	Ray Lee	Total
Capital, January 1	$ 28,000	$ 24,000	$ 52,000
Add: Additional investment	2,000		2,000
Net income	12,400	9,600	22,000
	42,400	33,600	76,000
Less: Drawings	7,000	5,000	12,000
Capital, December 31	**$35,400**	**$28,600**	**$64,000**

Illustration G-7 Partners' capital statement

Helpful Hint Partners' capital may change due to (1) additional investment, (2) drawings, and (3) net income or net loss.

The partners' capital statement is prepared from the income statement and the partners' capital and drawing accounts.

The balance sheet for a partnership is the same as for a corporation except for the owner's equity section. In a partnership, the capital balances of each partner are shown in the balance sheet. The owners' equity section for Kingslee Company is shown in Illustration G-8 (page G-10).

Illustration G-8 Owners' equity section of a partnership balance sheet

KINGSLEE COMPANY Balance Sheet (partial) December 31, 2007		
Total liabilities (assumed amount)		$115,000
Owners' equity		
Sara King, Capital	$35,400	
Ray Lee, Capital	28,600	
Total owners' equity		64,000
Total liabilities and owners' equity		$179,000

Admission and Withdrawal of Partners

We have seen how the basic accounting for a partnership works. Another issue relates to the accounting for the addition or withdrawal of a partner. From an economic standpoint, the admission or withdrawal of a partner is often of minor significance in the continuity of the business. For example, in large public accounting or law firms, partners are added or dropped without any change in operating policies. Because the accounting for the admission or withdrawal of a partner is complex, it is discussed in more advanced accounting courses.

Liquidation of a Partnership

STUDY OBJECTIVE
5

Explain the effects of the entries to record the liquidation of a partnership.

The liquidation of a partnership terminates the business. It involves selling the assets of the firm, paying liabilities, and distributing any remaining assets to the partners. Liquidation may result from the sale of the business by mutual agreement of the partners, from the death of a partner, or from bankruptcy. In contrast to partnership dissolution, **partnership liquidation** ends both the legal and economic life of the entity.

From an accounting standpoint, liquidation should be preceded by completing the accounting cycle for the final operating period. This includes preparing adjusting entries and financial statements. It also involves preparing closing entries and a post-closing trial balance. Thus, only balance sheet accounts should be open as the liquidation process begins.

In liquidation, the sale of noncash assets for cash is called **realization**. Any difference between book value and the cash proceeds is called the **gain or loss on realization**. To liquidate a partnership, it is necessary to:

1. Sell noncash assets for cash and recognize a gain or loss on realization.
2. Allocate gain/loss on realization to the partners based on their income ratios.
3. Pay partnership liabilities in cash.
4. Distribute remaining cash to partners on the basis of their **capital balances**.

Each of the steps must be performed in sequence. Creditors must be paid **before** partners receive any cash distributions. Each step also must be recorded by an accounting entry.

When a partnership is liquidated, all partners may have credit balances in their capital accounts. This situation is called **no capital deficiency**. Or, at least one partner's capital account may have a debit balance. This situation is termed a **capital deficiency**. To illustrate each of these conditions, assume that the Ace Company is liquidated when its ledger shows the assets, liabilities, and owners' equity accounts listed in Illustration G-9.

Assets		Liabilities and Owners' Equity	
Cash	$ 5,000	Notes payable	$15,000
Accounts receivable	15,000	Accounts payable	16,000
Inventory	18,000	R. Arnet, Capital	15,000
Equipment	35,000	P. Carey, Capital	17,800
Accum. depr.—equipment	(8,000)	W. Eaton, Capital	1,200
	$65,000		$65,000

Illustration G-9 Account balances prior to liquidation

NO CAPITAL DEFICIENCY

The partners of Ace Company agree to liquidate the partnership on the following terms: (1) The noncash assets of the partnership will be sold to Jackson Enterprises for $75,000 cash. And (2) the partnership will pay its partnership liabilities. The income ratios of the partners are 3:2:1, respectively. The steps in the liquidation process are as follows.

1. The noncash assets (accounts receivable, inventory, and equipment) are sold for $75,000. The book value of these assets is $60,000 ($15,000 + $18,000 + $35,000 − $8,000). Thus a gain of $15,000 is realized on the sale. The entry is:

(1)

Cash	75,000	
Accumulated Depreciation—Equipment	8,000	
Accounts Receivable		15,000
Inventory		18,000
Equipment		35,000
Gain on Realization		15,000
(To record realization of noncash assets)		

A = L + OE
+75,000   +15,000
+8,000
−15,000
−18,000
−35,000

Cash Flows
+75,000

2. The gain on realization of $15,000 is allocated to the partners on their income ratios, which are 3:2:1. The entry is:

(2)

Gain on Realization	15,000	
R. Arnet, Capital ($15,000 × 3/6)		7,500
P. Carey, Capital ($15,000 × 2/6)		5,000
W. Eaton, Capital ($15,000 × 1/6)		2,500
(To allocate gain to partners' capital accounts)		

A = L + OE
−15,000
+7,500
+5,000
+2,500

Cash Flows
no effect

3. Partnership liabilities consist of Notes Payable $15,000 and Accounts Payable $16,000. Creditors are paid in full by a cash payment of $31,000. The entry is:

(3)

Notes Payable	15,000	
Accounts Payable	16,000	
Cash		31,000
(To record payment of partnership liabilities)		

A = L + OE
−31,000 −15,000
−16,000

Cash Flows
−31,000

4. The remaining cash is distributed to the partners on the basis of **their capital balances**. After the entries in the first three steps are posted, all partnership accounts, including Gain on Realization, will have zero balances except for four accounts: Cash $49,000; R. Arnet, Capital $22,500; P. Carey, Capital $22,800; and W. Eaton, Capital $3,700, as shown in Illustration G-10 (page G-12).

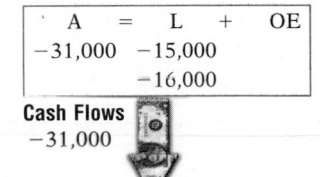

Cash		R. Arnet, Capital	P. Carey, Capital	W. Eaton, Capital
Bal. 5,000	(3) 31,000	Bal. 15,000	Bal. 17,800	Bal. 1,200
(1) 75,000		(2) 7,500	(2) 5,000	(2) 2,500
Bal. 49,000		**Bal. 22,500**	**Bal. 22,800**	**Bal. 3,700**

Illustration G-10
Ledger balances before distribution of cash

The entry to record the distribution of cash is as follows.

(4)

R. Arnet, Capital	22,500	
P. Carey, Capital	22,800	
W. Eaton, Capital	3,700	
Cash		49,000
(To record distribution of cash to partners)		

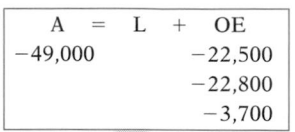

A   =   L   +   OE
−49,000   −22,500
                 −22,800
                 −3,700

Cash Flows
−49,000

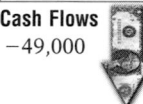

Helpful Hint Zero balances after posting is a quick proof of the accuracy of the cash distribution entry.

After this entry is posted, all partnership accounts will have zero balances.

A word of caution: **Cash should not be distributed to partners on the basis of their income-sharing ratios.** On this basis, Arnet would receive three-sixths, or $24,500, which would produce an erroneous debit balance of $2,000. The income ratio is the proper basis for allocating net income or loss. **It is not a proper basis for making the final distribution of cash to the partners.**

Schedule of Cash Payments

Some accountants prepare a cash payments schedule to determine the distribution of cash to the partners in the liquidation of a partnership. The **schedule of cash payments** is organized around the basic accounting equation. The schedule for the Ace Company is shown in Illustration G-11. The numbers in parentheses refer to the four required steps in the liquidation of a partnership. They also identify the accounting entries that must be made. The cash payments schedule is especially useful when the liquidation process extends over a period of time.

Illustration G-11
Schedule of cash payments, no capital deficiency

			Noncash			R. Arnet	P. Carey	W. Eaton
Item		Cash	+ Assets	= Liabilities	+ Capital	+ Capital	+ Capital
Balances before liquidation		5,000	+ 60,000	= 31,000	+ 15,000	+ 17,800	+ 1,200
Sales of noncash assets and							
allocation of gain	(1)&(2)	75,000	+ (60,000)	=	7,500	+ 5,000	+ 2,500
New balances		80,000	+ −0−	= 31,000	+ 22,500	+ 22,800	+ 3,700
Pay liabilities	(3)	(31,000)		= (31,000)			
New balances		49,000	+ −0−	= −0−	+ 22,500	+ 22,800	+ 3,700
Cash distribution to							
partners	(4)	(49,000)		=	(22,500)	+ (22,800)	+ (3,700)
Final balances		−0−	−0−	−0−	−0−	−0−	−0−

ACE COMPANY
Schedule of Cash Payments

CAPITAL DEFICIENCY

A capital deficiency may be caused by recurring net losses, excessive drawings, or losses from realization suffered during liquidation. To illustrate, assume that Ace Company is on the brink of bankruptcy. The partners decide to liquidate by having a "going-out-of-business" sale. Merchandise is sold at substantial discounts, and the equipment is sold at auction. Cash proceeds from these sales and collections from customers total only $42,000. Thus, the loss from liquidation is $18,000 ($60,000 − $42,000). The steps in the liquidation process are as follows.

1. The entry for the realization of noncash assets is:

(1)

Cash	42,000	
Accumulated Depreciation—Equipment	8,000	
Loss on Realization	18,000	
Accounts Receivable		15,000
Inventory		18,000
Equipment		35,000
(To record realization of noncash assets)		

A	=	L	+	OE
+42,000				−18,000
+8,000				
−15,000				
−18,000				
−35,000				

Cash Flows
+42,000

2. The loss on realization is allocated to the partners on the basis of their income ratios. The entry is:

(2)

R. Arnet, Capital ($18,000 × 3/6)	9,000	
P. Carey, Capital ($18,000 × 2/6)	6,000	
W. Eaton, Capital ($18,000 × 1/6)	3,000	
Loss on Realization		18,000
(To allocate loss on realization to partners)		

A	=	L	+	OE
				−9,000
				−6,000
				−3,000
				+18,000

Cash Flows
no effect

3. Partnership liabilities are paid. This entry is the same as in the previous example.

(3)

Notes Payable	15,000	
Accounts Payable	16,000	
Cash		31,000
(To record payment of partnership liabilities)		

A	=	L	+	OE
−31,000		−15,000		
		−16,000		

Cash Flows
−31,000

4. After posting the three entries, two accounts will have debit balances—Cash $16,000, and W. Eaton, Capital $1,800. Two accounts will have credit balances—R. Arnet, Capital $6,000, and P. Carey, Capital $11,800. All four accounts are shown below.

Illustration G-12 Ledger balances before distribution of cash

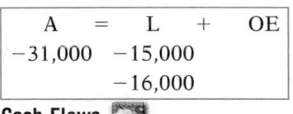

Cash			R. Arnet, Capital			P. Carey, Capital			W. Eaton, Capital		
Bal. 5,000	(3)	31,000	(2) 9,000	Bal. 15,000		(2) 6,000	Bal. 17,800		(2) 3,000	Bal. 1,200	
(1) 42,000				Bal. 6,000			Bal. 11,800		Bal. 1,800		
Bal. 16,000											

Eaton has a capital deficiency of $1,800, and thus owes the partnership $1,800. Arnet and Carey have a legally enforceable claim for that amount against Eaton's personal assets. The distribution of cash is still made on the basis of capital balances. But the amount will vary depending on how Eaton's deficiency is settled. Two alternatives are presented below.

Payment of Deficiency

If the partner with the capital deficiency pays the amount owed the partnership, the deficiency is eliminated. To illustrate, assume that Eaton pays $1,800 to the partnership. The entry is:

(a)

A	=	L	+	OE
+1,800				+1,800

Cash Flows
+1,800

Cash		1,800	
W. Eaton, Capital			1,800
(To record payment of capital deficiency by Eaton)			

After posting this entry, account balances are as follows.

Cash		R. Arnet, Capital		P. Carey, Capital		W. Eaton, Capital	
Bal. 5,000	(3) 31,000	(2) 9,000	Bal. 15,000	(2) 6,000	Bal. 17,800	(2) 3,000	Bal. 1,200
(1) 42,000							(a) 1,800
(a) 1,800			**Bal. 6,000**		**Bal. 11,800**		
Bal. 17,800							**Bal. –0–**

Illustration G-13 Ledger balances after paying capital deficiency

The cash balance of $17,800 is now equal to the credit balances in the capital accounts (Arnet $6,000 + Carey $11,800). Cash now is distributed on the basis of these balances. The entry is:

A	=	L	+	OE
−17,800				−6,000
				−11,800

Cash Flows
−17,800

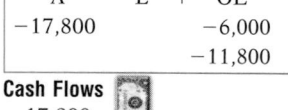

R. Arnet, Capital		6,000	
P. Carey, Capital		11,800	
Cash			17,800
(To record distribution of cash to the partners)			

After this entry is posted, all accounts will have zero balances.

Nonpayment of Deficiency

If a partner with a capital deficiency is unable to pay the amount owed to the partnership, the partners with credit balances must absorb the loss. The loss is allocated on the basis of the income ratios that exist between the partners with credit balances.

For example, the income ratios of Arnet and Carey are 3:2, or 3/5 and 2/5, respectively. Thus, the following entry would be made to remove Eaton's capital deficiency.

(a)

A	=	L	+	OE
				−1,080
				−720
				+1,800

R. Arnet, Capital ($1,800 × 3/5)		1,080	
P. Carey, Capital ($1,800 × 2/5)		720	
W. Eaton, Capital			1,800
(To record write-off of capital deficiency)			

Illustration G-14 Ledger balances after nonpayment of capital deficiency

After posting this entry, the cash and capital accounts will have the following balances.

Cash		R. Arnet, Capital		P. Carey, Capital		W. Eaton, Capital	
Bal. 5,000	(3) 31,000	(2) 9,000	Bal. 15,000	(2) 6,000	Bal. 17,800	(2) 3,000	Bal. 1,200
(1) 42,000		(a) 1,080		(a) 720			(a) 1,800
Bal. 16,000			**Bal. 4,920**		**Bal. 11,080**		**Bal. –0–**

The cash balance of $16,000 now equals the sum of the credit balances in the capital accounts (Arnet $4,920 + Carey $11,080). The entry to record the distribution of cash is:

R. Arnet, Capital	4,920	
P. Carey, Capital	11,080	
Cash		16,000
(To record distribution of cash to the partners)		

A = L + OE
−16,000   −4,920
              −11,080

Cash Flows
−16,000

After this entry is posted, all accounts will have zero balances.

Summary of Study Objectives

1 *Identify the characteristics of the partnership form of business organization.* The principal characteristics of a partnership are: (a) association of individuals, (b) mutual agency, (c) limited life, (d) unlimited liability, and (e) co-ownership of property.

2 *Explain the accounting entries for the formation of a partnership.* When a partnership is formed, each partner's initial investment should be recorded at the fair market value of the assets at the date of their transfer to the partnership.

3 *Identify the bases for dividing net income or net loss.* Net income or net loss is divided on the basis of the income ratio, which may be (a) a fixed ratio, (b) a ratio based on beginning or average capital balances, (c) salaries to partners and the remainder on a fixed ratio, (d) interest on partners' capital and the remainder on a fixed ratio, and (e) salaries to part-

ners, interest on partners' capital, and the remainder on a fixed ratio.

4 *Describe the form and content of partnership financial statements.* The financial statements of a partnership are similar to those of a corporation. The principal differences are: (a) the division of net income is shown on the income statement, (b) the owners' equity statement is called a partners' capital statement, and (c) each partner's capital is reported on the balance sheet.

5 *Explain the effects of the entries to record the liquidation of a partnership.* When a partnership is liquidated, it is necessary to record the (a) sale of noncash assets, (b) allocation of the gain or loss on realization, (c) payment of partnership liabilities, and (d) distribution of cash to the partners on the basis of their capital balances.

Glossary

Capital deficiency A debit balance in a partner's capital account after allocation of gain or loss. (p. G-10).

General partner A partner who has unlimited liability for the debts of the firm. (p. G-3).

Income ratio The basis for dividing net income and net loss in a partnership. (p. G-6).

Limited liability company A form of business organization, usually classified as a partnership and usually with limited life, in which partners, who are called *members*, have limited liability. (p. G-3).

Limited liability partnership A partnership of professionals in which partners are given limited liability and the public is protected from malpractice by insurance carried by the partnership. (p. G-3).

Limited partner A partner who has limited liability for the debts of the firm. (p. G-3).

Limited partnership A partnership in which one or more general partners have unlimited liability and one or more partners have limited liability for the obligations of the firm. (p. G-3).

No capital deficiency All partners have credit balances after allocation of gain or loss. (p. G-3).

Partners' capital statement The owners' equity statement for a partnership which shows the changes in each partner's capital balance and in total partnership capital during the year. (p. G-9).

Partnership An association of two or more persons to carry on as co-owners of a business for profit. (p. G-1).

Partnership agreement A written contract expressing the voluntary agreement of two or more individuals in a partnership. (p. G-4).

Partnership dissolution A change in partners due to withdrawal or admission, which does not necessarily terminate the business. (p. G-1).

Partnership liquidation An event that ends both the legal and economic life of a partnership. (p. G-10).

"S" corporation Corporation, with 75 or fewer stockholders, that is taxed like a partnership. (p. G-4).

Schedule of cash payments A schedule showing the distribution of cash to the partners in a partnership liquidation. (p. G-12).

Questions

1. The characteristics of a partnership include the following: (a) association of individuals, (b) limited life, and (c) co-ownership of property. Explain each of these terms.

2. Vera Cruz is confused about the partnership characteristics of (a) mutual agency and (b) unlimited liability. Explain these two characteristics for Vera.

3. Swen Varberg and Egor Karlstad are considering a business venture. They ask you to explain the advantages and disadvantages of the partnership form of organization.

4. Ginny Brown and Dorothy Fleming form a partnership. Brown contributes land with a book value of $50,000 and a fair market value of $75,000. Brown also contributes equipment with a book value of $52,000 and a fair market value of $57,000. The partnership assumes a $20,000 mortgage on the land. What should be the balance in Brown's capital account upon formation of the partnership?

5. Roy Orbison, S. Innis, and David Bowie have a partnership called Depeche Mode. A dispute has arisen among the partners. Orbison has invested twice as much in assets as the other two partners, and he believes net income and net losses should be shared in accordance with the capital ratios. The partnership agreement does not specify the division of profits and losses. How will net income and net loss be divided?

6. Leon Redbone and Elvis Costello are discussing how income and losses should be divided in a partnership they plan to form. What factors should be considered in determining the division of net income or net loss?

7. Doreen Shaffer and Quincy Jones have partnership capital balances of $40,000 and $80,000, respectively. The partnership agreement indicates that net income or net loss should be shared equally. If net income for the partnership is $24,000, how should the net income be divided?

8. Robben Ford and Gregg Allman share net income and net loss equally. (a) Which account(s) is (are) debited and credited to record the division of net income between the partners? (b) If Robben Ford withdraws $30,000 in cash for personal use in lieu of salary, which account is debited and which is credited?

9. Partners Reba McEntire and B. Zander are provided salary allowances of $30,000 and $25,000, respectively. They divide the remainder of the partnership income in a ratio of 60:40. If partnership net income is $50,000, how much is allocated to McEntire and Zander?

10. Are the financial statements of a partnership similar to those of a corporation? Discuss.

11. Phil Collins and Herb Alpert are discussing the liquidation of a partnership. Phil maintains that all cash should be distributed to partners on the basis of their income ratios. Is he correct? Explain.

12. In continuing their discussion, Herb says that even in the case of a capital deficiency, all cash should still be distributed on the basis of capital balances. Is Herb correct? Explain.

13. Erin, Cole, and Morgan have income ratios of 5:3:2 and capital balances of $34,000, $31,000, and $28,000, respectively. Noncash assets are sold at a gain. After creditors are paid, $119,000 of cash is available for distribution to the partners. How much cash should be paid to Cole?

14. Before the final distribution of cash, account balances are: Cash $25,000; B. Springsteen, Capital $19,000 (Cr.); L. Hamilton, Capital $12,000 (Cr.); and T. Zaret, Capital $6,000 (Dr.). Zaret is unable to pay any of the capital deficiency. If the income-sharing ratios are 5:3:2, respectively, how much cash should be paid to L. Hamilton?

Brief Exercises

Journalize entries in forming a partnership.
(SO 2)

BEG-1 Britney Spears and Pablo Cruise decide to organize the ALL-Star partnership. Britney Spears invests $15,000 cash, and Cruise contributes $10,000 cash and equipment having a book value of $3,500. Prepare the entry to record Cruise's investment in the partnership, assuming the equipment has a fair market value of $7,000.

Prepare portion of opening balance sheet for partnership.
(SO 2)

BEG-2 H. Tylo and R. Moss decide to merge their proprietorships into a partnership called Tylomoss Company. The balance sheet of Moss Co. shows:

Accounts receivable	$16,000	
Less: Allowance for doubtful accounts	1,200	$14,800
Equipment	20,000	
Less: Accumulated depreciation	8,000	12,000

The partners agree that the net realizable value of the receivables is $12,500 and that the fair market value of the equipment is $10,000. Indicate how the four accounts should appear in the opening balance sheet of the partnership.

BEG-3 Led Zeppelin Co. reports net income of $70,000. The income ratios are Led 60% and Zeppelin 40%. Indicate the division of net income to each partner, and prepare the entry to distribute the net income.

Journalize the division of net income using fixed income ratios.
(SO 3)

BEG-4 MET Co. reports net income of $65,000. Partner salary allowances are Moses $20,000, Evelyn $5,000, and Tom $5,000. Indicate the division of net income to each partner, assuming the income ratio is 50:30:20, respectively.

Compute division of net income with a salary allowance and fixed ratios.
(SO 3)

BEG-5 Bill&Til Co. reports net income of $24,000. Interest allowances are Bill $6,000 and Til $5,000; salary allowances are Bill $15,000 and Til $10,000; the remainder is shared equally. Show the distribution of income on the income statement.

Show division of net income when allowances exceed net income.
(SO 3)

BEG-6 After liquidating noncash assets and paying creditors, account balances in the Missouri Co. are Cash $21,000, A Capital (Cr.) $9,000, R Capital (Cr.) $7,000, and B Capital (Cr.) $5,000. The partners share income equally. Journalize the final distribution of cash to the partners.

Journalize final cash distribution in liquidation.
(SO 5)

Exercises

EG-1 Frank Voris has owned and operated a proprietorship for several years. On January 1, he decides to terminate this business and become a partner in the firm of Payne and Voris. Voris's investment in the partnership consists of $15,000 in cash, and the following assets of the proprietorship: accounts receivable $14,000 less allowance for doubtful accounts of $2,000, and equipment $20,000 less accumulated depreciation of $4,000. It is agreed that the allowance for doubtful accounts should be $3,000 for the partnership. The fair market value of the equipment is $17,500.

Journalize entry for formation of a partnership.
(SO 2)

Instructions
Journalize Voris's admission to the firm of Payne and Voris.

EG-2 B. Manilow and O. Newton have capital balances on January 1 of $50,000 and $40,000, respectively. The partnership income-sharing agreement provides for (1) annual salaries of $20,000 for Manilow and $12,000 for Newton, (2) interest at 10% on beginning capital balances, and (3) remaining income or loss to be shared 70% by Manilow and 30% by Newton.

Prepare schedule showing distribution of net income and closing entry.
(SO 3)

Instructions
(a) Prepare a schedule showing the distribution of net income, assuming net income is (1) $55,000 and (2) $30,000.
(b) Journalize the allocation of net income in each of the situations above.

EG-3 In Fleetwood Mac Co., beginning capital balances on January 1, 2007, are Ken Tucki $20,000 and Chris Cross $18,000. During the year, drawings were Tucki $8,000 and Cross $3,000. Net income was $32,000, and the partners share income equally.

Prepare partners' capital statement and partial balance sheet.
(SO 4)

Instructions
(a) Prepare the partners' capital statement for the year.
(b) Prepare the owners' equity section of the balance sheet at December 31, 2007.

EG-4 The Pips Company at December 31 has cash $20,000, noncash assets $100,000, liabilities $55,000, and the following capital balances: Agnes $45,000 and Mildred $20,000. The firm is liquidated, and $120,000 in cash is received for the noncash assets. Agnes and Mildred income ratios are 55% and 45%, respectively.

Prepare cash distribution schedule.
(SO 5)

Instructions
Prepare a cash distribution schedule.

EG-5 Data for The Pips partnership are presented in EG-4.

Journalize transactions in a liquidation.
(SO 5)

Instructions
Prepare the entries to record:
(a) The sale of noncash assets.
(b) The allocation of the gain or loss on liquidation to the partners.
(c) Payment of creditors.
(d) Distribution of cash to the partners.

*Journalize transactions with
a capital deficiency.
(SO 5)*

EG-6   Prior to the distribution of cash to the partners, the accounts in the MEL Company are: Cash $30,000, Maureen Capital (Cr.) $18,000, Ellen Capital (Cr.) $14,000, and Lou Capital (Dr.) $2000. The income ratios are 5 : 3 : 2, respectively.

Instructions

(a) Prepare the entry to record (1) Lou's payment of $2,000 in cash to the partnership and (2) the distribution of cash to the partners with credit balances.
(b) Prepare the entry to record (1) the absorption of Lou's capital deficiency by the other partners and (2) the distribution of cash to the partners with credit balances.

Problems

*Prepare entries for formation
of a partnership and a
balance sheet.
(SO 2, 4)*

PG-1   The post-closing trial balances of two proprietorships on January 1, 2007, are presented below.

	Mel Company		Gibson Company	
	Dr.	**Cr.**	**Dr.**	**Cr.**
Cash	$ 14,000		$13,000	
Accounts receivable	17,500		26,000	
Allowance for doubtful accounts		$ 3,000		$ 4,400
Merchandise inventory	26,500		18,400	
Equipment	45,000		28,000	
Accumulated depreciation—equipment		24,000		12,000
Notes payable		20,000		15,000
Accounts payable		20,000		31,000
Mel, Capital		36,000		
Gibson, Capital				23,000
	$103,000	$103,000	$85,400	$85,400

Mel and Gibson decide to form a partnership, Mel Gibson Company, with the following agreed upon valuations for noncash assets.

	Mel Company	Gibson Company
Accounts receivable	$17,500	$26,000
Allowance for doubtful accounts	4,500	4,000
Merchandise inventory	30,000	20,000
Equipment	25,000	18,000

All cash will be transferred to the partnership, and the partnership will assume all the liabilities of the two proprietorships. Further, it is agreed that Mel will invest $3,000 in cash, and Gibson will invest $18,000 in cash.

Instructions

(a) Mel, Capital $ 42,000
    Gibson, Capital $ 27,000

(c) Total assets $176,000

*Journalize divisions of net
income and prepare a
partners' capital statement.
(SO 3, 4)*

(a) Prepare separate journal entries to record the transfer of each proprietorship's assets and liabilities to the partnership.
(b) Journalize the additional cash investment by each partner.
(c) Prepare a balance sheet for the partnership on January 1, 2007.

PG-2   At the end of its first year of operations on December 31, 2007, MTC Company's accounts show the following.

Partner	Drawings	Capital
Teena Marie	$23,000	$48,000
Robin Tower	14,000	30,000
George Clinton	10,000	25,000

The capital balance represents each partner's initial capital investment. Therefore, net income or net loss for 2007 has not been closed to the partners' capital accounts.

Instructions

(a) Journalize the entry to record the division of net income for the year 2007 under each of the following independent assumptions.

   (1) Net income is $28,000. Income is shared 6:3:1.

   (2) Net income is $34,000. Marie and Tower are given salary allowances of $18,000 and $10,000, respectively. The remainder is shared equally.

   (3) Net income is $22,000. Each partner is allowed interest of 10% on beginning capital balances. Marie is given a $15,000 salary allowance. The remainder is shared equally.

(b) Prepare a schedule showing the division of net income under assumption (3) above.

(c) Prepare a partners' capital statement for the year under assumption (3) above.

(a) (1) Marie $16,800
(2) Marie $20,000
(3) Marie $18,700

(c) Marie $43,700

PG-3 The partners in Wilkowski Company decide to liquidate the firm when the balance sheet shows the following.

Prepare entries with a capital deficiency in liquidation of a partnership.
(SO 5)

GLS
Peachtree

WILKOWSKI COMPANY
Balance Sheet
May 31, 2007

Assets		Liabilities and Owners' Equity	
Cash	$ 27,500	Notes payable	$ 13,500
Accounts receivable	25,000	Accounts payable	27,000
Allowance for doubtful accounts	(1,000)	Wages payable	3,800
Merchandise inventory	34,500	S. Wilkowski, Capital	36,000
Equipment	21,000	J. Harkins, Capital	20,000
Accumulated depreciation—equipment	(5,500)	Mick Jagger, Capital	1,200
Total	$101,500	Total	$101,500

The partners share income and loss 5:3:2. During the process of liquidation, the following transactions were completed in the following sequence.

  1. A total of $53,000 was received from converting noncash assets into cash.

  2. Liabilities were paid in full.

  3. Mick Jagger paid his capital deficiency.

  4. Cash was paid to the partners with credit balances.

Instructions

(a) Prepare the entries to record the transactions.

(b) Post to the cash and capital accounts.

(c) Assume that Jagger is unable to pay the capital deficiency.

   (1) Prepare the entry to allocate Jagger's debit balance to Wilkowski and Harkins.

   (2) Prepare the entry to record the final distribution of cash.

Investments

STUDY OBJECTIVES

After studying this appendix,
you should be able to:

1 Identify the reasons corporations invest in stocks and debt securities.

2 Explain the accounting for debt investments.

3 Explain the accounting for stock investments.

4 Describe the purpose and usefulness of consolidated financial statements.

5 Indicate how debt and stock investments are valued and reported in the financial statements.

6 Distinguish between short-term and long-term investments.

Why Corporations Invest

Corporations purchase investments in debt or equity securities generally for one of three reasons. First, a corporation may **have excess cash** that it does not need for the immediate purchase of operating assets. For example, many companies experience seasonal fluctuations in sales. A Cape Cod marina has more sales in the spring and summer than in the fall and winter. The reverse is true for an Aspen ski shop. Thus, at the end of an operating cycle, many companies may have cash on hand that is temporarily idle until the start of another operating cycle. These companies may invest the excess funds to earn—through interest and dividends—a greater return than they would get by just holding the funds in the bank. The role that such temporary investments play in the operating cycle is depicted in Illustration H-1 on the next page.

A second reason some companies such as banks purchase investments is to generate **earnings from investment income**. Although banks make most of their earnings by lending money, they also generate earnings by investing in debt and equity securities. Banks purchase investment securities because loan demand

Illustration H-1
Temporary investments
and the operating cycle

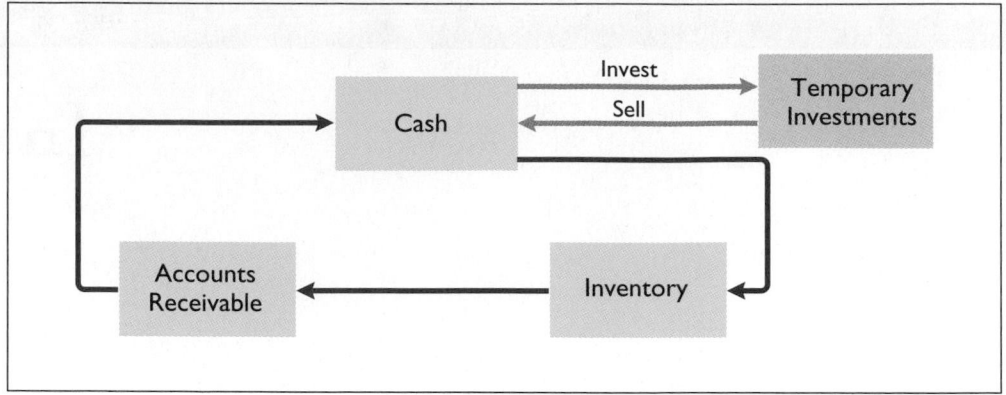

varies both seasonally and with changes in the economic climate. Thus, when loan demand is low, a bank must find other uses for its cash.

Pension funds and mutual funds are corporations that also regularly invest to generate earnings. However, they do so for *speculative reasons*. That is, they are speculating that the investment will increase in value and thus result in positive returns. Therefore, they invest primarily in the common stock of other corporations.

Third, companies also invest for **strategic reasons**. A company may purchase a noncontrolling interest in another company in a related industry in which it wishes to establish a presence. Alternatively, a company can exercise some influence over one of its customers or suppliers by purchasing a significant, but not controlling, interest in that company. Or, a corporation may choose to purchase a controlling interest in another company in order to enter a new industry without incurring the costs and risks associated with starting from scratch.

In summary, businesses invest in other companies for the reasons shown in Illustration H-2.

Illustration H-2 Why
corporations invest

Reason	Typical Investment
To house excess cash until needed	Low-risk, high-liquidity, short-term securities such as government-issued securities
To generate earnings (I need 1,000 Treasury bills by tonight)	Debt securities (banks and other financial institutions); and stock securities (mutual funds and pension funds)
To meet strategic goals	Stocks of companies in a related industry or in an unrelated industry that the company wishes to enter

Accounting for Debt Investments

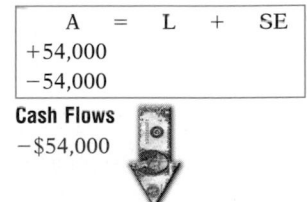

Debt investments are investments in government and corporation bonds. In accounting for debt investments, companies must make entries to record (1) the acquisition, (2) the interest revenue, and (3) the sale.

RECORDING ACQUISITION OF BONDS

At acquisition, the cost principle applies. Cost includes all expenditures necessary to acquire these investments, such as the price paid plus brokerage fees (commissions), if any.

For example, assume that Kuhl Corporation acquires 50 Doan Inc. 12%, 10-year, $1,000 bonds on January 1, 2007, for $54,000, including brokerage fees of $1,000. Kuhl records the investment as:

Jan. 1	Debt Investments		54,000	
	Cash			54,000
	(To record purchase of 50 Doan Inc.			
	bonds)			

A = L + SE
+54,000
−54,000

Cash Flows
−$54,000

RECORDING BOND INTEREST

The Doan Inc. bonds pay interest of $3,000 semiannually on July 1 and January 1 ($50,000 \times 12\% \times \frac{1}{2}$). The entry for the receipt of interest on July 1 is:

July 1	Cash		3,000	
	Interest Revenue			3,000
	(To record receipt of interest on Doan			
	Inc. bonds)			

A = L + SE
+3,000
          +3,000 Rev

Cash Flows
+$3,000

If Kuhl Corporation's fiscal year ends on December 31, it accrues the interest of $3,000 earned since July 1. The adjusting entry is:

Dec. 31	Interest Receivable		3,000	
	Interest Revenue			3,000
	(To accrue interest on Doan Inc. bonds)			

A = L + SE
+3,000
          +3,000 Rev

Cash Flows
no effect

Kuhl reports Interest Receivable as a current asset in the balance sheet. It reports Interest Revenue under "Other revenues and gains" in the income statement.

Kuhl records receipt of the interest on January 1 as follows.

Jan. 1	Cash		3,000	
	Interest Receivable			3,000
	(To record receipt of accrued interest)			

A = L + SE
+3,000
−3,000

Cash Flows
+$3,000

A credit to Interest Revenue at this time would be incorrect. Why? Because the company earned and accrued the interest revenue in the preceding accounting period.

RECORDING SALE OF BONDS

When Kuhl sells the bond investments, it credits the investment account for the cost of the bonds. The company records as a gain or loss any difference between the net proceeds from the sale (sales price less brokerage fees) and the cost of the bonds.

Assume, for example, that Kuhl Corporation receives net proceeds of $58,000 on the sale of the Doan Inc. bonds on January 1, 2008, after receiving the interest due. Since the securities cost $54,000, Kuhl has realized a gain of $4,000. It records the sale as follows.

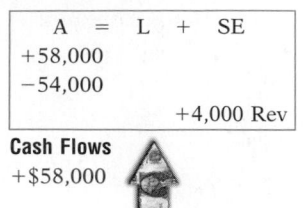

	A	=	L	+	SE
	+58,000				
	−54,000				
					+4,000 Rev

Cash Flows
+$58,000

Jan. 1	Cash	58,000	
	Debt Investments		54,000
	Gain on Sale of Debt Investments		4,000
	(To record sale of Doan Inc. bonds)		

Kuhl reports the gain on the sale of debt investments under "Other revenues and gains" in the income statement and reports losses under "Other expenses and losses."

Accounting for Stock Investments

STUDY OBJECTIVE
3
Explain the accounting for stock investments.

Stock investments are investments in the capital stock of corporations. When a company holds stock (and/or debt) of several different corporations, the group of securities is an **investment portfolio**.

The accounting for investments in common stock depends on the extent of the investor's influence over the operating and financial affairs of the issuing corporation (the **investee**). Illustration H-3 shows the general guidelines.

Illustration H-3
Accounting guidelines for stock investments

Investor's Ownership Interest in Investee's Common Stock	Presumed Influence on Investee	Accounting Guidelines
Less than 20%	Insignificant	Cost method
Between 20% and 50%	Significant	Equity method
More than 50%	Controlling	Consolidated financial statements

Companies are required to use judgment instead of blindly following the guidelines.[1] We explain and illustrate the application of each guideline next.

HOLDINGS OF LESS THAN 20%

In the accounting for stock investments of less than 20%, companies use the cost method. Under the **cost method**, companies record the investment at cost, and recognize revenue only when cash dividends are received.

---

[1]Among the factors that companies should consider in determining an investor's influence are whether (1) the investor has representation on the investee's board of directors, (2) the investor participates in the investee's policy-making process, (3) there are material transactions between the investor and the investee, and (4) the common stock held by other stockholders is concentrated or dispersed.

Recording Acquisition of Stock

At acquisition, the cost principle applies. Cost includes all expenditures necessary to acquire these investments, such as the price paid plus brokerage fees (commissions), if any.

Assume, for example, that on July 1, 2007, Sanchez Corporation acquires 1,000 shares (10% ownership) of Beal Corporation common stock at $40 per share plus brokerage fees of $500. The entry for the purchase is:

July 1	Stock Investments	40,500	
	Cash		40,500
	(To record purchase of 1,000 shares of Beal common stock)		

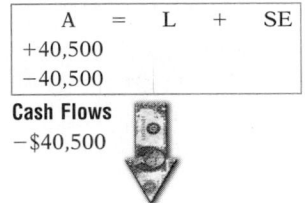

A	=	L	+	SE
+40,500				
−40,500				

Cash Flows
−$40,500

Recording Dividends

During the time the company holds the stock, it makes entries for any cash dividends received. Thus, if Sanchez Corporation receives a $2 per share dividend on December 31, the entry is:

Dec. 31	Cash (1,000 × $2)	2,000	
	Dividend Revenue		2,000
	(To record receipt of a cash dividend)		

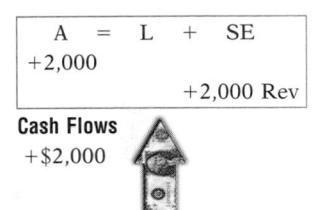

A	=	L	+	SE
+2,000				
				+2,000 Rev

Cash Flows
+$2,000

Sanchez reports Dividend Revenue under "Other revenues and gains" in the income statement.

Recording Sale of Stock

When a company sells a stock investment, it recognizes the difference between the net proceeds from the sale (sales price less brokerage fees) and the cost of the stock as a gain or a loss.

Assume, for instance, that Sanchez Corporation receives net proceeds of $39,500 on the sale of its Beal Corporation stock on February 10, 2008. Because the stock cost $40,500, Sanchez has incurred a loss of $1,000. It records the sale as:

Feb. 10	Cash	39,500	
	Loss on Sale of Stock Investments	1,000	
	Stock Investments		40,500
	(To record sale of Beal common stock)		

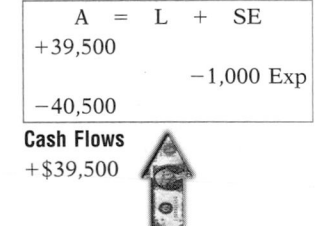

A	=	L	+	SE
+39,500				
				−1,000 Exp
−40,500				

Cash Flows
+$39,500

Sanchez reports the loss account under "Other expenses and losses" in the income statement, and would show a gain on sale under "Other revenues and gains."

HOLDINGS BETWEEN 20% AND 50%

When an investor company owns only a small portion of the shares of stock of another company, the investor cannot exercise control over the investee. But when an investor owns between 20% and 50% of the common stock of a corporation, it is presumed that the investor has significant influence over the financial and operating activities of the investee. The investor probably has a representative on the investee's board of directors. Through that representative, the investor begins to exercise some control over the investee—and the investee company in some sense becomes part of the investor company.

For example, even prior to purchasing all of Turner Broadcasting, Time Warner owned 20% of Turner. Because it exercised significant control over major decisions made by Turner, Time Warner used an approach called the equity method. Under the **equity method, the investor records its share of the net income of the investee in the year when it is earned**. An alternative might be to delay recognizing the investor's share of net income until a cash dividend is declared. But that approach would ignore the fact that the investor and investee are, in some sense, one company, making the investor better off by the investee's earned income.

Under the equity method, the company initially records the investment in common stock at cost. After that, it adjusts the investment account **annually** to show the investor's equity in the investee. Each year, the investor does the following: (1) It increases (debits) the investment account and increases (credits) revenue for its share of the investee's net income.[2] (2) The investor also decreases (credits) the investment account for the amount of dividends received. The investment account is reduced for dividends received because payment of a dividend decreases the net assets of the investee.

Recording Acquisition of Stock

Assume that Milar Corporation acquires 30% of the common stock of Beck Company for $120,000 on January 1, 2007. The entry to record this transaction is:

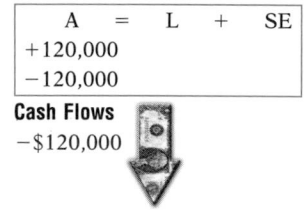

A	=	L	+	SE
+120,000				
−120,000				

Cash Flows
−$120,000

Jan. 1	Stock Investments		120,000	
	Cash			120,000
	(To record purchase of Beck common			
	stock)			

Recording Revenue and Dividends

For 2007 Beck reports net income of $100,000. It declares and pays a $40,000 cash dividend. Milar must record (1) its share of Beck's income, $30,000 (30% × $100,000), and (2) the reduction in the investment account for the dividends received, $12,000 ($40,000 × 30%). The entries are:

A	=	L	+	SE
+30,000				
				+30,000 Rev

Cash Flows
no effect

(1)

Dec. 31	Stock Investments		30,000	
	Revenue from Investment in Beck Company			30,000
	(To record 30% equity in Beck's 2007 net			
	income)			

A	=	L	+	SE
+12,000				
−12,000				

Cash Flows
+$12,000

(2)

Dec. 31	Cash		12,000	
	Stock Investments			12,000
	(To record dividends received)			

After Milar posts the transactions for the year, the investment and revenue accounts are as shown in Illustration H-4.

---

[2]Conversely, the investor increases (debits) a loss account and decreases (credits) the investment account for its share of the investee's net loss.

Stock Investments				Revenue from Investment in Beck Company		
Jan. 1	120,000	Dec. 31	12,000		Dec. 31	30,000
Dec. 31	**30,000**					
Dec. 31 Bal.	138,000					

Illustration H-4
Investment and revenue accounts after posting

During the year, the investment account increased by $18,000. This $18,000 is Milar's 30% equity in the $60,000 increase in Beck's retained earnings ($100,000 − $40,000). In addition, Milar reports $30,000 of revenue from its investment, which is 30% of Beck's net income of $100,000.

Note that the difference between reported income under the cost method and reported revenue under the equity method can be significant. For example, Milar would report only $12,000 of dividend revenue (30% × $40,000) if it used the cost method.

HOLDINGS OF MORE THAN 50%

A company that owns more than 50% of the common stock of another entity is known as the **parent company**. The entity whose stock is owned by the parent company is called the **subsidiary (affiliated) company**. Because of its stock ownership, the parent company has a **controlling interest** in the subsidiary company.

When a company owns more than 50% of the common stock of another company, it usually prepares **consolidated financial statements**. Consolidated financial statements present the assets and liabilities controlled by the parent company. They also present the total revenues and expenses of the subsidiary companies. Companies prepare consolidated statements **in addition to** the financial statements for the individual parent and subsidiary companies.

As noted earlier, prior to acquiring all of Turner Broadcasting, Time Warner accounted for its investment in Turner using the equity method. Time Warner's net investment in Turner was reported in a single line item—Other investments. After the merger, Time Warner instead consolidated Turner's results with its own. Under this approach, Time Warner included the individual assets and liabilities of Turner with its own assets. That is, Turner's plant and equipment were added to Time Warner's plant and equipment, its receivables were added to Time Warner's receivables, and so on. A similar sort of consolidation went on when AOL merged with Time Warner.

Consolidated statements are useful to the stockholders, board of directors, and management of the parent company. Consolidated statements indicate to creditors, prospective investors, and regulatory agencies the magnitude and scope of operations of the companies under common control. For example, regulators and the courts undoubtedly used the consolidated statements of AT&T to determine whether a breakup of AT&T was in the public interest. Listed here are three companies that prepare consolidated statements and some of the companies they have owned. Note that one, Disney, is Time Warner's arch rival.

> **STUDY OBJECTIVE**
> **4**
> Describe the purpose and usefulness of consolidated financial statements.

> **Helpful Hint** If the parent (A) has three wholly owned subsidiaries (B, C, and D), there are four separate legal entities but only one economic entity from the viewpoint of the shareholders of the parent company.

PepsiCo	Cendant	The Walt Disney Company
Frito-Lay	Howard Johnson	Capital Cities/ABC, Inc.
Tropicana	Ramada Inn	Disneyland, Disney World
Quaker Oats	Century 21	Mighty Ducks
Pepsi-Cola	Coldwell Banker	Anaheim Angels
Gatorade	Avis	ESPN

Valuing and Reporting Investments

STUDY OBJECTIVE

5

Indicate how debt and stock investments are valued and reported in the financial statements.

The value of debt and stock investments may fluctuate greatly during the time they are held. For example, in a 12-month period, the stock of Time Warner hit a high of $58\frac{1}{2}$ and a low of 9. In light of such price fluctuations, how should companies value investments at the balance sheet date? Valuation could be at cost, at fair value (market value), or at the lower-of-cost-or-market value.

Many people argue that fair value offers the best approach because it represents the expected cash realizable value of securities. **Fair value** is the amount for which a security could be sold in a normal market. Others counter that, unless a security is going to be sold soon, the fair value is not relevant because the price of the security will likely change again.

CATEGORIES OF SECURITIES

For purposes of valuation and reporting at a financial statement date, the accounting profession classifies debt and stock investments into three categories of securities:

1. **Trading securities** are bought and held primarily for sale in the near term to generate income on short-term price differences.
2. **Available-for-sale securities** are held with the intent of selling them sometime in the future.
3. **Held-to-maturity securities** are debt securities that the investor has the intent and ability to hold to maturity.[3]

Illustration H-5 shows the valuation guidelines for these securities. **These guidelines apply to all debt securities and all stock investments in which the holdings are less than 20%.**

Illustration H-5
Valuation guidelines

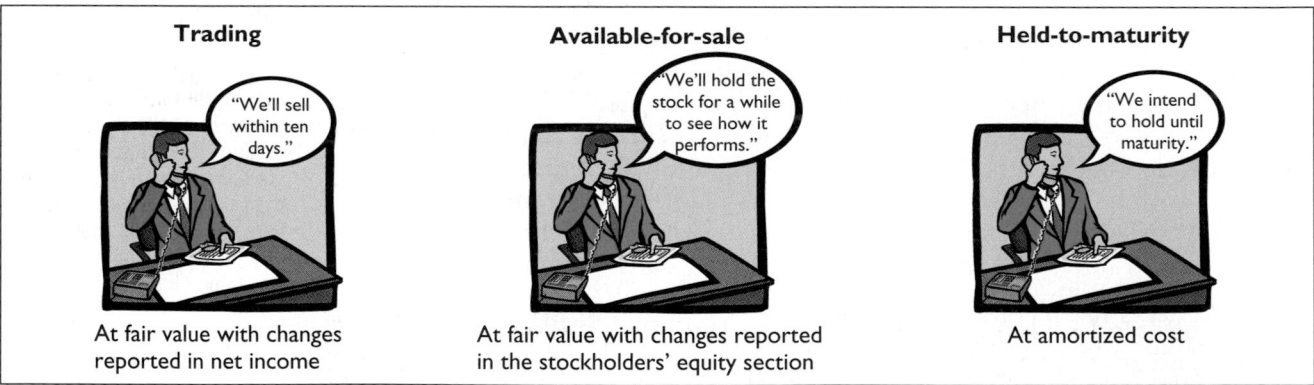

Trading	Available-for-sale	Held-to-maturity
"We'll sell within ten days."	"We'll hold the stock for a while to see how it performs."	"We intend to hold until maturity."
At fair value with changes reported in net income	At fair value with changes reported in the stockholders' equity section	At amortized cost

Trading Securities

Trading securities are held with the intention of selling them in a short period of time (generally less than a month). *Trading* means frequent buying and selling. As indicated in Illustration H-5, companies report trading securities at fair value (an approach referred to as **mark-to-market** accounting); they report changes from cost **as part of net income**. The changes are reported as **unrealized gains or losses** because the securities have not been sold. The unrealized gain or loss is the difference between the **total cost** of trading securities and their **total fair value**. Companies classify trading securities as a current asset.

---

[3]This category is provided for completeness. The accounting and valuation issues related to held-to-maturity securities are discussed in more advanced accounting courses.

As an example, Illustration H-6 shows the costs and fair values for investments classified as trading securities for Pace Corporation on December 31, 2007. Pace Corporation has an unrealized gain of $7,000 because total fair value ($147,000) is $7,000 greater than total cost ($140,000).

Trading Securities, December 31, 2007			
Investments	Cost	Fair Value	Unrealized Gain (Loss)
Yorkville Company bonds	$ 50,000	$ 48,000	$(2,000)
Kodak Company stock	90,000	99,000	9,000
Total	$140,000	$147,000	**$ 7,000**

Illustration H-6
Valuation of trading securities

The fact that trading securities are a short-term investment increases the likelihood that Pace will sell them at fair value for a gain. Pace records fair value and the unrealized gain through an adjusting entry at the time it prepares financial statements. In the entry, the company uses a valuation allowance account, Market Adjustment—Trading, to record the difference between the total cost and the total fair value of the securities. The adjusting entry for Pace Corporation is:

Helpful Hint Companies report an unrealized gain or loss in the income statement because of the likelihood that the securities will be sold at fair value since they are a short-term investment.

Dec. 31	Market Adjustment—Trading	7,000	
	Unrealized Gain—Income		7,000
	(To record unrealized gain on trading securities)		

A	= L	+	SE
+7,000			
			+7,000 Rev

Cash Flows
no effect

The use of the Market Adjustment—Trading account enables the company to maintain a record of the investment cost. Actual cost is needed to determine the gain or loss realized when the securities are sold. The company adds the Market Adjustment—Trading balance to the cost of the investments to arrive at a fair value for the trading securities.

The fair value of the securities is the amount companies report on the balance sheet. They report the unrealized gain on the income statement under "Other revenues and gains." The term *income* in the account title indicates that the gain affects net income. If the total cost of the trading securities is greater than total fair value, an unrealized loss has occurred. In such a case, the adjusting entry is a debit to Unrealized Loss—Income and a credit to Market Adjustment—Trading. Companies report the unrealized loss under "Other expenses and losses" in the income statement.

The market adjustment account is carried forward into future accounting periods. No entries are made to this account during the period. At the end of each reporting period, a company adjusts the balance in the account to the difference between cost and fair value at that time. It closes the Unrealized Gain—Income account or Unrealized Loss—Income account at the end of the reporting period.

Available-for-Sale Securities

As indicated earlier, available-for-sale securities are held with the intent of selling them sometime in the future. If the intent is to sell the securities within the next year or operating cycle, a company classifies the securities as current assets in the balance sheet. Otherwise, it classifies them as long-term assets in the investments section of the balance sheet.

Companies also report available-for-sale securities at fair value. The procedure for determining fair value and unrealized gain or loss for these securities is the same as that for trading securities. To illustrate, assume that Elbert Corporation has two securities that are classified as available-for-sale. Illustration H-7 provides information on the cost, fair value, and amount of the unrealized gain or loss on December 31, 2007. There is an unrealized loss of $9,537 because total cost ($293,537) is $9,537 more than total fair value ($284,000).

Illustration H-7
Valuation of available-for-sale securities

Available-for-Sale Securities, December 31, 2007			
Investments	Cost	Fair Value	Unrealized Gain (Loss)
Campbell Soup Corporation 8% bonds	$ 93,537	$103,600	$10,063
Hershey Foods stock	200,000	180,400	(19,600)
Total	$293,537	$284,000	$(9,537)

Both the adjusting entry and the reporting of the unrealized loss from Elbert's available-for-sale securities differ from those illustrated for trading securities. The differences result because these securities are not going to be sold in the near term. Thus, prior to actual sale it is much more likely that changes in fair value may reverse the unrealized loss. Therefore, Elbert does not report an unrealized loss in the income statement. Instead, it reports it as **a separate component of stockholders' equity**. In the adjusting entry, Elbert identifies the market adjustment account with available-for-sale securities, and identifies the unrealized gain or loss account with stockholders' equity. The adjusting entry for Elbert Corporation to record the unrealized loss of $9,537 is:

Helpful Hint The entry is the same regardless of whether the securities are considered short-term or long-term.

```
A   = L  +   SE
              -9,537 Eq
-9,537
```
Cash Flows
no effect

Dec. 31	Unrealized Gain or Loss—Equity	9,537	
	Market Adjustment—Available-for-Sale		9,537
	(To record unrealized loss on available-for-sale securities)		

If total fair value exceeds total cost, Elbert would record the adjusting entry as an increase (debit) to Market Adjustment—Available-for-Sale and a credit to Unrealized Gain or Loss—Equity.

For available-for-sale securities, the company carries forward the Unrealized Gain or Loss—Equity account to future periods. At each future balance sheet date, the account is adjusted with the market adjustment account to show the difference between cost and fair value at that time.

BALANCE SHEET PRESENTATION

For balance sheet presentation, companies must classify investments as either short-term or long-term.

Short-Term Investments

STUDY OBJECTIVE
6
Distinguish between short-term and long-term investments.

Short-term investments (also called **marketable securities**) are securities held by a company that are (1) **readily marketable** and (2) **intended to be converted into cash** within the next year or operating cycle, whichever is longer. Investments that do not meet **both criteria** are classified as long-term investments. In a recent survey of 600 large U.S. companies, 202 reported short-term investments.

READILY MARKETABLE.   **An investment is readily marketable when it can be sold easily whenever the need for cash arises.** Short-term paper[4] meets this criterion because a company can readily sell it to other investors. Stocks and bonds traded on organized securities markets, such as the New York Stock Exchange, are readily marketable because they can be bought and sold daily. In contrast, there may be only a limited market for the securities issued by small corporations and no market for the securities of a privately held company.

Helpful Hint Trading securities are always classified as short-term. Available-for-sale securities can be either short-term or long-term.

INTENT TO CONVERT.   **Intent to convert means that management intends to sell the investment within the next year or operating cycle, whichever is longer.** Generally, this criterion is satisfied when the investment is considered a resource that the company will use whenever the need for cash arises. For example, a ski resort may invest idle cash during the summer months with the intent to sell the securities to buy supplies and equipment shortly before the next winter season. This investment is considered short-term even if lack of snow cancels the next ski season and eliminates the need to convert the securities into cash as intended.

Because of their high liquidity, companies list short-term investments immediately below Cash in the current assets section of the balance sheet. Short-term investments are reported at fair value. For example, Weber Corporation would report its trading securities as shown in Illustration H-8.

WEBER CORPORATION Balance Sheet (partial)	
Current assets	
Cash	$21,000
Short-term investments, at fair value	**60,000**

Illustration H-8
Balance sheet presentation of short-term investments

Long-Term Investments

Companies generally report long-term investments in a separate section of the balance sheet immediately below "Current assets," as shown in Illustration H-9. Long-term investments in available-for-sale securities are reported at fair value. Investments in common stock accounted for under the equity method are reported at equity.

WEBER CORPORATION Balance Sheet (partial)		
Investments		
Bond sinking fund	$100,000	
Investments in stock of less than 20% owned companies, at fair value	**50,000**	
Investment in stock of 20%–50% owned company, at equity	**150,000**	
Total investments		$300,000

Illustration H-9
Balance sheet presentation of long-term investments

---

[4]Short-term paper includes (1) certificates of deposits (CDs) issued by banks, (2) money market certificates issued by banks and savings and loan associations, (3) Treasury bills issued by the U.S. government, and (4) commercial paper issued by corporations with good credit ratings.

PRESENTATION OF REALIZED AND UNREALIZED GAIN OR LOSS

Companies must present in the financial statements gains and losses on investments, whether realized or unrealized. In the income statement, companies report gains and losses, as well as interest and dividend revenue, in the nonoperating activities section under the categories listed in Illustration H-10.

Illustration H-10
Nonoperating items related to investments

Other Revenue and Gains	**Other Expenses and Losses**
Interest Revenue	Loss on Sale of Investments
Dividend Revenue	Unrealized Loss—Income
Gain on Sale of Investments	
Unrealized Gain—Income	

As indicated earlier, companies report an unrealized gain or loss on available-for-sale securities as a separate component of stockholders' equity. To illustrate, assume that Muzzillo Inc. has common stock of $3,000,000, retained earnings of $1,500,000, and an unrealized loss on available-for-sale securities of $100,000. Illustration H-11 shows the financial statement presentation of the unrealized loss.

Illustration H-11
Unrealized loss in stockholders' equity section

MUZZILLO INC. **Balance Sheet (partial)**	
Stockholders' equity	
Common stock	$3,000,000
Retained earnings	1,500,000
Total paid-in capital and retained earnings	4,500,000
Less: **Unrealized loss on available-for-sale securities**	**(100,000)**
Total stockholders' equity	$4,400,000

Note that the presentation of the loss is similar to the presentation of the cost of treasury stock in the stockholders' equity section. (It decreases stockholders' equity.) An unrealized gain would be added in this section. Reporting the unrealized gain or loss in the stockholders' equity section serves two important purposes: (1) It reduces the volatility of net income due to fluctuations in fair value. (2) It informs the financial statement user of the gain or loss that would occur if the company sold the securities at fair value.

Companies must report, as part of a more inclusive measure called *comprehensive income*, items such as unrealized gains and losses on available-for-sale securities, which affect stockholders' equity but are not included in the calculation of net income. For example, Tootsie Roll reported other comprehensive income in 2004 of $778,000. Note 11 to Tootsie Roll's financial statements shows that one component of this amount was unrealized gains and losses on investment securities. Comprehensive income is discussed more fully in Chapter 13.

STATEMENT OF CASH FLOWS PRESENTATION

As shown previously in Illustrations H-8, 9, and 11, the balance sheet presents a company's investment accounts at a point in time. The "Investing activities" section of the statement of cash flows reports information on the cash inflows and outflows during the period that resulted from investment transactions.

Illustration H-12 presents the cash flows from investing activities from the 2004 statement of cash flows of The Walt Disney Company. From this information we learn that during the year 2004 Disney received $14 million from the sale or redemption of investments and that it purchased $67 million of investments.

THE WALT DISNEY COMPANY Statement of Cash Flows (partial) September 30, 2004 (in millions)	
Investing Activities	
Investments in parks, resorts and other property	$(1,427)
Acquisitions (net of cash acquired)	(48)
Dispositions	—
Proceeds from sale of investments	**14**
Purchases of investments	**(67)**
Other	44
Cash used by investing activities	$(1,484)

Illustration H-12
Statement of cash flows presentation of investment activities

Summary of Study Objectives

1 *Identify the reasons corporations invest in stocks and debt securities.* Corporations invest for three common reasons: (a) They have excess cash. (b) They view investment income as a significant revenue source. (c) They have strategic goals such as gaining control of a competitor or supplier or moving into a new line of business.

2 *Explain the accounting for debt investments.* Entries for investments in debt securities are required when companies purchase bonds, receive or accrue interest, and sell bonds.

3 *Explain the accounting for stock investments.* Entries for investments in common stock are required when companies purchase stock, receive dividends, and sell stock. When ownership is less than 20%, the cost method is used—the investment is recorded at cost. When ownership is between 20% and 50%, the equity method should be used—the investor records its share of the net income of the investee in the year it is earned. When ownership is more than 50%, consolidated financial statements should be prepared.

4 *Describe the purpose and usefulness of consolidated financial statements.* When a company owns more than 50% of the common stock of another company, consolidated financial statements are usually prepared. These statements are especially useful to the stockholders, board of directors, and management of the parent company.

5 *Indicate how debt and stock investments are valued and reported in the financial statements.* Investments in debt and stock securities are classified as trading, available-for-sale, or held-to-maturity securities for valuation and reporting purposes. Trading securities are reported as current assets at fair value, with changes from cost reported in net income. Available-for-sale securities are also reported at fair value, with the changes from cost reported in stockholders' equity. Available-for-sale securities are classified as short-term or long-term depending on their expected realization.

6 *Distinguish between short-term and long-term investments.* Short-term investments are securities held by a company that are readily marketable and intended to be converted to cash within the next year or operating cycle, whichever is longer. Investments that do not meet both criteria are classified as long-term investments.

Glossary

Available-for-sale securities Securities that are held with the intent of selling them sometime in the future. (p. H-8)

Consolidated financial statements Financial statements that present the assets and liabilities controlled by the parent company and the aggregate profitability of the affiliated companies. (p. H-7)

Controlling interest Ownership of more than 50% of the common stock of another entity. (p. H-7)

Cost method An accounting method in which the investment in common stock is recorded at cost and revenue is recognized only when cash dividends are received. (p. H-4)

Debt investments Investments in government and corporation bonds. (p. H-3)

Equity method An accounting method in which the investment in common stock is initially recorded at cost, and the investment account is then adjusted annually to show the investor's equity in the investee. (p. H-6)

Fair value Amount for which a security could be sold in a normal market. (p. H-8)

Held-to-maturity securities Debt securities that the investor has the intent and ability to hold to their maturity date. (p. H-8)

Long-term investments Investments that are not readily marketable or that management does not intend to convert into cash within the next year or operating cycle, whichever is longer. (p. H-10)

Mark-to-market A method of accounting for certain investments that requires that they be adjusted to their fair value at the end of each period. (p. H-8)

Parent company A company that owns more than 50% of the common stock of another entity. (p. H-7)

Short-term investments (marketable securities) Investments that are readily marketable and intended to be converted into cash within the next year or operating cycle, whichever is longer. (p. H-10)

Stock investments Investments in the capital stock of corporations. (p. H-4)

Subsidiary (affiliated) company A company in which more than 50% of its stock is owned by another company. (p. H-7)

Trading securities Securities bought and held primarily for sale in the near term to generate income on short-term price differences. (p. H-8)

Self-Study Questions

Answers are at the end of the appendix.

(SO 2) **1.** Debt investments are initially recorded at:
  (a) cost.
  (b) cost plus accrued interest.
  (c) fair value.
  (d) None of the above

(SO 2) **2.** Stan Free Company sells debt investments costing $26,000 for $28,000 plus accrued interest that has been recorded. In journalizing the sale, credits are:
  (a) Debt Investments and Loss on Sale of Debt Investments.
  (b) Debt Investments, Gain on Sale of Debt Investments, and Bond Interest Receivable.
  (c) Stock Investments and Bond Interest Receivable.
  (d) The correct answer is not given.

(SO 3) **3.** Karen Duffy Company receives net proceeds of $42,000 on the sale of stock investments that cost $39,500. This transaction will result in reporting in the income statement a:
  (a) loss of $2,500 under "Other expenses and losses."
  (b) loss of $2,500 under "Operating expenses."

  (c) gain of $2,500 under "Other revenues and gains."
  (d) gain of $2,500 under "Operating revenues."

4. The equity method of accounting for long-term investments in stock should be used when the investor has significant influence over an investee and owns: (SO 3)
  (a) between 20% and 50% of the investee's common stock.
  (b) 20% or more of the investee's bonds.
  (c) more than 50% of the investee's common stock.
  (d) less than 20% of the investee's common stock.

5. Which of these statements is *not* true? Consolidated financial statements are useful to: (SO 4)
  (a) determine the profitability of specific subsidiaries.
  (b) determine the aggregate profitability of enterprises under common control.
  (c) determine the breadth of a parent company's operations.
  (d) determine the full extent of aggregate obligations of enterprises under common control.

(SO 5)   **6.** At the end of the first year of operations, the total cost of the trading securities portfolio is $120,000 and the total fair value is $115,000. What should the financial statements show?
   (a) A reduction of an asset of $5,000 and a realized loss of $5,000.
   (b) A reduction of an asset of $5,000 and an unrealized loss of $5,000 in the stockholders' equity section.
   (c) A reduction of an asset of $5,000 in the current assets section and an unrealized loss of $5,000 under "Other expenses and losses."
   (d) A reduction of an asset of $5,000 in the current assets section and a realized loss of $5,000 under "Other expenses and losses."

(SO 5)   **7.** In the balance sheet, Unrealized Loss—Equity is reported as a:
   (a) contra asset account.
   (b) contra stockholders' equity account.
   (c) loss in the income statement.
   (d) loss in the retained earnings statement.

8. If a company wants to increase its reported income by manipulating its investment accounts, which should it do?   (SO 5)
   (a) Sell its "winner" trading securities and hold its "loser" trading securities.
   (b) Hold its "winner" trading securities and sell its "loser" trading securities.
   (c) Sell its "winner" available-for-sale securities and hold its "loser" available-for-sale securities.
   (d) Hold its "winner" available-for-sale securities and sell its "loser" available-for-sale securities.

9. To be classified as short-term investments, debt investments must be readily marketable and be expected to be sold within: (SO 6)
   (a) 3 months from the date of purchase.
   (b) the next year or operating cycle, whichever is shorter.
   (c) the next year or operating cycle, whichever is longer.
   (d) the operating cycle.

Questions

1. What are the reasons that corporations invest in securities?

2. (a) What is the cost of an investment in bonds?
   (b) When is interest on bonds recorded?

3. Mary Cunningham is confused about losses and gains on the sale of debt investments. Explain these issues to Mary:
   (a) How the gain or loss is computed.
   (b) The statement presentation of gains and losses.

4. Nickle Company sells Craig's bonds that cost $40,000 for $45,000, including $2,000 of accrued interest. In recording the sale, Nickle books a $5,000 gain. Is this correct? Explain.

5. What is the cost of an investment in stock?

6. To acquire Alyssa Corporation stock, Elena Reuter pays $75,000 in cash plus $1,500 broker's fees. What entry should be made for this investment, assuming the stock is readily marketable?

7. (a) When should a long-term investment in common stock be accounted for by the equity method?
   (b) When is revenue recognized under the equity method?

8. Mack Corporation uses the equity method to account for its ownership of 25% of the common stock of Foley Packing. During 2007 Foley reported a net income of $80,000 and declares and pays cash dividends of $10,000. What recognition should Mack Corporation give to these events?

9. What constitutes "significant influence" when an investor's financial interest is less than 50%?

10. Distinguish between the cost and equity methods of accounting for investments in stocks.

11. What are consolidated financial statements?

12. What are the valuation guidelines for trading and available-for-sale investments at a balance sheet date?

13. Debbie Gocker is the controller of G-Products, Inc. At December 31 the company's investments in trading securities cost $74,000 and have a fair value of $72,000. Indicate how Debbie would report these data in the financial statements prepared on December 31.

14. Using the data in question 13, how would Debbie report the data if the investment were long-term and the securities were classified as available-for-sale?

15. Tundra Company's investments in available-for-sale securities at December 31 show total cost of $197,000 and total fair value of $210,000. Prepare the adjusting entry.

16. Using the data in question 15, prepare the adjusting entry assuming the securities are classified as trading securities.

17. Where is Unrealized Gain or Loss—Equity reported on the balance sheet?

18. What purposes are served by reporting Unrealized Gains (Losses)—Equity in the stockholders' equity section?

19. Reuter Wholesale Supply owns stock in Yount Corporation, which it intends to hold indefinitely because of some negative tax consequences if sold. Should the investment in Yount be classified as a short-term investment? Why?

Brief Exercises

Journalize entries for debt investments.
(SO 2)

BEH-1   Molina Corporation purchased debt investments for $41,500 on January 1, 2007. On July 1, 2007, Molina received cash interest of $1,660. Journalize the purchase and the receipt of interest. Assume no interest has been accrued.

Journalize entries for stock investments.
(SO 3)

BEH-2   On August 1 Alshare Company buys 1,000 shares of ABC common stock for $30,000 cash plus brokerage fees of $600. On December 1 the stock investments are sold for $38,000 in cash. Journalize the purchase and sale of the common stock.

Journalize transactions under the equity method.
(SO 3)

BEH-3   Morgan Company owns 40% of Holt Company. For the current year Holt reports net income of $150,000 and declares and pays a $50,000 cash dividend. Record Morgan's equity in Holt's net income and the receipt of dividends from Holt.

Prepare adjusting entry using fair value.
(SO 5)

BEH-4   Cost and fair value data for the trading securities of Shellankamp Company at December 31, 2007, are $62,000 and $57,000, respectively. Prepare the adjusting entry to record the securities at fair value.

Indicate statement presentation using fair value.
(SO 6)

BEH-5   For the data presented in BEH-4, show the financial statement presentation of the trading securities and related accounts.

Prepare adjusting entry using fair value.
(SO 5)

BEH-6   In its first year of operations Carpenter Corporation purchased available-for-sale stock securities costing $72,000 as a long-term investment. At December 31, 2007, the fair value of the securities is $68,000. Prepare the adjusting entry to record the securities at fair value.

Indicate statement presentation using fair value.
(SO 6)

BEH-7   For the data presented in BEH-6, show the financial statement presentation of the available-for-sale securities and related accounts. Assume the available-for-sale securities are noncurrent.

Prepare investments section of balance sheet.
(SO 6)

BEH-8   Bragg Corporation has these long-term investments: common stock of Sword Co. (10% ownership) held as available-for-sale securities, cost $108,000, fair value $115,000; common stock of Epee Inc. (30% ownership), cost $210,000, equity $250,000; and a bond sinking fund of $150,000. Prepare the investments section of the balance sheet.

Exercises

Journalize debt investment transactions, and accrue interest.
(SO 2)

EH-1   Pettengill Corporation had these transactions pertaining to debt investments:

Jan. 1   Purchased 60 10%, $1,000 Gant Co. bonds for $60,000 cash plus brokerage fees of $900. Interest is payable semiannually on July 1 and January 1.
July 1   Received semiannual interest on Gant Co. bonds.
July 1   Sold 30 Gant Co. bonds for $32,000 less $400 brokerage fees.

Instructions
(a) Journalize the transactions.
(b) Prepare the adjusting entry for the accrual of interest at December 31.

Journalize stock investment transactions, and explain income statement presentation.
(SO 3)

EH-2   Gonzalez Company had these transactions pertaining to stock investments:

Feb. 1   Purchased 1,000 shares of GET common stock (2% of outstanding shares) for $8,000 cash plus brokerage fees of $200.
July 1   Received cash dividends of $1 per share on GET common stock.
Sept. 1   Sold 500 shares of GET common stock for $5,500 less brokerage fees of $100.
Dec. 1   Received cash dividends of $1 per share on GET common stock.

Instructions
(a) Journalize the transactions.
(b) Explain how dividend revenue and the gain (loss) on sale should be reported in the income statement.

EH-3 Gocker Inc. had these transactions pertaining to investments in common stock:

Journalize transactions for investments in stock.
(SO 3)

Jan. 1 Purchased 1,500 shares of Sealey Corporation common stock (5% of outstanding shares) for $60,000 cash plus $1,400 broker's commission.

July 1 Received a cash dividend of $7 per share.

Dec. 1 Sold 900 shares of Sealey Corporation common stock for $38,000 cash less $800 broker's commission.

   31 Received a cash dividend of $7 per share.

Instructions
Journalize the transactions.

EH-4 On January 1 Didde Glaser Corporation purchased a 25% equity investment in Mortonsen Corporation for $150,000. At December 31 Mortonsen declared and paid a $60,000 cash dividend and reported net income of $320,000.

Journalize and post transactions under the equity method.
(SO 3)

Instructions
(a) Journalize the transactions.
(b) Determine the amount to be reported as an investment in Mortonsen stock at December 31.

EH-5 These are two independent situations:

Journalize entries under cost and equity methods.
(SO 3)

1. Ritter Cosmetics acquired 10% of the 250,000 shares of common stock of Lye Fashion at a total cost of $14 per share on March 18, 2007. On June 30 Lye declared and paid a $75,000 dividend. On December 31 Lye reported net income of $244,000 for the year. At December 31 the market price of Lye Fashion was $16 per share. The stock is classified as available-for-sale.

2. Hollandsworth Inc. obtained significant influence over Perez Corporation by buying 30% of Perez's 30,000 outstanding shares of common stock at a total cost of $11 per share on January 1, 2007. On June 15 Perez declared and paid a cash dividend of $35,000. On December 31 Perez reported a net income of $120,000 for the year.

Instructions
Prepare all the necessary journal entries for 2007 for (a) Ritter Cosmetics and (b) Hollandsworth Inc.

EH-6 At December 31, 2007, the trading securities for Winsor, Inc., are as follows.

Prepare adjusting entry to record fair value, and indicate statement presentation.
(SO 5, 6)

Security	Cost	Fair Value
A	$18,500	$16,000
B	12,500	14,000
C	23,000	20,000
Total	$54,000	$50,000

Instructions
(a) Prepare the adjusting entry at December 31, 2007, to report the securities at fair value.
(b) Show the balance sheet and income statement presentation at December 31, 2007, after adjustment to fair value.

EH-7 Data for investments in stock classified as trading securities are presented in EH-6. Assume instead that the investments are classified as available-for-sale securities with the same cost and fair value data. The securities are considered to be a long-term investment.

Prepare adjusting entry to record fair value, and indicate statement presentation.
(SO 5, 6)

Instructions
(a) Prepare the adjusting entry at December 31, 2007, to report the securities at fair value.
(b) Show the statement presentation at December 31, 2007, after adjustment to fair value.
(c) Karen Eaton, a member of the board of directors, does not understand the reporting of the unrealized gains or losses on trading securities and available-for-sale securities. Write a letter to Mrs. Eaton explaining the reporting and the purposes it serves.

Prepare adjusting entries for fair value, and indicate statement presentation for two classes of securities.
(SO 5, 6)

EH-8   Markowitz Company has these data at December 31, 2007:

Securities	Cost	Fair Value
Trading	$110,000	$125,000
Available-for-sale	100,000	90,000

The available-for-sale securities are held as a long-term investment.

Instructions
(a) Prepare the adjusting entries to report each class of securities at fair value.
(b) Indicate the statement presentation of each class of securities and the related unrealized gain (loss) accounts.

Problems

Journalize debt investment transactions and show financial statement presentation.
(SO 2, 5, 6)

PH-1   Hutchinson Farms is a grower of hybrid seed corn for DeKalb Genetics Corporation. It has had two exceptionally good years and has elected to invest its excess funds in bonds. The following selected transactions relate to bonds acquired as an investment by Hutchinson Farms, whose fiscal year ends on December 31.

2007

Jan.	1	Purchased at par $500,000 of Eldridge Corporation 10-year, 8% bonds dated January 1, 2007, directly from the issuing corporation.
July	1	Received the semiannual interest on the Eldridge bonds.
Dec. 31		Accrual of interest at year-end on the Eldridge bonds.

Assume that all intervening transactions and adjustments have been properly recorded and the number of bonds owned has not changed from December 31, 2007, to December 31, 2009.

2010

Jan.	1	Received the semiannual interest on the Eldridge bonds.
Jan.	1	Sold $300,000 of Eldridge bonds at 110. The broker deducted $7,000 for commissions and fees on the sale.
July	1	Received the semiannual interest on the Eldridge bonds.
Dec. 31		Accrual of interest at year-end on the Eldridge bonds.

Instructions
(a) Journalize the listed transactions for the years 2007 and 2010.
(b) Assume that the fair value of the bonds at December 31, 2007, was $470,000. These bonds are classified as available-for-sale securities. Prepare the adjusting entry to record these bonds at fair value.
(c) Show the balance sheet presentation of the bonds and interest receivable at December 31, 2007. Assume the investments are considered long-term. Indicate where any unrealized gain or loss is reported in the financial statements.

Journalize investment transactions, prepare adjusting entry, and show financial statement presentation.
(SO 2, 3, 6)

PH-2   In January 2007 the management of Mann Company concludes that it has sufficient cash to purchase some short-term investments in debt and stock securities. During the year, the following transactions occurred.

Feb.	1	Purchased 1,000 shares of PTI common stock for $40,000 plus brokerage fees of $1,000.
Mar.	1	Purchased 500 shares of ATF common stock for $20,000 plus brokerage fees of $500.
Apr.	1	Purchased 70 $1,000, 8% CRT bonds for $70,000 plus $1,200 brokerage fees. Interest is payable semiannually on April 1 and October 1.
July	1	Received a cash dividend of $0.60 per share on the PTI common stock.
Aug.	1	Sold 200 shares of PTI common stock at $42 per share less brokerage fees of $350.
Sept.	1	Received $2 per share cash dividend on the ATF common stock.

Oct. 1 Received the semiannual interest on the CRT bonds.
Oct. 1 Sold the CRT bonds for $75,000 less $1,000 brokerage fees.

At December 31 the fair values of the PTI and ATF common stocks were $39 and $30 per share, respectively.

Instructions
(a) Journalize the transactions and post to the accounts Debt Investments and Stock Investments. (Use the T account form.)
(b) Prepare the adjusting entry at December 31, 2007, to report the investments at fair value. All securities are considered to be trading securities.
(c) Show the balance sheet presentation of investment securities at December 31, 2007.
(d) Identify the income statement accounts and give the statement classification of each account.

PH-3 On December 31, 2006, Lank Associates owned the following securities that are held as long-term investments.

Journalize transactions, prepare adjusting entry for stock investments, and show balance sheet presentation.
(SO 3, 5, 6)

GLS

Common Stock	Shares	Cost
A Co.	1,000	$50,000
B Co.	6,000	36,000
C Co.	1,200	24,000

On this date the total fair value of the securities was equal to its cost. The securities are not held for influence or control over the investees. In 2007 the following transactions occurred.

July 1 Received $2.00 per share semiannual cash dividend on B Co. common stock.
Aug. 1 Received $0.50 per share cash dividend on A Co. common stock.
Sept. 1 Sold 500 shares of B Co. common stock for cash at $8 per share less brokerage fees of $100.
Oct. 1 Sold 400 shares of A Co. common stock for cash at $54 per share less brokerage fees of $600.
Nov. 1 Received $1 per share cash dividend on C Co. common stock.
Dec. 15 Received $0.50 per share cash dividend on A Co. common stock.
     31 Received $2.00 per share semiannual cash dividend on B Co. common stock.

At December 31 the fair values per share of the common stocks were: A Co. $47, B Co. $6, and C Co. $24.

Instructions
(a) Journalize the 2007 transactions and post to the account Stock Investments. (Use the T account form.)
(b) Prepare the adjusting entry at December 31, 2007, to show the securities at fair value. The stock should be classified as available-for-sale securities.
(c) Show the balance sheet presentation of the investments and the unrealized gain (loss) at December 31, 2007. At this date Lank Associates has common stock $2,000,000 and retained earnings $1,200,000.

PH-4 Grey Company acquired 20% of the outstanding common stock of Baden Inc. on January 1, 2007, by paying $1,400,000 for 50,000 shares. Baden declared and paid a $0.50 per share cash dividend on June 30 and again on December 31, 2007. Baden reported net income of $800,000 for the year.

Prepare entries under cost and equity methods, and prepare memorandum.
(SO 3)

Instructions
(a) Prepare the journal entries for Grey Company for 2007 assuming Grey cannot exercise significant influence over Baden. (Use the cost method.)
(b) Prepare the journal entries for Grey Company for 2007 assuming Grey can exercise significant influence over Baden. (Use the equity method.)
(c) The board of directors of Grey Company is confused about the differences between the cost and equity methods. Prepare a memorandum for the board that explains each method and shows in tabular form the account balances under each method at December 31, 2007.

Journalize stock transactions, and show balance sheet presentation.
(SO 3, 5, 6)

PH-5 Here is Railsback Company's portfolio of long-term available-for-sale securities at December 31, 2006:

	Cost
1,000 shares of Marquis Inc. common stock	$52,000
1,400 shares of B. Ogle Corporation common stock	84,000
800 shares of H. Aaron Corporation preferred stock	33,600

On December 31 the total cost of the portfolio equaled the total fair value. Railsback had the following transactions related to the securities during 2007.

Jan. 20 Sold 1,000 shares of Marquis Inc. common stock at $60 per share less brokerage fees of $600.

28 Purchased 400 shares of $10 par value common stock of M. DeVito Corporation at $78 per share plus brokerage fees of $480.

30 Received a cash dividend of $1.15 per share on B. Ogle Corporation common stock.

Feb. 8 Received cash dividends of $0.40 per share on H. Aaron Corporation preferred stock.

18 Sold all 800 shares of H. Aaron preferred stock at $30 per share less brokerage fees of $360.

July 30 Received a cash dividend of $1 per share on B. Ogle Corporation common stock.

Sept. 6 Purchased an additional 600 shares of the $10 par value common stock of M. DeVito Corporation at $82 per share plus brokerage fees of $800.

Dec. 1 Received a cash dividend of $1.50 per share on M. DeVito Corporation common stock.

At December 31, 2007, the fair values of the securities were:

B. Ogle Corporation common stock	$64 per share
M. DeVito Corporation common stock	$67 per share

Railsback uses separate account titles for each investment, such as Investment in B. Ogle Corporation Common Stock.

Instructions
(a) Prepare journal entries to record the transactions.
(b) Post to the investment accounts. (Use separate T accounts for each investment.)
(c) Prepare the adjusting entry at December 31, 2007, to report the portfolio at fair value.
(d) Show the balance sheet presentation at December 31, 2007.

Prepare a balance sheet.
(SO 6)

PH-6 The following data, presented in alphabetical order, are taken from the records of Wenger Corporation.

Accounts payable	$ 250,000
Accounts receivable	90,000
Accumulated depreciation—building	180,000
Accumulated depreciation—equipment	52,000
Allowance for doubtful accounts	6,000
Bond investments	400,000
Bonds payable (10%, due 2018)	380,000
Buildings	900,000
Cash	82,000
Common stock ($5 par value; 500,000 shares authorized, 300,000 shares issued)	1,500,000
Discount on bonds payable	20,000
Dividends payable	50,000
Equipment	275,000
Goodwill	230,000
Income taxes payable	70,000
Investment in Houston Inc. stock (30% ownership), at equity	240,000
Land	460,000

Merchandise inventory	170,000
Notes payable (due 2008)	70,000
Paid-in capital in excess of par value	200,000
Prepaid insurance	16,000
Retained earnings	310,000
Short-term stock investment, at fair value	185,000

Instructions
Prepare a balance sheet at December 31, 2007.

Answers to Self-Study Questions

1. a   2. b   3. c   4. a   5. a   6. c   7. b   8. c   9. c

PHOTO CREDITS

Chapter 20   Page 971: ©2000 Artville, Inc Page 974: Gary Conner/Index Stock Page 976: Gary Buss/Taxi/Getty Images Page 979: Photodisc/Getty Images, Inc. Page 983: Ralph Mercer/Stone/Getty Images Page 987: Corbis Digital Stock Page 991: PhotoDisc, Inc./Getty Images

Chapter 21   Page 1013: ©EyeWire Page 1026: ©2000 Artville, Inc Page 1029: ∏EyeWire

Chapter 22   Page 1065: Dick Luria/Taxi/Getty Images Page 1068: Wally McNamee/Corbis Images Page 1071: Hywit Dimyadi/iStockphoto Page 1076: Michel Tchervkoff Page 1083: iStockphoto Page 1086: PhotoDisc, Inc./Getty Images

Chapter 23   Page 1111: Royalty-Free/Corbis Images Page 1120: William Tautic/Corbis Stock Market Page 1126: Rebecca Ellis/iStockphoto

COMPANY INDEX

RECEIVABLES (Chapter 8)

Two Methods to Account for Uncollectible Accounts

Direct write-off method	Record bad debts expense when the company determines a particular account to be uncollectible.
Allowance method	At the end of each period estimate the amount of uncollectible receivables. Debit Bad Debts Expense and credit Allowance for Doubtful Accounts in an amount that results in a balance in the allowance account equal to the estimate of uncollectibles. As specific accounts become uncollectible, debit Allowance for Doubtful Accounts and credit Accounts Receivable.

Steps to Manage Accounts Receivable

1. Determine to whom to extend credit.
2. Establish a payment period.
3. Monitor collections.
4. Evaluate the receivables balance.
5. Accelerate cash receipts from receivables when necessary.

PLANT ASSETS (Chapter 9)

Computation of Annual Depreciation Expense

Straight-line	$\dfrac{\text{Cost} - \text{Salvage value}}{\text{Useful life (in years)}}$
*Units-of-activity	$\dfrac{\text{Depreciable cost}}{\text{Useful life (in units)}} \times \text{Units of activity during year}$
*Declining-balance	Book value at beginning of year × Declining balance rate* *Declining-balance rate = 1 ÷ Useful life (in years)

Note: If depreciation is calculated for partial periods, the straight-line and declining-balance methods must be adjusted for the relevant proportion of the year. Multiply the annual depreciation expense by the number of months expired in the year divided by 12 months.

BONDS (Chapter 10)

Premium	Market interest rate < Contractual interest rate
Face Value	Market interest rate = Contractual interest rate
Discount	Market interest rate > Contractual interest rate

Computation of Annual Bond Interest Expense

Interest expense = Interest paid (payable) + Amortization of discount
(OR − Amortization of premium)

*Straight-line amortization	$\dfrac{\text{Bond discount (premium)}}{\text{Number of interest periods}}$	
*Effective-interest amortization (preferred method)	Bond interest expense	Bond interest paid
	Carrying value of bonds at beginning of period × Effective interest rate	Face amount of bonds × Contractual interest rate

STOCKHOLDERS' EQUITY (Chapter 11)

No-Par Value vs. Par Value Stock Journal Entries

No-Par Value	Par Value

Cash
    Common Stock
	Cash
	    Common Stock (par value)
	    Paid-in Capital in Excess of Par Value

Comparison of Dividend Effects

	Cash	Common Stock	Retained Earnings
Cash dividend	↓	No effect	↓
Stock dividend	No effect	↑	↓
Stock split	No effect	No effect	No effect

STATEMENT OF CASH FLOWS (Chapter 12)

Cash flows from operating activities (**indirect method**)

Net income		
Add:	Amortization and depreciation	$ X
	Losses on disposals of assets	X
	Decreases in current assets	X
	Increases in current liabilities	X
Deduct:	Increases in current assets	(X)
	Decreases in current liabilities	(X)
	Gains on disposals of assets	(X)
Cash provided (used) by operating activities		$ X

Cash flows from operating activities (**direct method**)

Cash receipts	
(Examples: from sales of goods and services to customers, from receipts of interest and dividends on loans and investments)	$ X
Cash payments	
(Examples: to suppliers, for operating expenses, for interest, for taxes)	(X)
Cash provided (used) by operating activities	$ X

FINANCIAL STATEMENT ANALYSIS (Chapter 13)

Discontinued operations	Income statement (presented separately after "Income from continuing operations")
Extraordinary items	Income statement (presented separately after "Discontinued operations")
Changes in accounting principle	In most instances, use the new method in current period and restate previous years results using new method. For changes in depreciation and amortization methods, use the new method in the current period, but do not restate previous periods.

Income Statement and Comprehensive Income

Sales	$ XX
Cost of goods sold	XX
Gross profit	XX
Operating expenses	XX
Income from operations	XX
Other revenues (expenses) and gains (losses)	XX
Income before income taxes	XX
Income tax expense	XX
Income before irregular items	XX
Irregular items (net of tax)	**XX**
Net income	**XX**
Other comprehensive income items (net of tax)	**XX**
Comprehensive income	**$ XX**

INVESTMENTS (Appendix H)

Comparison of Long-Term Bond Investment and Liability Journal Entries

Event	Investor	Investee

Purchase / issue of bonds	Debt Investments
	    Cash
		Cash
		    Bonds Payable

Interest receipt / payment	Cash
	    Interest Revenue
		Interest Expense
		    Cash

Comparison of Cost and Equity Methods of Accounting for Long-Term Stock Investments

Event	Cost	Equity

Acquisition	Stock Investments
	    Cash
		Stock Investments
		    Cash

Investee reports earnings	No entry	Stock Investments Investment Revenue

Investee pays dividends	Cash
	    Dividend Revenue
		Cash
		    Stock Investments

*Items with asterisk are covered in appendix.

RAPID REVIEW
Chapter Content

MANAGERIAL ACCOUNTING (Chapter 14)

Characteristics of Managerial Accounting

Primary Users	Internal users
Reports	Internal reports issued as needed
Purpose	Special purpose for a particular user
Content	Pertains to subunits, may be detailed, use of relevant data
Verification	No independent audits

Types of Manufacturing Costs

Direct materials	Raw materials directly associated with finished product
Direct labor	Work of employees directly associated with turning raw materials into finished product
Manufacturing overhead	Costs indirectly associated with manufacture of finished product

JOB ORDER AND PROCESS COSTING (Chapters 15 and 16)

Types of Accounting Systems

Job order	Costs are assigned to each unit or each batch of goods
Process cost	Costs are applied to similar products that are mass-produced in a continuous fashion

Job Order and Process Cost Flow

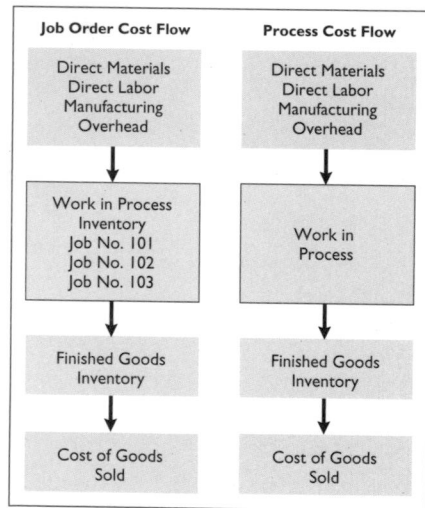

ACTIVITY-BASED COSTING (Chapter 17)

Activity-based costing involves the following four steps:
1. Identify and classify the major activities involved in the manufacture of specific products, and allocate the manufacturing overhead costs to the appropriate cost pools.
2. Identify the cost driver that has a strong correlation to the costs accumulated in the cost pool.
3. Compute the overhead rate for each cost driver.
4. Assign manufacturing overhead costs for each cost pool to products, using the overhead rates (cost per driver).

COST-VOLUME-PROFIT (Chapter 18)

Types of Costs

Variable costs	Vary in total directly and proportionately with changes in activity level
Fixed costs	Remain the same in total regardless of change in activity level
Mixed costs	Contain both a fixed and a variable element

CVP Income Statement Format

	Total	Per Unit
Sales	$xx	$xx
Variable costs	xx	xx
Contribution margin	xx	$xx
Fixed costs	xx	
Net income	$xx	

Breakeven Point

$$\text{Breakeven point in units} = \text{Fixed costs} \div \text{Contribution margin per unit}$$

Target Net Income

$$\text{Required sales in units} = (\text{Fixed costs} + \text{Target net income}) \div \text{Contribution margin per unit}$$

VARIABLE COSTING (Chapter 19)

Absorption Costing   **Variable Costing**

Product Cost ⟵ Fixed Manufacturing Overhead ⟶ Period Cost

Absorption Costing Income Statement

Sales		$X
Cost of goods sold		X
Gross profit		X
Variable selling and administrative expenses	$X	
Fixed selling and administrative expenses	X	X
Net income		$X

Variable Costing Income Statement

Sales		$X
Variable cost of goods sold	$X	
Variable selling and administrative expenses	X	X
Contribution margin		X
Fixed manufacturing overhead	X	
Fixed selling and administrative expenses	X	X
Net income		$X

Break-even Point with Multiple Products

$$\text{Break-even point in units} = \frac{\text{Fixed costs}}{\text{Weighted-average unit contribution margin}}$$

$$\text{Break-even point in dollars} = \frac{\text{Fixed costs}}{\text{Weighted-average contribution margin ratio}}$$

$$\text{Degree of operating leverage} = \frac{\text{Contribution margin}}{\text{Net income}}$$